MOON

OUTDOORS

WEST COAST
RV CAMPING

TOM STIENSTRA

WASHINGTON AND OREGON REGIONS

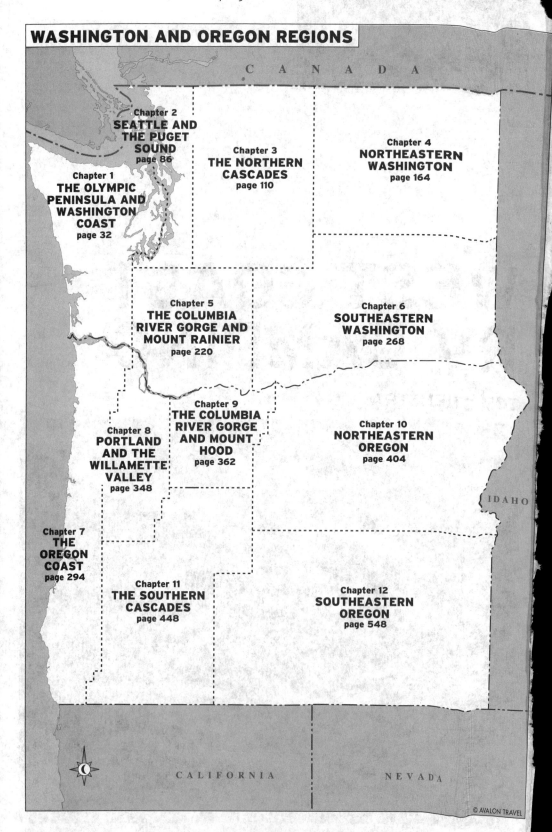

CANADA

Chapter 2
SEATTLE AND THE PUGET SOUND
page 86

Chapter 3
THE NORTHERN CASCADES
page 110

Chapter 4
NORTHEASTERN WASHINGTON
page 164

Chapter 1
THE OLYMPIC PENINSULA AND WASHINGTON COAST
page 32

Chapter 5
THE COLUMBIA RIVER GORGE AND MOUNT RAINIER
page 220

Chapter 6
SOUTHEASTERN WASHINGTON
page 268

Chapter 9
THE COLUMBIA RIVER GORGE AND MOUNT HOOD
page 362

Chapter 8
PORTLAND AND THE WILLAMETTE VALLEY
page 348

Chapter 10
NORTHEASTERN OREGON
page 404

IDAHO

Chapter 7
THE OREGON COAST
page 294

Chapter 11
THE SOUTHERN CASCADES
page 448

Chapter 12
SOUTHEASTERN OREGON
page 548

CALIFORNIA

NEVADA

© AVALON TRAVEL

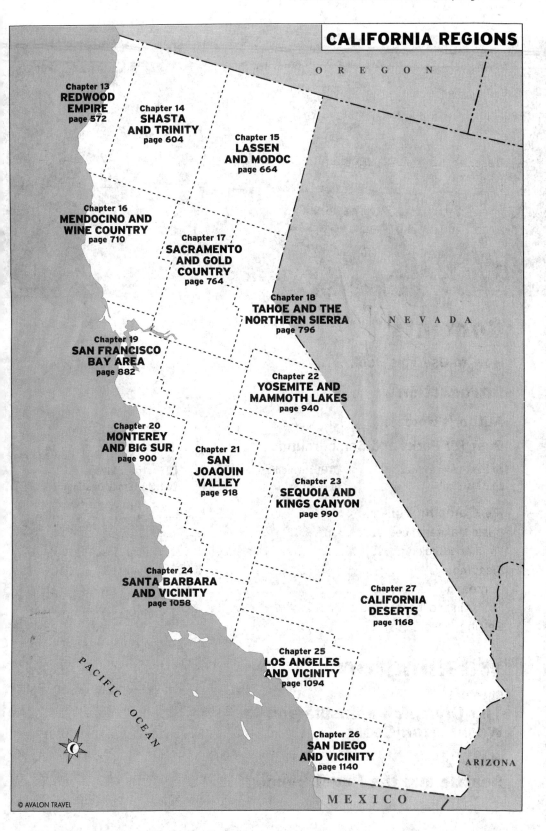

CALIFORNIA REGIONS

O R E G O N

Chapter 13
REDWOOD EMPIRE
page 572

Chapter 14
SHASTA AND TRINITY
page 604

Chapter 15
LASSEN AND MODOC
page 664

Chapter 16
MENDOCINO AND WINE COUNTRY
page 710

Chapter 17
SACRAMENTO AND GOLD COUNTRY
page 764

Chapter 18
TAHOE AND THE NORTHERN SIERRA
page 796

N E V A D A

Chapter 19
SAN FRANCISCO BAY AREA
page 882

Chapter 22
YOSEMITE AND MAMMOTH LAKES
page 940

Chapter 20
MONTEREY AND BIG SUR
page 900

Chapter 21
SAN JOAQUIN VALLEY
page 918

Chapter 23
SEQUOIA AND KINGS CANYON
page 990

Chapter 24
SANTA BARBARA AND VICINITY
page 1058

Chapter 27
CALIFORNIA DESERTS
page 1168

Chapter 25
LOS ANGELES AND VICINITY
page 1094

PACIFIC OCEAN

Chapter 26
SAN DIEGO AND VICINITY
page 1140

ARIZONA

M E X I C O

© AVALON TRAVEL

Contents

How to Use This Book

ABOUT THE CAMPGROUND PROFILES

The campgrounds are listed in a consistent, easy-to-read format to help you choose the ideal camping spot. If you already know the name of the specific campground you want to visit, or the name of the surrounding geological area or nearby feature (town, national or state park, forest, mountain, lake, river, etc.), look it up in the index and turn to the corresponding page. Here is a sample profile:

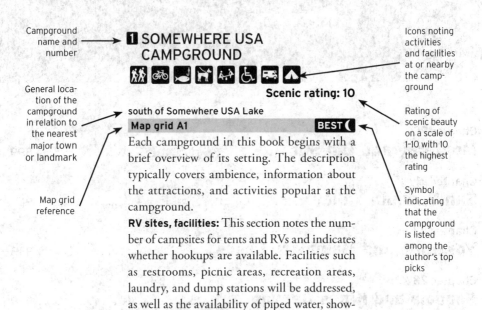

Campground name and number →

General location of the campground in relation to the nearest major town or landmark →

Map grid reference →

Icons noting activities and facilities at or nearby the campground

Rating of scenic beauty on a scale of 1-10 with 10 the highest rating

Symbol indicating that the campground is listed among the author's top picks

1 SOMEWHERE USA CAMPGROUND

Scenic rating: 10

south of Somewhere USA Lake

Map grid A1   BEST (

Each campground in this book begins with a brief overview of its setting. The description typically covers ambience, information about the attractions, and activities popular at the campground.

RV sites, facilities: This section notes the number of campsites for tents and RVs and indicates whether hookups are available. Facilities such as restrooms, picnic areas, recreation areas, laundry, and dump stations will be addressed, as well as the availability of piped water, showers, playgrounds, stores, and other amenities. The campground's pet policy and wheelchair accessibility is also mentioned here.

Reservations, fees: This section notes whether reservations are accepted, and provides rates for tent sites and RV sites. If there are additional fees for parking or pets, or discounted weekly or seasonal rates, they will also be noted here.

Directions: This section provides mile-by-mile driving directions to the campground from the nearest major town or highway.

Contact: This section provides an address, phone number, and website, if available, for the campground.

ABOUT THE ICONS

The icons in this book are designed to provide at-a-glance information on activities, facilities, and services available on-site or within walking distance of each campground.

- Hiking trails
- Biking trails
- Swimming
- Fishing
- Boating
- Canoeing and/or kayaking
- Winter sports

- Hot springs
- Pets permitted
- Playground
- Wheelchair accessible
- 5 Percent Club
- RV sites
- Tent sites

ABOUT THE SCENIC RATING

Each campground profile employs a scenic rating on a scale of 1 to 10, with 1 being the least scenic and 10 being the most scenic. A scenic rating measures only the overall beauty of the campground and environs; it does not take into account noise level, facilities, maintenance, recreation options, or campground management. The setting of a campground with a lower scenic rating may simply not be as picturesque that of as a higher rated campground, however other factors that can influence a trip, such as noise or recreation access, can still affect or enhance your camping trip. Consider both the scenic rating and the profile description before deciding which campground is perfect for you.

MAP SYMBOLS

━━━━━	Expressway	(80)	Interstate Freeway	✗	Airfield
━━━━━	Primary Road	(101)	U.S. Highway	✈	Airport
━━━━━	Secondary Road	(21)	State Highway	○	City/Town
⣀⣀⣀⣀	Unpaved Road	(66)	County Highway	▲	Mountain
············	Ferry	⬭	Lake	⬧	Park
━ ∙ ━ ∙ ━	National Border	⬭	Dry Lake	)(	Pass
━ ∙∙ ━	State Border	⬭	Seasonal Lake	◉	State Capital

INTRODUCTION

© SOLIDAGO / ISTOCKPHOTO.COM

Author's Note

"Moving is the closest thing to being free," wrote Billy Joe Shaver, an old Texas cowboy songwriter.

He got it.

It's not just the getaway destinations, adventures, and array of sights that makes roaming the West the greatest RV adventure in America. It's the way it makes you feel inside when you're on the road, the anticipation of the trip ahead, all the hopes and dreams that inspire road trips across the West—it's the closest thing to being free.

I understand these feelings. I've traveled more than a million miles across Washington, Oregon, and California in the past 25 years. Although I love hiking, boating, and fishing, the real underlying force is staying on the move, roaming around, free, always curious to see what is around the next bend in the road.

All along the Pacific Coast, from Mission Bay near San Diego to Orcas Island near the Canadian border north of the Olympic Peninsula, you can discover a series of beautiful park campgrounds that seem perfectly spaced for the trip. One of the greatest road trips anywhere is Highway 1 on the coast, the best of it venturing north along the slow, curving two-laner from Morro Bay to Fort Bragg, California. In the fall, the road is largely free of traffic, the skies often clear of fog, and the bluff-top perches furnish a procession of stunning views of the rocky coast, with unpeopled foothills on one side and an ocean that stretches to forever on the other. Traveling slowly, you'll discover, can be ecstasy.

Another option is to cruise up and down I-5, and then make side junctures into the Sierra Nevada in California, the Cascade Range in Oregon and Washington, or even a trip on a ferry boat out from Anacortes or Port Angeles in Washington to tour the San Juan Islands. Yosemite National Park is the No. 1 destination for most. Some of nature's most perfect artwork has been created in Yosemite and the adjoining eastern Sierra near Mammoth Lakes, as well as some of the most profound natural phenomena imaginable.

Cruising U.S. 395 along the Eastern Sierra is a preferred alternative for many, with the opportunity for easy side trips to many lakes. They include Bridgeport Reservoir, the June lakes, the Mammoth lakes, Convict Lake, and Crowley Lake. In addition, almost every lake's outlet stream provides prospects. This region has it all: beauty, variety, and a chance at the fish of a lifetime. There is also access to the Ansel Adams Wilderness, which features Banner and Ritter peaks, and lakes filled with fish.

Oregon and Washington feature similar stellar destinations, from pristine Crater Lake, a legend for its cobalt-blue waters, on north to Baker Lake in Mount Baker–Snoqualmie National Forest in Washington. These are just a handful amid more than a thousand lakes that provide RV access in Washington, Oregon, and California.

There's one catch. To make a road trip work, you have to be able to find a spot to stop every night. That's why this book is a must-have for every RV owner. You'll never get stuck again. One of the worst feelings imaginable is cruising down the road in the early evening without a clue where you will park for the night, without any knowledge of the array of spots available. I call that being a prisoner of hope. My advice is to never hope your way through a vacation.

This book details more than 2,300 campgrounds and parks with RV sites. The listings, directions, facilities, and highlights are far more detailed than any RV guide. To win your

5. Cutthroat trout in Omak Lake, Washington
Carl Precht RV Park, Northeastern Washington, page 177.

6. Steelhead in Bogachiel River, Washington
Bogachiel State Park, The Olympic Peninsula and Washington Coast, page 47.

7. Rainbow trout in Rufus Woods Lake, Washington
Bridgeport State Park, Northeastern Washington, page 180.

8. Bass in Lake San Antonio, California
North Shore/South Shore San Antonio, Santa Barbara and Vicinity, pages 1062–1063.

9. Salmon in Bodega Bay, California
Westside Regional Park, Mendocino and Wine Country, page 750.
Doran Regional Park, Mendocino and Wine Country, page 751.

**10. Rainbow trout in the Sacramento River
(Redding to Anderson), California**
Kangaroo Lake Walk-In, Shasta and Trinity, page 619.
Sacramento River RV Resort, Shasta and Trinity, page 659.

◖ Best Wildlife-Viewing

1. Tule elk, California
Olema Ranch Campground, San Francisco Bay Area, page 885.

2. Orcas, Washington
West Beach Resort Ferry-In, Seattle and the Puget Sound, page 92.

3. Roosevelt elk, California
Prairie Creek Redwoods State Park: Elk Prairie, Redwood Empire, page 586.

4. Gray whales, California
MacKerricher State Park, Mendocino and Wine Country, page 718.
Caspar Beach RV Park, Mendocino and Wine Country, page 722.
Ocean Cove Campground, Mendocino and Wine Country, page 746.

5. Bald eagles, Washington and California
Birch Bay State Park, Seattle and the Puget Sound, Washington, page 89.
Haag Cove, Northeastern Washington, Washington, page 190.
Indian Well, Lassen and Modoc, California page 668.

6. Black bears, California
White Wolf, Yosemite and Mammoth Lakes, page 946.
Tuolumne Meadows, Yosemite and Mammoth Lakes, page 946.
Dorst Creek, Sequoia and Kings Canyon, page 1029.

7. Roosevelt elk, Washington
Bay Center/Willapa Bay KOA, The Olympic Peninsula and Washington Coast, page 77.

8. Bighorn sheep, California
Borrego Palm Canyon, California Deserts, page 1205.

9. Antelope, Oregon
Hart Mountain National Antelope Refuge, Southeastern Oregon, page 564.

10. Deer and chukar, Oregon
Minam State Park, Northeastern Oregon, page 418.
Chukar Park, Southeastern Oregon, page 553.

◖ Prettiest Lakes

1. Lake Tahoe, California
D. L. Bliss State Park, Tahoe and the Northern Sierra, page 851.
Emerald Bay State Park and Boat-In, Tahoe and the Northern Sierra, page 852.

2. Crater Lake, Oregon
Crater Lake Resort, The Southern Cascades, page 543

3. Baker Lake, Washington
Horseshoe Cove, The Northern Cascades, page 115.

4. Sardine Lake, California
Sardine Lake, Tahoe and the Northern Sierra, page 811.

5. Crescent Lake, Oregon
Crescent Lake, The Southern Cascades, page 514.

6. Tenaya Lake, California
Tuolumne Meadows, Yosemite and Mammoth Lakes, page 946.

7. Lake Quinault, Washington
Falls Creek, The Olympic Peninsula and Washington Coast, page 56.

8. Lake Sabrina, California
Sabrina, Sequoia and Kings Canyon, page 1015.

9. Donner Lake, California
Donner Memorial State Park, Tahoe and the Northern Sierra, page 829.

10. Lake of the Woods, Oregon
Lake of the Woods Resort, The Southern Cascades, page 535.

◖ Prettiest Rivers

1. Umpqua River, Oregon
Umpqua Lighthouse State Park, The Oregon Coast, page 325.
Tyee, The Oregon Coast, page 329.
Susan Creek, The Southern Cascades, page 483.

2. McCloud River, Califorinia
Fowler's Camp, Shasta and Trinity, page 623.

3. Smith River, California
Panther Flat, Redwood Empire, page 579.
Grassy Flat, Redwood Empire, page 579.

4. Bogachiel River, Washington
Bogachiel State Park, The Olympic Peninsula and Washington Coast, page 47.

5. McKenzie River, Oregon
Olallie, The Southern Cascades, page 453.
Belknap Hot Springs Resort, The Southern Cascades, page 456

6. Owyhee River, Oregon
Birch Creek Historic Ranch, Southeastern Oregon, page 555.
Rome Launch, Southeastern Oregon, page 567.

7. Trinity River, California
Bigfoot Campground and RV Park, Shasta and Trinity, page 635.

8. Rogue River, Oregon
Indian Mary Park, The Southern Cascades, page 519.
Schroeder, The Southern Cascades, page 520.
Whitehorse, The Southern Cascades, page 521.

9. Yuba River, California
Moonshine Campground, Sacramento and Gold Country, page 776.
Indian Springs, Tahoe and the Northern Sierra, page 828.

10. Deschutes River, Oregon
Deschutes River State Recreation Area, The Columbia River Gorge and
    Mount Hood, page 390.
Tumalo State Park, The Southern Cascades, page 467.
Big River, The Southern Cascades, page 504.
LaPine State Park, The Southern Cascades, page 509.

◖ BEST FAMILY DESTINATIONS

One of the first lessons parents learn is that not everyone appreciates the philosophic release of mountain quiet. Many RVers will spend their time resting and gazing at epic scenery, watching the colors of the sky change minute by minute, or dreaming of the next day's adventure. But kids in the push-button video era, and a lot of adults too, want more. After all, "I'm on vacation. I want some fun."

It does not matter what your age is: Campers need options for fun. The following RV parks and campgrounds are sure to provide something for everyone.

WASHINGTON
Kitsap Memorial State Park, The Olympic Peninsula and Washington Coast,
    page 64.
Bay View State Park, Seattle and the Puget Sound, page 95.
Leavenworth KOA, The Northern Cascades, page 155.
Curlew Lake State Park, Northeastern Washington, page 182.
Shore Acres Resort, Northeastern Washington, page 205.
Henley's Silver Lake Resort, The Columbia River Gorge and Mount Rainier,
    page 225.

OREGON
Silver Falls State Park, Portland and the Willamette Valley, page 354.
Hoover Group Camp, The Columbia River Gorge and Mount Hood, page 394.
Wallowa Lake State Park, Northeastern Oregon, page 420.
Twin Lakes Resort, The Southern Cascades, page 501.
Abbott Creek, The Southern Cascades, page 527.
Drews Creek, Southeastern Oregon, page 562.

CALIFORNIA
Summit Lake: North, South, and Equestrian, Lassen and Modoc, page 689.
Dorst Creek, Sequioa and Kings Canyon, page 1029.
El Capitán State Beach, Santa Barbara and Vicinity, page 1074.
Newport Dunes Waterfront Resort, Los Angeles and Vicinity, page 1121.
Furnace Creek, California Deserts, page 1174.

RV Camping Tips

Many paths, one truth: There are nearly 40 styles of RVs in use, from the high-end 60-footers that resemble touring buses for rock stars, to the popular cab-over campers on pick-up trucks, to the pop-up trailers that can be towed by a small sedan. Regardless of what kind of rig you use, all share one similarity when you prepare for a trip: You must have good tires, brakes, and a cooling system for your engine.

During your trip, check fluid levels with every gas fill-up. These checks should include engine oil, brake fluid, engine coolant, transmission fluid, and power-steering fluid.

While these lists do not cover every imaginable item, they do serve as a checklist for primary items and a starting point to create your own list. My suggestion is to add items to these pages that are vital for your own vehicle.

BASIC MAINTENANCE

Here's a checklist for primary items; make sure that you have these and that they are in good working order before you go. Also be sure all mandatory routine maintenance is performed prior to your trip.

- All owner's manuals
- Batteries
- Brakes and brake fluid
- Cooling system and coolant
- Electrical system, lights
- Emergency flashers
- Fire extinguisher
- Gas filter
- Heater and air conditioner
- Lube
- Oil and filter
- Power-steering fluid
- Proof of insurance and registration
- Road service card
- Shocks
- Tire-changing equipment
- Tires (check air pressure, including spare tire)
- Transmission fluid
- Wheel bearings

Self-contained RVs
- Awning
- Dump valve and sewer hose
- Electrical system
- Extra battery if camping without hookups
- Fuses, including for slide-out motor
- Gray water tank and panel monitor
- Landing gear
- Lights
- Lube rollers or slider plates at the end of rams for slide-out rooms
- Pilot light
- Power converter
- Propane gas
- Refrigerator
- Stabilizer jacks
- Stove
- Toilet chemical and RV toilet paper
- Water system
- Windows and shades

Trailers and Fifth Wheels
- Lights
- Lube
- Perfect fit at tow junction
- Safety chains
- Self-adjusting brakes
- Wheel bearings

Safety on the Road

When you start your vehicle and then head down the road for a winter vacation—or in the high Sierra year-round—you may wonder, "What did I forget this time?"

The answer for some might be "plenty."

Engine trouble, tires and chains, road conditions, verified directions, and personal safety are all factors in road trips. Many people think they can handle whatever is thrown at them on a vacation. But what actually happens is that they are rewarded or punished for their level of preparation. To ensure you experience the former, rather than the latter, follow these simple tips before you head out on the road:

Verify directions: Just because MapQuest provides directions does not mean they are correct. Get independent verification of every destination and carry a detailed road map. Keep in mind that many Forest Service roads close in winter. For out-of-towners looking at a detailed map, it might appear that these roads could provide an alternate route; however, they could become a nightmare after a wrong turn at night for those unfamiliar with the area.

Check road conditions and weather: Just as pilots do, obtain all available information before taking off on your trip. Start by calling the state transportation agency road condition hot line or checking their information online. Detailed weather reports and forecasts are often available through newpaper websites.

Determine snow levels: If you're driving into the mountains in a storm, you can calculate the snow levels by subtracting 3.5 degrees for every 1,000 feet you gain in elevation. The magic number when snow starts to stick is usually 34°F. So if you're heading to Tahoe, it's raining in Sacramento (elevation 25 feet), and the temperature is 50°F, you will hit snow at an elevation of roughly 4,500 feet as you head up the Sierra.

Tires and chains: Never hope your way through a storm. Make sure your tires are in good condition and inflated properly. Carry the correct chains for your vehicle and know how to put them on so that doing so is fast and easy—don't think you can whip through anything. Even then, accelerate very cautiously uphill (when most spinouts occur), and brake very slowly; skids are the product of torque, not speed.

Get your vehicle checked: People often put undeserved trust in their vehicles these days, with the broad-brush assumption that paying a high price guarantees flawless operation. Unfortunately not. At the minimum, make sure your battery and oil are fresh, and brakes in perfect condition. (Hah! Back in the day, we didn't trust anything to work right and it seemed everybody had a coat hanger and duct tape to keep things together.)

Fuel up: Never set out at night or into bad weather without a full tank of gas. The worst traffic jams are caused when someone in a line of cars runs out of gas in a blizzard, then leaves their vehicle parked in the road to walk into town.

Emergency road equipment: Check to make sure you have complete tire-changing equipment (and know how to use it), emergency flashers, spotlight and cell phone, and that your spare tire is inflated. Other musts: a flashlight, a knife, and duct tape (hey, it still comes in handy!).

Never split up: Families should always stay together. According to a wise gent named Aristotle, "When two go upon journey, one sees before the other." If two adults split up, an individual, on their own, might not see the way out of trouble, and in addition, each adult might lose half of their reasoning power.

Personal safety: Don't put yourself in position for something bad to happen. If you feel that an area might be dangerous, then leave. Do not expect yourself to rise to the occasion. You will instead default to your level of training.

Ask directions: Nobody can explain this, but a lot of guys simply will not ask for directions. A key is to never ask directions at a gas station or a convenience store. The best bet is to stop at a restaurant, order dinner, and let the waitress work on your question.

File a trip plan: Again, just as pilots do, leave a trip plan and itinerary with a friend or family member back home. Then, if a search is necessary, they have a locator and timeline to shorten the search.

FOOD AND COOKING

When it comes to food, you are only limited by your imagination. So there is no reason to ever settle for less than what is ideal for you. Add to this list as necessary.

• Bottled water and drinks

- Can opener
- Charcoal
- Coffee maker and filters
- Cooking utensils
- Ice chest
- Kitchen towels
- Knives, forks, spoons
- Matches or lighters
- Napkins and paper towels
- Pots, pans, plates, glasses
- Primary foods for breakfasts, lunches, and dinners
- Seasonings, pepper and salt, spices
- Trash bags
- Wash rack and detergent

Protection Against Food Raiders

Bears, raccoons, and even blue jays specialize in the food-raiding business at camps. Bears, in particular, can be a real problem for people new to RV camping at parks with high bear populations. In rare cases, bears have even been known to break into unattended RVs in the pursuit of human goodies, especially Swiss Miss, Tang, butter, eggs, and ice cream. Raccoons can chew tiny holes in tents and destroy picnic baskets in their search. I've seen jays land on plastic bags hanging from tree limbs, rigged from rope as bear-proof food hangs, and then poke a hole in the plastic to get meat sticks. There are answers, of course. In the past few years, programs have been established at many state and national parks to reduce incidents with bears. The real problem, of course, is not bears, but the careless people who create incidents by not properly storing their food and disposing of garbage.

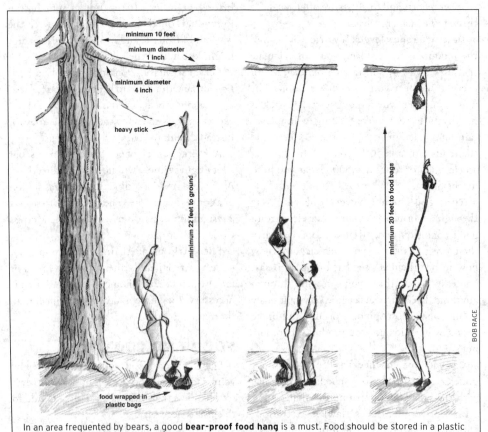

In an area frequented by bears, a good **bear-proof food hang** is a must. Food should be stored in a plastic bag 10 feet from the trunk of the tree and at least 20 feet from the ground.

In areas with high bear density, owners of small truck campers or pop-up camper trailers can use a bear-proof food hang or bear-proof food canisters. When creating a bear-proof food hang, use the counter-balance method with either double plastic bags or canvas bags. If no tree limb is suitable for the counter-balance method for a bear-proof food hang, put all your food in a double bag, hoist it up to a limb, and then tie the end off on a different tree.

Observe the following rules for proper food storage and disposal:

- Always use wildlife-proof metal food lockers available at major park campgrounds
- Do not leave food unattended on picnic tables or in camp
- Do not leave garbage unattended in camp
- Dispose of all garbage properly each day
- Do not leave food bags, cups, or anything that may appear as food within view of a bear who might peer into the window of an RV
- Do not put food inside a vehicle, under a vehicle, in a tent, or in a "hiding place"
- Report all aggressive bears to rangers

SLEEPING

Some things can't be compromised—ever. This is one of them. You must guarantee that you will get a good night's sleep. Your sleeping setup, whether in a bed or in a sleeping bag on a pad, must guarantee that you will be comfy, clean, dry, and warm—no matter what.

The problems RVers encounter come from two primary sources: lack of privacy and light intrusion. The lack of privacy stems from the natural restrictions of where a land yacht can go. Motor-home owners can often find themselves in parking-lot settings, jammed in with plenty of neighbors. Because RVs often have large picture windows, you lose your privacy, causing some late nights; then, come daybreak, light intrusion forces an early wake up. As a result, you get shorted on your sleep.

The answer is to carry inserts to fit over the inside of your windows. These close off the outside and retain your privacy. And if you don't

want to wake up with the sun at daybreak, you don't have to. It will still be dark.

To ensure a good night's sleep, start by making sure that the RV is level and solid, and then make sure that you have these essentials:

- Bed: sheets, blankets, or sleeping bag
- Blackout screens over windows
- Emergency ear plugs (snorers! hah!)
- Favorite pillows
- Sleeping surface: bed mattress, air bed, or foam pad
- Tent for children with foam pads, sleeping bags, and pillows

RECREATION

The most popular outdoor recreation activities on the West Coast are hiking, biking, wildlife-watching, swimming, fishing, golfing, boating, kayaking and canoeing, and hunting. America's wildlands are home to a remarkable abundance of fish and wildlife. Your RV camping adventures will evolve into premium outdoor experiences if you can work in a few good hikes and fishing trips.

For this checklist, you may wish to cross off items for activities that you do not take part in and add items essential for your favorites.

- Beach chair and towels
- Bike and tire repair kit
- Binoculars
- Boat with required safety equipment
- Camera, fresh battery, digital card or film
- Daypack
- Fishing rod, reel with fresh line, tackle, fishing license with appropriate tags, and state rulebook
- Flashlight and batteries
- Golf clubs and balls
- Hat
- Hiking boots and SmartWool (or equivalent) socks
- Identification guides
- Life vests
- Maps
- Rifle or shotgun with ammunition, hunting license with tags, and hunting regulations

- Sandals
- Sunglasses
- Sunscreen
- Swimsuit

Hiking
SELECTING THE RIGHT BOOTS
Every hiker eventually conducts a search for the perfect boot in the mission for ideal foot comfort and freedom from blisters. While there are many entries in this search, there is a way to find that perfect boot for you.here are different kinds of hiking footwear.

Hiking boots: Hiking boots can resemble low-cut leather/Gore-Tex hunting boots or Gore-Tex walking shoes. They are designed for day walks or short backpacking trips; for day hiking, they are the footwear of choice for most.

On the negative side, traction can be far from good on steep, slippery surfaces and they provide less than ideal ankle support, which can be a problem in rocky areas, such as along a stream where you might want to go trout fishing. For more support and traction, hunting boots or mountaineering boots might be your best bet.

Athletic shoes: Athletic shoes are frequently featherlight, so the long-term wear on your legs is minimal. For many short walks, they are ideal. For those with very strong feet and arches, they are popular even on multi-day trips that require only a small pack.

But there can be many problems with such a shoe. On steep sections, you can lose your footing, slip, and fall. If you stub your toe, you have little protection, and it hurts like heck. If you try to carry a backpack and don't have a strong arch, your arch can collapse or, at the minimum, overstress your ankles and feet. In addition, heavy socks usually are not a good fit in these lightweight shoes; if you go with a thin cotton sock and it folds over, you can rub up a blister in minutes.

BLISTERS
The key to treating blisters is fast work at the first sign of a hot spot. If you feel a hot spot, never keep walking, figuring that the problem will go away or that you will work through it. Wrong! Stop immediately and go to work.

Before you remove your socks, check to see if the sock has a wrinkle in it, a likely cause of the problem. If so, either change socks or pull them tight, removing the tiny folds, after taking care of the blister.

To take care of the blister, cut a piece of moleskin to cover the offending toe, securing the moleskin with white medical tape. If moleskin is not available, small Band-Aids can do the job, but these have to be replaced daily, and sometimes with even more frequency. At night, clean your feet and sleep without socks. That will allow your feet to dry and heal.

To stay blister-free, the most important factors are socks and boot flexibility. If there is any foot slippage from a thin sock or a stiff boot, you can rub up a blister in minutes.

Fishing
GEAR ESSENTIALS
Your fishing tackle selection should be as simple and clutter-free as possible. At home, I scan my tackle boxes for equipment and lures, make my selections, and bring just the essentials. Rod, reel, and tackle will fit into a side pocket of my backpack or a small carrying bag.

So what kind of rod should be used on an outdoor trip? For most anglers, I suggest the use of a light, multipiece spinning rod that will break down to a small size. The lowest-priced, quality six-piece rod on the market is the Daiwa 6.5-foot pack rod, number 6752, which is made of a graphite/glass composite that gives it the quality of a much more expensive model. And it comes in a hard plastic carrying tube for protection. Other major rod manufacturers, such as Fenwick, offer similar premium rods. It's tough to miss with any of them.

The use of graphite/glass composites in fishing rods has made them lighter and more sensitive, yet stronger. The only downside to graphite as a rod material is that it can be brittle. If you

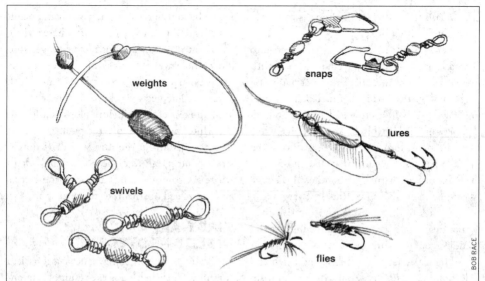

While camping, the only **fishing tackle** you should bring is the essentials: several varying weights, about 20 lures, and about 20 flies, splitshot, and snap swivels. These should all fit into a container just bigger than a deck of cards.

rap your rod against something, it can crack or cause a weak spot. That weak spot can eventually snap under even light pressure, like setting a hook or casting. Of course, a bit of care will prevent that from ever occurring.

If you haven't bought a fishing reel in some time, you will be surprised at the quality and price of micro spinning reels on the market. The reels come tiny and strong, with rear-control drag systems. Among others, Abu, Cardinal, Shimano, Sigma all make premium reels. They're worth it. With your purchase, you've just bought a reel that will last for years and years.

The one downside to spinning reels is that after long-term use, the bail spring will weaken. As a result, after casting and beginning to reel, the bail will sometimes not flip over and allow the reel to retrieve the line. Then you have to do it by hand. This can be incredibly frustrating, particularly when stream fishing, where instant line pickup is essential. The solution is to have a new bail spring installed every few years. This is a cheap, quick operation for a tackle expert.

You might own a giant tackle box filled with lures but, on your fishing trip, you are better off to fit just the essentials into a small container. One of the best ways to do that is to use the Plano Micro-Magnum 3414, a tiny two-sided tackle box for trout anglers that fits into a shirt pocket. In mine, I can fit 20 lures in one side of the box and 20 flies, splitshot, and snap swivels in the other. For bass lures, which are bigger, you need a slightly larger box, but the same principle applies.

There are more fishing lures on the market than you can imagine, but a few special ones can do the job. I make sure these are in my box on every trip. For trout, I carry a small black Panther Martin spinner with yellow spots, a small gold Kastmaster, a yellow Roostertail, a gold Z-Ray with red spots, a Super Duper, and a Mepps Lightning spinner.

The best trout catcher I've ever used on rivers is a small metal lure called a Met-L Fly. On days when nothing else works, it can be like going to a shooting gallery. The problem is that the lure is nearly impossible to find. Rambob and I consider the few we have remaining so valuable that if the lure is snagged on a rock, a cold swim is deemed mandatory for its retrieval. These lures are as hard to find in tackle shops as trout can be to catch without one.

For bass, you can also fit all you need into a small plastic tackle box. I have fished with many bass pros, and all of them actually use just a few lures: a white spinner bait, a small jig called a Gits-It, a surface plug called a Zara Spook, and plastic worms. At times, like when the bass move into shoreline areas during the spring, shad minnow imitations like those made by Rebel or Rapala can be dynamite. My favorite is the one-inch, blue-silver Rapala. Every spring as the lakes begin to warm and the fish snap out of their winter doldrums, I like to float and paddle around in my small raft. I'll cast that little Rapala along the shoreline and catch and release hundreds of bass, bluegill, and sunfish. The fish are usually sitting close to the shoreline, awaiting my offering.

FISHING TIPS

On every fishing trip, regardless of what you fish for, try to follow three hard-and-fast rules.

1. Always approach the fishing spot so you will be undetected. In order to fish undetected, you must walk softly, keep your shadow off the water, and keep your casting motion low. All of these key elements become easier at sunrise or sunset, when shadows are on the water. At midday, the sun is at its peak, causing a high level of light penetration in the water. This can make the fish skittish to any foreign presence.

2. Present your lure, fly, or bait in a manner so it appears completely natural, as if no line was attached. After you have sneaked up on a fishing spot, you should zip your cast upstream and start your retrieval as soon as it hits the water. If you let the lure sink to the bottom and then start the retrieval, you have no chance. When fishing on trout streams, always hike and cast upriver and retrieve as the offering drifts downstream in the current.

3. Stick and move, hitting one spot, working it the best you can, then moving to the next. The rule of the wild is that fish and wildlife will congregate wherever there is a distinct change

in the habitat. This is where you should begin your search. In a river, it can be where a riffle pours into a small pool, a rapid plunges into a deep hole and flattens, a big boulder in the middle of a long riffle, a shoreline point, a rock pile, a submerged tree. Look for the changes and zip your cast so the lure plops gently into the white water just above the pool. Start your retrieval instantly; the lure will drift downstream and plunk into the pool. Bang! That's where the trout will hit. Take a few more casts and then head upstream to the next spot.

FIRST AID AND INSECT PROTECTION

The most common injury on vacations is a sunburn. Close behind is the result of scratching a mosquito bite. Both are easily avoided. Although other mishaps are rare on vacations, campers should always be ready for them. In bright sun, always wear a hat that covers your ears, the tops of which can get singed quickly on a summer day. On trips to Central America, I learned that even on the hottest days, you can wear light long-sleeve shirts that provide sun protection, yet are cool and ventilated.

First Aid

A first-aid kit is a must in every RV. Here is a good starting list of basic sun and insect protection, plus basic first-aid supplies:
- Ace bandage
- Adhesive towels and medical tape
- AfterBite
- Aloe sunburn cream
- Antibiotic towels
- Aspirin
- Band-Aids
- Blood pressure monitoring equipment
- Burn ointment
- Chapstick
- Eye wash
- Moleskin or similar blister treatment
- Mosquito repellent
- Pain reliever such as Excedrin, Tylenol, Ibuprofen, Advil, Aleve, or similar

- Prescription medications (such as an inhaler for asthmatics)
- Scissors
- Sterile gloves
- Sun block
- Tums or other antacid
- Tweezers

Sunburn

The most common injury suffered on RV camping trips is sunburn, yet some people wear it as a badge of honor, believing that it somehow enhances their virility. Well, it doesn't. Neither do suntans. Too much sun can lead to serious burns or sunstroke.

Both are easy enough to avoid. When outdoors, use a high-level sunscreen on your skin, apply lip balm, and wear sunglasses and a hat. If any area gets burned, apply first-aid cream, which will soothe and provide moisture to the parched skin. The best advice is not to get even a suntan. Those who tan are involved in a practice that can eventually ruin their skin and possibly lead to cancer.

Mosquitoes

When it comes to mosquitoes, there are times when there is nothing you can do. However, in most situations, you can muster a defense to repel the attack. The first key with mosquitoes is to wear clothing too heavy for them to drill through. Expose a minimum of skin, wear a hat, and tie a bandanna around your neck, preferably one that has been sprayed with repellent. If you try to get by with just a cotton T-shirt, you will be declared a federal mosquito sanctuary.

So, first, your skin must be well covered, with only your hands and face exposed. Second, you should have your companion spray your clothes with repellent. Third, you should dab liquid repellent directly on your skin. Three citronella-based products—Avon's Skin-So-Soft, Buzz Away (manufactured by Quantum), and Natrapel (manufactured by Tender)—have received EPA registration and approval for sale as repellents against flies, gnats, midges, and mosquitoes. If you do get bit, a fluid called After Bite or a dab of ammonia should be applied immediately to the bite. To start the healing process, apply a first-aid gel (not a liquid), such as the one made by Campho-Phenique.

If you have horsefly or yellow jacket problems, you'd best just leave the area. One, two, or a few can be dealt with. More than that and your fun trip outdoors will be about as fun as being roped to a tree and stung by an electric shock rod.

Poison Oak

You can get poison oak only from direct contact with the oil residue from the plant's leaves. It can be passed in a variety of ways, as direct as skin-to-leaf contact or as indirect as leaf to dog, dog to sofa, sofa to skin. Once you have it, there is little you can do but feel horribly itchy. Applying Caladryl lotion or its equivalent can help because it contains antihistamines, which attack and dry the itch.

Reduce your exposure by staying on trails when you hike and making sure your dog does the same. Remember, the worst stands of poison oak are usually brush-infested areas just off the trail. Also protect yourself by dressing so your skin is completely covered, wearing long-sleeved shirts, long pants, and boots. If you suspect you've been exposed, immediately wash your clothes and then wash yourself with aloe vera, rinsing with a cool shower.

Remember that poison oak can disguise itself. In the spring, it is green; then it gradually turns reddish in the summer. By fall, it becomes a bloody, ugly-looking red. In the winter, it loses its leaves altogether and appears to be nothing more than the barren, brown sticks of a small plant. However, at any time and in any form, its contact with skin can quickly lead to infection.

GETTING ALONG

The most important element of any trip is the people you are with. That is why your choice of companions is so important. Your own behavior is equally consequential. Yet most people spend more time putting together their gear than considering why they enjoy or dislike the company of their chosen companions.

Here are a few rules of behavior for a great trip:

1. No whining: Nothing is more irritating than being around a whiner.

2. Activities must be agreed upon: Always have a meeting of the minds with your companions over the general game plan.

3. Nobody's in charge: It is impossible to be genuine friends if one person is always telling another what to do.

4. Equal chances at the fun stuff: There must be an equal distribution of the fun stuff and the not-fun stuff.

5. No heroes: Nobody cares about all your wonderful accomplishments. No gloating. The beauty of travel is simply how each person feels inside, the heart of the adventure.

6. Agree on a wake-up time: It is a good idea to agree on a general wake-up time before closing your eyes for the night. You can then proceed on course together without the risk of whining (see #1).

7. Think of the other guy: Count the number of times you say, "What do you think?"

8. Solo responsibilities: When it is time for you to cook, make a campfire, or clean a fish, it means you can do so without worrying about somebody else getting their mitts in the way.

9. Don't let money get in the way: Among friends, don't let somebody pay extra, because that person will likely try to control the trip, and yet at the same time, don't let somebody weasel out of paying a fair share.

10. Accordance on the food plan: Always have complete agreement on what you plan to eat each day, and always check for food allergies such as nuts, onions, or cheese.

Outdoors with Kids

How do you get kids excited about an RV trip to the great outdoors? How do you compete with the television, the DVD player, the video game, and get them *outside*?

The answer is in this list, put together with the help of my own kids, Jeremy and Kris, and their mother, Stephani. These are lessons that will get youngsters excited about the outdoors and that will make sure adults help the process along, not kill it. Some of the lessons are obvious, some are not, but all are important:

• Take children to places where there is a guarantee of action, such as a park with wildlife-viewing.

• Be enthusiastic. Enthusiasm is contagious—if you aren't excited about an adventure, you can't expect a child to be.

• Always be seated when talking to someone small, so the adult and child are on the same level.

• Always *show* how to do something—never tell.

• Let kids be kids by letting the adventure happen, rather than trying to force it within some preconceived plan.

• Use short attention spans to your advantage by bringing along a surprise bag of candy and snacks.

• Make absolutely certain the child's sleeping area is clean, dry, and warm, and that they feel safe, protected, and listened to.

• Introduce kids to outdoor ethics; they quickly relate to the concepts and long remember when they do something right that somebody else has done wrong.

• Take close-up photographs of them holding fish they have caught, trails they have hiked, or completing other tasks around the campground.

• Keep track of how often you say, "What do you think?"

Traveling with Pets

Many dogs and cats are considered members of the family. I recommend taking them along whenever possible. They always add to the trip. And after all, leaving them is a terrible moment, especially when they stare at you with those big, mournful eyes, and then you spend the next week thinking about them. My dog Rebel ended up traveling with me for 17 years. I believe one of the reasons he lived so long was because he was fit, happy, loved, had a job to do (camp security, or so he thought), and always had another adventure to look forward to. Of course, you just can't put your pet in the vehicle and figure everything will be fine. In addition, some pets are built for travel or camping, and some are not. Know the difference. A few precautions can prevent a lot of problems.

Start with your pet's comfort. Make certain your pet is cool, comfortable, and can sleep while you are driving. Once you arrive at your destination, create similar sleeping quarters at camp as at home. Be sure to make frequent stops for exercise, sniffing, and bathroom breaks.

To avoid frustration, always confirm that pets are permitted at planned destinations before you head out. Plus keep these items in the RV:

- Clean and filled water and food dishes
- ID collar labeled with your cell phone number
- Leash
- Pooper-scooper
- Records of shots, licenses, and the vet's phone number

PREDICTING WEATHER

Weather lore can be valuable on trips. Small signs provided by nature and wildlife can be translated to provide a variety of weather information. By paying attention, I can often provide weather forecasts for specific areas that are more reliable than the broad-brush approach provided by weather services. Here is the list I have compiled over the years:

When the grass is dry at morning light,
Look for rain before the night.

No dew on the grass at 7?
Expect sign of rain by 11.

Short notice, soon to pass.
Long notice, long it will last.

When the wind is from the east,
'Tis fit for neither man nor beast.

When the wind is from the south,
The rain is in its mouth.

When the wind is from the west,
Then it is the very best.

Red sky at night, sailors' delight.
Red sky in the morning, sailors take warning.

When all the cows are pointed north,
Within a day rain will come forth.

Onion skins very thin, mild winter coming in.
Onion skins very tough, winter's going to be
very rough.

When your boots make the squeak of snow,
Then very cold temperatures will surely show.

If a goose flies high, fair weather ahead.
If a goose flies low, foul weather will come
instead.

Washington

ROYALTY FREE / CORBIS

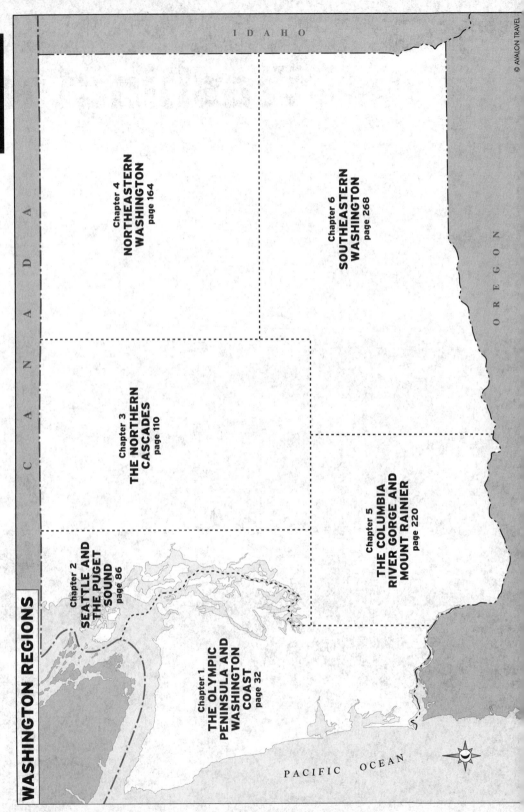

WASHINGTON

WASHINGTON REGIONS

CANADA

IDAHO

OREGON

PACIFIC OCEAN

© AVALON TRAVEL

Chapter 4
NORTHEASTERN WASHINGTON
page 164

Chapter 6
SOUTHEASTERN WASHINGTON
page 268

Chapter 3
THE NORTHERN CASCADES
page 110

Chapter 5
THE COLUMBIA RIVER GORGE AND MOUNT RAINIER
page 220

Chapter 2
SEATTLE AND THE PUGET SOUND
page 86

Chapter 1
THE OLYMPIC PENINSULA AND WASHINGTON COAST
page 32

THE OLYMPIC PENINSULA AND WASHINGTON COAST

◖ BEST RV PARKS AND CAMPGROUNDS

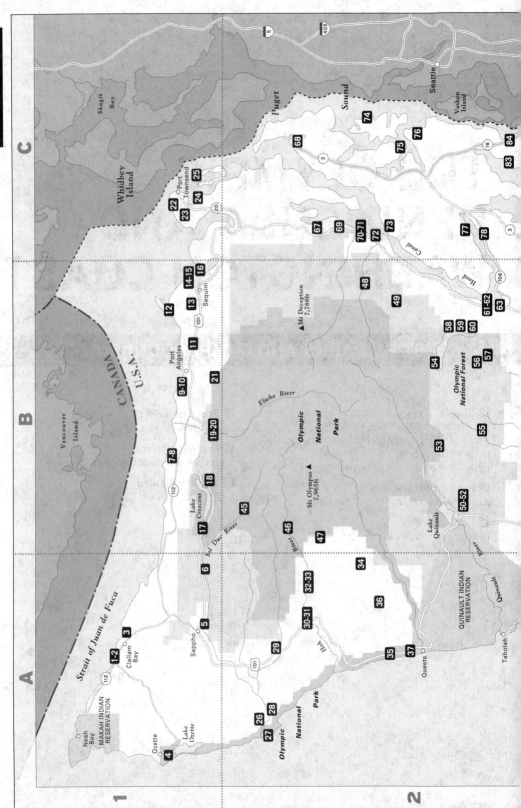

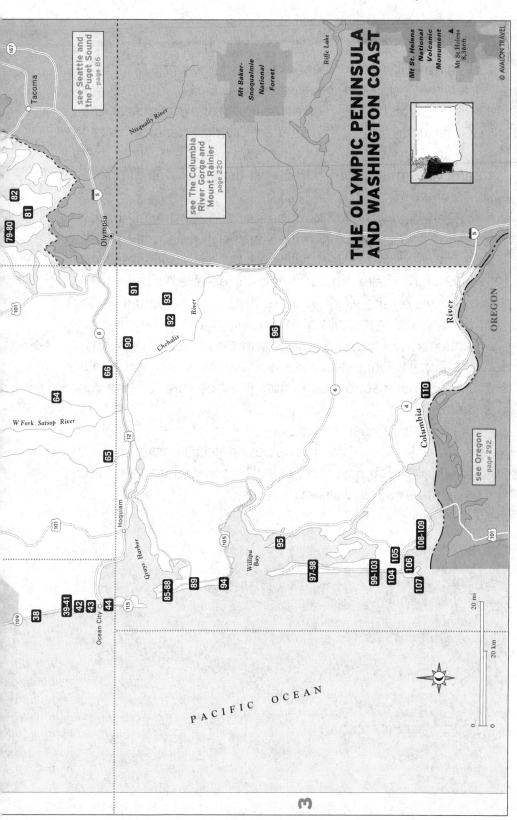

THE OLYMPIC PENINSULA AND WASHINGTON COAST

see Seattle and the Puget Sound
page 86

see The Columbia River Gorge and Mount Rainier
page 220

see Oregon
page 292

Mt St Helens National Volcanic Monument
▲ Mt St Helens 8,36oft

Mt Baker-Snoqualmie National Forest

Riffe Lake

OREGON

Tacoma

Olympia

Hoquiam

Ocean City

Nisqually River

Chehalis River

W Fork Satsop River

Grays Harbor

Willapa Bay

Columbia River

PACIFIC OCEAN

167

5

101

8

12

6

4

101

109

115

105

79-80 **81** **82**

64

65

66

90 **91** **92** **93**

96

110

38 **39-41** **42** **43** **44**

85-88 **89** **94** **95**

97-98 **99-103** **104** **105** **106** **107** **108-109**

20 mi

20 km

Vast, diverse, and beautiful, the Olympic Peninsula is like no other landscape in the world. Water borders the region on three sides: the Pacific Ocean to the west, the Strait of Juan de Fuca to the north, and the inlets of Hood Canal to the east. At its center are Olympic National Park and Mount Olympus, with rainforests on its slopes feeding rivers and lakes that make up the most dynamic river complex in America.

Only heavy rainfall for months on end from fall through spring and coastal fog in the summer have saved this area from a massive residential boom. At the same time, those conditions make it outstanding for getaways and virtually all forms of recreation. A series of stellar campgrounds ring the perimeter foothills of Mount Olympus, both in Olympic National Park and at the state parks and areas managed by the Department of Natural Resources. Your campsite can be your launch pad for adventure – just be sure to bring your rain gear.

In winter, campers can explore the largest array of steelhead rivers anywhere – there is no better place in America to fish for steelhead. Almost every one of these rivers provides campsites, often within walking distance of prime fishing spots.

1 VAN RIPER'S RESORT

Scenic rating: 7

on Clallam Bay in Sekiu
Map grid A1

Part of this campground hugs the waterfront and the other part sits on a hill overlooking the Strait of Juan de Fuca. Most sites are graveled, many with views of the strait. Other sites are grassy, without views. Note that some of the campsites are rented for the entire summer season. Hiking, fishing, and boating are among the options here, with salmon fishing being the principal draw. The beaches in the area, a mixture of sand and gravel, provide diligent rock hounds with agates and fossils.

RV sites, facilities: There are 100 sites with full or partial hookups (30 amps) for tents or RVs of any length. Some sites are pull-through. Other lodging includes two cabins, a mobile home, a house, and 12 motel rooms. Picnic tables are provided, and fire rings and cable TV are available at some sites. Restrooms with flush toilets and showers, drinking water, a dump station, firewood, and ice are available. A store, café, and coin laundry are located within one mile. Boat docks, launching facilities, and rentals are available. Leashed pets are permitted; no pets are allowed in cabins or other buildings.

Reservations, fees: Reservations are not accepted for campsites. Sites are $14–28 per night. Open April–September. Some credit cards are accepted.

Directions: Directions: From Port Angeles, take U.S. 101 west and drive 41 miles to Sappho Junction and Highway 113. Continue north on Highway 113 for nine miles to a fork with Highway 112. Take Highway 112 for two miles to Sekiu and Front Street. Turn right and drive 0.25 mile to the resort on the right.

Contact: Van Riper's Resort, 360/963-2334, www.vanripersresort.com.

2 OLSON'S RESORT

Scenic rating: 5

in Sekiu
Map grid A1

Olson's Resort is large with full services, and the nearby marina is salmon-fishing headquarters. In fact, the resort caters to anglers, offering all-day salmon fishing trips and boat moorage. Chartered trips can be arranged by reservation. A tackle shop, cabins, houses, and a motel are also available. Other recreation options include hiking, boating, and beachcombing for agates and fossils.

RV sites, facilities: There are 100 sites for tents or RVs of any length (no hookups), 45 sites with for tents or RVs of any length (full hookups), seven cabins, 14 motel rooms, and four houses available. Picnic tables are provided, and fire rings are available at some sites. Restrooms with flush toilets and showers, drinking water, a dump station, coin laundry, convenience store, bait and tackle, and ice are available. Boat docks, launching facilities, boat rentals, bait, tackle, fish-cleaning station, gear storage, gas, and diesel fuel are also available on-site. A restaurant is located one mile away. Leashed pets are allowed, with certain restrictions.

Reservations, fees: Reservations are not accepted. Sites are $18–28 per night, plus $2 per person per night for more than two people. Some credit cards are accepted. Open year-round.

Directions: From Port Angeles, drive 41 miles west on U.S. 101 to Sappho Junction and Highway 113. Continue north on Highway 113 for nine miles to a fork with Highway 112. Take Highway 112 for two miles to Sekiu and Front Street. Turn right and drive one block to the resort on the right.

Contact: Olson's Resort, 360/963-2311, www.olsonsresort.com.

WASHINGTON

3 SAM'S MOBILE HOME AND RV PARK

Scenic rating: 5

on Clallam Bay

Map grid A1

Sam's is an alternative to other resorts on Clallam Bay. It's a family-oriented park with grassy sites and many recreation options nearby. A mobile home park is adjacent to the RV park. Beaches are within walking distance. Those wanting to visit Cape Flattery, Hoh Rain Forest, or Port Angeles will find this a good central location.

RV sites, facilities: There are 21 sites, including some pull-through sites, with full hookups for RVs of any length and one tent site. Picnic tables are provided. Restrooms with flush toilets and showers, a dump station, cable TV, and coin laundry are available. Propane gas, gasoline, a store, café, and ice are located within one mile. Boat docks, launching facilities, and boat rentals are located within two miles. Leashed pets are permitted.

Reservations, fees: Reservations are accepted. RV sites are $24 per night, tent sites are $15 per night, $2 per person per night for more than two people. Credit cards are not accepted. Open year-round.

Directions: From Aberdeen, drive north on U.S. 101 for 119 miles to Sappho and Highway 113. Turn north on Highway 113 and drive nine miles to Clallam Bay and Highway 112. Continue straight on Highway 112 and drive into Clallam Bay. Just as you come into town, the park is on the right at 17053 Highway 112.

Contact: Sam's Mobile Home and RV Park, 360/963-2402.

4 OZETTE

Scenic rating: 6

on Lake Ozette in Olympic National Park

Map grid A1

Many people visit this site located on the shore of Lake Ozette just a few miles from the Pacific Ocean. Set close to a trailhead road and ranger station, with multiple trailheads nearby, this camp is a favorite for both hikers and boaters and is one of the first to fill in the park.

RV sites, facilities: There are 15 sites for tents or RVs up to 21 feet long. Picnic tables and fire grills are provided. Vault toilets, drinking water (summer season only), and garbage bins are available; pit toilets are available in winter. Some facilities are wheelchair accessible. Leashed pets are permitted.

Reservations, fees: Reservations are not accepted. Sites are $12 per night, plus a $15 national park entrance fee per vehicle. Open year-round, weather permitting.

Directions: From Port Angeles, drive west on U.S. 101 to the junction with Highway 112. Bear right on Highway 112 and drive to Hoko-Ozette Road. Turn left and drive 21 miles to the ranger station. The camp parking lot is across from the ranger station on the northwest corner of Lake Ozette.

Contact: Olympic National Park, 360/565-3130, fax 360/565-3147, www.nps.gov/olym.

5 BEAR CREEK MOTEL AND RV PARK

Scenic rating: 7

on Bear Creek

Map grid A1

This quiet little spot is set where Bear Creek empties into the Sol Duc River. It's private and developed, with a choice of sunny or shaded sites in a wooded setting. There are many recreation options in the area, including fishing, hunting, and nature and hiking trails leading to the ocean. Sol Duc Hot Springs is 25 miles north and well worth the trip. A restaurant next to the camp serves family-style meals.

RV sites, facilities: There are 10 pull-through sites for tents or RVs of any length (full hookups). Picnic tables and fire rings are provided. Restrooms with flush toilets and showers, drinking water, a dump station, a café, coin laundry, and firewood are available. A motel is also available on the premises. Boat-launching facilities are located within 0.5 mile. Leashed pets are permitted.

Reservations, fees: Reservations are not accepted. Sites are $25 per night. Some credit cards are accepted. Open year-round.

Directions: From Aberdeen, drive north on U.S. 101 to Forks. Continue past Forks for 15 miles to Milepost 205 (just past Sappho) to the park on the right at 205860 Highway 101 West.

Contact: Bear Creek Motel and RV Park, 360/327-3660, www.hungrybearcafémotel.com.

6 KLAHOWYA

Scenic rating: 9

on the Sol Duc River in Olympic National Forest
Map grid A1

Klahowya features great views of Lake Crescent and Mount Olympus. It's a good choice if you don't want to venture far from U.S. 101 yet want to retain the feel of being in Olympic National Forest. Set along the Sol Duc River, this 32-acre camp is pretty and wooded, with hiking trails in the area. A favorite, Kloshe Nanitch Trail, is across the river and leads up to a lookout on Snider Ridge overlooking Sol Duc Valley. Pioneer's Path Trail, an easy, wheelchair-accessible, 0.3-mile loop with interpretive signs, starts in the camp. Fishing for salmon and steelhead, in season, can be good about 0.25 mile downstream from camp; always check regulations. This camp gets medium use.

RV sites, facilities: There are 53 sites for tents or RVs up to 30 feet long and two walk-in sites requiring a 700-foot walk. Picnic tables and fire grills are provided. Drinking water, garbage bins, and vault and flush toilets are available. An amphitheater with summer interpretive programs is also available. A boat ramp is nearby. Some facilities are wheelchair accessible. Leashed pets are permitted.

Reservations, fees: Reservations are not accepted. Sites are $10 per night, $5 per night per additional vehicle. Open May–late September, weather permitting.

Directions: From U.S. 101 in Port Angeles, drive west for about 33 miles (10 miles west of Lake Crescent) to the campground on the right side of the road, close to Milepost 212. (Coming from the other direction on U.S. 101, drive eight miles east of Sappho to the campground.)

Contact: Olympic National Forest, Pacific Ranger District, 360/374-6522, fax 360/374-1250, www.fs.fed.us.

7 CRESCENT BEACH RV PARK

Scenic rating: 6

on the Strait of Juan de Fuca
Map grid B1

Set on a half-mile stretch of sandy beach, this campground makes a perfect weekend spot. Popular activities include swimming, fishing, surfing, sea kayaking, and beachcombing. It borders Salt Creek Recreation Area, with direct access available. Numerous attractions and recreation options are available in Port Angeles.

RV sites, facilities: There are 41 sites with full or partial hookups (30 and 50 amps) for tents or RVs of any length, and a grassy area for tent camping. Picnic tables and fire rings are provided. Restrooms with flush toilets and coin showers, coin laundry, pay phone, recreation field, and horseshoe pits are available. A dump station is nearby. Leashed pets are permitted.

Reservations, fees: Reservations are accepted. Sites are $35–40 per night, $5 per person per night for more than two people, $5 per extra vehicle (one-time fee per stay) unless towed, and $5 per night per pet. Weekly and monthly rates are available. Credit cards are accepted. Open year-round.

Directions: From U.S. 101 in Port Angeles, drive north five miles to a fork with Highway 112. Turn right (west) on Highway 112 and drive 10 miles to Camp Hayden Road (between Mileposts 53 and 54). Turn right on Camp Hayden Road and drive four miles to the park on the left, on the beach.

Contact: Crescent Beach RV Park, 360/928-3344, www.olypen.com/crescent.

8 SALT CREEK RECREATION AREA

Scenic rating: 8

near the Strait of Juan de Fuca

Map grid B1

The former site of Camp Hayden, a World War II–era facility, Salt Creek Recreation Area is a great spot for gorgeous ocean views, fishing, and hiking near Striped Peak, which overlooks the campground. Only a small beach area is available because of the rugged coastline, but there is an exceptionally good spot for tidepool viewing on the park's west side. The park covers 196 acres and overlooks the Strait of Juan de Fuca. It is known for its Tongue Point Marine Life Sanctuary. Recreation options include nearby hiking trails, swimming, fishing, horseshoes, and field sports. It's a good layover spot if you're planning to take the ferry out of Port Angeles to Victoria, British Columbia. The camp fills up quickly most summer weekends. Note that the gate closes at dusk.

RV sites, facilities: There are 92 sites, including 39 with partial hookups (30 and 50 amps) for tents or RVs of any length. Picnic tables and fire rings are provided. A restroom with flush toilets and coin showers, dump station, firewood, a playground, basketball and volleyball courts, and a covered picnic shelter that can be reserved are available. Some facilities are wheelchair accessible. Leashed pets are permitted.

Reservations, fees: Reservations are accepted only by downloading a reservation form at www.clallam.net/CountyParks. Sites are $18–24 per night, $5 per extra vehicle per night. Discount for Clallam County residents. Credit cards are not accepted. Open year-round.

Directions: From U.S. 101 in Port Angeles, drive north five miles to a fork with Highway 112. Turn right (west) on Highway 112 and drive 13 miles to Camp Hayden Road. Turn right (north) near Mile Marker 54 and drive 3.5 miles to the park entrance on the left.

Contact: Salt Creek Recreation Area, Clallam County, 360/928-3441, www.clallam.net/CountyParks.

9 PEABODY CREEK RV PARK

Scenic rating: 5

in Port Angeles

Map grid B1

This three-acre RV park is right in the middle of town but offers a wooded, streamside setting. Nearby recreation options include salmon fishing, an 18-hole golf course, marked biking trails, a full-service marina, and tennis courts. The park is within walking distance of shopping and ferry services.

RV sites, facilities: There is a grassy area for tents and 11 sites with full hookups (30 and 50 amps) for RVs of any length. Restrooms with flush toilets and coin showers, cable TV, ice, and a coin laundry are available. No open fires are allowed. A store and a café are located within one block. Boat docks and launching facilities are located within one mile. Leashed pets are permitted.

Reservations, fees: Reservations are accepted. RV sites are $25 per night, tent sites are $12 per night, $2 per person per night for more than two people. Credit cards are not accepted. Open year-round.

Directions: From U.S. 101 in Port Angeles, bear left on Lincoln Street and drive 0.5 mile to 2nd Street and the park entrance on the right.

Contact: Peabody Creek RV Park, tel./fax 360/457-7092 or 800/392-2361, www.peabodyrv.com.

10 AL'S RV PARK

Scenic rating: 8

near Port Angeles

Map grid B1

This campground is a good choice for RV owners. The campground is set in the country at about 1,000 feet elevation yet is centrally located and not far from the Strait of Juan de Fuca. Nearby recreation options include an 18-hole golf course and a full-service marina. Olympic National Park and the Victoria ferry are a short drive away.

RV sites, facilities: There are 31 sites with full hookups (20, 30, and 50 amps) for RVs up to 40 feet long and a grassy area for tents. No open fires are allowed. Picnic tables are provided. Restrooms with flush toilets and showers, drinking water, cable TV, modem access, and a coin laundry are available. A store, café, propane gas, and ice are located within 0.5 mile. Boat docks and launching facilities are located within two miles. Some facilities are wheelchair accessible. Leashed pets are permitted.

Reservations, fees: Reservations are not accepted. RV sites are $26 per night, tent sites are $18 per night, $3 per person per night for more than two people. Weekly and monthly rates available. Credit cards are not accepted. Open year-round.

Directions: From Port Angeles, take U.S. 101 east for two miles to North Brook Avenue. Turn left (north) on North Brook Avenue, then left (almost immediately) on Lees Creek Road, and drive 0.5 mile to the park on the right.

Contact: Al's RV Park, 360/457-9844.

11 KOA PORT ANGELES-SEQUIM

Scenic rating: 5

near Port Angeles

Map grid B1

This is a private, developed camp covering 13 acres in a country setting. A pleasant park, it features the typical KOA offerings, including a pool, recreation hall, and playground. Horseshoe pits and a sports field are also available. Hayrides are available in summer. Nearby recreation options include miniature golf, an 18-hole golf course, marked hiking trails, and tennis courts, and nearby side trips include Victoria, Butchart Gardens, and whale-watching tours.

RV sites, facilities: There are 24 tent sites, 82 sites with full and partial hookups (20, 30, and 50 amps) for tents or RVs of any length, 12 cabins, and one lodge. Some sites are pull-through. Picnic tables and fire pits are provided. Restrooms with flush toilets and showers, drinking water, cable TV, Wi-Fi and modem access, propane gas, firewood, dump station, convenience store, coin laundry, ice, a playground, miniature golf, organized activities, bicycle rentals, a recreation room, and a seasonal heated swimming pool and spa are available. A café is located within two miles. Some facilities are wheelchair accessible. Leashed pets are permitted.

Reservations, fees: Reservations are accepted at 800/562-7558. Sites are $25–90 per night, $6 per person per night for more than two people (ages six and older), and $6 per extra vehicle per night. Some credit cards are accepted. Open March–October.

Directions: In Port Angeles, go east on Highway 101 for seven miles to O'Brien Road. Turn right on O'Brien Road and drive half a block to the campground on the right.

Contact: KOA Port Angeles-Sequim, 360/457-5916, fax 360/452-4248, www.portangeleskoa.com.

12 DUNGENESS RECREATION AREA

Scenic rating: 5

near the Strait of Juan de Fuca

Map grid B1

This 216-acre park overlooks the Strait of Juan de Fuca and is set near the Dungeness National Wildlife Refuge. Quite popular, it fills up on summer weekends. A highlight, the refuge sits on a seven-mile spit with a historic lighthouse at its end. Bird-watchers often spot bald eagles in the wildlife refuge. There is a one-mile bluff trail, and equestrian trails are available. A 100-acre upland hunting area is open during season. Nearby recreation options include marked hiking trails, fishing, and golfing. The toll ferry at Port Angeles can take you to Victoria, British Columbia.

RV sites, facilities: There are 64 sites, including five pull-through sites, for tents or RVs of any length (no hookups) and eight hike-in/bike-in sites. Picnic tables and fire grills are provided. Restrooms with flush toilets and coin showers, drinking water, firewood, dump station, a playground, and a picnic area are available. A camp host is on-site. Some facilities are wheelchair accessible. Leashed pets are permitted.

Reservations, fees: Reservations are accepted only by downloading a reservation form at www.clallam.net/CountyParks. Sites are $18 per night, $5 per extra vehicle per night. Discount for Clallam County residents. Open February–September, with facilities limited to day use in the winter. Entrance gates close at dusk year-round.

Directions: From Sequim, drive north on U.S. 101 for four miles to Kitchen-Dick Road. Turn right (north) on Kitchen-Dick Road and drive three miles to the park on the left.

Contact: Dungeness Recreation Area, Clallam County, 360/683-5847, www.clallam.net/CountyParks/.

13 SEQUIM WEST INN & RV PARK

Scenic rating: 5

near the Dungeness River

Map grid B1

This two-acre camp is near the Dungeness River and within 10 miles of Dungeness National Wildlife Refuge. It's located in town and is a pleasant spot with full facilities and an urban setting. An 18-hole golf course and a full-service marina at Sequim Bay are close by.

RV sites, facilities: There are 27 pull-through sites for tents or RVs of any length (30 and 50 amp full hookups), 17 cabins, and 21 motel rooms. Picnic tables are provided. No open fires are allowed. Restrooms with flush toilets and showers, drinking water, cable TV, coin laundry, a pay phone, and ice are available. Propane gas, gasoline, a store, and a café are located within one mile. Leashed pets are permitted.

Reservations, fees: Reservations are accepted. Sites are $29–34 per night, $1 per person per night for more than two adults. Some credit cards are accepted. Open year-round.

Directions: From Sequim and U.S. 101, take the Washington Street exit and drive west on Washington Street for 2.7 miles to the park on the left.

Contact: Sequim West Inn & RV Park, 360/683-4144 or 800/528-4527, fax 360/683-6452, www.sequimwestinn.com

14 RAINBOW'S END RV PARK

Scenic rating: 6

on Sequim Bay

Map grid B1

This park on Sequim Bay is pretty and clean and features a pond (no fishing) and a creek running through the campground. There is a weekly potluck dinner in the summer, with free hamburgers and hot dogs, and a special landscaped area available for reunions, weddings, and other gatherings. Nearby recreation opportunities include an 18-hole golf course, marked bike trails, a full-service marina, and tennis courts.

RV sites, facilities: There are 10 tent sites and 42 sites with full hookups (30 and 50 amps), including some pull-through sites, for RVs of any length. Picnic tables are provided at all sites, and fire pits are provided at tent sites. Restrooms with flush toilets and showers, drinking water, dump station, cable TV, Wi-Fi and modem access, propane gas, firewood, coin laundry, and a clubhouse are available. A store, café, and ice are located within one mile. Leashed pets are permitted.

Reservations, fees: Reservations are accepted.

RV sites are $30–35 per night, tent sites are $17–20 per night, $2 per person per night for more than two people, $2 per extra vehicle per night. Weekly and monthly rates are available. Some credit cards are accepted. Open year-round.

Directions: From Sequim, drive west on U.S. 101 for one mile past the River Road exit to the park on the right (along the highway).

Contact: Rainbow's End RV Park, 360/683-3863, fax 360/683-2150, www.rainbowsend-rvpark.com.

15 SEQUIM BAY RESORT

Scenic rating: 5

on Sequim Bay
Map grid B1

This is Sequim Bay headquarters for salmon anglers. The camp is set in a wooded, hilly area, close to many activity centers and with an 18-hole golf course nearby.

RV sites, facilities: There are 42 sites with full hookups (15 and 30 amps) for RVs of any length (30 sites are pull-through) and eight cabins. Picnic tables are provided. Restrooms with flush toilets and showers, drinking water, cable TV, a community fire ring, Wi-Fi, and coin laundry are available. Boat docks and launching facilities are located across the street from the resort. Leashed pets are permitted, but not in cabins.

Reservations, fees: Reservations are accepted. Sites are $27–30 per night, $3 per person per night for more than two people. Credit cards are not accepted. Open year-round.

Directions: In Sequim, drive north 2.5 miles on U.S. 101 to Whitefeather Way (located between Mileposts 267 and 268). Turn right (north) on Whitefeather Way and drive 0.5 mile to West Sequim Bay Road. Turn left (west) and drive one block to the resort on the left.

Contact: Sequim Bay Resort, 360/681-3853, www.sequimbayresort.com.

16 SEQUIM BAY STATE PARK

Scenic rating: 8

on Sequim Bay
Map grid B1

Sequim translates to "quiet waters," which is an appropriate description of this area. Set in the heart of Washington's rain shadow, a region with far less rainfall than the surrounding areas, Sequim averages only 17 inches of rainfall a year. The 92-acre park features 4,909 feet of saltwater shoreline; two sandbars shield the park from the Strait of Juan de Fuca's rough waters. There is one mile of hiking trails.

RV sites, facilities: There are 60 sites for tents or RVs (no hookups), 16 sites with full hookups (30 amps) for RVs up to 40 feet long, three primitive tent sites, and one tent-only group site for up to 50 people (available mid-May–mid-September). Picnic tables and fire grills are provided. Restrooms with flush toilets and coin showers, drinking water, a dump station, a picnic area with kitchen shelters, an amphitheater, athletic fields, a basketball court, tennis courts, horseshoe pits, playground, and interpretive center are available. Boat docks, launching facilities, and boat mooring are also available. Some facilities are wheelchair accessible. Leashed pets are permitted.

Reservations, fees: Reservations are accepted at 888/CAMP-OUT (888/226-7688) or www.parks.wa.gov/reservations ($6.50–8.50 reservation fee). Sites are $21–28 per night, $14 per night for hike-in/bike-in sites, $10 per extra vehicle per night, and the group camp is $2.25 per person per night. Boat moorage is $0.50 per foot with a $10 minimum. Some credit cards are accepted. Open year-round.

Directions: From Olympia on I-5, turn north on U.S. 101 and drive 100 miles (near Sequim) to the park entrance on the right (along the highway). The park is located 3.5 miles southeast of the town of Sequim.

Contact: Sequim Bay State Park, 360/683-4235; state park information, 360/902-8844, www.parks.wa.gov.

WASHINGTON

17 FAIRHOLME

Scenic rating: 9

on Lake Crescent in Olympic National Park
Map grid B1

This camp is set on the shore of Lake Crescent, a pretty lake situated within the boundary of Olympic National Park, at an elevation of 580 feet. The campsites lie along the western end of the lake, in a cove with a boat ramp. Located less than one mile off U.S. 101, Fairholme gets heavy use during tourist months; some highway noise is audible at some sites. A naturalist program is often available in the summer. Waterskiing is permitted at Lake Crescent, but personal watercraft are prohibited.

RV sites, facilities: There are 88 sites for tents or RVs up to 21 feet long. Picnic tables and fire grills are provided. A dump station, restrooms with flush toilets (summer season), drinking water, and garbage bins are available. A store and café are located within one mile. Boat-launching facilities and rentals are nearby on Lake Crescent. Some facilities are wheelchair accessible. Leashed pets are permitted.

Reservations, fees: Reservations are not accepted. Sites are $12 per night, plus a $15 per vehicle national park entrance fee. Open April–October, weather permitting.

Directions: From Port Angeles, drive west on U.S. 101 for about 26 miles and continue along Lake Crescent to North Shore Road. Turn right and drive 0.5 mile to the camp on North Shore Road on the right.

Contact: Olympic National Park, 360/565-3130, fax 360/565-3147, www.nps.gov/olym.

18 LOG CABIN RESORT

Scenic rating: 10

on Lake Crescent in Olympic National Park
Map grid B1

Log Cabin Resort is one of my wife's favorite spots. This pretty camp along the shore of Lake Crescent is a good spot for boaters, as it features many sites near the water with excellent views. Fishing and swimming are two options at this family-oriented resort. It is home to a strain of Beardslee trout. Note the fishing is catch-and-release. Waterskiing is permitted, but no personal watercraft are allowed. A marked hiking trail traces the lake's 22-mile shoreline. This camp is extremely popular in the summer months; you may need to make reservations 6–12 months in advance.

RV sites, facilities: There are 38 sites with full hookups (20 and 30 amps) for RVs of any length, four tent sites, and 28 cabins. Some sites are pull-through. Picnic tables and fire barrels are provided. A dump station, restrooms with flush toilets and coin showers, a store, café, gift shop, coin laundry, Wi-Fi, firewood, ice, and a recreation field are available. Boat docks, launching facilities, and boat rentals and hydrobikes are available. Some facilities are wheelchair accessible. Leashed pets are permitted.

Reservations, fees: Reservations are accepted. RV sites are $40 per night, tent sites are $20 per night, $5 per person per night for more than two people, $2 per extra vehicle per night, $15 per pet per night. Some credit cards are accepted. Open Memorial Day weekend–September.

Directions: In Port Angeles, drive 18 miles north on U.S. 101 to East Beach Road. Turn right and drive three miles (along Lake Crescent) to the camp on the left.

Contact: Log Cabin Resort, 360/928-3325, fax 360/928-2088, www.logcabinresort.net.

19 ELWHA

Scenic rating: 7

on the Elwha River in Olympic National Park
Map grid B1

The Elwha River is the backdrop for this popular camp with excellent hiking trails close by in Olympic National Park. The elevation is 390 feet. Fishing is good in season at nearby Lake Mills; check regulations. Check at one of the visitors centers for maps and backcountry information.

RV sites, facilities: There are 40 sites for tents or RVs up to 21 feet long. Picnic tables and fire grills are provided. Restrooms with flush toilets, drinking water, and garbage bins are available. Some facilities are wheelchair accessible. Leashed pets are permitted.

Reservations, fees: Reservations are not accepted. Sites are $12 per night, plus a $15 national park entrance fee per vehicle. Open year-round.

Directions: From Port Angeles, drive west on U.S. 101 for about nine miles (just past Lake Aldwell) to the signed entrance road on the left. Turn left at the entrance road and drive three miles south along the Elwha River to the campground on the left.

Contact: Olympic National Park, 360/565-3130, fax 360/565-3147, www.nps.gov/olym.

20 ALTAIRE

Scenic rating: 8

on the Elwha River in Olympic National Park

Map grid B1

A pretty and well-treed camp with easy highway access, this camp is set on the Elwha River about one mile from Lake Mills. Fishing is good in season; check regulations. The elevation is 450 feet. Altaire also makes for a nice layover spot before taking the ferry at Port Angeles to Victoria, British Columbia.

RV sites, facilities: There are 30 sites for tents or RVs up to 21 feet long. Picnic tables and fire grills are provided. Restrooms with flush toilets, drinking water, and garbage bins are available. Some facilities are wheelchair accessible. Leashed pets are permitted.

Reservations, fees: Reservations are not accepted. Sites are $12 per night, plus a $15 national park entrance fee per vehicle. Open late May–October.

Directions: From Port Angeles, drive west on U.S. 101 for about nine miles (just past Lake Aldwell) to the signed entrance road on the left. Turn left at the signed entrance road and drive four miles south along the Elwha River.

Contact: Olympic National Park, 360/565-3130, fax 360/565-3147, www.nps.gov/olym.

21 HEART O' THE HILLS

Scenic rating: 9

in Olympic National Park

Map grid B1

Heart O' the Hills is nestled on the northern edge of Olympic National Park at an elevation of 1,807 feet. You can drive into the park on Hurricane Ridge Road and take one of numerous hiking trails. Little Lake Dawn is less than 0.5 mile to the west, but note that most of the property around this lake is privately owned. Naturalist programs are available in summer months.

RV sites, facilities: There are 105 sites for tents or RVs up to 21 feet long. Picnic tables and fire grills are provided. Restrooms with flush toilets, drinking water, and garbage bins are available. Some facilities are wheelchair accessible. Leashed pets are permitted.

Reservations, fees: Reservations are not accepted. Sites are $12 per night, plus a $15 national park entrance fee per vehicle. Open year-round, weather permitting.

Directions: From U.S. 101 in Port Angeles at Hurricane Ridge Road, turn left and drive five miles to the camp on the left. (Access roads can be impassable in severe weather.)

Contact: Olympic National Park, 360/565-3130, fax 360/565-3147, www.nps.gov/olym.

22 FORT WORDEN STATE PARK

Scenic rating: 9

in Port Townsend

Map grid C1

This park is set on the northeastern tip of the Olympic Peninsula, at the northern end of Port Townsend, on a high bluff with views of Puget Sound. Highlights here include great lookouts and two miles of beach trails over the Strait of Juan de Fuca as it feeds into Puget Sound. The park covers 433 acres at historic Fort Worden (on which construction was begun in 1897 and decommissioned in 1953) and includes buildings from the turn of the 20th century. It has 11,020 feet of saltwater shoreline. Recreation options include 12 miles of marked hiking and biking trails, including five miles of wheelchair-accessible trails. The Coast Artillery Museum, Rothschild House, Commanding Officers Quarters, and the Marine Science Center and Natural History Museum are open during the summer season. A ferry at Port Townsend will take you across the strait to Whidbey Island. Special note on reservations: This is an extremely popular park and campground and reservations are required online up to five months in advance or in person up to 11 months in advance.

RV sites, facilities: There are 80 sites with full or partial hookups (30 and 50 amps) for tents or RVs up to 75 feet long, including some pull-through sites, five hike-in/bike-in sites, one non-motorized boat-in site, and one group camp for up to 400 people. Other lodging includes 33 Victoria-era houses and three dormitories. Picnic tables and fire grills are provided. Restrooms with flush toilets and coin showers, drinking water, coin laundry, a store, dump station, and firewood are available. A restaurant, conference facilities, a sheltered amphitheater, athletic fields, and interpretive activities are available nearby. Boat docks, buoys, floats, and launching facilities are also nearby, as are several golf courses. Some facilities are wheelchair accessible. Leashed pets are permitted.

Reservations, fees: Reservations are accepted at 360/344-4431 or www.fortworden.net ($8 reservation fee). Sites are $36–42 per night, $13–22 per night for hike-in/bike-in and boat-in sites, $10 per extra vehicle per night, the group camp is $2.25 per person per night, and the dorms and houses are $135–408 per night. Boat moorage is $0.50 per foot with a $10 minimum. Open year-round.

Directions: From Port Townsend, take Highway 20 north through town to Kearney Street. Turn left on Kearney Street and drive to the first stop sign, at Blaine Street. Turn right on Blaine Street and drive to the next stop sign, on Cherry Street. Turn left at Cherry Street and drive 1.75 miles to the park entrance at the end of the road.

Contact: Fort Worden State Park, 360/344-4400, fax 360/385-7248; state park information, 360/902-8844, www.parks.wa.gov.

23 POINT HUDSON MARINA & RV PARK

Scenic rating: 5

in Port Townsend

Map grid C1

Point Hudson RV Park is located on the site of an old Coast Guard station near the beach in Port Townsend. This public facility is owned by the Port of Port Townsend. The park features ocean views and 2,000 feet of beach frontage. Known for its Victorian architecture, Port Townsend is called Washington's Victorian seaport. Fishing and boating are popular here, and nearby recreation opportunities include an 18-hole municipal golf course, a full-service marina, Old Fort Townsend State Park, Fort Flagler State Park, and Fort Worden State Park.

RV sites, facilities: There are 43 sites with full hookups (30 amps) for RVs of any length and two sites with no hookups. Some sites are pull-through. Picnic tables are provided at some sites. No fires are allowed. Restrooms with flush toilets and coin showers, drinking water, cable TV, Wi-Fi and modem access, three restaurants, and coin laundry are available. A 100-plus-slip marina is on-site. Leashed pets are permitted.

Reservations, fees: Reservations are accepted. Sites are $27–42 per night, $5 per extra vehicle per night. Some credit cards are accepted. Open year-round.

Directions: From Port Townsend on State Route 20, take the Water Street exit. Turn left (north) and continue (the road becomes Sims Way and then Water Street) to the end of Water Street at the marina. Turn left for registration.

Contact: Point Hudson Marina & RV Park, 360/385-2828 or 800/228-2803, fax 360/385-7331, www.portofpt.com.

24 OLD FORT TOWNSEND STATE PARK

Scenic rating: 10

near Quilcene

Map grid C1

This 367-acre park features a thickly wooded landscape, nearly 4,000 feet of saltwater shoreline on Port Townsend Bay, and 6.5 miles of hiking trails. Built in 1856, the historic fort is one of the oldest remaining in the state. The scenic campground has access to a good clamming beach (check regulations), and visitors can take two different short, self-guided walking tours. Note that the nearest boat ramps are at Port Townsend, Fort Flagler, and Hadlock. Mooring buoys are located just offshore of the park on the west side of Port Townsend Bay.

RV sites, facilities: There are 40 sites for tents or RVs up to 40 feet long, four hike-in/bike-in sites, and one group site for up to 80 people. Picnic tables and fire grills are provided. Restrooms with flush toilets and coin showers, drinking water, a playground, ball fields, boat buoys, firewood, a dump station, and a picnic area with a kitchen shelter are available. Some facilities are wheelchair accessible. Leashed pets are permitted.

Reservations, fees: Reservations are accepted at 360/344-4431 ($8.50 reservation fee). Sites are $19 per night, $10 per extra vehicle per night, hike-in/bike-in sites are $12 per night, and the group camp is $2.25 per person per night with a minimum of 20 people, plus $25 reservation fee. Open mid-April–mid-October, weather permitting.

Directions: From Port Townsend and State Route 20, drive south on State Route 20 for two miles to Old Fort Townsend Road. Turn left and drive 0.5 mile to the park entrance road.

Contact: Old Fort Townsend State Park, 360/344-4431 or 360/385-3595; state park information, 360/902-8844, www.parks. wa.gov.

25 FORT FLAGLER STATE PARK

Scenic rating: 10

near Port Townsend

Map grid C1

Historic Fort Flagler is a pretty and unique state park, set on Marrowstone Island east of Port Townsend. The camp overlooks Puget Sound and offers 19,100 feet of gorgeous saltwater shore. The park's 784 acres include five miles of trails for hiking and biking, an interpretive trail, and a military museum featuring gun batteries that are open in the summer. The RV sites are situated right on the beach, with views of the Olympic and Cascade Mountains. Anglers like this spot for year-round rockfish and salmon fishing, and crabbing and clamming are good in season (check regulations). Fort Flagler, under construction on some level from 1897 until its closure in 1953, offers summer tours. There is a youth hostel in the park.

RV sites, facilities: There are 116 tent sites, 57 sites with full hookups (30 amps) for RVs up to 50 feet long, two hike-in/bike-in sites, a vacation house, a group tent site for up to 40 people, and a group site for tents or RVs of any length for up to 100 people. Picnic tables and fire grills are provided. Restrooms with flush toilets and coin showers, drinking water, interpretive activities, a dump station, playground, picnic shelters that can be reserved, a camp store, boat buoys, moorage dock, and a launch are available. Some facilities are wheelchair accessible. Leashed pets are permitted.

Reservations, fees: Reservations are accepted at 888/CAMP-OUT (888/226-7688) or www. parks.wa.gov/reservations ($6.50–8.50 reservation fee). Sites are $21–28 per night, $10 per extra vehicle per night, $14 per night for hike-in/bike-in sites. The group sites are $2.25 per person per night, with a minimum of 20 people. The vacation house is $79–105 for up to four people and available year-round. Some credit cards are accepted. Open mid-May–October, weather permitting.

Directions: From Port Townsend at Highway 20, drive to Highway 19 (Airport cutoff) and make a slight left turn on Highway 19. Drive 3.5 miles to the traffic light at Ness Corner Road and turn left. Drive about one mile on Ness Corner Road to Oak Bay Road/Highway 116. Continue one mile on Highway 116 and turn left at Flagler Road to stay on Highway 116. Remain on Flagler Road and drive about 6.5 miles to the end of the road and the park and campground.

Contact: Fort Flagler State Park, 360/385-1259, fax 360/379-1746; state park information, 360/902-8844, www.parks.wa.gov.

26 MORA

Scenic rating: 8

in Olympic National Park
Map grid A2

At an elevation of 50 feet, this is a good out-of-the-way choice near the Pacific Ocean and the Olympic Coast Marine Sanctuary. The Quillayute River feeds into the ocean near the camp, and upstream lies the Bogachiel, a prime steelhead river in winter months. A naturalist program is available during the summer. This camp includes eight sites that require short walks, and several of them are stellar.

RV sites, facilities: There are 94 sites for tents or RVs up to 21 feet long and one walk-in site. Picnic tables and fire grills are provided. Restrooms with flush toilets, drinking water, garbage bins, and a dump station are available. Some facilities are wheelchair accessible. Leashed pets are permitted.

Reservations, fees: Reservations are not accepted. Sites are $12 per night, plus a $15 national park entrance fee per vehicle. Open year-round.

Directions: From Aberdeen, drive north on U.S. 101 for 108 miles to Forks. Continue past Forks for two miles to La Push Road/Highway 110. Turn left (west) and drive 12 miles to the campground on the left (well marked along the route).

Contact: Olympic National Park, 360/565-3130, fax 360/565-3147, www.nps.gov/olym.

27 LONESOME CREEK RV RESORT

Scenic rating: 8

near Forks
Map grid A2

This private, developed park is set along the Pacific Ocean and the coastal Dungeness National Wildlife Refuge. It has some of the few ocean sites available in the area and offers such recreation options as fishing, surfing, beachcombing, boating, whale-watching, and sunbathing.

RV sites, facilities: There are 42 sites for tents or RVs of any length (30 and 50 amp full hookups) and five tent sites; some sites are pull-through. Picnic tables and fire rings are provided. Restrooms with flush toilets and coin showers, a coin laundry, gasoline and propane gas, and a convenience store with a deli and ice are available. Boat docks, a marina, and launching facilities are located within one mile. Leashed pets are permitted.

Reservations, fees: Reservations are accepted and are recommended for the 18 oceanfront sites. Tent sites are $18 per night, and RV sites are $30–35 per night, with reduced rates in winter. Some credit cards are accepted. Open year-round.

Directions: From the town of Forks, drive north on U.S. 101 for two miles to La Push Road/Highway 110. Turn left (west) and drive 14 miles to the resort on the left.

Contact: Lonesome Creek RV Resort, 360/374-4338.

28 THREE RIVERS RESORT

Scenic rating: 8

on the Quillayute River
Map grid A2

Three Rivers Resort is a small, private camp is set at the junction of the Quillayute, Sol Duc, and Bogachiel Rivers. Situated above this confluence, about six miles upstream from the ocean, this pretty spot features wooded, spacious sites. Hiking and fishing are popular here, and there is a fishing guide service. Salmon and steelhead migrate upstream, best on the Sol Duc and Bogachiel Rivers; anglers should check regulations. The coastal Dungeness National Wildlife Refuge and Pacific Ocean, which often offer good whale-watching in the spring, are a short drive to the west. Hoh Rain Forest, a worthwhile side trip, is about 45 minutes away.

RV sites, facilities: There are 10 sites for tents or RVs of any length (no hookups), two sites with full or partial hookups (30 and 50 amps) for tents or RVs of any length, and six rental cabins. Picnic tables and fire rings are provided. Restrooms with flush toilets and coin showers, a convenience store, gas station, firewood, a café, coin laundry, firewood, and ice are available. Leashed pets are permitted.

Reservations, fees: Reservations are accepted. Tent sites are $14 per night, RV sites are $16–18 per night, $5 per pet per night. Some credit cards are accepted. Open year-round.

Directions: From Aberdeen, drive north on U.S. 101 for 108 miles to Forks. Continue past Forks for two miles to La Push Road/Highway 110. Turn left (west) and drive eight miles to the resort on the right.

Contact: Three Rivers Resort, 360/374-5300, www.northolympic.com/threerivers.

29 BOGACHIEL STATE PARK

Scenic rating: 6

on the Bogachiel River

Map grid A2 **BEST** (

A good base camp for salmon or steelhead fishing trips, this 123-acre park is set on the Bogachiel River, with marked hiking trails in the area. It can be noisy at times because a logging mill is located directly across the river from the campground. Also note that there is highway noise, and you can see the highway from some campsites. A one-mile hiking trail is nearby, and opportunities for wildlife-viewing are outstanding in the park. Hunting is popular

in the adjacent national forest. This region is heavily forested, with lush vegetation fed by an average of 140–160 inches of rain each year. This park was established in 1931.

RV sites, facilities: There are 36 sites for tents or RVs (no hookups), six sites with partial hookups (30 amps) for RVs up to 40 feet long, one hike-in/bike-in site, and one group tent camp with a covered shelter for up to 20 people. Picnic tables and fire grills are provided. Restrooms with flush toilets and coin showers, drinking water, dump station, and a picnic area are available. A primitive boat ramp is nearby. Some facilities are wheelchair accessible. Leashed pets are permitted.

Reservations, fees: Reservations are not accepted for individual sites but are required for the group camp at 360/374-6356. Sites are $19–25 per night, the hike-in/bike-in site is $12 per night, $10 per extra vehicle per night. The group site is $2.25 per person per night. Open year-round, with some sites closed in winter.

Directions: From Olympia on I-5, take Exit 104 and drive north on U.S. 101 to the Aberdeen/Highway 8 exit. Turn west on Highway 8 and drive 36 miles to Aberdeen. Continue through Aberdeen four miles to U.S. 101. Turn north on U.S. 101 and drive 102 miles to the park (six miles south of Forks) on the left side of the road.

Contact: Bogachiel State Park, Northwest Region, 360/374-6356; state park information, 360/902-8844, www.parks.wa.gov.

30 HOH RIVER RESORT

Scenic rating: 6

on the Hoh River

Map grid A2

This camp along U.S. 101 features a choice of grassy or graveled, shady sites and is most popular as a fishing camp. Although the Hoh River is nearby, you cannot see the river from the campsites. Marked hiking trails are in the area. This pleasant little park offers steelhead and salmon fishing in season as well as elk hunting in the fall. Horseshoe pits and a recreation field are available for campers.

RV sites, facilities: There are 23 sites with full or partial hookups for tents or RVs of any length and two cabins. Some sites are pull-through. Picnic tables and fire pits are provided. Restrooms with flush toilets and coin showers, a general store, propane gas, a gas station, firewood, and ice are available. A boat launch is available nearby. Leashed pets are permitted.

Reservations, fees: Reservations are accepted. RV sites are $15–25 per night, tent sites are $15 per night, $5 per person per night for more than two people. Some credit cards are accepted. Open year-round.

Directions: From Aberdeen, drive north on U.S. 101 for 90 miles to the resort (15 miles south of Forks) on the left.

Contact: Hoh River Resort, 360/374-5566, www.hohriverresort.com.

31 COTTONWOOD

Scenic rating: 8

on the Hoh River
Map grid A2

This primitive camp is set along the Hoh River, providing an alternative to Hoh Oxbow, Willoughby Creek, and Minnie Peterson campgrounds. Like Hoh Oxbow, Cottonwood offers the bonus of a boat launch. Its distance from the highway makes it quieter here. The camp is popular for anglers and hunters (in season).

RV sites, facilities: There are nine sites for tents or RVs up to 16 feet long. Picnic tables, fire grills, and tent pads are provided. There is no drinking water, and garbage must be packed out. Vault toilets and a boat launch are available. Some facilities are wheelchair accessible. Leashed pets are permitted.

Reservations, fees: Reservations are not accepted. There is no fee for camping. Open year-round.

Directions: From Olympia on I-5, take Exit 104 and drive north on U.S. 101 to the Aberdeen/Highway 8 exit. Turn west on Highway 8 and

drive 36 miles to Aberdeen. Continue through Aberdeen four miles to U.S. 101. Turn north on U.S. 101 and drive 92 miles to Oil City Road between Mileposts 177 and 178. Turn left (west) on Oil City Road and drive 2.3 miles. Turn left on Road H4060 (gravel) and drive one mile to the camp at the end of the road.

Contact: Department of Natural Resources, Olympic Region, 360/374-6131, fax 360/374-5446, www.dnr.wa.gov.

32 WILLOUGHBY CREEK

Scenic rating: 9

in Hoh Clearwater State Forest
Map grid A2

This little-known camp along Willoughby Creek and the Hoh River is tiny and rustic, with good fishing nearby for steelhead and salmon during peak migrations in season. The area gets heavy rainfall. Other campground options in the vicinity include Hoh Oxbow, Cottonwood, and Minnie Peterson.

RV sites, facilities: There are three campsites for tents or RVs up to 16 feet long. Picnic tables, fire grills, and tent pads are provided. Vault toilets are available. There is no drinking water, and garbage must be packed out. Leashed pets are permitted.

Reservations, fees: Reservations are not accepted. There is no fee for camping. Open year-round.

Directions: From Olympia on I-5, take Exit 104 and drive north on U.S. 101 to the Aberdeen/Highway 8 exit. Turn west on Highway 8 and drive 36 miles to Aberdeen. Continue through Aberdeen four miles to U.S. 101. Turn north on U.S. 101 and drive about 90 miles. Exit between Mileposts 178 and 179. At Hoh Rain Forest Road/Upper Hoh Valley Road, turn east and drive 3.5 miles to the campground on the right.

Contact: Department of Natural Resources, Olympic Region, 360/374-6131, fax 360/374-5446, www.dnr.wa.gov.

33 MINNIE PETERSON

Scenic rating: 9

on the Hoh River

Map grid A2

If location is everything, then it's why this campground has become popular. Minnie Peterson is set on the Hoh River on the edge of the Hoh Rain Forest. It's quite pretty, forested with Sitka spruce and western hemlock, and offers nice riverside sites. Bring your rain gear.

RV sites, facilities: There are eight sites for tents or RVs up to 16 feet long. Picnic tables, fire grills, and tent pads are provided. Vault toilets are available. There is no drinking water, and garbage must be packed out. Firing guns is prohibited. Some facilities are wheelchair accessible. Leashed pets are permitted.

Reservations, fees: Reservations are not accepted. There is no fee for camping. Open year-round.

Directions: From Olympia on I-5, take Exit 104 and drive north on U.S. 101 to the Aberdeen/ Highway 8 exit. Turn west on Highway 8 and drive 36 miles to Aberdeen. Continue through Aberdeen four miles to U.S. 101. Turn north on U.S. 101 and drive about 90 miles. Exit between Mileposts 178 and 179. At Hoh Rain Forest Road/Upper Hoh Valley Road, turn east and drive 4.5 miles to the campground on the left.

Contact: Department of Natural Resources, Olympic Region, 360/374-6131, fax 360/374-5446, www.dnr.wa.gov.

34 YAHOO LAKE

Scenic rating: 10

on Yahoo Lake

Map grid A2

Yahoo Lake is the most primitive and remote campground in the Olympic Region. A rustic trail surrounds the beautifully scenic and tranquil lake.

RV sites, facilities: There are three lakeside sites for tents or RVs up to 16 feet long. Picnic tables and fire grills are provided. A vault toilet is available. There is no drinking water. All garbage must be packed out. Leashed pets are permitted.

Reservations, fees: Reservations are not accepted. There is no fee for camping. Open year-round.

Directions: From Olympia on I-5, take Exit 104 and drive north on U.S. 101 to the Aberdeen/ Highway 8 exit. Turn west on Highway 8 and drive 36 miles to Aberdeen. Continue through Aberdeen four miles to U.S. 101. Turn north on U.S. 101 and drive about 60 miles to Milepost 147. Turn north on Clearwater Mainline Road and drive about 13 miles to C-3000 Road (a gravel one-lane road). Turn right and drive 0.8 mile to C-3100 Road. Turn right on C-3100 Road (paved one-lane, then gravel one-lane). Continue 6.1 miles to trailhead. This road is not recommended for motor home travel.

Contact: Department of Natural Resources, Olympic Region, 360/374-6131, www.dnr. wa.gov.

35 KALALOCH

Scenic rating: 10

in Olympic National Park

Map grid A2

This camp, located on a bluff above the beach, offers some wonderful oceanview sites—which explains its popularity. It can fill quickly. Like other camps set on the coast of the Olympic Peninsula, heavy rain in winter and spring is common, and it's often foggy in the summer. A naturalist program is offered in the summer months. There are several good hiking trails in the area; check out the visitors center for maps and information.

RV sites, facilities: There are 170 sites for tents or RVs up to 35 feet long, and one double site. The nearby Kalaloch Lodge offers a group site for tents or RVs that can accommodate up to 30 people. Picnic tables and fire grills are provided at Kalaloch Campground and the Kalaloch Lodge group camp. Restrooms with flush toilets, drinking water, garbage bins, and a dump station are available at Kalaloch Campground. A water tap and a pit toilet are available at the Kalaloch Lodge group site. A store and a restaurant are located within one mile of both campgrounds. Some facilities are wheelchair accessible. Leashed pets are permitted in the campground.

Reservations, fees: Reservations are accepted for the group site at 360/962-2271. Reservations are accepted June–September at 877/444-6777 or www.recreation.gov ($10 reservation fee). Single sites are $14–18 per night, the double site is $28–36 per night, and the national park entrance fee is $15 per vehicle. The group site is $20 per night for the first 10 people and $2 per person per night for each additional person, plus a $20 reservation fee. Open year-round.

Directions: From Aberdeen, drive north on U.S. 101 for 83 miles to the campground on the left. It is located near the mouth of the Kalaloch River five miles north of the U.S. 101 bridge over the Queets River.

Contact: Olympic National Park, 360/565-3130, fax 360/565-3147, www.nps.gov/olym.

36 COPPERMINE BOTTOM

Scenic rating: 9

on the Clearwater River

Map grid A2

Few tourists ever visit this primitive, hidden campground set on the Clearwater River, a tributary of the Queets River, which runs to the ocean. The river dory–launching facility is a bonus and makes this a perfect camp for anglers and river runners who want to avoid the usual U.S. 101 crowds. Salmon fishing is popular here during the migratory journey of the anadromous fish.

RV sites, facilities: There are nine campsites for tents or RVs up to 16 feet long. Picnic tables, fire grills, and tent pads are provided. Vault toilets, a group shelter, and a hand boat launch are available. There is no drinking water, and

garbage must be packed out. Leashed pets are permitted.

Reservations, fees: Reservations are not accepted. There is no fee for camping. Open year-round.

Directions: From Olympia on I-5, take Exit 104 and drive north on U.S. 101 to the Aberdeen/Highway 8 exit. Turn west on Highway 8 and drive 36 miles to Aberdeen. Continue through Aberdeen four miles to U.S. 101. Turn north on U.S. 101 and drive about 60 miles to Milepost 147. Turn north on Clearwater Mainline Road and drive about 14 miles to C-3000 Road. Turn right (east) on C-3000 Road (a gravel one-lane road) and drive two miles to C-1010 Road. Turn right on C-1010 Road and drive one mile. The camp is on the left.

Contact: Department of Natural Resources, Olympic Region, 360/374-6131, fax 360/374-5446, www.dnr.wa.gov.

37 SOUTH BEACH

Scenic rating: 6

in Olympic National Park

Map grid A2

Little South Beach campground is located in an open field with little shade or privacy, but the payoff is that it is just a stone's throw from the ocean.

RV sites, facilities: There are 50 sites for tents or RVs up to 21 feet long. Picnic tables and fire grills are provided. Drinking water and non-accessible restrooms with flush toilets are available during summer. In winter, only pit toilets are available, and there is no drinking water. Leashed pets are permitted in the campground.

Reservations, fees: Reservations are not accepted. Sites are $10 per night, plus a $15 national park entrance fee per vehicle. Open late May–mid-September.

Directions: From Aberdeen, drive north on U.S. 101 for 65 miles to the campground.

Contact: Olympic National Park, 360/565-3130, fax 360/565-3147, www.nps.gov/olym.

38 PACIFIC BEACH STATE PARK

Scenic rating: 10

near Pacific Beach

Map grid A2   **BEST (**

This is the only state park campground in Washington where you can see the ocean from your campsite. Set on just nine acres, within the town of Pacific Beach, it boasts 2,300 feet of beachfront. This spot is great for long beach walks, although it can be windy, especially in the spring and early summer. Because of those winds, this is a great place for kite-flying. Clamming (for razor clams) is permitted only in season. Note that rangers advise against swimming or body surfing because of strong riptides. Vehicle traffic is allowed seasonally on the uppermost portions of the beach, but ATVs are not allowed in the park, on the beach, or on sand dunes. This camp is popular and often fills up quickly.

RV sites, facilities: There are 32 developed tent sites and 32 sites with partial hookups (30 amps) for RVs up to 60 feet long. Picnic tables are provided. Restrooms with flush toilets and coin showers, drinking water, a dump station, and a picnic area are available. No fires are permitted, except on the beach; charcoal and propane barbecues are allowed in campsites. Some facilities are wheelchair accessible. Leashed pets are permitted.

Reservations, fees: Reservations are accepted at 888/CAMP-OUT (888/226-7688) or www. parks.wa.gov/reservations ($6.50–8.50 reservation fee). Sites are $21–27 per night, $10 per night for hike-in/bike-in sites, and $10 per extra vehicle per night. Some credit cards are accepted. Open year-round.

Directions: From Hoquiam, drive north on State Route 109 for 37 miles to Pacific Beach and Main Street. Turn left on Main Street and drive 0.5 mile to 2nd Street. Turn left on 2nd Street and continue to the park entrance.

Contact: Pacific Beach State Park, 360/276-4297; state park information, 360/902-8844, www.parks.wa.gov.

39 DRIFTWOOD ACRES OCEAN CAMPGROUND

Scenic rating: 7

in Copalis Beach

Map grid A2

Driftwood Acres spreads over some 150 acres and features secluded tent sites and large RV sites. It is located along a tidal river basin, out of the wind. Most find the rustic camp family friendly, with its beach access, old-growth forest, and marked hiking trails. A bundle of firewood is provided for each night's stay. Clamming in season is often good in the area. Additional facilities within seven miles include an 18-hole golf course and a riding stable.

RV sites, facilities: There are 20 tent sites and 17 sites with partial hookups (20 and 30 amps) for tents or RVs of any length. Restrooms with flush toilets and coin showers, drinking water, a free bundle of firewood per day, a recreation hall, and dump station are available. A clam-cleaning station is nearby. Propane gas, a store, café, and ice are located within one mile. Leashed pets are permitted with certain restrictions.

Reservations, fees: Reservations are accepted. Sites are $30 per night, $5 per extra vehicle per night. Some credit cards are accepted. Open year-round.

Directions: From Hoquiam, drive west on State Route 109 for 21 miles to Copalis Beach. Continue 0.5 mile north to the camp on the left, between Mileposts 21 and 22.

Contact: Driftwood Acres Ocean Campground, 360/289-3484 or 877/298-1916, www.drift-woodacres.com.

40 SURF AND SAND RV PARK

Scenic rating: 4

in Copalis Beach

Map grid A2

Although not particularly scenic, this five-acre park is a decent layover for an RV vacation and will do the job if you're tired and ready to get off U.S. 101. It has beach access, possible with a 15-minute walk; the surrounding terrain is flat and grassy. Facilities are serviceable, but in need of updating.

RV sites, facilities: There are 16 tent sites and 50 sites with full or partial hookups (30 amps) for RVs of any length. Some sites are pull-through. Picnic tables and fire grills are provided. Restrooms with flush toilets and showers, drinking water, cable TV, coin laundry, a recreation room with kitchen facilities, and ice are available. Propane gas is available within one mile. Leashed pets are permitted.

Reservations, fees: Reservations are accepted. RV sites are $27–40 per night, tent sites are $15 per night, $4 per extra vehicle per night. Some credit cards are accepted. Open year-round.

Directions: From Hoquiam, drive west on State Route 109 for 21 miles to Copalis Beach and Heath Road. Turn left (west) on Heath Road and drive 0.2 mile to the park.

Contact: Surf and Sand RV Park, 360/289-2707 or 866/787-2751.

41 RIVERSIDE RV RESORT

Scenic rating: 8

near Copalis Beach
Map grid A2

River access is a bonus at this nice and clean six-acre resort. Most sites have a river view. Salmon fishing can be good in the Copalis River, and a boat ramp is available nearby for anglers. Other options include swimming and beachcombing.

RV sites, facilities: There are 56 sites with full hookups (30 amps) for RVs of any length and 15 tent sites. Some sites are pull-through. Picnic tables and fire grills are provided. Restrooms with flush toilets and coin showers, drinking water, a dump station, a spa, modem access, firewood, and a recreation hall are available. A café is located within one mile. A boat dock, launching facilities, and boat rentals are nearby. Leashed pets are permitted.

Reservations, fees: Reservations are accepted. Tent sites are $16 per night, RV sites are $21 per night, $2 per person per night for more than two people. Some credit cards are accepted. Open year-round.

Directions: From Hoquiam, drive west on State Route 109 for 22 miles to Copalis Beach. The park is off the highway on the left.

Contact: Riverside RV Resort, 360/289-2111 or 800/500-2111, www.riversidervresort.net.

42 TIDELANDS RESORT

Scenic rating: 7

near Copalis Beach
Map grid A2

This flat, wooded resort covers 47 acres and provides beach access and a great ocean view. It's primarily an RV park, and the sites are pleasant. Ten sites are set on sand dunes, while the rest are in a wooded area. In the spring, azaleas and wildflowers abound. Horseshoe pits and a sports field offer recreation possibilities. Though more it's remote than at the other area campgrounds, clamming is an option in season. Various festivals are held in the area from spring through fall.

RV sites, facilities: There are 25 sites for tents or RVs (no hookups), 35 sites with full or partial hookups (20 and 30 amps) for tents or RVs of any length, one rental trailer, and three cottages. Some sites are pull-through. Picnic tables and fire pits are provided. Restrooms with flush toilets and coin showers, drinking water, a dump station, firewood, ice, cable TV, and a playground are available. A café is located within one mile. A casino and horseback riding are within five miles. A golf course is within six miles. Leashed pets are permitted.

Reservations, fees: Reservations are accepted. RV sites are $26–30 per night, tent sites are $20–21. Some credit cards are accepted. Open year-round.

Directions: From Hoquiam, drive west on State Route 109 for about 20 miles to the resort on the left. It is located between Mileposts 20 and 21, about one mile south of Copalis Beach.

Contact: Tidelands Resort, 360/289-8963, www.tidelandsresort.com.

43 OCEAN MIST RESORT

Scenic rating: 9

on Conners Creek

Map grid A2

Always call to determine whether space is available before planning a stay here. This is a membership resort RV campground, and members always come first. If space is available, they will rent sites to the public. Surf fishing is popular in the nearby Pacific Ocean, while the Copalis River offers salmon fishing and canoeing opportunities. It's about a one-block walk to the beach. There's a golf course within five miles.

RV sites, facilities: There are 107 sites for RVs up to 40 feet long, most with full hookups (30 amps), a grassy area for tents, and two trailers. Picnic tables are provided. Restrooms with flush toilets and showers, drinking water, cable TV, modem access, dump station, two community fire pits, a spa, clubhouse, and coin laundry are available. A grocery store is within one mile in Ocean City. Leashed pets are permitted.

Reservations, fees: Reservations are accepted in the summer. Tent sites are $15 per night, and RV sites are $35 per night. Some credit cards are accepted. Open year-round.

Directions: From Hoquiam, drive west on State Route 109 for 19 miles to the resort on the left (one mile north of Ocean City).

Contact: Ocean Mist Resort, 360/289-3656, fax 360/289-2807, www.kmresorts.com.

44 OCEAN CITY STATE PARK

Scenic rating: 9

near Hoquiam

Map grid A2

This 170-acre oceanfront camp, an excellent example of coastal wetlands and dune succession, features ocean beach, dunes, and dense thickets of pine surrounding freshwater marshes. The Ocean Shores Interpretive Center is located on the south end of Ocean Shores near the marina (open summer season only). This area is part of the Pacific Flyway, and the migratory route for gray whales and other marine mammals lies just offshore. Spring wildflowers are excellent and include lupine, buttercups, and wild strawberry. This is also a good area for surfing and kite-flying, with springs typically windy. Beachcombing, clamming, and fishing are possibilities at this park. An 18-hole golf course is nearby.

RV sites, facilities: There are 149 sites for tents or self-contained RVs (no hookups), 29 sites with full hookups (30 amps) for RVs up to 50 feet long; some sites are pull-through. There are also three hike-in/bike-in sites, and two group camps for tents only for 20–30 people each. Picnic tables and fire rings are provided. Restrooms with flush toilets and coin showers, drinking water, dump station, sheltered picnic area, and firewood are available. A ball field and amphitheater are available nearby. A camp host is on-site. Some facilities are wheelchair accessible. Leashed pets are permitted.

Reservations, fees: Reservations are accepted at 888/226-7688 (CAMP-OUT) or www.parks. wa.gov/reservations ($6.50–8.50 reservation fee). Sites are $21–28 per night, $10 per extra vehicle per night, hike-in/bike-in sites are $14 per night, and group sites are $2.25 per person, plus $25 for reservations. Some credit cards are accepted. Open year-round.

Directions: From Hoquiam, drive northwest on State Route 109 for 16 miles to State Route 115. Turn left and drive 1.2 miles south to the park on the right (1.5 miles north of Ocean Shores).

Contact: Ocean City State Park, 360/289-3553, fax 360/289-9405; state park information, 360/902-8844, www.parks.wa.gov.

45 SOL DUC

Scenic rating: 10

on the Sol Duc River in Olympic National Park

Map grid B2

This site is a nice hideaway, with nearby Sol Duc Hot Springs a highlight. The problem is that this camp is very popular. It fills up quickly on weekends, and a fee is charged to use the hot springs, which have been fully developed since the early 1900s. The camp is set at 1,680 feet along the Sol Duc River.

RV sites, facilities: There are 82 sites for tents or RVs up to 21 feet long, and one group site for up to 24 people. Picnic tables and fire grills are provided. Restrooms with flush toilets and drinking water are available in the summer season; there is no water in the winter season, but pit toilets are available. A dump station is available nearby, and a store and café are within one mile. Some facilities are wheelchair accessible. Leashed pets are permitted.

Reservations, fees: Reservations accepted for the group site only at 360/327-3534 (Apr. 16–Oct. 31) and at 360/928-3380 (Mar. 1–Apr. 15). Sites are $14 per night, plus a $15 national park entrance fee per vehicle. The group site is $1 per person per night, plus a $20 reservation fee. Open May–late October, with limited facilities in winter.

Directions: From Port Angeles, continue on U.S. 101 for 27 miles, just past Lake Crescent. Turn left at the Sol Duc turnoff and drive 12 miles to the camp.

Contact: Olympic National Park, 360/565-3130, fax 360/565-3147, www.nps.gov/olym.

46 HOH

Scenic rating: 10

in Olympic National Park

Map grid B2

This camp at a trailhead leading into the interior of Olympic National Park is located in the beautiful heart of a temperate, old-growth rainforest. Hoh Oxbow, Cottonwood, Willoughby Creek, and Minnie Peterson campgrounds are nearby, set downstream on the Hoh River, outside national park boundaries. In the summer, there are naturalist programs, and a visitors center is nearby. This is one of the most popular camps in the park. The elevation is 578 feet.

RV sites, facilities: There are 88 sites for tents or RVs up to 21 feet long. Picnic tables and

fire grills are provided. Garbage bins and restrooms with flush toilets and drinking water are available. A dump station is nearby. Some facilities are wheelchair accessible. Leashed pets are permitted.

Reservations, fees: Reservations are not accepted. Sites are $12 per night, plus a $15 national park entrance fee per vehicle. Open year-round.

Directions: From Aberdeen, drive north on U.S. 101 for about 90 miles to Milepost 176. Turn east on Hoh River Road and drive 19 miles to the campground on the right (near the end of the road).

Contact: Olympic National Park, 360/565-3130, fax 360/565-3147, www.nps.gov/olym.

47 SOUTH FORK HOH

Scenic rating: 10

in Hoh Clearwater State Forest

Map grid B2

This rarely used, beautiful camp set along the cascading South Fork of the Hoh River is way out there. It's tiny and primitive but offers a guarantee of peace and quiet, something many U.S. 101 cruisers would cheerfully give a limb for after a few days of fighting crowds. The South Fork Trailhead in Olympic National Park is two miles away. When conditions are right, fishing for steelhead can be excellent (check regulations).

RV sites, facilities: There are three sites for tents or RVs up to 16 feet long. Picnic tables, fire grills, and tent pads are provided. Vault toilets are available. There is no drinking water, and garbage must be packed out. Leashed pets are permitted.

Reservations, fees: Reservations are not accepted. There is no fee for camping. Open year-round.

Directions: From Olympia on I-5, take Exit 104 and drive north on U.S. 101 to the Aberdeen/Highway 8 exit. Turn west on Highway 8 and drive 36 miles to Aberdeen. Continue through Aberdeen four miles to U.S. 101. Turn north on U.S. 101 and drive about 94 miles. Exit at Milepost 176. At Hoh Mainline Road turn east and drive 6.5 miles. Turn left on Road H1000 and drive 7.5 miles to the campground on the right. Obtaining a Department of Natural Resources (DNR) map is advised.

Contact: Department of Natural Resources, Olympic Region, 360/374-6131, fax 360/374-5446, www.dnr.wa.gov.

48 COLLINS

Scenic rating: 7

on the Duckabush River in Olympic National Forest

Map grid B2

Most vacationers cruising U.S. 101 don't have a clue about this quiet spot set on a great launch point for adventure, yet it's only five or six miles from the highway. This four-acre camp is located on the Duckabush River at 200 feet elevation. It has small, shaded sites, river access nearby, and plenty of fishing and hiking; check fishing regulations. Just one mile from camp is Duckabush Trail, which connects to trails in Olympic National Park. Murhut Falls Trail starts about three miles from the campground, providing access to a 0.8-mile trail to the falls. It's a 1.5-mile drive to Dosewallips State Park and a 30- to 35-minute drive to Olympic National Park.

RV sites, facilities: There are six tent sites and 10 sites for RVs up to 21 feet long. Picnic tables and fire rings are provided. Vault toilets are available, but there is no drinking water. Garbage must be packed out. Leashed pets are permitted.

Reservations, fees: Reservations are not accepted. Sites are $14 per night. Open May–September, weather permitting.

Directions: From Olympia on I-5, drive north on U.S. 101 for 59 miles to Forest Road 2510 (near Duckabush). Turn left on Forest Road 2510 and drive six miles west to the camp on the left.

Contact: Olympic National Forest, Hood Canal Ranger District, Quilcene Office, 360/765-2200, fax 360/765-2202, www.fs.fed.us.

49 HAMMA HAMMA

Scenic rating: 7

on the Hamma Hamma River in Olympic National Forest

Map grid B2

This camp is set on the Hamma Hamma River at an elevation of 600 feet. It's small and primitive, but it can be preferable to some of the developed camps on the U.S. 101 circuit. The Civilian Conservation Corps is memorialized in a wheelchair-accessible interpretive trail that begins in the campground and leads 0.25 mile along the river. The sites are set among conifers and hardwoods.

RV sites, facilities: There are 15 sites for tents or RVs up to 22 feet long. Picnic tables and fire rings are provided. Vault toilets are available. There is no drinking water, and garbage must be packed out. (In season, drinking water is available two miles away at Lena Creek Campground.) Some facilities are wheelchair accessible. Leashed pets are permitted.

Reservations, fees: Reservations are not accepted. Sites are $10 per night, $5 per night per additional vehicle. Open May–September, weather permitting.

Directions: From Olympia on I-5, turn north on U.S. 101 and drive 37 miles to Hoodsport. Continue on U.S. 101 for 14 miles north to Forest Road 25. Turn left on Forest Road 25 and drive seven miles to the camp on the left side of the road.

Contact: Olympic National Forest, Hood Canal Ranger District, Quilcene Office, 360/765-2200, fax 360/765-2202, www.fs.fed.us.

50 WILLABY

Scenic rating: 8

on Lake Quinault in Olympic National Forest

Map grid B2

This pretty, 14-acre wooded camp is set on the shore of Lake Quinault, which covers about six square miles. Part of the Quinault Indian Reservation, the camp is at 200 feet elevation, adjacent to where Willaby Creek empties into the lake. A boating permit and fishing license are required before fishing on the lake. The campsites vary, with some open and featuring lake views, while others are more private, with no views. The tree cover consists of Douglas fir, western red cedar, western hemlock, and big leaf maple. The forest floor is covered with wall-to-wall greenery, with exceptional moss growth. Quinault Rain Forest Nature Trail and the Quinault National Recreation Trail System are nearby. This camp is operated by a concessionaire.

RV sites, facilities: There are 32 sites for tents or RVs up to 16 feet long and two walk-in sites. Picnic tables and fire pits are provided. Drinking water, garbage bins, and restrooms with flush toilets are available. Launching facilities and rentals are available at nearby Lake Quinault. Some facilities are wheelchair accessible. Leashed pets are permitted.

Reservations, fees: Reservations are not accepted. Sites are $14 per night, $5 per extra vehicle per night. Open Memorial Day weekend–September.

Directions: From Aberdeen, drive north on U.S. 101 for 42 miles to the Lake Quinault-South Shore turnoff. Turn right (northeast) on South Shore Road and drive 1.5 miles to the camp on the southern shore of the lake.

Contact: Olympic National Forest, Pacific Ranger District, Quinault Office, 360/288-2525, fax 360/288-0286, www.fs.fed.us.

51 FALLS CREEK

Scenic rating: 8

on Lake Quinault in Olympic National Forest

Map grid B2   **BEST (**

This scenic, wooded three-acre camp is set where Falls Creek empties into Quinault Lake. A canopy of lush big leaf maple hangs over the campground. The campground features both drive-in and walk-in sites, with the latter requiring about a 125-yard walk. Quinault Rain Forest Nature Trail and the Quinault National

Recreation Trail System are nearby. The camp is located adjacent to the Quinault Ranger Station and historic Lake Quinault Lodge at an elevation of 200 feet.

RV sites, facilities: There are 10 walk-in sites and 21 sites for tents or RVs up to 16 feet long. Picnic tables and fire pits are provided. Drinking water and restrooms with flush toilets are available. A camp host has firewood for sale nearby. A picnic area, boat launching facilities, and boat rentals are available at Lake Quinault. Some facilities are wheelchair accessible. Leashed pets are permitted.

Reservations, fees: Reservations are not accepted. Sites are $12–15 per night, $5 per extra vehicle per night. Open Memorial Day weekend–Labor Day weekend.

Directions: From Aberdeen, drive north on U.S. 101 for 42 miles to the Lake Quinault-South Shore turnoff. Turn right (northeast) on South Shore Road and drive 2.5 miles to the camp on the southeast shore of Lake Quinault. Make a very sharp left turn into the campground.

Contact: Olympic National Forest, Pacific Ranger District, Quinault Office, 360/288-2525, fax 360/288-0286, www.fs.fed.us.

52 GATTON CREEK WALK-IN

Scenic rating: 9

on Lake Quinault in Olympic National Forest

Map grid B2

This five-acre wooded camp is set on the shore of Lake Quinault (elevation 200 feet), where Gatton Creek empties into it. Reaching the campsites requires about a 100-yard walk from the parking area. The camp features great views across the lake to the forested slopes of Olympic National Park. The lake is part of the Quinault Indian Nation, which has jurisdiction here. Rules allow a 24-mph speed limit on the lake, but no towing and no personal watercraft. Salmon fishing is catch-and-release only, and fishing opportunities vary from year to year—always check regulations. Lake Quinault covers about six square miles. Quinault Rain Forest

Nature Trail and the Quinault National Recreation Trail System are nearby. About nine miles of loop trails are accessible here. This camp, like the others on the lake, is concessionaire operated.

RV sites, facilities: There are 15 walk-in sites for tents and 10 overflow sites for RVs up to 24 feet long. Picnic tables and fire pits are provided at the tent sites. Vault toilets, firewood, and a picnic area are available. Some facilities are wheelchair accessible. Leashed pets are permitted.

Reservations, fees: Reservations are not accepted. Sites are $12 per night. Open late May–early October, weather permitting.

Directions: From Aberdeen, drive north on U.S. 101 for 42 miles to the Lake Quinault-South Shore turnoff. Turn right (northeast) on South Shore Road and drive three miles to the camp on the southeast shore of Lake Quinault.

Contact: Olympic National Forest, Pacific Ranger District, Quinault Office, 360/288-2525, fax 360/288-0286, www.fs.fed.us.

53 CAMPBELL TREE GROVE

Scenic rating: 8

on the Humptulips River in Olympic National Forest

Map grid B2

This 14-acre camp is set amid dense, old-growth forest featuring stands of both conifers and hardwoods, with licorice ferns growing on the trunks and branches of the big leaf maples. The camp is a favorite for hikers, with trailheads nearby that provide access to the Colonel Bob Wilderness. One of the best, the 3,400-foot climb to the Colonel Bob Summit provides an 8.5-mile round-trip accessible from the Pete's Creek Trailhead, which is located a couple of miles south of camp on Forest Road 2204. Note that much of this summit hike is a great butt-kicker. The West Fork of the Humptulips River runs near the camp, and Humptulips Trail provides access. Fishing is an option here as well; check state regulations.

RV sites, facilities: There are eight tent sites

and three sites for RVs up to 16 feet long. Picnic tables and fire grills are provided. Vault toilets, garbage bins and drinking water (well water) are available. Some facilities are wheelchair accessible. Leashed pets are permitted.

Reservations, fees: Reservations are not accepted. There is no fee for camping. Open May–October, weather permitting.

Directions: From Aberdeen, drive north on U.S. 101 for 22 miles to Humptulips and continue for another five miles to Forest Road 22 (Donkey Creek Road). Turn right and drive eight miles to Forest Road 2204. Turn left (north) and drive nine miles to the campground.

Contact: Olympic National Forest, Pacific Ranger District, Quinault Office, 360/288-2525, fax 360/288-0286, www.fs.fed.us.

54 STAIRCASE

Scenic rating: 9

on the North Fork of the Skokomish River in Olympic National Park

Map grid B2

This camp is located near the Staircase Rapids of the North Fork of the Skokomish River, about one mile from where it empties into Lake Cushman. The elevation is 765 feet. A major trailhead at the camp leads to the backcountry of Olympic National Park, and other trails are nearby. Hiking trails along the river can be accessed nearby. Stock facilities are also available nearby. Note that Staircase Road is closed in winter.

RV sites, facilities: There are 47 sites for tents or RVs up to 21 feet long. Picnic tables and fire grills are provided. Restrooms with flush toilets and drinking water are available during the summer season. In winter, pit toilets are available, but there is no drinking water. Leashed pets are permitted in camp.

Reservations, fees: Reservations are not accepted. Sites are $12 per night, plus a $15 national park entrance fee per vehicle. Open year-round, with limited winter services.

Directions: From Olympia on I-5, take U.S. 101

and drive north about 37 miles to the town of Hoodsport and Lake Cushman Road (County Road 119). Turn left (west) and drive 17 miles to the camp at the end of the road (set about one mile above the inlet of Lake Cushman). The last several miles of the road are unpaved.

Contact: Olympic National Park, 360/565-3130, fax 360/565-3147, www.nps.gov/olym.

55 COHO

Scenic rating: 10

on Wynoochee Lake in Olympic National Forest
Map grid B2

This eight-acre camp sits on the shore of Wynoochee Lake, which is 4.4 miles long and covers 1,140 acres. The camp is set at an elevation of 900 feet. The fishing season opens June 1 and closes October 31. Powerboats, waterskiing, and personal watercraft are permitted. Points of interest include Working Forest Nature Trail, Wynoochee Dam Viewpoint and exhibits, and 12-mile Wynoochee Lake Shore Trail, which circles the lake. This is one of the most idyllic drive-to settings you could hope to find.

RV sites, facilities: There are 46 sites for tents or RVs up to 36 feet long and 10 walk-in sites. Picnic tables are provided. Vault toilets are available. There is no drinking water. A dump station is nearby. Boat docks and launching facilities are available at Wynoochee Lake. Leashed pets are permitted.

Reservations, fees: Reservations are not accepted. Sites are $18 per night, $14 per night for walk-in sites, $5 per extra vehicle per night. Open May–November, weather permitting.

Directions: From Olympia on I-5, take Exit 104 and drive north on U.S. 101 to the Aberdeen/Highway 8 exit. Turn west on Highway 8 and drive 36 miles (it becomes Highway 12 at Elma) to Montesano. Continue two miles on Highway 12 to Wynoochee Valley Road. Turn right (north) on Wynoochee Valley Road and drive 12 miles to Forest Road 22. Continue north on Forest Road 22 (a gravel road) for 23 miles to Wynoochee Lake. Just south of the lake, bear

left and drive on Forest Road 2294 (which runs along the lake's northwest shore) for one mile to the camp on the west shore of Wynoochee Lake. Obtaining a U.S. Forest Service map is helpful.

Contact: Olympic National Forest, Hood Canal Ranger District, Quilcene Office, 360/765-2200, fax 360/765-2202, www.fs.fed.us.

56 BROWN CREEK

Scenic rating: 9

on Brown Creek in Olympic National Forest
Map grid B2

Brown Creek is little known among out-of-town visitors. While this camp is accessible to two-wheel-drive vehicles, the access road connects to a network of primitive, backcountry forest roads. The campground was moved out of the riparian habitat and expanded to 60 sites. It is situated within the vast Olympic National Forest, which offers many opportunities for outdoor recreation. Wheelchair-accessible Brown Creek Nature Trail begins at the hand pump and makes a one-mile loop around the camp, featuring views of an active beaver pond. Obtain a U.S. Forest Service map to expand your trip.

RV sites, facilities: There are 20 sites for tents or RVs up to 20 feet long. Picnic tables and fire rings are provided. Drinking water and vault toilets are available. Garbage must be packed out. Some facilities are wheelchair accessible. Leashed pets are permitted.

Reservations, fees: Reservations are not accepted. Sites are $14 per night, $5 per extra vehicle per night. Open May–September, weather permitting.

Directions: From Olympia on I-5, take Exit 104 for U.S. 101/Highway 8. Drive north on U.S. 101 for 31 miles (about six miles past Shelton) to Skokomish Valley Road. Turn left (west) and drive 5.3 miles to Forest Road 23. Turn right on Forest Road 23 and drive nine miles to Forest Road 2353. Turn right on Forest Road 2353 and drive one mile to the South Fork

Skokomish River Bridge. Cross the bridge, turn right sharply onto Forest Road 2340 and drive 0.25 mile to the camp. Obtaining a U.S. Forest Service map is advisable.

Contact: Olympic National Forest, Hood Canal Ranger District, Quilcene Office, 360/765-2200, fax 360/765-2202, www.fs.fed.us.

57 LEBAR HORSE CAMP

Scenic rating: 9

in Olympic National Forest

Map grid B2

This camp is exclusively for people with horses or pack animals, such as mules, mollies, llamas, and goats. The camp provides access to Lower South Fork Skokomish Trail, a 10.9-mile trip, one-way. The camp features beautiful old-growth forest, with western hemlock and Douglas fir.

RV sites, facilities: There are 13 sites for tents or RVs up to 28 feet long for the exclusive use of campers with pack animals. Picnic tables, fire grills, hitching posts, and high lines are provided. Vault toilets are available. There is no drinking water, and garbage must be packed out. A day-use area with a picnic shelter is available nearby. Leashed pets are permitted.

Reservations, fees: Reservations are not accepted. Sites are $10 per night, $5 per extra vehicle per night. Open May–September, weather permitting.

Directions: From Olympia on I-5, take Exit 104 for U.S. 101/Highway 8. Drive north on U.S. 101 for 31 miles (about six miles past Shelton) to Skokomish Valley Road. Turn left (west) and drive 5.3 miles to Forest Road 23. Turn right on Forest Road 23 and drive nine miles to Forest Road 2353. Turn right on Forest Road 2353 and drive one mile to the South Fork Skokomish River Bridge. Cross the bridge, turn left sharply to remain on Forest Road 2353, and drive 0.5 mile to the camp. Obtaining a U.S. Forest Service map is advisable.

Contact: Olympic National Forest, Hood Canal Ranger District, 360/765-2200, fax 360/765-2202, www.fs.fed.us.

58 BIG CREEK

Scenic rating: 7

near Lake Cushman in Olympic National Forest

Map grid B2

Big Creek is an alternative to Staircase camp on the North Fork of Skokomish River and Camp Cushman and Recreation Park, both of which get heavier use. The sites here are large and well spaced for privacy over 30 acres, primarily of second-growth forest. Big Creek runs adjacent to the campground. A four-mile loop trail extends from camp and connects to Mount Eleanor Trail. A bonus: two walk-in sites are located along the creek.

RV sites, facilities: There are 23 sites for tents or RVs up to 30 feet long. Picnic tables and fire grills are provided. Drinking water, vault toilets, and a sheltered picnic area are available. A boat dock and ramp are located at nearby Lake Cushman. Garbage must be packed out. Leashed pets are permitted.

Reservations, fees: Reservations are not accepted. Sites are $14 per night, $5 per extra vehicle per night. Open May–September, weather permitting.

Directions: From Olympia on I-5, take Exit 104 for U.S. 101/Highway 8. Drive north on U.S. 101 for 37 miles to Hoodsport and Lake Cushman Road (Highway 119). Turn left on Lake Cushman Road and drive nine miles (two miles north of Camp Cushman) to the T intersection with Forest Road 24. Turn left and the campground is on the right.

Contact: Olympic National Forest, Hood Canal Ranger District, Quilcene Office, 360/765-2200, www.fs.fed.us; visitors center, 360/877-2021.

59 CAMP CUSHMAN AND RECREATION PARK

Scenic rating: 10

on Lake Cushman

Map grid B2

Set in the foothills of the Olympic Mountains on the shore of Lake Cushman, this 500-acre park features a 10-mile-long blue-water mountain lake, eight miles of park shoreline, forested hillsides, and awesome views of snowcapped peaks. Beach access and good trout fishing are other highlights. The park has eight miles of hiking trails. Windsurfing, waterskiing, and swimming are all popular here. A nine-hole golf course is nearby.

RV sites, facilities: There are 50 sites for tents or RVs up to 30 feet long (no hookups), 30 sites with full hookups (30 amps) for RVs up to 30 feet long, two hike-in/bike-in sites, and one group camp for up to 72 people. Picnic tables and fire grills are provided. Restrooms with flush toilets and coin showers, drinking water, a camp store, picnic area, amphitheater, horseshoe pits, badminton, ice, and firewood are available. A restaurant is within three miles. Boat docks and launching facilities are located nearby on Lake Cushman. Some facilities are wheelchair accessible. Leashed pets are permitted.

Reservations, fees: Reservations are accepted. Sites are $20–26 per night, $6 per extra vehicle per night, $10 per pet per stay. The group camp is a minimum of $135 per night. Some credit cards are accepted. Open mid-April–October, weather permitting.

Directions: From Olympia on I-5, take the U.S. 101 exit and drive north 37 miles to Hoodsport and Highway 119 (Lake Cushman Road). Turn left (west) on Lake Cushman Road and drive 7.5 miles to the park on the left.

Contact: Camp Cushman and Recreation Park, 360/877-6770 or 866/259-2900, fax 360/877-6550, www.lakecushman.com.

60 LAKE CUSHMAN RESORT

Scenic rating: 10

on Lake Cushman

Map grid B2

This campground on Lake Cushman has full facilities for water sports, including boat launching and rentals. Waterskiing and fishing are popular. Lake Cushman Dam makes a good side trip. A nine-hole golf course is nearby.

RV sites, facilities: There are 50 sites for tents or RVs up to 22 feet long (no hookups), 21 sites with partial hookups (20 amps) for RVs up to 40 feet long, and 11 cabins. Picnic tables and fire grills are provided. Drinking water, flush and portable toilets, firewood, a convenience store, boat docks and launching facilities, mooring, and boat rentals are available. Groups can be accommodated. Some facilities are wheelchair accessible. Leashed pets are permitted.

Reservations, fees: Reservations are accepted. Tent sites are $15–25.50 per night, RV sites are $20–29.50 per night, $10 per pet per stay, and mooring is $10–15 per day. Some credit cards are accepted. Open year-round.

Directions: From Olympia on I-5, take the U.S. 101 exit and drive north 37 miles to Hoodsport and Highway 119/Lake Cushman Road. Turn left (west) on Lake Cushman Road and drive 4.5 miles to the resort on the left.

Contact: Lake Cushman Resort, 360/877-9630 or 800/588-9630, fax 360/877-9356, www.lakecushman.com.

61 REST-A-WHILE RV PARK

Scenic rating: 5

on Hood Canal

Map grid B2

This seven-acre park, located at sea level on Hood Canal, offers waterfront sites and a private beach for clamming and oyster gathering, not to mention plenty of opportunities to fish, boat, and scuba dive. It's an alternative to Potlatch State Park and Glen-Ayr RV Park.

RV sites, facilities: There are 80 sites for tents

or RVs of any length (30 amp full hookups), two tent sites, two rental trailers, and a bunkhouse. Some sites are pull-through. Picnic tables and fire rings are provided. Restrooms with flush toilets and showers, drinking water, cable TV, modem access, propane gas, firewood, a clubhouse, convenience store, drive-in restaurant, coin laundry, and ice are available. A café is within walking distance. Boat docks, launching facilities, a scuba diving shop, seasonal boat and kayak rentals, and a private beach for clamming and oyster gathering (in season) are also available. Leashed pets are permitted.

Reservations, fees: Reservations are accepted. Sites are $30–35 per night, $2 per extra vehicle per night, and $4 per person per night for more than two people. Some credit cards are accepted. Open year-round.

Directions: From Olympia on I-5, take Exit 104 for U.S. 101/Highway 8. Drive north on U.S. 101 for 37 miles to Hoodsport. Continue 2.5 miles north on U.S. 101 to the park located at Milepost 329.

Contact: Rest-A-While RV Park, 360/877-9474 or 866/637-9474, www.restawhile.com.

62 GLEN-AYR RV PARK & MOTEL

Scenic rating: 5

on Hood Canal
Map grid B2

This fully developed, nine-acre park is located at sea level on Hood Canal, where there are opportunities to fish and scuba dive. Salmon fishing is especially excellent. Swimming and boating round out the options. The park has a spa, moorage, horseshoe pits, recreation field, and a motel.

RV sites, facilities: There are 38 sites with full hookups (five with 50 amps and 33 with 30 amps) for RVs of any length, 18 motel rooms, a townhouse, and two suites with kitchens. Some sites are pull-through. No open fires are allowed. Picnic tables are provided. Restrooms with flush toilets and showers, drinking water, cable TV, Wi-Fi, propane gas, a spa, recreation

hall, horseshoe pits, seasonal organized activities, and coin laundry are available. A store, café, and ice are within one mile. A boat dock is located across the street from the park. Leashed pets are permitted.

Reservations, fees: Reservations are accepted. Sites are $30–40 per night, $5 per person per night for more than two people, $5 per extra vehicle per night. Some credit cards are accepted. Open year-round.

Directions: From Olympia on I-5, take Exit 104 for U.S. 101/Highway 8. Drive north on U.S. 101 for 37 miles to Hoodsport. Continue one mile north on U.S. 101 to the park on the left.

Contact: Glen-Ayr RV Park & Motel, 360/877-9522 or 866/877-9522, www.glen-ayr.com.

63 POTLATCH STATE PARK

Scenic rating: 8

on Hood Canal
Map grid B2

This state park features good shellfish harvesting in season. The park has 9,570 feet of shoreline on Hood Canal. There are 1.5 miles of trails for hiking and biking, but the shoreline and water bring people here for the good kayaking, windsurfing, scuba diving, clamming, and fishing. The park is named for the potlatch, a Skyhomish gift-giving ceremony. There are four major rivers, the Skokomish, Hamma Hamma, Duckabush, and Dosewallips, within a 30-mile radius of the park. The park receives an annual rainfall of 64 inches.

RV sites, facilities: There are 18 sites with full hookups (30 and 50 amps) for RVs up to 60 feet long, 19 developed tent sites, and two hike-in/bike-in sites. Picnic tables and fire grills are provided. Restrooms with flush toilets and coin showers, drinking water, a dump station, firewood, an amphitheater, a picnic area, and seasonal interpretive programs are available. Five mooring buoys are located at the park, and a boat launch and dock are available nearby. Groceries, gas, and propane are available three miles away. Some facilities are wheelchair accessible. Leashed pets are permitted.

Reservations, fees: Reservations are accepted in summer at 888/226-7688 or www.parks. wa.gov. Sites are $19–26 per night, $12 per night for hike-in/bike-in sites, $10 per extra vehicle per night. Open year-round.

Directions: From Olympia on I-5, take Exit 104 for U.S. 101/Highway 8. Drive north on U.S. 101 for 22 miles to Shelton. Continue north on U.S. 101 for 12 miles to the park on the right (located along the shoreline of Annas Bay on Hood Canal).

Contact: Potlatch State Park, 360/877-5361, fax 360/877-6346; state park information, 360/902-8844, www.parks.wa.gov.

64 SCHAFER STATE PARK

Scenic rating: 8

on the Satsop River
Map grid B2

This unique destination boasts many interesting features, including buildings constructed from native stone. A heavily wooded, rural camp, Schafer State Park covers 119 acres along the East Fork of the Satsop River. The river is well known for fishing and rafting. Fish for sea-run cutthroat in summer, salmon in fall, and steelhead in late winter. There are good canoeing and kayaking spots, some with Class II and III rapids, along the Middle and West Forks of the Satsop. Three miles of hiking trails are also available. At one time, this park was the Schafer Logging Company Park and was used by employees and their families.

RV sites, facilities: There are 32 developed tent sites, 10 sites with partial hookups (30 amps) for RVs up to 40 feet long, two hike-in/bike-in sites, and two group camps for up to 50 and 100 people. Picnic tables and fire grills are provided. Restrooms with flush toilets and coin showers, drinking water, picnic shelters that can be reserved, a dump station, and horseshoe pits are available. Some facilities are wheelchair accessible. Leashed pets are permitted.

Reservations, fees: Reservations are not accepted for individual sites but are required for the group camp at 360/482-3852. Sites are $19–25 per night, $10 per extra vehicle per night; hike-in/bike-in sites are $12 per night. The group area is $2.25 per person per night with a $25 reservation fee. Open late April–early October, weather permitting.

Directions: From Olympia on I-5, take Exit 104 to U.S. 101. Drive west on U.S. 101 for six miles to Highway 8. Turn west on Highway 8 and drive to Elma (Highway 8 becomes Highway 12). Continue west on Highway 12 for five miles to the Brady exit/West Satsop Road (four miles east of Montesano). Turn right (north) on West Satsop Road and drive eight miles to Schafer Park Road. Turn right and drive two miles to the park.

Contact: Schafer State Park, tel./fax 360/482-3852; state park information, 360/902-8844, www.parks.wa.gov.

65 LAKE SYLVIA STATE PARK

Scenic rating: 8

on Lake Sylvia
Map grid B2

This 234-acre state park on the shore of Lake Sylvia features nearly three miles of freshwater shoreline. The park is located in a former logging camp in a wooded area set midway between Olympia and the Pacific Ocean. Expect plenty of rustic charm, with displays of old logging gear, a giant ball carved out of wood from a single log, and some monstrous stumps. The lake is good for fishing and ideal for canoes, prams, or small boats with oars or electric motors; no gas motors are permitted. Five miles of hiking trails and a 0.5-mile wheelchair-accessible trail meander through the park. Additional recreation options include trout fishing and swimming.

RV sites, facilities: There are 35 sites for tents or RVs up to 30 feet long (no hookups), two hike-in/bike-in sites, and one group site for up to 60 people and 10 vehicles. Picnic tables and fire grills are provided. Restrooms with flush toilets and coin showers, drinking water, a dump station, boat launch, picnic area, a kitchen shelter that can be reserved, firewood, and a playground are available. A coin laundry and grocery store are located within two miles. Some facilities are wheelchair accessible. Leashed pets are permitted.

Reservations, fees: Reservations are accepted for individual sites and are required for the group site at 888/CAMP-OUT (888/226-7688) or www.parks.wa.gov/reservations ($6.50–8.50 reservation fee). Sites are $21 per night, $10 per extra vehicle per night; hike-in/bike-in sites are $14 per night. The group site is $2.25 per person, with a 20-person minimum. Open early April–mid-October, weather permitting.

Directions: From Olympia on I-5, take Exit 104 to U.S. 101. Drive west on U.S. 101 six miles to Highway 8. Turn west on Highway 8 (becomes Highway 12) and drive 26 miles to Montesano and West Pioneer Street (the only stoplight in town). Turn left on West Pioneer Street and drive three blocks to 3rd Street. Turn right and drive two miles to the park entrance (route is well signed).

Contact: Lake Sylvia State Park, 360/249-3621, fax 360/249-5571; state park information, 360/902-8844, www.parks.wa.gov.

66 TRAVEL INN RESORT

Scenic rating: 7

on Lake Sylvia

Map grid B2

This is a membership campground, which means sites for RV travelers are available only if there is extra space. It can be difficult to get a spot May–September, but the park opens up significantly in the off-season. There are five major rivers or lakes within 15 minutes of this camp (Satsop, Chehalis, Wynoochee, Black River, and Lake Sylvia). Nearby Lake Sylvia State Park provides multiple marked hiking trails. Additional recreation options include trout fishing, swimming, and golf (three miles away).

RV sites, facilities: There are 200 sites with full or partial hookups (30 and 50 amps) for RVs of any length and three tent sites. Picnic tables are provided. Restrooms with flush toilets and showers, drinking water, coin laundry, two community fire pits, a gazebo, a seasonal heated swimming pool, game room, cable TV, Wi-Fi and modem access, seasonal organized activities, and a clubhouse are available. A grocery store, gas station, propane, and restaurant are available within one mile. Some facilities are wheelchair accessible. Leashed pets are permitted.

Reservations, fees: Reservations are accepted May–September. Sites are $35 per night. No credit cards are accepted. Open year-round.

Directions: From Olympia on I-5, take Exit 104 to U.S. 101. Drive west on U.S. 101 for six miles to Highway 8. Turn west on Highway 8 and drive to Elma (Highway 8 becomes Highway 12). Take the first Elma exit and drive to the stop sign and Highway 12/East Main Street. Turn right and drive about 200 yards to the end of the highway and a stop sign. Turn right and drive another 200 yards to the resort on the right.

Contact: Travel Inn Resort, 360/482-3877 or 800/871-2888, www.kmresorts.com.

67 FALLS VIEW

Scenic rating: 8

on the Big Quilcene River in Olympic National Forest

Map grid C2

A viewing area to a pretty waterfall on the Big Quilcene River, where you see a narrow, 100-foot cascade, is only a 150-foot walk from the campground. That explains why, despite the rustic setting, this spot on the edge of the Olympic National Forest has a host of facilities and is popular. Enjoy the setting of mixed conifers and rhododendrons along a one-mile scenic loop trail, which overlooks the river and provides views of the waterfall. A picnic area is also located near the waterfall.

RV sites, facilities: There are 30 sites for tents or RVs up to 35 feet long. Picnic tables and fire pits are provided. Vault toilets are available. There is no drinking water. Leashed pets are permitted.

Reservations, fees: Reservations are not accepted. Sites are $10 per night, $5 per extra vehicle per night. Open May–September, weather permitting.

Directions: From Olympia on I-5, turn north on U.S. 101 and drive approximately 70 miles to the campground entrance on the left (located about four miles south of Quilcene).

Contact: Olympic National Forest, Hood Canal Ranger District, Quilcene Office, 360/765-2200, fax 360/765-2202, www.fs.fed.us.

68 KITSAP MEMORIAL STATE PARK

Scenic rating: 10

on Hood Canal

Map grid C2   **BEST (**

Kitsap Memorial State Park is a beautiful spot for campers along Hood Canal. The park covers only 58 acres but features sweeping views of Puget Sound and 1,797 feet of shoreline. The park has 1.5 miles of hiking trails and two open grassy fields for family play. Note that the nearest boat launch is four miles away, north on State Route 3 at Salisbury County Park. An 18-hole golf course and swimming, fishing, and hiking at nearby Anderson Lake Recreation Area are among the activities available. A short drive north will take you to historic Old Fort Townsend, which makes an excellent day trip.

RV sites, facilities: There are 21 sites for tents or RVs up to 30 feet long, 18 sites with partial hookups (30 amps) for RVs, three hike-in/bike-in sites, a group camp for 20 to 56 people, four cabins, and a vacation house. Picnic tables and fire grills are provided. Restrooms with flush toilets and showers, drinking water, a dump station, sheltered picnic area, firewood, a playground, ball fields, and a community meeting hall are available. Two gas stations with mini-marts are located just outside the park. Two boat buoys are available. Some facilities are wheelchair accessible. Leashed pets are permitted.

Reservations, fees: Reservations are not accepted for individual campsites but are required for the group camp at 888/CAMP-OUT (888/226-7688) or www.parks.wa.gov/reservations ($6.50–8.50 reservation fee). Sites are $21–27 per night, $14 per night for hike-in/bike-in sites, $10 per extra vehicle per night. The group camp is $102 per night. Cabins are $60 per night, and the vacation house is $117–156 per night. Open year-round.

Directions: From Tacoma on I-5, turn north on Highway 16 and drive 44 miles (Highway 16 turns into Highway 3). Continue north on Highway 3 and drive six miles to Park Street. Turn left and drive 200 yards to the park entrance on the right (well marked). The park is located four miles south of the Hood Canal Bridge.

Contact: Kitsap Memorial State Park, 360/779-3205, fax 360/779-3161; state park information, 360/902-8844, www.parks.wa.gov.

69 RAINBOW GROUP CAMP

Scenic rating: 7

near Quilcene in Olympic National Forest

Map grid C2

Rainbow Group Camp is in a rugged, primitive setting on the edge of Olympic National Forest. This area is heavily wooded with old-growth and new-growth forest, a variety of wildflowers, and spring-blooming rhododendrons. The Rainbow Canyon Trailhead, located at the far side of the campground, provides a short hike to the Big Quicene River and a waterfall. It is fairly steep, but it's not a butt-kicker. Forest roads provide considerable backcountry access (obtaining a U.S. Forest Service map is advisable). The nearest is Forest Road 2730, just 0.10 mile away, which leads to spectacular scenery at the Mount Walker Observation Area. Olympic National Park is also just a short drive away.

RV sites, facilities: This is a group campground only. There are nine sites for tents or pickup campers that can accommodate up to 50 people. Picnic tables and fire grills are provided. Vault toilets are available. There is no drinking water. A store, café, coin laundry, and ice are within five miles. Leashed pets are permitted.

Reservations, fees: Reservations are accepted at 360/765-2200. The camp is $50 per night. Open May–September, weather permitting.

Directions: From I-5 at Olympia, drive north on U.S. 101 and drive approximately 69 miles to the campground (about six miles past Dosewallips State Park) on the left (near Walker Pass).

Contact: Olympic National Forest, Hood Canal Ranger District, Quilcene Office, 360/765-2200, fax 360/765-2202, www.fs.fed.us.

70 COVE RV PARK

Scenic rating: 5

near Dabob Bay
Map grid C2

This five-acre private camp enjoys a rural setting close to the shore of Dabob Bay, yet it is fully developed. Sites are grassy and graveled with a few trees. Scuba diving is popular in this area, and the park sells air for scuba tanks. Dosewallips State Park is a short drive away and a possible side trip.

RV sites, facilities: There are 32 sites with full hookups (30 and 50 amps) for RVs up to 40 feet long and six tent sites. Some sites are pull-through. Picnic tables and fire rings are provided. Restrooms with flush toilets and coin showers, drinking water, cable TV, modem access, propane gas, a convenience store, bait and tackle, coin laundry, a sheltered picnic area, and ice are available. Boat docks and launching facilities are on Hood Canal 2.2 miles from the park. Leashed pets are permitted.

Reservations, fees: Reservations are accepted. Tent sites are $17 per night; RV sites are $27 per night. Some credit cards are accepted. Open year-round.

Directions: From Olympia on I-5, drive north on U.S. 101 for 60 miles to Brinnon (located about one mile north of Dosewallips State Park). Continue three miles north on U.S. 101 to the park on the right (before Milepost 303).

Contact: Cove RV Park, 360/796-4723 or 866/796-4723, fax 360/796-3452.

71 SEAL ROCK

Scenic rating: 9

on Dabob Bay in Olympic National Forest
Map grid C2

Seal Rock is a 30-acre camp set along the shore near the mouth of Dabob Bay. This is one of the few national forest campgrounds anywhere located on saltwater. It brings with it the opportunity to harvest oysters and clams in season, and it is an outstanding jumping-off point for scuba diving. Most campsites are set along the waterfront, spaced among trees. Carry-in boats, such as kayaks and canoes, can be launched from the north landing. Native American Nature Trail and Marine Biology Nature Trail begin at the day-use area. These are short walks, each less than 0.5 mile. This camp is extremely popular in the summer, often filling up quickly.

RV sites, facilities: There are 41 sites for tents or RVs up to 21 feet long. Picnic tables and fire rings are provided. Restrooms with flush toilets, drinking water, garbage bins, and a picnic area are available. A camp host is on-site in summer. Boat docks and launching facilities are nearby on Hood Canal and in Dabob Bay. Some facilities, including viewing areas and trails, are wheelchair accessible. Leashed pets are permitted.

Reservations, fees: Reservations are not accepted. Sites are $18 per night. Open May–September, weather permitting.

Directions: From Olympia on I-5, drive north on U.S. 101 for 62 miles to Brinnon (located about one mile north of Dosewallips State Park). Continue two miles north on U.S. 101 to Seal Rock and the camp on the right.

Contact: Olympic National Forest, Hood Canal Ranger District, Quilcene Office, 360/765-2200, fax 360/765-2202, www.fs.fed.us.

72 DOSEWALLIPS STATE PARK

Scenic rating: 8

on Dosewallips Creek

Map grid C2

This 425-acre park is set on the shore of Hood Canal at the mouth of Dosewallips River. It features 5,500 feet of saltwater shoreline on Hood Canal and 5,400 feet of shoreline on both sides of the Dosewallips River. Most campsites are grassy and located in scenic, rustic settings. Mushrooming is available in season. Check regulations for fishing and clamming, which fluctuate according to time, season, and supply. The park hosts an annual "Shrimp Fest," often in April. This camp is popular because it's set right off a major highway; reservations or early arrival are advised. Access is not affected by the nearby slide area.

RV sites, facilities: There are 140 sites for tents or RVs up to 60 feet long (no hookups), 40 sites with full hookups (30 amps) for RVs up to 60 feet long, two hike-in/bike-in sites, three platform tent rentals, two group camps for up to 50 and 80 people, and three cabins. Picnic tables and fire rings are provided. Restrooms with flush toilets and coin showers, drinking water, a sheltered picnic area, interpretive activities, and a summer Junior Ranger Program are available. A wildlife-viewing platform, horseshoe pits, and saltwater boat-launching facilities are available within the park. A store and café are available nearby. Some facilities are wheelchair accessible. Leashed pets are permitted.

Reservations, fees: Reservations are accepted at 888/CAMP-OUT (888/226-7688) or www.parks.wa.gov/reservations ($6.50–8.50 reservation fee). Sites are $21–27 per night, $10 per extra vehicle per night; hike-in/bike-in sites are $14 per night, platform tent rentals are $50–55 per night, group camps are $2.25 per person per night with a $25 reservation fee, and cabins are

$60 per night. Some credit cards are accepted. Open year-round.

Directions: From Olympia on I-5, drive north on U.S. 101 for 61 miles (one mile south of Brinnon) to the state park entrance on the left.

Contact: Dosewallips State Park, 360/796-4415; state park information, 360/902-8844, www.parks.wa.gov.

73 SCENIC BEACH STATE PARK

Scenic rating: 10

on Hood Canal

Map grid C2

Scenic Beach is an exceptionally beautiful state park with beach access and superb views of the Olympic Mountains. It features 1,500 feet of saltwater beachfront on Hood Canal. The park is also known for its wild rhododendrons in spring. Wheelchair-accessible paths lead to a country garden, gazebo, rustic bridge, and large trees. Many species of birds and wildlife can often be seen here. This camp is also close to Green Mountain Forest, where there is extensive hiking. A boat ramp is 0.5 mile east of the park. A nice touch here is that park staff will check out volleyballs and horseshoes during the summer.

RV sites, facilities: There are 52 sites for tents or RVs up to 60 feet long (some pull-through), two hike-in/bike-in sites, and a group camp for 20–50 people. Picnic tables and fire grills are provided. Restrooms with flush toilets and coin showers, drinking water, and a dump station are available. A sheltered picnic area, playground, horseshoe pits, and volleyball fields are nearby. A boat ramp, dock, and moorage are available within one mile. Some facilities are wheelchair accessible. Leashed pets are permitted.

Reservations, fees: Reservations are accepted at 888/CAMP-OUT (888/226-7688) or www.parks.wa.gov/reservations ($6.50–8.50 reservation fee). Sites are $21 per night, $10 per extra vehicle per night, hike-in/bike-in sites are $14 per night, and the group site is $2.25 per person per night plus a $25 reservation fee. Open year-round, weather permitting.

Directions: From the junction at Highway 16 and Highway 3 in Bremerton, turn north on Highway 3 and drive about nine miles and take the first Silverdale exit (Newberry Hill Road). Turn left and drive approximately three miles to the end of the road. Turn right on Seabeck Highway and drive six miles to Scenic Beach Road. Turn right and drive one mile to the park.

Contact: Scenic Beach State Park, 360/830-5079, fax 360/830-2970; state park information, 360/902-8844, www.parks.wa.gov.

74 FAY BAINBRIDGE STATE PARK

Scenic rating: 10

on Bainbridge Island

Map grid C2

A beach park that offers beauty and great recreation, this camp is set on the edge of Puget Sound. The park covers just 17 acres but features 1,420 feet of saltwater shoreline on the northeast corner of the island. You can hike several miles along the beach at low tide; the water temperature is typically about 55°F in summer. The primitive walk-in sites are heavily wooded, and the developed sites have great views of the sound. On clear days, campers can enjoy views of Mount Rainier and Mount Baker to the east, and at night the park provides beautiful vistas of the lights of Seattle. Clamming, diving, picnicking, beachcombing, and kite-flying are popular here. In the winter months, there is excellent salmon fishing just offshore of the park.

RV sites, facilities: There are 26 sites for tents or RVs up to 40 feet long (no hookups), 10 sites for tents only, and four hike-in/bike-in sites. Picnic tables and fire grills are provided. Restrooms with flush toilets and coin showers, drinking water, a dump station, sheltered picnic areas, firewood, horseshoes, and playground are available. Mooring buoys are available nearby. A store and café are located within three

miles. Some facilities are wheelchair accessible. Leashed pets are permitted.

Reservations, fees: Reservations are not accepted. Sites are $17 per night, $10 per extra vehicle per night, hike-in/bike-in sites are $14 per night, and moorage is $0.50 per foot, with a $10 per night minimum. Open year-round, weather permitting.

Directions: From Tacoma at I-5, turn north on Highway 16 and drive 30 miles to Bremerton to the junction with Highway 3. Turn north on Highway 3 and drive 18 miles to Highway 305. Turn south on Highway 305 and drive over the bridge to Bainbridge Island and continue three miles to Day Road. Turn left and drive 1.5 miles to Sunrise Drive. Turn left and drive two miles to the park on the right.

Note: From Seattle, this camp can be more easily accessed by taking the Bainbridge Island ferry and then Highway 305 north to Day Road at the northeast end of the island. From there, follow the directions above.

Contact: Fay Bainbridge State Park, 206/842-3931; state park information, 360/902-8844, www.parks.wa.gov.

75 ILLAHEE STATE PARK

Scenic rating: 9

near Bremerton

Map grid C2

This 75-acre park, named for a Native American word for earth or country, features the last stand of old-growth forest in Kitsap County, including one of the largest yew trees in America. The park also features 1,785 feet of saltwater frontage. The campsites are located in a pretty, forested area, and some are grassy. The shoreline is fairly rocky, set on the shore of Port Orchard Bay, although there is a small sandy area for sunbathers. Clamming is popular here. A fishing pier is available for anglers. Note that large vessels can be difficult to launch at the ramp here.

RV sites, facilities: There are 23 sites for tents or RVs up to 40 feet long (no hookups), two sites for tents or RVs up to 35 feet long (50 amp full hookups), and two hike-in/bike-in sites. Picnic tables and fire grills are provided. Restrooms with flush toilets and coin showers, drinking water, firewood, dump station, and a pier are available. Boat docks, launching facilities, five mooring buoys, and 356 feet of moorage float space are also available. A sheltered picnic area, horseshoes, volleyball, a field, and a playground are nearby. A coin laundry and ice are located within one mile. Some facilities are wheelchair accessible. Leashed pets are permitted.

Reservations, fees: Reservations are not accepted. Sites are $19–26 per night, $12 per night for hike-in/bike-in sites, $10 per extra vehicle per night. Moorage is a $0.50 per foot, with a $10 per night minimum. Open year-round.

Directions: On Highway 3, drive to Bremerton and the East Bremerton exit. Drive east for 7.5 miles to Sylvan Way. Turn left and drive 1.5 miles to the park entrance road.

Contact: Illahee State Park, 360/478-6460; state park information, 360/902-8844, www.parks.wa.gov.

76 MANCHESTER STATE PARK

Scenic rating: 9

near Port Orchard
Map grid C2

Manchester State Park is set on the edge of Port Orchard, providing excellent lookouts across Puget Sound. The park covers 111 acres, with 3,400 feet of saltwater shoreline on Rich Passage in Puget Sound. The landscape is filled with fir maple, hemlock, cedar, alder, and ash, which are very pretty in the fall. There are approximately 2.5 miles of hiking trails, including an interpretive trail. Group and day-use reservations are available. Note that the beach is closed to shellfish harvesting. In the early 1900s, this park site was used as a U.S. Coast Guard defense installation. A gun battery remains from the park's early days, along with two other buildings that are on the register of National Historical Monuments.

RV sites, facilities: There are 35 tent sites, 15 sites with partial hookups (30 amps) for tents or RVs up to 60 feet long, three hike-in/bike-in sites, and one group site with hookups (30 amps) for tents or RVs for up to 130 people. Picnic tables and fire grills are provided. Restrooms with flush toilets and coin showers, drinking water, dump station, firewood, sheltered picnic area, volleyball field, and horseshoe pit are available. Some facilities are wheelchair accessible. Leashed pets are permitted.

Reservations, fees: Reservations are accepted for individual sites (mid-May–mid-Sept.) and the group site at 888/CAMP-OUT (888/226-7688) or www.parks.wa.gov/reservations ($6.50–8.50 reservation fee). Sites are $21–28 per night, $10 per extra vehicle per night, and hike-in/bike-in sites are $14 per night. The group site is $2.25 per person per night with a minimum of 20 people and a $25 reservation fee. Some credit cards are accepted. Open year-round, with limited winter facilities.

Directions: From Tacoma on I-5, turn north on Highway 16 and drive to the Port Orford/Sedgwick Road exit and Highway 160. Turn right (east) and drive one mile to Long Lake Road. Turn left and drive six miles to Milehill. Turn right on Milehill and drive about one mile to Colchester Road. Turn left on Colchester Road and drive through Manchester, continuing for two miles to the park.

Note: Directions to this park are flawed on most website maps and in other books. Use the directions above, and when nearing the camp, you will note the route is signed.

Contact: Manchester State Park, 360/871-4065; state park information, 360/902-8844, www.parks.wa.gov.

77 BELFAIR STATE PARK

Scenic rating: 8

on Hood Canal
Map grid C2

Belfair State Park is situated along the southern edge of Hood Canal, spanning 65 acres with

3,720 feet of saltwater shoreline. This park is known for its saltwater tidal flats, wetlands, and wind-blown beach grasses. Beach walking and swimming are good. The camp is set primarily amid conifer forest and marshlands on Hood Canal with nearby streams, tideland, and wetlands. A gravel-rimmed pool that is separate from Hood Canal creates a unique swimming area; water level is determined by the tides. Note that the DNR Tahuya Multiple-Use Area is nearby with trails for motorcycles, mountain biking, hiking, horseback riding, and off-road vehicles. Big Mission Creek and Little Mission Creek, both located in the park, are habitat for chum salmon during spawning season in fall.

RV sites, facilities: There are 137 sites for tents, 47 sites with full hookups (30 amps) for RVs up to 60 feet long, three hike-in/bike-in sites, and one water trail site. Picnic tables and fire grills are provided. Restrooms with flush toilets and coin showers, drinking water, firewood, a bathhouse, dump station, swimming lagoon, playground, badminton, volleyball court, and horseshoe pits are available. A store and restaurant are located nearby. Some facilities are wheelchair accessible. Leashed pets are permitted.

Reservations, fees: Reservations are accepted at 888/CAMP-OUT (888/226-7688) or www. parks.wa.gov/reservations ($6.50–8.50 reservation fee). Sites are $21–28 per night, $10 per extra vehicle per night, hike-in/bike-in sites are $14 per night, and the water trail site is $14 per night. Some credit cards are accepted. Open year-round.

Directions: From Tacoma on I-5, drive to the Highway 16 west exit. Take Highway 16 northwest and drive about 27 miles toward Bremerton and Belfair (after the Port Orchard exits, note that the highway merges into three lanes). Get in the left lane for the Belfair/State Route 3 south exit. Take that exit and turn left at the traffic signal. Take State Route 3 eight miles south to Belfair to State Route 300 (at the signal just after the Safeway). Turn right and drive three miles to the park entrance.

Contact: Belfair State Park, 360/275-0668;

state park information, 360/902-8844, www. parks.wa.gov.

78 TWANOH STATE PARK

Scenic rating: 8

near Union

Map grid C2

This state park is set on the shore of Hood Canal at one of the warmest saltwater bodies in Puget Sound—and likely the warmest saltwater beach in the state. Twanoh, from a Native American word meaning gathering place, covers 182 acres, with 3,167 feet of saltwater shoreline. Swimming and oyster, clam, and crab harvesting are popular here. Winter smelting is also popular; check regulations. In late fall, the chum salmon can be seen heading up the small creek; fishing for them is prohibited. Most of the park buildings are made of brick, stone, and round logs, built by the Civilian Conservation Corps in the 1930s. You'll also see extensive evidence of logging from the 1890s. Amenities include a tennis court, horseshoe pits, and a concession stand.

RV sites, facilities: There are 25 sites for tents or RVs (no hookups), 22 sites with full hookups (30 and 50 amps) for RVs up to 35 feet long, and a group tent camp for up to 50 people. Picnic tables and fire grills are provided. Restrooms with flush toilets and coin showers and drinking water are available. A seasonal snack bar, sheltered picnic area, firewood, boat ramp, boat dock, moorage buoys, marine pump-out station, wading pool, horseshoes, badminton, and volleyball are available nearby. Some facilities are wheelchair accessible. Leashed pets are permitted.

Reservations, fees: Reservations are accepted only for the group site at 888/226-7688 or www.parks.wa.gov. Sites are $21–28 per night, $10 per extra vehicle per night. The group camp is $2.25 per person per night with a minimum of 20 people, plus a $25 reservation fee. Open April–October, weather permitting.

Directions: From Bremerton, take Highway 3

southwest to Belfair and Highway 106. Turn right (west) and drive eight miles to the park. If driving from U.S. 101, turn east on Highway 106 and drive 12 miles to the park.

Contact: Twanoh State Park, 360/275-2222; state park information, 360/902-8844, www.parks.wa.gov.

79 JARRELL COVE STATE PARK

Scenic rating: 8

on Harstine Island
Map grid C2

Most visitors to this park arrive by boat. Campsites are near the docks, set on a rolling, grassy area. The park covers just 43 acres but boasts 3,500 feet of saltwater shoreline on the northeast end of Harstine Island in South Puget Sound. The park's dense forest presses nearly to the water's edge at high tides—a beautiful setting. At low tides, tideland mud flats are unveiled. The beach is rocky and muddy—not exactly Hawaii. Hiking and biking are limited to just one mile of trail.

RV sites, facilities: There are 22 sites for tents or RVs up to 34 feet long, one boat-in site (non-motorized boats only), and a group camp for up to 64 people. Picnic tables and fire grills are provided. Restrooms with flush toilets and coin showers and drinking water are available. Boat docks, a marine pump-out station, and 14 mooring buoys are available. A picnic area and a horseshoe pit are nearby. Some facilities are wheelchair accessible. Leashed pets are permitted.

Reservations, fees: Reservations are accepted and are required for the group camp at 888/CAMP-OUT (888/226-7688) or www.parks.wa.gov/reservations ($7 reservation fee). Sites are $12–25 per night, $10 per extra vehicle per night, and the group site is $2 per person per night with a 20-person minimum. Open year-round.

Directions: From Olympia on I-5, turn north on U.S. 101 and drive 22 miles to Shelton and Highway 3. Turn north on Highway 3 and

drive about eight miles to Pickering Road. Turn right and drive to the Harstine Bridge. Cross the bridge and continue to North Island Drive. Turn left and drive four miles to Wingert Road. Turn left and drive 0.25 mile to the park on the left.

Contact: Jarrell Cove State Park, 360/426-9226; state park information, 360/902-8844, www.parks.wa.gov.

80 JARRELL'S COVE MARINA

Scenic rating: 6

near Shelton
Map grid C2

The marina and nearby Puget Sound are the big draws here. This small camp features 1,000 feet of shoreline and 0.5 mile of public beach. Clamming is available in season.

RV sites, facilities: There are three sites with partial hookups for RVs up to 40 feet long. Picnic tables and barbecues are provided. Restrooms with flush toilets and coin showers, drinking water, propane gas, a dump station, a seasonal convenience store, fishing licenses, bait and tackle, coin laundry, gasoline, marine fuel, boat docks, and moorage are available. Leashed pets are permitted.

Reservations, fees: Reservations are accepted. Sites are $26 per night. Some credit cards are accepted. Open year-round, with limited winter facilities.

Directions: From Olympia on I-5, turn north on U.S. 101 and drive 22 miles to Shelton and Highway 3. Turn north on Highway 3 and drive about eight miles to Pickering Road. Turn right and drive to the Harstine Bridge. Cross the bridge and continue to North Island Drive. Turn left on North Island Drive and drive 2.8 miles to Haskell Hill Road. Turn left (west) on Haskell Hill Road and drive one mile to the marina.

Contact: Jarrell's Cove Marina, 360/426-8823 or 800/362-8823.

81 JOEMMA BEACH STATE PARK

Scenic rating: 8

on Puget Sound

Map grid C2

This beautiful camp set along the shore of the peninsula provides an alternative to nearby Penrose Point State Park. It covers 122 acres and features 3,000 feet of saltwater frontage on the southeast Kitsap Peninsula. This area is often excellent for boating, fishing, and crabbing. It is a forested park with the bonus of boat-in campsites. Hiking is limited to a trail less than a mile long.

RV sites, facilities: There are 19 sites for tents or RVs up to 40 feet long, two hike-in/bike-in sites, and two boat-in sites (non-motorized boats only). Picnic tables and fire grills are provided. Vault toilets, drinking water, boat-launching facilities, a dock and mooring buoys, and a picnic shelter that can be reserved are available. A grocery store is approximately five miles away. Some facilities are wheelchair accessible. Leashed pets are permitted.

Reservations, fees: Reservations are not accepted. Sites are $19 per night, $12 per night for hike-in/bike-in and boat-in sites, $10 per extra vehicle per night. Moorage is $0.50 per foot with a $10 per night minimum. Open year-round.

Directions: From Tacoma, drive north on Highway 16 for about 10 miles to Highway 302/Purdy exit. At the light turn left onto Highway 302, which changes into Key Peninsula Highway. Stay on Key Peninsula Highway and drive about 15 miles to Whiteman Road. Turn right on Whiteman Road and drive four miles to Bay Road. Turn right and drive one mile to the park entrance (stay on the asphalt road when entering the park).

Contact: Joemma Beach State Park, 253/884-1944; state park information, 360/902-8844, www.parks.wa.gov.

82 PENROSE POINT STATE PARK

Scenic rating: 8

on Puget Sound

Map grid C2

This park on Carr Inlet on Puget Sound, overlooking Lake Bay, has a remote feel, but it's actually not far from Tacoma. The park covers 162 acres, with two miles of saltwater frontage on Mayo Cove and Carr Inlet. The camp has impressive stands of fir and cedars nearby, along with ferns and rhododendrons. The park has 2.5 miles of trails for biking and hiking. Bay Lake is a popular fishing lake for trout and is located one mile away; a boat launch is available there. Penrose is known for its excellent fishing, crabbing, clamming, and oysters. The nearest boat launch to Puget Sound is located three miles away in the town of Home.

RV sites, facilities: There are 82 sites for tents or RVs up to 35 feet (no hookups), one marine trail boat-in site, and a group camp for tents or RVs for 20–50 people. Picnic tables and fire grills are provided. Restrooms with flush toilets and coin showers, drinking water, a dump station, firewood, horseshoe pits, sheltered picnic areas, an interpretive trail, and a beach are available. Boat docks, a marine pump-out station, and mooring buoys are nearby. Some facilities are wheelchair accessible. Leashed pets are permitted.

Reservations, fees: Reservations are accepted (and required for the group camp) at 888/CAMP-OUT (888/226-7688) or www.parks.wa.gov/reservations ($6.50–8.50 reservation fee). Sites are $21 per night, $10 per extra vehicle per night, and the group site is $2.25 per person per night, with a minimum of 20 people per night. Boat mooring is $0.50 per foot with a $10 minimum. Some credit cards are accepted. Open year-round.

Directions: From Tacoma, drive north on Highway 16 for about 10 miles to Highway 302/Purdy exit. At the light turn left onto Highway 302, which changes into Key Peninsula Highway. Stay on Key Peninsula Highway and drive south nine miles through the towns of

Key Center and Home to Cornwall Road KPS (second road after crossing the Home Bridge). Drive 1.25 miles more to 158 Avenue KPS. Turn left and continue on 158 Avenue KPS to the park entrance.

Contact: Penrose Point State Park, 253/884-2514; state park information, 360/902-8844, www.parks.wa.gov.

83 KOPACHUCK STATE PARK

Scenic rating: 8

on Puget Sound

Map grid C2

This park is located on Henderson Bay on Puget Sound near Tacoma. Noteworthy are the scenic views and dramatic sunsets across Puget Sound and the Olympic Mountains. The park covers 109 acres, with 5,600 feet of saltwater shoreline. A unique element of this park is Cutts Island (also called Deadman's Island), which is located 0.5 mile from shore and is accessible only by boat. (There is no camping on the island.) The park has sandy beaches, located about 250 yards down the hill from the camp. Two miles of hiking trails are available. Fishing access is by boat only; a boat launch is located not far from camp.

RV sites, facilities: There are 41 sites for tents or RVs up to 35 feet (no hookups), one primitive boat-in site (no motorized boats permitted), and two group sites for up to 20 and 35 people, respectively. Picnic tables and fire grills are provided. Restrooms with flush toilets and coin showers, drinking water, a dump station, covered picnic areas, a Junior Ranger Program (seasonal), interpretive activities, and boat buoys are available. A small store is approximately one mile away. Some facilities are wheelchair accessible. Leashed pets are permitted.

Reservations, fees: Reservations are not accepted for individual sites but are required for the group site at 253/265-3606. Sites are $21 per night, $10 per extra vehicle per night; the boat-in site is $14 per night. The group site is $2.25 per person per night with a 20-person minimum. Open year-round.

Directions: From Tacoma on I-5, turn north on Highway 16. Drive seven miles north to the third Gig Harbor exit (Wollochet Drive NW). Take that exit and follow the signs for about seven miles to Kopachuck State Park. Note: The road changes names several times, but the route is well signed.

Contact: Kopachuck State Park, 253/265-3606; state park information, 360/902-8844, www.parks.wa.gov.

84 GIG HARBOR RV RESORT

Scenic rating: 7

near Tacoma

Map grid C2

This is a popular layover spot for folks heading up to Bremerton. Just a short jaunt off the highway, it's pleasant, clean, and friendly. An 18-hole golf course, full-service marina, and tennis courts are located nearby. Look for the great view of Mount Rainier from the end of the harbor.

RV sites, facilities: There are 93 sites, most with full or partial hookups (30 and 50 amps), including some long-term rentals, for tents or RVs of any length and one cabin. Some sites are pull-through. Restrooms with flush toilets and showers, drinking water, cable TV, modem access, propane gas, a dump station, a clubroom, coin laundry, ice, playground, horseshoe pits, sports field, and a seasonal heated swimming pool are available. Leashed pets are permitted.

Reservations, fees: Reservations are accepted. Tent sites are $21–26 per night, and RV sites are $32–35 per night. Some credit cards are accepted. Open year-round.

Directions: From Tacoma, drive northwest on Highway 16 for 12 miles to the Burnham Drive NW exit. Take that exit and enter the roundabout to the first right and Burnham Drive NW. Turn right on Burnham Drive NW and drive 1.25 miles to the resort on the left.

Contact: Gig Harbor RV Resort, 253/858-8138 or 800/526-8311, fax 253/858-8399.

85 AMERICAN SUNSET RV AND TENT RESORT

Scenic rating: 8

near Westport Harbor
Map grid B3   BEST (

If location is everything, then this RV camp, set on a peninsula, is a big winner. It covers 32 acres and is 10 blocks from the ocean; hiking and biking trails are nearby. The park is divided into two areas: one for campers, another for long-term rentals. Nearby are Westhaven and Westport Light State Parks, popular with hikers, rockhounds, scuba divers, and surf anglers. Fishing and crabbing off the docks are also options; you can also swim, but not off the docks. Monthly rentals are available in summer.

RV sites, facilities: There are 120 sites with full hookups (20, 30, and 50 amps) for RVs up to 45 feet long, 50 sites for tents or RVs up to 30 feet (no hookups), one lighthouse unit, one beach house, one cabana, and one rental trailer. Some sites are pull-through. Picnic tables and fire rings are provided. Restrooms with flush toilets and showers, drinking water, satellite TV, Wi-Fi, coin laundry, a convenience store, propane, a seasonal heated swimming pool, horseshoe pits, a playground, fish-cleaning station, and recreation hall are available. A marina is located three blocks away. Leashed pets are permitted.

Reservations, fees: RV Sites are $30–32 per night, and tent sites are $21–22. Some discounts are available. Some credit cards are accepted. Open year-round.

Directions: From Aberdeen, drive south on State Route 105 for 22 miles to Westport and Montesano Street (the first exit in Westport). Turn right (northeast) on Montesano Street and drive three miles to the resort on the left.

Contact: American Sunset RV and Tent Resort, 360/268-0207 or 800/569-2267, www.americansunsetrv.com.

86 TOTEM RV PARK

Scenic rating: 8

in Westport
Map grid B3

This 3.2-acre park is set 300 yards from the ocean and features an expanse of sand dunes between the park and the ocean. It has large, grassy sites close to Westhaven State Park, which offers day-use facilities. The owner is a fishing guide and can provide detailed fishing information. The salmon fishing within 10 miles of this park is often excellent in summer. Marked biking trails and a full-service marina are within five miles of the park.

RV sites, facilities: There are 80 sites with full or partial hookups (30 and 50 amps) for tents or RVs of any length. Some sites are pull-through. Restrooms with flush toilets and coin showers, drinking water, cable TV, Wi-Fi, a dump station, coin laundry, and ice are available. A pavilion, barbecue facilities with kitchen, and a fish-cleaning station are also available. Boat docks, launching facilities, and fishing charters are nearby. Propane gas, a store, and café are within 0.5 mile. Some facilities are wheelchair accessible. Leashed pets are permitted.

Reservations, fees: Reservations are accepted. Sites are $24–27 per night. Some credit cards are accepted. Open year-round.

Directions: From Aberdeen, drive south on State Route 105 for 20 miles to the turnoff for Westport. Turn right (north) on the State Route 105 spur and drive 4.3 miles to the docks and Nyhus Street. Turn left on Nyhus Street and drive two blocks to the park on the left.

Contact: Totem RV Park, 360/268-0025 or 888/TOTEM-RV (888/868-3678).

87 HOLAND CENTER

Scenic rating: 6

in Westport
Map grid B3

This pleasant, 18-acre RV park is one of several in the immediate area. The sites are graveled or grassy, with ample space and pine trees in between. There is no beach access from the park, but full recreational facilities are available nearby. About half of the sites are long-term rentals.

RV sites, facilities: There are 85 sites with full hookups for RVs up to 40 feet long. Picnic tables are provided. No open fires are allowed. Restrooms with flush toilets and coin showers, cable TV, coin laundry, and storage sheds are available. Propane gas, a store, café, and ice are located within one mile. Boat docks and launching facilities are nearby. Leashed pets are permitted.

Reservations, fees: Reservations are accepted. Sites are $30 per night. Credit cards are not accepted. Open year-round.

Directions: From Aberdeen, drive south on State Route 105 for 22 miles to Westport. Continue on State Route 105 to a Y intersection. Bear right on Montesano Street and drive approximately two miles to Wilson Street. The park is on the left, at the corner of State Route 105 and Wilson Street.

Contact: Holand Center, phone/fax 360/268-9582.

88 PACIFIC MOTEL AND RV PARK

Scenic rating: 5

near Twin Harbors
Map grid B3

This five-acre park has shaded sites in a wooded setting. It's near Twin Harbors and Westport Light State Park, a day-use park nearby. Both parks have beach access. A full-service marina is located within two miles. About 25 percent of the sites are occupied with long-term rentals.

RV sites, facilities: There are 80 sites with full hookups (20 and 30 amps) for RVs of any length and 12 tent sites. Picnic tables and fire rings are provided. Restrooms with flush toilets and coin showers, drinking water, propane gas, a dump station, fish-cleaning station, recreation hall with a kitchen, cable TV, modem access, pay phone, coin laundry, and a seasonal heated

swimming pool are available. A store, café, and ice are located within one mile. Boat-launching and boat docks are nearby in a full-service marina. Leashed pets are permitted.

Reservations, fees: Reservations are accepted. RV sites are $27 per night, tent sites are $20 per night, $2 per person per night for more than two people. Some credit cards are accepted. Open year-round.

Directions: From Aberdeen, drive south on State Route 105 for approximately 21 miles to Westport. Go past the first Westport exit to a stop sign. Turn right onto the State Route 105 spur (becomes Forrest Street in Westport) and drive 1.8 miles to the park on the right.

Contact: Pacific Motel and RV Park, 360/268-9325, fax 360/268-6227, www.pacificmotelan-drv.com.

89 TWIN HARBORS STATE PARK

Scenic rating: 8

near Westport
Map grid B3

The park covers 172 acres and is located four miles south of Westhaven. It was a military training ground in the 1930s. The campsites are close together and often crammed to capacity in the summer. Highlights include beach access and marked hiking trails, including Shifting Sands Nature Trail. The most popular recreation activities are surf fishing, surfing, beachcombing, and kite-flying. Fishing boats can be chartered nearby in Westport.

RV sites, facilities: There are 250 tent sites, 49 sites with for tents or RVs up to 35 feet long (30 amp full hookups), four hike-in/bike-in sites, and one group site for up to 60 people. Picnic tables and fire grills are provided. Restrooms with flush toilets and coin showers, drinking water, a dump station, a picnic area with a kitchen shelter, and horseshoe pits are available. A store, café, and ice are available within one mile. Some facilities are wheelchair accessible. Leashed pets are permitted.

Reservations, fees: Reservations are accepted

for individual sites and are required for the group site at 888/CAMP-OUT (888/226-7688) or www.parks.wa.gov/reservations ($6.50–8.50 reservation fee). Sites are $21–28 per night, $10 per extra vehicle per night, and hike-in/bike-in sites are $14 per night. The group site is $2.25 per person per night with a 20-person minimum. Some credit cards are accepted. Open year-round.

Directions: From Aberdeen, drive south on State Route 105 for 17 miles to the park entrance on the left (three miles south of Westport).

Contact: Twin Harbors State Park, 360/268-9717; state park information, 360/902-8844, www.parks.wa.gov.

90 PORTER CREEK

Scenic rating: 7

on Porter Creek in Capitol Forest
Map grid B3

This primitive, rustic campground is located about 30 miles from Olympia. It is set in the Capitol Forest along the shore of Porter Creek and is managed by the Department of Natural Resources. It offers trails for hiking, horseback riding, or motorbikes. The camp serves as a launch point for a variety of trips. Most campers take the 0.5-mile trail to Porter Falls, departing from the trailhead just across the road. Within three miles, you can also access trails that lead to a network of 87 miles of off-road vehicle trails and 84 miles of trails for non-motorized use—mountain biking is popular here. With corrals and hitching posts available, this camp is popular among horseback riders.

Note: As of 2010, access from Porter Creek Campground to Capitol Forest was closed because of flood damage and slides; check conditions before attempting a visit.

RV sites, facilities: There are 16 sites for tents or RVs up to 16 feet (no hookups). Picnic tables and fire grills are provided. There is no drinking water, and garbage must be packed out. Vault toilets, corrals, hitching posts, and horse-loading ramps are available. All-terrain vehicles

are permitted. Some facilities are wheelchair accessible. Leashed pets are permitted.

Reservations, fees: Reservations are not accepted. There is no fee for camping. Open May–November, weather permitting.

Directions: On I-5, drive to Exit 88 (10 miles north of Chehalis) and U.S. 12. Turn west on U.S. 12 and drive 21 miles to Porter and Porter Creek Road. Turn right (northeast) on Porter Creek Road and drive 3.4 miles (last half mile is gravel) to a junction. Continue straight on B-Line Road for 0.6 mile to the campground on the left.

Contact: Department of Natural Resources, Pacific Cascade Region North, 360/577-2025, fax 360/274-4196, www.dnr.wa.gov.

91 MIDDLE WADDELL

Scenic rating: 7

on Waddell Creek in Capitol Forest
Map grid B3

This wooded campground is nestled along Waddell Creek in Capitol Forest. The trails in the immediate vicinity are used primarily for all-terrain vehicles (ATVs), making for some noise. There is an extensive network of ATV trails in the area. Mountain bikers tend to prefer Fall Creek camp.

RV sites, facilities: There are 24 sites for tents or RVs of any length. Picnic tables and fire grills are provided. Vault toilets are available. There is no drinking water, and garbage must be packed out. A camp host is on-site. Some facilities are wheelchair accessible. Leashed pets are permitted.

Reservations, fees: Reservations are not accepted. There is no fee for camping. Open May–November, weather permitting.

Directions: From Olympia on I-5, drive south for about 10 miles to Exit 95 and Highway 121. Turn west on Highway 121 and drive four miles to Littlerock. Continue west for one mile to Waddell Creek Road. Turn right and drive three miles and look for the campground entrance road on the left.

WASHINGTON

Contact: Department of Natural Resources, Pacific Cascade Region North, 360/577-2025, fax 360/274-4196, www.dnr.wa.gov.

92 NORTH CREEK/ SHERMAN VALLEY

Scenic rating: 8

on Cedar Creek

Map grid B3

This little-known, wooded campground managed by the Department of Natural Resources is set along Cedar Creek, which offers fishing. There are trails for hikers only (no horses or mountain bikes are allowed). A four-mile loop trail leads to Sherman Valley (a bridge has been out on this trail, with a longer alternative route available; call before planning a hike). Hunters use this camp in the fall. For a side trip, visit the Chehalis River, a five-mile drive to the west. A canoe launch off U.S. 12 is available north of Oakville.

RV sites, facilities: There are five primitive sites for tents or RVs up to 25 feet long. Picnic tables and fire grills are provided. Vault toilets are available. There is no drinking water, and garbage must be packed out. Mountain bikes are permitted on the roads only; trails are reserved for hikers. Some facilities are wheelchair accessible. Leashed pets are permitted.

Reservations, fees: Reservations are not accepted. There is no fee for camping. Open May–November, weather permitting.

Directions: From Olympia, take I-5 to to Exit 95 onto Maytown Road SW. Take that exit and turn southwest on Maytown Road drive to Littlerock (where the road becomes 128th Ave. SW) and continue on 128th to where it ends at Waddell Creek Road SW. Turn right on Waddell Creek Road SW and drive two miles to the Triangle. Turn left (the road will become Sherman Valley Road SW) and drive one mile (the pavement ends and the road become C-Line Road and enters Capitol Forest), and continue four miles to Road C-6000. Turn left (signed Falls Creek Campground) and drive three miles (just beyond a small bridge) to the campgrounds.

Contact: Department of Natural Resources, Pacific Cascade Region North, 360/577-2025, fax 360/274-4196, www.dnr.wa.gov.

93 MIMA FALLS TRAILHEAD

Scenic rating: 10

near Mima Falls

Map grid B3

The highlight here is the five-mile loop trail for hikers and horseback riders that leads to beautiful 90-foot Mima Falls. The campground is quiet and pretty. This spot can be a first-rate choice. One of the unique qualities of this campground is that it provides facilities for both wheelchair users and horseback riders. The trail is not wheelchair accessible, but wheelchair users on horses can access the trip to Mima Falls. The trail runs across the brink of the falls.

RV sites, facilities: There is a primitive, dispersed camping area for about five tents or RVs up to 25 feet long. Picnic tables and fire grills are provided. Vault toilets and a horse-loading ramp are available. There is no drinking water, and garbage must be packed out. Some facilities are wheelchair accessible. Leashed pets are permitted.

Reservations, fees: Reservations are not accepted. There is no fee for camping. Open May–November, weather permitting.

Directions: From Olympia, drive south on I-5 for 10 miles to Highway 121. Turn west on Highway 121 and drive four miles west to Littlerock. Continue west for one mile to Mima Road. Turn left on Mima Road and drive 1.5 miles to Bordeaux Road. Turn right on Bordeaux Road and drive 0.5 mile to Marksman Road. Turn right and drive about 0.6 mile to the campground access road on the left. Turn left and drive 200 yards to the campground.

Contact: Department of Natural Resources, Pacific Cascade Region North, 360/577-2025, fax 360/274-4196, www.dnr.wa.gov.

94 GRAYLAND BEACH STATE PARK

Scenic rating: 8

near Grayland

Map grid B3

This state park features 7,500 feet of beach frontage. All the campsites are within easy walking distance of the ocean. The campsites are relatively spacious for a state park, but they are not especially private. This park is popular with out-of-towners, especially during summer. Recreation options include fishing, beachcombing, and kite-flying. The best spot for surfing is five miles north at Westhaven State Park.

RV sites, facilities: There are 100 sites, including 58 with full-hookups (30 and 50 amps) for tents and RVs up to 40 feet long, four hike-in/bike-in sites, and 16 yurts. Picnic tables and fire grills are provided. Drinking water and restrooms with flush toilets and coin showers, an amphitheater, and a dump station are available. Some facilities are wheelchair accessible. Leashed pets are permitted.

Reservations, fees: Reservations are accepted at 888/CAMP-OUT (888/226-7688) or www.parks.wa.gov/reservations ($6.50–8.50 reservation fee). Sites are $27–28 per night, $10 per extra vehicle per night, hike-in/bike-in sites are $14 per night, and yurts are $55–60 per night. Some credit cards are accepted. Open year-round.

Directions: From Aberdeen, drive south on State Route 105 for 22 miles to the park entrance. The park is just south of the town of Grayland on the right (west).

Contact: Grayland Beach State Park, 360/267-4301; state park information, 360/902-8844, www.parks.wa.gov.

95 BAY CENTER/ WILLAPA BAY KOA

Scenic rating: 7

on Willapa Bay

Map grid B3   BEST (

This KOA is 200 yards from Willapa Bay, within walking distance of a beach that seems to stretch to infinity. A trail leads to the beach and from here you can walk for miles in either direction. The beach sand is mixed with agates, driftwood, and seaweed. Dungeness crabs, clams, and oysters all live near shore. Another bonus is that herds of Roosevelt elk roam the nearby woods. Believe it or not, there are also black bear, although they are seldom seen here. The park covers five acres, and the campsites are graveled and shaded.

RV sites, facilities: There are 42 sites with full or partial hookups (20, 30, and 50 amps) for RVs of any length, 23 tent sites, and two cabins. Some sites are pull-through. Picnic tables and fire rings are provided. Restrooms with flush toilets and showers, drinking water, propane gas, dump station, cable TV, modem access, a recreation hall, camp store, firewood, coin laundry, and ice are available. A café, boat docks, and launching facilities are nearby. Some facilities are wheelchair accessible. Leashed pets are permitted, with certain restrictions.

Reservations, fees: Reservations are accepted at 800/562-7810. Sites are $30–37 per night, $4 per person per night for more than two people, $4 per extra vehicle per night. Some credit cards are accepted. Open mid-March–late October.

Directions: From Nemah on U.S. 101, drive north for five miles to Bay Center/Dike exit (located between Mileposts 42 and 43, 16 miles south of Raymond). Turn left (west) and drive three miles to the campground.

Contact: Bay Center/Willapa Bay KOA, 360/875-6344, www.koa.com.

WASHINGTON

96 RAINBOW FALLS STATE PARK

Scenic rating: 8

on the Chehalis River Bay

Map grid B3

This 139-acre park is set on the Chehalis River and boasts 3,400 feet of shoreline. The camp features stands of old-growth cedar and fir and is named after a few small cascades with drops of about 10 feet. The park has 10 miles of hiking trails, including an interpretive trail, seven miles of bike trails, and seven miles of horse trails. A pool at the base of Rainbow Falls is excellent for swimming. Another attraction, a small fuchsia garden, has more than 40 varieties. There are also several log structures built by the Civilian Conservation Corps in 1935.

RV sites, facilities: There are 45 sites for tents or RVs up to 32 feet (no hookups), eight sites with partial hookups (30 and 50 amps) for tents or RVs up to 60 feet long, three hike-in/bike-in sites, three equestrian sites with hitching points and stock water, and one group site for up to 60 people. Picnic tables and fire rings are provided. Restrooms with flush toilets and coin showers, drinking water, a dump station, firewood, a picnic area, interpretive activities, a playground, horseshoe pits, and a softball field are available. Some facilities are wheelchair accessible. Leashed pets are permitted.

Reservations, fees: Reservations are accepted for only for group site at 360/291-3767. Sites are $21–27 per night, $10 per extra vehicle per night, and hike-in/bike-in sites are $10 per night. Open year-round.

Directions: From Chehalis on I-5, take Exit 77 to drive west 11.7 miles on Highway 6 to milepost 40. Drive 0.4 miles past the marker to River Road. Turn right (west) on River Road and drive 2.7 miles to the Bailey Bridge. Turn right to cross the bridge and immediately turn left onto Leudinghaus Road. Drive 2.2 miles west on Leudinghaus Road to the park entrance on the left. Once inside the park, the campground is on the right.

Contact: Rainbow Falls State Park, 360/291-3767 or 360/902-8844, www.parks.wa.gov.

97 OCEAN PARK RESORT

Scenic rating: 5

on Willapa Bay

Map grid B3

This wooded, 10-acre campground is located 0.5 mile from Willapa Bay. With grassy, shaded sites, it caters primarily to RVs. Fishing, crabbing, and clamming are popular in season. Ocean Park has several festivals during the summer season. During these festivals, this resort fills up. To the north, Leadbetter Point State Park provides a side-trip option.

RV sites, facilities: There are 70 sites with full hookups for RVs of any length, seven tent sites, and two park-model cottages. Some sites are pull-through. Picnic tables are provided. Fire pits are provided at tent sites. Restrooms with flush toilets and coin showers, drinking water, propane gas, a recreation hall, coin laundry, playground, firewood, a spa, and a seasonal heated swimming pool are available. A store and café are available within one mile. Boat docks and launching facilities are located nearby on Willapa Bay. Leashed pets are permitted, with certain restrictions.

Reservations, fees: Sites are $25–30 per night, plus $3 per person per night for more than two people. Some credit cards are accepted. Open year-round.

Directions: From Kelso/Longview on I-5, turn west on Highway 4 and drive 63 miles to U.S. 101. Turn south on U.S. 101 and drive 13 miles to the junction with Highway 103. Turn right (north) on Highway 103 and drive 11 miles to the town of Ocean Park and 259th Street. Turn right (east) on 259th Street and drive two blocks to the resort at the end of the road.

Contact: Ocean Park Resort, 360/665-4585 or 800/835-4634, www.opresort.com.

98 WESTGATE CABIN & RV PARK

Scenic rating: 9

near Long Beach

Map grid B3

Highlights at this pretty and clean four-acre camp include beach access, oceanfront sites, and all the amenities. There are 28 miles of beach that can be driven on. Additional facilities within five miles of the park include an 18-hole golf course.

RV sites, facilities: There are 38 sites with full hookups (30 amps) for RVs up to 50 feet long and six cabins. Some sites are pull-through. Picnic tables are provided. Restrooms with flush toilets and showers, drinking water, cable TV, modem access, coin laundry, gas station, a recreation hall, and ice are available. A store and café are available about four miles away. Boat docks and launching facilities are located nearby on Willapa Bay. Leashed pets are permitted, but not in cabins.

Reservations, fees: Reservations are accepted. Sites are $35–42 per night, plus $2 per person per night for more than two people. Some credit cards are accepted. Open year-round.

Directions: From Kelso/Longview on I-5, turn west on Highway 4 and drive 63 miles to U.S. 101. Turn left (south) on U.S. 101 and drive 13 miles to the junction with Highway 103. Turn right (north) on Highway 103 and drive nine miles to the park on the left (located at the south edge of the town of Ocean Park).

Contact: Westgate Cabin & RV Park, 360/665-4211, fax 360/665-2451.

99 ANDERSEN'S RV PARK ON THE OCEAN

Scenic rating: 7

near Long Beach

Map grid B3

Timing is everything here. When the dates are announced for the local festivals, reservations start pouring in and the sites at this park can be booked a year in advance. Located near the city limits of Long Beach, this five-acre camp features a path through the dunes that will get you to the beach in a flash. It is set in a flat, sandy area with gravel sites. Recreation options include beach bonfires, beachcombing, surf fishing, and clamming (seasonal). Additional facilities found within five miles of the park include marked dune trails, a nine-hole golf course, a riding stable, and tennis courts. The park is big-rig friendly.

RV sites, facilities: There are 60 sites for tents or RVs of any length (20, 30, and 50 amp full hookups). Picnic tables and fire pits are provided. Restrooms with flush toilets and showers, drinking water, cable TV, Wi-Fi, modem access, a dump station, coin laundry, ice, propane gas, fax machine, group facilities, a horseshoe pit, and a playground are available. A store and café are available within two miles. Leashed pets are permitted.

Reservations, fees: Reservations are accepted. Sites are $28–36 per night, plus $2 per person per night for more than two people. Some credit cards are accepted. Open year-round.

Directions: From Kelso/Longview on I-5, turn west on Highway 4 and drive 63 miles to U.S. 101. Turn left (south) on U.S. 101 and drive 13 miles to the junction with Highway 103. Turn right (north) on Highway 103 and drive five miles to the park on the left.

Contact: Andersen's RV Park on the Ocean, 360/642-2231 or 800/645-6795, www.andersensrv.com.

100 OCEANIC RV PARK

Scenic rating: 3

in Long Beach

Map grid B3

This two-acre park is located in the heart of downtown, within walking distance of restaurants and stores. It is also within five miles of an 18-hole golf course, marked bike trails, and a full-service marina.

RV sites, facilities: There are 18 pull-through sites with full hookups (30 and 50 amps) for RVs of any length. No open fires are allowed. Restrooms with flush toilets and showers, cable TV, a restaurant, and propane gas are available. A store, coin laundry, and ice are located within one mile. Boat docks, launching facilities, and boat rentals are nearby. Leashed pets are permitted.

Reservations, fees: Reservations are accepted. Sites are $35 per night, plus $2 per person per night for more than two people. Some credit cards are accepted. Open year-round.

Directions: From Kelso/Longview on I-5, turn west on Highway 4 and drive 63 miles to U.S. 101. Turn left (south) on U.S. 101 and drive 13 miles to the junction with Highway 103. Turn right (north) on Highway 103 and drive two miles to Long Beach. Continue to the park at the south junction of Pacific Highway (Highway 103) and 5th Avenue on the right.

Contact: Oceanic RV Park, 360/642-3836.

101 MERMAID INN AND RV PARK

Scenic rating: 3

near Long Beach
Map grid B3

Situated along the highway, this three-acre park is within four blocks of the beach. It is also within five miles of an 18-hole golf course, a full-service marina, and a riding stable.

RV sites, facilities: There are 11 sites with full hookups (20 and 30 amps) for RVs of any length and 10 motel rooms. Picnic tables are provided. Restrooms with flush toilets and showers, drinking water, cable TV, a picnic area, and coin laundry are available. Propane gas, a gas station, store, restaurant, and ice are located within one mile.

Reservations, fees: Reservations are accepted. Sites are $21–30, plus $1.50 per person per night for more than two people. Some credit cards are accepted. Open year-round.

Directions: From Kelso/Longview on I-5, turn west on Highway 4 and drive 63 miles to U.S. 101. Turn left (south) on U.S. 101 and drive 13 miles to the junction with Highway 103. Turn right (north) on Highway 103 and drive three miles to the park on the right.

Contact: Mermaid Inn and RV Park, 360/642-2600, www.mermaidinnatlongbeachwa.com.

102 DRIFTWOOD RV PARK

Scenic rating: 2

near Long Beach
Map grid B3

This two-acre park features grassy, shaded sites and beach access close by. A fenced pet area is a bonus. Additional facilities within five miles of the park include a nine-hole golf course and a full-service marina.

RV sites, facilities: There are 56 sites with full hookups (30 amps) for RVs of any length. Many sites are pull-through. Picnic tables are provided and portable fire pits can be rented. Restrooms with flush toilets and showers, drinking water, coin laundry, cable TV, Wi-Fi, modem access, group facilities, and a fenced pet area are available. Propane gas, a gas station, store, and restaurant are available within one mile. Leashed pets are permitted, with certain restrictions.

Reservations, fees: Reservations are accepted. Sites are $25–33 per night, plus $3 per person per night for more than two people. Some credit cards are accepted. Open year-round.

Directions: From Kelso/Longview on I-5, turn west on Highway 4 and drive 63 miles to U.S. 101. Turn left (south) on U.S. 101 and drive 13 miles to the junction with Highway 103. Turn right (north) on Highway 103 and drive 2.25 miles to the park on the right, at 14th Street North and Pacific Avenue.

Contact: Driftwood RV Park, 360/642-2711 or 888/567-1902, www.driftwood-rvpark.com.

103 SAND CASTLE RV PARK

Scenic rating: 3

in Long Beach
Map grid B3

This park is set across the highway from the ocean. Although not particularly scenic, it is clean and does provide nearby beach access.

The park covers two acres, has grassy areas, and is one of several in the immediate area. Additional facilities found within five miles of the park include a nine-hole golf course, marked bike trails, a full-service marina, and two riding stables.

RV sites, facilities: There are 38 sites with full hookups (30 and 50 amps) for RVs of any length. Some sites are pull-through. Tents are permitted only with RVs. Picnic tables are provided. Restrooms with flush toilets and coin showers, drinking water, cable TV, Wi-Fi, a dump station, coin laundry, and pay phone are available. Propane gas, a gas station, a store, ice, and a café are available within one mile. Boat docks, launching facilities, and rentals are within five miles. Leashed pets are permitted.

Reservations, fees: Reservations are accepted. Sites are $28.50–30.50 per night, $2 per person per night for more than two people, $2 per extra vehicle per night. Some credit cards are accepted. Open year-round.

Directions: From Kelso/Longview on I-5, turn west on Highway 4 and drive 63 miles to U.S. 101. Turn left (south) on U.S. 101 and drive 13 miles to the junction with Highway 103. Turn right (north) on Highway 103 and drive two miles to the park on the right.

Contact: Sand Castle RV Park, 360/642-2174, www.sandcastlerv.com.

104 SOU'WESTER LODGE

🥾 🚵 🎣 🛶 🐕 🚙 ⛺

Scenic rating: 7

in Seaview on the Long Beach Peninsula

Map grid B3

This one-of-a-kind place features a lodge that dates back to 1892, vintage trailers available for rent, and cottages. Various cultural events are held at the park throughout the year, including fireside evenings with theater and chamber music. The park covers three acres, provides beach access, and is one of the few sites in the immediate area that provides spots for tent camping. This park often attracts creative people such as musicians and artists, and some

arrive for vacations in organized groups. It is definitely not for Howie and Ethel from Iowa. Fishing is a recreation option. The area features the Lewis and Clark Interpretive Center, a lighthouse, museums, fine dining, bicycle and boat rentals, bicycle and hiking trails, and bird sanctuaries. Additional facilities found within five miles of the park include an 18-hole golf course, a full-service marina, and a riding stable. The lodge was originally built for U.S. Senator Henry Winslow Corbett. Two side notes: Tch-Tch stands for "trailers, classic, hodge-podge." The park owners also boast of a "t'ink tank," which they say is not quite a think tank. Like I said, the place is unique—and management has a great sense of humor.

RV sites, facilities: There are 60 sites with full hookups (20 and 30 amps) for RVs of any length, 10 tent sites, a historic lodge, four cottages, and 12 1950s-style trailers in vintage condition. Some RV sites are pull-through. Picnic tables are provided at some sites. Restrooms with flush toilets and showers, drinking water, cable TV, modem access, coin laundry, a classic video library, picnic area with pavilion, and community fire pits and grills are available. Propane gas, dump station, a store, gas station, café, and ice are located within one mile. Boat-launching facilities are nearby. Leashed pets are permitted.

Reservations, fees: Reservations are accepted. Sites are $25.75–42.75 per night, plus $3–4 per person per night for more than two people. Some credit cards are accepted. Open year-round.

Directions: From Kelso/Longview on I-5, turn west on Highway 4 and drive 63 miles to U.S. 101. Turn left (south) on U.S. 101 and drive 13 miles to the junction with Highway 103 (flashing light). Turn left to stay on U.S. 101 and drive one block to Seaview Beach Access Road (38th Place). Turn right and drive toward the ocean. Look for the campground on the left.

Contact: Sou'Wester Lodge, 360/642-2542, www.souwesterlodge.com.

WASHINGTON

105 ILWACO KOA

Scenic rating: 5

near Fort Canby State Park

Map grid B3 · · · · · · · · · · · · **BEST (**

This 17-acre camp is about nine miles from the beach and includes a secluded area for tents. You'll find a boardwalk nearby, as well as the Lewis and Clark Museum, lighthouses, an amusement park, and fishing from a jetty or charter boats. The Washington State International Kite Festival is held in Long Beach the third week of August. The World Kite Museum and Hall of Fame, also in Long Beach, is open year-round. Additional facilities found within five miles of the campground include a maritime museum, hiking trails, and a nine-hole golf course. In my experience, attempts to phone this park were thwarted by a busy signal for weeks.

RV sites, facilities: There are 114 sites with full hookups for RVs of any length, a tent area for up to 50 tents, and four cabins. Some sites are pull-through. Picnic tables are provided. Restrooms with flush toilets and showers, drinking water, cable TV, propane gas, a dump station, recreation hall, seasonal organized activities and tours, a camp store, coin laundry, ice, and a playground are available. Leashed pets are permitted.

Reservations, fees: Reservations are accepted at 800/562-3258. Sites are $26–40 per night, plus $5 per person per night for more than two people, and $6.50 per extra vehicle per night. Some credit cards are accepted. Open mid-May–mid-October.

Directions: From Kelso/Longview on I-5, turn west on Highway 4 and drive 63 miles to U.S. 101. Turn left (south) on U.S. 101 and drive 13 miles to the junction with Highway 103. The campground is located at the junction.

Contact: Ilwaco KOA, phone/fax 360/642-3292, www.koa.com.

106 FISHERMAN'S COVE RV PARK

Scenic rating: 7

near Fort Canby State Park

Map grid B3 · · · · · · · · · · · · **BEST (**

This five-acre park is located by the docks, near where the Pacific Ocean and the Columbia River meet. It has fishing access nearby and caters to anglers. Fish- and clam-cleaning facilities are available in the park. Beach access is approximately one mile away. A maritime museum, hiking trails, a full-service marina, and a riding stable are located within five miles of the park. About 15 percent of the sites are taken by monthly renters.

RV sites, facilities: There are 53 sites with full hookups (30 and 50 amps) for RVs of any length and two tent sites. Picnic tables are provided. Restrooms with flush toilets and coin showers, drinking water, cable TV, modem access, a dump station, and coin laundry are available. Propane gas, a gas station, store, and café are located within one mile. Boat docks, launching facilities, and rentals are nearby. Leashed pets are permitted.

Reservations, fees: Reservations are accepted. RV sites are $30 per night, tent sites are $15 per night. Credit cards are not accepted. Open year-round.

Directions: From Kelso/Longview on I-5, turn west on Highway 4 and drive 63 miles to U.S. 101. Turn left (south) on U.S. 101 and drive 13 miles to the junction with Highway 103. Turn right (north) on Highway 103 and drive two miles to Highway 100/Spruce Street exit. Turn right (south) and drive into the town of Ilwaco. At the junction of Spruce Street SW and 1st Street, turn right (west) on Spruce Street and drive one block to 2nd Avenue SW. Turn left (south) on 2nd Avenue SW and drive four blocks south to the park on the right.

Contact: Fisherman's Cove RV Park, 360/642-3689.

107 CAPE DISAPPOINTMENT STATE PARK

Scenic rating: 10

near Ilwaco

Map grid B3

This park covers 1,882 acres on the Long Beach Peninsula and is fronted by the Pacific Ocean. There is access to 27 miles of ocean beach and two lighthouses. The park contains old-growth forest, lakes, both freshwater and saltwater marshes, streams, and tidelands. It is the choice spot in the area for tent campers. There are two places to camp: a general camping area and the Lake O'Neil area, which offers sites right on the water. Highlights at the park include hiking trails and opportunities for surf, jetty, and ocean fishing. An interpretive center highlights the Lewis and Clark expedition as well as maritime and military history. North Head Lighthouse is open for touring. Colbert House Museum is open during the summer.

RV sites, facilities: There are 83 sites with full or partial hookups (20 and 30 amps) for tents or RVs of any length, 152 sites for tents or RVs of any length (no hookups), five primitive tent sites, three cabins, 14 yurts, and three vacation homes. Picnic tables and fire grills are provided. Restrooms with flush toilets and coin showers, drinking water, a dump station, boat ramp, dock (135 feet), a picnic area, interpretive activities, a horseshoe pit, athletic fields, a small store, and firewood are available. Some facilities are wheelchair accessible. Leashed pets are permitted.

Reservations, fees: Reservations are accepted at 888/CAMP-OUT (888/226-7688) or www. parks.wa.gov/reservations ($6.50–8.50 reservation fee). Sites are $21–28 per night, primitive tent sites are $14 per night, cabins and yurts are $55–60 per night, and vacation homes are $206–388 per night. Some credit cards are accepted. Open year-round.

Directions: From the junction of Highway 4 and Highway 103 (a flashing light, south of Nemah), turn west on Highway 103 (toward Ilwaco) and drive two miles to Ilwaco and Highway 100. Turn right and drive three miles to the park entrance on the right.

Contact: Cape Disappointment State Park, 360/642-3078; state park information, 360/902-8844, www.parks.wa.gov.

108 RIVER'S END RV PARK

Scenic rating: 6

near Fort Columbia State Park

Map grid B3

This wooded park spreads over five acres and has riverside access. Salmon fishing is available here. Additional facilities found within five miles of the campground include marked bike trails and a full-service marina. Also nearby is Fort Columbia State Park.

RV sites, facilities: There are 75 sites with full or partial hookups (30 amps) for tents or RVs of any length. Some sites are pull-through. Picnic tables are provided, and fire pits are available at some sites. Restrooms with flush toilets and coin showers, drinking water, cable TV, a dump station, a recreation hall, coin laundry, firewood, a fish-cleaning station, and ice are available. Propane gas, a gas station, store, and café are located within one mile. Boat docks and launching facilities are nearby on the Columbia River. Leashed pets are permitted.

Reservations, fees: Reservations are accepted. Sites are $26 per night, plus $5 per person per night for more than two people. Credit cards are not accepted. Open April–late October.

Directions: From Kelso/Longview on I-5, turn west on Highway 4 and drive 60 miles to Highway 401. Turn left (south) on Highway 401 and drive 14 miles to the park entrance (just north of Chinook) on the left.

Contact: River's End Campground and RV Park, 360/777-8317.

109 MAUCH'S SUNDOWN RV PARK

Scenic rating: 5

near Fort Columbia State Park

Map grid B3

This park has about 50 percent of the sites rented monthly, usually throughout the summer. The park covers four acres, has riverside access, and is in a wooded, hilly setting with grassy sites. Nearby fishing from shore is available. It's near Fort Columbia State Park.

RV sites, facilities: There are 44 sites with full or partial hookups (30 amps) for tents or RVs of any length. Some sites are pull-through. Small pets are permitted. Picnic tables are provided. No open fires are allowed. Restrooms with flush toilets and coin showers, drinking water, a dump station, cable TV, coin laundry, a convenience store, propane gas, and ice are available. A café is located within three miles. Boat docks and launching facilities are nearby on the Columbia River.

Reservations, fees: Reservations are accepted. Sites are $10–25 per night, plus $2 per person per night for more than two people. Credit cards are not accepted. Open year-round.

Directions: From Kelso/Longview on I-5, turn west on Highway 4 and drive 60 miles to Highway 401. Turn left (south) on Highway 401 and drive to U.S. 101. Take U.S. 101 to the right and continue for 0.5 mile (do not go over the bridge) to the park on the right.

Contact: Mauch's Sundown RV Park, 360/777-8713.

110 SKAMOKAWA VISTA PARK

Scenic rating: 7

near the Columbia River

Map grid B3

This public camp covers 70 acres and features a half mile of sandy beach and a Lewis and Clark interpretive site. A short hiking trail is nearby. The camp also has nearby access to the Columbia River, where recreational options include fishing, swimming, and boating. Additional facilities found within five miles of the park include a full-service marina and tennis courts. In Skamokawa, River Life Interpretive Center stays open year-round.

RV sites, facilities: There are seven RV sites with full hookups, 24 sites with partial hookups for RVs of any length, nine sites for tents or RVs of any length (no hookups), four tent sites, and five yurts. Picnic tables and fire grills are provided. Restrooms with flush toilets and coin showers, drinking water, a dump station, firewood, tennis courts, basketball courts, and a playground are available. A café and ice are located within one mile. Boat docks, launching facilities, and canoe and kayak rentals are nearby. Leashed pets are permitted, with some restrictions.

Reservations, fees: Reservations are accepted. Tent sites are $18 per night, and RV sites are $21–28 per night. Some credit cards are accepted. Open year-round.

Directions: From Kelso/Longview on I-5, turn west on Highway 4 and drive 35 miles to Skamokawa. Continue west on Highway 4 for 0.5 mile to the park on the left.

Contact: Skamokawa Vista Park, Port of Wahkiakum No. 2, 360/795-8605, fax 360/795-8611.

SEATTLE AND THE PUGET SOUND

(BEST RV PARKS AND CAMPGROUNDS

(Family Destinations
Bay View State Park, page 95.

(Wildlife-Viewing
Birch Bay State Park, page 89.
West Beach Resort Ferry-In, page 92.

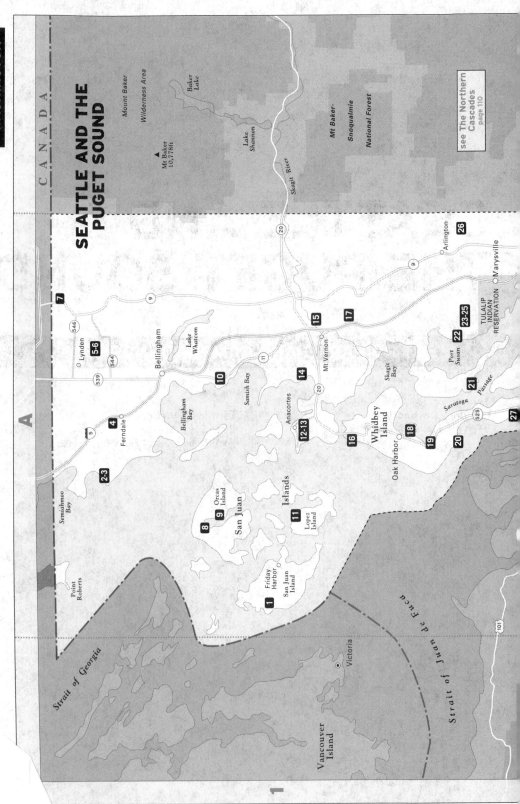

SEATTLE AND THE PUGET SOUND

see The Northern Cascades page 110

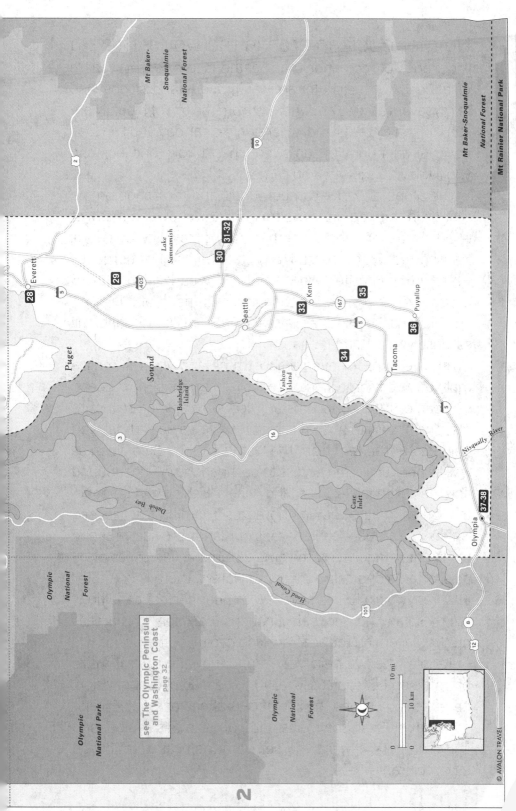

see The Olympic Peninsula
and Washington Coast
page 32

WASHINGTON

Mt Baker-
Snoqualmie
National Forest

Mt Baker-Snoqualmie
National Forest

Mt Rainier National Park

2

90

Lake
Sammamish

31-32

30

29

405

Everett

28

5

33 Kent

167

35

5

Puyallup

36

Seattle

34

Tacoma

Puget

Sound

Bainbridge
Island

Vashon
Island

3

16

5

Case
Inlet

Nisqually River

Dabob Bay

37-38

Olympia

Hood Canal

101

8

12

Olympic
National
Forest

Olympic
National
Forest

Olympic

National Park

10 mi

10 km

0

0

© AVALON TRAVEL

2

No metropolitan area in the world offers a wider array of recreation than Seattle-Tacoma and its sphere of influence. At the center are water, woods, and islands. One of my favorite views anywhere is from the top of Mount Constitution on Orcas Island, where on a clear day you can look out over an infinity of sun-swept charm. Take one look and you'll know this is why you came.

The scope of parks, campgrounds, and recreation on the islands in this region is preeminent. You have an array of excellent destinations, whether you're traveling by car or transported by transport. Many state parks offer gorgeous water-view campsites. Well-furnished RV parks along the I-5 corridor offer respite for vacationers in need of a layover, and hidden lakes, such as Cascade Lake on Orcas Island, will surprise you with their beauty.

But live here for even a short time and you will realize that you need some kind of boat to do it right. A powerboat, sailboat, or kayak offers instant access to adventure, not to mention access to boat-in campsites. With a powerboat, you get instant freedom from the traffic on the I-5 corridor, as well as near-unlimited access to destinations in Puget Sound and the linked inlets, bays, and canals. Fishing can be good, too. On calm days with light breezes, roaming the peaceful waters in a sailboat amid dozens of islands provides a segue to instant tranquility. With some 25 boat-in campsites available, often along calm, sheltered waters, there is no better place anywhere to sea kayak. With near-perfect conditions like these and gorgeous destinations to explore, this area is quickly becoming the sea kayaking capital of the world.

People who live here year-round, fighting the rat maze of traffic on I-5, can easily fall into the trap of tunnel vision, never seeing beyond the line of cars ahead of them. Escape that tunnel. Scan the maps and pages in this region, and in the process, reward yourself with the best water-based adventure anywhere.

1 LAKEDALE RESORT FERRY-IN

Scenic rating: 7

on San Juan Island

Map grid A1

This is a nice spot on 82 acres for visitors who want the solitude of an island camp, yet all the amenities of a privately run campground. Fishing, swimming, and boating are available at the three Lakedale lakes. A sand volleyball court, a half-court basketball area, and a grassy sports field are also on-site. Roche Harbor and Wescott Bay are nearby to the north, and Friday Harbor and its restaurants are nearby to the south.

RV sites, facilities: There are 102 sites for tents and seven sites with partial hookups for tents or RVs up to 40 feet long. There are also six log cabins, one lake house, and 10 luxury lodge rooms. Picnic tables and fire rings are provided. Restrooms with flush toilets and coin showers, drinking water, and firewood are available. A convenience store and ice are available. Boat docks, a swimming beach, and boat and fishing gear rentals are available on-site. Leashed pets are permitted.

Reservations, fees: Reservations are accepted. Tent sites are $20–42 per night, RV sites are $47–57 per night, $7 per extra vehicle per night, and $3 per pet per night. Discounts are offered off-season. Some credit cards are accepted. Open mid-March–mid-October for camping; cabins and lodge rooms are available year-round.

Directions: From Burlington and Highway 20, turn west on Highway 20 and drive 12 miles to the Highway 20 North spur, following signs to the San Juan Islands Ferry Terminal in Anacortes. Take the ferry to Friday Harbor on San Juan Island. From the ferry landing at Friday Harbor, drive two blocks on Spring Street to 2nd Street. Turn right (northwest) on 2nd Street and drive a 0.5 mile to Tucker Avenue (it becomes Roche Harbor Road). Continue 4.5 miles to the resort on the left.

Contact: Lakedale Resort, 360/378-2350 or 800/617-CAMP (800/617-2267), fax 360/378-0944, www.lakedale.com; Washington State Ferries information, 206/464-6400 or 888/808-7977 (Washington state only).

2 BIRCH BAY STATE PARK

Scenic rating: 8

on Birch Bay

Map grid A1   **BEST (**

Birch Bay State Park covers 194 acres and features nearly two miles of beach as well as great views of the Canadian coast range and some of the San Juan Islands. For water lovers it has the best of both worlds, with 8,255 feet of saltwater shoreline and 14,923 feet of freshwater shoreline on Terrell Creek. More than 100 different species of birds, many of which migrate on the Pacific Flyway, can be seen here. Terrell Creek Marsh Interpretive Trail extends 0.5 mile through a forest of black birch trees, Douglas fir, and western hemlock and one of the few remaining saltwater/freshwater estuaries in northern Puget Sound. Bald eagles and great blue herons feed along the banks of Terrell Creek. Several 18-hole golf courses are located nearby. The campground is divided into two loops; hookups for RVs are in the North Loop.

RV sites, facilities: There are 147 sites for tents or self-contained RVs, 20 sites with full or partial hookups (30 amps) for RVs up to 60 feet long, and one primitive group site for tents and RVs that can accommodate up to 40 people, plus two group camps with five sites each. Picnic tables and fire grills are provided. Restrooms with flush toilets and coin showers and a dump station are available. A boat ramp (for boats less than 16 feet only), a picnic area with a sheltered kitchen with electricity, an amphitheater, basketball court, interpretive activities, and a camp host are available. A store, restaurant, coin laundry, and ice are located within one mile. Some facilities are wheelchair accessible. Leashed pets are permitted.

Reservations, fees: Reservations are accepted and are required for groups at 888/CAMP-OUT (888/226-7688) or www.parks.wa.gov/

WASHINGTON

reservations ($6.50–8.50 reservation fee for individual sites, $25 reservation fee for groups). Sites are $21–28 per night, $10 per extra vehicle per night. The group site is $2.25 per person per night. Some credit cards are accepted. Open year-round.

Directions: From Bellingham, drive north on I-5 to Exit 266. At Exit 266 take Grandview west and continue seven miles to Jackson Road. Turn right on Jackson Road and drive one mile to Helweg Road. Turn left and drive 0.25 mile to the reservation office.

Contact: Birch Bay State Park, 360/371-2800, fax 360/371-0455; state park information, 360/902-8844, www.parks.wa.gov.

🖹 BEACHSIDE RV PARK

Scenic rating: 8

on Birch Bay
Map grid A1

This pretty park is surrounded by evergreens and bay views. Hiking, fishing, mountain biking, and nearby golf are also options. Note that most sites are filled with monthly renters.

RV sites, facilities: There are 74 pull-through sites with full hookups (30 and 50 amps) for RVs and five tent sites. Picnic tables are provided. Restrooms with flush toilets and showers, drinking water, a group fire pit, modem access, barbecue area, and coin laundry are available. A boat launch, grocery store, and restaurant are located within one mile. Leashed pets are permitted with certain restrictions.

Reservations, fees: Reservations are recommended at 800/596-9586. Sites are $20–33 per night, $4 per person per night for more than four people. Some credit cards are accepted. Open year-round.

Directions: From Bellingham, drive north on I-5 to Exit 270. Turn west on Birch Bay-Lynden Road and drive five miles to Birch Bay Drive. Turn left and drive one mile to the park on the left.

Contact: Beachside RV Park, tel./fax 360/371-

🖹 THE CEDARS RV RESORT

Scenic rating: 5

in Ferndale
Map grid A1

This resort provides more direct access from I-5 than nearby Windmill Inn or KOA Lynden, and you can usually get a site here. It's a nice, clean park covering 22 acres with spacious sites and trees. Horseshoe pits, a game room, and a recreation field provide possible activities for campers. Several golf courses are nearby.

RV sites, facilities: There are 165 sites with full or partial hookups (20, 30, and 50 amps), including pull-through sites, for tents or RVs of any length and a dispersed tent camping area on grass. Picnic tables and fire pits are provided. Restrooms with flush toilets and showers, drinking water, cable TV, Wi-Fi, modem access, two dump stations, coin laundry, a playground, horseshoe pits, badminton, volleyball, recreation room, arcade, a seasonal heated pool, convenience store, and ice are available. Leashed pets are permitted.

Reservations, fees: Reservations are accepted. Tent sites are $25–30 per night, RV sites are $30–33 per night, and it's $2 per pet per night. Some credit cards are accepted. Open year-round.

Directions: From Bellingham on I-5, drive north to Ferndale and Exit 263. Take Exit 263 and turn right (north) on Portal Way. Drive less than one mile to the resort on the left.

Contact: The Cedars RV Resort, 360/384-2622, fax 360/380-6365.

🖹 WINDMILL INN

Scenic rating: 7

near the Nooksack River
Map grid A1

This nice little spot, only 15 minutes from Puget Sound, is set near the Nooksack River and Wiser Lake. As the last stop before the U.S./Canada border, the camp serves primarily as a layover for people heading north. The quiet and pretty setting abounds with trees and flowers. Area attractions include Mount Baker, the quaint little shops of Lynden, and the nearby Birch Bay area, which offers many recreation options.

RV sites, facilities: There are eight sites for tents or RVs of any length, as well as 15 motel rooms. Picnic tables are provided. Restrooms with flush toilets and coin showers, drinking water, cable TV, modem access, and a park are available. A store, propane gas, a café, coin laundry, and ice are available within one mile. Boat-launching facilities are located within 1.5 miles.

Reservations, fees: Reservations are not accepted. Sites are $18–25 per night, plus $1 per person per night for more than two people. Some credit cards are accepted. Open year-round.

Directions: In Bellingham on I-5, take Exit 256 for Highway 539 (called Meridian Street in Bellingham). Turn north on Highway 539 and drive 10 miles to Lynden. The RV park is on the right side of the road as you enter Lynden.

Contact: Windmill Inn, 360/354-3424, fax 360/354-8138.

6 KOA LYNDEN/BELLINGHAM

Scenic rating: 9

in Lynden

Map grid A1

Lynden is a quaint Dutch town with a windmill and the Pioneer Museum. The park features green lawns, flowers, and trees surrounding a miniature golf course and three fishing ponds, where you can fish for trout. This KOA stars as a unique layover spot for vacationers heading north to Canada via Highway 539 and Highway 546. Nearby recreational options include several golf courses. Bellingham, a historic waterfront town with good restaurants and Victorian mansions, is also close by.

RV sites, facilities: There are 31 sites for tents or RVs (no hookups), 107 sites with full or partial hookups (30 and 50 amps) for RVs

of any length, and 12 cabins. Some sites are pull-through. Picnic tables are provided, and most sites have fire pits. Restrooms with flush toilets and showers, drinking water, modem access, propane gas, a dump station, firewood, a recreation hall, convenience store, café (summer season only), espresso bar, ice cream parlor, coin laundry, ice, a playground, miniature golf, horseshoe pits, volleyball, bicycle rentals, and a seasonal heated swimming pool are available. Fishing tackle and boat rentals are available. Leashed pets are permitted.

Reservations, fees: Reservations are not accepted. Sites are $32–41 per night, $5 per person per night for more than two people. Some credit cards are accepted. Open year-round.

Directions: From I-5 at Bellingham, take Exit 256 to Highway 539. Turn north and drive 12 miles to Highway 546. Turn east on Badger Road and drive three miles to Line Road. Turn right on Line Road and drive 0.5 mile to the campground on the right.

Contact: KOA Lynden/Bellingham, 360/354-4772, fax 360/354-7050, www.koa.com.

7 SUMAS RV PARK

Scenic rating: 5

in Sumas

Map grid A1

Located near the U.S./Canada border, this campground is a layover spot to spend American dollars before heading into British Columbia and making the conversion. The camp is set in the grassy flatlands; it has graveled sites and a few trees. Nearby recreation options include an 18-hole golf course.

RV sites, facilities: There is a grassy area for tents and 50 sites with full or partial hookups (20, 30, and 50 amps) for tents or RVs of any length. Some sites are pull-through. Picnic tables are provided, and fire rings are at most sites. Restrooms with flush toilets and coin showers, drinking water, modem access, a dump station, coin laundry, and firewood are available. A store, ice, café, and a ballpark are located within one mile. Leashed pets are permitted.

Reservations, fees: Reservations are accepted. Tent sites are $10 per night, RV sites are $20–25 per night, plus $4 per person per night for more than two people. Some credit cards are accepted. Open year-round.

Directions: From I-5 at Bellingham, take Exit 256 to Highway 539. Turn north on Highway 539 and drive 12 miles to Highway 546. Turn right (east) on Highway 546 (Badger Road) and drive 14 miles (the road becomes Highway 9) to Sumas and look for Cherry Street. Turn right (south) at Cherry Street (the road becomes Easterbrook Road) and drive two blocks to the park on the left.

Contact: Sumas RV Park, 360/988-8875 or 866/213-5180.

8 WEST BEACH RESORT FERRY-IN

Scenic rating: 9

on Orcas Island

Map grid A1   **BEST (**

Right on the beach, this resort offers salmon fishing, boating, swimming, and an apple orchard. Some sites have ocean views and rent by the week in July and August. An excellent alternative to Moran State Park, which is often full, it offers the same recreation opportunities. There is excellent fishing, crabbing, and scuba diving at the resort, and fishing charters and guided kayak tours are available. The beaches at Orcas Island are prime spots for whale-watching and beautiful views, especially at sunrise and sunset.

RV sites, facilities: There are 11 sites with tents or RVs of any length (20 and 30 amp full hookups), 18 tent sites, and eight overflow tent sites. There are also 20 cabins. Picnic tables and fire pits are provided. Restrooms with flush toilets and coin showers (April–October only), a pay phone, convenience store, seasonal café, play-ound, coin laundry, ice, propane gas, modem ~s, fish-cleaning station, and firewood are ~e. A spa is available for a fee. Also on-site

are a boat ramp, dock, full-service marina, rentals, moorage, and dry storage. A dump station is nearby. Leashed pets are permitted.

Reservations, fees: Reservations are accepted by phone or online. Sites are $38–43 per night for up to three people, $5 for each additional person to a maximum of six, $7 per extra vehicle per night, and $5 per pet per night. Some credit cards are accepted. Open year-round.

Directions: From Burlington and I-5, take exit 230 (San Juan Islands) for Highway 20. Turn west on Highway 20 and drive 12 miles to the Highway 20 North spur, following signs to the San Juan Islands Ferry Terminal in Anacortes. Take the ferry to Orcas Island. From the ferry landing, turn left and drive nine miles on Horseshoe Highway/Orcas Road to the entrance of Eastsound. Continue 0.25 mile to Enchanted Forest Road. Turn left and drive 2.4 miles to the end of Enchanted Forest Road and the resort.

Contact: West Beach Resort, 360/376-2240 or 877/WEST-BCH (877/937-8224), fax 360/376-4746, www.westbeachresort.com; Washington State Ferries, 206/464-6400 or 888/808-7977 (Washington state only).

9 MORAN STATE PARK FERRY-IN

Scenic rating: 10

on Orcas Island

Map grid A1

This state park is drop-dead gorgeous. It covers 5,252 acres, with surprise lakes, hiking trails, and the best mountaintop views anywhere in the chain of islands. There are actually four separate campgrounds plus a primitive area. You can drive to the summit of Mount Constitution, which tops out at 2,409 feet, then climb up the steps to a stone observation tower (built in 1936 by the Civilian Conservation Corps). The tower provides sensational 360-degree views of Vancouver, Mount Baker, the San Juan Islands, the Cascade Mountains, and several cities on the distant shores of mainland America and Canada. No RVs are allowed on the winding road to the top. There are five freshwater lakes (no gas motors boats permitted) with fishing for rainbow trout, cutthroat trout, and kokanee salmon, 33 miles of hiking trails, 11 miles of biking trails, and six miles of horse trails. The landscape features old-growth forest, primarily lodgepole pine, and several small waterfalls. Nearby recreation options include a nine-hole golf course.

RV sites, facilities: There are 136 sites for tents or RVs up to 45 feet (no hookups), including some pull-through sites, 15 primitive hike-in/bike-in tent sites, and one vacation house for up to 10 people. Picnic tables and fire grills are provided. Restrooms with flush toilets and coin showers, drinking water, a dump station, a picnic area with log kitchen shelter, firewood, and a snack bar are available. Boat docks, limited fishing supplies, launching facilities, and boat rentals are located at the concession stand in the park. Some facilities are wheelchair accessible. Leashed pets are permitted.

Reservations, fees: Reservations are accepted at 888/CAMP-OUT (888/226-7688) or www.parks.wa.gov/reservations ($6.50–8.50 reservation fee); sites are $16–21 per night, $14 per night for bike-in/hike-in sites, and $10 per extra vehicle per night. Reserve the vacation house at 800/360-4240. Some credit cards are accepted. Open year-round. Note that some campers consider the ferry-crossing fee for RVs very high; call ahead for prices.

Directions: From Seattle on I-5, drive north to Burlington and Highway 20. Turn west on Highway 20 and drive 12 miles to the Highway 20 North spur, following signs to the San Juan Islands Ferry Terminal in Anacortes. Take the ferry to Orcas Island. From the ferry landing, turn left on Horseshoe Highway/Orcas Road and drive 13 miles to Moran State Park (well marked). Stop at the campground registration booth for directions to your site.

Contact: Moran State Park Ferry-In, 360/376-2326; state park information, 360/902-8844, www.parks.wa.gov; Washington State Ferries, 206/464-6400 or 888/808-7977 (Washington state only).

10 LARRABEE STATE PARK

Scenic rating: 9

on Samish Bay

Map grid A1

Larrabee State Park—the first state park established in Washington—sits on Samish Bay in Puget Sound and boasts 8,100 feet of saltwater shoreline. The park's 2,683-acres include two freshwater lakes, coves, and tidelands, as well as 13.7 miles of hiking trails and 11.7 miles of mountain-biking trails. A setting of conifers and thick forests mixes with waterways, streams, and marsh before concluding at a beautiful stretch of coastline, a prime spot for sunsets and wildlife-viewing. Fishing is available on Fragrance Lake and Lost Lake, which are hike-in lakes. Chuckanut Mountain is nearby. A relatively short drive south will take you to Anacortes, where you can catch a ferry to islands in the San Juan chain.

RV sites, facilities: There are 51 tent sites, 26 sites for tents or RVs up to 60 feet long (30 amp full hookups), eight primitive tent sites, and a group site for up to 40 people. Picnic tables and fire grills are provided. Restrooms with flush toilets and coin showers, drinking water, a dump station, a picnic area with electricity and a covered shelter, amphitheater, and firewood are available. Boat-launching facilities are available nearby. Some facilities are wheelchair accessible. Leashed pets are permitted.

Reservations, fees: Reservations are accepted at 888/CAMP-OUT (888/226-7688) or www.parks.wa.gov/reservations ($6.50–8.50 reservation fee). Primitive tent sites are $14 per night, tent sites are $21 per night, hookup sites are $28 per night, $10 per extra vehicle per night. Group site fees vary with size of group. Some credit cards are accepted. Open year-round with limited winter facilities.

Directions: From Bellingham on I-5, take Exit 250 to Fairhaven Parkway. Turn right on Fairhaven Parkway. Drive less than a mile to State Route 11/Chuckanut Drive (second stoplight). Turn left (stay left at the next stoplight) and drive six miles to the park entrance on the right.

WASHINGTON

Contact: Larrabee State Park, 360/676-2093, fax 360/676-2061; state park information, 360/902-8844, www.parks.wa.gov.

11 SPENCER SPIT STATE PARK FERRY-IN

Scenic rating: 9

on Lopez Island

Map grid A1

Spencer Spit State Park offers one of the few island campgrounds accessible to cars via ferry. It also features walk-in sites for privacy, which require anywhere from a 50-foot to a 200-yard walk to the tent sites. A sand spit extends far into the water and provides a lagoon and good access to prime clamming areas. The park covers 138 acres. Picnicking, beachcombing, and sunbathing are some pleasant activities for campers looking for relaxation.

RV sites, facilities: There are 37 sites for tents or self-contained RVs up to 20 feet long (no hookups), seven primitive walk-in sites, seven hike-in/bike-in sites, three marine trail sites, one Adirondack for up to eight people, and three group sites for up to 50 people each. Picnic tables and fire grills are provided. Restrooms with flush toilets, drinking water, a picnic area, two kitchen shelters, and a dump station are available, and 12 mooring buoys are available on the Cascadia Marine Trail. Boat docks and a launch are within two miles, and showers are approximately three miles away. Some facilities are wheelchair accessible. Leashed pets are permitted.

Reservations, fees: Reservations are accepted at 888/CAMP-OUT (888/226-7688) or www.parks.wa.gov/reservations ($6.50–8.50 reservation fee, $25 for groups). Sites are $21 per night, $14 per night for primitive and marine trail sites, $25–30 per night for the Adirondack, $10 per extra vehicle per night, and $10 per night for mooring buoys. Group site fees vary with size of group. Open year-round with limited winter facilities.

Directions: From Seattle on I-5, drive north to Burlington and Highway 20. Turn west on Highway 20 and drive 12 miles to the Highway 20 North spur, following signs to the San Juan Islands Ferry Terminal in Anacortes. Take the ferry to Lopez Island. The park is within four miles of the ferry terminal.

Contact: Spencer Spit State Park, 360/468-2251, fax 360/468-3176; state park information, 360/902-8844, www.parks.wa.gov; Washington State Ferries, 206/464-6400 or 888/808-7977 (Washington state only).

12 PIONEER TRAILS RV RESORT & CAMPGROUND

Scenic rating: 9

near Anacortes on Fidalgo Island

Map grid A1

This site offers resort camping in the beautiful San Juan Islands. Tall trees, breathtaking views, cascading waterfalls, and country hospitality can all be found here. Side trips include nearby Deception Pass State Park (eight minutes away) and ferries to Victoria (British Columbia), Friday Harbor, Orcas Island, and other nearby islands (it is imperative to arrive early at the ferry terminal). Nearby recreation activities include horseshoes, an 18-hole golf course, relaxing spas, and lake fishing. Those familiar with this park may remember the group of old covered wagons that were here; they're gone now.

RV sites, facilities: There are 150 sites with full hookups (30 and 50 amps), including some pull-through sites, for RVs of any length, and five cabins. Picnic tables and fire rings are provided. Restrooms with flush toilets and showers, drinking water, a dump station, cable TV, modem and Wi-Fi access, a pay phone, and coin laundry are available. A recreation hall, playground, horseshoe pits, and a basketball court are available nearby. Leashed pets are permitted (no fee) with certain restrictions.

Reservations, fees: Reservations are recommended. A three-night minimum on holidays is required. Sites are $32–59 per night, $5 per extra vehicle per night. Some credit cards are accepted. Open year-round.

Directions: From Burlington and I-5, take Exit 230 for Highway 20 West. Drive west and cross over the Padilla Bridge onto Fidalgo Island. Watch for the Highway 20 sign and turn left at Mile Post 48. Go up the hill and take the first road on the right (Miller Road). Drive 0.25 mile, and look for the park on the right side of the road.

Contact: Pioneer Trails RV Resort & Campground, 360/293-5355 or 888/777-5355, fax 360/299-2240, www.pioneertrails.com.

13 WASHINGTON PARK

Scenic rating: 6

in Anacortes

Map grid A1

This 220-acre city park is set in the woods on a peninsula at the west end of Fidalgo Island. It features many hiking trails. A 2.2-mile paved loop route for vehicles, hikers, and bicyclists stretches around the perimeter of the park. The Washington State Ferry terminals are located 0.5 mile away, providing access to the San Juan Islands. This is a popular camp, and it's a good idea to arrive early to claim your spot.

RV sites, facilities: There are 63 sites, including 46 with partial hookups, for tents or RVs of any length and one group tent site for up to 30 people. Some sites are pull-through. Restrooms with flush toilets and coin showers, drinking water, a playground, recreation field, dump station, a picnic area that can be reserved, a boat launch, and coin laundry are available. Some facilities are wheelchair accessible. Leashed pets are permitted.

Reservations, fees: Reservations are accepted for residents of Anacortes only. Sites are $17–23 per night; the group site is $84 per night. Open year-round.

Directions: From Burlington and I-5, turn west on Highway 20 and drive to Anacortes and Commercial Avenue. Turn right on Commercial Avenue and drive approximately 0.5 mile to 12th Street. Turn left and drive about three miles (west of the ferry landing the road changes names several times) to Sunset Avenue. Turn left on Sunset Avenue. The park entrance and campground will be on the left.

Contact: Washington Park, City of Anacortes, 360/293-1927; Parks and Recreation, 360/293-1918, www.cityofanacortes.org.

14 BAY VIEW STATE PARK

Scenic rating: 10

on Padilla Bay

Map grid A1   BEST (

This campground set on Padilla Bay has a large, grassy area for kids, making it a good choice for families. Bordering 11,000 acres of Padilla Bay and the National Estuarine Sanctuary, this 25-acre park boasts 1,285 feet of saltwater shoreline. From the park, you can enjoy views of the San Juan Islands fronting Padilla Bay. On a clear day, you can see the Olympic Mountains to the west and Mount Rainier to the south. Kayakers should note that Padilla Bay becomes a large mud flat during low tides. Windsurfing is becoming popular, but tracking tides and wind is required. The Breazeale Padilla Bay Interpretive Center is located 0.5 mile north of the park. For a nice day trip, take the ferry at Anacortes to Lopez Island (there are several campgrounds there as well).

RV sites, facilities: There are 46 sites for tents or self-contained RVs, 29 sites with full hookups for RVs up to 60 feet long, one group tent site for up to 20–64 people, and four cabins. Picnic tables and fire rings are provided. Restrooms with flush toilets and coin showers, drinking water, firewood, a dump station, and a picnic area with a beach shelter are available. Horseshoes, volleyball, interpretive activities, windsurfing, waterskiing, swimming, and boating are available. A store and coin laundry are eight miles away in Burlington. Some facilities are wheelchair accessible. Leashed pets are permitted.

Reservations, fees: Reservations are accepted

for individual sites and are required for groups at 888/226-7688 (CAMP-OUT) or www.parks. wa.gov/reservations ($6.50–8.50 reservation fee). Sites are $21–28 per night, $10 per extra vehicle per night. The group site is $2.25 per person per night with a minimum of 20 people. Cabins are $55–65 per night. Some credit cards are accepted. Open year-round, but some campsites are closed in winter.

Directions: From Seattle on I-5, drive north to Burlington and Exit 230 for Highway 20. Turn west on Highway 20 and drive seven miles west (toward Anacortes) to Bay View-Edison Road. Turn right (north) on Bay View-Edison Road and drive four miles to the park on the right.

Contact: Bay View State Park, 360/757-0227, fax 360/757-1967; state park information, 360/902-8844, www.parks.wa.gov.

15 BURLINGTON/ ANACORTES KOA

Scenic rating: 5

in Burlington

Map grid A1

This is a fine KOA campground, complete with all the amenities. The sites are spacious and comfortable. Possible side trips include tours of the Boeing plant in Everett, about 30 miles away, Victoria, Vancouver Island, and the San Juan Islands.

RV sites, facilities: There are 110 sites, most with full or partial hookups for tents or RVs of any length and 11 cabins. Some sites are pull-through. Restrooms with flush toilets and showers, drinking water, a dump station, cable TV, modem access, a pay phone, coin laundry, limited groceries, ice, propane gas, firewood, and a barbecue area are available. There are also an indoor heated pool, spa, recreation hall, game room, playground, nine-hole miniature golf, bicycle rentals, horseshoe pits, and a sports field. Leashed pets are permitted.

Reservations, fees: Reservations are recommended in the summer, 800/562-9154. Sites are $32–45 per night, plus $2.50–4 per person

per night for more than two people. Some credit cards are accepted. Open year-round.

Directions: From Burlington and I-5, take Exit 232/Cook Road. Turn right on Cook Road and drive 100 feet to Old Highway 99. Turn left and drive 3.5 miles to the campground on the right.

Contact: Burlington/Anacortes KOA, 360/724-5511, www.koa.com.

16 DECEPTION PASS STATE PARK

Scenic rating: 10

on Whidbey Island

Map grid A1

This state park is located at beautiful Deception Pass on the west side of Whidbey Island. It features 4,134 acres with almost 15 miles of saltwater shoreline and six miles of freshwater shoreline on three lakes. The landscape ranges from old-growth forest to sand dunes. This diverse habitat has attracted 174 species of birds. An observation deck overlooks the Cranberry Lake wetlands. The park also features spectacular views of shoreline, mountains, and islands, often with dramatic sunsets. At one spot, rugged cliffs drop to the turbulent waters of Deception Pass. Recreation options include fishing at Pass Lake, a freshwater lake within the park. Fly-fishing for trout is a unique bonus for anglers. Note that each lake has different regulations for boating. Scuba diving is also popular. The park provides 38 miles of hiking trails, 1.2 miles of wheelchair-accessible trails, and six miles of biking trails. There are several historic Civilian Conservation Corps buildings throughout the park.

RV sites, facilities: There are 167 sites for tents or self-contained RVs up to 50 feet (no hookups), 143 sites with partial hookups (30 amps) for RVs up to 50 feet long, five primitive tent sites, and three group sites for up to 50 people each. Some sites are pull-through. Picnic tables and fire rings are provided. Restrooms with flush toilets and coin showers, drinking water, and a dump station are available. A concession stand, park store, firewood, horseshoe pit, an amphitheater, interpretive activities, a sheltered picnic area with electricity and a kitchen, a boat launch, boat rentals, and mooring buoys are available nearby. Some facilities are wheelchair accessible. Leashed pets are permitted.

Reservations, fees: Reservations are accepted at 888/CAMP-OUT (888/226-7688) or www. parks.wa.gov/reservations ($6.50–8.50 reservation fee). Primitive tent sites are $12 per night, sites without hookups are $21 per night, sites with hookups are $28 per night, $10 per extra vehicle per night. Some credit cards are accepted. Open year-round, with limited winter services.

Directions: From Seattle on I-5, drive north to Burlington and Exit 230/Highway 20. Take that exit and drive west on Highway 20 for 12 miles to Highway 20 South. Turn south on Highway 20 South and drive six miles (across the bridge at Deception Pass) and continue to the park entrance (three miles south of the bridge) on the right.

Contact: Deception Pass State Park, 360/675-2417, fax 360/675-8991; state park information, 360/902-8844, www.parks.wa.gov.

17 RIVERBEND RV PARK

Scenic rating: 5

on the Skagit River

Map grid A1

Riverbend RV Park is a pleasant layover spot for I-5 travelers. While not particularly scenic, it is clean and spacious. Access to the Skagit River here is a high point, with fishing for salmon, trout, and Dolly Varden in season; check regulations. Nearby recreational options include a casino and an 18-hole golf course. Note that about half of the sites are filled with monthly renters.

RV sites, facilities: There are 90 sites with full hookups (30 and 50 amps) for RVs of any length and 25 tent sites. Most sites are pull-through. Picnic tables are provided at RV sites, and fire pits are at some tent sites. Restrooms with flush toilets and coin showers, drinking water, a dump station, coin laundry, a playground, and horseshoe pits are available. A store, café, and ice are located within 0.25 mile. Leashed pets are permitted with certain restrictions.

Reservations, fees: Reservations are accepted. RV sites are $15–21.84 per night; tent sites are $13 per night. Some credit cards are accepted. Open year-round.

Directions: From Seattle on I-5, drive north to Mount Vernon and the College Way exit. Take the College Way exit and drive one block west to Freeway Drive. Turn right (north) and drive 0.25 mile to Stewart Road. Turn left and drive a short distance to the park entrance on the right.

Contact: Riverbend RV Park, 360/428-4044.

18 STAYSAIL RV

Scenic rating: 4

in Oak Harbor on Whidbey Island

Map grid A1

This popular city park fills quickly on summer weekends. With graveled sites, it is geared toward RVers but is also suitable for tent campers. Fishing, swimming, boating, and sunbathing are all options in the vicinity. Several miles of paved trails run along the waterfront. A full-service marina is nearby. Within a few miles are an 18-hole golf course and tennis courts. Fort Ebey and Fort Casey State Parks are both a short drive away and make excellent side trips.

RV sites, facilities: There are 56 sites with full hookups for RVs of any length and 30 tent sites. Picnic tables are provided. No campfires are allowed. Restrooms with flush toilets and coin showers, drinking water, and a dump station are available. A playground, picnic shelter, ball fields, volleyball, basketball and tennis courts, and horseshoe pits are also available. Propane gas, a store, café, coin laundry, and ice are available within one mile. Boat-launching facilities, swimming, a lagoon, wading pools, a day-use area, and walking trails are at Oak

Harbor. Some facilities are wheelchair accessible. Leashed pets are permitted.

Reservations, fees: Reservations are not accepted. Sites are $12–20 per night. Open year-round.

Directions: From Burlington and I-5, turn west on Highway 20 and drive 28 miles to the intersection of Highway 20 and Pioneer Way in the town of Oak Harbor on Whidbey Island. Drive straight through the intersection onto Beeksma Drive and continue about one block to the park on the left.

Contact: Windjammer Park, City of Oak Harbor, 360/279-4500, www.oakharbor.org.

19 FORT EBEY STATE PARK

Scenic rating: 9

on Whidbey Island

Map grid A1

This park is situated on the west side of Whidbey Island at Point Partridge. It covers 645 acres and has access to a rocky beach that is good for exploring. There are also 28 miles of trails for hiking and biking. Fort Ebey is the site of a historic World War II bunker, where concrete platforms mark the locations of the historic gun batteries. Other options here include fishing and wildlife viewing. There is limited fishing available for smallmouth bass at Lake Pondilla, which is only about 100 yards away from the campground and a good place to see bald eagles. The saltwater shore access provides a good spot for surfing and paragliding.

RV sites, facilities: There are 50 developed campsites, including 10 sites with electricity, for tents or self-contained RVs up to 70 feet long, one boat-in site, and four hike-in/bike-in sites. Picnic tables and fire grills are provided. Restrooms with flush toilets and coin showers, drinking water, firewood, amphitheater, and picnic area are available. Some facilities are wheelchair accessible. Leashed pets are permitted.

Reservations, fees: Reservations are accepted at 888/CAMP-OUT (888/226-7688) or parks.wa.gov/reservations ($6.50–8.50

reservation fee). Sites are $14 per night for primitive sites, $21–28 per night for developed sites, $10 per extra vehicle per night. Some credit cards are accepted. Open year-round.

Directions: From Burlington and I-5, turn west on Highway 20 and drive 23 miles (Whidbey Island) to Libbey Road (eight miles past Oak Harbor). Turn right and drive 1.5 miles to Hill Valley Drive. Turn left and enter the park.

Contact: Fort Ebey State Park, 360/678-4636; state park information, 360/902-8844, www.parks.wa.gov.

20 FORT CASEY STATE PARK

Scenic rating: 10

on Whidbey Island

Map grid A1

Fort Casey State Park offers more than 10,000 feet of shoreline on Puget Sound at Admiralty Inlet; fishing is often good in this area, in season. The park's 467 acres include a lighthouse, Keystone Spit, and 1.8 miles of hiking trails. As part of Ebey's Landing National Historic Reserve, there is a coast artillery post featuring two historic guns on display. The lighthouse and interpretive center are open seasonally. Remote-control glider flying is allowed in a designated area, and there is a parade field perfect for kite-flying. The underwater park, another highlight, attracts divers. You can also take a ferry from here to Port Townsend on the Olympic Peninsula.

RV sites, facilities: There are 35 developed campsites for tents or self-contained RVs up to 40 feet long. Picnic tables and fire grills are provided. Restrooms with flush toilets and coin showers, drinking water, a seasonal interpretive center, a picnic area, firewood, and an amphitheater are available. Boat-launching facilities are located in the park. Some facilities are wheelchair accessible. Leashed pets are permitted.

Reservations, fees: Reservations are not accepted. Sites are $21 per night, $10 per extra vehicle per night. Open year-round.

Directions: From Burlington and I-5, turn west on Highway 20 and drive 35 miles to Coupeville. Continue south on Highway 20 (adjacent to Whidbey Island Naval Air Station) and then turn right (still Highway 20, passing Crockett Lake and the Camp Casey barracks) to the park entrance.

Contact: Fort Casey State Park, 360/678-4519; state park information, 360/902-8844, www. parks.wa.gov.

21 CAMANO ISLAND STATE PARK

Scenic rating: 10

on Camano Island

Map grid A1

This park features panoramic views of Puget Sound, the Olympic Mountains, and Mount Rainier. Set on the southwest point of Camano Island, near Lowell Point and Elger Bay along the Saratoga Passage, this wooded camp offers quiet and private campsites. The park covers 134 acres and features 6,700 feet of rocky shoreline and beach, three miles of hiking trails, and just one mile of bike trails. Good inshore angling for rockfish is available year-round, and salmon fishing is also good in season. A diving area with kelp is available. There is also a self-guided nature trail.

RV sites, facilities: There are 88 developed campsites for tents or self-contained RVs up to 40 feet long, one group camp for up to 100 people, and five cabins. Picnic tables and fire grills are provided. Restrooms with flush toilets and coin showers, drinking water, a dump station, firewood, a playground, a sheltered picnic area with a kitchen, summer interpretive programs, an amphitheater, and a large grassy play area in the day-use area are available. Boat-launching facilities are located in the park. An 18-hole golf course is nearby. Some facilities are wheelchair accessible. Leashed pets are permitted.

Reservations, fees: Reservations are not accepted for individual sites but are required for the group camp and the cabins May–September at 360/387-1550. Sites are $21 per night, $10 per extra vehicle per night. The group reservation fee is $25, plus $2.25 per person per night for tents and $8.66 per night per RV. Cabins are $23–62 per night. Open year-round.

Directions: From Seattle on I-5, drive north (17 miles north of Everett) to Exit 212. Take Exit 212 to Highway 532. Drive west on Highway 532 to Stanwood and continue three miles (to Camano Island) to a fork. Bear left at the fork and continue south for six miles on East Camano Drive, bearing to the right where the road becomes Elger Bay Road, to Mountain View Road. Turn right and drive two miles (climbs a steep hill) and continue to Lowell Point Road. Turn left and continue to the park entrance road. (The park is 14 miles southwest of Stanwood).

Contact: Camano Island State Park, 360/387-3031; state park information, 360/902-8844, www.parks.wa.gov.

22 KAYAK POINT REGIONAL PARK

Scenic rating: 5

near Tulalip Indian Reservation on Puget Sound

Map grid A1

This camp usually fills on summer weekends. Set on the shore of Puget Sound, this large, wooded county park covers 428 acres on Port Susan. It provides good windsurfing and whale-watching as well as hiking; there's an 18-hole golf course nearby. Good for crabbing and fishing, a pier is also available.

RV sites, facilities: There are 34 sites with partial hookups, including some pull-through sites, for tents or RVs up to 32 feet long, and 10 yurts with heat and electricity for up to five people. Picnic tables and fire rings are provided. Restrooms with flush toilets and showers, drinking water, firewood, a picnic area with covered shelter, and a 300-foot fishing pier are available. Boat docks and launching facilities are located in the park. Some facilities are wheelchair accessible. Leashed pets are permitted.

Reservations, fees: Reservations are accepted at 425/388-6600 or www1.co.snohomish.wa.us/. Sites are $20–25 per night, additional tents are $6 per tent per night, and yurts are $40–60 per night. Some credit cards are accepted. Open year-round.

Directions: From Everett and I-5, drive north to Exit 199 (Tulalip) at Marysville. Take Exit 199, bear left on Tulalip Road, and drive west for 13 miles (road name changes to Marine Drive) through the Tulalip Indian Reservation to the park entrance road on the left (marked for Kayak Point). Turn left and drive mile to the park.

Contact: Kayak Point Regional Park, Snohomish County, 425/388-6600 or 360/652-7992, fax 425/377-9509, www1.co.snohomish.wa.us/.

23 WENBERG COUNTY PARK

Scenic rating: 8

on Lake Goodwin

Map grid A1

Wenberg County Park is set along the east shore of Lake Goodwin, where the trout fishing can be great. The park covers 46 acres with 1,140 feet of shoreline frontage on the lake. Powerboats are allowed, and a seasonal concession stand provides food. Hiking is limited to a 0.5-mile trail. This is a popular weekend spot for Seattle-area residents.

Management of Wenberg Park was transferred from the state to Snohomish County, and with that came several significant changes. The reservation protocol is different, of course, and no alcohol is permitted.

RV sites, facilities: There are 45 developed tent sites and 30 sites with partial hookups (30 amps) for RVs up to 50 feet long. Some sites are pull-through. Picnic tables and fire grills are provided. Restrooms with flush toilets and coin showers, drinking water, a dump station, two sheltered picnic areas, concession stand, firewood, swimming beach with bathhouse, ⌐d a playground are available. Boat-launching

facilities and docks are located on Lake Goodwin. Some facilities are wheelchair accessible. Leashed pets are permitted.

Reservations, fees: Reservations are accepted at 425/388-6600. Sites are $20–25 per night, $10 per extra vehicle per night. Some credit cards are accepted. Open year-round.

Directions: From Everett on I-5, drive north to Exit 206. Take Exit 206/Smokey Point, turn west, and drive 2.4 miles to Highway 531. Bear right on Highway 531 and drive 2.7 miles to East Lake Goodwin Road. Turn left and drive 1.6 miles to the park entrance on the right.

Contact: Wenberg County Park, 425/388-6600, www1.co.snohomish.wa.us.

24 CEDAR GROVE SHORES RV PARK

Scenic rating: 5

on Lake Goodwin

Map grid A1

This wooded resort is set on the shore of Lake Goodwin near Wenberg County Park. The camp is a busy place in summer, with highlights including trout fishing, waterskiing, and swimming. A security gate is closed at night. Tent campers should try Lake Goodwin Resort. An 18-hole golf course is nearby.

RV sites, facilities: There are 48 sites with full hookups (30 and 50 amps), some pull-through, for RVs of any length. Restrooms with flush toilets and coin showers, drinking water, coin laundry, a dump station, modem access, propane gas, ice, a clubhouse, a recreation room, horseshoe pits, and firewood are available. A store and café are located within one mile. Boat docks and launching facilities are nearby on Lake Goodwin. Some facilities are wheelchair accessible. Leashed pets are permitted.

Reservations, fees: Reservations are accepted. Sites are $24.55–42 per night, plus $5 per adult per night for more than two people. Some credit cards are accepted. Open year-round.

Directions: From Everett on I-5, drive north for 10 miles to Exit 206. Take Exit 206/Smokey

Point and drive west for 2.2 miles to Lakewood Road. Turn right and drive 3.2 miles to Westlake Goodwin Road. Turn left (the park is marked) and drive 0.75 mile to the resort on the left.

Contact: Cedar Grove Shores RV Park, 360/652-7083 or 866/342-4981, www.cgsrvpark.com.

25 LAKE GOODWIN RESORT

Scenic rating: 5

on Lake Goodwin
Map grid A1

This private campground is set on Lake Goodwin, which is known for good trout fishing. Motorboats are permitted on the lake, and an 18-hole golf course is located nearby. Other activities include swimming in the lake, horseshoe pits, shuffleboard, and a recreation field.

RV sites, facilities: There are 85 sites with full or partial hookups (30 and 50 amps) for RVs of any length, 11 tent sites, and four cabins. Some sites are pull-through. Picnic tables and fire grills are provided. Restrooms with flush toilets and coin showers, drinking water, propane gas, a convenience store with recreation equipment, coin laundry, ice, Wi-Fi, a playground, and firewood are available. Boat moorage and a fishing pier are located nearby on Lake Goodwin.

Reservations, fees: Reservations are accepted at 800/242-8169. RV sites are $40–55 per night, and tent sites are $26 per night. Some credit cards are accepted. Open year-round.

Directions: From Everett on I-5, drive north for 10 miles to Exit 206. Take Exit 206/Smokey Point, turn west, and drive two miles to Highway 531/Lakewood Road. Bear right on Highway 531 and drive 3.5 miles to the resort on the left.

Contact: Lake Goodwin Resort, 360/652-8169, fax 360/652-4025, www.lakegoodwinresort.com.

26 RIVER MEADOWS COUNTY PARK WALK-IN

Scenic rating: 6

on the Stillaguamish River
Map grid A1

This Snohomish County park has 150 acres of open meadows and forests along the banks of the Stillaguamish River. The campground gets light to average use. This area of the river is popular for non-motorized boating such as canoeing, kayaking and inner tubing. Hiking trails meander through the park, and other activities include cycling, bird-watching, and fishing for steelhead in season. The Festival of the River is held in August. Native Americans once occupied the property, and ancient Olcott artifacts have been found here.

RV sites, facilities: There are six sites for RVs up to 20 feet long, 23 walk-in tent sites, an overflow area (parking lot) for RVs of any length (no hookups), and six yurts. Picnic tables and fire pits are provided at the tent sites. Flush toilets, drinking water, picnic tables, picnic shelters that can be reserved, a primitive boat launch, and a swimming beach are available. Some facilities are wheelchair accessible. Leashed pets are permitted.

Reservations, fees: Reservations are accepted for RV sites and yurts at 360/388-6600 or www1.co.snohomish.wa.us. Sites are $20–25 per night; yurts are $40–60 per night. No credit cards are accepted. Open year-round.

Directions: From Seattle, drive north on I-5 to Exit 203 and the junction with Highway 530. Turn east on Highway 530 and drive approximately 3.5 miles to the town of Arlington and Highway 9. Turn left (north) and drive a short distance to Highway 530. Turn right (east) on Highway 530 and drive approximately one mile to Arlington Heights Road. Turn right (south) and drive two miles to Jordan Road. Bear right and drive approximately three miles to the park entrance on the right.

Contact: River Meadows County Park, 360/435-3441; Snohomish County Parks, 425/388-6600, www1.co.snohomish.wa.us.

WASHINGTON

27 SOUTH WHIDBEY STATE PARK

Scenic rating: 10

on Whidbey Island

Map grid A1

This park is located on the southwest end of Whidbey Island. It covers 347 acres and provides opportunities for hiking, picnicking, and beachcombing along a sandy beach. There are spectacular views of Puget Sound and the Olympic Mountains. The park features old-growth forest, tidelands for clamming and crabbing (check current regulations), and campsites set in the seclusion of lush forest undergrowth. The park has 4,500 feet of saltwater shoreline on Admiralty Inlet and 3.5 miles of hiking trails.

RV sites, facilities: There are 46 sites for tents or RVs up to 45 feet (no hookups), eight sites with partial hookups (30 amps) for tents or RVs up to 45 feet long, three hike-in/bike-in sites, and one group site for tents and RVs up to 28 feet long for up to 100 people. Picnic tables and fire grills are provided. Restrooms with flush toilets and coin showers, drinking water, a dump station, convenience store, a picnic area with a log kitchen shelter, an amphitheater, interpretive activities, a seasonal Junior Ranger program, and firewood are available. Some facilities are wheelchair accessible. Leashed pets are permitted.

Reservations, fees: Reservations are accepted at 888/CAMP-OUT (888/226-7688) or www.parks.wa.gov/reservations ($6.50–8.50 reservation fee). Sites are $21–28 per night, $10 per night for hike-in/bike-in sites, $10 per extra vehicle per night, and the group site is $2.25 per person per night with a minimum of 20 people. Some credit cards are accepted. Open February–November.

Directions: From Seattle on I-5, drive north to Burlington and the Highway 20 exit. Take Highway 20 west and drive 28 miles (past Coupeville on Whidbey Island) until it becomes Highway 525. Continue south on Highway 525 to Smugglers Cove Road (the park access road,

well marked). Turn right and drive six miles to the park entrance. The park can also be reached easily with a ferry ride from Mukilteo (located southwest of Everett) to Clinton (this also makes a great bike trip to the state park).

Contact: South Whidbey State Park, 360/331-4559, fax 360/331-7669; state park information, 360/902-8844, www.parks.wa.gov.

28 LAKESIDE RV PARK

Scenic rating: 6

in Everett

Map grid A2

With 75–100 of the 150 RV spaces dedicated to permanent rentals, this camp can be a crapshoot for vacationers in summer; the remaining spaces get filled nightly with vacationers all summer. The park is landscaped with annuals, roses, other perennials, and shrubs, which provide privacy and gardens for each site. There's a pond stocked with trout year-round, providing fishing for a fee.

RV sites, facilities: There are 150 sites, including some pull-through, with full hookups (20, 30, and 50 amps) for RVs of any length and nine tent sites. Restrooms with flush toilets and showers, drinking water, cable TV, coin laundry, propane gas, a playground, off-leash dog area, horseshoe pits, modem access, and pay phones are available. Some facilities are wheelchair accessible. Leashed pets are permitted.

Reservations, fees: Reservations are recommended at 800/468-7275. Tent sites are $13.83–15.37 per night, and RV sites are $34.73–38.59 per night. Some credit cards are accepted. Open year-round.

Directions: From Everett on I-5, drive north to Exit 186. Take Exit 186 and turn west on 128th Street. Drive about two miles to Old Highway 99. Turn left and drive 0.25 mile to the park on the left.

Contact: Lakeside RV Park, 425/347-2970 or 800/468-7275, fax 425/347-9052.

29 LAKE PLEASANT RV PARK

Scenic rating: 6

on Lake Pleasant

Map grid A2

A large, developed camp geared primarily toward RVers, this park is set on Lake Pleasant. The setting is pretty, with lakeside sites and plenty of trees. Just off the highway, it's a popular camp, so expect lots of company, especially in summer. This is a good spot for a little trout fishing. The lake is not suitable for swimming. Note that half of the 196 sites are monthly rentals. All sites are paved.

RV sites, facilities: There are 196 sites with full hookups (30 and 50 amps) for RVs up to 45 feet long; half of these are available for overnight use. Some sites are pull-through. No campfires are allowed. Picnic tables are provided. Restrooms with flush toilets and showers, drinking water, cable TV, modem and Wi-Fi access, a dump station, pay phone, coin laundry, a playground, and propane gas are available. Some facilities are wheelchair accessible. Leashed pets are permitted with certain restrictions.

Reservations, fees: Reservations are recommended. Sites are $44 per night. Some credit cards are accepted. Open year-round.

Directions: From the junction of I-5 and I-405 (just south of Seattle), take I-405 and drive to Exit 26. Take that exit to the Bothell/Everett Highway over the freeway and drive south for about one mile; look for the park on the left side.

Contact: Lake Pleasant RV Park, 425/487-1785 or 800/742-0386.

30 VASA PARK RESORT

Scenic rating: 5

on Lake Sammamish

Map grid A2

I was giving a seminar in Bellevue one evening when a distraught-looking couple walked in and pleaded, "Where can we camp tonight?" I answered, "Just look in the book," and they ended up staying at this camp. It was the easiest sale I ever made. This is the most rustic of the parks in the immediate Seattle area. The resort is on the western shore of Lake Sammamish, and the state park is at the south end of the lake. Lake activities include fishing for smallmouth bass, waterskiing, and personal watercraft riding. There is a two-week maximum stay during the summer. An 18-hole golf course, hiking trails, and marked bike trails are close by. The park is within easy driving distance of Seattle.

RV sites, facilities: There are 16 sites for tents or RVs of any length (partial hookups) and six sites with full hookups for RVs of any length. Picnic tables are provided. Restrooms with flush toilets and coin showers, drinking water, a dump station, coin laundry, a playground, and a boat-launching facility are available. Propane gas, firewood, a store, and a café are located within one mile. Leashed pets are permitted.

Reservations, fees: Reservations are accepted. Sites are $24–29 per night, plus $4 per adult per night for more than two people, $1.50 per child. Some credit cards are accepted. Open mid-May–mid-October.

Directions: From Bellevue, drive east on I-90 to Exit 13. Take Exit 13 to West Lake Sammamish Parkway SE and drive north for one mile; the resort is on the right. Note: Larger rigs should pull into the parking lot on the left.

Contact: Vasa Park Resort, 425/746-3260, fax 425/746-0301, www.vasaparkresort.com.

31 ISSAQUAH VILLAGE RV PARK

Scenic rating: 7

in Issaquah

Map grid A2

Although Issaquah Village RV Park doesn't allow tents, it's set in a beautiful environment ringed by the Cascade Mountains, making it a scenic choice in the area. Lake Sammamish State Park is just a few miles north. Most of the sites are asphalt, and 20 percent are long-term rentals.

RV sites, facilities: There are 58 sites, including

two pull-through sites, with full hookups (30 and 50 amps) for RVs of any length. Picnic tables are provided. Restrooms with flush toilets and showers, drinking water, cable TV, a dump station, pay phone, coin laundry, picnic areas, playground, and propane gas are available. Some facilities are wheelchair accessible. Leashed pets are permitted.

Reservations, fees: Reservations are recommended. Sites are $42–55 per night. Some credit cards are accepted. Open year-round.

Directions: From Seattle on I-405 (preferred) or I-5, drive to the junction of I-90. Take I-90 east and drive 17 miles to Exit 17 (Front Street). Drive under the freeway and turn right at 229th Avenue SE. Turn right on SE 66th Street (about 50 feet from the first right turn). Proceed on 66th, as it turns into 1st Avenue and brings you to the park entrance.

Contact: Issaquah Village RV Park, 425/392-9233 or 800/258-9233, http://home.earthlink.net/issaquahrv.

32 BLUE SKY RV PARK

Scenic rating: 5

near Lake Sammamish State Park
Map grid A2

Blue Sky RV Park is situated in an urban setting just outside of Seattle. It provides a good off-the-beaten-path alternative to the more crowded metro area, yet it is still only a short drive from the main attractions in the city. Nearby Lake Sammamish State Park provides more rustic recreation opportunities, including hiking and fishing. All sites are paved and level, and about half of the sites are filled with monthly renters.

RV sites, facilities: There are 51 sites with full hookups for RVs of any length. Some sites are pull-through. Picnic tables are provided at some sites. Restrooms with flush toilets and showers, drinking water, cable TV, coin laundry, modem access, and a covered picnic pavilion with barbecue are available. Leashed pets are permitted.

Reservations, fees: Reservations are accepted. Sites are $35 per night, plus $5 per person per night for more than two people. Open year-round.

Directions: From Seattle on I-5, drive to the junction with Highway 90. Go east on Highway 90 and drive 22 miles to Exit 22 (Preston/Falls City exit) and turn right at stop sign. Turn left onto 302nd Avenue SE and proceed 0.5 mile to the campground entrance at the end of the road.

Contact: Blue Sky RV Park, 425/222-7910, www.blueskypreston.com.

33 SEATTLE/TACOMA KOA

Scenic rating: 5

in Kent on the Green River
Map grid A2

This is a popular urban campground, not far from the highway yet in a pleasant setting. The sites are spacious, and many are pull-throughs that accommodate large RVs. A public golf course is located nearby. During the summer, take a tour of Seattle from the campground. The tour highlights include the Space Needle, Pike Place Market, Pioneer Square, Woodland Park Zoo, Seattle Aquarium, Boeing Museum of Flight, Safeco Field, and Puget Sound.

RV sites, facilities: There are 134 sites with full or partial hookups (30 and 50 amps) for RVs up to 50 feet long and 10 tent sites. Cable TV is provided at some sites. Restrooms with flush toilets and showers, drinking water, a dump station, pay phone, coin laundry, modem and Wi-Fi access, limited groceries, espresso bar, propane gas, ice, RV supplies, free movies, and a seasonal pancake breakfast are available. A large playground, a seasonal heated swimming pool, three-wheel fun-cycle rentals, and a recreation room are also available. No campfires are allowed. Some facilities are wheelchair accessible. Leashed pets are permitted with certain restrictions.

Reservations, fees: Reservations are recommended at 800/562-1892. Sites are $31.95–54.95

per night, plus $3.50 per person per night for more than two people. Some credit cards are accepted. Open year-round.

Directions: From Seattle, drive south on I-5 for 10 miles to Exit 152 for 188th Street/Orillia Road. Drive east on Orillia Road for three miles (the road becomes 212th Street) to the campground on the right.

Contact: Seattle/Tacoma KOA, 253/872-8652, fax 253/395-1782, www.koa.com.

34 DASH POINT STATE PARK

Scenic rating: 8

near Federal Way

Map grid A2

This urban state park set on Puget Sound features unobstructed water views. The park covers 388 acres, with 3,300 feet of saltwater shoreline and 12 miles of trails for hiking and biking. Fishing, windsurfing, swimming, boating, and mountain biking are all popular. Tacoma offers a variety of activities and attractions, including the Tacoma Art Museum (with a children's gallery); the Washington State Historical Society Museum; the Seymour Botanical Conservatory at Wrights Park; Point Defiance Park, Zoo, and Aquarium; the Western Washington Forest Industries Museum; and the Fort Lewis Military Museum.

RV sites, facilities: There are 114 tent sites, 27 sites with partial hookups for RVs up to 40 feet long, and a group site for up to 80 people. Picnic tables and fire grills are provided. Restrooms with flush toilets and coin showers, drinking water, an amphitheater, two sheltered picnic areas, and firewood are available. Some facilities are wheelchair accessible. Leashed pets are permitted.

Reservations, fees: Reservations are accepted for individual sites at 888/CAMP-OUT (888/226-7688) or www.parks.wa.gov/reservations ($6.50–8.50 reservation fee); reservations are required for group site at 253/661-4955. Sites are $21–28 per night, $10 per extra vehicle per night; the group site is $2.25 per

person with a minimum of 20 people. Open year-round.

Directions: On I-5 in Tacoma, drive to Exit 143/320th Street. Take that exit and turn west on 320th Street and drive four miles to 47th Street (a T intersection). Turn right on 47th Street and drive to Highway 509 (another T intersection). Turn left on Highway 509/Dash Point Road and drive one mile to the park. Note: The camping area is on the south side of the road; the day-use area is on the north side of the road.

Contact: Dash Point State Park, 253/661-4955, fax 253/661-4995; state park information, 360/902-8844, www.parks.wa.gov.

35 GAME FARM WILDERNESS PARK CAMP

Scenic rating: 6

on the Stuck River in Auburn

Map grid A2

The Game Farm Wilderness Park is just minutes from downtown Auburn and centrally located to Mount Rainier, Seattle, and the Cascade Mountains. The campground is located along the scenic Stuck River and is adjacent to an 18-hole disc golf course.

RV sites, facilities: There are 18 sites with partial hookups for tents or RVs of any length. Picnic tables and fire grills are provided. Restrooms with flush toilets, drinking water, a picnic shelter, and a dump station are available. Some facilities are wheelchair accessible. Leashed pets are permitted.

Reservations, fees: Reservations are accepted. Sites are $25 per night, with a discount for Auburn residents and a one-week maximum stay limit. Some credit cards are accepted. Open April–mid-October.

Directions: On I-5 (north of Tacoma), drive to Exit 142 and Highway 18. Turn east on Highway 18 and drive to the Auburn/Enumclaw exit. Take that exit and drive to the light at Auburn Way. Turn left on Auburn Way South and drive one mile to Howard Road. Exit to the right on

WASHINGTON

Howard Road and drive 0.2 mile to the stop sign at R Street. Turn right on R Street and drive 1.5 miles to Stuck River Drive SE (just over the river). Turn left and drive 0.25 mile upriver to the park on the left at 2401 Stuck River Drive.

Contact: City of Auburn Parks and Recreation Department, 253/931-3043, fax 253/931-4005, www.auburnwa.gov.

36 MAJESTIC MOBILE MANOR RV PARK

Scenic rating: 7

on the Puyallup River near Tacoma
Map grid A2

This clean, pretty park along the Puyallup River and with views of Mount Rainier caters to RVers. (Note that at least half of the sites are filled with monthly renters.) Recreation options within 10 miles include an 18-hole golf course, a full-service marina, and tennis courts. Tacoma offers a variety of activities and attractions, including the Tacoma Art Museum (with a children's gallery); the Washington State Historical Society Museum; the Seymour Botanical Conservatory at Wrights Park; Point Defiance Park, Zoo, and Aquarium; the Western Washington Forest Industries Museum; and the Fort Lewis Military Museum.

RV sites, facilities: There are 118 sites with full hookups for RVs of any length and 12 tent sites (May–Sept. only). Restrooms with flush toilets and showers, drinking water, cable TV, Wi-Fi access, propane gas, a dump station, a recreation hall, a convenience store, coin laundry, ice, and a seasonal heated swimming pool are available. Leashed pets are permitted.

Reservations, fees: Reservations are accepted. Tent sites are $18 per night, RV sites $18–26 per night, $2 per person per night for more than two people. Open year-round.

Directions: From the north end of Tacoma on I-5, take Exit 135 to Highway 167. Drive east on Highway 167 (River Road) for four miles to the park on the right.

Contact: Majestic Mobile Manor RV Park, 253/845-3144 or 800/348-3144, fax 253/841-2248, www.majesticrvpark.com.

37 OLYMPIA CAMPGROUND

Scenic rating: 7

near Olympia
Map grid A2

This campground in a natural, wooded setting has all the comforts. Nearby recreation options include an 18-hole golf course, hiking trails, marked bike trails, and tennis courts.

RV sites, facilities: There are 95 sites with full or partial hookups for tents or RVs of any length and two cabins. Some sites are pull-through. Picnic tables are provided and fire rings are at some sites. Restrooms with flush toilets and showers, drinking water, modem and Wi-Fi access, propane gas, a dump station, recreation hall, convenience store, coin laundry, ice, a playground, seasonal heated swimming pool, gas station, and firewood are available. A café is located within two miles. Leashed pets are permitted.

Reservations, fees: Reservations are accepted. Sites are $19–28 per night, plus $4 for each child and $8 per adult per night for more than two people. Some credit cards are accepted. Open year-round.

Directions: From Olympia on I-5, take Exit 101 to Tumwater Boulevard. Turn left and drive 0.25 mile to Center Street. Turn right and drive one mile to 83rd Avenue (Center ends at 83rd). Turn right and drive an eighth of a mile to the park on the left. Turn in at the Texaco station entrance (the campground is behind the store)

Contact: Olympia Campground, 360/352-2551, www.olympiacampground.com.

38 NISQUALLY PLAZA RV PARK

Scenic rating: 5

on McAlister Creek

Map grid A2

Nisqually Plaza is located near McAlister Creek, where salmon fishing and boating are popular. Nearby recreation opportunities include an 18-hole golf course and the Nisqually National Wildlife Refuge (admission is charged), which offers seven miles of foot trails for viewing a great variety of flora and fauna.

RV sites, facilities: There are 65 sites with full hookups (20, 30, and 50 amps) for RVs of any length. Some sites are pull-through. Picnic tables are provided. Restrooms with flush toilets and coin showers, drinking water, cable TV, Wi-Fi access, a convenience store, café, coin laundry, ice, and a seasonal swimming pool are available. Some facilities are wheelchair accessible. Small, hand-launched boat facilities are nearby. Leashed pets are permitted.

Reservations, fees: Reservations are accepted. Sites are $28 per night, plus $2 per person per night for more than two people. Weekly and monthly rates are available. Open year-round.

Directions: In Olympia on I-5, take Exit 114 and drive a short distance to Martin Way. Turn right and proceed to the first road (located between two gas stations), a private access road for the park. Turn right and drive a short distance to the park.

Contact: Nisqually Plaza RV Park, 360/491-3831.

THE NORTHERN CASCADES

BEST RV PARKS AND CAMPGROUNDS

Family Destinations
Leavenworth KOA, page 155.

Prettiest Lakes
Horseshoe Cove, page 115.

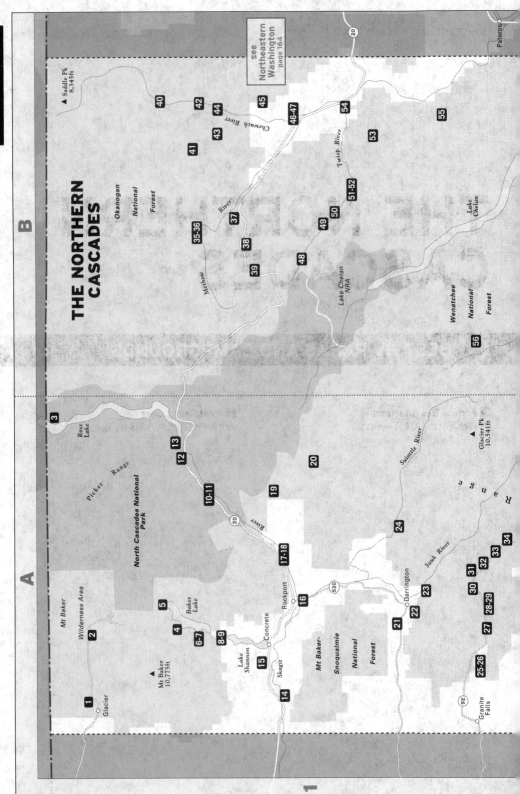

THE NORTHERN CASCADES

see Northeastern Washington page 164

▲ Saddle Pk 8,345ft

Okanogan National Forest

Chewuch River

Methow River

Twisp River

Lake Chelan

Lake Chelan NRA

Wenatchee National Forest

Picket Range

North Cascades National Park

Ross Lake

Mt Baker Wilderness Area

Glacier

▲ Mt Baker 10,775ft

Baker Lake

Lake Shannon

Concrete

Skagit River

Rockport

Darrington

Sauk River

Suiattle River

▲ Glacier Pk 10,541ft

Mt Baker-Snoqualmie National Forest

Granite Falls

Pateros

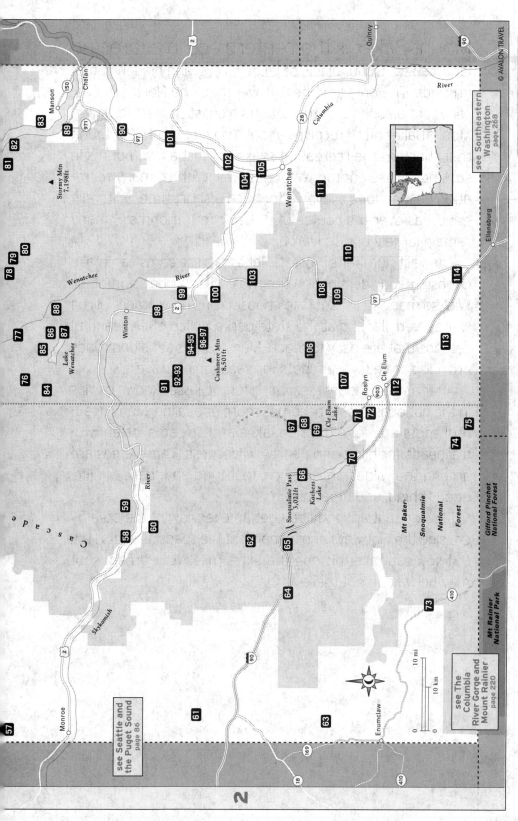

see Southeastern Washington page 268

see The Columbia River Gorge and Mount Rainier page 220

see Seattle and the Puget Sound page 86

© AVALON TRAVEL

Mount Baker is the centerpiece in a forested landscape with hundreds of lakes, rivers, and hidden campgrounds. The only limit here is weather. The Northern Cascades are deluged with the nation's highest snowfall in winter; Mount Baker often receives a foot a day for weeks. Although that shortens the recreation season to just a few months in summer, it has another effect as well: With so many recreation destinations available for such a short time – literally hundreds over the course of three or four months – many remain largely undiscovered.

The vast number of forests, lakes, and streams can make choosing your destination the most difficult decision of all. With so many stellar spots to choose from, newcomers will be well served starting at the state parks, which offer beautiful settings that are easy to reach. Many camps set along roads provide choice layover spots for vacationing travelers.

After a while, though, searching for the lesser-known camps in the national forests becomes more appealing. Many beautiful spots are set alongside lakes and streams, often with trailheads for hikes into nearby wilderness. These areas are among the wildest in America, featuring abundant wildlife, good fishing, and great hiking.

It's true that anybody can get an overview of the area by cruising the highways and camping at the roadside spots I list. But you can take this one the extra mile. Your dream spot may be waiting out there.

1 DOUGLAS FIR

Scenic rating: 10

on the Nooksack River in
Mount Baker–Snoqualmie National Forest

Map grid A1

Set along the Nooksack River, this camp features river views from some campsites. It is a beautiful camp, surrounded by old-growth Douglas fir, silver fir, and western hemlock. Trout fishing is available on the river, and there are hiking trails in the area.

RV sites, facilities: There are 30 sites for tents or RVs up to 55 feet long. Picnic tables and fire grills are provided. Drinking water, vault toilets, and a picnic shelter are available. A store, café, coin laundry, and ice are located within five miles at Glacier. Some facilities are wheelchair accessible. Leashed pets are permitted.

Reservations, fees: Reservations are accepted at 877/444-6777 or www.recreation.gov ($10 reservation fee). Sites are $16–18 per night, $8 per night per additional vehicle. Open May–September, weather permitting.

Directions: From Bellingham on I-5, take the Highway 542 exit and drive 33 miles to Glacier. Continue two miles northeast on Highway 542 to the campground on the left.

Contact: Mount Baker–Snoqualmie National Forest, Mount Baker Ranger District, 360/856-5700, fax 360/856-1934, www.fs.fed.us.

2 SILVER FIR

Scenic rating: 9

on the North Fork of the Nooksack River in
Mount Baker–Snoqualmie National Forest

Map grid A1

This campground is set on the North Fork of the Nooksack River. It is within 30 minutes of the Heather Meadows area, which provides some of the best hiking trails in the entire region. In addition, a one-mile round-trip to Artist Ridge promises views of Mount Baker and Mount Shuksan. The first part of the trail to the first viewpoint is wheelchair accessible.

Fishing is available nearby, and in the winter the area offers cross-country skiing. You're strongly advised to obtain a U.S. Forest Service map in order to take maximum advantage of the recreational opportunities in the area.

RV sites, facilities: There are 16 sites for tents or RVs of any length. Picnic tables and barbecue grills are provided. Drinking water, vault toilets, garbage bins, and a group picnic shelter are available. Some facilities are wheelchair accessible. Leashed pets are permitted.

Reservations, fees: Reservations are accepted at 877/444-6777 or www.recreation.gov ($10 reservation fee). Sites are $16–17 per night, $8 per night per additional vehicle. Open May–early September, weather permitting.

Directions: From I-5 at Bellingham, turn east on Highway 542 and drive 33 miles to Glacier. Continue east on Highway 542 for 12.5 miles to the campground on the right.

Contact: Mount Baker–Snoqualmie National Forest, Mount Baker Ranger District, 360/856-5700, fax 360/856-1934, www.fs.fed.us.

3 HOZOMEEN

Scenic rating: 9

on Ross Lake in
Ross Lake National Recreation Area

Map grid A1

Hozomeen campground, at 1,600 feet elevation, is just inside the U.S./Canada border at the northeast end of Ross Lake. It takes quite an effort to get here, which tends to weed out all but the most stalwart campers. This is good news for those few, for they will find a quiet, uncrowded camp in a beautiful setting. No firewood gathering is permitted here.

RV sites, facilities: There are 122 sites for tents or RVs of any length (but getting there requires traveling over 39 miles of rough road). Picnic tables and fire grills are provided. Vault toilets and drinking water are available. Garbage must be packed out. A boat launch on nearby Ross Lake is available. Leashed pets are permitted.

Reservations, fees: Reservations are not

accepted. There is no fee for camping. Open late May–September.

Directions: This campground is accessible only through Canada. From the town of Hope, British Columbia, turn south on Silver-Skagit Road; it is a narrow dirt/gravel road, which is often rough. Drive south for 39 miles to the campground at the north end of Ross Lake.

Contact: North Cascades National Park, 360/856-5700, fax 360/856-1934, www.nps.gov/noca/.

◢ PARK CREEK

Scenic rating: 6

near Baker Lake in
Mount Baker-Snoqualmie National Forest

Map grid A1

This pretty camp is set at an elevation of 800 feet on Park Creek amid a heavily wooded area comprising old-growth Douglas fir and western hemlock. Park Creek is a feeder stream to nearby Baker Lake. The camp is primitive and small but gets its fair share of use.

RV sites, facilities: There are 12 sites for tents or RVs up to 40 feet long. Picnic tables and fire grills are provided. Vault toilets are available, but there is no drinking water. Boat docks, launching facilities, and rentals are nearby on Baker Lake. Leashed pets are permitted.

Reservations, fees: Reservations are accepted at 877/444-6777 or www.recreation.gov ($10 reservation fee). Sites are $12 per night, $6 per night per additional vehicle. Open mid-May–early September, weather permitting.

Directions: From I-5 at Burlington, turn east on Highway 20 and drive approximately 24 miles to Milepost 82 and Baker Lake Highway (Forest Road 11). Turn north on Baker Lake Highway and drive about 19.5 miles to Forest Road 1144. Turn left (northwest) and drive about 200 yards to the campground on the left. Obtaining a U.S. Forest Service map is helpful.

Contact: Mount Baker–Snoqualmie National Forest, Mount Baker Ranger District, 360/856-5700, fax 360/856-1934, www.fs.fed.us.

◢ SHANNON CREEK

Scenic rating: 9

near Baker Lake in
Mount Baker-Snoqualmie National Forest

Map grid A1

This pretty camp is set at an elevation of 909 feet at the north end of Baker Lake.

RV sites, facilities: There are 19 sites, including two double sites, for tents or RVs up to 36 feet long. Picnic tables and fire grills are provided. Drinking water, garbage bins, firewood, a picnic shelter, and vault toilets are available. A boat launch is available, and docks and rentals are nearby on Baker Lake. Some facilities are wheelchair accessible. Leashed pets are permitted.

Reservations, fees: Reservations are accepted at 877/444-6777 or recreation.gov ($10 reservation fee). Sites are $14–16 per night, $25 per night for the double sites, and $7 per night per additional vehicle. Open mid-May–mid September, weather permitting.

Directions: From I-5 at Burlington, turn east on Highway 20 and drive approximately 24 miles to Milepost 82 and Baker Lake Highway (Forest Road 11). Turn north on Baker Lake Highway and drive. Obtaining a U.S. Forest Service map is helpful.

Contact: Mount Baker–Snoqualmie National Forest, Mount Baker Ranger District, 360/856-5700, fax 360/856-1934, www.fs.fed.us.

◢ BOULDER CREEK

Scenic rating: 8

near Baker Lake in
Mount Baker-Snoqualmie National Forest

Map grid A1

This camp provides an alternative to Horseshoe Cove. It is set on Boulder Creek about one mile from the shore of Baker Lake. Fishing is fair here for rainbow trout, but typically far better at Baker Lake. A boat launch is located at Panorama Point, about 15 minutes away. Wild berries can be found in the area in season.

The campground offers prime views of Mount Baker.

RV sites, facilities: There are eight sites for tents or RVs up to 22 feet long and one group site for up to 25 people. Picnic tables and fire grills are provided. Vault toilets are available, but there is no drinking water. Boat docks and launching facilities are nearby on Baker Lake. Leashed pets are permitted.

Reservations, fees: Reservations are required for the group site and are available for some family sites at 877/444-6777 or www.recreation.gov ($10 reservation fee). Family sites are $14 per night, $7 per night per additional vehicle; the group site is $40 per night. Open mid-May–early September, weather permitting.

Directions: From I-5 at Burlington, turn east on Highway 20 and drive approximately 24 miles to Milepost 82 and Baker Lake Highway (Forest Road 11). Turn north on Baker Lake Highway and drive 17.4 miles to the campground on the right.

Contact: Mount Baker–Snoqualmie National Forest, Mount Baker Ranger District, 360/856-5700, fax 360/856-1934, www.fs.fed.us.

7 PANORAMA POINT

Scenic rating: 10

on Baker Lake in
Mount Baker-Snoqualmie National Forest

Map grid A1

With incredible scenic views of Mount Baker, Mount Shuk, Baker Lake, and Anderson Mountain, this camp is true to its name. Panorama Point is a well-maintained campground on the northwest shore of Baker Lake. The reservoir is one of the better fishing lakes in the area, often with good prospects for rainbow trout. Powerboating and waterskiing are permitted. Hiking trails are nearby.

RV sites, facilities: There are nine sites for tents or RVs up to 45 feet long. Picnic tables are provided. Drinking water, vault toilets, firewood and garbage bins are available. A convenience store and ice are located within one mile. A boat

ramp is adjacent to the camp. Boat docks and rentals are nearby. Some facilities are wheelchair accessible. Leashed pets are permitted.

Reservations, fees: Reservations are accepted for some sites at 877/444-6777 or www.recreation.gov ($10 reservation fee). Sites are $14–17 per night, $7 per night per additional vehicle. Open mid-May–mid-September, weather permitting.

Directions: From I-5 at Burlington, turn east on Highway 20 and drive approximately 24 miles to Milepost 82 and Baker Lake Highway (Forest Road 11). Turn north on Baker Lake Highway and drive 18.7 miles to the campground entrance on the right on the shore of Baker Lake.

Contact: Mount Baker–Snoqualmie National Forest, Mount Baker Ranger District, 360/856-5700, fax 360/856-1934, www.fs.fed.us.

8 HORSESHOE COVE

Scenic rating: 9

on Baker Lake in
Mount Baker-Snoqualmie National Forest

Map grid A1   BEST ❬

This camp is set along 5,000-acre Baker Lake. Anglers will often find good fishing for rainbow trout and kokanee salmon. Other highlights include swimming access from the campground and a boat ramp. Some hiking trails can be found nearby. The Baker Lake Basin has many trails, and the Mount Baker National Recreation area is located within 30 minutes.

RV sites, facilities: There are 37 sites for tents or RVs up to 60 feet long and three group sites for up to 25 people each. Picnic tables and fire grills are provided. Drinking water, flush toilets, garbage bins, and firewood are available. A boat ramp and swimming beach are adjacent to camp. Canoes, kayaks, and paddleboats are available for rent; check with the camp host. Some facilities are wheelchair accessible. Leashed pets are permitted.

Reservations, fees: Reservations are required for group sites and accepted for family sites at

877/444-6777 or www.recreation.gov ($10 reservation fee). Sites are $16 per night and group sites are $75 per night. Open May–September, weather permitting.

Directions: From I-5 at Burlington, turn east on Highway 20 and drive approximately 24 miles to Milepost 82 and the Baker Lake Highway (Forest Road 11). Turn north on Baker Lake Highway and drive about 14.8 miles to Forest Road 1118. Turn right (east) on Forest Road 1118 and drive two miles to the campground. A U.S. Forest Service map is recommended.

Contact: Mount Baker–Snoqualmie National Forest, Mount Baker Ranger District, 360/856-5700, fax 360/856-1934, www.fs.fed.us.

9 BAY VIEW NORTH/ SOUTH GROUP

Scenic rating: 9

on Baker Lake in
Mount Baker–Snoqualmie National Forest

Map grid A1

These are both group camps set along Baker Lake. They are located in forest, though not a dense one, and there is an open feel to the area here. Many sites are close to the water. Baker Lake covers 5,000 acres and offers fishing for rainbow trout and kokanee salmon.

RV sites, facilities: There are two group sites for tents or RVs up to 30 feet long for up to 100 people each. Picnic tables and fire grills are provided. Vault toilets, garbage bins, and firewood are available. There is no drinking water. A boat ramp is located nearby near Horseshoe Cove Camp. Leashed pets are permitted.

Reservations, fees: Reservations are accepted at 877/444-6777 or www.recreation.gov ($10 reservation fee). Sites are $75 per night. Some credit cards are accepted. Open mid-May–mid-September, weather permitting.

Directions: From I-5 at Burlington, turn east on Highway 20 and drive approximately 24 miles to Milepost 82 and the Baker Lake Highway (Forest Road 11). Turn north on Baker Lake Highway and drive about 14.8 miles to

Forest Road 1118. Turn right (east) on Forest Road 1118 and drive 1.75 miles to Forest Road 1118.011. Turn left and drive 0.75 mile to the campground. A U.S. Forest Service map is recommended.

Contact: Mount Baker–Snoqualmie National Forest, Mount Baker Ranger District, 360/856-5700, fax 360/856-1934, www.fs.fed.us.

10 GOODELL CREEK

Scenic rating: 7

on Goodell Creek and the Skagit River in
Ross Lake National Recreation Area

Map grid A1

Goodell Creek Campground is an alternative to nearby, larger Newhalem Creek campground. This one is set at 500 feet elevation, where Goodell Creek pours into the Skagit River in the Ross Lake National Recreation Area. It's a popular put-in camp for raft trips downriver; that makes the group sites popular here. No firewood gathering is permitted.

RV sites, facilities: There are 21 campsites for tents or RVs up to 22 feet long and two group sites (Upper and Lower Goodell) for tents or RVs up to 30 feet long. Picnic tables and fire rings are provided. Drinking water is available in the family sites, but not in the group sites. Vault toilets, garbage bins, and a picnic shelter are available. Some facilities are wheelchair accessible. Leashed pets are permitted.

Reservations, fees: Reservations are not accepted for family sites. Reservations are required for group sites only at 877/444-6777 or www.recreation.gov ($10 reservation fee). Family sites are $10 per night, and group sites are $25 per night. Family sites are open year-round, but there are no services (and no fees) in the winter; group sites are open Memorial Day weekend–September.

Directions: On I-5, drive to Exit 230/Highway 20 at Burlington. Turn east on Highway 20, and drive 46 miles to Marblemount. Continue east on Highway 20 for 13 miles to the campground entrance.

Contact: North Cascades National Park, 360/856-5700, fax 360/856-1934, www.nps. gov/noca/.

11 NEWHALEM CREEK

Scenic rating: 7

near the Skagit River in
Ross Lake National Recreation Area

Map grid A1

This spot is set along the Skagit River west of Newhalem at 500 feet elevation. Good hiking possibilities abound in the immediate area, and naturalist programs are available. Be sure to visit the North Cascades Visitor Center at the top of the hill from the campground. No firewood gathering is permitted here. If this camp is full, try Goodell Creek Campground, located just one mile west on Highway 20.

RV sites, facilities: There are 111 sites for tents or RVs of any length, and two group sites for tents or RVs up to 45 feet long for up to 25 people each. Picnic tables and fire grills are provided. Restrooms with flush toilets, drinking water, and a dump station are available. The group camp has a covered pavilion. Some facilities are wheelchair accessible. Leashed pets are permitted.

Reservations, fees: Reservations are accepted for family sites and required for group camps at 877/444-6777 or www.recreation.gov ($10 reservation fee). Family sites are $12 per night; group sites are $32 per night. Open mid-May to mid-October.

Directions: On I-5, drive to Exit 230/Highway 20 at Burlington. Turn east on Highway 20, and drive 46 miles to Marblemount. Continue 14 miles east on Highway 20 to the camp.

Contact: North Cascades National Park, 360/856-5700, fax 360/856-1934, www.nps. gov/noca/.

12 GORGE LAKE

Scenic rating: 9

on Gorge Lake on the Skagit River in
Ross Lake National Recreation Area

Map grid A1

This small camp is set near the north shore of Gorge Lake, with lake views from many sites, and close to Colonial Creek and Goodell Creek. There is some tree cover. Gorge Lake is very narrow and has trout fishing (check regulations). The camp is not well known and gets low use. One problem here is that the lake level can fluctuate (but not as much as Ross Lake), leaving the camps high and dry. No firewood gathering is permitted. There are two other lakes nearby on the Skagit River—Diablo Lake and Ross Lake. The elevation is 900 feet.

RV sites, facilities: There are six sites for tents or RVs up to 22 feet long. Picnic tables and fire grills are provided. Vault toilets are available. There is no drinking water, and garbage must be packed out. A boat ramp is nearby. Leashed pets are permitted.

Reservations, fees: Reservations are not accepted. There is no fee for camping. Open year-round.

Directions: From I-5 near Burlington, take exit 230 for Highway 20. Turn east on Highway 20 and drive 46 miles to Marblemount. Continue east on Highway 20 for another 20 miles to the junction with Diablo Road. Bear left and drive 0.6 mile to the campground on the right.

Contact: North Cascades National Park, 360/856-5700, fax 360/856-1934, www.nps. gov/noca/.

13 COLONIAL CREEK

Scenic rating: 7

on Diablo Lake in
Ross Lake National Recreation Area

Map grid A1

Colonial Creek Campground sits at an elevation of 1,200 feet along the shore of Diablo Lake in the Ross Lake National Recreation Area. The five-mile-long lake offers many hiking and fishing opportunities. A naturalist program and guided walks are available during the summer months. No firewood gathering is permitted at this campsite.

RV sites, facilities: There are 142 campsites for tents or RVs up to 45 feet long, including a few walk-in tent sites. Picnic tables and fire grills are provided. Restrooms with flush toilets, drinking water, garbage bins, a dump station, three boat docks, and a boat ramp are available. Some facilities are wheelchair accessible, including a fishing pier. Leashed pets are permitted.

Reservations, fees: Reservations are not accepted. Sites are $12 per night. Open mid-April to mid-October; 18 lakefront sites are open through the winter (no services provided).

Directions: From I-5 at Burlington, take Exit 230 and drive east to Highway 20. Turn east on Highway 20 and drive 46 miles to Marblemount. Continue east on Highway 20 for 24 miles to the campground entrance.

Contact: North Cascades National Park, 360/856-5700, fax 360/856-1934, www.nps.gov.noca/.

14 RASAR STATE PARK

Scenic rating: 8

on the Skagit River

Map grid A1

This park borders North Cascade National Park and is also near 10,778-foot Mount Baker and the Baker River watershed. Fishing the 4,000 feet of shoreline and hiking are the attractions here, as is bird-watching.

RV sites, facilities: There are 20 sites with partial hookups (30 amps) for tents or RVs up to 40 feet long, three primitive hike-in/bike-in sites, 18 walk-in sites, two four-person Adirondack shelters, and three group sites, two for 20–80 people and one for 20–100 people. Picnic tables and fire grills are provided. Restrooms with flush toilets and coin showers, drinking water, dump station, a kitchen shelter, an amphitheater, playground, and park store are available.

Firewood gathering is prohibited, but firewood is available for sale. Some facilities are wheelchair accessible. Leashed pets are permitted.

Reservations, fees: Reservations are required for the group site and accepted for the other sites at 888/CAMP-OUT (888/226-7688) or www.parks.wa.gov/reservations ($6.50–8.50 reservation fee). Sites are $10–22 per night, $10 per extra vehicle per night. Group sites are $2.25 per person per night. Open year-round.

Directions: From I-5 at Burlington, take Exit 232 (Cook Road) and drive six miles (to a traffic light) to Highway 20 in Sedro-Woolley. Turn left (east) on Highway 20 and drive 15 miles to Lusk Road. Turn right on Lusk Road and drive 0.75 mile to Cape Horn Road. Turn left on Cape Horn Road and drive one mile to the park entrance.

Contact: Rasar State Park, 360/826-3942; state park information, 360/902-8844, www.parks.wa.gov.

15 CREEKSIDE CAMPGROUND

Scenic rating: 6

near the Skagit River

Map grid A1

This pretty, wooded campground is centrally located to nearby recreational opportunities at Baker Lake and the Skagit River. Trout fishing is good here, and tackle is available nearby. Horseshoe pits and a recreation hall are also available. About half of the sites are filled with monthly renters.

RV sites, facilities: There are 29 sites with full or partial hookups (20 and 30 amp) for tents, trailers, or RVs up to 40 feet long. Picnic tables and fire rings are provided. Restrooms with flush toilets and showers, drinking water, a dump station, coin laundry, and horseshoe pits are available. A café is located within one mile. Leashed pets are permitted.

Reservations, fees: Reservations are accepted. RV sites are $25 per night; tent sites are $16 per night. Open year-round.

Directions: From Seattle, drive north on I-5

to Exit 232 (Cook Road). Take the exit up and over the highway to the flashing light and Highway 20. Turn left on Cook Road/Highway 20 and drive four miles to the light at Highway 20. Turn left at Highway 20 and drive 17 miles to Baker Lake Road, between Mileposts 182 and 183. Turn left on Baker Lake Road and drive 0.25 mile to the camp on the right.

Contact: Creekside Campground, 360/826-3566.

16 HOWARD MILLER STEELHEAD PARK

Scenic rating: 5

on the Skagit River

Map grid A1

This Skagit County Park provides grassy sites and access to the Skagit River. The river is designated a Wild and Scenic River. The steelhead fishing is often good in season. Campsites at this spot are sunny and spacious. Groups can be accommodated. A bald eagle sanctuary is located at the east end of the park. November–January is the best time to see bald eagles here. This camp is most popular in July, August, and September, when the weather is best, but also attracts visitors in early winter who arrive primarily for bald eagle–watching.

RV sites, facilities: There are 54 sites with full or partial hookups for tents or RVs of any length, 10 walk-in tent sites, and two Adirondack sleeping shelters. Picnic tables and fire pits are provided. Restrooms with flush toilets and coin showers, drinking water, a dump station, a clubhouse, picnic shelter, playground, interpretive center, and horseshoe pits are available. A store and ice are located within one mile. Boat-launching facilities are located on the Skagit River. Some facilities are wheelchair accessible. Leashed pets are permitted.

Reservations, fees: Reservations are recommended ($6 reservation fee). RV sites are $22–24 per night, tent sites are $16 per night, Adirondacks are $22 per night, and it's $5 per

extra vehicle per night. Some credit cards are accepted. Open year-round.

Directions: On I-5, drive to Exit 230/Highway 20 at Burlington. Turn east on Highway 20, and drive 44 miles to Rockport and Rockport-Darrington Road (Highway 530). Turn right (south) and drive three blocks to the camp on the right.

Contact: Howard Miller Steelhead Park, 360/853-8808, fax 360/853-7315; Skagit County Parks, 360/336-9414, fax 360/336-9493, www.skagitparksfoundation.org.

17 WILDERNESS VILLAGE AND RV PARK

Scenic rating: 6

near the Skagit River

Map grid A1

This RV park is located near the Skagit River. Cool and wooded, it offers nice, grassy sites and nearby access to the river and fishing. Horseshoe pits and a sports field provide recreation alternatives. Rockport State Park and hiking trails are nearby. Bald eagles can often be viewed on the Skagit River in December and January. A one-mile trail (round-trip) can be accessed along the river.

RV sites, facilities: There are 32 pull-through sites with full hookups for RVs of any length and 20 tent sites. Picnic tables and fire rings are provided. Restrooms with flush toilets and coin showers, cable TV, a recreation hall, and coin laundry are available. A café and ice are located within two miles. Leashed pets are permitted.

Reservations, fees: Reservations are accepted. Sites are $12–21 per night. Open year-round.

Directions: From Burlington, drive east on Highway 20 for 44 miles to Rockport. Continue east on Highway 20 for five miles to the park. The park is between Mileposts 102 and 103 on the right.

Contact: Wilderness Village and RV Park, 360/873-2571 or 360/421-2976.

WASHINGTON

18 SKAGIT RIVER RESORT

Scenic rating: 9

on the Skagit River

Map grid A1

This beautiful camp is nestled in the trees along the Skagit River. The resort covers 125 acres, including 1.5 miles of river frontage. A restaurant called The Eatery has received awards for its pecan pie and is also known for its home-style meals. Fishing, river walks, and nearby hiking trails among the glaciers and waterfalls can be accessed close to the campground. There are also three hydroelectric plants nearby that offer tours. Recreational facilities include horseshoes and a sports field for volleyball, croquet, and badminton. This resort is popular July–September, when reservations are often required to get a spot.

RV sites, facilities: There are 48 sites for tents or RVs of any length (full hookups), 29 cabins, five chalets, and three mobile homes. Some sites are pull-through. Restrooms with flush toilets and coin showers, drinking water, a dump station, modem access, a pay phone, coin laundry, horseshoe pits, a restaurant, and a sports field for volleyball, croquet, and badminton are available. Leashed pets are permitted.

Reservations, fees: Reservations are recommended. RV sites are $30–35 per night, tent sites are $20–25, and it's $10 per pet per night (in cabins). Some credit cards are accepted. Open year-round.

Directions: From Burlington, drive east on Highway 20 for 44 miles to Rockport. Continue east on Highway 20 for six miles to the resort on the left (between Mileposts 103 and 104).

Contact: Skagit River Resort, 360/873-2250 or 800/273-2606, fax 360/873-4077, www.northcascades.com.

19 MARBLE CREEK

Scenic rating: 7

on Marble Creek in
Mount Baker-Snoqualmie National Forest

Map grid A1

This primitive campground is set on Marble Creek amid old-growth Douglas fir and western hemlock. Fishing for rainbow trout is possible here. A trailhead to Hidden Lake just inside the boundary of North Cascades National Park can be found about five miles from camp at the end of Forest Road 1540.

RV sites, facilities: There are 23 sites for tents or RVs of any length. Picnic tables and fire grills are provided. Vault toilets, garbage bins, and firewood are available. There is no drinking water. Some facilities are wheelchair accessible. Leashed pets are permitted.

Reservations, fees: Reservations are accepted at 877/444-6777 or www.recreation.gov ($10 reservation fee). Sites are $12 per night, $6 per night per additional vehicle. Open mid-May–mid-September, weather permitting.

Directions: From I-5 in Burlington, take Exit 230/Highway 20. Turn east on Highway 20 and drive 46 miles to Marblemount and Forest Road 15 (Cascade River Road). Cross the bridge, turn east on Cascade River Road, and drive eight miles to Forest Road 1530. Turn right (south) on Forest Road 1530 and drive to the campground. Obtaining a U.S. Forest Service map is advised.

Contact: Mount Baker-Snoqualmie National Forest, Mount Baker Ranger District, 360/856-5700, fax 360/856-1934, www.fs.fed.us.

20 MINERAL PARK

Scenic rating: 7

in Mount Baker-Snoqualmie National Forest

Map grid A1

This campground is just six miles from Cascade Pass along a narrow, bumpy gravel road. Campsites are near the Cascade River at the convergence of the North and South Forks.

RV sites, facilities: There are 22 sites, including two double sites, for tents or RVs up to 32 feet long. Picnic tables and fire grills are provided. Vault toilets, firewood, and garbage bins are available, but there is no drinking water. Leashed pets are permitted.

Reservations, fees: Reservations are accepted at 877/444-6777 or recreation.gov ($10 reservation fee). Sites are $12–14 per night, $6 per night per additional vehicle, and double sites are $20 per night. Open mid-May–mid-September, weather permitting.

Directions: From I-5 in Burlington, take Exit 230/Highway 20. Turn east on Highway 20 and drive 46 miles to Marblemount and Forest Road 15 (Cascade River Road). Cross the bridge over the Skagit River, turn east on Cascade River Road, and drive 16 miles to the campground. Obtaining a U.S. Forest Service map is advised.

Contact: Mount Baker–Snoqualmie National Forest, Mount Baker Ranger District, 360/856-5700, fax 360/856-1934, www.fs.fed.us.

21 SQUIRE CREEK COUNTY PARK

Scenic rating: 7

on Squire Creek

Map grid A1

This pretty park is set amid old-growth forest, primarily Douglas fir and cedar, along Squire Creek. A family-oriented park, it often fills on summer weekends. The park covers 53 acres and features several nearby trailheads. A trail from the park provides a 4.5-mile loop that heads toward White Horse Mountain. Other trailheads are located within five miles in nearby Mount Baker–Snoqualmie National Forest, about three miles from the boundaries of the Boulder River Wilderness. No alcohol is permitted in this park.

RV sites, facilities: There are 33 sites for tents or RVs of any length (no hookups). Picnic tables and fire rings are provided. Restrooms with flush toilets, drinking water, firewood, and picnic shelters that can be reserved are available. A store is located three miles east in

Darrington. Some facilities are wheelchair accessible. Leashed pets are permitted.

Reservations, fees: Reservations are accepted at 360/436-1283 or www.activenet10.active.com/snoco. Sites are $20 per night, $10 per night per additional vehicle. Open year-round, with limited winter services.

Directions: From Seattle, drive north on I-5 to Exit 208 and the junction with Highway 530. Turn east on Highway 530 and drive 26 miles to the park on the left. The park is at Milepost 45.2, approximately three miles west of the town of Darrington.

Contact: Squire Creek County Park, 360/436-1283; Snohomish County Parks, 425/388-6600, www1.co.snohomish.wa.us/.

22 CASCADE KAMLOOPS TROUT FARM AND RV PARK

Scenic rating: 5

in Darrington

Map grid A1

Campers will find a little bit of both worlds at this campground—a rustic quietness and a family atmosphere with all facilities available. A bonus is the trout pond, which is stocked year-round. No boats are allowed. Nearby recreation options include marked hiking trails, snowmobiling, cross-country skiing, river rafting, and tennis.

RV sites, facilities: There are 30 sites with full hookups for RVs of any length and 12 tent sites. A loft apartment is also available. Picnic tables and fire rings are provided. Restrooms with flush toilets and showers, drinking water, a dump station, firewood, coin laundry, Wi-Fi access, a community fire pit, trout pond, and recreation hall are available. Propane gas, a store, café, and ice are located within one mile. Leashed pets are permitted.

Reservations, fees: Reservations are accepted. Sites are $18–22 per night, $1 per person per night for more than two people, and $1 per pet per night. Some credit cards are accepted. Open year-round.

Directions: From Seattle, drive north on I-5 to Exit 208 and the junction with Highway 530. Turn east on Highway 530 and drive 32 miles to the Darrington/Madison Avenue exit. Turn right on Madison Avenue and drive about four blocks to Darrington Street. Turn right and drive two blocks to the park on the right.

Contact: Cascade Kamloops Trout Farm and RV Park, 360/436-1003.

23 CLEAR CREEK

🚶 🎣 🐕 ♿ 🚐 ⛺

Scenic rating: 8

on Clear Creek and the Sauk River in
Mount Baker-Snoqualmie National Forest

Map grid A1

This nice, secluded spot is set in old-growth fir on the water, but it doesn't get heavy use. It's located at the confluence of Clear Creek and the Sauk River, a designated Wild and Scenic River. Fishing is available for rainbow trout, Dolly Varden trout, whitefish, and steelhead in season. A trail from camp leads about one mile up to Frog Pond.

RV sites, facilities: There are 13 sites for tents or RVs up to 40 feet long. Picnic tables and fire grills are provided. Vault toilets, garbage bins, and firewood are available. There is no drinking water. A store, café, coin laundry, and ice are located within four miles. Some facilities are wheelchair accessible. Leashed pets are permitted.

Reservations, fees: Reservations are accepted at 877/444-6777 or www.recreation.gov ($10 reservation fee). Sites are $14 per night, $6 per extra vehicle per night. Open late May–mid-September, weather permitting.

Directions: From Seattle, drive north on I-5 to Exit 208 and the junction with Highway 530. Turn east on Highway 530 and drive 32 miles to Darrington and Forest Road 20 (Mountain Loop Highway). Turn right (south) on Forest Road 20 and drive 3.3 miles to the campground entrance on the left.

Contact: Mount Baker–Snoqualmie National Forest, Darrington Ranger District, 360/436-1155, fax 360/436-1309, www.fs.fed.us.

24 BUCK CREEK

🚶 🚴 🎣 🐕 ♿ 🚐 ⛺

Scenic rating: 9

near the Suiattle River in
Mount Baker-Snoqualmie National Forest

Map grid A1

Quiet and remote, this primitive campground is set along Buck Creek near its confluence with the Suiattle River in the Glacier Peak Wilderness. An interpretive trail runs along Buck Creek and provides access to fishing on the stream for rainbow trout, Dolly Varden, whitefish, and steelhead in season. There's a large (18 feet by 18 feet) Adirondack shelter by the creek and stands of old-growth timber. A zigzagging trail routed into the Glacier Peak Wilderness is accessible about one mile west of camp. See a U.S. Forest Service map for specifics.

Note: Buck Creek campground was closed in 2010 due to flood damage and is scheduled to reopen in 2011.

RV sites, facilities: There are 29 sites for tents or RVs of any length. Picnic tables and fire grills are provided. Vault toilets, garbage bins, and firewood are available. There is no drinking water. Some facilities are wheelchair accessible. Leashed pets are permitted.

Reservations, fees: Reservations are accepted at 877/444-6777 or www.recreation.gov ($10 reservation fee). Sites are $12 per night, $6 per extra vehicle per night. Open May–September, weather permitting.

Directions: From Seattle, drive north on I-5 to Exit 208 and the junction with Highway 530. Turn east on Highway 530 and drive 32 miles to Darrington. Continue 7.5 miles on Highway 530 to Forest Road 26 (Suiattle River Road). Turn right (southeast) on Forest Road 26 and drive 14 miles to the campground on the left. Obtaining a U.S. Forest Service map is essential.

Contact: Mount Baker–Snoqualmie National Forest, Darrington Ranger District, 360/436-1155, fax 360/436-1309, www.fs.fed.us.

25 TURLO

Scenic rating: 8

on the South Fork of the Stillaguamish River in
Mount Baker-Snoqualmie National Forest

Map grid A1

The westernmost camp on this stretch of Highway 92, Turlo is set at 900 feet elevation along
the South Fork of the Stillaguamish River. A
U.S. Forest Service Public Information Center
is nearby. Riverside campsites are available, and
the fishing can be good here. A few hiking trails
can be found in the area.

RV sites, facilities: There are 18 sites for tents
or RVs up to 40 feet long. Picnic tables and
fire rings are provided. Vault toilets, drinking
water, garbage bins, and firewood are available.
A camp host is on-site. A store, café, and ice are
located one mile away. Some facilities are wheelchair accessible. Leashed pets are permitted.

Reservations, fees: Reservations are accepted
at 877/444-6777 or www.recreation.gov ($10
reservation fee). Sites are $16–17 per night, $8
per extra vehicle per night. Open mid-May–
early September, weather permitting.

Directions: From I-5 and Everett, turn east on
U.S. 2 and drive five miles to Highway 9. Turn
north and drive four miles to Highway 92. Turn
east on Highway 92 and drive approximately 15
miles to the town of Granite Falls. Continue
another 11 miles east on Highway 92 to the
campground entrance on the right.

Contact: Mount Baker–Snoqualmie National
Forest, Darrington Ranger District, 360/436-
1155, fax 360/436-1309, www.fs.fed.us.

26 VERLOT

Scenic rating: 9

on the South Fork of the Stillaguamish River in
Mount Baker-Snoqualmie National Forest

Map grid A1

This pretty campground is set along the South
Fork of the Stillaguamish River. Some campsites provide river views. The camp is a short
distance from the Lake Twenty-Two Research

Natural Area and Maid of the Woods Trail.
Fishing is another recreation option.

RV sites, facilities: There are 26 sites for tents
or RVs up to 40 feet long. Picnic tables and fire
rings are provided. Restrooms with flush toilets,
drinking water, garbage bins, firewood, and a
visitors center are available. A store, café, and
ice are located within one mile. Some facilities
are wheelchair accessible. Leashed pets are
permitted.

Reservations, fees: Reservations are accepted
at 877/444-6777 or www.recreation.gov ($10
reservation fee). Sites are $16 per night, $8
per extra vehicle per night. Open mid-May–
October, weather permitting.

Directions: From I-5 and Everett, turn east on
U.S. 2 and drive five miles to Highway 9. Turn
north and drive four miles to Highway 92. Turn
east on Highway 92 and drive approximately 15
miles to the town of Granite Falls, and continue
another 11.6 miles east on Highway 92 to the
campground entrance on the right.

Contact: Mount Baker–Snoqualmie National
Forest, Darrington Ranger District, 360/436-
1155, fax 360/436-1309, www.fs.fed.us.

27 GOLD BASIN

Scenic rating: 9

on the South Fork of the Stillaguamish River in
Mount Baker-Snoqualmie National Forest

Map grid A1

This is the largest campground in Mount
Baker–Snoqualmie National Forest; since it's
loaded with facilities, it's a favorite with RVers.
Set at an elevation of 1,100 feet along the South
Fork of the Stillaguamish River, the campground features riverside sites, easy access, and
a wheelchair-accessible interpretive trail. This
area once provided good fishing, but a slide
upstream put clay silt into the water, and it
has hurt the fishing. Rafting and hiking are
options.

RV sites, facilities: There are 94 sites without
hook-ups for tents or RVs up to 45 feet long,
and one group site for up to 75 people. Picnic

tables and fire rings are provided. Drinking water, restrooms with flush toilets and coin showers, firewood, and garbage bins are available. A camp host is on-site. A store, café, and ice are located within 2.5 miles. Some facilities are wheelchair accessible. Leashed pets are permitted.

Reservations, fees: Reservations are accepted at 877/444-6777 or www.recreation.gov ($10 reservation fee). Sites are $20–40 per night, $10 per extra vehicle per night. The group site is $125 per night. Open mid-May–September, weather permitting.

Directions: From I-5 and Everett, turn east on Highway 92 and drive about 15 miles to the town of Granite Falls and Mountain Loop Highway. Continue east on Mountain Loop Highway for 13.5 miles to the campground entrance on the left.

Contact: Mount Baker–Snoqualmie National Forest, Darrington Ranger District, 360/436-1155, fax 360/436-1309, www.fs.fed.us.

28 MARTEN CREEK GROUP CAMP

Scenic rating: 7

in Mount Baker-Snoqualmie National Forest

Map grid A1

This campground is about 10 miles east of the Verlot Visitors Center, on the South Fork of the Stillaguamish River where it converges with Marten Creek. Sites are wooded and situated close to the river's bank, which is quite steep. The elevation is 1,420 feet.

RV sites, facilities: There is one group site for up to 25 people. Picnic tables and fire rings are provided. Vault toilets and garbage bins are available, but there is no drinking water. Leashed pets are permitted.

Reservations, fees: Reservations are accepted at 877/444-6777 or recreation.gov ($10 reservation fee). The site is $65 per night. Open mid-May–mid-September, weather permitting.

Directions: From I-5 and Everett, turn east on Highway 92 and drive about 15 miles to

the town of Granite Falls and Mountain Loop Highway. Continue east on Mountain Loop Highway for 20 miles to the campground.

Contact: Mount Baker–Snoqualmie National Forest, Darrington Ranger District, 360/436-1155, fax 360/436-1309, www.fs.fed.us.

29 ESSWINE GROUP CAMP

Scenic rating: 6

in Mount Baker-Snoqualmie National Forest

Map grid A1

This small, quiet camp is a great place for a restful group getaway. The only drawback? No drinking water. Fishing access is available nearby. The Boulder River Wilderness is located to the north; see a U.S. Forest Service map for trailhead locations.

RV sites, facilities: There is one group site for tents or RVs up to 35 feet long for up to 25 people. Picnic tables and fire pits are provided. Vault toilets, garbage bins, and firewood are available, but there is no drinking water. A store, café, and ice are located within seven miles. Leashed pets are permitted.

Reservations, fees: Reservations are accepted at 877/444-6777 or www.recreation.gov ($10 reservation fee). The sites is $75 per night. Open mid-May–September, weather permitting.

Directions: From I-5 and Everett, turn east on Highway 92 and drive about 15 miles to the town of Granite Falls and Mountain Loop Highway. Continue northeast on Mountain Loop Highway for 16 miles to the campground entrance on the left.

Contact: Mount Baker–Snoqualmie National Forest, Darrington Ranger District, 360/436-1155, fax 360/436-1309, www.fs.fed.us.

30 BOARDMAN CREEK GROUP CAMP

Scenic rating: 7

on the South Fork of the Stillaguamish River in Mount Baker-Snoqualmie National Forest

Map grid A1

Boardman is located at the far end of the Mountain Loop Road, about eight miles east of the Verlot Public Service Center on the Stillaguamish River. River access highlights this pretty camp, converted from a single-site into a group campground. The fishing near here can be excellent for rainbow trout, Dolly Varden, whitefish, and steelhead in season. The camp road parallels the Loop Road. Forest roads in the area will take you to several backcountry lakes, including Boardman Lake, Lake Evan, and Ashland Lakes. Get a U.S. Forest Service map, set up your camp, and go for it.

Insider's Tip: When not reserved by groups, Boardman is available for individuals on a first-come, first-serve basis; check with the Gold Basin host.

RV sites, facilities: There is one group camp for up to 35 people and RVs of any length. Picnic tables and fire pits are provided. Vault toilets, garbage bins, and firewood are available. There is no drinking water. A camp host is available Memorial Day–Labor Day. Some facilities are wheelchair accessible. Leashed pets are permitted.

Reservations, fees: Reservations are accepted at 877/444-6777 or recreation.gov ($25 reservation fee). The site is $60 per night. Open late May–early September, weather permitting.

Directions: From I-5 and Everett, turn east on Highway 92 and drive about 15 miles to the town of Granite Falls and Mountain Loop Highway. Continue northeast on Mountain Loop Highway for 16.5 miles to the campground entrance on the left.

Contact: Mount Baker–Snoqualmie National Forest, Darrington Ranger District, 360/436-1155, fax 360/436-1309, www.fs.fed.us.

31 BEDAL

Scenic rating: 9

on the Sauk River in Mount Baker-Snoqualmie National Forest

Map grid A1

A bit primitive, this campground is set at the confluence of the North and South Forks of the Sauk River. It offers shaded sites, river views, and good fishing. North Fork Falls is about one mile up the North Fork from camp and worth the trip.

RV sites, facilities: There are 22 sites for tents or RVs up to 21 feet long. Picnic tables and fire grills are provided. Vault toilets, garbage bins, firewood, and a picnic shelter are available. There is no drinking water. A U.S. Forest Service district office is located 19 miles from the campground, in Darrington. Some facilities are wheelchair accessible. Leashed pets are permitted.

Reservations, fees: Reservations are accepted at 877/444-6777 or www.recreation.gov ($10 reservation fee). Sites are $14 per night, $7 per extra vehicle per night. Open May–early September, weather permitting.

Directions: From Seattle, drive north on I-5 to Exit 208 and the junction with Highway 530. Turn east on Highway 530 and drive 32 miles to Darrington and Forest Road 20 (Mountain Loop Highway). Turn right (south) on Forest Road 20 and drive 19 miles to the campground on the right. Obtaining a U.S. Forest Service map is advised.

Contact: Mount Baker–Snoqualmie National Forest, Darrington Ranger District, 360/436-1155, fax 360/436-1309, www.fs.fed.us.

32 RED BRIDGE

Scenic rating: 9

on the South Fork of Stillaguamish River in Mount Baker-Snoqualmie National Forest

Map grid A1

Red Bridge is a classic spot, one of several in the vicinity, and a good base camp for a

WASHINGTON

backpacking expedition. The campground is set at 1,300 feet elevation on the South Fork of the Stillaguamish River near Mallardy Creek. It has pretty, riverside sites with old-growth fir. A trailhead two miles east of camp leads to Granite Pass in the Boulder River Wilderness.

RV sites, facilities: There are 15 sites for tents or RVs up to 40 feet long. Picnic tables and fire grills are provided. Vault toilets, drinking water, garbage bins, and firewood are available. Some facilities are wheelchair accessible. Leashed pets are permitted.

Reservations, fees: Reservations are accepted at 877/444-6777 or www.recreation.gov ($10 reservation fee). Sites are $14 per night, $7 per extra vehicle per night. Open mid-May–mid-September, weather permitting.

Directions: From I-5 and Everett, turn east on Highway 92 and drive about 15 miles to the town of Granite Falls and Mountain Loop Highway. Continue northeast on Mountain Loop Highway for 18 miles to the campground entrance on the right.

Contact: Mount Baker–Snoqualmie National Forest, Darrington Ranger District, 360/436-1155, fax 360/436-1309, www.fs.fed.us.

33 TULALIP MILLSITE GROUP CAMP

Scenic rating: 7

on the South Fork of the Stillaguamish River in Mount Baker-Snoqualmie National Forest

Map grid A1

This campground is set along the South Fork of the Stillaguamish River, close to several other camps: Turlo, Verlot, Gold Basin, Esswine, Boardman Creek, Coal Creek Bar, and Red Bridge. A trailhead about one mile east of camp leads north into the Boulder River Wilderness. Numerous creeks and streams crisscross this area, providing good fishing prospects.

RV sites, facilities: There is one group camp for tents or RVs up to 22 feet long for up to 60 people. Picnic tables and fire grills are provided. Vault toilets and garbage bins are available.

There is no drinking water. Some facilities are wheelchair accessible. Leashed pets are permitted.

Reservations, fees: Reservations are accepted at 877/444-6777 or www.recreation.gov ($10 reservation fee); note that for online reservations, this camp is mistakenly called Tulalip and not Tulalip Millsite. The site is $85 per night. Open mid-May–September, weather permitting.

Directions: From I-5 and Everett, turn east on Highway 92 and drive about 15 miles to the town of Granite Falls and Mountain Loop Highway. Continue east on Mountain Loop Highway for 18.5 miles to the campground entrance on the right.

Contact: Mount Baker–Snoqualmie National Forest, Darrington Ranger District, 360/436-1155, fax 360/436-1309, www.fs.fed.us.

34 COAL CREEK GROUP CAMP

Scenic rating: 8

on the South Fork of the Stillaguamish River in Mount Baker-Snoqualmie National Forest

Map grid A1

A U.S. Forest Service map will unlock the beautiful country around this campground set along the South Fork of the Stillaguamish River. Fishing access is available for rainbow trout, Dolly Varden, whitefish, and steelhead in season. Nearby forest roads lead to Coal Lake and a trailhead that takes you to other backcountry lakes.

RV sites, facilities: There is one group site for tents or RVs up to 30 feet long for up to 25 people. Picnic tables and fire grills are provided. Vault toilets, garbage bins, and firewood are available. There is no drinking water. Leashed pets are permitted.

Reservations, fees: Reservations are accepted at 877/444-6777 or www.recreation.gov ($10 reservation fee). The site is $75 per night. Open mid-May–late September, weather permitting.

Directions: From I-5 and Everett, turn east on Highway 92 and drive about 15 miles to the town of Granite Falls and Mountain Loop Highway. Continue northeast on Mountain Loop Highway for 23.5 miles to the campground entrance on the left.

Contact: Mount Baker–Snoqualmie National Forest, Darrington Ranger District, 360/436-1155, fax 360/436-1309, www.fs.fed.us.

35 BALLARD

Scenic rating: 6

near the Methow River in
Okanogan and Wenatchee National Forests

Map grid B1

Ballard is set at an elevation of 2,521 feet, about 0.5 mile from River Bend. Numerous hiking trails can be found in the area, as well as access to West Fork Methow and Lost River Monument Creek Trails. It is also possible to hike west and eventually hook up with the Pacific Crest Trail. Possible side trips include Winthrop to the south, which boasts a historical museum, a state fish hatchery, and Pearrygin Lake State Park. Livestock are not permitted in the campground, but a hitching rail and stock truck dock are available at the Robinson Creek Trailhead near the campground, where there are several primitive sites.

RV sites, facilities: There are seven sites for tents or RVs up to 28 feet long. Picnic tables and fire grills are provided. Vault toilets are available, but there is no drinking water. Garbage must be packed out. Some facilities are wheelchair accessible. Leashed pets are permitted. No livestock are permitted in camp.

Reservations, fees: Reservations are not accepted. Sites are $8 per night per vehicle. Open late May–October, weather permitting.

Directions: From Burlington, drive east on Highway 20 for 120 miles to Mazama Road. Turn left on Mazama Road and drive 0.25 mile to County Road 9140. Turn left and drive northwest for seven miles to Lost River, where the pavement ends and the road soon becomes Forest Road 5400. Continue northwest on Forest Road 5400 for two miles to the campground on the left.

Contact: Okanogan and Wenatchee National Forests, Methow Valley Ranger District, 509/996-4003, www.fs.fed.us; Methow Valley Visitor Center, 509/996-4000.

36 RIVER BEND

Scenic rating: 6

on the Methow River in
Okanogan and Wenatchee National Forests

Map grid B1

This campground is located along the Methow River at 2,600 feet elevation, about two miles from the boundary of the Pasayten Wilderness. Several trails near the camp provide access to the wilderness, and another trail follows the Methow River west for about eight miles before hooking up with the Pacific Crest Trail near Azurite Peak.

RV sites, facilities: There are five sites for tents, trailers, or RVs up to 24 feet long. Picnic tables and fire grills are provided. Vault toilets are available. There is no drinking water, and garbage must be packed out. Some facilities are wheelchair accessible. Leashed pets are permitted.

Reservations, fees: Reservations are not accepted. Sites are $5 per night per vehicle. Open late May–late October, weather permitting.

Directions: From Burlington, drive east on Highway 20 for 120 miles to Mazama Road. Turn left on Mazama Road and drive 0.25 mile to County Road 9140. Turn left and drive northwest for seven miles to Lost River, where the pavement ends and the road soon becomes Forest Road 5400. Continue northwest on Forest Road 5400 for two miles to Forest Road 5400-600. Continue straight on Forest Road 5400-600 and drive 0.5 mile to the campground on the left.

Contact: Okanogan and Wenatchee National Forests, Methow Valley Ranger District, 509/996-4003, www.fs.fed.us; Methow Valley Visitor Center, 509/996-4000.

WASHINGTON

37 EARLY WINTERS

Scenic rating: 6

on Early Winters Creek in
Okanogan and Wenatchee National Forests

Map grid B1

Located on each side of the highway, this campground has an unusual configuration. The confluence of Early Winters Creek and the Methow River mark the site of this campground. The elevation is 2,160 feet. You'll find great views of Goat Wall here. Campsites are flat, and the open landscape, set in a sparse lodgepole pine and fir forest, provides an arid feel to the area. Several hiking trails can be found within five miles, including one that leads south to Cedar Creek Falls. Other possible side trips include Goat Wall to the north and the town of Winthrop to the south, which boasts a historical museum, a state fish hatchery, and Pearrygin Lake State Park.

RV sites, facilities: There are 12 sites for tents or RVs up to 24 feet long. Picnic tables and fire grills are provided. Drinking water, vault toilets, and garbage bins are available. There is a small store and snack bar in Mazama, about two miles away. Some facilities are wheelchair accessible. Leashed pets are permitted.

Reservations, fees: Reservations are not accepted. Sites are $8 per night per vehicle. Open mid-May–October, weather permitting.

Directions: From Burlington, drive east on Highway 20 for 116 miles to the campground (if you reach County Road 1163 near Mazama, you have gone two miles too far).

Contact: Okanogan and Wenatchee National Forests, Methow Valley Ranger District, 509/996-4003, www.fs.fed.us; Methow Valley Visitor Center, 509/996-4000.

38 KLIPCHUCK

Scenic rating: 7

on Early Winters Creek in
Okanogan and Wenatchee National Forests

Map grid B1

This camp is located at an elevation of 3,000 feet along Early Winters Creek. The camp area is set amid majestic trees, primarily Douglas fir and subalpine firs. Klipchuck provides hiking aplenty, but note that rattlesnakes are occasionally seen in this area. A short loop trail from the camp leads about five miles up and over Delancy Ridge to Driveway Butte and down to the creek, although the trail is somewhat overgrown. Another trail starts nearby on Forest Road 200 (Sandy Butte-Cedar Creek Road) and goes two miles up Cedar Creek to lovely Cedar Creek Falls. Still another option from the campground is a four-mile trail along Early Winters Creek. This region is best visited in the spring and fall, with summer hot and dry.

RV sites, facilities: There are 46 sites for tents or RVs up to 34 feet long. Sites can be combined to accommodate groups. Picnic tables and fire grills are provided. Drinking water, vault toilets, and garbage bins are available. Some facilities are wheelchair accessible. Leashed pets are permitted.

Reservations, fees: Reservations are not accepted. Sites are $12 per night per vehicle. Open late May–late September, weather permitting.

Directions: From Burlington, drive east on Highway 20 for 115 miles to Forest Road 300. (If you reach the Methow River Valley, you have gone four miles past the turnoff.) Turn left (marked) and drive northwest one mile to the camp at the end of the road.

Contact: Okanogan and Wenatchee National Forests, Methow Valley Ranger District, 509/996-4003, www.fs.fed.us; Methow Valley Visitor Center, 509/996-4000.

39 LONE FIR

Scenic rating: 9

on Early Winters Creek in
Okanogan and Wenatchee National Forests

Map grid B1

Lone Fir is set at 3,640 feet elevation along the banks of Early Winters Creek. A loop trail through the campground woods is wheelchair accessible for 0.4 mile. The area has had some timber operations in the past, but there are no nearby clear-cuts. To the west, Washington Pass Overlook offers a spectacular view. Anglers can fish in the creek, and many hiking and biking trails crisscross the area, including the trailhead for Cutthroat Lake. Other possible side trips include Goat Wall to the north and the town of Winthrop to the south, which boasts a historical museum, a state fish hatchery, and Pearrygin Lake State Park.

RV sites, facilities: There are 27 sites for tents or RVs up to 20 feet long. Picnic tables and fire grills are provided. Drinking water, vault toilets, and garbage bins are available. Some facilities are wheelchair accessible. Leashed pets are permitted.

Reservations, fees: Reservations are not accepted. Sites are $12 per night per vehicle. Open late June–September, weather permitting.

Directions: From Burlington, drive east on Highway 20 for 107 miles to the campground (11 miles west of Mazama) on the right.

Contact: Okanogan and Wenatchee National Forests, Methow Valley Ranger District, 509/996-4003, www.fs.fed.us; Methow Valley Visitor Center, 509/996-4000.

40 CAMP 4

Scenic rating: 6

on the Chewuch River in
Okanogan and Wenatchee National Forests

Map grid B1

Camp 4 is the smallest and most primitive of the three camps along the Chewuch River (the others are Chewuch and Falls Creek). It is set at an elevation of 2,400 feet. Trailers are not recommended. There are three trailheads five miles north of camp: two at Lake Creek and another at Andrews Creek. They all have corrals, hitching rails, truck docks, and water for stock at the trailheads, but no livestock are permitted in the campground itself. Trails leading into the Pasayten Wilderness leave from both locations.

RV sites, facilities: There are three tent sites and two sites for tents or RVs up to 16 feet long. Fire grills and picnic tables are provided. Vault toilets are available, but there is no drinking water. Garbage must be packed out. Some facilities are wheelchair accessible. Leashed pets are permitted, but no livestock are permitted in camp.

Reservations, fees: Reservations are not accepted. Sites are $8 per vehicle per night. Open late May–October, weather permitting.

Directions: From Burlington, drive east on Highway 20 for 134 miles to Winthrop and County Road 1213/West Chewuch Road. Turn north on County Road 1213/West Chewuch Road and drive 6.5 miles (where it merges with Forest Road 51). Continue north on Forest Road 51 for 11 miles to the campground on the right.

Contact: Okanogan and Wenatchee National Forests, Methow Valley Ranger District, 509/996-4003, www.fs.fed.us; Methow Valley Visitor Center, 509/996-4000.

41 HONEYMOON

Scenic rating: 8

on Eightmile Creek in
Okanogan and Wenatchee National Forests

Map grid B1

This small camp is set along Eightmile Creek at an elevation of 3,280 feet. If you continue north seven miles to the end of Forest Road 5130, you'll reach a trailhead that provides access to the Pasayten Wilderness. Why is it named Honeymoon? Well, it seems that a forest ranger and his bride chose this quiet and secluded spot along the creek to spend their wedding night.

RV sites, facilities: There are five sites for tents or small RVs up to 18 feet long. Picnic tables and fire grills are provided. Vault toilets are available, but there is no drinking water. Garbage must be packed out. Some facilities are wheelchair accessible. Leashed pets are permitted.

Reservations, fees: Reservations are not accepted. Sites are $8 per vehicle per night. Open late May–September, weather permitting.

Directions: From Burlington, drive east on Highway 20 for 134 miles to Winthrop and County Road 1213/West Chewuch Road. Turn north on County Road 1213/West Chewuch Road and drive 6.5 miles (where it merges with Forest Road 5130). Continue north on Forest Road 5130 for 10 miles to the campground on the right.

Contact: Okanogan and Wenatchee National Forests, Methow Valley Ranger District, 509/996-4003, www.fs.fed.us; Methow Valley Visitor Center, 509/996-4000.

42 CHEWUCH

Scenic rating: 6

on the Chewuch River in
Okanogan and Wenatchee National Forests

Map grid B1

Chewuch Camp is set along the Chewuch River at an elevation of 2,278 feet and is surrounded by ponderosa pines. It is a small camp where catch-and-release fishing is a highlight. There are also hiking and biking trails in the area. By traveling north, you can access trailheads that lead into the Pasayten Wilderness. This camp provides an alternative to the more developed nearby Falls Creek campground.

RV sites, facilities: There are 16 sites for tents or RVs up to 35 feet long. Picnic tables and fire grills are provided. Drinking water, vault toilets, and garbage bins are available. Some facilities are wheelchair accessible. Leashed pets are permitted.

Reservations, fees: Reservations are not accepted. Sites are $12 per vehicle per night. Open late May–September, weather permitting.

Directions: From Burlington, drive east on Highway 20 for 134 miles to Winthrop and County Road 1213/West Chewuch Road. Turn north on County Road 1213/West Chewuch Road and drive 6.5 miles (where it merges with Forest Road 51). Continue north on Forest Road 51 for seven miles to the campground on the right.

Contact: Okanogan and Wenatchee National Forests, Methow Valley Ranger District, 509/996-4003, www.fs.fed.us; Methow Valley Visitor Center, 509/996-4000.

43 FLAT

Scenic rating: 6

on Eightmile Creek in
Okanogan and Wenatchee National Forests

Map grid B1

This campground is set along Eightmile Creek, two miles from where it empties into the Chewuch River. The elevation is 2,858 feet. Buck Lake is about three miles away. This is the closest of six camps to County Road 1213. Other options include Honeymoon, Nice, and Falls Creek.

RV sites, facilities: There are 12 sites for tents or RVs up to 36 feet long. Picnic tables and fire grills are provided. Vault toilets and drinking water are available. Garbage must be packed out. Some facilities are wheelchair accessible. Leashed pets are permitted.

Reservations, fees: Reservations are not accepted. Sites are $8 per night per vehicle. Open early May–September, weather permitting.

Directions: From Burlington, drive east on Highway 20 for 134 miles to Winthrop and County Road 1213 (West Chewuch Road). Turn north on West Chewuch Road and drive 6.5 miles (the road becomes Forest Road 51). Continue on Forest Road 51 and drive three miles to Forest Road 5130 (Eightmile Creek Road). Turn left (northwest) and drive two miles to the campground on the left.

Contact: Okanogan and Wenatchee National Forests, Methow Valley Ranger District,

509/996-4003, www.fs.fed.us; Methow Valley Visitor Center, 509/996-4000.

44 FALLS CREEK

Scenic rating: 7

on the Chewuch River in
Okanogan and Wenatchee National Forests

Map grid B1

About a 20-minute drive out of Winthrop, Falls Creek is a quiet and pretty campground located at the confluence of its namesake, Falls Creek, and the Chewuch River. The elevation is 2,100 feet. Highlights include fishing access and a 0.25-mile trail (wheelchair accessible) to a waterfall located across the road from the campground.

RV sites, facilities: There are seven sites for tents or RVs up to 18 feet long. Picnic tables and fire grills are provided. Vault toilets and drinking water are available. Garbage must be packed out. Some facilities are wheelchair accessible. Leashed pets are permitted.

Reservations, fees: Reservations are not accepted. Sites are $8 per vehicle per night. Open May–late September, weather permitting.

Directions: From Burlington, drive east on Highway 20 for 134 miles to Winthrop and County Road 1213 (West Chewuch Road). Turn north on West Chewuch Road and drive 6.5 miles (becomes Forest Road 51.) Continue on Forest Road 51 and drive 5.2 miles to the campground on the right. Obtaining a U.S. Forest Service map is advised.

Contact: Okanogan and Wenatchee National Forests, Methow Valley Ranger District, 509/996-4003, www.fs.fed.us; Methow Valley Visitor Center, 509/996-4000.

45 PEARRYGIN LAKE STATE PARK

Scenic rating: 8

on Pearrygin Lake

Map grid B1

Pearrygin Lake is fed from underground springs and Pearrygin Creek, the lifeblood for this setting and the adjacent 696-acre state park. Located in the beautiful Methow Valley, it's ringed by the Northern Cascade Mountains. The park is known for its expansive green lawns, which lead to 8,200 feet of waterfront and sandy beaches. The camp is frequented by red-winged and yellow-headed blackbirds, as well as by marmots. Wildflower- and wildlife-viewing are excellent in the spring. The campground has access to a sandy beach and facilities for swimming, boating, waterskiing, fishing, and hiking. The sites are set close together and don't offer much privacy, but they are spacious and shaded, and a variety of recreation options make it worth the crunch.

RV sites, facilities: There are 90 tent sites, 71 sites for tents or RVs up to 60 feet long (15 and 30 amp full hookups), two hike-in/bike-in sites, two cabins, a vacation house, and two group sites for up to 48 and 80 people. Picnic tables and fire grills are provided. Restrooms with flush toilets and coin showers, drinking water, a dump station, firewood, Junior Ranger program, horseshoe pits, swimming beach, and volleyball court are available. A store, deli, and ice are located within one mile. Boat launching and dock facilities and boat rentals are available. Some facilities are wheelchair accessible. Leashed pets are permitted.

Reservations, fees: Reservations are accepted for family sites and required for group camps at 888/CAMP-OUT (888/226-7688) or www.parks.wa.gov/reservations ($6.50–8.50 reservation fee). Tent sites are $21 per night, RV sites with hookups are $28 per night, $10 per extra vehicle per night, hike-in/bike-in sites are $14 per night, and group sites are $2.25 per person per night. Cabins are $65 per night, and the vacation house is $137 per night. Some credit cards are accepted. Open April–early November.

Directions: From Winthrop and Highway 20, drive north through town (road changes to East Chewuch Road). Continue 1.5 miles north from town to Bear Creek Road. Turn right and drive 1.5 miles to the end of the pavement and the park entrance on the right. Turn right, drive over the cattle guard, and continue 0.75 mile to the West Campground or 1.5 miles to the East Campground.

Contact: Pearrygin Lake State Park, 509/996-2370; state park information, 360/902-8844, www.parks.wa.gov.

46 KOA WINTHROP

Scenic rating: 7

on the Methow River

Map grid B1

Here's another campground set along the Methow River, which offers opportunities for fishing, boating, swimming, and rafting. The park has a free shuttle into Winthrop, an interesting town with many restored, early-1900s buildings lining the main street. One such building, the Shafer Museum, displays an array of period items. If you would like to observe wildlife, take a short, two-mile drive southeast out of Winthrop on County Road 9129 on the east side of the Methow River. Turn east on County Road 1631 into Davis Lake and follow the signs to the Methow River Habitat Management Area Headquarters. Depending on the time of year, you may see mule deer, porcupines, bobcats, mountain lions, snowshoe hares, black bears, red squirrels, and many species of birds. If you're looking for something tamer, other nearby recreation options include an 18-hole golf course and tennis courts.

RV sites, facilities: There are 60 sites with full or partial hookups for RVs of any length, 15 sites for RVs of any length (no hookups), and 35 tent sites. There are also 20 one- and two-room cabins. Some sites are pull-through. Picnic tables and fire grills are provided. Restrooms

with flush toilets and showers, drinking water, firewood, a dump station, recreation hall, high-speed modem and Wi-Fi access, bike and video rentals, a convenience store, coin laundry, ice, a playground, and a seasonal heated swimming pool are available. Propane gas and a café are located within one mile. There is a courtesy shuttle to and from Winthrop. Leashed pets are permitted.

Reservations, fees: Reservations are accepted at 800/562-2158. Sites are $27–38 per night, $2–4 per person per night for more than two people. Some credit cards are accepted. Open mid-April–October.

Directions: From Winthrop, drive east on Highway 20 for one mile to the camp on the left. The camp is between Mileposts 194 and 195.

Contact: KOA Winthrop, 509/996-2258, www.koa.com.

47 BIG TWIN LAKE CAMPGROUND

Scenic rating: 5

on Big Twin Lake

Map grid B1

As you might figure from the name, this campground is set along the shore of Big Twin Lake. With its sweeping lawn and shade trees, the camp features views of the lake from all campsites. No gas motors are permitted on the lake. Fly-fishing is good for rainbow trout, with special regulations in effect: one-fish limit, single barbless hook, artificial lures only. This is an ideal lake for a float tube, rowboat with a casting platform, or a pram. A short drive out of Winthrop (County Road 9129) leads to the Methow River Habitat Management Area Headquarters. Depending on the time of year, you may see mule deer, porcupines, bobcats, mountain lions, snowshoe hares, black bears, red squirrels, and many species of birds. Other recreation options include an 18-hole golf course and tennis courts.

RV sites, facilities: There are 50 sites with full or partial hookups for RVs of any length, and

35 tent sites. Some sites are pull-through. Picnic tables and fire grills are provided. Restrooms with flush toilets and coin showers, drinking water, a dump station, firewood, ice, and a playground are available. Boat docks, launching facilities, and boat rentals are on Big Twin Lake. Leashed pets are permitted.

Reservations, fees: Reservations are accepted. Sites are $27 per night for RVs, $21 for tents, $7 per person per night for more than two people, and $7 per extra vehicle per night. Weekly and monthly rates are available. Open mid-April–October.

Directions: From Winthrop, drive east on Highway 20 for three miles to Twin Lakes Road. Turn right (west) on Twin Lakes Road and drive two miles to the campground on the right.

Contact: Big Twin Lake Campground, 509/996-2650, www.methownet.com/bigtwin.

48 ROADS END

Scenic rating: 8

on the Twisp River in
Okanogan and Wenatchee National Forests

Map grid B1

This quiet trailhead camp is located at the end of Twisp River Road. Set at an elevation of 3,600 feet along the Twisp River, it features a major trailhead that provides fishing access and a chance to hike for mountain views and explore the Lake Chelan-Sawtooth Wilderness. The trail intersects with Copper Creek Trail and the Pacific Crest Trail about nine miles from the camp. A U.S. Forest Service map is essential. Note that this camp is closed in the off-season to protect bull trout, an endangered species.

RV sites, facilities: There are four sites for tents or small RVs up to 16 feet long. Picnic tables and fire grills are provided. Vault toilets are available. There is no drinking water, and garbage must be packed out. Some facilities are wheelchair accessible. Leashed pets are permitted.

Reservations, fees: Reservations are not

accepted. Sites are $8 per vehicle per night. Open late May–early September, weather permitting.

Directions: From Burlington, drive east on Highway 20 for 145 miles to Twisp and County Road 9114 (Twisp River Road). Turn west on County Road 9114 and drive 11 miles (becomes Forest Road 44, then eventually Forest Road 4440). Continue west for 13.5 miles to the campground. Obtaining a U.S. Forest Service map is advisable.

Contact: Okanogan and Wenatchee National Forests, Methow Valley Ranger District, 509/996-4003, www.fs.fed.us; Methow Valley Visitor Center, 509/996-4000.

49 SOUTH CREEK

Scenic rating: 6

on the Twisp River in
Okanogan and Wenatchee National Forests

Map grid B1

Although small, quiet, and little known, South Creek Campground packs a wallop with good recreation options. It's set at the confluence of the Twisp River and South Creek at a major trailhead that accesses the Lake Chelan-Sawtooth Wilderness. The South Creek Trailhead provides a hike to Louis Lake. The elevation at the camp is 3,100 feet.

RV sites, facilities: There are four sites for tents or RVs up to 24 feet long. Picnic tables and fire grills are provided. A vault toilet is available. There is no drinking water, and garbage must be packed out. Some facilities are wheelchair accessible. Leashed pets are permitted.

Reservations, fees: Reservations are not accepted. Sites are $8 per vehicle per night. Open late May–September, weather permitting.

Directions: From Burlington, drive east on Highway 20 for 145 miles to Twisp and County Road 9114 (Twisp River Road). Turn right on County Road 9114 and drive 17.5 miles (becomes Forest Road 44). Continue west (becomes Forest Road 4440 and a dirt road) for 4.5 miles to the campground on the left.

Contact: Okanogan and Wenatchee National Forests, Methow Valley Ranger District, 509/996-4003, www.fs.fed.us; Methow Valley Visitor Center, 509/996-4000.

50 POPLAR FLAT

Scenic rating: 7

on the Twisp River in
Okanogan and Wenatchee National Forests

Map grid B1

This campground is set at 2,900 feet elevation along the Twisp River. This area provides many wildlife-viewing opportunities for deer, black bears, and many species of birds. Several trails in the area, including Twisp River Trail, follow streams and some provide access to the Lake Chelan-Sawtooth Wilderness. Twisp River Horse Camp, across the river from the campground, has facilities for horses.

RV sites, facilities: There are 16 sites for tents or RVs up to 22 feet long. Picnic tables and fire grills are provided. Drinking water, vault toilets, and garbage bins are available. A day-use picnic area with a shelter is nearby. Some facilities are wheelchair accessible. Leashed pets are permitted.

Reservations, fees: Reservations are not accepted. Sites are $12 per vehicle per night. Open mid-May–September, weather permitting.

Directions: From Burlington, drive east on Highway 20 for 145 miles to Twisp and County Road 9114 (Twisp River Road). Turn west on County Road 9114 and drive 11 miles (becomes Forest Road 44 and then Forest Road 4440). Continue west for 9.5 miles to the campground on the left.

Contact: Okanogan and Wenatchee National Forests, Methow Valley Ranger District, 509/996-4003, www.fs.fed.us; Methow Valley Visitor Center, 509/996-4000.

51 TWISP RIVER HORSE CAMP

Scenic rating: 7

on the Twisp River in
Okanogan and Wenatchee National Forests

Map grid B1

This camp is only for horses and their owners. It is set on the Twisp River at an elevation of 3,000 feet. The camp features nearby access to trails, including North Fork Twisp River Trail, which leads to Copper Pass, and South Fork Twisp River Trail, which leads to Lake Chelan National Recreation Area and Twisp Pass. South Creek Trail is also available and leads from the camp to Lake Chelan National Recreation Area.

RV sites, facilities: There are 12 sites for tents or RVs up to 30 feet long. Picnic tables and fire grills are provided. Vault toilets are available. There is no drinking water, and garbage must be packed out. For horses, a loading ramp, hitching rails, and feed stations are available. Some facilities are wheelchair accessible. Leashed pets are permitted.

Reservations, fees: Reservations are not accepted. Northwest Forest Pass ($5 daily fee or $30 annual fee per parked vehicle) is required. Open May–September, weather permitting.

Directions: From Burlington, drive east on Highway 20 for 145 miles to Twisp and County Road 9114 (Twisp River Road). Turn west on County Road 9114 and drive 11 miles (becomes Forest Road 44). Continue west on Forest Road 44 for 3.5 miles to War Creek Campground on the left. Continue 250 yards to Forest Road 4430. Turn left (drive over the bridge) and drive approximately nine miles (the road becomes Forest Road 4435) to the campground on the right.

Contact: Okanogan and Wenatchee National Forests, Methow Valley Ranger District, 509/996-4003, www.fs.fed.us; Methow Valley Visitor Center, 509/996-4000.

52 WAR CREEK

Scenic rating: 6

on the Twisp River in
Okanogan and Wenatchee National Forests

Map grid B1

This trailhead camp is set at 2,400 feet elevation and provides several routes into the Lake Chelan-Sawtooth Wilderness. War Creek Trail, Eagle Creek Trail, and Oval Creek Trail all offer wilderness access and trout fishing. Backpackers can extend this trip into Lake Chelan National Recreation Area, for a 15-mile trek that finishes at the shore of Lake Chelan and the National Park Service outpost. Rattlesnakes are occasionally spotted in this region in the summer.

RV sites, facilities: There are 10 sites for tents or RVs up to 22 feet long. Picnic tables and fire grills are provided. Vault toilets, drinking water, and firewood are available. Garbage must be packed out. Some facilities are wheelchair accessible. Leashed pets are permitted.

Reservations, fees: Reservations are not accepted. Sites are $8 per vehicle per night. Open May–September, weather permitting.

Directions: From Burlington, drive east on Highway 20 for 145 miles to Twisp and County Road 9114 (Twisp River Road). Turn west on County Road 9114 and drive 11 miles (becomes Forest Road 44). Continue west on Forest Road 44 for 3.5 miles to the campground on the left.

Contact: Okanogan and Wenatchee National Forests, Methow Valley Ranger District, 509/996-4003, www.fs.fed.us; Methow Valley Visitor Center, 509/996-4000.

53 BLACKPINE LAKE

Scenic rating: 7

on Blackpine Lake in
Okanogan and Wenatchee National Forests

Map grid B1

This campground features great views of some local peaks. About one-third of the campsites have views; the rest are set in a forest of Douglas fir and ponderosa pine. This popular spot often fills up on summer weekends and occasionally even during the week. Fishing is available for stocked rainbow trout. Note that boating is permitted, but no gas motors are allowed, only electric motors. Less than 0.25 mile long, an interpretive trail leads around the north end of the lake.

RV sites, facilities: There are 23 sites for tents or RVs up to 24 feet long. Picnic tables and fire grills are provided. Drinking water, vault toilets, and garbage bins are available. A boat launch and two floating docks are available nearby. Some facilities are wheelchair accessible. Leashed pets are permitted.

Reservations, fees: Reservations are not accepted. Sites are $8 per night per vehicle. Open May–September, weather permitting.

Directions: From Burlington, drive east on Highway 20 for 145 miles to Twisp and County Road 9114 (Twisp River Road). Turn west on County Road 9114 and drive 10 miles to County Road 1090. Turn left and drive over a bridge (becomes Forest Road 43) and continue eight miles to the campground on the right.

Contact: Okanogan and Wenatchee National Forests, Methow Valley Ranger District, 509/996-4003, www.fs.fed.us; Methow Valley Visitor Center, 509/996-4000.

54 RIVERBEND RV PARK

Scenic rating: 6

on the Methow River

Map grid B1

The shore of the Methow River skirts this campground, and there is a nice separate area for tent campers set right along the river. Some of the RV sites are also riverfront. Trout fishing, river rafting, and swimming are popular here. The nearby Methow River Habitat Management Area Headquarters offers wildlife-viewing for mule deer, porcupines, bobcats, mountain lions, snowshoe hares, black bears, red squirrels, and many species of birds. Other recreation options include an 18-hole golf course and tennis courts.

WASHINGTON

RV sites, facilities: There are 69 sites with full hookups for RVs of any length, 35 tent sites, and one sleeping cabin. Some sites are pull-through. Picnic tables and fire pits are provided. Restrooms with flush toilets and coin showers, an RV dump station, firewood, a convenience store, coin laundry, ice, a playground, horseshoe pits, propane gas, Wi-Fi access, and RV storage are available. Groups can be accommodated. Leashed pets are permitted.

Reservations, fees: Reservations are accepted at 800/686-4498. Sites are $29–38 per night, $5 per person per night for more than two people, $5 per night per extra vehicle, and $5 per night per pet. Some credit cards are accepted. Open year-round.

Directions: From Twisp, drive west on Highway 20 for two miles to the park on the right, between Mileposts 199 and 200.

Contact: Riverbend RV Park, 509/997-3500 or 800/686-4498, www.riverbendrv.com.

55 FOGGY DEW

Scenic rating: 6

on Foggy Dew Creek in
Okanogan and Wenatchee National Forests

Map grid B1

This private, remote campground is set at the confluence of Foggy Dew Creek and the North Fork of Old Creek. The elevation is 2,400 feet. Several trails for hiking and horseback riding nearby provide access to various backcountry lakes and streams. To get to the trailheads, follow the forest roads near camp. Bicycles are allowed on Trails 417, 429, and 431. There is also access to a motorcycle-use area.

RV sites, facilities: There are 13 sites for tents or RVs up to 20 feet long. Picnic tables and fire grills are provided. Vault toilets are available. There is no drinking water, and garbage must be packed out. Some facilities are wheelchair accessible. Leashed pets are permitted.

Reservations, fees: Reservations are not accepted. Sites are $8 per night per vehicle. Open late May–September, weather permitting.

Directions: From Burlington, drive east on Highway 20 for 145 miles to Twisp. Continue east on Highway 20 for three miles to Highway 153. Turn south on Highway 153 and drive 12 miles to County Road 1029 (Gold Creek Road). Turn right (south) and drive one mile to Forest Road 4340. Turn right (west) and drive four miles to the campground on the left.

Contact: Okanogan and Wenatchee National Forests, Methow Valley Ranger District, 509/996-4003, www.fs.fed.us; Methow Valley Visitor Center, 509/996-4000.

56 PHELPS CREEK AND EQUESTRIAN

Scenic rating: 7

on the Chiwawa River in Wenatchee National Forest

Map grid B1

These camps are set at an elevation of 2,800 feet at the confluence of Phelps Creek and the Chiwawa River. There's a key trailhead for backpackers and horseback riders nearby that provides access to the Glacier Peak Wilderness and Spider Meadows. Phelps Creek Trail is routed out to Spider Meadows, a five-mile hike one-way, and Buck Creek Trail extends into the Glacier Peak Wilderness. The Chiwawa River is closed to fishing to protect endangered species. A U.S. Forest Service map is advisable.

RV sites, facilities: There are seven sites for tents or RVs up to 30 feet long at Phelps Creek and six sites for tents or RVs up to 30 feet long at Phelps Creek Equestrian. Picnic tables and fire grills are provided. Vault toilets are available. There is no drinking water, but stock water is available at Trinity Trailhead. Garbage must be packed out. Horse facilities, including loading ramps and high lines, are nearby. Leashed pets are permitted.

Reservations, fees: Reservations are not accepted. Sites are $8 per vehicle per night. Open mid-June–October, weather permitting.

Directions: From I-5 and Everett, turn east on U.S. 2 and drive 87 miles to State Route 207. Turn north on State Route 207 and drive four miles to Chiwawa Loop Road. Turn right (east) on Chiwawa Loop Road and drive 1.4 miles to Chiwawa River Road (Forest Road 6200). Bear left (north) and continue for 23.6 miles to the campground (the last 12 miles of road are gravel).

Contact: Okanogan and Wenatchee National Forests, Wenatchee River Ranger District, Lake Wenatchee Ranger Station, 509/763-3103, fax 509/763-3211, www.fs.fed.us.

57 FLOWING LAKE COUNTY PARK

Scenic rating: 6

near Snohomish

Map grid A2

This campground has a little something for everyone, including swimming, powerboating, waterskiing, and good fishing on Flowing Lake. The campsites are in a wooded setting (that is, no lake view), and it is a 0.25-mile walk to the beach. A one-mile nature trail is nearby. Note the private homes on the lake; all visitors are asked to respect the privacy of the owners.

RV sites, facilities: There are 29 sites, most with partial hookups for tents or RVs up to 40 feet long; some sites are pull-through. Four cabins are also available. Picnic tables and fire grills are provided. Restrooms with flush toilets and coin showers, drinking water, and firewood are available. Picnic shelters, a fishing dock, boat docks, launching facilities, swimming beach, playground, and interpretive programs are available nearby. Some facilities are wheelchair accessible. Leashed pets are permitted.

Reservations, fees: Reservations are accepted at 425/388-6600 or www.snoco.org ($7 reservation fee). Sites are $20–28 per night, $10 per night for a second vehicle. Cabins are $40–50 per night. Open year-round with limited winter facilities.

Directions: From I-5 and Everett, take the Snohomish-Wenatchee exit and turn east on U.S. 2; drive to Milepost 10, and look for 100th Street SE (Westwick Road). Turn left and drive

two miles (becomes 171st Avenue SE) to 48th Street SE. Turn right and drive about 0.5 mile into the park at the end of the road.

Contact: Flowing Lake County Park, 360/568-2274; Snohomish County Parks, 425/388-6600, www.snoco.org.

58 MONEY CREEK CAMPGROUND

Scenic rating: 5

on the Skykomish River in Mount Baker–Snoqualmie National Forest

Map grid A2

You have a little surprise waiting for you here. Trains go by regularly day and night, and the first time it happens while you're in deep sleep, you might just launch a hole right through the top of your tent. The Burlington Northern rail runs along the western boundary of the campground. By now you've got the picture: This can be a noisy camp. Money Creek Campground is on the Skykomish River, with hiking trails a few miles away. The best of these is Dorothy Lake Trail.

RV sites, facilities: There are 24 sites, including two double sites, for tents or RVs up to 35 feet long. Picnic tables and fire grills are provided. Vault toilets, drinking water, garbage bins, and firewood are available. A store, café, and ice are located 3.5 miles to the east. Some facilities are wheelchair accessible. Leashed pets are permitted.

Reservations, fees: Reservations are accepted at 877/444-6777 or www.recreation.gov ($10 reservation fee). Single sites are $16–18 per night, double sites are $32–40 per night, $8 per extra vehicle per night. Open mid-May–mid-September, weather permitting.

Directions: From I-5 and Everett, turn east on U.S. 2 and drive 46 miles to Old Cascade Highway, 11 miles east of Index. Turn right (south) on Old Cascade Highway and drive across the bridge to the campground.

Contact: Mount Baker–Snoqualmie National Forest, Skykomish Ranger District, 360/677-2414, www.fs.fed.us.

59 BECKLER RIVER

Scenic rating: 7

on the Beckler River in
Mount Baker-Snoqualmie National Forest

Map grid A2

Located on the Beckler River at an elevation of 900 feet, this camp has scenic riverside sites in second-growth timber, primarily Douglas fir, cedar, and big leaf maple. Fishing at the campground is poor; it's better well up the river. The Skykomish Ranger Station, which sells maps, is just a couple of miles away.

RV sites, facilities: There are 27 sites, including two double sites, for tents or RVs up to 40 feet long. Picnic tables and fire grills are provided. Vault toilets, drinking water, and firewood are available. A camp host is on-site. A store, café, and ice are located within two miles. Some facilities are wheelchair accessible. Leashed pets are permitted.

Reservations, fees: Reservations are accepted at 877/444-6777 or www.recreation.gov ($10 reservation fee). Single sites are $16 per night, double sites are $30 per night, $8 per extra vehicle per night. Open late May–early September, weather permitting.

Directions: From I-5 and Everett, turn east on U.S. 2 and drive 49 miles to Skykomish. Continue east on U.S. 2 for 0.5 mile to Forest Road 65. Turn left (north) on Forest Road 65 and drive 1.6 miles to the camp on the left.

Contact: Mount Baker–Snoqualmie National Forest, Skykomish Ranger District, 360/677-2414, www.fs.fed.us.

60 MILLER RIVER GROUP

Scenic rating: 8

near the Alpine Lakes Wilderness in
Mount Baker-Snoqualmie National Forest

Map grid A2

This campground is located along the Miller River, a short distance from the boundary of the Alpine Lakes Wilderness. If you continue another seven miles on Forest Road 6410, you'll get to a trailhead leading to Dorothy Lake, a 1.5-mile hike. This pretty lake is two miles long. The trail continues past the lake to many other backcountry lakes. Backpackers must limit their party to no more than 12 people per group. A U.S. Forest Service map is essential. The camp host at nearby Money Creek oversees this campground.

RV sites, facilities: There is one group camp with 18 sites for tents or RVs up to 30 feet long for up to 100 people. Picnic tables and fire grills are provided. Vault toilets, drinking water, and a group picnic area are available. A store, café, and ice are within five miles. Some facilities are wheelchair accessible. Leashed pets are permitted.

Reservations, fees: Reservations are accepted at 877/444-6777 or www.recreation.gov ($10 reservation fee). Sites are $75 for the first 30 people, $125 for 31–75 people, and $150 for 76–100 people. Open mid-May–mid-September, weather permitting.

Directions: From I-5 and Everett, turn east on U.S. 2 and drive 46 miles to Old Cascade Highway, 11 miles east of Index. Turn right (south) on Old Cascade Highway (across the bridge) and drive one mile to Forest Road 6410. Turn right (south) and drive two miles to the campground on the left.

Contact: Mount Baker–Snoqualmie National Forest, Skykomish Ranger District, 360/677-2414, www.fs.fed.us.

61 SNOQUALMIE RIVER RV PARK & CAMPGROUND

Scenic rating: 7

on the Snoqualmie River

Map grid A2

If you're in the Seattle area and stuck for a place for the night, this pretty 10-acre park set along the Snoqualmie River might be a welcome option. Approximately one-third of the sites are filled with monthly renters. Activities include fishing, swimming, road biking, and rafting. Nearby recreation options include several nine-hole golf courses. A worthwhile side trip is beautiful Snoqualmie Falls, 3.5 miles away in the famed Twin Peaks country.

RV sites, facilities: There are 92 sites with full or partial hookups for RVs of any length and 32 tent sites. Picnic tables and fire rings are provided. Restrooms with flush toilets and showers, drinking water, firewood, and a playground are available. Propane gas, a store, café, coin laundry, and ice are located within 3.5 miles. Boat-launching facilities are located within 0.5 mile. Leashed pets are permitted with certain restrictions.

Reservations, fees: Reservations are accepted. Sites are $26–38 per night, plus $5 per person per night for more than two people. Note that this RV park no longer charges for pets; after all, they're part of the family. Some credit cards are accepted. Open year-round with limited winter facilities.

Directions: From the junction of I-5 and I-90 south of Seattle, turn east on I-90. Drive east for 26 miles to Exit 22 (Preston-Fall City). Take that exit and turn north on Preston-Fall City Road and drive 4.5 miles to SE 44th Place. Turn right (east) and drive one mile to the park at the end of the road.

Contact: Snoqualmie River RV Park & Campground, 425/222-5545.

62 MIDDLE FORK

Scenic rating: 8

on the North Fork of the Snoqualmie River in Mount Baker-Snoqualmie National Forest

Map grid A2

Set at an elevation of 1,600 feet, this is one of the newest and most remote campgrounds in the Mount Baker-Snoqualmie National Forest. Getting there is a challenge, but this spot is popular with locals who tough out the graveled, potholed road to swim and fish here.

RV sites, facilities: There are 39 sites for tents or RVs up to 45 feet long and a group site for up to 25 people. Picnic tables and fire grills are provided. Drinking water, pit toilets, a camp

host, picnic shelter, and firewood are available. Some facilities are wheelchair accessible. Leashed pets are permitted.

Reservations, fees: Reservations are accepted at 877/444-6777 or recreation.gov ($10 reservation fee for individuals, $25 for groups). Sites are $14 per night, $7 per extra vehicle per night, and $40 per night for the group site. Open mid-May–early October, weather permitting.

Directions: In Seattle on I-5, turn east on I-90 and drive to North Bend and Exit 34. Take that exit and drive north on 468th Street for 0.6 mile to SE Middle Fork Road (Forest Service Road 56). Turn right and drive 12 miles to the campground (0.5 mile past the Middle Fork Trail trailhead). Obtaining a U.S. Forest Service map is advisable.

Contact: Mount Baker–Snoqualmie National Forest, Snoqualmie Ranger District, North Bend office, 425/888-1421, fax 425/888-1910, www.fs.fed.us.

63 KANASKAT-PALMER STATE PARK

Scenic rating: 8

on the Green River

Map grid A2

This wooded campground offers private campsites near the Green River. The park covers 320 acres with two miles of river frontage; the river can be accessed from the day-use area but not from the campground. It is set on a small, low, forested plateau. In summer, the river is ideal for expert-level rafting and kayaking, and the park is used as a put-in spot for the rafting run down the Green River Gorge. This area has much mining history, and coal mining continues, as does cinnabar mining (the base ore for mercury). Nearby Flaming Geyser gets its name from a coal seam. In winter, the river attracts a run of steelhead and salmon. The park has three miles of hiking trails.

RV sites, facilities: There are 31 tent sites, 19 pull-through sites with partial hookups (30 amps) for RVs up to 50 feet long, three yurts, and one group camp for up to 80 people, which includes two Adirondack shelters, a picnic shelter, and a community fire ring. Picnic tables are provided. Restrooms with flush toilets and showers, drinking water, a sheltered picnic area, horseshoe pits, and a dump station are available. A convenience store and deli are within two miles. Some facilities are wheelchair accessible. Leashed pets are permitted.

Reservations, fees: Reservations are accepted for individual sites in summer and are required for the group camp at 888/CAMP-OUT (888/226-7688) or www.parks.wa.gov/reservations ($6.50–8.50 reservation fee). Sites are $21–27 per night, $10 per extra vehicle per night, and yurts are $55–60 per night. Group camp fees vary with size of group and are based on a rate of $2.25 per person per night. Some credit cards are accepted. Open year-round, weather permitting.

Directions: From Puyallup at the junction of Highway 167 and Highway 410, turn southeast on Highway 410 and drive 25 miles to Enumclaw and Porter Street/Highway 169. Turn right and drive three miles to SE 400th Street. Turn right on SE 400th Street and drive one mile to SE 392nd Street. Veer right on SE 392nd Street and drive one mile to SE Vezie Cumberland Road. Turn left and drive three miles to Cumberland Kanasket Road SE and continue 2.5 miles to the park.

Contact: Kanaskat-Palmer State Park, 360/886-0148; state park information, 360/902-8844, www.parks.wa.gov.

64 TINKHAM

Scenic rating: 9

on the Snoqualmie River in
Mount Baker–Snoqualmie National Forest

Map grid A2

About half the campsites here face the Snoqualmie River, making this a pretty spot. Fishing can be good; check regulations. The camp is set at an elevation of 1,600 feet. The creek provides hiking options. This camp is often

used as an overflow for Denny Creek. Wilderness trails for the Alpines Lakes Wilderness are located 5–10 miles away from the camp.

RV sites, facilities: There are 47 sites for tents or RVs up to 40 feet long. Picnic tables and fire pits are provided. Drinking water, vault toilets, garbage bins, and firewood are available. A camp host is on-site. Some facilities are wheelchair accessible. Leashed pets are permitted.

Reservations, fees: Reservations are accepted at 877/444-6777 or www.recreation.gov ($10 reservation fee). Sites are $14–16 per night, $7 per extra vehicle per night. Open mid-May–mid-September, weather permitting.

Directions: In Seattle on I-5, turn east on I-90. Drive east on I-90 to Exit 42. Take that exit and turn right on Tinkham Road (Forest Road 55), and drive southeast 1.5 miles to the campground on the left. Obtaining a U.S. Forest Service map is advisable.

Contact: Mount Baker–Snoqualmie National Forest, Snoqualmie Ranger District, North Bend office, 425/888-1421, fax 425/888-1910, www.fs.fed.us.

65 DENNY CREEK

Scenic rating: 9

in Mount Baker-Snoqualmie National Forest

Map grid A2

This camp is set at 1,900 feet elevation along Denny Creek, which is pretty and offers nearby recreation access. The campground is secluded in an area of Douglas fir, hemlock, and cedar, with hiking trails available in addition to swimming opportunities. Denny Creek Trail starts from the campground and provides a 4.5-mile round-trip hike that features Keckwulee Falls and Denny Creek Waterslide. You can climb to Hemlock Pass and Melakwa Lake. There is access for backpackers into the Alpine Lakes Wilderness.

RV sites, facilities: There are 23 sites, some with partial hookups (30 amps), for tents or RVs up to 40 feet long, and one group site for up to 35 people. Picnic tables and fire grills are provided.

Drinking water, flush toilets, and firewood are available. Some facilities are wheelchair accessible. Leashed pets are permitted.

Reservations, fees: Reservations are accepted at 877/444-6777 or www.recreation.gov ($10 reservation fee). Sites are $20–24 per night, $10 per extra vehicle per night; double sites are $32 per night. The group site is $85 per night, plus $25 reservation fee. Open mid-May–mid-September, weather permitting.

Directions: In Seattle on I-5, turn east on I-90. Drive east on I-90 to Exit 47. Take that exit, cross the freeway, and at the T intersection turn right and drive 0.25 mile to Denny Creek Road (Forest Road 58). Turn left on Denny Creek Road and drive two miles to the campground on the left.

Contact: Mount Baker–Snoqualmie National Forest, Snoqualmie Ranger District, North Bend office, 425/888-1421, fax 425/888-1910, www.fs.fed.us.

66 KACHESS & KACHESS GROUP

Scenic rating: 8

on Kachess Lake in Wenatchee National Forest

Map grid A2

This is the only campground on the shore of Kachess Lake, but note that the water level can drop significantly in summer during low-rain years. It is the most popular campground in the local area, often filling in July and August, especially on weekends. Recreation opportunities include waterskiing, fishing, hiking, and bicycling. A trail from camp heads north into the Alpine Lakes Wilderness. The elevation is 2,300 feet.

RV sites, facilities: There are 75 single sites and 25 double sites for tents or RVs up to 32 feet long. A group site for up to 50 people is also available. Picnic tables and fire grills are provided. Drinking water, flush and vault toilets, firewood, and a camp host are available. Some facilities are wheelchair accessible. Leashed pets are permitted but aren't allowed in swimming areas.

Reservations, fees: Reservations are accepted for family sites and required for the group site at 877/444-6777 or www.recreation.gov ($10 reservation fee). Sites are $18–36 per night, $9 per extra vehicle per night. The group site is $100 per night. Open late May–mid-September, weather permitting.

Directions: In Seattle on I-5, turn east on I-90. Drive east on I-90 for 59 miles to Exit 62. Take that exit to Forest Road 49 and turn northeast; drive 5.5 miles to the campground on the right at the end of the paved road.

Contact: Okanogan and Wenatchee National Forests, Cle Elum Ranger District, 509/852-1100, fax 509/674-3800, www.fs.fed.us.

67 SALMON LA SAC

Scenic rating: 6

on the Cle Elum River in Wenatchee National Forest

Map grid A2

This is a base camp for backpackers and day hikers and is also popular with kayakers. It's located along the Cle Elum River at 2,400 feet elevation, about 0.25 mile from a major trailhead, the Salmon La Sac Trailhead. Hikers can follow creeks heading off in several directions, including into the Alpine Lakes Wilderness. A campground host is available for information.

RV sites, facilities: There are 68 sites, including eight double sites, for tents or RVs up to 21 feet long. Picnic tables and fire grills are provided. Drinking water and vault toilets are available. Some facilities are wheelchair accessible. Leashed pets are permitted.

Reservations, fees: Reservations are accepted at 877/444-6777 or www.recreation.gov ($10 reservation fee). Sites are $17–34 per night, $9 per extra vehicle per night. Open late May–mid-September, weather permitting.

Directions: In Seattle on I-5, turn east on I-90. Drive east on I-90 for 78 miles to Exit 80 (two miles before Cle Elum). Take that exit, turn north on Bullfrog Road, and drive four miles to Highway 903. Continue north on Highway 903 for 17 miles to the campground on the left.

WASHINGTON

Contact: Okanogan and Wenatchee National Forests, Cle Elum Ranger District, 509/852-1100, fax 509/674-3800, www.fs.fed.us.

68 RED MOUNTAIN

Scenic rating: 6

on the Cle Elum River in Wenatchee National Forest

Map grid A2

This alternative to nearby Wish Poosh has two big differences: There is no drinking water, and it's not on Cle Elum Lake. The camp sits along the Cle Elum River one mile from the lake, just above where the river feeds into it. The elevation is 2,200 feet.

RV sites, facilities: There are 10 sites for tents and small RVs up to 20 feet long. Picnic tables and fire grills are provided. Vault toilets and garbage bins are available, but there is no drinking water. Leashed pets are permitted.

Reservations, fees: Reservations are not accepted. Sites are $12 per night, $6 per night for extra vehicle with a two-vehicle maximum. Open mid-May–late November, weather permitting.

Directions: In Seattle on I-5, turn east on I-90. Drive east on I-90 for 78 miles to Exit 80 (two miles before Cle Elum). Take that exit and turn north on Bullfrog Road; drive four miles to Highway 903. Continue north on Highway 903 for 14 miles to the campground on the left.

Contact: Okanogan and Wenatchee National Forests, Cle Elum Ranger District, 509/852-1100, fax 509/674-3800, www.fs.fed.us.

69 CLE ELUM RIVER & CLE ELUM GROUP

Scenic rating: 6

on the Cle Elum River in Wenatchee National Forest

Map grid A2

The gravel roads in the campground make this setting a bit more rustic than nearby Salmon La Sac. It serves as a valuable overflow campground for Salmon La Sac and is similar in setting and

opportunities. The group site fills on most summer weekends. A nearby trailhead provides access into the Alpine Lakes Wilderness.

RV sites, facilities: There are 23 sites, including some pull-through, for tents or RVs up to 30 feet long and a group site for up to 100 people. Picnic tables and fire grills are provided. Drinking water, firewood, and vault toilets are available. Leashed pets are permitted.

Reservations, fees: Reservations are not accepted for family sites but are required for the group site at 877/444-6777 or www.recreation.gov ($10 reservation fee). Sites are $15–30 per night, $7 per extra vehicle per night. The group site is $100 per night. Open late May–mid-September, weather permitting.

Directions: In Seattle on I-5, turn east on I-90. Drive east on I-90 for 78 miles to Exit 80 (two miles before Cle Elum). Take that exit, turn north on Bullfrog Road, and drive four miles to Highway 903. Continue north on Highway 903 for 13 miles to the campground on the left.

Contact: Okanogan and Wenatchee National Forests, Cle Elum Ranger District, 509/852-1100, fax 509/674-3800, www.fs.fed.us.

70 LAKE EASTON STATE PARK

Scenic rating: 8

on Lake Easton

Map grid A2

This campground offers many recreational opportunities. For starters, it's set along the shore of Lake Easton on the Yakima River in the Cascade foothills. The landscape features old-growth forest, dense vegetation, and freshwater marshes, and the park covers 516 acres of the best of it. Two miles of trails for hiking and biking are available. The park provides opportunities for both summer and winter recreation, including swimming, fishing, boating, cross-country skiing, and snowmobiling. Note that high-speed boating is not recommended because Lake Easton is a shallow reservoir with stumps often hidden just below the water surface; the boat speed limit is 10 mph.

Nearby recreation options include an 18-hole golf course and hiking trails. Kachess Lake and Keechelus Lake are just a short drive away.

RV sites, facilities: There are 140 sites, including 45 sites with hookups (30 amps) for RVs up to 60 feet long, two primitive walk-in tent sites, and one group site for up to 50 people. Picnic tables and fire grills are provided. Restrooms with flush toilets and showers, drinking water, a dump station, an amphitheater, a playground, basketball, horseshoe pits, Junior Ranger program, movie nights, and a swimming beach are available. A store, café, and ice are located within one mile. Boat-launching facilities, dock, and floats are located on Lake Easton. Some facilities are wheelchair accessible. Leashed pets are permitted.

Reservations, fees: Reservations are accepted for all sites and are required for the group site at 888/CAMP-OUT (888/226-7688) or www.parks.wa.gov/reservations ($6.50–8.50 reservation fee). Sites are $21–28 per night, $10 per extra vehicle per night, walk-in sites are $10 per night, and the group site is $2.25 per person per night plus $25 reservation fee. Some credit cards are accepted. Open May–mid-October, with limited winter facilities.

Directions: From Seattle, drive east on I-90 for 68 miles to Exit 70. Take that exit to Lake Easton Road. Turn right and drive 1.5 miles to Lake Easton State Park Road. Turn right and enter park.

Contact: Lake Easton State Park, 509/656-2586, fax 509/656-2294; state park information, 360/902-8844, www.parks.wa.gov.

71 WISH POOSH

Scenic rating: 7

on Cle Elum Lake in Wenatchee National Forest
Map grid A2

This popular camp is set on the shore of Cle Elum Lake. It fills up on summer weekends and holidays. It is great midweek, when many sites are usually available. While the lake is near the camp, note that because it is an irrigation reservoir, the lake level falls rapidly each year. Waterskiing, sailing, fishing, and swimming are among recreation possibilities. The camp sits at an elevation of 2,400 feet.

RV sites, facilities: There are 34 sites, including four double sites, for tents or RVs up to 30 feet long. Picnic tables and fire grills are provided. Restrooms with flush toilets, drinking water, a camp host, and firewood are available. Boat-launching facilities are located on Cle Elum Lake. A restaurant and ice are available nearby. Leashed pets are permitted.

Reservations, fees: Reservations are not accepted. Sites are $18–36 per night, $9 per extra vehicle per night. Open mid-May–mid-September, weather permitting.

Directions: In Seattle on I-5, turn east on I-90. Drive east on I-90 for 78 miles to Exit 80 (two miles before Cle Elum). Take that exit, turn north on Bullfrog Road, and drive four miles to Highway 903. Continue north on Highway 903 for eight miles to the campground on the left.

Contact: Okanogan and Wenatchee National Forests, Cle Elum Ranger District, 509/852-1100, fax 509/674-3800, www.fs.fed.us.

72 CAYUSE HORSE CAMP

Scenic rating: 6

on the Cle Elum River in Wenatchee National Forest
Map grid A2

This camp is for horse campers only. It's located along the Cle Elum River at major trailheads for horses and hikers and marked trails for bikers. Hikers can follow creeks heading off in several directions, including into the Alpine Lakes Wilderness. The elevation is 2,400 feet.

RV sites, facilities: There are 13 sites for tents or RVs up to 35 feet long. Picnic tables and fire pits are provided. Drinking water, vault toilets, and a camp host are available. Stock facilities include corrals, troughs, and hitching posts. Bring your own stock feed. Leashed pets are permitted.

Reservations, fees: Reservations are accepted at 877/444-6777 or www.recreation.gov ($10 reservation fee). Sites are $17 per night, $9 per night for each additional vehicle. Open mid-May–mid-September, weather permitting.

Directions: In Seattle on I-5, turn east on I-90. Drive east on I-90 for 78 miles to Exit 80 (two miles before Cle Elum). Take that exit and turn north on Bullfrog Road; drive four miles to Highway 903. Continue north on Highway 903 for 17 miles to the campground on the right.

Contact: Okanogan and Wenatchee National Forests, Cle Elum Ranger District, 509/852-1100, fax 509/674-3800, www.fs.fed.us.

73 DALLES

Scenic rating: 10

in Mount Baker-Snoqualmie National Forest

Map grid A2

This campground is set at the confluence of Minnehaha Creek and the White River. Aptly, its name means "rapids." A nature trail is nearby, and the White River entrance to Mount Rainier National Park is about 14 miles south on Highway 410. The camp sits amid a grove of old-growth trees; a particular point of interest is a huge old Douglas fir that is 9.5 feet in diameter and more than 235 feet tall. This is one of the prettiest camps in the area. It gets moderate use in summer.

RV sites, facilities: There are 46 sites for tents or RVs up to 40 feet long. Picnic tables and fire grills are provided. Vault toilets, drinking water, and firewood are available. A camp host is onsite. There is a large shaded picnic area for day use. Some facilities are wheelchair accessible. Leashed pets are permitted.

Reservations, fees: Reservations are accepted for family sites and required for the group site at 877/444-6777 or www.recreation.gov ($10 reservation fee). Sites are $16–18 per night, $8 per extra vehicle per night. Open mid-May–late September, weather permitting.

Directions: From Enumclaw, drive east on Highway 410 for 25.5 miles to the campground (three miles inside the forest boundary) on the right.

Contact: Mount Baker–Snoqualmie National Forest, White River Ranger District, 360/825-6585, fax 360/825-0660, www.fs.fed.us.

74 CROW CREEK

Scenic rating: 5

on the Little Naches River in Wenatchee National Forest

Map grid A2

Set at an elevation of 2,900 feet, this campground on the Little Naches River is popular with off-road bikers and four-wheel-drive enthusiasts and is similar to Kaner Flat, except that there is no drinking water. A trail heading out from the camp leads into the backcountry and then forks in several directions. One route leads to the American River, another follows West Quartz Creek, and another goes along Fife's Ridge into the Norse Peak Wilderness (where no motorized vehicles are permitted). There is good seasonal hunting and fishing in this area.

RV sites, facilities: There are 15 sites for tents or RVs up to 30 feet long. Picnic tables and fire grills are provided. Vault toilets and garbage bins are available. There is no drinking water. Downed firewood may be gathered. Leashed pets are permitted.

Reservations, fees: Reservations are not accepted. Sites are $8 per night, $5 per extra vehicle per night. Open May–October, weather permitting.

Directions: From Yakima, drive northwest on U.S. 12 for 18 miles to Highway 410. Bear northwest on Highway 410 and drive 24.5 miles to Little Naches Road/Forest Road 1900. Turn northeast and drive 2.5 miles to Forest Road 1902. Turn left (west) and drive 0.5 mile to the campground on the right.

Contact: Okanogan and Wenatchee National Forests, Naches Ranger District, 509/653-1400, fax 509/653-2638, www.fs.fed.us.

75 KANER FLAT

Scenic rating: 7

near the Little Naches River in
Wenatchee National Forest

Map grid A2

This campground is set near the Little Naches River, at an elevation of 2,678 feet. It is located at the site of a wagon-train camp on the Old Naches Trail, a route used in the 1800s by wagon trains, Native Americans, and the U.S. Cavalry on their way to westside markets. The narrow-clearance Naches Trail is now used by motorcyclists and four-wheel-drive enthusiasts. Kaner Flat is popular among that crowd, and it is larger and more group-friendly than nearby Crow Creek campground.

RV sites, facilities: There are 41 sites for tents or RVs up to 30 feet long. Picnic tables and fire grills are provided. Restrooms with flush toilets, drinking water, and vault toilets are available. Some facilities are wheelchair accessible. Leashed pets are permitted.

Reservations, fees: Reservations are not accepted. Sites are $12 per night, $5 per night for each additional vehicle. Open mid-May–late November, weather permitting.

Directions: From Yakima, drive northwest on U.S. 12 for 18 miles to Highway 410. Bear northwest on Highway 410 and drive 24.5 miles to Little Naches Road/Forest Road 1900. Turn northeast and drive 2.5 miles to the campground on the right.

Contact: Okanogan and Wenatchee National Forests, Naches Ranger District, 509/653-1400, fax 509/653-2638, www.fs.fed.us.

76 NAPEEQUA CROSSING

Scenic rating: 8

on the White and Napeequa Rivers in
Wenatchee National Forest

Map grid B2

A trail across the road from this camp on the White River heads east for about 3.5 miles to Twin Lakes in the Glacier Peak Wilderness. It's definitely worth the hike, with scenic views and wildlife observation as your reward. But note that Twin Lakes is closed to fishing. Sightings of osprey, bald eagles, and golden eagles can brighten the trip. This is also an excellent spot for fall colors.

RV sites, facilities: There are five sites for tents or RVs up to 30 feet long. Picnic tables and fire grills are provided. Vault toilets are available, but you are advised to bring your own toilet paper. There is no drinking water, and garbage must be packed out. Leashed pets are permitted.

Reservations, fees: Reservations are not accepted. There is no fee for camping. Open year-round, weather and snow level permitting.

Directions: From Leavenworth, drive west on U.S. 2 for 14 miles to Coles Corner and State Route 207. Turn north and drive 10 miles to Forest Road 6400 (White River Road). Turn right and drive 5.9 miles to the campground on the left.

Contact: Okanogan and Wenatchee National Forests, Wenatchee River Ranger District, Lake Wenatchee Ranger Station, 509/763-3103, fax 509/763-3211, www.fs.fed.us.

77 CHIWAWA HORSE CAMP

Scenic rating: 8

in Wenatchee National Forest

Map grid B2

This camp is not designated solely for horse campers, as many horse camps are. Rather, it's for all users, but it features many facilities for horseback riding. It is seldom full but is popular among equestrians. Two short trails specifically designed for physically challenged visitors lead around the campground, covering about a mile. A trailhead at the camp also provides access to a network of backcountry trails. The elevation is 2,500 feet.

RV sites, facilities: There are 21 sites for tents or RVs up to 45 feet long. Some sites are pull-through. Picnic tables and fire grills are provided. Drinking water and vault toilets are available. Garbage must be packed out. Horse facilities include mounting ramps, high lines, water troughs, and a loading ramp. Some facilities are wheelchair accessible. Leashed pets are permitted.

Reservations, fees: Reservations are not accepted. Sites are $8 per vehicle per night. Open May–October, weather permitting.

Directions: From I-5 and Everett, turn east on U.S. 2 and drive 87 miles to State Route 207. Turn right on State Route 207 and drive 4.3 miles to Chiwawa Loop Road. Turn right and drive 1.2 miles to Chiwawa River Road/Forest Road 6200. Turn left and drive 14.8 miles to the campground on the right. Note: The last five miles are gravel.

Contact: Okanogan and Wenatchee National Forests, Wenatchee River Ranger District, Lake Wenatchee Ranger Station, 509/763-3103, fax 509/763-3211, www.fs.fed.us.

78 COTTONWOOD

Scenic rating: 8

on the Entiat River in Wenatchee National Forest
Map grid B2

Cottonwood Camp is set along the Entiat River, adjacent to a major trailhead leading into the Glacier Peak Wilderness. Note that dirt bikes are allowed on four miles of trail, Entiat River Trail to Myrtle Lake, but no motorcycles or mountain bikes are allowed inside the boundary of the Glacier Peak Wilderness; violators will be prosecuted by backcountry rangers. In other words, cool your jets. Let backpackers have some peace and quiet. A bonus near the camp is good berry picking in season. Trout fishing is another alternative. The camp is set at an elevation of 3,100 feet.

RV sites, facilities: There are 25 sites for tents or RVs up to 30 feet long. Picnic tables and fire grills are provided. Drinking water, vault toilets, and garbage bins are available. Some facilities are wheelchair accessible. Leashed pets are permitted.

Reservations, fees: Reservations are not

accepted. Sites are $8 per vehicle per night. Open June–mid-October, weather permitting.

Directions: From I-5 and Everett, turn east on U.S. 2 and drive 120 miles to U.S. 2/U.S. 97. Bear right on U.S. 2/U.S. 97 and drive one mile to Euclid Avenue/U.S. 97. Take that ramp and drive 18 miles on U.S. 97/U.S. 97-A to Entiat River Road. Turn left (northwest) and drive 37 miles to the campground.

Contact: Okanogan and Wenatchee National Forests, Entiat Ranger District, 509/784-1511, fax 509/784-1150, www.fs.fed.us.

79 NORTH FORK

Scenic rating: 8

on the Entiat River in Wenatchee National Forest
Map grid B2

One of eight campgrounds nestled along the Entiat River, North Fork is located near the confluence of the Entiat and the North Fork of the Entiat River. Highlights of this pretty, shaded camp include access to river fishing and Entiat Falls, which are located about 0.5 mile downstream. Note: No fishing is permitted in the vicinity of Entiat Falls to protect the bull trout; check regulations. The elevation is 2,500 feet.

RV sites, facilities: There are eight tent sites, including one site for small RVs up to 20 feet long. Picnic tables and fire grills are provided. Drinking water, pit toilets, and garbage bins are available. Leashed pets are permitted.

Reservations, fees: Reservations are not accepted. Sites are $10 per vehicle per night, $8 per night per additional vehicle. Open June–mid-October, weather permitting.

Directions: From I-5 and Everett, turn east on U.S. 2 and drive 120 miles to U.S. 2/U.S. 97. Bear right on U.S. 2/U.S. 97 and drive one mile to Euclid Avenue/U.S. 97. Take that ramp and drive 18 miles on U.S. 97/U.S. 97-A to Entiat River Road. Turn left (northwest) and drive 32 miles to the campground on the left.

Contact: Okanogan and Wenatchee National Forests, Entiat Ranger District, 509/784-1511, fax 509/784-1150, www.fs.fed.us.

80 SILVER FALLS

Scenic rating: 10

on the Entiat River in Wenatchee National Forest
Map grid B2

This campground is set in an enchanted spot at the confluence of Silver Creek and the Entiat River. A trail from camp leads 0.5 mile to the base of beautiful Silver Falls. This trail continues in a loop for another mile past the falls, parallel to the river. Fishing is available above Entiat Falls, located two to three miles upriver from Silver Falls. The elevation at the camp is 2,400 feet.

RV sites, facilities: There are 30 sites for tents or RVs up to 32 feet long, plus one group site for up to 40 people. Picnic tables and fire grills are provided. Drinking water, vault toilets, and garbage bins are available. A camp host is available in summer. Some facilities are wheelchair accessible. Leashed pets are permitted.

Reservations, fees: Reservations are not accepted for family sites but are required for the group site at 877/444-6777 or www.recreation. gov ($10 reservation fee). Sites are $12 per night, $10 per night per additional vehicle; the group site is $60 a night. Open mid-May–mid-October, weather permitting.

Directions: From I-5 and Everett, turn east on U.S. 2 and drive 120 miles to U.S. 2/U.S. 97. Bear right on U.S. 2/U.S. 97 and drive one mile to Euclid Avenue/U.S. 97. Take that ramp and drive 18 miles on U.S. 97/U.S. 97-A to Entiat River Road. Turn left (northwest) and drive 29 miles to the campground on the left.

Contact: Okanogan and Wenatchee National Forests, Entiat Ranger District, 509/784-1511, fax 509/784-1150, www.fs.fed.us.

81 SNOWBERRY BOWL

Scenic rating: 7

near Lake Chelan in Wenatchee National Forest
Map grid B2

Snowberry Bowl is set less than four miles from Twenty-Five Mile Creek State Park and Lake Chelan. Sites are nestled amid a forest of Douglas fir and ponderosa pine, which provide privacy screening. The elevation is 2,000 feet.

RV sites, facilities: There are seven sites for tents or RVs up to 40 feet long and two double sites for up to 15 people each. Picnic tables, fire rings, and tent pads on sand are provided. Drinking water, vault toilets, and garbage bins are available. Some facilities are wheelchair accessible. Leashed pets are permitted.

Reservations, fees: Reservations are not accepted. Sites are $10 per night, $20 per night for double sites, $8 per night per additional vehicle. Open year-round, with limited winter facilities.

Directions: From Chelan, drive south on U.S. 97-A for three miles to South Lakeshore Road. Turn right and drive 13.5 miles (passing the state park) to Shady Pass Road. Turn left and drive 2.5 miles to a Y intersection with Slide Ridge Road. Bear left and drive 0.5 mile to the campground on the right.

Contact: Okanogan and Wenatchee National Forests, Chelan Ranger District, 509/682-2576, fax 509/682-9004, www.fs.fed.us.

82 TWENTY-FIVE MILE CREEK STATE PARK

Scenic rating: 8

near Lake Chelan
Map grid B2

This campground is located on Twenty-Five Mile Creek near where it empties into Lake Chelan. A 235-acre marine camping park, it sits on the forested south shore of Lake Chelan between the mountains and the lake, surrounded by spectacular scenery, featuring a rocky terrain with forested areas. Known for its boat access, this park can serve as your launching point for exploring the up-lake wilderness portions of Lake Chelan. Fishing access for trout and salmon is close by, and fishing supplies, a dock, a modern marina, and boat moorage are available. There is also a small wading area for kids. Forest Road 5900, which heads west from the park, accesses several trailheads leading into the U.S. Forest Service lands of the Chelan Mountains.

RV sites, facilities: There are 46 sites for tents, 21 sites with full or partial hookups (30 amps) for RVs up to 30 feet long, and a group site for 20–50 people. Picnic tables and fire grills are provided. Restrooms with flush toilets, coin showers, and drinking water are available. A dump station, firewood, a boat dock, fishing pier, marina, boat ramp, boat moorage, a picnic area, gasoline, and a seasonal camp store are available at the park. Some facilities are wheelchair accessible. Leashed pets are permitted.

Reservations, fees: Reservations are accepted at 888/CAMP-OUT (888/226-7688) or www.parks.wa.gov/reservations ($6.50–8.50 reservation fee). Sites are $21–28 per night, and $10 per night per extra vehicle. The group site is $2.25 per person per night. Some credit cards are accepted. Open late March–October, weather permitting.

Directions: From Chelan, drive south on U.S. 97-A for three miles to South Lakeshore Road. Turn right and drive 15 miles to the park on the right.

Contact: Twenty-Five Mile Creek State Park, 509/687-3610; state park information, 360/902-8844, www.parks.wa.gov; Lake Chelan Boat Company, 509/682-4584, www.ladyofthelake.com.

83 KAMEI RESORT

Scenic rating: 6

on Lake Wapato

Map grid B2

This resort is on Lake Wapato, about two miles from Lake Chelan. Note that this is a seasonal lake that closes in early September. No open fires are allowed. If you have an extra day, take the ferry ride on Lake Chelan.

RV sites, facilities: There are 50 sites with partial hookups (30 amp) for tents or RVs of any length. A rental trailer is also available. Picnic tables are provided. Restrooms with flush toilets

and showers, drinking water, and ice are available. Boat docks, launching facilities, and rentals are nearby. Leashed pets are permitted.

Reservations, fees: Reservations are accepted beginning in January each year. Sites are $21–22 per night. Open late April–early September.

Directions: From Chelan, drive west on Highway 150 for seven miles to Wapato Lake Road. Turn right (north) on Wapato Lake Road and drive four miles to the resort on the right.

Contact: Kamei Resort, 509/687-3690.

84 LAKE CREEK/ LAKE WENATCHEE

Scenic rating: 6

on the Little Wenatchee River in Wenatchee National Forest

Map grid B2

Fishing for rainbow trout sometimes can be good, though difficult at this camp, which is set in a remote and primitive spot along the Little Wenatchee River. Berry picking is a bonus in late summer. The elevation is 2,300 feet. Note that there is another Lake Creek Camp in the Entiat Ranger District.

RV sites, facilities: There are eight sites for tents or RVs of any length. Picnic tables and fire grills are provided, but there is no drinking water. Vault toilets are available, but you are advised to bring your own toilet paper. Garbage must be packed out. Leashed pets are permitted.

Reservations, fees: Reservations are not accepted. There is no fee for camping. Open May–late October, weather permitting.

Directions: From I-5 and Everett, turn east on U.S. 2 and drive 87 miles to State Route 207. Turn left (north) on State Route 207 and drive 11 miles to Forest Road 6500. Turn left (west) on Forest Road 6500 and drive 9.5 miles to the campground on the left.

Contact: Okanogan and Wenatchee National Forests, Wenatchee River Ranger District, Lake Wenatchee Ranger Station, 509/763-3103, fax 509/763-3211, www.fs.fed.us.

85 LAKE WENATCHEE STATE PARK

Scenic rating: 8

on Lake Wenatchee

Map grid B2

Lake Wenatchee is the centerpiece for a 489-acre park with two miles of waterfront. Glaciers and the Wenatchee River feed Lake Wenatchee, and the river, which bisects the park, helps make it a natural wildlife area. Thanks to a nice location and pull-through sites that are spaced just right, you can expect plenty of company at this campground. The secluded campsites are set at the southeast end of Lake Wenatchee, which offers plenty of recreation opportunities, with a boat ramp nearby. A swimming beach is available at the north shore. There are eight miles of hiking trails, seven miles of bike trails, five miles of horse trails in and around the park, and a 1.1-mile interpretive snowshoe trail in winter. Note that no horse facilities are available right in the park, but horse rentals are nearby. In winter, there are 11 miles of multi-use trails and 23 miles of groomed cross-country skiing trails. Note: Bears are active in the park, so all food must be stored in bear-proof facilities.

RV sites, facilities: In the South Camp there are 100 sites for tents or RVs up to 25 feet (no hookups) and one group tent site for 20–50 people. In the North Camp there are 55 sites for tents or RVs of any length (no hookups), 42 sites with partial hookups (30 and 50 amps) for RVs of any length, and one group site for up to 30 people. Picnic tables and fire grills are provided. Restrooms with flush toilets and showers, drinking water, a dump station, a store, ice, firewood, two picnic shelters, amphitheater, volleyball, a restaurant, a playground, and guided horseback rides are available. Boat docks, launching facilities, rentals, and golf are nearby. Some facilities are wheelchair accessible. Leashed pets are permitted.

Reservations, fees: Reservations are accepted and required for the group camp at 888/CAMP-OUT (888/226-7688) or www.parks.wa.gov/reservations ($6.50–8.50 reservation fee). Sites are $21–27 per night, $10 per extra vehicle per night. The group site is $2.25 per person per night with a minimum of 20 people. Open year-round, with limited winter facilities.

Directions: From Leavenworth, drive west on U.S. 2 for 15 miles to State Route 207 at Coles Corner. Turn right (north) and drive 3.5 miles to Cedar Brae Road. Turn left on Cedar Brae Road and drive 2.5 miles to the south park entrance. For the north park entrance, continue past Cedar Brae Road for one mile.

Contact: Lake Wenatchee State Park, 509/763-3101; state park information, 360/902-8844, www.parks.wa.gov.

86 MIDWAY VILLAGE AND GROCERY

Scenic rating: 5

near Wenatchee River

Map grid B2

This private campground is located about 0.25 mile from the Wenatchee River, and one mile from Lake Wenatchee State Park and Fish Lake, which is noted for good fishing year-round. There is good hiking and mountain biking out of the camp. Nearby recreation options include boating, fishing, waterskiing, swimming, windsurfing, hiking, and bike riding. The average annual snowfall is 12 feet. There is a snowmobile trail across the road from Midway Village. Snowmobile races are held in winter months within 0.25 mile of the campground. Winter options include cross-country skiing, dogsledding (25 miles east of Stevens Pass Ski Area), snowshoeing, and ice fishing.

RV sites, facilities: There are 18 sites with full hookups (30 amp) for RVs up to 40 feet long. Restrooms with flush toilets and showers, a convenience store, gasoline, firewood, an espresso shop, coin laundry, ice, propane gas, picnic area, playground, horseshoe pits, and volleyball are available. Boat docks, launching facilities, and rentals are nearby. Leashed pets are permitted with certain restrictions.

Reservations, fees: Reservations are accepted.

Sites are $25 per night. Some credit cards are accepted. Open year-round.

Directions: From I-5 and Everett, turn east on U.S. 2 and drive 88 miles over Stevens Pass to Coles Corner at State Route 207. Turn left (north) on State Route 207 and drive four miles, crossing the bridge over the Wenatchee River to a Y intersection. Turn right at the Y and drive 0.25 mile to the campground on the right.

Contact: Midway Village and Grocery, 509/763-3344, fax 509/763-3519.

87 NASON CREEK

Scenic rating: 7

near Lake Wenatchee in Wenatchee National Forest
Map grid B2

This campground is located on Nason Creek near Lake Wenatchee, bordering Lake Wenatchee State Park. Recreation activities include swimming and waterskiing. Boat rentals, horseback riding, and golfing are available nearby.

RV sites, facilities: There are 73 sites for tents or RVs of any length. Some sites are pull-through. Picnic tables and fire grills are provided. Drinking water, restrooms with flush toilets and showers, and garbage bins are available. Boat-launching facilities are nearby. Some facilities are wheelchair accessible.

Reservations, fees: Reservations are not accepted. Sites are $16 per night, $11 per night per extra vehicle. Open mid-May–mid-October, weather permitting.

Directions: From I-5 and Everett, turn east on U.S. 2 and drive 87 miles to State Route 207, one mile west of Winton. Turn right on State Route 207 and drive 3.5 miles to Cedar Brae Road. Turn left (west) and drive 100 yards to the campground.

Contact: Okanogan and Wenatchee National Forests, Wenatchee River Ranger District, Lake Wenatchee Ranger Station, 509/763-3103, fax 509/763-3211, www.fs.fed.us.

88 GOOSE CREEK

Scenic rating: 7

on Goose Creek in Wenatchee National Forest
Map grid B2

With trails for dirt bikes available directly from the camp, Goose Creek is used primarily by motorcycle riders. A main trail links to the Entiat off-road vehicle trail system, so this camp gets high use during the summer. The camp is set near a small creek.

RV sites, facilities: There are 29 sites for tents or RVs of any length. Picnic tables and fire rings are provided. Drinking water, vault toilets, and garbage bins are available. Some facilities are wheelchair accessible. Leashed pets are permitted.

Reservations, fees: Reservations are not accepted. Sites are $8 per vehicle per night. Open mid-May–late October, weather permitting.

Directions: From I-5 and Everett, turn east on U.S. 2 and drive 87 miles to State Route 207, one mile west of Winton. Turn north on State Route 207 and drive 4.3 miles to Chiwawa Loop Road. Turn right and drive 1.5 miles to Chiwawa River Road/Forest Road 6200. Turn left and drive three miles to Forest Road 6100. Turn right and drive 0.6 mile to the camp on the right.

Contact: Okanogan and Wenatchee National Forests, Wenatchee River Ranger District, Lake Wenatchee Ranger Station, 509/763-3103, fax 509/763-3211, www.fs.fed.us.

89 LAKE CHELAN STATE PARK

Scenic rating: 10

on Lake Chelan
Map grid B2

This park is the recreation headquarters for Lake Chelan. It provides boat docks and concession stands on the shore of the 55-mile lake. The park covers 127 acres, featuring 6,000 feet of shoreline on the forested south shore. Water sports include fishing, swimming, scuba diving, and waterskiing. Summers tend to be hot and dry, but expansive lawns looking out on the lake provide a fresh feel, especially in the early evenings. A daily ferry service provides access to the roadless community at the head of the lake. The word "chelan" is a Chelan Indian word and translates to both "lake" and "blue water." Nearby attractions include the Holden Mine site and Holden Village and hiking in Glacier Peak Wilderness.

RV sites, facilities: There are 109 tent sites, 35 sites with full or partial hookups (30 and 50 amps) for RVs up to 30 feet long, and five hike-in/bike-in tent sites. Picnic tables and fire grills are provided. Restrooms with flush toilets and coin showers, drinking water, firewood, a picnic area with a kitchen shelter, a dump station, store, restaurant, ice, playground, horseshoe pits, ball field, beach area, boat dock, and launching facilities and moorage are available. Some facilities are wheelchair accessible. Leashed pets are permitted.

Reservations, fees: Reservations are accepted at 888/CAMP-OUT (888/226-7688) or www.parks.wa.gov/reservations ($6.50–8.50 reservation fee). Sites are $14 per night for primitive sites, tent sites are $21 per night, RV sites with hookups are $27–28 per night, $10 per extra vehicle per night. Some credit cards are accepted. Open year-round, weather permitting.

Directions: From Wenatchee, drive north on U.S. 97-A for nine miles to State Route 971 (Navarre Coulee Road). Turn left (north) and drive seven miles to the end of the highway at South Lakeshore Road. Turn right, then immediately look for the park entrance to the left.

Contact: Lake Chelan State Park, 509/687-3710; state park information, 360/902-8844, www.parks.wa.gov.

90 DAROGA STATE PARK

Scenic rating: 5

on the Columbia River

Map grid B2

This 90-acre state park is set along 1.5 miles of shoreline on the Columbia River. It sits on the elevated edge of the desert scablands. This camp fills up quickly on summer weekends. Desert Canyon Golf Course is two miles away. Fishing, along with walking and biking trails, are available out of the camp.

RV sites, facilities: There are 28 sites with partial hookups (30 amps) for tents or RVs up to 32 feet long, 17 walk-in or boat-in sites (requiring a 0.25-mile trip), and two group sites for up to 100 people each. Some sites are pull-through. Picnic tables and fire pits are provided. Restrooms with flush (near RV sites) and vault (near walk-in sites) toilets and coin showers, drinking water, a dump station, firewood, a swimming beach, boat-launching facilities and docks, a playground, baseball field, basketball courts, softball and soccer fields, and a picnic area with a kitchen shelter are available. Some facilities are wheelchair accessible. Leashed pets are permitted.

Reservations, fees: Reservations are not accepted for individual sites but are required for group sites at 888/CAMP-OUT (888/226-7688) or www.parks.wa.gov/reservations ($6.50–8.50 reservation fee). Sites are $14–27, $10 per extra vehicle per night; group sites are $2.25 per person per night for 20–100 people. Open mid-March–mid-October, weather permitting.

Directions: From East Wenatchee, drive north on U.S. 97 (east side of the Columbia River) for 18 miles to the camp. For boat-in camps, launch boats from the ramp at the park and drive 0.25 mile.

Contact: Daroga State Park, 509/664-6380; state park information, 360/902-8844, www.parks.wa.gov.

91 BLACKPINE CREEK HORSE CAMP

Scenic rating: 8

near the Alpine Lakes Wilderness in Wenatchee National Forest

Map grid B2

Note: This camp was closed because of a washout on the upper end of Icicle Road/7600 (closed just beyond the Ida Creek Campground); the camp is scheduled to reopen in fall 2010. Black-pine Creek Horse Camp is used primarily by horse campers for horse pack trips. It is set on Black Pine Creek near Icicle Creek at a major trailhead leading into the Alpine Lakes Wilderness. It's one of seven rustic camps on the creek, with the distinction of being the only one with facilities for horses. The elevation is 3,000 feet.

RV sites, facilities: There are eight sites for tents or RVs up to 60 feet long. Picnic tables and fire grills are provided. Drinking water, vault toilets, and garbage bins are available. Horse facilities, including a hitching rail and loading ramp, are also available. Leashed pets are permitted.

Reservations, fees: Reservations are not accepted. Sites are $12 per night, $8 per night per extra vehicle. Open mid-May–late October, weather permitting.

Directions: From I-5 and Everett, turn east on U.S. 2 and drive 103 miles to Leavenworth and County Road 76 (Icicle River Road). Turn south and drive 19.2 miles to the campground on the left. Note: Because of road washout, access may change in future.

Contact: Okanogan and Wenatchee National Forests, Wenatchee River Ranger District, Leavenworth Ranger Station, 509/548-6977, fax 509/548-5817, www.fs.fed.us.

92 ROCK ISLAND

Scenic rating: 8

near the Alpine Lakes Wilderness in Wenatchee National Forest

Map grid B2

The camp was closed because of a washout on the upper end of Icicle Road/7600 (closed just beyond the Ida Creek Campground); the camp is scheduled to reopen in fall 2010. Rock Island is one of several campgrounds in the immediate area along Icicle Creek and is located about one mile from the trailhead that takes hikers into the Alpine Lakes Wilderness. This is a pretty spot with good fishing access. The elevation is 2,900 feet.

RV sites, facilities: There are 22 sites for tents or RVs up to 22 feet long. Picnic tables and fire grills are provided. Drinking water, vault toilets, and garbage bins are available. Some facilities are wheelchair accessible. Leashed pets are permitted.

Reservations, fees: Reservations are not accepted. Sites are $13 per vehicle per night, $9 per night per extra vehicle. Open May–late October, weather permitting.

Directions: From I-5 and Everett, turn east on U.S. 2 and drive 103 miles to Leavenworth and County Road 7600/Icicle River Road. Turn right (south) and drive 17.7 miles to the campground. Note: Because of road washout, access may change in future.

Contact: Okanogan and Wenatchee National Forests, Wenatchee River Ranger District, Leavenworth Ranger Station, 509/548-6977, fax 509/548-5817, www.fs.fed.us.

93 CHATTER CREEK

Scenic rating: 8

near the Alpine Lakes Wilderness in Wenatchee National Forest

Map grid B2

Note: The camp was closed because of a wash-out on the upper end of Icicle Road/7600 (closed just beyond the Ida Creek Campground); the camp is scheduled to reopen in fall 2010. Icicle and Chatter Creeks are the backdrop for this creekside campground. The elevation is 2,800 feet. Trails lead out in several directions from the camp into the Alpine Lakes Wilderness.

RV sites, facilities: There are 12 sites for tents or RVs up to 22 feet long and one group site for up to 45 people. Picnic tables and fire grills are provided. Drinking water, vault toilets, garbage bins, firewood, and picnic shelter with fireplace are available. Some facilities are wheelchair accessible. Leashed pets are permitted.

Reservations, fees: Reservations are required for the group site at 877/444-6777 or www.

recreation.gov ($10 reservation fee). Sites are $13 per night, $9 per night per extra vehicle; the group site is $75 per night. Some credit cards are accepted. Open April–late October, weather permitting.

Directions: From I-5 and Everett, turn east on U.S. 2 and drive 103 miles to Leavenworth and County Road 7600/Icicle River Road. Turn right (south) and drive 16.1 miles to the campground on the right. Note: Because of road washout, access may change in future.

Contact: Okanogan and Wenatchee National Forests, Wenatchee River Ranger District, Leavenworth Ranger Station, 509/548-6977, fax 509/548-5817, www.fs.fed.us.

94 IDA CREEK

Scenic rating: 8

on Icicle Creek in Wenatchee National Forest

Map grid B2

This campground is one of several small, quiet camps along Icicle and Ida Creeks. Recreation options are similar to Chatter Creek and Rock Island campgrounds, hiking and fishing among them.

RV sites, facilities: There are 10 sites for tents or RVs up to 30 feet long. Picnic tables and fire grills are provided. Drinking water, vault toilets, and garbage bins are available. Some facilities are wheelchair accessible. Leashed pets are permitted.

Reservations, fees: Reservations are not accepted. Sites are $13 per night, $9 per night per extra vehicle. Open May–late October, weather permitting.

Directions: From I-5 and Everett, turn east on U.S. 2 and drive 103 miles to Leavenworth and County Road 7600/Icicle River Road. Turn right (south) and drive 14.2 miles to the campground on the left.

Contact: Okanogan and Wenatchee National Forests, Wenatchee River Ranger District, Leavenworth Ranger Station, 509/548-6977, fax 509/548-5817, www.fs.fed.us.

95 JOHNNY CREEK

Scenic rating: 8

on Icicle Creek in Wenatchee National Forest

Map grid B2

Johnny Creek campground is split into two parts, which sit on both sides of the road along Icicle and Johnny Creeks. It is fairly popular. Upper Johnny has a forest setting, whereas Lower Johnny is set alongside the creek, with adjacent forest. Nearby recreation opportunities include trail access into the Alpine Lakes Wilderness, horseback riding, and a golf course. The elevation is 2,300 feet.

RV sites, facilities: There are 65 sites for tents or RVs up to 50 feet long. Picnic tables and fire grills are provided. Drinking water, vault toilets, and garbage bins are available. Some facilities are wheelchair accessible. Leashed pets are permitted.

Reservations, fees: Reservations are not accepted. Sites are $13–15 per night, $9–10 per night per extra vehicle. Open May–late October, weather permitting.

Directions: From I-5 and Everett, turn east on U.S. 2 and drive 103 miles to Leavenworth and County Road 7600/Icicle River Road. Turn right (south) and drive 12.4 miles to the campground (with camps on each side of the road).

Contact: Okanogan and Wenatchee National Forests, Wenatchee River Ranger District, Leavenworth Ranger Station, 509/548-6977, fax 509/548-5817, www.fs.fed.us.

96 BRIDGE CREEK

Scenic rating: 8

on Icicle Creek in Wenatchee National Forest

Map grid B2

This camp is a small, quiet spot along Icicle and Bridge Creeks. The elevation is 1,800 feet. About two miles south of the camp at Eightmile Creek, a trail accesses the Alpine Lakes Wilderness. Horseback-riding opportunities are within four miles, and golf is within five miles.

RV sites, facilities: There are six sites for tents

or small RVs up to 19 feet long and one group site for up to 100 people. Picnic tables and fire grills are provided. Drinking water, vault toilets, garbage bins, and firewood are available. The group site does not have drinking water. Leashed pets are permitted.

Reservations, fees: Reservations are required for the group site at 877/444-6777 or www. recreation.gov ($10 reservation fee). Sites are $13 per night, $9 per night per extra vehicle. The group site is $80 per night. Open mid-April–late October, weather permitting.

Directions: From I-5 and Everett, turn east on U.S. 2 and drive 103 miles to Leavenworth and County Road 7600/Icicle River Road. Turn right (south) and drive 9.4 miles to the campground on the left.

Contact: Okanogan and Wenatchee National Forests, Wenatchee River Ranger District, Leavenworth Ranger Station, 509/548-6977, fax 509/548-5817, www.fs.fed.us.

97 EIGHTMILE

Scenic rating: 8

near the Alpine Lakes Wilderness in Wenatchee National Forest

Map grid B2

Trailheads are located within two miles of this campground along Icicle and Eightmile Creeks, providing access to fishing, as well as a backpacking route into the Alpine Lakes Wilderness. Horseback-riding opportunities are within four miles, and golf is within five miles. The elevation is 1,800 feet.

RV sites, facilities: There are 45 sites for tents or RVs up to 45 feet long and one group site for up to 70 people. Picnic tables and fire grills are provided. Drinking water, vault toilets, and garbage bins are available. Some facilities are wheelchair accessible. Leashed pets are permitted.

Reservations, fees: Reservations are required for the group site at 877/444-6777 or www. recreation.gov ($10 reservation fee). Sites are

$15 per night, $10 per night per extra vehicle, and $80 per night for the group site. Open mid-April–late October.

Directions: From I-5 and Everett, turn east on U.S. 2 and drive 103 miles to Leavenworth and County Road 7600/Icicle River Road. Turn right (south) and drive eight miles to the campground on the left.

Contact: Okanogan and Wenatchee National Forests, Wenatchee River Ranger District, Leavenworth Ranger Station, 509/548-6977, fax 509/548-5817, www.fs.fed.us.

98 TUMWATER

Scenic rating: 7

near the Alpine Lakes Wilderness in Wenatchee National Forest

Map grid B2

This large, popular camp provides a little bit of both worlds. It provides a good layover spot for campers cruising U.S. 2, but it also features two nearby forest roads, each less than a mile long, which end at trailheads that provide access to the Alpine Lakes Wilderness. The camp is on the Wenatchee River in Tumwater Canyon. This section of river is closed to fishing. The elevation is 2,050 feet.

RV sites, facilities: There are 84 sites for tents or RVs up to 50 feet long and one group site for up to 75 people. Picnic tables and fire grills are provided. Drinking water, restrooms with flush toilets, firewood, picnic shelter with fireplace, playground, horseshoes, and basketball court are available. Some facilities are wheelchair accessible. Leashed pets are permitted.

Reservations, fees: Reservations are required for the group site at 877/444-6777 or www. recreation.gov ($10 reservation fee). Sites are $16 per night, $11 per night per extra vehicle; the group site is $90 per night. Open May–mid-October, weather permitting.

Directions: From I-5 and Everett, turn east on U.S. 2 and drive 99 miles to the campground (10 miles west of Leavenworth).

Contact: Okanogan and Wenatchee National Forests, Wenatchee River Ranger District, Leavenworth Ranger Station, 509/548-6977, fax 509/548-5817, www.fs.fed.us.

99 LEAVENWORTH KOA

Scenic rating: 8

near the Wenatchee River

Map grid B2   **BEST**

This lovely resort on 30 acres is near the Bavarian-themed village of Leavenworth, to which the park provides a free shuttle in the summer. The spectacularly scenic area is surrounded by the Cascade Mountains and set among ponderosa pines. The camp has access to the Wenatchee River, not to mention many luxurious extras, including a spa and a heated pool. The park allows campfires and has firewood available. Nearby recreation options include an 18-hole golf course, horseback riding, white-water rafting, and hiking trails. Make a point to spend a day in Leavenworth if possible; it offers authentic German food and architecture, along with music and art shows in the summer.

RV sites, facilities: There are 60 sites with full hookups and 60 sites with partial hookups (30 and 50 amps) for RVs up to 65 feet long, 40 tent sites, 20 cabins, two cottages, and nine lodges. Some sites are pull-through. Picnic tables are provided, and fire grills are available at some sites. Restrooms with flush toilets and showers, drinking water, dump stations, modem and Wi-Fi access, bicycle rentals, firewood, a recreation hall, cable TV, a convenience store, coin laundry, ice, a playground, horseshoe pits, volleyball, a spa and sauna, a seasonal heated swimming pool, snack bar, and a beach area are available. Propane gas and a café are located within one mile. Some facilities are wheelchair accessible. Leashed pets are permitted.

Reservations, fees: Reservations are accepted at 800/562-5709. RV sites are $26–41 per night, tent sites are $21–34 per night, $5 per extra vehicle per night, and $4–5 per person per night

for more than two people. Some credit cards are accepted. Open April–November.

Directions: From I-5 and Everett, turn east on U.S. 2 and drive 103 miles to Leavenworth. Continue east on U.S. 2 for 0.25 mile to River Bend Drive. Turn left (north) and drive 0.5 mile to the campground on the right.

Contact: Leavenworth KOA/Leavenworth, tel./fax 509/548-7709, www.koa.com.

100 ICICLE RIVER RV RESORT

Scenic rating: 9

on Icicle River

Map grid B2

This pretty, wooded spot is set along the Icicle River, where fishing and swimming are available. The 50-acre resort is clean and scenic and even has its own putting green. An 18-hole golf course and hiking trails are nearby. Note that no tent camping is permitted here, but six cabins are available for rent.

RV sites, facilities: There are 108 sites with full or partial hookups for RVs of any length, six rustic cabins, and two full-service cabins. Picnic tables and fire pits (at some sites) are provided. Restrooms with flush toilets and coin showers, drinking water, cable TV, modem and Wi-Fi access, a spa, firewood, and propane gas are available. A putting green, horseshoe pits, and two pavilions are available nearby. Leashed pets are permitted in the campground.

Reservations, fees: Reservations are accepted. Sites are $30–42 per night, $5 per extra vehicle per night, $5 per person per night for more than two adults, $3 for each child. Some credit cards are accepted. Open April–mid-October, weather permitting.

Directions: From I-5 and Everett, turn east on U.S. 2 and drive 103 miles to Leavenworth and County Road 7600/Icicle Road. Turn right (south) and drive three miles to the resort on the left.

Contact: Icicle River RV Resort, 509/548-5420, fax 509/548-6207, www.icicleriverrv.com.

101 ENTIAT CITY PARK

Scenic rating: 8

on the Columbia River

Map grid B2

If you're hurting for a spot for the night, you can usually find a campsite here. The campground is on Lake Entiat, which is a dammed portion of the Columbia River. Access to nearby launching facilities makes this a good camping spot for boaters. Waterskiing and personal watercraft are allowed. A dirt trail leads from the lake to the town of Entiat.

RV sites, facilities: There are 25 tent sites and 31 sites with partial hookups for RVs of any length. Picnic tables and barbecue stands are provided. Restrooms with flush toilets and coin showers, drinking water, a dump station, and a playground are available. Boat docks and launching facilities are nearby. A store, café, propane gas, and coin laundry are available within 1.5 miles. Some facilities are wheelchair accessible. No open fires, dogs, or alcohol are permitted.

Reservations, fees: Reservations are available at 800/736-8428 ($5 reservation fee). Sites are $22–27.50 per night, $2 per extra vehicle per night. Open May–September.

Directions: From Wenatchee, drive north on U.S. 97-A for 16 miles to Entiat; the park entrance is on the right (Shearson Street is adjacent on the left). Turn right and drive a short distance to the park along the shore of Lake Entiat.

Contact: Entiat City Park, 800/736-8428, City Hall, 509/784-1500.

102 LINCOLN ROCK STATE PARK

Scenic rating: 5

on Lake Entiat

Map grid B2

Lincoln Rock State Park is an 80-acre park set along the shore of Lake Entiat, created by the Rocky Reach Dam on the Columbia River. The park features lawns and shade trees amid an arid landscape. There are two miles of paved, flat trails suitable for both hiking and biking. Water sports include swimming, boating, and waterskiing. Beavers are occasionally visible in the Columbia River. Oh, yeah, and the name? Look for a basalt outcropping in the shape of the former president's famous profile and you'll see why.

RV sites, facilities: There are 67 sites with partial or full hookups (30 amps) for RVs up to 65 feet long and 27 sites for tents or self-contained RVs up to 60 feet long. Picnic tables and fire grills are provided. Restrooms with flush toilets and coin showers, drinking water, dump station, playground, athletic fields, horseshoe pits, swimming beach, amphitheater, interpretive center, three picnic shelters, and firewood are available. Boat docks, moorage, and launching facilities are located on Lake Entiat. Some facilities are wheelchair accessible. Leashed pets are permitted.

Reservations, fees: Reservations are accepted at 888/CAMP-OUT (888/226-7688) or www.parks.wa.gov/reservations ($6.50–8.50 reservation fee). Sites are $21–28 per night, $10 per extra vehicle per night. Some credit cards are accepted. Open March–mid-October, weather permitting.

Directions: From East Wenatchee, drive northeast on U.S. 2 for seven miles to the park on the left.

Contact: Lincoln Rock State Park, 509/884-8702; state park information, 360/902-8844, www.parks.wa.gov.

103 BLU-SHASTIN RV RESORT

Scenic rating: 6

near Peshastin Creek

Map grid B2

This 13-acre park is set in a mountainous area near Peshastin Creek. Gold panning in the river is a popular activity here; during the gold rush, the Peshastin was the best-producing river in the state—and it still is. The camp has sites on the riverbank and plenty of shade trees. A heated pool, recreation field, and horseshoe pits provide possible activities in the park. Hiking trails and marked bike trails are nearby. Rafting and tubing nearby are popular in the summer. Snowmobiling is an option during the winter.

RV sites, facilities: There are 86 sites for tents or RVs of any length (20 and 30 amp full hookups); four sites are pull-through. Picnic tables and fire rings are provided. Restrooms with flush toilets and showers, drinking water, modem access, a recreation hall, firewood, coin laundry, ice, a playground, horseshoes, badminton, volleyball, and a seasonal heated swimming pool are available. Propane gas, a store, and a café are located within seven miles. Leashed pets are permitted.

Reservations, fees: Reservations are recommended at 888/548-4184. Sites are $23.64–28.18 per night. Some credit cards are accepted. Open year-round, weather permitting.

Directions: From Leavenworth, drive east on U.S. 2 for five miles to U.S. 97. Turn right (south) on U.S. 97 and drive seven miles to the park on the right.

Contact: Blu-Shastin RV Park, 509/548-4184 or 888/548-4184, www.blushastin.com.

104 WENATCHEE RIVER COUNTY PARK

Scenic rating: 5

on the Wenatchee River

Map grid B2

This camp is set along the Wenatchee River, situated between the highway and the river. Though not the greatest setting, with some highway noise, it is convenient for RV campers. You can usually get a tree-covered site in the campground, despite it being a small park. The adjacent river is fast moving and provides white-water rafting in season, with a put-in spot at the park.

RV sites, facilities: There are 43 sites with full hookups and three sites with partial hookups for RVs of any length. Several sites are pull-through. A cabin is also available. Picnic tables

and fire pits are provided. Drinking water, restrooms with flush toilets and coin showers, a recreation room, propane, coin laundry, dump station, sand volleyball court, and Wi-Fi are available. A convenience store and a restaurant are within 0.5 mile. Leashed pets are permitted.

Reservations, fees: Reservations are available at 509/667-7503. Sites are $19–29 per night, $5 per night per person for more than four people, and $5 per extra vehicle per night. The cabin is $200 per weekend. Some credit cards are accepted. Open April–September.

Directions: From Wenatchee and U.S. 2, take the State Route 285/N. Wenatchee exit, keeping left to merge onto State Route 285/N. Wenatchee Avenue. Drive 2.5 miles to N. Miller. Turn south and drive a short distance to Washington Street. Turn left and drive 0.5 mile to Orondo Avenue. Turn left and drive a short distance to the park entrance on the left.

Contact: Chelan County Commissioner, 509/667-6215, fax 509/667-6599; Wenatchee River County Park, 509/667-7503, www.co.chelan.wa.us/.

105 WENATCHEE CONFLUENCE STATE PARK

Scenic rating: 10

on the Columbia River

Map grid B2

This 197-acre state park is set at the confluence of the Wenatchee and Columbia Rivers. The park features expansive lawns shaded by deciduous trees and fronted by the two rivers. Wenatchee Confluence has something of a dual personality: The north portion of the park is urban and recreational, while the southern section is a designated natural wetland area. There are 10.5 miles of paved trail for hiking, biking, and in-line skating. A pedestrian bridge crosses the Wenatchee River. An interpretive hiking trail is available in the Horan Natural Area. Other recreation possibilities include fishing, swimming, boating, and waterskiing.

Sports enthusiasts will find playing fields as well as tennis and basketball courts. Daroga State Park and Lake Chelan to the north offer side-trip possibilities.

RV sites, facilities: There are 51 sites with full hookups (30 amps) for RVs up to 65 feet long, eight tent sites, and a group tent site for up to 300 people. Picnic tables and fire grills are provided. Restrooms with flush toilets and coin showers, drinking water, a boat launch, dump station, swimming beach, playground, horseshoe pits, a picnic shelter that can be reserved, and athletic fields are available. Some facilities are wheelchair accessible. Leashed pets are permitted.

Reservations, fees: Reservations are accepted at 888/CAMP-OUT (888/226-7688) or www.parks.wa.gov/reservations ($6.50–8.50 reservation fee). Tent sites are $21 per night, RV sites are $28 per night, $10 per extra vehicle per night. The group site is $2.25 per person per night. Some credit cards are accepted. Open year-round.

Directions: From Wenatchee and U.S. 2, take the Easy Street exit and drive south to Penny Road. Turn left and drive a short distance to Chester Kimm Street. Turn right and drive to a T intersection and Old Station Road. Turn left on Old Station Road and drive past the railroad tracks to the park on the right. The park is 1.3 miles from U.S. 2.

Contact: Wenatchee Confluence State Park, 509/664-6373, fax 509/662-0459; state park information, 360/902-8844, www.parks.wa.gov.

106 BEVERLY

Scenic rating: 8

on the North Fork of the Teanaway River in Wenatchee National Forest

Map grid B2

This primitive campground is set on the North Fork of the Teanaway River, a scenic area of the river. It is primarily a hiker's camp, with several trails leading up nearby creeks and into the Alpine Lakes Wilderness. Self-issued permits

(available at the trailhead) are required for wilderness hiking. The elevation is 3,100 feet.

RV sites, facilities: There are 13 sites for tents or RVs up to 21 feet long. Picnic tables and fire grills are provided. Vault toilets are available, but there is no drinking water. Garbage must be packed out. Leashed pets are permitted.

Reservations, fees: Reservations are not accepted. Sites are $8 per night per vehicle. Open June–mid-November, weather permitting.

Directions: In Seattle on I-5, turn east on I-90. Drive east on I-90 for 78 miles to Cle Elum and Exit 85. Take Exit 85 to Highway 970. Turn east on Highway 970 and drive seven miles to Teanaway Road (Highway 970). Turn left (north) on Teanaway Road and drive 13 miles to the end of the paved road. Bear right (north) on Forest Road 9737 and drive four miles to the campground on the left.

Contact: Okanogan and Wenatchee National Forests, Cle Elum Ranger District, 509/852-1100, fax 509/674-3800, www.fs.fed.us.

107 INDIAN HORSE CAMP

Scenic rating: 6

on the Middle Fork of the Teanaway River

Map grid B2

This campground along the Middle Fork of the Teanaway River is located in a primitive setting with sunny, open sites along the water. Fishing for brook trout is best here when the season first opens in June. Quiet and solitude are highlights of this little-used camp. It's an easy drive from here to trailheads accessing the Mount Stuart Range. Be sure to bring your own drinking water. This is a popular snowmobile area in winter.

RV sites, facilities: There are 10 sites for tents or RVs up to 35 feet long. Picnic tables, fire grills, and tent pads are provided. Pit toilets are available, but there is no drinking water. Garbage must be packed out. Some saddle-stock facilities are available, including hitching posts. Some facilities are wheelchair accessible. Leashed pets are permitted.

Reservations, fees: Reservations are not

accepted. There is no fee for camping. Open year-round, weather and snow level permitting.

Directions: From Seattle, drive east on I-90 for 80 miles to Cle Elum and Exit 85 and Highway 970. Turn east on Highway 970 and drive 6.9 miles to Teanaway Road. Turn left on Teanaway Road and drive 7.3 miles to West Fork Teanaway Road. Turn left and drive 0.6 mile to Middle Fork Teanaway Road. Turn right and drive 3.9 miles to the campground on the left.

Contact: Department of Natural Resources, Southeast Region, 509/925-8510, www.dnr.wa.gov.

108 SWAUK

🥾 🎣 ❄️ 🐾 🚐 ⛺

Scenic rating: 6

on Swauk Creek in Wenatchee National Forest
Map grid B2

Some decent hiking trails can be found at this campground along Swauk Creek. A short loop trail, about one mile round-trip, is the most popular. Fishing is marginal, and there is some highway noise from U.S. 97. The elevation is 3,200 feet. Three miles east of the camp on Forest Road 9716 is Swauk Forest Discovery Trail. This three-mile interpretive trail explains some of the effects of logging and U.S. Forest Service management of the forest habitat.

RV sites, facilities: There are 22 sites, including two double sites, for tents or RVs up to 25 feet long. Fire grills and picnic tables are provided. Flush and vault toilets and firewood are available. There is no drinking water. Leashed pets are permitted.

Reservations, fees: Reservations are not accepted. Sites are $15 per night, double sites are $30 per night, $7 per extra vehicle per night. Open late May–early September, weather permitting.

Directions: In Seattle on I-5, turn east on I-90. Drive east on I-90 for 80 miles to Cle Elum and Exit 85. Take Exit 85 to Highway 970. Turn east on Highway 970 and drive 20 miles north on Highway 970/U.S. 97 to the campground on the right (near Swauk Pass).

Contact: Okanogan and Wenatchee National Forests, Cle Elum Ranger District, 509/852-1100, fax 509/674-3800, www.fs.fed.us.

109 MINERAL SPRINGS

🥾 🎣 🐾 🚐 ⛺

Scenic rating: 6

on Swauk Creek in Wenatchee National Forest
Map grid B2

This campground is at the confluence of Medicine and Swauk Creeks. Note that this camp is set along a highway, so there is some highway noise. Fishing, berry picking, and hunting are good in season in this area. It is at an elevation of 2,800 feet. Most use the camp as a one-night layover spot.

RV sites, facilities: There are eight sites for tents or RVs up to 21 feet long and one group site for up to 50 people. Picnic tables and fire rings are provided. Drinking water, vault toilets, and a camp host are available. Leashed pets are permitted. A restaurant is nearby.

Reservations, fees: Reservations are not accepted for family sites but are required for the group site at 877/444-6777 or www.recreation.gov ($10 reservation fee). Sites are $15 per night, $7 per extra vehicle per night. The group site is $80 per night. Open mid-May–mid-September, weather permitting.

Directions: From Seattle, drive east on I-90 for 80 miles to Cle Elum and Exit 85 and Highway 970. Turn northeast on Highway 970 and drive 17 miles to the campground on the left.

Contact: Okanogan and Wenatchee National Forests, Cle Elum Ranger District, 509/852-1100, fax 509/674-3800, www.fs.fed.us.

110 KEN WILCOX HORSE CAMP

🥾 🚴 🚐 ⛺

Scenic rating: 8

near Swauk Creek at Haney Meadows in Wenatchee National Forest
Map grid B2

First note that the last couple miles of road are pretty rough, suitable only for high-clearance vehicles or pickups. The camp is set at an elevation of 5,500 feet, at the launch point for an extensive trail system. This scenic camp near Haney Meadows has been adopted by a local equestrian association that helps maintain the horse trails. Mountain bikers also use this camp; note that when bikers and horses meet on a trail, bikers must give way, even if it involves dismounting the bike and carrying it off the trail.

RV sites, facilities: There are 25 sites for tents or RVs up to 30 feet long. Picnic tables and fire pits are provided. Vault toilets are available. There is no drinking water, although stock water is available. Garbage must be packed out. Stock facilities include hitching equipment such as rails and rings for suspending a high line.

Reservations, fees: Reservations are not accepted. Northwest Forest Pass ($5 daily fee or $30 annual fee per parked vehicle) is required. Open early July–mid-October, weather permitting (the access road is not plowed).

Directions: In Seattle on I-5, turn east on I-90. Drive east on I-90 for 80 miles to Cle Elum and Exit 85. Take Exit 85 to Highway 970. Turn east on Highway 970 and drive 24 miles to the summit of Blewett (Swauk) Pass and Forest Road 9716. Turn right on Forest Road 9716 (gravel) and drive about four miles to Forest Road 9712. Turn left on Forest Road 9712 and drive about five miles to the camp on the left.

Contact: Okanogan and Wenatchee National Forests, Cle Elum Ranger District, 509/852-1100, fax 509/674-3800, www.fs.fed.us.

111 SQUILCHUCK STATE PARK

Scenic rating: 7

southwest of Wenatchee

Map grid B2

This 288-acre park sits at an elevation of 4,000 feet in a fir and pine forest. Recreation opportunities include 10 miles of hiking and biking trails; in winter, this park sees sledding, snowshoeing, and cross-country skiing. "Squilchuc" is Chinook language for "muddy water."

RV sites, facilities: There is one group site for 20–160 people in tents or RVs up to 30 feet long (no hookups). Picnic tables and fire rings are provided. A restroom with flush toilets and coin showers, drinking water, and a lodge with kitchen are available. Some facilities are wheelchair accessible. Leashed pets are permitted.

Reservations, fees: Reservations ($25 reservation fee) are required by calling Wenatchee Confluence State Park at 509/664-6373. The group site is $2.25 per person per night. Open May–mid-September, with limited winter facilities.

Directions: From U.S. 2 in Wenatchee, drive south on Wenatchee Avenue to Squilchuck Road and follow the signs for about eight miles to the park.

Contact: Wenatchee Confluence State Park, 509/664-6373; state park information, 360/902-8844, www.parks.wa.gov.

112 TRAILER CORRAL RV PARK

Scenic rating: 7

near the Yakima River

Map grid B2

This wooded campground about one mile from the Yakima River offers a choice of grassy or graveled sites. Nearby recreation options include an 18-hole golf course, marked hiking trails, and tennis courts.

RV sites, facilities: There are 23 sites with full or partial hookups for RVs of any length, three tent sites, and six cabins. Picnic tables and cable TV are provided, and fire rings are available on request. Restrooms with flush toilets and showers, firewood, and coin laundry are available. A store is located within one mile. Boat-launching facilities are nearby. Leashed pets are permitted.

Reservations, fees: Reservations are accepted. Sites are $17–22 per night, $2 per person per night for more than two people. Open year-round.

Directions: From Seattle, drive east on I-90 for 80 miles to Cle Elum and Exit 85 and Highway

970. Turn east on Highway 970 and drive 1.5 mile to the park on the left.

Contact: Trailer Corral, 509/674-2433.

113 ICEWATER CREEK

Scenic rating: 7

on Taneum Creek in Wenatchee National Forest
Map grid B2

Icewater Creek camp is most popular with off-road motorcyclists because there are two ORV trails leading from the camp, both of which network with an extensive system of off-road riding trails. The best route extends along the South Fork Taneum River area. The campground sports small trees and open sites. Fishing is fair, primarily for six- to eight-inch cutthroat trout.

RV sites, facilities: There are 14 sites for tents or RVs up to 26 feet long, including three double sites. Picnic tables and fire rings are provided. Drinking water and firewood are available. Leashed pets are permitted.

Reservations, fees: Reservations are not accepted. Single sites are $14 per night, double sites are $28 per night, $7 per night for each additional vehicle. Open May–late September, weather permitting.

Directions: From Seattle, take I-5 east on I-90. Drive east on I-90 for 80 miles to Cle Elum. Continue east for 9.3 miles to Exit 93/Elks Height Road. Take that exit and drive to the stop sign at Elks Height Road. Turn left and drive 0.3 mile to Taneum Road. Turn right on Taneum Road and drive 3.4 miles to East Taneum Road. Turn right on East Taneum Road and drive 0.1 miles to W. Taneum Road. Turn right on West Taneum Road and drive 8.4 miles to the campground on the left.

Contact: Okanogan and Wenatchee National Forests, Cle Elum Ranger District, 509/852-1100, www.fs.fed.us.

114 ELLENSBURG KOA

Scenic rating: 8

on the Yakima River
Map grid B2

This KOA is one of the few campgrounds in a 25-mile radius. Exceptionally clean and scenic, it offers well-maintained, shaded campsites along the Yakima River. Rafting and fly-fishing on the nearby Yakima River are popular. Other nearby recreation options include an 18-hole golf course and tennis courts. The Kittitas County Historical Museum is in town at 3rd and Pine Streets.

RV sites, facilities: There are 100 sites with full or partial hookups (30 and 50 amps) for RVs of any length and 30 tent sites. Some sites are pull-through. A trailer and an apartment are also available. Picnic tables are provided. Restrooms with flush toilets and showers, cable TV, a dump station, propane, Wi-Fi and modem access, firewood, bicycle rentals, a video arcade, convenience store, snack bar, coin laundry, ice, a playground, video rentals, a horseshoe pit, volleyball, a seasonal wading pool, and a seasonal heated swimming pool are available. Breakfast is available during the summer season. A café is located within one mile. Extra parking is available for horse trailers, vans, and boats. Leashed pets are permitted.

Reservations, fees: Reservations are accepted at 800/562-7616. Sites are $34–40 per night for RVs, $25 for tents, $3–4 per person per night for more than two people, and $3 per extra vehicle per night. Some credit cards are accepted. Open year-round.

Directions: From Seattle, drive east on I-90 for 106 miles to Exit 106 (near Ellensburg). Take that exit and continue mile to Thorp Highway. Turn right at Thorp Highway and drive a short distance to the KOA entrance (well marked).

Contact: Ellensburg KOA, 509/925-9319, fax 509/925-3607, www.koa.com.

NORTHEASTERN WASHINGTON

BEST RV PARKS AND CAMPGROUNDS

Family Destinations

Fishing

Wildlife-Viewing

see The Northern
Cascades
page 110

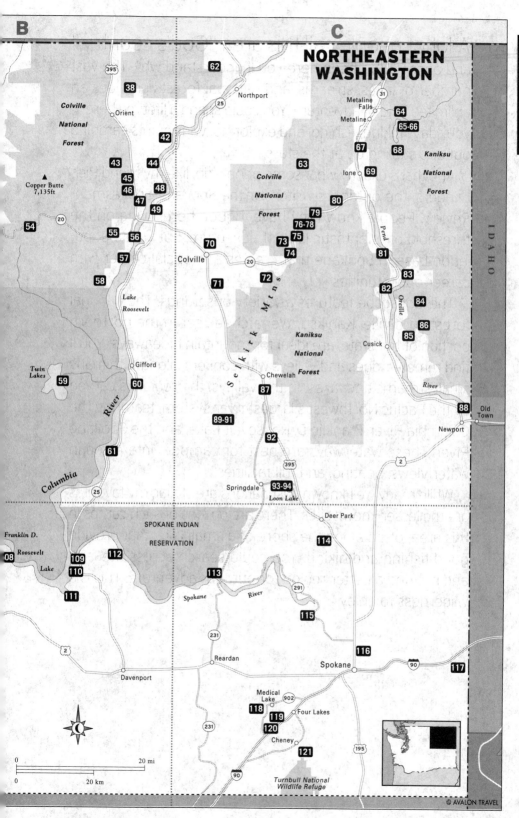

B

C

NORTHEASTERN WASHINGTON

Colville National Forest

Copper Butte 7,135ft

Colville National Forest

Kaniksu National Forest

Kaniksu National Forest

Selkirk Mtns

Pend

Oreille

Lake Roosevelt

Twin Lakes

Columbia River

Franklin D. Roosevelt Lake

SPOKANE INDIAN RESERVATION

Spokane River

IDAHO

62
38
42
43
44
45
46
47
48
49
54
55
56
57
58
59
60
61
70
71
72
73
74
75
76-78
79
80
81
82
83
84
85
86
87
88
89-91
92
93-94
108
109
110
111
112
113
114
115
116
117
118
119
120
121
63
64
65-66
67
68
69

Northport
Orient
Metaline Falls
Metaline
Ione
Colville
Gifford
Chewelah
Cusick
Old Town
Newport
Springdale
Loon Lake
Deer Park
Reardan
Davenport
Spokane
Medical Lake
Four Lakes
Cheney
Turnbull National Wildlife Refuge

395
25
31
20
20
2
291
231
231
195
902
90
25
2

0   20 mi
0   20 km

© AVALON TRAVEL

A lot of people call this area "God's country," and once you've been here you'll understand why. The vast number of lakes, streams, and national forests provides an unlimited land of adventure. You could spend a lifetime here – your days hiking, fishing, and exploring, your nights camping out and staring up at the stars.

And that's exactly what some people do, like my friend Rich Landers, the outdoors writer for the *Spokane Spokesman-Review*. People know they have it good here, living on the threshold of a fantastic land of adventure, but with a population base in Spokane that creates a financial center with career opportunities.

The landscape features a variety of settings. The national forests (Colville, Kaniksu, Wenatchee), set in the northern portion of the state, are ideal for mountain hideaways. You'll find remote ridges and valleys with conifers, along with many small streams and lakes. In the valleys, the region is carved by the Pacific Northwest's largest river system, featuring the Columbia River, Franklin D. Roosevelt Lake, and the Spokane River. These waterways are best for campers interested in water views, boating, and full facilities.

While many well-known destinations are stellar, my favorites are the lesser-known sites. There are dozens of such camps in this area, often along the shore of a small lake, that provide good fishing and hiking. You could search across the land and not find a better region for outdoor adventure. This is a wilderness to enjoy.

1 OSOYOOS LAKE STATE PARK

Scenic rating: 9

on Osoyoos Lake

Map grid A1

The park is set along the shore of Osoyoos Lake, a 14-mile-long lake created from the Okanogan River, located south of the Canadian Rockies. The park covers 47 acres and provides a base of operations for a fishing vacation. The lake has rainbow trout, kokanee salmon, small-mouth bass, crappie, and perch. Fishing gear and concessions are available. Water sports are also popular in the summer, and in winter, this is an ideal location for ice-skating, ice fishing, and snow play. Expansive lawns lead down to the sandy shore of the lake, which is a winter nesting area for geese. A nine-hole golf course is nearby. A historical note: Many years ago, the area was the site of the annual *okanogan* (rendezvous) of the Salish Indians from what are now Washington and British Columbia. They would gather and share supplies of fish and game for the year.

RV sites, facilities: There are 86 sites for tents or RVs up to 45 feet (no hookups) and six primitive tent sites. Picnic tables and fire grills are provided. Restrooms with flush toilets and coin showers, dump station, a store, café, firewood, horseshoes, and volleyball are available. A coin laundry and ice are located within one mile. Boat-launching and dock facilities are nearby. Leashed pets are permitted.

Reservations, fees: Reservations are accepted at 888/CAMP-OUT (888/226-7688) or www.parks.wa.gov/reservations ($7 reservation fee). Sites are $17–19 per night, $10 per extra vehicle per night. Some credit cards are accepted. Open year-round, with limited facilities in winter.

Directions: From Oroville, just south of the Canadian border, drive north on U.S. 97 for one mile to the park entrance on the right.

Contact: Osoyoos Lake State Park, 509/476-3321; state park information, 360/902-8844, www.parks.wa.gov.

2 CHOPAKA LAKE

Scenic rating: 8

on Chopaka Lake

Map grid A1

This campground provides a classic setting for the expert angler. It's nestled along the western shore of Chopaka Lake, which is extremely popular with trout anglers. No motorboats are permitted on the lake. That makes it a winner for fly fishers (barbless hooks required) using float tubes.

RV sites, facilities: There are 16 sites for tents or RVs up to 20 feet long. Picnic tables and fire grills are provided. Vault toilets, drinking water, a fishing platform, and primitive boat-launching facilities are available. Garbage must be packed out. Some facilities are wheelchair accessible. Leashed pets are permitted.

Reservations, fees: Reservations are not accepted. There is no fee for camping. Open year-round, weather permitting; drive-in access is usually passable mid-April–mid-November.

Directions: From Wenatchee, drive north on U.S. 97 for 120 miles to Tonasket and Forest Street. Turn left and drive 0.2 mile (crossing the Okanogan River) to Highway 7. Turn right (north) on Highway 7 (Loomis-Oroville Highway) and drive five miles. At the fork, continue on Loomis-Oroville Highway for about 12 miles to Toats Coulee Road, 2.1 miles north of Loomis. Turn left and drive 5.5 miles to Touts Coulee campground. Continue 2.1 miles to Nine Mile Road. Turn right and drive approximately 3.5 miles to Chopaka Road. Turn right and drive 3.5 miles to Chopaka Lake Road. Turn left and drive one mile to the camp on the left.

Contact: Department of Natural Resources, Northeast Region, 509/684-7474, fax 509/684-7484, www.dnr.wa.gov.

WASHINGTON

3 COLD SPRINGS

Scenic rating: 8

near Cold Creek

Map grid A1

It's quite a drive to get here, but you'll be happy you made the effort to reach this pretty forested camp. Campsites are located near a small stream amid a forest of lodgepole pine, western larch, and several species of fir, including Douglas fir. Trails for horseback riding, hiking, and snow-mobiling run through the area. Because the camp is little known and remote, it's advisable to obtain a map of the area from the Department of Natural Resources.

RV sites, facilities: There are nine campsites for tents or RVs up to 20 feet long. Picnic tables, fire grills, and tent pads are provided. Vault toilets and drinking water are available. Garbage must be packed out. Some facilities are wheelchair accessible. Leashed pets are permitted.

Reservations, fees: Reservations are not accepted. There is no fee for camping. Open year-round.

Directions: From Wenatchee, drive north on U.S. 97 for 120 miles to Tonasket and Forest Street. Turn left and drive 0.2 mile (crossing the Okanogan River) to Highway 7. Turn right (north) on Highway 7 (Loomis-Oroville Highway) and drive five miles. At the fork, continue on Loomis-Oroville Highway for about 12 miles to Toats Coulee Road, 2.1 miles north of Loomis. Turn left and drive 5.5 miles to the Toats Coulee camp. Continue on the main road for 2.1 miles to Nine Mile Road. Turn right and drive approximately 5.5 miles to the camp on the left.

Contact: Department of Natural Resources, Northeast Region, 509/684-7474, fax 509/684-7484, www.dnr.wa.gov.

4 NORTH FORK NINE MILE

Scenic rating: 6

on the North Fork of Toats Coulee Creek

Map grid A1

Deer and black bears frequent this campground situated in the forest along the North Fork of Toats Coulee Creek and Nine Mile Creek. This camp is popular in the fall with hunters. Trout fishing is fair at Toats Coulee Creek; check regulations. It's advisable to obtain a map from the Department of Natural Resources that details the area.

RV sites, facilities: There are 11 sites for tents or RVs up to 20 feet long. Picnic tables and fire grills are provided. Vault toilets and drinking water are available. Garbage must be packed out. Some facilities are wheelchair accessible. Leashed pets are permitted.

Reservations, fees: Reservations are not accepted. There is no fee for camping. Open year-round, weather permitting.

Directions: From Wenatchee, drive north on U.S. 97 for 120 miles to Tonasket and Forest Street. Turn left and drive 0.2 mile (crossing the Okanogan River) to Highway 7. Turn right (north) on Highway 7 (Loomis-Oroville Highway) and drive five miles. At the fork, continue on Loomis-Oroville Highway for about 12 miles to Toats Coulee Road, 2.1 miles north of Loomis. Turn left and drive 5.5 miles to the Toats Coulee camp. Continue 2.3 miles to the campground, 0.2 mile past Nine Mile Road.

Contact: Department of Natural Resources, Northeast Region, 509/684-7474, fax 509/684-7484, www.dnr.wa.gov.

5 TOATS COULEE

Scenic rating: 6

on Toats Coulee Creek

Map grid A1

Touts Coulee consists of two primitive campsites set a short distance apart. The camp is set in a wooded spot along Toats Coulee Creek. Trout fishing is available; check regulations.

The best hiking is located 10 miles northwest in the Pasayten Wilderness (to reach this trailhead, continue driving up the campground road). These camps are popular in the fall with hunters. In the winter, a road for snowmobile use follows the South Fork of Toats Coulee Creek, swinging south and then heading east along Cecil Creek.

RV sites, facilities: There are nine sites and two double sites for tents or RVs up to 20 feet long. Picnic tables and fire grills are provided. Vault toilets are available. There is no drinking water, and garbage must be packed out. Some facilities are wheelchair accessible. Leashed pets are permitted.

Reservations, fees: Reservations are not accepted. There is no fee for camping. Open year-round.

Directions: From Wenatchee, drive north on U.S. 97 for 120 miles to Tonasket and Forest Street. Turn left and drive 0.2 mile (crossing the Okanogan River) to Highway 7. Turn right (north) on Highway 7 (Loomis-Oroville Highway) and drive five miles. At the fork, continue on Loomis-Oroville Highway for about 12 miles to Toats Coulee Road, 2.1 miles north of Loomis. Turn left and drive 5.5 miles to the camp on the left.

Contact: Department of Natural Resources, Northeast Region, 509/684-7474, fax 509/684-7484, www.dnr.wa.gov.

₆ PALMER LAKE

Scenic rating: 9

on Palmer Lake

Map grid A1

This shorefront camp is the only one at Palmer Lake. The campsites are set close to the lake's very scenic shore. It fills up during the summer, even on weekdays, frequently with visitors from Canada. Fishing is often good for kokanee salmon and rainbow trout. Powerboating and waterskiing are permitted. There are numerous migration routes in the region; the Sinlahekin Valley to the south of Palmer Lake is part of

the winter range for deer. Endangered bighorn sheep, cougars, bald and golden eagles, black bears, and grouse are among the wildlife that can be spotted.

RV sites, facilities: There are eight sites for tents or RVs up to 20 feet long. Picnic tables and fire grills are provided. Vault toilets are available. There is no drinking water, and garbage must be packed out. Some facilities are wheelchair accessible. A primitive boat launch is located at the opposite end of the lake; four-wheel drive is required. Leashed pets are permitted.

Reservations, fees: Reservations are not accepted. There is no fee for camping. Open year-round, weather permitting.

Directions: From Wenatchee, drive north on U.S. 97 for 120 miles to Tonasket and Forest Street. Turn left and drive 0.2 mile, crossing the Okanogan River, to Highway 7. Turn right (north) on Highway 7 (Loomis-Oroville Highway) and drive 18.5 miles, 8.5 miles past Loomis. Stay to the right and drive to the camp at the north end of the lake.

Contact: Department of Natural Resources, Northeast Region, 509/684-7474, fax 509/684-7484, www.dnr.wa.gov.

₇ SUN COVE RESORT

Scenic rating: 9

on Wannacut Lake

Map grid A1

This beautiful resort is surrounded by trees and hills and set along the shore of Wannacut Lake, a spring-fed lake that doesn't get much traffic. The lake is approximately three miles long and 2.5 miles wide. An 8-mph speed limit is enforced for boats. Fishing, swimming, boating, and hiking are all summertime options. The park provides full facilities, including a heated pool, playground, and recreation hall. For the horse-riding set, a guided trail and overnight rides are available one mile from the resort.

RV sites, facilities: There are 22 sites for tents or RVs (no hookups), 28 pull-through sites with full hookups for RVs of any length, two cottages, and 10 motel units with kitchens. Picnic tables are provided. No wood fires are allowed. Restrooms with flush toilets and coin showers, a dump station, recreation hall, general store, café, coin laundry, ice, fishing supplies, a playground, and a seasonal heated swimming pool are available. Boat docks, launching facilities, and rentals are also available. Some facilities are wheelchair accessible. Leashed pets are permitted in the campground.

Reservations, fees: Reservations are accepted. Sites are $30 per night. Some credit cards are accepted. Open late April–mid-October.

Directions: From Oroville, just south of the Canadian border, drive west on Ellemehan Mountain Road for about six miles to Wannacut Lake Road. Turn left (south) and drive five miles to the resort at the end of the road.

Contact: Sun Cove Resort, tel./fax 509/476-2223.

8 SPECTACLE LAKE RESORT

Scenic rating: 7

on Spectacle Lake

Map grid A1

This pleasant resort on the shore of long, narrow Spectacle Lake has grassy, shaded sites. Space is usually available here, although reservations are accepted. Recreation options include boating, fishing, swimming, waterskiing, watercraft, and hunting (in season).

RV sites, facilities: There are 40 sites for tents or RVs of any length (20 and 30 amp full hookups) and 12 motel rooms with kitchenettes. Picnic tables and fire pits are provided. Restrooms with flush toilets and showers, propane gas, a dump station, a convenience store, coin laundry, ice, a playground, recreation hall, exercise room, and seasonal heated swimming pool are available. Boat docks, launching facilities, and rentals are also nearby. Leashed pets are permitted.

Reservations, fees: Reservations are accepted. Sites are $25 per night. Some credit cards are accepted. Open mid-April–late October.

Directions: In Tonasket on U.S. 97, turn west (left if arriving from the south), cross the bridge, and continue to Highway 7. Turn right on Highway 7 and drive about 12 miles to Holmes Road. Turn left (south) on Holmes Road and drive 0.5 mile to McCammon Road. Turn right (west) and drive one block to the resort at the end of the road.

Contact: Spectacle Lake Resort, 509/223-3433, www.spectaclelakeresort.com.

9 RAINBOW RESORT

Scenic rating: 7

on Spectacle Lake

Map grid A1

This resort on Spectacle Lake is an alternative to Spectacle Lake Resort. The camp features pretty lake views and full facilities. Nearby activities include swimming, fishing, hunting, and horseback riding, including overnight trail rides.

RV sites, facilities: There are 35 sites with full hookups (30 amps) for RVs of any length and 14 sites for tents or RVs of any length (partial hookups). Some sites are pull-through. Picnic tables are provided, and fire pits are available on request. Restrooms with flush toilets and showers, ice, a recreation room, horseshoe pits, volleyball, boat docks, and launching facilities are available. Leashed pets are permitted.

Reservations, fees: Reservations are accepted. Sites are $28 per night. Some credit cards are accepted. Open April–October.

Directions: From Ellisford, turn west on Ellisford Bridge Road. Drive 0.5 mile to Highway 7. Turn left (south) and drive one mile to Loomis Highway. Turn right and drive 6.5 miles to the resort on the left.

Contact: Rainbow Resort, 509/223-3700 or 800/347-4375.

10 SPECTACLE FALLS RESORT

Scenic rating: 8

on Spectacle Lake

Map grid A1

Spectacle Falls Resort is set on the shore of Spectacle Lake. It is open only as long as fishing is available, which means a closing in late July. Be sure to phone ahead of time to verify that the resort is open. Nearby recreation options include hiking, swimming, fishing, tennis, and horseback riding, including guided trails and overnight rides. Rainbow Resort provides an alternative.

RV sites, facilities: There are 10 pull-through sites with full hookups for RVs of any length and four mobile homes. Picnic tables are provided. Restrooms with flush toilets and showers, ice, boat docks, launching facilities, and boat rentals are available. Leashed pets are permitted.

Reservations, fees: Reservations are accepted. Sites are $20 per night, $2 per person per night for more than two people, $5 per extra vehicle per night. Open April–July.

Directions: From Tonasket on U.S. 97, turn northwest on Loomis Highway and drive 15 miles to the resort on the left.

Contact: Spectacle Falls Resort, 509/223-4141.

11 LOST LAKE

Scenic rating: 7

on Lost Lake in Okanogan National Forest

Map grid A1

This camp is set on the shore of Lost Lake at an elevation of 3,800 feet. As a launch point for fishing, swimming, hiking, hunting, and horseback riding, it keeps visitors happy. No gas motors are permitted on the lake. The lake is similar to Beth and Beaver Lakes, but rounder. The Big Tree Botanical Area is about one mile away. Note that the group site is often booked one year in advance.

RV sites, facilities: There are 19 sites for tents or

RVs up to 31 feet long. There is also one group site for up to 100 people. Picnic tables and fire rings are provided. Drinking water, vault toilets, and garbage bins are available. Boat-launching facilities and swimming platforms, a ball field, and horseshoe pits are nearby. Some facilities are wheelchair accessible. Leashed pets are permitted.

Reservations, fees: Reservations are not available for single and double sites but are required for the group site at 877/444-6777 or www.recreation.gov ($10 reservation fee). Sites are $12 per vehicle per night, $5 per night per additional vehicle; group sites are $40–80 per night. Open May–mid-October, weather permitting.

Directions: From East Wenatchee, drive north on U.S. 97 for 120 miles to Tonasket and Highway 20. Turn east on Highway 20 and drive 20 miles to Bonaparte Lake Road (County Road 4953). Turn left (north) and drive six miles to Forest Road 32. Turn right (north) and drive four miles to Forest Road 33. Bear left (northwest) and drive five miles to a four-way intersection. Turn left on Forest Road 33-050 and drive 0.3 mile to the campground on the right.

Contact: Okanogan and Wenatchee National Forests, Tonasket Ranger District, 509/486-2186, fax 509/486-5161, www.fs.fed.us.

12 BONAPARTE LAKE

Scenic rating: 7

on Bonaparte Lake in Okanogan National Forest

Map grid A1

This campground is located on the southern shore of Bonaparte Lake at an elevation of 3,600 feet. The lake is stocked with rainbow trout, brook trout, and mackinaw trout. A 10-mph speed limit keeps the lake quiet, ideal for fishing. Several trails nearby provide access to Mount Bonaparte Lookout.

RV sites, facilities: There are 28 single and multiple sites for tents or RVs of any length, one bike-in/hike-in site (requiring a walk of less than 100 feet), and one group site for up to 30 people. Picnic tables and fire grills are provided. Drinking water, vault toilets, and garbage bins are available. A store, café, gas, and ice are available within one mile. Boat docks and launching facilities are also available. Some facilities are wheelchair accessible. Leashed pets are permitted.

Reservations, fees: Reservations are not accepted for individual sites but are required for the group site at 877/444-6777 or www.recreation. gov ($10 reservation fee). Sites are $12 per night per vehicle, $5 per night per additional vehicle, and $8 for bike-in/hike-in sites. The group site is $40. Open mid-May–mid-October, weather permitting.

Directions: From East Wenatchee, drive north on U.S. 97 for 120 miles to Tonasket and Highway 20. Turn east on Highway 20 and drive 20 miles to Bonaparte Lake Road (County Road 4953). Turn left (north) and drive six miles to Bonaparte Lake and Forest Road 32 and the campground on the left.

Contact: Okanogan and Wenatchee National Forests, Tonasket Ranger District, 509/486-2186, fax 509/486-5161, www.fs.fed.us.

13 BONAPARTE LAKE RESORT

Scenic rating: 6

on Bonaparte Lake

Map grid A1

Fishing is popular at this resort, set on the southeast shore of Bonaparte Lake. A 10-mph speed limit keeps the lake quiet, ideal for fishing. Other recreational activities include hiking and hunting in the nearby U.S. Forest Service lands and snowmobiling, cross-country skiing, and ice fishing in the winter. Poker tournaments are held occasionally.

RV sites, facilities: There are 35 sites with full or partial hookups (20 and 30 amps) for RVs of any length, 10 tent sites, and 10 cabins. Some sites are pull-through. Picnic tables and fire rings are provided. Restrooms, flush toilets, showers, propane gas, a dump station, firewood, a recreation hall, convenience store, restaurant,

coin laundry, ice, a playground, boat docks, launching facilities, and boat rentals are available. Leashed pets are permitted.

Reservations, fees: Reservations are accepted. Sites are $10–22 per night. Some credit cards are accepted. Open year-round, with limited winter facilities.

Directions: From East Wenatchee, drive north on U.S. 97 for 20 miles to Tonasket and Highway 20. Turn east on Highway 20 and drive 20 miles to Bonaparte Lake Road (County Road 4953). Turn left (north) and drive six miles to Bonaparte Lake and the resort on the left.

Contact: Bonaparte Lake Resort, 509/486-2828, www.bonaparte-lake-resort.com.

14 TIFFANY SPRINGS
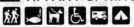

Scenic rating: 7

near Tiffany Lake in Okanogan National Forest

Map grid A1

Set at an elevation of 6,800 feet, this camp is less than a mile hike from Tiffany Lake. Tiffany Mountain rises 8,200 feet in the distance. The lake provides fishing for rainbow trout and brook trout. There are also some good hiking trails in the area. The Tiffany Mountain area provides a network of 26 miles of hiking trails, accessed from either here at Tiffany Springs or at Tiffany Lake.

RV sites, facilities: There are six sites for tents or small RVs up to 16 feet long. Picnic tables and fire grills are provided. Vault toilets are available. There is no drinking water, and garbage must be packed out. Some facilities are wheelchair accessible. Leashed pets are permitted.

Reservations, fees: Reservations are not accepted. There is no fee, but a Northwest Forest Pass is required. Open June–mid-October, weather permitting.

Directions: From East Wenatchee, drive north on U.S. 97 for 88 miles to Okanogan and County Road 9229. Turn north and drive 17.5 miles northwest to Conconully and County Road 2017. Turn left on County Road 2017 and drive two miles (road becomes Forest Road 42) to Forest Road 37. Turn right (northwest) on Forest Road 37 and drive 21 miles to Forest Road 39. Turn right (northeast) on Forest Road 39 and proceed eight miles to the campground on the left.

Contact: Okanogan and Wenatchee National Forests, Tonasket Ranger District, 509/486-2186, fax 509/486-5161, www.fs.fed.us.

15 SALMON MEADOWS

Scenic rating: 6

on Salmon Creek in Okanogan National Forest
Map grid A1

This camp is located along Salmon Creek at an elevation of 4,500 feet. Come in the spring for a spectacular wildflower display in an adjacent meadow. The camp features a forest setting, mainly Douglas fir, spruce, and some western larch. Trails from the campground are routed out to Angel Pass, two miles one-way, for views of the Tiffany area.

RV sites, facilities: There are seven sites for tents or small RVs up to 16 feet long. Picnic tables and fire grills are provided. Drinking water, vault toilets, and a horse corral are available. A gazebo is available at the day-use area. Garbage must be packed out. Leashed pets are permitted.

Reservations, fees: Reservations are not accepted. Sites are $8 per night, $5 per night per additional vehicle. Open mid-May–mid-October, weather permitting.

Directions: From East Wenatchee, drive north on U.S. 97 for 88 miles to Okanogan and County Road 9229. Turn left (north) on County Road 9229 and drive 17.5 miles to Conconully and County Road 2361. Continue northwest on County Road 2361 and drive five miles (becomes Forest Road 38) to Kerr Campground. Continue past Kerr for 4.5 miles to the campground on the right.

Contact: Okanogan and Wenatchee National Forests, Tonasket Ranger District, 509/486-2186, fax 509/486-5161, www.fs.fed.us.

16 KERR

Scenic rating: 6

on Salmon Creek in Okanogan National Forest
Map grid A1

This camp sits at an elevation of 3,100 feet along Salmon Creek, about four miles north of Conconully Reservoir, and is one of many campgrounds near the lake. Fishing prospects are marginal for trout here. There are numerous recreation options available at Conconully Reservoir, including far better fishing.

RV sites, facilities: There are 12 sites for tents or RVs up to 30 feet long. Picnic tables and fire grills are provided. Vault toilets are available. There is no drinking water, and garbage must be packed out. Some facilities are wheelchair accessible. Leashed pets are permitted.

Reservations, fees: Reservations are not accepted. Sites are $8 per night, $5 per night per additional vehicle. Open mid-May–mid-October, weather permitting.

Directions: From East Wenatchee, drive north on U.S. 97 for 88 miles to Okanogan and County Road 9229. Turn left (north) on County Road 9229 and drive 17.5 miles to Conconully and County Road 2361. Continue northwest on County Road 2361 and drive four miles (becomes Forest Road 38) to the campground on the left.

Contact: Okanogan and Wenatchee National Forests, Tonasket Ranger District, 509/486-2186, fax 509/486-5161, www.fs.fed.us.

17 ORIOLE

Scenic rating: 6

on Salmon Creek in Okanogan National Forest
Map grid A1

This camp is located at 2,900 feet elevation along Salmon Creek and offers a creek view from some of the campsites. This forest setting features well-spaced campsites among western larch and lodgepole pine. This is a primitive camp, similar to Kerr and Salmon Meadows, which are also set on Salmon Creek.

RV sites, facilities: There are 10 sites for tents or small trailers. Picnic tables and fire grills are provided. Drinking water, vault toilets, and garbage bins are available. Some facilities are wheelchair accessible. Leashed pets are permitted.

Reservations, fees: Reservations are not accepted. Sites are $8 per night, $5 per night per additional vehicle. Open mid-May–October, weather permitting.

Directions: From East Wenatchee, drive north on U.S. 97 for 88 miles to Okanogan and County Road 9229. Turn left (north) on County Road 9229 and drive 17.5 miles to Conconully and County Road 2361. Continue northwest on County Road 2361 and drive 2.5 miles to Forest Road 025. Turn left and drive 0.5 mile (crossing the creek) to the campground on the left.

Contact: Okanogan and Wenatchee National Forests, Tonasket Ranger District, 509/486-2186, fax 509/486-5161, www.fs.fed.us.

18 SUGARLOAF
🥾 🎣 🚐 🐕 🚙 ⛺

Scenic rating: 6

on Sugarloaf Lake in Okanogan National Forest
Map grid A1

Sugarloaf Lake is a small lake, about 20 acres, and this small camp is set near its shore. It provides fishing for rainbow trout, but the lake level often drops substantially during summer, so this camp gets little use in late summer and early fall. Conconully State Park and Information Center are nearby.

RV sites, facilities: There are four tent sites. Picnic tables and fire rings are provided. Vault toilets are available. There is no drinking water, and garbage must be packed out. Boat-launching facilities are available nearby. No boats with gas motors are permitted. Leashed pets are permitted.

Reservations, fees: Reservations are not accepted. Sites are $8 per night, $5 per night per additional vehicle. Open mid-May–mid-October, weather permitting.

Directions: From East Wenatchee, drive north on U.S. 97 for 88 miles to Okanogan and County Road 9229. Turn north and drive about 17.5 miles northwest to Conconully and County Road 4015. Turn right (northwest) on County Road 4015 and drive 4.5 miles to the campground on the left.

Contact: Okanogan and Wenatchee National Forests, Tonasket Ranger District, 509/486-2186, fax 509/486-5161, www.fs.fed.us.

19 KOZY KABINS AND RV PARK
🥾 🏊 🎣 🚐 ❄️ 🐕 🚙 ⛺

Scenic rating: 7

near Conconully Reservoir
Map grid A1

This quiet and private park in Conconully has a small creek running through it and plenty of greenery. A full-service marina is located close by. There is hunting in season, and snowmobiling is an option in the winter. If you continue northeast of town on County Road 4015, the road will get a bit narrow for a while but will widen again when you enter the Sinlahekin Habitat Management Area, which is managed by the Department of Fish and Wildlife. There are some primitive campsites in this valley, especially along the shores of the lakes in the area.

RV sites, facilities: There are 15 sites with full hookups (30 amps) for RVs up to 40 feet long, six tent sites, and seven cabins. Picnic tables are provided. Restrooms with flush toilets and coin showers, a community fire pit, and firewood are available. Propane gas, a dump station, general store, café, coin laundry, and ice are located within one block. Boat docks, launching facilities, and boat rentals are nearby. Leashed pets are permitted.

Reservations, fees: Reservations are accepted at 888/502-2246. RV sites are $22 per night, and tent sites are $10 per night. Some credit cards are accepted. Open year-round.

Directions: From U.S. 97 in Okanogan, turn north (left if arriving from the south) on Pine Street/Conconully Highway and drive 17.5

miles northwest to Conconully and Broadway Street. Turn right (east) and drive one block to A Avenue. The park is at the junction of A Avenue and Broadway Street.

Contact: Kozy Kabins and RV Park, 509/826-6780.

20 CONCONULLY STATE PARK

Scenic rating: 9

on Conconully Reservoir
Map grid A1

Conconully State Park, which dates to 1910, is set along Conconully Reservoir and covers 81 acres, with 5,400 feet of shoreline. Anglers will be happy here, with opportunities for trout, bass, and kokanee salmon. A boat launch, beach access, swimming, and fishing provide all sorts of water sports possibilities. A 0.5-mile nature trail is available. A side-trip option is Sinlahekin Habitat Management Area, which is accessible via County Road 4015. This route heads northeast along the shore of Conconully Reservoir on the other side of U.S. 97. The road is narrow at first, but it becomes wider as it enters the Habitat Management Area.

RV sites, facilities: There are 84 sites with for tents or RVs up to 60 feet long (no hookups) and one group site for up to 75 people. Picnic tables and fire grills are provided. Restrooms with flush toilets and coin showers, a dump station, firewood, and a playground are available. A store, café, coin laundry, and ice are located within one mile. Boat-launching and dock facilities are nearby. A sheltered picnic area, horseshoe pits, baseball field, and interpretive activities are available nearby. Some facilities are wheelchair accessible. Leashed pets are permitted.

Reservations, fees: Reservations are not accepted for individual sites but are required for group site at 509/826-7408. Sites are $17–19 per night, $10 per extra vehicle per night. The group site is $112.50 per night for 26–50 people or $168.75 per night for 51–75 people. Open year-round.

Directions: On U.S. 97 at Omak, take the North Omak exit. At the base of the hill, turn right and drive two miles until you reach Conconully Road. Turn right and drive 15 miles north to the park entrance.

Contact: Conconully State Park, 509/826-7408; state park information, 360/902-8844, www.parks.wa.gov.

21 CONCONULLY LAKE RESORT

Scenic rating: 6

on Upper Conconully Lake
Map grid A1

This is the only resort along the shore of Conconully Lake, which is 3.5 miles long. Tents are permitted, but this is a prime vacation destination for RVers. Trout fishing, swimming, boating, waterskiing, and riding personal watercraft are all options here. There are ATV trails in the area.

RV sites, facilities: There are 11 sites for tents or RVs of any length (30 amp full hookups), four cabins, and one apartment. Picnic tables and fire rings are provided. Restrooms with flush toilets and coin showers and ice are available. Propane gas, gasoline, a dump station, limited groceries, a gift shop, bait and tackle, café, and coin laundry are located within one mile. Boat docks, launching facilities, moorage, and a variety of boat rentals are available. Leashed pets are permitted.

Reservations, fees: Reservations are accepted. RV sites are $27 per night, tent sites are $17 per night, plus $2 per person per night for more than two people. Some credit cards are accepted. Open late April–October.

Directions: From U.S. 97 in Okanogan, turn north (left if arriving from the south) on Pine Street/Conconully Highway and drive 17.5 miles northwest to Conconully and Lake Street. Turn right on Lake Street and drive one mile to the resort on the right.

Contact: Conconully Lake Resort, 509/826-0813 or 800/850-0813, fax 509/826-1292.

WASHINGTON

22 LIAR'S COVE RESORT

Scenic rating: 6

on Conconully Reservoir

Map grid A1

Roomy sites for RVs can be found at this camp on the shore of Conconully Reservoir. Tents are allowed, too. Fishing, swimming, boating, and hiking opportunities are located nearby.

RV sites, facilities: There are 28 sites for tents or RVs of any length (30 amp full hookups), two cabins, one mobile home, and three motel rooms. Picnic tables and fire pits are provided. Restrooms with flush toilets and coin showers, cable TV, modem access, ice, boat docks, launching facilities, and boat rentals are available. Propane gas, a dump station, store, and café are within one mile. Some facilities are wheelchair accessible. Leashed pets are permitted.

Reservations, fees: Reservations are accepted. Sites are $25–30 per night, tent sites are $17 per night, plus $5 per person per night for more than two people. Some credit cards are accepted. Open April–October.

Directions: From U.S. 97 in Okanogan, turn north (left if arriving from the south) on Pine Street/Conconully Highway and drive 16.5 miles northwest to Conconully and look for the park on the left. It's located 0.25 mile south of Conconully.

Contact: Liar's Cove Resort, 509/826-1288 or 800/830-1288, www.omakchronicle.com/liarscove.

23 SHADY PINES RESORT

Scenic rating: 6

on Conconully Reservoir

Map grid A1

This camp is set on the western shore of Conconully Reservoir. It is near Conconully State Park and provides an option if the state park campground is full—a common occurrence in summer. But note that on summer weekends, this camp often fills as well. The nearby Sinlahekin Habitat Management Area, which is managed by the Department of Fish and Wildlife, offers a possible side trip.

RV sites, facilities: There are 21 sites with full hookups (20, 30, and 50 amps) for RVs of any length, two tent sites, and six cabins. Some sites are pull-through. Picnic tables and fire rings are provided. Restrooms with flush toilets and coin showers, ice, firewood, boat-launching facilities, and boat rentals are available. Propane gas, a dump station, store, café, and coin laundry are located within one mile. Leashed pets are permitted.

Reservations, fees: Reservations are accepted at 800/552-2287. RV sites are $25–27 per night, tent sites are $21 per night. Some credit cards are accepted. Open mid-April–late October.

Directions: From U.S. 97 in Okanogan, turn north (left if arriving from the south) on Pine Street/Conconully Highway and drive 16.5 miles northwest to Conconully and Broadway Street. Turn left (west) and drive one mile. The park is on the west shore of the lake.

Contact: Shady Pines Resort, 509/826-2287, www.shadypinesresort.com.

24 LYMAN LAKE

Scenic rating: 5

on Lyman Lake in Okanogan National Forest

Map grid A1

Little known and little used, this campground along the shore of Lyman Lake is an idyllic spot for those wanting solitude and quiet. The lake is quite small, just five acres at most, but fishing for stocked rainbow trout is an option.

RV sites, facilities: There are four sites for tents or RVs up to 30 feet long. Picnic tables and fire grills are provided. Vault toilets are available. There is no drinking water, and garbage must be packed out. Leashed pets are permitted.

Reservations, fees: Reservations are not accepted. There is no fee for camping. Open mid-May–mid-October, weather permitting.

Directions: From East Wenatchee, drive north on U.S. 97 for 120 miles to Tonasket and Highway

20. Turn east on Highway 20 and drive 12.5 miles to County Road 9455. Turn right (southeast) on County Road 9455 and drive 13 miles to County Road 3785. Turn right (south) on County Road 3785 and drive 2.5 miles to the campground entrance on the right.

Contact: Okanogan and Wenatchee National Forests, 509/486-2186, fax 509/486-5161, www.fs.fed.us.

25 ROCK LAKES

Scenic rating: 8

on Rock Lake

Map grid A1

This camp is set in a forested area along the shore of Rock Lake. Fishing for rainbow trout and brook trout is a plus at Rock Lake. A downer is that access for launching even cartop boats is difficult, requiring a 0.25-mile hike. That makes it a better bet for float tubes. Note that the best fishing is early in the season and that the lake level often drops because of irrigation use. Some roads in the area are used by hikers and bikers. A good bet is to combine a trip here with nearby Leader Lake. Highway 20 east of I-5 is a designated scenic route.

RV sites, facilities: There are eight sites for tents or RVs up to 20 feet long. Picnic tables and fire pits are provided. Vault toilets are available. There is no drinking water, and garbage must be packed out. Leashed pets are permitted.

Reservations, fees: Reservations are not accepted. There is no fee for camping. Open year-round.

Directions: From East Wenatchee, drive north on U.S. 97 for 88 miles to Okanogan and Highway 20. Turn west and drive 10 miles to Loup Loup Canyon Road. Turn left on Loup Loup Canyon Road and drive 4.8 miles to Rock Lakes Road. Turn left on Rock Lakes Road and drive 5.8 miles to the campground entrance. Turn left and drive 0.25 mile to the campground.

Contact: Department of Natural Resources, Northeast Region, 509/684-7474, fax 509/684-7484, www.dnr.wa.gov.

26 CARL PRECHT RV PARK

Scenic rating: 6

on the Okanogan River

Map grid A1 **BEST (**

East Side Park is in the town of Omak, along the shore of the Okanogan River. It covers about 76 acres and features the Carl Precht RV Park, with campsites positioned on concrete pads surrounded by grass. Fishing for cutthroat trout is often good here, and there is a boat ramp near the campground. Nearby recreation options include an 18-hole golf course, a swimming pool, and a sports field.

RV sites, facilities: There are 68 pull-through sites with full hookups (30 amps) for RVs of any length and five tent sites. Picnic tables are provided. Restrooms with flush toilets and coin showers, a dump station, a picnic area, gasoline, a seasonal heated swimming pool, a playground, horseshoe pits, a skateboarding park, and a fitness trail are available. A store, café, and ice are located within one mile. Boat-launching facilities are nearby. Some facilities are wheelchair accessible. Leashed pets are permitted.

Reservations, fees: Reservations are not accepted. RV sites are $20 per night, and tent sites are $11 per night. Open April–October, weather permitting.

Directions: From U.S. 97 in Omak, turn west (left, if coming from the south) on Highway 155 and drive 0.3 mile to the campground on the left.

Contact: City of Omak, 509/826-1170, fax 509/826-6531, www.omakcity.com.

27 CRAWFISH LAKE

Scenic rating: 8

on Crawfish Lake in Okanogan National Forest

Map grid A1

This pretty, remote, and primitive camp is set at 4,500 feet elevation along the shore of Crawfish Lake. Crawdads were once abundant here, but overfishing has depleted their numbers. Swimming and fishing for trout are more popular.

RV sites, facilities: There are 10 sites for tents or RVs up to 30 feet long. Picnic tables and fire grills are provided. Vault toilets are available. There is no drinking water, and garbage must be packed out. Boat-launching facilities are located on the lake. Some facilities are wheelchair accessible. Leashed pets are permitted.

Reservations, fees: Reservations are not accepted. There is no fee for camping. Open mid-May–mid-October, weather permitting.

Directions: From East Wenatchee, drive north on U.S. 97 for 102 miles to Riverside and County Road 9320. Turn right (east) on County Road 9320 and drive 20 miles (becomes Forest Road 30) to Forest Road 30-100. Turn right and drive 0.5 mile to the campground on the right.

Contact: Okanogan and Wenatchee National Forests, Tonasket Ranger District, 509/486-2186, fax 509/486-5161, www.fs.fed.us.

28 LOUP LOUP

Scenic rating: 6

near Loup Loup Ski Area in Okanogan National Forest

Map grid A1

This camp provides a good setup for large groups of up to 100 people. It is located next to the Loup Loup Ski Area at 4,200 feet elevation. The camp features a setting of western larch trees, along with good access to biking and hiking trails as well as the ski area.

RV sites, facilities: There are 25 sites for tents or RVs up to 36 feet long. Picnic tables and fire rings are provided. Drinking water, vault toilets, and garbage bins are available. Some facilities are wheelchair accessible. Leashed pets are permitted.

Reservations, fees: Reservations are not accepted. Sites are $8 per night per vehicle. Open May–mid-October, weather permitting.

Directions: From East Wenatchee, drive north on U.S. 97 for 88 miles to Okanogan and Highway 20. Turn west and drive 21 miles to Forest Road 42. Turn right (north) on Forest Road 42 and drive one mile to the campground on the left.

Contact: Okanogan and Wenatchee National Forests, Methow Valley Ranger District, 509/996-4003, fax 509/996-2208, www.fs.fed.us; Methow Valley Visitor Center, 509/996-4000, fax 509/996-4051.

29 SPORTSMAN'S CAMP

Scenic rating: 6

on Sweat Creek, in Lower Loomis State Forest

Map grid A1

In season, this is a popular camp with hunters, who may bring horses; although there are no livestock facilities, horses are allowed in the camp. The landscape is shady and grassy with a small stream. Some roads in the area can be used by hikers and bikers. Highway 20 east of I-5 is a designated scenic route.

RV sites, facilities: There are four sites for tents or RVs up to 20 feet long and a small, dispersed area for tents. Picnic tables and fire pits are provided. Vault toilets are available, but there is no drinking water. Garbage must be packed out. A gazebo shelter with a fire pit is also available. Some facilities are wheelchair accessible. Leashed pets are permitted.

Reservations, fees: Reservations are not accepted. There is no fee for camping. Open year-round, weather permitting.

Directions: From East Wenatchee, drive north on U.S. 97 for 88 miles to Okanogan and Highway 20. Turn west and drive 15 miles to Sweat Creek Road. Turn right on Sweat Creek Road and drive one mile to the campground on the right.

Contact: Department of Natural Resources, Northeast Region, 509/684-7474, fax 509/684-7484, www.dnr.wa.gov.

30 JR

Scenic rating: 7

on Frazier Creek in Okanogan National Forest

Map grid A1

This camp is located along Frazier Creek near the Loup Loup summit and ski area at an elevation of 3,900 feet. Recreation possibilities in the surrounding area include fishing, hunting, cross-country skiing, snowmobiling, hiking, and bicycling. This is a small layover for travelers looking for a spot on Highway 20.

RV sites, facilities: There are six sites for tents or RVs up to 16 feet long. Picnic tables and fire rings are provided. Vault toilets are available. There is no drinking water, and garbage must be packed out. Leashed pets are permitted.

Reservations, fees: Reservations are not accepted. Sites are $8 per night. Open late May–mid-October, weather permitting.

Directions: From East Wenatchee, drive north on U.S. 97 for 88 miles to Okanogan and Highway 20. Turn west and drive 22 miles to the campground on the right.

Contact: Okanogan and Wenatchee National Forests, Methow Valley Ranger District, 509/996-4003, fax 509/996-2208, www.fs.fed.us; Methow Valley Visitor Center, 509/996-4000, fax 509/996-4051.

31 ROCK CREEK

Scenic rating: 6

on Rock Creek and Loup Loup Creek
Map grid A1

This wooded campground is situated at the confluence of Rock and Loup Loup Creeks. A group picnic shelter with a barbecue is available. The camp is used primarily in the fall as a base camp for hunters and occasionally during the summer, mostly on weekends. It's advisable to obtain a map detailing the area from the Department of Natural Resources.

RV sites, facilities: There are five sites for tents or RVs up to 20 feet long. Picnic tables and fire pits are provided. Vault toilets, drinking water, and a picnic area are available. Some facilities are wheelchair accessible. Leashed pets are permitted.

Reservations, fees: Reservations are not accepted. There is no fee for camping. Open year-round.

Directions: From East Wenatchee, drive north on U.S. 97 for 88 miles to Okanogan and

Highway 20. Turn west and drive 10 miles to Loup Loup Canyon Road. Turn left on Loup Loup Canyon Road and drive 3.9 miles to the camp on the left.

Contact: Department of Natural Resources, Northeast Region, 509/684-7474, fax 509/684-7484, www.dnr.wa.gov.

32 LEADER LAKE

Scenic rating: 7

on Leader Lake
Map grid A1

This primitive but pretty camp is set along the shore of Leader Lake. It is just far enough off the beaten path to get missed by many travelers. The camp has forest cover. The boat ramp is a bonus, and trout fishing can be good in season. Note that the water level often drops in summer because of irrigation use.

RV sites, facilities: There are 16 sites for tents or RVs up to 30 feet long. Picnic tables and fire pits are provided. Vault toilets are available. There is no drinking water, and garbage must be packed out. Boat-launching facilities are nearby. Some facilities are wheelchair accessible. Leashed pets are permitted.

Reservations, fees: Reservations are not accepted. There is no fee for camping. Open year-round.

Directions: From East Wenatchee, drive north on U.S. 97 for 88 miles to Okanogan and Highway 20. Turn west and drive eight miles to Leader Lake Road. Turn left and drive 0.4 mile to the campground.

Contact: Department of Natural Resources, Northeast Region, 509/684-7474, fax 509/684-7484, www.dnr.wa.gov.

33 AMERICAN LEGION PARK

Scenic rating: 6

on the Okanogan River
Map grid A1

This city park is located along the shore of the Okanogan River in an urban setting. The sites are graveled and sunny. Anglers may want to try their hand at the excellent bass fishing here. There is a historical museum at the park. A local farmers market is held on summer weekends.

RV sites, facilities: There are 35 sites for tents or RVs of any length (no hookups). Picnic tables are provided. Restrooms with flush toilets and coin showers, drinking water, and a boat ramp are available. A store, café, coin laundry, gasoline, and ice are located within one mile. Some facilities are wheelchair accessible. Leashed pets are permitted.

Reservations, fees: Reservations are not accepted. Sites are $3.25 per tent and $5.50 per vehicle per night. Open May–October, weather permitting.

Directions: From East Wenatchee, drive north on U.S. 97 for 88 miles to Okanogan and Highway 215. Turn left (north) on Highway 215/2nd Avenue and drive about three miles to the campground on the right.

Contact: Okanogan City Hall, 509/422-3600, fax 509/422-0747.

34 ALTA LAKE STATE PARK

Scenic rating: 8

on Alta Lake

Map grid A1

This state park is nestled among the pines along the shore of Alta Lake. The park covers 186 acres, and the lake is two miles long and 0.25 mile wide. Alta Lake brightens a region where the mountains and pines meet the desert and features good trout fishing in summer, along with a boat launch and a 0.5-mile-long swimming beach. Windsurfing is often excellent on windy afternoons. Because of many hidden rocks just under the lake surface, waterskiing can be dangerous. An 18-hole golf course and a riding stable are close by, and a nice one-mile hiking trail leads up to a scenic lookout. Lake Chelan is about 30 minutes away.

RV sites, facilities: There are 91 developed tent sites, 32 sites with partial hookups for RVs up to 38 feet long, and two group sites for 20–85

people. Picnic tables and fire grills (campfires are not allowed after July 1) are provided. Restrooms with flush toilets and coin showers, firewood, a dump station, a small camp store, and ice are available. A sheltered picnic area is available nearby. Some facilities are wheelchair accessible. Boat-launching facilities are nearby. Leashed pets are permitted.

Reservations, fees: Reservations are not accepted for family sites but are required for the group site at 509/923-2473 ($25 reservation fee). Sites are $17–26 per night, and $10 per extra vehicle per night. The group site is $2.25 per person per night with a minimum of 20 people. Open April–October, weather permitting.

Directions: From East Wenatchee, drive north on U.S. 97 for 64 miles to Highway 153 (just south of Pateros). Turn left (northwest) on Highway 153 and drive two miles to Alta Lake Road. Turn left (southwest) and drive two miles to the park.

Contact: Alta Lake State Park, 509/923-2473; state park information, 360/902-8844, www. parks.wa.gov.

35 BRIDGEPORT STATE PARK

Scenic rating: 8

on Rufus Woods Lake

Map grid A1   BEST (

Bridgeport State Park is located along the shore of Rufus Woods Lake, a reservoir on the Columbia River above Chief Joseph Dam. It's a big place, covering 748 acres, including 7,500 feet of shoreline and 18 acres of lawn, with some shade amid the desert landscape. Highlights include beach access, a boat launch, and the aptly named "haystacks," unusual volcanic formations. Fishing is best by boat because shore fishing requires a Colville Tribe fishing license (for sale at the Bridgeport Hardware Store), in addition to a state fishing license. The lake has plenty of rainbow trout and walleye. Windsurfing in the afternoon wind and waterskiing are popular at the lake. Nearby recreation options include a nine-hole golf course.

RV sites, facilities: There are 14 sites for tents or RVs (no hookups), 20 sites with partial hookups for RVs up to 45 feet long, and one group site for up to 72 people. Picnic tables and fire grills are provided. Restrooms with flush toilets and coin showers, a picnic area, and a dump station are available. A store, café, and ice are located within two miles. Boat docks and launching facilities are nearby on both the upper and lower portions of the reservoir. Interpretive programs are available in summer. Some facilities are wheelchair accessible. Leashed pets are permitted.

Reservations, fees: Reservations are not accepted for individual sites but are required for group site at 509/686-7231 ($25 reservation fee). Sites are $19–27 per night, $10 per night per additional vehicle. Group sites are $2.25 per person per night with a minimum of 20 people. Open mid-March–October.

Directions: From East Wenatchee, drive north on U.S. 97 for 71 miles to Highway 17. Turn south on Highway 17 and drive eight miles southeast to the park entrance on the left.

Contact: Bridgeport State Park, 509/686-7231; state park information, 360/902-8844, www.parks.wa.gov.

36 BETH LAKE

Scenic rating: 7

on Beth Lake in Okanogan National Forest
Map grid B1

This campground is set between Beth Lake and Beaver Lake, both small, narrow lakes stocked with rainbow trout and brook trout. A 1.9-mile-long hiking trail (one-way) connects the two lakes. Other side trips in the area include Lost Lake, Bonaparte Lake, and several hiking trails, one of which leads up to the Mount Bonaparte Lookout. The elevation is 2,800 feet.

RV sites, facilities: There are 15 sites for tents or RVs up to 35 feet long, plus one multiple site. Picnic tables and fire rings are provided. Drinking water, vault toilets, and garbage bins are available. Boat-launching facilities are available

nearby. Some facilities are wheelchair accessible. Leashed pets are permitted.

Reservations, fees: Reservations are not accepted. Sites are $8 per night, $5 per night per additional vehicle. Open mid-May–mid-October, weather permitting.

Directions: From East Wenatchee, drive north on U.S. 97 for 120 miles to Tonasket and Highway 20. Turn east on Highway 20 and drive 20 miles to Bonaparte Lake Road (County Road 4953). Turn left (north) and drive six miles to Bonaparte Lake and Forest Road 32. Continue (north) on Forest Road 32 and drive six miles to County Road 9480. Turn left (northwest) and drive one mile to the campground on the left.

Contact: Okanogan and Wenatchee National Forests, Tonasket Ranger District, 509/486-2186, fax 509/486-5161, www.fs.fed.us.

37 BEAVER LAKE

Scenic rating: 7

on Beaver Lake in Okanogan National Forest
Map grid B1

This camp calls the southeastern shore of long, narrow Beaver Lake home. Situated at 2,700 feet elevation, it is one of several lakes in this area. Beth Lake is nearby and accessible with an hour-long hike. Both Beaver and Beth Lakes are stocked with trout. Fishing, swimming, hunting, and hiking are all possibilities here.

RV sites, facilities: There are nine single and two multiple sites for tents or RVs up to 21 feet long. Picnic tables are provided. Drinking water, vault toilets, and garbage bins are available. Boat-launching facilities are located within 100 yards of the campground. No boats with gas engines are permitted; electric motors are allowed. Leashed pets are permitted.

Reservations, fees: Reservations are not accepted. Sites are $8 per night, plus $5 per additional vehicle per night. Open mid-May–mid-October, weather permitting.

Directions: From East Wenatchee, drive north on U.S. 97 for 120 miles to Tonasket and Highway 20. Turn east on Highway 20 and drive 24

WASHINGTON

miles to Bonaparte Lake Road (County Road 4953). Turn left (north) and drive six miles to Bonaparte Lake and Forest Road 32. Continue (north) on Forest Road 32 and drive six miles to the campground on the left.

Contact: Okanogan and Wenatchee National Forests, Tonasket Ranger District, 509/486-2186, fax 509/486-5161, www.fs.fed.us.

38 PIERRE LAKE

Scenic rating: 8

on Pierre Lake in Colville National Forest

Map grid B1

At just 105 acres, Pierre Lake is a quiet jewel of a camp near the Canadian border and only a short drive from U.S. 395. It is popular and usually fills on summer weekends. The camp is set on the west shore of the lake where there is fishing for rainbow trout, cutthroat trout, brook trout, crappie, bass, and catfish. While there is no speed limit, the lake is too small for big, fast boats.

RV sites, facilities: There are 15 sites for tents or RVs up to 24 feet long. Picnic tables and fire grills are provided. Vault toilets are available. There is no drinking water, and garbage must be packed out. Boat docks and launching facilities are available on-site. A convenience store and ice are located within seven miles. Some facilities are wheelchair accessible. Leashed pets are permitted.

Reservations, fees: Reservations are not accepted. Sites are $6 per night. Open mid-April–mid-October, weather permitting.

Directions: From Spokane, drive north on U.S. 395 for 74 miles to Colville. Continue north on U.S. 395 for about 25 miles to Barstow and Pierre Lake Road (County Road 4013). Turn right (north) on Pierre Lake Road and drive nine miles to the campground on the west side of Pierre Lake.

Contact: Colville National Forest, Three Rivers Ranger District, 509/738-7700, fax 509/738-7780, www.fs.fed.us.

39 CURLEW LAKE STATE PARK

Scenic rating: 8

on Curlew Lake

Map grid B1   BEST (

Boredom is banned at this park, set on the eastern shore of Curlew Lake. The park covers 123 acres, and the lake is 5.5 miles long. Fishing is often good for trout and largemouth bass at the lake, and there are additional lakes and streams in the region. There is also beach access, swimming, waterskiing, and hiking, with two miles of hiking and biking trails in the park. The park is also used as a base for bicycle touring, with mountain biking available on a fairly steep trail that provides a view of the valley. There is an active osprey nest, and nearby recreation options include a nine-hole golf course. The park borders an airfield and is located in the heart of a historic gold-mining district.

RV sites, facilities: There are 25 sites with full or partial hookups (30 amps) for RVs up to 45 feet long, 57 developed tent sites, and two primitive tent sites. Picnic tables and fire rings are provided. Restrooms with flush toilets and coin showers, a dump station, drinking water, firewood, ice, and boat-launching and dock facilities are available. Boat fuel is available at the marina on the north side of the lake. Some facilities are wheelchair accessible. Leashed pets are permitted.

Reservations, fees: Reservations are not accepted. Sites are $12–26 per night, $10 per extra vehicle per night. Open April–October, weather permitting.

Directions: From Spokane on I-90, turn north on U.S. 395 and drive 87 miles to Kettle Falls and Highway 20. Turn west on Highway 20 and continue 34 miles to Highway 21 (two miles east of Republic). Turn right (north) and drive six miles to the park entrance on the left.

Contact: Curlew Lake State Park, 509/775-3592; state park information, 360/902-8844, fax 509/775-0822, www.parks.wa.gov.

40 TIFFANYS RESORT

Scenic rating: 7

on Curlew Lake

Map grid B1

Tiffanys Resort is located in a pretty, wooded setting along the western shore of Curlew Lake. This 6.5-mile-long lake is good for waterskiing. Fishing can be good for rainbow trout and largemouth bass. Most of the sites are fairly spacious. This is a smaller, more private alternative to Black Beach Resort.

RV sites, facilities: There are 15 sites for tents or RVs of any length (30 and 50 amp full hookups), four sites for tents or RVs up to 40 feet long (no hookups), and 19 cabins. Picnic tables are provided, and fire pits are available on request. Restrooms with flush toilets and showers, firewood, a convenience store, coin laundry, ice, a playground, and a swimming beach are available. Boat docks, launching facilities, and rentals are available. Leashed pets are permitted.

Reservations, fees: Reservations are accepted. Sites are $24–27 per night. Some credit cards are accepted. Open April–late October.

Directions: From Colville, drive west on Highway 20 for 36 miles into the town of Republic and Klondike Road. Turn right on Klondike Road and drive 10.2 miles (Klondike Road will turn into West Curlew Lake Road) to Tiffany Road. Turn right and drive 0.5 mile to the resort at the end of the road.

Contact: Tiffanys Resort, 509/775-3152, www.tiffanysresort.com.

41 BLACK BEACH RESORT

Scenic rating: 7

on Curlew Lake

Map grid B1

Here's another resort along Curlew Lake. This one is much larger than Tiffanys Resort, with beautiful waterfront sites and full facilities. Waterskiing, personal watercraft, swimming, and fishing are all options. Fossil digging near the town of Republic is also popular.

RV sites, facilities: There are 120 sites for tents or RVs of any length (20 and 30 amp full hookups), nine sites for tents or RVs of any length (no hookups), and 13 lodging units. Some sites are pull-through. Picnic tables are provided, and fire pits are available at some sites. Restrooms with flush toilets and coin showers, dump station, convenience store, coin laundry, ice, and a playground are available. Boat docks, launching facilities, and boat rentals are located at the resort. Leashed pets are permitted.

Reservations, fees: Reservations are accepted. RV sites are $24–28 per night, tent sites are $21 per night, $5 per pet per night. Some credit cards are accepted. Campground open April–October; two campsites and three cabins are available in winter.

Directions: From Colville, drive west on Highway 20 for approximately 36 miles to the town of Republic and Klondike Road. Turn right on Klondike Road (will become West Curlew Lake Road) and drive 7.5 miles to Black Beach Road. Turn right and drive 0.75 mile to the resort.

Contact: Black Beach Resort, tel./fax 509/775-3989, www.blackbeachresort.com.

42 NORTH GORGE

Scenic rating: 7

on Franklin Roosevelt Lake in
Lake Roosevelt National Recreation Area

Map grid B1

This is the first and northernmost of many campgrounds I discovered along the west shore of 130-mile-long Franklin Roosevelt Lake, which was formed by damming the Columbia River at Coulee. Recreation options include waterskiing and swimming, plus fishing for walleye, trout, bass, and sunfish. During the winter, the lake level lowers; for a unique trip, walk along the lake's barren edge. Note that this campground provides full facilities May 1–September 30, then limited facilities in the off-season. Lake Roosevelt National Recreation Area offers recreation options such as free ranger programs, guided canoe trips, historical tours, campfire talks, and guided hikes. Watch for bald eagles in winter. Side-trip options include visiting the Colville Tribal Museum and touring the Grand Coulee Dam Visitor Center.

RV sites, facilities: There are 12 sites for tents or RVs up to 26 feet long. Picnic tables and fire grills are provided. Drinking water, vault toilets, boat docks, and launching facilities are available. Note that if the lake level drops below an elevation of 1,272 feet, there is no drinking water. Some facilities are wheelchair accessible. Leashed pets are permitted.

Reservations, fees: Reservations are not accepted. Sites are $10 per night ($5 per night in off-season), $6 boat-launch fee (good for seven days). Open year-round, with limited winter access.

Directions: From Spokane on I-90, drive north on U.S. 395 for 84 miles to the town of Kettle Falls and Highway 25. Turn right (north) on Highway 25 and drive 20 miles to the campground entrance.

Contact: Lake Roosevelt National Recreation Area, 509/633-9441, fax 509/633-9332, www.nps.gov/laro.

43 DAVIS LAKE

Scenic rating: 8

on Davis Lake in Colville National Forest

Map grid B1

This tiny campground is set at 4,600 feet elevation at Little Davis Lake. It is a scenic spot, and the fishing for cutthroat trout is often good. Only small boats are permitted on the small, shallow lake, which covers just 17 acres. No gas motors are permitted, but the lake can be ideal for float tubes, canoes, and prams with electric motors or oars. A one-mile trail loops the lake.

RV sites, facilities: There are four sites for tents or RVs up to 16 feet long. Picnic tables and fire grills are provided. Vault toilets are available. There is no drinking water, and garbage must be packed out. A primitive boat ramp is available nearby. Leashed pets are permitted.

Reservations, fees: Reservations are not accepted. There is no fee for camping. Open mid-May–October, weather permitting.

Directions: From Spokane, drive north on U.S. 395 for 84 miles to Kettle Falls. Continue north on U.S. 395 for nine miles to Deadman Creek Road. Turn west on Deadman Creek Road and drive about three miles to County Road 465 (Jack Knife cutoff). Turn right and drive 2.5 miles. Bear right and drive about 0.5 mile to County Road 480. Turn left and drive about three miles to County Road 080. Turn right and drive about three miles to Davis Lake. Note: The access road is very rough; high-clearance vehicles are recommended.

Contact: Colville National Forest, Three Rivers Ranger District, 509/738-7700, fax 509/738-7780, www.fs.fed.us.

44 SNAG COVE

Scenic rating: 8

on Franklin Roosevelt Lake in Lake Roosevelt National Recreation Area

Map grid B1

Snag Cove has a setting similar to North Gorge campground. It is set amid ponderosa pines along the west shore of Franklin Roosevelt Lake. This small camp has just nine sites, but the nearby boat launch makes it a find.

RV sites, facilities: There are nine sites for tents or RVs up to 35 feet long. Picnic tables and fire grills are provided. Vault toilets are available. When the lake level drops (to elevation 1,265 feet), there is no drinking water. Boat-launching facilities and docks are nearby. Some facilities are wheelchair accessible. Leashed pets are permitted.

Reservations, fees: Reservations are not accepted. Sites are $5–10 per night, $6 boat-launch fee (good for seven days). Open year-round, weather permitting.

Directions: From Spokane, turn north on U.S. 395 and drive 84 miles to the town of Kettle Falls. Continue north on U.S. 395 (crossing the Columbia River) for seven miles to the Hedlund Bridge turnoff. Turn right, cross Hedlund Bridge, and drive 7.5 miles to the campground on the right.

Contact: Lake Roosevelt National Recreation Area, 509/633-9441, fax 509/633-9332, www. nps.gov/laro.

NORTH LAKE ROOSEVELT RESORT

Scenic rating: 7

on Franklin Roosevelt Lake
Map grid B1

This campground is set along the long, narrow Kettle River Arm of Franklin Roosevelt Lake. A country resort, it is usually quiet and peaceful. A highlight is easy access to the lake, with no steep walk like at so many other campgrounds. A one-mile loop nature trail is available along the lakeshore, where wild turkeys and deer are often spotted. It's close to marked bike trails, a full-service marina, and tennis courts. Riding stables are available 20 miles away, and a golf course is within 15 miles. Colville National Forest East Portal Interpretive Area, 10 miles away, is a good side trip. (Drive south to the junction of Highway 20 and continue southwest for about six miles.) Highlights include a nature trail and the Bangs Mountain auto tour, a five-mile drive that takes you through old-growth forest to Bangs Mountain Vista overlooking the Roosevelt Lake–Kettle Falls area.

RV sites, facilities: There are 31 sites for tents or RVs of any length (30 and 50 amp full hookups), two cabins, three rental trailers, and two motel rooms with kitchens. Some sites are pull-through. An overflow camping area is also available. Picnic tables and fire grills are provided. Restrooms with flush toilets and coin showers, drinking water, coin laundry, horseshoe pits, volleyball, modem hookups, a convenience store, and firewood are available. Lake swimming and fishing are on-site. Leashed pets are permitted. A restaurant is available within five miles.

Reservations, fees: Reservations are accepted. Sites are $15–25 per night. Weekly and monthly rates are available. Open year-round.

Directions: From Spokane, turn north on U.S.

395 and drive 84 miles to the town of Kettle Falls. Continue north on U.S. 395 for 6.5 miles (toward Canada) to Roosevelt Road. Turn right (east) and drive 300 yards to the resort on the right.

Contact: North Lake Roosevelt Resort, tel./fax 509/738-2593 or 800/597-4423.

KETTLE RIVER

Scenic rating: 7

on Franklin Roosevelt Lake in
Lake Roosevelt National Recreation Area

Map grid B1

Kettle River campground is set along the long, narrow Kettle River Arm of Franklin Roosevelt Lake; it features campsites amid ponderosa pines. The nearest boat launch is located at Napoleon Bridge.

RV sites, facilities: There are 13 sites for tents or RVs up to 40 feet long. Picnic tables and fire grills are provided. Vault toilets are available. When the lake level drops below an elevation of 1,272 feet, there is no drinking water. Boat docks are nearby. Some facilities are wheelchair accessible. Leashed pets are permitted.

Reservations, fees: Reservations are not accepted. Sites are $5–10 per night. Open year-round, weather permitting.

Directions: From Spokane, turn north on U.S. 395 and drive 84 miles to the town of Kettle Falls. Continue north on U.S. 395 (crossing the Columbia River) for seven miles to the campground on the right.

Contact: Lake Roosevelt National Recreation Area, 509/633-9441, fax 509/633-9332, www. nps.gov/laro.

KAMLOOPS ISLAND

Scenic rating: 10

on Franklin Roosevelt Lake in
Lake Roosevelt National Recreation Area

Map grid B1

This is one of the more primitive campgrounds located along Franklin Roosevelt Lake. Located at Kamloops Island, an optimum area for waterskiing and fishing, it features unbelievably beautiful views of water and mountains. It is located near the mouth of the Kettle River Arm of the lake. While the scenic beauty merits a 10, note that the nearest boat launch is way across the lake at Kettle Falls and that if the lake level drops below an elevation of 1,272 feet, there is no drinking water.

RV sites, facilities: There are 17 sites for tents or RVs to 40 feet long. Picnic tables and fire grills are provided. Vault toilets are available. When the lake level drops, there is no drinking water. Boat docks are nearby. Leashed pets are permitted.

Reservations, fees: Reservations are not accepted. Sites are $5–10 per night. Open year-round, weather permitting.

Directions: From Spokane, turn north on U.S. 395 and drive 84 miles to the town of Kettle Falls. Continue north on U.S. 395 (crossing the Columbia River) for seven miles to the Hedlund Bridge turnoff. Turn right, cross Hedlund Bridge, and drive to the campground on the left.

Contact: Lake Roosevelt National Recreation Area, 509/633-9441, fax 509/633-9332, www.nps.gov/laro.

48 EVANS

Scenic rating: 9

on Franklin Roosevelt Lake in
Lake Roosevelt National Recreation Area

Map grid B1

This campground is another in a series set along the shore of Franklin Roosevelt Lake. This one sits along the eastern shoreline, just south of the town of Evans. Fishing, swimming, and waterskiing are among the activities here. Lake Roosevelt National Recreation Area offers recreation options such as free ranger programs, guided canoe trips, historical tours, campfire talks, and guided hikes. Watch for bald eagles in winter. Side-trip options include visiting the Colville Tribal Museum and touring the Grand Coulee Dam Visitor Center.

RV sites, facilities: There are 43 sites for tents or RVs up to 55 feet long and one group site for tents or RVs up to 55 feet long for up to 25 people. Picnic tables and fire grills are provided. Drinking water and flush toilets are available. A boat dock, launch facilities, a dump station, amphitheater, playground, swimming beach, camp host, interpretive programs and a picnic area are available nearby. Some facilities are wheelchair accessible. Leashed pets are permitted.

Reservations, fees: Reservations are not accepted for individual sites but are required for the group site at 877/444-6777 or www.recreation.gov ($10 reservation fee). Sites are $5–10 per night, group site is $53 per night, $6 boat-launch fee (good for seven days). Open year-round, with limited facilities in the winter.

Directions: From Spokane on I-90, drive north on U.S. 395 for 84 miles to the town of Kettle Falls and Highway 25. Turn right (north) on Highway 25 and drive eight miles to the campground entrance on the left.

Contact: Lake Roosevelt National Recreation Area, 509/633-9441, fax 509/633-9332, www.nps.gov/laro.

49 MARCUS ISLAND

Scenic rating: 8

on Franklin Roosevelt Lake in
Lake Roosevelt National Recreation Area

Map grid B1

Located south of Evans camp on the eastern shore of Franklin Roosevelt Lake, this campground is quite similar to that camp. Waterskiing, fishing, and swimming are the primary recreation options. Lake Roosevelt National Recreation Area offers numerous recreation options, such as free programs conducted by rangers that include guided canoe trips, historical tours, campfire talks, and guided hikes. This lake is known as a prime location to view bald eagles, especially in winter. Side-trip options include visiting the Colville Tribal Museum in the town of Coulee Dam and touring the Grand Coulee Dam Visitor Center. Almost one mile long and twice as high as Niagara Falls, the dam is one of the largest concrete structures ever built; it is open for self-guided tours.

RV sites, facilities: There are 27 sites for tents or RVs up to 40 feet long. Picnic tables and fire grills are provided. Drinking water, vault toilets, and a picnic area are available. A boat launch and dock are available nearby. Note that if the lake level drops below an elevation of 1,265 feet, there is no drinking water. Leashed pets are permitted.

Reservations, fees: Reservations are not accepted. Sites are $5–10 per night, $6 boat-launch fee (good for seven days). Open year-round, weather permitting.

Directions: From Spokane on I-90, drive north on U.S. 395 for 84 miles to the town of Kettle Falls and Highway 25. Turn right (north) on Highway 25 and drive four miles to the campground entrance on the left.

Contact: Lake Roosevelt National Recreation Area, 509/633-9441, fax 509/633-9332, www.nps.gov/laro.

50 SWAN LAKE

Scenic rating: 8

on Swan Lake in Colville National Forest

Map grid B1

Scenic views greet visitors on the drive to Swan Lake and at the campground as well. The camp is set on the shore of Swan Lake, at an elevation of 3,700 feet. Swan Lake Trail, a beautiful hiking trail, circles the lake. Fishing for rainbow trout is an option. Swimming, boating (gas motors prohibited), mountain biking, and hiking are some of the possibilities here. This is a good out-of-the-way spot for RV cruisers seeking a rustic setting. It commonly fills on summer weekends.

RV sites, facilities: There are 25 sites for tents or RVs of any length, and a group site for up to 20 people. Picnic tables and fire grills are provided. Drinking water, vault toilets, and garbage bins are available. A picnic shelter with barbecue, a boat dock, and launching facilities

are available nearby. Gas motors are prohibited on the lake. Some facilities are wheelchair accessible. Leashed pets are permitted.

Reservations, fees: Reservations are not accepted. Sites are $10 per night, $2 per additional vehicle per night. Open May–November, weather permitting.

Directions: From Spokane on I-90, turn north on U.S. 395 and drive 87 miles to Highway 20. Turn west on Highway 20 and drive 36 miles to the town of Republic and Highway 21. Turn south on Highway 21 and drive seven miles to Forest Road 53 (Scatter Creek Road). Turn right (southwest) on Forest Road 53 and drive eight miles to the campground at the end of the road.

Contact: Colville National Forest, Republic Ranger District, 509/775-3305, fax 509/775-7401, www.fs.fed.us.

51 FERRY LAKE

Scenic rating: 7

on Ferry Lake in Colville National Forest

Map grid B1

Ferry Lake is one of three fishing lakes within a four-square-mile area; the others are Swan Lake and Long Lake. Swimming, boating (gas motors prohibited), mountain biking, and hiking are some of the possibilities here.

RV sites, facilities: There are nine sites for tents or RVs up to 20 feet long. Fire grills and picnic tables are provided. Vault toilets and garbage bins are available. No drinking water is available. Launching facilities are nearby. Leashed pets are permitted.

Reservations, fees: Reservations are not accepted. Sites are $6 per night, $2 per extra vehicle per night. Open May–October, weather permitting.

Directions: From Spokane on I-90, turn north on U.S. 395 and drive 87 miles to Highway 20. Turn west on Highway 20 and drive 36 miles to the town of Republic and Highway 21. Turn south on Highway 21 and drive seven miles to Forest Road 53 (Scatter Creek Road). Turn right (southwest) on Forest Road 53 and drive about seven miles to Forest Road 5330. Turn right (north) on Forest Road 5330 and drive one mile to Forest Road 100. Turn right and drive one mile to the campground on the left.

Contact: Colville National Forest, Republic Ranger District, 509/775-3305, fax 509/775-7401, www.fs.fed.us.

52 LONG LAKE

Scenic rating: 9

on Long Lake in Colville National Forest

Map grid B1

Long Lake is the third and smallest of the three lakes in this area; the others are Swan Lake and Ferry Lake. Expert anglers can have a quality experience here fly-fishing for cutthroat trout. No gas motors are allowed on the lake, and fishing is restricted (fly-fishing only), but it's ideal for a float tube or a pram. The lake is set adjacent to little Fish Lake, and a 0.5-mile trail runs between the two. The drive on Highway 21 south of Republic is particularly beautiful, with views of the Sanpoil River.

RV sites, facilities: There are 12 sites for tents or RVs up to 30 feet long. Picnic tables and fire grills are provided. Drinking water, vault toilets, and garbage bins are available. Primitive launching facilities are nearby. Leashed pets are permitted.

Reservations, fees: Reservations are not accepted. Sites are $8 per night, $2 per extra vehicle per night. Open May–October, weather permitting.

Directions: From Spokane on I-90, turn north on U.S. 395 and drive 87 miles to Highway 20. Turn west on Highway 20 and drive 36 miles to the town of Republic and Highway 21. Turn south on Highway 21 and drive seven miles to Forest Road 53 (Scatter Creek Road). Turn right (southwest) on Forest Road 53 and drive seven miles to Forest Road 400. Turn left (south) and drive 1.5 miles to the camp on the right.

Contact: Colville National Forest, Republic Ranger District, 509/775-3305, fax 509/775-7401, www.fs.fed.us.

53 TEN MILE

Scenic rating: 7

on the Sanpoil River in Colville National Forest

Map grid B1

This spot is secluded and primitive. Located about nine miles from Swan Lake, Ferry Lake, and Long Lake, this campground along the Sanpoil River is a good choice for a multi-day trip visiting each of the lakes. The Sanpoil River provides fishing for rainbow trout, and a hiking trail leads west from camp for about 2.5 miles.

RV sites, facilities: There are nine sites for tents or RVs up to 21 feet long. Picnic tables and fire rings are provided. Vault toilets and garbage bins are available. There is no drinking water. Leashed pets are permitted.

Reservations, fees: Reservations are not accepted. Sites are $6 per night, $2 per extra vehicle per night; fees are charged Memorial Day weekend–Labor Day weekend. Open mid-May–mid-October, weather permitting.

Directions: From Spokane on I-90, turn north on U.S. 395 and drive 87 miles to Highway 20. Turn west on Highway 20 and drive 36 miles to Republic and Highway 21. Turn south on Highway 21 and drive 10 miles to the campground entrance on the left.

Contact: Colville National Forest, Republic Ranger District, 509/775-3305, fax 509/775-7401, www.fs.fed.us.

54 SHERMAN PASS OVERLOOK

Scenic rating: 6

at Sherman Pass in Colville National Forest

Map grid B1

Sherman Pass Scenic Byway (Highway 20) runs through here, so the camp has some road noise. This roadside campground is located near Sherman Pass (5,575 feet elevation), one of the few high-elevation mountain passes open year-round in Washington. Several nearby trails provide access to various peaks and vistas in the area. One of the best is the Kettle Crest National Recreation Trail, with the trailhead located one mile from camp. This trail extends for 45 miles, generally running north to south, and provides spectacular views of the Cascades on clear days. No other campgrounds are in the immediate vicinity.

RV sites, facilities: There are nine sites for tents or RVs up to 24 feet long. Picnic tables and fire grills are provided. Vault toilets and garbage bins are available. There is no drinking water. Some facilities are wheelchair accessible. Leashed pets are permitted.

Reservations, fees: Reservations are not accepted. Sites are $6 per night. Open June–mid-September, weather permitting.

Directions: From Spokane on I-90, turn north on U.S. 395 and drive 87 miles to Highway 20. Turn west on Highway 20 and drive 19.5 miles to the campground on the right.

Contact: Colville National Forest, Three Rivers Ranger District, 509/738-7700, fax 509/738-7780, www.fs.fed.us.

55 CANYON CREEK

Scenic rating: 7

near the East Portal Historical Site in Colville National Forest

Map grid B1

This campground is located 0.4 mile from the highway, just far enough to keep it from road noise. It's a popular spot among campers looking for a layover, with the bonus of trout fishing in the nearby creek. Canyon Creek lies within hiking distance of the East Portal Historical Site. The camp is set in a pretty area not far from the Columbia River, which offers a myriad of recreation options. The Bangs Mountain Auto Tour, a scenic route with mountain vistas, is a good side trip.

RV sites, facilities: There are 12 sites for tents or RVs up to 30 feet long. Picnic tables and fire grills are provided. Vault toilets are available. There is no drinking water, and garbage must be packed out. Some facilities are wheelchair accessible. Leashed pets are permitted.

Reservations, fees: Reservations are not accepted. Sites are $6 per night. Open late April–early October, weather permitting.

Directions: From Spokane, drive north on U.S. 395 for 87 miles to Highway 20. Turn west on Highway 20 and drive 18 miles (crossing the Columbia River) to Forest Road 136. Turn left (south) and drive for 0.3 mile to the campground on the left.

Contact: Colville National Forest, Three Rivers, Ranger District, 509/738-7700, fax 509/738-7780, www.fs.fed.us.

56 KETTLE FALLS

Scenic rating: 8

on Franklin Roosevelt Lake in Lake Roosevelt National Recreation Area

Map grid B1

Kettle Falls campground is located along the eastern shore of Roosevelt Lake, about two miles south of the highway bridge near West Kettle Falls. The camp only fills occasionally. In the summer, rangers offer evening campfire programs. Waterskiing, swimming, and fishing are all options. Local side trips include St. Paul's Mission in Kettle Falls, which was built in 1846 and is one of the oldest churches in Washington.

RV sites, facilities: There are 76 sites for tents or RVs of any length and two group sites for tents or RVs up to 26 feet long that can accommodate up to 50 and 75 people respectively. Picnic tables and fire grills are provided. Restrooms with flush toilets and showers, drinking water, a dump station, firewood, a small marina (open June–August) with a store, and a playground are available. A store is located within one mile. Boat docks, fuel, and launching facilities are available. Some facilities are wheelchair accessible. Leashed pets are permitted.

Reservations, fees: Reservations are accepted

for individual sites and required for group sites at 877/444-6777 or www.recreation.gov ($10 reservation fee). Sites are $5–13 per night, $6 boat-launch fee (good for seven days). Some credit cards are accepted. Open year-round, with limited winter facilities.

Directions: From Spokane, drive north on U.S. 395 for 84 miles to the town of Kettle Falls. Continue on U.S. 395 for three miles to Kettle Park Road. Turn left and drive two miles to the campground on the right.

Contact: Lake Roosevelt National Recreation Area, 509/633-9441, fax 509/633-9332, www. nps.gov/laro.

57 HAAG COVE

Scenic rating: 8

on Franklin Roosevelt Lake in
Lake Roosevelt National Recreation Area

Map grid B1   BEST (

This campground is tucked away in a cove along the western shore of Franklin Roosevelt Lake (Columbia River), about two miles south of Highway 20. A good side trip is to the Sherman Creek Habitat Management Area, located just north of camp. It's rugged and steep, but a good place to see and photograph wildlife, including bald eagles, golden eagles, and 200 other species of birds, along with the occasional black bear, cougar, and moose. Note that no boat launch is available at this camp, but boat ramps are available at Kettle Falls and French Rock. Also note that no drinking water is available if the lake level drops below an elevation of 1,275 feet.

RV sites, facilities: There are 16 sites for tents or RVs up to 35 feet long. Picnic tables and fire grills are provided. Drinking water and vault toilets are available. Boat docks are available nearby. Some facilities are wheelchair accessible. Leashed pets are permitted.

Reservations, fees: Reservations are not accepted. Sites are $5–10 per night. Open year-round, weather permitting, with limited winter access.

Directions: From Spokane, drive north on U.S.

395 for 84 miles to the town of Kettle Falls and Highway 20. Continue on Highway 20 and drive 7.5 miles to Kettle Falls Road. Turn left (south) and drive two miles to the campground on the right.

Contact: Lake Roosevelt National Recreation Area, 509/633-9441, fax 509/633-9332, www. nps.gov/laro.

58 LAKE ELLEN & LAKE ELLEN WEST

Scenic rating: 7

on Lake Ellen in Colville National Forest

Map grid B1

This 82-acre lake is a favorite for power boating (with no speed limit) and fishing for rainbow trout, which are a good size and plentiful early in the season. There are two small camps available here. The boat launch is located at the west end of the lake. It is located about three miles west of the Columbia River and the Lake Roosevelt National Recreation Area.

RV sites, facilities: There are 11 sites at Lake Ellen and five sites at Lake Ellen West for tents or RVs up to 18 feet long. Picnic tables and fire grills are provided. Vault toilets and are available. There is no drinking water, and garbage must be packed out. Boat docks are available nearby. Some facilities are wheelchair accessible. Leashed pets are permitted.

Reservations, fees: Reservations are not accepted. Sites are $6 per night. Open mid-April–October, weather permitting.

Directions: From Spokane, drive north on U.S. 395 for 87 miles to Colville and Highway 20. Turn west on Highway 20 and drive 14 miles (crossing the Columbia River) to County Road 3. Turn left and drive south for 4.5 miles to County Road 412. Turn right on County Road 412 and drive five miles to the Lake Ellen Campground or continue another 0.7 mile to Lake Ellen West Campground.

Contact: Colville National Forest, Three Rivers Ranger District, 509/738-7700, fax 509/738-7780, www.fs.fed.us.

59 RAINBOW BEACH RESORT

Scenic rating: 8

on Twin Lakes Reservoir

Map grid B1

This quality resort is set along the shore of Twin Lakes Reservoir in the Colville Indian Reservation. Busy in summer, the camp fills up virtually every day in July and August. Nearby recreation options include hiking trails, marked bike trails, a full-service marina, and tennis courts.

RV sites, facilities: There are 11 sites with full hookups for RVs of any length, including five pull-through sites, seven tent sites, and 26 cabins. Picnic tables and fire pits are provided. Restrooms with flush toilets and coin showers, drinking water, propane gas, gasoline, a dump station, firewood, a recreation hall, a convenience store, coin laundry, ice, a roped swimming area, boat rentals, docks and launching facilities, a playground, volleyball, and horseshoe pits are available. Leashed pets are permitted.

Reservations, fees: Reservations are accepted. Sites are $17–22 per night, pets are $10 per entire stay. Some credit cards are accepted. Campsites are available April–October; cabins are available year-round.

Directions: From Spokane, drive north on U.S. 395 for 84 miles to the town of Kettle Falls and Highway 20. Turn east on Highway 20 and drive five miles to the turnoff for Inchelium Highway. Turn left (south) and drive about 20 miles to Inchelium and Bridge Creek-Twin Lakes County Road. Turn right (west) and drive two miles to Stranger Creek Road. Turn left and drive 0.25 mile to the resort on the right.

Contact: Rainbow Beach Resort, 509/722-5901, fax 509/722-7080.

60 GIFFORD

Scenic rating: 7

on Franklin Roosevelt Lake in
Lake Roosevelt National Recreation Area

Map grid B1

Fishing and waterskiing are two of the draws at this camp on the eastern shore of Franklin Roosevelt Lake (Columbia River). The nearby boat ramp is a big plus.

RV sites, facilities: There are 42 sites for tents or RVs up to 55 feet long and one group site for tents or RVs up to 20 feet long that can accommodate up to 50 people. Picnic tables and fire grills are provided. Drinking water and vault toilets are available. A camp host is on-site. Boat docks and launching facilities, a dump station, playground, ball field, and a picnic area are nearby. Some facilities are wheelchair accessible. Leashed pets are permitted.

Reservations, fees: Reservations are not accepted for individual sites but are required for the group site at 877/444-6777 or www.recreation.gov ($25 reservation fee). Sites are $5–10 per night, $6 boat-launch fee (good for seven days). Open year-round, with limited winter facilities.

Directions: From Spokane on I-90, drive west for four miles to U.S. 2. Turn west on U.S. 2 and drive 34 miles to Davenport and Highway 25. Turn right (north) on Highway 25 and drive 60 miles to the campground (located about three miles south of Gifford) on the left.

Contact: Lake Roosevelt National Recreation Area, 509/633-9441 or 509/738-2300, fax 509/633-9332, www.nps.gov/laro.

61 HUNTERS

Scenic rating: 8

on Franklin Roosevelt Lake in
Lake Roosevelt National Recreation Area

Map grid B1

This campground, on a shoreline point along Franklin Roosevelt Lake (Columbia River), offers good swimming, fishing, and waterskiing.

It is located on the east shore of the lake, adjacent to the mouth of Hunters Creek and near the town of Hunters. Note: No drinking water is available if the lake level drops below an elevation of 1,245 feet.

RV sites, facilities: There are 39 sites for tents or RVs up to 55 feet long and three group sites for tents or RVs up to 26 feet long that can accommodate up to 25 people each. Picnic tables and fire grills are provided. Drinking water, restrooms with flush toilets, vault toilets, a dump station, playground, and a picnic area are available. A camp host is on-site. A store and ice are available within one mile. Boat docks and launching facilities are nearby. Some facilities are wheelchair accessible. Leashed pets are permitted.

Reservations, fees: Reservations are not accepted for individual sites but are required for group sites at 877/444-6777 or www.recreation. gov ($10 reservation fee). Sites are $5–10 per night, $6 boat-launch fee (good for seven days), and the group site is $53 per night. Open year-round, with limited winter facilities. Call for group rates.

Directions: From Spokane on I-90, drive west for four miles to U.S. 2. Turn west on U.S. 2 and drive 34 miles to Davenport and Highway 25. Turn north on Highway 25 and drive 47 miles to Hunters and the campground access road on the left (west) side of the road (well marked). Turn left at the access road and drive two miles to the campground at the end of the road.

Contact: Lake Roosevelt National Recreation Area, 509/633-9441, fax 509/633-9332, www. nps.gov/laro.

62 SHEEP CREEK

Scenic rating: 8

near the Columbia River and the Canadian border
Map grid C1

This campground is in a forested area along Sheep Creek, about four miles from the Columbia River and close to the Canadian border.

Although a primitive camp, it has drinking water and is a "locals' spot" on the Fourth of July weekend. A wheelchair-accessible fishing platform and trail are available. Sheep Creek provides opportunities for trout fishing. Huckleberry picking is good in August.

Note: As of 2010, the Department of Natural Resource was considering decommissioning this campground; call ahead for status.

RV sites, facilities: There are 11 sites for tents or RVs up to 30 feet long. Picnic tables and fire grills are provided. Vault toilets, drinking water, and a group picnic shelter with barbecues are available. Garbage must be packed out. Restaurants and stores are located within five miles. Some facilities are wheelchair accessible. Leashed pets are permitted.

Reservations, fees: Reservations are not accepted. There is no fee for camping. Open mid-April–November, weather permitting.

Directions: From Spokane, drive north on U.S. 395 for 87 miles to Kettle Falls and Highway 25. Turn north on Highway 25 and drive 33 miles to Northport. Continue north on Highway 25 for 0.75 mile to Sheep Creek Road (across the Columbia River Bridge). Turn left on Sheep Creek Road and drive 4.3 miles (on a gravel road) to the campground entrance on the right.

Contact: Department of Natural Resources, Northeast Region, 509/684-7474, fax 509/684-7484, www.dnr.wa.gov.

63 BIG MEADOW LAKE

Scenic rating: 8

on Big Meadow Lake in Colville National Forest
Map grid C1

Big Meadow Lake is set at 3,400 feet elevation and has 71 surface acres. The camp, located in a scenic area, is quiet, remote, and relatively unknown, and the lake provides trout fishing. The U.S. Forest Service has built a wildlife-viewing platform, where osprey, ducks, geese, and occasionally even moose, elk, and cougars may be spotted.

RV sites, facilities: There are 16 sites for tents or RVs up to 32 feet long and a historic cabin nearby. Fire grills and picnic tables are provided. Vault toilets are available. There is no drinking water, and garbage must be packed out. A boat launch, restrooms, and a wheelchair-accessible nature trail and fishing pier are available nearby. Some facilities are wheelchair accessible. Leashed pets are permitted.

Reservations, fees: Reservations are not accepted. There is no fee for camping. Open May–November, weather permitting.

Directions: From Spokane, drive north on U.S. 395 for 87 miles to Colville and Highway 20. Turn east on Highway 20 and drive one mile to Colville-Aladdin Northpoint Road (County Road 9435). Turn north and drive 20 miles to Meadow Creek Road. Turn right (east) and drive six miles to the campground on the right. Note: The surface of the access road changes dramatically depending on the season.

Contact: Colville National Forest, Three Rivers Ranger District, Colville Office, 509/684-7000, fax 509/684-7780, www.fs.fed.us.

64 MILL POND

Scenic rating: 6

near Sullivan Lake in Colville National Forest

Map grid C1

Mill Pond campground, located along the shore of a small reservoir just north of Sullivan Lake, offers a good base camp for backpackers. Note that boat size is limited to crafts that can be carried and hand launched; about a 50-foot walk from the parking area to the lake is necessary. A 1.5-mile hiking trail (no bikes) circles Mill Pond and ties into a historical and wheelchair-accessible interpretive trail (located at the opposite end of the lake). For more ambitious hikes, nearby Hall Mountain Trail and Elk Creek Trail provide beautiful valley and mountain views. Nearby Sullivan Lake is well known for giant, but elusive, brown trout; it produced the state record. There are also rainbow trout in the lake.

RV sites, facilities: There are 10 sites for tents or RVs up to 25 feet long. Picnic tables and fire grills are provided. Drinking water and vault toilets are available. Boats can be hand launched after a 50-foot walk; no gas motors are permitted. Supplies are available in Metaline Falls. Some facilities are wheelchair accessible. Leashed pets are permitted.

Reservations, fees: Reservations are not accepted. Sites are $14 per night, $7 per night extra vehicle fee. Open late May–early September, weather permitting.

Directions: From Spokane, drive north on U.S. 395 for six miles to U.S. 2. Turn northeast on U.S. 2 and drive 30 miles to the Metaline turn-off and Highway 211 North. Turn northwest on Highway 211 and drive 15 miles to Usk and Highway 20. Turn left (northwest) and drive 31 miles to Tiger and Highway 31. Continue (north) on Highway 31 and drive three miles to the sign marking the Sullivan Lake Ranger Station. Turn right on Sullivan Lake Road/County Road 9345 and drive a short distance, cross the bridge over the Pend Oreille River, and continue 13 miles to the campground on the left.

Contact: Colville National Forest, Sullivan Lake Ranger District, 509/446-7500, fax 509/446-7580, www.fs.fed.us.

65 EAST SULLIVAN

Scenic rating: 7

on Sullivan Lake in Colville National Forest

Map grid C1

East Sullivan campground is the largest on Sullivan Lake and by far the most popular. It fills up in summer. The camp is located on the lake's north shore. Some come here to try to catch giant brown trout or smaller, more plentiful rainbow trout. The boating and hiking are also good. The beautiful Salmo-Priest Wilderness is located just three miles to the east. It gets light use, which means quiet, private trails. This is a prime place to view wildlife, so carry binoculars while hiking for a chance to spot the rare woodland caribou and Rocky Mountain bighorn sheep. A nearby grass airstrip provides an opportunity for fly-in camping, but pilots should note that there are chuck holes present and holes from lots of ground squirrels. Only planes suited for primitive landing conditions should be flown in; check FAA guide to airports.

RV sites, facilities: There are 38 sites, including some pull-through sites, for tents or RVs up to 55 feet long and one group site for up to 40 people. Picnic tables and fire grills are provided. Drinking water and vault toilets are available. A boat dock, launching facilities, a picnic area, swimming area and floating platform, camp host, and dump station are nearby. Some facilities are wheelchair accessible. Leashed pets are permitted.

Reservations, fees: Reservations are accepted for individual sites and are required for the group site at 877/444-6777 or www.recreation. gov ($10 reservation fee). (Note that the Forest Service names this campground East Sullivan, however, the website name is Sullivan Lake.) Sites are $14 per night, $7 per night extra vehicle fee, and the group site is $55 per night. Open mid- May–September, weather permitting.

Directions: From Spokane, drive north on U.S. 395 for six miles to U.S. 2. Turn northeast on U.S. 2 and drive 30 miles to the Metaline turnoff and Highway 211 North. Turn northwest on Highway 211 and drive 15 miles to Usk and Highway 20. Turn left (northwest) and drive 31 miles to Tiger and Highway 31. Continue (north) on Highway 31 and drive three miles to the sign marking the Sullivan Lake Ranger Station. Turn right on Sullivan Lake Road/ County Road 9345 and drive a short distance, cross the bridge over the Pend Oreille River, and continue 12 miles to the campground on the left.

Contact: Colville National Forest, Sullivan Lake Ranger District, 509/446-7500 or 801/226-3564, fax 509/446-7580, www.fs.fed.us.

66 WEST SULLIVAN

Scenic rating: 7

on Sullivan Lake in Colville National Forest

Map grid C1

If East Sullivan is full, this small campground set along the northwestern shore of Sullivan Lake can fit the bill. This is a popular destination for boating, fishing for trout, swimming, sailing, waterskiing, and hiking. Beautiful Salmo-Priest Wilderness, three miles to the east, provides quiet, private trails. Wildlife-viewing is prime here; carry binoculars to spot caribou and bighorn sheep.

RV sites, facilities: There are six sites for tents or RVs up to 30 feet long. Picnic tables and fire grills are provided. Drinking water and vault toilets, a picnic shelter, a developed swimming beach, and a floating swim platform are available. A camp host is on-site. A dump station is within one mile. Some facilities are wheelchair accessible. Leashed pets are permitted.

Reservations, fees: Reservations are accepted at 877/444-6777 or www.recreation.gov ($10 reservation fee). Sites are $12–14 per night, $6–7 per extra vehicle per night. Open mid-May–early September, weather permitting.

Directions: From Spokane, drive north on U.S. 395 for six miles to U.S. 2. Turn northeast on U.S. 2 and drive 30 miles to the Metaline turnoff and Highway 211 North. Turn northwest on Highway 211 and drive 15 miles to Usk and Highway 20. Turn left (northwest) and drive 31 miles to Tiger and Highway 31. Continue (north) on Highway 31 and drive three miles to the sign marking the Sullivan Lake Ranger Station. Turn right on Sullivan Lake Road/ County Road 9345 and drive a short distance, cross the bridge over the Pend Oreille River, and continue 12 miles to the campground on the left (set at the foot of Sullivan Lake, just across the road from the Sullivan Lake Ranger Station).

Contact: Colville National Forest, Sullivan Lake Ranger District, 509/446-7500, fax 509/446-7580, www.fs.fed.us.

67 EDGEWATER

Scenic rating: 6

on the Pend Oreille River in Colville National Forest

Map grid C1

Edgewater Camp is set on the shore of the Pend Oreille River about two miles downstream from the Box Canyon Dam. Although not far out of Ione, the camp has a primitive feel to it. Fishing for largemouth bass, rainbow trout, and brown trout is popular here, though suckers and squawfish present somewhat of a problem.

RV sites, facilities: There are 19 sites for tents or RVs up to 72 feet long. Picnic tables and fire grills are provided. Drinking water, vault toilets, garbage bins, and firewood are available. A boat launch and a picnic area are available nearby. Leashed pets are permitted.

Reservations, fees: Reservations are accepted at 877/444-6777 or www.recreation.gov ($10 reservation fee). Sites are $14 per night, $7 per extra vehicle per night. Open mid-May–early September, weather permitting.

Directions: From Spokane, drive north on U.S. 395 for six miles to U.S. 2. Turn northeast on U.S. 2 and drive 30 miles to the Metaline turn-off and Highway 211 North. Turn northwest on Highway 211 and drive 15 miles to Usk and Highway 20. Turn left (northwest) and drive 34 miles to Tiger and Highway 31. Continue on Highway 31 and drive 15 miles to the town of Metaline Falls (Highway 31 is known as Lehigh Avenue in town); continue 2.5 miles to Sullivan Lake Road (County Road 9345). Turn right (east) on Sullivan Lake Road and drive 0.25 mile to County Road 3669. Turn left (north) on County Road 3669 and drive two miles to the campground entrance road on the left. Turn left and drive 0.25 mile to the campground.

Contact: Colville National Forest, Sullivan Lake Ranger District, 509/446-7500, fax 509/446-7580, www.fs.fed.us.

68 NOISY CREEK & NOISY CREEK GROUP

Scenic rating: 7

on Sullivan Lake in Colville National Forest

Map grid C1

This campground is situated on the southeast end of Sullivan Lake, adjacent to where Noisy Creek pours into Sullivan Lake. Note that the lake level can be drawn down for irrigation, leaving this camp well above the lake. Noisy Creek Trail near camp heads east along Noisy Creek and then north up to Hall Mountain (elevation 6,323 feet), a distance of 5.3 miles; this is bighorn sheep country. The Lakeshore Trailhead is located at the nearby day-use area. Waterskiing is allowed on the 3.5-mile-long lake, and the boat ramp near the camp provides a good launch point.

RV sites, facilities: There are 20 sites for tents or RVs up to 45 feet long and one group camp for up to 50 people. If the group camp is not reserved, it is available as an overflow area. Picnic tables and fire grills are provided. Drinking water and flush toilets are available. A camp host is on-site. Boat-launching facilities and a picnic area are nearby. Some facilities are wheelchair accessible. Leashed pets are permitted.

Reservations, fees: Reservations are accepted for individual sites and required for the group camp at 877/444-6777 or www.recreation.gov ($10 reservation fee). Sites are $14 per night, $7 per night extra vehicle fee, and the group site is $55 per night. Open May–September, weather permitting.

Directions: From Spokane, drive north on U.S. 395 for six miles to U.S. 2. Turn northeast on U.S. 2 and drive 30 miles to the Metaline turn-off and Highway 211 North. Turn northwest on Highway 211 and drive 15 miles to Usk and Highway 20. Turn left (northwest) and drive 31 miles to Tiger and Highway 31. Continue (north) on Highway 31 and drive three miles to the sign marking the Sullivan Lake Ranger Station. Turn right on Sullivan Lake Road/County Road 9345 and drive a short distance, cross the bridge over the Pend Oreille River, and continue nine miles to the campground on the right (on the south end of Sullivan Lake).

Contact: Colville National Forest, Sullivan Lake Ranger District, 509/446-7500, fax 509/446-7580, www.fs.fed.us.

69 IONE RV PARK AND MOTEL

Scenic rating: 8

on the Pend Oreille River

Map grid C1

This camp is a good layover spot for campers with RVs or trailers who want to stay in town. The park sits on the shore of the Pend Oreille River, which offers fishing, swimming, several bike trails, and boating. The city park is adjacent to this property. In the winter, bighorn sheep may be spotted north of town.

RV sites, facilities: There are 19 sites for tents or RVs of any length (15, 20, and 30 amp full hookups), seven tent sites, and 11 motel rooms. Picnic tables are provided. Restrooms with flush toilets and showers, drinking water, dump station, pay phone, and coin laundry are available. A store, café, and ice are located within one mile. Boat docks, launching facilities, and a park with a playground are nearby. Leashed pets are permitted.

Reservations, fees: Reservations are accepted. RV sites are $18 per night and tents are $5 per night. Some credit cards are accepted. Open year-round.

Directions: From Spokane, drive north on U.S. 2 for 48 miles to the junction with Highway 211 at the Washington/Idaho border. Turn west on Highway 211 and drive 48 miles northwest to Tiger and Highway 31. Turn right (north) on Highway 31 and drive four miles to Ione. Cross a spillway (it looks like a bridge) on Highway 31 and continue a short distance to the park on the right.

Contact: Ione RV Park and Motel, 509/442-3213.

70 DOUGLAS FALLS

Scenic rating: 8

on Mill Creek

Map grid C1

This campground is just outside of Colville in a wooded area along Mill Creek. A 0.2-mile walk from the campground takes you to a beautiful overlook of Douglas Falls. Another unique highlight is a cabled free-span bridge. And best of all, this camp is free!

RV sites, facilities: There are 12 sites for tents or RVs up to 30 feet long. Picnic tables and fire grills are provided. Vault toilets, drinking water, and a group picnic shelter are available. Garbage must be packed out. A camp host is on-site. A baseball field is nearby. Some facilities are wheelchair accessible. Leashed pets are permitted.

Reservations, fees: Reservations are not accepted. There is no fee for camping. Open Memorial Day weekend–November, weather permitting.

Directions: From Spokane, drive north on U.S. 395 for 87 miles to Colville and Highway 20. Turn east on Highway 20 and drive 1.1 miles to Aladdin Road. Turn left (north) and drive two miles to Douglas Falls Road. Turn left and drive three miles to the campground on the left.

Contact: Department of Natural Resources, Northeast Region, 509/684-7474, fax 509/684-7484, www.dnr.wa.gov.

71 ROCKY LAKE

Scenic rating: 6

near Colville

Map grid C1

The campground is set on Rocky Lake, a shallow, weedy pond lined with a lot of rocks. This camp is good for overnight camping, but nearby Douglas Falls is better for a long-term stay. Fishing for rainbow trout is an option. If you backtrack about 10 miles on Rocky Lake Road, you'll see the entrance signs for the Little Pend Oreille Wildlife Refuge, a premium area for hiking, fishing, hunting, and wildlife photography.

RV sites, facilities: There are seven sites for tents or RVs up to 20 feet long. Picnic tables and fire grills are provided. Vault toilets, drinking water, and a boat launch are available. Garbage must be packed out. Some facilities are wheelchair accessible. Leashed pets are permitted.

Reservations, fees: Reservations are not accepted. There is no fee for camping. Open mid-April–September; at times, the camp is open only for day-use. Call ahead to confirm.

Directions: From Spokane, drive north on U.S. 395 for 87 miles to Colville and Highway 20. Turn east on Highway 20 and drive six miles to Artman-Gibson Road. Turn right on Artman-Gibson Road and drive 3.2 miles to a one-lane gravel road. Turn right on the gravel road (unnamed) and drive about 0.5 mile. Bear left and continue another two miles to the campground.

Contact: Department of Natural Resources, Northeast Region, 509/684-7474, fax 509/684-7484, www.dnr.wa.gov.

72 STARVATION LAKE

🎣 🛥 🐕 ♿ 🚐 ⛺

Scenic rating: 8

near Colville

Map grid C1

Starvation Lake is only 15 feet deep and has a weed problem, so it's OK for trout fishing but not for swimming. It is possible to drown here if you get your feet tangled in the weeds. Osprey and bald eagles frequent the area. It's advisable to obtain a detailed map of the area. The camp is used extensively by locals during the early fishing season (end of April–early June) but is not crowded thereafter, when the fishing becomes catch-and-release; check regulations. Boats must not exceed 16 feet.

RV sites, facilities: There are eight sites for tents or RVs up to 30 feet long. Some sites are pull-through. Picnic tables and fire grills are provided. Vault toilets, drinking water, primitive boat launch, and a fishing dock are available. A camp host is on-site. Garbage must

be packed out. Some facilities are wheelchair accessible. Leashed pets are permitted.

Reservations, fees: Reservations are not accepted. There is no fee for camping. Open mid-April–November, weather permitting.

Directions: From Spokane, drive north on U.S. 395 for 74 miles to Colville and Highway 20. Turn east on Highway 20 and drive 10.5 miles to a gravel road (sign says Starvation Lake). Turn right on the gravel road and drive 0.3 mile to the intersection. Turn left and drive 0.5 mile to the campground on the right.

Contact: Department of Natural Resources, Northeast Region, 509/684-7474, fax 509/684-7484, www.dnr.wa.gov.

73 LITTLE TWIN LAKES

🎣 🛥 🐕 🚐 ⛺

Scenic rating: 6

on Little Twin Lakes in Colville National Forest

Map grid C1

Sites at this pretty, wooded campground on the shore of Little Twin Lakes have lake views and are free. Fishing is best here for cutthroat trout. Nearby Lake Roosevelt National Recreation Area offers recreation options, and side-trip ideas include Colville Tribal Museum and Grand Coulee Dam Visitor Center.

RV sites, facilities: There are 20 sites for tents or RVs up to 16 feet long. Fire grills and picnic tables are provided. There is no drinking water. Vault toilets and firewood are available. Garbage must be packed out. Boat docks and launching facilities are located nearby. Leashed pets are permitted.

Reservations, fees: Reservations are not accepted. There is no fee for camping. Open May–early September, weather permitting.

Directions: From Spokane, drive north on U.S. 395 for 87 miles to Colville and Highway 20. Turn east on Highway 20 and drive 12.5 miles to County Road 4915. Turn left (northeast) and drive 1.5 miles to Forest Road 4939. Turn right (north) and drive 4.5 miles to the campground on the right.

Contact: Colville National Forest, Three Rivers

WASHINGTON

Ranger District, Colville Office, 509/684-7000, fax 509/684-7780, www.fs.fed.us.

74 FLODELLE CREEK

Scenic rating: 8

near Colville

Map grid C1

This campground is set where hiking, hunting, and fishing are quite good. It's advisable to obtain a detailed map of the area. Off-road vehicle trails are available at this camp and at nearby Sherry Creek camp, and they are often in use, so don't count on a particularly quiet camping experience. This spot can provide good fishing, best for brook trout. Wildlife includes black bears, moose, mosquitoes, and black gnats, the latter occasionally so prevalent that they are considered wildlife. Be prepared.

RV sites, facilities: There are eight sites for tents or RVs up to 30 feet long. Picnic tables and fire grills are provided. Vault toilets and drinking water are available. Garbage must be packed out. Some facilities are wheelchair accessible. Leashed pets are permitted.

Reservations, fees: Reservations are not accepted. There is no fee for camping. Open May–November, weather permitting.

Directions: From Spokane, drive north on U.S. 395 for 87 miles to Colville and Highway 20. Turn east on Highway 20 and drive 19.4 miles to an unnamed two-lane gravel road on the right. Turn right on that road and drive 0.25 mile to the campground entrance road on the left.

Contact: Department of Natural Resources, Northeast Region, 509/684-7474, fax 509/684-7484, www.dnr.wa.gov.

75 SHERRY CREEK

Scenic rating: 6

near Sherry Lake

Map grid C1

This old fire camp is set near the off-road vehicle (ORV) trail network of the Pend Oreille

Lake system. It is located on Sherry Creek, about three miles from Sherry Lake and is basically a fishing camp, with lots of brook trout and a few rainbow trout. It's advisable to obtain a detailed map of the area. Biking and hiking on the ORV trails is an option. The 78-mile network of ORV trails can be accessed from this campground. This area has good numbers of black bears and even some moose, and because it is set next to a wetland, there can be tons of mosquitoes in summer. Snowmobiling and cross-country skiing are popular in the winter.

RV sites, facilities: There are two sites for tents or RVs up to 30 feet long. Picnic tables and fire pits are provided. Vault toilets are available, but there is no drinking water. Garbage must be packed out. Leashed pets are permitted.

Reservations, fees: Reservations are not accepted. There is no fee for camping. Open May–November, weather permitting.

Directions: From Spokane, drive north on U.S. 395 for 74 miles to Colville and Highway 20. Turn east on Highway 20 and drive 23.8 miles to a gravel road. Turn right and drive approximately 0.5 mile to the campground.

Contact: Department of Natural Resources, Northeast Region, 509/684-7474, fax 509/684-7484, www.dnr.wa.gov.

76 LAKE GILLETTE

Scenic rating: 8

on Lake Gillette in Colville National Forest

Map grid C1

This pretty and popular camp is situated right on the shore of Lake Gillette. Like neighboring East Gillette Campground, it fills up quickly in the summer. The camp is popular with off-road vehicle (OHV) users, primarily motorcyclists. An OHV system can't be accessed directly from the campground, but is close. Note that OHV riding in and out of camp is prohibited. Fishing at Lake Gillette is best for cutthroat trout.

RV sites, facilities: There are 14 sites for tents or RVs up to 50 feet long. Fire grills and picnic tables are provided. Drinking water, vault toilets, garbage bins, firewood, and an amphitheater are available. A camp host is on-site. A store, ice, gas, and a café are located within one mile. Boat docks, launching facilities, and rentals are nearby. Some facilities are wheelchair accessible. Leashed pets are permitted.

Reservations, fees: Reservations are not accepted. Single sites are $14 per night, double sites are $28 per night, $6 per extra vehicle per night. Open mid-May–early September, weather permitting.

Directions: From Spokane, drive north on U.S. 395 for 74 miles to Colville and Highway 20. Turn east on Highway 20 and drive 20 miles to County Road 4987 (Lake Gillette Road). Turn right (east) on Lake Gillette Road and drive 0.5 mile to the campground on the left.

Contact: Colville National Forest, Three Rivers Ranger District, Colville Office, 509/684-7000, fax 509/684-7780, www.fs.fed.us.

77 GILLETTE

Scenic rating: 7

near Lake Gillette in Colville National Forest
Map grid C1

This beautiful and extremely popular campground, located just south of Beaver Lodge Resort and Lake Thomas, is near Lake Gillette, one in a chain of four lakes. There are a few hiking and biking trails in the area. In winter, downhill and cross-country skiing is available.

RV sites, facilities: There are 30 sites for tents or RVs up to 55 feet long. Picnic tables and fire grills are provided. Drinking water, vault toilets, restrooms with flush toilets, and garbage bins are available. A camp host is on-site. A store and ice are located within one mile. Boat docks, launching facilities, and rentals are nearby. Some facilities are wheelchair accessible. Leashed pets are permitted.

Reservations, fees: Reservations are not accepted. Sites are $14 per night, $6 per extra vehicle per night. Open late May–early September, weather permitting.

Directions: From Spokane, drive north on U.S. 395 for 74 miles to Colville and Highway 20. Turn east on Highway 20 and drive 20 miles to County Road 4987 (Lake Gillette Road). Turn right (east) on Lake Gillette Road and drive 0.5 mile to the campground on the right.

Contact: Colville National Forest, Three Rivers Ranger District, Colville Office, 509/684-7000, fax 509/684-7780, www.fs.fed.us.

78 BEAVER LODGE RESORT

Scenic rating: 9

on Lake Thomas
Map grid C1

This developed camp is set along the shore of Lake Gillette, one in a chain of four lakes. A highlight in this area: the numerous opportunities for off-road vehicles (OHVs) provided by a network of OHV trails. In addition, hiking trails and marked bike trails are close to the camp. In winter, downhill and cross-country skiing is available.

RV sites, facilities: There are 13 sites with full or partial hookups (30 amps) for tents or RVs up to 34 feet long, 24 sites for tents or RVs up to 40 feet (no hookups), and 10 cabins. Picnic tables and fire pits are provided. Restrooms with flush toilets and coin showers, drinking water, gasoline, propane gas, firewood, a convenience store, café, ice, boat rentals, and a playground are available. A dump station is located within one mile. Boat docks and launching facilities are nearby. Leashed pets are permitted.

Reservations, fees: Reservations are accepted. Sites are $20–30 per night, cabins are $55–75, $5 per extra vehicle per night. Some credit cards are accepted. Open year-round.

Directions: From Spokane, drive north on U.S. 395/Division Street for 74 miles to Colville and Highway 20. Turn east on Highway 20 and drive 25 miles to the resort on the right.

Contact: Beaver Lodge Resort, 509/684-5657, fax 509/685-9426, www.beaverlodgeresort.org.

79 LAKE THOMAS

Scenic rating: 6

on Lake Thomas in Colville National Forest
Map grid C1

This camp on the shore of Lake Thomas offers a less crowded alternative to the campgrounds at Lake Gillette. The lake provides fishing for cutthroat trout. Other nearby options include Lake Gillette and Beaver Lodge Resort, with trails, boating, and winter sports.

RV sites, facilities: There are 15 sites for tents or RVs up to 16 feet long. Picnic tables and fire grills are provided. Drinking water, vault toilets, and garbage bins are available. A camp host is on-site. Boat docks, launching facilities, and rentals are nearby. Some facilities are wheelchair accessible. Leashed pets are permitted.

Reservations, fees: Reservations are not accepted. Sites are $14 per night, $6 per extra vehicle per night. Open late May–early September, weather permitting.

Directions: From Spokane, drive north on U.S. 395 for 74 miles to Colville and Highway 20. Turn east on Highway 20 and drive 20 miles to County Road 4987 (Lake Gillette Road). Turn right (east) on Lake Gillette Road and drive one mile to the campground on the left.

Contact: Colville National Forest, Three Rivers Ranger District, Colville Office, 509/684-7000, fax 509/684-7780, www.fs.fed.us.

80 LAKE LEO

Scenic rating: 6

on Lake Leo in Colville National Forest
Map grid C1

Lake Leo is the northernmost and quietest camp on the chain of lakes in the immediate vicinity. This lake provides fishing for cutthroat trout. Frater and Nile Lakes, both fairly small, are located one mile north. In winter, a Nordic ski trail starts adjacent to the camp. Fishing and boating are two recreation options here.

RV sites, facilities: There are eight sites for tents or RVs up to 30 feet long. Picnic tables and fire grills are provided. Drinking water and vault toilets are available. A boat ramp and launching facilities are nearby. Some facilities are wheelchair accessible. Leashed pets are permitted.

Reservations, fees: Reservations are not accepted. Sites are $12 per night, $6 per extra vehicle per night. Open mid-April–September, with reduced services and fees after Labor Day weekend.

Directions: From Spokane on I-90, drive north on U.S. 395 for 74 miles to Colville and Highway 20. Turn east on Highway 20 and drive 23 miles to the campground entrance on the right.

Contact: Colville National Forest, Three Rivers Ranger District, Colville Office, 509/684-7000, fax 509/684-7780, www.fs.fed.us.

81 BLUESLIDE RESORT

Scenic rating: 7

on the Pend Oreille River
Map grid C1

This resort is situated along the western shore of the Pend Oreille River. It offers a headquarters for anglers and vacationers. Four or five bass tournaments are held each spring during May and June, and the river is stocked with both rainbow trout and bass. The resort offers full facilities for anglers, including tackle and a marina with the only boat gas for 53 miles. The park is lovely, with grassy, shaded sites, and is located along the waterfowl migratory path. Lots of groups camp here in the summer. Recreation options include bicycling nearby. The only other campground in the vicinity is The Outpost Resort.

RV sites, facilities: There are 49 sites with full or partial hookups (20, 30, and 50 amps), including four pull-through sites, for tents or RVs of any length, three tent sites, four motel units, and five cabins. Picnic tables and fire pits are provided. Restrooms with flush toilets and showers, drinking water, a dump station, a meeting hall, modem access, several sports fields, a convenience store, propane, coin laundry, ice, firewood, a playground, basketball, tetherball, volleyball, horseshoe pits, a seasonal heated swimming pool, boat docks, launching facilities, and boat fuel are available. Leashed pets are permitted.

Reservations, fees: Reservations are accepted. Sites are $24–45 per night. Some credit cards are accepted. Open year-round, but only cabins are available in the winter.

Directions: From Spokane, drive north on Division Street for six miles to U.S. 2. Turn north on U.S. 2 and drive 26 miles northeast to Highway 211. Turn left and drive 18 miles to Highway 20. Turn left and drive 22 miles to the park (located on the right at Milepost 400).

Contact: Blueslide Resort, 509/445-1327, fax 509/445-0202, www.blueslideresort.com.

82 THE OUTPOST RESORT

Scenic rating: 8

on the Pend Oreille River

Map grid C1

This comfortable campground in a pretty setting along the west shore of the Pend Oreille River has fairly spacious sites and views of snow-capped mountains. The tent sites are closer to the river than the RV sites. Winter sports, including snowmobiling, are available nearby. Blueslide Resort, the nearest alternative if this camp is full, is located about five miles north.

RV sites, facilities: There are 10 tent sites, 12 sites with full or partial hookups for tents or RVs of any length, four cabins, and a bunkhouse. Some sites are pull-through. Picnic tables are provided, and fire rings are available at some sites. Restrooms with flush toilets and coin showers, a dump station, convenience store, café, ice, drinking water, a swimming area, non-motorized boat rentals, boat docks, and launching facilities are available. Leashed pets are permitted.

Reservations, fees: Reservations are accepted. Sites are $10–20 per night, $5 per night per

extra vehicle or tent. Some credit cards are accepted. Open year-round, with limited winter facilities.

Directions: From Spokane, drive north on Division Street for six miles to U.S. 2. Turn north on U.S. 2 and drive 34 miles to Highway 211. Turn left and drive 18 miles to Highway 20. Turn left and drive 17 miles to the resort (located between Mileposts 405 and 406) on the right.

Contact: The Outpost Resort, 509/445-1531.

83 PANHANDLE

Scenic rating: 9

on the Pend Oreille River in Colville National Forest

Map grid C1

Among tall trees and with views of the river, this is a scenic spot to set up camp along the eastern shore of the Pend Oreille River. This camp makes a good base for a fishing or water-skiing trip. Fishing for largemouth and small-mouth bass is popular, with an annual bass tournament held every summer in the area. The campground is located in an area of mature trees directly across the river from the Outpost Resort. A network of hiking trails can be accessed by taking forest roads to the east.

RV sites, facilities: There are 13 sites for tents or RVs up to 33 feet long. Picnic tables and fire grills are provided. Drinking water, vault toilets, garbage bins (bear-proof), and firewood are available. A camp host is on-site. A small boat launch is nearby. Some facilities are wheelchair accessible. Leashed pets are permitted.

Reservations, fees: Reservations are accepted at 877/444-6777 or www.recreation.gov ($10 reservation fee). Sites are $14 per night, $7 per extra vehicle per night. Open late May–early September, weather permitting.

Directions: From Spokane, drive north on U.S. 395/Division Street for six miles to U.S. 2. Turn north on U.S. 2 and drive 30 miles to the Metaline turnoff and Highway 211 North. Take Highway 211 North and drive 15 miles to the junction of Highway 20. Cross Highway

20, driving through the town of Usk. Continue across the Pend Oreille River to Le Clerc Road. Turn left and drive 15 miles north on Le Clerc Road to the campground on the left.

Contact: Colville National Forest, Newport Ranger District, 509/447-7300, fax 509/447-7301, www.fs.fed.us; concessionaire, 509/445-0624.

84 BROWNS LAKE

Scenic rating: 8

on Browns Lake in Colville National Forest

Map grid C1

This campground is set along the shore of Browns Lake, with lakeside sites bordering old-growth hemlock and cedar. No motorized boats are permitted on the lake, and only fly-fishing is allowed, so it can be ideal for float tubes, canoes, and prams. A 1.25-mile hiking trail leaves the campground and ties into a wheelchair-accessible interpretive trail with beautiful views along the way. At the end of the trail sits a fishing-viewing platform in Browns Creek, which feeds into the lake. South Skookum Lake is about five miles away.

RV sites, facilities: There are 18 sites for tents or RVs up to 28 feet long. Picnic tables and fire grills are provided. Vault toilets are available. There is no drinking water. A primitive boat launch is available for small boats, such as canoes, rowboats, and inflatables. Some facilities are wheelchair accessible. Leashed pets are permitted.

Reservations, fees: Reservations are not accepted. Sites are $12 per night, $7 per extra vehicle per night. Open May–early September, weather permitting.

Directions: From Spokane, drive north on U.S. 395/Division Street for six miles to U.S. 2. Turn north on U.S. 2 and drive 30 miles to the Metaline turnoff and Highway 211 North. Turn northwest on Highway 211 and drive 15 miles to Usk and Highway 20. Drive north on Highway 20 a short distance to County Road 3389. Turn right (east) on Kings Lake-Boswell Road

(County Road 3389) and drive (over the Pend Oreille River) five miles to a fork with Forest Road 5030. Turn left and drive three miles to the campground at the end of the road.

Contact: Colville National Forest, Newport Ranger District, 509/447-7300, fax 509/447-7301, www.fs.fed.us.

85 SKOOKUM CREEK

Scenic rating: 5

near the Pend Oreille River

Map grid C1

Skookum Creek campground is set in a wooded area along Skookum Creek, about 1.5 miles from where it empties into the Pend Oreille River. It's a good canoeing spot, has drinking water, and gets little attention. And you can't beat the price of admission—free.

RV sites, facilities: There are 10 sites for tents or RVs up to 30 feet long. Picnic tables and fire grills are provided. Drinking water and vault toilets are available. Garbage must be packed out. A group picnic shelter with a barbecue is available nearby. Some facilities are wheelchair accessible. Leashed pets are permitted.

Reservations, fees: Reservations are not accepted. There is no fee for camping. Open mid-April–October, weather permitting.

Directions: From Spokane, drive north on U.S. 395 for six miles to U.S. 2. Turn north on U.S. 2 and drive 41 miles to Newport and Highway 20. Turn west on Highway 20 and drive 16 miles northwest to the town of Usk. Continue east across the bridge for 0.9 mile to Le Clerc Road. Turn right on Le Clerc Road and drive 2.2 miles to a one-lane gravel road. Turn left and drive a short distance to another gravel road. Turn left and drive 0.25 mile to the campground.

Contact: Department of Natural Resources, Northeast Region, 509/684-7474, fax 509/684-7484, www.dnr.wa.gov.

86 SOUTH SKOOKUM LAKE

Scenic rating: 7

on South Skookum Lake in Colville National Forest

Map grid C1

This camp is situated on the western shore of South Skookum Lake, at the foot of Kings Mountain (elevation 4,383 feet). This is a good fishing lake, stocked with cutthroat trout, and is popular with families. A 1.3-mile hiking trail circles the water. South Baldy Lookout is nearby.

RV sites, facilities: There are 25 sites for tents or RVs up to 30 feet long. Picnic tables and fire rings are provided. Drinking water and vault toilets are available. A camp host is on-site. A boat ramp for small boats and several docks, including a wheelchair-accessible fishing dock, are available nearby. Some facilities are wheelchair accessible. Leashed pets are permitted.

Reservations, fees: Reservations are not accepted. Sites are $14 per night, $7 per extra vehicle per night. Open late May–September, weather permitting.

Directions: From Spokane, drive north on U.S. 395/Division Street for six miles to U.S. 2. Turn north on U.S. 2 and drive 30 miles to the Metaline turnoff and Highway 211. Turn northwest on Highway 211 and drive 15 miles to Usk and Highway 20. Drive north on Highway 20 a short distance to Kings Lake-Boswell Road (County Road 3389). Turn right (east) on Kings Lake-Boswell Road and drive eight miles (over the Pend Oreille River) to the campground entrance road on the right. Turn right and drive 0.25 mile to the campground.

Contact: Colville National Forest, Newport Ranger District, 509/447-7300, fax 509/447-7301, www.fs.fed.us.

87 THE 49ER MOTEL & RV PARK

Scenic rating: 6

near Chewelah

Map grid C1

This region is the heart of mining country. The park has grassy sites and is located next to a motel in a mountainous setting. Nearby recreation options include a 27-hole golf course, hiking trails, and marked bike trails. This park is a good deal for RV cruisers—a rustic setting right in town. In winter, note that the 49 Degrees North Ski & Snowboard Park is located 12 miles to the east.

RV sites, facilities: There are 26 sites for tents or RVs up to 40 feet long (20 and 30 amp full hookups) and 13 motel rooms. Most sites are pull-through. Picnic tables are provided. Restrooms with flush toilets and showers, drinking water, a dump station, cable TV, a spa, recreation hall, and indoor heated swimming pool are available. Propane gas, gasoline, a store, café, ice, and coin laundry are within one mile. Leashed pets are permitted.

Reservations, fees: Reservations are accepted. RV sites are $20 per night, tent sites are $5 per person per night, and $5 per pet per night. Weekly and monthly rates available. Some credit cards are accepted. Open year-round.

Directions: From Spokane, drive north on U.S. 395 for 44 miles to Chewelah; the park is on the right (on U.S. 395 at the south edge of town, well marked).

Contact: The 49er Motel & RV Park, 509/935-8613 or 888/412-1994, fax 509/935-8705, www.49er-motel.com.

88 PIONEER PARK

Scenic rating: 8

on the Pend Oreille River in Colville National Forest

Map grid C1

Pioneer Park Campground is set along the shore of Box Canyon Reservoir on the Pend Oreille River near Newport. The launch and adjoining parking area are suitable for larger boats.

Waterskiing and water sports are popular here. There is a wheelchair-accessible interpretive trail with a boardwalk and beautiful views of the river. Signs along the way explain the history of the Kalispel tribe.

RV sites, facilities: There are 17 sites for tents or RVs up to 33 feet long. Picnic tables and fire rings are provided. Drinking water, vault toilets, garbage bins (bear-proof), firewood, and a sheltered picnic area are available. A camp host is on-site. Boat docks, launching facilities, and rentals are nearby. Some facilities are wheelchair accessible. Leashed pets are permitted.

Reservations, fees: Reservations are accepted at 877/444-6777 or www.recreation.gov ($10 reservation fee). Sites are $14 per night, $7 per extra vehicle per night. Open early May–early September, weather permitting.

Directions: From Spokane, drive north on U.S. 395 for six miles to U.S. 2. Turn north on U.S. 2 and drive 41 miles to Newport. Continue across the Pend Oreille River to Le Clerc Road (County Road 9305). Turn left on Le Clerc Road and drive two miles to the campground on the left.

Contact: Colville National Forest, Newport Ranger District, 509/447-7300, fax 509/447-7301, www.fs.fed.us.

89 WINONA BEACH RESORT

Scenic rating: 9

on Waitts Lake

Map grid C1

This beautiful and comfortable resort on the shore of Waitts Lake has spacious sites and friendly folks. The park fills up in July and August, and during this time cabins are available for rent (by the week, not the night). In the spring, fishing for brown trout and rainbow trout can be quite good. The trout head to deeper water in the summer, and bluegill and perch are easier to catch then. Waterskiing is also popular.

RV sites, facilities: There are 47 sites with full hookups (30 amps), including 20 lakeside sites,

and five sites with partial hookups (electricity and water) for tents or RVs up to 40 feet long, seven tent sites, and seven cabins. Picnic tables and fire rings are provided. Restrooms with flush toilets and coin showers, drinking water, a dump station, firewood, a snack bar, general store, playground, volleyball, horseshoe pits, basketball, a swimming beach, an antique store, and ice are available. Boat docks, launching facilities, and boat rentals are on-site. Leashed pets are permitted.

Reservations, fees: Reservations are accepted. RV sites are $25 per night, tent sites are $15 per night, $2 per extra vehicle per night, and $3 per pet per night. Some credit cards are accepted. Open April–September.

Directions: From Spokane, drive north on U.S. 395 for 42 miles to the Valley-Waitts Lake exit. Turn left (west) at that exit and drive one mile to Highway 231. Turn right (north) on Highway 231 and drive 1.5 to the town of Valley and Valley-Waitts Lake Road. Turn left and drive three miles to Winona Beach Road. Turn left and drive 0.25 mile to the resort at the end of the road.

Contact: Winona Beach Resort, 509/937-2231, fax 509/937-2215.

90 SILVER BEACH RESORT

Scenic rating: 6

on Waitts Lake

Map grid C1

Silver Beach Resort offers grassy sites on the shore of Waitts Lake, where fishing and waterskiing are popular. In the spring, fishing for brown trout and rainbow trout can be quite good.

RV sites, facilities: There are 53 sites for RVs up to 36 feet long (30 amp full hookups), including four pull-through sites, and seven cabins. Picnic tables are provided and fire pits can be rented. Restrooms with flush toilets and coin showers, drinking water, modem access, propane gas, a dump station, convenience store, restaurant, coin laundry, ice, a playground, boat docks, launching facilities, and boat rentals are available. Leashed pets are permitted.

Reservations, fees: Reservations are accepted. Sites are $32 per night, $2 per person per night for more than two people, and $2.50 per pet per night. Cabins are $107–120 per night. Some credit cards are accepted. Open mid-April–mid-September.

Directions: From Spokane, drive north on U.S. 395 for 42 miles to the Valley-Waitts Lake exit. Turn left (west) at that exit and drive six miles to Waitts Lake and the resort on the left-hand side near the shore of the lake.

Contact: Silver Beach Resort, 509/937-2811 or 800/937-2816, fax 509/937-2816, www. silverbeachresort.net.

91 TEALS WAITTS LAKE RESORT

Scenic rating: 7

on Waitts Lake
Map grid C1

The shore of Waitts Lake is home to this clean, comfortable resort, where lake views are available and ice fishing is popular in the winter. Hunting is possible in the fall. Waterskiing is also popular.

RV sites, facilities: There are 21 sites for tents or RVs up to 40 feet long (30 amp full hookups). Picnic tables and fire rings are provided. Restrooms with flush toilets and showers, drinking water, a camp store, restaurant, firewood, boat docks, boat rentals, launching facilities, and ice are available. Leashed pets are permitted.

Reservations, fees: Reservations are accepted. Sites are $25 per night, $5 per pet per night. Some credit cards are accepted. Open year-round.

Directions: From Spokane, drive north on U.S. 395 for 42 miles to the Valley-Waitts Lake exit. Turn left (west) at that exit and drive one mile to Highway 231. Turn right (north) on Highway 231 and drive 1.5 miles to the town of Valley and Valley-Waitts Lake Road. Turn left and drive three miles to the resort on the left.

Contact: Teals Waitts Lake Resort, 509/937-2400.

92 JUMP OFF JOE LAKE RESORT

Scenic rating: 7

on Jump Off Joe Lake
Map grid C1

Located on the edge of Jump Off Joe Lake, this wooded campground offers lake views and easy boating access. Recreational activities include boating, fishing, and swimming. Spokane and Grand Coulee Dam are both within a short drive and provide excellent side-trip options. Within 10 miles to the north are an 18-hole golf course and casino.

RV sites, facilities: There are 20 sites for tents, 20 sites for tents or RVs of any length (30 amp full hookups), and five cabins. Picnic tables and fire rings are provided. Restrooms with flush toilets and coin showers, drinking water, horseshoe pits, recreation field, a swimming beach, a convenience store, and a picnic area are available. The resort also rents boats and has a boat ramp and dock. Leashed pets are permitted.

Reservations, fees: Reservations are accepted. Sites are $23–25 per night, $2.50 per pet per night. Some credit cards are accepted. Open April–October.

Directions: From Spokane, drive north on U.S. 395 for about 40 miles (three miles south of the town of Valley) to the Jump Off Joe Road exit (Milepost 198). Take that exit, turn west, and drive 1.2 miles to the resort on the right.

Contact: Jump Off Joe Lake Resort, 509/937-2133.

93 SHORE ACRES RESORT

Scenic rating: 8

on Loon Lake
Map grid C1 BEST (

Located along the shore of Loon Lake at 2,400 feet elevation, this family-oriented campground has a long expanse of beach and offers an alternative to Granite Point Park across the lake. Some sites have lake views. Loon Lake is approximately four miles long, and waterskiing, wakeboarding, and personal watercraft are allowed. Fishing is best for mackinaw trout in spring (downriggers suggested) as well as kokanee salmon and rainbow trout. Warm weather brings perch, sunfish, and bass out of their hiding places.

RV sites, facilities: There are 30 sites for tents or RVs up to 40 feet long (full hookups) and 10 cabins. Picnic tables are provided. Restrooms with flush toilets and showers, drinking water, a dump station, cable TV, a general store, tackle, firewood, propane, marine fuel, ice, community fire pits, a playground, volleyball, a swimming area, boat docks, personal watercraft and boat rentals, moorage, and launching facilities are available. Leashed pets are permitted with certain restrictions.

Reservations, fees: Reservations are accepted. Sites are $35–40 per night, $5 per pet per night. Cabins are $115–140 per night. Some credit cards are accepted. Open mid-April–September.

Directions: From Spokane, drive north on U.S. 395 for 30 miles to Highway 292. Turn left (west) on Highway 292 and drive two miles to Shore Acres Road. Turn left and drive another two miles to the resort.

Contact: Shore Acres Resort, 509/233-2474 or 800/900-2474, www.shoreacresresort.com.

94 GRANITE POINT PARK

Scenic rating: 8

on Loon Lake

Map grid C1

This camp is located on the shore of Loon Lake, a clear, clean, spring-fed lake that covers 1,200 acres and features a sandy beach and swimming area. The RV park features grass sites—no concrete. In the spring, mackinaw trout range 4–30 pounds and can be taken by deepwater trolling (downriggers suggested). Easier to catch are kokanee salmon and rainbow trout in the 12- to 14-inch class. A sprinkling of perch, sunfish, and bass come out of their hiding places when the weather heats up. Waterskiing and windsurfing are popular in summer months, and personal watercraft are allowed.

RV sites, facilities: There are 80 sites with full hookups (30 amps) for RVs up to 40 feet long and 25 cottages with kitchens. Picnic tables are provided. Restrooms with flush toilets and showers, drinking water, a recreation hall, convenience store, café, coin laundry, ice, a playground, basketball and volleyball courts, horseshoe pits, three swimming areas with a 0.75-mile beach, two swimming docks, boat docks, boat rentals, and launching facilities are available. Propane gas is located within one mile.

Reservations, fees: Reservations are accepted. Sites are $33–35 per night, $4 per person per night for more than two people, $4 per night per additional vehicle. Open May–September.

Directions: From Spokane, drive north on U.S. 395/Division Street for 26 miles (eight miles past the town of Deer Park) to the park on the left.

Contact: Granite Point Park, 509/233-2100, www.granitepointpark.com.

95 LAKESHORE RV PARK AND MARINA

Scenic rating: 7

on Lake Chelan

Map grid A2

This municipal park and marina on Lake Chelan is a popular family camp, with fishing, swimming, boating, waterskiing, personal watercraft, and hiking among the available activities. City amenities are within walking distance. The camp fills up in the summer, including on weekdays in July and August. This RV park covers 22 acres, featuring a large marina and a 15-acre day-use area. An 18-hole championship golf course and putting green, lighted tennis courts, a water-slide park, and a visitors center are nearby. A casino is six miles west of Chelan. A trip worth taking, the ferry ride goes to several landings on the lake; the ferry terminal is 0.5 mile from the park.

RV sites, facilities: There are 165 sites for tents or RVs up to 40 feet long (30 and 50 amp full hookups). Some sites are pull-through. Picnic tables are provided. Restrooms with flush toilets and coin showers, Wi-Fi, cable TV, a dump station, a covered picnic area, swimming beaches, tennis courts, volleyball, and basketball are available. A store, café, coin laundry, playground, ice, and propane gas are available within one mile. Boat docks and launching facilities are on-site. Some facilities are wheelchair accessible. Leashed pets are permitted, except during some holiday periods.

Reservations, fees: Reservations are accepted at 509/628-8023 ($5 reservation fee). RV sites are $22–38 per night, $6 per night per additional vehicle; tent sites are $16–29 per night. Monthly rates available. Some credit cards are accepted. Open year-round.

Directions: From Wenatchee, drive north on U.S. 97-A for 38 miles to Chelan (after crossing the Dan Gordon Bridge, the road name changes to Saunders Street). Continue for 0.1 mile to Johnson Street. Turn left and drive 0.2 mile (becomes Highway 150/Manson Highway) to the campground on the left.

Contact: City of Chelan, Lakeshore RV Park and Marina, 509/682-8024, fax 509/682-8248, www.chelancityparks.com.

96 COULEE PLAYLAND RESORT

Scenic rating: 7

near the Grand Coulee Dam

Map grid A2

This park on North Banks Lake, south of the Grand Coulee Dam, is pretty and well treed, with spacious sites for both tents and RVs. The Grand Coulee Laser Light Show (seasonal) is just three miles away and is well worth a visit. Boating, fishing for many species, waterskiing, and personal watercraft are all popular. In addition, hiking trails, marked bike trails, a full-service marina, and tennis courts are close by.

RV sites, facilities: There are 65 sites with full or partial hookups (15 and 30 amps) for tents or RVs of any length, seven tent sites, and one yurt. Some sites are pull-through. Picnic tables and fire grills are provided. Restrooms with flush toilets and coin showers, a dump station, Wi-Fi and modem access, a general store, coin laundry, firewood, ice, a playground, boat docks, launching facilities, boat rentals, gas, and a bait and tackle shop are available. Propane gas and a café are located within one mile. Leashed pets are permitted.

Reservations, fees: Reservations are accepted. Sites are $30–36 per night, $15 per extra vehicle per night. The yurt is $95 per night. Some credit cards are accepted. Open year-round, with limited winter facilities.

Directions: From the junction of Highway 17 and U.S. 2 (north of Ephrata), drive east on U.S. 2 for five miles to Highway 155. Turn left (north) and drive 26 miles to Grand Coulee and Electric City. The resort is just off the highway on the left.

Contact: Coulee Playland Resort, 509/633-2671 or 888/633-2671, www.couleeplayland.com.

97 STEAMBOAT ROCK STATE PARK

Scenic rating: 10

on Banks Lake

Map grid A2

Steamboat Rock State Park is surrounded by desert. The park covers 3,522 acres and features nine miles of shoreline along Banks Lake, a reservoir created by the Grand Coulee Dam. A column of basaltic rock, with a surface area of 600 acres, rises 800 feet above the lake. Two campground areas and a large day-use area are set on green lawns sheltered by tall poplars. The park has 13 miles of hiking and biking trails, as well as 10 miles of horse trails. There is also a swimming beach. Fishing and waterskiing are popular; so is rock climbing. A hiking trail leads to Northrup Lake. Horse trails are also available in nearby Northrup Canyon. The one downer is mosquitoes, which are very prevalent in early summer. During the winter, the park is used by snowmobilers, cross-country skiers, and ice anglers.

RV sites, facilities: There are 100 sites with full hookups (50 amps) for RVs up to 50 feet long, 26 sites for tents or RVs up to 30 feet long (no hookups), 80 primitive sites (including five equestrian sites), 12 hike-in/boat-in sites, and a group site for 20–50 people. Picnic tables and fire grills are provided. Restrooms with flush toilets and coin showers, a dump station, firewood, a café, a playground, and volleyball are available. Boat-launching facilities, docks, moorage, and a marine dump station are nearby. Some facilities are wheelchair accessible. Leashed pets are permitted.

Reservations, fees: Reservations are accepted (except for primitive sites) at 888/CAMP-OUT (888/226-7688) or www.parks.wa.gov/reservations ($6.50–8.50 reservation fee). Sites are $17–26 per night, primitive sites are $12 per night, $10 per extra vehicle per night. Some credit cards are accepted. Open year-round, with limited winter facilities.

Directions: From East Wenatchee, drive north U.S. 2 for 70 miles to Highway 155 (five miles east of Coulee City). Turn north and drive 16 miles to the park on the left.

Contact: Steamboat Rock State Park, 509/633-1304, fax 509/633-1294; state park information, 360/902-8844, www.parks.wa.gov.

98 COULEE CITY PARK

Scenic rating: 6

on Banks Lake

Map grid A2

Coulee City Park is a well-maintained park located in shade trees on the southern shore of 30-mile-long Banks Lake. You can see the highway from the park, and there is some highway noise. Campsites are usually available. The busiest time of the year is Memorial Day weekend because of the local rodeo. Boating, fishing, waterskiing, and riding personal watercraft are popular. A one-mile walking trail leads from the campground and meanders along the eastern shore of the lake. An 18-hole golf course is close by.

RV sites, facilities: There is a large grassy area for tents and 55 sites for tents or RVs up to 35 feet long (30 and 50 amp full hookups). Some sites are pull-through. Picnic tables and fire rings are provided. Restrooms with flush toilets and showers, group fire pits, a dump station, and a playground are available. Propane gas, gasoline, firewood, a store, restaurant, coin laundry, and ice are located within one mile. Boat docks and launching facilities are on-site. Some facilities are wheelchair accessible. Leashed pets are permitted.

Reservations, fees: Reservations are not accepted. Sites are $15–20 per night, $2 per extra vehicle per night. Open April–late October, weather permitting.

Directions: From Coulee City, drive east on U.S. 2 for 0.5 mile to the park on the left. The park is within the city limits.

Contact: Coulee City Park, 509/632-5331, www.couleecity.com.

99 SUN LAKES STATE PARK

Scenic rating: 10

on Park Lake

Map grid A2

Sun Lakes State Park is situated on the shore of Park Lake, which is used primarily by anglers, boaters, and water-skiers. This 4,027-acre park features 12 miles of shoreline and nine lakes. A trail at the north end of Lake Lenore (a 15-minute car drive) leads to the Lake Lenore Caves. Dry Falls, a former waterfall, lies near the foot of the park. The cascades are history, however, and now only a barren 3.5-mile-wide, 400-foot climb awaits. An interpretive center at Dry Falls is open May–September. Nearby recreation possibilities include a nine-hole golf course and miniature golf.

RV sites, facilities: There are 152 sites for tents or RVs (no hookups), 39 sites for RVs up to 65 feet long (30 and 50 amp full hookups), and one group camp for up to 75 people. Picnic tables and fire pits are provided. Restrooms with flush toilets and coin showers, a dump station, snack bar, coin laundry, ice, horseshoe pits, playground, drinking water, and firewood are available. A store is located within one mile. Boat docks, launching facilities, moorage, and boat rentals are nearby. Some facilities are wheelchair accessible. Leashed pets are permitted.

Reservations, fees: Reservations are accepted at 888/CAMP-OUT (888/226-7688) or www.parks.wa.gov/reservations ($6.50–8.50 reservation fee). Sites are $17–26 per night. Call for the group rate. Some credit cards are accepted. Open year-round.

Directions: From Ephrata, drive northeast on Highway 28 to Soap Lake and Highway 17. Turn left (north) on Highway 17 and drive 17 miles to the park on the right.

Contact: Sun Lakes State Park, 509/632-5583, fax 509/632-5971; state park information, 360/902-8844, www.parks.wa.gov.

100 SUN LAKES PARK RESORT

🚶 🚴 🏊 🎣 🛶 🐕 🧗 ♿ 🚐 ⛺

Scenic rating: 6

Sun Lakes State Park

Map grid A2

Run by the concessionaire that operates within Sun Lakes State Park, this camp offers full facilities and is a slightly more developed alternative to the state park's campground.

RV sites, facilities: There are 119 sites for tents or RVs of any length (20, 30, and 50 amp full hookups) and 61 cabins. Some sites are pull-through. Picnic tables and fire grills are provided. Restrooms with flush toilets and coin showers, propane gas, dump station, convenience store, firewood, snack bar, coin laundry, ice, a playground, boat rentals, a seasonal heated swimming pool, miniature golf, and a nine-hole golf course are available. Boat docks and launching facilities are nearby. Some facilities are wheelchair accessible. Leashed pets are permitted.

Reservations, fees: Reservations are accepted. Sites are $23–36 per night, $5 per extra ve-

hicle per night. Open mid-April–mid-October, weather permitting.

Directions: From Ephrata, drive northeast on Highway 28 to Soap Lake and Highway 17. Turn left (north) on Highway 17 and drive 17 miles to the Sun Lakes Park on the right. Enter the park and drive to the resort (well marked).

Contact: Sun Lakes Park Resort, 509/632-5291, www.sunlakesparkresort.com.

101 BLUE LAKE RESORT

🚴 🏊 🛶 🚐 🐕 🧗 🚐 ⛺

Scenic rating: 6

on Blue Lake

Map grid A2

Blue Lake Resort is set in a desert-like area along the shore of Blue Lake between Sun Lakes State Park and Lake Lenore Caves State Park. Both parks make excellent side trips. Activities at Blue Lake include trout fishing, swimming, boating, waterskiing, and riding personal watercraft. Tackle and boat rentals are available at the resort.

RV sites, facilities: There are 80 sites with full or partial hookups, including six pull-through sites, for RVs of any length, 30 tent sites, and 10 cabins. Picnic tables and fire pits are provided. Restrooms with flush toilets and showers, a dump station, firewood, a store, ice, tackle, RV and boat storage, a roped swimming area, volleyball, a playground, horseshoe pits, badminton, a marina, boat docks, launching facilities, and boat rentals are available. Leashed pets are permitted.

Reservations, fees: Reservations are accepted. Sites are $20 per night, plus $5 per person per night for more than four people. Some credit cards are accepted. Open April–September.

Directions: From the junction of I-90 and Highway 17 (just south of Moses Lake), drive north on Highway 17 for 36 miles to the resort on the right. The resort is 15 miles south of Coulee City.

Contact: Blue Lake Resort, 509/632-5364 or 509/632-5388, www.bluelakeresortwashington.com.

WASHINGTON

102 LAURENT'S SUN VILLAGE RESORT

Scenic rating: 6

on Blue Lake

Map grid A2

Like Blue Lake Resort, this campground is situated along the shore of Blue Lake. The hot desert setting is perfect for swimming and fishing. Late July and early August are the busiest times of the year here. Nearby recreation possibilities include a nine-hole golf course and miniature golf.

RV sites, facilities: There are 95 sites, most with full hookups, for RVs of any length and four tent sites. Some sites are pull-through. Picnic tables are provided. Restrooms with flush toilets and coin showers, group fire pits, propane gas, dump station, coin laundry, a store, café, bait and tackle, ice, firewood, a playground, boat docks, launching facilities, and boat rentals are available. Leashed pets are permitted.

Reservations, fees: Reservations are accepted. Sites are $28 per night, $3 per person per night for more than four people, $4 per night for each additional vehicle. Some credit cards are accepted. Open late April–late September.

Directions: From the junction of I-90 and Highway 17 (just south of Moses Lake), drive north on Highway 17 for 36 miles to Blue Lake and Park Lake Road. Turn right (east) on Park Lake Road (the south entrance) and drive 0.5 mile to the resort on the right.

Contact: Laurent's Sun Village Resort, 509/632-5664, 509/632-5360, or 888/632-5664, www.laurentsresort.com.

103 COULEE LODGE RESORT

Scenic rating: 8

on Blue Lake

Map grid A2

This camp is set at Blue Lake, which often provides outstanding fishing for a mix of stocked rainbow trout and brown trout in early spring.

Blue Lake offers plenty of summertime recreation options, including a swimming beach. Nearby recreation possibilities include a nine-hole golf course and miniature golf.

RV sites, facilities: There are 18 sites for tents or RVs up to 35 feet long (30 amp full hookups) and 14 tent sites. Some sites are pull-through. Picnic tables and fire pits are provided. Restrooms with flush toilets and coin showers, propane gas, dump station, convenience store, firewood, coin laundry, boat docks, boat and personal watercraft rentals, launching facilities, and ice are available. A café is located within five miles. Leashed pets are permitted.

Reservations, fees: Reservations are accepted. Sites are $20–22 per night, $3 per extra vehicle per night, and $2 per pet per night. Some credit cards are accepted. Open mid-April–September.

Directions: From the junction of I-90 and Highway 17 (just south of Moses Lake), drive north on Highway 17 for 39 miles to the north end of Blue Lake.

Contact: Coulee Lodge Resort, 509/632-5565, fax 509/632-8607, www.couleelodgeresort.com.

104 SPRING CANYON

Scenic rating: 6

on Franklin Roosevelt Lake in Lake Roosevelt National Recreation Area

Map grid B2

This large, developed campground is a popular vacation destination. Fishing for bass, walleye, trout, and sunfish is popular at Franklin Roosevelt Lake, as is waterskiing. The campground is not far from Grand Coulee Dam. Lake Roosevelt National Recreation Area offers numerous activity options, such as free programs conducted by rangers that include guided canoe trips, historical tours, campfire talks, and guided hikes. This lake is known as a prime location to view bald eagles, especially in winter. Side-trip options include visiting the Colville Tribal Museum in the town of Coulee

Dam and touring the Grand Coulee Dam Visitor Center. Almost one mile long and twice as high as Niagara Falls, the dam is one of the largest concrete structures ever built. It is open for self-guided tours.

RV sites, facilities: There are 78 sites for tents or RVs up to 26 feet long and one group site for tents or RVs up to 26 feet long for up to 25 people. Picnic tables and fire grills are provided. Drinking water, restrooms with flush toilets, a dump station, picnic area, pay telephone, playground, amphitheater, and visitors center are available. A camp host is on-site. Boat docks, launching facilities, marine fuel, marine dump station, and fish-cleaning station are nearby. Some facilities are wheelchair accessible. Leashed pets are permitted.

Reservations, fees: Reservations are accepted for family sites and required for the group site sites at 877/444-6777 or www.recreation.gov ($10 reservation fee). Sites are $5–13 per night, $6 boat-launch fee (good for seven days), and the group site is $53 per night. Open year-round, weather permitting.

Directions: From the junction of I-90 and Highway 17 (just south of Moses Lake), drive north on Highway 17 for 45 miles to U.S. 2. Turn east on U.S. 2 and drive five miles to Highway 155. Turn left (north) and drive 26 miles to Grand Coulee and Highway 174. Turn right (east) on Highway 174 and drive three miles to the campground entrance on the left.

Contact: Lake Roosevelt National Recreation Area, 509/633-9441, fax 509/633-5125, www.nps.gov/laro.

105 LAKEVIEW TERRACE MOBILE AND RV PARK

Scenic rating: 6

near Franklin Roosevelt Lake

Map grid B2

This pleasant resort is situated near Franklin Roosevelt Lake, which was created by Grand Coulee Dam. It provides a slightly less crowded alternative to the national park camps in the vicinity. A mobile home park is also on the property. Nearby Spring Canyon offers a full-service marina and various recreation options on the water.

RV sites, facilities: There are 20 pull-through sites with full hookups (30 and 50 amps) for RVs of any length, 20 tent sites, and a group camp for up to 100 tents. Picnic tables are provided. Restrooms with flush toilets and coin showers, coin laundry, and a playground are available. Boat docks, launching facilities, and rentals are nearby. Leashed pets are permitted.

Reservations, fees: Reservations are accepted. Sites are $20–25 per night. The group site is $13 per tent. Credit cards are not accepted. Open year-round.

Directions: From Grand Coulee, drive east on Highway 174 for 3.5 miles to the park entrance on the left.

Contact: Lakeview Terrace Mobile and RV Park, 509/633-2169.

106 KELLER FERRY

Scenic rating: 7

on Franklin Roosevelt Lake in
Lake Roosevelt National Recreation Area

Map grid B2

This camp is set along the shore of Franklin Roosevelt Lake, a large reservoir created by Grand Coulee Dam, which sits about 15 miles west of camp. Franklin Roosevelt Lake is known for its walleye fishing; although more than 30 species live in this lake, 90 percent of the fish caught are walleye. They average 1–4 pounds and always travel in schools. Trout and salmon often swim below the bluffs near Keller Ferry. Waterskiing, fishing, and swimming are all recreation options here.

RV sites, facilities: There are 55 sites for tents or RVs up to 25 feet long and two group sites for tents or RVs up to 16 feet long for up to 50 people each. Picnic tables and fire grills are provided. Drinking water and restrooms with flush toilets are available. A dump station, ice, a picnic area, a pay telephone, and a playground are available nearby. Boat docks, launching facilities, fuel, and a marine dump station are also nearby. Some facilities are wheelchair accessible. Leashed pets are permitted.

Reservations, fees: Reservations are accepted for individual sites and required for group sites at 877/444-6777 or www.recreation.gov ($10 reservation fee). Sites are $5–13 per night, $6 boat-launch fee (good for seven days), and the group site is $53 per night. Open year-round, weather permitting.

Directions: From Spokane on U.S. 90, turn west on U.S. 2 and drive 71 miles to Wilbur and Highway 21. Turn north and drive 14 miles to the campground on the left.

Contact: Lake Roosevelt National Recreation Area, 509/633-9441, fax 509/633-9332, www.nps.gov/laro.

107 RIVER RUE RV PARK

Scenic rating: 7

near the Columbia River

Map grid B2

This camp is located in high desert terrain yet is surrounded by lots of trees. You can fish, swim, water ski, or rent a houseboat at Lake Roosevelt, one mile away. Personal watercraft are allowed. Another nearby side trip is to the Grand Coulee Dam. A nine-hole golf course is available in Wilbur.

RV sites, facilities: There are 48 sites with full or partial hookups (20 and 30 amps) for tents or RVs of any length and 29 sites for tents or RVs of any length (no hookups). Some sites are pull-through. Picnic tables and fire rings are provided. Restrooms with flush toilets and showers, a dump station, a pay phone, limited groceries, ice, a snack bar, RV supplies, fishing tackle, and propane gas are available. Recreational facilities include a playground, volleyball, and horseshoe pits. Some facilities are wheelchair accessible. Leashed pets are permitted.

Reservations, fees: Reservations are accepted. Sites are $27.50 per night, plus $3 per person

per night for more than two people. Some credit cards are accepted. Open April–October.

Directions: On U.S. 2 at Wilbur, drive west on U.S. 2 for one mile to Highway 174. Turn right (north) on Highway 174 and drive 0.25 mile to Highway 21. Turn right (north) on Highway 21 and drive 13 miles to the park on the right.

Contact: River Rue RV Park, 509/647-2647, www.riverrue.com.

108 JONES BAY

Scenic rating: 6

on Franklin Roosevelt Lake in
Lake Roosevelt National Recreation Area

Map grid B2

This small and primitive campground is set on Jones Bay on Franklin Roosevelt Lake. Well known by locals, it gets high use on summer weekends but is quiet most weekdays. The camp is located at the bottom of a canyon in a cove with ponderosa pines. Fishing for bass, walleye, trout, and sunfish is popular at Franklin Roosevelt Lake.

RV sites, facilities: There are nine sites for tents or RVs up to 30 feet long. Picnic tables and fire grills are provided. Vault toilets are available. There is no drinking water. A boat launch and dock are nearby. Leashed pets are permitted.

Reservations, fees: Reservations are not accepted. Sites are $5–10 per night; $6 boat-launch fee (good for seven days). Open year-round, weather permitting, with limited winter access.

Directions: From Spokane on U.S. 90, turn west on U.S. 2 and drive 71 miles to Wilbur and Highway 21. Turn right (north) on Highway 21 and drive seven miles to Jones Bay Road (a dirt road, marked). Turn right and drive eight miles to the campground entrance road on the right. A high-clearance vehicle is recommended.

Contact: Lake Roosevelt National Recreation Area, 509/633-9441, fax 509/633-9332, www.nps.gov/laro.

109 SEVEN BAYS RESORT AND MARINA

Scenic rating: 7

on Franklin Roosevelt Lake

Map grid B2

This resort is on the shore of Roosevelt Lake; highlights include manicured, grassy, lakeside sites among deciduous trees. This camp is an alternative to Fort Spokane and Hawk Creek. A full-service marina (run by an independent operator) sets this spot apart from the others.

RV sites, facilities: There are 48 sites for tents or RVs up to 50 feet long (30 amp full hookups) and 24 tent sites. Picnic tables are provided. Restrooms with flush toilets and coin showers, drinking water, propane gas, dump station, a general store, seasonal restaurant, coin laundry, and ice are available. Boat rentals, docks, and launching facilities are located at the resort. Leashed pets are permitted.

Reservations, fees: Reservations are accepted, but note that I had difficulty making contact with this park. Sites are $20 per night. Some credit cards are accepted. Open year-round.

Directions: From Spokane on I-90, drive west for four miles to U.S. 2. Turn west on U.S. 2 and drive 34 miles to Highway 25. Turn right (north) on Highway 25 and drive 23 miles to Miles-Creston Road. Turn left and drive five miles to the resort on the right.

Contact: Seven Bays Resort, 509/725-7124; Seven Bays Marina, 509/725-7229.

110 FORT SPOKANE

Scenic rating: 8

on Franklin Roosevelt Lake in
Lake Roosevelt National Recreation Area

Map grid B2

Rangers offer evening campfire programs and guided daytime activities at this modern campground on the shore of Roosevelt Lake. This park also hosts living-history demonstrations. Fort Spokane is one of more than two dozen campgrounds on the 130-mile-long lake. A 190-mile scenic vehicle route encircles most of the lake.

RV sites, facilities: There are 67 sites for tents or RVs of any length and two group sites for tents or RVs up to 26 feet long that can accommodate up to 30 people each. Picnic tables and fire grills are provided. Restrooms with flush toilets, drinking water, a dump station, and a playground are available. A camp host is on-site. A picnic area, pay telephone and visitors center are nearby. A store and ice are located within one mile. Boat docks, launching facilities, and a marine dump station are nearby. Some facilities are wheelchair accessible. Leashed pets are permitted.

Reservations, fees: Reservations are not accepted for individual sites but are required for group sites at 877/444-6777 or www.recreation.gov ($10 reservation fee). Sites are $5–13 per night, $6 boat-launch fee (good for seven days), the group site is $78 per night, plus $25 reservation fee. Open year-round, with limited winter facilities.

Directions: From Spokane on I-90, drive west for four miles to U.S. 2. Turn west on U.S. 2 and drive 34 miles to Davenport and Highway 25. Turn right (north) on Highway 25 and drive 22 miles to the campground entrance on the right.

Contact: Lake Roosevelt National Recreation Area, 509/633-9441 or 509/633-3830, fax 509/633-9332, www.nps.gov/laro.

111 HAWK CREEK

Scenic rating: 8

on Franklin Roosevelt Lake in
Lake Roosevelt National Recreation Area

Map grid B2

This pleasant camping spot is located along the shore of Roosevelt Lake (Columbia River), adjacent to the mouth of Hawk Creek. This is often a good fishing spot for walleye, trout, and bass. Note that there is no drinking water if the lake level drops below an elevation of 1,265 feet.

RV sites, facilities: There are 21 sites for tents or RVs up to 45 feet long. Picnic tables and fire grills are provided. Drinking water and vault toilets are available. Boat docks and launching facilities are nearby. Leashed pets are permitted.

Reservations, fees: Reservations are not accepted. Sites are $5–10 per night; there is a $6 boat-launch fee (good for seven days). Open year-round, with limited winter facilities.

Directions: From Spokane on I-90, drive west for four miles to U.S. 2. Turn west on U.S. 2 and drive 34 miles to Davenport and Highway 25. Turn right (north) on Highway 25 and drive 23 miles to Miles-Creston Road. Turn left (northwest) and drive 10 miles to the campground at the mouth of Hawk Creek on the left.

Contact: Lake Roosevelt National Recreation Area, 509/633-9441, fax 509/633-9332, www. nps.gov/laro.

112 PORCUPINE BAY

Scenic rating: 8

on Franklin Roosevelt Lake in
Lake Roosevelt National Recreation Area

Map grid B2

This camp is extremely popular, and the sites are filled most of the summer. Its proximity to a nearby dock and launch makes it an especially good spot for campers with boats. A swimming beach is located adjacent to the campground.

RV sites, facilities: There are 31 sites for tents or RVs up to 20 feet long. Picnic tables and fire grills are provided. Drinking water, vault toilets, restrooms with flush toilets, dump station, picnic area, pay telephone and playground are available. Boat docks and launching facilities are nearby. Some facilities are wheelchair accessible. Leashed pets are permitted.

Reservations, fees: Reservations are not accepted. Sites are $5–10 per night; $6 boat-launch fee (good for seven days). Open year-round, weather permitting, with limited winter access.

Directions: From Spokane on I-90, drive west

for four miles to U.S. 2. Turn west on U.S. 2 and drive 34 miles to Davenport and Highway 25. Turn right (north) on Highway 25 and drive 19 miles to Porcupine Bay Road. Turn right (east) and drive 4.3 miles to the campground at the end of the road.

Contact: Lake Roosevelt National Recreation Area, 509/633-9441, fax 509/633-9332, www. nps.gov/laro.

113 LAKE SPOKANE CAMPGROUND

Scenic rating: 8

on the Spokane River

Map grid C2

This campground is located about 45 minutes from Spokane. The camp is set on a terrace above Lake Spokane (Spokane River), where fishing can be good for rainbow trout and the occasional brown trout. This area is also popular for power boating, waterskiing, and personal watercraft. Crowded in summer, it gets a lot of use from residents of the Spokane area. Note that this campground and lake were previously known as Long Lake.

RV sites, facilities: There are 11 sites for tents or RVs up to 30 feet long. Picnic tables and fire grills are provided. Drinking water, vault toilets, and garbage bins are available. A camp host is on-site. A boat launch, dock, swimming beach, and a day-use area are nearby. Some facilities are wheelchair accessible. Leashed pets are permitted.

Reservations, fees: Reservations are not accepted. There is no fee for camping. Open May–September, weather permitting.

Directions: From Spokane on I-90, drive west for four miles to U.S. 2. Turn west on U.S. 2 and drive 21 miles to Reardan and Highway 231. Turn right (north) on Highway 231 and drive 14.2 miles to Highway 291. Turn right and drive 4.7 miles to the campground entrance on the right.

Contact: Department of Natural Resources, Northeast Region, 509/684-7474, fax 509/684-7484, www.dnr.wa.gov.

114 DRAGOON CREEK

Scenic rating: 5

near the Little Spokane River

Map grid C2

This spot is frequented by locals but is often missed by out-of-town vacationers. The camp is set along Dragoon Creek, a tributary to the Little Spokane River. Its campsites are situated in a forest of ponderosa pine and Douglas fir. Although fairly close to U.S. 395, it remains quiet and rustic.

Note: In 2010, the DNR was considering decommissioning this campground at some point in the future; call ahead for status.

RV sites, facilities: There are 22 sites for tents or RVs up to 30 feet long. Picnic tables and fire grills are provided. Vault toilets and drinking water are available. Garbage must be packed out. Some facilities are wheelchair accessible. Leashed pets are permitted.

Reservations, fees: Reservations are not accepted. There is no fee for camping. Open May–September, weather permitting.

Directions: From Spokane, drive north on U.S. 395 for 10.2 miles to North Dragoon Creek Road. Turn left on North Dragoon Creek Road and drive 0.4 mile to the campground entrance at the end of the road.

Contact: Department of Natural Resources, Northeast Region, 509/684-7474, fax 509/684-7484, www.dnr.wa.gov.

115 RIVERSIDE STATE PARK

Scenic rating: 8

near Spokane

Map grid C2

This 10,000-acre park is set along the Spokane and Little Spokane Rivers and features freshwater marshes in a beautiful setting. There are many recreation options, including fishing for bass, crappie, and perch, 55 miles of hiking and biking trails, and 25 miles of trails for horseback riding, as well as riding stables in the park. The 37-mile Centennial Trail can be accessed from the park. The park also has a 600-acre riding area for dirt bikes in summer and snowmobiles in winter. An 18-hole golf course is located nearby. A local point of interest is the unique Bowl and Pitcher rock formation in the Spokane River.

RV sites, facilities: There are 16 tent sites, 16 sites with partial hookups (30 and 50 amps) for tents or RVs up to 45 feet long, and two group tent sites for 40 and 60 people, respectively. Picnic tables and fire grills are provided. Restrooms with flush toilets and showers, drinking water, a picnic area with a kitchen shelter, dump station, interpretive center, camp store, firewood, and horse stable are available. A restaurant, gasoline, groceries and ice are located within three miles. Boat-launching facilities, a dock, and boat rentals are located on-site. Some facilities are wheelchair accessible. Leashed pets are permitted.

Reservations, fees: Reservations are accepted for individual sites and required for group sites at 888/CAMP-OUT (888/226-7688) or www.parks.wa.gov/reservations ($6.50–8.50 reservation fee). Sites are $17–25 per night, $10 per extra vehicle per night. The group sites are $2.25 per person per night with a minimum of 20 people, plus $25 reservation fee. Open year-round, with limited number of sites available in winter.

Directions: In Spokane on I-90, take Exit 280/Maple Street North (cross the Maple Street Bridge), and drive north 1.1 miles to Maxwell Street. Turn left (west) and drive 1.9 miles, bearing left along the Spokane River to the park entrance. From the park entrance, continue for 1.5 miles on Aubrey L. White Parkway to the campground.

Alternate route for long RVs: In Spokane on I-90, take Exit 280/Maple Street North (cross the Maple Street Bridge), and drive north 4.5 miles to Francis Avenue. Turn left and drive three miles to Rifle Club Road. Turn left and drive to Aubrey L. White Parkway and the park entrance. From the entrance, continue 1.5 miles to the campground.

Contact: Riverside State Park, 509/465-5064,

www.riversidestatepark.org; state park information, 360/902-8844, www.parks.wa.gov.

116 TRAILER INNS RV PARK/ SPOKANE

Scenic rating: 5

in Spokane

Map grid C2

This large RV park makes a good layover spot on the way to Idaho. It's as close to a hotel as an RV park can get. The pull-through sites are shaded. Nearby recreation options include an 18-hole golf course, a racquet club, and tennis courts. Note that when busy, many of the sites are taken by monthly campers.

RV sites, facilities: There are 93 sites for tents or RVs of any length (full hookups); in summer, only about 10 sites are available for overnight campers. Some sites are pull-through. Picnic tables are provided. Restrooms with flush toilets and showers, drinking water, propane gas, cable TV, Wi-Fi and modem access, TV room, coin laundry, ice, a picnic area, and a playground are available. A dump station, store, and café are within one mile. Leashed pets are permitted.

Reservations, fees: Reservations are accepted at 800/659-4864. Sites are $20–32 per night, plus $5 per person per night for more than two people. Some credit cards are accepted. Open year-round.

Directions: Note that your route will depend on the direction you're heading: In Spokane eastbound on I-90, take Exit 285 (Sprague Avenue/Eastern Road) to Eastern Road. Drive 0.1 mile on Eastern Road to 4th Avenue. Turn right (west) on 4th Avenue and drive two blocks to the park. In Spokane westbound on I-90, take Exit 284 (Havana Street). Drive one block south on Havana Street to 4th Avenue. Turn left (east) on 4th Avenue and drive one mile to the park.

Contact: Trailer Inns RV Park/Spokane, 509/535-1811 or 509/248-1142, www.trailer innsrv.com.

117 KOA SPOKANE

Scenic rating: 5

on the Spokane River

Map grid C2

This KOA campground is located close to the shore of the Spokane River. Nearby you'll find the 37-mile Centennial Trail along the river, as well as an 18-hole golf course and tennis courts. Other options include touring the gardens of Manito Park or visiting Riverfront Park, which has an IMAX theater and aerial gondola rides over the Spokane River.

RV sites, facilities: There are 150 sites with full hookups (30 and 50 amps) for RVs of any length, 50 tent sites, and three cabins. Some sites are pull-through. Picnic tables are provided. No wood fires are allowed. Restrooms with flush toilets and showers, drinking water, cable TV, a dump station, showers, a recreation hall, playground, convenience store, coin laundry, ice, modem access, pet walk, volleyball, horseshoe pits, basketball, and a seasonal heated swimming pool are available. A café and gasoline are located within two miles. Some facilities are wheelchair accessible. Leashed pets are permitted.

Reservations, fees: Reservations are accepted at 800/562-3309. Sites are $25–36 per night, plus $2–3 per night per person for more than two people. Some credit cards are accepted. Open year-round.

Directions: From Spokane, drive east on I-90 for 13 miles to Barker/Exit 293. Take that exit to Barker Road. Turn north on Barker Road and drive 1.5 miles to the campground on the left.

Contact: KOA Spokane, 509/924-4722, www.koa.com.

118 WEST MEDICAL LAKE RESORT

Scenic rating: 7

on West Medical Lake

Map grid C2

This resort functions primarily as a fish camp for anglers. There are actually two lakes: West

Medical is the larger of the two and has better fishing, with boat rentals available; Medical Lake is just 0.25-mile wide and 0.5-mile long, and boating is restricted to rowboats, canoes, kayaks, and sailboats. The lakes got their names from the wondrous medicinal powers once attributed to their waters. This family-operated shorefront resort, one of several campgrounds on these lakes, is a popular spot for Spokane locals.

RV sites, facilities: There are 20 tent sites and 20 sites for tents or RVs up to 40 feet long (full hookups). Picnic tables are provided at all sites and fire pits are provided at tent sites. Restrooms with flush toilets and showers, drinking water, a café, bait, tackle, and ice are available. Boat and fishing docks, launching facilities, a fish-cleaning station, and boat and barge rentals are nearby. Leashed pets are permitted.

Reservations, fees: Reservations are accepted. RV sites are $20 per night, tent sites are $15 per night. Some credit cards are accepted. Open late April–September.

Directions: In Spokane on I-90, drive west to Exit 264 and Salnave Road. Take that exit and turn north on Salnave Road; drive six miles to Fancher Road. Turn right (west) and drive 200 yards. Bear left on Fancher Road and drive 200 yards to the resort.

Contact: West Medical Lake Resort, 509/299-3921.

119 MALLARD BAY RESORT

Scenic rating: 8

on Clear Lake

Map grid C2

This popular fishing resort is on the shore of Clear Lake, which is two miles long, 0.5-mile wide, and used for waterskiing, personal watercraft, windsurfing, and sailing. Most of the campsites are lakeshore sites on a 20-acre peninsula. Marked bike trails are nearby.

RV sites, facilities: There are 50 sites with partial hookups (20 and 30 amps) for tents or RVs of any length. Picnic tables and fire pits are provided. Restrooms with flush toilets and showers, drinking water, propane gas, a dump station, camp store, bait and tackle, ice, swimming facilities with a diving board, a playground, basketball court, boat docks, launching facilities, fishing pier, fish-cleaning stations, and boat rentals are available. Leashed pets are permitted.

Reservations, fees: Reservations are accepted. Sites are $19.95 per night, plus $3.70 per person per night for more than four people. Open mid-April–Labor Day weekend.

Directions: In Spokane on I-90, drive west to Exit 264 and Salnave Road. Take that exit and turn north on Salnave Road; drive 1.5 miles to a junction and Mallard Bay Lane. Turn right on Mallard Bay Lane and drive 0.5 mile (bearing right at the intersection) on a dirt road to the resort at the end of the road.

Contact: Mallard Bay Resort, 509/299-3830.

120 DAN'S LANDING

Scenic rating: 7

on Clear Lake

Map grid C2

This resort at Clear Lake features a 300-foot dock with benches that can be used for fishing. If you figured that most people here are anglers, well, that is correct. Fishing can be good for rainbow trout, brown trout, largemouth bass, crappie, bullhead, and catfish. Most of the campsites are at least partially shaded. Summer weekends are often busy.

RV sites, facilities: There are 17 sites with full or partial hookups (30 and 50 amps) for RVs up to 40 feet long and seven tent sites. Picnic tables and fire pits are provided. Restrooms with flush toilets and coin showers, drinking water, a café, ice, bait and tackle, boat docks and launch, boat rentals, and moorage are available. Leashed pets are permitted.

Reservations, fees: Reservations are accepted. Sites are $25 per night, plus $5 per person per night for more than five people. Some credit cards are accepted. Open mid-April–mid-September.

Directions: In Spokane on I-90, drive west to Exit 264 and Salnave Road. Take that exit and turn right (north) on Salnave Road; drive a short distance to Clear Lake Road. Turn right (north) on Clear Lake Road and drive three miles to the resort on the left (well signed).

Contact: Dan's Landing, 509/299-3717.

121 YOGI BEAR'S CAMP RESORT

Scenic rating: 6

west of Spokane

Map grid C2

This resort is located 10 minutes from downtown Spokane, yet provides a wooded, rural setting. It features towering ponderosa pines. Highlights include an 18-hole golf course nearby and several other courses within 20 minutes of the resort.

RV sites, facilities: There are 168 sites for tents or RVs up to 40 feet long (30 and 50 amp full hookups), five cabins, and six bungalows. Some sites are pull-through. Picnic tables are provided. No open fires are allowed. Restrooms with flush toilets and showers, drinking water, cable TV, modem access, a dump station, propane, coin laundry, an RV wash station, and three playgrounds are available. Other facilities include a camp store, activity center with an indoor pool, spa, exercise room, game room, snack shack, dog walk, and various sports facilities (volleyball, basketball, badminton, miniature golf, and daily, organized recreational activities). Some facilities are wheelchair accessible. Leashed pets are permitted.

Reservations, fees: Reservations are accepted. RV sites are $35–40 per night, and tent sites are $25 per night. Some credit cards are accepted. Open year-round.

Directions: In Spokane on I-90, drive to Exit 272. Take that exit, turn east on Hayford Road (becomes Aero Road), and drive approximately two miles to Thomas Mallen Road. Turn right (south) on Thomas Mallen Road and drive 0.25 mile to the resort on the right.

Contact: Yogi Bear's Camp Resort, 509/747-9415 or 800/494-7275 (800/494-PARK), fax 509/459-0148, www.jellystonewa.com.

THE COLUMBIA RIVER GORGE AND MOUNT RAINIER

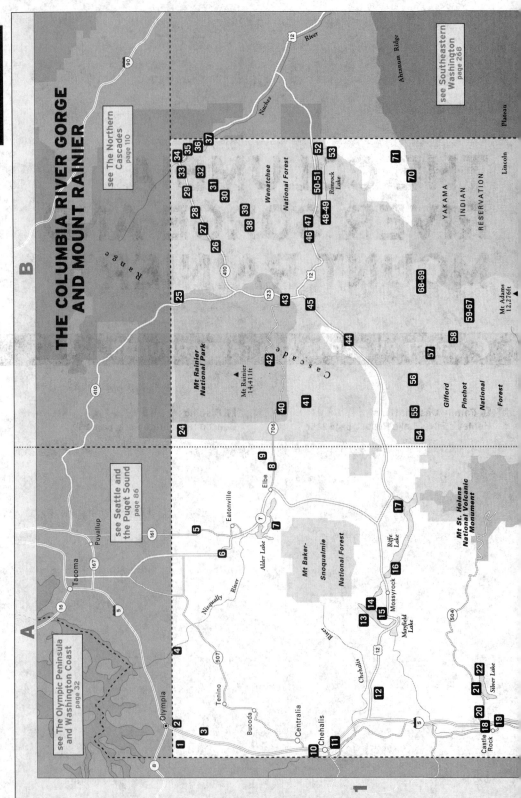

WASHINGTON

THE COLUMBIA RIVER GORGE AND MOUNT RAINIER

see The Olympic Peninsula and Washington Coast page 32

see Seattle and the Puget Sound page 86

see The Northern Cascades page 110

see Southeastern Washington page 268

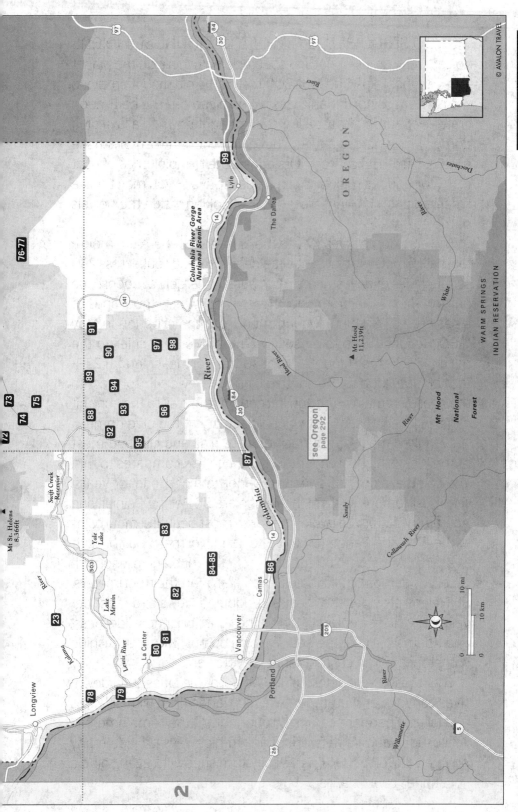

Columbia River Gorge
National Scenic Area

O R E G O N

Deschutes

River

▲ Mt Hood
11,239ft

WARM SPRINGS
INDIAN RESERVATION

see Oregon
page 292

Mt Hood

National

Forest

White

River

Sandy

Clackamas River

River

Lyle

The Dalles

Hood River

Columbia River

Columbia

Camas

Vancouver

Portland

La Center

Longview

Swift Creek
Reservoir

Yale
Lake

Lake
Merwin

Lewis River

Kalama
River

Willamette

River

▲ Mt St. Helens
8,366ft

76-77

73
74
72
75
88
89
90
91
92
93
94
95
96
97
98
99
87
86
84-85
83
82
81
80
79
78
23

141

503

5

205

26

97

30

84

97

99

14

14

30

84

10 mi

10 km

0

0

As you stand at the rim of the Mount St. Helens
volcano, the greatest natural spectacle anywhere on the planet
is at your boot tips. The top 1,300 feet of the old mountain, along
with the entire north flank, was blown clean off. The half-moon
crater walls drop almost 2,100 feet straight down to a lava plug
dome, a mile across and still building, where a wisp of smoke
emerges from its center. At its edges, the rising plumes of dust
from continuous rock falls can be deceptive – you may think a
small eruption is in progress. It's like looking inside the bowels
of the earth.

The plug dome gives way to the blast zone, where the mountain has completely blown out its side and spreads out across 230
square miles of devastation. From here, it's largely a moonscape
but for Spirit Lake on the northeast flank, where thousands of
trees are still floating, log-jammed from the eruption in May
1980. Beyond this scene rises 14,411-foot Mount Rainier to the
north, 12,276-foot Mount Adams to the northeast, and 11,239-
foot Mount Hood to the south, all pristine jewels in contrast to
the nearby remains. Though infrequent, the trail to the summit
can be closed because of volcanic activity at the plug dome.

I've hiked most of the Pacific Crest Trail and climbed most
of the West's highest mountains, but no view compares to this.
You could explore this sweeping panorama of a land for years.
The most famous spots in this region are St. Helens, Rainier, and
Adams; the latter are two of the three most beautiful mountains
in the Cascade Range (Mount Shasta in Northern California is
the third). All of them offer outstanding touring and hiking, with
excellent camps of all kinds available around their perimeters.
St. Helens provides the most eye-popping views and most developed visitors centers, Rainier the most pristine wilderness,
and Adams some of the best lakeside camps, with trout fishing
sometimes within casting range of your tent.

That's just the beginning. The Western Cascades span downriver canyons and up-mountain sub-ridges filled with streams
and lakes. There are camps throughout. At the same time, the
I-5 corridor and its network of linked highways provide many
privately developed RV parks fully furnished with everything a
vacationer could desire.

1 COLUMBUS PARK

Scenic rating: 8

on Black Lake

Map grid A1

This spot along the shore of Black Lake is pretty enough for special events, such as weddings and reunions. The campsites are wooded, and a stream (no fishing) runs through the campground. Black Lake is good for fishing, however. An 18-hole golf course is nearby.

RV sites, facilities: There are 29 sites for tents or RVs up to 40 feet long (30 amp partial hookups) and one tent site. There are also 46 sites with full hookups that are usually rented by the month. Picnic tables are provided. Restrooms with flush toilets and showers, drinking water, a dump station, coin laundry, ice, firewood, a playground, volleyball, horseshoe pits, boat docks, and launching facilities are available. A picnic area for special events is nearby. Propane gas and a store are located within one mile; there is a restaurant within three miles. Some facilities are wheelchair accessible. Leashed pets are permitted, but not on the swimming beach.

Reservations, fees: Reservations are accepted and are recommended during summer. Sites are $22 per night, $6 per night per additional car. Open year-round.

Directions: From I-5 in Olympia, take Exit 104, which merges onto U.S. 101. Drive northwest on U.S. 101 for 1.7 miles to Black Lake Boulevard. Turn left (south) on Black Lake Boulevard and drive 3.5 miles to the park on the left.

Contact: Columbus Park, 360/786-9460 or 866/848-9460, www.columbuspark.net.

2 AMERICAN HERITAGE CAMPGROUND

Scenic rating: 6

near Olympia

Map grid A1

This spacious, wooded campground situated just 0.5 mile off the highway is close to many activities, including an 18-hole golf course, hiking trails, marked bike trails, and tennis courts. The park features novelty cycle rentals, free wagon rides, and free nightly movies during the summer season. It's pretty and exceptionally clean, making for a pleasant layover on your way up or down I-5. The park has a 5,000-square-foot pavilion for special events or groups.

RV sites, facilities: There are 95 sites with full or partial hookups (30 amps) for tents or RVs of any length, 23 tent sites, and one cabin. Picnic tables and fire rings are provided. Restrooms with flush toilets and showers, drinking water, propane gas, dump station, recreation hall, group pavilion, seasonal recreation programs, a convenience store, coin laundry, ice, a playground, a seasonal heated swimming pool, and firewood are available. Leashed pets are permitted.

Reservations, fees: Reservations are accepted. Sites are $22–30 per night, plus $4 per person per night for more than two people. Some credit cards are accepted. Open year-round, with limited winter facilities.

Directions: From Olympia, drive five miles south on I-5 to Exit 99. Take that exit and drive 0.25 mile east to Kimmie Street. Turn right (south) on Kimmie Street and drive 0.25 mile to the end of the road to the campground on the left.

Contact: American Heritage Campground, 360/943-8778, www.americanheritagecampground.com.

3 MILLERSYLVANIA STATE PARK

Scenic rating: 8

on Deep Lake

Map grid A1

Millersylvania State Park is set on the shore of Deep Lake and features 3,300 feet of waterfront. The park has 8.6 miles of hiking trails amid an abundance of old-growth cedar and fir trees, of which 7.6 miles are open to bikes. Boating at Deep Lake is restricted to hand-launched boats, with a 5-mph speed limit. A fishing dock is available at the boat-launch area. Another highlight: a one-mile fitness trail. Look for the remains of a former railroad and skid trails dating from the 1800s, still present in the park.

RV sites, facilities: There are 120 developed tent sites, 48 sites with partial hookups (30 and 50 amps) for RVs up to 45 feet long, and four hike-in/bike-in sites. Picnic tables and fire grills are provided. Restrooms with flush toilets and coin showers, drinking water, a dump station, firewood boat docks and launching facilities, exercise trail, and amphitheater are available. A picnic area, boat rentals, summer interpretive activities, and horseshoe pits are nearby. A store, restaurant, and ice are located within one mile. Some facilities are wheelchair accessible. Leashed pets are permitted.

Reservations, fees: Reservations are accepted at 888/CAMP-OUT (888/226-7688) or www.parks.wa.gov/reservations ($6.50–8.50 reservation fee). Sites are $21–27 per night, $10 per night for hike-in/bike-in sites, $10 per extra vehicle per night. Some credit cards are accepted. Open year-round, with limited facilities mid-November–March.

Directions: From Olympia, drive south on I-5 for 10 miles to Exit 95 and Highway 121. Turn east on Maytown Road (Highway 121) and drive 2.7 miles to Tilley Road. Turn left (north) and drive 1.3 miles to the park.

Contact: Millersylvania State Park, 360/753-1519, fax 360/664-2180; state park information, 360/902-8844, www.parks.wa.gov.

4 OFFUT LAKE RESORT

Scenic rating: 8

on Offut Lake

Map grid A1

This wooded campground is set on Offut Lake, just enough off the beaten track to provide a bit of seclusion. Fishing, swimming, and boating are favorite activities here. Anglers will find everything they need, including tackle and

boat rentals, at the resort. Boating is restricted to a 5-mph speed limit, and no gas motors are permitted on the lake. Several fishing derbies are held here every year.

RV sites, facilities: There are 31 sites with full hookups (30 and 50 amps) for RVs up to 40 feet long, 25 tent sites, and seven cabins. Picnic tables, fire rings, and cable TV are provided. Restrooms with flush toilets and coin showers, drinking water, modem access, a picnic shelter, dump station, firewood, a convenience store, bait and tackle, propane gas, coin laundry, ice, a playground, basketball, and horseshoe pits are available. Boat rentals and docks are available; no gas motors are permitted. Some facilities are wheelchair accessible. Leashed pets are permitted.

Reservations, fees: Reservations are accepted. Sites are $20–30 per night, plus $5 per person per night for more than two adults and two children, $2 per extra vehicle per night, and $2 per pet per night. Some credit cards are accepted. Open year-round.

Directions: From Olympia, drive south on I-5 for seven miles to Exit 99. Take that exit and turn east on 93rd Avenue; drive four miles to Old Highway 99. Turn right (south) and drive four miles to Offut Lake Road. Turn left (east) and drive 1.5 miles to the resort.

Contact: Offut Lake Resort, 360/264-2438, www.offutlakeresort.com.

5 RAINBOW RV RESORT

Scenic rating: 8

on Tanwax Lake

Map grid A1

This wooded park along the shore of Tanwax Lake has spacious sites with views of mountains, forest, and lake. Highlights include good fishing for trout, perch, crappie, bass, bluegill, catfish, and bullhead. Powerboating and water-skiing are popular on hot summer weekends.

RV sites, facilities: There are about 50 sites with full hookups for RVs up to 40 feet long and eight tent sites. Picnic tables are provided at most sites, and portable fire pits are available. Restrooms with flush toilets and coin showers, drinking water, propane gas, recreation hall, convenience store, coin laundry, a café, ice, cable TV, boat docks and launch, boat rentals, and boat moorage are available. Leashed pets are permitted.

Reservations, fees: Reservations are accepted. RV sites are $25–28 per night, and tent sites are $15 per night. Some credit cards are accepted. Open year-round.

Directions: From Tacoma, drive south on I-5 to Exit 127 and Highway 512. Turn east on Highway 512 and drive to Highway 161. Turn right (south) on Highway 161 and drive to Tanwax Drive. Turn left (east) on Tanwax Drive and continue 200 yards to the resort.

Contact: Rainbow RV Resort, 360/879-5115, fax 360/879-5116, www.rainbowrvresort. com.

6 HENLEY'S SILVER LAKE RESORT

Scenic rating: 8

on Silver Lake

Map grid A1   BEST

Silver Lake is a 150-acre, spring-fed lake that can provide good trout fishing. This full-facility resort is set up as a family vacation destination. A rarity, this private campground caters both to tent campers and RVers. Silver Lake is beautiful and stocked with trout. Highlights include a 250-foot fishing dock and rental rowboats.

RV sites, facilities: There are 36 sites with full hookups, including two pull-through, for RVs, a very large area for dispersed tent camping, and six cabins. Picnic tables are provided, and fire pits are available at most sites. Restrooms with flush toilets, drinking water, snacks, bait and tackle, boat rentals, a boat ramp, and a dock are available. No showers are available. A grocery store, gasoline, and supplies are available within 3.5 miles. Leashed pets are permitted except in the cabins.

Reservations, fees: Reservations are accepted.

RV sites are $20–27 per night, and tent sites are $18 per night. Open the first day of fishing season in late April through October, weather permitting.

Directions: From Tacoma, drive south on I-5 for five miles to Exit 127 and Highway 512. Turn east on Highway 512 and drive two miles to Highway 7. Turn right (south) on Highway 7 and drive 19 miles (two miles straight beyond the blinking light) to Silver Lake Road on the right (well marked). Turn right and drive 0.25 mile to the resort entrance on the left.

Contact: Henley's Silver Lake Resort, 360/832-3580, www.henleyssilverlakeresort.zoomshare. com.

7 ALDER LAKE PARK

Scenic rating: 6

on Alder Lake

Map grid A1

The 161-acre recreation area at Alder Lake features four camping areas and a group camp; one of the camps is located four miles east of the main park entrance. Alder Lake is a 3,065-acre lake (7.5 miles long) often with good fishing for kokanee salmon, rainbow trout, and cutthroat trout. Rocky Point features a sunny beach and is set near the mouth of feeder streams, often the best fishing spots on the lake. At the west end of the lake, anglers can catch catfish, perch, and crappie. The campsites have lots of trees and shrubbery. On clear, warm summer weekends, these camps can get crowded. The camps are always booked full for summer holiday weekends as soon as reservations are available in January. Another potential downer, the water level fluctuates here. Powerboating, waterskiing, and personal watercraft are allowed at this lake. Mount Rainier Scenic Railroad leaves from Elbe regularly and makes its way through the forests to Mineral Lake. It features open deck cars, live music, and restored passenger cars.

RV sites, facilities: There are four camping areas with approximately 111 sites with full or partial hookups (30 and 50 amps) for tents or

RVs up to 40 feet, 62 tent sites, and one group area of 20 sites for tents or RVs (full hookups). Picnic tables and fire rings are provided. Restrooms with flush toilets and coin showers, drinking water, vault toilets, and a dump station are available. Boat docks and launching facilities are available nearby. A swimming beach, picnic area, playground, and fishing dock are also available nearby. Some facilities are wheelchair accessible. Leashed pets are permitted.

Reservations, fees: Reservations are accepted at 888/CAMP-OUT (888/226-7688) or www.mytpu.org/tacomapower ($6.50–8.50 reservation fee). For group reservations, phone 360/569-2778 ($15 group reservation fee). Sites are $19–26 per night, $10 per extra vehicle per night. The group camp is $26 per site per night, with a five-site minimum. Some credit cards are accepted. Open year-round, excluding December 20–January 1.

Directions: From Chehalis, drive south on I-5 for six miles to U.S. 12. Turn east and drive 31 miles to Morton and Highway 7. Turn north on Highway 7 and drive 17 miles to Elbe. Bear left on Highway 7 and drive to the park entrance road on the left (on the east shore of Alder Lake). Turn left and drive 0.2 mile to the park entrance gate.

Contact: Alder Lake Park, Tacoma Power, 360/569-2778, fax 253/502-8631, www.mytpu. org/tacomapower.

8 SAHARA CREEK HORSE CAMP

Scenic rating: 6

near Elbe

Map grid A1

While this camp is called a "horse camp," it is actually a multiple-use camp open to campers without horses. This pretty camp is set near the foot of Mount Rainier and features multiple trailheads and a camp host on-site. Note that no motorized vehicles or mountain bikes are allowed on trails. In winter, miles of groomed cross-country ski trails are available in the area.

RV sites, facilities: There are 18 sites for tents or RVs up to 25 feet long. Picnic tables and fire pits are provided. Drinking water, stock water, a covered pavilion, vault toilets, high lines, and hitching posts are available. Garbage must be packed out. Leashed pets are permitted.

Reservations, fees: Reservations are not accepted. There is no fee for camping. Open year-round.

Directions: From Chehalis, drive south on I-5 for six miles to U.S. 12. Turn east and drive 31 miles to Morton and Highway 7. Turn north on Highway 7 and drive 17 miles to Elbe and Highway 706. Turn right (east) and drive five miles to the campground on the left.

Contact: Department of Natural Resources, South Puget Sound Region, 360/825-1631, fax 360/825-1672, www.dnr.wa.gov.

9 ELBE HILLS

Scenic rating: 6

near Elbe

Map grid A1

Elbe Hills is not an official, designated campground, but rather a trailhead with room for three campsites for four-wheelers, equestrians, or hikers. The Department of Natural Resources manages this wooded campground and provides eight miles of trails for short-wheelbase four-wheel-drive vehicles. The area features a technical obstacle course. In some places, you must have a winch to make it through the course. In winter, groomed cross-country ski trails are available in the area. Note: The area is always gated, and arrangements for access must be made in advance.

RV sites, facilities: There are three primitive sites for tents or RVs up to 25 feet long. Picnic tables and fire grills are provided. Vault toilets and a group shelter are available. There is no drinking water, and garbage must be packed out. Leashed pets are permitted.

Reservations, fees: Reservations are not accepted. There is no fee for camping. Open year-round, weather permitting.

Directions: From Chehalis, drive south on I-5 for six miles to U.S. 12. Turn east and drive 31 miles to Morton and Highway 7. Turn north on Highway 7 and drive 17 miles to Elbe and Highway 706. Turn right (east) and drive six miles to Stoner Road (a Department of Natural Resources access road). Turn left and drive 2.5 miles to The 9 Road. Bear right on The 9 Road and drive one mile; look for a spur road on the left. Turn left and drive about 100 yards to the four-wheel-drive trailhead.

Contact: Department of Natural Resources, South Puget Sound Region, 360/825-1631, fax 360/825-1672, www.dnr.wa.gov.

10 PEPPERTREE WEST MOTOR INN & RV PARK

Scenic rating: 5

in Centralia
Map grid A1

If you're driving I-5 and looking for a stopover, this spot is a good choice for tent campers and RVers. Surrounded by Chehalis Valley farmland, it's near an 18-hole golf course, hiking trails, and tennis courts.

RV sites, facilities: There are 42 sites with full or partial hookups (30 amps) for RVs of any length, a grassy area for tents, and 26 motel rooms. Most sites are pull-through. Restrooms with flush toilets and coin showers, drinking water, cable TV, a dump station, coin laundry, and ice are available. Boat-launching facilities are nearby. A store, propane, and a café are also nearby. Leashed pets are permitted.

Reservations, fees: Reservations are accepted. RV sites are $20 per night, and tent sites are $6 per night. Some credit cards are accepted. Open year-round.

Directions: From Centralia on I-5, take Exit 81 to Melon Street. Turn west and then take the first right (Alder Street) to the park (located in the southeast corner of Centralia).

Contact: Peppertree West Motor Inn & RV Park, 360/736-1124, fax 360/807-9779.

11 STAN HEDWALL PARK

Scenic rating: 5

on the Newaukum River
Map grid A1

This park is set along the Newaukum River, and its proximity to I-5 makes it a good layover spot for vacation travelers. Recreational opportunities include fishing, hiking, and golf; an 18-hole course and hiking trails are nearby.

RV sites, facilities: There are 29 sites with partial hookups (30 and 50 amps) for tents or RVs of any length. Picnic tables are provided, and some sites have fire pits. Restrooms with flush toilets and coin showers, drinking water, a dump station, satellite TV, and a playground are available. Propane gas, a store, café, and coin laundry are located within one mile. Leashed pets are permitted.

Reservations, fees: Reservations are accepted. Sites are $15 per night. Open April–November, weather permitting.

Directions: From Chehalis on I-5, take Exit 76 to Rice Road. Turn south and drive 0.13 mile to the park.

Contact: Stan Hedwall Park, City of Chehalis, 360/748-0271, fax 360/748-6993, www.ci.chehalis.wa.us.

12 LEWIS AND CLARK STATE PARK

Scenic rating: 8

near Chehalis
Map grid A1

The highlight of this state park is an immense old-growth forest that contains some good hiking trails and a 0.5-mile nature trail. This famous grove lost half of its old-growth trees along the highway when they were blown down in the legendary 1962 Columbus Day storm. This was a cataclysmic event for this one of the last major stands of old-growth forest in the state. The park covers 621 acres and features primarily Douglas fir and red cedar, wetlands, and dense vegetation. There are eight miles of trails, including five miles of horse trails. June is

Youth Fishing Month, when youngsters age 14 and younger can fish the creek. Jackson House tours, in which visitors can see a pioneer home built in 1845 north of the Columbia River, are available year-round by appointment.

RV sites, facilities: There are 25 sites for tents or self-contained RVs (no hookups), eight sites with full hookups (30 amps) for RVs up to 35 feet long, five equestrian sites, and two group camps for up to 50 people each. A bunkhouse is also available. Picnic tables and fire grills are provided. Restrooms with flush toilets and coin showers, drinking water, a small store, firewood, a picnic area, an amphitheater, day-use area that can be reserved, playground, horseshoe pits, volleyball, and badminton, and interpretive activities are available. Leashed pets are permitted.

Reservations, fees: Reservations are not accepted for family sites but are required for the bunkhouse at 360/902-8600 or 800/360-4240. Sites are $21 per night, equestrian sites are $14 per night, $10 per extra vehicle per night. The bunkhouse is $13.95 per person with a 15-person minimum. Group sites are $2.15 per person per night with a 20-person minimum. Open April–September.

Directions: From Chehalis, drive south on I-5 six miles to Exit 68 and U.S. 12. Turn east on U.S. 12 for three miles to Jackson Highway. Turn right and drive three miles to the park entrance on the right.

Contact: Lewis and Clark State Park, 360/864-2643, fax 360/864-2515; state park information, 360/902-8844, www.parks.wa.gov.

13 IKE KINSWA STATE PARK

Scenic rating: 8

on Mayfield Lake

Map grid A1

This state park is set alongside the north shore of Mayfield Lake. The park features 8.5 miles of shore, forested campsites, 2.5 miles of hiking trails, and two miles of bike trails. Mayfield Lake is a treasure trove of recreational possibilities. Fishing is a year-round affair here,

with trout and tiger muskie often good. Boating, waterskiing, swimming, and driftwood collecting are all popular. The park is named after a prominent member of the Cowlitz tribe. Two fish hatcheries are located nearby. A spectacular view of Mount St. Helens can be found at a vista point 11 miles east. This popular campground often fills on summer weekends. Be sure to reserve well in advance.

RV sites, facilities: There are 31 developed tent sites, 72 sites with full or partial hookups (30 amps) for RVs up to 36 feet long, two primitive tent sites, and five cabins. Picnic tables and fire grills are provided. Restrooms with flush toilets and coin showers, drinking water, a dump station, store, playground, picnic area, horseshoe pits, and firewood are available. Boat docks and launching facilities are nearby. Some facilities are wheelchair accessible. Leashed pets are permitted.

Reservations, fees: Reservations are accepted at 888/CAMP-OUT (888/226-7688) or www.parks.wa.gov/reservations ($6.50–8.50 reservation fee). Sites are $21 per night for tent sites, $27–28 per night for RV sites, $14 per night for primitive sites, $10 per extra vehicle per night, and cabins are $55 per night. Some credit cards are accepted. Open year-round.

Directions: From Chehalis, drive south on I-5 six miles to Exit 68 and U.S. 12. Turn east on U.S. 12 and drive 14 miles to Silver Creek Road (State Route 122). Turn left (north) and drive 1.9 miles to a Y intersection. Bear right on State Route 122/Harmony Road and drive 1.6 miles to the park entrance.

Contact: Ike Kinswa State Park, 360/983-3402, fax 360/983-3332; state park information, 360/902-8844, www.parks.wa.gov.

14 HARMONY LAKESIDE RV PARK

Scenic rating: 6

on Mayfield Lake

Map grid A1

This park fills up on weekends in July, August, and September. It is set on Mayfield Lake, a

10-mile-long lake with numerous recreational activities, including fishing, boating, riding personal watercraft, and waterskiing. Some sites feature lake views. Nearby Ike Kinswa State Park is a side-trip option.

RV sites, facilities: There are 80 sites with full hookups (30 and 50 amps) for RVs of any length; some sites are pull-through. Picnic tables and fire grills are provided. Restrooms with drinking water and coin showers, drinking water, a dump station, ice, firewood, a pay phone, boat docks, and launching facilities are available. Group facilities, including a banquet and meeting room, are also available. Leashed pets are permitted.

Reservations, fees: Reservations are recommended. Sites are $32–52.50 per night, and $2.50 per pet per night. Winter and monthly rates are available. Some credit cards are accepted. Open year-round.

Directions: From Chehalis, drive south on I-5 for six miles to Exit 68 and U.S. 12. Turn east on U.S. 12 and drive 21 miles to Mossyrock (Highway 122). Turn left (north) and drive 3.5 miles to the park on the left.

Contact: Harmony Lakeside RV Park, 360/983-3804, fax 360/983-8345, www.mayfieldlake.com.

15 MAYFIELD LAKE PARK

Scenic rating: 7

on Mayfield Lake

Map grid A1

Mayfield Lake is the centerpiece of this 50-acre park. Insider's tip: Campsites 42–54 are set along the lake's shoreline. The camp has a relaxing atmosphere and comfortable, wooded sites. Fishing is primarily for trout, bass, and silver salmon. Other recreational activities include waterskiing, swimming, and boating. For a great side trip, tour nearby Mount St. Helens.

RV sites, facilities: There are 55 sites with partial hookups for tents or RVs of any length and a group camp (12 sites) for tents or RVs up to 45 feet long. Picnic tables and fire rings are provided. Restrooms with flush toilets and coin showers,

drinking water, a pay phone, dump station, and a day-use area with a picnic shelter that can be reserved, playground, horseshoe pits, and a volleyball court are available. Some facilities are wheelchair accessible. Leashed pets are permitted.

Reservations, fees: Reservations are accepted at 888/CAMP-OUT (888/226-7688) or www.mytpu.org/tacomapower ($6.50–8.50 reservation fee, $15 group reservation fee). Sites are $25–27 per night, $10 per extra vehicle per night. The group camp is $150 per night. Open mid-April–mid-October; the group camp is open Memorial Day weekend–mid-October.

Directions: From Longview, drive north on I-5 to Exit 68 and U.S. 12. Turn east on U.S. 12 and drive approximately 17 miles to Beach Road. Turn left and drive 0.25 mile to the park entrance.

Contact: Mayfield Lake Park, 360/985-2364, fax 360/985-7825, www.mytpu.org/tacomapower.

16 MOSSYROCK PARK

Scenic rating: 8

on Riffe Lake

Map grid A1

This park is located along the southwest shore of Riffe Lake. It is an extremely popular campground. For anglers, it provides the best of both worlds: a boat launch on Riffe Lake, which offers coho salmon, rainbow trout, and bass, and nearby Swofford Pond, a 240-acre pond stocked with rainbow trout, brown trout, bass, catfish, and bluegill. Swofford Pond is located south of Mossyrock on Swofford Road; no gas motors are permitted. This campground provides access to a 0.5-mile loop nature trail. Bald eagles and osprey nest on the north side of the lake in the 14,000-acre Cowlitz Wildlife Area.

RV sites, facilities: There are 152 sites with partial hookups for tents or RVs of any length, 12 walk-in sites, one group camp (60 sites) with partial hookups for tents or RVs of any length, and a primitive group camp (10 sites) for tents or RVs of any length. Picnic tables and fire rings are provided. Restrooms with flush toilets and coin showers, drinking water, a dump station, seasonal convenience store, seasonal snack bar, coin laundry, fish-cleaning stations, boat launch, playground, picnic area that can be reserved, a swimming area, horseshoe pit, volleyball net, BMX track, camp host, and interpretive displays are available. Some facilities are wheelchair accessible. Leashed pets are permitted.

Reservations, fees: Reservations are accepted at 888/CAMP-OUT (888/226-7688) or www.mytpu.org/tacomapower ($6.50–8.50 reservation fee, $15 group reservation fee). Sites are $19–25 per night, $10 per extra vehicle per night. The primitive group camp is $150 per night, and the other group camp is $23 per site per night with a minimum of five sites. Some credit cards are accepted in summer. Open year-round, excluding December 20–January 1.

Directions: From Chehalis, drive south on I-5 six miles to Exit 68 and Highway 12 East. Take Highway 12 East and drive 21 miles to Williams Street (flashing yellow light). Turn right and drive several blocks in the town of Mossyrock to a T intersection with State Street. Turn left and drive 3.5 miles (becomes Mossyrock Road East, then Ajlune Road) to the park. Ajlune Road leads right into the park.

Contact: Mossyrock Park, Tacoma Power, 360/983-3900, fax 360/983-3906, www.mytpu.org/tacomapower.

17 TAIDNAPAM PARK

Scenic rating: 8

on Riffe Lake

Map grid A1

This 50-acre park is located at the east end of Riffe Lake. Nestled in a cover of Douglas fir and maple, it is surrounded by thousands of acres of undeveloped greenbelt. Fishing is permitted year-round at the lake, with coho salmon, rainbow trout, and bass available. This camp was named after the Upper Cowlitz Indians, also known as Taidnapam.

RV sites, facilities: There are 52 sites with full or partial hookups for tents or RVs of any length, 16 walk-in sites, and two group camps (one with 22 sites and one with 12 primitive sites) with full or partial hookups for tents or RVs or any length. Picnic tables and fire rings are provided. Restrooms with flush toilets and coin showers, drinking water, dump station, a fishing bridge, fish-cleaning stations, boat launch, picnic shelter, playground, swimming beach, horseshoe pit, volleyball net, and interpretive displays are available. Some facilities are wheelchair accessible. Leashed pets are permitted.

Reservations, fees: Reservations for individual sites are accepted at 888/CAMP-OUT (888/226-7688) or www.mytpu.org/tacomapower ($6.50–8.50 reservation fee, $15 fee for group reservation). Group reservations are accepted at 360/497-7707 ($15 group reservation fee). Sites are $25–26 per night, $10 per extra vehicle per night, and walk-in sites are $14 per night. The developed group camp is $25–26 per site per night with a minimum of 10 sites; the primitive group camp is $180 per night for all 12 sites. Some credit cards are accepted in summer season. Open year-round, excluding December 20–January 1.

Directions: From Chehalis, drive south on I-5 to Exit 68 and Highway 12 East. Take Highway 12 East and drive 37 miles (five miles past Morton) to Kosmos Road. Turn right and drive 200 yards to No. 100 Champion Haul Road. Turn left and drive four miles to the park entrance on the right.

Contact: Taidnapam Park, Tacoma Power, 360/497-7707, fax 360/497-7708, www.mytpu.org/tacomapower.

18 RIVER OAKS RV PARK & CAMPGROUND

Scenic rating: 8

on the Cowlitz River

Map grid A1

This camp is set right on the Cowlitz River, with opportunities for boating and fishing for sturgeon, steelhead, and salmon in season. Swimming is not recommended because of the cold water. The park provides nearby access to Mount St. Helens. Note that some sites are filled with monthly renters.

RV sites, facilities: There are 30 sites with full hookups (30 and 50 amps) for RVs of any length; some sites are pull-through. Picnic tables and fire rings are provided. Restrooms with flush toilets and showers, drinking water, firewood, and horseshoe pits are available. Propane gas, bait and tackle, a store, and a café are located within 0.3 mile. Boat-launching facilities, mooring buoys, and a fishing shelter are nearby. Leashed pets are permitted.

Reservations, fees: Reservations are accepted. Sites are $15–25 per night, $2.50 per person per night for more than two people. Weekly and monthly rates available. Open year-round.

Directions: From Castle Rock on I-5, take Exit 59 for Highway 506. Turn west on Highway 506 and drive 0.3 mile to the park on the left.

Contact: River Oaks RV Park & Campground, 360/864-2895, www.riveroaksrvpark.com.

19 PARADISE COVE RESORT & RV PARK

Scenic rating: 7

near the Toutle River

Map grid A1

This wooded park is situated about 400 yards from the Toutle River and 0.5 mile from the Cowlitz River. Take your pick: Seaquest State Park and Silver Lake to the east provide two excellent, activity-filled side-trip options. This is a major stopover for visits to Mount St. Helens.

RV sites, facilities: There are 48 sites for tents or RVs of any length (20, 30, and 50 amp full hookups) and a large dispersed tent camping area. Some sites are pull-through. Picnic tables are provided. Restrooms, drinking water, flush toilets, showers, coin laundry, a general store with video rentals, and ice are available. Boat-launching facilities are nearby. Leashed pets are permitted.

Reservations, fees: Reservations are accepted. Sites are $12–30 per night. Some credit cards are accepted. Open year-round.

Directions: From Longview, drive 10 miles north on I-5 to Castle Rock and Exit 52. Take Exit 52 and turn right on the frontage road and drive a short distance to Burma Road. Turn left and drive a short distance to the resort, just off the freeway (within view of the freeway).

Contact: Paradise Cove Resort & RV Park, 360/274-6785, fax 360/274-4031.

20 MOUNT ST. HELENS RV PARK

Scenic rating: 6

near Silver Lake

Map grid A1

This RV park is located just outside Castle Rock, only three miles from the Mount St. Helens Visitor Center. It is close to the highway. Fishing and boating are available nearby on Silver Lake. Note that some sites are filled with monthly renters.

RV sites, facilities: There are 88 sites with full or partial hookups (20 and 30 amps) for tents or RVs up to 45 feet long. Picnic tables are provided. Restrooms with flush toilets and coin showers, drinking water, cable TV, modem access, coin laundry, horseshoe pits, a meeting room, and dump station are available. A convenience store and gasoline are nearby. Some facilities are wheelchair accessible. Leashed pets are permitted.

Reservations, fees: Reservations are recommended in the summer. RV sites are $20–30 per night, tent sites are $20 per night, $2 per person per night for more than two people. Some credit cards are accepted. Open year-round.

Directions: From Longview, drive 10 miles north on I-5 to Castle Rock and Exit 49 and Highway 504. Take Exit 49 and drive east on Highway 504 for two miles to Tower Road. Turn left (well signed) and drive a short distance to a Y intersection and Schaffran Road. Bear right and drive approximately 300 yards to the park on the right

WASHINGTON

Contact: Mount St. Helens RV Park, 360/274-8522, fax 360/274-4529, www.mtsthelensrv-park.com.

21 SEAQUEST STATE PARK

Scenic rating: 6

near Silver Lake

Map grid A1

This camp fills nightly because it is set along the paved road to the awesome Johnston Ridge Observatory, the premier lookout of Mount St. Helens. This state park is adjacent to Silver Lake, one of western Washington's finest fishing lakes for bass and trout. But that's not all: The Mount St. Helens Visitor Center is located across the road from the park entrance. This heavily forested, 475-acre park features more than one mile of lake shoreline and 5.5 miles of trails for hiking and biking. The park is popular for day use as well as camping. No hunting or fishing is allowed.

The irony of the place is that some out-of-towners on vacation think that this park is located on the ocean because of its name, Seaquest. The park has nothing to do with the ocean, of course; it is named after Alfred L. Seaquest, who donated the property to the state for parkland. One interesting fact: He stipulated in his will that if liquor were ever sold on the property that the land would be transferred to Willamette University.

RV sites, facilities: There are 93 sites, including 33 with partial hookups (30 amps) for tents or RVs, four hike-in/bike-in sites, and five yurts. Picnic tables and fire grills are provided. Restrooms with flush toilets and coin showers, drinking water, a picnic area, playground, horseshoe pits, dump station, firewood, and a volleyball court are available. A store is within three miles. Some facilities are wheelchair accessible. Leashed pets are permitted.

Reservations, fees: Reservations are accepted at 888/CAMP-OUT (888/226-7688) or www.parks.wa.gov/reservations ($6.50–8.50 reservation fee). Sites are $21–28 per night, $12 per

night for hike-in/bike-in sites, $10 per extra vehicle per night, and yurts are $55 per night. Some credit cards are accepted. Open year-round.

Directions: From Longview, drive 10 miles north on I-5 to Castle Rock and Exit 49 and Highway 504. Take Exit 49 and drive east on Highway 504 for 5.5 miles to the park.

Contact: Seaquest State Park, 360/274-8633, fax 360/274-0962; state park information, 360/902-8844, www.parks.wa.gov.

22 SILVER LAKE MOTEL AND RESORT

Scenic rating: 8

on Silver Lake

Map grid A1

This park is set near the shore of Silver Lake and features a view of Mount St. Helens. One of Washington's better lakes for largemouth bass and trout, Silver Lake also has perch, crappie, and bluegill. Powerboating, personal watercraft riding, and waterskiing are popular. This spot is considered a great anglers' camp. The sites are set along a horseshoe-shaped driveway on grassy sites. Access is quick to Mount St. Helens, nearby to the east.

RV sites, facilities: There are 19 sites with full or partial hookups (30 amps) for RVs of any length, 11 tent sites, five cabins, and six motel rooms. Picnic tables are provided. Restrooms with flush toilets and coin showers, drinking water, a convenience store, bait and tackle, fish-cleaning station, ice, boat docks, boat rentals, launching facilities, and a playground are available. A dump station is within one mile, and a café is within four miles. Leashed pets are permitted in the campground.

Reservations, fees: Reservations are accepted. RV sites are $23–27 per night, tent sites are $13–17 per night, $5 per extra vehicle per night. Cabins are $70–125. Some credit cards are accepted. Open mid-March–mid-November.

Directions: From Longview, drive 10 miles north on I-5 to Castle Rock and Exit 49 and Highway

504. Take Exit 49 and drive east on Highway 504 for six miles to the resort on the right.

Contact: Silver Lake Motel and Resort, 360/274-6141, fax 360/274-2183, www.silver-lake-resort.com.

23 KALAMA HORSE CAMP

Scenic rating: 8

near Mount St. Helens
Map grid A1

The most popular horse camp in the area, Kalama Horse Camp receives the enthusiastic volunteer support of local equestrians. The camp fills on weekends partly because of a network of 53 miles of horse trails accessible from camp. It is located very near Mount St. Helens.

RV sites, facilities: There are 17 sites for tents or RVs up to 25 feet long and two double sites. Picnic tables and fire grills are provided. Vault toilets are available. No drinking water is provided. Garbage must be packed out. Horse facilities include 10- by 10-foot corrals, a staging and mounting assist area, stock water, a stock-loading ramp, hitching rails, and manure disposal bins. A 24- by 36-foot log cabin shelter with a picnic area with horseshoe pits is also available. Boat-launching facilities are located on Lake Merrill. Some facilities are wheelchair accessible. Leashed pets are permitted.

Reservations, fees: Reservations are not accepted. Sites are $12 per night, $16 per night for double sites, $5 per night per extra vehicle. Open April–mid-December, weather permitting.

Directions: From Woodland on I-5, take Exit 21 for Highway 503. Drive east on Highway 503 for 23 miles to the Highway 503 spur. Continue northeast on the Highway 503 spur to Forest Road 81 (at Yale Lake, one mile south of Cougar). Turn left on Forest Road 81 and drive about eight miles to the camp on the right.

Contact: Gifford Pinchot National Forest, Mount St. Helens National Volcanic Monument, 360/449-7800, fax 360/449-7801, www.fs.fed.us/gpnf/recreation.

24 LONE FIR RESORT

Scenic rating: 4

near Yale Lake
Map grid B1

This private campground is located near Yale Lake (the smallest of four lakes in the area) and, with grassy sites and plenty of shade trees, is designed primarily for RV use. Mount St. Helens provides a side-trip option. The trailhead for the summit climb is located nearby at Climber's Bivouac on the south flank of the volcano; a primitive campground with dispersed sites for hikers only is available there. Note: This trailhead is the only one available for the summit climb. Though infrequent, the trail to the summit can be closed because of volcanic activity at the plug dome.

RV sites, facilities: There are 38 sites with full hookups (30 and 50 amps) for RVs of any length, a grassy area for tents, six cabins, and 12 motel rooms. Some sites are pull-through. Picnic tables are provided, and fire pits are at some sites. Restrooms with flush toilets and coin showers, satellite TV, drinking water, coin laundry, clubhouse, playground, Wi-Fi, community fire pit, horseshoe pits, ice, a snack bar, snowshoe rentals, restaurant, and a seasonal heated swimming pool are available. Propane gas, a store, boat docks, and launching facilities are nearby. Leashed pets are permitted.

Reservations, fees: Reservations are accepted. RV sites are $27 per night, and tent sites are $15 per night. Some credit cards are accepted. Open year-round.

Directions: In Woodland on I-5, take Exit 21 for Highway 503. Drive east on Highway 503 for 29 miles to Cougar and the resort turnoff (marked, in town, with the park visible from the road) on the left.

Contact: Lone Fir Resort, 360/238-5210, fax 360/238-5120, www.lonefirresort.com.

25 WHITE RIVER

Scenic rating: 7

on the White River in Mount Rainier National Park
Map grid B1

This campground is set on the White River at 4,400 feet elevation. The Glacier Basin Trail, a seven-mile round-trip, starts at the campground and leads along the Emmons Moraine for a short distance before ascending above it. A view of the Emmons Glacier, the largest glacier in the continental United States, is possible by hiking the spur trail, the Emmons Moraine Trail. It is sometimes possible to spot mountain goats, as well as mountain climbers, on the surrounding mountain slopes. Note that another trail near camp leads a short distance (but vertically, for a rise of 2,200 feet) to the Sunrise Visitor Center. Local rangers recommend that trailers be left at the White River Campground and the 11-mile road trip to Sunrise be made by car. From there, you can take several trails that lead to backcountry lakes and glaciers. Also note that this campground is located in what is considered a geo-hazard zone, where there is risk of a mudflow, although it hasn't happened in recent years.

RV sites, facilities: There are 112 sites for tents or RVs up to 27 feet long. Picnic tables and fire grills are provided. Flush toilets and drinking water are available. A small amphitheater is nearby. Some facilities are wheelchair accessible. Leashed pets are permitted in camp, but not on trails or in the wilderness.

Reservations, fees: Reservations are not accepted. Sites are $12 per night, plus $15 per vehicle park entrance fee. Some credit cards are accepted. Open July–mid-September.

Directions: From Enumclaw, drive southeast on Highway 410 to the entrance of Mount Rainier National Park and White River Road. Turn right and drive seven miles to the campground on the left.

Contact: Mount Rainier National Park, 360/569-2211, fax 360/569-2170, www.nps.gov/mora.

26 SILVER SPRINGS

Scenic rating: 9

in Mount Baker-Snoqualmie National Forest
Map grid B1

Silver Springs campground along the White River on the northeastern border of Mount Rainier National Park offers a good alternative to the more crowded camps in the park. It's located in a beautiful section of old-growth forest, primarily with Douglas fir, cedar, and hemlock. Recreational options are limited to hiking. A U.S. Forest Service information center is located one mile away from the campground entrance on Highway 410.

RV sites, facilities: There are 56 sites for tents or RVs up to 40 feet long and one group site for up to 50 people. Picnic tables and fire grills are provided. Flush toilets, drinking water, and downed firewood for gathering are available. The group site has a picnic shelter. Some facilities are wheelchair accessible. Leashed pets are permitted.

Reservations, fees: Reservations are accepted for all sites and are required for the group site at 877/444-6777 or www.recreation.gov ($10 reservation fee). Sites are $18–32 per night, $9 per night extra vehicle fee. The group site is $50 per night. Open mid-May–late September, weather permitting.

Directions: From Enumclaw, drive east on Highway 410 for 31 miles (one mile south of the turnoff for Corral Pass) to the campground entrance on the right.

Contact: Mount Baker–Snoqualmie National Forest, White River Ranger District, 360/825-6585, fax 360/825-0660, www.fs.fed.us.

27 LODGEPOLE

Scenic rating: 6

on the American River in Wenatchee National Forest
Map grid B1

This campground is set at an elevation of 3,500 feet along the American River, just eight miles east of the boundary of Mount Rainier

National Park. Winter activities in the park include cross-country skiing, snowshoeing, and inner-tube sledding down slopes. Fishing access is available nearby.

RV sites, facilities: There are 33 sites for tents or RVs up to 20 feet long. Picnic tables and fire grills are provided. Drinking water, vault toilets, garbage service, and firewood are available. A camp host is on-site. Some facilities are wheelchair accessible. Leashed pets are permitted.

Reservations, fees: Reservations are accepted at 877/444-6777 or www.recreation.gov ($10 reservation fee). Sites are $17–19 per night, $5 per night for each additional vehicle. Open mid-May–mid-September, weather permitting.

Directions: From Yakima, drive northwest on U.S. 12 for 18 miles to Highway 410. Bear northwest on Highway 410 and drive 40.5 miles (eight miles east of the national park boundary) to the campground on the right.

Contact: Okanogan and Wenatchee National Forests, Naches Ranger District, 509/653-1401, fax 509/653-2638, www.fs.fed.us.

28 PLEASANT VALLEY

Scenic rating: 7

on the American River in Wenatchee National Forest

Map grid B1

It's always strange how campgrounds get their names. Pleasant Valley? More like Camp Thatcher, as in Thatcher ants, which have infested the campground and can inflict painful bites on you and your pet. Even the Forest Service advises, "Camp at your own risk. No refunds." If still set on camping here, plan to stay off the ground or bring an RV. That said, the campground (elevation of 3,300 feet) does provide a good base camp for a hiking or fishing trip. A trail from the camp follows Kettle Creek up to the American Ridge and Kettle Lake in the William O. Douglas Wilderness. It joins another trail that follows the ridge and then drops down to Bumping Lake (a U.S. Forest Service map is essential). You can fish here for

whitefish, steelhead, trout, and salmon in season; check regulations. In the winter, the area is popular with cross-country skiers.

RV sites, facilities: There are 16 sites for tents or RVs up to 32 feet long. Picnic tables and fire grills are provided. Drinking water, garbage service, vault toilets, and a picnic shelter are available. Downed firewood may be gathered. A camp host is on-site. Some facilities are wheelchair accessible. Leashed pets are permitted.

Reservations, fees: Reservations are accepted at 877/444-6777 or www.recreation.gov ($10 reservation fee). Sites are $17–38 per night, $5 per night for each additional vehicle. Open mid-May–mid-September, weather permitting.

Directions: From Yakima, drive northwest on U.S. 12 for 18 miles to Highway 410. Bear northwest on Highway 410 and drive 37 miles to the campground on the left.

Contact: Okanogan and Wenatchee National Forests, Naches Ranger District, 509/653-1401, fax 509/653-2638, www.fs.fed.us.

29 HELLS CROSSING

Scenic rating: 7

on the American River in Wenatchee National Forest

Map grid B1

Hells Crossing campground lies along the American River at an elevation of 3,250 feet. A steep trail from the camp leads up to Goat Peak and follows the American Ridge in the William O. Douglas Wilderness. Other trails join the ridgeline trail and connect with lakes and streams. Fishing here is for trout, steelhead, salmon, and whitefish in season; check regulations.

RV sites, facilities: There are 18 sites, including three multi-family sites, for tents or RVs up to 20 feet long. Picnic tables and fire grills are provided. Drinking water (at the west end of camp) and vault toilets are available. Downed firewood may be gathered. Leashed pets are permitted.

Reservations, fees: Reservations are accepted at 877/444-6777 or www.recreation.gov ($10 reservation fee). Sites are $17–19 per night for single sites, $34 per night for double sites, and $5 per night for each additional vehicle. Open mid-May–mid-September, weather permitting.

Directions: From Yakima, drive northwest on U.S. 12 for 18 miles to Highway 410. Bear northwest on Highway 410 and drive 33.5 miles to the campground on the right.

Contact: Okanogan and Wenatchee National Forests, Naches Ranger District, 509/653-1401, fax 509/653-2638, www.fs.fed.us.

30 PINE NEEDLE GROUP CAMP

Scenic rating: 7

on the American River in Wenatchee National Forest

Map grid B1

This reservations-only group campground sits on the edge of the William O. Douglas Wilderness along the American River at an elevation of 3,000 feet. There are trails leading south into the backcountry at nearby camps; consult a U.S. Forest Service map. The camp is easy to reach, rustic, and beautiful. Fishing is available for whitefish, trout, steelhead, and salmon in season. For a side trip, visit Bumping Lake to the south, where recreation options include boating, fishing, and swimming.

RV sites, facilities: There is one group site for tents or RVs up to 30 feet long that can accommodate up to 60 people. Picnic tables and fire grills are provided. Vault toilets are available. There is no drinking water here, but it is available 2.5 miles west at Hells Crossing campground. Garbage must be packed out. Downed firewood may be gathered. Leashed pets are permitted.

Reservations, fees: Reservations are accepted at 877/444-6777 or www.recreation.gov ($10 reservation fee). The camp is $50 per night. Open mid-May–mid-November, weather permitting.

Directions: From Yakima, drive northwest on U.S. 12 for 18 miles to Highway 410. Bear northwest on Highway 410 and drive 30.5 miles to the campground on the left.

Contact: Okanogan and Wenatchee National Forests, Naches Ranger District, 509/653-1401, fax 509/653-2638, www.fs.fed.us.

31 COUGAR FLAT

Scenic rating: 5

on the Bumping River in Wenatchee National Forest

Map grid B1

One of several camps in the immediate vicinity, this spot along the Bumping River is close to good fishing; a trail from the camp follows the river and then heads up the tributaries. The elevation is 3,100 feet.

RV sites, facilities: There are 12 sites for tents or RVs up to 40 feet long. Picnic tables and fire grills are provided. Drinking water, vault toilets, and garbage bins are available. Some facilities are wheelchair accessible. Leashed pets are permitted.

Reservations, fees: Reservations are accepted at 877/444-6777 or www.recreation.gov ($10 reservation fee). Sites are $15–17 per night, $5 per night for each additional vehicle. Open mid-May–mid-September, weather permitting.

Directions: From Yakima, drive northwest on U.S. 12 for 18 miles to Highway 410. Turn left (northwest) on Highway 410 and drive 28.5 miles to Forest Road 1800. Turn left (southwest) and drive six miles (along the Bumping River) to the campground on the left.

Contact: Okanogan and Wenatchee National Forests, Naches Ranger District, 509/653-1401, fax 509/653-2638, www.fs.fed.us.

32 SODA SPRINGS

Scenic rating: 6

on the Bumping River in Wenatchee National Forest

Map grid B1

Highlights at this camp along Bumping River include natural mineral springs and a nature trail. The mineral spring is located next to a trail across the river from the campground, where the water bubbles up out of the ground. This cold-water spring is popular with some campers for soaking and drinking. Many campers use this camp for access to nearby Bumping Lake. Fishing access is available. A sheltered picnic area is provided.

RV sites, facilities: There are 26 sites for tents or RVs up to 30 feet in length. Picnic tables and fire grills are provided. Drinking water, vault toilets, firewood, a picnic shelter with a fireplace, and garbage service are available. A camp host is on-site. Some facilities are wheelchair accessible. Leashed pets are permitted.

Reservations, fees: Reservations are accepted at 877/444-6777 or www.recreation.gov ($10 reservation fee). Sites are $17–19 per night, $5 per night for each additional vehicle. Open mid-May–mid-September, weather permitting.

Directions: From Yakima, drive northwest on U.S. 12 for 18 miles to Highway 410. Turn left (northwest) on Highway 410 and drive 28.5 miles to Forest Road 1800. Turn left (southwest) and drive five miles (along the Bumping River) to the campground on the left.

Contact: Okanogan and Wenatchee National Forests, Naches Ranger District, 509/653-1401, fax 509/653-2638, www.fs.fed.us.

33 CEDAR SPRINGS

Scenic rating: 6

on the Bumping River in Wenatchee National Forest
Map grid B1

The Bumping River runs alongside this camp, set at an elevation of 2,800 feet. Fishing here follows the seasons for trout, steelhead, and whitefish; check regulations. If you continue driving southwest for 11 miles on Forest Road 1800/Bumping River Road, you'll reach Bumping Lake, where recreation options abound.

RV sites, facilities: There are 15 sites for tents or RVs up to 22 feet long, including two double sites. Picnic tables and fire grills are provided. Drinking water and vault toilets are available. Leashed pets are permitted.

Reservations, fees: Reservations are accepted at 877/444-6777 or www.recreation.gov ($10 reservation fee). Single sites are $14–18 per night,

$34 per night for double sites, and $5 per night for each additional vehicle. Open mid-May–mid-September, weather permitting.

Directions: From Yakima, drive northwest on U.S. 12 for 18 miles to Highway 410. Bear northwest on Highway 410 and drive 28.5 miles to the campground access road (Forest Road 1800/Bumping River Road). Turn left (southwest) and drive 0.5 mile to the campground on the left.

Contact: Okanogan and Wenatchee National Forests, Naches Ranger District, 509/653-1401, fax 509/653-2638, www.fs.fed.us.

34 INDIAN FLAT GROUP CAMP

Scenic rating: 7

on the American River in Wenatchee National Forest
Map grid B1

This reservations-only group campground is set along the American River at an elevation of 2,600 feet. Fishing access is available for trout, steelhead, and whitefish in season; check regulations. A trail starts just across the road from camp and leads into the backcountry, west along Fife's Ridge, and farther north to the West Quartz Creek drainage.

RV sites, facilities: There is one group site for tents or RVs up to 30 feet long, with a maximum capacity of 65 campers and 22 vehicles. Picnic tables and fire grills are provided. Drinking water, vault toilets, and firewood are available. Garbage must be packed out. Leashed pets are permitted.

Reservations, fees: Reservations are accepted at 877/444-6777 or www.recreation.gov ($10 reservation fee). The camp is $70 per night on weekdays and $100 per night on weekends. Open late May–mid-November, weather permitting.

Directions: From Yakima, drive northwest on U.S. 12 for 18 miles to Highway 410. Bear northwest on Highway 410 and drive 27 miles to the campground on the left.

Contact: Okanogan and Wenatchee National Forests, Naches Ranger District, 509/653-1401, fax 509/653-2638, www.fs.fed.us.

35 LITTLE NACHES

Scenic rating: 5

on the Little Naches River in
Wenatchee National Forest

Map grid B1

This campground on the Little Naches River
near the American River is just 0.1 mile off the
road and 24 miles from Mount Rainier. The
easy access is a major attraction for highway
cruisers, but the location also means you can
sometimes hear highway noise, and at four sites,
you can see highway vehicles. Trees act as a buffer between the highway and the campground
at other sites. Fishing access is available from
camp. The elevation is 2,562 feet.

RV sites, facilities: There are 17 sites for tents
or RVs up to 49 feet long and one double site.
Picnic tables and fire grills are provided. Drinking water, vault toilets, firewood, and garbage
service are available. A camp host is on-site.
Leashed pets are permitted.

Reservations, fees: Reservations are accepted at
877/444-6777 or www.recreation.gov ($10 res-
ervation fee). Sites are $17–34 per night, $5 per
night for each additional vehicle. Open mid-
May–mid-September, weather permitting.

Directions: From Yakima, drive northwest on
U.S. 12 for 18 miles to Highway 410. Bear
northwest on Highway 410 and drive 25 miles
to the campground access road (Forest Road
1900). Turn left and drive 100 yards to the
campground on the left.

Contact: Okanogan and Wenatchee National
Forests, Naches Ranger District, 509/653-1401,
fax 509/653-2638, www.fs.fed.us.

36 COTTONWOOD

Scenic rating: 7

on the Naches River in Wenatchee National Forest

Map grid B1

Pretty, shaded sites and river views are the main
draw at this camp along the Naches River. The
fishing is similar to that of the other camps
in the area—primarily for trout in summer

and whitefish in winter. The elevation here is
2,300 feet.

RV sites, facilities: There are 16 sites for tents
or RVs up to 22 feet long. Picnic tables and fire
grills are provided. Drinking water, vault toilets, and garbage service are available. A store,
café, and ice are available nearby. Leashed pets
are permitted.

Reservations, fees: Reservations are not accepted. Sites are $17–19 per night, $5 per night
for each additional vehicle. Open mid-May–
mid-September, weather permitting.

Directions: From Yakima, drive northwest on
U.S. 12 for 18 miles to Highway 410. Turn left
(northwest) on Highway 410 and drive 17.5
miles to the campground on the left.

Contact: Okanogan and Wenatchee National
Forests, Naches Ranger District, 509/653-1401,
fax 509/653-2638, www.fs.fed.us.

37 SAWMILL FLAT

Scenic rating: 6

on the Naches River in Wenatchee National Forest

Map grid B1

This campground on the Naches River near
Halfway Flat is used by motorcyclists more
than any other types of campers. It offers fishing access and a hiking trail that leads west
from Halfway Flat campground for several
miles into the backcountry. Fishing is primarily for trout in summer, whitefish in winter—
check regulations. Another trailhead is located
at Boulder Cave to the south.

RV sites, facilities: There are 24 sites for tents
or RVs up to 24 feet long. Picnic tables and
fire grills are provided. Drinking water, vault
toilets, garbage bins, firewood, and an Adirondack group shelter are available. A camp host
is on-site in summer. Downed firewood may
be gathered. Some facilities are wheelchair accessible. Leashed pets are permitted.

Reservations, fees: Reservations are accepted at 877/444-6777 or www.recreation.gov
($10 reservation fee). Sites are $15–21 per
night, $5 per night for each additional vehicle.

Open mid-May–mid-September, weather permitting.

Directions: From Yakima, drive northwest on U.S. 12 for 18 miles to Highway 410. Bear northwest on Highway 410 and drive 23.5 miles to the campground on the left.

Contact: Okanogan and Wenatchee National Forests, Naches Ranger District, 509/653-1401, fax 509/653-2638, www.fs.fed.us.

38 HALFWAY FLAT

Scenic rating: 7

on the Naches River in Wenatchee National Forest

Map grid B1

Fishing, hiking, and off-road vehicle (OHV) opportunities abound at this campground along the Naches River. A motorcycle trail leads from the campground into the backcountry adjacent to the William O. Douglas Wilderness; no motorized vehicles are permitted in the wilderness itself, however. Do not expect peace and quiet. This campground is something of a chameleon—sometimes primarily a family campground, but at other times dominated by OHV users.

RV sites, facilities: There are nine sites for tents or RVs up to 27 feet long and an area for dispersed tent or RV camping. Picnic tables and fire grills are provided. Drinking water, vault toilets, and garbage service are available. Some facilities are wheelchair accessible. Leashed pets are permitted.

Reservations, fees: Reservations are not accepted. Sites are $10 per night, dispersed campsites are $8 per night, $5 per night per additional vehicle. Open mid-May–mid-September, weather permitting.

Directions: From Yakima, drive northwest on U.S. 12 for 18 miles to Highway 410. Turn left (northwest) on Highway 410 and drive 17 miles to Forest Road 1704. Turn left and drive one mile to the campground.

Contact: Okanogan and Wenatchee National Forests, Naches Ranger District, 509/653-1401, fax 509/653-2638, www.fs.fed.us.

39 LOWER BUMPING LAKE

Scenic rating: 7

on Bumping Lake in Wenatchee National Forest

Map grid B1

This popular campground is set at an elevation of 3,200 feet near Bumping Lake amid a forest of primarily lodgepole pine. Bumping Lake features a variety of water activities, including waterskiing, fishing for salmon and trout, and swimming. A boat ramp is available near the camp. There are also several hiking trails that go into the William O. Douglas Wilderness surrounding the lake.

RV sites, facilities: There are 17 sites for tents or RVs up to 40 feet long. Picnic tables and fire grills are provided. Drinking water, vault toilets, and a dump station are available. Boat-launching facilities are nearby at Upper Bumping Lake campground. Some facilities are wheelchair accessible. Leashed pets are permitted.

Reservations, fees: Reservations are accepted at 877/444-6777 or www.recreation.gov ($10 reservation fee). Note that the website combines Lower and Upper Bumping Lake campgrounds into one listing; use the facility map to confirm your site. Sites are $15–17 per night, $34 for a double site, and $5 per night for each additional vehicle. Open June–mid-September, weather permitting.

Directions: From Yakima, drive northwest on U.S. 12 for 18 miles to Highway 410. Turn left (northwest) on Highway 410 and drive 28.5 miles to Forest Road 1800. Turn left (southwest) and drive 11 miles (along the Bumping River); look for the campground entrance road on the right.

Contact: Wenatchee National Forest, Naches Ranger District, 509/653-1401, fax 509/653-2638, www.fs.fed.us.

40 UPPER BUMPING LAKE

Scenic rating: 7

on Bumping Lake in Wenatchee National Forest

Map grid B1

Woods and water—this spot has them both. The cold lake is stocked with trout, and the nearby boat launch makes it a winner for campers with boats. This popular camp fills up quickly on summer weekends. A variety of water activities are allowed at Bumping Lake, including waterskiing, fishing (for salmon and trout), and swimming. A picnic area is adjacent to the boat facilities. In addition, several hiking trails lead into the William O. Douglas Wilderness surrounding the lake. This is one of the more developed camps in the area.

RV sites, facilities: There are 48 sites for tents or RVs up to 30 feet long. Picnic tables and fire grills are provided. Drinking water, vault toilets, and firewood are available. A camp host is on-site. Boat docks, launching facilities, and a dump station are nearby. Some facilities are wheelchair accessible. Leashed pets are permitted.

Reservations, fees: Reservations are accepted at 877/444-6777 or www.recreation.gov ($10 reservation fee). Note that the website combines Lower and Upper Bumping Lake campgrounds into one listing. Sites are $15–17 per night, $5 per night for each additional vehicle. Open June–late September, weather permitting.

Directions: From Yakima, drive northwest on U.S. 12 for 18 miles to Highway 410. Turn left (northwest) on Highway 410 and drive 28.5 miles to Forest Road 1800. Turn left (southwest) and drive 11 miles (along the Bumping River); look for the campground entrance road on the right.

Contact: Okanogan and Wenatchee National Forests, Naches Ranger District, 509/653-1401, fax 509/653-2638, www.fs.fed.us.

41 MOUNTHAVEN RESORT

Scenic rating: 6

near Mount Rainier National Park
Map grid B1

This campground is located within 0.5 mile of the Nisqually (southwestern) entrance to Mount Rainier National Park. In turn, it can provide a launching point for your vacation. One option: Enter the park at the Nisqually entrance, then drive on Nisqually Paradise Road for about five miles to Longmire Museum; general park information and exhibits about the plants and geology of the area are available. If you then continue into the park for 10 more miles, you'll arrive at the Jackson Visitor Center in Paradise, which has more exhibits and an observation deck. This road is the only one into the park that's open year-round. Winter activities in the park include cross-country skiing, snowshoeing, and inner-tube sledding down slopes. A creek runs through this wooded camp.

RV sites, facilities: There are 16 sites with full hookups (20 and 30 amps) for RVs of any length and eight furnished cabins. Picnic tables and fire grills are provided. A restroom with a toilet and shower, drinking water, coin laundry, firewood, and a playground are available. A restaurant and a store are within one mile. Leashed pets are permitted.

Reservations, fees: Reservations are accepted at 800/456-9380. Sites are $30 per night, $3 per pet per night. Some credit cards are accepted. Open year-round.

Directions: From Chehalis, drive south on I-5 for 10 miles to U.S. 12. Turn east and drive 31 miles to Morton and Highway 7. Turn left (north) on Highway 7 and drive 17 miles to Elbe and Highway 706. Turn right (east) on Highway 706 and drive to Ashford; continue for six miles to the resort on the right.

Contact: Mounthaven Resort, 360/569-2594, fax 360/569-2949, www.mounthaven.com.

42 BIG CREEK

Scenic rating: 8

on Big Creek in Gifford Pinchot National Forest
Map grid B1

This camp is useful as an overflow spot for Mount Rainier Sound–area campers. It is set along a stream next to a rural residential area in a forest setting made up of Douglas fir, western hemlock, western red cedar, and big leaf and vine maple.

RV sites, facilities: There are 24 sites for tents

or RVs up to 20 feet long. Picnic tables and fire rings are provided. Drinking water, firewood, and vault toilets are available. A camp host is on-site. Some facilities are wheelchair accessible. Leashed pets are permitted.

Reservations, fees: Reservations are accepted at 877/444-6777 or www.recreation.gov ($10 reservation fee). Sites are $17 per night, $34 for a double site per night, and $5 per night for each additional vehicle. Open May–mid-September.

Directions: On I-5, drive to Exit 68 (south of Chehalis) and U.S. 12. Turn east on U.S. 12 and drive 62 miles to Packwood and Forest Road 52/Skate Creek Road. Turn left (northwest) and drive 23 miles to the campground on the left.

Contact: Gifford Pinchot National Forest, Cowlitz Valley Ranger District, 360/497-1100, fax 360/497-1102, www.fs.fed.us.

43 COUGAR ROCK

Scenic rating: 9

in Mount Rainier National Park

Map grid B1

Cougar Rock is a national park campground at 3,180 feet elevation at the foot of awesome Mount Rainier. To the east lies the Nisqually Vista Trail, a beautiful 1.2-mile loop trail. It begins at the visitors center at Paradise and provides stellar views of Mount Rainier and the Nisqually Glacier. Fishing tends to be marginal. As in all national parks, no trout are stocked, and lakes without natural fisheries provide zilch. Nearby Mounthaven Resort offers winter activities in Mount Rainier Park, such as cross-country skiing, snowshoeing, and inner-tube sledding down slopes.

RV sites, facilities: There are 173 sites for tents or RVs up to 35 feet long and five group sites for up to 24–40 people each. Picnic tables and fire rings are provided. Restrooms with flush toilets, drinking water, a dump station, and an amphitheater are available. A general store is located two miles away at Longmire. Some

facilities are wheelchair accessible. Leashed pets are permitted.

Reservations, fees: Reservations are accepted at 877/444-6777 or www.recreation.gov ($10 reservation fee). Sites are $12–15 per night, plus a $15 per vehicle park entrance fee. Group sites are $40–64 per night. Open late May–mid-October.

Directions: From Tacoma, drive south on I-5 for five miles to Highway 512. Turn east on Highway 512 and drive two miles to Highway 7. Turn right (south) on Highway 7 and drive to Elbe and Highway 706. Continue east on Highway 706 and drive 12 miles to the park entrance. Continue 11 miles to the campground entrance on the left (about two miles past the Longmire developed area).

Contact: Mount Rainier National Park, 360/569-2211, fax 360/569-2170, www.nps.gov/mora.

44 OHANAPECOSH

Scenic rating: 8

on the Ohanapecosh River in Mount Rainier National Park

Map grid B1

This camp is set at an elevation of 1,914 feet at the foot of North America's most beautiful volcano, 14,410-foot Mount Rainier. It is also set along the Ohanapecosh River, adjacent to the Ohanapecosh Visitor Center, which features exhibits on the history of the forest, plus visitor information. A 0.5-mile loop trail leads from the campground, behind the visitors center, to Ohanapecosh Hot Springs. The Silver Falls Trail, a three-mile loop trail, follows the Ohanapecosh River to 75-foot Silver Falls. Warning: Do not climb on the wet rocks near the waterfall; they are wet and slippery. Note that Stevens Canyon Road heading west and Highway 123 heading north are closed by snowfall in winter.

RV sites, facilities: There are 195 sites for tents or RVs up to 32 feet long and two group sites for up to 25 people each. Picnic tables and fire rings are provided. Flush toilets, drinking water, and a dump station are available. An amphitheater is nearby. Some facilities are wheelchair accessible. Leashed pets are permitted in camp, but not on trails.

Reservations, fees: Reservations are accepted at 877/444-6777 or www.recreation.gov ($10 reservation fee). Sites are $15 per night, plus a $15 per vehicle park entrance fee. The group site is $40 per night. Some credit cards are accepted. Open mid-May–October.

Directions: On I-5, drive to Exit 68 (south of Chehalis) and U.S. 12. Turn east on U.S. 12 and drive 72 miles (seven miles past Packwood) to Highway 123. Turn left (north) and drive 6.5 miles to the Ohanapecosh entrance to the park. As you enter the park, the camp is on the left, next to the visitors center.

Contact: Mount Rainier National Park, 360/569-2211, fax 360/569-2170, www.nps.gov/mora.

45 PACKWOOD RV PARK

Scenic rating: 6

in Packwood

Map grid B1

This is a pleasant campground, especially in the fall when the maples turn color. Groups are welcome. Mount Rainier National Park is located just 25 miles north, and this camp provides a good alternative if the park is full. Nearby recreation options include a riding stable. Note that some sites are filled with monthly renters.

RV sites, facilities: There are 88 sites, most with full hookups (30 amps), for RVs of any length and 15 tent sites. Some sites are pull-through. Picnic tables are provided at some sites and portable fire pits are available on request. Restrooms with flush toilets and showers, a dump station, cable TV, and coin laundry are available. A café, store, and propane gas are within walking distance. Leashed pets are permitted.

Reservations, fees: Reservations are accepted. Sites are $16–21 per night, $3 per person per

night for more than two people. Open year-round.

Directions: On I-5, drive to Exit 68 (south of Chehalis) and U.S. 12. Turn east on U.S. 12 and drive 65 miles to Packwood. The park is on the left (north) side of the highway in town at 12985 U.S. Highway 12.

Contact: Packwood RV Park, 360/494-5145.

46 LA WIS WIS

Scenic rating: 9

on the Cowlitz River in Gifford Pinchot National Forest

Map grid B1

This camp is ideally located for day trips to Mount Rainier and Mount St. Helens. It's set at an elevation of 1,400 feet along the Clear Fork of the Cowlitz River, near the confluence with the Ohanapecosh River. Trout fishing is an option. The landscape features an old-growth forest of Douglas fir, western hemlock, western red cedar, and Pacific yew, with undergrowth of big leaf maple. A 200-yard trail provides access to the Blue Hole on the Ohanapecosh River, a deep pool designated by an observation point and interpretive signs. Another trail leads less than 0.25 mile to Purcell Falls. The entrance to Mount Rainier National Park is about seven miles south of the camp.

RV sites, facilities: There are 122 sites for tents or RVs up to 60 feet long. Picnic tables and fire rings are provided. Flush and vault toilets, drinking water, garbage bins, and firewood are available. Some facilities are wheelchair accessible. Leashed pets are permitted.

Reservations, fees: Reservations are accepted at 877/444-6777 or www.recreation.gov ($10 reservation fee). RV sites are $18 per night, tent sites are $16 per night, $5 per extra vehicle per night. Open late May–early September, weather permitting.

Directions: On I-5, drive to Exit 68 (south of Chehalis) and U.S. 12. Turn east on U.S. 12 and drive 69 miles (about six miles past

Packwood) to Forest Road 1272. Turn left and drive 0.5 mile to the campground on the left.

Contact: Gifford Pinchot National Forest, Cowlitz Valley Ranger District, 360/497-1100, fax 360/497-1102, www.fs.fed.us.

47 WHITE PASS

Scenic rating: 7

on Leech Lake in Wenatchee National Forest
Map grid B1

This campground on the shore of Leech Lake sits at an elevation of 4,500 feet and boasts nearby trails leading into the Goat Rocks Wilderness to the south and the William O. Douglas Wilderness to the north. A trailhead for the Pacific Crest Trail is also nearby. Beautiful Leech Lake is popular for fly-fishing for rainbow trout. Note that this is the only type of fishing allowed here—check regulations. No gas motors are permitted on Leech Lake. White Pass Ski Area is located across the highway, 0.2 mile away.

RV sites, facilities: There are 16 sites for tents or RVs up to 20 feet long. Picnic tables and fire grills are provided. Vault toilets, garbage bins, and firewood are available, but there is no drinking water. A store and ice are located within one mile. Boat-launching facilities are nearby. No gas motors on boats are allowed; electric motors are permitted. Leashed pets are permitted.

Reservations, fees: Reservations are not accepted. Sites are $8 per night, $5 per night per additional vehicle. Open mid-May–mid-September, weather permitting.

Directions: On I-5, drive to Exit 68 (south of Chehalis) and U.S. 12. Turn east on U.S. 12 and drive 81 miles (one mile past the White Pass Ski Area) to the campground entrance road on the left side. Turn left (north) and drive 200 yards to Leech Lake and the campground.

Contact: Okanogan and Wenatchee National Forests, Naches Ranger District, 509/653-1401, fax 509/653-2638, www.fs.fed.us.

48 DOG LAKE

Scenic rating: 5

on Dog Lake in Wenatchee National Forest
Map grid B1

Set on the shore of Dog Lake at 3,400 feet elevation is little Dog Lake campground. Fishing can be good for native rainbow trout, and the lake is good for hand-launched boats, such as canoes and prams. Nearby trails lead into the William O. Douglas Wilderness.

RV sites, facilities: There are 11 sites for tents or RVs up to 24 feet long. Picnic tables and fire grills are provided. Vault toilets and garbage bins are available, but there is no drinking water. No horses are allowed in the campground. Leashed pets are permitted.

Reservations, fees: Reservations are not accepted. Sites are $8 per night, $5 per extra vehicle per night. Open mid-May–early September, weather permitting.

Directions: On I-5, drive to Exit 68 (south of Chehalis) and U.S. 12. Turn east on U.S. 12 and drive 84 miles (three miles past the White Pass Ski Area) to the campground entrance road on the left side.

Contact: Okanogan and Wenatchee National Forests, Naches Ranger District, 509/653-1401, fax 509/653-2638, www.fs.fed.us.

49 CLEAR LAKE NORTH

Scenic rating: 7

on Clear Lake in Wenatchee National Forest
Map grid B1

This primitive campground is set along the shore of Clear Lake at an elevation of 3,100 feet; it gets relatively little use. A 5-mph speed limit keeps the lake quiet and ideal for fishing, which is often good for rainbow trout. It is stocked regularly in the summer. Clear Lake is the forebay for Rimrock Lake. Swimming is allowed.

RV sites, facilities: There are 33 sites for tents or RVs up to 22 feet long. Picnic tables and fire grills are provided. Vault toilets and garbage service are available. There is no drinking water at Clear Lake North, but there is drinking water at Clear Lake South campground. Boat docks and launching facilities are nearby. Some facilities are wheelchair accessible. Leashed pets are permitted.

Reservations, fees: Reservations are not accepted. Sites are $10 per night, $5 per extra vehicle per night. Open mid-May–mid-November, weather permitting.

Directions: From Yakima, drive northwest on U.S. 12 for 17 miles to the junction with Highway 410. Turn west on U.S. 12 and drive 31 miles to Forest Road 1200. Turn left (south) and drive 0.25 mile to Forest Road 1200-740. Continue south for 0.5 mile to the campground.

Contact: Okanogan and Wenatchee National Forests, Naches Ranger District, 509/653-1401, fax 509/653-2638, www.fs.fed.us.

50 CLEAR LAKE SOUTH

Scenic rating: 7

in Wenatchee National Forest

Map grid B1

This campground (elevation 3,100 feet) is located near the east shore of Clear Lake, which is the forebay for Rimrock Lake. Fishing and swimming are recreation options. For winter travelers, several Sno-Parks in the area offer snowmobiling and cross-country skiing. Many hiking trails lie to the north.

RV sites, facilities: There are 22 sites for tents or RVs up to 22 feet long. Picnic tables and fire grills are provided. Drinking water, vault toilets, and garbage bins are available. Downed firewood may be gathered. Boat-launching facilities are nearby. Some facilities are wheelchair accessible. Leashed pets are permitted.

Reservations, fees: Reservations are not accepted. Sites are $10 per night, $5 per extra vehicle per night. Open mid-May–mid-November, weather permitting.

Directions: From Yakima, drive northwest on I-82 for 17 miles to the junction with Highway 410. Turn west on U.S. 12 and drive 31 miles to

Forest Road 1200. Turn left (south) and drive one mile to Forest Road 1200-740. Continue south and drive 0.25 mile to the campground.

Contact: Okanogan and Wenatchee National Forests, Naches Ranger District, 509/653-1401, fax 509/653-2638, www.fs.fed.us.

51 SILVER BEACH RESORT

Scenic rating: 8

on Rimrock Lake

Map grid B1

This resort along the shore of Rimrock Lake is one of several camps in the immediate area. It's very scenic, with beautiful lakefront sites. Hiking trails, marked bike trails, a full-service marina, a sandy swimming beach, and a riding stable are close by.

RV sites, facilities: There are 46 sites with full or partial hookups for tents or RVs up to 40 feet long, 46 sites for tents or RVs up to 40 feet long (no hookups), three cabins with kitchens, and 16 motel rooms. Some sites are pull-through. Picnic tables and fire pits are provided. Restrooms with flush toilets and coin showers, a café, convenience store, dump station, bait and tackle, bottled gas, ice, a playground, boat docks, launching facilities, and boat and personal watercraft rentals are available. Leashed pets are permitted.

Reservations, fees: Reservations are accepted. Sites are $17–23 per night, $5 per extra vehicle per night. Some credit cards are accepted. Open year-round, with limited winter facilities.

Directions: From Yakima, drive northwest on U.S. 12 for 40 miles to the resort on the left.

Contact: Silver Beach Resort, 509/672-2500, www.campingatsilverbeach.com.

52 INDIAN CREEK

Scenic rating: 7

on Rimrock Lake in Wenatchee National Forest

Map grid B1

Fishing, swimming, and waterskiing are among the activities at this shorefront campground on

Rimrock Lake (elevation 3,000 feet). The camp is adjacent to Rimrock Lake Marina and Silver Beach Resort. This is a developed lake and an extremely popular campground, often filling on summer weekends. Fishing is often good for rainbow trout. The treasured Indian Creek Trail and many other excellent hiking trails about 5–10 miles north of the campground lead into the William O. Douglas Wilderness.

RV sites, facilities: There are 39 sites for tents or RVs up to 45 feet long. Picnic tables and fire grills are provided. Drinking water, vault toilets, and garbage bins are available. Downed firewood may be gathered. A camp host is on-site. A café, store, ice, boat docks, launching facilities, and rentals are nearby. Leashed pets are permitted.

Reservations, fees: Reservations are accepted at 877/444-6777 or www.recreation.gov ($10 reservation fee). Sites are $15–19 per night, $5 per extra vehicle per night. Open mid-May–mid-September, weather permitting.

Directions: From Yakima, drive northwest on I-82 for 17 miles to the junction with Highway 410. Turn west on U.S. 12 and drive 20 miles to Rimrock Lake and the campground entrance at the lake.

Contact: Okanogan and Wenatchee National Forests, Naches Ranger District, 509/653-1401, fax 509/653-2638, www.fs.fed.us.

53 PENINSULA

Scenic rating: 7

on Rimrock Lake in Wenatchee National Forest

Map grid B1

Fishing for silvers and rainbow trout, swimming, and waterskiing are all allowed at Rimrock Lake (elevation 3,000 feet), where this shorefront recreation area and camp are located. The lake is stocked regularly in summer and is popular, in part because of the nearby boat ramp. This camp is one of several on the lake. A point of interest, the nearby emergency airstrip here features a grass runway. A nearby Sno-Park offers wintertime fun, including cross-country skiing and snowmobiling.

RV sites, facilities: There is a dispersed camping area for tents or RVs up to 20 feet long. Picnic tables are provided. Vault toilets and garbage bins are available. There is no drinking water. Boat docks and launching facilities are nearby. Some facilities are wheelchair accessible. Leashed pets are permitted.

Reservations, fees: Reservations are not accepted. Sites are $8 per night, $5 per night per additional vehicle. Open May–mid-November, weather permitting.

Directions: From Yakima, drive northwest on I-82 for 17 miles to the junction with Highway 410. Turn west on U.S. 12 and drive 22 miles to Forest Road 1200. Turn left (south) and drive three miles (across the cattle guard) to Forest Road 711. Turn right (west) and drive a short distance to the campground.

Contact: Okanogan and Wenatchee National Forests, Naches Ranger District, 509/653-1401, fax 509/653-2638, www.fs.fed.us.

54 SOUTH FORK GROUP CAMP

Scenic rating: 8

on the South Fork of the Tieton River in Wenatchee National Forest

Map grid B1

South Fork Group Camp is set at 3,000 feet elevation along the South Fork of the Tieton River, less than one mile from where it empties into Rimrock Lake. Note that fishing is prohibited to protect the bull trout. By traveling a bit farther south on Tieton River Road, you can see huge Blue Slide, an enormous prehistoric rock and earth slide that has a curious blue tinge to it. Note: In 2009, a fire burned south of this area.

RV sites, facilities: There is one group site for up to 80 people for tents or RVs up to 40 feet long. Picnic tables and fire grills are provided. Vault toilets are available. There is no drinking water, and garbage must be packed out. Some facilities are wheelchair accessible. Leashed pets are permitted.

Reservations, fees: Reservations are accepted

at 877/444-6777 or www.recreation.gov ($25 reservation fee). The site is $60 per night. Open May–mid-November, weather permitting.

Directions: From Yakima, drive northwest on I-82 for 17 miles to the junction with Highway 410. Turn west on U.S. 12 and drive 22 miles to Forest Road 1200. Turn left (south) and drive four miles to Forest Road 1203. Bear left and drive 0.75 mile to Forest Road 1203-517. Turn right and drive 200 feet to the campground.

Contact: Okanogan and Wenatchee National Forests, Naches Ranger District, 509/653-1401, fax 509/653-2638, www.fs.fed.us.

55 IRON CREEK

Scenic rating: 7

on the Cispus River in
Gifford Pinchot National Forest

Map grid B1

This popular U.S. Forest Service campground is set along the Cispus River near its confluence with Iron Creek. Trout fishing is available. The landscape features primarily Douglas fir, western red cedar, and old-growth forest on fairly flat terrain. The camp is also located along the access route that leads to the best viewing areas on the eastern flank for Mount St. Helens. Take a 25-mile drive to Windy Ridge Vista Point for a breathtaking view of Spirit Lake and the blast zone of the volcano.

RV sites, facilities: There are 99 sites for tents or RVs up to 40 feet long. Picnic tables and fire rings are provided. Drinking water, vault toilets, firewood, and an amphitheater are available. A camp host is on-site. Some facilities are wheelchair accessible. Leashed pets are permitted.

Reservations, fees: Reservations are accepted at 877/444-6777 or www.recreation.gov ($10 reservation fee). Sites are $18–36 per night, $32 per night for a double site, $5 per extra vehicle per night. Open mid-May–early September, weather permitting.

Directions: From Chehalis, drive south on I-5 for six miles to Exit 68 and U.S. 12. Turn east

on U.S. 12 and drive 48 miles to Randle and Highway 131. Turn south on Highway 131 and drive one mile (becomes Forest Road 25). Continue south on Forest Road 25 and drive nine miles to a fork. Bear left at the fork, continue across the bridge, turn left, and drive two miles to the campground entrance on the left (along the south shore of the Cispus River).

Contact: Gifford Pinchot National Forest, Cowlitz Valley Ranger District, 360/497-1100, fax 360/497-1102, www.fs.fed.us.

56 TOWER ROCK

Scenic rating: 5

on the Cispus River in
Gifford Pinchot National Forest

Map grid B1

Tower Rock campground along the Cispus River is an alternative to nearby Iron Creek and North Fork. It has shaded and sunny sites, with lots of trees and plenty of room. The camp is set fairly close to the river; some sites feature river frontage. It is also fairly flat and forested with Douglas fir, western hemlock, red cedar, and big leaf maple. Fishing for trout is popular here.

RV sites, facilities: There are 22 sites for tents or RVs up to 40 feet long. Picnic tables and fire grills are provided. Drinking water, vault toilets, and firewood are available. Leashed pets are permitted.

Reservations, fees: Reservations are accepted at 877/444-6777 or www.recreation.gov ($10 reservation fee). Sites are $18–20 per night, $5 per extra vehicle per night. Open mid-May–mid-September, weather permitting.

Directions: From Chehalis, drive south on I-5 for six miles to Exit 68 and U.S. 12. Turn east on U.S. 12 and drive 48 miles to Randle and Highway 131. Turn right (south) on Highway 131 and drive one mile to Forest Road 23. Turn left on Forest Road 23 and drive eight miles to Forest Road 28. Turn right and drive two miles to Forest Road 76. Turn right and drive two miles to the campground entrance road on the right.

Contact: Gifford Pinchot National Forest, Cowlitz Valley Ranger District, 360/497-1100, fax 360/497-1102, www.fs.fed.us.

57 NORTH FORK & NORTH FORK GROUP

Scenic rating: 6

on the Cispus River in
Gifford Pinchot National Forest

Map grid B1

This campground offers single sites, double sites, and group camps, with the North Cispus River flowing between the sites for individual and group use. The elevation is 1,500 feet. The campsites are set back from the river in a well-forested area. A national forest map details the backcountry access to the Valley Trail, which is routed up the Cispus River Valley for 16.7 miles. This trailhead provides access for hikers, bikers, all-terrain vehicles, and horses. Note that if you explore Road 2300-083 15 miles west you will find Layser Cave, a Native American archeological site that is open to the public.

RV sites, facilities: There are 33 sites for tents or RVs up to 31 feet long and three group camps for up to 35 people each. Picnic tables and fire grills are provided. Drinking water, vault toilets, garbage bins, and firewood are available. Leashed pets are permitted.

Reservations, fees: Reservations are accepted at 877/444-6777 or www.recreation.gov ($10 reservation fee). Sites are $18–20 per night, $36 per night for double sites, $5 per extra vehicle per night, and $70–90 per night for group sites. Open mid-May–mid-September, weather permitting.

Directions: From Chehalis, drive south on I-5 for six miles to Exit 68 and U.S. 12. Turn east on U.S. 12 and drive 48 miles to Randle and Highway 131. Turn right (south) on Highway 131 and drive one mile to Forest Road 23. Bear left and drive 11 miles to the campground on the left.

Contact: Gifford Pinchot National Forest, Cowlitz Ranger District, 360/497-1100, fax 360/497-1102, www.fs.fed.us.

58 BLUE LAKE CREEK

Scenic rating: 7

near Blue Lake in Gifford Pinchot National Forest

Map grid B1

This camp is set at an elevation of 1,900 feet along Blue Lake Creek. With access to a network of all-terrain vehicle (ATV) trails, it is a significant camp for ATV owners. There is nearby access to 16.7-mile Valley Trail. This camp is also near the launch point for the 3.5-mile hike to Blue Lake; the trailhead lies about a half mile from camp.

RV sites, facilities: There are 11 sites for tents or RVs up to 22 feet long. Picnic tables and fire rings are provided. Drinking water, vault toilets, and garbage bins are available. Firewood can be gathered outside of the campground area. A camp host is on-site. Some facilities are wheelchair accessible. Leashed pets are permitted.

Reservations, fees: Reservations are accepted at 877/444-6777 or www.recreation.gov ($10 reservation fee). Sites are $15–16 per night, $5 per extra vehicle per night. Open mid-May–mid-September, weather permitting.

Directions: From Chehalis, drive south on I-5 for six miles to Exit 68 and U.S. 12. Turn east on U.S. 12 and drive 48 miles to Randle and Highway 131. Turn right (south) on Highway 131 and drive one mile to Forest Road 23. Turn south and drive about 10 miles to the campground on the left.

Contact: Gifford Pinchot National Forest, Cowlitz Ranger District, 360/497-1100, fax 360/497-1102, www.fs.fed.us.

59 ADAMS FORK

Scenic rating: 7

on the Cispus River in
Gifford Pinchot National Forest

Map grid B1

Adams Fork campground is set at 2,600 feet elevation along the Upper Cispus River near Adams Creek and is popular with off-road vehicle (ORV) enthusiasts. There are many miles of trails designed for use by ORVs. A trail just 0.5 mile away leads north to Blue Lake, which is about a five-mile hike (one-way) from the camp. Most of the campsites are small, but a few are large enough for comfortable RV use. The area has many towering trees. The Cispus River provides trout fishing.

RV sites, facilities: There are 24 sites for tents or RVs up to 22 feet long and three group camps for up to 20 people each. Picnic tables and fire grills are provided. Drinking water and vault toilets are available. Firewood may be gathered outside the campground area. Leashed pets are permitted.

Reservations, fees: Reservations are accepted at 877/444-6777 or www.recreation.gov ($10 reservation fee). Sites are $18 per night, group sites are $25–35 per night, $5 per extra vehicle per night. Open May–mid-September, weather permitting.

Directions: On I-5, drive to Exit 68 (south of Chehalis) and U.S. 12. Turn east on U.S. 12 and drive 48 miles to Randle and U.S. 131. Turn right (south) and drive one mile to Forest Road 23. Turn left (southeast) and drive 18 miles to Forest Road 21. Turn left (southeast) on Forest Road 21 and drive five miles to Forest Road 56. Turn right on Forest Road 56 and drive 200 yards to the campground on the left.

Contact: Gifford Pinchot National Forest, Cowlitz Valley Ranger District, 360/497-1100, fax 360/497-1102, www.fs.fed.us.

60 OLALLIE LAKE

Scenic rating: 9

on Olallie Lake in Gifford Pinchot National Forest
Map grid B1

Located at an elevation of 4,200 feet, this campground lies on the shore of Olallie Lake, one of several small alpine lakes in the area fed by streams coming off the glaciers on nearby Mount Adams (elevation 12,276 feet). Trout fishing is good here in early summer. The campsites are situated close to the lake and feature gorgeous views of Mount Adams across

the lake. Several of the campsites are small, and there is one larger area with room for RVs. A word to the wise: Mosquitoes can be a problem in the spring and early summer.

RV sites, facilities: There are five sites for tents or RVs up to 22 feet long. Picnic tables and fire rings are provided. Vault toilets are available, but there is no drinking water. Firewood may be gathered outside the campground area. Boat-launching facilities are nearby, but gasoline motors are prohibited on the lake. Some facilities are wheelchair accessible. Leashed pets are permitted.

Reservations, fees: Reservations are not accepted. Sites are $14 per night, $5 per night per additional vehicle. Open June–September, weather permitting.

Directions: From Chehalis, drive south on I-5 for 10 miles to Exit 68 and U.S. 12. Turn east on U.S. 12 and drive 48 miles to Randle and U.S. 131. Turn right (south) and drive one mile to Forest Road 23. Turn left (southeast) and drive 29 miles to Forest Road 2329. Turn left (northeast) and drive one mile to a junction with Forest Road 5601. Bear left and drive 0.5 mile to the campground on the right.

Contact: Gifford Pinchot National Forest, Cowlitz Valley Ranger District, 360/497-1100, fax 360/497-1102, www.fs.fed.us.

61 TAKHLAKH LAKE

Scenic rating: 9

on Takhlakh Lake in Gifford Pinchot National Forest
Map grid B1

This campground is situated along the shore of Takhlakh Lake, one of five lakes in the area, all accessible by car. It's a beautiful place, set at 4,500 feet elevation, but, alas, mosquitoes abound until late July. A viewing area (Mount Adams is visible across the lake) is available for visitors, while the more ambitious can go berry picking, fishing, and hiking. This lake is much better than nearby Horseshoe Lake, and the fishing is much better, especially for trout early in the season. The Takhlakh Meadow

Loop Trail, a barrier-free trail, provides a 1.5-mile hike.

RV sites, facilities: There are 54 sites for tents or RVs up to 40 feet long. Picnic tables are provided. Vault toilets and garbage bins are available. There is no drinking water. Firewood may be gathered outside the campground area. A camp host is on-site. Boat-launching facilities are available in the day-use area, but gasoline motors are prohibited on the lake. Some facilities are wheelchair accessible. Leashed pets are permitted.

Reservations, fees: Reservations are accepted at 877/444-6777 or www.recreation.gov ($10 reservation fee). Single sites are $15–16 per night, double sites are $32 per night, $5 per night for each additional vehicle. Open mid-June–late September, weather permitting.

Directions: From Chehalis, drive south on I-5 for 10 miles to Exit 68 and U.S. 12. Turn east on U.S. 12 and drive 48 miles to Randle and U.S. 131. Turn right (south) and drive one mile to Forest Road 23. Turn left (southeast) and drive 29 miles to Forest Road 2329. Turn left (northeast) and drive 1.5 miles to the campground entrance road on the right.

Contact: Gifford Pinchot National Forest, Cowlitz Valley Ranger District, 360/497-1100, fax 360/497-1102, www.fs.fed.us.

62 CAT CREEK

Scenic rating: 5

on Cat Creek and the Cispus River in Gifford Pinchot National Forest

Map grid B1

This small, rustic camp is set along Cat Creek at its confluence with the Cispus River, about 10 miles from the summit of Mount Adams. The camp, which features a forested setting, gets a lot of all-terrain vehicle (ATV) use. A trail starts less than one mile from camp and leads up along Blue Lake Ridge to Blue Lake. The area has many towering trees and the Cispus River provides trout fishing.

RV sites, facilities: There are five sites for tents or RVs up to 15 feet long. Picnic tables and fire

grills are provided. Vault toilets and firewood are available. There is no drinking water, and garbage must be packed out. Firewood may be gathered outside the campground area. Some facilities are wheelchair accessible. Leashed pets are permitted.

Reservations, fees: Reservations are not accepted. There is no fee. Open June–mid-September, weather permitting.

Directions: On I-5, drive to Exit 68 (south of Chehalis) and U.S. 12. Turn east on U.S. 12 and drive 48 miles to Randle and U.S. 131. Turn right (south) and drive one mile to Forest Road 23. Turn left (southeast) and drive 18 miles to Forest Road 21. Turn left (southeast) on Forest Road 21 and drive six miles to the campground on the right.

Contact: Gifford Pinchot National Forest, Cowlitz Valley Ranger District, 360/497-1100, fax 360/497-1102, www.fs.fed.us.

63 HORSESHOE LAKE

Scenic rating: 9

on Horseshoe Lake in Gifford Pinchot National Forest

Map grid B1

This camp is set on the shore of picturesque, 10-acre Horseshoe Lake. The campsites are poorly defined, more like camping areas, though some are close to the lake. A trail runs partway around the lake and is open to mountain bikers and horseback riders (who occasionally come from a nearby camp). Fishing for trout is just fair in the lake, which is stocked infrequently. The water is too cold for swimming. A trail from the camp, about a three-mile round-trip, goes up to nearby Green Mountain (elevation 5,000 feet). This is a multi-use trail that ties into the High Lakes Trail system. Another trail heads up the north flank of Mount Adams. Berry picking is an option in the late summer months.

RV sites, facilities: There are 10 sites for tents or RVs up to 16 feet long. Picnic tables and fire rings are provided. Vault toilets are available. There is no drinking water, and garbage must be packed out. Firewood may be gathered outside the campground area. Primitive launching facilities are located on the lake, but gasoline motors are prohibited on the water. Leashed pets are permitted.

Reservations, fees: Reservations are not accepted. There is no fee. Open mid-June–late September, weather permitting.

Directions: From Chehalis, drive south on I-5 for 10 miles to Exit 68 and U.S. 12. Turn east on U.S. 12 and drive 48 miles to Randle and U.S. 131. Turn right (south) and drive one mile to Forest Road 23. Turn left (southeast) and drive 29 miles to Forest Road 2329. Turn left (northeast) and drive seven miles (bearing right at the junction with Forest Road 5601) to Forest Road 078. Turn left on Forest Road 078 and drive 1.5 miles to the campground on the left.

Contact: Gifford Pinchot National Forest, Cowlitz Valley Ranger District, 360/497-1100, fax 360/497-1102, www.fs.fed.us.

64 KEENE'S HORSE CAMP

Scenic rating: 7

on the South Fork of Spring Creek in
Gifford Pinchot National Forest

Map grid B1

This equestrians-only camp is set at 4,200 feet elevation along the South Fork of Spring Creek on the northwest flank of Mount Adams (elevation 12,276 feet). The Pacific Crest Trail passes within a couple miles of the camp. Several trails lead from here into the backcountry and to several alpine meadows. The meadows are fragile, so walk along their outer edges. Nearby Goat Rocks Wilderness has 50 miles of trails open to horses; other trails meander outside of the wilderness boundary.

RV sites, facilities: There are 16 sites in two areas for tents or RVs up to 22 feet long. Picnic tables and fire grills are provided. Vault toilets, water troughs, a mounting ramp, manure bins, and hitching facilities (high lines) are available, but there is no drinking water. Firewood may be gathered outside the campground area. Some

facilities are wheelchair accessible. Leashed pets are permitted.

Reservations, fees: Reservations are not accepted. There is no fee. Open mid-June–late September.

Directions: On I-5, drive to Exit 68 (south of Chehalis) and U.S. 12. Turn east on U.S. 12 and drive 48 miles to Randle and U.S. 131. Turn right (south) and drive one mile to Forest Road 23. Turn left (southeast) and drive 18 miles to Forest Road 21. Turn left (southeast) on Forest Road 21 and drive five miles to Forest Road 56. Turn right on Forest Road 56 and drive five miles to Forest Road 5603. Turn right and drive five miles to Forest Road 2329. Turn right and drive two miles to the camp on the right.

Contact: Gifford Pinchot National Forest, Cowlitz Valley Ranger District, 360/497-1100, fax 360/497-1102, www.fs.fed.us.

67 KILLEN CREEK

Scenic rating: 7

near Mount Adams in
Gifford Pinchot National Forest

Map grid B1

This wilderness trailhead camp is ideal as a launch point for backpackers. The campground, set along Killen Creek at the foot of 12,276-foot Mount Adams, marks the start of a three-mile trail that leads up the mountain and connects with the Pacific Crest Trail. It's worth the effort. The Killen Trail goes up to secondary ridges and shoulders of Mount Adams for stunning views. Berry picking is a summertime option.

RV sites, facilities: There are nine sites for tents or RVs up to 22 feet long. Picnic tables and fire grills are provided. Vault toilets are available, but there is no drinking water. Garbage must be packed out. Firewood may be gathered outside the campground area. Leashed pets are permitted.

Reservations, fees: Reservations are not accepted. There is no fee. Open June–mid-September, weather permitting.

Directions: On I-5, drive to Exit 68 (south of Chehalis) and U.S. 12. Turn east on U.S. 12 and drive 48 miles to Randle and U.S. 131. Turn right (south) and drive one mile to Forest Road 23. Turn left (southeast) and drive 29 miles to Forest Road 2329. Turn left (northeast) and drive six miles to Forest Road 073. Turn left (west) and drive 200 yards to the campground.

Contact: Gifford Pinchot National Forest, Cowlitz Valley Ranger District, 360/497-1100, fax 360/497-1102, www.fs.fed.us.

68 WALUPT LAKE

Scenic rating: 8

on Walupt Lake in Gifford Pinchot National Forest

Map grid B1

This popular spot, set at 3,900 feet elevation along the shore of Walupt Lake, is a good base camp for a multi-day vacation. The trout fishing is often good here; check regulations. But note that only small boats are advisable here because the launch area at the lake is shallow and it can take a four-wheel-drive vehicle to get a boat in and out. A small swimming beach is nearby. In addition, several nearby trails lead into the backcountry and to other smaller alpine lakes. One trail out of the campground leads to the upper end of the lake, then launches off to the Goat Rocks Wilderness; it's an outstanding hike, and the trail is also excellent for horseback rides.

RV sites, facilities: There are 34 sites for tents or RVs up to 22 feet long and 10 walk-in sites. Picnic tables are provided. Drinking water and vault toilets are available. Fire rings are located next to the campground. There is primitive boat access with a 10-mph speed limit; no waterskiing is allowed. Leashed pets are permitted.

Reservations, fees: Reservations are accepted at 877/444-6777 or www.recreation.gov ($10 reservation fee). Sites are $18–36 per night, $5 per night for each additional vehicle. Open mid-June–mid-September.

Directions: On I-5, drive to Exit 68 (south of Chehalis) and U.S. 12. Turn east on U.S.

12 and drive 62 miles to Forest Road 21 (2.5 miles southwest of Packwood). Turn right (southeast) and drive 20 miles to Forest Road 2160. Turn left (east) and drive 4.5 miles to the campground.

Contact: Gifford Pinchot National Forest, Cowlitz Valley Ranger District, 360/497-1100, fax 360/497-1102, www.fs.fed.us.

69 WALUPT HORSE CAMP

Scenic rating: 7

near the Goat Rocks Wilderness in Gifford Pinchot National Forest

Map grid B1

This camp is for horse campers only and is set about one mile from Walupt Lake, which is good for trout fishing. Several trails lead from the lake into the backcountry of the southern Goat Rocks Wilderness, which has 50 miles of trails that can be used by horses; other trails meander outside of the wilderness boundary. If you have planned a multi-day horse-packing trip, you should bring in your own feed for the horses. Feed must be pellets or processed grain only. Hay is not permitted in the wilderness. The lake has a 10-mph speed limit for boats.

RV sites, facilities: There are nine sites for equestrians in tents or RVs up to 22 feet long. Picnic tables and fire grills are provided. Drinking water, vault toilets, and firewood are available. Garbage must be packed out. A horse ramp and high lines are available. Leashed pets are permitted.

Reservations, fees: Reservations are not accepted. There is no fee. Open June–late September, weather permitting.

Directions: On I-5, drive to Exit 68 (south of Chehalis) and U.S. 12. Turn east on U.S. 12 and drive 62 miles to Forest Road 21 (2.5 miles southwest of Packwood). Turn right (southeast) and drive 20 miles to Forest Road 2160. Turn left (east) and drive 3.5 miles to the campground on the right.

Contact: Gifford Pinchot National Forest, Cowlitz Valley Ranger District, 360/497-1100, fax 360/497-1102, www.fs.fed.us.

70 CLOVER FLATS

Scenic rating: 8

near the Goat Rocks Wilderness

Map grid B1

Clover Flats campground is located in the sub-alpine zone on the slope of Darland Mountain, which peaks at 6,982 feet. Trails connect the area with the Goat Rocks Wilderness, six miles to the west. This is a popular area for winter sports.

RV sites, facilities: There are eight campsites for tents or RVs up to 16 feet long. Picnic tables and fire grills are provided. Vault toilets, drinking water, and garbage bins are available. Leashed pets are permitted.

Reservations, fees: Reservations are not accepted. There is no fee for camping. Open June–September, weather permitting.

Directions: From Yakima, drive south on I-82 for two miles to the Union Gap exit. Take that exit and turn right on East Valley Mall Road. Drive one mile to 3rd Avenue. Turn left and drive 0.25 mile to Ahtaman Road. Turn right (west) and drive 20 miles to Tampico and Road A-3000 (North Fork Road). Turn right (west) and drive 9.5 miles to the Ahtaman Camp. Continue to a junction with A-2000 (Middle Fork Road). Bear left and drive nine miles to the camp on the left. Note: The last few miles of Road A-2000 are very steep and unpaved, with a 12 percent grade. Only high-clearance vehicles are recommended.

Contact: Department of Natural Resources, Southeast Region, 509/925-8510, fax 509/925-8522, www.dnr.wa.gov.

71 TREE PHONES

Scenic rating: 7

on the Middle Fork of Ahtanum Creek

Map grid B1

Forested Tree Phones campground is set along the Middle Fork of Ahtanum Creek at an elevation of 4,800 feet. It is close to hiking, motor-biking, and horseback-riding trails. A shelter with a wood stove is available year-round for picnics. During summer, there are beautiful wildflower displays.

RV sites, facilities: There are nine sites for tents or RVs up to 40 feet long. Picnic tables, fire grills, and tent pads are provided. Vault toilets are available. A 20- by 40-foot snow shelter and hitching rails are also available. There is no drinking water. Stock are permitted to drink from the creek. Some facilities are wheelchair accessible. Leashed pets are permitted.

Reservations, fees: Reservations are not accepted. There is no fee for camping. Open year-round, weather permitting (heavy snows are expected late November–March).

Directions: From Yakima, drive south on I-82 for two miles to the Union Gap exit. Take that exit and turn right on East Valley Mall Road. Drive one mile to 3rd Avenue. Turn left and drive 0.25 mile to Ahtaman Road. Turn right (west) and drive 20 miles to Tampico and Road A-3000 (North Fork Road). Turn right (west) and drive 9.5 miles to the Ahtaman Camp. Continue to a junction with A-2000 (Middle Fork Road). Bear left and drive six miles to the camp. Note: Only high-clearance vehicles are recommended.

Contact: Department of Natural Resources, Southeast Region, 509/925-8510, fax 509/925-8522, www.dnr.wa.gov.

72 GREEN RIVER HORSE CAMP

Scenic rating: 8

near Green River in Gifford Pinchot National Forest

Map grid B1

This premier equestrians-only horse camp is set on the Green River near an area of beautiful, old-growth timber, but the campsites themselves are in a reforested clear-cut area with trees about 25–40 feet tall. The camp features access to great trails into the Mount St. Helens blast area. The lookout from Windy Ridge is one of the most drop-dead awesome views in North America, spanning Spirit Lake, the blast zone, and the open crater of Mount St. Helens. The campground features high lines at each site, and the access is designed for easy turning and parking with horse trailers.

RV sites, facilities: There are eight sites for up to two trailer rigs or three vehicles each. Picnic tables, fire grills, and high lines are provided. Vault toilets are available. No drinking water is provided, but it is available five miles north at Norway Pass Trailhead. In the past, stock water had to be hand-carried from the river, but new facilities are expected to solve this in 2010. Garbage must be packed out. Some facilities are wheelchair accessible. Leashed pets are permitted.

Reservations, fees: Reservations are not accepted. There is no fee. Open mid-May–November, weather permitting.

Directions: From Chehalis, drive south on I-5 for six miles to Exit 68 and U.S. 12. Turn east on U.S. 12 and drive 48 miles to Randle and Highway 131. Turn right (south) and drive one mile (becomes Forest Road 25). Continue south and drive 19 miles to Forest Road 99. Turn right (west, toward Windy Ridge) and drive 8.5 miles to Forest Road 26. Turn right (north) and drive five miles to Forest Road 2612 (gravel). Turn left (west) and drive about two miles to the campground entrance on the left.

Contact: Gifford Pinchot National Forest, Mount St. Helens National Volcanic Monument, 360/449-7800, fax 360/449-7801.

73 LEWIS RIVER HORSE CAMP

🚶 🚲 🎣 🐕 ♿ 🚐 ⛺

Scenic rating: 7

near the Lewis River and Quartz Creek in Gifford Pinchot National Forest

Map grid B1

During summer, this camp caters to equestrians only. The camp is not particularly scenic, but the area around it is: There are six waterfalls nearby on the Lewis River. There are also many trails, all of which are open to mountain bikers and some to motorcycles. The spectacular Lewis River Trail is available for hiking, mountain biking, or horseback riding, and there is a wheelchair-accessible loop. Several other hiking

trails in the area branch off along backcountry streams.

RV sites, facilities: There are nine sites for tents or RVs up to 35 feet long. Picnic tables and fire rings are provided. A composting toilet is available. No drinking water is provided. Garbage must be packed out. Horse facilities include high lines, mounting ramp, stock water, and three corrals. Some facilities are wheelchair accessible. Leashed pets are permitted.

Reservations, fees: Reservations are not accepted. There is no fee. Open May–November, weather permitting.

Directions: From Woodland on I-5, take Exit 21 for Highway 503. Drive east on Highway 503 and drive 23 miles to the Highway 503 spur. Drive northeast on the Highway 503 spur road for seven miles (becomes Forest Road 90). Continue east on Forest Road 90 for 33 miles to Forest Road 93. Turn left and drive a short distance to the campground (along the Lewis River) on the right.

Contact: Gifford Pinchot National Forest, Mount St. Helens National Volcanic Monument, 360/449-7800, fax 360/449-7801.

74 LOWER FALLS

🚶 🚲 🎣 🐕 ♿ 🚐 ⛺

Scenic rating: 10

on the Lewis River in Gifford Pinchot National Forest

Map grid B1

This camp is set at 1,400 feet elevation in the primary viewing area for six major waterfalls on the Lewis River. The spectacular Lewis River Trail is available for hiking or horseback riding, and it features a wheelchair-accessible loop. Several other hiking trails in the area branch off along backcountry streams. The sites are paved and set among large fir trees on gently sloping ground; access roads were designed for easy RV parking. Note that above the falls, the calm water in the river looks safe, but it is not! Stay out. In addition, the Lewis River Trail goes along cliffs, providing beautiful views but potentially dangerous hiking.

RV sites, facilities: There are 42 sites for tents or RVs up to 60 feet long and two group sites for up to 20 people each. Picnic tables and fire grills are provided. Drinking water and composting toilets are available. Some facilities are wheelchair accessible. Leashed pets are permitted.

Reservations, fees: Reservations are not accepted. Single sites are $15 per night for single sites, $30 per night for double sites, and $5 per extra vehicle per night. Group sites are $35 per night. Open May–November, weather permitting.

Directions: From Woodland on I-5, take Exit 21 for Highway 503. Drive east on Highway 503 for 23 miles to the Highway 503 spur. Drive northeast on the Highway 503 spur for seven miles (becomes Forest Road 90). Continue east on Forest Road 90 for 30 miles to the campground (along the Lewis River) on the right.

Contact: Gifford Pinchot National Forest, Mount St. Helens National Volcanic Monument, 360/449-7800, fax 360/449-7801.

75 TILLICUM AND SADDLE

🚶 🚲 🏊 🎣 🐕 ♿ 🚐 ⛺

Scenic rating: 8

near Meadow Lake in
Gifford Pinchot National Forest

Map grid B1

Remote Tillicum and Saddle campgrounds are grouped together because of their location close to one another. These two pretty camps are primitive but well forested and within walking distance of several recreation options. Tillicum has a wheelchair-accessible vault toilet, but Saddle, a tiny and primitive camp, has no toilet facilities at all. A 4.5-mile trail from the Tillicum camp leads southwest past little Meadow Lake to Squaw Butte, then over to Big Creek. It's a nice hike, as well as an excellent ride for mountain bikers. This is a premium area for picking huckleberries in August and early September. The Lone Butte area about five miles to the south provides a side trip. Nearby Saddle camp, located one mile to the east, receives little use. There are two lakes nearby, Big and Little Mosquito Lakes, which

are fed by Mosquito Creek. So, while we're on the subject, mosquito attacks in late spring and early summer can be like squadrons of World War II bombers moving in. The Pacific Crest Trail passes right by camp.

RV sites, facilities: Tillicum has 24 sites for tents or RVs up to 18 feet long. Saddle has three primitive sites for tents only. Picnic tables and fire grills are provided. Tillicum has a wheelchair-accessible vault toilet. There is no drinking water, and garbage must be packed out. Leashed pets are permitted.

Reservations, fees: Reservations are not accepted. Sites are $5 per night. Open June–late September, weather permitting.

Directions: From Vancouver, Washington on I-205, take Highway 14 and drive east for 66 miles to Highway 141. Turn left (north) on Highway 141 and drive 25 miles to Trout Lake and County Road 141 (Forest Road 24). Turn left (west) and drive two miles to a fork. Bear left at the fork and drive 20 miles (becomes Forest Road 24) to the campground on the left.

Contact: Gifford Pinchot National Forest, Mount St. Helens National Volcanic Monument, 360/449-7800, fax 360/449-7801.

76 ISLAND CAMP

🚶 🎣 ❄ 🐕 🚐 ⛺

Scenic rating: 8

on Bird Creek

Map grid B1

Island campground sits in a forested area along Bird Creek and is close to lava tubes and blowholes. A strange one-foot-wide slit in the ground (too small to climb into and explore) can be reached by walking about 0.75 mile. Bird Creek provides a chance to fish for brook trout in late spring. In the winter, the roads are used for snowmobiling. A snowmobile shelter with a wood stove is available year-round for picnics.

RV sites, facilities: There are six campsites for tents or RVs up to 16 feet long. Picnic tables, fire grills, and tent pads are provided. Vault toilets are available, but there is no drinking water. Garbage must be packed out. Leashed pets are permitted.

Reservations, fees: Reservations are not accepted. There is no fee for camping. Open May–October, with limited winter access.

Directions: From Yakima, drive south on I-82 for 15 miles to U.S. 97. Turn south and drive 49 miles to Goldendale and Highway 142. Turn right (west) and drive 10 miles to Counts Road. Turn right (northwest) and drive 26 miles to Glendale; continue for 0.25 mile to Bird Creek Road. Turn right and drive 0.9 mile to K-3000 Road (still Bird Creek Road). Turn left, drive over the cattle guard, and drive 1.2 miles to Road S-4000. Turn right and drive 1.3 miles to Road K-4000. Turn left and drive 3.4 miles to Road K-4200. Turn left and drive 1.1 miles to the campground entrance on the left. Turn left and drive 0.25 mile to the campground.

Contact: Department of Natural Resources, Southeast Region, 509/925-8510, fax 509/925-8522, www.dnr.wa.gov.

77 BIRD CREEK

Scenic rating: 7

near the Mount Adams Wilderness

Map grid B1

Bird Creek campground is set in a forested area of old-growth Douglas fir and ponderosa pine along Bird Creek. This spot lies just east of the Mount Adams Wilderness and is one of two camps in the immediate area. (The other, Island Camp, is within three miles. It is also a primitive site, but it features snowmobile trails.)

RV sites, facilities: There are 10 sites for tents or RVs up to 22 feet long and one group camp for tents or RVs up to 35 feet long that can accommodate up to 25 people. Picnic tables, fire grills, and tent pads are provided. Pit and vault toilets are available, but there is no drinking water. Garbage must be packed out. Some facilities are wheelchair accessible. Leashed pets are permitted.

Reservations, fees: Reservations are not accepted. There is no fee for camping. Open May–mid-October, weather permitting.

Directions: From Yakima, drive south on I-82 for 15 miles to U.S. 97. Turn south and drive

49 miles to Goldendale and Highway 142. Turn right (west) and drive 10 miles to Counts Road. Turn right (northwest) and drive 26 miles to Glenwood. From the post office in Glenwood, continue 0.25 mile to Bird Creek Road. Turn right and drive 0.9 mile. Turn left (still Bird Creek Road), cross the cattle guard to Road K-3000, and drive 1.2 miles to Road S-4000 (gravel). Turn right and drive 1.3 miles to Road K-4000. Turn left and drive two miles to the campground on the left.

Contact: Department of Natural Resources, Southeast Region, 509/925-8510, fax 509/925-8522, www.dnr.wa.gov.

78 CAMP KALAMA RV PARK AND CAMPGROUND

Scenic rating: 6

on the Kalama River

Map grid A2

This campground has a rustic setting, with open and wooded areas and some accommodations for tent campers. It's set along the Kalama River, where salmon and steelhead fishing is popular. A full-service marina is nearby. Note that some sites are filled with monthly renters.

RV sites, facilities: There are 113 sites with full or partial hookups (30 and 50 amps) for RVs of any length and 50 tent sites. Some sites are pull-through. Picnic tables and fire pits are provided. Restrooms with flush toilets and coin showers, drinking water, cable TV, propane gas, a dump station, general store, café, banquet room, firewood, coin laundry, ice, boat-launching facilities, a beach area, and a playground are available. Some facilities are wheelchair accessible. Leashed pets are permitted.

Reservations, fees: Reservations are accepted. RV sites are $29–32 per night, tent sites are $19–21, $1.50 per person per night for more than two adults, $1.50 per night per extra vehicle, and $1 per pet per night. Weekly and monthly rates are available. Some credit cards are accepted. Open year-round.

Directions: From the north end of Kalama

(between Kelso and Woodland) on I-5, take Exit 32 and drive south on the frontage road for one block to the campground.

Contact: Camp Kalama RV Park and Campground, 360/673-2456 or 800/750-2456, fax 360/673-2324, www.kalama.com/campkalama.

79 PARADISE POINT STATE PARK

Scenic rating: 8

on the East Fork of the Lewis River
Map grid A2

Paradise Point is named for the serenity that once blessed this area. Alas, it has lost much of that peacefulness since the freeway went in next to the park. To reduce traffic noise, stay at one of the wooded sites in the small apple orchard. The sites in the grassy areas have little noise buffer. This park covers 88 acres and features 1,680 feet of river frontage. The two-mile hiking trail is good for families and children. Note that the dirt boat ramp is primitive and nonfunctional when the water level drops; it is recommended for car-top boats only. Fishing on the East Fork of the Lewis River is a bonus.

RV sites, facilities: There 58 sites for tents or RVs up to 50 feet long (no hookups), 18 sites with partial hookups (30 and 50 amps) for tents or RVs up to 40 feet long, nine hike-in/bike-in sites, and two yurts. Picnic tables and fire grills are provided. Restrooms with flush toilets and coin showers, drinking water, a dump station, firewood, an amphitheater, and summer interpretive programs are available. A primitive, dirt boat-launching area is located nearby on East Fork Lewis River. Some facilities are wheelchair accessible. Leashed pets are permitted.

Reservations, fees: Reservations are accepted at 888/CAMP-OUT (888/226-7688) or www.parks.wa.gov/reservations ($6.50–8.50 reservation fee). Sites are $21–28 per night, $12 per night for hike-in/bike-in sites, $10 per extra vehicle per night, and yurts are $55 per night. Some credit cards are accepted. Open year-round, with some sites closed October–April.

Directions: From Vancouver, Washington, drive north on I-5 for 15 miles to Exit 16 (La Center/Paradise Point State Park exit). Take that exit and turn right, then almost immediately at Paradise Park Road, turn left and drive one mile to the park.

Contact: Paradise Point State Park, tel./fax 360/263-2350; state park information, 360/902-8844, www.parks.wa.gov.

80 BIG FIR CAMPGROUND AND RV PARK

Scenic rating: 6

near Paradise Point State Park
Map grid A2

Big Fir campground is set in a heavily wooded, rural area not far from Paradise Point State Park. It's nestled among hills and features shaded gravel sites and wild berries. Recreation opportunities include hiking and fishing on the East Fork of the Lewis River.

RV sites, facilities: There are 37 sites with full hookups (30 and 50 amps) for RVs of any length and 33 tent sites. Some sites are pull-through. Picnic tables and barbecues are provided; no wood fires are allowed. Restrooms with flush toilets and coin showers, drinking water, volleyball, croquet, a horseshoe pit, board games, limited groceries, and ice are available. Boat-launching facilities are located within 1.5 miles. Leashed pets are permitted.

Reservations, fees: Reservations are accepted. Sites are $18–24 per night, $2 per night per extra vehicle, $4 per person per night for more than four people. Some credit cards are accepted. Open year-round, except for the tent area, which is open Memorial Day weekend–Labor Day weekend.

Directions: From Vancouver, Washington, drive north on I-5 to Exit 14 (Ridgefield exit). Take that exit to Highway 269. Drive east on Highway 269 (the road's name changes several times) for two miles to 10th Avenue. Turn right and drive to the first intersection at 259th Street. Turn left and drive two miles to the park on the right (route is well marked).

Contact: Big Fir Campground and RV Park, 360/887-8970 or 800/532-4397.

81 COLUMBIA RIVERFRONT RV PARK

Scenic rating: 8

near Portland

Map grid A2

Columbia Riverfront RV Park is located directly on the Columbia River, north of Portland. That means it is away from freeway noise, airports, and train tracks. Quiet? Oh yeah. The park encompasses 10 acres and boasts 900 feet of sandy beach, perfect for fishing for steelhead or salmon and beachcombing.

RV sites, facilities: There are 76 sites with for RVs up to 78 feet (full hookups); some sites are pull-through. Picnic tables are provided, but only beach sites have fire rings. Drinking water, restrooms with flush toilets and coin showers, a park store (with groceries, propane, and ice), horseshoe pits, Wi-Fi, cable TV, coin laundry, and a playground are available. Some facilities are wheelchair accessible. Leashed pets are permitted.

Reservations, fees: Reservations are accepted. Sites are $32–38 per night.

Directions: From I-5 in Woodland, take Exit 22 and turn south onto Dike Access Road. Drive two miles on Dike Access Road to the T intersection and turn left onto Dike Road. Drive one mile on Dike Road to the campground on the right.

Contact: Columbia Riverfront RV Park, 360/225-2327 or 800/845-9842, www.columbiariverfrontrvpark.com.

82 BATTLE GROUND LAKE STATE PARK

Scenic rating: 8

on Battle Ground Lake

Map grid A2

The centerpiece of this state park is Battle Ground Lake, a spring-fed lake that is stocked with trout but popular for bass and catfish fishing as well.

Underground lava tubes feed water into the lake, which is similar to Crater Lake in Oregon, though smaller. The park covers 280 acres, primarily forested with conifers, in the foothills of the Cascade Mountains. There are 10 miles of trails for hiking and biking, including a trail around the lake, and an additional five miles of trails open to horses; a primitive equestrian camp is also available. The lake is good for swimming and fishing, and it has a nice beach area; boats with gas motors are not allowed. If you're traveling on I-5 and looking for a layover, this camp, just 15 minutes from the highway, is ideal. In July and August, the area hosts several fairs and celebrations. Like many of the easy-access state parks on I-5, this one fills up quickly on weekends. The average annual rainfall is 35 inches.

RV sites, facilities: There are 25 sites for tents or RVs up to 35 feet long (no hookups), six sites with partial hookups (50 amps) for RVs, 15 hike-in/bike-in sites, one group site for 25–32 people, a horse camp for 10–16 people, and four cabins. Picnic tables and fire grills are provided. Restrooms with flush toilets and coin showers, drinking water, a dump station, a store, firewood, a seasonal snack bar, sheltered picnic area, amphitheater, summer interpretive programs, a playground, horseshoe pits, and an athletic field are available. Boat-launching facilities and rentals are nearby. Some facilities are wheelchair accessible. Leashed pets are permitted.

Reservations, fees: Reservations are accepted at 888/CAMP-OUT (888/226-7688) or www.parks.wa.gov/reservations ($6.50–8.50 reservation fee). Sites are $21–28 per night, $12 per night for hike-in/bike-in sites, $10 per night per extra vehicle, $55–60 per night for cabins. Some credit cards are accepted. Open year-round.

Directions: From I-5 southbound, take Exit 11; from I-5 northbound, take Exit 9. Drive to the city of Battle Ground (well marked); continue to the east end of town to Grace Avenue. Turn left on NE Grace Avenue and drive three miles (a marked route) to the park.

Contact: Battle Ground Lake State Park, tel./fax 360/687-4621; state park information, 360/902-8844, www.parks.wa.gov.

83 SUNSET FALLS

Scenic rating: 9

on the East Fork of the Lewis River in
Gifford Pinchot National Forest

Map grid A2

This campground is located at an elevation of
1,000 feet along the East Fork of the Lewis
River. Fishing, hiking, and huckleberry and
mushroom picking are some of the favored pursuits of visitors. Scenic Sunset Falls is located
just upstream of the campground. A barrier-free
viewing trail leads to an overlook.

RV sites, facilities: There are 16 sites for tents
or RVs up to 22 feet long. Picnic tables and fire
grills are provided. Vault toilets are available.
There is no drinking water, and garbage must
be packed out. Some facilities are wheelchair
accessible. Leashed pets are permitted.

Reservations, fees: Reservations are not accepted. Sites are $12 per night, $5 per extra
vehicle per night. Open year-round.

Directions: From Vancouver, Washington,
drive north on I-5 about seven miles to County
Road 502. Turn east on Highway 502 and
drive six miles to Highway 503. Turn left and
drive north for five miles to Lucia Falls Road.
Turn right and drive eight miles to Moulton
Falls and Old County Road 12. Turn right on
Old County Road 12 and drive seven miles
to the Forest Boundary and the campground
entrance on the right.

Contact: Gifford Pinchot National Forest,
Mount St. Helens National Volcanic Monument, 360/449-7800, fax 360/449-7801.

84 COLD CREEK CAMP

Scenic rating: 6

on Cedar Creek

Map grid A2

The late Waylon Jennings once told me that few
things worth remembering come easy, right?
Well, sometimes. First, don't expect to find a
"cold creek" here. There just is no such thing.

And second, the directions are complicated.
This campground is set in a forested area with
plenty of trails nearby for hiking and horseback
riding. The camp gets minimal use. A large
shelter is available at the day-use area. There is
a seven-day stay limit.

RV sites, facilities: There are seven sites for
tents or RVs up to 20 feet long. Picnic tables,
fire grills, and tent pads are provided. Vault
toilets are available. There is no drinking water,
and garbage must be packed out. A camp host
is on-site. Some facilities are wheelchair accessible. Leashed pets are permitted.

Reservations, fees: Reservations are not accepted. There is no fee for camping. Open
year-round, weather permitting.

Directions: From Vancouver, Washington, drive
north on I-5 to Exit 9 and NE 179th Street. Turn
east and drive 5.5 miles to Highway 503. Turn
right and drive 1.5 miles to NE 159th Street.
Turn left on NE 159th Street and drive three
miles to 182nd Avenue. Turn right and drive one
mile to NE 139th. Turn left and drive eight miles
(becomes Rawson, then Road L-1400) to Road
L-1000. Turn left and drive four miles to the
campground entrance road. Turn left, past the
yellow gate, and drive one mile to the camp.

Contact: Department of Natural Resources,
Pacific Cascade Region South, 360/577-2025,
fax 360/274-4196, www.dnr.wa.gov.

85 ROCK CREEK CAMPGROUND AND HORSE CAMP

Scenic rating: 6

on Rock Creek

Map grid A2

This camp is located in a wooded area along
Rock Creek. It is popular among equestrians
and mountain bikers, especially on weekends,
because of the Tarbell Trail, a 25-mile loop trail
that is accessible from the campground and goes
to the top of Larch Mountain (this road becomes
Rawson, then L-1400). Camping is limited to
seven days.

RV sites, facilities: There are 19 sites for tents or RVs up to 20 feet long. Picnic tables, fire grills, and tent pads are provided. Vault toilets, a horse-loading ramp, and corrals are available. There is no drinking water, and garbage must be packed out. There is a campground host on-site. Some facilities are wheelchair accessible. Leashed pets are permitted.

Reservations, fees: Reservations are not accepted. There is no fee for camping. Open year-round, weather permitting.

Directions: From Vancouver, Washington, drive north on I-5 to Exit 9 and NE 179th Street. Turn east and drive 5.5 miles to Highway 503. Turn right and drive 1.5 miles to NE 159th Street. Turn left on NE 159th Street and drive three miles to 182nd Avenue. Turn right and drive one mile to NE 139th (Road L-1400). Turn left and drive eight miles (road becomes Rawson, then L-1400) to Road L-1000. Turn left and drive 4.5 miles (passing Cold Creek Campground after three miles) to Road L-1200/Dole Valley Road. Turn left and drive 200 yards to the campground on your right.

Contact: Department of Natural Resources, Pacific Cascade Region South, 360/577-2025, fax 360/274-4196, www.dnr.wa.gov.

86 DOUGAN CREEK

Scenic rating: 7

near the Washougal River

Map grid A2

Insider's note: Dougan Creek campground is available only when a camp host is on-site. Located on Dougan Creek where it empties into the Washougal River, this campground is small and remote. Heavily forested with second-growth Douglas fir, it features pretty sites with river views.

RV sites, facilities: There are seven sites for tents or RVs up to 20 feet long. Picnic tables, fire grills, and tent pads are provided. Vault toilets are available. There is no drinking water,

and garbage must be packed out. Some facilities are wheelchair accessible. Leashed pets are permitted.

Reservations, fees: Reservations are not accepted. There is no fee for camping. Open mid-May–mid-October, weather permitting.

Directions: From Vancouver, Washington, on I-205, take Highway 14 and drive east for 20 miles to Highway 140. Turn north on Highway 140 and drive five miles to Washougal River Road. Turn right on Washougal River Road and drive about seven miles until you come to the end of the pavement and pass the picnic area on the left. The campground is 0.25 mile beyond the picnic area.

Contact: Department of Natural Resources, Pacific Cascade Region South, 360/577-2025, fax 360/274-4196, www.dnr.wa.gov.

87 BEACON ROCK STATE PARK

Scenic rating: 8

in Columbia River Gorge National Scenic Area

Map grid A2   BEST (

This state park features Beacon Rock, the second-largest monolith in the world, which overlooks the Columbia River Gorge. Lewis and Clark gave Beacon Rock its name on their expedition to the Pacific Ocean in 1805. The Beacon Rock Summit Trail, a 1.8-mile round-trip hike, provides excellent views of the gorge. The park is excellent for rock climbing, with the climbing season running mid-July–January. The park covers nearly 5,000 acres and includes 9,500 feet of shoreline along the Columbia River and more than 22 miles of nearby trails open for hiking, mountain biking, and horseback riding. An eight-mile loop trail to Hamilton Mountain (2,300 feet elevation) is one of the best hikes, featuring even better views than from Beacon Rock. Fishing for sturgeon, salmon, steelhead, smallmouth bass (often excellent), and walleye is available in season on the Lower Columbia River below Bonneville Dam; check regulations.

RV sites, facilities: There are 28 sites for tents or small RVs (no hookups), five sites with full hookups (30 amps) for RVs, one hike-in/bike-in site, and one group site for up to 200 people. Picnic tables and fire grills are provided. Restrooms with flush toilets and coin showers, drinking water, picnic areas, and a playground are available. Boat docks and launching facilities, moorage, and boat pumpout are available. Some facilities are wheelchair accessible. Leashed pets are permitted.

Reservations, fees: Reservations are not accepted for family sites but are required for the group camp at 888/CAMP-OUT (888/226-7688) or www.parks.wa.gov/reservations ($6.50–8.50 reservation fee). Sites are $16–22 per night, $10 per night for hike-in/bike-in sites, $10 per night per extra vehicle. The group site is $2.45 per person per night with a 20-person minimum. Boat launch fee is $7, and daily mooring fee is $0.50 per foot with a $10 minimum. Open April–October, with two sites available year-round.

Directions: From Vancouver, Washington, take Highway 14 and drive east for 35 miles. The park straddles the highway; follow the signs to the campground.

Contact: Beacon Rock State Park, 509/427-8265, fax 509/427-4471; state park information, 360/902-8844, www.parks.wa.gov.

88 CULTUS CREEK

Scenic rating: 7

near the Indian Heaven Wilderness in Gifford Pinchot National Forest

Map grid B2

This camp is set at an elevation of 4,000 feet along Cultus Creek on the edge of the Indian Heaven Wilderness. It offers nearby access to trails that will take you into the backcountry, which has numerous small meadows and lakes among old-growth stands of fir and pine. Horse trails are available as well. Access to the Pacific Crest Trail requires a two-mile climb. This camp is popular during the fall huckleberry season,

when picking is good, but gets light use the rest of the year. Situated amid gentle terrain, the sites are graveled and level.

RV sites, facilities: There are 51 sites for tents or RVs up to 32 feet long. Picnic tables and fire grills are provided. Vault toilets and firewood are available. There is no drinking water, and garbage must be packed out. Some facilities are wheelchair accessible. Leashed pets are permitted.

Reservations, fees: Reservations are not accepted. Sites are $10 per night, $5 per night per additional vehicle. Open late June–late September, weather permitting.

Directions: From Vancouver, Washington, on I-205, take Highway 14 east and drive 66 miles to State Route 141-A. Turn left (north) on State Route 141-A and drive 28 miles (becomes Forest Road 24); continue two miles to a junction. Turn right (staying on Forest Road 24) and drive 13.5 miles to the campground.

Contact: Gifford Pinchot National Forest, Mount Adams Ranger District, 509/395-3400, fax 509/395-3424, www.fs.fed.us.

89 LITTLE GOOSE AND HORSE CAMP

Scenic rating: 5

on Little Goose Creek in Gifford Pinchot National Forest

Map grid B2

This campground is near Little Goose Creek (located between Smokey and Cultus campgrounds). Huckleberry picking is quite good in August and early September. The camp sits close to the road and is sometimes dusty. Note that the access road is paved but rough and not recommended for RVs or trailers. Campers with horse trailers must drive slowly. This camp has sites ranging from good to poor and is lightly used in fall. Several trails are available leading out from the campground. The elevation is 4,000 feet.

RV sites, facilities: There are eight sites for tents or RVs up to 32 feet long and three sites for campers with stock animals. Picnic tables and fire grills are provided. Vault toilets are available. There is no drinking water, and garbage must be packed out. Leashed pets are permitted.

Reservations, fees: Reservations are not accepted. There is no fee. Open late June–late September, weather permitting.

Directions: From Vancouver, Washington, on I-205, take Highway 14 east and drive 66 miles to State Route 141-A. Turn left (north) on State Route 141-A and drive 28 miles (becomes Forest Road 24); continue two miles to a junction. Turn right (staying on Forest Road 24) and drive eight miles (one mile past Smokey Creek) to the campground.

Contact: Gifford Pinchot National Forest, Mount Adams Ranger District, 509/395-3400, fax 509/395-3424, www.fs.fed.us.

90 PETERSON PRAIRIE AND GROUP

Scenic rating: 8

near the town of Trout Lake in
Gifford Pinchot National Forest

Map grid B2

Here's a good base camp if you want a short ride to town as well as access to the nearby wilderness areas. Peterson Prairie is a prime spot for huckleberry picking in the fall. A trail from the camp leads about one mile to nearby ice caves; a stairway into the caves provides access to a variety of ice formations. An area Sno-Park with snowmobiling and cross-country skiing trails is open for winter recreation. The elevation is 2,800 feet.

RV sites, facilities: There are 30 sites for tents or RVs up to 40 feet long, and one group site for up to 50 people. Picnic tables and fire grills are provided. Drinking water, vault toilets, and firewood are available. A camp host is available in summer. Leashed pets are permitted.

Reservations, fees: Reservations are accepted and are required for the group site at 877/444-6777 or www.recreation.gov ($10 reservation fee). Single sites are $15 per night, $34 per night for double sites, $5 per extra vehicle per night.

The group site is $70 per night. Open May–mid-September, weather permitting.

Directions: From White Salmon, take Grangeview Loop Road to W. Jewett Boulevard/WA-141. Turn right on WA-141 and drive 26 miles to Carson Guler Road/NF Development Road 24. Follow Carson Guler Road/NF Development Road 24 two miles to the campground.

Alternately, from Hood River, Oregon, drive north on Highway 35 (over the Columbia River) to Highway 14. Turn left and drive two miles to Highway 141-A. Turn right (north) on Highway 141-A and drive 25.5 miles to Forest Road 24 (5.5 miles beyond and southwest of the town of Trout Lake). Bear right (west) and drive 2.5 miles to the campground on the left.

Contact: Gifford Pinchot National Forest, Mount Adams Ranger District, 509/395-3400, fax 509/395-3424, www.fs.fed.us.

91 TROUT LAKE CREEK

Scenic rating: 7

on Trout Lake Creek in
Gifford Pinchot National Forest

Map grid B2

This spot makes a popular base camp for folks fishing at Trout Lake (five miles away). Many anglers will spend the day at the lake, where fishing is good for stocked rainbow trout, then return to this camp for the night. Some bonus brook trout are occasionally caught at Trout Lake. The camp is set along a creek in a forest of Douglas fir. In season, berry picking can be good here.

RV sites, facilities: There are 16 sites for tents or RVs up to 28 feet long. Picnic tables and fire rings are provided. Vault toilets are available. There is no drinking water, and garbage must be packed out. Leashed pets are permitted.

Reservations, fees: Reservations are not accepted. Sites are $10 per night, $5 per night per additional vehicle. Open mid-May–mid-September, weather permitting.

Directions: From White Salmon, take Grangeview Loop Road to W. Jewett Boulevard/

WA-141. Turn right on WA-141 and drive 22 miles to Trout Creek Road/Trout Lake Creek Road. Turn right on Trout Creek Road/Trout Lake Creek Road and drive four miles to National Forest Development Road 010. Take a slight right and drive about 0.5 mile to the campground on the left.

Alternately, from Hood River, Oregon, drive north on Highway 35 (over the Columbia River) to Highway 14. Turn left and drive two miles to Highway 141-A. Turn right (north) on Highway 141-A and drive 25 miles north to Forest Road 88. Turn right and drive four miles to Forest Road 8810. Turn right and drive 1.5 miles to Forest Road 8810-010. Turn right and drive 0.25 mile to the campground on the right. Note that the access road is rough.

Contact: Gifford Pinchot National Forest, Mount Adams Ranger District, 509/395-3400, fax 509/395-3424, www.fs.fed.us.

92 PARADISE CREEK

Scenic rating: 9

on Paradise Creek and the Wind River in Gifford Pinchot National Forest

Map grid B2

This camp is located deep in Gifford Pinchot National Forest at the confluence of Paradise Creek and the Wind River. It gets light use despite easy access and easy RV parking. The well-shaded campsites are set among old-growth woods, primarily Douglas fir, cedar, and western hemlock. Lava Butte, located a short distance from the camp, is accessible by trail; the 1.2-mile round-trip hike from the campground provides a good view of the valley. Fishing is closed here. The elevation is 1,500 feet.

RV sites, facilities: There are 42 sites for tents or RVs up to 40 feet long. Picnic tables and fire grills are provided. Drinking water, vault toilets and firewood are available. A camp host is on-site. Some facilities are wheelchair accessible. Leashed pets are permitted.

Reservations, fees: Reservations are accepted

at 877/444-6777 or www.recreation.gov ($10 reservation fee). Sites are $15 per night, double sites are $34 per night, $5 per extra vehicle per night. Open mid-May–mid-September, weather permitting.

Directions: From Vancouver, Washington, take Highway 14 east and drive 50 miles to Carson and the Wind River Highway (County Road 30). Turn left (north) on the Wind River Highway and drive 20 miles to the camp on the right.

Contact: Gifford Pinchot National Forest, Mount Adams Ranger District, 509/395-3400, fax 509/395-3424, www.fs.fed.us.

93 FALLS CREEK HORSE CAMP

Scenic rating: 5

near the Pacific Crest Trail in Gifford Pinchot National Forest

Map grid B2

This camp sits at the threshold of a great launch point for hiking, horseback riding, and mountain biking. There are 90 miles of trail for horses and hiking and 40 miles for mountain bikes. The camp is set along Race Track Trail, adjacent to the western border of Indian Heaven Wilderness. A wilderness trailhead is available right at the camp. Although this is a multiple-use campground, note that the sites are small and the turnaround is tight for RVs.

RV sites, facilities: There are six sites for tents or RVs up to 15 feet long. Picnic tables and fire grills are provided. Pit toilets are available. A loading ramp for horses is available. There is no drinking water, and garbage must be packed out. Some facilities are wheelchair accessible. Leashed pets are permitted.

Reservations, fees: Reservations are not accepted. There is no fee. Open mid-June–November.

Directions: From Vancouver, Washington, on I-205, take Highway 14 and drive east for 50 miles to Carson and the Wind River Highway (County Road 30). Turn left (north) on the Wind River Highway and drive 9.5 miles to Forest Road 6517. Continue 1.5 miles to Forest

Road 65. Turn left and drive 15 miles to the campground on the left.

Contact: Gifford Pinchot National Forest, Mount Adams Ranger District, 509/395-3400, fax 509/395-3424, www.fs.fed.us.

94 CREST HORSE CAMP

Scenic rating: 6

bordering Big Lava Bed in
Gifford Pinchot National Forest

Map grid B2

Crest Horse Camp is a small, primitive, multiple-use camp set near the Pacific Crest Trail, adjacent to the eastern boundary of the Indian Heaven Wilderness. It is an excellent jumping-off spot for wilderness treks with horses or other stock animals. The camp features a forested setting, primarily second-growth Douglas fir. Adjacent to the camp is the Big Lava Bed, a volcanic flow known for its lava tubes and lava tube caves.

RV sites, facilities: There are three sites for tents or RVs up to 16 feet long. Picnic tables and fire pits are provided. A vault toilet is available. A loading ramp and high lines for horses are available. There is no drinking water, and garbage must be packed out. Some facilities are wheelchair accessible. Leashed pets are permitted.

Reservations, fees: Reservations are not accepted. There is no fee. Open mid-May–mid-October, weather permitting.

Directions: From Vancouver, Washington, take Highway 14 east and drive 50 miles to Carson and the Wind River Highway (County Road 30). Turn left (north) and drive nine miles to Forest Road 6517. Turn right (east) on Forest Road 6517 and drive 1.5 miles to Forest Road 65. Turn left (north) on Forest Road 65 and drive about 10 miles to Forest Road 60. Turn right and drive two miles to the camp on the right.

Contact: Gifford Pinchot National Forest, Mount Adams Ranger District, 509/395-3400, fax 509/395-3424, www.fs.fed.us.

95 BEAVER

Scenic rating: 7

on the Wind River in Gifford Pinchot National Forest

Map grid B2

This is the closest campground north of Stevenson in the Columbia Gorge. Set along the Wind River at an elevation of 1,100 feet, it features pretty, shaded sites. No fishing is permitted. The campsites are paved, and a large grassy day-use area is nearby. Hiking highlights include two nearby trailheads. Two miles north lies the trailhead for the Trapper Creek Wilderness, with 30 miles of trails, including a loop possibility. Three miles north is the Falls Creek Trail.

RV sites, facilities: There are 24 sites for tents or RVs up to 25 feet long and one group site for up to 40 people. Picnic tables and fire grills are provided. Drinking water, firewood, and flush and vault toilets are available. A camp host is on-site. Some facilities are wheelchair accessible. Leashed pets are permitted.

Reservations, fees: Reservations are accepted and are required for the group site at 877/444-6777 or www.recreation.gov ($10 reservation fee). Sites are $15.60–31.20 per night, $30 per night for double sites, $5 per extra vehicle per night. The group site is $91.75 per night. Open early May–late September.

Directions: From Vancouver, Washington, take Highway 14 east and drive 50 miles to Carson and the Wind River Highway (County Road 30). Turn left (north) and drive 12 miles to the campground entrance (five miles past Stabler) on the left.

Contact: Gifford Pinchot National Forest, Mount Adams Ranger District, 509/395-3400, fax 509/395-3424, www.fs.fed.us.

WASHINGTON

96 PANTHER CREEK AND HORSE CAMP

Scenic rating: 8

on Panther Creek in Gifford Pinchot National Forest

Map grid B2

This campground is set along Panther Creek in a second-growth forest of Douglas fir and western hemlock, adjacent to an old-growth forest. The sites are well defined, but despite a paved road to the campground and easy parking and access, it gets light use. The camp lies 3.5 miles from the Wind River, an option for those who enjoy fishing, hiking, and horseback riding. The Pacific Crest Trail is accessible from the adjacent Panther Creek Horse Camp. The elevation is 1,000 feet.

RV sites, facilities: There are 33 sites for tents or RVs up to 25 feet long and one equestrian site with a stock loading ramp at the adjacent horse camp. Picnic tables and fire rings are provided. Drinking water, pit toilets, garbage bins, and firewood are available. A camp host is on-site. Some facilities are wheelchair accessible. Leashed pets are permitted.

Reservations, fees: Reserve at 877/444-6777 or www.recreation.gov ($10 reservation fee). Sites are $15–34 per night, $5 per extra vehicle per night. Open mid-May–mid-September.

Directions: From Vancouver, Washington, take Highway 14 east and drive 50 miles to Carson and the Wind River Highway (County Road 30). Turn north and drive nine miles to Forest Road 6517 (just past Stabler). Turn right (east) on Forest Road 6517 and drive 1.5 miles to the campground entrance road on the right.

Contact: Gifford Pinchot National Forest, Mount Adams Ranger District, 509/395-3400, fax 509/395-3424, www.fs.fed.us.

97 OKLAHOMA

Scenic rating: 7

on the Little White Salmon River in Gifford Pinchot National Forest

Map grid B2

Pretty Oklahoma campground is set along the Little White Salmon River at an elevation of 1,700 feet. Fishing can be excellent in this area and the river is stocked in the spring with rainbow trout. The camp gets light use. It features some open meadow but is generally flat. Close to the Columbia River Gorge, it features paved road all the way into the campground and easy RV parking. As to why they named the camp Oklahoma, who knows? If you do, drop me a line.

RV sites, facilities: There are 23 sites for tents or RVs up to 40 feet long. Drinking water, fire rings, and picnic tables are provided. Vault toilets are available. Some facilities are wheelchair accessible. Leashed pets are permitted.

Reservations, fees: Reservations are accepted at 877/444-6777 or www.recreation.gov ($10 reservation fee). Sites are $15–17 per night, $5 per night for each additional vehicle. Open mid-May–mid-September, weather permitting.

Directions: From White Salmon, take N. Main Avenue to E. Jewett Boulevard. Turn left on E. Jewett Boulevard and drive 0.5 mile to SE 6th Avenue/Dock Grade Road. Turn right on SE 6th Avenue/Dock Grade Road and drive 0.8 mile to Lewis and Clark Highway/WA-14W. Turn right on Lewis and Clark Highway/WA-14W and drive 1.5 miles to Cook Underwood Road. Turn right on Cook Underwood Road and drive 8.3 miles to Willard Road. Turn right on Willard Road and drive two miles to Oklahoma Road. Turn right on Oklahoma Road and drive five miles to National Forest Development Road 18/Oklahoma Road. Turn right on National Forest Development Road 18/Oklahoma Road and drive three miles to the campground on the left.

Alternately, From Hood River, Oregon, drive north on Highway 35 for one mile over the

Columbia River to Highway 14. Turn left on Highway 14 and drive about five miles to Cook and County Road 1800. Turn right (north) and drive 14 miles (becomes Cook-Underwood Road, then Willard Road, then Oklahoma Road) to the campground entrance at the end of the paved road.

Contact: Gifford Pinchot National Forest, Mount Adams Ranger District, 509/395-3400, fax 509/395-3424, www.fs.fed.us.

98 MOSS CREEK

Scenic rating: 7

on the Little White Salmon River in Gifford Pinchot National Forest

Map grid B2

This campground is set at 1,400 feet elevation, about one mile from the Little White Salmon River. Although it's a short distance from Willard and Big Cedars County Park, the camp gets light use. The river provides good fishing prospects for trout in the spring, usually with few other people around. The sites are generally small but are shaded and still functional for most RVs. The road is paved all the way to the campground.

RV sites, facilities: There are 18 sites for tents or RVs up to 32 feet long. Picnic tables and fire grills are provided. Drinking water, vault toilets, and firewood are available. A camp host is available in the summer. Some facilities are wheelchair accessible. Leashed pets are permitted.

Reservations, fees: Reservations are accepted at 877/444-6777 or www.recreation.gov ($10 reservation fee). Sites are $17 per night, and $5 per night for each additional vehicle. Open mid-May–mid-September, weather permitting.

Directions: From White Salmon, take N. Main Avenue to E. Jewett Boulevard. Turn left on E. Jewett Boulevard and drive 0.5 mile to SE 6th Avenue/Dock Grade Road. Turn right on SE 6th Avenue/Dock Grade Road and drive 0.8 mile to Lewis and Clark Highway/WA-14W.

Turn right on Lewis and Clark Highway/WA-14W and drive 1.5 miles to Cook Underwood Road. Turn right on Cook Underwood Road and drive 8.3 miles to Willard Road. Turn right on Willard Road and drive two miles to Oklahoma Road. Turn right on Oklahoma Road and drive 1.3 miles to the campground on the left.

Alternately, from Hood River, Oregon, drive north on Highway 35 for one mile over the Columbia River to Highway 14. Turn left on Highway 14 and drive about five miles to Cook and County Road 1800. Turn right (north) and drive 10 miles (becomes Cook-Underwood Road, then Willard road, then Oklahoma Road) to the campground entrance on the right.

Contact: Gifford Pinchot National Forest, Mount Adams Ranger District, 509/395-3400, fax 509/395-3424, www.fs.fed.us.

99 COLUMBIA HILLS STATE PARK

Scenic rating: 10

near the Dalles Dam

Map grid B2

You may remember this park by its former name: Horsethief Lake State Park. The 338-acre park boasts 7,500 feet of Columbia River shoreline. It also adjoins the 3,000-acre Dalles Mountain Ranch State Park. Horsethief Lake, created by the Dalles Dam, covers approximately 100 acres and is part of the Columbia River. Horsethief Butte, adjacent to the lake, dominates the skyline. The bloom of lupine and balsamroot in mid-April create stunning views. Rock climbing in the park is popular, but the river canyon is often windy, especially in late spring and early summer. Most people find the place as a spot to camp while driving along the Columbia River Highway. There are hiking trails and access to both the lake and the Columbia River. The boat speed limit is 5 mph, and anglers can try for trout and bass.

Guided tours on weekends feature pictographs and petroglyphs; reservations are required at 509/767-1159.

RV sites, facilities: There are eight sites with partial hookups (15 amps, converters available) for tents or RVs up to 30 feet long, four sites for tents or RVs up to 30 feet long (no hookups), six primitive tent sites, and one hike-in/bike-in site. Picnic tables and fire grills are provided. Drinking water, restrooms with flush toilets and coin showers, firewood, a dump station, a horseshoe pit, and a picnic area are available. A store is within three miles. Boat-launching facilities are located on both the lake and the river. Leashed pets are permitted.

Reservations, fees: Reservations are not accepted. Sites are $19–25 per night, $12 per night for primitive sites and the hike-in/bike-in site, $10 per extra vehicle per night. Open April–late October.

Directions: From Dallesport, drive east on 6th Avenue to Dallesport Road. Turn left on Dallesport Road and drive 2.3 miles to Lewis and Clark Highway/WA-14E. Turn right at Lewis and Clark Highway/WA-14E and drive four miles to the campground on the left.

Alternately, from The Dalles in Oregon, turn north on Highway 197, cross over the Columbia River, and drive four miles to Highway 14. Turn right (east) and drive two miles to Milepost 85 and the park entrance on the right.

Contact: Columbia Hills State Park, 509/767-1159, fax 509/767-4304; state park information, 360/902-8844, www.parks.wa.gov.

SOUTHEASTERN WASHINGTON

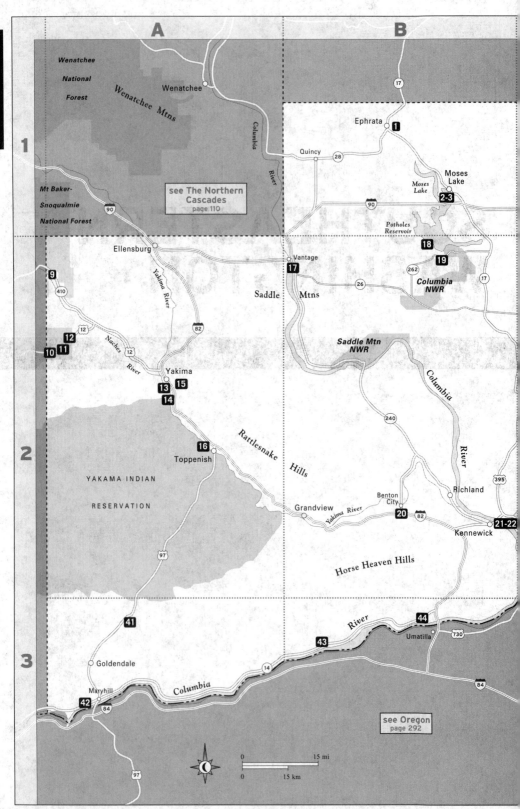

WASHINGTON

A

B

Wenatchee
National
Forest

Wenatchee Mtns

Wenatchee

Columbia River

1

17

Ephrata **1**

Quincy 28

Moses Lake

Moses Lake

2-3

see The Northern
Cascades
page 110

Mt Baker-
Snoqualmie
National Forest

90

Potholes Reservoir

18

19

Columbia
NWR

262

17

Ellensburg

Vantage

Saddle Mtns

26

17

9

410

Yakima River

82

Saddle Mtn
NWR

12

12

Naches River

Columbia River

10 **11**

12

Yakima

13 **15**

14

240

395

Richland

2

16

Toppenish

Rattlesnake Hills

YAKAMA INDIAN

RESERVATION

Grandview

Yakima River

Benton City

20

82

21-22

Kennewick

97

Horse Heaven Hills

41

3

44

River

43

Umatilla

730

Goldendale

14

84

Maryhill

Columbia

42

84

see Oregon
page 292

97

0   15 mi

0   15 km

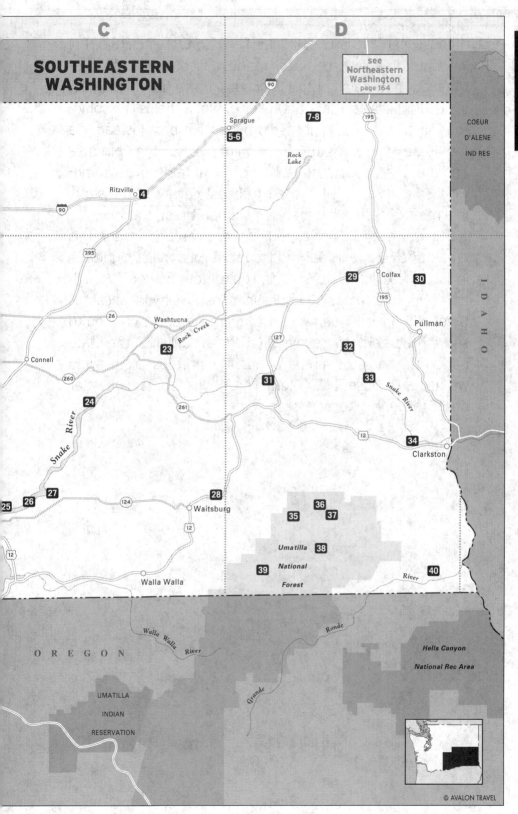

The expansive domain of southeastern Washington is a surprise for many newcomers. Instead of the high mountains of the Cascades, there are rolling hills. Instead of forests, there are miles of wheat fields (Washington's second-largest export crop behind lumber). Instead of a multitude of streams, there are giant rivers – the Columbia and the Snake. Just one pocket of mountains and a somewhat sparse forest sit in the southeast corner of the state, in a remote sector of Umatilla National Forest.

The Lewis and Clark expedition was routed through this area some 200 years ago, and today, several major highways, including I-82 and U.S. 395, bring out-of-town visitors through the region en route to other destinations. A network of camps is set along these highways, including RV parks created to serve the needs of travelers. Of the area parks, the state parks offer the best campgrounds. The prettiest picture you will find is Palouse Falls, where a gorgeous fountain of water pours through a desert gorge.

1 OASIS RV PARK AND GOLF

Scenic rating: 5

near Soap Lake

Map grid B1

This area can be extremely warm and arid during the summer months, but, fortunately, Oasis RV Park offers shaded sites. There are two fishing ponds at the resort: One has crappie, while the other is for kids and has trout and bass. There is also a nine-hole golf course at the park. Mineral baths are located just a few miles north.

RV sites, facilities: There are 12 tent sites and 69 sites with full or partial hookups (30 amps) for tents or RVs of any length. Some sites are pull-through. Picnic tables are provided. Restrooms with flush toilets and coin showers, cable TV, Wi-Fi, a playground, horseshoe pits, picnic areas, a nine-hole golf course, an 18-hole miniature golf course, dump station, a store, propane gas, coin laundry, ice, a seasonal heated swimming pool, and two fishing ponds are available. A café is located within one mile. Leashed pets are permitted.

Reservations, fees: Reservations are recommended. Sites are $20–25 per night, $5 per night per extra vehicle. Some credit cards are accepted. Open year-round, with limited winter facilities.

Directions: From Spokane, take I-90 west to the Moses Lake exit and Highway 17. Turn northeast on Highway 17 and drive 32.7 miles to the Y junction with Highway 282. Take Highway 282 and drive four miles to Highway 281/283 (a stoplight). Turn left and drive 1.9 miles to the park on the right (just before reaching the town of Ephrata).

Contact: Oasis RV Park and Golf, 509/754-5102 or 877/754-5102, www.oasisrvandgolfresort.com.

2 LAKEFRONT RV PARK

Scenic rating: 5

near Moses Lake State Park

Map grid B1

This park sits a short distance from Moses Lake State Park, which is open for day-use only. The primary appeal is Moses Lake, Washington's largest freshwater lake, where you will find shady picnic spots with tables and fire grills, beach access, and moorage floats. Waterskiing and personal watercraft are allowed on the lake. Bird hunting is popular in season. Sand dunes are located a few miles away and can be used for all-terrain-vehicle (ATV) activities.

RV sites, facilities: There are 42 sites with full hookups (30 amps) for RVs of any length. Some sites are pull-through. Picnic tables are provided. A restroom with flush toilets and coin showers is available. Coin laundry, ice, cable TV, community fire pits, and boat docks and launch are available. A dump station, store, and restaurant are located within one mile. Leashed pets are permitted with certain restrictions.

Reservations, fees: Reservations are accepted. Sites are $30 per night. Open year-round.

Directions: From Spokane, drive west on I-90 to Moses Lake and Exit 176. Take that exit to Broadway, turn right, and drive 0.75 mile to Burress Avenue. Turn left (west) on Burress Avenue and drive one block to the park.

Contact: Lakefront RV Park, 509/765-8294.

3 WILLOWS TRAILER VILLAGE

Scenic rating: 5

near Moses Lake State Park

Map grid B1

One of two campgrounds in the area, Willows Trailer Village has grassy, shaded sites, horseshoe pits, barbecues, and a recreation field. Most recreation opportunities can be found at Moses Lake, including picnicking, beach access, waterskiing, and moorage floats. Birdwatching and sand dunes for ATV riding are nearby. Note that there are some permanent site rentals at this RV park, but a landscape barrier separates them from the other sites.

RV sites, facilities: There are 20 tent sites and 68 pull-through sites for RVs of any length, most with full hookups (30 and 50 amps). Picnic tables are provided. A restroom with flush toilets and coin showers, propane gas, a convenience store, ice, coin laundry, playground, and horseshoe pits are available. There is also a hair salon on-site. Leashed pets are permitted.

Reservations, fees: Reservations are accepted. Sites are $28.50–34.50 per night, $3 per person per night for more than two people. Open year-round.

Directions: From Spokane, drive west on I-90 to Moses Lake and Exit 179 and Highway 17. Turn south on Highway 17 and drive 2.5 miles to Road M SE. Turn right and drive 0.5 mile to the park on the left.

Contact: Willows Trailer Village, tel./fax 509/765-7531.

4 LA QUINTA INN/ RITZVILLE RV PARK

Scenic rating: 7

in Ritzville

Map grid C1

If you have an RV, well, this might be the only site to stake it on within a radius of 25 miles. Ritzville RV Park is adjacent to La Quinta motel. A nine-hole golf course and tennis courts are just across the street. Burroughs Historical Museum is a possible side trip in town. The nearest fishing is at Sprague Lake, 22 miles north on U.S. 395.

RV sites, facilities: There are 39 pull-through sites for tents or RVs of any length (30 and 50 amps full hookups). Picnic tables are provided. Restrooms with flush toilets and showers, cable TV, a dump station, coin laundry, modem access, ice, a playground, spa, and seasonal heated swimming pool are available. Propane gas, a store, gift shop, café, and restaurant are located within one mile. Some facilities are wheelchair accessible. Leashed pets are permitted.

Reservations, fees: Reservations are accepted for groups only. Sites are $15–30 per night. Some credit cards are accepted. Open year-round, with limited winter facilities.

Directions: From Pasco, take U.S. 395 north and drive 85 miles to Ritzville and I-90. Take

I-90 east and drive 0.5 mile to Exit 221. Take that exit and drive 0.25 mile to Smitty's Boulevard. Turn right and drive a short distance to the motel/RV check-in on the left.

Contact: La Quinta Inn/Ritzville RV Park, 509/659-1007, fax 509/659-1025.

5 FOUR SEASONS CAMPGROUND & RESORT

Scenic rating: 7

on Sprague Lake

Map grid D1

This campground along the shore of Sprague Lake, one of the top fishing waters in the state, has spacious sites with plenty of vegetation. The fishing for rainbow trout is best in May and June, with some bass in spring and fall. Because there is an abundance of natural feed in the lake, the fish reach larger sizes here than in neighboring lakes. Walleye up to 10 pounds are taken here. Crappie and catfish are also abundant, with a sprinkling of perch and bluegill. In late July–August, a fair algae bloom is a turnoff for swimmers and water-skiers.

RV sites, facilities: There are 38 sites with full or partial hookups, including some pull-through sites, for RVs of any length, and four cabins. Tent camping is allowed when space is available. Picnic tables and fire pits are provided. Restrooms with flush toilets and coin showers, drinking water, a dump station, firewood, ice, a convenience store with fishing tackle, a fish-cleaning station, a small basketball court, and a seasonal swimming pool are available. Boat and fishing docks, launching facilities, slips, and rentals are nearby. Leashed pets are permitted.

Reservations, fees: Reservations are accepted. Sites are $21–26 per night, $1 per pet per night. Open late March–mid-October, weather permitting.

Directions: From Spokane, drive west on I-90 for 35 miles to Exit 245. Take Exit 245 and drive south to 4th Street. Turn right and drive one block to B Street. Turn left and drive two blocks to 1st Street. Turn right and drive one mile through the town of Sprague to a Y intersection (from here, the resort is six miles away). Continue (over the railroad tracks and then under I-90) to Lake Road. Turn left and drive (parallel to the freeway) until the road bears to the right to Bob Lee Road. Turn left on Bob Lee Road and drive (over I-90) to the resort.

Contact: Four Seasons Campground and Resort, 509/257-2332, www.fourseasonscampground.com.

⑥ SPRAGUE LAKE RESORT

Scenic rating: 5

on Sprague Lake

Map grid D1

This developed campground is located on the shore of Sprague Lake, about 35 miles from Spokane. It offers a pleasant, grassy setting with about 50 cottonwood and native trees on the property. Sprague Lake is one of the top fishing waters in the state—look for rainbow trout, bass, walleye, crappie, catfish, perch, and bluegill. A late-summer algae bloom tends to leave swimmers and water-skiers landlocked.

RV sites, facilities: There are 30 pull-through sites with full or partial hookups for RVs of any length and 50 tent sites. Picnic tables and fire grills are provided. Restrooms with flush toilets and coin showers, drinking water, a small store, coin laundry, ice, firewood, a playground, boat docks, launching facilities, and rentals are available. Leashed pets are permitted.

Reservations, fees: Reservations are accepted. Sites are $22–32 per night, plus $2 per person per night for more than two people. Open April–mid-October.

Directions: From Spokane, drive west on I-90 to the Sprague Business Center exit. Take that exit to Sprague Lake Road and continue two miles to the resort on the left (well signed).

Contact: Sprague Lake Resort, 509/257-2864, www.spraguelakeresort.com.

⑦ KLINK'S WILLIAMS LAKE RESORT

Scenic rating: 6

on Williams Lake

Map grid D1

This family-oriented resort is set on the shore of Williams Lake, which is less than three miles long and is popular for swimming and waterskiing. The resort has a swimming area with a floating dock and slide. This lake is also one of the top fishing lakes in the region for rainbow and cutthroat trout. Rocky cliffs border the lake in some areas. Note that about 100 permanent residents live at the resort.

An option for a side trip is Turnbull National Wildlife Refuge, an expanse of marsh and pine that is a significant stopover point for migratory birds on the Pacific Flyway. This is a prime spot and only a 30-minute drive out of Spokane, yet it is relatively unknown.

RV sites, facilities: There are 60 sites with full or partial hookups (30 and 50 amps) for RVs of any length, 15 tent sites, and five log cabins. Picnic tables and fire grills are provided. Restrooms with flush toilets and coin showers, drinking water, modem access, propane gas, a dump station, firewood, a general store, café, restaurant, ice, a playground, boat docks, launching facilities, and boat rentals are available. Leashed pets are permitted.

Reservations, fees: Reservations are recommended. Sites are $20.95–29.95 per night. Some credit cards are accepted. Open mid-April–October.

Directions: From Spokane, drive west on I-90 for 10 miles to Exit 270 and Highway 904. Turn south on Highway 904 and drive four miles to Cheney and Cheney Plaza Road. Turn left (south) on Cheney Plaza Road and drive 12 miles to Williams Lake Road. Turn right (west) and drive two miles to the resort on the left.

Contact: Klink's Williams Lake Resort, 509/235-2391, www.klinksresort.com.

8 BUNKER'S RESORT

Scenic rating: 8

on Williams Lake

Map grid D1

Bunker's Resort is set on the shore of Williams Lake. The lake is stocked with rainbow, cutthroat, and triploid trout; fishing season is from the last Saturday in April through September. Waterskiing, wakeboarding, and personal watercraft are allowed; swimming is also popular.

RV sites, facilities: There are 10 sites with full or partial hookups (30 amps) for RVs up to 32 feet long, seven tent sites, and four cottages. Picnic tables and fire pits are provided. Restrooms with flush toilets and coin showers, drinking water, propane gas, dump station, a restaurant, convenience store, bait and tackle, ice, boat and fishing docks, launching facilities, and boat rentals are available. Leashed pets are permitted.

Reservations, fees: Reservations are accepted. Sites are $25–35 per night. Some credit cards are accepted. Open mid-April–September.

Directions: From Spokane, drive west on I-90 for 10 miles to Exit 270 and Highway 904. Turn south on Highway 904 and drive six miles to Cheney and Mullinex Road. Turn left (south) on Mullinex Road and drive 12 miles to the resort.

Contact: Bunker's Resort, 509/235-5212 or 800/404-6674, www.bunkersresort.com.

9 SQUAW ROCK RESORT

Scenic rating: 8

on the Naches River

Map grid A2

This park, situated in a stand of old-growth fir and pine on the Naches River, is close to a host of activities, including trout fishing, hiking trails, marked bike trails, and a riding stable. The park has a pool and spa. The nearby town of Naches, located southeast of the campground on State Route 410, offers all services.

RV sites, facilities: There are 65 sites with full or partial hookups (20, 30, and 50 amps) for RVs of any length, 10 tent sites, six cabins, and four motel rooms. Picnic tables and fire pits are provided. Restrooms with flush toilets and showers, propane gas, gasoline, diesel, a dump station, cable TV, a recreation hall, convenience store, café, ice, a playground, spa, and a seasonal heated swimming pool are available. Leashed pets are permitted.

Reservations, fees: Reservations are accepted. Sites are $35–40 per night, $3 per person per night for more than two people, $10 per pet per stay in the cabins and motel rooms. Some credit cards are accepted. Open year-round.

Directions: From Yakima, drive northwest on U.S. 12 for 18 miles to State Route 410. Continue straight on State Route 410 and drive 15 miles to the resort on the left.

Contact: Squaw Rock Resort, 509/658-2926, fax 509/658-2927, www.squawrockresort.net.

10 HAUSE CREEK

Scenic rating: 7

on the Tieton River in Wenatchee National Forest

Map grid A2

Several creeks converge at this campground along the Tieton River (elevation 2,500 feet). The Tieton Dam, which creates Rimrock Lake, is located just upstream. Hause Creek is one of the larger, more developed camps in the area. Willows campground provides a primitive alternative.

RV sites, facilities: There are 42 sites for tents or RVs up to 49 feet. Picnic tables and fire grills are provided. Drinking water, flush toilets, firewood, and garbage bins are available. A camp host is on-site. Boat docks, launching facilities, and rentals are located on Rimrock Lake. Some facilities are wheelchair accessible. Leashed pets are permitted.

Reservations, fees: Reservations are accepted at 877/444-6777 or www.recreation.gov ($10 reservation fee). Sites are $15–19 per night, $34 per night for double sites, and $5 per extra vehicle per night. Open late May–September, weather permitting.

Directions: From Yakima, drive northwest on U.S. 12 for 18 miles to the junction with Highway 410. Turn west on U.S. 12 and drive 22 miles to the campground on the left.

Contact: Okanogan and Wenatchee National Forests, Naches Ranger District, 509/653-1400, fax 509/653-2638, www.fs.fed.us.

11 WILLOWS

Scenic rating: 5

on the Tieton River in Wenatchee National Forest
Map grid A2

This primitive, beautiful, and easily accessible camp can be found on the Tieton River at 2,400 feet elevation. Rimrock Lake to the west provides many recreation options, and hiking trails leading into the William O. Douglas Wilderness are within driving distance.

RV sites, facilities: There are 16 sites for tents or RVs up to 35 feet. Picnic tables and fire grills are provided. Drinking water, pit toilets, firewood and garbage service are available. Some facilities are wheelchair accessible. Leashed pets are permitted.

Reservations, fees: Reservations are accepted at 877/444-6777 or www.recreation.gov ($10 reservation fee). Sites are $17–19 per night, $5 per night per extra vehicle. Open mid-May–September, weather permitting.

Directions: From Yakima, drive northwest on I-82 for 17 miles to the junction with Highway 410. Turn west on U.S. 12 and drive 16 miles to the campground on the left.

Contact: Okanogan and Wenatchee National Forests, Naches Ranger District, 509/653-1400, fax 509/653-2638, www.fs.fed.us.

12 WINDY POINT

Scenic rating: 5

on the Tieton River in Wenatchee National Forest
Map grid A2

This campground, located along the Tieton River at an elevation of 2,000 feet, is more isolated than the camps set westward toward Rimrock Lake. Drinking water is a bonus. Fishing access is available.

RV sites, facilities: There are 15 sites for tents or RVs up to 37 feet. Picnic tables and fire grills are provided. Drinking water and vault toilets are available. Garbage service and firewood are available nearby. Some facilities are wheelchair accessible. Leashed pets are permitted.

Reservations, fees: Reservations are not accepted. Sites are $15–19 per night, $5 per extra vehicle per night. Open mid- May–September, weather permitting.

Directions: From Yakima, drive northwest on I-82 for 17 miles to the junction with Highway 410. Turn west on U.S. 12 and drive nine miles to the campground on the left.

Contact: Okanogan and Wenatchee National Forests, Naches Ranger District, 509/653-1400, fax 509/653-2638, www.fs.fed.us.

13 CIRCLE H RV RANCH

Scenic rating: 8

in Yakima
Map grid A2

This pleasant, centrally located, and clean park with a Western flavor has comfortable, spacious sites among ornamental trees and roses. Nearby recreation options include an 18-hole golf course, hiking trails, and marked bike trails.

RV sites, facilities: There are 69 sites with full hookups (30 and 50 amps) for RVs of any length, and 12 tent sites. Some sites are pull-through. Picnic tables and barbecues are provided. Restrooms with flush toilets and showers, a recreation hall, coin laundry, a spa, modem and Wi-Fi access, clubhouse, playgrounds, horseshoes, a tennis court, volleyball and basketball, a video arcade, an 18-hole miniature golf course, and a seasonal heated swimming pool are available. Propane gas, a store, casino, and shopping center are located within one mile. Mini-storage units are available for a fee. Leashed pets are permitted.

Reservations, fees: Reservations are accepted.

Sites are $25–28 per night, $4 per person per night for more than two people. Some credit cards are accepted. Open year-round.

Directions: In Yakima on I-82, take Exit 34 West and drive one block to South 18th Street. Turn right (north) and drive 0.25 mile to the campground on the right.

Contact: Circle H RV Ranch, 509/457-3683, www.circlehrvranch.com.

14 TRAILER INNS RV PARK/YAKIMA

Scenic rating: 7

in Yakima

Map grid A2

This spot has many of the luxuries you'd find in a hotel, including a pool, spa, on-site security, and a large-screen TV. An 18-hole golf course, hiking trails, marked bike trails, and tennis courts are close by. Local pond fishing, as well as fishing in the Yakima River, is available. It's especially pretty in the fall when the sycamores turn color. The region has become known for its wineries and breweries. A variety of fresh produce is available in the local area in season.

RV sites, facilities: There are 135 sites for tents or RVs of any length (20, 30, and 50 amp full hookups). Some sites are pull-through. Picnic tables are provided and some sites have gas barbecues. Restrooms with flush toilets and showers, cable TV, Wi-Fi and modem access, propane gas, a dump station, a recreation hall, coin laundry, ice, an indoor heated swimming pool, a whirlpool, TV room, dog walk, enclosed barbecue area (no open fires permitted), and a playground are available. A store and café are within one block. Leashed pets are permitted.

Reservations, fees: Reservations are accepted. Sites are $20–40 per night, $5 per person per night for more than two people, and $5 per extra vehicle per night. Some credit cards are accepted. Open year-round.

Directions: In Yakima on I-82, take Exit 31 and drive south for one block on North 1st Street to the park on the right (west side of the road).

Contact: Trailer Inns RV Park, 509/452-9561; corporate office, 509/248-1142, www.trailerinnsrv.com.

15 YAKIMA SPORTSMAN STATE PARK

Scenic rating: 8

on the Yakima River

Map grid A2

Yakima Sportsman State Park is popular with visitors to the Yakima area. Campsites and picnic areas are shaded, thanks to the park's location on the Yakima River floodplain. There is a fishing pond for children (no anglers over age 15 are allowed), access to the river for adult anglers, and an unpaved roadway on the river dike for hikers and horseback riders. A put-in for kayaking and rafting is an approximately 20-minute drive away. No swimming is allowed. Nearby recreation options include bird-watching, an 18-hole golf course, and hiking trails.

RV sites, facilities: There are 30 sites for tents and 37 sites with full hookups (50 amps) for RVs up to 60 feet long; some sites are pull-through. Picnic tables and fire grills are provided. Restrooms with flush toilets and coin showers, a dump station, firewood, playground, horseshoe pit, and picnic shelter are available. A store and ice are within one mile. Some facilities are wheelchair accessible. Leashed pets are permitted.

Reservations, fees: Reservations are accepted at 888/CAMP-OUT (888/226-7688) or www.parks.wa.gov/reservations ($6.50–8.50 reservation fee). Sites are $21–28 per night, $10 per extra vehicle per night. Some credit cards are accepted. Open year-round.

Directions: In Yakima, drive on I-82 to Milepost 34 and the Highway 24 exit. Turn east on Highway 24 and drive one mile to Keys Road. Turn left and drive 0.75 mile to South 33rd Street. Turn left and drive approximately 300 feet to the park entrance on the left.

Contact: Yakima Sportsman State Park, 509/575-2774, fax 509/454-4114; state park information, 360/902-8844, www.parks.wa.gov.

16 YAKAMA NATION RV RESORT

Scenic rating: 3

near the Yakima River

Map grid A2

The park is set within the Yakama Indian Reservation (the tribe spells its name differently from the river and town), close to a casino and movie theater. The Toppenish National Wildlife Refuge (509/545-8588), the best side trip, is almost always a good spot to see a large variety of birds. Nearby Toppenish, a historic Old West town with a museum, is also worth a side trip.

RV sites, facilities: There are 125 sites with full hookups (20, 30, and 50 amps) for RVs of any length, one tent site, and several tepees (both permanent and portable) for up to 10 people each. Picnic tables and fire pits are provided. Restrooms with flush toilets and showers, cable TV, modem and Wi-Fi access, a dump station, playground, recreation room, exercise room, jogging track, basketball, volleyball, tennis courts, a seasonal heated swimming pool, spa, sauna, and coin laundry are available. A picnic shelter is available in the tent area. A restaurant and grocery store are located within 1.5 miles. Some facilities are wheelchair accessible. Leashed pets are permitted.

Reservations, fees: Reservations are accepted at 800/874-3087. Tent sites are $20 per night, RV sites are $29–30 per night, $2 per person per night for more than two people. Tepees are $20–30 per night for five campers, plus $5 per night for each additional person. Some credit cards are accepted. Open year-round.

Directions: From Yakima, drive south on U.S. 97 for 16 miles to the resort on the right.

Contact: Yakama Nation RV Resort, 509/865-2000 or 800/874-3087, www.yakamanation.com.

17 WANAPUM STATE RECREATION AREA

Scenic rating: 7

on the Columbia River and Wanapum Lake

Map grid B2

The site of an ancient petrified forest, Ginkgo Petrified Forest State Park is a National Natural Landmark. This fossilized forest is set along Wanapum Lake in the course of the Columbia River. Ginkgo is a huge park, covering 7,740 acres and surrounding the 27,000 feet of shoreline of Wanapum Lake. The park features an interpretive center and trail.

Although completely separate, Wanapum State Recreation Area is linked to Ginkgo Petrified Forest State Park. Camping, however, is permitted only at the Wanapum Recreation Area, which is three miles south of I-90. Recreation options include hiking (three miles of trails), swimming, boating, waterskiing, and fishing. There are also several historical Civilian Conservation Corps structures from the 1930s. The Wanapum campground is set up primarily for RVs, with full hookups, restrooms, and showers. Note that the park always fills up during the Gorge concert season.

RV sites, facilities: There are 50 sites with full hookups (30 amps) for RVs up to 50 feet long. Picnic tables and fire grills are provided. Restrooms with flush toilets and coin showers and firewood are available. Boat docks, launching facilities, a museum, and a picnic area are nearby. Some facilities are wheelchair accessible. Leashed pets are permitted.

Reservations, fees: Reservations are accepted in season at 888/CAMP-OUT (888/226-7688) or www.parks.wa.gov/reservations ($6.50–8.50 reservation fee). Sites are $28 per night, $10 per extra vehicle per night. Open year-round, weather permitting; weekends and holidays only Nov.–Mar.

Directions: From Ellensburg, drive east on I-90 to the Vantage Highway/Huntzinger Road (Exit 136). Take that exit, turn south on Huntzinger Road, and drive three miles to the campground on the left.

Contact: Wanapum State Recreation Area, 509/856-2700; state park information, 360/902-8844, www.parks.wa.gov.

18 POTHOLES STATE PARK

Scenic rating: 8

on Potholes Reservoir
Map grid B2

This park is set on Potholes Reservoir, also known as O'Sullivan Reservoir (because of the O'Sullivan Dam), where fishing is the highlight. Trout, walleye, bass, crappie, and perch are among the species taken here. Waterskiing and hiking (on one mile of hiking trails) are other recreation options. A side trip to the Columbia Wildlife Refuge, located two miles southeast of the park, is recommended. Note: Do not confuse Potholes Reservoir with the Potholes Lakes, a 30- to 45-minute drive away.

RV sites, facilities: There are 61 sites for tents or RVs up to 50 feet long (no hookups), 60 sites for tents or RVs up to 50 feet long (30 amp full hookups), and a group site for up to 50 people. Picnic tables and fire grills are provided. Restrooms with flush toilets and showers, a dump station, a playground, volleyball courts, firewood, and a sheltered picnic area are available. Boat-launching facilities and rentals are nearby. Some facilities are wheelchair accessible. Leashed pets are permitted.

Reservations, fees: Reservations are accepted at 888/CAMP-OUT (888/226-7688) or www. parks.wa.gov/reservations ($6.50–8.50 reservation fee). Tent sites are $21 per night, RV sites are $28 per night, $10 per night per extra vehicle. Open year-round.

Directions: From I-90 at Moses Lake, take Exit 179 and Highway 17. Turn south and drive nine miles to Highway 262. Turn right (west) and drive 11 miles to the resort on the southern shore of Potholes Reservoir (well signed).

Contact: Potholes State Park, 509/346-2759, fax 509/346-1732; state park information, 360/902-8844, www.parks.wa.gov.

19 MAR DON RESORT

Scenic rating: 7

on Potholes Reservoir
Map grid B2

This resort is located on Potholes Reservoir and provides opportunities for fishing, swimming, and boating. A marina, tackle, and boat rentals are all available. Hiking trails and marked bike trails are close by. Many visitors find the café and cocktail lounge a nice bonus. The Columbia National Wildlife Refuge is located nearby to the south and provides exceptional bird-watching; pelicans and kingfishers are common, and bald eagles and migratory sandhill cranes are often seen as well.

RV sites, facilities: There are 88 sites for tents or RVs of any length (no hookups) and 187 sites with full or partial hookups for tents or RVs of any length; some sites are pull-through. Three rental homes, nine cottages, and 18 motel rooms are also available. Picnic tables and fire rings are provided. A restroom with flush toilets and coin showers, drinking water, propane gas, a dump station, a small convenience store, a boutique, coin laundry, ice, a playground, fish-cleaning station, boat moorage, boat rentals, and launching facilities are available. Some facilities are wheelchair accessible. Leashed pets are permitted.

Reservations, fees: Reservations are accepted. RV sites are $20–35 per night, tent sites are $15–30, $5 per extra vehicle per night, and $3 per pet per night. Some credit cards are accepted. Open year-round.

Directions: From Highway 17 in Moses Lake, drive south nine miles to Highway 262. Turn right (west) and drive 10 miles to the resort on the southern shore of Potholes Reservoir.

Contact: Mar Don Resort, 509/346-2651 or 800/416-2736, www.mardonresort.com.

20 BEACH RV PARK

Scenic rating: 8

on the Yakima River

Map grid B2

This park along the shore of the Yakima River is a pleasant spot with spacious RV sites, a large grassy area, and poplar trees and shrubs that provide privacy between many of the sites. Note that Beach RV is the only park in the area that has tent camping available. Fishing for bass and trout is available in season. Nearby recreation options include an 18-hole golf course and a full-service marina, both within 12 miles.

RV sites, facilities: There are 59 sites with full hookups (30 and 50 amps) for RVs of any length, including some pull-through sites, and 10 sites for tents. Picnic tables are provided. Restrooms with flush toilets and coin showers, cable TV, Wi-Fi, and coin laundry are available. Propane gas, a dump station, a store, and a café are located within one mile. Boat-launching facilities are nearby. Leashed pets are permitted.

Reservations, fees: Reservations are accepted. RV sites are $29–35 per night, tent sites are $21.95 per night, $4 per person per night for more than two people, $2 per night per extra vehicle, and $2 per night per pet. Some credit cards are accepted. Open year-round.

Directions: From Pasco, drive west on U.S. 12 past Richland and continue eight miles to Exit 96 and the Benton City/West Richland exit. Take that exit and drive one block north to Abby Avenue. Turn left (west) and drive 1.5 blocks to the park.

Contact: Beach RV Park, tel./fax 509/588-5959, www.beachrv.net.

21 GREENTREE RV & MOBILE HOME PARK

Scenic rating: 6

in Pasco

Map grid B2

This shady park in urban Pasco is close to an 18-hole golf course, hiking trails, and a full-

service marina. The Franklin County Historical Museum, which is located in town, and the Sacajawea State Park Museum and Interpretive Center, located three miles southeast of town, both offer extensive collections of Native American artifacts. Note that most sites are filled with monthly rentals.

RV sites, facilities: There are 40 sites with full hookups for RVs of any length. A coin laundry and coin showers are available, but there are no toilets. A mini-storage facility is on-site. Propane gas, a store, café, and ice are located within one mile. Boat docks, launching facilities, and rentals are nearby. Leashed pets are permitted, with certain restrictions.

Reservations, fees: Reservations are accepted. Sites are $20 per night. Weekly and monthly rates available. Open year-round.

Directions: In Pasco on I-82, take Exit 13 onto 4th Avenue and continue a short distance to the park entrance driveway on the right.

Contact: Greentree RV & Mobile Home Park, tel./fax 509/547-6220.

22 ARROWHEAD RV PARK

Scenic rating: 5

near the Columbia River

Map grid B2

Arrowhead provides a decent layover spot in Pasco. The park has both trees and grassy areas. Nearby recreation options include an 18-hole golf course, a full-service marina, and tennis courts. Some sites are filled with monthly renters.

RV sites, facilities: There are 80 sites for tents or RVs of any length (20, 30, and 50 amp full hookups) and a large grassy area for tents. Some sites are pull-through. Picnic tables are provided. Restroom with flush toilets and showers, drinking water, TV hookups, a pay phone, and coin laundry are available. A store and café are located within walking distance. Leashed pets are permitted, with certain restrictions.

Reservations, fees: Reservations are accepted. Sites are $30 per night, $7 per person per night for more than two people, and $1 per pet per night. Open year-round.

Directions: In Pasco on U.S. 395 North, take the Kartchner Street exit, turn east, and drive a short distance to Commercial Avenue. Turn right (south) and drive 0.25 mile to the park entrance on the right.

Contact: Arrowhead RV Park, 509/545-8206.

23 PALOUSE FALLS STATE PARK

Scenic rating: 10

on the Snake and Palouse Rivers
Map grid C2

This remote state park is well worth the trip. Spectacular 198-foot Palouse Falls is a sight not to miss. A 0.25-mile wheelchair-accessible trail leads to a waterfall overlook. The park is set at the confluence of the Snake and Palouse Rivers, and it does not receive heavy use, even in summer. The park covers 1,282 acres and features a waterfall observation shelter, shaded picnic facilities, historical displays, and an abundance of wildlife.

RV sites, facilities: There are 10 sites for tents or RVs up to 40 feet long (no hookups). Picnic tables and fire grills are provided. Drinking water (in summer), pit toilets, and a picnic area are available. Some facilities are wheelchair accessible. Leashed pets are permitted.

Reservations, fees: Reservations are not accepted. Sites are $19 per night, $10 per extra vehicle per night. Open year-round, weather permitting, with limited winter facilities.

Directions: From Starbuck, drive northwest on Highway 261 for 15 miles (crossing the river) to the park entrance and Palouse Falls Road. Turn right and drive to the park.

Contact: Palouse Falls State Park, 360/902-8844, www.parks.wa.gov.

24 WINDUST

Scenic rating: 6

on Lake Sacajawea
Map grid C2

With no other campgrounds within a 30-mile radius, Windust is the only game in town. The camp is located along the shore of Lake Sacajawea near the Lower Monumental Dam on the Snake River. The park covers 54 acres. Swimming, waterskiing, and fishing are popular.

RV sites, facilities: There are 24 sites for tents or RVs of any length (no hookups). Picnic tables and fire grills are provided. Flush toilets are available May–September, and pit toilets are provided the rest of the year. Drinking water, garbage bins, dump station, a playground, and a swimming beach are available nearby. No alcohol is permitted. Boat docks and launching facilities are nearby. Some facilities are wheelchair accessible. Leashed pets are permitted.

Reservations, fees: Reservations are not accepted. There is no fee for camping. Open year-round.

Directions: From Pasco, drive east on U.S. 12 for 2.5 miles to Pasco/Kahlotus Highway. Turn east and drive 28 miles to Burr Canyon Road. Turn right on Burr Canyon Road and drive 5.2 miles to the park (from the north, Burr Canyon Road becomes Highway 263).

Contact: U.S. Army Corps of Engineers, Walla Walla District, 509/547-2048, www.nww.usace.army.mil; City of Pasco, 509/547-2048.

25 HOOD PARK

Scenic rating: 6

on Lake Wallula
Map grid C2

This 99-acre developed park on Lake Wallula provides access for swimming and boating. Some sites are situated near the shoreline, and shaded sites are available. No alcohol is permitted. There are hiking trails throughout the park, along with fishing ponds. Other recreation options include basketball and horseshoes.

McNary Wildlife Refuge is right next door, and Sacajawea State Park is within four miles.

RV sites, facilities: There are 69 sites with partial hookups for tents or RVs of any length, and an overflow camping area with some pull-through sites. Picnic tables and fire grills are provided. Drinking water, restrooms with flush toilets and showers, a dump station, a playground, horseshoe pits, a basketball court, swimming beach, covered picnic area, pay phone, and an amphitheater are available. A restaurant and convenience store are located within two miles. Boat docks and launching facilities are nearby. Some facilities are wheelchair accessible. Leashed pets are permitted.

Reservations, fees: Reservations are accepted at 877/444-6777 or www.recreation.gov ($10 reservation fee). Sites are $11–22 per night, $4 per night per additional vehicle, and $8 per night in the overflow area and for boat camping. Open May–September.

Directions: In Pasco, drive southeast on U.S. 12 for five miles to the junction with Highway 124. Turn left (east) on Highway 124 and drive to the park entrance on the left (just before the town of Burbank). Drive 0.5 mile to the gate entrance.

Contact: U.S. Army Corps of Engineers, Walla Walla District, 509/547-2048, www.nww.usace. army.mil.

26 CHARBONNEAU PARK

Scenic rating: 6

on the Snake River

Map grid C2

This shorefront camp is the centerpiece of a 244-acre park set along the Snake River just above Ice Harbor Dam. It is a good spot for fishing, boating, swimming, and waterskiing. An overflow camping area provides an insurance policy if the numbered sites are full. No alcohol is permitted. At Lake Sacajawea, the dam's visitors center (open daily April–October) features exhibits and a view through Lucite of a salmon fish ladder.

RV sites, facilities: There are 55 sites with full or partial hookups for tents or RVs up to 45 feet long and an overflow camping area. Some sites are pull-through. Picnic tables and fire grills are provided. Restrooms with flush toilets and showers, a dump station, pay telephone, playground, and volleyball net are available. A camp host is on-site. A marina with boat docks, launching facilities, a marine dump station, a swimming beach, fishing tackle, seasonal snack bar, ice, and a day-use area and picnic shelters are nearby. Some facilities are wheelchair accessible. Leashed pets are permitted.

Reservations, fees: Reservations are accepted at 877/444-6777 or www.recreation.gov ($10 reservation fee). Sites are $18–22 per night. Overflow camping is $8 per night. Open April–October with full facilities; there are limited facilities and no fee the rest of the year.

Directions: From Pasco, drive southeast on U.S. 12 for five miles to Highway 124. Turn left (east) and drive eight miles to Sun Harbor Road. Turn left (north) and drive two miles to the park.

Contact: U.S. Army Corps of Engineers, Walla Walla District, 509/547-2048, www.nww.usace. army.mil.

27 FISHHOOK PARK

Scenic rating: 6

on Lake Sacajawea

Map grid C2

If you're driving along Highway 124 and you need a spot for the night, check out this wooded camp along the Snake River. It is a nice spot within a 46-acre park set on Lake Sacajawea, which is a dammed portion of the Snake River. The park provides some lawn area, along with places to swim, fish, and water ski. A one-mile walk along railroad tracks will take you to a fishing pond. This park is popular on summer weekends.

RV sites, facilities: There are 20 tent sites, 41 sites with partial hookups for tents or RVs up to 65 feet long, and one group tent site that can

WASHINGTON

accommodate up to 16 people. Some sites are pull-through. Picnic tables and fire grills are provided. Drinking water, restrooms with flush toilets and showers, a dump station, and playgrounds are available. Boat docks, launching facilities, a swimming beach, and group picnic shelters that can be reserved are nearby. Some facilities are wheelchair accessible. Leashed pets are permitted.

Reservations, fees: Reservations are accepted at 877/444-6777 or www.recreation.gov ($10 reservation fee). Tent sites are $8 per night, hookup sites are $14–22 per night, $4 per night per additional vehicle; the group tent site is $22 per night, and boat camping is $8 per night. Open May–September. Park gates are locked 10 P.M.–6 A.M.

Directions: From Pasco, drive southeast on U.S. 12 for five miles to Highway 124. Turn left (east) and drive 18 miles to Fishhook Park Road. Turn left on Fishhook Park Road and drive four miles to the park.

Contact: U.S. Army Corps of Engineers, Walla Walla District, 509/547-2048, www.nww.usace.army.mil.

28 LEWIS AND CLARK TRAIL STATE PARK

Scenic rating: 8

on the Touchet River

Map grid C2

Lewis and Clark features an unusual mixture of old-growth forest and riparian habitat, with long-leafed ponderosa pine and cottonwood amid the prairie grasslands. The park is set on 37 acres with frontage along the Touchet River. Fishing for rainbow trout and brown trout can be excellent here. An interpretive display explains much of the history of the area. A seasonal Saturday evening living-history program depicts the story of Lewis and Clark and the site's history here on the original Lewis and Clark Trail. In winter, cross-country skiing and snowshoeing are good here. Note: If it's getting late and you need to stop, consider this camp because it's the only one within 20 miles.

RV sites, facilities: There are 24 sites for tents or self-contained RVs up to 28 feet long, 17 sites for tents or RVs of any length available (in the day-use area) for winter use only, and two group sites for up to 100 people each. Picnic tables and fire grills are provided. Restrooms with flush toilets and coin showers, firewood, and a dump station are available. Two fire circles, an amphitheater, interpretive programs, a picnic area, badminton, a baseball field, and a volleyball court are available nearby. A store, café, and ice are located within four miles. Leashed pets are permitted.

Reservations, fees: Reservations are not accepted for individual sites but are required at group sites at 509/337-6457. Sites are $12–19 per night, $10 per extra vehicle per night. Group site fees vary according to the size of the group. Open April–mid-September, with primitive sites open mid-September–March.

Directions: From Walla Walla, drive east on U.S. 12 for 22 miles to Waitsburg. Bear right on U.S. 12 and drive east for 4.5 miles to the park entrance on the left.

Contact: Lewis and Clark Trail State Park, 509/337-6457; state park information, 360/902-8844, www.parks.wa.gov.

29 PALOUSE EMPIRE FAIRGROUNDS & HORSE CAMP

Scenic rating: 6

west of Colfax

Map grid D2

The camp consists primarily of a large lawn area with shade trees. It is set just off the road, but the highway noise, surprisingly, is relatively limited. All sites are on grass. The park covers 47 acres, with paved trails available around the adjacent fairgrounds. This area is agricultural, with rolling hills, and it is considered the "Lentil Capital of the World." With wash racks, corrals, arenas, and water troughs, the camp encourages horse campers to stay here. It fills up for the Whitman County Fair in mid-September. They turn back the clock every Labor Day weekend with the annual Threshing Bee, where there are demonstrations of historical farming practices dating back to the early 1900s, including the use of draft horses.

RV sites, facilities: There are 60 sites with partial hookups for tents or RVs of any length. Large groups can be accommodated. Restrooms with flush toilets and showers, drinking water, and a dump station are available. Restaurants, gas, and supplies are available 4.5 miles away in Colfax. Some facilities are wheelchair accessible. Leashed pets are permitted.

Reservations, fees: Reservations are accepted for groups only. Sites are $15 per night, horse stalls $10 per night. Open year-round with limited winter facilities.

Directions: From Colfax and Highway 26, drive west on Highway 26 for 4.5 miles to the fairgrounds on the right.

Contact: Palouse Empire Fairgrounds & Horse Camp, Whitman County, 509/397-6238 or 509/397-3753, www.palouseempirefair.org.

30 KAMIAK BUTTE COUNTY PARK

Scenic rating: 8

east of Colfax

Map grid D2

This quiet and peaceful park gets medium use. Kamiak Butte is a National Natural Landmark with more than five miles of wooded hiking trails. The 3.5-mile Pine Ridge Trail is part of the national trails system, and hikers can obtain excellent views of the Palouse region by walking to the highest point at 3,641 feet. The park gate closes at dusk each night and reopens at 7 A.M.

RV sites, facilities: There are nine sites for tents or RVs up to 18 feet long (no hookups). Overflow camping for RVs of any length is available in the parking lot. Picnic tables and fire grills are provided. Drinking water (mid-April–mid-October) and vault and pit toilets are available. A playground, picnic area, amphitheater, and

group facilities that can be reserved are available. Some facilities are wheelchair accessible. Leashed pets are permitted.

Reservations, fees: Reservations are not accepted. Sites are $15 per night, $5 per night per extra vehicle. Open year-round, with limited winter facilities.

Directions: From Colfax, drive east on Highway 272 for five miles to Clear Creek Road. Turn right and drive seven miles to Fugate Road. Turn right and drive 0.5 mile to the park entrance on the left.

Contact: Whitman County Parks and Recreation, 509/397-6238, www.whitmancounty.org.

31 CENTRAL FERRY PARK

Scenic rating: 8

on the Snake River

Map grid D2

This campground is the only one within a 20-mile radius, yet it's a great spot to hunker down and enjoy the world. This 185-acre park is set near 10,000-acre Lake Bryan, a reservoir situated on the Snake River and created by Little Goose Dam. With summer daytime temperatures in the 90s and even 100s occasionally, boating is popular at the desert lake. The surrounding terrain is dry, courtesy of just eight inches of average rainfall per year, as well as basaltic lava flows, according to geologic evidence. The park is named after a ferry that once operated in this area. A beach, swimming, boating, waterskiing, and fishing for bass and catfish are all options here. This was formerly a state park but is now owned by the U.S. Army Corps of Engineers.

RV sites, facilities: There are 60 sites with full hookups (30 amps) for RVs up to 40 feet and eight primitive tent sites. There is also one group camp for up to 160 people. Picnic tables and fire grills are provided. Restrooms with flush toilets and coin showers, drinking water, a dump station, a group fire ring, a day-use picnic area, covered shelters, a swimming beach and bathhouse, beachside shade structures, volleyball courts, horseshoe pits, firewood, fishing supplies, and a convenience store are available. A camp host is on-site. A store and restaurant are within five miles. Boat docks, launching facilities, and a fishing pier are within the park. Some facilities are wheelchair accessible. Leashed pets are permitted.

Reservations, fees: Reservations are accepted at 877/444-6777 or www.recreation.gov ($10 reservation fee). Sites are $22–28 per night, $5 per extra vehicle per night. The group camp is $120 per night. Some credit cards are accepted. Open May–October, weather permitting.

Directions: From Spokane, drive south on U.S. 195 for 59 miles to Highway 26. Turn west on Highway 26 and drive 17 miles southwest to the town of Dusty and Highway 127. Turn south on Highway 127 and drive 17 miles to the park entrance on the right (set on the north shore of the Snake River).

Contact: Central Ferry Park, 509/549-3551; U.S. Army Corps of Engineers, Walla Walla District, 509/547-7781, www.nww.usace.army. mil.

provided. Restrooms with flush toilets and coin showers, drinking water, and a dump station are available. A coin laundry, covered shelters, a swimming area, snack bar, convenience store, ice, gas, and pay phones are available. A marina, boat docks, a boat launch, moorage, and a marine dump station are nearby. Some facilities are wheelchair accessible. Leashed pets are permitted.

Reservations, fees: Reservations are accepted at 509/397-3208 ($10 reservation fee). Tent sites are $12.50–13.50 per night, $8 per night per additional tent. RV sites are $26.50–31.50 per night, $8 per night per extra vehicle; moorage is $13–17 per night. Winter rates are available. Some credit cards are accepted. Open year-round, with limited winter facilities.

Directions: From U.S. 195 at Colfax, turn southwest on Almota Road and drive 17 miles to the park and campground.

Contact: Boyer Park, 509/397-3208, fax 509/397-3181; Port of Whitman County, 509/397-3791, fax 509/397-4758, www.port-whitman.com.

32 BOYER PARK AND MARINA

🚶 🚴 🏊 ⛵ 🛥️ 🐕 ♿ 🚐 ⛺

Scenic rating: 7

on Lake Bryan on the Snake River

Map grid D2

This 99-acre park on the north shore of Lake Bryan is located two miles from the Lower Granite Dam. It features 3.5 miles of trails for hiking and biking, and the lake is popular for waterskiing and fishing for sturgeon, steelhead, and salmon. Most campsites are shaded, and all are paved and bordered by a grassy day-use area. The landscape is flat and open, and it gets hot here in summer. The camp is well above the water level, typically about 100 feet above the lakeshore. The camp commonly fills on summer weekends.

RV sites, facilities: There are 28 sites with full or partial hookups for tents or RVs up to 70 feet long and seven tent sites. Four motel rooms are also available. Picnic tables and fire grills are

33 WAWAWAI COUNTY PARK

⛵ 🛥️ 🐕 ♿ 🚐 ⛺

Scenic rating: 7

on Lower Granite Lake

Map grid D2

This park covers 49 acres and is set near the inlet to Lower Granite Lake, about 0.25 mile from the lake. The camp itself is situated on a hillside, and all sites are paved. Some sites have views of a bay, but not the entire lake. Tree cover is a plus. So is a 0.5-mile loop trail that leads to a bird-viewing platform, and a diverse mix of wildlife and geology, making interpretive hikes with naturalists popular. One strange note: An underground house built in 1980 has been converted to a ranger's residence. This camp often fills on summer weekends. No campfires are permitted during the summer season.

RV sites, facilities: There are nine sites for tents or RVs up to 24 feet long (no hookups). Some sites are pull-through. Picnic tables and fire grills are provided; fires are restricted in Hells Canyon mid-June–mid-October. Drinking water (mid-April–mid-October) and pit toilets are available. A group picnic shelter that can be reserved and a boat launch are nearby. Some facilities are wheelchair accessible. Leashed pets are permitted.

Reservations, fees: Reservations are not accepted. Sites are $15 per night, $5 per extra vehicle per night. Open year-round, with limited winter facilities.

Directions: From Colfax, drive south on U.S. 195 for 15 miles to Wawawai-Pullman Road (located just west of Pullman). Turn right (west) and drive approximately 9.5 miles to Wawawai Road. Turn right on Wawawai Road (signed) and drive 5.5 miles to the park.

Contact: Wawawai County Park, Whitman County Parks and Recreation, 509/397-6238, www.whitmancounty.org.

34 CHIEF TIMOTHY PARK

Scenic rating: 8

on the Snake River

Map grid D2

This unusual park is set on an island composed of glacial tills in the Snake River; it is accessible by car over a bridge. The park covers 282 acres with two miles of shoreline and features a desert landscape. There are 2.5 miles of hiking trails, plus docks for boating campers and a beach area. Water sports include fishing, swimming, boating, waterskiing, and sailing. Outfitters in Clarkston will take you sightseeing up Hells Canyon. (Call the Clarkston Chamber of Commerce at 509/758-7712 for details.) This was formerly a state park but is now a U.S. Army Corps of Engineers facility.

RV sites, facilities: There are 66 sites, including 33 with full or partial hookups (30 amps) for tents or RVs up to 60 feet long, two primitive tent sites, and four camping cabins. Picnic tables and fire grills are provided. Restrooms with flush toilets and coin showers, dump station, a picnic area, a small store, firewood,

a playground, volleyball court, and horseshoe pits are available. A camp host is on-site. Boat docks and launching facilities, a swimming beach, and beach house are nearby. Some facilities are wheelchair accessible. Leashed pets are permitted.

Reservations, fees: Reservations are accepted at 877/444-6777 or www.recreation.gov ($10 reservation fee). Sites are $20–28.50 per night, $5 per night per extra vehicle. Cabins are $66 per night. Some credit cards are accepted. Open May–November, weather permitting; only walk-in camping is permitted in November.

Directions: From Clarkston on the Washington/Idaho border, drive west on U.S. 12 for seven miles to the signed park entrance road on the right. Turn right (north) and drive one mile to the park, which is set on a bridged island in the Snake River.

Contact: Chief Timothy Park, 509/758-9580; U.S. Army Corps of Engineers, Walla Walla District, 509/547-7781, www.nww.usace.army.mil.

35 TUCANNON

Scenic rating: 8

in Umatilla National Forest

Map grid D2

For people willing to rough it, this backcountry camp in Umatilla National Forest is the place. It has plenty of hiking, fishing, and hunting, all in a rugged setting. The camp is set along the Tucannon River, which offers a myriad of recreation options for vacationers. It is popular from early spring (the best time for fishing) through fall (when it makes a good hunting camp). In summer, several nearby ponds are stocked with trout, making it a good family destination. There is some tree cover. The elevation is 2,600 feet.

RV sites, facilities: There are 18 sites for tents or RVs up to 21 feet long. Picnic tables and fire grills are provided. Vault toilets are available, but there is no drinking water. Garbage must be packed out. Two covered shelters are available nearby. Some facilities are wheelchair accessible. Leashed pets are permitted.

Reservations, fees: Reservations are not accepted. Sites are $8 per night, $5 per night per additional vehicle. Open year-round, weather permitting.

Directions: From Clarkston, drive west on U.S. 12 for 37 miles to Pomeroy. Continue west for five miles to Tatman Mountain Road (signed for Camp Wooten). Turn left (south) and drive 19 miles (becomes Forest Road 47). Once inside the national forest boundary, continue southwest on Forest Road 47 for four miles to the campground on the left.

Contact: Umatilla National Forest, Pomeroy Ranger District, 509/843-1891, fax 509/843-4621, www.fs.fed.us.

36 ALDER THICKET

Scenic rating: 7

in Umatilla National Forest
Map grid D2

This is probably the first time you've heard of this place. Hardly anybody knows about it, including people who live relatively nearby in Walla Walla. It is set at an elevation of 5,100 feet, making it a prime base camp for a backcountry hiking adventure in summer or a jumping-off point for a hunting trip in the fall. This is a primitive camp, but it's great if you're looking for quiet and solitude.

RV sites, facilities: There are five sites for tents or RVs up to 21 feet long. Picnic tables and fire grills are provided. Vault toilets are available, but there is no drinking water. Garbage must be packed out. Some facilities are wheelchair accessible. Leashed pets are permitted.

Reservations, fees: Reservations are not accepted. There is no fee for camping. Open mid-May–mid-November, weather permitting.

Directions: From Clarkston, drive west on U.S. 12 for 37 miles to Pomeroy and Highway 128. Turn south and drive seven miles to a fork. At the fork, continue straight to Forest Road 40 (15 miles from Pomeroy to the national forest

boundary) and drive 3.5 miles to the campground on the right.

Contact: Umatilla National Forest, Pomeroy Ranger District, 509/843-1891, fax 509/843-4621, www.fs.fed.us.

37 BIG SPRINGS

Scenic rating: 8

in Umatilla National Forest
Map grid D2

This camp is set at an elevation of 5,000 feet. In the fall, primarily hunters use Big Springs; come summer, this nice, cool site becomes a possible base camp for backpacking trips. Although quite primitive with little in the way of activity options, this is a perfect spot to get away from it all. It's advisable to obtain a U.S. Forest Service map.

RV sites, facilities: There are eight sites for tents or self-contained RVs up to 16 feet. Picnic tables are provided. Vault toilets are available, but there is no drinking water. Some facilities are wheelchair accessible. Leashed pets are permitted.

Reservations, fees: Reservations are not accepted. There is no fee for camping. Open mid-May–mid-November, weather permitting.

Directions: From Clarkston, drive west on U.S. 12 for 37 miles to Pomeroy and Highway 128. Turn south and drive 25 miles to Forest Road 42 (to the Clearwater Lookout Tower). Turn left and continue on Forest Road 42 for five miles to the campground entrance road (Forest Road 4225). Turn left and drive to the campground at the end of the road.

Contact: Umatilla National Forest, Pomeroy Ranger District, 509/843-1891, fax 509/843-4621, www.fs.fed.us.

38 TEAL SPRING

Scenic rating: 8

in Umatilla National Forest
Map grid D2

The views of the Tucannon drainage and the Wenaha-Tucannon Wilderness are astonishing from the nearby lookout. Teal Spring Camp is set at 5,600 feet elevation and is one of several small, primitive camps in the area. Trails in the immediate area provide a variety of good day-hiking options. Hunting is popular in the fall.

RV sites, facilities: There are six sites for tents or RVs up to 35 feet. Vault toilets are available, but there is no drinking water. Picnic tables and fire grills are provided. Garbage must be packed out. Some facilities are wheelchair accessible. Leashed pets are permitted.

Reservations, fees: Reservations are not accepted. There is no fee for camping. Open late May–mid-November, weather permitting.

Directions: From Clarkston, drive west on U.S. 12 for 37 miles to Pomeroy and Highway 128. Turn left (south) and drive 25 miles to Forest Road 42 (to the Clearwater Lookout Tower). Turn left and continue on Forest Road 42; drive one mile to the campground entrance road. Turn right and drive 200 yards to the campground.

Contact: Umatilla National Forest, Pomeroy Ranger District, 509/843-1891, fax 509/843-4621, www.fs.fed.us.

39 GODMAN

Scenic rating: 8

near the Wenaha-Tucannon Wilderness in Umatilla National Forest

Map grid D2

This tiny, little-known spot bordering a wilderness area is set at 6,050 feet elevation and features drop-dead gorgeous views at sunset, as well as a wilderness trailhead. It is used primarily as a base camp for backcountry expeditions. A trailhead provides access to the Wenaha-Tucannon Wilderness for both hikers and horseback riders. Horse facilities are available 0.2 mile away. There are also opportunities for mountain biking, but note that bikes are forbidden past the wilderness boundary. A bonus here is the primitive cabin, the Godman Guard Station, available year-round, including in winter when it's accessible only by snowmobile.

RV sites, facilities: There are eight sites for tents or RVs up to 16 feet long, plus one cabin that can accommodate up to eight people. Picnic tables and fire grills are provided. Vault toilets and a group picnic shelter are available, but there is no drinking water. Garbage must be packed out. Facilities, including hitching rails and a spring, are available nearby for up to six people with horses, with an additional fee for more than six. Some facilities are wheelchair accessible, but assistance may be required. Leashed pets are permitted.

Reservations, fees: Reservations are not accepted for campsites. The Godman Guard Station can be reserved at 877/444-6777 or www.recreation.gov ($25 reservation fee). There is no fee for the campsites. The cabin starts at $40 a night. Open mid-June–late October; cabin is available year-round.

Directions: From Walla Walla, drive northeast on U.S. 12 for 32 miles to Dayton and North Fork Touchet River Road. Turn right on North Fork Touchet River Road and drive 14 miles southeast to the national forest boundary; continue to Kendall Skyline Road. Turn left (south) and drive 11 miles to the campground on the left.

Contact: Umatilla National Forest, Pomeroy Ranger District, 509/843-1891, fax 509/843-4621, www.fs.fed.us.

40 FIELDS SPRING STATE PARK

Scenic rating: 8

near Puffer Butte

Map grid D2

Not many people know about this spot, yet it's a good one, tucked away in the southeast corner of the state. This 792-acre state park is located in the Blue Mountains, set in a forested landscape covering Puffer Butte, with views of Oregon, Idaho, and the Grande Ronde. Basalt dominates the landscape. Two hiking trails lead up to Puffer Butte at 4,500 feet elevation, providing a panoramic view of the Snake River Canyon and the Wallowa Mountains.

The park is noted for its variety of birdlife and wildflowers, and there are seven miles of mountain-biking trails, along with three miles of hiking trails. In winter, non-motorized recreation opportunities include cross-country skiing (groomed trails), snowmobiling, snowshoeing, and general snow play; warming huts are available. There is also a retreat center with lodges that can be reserved. Two day-use areas with boat launches, managed by the Department of Fish and Wildlife, are within about 25 miles of the park.

RV sites, facilities: There are 20 sites for tents or RVs up to 30 feet long (no hookups), two primitive tent sites, and two tepees. Picnic tables and fire grills are provided. Drinking water, restrooms with flush toilets and coin showers, firewood, a dump station, two picnic shelters, two sheltered fire circles, a playground, horseshoe pits, a softball field, and volleyball courts are available. Some facilities are wheelchair accessible. Leashed pets are permitted.

Reservations, fees: Reservations are not accepted for campsites but are accepted for tepees at 509/256-3332. Sites are $19 per night, primitive sites are $12 per night, tepees are $20 per night, $10 per extra vehicle per night. Open year-round, with limited winter facilities.

Directions: From Clarkston, turn south on Highway 129 and drive 30 miles (just south of Rattlesnake Pass) to the park entrance on the left (east) side of the road.

Contact: Fields Spring State Park, 509/256-3332; state park information, 360/902-8844, www.parks.wa.gov.

41 BROOKS MEMORIAL STATE PARK

Scenic rating: 7

near the Goldendale Observatory
Map grid A3

Brooks Memorial State Park sits near the South Yakima Valley at an elevation of nearly 3,000 feet. The campground is located on the Little Klickitat River amid the pines of the Simcoe Mountains. The park's 700 acres include nine miles of hiking trails, and occasionally excellent fishing for trout. You can extend your trip into the mountains, where you'll find open meadows with a panoramic view of Mount Hood. Nearby side trips include the Goldendale Observatory and a replica of Stonehenge on State Route 14. Note that the Yakama Indian Nation is two miles north.

RV sites, facilities: There are 22 sites for tents or RVs (no hookups), 23 sites with partial hookups (50 amps) for RVs up to 30 feet long, and a group site for 20–50 people. Picnic tables and fire grills are provided. Restrooms with flush toilets and coin showers, a dump station, and a playground with horseshoe pits and volleyball court are available. A sheltered picnic area, ball field, and store are nearby. Leashed pets are permitted.

Reservations, fees: Reservations are not accepted; campers must self-register. Sites are $19–25 per night, $10 per extra vehicle per night. Group sites vary; call for rates. Open year-round, with limited winter facilities.

Directions: From Toppenish, drive south on U.S. 97 for 40 miles to the park on the right (well signed).

Contact: Brooks Memorial State Park, 509/773-4611, fax 509/773-6428; state park information, 360/902-8844, www.parks.wa.gov.

42 MARYHILL STATE PARK

Scenic rating: 8

on the Columbia River
Map grid A3

This 99-acre park has 4,700 feet of frontage along the Columbia River. Fishing, waterskiing, and windsurfing are among the recreation possibilities. The climate here is pleasant March–mid-November. Two interesting places can be found near Maryhill: a full-scale replica of Stonehenge, located on a bluff overlooking the Columbia River about one mile from the park and the historic Mary Hill home, which is open to the public. Mary Hill's husband, Sam Hill, constructed the Stonehenge replica.

RV sites, facilities: There are 50 sites with full hookups (30 and 50 amps) for RVs up to 60 feet long, 20 tent sites, two hike-in/bike-in sites, and one group camp for up to 200 people. Picnic tables and fire pits are provided. Restrooms with flush toilets and showers, a dump station, and a picnic area with covered shelters are available. A café and store are within one mile. Boat docks and launching facilities are nearby. Some facilities are wheelchair accessible. Leashed pets are permitted.

Reservations, fees: Reservations are accepted and are required for the group camp at 888/CAMP-OUT (888/226-7688) or www.parks.wa.gov/reservations ($6.50–8.50 reservation fee). Sites are $21–28 per night, $10 per night for hike-in/bike-in sites, $10 per extra vehicle per night. The group camp is $100–200 per night, plus a $25 reservation fee. Some credit cards are accepted. Open year-round.

Directions: From Goldendale and U.S. 97, drive 12 miles south to the park on the left.

Contact: Maryhill State Park, 509/773-5007, fax 509/773-6337; state park information, 360/902-8844, www.parks.wa.gov.

43 CROW BUTTE PARK

Scenic rating: 8

on the Columbia River

Map grid B3

How would you like to be stranded on a romantic island? Well, this park offers that possibility. The park is set on an island in the Columbia River and is the only campground in a 25-mile radius. Sometimes referred to as the "Maui of the Columbia," the park covers 1,312 acres and has several miles of shoreline. It is set on the Lewis and Clark Trail, with the camp situated in a partially protected bay. The highlight of 3.5 miles of hiking trails is a mile-long path that leads to the top of a butte, where you can see Mount Hood, Mount Adams, and the Columbia River Valley. Waterskiing, sailboarding, fishing, swimming, and hiking are among the possibilities here. One downer: Keep an eye out

for rattlesnakes, which are occasionally spotted. The Umatilla National Wildlife Refuge is adjacent to the park and allows fishing and hunting in specified areas. Note that Crow Butte Park was formerly a state park but is now run by the Crow Butte Park Association.

RV sites, facilities: There are 50 sites for tents or RVs up to 60 feet long (30 amp full hookups), one primitive tent site, and one group camp for up to 100 people. Some sites are pull-through. Fire grills and picnic tables are provided. Restrooms with flush toilets and coin showers, a sheltered picnic area, a swimming beach, and a dump station are available. Boat-launching and moorage facilities are nearby. A store is open on weekends. Some facilities are wheelchair accessible. Leashed pets are permitted.

Reservations, fees: Reservations are accepted at 509/875-2644. Sites are $25 per night, $5 per extra vehicle per night. The group site is $60 per night. Open year-round, with limited winter facilities.

Directions: From the junction of I-82/U.S. 395 and Highway 20 at Plymouth, just north of the Columbia River, turn west on State Route 14. Drive to Paterson and continue west for 13 miles to the park entrance road at Milepost 155 on the right. Turn right and drive one mile (across the bridge) to the park on the island.

Contact: Crow Butte Park, 509/875-2644, www.crowbutte.com.

44 PLYMOUTH PARK

Scenic rating: 7

near Lake Umatilla

Map grid B3

Plymouth Park is a family- and RV-style campground set near Lake Umatilla on the Columbia River. The 112-acre park is not located on the shore of the lake, rather about a quarter-mile drive from the water. The camp has tree cover, which is a nice plus, and it fills up on most summer weekends. Each campsite has a tent pad.

RV sites, facilities: There are 32 sites with full or partial hookups (30 amps) for tents or RVs up to 40 feet long. Most sites are pull-through. Picnic tables and fire grills are provided. Restrooms with flush toilets and showers, drinking water, a dump station, playground, and coin laundry are available. A boat dock, boat launch, swimming areas, and covered picnic shelters are available nearby. A store and a restaurant are within two miles. Some facilities are wheelchair accessible. Leashed pets are permitted.

Reservations, fees: Reservations are accepted at 877/444-6777 or www.recreation.gov ($10 reservation fee). Sites are $18–24 per night, $5 per night per extra vehicle. Some credit cards are accepted. Open April–October.

Directions: From Richland and I-82, drive south on I-82 for about 30 miles to State Route 14. Turn west on State Route 14 and drive two miles to the Plymouth exit. Take that exit and drive south 1.5 miles to Christy Road; turn right and continue 200 yards to the campground entrance on the left.

Contact: U.S. Army Corps of Engineers, Walla Walla District, 541/506-7818, www.nww.usace. army.mil; gate attendant 509/783-1270.

Oregon

ROYALTY FREE / GETTY IMAGES

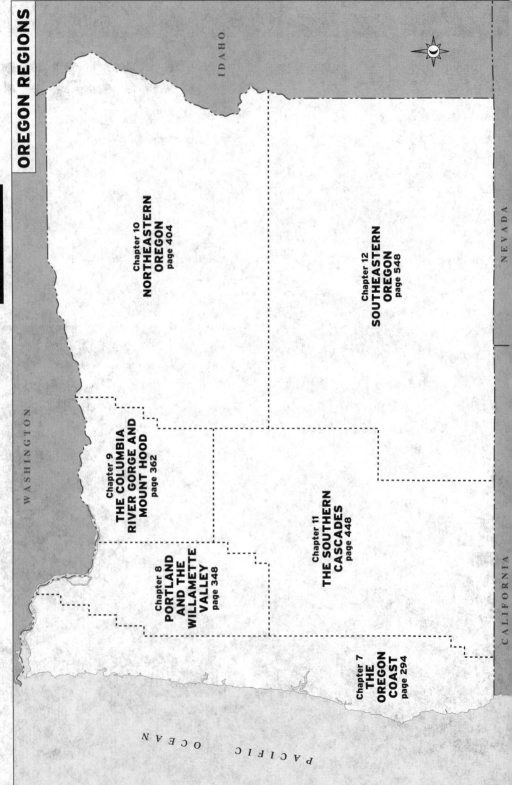

OREGON REGIONS

OREGON

IDAHO

NEVADA

CALIFORNIA

WASHINGTON

PACIFIC OCEAN

Chapter 10
NORTHEASTERN
OREGON
page 404

Chapter 12
SOUTHEASTERN
OREGON
page 548

Chapter 9
THE COLUMBIA
RIVER GORGE AND
MOUNT HOOD
page 362

Chapter 8
PORTLAND
AND THE
WILLAMETTE
VALLEY
page 348

Chapter 11
THE SOUTHERN
CASCADES
page 448

Chapter 7
THE
OREGON
COAST
page 294

THE OREGON COAST

◖ BEST RV PARKS AND CAMPGROUNDS

OREGON

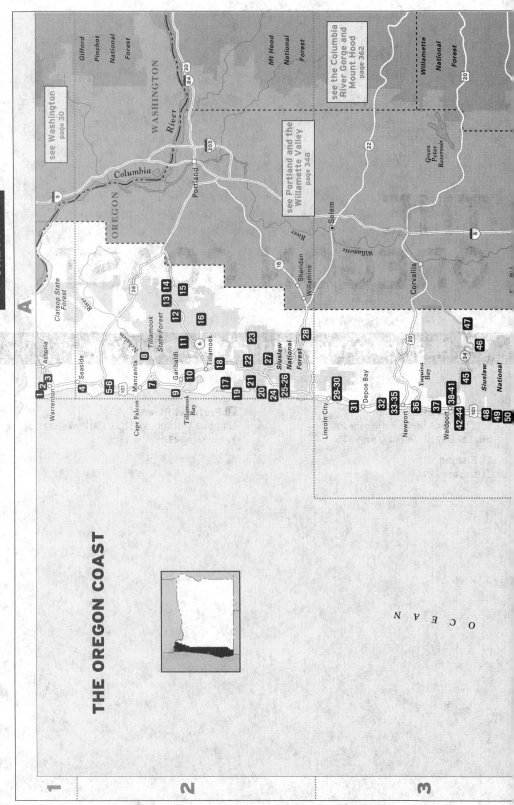

THE OREGON COAST

see Washington page 30

see the Columbia River Gorge and Mount Hood page 362

see Portland and the Willamette Valley page 348

OCEAN

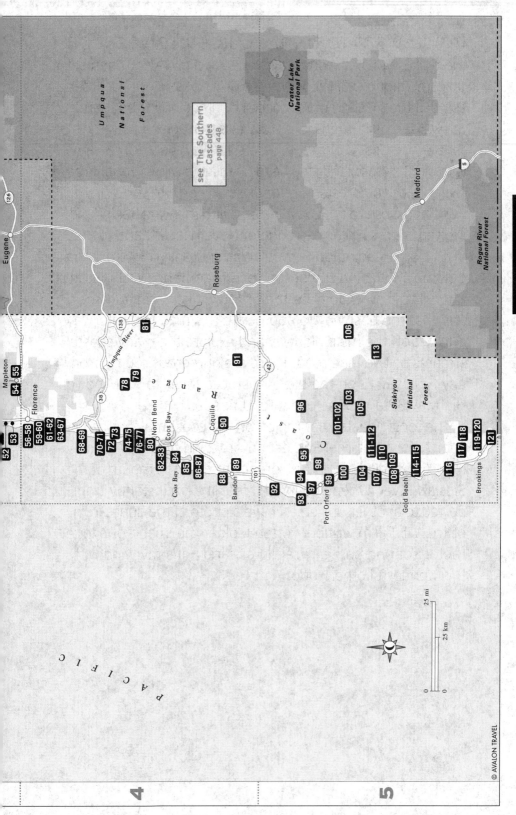

OREGON

© AVALON TRAVEL

If you want to treat yourself to vacation memories you'll treasure forever, take a drive and then set up camp along U.S. 101 on the Oregon Coast. Here you'll see some of the most dramatic coastal frontage in North America: tidewater rock gardens, cliff-top views that seem to stretch to forever, vast sand dunes, protected bays, beautiful streams with giant salmon and steelhead (in fall and winter), and three major national forests. I prefer cruising north to south, in the right lane close to the coastline and with the wind behind me; it often seems I'm on the edge of Never Never Land.

If you're heading down from Washington, you'll cross the Columbia River on the border of Oregon and Washington. The river is so wide here that it looks like an inland sea. I find that the best way to appreciate this massive waterway is to get off the main highway and explore the many coastal streams by two-lane road. There are numerous routes, from tiny Highway 15 on the Little Nestucca River to well-known Highway 38 along the beautiful Umpqua.

The most spectacular region on the coast may be the Oregon Dunes National Recreation Area, which spans roughly from Coos Bay north past Florence to near the mouth of the Siuslaw River. Whenever I visit, I feel like I'm instantly transported to another universe. I have a photo of the dunes in my office. While I'm writing, I often look at the image of a lone raptor soaring past a pyramid of sand – it's my window to this wonderful otherworld.

◼ FORT STEVENS STATE PARK

Scenic rating: 8

at the mouth of the Columbia River

Map grid A1   **BEST (**

This classic spot is set at the northern tip of Oregon, right where the Columbia River enters the Pacific Ocean. At 3,700 acres, the park offers nine miles of biking trails, six miles of hiking trails, swimming, boating, fishing, and wildlife-viewing in a landscape of forests, wetlands, and dunes. The trailhead for the Oregon Coast Trail is here as well. History buffs will find a museum, tours of the fort and artillery batteries, and the remains of the *Peter Iredale* shipwreck.

RV sites, facilities: There are 476 sites with full or partial hookups for tents or RVs up to 60 feet long, 19 sites for tents or small RVs (no hookups), a camping area for hikers and bicyclists, and 15 yurts. Picnic tables and fire grills are provided. Drinking water, restrooms with flush toilets and showers, dump station, a transfer and recycling station, two picnic shelters, firewood, and a playground are available. Boat docks and launching facilities are nearby. Some facilities are wheelchair accessible. Leashed pets are permitted.

Reservations, fees: Reservations are accepted at 800/452-5687 or www.oregonstateparks.org ($8 reservation fee). RV sites are $18–27 per night, tent sites are $13–21 per night, $4–6 per night per person for hikers/bikers, yurts are $30–41 per night, $5 per night per additional vehicle. Some credit cards are accepted. Open year-round.

Directions: From Portland, turn west on U.S. 26 and drive 73 miles to the junction with U.S. 101. Turn right (north) on U.S. 101 and drive about 15 miles (about 0.25 mile past the Camp Rilea Army Base). Turn west on Perkins Road/Highway 104 at the sign for Fort Stevens State Park and drive about one mile to Ocean View Cemetery Road. Turn left and drive about 2.5 miles (Ocean View Cemetery Road becomes Ridge Road) to the park entrance.

Contact: Fort Stevens State Park, 503/861-1671 or 800/551-6949, www.oregonstateparks.org.

◼ ASTORIA/WARRENTON SEASIDE KOA

Scenic rating: 3

near Fort Stevens State Park

Map grid A1

This campground is nestled in a wooded area adjacent to Fort Stevens State Park, and tours of that historical military site can be arranged. This camp provides an excellent alternative if the state park campground is full. A host of activities are available in the immediate area, including beachcombing, bicycling, deep-sea fishing, hiking, and kayaking. Horse stables are within 10 miles.

RV sites, facilities: There are 311 sites with full or partial hookups for tents or RVs of any length, 54 cabins, and two lodges. Some sites are pull-through. Picnic tables and fire pits are provided. Cable TV, 30- and 50-amp service, modem hookups, wireless Internet service, restrooms with showers, security, public phone, coin laundry, meeting room, firewood, limited groceries, ice, snack bar, RV supplies, propane gas, and a picnic area are available. Recreational facilities include a playground, game room, recreation field, bicycle rentals, miniature golf, horseshoe pits, spa, and a heated indoor swimming pool. Some facilities are wheelchair accessible. Leashed pets are permitted with some restrictions.

Reservations, fees: Reservations are accepted at 800/562-8506. Sites are $39.55–199 per night, $6.50 per person per night for more than two people, $2 per pet per night, $5 per night per additional vehicle unless towed. Some credit cards are accepted. Open year-round.

Directions: From Portland, turn west on U.S. 26 and drive 73 miles to the junction with U.S. 101. Turn right (north) on U.S. 101 and drive about 15 miles (about 0.25 mile past the Camp Rilea Army Base). Turn west on Perkins Road/Highway 104 at the sign for Fort Stevens State Park and drive about one mile to Ocean View Cemetery Road. Turn left and drive about 2.5 miles (Ocean View Cemetery Road becomes Ridge Road) to the campground directly across from the state park.

OREGON

Contact: Astoria/Warrenton Seaside KOA, 503/861-2606, fax 503/861-3209, www.koa.com.

3 KAMPERS WEST RV PARK

Scenic rating: 7

near Fort Stevens State Park
Map grid A1

Just four miles from Fort Stevens State Park, this privately run camp offers full RV services. Nearby recreation possibilities include an 18-hole golf course, hiking trails, and marked bike trails.

RV sites, facilities: There are 163 sites with full or partial hookups for RVs of any length, a small area for tents only, and three park-model cabins. Drinking water and picnic tables are provided, and some sites have fire pits. Restrooms with flush toilets and showers, propane gas, dump station, coin laundry, and ice are available. A store and a café are within one mile. Leashed pets are permitted.

Reservations, fees: Reservations are accepted. RV sites are $36 per night, and tent sites are $28 per night. Some credit cards are accepted. Open year-round.

Directions: From Portland, turn west on U.S. 30 and drive 105 miles north and west to Astoria and the junction of U.S. 101. Turn south and drive 6.5 miles to the Warrenton/ Hammond Junction. Turn right (west) on Warrenton and drive 1.5 miles to the campground on the right.

Contact: Kampers West RV Park, 503/861-1814, fax 503/861-3620, www.kamperswest.com.

4 VENICE RV PARK

Scenic rating: 3

on the Neawanna River
Map grid A2

This park along the Neawanna River—one of two rivers running through Seaside—is less than a mile from the beach. A great bonus: Crab pot rentals are available. Seaside offers beautiful ocean beaches for fishing and surfing, moped and bike rentals, shops, and a theater. The city provides swings and volleyball nets on the beach. An 18-hole golf course is nearby.

RV sites, facilities: There are 26 sites for RVs of any length (full hookups, some pull-through) and six tent sites. Drinking water, cable TV, and picnic tables are provided. Restrooms with flush toilets and showers, picnic area and a coin laundry are available. A store and a café are within one mile. Leashed pets are permitted.

Reservations, fees: Reservations are accepted. RV sites are $27.25 per night (with camp membership), tent sites are $18 per night, $2 per person per night for more than two people, $2 per night per additional vehicle, and $2 per pet per night. Some credit cards are accepted. Open year-round.

Directions: From Portland on I-5, turn west on U.S. 26 and drive 73 miles to the junction with U.S. 101. Turn north on U.S. 101 and drive 5.25 miles to Seaside. Continue to the north end of town and bear left (west) on 24th Avenue. The campground is on the corner (do not cross the bridge) at 1032 24th Avenue.

Contact: Venice RV Park, 503/738-8851, www.shopseaside.com/vrv.

5 SEA RANCH RV PARK

Scenic rating: 9

in Cannon Beach
Map grid A2

This park is set in a wooded area with nearby access to the beach. Activities at the camp include stream fishing, horseback riding, and swimming on the seashore. A golf course is six miles away, and the historic Lewis and Clark Trail is nearby. Elk hunters camp here in season. The beach and the town of Cannon Beach are within walking distance of the park.

RV sites, facilities: There are 80 sites with full or partial hookups for tents or RVs up to 40 feet long and seven cabins. Picnic tables and fire rings are provided. Restrooms with showers, horse rentals, and a dump station are available.

Supplies are available within two miles. Leashed pets are permitted.

Reservations, fees: Reservations are accepted. RV sites are $30–90 per night, tent sites are $23 per night; and it costs $2 per person per night for more than two people, $3 per night per additional vehicle, and $10 per pet per night. Some credit cards are accepted. Open year-round.

Directions: From Portland on I-5, turn west on U.S. 26 and drive 73 miles to the junction with U.S. 101. Turn south on U.S. 101 and drive three miles to the Cannon Beach exit. Take that exit and drive on Fir Street for 0.3 mile to the park on the left.

Contact: Sea Ranch RV Park, 503/436-2815, www.searanchrv.com.

⬛ RV RESORT AT CANNON BEACH

Scenic rating: 9

near Ecola State Park

Map grid A2

This private resort is located about seven blocks from one of the nicest beaches in the region and about two miles from Ecola State Park. From the town of Cannon Beach, you can walk for miles in either direction. Nearby recreational facilities include marked bike trails, a riding stable, and tennis courts. The city shuttle service stops here.

RV sites, facilities: There are 100 sites with full hookups for RVs of any length; some are pull-through sites. Picnic tables and fire pits are provided. Restrooms with flush toilets and showers, cable TV, propane gas, firewood, recreation hall, playground, horseshoe pits, basketball court, convenience store, spa, coin laundry, ice, gasoline, playground, and a heated swimming pool (year-round) are available. Leashed pets are permitted.

Reservations, fees: Reservations are accepted at 800/847-2231. Sites are $32–44 per night, $3 per person per night for more than two people, $3 per night per additional vehicle. Some credit cards are accepted. Open year-round.

Directions: From Portland on I-5, turn west on U.S. 26 and drive 73 miles to the junction with

U.S. 101. Turn south on U.S. 101 and drive four miles to the second Cannon Beach exit at Milepost 29.5. Exit on the left (east) and drive 200 feet to the resort.

Contact: RV Resort at Cannon Beach, 503/436-2231, fax 503/436-1527, www.cbrvresort.com.

⬛ NEHALEM BAY STATE PARK

Scenic rating: 7

on Nehalem Bay

Map grid A2

This state park on a sandy point separating the Pacific Ocean from Nehalem Bay features six miles of beach frontage. There is no ocean view from the campsites, but the sites are about 150 yards from the ocean. In 2008, beachcombers discovered a pair of historic cannons at low tide, likely dating back to an 1846 shipwreck. Crabbing and fishing on the bay are popular. The Oregon Coast Trail passes through the park. A horse camp with corrals and a 7.5-mile equestrian trail are available. There is also a two-mile bike trail. The neighboring towns of Manzanita and Nehalem offer fine dining and shopping. An airport is adjacent to the park, and there are airstrip fly-in campsites.

RV sites, facilities: There are 265 sites with partial hookups for tents or RVs up to 60 feet long, a camping area for hikers and bicyclists, and six primitive fly-in sites next to the airport. There are also 18 yurts and 17 equestrian sites with stock corrals. Drinking water, picnic tables, and fire grills are provided. Restrooms with flush toilets and showers, dump station, playgrounds, firewood, and a meeting hall are available. Boat-launching facilities are nearby on Nehalem Bay, and an airstrip is adjacent to the park. Some facilities are wheelchair accessible. Leashed pets are permitted.

Reservations, fees: Reservations are accepted at 800/452-5687 or www.oregonstateparks.org ($8 reservation fee). Sites are $16–24 per night, $5 per night per additional vehicle, and $4–5 per person per night for hikers/bikers. Yurts are $27–36 per night; horse sites are $12–19 per night. Fly-in sites are $8–10 per night, not including tie-down. Some credit cards are accepted. Open year-round.

Directions: From Portland, drive west on U.S. 26 for 73 miles to the junction with U.S. 101. Turn south on U.S. 101 and drive 19 miles to Manzanita. Continue south on U.S. 101 for 0.75 mile to Necarney City Road. Turn right and drive 0.2 mile to a stop sign. Turn right and drive 0.75 mile to the park entrance.

Contact: Nehalem Bay State Park, 503/368-5154 or 800/551-6949, www.oregonstateparks.org.

8 NEHALEM FALLS

Scenic rating: 10

in Tillamook State Forest
Map grid A2

This beautiful campground, amid old-growth hemlock and spruce, is located within a two-minute walk of lovely Nehalem Falls. Note that swimming in the pool below the falls is hazardous and not advised. A half-mile loop trail follows the Nehalem River, where fishing and swimming are options.

RV sites, facilities: There are 14 sites for tents or RVs up to 40 feet long, four walk-in tent sites, and one group site for up to 20 people. Drinking water, picnic tables, garbage bins, recycling center, fire grills, and vault toilets are available. A camp host is on-site. Some facilities are wheelchair accessible. Leashed pets are permitted.

Reservations, fees: Reservations are accepted only for the group site at 503/842-2545. Sites are $10 per night, $2 per night per additional vehicle, walk-in sites are $5 per night, and the group site is $25 per night. Open May–October.

Directions: From Tillamook on U.S. 101 northbound, drive 22 miles to Highway 53. Turn right (east) and drive 1.3 miles to Miami Foley Road. Turn right (south) and drive one mile to Foss Road (narrow and rough). Turn left and drive seven miles to the campground on the left.

Contact: Tillamook State Forest, Tillamook District, 503/842-2545, fax 503/842-3143, www.oregon.gov.

9 BARVIEW JETTY PARK

Scenic rating: 7

near Garibaldi
Map grid A2

This Tillamook County park covers 160 acres and is located near the beach, in a wooded area adjacent to Tillamook Bay. The sites are set on grassy hills. Nearby recreation options include an 18-hole golf course, surf and scuba fishing, and a full-service marina.

RV sites, facilities: There are 224 tent sites, 69 sites for tents or RVs of any length (full hookups), and four hiker/bicyclist sites. Some sites are pull-through. Drinking water, picnic tables, and fire pits are provided. Restrooms with flush toilets and showers, a dump station, fish-cleaning station, and day-use area are available. Groups can be accommodated. Propane gas, store, café, and ice are within one mile. Some facilities are wheelchair accessible. Leashed pets are permitted.

Reservations, fees: Reservations are accepted ($5 reservation fee) at 503/322-3522 or www.co.tillamook.or.us. Sites are $10–30 per night, $3–5 per night per each additional vehicle or tent, $5 per person per night for hikers/bikers. Some credit cards are accepted. Open year-round.

Directions: From Tillamook, drive north on U.S. 101 for 12 miles to the park on the left (two miles north of the town of Garibaldi).

Contact: Barview Jetty Park, Tillamook County, 503/322-3522, www.co.tillamook.or.us/gov/parks.

10 BIAK-BY-THE-SEA RV PARK

Scenic rating: 7

on Tillamook Bay
Map grid A2

This park along the shore of Tillamook Bay is a prime retreat for beachcombing, clamming, crabbing, deep-sea fishing, scuba diving, and surf fishing. The nearby town of Tillamook is home to a cheese factory and a historical museum. Cape Meares State Park, where you can hike through the national wildlife preserve and see how the seabirds nest along the cliffs, makes a good side trip. There is also a golf course nearby. Note that most of the sites are monthly rentals.

RV sites, facilities: There are 45 pull-through sites with full hookups for RVs of any length and a grassy area for tents. Drinking water and cable TV are provided. Restrooms with flush toilets and coin showers and a coin laundry are available. Propane gas, a store, café, and ice are within one mile. Boat docks, launching facilities, and rentals are nearby. Leashed pets are permitted.

Reservations, fees: Reservations are accepted. Sites are $25 per night. Some credit cards are accepted. Open year-round.

Directions: From Tillamook and U.S. 101, drive north for 10 miles to 7th Street. Turn left on 7th Street and drive to the park on the left (just over the tracks).

Contact: Biak-by-the-Sea RV Park, 503/322-2111.

11 KILCHIS RIVER PARK

Scenic rating: 8

on the Kilchis River

Map grid A2

Riverfront campsites are the highlight at this Tillamook County campground. The campground is forested and gets moderate use. Hiking trails are available. Other recreational options include boating, fishing, and swimming.

RV sites, facilities: There are 63 sites for tents or RVs of any length (no hookups), hiker/bicyclist sites, and group sites. Picnic tables, drinking water, flush toilets, and fire pits are provided. A playground, garbage bins, boat launch, day-use area, pay phone, coin showers, dump station, basketball court, and a volleyball court are available. A camp host is on-site. Leashed pets are permitted.

Reservations, fees: Reservations are accepted ($5 reservation fee) at 503/842-6694 or www.

co.tillamook.or.us. Sites are $12–15 per night, $3 per night per additional vehicle, and $5 per person per night for hikers and bicyclists. Open May–September.

Directions: From Tillamook and U.S. 101, take the Alderbrook Loop/Kilches Park exit. Turn onto Alderbrook Loop and drive northeast for approximately one mile to Kilches River Road. Turn right and drive approximately four miles to the park at the end of the road.

Contact: Kilchis River Park, Tillamook County, 503/842-6694, www.co.tillamook.or.us/gov/parks.

12 JONES CREEK

Scenic rating: 7

on the Wilson River in Tillamook State Forest

Map grid A2

Set in a forest of alder, fir, hemlock, and spruce, campsites here are spacious and private. The adjacent Wilson River provides opportunities for steelhead and salmon fishing (artificial lures only). A scenic 3.8-mile trail runs along the riverfront. The camp fills up on weekends July–Labor Day.

RV sites, facilities: There are 29 sites for tents or RVs (27 sites are 50 feet long and one is 72 feet long and pull-through), nine walk-in tent sites, and one group site for up to 80 people. Drinking water, picnic tables, and fire grills are provided. Vault toilets, garbage bins, firewood, and a horseshoe pit are available. A camp host is on-site. Some facilities are wheelchair accessible. Leashed pets are permitted.

Reservations, fees: Reservations are accepted only for the group site at 503/842-2545. Sites are $10 per night, $2 per night per additional vehicle, walk-in sites are $5 per night, and the group site is $25 per night. Open May–October.

Directions: From Portland, turn west on U.S. 26 and drive 24 miles to Highway 6. Turn west on Highway 6 and drive 28 miles to Milepost 22.7 and North Fork Road. Turn right and drive 0.25 mile to the campground on the left.

Contact: Tillamook State Forest, Tillamook

District, 503/842-2545, fax 503/842-3143, www.oregon.gov.

13 JORDAN CREEK OHV

Scenic rating: 6

near Jordan Creek in Tillamook State Forest

Map grid A2

This off-highway vehicle (OHV) camp is set at the bottom of a scenic, steep canyon next to Jordan Creek. Wooded campsites are clustered around a central parking area, and the park caters to OHV campers. There are almost 40 miles of OHV trails, varying from moderate to difficult. Note that in order to ride an ATV on roads, you need an ATV sticker, a driver's license, and a spark arrestor. There's no fishing in Jordan Creek.

RV sites, facilities: There are six sites for tents or RVs of any length. Overflow RV camping is allowed in the main parking lot. There is no drinking water. Picnic tables, fire grills, garbage bins, and vault toilets are available. Leashed pets are permitted.

Reservations, fees: Reservations are not accepted. Sites are $10 per night, $2 per night per additional vehicle. Open March–November.

Directions: From Tillamook on U.S. 101, turn east on Highway 6 and drive 17.9 miles to Jordan Creek Road. Turn right and drive 2.2 miles to the campground on the right.

Contact: Tillamook State Forest, Tillamook District, 503/842-2545, fax 503/842-3143, www.oregon.gov.

14 GALES CREEK

Scenic rating: 7

on Gales Creek in Tillamook State Forest

Map grid A2

Gales Creek runs through this heavily forested camp. The Gales Creek Trailhead is accessible from camp, providing access to hiking and mountain biking opportunities. A day-use picnic area is also available.

RV sites, facilities: There are 19 sites for tents or RVs up to 35 feet long and four walk-in tent sites. Drinking water, picnic tables, fire grills, garbage bins, and vault toilets are available. Some facilities are wheelchair accessible. Leashed pets are permitted.

Reservations, fees: Reservations are not accepted. RV sites are $10 per night, walk-in tent sites are $5 per night, and an additional vehicle is $2 per night. Open early May–October.

Directions: From Portland, turn west on U.S. 26 and drive 24 miles to Highway 6. Turn west on Highway 6 and drive 17 miles to the campground entrance road (Rogers Road) on the right at Milepost 35. Turn right on Rogers Road and drive one mile to the campground.

Contact: Tillamook State Forest, Forest Grove District, 503/357-2191, www.oregon.gov.

15 BROWNS CAMP OHV

Scenic rating: 6

in Tillamook State Forest

Map grid A2

This camp is located next to the Devil's Lake Fork of the Wilson River and has sites with and without tree cover. Surrounded by miles of OHV trails, it caters to off-highway vehicle campers. Don't expect peace and quiet. No fishing is allowed here.

RV sites, facilities: There are 29 sites for tents or RVs up to 45 feet long. Drinking water, picnic tables, fire grills, garbage bins, and vault toilets are available. Some facilities are wheelchair accessible. Leashed pets are permitted.

Reservations, fees: Reservations are not accepted. Sites are $10 per night, $2 per night per additional vehicle. Open March–November.

Directions: From Portland, turn west on U.S. 26 and drive 24 miles to Highway 6. Turn west on Highway 6 and drive 19 miles to Beaver Dam Road. Turn left (south) and drive 2.5 miles to Scoggins Road. Turn left (southeast) and drive 0.5 mile to the campground.

Contact: Tillamook State Forest, Forest Grove District, 503/357-2191, www.oregon.gov.

OREGON

16 TRASK RIVER PARK

Scenic rating: 7

on the Trask River

Map grid A2

This is a popular campground and park that gets moderate use primarily from the locals in Tillamook County. Some campsites are shaded. Fishing for trout and steelhead is available in season; check current fishing regulations.

RV sites, facilities: There are 63 sites for tents or RVs of any length (no hookups) and a hiker/bicyclist area. Picnic tables, garbage service, and fire pits are provided. Drinking water, vault toilets, and a day-use area are available. A camp host is on-site. Some facilities are wheelchair accessible. Leashed pets are permitted.

Reservations, fees: Reservations are accepted ($5 reservation fee) at 503/842-4559 or www.co.tillamook.or.us. Sites are $10–15 per night, $3 per night for additional vehicle, and $5 per person per night for hikers/bicyclists. Some credit cards are accepted. Open year-round.

Directions: From Tillamook and U.S. 101, turn east on 3rd Street. Drive 2.5 miles to Trask River Road. Turn right and drive 1.5 miles, turning left to stay on Trask River Road. Continue 10 miles to the park.

Contact: Trask River Park, Tillamook County, 503/842-4559, www.co.tillamook.or.us/gov/parks.

17 NETARTS BAY RV PARK & MARINA

Scenic rating: 8

on Netarts Bay

Map grid A2

This camp is one of three on the east shore of Netarts Bay. A golf course is eight miles away. Sunsets and wildlife-viewing are notable here. Some sites are filled with rentals for the summer season.

RV sites, facilities: There are 88 sites with full hookups for RVs of any length; some are pull-through sites. Drinking water and picnic tables are provided, and fire rings are available at some sites.

Restrooms with flush toilets and showers, propane gas, a meeting room, coin laundry, playground, horseshoe pits, crab-cooking facilities, crab bait, and ice are available. Boat docks, launching facilities, and rentals are available on-site. A store and a café are within one mile. Leashed pets are permitted, with a two-pet maximum.

Reservations, fees: Reservations are recommended. Sites are $28–35 per night, $5 per night per additional vehicle. Some credit cards are accepted. Monthly rentals are available. Open year-round.

Directions: From Tillamook and Netarts Highway/Highway 131, drive west on Netarts Highway for six miles to the campground entrance.

Contact: Netarts Bay RV Park & Marina, 503/842-7774, www.netartsbay.com.

18 PLEASANT VALLEY RV PARK

Scenic rating: 8

on the Tillamook River

Map grid A2

Pleasant Valley RV Park sits along the Tillamook River. The park is very clean and provides easy access to many recreation options in the immediate area.

RV sites, facilities: There are 10 tent sites and 76 pull-through sites with full or partial hookups for RVs of any length, plus two cabins. Drinking water and picnic tables are provided and some sites have fire rings. Restrooms with flush toilets and showers, propane gas, dump station, firewood, a meeting room, cable TV, modem access, convenience store, coin laundry, ice, and a playground are available. Boat-launching facilities are nearby. Leashed pets are permitted.

Reservations, fees: Reservations are accepted. RV sites are $28–32 per night, tent sites are $18 per night, $2 per person per night for more than two people; cabins are $29 per night. Some credit cards are accepted. Open year-round.

Directions: From Tillamook and U.S. 101, drive south on U.S. 101 for 7 miles to the campground entrance on the right (west).

Contact: Pleasant Valley RV Park, 503/842-4779,

fax 503/842-2293, www.pleasantvalleyrvpark. com.

19 CAPE LOOKOUT STATE PARK

Scenic rating: 8

near Netarts Bay

Map grid A2

This park is set on a sand spit between Netarts Bay and the Pacific. There are more than eight miles of wooded trails, including the Cape Lookout Trail which follows the headland for more than two miles. Another walk will take you out through a variety of estuarine habitats along the five-mile sand spit that extends between the ocean and Netarts Bay. With many species to view, this area is a paradise for bird-watchers. You might also catch the local hang gliders and paragliders that frequent the park. Fishing is another option here.

RV sites, facilities: There are 173 sites for tents or RVs (no hookups), 38 sites with full hook-ups for RVs up to 60 feet long, a tent camping area for hikers and bicyclists, two group tent sites for up to 25 people each, three cabins, and 13 yurts. Picnic tables and fire grills are provided. Restrooms with flush toilets and showers, dump station, garbage bins, meeting hall and picnic shelter, summer interpretive programs, and firewood are available. Some facilities are wheelchair accessible. Leashed pets are permitted.

Reservations, fees: Reservations are accepted at 800/452-5687 or www.oregonstateparks.org ($8 reservation fee). RV sites are $16–24 per night, tent sites are $12–19 per night, $4–5 per person per night for hikers/bikers, $40–71 per night for group sites, $45–76 per night for cabins, and $27–36 per night for yurts, $5 per night per additional vehicle. Some credit cards are accepted. Open year-round.

Directions: From Tillamook and U.S. 101, turn east on 3rd Street (becomes Netarts Highway). Drive approximately five miles to Whiskey Creek Road. Turn left and drive approximately seven miles to the park on the right.

Contact: Cape Lookout State Park, 503/842-4981, www.oregonstateparks.org.

20 WHALEN ISLAND PARK

Scenic rating: 6

in the Sandlake Estuary

Map grid A2

This park is located in the Sandlake Estuary and is close to the beach and Nestucca Bay. The campground is fairly open and has a few trees.

RV sites, facilities: There are 34 sites for tents or RVs of any length (no hookups) and two hiker/bicyclist sites. Picnic tables and fire pits are provided. Drinking water, flush and chemical toilets, dump station, a day-use area, and a boat launch are available. A camp host is on-site during the summer. Some facilities are wheelchair accessible. Leashed pets are permitted.

Reservations, fees: Reservations are accepted ($5 reservation fee). Sites are $10–15 per night, $3 per night per additional vehicle, and $5 per person per night for hikers and bicyclists. Open March–November; check for current status at other times of year.

Directions: From Tillamook and U.S. 101, drive south for 11 miles to Sand Lake Road. Turn right (west) and drive approximately 55 miles to a stop sign. Turn left to stay on Sand Lake Road. Continue 4.75 miles south to the park entrance road on the right.

Contact: Whalen Island Park, Tillamook County, 503/965-6085, www.co.tillamook. or.us/gov/parks.

21 SANDBEACH, EAST DUNES, AND WEST WINDS OHV

Scenic rating: 5

in Siuslaw National Forest

Map grid A2

Sandbeach campground is set along the shore of Sand Lake, which is actually more like an estuary than a lake since the ocean is just around the bend. This area is known for its beaches with large sand dunes, which are popular with off-road-vehicle enthusiasts. It's noisy and can be windy. East Dunes and West Winds, which used to be the overflow parking area, are nearby. This is the only coastal U.S. Forest Service camping area for many miles, and it's quite popular. If you're planning a trip for midsummer, be sure to reserve far in advance. Holiday permits are required ($10 at the district office) for three-day holiday weekends.

RV sites, facilities: At Sandbeach, there are 101 sites for tents or RVs; West Winds has 51 sites for tents or RVs; and East Dunes has 51 sites for tents or RVs. There are no hookups and RV length limit is 60 feet long. Picnic tables and fire pits are provided. Drinking water, garbage bins, and flush toilets are available. A camp host is on-site at each campground. Leashed pets are permitted.

Reservations, fees: Reservations are accepted during the summer season at 877/444-6777 or www.recreation.gov ($10 reservation fee). Sites at Sandbeach are $20 per night; sites at East Dunes and West Winds are $15 per night. Additional vehicles cost $8 per night at all campgrounds. Open year-round.

Directions: From Tillamook on U.S. 101, drive south for 11 miles to County Road 8. Turn right (west) on County Road 8 and drive approximately 12 miles to the campground.

Contact: Siuslaw National Forest, Hebo Ranger District, 503/392-3161, fax 503/392-4203, www.fs.fed.us.

22 CAMPER COVE RV PARK AND CAMPGROUND

Scenic rating: 6

on Beaver Creek

Map grid A2

This small, wooded campground along Beaver Creek is set just far enough off the highway to provide quiet. The park can be used as a base camp for anglers, with seasonal steelhead and salmon fishing in the nearby Nestucca River. It gets crowded here, especially in the summer, so be sure to make a reservation if possible. Ocean beaches are four miles away.

RV sites, facilities: There are 50 sites with full hookups for RVs up to 40 feet long, five tent sites, and three cabins. Drinking water, fire pits, and picnic tables are provided. Restrooms with flush toilets and coin showers, dump station, firewood, recreation hall, coin laundry, and ice are available. Leashed pets are permitted.

Reservations, fees: Reservations are accepted. RV sites are $28 per night, tent sites are $20 per night, $3 per person per night for more than two people and $3 per night per additional vehicle. Open year-round.

Directions: From Tillamook and U.S. 101, drive south on U.S. 101 for 12 miles to the park entrance on the right (west), three miles north of Beaver.

Contact: Camper Cove RV Park and Campground, 503/398-5334, www.campercovecampground.com.

23 DOVRE, FAN CREEK, ALDER GLEN

Scenic rating: 5

on the Nestucca River

Map grid A2

This is a series of three BLM campgrounds set along the Nestucca River. The camps, separated by alder trees and shrubs, are near the river, and some have river views. Tourists don't know about these spots. The Nestucca is a gentle river, with the water not deep enough for swimming.

RV sites, facilities: Dovre has 10 sites, Fan Creek has 11 sites, and Alder Glen has 11 sites—all for tents or small RVs. Picnic tables and fire grills are provided. Drinking water and vault toilets are available. Garbage must be packed out. Some facilities, including a fishing pier at Alder Glen, are wheelchair accessible. Leashed pets are permitted.

Reservations, fees: Reservations are not accepted. Sites are $10 per night, $4 per night per additional vehicle with a limit of two vehicles per site. Open year-round.

Directions: On U.S. 101 southwest of Portland, drive to the tiny town of Beaver and Blaine Road. Turn east on Blaine Road (keep right; Blaine Road turns into Nestucca River Access Road) and drive 17.5 miles to Alder Glen. Continue east for seven more miles to reach Fan Creek and nine more miles to reach Dovre.

Contact: Bureau of Land Management, Salem District, 503/375-5646, fax 503/375-5622, www.blm.gov.

24 WOODS COUNTY PARK

Scenic rating: 6

on the Kilchis River
Map grid A2

This small Tillamook County park is not well known outside the local area and gets fairly light use. The campground is grassy with few trees. Salmon fishing is a possibility; check current regulations.

RV sites, facilities: There are seven tent sites and five sites for RVs up to 40 feet long. Picnic tables and fire pits are provided. Drinking water, flush toilets, garbage containers, and a day-use area are available. A camp host is on-site. Leashed pets are permitted.

Reservations, fees: Reservations are accepted ($5 reservation fee) at 503/965-5001 or www.co.tillamook.or.us. Sites are $15–25 per night, $3 per night per additional vehicle. Open May–October, weather permitting.

Directions: From Tillamook and U.S. 101, drive approximately 25 miles south to Resort Drive. Turn right (west) and drive three miles (road changes to Brooten Drive) to the park on the right.

Contact: Woods County Park, Tillamook County, 503/965-5001, www.co.tillamook.or.us/gov/parks.

25 CAPE KIWANDA RV RESORT

Scenic rating: 8

near Cape Kiwanda State Park
Map grid A2

This park is set a short distance from Cape Kiwanda State Park, which is open for day use only. Highlights at the park include a boat launch and hiking trails that lead out to the cape. Four miles south at Nestucca Spit, there is another day-use park, providing additional recreational options. The point extends about three miles and is a good spot for bird-watching. The campsites do not have ocean views, but the ocean is across the road and within walking distance. Surfing is an option.

RV sites, facilities: There are 150 sites with full hookups for RVs up to 65 feet long, 13 tent sites, and 14 camping cabins. Some sites are pull-through. Drinking water, fire rings, and picnic tables are provided. Restrooms with flush toilets and showers, dump station, modem access, a heated swimming pool (year-round), hot tub, an exercise room, firewood, a recreation hall, coin laundry, propane, a seafood market, deli, gift shop, automated teller machine (ATM), sandboard rentals, and a playground are available. Gasoline, a store, and a café are within one mile. Boat docks, launching facilities, and rentals are nearby. Leashed pets are permitted.

Reservations, fees: Reservations are accepted. RV sites are $40.95–43.95 per night, tent sites are $26 per night, $2–4 per person per night for more than two people, and $4 per night per additional vehicle. Some credit cards are accepted. Open year-round.

Directions: From Tillamook and U.S. 101, drive south on U.S. 101 for 25 miles to the Pacific City exit and Brooten Road. Turn right on Brooten Road and drive three miles toward Pacific City and Three Capes Drive. Turn left, cross the bridge, and bear right on Three Capes Drive. Continue one mile north to the park on the right.

Contact: Cape Kiwanda RV Resort, 503/965-6230, fax 503/965-6235, www.capekiwandarv-park.com.

26 WEBB PARK

Scenic rating: 7

near Cape Kiwanda

Map grid A2

This public campground provides an excellent alternative to the more crowded commercial RV parks off U.S. 101. Although not as developed, it offers a quiet, private setting and access to the ocean. Fishing and swimming are among your options here. The camp is adjacent to Cape Kiwanda and provides convenient access to the beach.

RV sites, facilities: There are 31 sites for tents or RVs (no hookups), seven sites with partial hookups for RVs up to 40 feet long, and a hiker/bicyclist site. Picnic tables and fire pits are provided. Drinking water, a dump station, fish-cleaning station, and restrooms with flush toilets and showers are available. Beach launching is nearby. Leashed pets are permitted.

Reservations, fees: Reservations are accepted ($5 reservation fee) at 503/965-5001 or www.co.tillamook.or.us. Sites are $15–25 per night, $3 per night per additional vehicle, and $5 per person per night for hikers/bikers. Some credit cards are accepted. Open May–September.

Directions: From Tillamook and U.S. 101, drive south on U.S. 101 for 25 miles to the Pacific City exit and Highway 30. From Pacific City, turn right (north) and drive to the four-way stop at McPhillips Drive. Turn left on McPhillips Drive and drive 0.5 mile to Cape Kiwanda and the park on the right.

Contact: Webb Park, Tillamook County Parks, 503/965-5001, www.co.tillamook.or.us/gov/parks.

27 HEBO LAKE

Scenic rating: 7

on Hebo Lake in Siuslaw National Forest

Map grid A2

This U.S. Forest Service campground along the shore of Hebo Lake is a secluded spot with sites nestled under trees. The trailhead for the eight-mile-long Pioneer-Indian Trail is located in the campground. The trail around the lake is wheelchair accessible.

RV sites, facilities: There are 15 sites for tents or RVs up to 18 feet long. Picnic tables and fire pits are provided. Drinking water, garbage bins, and vault toilets are available. Boats with electric motors are allowed on the lake, but gas motors are not. Some facilities are wheelchair accessible. Leashed pets are permitted.

Reservations, fees: Reservations are not accepted. Sites are $12 per night, $5 per night per additional vehicle. Open from mid-April to mid-November, weather permitting.

Directions: On U.S. 101 southwest of Portland, drive to the town of Hebo and Highway 22. Turn east on Highway 22 and drive 0.25 mile to Forest Road 14. Turn left (east) and drive five miles to the campground on the right.

Contact: Siuslaw National Forest, Hebo Ranger District, 503/392-5100, fax 503/392-5143, www.fs.fed.us.

28 WANDERING SPIRIT RV PARK

Scenic rating: 6

on Rock Creek

Map grid A2

The major draw here is the nearby casino, but there is the added benefit of shaded sites next to Rock Creek, which provides fishing and swimming options. The Yamhill River is 0.5 mile away. Fishing is good for steelhead and salmon in season. Golf courses and wineries are available within 10 miles. There is a combination of monthly rentals and overnighters at this park.

RV sites, facilities: There are 129 sites with full hookups for RVs up to 45 feet long, 10 tent sites, and four park-model cabins. Some sites are pull-through. Drinking water, cable TV, wireless Internet service, modem access, restrooms with showers, dump station, coin laundry, RV storage, RV supplies, and a convenience store are available. Propane, a clubhouse, basketball hoop, an exercise room, and a game room are also available on-site. A 24-hour free bus

OREGON

shuttles campers to and from the Spirit Mountain Casino, restaurants, and shops less than two miles away. Some facilities are wheelchair accessible. Leashed pets are permitted.

Reservations, fees: Reservations are accepted at 800/390-6980. RV sites are $26 per night, tent sites are $16 per night, $2 per person per night for more than two people. Monthly rates are available. Some credit cards are accepted. Open year-round.

Directions: From Salem, drive west on Highway 22 about 25 miles to Highway 18. Turn west on Highway 18 and drive seven miles to the park on the left.

Contact: Wandering Spirit RV Park, 503/879-5700, fax 503/879-5171.

29 DEVIL'S LAKE STATE PARK

Scenic rating: 7

on Devil's Lake

Map grid A3

Oregon's only coastal camp in the midst of a city, Devil's Lake is the center of summertime activity. A take-your-pick deal: You can boat, canoe, fish, kayak, or water ski. A walking path extends from the campground to the boat launch 0.25 mile away. For something different, head west and explore the seven miles of beaches. Lincoln City also has a number of arts and crafts galleries and a weekend farmers market during the summer. East Devil's Lake is two miles east and offers a boat ramp and picnic facilities.

RV sites, facilities: There are 54 sites for tents or small RVs (no hookups), 33 sites for tents or RVs up to 55 feet long (full hookups), 10 yurts, and a separate area for hikers and bikers. Picnic tables and fire grills are provided. Drinking water, cable TV, garbage bins, restrooms with flush toilets and showers, an amphitheater, and firewood are available. Boat docks and launching facilities are nearby. Some facilities are wheelchair accessible. Leashed pets are permitted.

Reservations, fees: Reservations are accepted

at 800/452-5687 or www.oregonstateparks.org ($8 reservation fee). RV sites are $17–23 per night, $5 per night per additional vehicle, tent sites are $13–17 per night, $4 per person per night for hikers/bikers, and yurts are $29 per night. Boat mooring is $7 per night. Some credit cards are accepted. Open year-round.

Directions: From Lincoln City and U.S. 101, take the 6th Street exit. Drive east on 6th Street for one block to the park on the right.

Contact: Devil's Lake State Park, 503/994-2002 or 800/551-6949, www.oregonstateparks.org.

30 KOA LINCOLN CITY

Scenic rating: 7

on Devils Lake

Map grid A3

This area offers opportunities for beachcombing, fishing, and tidepool-viewing along a seven-mile stretch of beach. Nearby recreation options include a casino, factory outlets, a golf course, skateboard park, and tennis courts.

RV sites, facilities: There are 15 tent sites and 81 sites with full or partial hookups for RVs up to 60 feet long, including some pull-through sites, and 30- and 50-amp service is available. There are also 14 cabins. Picnic tables and fire pits are provided. Drinking water, cable TV, modem access, restrooms with flush toilets and showers, dump station, public phones, convenience store, snack bar, gift shop, propane gas, ice, RV supplies, video and DVD rentals, game room, coin laundry, meeting room, firewood, and a playground are available. Leashed pets are permitted.

Reservations, fees: Reservations are accepted at 800/562-2791. RV sites are $20–32 per night, tent sites are $20–25 per night, $3 per person per night for more than two people, $7.50 per night per additional vehicle. Some credit cards are accepted. Open year-round.

Directions: From Portland, drive south on Highway 99 West to Highway 18. Turn west on Highway 18 and drive 47 miles to U.S. 101. Turn south on U.S. 101 and drive 1.5 miles to East Devil's Lake Road. Turn east on East Devil's Lake Road and drive one mile to the park on the left.

Contact: KOA Lincoln City, 541/994-2961, fax 541/994-9454, www.koa.com.

31 SEA AND SAND RV PARK

Scenic rating: 9

near Siletz Bay

Map grid A3

Beachcombing for fossils and agates is popular at this oceanfront park near Gleneden Beach on Siletz Bay. Some sites have ocean views and pleasant terraces. The Siletz River and numerous small creeks are in the area. The park is located 3.5 miles north of Depoe Bay.

RV sites, facilities: There are 109 sites with full hookups for RVs up to 35 feet long. Drinking water, cable TV, fire pits, and picnic tables are provided. Restrooms with flush toilets and showers, dump station, firewood, and a coin laundry are available. A store, café, and ice are within one mile. Leashed pets are permitted.

Reservations, fees: Reservations are accepted. Sites are $29–57 per night, $2 per person per night for more than two people, and $5 per night per additional vehicle unless towed. Open year-round.

Directions: From Lincoln City and U.S. 101, drive south for nine miles on U.S. 101 to the park entrance (on the beach side of the highway).

Contact: Sea and Sand RV Park, 541/764-2313.

32 BEVERLY BEACH STATE PARK

Scenic rating: 7

near Newport

Map grid A3

This beautiful campground is set in a wooded, grassy area on the east side of U.S. 101. Treed campsites sit along Spencer Creek. A tunnel leads under the roadway to a beach that stretches from Yaguna Head to the Otter Rock headlands. A one-mile hiking trail is available. Just a mile to the north lies a small day-use state park called Devil's Punchbowl, named for an unusual bowl-shaped rock formation with caverns under it where the waves rumble about. For some great ocean views, head north one more mile to the Otter Crest Wayside. The Oregon Coast Aquarium is within a few minutes' drive.

RV sites, facilities: There are 128 sites for tents or small RVs, 128 sites with full or partial hookups for tents or RVs up to 65 feet long, a special camping area for hikers and bicyclists, and five group sites for tents or RVs (no hookups) that can accommodate up to 25 people each. There is also a village of 21 yurts. Picnic tables and fire grills are provided. Drinking water, restrooms with flush toilets and showers, cable TV, a playground, a day-use area, garbage bins, and a dump station are available. Some facilities are wheelchair accessible. Leashed pets are permitted.

Reservations, fees: Reservations are accepted at 800/452-5687 or www.oregonstateparks.org ($8 reservation fee). Sites are $13–26 per night, $5 per night per additional vehicle, $4–6 per person per night for hikers/bikers, $30–40 per night for yurts, and $44–77 for group sites. Some credit cards are accepted. Open year-round.

Directions: From Newport and U.S. 101, drive north on U.S. 101 for seven miles to the park entrance on the east side.

Contact: Beverly Beach State Park, 541/265-9278 or 800/551-6949, www.oregonstateparks.org.

33 AGATE BEACH RV PARK

Scenic rating: 6

near Newport

Map grid A3

This park is located about half a mile from Agate Beach Wayside, a small state park with beach access. Agate hunting can be good. Sometimes, a layer of sand covers the agates, and you have to dig a bit. But other times, wave action clears the

OREGON

sand, unveiling the agates at low tides. Beverly Beach State Park is 4.5 miles north. About half of the sites are filled with monthly rentals. There are no ocean views from the campsites.

RV sites, facilities: There are 32 sites with full or partial hookups for RVs up to 40 feet long. Drinking water, cable TV, and picnic tables are provided. Restroom with flush toilets and showers, dump station, and a coin laundry room are available. A store and ice are within one mile. Leashed pets are permitted, with some restrictions.

Reservations, fees: Reservations are accepted. Sites are $22.50 per night, $1 per person per night for more than two people, and $1 per night per additional vehicle. Some credit cards are accepted. Open year-round.

Directions: From Newport and U.S. 101, drive to the north end of town. The park is on the east side of the road.

Contact: Agate Beach RV Park, 541/265-7670.

34 HARBOR VILLAGE RV PARK

Scenic rating: 6

on Yaquina Bay
Map grid A3

This wooded and landscaped park is set near the shore of Yaquina Bay. Nearby recreation options include clamming, crabbing, deep-sea fishing, an 18-hole golf course, hiking trails, and a full-service marina.

RV sites, facilities: There are 40 sites with full hookups for RVs up to 35 feet long. Note that there are also 100 sites for full-time renters and a mobile-home park for ages 55 and up. Drinking water, cable TV, wireless Internet service, modem access, and picnic tables are provided. Restrooms with flush toilets and showers and a coin laundry are available. Propane gas, a store, and a café are within one mile. Boat docks, launching facilities, and rentals are nearby. Leashed pets are permitted.

Reservations, fees: Reservations are accepted at 888/818-0002. Sites are $30 per night, $5 per person per night for more than two people. Some credit cards are accepted. Open year-round.

Directions: In Newport, drive south on John Moore Road for 0.5 mile to the bay and Bay Boulevard. Bear left and drive a short distance to the park entrance on the left.

Contact: Harbor Village RV Park, 541/265-5088, fax 541/265-5895, www.harborvillagervpark.com.

35 PORT OF NEWPORT MARINA AND RV PARK

Scenic rating: 7

on Yaquina Bay
Map grid A3

This public park is set along the shore of Yaquina Bay near Newport, a resort town that offers a variety of attractions. Among them are ocean fishing, a museum and aquarium at the nearby Hatfield Marine Science Center, the Undersea Garden, the Waxworks, Ripley's Believe It or Not, and the Lincoln County Historical Society Museum. Nearby recreation options include an 18-hole golf course, hiking trails, and a full-service marina.

RV sites, facilities: There are 143 sites with full hookups for RVs up to 45 feet long. Restrooms with flush toilets and showers, cable TV, Wi-Fi, modem access, dump station, convenience store, coin laundry, fish-cleaning station, and ice are available. A marina with boat docks and launching facilities is available on-site. Some facilities are wheelchair accessible. Leashed pets are permitted.

Reservations, fees: Reservations are accepted at 541/867-3321. Sites with hookups are $29.73–40.78 per night, sites without hookups are $17.68 per night, $1 per person per night for more than two people. Weekly rates are available. Some credit cards are accepted. Open year-round.

Directions: From Newport and U.S. 101, drive south for 0.5 mile (over the bridge) to Marine Science Drive. Turn right (east) and drive 0.5 mile to the park entrance on the left.

Contact: Port of Newport Marina and RV Park, 541/867-3321, fax 541/867-3352, www.portofnewport.com.

OREGON

36 SOUTH BEACH STATE PARK

Scenic rating: 7

near Newport

Map grid A3

This park along the beach offers opportunities for beachcombing, boating, crabbing, fishing, hiking, and windsurfing. The Oregon Coast Trail passes right through the park. A nature trail circles the campground, and there are hiking and bicycling trails to the beach. A primitive hike-in campground is also available. A naturalist provides campground talks during the summer season. Kayak trips are an option during the summer. The park is within walking distance of Oregon Aquarium. Newport attractions include the Hatfield Marine Science Center, the Undersea Garden, the Waxworks, Ripley's Believe It or Not, and the Lincoln County Historical Society Museum.

RV sites, facilities: There are 228 sites with partial hookups for tents or RVs up to 45 feet long, six primitive tent sites, a dispersed camping area (without designated sites) for hikers and bicyclists, and an overflow area for RVs. There are also three group sites for up to 25 people each and 27 yurts. Picnic tables and fire grills are provided. Drinking water, restrooms with flush toilets and showers, garbage bins, recycling, a dump station, Wi-Fi, horseshoe pits, playground, a day-use area, meeting hall, and firewood are available. A camp host is onsite. Some facilities are wheelchair accessible. Leashed pets are permitted.

Reservations, fees: Reservations are accepted at 800/452-5687 or www.oregonstateparks.org ($8 reservation fee). Sites are $18–27 per night, $5 per night per additional vehicle, $4–6 per person per night for hikers/bicyclists (three-night limit), $10 for primitive tent sites, $44–77 per night for group sites, and $30–40 per night for yurts. Some credit cards are accepted. Open year-round.

Directions: From Newport and U.S. 101, drive south for three miles to the park entrance on the right.

Contact: South Beach State Park, 541/867-4715 or 800/551-6949, www.oregonstateparks.org.

37 SEAL ROCKS RV COVE

Scenic rating: 8

near Seal Rock State Park

Map grid A3

This RV park is situated on the rugged coastline near Seal Rock State Park (open for day use only), where you may find seals, sea lions, and a variety of birds. The ocean views are stunning, and some sites have views.

RV sites, facilities: There are 28 sites with full hookups for RVs of any length and 16 tent sites with electricity. Drinking water, picnic tables, and fire rings are provided. Firewood and restrooms with flush toilets and showers are available. A store, a café, and ice are within one mile. Leashed pets are permitted.

Reservations, fees: Reservations are accepted. RV sites are $29–36 per night, tent sites are $20–24 per night, $1–3 per person per night for more than two people, and there's a $3 one-time fee for an additional vehicle unless towed. Winter rates are available. Open year-round.

Directions: From Newport and U.S. 101, drive south for 10 miles to the town of Seal Rock. Continue south on U.S. 101 for 0.25 mile to the park entrance on the left.

Contact: Seal Rocks RV Cove, 541/563-3955, www.sealrocksrv.com.

38 DRIFT CREEK LANDING

Scenic rating: 6

on the Alsea River

Map grid A3

Drift Creek Landing is set along the shore of the Alsea River in a heavily treed and mountainous area. The Oregon Coast Aquarium is 15 miles away, and an 18-hole golf course is nearby. There are 10 mobile homes with long-term renters on this property, and more than one-third of the RV sites are taken by monthly renters.

RV sites, facilities: There are 49 sites with full hookups for RVs of any length, five sites for tents, and three cabins. Drinking water and picnic tables are provided. Restroom with flush toilets

OREGON

and showers, cable TV, propane gas, recreation hall, convenience store, snack bar, coin laundry, boat docks, boat rentals, and launching facilities are available. Leashed pets are permitted.

Reservations, fees: Reservations are accepted. RV sites are $22 per night, and tent sites are $15 per night; it's $2 per person per night for more than two people and $5 per night per additional vehicle. Some credit cards are accepted. Open year-round.

Directions: From Newport and U.S. 101, drive south for 14 miles to Waldport and Highway 34. Turn east on Highway 34 and drive 3.8 miles to the campground.

Contact: Drift Creek Landing, 541/563-3610, fax 541/563-5234.

39 FISHIN' HOLE RV PARK & MARINA

Scenic rating: 6

on the Alsea River
Map grid A3

This campground is one of several along the shore of the Alsea River. Kayaking and canoeing are popular. Some of the sites here are filled with monthly rentals.

RV sites, facilities: There are 24 sites with full or partial hookups for RVs of any length, six sites for tents, one rental home, and one cabin. Drinking water and picnic tables are provided, and fire pits are available on request. Restrooms with flush toilets and showers, coin laundry, recreation room, bait and tackle, boat docks, boat rentals, and launching facilities are available. Leashed pets are permitted.

Reservations, fees: Reservations are accepted at 877/770-6137. Tent sites are $17 per night, RV sites are $21-23 per night, and it's $5 per person per night for more than two people and $5 per night per additional vehicle. Some credit cards are accepted. Open year-round.

Directions: From Newport and U.S. 101, drive south for 14 miles to Waldport and Highway 34. Turn east on Highway 34 and drive four miles to the entrance on the left.

Contact: Fishin' Hole RV Park & Marina, 541/563-3401.

40 CHINOOK RV PARK

Scenic rating: 7

on the Alsea River
Map grid A3

This park is set along the shore of the Alsea River, about 3.5 miles from the ocean. The park is filled primarily with monthly rentals, although several RV sites are reserved for short-term campers. Campsites are rented on a space-available basis.

RV sites, facilities: There are six sites for tents and 34 sites with full or partial hookups for RVs up to 40 feet long. Picnic tables are provided. Drinking water, cable TV, wireless Internet service, restrooms with flush toilets and showers, a picnic area, ice, and a coin laundry are available. A store is within 1.5 miles. Boat docks are nearby. Propane gas and boat launching facilities are available 3.5 miles away. Leashed pets are permitted.

Reservations, fees: Reservations are accepted. RV sites are $22-27 per night, tent sites are $15.75-17.50 per night, $3 per person per night for more than two people. Open year-round.

Directions: From Newport and U.S. 101, drive south for 14 miles to Waldport and Highway 34. Turn east on Highway 34 and drive 3.3 miles to the park entrance on the left.

Contact: Chinook RV Park, 541/563-3485, www.chinookrvpark.com.

41 TAYLOR'S LANDING RV PARK

Scenic rating: 9

on the Alsea River
Map grid A3

This wooded campground is set along the scenic Alsea River. Fall, when the salmon fishing is best, is the prime time here, and the park often fills up. Recreation options include hiking trails, marked bike trails, the Oregon Coast Aquarium, the Sea Lion Caves, and a marina.

RV sites, facilities: There are 81 sites for tents

or RVs of any length (full hookups). Drinking water, cable TV, and picnic tables are provided. Restrooms with flush toilets and showers, propane gas, a café, coin laundry, community fire ring, and boat docks and rentals are available. Boat launching facilities are nearby. Leashed pets are permitted.

Reservations, fees: Reservations are accepted. Sites are $27 per night, $1 per person per night for more than two people. Monthly rates are available. Open year-round.

Directions: From Newport and U.S. 101, drive south for 14 miles to Waldport and Highway 34. Turn east on Highway 34 and drive seven miles to the entrance on the right.

Contact: Taylor's Landing RV Park, phone/fax 541/528-3388, www.taylorslandingrvparkmarina.com.

42 WALDPORT/NEWPORT KOA

Scenic rating: 8

on Alsea Bay

Map grid A3

This pretty park, set amid some of the oldest pine trees in Oregon, is located within walking distance of the beach, the bay, and downtown Waldport—and to top it off, some of the campsites have beautiful ocean views. Alsea Bay's sandy and rocky shoreline makes this area a favorite with anglers. The crabbing and clamming can also be quite good. Kite flying is popular. South Beach State Park, about five miles north on U.S. 101, offers more fishing and a boat ramp along Beaver Creek. It's open for day use only. Other nearby recreation options include hiking trails, marked bike trails, the Oregon Coast Aquarium, the Sea Lion Caves, and a marina.

RV sites, facilities: There are 10 tent sites and 66 sites for RVs up to 45 feet long (full hookups), and 15 cabins. Picnic tables and fire pits are provided; drinking water and cable TV are also available. Restrooms with flush toilets and showers, wireless Internet service, modem access, recreation room, propane gas, dump

station, store, café, coin laundry, playground, and ice are available. Boat docks, launching facilities, and boat rentals are nearby. A café is within one mile. Leashed pets are permitted, with certain restrictions.

Reservations, fees: Reservations are accepted at 800/562-3443. RV sites are $46.50–59.50 per night, tent sites are $25–26 per night, $2–5 per person per night for more than two people. Some credit cards are accepted. Open year-round.

Directions: From Newport and U.S. 101, drive south for approximately 14 miles to Milepost 155 at the north end of the Alsea Bay Bridge. The park is on the west side of the bridge.

Contact: Waldport/Newport KOA, 541/563-2250, fax 541/563-4098, www.koa.com.

43 BEACHSIDE STATE RECREATION SITE

Scenic rating: 7

near Alsea Bay

Map grid A3

This state park offers about nine miles of beach and is not far from Alsea Bay and the Alsea River. Sites are close to the beach. Nearby attractions include clamming, crabbing, and fishing, as well as hiking and driving tours, tidepools, an aquarium, three lighthouses, science centers, and visitors centers. South Beach State Park, about five miles north on U.S. 101, offers more fishing and a boat ramp along Beaver Creek (day use only).

RV sites, facilities: There are 42 sites for tents, 32 sites with partial hookups for RVs up to 30 feet long, two yurts, and a special camping area for hikers and bicyclists. Picnic tables and fire grills are provided. Drinking water, garbage bins, restrooms with flush toilets and showers, recycling, and firewood are available. A horseshoe pit is available nearby. Some facilities are wheelchair accessible. Leashed pets are permitted.

Reservations, fees: Reservations are accepted at 800/452-5687 or www.oregonstateparks.org ($8 reservation fee). RV sites are $18–21 per night, $5 per night per additional vehicle, tent

OREGON

sites are $13–17 per night, $4 per person per night for hikers/bicyclists, and yurts are $30 per night. Some credit cards are accepted. Open mid-March–October, weather permitting.

Directions: From Newport and U.S. 101, drive south for 16 miles to Waldport. Continue south on U.S. 101 for four miles to the park entrance on the west side of the road.

Contact: Beachside State Recreation Site, 541/563-3220, fax 541/563-3657, www.oregonstateparks.org.

44 TILLICUM BEACH

Scenic rating: 8

in Siuslaw National Forest

Map grid A3

Oceanview campsites are a big draw at this campground just south of Beachside State Park. Since it's just off the highway and along the water, this camp fills up very quickly in the summer, so expect crowds. Nearby forest roads provide access to streams in the mountains east of the beach area.

RV sites, facilities: There are 61 sites for tents or RVs up to 60 feet long; some sites have partial hookups. Picnic tables and fire grills are provided. Flush toilets, garbage bins, firewood, and drinking water are available. Leashed pets are permitted.

Reservations, fees: Reservations are accepted at 877/444-6777 or www.recreation.gov ($10 reservation fee). Sites are $22 per night, $6 per night per additional vehicle. Open year-round, with reduced capacity in winter.

Directions: From Newport and U.S. 101, drive south for 14 miles to Waldport. Continue south on U.S. 101 for 4.5 miles to the campground entrance on the right.

Contact: Siuslaw National Forest, Waldport Ranger District, 541/563-3211 or 541/547-3679 (concessionaire), fax 541/563-8449, www.fs.fed.us.

45 CANAL CREEK

Scenic rating: 5

on Canal Creek in Siuslaw National Forest

Map grid A3

There's one key thing you must know: Vehicles must be able to cross a small creek to access this site. That accomplished, this pleasant little campground is just off the beaten path in a large, wooded, open area along Canal Creek. It feels remote because of the creek that runs through the campground and the historic homesites nearby, with old fruit trees on the grounds. Yet it has easy access and is close to the coast and all the amenities. The climate here is relatively mild, but, on the other hand, there is the rain in winter—lots of it.

RV sites, facilities: There are 11 sites for tents or RVs up to 22 feet long, plus a group area for up to 100 people. Picnic tables and fire grills are provided. Vault toilets are available. There is no drinking water and garbage must be packed out. The group site has a picnic shelter and a play area. Leashed pets are permitted.

Reservations, fees: Reservations are not accepted for family sites but are required for group sites at 877/444-6777 or www.recreation.gov ($10 reservation fee). Sites are $17 per night, $6 per night per additional vehicle; group sites are $115–165 per night. Open year-round for individual camping. The group sites are open mid-May–mid-September.

Directions: From Albany, drive west on U.S. 20 for 15 miles to Philomath and Highway 34. Turn south on Highway 34 and drive 52 miles to Forest Road 3462. Turn left (south) and drive four miles to the camp.

Contact: Siuslaw National Forest, Waldport Ranger District, 541/563-3211 or 541/547-3679, fax 541/563-3124, www.fs.fed.us.

46 BLACKBERRY

Scenic rating: 7

on the Alsea River in Siuslaw National Forest

Map grid A3

Blackberry makes a good base camp for a fishing trip on the Alsea River. The U.S. Forest Service provides boat launches and picnic areas at several spots along this stretch of river. Often, there is a camp host who can give you inside information on nearby recreational opportunities. Large fir trees and lawns separate the sites.

RV sites, facilities: There are 32 sites for tents or RVs of any length. Picnic tables and fire grills are provided. Drinking water, garbage bins, and flush toilets are available. There is no firewood. A boat ramp is on-site. Leashed pets are permitted.

Reservations, fees: Reservations are not accepted. Sites are $20 per night, $6 per night per additional vehicle. Open year-round.

Directions: From Albany, drive west on U.S. 20 for 15 miles to Philomath and Highway 34. Turn south on Highway 34 and drive 41 miles to the campground entrance on the left.

Contact: Siuslaw National Forest, Waldport Ranger District, 541/563-3211, fax 541/563-3124, www.fs.fed.us.

47 ALSEA FALLS

Scenic rating: 8

adjacent to the south fork of the Alsea River

Map grid A3

Enjoy the beautiful surroundings of Alsea Falls by exploring the trails that wander through this park and lead to a picnic area by the falls. Trails to McBee Park and Green Peak Falls are accessible from the campground along the south fork of the river. The campsites are situated in a 40-year-old forest of Douglas fir and vine maple. On a warm day, Alsea Falls offers cool relief along the river. The area was named after its original inhabitants, the Alsea people.

RV sites, facilities: There are 16 sites for tents

or RVs up to 30 feet long. Picnic tables and fire pits are provided. Drinking water, vault toilets, and garbage bins are available. Leashed pets are permitted.

Reservations, fees: Reservations are not accepted. Sites are $10 per night, $5 per night per additional vehicle. Open late May-early September.

Directions: From Albany, drive west on U.S. 20 for nine miles to Corvallis. Turn left (south) onto Highway 99 and drive 15 miles to County Road 45120. Turn right (west) and drive five miles to Alpine Junction. Continue along the South Fork Alsea Access Road for nine miles to the campground on the right.

Contact: Bureau of Land Management, Salem District Office, 503/375-5646, fax 503/375-5622, www.blm.gov.

48 CAPE PERPETUA

Scenic rating: 8

on Cape Creek in Siuslaw National Forest

Map grid A3

This U.S. Forest Service campground is set along Cape Creek in the Cape Perpetua Scenic Area. The visitor information center provides hiking and driving maps to guide you through this spectacular region; maps highlight the tidepools and picnic spots. The coastal cliffs are perfect for whale-watching December–March. Neptune State Park is just south and offers additional rugged coastline vistas.

RV sites, facilities: There are 38 sites for tents or RVs up to 45 feet long, plus one group site that can accommodate up to 50 people and 12 vehicles. Picnic tables and fire grills are provided. Flush toilets, drinking water, dump station, firewood, and garbage bins are available. A camp host is on-site. Some facilities are wheelchair accessible. Leashed pets are permitted.

Reservations, fees: Reservations are accepted at 877/444-6777 or www.recreation.gov ($10 reservation fee). Sites are $22 per night, $6 per night per additional vehicle; group sites are $115 per night. Open May–September.

Directions: From Newport and U.S. 101, drive south for 23 miles to Yachats. Continue three miles south on U.S. 101 to the entrance on the left.

Contact: Siuslaw National Forest, Waldport Ranger District, 541/563-3211 or 541/547-3676 (concessionaire), fax 541/563-3124, www.fs.fed. us; Cape Perpetua Visitors Center, 541/547-3289.

49 SEA PERCH RV PARK

Scenic rating: 8

near Cape Perpetua

Map grid A3

Sea Perch sits right in the middle of one of the most scenic areas on the Oregon coast. This private park just south of Cape Perpetua has sites 75 feet from the beach and lawn areas, plus its own shell museum and gift shop. Surf fishing and windsurfing are options here, or head to Cape Perpetua for whale-watching and tidepooling. Big rigs are welcome here.

RV sites, facilities: There are 29 sites with full or partial hookups for RVs of any length. Some sites are pull-through. Drinking water and picnic tables are provided. Restrooms with flush toilets and coin showers, dump station, firewood, recreation hall, coin laundry, ice, convenience store, wireless Internet access, modem hookups, picnic area, and a beach are available. Leashed pets are permitted.

Reservations, fees: Reservations are accepted. Sites are $45–60 per night, $5 per person per night for more than four, $15 per night for an additional vehicle if it cannot be parked on your site. Some credit cards are accepted. Open year-round.

Directions: From Newport and U.S. 101, drive south for 23 miles to Yachats. Continue south on U.S. 101 for 6.5 miles to the campground at Milepost 171 on the right.

Contact: Sea Perch RV Park, 541/547-3505, fax 541/547-3368, www.seaperchrvpark.com.

50 ROCK CREEK

Scenic rating: 7

on Rock Creek in Siuslaw National Forest

Map grid A3

This little campground is set along Rock Creek just 0.25 mile from the ocean. It's a premium spot for coastal-highway travelers, although it can get packed very quickly. An excellent side trip is to Cape Perpetua, a designated scenic area a few miles up the coast. The cape offers beautiful ocean views and a visitors center that will supply you with information on nature trails, picnic spots, tidepools, and where to find the best viewpoints in the area.

RV sites, facilities: There are 15 sites for tents or RVs up to 22 feet long. Fire grills and picnic tables are provided. Flush toilets, garbage bins, and drinking water are available. Leashed pets are permitted.

Reservations, fees: Reservations are not accepted. Sites are $22 per night, $6 per night per additional vehicle. Open mid-May–September.

Directions: From Newport and U.S. 101, drive south for 23 miles to Yachats. Continue south on U.S. 101 for 10 miles to the campground entrance on the left.

Contact: Siuslaw National Forest, Waldport Ranger District, 541/563-3211 or 541/547-3679 (concessionaire), fax 541/563-3124, www. fs.fed.us.

51 CARL G. WASHBURNE STATE PARK

Scenic rating: 7

near Florence

Map grid A3

Even though busy Highway 101 lies right next to Washburne State Park, a bank of native plants shields campers from most road noise, so you hear the roar of the ocean instead of traffic. Sites are spacious, with some abutting China Creek, and elk are frequent visitors. Short hikes lead from the campground to a two-mile-long beach, extensive tidepools along the base of the cliffs, and a three-

OREGON

mile trail to Heceta Head Lighthouse. Just three miles south of the park are the Sea Lion Caves, where an elevator takes visitors down into a cavern for an insider's view of the life of a sea lion.

RV sites, facilities: There are 56 sites for tents or RVs up to 45 feet long (full hookups), seven primitive walk-in sites, two yurts, and a hiker/biker camping area. Picnic tables, fire pits, drinking water, garbage bins, and a dump station are provided. Firewood and restrooms with flush toilets and showers are available. Leashed pets are permitted.

Reservations, fees: Reservations are not accepted, except for yurts. RV sites are $17–26 per night, tent sites are $13–21 per night, $4–5 per person per night for hikers/bicyclists, and yurts are $29–39 per night; $5 per night per additional vehicle. Some credit cards are accepted. Open year-round.

Directions: From Florence and U.S. 101, drive north for 12.5 miles to the park entrance road (it is well signed, 10 miles south of the town of Yachats). Turn east and drive a short distance to the park.

Contact: Carl G. Washburne State Park, 541/547-3416 or 800/551-6949, www.oregon-stateparks.org.

52 ALDER DUNE

Scenic rating: 7

near Alder Lake in Siuslaw National Forest
Map grid A3

This wooded campground is situated near four lakes—Alder Lake, Dune Lake, Mercer Lake (the largest), and Sutton Lake. A boat launch is available at Sutton Lake. An excellent recreation option is to explore the expansive sand dunes in the area by foot (there is no off-road-vehicle access here). Side trips include the Sea Lion Caves, Darlington State Park, Jessie M. Honeyman Memorial State Park, and the Indian Forest, just four miles north.

RV sites, facilities: There are 39 sites for tents or self-contained RVs (no hookups) up to 62 feet long. Picnic tables and fire grills are provided.

Flush toilets, garbage bins, and drinking water are available. Leashed pets are permitted.

Reservations, fees: Reservations are accepted at 877/444-6777 or www.recreation.gov ($10 reservation fee). Sites are $20 per night. Open year-round, weather permitting.

Directions: From Florence and U.S. 101, drive north for eight miles to the campground on the left.

Contact: Siuslaw National Forest, Reedsport Ranger District, 541/271-6000, fax 541/271-1563, www.fs.fed.us.

53 SUTTON

Scenic rating: 7

near Sutton Lake in Siuslaw National Forest
Map grid A3

This campground is located adjacent to Sutton Creek, not far from Sutton Lake. Vegetation provides some privacy between sites. Holman Vista on Sutton Beach Road offers a beautiful view of the dunes and ocean. Wading and fishing are both popular. A hiking trail system leads from the camp out to the dunes. There is no off-road-vehicle access here. An alternative camp is Alder Dune to the north.

RV sites, facilities: There are 80 sites, 20 with partial hookups, for tents or RVs up to 30 feet long and two group sites for up to 50 and 100 people, respectively. Picnic tables and fire grills are provided. Flush toilets, garbage bins, and drinking water are available. A boat ramp is nearby. Leashed pets are permitted.

Reservations, fees: Reservations are accepted at 877/444-6777 or www.recreation.gov ($10 reservation fee). Sites are $20–22 per night and $50–75 per night for group sites. Open May–December.

Directions: From Eugene, drive west on Highway 126 for 61 miles to Florence and U.S. 101. Turn north on U.S. 101 and drive six miles to Sutton Beach Road (Forest Road 794). Turn left (northwest) and drive 1.5 miles to the campground entrance.

Contact: Siuslaw National Forest, Reedsport

OREGON

Ranger District, 541/271-6000, fax 541/271-1563, www.fs.fed.us.

54 MAPLE LANE RV PARK AND MARINA

Scenic rating: 5

on the Siuslaw River
Map grid A3

This park along the shore of the Siuslaw River in Mapleton is close to hiking trails. The general area is surrounded by Siuslaw National Forest land. A U.S. Forest Service map details nearby backcountry side-trip options. Fall is the most popular time of the year here, as it's prime time for salmon fishing on the Siuslaw. Most sites are taken by monthly renters.

RV sites, facilities: There are five tent sites and 39 sites with full hookups for RVs up to 35 feet long. Some sites are pull-through. Drinking water, restrooms with flush toilets and showers, and propane gas are available. A bait and tackle shop is open during the fishing season. Boat docks and launching facilities are on-site. A store, café, and ice are nearby. Small pets (under 15 pounds) are permitted.

Reservations, fees: Reservations are accepted. RV sites are $25–30 per night, tent sites are $18 per night, $1.50 per night for more than two people, and $2 per night per additional vehicle. Monthly rates are available. Open year-round.

Directions: From Eugene, drive west on Highway 126 for 47 miles to Mapleton. Continue on Highway 126 for 0.25 mile past the business district to the park entrance on the left.

Contact: Maple Lane RV Park and Marina, 541/268-4822.

55 ARCHIE KNOWLES

Scenic rating: 6

on Knowles Creek in Siuslaw National Forest
Map grid A3

This little campground along Knowles Creek about three miles east of Mapleton is rustic,

with a mix of forested and lawn areas, yet it offers easy proximity to the highway.

RV sites, facilities: There are nine sites for tents or RVs up to 16 feet long. Picnic tables and fire grills are provided. Flush toilets, garbage bins, and drinking water are available. Leashed pets are permitted.

Reservations, fees: Reservations are not accepted. Sites are $15 per night. Open May–early September, weather permitting.

Directions: From Eugene, drive west on Highway 126 for 44 miles to the campground entrance (three miles east of Mapleton).

Contact: Siuslaw National Forest, Reedsport Ranger District, 541/271-6000, fax 541/271-1563, www.fs.fed.us.

56 HARBOR VISTA COUNTY PARK

Scenic rating: 6

near Florence
Map grid A4

This county park out among the dunes near the entrance to the harbor offers a great lookout point from its observation deck. The park is perched above the North Jetty of the Siuslaw River and encompasses 15 acres. Beach access is one mile away. A number of side trips are available, including to the Sea Lion Caves, Darlington State Park, Jessie M. Honeyman Memorial State Park, and the Indian Forest, just four miles north. Florence also has displays of Native American dwellings and crafts.

RV sites, facilities: There are 38 sites with partial hookups for tents or RVs up to 60 feet long. Picnic tables, fire rings, and garbage bins are provided. Restrooms with flush toilets and coin showers, dump station, drinking water, pay phone, and a playground are available. A camp host is on-site. Some facilities are wheelchair accessible. Leashed pets are permitted.

Reservations, fees: Reservations are accepted at 541/682-2000 ($10 reservation fee). Sites are $20 per night, $6.50 per night per additional vehicle. Some credit cards are accepted. Open year-round.

Directions: From Florence and U.S. 101, drive north for four miles to 35th Street. Turn left and drive to where it dead-ends into Rhododendron Drive. Turn right and drive 1.4 miles to North Jetty Road. Turn left and drive half a block to Harbor Vista Road. Turn left and continue to the campground at 87658 Harbor Vista Road.

Note: Follow these exact directions. Previous visitors to this park taking a different route will discover that part of Harbor Vista Road is now gated.

Contact: Harbor Vista County Park, 541/997-5987, www.co.lane.or.us/.

57 B AND E WAYSIDE MOBILE HOME AND RV PARK

Scenic rating: 5

near Florence

Map grid A4

Adjacent to this landscaped RV park is a 28-unit mobile home park for ages 55 and up. Some sites at the RV park are taken by monthly rentals. Nearby recreation options include two golf courses and a riding stable, two miles away.

RV sites, facilities: There are 24 sites with full hookups for RVs of any length. Picnic tables are provided. Restrooms with flush toilets and showers, dump station, recreation room, modem access, and a coin laundry are available. Propane gas, a store, ice, a café, and a restaurant are within two miles. Boat-launching facilities are nearby. Small, leashed pets are permitted.

Reservations, fees: Reservations are accepted. Sites are $24 per night, $2 per person per night for more than two people. Weekly and monthly rates are available. Open year-round.

Directions: From Florence and U.S. 101, drive north for 1.8 miles to the park on the right.

Contact: B and E Wayside Mobile Home and RV Park, 541/997-6451.

58 PORT OF SIUSLAW RV PARK AND MARINA

Scenic rating: 8

on the Siuslaw River

Map grid A4

This public resort can be found along the Siuslaw River in a grassy, urban setting. Anglers with boats will find that the U.S. 101 bridge support pilings make good spots for crabbing, as well as fishing for perch and flounder. A new set of docks with drinking water, electricity, gasoline, security, and a fish-cleaning station are available. The Sea Lion Caves and estuary are a bonus for wildlife lovers, and nearby lakes make swimming and waterskiing a possibility. Golf is within driving distance, and horses can be rented about nine miles away.

RV sites, facilities: There are 10 tent sites and 92 sites with full or partial hookups for tents or RVs of any length. Drinking water, cable TV, and picnic tables are provided. Restrooms with flush toilets and showers, dump station, coin laundry, wireless Internet service, and boat docks are available. A café, grocery store, and ice are within one mile. Some facilities are wheelchair accessible. Leashed pets are permitted.

Reservations, fees: Reservations are accepted at 541/997-3040 or www.portofsiuslaw.com ($10 reservation fee). Sites are $22–30 per night, $2 per night per additional vehicle. Weekly rates available. Some credit cards are accepted. Open year-round.

Directions: From Florence and U.S. 101, drive south to Nopal Street. Turn left (east) and drive two blocks to 1st Street. Turn left and drive 0.25 mile to the park at the end of the road.

Contact: Port of Siuslaw RV Park and Marina, 541/997-3040, www.portofsiuslaw.com.

59 JESSIE M. HONEYMAN MEMORIAL STATE PARK

Scenic rating: 7

near Cleowax Lake

Map grid A4

This popular state park is within walking distance of the shore of Cleawox Lake and adjacent to the dunes of the Oregon Dunes National Recreation Area. Dunes stretch for two miles between the park and the ocean. The dunes here are quite impressive, with some reaching to 500 feet. In the winter, the area is open to OHV use. For thrill-seekers, sandboard rentals (for sand-boarding on the dunes) are available in nearby Florence. The two lakes in the park offer facilities for boating, fishing, and swimming. A one-mile hiking trail with access to the dunes is available in the park, and off-road-vehicle trails are nearby in the sand dunes.

RV sites, facilities: There are 187 sites for tents or RVs (no hookups) up to 60 feet long, 168 sites with full or partial hookups for RVs, a camping area for hikers and bicyclists, six group tent areas for up to 25 people and 10 vehicles each, and 10 yurts. Picnic tables, garbage bins, and fire grills are provided. Drinking water, restrooms with flush toilets and showers, a dump station, seasonal interpretive programs, a playground, an amphitheater, and firewood are available. A meeting hall and picnic shelters can be reserved. Boat docks and launching facilities are nearby. Some facilities are wheelchair accessible. Leashed pets are permitted.

Reservations, fees: Reservations are accepted at 800/452-5687 or www.oregonstateparks.org ($8 reservation fee). RV sites are $17–26 per night, tent sites are $13–21 per night, $5 per night per additional vehicle, $4–5 per person per night for hikers/bicyclists, $29–39 per night for yurts, and $43–76 per night for group sites. Some credit cards are accepted. Open year-round.

Directions: From Florence and U.S. 101, drive south for three miles to the park entrance on the west side of the road.

Contact: Jessie M. Honeyman Memorial State Park, 541/997-3641 or 800/551-6949, www.oregonstateparks.org.

60 LAKESHORE RV PARK

Scenic rating: 5

on Woahink Lake

Map grid A4

Here's a prime area for vacationers. This park is set along the shore of Woahink Lake, a popular spot to fish for bass, bluegill, catfish, crappie, perch, and trout. It's adjacent to Jessie M. Honeyman Memorial State Park and the Oregon Dunes National Recreation Area. Off-road-vehicle access to the dunes is four miles northeast and three miles south of the park. Hiking trails through the dunes can be found at Honeyman Memorial State Park. Some sites are filled with monthly rentals.

RV sites, facilities: There are 20 sites with full hookups for RVs of any length; some are pull-through sites. Picnic tables and cable TV are provided. Drinking water, restrooms with flush toilets and showers, modem access, wireless Internet service, and a coin laundry are available. A café is within three miles. Boat docks are nearby. Leashed pets are permitted.

Reservations, fees: Reservations are accepted at 866/240-4269. Sites are $29 per night, $2 per person per night for more than two people. Monthly rentals are available. Open year-round.

Directions: From Florence and U.S. 101, drive south for four miles to Milepost 195. The park is on the left (east side of road).

Contact: Lakeshore RV Park, 541/997-2741, www.lakeshorerv.com.

61 MERCER LAKE RESORT

Scenic rating: 7

on Mercer Lake

Map grid A4

This resort is in a forested setting situated above the shore of Mercer Lake, one of a number of lakes that have formed among the ancient dunes in this area. The 375-acre lake has 11 miles of shoreline and numerous coves. Fishing for rainbow trout and largemouth bass in the stocked lake is the most popular activity. A sandy swimming beach is also available, and the ocean is four miles away.

RV sites, facilities: There are 10 sites with full or partial hookups for RVs up to 40 feet long and 10 cabins. Some sites are pull-through. No open fires are allowed. Drinking water, cable TV, and picnic tables are provided. Restrooms with flush toilets and showers, dump station, convenience store, coin laundry, and ice are available. Boat docks, launching facilities, and fishing boat rentals are on-site. Leashed pets are permitted.

Reservations, fees: Reservations are accepted at 800/355-3633. Sites are $22–35 per night, $2 per night per additional vehicle, $5 per night per pet. Some credit cards are accepted. Open year-round.

Directions: From Florence and U.S. 101, drive north for five miles to Mercer Lake Road. Turn east and drive just under one mile to Bay Berry Lane. Turn left and drive to the resort.

Contact: Mercer Lake Resort, 541/997-3633, www.mlroregon.com.

62 CARTER LAKE

Scenic rating: 9

on Carter Lake in
Oregon Dunes National Recreation Area

Map grid A4

This campground sits on the north shore of Carter Lake, and you can fish almost right from your campsite. Boating and fishing are permitted on this long, narrow lake, which is set among dunes overgrown with vegetation. The nearby Taylor Dunes Trail is a half-mile, wheelchair-accessible trail to the dunes past Taylor Lake. Hiking is allowed in the dunes, but there is no off-road-vehicle access here. If you want off-road access, head north one mile to Siltcoos Road, turn west, and drive 1.3 miles to Driftwood II.

RV sites, facilities: There are 22 sites for tents or RVs up to 30 feet long. Picnic tables, garbage service, and fire grills are provided. Drinking water,

flush toilets, and firewood are available. A camp host is on-site. Leashed pets are permitted.

Reservations, fees: Reservations are accepted at 877/444-6777 or www.recreation.gov ($10 reservation fee). Sites are $17–20 per night, $5 per night per additional vehicle. Open May–September.

Directions: From Florence and U.S. 101, drive south for 8.5 miles to Forest Road 1084. Turn right on Forest Road 1084 and drive west 200 yards to the camp.

Contact: Oregon Dunes National Recreation Area, Visitors Center, 541/271-3611, fax 541/750-7244.

63 DRIFTWOOD II

Scenic rating: 6

near Siltcoos Lake in
Oregon Dunes National Recreation Area

Map grid A4

Primarily a campground for off-road vehicles, Driftwood II is set near the ocean, but without an ocean view, in the Oregon Dunes National Recreation Area. It has off-road-vehicle access. Several small lakes, the Siltcoos River, and Siltcoos Lake are nearby. Note that ATV use is prohibited between 10 p.m. and 6 a.m.

RV sites, facilities: There are 68 sites for tents or RVs up to 59 feet long, including 10 pull-through sites. Picnic tables, garbage service, and fire grills are provided at back-in sites but not at the 10 pull-through sites. Drinking water and restrooms with flush toilets and showers are available. A dump station is within five miles. Boat docks, launching facilities, and rentals can be found about four miles away on Siltcoos Lake. Some facilities are wheelchair accessible. Leashed pets are permitted.

Reservations, fees: Reservations are accepted at 877/444-6777 or www.recreation.gov ($10 reservation fee). Sites are $20 per night. Open year-round.

Directions: From Florence and U.S. 101, drive south for seven miles to Siltcoos Beach Road. Turn right and drive 1.5 miles west to the campground.

OREGON

64 LAGOON

Scenic rating: 9

near Siltcoos Lake in
Oregon Dunes National Recreation Area

Map grid A4

One of several campgrounds in the area, this camp is located along the lagoon, about one mile from Siltcoos Lake and set 0.5 mile inland. The Lagoon Trail offers prime wildlife-viewing for marine birds and other aquatic species.

RV sites, facilities: There are 41 sites for tents or RVs of any length. Picnic tables, garbage service, and fire grills are provided. Drinking water and flush and vault toilets are available. A camp host is on-site. Boat docks, launching facilities, and rentals are nearby on Siltcoos Lake. A telephone and a dump station are within five miles. Some facilities are wheelchair accessible. Leashed pets are permitted.

Reservations, fees: Reservations are accepted at 877/444-6777 or www.recreation.gov ($10 reservation fee). Sites are $20 per night. Open year-round.

Directions: From Florence and U.S. 101, drive south for seven miles to Siltcoos Beach Road. Turn right on Siltcoos Beach Road and drive west for 1.2 miles to the campground.

Contact: Oregon Dunes National Recreation Area, Visitors Center 541/271-6000 or 541/271-3611, fax 541/750-7244.

65 DARLINGS RESORT AND MARINA

Scenic rating: 7

on Siltcoos Lake

Map grid A4

This park, in a rural area along the north shore of Siltcoos Lake, is adjacent to the extensive Oregon Dunes National Recreation Area. Sites are right on the lake; fish from your picnic table. An access point to the dunes for hikers and off-road vehicles is just across the highway. The lake has a full-service marina. About half the sites are taken by monthly rentals.

RV sites, facilities: There are 14 sites with partial hookups for RVs up to 38 feet long. Cable TV, drinking water, fire pits, and picnic tables are provided. Restrooms with flush toilets and coin showers, firewood, convenience store, tavern, deli, boat docks, boat rentals, launching facilities, and a coin laundry are available. Leashed pets are permitted.

Reservations, fees: Reservations are accepted. Sites are $29.96 per night, $5 per night per additional vehicle. Some credit cards are accepted. Open year-round.

Directions: From Florence and U.S. 101, drive south for five miles to North Beach Road. Turn left (east) and drive 0.25 mile to Darlings Loop Road. Turn right and drive 0.25 mile to the resort.

Contact: Darlings Resort and Marina, 541/997-2841, www.darlingsresortrv.com.

66 TYEE

Scenic rating: 6

on the Siltcoos River in
Oregon Dunes National Recreation Area

Map grid A4

This wooded campground along the shore of the Siltcoos River provides an alternative to Driftwood II and Lagoon. Fishing is permitted at the nearby lake, where there is a canoe portage trail and a boat ramp. Off-road-vehicle access to the dunes is available from Driftwood II, and there are hiking trails in the area.

RV sites, facilities: There are 16 sites for tents or RVs up to 30 feet long. Picnic tables, garbage service, and fire grills are provided. Drinking water, vault toilets, firewood, and a day-use area with horseshoe pits are available. A camp host is on-site. A store, boat docks, launching facilities, and rentals are nearby. Some facilities are wheelchair accessible. Leashed pets are permitted.

Reservations, fees: Reservations are accepted at 877/444-6777 or www.recreation.gov ($10 reservation fee). Sites are $17–18.35 per night, $5 per night per each additional vehicle. Open May–September.

Directions: From Florence and U.S. 101, drive south for six miles to the Westlake turnoff. Take that exit and continue a short distance to the campground.

Contact: Oregon Dunes National Recreation Area, Visitors Center 541/271-6000 or 541/271-3611, fax 541/750-7244; campground management 541/997-4479.

67 WAXMYRTLE

Scenic rating: 7

near Siltcoos Lake in
Oregon Dunes National Recreation Area

Map grid A4

One of three camps in the immediate vicinity, Waxmyrtle is adjacent to Lagoon and less than a mile from Driftwood II. The camp is near the Siltcoos River and a couple of miles from Siltcoos Lake, a good-sized lake with boating facilities where you can fish. A pleasant hiking trail here meanders through the dunes and along the estuary.

RV sites, facilities: There are 57 sites for tents or RVs of any length. Picnic tables, garbage service, and fire grills are provided. Drinking water and flush toilets are available. A camp host is on-site. Boat docks, launching facilities, and rentals are nearby on Siltcoos Lake. Leashed pets are permitted.

Reservations, fees: Reservations are accepted at 877/444-6777 or www.recreation.gov ($10 reservation fee). Sites are $20 per night. Open year-round.

Directions: From Florence and U.S. 101, drive south for seven miles to Siltcoos Beach Road. Turn right and drive 1.3 miles west to the campground.

Contact: Oregon Dunes National Recreation Area, Visitors Center 541/271-6000 or 541/271-3611, fax 541/750-7244.

68 TAHKENITCH LANDING

Scenic rating: 6

near Tahkenitch Lake in
Oregon Dunes National Recreation Area

Map grid A4

This camp overlooking Tahkenitch Lake (Lake of Many Fingers) has easy access to excellent fishing.

RV sites, facilities: There are 29 sites for tents or RVs up to 40 feet long. Picnic tables and garbage service are provided. Vault toilets, boat-launching facilities, and a floating dock are available, but there is no drinking water. A camp host is on-site. Leashed pets are permitted.

Reservations, fees: Reservations are accepted at 877/444-6777 or www.recreation.gov ($10 reservation fee). Sites are $17–19 per night, $5 per night per additional vehicle. Open year-round.

Directions: From Florence and U.S. 101, drive south for 14 miles to the campground on the east side of the road.

Contact: Oregon Dunes National Recreation Area, Visitors Center 541/271-6000 or 541/271-3611, fax 541/750-7244; campground management 541/997-4479.

69 TAHKENITCH

Scenic rating: 7

near Tahkenitch Lake in
Oregon Dunes National Recreation Area

Map grid A4

This very pretty campground with dense vegetation is set in a wooded area across the highway from Tahkenitch Lake, which has numerous coves and backwater areas for fishing. A hiking trail close to the camp goes through the dunes out to the beach, as well as to Threemile Lake. If this camp is full, Tahkenitch Landing provides space nearby.

RV sites, facilities: There are 26 sites for tents or RVs up to 30 feet long. Picnic tables, garbage service, and fire grills are provided. Drinking water, firewood, and flush toilets are available.

A camp host is on-site. Boat docks and launching facilities are on the lake across the highway. Some facilities are wheelchair accessible. Leashed pets are permitted.

Reservations, fees: Reservations are accepted at 877/444-6777 or www.recreation.gov ($10 reservation fee). Sites are $16.83–19.80 per night, $5 per night per additional vehicle. Open mid-May–September.

Directions: From Florence and U.S. 101, drive south for 14 miles. The campground entrance is on the right.

Contact: Oregon Dunes National Recreation Area, Visitors Center 541/271-6000 or 541/271-3611, fax 541/750-7244; campground management 541/997-4479.

70 DISCOVERY POINT RESORT & RV PARK

Scenic rating: 7

on Winchester Bay

Map grid A4

This resort sits on the shore of Winchester Bay, adjacent to sandy dunes, in a fishing village near the mouth of the Umpqua River. The park was designed around motor sports, and ATVs are available for rent. It is somewhat noisy, but that's what most people come for.

RV sites, facilities: There are five tent sites, 60 sites with full hookups for RVs of any length, 13 cabins, and two condos. Some sites are pull-through. Picnic tables and fire pits are provided at most sites. Restrooms with flush toilets and showers, drinking water, cable TV, convenience store, coin laundry, a weekend snack bar, and ice are available. A dump station and propane gas are within one mile. Boat docks and launching facilities are nearby. Leashed pets are permitted.

Reservations, fees: Reservations are accepted. RV sites are $28–33 per night, tent sites are $14–16 per night, condos are $260–275 per night, $7 per night per each additional vehicle. Call for cabin rates. Some credit cards are accepted. Open year-round.

Directions: From Reedsport and U.S. 101, drive south for two miles to Winchester Bay and Salmon Harbor Drive. Turn right at Salmon Harbor Drive and proceed west for one mile to the resort on the left.

Contact: Discovery Point Resort & RV Park, 541/271-3443, www.discoverypointresort.com; ATV rentals, 541/271-9357.

71 WINDY COVE COUNTY PARK

Scenic rating: 7

adjacent to Salmon Harbor at Winchester Bay

Map grid A4

This Douglas County park actually comprises two campgrounds, Windy Cove A and B. Set near ocean beaches and sand dunes, both offer a variety of additional recreational opportunities, including an 18-hole golf course, hiking trails, and a lighthouse.

RV sites, facilities: There are 33 tent sites and 64 sites with full or partial hookups for RVs up to 60 feet long. Drinking water and picnic tables are provided. Fire pits are provided at some Windy A sites, but not at Windy B sites. Restrooms with flush toilets and showers and cable TV are available. Propane gas, dump station, a store, café, coin laundry, and ice are within one mile. Boat docks, launching facilities, boat charters, and rentals are nearby. Some facilities are wheelchair accessible. Leashed pets are permitted.

Reservations, fees: Reservations are accepted for selected Windy B sites only at 541/957-7001. Sites are $15–20 per night, $3 per night per additional vehicle. Some credit cards are accepted. Open year-round.

Directions: From Reedsport and U.S. 101, drive south for three miles to the Windy Cove exit near Winchester Bay. Take that exit and drive west to the park on the left.

Contact: Windy Cove County Park, Windy B, 541/271-5634; Windy A, 541/271-4138, www.co.douglas.or.us/parks.

OREGON

72 UMPQUA LIGHTHOUSE STATE PARK

Scenic rating: 7

on the Umpqua River

Map grid A4   BEST (

This park is located near Lake Marie and less than a mile from Salmon Harbor on Winchester Bay. A one-mile trail circles Lake Marie, and swimming and non-motorized boating are allowed. Near the mouth of the scenic Umpqua River, this unusual area features dunes as high as 500 feet. Hiking trails lead out of the park and into the Oregon Dunes National Recreation Area. The park offers more than two miles of beach access on the ocean and 0.5 mile along the Umpqua River. The adjacent lighthouse is still in operation, and tours are available during the summer season.

RV sites, facilities: There are 24 sites for tents or RVs up to 45 feet long (no hookups), 20 sites with full hookups for RVs up to 45 feet long, a hiker/bicyclist camp, two cabins, two rustic yurts, and six deluxe yurts. Picnic tables and fire pits are provided. Drinking water, garbage bins, restrooms with flush toilets and showers, and firewood are available. Boat docks and launching facilities are on the Umpqua River. Leashed pets are permitted.

Reservations, fees: Reservations are accepted at 800/452-5687 or www.oregonstateparks.org ($8 reservation fee). RV sites are $16–24 per night, tent sites are $12–19 per night, $5 per night for an additional vehicle, $4–5 per person per night for hikers/bikers, $35–39 per night for cabins, $27–36 per night for rustic yurts, and $45–76 for deluxe yurts. Some credit cards are accepted. Open year-round.

Directions: From Reedsport and U.S. 101, drive south for six miles to Umpqua Lighthouse Road. Turn right (west) and drive one mile to the park.

Contact: Umpqua Lighthouse State Park, 541/271-4118 or 800/551-6949, www.oregon-stateparks.org.

73 WILLIAM M. TUGMAN STATE PARK

Scenic rating: 7

on Eel Lake

Map grid A4

This campground is set along the shore of Eel Lake, which offers almost five miles of shoreline for boating, fishing, sailing, and swimming. It's perfect for bass fishing. A boat ramp is available, but there is a 10-mph speed limit for boats. Oregon Dunes National Recreation Area is across the highway. Hiking is available just a few miles north at Umpqua Lighthouse State Park. A developed, 2.5-mile trail along the south end of the lake allows hikers to get away from the developed areas of the park and explore the lake's many outlets.

RV sites, facilities: There are 94 sites with partial hookups for tents or RVs up to 50 feet long, a camping area for hikers and bicyclists, and 16 yurts. Drinking water, fire rings, and picnic tables are provided. Restrooms with flush toilets and showers, dump station, firewood, and a picnic shelter are available. Boat docks and launching facilities are nearby. Some facilities are wheelchair accessible. Leashed pets are permitted.

Reservations, fees: Reservations are accepted at 800/452-5687 or www.oregonstateparks.org ($8 reservation fee). Sites are $12–20 per night, $5 per night per additional vehicle, $4–5 per person per night for hikers/bicyclists, and $27–39 per night for yurts. Some credit cards are accepted. Open year-round.

Directions: From Reedsport and U.S. 101, drive south for eight miles to the park entrance on the left (east side of the road).

Contact: Sunset Bay State Park, 541/759-3604 or 800/551-6949, www.oregonstateparks.org.

OREGON

OREGON

74 NORTH LAKE RESORT AND MARINA

Scenic rating: 8

on Tenmile Lake

Map grid A4

This 40-acre resort along the shore of Tenmile Lake is wooded and secluded, has a private beach, and makes the perfect layover spot for U.S. 101 travelers. The lake has a full-service marina, and bass fishing can be good here. About 25 percent of the sites are taken by summer season rentals.

RV sites, facilities: There are 20 tent sites and 75 sites with full or partial hookups for RVs of any length. Picnic tables are provided and there are fire pits at most sites. Restrooms with flush toilets and coin showers, dump station, firewood, convenience store, ice, phone/modem hookups, cable TV, drinking water, coin laundry, horseshoe pits, and a volleyball court are available. Boat docks, launching facilities, and a marina are also available. A café and boat rentals are nearby. Leashed pets are permitted.

Reservations, fees: Reservations are accepted. Tent sites are $20 per night; RV sites are $25 per night. Some credit cards are accepted. Open April–October.

Directions: From Reedsport and U.S. 101, drive south on U.S. 101 for 11 miles to the Lakeside exit. Take that exit east into town for 0.75 mile (across the railroad tracks) to North Lake Road. Turn left (north) and drive 0.5 mile to the resort on the left.

Contact: North Lake Resort and Marina, 541/759-3515, fax 541/759-3326, www.north-lakeresort.com.

75 OSPREY POINT RV RESORT

Scenic rating: 7

on Tenmile Lake

Map grid A4

Tenmile is one of Oregon's premier bass fishing lakes and yet is located only three miles from the ocean. The resort is situated in a large, open area adjacent to Tenmile Lake and 0.5 mile from North Lake. A navigable canal connects the lakes. The Oregon Dunes National Recreation Area provides nearby hiking trails, and Elliot State Forest offers wooded trails. With weekend barbecues and occasional live entertainment, Osprey Point is more a destination resort than an overnight stop.

RV sites, facilities: There are 132 sites for tents or RVs of any size (full hookups), a grassy area for tents, and five park-model cabins. Drinking water, picnic tables, and fire pits are provided. Cable TV, modem access, restrooms with flush toilets and showers, dump station, coin laundry, restaurant, cocktail lounge, convenience store, full-service marina with boat docks, launch, fishing pier, fish-cleaning station, horseshoe pits, volleyball, tetherball, recreation hall, video arcade, and a pizza parlor are available. Leashed pets are permitted.

Reservations, fees: Reservations are accepted. RV sites are $25–36 per night, tent sites are $18 per night, $3.50 per person per night for more than two people. Monthly rates are available. Some credit cards are accepted. Open year-round.

Directions: From Reedport, drive north on U.S. 101 for 11 miles to the Lakeside exit. Take that exit east into town for 0.75 mile (across the railroad tracks) to North Lake Road. Turn left (north) on North Lake Road and drive 0.5 mile to the resort on the right.

Contact: Osprey Point RV Resort, 541/759-2801, fax 541/759-3198, www.ospreypoint.net.

76 EEL CREEK

Scenic rating: 8

near Eel Lake in
Oregon Dunes National Recreation Area

Map grid A4

This campground along Eel Creek is located near both Eel and Tenmile Lakes. Although Tenmile Lake allows waterskiing, Eel Lake does not. Nearby trails offer access to the Umpqua

Dunes Scenic Area, where you'll find spectacular scenery in an area closed to off-road vehicles. Off-road access is available at Spinreel.

RV sites, facilities: There are 38 sites for tents or RVs up to 50 feet long. Picnic tables, garbage service, and fire grills are provided. Drinking water, flush toilets, and firewood are available. A camp host is on-site. Boat docks, launching facilities, and rentals are nearby. Leashed pets are permitted.

Reservations, fees: Reservations are accepted at 877/444-6777 or www.recreation.gov ($10 reservation fee). Sites are $20 per night, $5 per night per additional vehicle. Open mid-May–September.

Directions: From Reedsport and U.S. 101, drive south for 10.5 miles to the park entrance.

Contact: Oregon Dunes National Recreation Area, Visitors Center 541/271-6000 or 541/271-3611, fax 541/750-7244.

77 SPINREEL

Scenic rating: 6

on Tenmile Creek in
Oregon Dunes National Recreation Area

Map grid A4

Spinreel campground is set several miles inland at the outlet of Tenmile Lake in the Oregon Dunes National Recreation Area. A boat launch (for drift boats and canoes) is near the camp. Primarily for off-road-vehicle enthusiasts, Spinreel's other recreational opportunities include hiking trails and off-road-vehicle access to the dunes. Off-road-vehicle rentals are available adjacent to the camp.

RV sites, facilities: There are 37 sites for tents or RVs up to 61 feet long. Drinking water, garbage service, and flush toilets are available. Picnic tables and fire grills are provided. Firewood, store, and a coin laundry are nearby. Boat docks, launching facilities, and rentals are on Tenmile Lake. Some facilities are wheelchair accessible. Leashed pets are permitted.

Reservations, fees: Reservations are accepted at 877/444-6777 or www.recreation.gov ($10

reservation fee). Sites are $20 per night. Open year-round.

Directions: From Coos Bay, drive north on U.S. 101 for 10 miles to the campground entrance road (well signed). Turn northwest and drive one mile to the campground.

Contact: Oregon Dunes National Recreation Area, Visitors Center 541/271-6000 or 541/271-3611, fax 541/750-7244.

78 LOON LAKE RECREATION AREA

Scenic rating: 8

on Loon Lake

Map grid A4

Loon Lake was created 1,400 years ago when a nearby mountain crumbled and slid downhill, damming a creek with house-sized boulders. Today, the lake is half a mile wide and nearly two miles long, covers 260 acres, and is more than 100 feet deep in places. Its ideal location provides a warm, wind-sheltered summer climate for various water activities. A nature trail leads to a waterfall about half a mile away. Evening interpretive programs are held during summer weekends.

RV sites, facilities: There are 57 sites for tents or RVs of any length; some sites can be combined into a group site for up to 12 people. Picnic tables and fire pits are provided. Drinking water, restrooms with flush toilets and showers, garbage bins, dump station, basketball court, firewood, playground, horseshoe pits, volleyball, fish-cleaning station, a sand beach, and a boat ramp and moorings are available. Some facilities are wheelchair accessible, including the fishing pier. Leashed pets are permitted in the campground, but not on the beach or in the day-use area.

Reservations, fees: Reservations are accepted at 877/444-6777 or www.recreation.gov ($10 reservation fee). Sites are $18 per night, $7 per night per additional vehicle, and $36 per night for group sites. Open late May–November, weather permitting.

Directions: From Eugene, drive south on I-5 to Exit 162 and Highway 38. Turn west on Highway 38 and drive 43 miles to Milepost 13.5 and the County Road 3 exit. Turn left (south) and drive 7.5 miles to the campground on the right.

Contact: Bureau of Land Management, Coos Bay District Office, 541/756-0100, fax 541/751-4303, www.blm.gov.

79 LOON LAKE LODGE AND RV

Scenic rating: 8

on Loon Lake

Map grid A4

This resort boasts one mile of lake frontage and nestles among the tall trees on pretty Loon Lake. It's not a long drive from either U.S. 101 or I-5, making it an ideal layover spot for travelers eager to get off the highway. The lake offers good bass fishing, boating, swimming, and waterskiing.

RV sites, facilities: There are 25 tent sites, 40 sites with full or partial hookups for tents or RVs up to 40 feet long, four group sites for up to 20–30 people each, eight cabins, and a six-unit motel. Some RV sites are pull-through. Picnic tables and fire rings are provided. Pit toilets and drinking water are available. A restaurant, general store, wireless Internet service, ice, gas, a beach, boat ramp, dock, marina, and boat rentals are also available. Leashed pets are permitted, with certain restrictions.

Reservations, fees: Reservations are accepted. Tent sites are $19 per night, RV sites are $35 per night, $7 per person per night for more than five, $5 per night per additional vehicle. Some credit cards are accepted. Open year-round.

Directions: From Eugene, drive south on I-5 to Exit 162 and Highway 38. Turn west on Highway 38 and drive 20 miles through the town of Elkton. Continue on Highway 38 for another 22 miles until you cross a large bridge and reach Loon Lake Road. Turn left at Loon Lake Road and drive nine miles to the resort.

Contact: Loon Lake Lodge and RV Resort, 541/599-2244, fax 541/599-2274, www.loon-lakerv.com.

80 OREGON DUNES KOA

Scenic rating: 5

north of North Bend, next to the Oregon Dunes National Recreation Area

Map grid A4

This ATV-friendly park has direct access to Oregon Dunes National Recreation Area, which offers miles of ATV trails. The fairly open campground features a landscape of grass, young trees, and a small lake. The ocean is a 15-minute drive away. Mill Casino is about six miles south on U.S. 101. Freshwater and ocean fishing are nearby. A golf course is about five miles away.

RV sites, facilities: There are 51 sites for tents or RVs of any size (full hookups), six tent sites, and nine cabins. Most sites are pull-through, and 30- and 50-amp service is available. RV sites have drinking water, picnic tables, fire pits, and cable TV provided. Drinking water, restrooms with flush toilets and showers, wireless Internet service, modem access, coin laundry, convenience store, game room, playground, seasonal organized activities, a snack bar, firewood, propane gas, horseshoe pits, volleyball, and a picnic shelter are available. ATV rentals are nearby. Some facilities are wheelchair accessible. Leashed pets are permitted, except in cabins.

Reservations, fees: Reservations are accepted at 800/562-4236. Tent sites are $18–32 per night, RV sites are $25–55 per night, and it costs $3.25–5 per person per night for more than two people and $4.50 per night per additional vehicle. Some credit cards are accepted. Open year-round.

Directions: From Coos Bay, drive north on U.S. 101 past North Bend for nine miles to Milepost 229. The campground entrance road is on the left.

Contact: Oregon Dunes KOA, 541/756-4851, fax 541/756-8838, www.koa.com.

OREGON

81 TYEE

Scenic rating: 7

on the Umpqua River

Map grid A4　　　　　　　　　　**BEST**

Here's a classic spot along the Umpqua River with great salmon, smallmouth bass, and steelhead fishing in season. Boat launches are available a few miles upstream and downstream of the campground. Eagleview Group camp, a BLM campground, is one mile away.

RV sites, facilities: There are 15 sites for tents or RVs up to 70 feet long. Drinking water, garbage service, fire grills, and picnic tables are provided. Vault toilets, a day-use area with horseshoe pits, and a pavilion are available. A camp host is on-site. A store is within one mile. Some facilities are wheelchair accessible. Leashed pets are permitted.

Reservations, fees: Reservations are not accepted. Sites are $10 per night, $4 per night for each additional vehicle. Open mid-March–November.

Directions: From Roseburg, drive north on I-5 to Exit 136 and Highway 138. Take that exit and drive west on Highway 138 for 12 miles. Cross Bullock Bridge and continue to County Road 57. Turn right and drive 0.5 mile to the campground entrance.

Contact: Bureau of Land Management, Roseburg District, 541/440-4930, fax 541/440-4948, www.blm.gov.

82 WILD MARE HORSE CAMP

Scenic rating: 7

in Oregon Dunes National Recreation Area

Map grid A4

This horse camp has paved parking, with single and double corrals. No off-road vehicles are allowed within the campground. Horses can be ridden straight out into the dunes and to the ocean; they cannot be ridden on developed trails, such as Bluebill Lake Trail. The heavily treed shoreline gives rise to treed sites with some bushes.

RV sites, facilities: There are 11 horse camp-sites for tents or RVs up to 61 feet long. There is a maximum of two vehicles per site. Picnic tables and fire pits are provided. Drinking water, vault toilets, and garbage bins are available. Leashed pets are permitted.

Reservations, fees: Reservations are accepted at 877/444-6777 or www.recreation.gov ($10 reservation fee). Sites are $20 per night. Some credit cards are accepted. Open year-round.

Directions: From Coos Bay, drive north on U.S. 101 for 1.5 miles to Horsfall Dunes and Beach Access Road. Turn left and drive west for one mile to the campground access road. Turn right and drive 0.75 mile to the campground on the left.

Contact: Oregon Dunes National Recreation Area, Visitors Center 541/271-6000 or 541/271-3611, fax 541/750-7244.

83 BLUEBILL

Scenic rating: 6

on Bluebill Lake in
Oregon Dunes National Recreation Area

Map grid A4

This campground gets very little camping pressure, although there are some good hiking trails available. It's located next to little Bluebill Lake, which sometimes dries up during the summer. A one-mile trail goes around the lake bed. The camp is a short distance from Horsfall Lake, which is surrounded by private property. If you continue west on the forest road, you'll come to a picnicking and parking area near the beach. This spot provides off-road-vehicle access to the dunes at the Horsfall day-use area and Horsfall Beach.

RV sites, facilities: There are 19 sites for tents or RVs of any length. Picnic tables, garbage service, and fire grills are provided. Flush toilets and drinking water are available. Leashed pets are permitted.

Reservations, fees: Reservations are accepted at 877/444-6777 or www.recreation.gov ($10 reservation fee). Sites are $20 per night. Open May–September.

Directions: From Coos Bay, drive north on U.S. 101 for 1.5 miles north to Horsfall Dunes and Beach Access Road. Turn west and drive one mile to Horsfall Road. Turn northwest and drive two miles to the campground entrance.

Contact: Oregon Dunes National Recreation Area, Visitors Center 541/271-6000 or 541/271-3611, fax 541/750-7244.

84 HORSFALL

Scenic rating: 4

in Oregon Dunes National Recreation Area

Map grid A4

Horsfall campground is actually a nice, large paved area for parking RVs; it's the staging area for off-road-vehicle access into the southern section of Oregon Dunes National Recreation Area. If Horsfall is full, try nearby Horsfall Beach, an overflow area with 34 tent and RV sites.

RV sites, facilities: There are 69 sites for RVs up to 52 feet in length. Picnic tables and fire rings are provided. Drinking water, garbage service, restrooms with flush toilets and coin showers, and a pay phone are available. Some facilities are wheelchair accessible. Leashed pets are permitted.

Reservations, fees: Reservations are accepted at 877/444-6777 or www.recreation.gov ($10 reservation fee). Sites are $20 per night. Open year-round.

Directions: From Coos Bay, drive north on U.S. 101 for 1.5 miles to Horsfall Road. Turn west on Horsfall Road and drive about one mile to the campground access road. Turn on the campground access road (well signed) and drive 0.5 mile to the campground.

Contact: Oregon Dunes National Recreation Area, Visitors Center 541/271-6000541/271-3611, fax 541/750-7244.

85 SUNSET BAY STATE PARK

Scenic rating: 8

near Sunset Bay

Map grid A4   **BEST (**

Scenic Sunset Bay sits on the beautiful Oregon Coast, amid coastal forest and headlands. The sandy beach is secluded, protected by cliffs and confiers, and tidepooling is a popular activity. A series of hiking trails leads to Shore Acres and Cape Arago Parks. Clamming and fishing is available in nearby Charleston. Golfing and swimming are some of the recreation options here.

RV sites, facilities: There are 66 sites for tents or self-contained RVs, 63 sites with full or partial hookups for tents or RVs up to 47 feet long, a separate area for hikers and bicyclists, eight yurts, and two group camps for up to 25 and 250 people, respectively. Drinking water, picnic tables, garbage bins, and fire grills are provided. Restrooms with flush toilets and showers, a fish-cleaning station, boat ramp, and firewood are available. A camp host is on-site. A gazebo and meeting hall can be reserved at nearby Shore Acres. A restaurant is within three miles. Some facilities are wheelchair accessible. Leashed pets are permitted, except in yurts.

Reservations, fees: Reservations are accepted at 800/452-5687 or www.oregonstateparks.org ($8 reservation fee). RV sites are $16–24 per night, tent sites are $12–19 per night, $5 per night per additional vehicle, $4–5 per person per night for hikers/bicyclists, $27–36 per night for yurts, $40–71 per night for group camps, and $2.40 per person per night for more than 25 people. Some credit cards are accepted. Open year-round.

Directions: In Coos Bay, take the Charleston/State Parks exit to Empire Coos Bay Highway. Drive west to Newmark Avenue. Bear left and continue to Cape Arago Highway. Turn left and drive about five miles south to Charleston and cross the South Slough Bridge. Continue on Cape Arago Highway about three miles to the park entrance on the left.

Contact: Sunset Bay State Park, 541/888-4902 or 800/551-6949, www.oregonstateparks.org.

86 BASTENDORFF BEACH PARK

Scenic rating: 8

near Cape Arago State Park

`Map grid A4`

This campground is surrounded by large trees and provides access to the ocean and a small lake. Nearby activities include boating, clamming, crabbing, dune buggy riding, fishing, golfing, swimming, and whale-watching. Swimmers should be aware of undertows and sneaker waves. Horses may be rented near Bandon. A nice side trip is to Shore Acres State Park and Botanical Gardens, about 2.5 miles away.

RV sites, facilities: There are 35 tent sites, 56 sites with partial hookups for tents or RVs (of any length), and two cabins. Group camping is available. Picnic tables and fire pits are provided. Drinking water, restrooms with flush toilets and coin showers, and a dump station are available. A fish-cleaning station, horseshoe pits, playground, basketball courts, and a picnic area are also available. Some facilities are wheelchair accessible. Leashed pets are permitted.

Reservations, fees: Reservations are accepted for groups, cabins, and the picnic area only at 541/396-3121, ext. 354 ($10 reservation fee). Sites are $15–20 per night, $5 per night per additional vehicle, and cabins are $30 per night. Some credit cards are accepted. Open year-round.

Directions: In Coos Bay, take the Charleston/State Parks exit to Empire Coos Bay Highway. Drive west to Newmark Avenue. Bear left and continue to Cape Arago Highway. Turn left and drive about five miles south to Charleston and cross the South Slough Bridge. Continue on Cape Arago Highway for 1.25 miles to the park entrance.

Contact: Bastendorff Beach Park, 541/888-5353, www.co.coos.co.or.us/ccpark.

87 CHARLESTON MARINA RV PARK

Scenic rating: 7

on Coos Bay

`Map grid A4`

This large, developed public park and marina is located near Charleston on the Pacific Ocean. Recreational activities in and near the campground include boating, clamming, crabbing, fishing (halibut, salmon, and tuna), hiking, huckleberry and blackberry picking, and swimming.

RV sites, facilities: There are 100 sites for tents or RVs up to 50 feet long (full hookups), six tent sites, and two yurts. Picnic tables are provided. No open fires are allowed. Drinking water, satellite TV, modem access, restrooms with showers, dump station, public phone, coin laundry, playground, fish-cleaning station, crab-cooking facilities, and propane gas are available. A marina with a boarding dock and launch ramp are on-site. Some facilities are wheelchair accessible. Leashed pets are permitted.

Reservations, fees: Reservations are accepted at 541/888-9512 or rvpark@charlestonmarina.com. RV sites are $22–25 per night, tent sites are $13 per night, and yurts are $31 per night. Weekly and monthly rates are available. Some credit cards are accepted. Open year-round.

Directions: In Coos Bay, take the Charleston/State Parks exit to Empire Coos Bay Highway. Drive west to Newmark Avenue. Bear left and continue to Cape Arago Highway. Turn left and drive about five miles south to Charleston and cross the South Slough Bridge. Continue to Boat Basin Drive. Turn right and drive 0.2 mile to Kingfisher Drive. Turn right and drive 200 feet to the campground on the left.

Contact: Charleston Marina RV Park, 541/888-9512, fax 541/888-6111, www.charlestonmarina.com.

OREGON

OREGON

88 BULLARDS BEACH STATE PARK

Scenic rating: 7

on the Coquille River

Map grid A4

The Coquille River, which has good fishing in season for both boaters and crabbers, is the centerpiece of this park with four miles of shore access. If fishing is not your thing, the park also has several hiking trails. The Coquille River Lighthouse is at the end of the road that wanders through the park; during the summer, there are tours to the tower. Equestrians can explore the seven-mile horse trail.

RV sites, facilities: There are 185 sites with full or partial hookups for tents or RVs up to 64 feet long, a hiker/bicyclist camping area, a primitive horse camp with eight sites and three corrals, and 13 yurts. Drinking water, garbage bins, picnic tables, and fire grills are provided. Restrooms with flush toilets and showers, dump station, playground, firewood, a yurt meeting hall, and picnic shelters are available. Boat docks and launching facilities are in the park on the Coquille River. Some facilities are wheelchair accessible. Leashed pets are permitted.

Reservations, fees: Reservations are accepted at 800/452-5687 or www.oregonstateparks. org ($8 reservation fee). Sites are $16–24 per night, $5 per vehicle per night, $4–5 per person per night for hikers/bicyclists, and yurts are $27–36 per night. Horse camping is $12–19 per night. Some credit cards are accepted. Open year-round.

Directions: In Coos Bay, drive south on U.S. 101 for about 22 miles to the park on the right (west side of road), two miles north of Bandon.

Contact: Bullards Beach State Park, 541/347-3501 or 800/551-6949, www.oregonstateparks. org.

89 BANDON RV PARK

Scenic rating: 6

near Bullards Beach State Park

Map grid A4

This in-town RV park is a good base for many adventures. Some sites are filled with renters, primarily anglers, for the summer season. Rock hounds will enjoy combing for agates and other semiprecious stones hidden along the beaches, while kids can explore the West Coast Game Park Walk-Through Safari petting zoo seven miles south of town. Bandon State Park, four miles south of town, has a nice wading spot in the creek at the north end of the park. Nearby recreation opportunities include two 18-hole golf courses, a riding stable, and tennis courts. Bullards Beach is about 2.5 miles north. Nice folks run this place.

RV sites, facilities: There are 44 sites with full hookups for RVs of any length; some are pull-through sites. Picnic tables are provided at most sites. No open fires are allowed. Restrooms with flush toilets and showers, dump station, cable TV, modem access, and a coin laundry are available. Propane gas and a store are within two blocks. Boat docks and launching facilities are nearby. Leashed pets are permitted.

Reservations, fees: Reservations are accepted at 800/393-4122. Sites are $22–24 per night, $2 per person per night for more than two people. Some credit cards are accepted. Open year-round.

Directions: From Coos Bay, drive south on U.S. 101 for 26 miles to Bandon and the Highway 42S junction. Continue south on U.S. 101 for one block to the park (located on the right at 935 2nd Street Southeast).

Contact: Bandon RV Park, 541/347-4122.

90 LAVERNE AND WEST LAVERNE GROUP CAMP

Scenic rating: 9

in Fairview on the north fork of the Coquille River

Map grid A4

This beautiful, 350-acre park sits on a river with a small waterfall and many trees, including a myrtle grove and old-growth Douglas fir. Mountain bikers can take an old wagon road, and golfers can enjoy any of several courses. There are a few hiking trails and a very popular swimming hole. You can fish for salmon, steelhead, and trout, and the wildlife includes bears, cougars, deer, elk, and raccoons. You can take a side trip to the museums at Myrtle Point and Coos Bay, which display local indigenous items, or an old stagecoach house in Dora.

RV sites, facilities: There are 30 tent sites and 46 RV sites with partial hookups for RVs of any length. There is also a large group site at West Laverne B that includes 22 RV sites with partial hookups. One cabin is also available. Drinking water, picnic tables, and fire pits are provided. Restrooms with flush toilets and coin showers, garbage bins, dump station, ice, playground, a picnic area that can be reserved, swimming hole (unsupervised), horseshoe pits, and volleyball and softball areas are available. A restaurant is within 1.5 miles. Propane gas, a store, and gasoline are within five miles. Some facilities are wheelchair accessible. Leashed pets are permitted.

Reservations, fees: Reservations are not accepted for family sites but are accepted for the group site and cabin ($10 reservation fee) at 541/396-3121, ext. 354. RV sites are $12–16 per night, tent sites are $10–11 per night, $5 per night per each additional vehicle. The group site is $140 per night for the first six camping units, plus $16 per night for each additional unit. The cabin is $30 per night. Some credit cards are accepted. Open year-round.

Directions: From Coos Bay, drive south on U.S. 101 for six miles to the junction with Highway 42. Turn east and drive 11 miles to Coquille and West Central. Turn left and drive 0.5 mile to Fairview McKinley Road. Turn right and drive eight miles to the Fairview Store. Continue east another five miles (past the store) to the park on the right.

Contact: Laverne County Park, Coos County, 541/396-2344, www.co.coos.or.us/ccpark.

91 PARK CREEK

🐕 🚐 ⛺

Scenic rating: 7

near Coquille
Map grid A4

Want to be by yourself? You came to the right place. This pretty little campground offers peaceful, shady campsites under an old-growth canopy of Douglas fir, myrtle, red cedar, and western hemlock. Relax and enjoy nearby Park Creek and Middle Creek.

RV sites, facilities: There are 15 sites for tents or small RVs. Picnic tables and fire grills are provided. Vault toilets and garbage bins are available. There is no drinking water. Leashed pets are permitted.

Reservations, fees: Reservations are not accepted. There is no fee, but the stay limit is 14 days. Open year-round.

Directions: From Coos Bay, drive south on U.S. 101 for six miles to the junction with Highway 42. Turn east and drive 11 miles to Coquille and Coquille Fairview Road. Turn left (east) on Coquille Fairview Road and drive 7.5 miles to Fairview and Coos Bay Wagon Road. Turn right and drive four miles to Middle Creek Access Road. Turn left (east) and drive nine miles to the campground on the right.

Contact: Bureau of Land Management, Coos Bay District, 541/756-0100, fax 541/751-4303, www.or.blm.gov/coosbay.

92 KOA BANDON/PORT ORFORD

🥾 🏊 🐕 🧑‍🤝‍🧑 🚐 ⛺

Scenic rating: 7

near the Elk River
Map grid A5

This spot is considered just a layover camp, but it offers large, secluded sites nestled among big trees and coastal ferns. A pool and spa are available. During the summer season, a daily pancake breakfast and ice cream social are held. The Elk and Sixes Rivers, where the fishing can be good, are minutes away, and Cape Blanco State Park is just a few miles down the road.

RV sites, facilities: There are 46 tent sites

OREGON

and 26 pull-through sites with full hookups (20-, 30-, and 50-amp) for RVs of any length. Six cabins are also available. Picnic tables and fire rings are provided. Restrooms with flush toilets and showers, cable TV, modem access, snack bar, propane gas, dump station, firewood, recreation hall, convenience store, coin laundry, seasonal heated swimming pool, hot tub, horseshoe pits, basketball court, ice, and a playground are available. Leashed pets are permitted.

Reservations, fees: Reservations are accepted at 800/562-3298. Sites are $24–32 per night, $3 per person per night for more than two people, and $5 per night per additional vehicle. Some credit cards are accepted. Open March–November.

Directions: From Bandon, drive south on U.S. 101 for 16 miles to the campground at Milepost 286 near Langlois, on the west side of the highway.

Contact: KOA Bandon/Port Orford, 541/348-2358, www.koa.com.

93 CAPE BLANCO STATE PARK

Scenic rating: 8

between the Sixes and Elk Rivers
Map grid A5

This large park is named for the white (*blanco*) chalk appearance of the sea cliffs here, which rise 200 feet above the ocean. Sea lions inhabit the offshore rocks, and trails and a road lead to the black sand beach below the cliffs. The park offers good fishing access to the Sixes River, which runs for more than two miles through meadows and forests. There are seven miles of trails for horseback riding available and more than eight miles of hiking trails, some with ocean views. Tours of the lighthouse and historic Hughes House are available.

RV sites, facilities: There are 53 sites with partial hookups for tents or RVs up to 65 feet long. Other options include an equestrian camp with eight sites, a hiker/bicyclist camping area, four cabins, and four primitive group sites for tents or RVs for up to 25 people. Garbage bins, picnic tables, drinking water, and fire grills are provided. Firewood and restrooms with flush toilets and showers are available. Some facilities are wheelchair accessible. Leashed pets are permitted.

Reservations, fees: Reservations are not accepted for single sites, but are accepted for cabins, the group site, and the horse camp at 800/452-5687 or www.oregonstateparks.org ($8 reservation fee). Single sites are $12–20 per night, $5 per night per additional vehicle. The horse camp is $10–17 per night; the hiker/biker sites are $4–5 per person per night. The group site is $40–71 per night for the first 25 people, then $2.40–3 per additional person per night. Some credit cards are accepted. Open year-round.

Directions: From Coos Bay, turn south on U.S. 101 and drive approximately 46 miles (south of Sixes, five miles north of Port Orford) to Cape Blanco Road. Turn right (northwest) and drive five miles to the campground on the left.

Contact: Humbug Mountain State Park, 541/332-6774 or 800/551-6949, www.oregon-stateparks.org. (This park is under the same management as Humbug Mountain State Park.)

94 EDSON

Scenic rating: 6

on the Sixes River
Map grid A5

This is a popular campground along the banks of the Sixes River. Edson is similar to Sixes River Campground, except it has less tree cover and Sixes River has the benefit of a boat ramp.

RV sites, facilities: There are 25 sites for tents or RVs up to 30 feet long, and four group sites for up to 50 people. Picnic tables and fire grills are provided. Drinking water, vault toilets, garbage service, a boat launch, and a camp host are available. Some facilities are wheelchair accessible. Leashed pets are permitted.

Reservations, fees: Reservations are not

accepted for single sites but are required for group sites at 541/332-8027. Sites are $8 per night and $4 per night for each additional vehicle, with a 14-day stay limit. Open May–November, weather permitting.

Directions: From Coos Bay, drive south on U.S. 101 for 40 miles to Sixes and Sixes River Road/County Road 184. Turn left (east) on Sixes River Road and drive four miles to the campground entrance on the left. It's located before the Edson Creek Bridge.

Contact: Bureau of Land Management, Coos Bay District, 541/756-0100 or 541/332-8027, fax 541/751-4303, www.blm.gov.

95 SIXES RIVER

Scenic rating: 6

on the Sixes River
Map grid A5

Set along the banks of the Sixes River at an elevation of 4,303 feet, this camp is a favorite of anglers, miners, and nature lovers. There are opportunities to pan or sluice for gold year-round or through a special limited permit. Dredging is permitted from July 15 through September. The camp roads are paved.

RV sites, facilities: There are 19 sites for tents or RVs up to 30 feet long. Picnic tables, garbage service, and fire grills are provided. Drinking water and vault toilets are available. Some facilities are wheelchair accessible. Leashed pets are permitted.

Reservations, fees: Reservations are not accepted. Sites are $8 per night, $4 per night for an additional vehicle, with a 14-day stay limit. Open May–November, weather permitting.

Directions: From Coos Bay, drive south on U.S. 101 for 40 miles to Sixes and Sixes River Road/County Road 184. Turn left (east) on Sixes River Road and drive 11 miles to the campground on the right. The last 0.5 mile is an unpaved road.

Contact: Bureau of Land Management, Coos Bay District, 541/756-0100, fax 541/751-4303, www.blm.gov.

96 POWERS COUNTY PARK

Scenic rating: 9

near the south fork of the Coquille River
Map grid A5

This private and secluded public park in a wooded, mountainous area is a great stop for travelers going between I-5 and the coast. A 30-acre lake at the park provides a spot for visitors to boat and fish for trout. The lake is stocked with bass, catfish, crappie, and trout. Only electric boat motors are allowed. Swimming is not recommended because of the algae in the lake. A bike trail is available. On display at the park are an old steam donkey and a hand-carved totem pole. The biggest cedar tree in Oregon is reputed to be about 12 miles away.

RV sites, facilities: There are 30 sites for tents or RVs up to 54 feet long and 40 sites with partial hookups (20- and 30-amp). One cabin is also available. Picnic tables, fire pits, drinking water, restrooms with flush toilets and showers, a dump station, fish-cleaning station, picnic shelters, and a public phone are provided. Recreational facilities include a boat ramp, horseshoe pits, playground, basketball and volleyball courts, tennis courts, and a softball field. Supplies are available within one mile. Some facilities are wheelchair accessible. Leashed pets are permitted.

Reservations, fees: Reservations ($10 reservation fee) are accepted for the cabin only at 541/396-3121, ext. 354. RV sites are $12–16 per night, tent sites are $10–11 per night, and cabins are $30 per night. Some credit cards are accepted. Open year-round.

Directions: From Coos Bay, drive south on U.S. 101 for six miles to the junction with Highway 42. Turn east and drive 20 miles to Myrtle Point. Continue on Highway 42 to the Powers Highway (Highway 242) exit. Turn right (southwest) and drive 19 miles to the park on the right.

Contact: Powers County Park, Coos County, 541/439-2791, www.co.coos.or.us/ccpark/.

OREGON

97 ELK RIVER CAMPGROUND

Scenic rating: 7

near the Elk River

Map grid A5

This quiet and restful camp makes an excellent base for fall and winter fishing on the Elk River, which is known for its premier salmon fishing. A one-mile private access road goes to the river, so guests get their personal fishing holes. About half of the sites are taken by monthly rentals.

RV sites, facilities: There are 50 sites with full hookups for RVs up to 40 feet long; some sites are pull-through. Picnic tables are provided. No open fires are allowed. Drinking water, restrooms with showers, dump station, public phone, modem hookups, cable TV, and a coin laundry are available. Recreational facilities include a sports field, horseshoe pits, recreation hall, and a boat ramp. Some facilities are wheelchair accessible. Leashed pets are permitted.

Reservations, fees: Reservations are recommended. Sites are $20.20 per night. Weekly and monthly rates are available. Open year-round.

Directions: From Port Orford, drive north on U.S. 101 for 1.5 miles to Elk River Road (Milepost 297). Turn right (east) on Elk River Road and drive 1.8 miles to the campground on the left.

Contact: Elk River Campground, 541/332-2255.

98 LAIRD LAKE

Scenic rating: 8

on Laird Lake in Siskiyou National Forest

Map grid A5

This secluded campground is set at 1,600 feet elevation, along the shore of pretty Laird Lake (six feet at its deepest point). Some old-growth cedar logs are in the lake. Most campers have no idea such a place exists in the area. This very private and scenic spot can be just what you're looking for if you're tired of fighting the crowds at the more developed camps along U.S. 101.

RV sites, facilities: There are four sites for tents or RVs up to 25 feet long. There is no drinking water, and garbage must be packed out. Leashed pets are permitted.

Reservations, fees: Reservations are not accepted. There is no fee for camping. Open year-round.

Directions: From Port Orford, drive north on U.S. 101 for three miles to County Road 208. Turn right and drive 7.5 miles southeast (the road becomes Forest Road 5325). Continue for 15.5 miles (the road bears to the right when you reach the gravel) to the campground. The road is paved for 11 miles and is gravel for the last 4.5 miles to the campground.

Contact: Siskiyou National Forest, Powers Ranger District, 541/439-6200, fax 541/439-6217, www.fs.fed.us.

99 PORT ORFORD RV VILLAGE

Scenic rating: 5

near the Elk and Sixes Rivers

Map grid A5

Each evening, an informal group campfire and happy hour enliven this campground. Other nice touches include a small gazebo where you can get free coffee each morning and a patio where you can sit. Fishing is good during the fall and winter on the nearby Elk and Sixes Rivers, and the campground has a smokehouse, freezer, and fish-cleaning station. Some sites here are taken by summer season rentals or permanent residents.

RV sites, facilities: There are 47 sites with full or partial hookups for RVs of any length. Some sites are pull-through. Picnic tables are provided, and fire pits are available on request. Restrooms with flush toilets and showers, propane gas, dump station, horseshoe pits, recreation hall, and a coin laundry are available. Boat docks and launching facilities are nearby. Lake, river, and ocean are all within 1.5 miles. Leashed pets are permitted.

Reservations, fees: Reservations are accepted. Sites are $26 per night, plus $2 per person per night for more than two people. Open year-round.

Directions: In Port Orford on U.S. 101, drive to Madrona Avenue. Turn east and drive one block to Port Orford Loop. Turn left (north) and drive 0.5 mile to the camp on the left side.

Contact: Port Orford RV Village, 541/332-1041, www.portorfordrv.com.

100 HUMBUG MOUNTAIN STATE PARK

Scenic rating: 7

near Port Orford

Map grid A5

Humbug Mountain, at 1,756 feet elevation, looms over its namesake state park. Fortunately, this natural guardian affords the campground some of the warmest weather on the coast by blocking cold winds from the ocean. Windsurfing and scuba diving are popular, as is hiking the three-mile trail to Humbug Peak. Both ocean and freshwater fishing are accessible nearby.

RV sites, facilities: There are 62 sites for tents or RVs (no hookups), 32 sites with partial hookups for RVs up to 55 feet long, and a hiker/bicyclist camp. Some sites are pull-through. Fire grills, picnic tables, garbage bins, and drinking water are provided. Firewood and restrooms with flush toilets and showers are available. A camp host is on-site. Some facilities are wheelchair accessible. Leashed pets are permitted.

Reservations, fees: Reservations are not accepted. RV sites are $12–20 per night, tent sites are $10–17 per night, $5 per night per additional vehicle, and $4–5 per person per night for hikers/bicyclists. The group camp is $60 per night for up to 25 people, plus $2.40 per person per night for additional persons. Some credit cards are accepted. Open year-round.

Directions: From Port Orford, drive south on U.S. 101 for six miles to the park entrance on the left.

Contact: Humbug Mountain State Park, 541/332-6774 or 800/551-6949, www.oregonstateparks.org.

101 DAPHNE GROVE

Scenic rating: 7

on the south fork of the Coquille River in Siskiyou National Forest

Map grid A5

This prime spot is far enough out of the way to attract little attention. At 1,000 feet elevation, it sits along the south fork of the Coquille River and is surrounded by old-growth cedar, Douglas fir, and maple. No fishing is allowed. The road is paved all the way to, and in, the campground, a plus for RVs and "city cars."

RV sites, facilities: There are 15 sites for tents or RVs up to 35 feet long. Picnic tables, garbage bins, and fire grills are provided. Vault toilets are available. There is no drinking water. Some facilities are wheelchair accessible. Leashed pets are permitted.

Reservations, fees: Reservations are not accepted. Sites are $6 per night, $3 per night per additional vehicle. Open year-round.

Directions: From Coos Bay, drive south on U.S. 101 for six miles to the junction with Highway 42. Turn east and drive 20 miles to Myrtle Point. Continue on Highway 42 to Powers Highway (Highway 242). Turn right (southwest) and drive 18 miles (the road becomes County Road 90) to Powers. Continue for 4.3 miles (the road becomes Forest Road 33). Continue for 10.5 miles to the campground entrance.

Contact: Siskiyou National Forest, Powers Ranger District, 541/439-6200, fax 541/439-6217, www.fs.fed.us.

102 ISLAND

Scenic rating: 7

near Coquille River Falls

Map grid A5

Island Camp is an excellent base camp for hikers with many trailheads nearby. It is located along the south fork of the Coquille River at 1,000-foot elevation in Siskiyou National Forest. Nearby hiking opportunities include the Azalea Lake

Trail, Panther Ridge Trail, Coquille River Falls Trail, and Sucker Creek Trail. Note: Do not confuse this Island Campground with the Island Campground in Umpqua National Forest.

RV sites, facilities: There are five sites for tents or RVs to 16 feet. Picnic tables and fire rings are provided. Vault toilets and garbage bins are available, but there is no drinking water. Leashed pets are permitted.

Reservations, fees: Reservations are not accepted. Sites are $6 per night. Open year-round.

Directions: From Coos Bay, drive south on U.S. 101 for six miles to the junction with Highway 42. Turn east and drive 20 miles to Myrtle Point. Continue on Highway 42 to Powers Highway (Highway 242). Turn right (southwest) and drive 18 miles (the road becomes County Road 90) to Powers. Drive south 17 miles on Forest Service Road 3300 to the campground.

Contact: Siskiyou National Forest, Powers Ranger District, 541/439-6200, fax 541/439-6217, www.fs.fed.us.

103 SRU LAKE
🥾 🎣 🐕 🚐 ⛺

Scenic rating: 8

on Squaw Lake in Siskiyou National Forest

Map grid A5

Sru (pronounced "Shrew") campground is set along the shore of one-acre Sru Lake at 2,200 feet elevation in rich, old-growth forest. Sru is more of a pond than a lake, but it is stocked with trout in the spring. Get there early—the fish are generally gone by midsummer. The trailheads for the Panther Ridge Trail and Coquille River Falls Trail are a 10-minute drive from the campground. It's strongly advised that you obtain a U.S. Forest Service map detailing the backcountry roads and trails.

RV sites, facilities: There are seven sites for tents or RVs up to 21 feet long. Picnic tables and fire rings are provided. Vault toilets are available. There is no drinking water, and garbage must be packed out. Leashed pets are permitted.

Reservations, fees: Reservations are not accepted. There is no fee for camping. Open year-round.

Directions: From Coos Bay, drive south on U.S. 101 for six miles to the junction with Highway 42. Turn east and drive 20 miles to Myrtle Point. Continue on Highway 42 to Powers Highway (Highway 242). Turn right (southwest) and drive 18 miles (the road becomes County Road 90) to Powers. Continue for 4.3 miles (the road becomes Forest Road 33). Continue on Forest Road 33 for 15 miles to the South Fork Coquille River Bridge. Continue on Forest Road 33 for 0.5 mile to Forest Road 3347 (paved road). Turn right and drive one mile to the camp.

Contact: Siskiyou National Forest, Powers Ranger District, 541/439-6200, fax 541/439-6217, www.fs.fed.us.

104 HONEY BEAR CAMPGROUND & RV RESORT

Scenic rating: 10

near Gold Beach

Map grid A5

This campground offers wooded sites with ocean views. The owners have built a huge, authentic chalet, which contains a German deli, recreation area, and a big dance floor. On summer nights, they hold dances with live music. A restaurant is available on-site with authentic German food. A fishing pond is stocked with trout.

RV sites, facilities: There are 20 sites for tents or RVs (no hookups) and 65 sites with full hookups for RVs of any length. Thirty are pull-through sites with full hookups and 15 have patios. Picnic tables and fire rings are provided. Restrooms with flush toilets and showers, drinking water, cable TV, modem access, dump station, firewood, recreation hall, restaurant, convenience store, coin laundry, ice, and a playground are available. Leashed pets are permitted.

Reservations, fees: Reservations are accepted at 800/822-4444. Sites are $21.95 per night, $3 per person per night for more than two people, and $1 per night per additional vehicle. Open year-round, weather permitting.

Directions: From Gold Beach, drive north on U.S. 101 for eight miles to Ophir Road near Milepost 321. Turn right and drive two miles to the campground on the right side of the road.

Contact: Honey Bear Campground & RV Resort, 541/247-2765, www.honeybearrv.com.

105 ROCK CREEK

Scenic rating: 6

near the south fork of the Coquille River in Siskiyou National Forest

Map grid A5

This little-known camp (elevation 1,400 feet) in a tree-shaded canyon is surrounded by old-growth forest and some reforested areas. It is set near Rock Creek, just upstream from its confluence with the south fork of the Coquille River. No fishing is allowed. For a good side trip, take the one-mile climb to Azalea Lake, a small, shallow lake where there are some hike-in campsites. In July, the azaleas are spectacular.

RV sites, facilities: There are seven sites for tents or RVs up to 16 feet long. Picnic tables and fire grills are provided. Vault toilets, garbage bins, and firewood are available. There is no drinking water. Leashed pets are permitted.

Reservations, fees: Reservations are not accepted. Sites are $6 per night, $3 per night per additional vehicle. Open year-round, with limited winter facilities.

Directions: From Coos Bay, drive south on U.S. 101 for six miles to the junction with Highway 42. Turn east and drive 20 miles to Myrtle Point. Continue on Highway 42 to Powers Highway (Highway 242). Turn right (southwest) and drive 18 miles (the road becomes County Road 90) to Powers. Continue for 4.3 miles (the road becomes Forest Road 33). Continue on Forest Road 33 for 15 miles to the South Fork Coquille River Bridge. Continue on Forest Road 33 for 0.5 mile to Forest Road 3347 (paved road). Turn right and drive 0.5 mile to the camp.

Contact: Siskiyou National Forest, Powers Ranger District, 541/439-6200, fax 541/439-6217, www.fs.fed.us.

106 ALMEDA PARK

Scenic rating: 6

on the Rogue River

Map grid A5

This rustic park, located along the Rogue River and featuring a grassy area, is popular for rafting and swimming. One of the main put-in points for floating the lower section of the river can be found right here. Fishing is also available. The Rogue River Trail is four miles west.

RV sites, facilities: There are 34 sites for tents or RVs of any length (no hookups), two group sites for tents or RVs for up to 30 people, and one yurt. Some sites are pull-through. Picnic tables and fire pits are provided. Drinking water, vault toilets, garbage bins, and a boat ramp are available. A seasonal camp host is on-site. Leashed pets are permitted.

Reservations, fees: Reservations are accepted. Sites are $19 per night, $5 per night per additional vehicle, and the yurt is $30 per night. The group site is $32 per night for up to 12 people, and $3 per person per night for more than 12 people. Open year-round.

Directions: From Grants Pass, drive north on I-5 for 3.5 miles to Exit 61 (Merlin-Galice Road). Take that exit and drive on Merlin-Galice Road for 19 miles to the park on the right. The park is approximately 16 miles west of Merlin.

Contact: Josephine County Parks, 541/474-5285, fax 541/474-5288, www.co.josephine.or.us/parks/index.htm.

107 NESIKA BEACH RV PARK

Scenic rating: 7

near Gold Beach

Map grid A5

This RV park next to Nesika Beach is a good layover spot for U.S. 101 cruisers. An 18-hole

OREGON

golf course is close by. There are many long-term rentals here.

RV sites, facilities: There are six tent sites and 32 sites with full or partial hookups for RVs of any length; some sites are pull-through. Drinking water, cable TV, and picnic tables are provided; some tent sites have fire rings. Restrooms with flush toilets and showers, a dump station, convenience store, coin laundry, and ice are available. Leashed pets are permitted.

Reservations, fees: Reservations are accepted. RV sites are $20–24 per night, tent sites are $15 per night, $1 per person per night for more than two people. Monthly rates are available. Open year-round.

Directions: From Gold Beach, drive north on U.S. 101 for six miles to Nesika Road. Turn left and drive 0.75 mile west to the park on the right.

Contact: Nesika Beach RV Park, 541/247-6077, www.nesikarv.com.

108 INDIAN CREEK RESORT

Scenic rating: 7

on the Rogue River

Map grid A5

This campground is set along the Rogue River on the outskirts of the town of Gold Beach. A few sites have river views. Nearby recreation options include boat trips on the Rogue.

RV sites, facilities: There are 26 tent sites and 90 sites with full hookups for RVs of any length; some sites are pull-through. Five park-model cabins are also available. Drinking water, cable TV hookups, and picnic tables are provided. Fire pits are provided at some sites. Restrooms with flush toilets and showers, modem access, firewood, recreation hall, convenience store, sauna, café, coin laundry, ice, and a playground are available. Propane gas is within two miles. Boat docks, launching facilities, and rentals are nearby. Leashed pets are permitted.

Reservations, fees: Reservations are accepted at 877/537-7704. RV sites are $27 per night, tent

sites are $18 per night, $2 per person per night for more than two people. Some credit cards are accepted. Open year-round, with limited winter facilities.

Directions: On U.S. 101, drive to the northern end of Gold Beach to Jerry's Flat Road (just south of the Patterson Bridge). Turn left (east) on Jerry's Flat Road and drive 0.5 mile to the resort.

Contact: Indian Creek Resort, 541/247-7704, www.indiancreekrv.com.

109 LUCKY LODGE RV PARK

Scenic rating: 6

on the Rogue River

Map grid A5

Lucky Lodge is a good layover spot for U.S. 101 travelers who want to get off the highway circuit. Set on the shore of the Rogue River, it offers opportunities for boating, fishing, and swimming. Most sites have a view of the river. Nearby recreation options include hiking trails. About one-third of the sites are occupied by monthly renters.

RV sites, facilities: There are 31 sites with full hookups for RVs of any length, three tent sites, and two cabins. Most sites are pull-through. Drinking water and picnic tables are provided. Restrooms with flush toilets and showers, propane gas, a recreation hall, and coin laundry are available. Boat docks and rentals are within eight miles. Leashed pets are permitted.

Reservations, fees: Reservations are accepted. RV sites are $27–30 per night, tent sites are $20 per night, $4 per person per night for more than two people. Open year-round.

Directions: From Gold Beach, drive north on U.S. 101 for four miles (on the north side of the Rogue River) to Rogue River Road. Turn right (east) and drive 3.5 miles to North Bank River Road. Turn right and drive 4.5 miles to the park on the right.

Contact: Lucky Lodge RV Park, 541/247-7618.

110 KIMBALL CREEK BEND RV RESORT

Scenic rating: 6

on the Rogue River

Map grid A5

Kimball Creek campground on the scenic Rogue River is just far enough from the coast to provide quiet and its own distinct character. The resort offers guided fishing trips and sells tickets for jet boat tours. Nearby recreation options include an 18-hole golf course, hiking trails, and boating facilities. Note that about one-third of the sites are monthly rentals.

RV sites, facilities: There are 62 sites with full hookups for RVs of any length, 13 tent sites, one park-model cabin, and three motel rooms. Drinking water and picnic tables are provided, and fire rings are at some sites. Restrooms with flush toilets and showers, modem access, propane gas, dump station, recreation hall, store, coin laundry, ice, and a playground are available. Boat docks are on-site, and launching facilities are nearby. Leashed pets are permitted.

Reservations, fees: Reservations are accepted at 888/814-0633. RV sites are $27–39 per night, tent sites are $25 per night, $3 per person per night for more than two people. Some credit cards are accepted. Open year-round.

Directions: From Gold Beach, drive north on U.S. 101 for one mile (on the north side of the Rogue River) to Rogue River Road. Turn right (east) and drive about eight miles to the resort on the right.

Contact: Kimball Creek Bend RV Resort, 541/247-7580, www.kimballcreek.com.

111 QUOSATANA

Scenic rating: 6

on the Rogue River in Siskiyou National Forest

Map grid A5

This campground is set along the banks of the Rogue River, upstream from the much smaller Lobster Creek Campground. The campground features a large, grassy area and a barrier-free trail around the campground. Ocean access is just a short drive away, and the quaint town of Gold Beach offers a decent side trip. Nearby Otter Point State Park (day-use only) has further recreation options. The Shrader Old-Growth Trail, Lower Rogue River Trail, and Myrtle Tree Trail provide nearby hiking opportunities. Quosatana makes a good base camp for a hiking or fishing trip.

RV sites, facilities: There are 42 sites for tents or RVs up to 32 feet long. Drinking water, fire grills, garbage bins, and picnic tables are provided. Flush toilets, dump station, fish-cleaning station, and a boat ramp are available. A camp host is on-site. Some facilities are wheelchair accessible. Leashed pets are permitted.

Reservations, fees: Reservations are not accepted. Sites are $10 per night, $3 per night per additional vehicle. Open year-round.

Directions: From Gold Beach on U.S. 101, turn east on County Road 595 and drive 14.5 miles (it becomes Forest Road 33) to the campground on the left.

Contact: Rogue River Siskiyou National Forest, Gold Beach Ranger District, 541/247-3600, fax 541/247-3617, www.fs.fed.us.

112 LOBSTER CREEK

Scenic rating: 6

on the Rogue River in Siskiyou National Forest

Map grid A5

This small campground on a river bar along the Rogue River is about a 15-minute drive from Gold Beach, and it makes a good base for a fishing or hiking trip. The area is heavily forested with myrtle and Douglas fir, and the Shrader Old-Growth Trail and Myrtle Tree Trail are nearby.

RV sites, facilities: There are six sites for tents or RVs up to 21 feet long. Fire rings and picnic tables are provided. Drinking water, flush toilets, and garbage bins are available, as is a boat launch. A camp host is on-site. Leashed pets are permitted.

Reservations, fees: Reservations are not accepted. Sites are $6 per night, $3 per night per additional vehicle. Camping is also permitted

OREGON

on a gravel bar area for $5 per night. Open year-round, weather permitting.

Directions: From Gold Beach on U.S. 101, turn east on County Road 595 and drive 10 miles (it becomes Forest Road 33) to the campground on the left.

Contact: Rogue River Siskiyou National Forest, Gold Beach Ranger District, 541/247-3600, fax 541/247-3617, www.fs.fed.us.

113 SAM BROWN

Scenic rating: 4

near Grants Pass in Siskiyou National Forest

Map grid A5

This campground is located in an isolated area near Grants Pass along Briggs Creek in a valley of pine and Douglas fir. It is set at an elevation of 2,500 feet. Many sites lie in the shade of trees, and a creek runs along one side of the campground. Briggs Creek Trail, Dutchy Creek Trail, and Taylor Creek Trail are nearby and are popular for hiking and horseback riding. An amphitheater is available for small group presentations. Although the campground was spared, the Biscuit Fire of 2002 did burn nearby areas.

RV sites, facilities: There are 27 sites for tents or RVs of any length at Sam Brown and seven equestrian tent sites with small corrals across the road at Sam Brown Horse Camp. Picnic tables and fire rings or grills are provided. Drinking water and vault toilets are available. A picnic shelter, solar shower, and an amphitheater are available. Some facilities are wheelchair accessible. Leashed pets are permitted.

Reservations, fees: Reservations are not accepted. Sites are $5 per night, $2 per night per additional vehicle. Open late May–mid-October, weather permitting.

Directions: From Grants Pass, drive north on I-5 for 3.5 miles to Exit 61 (Merlin-Galice Road). Take that exit and drive northwest for 12.5 miles to Forest Road 25. Turn left on Forest Road 25 and head southwest for 14 miles to the campground.

Contact: Siskiyou National Forest, Galice

Ranger District, 541/471-6500, fax 541/471-6514, www.fs.fed.us.

114 IRELAND'S OCEAN VIEW RV PARK

Scenic rating: 8

in Gold Beach

Map grid A5

This spot is situated on the beach in the quaint little town of Gold Beach, only one mile from the famous Rogue River. The park is very clean and features blacktop roads and grass beside each site. Recreation options include beachcombing, boating, and fishing. Great ocean views are possible from the observatory/lighthouse.

RV sites, facilities: There are 33 sites with full hookups (20-, 30-, and 50-amp) for RVs up to 40 feet long; some sites are pull-through. Picnic tables are provided. No open fires are allowed. Cable TV, restrooms with showers, coin laundry, recreation room, horseshoe pits, and modem access are available. Leashed pets are permitted.

Reservations, fees: Reservations are recommended. Sites are $24 per night, $1 per person per night for more than two people. Monthly rates are available. Open year-round.

Directions: On U.S. 101, drive to the southern end of Gold Beach (U.S. 101 becomes Ellensburg Avenue). The park is located at 20272 Ellensburg Avenue, across from the U.S. Forest Service office.

Contact: Ireland's Ocean View RV Park, 541/247-0148, www.irelandsrvpark.com.

115 OCEANSIDE RV PARK

Scenic rating: 5

in Gold Beach

Map grid A5

Set 100 yards from the ocean, this park is close to beachcombing terrain, marked bike trails, and boating facilities. The park is also adjacent to the mouth of the Rogue River, in the Port of Gold Beach.

RV sites, facilities: There are 80 sites with full or partial hookups for RVs up to 40 feet long and two yurts; some sites are pull-through. Drinking water and picnic tables are provided. Restrooms with flush toilets and showers, coin laundry, cable TV, a convenience store, picnic area, and ice are available. Propane gas, a store, and a café are within two miles. Boat docks, launching facilities, and rentals are nearby. Leashed pets are permitted.

Reservations, fees: Reservations are recommended. Sites are $25 –29, $1 per person per night for more than two people; yurts are $35 per night. Some credit cards are accepted. Open year-round.

Directions: On U.S. 101, drive to central Gold Beach and the intersection with Moore Street. Turn west and drive two blocks to Airport Way. Turn right and drive three blocks to South Jetty Road. Turn left and look for the park on the left.

Contact: Oceanside RV Park, 541/247-2301, www.oceansiderv1.com.

116 WHALESHEAD BEACH RESORT

Scenic rating: 7

near Brookings

Map grid A5

This resort, about 0.25 mile from the beach, is set in a forested area with a small stream nearby. Activities at and around the camp include ocean and river fishing, jet boat trips, whale-watching excursions, and a golf course (13 miles away). Each campsite has a deck, and many cabins have an ocean view. One unique feature, a tunnel connects the campground to a trail to the beach.

RV sites, facilities: There are 45 sites with full hookups for RVs up to 60 feet long and 36 cabins. Picnic tables are provided and fire rings are available on request. Cable TV, restrooms with showers, coin laundry, modem access, limited

groceries, ice, snacks, RV supplies, propane gas, and a restaurant are available. A dump station is six miles away. Some facilities are wheelchair accessible. Leashed pets are permitted.

Reservations, fees: Reservations are recommended. Sites are $25 per night, $2 per person per night for more than two people; cable TV is $1.50 per night. Some credit cards are accepted. Open year-round.

Directions: From Brookings, drive seven miles north on U.S. 101 until you pass Harris Beach. Look for the resort on the right.

Contact: Whaleshead Beach Resort, 541/469-7446, fax 541/469-7447, www.whaleshead-resort.com.

117 ALFRED A. LOEB STATE PARK

Scenic rating: 8

near the Chetco River

Map grid A5

This park is set in a canyon formed by the Chetco River. The campsites are set in a beautiful old myrtle grove. The 0.75-mile River View Trail follows the Chetco River to a redwood grove. Swimming, fishing, and rafting are popular activities. Nature programs and interpretive tours are available by request.

RV sites, facilities: There are 48 sites with partial hookups for tents or RVs up to 50 feet long and three log cabins. Picnic tables, drinking water, garbage bins, and fire grills are provided. Restrooms with flush toilets and showers and firewood are available. A camp host is onsite. Some facilities are wheelchair accessible. Leashed pets are permitted.

Reservations, fees: Reservations are accepted for cabins only at 800/452-5687 or www.oregonstateparks.org ($8 reservation fee). Sites are $12–20 per night, $5 per night per additional vehicle; cabins are $35–39 per night. Some credit cards are accepted. Open year-round.

Directions: On U.S. 101, drive south to Brookings and County Road 784 (North Bank Chetco River Road). Turn northeast and drive eight miles northeast on North Bank Road to the park entrance on the right.

Contact: Harris Beach State Park, 541/469-2021 or 800/551-6949, www.oregonstateparks.org.

118 HARRIS BEACH STATE PARK

Scenic rating: 8

near Brookings
Map grid A5

This park is prime with wildlife-watching opportunities. Not only is it home to Bird Island, a breeding site for the tufted puffin and other rare birds, but gray whales, harbor seals, and sea lions can be spotted here as well. Tidepooling is also popular. Sites are shaded and well-spaced with plenty of beach and nature trails leading from the campground. In the fall and winter, the nearby Chetco River attracts good runs of salmon and steelhead, respectively.

RV sites, facilities: There are 63 sites for tents or RVs up to 50 feet (no hookups), 86 sites with full or partial hookups for RVs up to 60 feet long, a hiker/biker camp, and six yurts. Picnic tables, garbage bins, and fire grills are provided. Drinking water, cable TV, Wi-Fi, restrooms with flush toilets and showers, a dump station, coin laundry, and firewood are available. A camp host is on-site. Some facilities are wheelchair accessible. Leashed pets are permitted.

Reservations, fees: Reservations are accepted at 800/452-5687 or www.oregonstateparks.org ($8 reservation fee). RV sites are $17–26 per night, tent sites are $13–20 per night, $5 per night per additional vehicle, $4–5 per night per person for hikers/bikers, $17 per night for group tent sites, and $29–39 per night for yurts. Some credit cards are accepted. Open year-round.

Directions: From Brookings, drive north on U.S. 101 for two miles to the park entrance on the left (west side of road).

Contact: Harris Beach State Park, 541/469-2021, www.oregonstateparks.org.

119 BEACHFRONT RV PARK

Scenic rating: 8

near Brookings
Map grid A5

Beachfront RV, located just this side of the Oregon/California border on the Pacific Ocean, makes a great layover spot. Oceanfront sites are available, and recreational activities include boating, fishing, and swimming. Beach access is available from the park. Plan your trip early, as sites usually book up for the entire summer season. Nearby Harris Beach State Park, with its beach access and hiking trails, makes a good side trip.

RV sites, facilities: There are 25 tent sites and 138 sites with full or partial hookups for RVs of any length; some sites are pull-through. Picnic tables and fire rings are provided. Restrooms with showers, dump station, public phone, modem access, coin laundry, restaurant, ice, and a marina with a boat ramp, boat dock, and snacks are available. Supplies are available nearby. Some facilities are wheelchair accessible. Leashed pets are permitted.

Reservations, fees: Reservations are accepted at 800/441-0856. Tent sites are $14 per night and RV sites are $22–28.28 per night. Some credit cards are accepted. Open year-round.

Directions: From Brookings, drive south on U.S. 101 for 2.5 miles to Benham Lane. Turn west on Benham Lane and drive 1.5 miles (it becomes Lower Harbor Road) to Boat Basin Road. Turn left and drive two blocks to the park on the right.

Contact: Beachfront RV Park, 541/469-5867 or 800/441-0856; Port of Brookings Harbor, 541/469-2218, www.port-brookings-harbor.org.

120 ATRIVERS EDGE RV RESORT

Scenic rating: 7

on the Chetco River

Map grid A5

This resort lies along the banks of the Chetco River, just upstream from Brookings Harbor. A favorite spot for anglers, it features salmon and steelhead trips on the Chetco in the fall and winter. Deep-sea trips for salmon or rockfish are available nearby in the summer. This resort looks like the Rhine Valley in Germany, a pretty canyon between the trees and the river. A golf course is nearby.

RV sites, facilities: There are 110 sites with full hookups for RVs of any length; some are pullthrough. Nine cabins are also available. Picnic tables are provided and fire rings are at most sites. Restrooms with flush toilets and showers, wireless Internet service, modem access, propane gas, dump station, recreation hall with exercise equipment, coin laundry, recycling station, small boat launch, and cable TV are available. Leashed pets are permitted.

Reservations, fees: Reservations are recommended at 888/295-1441. Sites are $30–33 per night, $2 per person per night for more than two people. Some credit cards are accepted. Open year-round.

Directions: On U.S. 101, drive to the southern end of Brookings (harbor side) and to South Bank Chetco River Road (a cloverleaf exit). Turn east on South Bank Chetco River Road and drive 1.5 miles to the resort entrance on the left (a slanted left turn, through the pillars, well signed).

Contact: AtRivers Edge RV Resort, 541/469-3356, www.atriversedge.com.

121 SEA BIRD RV PARK

Scenic rating: 5

near Brookings

Map grid A5

Sea Bird is one of several parks in the area. Nearby recreation options include marked bike trails, a full-service marina, and tennis courts. A nice, neat park, it features paved roads and gravel/granite sites. There is also a beach for surfing near the park. In summer, most of the sites are reserved for the season. An 18-hole golf course is within 2.5 miles.

RV sites, facilities: There are 60 sites with full or partial hookups for RVs of any length; some are pull-through sites. Picnic tables are provided. No open fires are allowed. Restrooms with flush toilets and showers, dump station, highspeed modem access, recreation hall, and a coin laundry are available. Boat docks, launching facilities, and rentals are nearby. Leashed pets are permitted.

Reservations, fees: Reservations are accepted. Sites are $18 per night, $2 per person per night for more than two people. Open year-round.

Directions: In Brookings, drive south on U.S. 101 to the Chetco River Bridge. Continue 0.25 mile south on U.S. 101 to the park entrance on the left.

Contact: Sea Bird RV Park, 541/469-3512, www.seabirdrv.com.

OREGON

PORTLAND AND THE WILLAMETTE VALLEY

( ) **Family Destinations**
Silver Falls State Park, page 354.

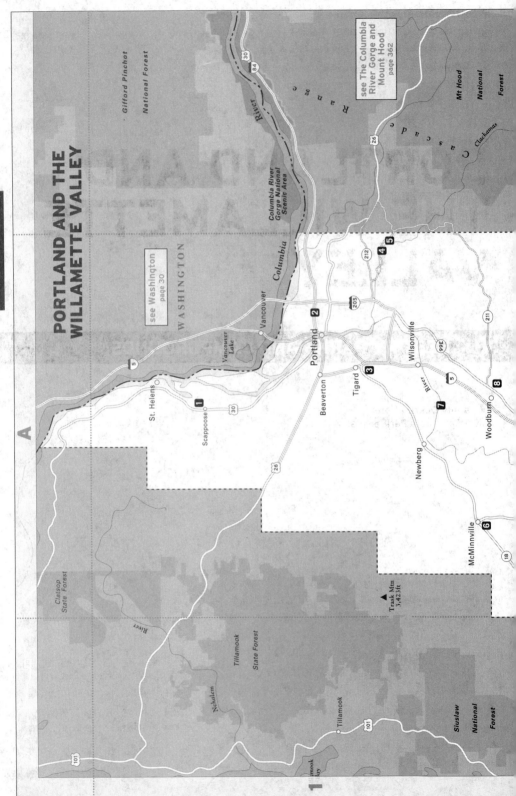

PORTLAND AND THE WILLAMETTE VALLEY

see Washington
page 30

see The Columbia
River Gorge and
Mount Hood
page 362

WASHINGTON

Gifford Pinchot

National Forest

Columbia River
Gorge National
Scenic Area

Cascade Range

Mt Hood

National

Forest

Clackamas

Columbia River

Vancouver

Vancouver Lake

Portland

Beaverton

Tigard

Wilsonville

Newberg

Woodburn

McMinnville

St. Helens

Scappoose

Clatsop
State Forest

Tillamook
State Forest

Nehalem River

Tillamook

Siuslaw

National

Forest

Trask Mtn
3,423ft

1   2   3   4   5   6   7   8

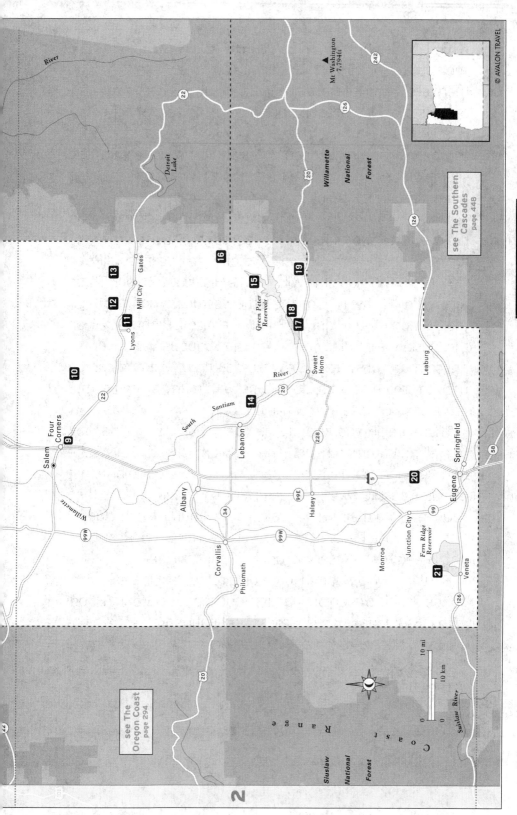

see The Southern Cascades
page 448

see The Oregon Coast
page 294

OREGON

© AVALON TRAVEL

Mt Washington
7,794ft

Willamette National Forest

Detroit Lake

River

Gates

Mill City

Lyons

Four Corners

Salem

Willamette

Green Peter Reservoir

Sweet Home

South Santiam River

Lebanon

Leaburg

Albany

Halsey

Corvallis

Philomath

Monroe

Junction City

Fern Ridge Reservoir

Veneta

Springfield

Eugene

Siuslaw National Forest

Coast Range

Siuslaw River

10 mi

10 km

Most visitors to the Willamette Valley only

see a stretch of I-5 from Portland to Cottage Grove. Although there are some interesting things about this particular part of the state – it's Oregon's business center and most of my relatives and pals live there – the glimpse provided from I-5 doesn't capture its beauty. Residents, however, know the secret: Not only can you earn a good living here, it's also a great jumping-off point to adventure.

To discover what the locals know, venture east to west on the slow two-lane highways that border the streams. Among the most notable are Highway 26 along the Nacanticum River, little Highway 6 along the Wilson, little Highway 22 along Three Rivers, tiny Highway 15 on the Little Nestucca, Highway 18 on the Salmon River, Highway 34 on the Alsea, Highway 126 on the Siuslaw, and Highway 38 on the Umpqua (my favorite). These roads provide routes to reach the coast and can be used to create beautiful loop trips, with many hidden campgrounds to choose from while en route.

There are also parks and a number of lakes set in the foothills along dammed rivers. The highlight is Silver Falls State Park, Oregon's largest state park, with a seven-mile hike that is routed past 10 awesome waterfalls, some falling more than 100 feet from their brinks. Lakes are plentiful, too, including Cottage Grove Reservoir, Dorena Lake, Fall Creek Reservoir, and Green Peter Reservoir on the Santiam River.

Portland is a great hub for finding recreation in the region. To the east is the Columbia River corridor and Mount Hood, with its surrounding wilderness and national forest. To the south is Eugene, which leads to the McKenzie and Willamette Rivers and offers a good launch station to the Three Sisters in the east.

OREGON

1 SCAPPOOSE RV PARK

Scenic rating: 6

in Scappoose

Map grid A1

This county-operated RV park neighbors the rural Scappoose airport, making it a convenient spot for private pilots. The sites are partially shaded with maple, oak, and spruce trees. Set on the edge of a dike, it is less than a mile from the Columbia River and about a 30-minute drive from Portland.

RV sites, facilities: There are four tent sites in dispersed areas and seven sites for RVs up to 41 feet long, six with full hookups. Picnic tables and fire grills are provided. Drinking water, a restroom with flush toilets and showers, a dump station, firewood, a playground, and horseshoe pits are available. Some facilities are wheelchair accessible. Leashed pets are permitted.

Reservations, fees: Reservations are accepted at 503/366-3984. RV sites are $17–20 per night, tent sites are $12–15 per night, $5–7 per night for an additional vehicle. Open year-round.

Directions: From Portland, turn west on U.S. 30 and drive to Scappoose. Continue one mile north on U.S. 30 to West Lane Road. Turn right (east) and drive 0.75 mile to Honeyman Road. Turn left and drive one block to the park on the right.

Contact: Columbia County, Parks and Recreation, 503/397-2353; Scappoose RV Park, 503/543-3225.

2 PORTLAND FAIRVIEW RV PARK

Scenic rating: 7

east of Portland

Map grid A1

This is a massive yet pretty RV park located eight miles east of downtown Portland. The setting is peaceful, with the entire park landscaped, edged by tall conifers. A small brook runs nearby. Many I-5 ramblers have a chance to unwind for a spell here.

RV sites, facilities: There are 407 sites with full hookups for RVs of any length; most sites are pull-through. Picnic tables are provided. Drinking water and restrooms with flush toilets and coin showers, a barbecue and picnic area, horseshoe pits, seasonal swimming pool, basketball, recreation and fitness centers, Wi-Fi, satellite TV, coin laundry, a playground, and parking for boats and tow vehicles are available. Some facilities are wheelchair accessible. Leashed pets are permitted, with some breed restrictions.

Reservations, fees: Reservations are accepted online at www.portlandfairviewrv.com. Sites are $40 per night. Open year-round.

Directions: From I-84/Highway 30 in Portland, take Exit 14 and turn north on NE 207th Avenue. Drive on NE 207th Avenue to NE Sandy Boulevard. Turn right on NE Sandy Boulevard and drive a short distance to the park.

Contact: Portland Fairview RV Park, 877/777-1047, www.portlandfairviewrv.com.

3 RV PARK OF PORTLAND

Scenic rating: 6

in Tualatin

Map grid A1

This park, just south of Portland in a wooded setting, has spacious sites, all with access to lawn areas. More than half of the sites are taken by monthly rentals.

RV sites, facilities: There are 112 sites, most with full hookups and pull-throughs for RVs of any length. Cable TV and picnic tables are provided. Restrooms with flush toilets and showers, a dump station, coin laundry, modem access, and wireless Internet service are available. A store, café, and ice are within one mile. Leashed pets are permitted.

Reservations, fees: Reservations are accepted at 800/856-2066. Sites are $39.75 per night, plus $2.50 per person per night for more than two people. Some credit cards are accepted. Open year-round.

Directions: From Portland, drive south on I-5 to Tualatin and Exit 289. Take Exit 289 and turn left (east) on Nyberg Road. Drive 0.25

mile to Nyberg Lane. Turn left and drive a short distance to the park on the left.

Contact: RV Park of Portland, 503/692-0225 or 800/856-2066, www.rvparkofportland.com.

4 BARTON PARK

Scenic rating: 6

near the Clackamas River

Map grid A1

Getting here may seem a bit of a maze, but the trip is well worth it. This camp is set on the Clackamas River and is surrounded by woods and tall trees. The river can provide good salmon and steelhead fishing.

RV sites, facilities: There are 98 sites for tents or RVs up to 40 feet; sites have partial hookups, and some sites are pull-through. Picnic tables and fire rings are provided. Restrooms with showers, a dump station, picnic area, and picnic shelters are available. Recreational facilities include horseshoe pits, a playground, volleyball court, softball field, and boat ramp. Supplies are available within one mile. A camp host is on-site. Some facilities are wheelchair accessible. Leashed pets are permitted.

Reservations, fees: Reservations are recommended. Sites are $16–19 per night, $5 per night per additional vehicle. Some credit cards are accepted for reservations. Open May–September.

Directions: From Portland, drive south on I-5 to I-205. Turn east and drive about 20 miles to Exit 12, the Clackamas/Estacada exit (Highway 212). Turn east on Highway 212/224 and drive 3.2 miles to the Carver exit/Rock Creek junction. Turn right on Highway 224 and drive about 6.5 miles to the town of Barton and Baker's Ferry Road. Turn right and drive 0.2 mile to Barton Park Road. Turn left and drive to the park on the left.

Contact: Clackamas County Parks Department, 503/742-4414, fax 503/742-4420, www.co.clackamas.or.us.

5 METZLER PARK

Scenic rating: 8

on Clear Creek

Map grid A1

This county campground on a small stream not far from the Clackamas River is a hot spot for fishing, picnicking, and swimming. Be sure to make your reservation early at this very popular park.

RV sites, facilities: There are 75 sites with partial hookups for tents or RVs up to 40 feet long. Picnic tables and fire pits are provided. Restrooms with flush toilets and showers, a dump station, playground, picnic areas, and a recreation field with baseball, basketball, and volleyball are available. Propane and ice are within five miles. Some facilities are wheelchair accessible. Leashed pets are permitted.

Reservations, fees: Reservations are recommended. Sites are $12–19 per night. Some credit cards are accepted with reservations. Open May–September.

Directions: From Portland, drive south on I-5 to I-205. Turn east and drive about 20 miles to Exit 12, the Clackamas/Estacada exit (Highway 212). Turn east on Highway 212/224 and drive 3.2 miles to the Carver exit/Rock Creek junction. Turn right on Highway 224 and drive approximately 15 miles to Estacada and Highway 211. Turn right, crossing a bridge, and drive four miles to Tucker Road. Turn right and drive 0.5 mile to Metzler Park Road. Turn left and drive 1.6 miles to the park entrance.

Contact: Clackamas County Parks Department, 503/742-4414, fax 503/742-4420, www.co.clackamas.or.us.

6 MULKEY RV PARK

Scenic rating: 7

near the South Yamhill River

Map grid A1

This wooded park sits near the South Yamhill River. Nearby recreation options include an 18-hole golf course, tennis courts, and the

OREGON

Western Deer Park and Arboretum, which has a playground. Note that most sites are taken by monthly renters.

RV sites, facilities: There are 70 sites with full hookups for RVs of any length; some sites are pull-through. Drinking water and picnic tables are provided. Restrooms with flush toilets and showers, a grocery store, propane gas, ice, and coin laundry are available. Some facilities are wheelchair accessible. Leashed pets are permitted.

Reservations, fees: Reservations are advised at 877/472-2475. RV sites are $28 per night, $5 per person per night for more than two people. Monthly rates are available. Some credit cards are accepted. Open year-round.

Directions: From Portland, turn south on Highway 99 and drive about 31 miles to McMinnville and Highway 18. Turn southwest on Highway 18 and drive 3.5 miles to the park entrance.

Contact: Mulkey RV Park, 503/472-2475, fax 503/472-0718.

7 CHAMPOEG STATE HERITAGE AREA

Scenic rating: 7

on the Willamette River

Map grid A1

Champoeg State Heritage Area lies on the south bank of the Willamette River and features an interpretive center, a botanical garden with native plants, and hiking and bike trails. A junior ranger program is available during the summer. The log cabin museum, the historic Newell House, and the visitors center are also worth a tour. Some of the best sturgeon fishing in North America is on the Willamette River below Oregon City Falls (also called Willamette Falls). I caught my biggest fish here in 2009, a nine-foot sturgeon that weighed 400 pounds. The best fishing guide to the area is Charlie Foster.

RV sites, facilities: There are 79 sites with full or partial hookups for tents or RVs up to 50

feet long. There are also three group tent areas that accommodate a maximum of 25 people each, six walk-in sites, six cabins, six yurts, a hiker/biker camp, and a 10-site tent and RV group area with electric hookups only. Picnic tables and fire grills are provided. Restrooms with flush toilets and showers, drinking water, garbage bins, a dump station, meeting hall, picnic area, off-leash dog park, disc golf, ice, and firewood are available. Boat docking facilities are nearby. Some facilities are wheelchair accessible. Leashed pets are permitted.

Reservations, fees: Reservations are accepted at 800/452-5687 or www.oregonstateparks.org ($8 reservation fee). Sites are $16–24 per night, $4–5 per person per night for hiker/biker sites, the group tent camps are $40–71 per night, the group RV/tent camp is $81–101 per night and $8–10 per RV after the first 10 units; yurts are $27–36 per night, and cabins are $35–39 per night. It costs $5 per night for an additional vehicle. Some credit cards are accepted. Open year-round.

Directions: From Portland, drive south on I-5 to Exit 278, the Donald/Aurora exit. Take that exit and turn right (west) on Ehlen Road and drive three miles to Case Road. Turn right (north) and drive 4.5 miles (the road becomes Champoeg Road) to the park on the right.

Contact: Champoeg State Heritage Area, 503/678-1251 or 800/551-6949, www.oregonstateparks.org; Charlie Foster's NW Sturgeon Adventures, 503/820-1189, www.nwsturgeonadventures.com.

8 FEYRER MEMORIAL PARK

Scenic rating: 5

on the Molalla River

Map grid A1

On the scenic Molalla River, this county park offers swimming and excellent salmon fishing. A superb option for weary I-5 cruisers, the park is only 30 minutes off the highway and provides a peaceful, serene environment.

RV sites, facilities: There are 20 sites with

partial hookups for tents or RVs up to 40 feet long. Picnic tables and fire rings are provided. Drinking water, restrooms with showers, a dump station, and picnic areas are available. There are also a playground, horseshoe pits, volleyball, and softball. A boat ramp is nearby. Supplies are available within three miles. Some facilities are wheelchair accessible. Leashed pets are permitted.

Reservations, fees: Reservations are recommended. Sites are $16–19 per night. Some credit cards are accepted with reservations. Open May–September.

Directions: From Portland, drive south on I-5 to Woodburn. Take Exit 271 and drive east on Highway 214; continue (the road changes to Highway 211 at the crossing with Highway 99E) to Molalla and Mathias Road. Turn right and drive 0.25 mile to Feyrer Park Road. Turn right and drive three miles to the park on the left.

Contact: Clackamas County Parks Department, 503/742-4414, fax 503/742-4420, www.co.clackamas.or.us.

9 SALEM CAMPGROUND & RVS

Scenic rating: 5

in Salem

Map grid A2

This park with shaded sites is located next to I-5 in Salem; expect to hear traffic noise. A picnic area and a lake for swimming are within walking distance, and a nine-hole golf course, hiking trails, riding stable, and tennis courts are nearby. This is a good overnight campground, but not a destination place.

RV sites, facilities: There are 144 sites with full hookups (20-, 30-, and 50-amp) for RVs of any length; most sites are pull-through. There are also 25 tent sites. Picnic tables are provided, and there are fire pits at the tent sites; barbecues are available upon request. Restrooms with flush toilets and showers, propane gas, a dump station, recreation hall with a game room, convenience store, coin laundry, ice, a playground, cable TV, modem hookups, and drinking water

are available. A café is within one mile. Some facilities are wheelchair accessible. Leashed pets are permitted; no pit bulls or rottweilers are allowed.

Reservations, fees: Reservations are accepted at 800/826-9605. Sites are $16–25 per night, $2 per person per night for more than two people. Weekly, monthly, and group rates are available. Some credit cards are accepted. Open year-round.

Directions: From Salem on I-5, take Exit 253 to Highway 22. Turn east and drive 0.25 mile to Lancaster Drive. Turn right on Lancaster Drive and continue 0.1 mile to Hagers Grove Road. Turn right on Hagers Grove Road and drive a short distance to the campground at the end of the road.

Contact: Salem Campground & RVs, 503/581-6736 or 800/826-9605, fax 503/581-9945, www.salemrv.com.

10 SILVER FALLS STATE PARK

Scenic rating: 8

near Salem

Map grid A2   BEST (

Oregon's largest state park, Silver Falls covers more than 8,700 acres. Numerous trails crisscross the area, one of which is a seven-mile jaunt that meanders past 10 majestic waterfalls (some more than 100 feet high) in the rainforest of Silver Creek Canyon. Four of these falls have an amphitheater-like surrounding where you can walk behind the falls and feel the misty spray. A horse camp and a 14-mile equestrian trail are available in the park. Fitness-conscious campers can check out the three-mile jogging trail or the four-mile bike trail. There are also a rustic nature lodge and group lodging facilities. Pets are not allowed on the Canyon Trail.

RV sites, facilities: There are 45 sites for tents or self-contained RVs (no hookups), 52 sites with partial hookups for tents or RVs up to 60 feet long, three group tent sites for up to 50–75 people each, two group RV areas, five horse sites, a group horse camp, and 14 cabins. Picnic tables and fire grills are provided.

Drinking water, garbage bins, restrooms with flush toilets and showers, a dump station, an amphitheater, firewood, ice, and a playground are available. Some facilities are wheelchair accessible. Leashed pets are permitted in the campground.

Reservations, fees: Reservations are accepted at 800/452-5687 or www.oregonstateparks. org ($8 reservation fee). Sites are $12–24 per night, $5 per night for an additional vehicle. The group tent site is $40–71 per night; the group RV sites are $60–101 per night for the first 10 units and then $10 per additional unit. Horse campsites are $12–19 per night, the group horse camp is $36–58 per night. Cabins are $35–39 per night. Some credit cards are accepted. RV sites are open year-round, tent sites April–October.

Directions: From Salem on I-5, take Exit 253 to Highway 22. Turn east and drive five miles to Highway 214. Turn left (east) and drive 15 miles to the park.

Contact: Silver Falls State Park, 503/873-8681, 503/873-4395, or 800/551-6949, 503/873-3890 (trail rides), www.oregonstateparks.org.

11 JOHN NEAL MEMORIAL PARK

Scenic rating: 6

on the North Santiam River
Map grid A2

This camp is set on the banks of the North Santiam River, offering good boating and trout fishing possibilities. The park covers about 27 acres, and there are hiking trails. Other recreation options include exploring lakes and trails in the adjacent national forest land or visiting Silver Falls State Park.

RV sites, facilities: There are 23 sites for tents or self-contained RVs up to 30 feet long, and 12 group sites for up to 100 people. Picnic tables and fire pits are provided. Restrooms with flush toilets and showers, garbage bins, and drinking water are available. Recreational facilities include a boat ramp, playground, horseshoe pits, picnic area, and a recreation field. Ice

and a grocery store are within one mile. Some facilities are wheelchair accessible. Leashed pets are permitted.

Reservations, fees: Reservations are accepted. Sites are $11 per night for tent sites, $20 per night for RV sites, $5 per night per additional vehicle, and $200 per night for group sites plus a $50 reservation fee. Some credit cards are accepted for reservations. Open mid-April–mid-September, weather permitting.

Directions: From Salem, drive east on Highway 22 for about 20 miles to Highway 226. Turn right and drive south for two miles to Lyons and John Neal Park Road. Turn left (east) and drive a short distance to the campground on the left.

Contact: Linn County Parks Department, 541/967-3917, fax 541/924-6915, www.co.linn.or.us.

12 FISHERMEN'S BEND

Scenic rating: 7

on the North Santiam River
Map grid A2

Fishermen's Bend is a popular spot for anglers of all ages, and the sites are spacious. The campground was renovated in 2005. A barrier-free fishing and river viewing area and a network of trails provide access to more than a mile of river. There's a one-mile, self-guided nature trail, and the nature center has a variety of displays. The amphitheater has films and activities on weekends. The front gate closes at 10 P.M.

RV sites, facilities: There are 51 sites for tents and RVs up to 38 feet long; some sites are pull-through, some have full hookups. There are also three group sites (for up to 60 people each) and two cabins. Drinking water, picnic tables, and fire pits are provided. Restrooms with flush toilets and showers, a dump station, and garbage containers are available. A boat ramp, fishing pier, day-use area with playgrounds, baseball fields, volleyball and basketball courts, horseshoe pits, firewood, and a picnic shelter are also available. Some facilities are wheelchair accessible. Leashed pets are permitted.

Reservations, fees: Reservations are accepted for cabins and the group site at 888/444-6777 or www.recreation.gov ($10 reservation fee). Sites are $12–22 per night, $5 per night per each additional vehicle. Group sites are $65–85 per night. Cabins are $40 per night. Open April–October.

Directions: From Salem on I-5, take Exit 253 to Highway 22. Turn east and drive 30 miles to the campground on the right.

Contact: Bureau of Land Management, Salem District Office, 503/897-2406, fax 503/375-5622, www.blm.gov/or/resources/recreation.

13 ELKHORN VALLEY

Scenic rating: 7

on the Little North Santiam River

Map grid A2

This pretty campground along the Little North Santiam River, not far from the north fork of the Santiam River, has easy access and on-site hosts and is only a short drive away from a major metropolitan area. Swimming is good here during the summer, and the campground is popular with families. The front gate is locked 10 P.M.–7 A.M. daily. This site offers an alternative to Shady Cove, which is about 10 miles to the east.

RV sites, facilities: There are 24 sites for tents or RVs up to 24 feet long. Picnic tables, garbage bins, fire grills, vault toilets, and drinking water are available. Firewood is available for purchase. Leashed pets are permitted.

Reservations, fees: Reservations are not accepted. Sites are $10 per night, $5 per night per additional vehicle. There is a 14-day stay limit. Open late May–early September.

Directions: From Salem on I-5, take Exit 253 to Highway 22. Turn east and drive 25 miles to Elkhorn Road (Little North Fork Road). Turn left (northeast) and drive nine miles to the campground on the left.

Contact: Bureau of Land Management, Salem District Office, 503/375-5646, fax 503/375-5622, www.blm.gov/or/resources/recreation.

14 WATERLOO COUNTY PARK

Scenic rating: 8

on the South Santiam River

Map grid A2

This campground features more than a mile of South Santiam River frontage. Field sports, fishing, picnicking, and swimming are options here. Small boats with trolling motors are the only boats allowed here.

RV sites, facilities: There are 120 sites for tents or RVs of any length; most have partial hook-ups. Drinking water, fire pits, and picnic tables are provided. Restrooms with showers, a dump station, boat ramps, a playground, day-use area, off-leash dog park, and picnic shelters are available. Some facilities are wheelchair accessible. Leashed pets are permitted.

Reservations, fees: Reservations are accepted at 541/967-3917 or www.co.linn.or.us ($11 reservation fee). Sites are $20–24 per night, $6 per night for an additional vehicle. Some credit cards are accepted for reservations. Open year-round.

Directions: From Albany, drive east on U.S. 20 for about 20 miles through Lebanon to the Waterloo exit. Turn left (north) at the Waterloo exit and drive approximately two miles to the camp on the right. The camp is on the south side of the South Santiam River, five miles east of Lebanon.

Contact: Linn County Parks Department, 541/967-3917, fax 541/924-6915, www.co.linn.or.us.

15 WHITCOMB CREEK COUNTY PARK

Scenic rating: 8

on Green Peter Reservoir

Map grid A2

This camp, located on the north shore of Green Peter Reservoir, is in a wooded area with lots of ferns, which gives it a rainforest feel. Recreation options include hiking, picnicking, sailing, swimming, and waterskiing. Two boat ramps are on the reservoir about a mile from camp.

RV sites, facilities: There are 39 sites for tents or RVs up to 30 feet long (no hookups) and one group tent and RV area for up to 100 people. Picnic tables and fire pits are provided. Drinking water is available to haul; vault toilets, garbage bins, and a boat ramp are also available. Supplies are within 15 miles. Leashed pets are permitted.

Reservations, fees: Reservations are accepted at 541/967-3917 or www.co.linn.or.us ($11 reservation fee). Sites are $18 per night, $6 per night per additional vehicle; the group site is $200 per night, plus a $50 reservation fee. Some credit cards are accepted. Open mid-April–mid-September.

Directions: From Albany, drive east on U.S. 20 for about 35 miles (through Lebanon and Sweet Home) to the Quartzville Road exit (near Foster Reservoir). Turn left (north) on Quartzville Road and drive 15 miles to the park.

Contact: Linn County Parks Department, 541/967-3917, fax 541/924-6915, www.co.linn.or.us.

16 YELLOWBOTTOM

Scenic rating: 7

on Quartzville Creek

Map grid A2

Out-of-town visitors always miss this campground across the road from Quartzville Creek. It's nestled under a canopy of old-growth forest. The Rhododendron Trail, which is just under a mile, provides a challenging hike through forest and patches of rhododendrons. Some folks pan for gold here, and swimming is popular in the creek. Though primitive, the camp is ideal for a quiet getaway weekend.

RV sites, facilities: There are 28 sites for tents or RVs up to 28 feet long, including 22 pull-through sites. Picnic tables, garbage bins, and fire grills are provided. Drinking water, vault toilets, and firewood are available. A camp host is on-site seasonally. Some facilities are wheelchair accessible. Leashed pets are permitted.

Reservations, fees: Reservations are not

accepted. Sites are $8 per night, with a 14-day stay limit, and $5 per night for an additional vehicle. Open late May–early September.

Directions: From Albany, drive east on U.S. 20 for about 35 miles (through Sweet Home) to Quartzville Road. Turn left (northeast) on Quartzville Road and drive 24 miles to the campground on the left.

Contact: Bureau of Land Management, Salem District, 503/375-5646, fax 503/375-5622, www.blm.gov/or/resources/recreation.

17 RIVER BEND COUNTY PARK

Scenic rating: 8

on the South Santiam River

Map grid A2

When River Bend opened in 2005, it was an instant hit. The park has plenty of hiking trails, the river current is calm in summer, and there are swimming beaches. The campground is in a woodsy setting of firs and ferns. Additional water activities include fishing and inner tubing, a favorite.

RV sites, facilities: There are 20 sites for tents and self-contained RVs (no hookups) and 60 sites with partial hookups for tents and RVs of any length. Picnic tables and fire pits are provided. Drinking water, restrooms with flush toilets and showers, a dump station, picnic area, athletic field, interpretive display, fishing area, and swimming and tubing area are available. An enclosed group shelter is also available. Some facilities are wheelchair accessible. Leashed pets are permitted.

Reservations, fees: Reservations are accepted at 541/967-3917 or www.co.linn.or.us ($11 reservation fee). Sites are $20–24 per night, $6 per night per additional vehicle. Some credit cards are accepted for reservations. Open year-round.

Directions: From Albany, drive east on U.S. 20 to Sweet Home. Continue east on U.S. 20 for five miles to the park on the left.

Contact: Linn County Parks Department, 541/967-3917, fax 541/924-6915, www.co.linn.or.us.

OREGON

18 SUNNYSIDE COUNTY PARK

Scenic rating: 8

on Foster Reservoir

Map grid A2

Sunnyside is Linn County's most popular park. Recreation options at this 98-acre park include boating, fishing, swimming, and waterskiing. A golf course is within 15 miles.

RV sites, facilities: There are 165 sites for tents or RVs of any length; most sites have partial hookups. There are also three group sites for up to 80 people each. Picnic tables and fire rings are provided; there is also a community fire ring. Drinking water, restrooms with flush toilets and showers, a dump station, playground, dog park, stocked fishing ponds, fish-cleaning station, picnic shelter (available by reservation), volleyball courts, firewood, a boat ramp, and moorage are available. Supplies are available within three miles. Some facilities are wheelchair accessible. Leashed pets are permitted.

Reservations, fees: Reservations are accepted at 541/967-3917 or www.co.linn.or.us ($11 reservation fee, $50 reservation fee for group site). Sites are $20–24 per night, $6 per night for an additional vehicle. Open mid-March–early November.

Directions: From Albany, drive east on U.S. 20 for about 35 miles (through Lebanon and Sweet Home) to the Quartzville Road exit (near Foster Reservoir). Turn left (north) on Quartzville Road and drive one mile to the campground on the right. The camp is on the south side of Foster Reservoir.

Contact: Linn County Parks Department, 541/967-3917, fax 541/924-6915, www.co.linn.or.us.

19 CASCADIA STATE PARK

Scenic rating: 7

on the Santiam River

Map grid A2

Cascadia State Park is set along the banks of the Santiam River. The highlight of this 258-acre park is Soda Creek Falls, with a fun 0.75-mile hike to reach it. Another riverside trail leads through groves of Douglas fir and provides good fishing access. This is a choice spot for a less crowded getaway, and also for reunions and meetings for families, Boy Scouts, and other groups.

RV sites, facilities: There are 25 primitive sites for tents or self-contained RVs up to 35 feet long, and two group tent areas for up to 100 people each. Picnic tables, garbage bins, and fire grills are provided. Drinking water, flush and vault toilets, and firewood are available. A camp host is on-site. Some facilities are wheelchair accessible. Leashed pets are permitted.

Reservations, fees: Reservations are accepted for group tent areas only at 800/452-5687. Sites are $17 per night, $5 per night for an additional vehicle. Group sites are $71 per night for up to 25 people and $3 per night for each additional person. Some credit cards are accepted. Open May–September, weather permitting.

Directions: From Albany, drive east on U.S. 20 for 40 miles to the park on the left (14 miles east of the town of Sweet Home).

Contact: Cascadia State Park, 541/367-6021 or 800/551-6949, www.oregonstateparks.org.

20 ARMITAGE PARK

Scenic rating: 7

north of Eugene

Map grid A2

This 57-acre county park sits along on the banks of the McKenzie River outside Eugene. Hiking opportunities include the 0.5-mile Crilly Nature Trail through deciduous forest common around this river. Over the years, my brother Rambob, cousins Andy and Neil, and I have caught a lot of trout on the McKenzie in this area. Hopefully you will too.

RV sites, facilities: There are 37 sites for tents or RVs and two group sites for up to 40 people each. Picnic tables and fire rings are provided. Drinking water and restrooms with flush toilets are available. A boat ramp, volleyball courts, horseshoe pits, Wi-Fi, and a two-acre dog park are available. Some facilities are wheelchair accessible. Leashed pets are permitted.

Reservations, fees: Reservations are accepted ($10 reservation fee) for the group sites at 541/682-2000. Single sites are $25 per night, group sites are $100–150 per night, $6.50 for each additional vehicle, $3 parking fee. Open year-round.

Directions: From Portland, take I-5 to the Eugene area. Take Exit 195A-B and drive 0.7 mile toward Florence/Junction City. Merge onto Belt Line Highway and drive one mile to the Coburg exit. Take that exit and drive 0.2 mile to N. Coburg Road. Turn right on N. Coburg Road and drive 1.8 miles to the campground at 90064 Coburg Road.

Contact: Lane County Parks, 541/682-2000, http://ecomm.lanecounty.org/parks.

21 RICHARDSON PARK

Scenic rating: 7

on Fern Ridge Reservoir

Map grid A2

This pretty Lane County park is a favorite for sailing and sailboarding, as the wind is consistent. Boating and waterskiing are also popular. There is a walking trail that doubles as a bike trail. A kiosk display in the park features the historic Applegate Trail. Additional activities include fishing, swimming (unsupervised), and wildlife-viewing. The Corps of Engineers has wildlife areas nearby.

RV sites, facilities: There are 88 sites with partial hookups for tents or RVs of any length; some sites are pull-through. Group sites are double campsites. Drinking water, picnic tables, and fire pits are provided. A dump station, picnic areas, sand volleyball area, swimming area, playground, amphitheater, and restrooms with flush toilets, garbage bins, and coin showers are available. A seasonally attended marina offers minimal supplies including ice, a boat launch, and transient boat docks. There is a small town within five miles. Some facilities are wheelchair accessible. Leashed pets are permitted.

Reservations, fees: Reservations are accepted at 541/682-2000 or www.lanecounty.org/parks, ($10 reservation fee). Sites are $20 per night, plus $6.50 per night per additional vehicle. Maximum stay is 14 days within a 30-day period. Some credit cards are accepted. Open mid-April–mid-October.

Directions: In Eugene on I-5, drive to Exit 195B and Belt Line Road. Turn west on Belt Line Road and drive 6.5 miles to the Junction City Airport exit and Highway 99. Take that exit, turn left on Highway 99, and drive north for 0.5 mile to Clear Lake Road (the first stoplight). Turn left and drive 8.25 miles to the campground on the left.

Contact: Richardson Park, 541/935-2005 or 541/682-2000, www.co.lane.or.us/parks.

THE COLUMBIA RIVER GORGE AND MOUNT HOOD

(BEST RV PARKS AND CAMPGROUNDS

(**Family Destinations**
Hoover Group Camp, page 394.

(**Prettiest Rivers**
Deschutes River State Recreation Area, page 390.

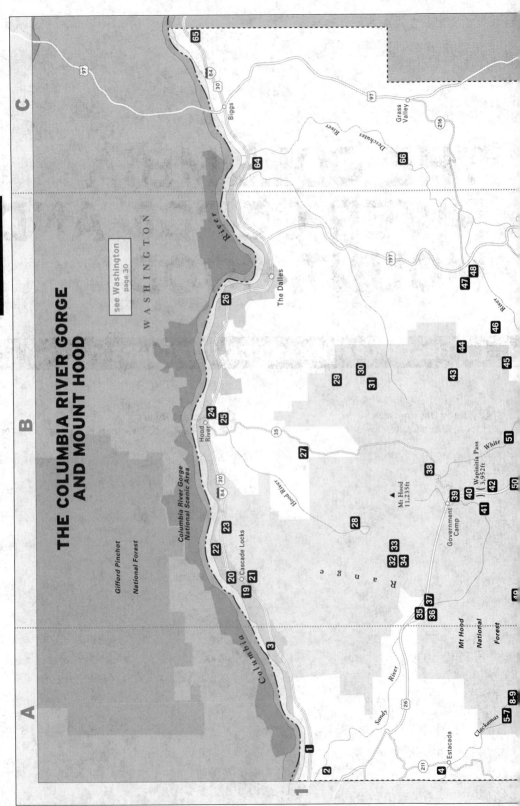

OREGON

THE COLUMBIA RIVER GORGE
AND MOUNT HOOD

Gifford Pinchot
National Forest

Columbia River Gorge
National Scenic Area

see Washington
page 30

WASHINGTON

Biggs

The Dalles

Hood River

Mt Hood
11,235ft

Government
Camp

Wapinitia Pass
3,952ft

Cascade Locks

Estacada

Mt Hood
National
Forest

Sandy River

Clackamas

Columbia

R a n g e

Deschutes River

Grass Valley

White River

Hood River

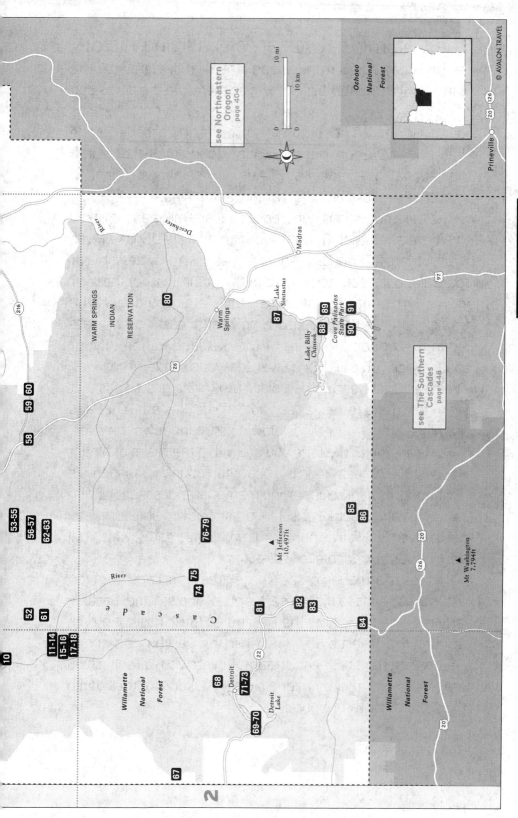

see Northeastern Oregon
page 404

see The Southern Cascades
page 448

OREGON

© AVALON TRAVEL

10 mi

10 km

Prineville

20 126

Ochoco
National
Forest

97

Madras

126

20

Mt Washington
7,794ft

20

Lake
Simtustus

87

Lake Billy
Chinook

88 89

Cove Palisades
State Park

90 91

85

86

Mt Jefferson
10,497ft

WARM SPRINGS

INDIAN

RESERVATION

80

Warm
Springs

216

26

58

59 60

53-55

56-57

62-63

76-79

Deschutes

River

River

C a s c a d e

52

61

75

74

81

82 83

84

22

10

11-14

15-16

17-18

Willamette
National
Forest

68

Detroit

71-73

69-70

Detroit
Lake

Willamette
National
Forest

67

2

The Columbia River area is a living history

lesson, a geological wonder, and a recreation paradise. The waterway is probably best known as the route the Lewis and Clark expedition followed two centuries ago. It's also famous for carving out a deep gorge through the Cascade Range that divides Oregon. Nearby Mount Hood and its surrounding national forest and many lakes provide almost unlimited opportunities for camping, fishing, and hiking.

The Columbia spans hundreds of square miles and is linked to a watershed that in turn is connected to the Snake River, which covers thousands of square miles. I-84 provides a major route along the southern shore of the Columbia, but the river view is not what you will remember. After you depart the traffic of the Portland area, driving west to east, you will pass along the wooded foothills of the Cascade Range to your south. When you pass Hood River, the world suddenly changes. The trees disappear. In their place are rolling grasslands that seem to extend for as far as you can see. It is often hot and dry here, with strong winds blowing straight down the river.

However, the entire time you are within the realm of Mount Hood. At 11,239 feet, Hood is a beautiful mountain, shaped like a diamond, its flanks supporting many stellar destinations with campsites and small lakes set in forest. Snowmelt feeds many major rivers as well as numerous smaller streams, which roll down Mount Hood in every direction.

The transformation of the Gorge-area landscape from forest to grasslands to high desert is quick and striking. Particularly remarkable is how the Deschutes River has cut a path through the desert bluffs. And while the Deschutes is one of Oregon's better steelhead streams, unless you're fishing, you are more likely to encounter a desert chukar on a rock perch than anything water-bound.

1 CROWN POINT RV PARK

Scenic rating: 6

near the Columbia River

Map grid A1

This little park is located near the Columbia River along scenic U.S. 30. Nearby Crown Point State Park is open during the day and offers views of the Columbia River Gorge and the historic Vista House, a memorial built in 1918 to honor Oregon's pioneers. Multnomah Falls offers another possible side trip.

RV sites, facilities: There are 22 sites with full or partial hookups for RVs of any length; some sites are pull-through. Drinking water and picnic tables are provided. Restrooms with flush toilets and coin showers, modem access, horseshoe pits, a hair salon, and a coin laundry are available. A store and ice are within walking distance. Leashed pets are permitted.

Reservations, fees: Reservations are accepted. Sites are $30 per night. Open year-round.

Directions: From Portland on I-84 eastbound, drive 16 miles to Exit 22 and Corbett. Take that exit and turn right on Corbett Hill Road. Drive 1.5 miles to a Y intersection with East Historic Columbia River Highway. Bear left and drive 0.25 mile to the park on the right.

Note: The recommended route has a 10 percent grade for 1.5 miles. An alternate route: From Portland on I-84 eastbound, drive to Exit 18/Lewis and Clark State Park. Take that exit and drive to East Historic Columbia River Highway and continue seven miles to the park on the right.

Contact: Crown Point RV Park, 503/695-5207, fax 503/695-3217.

2 OXBOW REGIONAL PARK

Scenic rating: 7

on the Sandy River

Map grid A1

This 1,200-acre park along the Sandy River, a short distance from the Columbia River Gorge, is a designated national scenic waterway.

Fishing, non-motorized boating, and swimming are permitted here. The water is usually calm, and canoes, kayaks, and rafts are allowed. About 200 acres of the park are old-growth Douglas fir forest. There are several miles of hiking trails.

RV sites, facilities: There are 67 sites for tents or RVs up to 35 feet long; some sites are pull-through. Picnic tables, fire pits, and barbecues are provided. Drinking water, flush and vault toilets, coin showers, firewood, and a playground are available. Boat-launching facilities are nearby. Gates lock at sunset and open at 6:30 A.M. Services are approximately 10 miles away. Some facilities are wheelchair accessible. No pets are permitted.

Reservations, fees: Reservations are not accepted. Sites are $15 per night, $4 per night per additional vehicle. There is a park entrance fee of $4 per vehicle for the first day only. Open year-round.

Directions: From Portland on I-84, drive to Exit 17/Troutdale. Take that exit and drive on the frontage road for 0.5 mile to 257th Street. Turn right (south) on 257th Street and drive three miles to Division Street. Turn left and drive seven miles to the park entrance on the left.

Contact: Metro Regional Parks and Greenspaces, Oxbow Regional Park, 503/663-4708, www.oregonmetro.gov.

3 AINSWORTH STATE PARK

Scenic rating: 8

along the Columbia River Gorge

Map grid A1

Set along the scenic Columbia River Gorge, Ainsworth State Park is waterfall central, with famous Multnomah Falls a highlight. A 1.3-mile trail leads from the campground to Horsetail Falls and the Nesmith Point Trail shares a great view of St. Peter's Dome. Anglers should check out the Bonneville Fish Hatchery about five miles away.

RV sites, facilities: There are 45 sites with full hookups for RVs up to 60 feet long and four walk-in tent sites. Picnic tables and fire grills are provided. Drinking water, restrooms with flush toilets and showers, garbage bins, a dump station, playground, camp host, amphitheater with occasional interpretive programs, and firewood are available. Some facilities are wheelchair accessible. Leashed pets are permitted.

Reservations, fees: Reservations are not accepted. Sites are $12–20 per night, $10–17 per night for walk-in tent sites, and $5 per night per additional vehicle. Some credit cards are accepted. Open mid-March–late October, weather permitting.

Directions: From Portland on I-84 eastbound, drive 35 miles to Exit 35. Turn southwest on the Columbia River Scenic Highway and continue a short distance to the park; the park is 17 miles east of Troutdale. An alternate route is to take the historic Columbia River Highway, a designated scenic highway, all the way from Portland (37 miles).

Contact: Ainsworth State Park, 503/695-2301 or 800/551-6949, www.oregonstateparks.org.

4 MILO McIVER STATE PARK

Scenic rating: 7

on the Clackamas River
Map grid A1

Though only 45 minutes from Portland, this park is far enough off the beaten track to provide a feeling of separation from the metropolitan area. It sits along the banks of the Clackamas River and has a boat ramp. There is fishing for salmon and steelhead in season; check current regulations. Trails for hiking are available, and a 4.5-mile equestrian trail is also accessible; bicycles are not allowed on trails. A fish hatchery is a nearby point of interest. Every September, actors participate in a Civil War reenactment here.

RV sites, facilities: There are 44 sites with partial hookups for RVs up to 50 feet long, nine primitive tent sites, one hiker/bicyclist site, and three group tent areas for up to 50 people each. Picnic tables and fire grills are provided. Drinking water, garbage bins, restrooms with

flush toilets and showers, a dump station, picnic shelters, and firewood are available. Boat-launching facilities (canoes, inflatables, and kayaks), a model airplane field, and a 27-hole disc golf course are nearby. Group facilities are available. Some facilities are wheelchair accessible. Leashed pets are permitted, and there is a designated area for off-leash dog runs.

Reservations, fees: Reservations are accepted at 800/452-5687 or www.oregonstateparks.org ($8 reservation fee). Tent sites are $11–18 per night, RV sites are $13–27 per night, $5 per night per each additional vehicle. Hiker/biker sites are $4 per person per night, and group sites are $64–128.25 per night in summer, $43–103 the rest of the year. Some credit cards are accepted. Open mid-March–October.

Directions: From Portland, drive east on U.S. 26 to Gresham. Continue 11 miles to Sandy and Highway 211. Turn right (south) and drive six miles to a junction. Turn south (still Highway 211) and drive one mile to Hayden Road. Turn right and drive one mile to Springwater Road. Turn right and drive one mile to the park on the right.

Contact: Milo McIver State Park, 503/630-6147, 503/630-7150, or 800/551-6949, www.oregonstateparks.org.

5 PROMONTORY

Scenic rating: 7

on North Fork Reservoir
Map grid A1

This Portland General Electric camp on North Fork Reservoir is part of a large recreation area and park. The reservoir, actually a dammed-up overflow of the Clackamas River, encompasses 350 acres. The water is calm and ideal for boating, and the trout fishing is excellent. A trail connects the campground to the marina. A one-acre lake is available for children's fishing.

RV sites, facilities: There are 35 sites for tents or RVs up to 35 feet long and 14 yomes (which are a cross between a yurt and a dome). There is also a group area for up to 35 people for tents or small self-contained RVs. There are no RV hookups. Picnic tables and fire rings are provided. Restrooms with flush toilets and showers, garbage bins, limited groceries, ice, a playground, horseshoes, covered picnic shelters, and snacks are available. A fish-cleaning station, a fishing pier, a children's fishing pond, boat ramp, dock, and boat rentals are also on-site. Some facilities, including the boat ramp and fishing pier, are wheelchair accessible. Leashed pets are permitted.

Reservations, fees: Reservations are accepted at 503/630-7229 or www.portlandgeneral.com. Sites are $16 per night, $25 per night for a yome. Some credit cards are accepted. Open mid-May–September.

Directions: From Portland, drive east on U.S. 26 to Gresham. Continue 11 miles to Sandy and Highway 211. Turn right (south) and drive six miles to a junction. Turn south (still Highway 211) and drive six miles to Estacada. Continue south on Highway 224 and drive seven miles to the campground on the right. The route is well signed.

Contact: Portland General Electric, 503/464-8515, fax 503/464-2944, www.portlandgeneral.com; store and marina, 503/630-5152; campground, 503/630-7229.

6 LAZY BEND

Scenic rating: 8

on the Clackamas River in
Mount Hood National Forest

Map grid A1

This campground is situated at 800 feet elevation along the banks of the Clackamas River near the large North Fork Reservoir. It's far enough off the highway to provide a secluded, primitive feeling, though it fills quickly on weekends and holidays. There's only catch-and-release fishing in the Clackamas.

RV sites, facilities: There are 23 sites for tents or RVs up to 52 feet long. Picnic tables, garbage service, and fireplaces are provided. Drinking water and flush toilets are available. Leashed pets are permitted.

Reservations, fees: Reservations are accepted at 877/444-6777 or www.recreation.gov ($10 reservation fee). Sites are $17 per night, $8 per night per additional vehicle. Open late early May–late September, weather permitting.

Directions: From Portland, drive south on U.S. 205 to the junction with Highway 24. Take the Highway 224/Estacada exit and turn left (south) onto Highway 224. Drive approximately 13 miles to Estacada. Continue south on Highway 224 for 10.5 miles to the campground on the right.

Contact: Mount Hood National Forest, Clackamas River Ranger District, 503/630-6861, fax 503/630-2299, www.fs.fed.us.

7 ARMSTRONG

Scenic rating: 5

on the Clackamas River in
Mount Hood National Forest

Map grid A1

Armstrong campground is set at an elevation of 900 feet along the banks of the Clackamas River and offers good fishing access. Fishing is catch-and-release only.

RV sites, facilities: There are 11 sites for tents or RVs up to 40 feet long. Picnic tables and fire rings are provided. Vault toilets and drinking water are available. Garbage service is available in the summer only. Some facilities are wheelchair accessible. Leashed pets are permitted.

Reservations, fees: Reservations are accepted at 877/444-6777 or www.recreation.gov ($10 reservation fee). Sites are $16 per night, $8 per night per additional vehicle. Open year-round, with limited winter services.

Directions: From Portland, drive south on U.S. 205 to the junction with Highway 24. Take the Highway 224/Estacada exit and turn left (south) onto Highway 224. Drive approximately 13 miles to Estacada. Continue south on Highway 224 for 15 miles to the campground on the right.

Contact: Mount Hood National Forest, Clack-

OREGON

amas River Ranger District, 503/630-6861, fax 503/630-2299, www.fs.fed.us.

8 CARTER BRIDGE

Scenic rating: 5

on the Clackamas River in Mount Hood National Forest

Map grid A1

This small, flat campground is popular with anglers. The Clackamas River flows along one end, and the other end borders the highway, with peripheral traffic noise.

RV sites, facilities: There are 15 sites for tents or RVs up to 28 feet long. Picnic tables and fire pits are provided. Vault toilets and garbage bins are available. There is no drinking water. Some facilities are wheelchair accessible. Leashed pets are permitted.

Reservations, fees: Reservations are not accepted. Sites are $14 per night, $7 per night per additional vehicle. Open late May–early September, weather permitting.

Directions: From Portland, drive south on U.S. 205 to the junction with Highway 24. Take the Highway 224/Estacada exit and turn left (south) onto Highway 224. Drive approximately 13 miles to Estacada. Continue south on Highway 224 for 15.2 miles to the campground on the left.

Contact: Mount Hood National Forest, Clackamas River Ranger District, 503/630-6861, fax 503/630-2299, www.fs.fed.us.

9 LOCKABY

Scenic rating: 6

on the Clackamas River in Mount Hood National Forest

Map grid A1

This campground sits at an elevation of 900 feet along the banks of the Clackamas River, next to Armstrong. Fishing in the Clackamas River is catch-and-release only.

RV sites, facilities: There are 30 sites for tents or RVs up to 15 feet long. Picnic tables, fireplaces, drinking water, garbage service, vault toilets, and firewood are available. A camp host is on-site. Leashed pets are permitted.

Reservations, fees: Reservations are accepted at 877/444-6777 or www.recreation.gov ($10 reservation fee). Sites are $16 per night, $8 per night per additional vehicle. Open late May–early September.

Directions: From Portland, drive south on U.S. 205 to the junction with Highway 24. Take the Highway 224/Estacada exit and turn left (south) onto Highway 224. Drive approximately 13 miles to Estacada. Continue south on Highway 224 for 15.3 miles to the campground on the left.

Contact: Mount Hood National Forest, Clackamas River Ranger District, Estacada Ranger Station, 503/630-6861, fax 503/630-2299, www.fs.fed.us.

10 ROARING RIVER

Scenic rating: 8

on the Roaring River in Mount Hood National Forest

Map grid A1

Set among old-growth cedars at the confluence of the Roaring and Clackamas Rivers at an elevation of 1,000 feet, this campground has access to the Dry Ridge Trail. The trail starts in camp, and it's a butt-kicker of an uphill climb. Several other trails into the adjacent roadless area are accessible from camp.

RV sites, facilities: There are 14 sites for tents or RVs up to 16 feet long. Picnic tables and fireplaces are provided. Garbage service, drinking water, and vault toilets are available. Leashed pets are permitted.

Reservations, fees: Reservations are accepted at 877/444-6777 or www.recreation.gov ($10 reservation fee). Sites are $16 per night, $8 per night per additional vehicle. Open mid-May–mid-September, weather permitting.

Directions: From Portland, drive south on U.S. 205 to the junction with Highway 24. Take the Highway 224/Estacada exit and turn left (south) onto Highway 224. Drive approximately 13 miles to Estacada. Continue south on Highway 224 for 18 miles to the campground on the left.

Contact: Mount Hood National Forest, Clackamas River Ranger District, 503/630-6861, fax 503/630-2299, www.fs.fed.us.

11 SUNSTRIP

Scenic rating: 3

on the Clackamas River in
Mount Hood National Forest

Map grid A1

This campground on the banks of the Clackamas River offers fishing and rafting access. One of several camps along the Highway 224 corridor, Sunstrip is a favorite with rafting and kayaking enthusiasts and can fill up quickly on weekends. The elevation is 1,000 feet. Note: This campground, squeezed between the river and the highway and traversed by power lines, may be a turnoff for those wanting another kind of experience.

RV sites, facilities: There are nine sites for tents or RVs up to 60 feet long. Picnic tables and fireplaces are provided. Garbage service, drinking water, firewood, and vault toilets are available. A camp host is on-site. Leashed pets are permitted.

Reservations, fees: Reservations are accepted at 877/444-6777 or www.recreation.gov ($10 reservation fee). Sites are $16 per night, $8 per night per additional vehicle. Open year-round, with limited winter services.

Directions: From Portland, drive south on U.S. 205 to the junction with Highway 24. Take the Highway 224/Estacada exit and turn left (south) onto Highway 224. Drive approximately 13 miles to Estacada. Continue south on Highway 224 for 19 miles to the campground.

Contact: Mount Hood National Forest, Clackamas River Ranger District, 503/630-6861, fax 503/630-2299, www.fs.fed.us.

12 RAINBOW

Scenic rating: 6

on the Oak Grove Fork of the Clackamas River in
Mount Hood National Forest

Map grid A1

Rainbow campground sits at an elevation of 1,400 feet along the banks of the Oak Grove Fork of the Clackamas River, not far from where it empties into the Clackamas River. The camp is less than a quarter mile from Ripplebrook Campground.

RV sites, facilities: There are 17 sites for tents or RVs up to 62 feet long. Picnic tables and fire grills are provided. Vault toilets are available. Garbage service is available during the summer. There is no drinking water. Leashed pets are permitted.

Reservations, fees: Reservations are accepted at 877/444-6777 or www.recreation.gov ($10 reservation fee). Sites are $14 per night, $8 per night per additional vehicle. Open year-round, with limited winter services.

Directions: From Portland, drive south on U.S. 205 to the junction with Highway 24. Take the Highway 224/Estacada exit and turn left (south) onto Highway 224. Drive approximately 13 miles to Estacada. Continue south on Highway 224 and drive 27 miles in national forest (the road becomes Forest Road 46). Continue south and drive about 100 yards to the campground on the right.

Contact: Mount Hood National Forest, Clackamas River Ranger District, 595 N.W. Industrial Way, Estacada, OR 97023, 503/630-6861, fax 503/630-2299, www.fs.fed.us.

13 INDIAN HENRY

Scenic rating: 8

on the Clackamas River in
Mount Hood National Forest

Map grid A1

One of the most popular campgrounds in the Clackamas River Ranger District, Indian Henry hugs the banks of the Clackamas River at an

OREGON

elevation of 1,250 feet and has a wheelchair-accessible trail. Group campsites and an amphitheater are available. The nearby Clackamas River Trail has fishing access.

RV sites, facilities: There are 84 sites for tents or RVs up to 40 feet long and eight group tent sites for up to 30 people. Picnic tables, garbage service, and fire grills are provided. Flush toilets, firewood, and drinking water are available. A camp host is on-site. Some facilities are wheelchair accessible. Leashed pets are permitted.

Reservations, fees: Reservations are accepted at 877/444-6777 or www.recreation.gov ($10 reservation fee). Sites are $17 per night, $8 per night per additional vehicle; group sites are $46–50 per night. Open late May–early September, weather permitting.

Directions: From Portland, drive south on U.S. 205 to the junction with Highway 24. Take the Highway 224/Estacada exit and turn left (south) onto Highway 224. Drive approximately 13 miles to Estacada. Continue south on Highway 224 for 23 miles to Forest Road 4620. Turn right and drive 0.5 mile southeast to the campground on the left.

Contact: Mount Hood National Forest, Clackamas River Ranger District, 503/630-6861, fax 503/630-2299, www.fs.fed.us.

14 RIPPLEBROOK

Scenic rating: 7

on the Oak Grove Fork of the Clackamas River in Mount Hood National Forest

Map grid A1

Shaded sites with river views are a highlight at this campground along the banks of the Oak Grove Fork of the Clackamas River, where anglers are limited to artificial lures and catch-and-release only. Note: The road to this camp experiences slides and washouts; check current status before making a trip.

RV sites, facilities: There are 14 sites for RVs up to 45 feet long. Picnic tables, garbage service, and fire grills are provided. Vault toilets

are available, but there is no drinking water. Leashed pets are permitted.

Reservations, fees: Reservations are accepted at 877/444-6777 or www.recreation.gov ($10 reservation fee). Sites are $14 per night, $8 per night per additional vehicle. Open late April–late September, weather permitting.

Directions: From Portland, drive south on U.S. 205 to the junction with Highway 24. Take the Highway 224/Estacada exit and turn left (south) onto Highway 224. Drive approximately 13 miles to Estacada. Continue south on Highway 224 for 26.5 miles to the campground entrance on the left.

Contact: Mount Hood National Forest, Clackamas River Ranger District, 503/630-6861, fax 503/630-2299, www.fs.fed.us.

15 RIVERSIDE

Scenic rating: 8

on the Clackamas River in Mount Hood National Forest

Map grid A1

The banks of the Clackamas River are home to this campground (elevation 1,400 feet). A worthwhile trail leaves the camp and follows the river for four miles north. Fishing is another option here, and several old forest roads in the vicinity make excellent mountain-biking trails.

RV sites, facilities: There are 16 sites for tents or RVs up to 40 feet long. Picnic tables, garbage service, and fire grills are provided. Vault toilets and drinking water are available. Some facilities are wheelchair accessible. Leashed pets are permitted; no horses are allowed in the campground.

Reservations, fees: Reservations are accepted at 877/444-6777 or www.recreation.gov ($10 reservation fee). Sites are $16 per night, $8 per night per additional vehicle. Open mid-May–late September, weather permitting.

Directions: From Portland, drive south on U.S. 205 to the junction with Highway 24. Take the Highway 224/Estacada exit and turn left (south) onto Highway 224. Drive approximately 13 miles to Estacada. Continue south on Highway 224 for 27 miles and into national forest (Highway 224 becomes Forest Road 46). Continue 2.5 miles south on Forest Road 46 to the campground on the right.

Contact: Mount Hood National Forest, Clackamas River Ranger District, 503/630-6861, fax 503/630-2299, www.fs.fed.us.

16 RIVERFORD

Scenic rating: 4

on the Clackamas and Collawash Rivers in Mount Hood National Forest

Map grid A1

This campground, just a two-minute walk from the confluence of the Clackamas and Collawash Rivers, offers access to good fishing. Otherwise, it's small, and the sites provide little privacy. It is set at an elevation of 1,500 feet. Although there is no drinking water at this camp, drinking water is available 0.75 mile away at Riverside Campground.

RV sites, facilities: There are eight sites for tents and two sites for RVs up to 20 feet long. Picnic tables and fire grills are provided. Vault toilets are available. Garbage service is provided in the summer. There is no drinking water. Leashed pets are permitted.

Reservations, fees: Reservations are not accepted. Sites are $16 per night, $7 per night per additional vehicle. Open year-round, with limited winter services.

Directions: From Portland, drive south on U.S. 205 to the junction with Highway 24. Take the Highway 224/Estacada exit and turn left (south) onto Highway 224. Drive approximately 13 miles to Estacada. Continue south on Highway 224 for 27 miles in national forest (the road becomes Forest Road 46). Continue south on Forest Road 46 for 3.5 miles to the campground on the right.

Contact: Mount Hood National Forest, Clackamas River Ranger District, 503/630-6861, fax 503/630-2299, www.fs.fed.us.

17 RAAB GROUP

Scenic rating: 7

on the Collawash River in Mount Hood National Forest

Map grid A1

Raab Group camp (1,500 feet elevation) is located along the banks of the Collawash River, about a mile from its confluence with the Clackamas River. Raab gets moderate use, but it's usually quiet and has a nice, secluded atmosphere with lots of privacy among the sites.

RV sites, facilities: There are 27 sites for tents or RVs up to 16 feet long. Picnic tables, garbage service, and fire grills are provided. Vault toilets are available. There is no drinking water in the campground; water is available one mile away at Two Rivers Picnic Area. Leashed pets are permitted.

Reservations, fees: Reservations are accepted at 877/444-6777 or www.recreation.gov ($10 reservation fee). Sites are $35–42 per night. Open late May–early September, weather permitting.

Directions: From Portland, drive south on U.S. 205 to the junction with Highway 24. Take the Highway 224/Estacada exit and turn left (south) onto Highway 224. Drive approximately 13 miles to Estacada. Continue south on Highway 224 for 27 miles in national forest (the road becomes Forest Road 46). Continue south on Forest Road 46 for 2.5 miles to Forest Road 63. Turn right and drive 1.5 miles to the campground on the right.

Contact: Mount Hood National Forest, Clackamas River Ranger District, 503/630-6861, fax 503/630-2299, www.fs.fed.us; park concessionaire, 503/668-1700.

18 KINGFISHER

Scenic rating: 7

on the Hot Springs Fork of the Collawash River in Mount Hood National Forest

Map grid A1

This pretty campground, surrounded by old-growth forest, sits on the banks of the Hot

OREGON

Springs Fork of the Collawash River and provides fishing access. It's about three miles from Bagby Hot Springs, a U.S. Forest Service day-use area. The hot springs are an easy 1.5-mile hike from the day-use area. The camp sits at 1,250 feet elevation.

RV sites, facilities: There are 23 sites for tents or RVs up to 66 feet long. Picnic tables and fireplaces are provided. Garbage service is provided during the summer. Vault toilets and drinking water are available. Leashed pets are permitted.

Reservations, fees: Reservations are accepted at 877/444-6777 or www.recreation.gov ($10 reservation fee). Sites are $16 per night, $8 per night per additional vehicle. Open year-round, weather permitting, with limited winter facilities.

Directions: From Portland, drive south on U.S. 205 to the junction with Highway 24. Take the Highway 224/Estacada exit and turn left (south) onto Highway 224. Drive approximately 13 miles to Estacada. Continue south on Highway 224 for 27 miles in national forest (the road becomes Forest Road 46). Continue south on Forest Road 46 for 3.5 miles to Forest Road 63. Turn right and drive three miles to Forest Road 70. Turn right again and drive one mile to the campground on the left.

Contact: Mount Hood National Forest, Clackamas River Ranger District, 503/630-6861, fax 503/630-2299, www.fs.fed.us.

19 EAGLE CREEK

Scenic rating: 8

near the Columbia Wilderness in Mount Hood National Forest

Map grid B1

Eagle Creek is the oldest Forest Service Camp in America. Set at 400 feet elevation among old-growth Douglas fir and hemlock, it makes a good base camp for a hiking trip. The Eagle Creek Trail leaves the campground and travels 13 miles to Wahtum Lake, where it intersects with the Pacific Crest Trail. A primitive

campground sits at the 7.5-mile point. The upper seven miles of the trail pass through the Hatfield Wilderness.

RV sites, facilities: There are 20 sites for tents or RVs up to 20 feet long and one group site for up to 90 people. Picnic tables and fire grills are provided. Drinking water, garbage bins, and flush toilets are available. A camp host is on-site. Boat docks and launching facilities are nearby on the Columbia River. Some facilities are wheelchair accessible. Leashed pets are permitted.

Reservations, fees: Reservations are not accepted for single sites, but are required for the group site at 877/444-6777 or www.recreation.gov ($10 reservation fee). Sites are $10 per night, $5 per night per additional vehicle; the group site is $75–125. Open May–September.

Directions: From Portland, drive east on I-84 for 41 miles to Bonneville. Continue east for two miles to the campground.

Contact: Columbia River Gorge National Scenic Area, 541/308-1700, fax 541/386-1916, www.fs.fed.us/r6/columbia.

20 CASCADE LOCKS MARINE PARK

Scenic rating: 8

in Cascade Locks

Map grid B1

This public riverfront park covers 23 acres and offers a museum and boat rides. The salmon fishing is excellent here. Stern-wheeler dinner cruises are available. Hiking trails and tennis courts are nearby; the Pacific Crest Trail is within one mile.

RV sites, facilities: There are 16 sites for tents or RVs of any length; some sites have partial hookups. Picnic tables are provided. Drinking water, restrooms with flush toilets and showers, a dump station, boat docks, launching facilities, a picnic area, and a playground are available. A camp host is on-site. Propane gas, gasoline, a store, café, coin laundry, and ice are within one mile. Some facilities are wheelchair accessible. Leashed pets are permitted.

Reservations, fees: Reservations are accepted at 541/374-8619. Sites are $15–25 per night. Some credit cards are accepted. Open year-round, with limited winter facilities.

Directions: From Portland, drive east on I-84 for 44 miles to Cascade Locks. Take Exit 44/ Cascade Locks to Wanapa Street. Turn left and drive 0.5 mile to the sign for the park on the left (well signed).

Contact: Port of Cascade Locks, Cascade Locks Marine Park, 541/374-8619, fax 541/374-8428, www.portofcascadelocks.org.

21 KOA CASCADE LOCKS

Scenic rating: 5

near the Columbia River

Map grid B1

This KOA is a good layover spot for RVers touring the Columbia River corridor. The campground offers level, shaded RV sites and grassy tent sites. A pancake breakfast is available on weekends during the summer season. Nearby recreation options include bike trails, hiking trails, and tennis courts. The 200-acre Cascade Locks Marine Park is close by and offers everything from museums to boat trips.

RV sites, facilities: There are 33 sites for tents, 78 sites with full or partial hookups for RVs of any length, nine cabins, and two cottages. Most RV sites are pull-through. Picnic tables and fire pits are provided. Restrooms with flush toilets and showers, drinking water, propane gas, a dump station, firewood, a spa, cable TV, wireless Internet service, a recreation hall, convenience store, coin laundry, ice, a playground, bicycle rentals, and a heated seasonal swimming pool are available. A café is within one mile. Some facilities are wheelchair accessible. Leashed pets are permitted.

Reservations, fees: Reservations are accepted at 800/562-8698. Sites are $27–36 per night, $5 per person per night for more than two people. Cabins are $45–55 per night; cottages are $55–89 per night. Some credit cards are accepted. Open February–November.

Directions: From Portland, drive east on I-84 for 44 miles to Cascade Locks and Exit 44. Take that exit to Forest Lane. Turn east on Forest Lane and drive one mile to the campground on the left.

Contact: KOA Cascade Locks, 541/374-8668, www.koa.com.

22 HERMAN CREEK HORSE CAMP

Scenic rating: 9

near the Pacific Crest Trail in Mount Hood National Forest

Map grid B1

This rustic campground sits at 300 feet elevation and is about half a mile from Herman Creek, not far from the Pacific Crest Trail. This area, separated from Washington by the Columbia River, is particularly beautiful. The campsites are spacious, and the many recreation options include biking, boating, fishing, and hiking. Note that new rules regarding stock feed require certified weed-free hay, feed, and crop products on national forest land.

RV sites, facilities: There are seven sites for tents or RVs up to 20 feet long. Drinking water, garbage bins, fire grills, and picnic tables are provided. Restrooms with flush toilets and showers, stock-handling facilities, a store, a café, a coin laundry, and ice are available. Leashed pets are permitted.

Reservations, fees: Reservations are not accepted. Sites are $10 per night, $5 per night per additional vehicle. Open May–September.

Directions: From Portland, drive east on I-84 for 44 miles to Cascade Locks and Exit 44. Take that exit and drive straight ahead (east) onto Wanapa Street and drive back under the highway. Continue 1.5 miles (the road becomes Herman Creek Road) to the campground on the right.

Contact: Columbia River Gorge National Scenic Area, 541/308-1700, fax 541/386-1916, www.fs.fed.us/r6/columbia.

OREGON

23 WYETH

Scenic rating: 5

on Gordon Creek in Mount Hood National Forest
Map grid B1

Wyeth makes a good layover spot for Columbia River corridor cruisers. The camp (100 feet elevation) borders Gordon Creek, near the Columbia River. Recreation options include biking, boating, fishing, and hiking.

RV sites, facilities: There are 16 sites for tents or RVs up to 30 feet long and three group sites. Fire grills and picnic tables are provided. Drinking water and flush toilets are available. A camp host is on-site. Leashed pets are permitted.

Reservations, fees: Reservations are not accepted. Sites are $15 per night, $5 per night per additional vehicle, group sites are $30 per night. Open April–mid-October.

Directions: From Portland, drive east on I-84 for 44 miles to Cascade Locks. Continue east on I-84 for seven miles to Wyeth and Exit 51. Turn right and drive 0.25 mile to the campground entrance.

Contact: Columbia River Gorge National Scenic Area, 541/308-1700, fax 541/386-1916, www.fs.fed.us/r6/columbia.

24 VIENTO STATE PARK

Scenic rating: 8

along the Columbia River Gorge
Map grid B1

This park along the Columbia River Gorge offers scenic hiking trails and some of the best windsurfing in the Gorge. Just 12 miles to the east, old U.S. 30 skirts the Columbia River, offering a picturesque drive. Viento has a day-use picnic area right next to a babbling creek. Look for weekend interpretive programs during the summer. There are several other day-use state parks along I-84 just west of Viento, including Seneca Fouts, Vinzenz Lausmann, and Wygant. All offer quality hiking trails and scenic views.

RV sites, facilities: There are 56 sites with partial hookups for RVs up to 30 feet long (with some up to 40 feet long) and 18 tent sites. Picnic tables and fire grills are provided. Drinking water, garbage bins, restrooms with flush toilets and showers, firewood, and a playground are available. Some facilities are wheelchair accessible. Leashed pets are permitted.

Reservations, fees: Reservations are not accepted. RV sites are $12–20 per night, tent sites are $10–17 per night, $5 per night per additional vehicle. Some credit cards are accepted. Open mid-March–October, weather permitting.

Directions: From Portland, drive east on I-84 for 56 miles to Exit 56 (eight miles west of Hood River). Take Exit 56 and drive to the park entrance. The park is set on both sides of I-84.

Contact: Viento State Park, 541/374-8811 or 800/551-6949, www.oregonstateparks.org.

25 TUCKER COUNTY PARK

Scenic rating: 6

on the Hood River
Map grid B1

This county park along the banks of the Hood River is just far enough out of the way to be missed by most of the tourist traffic. Many people who choose this county park come for the windsurfing. Other recreation opportunities include rafting and kayaking. Fishing is not allowed at the park.

RV sites, facilities: There are 84 tent sites and 14 sites with partial hookups for tents or RVs up to 30 feet long. Picnic tables and fire rings are provided. Drinking water, restrooms with flush toilets and showers, and a playground are available. A store, café, gasoline, and ice are within two miles. Leashed pets are permitted.

Reservations, fees: Reservations are not accepted. Sites are $18–20 per night, and it costs $8 per night per additional tent and $5 per night per additional vehicle. Open April–October.

Directions: From Portland, turn east on I-84

and drive about 65 miles to the town of Hood River and Exit 62. Take the exit and drive east on Cascade Street, continuing to 13th Street (first light). Turn right (south) and drive through and out of town; 13th Street becomes Tucker Road and then Dee Highway (Highway 281). Follow the signs to Parkdale. The park is four miles out of town on the right.

Contact: Hood River County Parks, 541/387-6889 or 541/386-4477, fax 541/386-6325, www.co.hood-river.or.us.

26 MEMALOOSE STATE PARK

Scenic rating: 7

in the Columbia River Gorge

Map grid B1

This park borrows its name from nearby Memaloose Island, which Native Americans used as a sacred burial ground. Situated along the hottest part of the scenic Columbia River Gorge, the campground makes a prime layover spot for campers cruising the Oregon/Washington border. Nature programs and interpretive events are held here. This popular camp receives a good deal of traffic, so plan on arriving early to claim a spot, even if you have a reservation.

RV sites, facilities: There are 66 tent sites and 44 sites with full hookups for RVs up to 60 feet long. Picnic tables and fire grills are provided. Drinking water, garbage bins, restrooms with flush toilets and showers, a dump station, playground, and firewood are available. Leashed pets are permitted.

Reservations, fees: Reservations are accepted at 800/452-5687 or www.oregonstateparks.org ($8 reservation fee). RV sites are $16–20 per night, tent sites are $12–24 per night, $5 per night per additional vehicle. Some credit cards are accepted. Open mid-March–October.

Directions: Memaloose State Park is accessible only to westbound traffic on I-84. From The Dalles, drive west on I-84 for 11 miles to the signed turnoff. (The park is about 75 miles east of Portland.)

If eastbound on I-84, take Exit 76. Drive under the freeway to the I-84 west on-ramp. Once on I-84 west, drive 2.5 miles to the sign for Rest Area/Memaloose State Park. Drive into the rest area and take an immediate right into the campground.

Contact: Memaloose State Park, 541/478-3008 or 800/551-6949, www.oregonstateparks.org.

27 KINNICKKINNICK

Scenic rating: 5

on Laurence Lake in Mount Hood National Forest

Map grid B1

Kinnickkinnick campground sits on a peninsula that juts into Laurence Lake; only non-motorized boats are allowed on the lake. Campsite privacy varies because of the fairly sparse tree cover, and more than half of the sites are a short walk from your vehicle.

RV sites, facilities: There are 20 sites for tents or RVs up to 16 feet long. Picnic tables and fire rings with fire grills are provided. There is no drinking water. Vault toilets, garbage bins, and a boat ramp are available. Some facilities are wheelchair accessible. Leashed pets are permitted.

Reservations, fees: Reservations are not accepted. Sites are $12 per night, $7 per night per additional vehicle. Open May–September, weather permitting.

Directions: From Portland, drive 62 miles west on I-84 to the city of Hood River. Take Exit 64 and drive about 14 miles south on Highway 35 to the town of Mount Hood and Cooper Spur Road. Turn right and drive three miles to Parkdale and Clear Creek Road. Turn left (south) and drive three miles to the Laurence Lake turnoff. Turn right on Forest Road 2840 (Laurence Lake Road) and drive four miles to the campground on the right.

Contact: Mount Hood National Forest, Hood River Ranger District, 541/352-6002, fax 541/352-7365, www.fs.fed.us.

OREGON

28 LOST LAKE

Scenic rating: 9

on Lost Lake in Mount Hood National Forest

Map grid B1

Only non-motorized boats are allowed on this clear, 240-acre lake set against the Cascade Range. The campground is nestled in an old-growth forest of cedar, Douglas fir, and hemlock trees at 3,200 feet elevation. Many sites have a lake view, and the campground affords a great view of Mount Hood.

RV sites, facilities: There are 125 sites for tents or RVs up to 32 feet long and several group sites. A horse camp with a corral is also available. Picnic tables and fire rings with grills are provided. Drinking water, vault toilets, garbage containers, a dump station, and a covered picnic shelter are available. Cabins, a grocery store, showers, beach picnic areas, a boat launch, and boat rentals are nearby. Some facilities are wheelchair accessible, including a barrier-free boat launch and fishing pier, as well as 3.5 miles of barrier-free trails. Leashed pets are permitted.

Reservations, fees: Reservations are not accepted for single sites but are required for the group sites at 541/386-6366. Single sites are $25 per night, $7 per night per additional vehicle. There are three group sites that can accommodate up to 15 people and five vehicles each. The group sites are $75–125 per night. Some credit cards are accepted. Open mid-May–mid-October, weather permitting.

Directions: From Portland, drive 62 miles east on I-84 to the city of Hood River. Take Exit 62/Westcliff to Cascade Street. Drive east on Cascade Street to 13th Street. Turn right on 13th Street and drive through Hood River Heights. The road turns into Dee Highway. Continue seven miles to Lost Lake Road/Forest Road 13. Turn right and drive seven miles to the campground.

Contact: Mount Hood National Forest, Hood River Ranger District, 541/352-6002, fax 541/352-7365; Lost Lake Resort, 541/6366, www.fs.fed.us.

29 KNEBAL SPRINGS

Scenic rating: 6

near Knebal Springs in Mount Hood National Forest

Map grid B1

This spot (4,000 feet elevation) is in a semi-primitive area near Knebal Springs, an ephemeral water source. The Knebal Springs Trail begins at the campground. A nice, level family bike trail is available here. Another trail from the camp provides access to a network of trails in the area. A U.S. Forest Service map is advised.

RV sites, facilities: There are eight sites for tents or RVs up to 22 feet long. Picnic tables and fire grills are provided. There is no drinking water. Vault toilets and horse-loading and -tending facilities are available. Garbage must be packed out. Leashed pets are permitted.

Reservations, fees: Reservations are not accepted. Sites are $10 per night. Open mid-May–October, weather permitting.

Directions: From Portland, turn east on I-84 and drive about 90 miles to Exit 87. Take Exit 87 and turn south on U.S. 197; drive 13 miles to Dufur and Dufur Valley Road. Turn right on Dufur Valley Road and drive west for 12 miles to Forest Road 44. Continue west on Forest Road 44 for four miles to Forest Road 4430. Turn right and drive four miles to Forest Road 1720. Turn left (southwest) and drive one mile to the campground.

Contact: Mount Hood National Forest, Barlow Ranger District, 541/467-2291, fax 541/467-2271, www.fs.fed.us.

30 EIGHTMILE CROSSING

Scenic rating: 7

on Eightmile Creek in Mount Hood National Forest

Map grid B1

This campground sits at an elevation of 4,200 feet along Eightmile Creek. Although pretty and shaded, with sites scattered along the banks of the creek, it gets relatively little camping pressure. From the day-use area, you have access to a nice hiking trail that runs along Eightmile Creek. In addition, a 0.75-mile wheelchair-accessible trail links Eightmile Campground to Lower Crossing Campground. The fishing can be good here, so bring your gear.

RV sites, facilities: There are 21 sites for tents or RVs up to 30 feet long. Picnic tables and fire grills are provided. Vault toilets are available. No drinking water is available, and garbage must be packed out. Some facilities are wheelchair accessible. Leashed pets are permitted.

Reservations, fees: Reservations are not accepted. Sites are $10 per night. Open June–mid-October, weather permitting.

Directions: From Portland, turn east on I-84 and drive about 90 miles to Exit 87. Take Exit 87 and turn south on U.S. 197; drive 13 miles to Dufur and Dufur Valley Road. Turn right on Dufur Valley Road and drive west for 12 miles to Forest Road 44. Continue west on Forest Road 44 for four miles to Forest Road 4430. Turn right and drive 0.5 mile to the campground.

Contact: Mount Hood National Forest, Barlow Ranger District, 541/467-2291, fax 541/467-2271, www.fs.fed.us.

31 PEBBLE FORD

Scenic rating: 6

in Mount Hood National Forest

Map grid B1

This is just a little camping spot by the side of a gravel forest road. Primitive and quiet, it's an alternative to the better-known Eightmile Crossing. There are some quality hiking trails in the area if you're willing to drive two or three miles. The elevation is 4,200 feet.

RV sites, facilities: There are three sites for tents or RVs up to 16 feet long. Picnic tables and fire grills are provided. Vault toilets are available. There is no drinking water. Leashed pets are permitted.

Reservations, fees: Reservations are not accepted. Sites are $10 per night. Open June–early October, weather permitting.

Directions: From Portland, turn east on I-84 and drive about 90 miles to Exit 87. Take Exit 87 and turn south on U.S. 197; drive 13 miles to Dufur and Dufur Valley Road. Turn right on Dufur Valley Road and drive west for 12 miles to Forest Road 44. Continue west on Forest Road 44 for five miles to Forest Road 130. Turn left (south) and drive a short distance to the campground on the left.

Contact: Mount Hood National Forest, Barlow Ranger District, 541/467-2291, fax 541/467-2271, www.fs.fed.us.

32 MCNEIL

Scenic rating: 5

on the Clear Fork of the Sandy River in Mount Hood National Forest

Map grid B1

McNeil campground (2,040 feet elevation) is located in Old Maid Flat, a special geological area along the Clear Fork of the Sandy River. There's a good view of Mount Hood from the campground entrance. Several trails nearby provide access to the wilderness backcountry.

RV sites, facilities: There are 34 sites for tents or RVs up to 22 feet long. Picnic tables and vault toilets are provided. There is no drinking water. Leashed pets are permitted.

Reservations, fees: Reservations are not accepted. Sites are $12 per night, $6 per night per additional vehicle. Open May–October, weather permitting.

Directions: From Portland, drive 40 miles east on U.S. 26 to Zigzag. Turn left on County Road 18/East Lolo Pass Road and drive 4.5 miles to Forest Road 1825. Turn right on Forest Road 1825, drive less than one mile, bear right onto a bridge to stay on Forest Road 1825, and drive 0.25 mile to the campground on the left.

Contact: Mount Hood National Forest, Zigzag Ranger District, 503/622-3191, fax 503/622-5622, www.fs.fed.us.

33 RILEY HORSE CAMP

Scenic rating: 6

near the Clear Fork of the Sandy River in
Mount Hood National Forest

Map grid B1

Riley Horse Camp is close to McNeil and
offers the same opportunities, except Riley
provides stock facilities and is reserved for
horse camping only on holidays. Secluded in an area of Douglas fir and lodgepole pine at 2,100 feet elevation, Riley is a
popular base camp for horse-packing trips.

RV sites, facilities: There are 14 sites for tents
or RVs up to 45 feet long. Picnic tables and
fire grills are provided. Drinking water, vault
toilets, garbage bins, and firewood are available.
Corrals and hitching posts for horses are available. Leashed pets are permitted.

Reservations, fees: Reservations are accepted
at 877/444-6777 or www.recreation.gov ($10
reservation fee). Sites are $16 per night, $8
per night per additional vehicle. Open May–
September, weather permitting.

Directions: From Portland, drive 40 miles east
on U.S. 26 to Zigzag. Turn left (northeast) on
County Road 18/East Lolo Pass Road and drive
4.5 miles to Forest Road 1825. Turn right and
drive 0.5 mile to Forest Road 380. Turn right
and drive 100 yards to the camp.

Contact: Mount Hood National Forest, Zigzag
Ranger District, 503/622-3191, fax 503/622-
5622, www.fs.fed.us.

34 LOST CREEK

Scenic rating: 8

on Lost Creek in Mount Hood National Forest

Map grid B1

This campground near McNeil and Riley has
some of the same opportunities. Set in a cool,
lush area on a creek at 2,600 feet elevation, it's
barrier-free and offers an interpretive nature
trail about one mile long, as well as a wheelchair-accessible fishing pier.

RV sites, facilities: There are 14 sites for tents
or RVs up to 40 feet long, including some pull-
through sites and some walk-in sites. Picnic
tables and fire grills are provided. Drinking
water, garbage service, and vault toilets are
available. Some facilities are wheelchair accessible. Leashed pets are permitted.

Reservations, fees: Reservations are accepted
at 877/444-6777 or www.recreation.gov ($10
reservation fee). Sites are $16 for a single site,
$32 for a double site, and $8–9 per night per additional vehicle. Open May–late September.

Directions: From Portland, drive 40 miles east
on U.S. 26 to Zigzag. Turn left (northeast) on
County Road 18/East Lolo Pass Road and drive
4.5 miles to Forest Road 1825. Turn right and
drive two miles to a fork. Bear right and drive
0.25 mile to the campground on the right.

Contact: Mount Hood National Forest, Zigzag
Ranger District, 503/622-3191, fax 503/622-
5622, www.fs.fed.us.

35 TOLL GATE

Scenic rating: 8

on the Zigzag River in Mount Hood National Forest

Map grid B1

This shady campground along the banks of the
Zigzag River near Rhododendron is extremely
popular, and finding a site on a summer weekend can be next to impossible. Luckily, you can
make a reservation. There are numerous hiking
trails in the area. The nearest one leads east for
several miles along the river. The campground
features a historic Civilian Conservation Corps
shelter from the 1930s, which can be used by
campers for day use.

RV sites, facilities: There are 15 sites for tents
or RVs up to 40 feet long. Picnic tables and
fire grills are provided. Drinking water, garbage service, firewood, a group picnic area
(available by reservation), and vault toilets are
available. A camp host is on-site. Leashed pets
are permitted.

Reservations, fees: Reservations are accepted

at 877/444-6777 or www.recreation.gov ($10 reservation fee). Sites are $16 per night, $8 per night per additional vehicle. Open late May–early September, weather permitting.

Directions: From Portland, drive east on U.S. 26 for 40 miles to Zigzag. Continue 2.5 miles southeast on U.S. 26 to the campground entrance.

Contact: Mount Hood National Forest, Zigzag Ranger District, 503/622-3191, fax 503/622-5622, www.fs.fed.us.

36 GREEN CANYON

Scenic rating: 8

on the Salmon River in Mount Hood National Forest
Map grid B1

Few out-of-towners know about this winner. But the locals do, and they keep the place hopping in the summer. The camp sits at 1,600 feet elevation along the banks of the Salmon River. A long trail cuts through the area and parallels the river, passing through a magnificent old-growth forest.

RV sites, facilities: There are 15 sites for tents or RVs up to 22 feet long. Picnic tables and fire grills are provided. Drinking water, garbage bins, and vault toilets are available. A store, café, and ice are within five miles. Leashed pets are permitted.

Reservations, fees: Reservations are not accepted. Sites are $16–18 per night, $8–9 per night per additional vehicle. Open May–October, weather permitting.

Directions: From Portland, drive east on U.S. 26 for 39 miles to Forest Road 2618 (Salmon River Road) near Zigzag. Turn right and drive 4.5 miles to the campground on the right.

Contact: Mount Hood National Forest, Zigzag Ranger District, 503/622-3191, fax 503/622-5622, www.fs.fed.us.

37 CAMP CREEK

Scenic rating: 8

near the Zigzag River in Mount Hood National Forest
Map grid B1

This campground (2,200 feet elevation) sits along Camp Creek, not far from the Zigzag River. It looks similar to Toll Gate, but larger and farther from the road. A hiking trail runs through camp and along the river; another one leads south to Still Creek. This campground, along with Toll Gate to the west, is very popular—you'll probably need a reservation.

RV sites, facilities: There are 25 sites for tents or RVs up to 45 feet long. Picnic tables and fire grills are provided. Drinking water, vault toilets, and garbage bins are available. A camp host is on-site. Some facilities are wheelchair accessible. Leashed pets are permitted.

Reservations, fees: Reservations are accepted at 877/444-6777 or www.recreation.gov ($10 reservation fee). Sites are $16 per night, $32 for a double site, and $8 per night per additional vehicle. Open May–September, weather permitting.

Directions: From Portland, drive east on U.S. 26 for 40 miles to Zigzag. Continue southeast on U.S. 26 for about four miles to the camp on the right.

Contact: Mount Hood National Forest, Zigzag Ranger District, 503/622-3191, fax 503/622-5622, www.fs.fed.us.

38 NOTTINGHAM

Scenic rating: 7

near the East Fork of the Hood River
Map grid B1

Nottingham campground, situated at 3,300 feet in elevation on the East Fork of the Hood River, has a variety of shady and sunny spots. The primary tree cover is Douglas fir and ponderosa pine. The Tamanawas Falls Trail (near Sherwood Camp) is three miles away, and the Gumjuwac Trail is 1.5 miles north. Fishing is

OREGON

only fair because of the swift water and lack of pools.

RV sites, facilities: There are 23 sites for tents or RVs up to 32 feet long. Picnic tables and fire rings are provided. Vault toilets and garbage bins are available. There is no drinking water. Some facilities are wheelchair accessible. Leashed pets are permitted.

Reservations, fees: Reservations are not accepted. Sites are $12 per night, $7 per night per additional vehicle. Open May–October, weather permitting.

Directions: From Mount Hood, drive south on Highway 35 for 13 miles to the camp on the right.

Contact: Mount Hood National Forest, Hood River Ranger District, 541/352-6002, fax 541/352-7365, www.fs.fed.us.

39 STILL CREEK

Scenic rating: 6

on Still Creek in Mount Hood National Forest

Map grid B1

This primitive camp, shaded primarily by fir and hemlock, sits along Still Creek where the creek pours off Mount Hood's south slope. Adjacent to Summit Meadows and the site of a pioneer gravesite from the Oregon Trail days, it's a great place for mountain views, sunsets, and wildlife. Anglers should bring along their rods: The fishing in Still Creek can be excellent. The camp sits at 3,600 feet elevation.

RV sites, facilities: There are 27 sites for tents or RVs up to 40 feet long. Picnic tables and fire grills are provided. Vault toilets, drinking water, and garbage service are available. Leashed pets are permitted.

Reservations, fees: Reservations are accepted at 877/444-6777 or www.recreation.gov ($10 reservation fee). Sites are $16–18 per night, $8–9 per night per additional vehicle. Open mid-June–mid-September, weather permitting.

Directions: From Portland, drive 55 miles east on U.S. 26 to Government Camp. Continue east on U.S. 26 for one mile to Forest Road

2650. Turn right and drive south for 500 yards to the campground.

Contact: Mount Hood National Forest, Zigzag Ranger District, 503/622-3191, fax 503/622-5622, www.fs.fed.us.

40 DEVIL'S HALF ACRE MEADOW

Scenic rating: 8

on Barlow Creek in Mount Hood National Forest

Map grid B1

On a site used by the pioneers, this campground is situated a few miles upstream from Grindstone Campground on Barlow Creek. Several hiking trails close to camp, including the Pacific Crest Trail, provide access to small lakes in the area. There are many historic points of interest in the vicinity. High-clearance vehicles are recommended. The camp is at 3,600 feet elevation.

RV sites, facilities: There are two sites for tents or RVs up to 16 feet long. Picnic tables and fire grills are provided. Vault toilets are available. There is no drinking water, and garbage must be packed out. Leashed pets are permitted.

Reservations, fees: Reservations are not accepted. There is no fee. Open May–October, weather permitting.

Directions: From Portland, drive east on U.S. 26 for 57 miles (just past the town of Government Camp) to the junction with Highway 35. Take that exit, bear right on Highway 35, and drive 4.5 miles to Forest Road 3530. Turn southeast and drive one mile to the campground.

Contact: Mount Hood National Forest, Hood River Ranger District, 541/352-6002, fax 541/352-7365, www.fs.fed.us

41 TRILLIUM LAKE

Scenic rating: 9

on Trillium Lake in Mount Hood National Forest

Map grid B1

This campground (3,600 feet elevation) hugs the shores of Trillium Lake, which is about half a mile long and a quarter mile wide. Fishing is good in the evening here, and the nearby boat ramp makes this an ideal camp for anglers. The lake is great for canoes, rafts, and small rowboats. Trillium Lake is an extremely popular vacation destination, so expect plenty of company. Reservations are highly recommended.

RV sites, facilities: There are 57 sites for tents or RVs of any length. Picnic tables and fire grills are provided. Vault toilets and drinking water are available. Boat docks and launching facilities are available on the lake, but no motors are allowed. Some facilities are wheelchair accessible. Leashed pets are permitted.

Reservations, fees: Reservations are accepted at 877/444-6777 or www.recreation.gov ($10 reservation fee). Sites are $17 per night; double sites are $34 per night, $8–9 per night per additional vehicle. Open late May–late September, weather permitting.

Directions: From Portland, drive east on U.S. 26 for 55 miles to the small town of Government Camp. Continue east on U.S. 26 for 1.5 miles to Forest Road 2656. Turn right and drive 1.3 miles to the campground on the right.

Contact: Mount Hood National Forest, Zigzag Ranger District, 503/622-3191, fax 503/622-5622, www.fs.fed.us.

42 FROG LAKE

Scenic rating: 6

near the Pacific Crest Trail in
Mount Hood National Forest

Map grid B1

This classic spot in the Cascade Range is situated on the shore of little Frog Lake (more of a pond than a lake), at an elevation of 3,800 feet and a short distance from the Pacific Crest Trail. Several other trails lead to nearby lakes. Clear Lake, to the south, provides a possible day trip and offers more recreation options.

RV sites, facilities: There are 33 sites for tents or RVs up to 35 feet long. Picnic tables and fire rings are provided. Drinking water, vault toilets, garbage bins, and firewood are available.

A camp host is on-site. Boat-launching facilities are nearby; no motorized boats are allowed. Some facilities are wheelchair accessible. Leashed pets are permitted.

Reservations, fees: Reservations are accepted at 877/444-6777 or www.recreation.gov ($10 reservation fee). Sites are $15–18 per night, $8–9 per night per additional vehicle. Open mid-May–mid-September, weather permitting.

Directions: From Portland, drive east on U.S. 26 for 57 miles to the junction with Highway 35 (two miles past Government Camp). Take that exit, bear right onto Highway 35, and drive seven miles to Forest Road 2610. Turn left and drive 0.5 mile to the campground.

Contact: Mount Hood National Forest, Hood River Ranger District, 541/352-6002, fax 541/352-7365, www.fs.fed.us; park phone, 503/622-3191.

43 BONNEY MEADOW

Scenic rating: 9

in Mount Hood National Forest

Map grid B1

This primitive campground is on the east side of the Cascade Range at an elevation of 4,800 feet. As a result, there is little water in the area, and also very few people, so you're liable to have the place all to yourself. Bonney Meadow Trail leaves from the campground and travels 1.5 miles up to a group of small lakes. This trail provides great mountain views.

RV sites, facilities: There are six sites for tents or RVs up to 16 feet long. Picnic tables and fire grills are provided. Vault toilets are available. There is no drinking water and garbage must be packed out. Leashed pets are permitted.

Reservations, fees: Reservations are not accepted. Sites are $10 per night. Open June–early October, weather permitting.

Directions: From Portland, turn east on I-84 and drive 65 miles to the town of Hood River, Exit 64 and Highway 35. Turn right (south) on Highway 35 and drive 37 miles to Forest Road 48. Turn left and drive 14 miles to Forest Road

4890. Turn left and drive four miles north to Forest Road 4891. Turn right and drive a short distance to the campground.

Contact: Mount Hood National Forest, Barlow Ranger District, 541/467-2291, fax 541/467-2271, www.fs.fed.us.

44 BONNEY CROSSING

Scenic rating: 7

on Badger Creek in Mount Hood National Forest

Map grid B1

Bonney Crossing campground at 2,200 feet elevation along Badger Creek is the trailhead for the Badger Creek Trail, which provides access to the Badger Creek Wilderness. The camp gets fairly light use and is usually very quiet. Fishing is available in the creek and is usually pretty good. Horse campers are welcome here.

RV sites, facilities: There are eight sites for tents or RVs up to 16 feet long. Picnic tables and fire grills are provided. Vault toilets are available. There is no drinking water, and garbage must be packed out. Stock facilities include horse corrals. Leashed pets are permitted.

Reservations, fees: Reservations are not accepted. Sites are $10 per night. Open mid-April–mid-October, weather permitting.

Directions: From The Dalles, drive south on U.S. 197 for 32 miles to Tygh Valley. Take the Tygh Valley exit to Tygh Valley Road. Turn west and drive 0.25 mile to Wamic Market Road (County Road 226). Turn right (west) and drive eight miles to Wamic. Continue through Wamic and drive seven miles to Forest Road 4810. Bear right and drive three miles to Forest Road 4811. Turn right and drive two miles to a junction with Forest Road 2710. Turn right and drive three miles to the campground on the right.

Contact: Mount Hood National Forest, Barlow Ranger District, 541/467-2291, fax 541/467-2271, www.fs.fed.us.

45 FOREST CREEK

Scenic rating: 6

on Forest Creek in Mount Hood National Forest

Map grid B1

This is a very old camp that borders Forest Creek on the original Barlow Trail, once used by early settlers. Shaded by an old-growth Douglas fir and ponderosa pine forest, you'll camp amid solitude. The elevation here is 3,000 feet. See a U.S. Forest Service map for specific roads and trails.

RV sites, facilities: There are eight sites for tents or RVs up to 16 feet long. Picnic tables and fire grills are provided. No drinking water is available. Vault toilets are available. Garbage must be packed out. Leashed pets are permitted.

Reservations, fees: Reservations are not accepted. Sites are $10 per night. Open June–early October, weather permitting.

Directions: From Portland, turn east on I-84 and drive 91 miles to The Dalles/Exit 87/Highway 197. Turn south and drive 31 miles to Tygh Valley and Wamic Market Road. Turn right and drive west for six miles to Forest Road 48. Continue west and drive 12.5 miles southwest to Forest Road 4885. Turn left and drive one mile to Forest Road 3530. Turn left and drive a short distance to the campground.

Contact: Mount Hood National Forest, Barlow Ranger District, 541/467-2291, fax 541/467-2271, www.fs.fed.us.

46 ROCK CREEK RESERVOIR

Scenic rating: 7

on Rock Creek Reservoir in Mount Hood National Forest

Map grid B1

Fishing is excellent, and the environment is perfect for canoes or rafts at this campground along the shore of Rock Creek Reservoir. Enjoy views of Mount Hood from the day-use area (Northwest Forest Pass required). No hiking trails are in the immediate vicinity, but there are many old forest roads that are ideal for walking or mountain biking. The camp sits at 2,200 feet elevation.

RV sites, facilities: There are 33 sites for tents or RVs up to 18 feet long. Picnic tables, garbage service, and fire grills are provided. Vault toilets, drinking water, and firewood are available. There are boat docks nearby, but no motorboats are allowed on the reservoir. Some facilities are wheelchair accessible. Leashed pets are permitted.

Reservations, fees: Reservations are accepted at 877/444-6777 or www.recreation.gov ($10 reservation fee). Sites are $14–16 per night, $7–8 per night per additional vehicle. Open late May–early October.

Directions: From Portland, turn east on I-84 and drive 91 miles to The Dalles/Exit 87/Highway 197. Turn south and drive 31 miles to Tygh Valley and Wamic Market Road. Turn right and drive west for six miles to Forest Road 48. Turn west and drive one mile to Forest Road 4820. Turn west and drive a short distance to the campground.

Contact: Mount Hood National Forest, Barlow Ranger District, 541/467-2291, fax 541/467-2271, www.fs.fed.us.

47 PINE HOLLOW LAKESIDE RESORT

Scenic rating: 8

on Pine Hollow Reservoir
Map grid B1

This resort on the shore of Pine Hollow Reservoir is the best game in town for RV campers, with some shaded lakefront sites and scenic views. Year-round boating, fishing, swimming, and waterskiing are some recreation options here.

RV sites, facilities: There are 35 tent sites, 78 sites with partial hookups for RVs of any length, and 10 cabins. Picnic tables and fire pits are provided. Drinking water, restrooms with flush toilets and coin showers, propane gas, a dump station, firewood, a convenience store, café, coin laundry, and ice are available.

Boat docks, launching facilities, and boat and personal watercraft rentals are nearby. Leashed pets are permitted.

Reservations, fees: Reservations are accepted. Sites are $25 per night, $2 per person per night for more than two people, $2 per night per additional vehicle, and $2 per pet per night. Some credit cards are accepted. Open mid-March–October.

Directions: From Portland, turn east on I-84 and drive 91 miles to The Dalles/Exit 87/Highway 197. Turn south on Highway 197 and drive 31 miles to Tygh Valley and Wamic Market Road. Turn right (west) and drive four miles to Ross Road. Turn right (north) and drive 3.5 miles to the resort on the right.

Contact: Pine Hollow Lakeside Resort, 541/544-2271, www.pinehollowlakeside.com.

48 HUNT PARK

Scenic rating: 6

near Badger Creek
Map grid B1

This Wasco County campground is set near the confluence of Badger and Tygh Creeks. Hiking trails, marked bike trails, and tennis courts are nearby, and fishing and rafting are available on the Deschutes River.

RV sites, facilities: There are 150 tent sites, 120 pull-through sites with partial hookups for RVs of any length, and a group site for tents only. Picnic tables are provided. Drinking water, restrooms with flush toilets and coin showers, a dump station, garbage bins, a basketball court, wireless Internet, and picnic shelters (which can be reserved) are available. Horse facilities, including stalls and an arena, are also available. A camp host is on-site. A store, café, and ice are within one mile. Some facilities are wheelchair accessible. Leashed pets are permitted.

Reservations, fees: Reservations are accepted at 541/483-2288. Sites are $12–15 per night, $3 per night per additional vehicle. The group site is $5 per person per night for up to 100 people, $3 per person thereafter. Open May–October.

OREGON

Directions: From Portland, turn east on I-84 and drive 91 miles to The Dalles/Exit 87/Highway 197. Turn south on Highway 197 and drive 31 miles to Tygh Valley and Main Street. Turn right on Main Street and drive two blocks to Fairgrounds Road. Turn right and drive one mile to the fairgrounds on the right.

Contact: Wasco County, 541/483-2288, http://co.wasco.or.us.

49 HIDEAWAY LAKE

Scenic rating: 9

near the Rock Lakes Basin in Mount Hood National Forest

Map grid B1

This jewel of a spot features a small, deep lake where non-motorized boats are allowed, but they must be carried about 100 yards to the lake. The campsites are separate and scattered around the shore. At the north end of the lake, an 8.5-mile loop trail passes a number of lakes in the Rock Lakes Basin, all of which support populations of rainbow and brook trout. If you don't want to make the whole trip in a day, you can camp overnight at Serene Lake. See a U.S. Forest Service map for information.

RV sites, facilities: There are nine sites for tents or small RVs up to 16 feet long. Picnic tables and fire grills are provided. Vault toilets are available. There is no drinking water. Leashed pets are permitted.

Reservations, fees: Reservations are not accepted. Sites are $14 per night, $7 per night per additional vehicle. Open mid-June–late September, weather permitting.

Directions: From Portland, drive south on U.S. 205 to the junction with Highway 224/Estacada. Take the exit and turn left onto Highway 224, heading south. Drive approximately 13 miles to Estacada. Continue south on Highway 224 and drive 27 miles to Forest Road 57. Turn left (east) and drive 7.5 miles to Forest Road 58. Turn left (north) and drive three miles to Forest Road 5830. Turn left (northwest) and drive 5.5 miles to the campground on the left.

Contact: Mount Hood National Forest, Clackamas River Ranger District, 503/630-6861, fax 503/630-2299, www.fs.fed.us.

50 CLEAR LAKE

Scenic rating: 4

near the Pacific Crest Trail in Mount Hood National Forest

Map grid B1

This campground is located along the shore of Clear Lake, a spot favored by anglers, swimmers, and windsurfers, but as a reservoir, it is subject to water-level fluctuations. The boating speed limit is 10 mph. This wooded camp features shady sites and is set at 3,600 feet elevation. The camp sometimes gets noisy from the revels of the party set. If you want quiet, this spot is probably not for you. A nearby trail heads north from the lake and provides access to the Pacific Crest Trail and Frog Lake, both good recreation options.

RV sites, facilities: There are 28 sites for tents or RVs up to 30 feet long and one lookout cabin. Picnic tables and fire grills are provided. Drinking water, garbage bins, firewood, and vault toilets are available. Some facilities are wheelchair accessible. Boat-launching facilities are nearby. Leashed pets are permitted.

Reservations, fees: Reservations are accepted at 877/444-6777 or www.recreation.gov ($10 reservation fee). Sites are $16–18 per night, $8–9 per night per additional vehicle. The lookout cabin is $30 per night. Open mid-May–late September, weather permitting.

Directions: From Portland, drive east on U.S. 26 for 57 miles to the junction with Highway 35 (two miles past Government Camp). Bear right (southeast) on U.S. 26 and drive nine miles to Forest Road 2630. Turn right (south) and drive one mile to the campground on the right.

Contact: Mount Hood National Forest, Hood River Ranger District, 541/352-6002, fax 541/352-7365, www.fs.fed.us.

51 WHITE RIVER STATION

Scenic rating: 9

on the White River in Mount Hood National Forest
Map grid B1

This tiny campground is set along the White River at an elevation of 3,000 feet. It is on Old Barlow Road, an original wagon trail used by early settlers. One of several small, secluded camps in the area, White River Station is quiet and private, but with poor fishing prospects.

RV sites, facilities: There are five sites for tents or RVs up to 32 feet long. Picnic tables and fire grills are provided. Vault toilets are available. There is no drinking water, and garbage must be packed out. Leashed pets are permitted.

Reservations, fees: Reservations are not accepted. Sites are $10 per night, $5 per night per additional vehicle. Open May–September, weather permitting.

Directions: From Portland, drive east on U.S. 26 for 57 miles to the junction with Highway 35 (two miles past Government Camp). Stay on U.S. 26 and continue 12 miles to Forest Road 43. Turn left and drive five miles to Forest Road 3530. Turn right and drive approximately 1.5 miles to the campground on the left. (White River is less than one mile away from Barlow Creek.)

Contact: Mount Hood National Forest, Barlow Ranger District, 541/467-2291, fax 541/467-2271, www.fs.fed.us.

52 LAKE HARRIET

Scenic rating: 5

on Lake Harriet in Mount Hood National Forest
Map grid B1

Formed by a dam on the Oak Grove Fork of the Clackamas River, this little lake is a popular spot during the summer. Rowboats and boats with small motors are permitted, but only non-motorized boats are encouraged. The lake is stocked regularly and can provide good fishing for a variety of trout, including brook, brown, cutthroat, and rainbow. Anglers often stand shoulder to shoulder in summer.

RV sites, facilities: There are 11 sites for tents or RVs up to 40 feet long. Picnic tables and fire grills are provided. Drinking water and vault toilets are available. Garbage service is provided in the summer. A fishing pier and boat-launching facilities are on the lake. Some facilities are wheelchair accessible. Leashed pets are permitted.

Reservations, fees: Reservations are accepted at 877/444-6777 or www.recreation.gov ($10 reservation fee). Sites are $16 per night, $8 per night per additional vehicle. Open year-round, weather permitting, with limited winter services.

Directions: From Portland, drive south on U.S. 205 to the junction with Highway 224/Estacada. Take the exit and turn left onto Highway 224, heading south. Drive approximately 13 miles to Estacada. Continue south on Highway 224 and drive 27 miles to Forest Road 57. Turn east and drive 7.5 miles to Forest Road 4630. Turn left and drive two miles to the campground on the left.

Contact: Mount Hood National Forest, Clackamas River Ranger District, 503/630-6861, fax 503/630-2299, www.fs.fed.us.

53 GONE CREEK

Scenic rating: 8

on Timothy Lake in Mount Hood National Forest
Map grid B1

This campground, set along the south shore of Timothy Lake at 3,200 feet elevation, is one of five camps at the lake. Timothy Lake provides good fishing for brook trout, cutthroat trout, kokanee salmon, and rainbow trout. Boats with motors are allowed, but a 10-mph speed limit keeps it quiet. Several trails in the area—including the Pacific Crest Trail—provide access to a number of small mountain lakes.

RV sites, facilities: There are 49 sites for tents or RVs up to 45 feet long. Picnic tables and fire grills are provided. Drinking water, garbage service, vault toilets, and firewood are available. A boat ramp is nearby. Leashed pets are permitted.

OREGON

Reservations, fees: Reservations are accepted at 877/444-6777 or www.recreation.gov ($10 reservation fee). Sites are $17–18 per night, $8–9 per night per additional vehicle. Open mid-May–early September, weather permitting.

Directions: From Portland, drive on U.S. 26 for 55 miles (just past the town of Government Camp) to the junction with Highway 35. Bear southeast, staying on U.S. 26, and drive 15 miles to Forest Road 42 (Skyline Road). Turn right and drive eight miles to Forest Road 57. Turn right and drive one mile west to the campground on the right.

Contact: Mount Hood National Forest, Zigzag Ranger District, 503/622-3191, fax 503/622-5622, www.fs.fed.us.

54 OAK FORK

Scenic rating: 8

on Timothy Lake in Mount Hood National Forest
Map grid B1

Heavy timber and bear grass surround this forested camp along the south shore of Timothy Lake, where fishing is good for brook trout, cutthroat trout, kokanee salmon, and rainbow trout. Boats with motors are allowed, but a 10-mph speed limit is enforced. Oak Fork is located just east of Hoodview and Gone Creek campgrounds, at an elevation of 3,200 feet. Several area trails—including the Pacific Crest—provide access to various small mountain lakes.

RV sites, facilities: There are 46 sites for tents or RVs up to 45 feet long. Picnic tables and fire grills are provided. Drinking water, firewood, and vault toilets are available. A boat ramp and launching facilities are nearby; the speed limit on the lake is 10 mph. Leashed pets are permitted.

Reservations, fees: Reservations are accepted at 877/444-6777 or www.recreation.gov ($10 reservation fee). Sites are $17–18 per night, $8–9 per night per additional vehicle. Open May–early October, weather permitting.

Directions: From Portland, turn east on U.S.

26 and drive 57 miles (just past the town of Government Camp) to the junction with Highway 35. Bear southeast, staying on U.S. 26, and drive 15 miles to Forest Road 42 (Skyline Road). Turn right and drive eight miles to Forest Road 57. Turn right and drive three miles to the camp on the right.

Contact: Mount Hood National Forest, Zigzag Ranger District, 503/622-3191, fax 503/622-5622, www.fs.fed.us.

55 PINE POINT

Scenic rating: 8

on Timothy Lake in Mount Hood National Forest
Map grid B1

One of five camps on Timothy Lake, Pine Point spot sits at an elevation of 3,400 feet on the southwest shore. This camp has lake access and more open vegetation than the other Timothy Lake campgrounds. There's good fishing for brook trout, cutthroat trout, kokanee salmon, and rainbow trout, and a 10-mph speed limit keeps it pleasant for everyone. The trail that leads around the lake and to the Pacific Crest Trail passes along this campground.

RV sites, facilities: There are 25 sites for tents or RVs up to 45 feet long, including 12 single sites, eight double sites, and five group sites for up to 25 people each. Picnic tables, garbage service, and fire grills are provided. Drinking water and vault toilets are available. A boat ramp, launching facilities, and fishing pier are nearby; the speed limit on the lake is 10 mph. Leashed pets are permitted.

Reservations, fees: Reservations are accepted at 877/444-6777 or www.recreation.gov ($10 reservation fee). Single sites are $17 per night, $34 per night for a double site, and $8–9 per night per additional vehicle. Group sites are $50 per night. Open late May–mid-September, weather permitting.

Directions: From Portland, turn east on U.S. 26 and drive 57 miles (just past the town of Government Camp) to the junction with Highway 35. Bear southeast, staying on U.S. 26, and drive 15 miles to Forest Road 42 (Skyline Road). Turn right and drive eight miles to Forest Road 57. Turn right and drive four miles to the park on the right.

Contact: Mount Hood National Forest, Zigzag Ranger District, 503/622-3191, fax 503/622-5622, www.fs.fed.us.

56 HOODVIEW

Scenic rating: 9

Map grid B1

Here's another camp along the south shore of Timothy Lake; this one is set at 3,200 feet elevation. Timothy Lake provides good fishing for brook trout, cutthroat trout, kokanee salmon, and rainbow trout. Motorized boats are allowed, and the speed limit is 10 mph. A trail out of camp branches south for a few miles and, if followed to the east, eventually leads to the Pacific Crest Trail.

RV sites, facilities: There are 41 sites for tents or RVs up to 45 feet long. Picnic tables and fire grills are provided. Vault toilets, drinking water, garbage service, and firewood are available. A boat ramp is nearby. Leashed pets are permitted.

Reservations, fees: Reservations are accepted at 877/444-6777 or www.recreation.gov ($10 reservation fee). Sites are $17–18 per night, $8–9 per night per additional vehicle. Open mid-May–mid-September, weather permitting.

Directions: From Portland, turn east on U.S. 26 and drive 57 miles (just past the town of Government Camp) to the junction with Highway 35. Bear southeast, staying on U.S. 26, and drive 15 miles to Forest Road 42 (Skyline Road). Turn right and drive eight miles to Forest Road 57. Turn right and drive three miles to the campground on the right.

Contact: Mount Hood National Forest, Zigzag Ranger District, 503/622-3191, fax 503/622-5622, www.fs.fed.us.

57 LITTLE CRATER LAKE

Scenic rating: 7

Map grid B1

Little Crater campground (3,200 feet elevation) nestles against Crater Creek and scenic Little Crater Lake. This camp is popular with hunters in the fall. Both the drinking water and the lake water are spring fed, and the water is numbingly cold. The Pacific Crest Trail is located near camp, providing hiking trail access. Fishing is poor at Little Crater Lake. Little Timothy Lake lies about 10 miles away; note the 10-mph speed limit for boats. Bring your mosquito repellent—you'll need it.

RV sites, facilities: There are 16 sites for tents or RVs up to 35 feet long. Picnic tables, garbage bins, and fire grills are provided. Vault toilets, firewood, and drinking water are available. Leashed pets are permitted.

Reservations, fees: Reservations are accepted at 877/444-6777 or www.recreation.gov ($10 reservation fee). Sites are $16 per night, $8 per night per additional vehicle. Open May–mid-September, weather permitting.

Directions: From Portland, drive east on U.S. 26 for 57 miles to the junction with Highway 35 (two miles past Government Camp). Bear right (southeast), staying on U.S. 26, and drive 15 miles to Forest Road 42 (Skyline Road). Turn right and drive about six miles to Forest Road 58. Turn right and drive about 2.5 miles to the campground on the left.

Contact: Mount Hood National Forest, Zigzag Ranger District, 503/622-3191, fax 503/622-5622, www.fs.fed.us.

58 CLEAR CREEK CROSSING

Scenic rating: 7

Map grid B1

This secluded, little-known spot hugs the banks of Clear Creek at an elevation of 3,600 feet. Clear Creek Trail, a very pretty walk, begins at the campground. Fishing and hiking are two recreation options here.

RV sites, facilities: There are seven sites for tents or RVs up to 16 feet long. Picnic tables and fire grills are provided. Vault toilets are available. There is no drinking water, and garbage must be packed out. Leashed pets are permitted.

Reservations, fees: Reservations are not accepted. Sites are $10 per night. Open May–September, weather permitting.

Directions: From Portland, drive east on U.S. 26 for 55 miles to Government Camp. Continue three miles to a junction and bear right, staying on U.S. 26, and drive south for 12 miles to Highway 216. Turn left (east) on Highway 216 and drive two miles to Forest Road 2130. Turn left (north) on Forest Road 2130 and drive three miles to the campground.

Contact: Mount Hood National Forest, Barlow Ranger District, 541/467-2291, fax 541/467-2271, www.fs.fed.us.

59 BEAR SPRINGS

Scenic rating: 6

on Indian Creek in Mount Hood National Forest

Map grid B1

This campground is set along the banks of Indian Creek on the border of the Warm Springs Indian Reservation and features both secluded and open sites set in old-growth forest. The elevation is 3,000 feet.

RV sites, facilities: There are 21 sites for tents or RVs up to 32 feet long. Picnic tables and fire grills are provided. Drinking water, garbage bins, vault toilets, and firewood are available. Leashed pets are permitted.

Reservations, fees: Reservations are not accepted. Sites are $12 per night and $6 per night for each additional vehicle. Open June–September, weather permitting.

Directions: From Portland, drive east on U.S. 26 for 55 miles to Government Camp. Continue three miles to a junction and bear right,

staying on U.S. 26, and drive south for 12 miles to Highway 216. Turn left (east) on Highway 216 and drive four miles to Reservation Road. Turn right (east) on Reservation Road and look for the campground on the right.

Contact: Mount Hood National Forest, Barlow Ranger District, 541/467-2291, fax 541/467-2271, www.fs.fed.us.

60 McCUBBINS GULCH

Scenic rating: 5

in Mount Hood National Forest

Map grid B1

This small, primitive camp sits alongside a small creek at 3,000 feet in elevation and offers decent fishing and OHV (off-highway vehicle) recreation. A 40-mile network of OHV trails runs through the surrounding forest, with access right from camp. So, though out of the way, this camp gets heavy use; claim a spot early in the day. To the south is the Warm Springs Indian Reservation; do not trespass, as large fines are assessed to those prosecuted. Bear Springs provides a nearby camping alternative.

RV sites, facilities: There are 15 sites for tents and RVs up to 25 feet long. Picnic tables and fire grills are provided. Vault toilets are available. There is no drinking water, and garbage must be packed out. Leashed pets are permitted.

Reservations, fees: Reservations are not accepted. Sites are $10 per night. Open May–September, weather permitting.

Directions: From Portland, drive east on U.S. 26 for 55 miles to Government Camp. Continue three miles to a junction and bear right, staying on U.S. 26, and drive south for 12 miles to Highway 216. Turn left (east) on Highway 216 and drive six miles to Forest Road 2110. Take a sharp left and drive 1.5 miles to the campground entrance on the right.

Contact: Mount Hood National Forest, Barlow Ranger District, 541/467-2291, fax 541/467-2271, www.fs.fed.us.

61 SHELLROCK CREEK

Scenic rating: 6

on Shellrock Creek in Mount Hood National Forest

Map grid B1

This quiet little campground (2,200 feet elevation) occupies a nice spot on Shellrock Creek and has been used primarily as an overflow area for Lake Harriet campground. Small trout can be caught here, but remember that on the Clackamas River it's catch-and-release only. Obtain a U.S. Forest Service map for details on the backcountry roads and trails.

RV sites, facilities: There are eight sites for tents or RVs up to 16 feet long. Picnic tables and fire grills are provided. Vault toilets are available. There is no drinking water and garbage must be packed out. Leashed pets are permitted.

Note: In 2010, the Forest Service plans some changes to several campgrounds in the Estacada Ranger District.

Reservations, fees: Reservations are not accepted. Sites are $14 per night, $7 per night per additional vehicle. Open year-round, with limited winter services.

Directions: From Portland, drive south on U.S. 205 to the junction with Highway 24. Take the Highway 224/Estacada exit and turn left (south) onto Highway 224. Drive approximately 13 miles to Estacada. Continue south on Highway 224 for 27 miles in national forest (the road becomes Forest Road 46) to Forest Road 57. Turn left (east) and drive 7.5 miles to Forest Road 58. Turn left and drive north one mile to the campground on the left.

Contact: Mount Hood National Forest, Clackamas River Ranger District, Estacada Ranger Station, 503/630-6861, fax 503/630-2299, www.fs.fed.us.

62 JOE GRAHAM HORSE CAMP

Scenic rating: 8

near Clackamas Lake in
Mount Hood National Forest

Map grid B1

Named for a forest ranger, this campground sits at 3,250 feet elevation among majestic Douglas fir and hemlock, just north of tiny Clackamas Lake. It's one of two campgrounds in the area that allow horses. Timothy Lake (the setting for the Gone Creek, Hoodview, Meditation Point, Oak Fork, and Pine Point camps) provides a nearby alternative to the northwest. The Pacific Crest Trail is just east of camp.

RV sites, facilities: There are 15 sites for tents, horse trailers, or RVs up to 45 feet long; 11 have corrals, and two have hitching rails. Picnic tables, hitching posts, garbage service, and fire grills are provided. Drinking water and vault toilets are available. Leashed pets are permitted.

Reservations, fees: Reservations are accepted at 877/444-6777 or www.recreation.gov ($10 reservation fee). Sites are $17 per night, $8.50 per night per additional vehicle. Open mid-May–mid-October, weather permitting.

Directions: From Portland, turn east on U.S. 26 and drive 57 miles (just past the town of Government Camp) to the junction with Highway 35. Bear right, continuing southeast on U.S. 26, and drive 15 miles to Forest Road 42 (Skyline Road). Turn right and drive eight miles to the campground on the left.

Contact: Mount Hood National Forest, Zigzag Ranger District, 503/622-3191, fax 503/622-5622, www.fs.fed.us.

63 CLACKAMAS LAKE

Scenic rating: 7

near the Clackamas River in
Mount Hood National Forest

Map grid B1

This camp, set at 3,400 feet elevation, is a good place to go to escape the hordes of people at the

OREGON

lakeside sites in neighboring camps. The Pacific Crest Trail passes nearby, and Timothy Lake requires little more than a one-mile hike from camp. The Clackamas Lake Historic Ranger Station, a visitors center, is worth a visit and is still using the old, hand crank–style phones once used in lookout towers and guard stations. This is a popular spot for campers with horses, although the facilities could use some updating and repairs.

RV sites, facilities: There are 46 sites for tents, trailers, horse trailers, or RVs up to 45 feet long. Some sites have hitch rails, and horses are permitted at the first 19 sites. Drinking water, garbage service, fire grills, and picnic tables are provided. Vault toilets are available. Boat docks and launching facilities are nearby at Timothy Lake, but only non-motorized boats are allowed. Leashed pets are permitted.

Reservations, fees: Reservations are accepted at 877/444-6777 or www.recreation.gov ($10 reservation fee). Sites are $16 per night, $8 per night per additional vehicle. Open May–mid-September, weather permitting.

Directions: From Portland, turn east on U.S. 26 and drive 57 miles (just past the town of Government Camp) to the junction with Highway 35. Bear southeast, staying on U.S. 26, and drive 15 miles to Forest Road 42 (Skyline Road). Turn right and drive eight miles to Forest Road 57. Continue 500 feet (on Forest Road 42) past the Clackamas Lake Historic Ranger Station to Forest Road 4270. Turn left and drive 0.5 mile to the campground on the left.

Contact: Mount Hood National Forest, Zigzag Ranger District, 503/622-3191, fax 503/622-5622, www.fs.fed.us.

64 DESCHUTES RIVER STATE RECREATION AREA

Scenic rating: 7

on the Deschutes River

Map grid C1   **BEST** (

This tree-shaded park along the Deschutes River in the Deschutes Canyon offers bicycling

and hiking trails and good steelhead fishing in season. The river-level Atiyeh Deschutes River Trail is a favorite jaunt for hikers. A small day-use state park called Heritage Landing, which has a boat ramp and restroom facilities, is located across the river. The U.S. Army Corps of Engineers offers a free train ride and tour of the dam at The Dalles during the summer. Good rafting is a bonus here. For 25 miles upstream, the river is mostly inaccessible by car. Many anglers launch boats here and then go upstream to steelhead fishing grounds. Note that boat fishing is not allowed here; you must wade into the river or fish from shore.

RV sites, facilities: There are 34 sites with partial hookups for tents or RVs up to 50 feet, 25 primitive sites for tents or self-contained RVs up to 30 feet, and four group areas for RVs and tents, which can hold up to 25 people and five RVs each. Picnic tables and fire grills are provided, but campfires are prohibited July 1–September 30. Drinking water, garbage bins, and flush toilets are available. Leashed pets are permitted.

Reservations, fees: Reservations are accepted at 800/452-5687 or www.oregonstateparks.org ($8 reservation fee). Sites with partial-hookup are $12–20 per night, primitive sites are $5–9 per night, $5 per night per additional vehicle. Group sites are $40–71 per night. Some credit cards are accepted. Open year-round, with limited services November–March.

Directions: From Portland, turn east on I-84 and drive about 90 miles to The Dalles. Continue east on I-84 for 12 miles to Exit 97/Deschutes State Recreation Area, turn right, and drive 50 feet to Biggs-Rufus Highway. Turn left and drive about three miles, cross the Deschutes River, and turn right to the campground entrance.

Contact: Deschutes River State Recreation Area, 541/739-2322 or 800/452-5687, www.oregonstateparks.org.

65 LEPAGE PARK

Scenic rating: 6

on the John Day River
Map grid C1

Half of the campsites are adjacent to the John Day River and the other half are on the opposite side of the road at this partially shaded campground. The John Day River feeds into the Columbia just 0.12 mile north of the campground. Rattlesnakes are occasionally seen in the area but are not abundant. Anglers come for the smallmouth bass and catfish during the summer. The day-use area has a swimming beach, lawn, boat launch, and boat docks. There are several other campgrounds nearby.

RV sites, facilities: There is a grassy area with 20 walk-in sites for tents and 22 sites with partial hookups for tents or RVs up to 56 feet long; some sites are pull-through. Picnic tables and fire pits are provided. Drinking water, restrooms with flush toilets and showers, and pit toilets are available. A boat ramp, docks, dump station, fish-cleaning station, and garbage containers are also available. Food, gasoline, and coin laundry are available five miles away in the town of Rufus. Leashed pets are permitted.

Reservations, fees: Reservations are accepted at 877/444-6777 or www.recreation.gov ($10 reservation fee). RV sites are $18–20 per night, and tent sites are $12–14 per night. Some credit cards are accepted. Open April–October.

Directions: From Portland on I-84, drive east 120 miles (30 miles past The Dalles) to Exit 114, the John Day River Recreation Area. The campground is just off I-84.

Contact: Army Corps of Engineers, Portland District, 503/808-5150, fax 503/808-4515; LePage Park, 541/739-2713.

66 BEAVERTAIL

Scenic rating: 6

on the Deschutes River
Map grid C1

This isolated campground is set at an elevation of 2,900 feet along the banks of the Deschutes River, one of the classic steelhead streams in the Pacific Northwest. The camp provides fishing and rafting options. The open landscape affords canyon views. This is my favorite put-in spot for a drift boat for fishing float trips on the Deschutes. I've made the trip from Beavertail to the mouth of the Deschutes, ideal in four days, camping at BLM boat-in sites along the river and fly-fishing for steelhead. A boating pass is required to float the river. There are 12 other BLM campgrounds along upper and lower Deschutes River Road. The hardest part is getting used to the freight trains that rumble through the canyon at night.

RV sites, facilities: There are 17 sites for tents or RVs up to 30 feet long and two group sites for up to 16 people. Picnic tables, garbage bins, and fire grills are provided. No campfires are allowed June 1–October 15. Drinking water and vault toilets are available. Boat-launching facilities are nearby. Some facilities are wheelchair accessible. Leashed pets are permitted.

Reservations, fees: Reservations are not accepted. Sites are $8–12 per night, with a 14-day stay limit. Group sites are $25–35 per night. Open year-round.

Directions: From Portland, drive east on U.S. 84 to The Dalles and Highway 197. Turn south and drive to Maupin. Continue through Maupin, cross the bridge, and within a mile look for Deschutes River Road on your left. Turn left on Deschutes River Road and drive 21 miles northeast to the campground.

Contact: Bureau of Land Management, Prineville District, 541/416-6700, fax 541/416-6798, www.blm.gov.

OREGON

67 SHADY COVE

Scenic rating: 7

on the Little North Santiam River in
Willamette National Forest

Map grid A2

Shady Cove campground is on the Little
North Santiam River in the recently designated Opal Creek Scenic Recreation Area. The
Little North Santiam Trail runs adjacent to the
campground.

RV sites, facilities: There are 12 sites for tents
or RVs up to 16 feet long. Picnic tables, garbage
service (summer only), fire grills, and vault
toilets are available. There is no drinking water.
Leashed pets are permitted.

Reservations, fees: Reservations are not accepted. Sites are $8–10 per night, $5 per night per
additional vehicle. Open year-round, weather
permitting.

Directions: From Salem on I-5, take Exit 253
to Highway 22. Turn east and drive 23 miles
to Mehama and North Fork Road (Marion
County Road). Turn left and drive 17 miles
northeast to the fork. Bear right on Forest
Road 2207 and continue for two miles to the
campground on the right.

Contact: Willamette National Forest, Detroit
Ranger District, 503/854-3366, fax 503/854-
4239, www.fs.fed.us.

68 HUMBUG

Scenic rating: 9

on the Breitenbush River in
Willamette National Forest

Map grid A2

Fishing and hiking are popular at this campground along the banks of the Breitenbush
River, about four miles from where it empties
into Detroit Lake. The lake offers many other
recreation opportunities. The Humbug Flat
Trailhead is behind Sites 9 and 10, and a scenic
stroll through an old-growth forest follows the
Breitenbush River. The rhododendrons put on
a spectacular show May–July.

RV sites, facilities: There are 22 sites for tents
or RVs up to 30 feet long. Picnic tables and fire
grills are provided. Garbage service (summer
only), drinking water, firewood, and vault toilets are available. Leashed pets are permitted.

Reservations, fees: Reservations are not accepted. Sites are $12 per night, $5 per night per
additional vehicle. Open year-round, weather
permitting, with limited winter facilities.

Directions: From Salem on I-5, take Exit 253,
turn east on Highway 22, and drive 52 miles
to Detroit. Turn left on Forest Road 46/Breit-
enbush Road and drive five miles northeast to
the campground on the right.

Contact: Willamette National Forest, Detroit
Ranger District, 503/854-3366, fax 503/854-
4239, www.fs.fed.us.

69 DETROIT LAKE STATE RECREATION AREA

Scenic rating: 7

on Detroit Lake

Map grid A2

This campground is set at 1,600 feet elevation
along the shore of Detroit Lake, which is 400
feet deep, nine miles long, and has more than
32 miles of shoreline. The park offers a fishing
dock and a moorage area, and a boat ramp and
bathhouse are available nearby at the Mongold
Day Use Area. The heavily stocked lake is
crowded on the opening day of trout season
in late April.

RV sites, facilities: There are 178 sites with
full or partial hookups for RVs up to 60 feet
long, 133 tent sites, and 82 boat slips. Drinking water, garbage bins, fire grills, and picnic
tables are provided. Firewood and restrooms
with flush toilets and showers are available.
Recreation facilities include two playgrounds,
swimming areas, horseshoe pits, basketball and
volleyball courts, an amphitheater, a gift shop,
and a visitors center. A camp host is on-site.
Two boat docks and launching facilities are
nearby. Some facilities are wheelchair accessible.
Leashed pets are permitted.

OREGON

Reservations, fees: Reservations are accepted at 800/452-5687 or www.oregonstateparks.org ($8 reservation fee). RV sites are $16–24 per night, tent sites are $12–19 per night, $5 per night per additional vehicle. Boating moorage is $7 per night. Some credit cards are accepted. Open mid-March–September, weather permitting.

Directions: From Salem, drive east on Highway 22 for 50 miles to the park entrance on the right (located two miles west of Detroit).

Contact: Detroit Lake State Recreation Area, 503/854-3406 or 503/854-3346, www.oregonstateparks.org.

70 SOUTHSHORE

Scenic rating: 9

on Detroit Lake in Willamette National Forest

Map grid A2

This popular camp hugs the south shore of Detroit Lake, where fishing, swimming, and waterskiing are some of the recreation options. The Stahlman Point Trailhead is about half a mile from camp. There's a day-use area for picnicking and swimming. The views of the lake and surrounding mountains are outstanding.

RV sites, facilities: There are eight walk-in tent sites and 22 sites for tents or RVs up to 30 feet long. Fire grills, garbage service, and picnic tables are provided. Vault toilets, drinking water, and firewood are available. Boat-launching facilities are nearby at a day-use area. Some facilities are wheelchair accessible. Leashed pets are permitted.

Reservations, fees: Reservations are not accepted. Sites are $16 for a single site, $32 for double site, and $5 per night per additional vehicle. Open May–late September, with a gate preventing access during the off-season.

Directions: From Salem, drive east on Highway 22 for 52 miles to Detroit. Continue southeast on Highway 22 for 2.5 miles to Forest Road 10 (Blowout Road). Turn right and drive four miles to the campground on the right.

Contact: Willamette National Forest, Detroit

Ranger District, 503/854-3366, fax 503/854-4239, www.fs.fed.us.

71 COVE CREEK

Scenic rating: 10

on Detroit Lake in Willamette National Forest

Map grid A2

Cove Creek is a popular campground, and it gets high use in the summer. Situated in a forest, the campground is located on the south side of the lake, about one mile from both Hoover and Southshore campgrounds. Water sports are popular, and both waterskiing and personal watercraft are allowed.

RV sites, facilities: There are 63 sites for tents or RVs of any length and one group site for up to 70 people. Picnic tables and fire rings are provided. Drinking water, restrooms with flush toilets and coin showers, garbage bins, firewood, and a boat ramp are available. Some facilities are wheelchair accessible. Leashed pets are permitted.

Reservations, fees: Reservations are accepted only for the group site at 877/444-6777 or www.recreation.gov ($10 reservation fee). Single sites are $18 per night, double sites are $36 per night, $5 per night per additional vehicle. Group sites are $150 per night and require a two-night minimum stay on weekends. Open May–September, with a gate preventing access in the off-season.

Directions: From Salem, drive east on Highway 22 for 52 miles to Detroit. Continue southeast on Highway 22 for 2.5 miles to Forest Road 10 (Blowout Road). Turn right and drive three miles to the campground on the right.

Contact: Willamette National Forest, Detroit Ranger District, 503/854-3366, fax 503/854-4239, www.fs.fed.us; park information, 503/854-3251.

OREGON

OREGON

HOOVER

Scenic rating: 9

on Detroit Lake in Willamette National Forest

Map grid A2

Hoover campground is located along the eastern arm of Detroit Lake at an elevation of 1,600 feet, near the mouth of the Santiam River. The camp features a wheelchair-accessible fishing area and interpretive trail; fishing, swimming, and waterskiing are some of the recreation options. You're likely to see osprey fishing during the day, a truly special sight.

RV sites, facilities: There are 37 sites for tents or RVs up to 30 feet long. Picnic tables, garbage service, and fire grills are provided. Flush toilets and drinking water are available. Boat docks and launching facilities are nearby. Some facilities are wheelchair accessible. Leashed pets are permitted.

Reservations, fees: Reservations are not accepted. Single sites are $16 per night, double sites are $32 per night, $5 per night per additional vehicle. Open mid-May–mid-September; a gate prevents access in the off-season.

Directions: From Salem, drive east on Highway 22 for 52 miles to Detroit. Continue southeast on Highway 22 for 2.5 miles to Forest Road 10 (Blowout Road). Turn right and drive one mile to the campground on the right.

Contact: Willamette National Forest, Detroit Ranger District, 503/854-3366, fax 503/854-4239, www.fs.fed.us.

73 HOOVER GROUP CAMP

Scenic rating: 9

on Detroit Lake in Willamette National Forest

Map grid A2   BEST (

This is a perfect spot for a family reunion or club trip. Detroit Lake offers a myriad of activities, including boating, fishing, hiking, and swimming, just to name a few. The campground has nice, open sites and direct access to the lake.

RV sites, facilities: There is one group camp

for tents or RVs up to 30 feet long, for up to 70 people and 20 vehicles. Drinking water, fire rings, and picnic tables are provided. Flush toilets, garbage bins, firewood, and a group picnic shelter are available. Boat docks, launching facilities, and rentals are nearby. Some facilities are wheelchair accessible. Leashed pets are permitted.

Reservations, fees: Reservations are accepted at 877/444-6777 or www.recreation.gov ($10 reservation fee). The site is $150 per night, with a two-night minimum for weekend reservations. Open mid-April–late September; a gate prevents access during the off-season.

Directions: From Salem, drive east on Highway 22 for 52 miles to Detroit. Continue southeast on Highway 22 for 2.5 miles to Forest Road 10 (Blowout Road). Turn right and drive 0.5 mile to the campground on the right.

Contact: Willamette National Forest, Detroit Ranger District, 503/854-3366, fax 503/854-4239, www.fs.fed.us; park information, 503/854-3251.

74 CLEATER BEND

Scenic rating: 8

near the Breitenbush River in Willamette National Forest

Map grid B2

Creek views and pretty, shaded sites are the highlights of Cleater Bend, situated on the banks of the Breitenbush River at 2,200 feet elevation. This camp is 0.25 mile from Breitenbush and is a good option if that campground is full. Nearby recreation options include fishing access along the Breitenbush River, the South Breitenbush Gorge National Recreation Trail (three miles away), and Breitenbush Hot Springs (just over a mile away).

RV sites, facilities: There are nine sites for tents or RVs up to 24 feet long. Picnic tables and fire grills are provided. Garbage service, drinking water, vault toilets, and firewood are available. Some facilities are wheelchair accessible. Leashed pets are permitted.

Reservations, fees: Reservations are not accepted. Sites are $12 per night, $5 per night per additional vehicle. Open May–September, with a gate preventing access during the off-season.

Directions: From Salem on I-5, take Exit 253, turn east on Highway 22, and drive 50 miles to Detroit. Turn left on Forest Road 46/Breitenbush Road and drive nine miles to the campground on the right.

Contact: Willamette National Forest, Detroit Ranger District, 503/854-3366, fax 503/854-4239, www.fs.fed.us.

75 BREITENBUSH

Scenic rating: 8

on the Breitenbush River in
Willamette National Forest

Map grid B2

There is fishing access at this campground along the Breitenbush River. Nearby recreation options include the South Breitenbush Gorge National Recreation Trail, three miles away, and Breitenbush Hot Springs, just over a mile away. If this campground is crowded, try nearby Cleater Bend.

RV sites, facilities: There are 30 sites for tents or RVs up to 24 feet long (longer trailers may be difficult to park and turn). Picnic tables and fire grills are provided. Drinking water, vault toilets, garbage service, and firewood are available. Some facilities are wheelchair accessible. Leashed pets are permitted.

Reservations, fees: Reservations are not accepted. Sites are $12 per night for a single site, $24 per night for a double site, and $5 per night per additional vehicle. Open May–September; a gate prevents access during the off-season.

Directions: From Salem on I-5, take Exit 253, turn east on Highway 22, and drive 50 miles to Detroit. Turn left (north) on Forest Road 46/Breitenbush Road and drive 10 miles to the campground on the right.

Contact: Willamette National Forest, Detroit Ranger District, 503/854-3366, fax 503/854-4239, www.fs.fed.us.

76 CAMP TEN

Scenic rating: 9

on Olallie Lake in Mount Hood National Forest

Map grid B2

Here's a camp along the shore of Olallie Lake, a popular area. Camp Ten sits at an elevation of 5,000 feet, on the lake's western shore in the midst of the Olallie Lake Scenic Area, which is home to a number of pristine mountain lakes and a network of hiking trails. (See a U.S. Forest Service map for trail locations.) Boats without motors—including canoes, kayaks, and rafts—are permitted on the lake.

RV sites, facilities: There are 10 sites for tents or RVs up to 16 feet long. Picnic tables, garbage service, and fire grills are provided. Vault toilets are available. There is no drinking water. Leashed pets are permitted.

Reservations, fees: Reservations are not accepted. Sites are $12 per night. Open July–October, weather permitting.

Directions: From Portland, drive south on U.S. 205 to the junction with Highway 24. Take the Highway 224/Estacada exit and turn left (south) onto Highway 224. Drive approximately 13 miles to Estacada. Continue south on Highway 224 and drive 27 miles in national forest (the road becomes Forest Road 46). Continue south on Forest Road 46 for 20 miles to Forest Road 4690. Turn left on Forest Road 4690 and drive southeast for 8.2 miles to Forest Road 4220. Turn right (south) and drive about six miles of rough road to the campground.

Contact: Mount Hood National Forest, Clackamas River Ranger District, 503/630-6861, fax 503/630-2299, www.fs.fed.us.

77 PAUL DENNIS

Scenic rating: 10

on Olallie Lake in Mount Hood National Forest

Map grid B2

This campground, set at an elevation of 5,000 feet, borders the north shore of Olallie Lake. From here, you can see the reflection of Mount

OREGON

Jefferson (10,497 feet). Boats with motors are not permitted on the lake. A trail from camp leads to Long Lake (just east of the border of the Warm Springs Indian Reservation), Monon Lake, and Nep-Te-Pa Lake. It's advisable to obtain a U.S. Forest Service map.

RV sites, facilities: There are 17 sites for tents or RVs up to 16 feet long (trailers not recommended) and three hike-in tent sites. Picnic tables, garbage service, and fire grills are provided. Pit toilets are available. There is no drinking water. A store and ice are nearby. Leashed pets are permitted.

Reservations, fees: Reservations are not accepted. Sites are $12 per night. Open July–October, weather permitting.

Directions: From Portland, drive south on U.S. 205 to the junction with Highway 24. Take the Highway 224/Estacada exit and turn left (south) onto Highway 224. Drive approximately 13 miles to Estacada. Continue south on Highway 224 and drive 27 miles in national forest (the road becomes Forest Road 46). Continue south on Forest Road 46 for 20 miles to Forest Road 4690. Turn left and drive southeast for 8.2 miles to Forest Road 4220. Turn right (south) and drive 6.2 miles to Forest Road 4220-170. Turn left and drive 0.12 mile to the campground.

Contact: Mount Hood National Forest, Clackamas River Ranger District, 503/630-6861, fax 503/630-2299, www.fs.fed.us.

78 PENINSULA

🥾 🎣 🛶 🐕 🚐 ⛺

Scenic rating: 10

on Olallie Lake in Mount Hood National Forest

Map grid B2

Peninsula, the largest of several campgrounds along Olallie Lake, is set at an elevation of 5,000 feet on the south shore. An amphitheater is located near the campground, and rangers present campfire programs during the summer. Nonmotorized boats are permitted on the lake, and nearby trails lead to a number of smaller

lakes in the area, such as Long Lake, Monon Lake, and Nep-Te-Pa Lake.

RV sites, facilities: There are 35 sites for tents or RVs up to 24 feet long and six walk-in tent sites. Picnic tables, garbage service, and fire grills are provided. Vault toilets are available. There is no drinking water. Leashed pets are permitted.

Reservations, fees: Reservations are not accepted. Sites are $12 per night, $6 per night per additional vehicle, and $6 per night for walk-in sites. Open July–October, weather permitting.

Directions: From Portland, drive south on U.S. 205 to the junction with Highway 24. Take the Highway 224/Estacada exit and turn left (south) onto Highway 224. Drive approximately 13 miles to Estacada. Continue south on Highway 224 and drive 27 miles in national forest (the road becomes Forest Road 46). Continue south on Forest Road 46 for 20 miles to Forest Road 4690. Turn left and drive southeast for 8.2 miles to Forest Road 4220. Turn right (south) and drive 6.5 miles of rough road to the campground on the left.

Contact: Mount Hood National Forest, Clackamas River Ranger District, 503/630-6861, fax 503/630-2299, www.fs.fed.us.

79 OLALLIE MEADOWS

🥾 🎣 🛶 🐕 🚐 ⛺

Scenic rating: 8

near Olallie Lake in Mount Hood National Forest

Map grid B2

Olallie Meadows is set at 4,500 feet elevation along a large and peaceful alpine meadow about three miles from Olallie Lake. Nonmotorized boats are allowed on Olallie Lake. The Pacific Crest Trail passes very close to the campground.

RV sites, facilities: There are seven sites for tents or RVs up to 16 feet long. Picnic tables, garbage service, and fire grills are provided. Vault toilets are available. There is no drinking water. Leashed pets are permitted.

Reservations, fees: Reservations are not accepted. Sites are $12 per night. Open July–October, weather permitting.

Directions: From Portland, drive south on U.S. 205 to the junction with Highway 24. Take the Highway 224/Estacada exit and turn left (south) onto Highway 224. Drive approximately 13 miles to Estacada. Continue south on Highway 224 and drive 27 miles in national forest (the road becomes Forest Road 46). Continue south on Forest Road 46 for 20 miles to Forest Road 4690. Turn left and drive southeast for 8.2 miles to Forest Road 4220. Turn right (south) and drive 1.5 miles to the campground on the left.

Contact: Mount Hood National Forest, Clackamas River Ranger District, 503/630-6861, fax 503/630-2299, www.fs.fed.us.

80 KAH-NEE-TA RESORT

Scenic rating: 7

on the Warm Springs Indian Reservation

Map grid B2

This resort features a stellar-rated, full-concept spa, with the bonus of a nearby casino. It is also the only public camp on the east side of the Warm Springs Indian Reservation; there are no other camps within 30 miles. The Warm Springs River runs nearby. Recreation options in the area include an 18-hole golf course, miniature golf, biking and hiking trails, a riding stable, and tennis courts.

RV sites, facilities: There are 55 pull-through sites with full hookups for RVs of any length. A motel and cottage are also available. Cable TV, restrooms with flush toilets and coin showers, propane gas, a dump station, concession stand, coin laundry, ice, a playground, a spa, mineral baths, and an Olympic-sized, spring-fed swimming pool with a 140-foot water slide are available. Some facilities are wheelchair accessible. Leashed pets are permitted, but some areas are restricted.

Reservations, fees: Reservations are accepted at 800/554-4786. Sites are $45 per night for three people. There is a two-night minimum on weekends, and a three-night minimum on holiday weekends. Some credit cards are accepted. Open year-round.

Directions: From Portland, turn east on U.S. 26 and drive about 105 miles to Warm Springs and Agency Hot Springs Road on the left. Turn left and drive 11 miles northeast to Kah-Nee-Ta and the resort on the right.

Contact: Kah-Nee-Ta Resort, 541/553-1112, http://kahneetaresort.com.

81 WHISPERING FALLS

Scenic rating: 10

on the North Santiam River near Detroit Lake in Willamette National Forest

Map grid B2

This popular campground sits on the banks of the North Santiam River, where you can fish. If the campsites at Detroit Lake are crowded, this camp provides a more secluded option, and it's only about a 10-minute drive from the lake. Ospreys sometimes nest near the campground.

RV sites, facilities: There are 16 sites for tents or RVs up to 30 feet long. Picnic tables, garbage service, and fire grills are provided. Drinking water and flush toilets are available. Bring your own firewood. Leashed pets are permitted.

Reservations, fees: Reservations are not accepted. Sites are $12 per night, $5 per night per additional vehicle. Open late April–mid-September; a gate prevents access in the off-season.

Directions: From Salem, drive east on Highway 22 for 50 miles to Detroit. Continue east on Highway 22 for eight miles to the campground on the right.

Contact: Willamette National Forest, Detroit Ranger District, 503/854-3366, fax 503/854-4239, www.fs.fed.us.

OREGON

82 RIVERSIDE

Scenic rating: 7

on the North Santiam River in
Willamette National Forest

Map grid B2

This campground is set at an elevation of 2,400 feet along the banks of the North Santiam River, where the fishing can be good. A point of interest, the Marion Forks Fish Hatchery and interpretive site lies just 2.5 miles south. Other day-trip options include the Mount Jefferson Wilderness, directly to the east in Willamette National Forest, and Minto Mountain Trail, three miles east.

RV sites, facilities: There are 37 sites for tents or RVs up to 24 feet long. Picnic tables and fire grills are provided. Drinking water and vault toilets are available. Leashed pets are permitted.

Reservations, fees: Reservations are not accepted. Sites are $12 per night, $5 per night per additional vehicle. Open late May–September; a gate prevents access during the off-season.

Directions: From Salem, drive east on Highway 22 for 50 miles to Detroit. Continue southeast on Highway 22 for 14 miles to the campground on the right.

Contact: Willamette National Forest, Detroit Ranger District, 503/854-3366, fax 503/854-4239, www.fs.fed.us.

83 MARION FORKS

Scenic rating: 8

on the Santiam River in Willamette National Forest

Map grid B2

Situated along Marion Creek at 2,500 feet in elevation, this campground is adjacent to the Marion Forks Fish Hatchery. A U.S. Forest Service guard station and a restaurant are across Highway 22. The area boasts some quality hiking trails; the nearest is Independence Rock Trail, 0.25 mile north of the campground.

RV sites, facilities: There are 15 sites for tents or RVs up to 24 feet long. Picnic tables, fire grills, and garbage containers are provided. Vault toilets are available. There is no drinking water. Leashed pets are permitted.

Reservations, fees: Reservations are not accepted. Sites are $10 per night, $5 per night per additional vehicle. Open year-round, weather permitting, with no winter services.

Directions: From Salem, drive east on Highway 22 for 50 miles to Detroit. Continue southeast on Highway 22 for 16 miles to the campground on the left.

Contact: Willamette National Forest, Detroit Ranger District, 503/854-3366, fax 503/854-4239, www.fs.fed.us.

84 BIG MEADOWS HORSE CAMP

Scenic rating: 10

near Mount Jefferson Wilderness in
Willamette National Forest

Map grid B2

Built by the U.S. Forest Service with the support of a horse club, this camp is used heavily by equestrians riding into the Big Meadows area and the adjacent Mount Jefferson Wilderness. If you're not a horse lover, you may want to stick with Riverside or Marion Forks.

RV sites, facilities: There are nine sites for tents or RVs up to 36 feet long. Picnic tables, garbage service, fire grills, and enclosed four-horse corrals are provided at each site. Drinking water, vault toilets, firewood, and stock water troughs are available. Some facilities are wheelchair accessible. Leashed pets are permitted.

Reservations, fees: Reservations are not accepted. Sites are $14 per night, $5 per night per additional vehicle. Open June–October, weather permitting.

Directions: From Salem, drive east on Highway 22 for 50 miles to Detroit. Continue southeast on Highway 22 for 27 miles to Big Meadows Road (Forest Road 2267). Turn left and drive one mile to Forest Road 2257. Turn left and drive 0.5 mile to the campground on the left.

Contact: Willamette National Forest, Detroit Ranger District, 503/854-3366, fax 503/854-4239, www.fs.fed.us.

85 SHEEP SPRINGS HORSE CAMP

Scenic rating: 7

near the Mount Jefferson Wilderness in Deschutes National Forest

Map grid B2

This well-shaded equestrian camp with privacy screening between sites is near the trailhead for the Metolius-Windigo Horse Trail, which heads northeast into the Mount Jefferson Wilderness and south to Black Butte. Contact the U.S. Forest Service for details and maps of the backcountry. The camp is set at an elevation of 3,200 feet.

RV sites, facilities: There are 11 sites for tents or RVs up to 45 feet long. Fire grills are provided. Drinking water, vault toilets, garbage bins, and corrals and box stalls for horses are available.

Reservations, fees: Reservations are accepted at 877/444-6777 or www.recreation.gov ($10 reservation fee). Sites are $14–16 per night, $8 per night per additional vehicle. Open early May–mid-September, weather permitting.

Directions: From Albany, drive east on U.S. 20 for 87 miles to the sign for Jack Lake (located one mile east of Suttle Lake) and Suttle-Sherman Road. Turn left on Forest Road 12 and drive eight miles to Forest Road 1260. Turn left and drive 1.5 miles to Forest Road 1260-200. Turn right and drive 1.5 miles to the campground on the right.

Contact: Deschutes National Forest, Sisters Ranger District, 541/549-7700, fax 541/549-7746; Hoodoo District, 541/822-3799, www.fs.fed.us.

86 JACK CREEK

Scenic rating: 5

near Mount Jefferson Wilderness in Deschutes National Forest

Map grid B2

A more primitive alternative to the other camps in the area, this campground sits along the banks of Jack Creek in an open setting among ponderosa pine. The elevation is 3,100 feet. To protect the bull trout habitat, no fishing is permitted here.

RV sites, facilities: There are 20 sites for tents or RVs up to 40 feet long. Picnic tables and fire grills are provided. Vault toilets and garbage bins are available. There is no drinking water. Leashed pets are permitted.

Reservations, fees: Reservations are not accepted. Sites are $12 per night, $6 per night per additional vehicle. Open mid-April–mid-October.

Directions: From Albany, drive east on U.S. 20 for 87 miles to the sign for Jack Lake (located one mile east of Suttle Lake) and Suttle-Sherman Road. Turn left on Forest Road 12 and drive five miles to Forest Road 1230. Turn left and drive 0.75 mile to Forest Road 1232. Turn left and drive 0.25 mile to the campground on the left.

Contact: Deschutes National Forest, Sisters Ranger District, 541/549-7700, fax 541/549-7746, www.fs.fed.us.

87 PELTON

Scenic rating: 8

on Lake Simtustus in Deschutes National Forest

Map grid B2

This campground claims 0.5 mile of shoreline along the north side of Lake Simtustus. Campsites here are shaded with juniper in an area of rolling hills and sagebrush. One section of the lake is accessible for water skis and personal watercraft. Simtustus is a trophy fishing lake for kokanee and brown, bull, and rainbow trout.

OREGON

Just north of the park is the Pelton Wildlife Overlook, where you can view a variety of waterfowl, such as great blue herons, ducks, geese, and shorebirds, as well as eagles and other raptors. Cove Palisades State Park, about 15 miles south, provides additional recreational opportunities.

RV sites, facilities: There are 69 sites, some with partial hookups, for tents or RVs up to 56 feet long, three group sites for up to 12–35 people, and 10 yomes (which are a cross between a yurt and a dome). Drinking water, picnic tables, garbage service, and fire grills are provided. Restrooms with flush toilets and showers, a restaurant, snack bar, general store, ice, fishing supplies, gasoline, and a picnic shelter are available. Also, a full-service marina with boat rentals, marine fuel, a boat launch, boat dock, fishing pier, moorage, swimming beach, volleyball courts, horseshoe pits, and a playground are available. Some facilities are wheelchair accessible. Leashed pets are permitted, and a dog run area is available.

Reservations, fees: Reservations are accepted at 541/475-0517 or www.portlandgeneral.com. Sites are $16–21 per night; the group site is $42–65 per night; yomes are $25 per night. Some credit cards are accepted. Open mid-April–September.

Directions: From Portland, drive south on U.S. 26 for 108 miles to the town of Warm Springs. Continue south two miles to Pelton Dam Road. Turn right and drive three miles to the campground on the right.

Contact: Portland General Electric, 503/464-8515 or 541/475-0516 (store and marina), fax 503/464-2944, www.portlandgeneral.com/parks; campground, 541/475-0517.

Chinook. The lake borders the Warm Springs Indian Reservation and can get very crowded and noisy, as it attracts powerboat/water-ski enthusiasts. Recreation options include water-skiing and fishing for bass and panfish, and one of Oregon's nicest golf courses is nearby.

RV sites, facilities: There are 63 sites for tents or RVs up to 95 feet long. Picnic tables, garbage service, and fire grills are provided. Drinking water, vault toilets, firewood, a fish-cleaning station, boat docks, and launching facilities are available. A camp host is on-site. Some facilities are wheelchair accessible. Leashed pets are permitted.

Reservations, fees: Reservations are accepted at 877/444-6777 or www.recreation.gov ($10 reservation fee). Sites are $16–18 per night, $8 per night per additional vehicle. Open May–September, weather permitting.

Directions: From Bend, drive north on U.S. 97 to Redmond, then continue north for 15 miles to the Culver Highway. Take the Culver Highway north to Culver, and continue two miles to Gem Lane. Turn left and drive two miles to Frazier Drive. Turn left and drive a short distance to Peck Road. Turn right and drive through Cove Palisades State Park to Jordan Road at the shore of Lake Billy Chinook. Turn left on Jordan Road and drive about 10 miles (over the bridge) to County Road 64. Continue (bearing left) and drive about eight miles to the campground entrance on the left (on the upper end of the Metolius Fork of Lake Billy Chinook).

Contact: Deschutes National Forest, Sisters Ranger District, 541/549-7700, fax 541/549-7746, www.fs.fed.us.

88 PERRY SOUTH

🏊 🎣 🚙 🏕 ♿ 🚐 ⛺

Scenic rating: 6

on Lake Billy Chinook in Deschutes National Forest
Map grid B2

Perry South campground is located near the shore of the Metolius arm of Lake Billy

89 MONTY

🥾 🎣 🏕 🚐 ⛺

Scenic rating: 5

on the Metolius River in Deschutes National Forest
Map grid B2

Remote Monty campground is set at 2,000 feet elevation and gets light use. Trout fishing can be good along the banks of the Metolius River, near where it empties into Lake Billy Chinook. Warm Springs Indian Reservation is across the river.

RV sites, facilities: There are 20 sites for tents or RVs up to 20 feet long. Picnic tables, garbage service, and fire grills are provided. Firewood and pit toilets are available. There is no drinking water. Boat docks and launching facilities are nearby at Perry South. Leashed pets are permitted.

Reservations, fees: Reservations are not accepted. Sites are $14 per night, $7 per night per additional vehicle. Open June–mid-September, weather permitting.

Directions: From Bend, drive north on U.S. 97 to Redmond and continue north for 15 miles to the Culver Highway. Take the Culver Highway north to Culver and continue two miles to Gem Lane. Turn left and drive two miles to Frazier Drive. Turn left and drive a short distance to Peck Road. Turn right and drive through Cove Palisades State Park to Jordan Road at the shore of Lake Billy Chinook. Turn left on Jordan Road and drive about 10 miles (over the bridge) to County Road 64. Turn left and drive about 13 miles to the campground entrance (on the Metolius River above the headwaters of Lake Billy Chinook). The last five miles are very rough.

Contact: Deschutes National Forest, Sisters Ranger District, 541/549-7700, fax 541/549-7746, www.fs.fed.us.

90 COVE PALISADES STATE PARK

Scenic rating: 7

on Lake Billy Chinook

Map grid B2

This park is a mile away from the shore of Lake Billy Chinook, where some lakeshore cabins are available. Here in Oregon's high-desert region, summers are warm and sunny with fairly mild but cold winters. Lofty cliffs surround the lake, and about 10 miles of hiking trails crisscross the area. Two popular special events are held here annually: Lake Billy Chinook Day in September and the Eagle Watch in February.

RV sites, facilities: There are two campgrounds: Crooked River Campground offers 91 sites with partial hookups for tents or RVs and three deluxe cabins; Deschutes Campground has 92 tent sites, 82 sites with full hookups for RVs up to 60 feet long, and three group tent areas for up to 25 people each. Picnic tables and fire grills are provided. Drinking water, garbage bins, restrooms with flush toilets and showers, a dump station, firewood, a convenience store, amphitheater, horseshoe pit, playground, and ice are available. Boat docks, launching facilities, a marina, boat rentals, fish-cleaning station, and a restaurant are nearby. Some facilities are wheelchair accessible. Leashed pets are permitted, and there is a designated pet exercise area.

Reservations, fees: Reservations are accepted at 800/452-5687 or www.oregonstateparks. org ($8 reservation fee). RV sites are $17–26 per night, tent sites are $13–20 per night, cabins are $48–80 per night, the group areas are $43–75 per night, $5 per night per additional vehicle. Some credit cards are accepted. Crooked River Campground is open year-round; Deschutes Campground is open May–mid-September.

Directions: From Bend, drive north on U.S. 97 for 13 miles to Redmond and continue north for 15 miles to the Culver Highway. Take the Culver Highway north to Culver and continue two miles to Gem Lane. Turn left and drive two miles to Frazier Drive. Turn left and drive a short distance to Peck Road. Turn right and drive to the park entrance.

Contact: Cove Palisades State Park, 541/546-3412 or 800/551-6949, www.oregonstateparks. org.

91 KOA MADRAS/CULVER

Scenic rating: 6

near Lake Billy Chinook

Map grid B2

This KOA has a relaxing atmosphere, with some mountain views. It is set about three miles from Lake Billy Chinook, a steep-sided reservoir formed where the Crooked River, Deschutes River, Metolius River, and Squaw Creek all merge. Like much of the country east of the Cascades, this is a high-desert area.

RV sites, facilities: There are 22 tent sites and 58 pull-through sites with full or partial hookups for RVs of any length; most sites are pull-through. There are also three cabins. Drinking water, fire pits, and picnic tables are provided. Restrooms with flush toilets and showers, propane gas, a dump station, firewood, a convenience store, coin laundry, ice, and a playground are available. Recreational activities include a recreation hall, seasonal heated pool, bicycle rentals, volleyball, horseshoe pits, and tetherball. Boat docks and launching facilities are nearby. Leashed pets are permitted.

Reservations, fees: Reservations are accepted at 800/562-1992. Sites are $21–30 per night, $2–4 per person per night for more than two people. Some credit cards are accepted. Open year-round.

Directions: From Madras, drive south on U.S. 97 for nine miles to Jericho Lane. Turn left (east) and drive 0.5 mile to the campground on the right.

Contact: KOA Madras/Culver, 541/546-3046, fax 541/546-7972, www.koa.com.

NORTHEASTERN OREGON

◖ BEST RV PARKS AND CAMPGROUNDS

◖ **Family Destinations**
Wallowa Lake State Park, page 420.

◖ **Wildlife-Viewing**
Minam State Park, page 418.

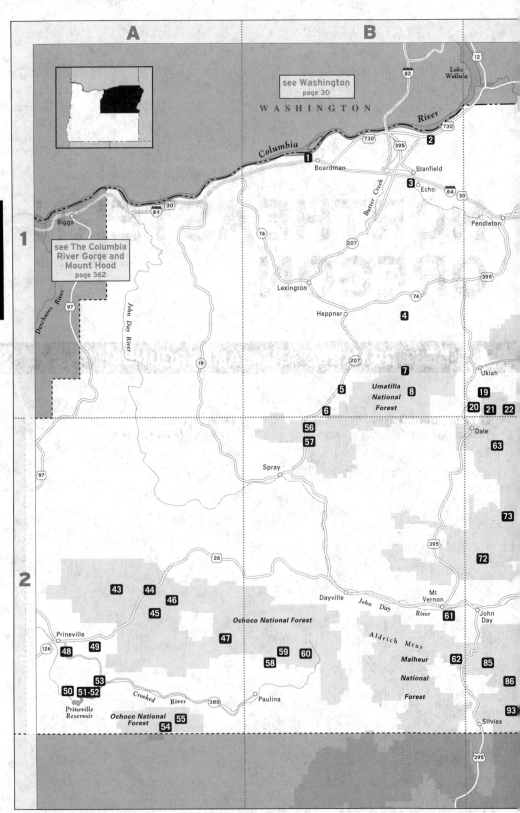

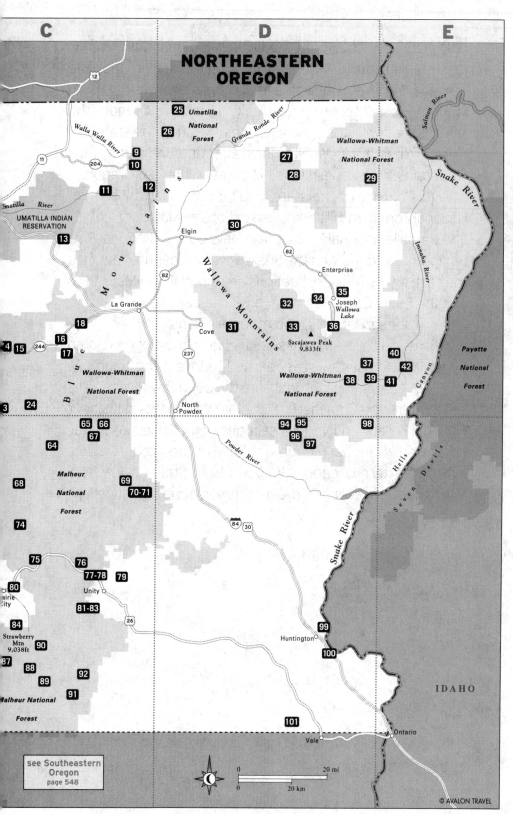

NORTHEASTERN OREGON

see Southeastern Oregon page 548

OREGON

© AVALON TRAVEL

It might be difficult to believe that there are many places left in America that are little known and little traveled. Yet that is how it is in northeastern Oregon. Even longtime residents often overlook this area of Oregon (the same is true with the southeastern portion of the state, detailed in Chapter 6). With its high desert abutting craggy Blue Mountains, it just doesn't look like the archetypal Oregon.

In this corner of the state, you'll find Wallowa-Whitman National Forest and little-known sections of Malheur, Ochoco, and Umatilla National Forests. The Hells Canyon National Recreation Area, Idaho, and the Snake River border this region to the east. My favorite destinations are the Wallowa Mountains and the Eagle Cap Wilderness, a wildlife paradise with bears, bighorn sheep, deer, elk, and mountain lions.

This region covers a huge swatch of land, most of it explored by few. But those few have learned to love it for its unique qualities. Among the highlights are the John Day River and its headwaters, the Strawberry Mountain Wilderness in Malheur National Forest, and various sections of the linked John Day Fossil Beds National Monument. One of the prettiest spots in northeastern Oregon is Wallowa Lake State Park, where 9,000-foot snowcapped mountains surround a pristine lake on three sides.

1 BOARDMAN MARINA AND RV PARK

Scenic rating: 7

on the Columbia River

Map grid B1

This public campground is set on the Columbia River among linden, maple, and sycamore trees. Some sites are located along the riverbank. In addition to fishing for bass, crappie, and walleye, nearby recreation options include a marina and golf course (five miles away).

RV sites, facilities: There are four tent sites and 63 sites for tents or RVs of any length; most sites have full hookups, some are pull-through. Drinking water, picnic tables, and fire pits are provided. Restrooms with flush toilets and showers, fire pits, a dump station, garbage bins, coin laundry, a day-use area with picnic shelters, a pay phone, Wi-Fi, seasonal firewood and ice for sale, and a boat dock and launch are available. Recreational facilities include a basketball court, horseshoe pits, sand volleyball, and a hiking/biking path along the river. A boat marina and grocery store are available within one mile. Leashed pets are permitted.

Reservations, fees: Reservations are accepted at 888/481-7217. Tent sites are $15.90 per night; RV sites are $26.50 per night. Some credit cards are accepted. Discounts are sometimes available. Open year-round, with limited winter facilities.

Directions: From Portland on I-84 eastbound, drive 164 miles to Boardman and Exit 164. Take that exit and turn left (north) on Main Street. Drive 0.25 mile over the railroad bridge, bear left, and continue 0.2 mile to the Y intersection and the park on the right.

Contact: Boardman Marina Park, Boardman Park and Recreation District, 541/481-7217, fax 541/481-2828, www.boardmanmarinapark.com.

2 HAT ROCK CAMPGROUND

Scenic rating: 7

near the Columbia River

Map grid B1

Hat Rock State Park is a day-use area with a boat launch along the banks of the Columbia River. The campground itself is very pretty, with lots of trees, and offers close access to the river and fishing.

RV sites, facilities: There are eight tent sites and 60 sites with full or partial hookups for RVs of any length. Drinking water and picnic tables are provided. Fire pits are provided at some sites. Restrooms with flush toilets and showers, a dump station, convenience store, café, coin laundry, seasonal swimming pool, and ice are available. Boat docks and launching facilities are nearby. Some facilities are wheelchair accessible. Leashed pets are permitted.

Reservations, fees: Reservations are accepted at 541/567-4188 or 541/567-0917. Sites are $18–22 per night, $2 per person per night for more than two people. Some credit cards are accepted. Open year-round.

Directions: From Portland, drive east on U.S. 84 for roughly 170 miles past Boardman to the junction of U.S. 84 and U.S. 730. Turn northeast on U.S. 730 and drive 18 miles to the junction with I-82. Continue east on U.S. 730 for seven miles to the state park access road. Turn left (north) and drive 0.5 mile to the park on the left.

Contact: Hat Rock Campground, 541/567-4188 or 541/567-0917 (Hat Rock Store).

3 FORT HENRIETTA RV PARK

Scenic rating: 7

on the Umatilla River

Map grid B1

This park, located in the historic community of Echo, sits along the Umatilla River. It provides a quiet, pleasant layover spot for travelers cruising I-84. The river has some good trout fishing.

RV sites, facilities: There are seven sites with

full or partial hookups for RVs of any length, two pull-through sites with partial hookups, and an area for dispersed tent camping. Picnic tables are provided, and cable TV is available at some sites. Drinking water, restrooms with showers, and a dump station are available. The camp is within walking distance of two restaurants. Some facilities are wheelchair accessible. Leashed pets are permitted.

Reservations, fees: Reservations available at 541/571-3597. Sites are $16–19 per night, $2 per person per night for more than two people. Open year-round.

Directions: From Pendleton, drive west on I-84 to Exit 188 and the Echo Highway. Take the exit, turn left (southeast), and drive one mile; cross the railroad tracks and continue 0.5 mile to Dupont Street. Turn right (south) and drive 0.3 mile to Main Street. Turn left (west) and drive one block to the park on the left.

Contact: Echo City Hall, 541/571-3597, fax 541/376-8218.

4 CUTSFORTH PARK

Scenic rating: 8

on Willow Creek

Map grid B1

Cutsforth is a secluded and private county park set beside a small, wheelchair-accessible pond in a quiet, wooded area. Unfortunately, the pond was closed to fishing in 2009 and it is unknown if it will reopen. In winter, the park serves as a staging area for snowmobilers, and in spring mushroom hunting is an attraction.

RV sites, facilities: There are 52 sites, most with full or partial hookups for tents or RVs up to 36 feet long. Three of the campsites have horse pens available for rent. A large building with kitchen facilities is available for rent by groups. Picnic tables and fire rings are provided. Restrooms with coin showers, a dump station, horseshoe pits, firewood, ice, and a playground are available. Supplies are available in Heppner (22 miles away). Some facilities are wheelchair accessible. Leashed pets are permitted.

Reservations, fees: Reservations are accepted at 541/989-8214. Sites are $10–15 per night, $2 per night per additional vehicle, and $3 per night per horse. Weekly rates are available. Open mid-May–November, weather permitting.

Directions: From Pendleton on I-84, drive west for 27 miles to Exit 182 and Highway 207 (Heppner Highway). Turn south and drive 32 miles to Lexington and Highway 74. Turn left (southeast) on Highway 74 (becomes Highway 207) and drive 10 miles to Heppner. Continue south on Highway 207 for 0.5 mile to Willow Creek Road. Turn left on Willow Creek Road and drive 23 miles to the park.

Contact: Morrow County Public Works, 541/989-8214, fax 541/989-8352, www.morrowcountyparks.org.

5 ANSON WRIGHT MEMORIAL PARK

Scenic rating: 7

on Rock Creek

Map grid B1

Set among wooded hills along a small stream, this county park offers visitors prime trout fishing in several stocked ponds, as well as hiking opportunities. One of the fishing ponds is wheelchair accessible. Attractions in the area include Emigrant Springs State Park, Hardman Ghost Town (10 miles away), and the Pendleton Mills. There's also a nearby opal mine.

RV sites, facilities: There are 44 sites for tents or RVs up to 42 feet long and one cabin. Some sites have full hookups and/or are pull-through. Picnic tables and fire rings are provided. Restrooms with coin showers, a picnic area, dump station, firewood, ice, and a playground are provided. Some facilities are wheelchair accessible. Leashed pets are permitted.

Reservations, fees: Reservations are accepted at 541/989-8214. Sites are $10–15 per night, $2 per night per additional vehicle. Open mid-May–mid-November, weather permitting.

Directions: From Pendleton, drive west on I-84 for 27 miles to Exit 182 and Highway 207

(Heppner Highway). Turn south and drive 32 miles to Lexington and Highway 74. Turn left (south) on Highway 74 (becomes Highway 20) and drive 10 miles to Heppner. Continue south on Highway 207 for 11 miles to Ruggs and a fork. Bear left at the fork (still Highway 207) and drive 12 miles to the park on the right.

Contact: Morrow County Public Works, 541/989-8214, fax 541/989-8352, www.morrowcountyparks.org.

6 OHV PARK

Scenic rating: 5

in Morrow County Park

Map grid B1

This 6,200-acre park is very popular. It is designed primarily for OHV use and has more than 150 miles of trails specifically for off-highway vehicles. There is a day-use area, and the campground itself is wooded. Campers are allowed to use the showers at Anson Wright campground, 10 miles away.

RV sites, facilities: There are 67 sites for tents or RVs up to 42 feet long, three group sites, and six cabins. Picnic tables and fire rings are provided at some sites. Drinking water, portable toilets, dump station, firewood, coin wash rack, helmet rental, propane, a seasonal snack bar, and a day-use area are available. Some facilities are wheelchair accessible. Leashed pets are permitted.

Reservations, fees: Reservations accepted at 541/989-8214. Sites are $10–15 per night; it's $35 per night for the group site, and $2 per night per additional vehicle. Open year-round, weather permitting; call ahead December–February.

Directions: From Pendleton, drive west on I-84 for 27 miles to Exit 182 and Highway 207 (Heppner Highway). Turn south and drive 32 miles to Lexington and Highway 74. Turn left (south) on Highway 74 (becomes Highway 20) and drive 10 miles to Heppner. Continue south on Highway 207 for 11 miles to Ruggs and a fork. Bear left at the fork (still Highway 207) and drive 22 miles to the park on the right.

Contact: Morrow County Public Works, 541/989-8214, fax 541/989-8352, www.morrowcountyparks.org

7 PENLAND LAKE

Scenic rating: 10

near Penland Lake in the Umatilla National Forest

Map grid B1

This campground (4,950 feet elevation) has partial tree cover, so there are many open spaces. The lake is small, and electric-motor boats are allowed. The fishing can be good at times, with rainbow trout and bluegill the primary fish species. Hiking and bicycling are popular on the nearby trails. The wildlife viewing can be outstanding; species include bear, deer, and elk, as well as grouse and other birds.

RV sites, facilities: There are eight sites for tents or RVs up to 50 feet long. Picnic tables and fire rings are provided. Vault toilets are available. There is no drinking water. Garbage must be packed out. A boat ramp is nearby. Leashed pets are permitted.

Reservations, fees: Reservations are not accepted. There is no fee. Open May–October, weather permitting. A 14-day stay limit is enforced.

Directions: From Heppner, drive south on Highway 207 to Willow Creek Road (Forest Road 54/County Road 678). Turn left (east) and drive 23 miles to Forest Road 21. Turn right (gravel road) and drive three miles to Forest Road 2103. Turn left and drive two miles to the lake and campground.

Contact: Umatilla National Forest, Heppner Ranger District, 541/676-9187, fax 541/676-2105, www.fs.fed.us.

8 DIVIDE WELLS

Scenic rating: 5

in Umatilla National Forest

Map grid B1

Divide Wells is a primitive campground, but it is busy in the summer, and even occasionally used for reunions. Set at 4,700 feet elevation, it can serve as a good base camp for a hunting trip. Mule deer and Rocky Mountain elk can be spotted in the surrounding ponderosa pine and fir forest. Potamus Point Scenic Overlook, offering a spectacular view of the John Day River drainage, is 11 miles south of the camp on Forest Road 5316 and provides a good opportunity to see bighorn sheep.

RV sites, facilities: There are eight sites for tents or RVs up to 20 feet long and three group sites. A vault toilet is provided. There is no drinking water, and garbage must be packed out. Leashed pets are permitted.

Reservations, fees: Reservations are not accepted. Sites are $8 per night, $5 per night per additional vehicle. Open late May–November, weather permitting. A 14-day stay limit is enforced.

Directions: From Pendleton, drive south on U.S. 395 for 48 miles to Ukiah and Highway 244. Turn right (the road becomes Forest Road 53) and drive west on Forest Road 53 for about 14 miles to Forest Road 5327. Turn left (south) and drive seven miles to the campground on the right. A U.S. Forest Service map is recommended.

Contact: Umatilla National Forest, North Fork John Day Ranger District, 541/427-3231, fax 541/427-3018, www.fs.fed.us.

⑨ WOODWARD

Scenic rating: 7

near Langdon Lake in Umatilla National Forest

Map grid C1

Nestled among the trees at an elevation of 4,950 feet, this popular campground has a view of Langdon Lake (though campers do not have access to the private lake). A flat trail encircles the campground, and there is some privacy screening between the sites.

RV sites, facilities: There are 18 sites for tents or RVs up to 28 feet long. Picnic tables, garbage bins, fire grills, and vault toilets are provided. There is no drinking water. Leashed pets are permitted.

Reservations, fees: Reservations are not accepted. Sites are $12 per night. Open late June–September, weather permitting. A 14-day stay limit is enforced.

Directions: From Pendleton on I-84, turn north on Highway 11 and drive approximately 27 miles to Weston and Highway 204. Turn right (southeast) on Highway 204 and drive 17 miles to the campground on the right (near Langdon Lake).

Contact: Umatilla National Forest, Walla Walla Ranger District, 509/522-6290, fax 509/522-6000, www.fs.fed.us.

⑩ TARGET MEADOWS

Scenic rating: 6

near the south fork of the Walla Walla River in Umatilla National Forest

Map grid C1

This quiet campground with shady sites and a sunny meadow is situated at 4,800 feet elevation. The camp is adjacent to the Burnt Cabin Trailhead, which leads to the south fork of the Walla Walla River Trail and an old military site.

RV sites, facilities: There are 16 sites for tents or RVs up to 28 feet long. Picnic tables and fire grills are provided. Garbage bins and vault toilets are available. There is no drinking water. Leashed pets are permitted.

Reservations, fees: Reservations are not accepted. Sites are $12 per night. Open late June–mid-November, weather permitting. A 14-day stay limit is enforced.

Directions: From Pendleton, drive north on Highway 11 for 16 miles to Highway 204 near Weston. Turn right (southeast) on Highway 204 and drive 17.5 miles to Forest Road 64. Turn left and drive 0.5 mile to Forest Road 6401. Turn left (north) and drive two miles to Road 6401-050. Turn right (north) and drive 0.5 mile to the camp.

Contact: Umatilla National Forest, Walla Walla Ranger District, 509/522-6290, fax 509/522-6000, www.fs.fed.us.

11 UMATILLA FORKS

Scenic rating: 3

along the Umatilla River in Umatilla National Forest

Map grid C1

Umatilla Forks campground lies in a canyon between the South and North Forks of the Umatilla River at an elevation of 2,400 feet. Expect warm temperatures in mid- to late summer; tree cover provides some relief. Fishing on the Umatilla River is catch-and-release only, and hiking is possible in the North Fork Umatilla Wilderness.

RV sites, facilities: There are 15 sites for tents or RVs up to 28 feet long. Picnic tables and fire grills are provided. Vault toilets are available. There is no drinking water. Garbage must be packed out. Leashed pets are permitted.

Reservations, fees: Reservations are not accepted. Sites are $10 per night. Open May–October, weather permitting. A 14-day stay limit is enforced.

Directions: From Pendleton, drive north on Highway 11 for about 25 miles to Athena and Pambrun Road. Turn right on Pambrun Road and drive five miles to Spring Hollow Road. Turn left on Spring Hollow Road (it becomes Thorn Hollow Road) and drive about 6.5 miles to Bingham Road (River Road). Turn left on Bingham Road (River Road), cross the railroad tracks, and follow signs for about five miles to Gibbon. Cross the railroad tracks at Gibbon and continue on Bingham Road (it becomes Forest Road 32) about 11 miles to the campground on the right.

Contact: Umatilla National Forest, Walla Walla Ranger District, 509/522-6290, fax 509/522-6000, www.fs.fed.us.

12 WOODLAND

Scenic rating: 4

in Umatilla National Forest

Map grid C1

Primitive Woodland campground is set at 5,200 feet elevation with easy highway access—and related road noise. The camp has both shaded and sunny sites and can be a perfect spot for I-84 cruisers looking for a short detour. During fall, the area is popular with hunters; hikers and mountain bikers will enjoy the area the rest of the year.

RV sites, facilities: There are seven sites for tents or RVs up to 28 feet long. Picnic tables, fire grills, and vault toilets are provided. There is no drinking water. Garbage must be packed out. Leashed pets are permitted.

Reservations, fees: Reservations are not accepted. Sites are $8 per night. Open mid-June–mid-November, weather permitting. A 14-day stay limit is enforced.

Directions: From Pendleton, drive north on Highway 11 for 16 miles to Highway 204 near Weston. Turn right (southeast) on Highway 204 and drive 23 miles. The campground is just off the highway on the left.

Contact: Umatilla National Forest, Walla Walla Ranger District, 509/522-6290, fax 509/522-6000, www.fs.fed.us.

13 EMIGRANT SPRINGS STATE HERITAGE AREA

Scenic rating: 7

near the Umatilla Indian Reservation

Map grid C1

Emigrant Springs sits in old-growth forest at the summit of the Blue Mountains. The campground is popular with horse campers and offers wildlife-watching opportunities. The nearby Oregon Trail and Pendleton Woolen Mills provide interesting side-trips.

RV sites, facilities: There are 32 tent sites, 19 sites with full hookups for RVs of any length, a designated horse camp (closed in winter), group tent site, and eight cabins. Picnic tables, fire grills, and horse corrals are provided. Drinking water, garbage bins, restrooms with flush toilets and showers, firewood, some horse facilities, a community building with kitchen, basketball court, amphitheater, and baseball field are available. Some facilities are wheelchair accessible. Leashed pets are permitted.

OREGON

Reservations, fees: Reservations are accepted at 800/452-5687 or www.reserveamerica.com ($8 reservation fee). Tent sites are $10–17 per night, RV sites are $12–20 per night, cabins are $35–39 per night, equestrian sites are $10–17 per night, and the group site is $71 for up to 25 people. Additional vehicles cost $5 per night. Some credit cards are accepted. Open year-round (water is off mid-Oct.–mid-April).

Directions: From Pendleton, drive southeast on I-84 for 26 miles to Exit 234. Take that exit to Old Oregon Trail Road (frontage road) and drive 0.5 mile to the park on the right.

Contact: Emigrant Springs State Heritage Area, 541/983-2277 or 800/551-6949, www.oregonstateparks.org.

14 LANE CREEK

Scenic rating: 4

on Camas Creek in Umatilla National Forest

Map grid C1

This primitive campground (3,850 feet elevation) borders Camas Creek and Lane Creek, just inside the forest boundary, and provides easy access to all the amenities of town. It's a popular stop for overnighters passing through the area. Some of the sites close to the highway get traffic noise. Highlights in the area include hot springs (privately owned) and good hunting and fishing. A U.S. Forest Service map details the back roads.

RV sites, facilities: There are six sites for tents or RVs up to 28 feet long and one group site. Picnic tables and fire grills are provided. Vault toilets are available. There is no drinking water, and garbage must be packed out. Leashed pets are permitted.

Reservations, fees: Reservations are not accepted. Sites are $8 per night, $25 per night for the group site. Open April–November, weather permitting. A 14-day stay limit is enforced.

Directions: From Pendleton, drive south on U.S. 395 for 50 miles to Ukiah and Highway 244. Turn east on Highway 244 and drive nine miles to the campground on the left.

Contact: Umatilla National Forest, North Fork John Day Ranger District, 541/427-3231, fax 541/427-3018, www.fs.fed.us.

15 BEAR WALLOW CREEK

Scenic rating: 5

on Bear Wallow Creek in Umatilla National Forest

Map grid C1

Situated near the confluence of Bear Wallow and Camus Creeks at an elevation of 3,900 feet, Bear Wallow is one of three off Highway 244 (the others are Lane Creek and Frazier). Quiet and primitive, the camp is used primarily in the summer. A 0.5-mile, wheelchair-accessible, interpretive trail meanders next to Bear Wallow Creek, highlighting the steelhead habitat.

RV sites, facilities: There are seven sites for tents or RVs up to 28 feet long and one group site. Picnic tables and fire grills are provided. Vault toilets are available. No drinking water is available, and garbage must be packed out. Some facilities are wheelchair accessible. Leashed pets are permitted.

Reservations, fees: Reservations are not accepted. Sites are $8 per night, and the group site is $25 per night. Open April–November, weather permitting. A 14-day stay limit is enforced.

Directions: From Pendleton, drive south on U.S. 395 for 50 miles to Ukiah and Highway 244. Turn east on Highway 244 and drive 10 miles to the camp on the left.

Contact: Umatilla National Forest, North Fork John Day Ranger District, 541/427-3231, fax 541/427-3018, www.fs.fed.us.

16 FRAZIER

Scenic rating: 5

on Frazier Creek in Umatilla National Forest

Map grid C1

With nearly 130 miles of OHV and motorcycle trails at the Winom-Frazier Off-Highway-Vehicle Complex, this camp is popular in the summer with the OHV crowd. The campground is set at 4,300 feet elevation along the banks of Frazier Creek. It is a popular hunting area in the fall, and some fishing is available in the area. It's advisable to obtain a map of Umatilla National Forest. On weekends, it's not a good spot for the traditional camper looking for quiet and solitude. Lehman Hot Springs, one mile away, provides a side-trip option.

RV sites, facilities: There are 14 sites for tents or RVs up to 28 feet long and four group sites. Picnic tables and fire grills are provided. An OHV loading ramp and vault toilets are available. There is no drinking water, and garbage must be packed out. Some facilities are wheelchair accessible. Leashed pets are permitted. A 14-day stay limit is enforced.

Reservations, fees: Reservations are not accepted. Sites are $8 per night; group sites are $25 per night. Open April–November, weather permitting.

Directions: From Pendleton, drive south on U.S. 395 for 50 miles to Ukiah and Highway 244. Turn left (east) on Highway 244 and drive 18 miles to Forest Road 5226. Turn right (south) and drive 0.5 mile to the campground.

Contact: Umatilla National Forest, North Fork John Day Ranger District, 541/427-3231, fax 541/427-3018, www.fs.fed.us.

17 SPOOL CART

Scenic rating: 6

on the Grande Ronde River in
Wallowa-Whitman National Forest

Map grid C1

Spool Cart gets its name from the large cable spools that were left on a cart here for some years. The wooded campground sits at 3,500 feet elevation on the banks of the Grande Ronde River; sites offer privacy. The camp is popular with hunters in the fall, and the gurgling Grande Ronde offers fishing for bull trout. Hilgard Junction State Park to the north provides numerous recreation options, and the Oregon Interpretive Trail Park at Blue Crossing is nearby.

RV sites, facilities: There are nine sites for tents

or RVs up to 22 feet long. Picnic tables and fire grills are provided. Vault toilets are available. There is no drinking water, and garbage must be packed out. Some facilities are wheelchair accessible. Leashed pets are permitted.

Reservations, fees: Reservations are not accepted. Sites are $5 per night per vehicle. Open late May–late November.

Directions: From Pendleton, drive southeast on U.S. 84 for 42 miles to Highway 244. Turn southwest on Highway 244 and drive 13 miles to Forest Road 51. Turn left (south) and drive five miles to the campground on the right.

Contact: Wallowa-Whitman National Forest, LaGrande Ranger District, 541/963-7186, fax 541/962-8580, www.fs.fed.us.

18 BIRD TRACK SPRINGS

Scenic rating: 7

near the Grande Ronde River in
Wallowa-Whitman National Forest

Map grid C1

Bird Track Springs is located at 3,100 feet elevation and is about a five-minute walk from the Grande Ronde River. The spacious campsites are right off the highway in surrounding woods of primarily ponderosa pine and white fir. The Bird Track Springs Interpretive Trail, across the campground, offers a hiking and bird-watching opportunity.

RV sites, facilities: There are 21 sites for tents or RVs up to 22 feet long. Picnic tables and fire rings are provided. Vault toilets are available. There is no drinking water, and garbage must be packed out. A camp host is on-site in the summer. Some facilities are wheelchair accessible. Leashed pets are permitted.

Reservations, fees: Reservations are not accepted. Sites are $5 per night per vehicle. Open mid-May–November, weather permitting.

Directions: From Pendleton, drive southeast on U.S. 84 for 42 miles to Highway 244. Turn right (southwest) and drive seven miles to the campground on the left.

Contact: Wallowa-Whitman National Forest,

LaGrande Ranger District, 541/963-7186, fax 541/962-8580, www.fs.fed.us.

19 DRIFT FENCE

Scenic rating: 5

near Ross Springs in Umatilla National Forest

Map grid C1

Get this: Drift Fence is not marked on the Umatilla National Forest Map. The camp, set at 4,250 feet elevation, is adjacent to Blue Mountain National Forest Scenic Byway. With some elk and deer in the area, hunting is a highlight here. The Bridge Creek Interpretive Trail, three miles northwest of the campground off Forest Road 52, leads to a beautiful view of open meadow with various wildflowers and wildlife. Elk may be seen roaming in the Bridge Creek area.

RV sites, facilities: There are four sites for tents or RVs up to 30 feet long and one group site. Picnic tables are provided. A pit toilet is available. There is no drinking water, and garbage must be packed out. Leashed pets are permitted.

Reservations, fees: Reservations are not accepted. There is no fee for camping. Open May–November, weather permitting. A 14-day stay limit is enforced.

Directions: From Pendleton, drive south on U.S. 395 for 50 miles to Highway 244. Turn east on Highway 244 and drive one mile to Ukiah and Forest Road 52. Turn right (south) on Forest Road 52 and drive eight miles to the campground on the right.

Contact: Umatilla National Forest, North Fork John Day Ranger District, 541/427-3231, fax 541/427-3018, www.fs.fed.us.

20 UKIAH-DALE FOREST STATE SCENIC CORRIDOR

Scenic rating: 7

near the North Fork of the John Day River

Map grid C1

Fishing is a prime activity at this Camas Creek campground, nestled near the banks of the

north fork of the John Day River at an elevation of 3,140 feet. It's a good layover for visitors cruising U.S. 395 looking for a shady spot for the night. Emigrant Springs State Park near Pendleton is a possible side trip.

RV sites, facilities: There are 27 sites for tents or self-contained RVs of any length. Picnic tables and fire pits are provided. Drinking water, firewood, and restrooms with flush toilets are available. Leashed pets are permitted.

Reservations, fees: Reservations are not accepted. Sites are $5–9 per night, $5 per night per additional vehicle. Open May–late October.

Directions: From Pendleton, drive south on U.S. 395 for 50 miles to Highway 244 (near Ukiah). Continue south on U.S. 395 for three miles to the park.

Contact: Emigrant Springs State Heritage Park, 541/983-2277 or 800/551-6949, www.oregonstateparks.org.

21 TOLLBRIDGE

Scenic rating: 4

on the north fork of the John Day River in Umatilla National Forest

Map grid C1

This small, secluded campground (elevation 3,800 feet) lies at the confluence of Desolation Creek and the north fork of the John Day River and is adjacent to the Bridge Creek Wildlife Area. It can be beautiful or ugly, depending upon which direction you look. It's dusty in the summer, and there's sparse tree cover. Hunting and fishing are two options here, or explore the geological interpretive sign in the camp.

RV sites, facilities: There are seven sites for tents or RVs up to 26 feet long. Picnic tables and fire grills are provided. A vault toilet is available. There is no drinking water, and garbage must be packed out. Leashed pets are permitted.

Reservations, fees: Reservations are not accepted. Sites are $8 per night, with a 14-day stay limit. Open April–November, weather permitting. A 14-day stay limit is enforced.

Directions: From Pendleton, drive south on

U.S. 395 for 50 miles to the intersection with Highway 244. Continue south on U.S. 395 for 18 miles to Forest Road 55 (one mile north of Dale). Turn left and drive 0.5 mile southeast to Forest Road 10 and the campground access road. Drive a short distance to the campground.

Contact: Umatilla National Forest, North Fork John Day Ranger District, 541/427-3231, fax 541/427-3018, www.fs.fed.us.

22 GOLD DREDGE CAMP

Scenic rating: 7

on the north fork of the John Day River in Umatilla National Forest

Map grid C1

Gold Dredge lies along the banks of the north fork of the John Day River, a federally designated Wild and Scenic River. This camp is an excellent launch point for recreation: swimming, fishing, rafting (spring only), float-tubing, and hunting (fall) are among the many activities. Dredge tailings from old mining activity are visible from the camp. At the end of Forest Road 5506, you can access a trailhead that heads into the adjacent North Fork John Day Wilderness. Special fishing regulations are in effect for the North Fork John Day River; check Oregon fishing regulations before heading out.

Parking is provided at Big Creek Bridge for the North Fork John Day Wilderness Trailhead and the OHV trail that leads to the Winom-Frazier OHV Complex. Those driving to the end of Forest Road 5506 will need a high-clearance vehicle.

RV sites, facilities: There are six sites for tents or RVs up to 28 feet long. Picnic tables are provided. Vault toilets are available. There is no drinking water, and garbage must be packed out. Leashed pets are permitted.

Reservations, fees: Reservations are not accepted. There is no fee for camping. Open May–November, weather permitting. A 14-day stay limit is enforced.

Directions: From Pendleton, drive south on U.S. 395 for 62 miles to Forest Road 55 (one mile north of Dale). Turn left and drive six miles to the crossroads. Continue straight onto Forest Road 5506 and drive 2.5 miles to the campground on the right. Note: The last two miles of road are very rough.

Contact: Umatilla National Forest, North Fork John Day Ranger District, 541/427-3231, fax 541/427-3018, www.fs.fed.us.

23 DRIFTWOOD

Scenic rating: 6

on the north fork of the John Day River in Umatilla National Forest

Map grid C1

This tiny campground with ponderosa pine and Douglas fir cover sits on the banks of the north fork of the John Day River at an elevation of 2,500 feet. Recreational opportunities at this remote spot include fishing, float tubing, hunting, rafting, and swimming.

RV sites, facilities: There are five sites for tents or RVs up to 28 feet long. Fire grills and picnic tables are provided. A vault toilet is available. No drinking water is available. Garbage must be packed out. Leashed pets are permitted. A 14-day stay limit is enforced.

Reservations, fees: Reservations are not accepted. Sites are $8 per night. Open April–November, weather permitting.

Directions: From Pendleton, drive south on U.S. 395 for 62 miles to Forest Road 55 (one mile north of Dale; it's easier to find if you know the marker, Texas Bar Road). Turn left and drive six miles to the crossroads. Continue straight ahead onto Forest Road 5506 and drive one mile to the campground on the right. Note: The last two miles of road are very rough.

Contact: Umatilla National Forest, North Fork John Day Ranger District, 541/427-3231, fax 541/427-3018, www.fs.fed.us.

OREGON

24 WINOM CREEK

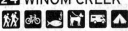

Scenic rating: 2

on Winom Creek in Umatilla National Forest

Map grid C1

Winom Creek campground is set at 5,000 feet elevation and provides access to the Winom-Frazier Off-Highway Vehicle Complex, with 130 miles of OHV trails of varying difficulty. The complex was developed in the late 1980s for OHV enthusiasts and has worn in well. The camp is also near the North Fork John Day Wilderness, perfect for hikers. (Check the campground bulletin boards for detailed maps of the terrain.)

RV sites, facilities: There are five sites for tents or RVs up to 28 feet long and three group sites. Picnic tables and fire rings are provided. Vault toilets and an OHV loading ramp are available. There is no drinking water, and garbage must be packed out. Two of the group sites have picnic shelters. Leashed pets are permitted.

Reservations, fees: Reservations are not accepted. Sites are $8 per night, $25 per night for group sites. Open May–early November, weather permitting. A 14-day stay limit is enforced.

Directions: From Pendleton, drive south on U.S. 395 for 50 miles to Highway 244. Turn east on Highway 244 and drive one mile to Ukiah and Forest Road 52. Turn right (south) on Forest Road 52 and drive 20 miles to Forest Road 440. Turn right and drive one mile to the campground on the right. The last mile of the access road is narrow and steep.

Contact: Umatilla National Forest, North Fork John Day Ranger District, 541/427-3231, fax 541/427-3018, www.fs.fed.us.

25 MOTTET

Scenic rating: 6

near the south fork of the Walla Walla River in Umatilla National Forest

Map grid D1

Mottet sits perched at 5,200 feet elevation along a ridge top, surrounded by a heavily timbered forest. Far from the beaten path, it's quite primitive and relatively unknown, so you're almost guaranteed privacy. A trailhead across the road leads down to the south fork of the Walla Walla River.

RV sites, facilities: There are seven sites for tents or RVs up to 22 feet. Picnic tables and fire grills are provided. Spring water and vault toilets are available. Garbage must be packed out. Leashed pets are permitted.

Reservations, fees: Reservations are not accepted. Sites are $8 per night. Open early July–November, weather permitting. A 14-day stay limit is enforced.

Directions: From Pendleton, drive north on Highway 11 for 16 miles to Highway 204 near Weston. Turn right (southeast) on Highway 204 and drive 17.5 miles to Forest Road 64. Turn left and drive about 15 miles to Forest Road 6403. Turn left and drive about two miles to the campground on the left. The road is rough for the last two miles.

Contact: Umatilla National Forest, Walla Walla Ranger District, 509/522-6290, fax 509/522-6000, www.fs.fed.us.

26 JUBILEE LAKE

Scenic rating: 8

on Jubilee Lake in Umatilla National Forest

Map grid D1

Jubilee Lake is the largest and most popular campground in Umatilla National Forest, and it fills up on weekends and holidays. Located along the shore of 90-acre Jubilee Lake (elevation 4,800 feet), this spot offers good fishing, hiking, and swimming. Electric boat motors are permitted on the lake, but gas-powered motors are prohibited. A 2.8-mile trail loops around the lake and provides different levels of accessibility for those in wheelchairs; fishing access is available along the trail.

RV sites, facilities: There are 50 sites for tents and RVs up to 28 feet long. Picnic tables and fire grills are provided. Drinking water, firewood, picnic areas, and restrooms with flush toilets are available. Boat docks and launching facilities are nearby. Garbage bins are available during the summer. Some facilities are wheelchair accessible. Leashed pets are permitted.

Reservations, fees: Reservations are not accepted. Sites are $17 per night, $5 per night for each additional vehicle. Open late June–mid-October, weather permitting. A 14-day stay limit is enforced.

Directions: From Pendleton, drive north on Highway 11 for 16 miles to Highway 204 near Weston. Turn right (southeast) on Highway 204 and drive 17.5 miles to Forest Road 64. Turn left and drive 12 miles northeast to Forest Road 6400-250. Turn right (south) and drive 0.5 mile to the camp.

Contact: Umatilla National Forest, Walla Walla Ranger District, 509/522-6290, fax 509/522-6000, www.fs.fed.us.

27 DOUGHERTY SPRINGS

Scenic rating: 5

near Dougherty Springs in
Wallowa-Whitman National Forest

Map grid D1

This wooded, primitive campground (elevation 5,100 feet) adjacent to Dougherty Springs is one in a series of remote camps set near natural springs. The camp is in an open area with sparse Douglas and white fir. Birds, deer, elk, and small mammals can be seen in the area. Hells Canyon National Recreation Area to the east provides many recreation options.

RV sites, facilities: There are 12 sites for tents or RVs up to 22 feet long. Picnic tables and fire rings are provided. Vault toilets are available. There is no drinking water, and garbage must be packed out. Leashed pets are permitted.

Reservations, fees: Reservations are not accepted. There is no fee for camping. Open June–late November, weather permitting.

Directions: From LaGrande, drive northeast on Highway 82 for 64 miles to Enterprise and Highway 3. Turn north on Highway 3 and drive 15 miles to Forest Road 46. Turn right

(northeast) and drive 30 miles to the campground on the left.

Contact: Hells Canyon National Recreation Area, Wallowa Mountains Visitors Center, 541/426-5546, fax 541/426-5522, www.fs.fed.us/r6/w-w.

28 COYOTE

Scenic rating: 4

near Coyote Springs in
Wallowa-Whitman National Forest

Map grid D1

Coyote campground is set at 4,800 feet elevation and adjacent to Coyote Springs. This is the largest of the three primitive camps in the vicinity, offering open sites and privacy.

RV sites, facilities: There are 30 sites for tents or RVs up to 22 feet long. Picnic tables and fire rings are provided. Vault toilets are available. There is no drinking water, and garbage must be packed out. Leashed pets are permitted.

Reservations, fees: Reservations are not accepted. There is no fee for camping. Open May–November, weather permitting.

Directions: From LaGrande, drive northeast on Highway 82 for 64 miles to Enterprise and Highway 3. Turn north on Highway 3 and drive 15 miles to Forest Road 46. Turn right (northeast) and drive 25 miles to the campground on the left.

Contact: Wallowa-Whitman National Forest, Wallowa Valley Ranger District, Wallowa Mountains Visitors Center, 541/426-5546, fax 541/426-5522, www.fs.fed.us.

29 VIGNE

Scenic rating: 5

on Chesnimnus Creek in
Wallowa-Whitman National Forest

Map grid D1

Vigne campground sits at 3,500 feet elevation on the banks of Chesnimnus Creek. The campground has pretty riverside sites shaded by

Douglas and white fir. Recreation opportunities include fishing and exploring a few of the many hiking trails in the area.

RV sites, facilities: There are seven sites for tents or RVs up to 22 feet long. Picnic tables and fire rings are provided. Drinking water and vault toilets are available. Garbage must be packed out. Leashed pets are permitted.

Reservations, fees: Reservations are not accepted. Sites are $6 per night. Open May–November, weather permitting.

Directions: From LaGrande, drive northeast on Highway 82 for 64 miles to Enterprise and Highway 3. Turn north on Highway 3 and drive 15 miles to Forest Road 46. Turn right (northeast) and drive 10 miles to Forest Road 4625. Turn right (east) and drive 10 miles to the campground. The last 10 miles are potholed and rough.

Contact: Wallowa-Whitman National Forest, Wallowa Valley Ranger District, Wallowa Mountains Visitors Center, 541/426-5546, fax 541/426-5522, www.fs.fed.us.

30 MINAM STATE PARK

Scenic rating: 7

near the Grande Ronde River

Map grid D1   **BEST**

This small and pretty park is well worth the detour off I-84 necessary to get there. Once you do, you'll be greeted by large pines towering above the sharp valley, cut through by the Wallowa River. Rafting and fishing for steelhead are popular activities, and the area is teeming with wildlife, including bears, cougars, deer, elk, and the occasional mountain sheep downriver.

RV sites, facilities: There are 12 primitive sites for tents or self-contained RVs up to 71 feet. Picnic tables and fire grills are provided. Drinking water is available May–mid-October. Garbage bins and vault toilets are available. Raft rentals are available nearby. Leashed pets are permitted.

Reservations, fees: Reservations are not

accepted. Sites are $5–9 per night, $5 per night for an additional vehicle. Open April–October.

Directions: From LaGrande, drive northeast on Highway 82 for 18 miles to Elgin, then continue 14 miles to the park entrance road. Turn left (north) and drive two miles to the park.

Contact: Wallowa Lake State Park, 541/432-8855 or 800/551-6949, www.oregonstateparks.org.

31 MOSS SPRINGS

Scenic rating: 7

near the Eagle Cap Wilderness in Wallowa-Whitman National Forest

Map grid D1

At 6,000 feet elevation, Moss Springs campground is heavily forested with spruce and fir and has good views of the Grande Ronde Valley in some locations. The camp is popular with horse packers, and there is a loading ramp on-site. A trailhead provides access to the Eagle Cap Wilderness, a good jumping-off point for a multi-day backpacking trip. (Obtain a map of Wallowa-Whitman National Forest for detailed trail information.) The Breshears OHV Trail and the Mount Fanny Mountain bike trails are just north of the camp.

RV sites, facilities: There are seven sites for tents and RVs up to 16 feet long. Picnic tables and fire grills are provided. No drinking water is provided, but water is available for stock. Horse facilities and vault toilets are available. Garbage must be packed out. Some facilities are wheelchair accessible. Leashed pets are permitted.

Reservations, fees: Reservations are not accepted. Sites are $5 per night per vehicle. Open June–mid-October, weather permitting.

Directions: From LaGrande, drive east on Highway 237 for 15 miles to Cove and County Road 65 (signed for Moss Springs). Turn right (southeast) and drive 1.5 miles to Forest Road 6220. Turn left (east) and drive eight miles to the camp entrance. Note: The last five miles are on a steep gravel road.

Contact: Wallowa-Whitman National Forest, LaGrande Ranger District, 541/963-7186, fax 541/962-8580, www.fs.fed.us.

32 SHADY

Scenic rating: 6

on the Lostine River in
Wallowa-Whitman National Forest

Map grid D1

Shady campground sits along the banks of the Lostine River at an elevation of 5,400 feet. The camp has wooded as well as meadow areas. It is close to trails that provide access to the Eagle Cap Wilderness, a beautiful and pristine area that's perfect for an extended backpacking trip. You can sometimes spot mountain sheep in the area.

RV sites, facilities: There are 12 sites for tents or RVs up to 16 feet long. Picnic tables and fire grills are provided. Vault toilets are available. There is no drinking water, and garbage must be packed out. Leashed pets are permitted.

Reservations, fees: Reservations are not accepted. Sites are $6 per night. Open mid-June–November, weather permitting.

Directions: From LaGrande, turn north on Highway 82 and drive 52 miles to Lostine and Forest Road 8210. Turn right (south) and drive 15 miles to the campground.

Contact: Wallowa-Whitman National Forest, Eagle Cap Ranger District, 541/426-5546, www.fs.fed.us.

33 TWO PAN

Scenic rating: 6

on the Lostine River in
Wallowa-Whitman National Forest

Map grid D1

Two Pan lies at the end of a forest road on the banks of the Lostine River. At 5,600 feet elevation, this camp is a prime jumping-off spot for a multi-day wilderness adventure. Adjacent trails provide access to numerous lakes and streams in the Eagle Cap Wilderness. If full, another

campground option is Williamson, seven miles north on Forest Road 8210.

RV sites, facilities: There are nine sites for tents or RVs up to 16 feet. Picnic tables and fire grills are provided. Vault toilets are available. There is no drinking water, and garbage must be packed out. Leashed pets are permitted.

Reservations, fees: Reservations are not accepted. A Northwest Forest Pass is required, but there is no camping fee. Open mid-June–November, weather permitting.

Directions: From LaGrande, turn north on Highway 82 and drive 52 miles to Lostine and Forest Road 8210. Turn right (south) and drive 17 miles to the campground.

Contact: Wallowa-Whitman National Forest, Eagle Cap Ranger District, Wallowa Mountains Visitors Center, 541/426-5546, www.fs.fed.us.

34 HURRICANE CREEK

Scenic rating: 5

near the Eagle Cap Wilderness in
Wallowa-Whitman National Forest

Map grid D1

Set along Hurricane Creek at an elevation of 5,000 feet, this campground is on the edge of the Eagle Cap Wilderness and provides a good place to begin a backcountry backpacking trip. Sites are wooded, and some sit close to the creek—perfect for fishing. There is no access for medium to large RVs, which gives the camp more of a wilderness environment. Obtaining maps of the area from the ranger district is essential.

RV sites, facilities: There are 12 sites for tents or RVs up to 16 feet long. Picnic tables and fire grills are provided. Vault toilets are available. There is no drinking water, and garbage must be packed out. Leashed pets are permitted.

Reservations, fees: Reservations are not accepted. Sites are $6 per night. Open mid-June–November, weather permitting.

Directions: From LaGrande, turn north on Highway 82 and drive 62 miles to Enterprise and Hurricane Creek Road. Turn right (south) on Hurricane Creek Road and drive five miles to Hurricane Grange Hall and Forest Road 8205; bear right (off the paved road) and drive two miles to the campground on the left.

Contact: Wallowa-Whitman National Forest, Eagle Cap Ranger District, 541/426-5546, www.fs.fed.us.

35 MOUNTAIN VIEW MOTEL AND RV PARK

Scenic rating: 3

near Wallowa Lake

Map grid D1

Mountain View is centrally located for exploring the greater Wallowa Lake area. Fishing and jet boating are available only a mile away at Wallowa Lake, and nearby recreational facilities include bike paths, a golf course, hiking trails, and a riding stable. The park has a fish pond and creek and offers views of the Seven Devils Mountains and of the Eagle Cap Wilderness.

RV sites, facilities: There are 30 sites with full hookups (some pull-through) for RVs of any length, a grassy area for tents, and nine cabins. Picnic tables and fire pits are provided. Restrooms with flush toilets and showers, a dump station, Wi-Fi, firewood, and coin laundry are available. Propane gas, a store, and café are within two miles. Leashed pets are permitted, but pit bulls and rottweilers are not allowed.

Reservations, fees: Reservations are accepted. RV sites are $24.95 per night, tent sites are $19.95 per night, $3.50 per person per night for more than two people. Some credit cards are accepted. Open year-round.

Directions: From LaGrande, turn north on Highway 82 and drive 62 miles to Enterprise and the junction with Highway 3. Continue north on Highway 82 for four miles to the campground on the right (1.5 miles north of Joseph).

Contact: Mountain View Motel and RV Park, 866/262-9891 (toll free) or 541/432-2982 (phone or fax), www.rvmotel.com.

36 WALLOWA LAKE STATE PARK

Scenic rating: 8

on Wallowa Lake

Map grid D1   **BEST (**

Surrounded by snowy peaks, Wallowa Lake is a large lake with plenty of fishing and boating, including waterskiing and parasailing. Recreational activities include canoeing, horseback riding, and hiking. Bumper boats, miniature golf, and an artist community provide other diversions. Other highlights include a pretty one-mile nature trail and trailheads that provide access into the Eagle Cap Wilderness and Hells Canyon gorge. A marina is nearby for boaters and anglers. Picnicking, swimming, and wildlife-viewing are a few of the other activities available to visitors.

RV sites, facilities: There are 121 sites with full hookups for RVs of any length, 89 tent sites, three group tent areas for up to 25 people each, two yurts, and one cabin. Picnic tables and fire rings are provided. Garbage bins, drinking water, restrooms with flush toilets and showers, a dump station, and firewood are available. A store, café, and ice are within one mile. Boat docks, launching facilities, and rentals are nearby. Some facilities are wheelchair accessible. Leashed pets are permitted.

Reservations, fees: Reservations are accepted at 800/452-5687 or www.reserveamerica.com ($8 reservation fee). RV sites are $17–25 per night, tent sites are $13–20 per night, hiker/biker sites are $4–5 per person per night, group areas are $42–74 per night, yurts are $29–38 per night, the cabin is $58–90 per night, and $5 per night per additional vehicle. Some credit cards are accepted. Open year-round, with limited availability in winter (no water).

Directions: From LaGrande, turn north on Highway 82 and drive 62 miles to Enterprise and the junction with Highway 3. Continue south on Highway 82 to Joseph. Continue for six miles to the south shore of the lake and the campground.

Contact: Wallowa Lake State Park, 541/432-4185, www.oregonstateparks.org.

37 LICK CREEK

Scenic rating: 7

on Lick Creek in Wallowa-Whitman National Forest
Map grid D1

Located along the banks of Lick Creek in Hells Canyon National Recreation Area, this secluded and pretty campground sits in park-like surroundings at an elevation of 5,400 feet. Interspersed throughout the campground, tall Douglas fir, lodgepole pine, tamarack, and white fir provide a wildlife habitat for the area's birds and small animals.

RV sites, facilities: There are seven tent sites and five sites for RVs up to 30 feet long. Picnic tables and fire rings are provided. Vault toilets are available. There is no drinking water, and garbage must be packed out. Leashed pets are permitted.

Reservations, fees: Reservations are not accepted. Sites are $6 per night. Open mid-June–late November, weather permitting.

Directions: From LaGrande, turn north on Highway 82 and drive 64 miles to Enterprise. Continue south on Highway 82 to Joseph and Highway 350. Turn left (east) and drive 7.5 miles to Forest Road 39. Turn right (south) and drive 15 miles to the campground.

Contact: Hells Canyon National Recreation Area, Wallowa Mountains Visitors Center, 541/426-5546, fax 541/426-5522, www.fs.fed.us/r6/w-w.

38 COVERDALE

Scenic rating: 7

near the Imnaha River
Map grid D1

Located at 4,300 feet in elevation along the Imnaha River, this campground is in a lushly forested drainage area. Wildflower viewing can be spectacular and fishing can be good. Hiking trails are nearby.

RV sites, facilities: There are four sites for tents and two sites for RVs up to 24 feet long. Picnic tables and fire rings are provided. There is no drinking water. Garbage must be packed out. Some facilities are wheelchair accessible. Leashed pets are permitted.

Reservations, fees: Reservations are not accepted. Sites are $6 per night. Open June–October, weather permitting.

Directions: From Joseph, drive east on Highway 350 for eight miles to Wallowa Mountain Loop Road (Forest Road 39). Turn right and drive approximately 38 miles to Forest Road 3960. Turn right and drive four miles to the campground on the left.

Contact: Hells Canyon National Recreation Area, Wallowa Mountains Visitors Center, 541/426-5546, fax 541/426-5522.

39 OLLOKOT

Scenic rating: 5

on the Imnaha River in
Wallowa-Whitman National Forest
Map grid D1

This campground sits on the banks of the Imnaha River in Hells Canyon National Recreation Area at an elevation of 4,000 feet. It's named for Chief Joseph's brother, a member of the Nez Perce tribe. For those seeking a little more solitude, this could be the spot.

RV sites, facilities: There are 12 sites for tents or RVs up to 30 feet long. Picnic tables and fire rings are provided. Vault toilets are available. There is no drinking water, and garbage must be packed out. Leashed pets are permitted.

Reservations, fees: Reservations are not accepted. Sites are $8 per night. Open June–late November, weather permitting.

Directions: From I-84 at LaGrande, turn north on Highway 82 and drive 64 miles to Enterprise. Continue six miles south to Joseph and Highway 350. Turn left (east) on Highway 350 and drive eight miles to Forest Road 39. Turn right (south) on Forest Road 39 and drive 30 miles to the campground on the left.

Contact: Hells Canyon National Recreation Area, Wallowa Mountains Visitors Center, 541/426-5546, fax 541/426-5522, www.fs.fed.us/r6/w-w.

OREGON

40 BLACKHORSE

Scenic rating: 7

on the Imnaha River in
Wallowa-Whitman National Forest

Map grid E1

This campground along the banks of the Imnaha River in Hells Canyon National Recreation Area is located in a secluded section of Wallowa-Whitman National Forest at an elevation of 4,000 feet.

RV sites, facilities: There are 15 sites for tents or RVs up to 30 feet long. Picnic tables and fire rings are provided. Vault toilets are available. There is no drinking water, and garbage must be packed out. Leashed pets are permitted.

Reservations, fees: Reservations are not accepted. Sites are $8 per night. Open June–late November, weather permitting.

Directions: From I-84 at LaGrande, turn north on Highway 82 and drive 64 miles to Enterprise. Continue six miles south to Joseph and Highway 350. Turn left (east) and drive eight miles on Highway 350 to Forest Road 39. Turn right (south) on Forest Road 39 and drive 29 miles to the campground.

Contact: Hells Canyon National Recreation Area, Wallowa Mountains Visitors Center, 541/426-5546, fax 541/426-5522, www.fs.fed.us/r6/w-w.

41 HIDDEN

Scenic rating: 6

on the Imnaha River in
Wallowa-Whitman National Forest

Map grid E1

River views and spacious sites can be found at this campground in a pretty spot along the banks of Imnaha River in the Hells Canyon National Recreation Area. It's essential to obtain a map of Wallowa-Whitman National Forest that details back roads and hiking trails. If full, Coverdale Campground is an option, just four miles northeast on Forest Road 3960.

RV sites, facilities: There are 10 tent sites and three sites for tents or small, self-contained RVs. Picnic tables and fire rings are provided. Vault toilets are available. There is no drinking water, and garbage must be packed out. Leashed pets are permitted.

Reservations, fees: Reservations are not accepted. Sites are $6 per night. Open June–late November, weather permitting.

Directions: From LaGrande, drive east on Highway 82 for 64 miles to Enterprise. Continue six miles south to Joseph and Highway 350. Turn left (east) and drive eight miles to Wallowa Mountain Loop Road (Forest Road 39). Turn right (south) and drive 30 miles to Forest Road 3960. Turn right (southwest) and drive seven miles to the campground.

Contact: Hells Canyon National Recreation Area, Wallowa Mountains Visitors Center, 541/426-5546, fax 541/426-5522, www.fs.fed.us/r6/w-w.

42 INDIAN CROSSING

Scenic rating: 6

on the Imnaha River in
Wallowa-Whitman National Forest

Map grid E1

Indian Crossing is situated at an elevation of 4,500 feet and is more developed than nearby Hidden Campground. A trailhead for the Eagle Cap Wilderness is near; obtain a U.S. Forest Service map for trail options.

RV sites, facilities: There are 14 sites for tents or RVs up to 30 feet long. Picnic tables and fire rings are provided. Drinking water, vault toilets, and horse facilities are available. Garbage must be packed out. Leashed pets are permitted.

Reservations, fees: Reservations are not accepted. Sites are $8 per night. Open June–late November, weather permitting.

Directions: From LaGrande, turn north on Highway 82 and drive 62 miles to Enterprise. Continue on Highway 82 for six miles to Joseph and Highway 350. Turn left (east) on

Highway 350 and drive eight miles to Forest Road 39. Turn right (south) and drive about 30 miles to Forest Road 3960. Turn right and drive 10 miles to the campground at the end of the road.

Contact: Hells Canyon National Recreation Area, Wallowa Mountains Visitors Center, 541/426-5546, fax 541/426-5522, www.fs.fed.us/r6/w-w.

43 WILDCAT

Scenic rating: 4

on the east fork of Mill Creek in Ochoco National Forest

Map grid A2

Surrounded by conifer forest, Wildcat campground sits at an elevation of 3,700 feet in a cool canyon. Situated along the east fork of Mill Creek, the quiet camp is near the Twin Pillars Trailhead, which provides access into the Mill Creek Wilderness. No climbing is allowed in the wilderness. Ochoco Lake and Ochoco Lake State Park to the south provide side-trip possibilities.

RV sites, facilities: There are 17 sites for tents or RVs up to 30 feet long. Picnic tables and fire grills are provided. Drinking water and vault toilets are available. Garbage must be packed out. Leashed pets are permitted.

Reservations, fees: Reservations are not accepted. Sites are $8 per night, $3 per night for each additional vehicle. Open mid-May–late October, weather permitting.

Directions: From Prineville, drive east on U.S. 26 for nine miles to Mill Creek Road (Forest Road 33). Turn left on Mill Creek Road and drive about 10 miles to the campground.

Contact: Ochoco National Forest, Lookout Mountain Ranger District, 541/416-6500, fax 541/416-6695, www.fs.fed.us.

44 OCHOCO DIVIDE

Scenic rating: 5

in Ochoco National Forest

Map grid A2

This quiet campground is set at an elevation of 4,700 feet in a ponderosa pine forest. Hiking is available along a forest road near the camp and at nearby Marks Creek and Bandit Springs. This is a quick jump off U.S. 26; campers tend to set up in the afternoon and leave early in the morning, so you may get the place to yourself.

RV sites, facilities: There are 28 sites for tents or RVs up to 30 feet long, with a separate area of walk-in and bike-in sites. Picnic tables and fire pits are provided. Vault toilets are available. There is no drinking water, and garbage must be packed out. Some facilities are wheelchair accessible. Leashed pets are permitted.

Reservations, fees: Reservations are not accepted. Sites are $13 per night, plus $6.50 per night for an additional vehicle. Hike-in/bike-in sites are $13 per person per night. Open late May–mid-October, weather permitting.

Directions: From Prineville, drive east on U.S. 26 for 30 miles to the campground at the summit of Ochoco Pass.

Contact: Ochoco National Forest, Lookout Mountain Ranger District, 541/416-6500, fax 541/416-6695, www.fs.fed.us.

45 OCHOCO CAMPGROUND

Scenic rating: 4

in Ochoco National Forest

Map grid A2

Ochoco Campground sits at an elevation of 4,000 feet along Ochoco Creek amid pine and aspen trees. There's fair fishing for rainbow trout, and hiking is nearby in the Lookout Mountain Recreation Area—that's 15,000 acres without roads. But hey, the truth is: don't expect privacy and solitude at this campground. The log shelter and picnic area are often reserved for weddings, family reunions, and other group events.

OREGON

RV sites, facilities: There are six sites for tents or RVs up to 24 feet long and one group site. Picnic tables and fire rings are provided. Drinking water, garbage bins, vault toilets, and a picnic shelter (by reservation) are available. Some facilities are wheelchair accessible. Leashed pets are permitted.

Reservations, fees: Reservations are only accepted for the group site at 877/444-6777 or www.recreation.gov. Sites are $13 per night, the group site is $60 per night, $6.50 per night for an additional vehicle. Open mid-May–October, weather permitting.

Directions: From Prineville, drive east on U.S. 26 for 16.5 miles to County Road 23. Turn right on County Road 23 and drive nine miles (County Road 23 becomes Forest Road 42) to the campground, across from the Ochoco Ranger Station.

Contact: Ochoco National Forest, Lookout Mountain Ranger District, 541/416-6500, fax 541/416-6695, www.fs.fed.us.

46 WALTON LAKE

Scenic rating: 7

on Walton Lake in Ochoco National Forest

Map grid A2

This campground, surrounded by meadows and ponderosa pine, borders the shore of small Walton Lake. Fishing and swimming are popular; the lake is stocked with rainbow trout, and the fishing can range from middle-of-the-road right up to downright excellent. Only non-motorized boats or boats with electric motors are allowed on the lake. Hikers can explore a nearby trail that leads south to Round Mountain.

RV sites, facilities: There are 30 sites for tents or RVs up to 28 feet long and two group sites. Picnic tables, garbage bins, and fire grills are provided. Drinking water and vault toilets are available. Boat-launching facilities are nearby (only electric motors are allowed). Some facilities are wheelchair accessible. Leashed pets are permitted.

Reservations, fees: Reservations accepted only

for the group sites at 877/444-6777 or www.recreation.gov ($10 reservation fee). Sites are $15 per night, $7.50 per night per additional vehicle. Group sites are $50 per night. Open mid-May–mid-September, weather permitting.

Directions: From Prineville, drive east on U.S. 26 for 16.5 miles to County Road 23. Turn right (northeast) and drive nine miles (County Road 23 becomes Forest Road 42) to the Ochoco Ranger Station and Forest Road 22. Turn left and drive north on Forest Road 22 for seven miles to the campground.

Contact: Ochoco National Forest, Lookout Mountain Ranger District, 541/416-6500, fax 541/416-6695, www.fs.fed.us.

47 DEEP CREEK

Scenic rating: 5

on the north fork of the Crooked River in Ochoco National Forest

Map grid A2

This small camp on the edge of high desert (4,200 feet elevation) gets little use, but it's in a nice spot. Located right at the confluence of Deep Creek and the north fork of the Crooked River, the pretty, shady sites allow for river access and fishing.

RV sites, facilities: There are six sites for tents or RVs up to 22 feet long. Picnic tables and fire grills are provided. Drinking water and vault toilets are available. Garbage must be packed out. Leashed pets are permitted.

Reservations, fees: Reservations are not accepted. Sites are $8 per night, $3 per night per additional vehicle. Open mid-May–mid-October, weather permitting.

Directions: From Prineville, drive east on U.S. 26 for 16.5 miles to County Route 23. Turn right (northeast) and drive 8.5 miles (it becomes Forest Road 42). Continue east on Forest Road 42 (paved road) for 23.5 miles to the campground on the right.

Contact: Ochoco National Forest, Lookout Mountain Ranger District, 541/416-6500, fax 541/416-6695, www.fs.fed.us.

48 CROOK COUNTY RV PARK

Scenic rating: 6

near the Crooked River

Map grid A2

This five-acre public campground sits in a landscaped, grassy area near the Crooked River, where fly-fishing is popular. The camp is located right next to the Crook County Fairgrounds, which offers seasonal expositions, horse races, and rodeos.

RV sites, facilities: There are 81 sites for tents or RVs up to 70 feet long (full hookups); most sites are pull-through. In addition, there are nine tent sites and two log cabins available. Picnic tables are provided. Fire pits are provided at the tent sites. Restrooms with flush toilets and showers, a dump station, cable TV, and modem access are available. A convenience store, restaurant, ice, gasoline, and propane are available within one mile. Some facilities are wheelchair accessible. Leashed pets are permitted with restrictions on some breeds.

Reservations, fees: Reservations are accepted at 800/609-2599. Tent sites are $10 per night, RV sites are $28–30 per night, $5 per night per additional vehicle. Weekly and monthly rates are available. Some credit cards are accepted. Open year-round.

Directions: From Redmond, drive east on Highway 126 for 18 miles to Prineville (Highway 126 becomes 3rd Street) and Main Street. Turn right on Main Street and drive about 0.5 mile south to the campground on the left, before the fairgrounds.

Contact: Crook County RV Park, 541/447-2599, fax 541/416-9022, www.ccprd.org/parks_rv.cfm.

49 OCHOCO LAKE

Scenic rating: 6

on Ochoco Lake

Map grid A2

This is one of the nicer camps along U.S. 26 in eastern Oregon. The campground is located on the shore of Ochoco Lake, where boating and fishing are popular pastimes. Some quality hiking trails can be found in the area.

RV sites, facilities: There are 21 primitive sites for tents or self-contained RVs up to 50 feet long and a special area for hikers and bicyclists. Picnic tables, garbage bins, and fire grills are provided. Drinking water, firewood, restrooms with showers and flush toilets, ice, a fish-cleaning station, and boat-launching facilities are available. Leashed pets are permitted.

Reservations, fees: Reservations are not accepted. Sites are $16 per night, $5 per person per night for hike-in/bike-in sites, and $7 per night per additional vehicle. Some credit cards are accepted. Open April–October, weather permitting.

Directions: From Prineville, drive east on U.S. 26 for seven miles to the park entrance on the right.

Contact: Crook County Parks and Recreation, 541/447-1209, fax 541/447-9894, www.ccprd.org/parks_ochoco.cfm.

50 CHIMNEY ROCK

Scenic rating: 6

on the Crooked River

Map grid A2

Chimney Rock Campground is one of eight BLM camps along a six-mile stretch of Highway 27. This well-spaced campground is a favorite for picnicking and wildlife-viewing. The Chimney Rock Trailhead, just across the highway, is the jumping-off point for the 1.7-mile, moderately difficult hike to Chimney Rock. There are numerous scenic overlooks along the trail, and wildlife sightings are common. The elevation here is 3,000 feet.

RV sites, facilities: There are 20 sites for tents or RVs of any length. Picnic tables are provided. Vault toilets, drinking water, and garbage bins are available. Some facilities are wheelchair accessible, including a fishing dock. Leashed pets are permitted.

Reservations, fees: Reservations are not accepted. Sites are $8 per night, $2 per night for an additional vehicle. Open year-round.

Directions: In Prineville, drive south on Highway 27 for 16.4 miles to the campground.

OREGON

Contact: Bureau of Land Management, Prineville District, 541/416-6700, fax 541/416-6798, www.blm.gov.

51 PRINEVILLE RESERVOIR STATE PARK

Scenic rating: 7

on Prineville Reservoir

Map grid A2

This state park is set along the shore of Prineville Reservoir, which formed with the damming of the Crooked River. This is one of two campgrounds on the reservoir (the other is Prineville Reservoir Resort). Boating, fishing, swimming, and waterskiing are popular activities here; the nearby boat docks and ramp are a bonus. The reservoir supports rainbow and cutthroat trout, small and largemouth bass, catfish, and crappie; you can even ice fish in the winter.

RV sites, facilities: There are 44 sites with partial hookups for RVs up to 40 feet long, 23 tent sites, two rustic cabins, and three deluxe cabins. Picnic tables and fire pits are provided. Drinking water, garbage bins, restrooms with flush toilets and showers, ice, and firewood are available. Boat docks, launching facilities, and moorings that can be reserved are nearby. Some facilities are wheelchair accessible. Leashed pets are permitted.

Reservations, fees: Reservations are accepted at 800/452-5687 or www.reserveamerica.com ($8 reservation fee). RV sites are $18–26, tent sites are $13–21 per night, cabins are $38–82 per night, boat moorage is $7–10, and $5 per night per additional vehicle. Some credit cards are accepted. Open year-round.

Directions: From Prineville, drive east on U.S. 26 for one mile to Combs Flat Road. Turn right (south) and drive one mile to Juniper Canyon Road. Turn right (south) and drive 18 miles to the campground.

Contact: Prineville Reservoir State Park, 541/447-4363 or 800/551-6949, www.oregonstateparks.org.

52 PRINEVILLE RESERVOIR RESORT

Scenic rating: 6

on Prineville Reservoir

Map grid A2

This resort sits on the shore of Prineville Reservoir in the high desert, a good spot for water sports and fishing. The mostly shaded sites are a combination of dirt and gravel. The camp features easy access to the reservoir and some colorful rock formations to check out.

RV sites, facilities: There are 70 sites with partial hookups (including four pull-through sites) for tents or RVs of any length, seven motel rooms, and one primitive cabin. Drinking water, fire pits, and picnic tables are provided. Restrooms with flush toilets and coin showers, propane gas, a dump station, firewood, a convenience store, a café, and ice are available. A full-service marina, boat ramp, boat rentals, fish-cleaning station, and fishing licenses are on-site. Some facilities are wheelchair accessible. Leashed pets are permitted.

Reservations, fees: Reservations are accepted at 541/447-7468 ($7 reservation fee). Sites are $16–24 per night. Some credit cards are accepted. Open May–mid-October, weather permitting.

Directions: From Prineville, drive east on U.S. 26 for one mile to Combs Flat Road. Turn right (south) and drive one mile to Juniper Canyon Road. Turn right (south) and drive 18 miles to the resort at the end of the road.

Contact: Prineville Reservoir Resort, tel./fax 541/447-7468, www.prinevillereservoirresort.com.

53 JASPER POINT STATE PARK

Scenic rating: 7

on Prineville Reservoir

Map grid A2

Jasper Point is a quiet alternative to Prineville Reservoir State Park. The park is not as popular as Prineville; although it does fill up on summer weekends, it's used mainly by locals. Although the park is named Jasper Point, the setting is in a cove and the views are not as good as those at Prineville Reservoir State Park. A 1.75-mile trail connects the two campgrounds, and another 0.7-mile trail runs along the shoreline.

RV sites, facilities: There are 30 sites for tents or RVs of any length. Picnic tables and fire pits are provided. Drinking water, vault toilets, garbage containers, a day-use area, and a boat launch are available. Leashed pets are permitted.

Reservations, fees: Reservations are not accepted. Sites are $22–26 per night, $5 per night per additional vehicle. Open May–September.

Directions: From Prineville, drive east on U.S. 26 for one mile to Combs Flat Road. Turn right (south) and drive one mile to Juniper Canyon Road. Turn right (south) and drive 21 miles to the campground.

Contact: Prineville Reservoir State Park, 541/447-4363 or 800/551-6949, www.oregonstateparks.org.

54 ANTELOPE FLAT RESERVOIR

Scenic rating: 6

on Antelope Flat Reservoir in
Ochoco National Forest

Map grid A2

This pretty spot is situated along the west shore of Antelope Flat Reservoir amid ponderosa pine and juniper. The campground is on the edge of the high desert at an elevation of 4,600 feet. It features wide sites and easy access to the lake. Trout fishing can sometimes be good in the spring, and boating with motors is permitted. This is also a good lake for canoes.

RV sites, facilities: There are 25 sites for tents or RVs up to 30 feet long. Picnic tables and fire grills are provided. Drinking water and vault toilets are available. Garbage must be packed out. Boat-launching facilities are nearby. Leashed pets are permitted.

Reservations, fees: Reservations are not accepted. Sites are $8 per night, $3 per night for each additional vehicle. Open early May–late October, weather permitting.

Directions: From Prineville, drive southeast on Combs Flat Road (Paulina Highway) for 30 miles to Forest Road 17 (Antelope Reservoir Junction). Turn right on Forest Road 17 and drive about 10 miles to Forest Road 1700-600. Drive 0.25 mile on Forest Road 1700-600 to the campground.

Contact: Ochoco National Forest, Lookout Mountain Ranger District, 541/416-6500, fax 541/416-6695, www.fs.fed.us.

55 WILEY FLAT

Scenic rating: 3

on Wiley Creek in Ochoco National Forest

Map grid A2

Wiley Flat campground is set along Wiley Creek in a nice, hidden spot with minimal crowds. It is popular with horseback riders and seasonal hunters. Tower Point Lookout is one mile north of the camp. A map of Ochoco National Forest details nearby access roads.

RV sites, facilities: There are five sites for tents or RVs up to 30 feet long. Picnic tables and fire grills are provided. Vault toilets are available. There is no drinking water, and garbage must be packed out. Leashed pets are permitted.

Reservations, fees: Reservations are not accepted. There is no fee for camping. Open mid-June–late October, weather permitting.

Directions: From Prineville, drive southeast on the Paulina Highway (Combs Flat Road) for 34 miles to Forest Road 16. Turn right (southeast) and drive 10 miles to Forest Road 1600-400. Turn right (west) and drive one mile to the camp.

Contact: Ochoco National Forest, Lookout Mountain Ranger District, 541/416-6500, fax 541/416-6695, www.fs.fed.us.

56 BULL PRAIRIE LAKE

Scenic rating: 8

on Bull Prairie Lake in Umatilla National Forest

Map grid B2

Set on the shore of Bull Prairie Lake, a 28-acre lake at 4,000 feet elevation, this spot attracts little attention from out-of-towners, yet it offers plenty of recreation opportunities, making it an ideal vacation destination. Boating (no motors permitted), fishing for blue gill and trout, hunting, and swimming are some of the attractions here. A hiking trail circles the lake.

RV sites, facilities: There are 28 sites for tents or RVs up to 31 feet long and one group site for up to 25 people. Picnic tables and fire grills are provided. Vault toilets are available. Drinking water and garbage bins are available late May–mid-October. Boat docks and a boat ramp are on-site. Some facilities are wheelchair accessible, including the boat ramp. Leashed pets are permitted.

Reservations, fees: Reservations are not accepted. Single sites are $14, double sites are $19, the group site is $28, $5–8 per night for an additional vehicle. Open year-round, weather permitting.

Directions: From Heppner, drive south on Highway 207 for roughly 35 miles to the national forest boundary and continue four miles to Forest Road 2039 (paved). Turn left and drive three miles northeast to the campground on the right.

Contact: Umatilla National Forest, Heppner Ranger District, 541/676-9187, fax 541/676-2105, www.fs.fed.us.

57 FAIRVIEW

Scenic rating: 5

near Bull Prairie Lake in Umatilla National Forest

Map grid B2

This small, rugged campground is located in a remote area at 4,300 feet elevation near Mahogany Butte and adjacent to Fairview Springs. Known by very few people, it's very easy to miss and not even marked on Umatilla National Forest maps. Hunters use it primarily as a base camp. Bull Prairie Lake is only four miles away.

RV sites, facilities: There are five sites for tents or RVs up to 16 feet long. Picnic tables and fire grills are provided. Vault toilets are available. Drinking water is available May–October. Garbage must be packed out. Boat docks and launching facilities are nearby at Bull Prairie Lake. Leashed pets are permitted.

Reservations, fees: Reservations are not accepted. There is no fee for camping. Open May–October, weather permitting.

Directions: From Heppner, drive south on Highway 207 for roughly 35 miles to the national forest boundary. Continue four miles to Forest Road 2039 (the turnoff for Bull Prairie Lake). Continue on Highway 207 for one mile to Forest Road 400 (if you pass through an immediate series of hairpin turns, you have gone too far). Turn west and drive 500 yards to the campground.

Contact: Umatilla National Forest, Heppner Ranger District, 541/676-9187, fax 541/676-2105, www.fs.fed.us.

58 WOLF CREEK

Scenic rating: 5

on Wolf Creek in Ochoco National Forest

Map grid B2

This campground, at 4,000 feet elevation, is set along the banks of Wolf Creek, a nice trout stream that runs through Ochoco National Forest.

RV sites, facilities: There are 10 sites for tents or RVs up to 20 feet long. Picnic tables and fire grills are provided. Vault toilets are available. There is no drinking water, and garbage must be packed out. Leashed pets are permitted.

Reservations, fees: Reservations are not accepted. Sites are $6 per night, with a 14-day stay limit, and $3 per night for an additional vehicle. Open May–November, weather permitting.

Directions: From Prineville, drive southeast on

Combs Flat Road (Paulina Highway) for 55 miles to Paulina. Continue east for 3.5 miles to County Road 112. Turn left (north) and drive 6.5 miles to Forest Road 42. Turn left (north) and drive 1.5 miles to the campground on the right.

Contact: Ochoco National Forest, Paulina Ranger District, 541/477-6900, fax 541/477-6949, www.fs.fed.us.

59 SUGAR CREEK

Scenic rating: 6

on Sugar Creek in Ochoco National Forest
Map grid B2

This small, quiet, and remote campground sits along the banks of Sugar Creek at an elevation of 4,000 feet in a forest of ponderosa pine. A 0.5-mile trail loops along the creek. The camp also offers a covered group shelter in the day-use area and a wheelchair-accessible trail. Bald eagles occasionally nest in the area.

RV sites, facilities: There are 17 sites for tents or RVs up to 22 feet long. Picnic tables and fire grills are provided. Drinking water, a picnic shelter, and vault toilets are available. Garbage must be packed out. Some facilities are wheelchair accessible. Leashed pets are permitted.

Reservations, fees: Reservations are not accepted. Sites are $8 per night, with a 14-day stay limit, and $3 per night for an additional vehicle. Open May–November.

Directions: From Prineville, drive southeast on Combs Flat Road (Paulina Highway) for 55 miles to Paulina. Continue east and drive 3.5 miles to a fork with County Road 112. Bear left at the fork onto County Road 112 and drive 7.5 miles to Forest Road 58. Bear right on Forest Road 58 and continue for 1.3 miles to the campground on the right.

Contact: Ochoco National Forest, Paulina Ranger District, 541/477-6900, fax 541/477-6949, www.fs.fed.us.

60 FRAZIER

Scenic rating: 4

on Frazier Creek in Ochoco National Forest
Map grid B2

Frazier is a small, remote, and little-used campground located at an elevation of 4,600 feet. The landscape is open, grassy, and sprinkled with a few large pine trees. Some dirt roads adjacent to the camp are good for mountain biking in summer, and the camp's meadow setting is occasionally the site of family reunions during summer holidays.

RV sites, facilities: There are seven sites for tents or RVs up to 22 feet long. Picnic tables and fire grills are provided. Vault toilets are available. There is no drinking water, and garbage must be packed out. Leashed pets are permitted.

Reservations, fees: Reservations are not accepted. There is no fee for camping. The stay limit is 14 days. Open May–November, weather permitting.

Directions: From Prineville, drive southeast on Combs Flat Road (Paulina Highway) for 55 miles to Paulina. Continue east and drive 3.5 miles to a fork with County Road 112. Bear left at the fork onto County Road 112 and drive 2.5 miles to County Road 135/Puett Road. Turn right (east) and drive 10 miles to Forest Road 58. Turn right and drive six miles to Forest Road 58-500. Turn left and drive two miles (bearing to the left) to the campground.

Contact: Ochoco National Forest, Paulina Ranger District, 541/477-6900, fax 541/477-6949, www.fs.fed.us.

61 CLYDE HOLLIDAY STATE RECREATION SITE

Scenic rating: 7

near the John Day River
Map grid B2

Clyde Holliday campground borders the John Day River, a spawning site for steelhead. Sites are private and shaded with cottonwood trees. Wildlife is prevalent in the area; watch for mule deer and elk near the campsites.

RV sites, facilities: There are 31 sites with partial hookups for tents or RVs up to 60 feet long, a hiker/biker tent area, and two tepees. Picnic tables and fire grills are provided. Drinking water, firewood, a dump station, and restrooms with showers and flush toilets are available. Leashed pets are permitted.

Reservations, fees: Reservations are not accepted for campsites but are advised for the tepees at 541/932-4453 or 800/932-4953. Sites are $13–22 per night, $4–5 per person per night for hike-in/bike-in sites, $29–39 per night for tepees, $5 per night for an additional vehicle. Open March–November, weather permitting.

Directions: From John Day, drive west on U.S. 26 for six miles to the park on the left.

Contact: Clyde Holliday State Recreation Site, 541/932-4453 or 800/551-6949, www.oregonstateparks.org.

62 STARR

Scenic rating: 4

on Starr Ridge in Malheur National Forest

Map grid B2

A good layover spot for travelers on U.S. 395, Starr happens to be adjacent to Starr Ridge, a snow play area popular in winter for skiing and sledding. The camp itself doesn't offer much in the way of recreation, but to the northeast is the Strawberry Mountain Wilderness, which has a number of lakes, streams, and trails. The camp sits at an elevation of 5,100 feet.

RV sites, facilities: There are eight sites for tents or RVs up to 22 feet long. Picnic tables and fire rings are provided. Vault toilets are available. There is no drinking water, and garbage must be packed out. Some facilities are wheelchair accessible. Leashed pets are permitted.

Reservations, fees: Reservations are not accepted. Sites are $6 per night, $3 per night for an additional vehicle. Open late May–November, weather permitting.

Directions: From John Day, drive south on U.S. 395 for 15 miles to the campground on the right.

Contact: Malheur National Forest, Blue

Mountain Ranger District, 541/575-3000, fax 541/575-3319, www.fs.fed.us.

63 WELCH CREEK

Scenic rating: 4

on Desolation Creek in Umatilla National Forest

Map grid C2

Welch Creek is a primitive camp set on the banks of Desolation Creek. Road noise and dust may be a problem for some, and there's little privacy among sites. The camp features trail access to the Desolation Area, both for non-motorized and motorized traffic. Hunting and fishing are popular here.

RV sites, facilities: There are five sites for tents or RVs up to 30 feet long and one group site. Picnic tables and fire rings are provided. A vault toilet is available. There is no drinking water. Garbage must be packed out. Leashed pets are permitted.

Reservations, fees: Reservations are not accepted. Sites are $8 per night, $25 for the group site, $5 per night for an additional vehicle. Open late May–early November, weather permitting. A 14-day stay limit is enforced.

Directions: From Pendleton, drive south on U.S. 395 for 62 miles to Forest Road 55 (one mile north of Dale; it's easier to find if you know the marker, Texas Bar Road). Turn left and drive one mile to Forest Road 10. Turn right and drive 13 miles to the campground on the right.

Contact: Umatilla National Forest, North Fork John Day Ranger District, 541/427-3231, fax 541/276-5026, www.fs.fed.us.

64 NORTH FORK JOHN DAY

Scenic rating: 6

on the north fork of the John Day River in Umatilla National Forest

Map grid C2

Set along the banks of the north fork of the John Day River at an elevation of 5,200 feet, this campground sits in a stand of lodgepole pine at the intersection of Elkhorn and Blue Mountain National Forest Scenic Byways. The campground has a great view of salmon spawning in the river in spring and fall and also makes an ideal launch point for a wilderness backpacking trip. Trails from camp lead into the North Fork John Day Wilderness. A horse-handling area is also available for wilderness users. No mountain bikes or motorcycles are permitted in the wilderness.

RV sites, facilities: There are 12 sites for tents or RVs up to 28 feet long, five sites for tents only, and one group site. Picnic tables and fire rings are provided. Vault toilets are available. There is no drinking water. Garbage must be packed out. Leashed pets are permitted.

Reservations, fees: Reservations are not accepted. Sites are $8 per night, $25 for the group site, $5 per night for an additional vehicle. Open June–November, weather permitting. A 14-day stay limit is enforced.

For trailhead use, a Northwest Forest Pass is required ($5 daily fee or $30 annual fee per parked vehicle).

Directions: From Pendleton, drive south on U.S. 395 for 50 miles to Highway 244. Turn east on Highway 244 and drive one mile to Ukiah and Forest Road 52. Turn right (south) on Forest Road 52 and drive 36 miles to the campground on the right.

Contact: Umatilla National Forest, North Fork John Day Ranger District, 541/427-3231, fax 541/427-3018, www.fs.fed.us.

65 ANTHONY LAKES

Scenic rating: 10

on Anthony Lake in Wallowa-Whitman National Forest

Map grid C2

This campground (7,100 feet elevation) is adjacent to Anthony Lake, where non-motorized boating is permitted. Sites are wooded, providing good screening between them. Alas, mosquitoes are often in particular abundance. Several smaller lakes within two miles by car

or trail are ideal for trout fishing from a canoe, float tube, or raft. Sometimes mountain goats can be seen from the Elkhorn Crest Trail, which begins near here. Weekends and holidays the campground tends to fill up.

RV sites, facilities: There are 10 sites for tents, 32 sites for RVs up to 22 feet long, and one group site for up to 75 people. Drinking water, fire grills, garbage bins (summer only), and picnic tables are provided. Vault toilets are available. Garbage must be packed out the rest of the year. Boat-launching facilities are nearby. Some facilities are wheelchair accessible. Leashed pets are permitted.

Reservations, fees: Reservations are not accepted for tent or RV sites but are required for the group site at 541/894-2404. Sites are $8–12 per night, $50 per night for the group site, and $6 per night per additional vehicle. Open June–late September, weather permitting.

Directions: From Baker City on I-84, turn north on U.S. 30. Drive north for 10 miles to Haines and County Road 1146 (signed for Anthony Lakes Ski Resort). Turn left on County Road 1146 and drive 20 miles (the road becomes Forest Road 73) to the campground on the left.

Contact: Wallowa-Whitman National Forest, Whitman Ranger District, 541/523-4476, fax 541/523-1965, www.fs.fed.us; Aud & Di Campground Services, 541/894-2404.

66 GRANDE RONDE LAKE

Scenic rating: 8

on Grande Ronde Lake in Wallowa-Whitman National Forest

Map grid C2

Grande Ronde campground sits amid Douglas and white fir at an elevation of 6,800 feet along the shore of Grande Ronde Lake. Trout fishing can be good at this small lake, and mountain goats are sometimes seen in the area. Several trails lie to the south, near Anthony Lake.

RV sites, facilities: There are eight sites for tents or RVs up to 16 feet long. Picnic tables and fire grills are provided. Drinking water and vault toilets are available. Garbage must be packed out. Boat launching facilities are nearby. Some facilities are wheelchair accessible. Leashed pets are permitted.

Reservations, fees: Reservations are not accepted. Sites are $8 per night, $4 per night per additional vehicle. Open late June–September, weather permitting.

Directions: Drive on I-84 to Baker City and U.S. 30. From Baker City, drive north on U.S. 30 for 10 miles to Haines and County Road 1146 (signed for Anthony Lakes Ski Resort). Turn left on County Road 1146 and drive 20 miles (the road becomes Forest Road 73) to the campground on the right.

Contact: Wallowa-Whitman National Forest, Whitman Ranger District, 541/523-4476, www.fs.fed.us; Aud & Di Campground Services, 541/894-2404.

67 MUD LAKE

Scenic rating: 7

on Mud Lake in Wallowa-Whitman National Forest

Map grid C2

Set at an elevation of 7,100 feet, tiny yet pleasant Mud Lake campground is filled with lots of vegetation and sees relatively little use. The campground is situated in fir forest on the shore of small Mud Lake, where the trout fishing can be fairly good. Mud Lake is shallow and more marshy than muddy. Bring your mosquito repellent.

RV sites, facilities: There are eight sites for tents or RVs up to 16 feet long. Picnic tables and fire grills are provided. Drinking water and vault toilets are available. Garbage must be packed out. Boat launching facilities are nearby at Anthony Lake. Leashed pets are permitted.

Reservations, fees: Reservations are not accepted. Sites are $8 per night, $4 per night per additional vehicle. Open June–late September, weather permitting.

Directions: Drive on I-84 to Baker City and U.S. 30. From Baker City, drive north on U.S.

30 for 10 miles to Haines and County Road 1146 (signed for Anthony Lakes Ski Resort). Turn left on County Road 1146 and drive 21 miles (the road becomes Forest Road 73) to the campground on the right.

Contact: Wallowa-Whitman National Forest, Whitman Ranger District, 541/523-4476, www.fs.fed.us; Aud & Di Campground Services, 541/894-2404.

68 OLIVE LAKE

Scenic rating: 9

on Olive Lake in Umatilla National Forest

Map grid C2

This campground (6,100 feet elevation) is nestled along the shore of Olive Lake, between two sections of the North Fork John Day Wilderness. Dammed to hold an increased volume of water, the glacial lake is a beautiful tint of blue. Motorized boats are allowed, but waterskiing is prohibited. Fishing is fair for kokanee salmon and brook, cutthroat, and rainbow trout. A 2.5-mile trail circles the lake. Nearby trails provide access to the wilderness; motorbikes and mountain bikes are not permitted in the wilderness. Sections of the old wooden pipeline for the historic Fremont Powerhouse can still be seen. The old mining town of Granite is 12 miles east of camp.

RV sites, facilities: There are 22 sites for tents or RVs up to 28 feet long, four sites for tents only, and two group sites. Picnic tables and fire grills are provided. Vault toilets are available. There is no drinking water, and garbage must be packed out. Two boat docks, launching facilities, and picnic areas are available. A camp host is on-site. Some facilities are wheelchair accessible. Leashed pets are permitted.

Reservations, fees: Reservations are not accepted. Sites are $12 per night, $25 per night for the group camp, $5 per night per additional vehicle. Open June–early October, weather permitting. A 14-day stay limit is enforced.

Directions: From Pendleton, drive south on U.S. 395 for 62 miles to Forest Road 55 (one mile north of Dale). Turn right and drive 0.5 mile

to Forest Road 10. Turn right on Forest Road 10 and drive 26 miles to Forest Road 480. Turn right and drive 0.5 mile to the campground.
Contact: Umatilla National Forest, North Fork John Day Ranger District, 541/427-3231, fax 541/427-3018, www.fs.fed.us.

69 UNION CREEK

Scenic rating: 8

on Phillips Lake in Wallowa-Whitman National Forest
Map grid C2

Union Creek campground along the north shore of Phillips Lake is easy to reach, yet missed by most I-84 travelers. It's the largest of three camps on the lake and the only one with drinking water. An old narrow-gauge railroad has been restored and runs up the valley from McEwen Depot (six miles from the campground) to Sumpter (10 miles away). Visit Sumpter to see an old dredge.
RV sites, facilities: There are 70 sites for tents or RVs up to 32 feet long and one group site; some sites have full hookups. Drinking water, garbage bins (summer only), and picnic tables are provided. Flush toilets, a dump station, firewood, and ice are available. There is a seasonal concession stand for packaged goods and fishing tackle. Boat docks and launching facilities are adjacent to the campground. Some facilities are wheelchair accessible. Leashed pets are permitted.
Reservations, fees: Reservations are not accepted for tent or RV sites but are required for the group site at 541/894-2404. Sites are $12–20 per night, additional fee for hookups, $50 per night for group sites, $6 per night per additional vehicle. Open May–September, weather permitting.
Directions: From Baker City, drive southwest on Highway 7 for 20 miles to the campground on the left.
Contact: Wallowa-Whitman National Forest, Whitman Ranger District, 541/523-4476 or 541/894-2505, www.fs.fed.us; Aud & Di Campground Services, 541/894-2404.

70 SOUTHWEST SHORE

Scenic rating: 7

on Phillips Lake in Wallowa-Whitman National Forest
Map grid C2

Southwest Shore is one of two primitive campgrounds on Philips Lake, a four-mile-long reservoir created by the Mason Dam on the Powder River. Set at 4,120 feet elevation, the camp borders the south shore of the lake; the boat ramp here is usable only when water is high in the reservoir. An old narrow-gauge railroad runs out of McEwen Depot (six miles from the campground) to Sumpter (10 miles away) for an interesting side-trip.
RV sites, facilities: There are 17 sites for tents or RVs up to 24 feet long. Fire grills and vault toilets are available. There is no drinking water, and garbage must be packed out. A boat ramp is adjacent to the campground. Leashed pets are permitted.
Reservations, fees: Reservations are not accepted. Sites are $8 per night, $4 per night per additional vehicle. Open May–October, weather permitting.
Directions: From Baker City, drive southwest on Highway 7 for 24 miles (just past Philips Lake) to Hudspeth Lane (County Road 667). Turn left (south) on Hudspeth Lane and drive two miles to Forest Road 2220. Turn left (southeast) and drive 2.5 miles to the campground on the left.
Contact: Wallowa-Whitman National Forest, Whitman Ranger District, 541/523-4476, www.fs.fed.us; Aud & Di Campground Services, 541/894-2404.

71 MILLERS LANE

Scenic rating: 7

on Phillips Lake in Wallowa-Whitman National Forest
Map grid C2

Millers Lane is one of two primitive camps on Philips Lake (the other is Southwest Shore). Phillips Lake is a long, narrow reservoir (and the largest in the region), and this small

OREGON

campground is situated along the south shore at an elevation of 4,120 feet. The camp is also near an old narrow-gauge railroad that runs out of McEwen Depot.

RV sites, facilities: There are seven sites for tents or RVs up to 20 feet long. Picnic tables and fire grills are provided. Vault toilets are available. There is no drinking water, and garbage must be packed out. A boat ramp is at Southwest Shore. Leashed pets are permitted.

Reservations, fees: Reservations are not accepted. Sites are $8 per night, $4 per night per additional vehicle. Open May–October, weather permitting.

Directions: From Baker City, drive southwest on Highway 7 for 24 miles (just past Phillips Lake) to Hudspeth Lane (County Road 667). Turn left (south) on Hudspeth Lane and drive two miles to Forest Road 2220. Turn left (southeast) and drive 3.5 miles to the campground on the left.

Contact: Wallowa-Whitman National Forest, Whitman Ranger District, 541/523-4476, www.fs.fed.us; Aud & Di Campground Services, 541/894-2404.

72 MAGONE LAKE

Scenic rating: 8

on Magone Lake in Malheur National Forest

Map grid C2

This campground is set along the shore of little Magone Lake at an elevation of 5,500 feet. A 1.8-mile trail rings the lake, and the section extending from the beach area to the campground (about 0.25 mile) is wheelchair accessible. A 0.5-mile trail leads to Magone Slide, an unusual geological formation. Canoeing, fishing, sailing, and swimming are some of the popular activities at this lake. Easy-access bike trails can be found within 0.25 mile of the campground. Just so you know, Magone is pronounced "Ma-Goon." Got it?

RV sites, facilities: There are 22 sites for tents or RVs up to 40 feet long (some pull-through),

eight tent sites, and a separate group camp designed for 10 families and a picnic shelter. Picnic tables and fire grills are provided. Drinking water, flush toilets, a boat ramp, and a beach area are available. A camp host is on-site. Boat docks are nearby. Some facilities, including a fishing pier, are wheelchair accessible. Leashed pets are permitted.

Reservations, fees: Reservations are required for the group site and group picnic shelter at 877/444-6777 or www.recreation.gov ($10 reservation fee). Sites are $13 per night, $60 per night for the group site, $6.50 per night per additional vehicle. Open late May–November, weather permitting.

Directions: From John Day, drive east on U.S. 26 for eight miles to County Road 18. Turn north and drive 10 miles to Forest Road 3620. Turn left (west) on Forest Road 3620 and drive 1.5 miles to Forest Road 3618. Turn right (northwest) and drive 1.5 miles to the campground. Note: The road is paved all the way.

Contact: Malheur National Forest, Blue Mountain Ranger District, 541/575-3000, fax 541/575-3319, www.fs.fed.us.

73 LOWER CAMP CREEK

Scenic rating: 5

in Malheur National Forest

Map grid C2

Lower Camp Creek is set at 5,026 feet elevation on the edge of a remote national forest. The camp is small and primitive, with a creek nearby, and is often overlooked, so you may have the place to yourself. In fall, a few hunters will often hunker down here and use it as their base camp.

RV sites, facilities: There are six sites for tents or RVs up to 40 feet long. Picnic tables, fire rings, and vault toilets are provided. There is no drinking water. Garbage must be packed out. Some facilities are wheelchair accessible. Leashed pets are permitted.

Reservations, fees: Reservations are not

accepted. Sites are $6 per night for single sites, $3 per night per additional vehicle. Open late May–November, weather permitting.

Directions: From John Day, drive east on U.S. 26 for eight miles to County Road 18. Turn north and drive eight miles to Four Corners. Turn right on Forest Road 36 and drive 12 miles to the campground on the left.

Contact: Malheur National Forest, Blue Mountain Ranger District, 541/573-4300, fax 541/573-4398, www.fs.fed.us.

74 MIDDLE FORK

Scenic rating: 6

on the Middle Fork of the John Day River in Malheur National Forest

Map grid C2

Scattered along the banks of the Middle Fork of the John Day River at 4,100 feet elevation, these rustic campsites are easy to reach off a paved road. Besides wildlife-viewing and berry picking, the main activity at this camp is fishing, so bring along your fly rod and pinch down your barbs for catch-and-release. The John Day is a state scenic waterway.

RV sites, facilities: There are 12 sites for tents or RVs up to 22 feet long. Picnic tables and fire rings are provided. Vault toilets are available. There is no drinking water, and garbage must be packed out. Some facilities are wheelchair accessible. Leashed pets are permitted.

Reservations, fees: Reservations are not accepted. Sites are $8 per night, $4 per night per additional vehicle. Open late May–November, weather permitting.

Directions: From John Day, drive northeast on U.S. 26 for 28 miles to Highway 7. Turn left (north) and drive one mile to County Road 20. Turn left and drive five miles to the campground on the left.

Contact: Malheur National Forest, Blue Mountain Ranger District, 541/575-3000, fax 541/575-3319, www.fs.fed.us.

75 DIXIE

Scenic rating: 5

near Dixie Summit in Malheur National Forest

Map grid C2

Perched at Dixie Summit (elevation 5,000 feet), this camp, just off U.S. 26, is close enough to provide easy access to nearby Bridge Creek, where you can toss in a fishing line. Dixie draws overnighters but otherwise gets light use. The Sumpter Valley Railroad interpretive site is one mile west on U.S. 26.

RV sites, facilities: There are 11 sites for tents or RVs up to 22 feet long. Picnic tables, vault toilets, and fire rings are provided. No drinking water is available, and garbage must be packed out. A store, café, gas, and ice are available within nine miles. Some facilities are wheelchair accessible. Leashed pets are permitted.

Reservations, fees: Reservations are not accepted. Sites are $8 per night, $4 per night for an additional vehicle. Open late May–November, weather permitting.

Directions: From John Day, drive northeast on U.S. 26 for 24 miles to Forest Road 365. Turn left and drive 0.25 mile to the campground on the left.

Contact: Malheur National Forest, Blue Mountain Ranger District, 541/575-3000, fax 541/575-3319, www.fs.fed.us.

76 WETMORE

Scenic rating: 7

on the Middle Fork of the Burnt River in Wallowa-Whitman National Forest

Map grid C2

This campground, set at an elevation of 4,320 feet near the Middle Fork of the Burnt River, makes a nice base camp for a fishing or hiking trip. The stream can provide good trout fishing. (Trails are detailed on maps of Wallowa-Whitman National Forest.) An excellent 0.5-mile, wheelchair-accessible trail passes through old-growth forest—watch for bald eagles.

RV sites, facilities: There are 10 sites for tents or RVs up to 16 feet long. Picnic tables and fire grills are provided. Vault toilets and drinking water (seasonal) are available. Garbage must be packed out. Some facilities are wheelchair accessible. Leashed pets are permitted.

Reservations, fees: Reservations are not accepted. Sites are $6 per night, $5 per night per additional vehicle. Open mid-May–mid-October, weather permitting.

Directions: From John Day, drive east on U.S. 26 for 29 miles to Austin Junction. Continue east on U.S. 26 for 10 miles to the campground on the left.

Contact: Wallowa-Whitman National Forest, Whitman Ranger District, 541/523-4476, fax 541/523-1965, www.fs.fed.us.

77 OREGON

Scenic rating: 6

near Austin Junction in
Wallowa-Whitman National Forest

Map grid C2

Oregon campground sits at 4,880 feet elevation just off U.S. 26 surrounded by hillside as well as Douglas fir, tamarack, and white fir. It is the staging area for ATV enthusiasts, and the popular Blue Mountain OHV Trailhead is here; several trails crisscross the area. Bald eagles nest in the area.

RV sites, facilities: There are eight sites for tents or RVs up to 28 feet long. Picnic tables and fire grills are provided. Vault toilets are available. There is no drinking water, and garbage must be packed out. Leashed pets are permitted.

Reservations, fees: Reservations are not accepted. Sites are $6 per night, $5 per night per additional vehicle. Open mid-May–mid-October, weather permitting.

Directions: From John Day, drive east on U.S. 26 for 29 miles to Austin Junction. Continue east for 20 miles to the campground.

Contact: Wallowa-Whitman National Forest, Whitman Ranger District, 541/523-4476, fax 541/523-1965, www.fs.fed.us.

78 YELLOW PINE

Scenic rating: 7

near Middle Fork Burnt River

Map grid C2

Yellow Pine is similar to Oregon Campground, but larger; highlights include easy access and good recreation potential. The camp offers a number of hiking trails, including a 0.5-mile-long, wheelchair-accessible trail that connects to the Wetmore Campground. Keep an eye out for bald eagles in this area.

RV sites, facilities: There are 21 sites for tents or RVs up to 28 feet long. Picnic tables and fire grills are provided. Vault toilets and drinking water (seasonal) are available. Garbage must be packed out. Some facilities are wheelchair accessible. Leashed pets are permitted.

Reservations, fees: Reservations are not accepted. Sites are $6 per night. Open late mid-May–mid-October, weather permitting.

Directions: From John Day, drive east on U.S. 26 for 29 miles to Austin Junction. Continue east for 21 miles to the campground.

Contact: Wallowa-Whitman National Forest, Whitman Ranger District, 541/523-4476, fax 541/523-1965, www.fs.fed.us.

79 UNITY LAKE STATE RECREATION SITE

Scenic rating: 7

on Unity Reservoir

Map grid C2

The grassy setting of Unity Lake contrasts nicely with the bordering sagebrush and cheatgrass of the high desert. This camp, set along the east shore of Unity Reservoir, is a popular spot in good weather. Campers can choose from boating, fishing, hiking, picnicking, swimming, or enjoying the scenic views.

RV sites, facilities: There are 35 sites with partial hookups for tents or RVs up to 40 feet long, a separate area for hikers and bicyclists, and two rustic cabins. Picnic tables, garbage bins, and fire rings are provided. Drinking water, restrooms with flush toilets and showers, a dump station, horseshoe pits, and firewood are available. Boat docks and launching facilities are nearby. Some facilities are wheelchair accessible. Leashed pets are permitted.

Reservations, fees: Reservations are not accepted. Sites are $13–22 per night, $4 per person per night for hike-in/bike-in sites, $38–42 per night for rustic cabins, and $5 per night for an additional vehicle. Open April–late October.

Directions: From John Day, drive east on U.S. 26 for 50 miles to Highway 245. Turn left (north) on Highway 245 and drive three miles to the park on the left.

Contact: Clyde Holliday State Recreation Site, 541/932-4453 or 800/551-6949, www.oregonstateparks.org.

80 DEPOT PARK

Scenic rating: 6
on the John Day River
Map grid C2

Depot Park is a more developed alternative to the many U.S. Forest Service campgrounds in the area. This urban park sits on grassy flatlands and provides access to the John Day River, a good trout fishing spot. The camp features a historic rail depot on the premises, as well as a related museum. A nearby attraction, the Strawberry Mountain Wilderness, has prime hiking trails.

RV sites, facilities: There are 20 sites for tents or RVs up to 35 feet long (full hookups); some sites are pull-through. There is also a grassy area for hikers/bikers. Picnic tables and fire rings are provided. Restrooms with showers, a dump station, gazebo, playground, and picnic area are provided. A camp host is on-site seasonally. Some facilities are wheelchair accessible. Leashed pets are permitted.

Reservations, fees: Reservations are not accepted. Sites are $12–16 per night, $6 per night for the hike-in/bike-in area. Open May–November, weather permitting.

Directions: From John Day, drive east on U.S.

26 for 13 miles to Prairie City and the junction of U.S. 26 and Main Street. Turn right (south) on Main Street and drive 0.5 mile to the park (well signed).

Contact: Prairie City Hall, 541/620-2790 or 541/820-3605, www.prairiecityoregon.com.

81 ELK CREEK CAMPGROUND

Scenic rating: 5
in Wallowa-Whitman National Forest
Map grid C2

Elk Creek campground is small, primitive, and remote. It has no designated campsites, but rather an area for dispersed-style tent camping. Its primary use is for OHV riders, with nearby OHV trail access.

RV sites, facilities: There are no specific sites, only dispersed camping areas for tents or small RVs. Picnic tables and fire rings are provided. Vault toilets are available. There is no drinking water. Garbage must be packed out. Leashed pets are permitted.

Reservations, fees: Reservations are not accepted. Sites are $6 per night. Open mid-May–mid-October, weather permitting.

Directions: From John Day, drive east on U.S. 26 for 49 miles to Unity and County Road 600. Turn right on County Road 600 and drive west for six miles (the road becomes Forest Road 6005/South Fork Road). Continue past the forest boundary for three miles to the campground on the right.

Contact: Wallowa-Whitman National Forest, Whitman Ranger District, 541/523-4476, fax 541/523-1965, www.fs.fed.us.

82 STEVENS CREEK

Scenic rating: 5
on the south fork of the Burnt River in Wallowa-Whitman National Forest
Map grid C2

This campground sits at an elevation of 4,480 feet along the banks of the south fork of the

OREGON

Burnt River and provides an alternative to the other small camps along the river. The trout fishing is often good here.

RV sites, facilities: There are seven sites for tents or RVs up to 30 feet. Picnic tables and fire grills are provided. There is no drinking water, and garbage must be packed out. Vault toilets are available. Leashed pets are permitted.

Reservations, fees: Reservations are not accepted. Sites are $6 per night, $5 per night per additional vehicle. Open mid-May–mid-October, weather permitting.

Directions: From John Day, drive east on U.S. 26 for 49 miles to Unity and County Road 600. Turn right on County Road 600 and drive west for six miles (the road becomes Forest Road 6005/South Fork Road). Continue past the forest boundary for two miles to the campground on the right.

Contact: Wallowa-Whitman National Forest, Whitman Ranger District, 541/523-4476, fax 541/523-1965, www.fs.fed.us.

83 SOUTH FORK

Scenic rating: 5

on the south fork of the Burnt River in Wallowa-Whitman National Forest

Map grid C2

A gem of a spot, South Fork offers drinking water, privacy, and scenery. The campground (4,400 feet elevation) is set on the banks of the south fork of the Burnt River, a nice trout creek with good evening bites for anglers who know how to sneak-fish. An OHV staging area with trail access is across the road from the campground.

RV sites, facilities: There are 12 sites for tents or RVs up to 28 feet long; most sites are pull-through. Picnic tables and fire grills are provided. There are vault toilets, and drinking water is available seasonally. Garbage must be packed out. Some facilities are wheelchair accessible. Leashed pets are permitted.

Reservations, fees: Reservations are not accepted. Sites are $6 per night, $5 per night

per additional vehicle. Open mid-May–mid-October, weather permitting.

Directions: From John Day, drive east on U.S. 26 for 49 miles to Unity and County Road 600. Turn right on County Road 600 and drive west for six miles (the road becomes Forest Road 6005/South Fork Road). Continue past the forest boundary for one mile to the campground on the left.

Contact: Wallowa-Whitman National Forest, Whitman Ranger District, 541/523-4476, fax 541/523-1965, www.fs.fed.us.

84 SLIDE CREEK

Scenic rating: 5

in Malheur National Forest

Map grid C2

Slide Creek has tiny, overlooked sites known by a handful of backcountry horsemen. It is set at 4,900 feet in Malheur National Forest with a nearby creek to provide water for horses.

RV sites, facilities: There are three sites for tents or RVs up to 40 feet long. Picnic tables and fire rings are provided. Vault toilets, corrals, and hitching posts are available. There is no drinking water, and garbage must be packed out. Some facilities are wheelchair accessible. Leashed pets are permitted.

Reservations, fees: Reservations are not accepted. Sites are $8 per night, $4 per night for an additional vehicle. Open late May–November, weather permitting.

Directions: From John Day, drive east on U.S. 26 for 13 miles to Prairie City and County Road 62. Turn right (southeast) and drive 0.5 mile to County Road 60. Turn right and drive south on County Road 60 for 8.5 miles (County Road 60 becomes Forest Road 6001). Continue on Forest Road 6001 to the campground on the right.

Contact: Malheur National Forest, Prairie City Ranger District, 541/820-3311, fax 541/820-3838, www.fs.fed.us.

OREGON

85 WICKIUP

Scenic rating: 5

on Wickiup Creek in Malheur National Forest

Map grid C2

This campground sits at an elevation of 4,300 feet along the forks of Wickiup Creek and Canyon Creek at a historic site; many of its original Civilian Conservation Corps structures are still in place. There is limited fishing in the creek. To the north are numerous trails that lead into the Strawberry Mountain Wilderness.

RV sites, facilities: There are four sites for tents or RVs up to 22 feet long. Picnic tables and fire rings are provided. A vault toilet is available. There is no drinking water, and garbage must be packed out. Some facilities are wheelchair accessible. Leashed pets are permitted.

Reservations, fees: Reservations are not accepted. Sites are $6 per night, $3 per night per additional vehicle. Open late May–November, weather permitting.

Directions: From John Day, drive south on U.S. 395 for 10 miles to Forest Road 15. Turn left (southeast) and drive eight miles to the campground on the right.

Contact: Malheur National Forest, Blue Mountain Ranger District, 541/575-3000, fax 541/575-3319, www.fs.fed.us.

86 PARISH CABIN

Scenic rating: 6

on Little Bear Creek in Malheur National Forest

Map grid C2

Parish Cabin campground sits along the banks of Little Bear Creek at an elevation of 4,900 feet. This is a pretty spot that's not heavily used, and the road is paved all the way to the campground. The creek offers limited fishing. The place is popular with groups of families and hunters in season.

RV sites, facilities: There are 19 sites for tents or RVs up to 22 feet long and one group site for up to 50 people. Picnic tables and fire rings are provided. Drinking water and vault toilets are available. Garbage must be packed out. Some facilities are wheelchair accessible. Leashed pets are permitted.

Reservations, fees: Reservations are not accepted. Sites are $8 per night, $4 per night per additional vehicle. Open late May–November, weather permitting.

Directions: From John Day, drive south on U.S. 395 for 10 miles to Forest Road 15. Turn left and drive 16 miles southeast to Forest Road 16. Turn right onto Forest Road 16 and drive a short distance to the campground on the right.

Contact: Malheur National Forest, Blue Mountain Ranger District, 541/575-3000, fax 541/575-3319, www.fs.fed.us.

87 CANYON MEADOWS

Scenic rating: 5

on Canyon Meadows Reservoir in Malheur National Forest

Map grid C2

Canyon Meadows campground sits on the shore of Canyon Meadows Reservoir, where non-motorized boating, fishing, hiking, sailing, and swimming are recreation options. However, this reservoir dries up by the Fourth of July because of a leak in the dam. Several hiking trails nearby lead north into the Strawberry Mountain Wilderness.

RV sites, facilities: There are five sites for tents or RVs up to 25 feet long. Picnic tables and fire grills are provided. A vault toilet is available. There is no drinking water, and garbage must be packed out. Some facilities are wheelchair accessible. Leashed pets are permitted.

Reservations, fees: Reservations are not accepted. There is no fee. Open late May–November, weather permitting.

Directions: From John Day, drive south on U.S. 395 for 10 miles to Forest Road 15. Turn left and drive nine miles southeast to Forest Road 1520. Turn left and drive five miles to the campground on the left.

Contact: Malheur National Forest, Blue

OREGON

Mountain Ranger District, 541/575-3000, fax 541/575-3319, www.fs.fed.us.

88 MURRAY CAMPGROUND

Scenic rating: 7

in Malheur National Forest

Map grid C2

Murray Elk Creek is set at an elevation of 5,200 feet with nearby Forest Service roads that provide access to the Strawberry Mountain Wilderness. The camp is used primarily as a layover for those heading into the wilderness to fish or hunt. Note that fishing is restricted to the use of artificial lures with a single, barbless hook.

RV sites, facilities: There are six sites for tents or RVs up to 40 feet long. Picnic tables and fire rings are provided. Vault toilets are available. There is no drinking water, and garbage must be packed out. Some facilities are wheelchair accessible. Leashed pets are permitted.

Reservations, fees: Reservations are not accepted. Sites are $8 per night, $4 per night for an additional vehicle. Open late May–November, weather permitting.

Directions: From John Day, drive east on U.S. 26 for 13 miles to Prairie City and County Road 62. Turn right and drive 24 miles to Forest Road 16. Turn right and follow signs to the campground on the right.

Contact: Malheur National Forest, Prairie City Ranger District, 541/820-3311, fax 541/820-3838, www.fs.fed.us.

89 BIG CREEK

Scenic rating: 6

near the Strawberry Mountain Wilderness in Malheur National Forest

Map grid C2

At 5,100 feet elevation, this campground hugs the banks of Big Creek. Nearby forest roads provide access to the Strawberry Mountain Wilderness. Other recreation options include fishing and mountain biking. Note that fishing

is restricted to the use of artificial lures with a single, barbless hook. In the appropriate seasons, bear, coyote, deer, and elk are hunted here.

RV sites, facilities: There are 15 sites for tents or RVs up to 40 feet long. Picnic tables and fire rings are provided. Drinking water and vault toilets are available. Garbage must be packed out. Some facilities are wheelchair accessible. Leashed pets are permitted.

Reservations, fees: Reservations are not accepted. Sites are $8 per night, $4 per night for an additional vehicle. Open late May–November, weather permitting.

Directions: From John Day, take U.S. 395 south for 10 miles to Forest Road 15. Turn left and on Forest Road 15 drive 16 miles to Forest Road 16. Turn right on Forest Road 16 and drive six miles to Forest Road 815. Turn right and drive 0.5 mile to the campground on the right.

Contact: Malheur National Forest, Prairie City Ranger District, 541/820-3311, fax 541/820-3838, www.fs.fed.us.

90 TROUT FARM

Scenic rating: 6

near Prairie City in Malheur National Forest

Map grid C2

Trout Farm campground (4,900 feet elevation) is situated on the Upper John Day River, which provides good trout fishing with easy access for people who don't wish to travel off paved roads. A picnic shelter is available for family picnics, and a small pond at the campground has a wheelchair-accessible trail.

RV sites, facilities: There are six sites for tents or RVs up to 21 feet long. Picnic tables and fire rings are provided. Drinking water and vault toilets are available. Garbage must be packed out. Some facilities are wheelchair accessible. Leashed pets are permitted.

Reservations, fees: Reservations are not accepted. Sites are $8 per night, $4 per night per additional vehicle. Open June–mid-October, weather permitting.

Directions: From John Day, drive east on U.S. 26 for 13 miles to Prairie City and Front Street. Turn right on Front Street and drive 0.5 mile to County Road 62. Turn left on County Road 62 and drive 15 miles to the campground entrance on the right.

Contact: Malheur National Forest, Prairie City Ranger District, 541/820-3311, fax 541/820-3838, www.fs.fed.us.

91 LITTLE CRANE

Scenic rating: 5

on Little Crane Creek in Malheur National Forest

Map grid C2

Quiet, primitive, private, and small: all these words describe this camp along the banks of Little Crane Creek at an elevation of 5,500 feet. The creek provides good trout fishing (only artificial bait and artificial lures are allowed). There are also some nice hiking trails in the area, the closest one at the north fork of the Malheur River, about 10 miles away.

RV sites, facilities: There are four sites for tents or RVs up to 20 feet long. Picnic tables and fire rings are provided. Vault toilets are available. There is no drinking water, and garbage must be packed out. Leashed pets are permitted.

Reservations, fees: Reservations are not accepted. There is no fee for camping. Open late May–November, weather permitting.

Directions: From John Day, drive east on U.S. 26 for 13 miles to Prairie City and County Road 62. Turn right and drive 8.5 miles to Forest Road 13. Turn left and drive 16 miles to Forest Road 16. Turn right and drive 5.5 miles south to the campground on the left.

Contact: Malheur National Forest, Prairie City Ranger District, 541/820-3311, fax 541/820-3838, www.fs.fed.us.

92 NORTH FORK MALHEUR

Scenic rating: 7

on the north fork of the Malheur River in Malheur National Forest

Map grid C2

The secluded North Fork Malheur campground sits at an elevation of 4,700 feet along the banks of the north fork of the Malheur River, a designated Wild and Scenic River. Hiking trails and dirt roads provide additional access to the river and backcountry streams. (It's essential to obtain a U.S. Forest Service map.) Good fishing, hunting, and mountain biking opportunities abound in the area. Fishing is restricted to the use of artificial lures with a single, barbless hook.

RV sites, facilities: There are five sites for tents or RVs up to 21 feet long. Picnic tables and fire rings are provided. Vault toilets are available. There is no drinking water, and garbage must be packed out. Leashed pets are permitted.

Reservations, fees: Reservations are not accepted. There is no fee for camping. Open late May–November, weather permitting.

Directions: From John Day, drive east on U.S. 26 for 13 miles to Prairie City and County Road 62. Turn right and drive 8.5 miles to Forest Road 13. Turn left and drive 16 miles to Forest Road 16. Turn right and drive two miles south to a fork with Forest Road 1675. Take the left fork to Forest Road 1675 and drive two miles to the camp on the right.

Contact: Malheur National Forest, Prairie City Ranger District, 541/820-3311, fax 541/820-3838, www.fs.fed.us.

93 ROCK SPRINGS FOREST CAMP

Scenic rating: 5

at Rock Springs in Malheur National Forest

Map grid C2

If you want to camp in a big forest filled with the scent of ponderosa pines, Rock Springs Forest Camp is for you. This primitive camp has a sprinkling of pretty aspens and several little springs—in fact, it's located right on Rock Springs, with Cave Spring, House Creek Spring, and Sunshine Spring within a few miles. Do not count on the springs for drinking water, however, without a water filter. The elevation is 4,800 feet.

RV sites, facilities: There are 12 sites for tents or RVs up to 40 feet long. Picnic tables and fire grills are provided. Vault toilets are available. Drinking water is available from a spring (you must filter it first). Garbage must be packed out. Leashed pets are permitted.

Reservations, fees: Reservations are not accepted for single sites, but a permit is required for groups. Sites are $6 per night for first two vehicles, $3 per night for each additional vehicle. Open late May–mid-October, weather permitting.

Directions: From Burns, drive north on U.S. 395 for 30 miles to Van-Silvies Highway (County Road 73). Turn right on Van-Silvies Highway (which turns into Forest Road 17) and drive four miles to Forest Road 054. Turn right (south) and drive 0.75 mile to the camp on the left.

Contact: Malheur National Forest, Emigrant Creek Ranger District, 541/573-4300, fax 541/573-4398, www.fs.fed.us.

94 WEST EAGLE MEADOW

Scenic rating: 7

near West Eagle Creek in
Wallowa-Whitman National Forest

Map grid D2

West Eagle campground sits in a big, open meadow (5,200 feet elevation) about a five-minute walk from West Eagle Creek. The West Eagle Trail starts at the camp, providing access to the Eagle Cap Wilderness and offering a good opportunity to observe wildlife. The adjacent meadow fills with wildflowers in the summer. For campers with horses, there are new stock facilities with water available in a separate, adjacent campground.

RV sites, facilities: There are 24 sites for tents or RVs up to 30 feet long and an adjacent campground with six sites for campers with horses. Picnic tables and fire rings are provided. Vault toilets are available. There is no drinking water, and garbage must be packed out. Stock facilities include corrals and hitching rails. Some facilities are wheelchair accessible. Leashed pets are permitted.

Reservations, fees: Reservations are not accepted. Sites are $5 per night per vehicle. Open mid-June–late October, weather permitting.

Directions: From Baker City, drive north on I-84 for six miles to Highway 203. Turn east and drive 17 miles to the town of Medical Springs and County Road 71. Turn right (south) and drive two miles to Forest Road 67. Turn left and drive 12 miles to Forest Road 77. Turn left (north) and drive five miles to the camp on the right. Note: Segments of the road are narrow and steep.

Contact: Wallowa-Whitman National Forest, LaGrande Ranger District, 541/963-7186, fax 541/962-8580, www.fs.fed.us.

95 EAGLE FORKS

Scenic rating: 6

on Eagle Creek in Wallowa-Whitman National Forest

Map grid D2

This campground (3,000 feet elevation) is located at the confluence of Little Eagle Creek and Eagle Creek. A trail follows the creek northwest for several miles, making for a prime day hike, yet the spot attracts few people. It's quite pretty and perfect for a weekend getaway or an extended layover.

RV sites, facilities: There are seven sites for tents or RVs up to 21 feet long. Picnic tables and fire rings are provided. Drinking water and vault toilets are available. Garbage must be packed out. Leashed pets are permitted.

Reservations, fees: Reservations are not accepted. Sites are $6 per night. Open May–late October, weather permitting.

Directions: From Baker City, drive east on

Highway 86 for 42 miles to Richland and Newbridge. Turn north on Newbridge (after two miles on paved roads, it becomes Eagle Creek Rd.); then continue on Forest Road 7735 for seven miles to the campground entrance on the left.

Contact: Wallowa-Whitman National Forest, Pine Ranger District, 541/742-7511, fax 541/742-6705, www.fs.fed.us.

96 TWO COLOR

Scenic rating: 6

on Eagle Creek in Wallowa-Whitman National Forest
Map grid D2

Two Color campground (4,800 feet elevation) sits on the banks of Eagle Creek, about a mile north of Tamarack. Evergreens shade the spacious campsites, and the creek is stocked with rainbow trout. If full, another option for campers is nearby Boulder Park campground, three miles northeast on Forest Road 7755.

RV sites, facilities: There are 14 sites for tents or RVs up to 16 feet long. Picnic tables and fire grills are provided. Vault toilets are available. There is no drinking water, and garbage must be packed out. Leashed pets are permitted.

Reservations, fees: Reservations are not accepted. Sites are $5 per night per vehicle. Open mid-June–late October, weather permitting.

Directions: From Baker City, drive north on I-84 for six miles to Highway 203. Turn east on Highway 203 and drive 17 miles to Medical Springs and County Road 71. Turn right (south) and drive two miles to Forest Road 67. Turn left and drive 12 miles to Forest Road 77. Turn left and drive one mile to Forest Road 7755. Turn right and drive one mile north to the camp.

Contact: Wallowa-Whitman National Forest, LaGrande Ranger District, 541/963-7186, fax 541/962-8580, www.fs.fed.us.

97 TAMARACK

Scenic rating: 5

on Eagle Creek in Wallowa-Whitman National Forest
Map grid D2

On the banks of Eagle Creek in a beautiful area with lush vegetation and abundant wildlife sits Tamarack campground at 4,600 feet elevation. This is a good spot for fishing and hiking in a remote setting.

RV sites, facilities: There are 12 sites for tents or RVs up to 25 feet long. Picnic tables and fire rings are provided. Drinking water and vault toilets are available. Garbage must be packed out. Some facilities are wheelchair accessible. Leashed pets are permitted.

Reservations, fees: Reservations are not accepted. Sites are $6 per night. Open June–late October, weather permitting.

Directions: From Baker City, drive east on Highway 86 for 42 miles to Richland and Newbridge. Turn north on Newbridge (after two miles on paved roads, it becomes Eagle Creek Road); then continue on Forest Road 7735 for 20 miles to the campground entrance.

Contact: Wallowa-Whitman National Forest, Pine Ranger District, 541/742-7511, fax 541/742-6705, www.fs.fed.us.

98 FISH LAKE

Scenic rating: 6

on Fish Lake in Wallowa-Whitman National Forest
Map grid D2

This is a pretty, well-forested camp with comfortable sites along the shore of 20-acre Fish Lake at an elevation of 6,600 feet. Fish Lake makes a good base for a fishing trip; side-trip options include hiking on nearby trails that lead to mountain streams. Sites on the upper loop accommodate longer RVs.

RV sites, facilities: There are 21 sites for tents or RVs up to 20 feet long. Picnic tables and fire rings are provided. Drinking water and vault toilets are available. Garbage must be packed

OREGON

out. Boat-launching facilities (for small boats only) are nearby. Leashed pets are permitted.

Reservations, fees: Reservations are not accepted. Sites are $6 per night. Open July–late October, weather permitting.

Directions: From Baker City, take I-84 north for four miles to Highway 86. Turn east on Highway 86 and drive 52 miles to Halfway and Main Street. Turn left (north) on Main Street and drive to Fish Lake Road. Turn right on Fish Lake Road, then drive five miles to Forest Road 66. Continue north on Forest Road 66 for 18.5 miles to the campground on the left.

Contact: Wallowa-Whitman National Forest, Pine Ranger District, 541/742-7511, fax 541/742-6705, www.fs.fed.us.

99 SPRING RECREATION SITE

Scenic rating: 5

on the Snake River
Map grid D2

One of two camps in or near Huntington, this campground hugs the banks of the Brownlee Reservoir. Fishing is popular at this reservoir; it's known for large channel catfish. A more developed alternative, Farewell Bend State Recreation Area offers showers and all the other luxuries a camper could want.

RV sites, facilities: There are 35 sites for tents or RVs of any length. Picnic tables, garbage service, and fire grills are provided. Drinking water (summer only), a dump station, and vault toilets are available. Boat-launching facilities and a fish-cleaning station are on-site. A seasonal camp host is on-site. Leashed pets are permitted.

Reservations, fees: Reservations are not accepted. Sites are $5 per night per vehicle, with a 14-day stay limit. Open year-round, weather permitting.

Directions: From Ontario (near the Oregon/Idaho border), drive northwest on I-84 for 28 miles to Huntington and Snake River Road. Turn right (northeast) on Snake River Road and drive three miles (paved road) to the campground.

Contact: Bureau of Land Management, Baker City Office, 541/523-1256, fax 541/523-1965, www.blm.gov.

100 FAREWELL BEND STATE RECREATION AREA

Scenic rating: 7

on the Snake River
Map grid D2

Farewell Bend campground offers a green desert experience on the banks of the Snake River's Brownlee Reservoir. Situated along the Oregon Trail, the camp has historic interpretive displays and an evening interpretive program at the amphitheater during the summer. The lake provides good numbers of catfish.

RV sites, facilities: There are 101 sites with partial hookups for RVs up to 56 feet long, 30 tent sites, a hiker-biker camp, two cabins, and one group site for up to 25 people. Drinking water, garbage bins, fire rings, and picnic tables are provided. Restrooms with flush toilets and showers, a dump station, firewood, a fish-cleaning station, basketball hoops, horseshoe pits, sand volleyball court, and boat-launching facilities are available. Some facilities are wheelchair accessible. Leashed pets are permitted.

Reservations, fees: Reservations are accepted at 800/452-5687 or www.reserveamerica.com ($8 reservation fee). Tent sites are $11–18 per night, RV sites are $13–22, $4–5 per person per night for the hiker/biker camp, $43–76 per night for group sites, $38–42 per night for cabins, and $5 per night per extra vehicle. Some credit cards are accepted. Open year-round, with limited winter facilities.

Directions: From Ontario (near the Oregon/Idaho border), drive northwest on I-84 for 21 miles to Exit 353. Take that exit and drive one mile to the park.

Contact: Farewell Bend State Recreation Area, 541/869-2365 or 800/551-6949, www.oregonstateparks.org.

101 BULLY CREEK PARK

Scenic rating: 7

on Bully Creek Reservoir
Map grid D2

Bully Creek reservoir is located in a kind of high desert area with sagebrush and poplar trees for shade. It's beautiful if you like the desert, and the sunsets are worth the trip. People come here to boat, fish (mostly for warm-water fish, such as crappie and large and smallmouth bass), swim, and water ski, and there is biking on the gravel roads. At 2,300 feet elevation, the primitive setting is home to deer, jackrabbits, squirrels, and many birds. No monthly rentals are permitted here—a big plus for overnighters.

RV sites, facilities: There are 40 double sites with partial hookups for tents or RVs up to 40 feet in length; some sites are pull-through. There are also three group sites. Picnic tables and fire pits are provided. Drinking water, restrooms with flush toilets and showers, ice, garbage bins, a dump station, picnic area, and boat ramp and dock are available. A camp host is on-site. A restaurant, café, convenience store, gasoline, propane gas, charcoal, and coin laundry are within 10 miles. Bring your own firewood. Some facilities are wheelchair accessible. Leashed pets are permitted.

Reservations, fees: Reservations are accepted at 541/473-2969 ($15 deposit). Sites are $15 per night. Open mid-April–mid-November, weather permitting.

Directions: From Ontario (near the Oregon/Idaho border), drive west on U.S. 20/26 for 12 miles to Vale and Graham Boulevard. Turn right (northwest) on Graham Boulevard and drive five miles to Bully Creek Road. Turn right (west) and drive three miles to the park on the left.

Contact: Bully Creek Park, 541/473-2969, fax 541/473-9462; Malheur County Parks Department, 541/473-5191, fax 541/473-3701, www.malheurco.org.

OREGON

THE SOUTHERN CASCADES

BEST RV PARKS AND CAMPGROUNDS

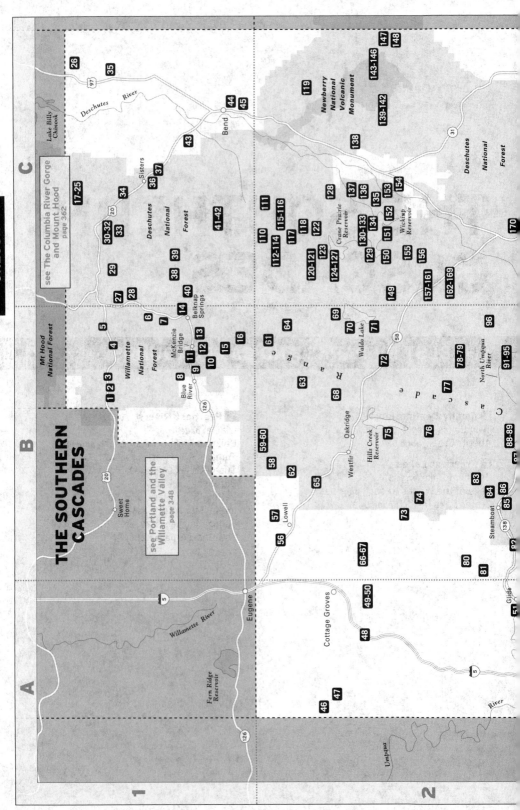

OREGON

THE SOUTHERN CASCADES

see The Columbia River Gorge and Mount Hood page 362

see Portland and the Willamette Valley page 348

Lake Billy Chinook

Deschutes River

Sisters

Bend

Newberry National Volcanic Monument

Deschutes National Forest

Crane Prairie Reservoir

Wickiup Reservoir

Deschutes National Forest

Mt Hood National Forest

Willamette National Forest

McKenzie Bridge

Belknap Springs

Blue River

Sweet Home

Willamette River

Eugene

Fern Ridge Reservoir

Westfir

Oakridge

Hills Creek Reservoir

Waldo Lake

Cascade Range

North Umpqua River

Steamboat

Glide

Lowell

Cottage Groves

Umpqua River

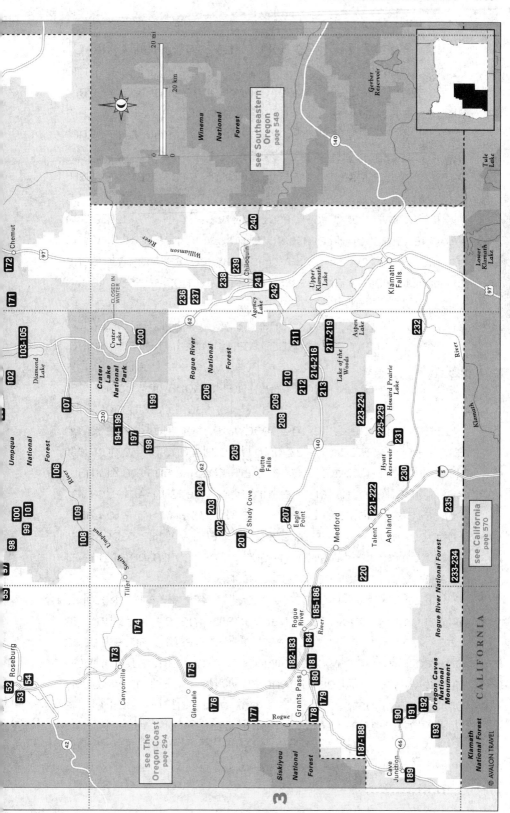

see Southeastern Oregon
page 548

see California
page 570

see The Oregon Coast
page 294

OREGON

© AVALON TRAVEL

3

This region of Oregon is famous for one of its lakes, but it holds many fantastic recreation secrets. The crown jewel is Crater Lake, of course, and visitors come from all over the world to see its vast cobalt-blue waters within cliff-like walls. The lake's Rim Drive is one of those trips that everybody should have on their life's to-do list.

Beyond the lake, though, you'll find stellar camping, fishing, and hiking spots. The best among them are neighboring Mount Washington Wilderness and Three Sisters Wilderness in Willamette National Forest, accessible via a beautiful drive on the McKenzie River Highway (Highway 126) east from Eugene and Springfield. Many ideal trailhead camps are detailed in this chapter for these areas.

But wait, there's more: Crane Prairie, Waldo Lake, and Wickiup Reservoir provide boating, camping, and good fishing. Wickiup, in turn, feeds into the headwaters of the Deschutes River, a prime steelhead locale. The Umpqua and Rogue National Forests offer some great water-sport destinations, including Diamond Lake, the headwaters of the Rogue River, and the headwaters of the North Umpqua, one of the prettiest rivers in North America. Upper Klamath Lake and the Klamath Basin are the number-one wintering areas in America for bald eagles. Klamath Lake also provides a chance to catch huge but elusive trout, as does the nearby Williamson River out of Chiloquin. All of this is but a small sampling of one of Oregon's best regions for adventure.

This region is all the more special for me because it evokes powerful personal memories. One of these is of a time at Hills Creek Reservoir southeast of Eugene. My canoe flipped on a cold winter day and I almost drowned after 20 minutes in the icy water. After I'd gone down for the count twice, my brother Bob jumped in, swam out, grabbed the front of the flipped canoe, and towed me to shore. Then, once ashore, he kept me awake, preventing me from lapsing into a coma from hypothermia.

Thanks, Bob.

1 TROUT CREEK

Scenic rating: 8

on the South Santiam River in
Willamette National Forest

Map grid B1

Trout Creek campground is set along the banks
of the South Santiam River at 1,200 feet in
elevation, about seven miles east of Cascadia.
Fishing and swimming are some of the recreation possibilities here. There is a historic
shelter and the remains of stonework from the
era of the Civilian Conservation Corps. The
Trout Creek Trail, just across the highway,
leads into the Menagerie Wilderness. The Long
Ranch Elk Viewing Area is immediately west
of the campground, and, at the Trout Creek
Trailhead, you'll also find a short trail leading
to an elk-viewing platform. Nearby is the Old
Santiam Wagon Road.

RV sites, facilities: There are 24 sites for tents
or RVs up to 32 feet long. Picnic tables, garbage
bins, and fire rings are provided. Drinking
water and vault toilets are available. Some facilities are wheelchair accessible. Leashed pets
are permitted.

Reservations, fees: Reservations are not accepted. Sites are $12 per night, $5 per night
per additional vehicle. Open May–October,
weather permitting.

Directions: From Albany, drive east on U.S. 20
for 45 miles (19 miles past Sweet Home) to the
campground entrance on the right.

Contact: Willamette National Forest, Sweet
Home Ranger District, 541/367-5168, fax
541/367-2367, www.fs.fed.us.

2 YUKWAH

Scenic rating: 7

on the Santiam River in Willamette National Forest

Map grid B1

Yukwah campground is nestled in a second-
growth Douglas fir forest on the banks of the
Santiam River. The camp is 0.25 mile east
of Trout Creek Campground and offers the
same recreation possibilities, including a 0.5-
mile, compacted-surface interpretive trail that's
barrier-free.

RV sites, facilities: There are 20 sites for tents
or RVs up to 32 feet long, including a deluxe
group site for up to 20 people. Picnic tables, garbage bins, and fire grills are provided. Drinking
water, vault toilets, a picnic area, and a fishing
platform are available. Some facilities, including
the fishing platform, are wheelchair accessible.
Leashed pets are permitted.

Reservations, fees: Reservations are not accepted. Sites are $12 per night, $5 per night
per additional vehicle. The deluxe site is $24
per night. Open May–October, weather
permitting.

Directions: From Albany, drive east on U.S. 20
for 45 miles (19 miles past Sweet Home) to the
campground.

Contact: Willamette National Forest, Sweet
Home Ranger District, 541/367-5168, fax
541/367-2367, www.fs.fed.us.

3 FERNVIEW

Scenic rating: 7

on the Santiam River in Willamette National Forest

Map grid B1

This campground is perched high above the
confluence of Boulder Creek and the Santiam
River, just south of the Menagerie Wilderness.
A stepped walkway leads down to the river.
Just across U.S. 20 lies the Rooster Rock Trail,
which leads to—where else?—Rooster Rock,
the site of an old lookout tower. The Old Santiam Wagon Road runs through the back of the
campground. The camp is best suited for tent
and small RV camping: The sites are small. The
elevation is 1,400 feet.

RV sites, facilities: There are nine sites for tents
or RVs up to 22 feet long and two tent-only
sites. Picnic tables, garbage bins, and fire grills
are provided. Drinking water and vault toilets
are available. Some facilities are wheelchair accessible. Leashed pets are permitted.

Reservations, fees: Reservations are not

OREGON

accepted. Sites are $12 per night, $5 per night per additional vehicle. Open mid-May–mid-September, weather permitting.

Directions: From Albany drive east on U.S. 20 for 49 miles (23 miles past Sweet Home) to the campground entrance on the right.

Contact: Willamette National Forest, Sweet Home Ranger District, 541/367-5168, fax 541/367-2367, www.fs.fed.us.

4 HOUSE ROCK

Scenic rating: 8

on the Santiam River in Willamette National Forest

Map grid B1

House Rock campground is situated at the confluence of Sheep Creek and the South Santiam River. The camp is set in the midst of an old-growth forest and is surrounded by huge, majestic Douglas fir. Trout fishing can be good, particularly during summer evenings. Botany students come here from long distances to see firsthand many uncommon and spectacular specimens of plantlife. History buffs should explore the short loop trail out of camp, which passes by House Rock, a historic rock shelter for Native Americans, and continues to the historic Old Santiam Wagon Road.

RV sites, facilities: There are 12 sites for tents or RVs up to 22 feet long and five tent-only sites. Picnic tables, garbage bins, and fire grills are provided. Vault toilets and drinking water are available. Some facilities are wheelchair accessible. Leashed pets are permitted.

Reservations, fees: Reservations are not accepted. Sites are $12 per night, $5 per night per additional vehicle. Open May–October, weather permitting.

Directions: From Albany drive east on U.S. 20 for 52.5 miles (26 miles past Sweet Home) to Latiwi Road (Forest Road 2044). Turn right and drive a short distance to the campground.

Contact: Willamette National Forest, Sweet Home Ranger District, 541/367-5168, fax 541/367-2367, www.fs.fed.us.

5 LOST PRAIRIE

Scenic rating: 7

on Hackleman Creek in Willamette National Forest

Map grid B1

Lost Prairie campground hugs the banks of Hackleman Creek at 3,200 feet elevation in an area of Douglas fir and spruce. Three excellent hiking trails can be found within five miles of the camp: Hackleman Old-Growth Grove, Cone Peak, and Iron Mountain. The last two offer spectacular wildflower-viewing in the late spring and early summer. This camp provides an alternative to nearby Fish Lake.

RV sites, facilities: There are 10 sites for tents or RVs up to 28 feet long (eight are walk-in sites). Picnic tables, garbage bins, and fire grills are provided. Drinking water and vault toilets are available. Some facilities are wheelchair accessible. Leashed pets are permitted.

Reservations, fees: Reservations are not accepted. Sites are $14 per night, $7 per night per additional vehicle. Open May–October, weather permitting.

Directions: From Albany, drive east on U.S. 20 for 63 miles (approximately 38 miles past Sweet Home) to the camp on the right.

Contact: Willamette National Forest, Sweet Home Ranger District, 541/367-5168, fax 541/367-2367, www.fs.fed.us; Hoodoo Recreation, 541/822-3799.

6 TRAIL BRIDGE

Scenic rating: 6

on Trail Bridge Reservoir in Willamette National Forest

Map grid B1

Set along the shore of Trail Bridge Reservoir (2,000 feet elevation), this campground offers boating, fishing, and hiking among its recreation options. From the camp, there is access to the McKenzie River National Recreation Trail. Highway 126 east of McKenzie Bridge is a designated scenic route, providing a pleasant trip to the camp and making Trail Bridge an exceptional spot for car campers. For a good side trip, take the beautiful 40-minute drive east to the little town of Sisters.

RV sites, facilities: There are 46 sites for tents or RVs up to 45 feet long and a large camping area at Trail Bridge Flats. Picnic tables, garbage service, and fire grills are provided. Drinking water and vault and flush toilets are available. Boat ramps are nearby. Some facilities are wheelchair accessible. Leashed pets are permitted.

Reservations, fees: Reservations are not accepted. Sites are $10 per night, $5 per night per additional vehicle. Open late April–September, weather permitting.

Directions: From Eugene, drive east on Highway 126 for 47 miles to the town of McKenzie Bridge. Continue on Highway 126 for 13 miles to Forest Road 1477. Turn left on Forest Road 1477 and drive a short distance; then bear left and continue 0.25 mile to the campground on the left.

Contact: Willamette National Forest, McKenzie River Ranger District, 541/822-3381, fax 541/822-7254, www.fs.fed.us.

7 OLALLIE

Scenic rating: 7

on the McKenzie River in
Willamette National Forest

Map grid B1 **BEST (**

Olallie campground sits at an elevation of 2,000 feet elevation along the banks of the gorgeous McKenzie River. Boating, fishing, and hiking are among its recreational opportunities, and fishing for rainbow trout usually is good. Other bonuses include easy access from Highway 126. The campground is two miles southwest of Trail Bridge Reservoir off Highway 126.

RV sites, facilities: There are 16 sites for tents or RVs up to 35 feet long. Picnic tables and fire grills are provided. Vault toilets, drinking water, and garbage service are available. A boat launch is nearby (non-motorized boats only). Leashed pets are permitted.

Reservations, fees: Reservations are accepted

at 877/444-6777 or www.recreation.gov ($10 reservation fee). Sites are $12–14 per night, $7 per night per additional vehicle. Open late April–October, weather permitting.

Directions: From Eugene, drive east on Highway 126 for 47 miles to the town of McKenzie Bridge. Continue on Highway 126 for 11 miles to the campground on the left.

Contact: Willamette National Forest, McKenzie River Ranger District, 541/822-3381, fax 541/822-7254, www.fs.fed.us; Hoodoo Recreation, 541/822-3799.

8 MONA

Scenic rating: 8

near Blue River Reservoir in
Willamette National Forest

Map grid B1

This forested campground (1,360 feet elevation) is set along the shore of Blue River Reservoir, close to where the Blue River joins it. A boat ramp is located across the river from the campground (at Lookout Campground); another boat ramp is situated at the south end of the reservoir. After launching a boat, campers can ground it near their campsite. Note that this camp is extremely popular when the reservoir is full.

RV sites, facilities: There are 23 sites for tents or RVs up to 36 feet long. Picnic tables, garbage bins, and fire grills are provided. Drinking water and flush toilets are available. Some facilities are wheelchair accessible. Leashed pets are permitted.

Reservations, fees: Reservations are not accepted. Single sites are $16 per night, $30 per night for double sites, $8 per night per additional vehicle. Open May–mid-September, weather permitting.

Directions: From Eugene, drive east on Highway 126 for 41 miles to Blue River. Continue east on Highway 126 for three miles to Forest Road 15. Turn left (north) and drive three miles to the campground on the left.

Contact: Willamette National Forest, McKenzie River Ranger District, 541/822-3381, fax

541/822-7254, www.fs.fed.us; Hoodoo Recreation, 541/822-3799.

9 PATIO RV PARK

Scenic rating: 7

near the South Fork of the McKenzie River

Map grid B1

This RV park is situated near the banks of the South Fork of the McKenzie River, not far from Cougar Lake, which offers opportunities for fishing, swimming, and waterskiing. Nearby recreation options include a golf course, hiking trails, and bike paths. The Hoodoo Ski Area is approximately 30 miles away.

RV sites, facilities: There are 60 sites with full hookups for RVs of any length and a grassy area for tents. Picnic tables are provided. Restrooms with flush toilets and coin showers, ice, firewood, a recreation hall, video rentals, group kitchen facilities, cable TV, modem access, a community fire pit, horseshoe pits, and a coin laundry are available. A store, gasoline, propane, and a café are within two miles. Leashed pets are permitted.

Reservations, fees: Reservations are accepted at 800/650-0290 or via email at reservations@patiorv.com. RV sites are $26–31 per night, tent sites are $20 per night, $2 per person per night for more than two people, and $8 per night per additional vehicle. Some credit cards are accepted. Open year-round, weather permitting.

Directions: From Eugene, drive east on Highway 126 for 37 miles to the town of Blue River. Continue east on Highway 126 for six miles to McKenzie River Drive. Turn right and drive two miles to the park on the right.

Contact: Patio RV Park, 541/822-3596, fax 541/822-8392, www.patiorv.com.

10 DELTA

Scenic rating: 8

on the McKenzie River in Willamette National Forest

Map grid B1

This popular campground sits along the banks of the McKenzie River in a spot heavily forested primarily with old-growth Douglas fir. The Delta Old Growth Nature Trail, a 0.5-mile wheelchair-accessible interpretive trail, is adjacent to the campground. The camp also features an amphitheater. Nearby are Blue River and Cougar Reservoirs (seven and five miles away, respectively), both of which offer swimming, trout fishing, and waterskiing.

RV sites, facilities: There are 38 sites for tents or RVs up to 36 feet long. Picnic tables, garbage bins, and fire grills are provided. Drinking water and vault toilets are available. Some facilities are wheelchair accessible. Leashed pets are permitted.

Reservations, fees: Reservations are not accepted. Single sites are $14 per night, $26 per night for double sites, and $7 per night per additional vehicle. Open late April–October, weather permitting.

Directions: From Eugene, drive east on Highway 126 for 37 miles to the town of Blue River. Continue east on Highway 126 for five miles to Forest Road 19 (Aufderheide Scenic Byway). Turn right (south) and drive 0.25 mile to Forest Road 400. Turn right and drive one mile to the campground.

Contact: Willamette National Forest, McKenzie River Ranger District, 541/822-3381, fax 541/822-7254, www.fs.fed.us; Hoodoo Recreation, 541/822-3799.

11 McKENZIE BRIDGE

Scenic rating: 8

on the McKenzie River in Willamette National Forest

Map grid B1

McKenzie campground is set at 1,400 feet elevation along the banks of the McKenzie

River, one mile from the town of McKenzie Bridge. During the summer, this stretch of river provides good evening fly-fishing for trout; only non-motorized boats are permitted on the river.

RV sites, facilities: There are 20 sites for tents or RVs up to 40 feet long. Picnic tables, garbage service, and fire rings are provided. Flush toilets and drinking water are available. A grocery store and restaurants are available within one mile. Some facilities are wheelchair accessible. Leashed pets are permitted.

Reservations, fees: Reservations are accepted at 877/444-6777 or www.recreation.gov ($10 reservation fee). Sites are $14 per night, $7 per night per additional vehicle. Open April–September, weather permitting.

Directions: From Eugene, drive east on Highway 126 for 46 miles to the campground entrance on the right (one mile west of the town of McKenzie Bridge).

Contact: Willamette National Forest, McKenzie River Ranger District, 541/822-3381, fax 541/822-7254, www.fs.fed.us; Hoodoo Recreation, 541/822-3799.

12 HORSE CREEK GROUP CAMP

Scenic rating: 9

on Horse Creek in Willamette National Forest
Map grid B1

This campground reserved for groups borders Horse Creek near the town of McKenzie Bridge. In spite of the name, no horse camping is permitted. Fishing is catch-and-release only; check current regulations. The camp sits at 1,400 feet elevation.

RV sites, facilities: This is a group camp with 21 sites for tents or RVs up to 27 feet long. Picnic tables and fire grills are provided. Vault toilets, drinking water, and garbage service are available. Leashed pets are permitted.

Reservations, fees: Reservations are accepted at 877/444-6777 or www.recreation.gov ($10 reservation fee). The fees are $40 per night for up to 49 people and $60 per night for 50–100 people. Open May–September, weather permitting.

Directions: From Eugene, drive east on Highway 126 for 47 miles to the town of McKenzie Bridge and Horse Creek Road. Turn right (south) on Horse Creek Road and drive one mile to the campground on the left.

Contact: Willamette National Forest, McKenzie River Ranger District, 541/822-3381, fax 541/822-7254, www.fs.fed.us.

13 PARADISE

Scenic rating: 9

on the McKenzie River in Willamette National Forest
Map grid B1

Paradise campground (1,600 feet elevation), along the banks of the McKenzie River, may be right off the highway, but it offers a rustic, streamside setting with access to the McKenzie River National Recreation Trail. Trout fishing can be good here.

RV sites, facilities: There are 64 sites for tents or RVs of any length. Picnic tables, garbage service, and fire rings are provided. Flush and vault toilets, drinking water, a boat ramp, and firewood are available. Some facilities are wheelchair accessible. Leashed pets are permitted.

Reservations, fees: Reservations are accepted at 877/444-6777 or www.recreation.gov ($10 reservation fee). Single sites are $18 per night, double sites are $32 per night, $9 per night per additional vehicle. Open May–September, weather permitting.

Directions: From Eugene, drive east on Highway 126 for 47 miles to the town of McKenzie Bridge. Continue east on Highway 126 for 3.5 miles to the campground on the left.

Contact: Willamette National Forest, McKenzie River Ranger District, 541/822-3381, fax 541/822-7254, www.fs.fed.us; Hoodoo Recreation, 541/822-3799.

OREGON

OREGON

14 BELKNAP HOT SPRINGS RESORT

Scenic rating: 9

on the McKenzie River

Map grid B1   **BEST (**

This beautiful park, with 60 acres of developed and landscaped gardens, has been featured on at least one magazine cover. It's in a wooded, mountainous area on the McKenzie River. Trout fishing can be excellent here. If you're looking for hiking opportunities, the McKenzie River Trail can be accessed from camp. Other hiking opportunities include the Three Sisters and Mount Washington Wilderness Areas, both accessible by driving west of Sisters on Highway 242. Exceptionally scenic and pristine expanses of forest, they are well worth exploring. The Pacific Crest Trail runs north and south through both wilderness areas.

RV sites, facilities: There are 62 sites with full or partial hookups for RVs of any length, 15 sites for tents, a lodge with 18 rooms, and six cabins. Picnic tables and fire pits are provided. Drinking water, restrooms with showers, and a dump station are available. Recreational facilities include two hot-spring fed swimming pools, massage therapy on weekends, and a recreation field. Some facilities are wheelchair accessible. Leashed pets are permitted at the campground and in some of the cabins; pets are not permitted in the other cabins and lodge rooms.

Reservations, fees: Reservations are accepted at 541/822-3512. Tent sites are $25–30 per night, RV sites are $35 per night, cabins are $65–400, $10 pet fee, lodge rooms are $100–185, $8 per person per night for more than two people. All fees include access to the hot springs. Some credit cards are accepted. Open year-round.

Directions: From Eugene, drive east on Highway 126 for 56 miles to Belknap Springs Road. Turn left and drive 0.5 mile until the road dead-ends at the lodge.

Contact: Belknap Hot Springs Resort, 541/822-3512, fax 541/822-3327, www.belkna-photsprings.com.

15 SLIDE CREEK

Scenic rating: 6

on Cougar Reservoir in Willamette National Forest

Map grid B1

Slide Creek campground sits on a hillside overlooking Cougar Reservoir, which covers about 1,300 acres, has a paved boat landing and offers opportunities for fishing, swimming, and waterskiing. This pretty lakeside camp at 1,700 feet in elevation is quite popular, so plan to arrive early on weekends. If the camp is full, Cougar Crossing (off Road 19) and Sunnyside (off Road 500) are nearby alternatives.

RV sites, facilities: There are 16 sites for tents or RVs up to 50 feet long. Picnic tables and fire grills are provided. Drinking water, garbage bins, and vault toilets are available. A boat ramp is also available. Leashed pets are permitted.

Reservations, fees: Reservations are not accepted. Single sites are $16 per night, $30 per night for double sites, $8 per night per additional vehicle. Open May–September, weather permitting.

Directions: From Eugene, drive east on Highway 126 for 41 miles to the town of Blue River. Continue east on Highway 126 for five miles to Aufderheide Scenic Byway. Turn right (south) and drive 11 miles (along the west shore of Cougar Reservoir, crossing the reservoir bridge) to Eastside Road (Forest Road 500). Turn left and drive 1.5 miles northeast to the campground set on the southeast shore of the lake.

Contact: Willamette National Forest, McKenzie River Ranger District, 541/822-3381, fax 541/822-7254, www.fs.fed.us; Hoodoo Recreation, 541/822-3799.

16 FRENCH PETE

Scenic rating: 8

on the South Fork of the McKenzie River in Willamette National Forest

Map grid B1

This quiet, wooded campground is set on the banks of the south fork of the McKenzie River and French Pete Creek at 1,800 feet in elevation. Fishing is catch-and-release only. A trail across the road from the campground provides access to the Three Sisters Wilderness (permit required; contact district office). French Pete is only two miles from Cougar Reservoir, and the camp attracts campers wanting to use Cougar Reservoir facilities. Two more primitive camps (Homestead and Frissell Crossing) are located a few miles southeast on the same road.

RV sites, facilities: There are 17 sites for tents or RVs up to 40 feet long. Picnic tables, garbage containers, and fire grills are provided. Drinking water and vault toilets are available. Leashed pets are permitted.

Reservations, fees: Reservations are not accepted. Sites are $14 per night, $5 per night per additional vehicle. Open May–September, weather permitting.

Directions: From Eugene, drive east on Highway 126 for 41 miles to the town of Blue River. Continue east on Highway 126 for five miles to Forest Road 19 (Aufderheide Scenic Byway). Turn right (south) and drive 12 miles to the campground on the right.

Contact: Willamette National Forest, McKenzie River Ranger District, 541/822-3381, fax 541/822-7254, www.fs.fed.us.

17 CAMP SHERMAN

Scenic rating: 6

on the Metolius River in Deschutes National Forest

Map grid C1

Camp Sherman is set at an elevation of 2,950 feet along the banks of the Metolius River, where you can fish for wild trout. This place is for expert fly anglers seeking a quality fishing experience. Camp Sherman is one of five camps in the immediate area. It's advisable to obtain a map of the Deschutes National Forest that details back roads, streams, and trails.

A personal note: My late pal, John Korb, named his dog Sherman after this camp.

RV sites, facilities: There are 14 sites for tents or RVs up to 40 feet long. Picnic tables and fire

grills are provided. Drinking water and garbage service is available mid-April–mid-October. Vault toilets and a picnic shelter are available. Leashed pets are permitted.

Reservations, fees: Reservations are accepted at 877/444-6777 or www.recreation.gov ($10 reservation fee). Sites are $12–16 per night, $6–8 per night per additional vehicle. Open year-round, weather permitting.

Directions: From Albany, drive east on U.S. 20 for 87 miles (near Black Butte) to the sign for Camp Sherman and Forest Road 14. Turn left on Forest Road 14 and drive five miles to Camp Sherman, the store, and Forest Road 900. Turn left on Forest Road 900 and drive 0.5 mile to the campground on the left.

Contact: Deschutes National Forest, Sisters Ranger District, 541/549-7700, fax 541/549-7746, www.fs.fed.us.

18 ALLINGHAM

Scenic rating: 5

on the Metolius River in Deschutes National Forest

Map grid C1

One of five camps in the immediate area, Allingham sits along the banks of the Metolius River. The river is perfect for trout fishing, and fly anglers will find a quality fishing experience.

RV sites, facilities: There are 10 sites for tents or RVs up to 40 feet long. Picnic tables and fire grills are provided. Vault toilets, drinking water, and garbage service are available. A dump station is nearby. Leashed pets are permitted.

Reservations, fees: Reservations are not accepted. Sites are $16 per night, $8 per night per additional vehicle. Open May–September, weather permitting.

Directions: From Albany, drive east on U.S. 20 for 87 miles (near Black Butte) to the sign for Camp Sherman and Forest Road 14. Turn left on Forest Road 14 and drive five miles to Camp Sherman, the store, and Forest Road 900. Turn left on Forest Road 900 and drive one mile to the campground on the left.

OREGON

OREGON

Contact: Deschutes National Forest, Sisters Ranger District, 541/549-7700, fax 541/549-7746, www.fs.fed.us.

19 BLACK BUTTE RESORT

Scenic rating: 6

near the Metolius River

Map grid C1

Black Butte offers a choice of graveled or grassy sites in a clean, scenic environment. Located near the Camp Sherman area, this is a nice spot for bird-watching, fishing, and hiking.

RV sites, facilities: There are 30 sites with full or partial hookups for RVs of any length and six motel rooms. Picnic tables and barbecues are provided. Restrooms with flush toilets and showers, a dump station, recreation room, firewood, and a coin laundry are available. Propane gas, an additional dump station, a store, café, and ice are within one block. Leashed pets are permitted.

Reservations, fees: Reservations are accepted. Sites are $26–28 per night, $3 per person per night for more than two people, $7 per additional vehicle (unless towed). Some credit cards are accepted. Open year-round.

Directions: From Albany, drive east on U.S. 20 for 87 miles (near Black Butte) to the sign for Camp Sherman. Turn left (north) on Forest Road 1419 and drive four miles to a stop sign and the resort access road. Turn right and drive 0.25 mile to the park on the right.

Contact: Black Butte Resort, 541/595-6514, fax 541/595-5971, http://blackbutterv.com.

20 GORGE

Scenic rating: 5

on the Metolius River in Deschutes National Forest

Map grid C1

Here is another of the camps set along the banks of the Metolius River near Camp Sherman. Gorge campground is located at an elevation of 2,900 feet and is more open, with less vegetation than many of the others. Fly-fishing and hiking trails provide recreation opportunities.

RV sites, facilities: There are 18 sites for tents or RVs up to 40 feet long. Picnic tables and fire grills are provided. Vault toilets, drinking water, and garbage service are available. Leashed pets are permitted.

Reservations, fees: Reservations are not accepted. Sites are $16 per night, $8 per night per additional vehicle. Open May–September, weather permitting.

Directions: From Albany, drive east on U.S. 20 for 87 miles (near Black Butte) to the sign for Camp Sherman and Forest Road 14. Turn left on Forest Road 14 and drive five miles to Camp Sherman, the store, and Forest Road 900. Turn left on Forest Road 900 and drive 2.5 miles to the campground on the left.

Contact: Deschutes National Forest, Sisters Ranger District, 541/549-7700, fax 541/549-7746, www.fs.fed.us.

21 SMILING RIVER

Scenic rating: 5

on the Metolius River in Deschutes National Forest

Map grid C1

Smiling River sits along the banks of the Metolius River at an elevation of 2,900 feet. Another campground in the popular Camp Sherman area, Smiling River has access to fly-fishing and nearby hiking trails.

RV sites, facilities: There are 35 sites for tents or RVs up to 50 feet long. Picnic tables and fire grills are provided. Vault toilets, drinking water, and garbage service are available. Leashed pets are permitted.

Reservations, fees: Reservations are accepted at 877/444-6777 or www.recreation.gov ($10 reservation fee). Sites are $16 per night, $8 per night per additional vehicle. Open May–October, weather permitting.

Directions: From Albany, drive east on U.S. 20 for 87 miles (near Black Butte) to the sign for Camp Sherman and Forest Road 14. Turn left on Forest Road 14 and drive five miles to Camp Sherman, the store, and Forest Road 900. Turn left on Forest Road 900 and drive one mile to the campground on the left.

Contact: Deschutes National Forest, Sisters Ranger District, 541/549-7700, fax 541/549-7746, www.fs.fed.us.

22 ALLEN SPRINGS

Scenic rating: 7

on the Metolius River in Deschutes National Forest
Map grid C1

Shady Allen Springs campground is nestled in a conifer forest along the banks of the Metolius River, where fishing and hiking can be good. For an interesting side trip, head to the Wizard Falls Fish Hatchery about a mile away.

RV sites, facilities: There are 16 sites for tents or RVs up to 36 feet long. Picnic tables and fire grills are provided. Vault toilets, drinking water, and garbage service are available. A store, café, and ice are within five miles. Leashed pets are permitted.

Reservations, fees: Reservations are not accepted. Single sites are $14 per night, double sites are $30 per night, $7 per night per additional vehicle. Open April–October, weather permitting.

Directions: From Albany, drive east on U.S. 20 for 87 miles (near Black Butte) to the sign for Camp Sherman and Forest Road 14. Turn left on Forest Road 14 and drive about nine miles to the campground on the left.

Contact: Deschutes National Forest, Sisters Ranger District, 541/549-7700, fax 541/549-7746, www.fs.fed.us.

23 LOWER BRIDGE

Scenic rating: 6

on the Metolius River in Deschutes National Forest
Map grid C1

Lower Bridge campground is set along the banks of the Metolius River at an elevation of

2,700 feet. The setting is similar to Pioneer Ford, but with less vegetation. A picnic area is located across the bridge.

RV sites, facilities: There are 12 sites for tents or RVs up to 30 feet long. Picnic tables and fire grills are provided. Vault toilets, drinking water, and garbage service are available. Leashed pets are permitted.

Reservations, fees: Reservations are not accepted. Sites are $16 per night, $8 per night per additional vehicle. Open May–October, weather permitting.

Directions: From Albany, drive east on U.S. 20 for 87 miles (near Black Butte) to the sign for Camp Sherman and Forest Road 14. Turn left on Forest Road 14 and drive 12 miles to the campground on the right.

Contact: Deschutes National Forest, Sisters Ranger District, 541/549-7700, fax 541/549-7746, www.fs.fed.us.

24 PIONEER FORD

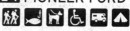

Scenic rating: 7

on the Metolius River in Deschutes National Forest
Map grid C1

Quiet and serene Pioneer Ford campground is set along the banks of the Metolius River at an elevation of 2,750 feet. The wooded campground features grassy sites north of the Camp Sherman area. Hiking and fly-fishing are activities here.

RV sites, facilities: There are 20 sites for tents or RVs up to 50 feet long. Picnic tables and fire grills are provided. Drinking water and garbage service are provided. Vault toilets are available. Some facilities are wheelchair accessible. Leashed pets are permitted.

Reservations, fees: Reservations are not accepted. Sites are $16 per night, $8 per night per additional vehicle. Open May–September, weather permitting.

Directions: From Albany, drive east on U.S. 20 for 87 miles (near Black Butte) to the sign for Camp Sherman and Forest Road 14. Turn left

OREGON

on Forest Road 14 and drive 11 miles to the campground on the left.

Contact: Deschutes National Forest, Sisters Ranger District, 541/549-7700, fax 541/549-7746, www.fs.fed.us.

25 COLD SPRINGS RESORT & RV PARK

Scenic rating: 7

on the Metolius River

Map grid C1

This pretty, wooded RV park on the Metolius River is world-famous for its fly-fishing and features an acre of riverfront lawn. Bird-watching is also popular. Recreation options in the area include boating, swimming, water-skiing, and windsurfing. In addition, nearby facilities include a golf course, hiking and biking trails, a riding stable, and tennis courts. Winter activities vary from alpine and Nordic skiing to sledding, snowmobiling, and winter camping. A private footbridge leads from the resort to Camp Sherman; the towns of Sisters and Bend are nearby (15 miles and 35 miles, respectively).

RV sites, facilities: There are 45 sites with full hookups for RVs of any length, a grassy area for tents, and five cabins on the river. Fire pits, picnic tables, and patios are provided. Restrooms with showers, coin laundry, wireless Internet service, firewood, and a riverfront picnic facility are available. Propane gas, a convenience store, fishing and sport supplies, a café, a post office, and ice are within 0.25 mile. Leashed pets are permitted.

Reservations, fees: Reservations are accepted. Sites are $30 per night, $2 per person per night for more than two people, and $2 per pet per night. Some credit cards are accepted. Open year-round.

Directions: From Albany, drive east on U.S. 20 for 87 miles (near Black Butte) to the sign for Camp Sherman/Metolius River. Turn left (north) on Forest Road 14 and drive 4.5 miles to a stop sign. Turn right (still Forest Road 14)

and drive about 300 feet to Cold Springs Resort Lane. Turn right and drive through the forest and the meadow, crossing Cold Springs Creek, to the resort.

Contact: Cold Springs Resort & RV Park, 541/595-6271, fax 541/595-1400, www.cold-springs-resort.com.

26 HAYSTACK RESERVOIR

Scenic rating: 5

on Haystack Reservoir in Crooked River National Grassland

Map grid C1

This campground can be found in the high desert along the shore of Haystack Reservoir, a bright spot in an expansive desert landscape. The camps feature a moderate amount of privacy, as well as views of nearby Mount Jefferson. Haystack Reservoir receives moderate numbers of people who boat, camp, fish, swim, and water ski.

RV sites, facilities: There are 24 sites for tents or RVs up to 32 feet long; some sites are pull-through. Picnic tables and fire grills are provided. Flush toilets, drinking water, and covered picnic shelters are available. A store, café, and ice are within five miles. Boat docks and launching facilities are nearby. Leashed pets are permitted.

Reservations, fees: Reservations are not accepted. Sites are $8 per night, $3 per night per additional vehicle. Open mid-May–mid-September.

Directions: From Madras, drive south on U.S. 97 for nine miles to Jericho Lane. Turn left and drive one mile to County Road 100. Turn right and drive two miles to Forest Road 96. Turn left (north) and drive 0.5 mile to the campground.

Contact: Crooked River National Grassland, 541/475-9272 or 541/416-6640, www.fs.fed.us.

27 COLD WATER COVE

Scenic rating: 10

on Clear Lake in Willamette National Forest

Map grid C1

Cold Water campground sits at 3,000 feet elevation on the south shore of Clear Lake, a spring-fed lake formed by a natural lava dam and the source of the McKenzie River. No motors are permitted on the lake, making it ideal for anglers in rowboats or canoes. The northern section of the McKenzie River National Recreation Trail passes by the camp.

RV sites, facilities: There are 35 sites for tents or RVs up to 40 feet long. Picnic tables and fire grills are provided. Vault toilets, drinking water, and garbage service are available. Boat docks, launching facilities, rowboats, a store, a café, and cabin rentals are available nearby at Clear Lake Resort. Some facilities are wheelchair accessible. Leashed pets are permitted.

Reservations, fees: Reservations are accepted at 877/444-6777 or www.recreation.gov ($10 reservation fee). Sites are $16 per night, $30 per night for double sites, $8 per night per additional vehicle. Open mid-May–mid-October, weather permitting.

Directions: From Eugene, drive east on Highway 126 for 47 miles to the town of McKenzie Bridge. Continue on Highway 126 for 14 miles to Forest Road 770. Turn right (east) and drive to the campground.

Contact: Willamette National Forest, McKenzie River Ranger District, 541/822-3381, fax 541/822-7254, www.fs.fed.us; Hoodoo Recreation, 541/822-3799.

28 ICE CAP

Scenic rating: 9

on Carmen Reservoir in Willamette National Forest

Map grid C1

Ice Cap campground is perched at 3,000 feet elevation on a hill above Carmen Reservoir, created by a dam on the McKenzie River. The McKenzie River National Recreation Trail passes by the camp, and Koosah Falls and Sahalie Falls are nearby. Clear Lake, a popular local vacation destination, is two miles away.

RV sites, facilities: There are 13 sites for tents or RVs up to 50 feet long, and nine walk-in sites. Picnic tables and fire grills are provided. Vault toilets, drinking water, and garbage service are available. Boat-launching facilities and boat rentals are about two miles away at Clear Lake Resort (541/967-5030). Only non-motorized boats are allowed on Carmen Reservoir. Leashed pets are permitted.

Reservations, fees: Reservations are not accepted. Sites are $16 per night, $8 per night per additional vehicle. Open mid-May–September, weather permitting.

Directions: From Eugene, drive east on Highway 126 for 47 miles to the town of McKenzie Bridge. Continue on Highway 126 for 19 miles to the campground entrance road on the left. Turn left and drive 200 yards to the campground.

Contact: Willamette National Forest, McKenzie River Ranger District, 541/822-3381, fax 541/822-7254, www.fs.fed.us; Hoodoo Recreation, 541/822-3799.

29 BIG LAKE

Scenic rating: 9

on Big Lake in Willamette National Forest

Map grid C1

This jewel of a spot on the north shore of Big Lake at 4,650 feet elevation offers a host of activities, including fishing, hiking, swimming, and waterskiing. Big Lake has heavy motorized boat use. One of the better hikes is the five-mile wilderness loop trail (Patjens Lakes Trail) that heads out from the south shore of the lake and cuts past a few small lakes before returning. There's a great view of Mount Washington from the lake. The Pacific Crest Trail is only 0.5 mile away.

RV sites, facilities: There are 49 sites for tents or RVs up to 35 feet long. Picnic tables and fire grills are provided. Drinking water, vault and

OREGON

flush toilets, and garbage service are available. Boat ramps are nearby. Some facilities are wheelchair accessible. Leashed pets are permitted.

Reservations, fees: Reservations are accepted at 877/444-6777 or www.recreation.gov ($10 reservation fee). Single sites are $18 per night, $32 for double sites, $9 per night per additional vehicle. Open late May–mid-October, weather permitting.

Directions: From Eugene, drive east on Highway 126 for 47 miles to the town of McKenzie Bridge. Continue northeast on Highway 126 for 40 miles to Big Lake Road (Forest Road 2690). Turn right and drive three miles to the campground on the left.

Contact: Willamette National Forest, McKenzie River Ranger District, 541/822-3381, fax 541/822-7254, www.fs.fed.us; Hoodoo Recreation, 541/822-3799.

30 SOUTH SHORE

Scenic rating: 6

on Suttle Lake in Deschutes National Forest

Map grid C1

This campground is at 3,500 feet elevation on the south shore of Suttle Lake, where waterskiing is permitted. A hiking trail winds around the lake and other popular activities include fishing and windsurfing. The camp often fills up on weekends and holidays, so reserve early.

RV sites, facilities: There are 38 sites for tents or RVs up to 40 feet long. Picnic tables and fire grills are provided. Vault toilets, drinking water, and garbage service are available. A fish-cleaning station, boat docks, launching facilities, and rentals are nearby. Leashed pets are permitted.

Reservations, fees: Reservations are accepted at 877/444-6777 or www.recreation.gov ($10 reservation fee). Sites are $16 per night, $8 per night per additional vehicle. Open May–September, weather permitting.

Directions: From Albany, drive east on U.S. 20 to the junction with Highway 126. Continue east on Highway 126 for 12 miles to Forest

Road 2070 (Suttle Lake). Turn right and proceed a short distance to the campground.

Contact: Deschutes National Forest, Sisters Ranger District, 541/549-7700, fax 541/549-7746, www.fs.fed.us.

31 LINK CREEK

Scenic rating: 6

on Suttle Lake in Deschutes National Forest

Map grid C1

Link Creek campground is set at the west end of Suttle Lake at an elevation of 3,450 feet. The high-speed boating area is located on this end of the lake, making it a popular spot with water-skiers. Other activities include fishing, swimming, and windsurfing.

RV sites, facilities: There are 33 sites for tents or RVs up to 50 feet long. Picnic tables and fire grills are provided. Vault toilets, drinking water, and garbage service are available. Boat docks, launching facilities, and rentals are nearby. Leashed pets are permitted.

Reservations, fees: Reservations are accepted at 877/444-6777 or www.recreation.gov ($10 reservation fee). Sites are $16–30 per night, $8 per night per additional vehicle. Open April–mid-October, weather permitting.

Directions: From Albany, drive east on U.S. 20 for 74 miles to the junction of U.S. 20 and Highway 126. Continue east on Highway 126 for 12 miles to Forest Road 2070 (Suttle Lake). Turn right and drive a short distance to the campground.

Contact: Deschutes National Forest, Sisters Ranger District, 541/549-7700, fax 541/549-7746, www.fs.fed.us.

32 BLUE BAY

Scenic rating: 7

on Suttle Lake in Deschutes National Forest

Map grid C1

Blue Bay campground is situated along the south shore of Suttle Lake at an elevation of

OREGON

3,450 feet. It's a quieter campground at the low-speed end of the lake, and with more tree cover than South Shore or Link Creek. Recreation activities include fishing, boating, and hiking.

RV sites, facilities: There are 21 single sites and three double sites for tents or RVs up to 50 feet long. Picnic tables and fire grills are provided. Vault toilets, drinking water, and garbage service are available. A fish-cleaning station, boat docks, launching facilities, and rentals are nearby. Leashed pets are permitted.

Reservations, fees: Reservations are accepted at 877/444-6777 or www.recreation.gov ($10 reservation fee). Sites are $16–30 per night, $8 per night per additional vehicle. Open May–mid-September, weather permitting.

Directions: From Albany, drive east on U.S. 20 for 74 miles to the junction of U.S. 20 and Highway 126. Continue east on Highway 126 for 12 miles to Forest Road 2070 (Suttle Lake). Turn right and drive a short distance to the campground.

Contact: Deschutes National Forest, Sisters Ranger District, 541/549-7700, fax 541/549-7746, www.fs.fed.us.

33 SCOUT LAKE GROUP

Scenic rating: 5

on Scout Lake in Deschutes National Forest

Map grid C1

Scout Lake is a group campground, with a mix of sunny and shady sites, at an elevation of 3,700 feet. The camp lies about 0.5 mile from Suttle Lake and is a good spot for swimming and hiking.

RV sites, facilities: There are nine sites—singles, doubles and triple sites—for tents or RVs up to 40 feet long. The triple group site can accommodate up to 100 people. Picnic tables and fire grills are provided. Vault toilets, drinking water, garbage service, a picnic shelter, a volleyball court, and horseshoe pits are available. Leashed pets are permitted in the campground only (not in the day-use area).

Reservations, fees: Reservations are accepted

at 877/444-6777 or www.recreation.gov ($10 reservation fee). Single sites are $16 per night, double sites are $30 per night, triple group site is $40 per night, $8 per night per additional vehicle. Open May–September, weather permitting.

Directions: From Eugene, drive east on Highway 126 for 74 miles to the junction of U.S. 20 and Highway 126. Continue east on Highway 126 for 12 miles to Forest Road 2070 (Suttle Lake). Turn right and drive to Forest Road 2066. Turn left and drive less than one mile to the campground.

Contact: Deschutes National Forest, Sisters Ranger District, 541/549-7700, fax 541/549-7746, www.fs.fed.us.

34 KOA SISTERS/BEND

Scenic rating: 7

on Branchwater Lake

Map grid C1

This park is located amid wooded mountains outside of Sisters at an elevation of 3,200 feet. Branchwater Lake, a three-acre lake at the campground, offers good trout fishing. (For hiking opportunities, explore the McKenzie River Trail or the Three Sisters and Mount Washington Wilderness Areas (west of Sisters on Hwy. 242). The Pacific Crest Trail runs north and south through both wilderness areas.

RV sites, facilities: There are 100 sites for tents or RVs of any length (full hookups); many sites are pull-through. There are also three cabins. Picnic tables and fire pits are provided. Drinking water, air-conditioning, cable TV, modem access, restrooms with showers, a dump station, coin laundry, convenience store, ice, RV supplies, and propane gas are available. Recreational facilities include a playground, game room, horseshoes, table tennis, a spa, and a seasonal heated swimming pool. Leashed pets are permitted.

Reservations, fees: Reservations are accepted at 800/562-0363. Sites are $48–65 per night,

$2–9 per person per night for more than two people, and $2 per night per additional vehicle. Some credit cards are accepted. Open late March–November, weather permitting.

Directions: From Eugene, drive east on Highway 126 to its junction with U.S. 20. Turn east on U.S. 20 and drive 26 miles to Sisters. Continue southeast on U.S. 20 for three miles to the park on the right side of the highway.

Contact: KOA Sisters/Bend, 541/549-3021, fax 541/549-8144, www.koa.com.

35 CROOKED RIVER RANCH RV PARK

Scenic rating: 6

near Smith Rock State Park

Map grid C1

Crooked River Ranch is a short distance from Smith Rock State Park, which contains unusual, colorful volcanic formations overlooking the Crooked River Canyon. Spectacular wildlife abounds in this area. Lake Billy Chinook to the north is a good spot for waterskiing and fishing for bass and panfish. The park has a basketball court and a softball field, and seasonal horseback riding is available. Nearby recreation options include fishing, golf, and tennis; one of Oregon's nicest golf courses is nearby.

RV sites, facilities: There are 90 sites with full or partial hookups for RVs of any length (some pull-through) and 20 tent sites. Picnic tables are provided. No open fires are allowed; propane is permitted. Restrooms with flush toilets and coin showers, a dump station, cable TV, Wi-Fi, a convenience store, coin laundry, ice, a covered picnic shelter, playground, horseshoe pits, a tennis court, and a seasonal swimming pool are available. A café is nearby. Leashed pets are permitted, with certain restrictions.

Reservations, fees: Reservations are accepted at 800/841-0563. RV sites are $25–34 per night; tent sites are $20–24 per night. Some credit cards are accepted. Open mid-March–October, weather permitting.

Directions: From Redmond, drive north on U.S. 97 for six miles to Terrebonne and Lower Bridge Road. Turn left (west) on Lower Bridge Road and drive approximately two miles to 43rd Street. Turn right and drive two miles to a T-intersection with Chinook. Turn left on Chinook and drive approximately 4.5 miles (becomes Clubhouse Road, then Hays Road) to the ranch on the right.

Contact: Crooked River Ranch RV Park, 541/923-1441 or 800/841-0563, www.crookedriverranch.com.

36 INDIAN FORD

Scenic rating: 4

on Indian Ford Creek in Deschutes National Forest

Map grid C1

This campground sits on the banks of Indian Ford Creek at an elevation of 3,250 feet. Used primarily by overnighters on their way to the town of Sisters, the camp is subject to a lot of traffic noise from U.S. 20. The grounds are sprinkled with aspen trees and great birdwatching opportunities are available.

RV sites, facilities: There are 25 sites for tents or RVs up to 50 feet long. Picnic tables, garbage service, and fire grills are provided. Vault toilets are available. There is no drinking water. Leashed pets are permitted.

Reservations, fees: Reservations are not accepted. Sites are $12 per night, $6 per night per additional vehicle. Open May–mid-October, weather permitting.

Directions: From Albany, drive east on U.S. 20 to the junction with Highway 126. Continue east on Highway 126 and drive 21 miles to the campground on the left.

Contact: Deschutes National Forest, Sisters Ranger District, 541/549-7700, fax 541/549-7746, www.fs.fed.us.

37 COLD SPRINGS

Scenic rating: 7

in Deschutes National Forest

Map grid C1

Wooded Cold Springs campground is set at 3,400 feet elevation at the source of a small seasonal creek. It's just far enough off the main drag to be missed by many campers. Spring and early summer are the times to come for great bird-watching in the area's abundant aspen trees.

RV sites, facilities: There are 22 sites for tents or RVs up to 50 feet long. Picnic tables, fire grills, and garbage service are provided. Vault toilets and drinking water are available. Leashed pets are permitted.

Reservations, fees: Reservations are not accepted. Sites are $14 per night, $7 per night per additional vehicle. Open May–October, weather permitting.

Directions: From Albany, drive east on U.S. 20 to the junction with Highway 126. Continue east on Highway 126 and drive 26 miles to Sisters and Highway 242. Turn right and drive 4.2 miles to the campground on the right.

Contact: Deschutes National Forest, Sisters Ranger District, 541/549-7700, fax 541/549-7746, www.fs.fed.us.

38 LAVA CAMP LAKE

Scenic rating: 4

near the Pacific Crest Trail in Deschutes National Forest

Map grid C1

Lava campground sits at an elevation of 5,300 feet among subalpine fir in the McKenzie Pass. It's not far from the Pacific Crest Trail, and a number of other trails provide additional hiking possibilities. Fishing is allowed, but don't expect to catch anything—perhaps that is why this campground gets such light use!

RV sites, facilities: There are 10 sites for tents or RVs up to 20 feet long. Picnic tables and fire grills are provided. Vault toilets are available.

There is no drinking water, and garbage must be packed out. Leashed pets are permitted.

Reservations, fees: Reservations are not accepted. There is no fee for camping. Open June–October, weather permitting.

Directions: From Eugene, drive east on Highway 126 for 47 miles to the town of McKenzie Bridge. Continue east on Highway 126 for five miles to Highway 242. Turn right (east) and drive 14.6 miles on Highway 242 to the campground entrance on the right. Note: Highway 242 is spectacularly scenic, but also very narrow, winding, and steep. RVs and trailers are strictly held to a 35-foot length limit.

Contact: Deschutes National Forest, Sisters Ranger District, 541/549-7700, fax 541/549-7746, www.fs.fed.us.

39 WHISPERING PINE HORSE CAMP

Scenic rating: 5

near the Trout Creek Swamp in Deschutes National Forest

Map grid C1

This wooded campground (elevation 4,400 feet) near Trout Creek Swamp is pretty, isolated, and private. Although generally not crowded, it's set up as a horse camp with corrals and is gaining in popularity; groups of horse users occasionally fill it up. Hikers, beware: You'll be sharing the trails with horses.

RV sites, facilities: There are nine primitive sites for tents or RVs up to 30 feet long. Picnic tables and fire grills are provided. Vault toilets and garbage service are available. There is no drinking water. Leashed pets are permitted.

Reservations, fees: Reservations are not accepted. Sites are $16 per night, $8 per night per additional vehicle. Open May–October, weather permitting.

Directions: From Albany, drive east on U.S. 20 to the junction with U.S. 126. Turn east on U.S. 126 and drive for 26 miles to Sisters and Highway 142. Turn right (east) and drive six miles on Highway 242 to Forest Road 1018.

OREGON

Turn left and drive four miles to the campground entrance. Note: Highway 242 is spectacularly scenic, but also very narrow, winding, and steep. RVs and trailers are discouraged (a 35-foot length limit is in effect).

Contact: Deschutes National Forest, Sisters Ranger District, 541/549-7700, fax 541/549-7746, www.fs.fed.us or www.hoodoo.com.

40 LIMBERLOST

Scenic rating: 9

on Lost Creek in Willamette National Forest

Map grid C1

Limberlost is a secluded campground set at 1,800 feet elevation along Lost Creek, about two miles from where it empties into the McKenzie River. Relatively unknown, the camp gets light use; it makes a good base camp for a trout-fishing trip.

RV sites, facilities: There are 12 sites for tents or RVs up to 16 feet long. Picnic tables, garbage service, and fire grills are provided. Vault toilets are available, but there is no drinking water. Some facilities are wheelchair accessible. Leashed pets are permitted.

Reservations, fees: Reservations are not accepted. Sites are $12 per night, $6 per night per additional vehicle. Open May–September, weather permitting.

Directions: From Eugene, drive east on Highway 126 for 47 miles to the town of McKenzie Bridge. Continue east on Highway 126 for five miles to Highway 242. Turn right (east) and drive 1.5 miles on Highway 242 to the camp. Note: Highway 242 is spectacularly scenic, but also very narrow, winding, and steep. RVs and trailers are discouraged (a 35-foot length limit is in effect).

Contact: Willamette National Forest, McKenzie River Ranger District, 541/822-3381, fax 541/822-7254, www.fs.fed.us.

41 DRIFTWOOD

Scenic rating: 9

on Three Creek Lake in Deschutes National Forest

Map grid C1

This wooded campground, at 6,600 feet elevation, is often blocked by snowdrifts until early July. At this high elevation, the views of Tam McArthur Rim are spectacular. Although located on the lakeshore and hidden from outsiders, the area can get very crowded, and the campground is full most weekends from the Fourth of July through Labor Day. Some recreation options include boating (non-motorized only), fishing, hiking, and swimming.

RV sites, facilities: There are 18 sites for tents or RVs up to 40 feet long. Picnic tables and fire grills are provided. Vault toilets and garbage service are available. There is no drinking water. Boats with motors are not allowed. Leashed pets are permitted.

Reservations, fees: Reservations are not accepted. Sites are $14 per night, $7 per night per additional vehicle. Open June–October, weather permitting.

Directions: From Eugene, drive east on Highway 126 to its junction with U.S. 20. Turn east and drive 26 miles to Sisters and Forest Road 16. Turn right and drive 16.4 miles to the campground.

Contact: Deschutes National Forest, Sisters Ranger District, 541/549-7700, fax 541/549-7746, www.fs.fed.us.

42 THREE CREEK LAKE

Scenic rating: 8

on Three Creek Lake in Deschutes National Forest

Map grid C1

Three Creek Lake is in a pretty spot at 6,600 feet elevation; this forested campground lies along the south shore of its namesake lake. Boating (non-motorized only), fishing, hiking, and swimming are the highlights.

RV sites, facilities: There are 11 sites for tents

or RVs up to 40 feet long. Picnic tables and fire grills are provided. Vault toilets and garbage service are available. There is no drinking water. Boats with motors are not allowed. Leashed pets are permitted.

Reservations, fees: Reservations are not accepted. Sites are $14 per night, $7 per night per additional vehicle. Open June–October, weather permitting.

Directions: From Eugene, drive east on Highway 126 to its junction with Highway 20. Turn east and drive 26 miles to Sisters and Forest Road 16. Turn right and drive 17 miles to the campground.

Contact: Deschutes National Forest, Sisters Ranger District, 541/549-7700, fax 541/549-7746, www.fs.fed.us.

43 TUMALO STATE PARK

Scenic rating: 7

on the Deschutes River

Map grid C1   BEST (

Tumalo State Park sits along the banks of the Deschutes River, just four miles from Bend. Trout fishing can be good, and bird-watching is popular. The swimming area is generally safe and a good spot for children. Rafting is also an option here. Mount Bachelor is just up the road and provides plenty of winter recreation opportunities.

RV sites, facilities: There are 54 sites for tents or self-contained RVs, 23 sites with full hookups for RVs up to 44 feet long, a hiker/bicyclist area, seven yurts, and two group tent areas for up to 25 people each. Drinking water, fire grills, and picnic tables are provided. Restrooms with flush toilets and showers, firewood, and a playground are available. A store, café, and ice are within one mile. Some facilities are wheelchair accessible. Leashed pets are permitted.

Reservations, fees: Reservations are accepted at 800/452-5687 or www.reserveamerica.com ($8 reservation fee). RV sites are $17–26 per night, tent sites are $13–21, $4–5 per person per night

for hikers/bikers, $29–39 per night for yurts, $43–76 per night for the group areas, and $5 per night per additional vehicle. Some credit cards are accepted. Open year-round.

Directions: From Bend, drive north on U.S. 97 for two miles to U.S. 20 West. Turn west and drive five miles to Tumalo Junction. Turn left at Tumalo Junction onto Cook Avenue (the road becomes O. B. Riley), and drive one mile to the campground.

Contact: High Desert Management Unit, Oregon State Parks, 541/388-6055 or 800/551-6949, www.oregonstateparks.org.

44 SCANDIA RV AND MOBILE PARK

Scenic rating: 5

near the Deschutes River

Map grid C1

This in-town park near the Deschutes River is close to bike paths, a golf course, a stable, and tennis courts.

RV sites, facilities: There are 97 sites for tents or RVs of any length (full hookups); some are pull-through sites. Picnic tables and cable TV are provided. Restrooms with flush toilets and showers, modem access, a picnic area, and a coin laundry are available. Propane gas, a dump station, store, café, and ice are within one mile. Leashed pets are permitted.

Reservations, fees: Reservations are accepted. Sites are $28–32 per night, plus $2.50 per person per night for more than two people. Some credit cards are accepted. Open year-round.

Directions: In Bend, drive south on Business U.S. 97 (3rd Street) for 0.5 mile to the park entrance on the right.

Contact: Scandia RV and Mobile Park, 541/382-6206, fax 541/382-4087.

OREGON

45 CROWN VILLA RV RESORT

Scenic rating: 6

near Bend

Map grid C1

This RV park offers large and landscaped grassy sites. Nearby recreation options include horseback riding and golf.

RV sites, facilities: There are 116 sites with full or partial hookups for RVs of any length; some sites are pull-through. Picnic tables are provided. Restrooms with flush toilets and showers, cable TV, wireless Internet service, a coin laundry, a bistro, propane gas, and ice are available. A store and a café are within one mile. Some facilities are wheelchair accessible. Leashed pets are permitted.

Reservations, fees: Reservations are accepted. Sites are $35–70 per night, $3 per person per night for more than four people. Some credit cards are accepted. Open year-round.

Directions: From Bend, drive south on Business U.S. 97 (3rd Street) for two miles to Brosterhous Road. Turn left (east) and drive approximately one mile to a T intersection. Bear right to stay on Brosterhous Road. Continue about one mile to the park on the right.

Contact: Crown Villa RV Resort, 541/388-1131, www.crownvillarvresort.com.

46 WHITTAKER CREEK

Scenic rating: 7

near the Siuslaw River

Map grid A2

Whittaker Creek campground is home to one of the area's premier salmon spawning grounds, where annual runs of chinook, coho salmon, and steelhead can be viewed. The (Whitaker Creek) Old Growth Ridge Trail, a national recreation trail, is accessible from the campground. This moderately difficult trail ascends 1,000 feet above the Siuslaw River through a stand of old-growth Douglas fir.

RV sites, facilities: There are 31 sites for tents or RVs up to 35 feet long. Picnic tables and fire

pits are provided. Drinking water, vault toilets, garbage bins, a boat ramp, swimming beach, playground, and picnic shelter are available. A camp host is on-site. Some facilities are wheelchair accessible. Leashed pets are permitted.

Reservations, fees: Reservations are not accepted. Sites are $10 per night, $5 per night for each additional vehicle. Open mid-May–September, weather permitting.

Directions: From Eugene, drive west on Highway 126 for 33 miles to Siuslaw River Road. Turn left (south) and drive two miles to the first junction. Turn right and drive a short distance across Siuslaw River to the campground on the right.

Contact: Bureau of Land Management, Eugene District Office, 541/683-6600 or 888/442-3061, fax 541/683-6981, www.blm.gov.

47 CLAY CREEK

Scenic rating: 7

near the Siuslaw River

Map grid A2

This campground gets a medium amount of use. Sites are situated in a forest of cedar, Douglas fir, and maple trees. Clay Creek Trail, a two-mile loop, takes you to a ridge overlooking the river valley and is well worth the walk. Fishing for trout and crayfish is popular.

RV sites, facilities: There are 21 sites for tents or RVs up to 35 feet long. Picnic tables and fire pits are provided. Drinking water, vault toilets, garbage bins, a swimming beach with changing rooms, a softball field, horseshoe pits, and two group picnic shelters with fireplaces are available. There is a camp host. Some facilities are wheelchair accessible. Leashed pets are permitted.

Reservations, fees: Reservations are not accepted. Sites are $10 per night, $5 per night for each additional vehicle. Open mid-May–September, weather permitting.

Directions: From Eugene, drive west on Highway 126 for 33 miles to Siuslaw River Road. Turn left (south) and drive 16 miles to BLM

Road 19-7-2001 (signed for Clay Creek). Turn right and drive a short distance to the campground on the right.

Contact: Bureau of Land Management, Eugene District Office, 541/683-6600 or 888/442-3061, fax 541/683-6981, www.blm.gov.

48 PASS CREEK COUNTY PARK

Scenic rating: 7

near Cottage Grove

Map grid A2

Pass Creek provides a decent layover spot for travelers on I-5. Situated in a wooded, hilly area, the camp features many shaded sites, and mountain views give the park scenic value. There is a covered pavilion and gazebo with barbecue grills for get-togethers. A bonus is the fishing pond with bluegill, crappie, and largemouth bass. There are no other campgrounds in the immediate area, so if it's late and you need a place to stay, grab this one.

RV sites, facilities: There is a grassy area for tents and 30 sites with full hookups (50-amp) for RVs up to 45 feet long. Picnic tables and fire rings or barbecues are provided. Drinking water, restrooms with flush toilets and showers, a coin laundry, and a playground are available. A store and ice are within one mile. Some facilities are wheelchair accessible. Leashed pets are permitted.

Reservations, fees: Reservations are not accepted. Sites are $15–20 per night, $3 per night for an additional vehicle unless towed. Open year-round.

Directions: On I-5, drive to Exit 163 (between Roseburg and Eugene). Take Exit 163 and turn west on Curtin Park Road. Drive west (under the freeway) for a very short distance to the park entrance.

Contact: Pass Creek County Park, 541/942-3281, www.co.douglas.or.us.

49 PINE MEADOWS

Scenic rating: 6

on Cottage Grove Reservoir

Map grid A2

Pine Meadows campground is surrounded by a varied landscape of forest, grassland, and marsh near the banks of Cottage Grove Reservoir. Campsites are within 200 feet of the water. Boating, fishing, swimming, and waterskiing are among the recreation options. It's an easy hop from I-5.

RV sites, facilities: There are 93 sites for tents or RVs of any length, with some pull-through sites. Drinking water, picnic tables, garbage bins, and fire rings are provided. Restrooms with flush toilets and showers, a dump station, a children's play area, an amphitheater, interpretive displays, and a swimming area are available. A boat dock, launching facilities, and a small store are nearby. Leashed pets are permitted.

Reservations, fees: Reservations are accepted at 877/444-6777 or www.recreation.gov ($10 reservation fee). Sites are $15 per night, $5 per night for an additional vehicle. Open mid-May–mid-September.

Directions: From Eugene, drive south on I-5 past Cottage Grove to Exit 172. Take that exit to London Road and drive south for 4.5 miles to Reservoir Road. Turn left and drive three miles to the camp entrance on the right.

Contact: U.S. Army Corps of Engineers, Recreation Information, Cottage Grove, 541/942-8657 or 541/942-5631, fax 541/942-1305, www.nwp.usace.army.mil.

50 PINE MEADOWS PRIMITIVE SITES

Scenic rating: 6

on Cottage Grove Reservoir

Map grid A2

Located adjacent to Pine Meadows, this primitive campground offers the same boating, fishing, swimming, and waterskiing activities on Cottage Grove Reservoir.

OREGON

RV sites, facilities: There are 15 primitive sites for tents or small, self-contained RVs. Picnic tables, vault toilets, drinking water, garbage bins, and fire rings are provided. Boat docks, launching facilities, and a mini-market are nearby. Leashed pets are permitted.

Reservations, fees: Reservations are accepted at 877/444-6777 or www.recreation.gov ($10 reservation fee). Sites are $10 per night, $5 per night for an additional vehicle. Campers must have a permit, obtained at the entrance booth. Open late May–early September.

Directions: From Eugene, drive south on I-5 past Cottage Grove to Exit 172. Take that exit to London Road and drive south for 4.5 miles to Reservoir Road. Turn left and drive three miles to the camp entrance.

Contact: U.S. Army Corps of Engineers, Recreation Information, Cottage Grove, 541/942-8657 or 541/942-5631, fax 541/942-1305, www.nwp.usace.army.mil.

51 WHISTLER'S BEND PARK

Scenic rating: 7

on the North Umpqua River

Map grid A2

This 175-acre county park along the banks of the North Umpqua River is an idyllic spot because it gets little pressure from outsiders, yet it is just a 20-minute drive from I-5. Two boat ramps accommodate boaters, and fishing is a plus. A wildlife reserve provides habitat for deer.

RV sites, facilities: There are 23 sites for tents or RVs up to 35 feet long (no hookups) and two yurts. Two group camps are available. Picnic tables and fire grills are provided. Drinking water, restrooms with flush toilets and showers, a playground, disc golf, and launching facilities are available. Some facilities are wheelchair accessible. Leashed pets are permitted.

Reservations, fees: Reservations are accepted for yurts and group camps at 541/957-7001 ($10 reservation fee) but not for tent or RV

sites. Single sites are $15 per night, $3 per night per additional vehicle, $32 per night for yurts, $50 per night for the group camp for up to 50 people, $100 per night for the group camp for up to 100 people. Some credit cards are accepted. Individual sites are open April–November; group sites are open year-round.

Directions: From Roseburg, drive east on Highway 138 for 12 miles to Whistler's Bend Park Road (well signed). Turn left and drive two miles to the end of the road and the park entrance.

Contact: Whistler's Bend Park, 541/673-4863, www.co.douglas.or.us.

52 AMACHER PARK

Scenic rating: 5

on the Umpqua River

Map grid A2

A wooded Douglas County park set along the banks of the North Umpqua River, Amacher is a prime layover spot for I-5 RV cruisers. This park has one of the few Myrtlewood groves in the country. Tent sites are located underneath the freeway next to the railroad tracks; trains come by intermittently. An 18-hole golf course and tennis courts are close by, riding stables are within a 20-minute drive, and Winchester Dam is within 0.25 mile.

RV sites, facilities: There are 10 sites for tents or self-contained RVs and 20 sites with full or partial hookups (20-amp service only) for RVs up to 30 feet long. Picnic tables are provided; some sites have fire rings. Drinking water, restrooms with flush toilets and showers, a gazebo, and picnic area are available. Propane gas, a store, café, coin laundry, and ice are within one mile. Boat-launching facilities are available. Some facilities are wheelchair accessible. Leashed pets are permitted.

Reservations, fees: Reservations are not accepted. Sites are $15–20 per night, $3 per night per additional vehicle. Cash only. Open March–October (closed in winter).

Directions: From Roseburg, drive five miles north on I-5 to Exit 129. Take that exit and drive south on Old Highway 99 for 0.25 mile to the park on the right (just across Winchester Bridge).

Contact: Amacher Park, 541/672-4901; Douglas County, 541/672-4901, www.co.douglas.or.us.

53 TWIN RIVERS VACATION PARK

Scenic rating: 6

near the Umpqua River
Map grid A2

This wooded campground is near the Umpqua River. It features large shaded pull-through sites and more than 100 kinds of trees on the property. Groups are welcome and clubhouses are available for group use. Nearby recreation options include bike paths, a county park, and a golf course.

RV sites, facilities: There are 82 sites with full or partial hookups for RVs of any length; many are pull-through sites. Cable TV, fire pits, and picnic tables are provided. Restrooms with flush toilets and showers, modem access, propane gas, firewood, a convenience store, a coin laundry, ice, and a playground are available. Boat-launching facilities are nearby. Leashed pets are permitted.

Reservations, fees: Reservations are accepted. Sites are $22–33 per night, $3 per person per night for more than two people. Some credit cards are accepted. Open year-round.

Directions: In Roseburg on I-5, take Exit 125 to Garden Valley Road. Drive west for five miles (over the river) to Old Garden Valley Road. Turn left and drive 1.5 miles to River Forks Road. Turn left and drive a short distance to the park entrance on the left.

Contact: Twin Rivers Vacation Park, 541/673-3811, www.twinriversrvpark.com.

54 DOUGLAS COUNTY FAIRGROUNDS RV PARK

Scenic rating: 8

on the South Umpqua River
Map grid A2

This 74-acre county park is very easily accessible off the highway. Nearby Umpqua River, one of Oregon's prettiest rivers, often has good fishing in season. Bike paths, a golf course, and tennis courts are nearby. Horse stalls and a boat ramp are available at the nearby fairgrounds. The campground fills up the third weekend in March, during the annual fiddlers' convention.

RV sites, facilities: There are 50 sites with partial hookups for tents or RVs of any length. Drinking water and picnic tables are provided. Restrooms with flush toilets and showers and a dump station are available. A store, café, coin laundry, and ice are within one mile. Some facilities are wheelchair accessible. Leashed pets are permitted.

Reservations, fees: Reservations are not accepted. Sites are $15–20 per night, with a 14-day stay limit. Tent camping is limited to two nights. Open year-round, except one week in August during the county fair. Phone ahead to confirm current status.

Directions: Heading south on I-5 in Roseburg, take Exit 123 and drive south under the freeway to Frear Street. Turn right and enter the park.

Contact: Douglas County Fairgrounds & Speedway, 541/957-7010, fax 541/440-6023, www.co.douglas.or.us/dcfair.

55 CAVITT CREEK FALLS

Scenic rating: 8

west of Roseburg
Map grid A2

The locals might try to hunt me down for revealing this spot, but here it is. This campground is located near a sensational swimming hole at the base of a 10-foot waterfall on Cavitt

OREGON

Creek. The elevation is 1,040 feet, and an abundant forest of fir, maple, and oak trees surrounds the campground. It is overlooked because it is set on land run by the Bureau of Land Management, not the Park Service or Forest Service. Fishing is closed on Cavitt Creek by the Oregon Department of Fish and Wildlife.

RV sites, facilities: There are 10 sites for tents or RVs up to 20 feet long. Picnic tables, garbage bins, and fire rings are provided. Drinking water and vault toilets are available. A camp host is on-site. Some facilities are wheelchair accessible. Leashed pets are permitted.

Reservations, fees: Reservations are not accepted. Sites are $8 per night, $4 per night for an additional vehicle. Open mid-May–mid-October, weather permitting.

Directions: From Roseburg, drive east on Highway 138 for 16.5 miles to Little River Road. Turn right (south) on Little River Road and drive 6.7 miles to the covered bridge. Turn right onto Cavitt Creek Road and drive 3.2 miles to Cavitt Creek Falls Recreation Site.

Contact: Bureau of Land Management, Roseburg District, 541/440-4930, fax 541/440-4948, www.or.blm.gov/or/resources/recreation.

56 DEXTER SHORES RV PARK

Scenic rating: 7

near Dexter Reservoir
Map grid B2

If you're traveling on I-5, this RV park is well worth the 15-minute drive out of Springfield. It's across the street from Dexter Reservoir, where fishing and boating are permitted year-round. Speedboat races are held at Dexter in the summer. There is seasonal fishing for salmon and steelhead below Dexter dam. The local area is good for bird-watching. Nearby Lookout and Fall Creek Lakes offer sailing, swimming, waterskiing, and windsurfing. There are three authentic Sioux tepees on the property in the summer and two cabins. Many of the campsites have a lake view.

RV sites, facilities: There are 56 sites with full or partial hookups for RVs up to 40 feet long; 12 sites are pull-through. There are also eight tent sites, three tepees, and two one-bedroom cabins. Drinking water, cable TV and telephone hookups, picnic tables, and fire pits are provided. Restrooms with flush toilets and showers, a dump station, modem access, a clubhouse, lending library, video rentals, firewood, horseshoe pits, and a coin laundry are available. Propane gas, a café, restaurant, and ice are within one mile. Boat docks and launching facilities are nearby. Leashed pets are permitted in the campground, but not in the cabins or tepees.

Reservations, fees: Reservations are accepted at 866/558-9777. RV sites are $30–45 per night, tent sites are $20 per night, tepees are $25–35 per night, $3 per person per night for more than four people, and $1 per pet per night. Some credit cards are accepted. Open year-round.

Directions: From south Eugene on I-5, drive to Exit 188A and Highway 58. Take Highway 58 east and drive 11.5 miles to Lost Creek Road. Turn right (south) and drive several hundred feet to Dexter Road. Turn left (in front of the café) and drive east for half a block to the park on the right.

Contact: Dexter Shores RV Park, 866/558-9777 or 541/937-3711, fax 541/937-1724, www.dextershoresrv.com.

57 FALL CREEK STATE RECREATION AREA

Scenic rating: 7

in Fall Creek State Recreation Area
Map grid B2

There are two campgrounds here: Cascara and the group camp area, Fisherman's Park. Most of these spacious sites have Douglas fir and white fir tree cover. Water recreation is the primary activity here; boating and water skis are allowed. The lake level drops in August, and water temperatures are ideal for summer swimming.

RV sites, facilities: There are 42 primitive sites

for tents or RVs up to 45 feet, five walk-in sites for tents, and a group area for RVs of any length up to 16 vehicles; there are no pull-through sites. Picnic tables and fire rings are provided. Drinking water, vault toilets, garbage service, and firewood are available. A camp host is on-site. A boat launch, dock, and swimming area are also available. Leashed pets are permitted.

Reservations, fees: Reservations are accepted for the RV group area only at 800/452-5687. Sites are $19 per night, $10 per night for primitive sites, $5 per night for an additional vehicle. The group RV area is $109 per night for up to 10 RVs. Some credit cards are accepted. Open May–September.

Directions: From south Eugene on I-5, take Exit 188 to Highway 58. Drive 11 miles south to Lowell and Pioneer Street (at the covered bridge). Turn left on Pioneer Street and drive less than 0.25 mile to West Boundary Road. Turn left and drive one block to Lowell Jasper Road. Turn right and drive 1.5 miles to Unity and Place Road. Turn right and drive about one mile to a fork with North Shore Road (Big Fall Creek Road). Bear left onto Big Fall Creek Road and drive about eight miles to the head of Fall Creek Reservoir and Peninsula Road (Forest Road 6250). Turn right and drive 0.5 mile to the campground. The park is approximately 27 miles southeast of Eugene.

Contact: Fall Creek State Recreation Area, 541/937-1173 or 800/551-6949, www.oregon-stateparks.org.

58 BIG POOL

Scenic rating: 6

on Fall Creek in Willamette National Forest

Map grid B2

Big Pool campground is quiet, secluded, and primitive. The camp sits along Fall Creek at about 1,000 feet elevation, and the scenic Fall Creek National Recreation Trail passes the camp on the other side of the creek, providing hiking opportunities.

RV sites, facilities: There are three tent sites

and two sites for tents or RVs up to 24 feet long. Picnic tables, garbage containers, and fire grills are provided. Vault toilets and drinking water are available. Leashed pets are permitted.

Reservations, fees: Reservations are not accepted. Sites are $12 per night, $6 per night per additional vehicle. Open late May–September, weather permitting.

Directions: From south Eugene on I-5, take Exit 188 to Highway 58. Drive 11 miles south to Lowell and Pioneer Street (at the covered bridge). Turn left and drive 0.2 mile to West Boundary Road. Turn left and drive one block to Lowell Jasper Road. Turn right and drive 1.5 miles to Unity and Place Road. Turn right and drive about one mile to a fork with North Shore Road. Bear left onto North Shore Road (Big Fall Creek Road) and drive about 12 miles (the road becomes Forest Road 18) to the campground on the right.

Contact: Willamette National Forest, Middle Fork Ranger District, 541/782-2283, fax 541/782-5306, www.fs.fed.us; Hoodoo Recreation, 541/822-3799.

59 BEDROCK

Scenic rating: 6

on Fall Creek in Willamette National Forest

Map grid B2

Bedrock lies along the banks of Fall Creek amid Douglas firs and cedars. This is one of the access points for the scenic Fall Creek National Recreation Trail, which in turn offers access to Jones Trail, a six-mile uphill climb. Swimming holes offer relief in summer. Note that the campground suffered previous fire damage, but it is recovering.

RV sites, facilities: There are 18 single sites and one multiple site for tents or RVs up to 36 feet long. Picnic tables and fire grills are provided. Vault toilets and garbage service are available. There is no drinking water. Some facilities are wheelchair accessible. Leashed pets are permitted.

Reservations, fees: Reservations are not

accepted. Single sites are $14 per night, $22 per night for double sites, and $7 per night per additional vehicle. Open May–mid-September, weather permitting.

Directions: From south Eugene on I-5, take Exit 188 to Highway 58. Drive 11 miles south to Lowell and Pioneer Street (at the covered bridge). Turn left and drive 0.2 mile to West Boundary Road. Turn left and drive one block to Lowell Jasper Road. Turn right and drive 1.5 miles to Unity and Place Road. Turn right and drive about one mile to a fork with North Shore Road. Bear left onto North Shore Road (Big Fall Creek Road) and drive about 14 miles (the road becomes Forest Road 18) to the campground on the left.

Contact: Willamette National Forest, Middle Fork Ranger District, 541/782-2283, fax 541/782-5306, www.fs.fed.us; Hoodoo Recreation, 541/822-3799.

60 PUMA

Scenic rating: 6

on Fall Creek in Willamette National Forest

Map grid B2

Puma campground hugs the banks of Fall Creek at an elevation of 1,100 feet. This is one of four camps in the immediate area, located across from the popular Fall Creek National Recreation Trail. The trail offers hiking opportunities, while Fall Creek provides a nice spot to cool off in summer.

RV sites, facilities: There are 11 sites for tents or RVs up to 36 feet long. Picnic tables and fire grills are provided. Vault toilets, drinking water, and garbage bins are available. Leashed pets are permitted.

Reservations, fees: Reservations are not accepted. Sites are $14 per night, $7 per night per additional vehicle. Open late May–September, weather permitting.

Directions: From I-5 south of Eugene, take Exit 188 to Highway 58. Drive about 11 miles to Lowell. Turn left at Pioneer Street (at the covered bridge), drive 0.2 mile, and turn left on West Boundary Road. Drive one block and turn right at Lowell Jasper Road. Drive 1.5 miles to Place Road and turn right. Drive about one mile to a fork and bear left onto North Shore Road (Big Fall Creek Road). Drive about 16 miles (the road becomes Forest Road 18) to the campground on the left.

Contact: Willamette National Forest, Middle Fork Ranger District, 541/782-2283, fax 541/782-5306, www.fs.fed.us.

61 FRISSELL CROSSING

Scenic rating: 8

near the Three Sisters Wilderness in Willamette National Forest

Map grid B2

If you're looking for solitude, this place should be heaven to you. Frissell campground (elevation 2,600 feet) sits on the banks of the South Fork of the McKenzie River, adjacent to a trailhead that provides access to the backcountry of the Three Sisters Wilderness. Note that Frissell Crossing is the only camp in the immediate area that has drinking water.

RV sites, facilities: There are 12 sites for tents or RVs up to 36 feet long. Picnic tables, garbage bins, and fire grills are provided. Drinking water and vault toilets are available. Leashed pets are permitted.

Reservations, fees: Reservations are not accepted. Sites are $12 per night, $6 per night per additional vehicle. Open mid-May–mid-September, weather permitting.

Directions: From Eugene, drive east on Highway 126 for 37 miles to Blue River. Continue east on Highway 126 for five miles to Forest Road 19 (Aufderheide Scenic Byway). Turn right (south) and drive 21.5 miles to the camp on the left.

Contact: Willamette National Forest, McKenzie River Ranger District, 541/822-3381, fax 541/822-7254, www.fs.fed.us; Hoodoo Recreation, 541/822-3799.

62 WINBERRY

Scenic rating: 6

on Winberry Creek in Willamette National Forest

Map grid B2

This campground is on Winberry Creek in a tree-shaded area at 1,900 feet elevation. The closest hiking option is Station Butte Trail, just downstream from the campground on Forest Road 1802-150. Be cautious: Poison oak grows at the top of the butte.

RV sites, facilities: There are six sites for tents or RVs up to 14 feet long. Picnic tables and fire grills are provided. Drinking water, vault toilets, garbage service, and two A-frame shelters are available. Some facilities are wheelchair accessible. Leashed pets are permitted.

Reservations, fees: Reservations are not accepted. Sites are $5 per night, $2 per night per additional vehicle. Open late May–early September, weather permitting.

Directions: From south Eugene on I-5, take Exit 188 to Highway 58. Drive 11 miles south to Lowell and Pioneer Street (at the covered bridge). Turn left and drive 0.2 mile to West Boundary Road. Turn left and drive one block to Lowell Jasper Road. Turn right and drive 1.5 miles to Unity and Place Road. Turn right and drive about one mile to a fork with Winberry Road. Bear right and drive six miles (the road becomes Forest Road 1802). Continue 3.5 miles to the campground.

Contact: Willamette National Forest, Middle Fork Ranger District, 541/782-2283, fax 541/782-5306, www.fs.fed.us.

63 KIAHANIE

Scenic rating: 5

on the North Fork of the Willamette River in Willamette National Forest

Map grid B2

This is one heck of a spot for fly-fishing (and the only kind of fishing allowed). Kiahanie is a remote campground that sits at 2,200 feet elevation along the North Fork of the Willamette

River, a designated Wild and Scenic River. If you want beauty and quiet among enormous Douglas fir trees, you came to the right place. An even more remote campground, Box Canyon Horse Camp, is farther north on Forest Road 19.

RV sites, facilities: There are 19 sites for tents or RVs up to 24 feet long. Picnic tables and fire rings are provided. Drinking water, vault toilets, garbage bins, and a recycling center are available. Some facilities are wheelchair accessible. Leashed pets are permitted.

Reservations, fees: Reservations are not accepted. Sites are $10 per night, $5 per night per additional vehicle. Open late May–late October, weather permitting.

Directions: From south Eugene on I-5, take Exit 188 to Highway 58. Drive 31 miles southeast on Highway 58 to Westfir. Take the Westfir exit and drive two miles to Westfir and the junction with Aufderheide Scenic Byway (Forest Road 19). Bear left (northeast) and drive 19 miles to the campground.

Contact: Willamette National Forest, Middle Fork Ranger District, 541/782-2283, fax 541/782-5306, www.fs.fed.us.

64 BOX CANYON HORSE CAMP

Scenic rating: 4

near Chucksney Mountain in Willamette National Forest

Map grid B2

Only 80 miles from Eugene, this secluded campground with sparse tree cover offers wilderness trails, including the Chucksney Mountain Trail, Crossing-Way Trail, and Grasshopper Trail. It's a good base camp for a backpacking trip and is at 3,600 feet in elevation.

RV sites, facilities: There are 13 sites for tents or RVs up to 30 feet long that allow horse and rider to camp close together. Picnic tables, fire grills, stock water, and corrals are provided. Vault toilets are available. There is no drinking water, and garbage must be packed out. Leashed pets are permitted.

Reservations, fees: Reservations are not accepted. There is no fee for camping. Open June–November, weather permitting.

Directions: From Eugene, drive east on Highway 126 for 41 miles to Blue River. Continue east on Highway 126 for five miles to Forest Road 19 (Aufderheide Scenic Byway). Turn right (south) and drive 33 miles to the camp on the right.

Contact: Willamette National Forest, McKenzie River Ranger District, 541/822-3381, fax 541/822-7254, www.fs.fed.us.

65 BLACK CANYON

Scenic rating: 7

on the Middle Fork of the Willamette River in Willamette National Forest

Map grid B2

Black Canyon campground is set along the banks of the Middle Fork of the Willamette River, not far above Lookout Point Reservoir, where fishing and boating are available. The elevation is 1,000 feet. The camp is pretty and wooded and has comfortable sites. Within the camp is a one-mile-long nature trail with interpretive signs. You will hear train noise from the other side of the river.

RV sites, facilities: There are 70 sites for tents or RVs up to 40 feet long, and one group site is available. Picnic tables, garbage service, and fire grills are provided. Drinking water, vault toilets, and firewood are available. A dump station, café, and coin laundry are within six miles. Launching facilities are nearby at the south end of Lookout Point Reservoir. Some facilities are wheelchair accessible. Leashed pets are permitted.

Reservations, fees: Reservations are accepted at 877/444-6777 or www.recreation.gov ($10 reservation fee). Single sites are $16 per night, $30 per night for double site, $8 per night per additional vehicle, $75 for the group site. Open late April–early October, weather permitting.

Directions: From south Eugene on I-5, take Exit 188 to Highway 58. Drive southeast on Highway 58 for 27 miles to the camp on the left (six miles west of Oakridge).

Contact: Willamette National Forest, Middle Fork Ranger District, 541/782-2283, fax 541/782-5306, www.fs.fed.us.

66 BAKER BAY COUNTY PARK

Scenic rating: 6

on Dorena Lake

Map grid B2

Baker Bay is set along the shore of Dorena Lake, where boating, canoeing, fishing, sailing, swimming, and waterskiing are among the recreation options. Row River Trail follows part of the lake for a hike or bike ride, and there are covered bridges in the area. For golf, head to Cottage Grove.

RV sites, facilities: There are 49 sites for tents or self-contained RVs up to 35 feet, plus two group sites for up to 25 people each. Picnic tables and fire grills are provided. Drinking water, restrooms with flush toilets and coin showers, firewood, garbage bins, and a dump station are available. A concession stand with ice is in the park, and a store is within two miles. Boat docks, launching, and rentals are nearby, with seasonal onshore facilities for catamarans. Some facilities are wheelchair accessible. Leashed pets are permitted.

Reservations, fees: Reservations are accepted for group sites only at 541/682-2000 ($10 reservation fee). Single sites are $16 per night, $6.50 for an additional vehicle. Group sites are $50 per night. Open April–October.

Directions: From Eugene, drive south on I-5 for 22 miles to Cottage Grove and Exit 174 (Dorena Lake exit). Take that exit to Row River Road and drive east for 4.4 miles (the road becomes Shore View Drive). Bear right on Shore View Drive and continue 2.8 miles to the campground entrance on the left.

Contact: Baker Bay Park, 541/942-7669, www.co.lane.or.us/parks.

67 SCHWARZ PARK

Scenic rating: 7

on Dorena Lake

Map grid B2

This large campground sits below Dorena Lake on the Row River, where boating, fishing, swimming, and waterskiing are among the recreation options at the lake. Note that chances of rain are high May to mid-June and that there is a posted warning against consumption of fish from Dorena Lake. The Row River Trail, a paved trail for biking, walking, and shoreline access, parallels Dorena Lake's north shoreline and then extends 12 miles.

RV sites, facilities: There are 69 sites for tents or RVs of any length and six group sites for up to 15–50 people. Drinking water, garbage bins, picnic tables, and fire rings are provided. Restrooms with flush toilets and showers and a dump station are available. Boat-launching facilities are on the lake about two miles upstream. Some facilities are wheelchair accessible. Leashed pets are permitted.

Reservations, fees: Reservations are accepted at 877/444-6777 or www.recreation.gov ($10 reservation fee). Sites are $13 per night, group sites are $130 per night, and an additional vehicle is $5 per night. Open late April–late September.

Directions: From Eugene, drive south on I-5 for 22 miles to Cottage Grove and Exit 174. Take that exit to Shoreview Drive and drive one mile to Row River Road. Turn left and drive four miles east to the campground entrance.

Contact: U.S. Army Corps of Engineers, Recreation Information, Cottage Grove, 541/942-1418 or 541/942-5631, fax 541/942-1305, http://corpslakes.usace.army.mil.

68 SALMON CREEK FALLS

Scenic rating: 8

on Salmon Creek in Willamette National Forest

Map grid B2

This pretty campground sits in a lush, old-growth forest, right along Salmon Creek at 1,500 feet in elevation. The rocky gorge area creates two small but beautiful waterfalls and several deep pools in the clear, blue-green waters. Springtime brings a full range of wildflowers and wild thimbleberries; hazelnuts abound in the summer. This area is a popular recreation spot.

RV sites, facilities: There are 14 sites for tents or RVs up to 40 feet long. Picnic tables, garbage bins, and fire grills are provided. Drinking water and vault toilets are available. A store, café, coin laundry, and ice are available within five miles. Leashed pets are permitted.

Reservations, fees: Reservations are not accepted. Sites are $14 per night, $7 per night per additional vehicle. Open late April–mid-September, weather permitting.

Directions: From south Eugene on I-5, take Exit 188 to Highway 58. Drive southeast on Highway 58 for 35 miles to Oakridge and the signal light for downtown. Turn left on Crestview Street and drive 0.25 mile to 1st Street. Turn right and drive five miles (the road becomes Forest Road 24, then Salmon Creek Road) to the campground entrance on the right.

Contact: Willamette National Forest, Middle Fork Ranger District, 541/782-2283, fax 541/782-5306, www.fs.fed.us; Hoodoo Recreation, 541/822-3799.

69 NORTH WALDO

Scenic rating: 10

on Waldo Lake in Willamette National Forest

Map grid B2

North Waldo is the most popular of the Waldo Lake campgrounds. Set at an elevation of 5,400 feet, Waldo Lake has the special distinction of being one of the three purest lakes in the world. The boat launch here is deeper than the others on the lake, which makes it more accommodating for large sailboats (gas motors are not allowed on the lake). Amphitheater programs are presented here on weekends late July–Labor Day. North Waldo is also a popular starting point to many wilderness trails and lakes, most notably Rigdon, Torrey, and Wahanna lakes. The drier environment supports fewer mosquitoes, but they can still be plentiful in season.

RV sites, facilities: There are 56 sites for tents or RVs up to 40 feet long. Picnic tables and fire rings are provided. Drinking water, composting toilets, garbage bins, recycling center, swimming area, and amphitheater are available. Boat-launching facilities are available. Leashed pets are permitted.

Reservations, fees: Reservations are not accepted. Single sites are $18 per night, double sites $20 per night, $9 per night per additional vehicle. A Northwest Forest Pass ($5 daily fee or $30 annual fee per vehicle) is required at the nearby boat launch and trailheads. Open early June–early October, weather permitting.

Directions: From Eugene, drive south on I-5 for four miles to Exit 188 and Highway 58. Turn southeast and drive about 60 miles to Waldo Lake Road (Forest Road 5897). Turn left and drive north on Waldo Lake Road for 14 miles to Forest Road 5898. Turn left and drive about two miles to the campground at the northeast end of Waldo Lake.

Contact: Willamette National Forest, Middle Fork Ranger District, 541/782-2283, fax 541/782-5306, www.fs.fed.us; Hoodoo Recreation, 541/822-3799.

70 ISLET

🥾 🚴 🏊 🎣 🛥 🐕 🚐 ⛺

Scenic rating: 10

on Waldo Lake in Willamette National Forest

Map grid B2

You'll find sandy beaches and an interpretive sign at this campground at the north end of Waldo Lake. The winds blow consistently every afternoon, great for sailing. A picnic table placed strategically on the rock jetty provides a great spot to enjoy a sunset. A one-mile shoreline trail stretches between Islet and North Waldo Campground. Bring your mosquito repellent June–August—you'll need it.

RV sites, facilities: There are 55 sites, including

four multiple sites, for tents or RVs up to 40 feet long. Picnic tables, garbage bins, a recycling center, and fire rings are provided. Drinking water and composting toilets are available. Boat-launching facilities are available nearby. Leashed pets are permitted.

Reservations, fees: Reservations are not accepted. Single sites are $18 per night, $9 per night per additional vehicle. Double sites are $25 per night. A Northwest Forest Pass ($5 daily fee or $30 annual fee per parked vehicle) is required at the nearby boat launch and trailheads. Open July–October, weather permitting.

Directions: From Eugene, drive south on I-5 for four miles to Exit 188 and Highway 58. Turn southeast and drive about 60 miles to Waldo Lake Road (Forest Road 5897). Turn left and drive north on Waldo Lake Road for 14 miles to Forest Road 5898. Turn left and continue 1.5 miles to the campground at the northeast end of Waldo Lake.

Contact: Willamette National Forest, Middle Fork Ranger District, 541/782-2283, fax 541/782-5306, www.fs.fed.us; Hoodoo Recreation, 541/822-3799.

71 SHADOW BAY

🥾 🚴 🏊 🎣 🛥 🐕 🚐 ⛺

Scenic rating: 10

on Waldo Lake in Willamette National Forest

Map grid B2

Shadow Bay campground, at 5,400 in elevation, is situated on a large bay at the south end of Waldo Lake. It has a considerably wetter environment than either North Waldo or Islet, supporting a more diverse and prolific ground cover—as well as more mosquitoes. The camp receives considerably lighter use than North Waldo. You have access to the Shore Line Trail and then the Waldo Lake Trail from here. Note that gas motors are not permitted on Waldo Lake.

RV sites, facilities: There are 92 sites, including several multiple sites, for tents or RVs up to 44 feet long. Picnic tables, garbage bins, a recycling center, and fire grills are provided. Drinking water and vault and composting toilets are available. A camp host is on-site in season. Boat-launching facilities and a swimming area are nearby. Leashed pets are permitted.

Reservations, fees: Reservations are accepted at 877/444-6777 or www.recreation.gov ($10 reservation fee). Single sites are $18 per night, $32 per night for double sites, $9 per night per additional vehicle. A Northwest Forest Pass ($5 daily fee or $30 annual fee per vehicle) is required at the nearby boat launch and trailheads. Open July–October, weather permitting.

Directions: From Eugene, drive south on I-5 for four miles to Exit 188 and Highway 58. Turn southeast and drive about 60 miles to Waldo Lake Road (Forest Road 5897). Turn left on Waldo Lake Road and drive north for 6.5 miles to the Shadow Bay turnoff. Turn left and drive on Forest Road 5896 to the campground at the south end of Waldo Lake.

Contact: Willamette National Forest, Middle Fork Ranger District, 541/782-2283, fax 541/782-5306, www.fs.fed.us; Hoodoo Recreation, 541/822-3799.

72 BLUE POOL

Scenic rating: 4

on Salt Creek in Willamette National Forest
Map grid B2

This campground is situated in an old-growth forest alongside Salt Creek at 1,900 feet elevation. The camp features a large picnic area along the creek with picnic tables, a large grassy area, and fire stoves built in the 1930s by the Civilian Conservation Corps. One-half mile east of the campground on Highway 58 is McCredie Hot Springs. This spot is undeveloped, without any facilities. Exercise caution when using the hot springs; they can be very hot.

RV sites, facilities: There are 24 sites for tents or RVs up to 36 feet long. Picnic tables, garbage bins, a recycling center, and fire rings are provided. Drinking water and vault and flush toilets are available. Leashed pets are permitted.

Reservations, fees: Reservations are not accepted. Sites are $14 per night, $7 per night per additional vehicle. Open mid-May–September, weather permitting.

Directions: From Eugene, drive south on I-5 for four miles to Exit 188 and Highway 58. Turn southeast and drive 35 miles to Oakridge. Continue east on Highway 58 for eight miles to the campground on the right.

Contact: Willamette National Forest, Middle Fork Ranger District, 541/782-2283, fax 541/782-5306, www.fs.fed.us; Hoodoo Recreation, 541/822-3799.

73 SHARPS CREEK

Scenic rating: 5

on Sharps Creek
Map grid B2

Like nearby Rujada, this camp on the banks of Sharps Creek is just far enough off the beaten path to be missed by most campers. It's quiet, primitive, and remote, and fishing, gold-panning, and swimming are popular activities in the day-use area.

RV sites, facilities: There are 10 sites for tents or RVs up to 30 feet long. Picnic tables and fire pits are provided. Drinking water and vault toilets are available. A camp host is here in summer. Some facilities are wheelchair accessible. Leashed pets are permitted.

Reservations, fees: Reservations are not accepted. Sites are $8 per night, with a 14-day stay limit, and $3 per night per additional vehicle. Open mid-May–September, weather permitting.

Directions: From Eugene, drive south on I-5 to Cottage Grove and Exit 174. Take that exit and drive east on Row River Road for 18 miles to Sharps Creek Road. Turn right (south) and drive four miles to the campground.

Contact: Bureau of Land Management, Eugene District, 541/683-6600 or 888/442-3061, fax 541/683-6981, www.blm.gov.

OREGON

74 RUJADA

Scenic rating: 7

on Layng Creek in Umpqua National Forest

Map grid B2

Rujada campground is nestled on a river terrace on the banks of Layng Creek, right at the national forest border. The Swordfern Trail follows Layng Creek through a beautiful forest within a lush fern grotto. There is a fair swimming hole near the campground. Those with patience and persistence can fish in the creek. By continuing east on Forest Road 17, you reach a trailhead that leads 0.5 mile to beautiful Spirit Falls, a spectacular 60-foot waterfall. A bit farther east is another easy trail, which leads to Moon Falls, even more awe-inspiring at 125 feet. Another campground option is Cedar Creek, about six miles southeast on Brice Creek Road (County Road 2470).

RV sites, facilities: There are 15 sites for tents or RVs up to 22 feet long. Picnic tables, garbage bins, and fire pits are provided. Flush and vault toilets, drinking water, and a softball field are available. Some facilities are wheelchair accessible. Leashed pets are permitted.

Reservations, fees: Reservations are not accepted. Sites are $8 per night, $3 per night per additional vehicle. Open late May–late September, weather permitting.

Directions: From Eugene, drive south on I-5 to Cottage Grove and Exit 174. Take that exit and drive east on Row River Road for 19 miles to Layng Creek Road (Forest Road 17). Turn left and drive two miles to the campground on the right.

Contact: Umpqua National Forest, Cottage Grove Ranger District, 541/767-5000, fax 541/767-5075, www.fs.fed.us.

75 PACKARD CREEK

Scenic rating: 6

on Hills Creek Reservoir in Willamette National Forest

Map grid B2

Packard Creek campground is located on a large flat beside Hills Creek Reservoir. This camp is extremely popular with families and fills up on weekends and holidays. The mix of vegetation in the campground unfortunately includes an abundance of poison oak. The speed limit around the swimming area and boat ramp is 5 mph. The elevation is 1,600 feet.

RV sites, facilities: There are 37 sites, including two multiple sites, for tents or RVs up to 40 feet long, and a group area for up to 75 people. Picnic tables and fire rings are provided. Drinking water, vault toilets, garbage bins, a recycling center, and firewood are available. Fishing and boat docks, boat-launching facilities, a roped swimming area, picnic shelter, and an amphitheater are available. Some sites have their own docks. Some facilities are wheelchair accessible. Leashed pets are permitted.

Reservations, fees: Reservations are accepted at 877/444-6777 or www.recreation.gov ($10 reservation fee). Single sites are $16 per night, $30 per night for double sites, $8 per night per additional vehicle, $125 for the group site. Open mid-April–mid-September, weather permitting.

Directions: From Eugene, drive south on I-5 for four miles to Exit 188 and Highway 58. Turn southeast and drive 35 miles to Oakridge. Continue east on Highway 58 for two miles to Kitson Springs Road. Turn right and drive 0.5 mile to Forest Road 21. Turn right and continue six miles to the campground on the left.

Contact: Willamette National Forest, Middle Fork Ranger District, 541/782-2283, fax 541/782-5306, www.fs.fed.us; Hoodoo Recreation, 541/822-3799.

76 SAND PRAIRIE

Scenic rating: 6

on the Willamette River in
Willamette National Forest

Map grid B2

Situated at 1,600 feet elevation in a mixed stand of cedar, dogwood, Douglas fir, hazelnut, and western hemlock, this campground provides easy access to the Middle Fork of the Willamette River. An access road leads to the south (upstream) end of the Hills Creek Reservoir. The 27-mile Middle Fork Trail begins at the south end of the campground. Fishing is good here; you can expect to catch large cutthroat trout, rainbow trout, and suckers in the Middle Fork.

RV sites, facilities: There are 21 sites for tents or RVs up to 40 feet long. Picnic tables, garbage bins, and fire rings are provided. Vault and flush toilets, a group picnic area, and drinking water are available. A camp host is on-site. A boat launch is nearby on Hills Creek Reservoir. Some facilities are wheelchair accessible. Leashed pets are permitted.

Reservations, fees: Reservations are not accepted. Sites are $12 per night, $6 per night per additional vehicle. Open late May–early September, weather permitting.

Directions: From Eugene, drive south on I-5 for four miles to Exit 188 and Highway 58. Turn southeast and drive 35 miles to Oakridge. Continue east on Highway 58 for two miles to Kitson Springs Road. Turn right and drive 0.5 mile to Forest Road 21. Turn right and continue 11 miles to the campground on the right.

Contact: Willamette National Forest, Middle Fork Ranger District, 541/782-2283, fax 541/782-5306, www.fs.fed.us.

77 SACANDAGA

Scenic rating: 5

on the Willamette River in
Willamette National Forest

Map grid B2

Sacandaga campground sits along the middle fork of the Willamette River, where a segment of the historic Oregon Central Military Wagon Road is visible. Two trails from the campground access the Willamette River, and the Middle Fork Trail is in close proximity. Also, a short trail leads to a viewpoint with a bench, great for a short break. This campground gets low use, and the sites are well separated by vegetation. Count on solitude here. The elevation is 2,400 feet.

RV sites, facilities: There are 17 sites for tents or RVs up to 24 feet long. Picnic tables and fire rings are provided. Drinking water, vault toilets, and firewood are available. Leashed pets are permitted.

Reservations, fees: Reservations are not accepted. Sites are $8 per night, $4 per night per additional vehicle. Open mid-May–mid-November, weather permitting.

Directions: From Eugene, drive south on I-5 for four miles to Exit 188 and Highway 58. Turn southeast and drive 35 miles to Oakridge. Continue east on Highway 58 for two miles to Kitson Springs Road. Turn right and drive 0.5 mile to Forest Road 21. Turn right and drive 24 miles to the campground on the right.

Contact: Willamette National Forest, Middle Fork Ranger District, 541/782-2283, fax 541/782-5306, www.fs.fed.us.

78 CAMPERS FLAT

Scenic rating: 5

on the Willamette River in
Willamette National Forest

Map grid B2

Small, pretty Campers Flat campground sits adjacent to the Middle Fork Willamette River, near Deadhorse Creek. Though the camp is

OREGON

right next to Forest Road 21, you're likely to hear more river than road. Fishing is a popular activity here, with good river access. For mountain bikers, the Young's Rock Trailhead awaits on the other side of the road. While at camp, be sure to check out the interpretive sign detailing the history of the Oregon Central Military Wagon Road.

RV sites, facilities: There are five sites for tents or RVs up to 40 feet long. Picnic tables, garbage bins, and fire grills are provided. Vault toilets and firewood are available. Well water may be available for drinking, but bring your own just in case. Leashed pets are permitted.

Reservations, fees: Reservations are not accepted. Sites are $12 per night, $6 per night per additional vehicle. Open late May–September.

Directions: From Eugene, drive south on I-5 for five miles to Exit 188 and Highway 58. Turn east and drive 35 miles to the town of Oakridge. From Oakridge, continue east on Highway 58 about two miles to Kitson Springs Road. Turn right and drive 0.5 mile to Forest Road 21. Turn right and drive 19 miles to the campground on the right.

Contact: Willamette National Forest, Middle Fork Ranger District, 541/782-2283, fax 541/782-5306, www.fs.fed.us.

79 SECRET

Scenic rating: 5

on the Willamette River in Willamette National Forest

Map grid B2

This small campground, set on the middle fork of the Willamette River, gets regular use from locals in the know. The tree cover is scant, but there is adequate vegetation to buffer the campsites from the nearby road noise. Fishing the Middle Fork Willamette is generally fair.

RV sites, facilities: There are six sites for tents or RVs up to 36 feet long. Picnic tables, garbage bins, and fire rings are provided. Pit toilets are available, but there is no drinking water. Leashed pets are permitted.

Reservations, fees: Reservations are not accepted. Sites are $12 per night, $6 per night per additional vehicle. Open May–late September, weather permitting.

Directions: From Eugene, drive south on I-5 for five miles to Exit 188 and Highway 58. Turn east and drive 35 miles to the town of Oakridge. From Oakridge, continue east on Highway 58 about two miles to Kitson Springs Road. Turn right and drive 0.5 mile to Forest Road 21. Turn right and drive 18 miles to the campground.

Contact: Willamette National Forest, Middle Fork Ranger District, 541/782-2283, fax 541/782-5306, www.fs.fed.us; Hoodoo Recreation, 541/822-3799.

80 ROCK CREEK

Scenic rating: 8

on Rock Creek

Map grid B2

Since I started roaming around the state 20 years ago, this campground on the banks of Rock Creek in a relatively obscure spot has been considerably improved by the BLM. It's not well known, either, so you're likely to have privacy as a bonus. No fishing is allowed in Rock Creek.

RV sites, facilities: There are 17 sites for tents or RVs up to 40 feet long. Picnic tables and fire grills are provided. A camp host is on-site, and vault toilets, drinking water, a pavilion, and firewood are available. Some facilities are wheelchair accessible. Leashed pets are permitted.

Reservations, fees: Reservations are not accepted. Sites are $10 per night, with a 14-day stay limit, and $4 per night per additional vehicle. Open mid-May–mid-September.

Directions: From Roseburg, drive east on Highway 138 for 22 miles to Rock Creek Road. Turn right (north) and drive seven miles to the campground on the right.

Contact: Bureau of Land Management, Roseburg District, 541/440-4930, fax 541/440-4948, www.blm.gov.

81 MILLPOND

Scenic rating: 8

on Rock Creek

Map grid B2

Rock Creek flows past Millpond and empties into the North Umpqua River five miles downstream. Just above this confluence is the Rock Creek Fish Hatchery, which is open year-round to visitors, with free access. This campground along the banks of Rock Creek is the first camp you'll see along Rock Creek Road, which accounts for its relative popularity in the area. Like Rock Creek Campground, it's primitive and remote. No fishing is allowed in Rock Creek.

RV sites, facilities: There are 12 sites for tents or RVs up to 45 feet long. Picnic tables, garbage service, and fire grills are provided. A camp host is on-site, and flush and vault toilets, drinking water, firewood, a ball field, playground, and pavilion are available. Some facilities are wheelchair accessible. Leashed pets are permitted.

Reservations, fees: Reservations are not accepted. Sites are $10 per night, with a 14-day stay limit, and $4 per night per additional vehicle. Open early May–early November.

Directions: From Roseburg, drive east on Highway 138 for 22 miles to Rock Creek Road. Turn right (north) and drive five miles to the campground on the right.

Contact: Bureau of Land Management, Roseburg District, 541/440-4930, fax 541/440-4948, www.blm.gov.

82 SUSAN CREEK

Scenic rating: 9

on the North Umpqua River

Map grid B2   **BEST (**

This popular and pretty campground borders the North Umpqua Wild and Scenic River. This lush setting features plenty of trees and river access. Highlights include two barrier-free trails, one traveling 0.5 mile to the day-use area. From there, a hike of about 0.75 mile leads to the 50-foot Susan Creek Falls. Another 0.4

mile up the trail are the Susan Creek Indian Mounds. These moss-covered rocks are believed to be a spiritual site and are visited by Native Americans in search of guardian spirit visions. This area also boasts an excellent osprey interpretive site with a viewing platform along the river.

RV sites, facilities: There are 29 sites for RVs up to 65 feet long. Picnic tables, garbage service, and fire grills are provided. Restrooms with flush toilets and showers, drinking water, and firewood are available, and there is a camp host. Some facilities and trails are wheelchair accessible. Leashed pets are permitted.

Reservations, fees: Reservations are not accepted. Sites are $14 per night, with a 14-day stay limit, and $4 per night per additional vehicle. Open late April–mid-November.

Directions: From Roseburg, drive east on Highway 138 for 29.5 miles to the campground (turnoff well signed).

Contact: Bureau of Land Management, Roseburg District, 541/440-4930, fax 541/440-4948, www.blm.gov.

83 STEAMBOAT FALLS

Scenic rating: 8

on Steamboat Creek in Umpqua National Forest

Map grid B2

This Steamboat Creek campground boasts some excellent scenery. Beautiful Steamboat Falls features a fish ladder that provides passage for steelhead and salmon on their upstream migration. No fishing is permitted in Steamboat Creek. Other nearby camping options are Island and Canton Creek.

RV sites, facilities: There are 10 sites for tents or RVs up to 24 feet long. Picnic tables, garbage bins, vault toilets, and fire grills are provided. There is no drinking water. Leashed pets are permitted.

Reservations, fees: Reservations are not accepted. Sites are $7 per night, $4 per night per additional vehicle. Open year-round, weather permitting.

Directions: From Roseburg on I-5, take Exit 120 to Highway 138. Drive east on Highway 138 to Steamboat and Forest Road 38. Turn left on Forest Road 38 (Steamboat Creek Road) and drive six miles to a fork with Forest Road 3810. Turn right and drive one mile on a paved road to the campground.

Contact: Umpqua National Forest, North Umpqua Ranger District, 541/496-3532, fax 541/496-3534, www.fs.fed.us.

84 SCAREDMAN

Scenic rating: 6

on Canton Creek

Map grid B2

Scaredman is a small campground along the banks of Canton Creek, virtually unknown to out-of-towners. Set in an old-growth forest, this private and secluded camp offers a chance to swim in the creek. Scaredman gets its name from an old legend that says some early settlers camped here, heard a pack of hungry wolves, and then ran off, scared to death. This is one of the few free camps left in the region. Although fishing is closed on Canton Creek and all Steamboat drainages, the North Umpqua River 3.5 miles downstream offers fly-fishing for steelhead or salmon.

RV sites, facilities: There are nine sites for tents or RVs up to 25 feet long. Picnic tables, garbage service, and fire grills are provided. Vault toilets and drinking water are available. A camp host is on-site in season. Leashed pets are permitted.

Reservations, fees: Reservations are not accepted. There is no fee for camping. The stay limit is 14 days. Open year-round.

Directions: From Roseburg, drive east on Highway 138 for 40 miles to Steamboat Creek Road. Turn left (north) and drive 0.5 mile to Canton Creek Road. Turn left (north) and drive three miles to the campground.

Contact: Bureau of Land Management, Roseburg District, 541/440-4930, fax 541/440-4948, www.blm.gov.

85 ISLAND

Scenic rating: 8

on the Umpqua River in Umpqua National Forest

Map grid B2

The North Umpqua is one of Oregon's most beautiful rivers, and this scenic campground borders its banks at a spot popular for both rafting and steelhead fishing. Note: Only fly-fishing is allowed here. A hiking trail that leads east and west along the river is accessible a short drive to the west.

RV sites, facilities: There are seven sites for tents or RVs up to 24 feet long. Picnic tables, garbage bins, and fire grills are provided. There is no drinking water. Some facilities are wheelchair accessible. Leashed pets are permitted.

Reservations, fees: Reservations are not accepted. Sites are $8 per night, $4 per night per additional vehicle. Open year-round, weather permitting.

Directions: From Roseburg, drive east on Highway 138 for 40 miles (just past Steamboat) to the camp on the right. The campground is along the highway.

Contact: Umpqua National Forest, North Umpqua Ranger District, 541/496-3532, fax 541/496-3534, www.fs.fed.us.

86 CANTON CREEK

Scenic rating: 8

near the North Umpqua River in Umpqua National Forest

Map grid B2

Set at an elevation of 1,195 feet at the confluence of Canton and Steamboat Creeks, this camp is less than a mile from the North Umpqua River and gets little overnight use—but lots of day swimmers come here in July and August. No fishing is permitted on Steamboat or Canton Creeks because they are spawning areas for steelhead and salmon. Steamboat Falls is six miles north on Forest Road 38.

RV sites, facilities: There are five sites for tents or RVs up to 22 feet long. Picnic tables, garbage bins, and fire grills are provided. Drinking water, a covered picnic gazebo, and flush toilets are available. Leashed pets are permitted.

Reservations, fees: Reservations are not accepted. Sites are $8 per night, $4 per night per additional vehicle. Open mid-May–mid-October, weather permitting.

Directions: From Roseburg, drive east on Highway 138 for 39 miles to Steamboat and Forest Road 38 (Steamboat Creek Road). Turn left and drive 0.25 mile to the campground on the right.

Contact: Umpqua National Forest, North Umpqua Ranger District, 541/496-3532, fax 541/496-3534, www.fs.fed.us.

87 HORSESHOE BEND/ DEER FLAT GROUP

Scenic rating: 8

on the Umpqua River in Umpqua National Forest

Map grid B2

This campground, set at an elevation of 1,300 feet, is in the middle of a big bend in the North Umpqua River. This spot is a major launching point for white-water rafting. Fly-fishing is popular here.

RV sites, facilities: There are 24 sites for tents or RVs up to 35 feet long and one group site, Deer Flat, for up to 70 people. Picnic tables, fire grills, garbage bins, drinking water, and flush toilets are provided. A store, gas, and propane are available one mile east. Raft-launching facilities are nearby. Some facilities are wheelchair accessible. Leashed pets are permitted.

Reservations, fees: Reservations are accepted for the group site (Deer Flat, not Horseshoe Bend) at 877/444-6777 or www.recreation.gov ($10 reservation fee) but are not accepted for family sites. Sites are $12 per night, $4 per night per additional vehicle, and $85 per night for group sites. Open mid-May–late September, weather permitting.

Directions: From Roseburg on I-5, take Exit 120. Drive east on Highway 138 for 47 miles to Forest Road 4750. Turn right and drive south

a short distance to the campground entrance road on the right.

Contact: Umpqua National Forest, North Umpqua Ranger District, 541/496-3532, fax 541/496-3534, www.fs.fed.us.

88 EAGLE ROCK

Scenic rating: 9

on the North Umpqua River in Umpqua National Forest

Map grid B2

Eagle Rock camp sits next to the North Umpqua River and adjacent to the Boulder Creek Wilderness. It is named after Eagle Rock, which, along with Rattlesnake Rock, towers above the campground. The camp offers outstanding views of these unusual rock formations. It gets moderate use, heavy on weekends. The camp sits at 1,676 feet elevation near Boulder Flat, a major launch point for rafting. Fishing here is restricted to the use of artificial lures with a single barbless hook.

RV sites, facilities: There are 25 sites for tents or RVs up to 30 feet long. Picnic tables and fire grills are provided. Vault toilets and garbage bins are available. There is no drinking water. A store, propane, and ice are within five miles. Some facilities are wheelchair accessible. Leashed pets are permitted.

Reservations, fees: Reservations are not accepted. Sites are $10 per night, $4 per night per additional vehicle. Open mid-May–October, weather permitting.

Directions: From Roseburg, drive east on Highway 138 for 53 miles to the campground on the left.

Contact: Umpqua National Forest, North Umpqua Ranger District, 541/496-3532, fax 541/496-3534, www.fs.fed.us.

OREGON

89 BOULDER FLAT

Scenic rating: 8

on the North Umpqua River in
Umpqua National Forest

Map grid B2

Boulder Flat campground is nestled along the banks of the North Umpqua River at the confluence with Boulder Creek. There's good trout fishing here (fly-fishing only) and outstanding scenery. The camp sits at a major launching point for white-water rafting. Across the river from the campground, a trail follows Boulder Creek north for 10.5 miles through the Boulder Creek Wilderness, a climb in elevation from 2,000 to 5,400 feet. It's a good thumper for backpackers. Access to the trail is at Soda Springs Dam, two miles east of the camp. A little over a mile to the east you can see some huge, dramatic pillars of volcanic rock, colored with lichen.

RV sites, facilities: There are nine sites for tents or RVs up to 24 feet long. Picnic tables, garbage bins, and fire grills are provided. Vault toilets are available. There is no drinking water. A store, propane, and ice are within five miles. A raft launch is on-site. Leashed pets are permitted.

Reservations, fees: Reservations are not accepted. Sites are $8 per night, $4 per night per additional vehicle. Open year-round.

Directions: From Roseburg, drive east on Highway 138 for 54 miles to the campground on the left.

Contact: Umpqua National Forest, North Umpqua Ranger District, 541/496-3532, fax 541/496-3534, www.fs.fed.us.

90 TOKETEE LAKE

Scenic rating: 7

on Toketee Lake in Umpqua National Forest

Map grid B2

Located just north of Toketee Lake, this campground sits at an elevation of 2,200 feet. The North Umpqua River Trail passes near camp and continues east along the river for many miles. Die-hard hikers can also take the trail west toward the Boulder Creek Wilderness. Toketee Lake, a 97-acre reservoir, offers a good population of brown and rainbow trout and many recreation options. A worthwhile point of interest is Toketee Falls, just west of the lake turnoff. Another is Umpqua Hot Springs, a few miles northeast of the camp. The area sustains a wide variety of wildlife; you might see bald eagles, beavers, a variety of ducks and geese, great blue herons, kingfishers, and otters in fall and winter.

RV sites, facilities: There are 33 sites for tents or RVs up to 22 feet long and one group site for up to 30 people. Picnic tables, garbage bins, and fire grills are provided. Vault toilets are available, but there is no drinking water. Boat docks and launching facilities are nearby. Leashed pets are permitted.

Reservations, fees: Reservations are accepted only for the group site at 541/498-2531. Sites are $7 per night, $3 per night per additional vehicle, and $25 per night for the group site. Open year-round.

Directions: From Roseburg, drive east on Highway 138 for 59 miles to Forest Road 34. Turn left (north) and drive 1.5 miles to the campground on the right.

Contact: Umpqua National Forest, Diamond Lake Ranger District, 541/498-2531, fax 541/498-2515, www.fs.fed.us.

91 EAST LEMOLO

Scenic rating: 8

on Lemolo Lake in Umpqua National Forest

Map grid B2

This campground is on the southeastern shore of Lemolo Lake, where boating and fishing are some of the recreation possibilities. Boats with motors and personal watercraft are allowed. The North Umpqua River and its adjacent trail lie just beyond the north shore of the lake. If you hike for two miles northwest of the lake, you can reach spectacular Lemolo Falls. Large

German brown trout, a wild, native fish, can be taken on troll and fly. Lemolo Lake also provides fishing for brook trout, kokanee, and a sprinkling of rainbow trout.

RV sites, facilities: There are 14 sites for tents or small RVs up to 22 feet long. No drinking water is available. Picnic tables, garbage bins, and fire rings are provided. Vault toilets are available. Boat docks, launching facilities, boat rentals, dump station, restaurants, a store, coin laundry, and showers are nearby. Leashed pets are permitted.

Reservations, fees: Reservations are not accepted. Sites are $7 per night, $3 per night per additional vehicle. Open mid-May–late October, weather permitting.

Directions: From Roseburg, drive east on Highway 138 for 73 miles to Forest Road 2610 (three miles east of Clearwater Falls). Turn left (north) and drive three miles to Forest Road 2614. Turn right and drive two miles to Forest Road 2614-430. Turn left and drive a short distance to the campground at the end of the road.

Contact: Umpqua National Forest, Diamond Lake Ranger District, 541/498-2531, fax 541/498-2515, www.fs.fed.us.

92 POOLE CREEK

Scenic rating: 8

on Lemolo Lake in Umpqua National Forest

Map grid B2

Poole Creek campground on the western shore of Lemolo Lake isn't far from Lemolo Lake Resort, which is open for recreation year-round. The camp is just south of the mouth of Poole Creek in a lodgepole pine, mountain hemlock, and Shasta red fir forest. This is by far the most popular U.S. Forest Service camp at the lake, especially with water-skiers, who are allowed to ski in designated areas of the lake.

RV sites, facilities: There are 60 sites for tents or RVs up to 35 feet long and a group site for up to 60 people. Picnic tables and fire grills are provided. Drinking water and vault toilets are available. A grocery store, a restaurant,

boat docks, launching facilities, and rentals are nearby. Leashed pets are permitted.

Reservations, fees: Reservations are not accepted for single sites but are required for the group camp at 877/444-6777 or www.recreation.gov ($10 reservation fee). Single sites are $11–14 per night, $4 per night per additional vehicle, and $72 per night for the group camp. Open late April–late October, weather permitting.

Directions: From Roseburg, drive east on Highway 138 for 73 miles to Forest Road 2610 (Bird's Point Road). Turn left (north) and drive four miles to the signed turnoff for the campground entrance on the right.

Contact: Umpqua National Forest, Diamond Lake Ranger District, 541/498-2531, fax 541/498-2515, www.fs.fed.us.

93 INLET

Scenic rating: 5

on Lemolo Lake in Umpqua National Forest

Map grid B2

Inlet campground sits on the eastern inlet of Lemolo Lake, hidden in the deep, green, and quiet forest where the North Umpqua River rushes into Lemolo Reservoir. The camp is just across the road from the North Umpqua River Trail, which is routed east into the Oregon Cascades Recreation Area and the Mount Thielsen Wilderness. Lemolo Lake exceeds 100 feet in depth in some spots; boating and fishing for brook trout, kokanee, and rainbow trout are some recreation possibilities. (Boats with motors and personal watercraft are allowed.) Two miles northwest of the lake lies spectacular Lemolo Falls, a good hike.

RV sites, facilities: There are 14 sites for tents or RVs up to 22 feet long. Vault toilets are available, but there is no drinking water. Picnic tables, garbage bins, and fire grills are provided. Boat docks, launching facilities, rentals, a restaurant, groceries, and a gas station are available nearby. Leashed pets are permitted.

Reservations, fees: Reservations are not accepted. Sites are $7 per night, $3 per night per additional vehicle. Open mid-May–late October, weather permitting.

Directions: From Roseburg, drive east on Highway 138 for 73 miles to Forest Road 2610. Turn left (north) and drive three miles to Forest Road 2614. Turn right (east) and drive three miles to the campground.

Contact: Umpqua National Forest, Diamond Lake Ranger District, 541/498-2531, fax 541/498-2515, www.fs.fed.us.

94 BUNKER HILL

Scenic rating: 7

on Crescent Lake in the Umpaqua National Forest

Map grid B2

Bunker Hill campground, on the northwest shore of Lemolo Reservoir, is in a heavily wooded area of lodgepole pine. Fishing is excellent for kokanee as well as brook, rainbow, and large native brown trout. Nearby hiking trails lead to Lemolo Falls, the North Umpqua River, and the Pacific Crest Trail.

RV sites, facilities: There are five sites for tents or RVs up to 22 feet long. Picnic tables and fire rings are provided. Vault toilets and garbage bins are available. There is no drinking water. A boat ramp, boat rentals, a dump station, a restaurant, coin laundry, and coin showers are available 1.5 miles away at Lemolo Lake Resort (541/643-0750). Leashed pets are permitted.

Reservations, fees: Reservations are not accepted. Sites are $7 per night, $3 per night per additional vehicle. Open May–October, weather permitting.

Directions: From Roseburg, drive east on Highway 138 for 73 miles to Bird's Point Road/Forest Road 2610. Turn left and drive 5.5 miles (crossing the dam) to Forest Road 2612. Turn right and drive to the camp at the north end of the lake.

Contact: Umpqua National Forest, Diamond Lake Ranger District, 541/498-2531, fax 541/498-2515, www.fs.fed.us.

95 LEMOLO LAKE RV PARK

Scenic rating: 7

in Umpqua National Forest

Map grid B2

Lemolo Lake is situated high in the Cascade Mountains at just over 4,000 feet elevation. This RV park is set up for folks to bring their own boats and enjoy the lake. Boating, waterskiing, wakeboarding, and Jet Skis are all popular, along, of course, with fishing and swimming, on the lake (40-mph speed limit). Each campground reservation includes free boat launch. There are also miles of hiking trails in the vicinity, plus Crater Lake National Park and Diamond Lake are a quick drive away. In winter, cross-country skiing is popular, and an extensive snowmobile loop runs through the property.

RV sites, facilities: There are 26 sites for tents or RVs; full hookups are available. Picnic tables and fire rings are provided. Drinking water, flush toilets, coin showers, and coin laundry are available. A restaurant and store are on the premises. Boat and ATV rentals are available.

Reservations, fees: Reservations are accepted at 541/643-0750. RV sites with full hookups are $25, tent sites are $12–16. Open year-round.

Directions: From Roseburg, drive east on Highway 138 (Diamond Lake Highway) for about 73 miles to Birds Point Road. Turn left on Birds Point Road and drive five miles to the resort.

Contact: Lemolo Lake RV Park, 541/643-0750, www.lemololakeresort.com.

96 TIMPANOGAS

Scenic rating: 8

on Timpanogas Lake in Willamette National Forest

Map grid B2

Timpanogas Lake is the headwaters of the Middle Fork Willamette River. This campground, at 5,200 feet elevation, is situated in a stand of grand, noble, and silver fir. Fishing for brook trout and cutthroat is good; only non-motorized boating is permitted. Nearby activities include 23 miles of hiking trails in the Timpanogas Basin trails, with views of the Cowhorn Mountains, Diamond Peak, and Sawtooth. Warning: Time it wrong (July–Aug.) and the mosquitoes will eat you alive if you forget insect repellent.

RV sites, facilities: There are 10 sites for tents or RVs up to 24 feet long. Picnic tables, garbage bins, and fire rings are provided. Drinking water, vault toilets, and firewood are available. A primitive boat ramp is nearby, but no boats with motors are allowed. Some facilities are wheelchair accessible. Leashed pets are permitted.

Reservations, fees: Reservations are not accepted. Sites are $8 per night, $4 per night per additional vehicle. Open June–October, weather permitting.

Directions: From Eugene, drive south on I-5 for five miles to Exit 188 and Highway 58. Turn east and drive 35 miles to the town of Oakridge. Continue east on Highway 58 for two miles to Kitson Springs Road. Turn right and drive 0.5 mile to Forest Road 21. Turn right and drive 32 miles to Forest Road 2154. Turn left and drive about 10 miles to the campground on the left.

Contact: Willamette National Forest, Middle Fork Ranger District, 541/782-2283, fax 541/782-5306, www.fs.fed.us.

97 WOLF CREEK

Scenic rating: 6

on the Little River in Umpqua National Forest
Map grid B2

This pretty Little River camp is located at the entrance to the national forest, near the Wolf Creek Civilian Conservation Center. It is set at an elevation of 1,100 feet, with easy access to civilization. The campground has abundant wildflowers in the spring. If you want to get deeper into the Cascades, Hemlock Lake and Lake of the Woods are about 21 and 15 miles east, respectively.

RV sites, facilities: There are eight sites for tents or RVs up to 30 feet long and one group

site for up to 130 people. Picnic tables and fire grills are provided. Flush toilets, drinking water, a covered pavilion for groups, garbage bins, horseshoe pits, a softball field, and a volleyball court are available. Note that if the group site is taken, some recreation facilities may not be available to single-site campers. Some facilities are wheelchair accessible. Leashed pets are permitted.

Reservations, fees: Reservations are accepted only for the group site at 877/444-6777 or www.recreation.gov ($10 reservation fee). Sites are $10 per night, $4 per night per additional vehicle, and $95 per night for the group site. Open mid-May–September, weather permitting.

Directions: From Roseburg on I-5, take Exit 120. Drive east on Highway 138 for 18 miles to Glide and County Road 17. Turn right (southeast) and drive 12 miles (the road becomes Little River Road) to the campground on the right.

Contact: Umpqua National Forest, North Umpqua Ranger District, 541/496-3532, fax 541/496-3534, www.fs.fed.us.

98 COOLWATER

Scenic rating: 6

on the Little River in Umpqua National Forest
Map grid B2

Coolwater campground (1,300 feet elevation) along the banks of the Little River gets moderate use. It features a pretty forest setting with some scenic hiking trails nearby. Overhang Trail is within 0.5 mile of the campground. Fishing and swimming are also options here. Scenic Grotto Falls can be reached by traveling north on Forest Road 2703 (across the road from the camp). Near the falls, you'll find Emile Grove, home of a thicket of old-growth Douglas firs and the huge "Bill Taft Tree," named after the former president.

RV sites, facilities: There are seven sites for tents or RVs up to 24 feet long. Picnic tables and fire grills are provided. Vault toilets are

OREGON

available. There is no drinking water. Leashed pets are permitted.

Reservations, fees: Reservations are not accepted. Sites are $6 per night, $4 per night per additional vehicle. Open year-round, weather permitting.

Directions: From Roseburg on I-5, take Exit 120. Drive east on Highway 138 for 18 miles to Glide and County Road 17. Turn right (southeast) and drive 17 miles (the road becomes Little River Road) to the campground on the right.

Contact: Umpqua National Forest, North Umpqua Ranger District, 541/496-3532, fax 541/496-3534, www.fs.fed.us.

99 WHITE CREEK

Scenic rating: 6

on the Little River in Umpqua National Forest
Map grid B2

Hiking and fishing are two of the recreation options at this campground set at the confluence of White Creek and the Little River. There is a sandy beach on shallow Little River, and waterfalls are in the area.

RV sites, facilities: There is an open parking area for tents or RVs up to 16 feet long. Picnic tables, fire grills, and garbage bins are provided. Vault toilets are available. There is no drinking water. Leashed pets are permitted.

Reservations, fees: Reservations are not accepted. Sites are $6 per night, $4 per night per additional vehicle. Open year-round, weather permitting.

Directions: From Roseburg on I-5, take Exit 120. Drive east on Highway 138 for 18 miles to Glide and County Road 17. Turn right (southeast) and drive 18 miles (the road becomes Little River Road) to Forest Road 2792 (Red Butte Road). Bear right and drive 0.25 mile to the campground on the left.

Contact: Umpqua National Forest, North Umpqua Ranger District, 541/496-3532, fax 541/496-3534, www.fs.fed.us.

100 LAKE IN THE WOODS

Scenic rating: 7

on Lake in the Woods in Umpqua National Forest
Map grid B2

The shore of little Lake in the Woods is the setting of this camp, which makes a nice home base for several good hikes. One of them leaves the camp and heads south for about three miles to the Hemlock Lake Campground. Two other nearby trails provide short, scenic hikes to either Hemlock Falls or Yakso Falls. The campground sits at 3,200 feet elevation. This is a man-made, four-acre lake, eight feet at its deepest point. Boats without motors are allowed.

RV sites, facilities: There are 11 sites for tents or RVs up to 35 feet long. Picnic tables, fire grills, and garbage bins are provided. Vault toilets are available. There is no drinking water. Leashed pets are permitted.

Reservations, fees: Reservations are not accepted. Sites are $10 per night, $4 per night per additional vehicle. Open late May–late October, weather permitting.

Directions: From Roseburg on I-5, take Exit 120. Drive east on Highway 138 for 18 miles to Glide and County Road 17. Turn right (southeast) and drive 18 miles (the road becomes Little River Road) to Forest Road 27. Continue 11 miles to the campground. The last seven miles are gravel.

Contact: Umpqua National Forest, North Umpqua Ranger District, 541/496-3532, fax 541/496-3534, www.fs.fed.us.

101 HEMLOCK LAKE

Scenic rating: 8

on Hemlock Lake in Umpqua National Forest
Map grid B2

This is a little-known jewel of a spot. For starters, it's set along the shore of Hemlock Lake at 4,400 feet elevation. This is a 28-acre, manufactured reservoir that is 33 feet at its deepest point. An eight-mile loop trail called the Yellow Jacket Loop is just south of the campground.

Another trail leaves camp and heads north for about three miles to the Lake in the Woods campground. From there, it's just a short hike to either Hemlock Falls or Yakso Falls, both spectacularly scenic.

RV sites, facilities: There are 13 sites for tents or RVs up to 35 feet long. Picnic tables, fire grills, and garbage bins are provided. Vault toilets are available, but there is no drinking water. Boat docks and launching facilities are nearby. No motors are allowed on the lake. Leashed pets are permitted.

Reservations, fees: Reservations are not accepted. Sites are $8 per night, $4 per night per additional vehicle. Open year-round, weather permitting.

Directions: From Roseburg on I-5, take Exit 120. Drive east on Highway 138 for 18 miles to Glide and County Road 17. Turn right (southeast) and drive 32 miles to the campground on the right.

Contact: Umpqua National Forest, North Umpqua Ranger District, 541/496-3532, fax 541/496-3534, www.fs.fed.us.

102 CLEARWATER FALLS

Scenic rating: 8

on the Clearwater River in Umpqua National Forest

Map grid B2

The main attraction at this campground along the banks of the Clearwater River is the nearby cascading section of stream called Clearwater Falls. Hiking and fishing opportunities abound. The camp sits at an elevation of 4,100 feet.

RV sites, facilities: There are nine sites for tents or RVs up to 30 feet long. Picnic tables, fire grills, and garbage bins are provided. Vault toilets are available. There is no drinking water. Leashed pets are permitted.

Reservations, fees: Reservations are not accepted. Sites are $7 per night, $3 per night per additional vehicle. Open mid-May–October, weather permitting.

Directions: From Roseburg, drive east on Highway 138 for 70 miles to a signed turn for

Clearwater Falls. Turn right and drive to the campground.

Contact: Umpqua National Forest, Diamond Lake Ranger District, 541/498-2531, fax 541/498-2515, www.fs.fed.us.

103 BROKEN ARROW

Scenic rating: 6

on Diamond Lake in Umpqua National Forest

Map grid B2

Broken Arrow campground sits at 5,190 feet elevation near the south shore of Diamond Lake, the largest natural lake in Umpqua National Forest. Set back from the lake, it is surrounded by lodgepole pine and features views of Mount Bailey and Mount Thielsen. Bicycling, boating, fishing, hiking, and swimming keep visitors busy here. Diamond Lake is adjacent to Crater Lake National Park, Mount Bailey, and the Mount Thielsen Wilderness, all of which offer a variety of recreation opportunities year-round. Diamond Lake is quite popular with anglers because of its good trout trolling, particularly in early summer.

RV sites, facilities: There are 117 sites for tents or RVs up to 40 feet long and group sites for 40–104 people. Picnic tables, fire grills, and garbage bins are provided. Restrooms with flush toilets and showers, a dump station, and drinking water are available. Boat docks, launching facilities, and rentals are nearby. Some facilities are wheelchair accessible. Leashed pets are permitted.

Reservations, fees: Reservations are accepted only for group sites at 877/444-6777 or www.recreation.gov ($10 reservation fee). Sites are $11–14 per night, $4 per night per additional vehicle, and $54–132 per night for group sites. Open June–mid-September.

Directions: From Roseburg, drive east on Highway 138 for 78.5 miles to Diamond Lake Loop (Forest Road 4795). Turn right (south) and drive four miles (along the east shore) to the campground turnoff road. Turn right and continue one mile to the camp on the left at the southern end of the lake.

OREGON

Contact: Umpqua National Forest, Diamond Lake Ranger District, 541/498-2531, fax 541/498-2515, www.fs.fed.us.

104 THIELSEN VIEW

Scenic rating: 7

on Diamond Lake in Umpqua National Forest

Map grid B2

This campground sits along the west shore of Diamond Lake in the shadow of majestic Mount Bailey. There is a beautiful view of Mount Thielsen from here. Diamond Lake is popular with anglers, and bicycling, boating, fishing, hiking, and swimming keep everyone else busy. Nearby Crater Lake National Park, Mount Bailey, and the Mount Thielsen Wilderness offer recreation opportunities year-round.

RV sites, facilities: There are 60 sites for tents or RVs up to 30 feet long. Picnic tables, fire grills, and garbage bins are provided. Drinking water and vault toilets are available. Boat docks and launching facilities are located adjacent to the campground, and boats can be rented at a resort five miles away. Some facilities are wheelchair accessible. Leashed pets are permitted.

Reservations, fees: Reservations are not accepted. Sites are $11–14 per night, $4 per night per additional vehicle. Open mid-May–mid-September, weather permitting.

Directions: From Roseburg, drive east on Highway 138 for 78.5 miles to Diamond Lake Loop (Forest Road 4795). Turn right and drive a short distance to the junction with the loop road. Continue on the loop road and drive four miles to the campground on the left.

Contact: Umpqua National Forest, Diamond Lake Ranger District, 541/498-2531, fax 541/498-2515, www.fs.fed.us.

105 DIAMOND LAKE

Scenic rating: 9

on Diamond Lake in Umpqua National Forest

Map grid B2

Diamond Lake is a true gem of the Cascades, and there's finally hope the trout fishing will return to its once famous status. This extremely popular camp along the east shore of Diamond Lake has all the luxuries: flush toilets, showers, and drinking water. There are campfire programs every Friday and Saturday night in the summer. Jet Skis and other motorized watercraft are not allowed.

RV sites, facilities: There are 238 sites for tents or RVs up to 45 feet long. Picnic tables, garbage bins, and fire grills are provided. Restrooms with flush toilets and showers, drinking water, a dump station, and an amphitheater are available. Boat docks, launching facilities, and a fish-cleaning station are available. Boat rentals are nearby. Leashed pets are permitted.

Reservations, fees: Reservations are accepted at 877/444-6777 or www.recreation.gov ($10 reservation fee). Sites are $12–24 per night, $6 per night per additional vehicle. Open late April–late October, weather permitting.

Directions: From Roseburg, drive east on Highway 138 for 78.5 miles to Diamond Lake Loop (Forest Road 4795). Turn right and drive a short distance to the junction with a loop road. Turn right (south) and drive two miles (along the east shore) to the campground on the right.

Contact: Umpqua National Forest, Diamond Lake Ranger District, 541/498-2531, fax 541/498-2515, www.fs.fed.us.

106 CAMP COMFORT

Scenic rating: 6

on the South Umpqua River in Umpqua National Forest

Map grid B2

Camp Comfort is located near the upper South Umpqua River, deep in the Umpqua National Forest, at an elevation of 2,000 feet. Large old-growth cedars shade the campsites. No fishing is permitted. South Umpqua Falls (you will pass the access point while driving to this camp) makes a good side trip. Nearby trailheads provide access to Rogue-Umpqua Divide Wilderness (a map of Umpqua National Forest will be helpful in locating them).

RV sites, facilities: There are five sites for tents or RVs up to 22 feet long. Picnic tables and fire grills are provided. A vault toilet and garbage bins are available. There is no drinking water. Some facilities are wheelchair accessible. Leashed pets are permitted.

Reservations, fees: Reservations are not accepted. Sites are $6 per night, $3 per night per additional vehicle. Open May–October.

Directions: At Canyonville on I-5, take Exit 99 to County Road 1. Drive east on County Road 1 for 25 miles to Tiller and County Road 46. Turn left and drive six miles northeast (County Road 46 turns into South Umpqua Road/Forest Road 28). Continue northeast and drive 22 miles to the camp on the right.

Contact: Umpqua National Forest, Tiller Ranger District, 541/825-3100, fax 541/825-3110, www.fs.fed.us.

107 HAMAKER

🥾 🎣 🐾 🚐 ⛺

Scenic rating: 8

near the Upper Rogue River in
Rogue River National Forest

Map grid B2

Set at 4,000 feet elevation near the Upper Rogue River, Hamaker is a beautiful little spot high in a mountain meadow. Wildflowers and wildlife abound in the spring and early summer. One of the least-used camps in the area, it's a prime camp for Crater Lake visitors.

RV sites, facilities: There are 10 sites for tents or RVs up to 30 feet long. Picnic tables, fire grills, garbage service, and stoves are provided. Drinking water and vault toilets are available. Firewood is available for purchase. Leashed pets are permitted.

Reservations, fees: Reservations are not accepted. Sites are $10 per night, $5 per night

per additional vehicle. Open late May–late October, weather permitting.

Directions: From Medford, drive northeast on Highway 62 for 57 miles (just past Union Creek) to Highway 230. Turn left (north) and drive 11 miles to a junction with Forest Road 6530. Continue on Forest Road 6530 for 0.5 mile to Forest Road 6530-900. Turn right and drive 0.5 mile to the campground.

Contact: Rogue River National Forest, Prospect Ranger District, 541/560-3400, fax 541/560-3444; Rogue Recreation, 541/560-3900, www.fs.fed.us.

108 BOULDER CREEK

🥾 🐾 ♿ 🚐 ⛺

Scenic rating: 4

on the South Umpqua River in
Umpqua National Forest

Map grid B2

Set at 1,400 feet elevation, this campground hugs the banks of the South Umpqua River near Boulder Creek. Unfortunately, no fishing is allowed here, but pleasant side trips include the fishing ladder and waterfall at nearby South Umpqua Falls.

RV sites, facilities: There are seven sites for tents or RVs up to 22 feet long. Picnic tables, fire grills, and garbage bins are provided. Vault toilets and drinking water are available. Some facilities are wheelchair accessible. Leashed pets are permitted.

Reservations, fees: Reservations are not accepted. Sites are $6 per night, $3 per night per additional vehicle. Open May–October, weather permitting.

Directions: At Canyonville on I-5, take Exit 99 to County Road 1. Drive east on County Road 1 for 25 miles to Tiller and County Road 46. Turn left, then drive six miles northeast (County Road 46 turns into South Umpqua Road/Forest Road 28). Continue northeast and drive seven miles to the camp.

Contact: Umpqua National Forest, Tiller Ranger District, 541/825-3100, fax 541/825-3110, www.fs.fed.us.

OREGON

109 COVER

Scenic rating: 4

on Jackson Creek in Umpqua National Forest
Map grid B2

If you want quiet, this camp set at 1,700 feet elevation along the banks of Jackson Creek is the right place, since hardly anyone knows about it. Cover gets light use during the summer. During the fall hunting season, however, it is known to fill. If you head east to Forest Road 68 and follow the road south, you'll have access to a major trail into the Rogue-Umpqua Divide Wilderness. Be sure not to miss the world's largest sugar pine tree, a few miles west of camp. No fishing is allowed here.

RV sites, facilities: There are seven sites for tents or RVs up to 22 feet long. Picnic tables, fire grills, and garbage bins are provided. Drinking water and vault toilets are available. Some facilities are wheelchair accessible. Leashed pets are permitted.

Reservations, fees: Reservations are not accepted. Sites are $6 per night, $2 per night per additional vehicle. Open May–October, weather permitting.

Directions: At Canyonville on I-5, take Exit 99 to County Road 1. Drive east on County Road 1 for 25 miles to Tiller and County Road 46. Turn left and drive five miles to Forest Road 29 (Jackson Creek Road). Turn right and drive east for 12 miles to the campground on the right.

Contact: Umpqua National Forest, Tiller Ranger District, 541/825-3100, fax 541/825-3110, www.fs.fed.us.

110 QUINN MEADOW HORSE CAMP

Scenic rating: 8

near Quinn Creek in the Deschutes National Forest
Map grid C2

This scenic campground (elevation 5,100 feet) is open only to horse camping and gets high use. The Elk-Devil's Trail and Wickiup Plains Trail offer access to the Three Sisters Wilderness.

There's also a horse route to Devil's Lake via Katsuk Trail.

RV sites, facilities: There are 26 sites for tents or RVs up to 40 feet long. Picnic tables and fire rings are provided. Horse corrals, stalls, and a manure disposal site are available. Drinking water, vault toilets, and garbage bins are also available. Some facilities are wheelchair accessible. Leashed pets are permitted.

Reservations, fees: Reservations are accepted at 877/444-6777 or www.recreation.gov ($10 reservation fee). Two-horse corral sites are $14 and four-horse sites are $18; it's $7 per night per additional vehicle. Open late June–September, weather permitting.

Directions: From Bend, drive southwest on Cascades Lakes Highway (also called Century Drive Highway and County Road 46) for 31.2 miles to the campground entrance on the left.

Contact: Deschutes National Forest, Bend-Fort Rock Ranger District, 541/383-4000, fax 541/383-4700, www.fs.fed.us.

111 SODA CREEK

Scenic rating: 5

near Sparks Lake in Deschutes National Forest
Map grid C2

This campground, nestled between two meadows in a pastoral setting, is on the road to Sparks Lake. Boating—particularly canoeing—is ideal at Sparks Lake, about a two-mile drive away. Also at the lake, a loop trail hugs the shore; about 0.5 mile of it is paved and barrier-free. Only fly-fishing is permitted. The camp sits at 5,450 feet elevation.

RV sites, facilities: There are six sites for tents or RVs up to 30 feet long and one multiple site. Picnic tables and fire grills are provided. Vault toilets are available. There is no drinking water, and garbage must be packed out. Leashed pets are permitted.

Reservations, fees: Reservations are not accepted. Single sites are $10 per night, multiple sites are $20 per night, $5 per night per extra vehicle. Open June–October, weather permitting.

OREGON

Directions: From Bend, drive southwest on Cascades Lakes Highway (also called Century Drive Highway and County Road 46) for 26.2 miles to Forest Road 400 (at sign for Sparks Lake). Turn left (east) and drive 25 yards to the campground.

Contact: Deschutes National Forest, Bend-Fort Rock Ranger District, 541/383-4000, fax 541/383-4700, www.fs.fed.us.

112 POINT

Scenic rating: 8

on Elk Lake in Deschutes National Forest

Map grid C2

Point campground is situated along the shore of Elk Lake at an elevation of 4,900 feet. Fishing for kokanee salmon and brook trout can be good; hiking is another option. Swimming and water sports are popular during warm weather.

RV sites, facilities: There are eight sites for tents or RVs up to 26 feet long, and one group site. Picnic tables and fire grills are provided. Vault toilets, drinking water, and garbage service are available. Boat docks and launching facilities are on-site. A store, restaurant, and propane are at Elk Lake Resort, one mile away. Leashed pets are permitted.

Reservations, fees: Reservations are not accepted. Sites are $12 per night, $6 per night per additional vehicle; the group site is $22 for up to 15 people and four vehicles. Open late May–late September, weather permitting.

Directions: From Bend, drive southwest on Cascades Lakes Highway (Century Drive Highway, which becomes County Road 46) for 34 miles to the campground on the left.

Contact: Deschutes National Forest, Bend-Fort Rock Ranger District, 541/383-4000, fax 541/383-4700, www.fs.fed.us.

113 ELK LAKE

Scenic rating: 8

on Elk Lake in Deschutes National Forest

Map grid C2

This campground hugs the shore of Elk Lake at 4,900 feet elevation. It is adjacent to Elk Lake Resort, which has a store, a restaurant, and propane. Elk Lake is popular for windsurfing and sailing.

RV sites, facilities: There are 22 sites for tents or RVs up to 30 feet long. Picnic tables and fire grills are provided. Vault toilets, drinking water, and garbage service are available. Boat-launching facilities are on-site. Boat rentals can be obtained nearby. Leashed pets are permitted.

Reservations, fees: Reservations are not accepted. Sites are $14 per night, $7 per night per additional vehicle. Open mid-May–mid-September, weather permitting.

Directions: From Bend, drive southwest on Cascades Lakes Highway (Century Drive Highway, which becomes County Road 46) and drive 33.1 miles to the campground at the north end of Elk Lake.

Contact: Deschutes National Forest, Bend-Fort Rock Ranger District, 541/383-4000, fax 541/383-4700, www.fs.fed.us.

114 LITTLE FAWN

Scenic rating: 5

on Elk Lake in Deschutes National Forest

Map grid C2

Choose between sites on the water's edge or nestled in the forest at this campground along the eastern shore of Elk Lake. Afternoon winds are common here, making this a popular spot for sailing and windsurfing. Fishing for kokanee salmon and brook trout can be good; hiking is another option. Swimming and water sports are popular during warm weather. A play area for children can be found at one of the lake's inlets. The camp sits at 4,900 feet elevation, with Little Fawn Group Camp located just beyond Little Fawn campground.

OREGON

RV sites, facilities: There are 20 sites for tents or RVs up to 36 feet long and one group site for up to 75 campers. Picnic tables and fire grills are provided. Vault toilets, drinking water, and garbage service are available. Boat-launching facilities and rentals are on-site. Leashed pets are permitted.

Reservations, fees: Reservations are accepted only for the group site at 877/444-6777 or www. recreation.gov ($10 reservation fee). Sites are $12 per night, $6 per night per additional vehicle, and $75 per night for the group site. Open late May–September, weather permitting.

Directions: From Bend, drive southwest on Cascades Lakes Highway (Century Drive Highway, which becomes County Road 46) and drive 35.5 miles to Forest Road 4625. Turn left (east) and drive 1.7 miles to the campground.

Contact: Deschutes National Forest, Bend-Fort Rock Ranger District, 541/383-4000, fax 541/383-4700, www.fs.fed.us.

115 MALLARD MARSH

Scenic rating: 8

on Hosmer Lake in Deschutes National Forest
Map grid C2

Quiet Mallard Marsh campground is located on the shore of Hosmer Lake, at an elevation of 5,000 feet. The lake is stocked with brook trout and Atlantic salmon and reserved for catch-and-release fly-fishing only. You'll get a pristine, quality fishing experience here. The lake is ideal for canoeing. Only non-motorized boats are allowed.

RV sites, facilities: There are 15 sites for tents or RVs up to 40 feet long. Picnic tables, garbage service, and vault toilets are provided. No drinking water is available. Boat-launching facilities are nearby. Leashed pets are permitted.

Reservations, fees: Reservations are not accepted. Sites are $10 per night, $5 per night per additional vehicle. Open May–October, weather permitting.

Directions: From Bend, drive southwest on Cascades Lakes Highway (Century Drive Highway, which becomes County Road 46) and

drive 35.5 miles to Forest Road 4625. Turn left (southeast) and drive 1.3 miles to the camp.

Contact: Deschutes National Forest, Bend-Fort Rock Ranger District, 541/383-4000, fax 541/383-4700, www.fs.fed.us.

116 SOUTH

Scenic rating: 8

on Hosmer Lake in Deschutes National Forest
Map grid C2

South campground is located along the shore of Hosmer Lake, adjacent to Mallard Marsh, and enjoys the same fishing experience. It's a good option if Mallard Marsh is full.

RV sites, facilities: There are 23 sites for tents or RVs up to 40 feet long. Picnic tables, garbage service, and fire grills are provided. Vault toilets and boat-launching facilities are available. No drinking water is provided. Leashed pets are permitted.

Reservations, fees: Reservations are not accepted. Sites are $10 per night, $5 per night per additional vehicle. Open late May–early October, weather permitting.

Directions: From Bend, drive southwest on Cascades Lakes Highway (Century Drive Highway, which becomes County Road 46) and drive 35.5 miles to Forest Road 4625. Turn left (east) and drive 1.2 miles to the campground on the right.

Contact: Deschutes National Forest, Bend-Fort Rock Ranger District, 541/383-4000, fax 541/383-4700, www.fs.fed.us.

117 LAVA LAKE

Scenic rating: 10

on Lava Lake in Deschutes National Forest
Map grid C2

This well-designed campground sits on the shore of pretty Lava Lake at 4,750 feet elevation. Mount Bachelor and the Three Sisters are in the background, making a classic picture. Boating and fishing are popular here. A bonus is nearby Lava Lake Resort, which has showers, laundry facilities, an RV dump station, store, gasoline, and propane.

RV sites, facilities: There are 44 sites for tents or RVs up to 40 feet long. Picnic tables, garbage service, and fire grills are provided. Vault toilets, drinking water, and a fish-cleaning station are available. Boat docks and launching facilities are on-site. Boat rentals are nearby. Some facilities are wheelchair accessible. Leashed pets are permitted.

Reservations, fees: Reservations are not accepted. Sites are $14 per night, $7 per night per additional vehicle. Open mid-April–October, weather permitting.

Directions: From Bend, drive southwest on Cascades Lakes Highway (Century Drive Highway), which becomes County Road 46) and drive 38.4 miles to Forest Road 4600-500. Turn left (east) and drive one mile to the campground.

Contact: Deschutes National Forest, Bend-Fort Rock Ranger District, 541/383-4000, fax 541/383-4700, www.fs.fed.us.

118 LITTLE LAVA LAKE

Scenic rating: 8

on Little Lava Lake in Deschutes National Forest

Map grid C2

Little Lake feeds into the Deschutes River; boating, fishing, hiking, and swimming are some of the recreation options here. Choose from lakeside or riverside sites set at an elevation of 4,750 feet.

RV sites, facilities: There are 15 sites for tents or RVs up to 40 feet long and a group site for up to 30 people. Picnic tables and fire grills are provided. Vault toilets, drinking water, and garbage service are available. A boat launch, docks, and rentals are nearby. There are also launching facilities on-site. Leashed pets are permitted.

Reservations, fees: Reservations are not accepted for the single sites. The group site can be reserved at 877/444-6777 or www.recreation.gov ($10 reservation fee). Sites are $12 per night,

$6 per night per additional vehicle. Open early May–late October, weather permitting.

Directions: From Bend, drive southwest on Cascades Lakes Highway (Century Drive Highway, which becomes County Road 46) and drive 38.4 miles to Forest Road 4600-500. Turn left (east) and drive 0.7 mile to Forest Road 4600-520. Continue east for 0.4 mile to the campground.

Contact: Deschutes National Forest, Bend-Fort Rock Ranger District, 541/383-4000, fax 541/383-4700, www.fs.fed.us.

119 SWAMP WELLS HORSE CAMP

Scenic rating: 3

near the Arnold Ice Caves in Deschutes National Forest

Map grid C2

If you look at the map, this campground may appear to be quite remote, but it's actually in an area less than 30 minutes from Bend. Set at an elevation of 5,450 feet, this camp is a good place for horseback riding, but you don't need a horse to enjoy this spot. Trails heading south re-enter the forested areas. The system of lava tubes at the nearby Arnold Ice Caves is fun to explore; bring a bicycle helmet, a flashlight, and knee pads.

RV sites, facilities: There are five primitive sites for tents or RVs up to 16 feet long. Picnic tables and fire grills are provided. There are vault toilets, but no drinking water, and garbage must be packed out. Manure bins are available for horses. Leashed pets are permitted.

Reservations, fees: Reservations are not accepted. There is no fee for camping. Open April–late November, weather permitting.

Directions: From Bend, drive south on U.S. 97 for four miles to Forest Road 18/China Hat Road. Turn left (southeast) and drive 5.4 miles to Forest Road 1810. Turn right (south) and drive 5.8 miles to Forest Road 1816. Turn left (east) and drive three miles to the campground. The last mile is rough and primitive.

Contact: Deschutes National Forest, Bend-

Fort Rock Ranger District, 541/383-4000, fax 541/383-4700, www.fs.fed.us.

120 CULTUS LAKE

Scenic rating: 7

on Cultus Lake in Deschutes National Forest

Map grid C2

Located along the east shore of Cultus Lake at 4,700 feet elevation, this camp is a popular spot for fishing, hiking, swimming, waterskiing, and windsurfing. The sites fill up early on weekends and holidays.

RV sites, facilities: There are 55 sites for tents or RVs up to 36 feet long. Picnic tables and fire grills are provided. Vault toilets, drinking water, and garbage service are available. Boat docks and launching facilities are on-site. Boat rentals are nearby. A restaurant, gasoline, and cabins are available nearby at Cultus Lake Resort. Leashed pets are permitted.

Reservations, fees: Reservations are not accepted. Sites are $16 per night, $8 per night per additional vehicle. Open mid-April–late September, weather permitting.

Directions: From Bend, drive southwest on Cascades Lakes Highway (Century Drive Highway, which becomes County Road 46) and drive 46 miles to Forest Road 4635. Turn right (west) and drive two miles to the campground.

Contact: Deschutes National Forest, Bend-Fort Rock Ranger District, 541/383-4000, fax 541/383-4700, www.fs.fed.us.

121 CULTUS CORRAL HORSE CAMP

Scenic rating: 3

near Cultus Lake in Deschutes National Forest

Map grid C2

Located at 4,450 feet elevation, about one mile from Cultus Lake, this camp sits in a stand of lodgepole pine. Several nearby trails provide access to backcountry lakes. This is a good overflow campground for Quinn Meadow Horse Camp.

RV sites, facilities: There are 11 sites for tents or RVs up to 40 feet long. Picnic tables, garbage service, fire grills, and four-horse corrals are provided. Drinking water and vault toilets are available. Leashed pets are permitted.

Reservations, fees: Reservations accepted at 877/444-6777 or www.recreation.gov ($10 reservation fee). Sites are $14 per night, $7 per night per additional vehicle. Open May–late September, weather permitting.

Directions: From Bend, drive southwest on Cascades Lakes Highway (Century Drive Highway, which becomes County Road 46) and drive 46 miles to Forest Road 4635. Turn right (west) and drive one mile to Forest Road 4630. Turn right and drive 0.75 mile to the campground on the right.

Contact: Deschutes National Forest, Bend-Fort Rock Ranger District, 541/383-4000, fax 541/383-4700, www.fs.fed.us.

122 DESCHUTES BRIDGE

Scenic rating: 5

on the Upper Deschutes River in the Deschutes National Forest

Map grid C2

Wooded Deschutes campground is set on the banks of the Deschutes River in a beautiful, green spot at 4,650 feet elevation. Fishing— the main activity—is often difficult and is restricted to artificial lures with a single barbless hook.

RV sites, facilities: There are 12 sites for tents or RVs up to 30 feet long. Picnic tables and fire grills are provided. Vault toilets, drinking water, and garbage service are available. Leashed pets are permitted.

Reservations, fees: Reservations are not accepted. Sites are $6 per night per vehicle. Open August–October.

Directions: From Bend, drive southwest on Cascades Lakes Highway (Century Drive Highway, which becomes County Road 46) and drive 41.1 miles to the campground on the left (just past the Deschutes River Bridge).

Contact: Deschutes National Forest, Bend-Fort Rock Ranger District, 541/383-4000, fax 541/383-4700, www.fs.fed.us.

123 LITTLE CULTUS LAKE

Scenic rating: 7

on Little Cultus Lake in Deschutes National Forest

Map grid C2

This campground is set near the shore of Little Cultus Lake at an elevation of 4,800 feet. It's a popular spot for boating (10-mph speed limit), fishing, hiking, and swimming. Nearby trails offer access to numerous backcountry lakes, and the Pacific Crest Trail passes about six miles west of the camp.

RV sites, facilities: There are 31 sites for tents or RVs up to 40 feet long. Picnic tables, garbage service, and fire grills are provided. Drinking water, vault toilets, and a boat launch are available. Leashed pets are permitted.

Reservations, fees: Reservations are not accepted. Sites are $14 per night, $7 per night per additional vehicle. Open May–September, weather permitting.

Directions: From Bend, drive southwest on Cascades Lakes Highway (Century Drive Highway, which becomes County Road 46) and drive 46 miles to Forest Road 4635. Turn right (west) and drive two miles to Forest Road 4630. Turn left (south) and drive 1.7 miles to Forest Road 4636. Turn left (west) and drive one mile to the campground.

Contact: Deschutes National Forest, Bend-Fort Rock Ranger District, 541/383-4000, fax 541/383-4700, www.fs.fed.us.

124 COW MEADOW

Scenic rating: 6

on Crane Prairie Reservoir in Deschutes National Forest

Map grid C2

Cow Meadow campground is located near the north end of Crane Prairie Reservoir and near the Deschutes River. It's a pretty spot (elevation is 4,450 feet), great for fly-fishing and bird-watching.

RV sites, facilities: There are 18 sites for tents or RVs up to 30 feet long. Picnic tables, garbage service, and fire grills are provided. Vault toilets are available. There is no drinking water. A boat launch for small boats is nearby. Leashed pets are permitted.

Reservations, fees: Reservations are not accepted. Sites are $10 per night, $5 per night per additional vehicle. Open May–mid-October, weather permitting.

Directions: From Bend, drive southwest on Cascades Lakes Highway (Century Drive Highway, which becomes County Road 46) for 44.7 miles to Forest Road 40. Turn left (east) on Forest Road 40 and drive 0.4 mile to Forest Road 4000-970. Turn right (south) and drive two miles to the campground on the right.

Contact: Deschutes National Forest, Bend-Fort Rock Ranger District, 541/383-4000, fax 541/383-4700, www.fs.fed.us.

125 CRANE PRAIRIE

Scenic rating: 6

on Crane Prairie Reservoir in Deschutes National Forest

Map grid C2

This campground along the north shore of Crane Prairie Reservoir is a good spot for anglers and boaters. World-renowned for rainbow trout fishing, this reservoir is also popular for bass fishing.

RV sites, facilities: There are 146 sites for tents or RVs of any length. There are also four group sites for up to 150 people each, depending on the site. Picnic tables and fire grills are provided. Vault toilets, drinking water, and garbage service are available. Boat docks, launching facilities, and a fish-cleaning station are available on-site. Boat rentals, showers, gas, and a coin laundry are nearby. Some facilities are wheelchair accessible. Leashed pets are permitted.

Reservations, fees: Reservations are accepted

for group sites only at 877/444-6777 or www. recreation.gov ($10 reservation fee). Single sites are $16 per night, multiple sites are $30 per night, group sites are $200 per night, $8 per night per additional vehicle. Open April–October, weather permitting.

Directions: From Bend, drive south on U.S. 97 for 26.8 miles to Wickiup Junction and County Road 43. Turn right (west) on County Road 43 and drive 11 miles to Forest Road 42. Continue west on Forest Road 42 for 5.4 miles to Forest Road 4270. Turn right (north) and drive 4.2 miles to the campground on the left.

Contact: Deschutes National Forest, Bend-Fort Rock Ranger District, 541/383-4000, fax 541/383-4700, www.fs.fed.us.

126 QUINN RIVER

Scenic rating: 5

on Crane Prairie Reservoir in
Deschutes National Forest

Map grid C2

Set along the western shore of Crane Prairie Reservoir, this campground is a popular spot for anglers and a great spot for bird-watching. A separate, large parking lot is available for boats and trailers. Boat speed is limited to 10 mph here. The elevation is 4,450 feet.

RV sites, facilities: There are 41 sites for tents or RVs up to 45 feet long. Picnic tables and fire grills are provided. Vault toilets, drinking water, and garbage service are available. Boat-launching facilities are available. Some facilities are wheelchair accessible. Leashed pets are permitted.

Reservations, fees: Reservations are not accepted. Sites are $14 per night, $7 per night per additional vehicle. Open late April–September, weather permitting.

Directions: From Bend, drive southwest on Cascade Lakes Highway (Century Drive Highway, which becomes County Road 46) for 48 miles to the campground.

Contact: Deschutes National Forest, Bend-Fort Rock Ranger District, 541/383-4000, fax 541/383-4700, www.fs.fed.us.

127 ROCK CREEK

Scenic rating: 5

on Crane Prairie Reservoir in
Deschutes National Forest

Map grid C2

Rock Creek campground is set along the west shore of Crane Prairie Reservoir at an elevation of 4,450 feet. The setting is similar to Quinn River campground, and provides another good spot for anglers when that camp is full.

RV sites, facilities: There are 31 sites for tents or RVs up to 40 feet long. Picnic tables, garbage service, and fire grills are provided. Drinking water, a fish-cleaning station, and vault toilets are available. Boat docks and launching facilities are on-site. Some facilities are wheelchair accessible. Leashed pets are permitted.

Reservations, fees: Reservations are not accepted. Sites are $14 per night, $7 per night per additional vehicle. Open April–September, weather permitting.

Directions: From Bend, drive southwest on Cascade Lakes Highway (Century Drive Highway, which becomes County Road 46) for 48.8 miles to the campground.

Contact: Deschutes National Forest, Bend-Fort Rock Ranger District, 541/383-4000, fax 541/383-4700, www.fs.fed.us.

128 FALL RIVER

Scenic rating: 5

on the Fall River in Deschutes National Forest

Map grid C2

Fall River is beautiful, crystal clear, and cold, and this campground is right on it at an elevation of 4,300 feet. Fishing is restricted to fly-fishing only, and it's wise to check the regulations for other restrictions. The Fall River Trail meanders along the river for 3.5 miles and is open for bicycling.

RV sites, facilities: There are 12 sites for tents or RVs up to 40 feet long. Picnic tables, garbage service, and fire grills are provided. Vault toilets are available. There is no drinking water. Leashed pets are permitted.

Reservations, fees: Reservations are not accepted. Sites are $10 per night, $5 per night per additional vehicle. Open early May–late October, weather permitting.

Directions: From Bend, drive south on U.S. 97 for 17.3 miles to the Vandevert Road exit. Take that exit and turn right on Vandevert Road. Drive 1.5 miles to Forest Road 42. Turn left and drive 12.2 miles to the campground.

Contact: Deschutes National Forest, Bend-Fort Rock Ranger District, 541/383-4000, fax 541/383-4700, www.fs.fed.us.

129 SHEEP BRIDGE

Scenic rating: 3

near Wickiup Reservoir in
Deschutes National Forest

Map grid C2

This campground is set along the north Deschutes River Channel of Wickiup Reservoir in an open, treeless area that has minimal privacy and is dusty in summer. Dispersed sites here are popular with group campers. The elevation is 4,350 feet.

RV sites, facilities: There are 20 sites and three group sites for tents or RVs up to 40 feet long. Picnic tables, garbage service, and fire grills are provided. Drinking water, vault toilets, boat-launching facilities, and a picnic area are available. Leashed pets are permitted.

Reservations, fees: Reservations are not accepted for single sites; group sites can be reserved at 877/444-6777 or www.recreation.gov ($10 reservation fee). Single sites are $12 per night, $22 for multiple sites, $6 per night per additional vehicle. Open early May–October, weather permitting.

Directions: From Bend, drive south on U.S. 97 for 26.8 miles to Wickiup Junction. Turn right (west) on County Road 43 and drive 11 miles to Forest Road 42. Continue 4.6 miles west on Forest Road 42 to Forest Road 4260. Turn left (south) and drive 0.75 mile to the campground on the right.

Contact: Deschutes National Forest, Bend-Fort Rock Ranger District, 541/383-4000, fax 541/383-4700, www.fs.fed.us.

130 NORTH TWIN LAKE

Scenic rating: 6

on North Twin Lake in Deschutes National Forest

Map grid C2

Although small and fairly primitive, North Twin Lake has lake access and a pretty setting. The campground is located on the shore of North Twin Lake and is a popular weekend spot for families. Only non-motorized boats are permitted. The elevation is 4,350 feet.

RV sites, facilities: There are 20 sites for tents or RVs up to 40 feet long. Picnic tables and fire grills are provided. Vault toilets are available. There is no drinking water. Boat-launching facilities are on-site. Leashed pets are permitted.

Reservations, fees: Reservations are not accepted. Sites are $12 per night, $6 per night per additional vehicle. Open April–October, weather permitting.

Directions: From Bend, drive southwest on Cascade Lakes Highway (Century Drive Highway, which becomes County Road 46) for 52 miles and drive past Crane Prairie Reservoir to Forest Road 42. Turn east and drive four miles to Forest Road 4260. Turn right (south) and drive 0.25 mile to the campground.

Contact: Deschutes National Forest, Bend-Fort Rock Ranger District, 541/383-4000, fax 541/383-4700, www.fs.fed.us.

131 TWIN LAKES RESORT

Scenic rating: 8

on Twin Lakes

Map grid C2 **BEST (**

Twin Lakes Resort is a popular family vacation destination with a full-service marina and all the amenities, including beach areas. Recreational activities vary from hiking to boating, fishing, and swimming on Wickiup

OREGON

Reservoir. Nearby South Twin Lake is popular with paddleboaters and kayakers; it's stocked with rainbow trout.

RV sites, facilities: There are 22 full-hookup sites for RVs of any length. There are also 14 cabins. Picnic tables and fire rings are provided. Restrooms with flush toilets and coin showers, a dump station, coin laundry, convenience store, restaurant, ice, snacks, some RV supplies, propane gas, and gasoline are available. A boat ramp, rentals, and a dock are provided; no motors are permitted on South Twin Lake. Leashed pets are permitted.

Reservations, fees: Reservations are recommended. Sites are $30 per night, $10 per tent in addition to RV. There are no tent-only sites. Some credit cards are accepted. Open late April–mid-October, weather permitting.

Directions: From Bend, drive south on U.S. 97 for 26.8 miles to Wickiup Junction. Turn right (west) on County Road 43 and drive 11 miles to Forest Road 42. Turn left and continue 4.6 miles west on Forest Road 42 to Forest Road 4260. Turn left (south) and drive two miles to the resort.

Contact: Twin Lakes Resort, 541/382-6432, fax 541/410-4688, www.twinlakesresortoregon. com.

132 SOUTH TWIN LAKE
🏃 🚲 🛶 🎣 🚤 🐕 ♿ 🚐 ⛺

Scenic rating: 6

on South Twin Lake in Deschutes National Forest
Map grid C2

This campground is on the shore of South Twin Lake, a popular spot for boating (non-motorized only), fishing, and swimming. The elevation is 4,350 feet.

RV sites, facilities: There are 21 sites for tents or RVs up to 40 feet long. Picnic tables, garbage service, and fire grills are provided. Drinking water, vault and flush toilets, and dump station are available. Boat-launching facilities (small boats only), boat rentals, showers, and laundry facilities are nearby. Some facilities are wheelchair accessible. Leashed pets are permitted.

Reservations, fees: Reservations are not accepted. Sites are $16 per night, $8 per night per additional vehicle. Open April–October, weather permitting.

Directions: From Bend, drive south on U.S. 97 for 26.8 miles to Wickiup Junction. Turn right (west) on County Road 43 and drive 11 miles to Forest Road 42. Continue west on Forest Road 42 for 4.6 miles to Forest Road 4260. Turn left (south) and drive two miles to the campground on the left.

Contact: Deschutes National Forest, Bend-Fort Rock Ranger District, 541/383-4000, fax 541/383-4700, www.fs.fed.us.

133 WEST SOUTH TWIN
🏃 🚲 🛶 🎣 🚤 🐕 🚐

Scenic rating: 4

on South Twin Lake in Deschutes National Forest
Map grid C2

A major access point to the Wickiup Reservoir, this camp is situated on South Twin Lake adjacent to the reservoir. It's a popular angling spot with very good kokanee salmon fishing. Twin Lakes Resort is adjacent to West South Twin. The elevation is 4,350 feet.

RV sites, facilities: There are 24 sites for RVs up to 40 feet long. Picnic tables and fire grills are provided. Vault toilets, drinking water, garbage service, and a dump station are available. Boat-launching facilities are on-site, and boat rentals, a restaurant, showers, coin laundry, gas, propane, cabins, and a store are nearby. Leashed pets are permitted.

Reservations, fees: Reservations are not accepted. Sites are $14 per night, $7 per night per additional vehicle. Open April–mid-October, weather permitting.

Directions: From Bend, drive southwest on Cascade Lakes Highway (Century Drive Highway, which becomes County Road 46) for 40 miles (past Crane Prairie Reservoir) to Forest Road 42. Turn left (east) and drive four miles to Forest Road 4260. Turn right (south) and drive 0.25 mile to the campground.

Contact: Deschutes National Forest, Bend-

Fort Rock Ranger District, 541/383-4000, fax 541/383-4700, www.fs.fed.us.

134 GULL POINT

Scenic rating: 5

on Wickiup Reservoir in Deschutes National Forest

Map grid C2

Gull Point campground sits in an open ponderosa stand on the north shore of Wickiup Reservoir. You'll find good fishing for kokanee salmon here. About two miles from West South Twin Campground, Gull Point is the most popular campground on Wickiup Reservoir.

RV sites, facilities: There are 73 sites for tents or RVs up to 40 feet long and two group sites for up to 30 people each. Picnic tables, garbage service, and fire grills are provided. Drinking water, a dump station, and flush and vault toilets are available. Boat-launching facilities and fish-cleaning stations are on-site. Coin showers and a small store are nearby. Some facilities are wheelchair accessible. Leashed pets are permitted.

Reservations, fees: Reservations are not accepted for single sites but can be made for the group sites at 877/444-6777 or www.recreation.gov ($10 reservation fee). Sites are $16 per night, $8 per night per additional vehicle, and $75 per night for group sites. Open mid-April–October, weather permitting.

Directions: From Bend, drive south on U.S. 97 for about 26.8 miles to County Road 43 (three miles north of LaPine). Turn right (west) on County Road 43 and drive 11 miles to Forest Road 42. Turn west on Forest Road 42 and drive 4.6 miles to Forest Road 4260. Turn left (south) and drive three miles to the campground on the right.

Contact: Deschutes National Forest, Bend-Fort Rock Ranger District, 541/383-4000, fax 541/383-4700, www.fs.fed.us.

135 BULL BEND

Scenic rating: 5

on the Deschutes River in Deschutes National Forest

Map grid C2

Bull Bend campground is located on the inside of a major bend in the Deschutes River at 4,300 feet elevation. For a mini-float trip, start at the upstream end of camp, float around the bend, and then take out at the downstream end of camp. This is a low-use getaway spot.

RV sites, facilities: There are 12 sites for tents or RVs up to 40 feet long. Picnic tables, garbage service, fire grills, vault toilets, and boat-launching facilities are available. There is no drinking water. Leashed pets are permitted.

Reservations, fees: Reservations are not accepted. Sites are $10 per night, $5 per night per additional vehicle. Open early May–late October, weather permitting.

Directions: From Bend, drive south on U.S. 97 for 26.8 miles to Wickiup Junction. Turn right (west) on County Road 43 and drive eight miles to Forest Road 4370. Turn left (south) and drive 1.5 miles to the campground.

Contact: Deschutes National Forest, Bend-Fort Rock Ranger District, 541/383-4000, fax 541/383-4700, www.fs.fed.us.

136 PRINGLE FALLS

Scenic rating: 4

on the Deschutes River in Deschutes National Forest

Map grid C2

This campground fringing the Deschutes River is less than a mile from Pringle Falls. The camp gets light use and is pretty and serene.

RV sites, facilities: There are seven sites for tents or RVs up to 30 feet long. Picnic tables, garbage service, and fire grills are provided. Vault toilets are available. There is no drinking water. Leashed pets are permitted.

Reservations, fees: Reservations are not accepted. Sites are $10 per night, $5 per night

OREGON

per additional vehicle. Open May–October, weather permitting.

Directions: From Bend, drive south on U.S. 97 for 26.8 miles to Wickiup Junction. Turn right (west) on County Road 43 and drive 7.4 miles to Forest Road 4330-500. Turn north (right) and drive one mile to the campground.

Contact: Deschutes National Forest, Bend-Fort Rock Ranger District, 541/383-4000, fax 541/383-4700, www.fs.fed.us.

137 BIG RIVER

Scenic rating: 4

on the Deschutes River in Deschutes National Forest

Map grid C2 **BEST(**

Big River is a good spot. Located between the banks of the Deschutes River and the road, it has easy access and is popular as an overnight camp. Fishing, motorized boating, and rafting are permitted.

RV sites, facilities: There are 10 sites for tents or RVs up to 40 feet long, and one group site for up to 40 people. Picnic tables, garbage service, and fire grills are provided. Vault toilets are available. There is no drinking water. Boat-launching facilities are on-site. Some facilities are wheelchair accessible. Leashed pets are permitted.

Reservations, fees: Reservations are not accepted. Sites are $10 per night, $5 per night per additional vehicle, and the group site is $30 per night. Open early May–late October, weather permitting.

Directions: From Bend, drive south on U.S. 97 for 17.3 miles to the Vandevert Road exit. Take that exit and turn right on Vandevert Road. Drive 1.5 miles to Forest Road 42. Turn left and drive 7.9 miles to the campground.

Contact: Deschutes National Forest, Bend-Fort Rock Ranger District, 541/383-4000, fax 541/383-4700, www.fs.fed.us.

138 PRAIRIE

Scenic rating: 4

on Paulina Creek in Deschutes National Forest

Map grid C2

Here's another good overnight campground that is quiet and private. Set along the banks of Paulina Creek, Prairie is located about 0.5 mile from the trailhead for the Peter Skene Ogden National Recreation Trail. The elevation is 4,300 feet.

RV sites, facilities: There are 16 sites for tents or RVs up to 40 feet long. Picnic tables, garbage service, and fire grills are provided. Drinking water, firewood, and vault toilets are available. Leashed pets are permitted.

Reservations, fees: Reservations are not accepted. Sites are $14 per night, $7 per night per additional vehicle. Open mid-May–late September, weather permitting.

Directions: From Bend, drive south on U.S. 97 for 23.5 miles to County Road 21 (Paulina/East Lake Road). Turn left (east) and drive 3.1 miles to the campground.

Contact: Deschutes National Forest, Bend-Fort Rock Ranger District, 541/383-4000, fax 541/383-4700, www.fs.fed.us.

139 PAULINA LAKE

Scenic rating: 8

on Paulina Lake in Deschutes National Forest

Map grid C2

This campground (6,350 feet elevation) is located along the south shore of Paulina Lake and within the Newberry National Volcanic Monument. The camp is adjacent to Paulina Lake Resort. The lake itself sits in a volcanic crater. Nearby trails provide access to the remains of volcanic activity, including craters and obsidian flows. My longtime friend, Guy Carl, caught the state's record brown trout here, right after I'd written a story about his unique method of using giant Rapala and Rebel bass lures for giant browns. The recreation options here include boating, fishing, hiking, mountain biking, and sailing. The boat speed limit is 10 mph. Note that food-raiding bears are common at all the campgrounds in the Newberry Caldera area and that all food must be kept out of reach. Do not store food in vehicles.

RV sites, facilities: There are 69 sites for RVs up to 30 feet long. Picnic tables, garbage service, and fire grills are provided. Drinking water and flush and vault toilets are available. Boat docks, launching facilities, boat rentals, coin showers, coin laundry, a small store, restaurant, cabins, gas, and propane are within five miles. The Newberry RV dump station is nearby. Some facilities are wheelchair accessible. Leashed pets are permitted.

Reservations, fees: Reservations are accepted at 877/444-6777 or www.recreation.gov ($10 reservation fee). Sites are $16–18 per night, $8 per night per additional vehicle. Open May–late October, weather permitting.

Directions: From Bend, drive south on U.S. 97 for 23.5 miles to County Road 21 (Paulina/East Lake Road). Turn left (east) and drive 12.9 miles to the campground on the left.

Contact: Deschutes National Forest, Bend-Fort Rock Ranger District, 541/383-4000, fax 541/383-4700, www.fs.fed.us.

140 CHIEF PAULINA HORSE CAMP
🥾 🚲 🐕 🚙 ⛺

Scenic rating: 4

on Paulina Lake in Deschutes National Forest

Map grid C2

Chief Paulina campground sits at an elevation of 6,400 feet, about 0.25 mile from the south shore of Paulina Lake, where fishing is good. Horse trails and a vista point are close by. Horse campers must use only certified weed-seed-free hay.

RV sites, facilities: There are 14 sites for tents or RVs up to 40 feet long. Picnic tables and fire grills are provided. A vault toilet, garbage service, and corrals are available. There is no drinking water. Boat docks and rentals are nearby. Leashed pets are permitted.

Reservations, fees: Reservations are accepted at 877/444-6777 or www.recreation.gov ($10 reservation fee). Sites are $14–18 per night, $7 per night per additional vehicle. Open May–late October, weather permitting.

Directions: From Bend, drive south on U.S. 97 for 23.5 miles to County Road 21 (Paulina/East Lake Road). Turn left (east) and drive 14 miles to the campground.

Contact: Deschutes National Forest, Bend-Fort Rock Ranger District, 541/383-4000, fax 541/383-4700, www.fs.fed.us.

141 LITTLE CRATER
🥾 🚲 🏊 🎣 🚤 🐕 ♿ 🚗 ⛺

Scenic rating: 8

near Paulina Lake in Deschutes National Forest

Map grid C2

Little Crater is a very popular campground (6,350 feet elevation) near the east shore of Paulina Lake in Newberry National Volcanic Monument, a caldera. Sites are situated on the scenic lake edge, perfect for fishing, and there are great hiking opportunities in the area. The place fills up most summer weekends.

RV sites, facilities: There are 50 sites for tents or RVs up to 40 feet long. Picnic tables and fire grills are provided. Vault toilets, drinking water, and garbage service are available. Boat docks and launching facilities are on-site, and boat rentals are nearby. Some facilities are wheelchair accessible. Leashed pets are permitted.

Reservations, fees: Reservations are not accepted. Sites are $16 per night, $8 per night for each additional vehicle. Parking at the nearby trailhead requires a Northwest Forest Pass ($5 daily fee or $30 annual fee per parked vehicle). Open early May–late October, weather permitting.

Directions: From Bend, drive south on U.S. 97 for 23.5 miles to County Road 21 (Paulina/East Lake Road). Turn left (east) and drive 14.5 miles to Forest Road 2100. Turn left (north) and drive 0.5 mile to the campground on the left.

Contact: Deschutes National Forest, 541/383-4000, fax 541/383-4700.

142 NEWBERRY GROUP CAMP

Scenic rating: 7

west of Roseburg

Map grid C2

Newberry Group has a great location on Paulina Lake and is the only area on Newberry Monument designed exclusively for group camping. The parking area and roads are paved, and the group sites are separated from one another, although group sites B and C can be joined to accommodate large groups. One site accommodates groups of up to 35 people, while the other two accommodate up to 50. The entire campground can be reserved as well. Cabins were renovated in 2009 for use starting 2010.

RV sites, facilities: There are three group sites for tents or RVs to 40 feet. Picnic tables and fire rings are provided. Drinking water and vault toilets are available. Leashed pets are permitted.

Reservations, fees: Reservations are accepted at 877/444-6777 or www.recreation.gov ($10 reservation fee). Sites are $75 per night for the smaller camp, $100 per night for the larger two camps. Open June–September, weather permitting.

Directions: From Bend, drive south on U.S. 97 for 23.5 miles to County Road 21 (Paulina/East Lake Road). Turn left (east) and drive 1.5 miles to the campground.

Contact: Deschutes National Forest, 541/383-4000, fax 541/383-4700.

143 CINDER HILL

Scenic rating: 7

on East Lake in Deschutes National Forest

Map grid C2

This campground hugs the northeast shore of East Lake at an elevation of 6,400 feet. Located within the Newberry National Volcanic Monument, Cinder Hill makes a good base camp for area activities. Boating, fishing, and hiking are

among the recreation options here. Boat speed is limited to 10 mph.

RV sites, facilities: There are 110 sites, including pull-through sites, for tents or RVs of any length. Picnic tables and fire grills are provided. Drinking water, flush and vault toilets, and garbage service are available. A camp host is on-site. Boat docks and launching facilities are on-site, and boat rentals, a store, restaurant, coin showers, coin laundry, and cabins are nearby at East Lake Resort. Some facilities are wheelchair accessible. Leashed pets are permitted.

Reservations, fees: Reservations are accepted at 877/444-6777 or www.recreation.gov ($10 reservation fee). Sites are $16 per night, $8 per night per additional vehicle. Parking at the nearby trailhead requires a Northwest Forest Pass ($5 daily fee or $30 annual fee per parked vehicle). Open mid-May–September, weather permitting.

Directions: From Bend, drive south on U.S. 97 for 23.5 miles to County Road 21 (Paulina/East Lake Road). Turn left (east) and drive 17.6 miles to Forest Road 2100-700. Turn left (north) and drive 0.5 mile to the campground.

Contact: Deschutes National Forest, Bend-Fort Rock Ranger District, 541/383-4000, fax 541/383-4700, www.fs.fed.us.

144 EAST LAKE

Scenic rating: 8

on East Lake in Deschutes National Forest

Map grid C2

This campground is set along the south shore of East Lake at an elevation of 6,400 feet. Boating and fishing are popular here, and hiking trails provide access to signs of former volcanic activity in the area. East Lake Campground is similar to Cinder Hill, but smaller. Boat speed is limited to 10 mph.

RV sites, facilities: There are 29 sites for tents or RVs up to 40 feet long. Picnic tables and fire grills are provided. Drinking water, flush and vault toilets, and garbage service are available. A camp host is on-site. Boat docks, launching facilities, and rentals are nearby. Some facilities are wheelchair accessible. Leashed pets are permitted.

Reservations, fees: Reservations are not accepted. Sites are $16 per night, $8 per night per additional vehicle. Open early May–late October, weather permitting.

Directions: From Bend, drive south on U.S. 97 for 23.5 miles to County Road 21 (Paulina/East Lake Road). Turn left (east) and drive 16.6 miles to the campground on the left.

Contact: Deschutes National Forest, Bend-Fort Rock Ranger District, 541/383-4000, fax 541/383-4700, www.fs.fed.us.

145 HOT SPRINGS

Scenic rating: 5

near East Lake in Deschutes National Forest
Map grid C2

Don't be fooled by the name: there are no hot springs at this campsite. It lies across the road from East Lake at 6,400 feet elevation, making it a good tent camping spot if you want to be near East Lake but farther away from RVs.

RV sites, facilities: There are 52 sites for tents or RVs up to 26 feet long. Picnic tables and fire grills are provided. Vault toilets, drinking water, and garbage service are available. Boat docks, launching facilities, and rentals are nearby. Leashed pets are permitted.

Reservations, fees: Reservations are not accepted. Sites are $10 per night and $5–7 per night per additional vehicle. Open July–late September, weather permitting.

Directions: From Bend, drive south on U.S. 97 for 23.5 miles to County Road 21 (Paulina/East Lake Road). Turn left (east) and drive 17.2 miles to the campground on the right.

Contact: Deschutes National Forest, Bend-Fort Rock Ranger District, 541/383-4000, fax 541/383-4700, www.fs.fed.us.

146 EAST LAKE RESORT AND RV PARK

Scenic rating: 7

on East Lake
Map grid C2

This resort offers shaded sites in a wooded, mountainous setting on the east shore of East Lake. Opportunities for boating, fishing, and swimming abound.

RV sites, facilities: There are 40 sites with partial hookups for tents or RVs up to 40 feet long and 16 cabins. Some sites are pull-through. Drinking water, barbecues, and picnic tables are provided. Restrooms with flush toilets and coin showers, propane gas, firewood, a dump station, convenience store, café, coin laundry, ice, boat-launching facilities, boat rentals, moorage, and a playground are available. Leashed pets are permitted.

Reservations, fees: Reservations are accepted. Sites are $27 per night. Some credit cards are accepted. Open mid-May–September, weather permitting.

Directions: From Bend, drive south on U.S. 97 for 23.5 miles to County Road 21 (Paulina/East Lake Road). Turn left (east) and drive 18 miles to the park at the end of the road.

Contact: East Lake Resort and RV Park, 541/536-2230, www.eastlakeresort.com.

147 CHINA HAT

Scenic rating: 3

in Deschutes National Forest
Map grid C2

Remote China Hat campground is located at 5,100 feet elevation in a rugged, primitive area. There is direct trail access here to the East Fort Rock OHV Trail System. Hunters use China Hat as a base camp in the fall, but in summer it is a base camp for off-road motorcyclists.

RV sites, facilities: There are 14 sites for tents or RVs up to 30 feet long. Picnic tables and fire grills are provided. Vault toilets are available.

OREGON

There is no drinking water, and garbage must be packed out. Leashed pets are permitted.

Reservations, fees: Reservations are not accepted. There is no fee for camping. Open April–early November, weather permitting.

Directions: From Bend, drive south on U.S. 97 for 29.6 miles to Forest Road 22. Turn left (east) and drive 26.4 miles to Forest Road 18. Turn left (north) and drive 5.9 miles to the campground on the left.

Contact: Deschutes National Forest, Bend-Fort Rock Ranger District, 541/383-4000, fax 541/383-4700, www.fs.fed.us.

148 CABIN LAKE

Scenic rating: 3

in Deschutes National Forest

Map grid C2

This remote campground (4,550 feet elevation) is adjacent to a bird blind that's more than 80 years old—it's a great place to watch birds. Primitive and secluded with sparse tree cover, this spot receives little use even in the busy summer months.

RV sites, facilities: There are 14 sites for tents or RVs up to 30 feet long. Picnic tables and fire grills are available, but not at each site. There are no toilets or drinking water, and garbage must be packed out. Leashed pets are permitted.

Reservations, fees: Reservations are not accepted. There is no fee for camping. Open April–late October, weather permitting.

Directions: From Bend, drive south on U.S. 97 for 29.6 miles to Forest Road 22. Turn left (east) and drive 26.4 miles to Forest Road 18. Turn left (north) and drive six miles to the campground on the left.

Contact: Deschutes National Forest, Bend-Fort Rock Ranger District, 541/383-4000, fax 541/383-4700, www.fs.fed.us.

149 GOLD LAKE

Scenic rating: 8

on Gold Lake in Willamette National Forest

Map grid C2

Gold Lake campground wins the popularity contest for high use. Although motors are not allowed on this small lake (100 acres, 25 feet deep), rafts and rowboats provide excellent fishing access. A primitive log shelter built in the early 1940s provides a dry picnic area. In the spring and summer, this area abounds with wildflowers and huckleberries. The Gold Lake Bog is another special attraction where one can often see deer, elk, and smaller wildlife.

RV sites, facilities: There are 21 sites for tents or RVs up to 32 feet long. Picnic tables, garbage bins, and fire grills are provided. Drinking water and vault toilets are available. Boat docks and launching facilities are nearby. Some facilities are wheelchair accessible. Leashed pets are permitted.

Reservations, fees: Reservations are not accepted. Sites are $16 per night, $8 per night per additional vehicle. Open mid-May–October, weather permitting.

Directions: From Eugene, drive south on I-5 for five miles to Exit 188 and Highway 58. Turn east and drive 35 miles to the town of Oakridge. From Oakridge, continue east on Highway 58 for 28 miles to Gold Lake Road (Forest Road 500). Turn left (north) and drive two miles to the campground on the right.

Contact: Willamette National Forest, Middle Fork Ranger District, 541/782-2283, fax 541/782-5306, www.fs.fed.us.

150 NORTH DAVIS CREEK

Scenic rating: 4

on North Davis Creek in Deschutes National Forest

Map grid C2

Set at an elevation of 4,350 feet, this remote, secluded campground is located along a western channel that feeds into Wickiup Reservoir. Fishing for brown and rainbow trout as well as kokanee salmon is good here. In late summer, the reservoir level tends to drop. The camp receives little use and makes a good overflow camp if campsites are filled at Wickiup.

RV sites, facilities: There are 14 sites for tents or RVs up to 40 feet long. Picnic tables and fire grills are provided. Vault toilets and garbage service are available. There is no drinking water. Boat-launching facilities are on-site. Leashed pets are permitted.

Reservations, fees: Reservations are not accepted. Sites are $10 per night, $5 per night per additional vehicle. Open April–early September.

Directions: From Bend, drive southwest on Cascade Lake Highway (Highway 46/Forest Road 46) for 56.2 miles to the campground on the left.

Contact: Deschutes National Forest, Bend-Fort Rock Ranger District, 541/383-4000, fax 541/383-4700, www.fs.fed.us.

151 RESERVOIR

Scenic rating: 4

on Wickiup Reservoir in Deschutes National Forest

Map grid C2

You'll find this campground along the south shore of Wickiup Reservoir, where the kokanee salmon fishing is good. The camp is best in early summer, before the lake level drops. This camp gets little use, so you won't find crowds here. The elevation is 4,350 feet.

RV sites, facilities: There are 28 sites for tents or RVs up to 24 feet long. Picnic tables, garbage service, and fire grills are provided. Boat-launching facilities and vault toilets are available, but there is no drinking water. Leashed pets are permitted.

Reservations, fees: Reservations are not accepted. Sites are $6 per night. Open April–September, weather permitting.

Directions: From Bend, drive southwest on Cascade Lakes Highway (Century Drive Highway, which becomes County Road 46) for 57.8 miles to Forest Road 44. Turn left (east) and drive 1.7 miles to the campground.

Contact: Deschutes National Forest, Bend-Fort Rock Ranger District, 541/383-4000, fax 541/383-4700, www.fs.fed.us.

152 WICKIUP BUTTE

Scenic rating: 4

on Wickiup Reservoir in Deschutes National Forest

Map grid C2

Wickiup Butte is more remote than the other campgrounds on Wickiup Reservoir, set at an elevation of 4,350 feet. This campground borders the southeast shore of Wickiup Reservoir, where kokanee salmon fishing is good during the early summer.

RV sites, facilities: There are eight sites for tents or RVs up to 22 feet long. Picnic tables, garbage service, and fire grills are provided. Vault toilets are available. There is no drinking water. Boat-launching facilities are nearby. Leashed pets are permitted.

Reservations, fees: Reservations are not accepted. Sites are $5 per night per vehicle. Open April–late September, weather permitting.

Directions: From Bend, drive south on U.S. 97 for 26.8 miles to Wickiup Junction. Turn right (west) on County Road 43 and drive 10.4 miles to Forest Road 4380. Turn left (south) and drive 3.6 miles to Forest Road 4260. Turn left (east) and drive three miles to the campground.

Contact: Deschutes National Forest, Bend-Fort Rock Ranger District, 541/383-4000, fax 541/383-4700, www.fs.fed.us.

153 LAPINE STATE PARK

Scenic rating: 7

on the Deschutes River

Map grid C2   BEST (

This peaceful and clean campground sits next to the trout-filled Deschutes River (a legendary fly-fishing spot) with many more high-mountain lakes in proximity. The camp is set in a subalpine pine forest populated by eagles or red-tailed hawks. Trails surround the campground;

be sure to check out Oregon's "Big Tree." Skiing is a popular wintertime option in the area.

RV sites, facilities: There are 128 sites with full or partial hookups for tents or RVs of any length; only 20-amp service is available. There are also 10 cabins. Picnic tables and fire grills are provided. Drinking water, restrooms with flush toilets and showers, garbage bins, a dump station, a seasonal store, a day-use area with a sandy beach, a meeting hall that can be reserved, ice, and firewood are available. A boat launch is nearby. Some facilities are wheelchair accessible. Leashed pets are permitted.

Reservations, fees: Reservations are accepted at 800/452-5687 or www.oregonstateparks.org ($8 reservation fee). Sites are $13–22 per night, $5 per night per additional vehicle. Cabins are $38–81 per night. Some credit cards are accepted. Open year-round, weather permitting.

Directions: From Bend, turn south on U.S. 97 and drive 23 miles to State Recreation Road. Turn right and drive four miles to the park.

Contact: LaPine State Park, 541/536-2071 or 800/551-6949, www.oregonstateparks.org.

154 HIDDEN PINES RV PARK

Scenic rating: 7

near the Little Deschutes River

Map grid C2

So you think you've come far enough, eh? If you want a spot in a privately run RV park two miles from the bank of the Little Deschutes River, you've found it. Within a 30-minute drive are two reservoirs, four lakes, and a golf course. The nearby town of LaPine is the gateway to the Newberry National Volcanic Monument.

RV sites, facilities: There is an area for tents, plus 25 sites with full or partial hookups for RVs of any length; most are pull-through sites. Drinking water, cable TV, and picnic tables are provided. Restrooms with flush toilets and showers, a dump station, coin laundry, RV supplies, propane gas, a community fire ring with firewood, and ice are available. The full-service

community of LaPine is about five miles away. Leashed pets are allowed.

Reservations, fees: Reservations are accepted. Sites are $19.44–25.92 per night, plus $2.50 per person per night for more than two people. Some credit cards are accepted. Open year-round.

Directions: From Bend, drive south on U.S. 97 for 24 miles to Wickiup Junction, Milepost 165, and County Road 43/Burgess Road. Turn right (west) on Burgess Road and drive 2.4 miles to Pine Forest Road. Turn left and drive 0.7 mile to Wright Avenue. Turn left and drive one block to the park on the left.

Contact: Hidden Pines RV Park, 541/536-2265.

155 NORTH LAVA FLOW

Scenic rating: 8

on Davis Lake in Deschutes National Forest

Map grid C2

North Lava Flow campground is surrounded by old-growth forest along the northeast shore of Davis Lake, a very shallow lake formed by lava flow. The water level fluctuates here, and this campground can sometimes be closed in summer. There's good duck hunting during the fall. Fishing can be decent, but only fly-fishing is allowed. Boat speed is limited to 10 mph.

RV sites, facilities: There are 25 sites for tents or RVs up to 30 feet long. Picnic tables and fire grills are provided. Vault toilets and firewood (which can be gathered from the surrounding area) are available. There is no drinking water, and garbage must be packed out. A primitive boat ramp is nearby. Leashed pets are permitted.

Reservations, fees: Reservations are not accepted. Sites are $9–11 per night, $5 per night per additional vehicle. Open April–December, weather permitting.

Directions: From Eugene, drive south on I-5 for five miles to Exit 188 and Highway 58.

Turn east on Highway 58 and drive 86 miles to County Road 61. Turn left and drive three miles to Forest Road 46. Turn left and drive 7.7 miles to Forest Road 850. Turn left and drive 1.8 miles to the campground.

Contact: Deschutes National Forest, Crescent Ranger District, 541/433-3200, fax 541/433-3224, www.fs.fed.us.

156 EAST DAVIS LAKE

Scenic rating: 9

on Davis Lake in Deschutes National Forest
Map grid C2

This campground is nestled in the lodgepole pines along the south shore of Davis Lake. Recreation options include boating (speed limit 10 mph), fly-fishing, and hiking. Leeches prevent swimming here. Bald eagles and sandhill cranes are frequently seen.

RV sites, facilities: There are 29 sites for tents or RVs up to 40 feet long. Picnic tables, garbage service, fire grills, drinking water, and vault toilets are provided. Firewood may be gathered from the surrounding area. Primitive boat-launching facilities are available on-site. Some facilities are wheelchair accessible. Leashed pets are permitted.

Reservations, fees: Reservations are not accepted. Sites are $12 per night, $6 per night per additional vehicle. Open mid-April–late September, weather permitting.

Directions: From Eugene, drive south on I-5 for five miles to Exit 188 and Highway 58. Turn east and drive 73 miles to County Road 61. Turn left (east) and drive three miles to Forest Road 46. Turn left and drive 7.7 miles to Forest Road 850. Turn left and drive 0.25 mile to the campground entrance road on the right.

Contact: Deschutes National Forest, Crescent Ranger District, 541/433-3200, fax 541/433-3224, www.fs.fed.us.

157 TRAPPER CREEK

Scenic rating: 8

on Odell Lake in Deschutes National Forest
Map grid C2

The west end of Odell Lake is the setting for this camp. Boat docks and rentals are available nearby at the Shelter Cove Resort. One of Oregon's prime fisheries for kokanee salmon and mackinaw (lake trout), this lake also has some huge brown trout.

RV sites, facilities: There are 26 sites for tents or RVs up to 40 feet long and three group sites. Picnic tables and fire grills are provided. Drinking water, vault toilets, garbage service and a boat launch are available. Firewood may be gathered from the surrounding area. A store, coin laundry, and ice are within one mile. Leashed pets are permitted.

Reservations, fees: Reservations are accepted at 877/444-6777 or www.recreation.gov ($10 reservation fee). Sites are $16–18 per night, $5 per night per additional vehicle; group sites are $30–34, $8 per night per additional vehicle. Open mid-May–October, weather permitting.

Directions: From Eugene, drive south on I-5 for five miles to Exit 188 and Highway 58. Turn east and drive 61 miles to the turnoff for Odell Lake and Forest Road 5810. Turn right on Forest Road 5810 and drive 1.9 miles to the campground on the left.

Contact: Deschutes National Forest, Crescent Ranger District, 541/433-3200, fax 541/433-3224, www.fs.fed.us.

158 SHELTER COVE RESORT
Scenic rating: 9

on Odell Lake
Map grid C2

Shelter Cove is a private resort along the north shore of Odell Lake, set at the base of the Diamond Peak Wilderness. The area offers opportunities for fishing, hiking, and swimming.

OREGON

The cabins sit right on the lakefront, and a general store and tackle shop are available.

RV sites, facilities: There are 64 sites with partial or full hookups for RVs up to 40 feet long; some sites are pull-through. There are also 13 cabins. Picnic tables and fire rings are provided. Drinking water, restrooms with flush toilets and showers, a dump station, wireless Internet service, an ATM, convenience store, coin laundry, and ice are available. Boat docks, launching facilities, and boat rentals are on-site. Leashed pets are permitted.

Reservations, fees: Reservations are accepted at 800/647-2729. Sites are $16–27 per night. Some credit cards are accepted. Open year-round.

Directions: From Eugene, drive south on I-5 for five miles to Exit 188 and Highway 58. Turn east and drive 61 miles to the turnoff for Odell Lake and West Odell Lake Road. Turn right and drive south for 1.8 miles to the resort at the end of the road.

Contact: Shelter Cove Resort, 541/433-2548, www.sheltercoveresort.com.

159 ODELL CREEK

Scenic rating: 9

on Odell Lake in Deschutes National Forest

Map grid C2

You can fish, hike, and swim at this campground (4,800 feet elevation) along the east shore of Odell Lake. A trail from the nearby Crater Buttes trailhead leads southwest into the Diamond Peak Wilderness and provides access to several small lakes in the backcountry. Another trail follows the north shore of the lake. Boat docks, launching facilities, and rentals are available at the Odell Lake Lodge and Resort, adjacent to the campground. Windy afternoons are common here.

RV sites, facilities: There are 26 sites for tents or RVs up to 50 feet long. Picnic tables and fire grills are provided. Vault toilets, drinking water, and garbage service are available. Firewood may be gathered from the surrounding area. Leashed pets are permitted.

Reservations, fees: Reservations are accepted

at 541/433-2540. Sites are $13–15 per night, $5 per night per additional vehicle. Open May–late September, weather permitting.

Directions: From Eugene, drive south on I-5 for five miles to Exit 188 and Highway 58. Turn east and drive 68 miles to Odell Lake and Forest Road 680 (at the east end of the lake). Turn right on Forest Road 680 and drive 400 yards to the campground on the right.

Contact: Deschutes National Forest, Crescent Ranger District, 541/433-3200, fax 541/433-3224, www.fs.fed.us; Odell Lake Lodge, 541/433-2540.

160 SUNSET COVE

Scenic rating: 8

on Odell Lake in Deschutes National Forest

Map grid C2

Sunset Cove campground borders the northeast shore of Odell Lake. Boat docks and rentals are available nearby at Odell Lake Lodge and Resort. Campsites are surrounded by large Douglas fir and some white pine trees. The camp backs up to the highway; expect to hear the noise.

RV sites, facilities: There are 20 sites for tents or RVs up to 22 feet long. Picnic tables and fire grills are provided. Drinking water, vault toilets, garbage service, a boat launch and day-use area, and fish-cleaning facilities are available. Firewood may be gathered from the surrounding area. Some facilities are wheelchair accessible. Leashed pets are permitted.

Reservations, fees: Reservations are not accepted. Sites are $13 per night, $5 per night per additional vehicle. Open mid-May–mid-October, weather permitting.

Directions: From Eugene, drive south on I-5 for five miles to Exit 188 and Highway 58. Turn east and drive 67 miles to the campground on the right.

Contact: Deschutes National Forest, Crescent Ranger District, 541/433-3200, fax 541/433-3224, www.fs.fed.us.

OREGON

161 PRINCESS CREEK

Scenic rating: 9

on Odell Lake in Deschutes National Forest

Map grid C2

This wooded campground is on the northeast shore of Odell Lake, but it backs up to the highway so expect traffic noise. Boat docks and rentals are available nearby at the Shelter Cove Resort. Fishing, hiking, and swimming are popular activities at the lake. A trail from the nearby Crater Buttes trailhead leads southwest into the Diamond Peak Wilderness and provides access to several small lakes in the backcountry.

RV sites, facilities: There are 44 sites for tents or RVs up to 30 feet long. Picnic tables and fire grills are provided. Vault toilets, garbage service, and boat-launching facilities are available. Drinking water is available at times, but not guaranteed. Firewood may be gathered from the surrounding area. Showers, a store, coin laundry, and ice are within five miles. Leashed pets are permitted.

Reservations, fees: Reservations are not accepted. Sites are $14 per night, $7 per night per additional vehicle. Open April–September, weather permitting.

Directions: From Eugene, drive south on I-5 for five miles to Exit 188 and Highway 58. Turn east and drive 64 miles to the campground on the right.

Contact: Deschutes National Forest, Crescent Ranger District, 541/433-3200, fax 541/433-3224, www.fs.fed.us.

162 CONTORTA FLAT

Scenic rating: 8

on Crescent Lake in the Deschutes National Forest

Map grid C2

This campground on Crescent Lake was named for the particular species of lodgepole pine (*Pinus contorta*) that grows here. The elevation is 4,850 feet.

RV sites, facilities: There are 19 sites for tents or RVs up to 40 feet long. Picnic tables and fire grills are provided. Vault toilets and garbage bins are available. There is no drinking water. Some facilities are wheelchair accessible. Leashed pets are permitted.

Reservations, fees: Reservations are not accepted. Sites are $12 per night, $6 per night per additional vehicle. Open June–October, weather permitting.

Directions: From Eugene, drive south on I-5 for five miles to Exit 188 and Highway 58. Turn east and drive 69 miles to County Road 60. Turn right (west) and drive 10 miles to the camp on the left.

Contact: Deschutes National Forest, Crescent Ranger District, 541/433-3200, fax 541/433-3224, www.fs.fed.us.

163 WINDY GROUP

Scenic rating: 8

on Crescent Lake in the Deschutes National Forest

Map grid C2

Windy Group is located near the beaches on Crescent Lake. The lake warms up more easily than many high-mountain lakes, making swimming and waterskiing two popular options. Mountain biking and hiking are also available.

RV sites, facilities: There is one group site for tents or RVs up to 60 feet long and up to 40 people. Picnic tables and fire rings are provided. Vault toilets and garbage bins are available. There is no drinking water. Some facilities are wheelchair accessible. Leashed pets are permitted.

Reservations, fees: Reservations are accepted at 877/444-6777 or www.recreation.gov ($10 reservation fee). The site is $65 per night. Open May–September, weather permitting.

Directions: From Eugene, drive south on I-5 for five miles to Exit 188 and Highway 58. Turn east and drive 69 miles to County Road 60. Turn right (west) and drive 7.5 miles to the camp.

Contact: Deschutes National Forest, Crescent Ranger District, 541/433-3200, fax 541/433-3224, www.fs.fed.us.

OREGON

164 SIMAX GROUP CAMP

Scenic rating: 8

on Crescent Lake in Deschutes National Forest

Map grid C2

This camp is set at an elevation of 4,850 feet on Crescent Lake and provides trails to day-use beaches. Fishing is variable year to year and is usually better earlier in the season. A boat launch is available at neighboring Crescent Lake, about two miles away. Nearby Diamond Peak Wilderness (free permit required) provides hiking options.

RV sites, facilities: There are three group campsites for 30–50 campers each. Drinking water, tent pads, restrooms with flush toilets and showers, picnic tables, garbage service, fireplaces, and a group shelter are available. Tents must be placed on tent pads. Some facilities are wheelchair accessible. Leashed pets are permitted.

Reservations, fees: Reservations are accepted at 877/444-6777 or www.recreation.gov ($10 reservation fee). Site A is $80–100 per night and Sites B and C are $100–120 per night. (Note that Site C is best for RVs.) The group shelter is $50 per day. Open mid-May–October, weather permitting.

Directions: From Eugene, drive south on I-5 for five miles to Exit 188 and Highway 58. Turn east and drive 70 miles to Crescent Lake Highway (Forest Road 60). Turn right and drive two miles to Forest Road 6005. Turn left and drive one mile to the campground on the right.

Contact: Deschutes National Forest, Crescent Ranger District, 541/433-3200, fax 541/433-3224, www.fs.fed.us.

165 CRESCENT LAKE

Scenic rating: 8

on Crescent Lake in Deschutes National Forest

Map grid C2   **BEST (**

This campground is set along the north shore of Crescent Lake. The lake warms up more easily than many high-mountain lakes, making swimming and waterskiing two popular options, but it is often windy here in the afternoon. Boat docks, launching facilities, and rentals are available at Crescent Lake Resort, adjacent to the campground. A trail from camp heads into the Diamond Peak Wilderness (free permit required; available on-site) and also branches north to Odell Lake.

RV sites, facilities: There are 46 sites for tents or RVs up to 36 feet long. Picnic tables and fire grills are provided. Drinking water, vault toilets, garbage service, and boat-launching facilities are available. Firewood may be gathered from the surrounding area. Leashed pets are permitted.

Reservations, fees: Reservations are not accepted. Sites are $16 per night, $8 per night per additional vehicle. Open April–late October, weather permitting.

Directions: From Eugene, drive south on I-5 for five miles to Exit 188 and Highway 58. Turn east and drive 70 miles to Crescent Lake Highway (Forest Road 60). Turn right (west) and drive 2.2 miles southwest. Bear right to remain on Forest Road 60, and drive another 0.25 mile to the campground on the left.

Contact: Deschutes National Forest, Crescent Ranger District, 541/433-3200, fax 541/433-3224, www.fs.fed.us.

166 SPRING

Scenic rating: 8

on Crescent Lake in Deschutes National Forest

Map grid C2

Spring campground is nestled in a lodgepole pine forest on the southern shore of Crescent Lake. Sites are open, with some on the lake offering Diamond Peak views. Boating, swimming, and waterskiing are popular activities, and the Windy-Oldenburg Trailhead provides access to the Oregon Cascades Recreation Area. The camp is at an elevation of 4,850 feet.

RV sites, facilities: There are five sites for tents only, 64 sites for tents or RVs up to 40 feet long, four multiple sites, and 12 sites that can be reserved together as a group site. Picnic tables and fire grills are provided. Drinking water, vault toilets, garbage service, boat-launching facilities, and firewood (may be gathered from the surrounding area) are available. Leashed pets are permitted.

Reservations, fees: Reservations are not accepted for single sites. Reservations are accepted for group sites at 877/444-6777 or www.recreation.gov ($10 reservation fee). Sites are $16 per night, $8 per night per additional vehicle; multiple sites are $30 per night, and the group site is $125 per night. Open May–September, weather permitting.

Directions: From Eugene, drive south on I-5 for five miles to Exit 188 and Highway 58. Turn east and drive 70 miles to Crescent Lake Highway (Forest Road 60). Turn right and drive eight miles west to the campground entrance road on the left. Turn left and drive one mile to the campground.

Contact: Deschutes National Forest, Crescent Ranger District, 541/433-3200, fax 541/433-3224, www.fs.fed.us.

167 CONTORTA POINT GROUP CAMP

Scenic rating: 8

on Crescent Lake in Deschutes National Forest

Map grid C2

This campground (4,850 feet elevation) sits on the southern shore of Crescent Lake, where boating, swimming, and waterskiing are among the summer pastimes. A number of trails from the nearby Windy-Oldenburg Trailhead provide access to lakes in the Oregon Cascades Recreation Area. Motorized vehicles are restricted to open roads only.

RV sites, facilities: There are two group sites for tents or RVs up to 30 feet long that can accommodate up to 40 people each. There is no drinking water. Picnic tables and fire rings are provided. Vault toilets and garbage bins are available. Firewood can be gathered in surrounding forest. Boat docks and launching

facilities are three miles away at Spring Campground. Leashed pets are permitted.

Reservations, fees: Reservations are accepted at 877/444-6777 or www.recreation.gov ($10 reservation fee). Sites are $65 per night. Open May–September, weather permitting.

Directions: From Eugene, drive south on I-5 for five miles to Exit 188 and Highway 58. Turn east and drive 70 miles to Crescent Lake Highway (Forest Road 60). Turn right and drive 9.9 miles to Forest Road 280. Turn left and drive one mile to the campground.

Contact: Deschutes National Forest, Crescent Ranger District, 541/433-3200, fax 541/433-3224, www.fs.fed.us.

168 WHITEFISH HORSE CAMP

Scenic rating: 5

on Whitefish Creek in Deschutes National Forest

Map grid C2

This just might be the best horse camp in the state. Only horse camping is allowed here, and manure removal is required. High lines are not allowed; horses must be kept in stalls. On Whitefish Creek at the west end of Crescent Lake, this campground is set in lodgepole pine and has shaded sites. Although located in a flat area across the road from the lake, the campground has no lake view. Moderately to heavily used, it has access to about 100 miles of trail, leading to Diamond Peak Wilderness, the Metolius-Windigo National Recreation Trail, the Oregon Cascades Recreation Area, and many high mountain lakes. The camp sits at 4,850 feet elevation.

RV sites, facilities: There are 19 sites for tents or RVs up to 40 feet long. Picnic tables and fire rings are provided. Drinking water, garbage bins, vault toilets, horse corrals, and manure disposal site are available are available. Firewood may be gathered from the surrounding area. Leashed pets are permitted.

Reservations, fees: Reservations are accepted at 877/444-6777 or www.recreation.gov ($10 reservation fee). Sites are $14 per night for two stalls, $18 per night for four stalls, and $7 per night per additional vehicle. Open May–September, weather permitting.

Directions: From Eugene, drive south on I-5 for five miles to Exit 188 and Highway 58. Turn east and drive 70 miles to Crescent Lake Highway (Forest Road 60). Turn right (west) and drive 2.2 miles southwest. Stay to the right to remain on Forest Road 60, and drive six miles to the campground on the right.

Contact: Deschutes National Forest, Crescent Ranger District, 541/433-3200, fax 541/433-3224, www.fs.fed.us.

169 CRESCENT CREEK

Scenic rating: 7

on Crescent Creek in Deschutes National Forest
Map grid C2

One of the Cascade's classic hidden campgrounds, Crescent Creek camp sits along the banks of its namesake at 4,500 feet elevation. The buzzwords here are pretty, developed, and private. A registered bird-watching area is nearby. Hunters are the primary users of this campground, mainly in the fall. Otherwise, it gets light use. There's some highway noise here, and even if you can't hear it, traffic is visible from some sites.

RV sites, facilities: There are nine sites for tents or RVs up to 40 feet long. Picnic tables and fire grills are provided. Vault toilets, drinking water, and garbage service are available. Firewood may be gathered from the surrounding area. Leashed pets are permitted.

Reservations, fees: Reservations are not accepted. Sites are $14 per night, $7 per night per additional vehicle. Open May–late September, weather permitting.

Directions: From Eugene, drive south on I-5 for five miles to Exit 188 and Highway 58. Turn east and drive 73 miles to County Road 61. Turn left (east) and drive three miles to the campground on the right.

Contact: Deschutes National Forest, Crescent Ranger District, 541/433-3200, fax 541/433-3224, www.fs.fed.us.

170 CORRAL SPRING

Scenic rating: 4

in Winema National Forest
Map grid C2

This flat campground with no water source is located next to Corral Spring at 4,900 feet elevation. The main attraction is solitude; it's primitive, remote, and quiet. The landscape features stands of lodgepole pine, interspersed by several small meadows.

RV sites, facilities: There are six sites for tents or RVs up to 50 feet long. Picnic tables and fire grills are provided. Vault toilets are available. There is no drinking water, and garbage must be packed out. A store, café, coin laundry, and ice are within five miles. Leashed pets are permitted.

Reservations, fees: Reservations are not accepted. There is no fee for camping. Open mid-May–late October, weather permitting.

Directions: From Eugene, drive southeast on Highway 58 for 86 miles to U.S. 97. Turn south and drive five miles to Forest Road 9774 (2.5 miles north of Chemult). Turn right and drive two miles west to the campground.

Contact: Winema National Forest, Chemult Ranger District, 541/365-7001, fax 541/365-2206, www.fs.fed.us.

171 DIGIT POINT

Scenic rating: 7

on Miller Lake in Winema National Forest
Map grid C2

This campground is nestled in a lodgepole pine and mountain hemlock forest at 5,600 feet elevation on the shore of Miller Lake, a popular spot for boating, fishing, and swimming. Nearby trails provide access to the Mount Thielsen Wilderness and the Pacific Crest Trail.

RV sites, facilities: There are 64 sites for tents or RVs up to 30 feet long. Picnic tables and fire grills are provided. Drinking water, flush toilets, garbage service and a dump station are available. Boat docks and launching facilities are nearby. Some facilities are wheelchair accessible. Leashed pets are permitted.

Reservations, fees: Reservations are not accepted. Sites are $12 per night, $5 per night per additional vehicle. Open Memorial Day–mid-October, weather permitting.

Directions: From Eugene, drive southeast on Highway 58 for 86 miles to U.S. 97. Turn south and drive seven miles to Forest Road 9772 (one mile north of Chemult). Turn right and drive 12 miles west to the campground.

Contact: Winema National Forest, Chemult Ranger District, 541/365-7001, fax 541/365-2206, www.fs.fed.us.

172 WALT HARING SNO-PARK

Scenic rating: 6

in Winema National Forest near Chemult

Map grid C2

For eons, this has been a tiny, unknown, and free campground used as a staging area for snowmobiling and cross-country skiing in winter. In summer, it has primarily been a picnic site and layover spot. Note: In 2009, the Forest Service began improving the site and may start charging fees in 2010. The elevation is 4,700 feet.

RV sites, facilities: There are five sites for tents or RVs. Picnic tables and fire rings are provided. Drinking water, vault toilets, and an RV dump station are available. Some facilities are wheelchair accessible. Leashed pets are permitted.

Reservations, fees: No reservations are accepted. There is no fee, however, the Forest Service may start charging fees starting in 2010. If this is critical to your trip, call first. A sno-park permit is required. Open year-round.

Directions: From Eugene, drive southeast on Highway 58 for 86 miles to U.S. 97. Turn south and drive seven miles to Forest Road 9772 (one mile north of Chemult). Turn right on Forest Road 9772 (Miller Lake Road) and drive 0.5 mile to the campground.

Contact: Winema National Forest, 541/365-7001, fax 541/365-2206.

173 CHARLES V. STANTON PARK

Scenic rating: 7

on the South Umpqua River

Map grid A3

Charles V. Stanton Park, along the banks of the South Umpqua River, is an all-season spot with a nice beach for swimming in the summer and good steelhead fishing in the winter.

RV sites, facilities: There are 20 sites for tents or self-contained RVs (no hookups), 20 sites with full hookups for RVs up to 60 feet long, and one group area for up to 13 camping units. Picnic tables and fire pits or barbecues are provided. Drinking water, restrooms with flush toilets and showers, a dump station, pavilion, picnic area, and playground are available. Propane gas, a store, café, coin laundry, and ice are within one mile. Some facilities are wheelchair accessible. Leashed pets are permitted.

Reservations, fees: No reservations are accepted for single sites; reservations are required for the group site ($10 reservation fee) at 541/957-7001. Sites are $15–20 per night for single sites, $200 per night for the group site. Some credit cards are accepted. Open year-round.

Directions: Depending on which direction you're heading on I-5, there are two routes to reach this campground. In Canyonville northbound on I-5, take Exit 99 and drive one mile north on the frontage road to the campground on the right. Otherwise: In Canyonville southbound on I-5, take Exit 101. Turn right at the first stop sign, and almost immediately turn right again onto the frontage road. Drive one mile south on the frontage road to the campground on the left.

Contact: Charles V. Stanton Park, Douglas County Parks, 541/839-4483, fax 541/440-4500, www.co.douglas.or.us/parks.

OREGON

174 CHIEF MIWALETA CAMPGROUND

Scenic rating: 7

on Galesville Reservoir, east of Azalea

Map grid A3

If location is everything, then this camp has got it. Wooded sites are set along the shore of beautiful Gales Reservoir, providing a base camp for a trip filled with fishing, boating, hiking, camping, and picnicking. A pavilion can be reserved in the day-use area.

RV sites, facilities: There are 20 sites with full hookups for RVs up to 60 feet long (some pull-through), dispersed sites for tents, and one cabin. Picnic tables and fire rings are provided. Drinking water, vault toilets, and a boat ramp are available. Some facilities are wheelchair accessible. Leashed pets are permitted.

Reservations, fees: Reservations are accepted only for the cabin ($10 reservation fee) at 541/957-7001. RV sites are $20 per night, $3 per night per additional vehicle, tent sites are $15 per night, and the cabin is $32 per night. Some credit cards are accepted for reservations only. Open year-round.

Directions: From Azalea, take I-5 north about 0.5 mile to Exit 88 east to Upper Cow Creek Road. Merge onto Upper Cow Creek and drive eight miles to the campground on the left.

Contact: Chief Miwaleta County Campground, 541/837-3302, www.co.douglas.or.us/parks/campgrounds.asp.

175 MEADOW WOOD RV PARK

Scenic rating: 6

in Glendale

Map grid A3

Meadow Wood is a good option for RVers looking for a camping spot along I-5. It features 80 wooded acres and all the amenities. Nearby attractions include a ghost town, gold panning, and Wolf Creek Tavern.

RV sites, facilities: There are 25 tent sites and 75 pull-through sites with full or partial hookups for RVs up to 40 feet long. Drinking water and picnic tables are provided. Restrooms with flush toilets and showers, propane gas, a dump station, modem access, firewood, a coin laundry, ice, a playground, and a seasonal heated swimming pool are available. Leashed pets are permitted.

Reservations, fees: Reservations are accepted at 800/606-1274. Sites are $12.50–25 per night. Monthly rentals are available. Open year-round.

Directions: From Grants Pass, drive north on I-5 to Exit 83 (near Glendale) and drive east for 0.25 mile to Autumn Lane. Turn right (south) on Autumn Lane and drive one mile to the park. Alternatively, if you are instead driving south from Roseburg, drive south on I-5 to Exit 86 (near Glendale). Take that exit and drive over the freeway and turn right onto the frontage road. Continue for three miles to Barton Road. Turn left (east) and drive one mile to Autumn Lane. Turn right (south) on Autumn Lane and drive 0.75 mile to the park.

Contact: Meadow Wood RV Park, 541/832-3114 or 800/606-1274, fax 541/832-2454.

176 WOLF CREEK PARK

Scenic rating: 6

near the town of Wolf Creek

Map grid A3

This rustic campground is located on Wolf Creek near the historic Wolf Creek Inn. A hiking trail leads to the top of London Peak through old-growth forest. Although close to I-5 and the town of Wolf Creek, this spot gets low to average use.

RV sites, facilities: There are 19 sites for tents or RVs (no hookups) and 15 sites for tents or RVs up to 40 feet long (partial hookups). Picnic tables and fire pits are provided. Drinking water, vault toilets, a dump station, softball field, playground, horseshoe pits, disc golf, and a picnic shelter are available. A camp host is on-site. Supplies are available nearby. Some facilities are wheelchair accessible. Leashed pets are permitted.

Reservations, fees: Reservations are accepted at 800/452-5687 or www.reserveamerica.com ($8 reservation fee). Sites are $19–20 per night, $5 per night per additional vehicle. Open year-round, but with no water November–early April.

Directions: From Grants Pass, drive north on I-5 for approximately 18 miles to exit 76/Wolf Creek. Take that exit to Wolf Creek Road. Turn left and drive 0.5 mile to the town of Wolf Creek and Main Street. Turn left and drive 0.25 mile to the park.

Contact: Josephine County Parks, 541/474-5285, fax 541/474-5288, www.co.josephine.or.us/parks/index.htm.

177 INDIAN MARY PARK

Scenic rating: 9

on the Rogue River

Map grid A3   **BEST (**

This park is the crown jewel of the Josephine County parks. Set right on the Rogue River at an elevation of 900–1,000 feet, the park offers disc golf (Frisbee golf), fishing, hiking trails, a historic mining town nearby, a picnic shelter, a swimming beach (unsupervised), and volleyball. Rogue River is famous for its rafting, which can be done with a commercial outfit or on your own.

RV sites, facilities: There are 34 sites for tents or self-contained RVs (no hookups), 58 sites for tents or RVs of up to 40 feet long (full or partial hookups), and two yurts. Picnic tables and fire pits are provided. Drinking water, restrooms with flush toilets and coin showers, garbage bins, a dump station, boat ramp, day-use area, a picnic shelter that can be reserved, playground, ice, and firewood are available. A camp host is on-site. A store and café are seven miles away, and a coin laundry is 16 miles away. Some facilities are wheelchair accessible. Leashed pets are permitted.

Reservations, fees: Reservations are accepted at 800/452-5687 or www.reserveamerica.com ($8 reservation fee). Sites are $19–22 per night, $5 per night per additional vehicle; yurts are $30 per night. Open year-round.

Directions: From Grants Pass, drive north on I-5 for 3.5 miles to Exit 61 (Merlin-Galice Road). Take that exit and drive west on Merlin-Galice Road for 19 miles to Indian Mary Park on the right.

Contact: Josephine County Parks, 541/474-5285, fax 541/474-5288, www.co.josephine.or.us/parks/index.htm.

178 GRIFFIN PARK

Scenic rating: 7

on the Rogue River

Map grid A3

This high-use campground and 16-acre park has grassy sites situated 100–150 yards from the Rogue River. The river current is slow in this area, so it is good for swimming and water play. Fishing and rafting are also popular. Hiking and bicycling are available nearby on Bureau of Land Management property.

RV sites, facilities: There are four sites for tents or RVs (no hookups), 15 sites for tents or RVs up to 40 feet long (full hookups), and one yurt. Picnic tables and fire pits are provided. Drinking water, restrooms with flush toilets and showers, a dump station, recreation field, playground, and horseshoe pits are available. A camp host is on-site. A boat ramp, convenience store, swimming area, and playground are within one mile. Some facilities are wheelchair accessible. Leashed pets are permitted.

Reservations, fees: Reservations are accepted at 800/452-5687 or www.reserveamerica.com ($8 reservation fee). Sites are $19–22 per night, $5 per night per additional vehicle; yurts are $30 per night. Open year-round, but with no water November–early April.

Directions: From Grants Pass on I-5, take the U.S. 199 exit. Turn south on U.S. 199 and drive 6.7 miles to Riverbanks Road. Turn right and drive 6.2 miles to Griffin Park Road. Turn right and drive 0.5 mile to the park.

Contact: Josephine County Parks, 541/474-5285, fax 541/474-5288, www.co.josephine.or.us/parks/index.htm.

OREGON

179 GRANTS PASS/ REDWOOD HIGHWAY

Scenic rating: 8

near Grants Pass

Map grid A3

This KOA campground along a stream in the hills outside of Grants Pass attracts bird-watchers. It also makes a perfect layover spot for travelers who want to get away from the highway for a while. For an interesting side trip, drive south down scenic U.S. 199 to Cave Junction or Illinois River State Park.

RV sites, facilities: There are 40 sites for tents or RVs of any length (full hookups); some sites are pull-through. There is also one cabin. Picnic tables are provided, and tent sites have fire pits. Restrooms with showers, drinking water, a dump station, coin laundry, convenience store, ice, RV supplies, propane gas, and modem access are available. There are also a recreation hall, playground, and recreation field. Leashed pets are permitted with certain restrictions.

Reservations, fees: Reservations are accepted at 888/476-6508 and receive a 10 percent discount. Sites are $35–39 per night, plus $4 per person per night for more than two people. Some credit cards are accepted. Open year-round.

Directions: In Grants Pass on I-5, take the U.S. 199 exit. Turn southwest on U.S. 199 and drive 14.5 miles to the campground on the right (at Milepost 14.5).

Contact: Grants Pass/Redwood Highway KOA, 541/476-6508 or 888/476-6508.

180 SCHROEDER

Scenic rating: 9

on the Rogue River

Map grid A3   **BEST (**

Steelhead and salmon fishing, swimming, and boating are among the possibilities at this popular camp along the Rogue River. Just a short jog off the highway, it makes an excellent layover for I-5 travelers. A bonus for RVers is 50-amp service. The park is set close to Hellgate Excursions, which provides jet boat trips on the Rogue River. Tennis courts are close by.

RV sites, facilities: There are 22 sites for tents and RVs (no hookups), 29 sites for tents or RVs of any length (full hookups), and two yurts. Picnic tables and fire pits are provided. Restrooms with flush toilets and coin showers and a picnic shelter that can be reserved are available. Recreational facilities include ball fields, tennis and basketball courts, horseshoe pits, volleyball court, a dog park, picnic area, playground, and boat ramp. A camp host is on-site. Some facilities, including a fishing pier, are wheelchair accessible. Leashed pets are permitted.

Reservations, fees: Reservations are accepted at 800/452-5687 or www.reserveamerica.com ($8 reservation fee). Sites are $19–22 per night, $5 per night per additional vehicle; yurts are $30 per night. Open year-round.

Directions: In Grants Pass on I-5, take Exit 55 to U.S. 199. Drive west on U.S. 199 for 0.7 mile to Redwood Avenue. Turn right and drive 1.5 miles to Willow Lane. Turn right and drive 0.9 mile to Schroeder Lane and the park.

Contact: Josephine County Parks, 541/474-5285, fax 541/474-5288, www.co.josephine.or.us/parks/index.htm.

181 ROGUE VALLEY OVERNITERS

Scenic rating: 5

near the Rogue River

Map grid A3

This park is just off the freeway in Grants Pass, the jumping-off point for trips down the Rogue River. The summer heat in this part of Oregon can surprise visitors in late June and early July. This is a nice, comfortable park with shade trees. About half of the sites are taken by monthly renters.

RV sites, facilities: There are 30 sites for tents or RVs of any length (full hookups); some are pull-through sites. Cable TV and picnic tables are provided. Restrooms with flush toilets and showers, modem access, a dump station, and coin laundry are available. Propane gas, a store, café, and ice are available within one mile. Leashed pets are permitted.

Reservations, fees: Reservations are accepted. Sites are $33.30 per night, plus $2 per person per night for more than two people. Weekly and monthly rates are available. Open year-round.

Directions: In Grants Pass on I-5, take Exit 58 to 6th Street. Drive south on 6th Street for 0.25 mile to the park on the right.

Contact: Rogue Valley Overniters, 541/479-2208.

182 WHITEHORSE

Scenic rating: 9

near the Rogue River

Map grid A3   BEST (

This pleasant county park is set about a quarter mile from the banks of the Rogue River. It is one of several parks in the Grants Pass area that provide opportunities for salmon and steelhead fishing, hiking, and boating. This is a popular bird-watching area. Wildlife Images, a wildlife rehabilitation center, is nearby. Possible side trips include Crater Lake National Park (two hours away), Kerby Museum, and Oregon Caves.

RV sites, facilities: There are 34 sites for tents or RVs of any length (no hookups), eight sites for RVs of any any length (full hookups), and one yurt. Picnic tables and fire pits are provided. Restrooms with flush toilets and coin showers, a boat ramp, horseshoe pits, volleyball, a picnic shelter, and a playground are available. A camp host is on-site. Some facilities are wheelchair accessible. Leashed pets are permitted.

Reservations, fees: Reservations are accepted at 800/452-5687 or www.reserveamerica.com ($8 reservation fee). Sites are $19–22 per night, $5 per night per additional vehicle, and $30 per night for the yurt. The group site is $30 per night for up to 12 people and $3 per person per night for additional people. Open year-round, but only to self-contained RVs in the winter.

Reservation note: When making a reservation for this campground, note that ReserveAmerica. com mistakenly lists it as White Horse, not Whitehorse, and its computer system will not recognize it as one word.

Directions: In Grants Pass on I-5, take Exit 58 to 6th Street. Drive south on 6th Street to G Street. Turn right (west) and drive approximately seven miles (the road becomes Upper River Road, then Lower River Road). The park is on the left at 7600 Lower River Road.

Contact: Josephine County Parks, 541/474-5285, fax 541/474-5288, www.co.josephine. or.us/parks/index.htm.

183 RIVER PARK RV RESORT

Scenic rating: 6

on the Rogue River

Map grid A3

This park has a quiet, serene riverfront setting, yet it is close to all the conveniences of a small city. Highlights here include 700 feet of Rogue River frontage for trout fishing and swimming. It's one of several parks in the immediate area.

RV sites, facilities: There are three tent sites and 47 sites with full or partial hookups for RVs up to 40 feet long. Picnic tables are provided. Cable TV, restrooms with showers, a dump station, public phone, coin laundry, and ice are available. Leashed pets are permitted.

Reservations, fees: Reservations are accepted at 800/677-8857. Sites are $31–38 per night, $3.50 per person per night for more than two people, and $2 per night for an additional vehicle if not towed. Some credit cards are accepted. Open year-round.

Directions: In Grants Pass on I-5, take Exit 55 west to Highway 199. Drive west on Highway 199 for two miles to Parkdale. Turn left on Parkdale and drive one block to Highway 99. Turn left on Highway 99 and drive two miles to the park on the left.

Contact: River Park RV Resort, 541/479-0046 or 800/677-8857.

OREGON

184 CHINOOK WINDS RV PARK

Scenic rating: 6

on the Rogue River

Map grid A3

This campground along the Rogue River is close to chartered boat trips down the Rogue and a golf course. Fishing and swimming access are available from the campground. (Note: This park was previously known as Circle W RV Park.)

RV sites, facilities: There are 25 sites with full or partial hookups for RVs of any length; some are pull-through sites. Picnic tables and cable TV are provided. Restrooms with flush toilets and showers, a dump station, coin laundry, and ice are available. A boat dock is nearby. Leashed pets are permitted.

Reservations, fees: Reservations are accepted. Sites are $27–40 per night, plus $1.50 per person per night for more than two people. Some credit cards are accepted. Open year-round.

Directions: From Grants Pass, drive south on I-5 for 10 miles to Exit 48 at Rogue River. Take that exit west (over the bridge) to Highway 99. Turn right and drive west one mile to the park on the right.

Contact: Chinook Winds RV Park, 541/582-1686.

185 VALLEY OF THE ROGUE STATE PARK

Scenic rating: 7

on the Rogue River

Map grid A3

With easy highway access, this popular campground along the banks of the Rogue River often fills to near capacity during the summer. Recreation options include fishing and boating. This spot makes a good base camp for taking in the Rogue Valley and surrounding attractions: Ashland's Shakespeare Festival, the Britt Music Festival, Crater Lake National Park, historic Jacksonville, and Oregon Caves National Monument.

RV sites, facilities: There are 147 sites with full or partial hookups for tents or RVs up to 75 feet long, some with pull-through sites, and 21 sites for tents. Three group tent areas for up to 25 people each and six yurts are available. Picnic tables and fire grills are provided. Restrooms with flush toilets and showers, drinking water, garbage bins, a dump station, firewood, Wi-Fi, coin laundry, a meeting hall, amphitheater, and playgrounds are available. A restaurant is nearby. Boat-launching facilities are nearby. Some facilities are wheelchair accessible. Leashed pets are permitted.

Reservations, fees: Reservations are accepted at 800/452-5687 or www.oregonstateparks.org ($8 reservation fee). Tent sites are $12–19 per night, RV sites are $16–24 per night, $5 per night per extra vehicle. Group areas are $40–71 per night; yurts are $27–36 per night. Some credit cards are accepted. Open year-round.

Directions: From Grants Pass, drive south on I-5 for 12 miles to Exit 45B/Valley of the Rogue State Park. Take that exit, turn right, and drive a short distance to the park on the right.

Contact: Valley of the Rogue State Park, 541/582-1118 or 800/551-6949, www.oregonstateparks.org.

186 KOA GOLD N' ROGUE

Scenic rating: 6

on the Rogue River

Map grid A3

This campground is set 0.5 mile from the Rogue River, with bike paths, a golf course, and the Oregon Vortex (the house of mystery) in the vicinity. It's one of the many campgrounds between Gold Hill and Grants Pass.

RV sites, facilities: There are 64 sites with full hookups for RVs of any length, 12 tent sites, and four cabins. Some sites are pull-through. Picnic tables are provided, and tent sites have fire rings. Restrooms with flush toilets and showers, modem access, propane gas, a dump station, firewood, a convenience store, coin laundry, ice, a playground, and a seasonal swimming pool are available. A café is within one mile, and boat-launching facilities are within five miles. Leashed pets are permitted.

Reservations, fees: Reservations are accepted at 800/562-7608. Sites are $25–38 per night, plus $2 per person per night for more than two people. Some credit cards are accepted. Open year-round.

Directions: From Medford, drive north on I-5 for 10 miles to South Gold Hill and Exit 40. Take that exit, turn right, and drive 0.25 mile to Blackwell Road. Turn right (on a paved road) and drive 0.25 mile to the park.

Contact: KOA Gold n' Rogue, 541/855-7710, www.koa.com.

187 LAKE SELMAC

Scenic rating: 9

on Lake Selmac

Map grid A3

Nestled in a wooded, mountainous area, this 300-acre park offers boating, hiking, sailing, swimming, and good trophy bass fishing on beautiful, 160-acre Lake Selmac. Horse trails are also available. There are seasonal hosts and an assistant park ranger on-site.

RV sites, facilities: There are 94 sites for tents or RVs up to 40 feet long, some with full or partial hookups, and a group area for up to 50 people. There are also six horse camps with corrals and two yurts. Picnic tables and fire pits are provided. Drinking water, restrooms with coin showers, a dump station, convenience store, picnic area, horseshoe pits, playground, ball fields, two boat ramps, and a dock are available. Some facilities are wheelchair accessible. Leashed pets are permitted.

Reservations, fees: Reservations are accepted at 800/452-5687 or www.reserveamerica.com ($8 reservation fee). Sites are $19–22 per night, $5 per night per additional vehicle, $19 per night for a horse site, $32 per night for a yurt, $32 per night for the first 12 people at the group site, and $3 per person per night for more than 12 people. Open year-round, with some facility limitations in winter.

Directions: In Grants Pass on I-5, take the U.S. 199 exit. Turn south on U.S. 199 and drive for 23 miles to Selma. Continue 0.5 mile to the Lake Selmac exit (Lakeshore Drive). Turn left (east) and drive 2.3 miles to the lake and the campground entrance.

Contact: Josephine County Parks, 541/474-5285, fax 541/474-5288, www.co.josephine.or.us/parks/index.htm.

188 LAKE SELMAC RESORT

Scenic rating: 7

on Lake Selmac

Map grid A3

This resort borders the shore of Lake Selmac, a 160-acre lake. Fishing is great for largemouth bass (the state record has been set here three times). Bluegill, catfish, crappie, and trout are also catchable here. Fishing derbies are held during the summer. There is a 5-mph speed limit on the lake. Watch for waterfowl, including eagles, geese, osprey, and swans. A trail circles the lake, and bikers, hikers, and horses are welcome. A disc golf course is 1.5 miles away at the county park, and a golf course is about six miles away. Oregon Caves National Monument, about 30 miles away, makes a good side trip.

RV sites, facilities: There are 29 sites with partial hookups for tents or RVs of any length; most sites are pull-through. Drinking water, fire rings, and picnic tables are provided. Restrooms with flush toilets and showers, firewood, a general store, café, coin laundry, ice, propane, bait and tackle, miniature golf, and a playground are available. Boat docks and launching facilities are nearby, and rentals are on-site. Leashed pets are permitted.

Reservations, fees: Reservations are accepted. Sites are $30–35 per night, $3 per night per additional vehicle. Some credit cards are accepted. Open year-round, with limited winter facilities.

Directions: In Grants Pass on I-5, take the U.S. 199 exit. Turn southwest on U.S. 199 and drive

23 miles to Selma and the Lake Selmac exit (Lakeshore Drive). Turn left (east) and drive 2.5 miles to the lake and the resort on the left.

Contact: Lake Selmac Resort, 541/597-2277, www.lakeselmacresort.com.

189 MOUNTAIN MAN RV PARK

Scenic rating: 7

on the Illinois River

Map grid A3

This park on the Illinois River provides good opportunities for swimming and boating (no motors are permitted). And yes, there is a mountain man here who often shows up in costume in the evening when camp groups build a fire. Great Cats World Park, a wildlife park, is 1.5 miles away. Other nearby side trips include Oregon Caves National Monument (21 miles) and Grants Pass (31 miles). Crescent City is 50 miles away. Note that a majority of the campground is taken by monthly rentals, with the remainder available for overnighters. This park was previously known as Town and Country RV Park.

RV sites, facilities: There are 51 sites for tents or RVs of any length (full hookups); some sites are pull-through. Picnic tables are provided, and some sites have fire rings. Cable TV, restrooms with showers, coin laundry, a community fire ring, and ice are available. Horseshoe pits and a clubhouse are also available. Leashed pets are permitted.

Reservations, fees: Reservations are accepted. Sites are $17–25 per night, plus $3 per person per night for more than two people. Monthly rates are available. Open year-round.

Directions: In Grants Pass on I-5, take the U.S. 199 exit. Go 30 miles west on U.S. 199 (past Cave Junction) to the park on the right.

Contact: Mountain Man RV Park, 541/592-2656 (phone or fax).

190 COUNTRY HILLS RESORT

Scenic rating: 7

near Oregon Caves National Monument

Map grid A3

Lots of sites at this wooded camp border Sucker Creek, a popular spot for swimming. Several wineries are located within two miles. Lake Selmac and Oregon Caves National Monument provide nearby side-trip options.

RV sites, facilities: There are 12 tent sites and 20 sites with partial or full hookups for RVs of any length; some are pull-through sites. There are also six cabins and a five-unit motel. Picnic tables and fire rings are provided. Restrooms with flush toilets and coin showers, a dump station, modem access, drinking water, firewood, a convenience store, coin laundry, motel, seasonal ice cream parlor, seasonal café, and ice are available. Leashed pets are permitted.

Reservations, fees: Reservations are accepted. Sites are $16–21 per night, $3 per night per additional vehicle. Some credit cards are accepted. Open year-round.

Directions: In Grants Pass on I-5, take the U.S. 199 exit. Go 28 miles on U.S. 199 to the junction of Cave Junction and Highway 46/Oregon Caves. Turn left on Highway 46 and drive eight miles to the resort on the right.

Contact: Country Hills Resort, 541/592-3406 (phone or fax).

191 GRAYBACK

Scenic rating: 7

near Oregon Caves National Monument in Siskiyou National Forest

Map grid A3

This wooded campground (2,000 feet elevation) along the banks of Sucker Creek has sites with ample shade. It's a good choice if you're planning to visit Oregon Caves National Monument, about 10 miles away. The camp, set in a grove of old-growth firs, is also a prime place for bird-watching. A 0.5-mile trail cuts through the camp.

RV sites, facilities: There are 39 sites for tents and one RV site with partial hookups. Picnic tables, garbage bins, and fire grills are provided. Flush toilets and drinking water are available. Some facilities are wheelchair accessible, including a 0.5-mile trail. Leashed pets are permitted.

Reservations, fees: Reservations are not accepted. Sites are $16 per night, $5 per night per additional vehicle. Open May–September, weather permitting.

Directions: In Grants Pass on I-5, take Exit 55 for U.S. 199. Bear southwest on U.S. 199 for 30 miles to Cave Junction and Highway 46. Turn east on Highway 46 and drive 12 miles to the campground on the right.

Contact: Siskiyou National Forest, Wild Rivers Ranger District, 541/592-4000, fax 541/592-4010, www.fs.fed.us.

192 CAVE CREEK

Scenic rating: 7

near Oregon Caves National Monument in Siskiyou National Forest

Map grid A3

No campground is closer to Oregon Caves National Monument than this U.S. Forest Service camp, a mere four miles away. There is even a two-mile trail out of camp that leads directly to the caves. The camp, at an elevation of 2,500 feet, lies in a grove of old-growth timber along the banks of Cave Creek, a small stream with some trout fishing opportunities (catch-and-release only). The sites are shaded, and an abundance of wildlife can be spotted in the area. Hiking opportunities abound.

RV sites, facilities: There are 18 sites for tents or RVs up to 16 feet long. Picnic tables and fire rings are provided. Drinking water, garbage bins, and vault toilets are available. Showers are within eight miles. Leashed pets are permitted.

Reservations, fees: Reservations are not accepted. Sites are $10 per night, $4 per night per additional vehicle. Open mid-May–mid-September, weather permitting.

Directions: In Grants Pass on I-5, take Exit 55 for U.S. 199. Bear southwest on U.S. 199 for 30 miles to Cave Junction and Highway 46. Turn east on Highway 46 and drive 16 miles to the campground on the right.

Contact: Siskiyou National Forest, Wild Rivers Ranger District, 541/592-4000, fax 541/592-4010, www.fs.fed.us.

193 BOLAN LAKE

Scenic rating: 9

on Bolan Lake in Siskiyou National Forest

Map grid A3

Very few out-of-towners know about this camp, with pretty, shaded sites along the shore of 15-acre Bolan Lake. The lake is stocked with trout, and the fishing can be good. Only non-motorized boats are allowed. A trail from the lake leads up to a fire lookout and ties into miles of other trails, including the Bolan Lake Trail. This spot is truly a bird-watcher's paradise, with a variety of species to view. The camp is set at 5,500 feet elevation.

RV sites, facilities: There are 12 sites for tents or RVs up to 16 feet long. Picnic tables and fire grills are provided. Vault toilets and firewood are available. There is no drinking water. Leashed pets are permitted.

Reservations, fees: Reservations are not accepted. Sites are $5 per night per vehicle. Open June–early October, weather permitting.

Directions: From Grants Pass, drive south on U.S. 199 for 30 miles to Cave Junction and Rockydale Road (County Road 5560). Turn left (southeast) on Rockydale Road and drive eight miles to County Road 5828 (also called Waldo Road and Happy Camp Road). Turn southeast and drive 14 miles to Forest Road 4812. Turn left (east) and drive four miles to Forest Road 4812-040. Turn left (south) and drive two miles to the campground. This access road is very narrow and rough. Large RVs are strongly discouraged.

Contact: Siskiyou National Forest, Wild Rivers Ranger District, 541/592-4000, fax 541/592-4010, www.fs.fed.us.

194 FAREWELL BEND

Scenic rating: 7

on the Upper Rogue River in
Rogue River National Forest

Map grid B3

Extremely popular Farewell Bend campground is set at an elevation of 3,400 feet along the banks of the Upper Rogue River near the Rogue River Gorge. A 0.25-mile barrier-free trail leads from camp to the Rogue Gorge Viewpoint and is definitely worth the trip. The Upper Rogue River Trail passes near camp. This spot attracts a lot of the campers visiting Crater Lake.

RV sites, facilities: There are 61 sites for tents or RVs up to 40 feet long. Picnic tables, fire grills, and fire rings are provided. Drinking water, firewood, and flush toilets are available. Some facilities are wheelchair accessible. Leashed pets are permitted.

Reservations, fees: Reservations are not accepted. Sites are $16 per night, $8 per night per additional vehicle. Open mid-May–late October, weather permitting.

Directions: From Medford, drive northeast on Highway 62 for 57 miles (near Union Creek) to the campground on the left.

Contact: Rogue River National Forest, Prospect Ranger District, 541/560-3400, fax 541/560-3444; Rogue Recreation, 541/560-3900, www.fs.fed.us.

195 UNION CREEK

Scenic rating: 8

near the Upper Rogue River in
Rogue River National Forest

Map grid B3

One of the most popular camps in the district, this spot is more developed than the nearby camps of Mill Creek, Natural Bridge, and River Bridge. It sits at 3,200 feet elevation along the banks of Union Creek, where the creek joins the Upper Rogue River. The Upper Rogue River Trail passes near camp. Interpretive programs are offered in the summer, and a convenience store and restaurant are within walking distance.

RV sites, facilities: There are 78 sites for tents or RVs up to 30 feet long, and three RV sites with full hookups. Picnic tables and fire grills are provided. A restroom with flush toilets, vault toilets, drinking water, and garbage service are available. Firewood is available for purchase. An amphitheater is available for programs. A store and restaurant are within walking distance. Some facilities are wheelchair accessible. Leashed pets are permitted.

Reservations, fees: Reservations are not accepted. Sites are $12 per night, $6 per night per additional vehicle. Open mid-May–mid-October, weather permitting.

Directions: From Medford, drive northeast on Highway 62 for 56 miles (near Union Creek) to the campground on the left.

Contact: Rogue River National Forest, Prospect Ranger District, 541/560-3400, fax 541/560-3444; Rogue Recreation, 541/560-3900, www.fs.fed.us.

196 NATURAL BRIDGE

Scenic rating: 8

on the Upper Rogue River Trail in
Rogue River National Forest

Map grid B3

Expect lots of company in midsummer at this popular camp, which sits at an elevation of 3,200 feet, where the Upper Rogue River runs underground. The Upper Rogue River Trail passes by the camp and follows the river for many miles to the Pacific Crest Trail in Crater Lake National Park. There is an interpretive area and a spectacular geological viewpoint adjacent to the camp. A 0.25-mile, barrier-free trail is also available.

RV sites, facilities: There are 17 sites for tents or RVs up to 30 feet long. Picnic tables, garbage service, and fire grills are provided. Vault toilets are available, but there is no drinking water. Some facilities are wheelchair accessible. Leashed pets are permitted.

Reservations, fees: Reservations are not accepted. Sites are $10 per night, $5 per night per additional vehicle. Open May–early November, weather permitting.

Directions: From Medford, drive northeast on Highway 62 for 55 miles (near Union Creek) to Forest Road 300. Turn left and drive one mile west to the campground on the right.

Contact: Rogue River National Forest, Prospect Ranger District, 541/560-3400, fax 541/560-3444; Rogue Recreation, 541/560-3900, www.fs.fed.us.

197 ABBOTT CREEK

Scenic rating: 8

on Abbott and Woodruff Creeks in
Rogue River National Forest

Map grid B3   BEST (

Situated at the confluence of Abbott and Woodruff Creeks about two miles from the Upper Rogue River, this camp is a better choice for visitors with children than some of the others along the Rogue River. Abbott Creek is small and tame compared to the roaring Rogue. The elevation here is 3,100 feet.

RV sites, facilities: There are 25 sites for tents or RVs up to 22 feet long. Picnic tables, garbage service, and fire grills are provided. Drinking water, vault toilets, and firewood are available. Leashed pets are permitted.

Reservations, fees: Reservations are not accepted. Sites are $10 per night, $6 per night per additional vehicle. Open mid-May–late October, weather permitting.

Directions: From Medford, drive northeast on Highway 62 for 50 miles (near Union Creek) to Forest Road 68. Turn left and drive 3.5 miles west to the campground on the left.

Contact: Rogue River National Forest, Prospect Ranger District, 541/560-3400, fax 541/560-3444; Rogue Recreation, 541/560-3900, www.fs.fed.us.

198 RIVER BRIDGE

Scenic rating: 7

on the Upper Rogue River in
Rogue River National Forest

Map grid B3

River Bridge campground, situated at 2,900 feet elevation along the banks of the Upper Rogue River, is particularly scenic, with secluded sites and river views. This is a calmer part of the Wild and Scenic Upper Rogue River, but swimming and rafting are not recommended. The Upper Rogue River Trail passes by the camp and follows the river for many miles to the Pacific Crest Trail in Crater Lake National Park.

RV sites, facilities: There are eight sites for tents or RVs up to 22 feet long. Picnic tables, garbage service, and fireplaces are provided. Vault toilets are available, but there is no drinking water. Leashed pets are permitted.

Reservations, fees: Reservations are not accepted. Sites are $8 per night, $4 per night per additional vehicle. Open early May–November, weather permitting.

Directions: From Medford, drive northeast on Highway 62 (Crater Lake Highway) for 42 miles (before reaching Union Creek) to Forest Road 6210. Turn left and drive one mile to the campground on the right.

Contact: Rogue River National Forest, Prospect Ranger District, 541/560-3400, fax 541/560-3444; Rogue Recreation, 541/560-3900, www.fs.fed.us.

199 HUCKLEBERRY MOUNTAIN

Scenic rating: 6

near Crater Lake National Park in
Rogue River National Forest

Map grid B3

Here's a hideaway for Crater Lake visitors. The camp is located at the site of an old 1930s Civilian Conservation Corps camp, and an OHV trail runs through and next to the campground. Set at an elevation of 5,400 feet, this spot, about 15 miles from the entrance to Crater Lake National Park, really does get overlooked by highway travelers, so you have a good shot at privacy. About 10 miles of rough roads keep traffic down most of the time.

RV sites, facilities: There are 25 sites for tents or RVs up to 26 feet long. Picnic tables and fireplaces are provided. Drinking water and vault toilets are available. Garbage must be packed out. Leashed pets are permitted.

Reservations, fees: Reservations are not accepted. There is no fee for camping. Open June–late October, weather permitting.

Directions: From Medford, drive north on Highway 62 for 50 miles (near Union Creek) to Forest Road 60. Turn right and drive 12 miles to the campground.

Contact: Rogue River National Forest, Prospect Ranger District, 541/560-3400, fax 541/560-3444; Rogue Recreation, 541/560-3900, www.fs.fed.us.

200 MAZAMA

Scenic rating: 6

near the Pacific Crest Trail in
Crater Lake National Park

Map grid B3

One of two campgrounds at Crater Lake—the other being Lost Creek—this camp sits at 6,000 feet elevation and is known for cold nights, even in late June and early September. I once got caught in a snowstorm here at the opening in mid-June. A nearby store is a great convenience. Seasonal boat tours and junior ranger programs are available. The Pacific Crest Trail passes through the park, but the only trail access down to Crater Lake is at Cleetwood Cove. Note that winter access to the park is from the west only on Highway 62 to Rim Village.

RV sites, facilities: There are 200 sites for tents or self-contained RVs up to 32 feet long; there are no hookups. Picnic tables, fire grills, bear-proof food lockers, and garbage bins are provided. Drinking water, restrooms with flush toilets and coin showers, a dump station, coin

laundry, gasoline, mini-mart, firewood, and ice are available. Some facilities are wheelchair accessible. Leashed pets are permitted in the campground and on paved roads only.

Reservations, fees: Reservations are not accepted. Sites are $14.75 per night, RV space is $15.75 per night, plus a $10 park-entrance fee per vehicle and $3 per person per night for more than two people. Some credit cards are accepted. Open early June–mid October, weather permitting.

Directions: From I-5 at Medford, turn east on Highway 62 and drive 72 miles into Crater Lake National Park and to Annie Springs junction. Turn left and drive a short distance to the national park entrance kiosk. Just beyond the kiosk, turn right to the campground and Mazama store entrance.

Contact: Crater Lake National Park, 541/594-3000, www.nps.gov/crla.

201 FLY CASTERS RV PARK

Scenic rating: 6

on the Rogue River

Map grid B3

This spot along the banks of the Rogue River is a good base camp for RVers who want to fish or hike. The county park, located across the river in Shady Cove, offers picnic facilities and a boat ramp. Lost Creek Lake is about a 15-minute drive northeast. Note that about half of the sites are taken by long-term rentals.

RV sites, facilities: There are 47 sites with full hookups for RVs of any length; two are pull-through sites. Picnic tables are provided. Restrooms with flush toilets and showers, propane gas, cable TV, wireless Internet service, a clubhouse, barbecue area, and coin laundry are available. A store, café, and ice are within one mile. Boat-launching facilities are nearby. Leashed pets are permitted.

Reservations, fees: Reservations are accepted. Sites are $25–38 per night. Some credit cards are accepted. Monthly rates are available. Open year-round.

Directions: From Medford, drive northeast on Highway 62 for 21 miles to the park on the left.

Contact: Fly Casters RV Park, 541/878-2749, fax 541/878-2742.

202 BEAR MOUNTAIN RV PARK

Scenic rating: 7

on the Rogue River

Map grid B3

This campground is set in an open, grassy area on the Rogue River about six miles from Lost Creek Lake, where boat ramps and picnic areas are available for day use. The campsites are spacious and shaded.

RV sites, facilities: There is a grassy area for tent sites and 37 sites with full or partial hookups for RVs of any length. Drinking water and picnic tables are provided. Restrooms with flush toilets and showers, propane gas, coin laundry, ice, and a playground are available. A store and café are within one mile. Boat docks and launching facilities are nearby. Leashed pets are permitted.

Reservations, fees: Reservations are accepted at 541/878-2400 (from Oregon) or 800/586-2327 (from outside Oregon). Sites are $20–24 per night, plus $2 per person per night for more than two adults. Some credit cards are accepted. Open year-round.

Directions: From Medford, drive northeast on Highway 62 to the junction with Highway 227. Continue east on Highway 62 for 2.5 more miles to the park on the left.

Contact: Bear Mountain RV Park, 541/878-2400.

203 ROGUE ELK CAMPGROUND

Scenic rating: 8

on the Rogue River east of the city of Trail

Map grid B3

Right on the Rogue River at an elevation of 1,476 feet, the park has creek swimming (unsupervised), a Douglas fir forest, fishing, hiking trails, rafting, and wildlife. With 33 acres of space and 0.75 mile of river frontage, this is Jackson County's most popular park. The forest is very beautiful here. Lost Creek Lake on Highway 62 makes a good side trip.

RV sites, facilities: There are 15 sites for tents or RVs of up to 25 feet long; some have partial hookups. Picnic tables and fire pits are provided. Drinking water, restrooms with flush toilets and coin showers, garbage bins, a dump station, boat ramp, and playground are available. A café, mini-mart, ice, coin laundry, and firewood are available within three miles. Some facilities are wheelchair accessible. Leashed pets are permitted.

Reservations, fees: Reservations are not accepted. Family sites are $18–32 per night and $1 per pet per night. Open mid-April–mid-October.

Directions: From Medford, take Exit 30 for the Crater Lake Highway (Highway 62) and drive northeast on Highway 62 for 29 miles to the park entrance on the right.

Contact: Jackson County Parks, 541/774-8183, fax 541/774-6320, www.jacksoncountyparks.com.

204 JOSEPH H. STEWART STATE PARK

Scenic rating: 7

on Lost Creek Reservoir

Map grid B3

This state park is on the shore of Lost Creek Reservoir, about 40 miles from Crater Lake National Park, and is home to 11 miles of hiking and biking trails, a lake with a beach, boat rentals, and a marina. Grassy sites are spacious and sprinkled with conifers. The Cole River Hatchery is available for tours.

Note: At time of publication, a blue-green algae health advisory was in effect.

RV sites, facilities: There are 151 sites with partial hookups for tents or self-contained RVs, including some sites for RVs of any length, and

50 sites with water for tents or self-contained RVs. There are also two group areas for tents for up to 50 people each. Picnic tables and fire grills are provided. Restrooms with flush toilets and showers, garbage bins, drinking water, a dump station, firewood, and a playground with volleyball and horseshoes are available. Boat rentals, launching facilities, a swimming area, and a picnic area that can be reserved are nearby. Some facilities are wheelchair accessible. Leashed pets are permitted.

Reservations, fees: Reservations are accepted for the group sites at 800/452-5687 or www.oregonstateparks.org ($8 reservation fee) but are not accepted for single sites. Tent sites are $10–17 per night, sites for tents or RVs are $12–20 per night, $5 per night per additional vehicle. The group site is $40–71, plus $2.40–3 per person per night for more than 25 people. Some credit cards are accepted. Open year-round, weather permitting.

Directions: From Medford, drive northeast on Highway 62 for 34 miles to the Lost Creek Reservoir and the campground on the left.

Contact: Joseph H. Stewart State Park, 541/560-3334 or 800/551-6949, www.oregonstateparks.org.

205 WHISKEY SPRINGS

Scenic rating: 9

near Butte Falls in Rogue River National Forest

Map grid B3

This campground at Whiskey Springs, near Fourbit Ford Campground, is one of the larger, more developed backwoods U.S. Forest Service camps in the area. A one-mile, wheelchair-accessible nature trail passes nearby. You can see beaver dams and woodpeckers here. The camp is set at 3,200 feet elevation.

RV sites, facilities: There are 36 sites for tents or RVs up to 30 feet long. Picnic tables, garbage service, and fire grills are provided. Drinking water and vault toilets are available. Some facilities are wheelchair accessible. Leashed pets are permitted.

Reservations, fees: Reservations are not accepted. Sites are $10 per night, $5 per night per additional vehicle. Open mid-May–September, weather permitting.

Directions: From Medford, drive northeast on Highway 62 for 14 miles to the Butte Falls Highway. Turn right and drive east for 16 miles to the town of Butte Falls. Continue southeast on Butte Falls Highway for nine miles to Forest Road 3065. Turn left on Forest Road 3065 and drive 300 yards to the campground on the left.

Contact: Rogue River National Forest, Butte Falls Ranger District, 541/865-2700, fax 541/865-2795, www.fs.fed.us.

206 SOUTH FORK

Scenic rating: 7

on the South Rogue River in Rogue River National Forest

Map grid B3

South Fork campground is set at an elevation of 4,000 feet along the South Rogue River. To the east, trails at the ends of the nearby forest roads provide access to the Sky Lakes Wilderness. The Southfork Trail, across the road from the campground, has a good biking trail in one direction and a hiking trail in the other. A map of Rogue River National Forest details all back roads, trails, and waters.

RV sites, facilities: There are two sites for tents and four sites for tents or RVs up to 16 feet long. Picnic tables, drinking water, garbage service, and fire grills are provided. Vault toilets are available. Leashed pets are permitted.

Reservations, fees: Reservations are not accepted. Sites are $10 per night, $5 per night per additional vehicle. Open early June–mid-November, weather permitting.

Directions: From Medford, drive northeast on Highway 62 for 14 miles to Butte Falls Highway. Turn right and drive 16 miles east to the town of Butte Falls. Continue one mile past Butte Falls to County Road 992 (Butte Falls Prospect Highway) and drive nine miles to

Forest Road 34. Turn right and drive 8.5 miles to the campground on the right.

Contact: Rogue River National Forest, Butte Falls Ranger District, 541/865-2700, fax 541/865-2795, www.fs.fed.us.

207 MEDFORD OAKS RV PARK

Scenic rating: 6

near Eagle Point
Map grid B3

This park is in a quiet, rural setting among the trees. Just a short hop off I-5, it's an excellent choice for travelers heading to or from California. The campground is located along the shore of a pond that provides good fishing. Most sites are filled with monthly renters.

RV sites, facilities: There are six sites for tents and 55 sites with full or partial hookups for RVs of any length; most sites are pull-through. There are also three cabins. Restrooms with coin showers, a dump station, modem access, coin laundry, limited groceries, ice, RV supplies, and propane gas are available. Recreational facilities include a seasonal, heated swimming pool, movies, horseshoe pits, table tennis, a recreation field for baseball and volleyball, and a playground. Leashed pets are allowed with certain restrictions.

Reservations, fees: Reservations are recommended. Sites are $28–33 per night. Group rates are available. Some credit cards are accepted. Open year-round.

Directions: From Medford, drive northeast on Highway 62 for five miles to Exit 30 and Highway 140. Turn east on Highway 140 and drive 6.8 miles to the park on the left.

Contact: Medford Oaks RV Park, 541/826-5103, fax 541/826-5984, www.medfordoaks.com.

208 WILLOW LAKE RESORT

Scenic rating: 9

on Willow Lake
Map grid B3

This campground sits on the shore of Willow Lake. Located at the base of Mount McLoughlin at an elevation of 3,200 feet, it encompasses 927 wooded acres. The lake has fishing opportunities for bass, crappie, and trout. A hiking trail starts near camp. Waterskiing is allowed at the lake.

RV sites, facilities: There are 26 sites for tents or RVs (no hookups), 54 sites for tents or RVs (full or partial hookups), and a group area with 11 sites. There are also four cabins. Picnic tables and fire rings are provided. Restrooms with flush toilets and coin showers, a dump station, and firewood are available. A store, boat ramp, and boat rentals are on-site. Leashed pets are permitted.

Reservations, fees: Reservations are accepted for groups and cabins only at 541/560-3900. Sites are $15–25 per night, and it's $1 per pet per night. The group area is $175 per night. Open April–October.

Directions: From Medford, drive northeast on Highway 62 for 15 miles to Butte Falls Highway. Turn east and drive 25 miles to Willow Lake Road. Turn right (south) and drive two miles to the campground.

Contact: Rogue Recreation, 541/560-3900.

209 PARKER MEADOWS

Scenic rating: 7

on Parker Meadow in Rogue River National Forest
Map grid B3

Fantastic views of nearby Mount McLoughlin are among the highlights of this rustic camp set at 5,000 feet elevation in a beautiful meadow. Trailheads at the ends of the forest roads lead into the Sky Lakes Wilderness. Parker Meadows is a nice spot, complete with water and lots of privacy between sites. Except during hunting season in the fall, this camp does not get much use.

OREGON

RV sites, facilities: There are eight sites for tents or RVs up to 16 feet long. Picnic tables and fire grills are provided. Vault toilets, drinking water, and garbage service are available. Leashed pets are permitted.

Reservations, fees: Reservations are not accepted. Sites are $10 per night, $5 per night per additional vehicle. Open mid-June–late October, weather permitting.

Directions: From Medford, drive northeast on Highway 62 for 14 miles to Butte Falls Highway. Turn right and drive 16 miles east to the town of Butte Falls and County Road 821. Turn left and drive 10 miles southeast to Forest Road 37. Turn left and drive 11 miles to the campground on the left.

Contact: Rogue River National Forest, Butte Falls Ranger District, 541/865-2700, fax 541/865-2795, www.fs.fed.us.

210 FOURMILE LAKE

Scenic rating: 8

at Fourmile Lake in Winema National Forest

Map grid B3

This beautiful spot is the only camp on the shore of Fourmile Lake. Several nearby trails provide access to the Sky Lakes Wilderness. The Pacific Crest Trail passes about two miles from camp. Primitive and with lots of solitude, it attracts a calm and quiet crowd. Afternoon winds can be a problem, and in the evening, if the wind isn't blowing, the mosquitoes often arrive. Although this campground is near the foot of Mount McLoughlin (9,495 feet), there is no view of the mountain from here. Go to the east side of the lake for a good view.

RV sites, facilities: There are 25 sites for tents or RVs up to 22 feet long. Picnic tables, garbage bins, and fire grills are provided. Drinking water and vault toilets are available. Leashed pets are permitted.

Reservations, fees: Reservations are not accepted. Sites are $11 per night, $5.50 per night per additional vehicle. Open June–late September, weather permitting.

Directions: From Medford, drive northeast on Highway 62 for five miles to Exit 30 and Highway 140. Turn east on Highway 140 and drive approximately 40 miles to Forest Road 3661. Turn left (north) and drive six miles to the campground.

Contact: Fremont-Winema National Forests, Klamath Ranger District, 541/885-3400, fax 541/885-3452, www.fs.fed.us.

211 ROCKY POINT RESORT

Scenic rating: 7

on Upper Klamath Lake

Map grid B3

Rocky Point Resort, at the Upper Klamath Wildlife Refuge, boasts 10 miles of canoe trails, along with opportunities for motorized boating and fishing. Ponderosa pines and Douglas firs create a quite picturesque setting for stellar sunsets and a peaceful retreat.

RV sites, facilities: There are 29 sites with partial or full hookups for RVs of any length, four tent sites, four cabins, and five motel rooms. Some sites are pull-through. Picnic tables and fire rings are provided. Restrooms with flush toilets and showers, drinking water, firewood, a convenience store, modem access, coin laundry, ice, a marina with boat gas, and boat and canoe rentals are available. There is a free boat launch and game area. A restaurant and lounge overlook the lake. Leashed pets are permitted.

Reservations, fees: Reservations are accepted. Sites are $28–30 per night, $4 per person per night for more than two people, $2 per pet per night, and $5 per night per additional vehicle. Some credit cards are accepted. Open April–November.

Directions: From Klamath Falls, drive northeast on Highway 140 for 25 miles to Rocky Point Road. Turn right and drive three miles to the resort on the right.

Contact: Rocky Point Resort, 541/356-2287, fax 541/356-2222, www.rockypointoregon.com.

212 WILLOW PRAIRIE

Scenic rating: 7

near Fish Lake in Rogue River National Forest

Map grid B3

There are two campgrounds here, including one for equestrian campers. This spot is located near the origin of the west branch of Willow Creek and next to a beaver swamp and several large ponds that attract deer, ducks, elk, geese, and sandhill cranes. A number of riding trails pass nearby. A map of Rogue River National Forest details the back roads and can help you get here. Fish Lake is four miles south.

RV sites, facilities: There are 10 sites for tents or RVs up to 16 feet long, one primitive cabin with cots, and 10 equestrian sites. Picnic tables and fire grills are provided. Drinking water, vault toilets, and garbage service are available. The equestrian camp has 10 sites for tents or small RVs, two stock water troughs, and horse corrals. A store, café, ice, boat docks, launching facilities, and rentals are nearby. A camp host is on-site. Leashed pets are permitted.

Reservations, fees: Reservations are accepted only for the horse camp and cabin at 877/444-6777 or www.recreation.gov ($10 reservation fee). Sites are $10 per night, $5 per night per additional vehicle. Open late May–late October, weather permitting.

Directions: From Medford, drive northeast on Highway 62 for five miles to Exit 30 and Highway 140. Turn east on Highway 140 and drive 31.5 miles to Forest Road 37. Turn left and drive north 1.5 miles to Forest Road 3738. Turn left and drive one mile west to Forest Road 3735. Turn left and drive 100 yards to the campground. For the equestrian camp, continue for 0.25 mile to the campground entrance.

Contact: Rogue River National Forest, Butte Falls Ranger District, 541/865-2700, fax 541/865-2795, www.fs.fed.us.

213 NORTH FORK

Scenic rating: 7

near Fish Lake in Rogue River National Forest

Map grid B3

Here is a small, pretty campground with easy access from the highway and proximity to Fish Lake. Situated on the north fork of Little Butte Creek at an elevation of 4,500 feet, it's fairly popular, so grab your spot early. Excellent fly-fishing can be found along the Fish Lake Trail, which leads directly out of camp.

RV sites, facilities: There are nine sites for tents or RVs up to 24 feet long. Picnic tables and fire grills are provided. Vault toilets and drinking water are available. Garbage must be packed out. A camp host is on-site. Boat docks, launching facilities, and rentals are nearby. Some facilities are wheelchair accessible. Leashed pets are permitted.

Reservations, fees: Reservations are not accepted. Sites are $8 per night, $4 per night per additional vehicle. Open May–mid-November, weather permitting.

Directions: From Medford, drive northeast on Highway 62 for five miles to Exit 30 and Highway 140. Turn east on Highway 140 and drive 31.5 miles to Forest Road 37. Turn right (south) and drive 0.5 mile to the campground.

Contact: Rogue River National Forest, Butte Falls District, 541/865-2700, fax 541/865-2795; Rogue Recreation, 541/560-3900, www.fs.fed.us.

214 FISH LAKE

Scenic rating: 8

on Fish Lake in Rogue River National Forest

Map grid B3

Bicycling, boating, fishing, and hiking are among the recreation options at this campground on the north shore of Fish Lake. Easy, one-mile access to the Pacific Crest Trail is also available. If this campground is full, Doe Point and Fish Lake Resort are nearby.

RV sites, facilities: There are 19 sites for tents

OREGON

or RVs up to 40 feet long and two walk-in tent sites. Picnic tables, fire grills, and garbage bins are provided. Drinking water, flush toilets, a picnic shelter that can be reserved, a store, café, firewood, and ice are available. A camp host is on-site. Boat docks, launching facilities, boat rentals, coin laundry, dump station, and coin showers are nearby. Some facilities are wheelchair accessible. Leashed pets are permitted.

Reservations, fees: Reservations are accepted only for the picnic shelter at 541/560-3900. Sites are $16 per night, $8 per night per additional vehicle. Open mid-May–mid-October, weather permitting.

Directions: From Medford, drive northeast on Highway 62 for five miles to Exit 30 and Highway 140. Turn east on Highway 140 and drive 30 miles to the campground on the right.

Contact: Rogue River National Forest, Butte Falls District, 541/865-2700, fax 541/865-2795; Rogue Recreation, 541/560-3900, www.fs.fed.us.

215 DOE POINT

Scenic rating: 8

on Fish Lake in Rogue River National Forest
Map grid B3

This campground (at 4,600 feet elevation) sits along the north shore of Fish Lake, nearly adjacent to Fish Lake Campground. Doe Point is slightly preferable because of its dense vegetation, offering shaded, quiet, well-screened sites. Privacy, rare at many campgrounds, can be found here. Recreation options include biking, boating, fishing, and hiking, plus an easy, one-mile access trail to the Pacific Crest Trail.

RV sites, facilities: There are five walk-in tent sites and 25 sites for tents or RVs up to 30 feet long. Picnic tables and fire grills are provided. Drinking water, garbage service, flush toilets, a store, café, firewood, and ice are available. Boat docks, launching facilities, boat rentals, showers, and a dump station are nearby. Some facilities are wheelchair accessible. Leashed pets are permitted.

Reservations, fees: Reservations are not accepted. Sites are $16 per night, $8 per night

per additional vehicle. Open mid-May–late September, weather permitting.

Directions: From Medford, drive northeast on Highway 62 for five miles to Exit 30 and Highway 140. Turn east on Highway 140 and drive 30 miles to the campground on the right.

Contact: Rogue River National Forest, Butte Falls District, 541/865-2700, fax 541/865-2795, www.fs.fed.us; Rogue Recreation, 541/560-3900, www.fs.fed.us.

216 FISH LAKE RESORT

Scenic rating: 7

on Fish Lake
Map grid B3

This resort along Fish Lake is privately operated under permit by the U.S. Forest Service and offers a resort-type feel, catering primarily to families. This is the largest and most developed of the three camps at Fish Lake. Bicycling, boating, fishing, and hiking are some of the activities here. Cozy cabins are available for rent. Boat speed on the lake is limited to 10 mph.

RV sites, facilities: There are 12 sites for tents, 46 sites with full hookups for RVs up to 38 feet long, and 11 cabins. Some sites are pull-through. Picnic tables, fire rings, drinking water, and garbage bins are provided. Restrooms with flush toilets and coin showers, propane gas, dump station, recreation hall, convenience store, café, coin laundry, ice, boat docks, boat rentals, and launching facilities are available. Leashed pets are permitted.

Reservations, fees: Reservations are accepted at 541/949-8500. Tent sites are $18–40 per night, and RV sites are $32–34 per night. Some credit cards are accepted. Open year-round, weather permitting, with limited winter facilities.

Directions: From Medford, take I-5 to Exit 30 and go to Highway 140. Turn east on Highway 140 and drive 30 miles to Fish Lake Road. Turn right (south) and drive 0.5 mile to the resort on the left.

Contact: Fish Lake Resort, 541/949-8500, www.fishlakeresort.net.

217 LAKE OF THE WOODS RESORT

Scenic rating: 9

on Lake of the Woods

Map grid B3   **BEST**

On beautiful Lake of the Woods, this resort offers fishing (four kinds of trout, catfish, and bass) and boating in a secluded forest setting. It's on one of the most beautiful lakes in the Cascade Mountains, surrounded by tall pine trees. A family-oriented campground, it has all the amenities. In the winter, snowmobiling and cross-country skiing are popular. Attractions in the area include the Mountain Lakes Wilderness and the Pacific Crest Trail.

RV sites, facilities: There are 27 sites with full or partial hookups for tents or RVs up to 35 feet long and 26 cabins. Picnic tables and fire rings are provided. Restrooms with showers, a dump station, coin laundry, ice, snacks, a restaurant, lounge, and propane gas are available. There are also a boat ramp, dock, marina, boat and mountain bike rentals, and a barbecue area. Leashed pets are permitted.

Reservations, fees: Reservations are accepted at 866/201-4194. Sites are $28–35 per night, $7 per night per additional vehicle, and $1 per pet per night. Some credit cards are accepted. Open during summer season; call for winter schedule.

Directions: In Medford on I-5, take Exit 14 to Highway 62. Go six miles on Highway 62 to Highway 140/Lake of the Woods. Drive 59.6 miles on Lake of the Woods Road to the resort on the left.

Contact: Lake of the Woods Resort, 541/949-8300, fax 541/949-8229, www.lakeofthewoodsresort.com.

218 ASPEN POINT

Scenic rating: 8

on Lake of the Woods in Winema National Forest

Map grid B3

This campground (at 5,000 feet elevation) is near the north shore of Lake of the Woods, adjacent to Lake of the Woods Resort. It's heavily timbered with old-growth fir and has a great view of Mount McLoughlin (9,495 feet). A hiking trail just north of camp leads north for several miles, meandering around Fourmile Lake and extending into the Sky Lakes Wilderness. Other trails nearby head into the Mountain Lakes Wilderness. Boating, fishing, swimming, and waterskiing are among the activities here. Note that of the 60 campsites, 20 are available by reservation; the rest are first-come, first-served.

RV sites, facilities: There are 18 single sites and two double sites for tents or RVs up to 55 feet long. Picnic tables, garbage bins, and fire grills are provided. Drinking water, a dump station, and flush toilets are available. Boat docks, launching facilities, and rentals are nearby. Some facilities are wheelchair accessible. Leashed pets are permitted.

Reservations, fees: Reservations are accepted at 877/444-6777 or www.recreation.gov ($10 reservation fee). Single sites are $16–17 per night, $34 for double sites, and $8 per night per additional vehicle. The group sites is $90–95 per night. Open late May–early September, weather permitting.

Directions: In Ashland on I-5, take Exit 14 to Highway 66. Drive east for less than a mile to Dead Indian Memorial Road. Turn left (east) and drive 40 miles to Lake of the Woods. Continue along the east shore to the campground turnoff on the left.

Contact: Fremont-Winema National Forests, Klamath Ranger District, 541/885-3400, fax 541/885-3452, www.fs.fed.us.

219 SUNSET

Scenic rating: 8

near Lake of the Woods in Winema National Forest

Map grid B3

Sunset campground (at 5,000 feet elevation) near the eastern shore of Lake of the Woods is fully developed and offers a myriad of recreation options. It's popular for both fishing and boating. Of the 67 sites, 20 are available by reservation.

RV sites, facilities: There are 67 sites for tents or RVs up to 50 feet long. Picnic tables, garbage bins, and fire grills are provided. Drinking water and flush toilets are available. Boat docks, launching facilities, and rentals are nearby. Some facilities are wheelchair accessible. Leashed pets are permitted.

Reservations, fees: Reservations are accepted at 877/444-6777 or www.recreation.gov ($10 reservation fee). Sites are $17 per night, $8 per night per additional vehicle. Open late May–early September.

Directions: In Ashland on I-5, take Exit 14 to Highway 66. Drive east for less than a mile to Dead Indian Memorial Road. Turn left (east) and drive 40 miles to Lake of the Woods. Continue along the east shore to Forest Road 3738. Turn left (west) and drive 0.5 mile to the camp.

Contact: Fremont-Winema National Forests, Klamath Ranger District, 541/885-3400, fax 541/885-3452, www.fs.fed.us.

220 CANTRALL-BUCKLEY PARK & GROUP CAMP

Scenic rating: 8

on the Applegate River

Map grid B3

This county park outside of Medford offers pleasant, shady sites in a wooded setting. Encompassing 88 acres of land, the camp has 1.75 miles of frontage along the Applegate River, which has good trout fishing.

RV sites, facilities: There are 42 sites for tents or self-contained RVs up to 25 feet long and one group area for 60–100 people. Picnic tables and fire pits are provided. Drinking water, restrooms with flush toilets and coin showers, and a picnic area that can be reserved are available. Recreational facilities include horseshoes, a playground, and a recreation field. Leashed pets are permitted.

Reservations, fees: Reservations are accepted only for the group site at 541/774-8183. Sites

are $12 per night, $1 per pet per night, and $65 per night for the group site. Some credit cards are accepted with reservations only. Open mid-April–mid-October.

Directions: In Medford on I-5, take the Jacksonville exit to the Jacksonville Highway. Drive west on the Jacksonville Highway (Highway 238) for seven miles to Jacksonsville. Bear left on Highway 238 and drive to Hamilton Road. Turn left (south) on Hamilton Road and drive approximately 0.4 mile to Cantrall Road. Turn right on Cantrall and drive approximately 0.5 mile to the campground.

Contact: Jackson County Parks, 541/774-8183, fax 541/774-6320, www.jacksoncountyparks.com.

221 THE WELLSPRINGS

Scenic rating: 5

near Ashland

Map grid B3

This wooded campground has mineral hot springs that empty into a swimming pool. Hot mineral baths are available in private rooms. Massages, sauna use, and swimming are also available for a fee. This is an old Native American birthing ground. Nearby recreation options include a bike path, a golf course, hiking trails, and tennis courts. Boating, fishing, and waterskiing are within 10 miles.

RV sites, facilities: There is a large grassy area for tents, 28 sites with full hookups for RVs of any length, and five tepees. Some sites are pull-through. Picnic tables and fire rings are provided. Restrooms with flush toilets and showers, coin laundry, ice, volleyball, massage therapists, a soaking pool, a swimming pool, and a sauna are available. Propane gas is within one mile. Leashed pets are permitted with deposit.

Reservations, fees: Reservations are not accepted. Tent sites are $15 per night, RV sites are $20 per night, $3–6 per person per night for more than two people, and tepees are $25 per night. Some credit cards are accepted. Open year-round.

Directions: From Ashland, drive north on I-5 to Exit 19. Take that exit and drive west for 0.25 mile to the stoplight at Highway 99. Turn right and drive 500 feet to the campground on the left.

Contact: The WellSprings, 541/482-3776.

222 GLENYAN CAMPGROUND OF ASHLAND

Scenic rating: 7

near Emigrant Lake

Map grid B3

This campground, located within seven miles of Ashland and less than one mile from Emigrant Lake, offers shady sites. Recreation options in the area include a golf course and tennis courts. It's an easy jump from I-5 at Ashland.

RV sites, facilities: There are 22 tent sites and 46 sites with full or partial hookups for tents or RVs of any length. Drinking water, fire rings, and picnic tables are provided. Restrooms with flush toilets and showers, propane gas, a dump station, wireless Internet service, firewood, a recreation hall, convenience store, coin laundry, ice, a playground, and a seasonal heated swimming pool are available. Leashed pets are permitted.

Reservations, fees: Reservations are accepted at 877/453-6926. Sites are $29–32 per night, plus $2 per person per night for more than five people. Some credit cards are accepted. Open year-round.

Directions: From Ashland, drive east on Highway 66 for 3.5 miles to the campground on the right.

Contact: Glenyan Campground of Ashland, 541/488-1785, www.glenyancampground.com.

223 DALEY CREEK

Scenic rating: 6

on Daley Creek in Rogue River National Forest

Map grid B3

Daley Creek campground is a primitive alternative to some of the more developed spots in the area. Situated at 4,500 feet elevation, the camp borders the banks of Daley Creek near the confluence of Beaver Dam and Daley Creek. Sites are scattered among old-growth Douglas and white fir, and the Beaver Dam Trail heads right out of camp, running along the creek. Fishing can be decent downstream from here.

RV sites, facilities: There are six sites for tents or RVs up to 18 feet long. Picnic tables and fire grills are provided. There is no drinking water, and garbage must be packed out. Some facilities are wheelchair accessible. Leashed pets are permitted.

Reservations, fees: Reservations are not accepted. Sites are $8 per night, $4 per night per additional vehicle. Open early May–mid-November, weather permitting.

Directions: In Ashland on I-5, take Exit 14 to Highway 66. Drive east for less than a mile to Dead Indian Memorial Road. Turn left (east) and drive 22 miles to Forest Road 37. Turn left (north) and drive 1.5 miles to the campground.

Contact: Rogue River National Forest, Ashland Ranger District, 541/552-2900, fax 541/552-2922, www.fs.fed.us.

224 BEAVER DAM

Scenic rating: 5

on Beaver Dam Creek in
Rogue River National Forest

Map grid B3

This campground sits at an elevation of 4,500 feet along Beaver Dam Creek. Look for beaver dams. There's not much screening between sites, but it's a pretty, rustic, and quiet spot, with unusual vegetation along the creek for botany fans. The trailhead for the Beaver Dam Trail is also here. The camp is adjacent to Daley Creek Campground.

RV sites, facilities: There are four sites for tents or RVs up to 16 feet long. Picnic tables and fire grills are provided. There is no drinking water, and garbage must be packed out. Leashed pets are permitted.

OREGON

Reservations, fees: Reservations are not accepted. Sites are $8 per night, $4 per night per additional vehicle. Open early May–early November, weather permitting.

Directions: In Medford on I-5, take Exit 14 to Highway 66. Drive east for less than a mile to Dead Indian Memorial Road. Turn left (east) and drive 22 miles to Forest Road 37. Turn left (north) and drive 1.5 miles to the campground.

Contact: Rogue River National Forest, Ashland Ranger District, 541/552-2900, fax 541/552-2922, www.fs.fed.us.

225 HOWARD PRAIRIE LAKE RESORT

Scenic rating: 7

on Howard Prairie Lake

Map grid B3

This wooded campground is located along the shore of Howard Prairie Lake, where boating, fishing, hiking, and swimming are among the recreation options. This is one of the largest campgrounds in over 100 miles.

RV sites, facilities: There are 150 sites with full or partial hookups for tents or RVs of any length and 20 furnished RV rentals. Some sites are pull-through. Picnic tables and fire rings are provided. Restrooms with flush toilets and showers, propane gas, a dump station, firewood, 24-hour security, a convenience store, café, coin laundry, boat docks, boat rentals, moorage, and launching facilities are available. Leashed pets are permitted.

Reservations, fees: Reservations are not accepted. Sites are $20–29 per night, plus $5 per person per night for more than two people. Some credit cards are accepted. Open mid-April–October.

Directions: In Ashland on I-5, take Exit 14 to Highway 66 and drive for less than a mile to Dead Indian Memorial Road. Turn left and drive 17 miles to Hyatt Prairie Road. Turn right and drive 3.5 miles to the resort.

Contact: Howard Prairie Lake Resort, 541/482-1979, fax 541/488-7485, www.howardprairie-resort.com.

226 HOWARD PRAIRIE LAKE: LILY GLEN

Scenic rating: 6

near Howard Prairie Lake

Map grid B3

Set along the shore of Howard Prairie Lake, this horse camp is a secluded, primitive getaway. Trout fishing is available. Tubb Springs Wayside State Park and the nearby Rogue River National Forest are possible side trips. There is also nearby access to the Pacific Crest Trail. The elevation is 4,500 feet.

RV sites, facilities: There are 26 sites for tents or self-contained RVs and two group sites for up to 75 people. Picnic tables and fire grills are provided. Drinking water, vault toilets, and corrals are available. Some facilities are wheelchair accessible. Leashed pets are permitted.

Reservations, fees: Reservations are accepted for group sites at 541/774-8183 but are not accepted for family sites. Sites are $16 per night, $6 per night per additional vehicle, $1 per pet per night, and $2 per horse per night for more than two horses; group sites are $75–150 per night. Some credit cards are accepted for reservations. Open mid-April–October, weather permitting.

Directions: In Ashland on I-5, take Exit 14 to Highway 66. Drive east for less than a mile to Dead Indian Memorial Road. Turn left (east) and drive 21 miles to the campground on the right.

Contact: Howard Prairie Lake Recreational Area, Jackson County Parks, 541/774-8183, fax 541/774-6320, www.jacksoncountyparks.com.

227 HOWARD PRAIRIE LAKE: GRIZZLY

Scenic rating: 7

near Howard Prairie Lake

Map grid B3

One of a series of four county campgrounds at Howard Prairie Lake, Grizzly features well-spaced campsites amid a forest and lake setting. The lake level is known to fluctuate; in low-water years, this camp is sometimes shut down. It gets moderate use. The elevation is 4,550 feet.

RV sites, facilities: There are 29 sites for tents or RVs (no hookups). Picnic tables and fire rings are provided. Drinking water, vault toilets, and garbage bins are available. A boat ramp is nearby. A store, café, laundry facilities, and boat rentals are available within two miles. Some facilities are wheelchair accessible. Leashed pets are permitted.

Reservations, fees: Reservations are not accepted. Sites are $14 per night, $6 per night per additional vehicle, and $1 per pet per night. Open mid-April–October, weather permitting.

Directions: In Ashland on I-5, take Exit 14 to Highway 66. Drive east for less than a mile to Dead Indian Memorial Road. Turn left (east) and drive 17 miles to Howard Prairie Road. Turn right (south) and drive eight miles to Howard Prairie Dam Road. Turn left (east) and drive 0.25 mile to the campground.

Contact: Howard Prairie Lake Recreational Area, Jackson County Parks, 541/774-8183, fax 541/774-6320, www.jacksoncountyparks.com.

228 HOWARD PRAIRIE LAKE: WILLOW POINT

Scenic rating: 7

near Howard Prairie Lake

Map grid B3

Willow Point is the most popular of the four county campgrounds on Howard Prairie Lake. Similar to Grizzly, it offers flat tent sites in an area well covered by trees. The lake is stocked with about 100,000 trout annually.

RV sites, facilities: There are 40 sites for tents or self-contained RVs. Picnic tables and fire rings are provided. Drinking water, vault toilets, and garbage bins are available. A boat ramp is nearby. A store, café, laundry facilities, and boat rentals are available within four miles. Some facilities are wheelchair accessible. Leashed pets are permitted.

Reservations, fees: No reservations are accepted. Sites are $16 per night, $6 per night per additional vehicle, and $1 per pet per night. Open mid-April–October.

Directions: In Ashland on I-5, take Exit 14 to Highway 66. Drive east for less than a mile to Dead Indian Memorial Road. Turn left (east) and drive 17 miles to Howard Prairie Road. Turn right (south) and drive three miles to the reservoir.

Contact: Howard Prairie Lake Recreational Area, Jackson County Parks, 541/774-8183, fax 541/774-6320, www.jacksoncountyparks. com.

229 HOWARD PRAIRIE LAKE: KLUM LANDING

Scenic rating: 7

near Howard Prairie Lake

Map grid B3

Klum Landing is one of four county campgrounds on Howard Prairie Lake. A bonus at this one is that coin-operated showers are available. Sugar Pine Group Camp is more primitive and is situated away from the lake.

RV sites, facilities: At Klum Landing, there are 32 sites for tents or self-contained RVs. Picnic tables and fire rings are provided. Drinking water, garbage bins, and restrooms with flush toilets and coin showers are available; some facilities are wheelchair accessible. Sugar Pine can accommodate up to 100 people in tents or self-contained RVs. Vault toilets are available, and the facilities are not wheelchair accessible. A boat ramp is nearby. A store, café, laundry facilities, and boat rentals are available at Howard Prairie Lake Resort. Leashed pets are permitted.

Reservations, fees: Reservations are not accepted for Klum Landing. Sites are $18 per night, $6 per night per additional vehicle, and $1 per pet per night. Reservations are accepted for Sugar Pine Group at 541/774-8183. The group camp is $150–200 per night. Open mid-April–October.

Directions: In Ashland on I-5, take Exit 14 to Highway 66. Drive east for less than a mile to

OREGON

Dead Indian Memorial Road. Turn left (east) and drive 17 miles to Howard Prairie Road. Turn right (south) and drive eight miles to Howard Prairie Dam Road. Turn left (east) and drive 0.25 mile to Sugar Pine Group Camp on the right. Continue 0.75 mile to reach Klum Landing.

Contact: Jackson County Parks, 541/774-8183, fax 541/774-6320, www.jacksoncountyparks. com.

230 EMIGRANT CAMPGROUND

Scenic rating: 8

on Emigrant Lake
Map grid B3

This camp is nestled among the trees above Emigrant Lake, a well-known recreational area. Activities at this park include boating, fishing, hiking, swimming, and waterskiing. There are also two 280-foot water slides. The park has its own swimming cove (unsupervised). Side-trip possibilities include exploring nearby Mount Ashland, where a ski area operates in the winter, as well as visiting Ashland's world-renowned Shakespeare Festival, the Britt Music Festival, and historic Jacksonville.

RV sites, facilities: There are 42 sites for tents or self-contained RVs, 32 sites for RVs of any length (50-amp full hookups), an overflow area, and one group camp area for up to 100 people. Restrooms with flush toilets, coin showers, a dump station, snacks in summer, and a barbecue are available. A group picnic and day-use area that can be reserved are also available. Recreational facilities include horseshoe pits, volleyball, and a playground. Two boat ramps are provided. Laundry and food are within six miles. Some facilities are wheelchair accessible. Leashed pets are permitted in designated areas only.

Reservations, fees: Reservations are accepted for RV sites and the group site at 541/774-8183. Tent sites are $18 per night, RV sites with full hookups are $26 per night, $6 per night per additional vehicle, and $1 per pet per night. The group site is $125–175 per night. Some credit cards are accepted for reservations. Open mid-March–mid-October, weather permitting.

Directions: From Ashland, drive east on Highway 66 for five miles to the campground on the left.

Contact: Jackson County Parks, 541/774-8183, fax 541/774-6320, www.jacksoncounty parks. com.

231 HYATT LAKE

Scenic rating: 8

on Hyatt Lake
Map grid B3

Hyatt Lake campground is situated on the south end of Hyatt Reservoir, which has six miles of shoreline. Fishing is good for brook and rainbow trout and smallmouth bass. The boat speed limit here is 10 mph. The Pacific Crest Trail runs next to the campground. Another campground option is Wildcat, about two miles north, with 12 semi-primitive sites.

RV sites, facilities: There are 54 sites for tents or RVs up to 40 feet long, five horse campsites, one group site for up to 50 people, and 12 walk-in tent sites. Picnic tables and fire grills are provided. Drinking water, restrooms with flush toilets and showers, garbage service, dump station, fish-cleaning station, group kitchen, day-use area, softball fields, volleyball, a playground, horseshoe pits, and two boat ramps are available. Some facilities are wheelchair accessible. Leashed pets are permitted.

Reservations, fees: Reservations are accepted only for the group camp or horse camp at 541/482-2031 or 541/618-2306. Sites are $12–15 per night, $3 per night per additional vehicle, with a 14-day stay limit. Campsites with horse facilities are $10 per night; the group site is $95 per night. Sites at nearby primitive Wildcat Campground are $7 per night. Pacific Crest Trail hikers pay $2 per person per night for camping. Open late April–October, weather permitting.

Directions: From Ashland, drive east on

Highway 66 for 17 miles to East Hyatt Lake Road. Turn north and drive three miles to the campground entrance on the left.

Contact: Bureau of Land Management, Ashland Resource Area, 541/618-2200, fax 541/618-2400, www.blm.gov.

232 TOPSY

Scenic rating: 7

on the Upper Klamath River

Map grid B3

This campground is on Boyle Reservoir near the Upper Klamath River, a good spot for trout fishing. Swimming is not recommended because of the murky water. This is a top river for rafters (experts only, or non-experts with professional, licensed guides). There are Class IV and V rapids about four miles southwest at Caldera, Hells Corner, and Satan's Gate. I flipped at Caldera and ended up swimming for it, finally getting out at an eddy. Luckily, I was wearing a dry suit and the best lifejacket available, perfect fitting, which saved my butt.

RV sites, facilities: There are 13 sites for RVs up to 40 feet long. Picnic tables and fire grills are provided. Drinking water, vault toilets, garbage service, and a dump station are available. Boat-launching facilities are nearby. A camp host is on-site in season. Some facilities are wheelchair accessible. Leashed pets are permitted.

Reservations, fees: Reservations are not accepted. Sites are $7 per night, $4 per night per additional vehicle, with a 14-day stay limit. Open mid-May–mid-September, weather permitting.

Directions: From Klamath Falls, drive west on Highway 66 for 20 miles to Topsy Road. Turn south on Topsy Road and drive 1.5 miles to the campground on the right.

Contact: Bureau of Land Management, Klamath Falls Resource Area, 541/883-6916, fax 541/884-2097, www.blm.gov.

233 HART-TISH RECREATION AREA WALK-IN

Scenic rating: 7

on Applegate Lake, Rogue River National Forest

Map grid B3

This concessionaire-managed campground on Applegate Lake has shaded sites and a great view of the lake. Bald eagles and osprey nest in the area, and it's a treat to watch them fish. A nearby boat launch and boat rentals are available. The walk-in sites are only 200 yards from the parking area.

RV sites, facilities: There are eight walk-in tent sites and eight parking-lot sites for RVs up to 45 feet long. Picnic tables and fire pits are provided. Drinking water, flush toilets, garbage bins, and firewood are available. A day-use area is nearby. A small general store and kayak and bicycle rentals are nearby. Some facilities are wheelchair accessible. Leashed pets are permitted.

Reservations, fees: Reservations are accepted at 877/444-6777 or www.recreation.gov ($10 reservation fee). Sites are $10 per night, $5 per night per additional vehicle. Open mid-April–September, weather permitting.

Directions: In Medford on I-5, take the Jacksonville exit to the Jacksonville Highway. Drive west on the Jacksonville Highway (Highway 238) for seven miles to Jacksonville. Bear left on Highway 238 and drive eight miles to the town of Ruch and Upper Applegate Road (County Road 10). Turn left (south) and drive 15.5 miles to the campground on the left.

Contact: Rogue River National Forest, Siskiyou Mountains District, 541/899-1812, fax 541/899-3888, www.fs.fed.us; concessionaire, 541/899-9220.

234 CARBERRY WALK-IN

Scenic rating: 5

near Applegate Reservoir in Rogue River National Forest

Map grid B3

You'll find recreational opportunities aplenty, including boating, fishing, hiking, mountain

OREGON

biking, and swimming, at this campground on Cougar Creek near the southwest shore of Applegate Reservoir. Dense forest covers the campsites, providing much-needed shade. This camp is similar to Watkins Walk-in.

RV sites, facilities: There are 11 walk-in sites for tents and three spaces in the parking lot for RVs up to 25 feet long. Picnic tables and fire grills are provided. Vault toilets and drinking water are available. A general store, firewood, boat docks, and launching facilities are within two miles. Some facilities are wheelchair accessible. Leashed pets are permitted.

Reservations, fees: Reservations are not accepted. Sites are $10 per night, $5 per night per additional vehicle. Open late May–early September, weather permitting.

Directions: In Medford on I-5, take the Jacksonville exit to the Jacksonville Highway. Drive west on the Jacksonville Highway (Highway 238) for seven miles to Jacksonville. Bear left on Highway 238 and drive eight miles to the town of Ruch and Upper Applegate Road (County Road 10). Turn left (south) and drive 18 miles to the campground parking area. A short walk is required.

Contact: Rogue River National Forest, Siskiyou Mountains District, 541/899-1812, fax 541/899-3888, www.fs.fed.us; concessionaire, 541/899-9220.

235 MOUNT ASHLAND

Scenic rating: 8

on the Pacific Crest Trail in
Klamath National Forest

Map grid B3

Set at 6,600 feet elevation along the Pacific Crest Trail, this beautiful camp is heavily wooded and has abundant wildlife. On a clear day, enjoy great lookouts from nearby Siskiyou Peak, particularly to the south, where California's 14,162-foot Mount Shasta is an awesome sight. Mount Ashland Ski Resort is one mile east of the campground.

RV sites, facilities: There are nine sites for tents

or RVs up to 15 feet long, with extremely limited space for RVs. Picnic tables and fire grills are provided. Vault toilets are available. There is no drinking water. Garbage must be packed out. Leashed pets are permitted.

Reservations, fees: Reservations are not accepted. There is no fee for camping but donations are accepted. Open May–late October, weather permitting.

Directions: From Ashland, drive south on I-5 for 12 miles to Mount Ashland Ski Park Road (County Road 993). Turn west and drive 10 miles (the road becomes Forest Road 20) to the campground.

Contact: Klamath National Forest, Happy Camp/Oak Knoll Ranger District, 530/493-2243, fax 530/493-1796, www.fs.fed.us.

236 JACKSON F. KIMBALL STATE PARK

Scenic rating: 7

on the Wood River

Map grid C3

This primitive state campground at the headwaters of the Wood River is another nice spot just far enough off the main drag to remain a secret. A trail from camp leads to a nearby spring. Fishing from canoe is good on the Wood River.

RV sites, facilities: There are 10 primitive sites for tents or self-contained RVs up to 45 feet long. Picnic tables, fire grills, and garbage bins are provided. Vault toilets are available. There is no drinking water. Leashed pets are permitted.

Reservations, fees: Reservations are not accepted. Sites are $6–10 per night, $5 per night per additional vehicle. Open year-round, weather permitting.

Directions: From Klamath Falls, drive north on U.S. 97 for 21 miles to Highway 62. Turn left (northwest) on Highway 62 and drive 10 miles to Highway 232/Sun Pass Road (near Fort Klamath). Turn right (north) and drive three miles to the campground.

Contact: Collier Memorial State Park, 541/783-

2471 or 800/551-6949, www.oregonstateparks. org. (Jackson F. Kimball is managed by Collier Memorial State Park.)

237 CRATER LAKE RESORT

Scenic rating: 6

on the Wood River

Map grid C3   **BEST**

The campground at Crater Lake Resort is dotted with huge pine trees on the banks of the beautiful, crystal-clear Fort Creek. It's located just outside Fort Klamath, the site of numerous military campaigns against the Modoc people in the late 1800s.

RV sites, facilities: There are 14 sites with full or partial hookups for RVs of any length, six tent sites, nine cabins, and one log cabin. Drinking water, picnic tables, and fire rings are provided. Restrooms with flush toilets and showers, modem access, a recreation hall, and coin laundry are available. Propane gas, a store, café, and ice are within one mile. Leashed pets are permitted.

Reservations, fees: Reservations are accepted. RV sites are $25 per night, $2 per person per night for more than two people, and $2 per pet per night. Tent sites are $5 per person per night. Some credit cards are accepted. Open mid-April–mid-October.

Directions: From Klamath Falls, drive north on U.S. 97 for 21 miles to Highway 62. Bear left on Highway 62 and drive 12.5 miles north to the resort (just before reaching Fort Klamath).

Contact: Crater Lake Resort, 541/381-2349, www.craterlakeresort.com.

238 COLLIER MEMORIAL STATE PARK

Scenic rating: 7

on the Williamson River

Map grid C3

This campground sits at the confluence of Spring Creek and the Williamson River, both of which are superior trout streams. An area for equestrian campers is situated at a trailhead for horses. A nature trail is also available. The park features a pioneer village and a logging museum. Movies about old-time logging and other activities are shown on weekend nights during the summer.

RV sites, facilities: There are 18 sites for tents or self-contained RVs up to 50 feet long (no hookups), 50 sites for tents or RVs of any length (full hookups), and an area for up to four groups of equestrian campers. Some sites are pull-through. Picnic tables, fire grills, garbage bins, and drinking water are provided. Restrooms with flush toilets and showers, a dump station, firewood, coin laundry, playground, and day-use hitching area are available. Some facilities are wheelchair accessible. Leashed pets are permitted.

Reservations, fees: Reservations are not accepted. Tent sites are $11–18 per night, RV sites are $13–21 per night, $5 per night per additional vehicle. The equestrian area is $12–18 per night and $1.50 per night per horse. Some credit cards are accepted. Open year-round, weather permitting.

Directions: From Klamath Falls, drive north on U.S. 97 for 28 miles to the park (well signed).

Contact: Collier Memorial State Park, 541/783-2471 or 800/551-6949, www.oregonstateparks. org.

239 WILLIAMSON RIVER

Scenic rating: 6

near Collier Memorial State Park in Winema National Forest

Map grid C3

Another great little spot is discovered, this one at 4,200 feet elevation, with excellent trout fishing along the banks of the Williamson River, a world-famous fly-fishing river. Mosquitoes are numerous in spring and early summer, which can drive people away. A map of Winema National Forest details the back roads and trails.

Collier Memorial State Park provides a nearby side-trip option.

RV sites, facilities: There are 10 sites for tents or RVs up to 30 feet long. Picnic tables, garbage bins, and fire grills are provided. Drinking water and vault toilets are available. A restaurant is within five miles. Some facilities are wheelchair accessible. Leashed pets are permitted.

Reservations, fees: Reservations are not accepted. Sites are $8 per night, $2 per night per additional vehicle. Open late April–late November, weather permitting.

Directions: From Klamath Falls, drive north on U.S. 97 for 30 miles to Chiloquin. Continue north on U.S. 97 for 5.5 miles to Forest Road 9730. Turn right (northeast) and drive one mile to the campground.

Contact: Fremont-Winema National Forests, Klamath Ranger District, 541/885-3400, fax 541/885-3452, www.fs.fed.us.

240 POTTER'S PARK

Scenic rating: 6

on the Sprague River

Map grid C3

This park on a bluff overlooking the Sprague River is in a wooded setting and bordered by the Winema National Forest. Canoeing and rafting are options here. For the most part, the area east of Klamath Lake doesn't get much attention.

RV sites, facilities: There are 17 tent sites and 22 sites with full hookups for RVs of any length. Drinking water, picnic tables, and fire pits are provided. Restrooms with flush toilets and showers, firewood, a convenience store, coin laundry, pay telephone, and ice are available. Leashed pets are permitted.

Reservations, fees: Reservations are accepted. Sites are $15 per night, plus $2.50 per person per night for more than one adult. Monthly

rates are available for RV sites. Open year-round, with limited winter facilities.

Directions: From Klamath Falls, drive north on U.S. 97 for 27 miles to Chiloquin and Sprague River Highway. Turn right (east) on Sprague River Highway and drive 12 miles to the park on the right.

Contact: Potter's Park, 541/783-2253.

241 WALT'S RV PARK

Scenic rating: 7

on the Williamson River

Map grid C3

This heavily treed campground, across the highway from the Williamson River near Collier Memorial State Park, is one of three camps in the immediate area. The Williamson River has excellent trout fishing. For those looking for a more remote setting, head east to Potter's Park.

RV sites, facilities: There are 20 tent sites and 16 sites with full or partial hookups for RVs up to 40 feet long; some are pull-through sites. Drinking water, picnic tables, and fire pits are provided. Restrooms with flush toilets and showers, firewood, coin laundry, and ice are available. A café is within 0.25 mile, and there is a store in Chiloquin. Leashed pets are permitted.

Reservations, fees: Reservations are accepted. Sites are $13.75–17.75 per night, $1 per person per night for more than two people, and $1 per night for air-conditioning. Open year-round, weather permitting.

Directions: From Klamath Falls, drive north on U.S. 97 for 24 miles to Chiloquin Junction. Continue north for 0.25 mile to the campground (adjacent to the Chiloquin Ranger Station) on the left.

Contact: Walt's RV Park, 541/783-2537, www.waltsrvpark.com.

242 AGENCY LAKE RESORT

Scenic rating: 5

on Agency Lake
Map grid C3

This campground sits along Agency Lake in an open, grassy area with some shaded sites. The resort has more than 700 feet of lakefront property, offering world-class trout fishing. Look across the lake and watch the sun set on the Cascades. Note that some sites are filled with monthly renters.

RV sites, facilities: There are 15 tent sites and 25 sites with full or partial hookups for tents or RVs of any length, three cabins, and one rental trailer. Drinking water and picnic tables are provided. Restrooms with flush toilets and showers, a general store, ice, boat docks, launching facilities, and marine gas are available. Leashed pets are permitted.

Reservations, fees: Reservations are accepted. RV sites are $16–20 per night; tent sites are $12–13 per night. Some credit cards are accepted. Open year-round, weather permitting.

Directions: From Klamath Falls, drive north on U.S. 97 for 17 miles to Modoc Point Road. Turn left and drive about 10 miles to the resort on the left.

Contact: Agency Lake Resort, 541/783-2489, www.agencylakeresort.net.

OREGON

SOUTHEASTERN OREGON

◖ BEST RV PARKS AND CAMPGROUNDS

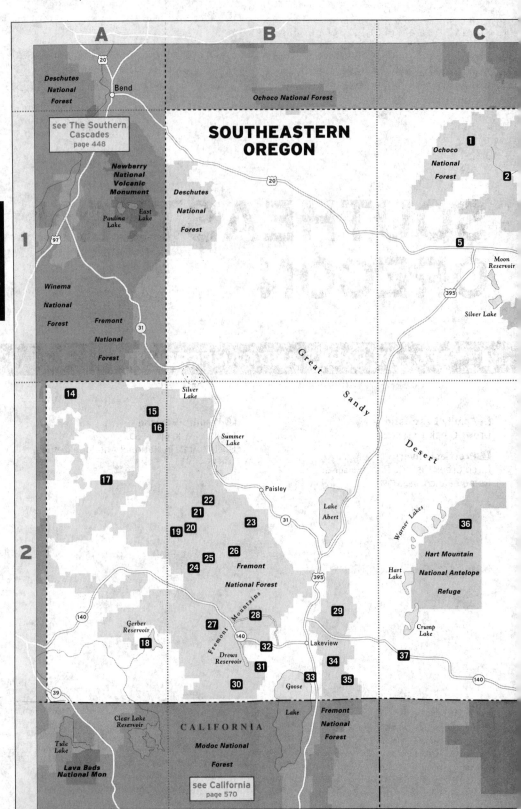

OREGON

A   B   C

20
Deschutes
National
Forest
Bend

Ochoco National Forest

see The Southern
Cascades
page 448

SOUTHEASTERN
OREGON

Ochoco
National
Forest

1

Newberry
National
Volcanic
Monument

Deschutes
National
Forest

20

2

97

Paulina
Lake

East
Lake

5

1

Moon
Reservoir

395

Winema

National

Forest

Silver Lake

Fremont

31

National

Forest

Great

Sandy

14

Silver
Lake

Desert

15
16

Summer
Lake

Paisley

17

22
21

Lake
Abert

Warner
Lakes

36

19
20

23

31

2

26

Hart Mountain

24
25

Fremont

395

Hart
Lake

National Antelope

Refuge

National Forest

Fremont
Mountains

28

29

Crump
Lake

Gerber
Reservoir

27

140

18

32

Lakeview

37

140

31

34

39

30

Drews
Reservoir

33

Goose

35

Clear Lake
Reservoir

CALIFORNIA

Lake

Fremont

Tule
Lake

Modac National

National

Forest

Forest

Lava Beds
National Mon

see California
page 570

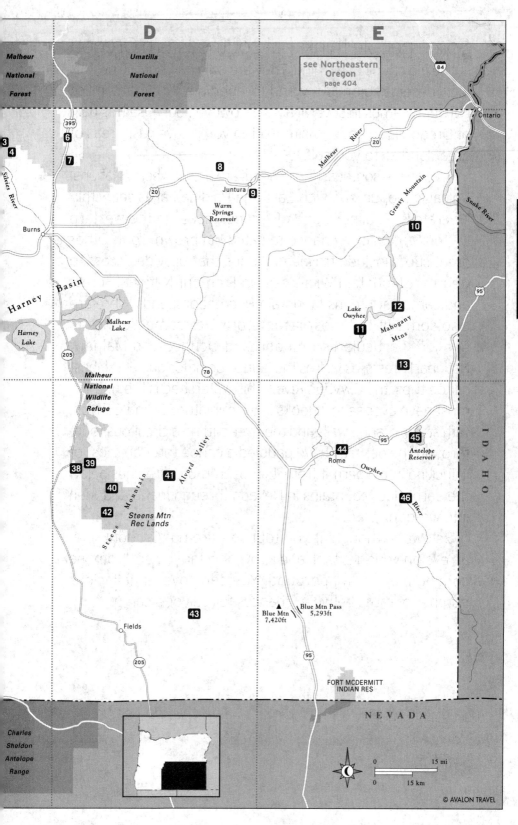

Malheur National Forest

Umatilla National Forest

see Northeastern Oregon page 404

84

Ontario

395

6

7

3

4

Silvies River

8

20

Juntura

9

Warm Springs Reservoir

Malheur River

20

Grassy Mountain

10

Snake River

Burns

95

Harney Basin

Malheur Lake

Harney Lake

205

Lake Owyhee

12

11

Mahogany Mtns

13

78

IDAHO

Malheur National Wildlife Refuge

Alvord Valley

45

44

Rome

Antelope Reservoir

Steens Mountain

38 39

40

41

42

Steens Mtn Rec Lands

95

Owyhee River

46

43

Blue Mtn 7,420ft

Blue Mtn Pass 5,293ft

Fields

205

95

FORT MCDERMITT INDIAN RES

NEVADA

Charles Sheldon Antelope Range

0   15 mi

0   15 km

OREGON

© AVALON TRAVEL

Some people think that southeastern Oregon is one big chunk of nothing. They are only half right. True, this high-desert region is dry and foreboding, with many miles between camps in several areas. However, because this part of Oregon is so under-visited, often you'll have vast areas of great land all to yourself.

Among the southeast's highlights are the Newberry National Volcanic Monument, with East and Paulina Lakes set within its craters; Paulina is one of the best lakes in the western United States for a chance to catch big brown trout. Other great spots include trailhead camps that provide access to Gearhart Mountain Wilderness in Fremont National Forest and camps at Steens Mountain Recreation Lands. Here are also some of the most remote drive-to campgrounds in Oregon, particularly in underused Ochoco and Malheur National Forests, as well as the launch point for one of the best canoe trips, the Owyhee River. This watershed is like nothing most have ever seen. It looks like a miniature Grand Canyon, with steep, orange walls and the river cutting a circuitous route through the desert. I have paddled a canoe through most of it, lucking into a permit from its most remote stretches below the Jarbridge Mountains in Nevada through Idaho and then into Oregon.

Be aware, though, if you tour this area of Oregon; keep an eye on your gas tank and know how far you are from the coming night's campground. You can cover a hellacious number of miles between chances for gas or a camp.

1 DELINTMENT LAKE

Scenic rating: 7

on Delintment Lake in Malheur National Forest

Map grid C1

This very pretty, forested camp skirts the shore of Delintment Lake. Originally a beaver pond, the lake was gradually developed to its current size of 62 acres. It is now pretty and blue and is stocked with trout, providing good bank and boat fishing. Note that electric motors only are allowed on the lake. Insider's note: Rainbow trout here average 12–18 inches.

RV sites, facilities: There are 29 sites for tents or RVs up to 30 feet long. Picnic tables and fire grills are provided. Drinking water, vault toilets, garbage service, a group picnic area, and boat-launching facilities are available. Some facilities are wheelchair accessible. Leashed pets are permitted.

Reservations, fees: Reservations are not accepted. Sites are $10 per night, $5 per night for an additional vehicle. Open May–October, weather permitting.

Directions: From Burns, drive southwest on U.S. 20 for three miles to County Road 127. Turn right (northwest) and drive 11 miles to Forest Road 41. Turn left on Forest Road 41 and drive about 26.5 miles (staying on Forest Road 41 at all junctions, paved all the way) to the campground at the lake.

Contact: Malheur National Forest, Emigrant Creek Ranger District, 541/573-4300, fax 541/573-4398, www.fs.fed.us.

2 EMIGRANT

Scenic rating: 4

near Emigrant Creek in Malheur National Forest

Map grid C1

One of two camps in the immediate area, Emigrant is set at an elevation of 5,200 feet in Malheur National Forest, in a meadow near Emigrant Creek. You'll get peace and quiet here, because this spot is usually not crowded. There's good fly-fishing in the spring and early summer,

and several nearby backcountry dirt roads are fun for mountain biking. Falls camp, two miles away, is busier but has drinking water.

RV sites, facilities: There are seven sites for tents or RVs up to 28 feet long. Picnic tables and fire grills are provided. Vault toilets and garbage service are available. There is no drinking water (but drinking water is available nearby at Falls campground). Some facilities are wheelchair accessible. Leashed pets are permitted.

Reservations, fees: Reservations are not accepted. Sites are $8 per night, $4 per night for an additional vehicle. Open May–October, weather permitting.

Directions: From Burns, drive southwest on U.S. 20 for three miles to County Road 127. Turn right (northwest) and drive 25 miles (passing Forest Road 41 on the left) to Forest Road 43 and the junction for Allison Guard Station, Delintment Lake, and Paulina. Turn left on Forest Road 43 and drive 9.75 miles to Forest Road 4340. Turn left and drive on Forest Road 4340-050 to the campground.

Contact: Malheur National Forest, Emigrant Creek Ranger District, 541/573-4300, fax 541/573-4398, www.fs.fed.us.

3 YELLOWJACKET

Scenic rating: 8

on Yellowjacket Lake in Malheur National Forest

Map grid C1

This quiet and crowd-free campground is set at an elevation of 4,800 feet in the ponderosa pines along the shore of Yellowjacket Lake. Fishing for rainbow trout can be very good in the summer; boats without motors are allowed.

RV sites, facilities: There are 20 sites for tents or RVs up to 22 feet long. Picnic tables are provided. Drinking water, vault toilets, and garbage service are available. A boat launch is nearby. Leashed pets are permitted.

Reservations, fees: Reservations are not accepted. Sites are $10 per night, $5 per night for an additional vehicle. Open late May–October, weather permitting.

OREGON

Directions: From Burns, drive southwest on U.S. 20 for three miles to County Road 127. Turn right (northwest) and drive 32 miles to Forest Road 47. Turn right and drive three miles to Forest Road 3745. Turn right and drive one mile to the campground on the right.

Contact: Malheur National Forest, Emigrant Creek Ranger District, 541/573-4300, fax 541/573-4398, www.fs.fed.us.

4 FALLS

Scenic rating: 5

near Emigrant Creek in Malheur National Forest
Map grid C1

Falls camp is set in a beautiful meadow next to Emigrant Creek and is surrounded by ponderosa pine forests. This is a great place to see wildflowers in the early summer. A short trail leads to a small waterfall on the creek, which gives the camp its name. Fly-fishing and mountain biking are good here, as well as at nearby Emigrant, located two miles down the road. The elevation is 5,200 feet.

RV sites, facilities: There are six sites for tents or RVs up to 28 feet long. Picnic tables and fire grills are provided. Drinking water, vault toilets, and garbage service are available. Some facilities are wheelchair accessible. Leashed pets are permitted.

Reservations, fees: Reservations are not accepted. Sites are $8 per night, $4 per night for an additional vehicle, except for towed vehicles. Open May–October, weather permitting.

Directions: From Burns, drive southwest on U.S. 20 for three miles to County Road 127. Turn right (northwest) and drive 25 miles (passing Forest Road 41 on the left) to Forest Road 43 and the junction for Allison Guard Station, Delintment Lake, and Paulina. Turn left on Forest Road 43 and drive eight miles to the campground on the left.

Contact: Malheur National Forest, Emigrant Creek Ranger District, 541/573-4300, fax 541/573-4398, www.fs.fed.us.

5 CHICKAHOMINY RESERVOIR

Scenic rating: 4

on Chickahominy Reservoir
Map grid C1

While a good spot for group camping, this camp is located in the high desert with no shade. Weather conditions can be extreme, so come prepared. The camp is used primarily as an overnight stop for travelers driving through the area. Boats with motors are allowed on the reservoir. There is an access road on the northwest side of the reservoir for day use. The nearest services are five miles east (via U.S. 20) in Riley.

RV sites, facilities: There are 28 sites for tents or RVs up to 35 feet long. Picnic tables, garbage bins, and fire grills are provided. Drinking water (summer season only, subject to fluctuations) and vault toilets are available. A fish-cleaning station is available nearby. Some facilities are wheelchair accessible. Leashed pets are permitted.

Reservations, fees: Reservations are not accepted. Sites are $8 per night per vehicle, with a stay limit of 14 days. Open year-round, with limited winter facilities.

Directions: From Burns, drive west on U.S. 20 for 30 miles to the campground on the right.

Contact: Bureau of Land Management, Burns District, 541/573-4400, fax 541/573-4411, www.blm.gov.

6 JOAQUIN MILLER HORSE CAMP

Scenic rating: 5

in Malheur National Forest
Map grid D1

Set among mature ponderosa pines and adjacent to a meadow, campsites here are spread out, and there's a fair amount of privacy at this camp. It does receive some highway noise, though. Lots of old logging roads are available for biking, horseback riding, and walking. The camp gets low use, and while it caters to horse campers, all are welcome. Campers with horses are strongly advised to arrive early, before the weekend, to claim the campsites nearest to the corrals.

RV sites, facilities: There are 12 sites for tents or RVs up to 28 feet long. Picnic tables and fire rings are provided. Drinking water, vault toilets, and garbage service are available. Stock facilities include four corrals and hitching rails. Leashed pets are permitted.

Reservations, fees: Reservations are not accepted. Sites are $8 per night, $4 per night per additional vehicle. Open mid-May–November, weather permitting.

Directions: From Burns, drive north on U.S. 395 for 19 miles to the campground on the left (this turnoff is easy to miss; watch for a very small green sign on the right that says Joaquin Miller Horse Camp).

Contact: Malheur National Forest, Emigrant Creek Ranger District, 541/573-4300, fax 541/573-4398, www.fs.fed.us.

7 IDLEWILD

Scenic rating: 8

in Devine Canyon in Malheur National Forest

Map grid D1

This campground sits at an elevation of 5,300 feet in Devine Canyon, a designated winter Sno-Park that's popular with locals for snowmobiling and cross-country skiing. Several hiking and biking trailheads start here, including the Divine Summit Interpretive Loop Trail and the Idlewild Loop Trail. Since it provides easy access and a pretty setting, it's also a popular spot for visitors traveling up U.S. 395 and in need of a stopover. Bird-watching for white-headed woodpeckers and goshawks is popular. Expect to hear some highway noise. But the ponderosa pine forest and area trails are so beautiful that this area can feel divine, even if Devine Canyon and neighboring Devine Ridge were named back in the good old days when nobody worried about spelling.

RV sites, facilities: There are 26 sites for tents and five sites for RVs up to 28 feet long. Picnic tables and fire grills are provided. Drinking water, vault toilets, picnic areas, and garbage

service are available. A group shelter can be reserved. Some facilities are wheelchair accessible. Leashed pets are permitted.

Reservations, fees: Reservations are not accepted. Sites are $10 per night, $5 per night for an additional vehicle, except for towed vehicles. Open late May–mid-October, weather permitting.

Directions: From Burns, drive north on U.S. 395 for 17 miles to the campground on the right.

Contact: Malheur National Forest, Emigrant Creek Ranger District, 541/573-4300, fax 541/573-4398, www.fs.fed.us.

8 CHUKAR PARK

Scenic rating: 7

on the north fork of the Malheur River

Map grid D1   BEST (

Chukar Park campground hugs the banks of the north fork of the Malheur River. The general area provides habitat for chukar, an upland game bird species. Hunting can be good in season during the fall but requires much hiking in rugged terrain. Trout fishing is also popular here. BLM asks that visitors please respect the surrounding private property.

RV sites, facilities: There are 18 sites for tents or RVs up to 28 feet long. Picnic tables, fire grills, and garbage service are provided. Drinking water (May–October only) and vault toilets are available. Firewood is not available. Leashed pets are permitted.

Reservations, fees: Reservations are not accepted. Sites are $5 per night per vehicle, with a 14-day stay limit. Open year-round, with limited winter facilities.

Directions: From Burns, drive north on U.S. 395 for three miles to U.S. 20. Take U.S. 20 east and drive 55 miles to Juntura and Beulah Reservoir Road. Turn northwest and drive six miles to the campground.

Contact: Bureau of Land Management, Vale District, 541/473-3144, fax 541/473-6213, www.blm.gov/or.

OREGON

OREGON

9 OASIS MOTEL & RV PARK

Scenic rating: 6

in Juntura

Map grid D1

One of the only camps in the area, this well-maintained RV park is close to Chukar Park. The general area provides habitat for chukar, an upland game bird species. Hunting during the fall and trout fishing are recreation opportunities here.

RV sites, facilities: There are 22 sites with full hookups for RVs of any length, two cabins, and seven motel rooms. Some sites are pull-through. Picnic tables are provided. Restrooms with flush toilets and showers, a café, and ice are available. Leashed pets are permitted.

Reservations, fees: Reservations are not accepted. Sites are $17 per night and $6 per night per pet. Some credit cards are accepted. Open year-round.

Directions: From Burns, drive north on U.S. 395 for three miles to U.S. 20. Turn east and drive 55 miles to Juntura (a very small town). The park is on the left along U.S. 20.

Contact: Oasis Motel & RV Park, 541/277-3605, fax 541/277-3434.

10 LAKE OWYHEE STATE PARK

Scenic rating: 7

on Owyhee Lake

Map grid E1

There are two campgrounds here: McCormack and Indian Creek, which are located 1.5 miles apart. This state park is situated along the shore of 53-mile-long Owyhee Lake, a good lake for waterskiing in the day and fishing for warm-water species in the morning and evening. Owyhee is famous for its superb bass fishing; the place even has floating restrooms. Other highlights include views of unusual geological formations and huge rock pinnacles. Bighorn sheep, coyotes, golden eagles, mountain lions, mule deer, pronghorn antelope, and wild horses live in the area.

RV sites, facilities: McCormack has 31 sites with partial hookups for tents and RVs of any length, eight tent sites, and two tepees. Indian Creek has 26 sites with partial hookups for tents or RVs up to 50 feet long and nine tent sites. Drinking water, picnic tables, and fire grills are provided. Vault toilets, garbage bins, firewood, a dump station, and a picnic area are available. Restrooms with flush toilets and showers are available at McCormack. Boat docks, launching facilities, fuel, and ice are available at the park. Marine fuel is available at Indian Creek. Some facilities are wheelchair accessible. Leashed pets are permitted.

Reservations, fees: Reservations are accepted at 800/452-5687 or www.reserveamerica.com ($8 reservation fee). RV sites are $12–20 per night, tent sites are $12–17 per night, tepees are $27–36 per night, and $5 per night for an additional vehicle. Some credit cards are accepted. Open April–October.

Directions: From Ontario (near the Oregon/Idaho border), drive south on U.S. 20/26 for six miles to the Nyssa exit. Turn south and drive eight miles to Nyssa and Highway 201. Turn left (southeast) on Highway 201 and drive eight miles to Owyhee. Turn east and drive about 20 miles to road's end and the entrance to the park, approximately 33 miles from Nyssa.

Contact: Lake Owyhee State Park, 541/339-2331 or 800/551-6949, www.oregonstateparks.org.

11 COW LAKES

Scenic rating: 6

near Cow Lakes

Map grid E1

Cow Lakes is a little-used campground adjacent to an old lava flow. The lake is shallow and murky, which makes fishing popular here. The campsites are open and treeless, and the road is rutted and rough in places.

RV sites, facilities: There are 10 sites for tents or small RVs. Picnic tables and fire rings are provided. A vault toilet and a primitive boat ramp are available. No drinking water or firewood is available, and garbage must be packed out. Leashed pets are permitted.

Reservations, fees: Reservations are not accepted. There is no fee for camping. Open year-round, weather permitting.

Directions: From Burns Junction, drive east on U.S. 95 for 30 miles to Danner Loop Road. Turn left (north) and drive 14 miles (past Danner) to Cow Lakes and the campground.

Contact: Bureau of Land Management, Vale District, 541/473-3144, fax 541/473-6213, www.blm.gov.

12 LESLIE GULCH

Scenic rating: 6

on Owyhee Lake

Map grid E1

This campground sits on the eastern shore of Owyhee Lake, about 20 miles from the Oregon/Idaho border. Hiking, warm-water fishing, and waterskiing are among the recreation options in this high-desert area. Lake Owyhee State Park provides the other developed recreation destination on the lake.

RV sites, facilities: There are 12 sites for tents or RVs up to 20 feet long. Picnic tables and garbage service are provided. Vault toilets are available. There is no drinking water. Boat-launching facilities (for boats less than 17 feet long) are available on-site. Leashed pets are permitted.

Reservations, fees: Reservations are not accepted. There is no fee for camping. Open mid-March–mid-November.

Directions: From U.S. 95 where it crosses the Idaho/Oregon border, drive north for five miles to McBride Creek Road. Turn west and drive 10 miles to Leslie Gulch Road. Turn left (west) and drive 15 miles to the campground.

Contact: Bureau of Land Management, Vale District, 541/473-3144, fax 541/473-6213, www.blm.gov.

13 BIRCH CREEK HISTORIC RANCH

Scenic rating: 9

near the Owyhee River

Map grid E1   BEST

This is one of the most remote campgrounds in Oregon. When I stayed here, it was known as "Hole in the Ground." The official name, Birch Creek Ranch, is the collective name for two ranches founded about 100 years ago. The remote setting is an oasis in the arid, scenic Owyhee River Canyon, its green fields contrasting strongly with the sun-drenched cream- and chocolate-colored formations and the red and black volcanic rocks that soar up from the edges of its narrow meadows. This section of the Owyhee River holds Class III, IV, and V+ rapids. Hiking options include the Jordan Crater, a 4,000-year-old caldera offering domes, kipukas, lava tubes, trenches, and more. The Owyhee Canyon rim looks like a miniature Grand Canyon. This camp/ranch's stone walls, water wheel, and barn contribute to its inclusion on the National Register of Historic Places. I canoed nearly the entire length of the Owhyee, from the headwaters below the Jarbridge Mountains in Nevada, through Idaho and into Oregon.

RV sites, facilities: There are five sites for tents or small RVs. Picnic tables and fire rings are provided. A vault toilet is available. There is no drinking water, and garbage must be packed out. A camp host is on-site. There is access to the Owyhee River by reservation for non-motorized boats only. Leashed pets are permitted.

Reservations, fees: Reservations are not accepted. There is no fee for camping. Open mid-March–mid-October, weather permitting.

Directions: From Jordan Valley, take U.S. 95 north for 10 miles to Cow Creek Road at the Jordan Craters sign. Turn left (west) on Cow Creek Road and follow BLM Owyhee River access signs 28 miles to campground. High-clearance 4WD vehicles recommended. Road may be impassable when wet.

OREGON

Contact: Bureau of Land Management, Vale District, 541/473-3144, fax 541/473-6213, www.blm.gov.

14 JACKSON CREEK

Scenic rating: 8

on Jackson Creek in the Winema National Forest
Map grid A2

Jackson Creek is a remote campground in a beautiful stand of old-growth ponderosa pine at an elevation of 4,600 feet. Horseback riding and mountain biking are popular. Wildlife-viewing can be outstanding some years. Note that there are many mosquitoes in spring and early summer, so bring repellent.

RV sites, facilities: There are 12 sites for tents or RVs up to 25 feet long. Picnic tables and fire grills are provided. Vault toilets are available. There is no drinking water. Garbage must be packed out. Leashed pets are permitted.

Reservations, fees: Reservations are not accepted. There is no fee. Open year-round, weather permitting.

Directions: From Chemult and Highway 97, drive south for 25 miles to Silver Lake Road (County Road 676). Turn left (northeast) and drive 22 miles to Forest Road 49. Turn right (southeast) and drive five miles to the camp.

Contact: Fremont-Winema National Forests, Chemult Ranger District, 541/365-7001, fax 541/365-7019, www.fs.fed.us.

15 THOMPSON RESERVOIR

Scenic rating: 3

on Thompson Reservoir in Fremont National Forest
Map grid A2

Located on the north shore of Thompson Reservoir among black-bark ponderosa pines the height of telephone poles, this simple and pretty camp features shaded sites close to the water. The area is popular for fishing and boating. Water in the reservoir fluctuates and sometimes nearly dries up altogether in late summer.

RV sites, facilities: There are 19 sites for tents or RVs up to 22 feet long, plus a separate group camping area. Picnic tables and fire grills are provided. Drinking water, garbage bins, and vault toilets are available. Boat-launching facilities are nearby. Leashed pets are permitted.

Reservations, fees: Reservations are not accepted. Sites are $6 per night, $2 per night per additional vehicle. Open May–mid-November, weather permitting.

Directions: From Bend, drive south on U.S. 97 for 32 miles to Highway 31. Turn southeast on Highway 31 and drive 48 miles to County Road 4-11 (one mile west of the town of Silver Lake). Turn right and drive six miles (the road becomes Forest Road 27) and continue south for nine miles to the campground entrance road. Turn left and drive one mile to the camp.

Contact: Fremont-Winema National Forests, Silver Lake Ranger District, 541/576-2107, fax 541/576-2450, www.fs.fed.us.

16 EAST BAY

Scenic rating: 3

on Thompson Reservoir in Fremont National Forest
Map grid A2

This campground on the east shore of Thompson Reservoir has paved roads, but it's still a long way from home, so be sure to bring all of your supplies with you. A day-use area is adjacent to the camp. Nearby Silver Creek Marsh Campground provides an even more primitive setting along a stream.

RV sites, facilities: There are 17 sites for tents or RVs up to 50 feet long. Picnic tables and fire grills are provided. Drinking water, garbage bins, vault toilets, and a fishing pier are available. Boat-launching facilities are nearby. Some facilities are wheelchair accessible. Leashed pets are permitted.

Reservations, fees: Reservations are not accepted. Sites are $10 per night, $4 per night per extra vehicle. Open May–mid-November, weather permitting.

Directions: From Bend, drive south on U.S. 97

for 32 miles to Highway 31. Turn southeast on Highway 31 and drive 49 miles to Silver Lake. Continue east a short distance on Highway 31 to Forest Road 28. Turn right on Forest Road 28 and drive 13 miles to Forest Road 014. Turn right on Forest Road 014 and drive two miles to the campground.

Contact: Fremont-Winema National Forests, Silver Lake Ranger District, 541/576-2107, fax 541/576-2450, www.fs.fed.us.

17 HEAD OF THE RIVER

Scenic rating: 8

on the Williamson River in Winema National Forest

Map grid A2

Almost nobody knows about this small, extremely remote spot on the edge of a meadow in the lodgepole and ponderosa pines, though hunters use it in the fall. The only camp for miles around, it's set at 4,500 feet elevation along the Williamson River headwaters, where you can actually see the beginning of the river bubbling up from underground springs.

RV sites, facilities: There are five sites for tents or RVs up to 30 feet long. Picnic tables, garbage bins, and fire pits are provided. Vault toilets are available. There is no drinking water. Leashed pets are permitted.

Reservations, fees: Reservations are not accepted. There is no fee for camping. Open Memorial Day weekend–late November, weather permitting.

Directions: From Klamath Falls, drive north on U.S. 97 for 30 miles to Chiloquin and Sprague River Highway. Turn right (east) on Sprague River Highway and drive five miles to Williamson River Road. Turn left (northeast) and drive 20 miles to Forest Road 4648. Turn left (north) on Forest Road 4648 and drive 0.5 mile to the campground.

Contact: Fremont-Winema National Forests, Klamath Ranger District, 541/885-3400, fax 541/885-3452, www.fs.fed.us.

18 GERBER RESERVOIR

Scenic rating: 6

on Gerber Reservoir

Map grid A2

This camp can be found at an elevation of 4,800 feet alongside the west shore of Gerber Reservoir. Off the beaten path, Gerber attracts mainly locals. Recreation options include boating (10-mph speed limit), fishing, and hiking. Swimming is not popular here because the water is murky with algae.

RV sites, facilities: There are 50 sites for tents or RVs up to 30 feet long. Picnic tables and fire grills are provided. Drinking water, a dump station, vault toilets, two boat ramps with docks, and a fish-cleaning station are available. Garbage service is available in summer only. Some facilities are wheelchair accessible. Leashed pets are permitted.

Reservations, fees: Reservations are not accepted. Sites are $7 per night, $4 per night for an additional vehicle. Open year-round, with drinking water and garbage service available May–mid-September, weather permitting.

Directions: From Klamath Falls, drive east on Highway 140 for 16 miles to Dairy and Highway 70. Turn right (south) on Highway 70 and drive seven miles to Bonanza and East Langell Valley Road. Turn left (east) on East Langell Valley Road and drive 11 miles to Gerber Road. Turn left on Gerber Road and drive eight miles to the campground on the right.

Contact: Bureau of Land Management, Klamath Falls Resource Area, 541/883-6916, fax 541/884-2097, www.blm.gov.

19 LEE THOMAS

Scenic rating: 6

near the north fork of the Sprague River in Fremont National Forest

Map grid B2

Lee Thomas is located near the trailhead that provides access to the Dead Horse Rim Trail. Nestled along the north fork of the Sprague

OREGON

River in the interior of Fremont National Forest, this small, cozy camp is a genuine hideaway, with all the necessities provided. It is set in a meadow at an elevation of 6,306 feet and, like Sandhill Crossing Campground (two miles downstream), it's popular with anglers and hunters in the fall.

RV sites, facilities: There are seven sites for tents or RVs up to 16 feet long. Picnic tables and fire grills are provided. Drinking water and vault toilets are available. Garbage must be packed out. Some facilities are wheelchair accessible. Leashed pets are permitted.

Reservations, fees: Reservations are not accepted. There is no fee for camping. Open June–late October, weather permitting.

Directions: From Lakeview, drive north on U.S. 395 for 23 miles to Highway 31. Turn northwest and drive 22 miles to Paisley. Continue on Highway 31 for 0.5 mile to Mill Street. Turn west on Mill Street and drive 20 miles (the road becomes Forest Road 33) and continue to the T intersection with Forest Road 28. Turn left on Forest Road 28 and drive 0.5 mile to Forest Road 3411. Turn right and drive one mile to the campground on the right.

Contact: Fremont-Winema National Forests, Paisley Ranger District, 541/943-3114, fax 541/943-4479, www.fs.fed.us.

20 SANDHILL CROSSING

Scenic rating: 6

on the north fork of the Sprague River in Fremont National Forest

Map grid B2

If you're looking for a combination of beauty and solitude, you've found it. This camp (6,306 feet elevation) sits on the banks of the designated Wild and Scenic North Fork Sprague River, where fishing is superior. Although a low-use camp, it is popular with anglers and hunters in the fall. A nearby trailhead leads into the Gearheart Wilderness.

RV sites, facilities: There are five sites for tents or RVs up to 25 feet long. Picnic tables and fire grills are provided. Vault toilets and drinking water are available. Garbage must be packed out. Some facilities are wheelchair accessible. Leashed pets are permitted.

Reservations, fees: Reservations are not accepted. There is no fee for camping. Open June–October, weather permitting.

Directions: From Lakeview, drive north on U.S. 395 for 23 miles to Highway 31. Turn northwest and drive 22 miles to Paisley. Continue on Highway 31 for 0.5 mile to Mill Street. Turn west on Mill Street and drive 20 miles (the road becomes Forest Road 33); continue to the T intersection with Forest Road 28. Turn right and drive 11 miles to Forest Road 3411. Turn left and drive eight miles to the campground on the left.

Contact: Fremont-Winema National Forests, Paisley Ranger District, 541/943-3114, fax 541/943-4479, www.fs.fed.us.

21 DEAD HORSE LAKE

Scenic rating: 9

on Dead Horse Lake in Fremont National Forest

Map grid B2

The shore of Dead Horse Lake is home to this camp sitting at 7,372 feet elevation; it generally fills up on most weekends and holidays. A hiking trail winds around the perimeter of the lake, hooking up with other trails along the way. One original Civilian Conservation Corps canoe, a relic of the 1930s, remains in the lake. No gas motors are permitted on the lake, and a 5-mph speed limit is in effect. Nearby Fremont National Forest provides good side trips.

RV sites, facilities: There are 16 sites for tents or RVs up to 25 feet long and a separate group area for up to 40 people. Picnic tables and fire grills are provided. Drinking water and vault toilets are available, but garbage must be packed out. A boat launch and day-use area are nearby. Leashed pets are permitted.

Reservations, fees: Reservations are not accepted. Sites are $6 per night, $2 per night per additional vehicle. Open July–October, weather permitting.

Directions: From Lakeview, drive north on U.S. 395 for 23 miles to Highway 31. Turn northwest and drive 22 miles to Paisley. Continue on Highway 31 for 0.5 mile to Mill Street. Turn west on Mill Street and drive 20 miles (the road becomes Forest Road 033); continue to the T intersection with Forest Road 28. Turn right and drive 11 miles (watch for the turn to Campbell-Dead Horse Lakes) to Forest Road 033. Turn left and drive three miles (gravel road) to the campground.

Contact: Fremont-Winema National Forests, Paisley Ranger District, 541/943-3114, fax 541/943-4479, www.fs.fed.us.

22 CAMPBELL LAKE

Scenic rating: 9

on Campbell Lake in Fremont National Forest

Map grid B2

This campground on the pebbled shore of Campbell Lake is located near Dead Horse Lake Campground. These high-elevation, crystal-clear lakes were formed during the glacier period, evidence of which can be found on the nearby Lakes Trail system. Both camps are very busy, filling up most weekends in July and August. No gas motors are permitted on Campbell Lake, and a 5-mph speed limit is in effect. A U.S. Forest Service map details the back roads.

RV sites, facilities: There are 16 sites for tents or RVs up to 25 feet long. Picnic tables and fire grills are provided. Drinking water and vault toilets are available. A boat launch and day-use area are adjacent to the camp. Boats with electric motors are permitted, but gas motors are prohibited. Garbage must be packed out. Leashed pets are permitted.

Reservations, fees: Reservations are not accepted. Sites are $6 per night, $2 per night per additional vehicle. Open July–late October, weather permitting.

Directions: From Lakeview, drive north on U.S. 395 for 23 miles to Highway 31. Turn northwest and drive 22 miles to Paisley. Continue on Highway 31 for 0.5 mile to Mill Street. Turn west on Mill Street and drive 20 miles (the road becomes Forest Road 33) and continue to the T intersection with Forest Road 28. Turn right and drive eight miles to Forest Road 033. Turn left and drive two miles to the campground.

Contact: Fremont-Winema National Forests, Paisley Ranger District, 541/943-3114, fax 541/943-4479, www.fs.fed.us.

23 MARSTER SPRING

Scenic rating: 6

on the Chewaucan River in Fremont National Forest

Map grid B2

The largest of several popular camps in this river corridor, Marster Spring sits right on the banks of the Chewaucan Riverr at an elevation of 4,845 feet. This pretty campground is set among ponderosa pine trees in a good fishing area, yet is close to the town of Paisley. The Fremont National Recreation Trail is accessible at the Chewaucan Crossing Trailhead, 0.25 mile to the south.

RV sites, facilities: There are 10 sites for tents or RVs up to 22 feet long. Picnic tables and fire grills are provided. Drinking water and vault toilets are available. Leashed pets are permitted.

Reservations, fees: Reservations are not accepted. Sites are $6 per night, $2 per night per additional vehicle. Open May–October, weather permitting.

Directions: From Lakeview, drive north on U.S. 395 for 23 miles to Highway 31. Turn northwest and drive 22 miles to Paisley. Continue on Highway 31 for 0.5 mile to Mill Street. Turn west on Mill Street and drive 7.5 miles (the road becomes Forest Road 33) to the campground on the left.

Contact: Fremont-Winema National Forests, Paisley Ranger District, 541/943-3114, fax 541/943-4479, www.fs.fed.us.

24 CORRAL CREEK

Scenic rating: 4

near the Gearhart Mountain Wilderness in Fremont National Forest

Map grid B2

Set along Corral Creek, this camp is adjacent to a trailhead that provides access into the Gearhart Mountain Wilderness, making it a prime base camp for a backpacking trip. Access is also available from camp to the Palisade Rocks, a worthwhile side trip. Another option is Quartz Mountain Sno-Park, which is 14 miles east of the campground. The elevation is 6,000 feet.

RV sites, facilities: There are six sites for tents or RVs up to 22 feet long. Picnic tables and fire grills are provided. Vault toilets are available. There is no drinking water, and garbage must be packed out. Stock facilities include hitching posts, stalls, and corrals. Some facilities are wheelchair accessible. Leashed pets are permitted.

Reservations, fees: Reservations are not accepted. There is no fee for camping. Open mid-May–late October, weather permitting.

Directions: From Klamath Falls, drive east on Highway 140 for 53 miles to the town of Bly. Continue east on Highway 140 for one mile to Campbell Road. Turn left and drive 0.5 mile to Forest Road 34. Turn right and drive 15 miles to Forest Road 012. Turn right and drive to the campground.

Contact: Fremont-Winema National Forests, Bly Ranger District, 541/947-6300, fax 541/947-6375, www.fs.fed.us.

25 DAIRY POINT

Scenic rating: 6

on Dairy Creek in Fremont National Forest

Map grid B2

This campground, elevation 5,200 feet, is situated next to the Dairy Creek Bridge in a stand of ponderosa pine and white fir at the edge of a large and open meadow. The setting is beautiful and peaceful, with a towering backdrop of mountains. In the spring, wildflowers are a sight to behold; bird-watching can also be excellent this time of year. Fishing and inner tubing are popular activities at Dairy Creek. Warning: This campground is suitable for large groups and is often full on holidays and most weekends.

RV sites, facilities: There are four sites for tents or self-contained RVs up to 25 feet long. Picnic tables and fire grills are provided. A vault toilet and drinking water are available. Garbage must be packed out. Leashed pets are permitted.

Reservations, fees: Reservations are not accepted. There is no fee for camping. Open mid-May–October, weather permitting.

Directions: From Lakeview, drive north on U.S. 395 for 23 miles to Highway 31. Turn northwest and drive 22 miles to Paisley. Continue on Highway 31 for 0.5 mile to Mill Street. Turn west on Mill Street and drive 20 miles (the road becomes Forest Road 33); continue to the T intersection with Forest Road 28. Turn left and drive two miles (crossing the Dairy Creek Bridge) to Forest Road 3428. Turn left and drive to the campground (just past the intersection on the left).

Contact: Fremont-Winema National Forests, Paisley Ranger District, 541/943-3114, fax 541/943-4479, www.fs.fed.us.

26 HAPPY CAMP

Scenic rating: 6

on Dairy Creek in Fremont National Forest

Map grid B2

Here's a pleasant spot with open sites along Dairy Creek, though only one site is close to the water. The camp features some old 1930s Civilian Conservation Corps shelters, preserved in their original state. Fishing is available for rainbow trout, though the creek is no longer stocked. The camp sits at 5,289 feet elevation.

RV sites, facilities: There are nine sites for tents or RVs up to 16 feet long. Picnic tables and fire grills are provided. Vault toilets, picnic shelters, and horseshoe pits are available. There is no drinking water (drinking water is available 1.5 miles west on Forest Road 047 at Clear Spring). Garbage must be packed out. Leashed pets are permitted.

Reservations, fees: Reservations are not accepted. There is no fee for camping. Open mid-May–late October, weather permitting.

Directions: From Lakeview, drive north on U.S. 395 for 23 miles to Highway 31. Turn northwest and drive 22 miles to Paisley. Continue on Highway 31 for 0.5 mile to Mill Street. Turn west on Mill Street and drive 20 miles (the road becomes Forest Road 33); continue to the T intersection with Forest Road 28. Turn left and drive two miles (just before Dairy Creek) to Forest Road 047. Turn right and drive two miles to the campground on the left.

Contact: Fremont-Winema National Forests, Paisley Ranger District, 541/943-3114, fax 541/943-4479, www.fs.fed.us.

27 LOFTON RESERVOIR

Scenic rating: 6

on Lofton Reservoir in Fremont National Forest

Map grid B2

This remote campground sits on the shore of Lofton Reservoir, a small lake that can provide the best trout fishing in this region. Other nearby lakes are accessible by forest roads. This area marks the beginning of the Great Basin, a high-desert area that extends to Idaho. A large fire burned much of the surrounding forest about 20 years ago, making this campground an oasis of sorts.

RV sites, facilities: There are 26 sites for tents or RVs up to 25 feet long. Picnic tables and fire grills are provided. Vault toilets and garbage bins are available. Garbage service may be discontinued, so prepared to pack out your trash. There is no drinking water. Boat docks and launching facilities are nearby. A camp host is on-site. Some facilities are wheelchair accessible. Leashed pets are permitted.

Reservations, fees: Reservations are not accepted. Sites are $6 per night, $2 per night

per additional vehicle. Open mid-May–late October, weather permitting.

Directions: From Klamath Falls, drive east on Highway 140 for 54 miles to Bly. Continue east on Highway 140 for 13 miles to Forest Road 3715. Turn right and drive seven miles to Forest Road 013. Turn left on Forest Road 013 and drive one mile to the campground.

Contact: Fremont-Winema National Forests, Bly Ranger District, 541/947-6300, fax 541/947-6375, www.fs.fed.us.

28 COTTONWOOD RECREATION AREA

Scenic rating: 6

on Cottonwood Meadow Lake in Fremont National Forest

Map grid B2

Cottonwood Recreation Area, along the upper shore of Cottonwood Meadow Lake, is one of the better spots in the vicinity for fishing and hiking. The camp is set at an elevation of 6,130 feet in a forested setting with aspen and many huge ponderosa pines. Boats with electric motors are allowed on the lake, but gas motors are prohibited. Three hiking trails wind around the lake, and facilities for horses include hitching posts, feeders, water, and corrals.

RV sites, facilities: There are 12 sites for tents or RVs up to 35 feet long and nine tent sites. Picnic tables and fire grills are provided. Drinking water and vault toilets are available, but garbage must be packed out. A camp host is on-site. Boat docks are nearby. No gasoline motors are allowed on the lake. The boating speed limit is 5 mph. Leashed pets are permitted.

Reservations, fees: Reservations are not accepted. Sites are $6 per night, $2 per night per additional vehicle. Open early June–mid-October, weather permitting.

Directions: From Lakeview, drive west on Highway 140 for 21 miles to Forest Road 3870. Turn right and drive about 10 miles to the campground.

Contact: Fremont-Winema National Forests,

Lakeview Ranger District, 541/353-2700, fax 541/947-6375, www.fs.fed.us.

29 MUD CREEK

Scenic rating: 4

on Mud Creek in Fremont National Forest

Map grid B2

Remote and quiet, this camp sits at 6,600 feet elevation in an isolated stand of lodgepole pines along the banks of Mud Creek. Fishing in Mud Creek is fairly good, and Drake Peak (8,405 feet elevation) is nearby. There are no other camps in the immediate vicinity.

RV sites, facilities: There are seven sites for tents or RVs up to 16 feet long. Picnic tables and fire grills are provided. Drinking water and vault toilets are available. Garbage must be packed out. Leashed pets are permitted.

Reservations, fees: Reservations are not accepted. There is no fee for camping. Open June–mid-October, weather permitting.

Directions: From Lakeview, drive five miles north on U.S. 395 to Highway 140. Turn right on Highway 140 and drive eight miles to Forest Road 3615. Turn left and drive seven miles to the campground.

Contact: Fremont-Winema National Forests, Lakeview Ranger District, 541/353-2700, fax 541/947-6375, www.fs.fed.us.

30 DOG LAKE

Scenic rating: 5

on Dog Lake in Fremont National Forest

Map grid B2

This campground is located on the west shore of Dog Lake at an elevation of 5,100 feet. Native Americans named the lake for its resemblance in shape to the hind leg of a dog. The lake provides a popular fishery for bass, crappie, and perch. Boats with motors are permitted, though speeds are limited to 5 mph. Prospects for seeing waterfowl and eagles are good.

RV sites, facilities: There are 17 sites for tents

or RVs up to 40 feet long. Picnic tables and fire grills are provided. Vault toilets are available. There is no drinking water. Garbage must be packed out. A boat launch is nearby. Leashed pets are permitted.

Reservations, fees: Reservations are not accepted. Sites are $6 per night, $2 per night per additional vehicle. Open mid-April–mid-October, weather permitting.

Directions: From Lakeview, drive west on Highway 140 for seven miles to County Road 1-13. Turn left on County Road 1-13 and drive four miles to County Road 1-11D (Dog Lake Road). Turn right and drive four miles (the road becomes Forest Road 4017) into national forest. Continue on Forest Road 4017 for 12 miles (two miles past Drew Reservoir) to Dog Lake and the campground entrance on the left.

Contact: Fremont-Winema National Forests, Lakeview Ranger District, 541/353-2700, fax 541/947-6375, www.fs.fed.us.

31 DREWS CREEK

Scenic rating: 9

near Lakeview in Fremont National Forest

Map grid B2 | **BEST (**

This exceptionally beautiful campground is set along Drews Creek at 4,900 feet elevation. Gorgeous wild roses grow near the creek, and several unmarked trails lead to nearby hills where campers can enjoy scenic views. A great spot for a family trip, Drews Creek features horseshoe pits, an area for baseball, and a large group barbecue, making it equally popular with group campers. Fishing is available in nearby Dog Lake, which also provides facilities for boating. Waterskiing is another option at Drews Reservoir, two miles to the west.

RV sites, facilities: There are five sites for tents or RVs up to 25 feet long. Picnic tables, fire grills, vault toilets, and drinking water are provided. Garbage must be packed out. Leashed pets are permitted.

Reservations, fees: Reservations are not accepted. There is no fee for camping. Open early mid-May–mid-October, weather permitting.

Directions: From Lakeview, drive west on Highway 140 for 10 miles to County Road 1-13. Turn left and drive four miles to County Road 1-11D. Turn right and drive six miles (the road will become Forest Road 4017) to the bridge that provides access to the campground.

Contact: Fremont-Winema National Forests, Lakeview Ranger District, 541/353-2700, fax 541/947-6375, www.fs.fed.us.

32 JUNIPERS RESERVOIR RV RESORT

Scenic rating: 6

on Junipers Reservoir
Map grid B2

This resort on an 8,000-acre cattle ranch is situated in a designated Oregon Wildlife Viewing Area, and campers may catch glimpses of seldom-seen species. Many nature-walking trails meander through the park, and guests can also take driving tours. Fishing for catfish and trout can be good and, because it is a private lake, no fishing license is required. The summer climate is mild and pleasant. Antelope and elk can be spotted in this area.

RV sites, facilities: There is a grassy area for tents and 40 pull-through sites with full or partial hookups (some 50-amp) for RVs of any length. Picnic tables are provided. Drinking water, restrooms with showers, a dump station, Wi-Fi and computer modem access, coin laundry, community fire pit, and ice are available. Recreational facilities include a recreation hall, a volleyball court, and horseshoe pits. Some of the facilities are wheelchair accessible. Leashed pets are permitted.

Reservations, fees: Reservations are recommended. Tent sites are $20 per night, and RV sites are $23.50–28.89 per night; weekly rates are available. Open May–mid-October.

Directions: From Lakeview, drive west on Highway 140 for 10 miles to the resort (at Milepost 86.5) on the right.

Contact: Junipers Reservoir RV Resort, 541/947-2050, fax 541/947-6788, www.junipersrv.com.

33 GOOSE LAKE STATE PARK

Scenic rating: 7

on Goose Lake
Map grid B2

This park is situated on the east shore of unusual Goose Lake, which lies half in Oregon and half in California. The fishing at the lake is poor, but better fishing is available in nearby streams. Waterfowl from the Pacific flyway frequent this out-of-the-way spot, as do many other species of birds and wildlife, like the mule deer that frequent the shaded campground. Note that only 15- and 20-amp service is available for RVs.

RV sites, facilities: There are 47 sites with partial hookups (water and electricity) for tents or RVs up to 50 feet long. Picnic tables, fire grills, garbage bins, and drinking water are provided. A camp host is on-site. Restrooms with flush toilets and showers, a dump station, ice, and firewood are available. Leashed pets are permitted.

Reservations, fees: Reservations are not accepted. Sites are $12–20 per night, $5 per night for an additional vehicle. Open mid-April–mid-October.

Directions: From Lakeview, drive south on U.S. 395 for 14 miles to the California border and Stateline Road. Turn right (west) and drive one mile to the campground.

Contact: Goose Lake State Park, 541/947-3111 or 800/551-6949, www.oregonstateparks.org.

34 WILLOW CREEK

Scenic rating: 4

near Willow Creek in Fremont National Forest
Map grid B2

This campground (at 5,800 feet elevation) is situated in a canyon among tall pines and quaking aspen not far from the banks of Willow Creek. Campsites are private, and some are located along the creek. Watch for wildflowers blooming in the spring. A hiking trail offers access to the Crane Mountain Trail, and a nearby dirt road heads north to Burnt Creek.

OREGON

RV sites, facilities: There are eight sites for tents or RVs up to 22 feet long. Picnic tables and fire grills are provided. There is no drinking water, and garbage must be packed out. Vault toilets are available. Leashed pets are permitted.

Reservations, fees: Reservations are not accepted. There is no fee for camping. Open June–mid-October, weather permitting.

Directions: From Lakeview, drive five miles north on U.S. 395 to Highway 140. Turn right (east) on Highway 140 and drive seven miles to Forest Road 3915. Turn right and drive nine miles to Forest Road 4011. Turn right and drive one mile to the campground on the right.

Contact: Fremont-Winema National Forests, Lakeview Ranger District, 541/353-2700, fax 541/947-6375, www.fs.fed.us.

35 DEEP CREEK

Scenic rating: 8

on Deep Creek in Fremont National Forest
Map grid B2

Shaded by huge ponderosa pines and cottonwoods and nestled on the banks of Deep Creek, this pretty, little-used campground is the place if you're after privacy. Deep Creek is a good fishing stream. Magnificent spring wildflowers are a highlight here. The camp sits at an elevation of 5,600 feet.

RV sites, facilities: There are six sites for tents or RVs up to 22 feet long. Picnic tables and fire grills are provided. Vault toilets are available. There is no drinking water, and garbage must be packed out. Leashed pets are permitted.

Reservations, fees: Reservations are not accepted. There is no fee for camping. Open June–mid-October, weather permitting.

Directions: From Lakeview, drive five miles north on U.S. 395 to Highway 140. Turn right (east) on Highway 140 and drive six miles to Forest Road 3915. Turn right on Forest Road 3915 and drive 14 miles to Deep Creek and the campground entrance road on the right (Forest Road 4015). Turn right and drive one mile to the campground on the right.

Contact: Fremont-Winema National Forests, Lakeview Ranger District, 541/353-2700, fax 541/947-6375, www.fs.fed.us.

36 HART MOUNTAIN NATIONAL ANTELOPE REFUGE

Scenic rating: 6

near Adel
Map grid C2   BEST (

The U.S. Fish and Wildlife Service operates very few areas with campgrounds—Hart Mountain is one of them. This unusual refuge features canyons and hot springs in a high-desert area. There are three primitive campgrounds: Hot Springs Campground, Post Meadows Horse Camp, and CCC Camp. Hot Springs gets the highest use in the summer. Some of Oregon's largest antelope herds roam this large area, and the campground is popular with hunters in the fall.

RV sites, facilities: Hot Springs Campground has 25 primitive sites for tents or RVs up to 20 feet long. Post Meadows Horse Camp has six primitive sites with corrals, hitching posts, and stock water (100 yards away) available; pellet feed is required for horses. CCC Camp has 20 primitive tent sites. Some sites have fire rings. Pit toilets are provided. There is no drinking water (but it can be obtained at headquarters, which you pass on the way in). Garbage must be packed out. Supplies are available in the town of Plush. Some facilities are wheelchair accessible. Leashed pets are permitted.

Reservations, fees: Reservations are not accepted. There is no fee for camping. Open year-round, weather permitting.

Directions: From Lakeview, drive north on U.S. 395 for five miles to Highway 140. Turn east on Highway 140 and drive 16 miles to the Plush-Hart Mountain Cutoff. Turn left (signed for Hart Antelope Refuge) and drive north for 43 miles (first paved, then gravel) to the refuge headquarters. Continue 0.5 mile to CCC Campground, four miles to Hot Springs Campground (the road is often impassable in the winter). For the Post Meadows Horse Camp, follow the above directions to the refuge headquarters. At headquarters, turn onto Blue Sky Road and drive 10 miles to the camp.

Contact: Hart Mountain National Antelope Refuge, 541/947-3315 or 541/947-2731, fax 541/947-4414, www.fws.gov/refuges.

37 ADEL STORE AND RV PARK

Scenic rating: 5

in Adel

Map grid C2

Remote Adel is the only game in town, so you'd better grab it while you can. Recreation options in the area include hang gliding, rock-hounding, and visiting hot springs at the Hart Mountain National Antelope Refuge, 40 miles north of Adel.

RV sites, facilities: There are eight sites for tents or RVs up to 40 feet (full hookups). Barbecues are provided. A store, a small café, gasoline, and ice are available. Leashed pets are permitted.

Reservations, fees: Reservations are accepted. Tent sites are $10 per night and RV sites are $18 per night; weekly rates are available. Some credit cards are accepted but not for the purchase of gasoline. Open year-round.

Directions: From Lakeview, drive five miles north on U.S. 395 to Highway 140. Turn right (east) on Highway 140 and drive 28 miles to Adel (a very small town). The RV park is in town along Highway 140 on the right.

Contact: Adel Store and RV Park, 541/947-3850.

38 STEENS MOUNTAIN RESORT

Scenic rating: 9

on the Blitzen River

Map grid D2

The self-proclaimed "gateway to the Steens Mountain," this resort is bordered by the Malheur National Wildlife Refuge on three sides, and it has great views. The mile-high mountain

and surrounding gorges make an excellent photo opportunity. Hiking and hunting are other possibilities in the area. Fishing is available on the Blitzen River, with easy access from the camp.

RV sites, facilities: There are 25 tent sites, 37 pull-through sites with full hookups (30 or 50 amps), and 39 sites with partial hookups for tents or RVs of any length, plus eight cabins and one rental home. Picnic tables and fire pits are provided. Drinking water, restrooms with showers, a dump station, coin laundry, limited groceries and fishing supplies, and ice are available. Leashed pets are permitted.

Reservations, fees: Reservations are accepted at 800/542-3765. Sites are $15–30 per night and $5 per person per night for more than two people. Some credit cards are accepted. Open year-round.

Directions: From Burns, drive east on Highway 78 for two miles to Highway 205. Turn right (south) on Highway 205 and drive 59 miles to Frenchglen and Steens Mountain Road. Turn left (east) and drive three miles to the resort on the right.

Contact: Steens Mountain Resort, 541/493-2415, fax 541/493-2484, www.steensmountainresort.com.

39 PAGE SPRINGS

Scenic rating: 7

near Malheur National Wildlife Refuge

Map grid D2

Page Springs campground lies adjacent to the Malheur National Wildlife Refuge at an elevation of 4,200 feet. Sites are shaded by juniper and cottonwood, with some near the Donner und Blitzen River. Activities include hiking on the area trails, bird-watching, fishing, hunting, and sightseeing. The Frenchglen Hotel (three miles away) is administered by the state parks department and offers overnight accommodations and meals.

RV sites, facilities: There are 36 sites for tents or RVs up to 35 feet long. Picnic tables and

OREGON

fire grills are provided. Drinking water, vault toilets, a day-use area with a shelter, and garbage bins are available. Some facilities are wheelchair accessible. Leashed pets are permitted.

Reservations, fees: Reservations are not accepted. Sites are $8 per vehicle per night, with a 14-day stay limit. Open year-round.

Directions: From Burns, drive east on Highway 78 for two miles to Highway 205. Turn south on Highway 205 and drive 60 miles to Frenchglen and Steens Mountain Loop Road. Turn left (east) and drive three miles to the campground.

Contact: Bureau of Land Management, Burns District, 541/573-4400, fax 541/573-4411, www.or.blm.gov/burns.

40 FISH LAKE

Scenic rating: 8

on Fish Lake
Map grid D2

The shore of Fish Lake is the setting for this primitive but pretty camp. Set among the aspens at 7,400 feet elevation, it can make an excellent weekend-getaway spot for sightseeing. Trout fishing is an option, made easier by the boat ramp near camp.

RV sites, facilities: There are 23 sites for tents or RVs up to 20 feet long. Picnic tables and fire grills are provided. Drinking water, garbage bins, and vault toilets are available. Boat-launching facilities are nearby (non-motorized boats only). Some facilities are wheelchair accessible. Leashed pets are permitted.

Reservations, fees: Reservations are not accepted. Sites are $8 per vehicle per night, with a 14-day stay limit. Open June–October, weather permitting.

Directions: From Burns, drive east on Highway 78 for two miles to Highway 205. Turn south on Highway 205 and drive 60 miles to Frenchglen and Steens Mountain Loop Road. Turn left (east) and drive 17 miles to the campground.

Contact: Bureau of Land Management, Burns District, 541/573-4400, fax 541/573-4411, www.or.blm.gov/burns.

41 MANN LAKE

Scenic rating: 8

on Mann Lake
Map grid D2

Mann Lake sits at the base of Steens Mountain. This scenic, high-desert camp is mainly used as a fishing camp—fishing can be very good for cutthroat trout. Wintertime ice fishing and wildlife-viewing are also popular. Sites are open, with sagebrush and no trees. There are two small boat ramps and a 10-horsepower limit on motors. Weather can be extreme. Nearby Alvord Desert is also an attraction.

Note: Please respect private property on parcels of land next to the lake.

RV sites, facilities: There are dispersed sites for tents or RVs of up to 35 feet long, and open areas on each side of the lake. Vault toilets are available. No drinking water is available. Garbage must be packed out. Some facilities are wheelchair accessible. Leashed pets are permitted.

Reservations, fees: Reservations are not accepted. There is no fee for camping. A 14-day stay limit is enforced. Open year-round.

Directions: From Burns, drive southeast on Highway 78 for 65 miles to East Steens Road. Turn right (south) and drive 22 miles to the campground at Mann Lake.

Contact: Bureau of Land Management, Burns District, 541/573-4400, fax 541/573-4411, www.or.blm.gov/burns.

42 SOUTH STEENS

Scenic rating: 6

near Steens Mountain Wilderness
Map grid D2

This campground hugs the edge of the Steens Mountain Wilderness. The area features deep, glacier-carved gorges, volcanic uplifts, stunning scenery, and a rare chance to see elk and bighorn sheep. Redband trout fishing is a mile away at Donner und Blitzen Wild and Scenic River and its tributaries, a designated reserve.

This campground is also good for horse campers, providing them with a separate area from the other campers. Trails are accessible from the campground.

RV sites, facilities: There are 36 sites for tents or RVs up to 25 feet long; 15 of the sites are designated for horse campers. Picnic tables, corrals, hitching posts, and fire grills are provided. Drinking water and vault toilets are available. Some facilities are wheelchair accessible. Leashed pets are permitted.

Reservations, fees: Reservations are not accepted. Sites are $6 per vehicle per night. There is a 14-day stay limit. Open May–October, weather permitting.

Directions: From Burns, drive east on Highway 78 for two miles to Highway 205. Turn south on Highway 205 and drive 60 miles to Frenchglen. Continue south on Highway 205 for 10 miles to Steens South Loop Road. Turn left (east) and drive 18 miles to the campground on the right.

Contact: Bureau of Land Management, Burns District, 541/573-4400, fax 541/573-4411, www.or.blm.gov/burns.

43 WILLOW CREEK HOT SPRINGS

Scenic rating: 7

near Whitehorse Butte

Map grid D2

A very small campground with no privacy, Willow Creek features campsites about 100 feet from the hot springs, which consist of two connected, smaller pools. This campground can be difficult to find, and only the adventurous should attempt this trip. Despite being out of the way, it still attracts travelers from far and wide. The surrounding scenery features rocky hills, not a flat expanse.

RV sites, facilities: There are four sites for tents or small RVs. Fire rings are provided. A vault toilet is available. Drinking water and firewood are not available, and garbage must be packed out. Leashed pets are permitted.

Reservations, fees: Reservations are not accepted. There is no fee for camping. Open year-round, weather permitting.

Directions: From Burns, drive southeast on Highway 78 for 105 miles to Burns Junction and U.S. 95. Turn right (south) on U.S. 95 and drive 20 miles to Whitehorse Road. Turn right (southwest) and drive 21 miles (passing Whitehorse Ranch); continue for 2.5 miles to a fork (look for the telephone pole). Bear left and drive two miles to the campground.

Contact: Bureau of Land Management, Vale District, 541/473-3144, fax 541/473-6213, www.blm.gov.

44 ROME LAUNCH

Scenic rating: 6

on the Owyhee River

Map grid E2   **BEST** (

Rome Launch campground is used mainly by folks rafting the Owyhee River and overnighters passing through. A few cottonwood trees and sagebrush dot the camp with some sites adjacent to the Owyhee River. Rome Launch is also good for wildlife-viewing; mountain lions and bobcats have been spotted, and there are some farms and ranches in the area.

The Owyhee Canyon is quite dramatic, like a miniature Grand Canyon. I have canoed most of the Owyhee from the headwaters in Nevada below the Jarbidge Mountains all the way through Idaho and into Oregon, and I would rate this river as one of the top canoeing destinations in North America. Note: No motorized boats are allowed on the river.

RV sites, facilities: There are five sites for tents or small RVs. Picnic tables and fire rings are provided. Drinking water, vault toilets, and a boat launch are available. No firewood is available. All garbage must be packed out. Leashed pets are permitted.

Reservations, fees: Reservations are not accepted. There is no fee for camping. Open March–November, weather permitting.

Directions: From Burns Junction, drive east on U.S. 95 for 15 miles to Jordan Valley and the

OREGON

signed turnoff for the Owyhee River and BLM-Rome boat launch. Turn south and drive 0.25 mile to the campground.

Contact: Bureau of Land Management, Vale District, 541/473-3144, fax 541/473-6213, www.blm.gov.

45 ANTELOPE RESERVOIR

Scenic rating: 3

on the Antelope Reservoir

Map grid E2

This campground gets little use, except during hunting season. An open area on a slope above the reservoir, the camp has no tree cover—be prepared for extreme weather. Water levels fluctuate at shallow Antelope Reservoir and it can dry up.

RV sites, facilities: There are four sites for tents or small RVs. Picnic tables and fire rings are provided. Vault toilets and primitive boat access are available. No drinking water is available, and all garbage must be packed out. Leashed pets are permitted.

Reservations, fees: Reservations are not accepted. There is no fee for camping. Open year-round, weather permitting.

Directions: From Burns Junction, drive east on U.S. 95 for 36 miles to the signed turnoff for Antelope Reservoir. Turn south and drive one mile to the campground on the left.

Contact: Bureau of Land Management, Vale District, 541/473-3144, fax 541/473-6213, www.blm.gov.

46 THREE FORKS

Scenic rating: 9

near the Owyhee River

Map grid E2

This remote camp is set along the east bank of the Owyhee River, where several warm streams snake through tall grass to the river. The area offers fishing for brown trout in the river and day hiking to secluded springs and a waterfall pool in the upper Owyhee Canyon (swimwear optional). Clusters of 95°F springs are located on both sides of the river, and the rugged Owyhee Canyon forms a magnificent backdrop. To the west are a number of wild horse herds. (The BLM recreation map has the general locations of the herds.)

RV sites, facilities: There are four sites for tents or small RVs. Picnic tables and fire rings are provided. Vault toilets are available. There is no drinking water, and garbage must be packed out. There is access to the Owyhee River by permit for non-motorized boats only. Leashed pets are permitted.

Reservations, fees: Reservations are not accepted. There is no fee for camping. Open year-round, weather permitting.

Directions: On U.S. 95 (15 miles southwest of Jordan Valley), turn south on Three Forks Road and drive 35 miles to the campground. High-clearance vehicles recommended. Road may be impassable when wet.

Contact: Bureau of Land Management, Vale District, 541/473-3144, fax 541/473-6213, www.blm.gov.

OREGON

California

CALIFORNIA

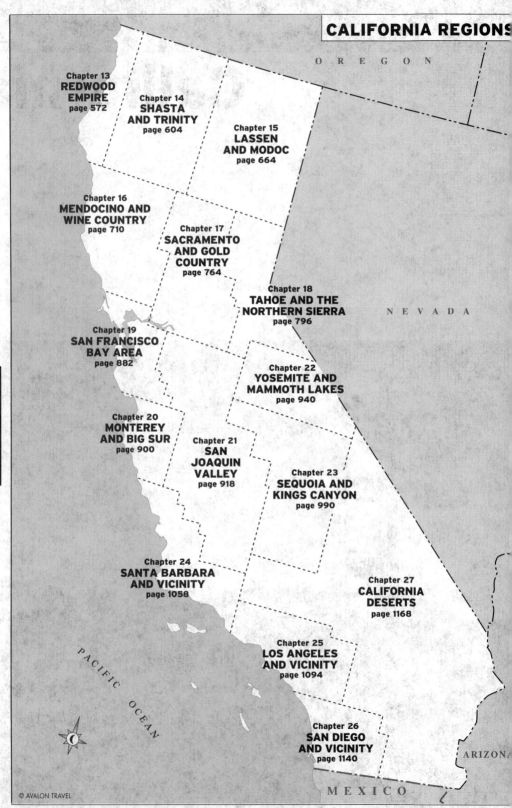

CALIFORNIA REGIONS

OREGON

Chapter 13
REDWOOD EMPIRE
page 572

Chapter 14
SHASTA AND TRINITY
page 604

Chapter 15
LASSEN AND MODOC
page 664

Chapter 16
MENDOCINO AND WINE COUNTRY
page 710

Chapter 17
SACRAMENTO AND GOLD COUNTRY
page 764

Chapter 18
TAHOE AND THE NORTHERN SIERRA
page 796

NEVADA

Chapter 19
SAN FRANCISCO BAY AREA
page 882

Chapter 22
YOSEMITE AND MAMMOTH LAKES
page 940

Chapter 20
MONTEREY AND BIG SUR
page 900

Chapter 21
SAN JOAQUIN VALLEY
page 918

Chapter 23
SEQUOIA AND KINGS CANYON
page 990

Chapter 24
SANTA BARBARA AND VICINITY
page 1058

Chapter 27
CALIFORNIA DESERTS
page 1168

Chapter 25
LOS ANGELES AND VICINITY
page 1094

PACIFIC OCEAN

Chapter 26
SAN DIEGO AND VICINITY
page 1140

ARIZONA

MEXICO

© AVALON TRAVEL

REDWOOD EMPIRE

(BEST RV PARKS AND CAMPGROUNDS

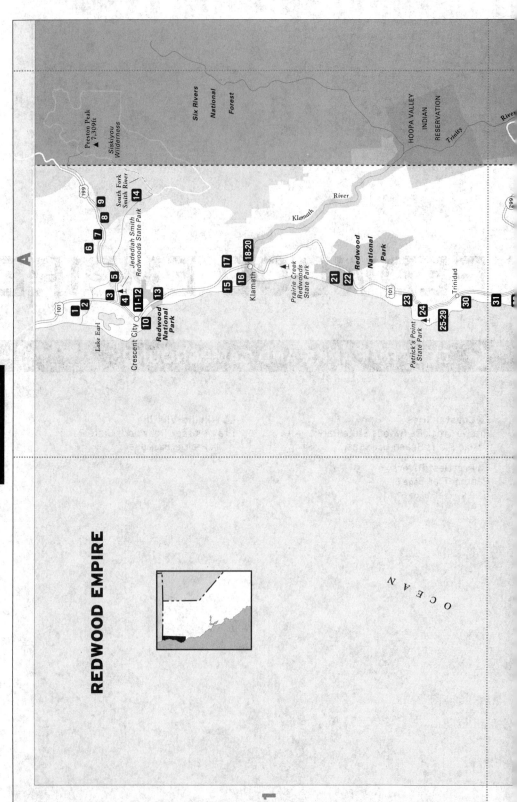

CALIFORNIA

REDWOOD EMPIRE

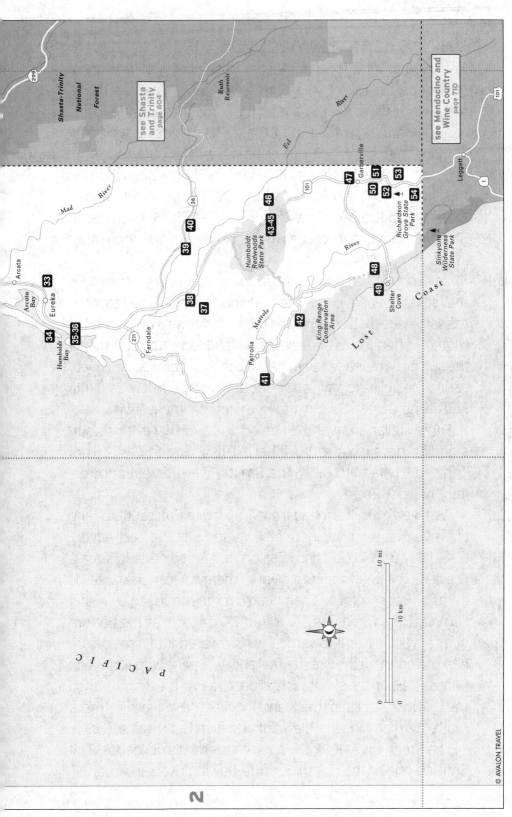

Visitors come from around the world to the Redwood Empire for one reason: to see the groves of giant redwoods, the tallest trees in the world. On a perfect day in the redwoods, refracted sunlight beams through the forest canopy, creating a solemn, cathedral-like effect. It feels as if you are standing in the center of the earth's pure magic.

But the redwood forests are only one of the attractions in this area. The Smith River canyon, Del Norte and Humboldt Coasts, and the remote edge of the Siskiyou Wilderness in Six Rivers National Forest all make this region like none other in the world.

On sunny days in late summer, some visitors are incredulous that so few people live in the Redwood Empire. The reason is the same one that explains why the trees grow so tall: rain in the winter – often for weeks at a time – and fog in the summer. If the sun does manage to appear, it's an event almost worthy of calling the police to say you've spotted a large, yellow Unidentified Flying Object. So most folks are content to just visit.

Three stellar areas should be on your must-see list for outstanding days of adventure here: the redwood parks from Trinidad to Klamath River, the Smith River Recreation Area, and the Lost Coast.

I've hiked every trailhead from Trinidad to Crescent City, and I believe that the hikes here feature some of the best adventuring day trips in Northern California. A good place to start is Prairie Creek Redwoods State Park, where you can see fantastic herds of Roosevelt elk. Then head over to the beach by hiking Fern Canyon, where you'll walk for 20 minutes at the bottom of a canyon adjacent to vertical walls covered with ferns before heading north on the Coastal Trail and its pristine woodlands and fantastic expanses of untouched beaches. All the trails through the redwoods north of the Klamath River are winners; it's just a matter of matching your level of ambition to the right hike.

The Smith River Recreation Area is equally gorgeous. The Smith is one of the last major free-flowing rivers in America.

Wild, pristine, and beautiful, it's set in a series of gorges and bordered by national forest. The centerpiece is Jedediah Smith Redwoods State Park and its grove of monster-sized redwoods. South Fork Road provides an extended tour into Six Rivers National Forest along the South Fork Smith River, with the option of visiting many of the largest trees in Jedediah Smith Redwoods State Park. The turnoff is on U.S. 199 just northeast of the town of Hiouchi. Turn right, cross two bridges, and you will arrive at a fork in the road. Turning left at the fork will take you along the South Fork Smith River and deep into Six Rivers National Forest. Turning right at the fork will take you to a series of trailheads for hikes into redwoods. Of these, the best is the Boy Scout Tree Trail.

The Lost Coast is often overlooked by visitors because of the difficulty in reaching it; your only access is via a slow, curvy road through the Mattole River Valley, past Petrolia, and out to a piece of coast. The experience is like being in suspended animation – your surroundings peaceful and pristine, with a striking lack of people. One of the best ways to capture the sensation is to drive out near the mouth of the Mattole, then hike south on the Coastal Trail long enough to get a feel for the area.

Compared to other regions in California, this corner of the state is somewhat one-dimensional. The emphasis here is primarily on exploring the redwoods and the coast, and to some extent, the Smith River. Most of the campgrounds here are designed with that in mind.

Many private campgrounds are set on U.S. 101 as well as near the mouths of the Smith and Klamath Rivers. These make fine base camps for fishing trips when the salmon are running. The state and national park campgrounds in the redwoods are in high demand, and reservations are often necessary in the peak vacation season. On the opposite end of the spectrum are primitive and remote settings, in Six Rivers National Forest, the Lost Coast, and even a few surprise nuggets in Redwood National Park.

CALIFORNIA

1 SALMON HARBOR RV RESORT

Scenic rating: 6

on the Smith River
Map grid A1

If location is everything, this privately operated campground rates high for salmon and steelhead anglers in the fall. It is set near the mouth of the Smith River, where salmon enter and school in the deep river holes in October. The fish are big, often in the 20-pound range, occasionally surpassing even 40 pounds. Year-round this is a good layover for RV cruisers looking for a spot near the Oregon border. It is actually an RV parking area with hookups, set within a mobile home park. Salmon Harbor RV Resort overlooks the ocean, with good beachcombing and driftwood and agate hunting nearby. Note that most sites are filled for the entire summer, but several sites are kept open for overnight campers.

RV sites, facilities: There are 93 sites for tents or RVs up to 40 feet; most sites have full hookups (30 and 50 amps) and are pull-through. Picnic tables and fire grills are provided. Drinking water, restrooms with flush toilets and showers, cable TV, coin laundry, storage sheds, modem hookups, and a recreation room are available. A grocery store, ice, gas, propane, a restaurant, boat ramp, fish cleaning station, RV storage, snack bar, and a bar are available within three miles. Leashed pets are permitted.

Reservations, fees: Reservations are accepted at 800/332-6139. Sites are $36 per night, $3 per person for more than two people. Monthly rates are available. Open year-round.

Directions: From Crescent City, drive north on U.S. 101 for 13 miles to the town of Smith River. Continue three miles north on U.S. 101 to the Salmon Harbor Road exit. Turn left on Salmon Harbor Road, drive a short distance, and look for Salmon Harbor Resort at the end of the road.

Contact: Salmon Harbor RV Resort, 707/487-3341 or 800/332-6139, www.salmonharbor-rvresort.com.

2 SHIP ASHORE RESORT

Scenic rating: 7

on the Smith River
Map grid A1

This is a famous spot for Smith River anglers in late fall and all through winter, when the tales get taller as the evening gets late. In the summer, the resort has become quite popular with people cruising the coast on U.S. 101. The park is set on five acres of land adjacent to the lower Smith River. Note that in addition to the 120 RV sites, another 80 sites have mobile homes. The salmon and steelhead seem to come in one size here—big—but they can be as elusive as Bigfoot. If you want to hear how big these fish can be, just check into the Captain's Galley restaurant any fall or winter evening. Salmon average 15–25 pounds, occasionally bigger, with 50-pounders caught each year, and steelhead average 10–14 pounds, with bigger fish occasionally hooked as well.

RV sites, facilities: There are 120 sites for RVs, and a separate area for 10–15 tents. Most RV sites have full hookups (30 amps); some sites are pull-through. Two houses and motel rooms are also available. Picnic tables are provided. Restrooms with flush toilets and showers, boat dock, boat ramp, coin laundry, propane, and a restaurant are available. A grocery store is two miles away. Leashed pets are permitted, with a maximum of two pets.

Reservations, fees: Reservations are not accepted. Sites are $10–18 per night, $1.50 per person per night for more than two people. Some credit cards accepted. Open year-round.

Directions: From Crescent City, drive north on U.S. 101 for 16 miles, three miles past the town of Smith River, to the Ship Ashore sign at Chinook Street. At Chinook Street, turn left and drive a short distance (less than half a block) to the motel lobby to register.

Contact: Ship Ashore Resort, 707/487-3141, fax 707/487-7070.

CALIFORNIA

❸ CRESCENT CITY REDWOODS KOA

Scenic rating: 6

five miles north of Crescent City

Map grid A1

This KOA camp is on the edge of a recreation wonderland, a perfect jump-off spot for a vacation. The park covers 17 acres, with 11 acres of redwood forest. A few farm animals live here, and guests are allowed to feed them. In addition, there are three golf courses nearby. The camp is only two miles from Redwood National Park, Jedediah Smith Redwoods State Park, and the Smith River National Recreation Area. It is also only a 10-minute drive to the beach and Tolowa Dunes Wildlife Area to the east, and to Crescent City Harbor to the south.

RV sites, facilities: There are 44 tent sites and 30 sites with full hookups (30 and 50 amps), including some pull-through sites for RVs of any length. Seventeen cabins and one cottage are also available. Picnic tables and fire grills are provided. A dump station, restrooms with flush toilets and showers, a coin laundry, free Wi-Fi, cable TV, playground, propane, convenience store, ice, firewood, recreation room, pool table, table tennis, horseshoes, go-carts, and volleyball are available. Leashed pets are permitted.

Reservations, fees: Reservations for RV sites are accepted at 800/562-5754. RV sites are $25–45 per night, $3.50 per person per night for more than two people, tent sites are $17–30 per night, $2.50 per person per night for more than two people. Some credit cards accepted. Open year-round.

Directions: From Crescent City, take U.S. 101 north for five miles to the campground entrance on the right (east) side of the road.

Contact: Crescent City Redwoods KOA, 707/464-5744, www.crescentcitykoa.com.

❹ JEDEDIAH SMITH REDWOODS STATE PARK

Scenic rating: 10

on the Smith River

Map grid A1

This is a beautiful park set along the Smith River, where the campsites are sprinkled amid a grove of old-growth redwoods. Reservations are usually a necessity during the summer. This park covers 10,000 acres on both sides of the Smith River, a jewel and California's last major free-flowing river. There are 20 miles of hiking and nature trails. The park has hiking trails that lead right out of the campground; one is routed along the beautiful Smith River, and another heads through forest, across U.S. 199, and hooks up with Simpson-Reed Interpretive Trail. In the summer, interpretive programs are available. There is also a good put-in spot at the park for river access in a drift boat, canoe, or raft. The fishing is best for steelhead from mid-January through March. In the summer, a seasonal footbridge connects the campground with more extensive trails. The best hikes are on the south side of the Smith River, accessible via Howland Hill Road, including the Boy Scout Tree Trail and Stout Grove (for access, see listing for *Hiouchi RV Resort*). Note that in winter, 100 inches of cumulative rainfall is common.

RV sites, facilities: There are 106 sites for tents or RVs up to 36 feet (no hookups) and trailers up to 31 feet, five hike-in/bike-in sites, and one group site for up to 15 vehicles and 50 people. Picnic tables, fire grills, and food lockers are provided. Drinking water, flush toilets, and a dump station are available. There is a visitors center with exhibits and a nature store. Propane gas and groceries are available within one mile. Some facilities are wheelchair-accessible. Leashed pets are permitted only in the campground and on roads.

Reservations, fees: Reservations are accepted ($8 reservation fee) at 800/444-PARK (800/444-7275) or www.reserveamerica.com. Sites are $45 per night, $8 per night for each additional vehicle, $300 per night for the group site, and $3 per person per night for hike-in/bike-in sites. Open year-round.

Directions: From Crescent City, drive north on U.S. 101 for four miles to the junction with U.S. 199. Turn east at U.S. 199 and drive five miles. Turn right at the well-signed entrance station.

Contact: Redwood National and State Parks, 707/465-2144 or 707/458-3018, fax 707/464-1812, www.parks.ca.gov.

5 HIOUCHI RV RESORT

Scenic rating: 7

near the Smith River

Map grid A1

This park is out of the wind and fog you get on the coast and set instead in the heart of the forest country. It makes a good base camp for a steelhead trip in winter. Insiders know that right next door, the fried chicken at the Hamlet's market is always good for a quick hit. An excellent side trip is to drive just east of Hiouchi on U.S. 199, turn right, and cross over two bridges, where you will reach a fork in the road. Turn left for a great scenic drive along the South Fork Smith River or turn right to get backdoor access to Jedediah Smith Redwoods State Park and three great trailheads for hiking in the redwoods. My favorite of the latter is the Boy Scout Tree Trail. Note that about one-fourth of the RV sites are filled with long-term renters, and many other sites fill up quickly with summer vacationers.

RV sites, facilities: There are 120 sites with full hookups (30 and 50 amps) for RVs of any length and six tent sites. Some sites are pull-through. Two park-model cabins and six furnished apartments are also available. Restrooms with flush toilets and showers, a dump station, coin laundry, Wi-Fi, high-speed modem hookups, cable TV, recreation room, fish cleaning station, horseshoe pits, grocery store, propane, and deli are available. A motel and café are nearby. A golf course is available within four miles. Some facilities are wheelchair-accessible. Leashed pets are permitted.

Reservations, fees: Reservations are accepted at 800/722-9468. RV sites are $26–34 per night, $2 per person per night for more than two

people; tent sites are $22–25 per night. Some credit cards accepted. Open year-round.

Directions: From Crescent City, drive five miles north on U.S. 101 to U.S. 199. Turn east (right) on U.S. 199 and drive about five miles (just past the entrance to Jedediah Smith Redwoods State Park) to the town of Hiouchi. In Hiouchi, turn left at the well-signed campground entrance.

Contact: Hiouchi RV Resort, 707/458-3321, fax 707/458-3521, www.hiouchi.com.

6 NORTH FORK

Scenic rating: 7

on the North Fork of the Smith River in Six Rivers National Forest

Map grid A1

This remote and primitive camp is a put-in for rafting and kayaking the North Fork Smith River in winter. Since there is no dam it can only be run in the rainy season, but this is a sensational Class III rafting trip in a rainstorm, including a spot at an overhanging rock along the northern shore where you can raft right through a waterfall. In the summer, the flows on the North Fork turn into a trickle and you can virtually walk down the stream. The campsites are primitive, open, and located within view of the river—not in the forest. Though there is space for RVs at the camp and the sites are wheelchair accessible, the road in can be impassable for RVs during wet weather and there is no additional access for wheelchairs.

RV sites, facilities: There are five sites for tents or RVs up to 18 feet (no hookups). Picnic tables and fire rings are provided. Vault toilets are available, but there is no drinking water. Garbage must be packed out. Some sites are wheelchair-accessible.

Reservations, fees: Reservations are not accepted. Sites are $8 per night. Open year-round.

Directions: From Crescent City, drive north on U.S. 101 (straight ahead past the Hwy. 199 turnoff) to Rowdy Creek Road. Turn right on Rowdy Creek Road (it becomes Forest Road 308) and drive about 4.5 miles on Rowdy Creek

Road/FR 308 to Forest Road 305. Turn left on Forest Road 305 (a dirt road) and drive 11 miles to the campground.

Contact: Smith River National Recreation Area, Six Rivers National Forest, 707/457-3131, fax 707/457-3794, www.fs.fed.us.

7 PANTHER FLAT

Scenic rating: 8

on the Smith River in Six Rivers National Forest

| Map grid A1 | BEST (|

This is an ideal alternative to the often-crowded Jedediah Smith Redwoods State Park. The park provides easy road access since it is set right along U.S. 199, the two-laner that runs beside the Smith River. This is the largest and one of the featured campgrounds in the Smith River National Recreation Area, with excellent prospects for salmon and steelhead fishing in the fall and winter respectively, and outstanding hiking and backpacking in the summer. A 0.25-mile interpretive trail and viewing area is one mile north of the campground, off U.S. 199. A great nearby hike is Stony Creek Trail, an easy walk along the North Fork Smith River; the trailhead is in nearby Gasquet on Stoney Creek Road. Redwood National Park is a short drive to the west. The Siskiyou Wilderness is a short drive to the southeast via forest roads detailed on Forest Service maps. The wild and scenic Smith River system provides fishing, swimming, sunbathing, kayaking for experts, and beautiful scenery.

RV sites, facilities: There are 39 sites for tents or RVs up to 40 feet (no hookups). Picnic tables and fire grills are provided. Drinking water and restrooms with flush toilets and coin showers are available. Propane gas, groceries, and coin laundry are available nearby. Some facilities are wheelchair-accessible. Leashed pets are permitted.

Reservations, fees: Reservations are accepted at 877/444-6777 or www.recreation.gov ($10 reservation fee). Sites are $15 per night, $5 per night for each additional vehicle. Open year-round.

Directions: From Crescent City, drive north on U.S. 101 for three miles to the junction with U.S. 199. At U.S. 199, turn east and drive 14.5 miles to Gasquet. From Gasquet, continue for 2.3 miles east on U.S. 199 and look for the entrance to the campground on the left side of the highway.

Contact: Smith River National Recreation Area, Six Rivers National Forest, 707/457-3131, fax 707/457-3794.

8 GRASSY FLAT

Scenic rating: 4

on the Smith River in Six Rivers National Forest

| Map grid A1 | BEST (|

This is one in a series of three easy-to-reach Forest Service camps set near U.S. 199 along the beautiful Middle Fork of the Smith River. It's a classic wild river, popular in the summer with kayakers, and the steelhead come huge in the winter for the crafty few. The camp itself is set directly across from a CalTrans waste area, and if you hit it when the crews are working, it can be noisy here. Most of the time, however, it is peaceful and quiet.

RV sites, facilities: There are four walk-in tent sites and 15 sites for tents or RVs up to 30 feet (no hookups). Picnic tables and fire grills are provided. Drinking water and vault toilets are available. Propane gas and groceries are available nearby. Some facilities are wheelchair-accessible. Leashed pets are permitted.

Reservations, fees: Reservations are accepted at 877/444-6777 or www.recreation.gov ($10 reservation fee). Sites are $10 per night, $5 per night for each additional vehicle. Open late May through mid-September.

Directions: From Crescent City, drive north on U.S. 101 for three miles to the junction with U.S. 199. Turn east on U.S. 199 and drive 14.5 miles to Gasquet. From Gasquet, continue east on U.S. 199 for 4.4 miles and look for the campground entrance on the right side of the road.

Contact: Smith River National Recreation Area, Six Rivers National Forest, 707/457-3131, fax 707/457-3794.

CALIFORNIA

CALIFORNIA

9 PATRICK CREEK

Scenic rating: 8

in Six Rivers National Forest
Map grid A1

This is one of the prettiest spots along U.S. 199, where Patrick Creek enters the upper Smith River. It is also a historic California Conservation Corps site that was built in the 1930s. This section of the Smith looks something like a large trout stream, rolling green past a boulder-lined shore, complete with forest canopy. There are small cutthroat trout in summer and salmon and steelhead in fall and winter. A big plus for this camp is its nearby access to excellent hiking in the Siskiyou Wilderness, especially the great day hike to Buck Lake. It is essential to have a map of Six Rivers National Forest, both for driving directions to the trailhead and for the hiking route. You can buy maps at the information center for the Smith River National Recreation Area on the north side of U.S. 199 in Gasquet. Patrick Creek Lodge, on the opposite side of the highway from the campground, has a restaurant and bar. A paved trail connects the campground to Patrick Creek Lodge.

RV sites, facilities: There are 13 sites for tents or RVs up to 35 feet (no hookups). Picnic tables and fire grills are provided. Drinking water and flush toilets are available. Some facilities are wheelchair-accessible, including a fishing area. Leashed pets are permitted.

Reservations, fees: Reservations are accepted for individual sites and are required for group sites at 877/444-6777 or www.recreation.gov ($10 reservation fee). Sites are $14 per night, $5 per night for each additional vehicle. Open May through September.

Directions: From Crescent City, drive north on U.S. 101 for three miles to the junction with U.S. 199. Turn east on U.S. 199 and drive 14.5 miles to Gasquet. From Gasquet, continue east on U.S. 199 for 7.5 miles and look for the campground entrance on the right side of the road.

Contact: Smith River National Recreation Area, Six Rivers National Forest, 707/457-3131, fax 707/457-3794.

10 BAYSIDE RV PARK

Scenic rating: 6

in Crescent City
Map grid A1

If you are towing a boat, you just found your personal heaven: This RV park is directly adjacent to the boat docking area in Crescent City Harbor. There are several walks in the immediate area, including exploring the harbor and ocean frontage. For a quick change of scenery, it is only a 15-minute drive to Redwood National Park and Jedediah Smith Redwoods State Park along U.S. 199 to the north. Note that about 20 sites are filled with long-term renters, and most of the spaces book up for the entire season.

RV sites, facilities: There are 110 sites for RVs up to 34 feet. Most sites have full hookups (30 amps) and/or are pull-through. No tents. Picnic tables are provided. Restrooms with flush toilets and showers, cable TV, Wi-Fi, and a coin laundry are available. A restaurant is adjacent to the park. Leashed pets are permitted.

Reservations, fees: Reservations are accepted at 800/446-9482. Sites are $20–24 per night, $3 per person per night for more than two people. Open year-round.

Directions: From U.S. 101 at the southern end of Crescent City, drive to Citizen Dock Road and continue one-half block south to the park office.

Contact: Bayside RV Park, 707/464-9482.

11 VILLAGE CAMPER INN RV PARK

Scenic rating: 7

in Crescent City
Map grid A1

Woods and water, that's what attracts visitors to California's north coast. Village Camper Inn provides nearby access to big woods and big water. This RV park is on 20 acres of wooded land, about a 10-minute drive away from the giant redwoods along U.S. 199. In addition, you'll find some premium beachcombing for driftwood and agates a mile away on the spectacular rocky beaches just west of town. Note that about half of the sites fill up for the entire summer season.

RV sites, facilities: There are 135 sites for RVs of any length, and a separate area for tents. Most RV sites have full hookups (30 and 50 amps); some sites are pull-through. Picnic tables are provided. Drinking water, a dump station, restrooms with flush toilets and showers, coin laundry, modem access, and cable TV are available. Leashed pets are permitted, with certain restrictions.

Reservations, fees: Reservations are accepted. Sites are $22.50–28.50 per night, $2 per person per night for more than two people. Some credit cards accepted. Open year-round.

Directions: From Crescent City, drive north on U.S. 101 to the Parkway Drive exit. Take that exit and drive 0.5 mile to the campground on the right.

On U.S. 101, driving south in Crescent City: Drive south on U.S. 101 to the Washington Boulevard exit. Turn left on Washington Boulevard and drive one block to Parkway Drive. Turn left on Parkway and drive one block to the campground on the right.

Contact: Village Camper Inn RV Park, 707/464-3544.

12 SUNSET HARBOR RV PARK

Scenic rating: 4

in Crescent City
Map grid A1

People camp here with their RVs to be close to the action in Crescent City and to the nearby harbor and beach frontage. For starters, drive a few minutes to the northwest side of town, where the sea is sprinkled with gigantic rocks and boulders, for dramatic ocean views and spectacular sunsets. For finishers, go down to the west side of town for great walks along the ocean parkway or south to the harbor and adjacent beach, which is long and expansive. About half of the sites are filled with long-term renters.

RV sites, facilities: There are 69 sites with full hookups (30 and 50 amps) for RVs up to 45 feet. No tents. Picnic tables are provided at some sites. Restrooms with flush toilets and showers, cable TV, coin laundry, and a recreation room are available. A grocery store is available nearby. Some facilities are wheelchair-accessible. Leashed pets are permitted.

Reservations, fees: Reservations are accepted. Sites are $28 per night, $3 per person per night for more than two people. Monthly rates are available. Some credit cards accepted. Open year-round.

Directions: In Crescent City on U.S. 101, drive to King Street. At King Street, turn east and drive one block to the park entrance at the end of the road.

Contact: Sunset Harbor RV Park, 707/464-3423.

13 DEL NORTE COAST REDWOODS STATE PARK

Scenic rating: 8

near Crescent City
Map grid A1

The campsites are set in a series of loops in the forest, so while there are a lot of camps, you still feel a sense of privacy here. In addition to redwoods, there are also good stands of alders, along with a rambling stream fed by several creeks. It makes for a very pretty setting, with four loop trails available right out of the camp. This park covers 6,400 acres, featuring 50 percent old-growth coastal redwoods and eight miles of wild coastline. Topography is fairly steep, with elevations ranging from sea level to 1,277 feet. This range is oriented in a north-to-south direction, with steep cliffs adjacent to the ocean. That makes most of the rocky seacoast generally inaccessible except by Damnation Trail and Footsteps Rock Trail. The best coastal access is at Wilson Beach or False Klamath Cove, where there is a half-mile of sandy beach bordered by excellent tide pools.

The forest interior is dense, with redwoods

and tanoaks, madrones, red alders, bigleaf maples, and California bay. One reason for the lush growth is what rangers call the "nurturing" coastal climate. Nurturing, in this case, means rain like you wouldn't believe in the winter—often more than 100 inches in a season—and lots of fog in the summer. Interpretive programs are conducted here. Insider's note: Hike-in and bike-in campers beware. There is a 900-foot elevation change over the course of two miles between the U.S. 101 access road and the campground.

RV sites, facilities: There are 38 tent sites and 107 sites for tents or RVs up to 31 feet (no hookups). Hike-in/bike-in sites are also available. Picnic tables, fire pits, and food lockers are provided. Drinking water, a dump station, and restrooms with flush toilets and coin showers are available. Some facilities are wheelchair-accessible. Leashed pets are permitted only in the campground.

Reservations, fees: Reservations are accepted ($8 reservation fee) at 800/444-PARK (800/444-7275) or www.reserveamerica.com. Sites are $35 per night, $8 per night for each additional vehicle, $3 per person per night for hike-in/bike-in sites. Open May through September.

Directions: From Crescent City, drive seven miles south on U.S. 101 to a signed access road for Del Norte Coast Redwoods State Park. Turn left at the park entrance.

Contact: Redwood National and State Parks, 1111 2nd Street, Crescent City, CA 95531, 707/465-2146, fax 707/464-1812, www.nps.gov/redw.

14 BIG FLAT

Scenic rating: 7

on Hurdygurdy Creek in Six Rivers National Forest
Map grid A1

This camp provides an ideal setting for those who know of it, which is why it gets quite a bit of use for a relatively remote camp. Set along Hurdygurdy Creek, near where the creek

enters the South Fork of the Smith River, it provides nearby access to South Kelsey Trail, an outstanding hiking route whether you are walking for a few hours or backpacking for days. In the summer, it is a good layover for rafters or kayakers paddling the South Fork of the Smith River.

RV sites, facilities: There are 25 sites for tents or RVs up to 22 feet (no hookups). Picnic tables and fire grills are provided. Vault toilets and food lockers are available. There is no drinking water and garbage must be packed out. Some facilities are wheelchair-accessible. Leashed pets are permitted.

Reservations, fees: Reservations are not accepted. Sites are $8 per night, $5 per night for each additional vehicle. Open May through mid-September.

Directions: From Crescent City, drive north on U.S. 101 for three miles to the junction with U.S. 199. Turn east on U.S. 199 and drive five miles to Hiouchi. Continue just past Hiouchi to South Fork Road. Turn right and cross two bridges. At the Y, turn left on South Fork Road and drive about 14 miles to Big Flat Road/County Road 405. Turn left and drive 0.25 mile to the campground entrance road (Forest Road 15N59) on the left. Turn left and drive a short distance to the camp on the left.

Contact: Smith River National Recreation Area, Six Rivers National Forest, 707/457-3131, fax 707/457-3794.

15 MYSTIC FOREST RV PARK

Scenic rating: 6

near the Klamath River
Map grid A1

The park features gravel roads, redwood trees, and grassy sites amid a 50-acre park designed primarily for RVs with a separate area for tents. A bonus here is the 18-hole miniature golf course. The Trees of Mystery is less than a mile away and features a nearly 50-foot-tall Paul Bunyan and his blue ox, Babe. (In the winter of 2008, you may recall the tale of Babe's head falling off in a storm. Have no fear—Babe again has a head.) The park is about 1.5 miles away from the ocean and 3.5 miles from the Klamath River. Jet-boat tours are available on the Klamath River.

RV sites, facilities: There are 30 sites with full hookups (30 amps) for RVs of any length and 14 tent sites. Some of the RV sites are pull-through. Picnic tables and fire rings are provided. Drinking water, restrooms with flush toilets and showers, Wi-Fi, cable TV, playground, recreation room, horseshoes, miniature golf, a coin laundry, modem access, convenience store and gift shop, group facilities, and firewood are available. Some facilities are wheelchair-accessible. Leashed pets are permitted.

Reservations, fees: Reservations are accepted. Sites are $16–28 per night, $4 per person per night for more than two people. Group rates available. Some credit cards accepted. Open year-round.

Directions: From Eureka, drive north on U.S. 101 to Klamath and continue north for four miles. Look for the entrance sign on the left side of the road. If you reach the Trees of Mystery, you have gone a mile too far north.

Contact: Mystic Forest RV Park, 707/482-4901, fax 707/482-0704, www.mysticforestrv.com.

16 CHINOOK RV RESORT

Scenic rating: 7

on the Klamath River
Map grid A1

The camping area at this park consists of grassy RV sites that overlook the Klamath River. Chinook RV Resort is one of the more well-known parks on the lower Klamath. A boat ramp and fishing supplies are available.

RV sites, facilities: There are 70 sites with full hookups (30 and 50 amps) for RVs of any length and a grassy area for tents. Some RV sites are pull-through. An apartment is also available. Picnic tables and fire grills are provided. Restrooms with flush toilets and showers, cable television, modem access, coin laundry, fish cleaning station, recreation room, propane, convenience store, RV supplies, boat ramp, boat rentals, and a tackle shop are available. Leashed pets are permitted.

Reservations, fees: Reservations are accepted at 866/482-3511. RV sites are $25–27 per night, tents are $16 per night, $3 per person per night for more than two people, $3 per night for each additional vehicle. Some credit cards accepted. Open year-round.

Directions: From Eureka, drive north on U.S. 101 to Klamath. After crossing the bridge at the Klamath River, continue north on U.S. 101 for a mile to the campground on the left.

Contact: Chinook RV Resort, 707/482-3511, fax 707/482-0493, www.chinookrvresort.com.

17 CAMP MARIGOLD

Scenic rating: 7

near the Klamath River
Map grid A1

Camp Marigold is surrounded by wonder: Redwood National Park, towering redwoods, Pacific Ocean beaches, driftwood, agates, fossilized rocks, blackberries, Fern Canyon, Lagoon Creek Park, and the Trees of Mystery. Fishing is available nearby, in season, for several species, including king salmon, steelhead, redtail perch, and candlefish. The camp has 3.5 acres of landscaped gardens with hiking trails… get the idea? Well, there's more: It is only two miles to the Klamath River, in case you can't find enough to do already. A few sites are filled with long-term renters.

RV sites, facilities: There are 40 sites with full hookups for RVs up to 35 feet. Twelve park-model cabins are also available. Picnic tables and barbecues are provided. Restrooms with showers, cable TV, group facilities, and a coin laundry are available. Small leashed pets are permitted.

Reservations, fees: Reservations are recommended. Sites are $28 per night. Monthly rates available. Some credit cards accepted. Open year-round.

Directions: From Eureka, drive 60 miles north on U.S. 101 to the campground at 16101 U.S. 101, four miles north of the Klamath River Bridge, on the right side of the road. The camp is a mile south of the Trees of Mystery.

Contact: Camp Marigold, 707/482-3585 or 800/621-8513.

18 KLAMATH'S CAMPER CORRAL RV RESORT AND CAMPGROUND

Scenic rating: 6

on the Klamath River

Map grid A1

This 50-acre resort offers 3,000 feet of Klamath River frontage, grassy tent sites, berry picking, access to the ocean, and hiking trails nearby. And, of course, in the fall it has salmon and steelhead, the main attraction on the lower Klamath. A boat launch is about 1.5 miles from the resort. Nature trails are on the property, and there is room for bike riding. River swimming is popular in summer. A nightly campfire is usually available. Organized recreation is available in summer. A free pancake breakfast is offered to campers on Sundays.

RV sites, facilities: There are 140 sites for RVs of any length and 60 tent sites. Many RV sites have full or partial hookups (30 amps) and are pull-through. Picnic tables and fire rings are provided at the tent sites. Drinking water, restrooms with flush toilets and showers, seasonal heated swimming pool, recreation hall, general store, playground, dump station, coin laundry, cable TV, ice, firewood, bait and tackle, fish-cleaning station, fishing guide service, group facilities, arcade, basketball, volleyball, badminton, shuffleboard, horseshoes, table tennis, croquet, and tetherball are available. Leashed pets are permitted.

Reservations, fees: Reservations are accepted at 800/701-7275. RV sites are $32–37.50 per night, $3 per night for each additional vehicle,

$3 per person per night for more than two people; tent sites are $19.50–24.50 per night. Weekly and monthly rates are available. Some credit cards accepted. Open April through October.

Directions: From Eureka, drive north on U.S. 101 to Klamath. Just after crossing the Klamath River/Golden Bear Bridge, take the Terwer Valley/Highway 169 exit. At the stop sign, turn left, drive under the highway and continue a short distance west to the campground.

Contact: Klamath's Camper Corral, 707/482-5741, www.campercorral.net.

19 STEELHEAD LODGE

Scenic rating: 6

on the Klamath River

Map grid A1

Many anglers use this park as headquarters when the salmon and steelhead get going in August. The park has grassy sites near the Klamath River.

RV sites, facilities: There are 24 sites for tents or RVs of any length (full hookups); some sites are pull-through. Picnic tables are provided. Drinking water, restrooms with flush toilets and showers, and ice are available. A bar, restaurant, and motel are also available. Some facilities are wheelchair-accessible. Leashed pets are permitted.

Reservations, fees: Reservations are required. RV sites are $20 per night, and tent sites are $10 per night. Weekly and monthly rates available. Some credit cards accepted. Open February through October.

Directions: From Eureka, drive north on U.S. 101 to Klamath and the junction with Highway 169. Turn east on Highway 169 and drive 3.2 miles to Terwer Riffle Road. Turn right (south) on Terwer Riffle Road and drive one block to Steelhead Lodge on the right.

Contact: Steelhead Lodge, 707/482-8145, www. steelheadlodge.klamath.com.

20 TERWER PARK

Scenic rating: 7

on the Klamath River

Map grid A1

This RV park is situated near the Terwer Riffle, one of the better shore-fishing spots for steelhead and salmon on the lower Klamath River. You'll find grassy sites, river access, and some fair trails along the Klamath. When the salmon arrive in late August and September, Terwer Riffle can be loaded with fish, as well as boaters and shore anglers—a wild scene. Note that at this park, tent campers are separated from the RV park, with tent camping at a grassy area near the river. Some sites are taken by monthly renters.

RV sites, facilities: There are 35 sites with full hookups (30 amps) for RVs up to 34 feet, and a separate tent area. Several sites are pull-through. Five cabins are also available. Picnic tables are provided. Restrooms with flush toilets and showers are available. A pulley boat launch is nearby. Leashed pets are permitted.

Reservations, fees: Reservations are accepted. Sites are $17–20 per night, $5 per night for each additional vehicle. Weekly and monthly rates available. Open April through October.

Directions: From Eureka, drive north on U.S. 101 to Klamath and the junction with Highway 169. Turn east on Highway 169 and drive 3.5 miles to Terwer Riffle Road. Turn right on Terwer Riffle Road and drive two blocks, then bear right on Terwer Riffle Road and continue five blocks (about 0.5 mile) to the park at the end of the road (641 Terwer Riffle Road).

Contact: Terwer Park, 707/482-3855.

21 PRAIRIE CREEK REDWOODS STATE PARK: GOLD BLUFFS BEACH

Scenic rating: 8

in Prairie Creek Redwoods State Park

Map grid A1　　　　　　　　　**BEST**

The campsites here are set in a sandy, exposed area with man-made windbreaks, with a huge, expansive beach on one side and a backdrop of 100- to 200-foot cliffs on the other side. You can walk for miles at this beach, often without seeing another soul, and there is a great trail routed north through forest, with many hidden little waterfalls. In addition, Fern Canyon Trail, one of the best 30-minute hikes in California, is at the end of Davison Road. Hikers walk along a stream in a narrow canyon, its vertical walls covered with magnificent ferns. There are some herds of elk in the area, often right along the access road. These camps are rarely used in the winter because of the region's heavy rain and winds. The expanse of beach here is awesome, covering 10 miles of huge, pristine ocean frontage. (See *Prairie Creek Redwoods State Park: Elk Prairie* in this chapter for more information about Prairie Creek Redwoods.)

RV sites, facilities: There are 26 sites for tents or RVs up to 24 feet (no hookups). No trailers or vehicles wider than eight feet. Fire grills, food lockers, and picnic tables are provided. Drinking water and restrooms with flush toilets and cold showers are available. Leashed pets are permitted.

Reservations, fees: Reservations are not accepted. Sites are $14–15 per night, $8 per night for each additional vehicle. Open March–November.

Directions: From Eureka, drive north on U.S. 101 for 45 miles to Orick. At Orick, continue north on U.S. 101 for three miles to Davison Road. Turn left (west) on Davison Road and drive six miles to the campground on the left. Note: No vehicles more than 24 feet long or eight feet wide are permitted on gravel Davison Road, which is narrow and very bumpy.

Contact: Prairie Creek Redwoods State Park, 707/465-7347; Visitors Center 707/465-7354, www.parks.ca.gov.

22 PRAIRIE CREEK REDWOODS STATE PARK: ELK PRAIRIE

Scenic rating: 9

in Prairie Creek Redwoods State Park

Map grid A1   BEST (

A small herd of Roosevelt elk wander free in this remarkable 14,000-acre park. Great opportunities for photographs abound, including a group of about five elk often found right along the highway and access roads. Where there are meadows, there are elk; it's about that simple. An elky here, an elky there, making this one of the best places to see wildlife in California. Remember that these are wild animals, they are huge, and they can be unpredictable; in other words, enjoy them, but don't harass them or get too close.

This park consists of old-growth coastal redwoods, prairie lands, and 10 miles of scenic, open beach (Gold Bluff Beach). The interior of the park can be reached by 75 miles of hiking, biking, and nature trails, including a trailhead for a great bike ride at the visitors center. There are many additional trailheads and a beautiful tour of giant redwoods along the Drury Scenic Parkway. A visitors center and summer interpretive programs with guided walks and junior ranger programs are available. The forest understory is very dense due to moisture from coastal fog. Western azalea and rhododendron blooms, peaking in May and June, are best seen from the Rhododendron Trail. November through May, always bring your rain gear. Summer temperatures range 40–75°F; winter temperatures range 35–55°F.

RV sites, facilities: There are 76 sites for tents or RVs up to 27 feet (no hookups), and one hike-in/bike-in site. Picnic tables, fire rings, and bear-proof food lockers are provided. Drinking water and restrooms with flush toilets and coin showers are available. Some facilities are wheelchair-accessible. Leashed pets are permitted.

Reservations, fees: Reservations are accepted during the summer ($8 reservation fee) at 800/444-PARK (800/444-7275) or www.reserveamerica.com. Sites are $35 per night,

$8 per night for each additional vehicle, $3 per person per night for hike-in/bike-in site. Open year-round.

Directions: From Eureka, drive 45 miles north on U.S. 101 to Orick. At Orick, continue north on U.S. 101 for five miles to the Newton B. Drury Scenic Parkway. Take the exit for the Newton B. Drury Scenic Parkway and drive north for a mile to the park. Turn left at the park entrance.

Contact: Prairie Creek Redwoods State Park, Elk Prairie Campground, 707/465-7347 or Visitors Center 707/465-7354, www.parks.ca.gov.

23 BIG LAGOON COUNTY PARK

Scenic rating: 7

north of Trinidad overlooking the Pacific Ocean

Map grid A1

This is a remarkable, huge lagoon that borders the Pacific Ocean. It provides good boating, excellent exploring, fair fishing, and good duck hunting in the winter. It's a good spot to paddle a canoe around on a calm day. A lot of out-of-towners cruise by, note the lagoon's proximity to the ocean, and figure it must be saltwater. Wrong! Not only is it freshwater, but it provides a long shot for anglers trying for rainbow trout. One reason not many RV drivers stop here is that most of them are drawn farther north (another eight miles) to Freshwater Lagoon.

RV sites, facilities: There are 25 sites for tents or RVs of any length (no hookups). Picnic tables and fire grills are provided. Drinking water and restrooms with flush toilets and coin showers are available. A boat ramp is also available. Some facilities are wheelchair-accessible. Leashed pets are permitted.

Reservations, fees: Reservations are not accepted. Sites are $15 per night per vehicle, $3 per night for a second vehicle, $3 per person per night for hike-in/bike-in, $1 per pet per night. Maximum stay is 10 days. Open year-round.

Directions: From Eureka, drive 22 miles north on U.S. 101 to Trinidad. At Trinidad, continue north on U.S. 101 for eight miles to Big Lagoon

CALIFORNIA

Park Road. Turn left (west) at Big Lagoon Park Road and drive two miles to the park.

Contact: Humboldt County Public Works, 707/445-7651, www.co.humboldt.ca.us; Humboldt Lagoons State Park Visitor Center, 707/488-2041.

24 PATRICK'S POINT STATE PARK

Scenic rating: 9

near Trinidad

Map grid A1

This pretty park covers 640 acres of coastal headlands and is filled with Sitka spruce, dramatic ocean lookouts, and several beautiful beaches, including one with agates, one with tidepools, and another with an expansive stretch of beachfront leading to a lagoon. You can see it best on the Rim Trail, which has many little cut-off routes to the lookouts and down to the beaches. The campground is sheltered in the forest, and while it is often foggy and damp in the summer, it is always beautiful. A Native American village, constructed by the Yurok tribe, is also here. At the north end of the park, a short hike to see the bizarre "Octopus Trees" is a good side trip, with trees that are growing atop downed logs, their root systems exposed like octopus tentacles; the trail here loops through a grove of old-growth Sitka spruce. In addition, there are several miles of pristine beach to the north that extends to the lagoons. Interpretive programs are available. The forest here is dense, with spruce, hemlock, pine, fir, and red alder covering an ocean headland. Night and morning fog are common almost year-round, and there are periods when it doesn't lift for days. This area gets 60 inches of rain per year on average. For camping, plan on making reservations.

RV sites, facilities: There are 85 sites for tents or RVs (no hookups), 39 sites for RVs up to 31 feet, and three group sites for up to 100 people. Fire grills, storage lockers, and picnic tables are provided. Drinking water and restrooms

with flush toilets and coin showers are available. Some facilities are wheelchair-accessible. Leashed pets are permitted at campsites, but not on trails or beaches.

Reservations, fees: Reservations are accepted ($8 reservation fee) at 800/444-PARK (800/444-7275) or www.reserveamerica.com. Sites are $35 per night, $8 per night for each additional vehicle, $110–300 per night for the group site. Open year-round.

Directions: From Eureka, drive north on U.S. 101 for 22 miles to Trinidad. At Trinidad, continue north on U.S. 101 for 5.5 miles to Patrick's Point Drive. Take that exit and at the stop sign turn left and drive 0.5 mile to the park entrance.

Contact: Patrick's Point State Park, 707/677-3570, www.parks.ca.gov.

25 SOUNDS OF THE SEA RV PARK

Scenic rating: 6

in Trinidad

Map grid A1

The Trinidad area, about 20 miles north of Eureka, is one of the great places on this planet. Nearby Patrick's Point State Park is one of the highlights, with a Sitka spruce forest, beautiful coastal lookouts, a great easy hike on the Rim Trail, and access to several secluded beaches. To the nearby south at Trinidad Head is a small harbor and dock, with deep-sea and salmon fishing trips available. A breezy beach is to the immediate north of the Seascape Restaurant. A bonus at this privately operated RV park is good berry picking in season.

RV sites, facilities: There are 70 sites with full hookups (30 and 50 amps) for RVs; some sites are pull-through. No tents. Four park-model cabins are also available. Picnic tables and fire rings are provided at most sites. Restrooms with showers, cable TV, Wi-Fi, exercise room and indoor spa (fee), bicycle rentals, dump station, coin laundry, convenience store, gift shop, propane, firewood, and ice are available. Leashed pets are permitted.

Reservations, fees: Reservations are accepted at 707/677-3271. Sites are $25–42 per night, $3–5 per person per night for more than two people. Some credit cards accepted. Open year-round.

Directions: From Eureka, drive north on U.S. 101 for 28 miles to Trinidad. In Trinidad, continue north on U.S. 101 for five miles to the Patrick's Point exit. Take the Patrick's Point exit, turn left, and drive 0.5 mile to the park.

Contact: Sounds of the Sea RV Park, 707/677-3271.

26 SYLVAN HARBOR RV PARK AND CABINS

Scenic rating: 8

in Trinidad

Map grid A1

This park is designed as an RV park and fish camp, with cleaning tables and canning facilities available on-site. It is a short distance from the boat hoist at the Trinidad pier. Beauty surrounds Sylvan Harbor on all sides for miles. Visitors come to enjoy the various beaches, go agate hunting, or look for driftwood on the beach. Nearby Patrick's Point State Park is an excellent side-trip getaway. This is one of several privately operated parks in the Trinidad area, offering a choice of shaded or open sites. (For more information about recreation options nearby, see *Sounds of the Sea RV Park* listing.)

RV sites, facilities: There are 73 sites with full hookups (30 amps) for RVs up to 35 feet. No tents. A storage shed and cable TV are provided. Three cabins are available. Restrooms with showers, fish-cleaning stations, fish smokers, canning facilities, coin laundry, and propane are available. Leashed pets are permitted.

Reservations, fees: Reservations are accepted for cabins only. Sites are $25 per night, $3 per person per night for more than two people. Monthly rates available during the summer. Open year-round, weather permitting.

Directions: From Eureka, drive north on U.S. 101 for 28 miles to the Trinidad exit. Take that exit to Main Street. Turn left on Main Street and drive 0.1 mile under the freeway to Patrick's Point Drive. Turn right on Patrick's Point Drive and drive one mile to the campground on the right at 875 Patrick's Point Drive.

Contact: Sylvan Harbor RV Park and Cabins, 707/677-9988, www.sylvanharbor.com.

27 VIEW CREST LODGE

Scenic rating: 8

in Trinidad

Map grid A1

View Crest Lodge is one of the premium spots in Trinidad, with pretty cottages available as well as campsites for RVs and tents. A bonus here is the remarkable flights of swallows, many of which have nests at the cottages. Recreation options include deep-sea and salmon fishing at Trinidad Harbor to the nearby south, and outstanding easy hiking at Patrick's Point State Park to the nearby north.

RV sites, facilities: There are 36 sites with full hookups (20 and 30 amps) for RVs of any length, and a separate area for tents. Some sites are pull-through. Twelve cottages are also available. Picnic tables and fire rings are provided. Restrooms with showers, cable TV, a coin laundry, and firewood are available. Leashed pets are permitted only in the campground.

Reservations, fees: Reservations are accepted. Sites are $16–26 per night, $1 per person per night for more than two people. Monthly rates available. Some credit cards accepted. Open year-round.

Directions: From Eureka, drive north on U.S. 101 for 28 miles to Trinidad. Take the Patrick's Point State Park exit. Continue north for five miles to Patrick's Point Drive. Turn left and drive 0.9 mile to the lodge on the left.

Contact: View Crest Lodge, 707/677-3393, fax 707/677-9363, www.viewcrestlodge.com.

28 MIDWAY RV PARK

Scenic rating: 6

in Trinidad

Map grid A1

This is one of several privately developed camp-grounds in Trinidad. In the summer, salmon fishing can be excellent just off Trinidad Head. In the fall, rock fishing is the way to go, and in winter, crabbing is tops. Patrick's Point State Park provides a nearby side-trip option to the north. Note that some sites have long-term rent-ers, and most of the remaining sites fill up for the entire summer season. It can be difficult to get a space here for overnight camping during the summer.

RV sites, facilities: There are 73 sites with full hookups (30 amps) for RVs up to 40 feet. No tents. Picnic tables are provided. Restrooms with showers, cable TV, club room, propane, coin laundry, and fish-cleaning station are available. Some facilities are wheelchair-acces-sible. Leashed pets are permitted.

Reservations, fees: Reservations are recom-mended in the summer. Sites are $25–28 per night. Some credit cards accepted. Open year-round.

Directions: From Eureka, drive north on U.S. 101 for 28 miles to the Trinidad exit. Take that exit to Main Street. Turn left on Main Street and drive 0.1 mile under the freeway to Patrick's Point Drive. Turn right on Patrick's Point Drive and drive 0.5 mile to Midway Drive. Turn right and drive 0.1 mile to the campground at 51 Midway Drive.

Contact: Midway RV Park, tel./fax 707/677-3934.

29 EMERALD FOREST

Scenic rating: 5

in Trinidad

Map grid A1

This campground is set on 12 acres of red-woods, often dark and wet, with the ocean at Trinidad Head only about a five-minute drive

away. The campground owners emphasize that they are a vacation and overnight park only, and not a mobile home or long-term park.

RV sites, facilities: There are 46 sites with full or partial hookups (30 amps) for RVs up to 45 feet, and 30 tent sites. Some sites are pull-through. There are also 19 cabins. Picnic tables, fire rings, and barbecues are provided. Restrooms, showers, free cable TV in RV sites, playground, convenience store, ice, firewood, coin laundry, group facilities, fish-cleaning station, dump station, propane, telephone and modem hookups, Wi-Fi, volleyball, horseshoes, badminton, and video arcade are available. Leashed pets are permitted, except in the tent sites or cabins.

Reservations, fees: Reservations are recom-mended in the summer. RV sites are $25–41 per night, $2.50–3 per person per night for more than two people; tent sites are $24–29 per night. Winter rates available. Some credit cards accepted. Open year-round.

Directions: From Eureka, drive north on U.S. 101 for 28 miles to the Trinidad exit. Take that exit to Main Street. Turn left on Main Street and drive 0.1 mile under the freeway to Patrick's Point Drive. Turn right on Patrick's Point Drive and drive 0.9 mile north to the campground at 753 Patrick's Point Drive.

Contact: Emerald Forest, 707/677-3554, fax 707/677-0963, www.rvintheredwoods.com.

30 HIDDEN CREEK

Scenic rating: 5

in Trinidad

Map grid A1

To tell you the truth, there really isn't much hidden about this RV park, but you might be hard-pressed to find year-round Parker Creek. Regardless, it is still in a pretty location in Trin-idad, with the Trinidad pier, adjacent harbor, restaurants, and beach all within a drive of just a minute or two. Deep-sea fishing for salmon, lingcod, and rockfish is available on boats out of Trinidad Harbor. Crab and albacore tuna are also caught here, and there's beachcombing for agates and driftwood on the beach to the immediate north. Note that half of the sites are filled with long-term renters.

RV sites, facilities: There are 56 sites with full or partial hookups (30 and 50 amps) for RVs up to 40 feet, and a grassy area for tents. Six park-model cabins are also available. Picnic tables are provided. Cable TV, restrooms with showers, fish-cleaning station, ice, picnic area, and a dump station are available. Leashed pets are permitted.

Reservations, fees: Reservations are recommended in the summer. Sites are $25–29 per night, $2 per person per night for more than two people. Long-term rates available. Open year-round.

Directions: From Eureka, drive north on U.S. 101 for 28 miles to Trinidad. Take the Trinidad exit to the stop sign. Turn right at Westhaven Drive and drive a short distance to the RV park on the left at 199 North Westhaven.

Contact: Hidden Creek RV Park, 707/677-3775, www.hiddencreekrvpark.com.

31 CLAM BEACH COUNTY PARK

Scenic rating: 7

near McKinleyville

Map grid A2

Here awaits a beach that seems to stretch on forever, one of the great places to bring a lover, dog, children, or, hey, all three. While the campsites are a bit exposed, making winds out of the north a problem in the spring, the direct beach access largely makes up for it. The park gets its name from the fair clamming that is available, but you must come equipped with a clam gun or special clam shovel, and then be out when minus low tides arrive at daybreak. Most people just enjoy playing tag with the waves, taking long romantic walks, or throwing sticks for the dog.

RV sites, facilities: There are 12 sites for tents and a parking lot for 15 RVs of any length (no hookups). Picnic tables and fire rings are provided. Drinking water and vault toilets are available. Propane gas, grocery store, and a coin laundry are available in McKinleyville. Leashed pets are permitted.

Reservations, fees: Reservations are not accepted. Sites are $10 per night per vehicle, $3 per person per night for hike-in/bike-in, $1 per pet per night. Maximum stay is three days. Open year-round.

Directions: From Eureka, drive north on U.S. 101 to McKinleyville. Continue past McKinleyville to the Clam Beach Park exit. Take that exit and turn west at the sign for Clam Beach. Drive two blocks to the campground, which is adjacent to Little River State Beach.

Contact: Humboldt County Public Works, 707/445-7651, www.co.humboldt.ca.us.

32 MAD RIVER RAPIDS RV PARK

Scenic rating: 7

in Arcata

Map grid A2

This park is near the farmlands on the outskirts of town, in a pastoral, quiet setting. There is a great bike ride nearby on a trail routed along the Mad River, and it is also excellent for taking a dog for a walk. Nearby Arcata is a unique town, a bit of the old and a bit of the new, and the Arcata Marsh at the north end of Humboldt Bay provides a scenic and easy bicycle trip, as well as an excellent destination for hiking, sightseeing, and bird-watching. About half of the sites are filled with long-term renters.

RV sites, facilities: There are 92 sites with full hookups (30 and 50 amps) for RVs of any length; some sites are pull-through. No tents. Picnic tables are provided. Fire grills are provided at two sites. Restrooms with showers, cable TV, Wi-Fi, a dump station, recreation room, tennis courts, fitness room, playground, basketball courts, jogging trail, arcade, table tennis, horseshoe pits, heated swimming pool, spa, group facilities, restaurant and bar, convenience store, RV supplies, and coin laundry are available. A motel is adjacent to the park. Some facilities are wheelchair-accessible. Leashed pets are permitted.

Reservations, fees: Reservations are accepted at 800/822-7776. Sites are $42.35 per night. Some credit cards accepted. Weekly and monthly rates available. Open year-round.

Directions: From the junction of U.S. 101 and Highway 299 in Arcata, drive 0.25 mile north on U.S. 101 to the Guintoli Lane/Janes Road exit. Take that exit and turn left (west) on Janes Road and drive two blocks to the park on the left.

Contact: Mad River Rapids RV Park, 707/822-7275, www.madriverrv.com.

33 EUREKA KOA

Scenic rating: 2

in Eureka

Map grid A2

This is a year-round KOA camp for U.S. 101 cruisers looking for a layover spot in Eureka. A bonus here is a few of those little KOA Kamping Kabins, the log-style jobs that win on cuteness alone. The closest significant recreation option is the Arcata Marsh on Humboldt Bay, a richly diverse spot with good trails for biking and hiking or just parking and looking at the water. Another option is excellent salmon fishing in June, July, and August.

RV sites, facilities: There are 140 sites with full or partial hookups (30 and 50 amps) for RVs of any length, 26 tent sites, and eight hike-in/bike-in sites. Most RV sites are pull-through. Ten camping cabins and two cottages are also available. Picnic tables and fire pits are provided. Drinking water, restrooms with flush toilets and showers, cable TV, playground, recreation room, heated swimming pool, two spas, convenience store, coin laundry, dump station, propane, ice, firewood, fax machine, and Wi-Fi are available. Some facilities are wheelchair-accessible. Leashed pets are permitted.

Reservations, fees: Reservations are accepted at 800/562-3136. Sites are $25–45 per night, $3 per person per night for more than two

people, $17 per night for hike-in/bike-in sites, $3 per pet per night, $2 per night for each additional vehicle. Some credit cards accepted. Open year-round.

Directions: From Eureka, drive north on U.S. 101 for four miles to KOA Drive (well signed on east side of highway). Turn right on KOA Drive and drive a short distance to the end of the road.

Contact: Eureka KOA, 707/822-4243, fax 707/822-0126, www.koa.com.

34 SAMOA BOAT LAUNCH COUNTY PARK

Scenic rating: 7

on Humboldt Bay

Map grid A2

The nearby vicinity of the boat ramp, with access to Humboldt Bay and the Pacific Ocean, makes this a star attraction for campers towing their fishing boats. Near the campground you'll find good beachcombing and clamming at low tides, and a chance to see a huge variety of seabirds, highlighted by egrets and herons. There's a reason: Directly across the bay is the Humboldt Bay National Wildlife Refuge. Adjacent to the park is the Samoa Dunes Recreation Area, which is popular with ATV enthusiasts who are allowed to ride on the beach. This park is set near the famed all-you-can-eat, logger-style Samoa Cookhouse. The park is on the bay, not on the ocean.

RV sites, facilities: There are 20 sites for tents or RVs of any length (no hookups). Overflow camping for tents or RVs of any length is also available in a parking lot. Picnic tables and fire grills are provided. Drinking water and restrooms with flush toilets and coin showers are available. A boat ramp, grocery store, propane, and a coin laundry are available in Eureka (about five miles away). Leashed pets are permitted.

Reservations, fees: Reservations are not accepted. Sites are $14 per night per vehicle, $3 per person per night for hike-in/bike-in, $3 per

CALIFORNIA

night for each additional vehicle, $1 per pet per night. Maximum stay is seven days. Open year-round.

Directions: From U.S. 101 in Eureka, turn west on Highway 255 and drive two miles until it dead-ends at New Navy Base Road. At New Navy Base Road, turn left and drive five miles to the end of the Samoa Peninsula and the campground entrance.

Contact: Humboldt County Public Works, 707/445-7651, www.co.humboldt.ca.us.

35 E-Z LANDING RV PARK AND MARINA

Scenic rating: 6

on Humboldt Bay
Map grid A2

This is a good base camp for salmon trips in July and August when big schools of king salmon often teem just west of the entrance of Humboldt Bay. A nearby boat ramp with access to Humboldt Bay is a bonus. It's not the prettiest camp in the world, with quite a bit of asphalt, but most people use this camp as a simple parking spot for sleeping and getting down to the business of the day: fishing. This spot is ideal for ocean fishing, clamming, beachcombing, and boating. There are a few long-term and seasonal renters here.

RV sites, facilities: There are 45 sites with full hookups (30 amps) for RVs; some sites are pull-through. Restrooms with flush toilets and showers, marine gas, ice, coin laundry, bait, and boat slips are available. Some facilities are wheelchair-accessible. Leashed pets are permitted.

Reservations, fees: Reservations are accepted. RV sites are $20 per night. Some credit cards accepted. Open year-round.

Directions: From Eureka, drive 3.5 miles south on U.S. 101 to King Salmon Avenue. Turn west (right) on King Salmon Avenue (it becomes Buhne Dr.) and drive for 0.5 mile to where the road turns. Turn left (south) on Buhne Drive and go 0.5 mile to the park on the left (1875 Buhne Dr.).

Contact: E-Z Landing RV Park and Marina, 707/442-1118, fax 707/442-1999.

36 JOHNNY'S MARINA AND RV PARK

Scenic rating: 5

on Humboldt Bay
Map grid A2

This is a good base camp for salmon fishing during the peak season—always call, since the season changes each year as set by the Department of Fish and Game. Mooring for private boats is available, a nice plus for campers trailering boats. Other recreation activities include beachcombing, clamming, and perch fishing from shore. The owners have run this place since 1948. Note that a number of sites are filled with long-term renters.

RV sites, facilities: There are 53 sites with full hookups (30 and 50 amps) for RVs up to 38 feet. No tents. Flush toilets and a dump station are available; there are no showers. A coin laundry and boat dock are available. Leashed pets are permitted.

Reservations, fees: Reservations are accepted. Sites are $23 per night, $1 per person per night for more than two people. Open year-round.

Directions: From Eureka, drive 3.5 miles south on U.S. 101 to King Salmon Avenue. Turn west (right) on King Salmon Avenue (it becomes Buhne Drive). Continue about 0.5 mile to the park on the left (1821 Buhne Drive).

Contact: Johnny's Marina and RV Park, 707/442-2284, fax 707/443-4608.

37 HONEYDEW CREEK

Scenic rating: 6

in the King Range National Conservation Area
Map grid A2

This little known and little used camp is located on Honeydew Creek, a tributary to the Mattole River in California's "Lost Coast." In summer, it's a hideaway that you can use a base camp to explore the Lost Coast and the King Range. In late winter, steelhead fishing can be good on the Mattole River between Honeydew and Petrolia, providing for good access and stream flows. One problem is rain. It can pound here and the river can get too high to fish; winters with 100 inches of rain are typical in average-to-wet years.

RV sites, facilities: There are five sites for tents or RVs (no hookups). Picnic tables and fire rings are provided. Vault toilets are available, but there is no drinking water. Some facilities are wheelchair accessible.

Reservations, fees: Reservations are not accepted. Sites are $8 per night.

Directions: From Garberville, drive north on U.S. 101 to the South Fork-Honeydew exit. Turn west on South Fork-Honeydew Road and drive to Wilder Ridge Road in Honeydew. Turn left (south) on Wilder Ridge Road and drive one mile to the campground.

Contact: Bureau of Land Management, Arcata Field Office, 707/825-2300, fax 707/825-2301.

38 HUMBOLDT REDWOOD STATE PARK: CUNEO CREEK EQUESTRIAN

Scenic rating: 7

in Humboldt Redwoods State Park

Map grid A2

This is a horse camp set within Humboldt Redwoods State Park near the South Fork Eel River. The site is woodsy and far enough away from other camps in the park to often make it feel all your own. Though it is primarily a camp set up for equestrians, you can also use it as a base camp for kayak trips on the nearby South Fork Eel, or for hiking and biking trips nearby.

RV sites, facilities: There are five individual and two group sites for tents and RVs, with parking space for horse trailers. Picnic tables and fire rings are provided. Drinking water, coin showers, and flush toilets are available. There are water troughs and corrals for horses.

Reservations, fees: Reservations are accepted at 800/444-7275 (800/444-PARK) or www. reserveamerica.com ($8 reservation fee). Individual sites are $35 per night, $8 per night for each additional vehicle, $135–200 for group sites. Open mid-April to mid-October.

Directions: From Eureka, drive south on U.S. 101 about 45 miles to the South Fork/Founders Tree exit. Turn left on the Avenue of the Giants and drive over the Eel River bridge. Turn left at the Honeydew/Rockefeller Forest sign onto Mattole Road. Drive about eight miles to the Cuneo Creek Horse Campground sign. Turn right onto the entrance road and continue to the campground.

Contact: Humboldt Redwoods State Park, 707/946-2472; Visitor Center, 707/946-2263, fax, 707/946-2326, www.parks.ca.gov.

39 VAN DUZEN COUNTY PARK: SWIMMER'S DELIGHT

Scenic rating: 6

on the Van Duzen River

Map grid A2

This campground is set near the headwaters of the Van Duzen River, one of the Eel River's major tributaries. The river is subject to tremendous fluctuations in flows and height, so low in the fall that it is often temporarily closed to fishing by the Department of Fish and Game, so high in the winter that only fools would stick their toes in. For a short period in late spring, it provides a benign run for rafting and canoeing, putting in at Grizzly Creek and taking out at Van Duzen. In October, you'll find an excellent salmon fishing spot where the Van Duzen enters the Eel.

RV sites, facilities: There are 30 sites for tents or RVs of any length; some sites have partial hookups (30 amps). Picnic tables and fire grills are provided. Drinking water and restrooms with flush toilets and coin showers are available. A grocery store and coin laundry are available nearby. Some facilities are wheelchair-accessible. Leashed pets are permitted in the campground, but not on the beach.

CALIFORNIA

Reservations, fees: Reservations are not accepted. Sites are $15–20 per night, $3 per person per night for hike-in/bike-in, $3 per night for each additional vehicle, $1 per pet per night. Maximum stay is 10 days. Open year-round.

Directions: From Eureka, drive south on U.S. 101 to the junction of Highway 36 at Alton. Turn east on Highway 36 and drive 12 miles to the campground.

Contact: Humboldt County Public Works, 707/445-7651, www.co.humboldt.ca.us.

40 GRIZZLY CREEK REDWOODS STATE PARK

Scenic rating: 8

near Bridgeville

Map grid A2

Most summer vacationers hit the campgrounds on the Redwood Highway, that is, U.S. 101. However, this camp is just far enough off the beaten path to provide some semblance of seclusion. It is set in redwoods, quite beautiful, with fair hiking and good access to the adjacent Van Duzen River. The park encompasses only a few acres, yet it is very intimate. There are 4.5 miles of hiking trails, a visitors center with exhibits, and a bookstore. The Cheatham Grove in this park is an exceptional stand of coast redwoods. Fishing is catch-and-release only with barbless hooks. Nearby attractions include the Victorian village of Ferndale and Fort Humboldt to the north, Humboldt Redwoods State Park to the south, and Ruth Lake to the more distant east. Insider's tip: Half of the park borders Highway 36, and you can hear highway noise from some campsites.

RV sites, facilities: There are 10 tent sites, nine sites for tents or small RVs, 11 sites for RVs up to 30 feet or trailers up to 24 feet, and one hike-in/bike-in site. No hookups. Picnic tables, food lockers, and fire grills are provided. Drinking water and restrooms with flush toilets and showers are available. A grocery store is available within 3.5 miles. Some facilities are wheelchair-accessible. Leashed pets are permitted in the campground, but not on trails or beach area.

Reservations, fees: Reservations are accepted ($8 reservation fee) at 800/444-PARK (800/444-7275) or www.reserveamerica.com. Sites are $35 per night, $8 per night for each additional vehicle, $3 per person per night for hike-in/bike-in site. Open year-round.

Directions: From Eureka, drive south on U.S. 101 to the junction of Highway 36 at Alton. Turn east on Highway 36 and drive about 17 miles to the campground on the right.

Contact: Grizzly Creek Redwoods State Park, 707/777-3683, www.parks.ca.gov.

41 MATTOLE

Scenic rating: 8

north of Garberville

Map grid A2

This is a little-known camp set at the mouth of the Mattole River, right where it pours into the Pacific Ocean. It is beautiful and isolated. An outstanding hike leads to the Punta Gorda Lighthouse. Hike from the campground to the ocean and head south. It's a level walk, and at low tide, there's a chance to observe tidepool life. Perch fishing is good where the Mattole flows into the ocean, best during low tides. In the winter, the Mattole often provides excellent steelhead fishing. Check the Department of Fish and Game regulations for closed areas. Be sure to have a full tank on the way out—the nearest gas station is quite distant.

RV sites, facilities: There are 14 sites for tents or RVs up to 16 feet (no hookups). Picnic tables and fire rings are provided. Vault toilets are available. No drinking water is available. Some facilities are wheelchair-accessible. Leashed pets are permitted.

Reservations, fees: Reservations are not accepted. Sites are $8 per night. Open year-round.

Directions: From U.S. 101 north of Garberville, take the South Fork-Honeydew exit and drive west to Honeydew. At Honeydew and Mattole Road, turn right on Mattole Road and drive toward Petrolia. At the second bridge over the Mattole River, one mile before Petrolia, turn west on Lighthouse Road and drive five miles to the campground at the end of the road.

Contact: Bureau of Land Management, Arcata Field Office, 707/825-2300, fax 707/825-2301; Department of Fish & Game, Low-Flow Fishing Information, 707/442-4502.

42 A. W. WAY COUNTY PARK

🏕 🛶 🐟 🐕 🚐 ⛺

Scenic rating: 8

on the Mattole River

Map grid A2

This secluded camp provides a home for visitors to the "Lost Coast," the beautiful coastal stretch of California far from any semblance of urban life. The highlight here is the Mattole River, a great steelhead stream when flows are suitable between January and mid-March. Nearby is excellent hiking in the King Range National Conservation Area. For the great hike out to the abandoned Punta Gorda Lighthouse, drive to the trailhead on the left side of Lighthouse Road (see the *Mattole* listing). This area is typically bombarded with monsoon-level rains in winter.

RV sites, facilities: There are 35 sites for tents or RVs of any length (no hookups). Overflow camping is also available. Picnic tables and fire grills are provided. Drinking water, restrooms with flush toilets, and cold showers are available. A grocery store, coin laundry, and propane gas are available nearby. Leashed pets are permitted.

Reservations, fees: Reservations are not accepted. Sites are $15 per night, $3 per person per night for hike-in/bike-in, $3 per night for each additional vehicle, $1 per pet per night. Maximum stay is 10 days. Open year-round.

Directions: From Garberville, drive north on U.S. 101 to the South Fork-Honeydew exit. Turn west on South Fork-Honeydew Road and drive 31 miles (the road changes between pavement, gravel, and dirt, and is steep and curvy) to the park entrance on the left side of the road. The park is 7.5 miles east of the town of Petrolia. (South Fork-Honeydew Road can be difficult for larger vehicles.)

Contact: Humboldt County Public Works, 707/445-7651, www.co.humboldt.ca.us.

43 HUMBOLDT REDWOODS STATE PARK: ALBEE CREEK

🏕 🛶 🐟 🐕 🚐 ♿ 🚍 ⛺

Scenic rating: 8

in Humboldt Redwoods State Park

Map grid A2

Humboldt Redwoods State Park is a massive sprawl of forest that is known for some unusual giant trees in the Federation Grove and Big Tree Area. The park covers nearly 53,000 acres, including more than 17,000 acres of old-growth coast redwoods. It has 100 miles of hiking trails, many excellent, both short and long. The camp is set in a redwood grove, and the smell of these trees has a special magic. Nearby Albee Creek, a benign trickle most of the year, can flood in the winter after heavy rains. Seasonal interpretive programs, campfire talks, nature walks, and junior ranger programs are available.

RV sites, facilities: There are 40 sites for tents or RVs up to 33 feet and trailers up to 24 feet (no hookups). Picnic tables, fire grills, and food lockers are provided. Drinking water, restrooms with flush toilets and showers, and firewood are available. Some facilities are wheelchair-accessible. Leashed pets are permitted.

Reservations, fees: Reservations are accepted ($8 reservation fee) at 800/444-PARK (800/444-7275) or www.reserveamerica.com. Sites are $45 per night, $8 per night for each additional vehicle, $3 per person per night for hike-in/bike-in sites. Open Memorial Day weekend through mid-October.

Directions: From Eureka, drive south on U.S. 101 about 11 miles to the Honeydew exit (if you reach Weott, you have gone two miles too far). At Mattole Road, turn west and drive five miles to the campground on the right.

Contact: Humboldt Redwoods State Park, 707/946-2472 or 707/946-2409, fax 707/946-

2326, Visitor Center, 707/946-2263, www.
parks.ca.gov.

44 HUMBOLDT REDWOODS STATE PARK: BURLINGTON

Scenic rating: 7

in Humboldt Redwoods State Park

Map grid A2

This camp is one of the centerpieces of Humboldt Redwoods State Park. Humboldt is California's largest redwood state park and also includes the largest remaining contiguous old-growth coastal redwood forest in the world: the Rockefeller Forest. The trees here are thousands of years old and have never been logged; they are as pristine now as 200 years ago. The average rainfall here is 65 inches per year, with most occurring between October and May. Morning and evening fog in the summer keeps the temperature cool in the river basin.

This camp is often at capacity during the tourist months. Sites are shady, with big redwood stumps that kids can play on, but packed close together with plenty of road noise from Avenue of the Giants a few feet away. There's good hiking on trails routed through the redwoods, and in winter, steelhead fishing is often good on the nearby Eel River. The park has 100 miles of trails, but it is little half-mile Founders Grove Nature Trail that has the quickest payoff and requires the least effort.

RV sites, facilities: There are 57 sites for tents or RVs up to 33 feet (no hookups) and trailers up to 24 feet, and three hike-in/bike-in sites. Picnic tables, fire grills, and food lockers are provided. Drinking water, restrooms with flush toilets and showers, and firewood are available. Some facilities are wheelchair-accessible. Leashed pets are permitted.

Reservations, fees: Reservations are accepted ($8 reservation fee) at 800/444-PARK (800/444-7275) or www.reserveamerica.com. Sites are $35 per night, $8 per night for each additional vehicle, $3 per person per night for hike-in/bike-in sites. Open year-round.

Directions: From Eureka, drive south on U.S. 101 for 45 miles to the Weott/Newton Road exit. Turn right on Newton Road and continue to the T junction where Newton Road meets the Avenue of the Giants. Turn left on the Avenue of the Giants and drive two miles to the campground entrance on the left.

Contact: Humboldt Redwoods State Park, 707/946-1811 or 707/946-2409, fax 707/946-2326, Visitor Center, 707/946-2263, www.parks.ca.gov.

45 HUMBOLDT REDWOODS STATE PARK: HIDDEN SPRINGS

Scenic rating: 7

in Humboldt Redwoods State Park

Map grid A2

This camp gets heavy use from May through September, but the campsites have been situated in a way that offers relative seclusion. Side trips include good hiking on trails routed through redwoods and a touring drive on Avenue of the Giants. The park has more than 100 miles of hiking trails, many of them amid spectacular giant redwoods, including Bull Creek Flats Trail and Founders Grove Nature Trail. Bears are occasionally spotted by mountain bikers on rides out to the park's outskirts. In winter, nearby High Rock on the Eel River is one of the better shoreline fishing spots for steelhead. (For more information on Humboldt Redwoods, see *Humboldt Redwoods State Park: Albee Creek* and *Humboldt Redwoods State Park: Burlington* listings.)

RV sites, facilities: There are 154 sites for tents or RVs up to 33 feet (no hookups) and trailers up to 24 feet. Picnic tables, fire grills, and food lockers are provided. Drinking water, restrooms with flush toilets and showers, and firewood are available. A grocery store and coin laundry are available within one mile in Myers Flat. Leashed pets are permitted.

Reservations, fees: Reservations are accepted ($8 reservation fee) at 800/444-PARK (800/444-7275) or www.reserveamerica.com.

CALIFORNIA

Sites are $35 per night, $8 per night for each additional vehicle. Open mid-April through Labor Day weekend.

Directions: From Eureka, drive south 50 miles on U.S. 101 to the Myers Flat/Avenue of the Giants exit. Continue south and drive less than a mile to the campground entrance on the left.

Contact: Humboldt Redwoods State Park, 707/943-3177 or 707/946-2409, fax 707/946-2326, Visitor Center, 707/946-2263, www.parks.ca.gov.

46 GIANT REDWOODS RV AND CAMP

Scenic rating: 8

on the Eel River

Map grid A2

This privately operated park is set in a grove of redwoods and covers 23 acres, much of it fronting the Eel River. Trip options include the scenic drive on Avenue of the Giants.

RV sites, facilities: There are 26 tent sites and 57 sites for RVs of any length. Many of the RV sites have full or partial hookups (30 amps) and are pull-through. Picnic tables and fire rings are provided. Restrooms with showers, free Wi-Fi, modem hookups, a convenience store, ice, coin laundry, playground, dog "freedom area," and a recreation room are available. Leashed pets are permitted.

Reservations, fees: Reservations are recommended in the summer. Sites are $25–40 per night, $3 per person per night for more than two people, $2 per pet per night. Seventh night free. Some credit cards accepted. Open year-round, with limited facilities in winter.

Directions: From Eureka, drive south 50 miles on U.S. 101 to the Myers Flat/Avenue of the Giants exit. Turn right on Avenue of the Giants and make a quick left onto Myers Avenue. Drive 0.25 mile on Myers Avenue to the campground entrance.

Contact: Giant Redwoods RV and Camp, 707/943-3198, www.giantredwoodsrvcamp.com.

47 DEAN CREEK RESORT

Scenic rating: 7

on the South Fork of the Eel River

Map grid A2

This year-round RV park is set on the South Fork of the Eel River. This is a very family-oriented resort. In the summer, it makes a good base camp for a redwood park adventure, with Humboldt Redwoods State Park (well north of here) providing 100 miles of hiking trails, many routed through awesome stands of giant trees. In the winter heavy rains feed the South Fork Eel, inspiring steelhead upstream on their annual winter journey. Fishing is good in this area, best by shore at nearby High Rock. Bank access is good at several other spots. Note that there is catch-and-release fishing only; check fishing regulations. Contact information for fishing guides is available at the resort, and they offer winter steelhead fishing specials. An excellent side trip is to drive three miles south to the Avenue of the Giants, a tour through giant redwood trees. The campground also offers volleyball, shuffleboard, badminton, and horseshoes. You get the idea.

RV sites, facilities: There are 64 sites with full or partial hookups (30 and 50 amps) for tents or RVs of any length; some sites are pull-through. Picnic tables and fire grills are provided. Restrooms with showers, recreation room, coin laundry, motel, convenience store, modem and Wi-Fi access, RV supplies, firewood, ice, giant spa, sauna, seasonal heated swimming pool, dump station, amphitheater, group facilities, arcade, basketball, tetherball, shuffleboard, volleyball, mini golf, and a playground are available. Some facilities are wheelchair-accessible. Leashed pets are permitted.

Reservations, fees: Reservations are recommended in the summer at 877/923-2555. Sites are $31–40 per night, $5 per person per night for more than two people, $1.50 per night for each additional vehicle. Some credit cards accepted. Open year-round.

Directions: From Eureka, drive 60 miles south on U.S. 101 to the Redwood Drive exit. Exit

CALIFORNIA

onto Redwood Drive and continue about one-half block to the motel/campground entrance on the right; check in at the motel.

Contact: Dean Creek Resort, 707/923-2555, www.deancreekresort.com.

48 TOLKAN

Scenic rating: 6

in the King Range
Map grid A2

This remote camp is set at 1,840 feet, a short drive south of Horse Mountain.

RV sites, facilities: There are nine sites for tents or RVs up to 20 feet (no hookups). Picnic tables and fire rings are provided. Vault toilets are available. No drinking water is available. Some facilities are wheelchair-accessible. Leashed pets are permitted.

Reservations, fees: Reservations are not accepted. Sites are $8 per night. Open year-round.

Directions: From Eureka, drive 60 miles south on U.S. 101 to the Redway exit. Take the Redway/Shelter Cove exit onto Redwood Drive into the town of Redway. Drive 2.5 miles (look on the right for the King Range Conservation Area sign) to Briceland-Thorne Road. Turn right on Briceland-Thorne Road (which will become Shelter Cove Road) and drive 17 miles to King Peak (Horse Mountain) Road. Turn right on King Peak Road and continue 3.5 miles to the campground on the right.

Contact: Bureau of Land Management, King Mountain Field Office, 707/986-5400, fax 707/825-2301.

49 SHELTER COVE CAMPGROUND AND DELI

Scenic rating: 8

in Shelter Cove overlooking the Pacific Ocean
Map grid A2

This is a prime oceanside spot to set up a base camp for deep-sea fishing, whale-watching,

tidepool gazing, beachcombing, and hiking. While this is a prime recreation area, the campground itself is rather uninspiring. Long-term renters occupy some of the campsites. A wide boat ramp makes it perfect for campers who have trailered boats and don't mind the long drive. Reservations are strongly advised here. The park's backdrop is the King Range National Conservation Area, offering spectacular views. The deli is well known for its fish-and-chips. The salmon, halibut, and rockfish fishing is quite good here in the summer; always call first for current regulations and seasons, which change every year. Clamming is best during winter's low tides; hiking is best in the King Mountain Range during the summer. Seasonal abalone diving and shore fishing for redtail perch are also available. There is heavy rain in winter. Insider's tip: Two miles north is one of the only black-sand beaches in the continental United States.

RV sites, facilities: There are 103 sites for tents or RVs; many have full hookups (30 amps); some sites are pull-through. Picnic tables and fire rings are provided. Restrooms with showers, dump station, coin laundry, grocery store, deli, propane, ice, and RV supplies are available. A boat ramp and marina are across the street. Leashed pets are permitted.

Reservations, fees: Reservations are recommended. Sites are $30–40 per night, $5 per person per night for more than two people, $1 per pet per night. Some credit cards accepted. Open year-round.

Directions: From Eureka, drive 60 miles south on U.S. 101 to the Redway/Shelter Cove exit. Take that exit and drive 2.5 miles north on Redwood Road to Briceland-Thorne Road (which will become Shelter Cove Road). Turn right (west) and drive 18 miles (following the truck/RV route signs) to Upper Pacific Drive. Turn left (south) on Upper Pacific Drive and proceed (it becomes Machi Road) 0.5 mile to the park on the right.

Contact: Shelter Cove Campground and Deli, 707/986-7474, fax 707/986-7865.

50 BENBOW LAKE STATE RECREATION AREA

Scenic rating: 7

on the Eel River

Map grid A2

This camp is set along the South Fork of the Eel River, with easy access from U.S. 101. It gets heavy use in the summer. In theory, Benbow Lake is created in summer when the river is dammed on a temporary basis, creating a 26-acre lake for swimming and light boating (no motors). This seasonal dam is projected to be installed in mid-June and kept in place until mid-September. However, there is no guarantee this will occur. Some years, the dam is not installed in order to provide passage of downstream migrating steelhead and salmon and the river becomes more of a creek. If you're planning a vacation around lake recreation, always call first. In the winter, this stretch of river can be quite good for catch-and-release steelhead fishing. Warning: Blue-green algae warnings are sometimes posted here in late summer; the algae can be dangerous to dogs.

RV sites, facilities: There are 77 sites for tents or RVs up to 30 feet; two sites have full hook-ups (30 amps). Picnic tables, food lockers, and fire grills are provided. Drinking water and restrooms with flush toilets and coin showers are available. A boat ramp (no motors) and seasonal boat rentals are available nearby. There is a dump station at the park entrance. Supplies and a coin laundry are available in Garberville. Leashed pets are permitted at campsites only.

Reservations, fees: Reservations are accepted ($8 reservation fee) at 800/444-PARK (800/444-7275) or www.reserveamerica.com. Sites are $35–45 per night, $8 per night for each additional vehicle. Open May through September, weather permitting.

Directions: From the junction of U.S. 101 and Highway 1 in Leggett, drive north on U.S. 101 past Richardson Grove State Park to the Benbow Drive exit (two miles south of Garberville). Take that exit and drive 2.7 miles to the park entrance.

Contact: Benbow Lake State Recreation Area, 707/923-3238; Richardson Grove State Park, 707/247-3318, www.parks.ca.gov.

51 BENBOW VALLEY RV RESORT AND GOLF COURSE

Scenic rating: 7

on the Eel River

Map grid A2

This is an RV park set along U.S. 101 and the South Fork Eel River, with both a pretty nine-hole regulation golf course and little Benbow Lake providing nearby recreation. It takes on a dramatically different character in the winter, when the highway is largely abandoned, the river comes up, and steelhead migrate upstream to the stretch of water here. Cooks Valley and Benbow provide good shore fishing access. Note that fishing restrictions for steelhead are extremely severe and subject to constant change; always check with DFG before fishing for steelhead. (See the *Benbow Lake State Recreation Area* listing for a note on the status of Benbow Lake.)

RV sites, facilities: There are 112 sites with full hookups (30 and 50 amps), including four "VIP" sites for RVs of any length. Many sites are pull-through. No tents. Cottages, park-model cabins, and trailer rentals are also available. Picnic tables and cable TV are provided. Restrooms with showers, coin laundry, convenience store, snack bar, playground, recreation room, seasonal heated swimming pool, seasonal spa, Wi-Fi, modem access, fax and copy services, group facilities, organized activities, shuffleboard, table tennis, horseshoes, game room, RV supplies, and a nine-hole golf course are available. A boat dock and boat rentals (in summer) are available within 100 feet at Benbow Lake. Leashed pets are permitted. A doggy playground and pet wash are available.

Reservations, fees: Reservations are accepted at 866/236-2697. Sites are $34–60 per night, $6 per person per night for more than two people, $3 per pet per night. Some credit cards accepted. Open year-round.

Directions: From the junction of U.S. 101 and Highway 1 in Leggett, drive north on U.S. 101 past Richardson Grove State Park to the Benbow Drive exit (two miles south of Garberville). Take that exit and turn right at the stop sign. Drive a short distance to the end of the road and Benbow Drive. Bear left on Benbow Drive and continue a short distance to the resort on the left.

Contact: Benbow Valley RV Resort and Golf Course, 707/923-2777, www.benbowrv.com.

52 RICHARDSON GROVE STATE PARK: MADRONE AND HUCKLEBERRY

Scenic rating: 8

in Richardson Grove State Park

Map grid A2

The highway cuts a swath right through Richardson Grove State Park, and everyone slows to gawk at the tallest trees in the world, one of the most impressive groves of redwoods you can drive through in California. To explore further, there are several campgrounds available at the park, as well as a network of outstanding hiking trails. The best of these are short Redwood Exhibit Trail, Settlers Loop, and Toumey Trail. The park is one of the prettiest and most popular state parks, making reservations a necessity from Memorial Day through Labor Day weekend. When arriving from points south on U.S. 101, this is the first park in the Redwood Empire where you will encounter significant old-growth redwood. There are nine miles of hiking trails, fishing in the winter for steelhead, and several trees of significant note. The Eel River runs through the park, providing swimming holes in summer.

RV sites, facilities: At Madrone Camp, there are 40 sites for tents or RVs up to 30 feet. At Huckleberry, there are 36 sites for tents or RVs up to 30 feet. Picnic tables, food lockers, and fire grills are provided. Drinking water and restrooms with flush toilets and coin showers are available. A minimart and dump station (three miles away) are available nearby. Some facilities are wheelchair-accessible. Leashed pets are permitted at campsites only.

Reservations, fees: Reservations are accepted ($8 reservation fee) at 800/444-PARK (800/444-7275) or www.reserveamerica.com. Sites are $35 per night, $8 per night for each additional vehicle. Open year-round, but subject to occasional winter closures.

Directions: From the junction of U.S. 101 and Highway 1 in Leggett, drive north on U.S. 101 for 16 miles (past Piercy) to the park entrance along the west (left) side of the road (eight miles south of Garberville).

Contact: Richardson Grove State Park, 707/247-3318, www.parks.ca.gov.

53 RICHARDSON GROVE STATE PARK: OAK FLAT

Scenic rating: 8

in Richardson Grove State Park

Map grid A2

Note: At time of publication, the Oak Flat campground was closed until July 2011. Usually, the campground is open summers only. Oak Flat is on the eastern side of the Eel River in the shade of forest and provides easy access to the river. (For side-trip information, see the *Richardson Grove State Park: Madrone and Huckleberry* listing.)

RV sites, facilities: There are 100 sites for tents or RVs up to 24 feet (no hookups) and trailers up to 18 feet. Picnic tables, food lockers, and fire grills are provided. Drinking water, restrooms with flush toilets and coin showers, and Wi-Fi are available. A grocery store and propane gas are available nearby. Leashed pets are permitted.

Reservations, fees: Reservations are accepted ($8 reservation fee) at 800/444-PARK (800/444-7275) or www.reserveamerica.com. Sites are $35–45 per night, $8 per night for each additional vehicle. Open mid-June through mid-September, weather permitting.

Directions: From the junction of U.S. 101 and

CALIFORNIA

Highway 1 in Leggett, drive north on U.S. 101 for 16 miles (past Piercy) to the park entrance on the west (left) side of the road (eight miles south of Garberville).

Contact: Richardson Grove State Park, 707/247-3318, www.parks.ca.gov.

54 RICHARDSON GROVE CAMPGROUND AND RV PARK

Scenic rating: 7

on the Eel River

Map grid A2

This private camp provides a nearby alternative to Richardson Grove State Park, complete with cabin rentals. The state park, with its grove of giant redwoods and excellent hiking, is the primary attraction. The RV park is family-oriented, with volleyball and basketball courts and horseshoe pits. The adjacent South Fork Eel River may look like a trickle in the summer, but there are some good swimming holes. It also provides good steelhead fishing in January and February, with especially good shore fishing access here as well as to the south in Cooks Valley (check DFG regulations before fishing). This campground is owned and operated by the Northern California/Nevada District Assemblies of God.

RV sites, facilities: There are 98 sites for tents or RVs; some sites are pull-through and many have full or partial hookups (30 amps). Two log cabins are also available. Picnic tables and fire rings are provided. Restrooms with showers, dump station, Wi-Fi, modem access, playground, coin laundry, convenience store, group facilities, propane, and ice are available. Leashed pets are permitted.

Reservations, fees: Reservations are recommended in the summer. Sites are $20–28 per night. Weekly, winter, and group rates available. Some credit cards accepted. Open year-round.

Directions: From the junction of U.S. 101 and Highway 1 in Leggett, drive north on U.S. 101 for 15 miles (one mile before reaching Richardson Grove State Park) to the camp entrance on the west (left) side of the road.

Contact: Richardson Grove Campground and RV Park, 707/247-3380, fax 707/247-9806, www.redwoodfamilycamp.com.

SHASTA AND TRINITY

(BEST RV PARKS AND CAMPGROUNDS

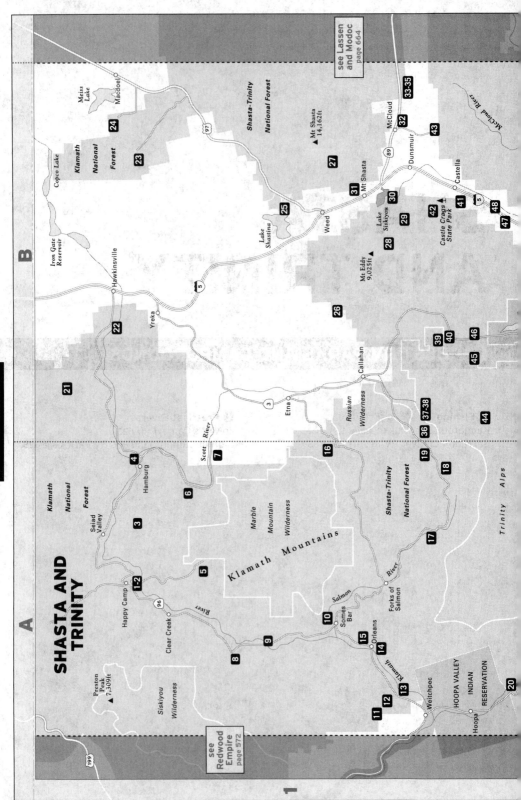

CALIFORNIA

see Lassen and Modoc page 664

see Redwood Empire page 572

SHASTA AND TRINITY

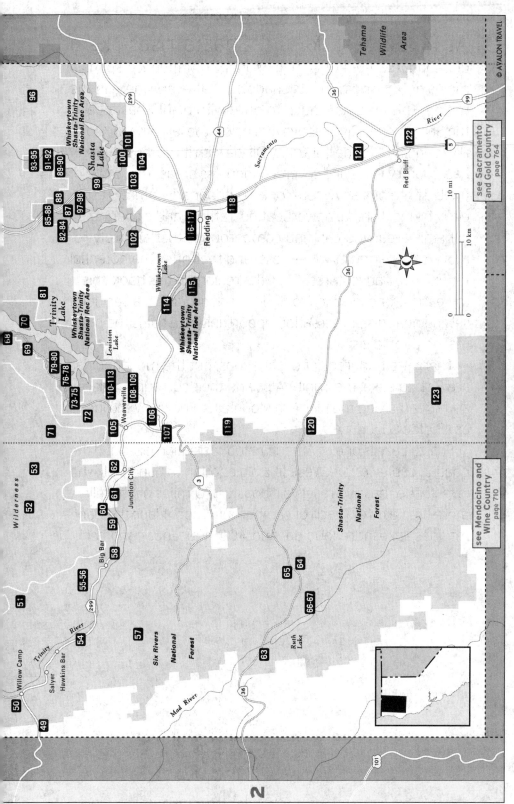

CALIFORNIA

© AVALON TRAVEL

see Sacramento and Gold Country
page 764

see Mendocino and Wine Country
page 710

At 14,162 feet, Mount Shasta rises like a diamond in a field of coal. Its sphere of influence spans a radius of 125 miles, and its shadow is felt everywhere in the region. This area has much to offer with giant Shasta Lake, the Sacramento River above and below the lake, the McCloud River, and the wonderful Trinity Divide with its dozens of pretty backcountry lakes and several wilderness areas. This is one of the best regions anywhere for an outdoor adventure – especially hiking, fishing, powerboating, rafting, and exploring.

In this area, you can find campgrounds that are truly remote, set near quiet wilderness, and that offer the potential for unlimited adventures. Of all the regions in this book, this is the easiest one in which to find a campground in a secluded setting near great recreation opportunities. That is the main reason people visit.

There are hundreds of destinations, but the most popular are Shasta Lake, the Trinity Alps and their surrounding lakes and streams, and the Klamath Mountains, known by the locals as "Bigfoot Country."

Shasta Lake is one of America's top recreation lakes and the boating capital of the West. It is big enough to handle all who love it. The massive reservoir boasts 370 miles of shoreline; more than a dozen each of campgrounds, boat launches, and marinas; lakeshore lodging; and 400 houseboat and cabin rentals. A remarkable 22 species of fish live in the lake. Many of the campgrounds feature lake views. In addition, getting here is easy – a straight shot off I-5.

At the charmed center of this beautiful region are the Trinity Alps, where lakes are sprinkled everywhere. It's also home to the headwaters for feeder streams to the Trinity River, Klamath River, New River, Wooley Creek, and others. Trinity Lake provides outstanding boating and fishing, and just downstream, smaller Lewiston Lake offers a quiet alternative. One advantage to Lewiston Lake is that it is always full of water, even all summer long, making for a very pretty scene. Downstream of Lewiston, the Trinity River provides low-cost rafting and outstanding shoreline access along Highway 299 for fishing for salmon and steelhead.

The neighboring Klamath Mountains are well known as Bigfoot Country. If you drive up the Forest Service road at Bluff Creek, just off Highway 96 upstream of Weitchpec, you can even find the spot where the famous Bigfoot movie was shot in the 1960s. Well, I haven't seen Bigfoot, but I have discovered tons of outdoor recreation. This remote region features miles of the Klamath and Salmon Rivers, as well as the Marble Mountain Wilderness. Options include canoeing, rafting, and fishing for steelhead on the Klamath River, or hiking to your choice of more than 100 wilderness lakes.

CALIFORNIA

1 CURLY JACK

Scenic rating: 7

on the Klamath River in Klamath National Forest

Map grid A1

This campground is set at 1,000 feet elevation on the Klamath River, providing opportunities for fishing, light rafting, and kayaking. What's special about Curly Jack, though, is that the water is generally warm enough through the summer for swimming.

RV sites, facilities: There are 16 sites for tents or RVs up to 22 feet, with some specially designed sites for RVs up to 45 feet, and three group sites for tents or RVs up to 22 feet that can accommodate up to 30 people each. No hookups. Fire grills and picnic tables are provided. Drinking water and vault toilets are available. Some facilities are wheelchair-accessible. Leashed pets are permitted.

Reservations, fees: Reservations are not accepted for individual sites but are required for group sites at 877/444-6777 or www.recreation. gov ($10 reservation fee). Sites are $10 per night, $30 per night for a group site. Open year-round, with limited winter facilities.

Directions: From the town of Happy Camp on Highway 96, turn south on Elk Creek Road and drive about one mile. Turn right on Curly Jack Road and drive one block to the campground entrance on the right.

Contact: Klamath National Forest, Happy Camp and Oak Knoll Ranger Districts, 530/493-2243, fax 530/493-1794.

2 ELK CREEK CAMPGROUND AND RV PARK

Scenic rating: 8

on the Klamath River

Map grid A1

Elk Creek Campground is a year-round RV park set where Elk Creek pours into the Klamath River. It is a beautiful campground, with sites right on the water in a pretty, wooded setting. The section of the Klamath River nearby is perfect for inflatable kayaking and rafting. Guided trips are available, with a wide scope of white water available, rated from the easy Class I stuff all the way to the Class V to-hell-and-back rapids. In addition, the water is quite warm in the summer and flows are maintained throughout the year, making it ideal for water sports. A swimming hole gets use in summer. The park is popular with anglers and hunters.

RV sites, facilities: There are 34 sites for RVs of any length, some with full or partial hookups (30 and 50 amps); some sites are pull-through. There is a separate area for tents. Three cabins and three rental trailers are available. Picnic tables and fire grills are provided. Restrooms with showers, cable TV, Wi-Fi, recreation room with billiards and table tennis, horseshoes, beach, coin laundry, dump station, propane, and firewood are available. Leashed pets are permitted.

Reservations, fees: Reservations are recommended. RV sites are $22–25 per night, $6 per night for each additional person, $15 per night for tent sites. Weekly, monthly, and group rates are available. Some credit cards accepted. Open year-round.

Directions: From Highway 96 in the town of Happy Camp, turn south on Elk Creek Road and drive 0.75 mile to the campground on the right.

Contact: Elk Creek Campground and RV Park, 530/493-2208, www.elkcreekcampground. com.

3 GRIDER CREEK

Scenic rating: 6

in Klamath National Forest

Map grid A1

This obscure little camp is used primarily by hikers, since a trailhead for the Pacific Crest Trail is available, and by deer hunters in the fall. The camp is set at 1,400 feet along Grider Creek. Access to the Pacific Crest Trail is provided from a bridge across the creek. From here, the PCT is routed uphill along Grider Creek into the Marble Mountain Wilderness, about an 11-mile ripper to Huckleberry Mountain at 6,303 feet. There are no lakes along the route, only small streams and feeder creeks.

RV sites, facilities: There are 10 sites for tents or RVs up to 16 feet (no hookups). Picnic tables and fire grills are provided. Vault toilets, horse corrals, and a loading ramp are available. No drinking water is provided. Garbage must be packed out. Some facilities are wheelchair-accessible. Leashed pets are permitted.

Reservations, fees: Reservations are not accepted. There is no fee for camping. Two vehicles maximum per site. Open May through October.

Directions: From Yreka, drive north on I-5 to the junction with Highway 96. At Highway 96, turn west and drive to Walker Creek Road/Forest Road 46N64, one mile before Seiad Valley. Turn left to enter Walker Creek Road and stay to the right as it runs adjacent to the Klamath River to Grider Creek Road. At Grider Creek Road, turn left and drive south for three miles to the camp entrance.

Contact: Klamath National Forest, Happy Camp and Oak Knoll Ranger Districts, 530/493-2243, fax 530/493-1794.

4 SARAH TOTTEN

Scenic rating: 7

on the Klamath River in Klamath National Forest
Map grid A1

This is one of the more popular Forest Service camps on the Klamath River, and it's no mystery why. In the summer, its placement is perfect for rafters (Class II+ and III), who camp here and use it as a put-in spot. In fall and winter, anglers arrive for the steelhead run. It's in the "banana belt," or good-weather area of the Klamath, in a pretty grove of oak trees. Fishing is often good here for salmon in early October and for steelhead from November through spring, providing there are fishable water flows.

RV sites, facilities: There are eight sites for

tents or RVs up to 22 feet, and two group sites for tents or RVs up to 22 feet that can accommodate up to 30 people each. No hookups. Picnic tables and fire grills are provided. Drinking water and vault toilets are available. A small grocery store is nearby. Some facilities are wheelchair-accessible. Leashed pets are permitted.

Reservations, fees: Reservations are not accepted for individual sites but are required for the group sites at 877/444-6777 or www.recreation.gov ($10 reservation fee). Sites are $10 per night, $30 per night for group sites. Open May through October.

Directions: From Yreka, drive north on I-5 to the junction with Highway 96. At Highway 96, turn west and drive to Horse Creek, continuing west for five miles to the campground on the right side of the road. If you reach the town of Hamburg, you have gone 0.5 mile too far.

Contact: Klamath National Forest, Happy Camp and Oak Knoll Ranger Districts, 530/493-2243, fax 530/493-1794.

5 NORCROSS

Scenic rating: 7

near Happy Camp in Klamath National Forest
Map grid A1

Set at 2,400 feet in elevation, this camp serves as a staging area for various trails that provide access into the Marble Mountain Wilderness. There is also access to the popular Kelsey Trail and to swimming and fishing activities.

RV sites, facilities: There are six sites for tents or RVs up to 25 feet (no hookups). Picnic tables and fire pits are provided. Vault toilets, a horse corral, stock water, and a loading ramp are available. No drinking water is available. Garbage must be packed out. Some facilities are wheelchair-accessible. Leashed pets are permitted.

Reservations, fees: Reservations are not accepted. There is no fee for camping. Open May through October.

Directions: From Yreka on I-5, drive north on

I-5 to the junction with Highway 96. Drive west on Highway 96 to the town of Happy Camp. In Happy Camp, turn south onto Elk Creek Road and drive 16 miles to the campground.

Contact: Klamath National Forest, Happy Camp and Oak Knoll Ranger Districts, 530/493-2243, fax 530/493-1794.

6 BRIDGE FLAT

Scenic rating: 7

in Klamath National Forest

Map grid A1

This camp is set at 2,000 feet along the Scott River. Though commercial rafting trips are only rarely available here, the river is accessible during the early spring for skilled rafters and kayakers, with a good put-in and take-out spot four miles downriver; others begin their trip at the Buker bridge or the Kelsey Creek bridge (popular swimming hole here). For backpackers, a trailhead for the Kelsey Trail is nearby, leading into the Marble Mountain Wilderness. A fish-spawning area is located on Kelsey Creek, upriver from camp.

RV sites, facilities: There are four sites for tents or RVs up to 22 feet (no hookups). Picnic tables and fire grills are provided. Vault toilets are available. There is no drinking water. Garbage must be packed out. Some facilities are wheelchair-accessible. Leashed pets are permitted.

Reservations, fees: Reservations are not accepted. There is no fee for camping. Open May through September.

Directions: From Redding, drive north on I-5 to Yreka. In Yreka, turn southwest on Highway 3 and drive 16.5 miles to Fort Jones. In Fort Jones, turn right on Scott River Road and drive 21 miles to the campground on the right side of the road, just after crossing a bridge.

Contact: Klamath National Forest, Scott River and Salmon River Ranger Districts, 530/468-5351, fax 530/468-1290.

7 INDIAN SCOTTY

Scenic rating: 7

on the Scott River in Klamath National Forest

Map grid A1

This popular camp provides direct access to the adjacent Scott River. Because it is easy to reach (no gravel roads) and shaded, it gets a lot of use. The camp is set at 2,400 feet. The levels, forces, and temperatures on the Scott River fluctuate greatly from spring to fall. In the spring, it can be a raging cauldron, but cold from snowmelt. Come summer it quiets, with some deep pools providing swimming holes. By fall, it can be reduced to a trickle. Keep your expectations flexible according to the season.

RV sites, facilities: There are 28 sites and a group site (parking lot) for tents or RVs up to 38 feet (no hookups). Picnic tables and fire grills are provided. Drinking water and vault toilets are available. There is a playground in the group-use area. Leashed pets are permitted.

Reservations, fees: Reservations are not accepted for individual sites but are required for the group site at 877/444-6777 or www.recreation.gov ($10 reservation fee). Individual sites are $10 per night, and the group site is $30 per night. Open May through October.

Directions: From Redding, drive north on I-5 to Yreka. In Yreka, turn southwest on Highway 3 and drive 16.5 miles to Fort Jones. In Fort Jones, turn right on Scott River Road and drive 14 miles to a concrete bridge and the adjacent signed campground entrance on the left.

Contact: Klamath National Forest, Scott River and Salmon River Ranger Districts, 530/468-5351, fax 530/468-1290.

8 DILLON CREEK

Scenic rating: 7

on the Klamath River in Klamath National Forest

Map grid A1

This is a prime base camp for rafting or a steelhead fishing trip. A put-in spot for rafting is adjacent to the camp, with an excellent river run available from here on down past Presido Bar to the takeout at Ti-Bar. If you choose to go on, make absolutely certain to pull out at Green Riffle river access and take-out, or risk death at Ishi Pishi Falls. The water is warm here in the summer, and there are also many excellent swimming holes in the area. In addition, this is a good stretch of water for steelhead fishing from September to February, best in early winter from Dillon Creek to Ti-Bar, with shoreline access available at Dillon Beach. The elevation is 800 feet.

RV sites, facilities: There are 21 sites for tents or RVs up to 30 feet (no hookups). Picnic tables, food lockers, and fire grills are provided. Drinking water and vault toilets are available. There is a dump station in Happy Camp 25 miles north of the campground, and at Aikens Creek nine miles west of the town of Orleans. Some facilities are wheelchair-accessible. Leashed pets are permitted.

Reservations, fees: Reservations are not accepted. Sites are $10 per night, $5 per night for each additional vehicle. Open mid-May through early November.

Directions: From Yreka, drive north on I-5 to the junction with Highway 96. At Highway 96, turn west and drive to Happy Camp. Continue south from Happy Camp for 35 miles and look for the campground on the right side of the road.

Coming from the west, from Somes Bar, drive 15 miles northeast on Highway 96.

Contact: Six Rivers National Forest, Orleans Ranger District, 530/627-3291, fax 530/627-3401.

⑨ MARBLE MOUNTAIN RANCH

🧍 🚴 ⛵ 🎣 🛶 🛥️ 🥾 🚗 ⛺

Scenic rating: 6

near the Klamath River

Map grid A1

The lodge is set just across the road from the Klamath River, an ideal location as headquarters for a rafting trip in the summer or a steelhead fishing trip in the fall. This ranch is considered a vacation destination, with most people staying for a week. The majority of people staying at the ranch are on a package deal with cabin lodging, but campers can participate in meals and organized activities if they make reservations. Commercial rafting or kayaking trips on the Klamath River and Trinity River are available here, with guided trips offered by the ranch. This piece of river is beautiful and fresh with lots of wildlife and birds, yet not dangerous. However, be absolutely certain to take out at Green Riffle boat access before reaching Ishi Pishi Falls, which cannot be run. There's a full pack station at the ranch for guided trail rides lasting from one hour to overnight. Riding lessons are available. Wilderness pack trips, salmon and steelhead drift-boat fishing, and nature walks are also available. In addition, there is a sporting clays trap course. Hiking trails and swimming holes are available on the property. This is a popular ranch for family reunions, conferences, and weddings.

RV sites, facilities: There are 30 tent sites and 10 sites with full hookups (30 amps) for RVs of any length; some sites are pull-through. Eleven housekeeping cabins and two houses are also available. Picnic tables and fire grills are provided. Restrooms with showers, drinking water, coin laundry, ice, firewood, recreation room, swimming pool, spa, fitness room, deli and gift shop, swimming and fishing pond, petting zoo, playground, horseshoe pits, and volleyball and basketball courts are available.

Reservations, fees: Reservations are recommended. RV sites are $20 per night, $5 per person per night for tent sites, $2 per person per night for more than two people. Some credit cards accepted. Open year-round, weather permitting.

Directions: From the junction of U.S. 101 and Highway 299 near Arcata, turn east on Highway 299 and drive to Willow Creek. In Willow Creek, turn north (left) on Highway 96 east and drive to Somes Bar. At Somes Bar, continue for 7.5 miles to Mile Marker 7.6 and Marble Mountain Ranch on the right.

Contact: Marble Mountain Ranch, 530/469-3322 or 800/KLAMATH (800/552-6284), www.marblemountainranch.com.

10 OAK BOTTOM

Scenic rating: 7

in Klamath National Forest on the Salmon River

Map grid A1

This camp is just far enough off Highway 96 that it gets missed by zillions of out-of-towners every year. It is set across the road from the lower Salmon River, a pretty, clean, and cold stream that pours out of the surrounding wilderness high country. Swimming is very good in river holes, though the water is cold, especially when nearby Wooley Creek is full of snowmelt pouring out of the Marble Mountains to the north. In the fall, there is good shoreline fishing for steelhead, though the canyon bottom is shaded almost all day and gets very cold.

RV sites, facilities: There are 26 sites for tents or RVs up to 25 feet (no hookups). Picnic tables and fire grills are provided. Drinking water and vault toilets are available. There is a dump station at the Elk Creek Campground in Happy Camp and at Aikens Creek, 13 miles southwest of the town of Orleans. Supplies are available in Somes Bar. Some facilities are wheelchair-accessible. Leashed pets are permitted.

Reservations, fees: Reservations are not accepted. Sites are $10 per night, $5 per night for each additional vehicle. Open April through mid-October, weather permitting.

Directions: From the junction of U.S. 101 and Highway 299 near Arcata, turn east on Highway 299 and drive to Willow Creek. In Willow Creek, turn north (left) on Highway 96 east and drive to Somes Bar-Etna Road (0.25 mile before Somes Bar). Turn right on Somes Bar-Etna Road and drive two miles to the campground on the left side of the road.

Contact: Six Rivers National Forest, Orleans Ranger District, 530/627-3291, fax 530/627-3401.

11 FISH LAKE

Scenic rating: 8

in Six Rivers National Forest

Map grid A1

This is a pretty little lake that provides good fishing for stocked rainbow trout from the season opener on Memorial Day weekend through July. The camp gets little pressure in other months. It's in the heart of Bigfoot Country, with numerous Bigfoot sightings reported near Bluff Creek. No powerboats are permitted on the lake, but it's too small for that anyway, being better suited for a canoe, float tube, raft, or pram. The elevation is 1,800 feet. The presence here of Port-Orford-cedar root disease, spread by spores in the mud, forces closure from October through May in some years; call for current status.

RV sites, facilities: There are 24 sites for tents or RVs up to 20 feet (no hookups). Picnic tables and fire grills are provided. Drinking water and vault toilets are available. Some facilities are wheelchair-accessible. Leashed pets are permitted.

Reservations, fees: Reservations are not accepted. Sites are $10 per night, $5 per night for each additional vehicle. Open late May through early October, weather permitting.

Directions: From I-5 in Redding, turn west on Highway 299 and drive to Willow Creek. In Willow Creek, turn north (left) on Highway 96 east and drive to Weitchpec, continuing seven miles north on Highway 96 to Fish Lake Road/Bluff Creek Road. Turn left on Fish Lake Road/Bluff Creek Road and drive five miles (stay to the right at the Y) to Fish Lake.

Contact: Six Rivers National Forest, Orleans Ranger District, 530/627-3291, fax 530/627-3401.

CALIFORNIA

12 E-NE-NUCK

Scenic rating: 7

in Six Rivers National Forest
Map grid A1

The campground gets its name from a Karuk chief who lived in the area in the late 1800s. It's a popular spot for anglers; Bluff Creek and the Klamath are within walking distance and Fish Lake is eight miles to the west. Bluff Creek is the legendary site where the Bigfoot film of the 1960s was shot. While it was finally admitted that the film was a phony, it still put Bluff Creek on the map. A unique feature at this campground is a smokehouse for lucky anglers.

RV sites, facilities: There are 11 sites for tents or RVs up to 30 feet (no hookups). Picnic tables, fire rings, and cast-iron firebox stoves are provided. Drinking water, vault toilets, and a smokehouse are available. Some facilities are wheelchair-accessible. Leashed pets are permitted.

Reservations, fees: Reservations are not accepted. Sites are $10 per night, $5 for each additional vehicle. Open late June through October.

Directions: From the junction of U.S. 101 and Highway 299 near Arcata, turn east on Highway 299 and drive to Willow Creek. In Willow Creek, turn north (left) on Highway 96 east and drive to Weitchpec, continuing on Highway 96 for about five miles to the campground. E-Ne-Nuck is just beyond Aikens Creek West campground.

Contact: Six Rivers National Forest, Orleans Ranger District, 530/627-3291, fax 530/627-3401.

13 AIKENS CREEK WEST

Scenic rating: 7

on the Klamath River in Six Rivers National Forest
Map grid A1

The Klamath River is warm and green here in summer, and this camp provides an ideal put-in spot for a day of easy rafting, especially for newcomers in inflatable kayaks. The camp is set at 340 feet in elevation along the Klamath. From here to Weitchpec is an easy paddle, with the take-out on the right side of the river just below the confluence with the Trinity River. The river is set in a beautiful canyon with lots of birds, and enters the Yurok Indian Reservation. The steelhead fishing can be good in this area from August through mid-November. Highway 96 is a scenic but slow cruise.

RV sites, facilities: There are dispersed sites for tents or RVs of any length (no hookups). Picnic tables and fire grills are provided. Vault toilets and a dump station are available, but there is no drinking water. There are reduced services in winter, and all garbage must be packed out. Leashed pets are permitted.

Reservations, fees: Sites are $8 per night, $5 per night for each additional vehicle; no fees during the winter. Open year-round, weather permitting.

Directions: From the junction of U.S. 101 and Highway 299 near Arcata, turn east on Highway 299 and drive to Willow Creek. In Willow Creek, turn north (left) on Highway 96 east and drive to Weitchpec, continuing on Highway 96 for five miles to the campground on the right side of the road.

Contact: Six Rivers National Forest, Orleans Ranger District, 530/627-3291, fax 530/627-3401.

14 KLAMATH RIVERSIDE RV PARK AND CAMPGROUND

Scenic rating: 8

on the Klamath River
Map grid A1

Klamath Riverside RV Park and Campground is an option for RV cruisers touring Highway 96—designated the Bigfoot Scenic Byway—and looking for a place in Orleans. The camp has large grassy sites set amid pine trees, right on the river. There are spectacular views of Mount Orleans and the surrounding hills. A 12-foot Bigfoot statue is on the property. Through the years, I've seen many changes at this park. It has been transformed from a dusty fishing spot to a park more resembling a rural resort that attracts hikers, cyclists, gold panners, river enthusiasts, anglers, and hunters. One big plus is that the park offers guided fishing trips during the season.

RV sites, facilities: There are 12 tent sites and 45 sites with full hookups (30 and 50 amps) for RVs of any length; some sites are pull-through. Two cabins and six rental trailers are also available. Picnic tables and fire rings are provided. Restrooms with showers, seasonal swimming pool, a spa, group pavilion, fish-cleaning station, coin laundry, horseshoes, playground, modem access, pay phone, and RV storage are available. Guided drift-boat fishing in season is available. Leashed pets are permitted.

Reservations, fees: Reservations are accepted. Sites are $18–24 per night, $5 per person per night for more than two people. Group, weekly, and monthly rates available. Open year-round.

Directions: From the junction of U.S. 101 and Highway 299 near Arcata, drive east on Highway 299 to Willow Creek, turn north (left) on Highway 96 east and drive past Weitchpec to Orleans. This campground is at the west end of the town of Orleans on Highway 96 on the right.

Contact: Klamath Riverside RV Park and Campground, 530/627-3239 or 800/627-9779, fax 530/627-3755, www.klamathriversidervpark.com.

15 PEARCH CREEK

Scenic rating: 7
on the Klamath River in Six Rivers National Forest
Map grid A1

This is one of the premium Forest Service camps on the Klamath River because of its easy access from the highway and easy access to the river. The camp is set on Pearch Creek, about a quarter mile from the Klamath at a deep bend in the river. Indeed, the fishing is often excellent for one- to five-pound steelhead

from August through November. The elevation is 400 feet.

RV sites, facilities: There are 10 sites for tents or RVs up to 22 feet (no hookups). Picnic tables and fire grills are provided. Drinking water and vault toilets are available. A grocery store, coin laundry, and propane gas are available within one mile. Leashed pets are permitted.

Reservations, fees: Reservations are not accepted. Sites are $10 per night, $5 per night for each additional vehicle. Open late May through early November.

Directions: From I-5 in Redding, turn west on Highway 299 and drive to Willow Creek. In Willow Creek, turn north (left) on Highway 96 east, drive past Weitchpec, and continue to Orleans. In Orleans, continue for one mile and look for the campground entrance on the right side of the road.

Contact: Six Rivers National Forest, Orleans Ranger District, 530/627-3291, fax 530/627-3401.

16 IDLEWILD

Scenic rating: 8
on the North Fork of the Salmon River in Klamath National Forest
Map grid A1

This is one of the prettiest drive-to camps in the region, set on the North Fork of the Salmon River, a beautiful, cold, clear stream and a major tributary to the Klamath River. Most campers use the camp for its nearby trailhead (two miles north on a dirt Forest Service road out of camp). The hike here is routed to the north, climbing alongside the Salmon River for miles into the Marble Mountain Wilderness (wilderness permits are required). It's a rugged 10-mile, all-day climb to Lake of the Island, with several other lakes (highlighted by Hancock Lake) to the nearby west, accessible on weeklong trips. The elevation is 2,600 feet.

RV sites, facilities: There are 18 sites for tents or RVs up to 22 feet (no hookups). Picnic tables and fire grills are provided. Drinking water and vault toilets are available, with limited winter facilities. Leashed pets are permitted.

Reservations, fees: Reservations are not accepted. Sites are $10 per night, with no fee during the winter. Open year-round.

Directions: From Yreka, turn southwest on Highway 3 and drive to Etna. In Etna, turn west on Etna-Somes Bar Road (Main Street in town) and drive about 16 miles to the campground on the right side of the road. Note: A shorter, more scenic, and more complex route is available from Gazelle (north of Weed on Old Highway 99). Take Gazelle-Callahan Road west over the summit and continue north to Etna.

Contact: Klamath National Forest, Salmon River and Scott River Ranger Districts, 530/468-5351, fax 530/468-1290.

17 MATTHEWS CREEK
🏊 🎣 🐕 🚐 ⛺

Scenic rating: 8

on the Salmon River in Klamath National Forest
Map grid A1

This camp is set in a dramatic river canyon, with the beautiful South Fork of the Salmon River nearby. Rafters call it the "Cal Salmon," and good put-in and take-out spots are found every few miles all the way to the confluence with the Klamath. In early summer the water is quite cold from snowmelt, but by midsummer it warms up significantly. The best fishing for steelhead on the Salmon is in December and January in the stretch of river downstream from the town of Forks of Salmon or upstream in the South Fork (check regulations for closed areas). In winter the mountain rims shield the canyon floor from sunlight and it gets so cold you'll feel like a human glacier. The elevation is 1,700 feet.

RV sites, facilities: There are 12 sites for tents or RVs up to 16 feet (no hookups). Picnic tables and fire grills are provided. Drinking water and vault toilets are available, with limited winter facilities. Leashed or controlled pets are permitted.

Reservations, fees: Reservations are not accepted. Sites are $10 per night. Open May through October.

Directions: From the junction of U.S. 101 and Highway 299 near Arcata, head east on Highway 299 and drive to Willow Creek. In Willow Creek, turn north on Highway 96 and drive past Orleans to Somes Bar. At Somes Bar, turn east on Salmon River Road/Forest Road 2B01 and drive to the town of Forks of Salmon. Turn right on Cecilville Road/Forest Road 1002 and drive about nine miles to the campground. Cecilville Road is very narrow.

Contact: Klamath National Forest, Salmon River and Scott River Ranger Districts, 530/468-5351, fax 530/468-1290.

18 EAST FORK
🏊 🎣 🐕 🚐 ⛺

Scenic rating: 6

on the Salmon River in Klamath National Forest
Map grid A1

This is one of the more spectacular areas in the fall when the leaves turn different shades of gold. It's set at 2,600 feet along the Salmon River, just outside the town of Cecilville. Directly adjacent to the camp is Forest Road 37N02, which leads to a Forest Service station four miles away, and to a trailhead for the Trinity Alps Wilderness three miles beyond that. Note to steelhead anglers: Check the Department of Fish and Game regulations for closed areas on the Salmon River.

RV sites, facilities: There are nine sites for tents or RVs up to 16 feet (no hookups). Picnic tables and fire grills are provided. Vault toilets are available. No drinking water is available. Garbage must be packed out. Leashed pets are permitted.

Reservations, fees: Reservations are not accepted. There is no fee for camping. Open May through October.

Directions: From Weed, drive north on I-5 to the Edgewood exit. Take the Edgewood exit, turn left at the stop sign, and drive a short distance under the freeway to another stop sign at

Old Highway 99. Turn right (north) and drive six miles to Gazelle and Gazelle-Callahan Road. Turn left (west) on Gazelle-Callahan Road, and drive to Callahan and Cecilville Road. Turn left (southwest) on Cecilville Road and drive about 30 miles to the campground on the right side of the road. If you reach the town of Cecilville, you have gone two miles too far.

Contact: Klamath National Forest, Salmon River and Scott River Ranger Districts, 530/468-5351, fax 530/468-1290.

19 SHADOW CREEK

Scenic rating: 7

in Klamath National Forest

Map grid A1

This tiny spot, secluded and quiet, is along little Shadow Creek where it enters the East Fork Salmon River, adjacent to a deep bend in the road. An unusual side trip is to take the Forest Service road out of camp (turn north off Cecilville Road) and follow it as it winds back and forth, finally arriving at Grouse Point, 5,409 feet elevation, for a view of the western slopes of the nearby Russian and Trinity Alps Wilderness Areas. There are three trailheads six miles to the east of the camp: Fish Creek, Long Gulch, and Trail Gulch. Note: The river adjacent to the campground is a spawning area and is closed to salmon and steelhead fishing, but you can take trout.

RV sites, facilities: There are five sites for tents or RVs up to 16 feet (no hookups). Picnic tables and fire grills are provided. Vault toilets are available. No drinking water is available. Garbage must be packed out. Leashed pets are permitted.

Reservations, fees: Reservations are not accepted. There is no fee for camping. Open May through October.

Directions: From Weed, drive north on I-5 to the Edgewood exit. Take the Edgewood exit, turn left at the stop sign, and drive a short distance under the freeway to another stop sign at Old Highway 99. Turn right (north) and

drive six miles to Gazelle and Gazelle-Callahan Road. Turn left (west) and drive to Callahan and Cecilville Road. Turn left (southwest) on Cecilville Road and drive about 25 miles to the campground on the left side of the road.

Contact: Klamath National Forest, Salmon River and Scott River Ranger Districts, 530/468-5351, fax 530/468-1290.

20 TISH TANG

Scenic rating: 8

in Six Rivers National Forest

Map grid A1

This campground is adjacent to one of the best swimming holes in all of Northern California. By late July the adjacent Trinity River is warm and slow, perfect for tubing, a quick dunk, and paddling a canoe. There is a large gravel beach, and some people will bring along their shorty lawn chairs and just take a seat on the edge of the river in a few inches of water. Though Tish Tang is a good put-in spot for rafting in the late spring and early summer, the flows are too slow and quiet for most rafters to even ruffle a feather during the summer. The elevation is 300 feet.

RV sites, facilities: There are 40 sites for tents or RVs up to 22 feet (no hookups). Picnic tables and fire grills are provided. Drinking water and vault toilets are available, and there is a camp host. Leashed pets are permitted.

Reservations, fees: Reservations are accepted at 530/625-4284. Sites are $10 per night, $3 per night for each additional vehicle, $15 per night for double sites. Open late May through September.

Directions: From the junction of U.S. 101 and Highway 299 near Arcata, turn east on Highway 299 and drive to Willow Creek. In Willow Creek, turn north (left) on Highway 96 east and drive eight miles north to the campground entrance on the right side of the road.

Contact: Hoopa Valley Tribal Council, Forestry Department, 530/625-4284, fax 530/625-4230.

21 BEAVER CREEK

Scenic rating: 8

in Klamath National Forest

Map grid B1

This camp is set along Beaver Creek, a feeder stream to the nearby Klamath River, with two small creeks entering Beaver Creek on the far side of the river near the campground. It is quiet and pretty. There are several historic mining sites in the area; you'll need a map of Klamath National Forest (available for a fee at the district office) to find them. In the fall, this campground is usually taken over by deer hunters. The elevation is 2,400 feet.

RV sites, facilities: There are eight sites for tents or RVs up to 16 feet (no hookups). Picnic tables and fire grills are provided. Vault toilets are available. There is no drinking water. Garbage must be packed out. Leashed pets are permitted.

Reservations, fees: Reservations are not accepted. There is no fee for camping. Open May through October.

Directions: From Yreka, drive north on I-5 to Highway 96. Turn west on Highway 96 and drive approximately 15 miles (if you reach the town of Klamath River, you have gone 0.5 mile too far) to Beaver Creek Road. Turn right on Beaver Creek Road/Forest Road 11 and drive four miles to the campground.

Contact: Klamath National Forest, Happy Camp and Oak Knoll Ranger Districts, 530/493-2243, fax 530/493-1796.

22 TREE OF HEAVEN

Scenic rating: 7

in Klamath National Forest

Map grid B1

This outstanding riverside campground provides excellent access to the Klamath River for fishing, rafting, and hiking. The best deal is to put in your raft, canoe, or drift boat upstream at the ramp below Iron Gate Reservoir, then make the all-day run down to the take-out at Tree of Heaven. This section of river is an easy paddle (Class II, II+, and III) and also provides excellent steelhead fishing in the winter. A 0.25 mile paved interpretive trail is near the camp. On the drive in from the highway, you can watch the landscape turn from high chaparral to forest.

RV sites, facilities: There are 20 sites for tents or RVs up to 35 feet (no hookups). Picnic tables and fire grills are provided. Drinking water and vault toilets are available. A river access spot for put-in and take-out for rafts and drift boats is available. Some facilities are wheelchair-accessible. Leashed pets are permitted.

Reservations, fees: Reservations are accepted at 877/444-6777 or www.recreation.gov ($10 reservation fee). Sites are $10 per night. Open year-round.

Directions: From Yreka, drive north on I-5 to Highway 96. Turn west on Highway 96 and drive seven miles to the campground entrance on the left side of the road.

Contact: Klamath National Forest, Happy Camp and Oak Knoll Ranger Districts, 530/493-2243, fax 530/493-1796.

23 MARTINS DAIRY

Scenic rating: 8

on the Little Shasta River in Klamath National Forest

Map grid B1

This camp is set at 6,000 feet, where the deer get big and the country seems wide open. A large meadow is nearby, directly across the road from this remote camp, with fantastic wildflower displays in late spring. This is one of the prettiest camps around in the fall, with dramatic color from aspens, elderberries, and willows. It also makes a good base camp for hunters in the fall. Before heading into the surrounding backcountry, obtain a map (fee) of Klamath National Forest at the Goosenest Ranger Station on Highway 97, on your way in to camp.

RV sites, facilities: There are eight sites for tents or RVs up to 30 feet (no hookups) and a horse campsite. Picnic tables and fire grills are provided. Drinking water and vault toilets are available. Leashed pets are permitted.

Reservations, fees: Reservations are not accepted. Sites are $8 per night. Open late May through early October, weather permitting.

Directions: From Weed and I-5, turn north on U.S. 97 (Klamath Falls exit) and drive to Grass Lake. Continue about seven miles to Forest Road 70/46N10 (if you reach Hebron Summit, you have driven about a mile too far). Turn left, drive about 10 miles to a Y, take the left fork, and drive three miles (including a very sharp right turn) to the campground on the right side of the road. A map of Klamath National Forest is advised.

Contact: Klamath National Forest, Goosenest Ranger District, 530/398-4391, fax 530/398-5749.

24 JUANITA LAKE

Scenic rating: 7

in Klamath National Forest
Map grid B1

Small and relatively unknown, this camp is set along the shore of Juanita Lake at 5,100 feet. Swimming is not recommended because the water is cold and mucky, and mosquitoes can be abundant as well. It is stocked with rainbow trout, brown trout, bass, and catfish, but a problem with golden shiners has cut into the lake's fishing productivity. It's a small lake and forested, set near the Butte Valley Wildlife Area in the plateau country just five miles to the northeast. The latter provides an opportunity to see waterfowl and, in the winter, bald eagles. Campers will discover a network of Forest Service roads in the area, providing an opportunity for mountain biking. There are designated fishing areas and a paved trail around the lake that is wheelchair-accessible and spans approximately 1.25 miles.

RV sites, facilities: There are 23 sites for tents or RVs up to 32 feet (no hookups), and a group tent site that can accommodate up to 50 people. Picnic tables and fire grills are provided.

Drinking water and vault toilets are available. Boating is allowed, but no motors are permitted on the lake. Many facilities are wheelchair-accessible. Leashed pets are permitted.

Reservations, fees: Reservations are not accepted for individual sites but are required for the group site at 530/398-4391. Individual sites are $10 per night, and the group site is $30 per night. Open late May through mid-October, weather permitting.

Directions: From Weed and I-5, turn north on U.S. 97 (Klamath Falls exit) and drive approximately 37 miles to Ball Mountain Road. Turn left on Ball Mountain Road and drive 2.5 miles, veer right at the fork, and continue to the campground entrance at the lake.

Contact: Klamath National Forest, Goosenest Ranger District, 530/398-4391, fax 530/398-5749.

25 LAKE SHASTINA

Scenic rating: 5

near Klamath National Forest and Weed
Map grid B1

Lake Shastina is set at the northern foot of Mount Shasta at 3,000 feet in elevation. The campground is located on the access road to the boat ramp, about 0.25 mile from the lake. It offers sweeping views, good swimming on hot summer days, waterskiing, and all water sports. There is fishing for catfish and bass in the spring and summer, an occasional opportunity for crappie, and good fishing for trout in late winter and spring. One reason the views of Mount Shasta are so good is that this is largely high sagebrush country with few trees. As such, it can get very dusty, windy, and, in the winter, nasty cold. When the lake is full, the wind is down, and the weather is good, there are few complaints. But that is only rarely the case. The lake level is often low, with the water drained for hay farmers to the north. This is one of the few lakes in Northern California that has property with lakeside housing. Lake Shastina Golf Course is nearby.

RV sites, facilities: There is a small primitive

area for tents or RVs of any length (no hookups). There is one faucet, but you should bring your own water just in case. A vault toilet is available and a boat launch is nearby; the boat ramp is nonfunctional when the lake level drops below the concrete ramp. Garbage service available May to September only. There is a 14-day limit for camping. Supplies can be obtained five miles away in Weed. Leashed pets are permitted.

Reservations, fees: Reservations are not accepted. There is no fee for camping. Open May through September.

Directions: From Redding, take I-5 north to the central Weed exit and U.S. 97. Take the exit to the stop sign, turn right, drive through Weed, exiting for U.S. 97/Klamath Falls. Merge right (north) on U.S. 97 and drive about five miles to Big Springs Road. Turn left (west) on Big Springs Road and drive about two miles to Jackson Ranch Road. Turn left (west) on Jackson Ranch Road and drive about one mile to Emerald Isle Road (watch for the signed turnoff). Turn right and drive one mile to the campground.

Contact: Siskiyou County Public Works, 530/842-8250.

26 KANGAROO LAKE WALK-IN

Scenic rating: 9

in Klamath National Forest

Map grid B1   **BEST (**

A remote paved road leads to the parking area for Kangaroo Lake, set at 6,500 feet. This provides a genuine rarity: a beautiful and pristine mountain lake with a campground, good fishing for brook and rainbow trout, and an excellent trailhead for hikers. The walk to the campsites is very short, 1–3 minutes, with many sites very close. Campsites are in a forested setting with no lake view. Reaching the lake requires another five minutes, but a paved wheelchair-accessible trail is available. In addition, a switchback ramp for wheelchairs makes it one of the best wheelchair-accessible fishing areas in California. The lake is small, 25 acres, but deep at 100 feet. No boat motors are allowed. A hiking trail rises

steeply out of the campground and connects to the Pacific Crest Trail, from which you turn left to gain a dramatic lookout of Northern California peaks as well as the lake below.

RV sites, facilities: There are 18 walk-in sites for tents, and RVs up to 25 feet (no hookups) are allowed in the parking lot. Picnic tables and fire grills are provided. Drinking water and vault toilets are available. Some facilities are wheelchair-accessible, including a nearby fishing pier. Leashed pets are permitted.

Reservations, fees: Reservations are not accepted. Sites are $10 per night. Open June through October, weather permitting.

Directions: From Weed, drive north on I-5 and take the Edgewood exit. At the stop sign, turn left and drive a short distance under the freeway to the stop sign at Old Highway 99. Turn right (north) on Old Highway 99 and drive six miles to Gazelle and Gazelle-Callahan Road. Turn left at Gazelle-Callahan Road and drive over the summit. From the summit, continue about five miles to Rail Creek Road. Turn left at Rail Creek Road and drive approximately eight miles to where the road dead-ends near the campground. Walk approximately 30–150 yards to reach the campsites.

Contact: Klamath National Forest, Scott River and Salmon River Ranger Districts, 530/468-5351, fax 530/468-1290.

27 McBRIDE SPRINGS

Scenic rating: 8

in Shasta-Trinity National Forest

Map grid B1

This camp is set at 4,880 feet on the slopes of the awesome Mount Shasta (14,162 feet), California's most majestic mountain. Stargazing is fantastic here, and during full moons, an eerie glow is cast on the adjoining high mountain slopes. A good side trip is to drive to the end of Everitt Memorial Highway, which tops out above 7,800 feet. You'll find great lookouts to the west, and a jump-off point for a Shasta expedition or day hike to Panther Meadows.

RV sites, facilities: There are nine sites for tents or RVs up to 16 feet (no hookups). Picnic tables and fire grills are provided. Drinking water (from a single well with a hand pump at the north end of the campground) and vault toilets are available. Supplies and a coin laundry are available in the town of Mount Shasta. Some facilities are wheelchair-accessible. Leashed pets are permitted.

Reservations, fees: Reservations are not accepted. Sites are $10 per night. Open Memorial Day weekend through October, weather permitting.

Directions: From Redding drive north on I-5 to the town of Mount Shasta and the Central Mount Shasta exit. Take that exit and drive to the stop sign and Lake Street. Turn right and continue on Lake Street through town; once out of town, the road becomes Everitt Memorial Highway. Continue on Everitt Memorial Highway for four miles to the campground entrance on the left side of the road.

Contact: Shasta-Trinity National Forest, Mount Shasta Ranger District, 530/926-4511, fax 530/926-5120.

28 GUMBOOT LAKE

Scenic rating: 9

in Shasta-Trinity National Forest
Map grid B1

This pretty spot at 6,080 feet elevation provides a few small camps set beside a small yet beautiful high mountain lake, the kind of place many think you can reach only with long hikes. Not so with Gumboot. In addition, the fishing is good here, with rainbow trout in the 12-inch class. The lake is small, almost too small for even a canoe, and better suited to a pram, raft, or float tube. No motors of any kind are permitted, including electric motors. When the fishing gets good, it can get crowded, with both out-of-towners and locals making casts from the shoreline. A better bet is floating in a pram or inflatable to the far end of the lake and flyfishing with black leeches and a sink-tip line.

Another option is hiking 10 minutes through forest to Upper Gumboot Lake, which is more of a pond with small trout. Another excellent hike is available here, tromping off-trail beyond Upper Gumboot Lake and up the back slope of the lake to the Pacific Crest Trail, then turning left and scrambling to a great lookout of Mount Shasta in the distance and Gumboot in the foreground.

RV sites, facilities: There are four sites for tents or RVs up to 16 feet (no hookups), and across the creek there are four walk-in tent sites. Picnic tables are provided. Vault toilets are available. No drinking water is available. Garbage must be packed out. Some facilities are wheelchair-accessible. Leashed pets are permitted.

Reservations, fees: Reservations are not accepted. There is no fee for camping. Open May through October, weather permitting.

Directions: From the town of Mount Shasta on I-5, take the Central Mount Shasta exit and drive to the stop sign. Turn west and continue less than a mile to Old Stage Road. Turn left and drive 0.25 mile to a Y intersection at W. A. Barr Road. Bear right on W. A. Barr Road and drive past Box Canyon Dam and the Lake Siskiyou Campground entrance. Continue 10 miles to a fork, signed for Gumboot Lake. Bear left and drive 0.5 mile to the lake and campsites. Note: Access roads may be closed because of flooding; call for current status.

Contact: Shasta-Trinity National Forest, Mount Shasta Ranger District, 530/926-4511, fax 530/926-5120.

29 CASTLE LAKE

Scenic rating: 10

in Shasta-Trinity National Forest
Map grid B1

Castle Lake is a beautiful spot, a deep blue lake set in a granite bowl with a spectacular wall on the far side. The views of Mount Shasta are great, fishing is decent (especially ice fishing in winter), canoeing or floating around on a raft is a lot of fun, and there is a terrific hike that loops around the left side of the lake, rising to the ridge overlooking the lake for dramatic views. Locals use this lake for ice-skating in winter. The campground is not right beside the lake, to ensure the pristine clear waters remain untouched, but is rather just a short distance downstream along Castle Lake Creek. The lake is only 47 acres, but 120 feet deep. The elevation is 5,280 at the camp, and 5,450 feet at the lake.

RV sites, facilities: There are six sites for tents or RVs up to 16 feet (no hookups). Picnic tables and fire grills are provided. Vault toilets are available. No drinking water is available. Garbage must be packed out. Leashed pets are permitted.

Reservations, fees: Reservations are not accepted. There is no fee for camping. Open May through October, weather permitting.

Directions: From the town of Mount Shasta on I-5, take the Central Mount Shasta exit and drive to the stop sign. Turn west and drive less than a mile to Old Stage Road. Turn left and drive 0.25 mile to a Y intersection at W. A. Barr Road. Bear right on W. A. Barr Road and drive past Box Canyon Dam. Turn left at Castle Lake Road and drive seven miles to the campground access road on the left. Turn left and drive a short distance to the campground. Note: Castle Lake is another 0.25 mile up the road; there are no legal campsites along the lake's shoreline.

Contact: Shasta-Trinity National Forest, Mount Shasta Ranger District, 530/926-4511, fax 530/926-5120.

30 LAKE SISKIYOU CAMP-RESORT

Scenic rating: 9

near Mount Shasta

Map grid B1

This is a true gem of a lake, a jewel set at the foot of Mount Shasta at 3,181 feet. The lake level is almost always full (because it was built for recreation, not water storage) and offers a variety of quality recreation options, with great swimming, low-speed boating, and fishing. The campground complexes are huge, yet they are tucked into the forest so visitors don't get their styles cramped. The water in this 435-acre lake is clean and fresh. There is an excellent beach and swimming area, the latter protected by a buoy line. In spring, the fishing is good for trout, and then as the water warms, for smallmouth bass. A good boat ramp and boat rentals are available, and a 10-mph speed limit is strictly enforced, keeping the lake pristine and quiet. The City of Mount Shasta holds its July 4 fireworks display above the lake.

RV sites, facilities: There are 150 sites with full or partial hookups (30 and 50 amps) for RVs of any length, including some pull-through sites, and 225 additional sites for tents, seven of which are group areas. There are also 20 cabins and 10 park-model cabins. Picnic tables and fire grills are provided. Drinking water, restrooms with flush toilets and showers, playground, propane, convenience store, gift shop, deli, coin laundry, and a dump station are available. There are also a marina, boat rentals (canoes, kayaks, pedal boats, motorized boats), free boat launching, fishing dock, fish-cleaning station, boat slips, swimming beach, horseshoes, volleyball, group facilities, and a recreation room. A free movie plays every night in the summer. Some facilities are wheelchair-accessible. Leashed pets are permitted at the campground only.

Reservations, fees: Reservations are accepted. RV sites are $29 per night, $3 per person per night for more than two people, $5 per night for each additional vehicle, $2 per pet per night; tent sites are $20 per night. Some credit cards accepted. Open April through October, weather permitting.

Directions: From the town of Mount Shasta on I-5, take the Central Mount Shasta exit and drive to the stop sign. Turn west and drive less than a mile to Old Stage Road. Turn left and drive 0.25 mile to a Y intersection at W. A. Barr Road. Bear right on W. A. Barr Road and drive past Box Canyon Dam. Two miles farther, turn right at the entrance road for Lake Siskiyou

Campground and Marina and drive a short distance to the entrance station.

Contact: Lake Siskiyou Camp-Resort, 530/926-2618 or 888/926-2618, www.lakesis.com.

31 KOA MOUNT SHASTA

Scenic rating: 7

in Mount Shasta City

Map grid B1

Despite this KOA camp's relative proximity to the town of Mount Shasta, the extended driveway, wooded grounds, and view of Mount Shasta offer some feeling of seclusion. There are many excellent side trips. The best is driving up Everitt Memorial Highway, which rises up the slopes of Mount Shasta to the tree line at Bunny Flat, where you can take outstanding, short day hikes with great views to the south of the Sacramento River Canyon and Castle Crags. In the winter, you can play in the snow, including heading up to Bunny Flat for snow-play or to the Mount Shasta Board and Ski Park for developed downhill and cross-country skiing. An ice skating rink is in Mount Shasta. One of the biggest events of the year in Mount Shasta is the Fourth of July Run for Fun (billed as the largest small-town foot race anywhere) and associated parade and fireworks display at nearby Lake Siskiyou.

RV sites, facilities: There are 47 sites with full or partial hookups (20, 30, and 50 amps) for RVs of any length, 50 additional sites with partial hookups for tents or RVs, and four camping cabins. All sites are pull-through. Picnic tables are provided, and fire grills are provided at tent sites only. Restrooms with showers, a playground, propane gas, a convenience store, recreation room with arcade, horseshoe pit, shuffleboard, a seasonal swimming pool, high-speed modem access and Wi-Fi, and coin laundry are available. Leashed pets are permitted.

Reservations, fees: Reservations are accepted at 800/562-3617. Sites are $25–40 per night, $3–4 per person per night for more than two people, $3.50 for each additional vehicle, and

a $5 site guarantee fee. Some credit cards accepted. Open year-round.

Directions: From Redding, drive north on I-5 to the town of Mount Shasta. Continue past the first Mount Shasta exit and take the Central Mount Shasta exit. At the stop sign, turn right (east) on Lake Street and drive 0.6 mile to Mount Shasta Boulevard. Turn left and drive 0.5 mile to East Hinckley Boulevard. Turn right (signed KOA) on East Hinckley, drive a very short distance, then turn left at the entrance to the extended driveway for KOA Mount Shasta.

Contact: KOA Mount Shasta, 530/926-4029, www.mtshastakoa.com or www.koa.com.

32 McCLOUD DANCE COUNTRY RV PARK

Scenic rating: 6

in McCloud

Map grid B1

McCloud Dance Country RV Park is very popular with square dancers in the summer. The town of McCloud is the home of McCloud Dance Country Hall, a large dance hall dedicated to square and round dancing. The park used to be affiliated with the dance hall, but now it is open to the public. The park is sprinkled with old-growth pine trees and bordered by Squaw Valley Creek, a pretty stream. The RV sites are grassy and manicured, many shaded. McCloud River's three waterfalls are accessible from the McCloud River Loop, five miles south of the park on Highway 89. Mount Shasta Board and Ski Park also offers summer activities such as biking, a rock-climbing structure, and chairlift rides to great views of the surrounding forests. The ski park access road is six miles west of McCloud off Highway 89 at Snowman's Hill Summit. The McCloud River Railroad runs an excursion and a dinner train on summer weekends out of McCloud; reservations are available in town. If you're lucky you might see "Old Engine No. 25," one of the few remaining steam engines in service. (For more information, see the Fowler's Camp listing.)

RV sites, facilities: There are 136 sites with full or partial hookups (30 and 50 amps) for RVs of any length, a grassy area for dispersed tent camping, and seven cabins. There are a few long-term rentals. Large groups are welcome. Picnic tables are provided. Drinking water, restrooms with hot showers (heated bathhouse), a central barbecue and campfire area, cable TV, pay telephone, coin laundry, dump station, propane, horseshoes, fish-cleaning station, and two pet walks are available. Some facilities are wheelchair-accessible. Leashed pets are permitted, except in cabins.

Reservations, fees: Reservations are recommended. Sites are $14–41 per night, $7 per person per night for more than two people. Weekly rates available. Some credit cards accepted. Open year-round.

Directions: From Redding, drive north on I-5 and continue just past Dunsmuir to the junction with Highway 89. Turn east on Highway 89 and drive nine miles to McCloud and Squaw Valley Road. Turn right on Squaw Valley Road and then turn immediately left into the park entrance.

Contact: McCloud Dance Country RV Park, 530/964-2252, www.mccloudrvpark.com.

33 FOWLER'S CAMP

Scenic rating: 10

on the McCloud River in
Shasta-Trinity National Forest

Map grid B1   **BEST**

This campground is set beside the beautiful McCloud River at 3,400 feet, providing the chance for an easy hike to two waterfalls, including one of the most dramatic in Northern California. From the camp, the trail is routed upstream through forest, a near-level walk for only 15 minutes, then arrives at awesome Middle Falls, a wide-sweeping and powerful cascade best viewed in April. By summer, the flows subside and warm to the point that some people will swim in the pool at the base of the falls. The trail is also routed from camp downstream

to Lower Falls, an outstanding swimming hole in midsummer. Fishing the McCloud River here is fair, with trout stocks made from Lakim Dam on downstream to the camp. If this camp is full, Cattle Camp and Algoma, described in this chapter, offer overflow areas.

RV sites, facilities: There are 38 sites and one double site for tents or RVs up to 30 feet (no hookups). Picnic tables and fire grills are provided. Drinking water and vault toilets are available. Some facilities are wheelchair-accessible. Leashed pets are permitted.

Reservations, fees: Reservations are not accepted. Sites are $12 per night. Open year-round, weather permitting.

Directions: From Redding, drive north on I-5 and continue just past Dunsmuir to the junction with Highway 89. Turn east on Highway 89 and drive 12 miles to McCloud. From McCloud, continue driving on Highway 89 for five miles to the campground entrance road on the right. Turn right and drive a short distance to a Y intersection, then turn left at the Y to the campground.

Contact: Shasta-Trinity National Forest, McCloud Ranger District, 530/964-2184, fax 530/964-2938.

34 ALGOMA

Scenic rating: 7

on the McCloud River in
Shasta-Trinity National Forest

Map grid B1

This little-known, undeveloped spot along the McCloud River at 3,800 feet elevation is quite dusty in August. It is an alternative to Fowler's Camp and Cattle Camp. (See the Fowler's Camp and Cattle Camp listings for side-trip options.) A dirt road out of Algoma (turn right at the junction) follows along the headwaters of the McCloud River, past Cattle Camp to Upper Falls. There is a parking area for a short walk to view Middle Falls and on to Fowler's Camp and Lower Falls.

RV sites, facilities: There are eight sites for

tents or RVs up to 27 feet (no hookups). Picnic tables and fire grills are provided. Drinking water and vault toilets are available. Leashed pets are permitted.

Reservations, fees: Reservations are not accepted. There is no fee for camping. Open year-round, weather permitting.

Directions: From Redding, drive north on I-5 and continue just past Dunsmuir to the junction with Highway 89. Turn east on Highway 89 and drive to McCloud. From McCloud, continue driving on Highway 89 for 14 miles to the campground entrance road on the right (signed). Turn right and drive one mile to the campground by the bridge.

Contact: Shasta-Trinity National Forest, McCloud Ranger District, 530/964-2184, fax 530/964-2938.

35 CATTLE CAMP

Scenic rating: 5

on the McCloud River in
Shasta-Trinity National Forest

Map grid B1

This campground, at 3,700 feet, is ideal for RV campers who want a rustic setting, or as an overflow area if the more attractive Fowler's Camp is filled. A small swimming hole in the McCloud River is near the camp, although the water is typically cold. There are several good side trips in the area, including fishing on the nearby McCloud River, visiting the three waterfalls near Fowler's Camp, and exploring the north slopes of Mount Shasta (a map of Shasta-Trinity National Forest details the back roads).

RV sites, facilities: There are 19 individual sites and four double sites for tents or RVs up to 32 feet (no hookups). Picnic tables and fire grills are provided. Drinking water and vault toilets are available. Some facilities are wheelchair-accessible. Leashed pets are permitted.

Reservations, fees: Reservations are not accepted. Sites are $12 per night. Open year-round, weather permitting.

Directions: From Redding, drive north on I-5

and continue just past Dunsmuir to the junction with Highway 89. Turn east on Highway 89 and drive to McCloud. From McCloud, continue driving on Highway 89 for 11 miles to the campground entrance road on the right. Turn right and drive 0.5 mile to the campground on the left side of the road.

Contact: Shasta-Trinity National Forest, McCloud Ranger District, 530/964-2184, fax 530/964-2938.

36 TRAIL CREEK

Scenic rating: 7

in Klamath National Forest

Map grid B1

This simple and quiet camp is set beside Trail Creek, a small tributary to the upper Salmon River, at an elevation of 4,700 feet. A trailhead is about a mile to the south, accessible via a Forest Service road, providing access to a two-mile trail routed along Fish Creek and leading to little Fish Lake. From Fish Lake the trail climbs steeply, switchbacking at times, for another two miles to larger Trail Gull Lake, a very pretty spot set below Deadman Peak (7,741 feet).

RV sites, facilities: There are 12 sites for tents or RVs up to 22 feet (no hookups). Picnic tables and fire grills are provided. Drinking water and vault toilets are available. Leashed pets are permitted.

Reservations, fees: Reservations are not accepted. Sites are $10 per night. Open May through October.

Directions: From Weed, drive north on I-5 to the Edgewood exit. Take the Edgewood exit, turn left at the stop sign, and drive a short distance under the freeway to another stop sign at Old Highway 99. Turn right (north) and drive six miles to Gazelle and Gazelle-Callahan Road. Turn left (west) on Gazelle-Callahan Road and continue to Callahan and Cecilville Road. Turn left (southwest) on Cecilville Road and drive 17 miles to the campground.

Contact: Klamath National Forest, Scott River Ranger District, 530/468-5351, fax 530/468-1290.

37 HIDDEN HORSE

Scenic rating: 7

in Klamath National Forest

Map grid B1

Hidden Horse provides an alternate horse camp to nearby Carter Meadows. The horse camps are in close proximity to the Pacific Crest Trail, which passes through the area and serves as access to the Russian Wilderness to the north and the Trinity Alps Wilderness to the south. Trail Creek and East Fork campgrounds are nearby. The elevation is 6,000 feet.

RV sites, facilities: There are six sites for tents or RVs up to 35 feet (no hookups). Picnic tables and fire grills are provided. Drinking water and vault toilets are available. A horse-mounting ramp and corrals are also available. There is no designated water for stock available, so bring a bucket. Some facilities are wheelchair-accessible. Leashed pets are permitted.

Reservations, fees: Reservations are not accepted. Sites are $10 per night. Open June through October, weather permitting.

Directions: From Weed, drive north on I-5 to the Edgewood exit. Take the Edgewood exit, turn left at the stop sign, and drive a short distance under the freeway to Old Highway 99. Turn right (north) and drive six miles to Gazelle and Gazelle-Callahan Road. Turn left (west) on Gazelle-Callahan Road, and continue to Callahan and Cecilville Road. Turn left (southwest) on Cecilville Road and drive 11 miles to Carter Meadows Horse Camp. Continue 0.25 mile to the campground on the left.

Contact: Klamath National Forest, Scott River and Salmon River Ranger Districts, 530/468-5351, fax 530/468-1290.

38 CARTER MEADOWS GROUP HORSE CAMP

Scenic rating: 7

in Klamath National Forest

Map grid B1

Carter Meadows offers an extensive trail network for riding and hiking. The Pacific Crest Trail passes through the area and serves as access to the Russian Wilderness to the north and the Trinity Alps Wilderness to the south. Stream fishing is another option here. Trail Creek and East Fork campgrounds are nearby.

RV sites, facilities: There is one disbursed group equestrian site for tents or RVs up to 35 feet (no hookups) that can accommodate up to 25 people and 25 horses. Group barbecues and picnic tables are provided. Drinking water, vault toilets, and 13 horse corrals are available. Leashed pets are permitted.

Reservations, fees: Reservations are required at 877/444-6777 or www.recreation.gov ($10 reservation fee). The camp is $30 per night. Open mid-May through October, weather permitting.

Directions: From Weed, drive north on I-5 to the Edgewood exit. Take the Edgewood exit, turn left at the stop sign, and drive a short distance under the freeway to Old Highway 99. Turn right (north) and drive six miles to Gazelle and Gazelle-Callahan Road. Turn left (west) on Gazelle-Callahan Road, and continue to Callahan and Cecilville Road. Turn left (southwest) on Cecilville Road and drive 11 miles to the campground.

Contact: Klamath National Forest, Scott River and Salmon River Ranger Districts, 530/468-5351, fax 530/468-1290.

39 HORSE FLAT

Scenic rating: 6

on Eagle Creek in Shasta-Trinity National Forest

Map grid B1

This camp is used by commercial pack operations as well as horse owners preparing for trips into the Trinity Alps. A trail starts right out of camp and is routed deep into the Trinity Alps Wilderness. It starts at 3,200 feet in elevation, then climbs all the way along Eagle Creek to Eagle Peak, where it intersects with the Pacific Crest Trail, then drops over the ridge to little Telephone Lake, a nine-mile hike. Note: Horse owners should call for the conditions of the corral and trail before making the trip.

RV sites, facilities: There are 16 sites for tents or RVs up to 16 feet (no hookups). Picnic tables and fire grills are provided. Vault toilets are available. No drinking water is available. Horse corrals are available. Garbage must be packed out. Leashed pets are permitted.

Reservations, fees: Reservations are not accepted. There is no fee for camping. Open mid-May through October.

Directions: From Redding, drive west on Highway 299 to Weaverville and Highway 3. Turn right (north) on Highway 3 and drive to Trinity Center at the north end of Trinity Lake. From Trinity Center, continue north on Highway 3 for 16.5 miles to Eagle Creek Campground (on the left) and Forest Road 38N27. Turn left on Forest Road 38N27 and drive two miles to the campground.

Contact: Shasta-Trinity National Forest, Weaverville Ranger Station, 530/623-2121, fax 530/623-6010.

40 EAGLE CREEK

Scenic rating: 7

in Shasta-Trinity National Forest

Map grid B1

This campground is set where little Eagle Creek enters the north Trinity River. Some campers use it as a base camp for a fishing trip, with the rainbow trout often abundant but predictably small in this stretch of water. The elevation is 2,800 feet.

RV sites, facilities: There are 17 sites for tents or RVs up to 35 feet (no hookups). Picnic tables and fire grills are provided. Drinking water and vault toilets are available. Leashed pets are permitted.

Reservations, fees: Reservations are not accepted. Sites are $10 per night. Open mid-May through October.

Directions: From Redding, drive west on Highway 299 to Weaverville and Highway 3. Turn right (north) on Highway 3 and drive to Trinity Center at the north end of Trinity Lake. From Trinity Center, continue north on Highway 3 for 16.5 miles to the campground on the left side of the road.

Contact: Shasta-Trinity National Forest, Weaverville Ranger Station, 530/623-2121, fax 530/623-6010.

41 RAILROAD PARK RV AND CAMPGROUND

Scenic rating: 7

south of Dunsmuir

Map grid B1

The resort adjacent to the RV park and campground was designed in the spirit of the railroad, when steam trains ruled the rails. The property features old stage cars (available for overnight lodging) and a steam locomotive. The railroad theme does not extend to the campground, however. What you'll find at the park is a classic campground set amid tall trees. There is a swimming hole in Little Castle Creek alongside the park. Many good side trips are available in the area, including excellent hiking and sightseeing at Castle Crags State Park (where there is a series of awesome granite spires) and outstanding trout fishing on the upper Sacramento River. At night, the sound of occasional passing trains soothes some, wakes others.

RV sites, facilities: There are 21 sites with full or partial hookups (30 amps) for RVs of any length, 31 sites with no hookups for tents or RVs. Some sites are pull-through. Cabins and a motel are next door at the resort. Picnic tables and fire rings are provided. Restrooms with showers, ice, coin laundry, group barbecue pit, game room, and horseshoes are available. A restaurant and lounge are within walking distance. Some facilities are wheelchair-accessible. Leashed pets are permitted.

Reservations, fees: Reservations are accepted. Sites are $22–30 per night, $3 per person per night for more than two people, $3 per night for each additional vehicle. Some credit cards accepted. Open April through November, weather permitting.

Directions: From Redding, drive north on I-5 for 45 miles to Exit 728 for Cragview Drive/Railroad Park Road. Take that exit and drive to the stop sign and Railroad Park Road. Turn left and drive under the freeway and continue to the campground on the left.

Contact: Railroad Park RV and Campground, 530/235-0420 or 800/974-7245 (California residents only), www.rrpark.com.

42 CASTLE CRAGS STATE PARK

Scenic rating: 9

on the Sacramento River

Map grid B1

This park is named for the awesome granite spires that tower 6,000 feet above the park. Beyond to the north is giant Mount Shasta (14,162 feet), making for a spectacular natural setting. The campsites are set in forest, shaded, very pretty, and sprinkled along a paved access road. But not a year goes by when people don't write in complaining of the highway noise from I-5 echoing in the Sacramento River Canyon, as well as of the occasional passing freight trains in the night. Pristine and quiet, this campground is not. (In the future, its location may be moved farther up the canyon for a quieter setting.) At the end of the access road is a parking area for the two-minute walk to the Crags Lookout, a beautiful view. Nearby is the trailhead (at 2,500 feet elevation) for hikes up the Crags, featuring a 5.4-mile round-trip that rises to the base of Castle Dome at 4,800 feet, the leading spire on the crag's ridge. Again, road noise echoing up the canyon provides a background once you clear the tree line. Trout fishing is good in the nearby Sacramento River and requires driving,

walking, and exploring to find the best spots. There are also some good swimming holes, but the water is cold. This is a popular state park, with reservations often required in summer, but with your choice of any campsite even in late spring.

RV sites, facilities: There are 52 sites for tents only, three sites for RVs up to 27 feet (no hookups), an overflow area with 12 sites and limited facilities, six walk-in environmental sites (100-yard walk required) with limited facilities, and a hike-in/bike-in site. Picnic tables, food lockers, and fire grills or fire rings are provided. Drinking water, restrooms with flush toilets and showers, and firewood are available. Leashed pets are permitted at campsites only.

Reservations, fees: Reservations are accepted ($8 reservation fee) at 800/444-PARK (800/444-7275) or www.reserveamerica.com. Sites are $25 per night, $9 per night for walk-in environmental sites, $8 per night for each additional vehicle. The hike-in/bike-in site is $3 per person per night. Open year-round.

Directions: From Redding, drive north on I-5 for 45 miles to the Castle Crags State Park exit. Take that exit, turn west, and drive a short distance to the well-signed park entrance on the right side of the road.

Contact: Castle Crags State Park, 530/235-2684, fax 530/235-1965, www.parks.ca.gov.

43 FRIDAY'S RV RETREAT AND McCLOUD FLY FISHING RANCH

Scenic rating: 7

near McCloud

Map grid B1

Friday's RV Retreat and McCloud Fly Fishing Ranch offers great recreation opportunities for every member of the family. The property features a small private fishing lake, two casting ponds, 1.5 miles of Squaw Valley Creek frontage, and five miles of hiking trails. The ranch specializes in fly-fishing packages, with both lodging and fly-fishing for one price. However, campers are welcome to stay here. In addition, the McCloud River's wild trout section is a 45-minute drive to the south, the beautiful McCloud Golf Course (nine holes) is within a five-minute drive, and a trailhead for the Pacific Crest Trail is also only five minutes away. Lake McCloud is three miles away and offers fishing and water-sports options. The park covers 400 wooded and grassy acres. Owner Bob Friday is quite a character, and he figured out that if he planted giant rainbow trout in the ponds for catch-and-release fishing, fly fishers would stop to catch a monster and take a photograph, and then tell people they caught the fish on the McCloud River, where they are smaller and elusive. Weeds are occasionally a problem at the ponds; call ahead if that is a concern. Also available is the dinner and excursion train that runs out of McCloud on summer weekends. (See McCloud Dance Country RV Park listing in this chapter for other information and side-trip options.)

RV sites, facilities: There are 30 sites with full hookups (30 and 50 amps) for RVs of any length, a large, grassy area for dispersed tent camping, and two cabins. Most RV sites are pull-through. Picnic tables and fire pits are provided. Drinking water, restrooms with showers and flush toilets, coin laundry, pay phone, propane gas, and a recreation room are available. A fly-fishing school is available by arrangement. Some facilities are wheelchair-accessible. Leashed pets are permitted.

Reservations, fees: Reservations are recommended. Sites are $16–24 per night, $3.50 per person per night for more than two people. Monthly rates available. Open early May through September.

Directions: From Redding, drive north on I-5 and continue just past Dunsmuir to the junction with Highway 89. Bear right on Highway 89 and drive nine miles to McCloud and Squaw Valley Road. Turn right at Squaw Valley Road and drive six miles to the park entrance on the right.

Contact: Friday's RV Retreat and McCloud Fly Fishing Ranch, 530/964-2878.

44 BIG FLAT

Scenic rating: 8

on Coffee Creek in Klamath National Forest

Map grid B1

This is a great jump-off spot for a wilderness backpacking trip into the adjacent Trinity Alps. An 11-mile hike will take you into the beautiful Caribou Lakes Basin for lakeside campsites, excellent swimming, dramatic sunsets, and fair trout fishing. The trail is routed out of camp, crosses the stream, then climbs a series of switchbacks to the ridge. From here it gets easier, rounding a mountain and depositing you in the basin. Bypass Little Caribou, Lower Caribou, and Snowslide Lakes, and instead head all the way to Caribou, the biggest and best of the lot. Big Flat is set at 5,000 feet elevation along Coffee Creek, and on the drive in, you'll see big piles of boulders along the stream, evidence of past gold mining activity.

RV sites, facilities: There are nine sites for tents or RVs up to 16 feet (no hookups). Picnic tables and fire grills are provided. Vault toilets are available. No drinking water is available. Garbage must be packed out. Leashed pets are permitted.

Reservations, fees: Reservations are not accepted. There is no fee for camping. Open May through October, weather permitting.

Directions: From Redding, turn east on Highway 299 and drive to Weaverville. In Weaverville, turn right (north) on Highway 3 and drive just past the north end of Trinity Lake to Coffee Creek Road/Forest Road 104, adjacent to a Forest Service ranger station. Turn left on Coffee Creek Road and drive 21 miles to the campground at the end of the road.

Contact: Klamath National Forest, Salmon River Ranger District, 530/468-5351, fax 530/468-1290.

45 GOLDFIELD

Scenic rating: 6

in Shasta-Trinity National Forest
Map grid B1

For hikers, this camp makes a perfect first stop after a long drive. You wake up, get your gear organized, and then take the trailhead to the south. It is routed along Boulder Creek, and with a left turn at the junction (about four miles in), will take you to Boulder Lake (another two miles), set inside the edge of the Trinity Alps Wilderness. Former 49er coach George Seifert first told me about the beauty of this place and how perfectly this campground is situated for the hike. Campground elevation is 3,000 feet.

RV sites, facilities: There are six sites for tents or RVs up to 16 feet (no hookups). Picnic tables and fire grills are provided. Vault toilets and hitching posts for horses are available. No drinking water is available. Garbage must be packed out. Leashed pets are permitted.

Reservations, fees: Reservations are not accepted. There is no fee for camping. Open year-round.

Directions: From Redding, head east on Highway 299 and drive to Weaverville. Turn right (north) on Highway 3 and drive just past the north end of Trinity Lake to Coffee Creek Road/Forest Road 104 (a Forest Service ranger station is nearby). Turn left on Coffee Creek Road/Forest Road 104 and drive 6.5 miles to the campground on the left side of the road.

Contact: Shasta-Trinity National Forest, Weaverville Ranger Station, 530/623-2121, fax 530/623-6010.

46 TRINITY RIVER

Scenic rating: 7

in Shasta-Trinity National Forest
Map grid B1

This camp offers easy access off Highway 3, yet it is fairly secluded and provides streamside access to the upper Trinity River. It's a good base camp for a fishing trip when the upper Trinity is loaded with small trout. The elevation is 2,500 feet.

RV sites, facilities: There are seven sites for tents or RVs up to 35 feet (no hookups). Picnic tables and fire grills are provided. Drinking water and vault toilets are available. Leashed pets are permitted.

Reservations, fees: Reservations are not accepted. Sites are $10 per night. Open May through October.

Directions: From Redding, drive west on Highway 299 to Weaverville and Highway 3. Turn right (north) on Highway 3 and drive to Trinity Center at the north end of Trinity Lake. From Trinity Center, continue north on Highway 3 for 9.5 miles to the campground on the left side of the road.

Contact: Shasta-Trinity National Forest, Weaverville Ranger Station, 530/623-2121, fax 530/623-6010.

47 BEST IN THE WEST RESORT

Scenic rating: 3

near Dunsmuir
Map grid B1

This is a good layover spot for RV cruisers looking to take a break. The proximity to Castle Crags State Park, the Sacramento River, and Mount Shasta make the location a winner. Meers Creek runs through the property, and the local area has outstanding swimming holes on the Sacramento River. Trains make regular runs every night in the Sacramento River Canyon and the noise is a problem for some visitors.

RV sites, facilities: There are 12 sites with full hookups (30 and 50 amps) for RVs, a separate grassy area for dispersed tent camping, eight cabins, and a lodge. Picnic tables are provided. Coin laundry, cable TV, and restrooms with showers are available. Leashed pets are permitted.

Reservations, fees: Reservations are accepted. Sites are $15–23 per night. Monthly rates available. Open year-round.

Directions: From Redding, drive north on I-5

for about 40 miles to the Sims Road exit. Take the Sims Road exit and drive one block west on Sims Road to the resort on the left.

Contact: Best in the West Resort, 530/235-2603, www.eggerbestwest.com.

48 SIMS FLAT

Scenic rating: 7

on the Sacramento River
Map grid B1

The upper Sacramento River is again becoming one of the best trout streams in the West, with easy and direct access off an interstate highway. This camp is a good example. Sitting beside the upper Sacramento River at an elevation of 1,600 feet, it provides access to some of the better spots for trout fishing, particularly from late April through July. The trout population has recovered since the devastating spill from a train derailment that occurred in 1991, and there's good trout fishing in this area. There is a wheelchair-accessible interpretive trail. If you want to literally get away from it all, there is a trailhead about three miles east on Sims Flat Road that climbs along South Fork, including a terrible, steep, one-mile section near the top, eventually popping out at Tombstone Mountain. The noise from passing trains can be a shock for newcomers.

RV sites, facilities: There are 20 sites for tents or RVs up to 24 feet (no hookups). Picnic tables and fire grills are provided. Drinking water and flush and vault toilets are available. A nearby seasonal grocery store is open intermittently. Supplies are available to the north in Castella and Dunsmuir. Some facilities are wheelchair-accessible. Leashed pets are permitted.

Reservations, fees: Reservations are not accepted. Sites are $12 per night. Open late April through October.

Directions: From Redding, drive north on I-5 for about 40 miles to the Sims Road exit. Take the Sims Road exit (on the east side of the highway) and drive south for a mile (crossing the railroad tracks and a bridge) to the campground on the right.

Contact: Shasta-Trinity National Forest, Mount Shasta Ranger District, 530/926-4511, fax 530/926-5120.

49 EAST FORK WILLOW CREEK

Scenic rating: 9

on Willow Creek
Map grid A2

This is a beautiful spot along Willow Creek. Set at a 2,000-foot elevation, it's one of the prettiest campgrounds in the area. While you can dunk into the cold creek, it's not really a good swimming area. Fishing is prohibited here.

RV sites, facilities: There are 10 sites for tents or RVs up to 20 feet (no hookups). Picnic tables and fire rings are provided. Vault toilets are available. No drinking water is available. Leashed pets are permitted.

Reservations, fees: Reservations are not accepted. Sites are $8 per night, $5 per night for each additional vehicle. Open late May through September, weather permitting.

Directions: From the junction of U.S. 101 and Highway 299 near Arcata, turn east on Highway 299 and drive 32 miles (six miles west of Willow Creek) and look for the camp's entrance road (well signed) on the right (south) side of the road.

Contact: Six Rivers National Forest, Lower Trinity Ranger District, 530/629-2118, fax 530/629-2102.

50 BOISE CREEK

Scenic rating: 7

in Six Rivers National Forest
Map grid A2

This camp features a 0.25-mile-long trail down to Willow Creek and nearby access to the Trinity River. If you have ever wanted to see Bigfoot, you can do it while camping here—there's a giant wooden Bigfoot on display in nearby Willow Creek. After your Bigfoot experience, your best bet during summer is to head north on nearby Highway 96 (turn north in Willow Creek) to the campground at Tish Tang, where there is excellent river access, swimming, and rafting in the late summer's warm flows. The Trinity River also provides good salmon and steelhead fishing during fall and winter, respectively. Note that fishing is prohibited in nearby Willow Creek.

RV sites, facilities: There are 17 sites for tents or RVs up to 35 feet (no hookups). Picnic tables and fire grills are provided. No drinking water. Vault toilets are available, and a camp host is on-site. A grocery store, gas station, restaurant, and propane gas are available nearby. Some facilities are wheelchair-accessible. Leashed pets are permitted.

Reservations, fees: Reservations accepted at 877/444-6777 or www.recreation.gov ($10 reservation fee). Sites are $10 per night, $5 per night for each additional vehicle. Open year-round.

Directions: From the intersection of U.S. 101 and Highway 299 near Arcata, drive 38 miles east on Highway 299 and look for the campground entrance on the left side of the road. If you reach the town of Willow Creek, you have gone 1.5 miles too far.

Contact: Six Rivers National Forest, Lower Trinity Ranger District, 530/629-2118, fax 530/629-2102.

51 DENNY

Scenic rating: 6

on the New River in Shasta-Trinity National Forest

Map grid A2

This is a secluded and quiet campground along the New River, a tributary to the Trinity River and a designated Wild and Scenic River. The stream here is OK for swimming but too cold to even dip a toe in until late summer. If you drive north from the camp on Denny Road, you will find several trailheads for trips into the Trinity Alps Wilderness. The best of them is at the end of the road, where there is a good parking area, with a trail that is routed along the East Fork

New River up toward Limestone Ridge. Note that the stretch of river near the camp is closed to fishing year-round. The campground is set at 1,400 feet.

RV sites, facilities: There are five sites for tents or RVs up to 22 feet (no hookups). Picnic tables and fire grills are provided. Vault toilets are available. No drinking water is available. Garbage must be packed out. Leashed pets are permitted. Supplies are available about one hour away in Sal-yers Bar.

Reservations, fees: Reservations are not accepted. There is no fee for camping. Open year-round.

Directions: From the junction of U.S. 101 and Highway 299 near Arcata, turn east on Highway 299 and drive to Willow Creek. In Willow Creek, continue east on Highway 299 and, after reaching Salyer, continue for four miles to Denny Road/County Road 402. Turn north (left) on Denny Road and drive about 14 miles on a paved but very windy road to the campground.

Contact: Shasta-Trinity National Forest, Big Bar Ranger Station, 530/623-6106, fax 530/623-6123.

52 HOBO GULCH

Scenic rating: 7

on the North Fork of the Trinity River in Shasta-Trinity National Forest

Map grid A2

Only the ambitious need apply. This is a trailhead camp set on the edge of the Trinity Alps Wilderness, and the reason only the ambitious show up is that it is a 20-mile uphill haul all the way to Grizzly Lake, set at the foot of the awesome Thompson Peak (8,663 feet), with no other lakes available en route. The camp is set at 2,200 feet along the North Fork of the Trinity River. The adjacent slopes of the wilderness are known for little creeks, woods, and a few pristine meadows, and are largely devoid of lakes.

RV sites, facilities: There are 10 sites for tents or RVs up to 16 feet (no hookups). Picnic tables and fire grills are provided. Vault toilets are available. No drinking water is available. Garbage must be packed out. Supplies can be obtained in Junction City, about one hour away. Leashed pets are permitted.

Reservations, fees: Reservations are not accepted. There is no fee for camping. Open year-round.

Directions: From Redding, turn on Highway 299 west and drive west past Weaverville, and continue 13 miles to Helena and County East Fork Road. Turn right on County East Fork Road and drive four miles to Hobo Gulch Road. At Hobo Gulch Road, turn left (north) and drive 16 miles (very rough road) to the end of the road at the campground.

Contact: Shasta-Trinity National Forest, Big Bar Ranger Station, 530/623-6106, fax 530/623-6123.

53 RIPSTEIN

Scenic rating: 8

on Canyon Creek in Shasta-Trinity National Forest

Map grid A2

This is one of the great trailhead camps for the neighboring Trinity Alps. It is set at 3,000 feet on the southern edge of the wilderness and is a popular spot for a late-night arrival followed by a backpacking trip the next morning. The Canyon Creek Lakes await via a six-mile uphill hike along Canyon Creek. The destination is extremely beautiful—two alpine lakes set in high granite mountains. The route passes Canyon Creek Falls, a set of two different waterfalls, about 3.5 miles out. This is one of the most popular backpacking destinations in Northern California. Seasonal guided rafting trips on Canyon Creek are also available.

RV sites, facilities: There are 10 sites for tents or RVs up to 22 feet (no hookups). Picnic tables and fire grills are provided. Vault toilets are available. No drinking water is available. Garbage must be packed out. Supplies can be obtained 25 minutes away in Junction City. Leashed pets are permitted.

Reservations, fees: Reservations are not accepted. There is no fee for camping. Open year-round.

Directions: From Redding, turn on Highway 299 west and drive west to Junction City and Canyon Creek Road. Turn right on Canyon Creek Road and drive 15 miles to the campground on the left side of the road.

Contact: Shasta-Trinity National Forest, Big Bar Ranger Station, 530/623-6106, fax 530/623-6123; Trinity River Rafting Company, 530/623-3033.

54 BURNT RANCH

Scenic rating: 7

on the Trinity River in Shasta-Trinity National Forest

Map grid A2

This campground is set on a bluff above the Trinity River and is one of its most compelling spots. This section of river is very pretty, with deep, dramatic canyons nearby. The elevation is 1,000 feet. Note that the trail to Burnt Ranch Falls is not maintained and is partially on private land—the landowners will not take kindly to anyone trespassing.

RV sites, facilities: There are 16 sites for tents or RVs up to 25 feet (no hookups). Picnic tables and fire grills are provided. Drinking water and vault toilets are available. Garbage must be packed out. Supplies can be obtained in Hawkins Bar about one hour away. Leashed pets are permitted.

Reservations, fees: Reservations are not accepted. Sites are $8 per night. Open year-round, weather permitting.

Directions: From Redding, take Highway 299 west and drive past Weaverville to Burnt Ranch. In Burnt Ranch, continue 0.5 mile and look for the campground entrance on the right side of the road.

Contact: Shasta-Trinity National Forest, Big Bar Ranger Station, 530/623-6106, fax 530/623-6123; Trinity River Rafting Company, 530/623-3033.

CALIFORNIA

55 DEL LOMA RV PARK AND CAMPGROUND

Scenic rating: 7

on the Trinity River

Map grid A2

RV cruisers looking for a layover spot near the Trinity River will find just that at Del Loma. Shady sites and sandy beaches are available here along the Trinity. Rafting and tubing trips are popular in this area during the summer. Salmon fishing is best in the fall, steelhead fishing in the winter. This camp is popular for family reunions and groups. Salmon fishing can be sensational on the Trinity in the fall, and some anglers will book a year in advance to make certain they get a spot. About two-thirds of the sites are rented for extended periods.

RV sites, facilities: There are 41 sites, including two pull-through, with full hookups (50 amps) for RVs and tents, five park-model cabins, and two apartments. Picnic tables and fire grills are provided. Restrooms with flush toilets and showers, dump station, convenience store, clubhouse, heated pool, deli, Wi-Fi, RV supplies, firewood, coin laundry, recreation room, volleyball, tetherball, 18-hole mini golf, and horseshoe pits are available. Leashed pets are permitted.

Reservations, fees: Reservations are accepted at 800/839-0194. Sites are $25 per night, $2 per person per night for more than two people. Group and monthly rates available. Some credit cards accepted. Open year-round.

Directions: From the junction of U.S. 101 and Highway 299 in Arcata, turn east on Highway 299 and drive to Burnt Ranch. From Burnt Ranch, continue 10 miles east on Highway 299 to the town of Del Loma and look for the campground entrance on the right.

Contact: Del Loma RV Park and Campground, 530/623-2834 or 800/839-0194, www.del-lomarv.com.

56 HAYDEN FLAT GROUP

Scenic rating: 7

on the Trinity River in Shasta-Trinity National Forest

Map grid A2

This campground is split into two pieces, with most of the sites grouped in a large, shaded area across the road from the river and a few on the river side. A beach is available along the river; it is a good spot for swimming as well as a popular put-in and take-out spot for rafters. The elevation is 1,200 feet.

RV sites, facilities: There are 36 sites for tents or RVs up to 25 feet (no hookups); it can also be used as a group camp with a three-site minimum. Picnic tables and fire grills are provided. Drinking water and vault toilets are available. Some facilities are wheelchair-accessible. Leashed pets are permitted.

Reservations, fees: Reservations are required for groups (minimum of three additional sites) at 530/623-6106. Sites are $10 per night. Open year-round.

Directions: From the junction of U.S. 101 and Highway 299 in Arcata, head east on Highway 299 and drive to Burnt Ranch. From Burnt Ranch, continue 10 miles east on Highway 299 and look for the campground entrance. If you reach the town of Del Loma, you have gone 0.5 mile too far.

Contact: Shasta-Trinity National Forest, Big Bar Ranger Station, 530/623-6106, fax 530/623-6123.

57 BIG SLIDE

Scenic rating: 7

on the South Fork of the Trinity River in Shasta-Trinity National Forest

Map grid A2

This camp is literally out in the middle of nowhere. Free? Of course it's free. Otherwise, someone would actually have to show up now and then to collect. It's a tiny, secluded, little-visited spot set along the South Fork of the Trinity River. The elevation is 1,250 feet.

RV sites, facilities: There are eight sites for tents or RVs up to 16 feet (no hookups). Picnic tables and fire grills are provided. Vault toilets are available. No drinking water is available. Leashed pets are permitted.

Reservations, fees: Reservations are not accepted. There is no fee for camping. Open late May to early October, weather permitting.

Directions: From Redding, turn on Highway 299 west and drive west over the Buckhorn Summit to the junction with Highway 3 near Douglas City. Turn south on Highway 3 and drive to Hayfork. From Hayfork, turn right on County Road 301 and drive about 20 miles to the town of Hyampom. In Hyampom, turn right on Lower South Fork Road/County Road 311 and drive five miles on County Road 311 to the campground on the right.

Contact: Shasta-Trinity National Forest, Hayfork Ranger Station, 530/628-5227, fax 530/628-5212.

58 BIG BAR

Scenic rating: 6

near the Trinity River in
Shasta-Trinity National Forest

Map grid A2

You name it, you got it—a quiet, small campground with easy access, and good fishing nearby (in the fall). In addition, there is a good put-in spot for inflatable kayaks and rafts. It is an ideal piece of water for newcomers, with Trinity River Rafting offering inflatable rentals for as low as $35. The elevation is 1,200 feet. If the shoe fits...

RV sites, facilities: There are three sites for tents or RVs up to 20 feet (no hookups). Picnic tables and fire grills are provided. Vault toilets are available. No drinking water is available. Garbage must be packed out. Supplies are available one mile away in Big Bar. Leashed pets are permitted.

Reservations, fees: Reservations are not accepted. There is no fee for camping. Open year-round.

Directions: From Redding, turn on Highway 299 west and drive west to Weaverville. Continue on Highway 299 for 25 miles to the ranger station one mile east of Big Bar, and look for Corral Bottom Road (across from the ranger station). Turn left on Corral Bottom Road and drive 0.25 mile to the campground on the left.

Contact: Shasta-Trinity National Forest, Big Bar Ranger Station, 530/623-6106, fax 530/623-6123; Trinity River Rafting, 530/623-3033, www.trinityriverrafting.com.

59 BIG FLAT

Scenic rating: 6

on the Trinity River in
Shasta-Trinity National Forest

Map grid A2

This level campground is set off Highway 299, just across the road from the Trinity River. The sites are close together, and it can be hot and dusty in midsummer. No problem. That is when you will be on the Trinity River, taking a rafting or kayaking trip—as low as $35 to rent an inflatable kayak from Trinity River Rafting in nearby Big Bar. It's fun, exciting, and easy (newcomers are welcome).

RV sites, facilities: There are 10 sites for tents or RVs up to 22 feet (no hookups). Picnic tables and fire grills are provided. Drinking water and vault toilets are available. Some facilities are wheelchair-accessible. Leashed pets are permitted.

Reservations, fees: Reservations are not accepted. Sites are $8 per night. Open year-round.

Directions: From Redding, turn on Highway 299 west, and drive west past Weaverville, Junction City, and Helena, and continue for about seven miles. Look for the campground entrance on the right side of the road. If you reach the town of Big Bar, you have gone three miles too far.

Contact: Shasta-Trinity National Forest, Big Bar Ranger Station, 530/623-6106, fax 530/623-6123; Trinity River Rafting Company, 530/623-3033, www.trinityriverrafting.com.

CALIFORNIA

60 PIGEON POINT AND GROUP

Scenic rating: 7

on the Trinity River in
Shasta-Trinity National Forest

Map grid A2

In the good old days, huge flocks of bandtail pigeons flew the Trinity River Canyon, swooping and diving in dramatic shows. Nowadays you don't see too many pigeons, but this camp still keeps its namesake. It is better known for its access to the Trinity River, with a large beach for swimming. The elevation is 1,100 feet.

RV sites, facilities: There are 10 sites for tents or RVs up to 22 feet, two multi-family sites, and one group site that can accommodate up to 50 people with tents or RVs up to 16 feet. No hookups. Picnic tables and fire grills are provided. Vault toilets are available. No drinking water is available. Supplies can be obtained within 10 miles in Big Bar or Junction City. Some facilities are wheelchair-accessible. Leashed pets are permitted.

Reservations, fees: Reservations are not accepted for individual sites but are required for the group site at 530/623-6106. Sites are $8 per night, $12 for multi-family sites, and $50 per night for the group site. Open year-round.

Directions: From Redding, turn on Highway 299 west and drive west to Weaverville. Continue west on Highway 299 to Helena and continue 0.5 mile to the campground on the left (south) side of the road.

Contact: Shasta-Trinity National Forest, Big Bar Ranger Station, 530/623-6106, fax 530/623-6123.

61 BIGFOOT CAMPGROUND AND RV PARK

Scenic rating: 8

on the Trinity River

Map grid A2   **BEST(**

This private RV park is set along the Trinity River and has become one of the most popular spots on the Trinity River. Rafting and fishing trips are a feature, along with cabin rentals. It is also a popular layover for Highway 299 cruisers but provides the option for longer stays with rafting, gold panning, and in the fall and winter, fishing for salmon and steelhead, respectively. RV sites are exceptionally large, and a bonus is that a storage area is available. A three-acre site for tent camping is set along the river.

RV sites, facilities: There are 46 sites with full or partial hookups (30 and 50 amps) for RVs of any length, a separate area for tent camping, and four cabins. Tent camping is not allowed during the winter. Picnic tables and barbecues are provided. Restrooms with flush toilets and coin showers, coin laundry, convenience store, dump station, propane gas, solar-heated swimming pool (summer only), and horseshoe pits are available. Modem hookups, television hookups, fishing licenses, and a tackle shop are also available. Some facilities are wheelchair-accessible. Leashed pets are permitted.

Reservations, fees: Reservations are recommended from June through October. Sites are $16–25.50 per night, $2 per night per person for more than two people. Some credit cards accepted. Open year-round.

Directions: From Redding, turn on Highway 299 west and drive west to Junction City. Continue west on Highway 299 for three miles to the camp on the left.

Contact: Bigfoot Campground and RV Park, 530/623-6088 or 800/422-5219, www.bigfoot-rvcabins.com.

62 JUNCTION CITY

Scenic rating: 7

on the Trinity River

Map grid A2

Some of the Trinity River's best fall salmon fishing is in this area in September and early October, with steelhead following from mid-October into the winter. That makes it an ideal base camp for a fishing or camping trip.

RV sites, facilities: There are 22 sites for tents or RVs up to 40 feet (no hookups). Picnic tables, fire grills, and bearproof food lockers are provided. Drinking water and vault toilets are available. Groceries and propane gas are available within two miles in Junction City. Some facilities are wheelchair-accessible. Leashed pets are permitted.

Reservations, fees: Reservations are not accepted. Sites are $10 per night per vehicle. Open May through November.

Directions: From Redding, turn on Highway 299 west and drive west to Junction City. At Junction City, continue west on Highway 299 for 1.5 miles to the camp on the right.

Contact: Bureau of Land Management, Redding Field Office, 530/224-2100, fax 530/224-2172.

63 MAD RIVER

Scenic rating: 7

in Six Rivers National Forest

Map grid A2

This Forest Service campground is set along an alluvial flood terrace, a unique landscape for this region, featuring a forest of manzanita and Douglas fir. It is often hot, always remote, in a relatively unknown section of Six Rivers National Forest at an elevation of 2,600 feet. The headwaters of the Mad River pour right past the campground, about two miles downstream from the Ruth Lake Dam. People making weekend trips to Ruth Lake sometimes end up at this little-used camp. Ruth Lake is a designated Watchable Wildlife Site and is the only major recreation lake within decent driving range of Eureka, offering a small marina with boat rentals and a good boat ramp for access to trout and bass fishing and waterskiing. Swimming and all water sports are allowed at Ruth Lake.

RV sites, facilities: There are 40 sites for tents or RVs up to 22 feet (no hookups). Picnic tables and fire grills are provided. Drinking water and vault toilets are available. Leashed pets are permitted.

Reservations, fees: Reservations are not accepted. Sites are $12 per night, $5 per night for each additional vehicle. Open late May through mid-September.

Directions: From Eureka, drive south on U.S. 101 to Alton. Turn east on Highway 36 and drive about 50 miles to the town of Mad River. Turn southeast on Lower Mad River Road and drive four miles to the camp on the right side of the road.

Contact: Six Rivers National Forest, Mad River Ranger District, 707/574-6233, fax 707/574-6273.

64 HELLS GATE

Scenic rating: 7

on the South Fork of the Trinity River in Shasta-Trinity National Forest

Map grid A2

This is a pretty spot bordering the South Fork of the Trinity River. The prime feature is for hikers. The South Fork National Recreation Trail begins at the campground and follows the river for many miles. Additional trails branch off and up into the South Fork Mountains. This area is extremely hot in summer. The elevation is 2,300 feet. It gets moderate use and may even fill on three-day weekends. Insider's note: If Hells Gate is full, there are seven primitive campsites at Scott's Flat Campground, 0.5 mile beyond Hells Gate, that can accommodate RVs up to 20 feet.

RV sites, facilities: There are 15 sites for tents or RVs up to 16 feet (no hookups). Picnic tables and fire grills are provided. Drinking water and vault toilets are available. Some facilities are wheelchair-accessible. Leashed pets are permitted.

Reservations, fees: Reservations are not accepted. Sites are $6 per night. Open late May through early November, weather permitting.

Directions: From Red Bluff, turn west on Highway 36 (very twisty) and drive past Platina to the junction with Highway 3. Continue west on Highway 36 for 10 miles to the campground entrance on the left side of the road. If you reach Forest Glen, you have gone a mile too far.

Contact: Shasta-Trinity National Forest, Hayfork Ranger Station, 530/628-5227, fax 530/628-5212.

65 FOREST GLEN

Scenic rating: 7

on the South Fork of the Trinity River in Shasta-Trinity National Forest

Map grid A2

If you get stuck for a spot in this region, this camp almost always has sites open, even during three-day weekends. It is on the edge of a forest near the South Fork of the Trinity River. If you hit it wrong, during a surprise storm, a primitive shelter is available at the nearby Forest Glen Guard Station—a historic cabin that sleeps eight and rents out from the Forest Service for $35 a night.

RV sites, facilities: There are 15 sites for tents or RVs up to 15 feet (no hookups). Picnic tables and fire grills are provided. Vault toilets are available. No drinking water is available. Some facilities are wheelchair-accessible. Leashed pets are permitted.

Reservations, fees: Reservations are not accepted. Sites are $6 per night. Open late May through early November, weather permitting.

Directions: From Red Bluff, turn west on Highway 36 (very twisty) and drive past Platina to the junction with Highway 3. Continue west on Highway 36 for 11 miles to Forest Glen. The campground is at the west end of town on the right side of the road.

Contact: Shasta-Trinity National Forest, Hayfork Ranger Station, 530/628-5227, fax 530/628-5212.

66 FIR COVE CAMP

Scenic rating: 7

on Ruth Lake in Six Rivers National Forest

Map grid A2

This spot is situated along Ruth Lake adjacent to Bailey Cove. The elevation is 2,600 feet, and the lake covers 1,200 acres. Swimming and all water sports are allowed on Ruth Lake, and there are three boat ramps. In the summer the warm water makes this an ideal place for families to spend some time swimming. Fishing is decent for rainbow trout in the spring and for bass in the summer.

RV sites, facilities: There 19 sites for tents or RVs up to 22 feet (no hookups). Picnic tables and fire grills are provided. Drinking water and vault toilets are available. Some facilities are wheelchair-accessible. Leashed pets are permitted.

Reservations, fees: Reservations are not accepted. Sites are $12 per night, $5 per night for each additional vehicle. Open late May through mid-September.

Directions: From Eureka, drive south on U.S. 101 to Alton and the junction with Highway 36. Turn east on Highway 36 and drive about 50 miles to the town of Mad River. Turn right at the sign for Ruth Lake/Lower Mad River Road and drive 12 miles to the campground on the right side of the road.

Contact: Six Rivers National Forest, Mad River Ranger District, 707/574-6233, fax 707/574-6273.

67 BAILEY CANYON

Scenic rating: 7

on Ruth Lake in Six Rivers National Forest

Map grid A2

Ruth Lake is the only major lake within a reasonable driving distance of U.S. 101, although some people might argue with you over how reasonable this twisty drive is. Regardless, you end up at a camp along the east shore of Ruth Lake, where fishing for trout or bass and waterskiing are popular. What really wins out is that it is hot and sunny all summer, the exact opposite of the fogged-in Humboldt coast. The elevation is 2,600 feet.

RV sites, facilities: There are 25 sites for tents or RVs up to 22 feet (no hookups). Picnic tables and fire grills are provided. Drinking water

and vault toilets are available. A boat ramp and small marina are available nearby. Some facilities are wheelchair-accessible. Leashed pets are permitted.

Reservations, fees: Reservations are not accepted. Sites are $12 per night, $5 per night for each additional vehicle. Open late May through mid-September.

Directions: From Eureka, drive south on U.S. 101 to Alton and the junction with Highway 36. Turn east on Highway 36 and drive about 50 miles to the town of Mad River. Turn right at the sign for Ruth Lake/Lower Mad River Road and drive 13 miles to the campground on the right side of the road.

Contact: Six Rivers National Forest, Mad River Ranger District, 707/574-6233, fax 707/574-6273.

68 TRINITY LAKE KOA

🚶 🚲 🏊 🎣 🛶 🐕 🏕 ♿ 🚐 ⛺

Scenic rating: 8

on Trinity Lake

Map grid B2

This huge resort (some may remember this as the former Wyntoon Resort) is an ideal family vacation destination. Set in a wooded area covering 90 acres on the north shore of Trinity Lake, it provides opportunities for fishing, boating, swimming, and waterskiing, with access within walking distance. The lake boasts a wide variety of fish, including smallmouth bass and rainbow trout. The tent sites are spread out on 20 forested acres. The lake sits at the base of the dramatic Trinity Alps, one of the most beautiful regions in the state.

RV sites, facilities: There are 77 tent sites, 136 sites with full hookups (30 and 50 amps) for RVs of any length, and 19 cottages. Some RV sites are pull-through. Picnic tables and fire rings are provided. Drinking water, restrooms with showers, coin laundry, playground, seasonal heated pool, dump station, gasoline, convenience store, ice, snack bar, fish-cleaning area, boat rentals, and slips are available. Some facilities are wheelchair-

accessible. Leashed pets are permitted, with certain restrictions.

Reservations, fees: Reservations are accepted. Sites are $30–52 per night, $3–6 per person per night for more than two people. Some credit cards accepted. Open year-round.

Directions: From Redding, drive west on Highway 299 to Weaverville and Highway 3. Turn right (north) on Highway 3 and drive approximately 30 miles to Trinity Lake. At Trinity Center, continue 0.5 mile north on Highway 3 to the resort on the right.

Contact: Trinity Lake KOA, 530/266-3337 or 800/562-7706, www.trinitylakekoa.com or www.koa.com.

69 PREACHER MEADOW

🚶 🐕 🚐 ⛺

Scenic rating: 7

in Shasta-Trinity National Forest

Map grid B2

The view of the Trinity Alps can be excellent here from the right vantage point. Otherwise, compared to all the other camps in the area so close to Trinity Lake, it has trouble matching up in the quality department. If the lakeside camps are full, this camp provides an overflow option. The winter of 2000 was one of the strangest on record, where a localized wind storm knocked down 66 trees at this campground.

RV sites, facilities: There are 45 sites for tents or RVs up to 40 feet (no hookups). Picnic tables and fire grills are provided. Drinking water and vault toilets are available. Supplies, a coin laundry, and a small airport are available nearby. Leashed pets are permitted.

Reservations, fees: Reservations are not accepted. Sites are $12 per night. Open mid-May through October.

Directions: From Redding, drive west on Highway 299 to Weaverville at Highway 3. Turn right (north) on Highway 3 and drive to Trinity Lake. Continue toward Trinity Center and look for the campground entrance on the left side of the road (if you reach Trinity Center you have gone two miles too far).

Contact: Shasta-Trinity National Forest, Weaverville Ranger Station, 530/623-2121, fax 530/623-6010.

70 JACKASS SPRINGS

Scenic rating: 6

near Trinity Lake in Shasta-Trinity National Forest
Map grid B2

If you're poking around for a more secluded campsite on this end of the lake, halt your search and pick the best spot you can find at this campground, since it's the only one in this area of Trinity Lake. The campground is 0.5 mile from Trinity Lake, but you can't see the lake from the camp. It is most popular in the fall as a base camp for deer hunters. The elevation is 2,500 feet.

RV sites, facilities: There are 21 sites for tents or RVs up to 32 feet (no hookups). Picnic tables and fire grills are provided. Vault toilets are available. No drinking water is available. Garbage must be packed out. Leashed pets are permitted.

Reservations, fees: Reservations are not accepted. There is no fee for camping. Open year-round, weather permitting.

Directions: From Redding, drive west on Highway 299 to Weaverville and the junction with Highway 3. Turn right (north) on Highway 3 and drive 29 miles to Trinity Center. Continue five miles past Trinity Center to County Road 106. Turn right on County Road 106 and drive 12 miles to the Jackass Springs/County Road 119 turnoff. Turn right on County Road 119 and drive five miles to the campground near the end of the road.

Contact: Shasta-Trinity National Forest, Weaverville Ranger Station, 530/623-2121, fax 530/623-6010.

71 BRIDGE CAMP

Scenic rating: 8

on Stuarts Fork in Shasta-Trinity National Forest
Map grid B2

This remote spot is an ideal jump-off point for backpackers. It's at the head of Stuarts Fork Trail, about 2.5 miles from the western shore of Trinity Lake. The trail leads into the Trinity Alps Wilderness, along Stuarts Fork, past Oak Flat and Morris Meadows, and up to Emerald Lake and the Sawtooth Ridge. It is a long and grueling climb, but fishing is excellent at Emerald Lake as well as at neighboring Sapphire Lake. There's a great view of the Alps from this camp. It is set at 2,700 feet and remains open year-round, but there's no piped water in the winter and it gets mighty cold up here.

RV sites, facilities: There are 10 sites for tents or RVs up to 20 feet (no hookups). Picnic tables and fire grills are provided. Drinking water (summer season), vault toilets, and horse corrals are available. Leashed pets are permitted.

Reservations, fees: Reservations are not accepted. Sites are $12 per night in the summer, $5 per night in the winter. Open year-round.

Directions: From Redding, drive west on Highway 299 to Weaverville. In Weaverville, turn right (north) on Highway 3 and drive 17 miles to Trinity Alps Road (at Stuarts Fork of Trinity Lake). Turn left at Trinity Alps Road and drive about two miles to the campground on the right side of the road.

Contact: Shasta-Trinity National Forest, Weaverville Ranger Station, 530/623-2121, fax 530/623-6010.

72 RUSH CREEK

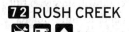

Scenic rating: 4

in Shasta-Trinity National Forest,
north of Weaverville

Map grid B2

This small, primitive camp provides overflow space during busy holiday weekends when the camps at Lewiston and Trinity Lakes are near capacity. It may not be much, but hey, at least if you know about Rush Creek you'll never get stuck for a spot. The camp borders Rush Creek and is secluded, but again, it's nearly five miles to the nearest access point to Trinity Lake.

RV sites, facilities: There are 10 sites for tents or RVs up to 20 feet (no hookups). Picnic tables and fire pits are provided. Vault toilets are available. No drinking water is available. Leashed pets are permitted.

Reservations, fees: Reservations are not accepted. Sites are $7 per night. Open mid-May through mid-September.

Directions: From Redding, drive west on Highway 299 to Weaverville. In Weaverville, turn right (north) on Highway 3 and drive about eight miles to the signed turnoff on the left side of the road. Turn left and drive 0.25 mile on the short spur road to the campground on the left side of the road. If you get to Forest Road 113, you've gone too far.

Contact: Shasta-Trinity National Forest, Weaverville Ranger Station, 530/623-2121, fax 530/623-6010.

73 PINEWOOD COVE RESORT

Scenic rating: 7

on Trinity Lake
Map grid B2

This is a privately operated camp with full boating facilities at Trinity Lake. If you don't have a boat but want to get on Trinity Lake, this can be a good starting point. A reservation is advised during the peak summer season. The elevation is 2,300 feet.

RV sites, facilities: There are 50 sites with full or partial hookups (30 and 50 amps) for RVs up to 40 feet, including 10 RV sites rented for the entire season and wait-listed, and 28 tent sites. There are also 15 park-model cabins. Picnic tables and fire grills are provided. Restrooms with showers, coin laundry, dump station, RV supplies, seasonal heated swimming pool, playground, children's treehouse, volleyball, badminton, free movies three nights a week in summer, modem access, video rentals, recreation room with billiards and video arcade, convenience store, ice, fishing tackle, library, boat dock with 32 slips, beach, and canoe and kayak rentals are available. Some facilities are wheelchair-accessible. Leashed pets are permitted.

Reservations, fees: Reservations are recommended in the summer. Sites are $27.50–37.50 per night, $4 per person per night for more than two people, $4 per pet per night. Some credit cards accepted. Open mid-April through October.

Directions: From Redding, drive west on Highway 299 to Weaverville. In Weaverville, turn north (right) on Highway 3 and drive 14 miles to the campground entrance on the right.

Contact: Pinewood Cove Resort, 530/286-2201 or 800/988-5253, www.pinewoodcove.com.

74 FAWN GROUP CAMP

Scenic rating: 7

on Trinity Lake in Shasta-Trinity National Forest
Map grid B2

If you want Trinity Lake all to yourself, one way to do it is to get a group together and then reserve this camp near the shore of Trinity Lake. The elevation is 2,500 feet.

RV sites, facilities: There are two group sites for tents or RVs up to 37 feet (no hookups) that can accommodate up to 100 people each. Picnic tables and fire grills are provided. Drinking water and flush toilets are available. A marina is nearby. Leashed pets are permitted.

Reservations, fees: Reservations are required at 877/444-6777 or www.recreation.gov ($10 reservation fee). Sites are $100 per night. Open early May through late September.

Directions: From Redding, drive west on Highway 299 to Weaverville. In Weaverville, turn right (north) on Highway 3 and drive 15 miles to the campground.

Contact: Shasta-Trinity National Forest, Weaverville Ranger Station, 530/623-2121, fax 530/623-6010.

CALIFORNIA

75 TANNERY GULCH

Scenic rating: 8

on Trinity Lake in Shasta-Trinity National Forest

Map grid B2

This is one of the more popular Forest Service camps on the southwest shore of huge Trinity Lake. There's a nice beach near the campground, provided the infamous Bureau of Reclamation hasn't drawn the lake level down too far. It can be quite low in the fall. The elevation is 2,400 feet. Side note: This campground was named by the tannery that once operated in the area; bark from local trees was used in the tanning process.

RV sites, facilities: There are 72 sites and four double sites for tents or RVs up to 40 feet (no hookups). Picnic tables and fire grills are provided. Drinking water, flush and vault toilets, and a boat ramp are available. Leashed pets are permitted.

Reservations, fees: Reservations are accepted at 877/444-6777 or www.recreation.gov ($10 reservation fee). Sites are $17–23 per night, $5 per night for each additional vehicle. Open early May through late September.

Directions: From Redding, drive west on Highway 299 to Weaverville. In Weaverville, turn right (north) on Highway 3 and drive 13.5 miles north to County Road 172. Turn right on County Road 172 and drive 1.5 miles to the campground entrance.

Contact: Shasta-Trinity National Forest, Weaverville Ranger Station, 530/623-2121, fax 530/623-6010.

76 BUSHY TAIL AND BUSH TAIL GROUP

Scenic rating: 7

on Trinity Lake in Shasta-Trinity National Forest

Map grid B2

This is a great spot for families and water-sports enthusiasts. It's pretty here on Trinity Lake, and the nearby boat launch is a bonus. The elevation is 2,500 feet.

RV sites, facilities: There are 11 sites with partial hookups (30 amps) for tents or RVs up to 40 feet. The sites are single, double, and triple sizes. Picnic tables and fire grills are provided. Drinking water and restrooms with flush toilets and coin showers are available. Supplies, a swimming beach, and a boat ramp are available nearby. Leashed pets are permitted.

Reservations, fees: Reservations are required at 877/444-6777 or www.recreation.gov ($10 reservation fee). Sites are $16–24 per night for single sites, $40 per night for double sites, $55 per night for triple sites, $80 per night for group camp. Open mid-May through late September.

Directions: From Redding, drive west on Highway 299 to Weaverville. In Weaverville, turn right (north) on Highway 3 and drive 16.2 miles (approximately 3.5 miles past the Stuarts Fork Bridge) to the campground entrance road on the right. Turn right and drive a short distance to the camp on the left side of the road.

Contact: Shasta-Trinity National Forest, Weaverville Ranger Station, 530/623-2121, fax 530/623-6010.

77 MINERSVILLE

Scenic rating: 7

on Trinity Lake in Shasta-Trinity National Forest

Map grid B2

The setting is near lakeside, quite beautiful when Trinity Lake is fullest in the spring and early summer. This is a good camp for boaters, with a boat ramp in the cove a short distance to the north. But note that the boat ramp is not always functional. When the lake level drops to 65 feet below full, the ramp is not usable. The elevation is 2,400 feet.

RV sites, facilities: There are 14 sites for tents or RVs up to 36 feet (no hookups). Picnic tables and fire grills are provided. Drinking water, flush toilets, and a low-water boat ramp are provided. Leashed pets are permitted.

Reservations, fees: Reservations are not accepted. Sites are $13–24 per night, $7–12 per night during the winter season. Open year-round, with limited winter services.

Directions: From Redding, drive west on Highway 299 to Weaverville. Turn right (north) on Highway 3 and drive about 18 miles (if you reach the Mule Creek Ranger Station, you have gone 0.5 mile too far). Turn right at the signed campground access road and drive 0.5 mile to the camp.

Contact: Shasta-Trinity National Forest, Weaverville Ranger Station, 530/623-2121, fax 530/623-6010.

78 CLARK SPRINGS

Scenic rating: 7

on Trinity Lake in Shasta-Trinity National Forest
Map grid B2

This used to be a day-use-only picnic area, but because of popular demand, the Forest Service opened it for camping. That makes sense because people were bound to declare it a campground anyway, since it has a nearby boat ramp and a beach. The elevation is 2,400 feet.

RV sites, facilities: There are 21 sites for tents or RVs up to 25 feet (no hookups). Picnic tables and fire grills are provided. Drinking water and flush toilets are available, with limited facilities in the winter. Supplies are available in Weaverville. Leashed pets are permitted.

Reservations, fees: Reservations are not accepted. Sites are $12 per night. Open early April through October.

Directions: From Redding, drive west on Highway 299 to Weaverville. In Weaverville, turn right (north) on Highway 3 and drive 16.5 miles (about four miles past the Stuarts Fork Bridge) to the campground entrance road on the right.

Contact: Shasta-Trinity National Forest, Weaverville Ranger Station, 530/623-2121, fax 530/623-6010.

79 HAYWARD FLAT

Scenic rating: 7

on Trinity Lake in Shasta-Trinity National Forest
Map grid B2

When giant Trinity Lake is full of water, Hayward Flat is one of the prettiest places you could ask for. The camp has become one of the most popular Forest Service campgrounds on Trinity Lake because it sits right along the shore and offers a beach. The elevation is 2,400 feet.

RV sites, facilities: There are 98 sites for tents or RVs up to 40 feet (no hookups) and four double sites. Picnic tables and fire grills are provided. Drinking water and flush toilets are available, and there is usually a camp host. Supplies and a boat ramp are nearby. Some facilities are wheelchair-accessible. Leashed pets are permitted.

Reservations, fees: Reservations are accepted at 877/444-6777 or www.recreation.gov ($10 reservation fee). Sites are $17–23 per night, $5 per night for each additional vehicle. Open mid-May through mid-September.

Directions: From Redding, drive west on Highway 299 to Weaverville. In Weaverville, turn right (north) on Highway 3 and drive 19.5 miles, approximately three miles past the Mule Creek Ranger Station. Turn right at the signed access road for Hayward Flat and drive about three miles to the campground at the end of the road.

Contact: Shasta-Trinity National Forest, Weaverville Ranger Station, 530/623-2121, fax 530/623-6010.

80 ALPINE VIEW

Scenic rating: 9

on Trinity Lake in Shasta-Trinity National Forest
Map grid B2

This is an attractive area, set on the shore of Trinity Lake at a creek inlet. The boat ramp nearby provides a bonus. It's a very pretty spot, with views to the west across the lake arm and to the Trinity Alps, featuring Granite Peak. The

Forest Service occasionally runs tours from the campground to historic Bowerman Barn, which was built in 1894. The elevation is 2,400 feet.

RV sites, facilities: There are 53 sites for tents or RVs up to 32 feet (no hookups). Picnic tables and fire grills are provided. Drinking water and flush toilets are available. Some facilities are wheelchair-accessible. The Bowerman boat ramp is nearby. Leashed pets are permitted.

Reservations, fees: Reservations are not accepted. Sites are $17–23 per night, $5 per night for each additional vehicle. Open mid-May through mid-September.

Directions: From Redding, drive west on Highway 299 to Weaverville. In Weaverville, turn right (north) on Highway 3 and drive 22.5 miles to Covington Mill (south of Trinity Center). Turn right (south) on Guy Covington Drive and drive three miles to the camp (one mile past Bowerman boat ramp) on the right side of the road.

Contact: Shasta-Trinity National Forest, Weaverville Ranger Station, 530/623-2121, fax 530/623-6010.

81 CLEAR CREEK

Scenic rating: 6

in Shasta-Trinity National Forest

Map grid B2

This is a primitive, little-known camp that gets little use. It is set near Clear Creek at 3,500 feet elevation. In fall hunters will occasionally turn it into a deer camp, with the adjacent slopes of Blue Mountain and Damnation Peak in the Trinity Divide country providing fair numbers of large bucks three points or better. Trinity Lake is only seven miles to the west, but it seems as if it's in a different world.

RV sites, facilities: There are eight sites for tents or RVs up to 22 feet (no hookups). Picnic tables and fire grills are provided. Vault toilets are available. No drinking water is available. Garbage must be packed out. Leashed pets are permitted.

Reservations, fees: Reservations are not accepted. There is no fee for camping. Open year-round.

Directions: From Redding, drive west on Highway 299 for 17 miles to Trinity Mountain Road. Turn right (north) on Trinity Mountain Road and continue past the town of French Gulch for about 12 miles to East Side Road/County Road 106. Turn right on the gravel road and drive north for about 11 miles to the campground access road (dirt) on right. Turn right on the access road and drive two miles to the campground.

Contact: Shasta-Trinity National Forest, Weaverville Ranger District, 530/623-2121, fax 530/623-6010.

82 LAKESHORE VILLA RV PARK

Scenic rating: 7

on Shasta Lake

Map grid B2

This is a large campground with level, shaded sites for RVs, set near the northern Sacramento River arm of giant Shasta Lake. Most of the campers visiting here are boaters coming for the water sports—waterskiing, wakeboarding, or tubing. The sites are level and graveled.

RV sites, facilities: There are 92 sites with full or partial hookups (20, 30, and 50 amps) for RVs up to 45 feet; some sites are pull-through. There are also two RV rentals. No tents. Restrooms with showers, ice, dump station, cable TV, modem access, playground, group facilities, and a boat dock are available. Boat ramp, store, restaurant, and bar are nearby. Some facilities are wheelchair-accessible. Leashed pets are permitted.

Reservations, fees: Reservations are accepted. Sites are $25–38 per night. Some credit cards accepted. Open year-round.

Directions: From Redding, drive north on I-5 for 24 miles to Exit 702 for Lakeshore Drive/Antlers Road in Lakehead. Take that exit, turn left at the stop sign, and drive under the freeway to Lakeshore Drive. Turn left on Lakeshore Drive and drive 0.5 mile to the campground on the right.

Contact: Lakeshore Villa RV Park, 530/238-8688, www.lakeshorevillarvpark.com.

83 LAKESHORE INN AND RV

Scenic rating: 7

on Shasta Lake

Map grid B2

Shasta Lake is a boater's paradise and an ideal spot for campers with boats. The nearest marina is 2.75 miles away. It is on the Sacramento River arm of Shasta Lake. Shasta Lake Caverns are 10 miles away, and Shasta Dam tours are available about 20 miles away.

RV sites, facilities: There are 40 sites with full or partial hookups (30 and 50 amps) for tents or RVs of any length; some sites are pull-through. Ten cabins are also available. Picnic tables are provided. Restrooms with showers, cable TV, dump station, seasonal swimming pool, playground, video arcade, coin laundry, seasonal bar and restaurant, and a small seasonal convenience store are available. Family barbecues are held on Sunday in season, 5 P.M.–9 P.M. Live music is scheduled most Friday and Saturday nights. Some facilities are wheelchair-accessible. Leashed pets are permitted in the campground only.

Reservations, fees: Reservations are recommended at 530/238-2003. Sites are $29–33 per night, $2.50 per person per night for more than two people, $1 per pet per night. Some credit cards accepted. Open year-round, with limited winter facilities.

Directions: From Redding, drive north on I-5 for 24 miles to Exit 702 for Lakeshore Drive/Antlers Road in Lakehead. Take that exit, turn left at the stop sign, and drive under the freeway to Lakeshore Drive. Turn left on Lakeshore Drive and drive one mile to the campground.

Contact: Lakeshore Inn and RV, 530/238-2003, www.shastacamping.com.

84 SHASTA LAKE RV RESORT AND CAMPGROUND

Scenic rating: 7

on Shasta Lake

Map grid B2

Shasta Lake RV Resort and Campground is one of a series on the upper end of Shasta Lake with easy access off I-5 by car, then easy access by boat to premium trout or bass fishing as well as waterskiing and water sports.

RV sites, facilities: There are 53 sites with full hookups (30 amps) for RVs up to 40 feet, 21 tent sites, one trailer rental, and three cabins. Some sites are pull-through. Picnic tables, barbecues, and fire rings are provided. Restrooms with showers, seasonal convenience store, firewood, bait, coin laundry, playground, table tennis, horseshoes, trailer and boat storage, modem access, and a seasonal swimming pool are available. There is also a private dock with 36 boat slips. Leashed pets are permitted.

Reservations, fees: Reservations are accepted at 800/374-2782. Sites are $22–32 per night, $2 per pet per night. Some credit cards accepted. Open year-round.

Directions: From Redding, drive north on I-5 for 24 miles to the Lakeshore Drive/Antlers Road exit in Lakehead. Take that exit, turn left at the stop sign, and drive under the freeway to Lakeshore Drive. Turn left on Lakeshore Drive and drive 1.5 miles to the campground on the right.

Contact: Shasta Lake RV Resort and Campground, 530/238-2370, www.shastalakerv.com.

85 ANTLERS RV PARK AND CAMPGROUND

Scenic rating: 7

on Shasta Lake

Map grid B2

Antlers Park is set along the Sacramento River arm of Shasta Lake at 1,215 feet. The park is set on 20 acres and has shady sites. This is a full-service spot for campers, boaters, and anglers, with access to the beautiful Sacramento River arm. The camp often fills in summer, including on weekdays.

RV sites, facilities: There are 70 sites with full hookups (30 and 50 amps) for RVs of any length (several are pull-through), 40 sites for tents, and several rental trailers. Picnic tables and fire rings or fire grills are provided. Tent sites also have food lockers. Restrooms with showers, seasonal convenience store and snack bar, ice, coin laundry, Sunday pancake breakfasts, video games, playground, volleyball court, table tennis, horseshoes, basketball, and seasonal swimming pool. Boat rentals, houseboats, moorage, and a complete marina with recreation room are adjacent to the park. Some facilities are wheelchair-accessible. Leashed pets are permitted, with a limit of two.

Reservations, fees: Reservations are recommended. Sites are $22.50–33.50 per night, $4 per person per night for more than two people, $2 per pet per night. Some credit cards accepted. Open year-round.

Directions: From Redding, drive north on I-5 for 24 miles to the Lakeshore Drive/Antlers Road exit in Lakehead. Take that exit, turn right at the stop sign, and drive a short distance to Antlers Road. At Antlers Road, turn right and drive 1.5 miles south to the campground on the left.

Contact: Antlers RV Park and Campground, 530/238-2322 or 800/642-6849, www.antlersrvpark.com.

86 ANTLERS

Scenic rating: 7

on Shasta Lake in Shasta-Trinity National Forest

Map grid B2

This spot is set on the primary Sacramento River inlet of giant Shasta Lake. Antlers is a well-known spot that attracts returning campers and boaters year after year. It is the farthest upstream marina/camp on the lake. Lake levels can fluctuate greatly from spring through fall,

and the operators will move their docks to compensate. Easy access off I-5 is a big plus for boaters.

RV sites, facilities: There are 41 individual sites and 18 double sites for tents or RVs up to 30 feet (no hookups). Picnic tables, food lockers, and fire grills are provided. Drinking water and flush and vault toilets are available. A boat ramp, amphitheater with summer interpretive programs, grocery store, and coin laundry are nearby. Some facilities are wheelchair-accessible. Leashed pets are permitted.

Reservations, fees: Reservations are accepted at 877/444-6777 or www.recreation.gov ($10 reservation fee). Sites are $18 per night, $30 per night for a double site, $5 per night for each additional vehicle. Open year-round.

Directions: From Redding, drive north on I-5 for 24 miles to the Lakeshore Drive/Antlers Road exit in Lakehead. Take that exit, turn right at the stop sign, and drive a short distance to Antlers Road. At Antlers Road, turn right and drive one mile south to the campground.

Contact: Shasta-Trinity National Forest, Shasta Lake Ranger District, 530/275-1587, fax 530/275-1512; Shasta Lake Visitor Center, 530/275-1589; Shasta Recreation Company, 530/275-8113.

87 LAKESHORE EAST

Scenic rating: 7

on Shasta Lake in Shasta-Trinity National Forest

Map grid B2

Lakeshore East is near the full-service community of Lakehead and is on the Sacramento arm of Shasta Lake. It's a nice spot, with a good boat ramp and marina nearby at Antlers or Sugarloaf.

RV sites, facilities: There are 20 individual sites and six double sites for tents or RVs up to 30 feet (no hookups). Picnic tables and fire grills are provided. Drinking water and flush toilets are available. A boat ramp, grocery store, and coin laundry are available nearby. Some facilities are wheelchair-accessible. Leashed pets are permitted.

Reservations, fees: Reservations are accepted at 877/444-6777 or www.recreation.gov ($10 reservation fee). Sites are $18 per night for a single site, $30 for a double site, $5 per night for each additional vehicle. Open year-round.

Directions: From Redding, drive north on I-5 for 24 miles to the Lakeshore Drive/Antlers Road exit at Lakehead. Take the Antlers exit, turn left at the stop sign, and drive under the freeway to Lakeshore Drive. Turn left on Lakeshore Drive and drive three miles. Look for the campground entrance on the left side of the road.

Contact: Shasta-Trinity National Forest, Shasta Lake Ranger District, 530/275-1587, fax 530/275-1512; Shasta Lake Visitor Center, 530/275-1589; Shasta Recreation Company, 530/275-8113.

88 GREGORY CREEK

Scenic rating: 7

on Shasta Lake in Shasta-Trinity National Forest
Map grid B2

This is one of the more secluded Forest Service campgrounds on Shasta Lake, and it has become extremely popular with the younger crowd. It is set just above lakeside, on the eastern shore of the northern Sacramento River arm of the lake. When the lake is fullest in the spring and early summer, this is a great spot. Note: This is a bald eagle nesting area and the campground is subject to closures for habitat protection.

RV sites, facilities: There are 18 sites for tents or RVs up to 16 feet (no hookups). Picnic tables and fire grills are provided. Drinking water and flush toilets are available. Leashed pets are permitted.

Reservations, fees: Reservations are not accepted. Sites are $14 per night, $5 per night for each additional vehicle. Open early August through September; call to verify current status.

Directions: From Redding, drive north on I-5 for 21 miles to the Salt Creek/Gilman Road exit. Take that exit and drive over the freeway to Gregory Creek Road. Turn right and drive 10 miles to the campground at the end of the road.

Contact: Shasta-Trinity National Forest, Shasta Lake Ranger District, 530/275-1587, fax 530/275-1512; Shasta Lake Visitor Center, 530/275-1589; Shasta Recreation Company, 530/275-8113.

89 HIRZ BAY GROUP CAMP

Scenic rating: 8

on Shasta Lake in Shasta-Trinity National Forest
Map grid B2

This is the spot for your own private party—provided you get a reservation—set on a point at the entrance of Hirz Bay on the McCloud River arm of Shasta Lake. A boat ramp is only 0.5 mile away on the camp access road, giving access to the McCloud River arm. This is an excellent spot to make a base camp for a fishing trip, with great trolling for trout in this stretch of the lake.

RV sites, facilities: There are two group sites for tents or RVs up to 30 feet (no hookups) that can accommodate 80–120 people each. Picnic tables and fire grills are provided. Drinking water, vault toilets, and a group picnic area are available. Leashed pets are permitted.

Reservations, fees: Reservations are required at 877/444-6777 or www.recreation.gov ($10 reservation fee). Sites are $80–110 per night. Open April through late September.

Directions: From Redding, drive north on I-5 for about 20 miles to the Salt Creek/Gilman exit. Turn right on Gilman Road/County Road 7H009 and drive northeast for 10 miles to the campground/boat launch access road. Turn right and drive 0.5 mile to the camp on the left side of the road. The group camp is past the family campground.

Contact: Shasta-Trinity National Forest, Shasta Lake Ranger District, 530/275-1587, fax 530/275-1512; Shasta Lake Visitor Center, 530/275-1589; Shasta Recreation Company, 530/275-8113.

CALIFORNIA

90 HIRZ BAY

Scenic rating: 8

on Shasta Lake in Shasta-Trinity National Forest
Map grid B2

This is one of two camps in the immediate area (the other is Hirz Bay Group Camp) that provides nearby access to a boat ramp (0.5 mile down the road) and the McCloud River arm of Shasta Lake. The camp is set on a point at the entrance of Hirz Bay. This is an excellent spot to make a base camp for a fishing trip, with great trolling for trout in this stretch of the lake.

RV sites, facilities: There are 37 individual sites and 10 double sites for tents or RVs up to 40 feet (no hookups). Picnic tables and fire grills are provided. Drinking water and flush and vault toilets are available. A camp host is usually available in the summer. A boat ramp is nearby. Some facilities are wheelchair-accessible. Leashed pets are permitted.

Reservations, fees: Reservations are accepted at 877/444-6777 or www.recreation.gov ($10 reservation fee). Sites are $18 per night, $30 per night for a double site, $5 per night for each additional vehicle. Open year-round.

Directions: From Redding, drive north on I-5 for about 20 miles to the Salt Creek/Gilman exit. Turn right on Gilman Road/County Road 7H009 and drive northeast for 10 miles to the campground/boat launch access road. Turn right and drive 0.5 mile to the camp on the left side of the road.

Contact: Shasta-Trinity National Forest, Shasta Lake Ranger District, 530/275-1587, fax 530/275-1512; Shasta Lake Visitor Center, 530/275-1589; Shasta Recreation Company, 530/275-8113.

91 DEKKAS ROCK GROUP CAMP

Scenic rating: 8

on Shasta Lake in Shasta-Trinity National Forest
Map grid B2

The few people who know about this camp love this little spot. It is an ideal group camp, set on

a flat above the McCloud arm of Shasta Lake, shaded primarily by bays and oaks, with a boat ramp two miles to the south at Hirz Bay. The views are pretty here, looking across the lake at the limestone ridge that borders the McCloud arm. In late summer and fall when the lake level drops, it can be a hike from the camp down to water's edge.

RV sites, facilities: There is one group site for tents or RVs up to 16 feet (no hookups) that can accommodate up to 60 people. A central meeting area with preparation tables, picnic tables, two pedestal grills, and a large barbecue is provided. Drinking water and vault toilets are available. Leashed pets are permitted.

Reservations, fees: Reservations are required at 877/444-6777 or www.recreation.gov ($10 reservation fee). The camp is $110 per night.

Directions: From Redding, drive north on I-5 for about 20 miles to the Salt Creek/Gilman exit. Turn right on Gilman Road/County Road 7H009 and drive northeast for 11 miles to the campground on the right side of the road.

Contact: Shasta-Trinity National Forest, Shasta Lake Ranger District, 530/275-1587, fax 530/275-1512; Shasta Lake Visitor Center, 530/275-1589; Shasta Recreation Company, 530/275-8113.

92 MOORE CREEK GROUP AND OVERFLOW

Scenic rating: 8

on Shasta Lake in Shasta-Trinity National Forest
Map grid B2

The McCloud arm of Shasta Lake is the most beautiful of the five arms at Shasta, with its emerald-green waters and limestone canyon towering overhead to the east. That beautiful setting is taken advantage of at this camp, with a good view of the lake and limestone, along with good trout fishing on the adjacent section of water. Moore Creek is rented as a group camp most of the summer, except during holidays when individual sites are available on a first-come, first-served basis.

RV sites, facilities: There are 12 sites for tents or RVs up to 16 feet (no hookups) that are usually rented as one group site for up to 90 people. Picnic tables and fire grills are provided. Drinking water and vault toilets are available. Leashed pets are permitted.

Reservations, fees: Reservations are required for the group site at 877/444-6777 or www.recreation.gov ($10 reservation fee). Sites are $14 per night for individual sites, $5 per night for each additional vehicle, $110 per night for group site. Open late May through early September.

Directions: From Redding, drive north on I-5 for about 20 miles to the Salt Creek/Gilman exit. Take that exit and turn right on Gilman Road/County Road 7H009 and drive northeast for 14 miles to the campground on the right side of the road.

Contact: Shasta-Trinity National Forest, Shasta Lake Ranger District, 530/275-1587, fax 530/275-1512; Shasta Lake Visitor Center, 530/275-1589; Shasta Recreation Company, 530/275-8113.

93 ELLERY CREEK

Scenic rating: 7

on Shasta Lake in Shasta-Trinity National Forest

Map grid B2

This camp is set at a pretty spot where Ellery Creek empties into the upper McCloud arm of Shasta Lake. Several sites are set on the pavement with an unobstructed view of the beautiful McCloud arm. This stretch of water is excellent for trout fishing in the summer, with bank-fishing access available two miles upstream at the McCloud Bridge. In the spring, there are tons of small spotted bass along the shore from the camp continuing upstream to the inlet of the McCloud River. Boat-launching facilities are available five miles south at Hirz Bay.

RV sites, facilities: There are 19 sites for tents or RVs up to 25 feet (no hookups). Picnic tables, food lockers, and fire grills are provided. Drinking water and vault toilets are available. Leashed pets are permitted.

Reservations, fees: Reservations are accepted at 877/444-6777 or www.recreation.gov ($10 reservation fee). Sites are $16 per night, $5 per night for each additional vehicle. Open early May through September.

Directions: From Redding, drive north on I-5 for about 20 miles to the Salt Creek/Gilman exit. Turn right on Gilman Road/County Road 7H009 and drive northeast for 15 miles to the campground on the right side of the road.

Contact: Shasta-Trinity National Forest, Shasta Lake Ranger District, 530/275-1587, fax 530/275-1512; Shasta Lake Visitor Center, 530/275-1589; Shasta Recreation Company, 530/275-8113.

94 PINE POINT AND GROUP CAMP

Scenic rating: 7

on Shasta Lake in Shasta-Trinity National Forest

Map grid B2

Pine Point is a pretty little camp, set on a ridge above the McCloud arm of Shasta Lake amid oak trees and scattered ponderosa pines. The view is best in spring, when lake levels are generally highest. Boat-launching facilities are available at Hirz Bay; boaters park their boats on shore below the camp while the rest of their party arrives at the camp by car. That provides a chance not only for camping, but also for boating, swimming, waterskiing, and fishing. Note: From July through September, this campground can be reserved as a group site only. It is also used as a summer overflow camping area on weekends and holidays.

RV sites, facilities: There are 14 sites for tents or RVs up to 24 feet (no hookups), which can also be used as a group camp for up to 100 people. Picnic tables, food lockers, and fire rings are provided. Drinking water and vault toilets are available. Leashed pets are permitted.

Reservations, fees: Reservations are required for group site at 877/444-6777 or www.recreation.gov ($10 reservation fee). Sites are $14 per night, $5 per night for each additional vehicle,

$110 per night for a group site. Open May through early September.

Directions: From Redding, drive north on I-5 for about 20 miles to the Salt Creek/Gilman exit. Turn right on Gilman Road/County Road 7H009 and drive northeast for 17 miles to the campground entrance road on the right.

Contact: Shasta-Trinity National Forest, Shasta Lake Ranger District, 530/275-1587, fax 530/275-1512; Shasta Lake Visitor Center, 530/275-1589; Shasta Recreation Company, 530/275-8113.

95 McCLOUD BRIDGE

Scenic rating: 7

on Shasta Lake in Shasta-Trinity National Forest

Map grid B2

Even though reaching this camp requires a long drive, it remains popular. That is because the best shore-fishing access at the lake is available at nearby McCloud Bridge. It is common to see 15 or 20 people shore fishing here for trout on summer weekends. In the fall, big brown trout migrate through this section of lake en route to their upstream spawning grounds.

RV sites, facilities: There are 11 individual sites and three double sites for tents or RVs up to 16 feet (no hookups). Picnic tables and fire grills are provided. Drinking water, vault toilets, and a group picnic area are available. Some facilities are wheelchair-accessible. Leashed pets are permitted.

Reservations, fees: Reservations are not accepted. Sites are $18 per night, $30 per night for double sites, $5 per night for each additional vehicle. Open early May through September.

Directions: From Redding, drive north on I-5 for about 20 miles to the Salt Creek/Gilman exit. Turn right on Gilman Road/County Road 7H009 and drive northeast for 18.5 miles. Cross the McCloud Bridge and drive one mile to the campground entrance on the right.

Contact: Shasta-Trinity National Forest, Shasta Lake Ranger District, 530/275-1587, fax 530/275-1512; Shasta Lake Visitor Center,

530/275-1589; Shasta Recreation Company, 530/275-8113.

96 MADRONE CAMP

Scenic rating: 7

on Squaw Creek in Shasta-Trinity National Forest

Map grid B2

Tired of people? Then you've come to the right place. This remote camp is set along Squaw Creek, a feeder stream of Shasta Lake, which lies to the southwest. It's way out there, far away from anybody. Even though Shasta Lake is relatively close, about 10 miles away, it is in another world. A network of four-wheel-drive roads provides a recreation option, detailed on a map of Shasta-Trinity National Forest.

RV sites, facilities: There are 10 sites for tents or RVs up to 16 feet (no hookups). Picnic tables and fire grills are provided. Vault toilets are available. No drinking water is available. Garbage must be packed out. Leashed pets are permitted.

Reservations, fees: Reservations are not accepted. There is no fee for camping. Open year-round.

Directions: From Redding, drive 31 miles east on Highway 299 to the town of Montgomery Creek. Turn left on Fenders Ferry Road/Forest Road 27 and drive 18 miles to the camp (the road starts as gravel and then becomes dirt). Note: The access road is rough and RVs are not advised.

Contact: Shasta-Trinity National Forest, Shasta Lake Ranger District, 530/275-1587, fax 530/275-1512; Shasta Lake Visitor Center, 530/275-1589.

97 TRAIL IN RV PARK AND CAMPGROUND

Scenic rating: 7

near Shasta Lake

Map grid B2

This is a privately operated campground near the Salt Creek arm of giant Shasta Lake. Open, level sites are available. Many of the sites are filled with long-term renters. The nearest boat launch is one mile away and the lake offers fishing, boating, and swimming. Its proximity to I-5 makes this a popular spot, fast and easy to reach, which is extremely attractive for drivers of RVs and trailers who want to avoid the many twisty roads surrounding Shasta Lake.

RV sites, facilities: There are 39 sites with full hookups (30 and 50 amps) for RVs of any length and four tent sites; some sites are pull-through. Picnic tables and fire grills are provided. Restrooms with showers, satellite TV hookups, seasonal heated swimming pool, playground, convenience store, ice, firewood, Wi-Fi, full-service deli, Saturday night barbecue, and coin laundry are available. Leashed pets are permitted.

Reservations, fees: Reservations are accepted. Sites are $28 per night for RV camping, $17 per night for tent camping, $2 per person per night for more than two people, $1 per pet per night. Monthly rates available. Some credit cards accepted. Open year-round.

Directions: From Redding, drive 22 miles north on I-5 to Exit 698/Gilman Road/Salt Creek Road exit. Take that exit and turn left on Salt Creek Road and drive a short distance to Gregory Creek Road. Turn right and drive 0.25 mile to the campground on the right.

Contact: Trail In RV Park and Campground, tel./fax 530/238-8533.

98 NELSON POINT AND GROUP CAMP

Scenic rating: 7

on Shasta Lake in Shasta-Trinity National Forest

Map grid B2

This is an easy-to-reach campground, only a few minutes from I-5. It's set beside the Salt Creek inlet of Shasta Lake, deep in a cove. In low-water years, or when the lake level is low in the fall and early winter, this camp can seem quite distant from water's edge. This campground can be reserved as a group camp July through September.

RV sites, facilities: There are eight sites for tents or RVs up to 16 feet, and a group site for tents or RVs up to 16 feet that can accommodate up to 60 people. No hookups. Vault toilets, picnic tables, and fire grills are provided. No drinking water is available. A grocery store and coin laundry are nearby in Lakehead. Leashed pets are permitted.

Reservations, fees: Reservations are required for group sites only at 877/444-6777 or www.recreation.gov ($10 reservation fee). Sites are $10 per night, $5 per night for each additional vehicle, and $80 per night for a group site. Open May through early September.

Directions: From Redding, drive north on I-5 for about 20 miles to the Salt Creek Road/ Gilman Road exit. Take that exit, turn left and drive 0.25 mile to Gregory Creek Road. Turn right and drive one mile to Conflict Point Road. Turn left and drive one mile to the campground on the left.

Contact: Shasta-Trinity National Forest, Shasta Lake Ranger District, 530/275-1587, fax 530/275-1512; Shasta Lake Visitor Center, 530/275-1589; Shasta Recreation Company, 530/275-8113.

99 HOLIDAY HARBOR RESORT

Scenic rating: 7

on Shasta Lake

Map grid B2

This camp is one of the more popular family-oriented, all-service resorts on Shasta Lake, which has the second-largest dam in the United States. It is set on the lower McCloud arm of the lake, which is extremely beautiful, with a limestone mountain ridge off to the east. It is an ideal jump-off point for all water sports, especially waterskiing, houseboating and boating, and fishing. A good boat ramp, boat rentals, and store with all the goodies are bonuses. The place is full service and even offers boat-launching service. Campers staying here also get a 15 percent discount on boat rentals. Another plus is the nearby side trip to Shasta Caverns, a privately guided adventure (fee charged) into limestone caves. This camp often fills in summer, even on weekdays.

RV sites, facilities: There are 28 sites with full hookups (50 amps) for RVs up to 40 feet, with tents allowed in several sites. Picnic tables and barbecues are provided. Restrooms with showers, general store, seasonal café, gift shop, coin laundry, marina, marine repair service, boat moorage, swim area, playground, propane gas, and houseboat and boat and personal watercraft rentals are available. Some facilities are wheelchair-accessible. Leashed pets are permitted.

Reservations, fees: Reservations are recommended. Sites are $22.75–36 per night, $6 per person per night for more than two people, $4.50–6 per night for each additional vehicle, and $7.75–12.50 per night for boat moorage. Some credit cards accepted. Open April through October.

Directions: From Redding, drive 18 miles north on I-5 to Exit 695 and the O'Brien Road/Shasta Caverns Road exit. Turn right (east) at Shasta Caverns Road and drive one mile to the resort entrance on the right; check in at the store (20061 Shasta Caverns Road).

Contact: Holiday Harbor Resort, 530/238-2383 or 800/776-2628, www.lakeshasta.com.

100 JONES VALLEY INLET

Scenic rating: 4

on Shasta Lake in Shasta-Trinity National Forest
Map grid B2

This is one of the few primitive camp areas on Shasta Lake, set on the distant Pit River arm of the lake. It is an ideal camp for hiking and biking, with nearby Clickapudi Trail routed for miles along the lake's shore, in and out of coves, and then entering the surrounding foothills and oak/bay woodlands. The camp is pretty, if a bit exposed, with two nearby resorts, Jones Valley and Silverthorn, providing boat rentals and supplies.

RV sites, facilities: There is an area for dispersed, primitive camping for tents or RVs up

to 40 feet (no hookups). Portable toilets are available. No drinking water is available. Garbage must be packed out. A boat ramp at Jones Valley is two miles from camp. Groceries are available nearby. Leashed pets are permitted.

Reservations, fees: Reservations are not accepted. Sites are $8 per vehicle per night. Open year-round.

Directions: From Redding, turn east on Highway 299 and drive 7.5 miles just past the town of Bella Vista. At Dry Creek Road turn left and drive nine miles to a Y intersection. Bear right at the Y (left will take you to Silverthorn Resort) and drive a short distance to the campground entrance on the left side of the road.

Contact: Shasta-Trinity National Forest, Shasta Lake Ranger District, 530/275-1587, fax 530/275-1512; Shasta Lake Visitor Center, 530/275-1589; Shasta Recreation Company, 530/275-8113.

101 UPPER AND LOWER JONES VALLEY CAMPS

Scenic rating: 3

on Shasta Lake in Shasta-Trinity National Forest
Map grid B2

Lower Jones is a small camp set along a deep cove in the remote Pit River arm of Shasta Lake. The advantage of Lower Jones Valley is that it is closer to the lake than Upper Jones Valley. Unfortunately, the Bear Fire of 2004 burned the trees and vegetation around these campgrounds. There is a trailhead at the camp that provides access to Clickapudi Trail, a great hiking and biking trail that traces the lake's shore, routed through woodlands. Two nearby resorts, Jones Valley and Silverthorn, provide boat rentals and supplies.

RV sites, facilities: There are 18 sites and three double sites for tents or RVs up to 16 feet (no hookups) in two adjacent campgrounds. Picnic tables and fire grills are provided. Drinking water, food lockers, and vault toilets are available. Some facilities are wheelchair-accessible. A boat ramp at Jones Valley is two miles from camp. Leashed pets are permitted.

Reservations, fees: Reservations are not accepted. Upper Jones sites are $18 per night, Lower Jones sites are $18 per night and $30 per night for a double site, $5 per night for each additional vehicle. Lower Jones is open year-round. Upper Jones is open May through September.

Directions: From Redding, turn east on Highway 299 and drive 7.5 miles just past the town of Bella Vista. At Dry Creek Road, turn left and drive nine miles to a Y intersection. Bear right at the Y (left will take you to Silverthorn Resort) and drive a short distance to the campground entrances, on the left side for Lower Jones and the right side for Upper Jones.

Contact: Shasta-Trinity National Forest, Shasta Lake Ranger District, 530/275-1587, fax 530/275-1512; Shasta Lake Visitor Center, 530/275-1589; Shasta Recreation Company, 530/275-8113.

102 SHASTA

Scenic rating: 6

on the Sacramento River in Shasta-Trinity National Forest

Map grid B2

Because campers must drive across Shasta Dam to reach this campground, general access was closed in 2002 for national security reasons. Call at least one week in advance (Bureau of Reclamation, Security Office, 530/275-4253) to get approval to cross the dam and make arrangements before planning a visit. The closed road also provides access to an adjacent OHV area, one of the few in the north state. Thus when open this place is for quads and dirt bikes—loud and wild and hey, it's a perfect spot for them. Because of past mining in the area, it's barren with almost no shade, but the views of the river and Shasta Dam are incredible. Nearby dam tours are unique and memorable.

RV sites, facilities: There are 22 sites for tents or RVs up to 30 feet (no hookups). Picnic tables and fire rings are provided. Drinking water and vault toilets are available. A boat ramp is nearby.

Groceries and bait are available in Shasta Lake City. Leashed pets are permitted.

Reservations, fees: Reservations are not accepted. Sites are $10 per night, $5 per night for each additional vehicle. Open year-round.

Directions: From I-5 in Redding, drive north for three miles to the exit for the town of Shasta Lake City and Shasta Dam Boulevard. Take that exit and bear west on Shasta Dam Boulevard and drive three miles to Lake Boulevard. Turn right on Lake Boulevard and drive two miles. Cross Shasta Dam and continue four miles to the signed campground.

Contact: Bureau of Reclamation, Shasta Dam Visitor Center, 530/275-4463; Shasta-Trinity National Forest, Shasta Lake Ranger District, 530/275-1587, fax 530/275-1512; Shasta Lake Visitor Center, 530/275-1589.

103 FAWNDALE OAKS RV PARK

Scenic rating: 5

near Shasta Lake

Map grid B2

This park is midway between Shasta Lake and Redding, so it's close to many recreational activities. Toward Redding, the options include Turtle Bay Exploration Park, WaterWorks Park, public golf courses, and Sacramento River trails, which are paved, making them accessible for wheelchairs and bicycles. Toward Shasta Lake, there are tours of Shasta Caverns, via a short drive to Holiday Harbor. The RV park is on 40 acres and has shaded sites.

RV sites, facilities: There are 10 tent sites and 15 sites with full hookups (30 and 50 amps) and cable TV for RVs up to 45 feet. Some sites are pull-through. A cabin and trailer are also available for rent. Picnic tables are provided and some sites have barbecues. Phone/modem hookups, coin laundry, boat and RV storage, a general store, picnic area, playground, seasonal swimming pool, club room, game room, propane, and group facilities are available. Some facilities are wheelchair-accessible. Leashed pets are permitted.

Reservations, fees: Reservations are accepted by telephone or website. RV sites are $25–27.50 per night for two people, tent sites are $19 per night for a family of four, $2 per person per night for any additional people, $1 per pet per night, $1 per night for each additional vehicle. Weekly and monthly rates are available. Some credit cards accepted. Open year-round.

Directions: From Redding, drive north on I-5 for nine miles to the Fawndale Road exit (Exit 689). Take that exit and turn right (east) on Fawndale Road. Drive 0.5 mile to the second RV park at the end of the road at 15015 Fawndale Road.

Contact: Fawndale Oaks RV Park, 530/275-0764 or 888/838-2159, www.fawndaleoaks.com.

104 BEAR MOUNTAIN RV RESORT AND CAMPGROUND
🚶 🏊 🎣 🚤 🐕 🚵 ♿ 🚐 ⛺

Scenic rating: 5

near Shasta Lake

Map grid B2

This is a privately operated park in the remote Jones Valley area five miles from Shasta Lake. It is set on 52 acres. A hiking trail leaves from the campground, rises up a hill, and provides a great view of Redding. The resort emphasizes that there is no train noise here, as there often is at campgrounds closer to Shasta Lake.

RV sites, facilities: There are 70 sites with full or partial hookups (30 amps) for RVs up to 40 feet, 24 tent sites, and four park-model cabins. Some RV sites are pull-through. Picnic tables and fire rings are provided. Drinking water, restrooms with flush toilets and coin showers, coin laundry, modem access, convenience store, dump station, a seasonal swimming pool, recreation hall, arcade, table tennis, two playgrounds, volleyball, and horseshoe pit are available. Some facilities are wheelchair-accessible. A boat ramp is within three miles. Leashed pets are permitted.

Reservations, fees: Reservations are accepted at 800/952-0551. Tent sites are $14 per night,

RV sites are $16–20 per night, $2 per person per night for more than two people, $2 per night for each additional vehicle. Weekly and monthly rates available. Some credit cards accepted. Open year-round.

Directions: From Redding, drive north on I-5 for three miles to Exit 682 for Oasis Road. Take that exit and drive to Oasis Road. Turn right on Oasis Road and drive 3.5 miles to Bear Mountain Road. Turn right on Bear Mountain Road and drive 3.5 miles to the campground on the left.

Contact: Bear Mountain RV Resort and Campground, 530/275-4728, www.campshasta.com.

105 EAST WEAVER
🚶 🎣 🏕 🚵 ⛺

Scenic rating: 6

on the east branch of Weaver Creek in Shasta-Trinity National Forest

Map grid B2

This camp is set along East Weaver Creek. Another mile to the west on East Weaver Road, the road dead-ends at a trailhead, a good side trip. From here, the hiking trail is routed four miles, a significant climb, to tiny East Weaver Lake, set to the southwest of Monument Peak (7,771 feet elevation). The elevation at East Weaver is 2,700 feet.

RV sites, facilities: There are 11 sites for tents or RVs up to 25 feet (no hookups). Picnic tables and fire grills are provided. Drinking water and vault toilets are available. Supplies and a coin laundry are available in Weaverville. Leashed pets are permitted.

Reservations, fees: Reservations are not accepted. Sites are $11 per night, $5 per night in the winter. Open year-round.

Directions: From Redding, drive west on Highway 299 to Weaverville. In Weaverville, turn right (north) on Highway 3 and drive about two miles to East Weaver Road. Turn left on East Weaver Road and drive 3.5 miles to the campground.

Contact: Shasta-Trinity National Forest,

Weaverville Ranger Station, 530/623-2121, fax 530/623-6010.

106 STEELBRIDGE

Scenic rating: 7

on the Trinity River
Map grid B2

Very few people know of this spot, yet it can be a prime spot for anglers and campers. It's one of the better stretches of water in the area for steelhead, with good shore-fishing access. The prime time is from October through December. In the summer, the shade of conifers will keep you cool. Don't forget to bring your own water. The elevation is 1,700 feet.

RV sites, facilities: There are nine sites for tents or RVs up to 20 feet (no hookups). Picnic tables and fire grills are provided. Vault toilets are available. No drinking water is available. Supplies are available within three miles in Douglas City. Some facilities are wheelchair-accessible. Leashed pets are permitted.

Reservations, fees: Reservations are not accepted. Sites are $5 per night. Open year-round, weather permitting.

Directions: From Redding, turn west on Highway 299 and drive over Buckhorn Summit. Continue toward Douglas City to Steel Bridge Road (if you reach Douglas City, you have gone 2.3 miles too far). At Steel Bridge Road, turn right and drive about four miles to the campground at the end of the road.

Contact: Bureau of Land Management, Redding Field Office, 530/224-2100, fax 530/224-2172.

107 DOUGLAS CITY AND STEINER FLAT

Scenic rating: 7

on the Trinity River
Map grid B2

If you want to camp along this stretch of the main Trinity River, these camps are your best

bet (they're along the river about two miles from each other). They are set off the main road, near the river, with good bank fishing access (the prime season is from mid-August through winter for salmon and steelhead). There's paved parking and two beaches at Douglas City Campground. Steiner Flat, a more primitive camp, provides better access for fishing. This can be a good base camp for an off-season fishing trip on the Trinity River or a lounging spot during the summer. The elevation is 1,700 feet.

RV sites, facilities: There are 20 sites for tents or RVs up to 28 feet at Douglas City, and dispersed camping for tents and small RVs at Steiner Flat. No hookups. At Douglas City, picnic tables and fire grills are provided. Drinking water and restrooms with sinks and flush toilets are available. At Steiner Flat, no drinking water or toilets are available. Supplies are available within one mile in the town of Douglas City. Leashed pets are permitted.

Reservations, fees: Reservations are not accepted. Sites are $10 per night at Douglas City; no fee at Steiner Flat. Open mid-May through November.

Directions: From Redding, turn on Highway 299 west and drive west (toward Weaverville). Continue over the bridge at the Trinity River near Douglas City to Steiner Flat Road. Turn left on Steiner Flat Road and drive 0.5 mile to Douglas City campground on the left. To reach Steiner Flat, continue two more miles and look for the campground on the left.

Contact: Bureau of Land Management, Redding Field Office, 530/224-2100, fax 530/224-2172.

108 OLD LEWISTON BRIDGE RV RESORT

Scenic rating: 7

on the Trinity River
Map grid B2

This is a popular spot for calm-water kayaking, rafting, and fishing. Though much of the water from Trinity and Lewiston Lakes is diverted via tunnel to Whiskeytown Lake (en route to the valley and points south), enough escapes downstream to provide a viable stream here near the town of Lewiston. This upstream section below Lewiston Lake is prime in the early summer for trout, particularly the chance for a huge brown trout (special regulations in effect). A fishing shuttle service is available. The campground is in a hilly area but has level sites, with nearby Lewiston Lake also a major attraction. Some sites are occupied by long-term renters.

RV sites, facilities: There are 52 sites with full hookups (30 amps) for RVs up to 45 feet, a separate area for tents, and five rental trailers. Picnic tables are provided. Restrooms with showers, coin laundry, grocery store, modem access, ice, bait and tackle, and propane gas refills are available. A group picnic area is available by reservation. A restaurant is within 0.5 mile. Leashed pets are permitted.

Reservations, fees: Reservations are accepted by phone or website. Sites are $26 per night for RVs, $14 per night per vehicle for tent campers, $2 per person per night for more than two people. Monthly rates available. Some credit cards accepted. Open year-round.

Directions: From Redding, turn on Highway 299 and drive west over Buckhorn Summit, and continue for five miles to Trinity Dam Boulevard. Turn right on Trinity Dam Boulevard and drive four miles to Lewiston, and continue north to Rush Creek Road. Turn left (west) on Rush Creek Road and drive 0.25 mile to the resort on the left.

Contact: Old Lewiston Bridge RV Resort, 800/922-1924 or tel./fax 530/778-3894, www.lewistonbridgerv.com.

109 TRINITY RIVER LODGE RV RESORT

Scenic rating: 7

on the Trinity River

Map grid B2

For many, this privately operated park has an ideal location. You get level, grassy sites with shade trees along the Trinity River, yet it is just a short drive north to Lewiston Lake or a bit farther to giant Trinity Lake. Lake or river, take your pick. The resort covers nearly 14 acres, and about half the sites are rented for the entire summer.

RV sites, facilities: There are 60 sites with full hookups (30 and 50 amps) for RVs up to 40 feet, five tent sites, and one cottage. Restrooms with showers, a coin laundry, cable TV, modem access, recreation room, lending library, clubhouse, athletic field, propane gas, camp store, ice, firewood, boat and trailer storage, horseshoes, and picnic area are available. Some facilities are wheelchair-accessible. Leashed pets are permitted.

Reservations, fees: Reservations are recommended. Tent sites are $15.75 per night, and RV sites are $28.35 per night. Some credit cards accepted. Open year-round.

Directions: From Redding, turn on Highway 299 west and drive west over Buckhorn Summit. Continue for five miles to Trinity Dam Boulevard. Turn right on Trinity Dam Boulevard and drive four miles to Lewiston. Continue on Trinity Dam Boulevard to Rush Creek Road. Turn left on Rush Creek Road and drive 2.3 miles to the campground on the left.

Contact: Trinity River Lodge RV Resort, 530/778-3791, www.trinityriverresort.com.

110 COOPER GULCH

Scenic rating: 8

on Lewiston Lake in Shasta-Trinity National Forest

Map grid B2

Here is a nice spot along a beautiful lake, featuring a short trail to Baker Gulch, where a pretty creek enters Lewiston Lake. The trout fishing is good on the upper end of the lake (where the current starts) and upstream. The lake speed limit is 10 mph. Swimming is allowed, although the water is cold because it flows in from the bottom of Trinity Lake. The lake is designated a wildlife-viewing area, with large numbers of waterfowl and other birds often spotted near the tules off the shore of Lakeview Terrace. Bring all of your own supplies and plan on hunkering down here for a while.

RV sites, facilities: There are five sites for tents or RVs up to 16 feet (no hookups). Picnic tables and fire grills are provided. Vault toilets and drinking water are available. Boat launching and rentals are nearby at Pine Cove Marina. Supplies and a coin laundry are available in Lewiston. Some facilities are wheelchair-accessible. Leashed pets are permitted.

Reservations, fees: Reservations are not accepted. Sites are $13 per night. Open early April through late October.

Directions: From Redding, turn on Highway 299 west and drive west over Buckhorn Summit. Continue for five miles to Trinity Dam Boulevard. Turn right on Trinity Dam Boulevard, drive four miles to Lewiston, and then continue on Trinity Dam Boulevard another four miles north to the campground.

Contact: Shasta-Trinity National Forest, Weaverville Ranger Station, 530/623-2121, fax 530/623-6010; Pine Cove Marina, 530/778-3770.

111 LAKEVIEW TERRACE RESORT

Scenic rating: 8

on Lewiston Lake
Map grid B2

This might be your Golden Pond. It's a terraced RV park—with cabin rentals also available—that overlooks Lewiston Lake, one of the prettiest drive-to lakes in the region. Fishing for trout is excellent from Lakeview Terrace continuing upstream toward the dam. Lewiston Lake is perfect for fishing, with a 10-mph speed limit in effect (all the hot boats go to nearby Trinity Lake), along with excellent prospects for rainbow and brown trout. Other fish species include brook trout and kokanee salmon. The topper is that Lewiston Lake is always full to the brim, just the opposite of the up-and-down nightmare of its neighboring big brother, Trinity.

RV sites, facilities: There are 40 sites with full hookups (50 amps) for RVs up to 40 feet; some sites are pull-through. No tents. Cabins are also available. Picnic tables and barbecues are provided. Restrooms with showers, coin laundry, seasonal heated pool, propane gas, ice, horseshoes, playground, bait, and boat and patio-boat rentals are available. Supplies are available within five miles. Leashed pets are permitted.

Reservations, fees: Reservations are recommended. Sites are $26 per night, $3 per person per night for more than two people, $2 per additional vehicle per night. Weekly and monthly rates available. Some credit cards accepted. Open year-round.

Directions: From Redding, turn on Highway 299 west and drive west over Buckhorn Summit. Continue for five miles to Trinity Dam Boulevard. Turn right on Trinity Dam Boulevard and drive 10 miles (five miles past Lewiston) to the resort on the left side of the road.

Contact: Lakeview Terrace Resort, 530/778-3803, fax 530/778-3960, www.lakeviewterraceresort.com.

112 TUNNEL ROCK

Scenic rating: 7

on Lewiston Lake in Shasta-Trinity National Forest
Map grid B2

This is a very small, primitive alternative to Ackerman, which is more developed and another mile up the road to the north. The proximity to the Pine Cove boat ramp and fish-cleaning station, less than two miles to the south, is a primary attraction. Pine Cove Marina is full service and rents fishing boats. The elevation is 1,700 feet.

RV sites, facilities: There are six sites for tents or RVs up to 15 feet (no hookups). Picnic tables and fire grills are provided. Vault toilets are available. No drinking water is available. Leashed pets are permitted.

Reservations, fees: Reservations are not accepted. Sites are $7 per night. Open year-round.

Directions: From Redding, turn on Highway 299 west and drive over Buckhorn Summit. Continue for five miles to County Road 105/ Trinity Dam Road. Turn right on Trinity Dam Road and drive four miles to Lewiston, and then continue another seven miles north on Trinity Dam Boulevard to the campground.

Contact: Shasta-Trinity National Forest, Weaverville Ranger Station, 530/623-2121, fax 530/623-6010.

113 ACKERMAN

Scenic rating: 7

on Lewiston Lake in Shasta-Trinity National Forest
Map grid B2

Of the camps and parks at Lewiston Lake, Ackerman is closest to the lake's headwaters. This stretch of water below Trinity Dam is the best area for trout fishing on Lewiston Lake. Nearby Pine Cove boat ramp, two miles south of the camp, offers the only boat launch on Lewiston Lake with docks and a fish-cleaning station—a popular spot for anglers. When the Trinity powerhouse is running, trout fishing is excellent in this area. The elevation is 2,000 feet.

RV sites, facilities: There are 66 sites for tents or RVs up to 40 feet (no hookups). Picnic tables and fire grills are provided. Drinking water, flush toilets, and a dump station are available. Leashed pets are permitted.

Reservations, fees: Reservations are not accepted. Sites are $13 per night, and $7 per night during the winter. Open year-round.

Directions: From Redding, turn on Highway 299 west and drive west over Buckhorn Summit. Continue for five miles to Trinity Dam Boulevard. Turn right on Trinity Dam Boulevard and drive four miles to Lewiston. Continue north on Trinity Dam Boulevard for eight miles to the campground.

Contact: Shasta-Trinity National Forest, Weaverville Ranger Station, 530/623-2121, fax 530/623-6010.

114 OAK BOTTOM

Scenic rating: 7

on Whiskeytown Lake
Map grid B2

The prettiest hiking trails at Whiskeytown Lake are at the far western end of the reservoir, and this camp provides excellent access to them. One hiking and biking trail skirts the north shoreline of the lake and is routed to the lake's inlet at the Judge Carr Powerhouse. The other, with the trailhead just a short drive to the west, is routed along Mill Creek, a pristine, clear-running stream with the trail jumping over the water many times. The campground sites seem a little close, but the camp is next to a beach area. There are junior ranger programs, and evening ranger programs at the Oak Bottom Amphitheater are available several nights per week from mid-June through Labor Day. A self-guided nature trail is five miles away at the visitors center.

RV sites, facilities: There are 100 walk-in tent sites with picnic tables and fire grills. There are 22 sites for RVs up to 32 feet (no hookups) in the large parking area near the launch ramp. Drinking water, restrooms with flush toilets and coin showers, storage lockers, convenience store, ice, firewood, dump station, boat ramp, and boat rentals are available. Some facilities are wheelchair-accessible. Leashed pets are permitted.

Reservations, fees: Reservations accepted during summer at 877/444-6777 or www. recreation.gov ($10 reservation fee). Sites are $16–18 per night, plus a park-use permit of $5 per day, $10 per week, or $25 per year. Open year-round.

Directions: From Redding, turn on Highway 299 west and drive west for 15 miles (past the visitors center) to the campground entrance road on the left. Turn left and drive a short distance to the campground.

Contact: Whiskeytown National Recreation Area, 530/242-3400 or 530/242-3412, fax 530/246-5154; Whiskeytown Visitor Center, 530/246-1225, www.nps.gov/whis; Oak Bottom

Campground Store, 530/359-2269; Forever Resorts, www.whiskeytownmarinas.com.

115 BRANDY CREEK

Scenic rating: 7

on Whiskeytown Lake

Map grid B2

For campers with boats, this is the best place to stay at Whiskeytown Lake, with a boat ramp less than a quarter mile away. Whiskeytown is popular for sailing and sailboarding, as it gets a lot more wind than other lakes in the region. Personal watercraft have been banned from this lake. Fishing for kokanee salmon is good in the early morning before the wind comes up; trout fishing is pretty good as well. The lake has 36 miles of shoreline.

RV sites, facilities: There are 37 sites for RVs up to 35 feet (no hookups). No tents. Drinking water and a dump station are available. Leashed pets are permitted.

Reservations, fees: Reservations are not accepted. Sites are $14 per night, $7 per night during off-season, plus a park-use permit of $5 per day, $10 per week, or $25 per year. Open year-round.

Directions: From Redding, drive west on Highway 299 for eight miles to the visitors center and Kennedy Memorial Drive. Turn left at the visitors center (Kennedy Memorial Drive) and drive five miles to the campground entrance road on the right. Turn right and drive a short distance to the camp.

Contact: Whiskeytown National Recreation Area, 530/242-3400 or 530/242-3412, fax 530/246-5154; Whiskeytown Visitor Center, 530/246-1225, www.nps.gov/whis.

116 PREMIER RV RESORT

Scenic rating: 2

in Redding

Map grid B2

If you're stuck with no place to go, this large park could be your savior. Nearby recreation options include a waterslide park and the Turtle Bay Museum and Exploration Park on the Sacramento River. The newest attraction is Sundial Bridge, with its glass walkway that allows users to look down into the river, a stunning feat of architecture—where the experience simulates walking on air. In addition, Whiskeytown Lake is nearby to the west, and Shasta Lake to the north. A casino and several golf courses are nearby.

RV sites, facilities: There are 111 sites with full or partial hookups (30 and 50 amps) for RVs of any length, and two yurts. A flat cut-out area on a hillside provides space for dispersed tent sites. Picnic tables and fire grills are provided. Drinking water, restrooms with flush toilets and showers, playground, seasonal swimming pool, coin laundry, dump station, satellite TV hookups, modem access, a convenience store, propane gas, and recreation room are available. Some facilities are wheelchair accessible. Leashed pets are permitted.

Reservations, fees: Reservations are accepted. RV sites are $47.50 per night, $3 per person per night for more than two people; tent sites are $37 per night. Some credit cards accepted. Open year-round.

Directions: In Redding, drive north on I-5 to the Lake Boulevard/Burney-Alturas exit. Turn west (left) on Lake Boulevard and drive 0.25 mile to North Boulder Drive. Turn right (north) on North Boulder Drive and drive one block to the resort on the left.

Contact: Premier RV Resort, 530/246-0101 or 888/710-8450, fax 530/246-0123, www.premierrvresorts.com.

117 MARINA RV PARK

Scenic rating: 6

on the Sacramento River

Map grid B2

The riverside setting is a highlight here, with the Sacramento River providing relief from the dog days of summer. An easy, paved walking and bike trail is available nearby at the Sacramento

River Parkway, providing river views and sometimes a needed breeze on hot summer evenings. It is also two miles away from the Turtle Bay Museum, and close to a movie theater. A golf driving range is nearby. This park includes an area with long-term RV renters.

RV sites, facilities: There are 42 sites with full or partial hookups (30 amps) for RVs up to 40 feet. Picnic tables, restrooms with showers, a coin laundry, small store, modem access, seasonal swimming pool, spa, boat ramp, and a dump station are available. Leashed pets are permitted.

Reservations, fees: Reservations are accepted. Sites are $31.90 per night, $2 per person per night for more than two people. Weekly and monthly rates available. Open year-round.

Directions: In Redding, turn west on Highway 44 and drive 1.5 miles to the exit for Convention Center/Marina Park Drive. Take that exit, turn left, and drive over the highway to a stoplight and Marina Park Drive. Turn left (south) on Marina Park Drive and drive 0.8 mile to the park on the left.

Contact: Marina RV Park, 530/241-4396, www.marinapark.com.

118 SACRAMENTO RIVER RV RESORT

Scenic rating: 7

south of Redding

Map grid B2   **BEST (**

This makes a good headquarters for a fall fishing trip on the Sacramento River, where the salmon come big from August through October. In the summer, trout fishing is very good from this area as well, but a boat is a must. No problem; there's a boat ramp at the park. In addition, you can hire fishing guides who launch from here daily. The park is open year-round, and if you want to stay close to home, a three-acre pond with bass, bluegill, and perch is also available at the resort. You also get great long-distance views of Mount Shasta and Mount Lassen.

RV sites, facilities: There are 140 sites with full hookups (30 and 50 amps) for RVs of any length and 10 sites for tents in a shaded grassy area. Some RV sites are pull-through. Picnic tables, restrooms with showers, coin laundry, dump station, cable TV, Wi-Fi, modem access, bait, boat launch, playground, two tennis courts, horseshoes, golf driving range, and a large seasonal swimming pool are available. A clubhouse is available by reservation. Some facilities are wheelchair-accessible. Leashed pets are permitted.

Reservations, fees: Reservations are accepted. Sites are $16.50–28 per night. Some credit cards accepted. Open year-round.

Directions: From Redding, drive south on I-5 for five miles to the Knighton Road exit. Turn west (right) and drive a short distance to Riverland Drive. Turn left on Riverland Drive and drive two miles to the park at the end of the road.

Contact: Sacramento River RV Resort, 530/365-6402, fax 530/365-2601, www.sacramentoriverrvresort.com.

119 DEERLICK SPRINGS

Scenic rating: 8

on Browns Creek in Shasta-Trinity National Forest

Map grid B2

It's a long, twisty drive to this remote and primitive camp set on the edge of the Chanchelulla Wilderness in the transition zone where the valley's oak grasslands give way to conifers. This quiet little spot is set along Browns Creek. A trailhead just north of camp provides a streamside walk. The elevation is 3,100 feet.

RV sites, facilities: There are 13 sites for tents or RVs up to 20 feet (no hookups). Picnic tables and fire grills are provided. Vault toilets are available. No drinking water is available. Garbage must be packed out. Leashed pets are permitted.

Reservations, fees: Reservations are not accepted. There is no fee for camping. Open May through October.

Directions: From Red Bluff, turn west on Highway 36 (very twisty) and drive to the Forest Service ranger station in Platina. In Platina, turn right (north) on Harrison Gulch Road and drive 10 miles to the campground on the left.
Contact: Shasta-Trinity National Forest, Yolla Bolly Ranger Station, 530/352-4211, fax 530/352-4312.

120 BASIN GULCH

Scenic rating: 5

in Shasta-Trinity National Forest

Map grid B2

This is one of two little-known campgrounds in the vicinity that rarely gets much use. A trail out of this camp climbs Noble Ridge, eventually rising to a good lookout at 3,933 feet, providing sweeping views of the north valley. Of course, you could also just drive there, taking a dirt road out of Platina. There are many backcountry Forest Service roads in the area, so your best bet is to get a Shasta-Trinity National Forest map, which details the roads. The elevation is 2,600 feet. There is evidence in the area of a wildfire that occurred in 2001.
RV sites, facilities: There are 13 sites for tents or RVs up to 20 feet (no hookups). Picnic tables and fire grills are provided. Vault toilets are available. No drinking water is available. Leashed pets are permitted.
Reservations, fees: Reservations are not accepted. Sites are $6 per night. Open May through October.
Directions: From Red Bluff, drive about 45 miles west on Highway 36 to the Yolla Bolly District Ranger Station. From the ranger station, turn south on Stuart Gap Road and drive two miles to the campground on the left.
Contact: Shasta-Trinity National Forest, Yolla Bolly Ranger Station, 530/352-4211, fax 530/352-4312.

121 BEND RV PARK AND FISHING RESORT

Scenic rating: 7

on the Sacramento River

Map grid B2

Here's a spot for RV cruisers to rest their rigs for a while. Bend RV Park and Fishing Resort is open year-round and is set beside the Sacramento River. The salmon average 15–25 pounds in this area, and anglers typically have the best results from mid-August through October. In recent years, the gates of the Red Bluff Diversion Dam have been raised in early September. When that occurs, huge numbers of salmon charge upstream from Red Bluff to Anderson, holding in each deep river hole. Expect very hot weather in July and August.
RV sites, facilities: There are 14 sites with full or partial hookups (30 amps) for RVs up to 40 feet. In addition, there is a separate area for tents only. Picnic tables are provided. Drinking water, restrooms with showers and flush toilets, convenience store, bait and tackle, boat ramp, boat dock, coin laundry, and a dump station are available. Leashed pets are permitted.
Reservations, fees: Reservations are accepted. Sites are $21.50–24 per night, $3.50 per person per night for more than two people. Open year-round.
Directions: From I-5 in Red Bluff, drive four miles north on I-5 to the Jelly's Ferry Road exit. Take that exit and turn northeast on Jelly's Ferry Road and drive 2.5 miles to the resort at 21795 Bend Ferry Road.
Contact: Bend RV Park and Fishing Resort, 530/527-6289.

122 LAKE RED BLUFF

Scenic rating: 6

on the Sacramento River near Red Bluff

Map grid B2

Lake Red Bluff is created by the Red Bluff Diversion Dam on the Sacramento River, and waterskiing, bird-watching, hiking, and fishing are the most popular activities. A three-mile-long paved trail parallels the river, and cycling and skating are allowed on the trail. It has become a backyard swimming hole for local residents in the summer when the temperatures reach the high 90s and low 100s almost every day. In early September, the Bureau of Reclamation raises the gates at the diversion dam to allow migrating salmon an easier course on the upstream journey, and in the process, Lake Red Bluff reverts to its former self as the Sacramento River.

RV sites, facilities: At Sycamore Camp, there are 30 sites for tents or RVs up to 35 feet (no hookups). There is also a tent-only group camp (Camp Discovery) that has 11 screened cabins and can accommodate up to 100 people. Drinking water, restrooms with coin showers and flush toilets, vault toilets, picnic areas, visitors center, two boat ramps, and a fish-viewing plaza are available. There are two large barbecues, electrical outlets, lockable storage, five large picnic tables, restroom with showers and sinks, and an amphitheater in the group camp area. Some facilities are wheelchair-accessible. Leashed pets are permitted.

Reservations, fees: Reservations are not accepted for individual sites but are required for the group camp at 530/527-1196. Sites are $12–24 per night for individual sites; the group camp is $150 per night. Open April through October.

Directions: From I-5 at Red Bluff, turn east on Highway 36 and drive 100 yards to the first turnoff at Sale Lane. Turn right (south) on Sale Lane and drive 2.5 miles to the campground at the end of the road.

Contact: Mendocino National Forest, Red Bluff Recreation Area, 530/527-2813, fax 530/527-1312; Discovery Center, 530/527-1196.

123 TOMHEAD SADDLE

Scenic rating: 4

in Shasta-Trinity National Forest

Map grid B2

This one is way out there in remote wildlands. Little known and rarely visited, it's primarily a jump-off point for ambitious backpackers. The camp is on the edge of the Yolla Bolly-Middle Eel Wilderness. A trailhead here is routed to the South Fork of Cottonwood Creek, a trek that entails hiking eight miles in dry, hot terrain. The elevation is 5,700 feet.

RV sites, facilities: There are five sites for tents or RVs up to 16 feet (no hookups). Picnic tables and fire grills are provided. Vault toilets are available. No drinking water is available. Garbage must be packed out. Leashed pets are permitted.

Reservations, fees: Reservations are not accepted. There is no fee for camping. Open late June through mid-September, weather permitting.

Directions: From I-5 in Red Bluff, turn west on Highway 36 and drive about 13 miles to Cannon Road. Turn left on Cannon Road and drive about five miles to Pettyjohn Road. Turn west on Pettyjohn Road, drive to Saddle Camp and Forest Road 27N06. Turn south on Forest Road 27N06 and drive three miles to the campground on the left. It is advisable to obtain a map of Shasta-Trinity National Forest.

Contact: Shasta-Trinity National Forest, Yolla Bolly Ranger Station, 530/352-4211, fax 530/352-4312.

LASSEN
AND MODOC

(Family Destinations
Summit Lake: North, South, and Equestrian, page 689.

(Wildlife-Viewing
Indian Well, page 668.

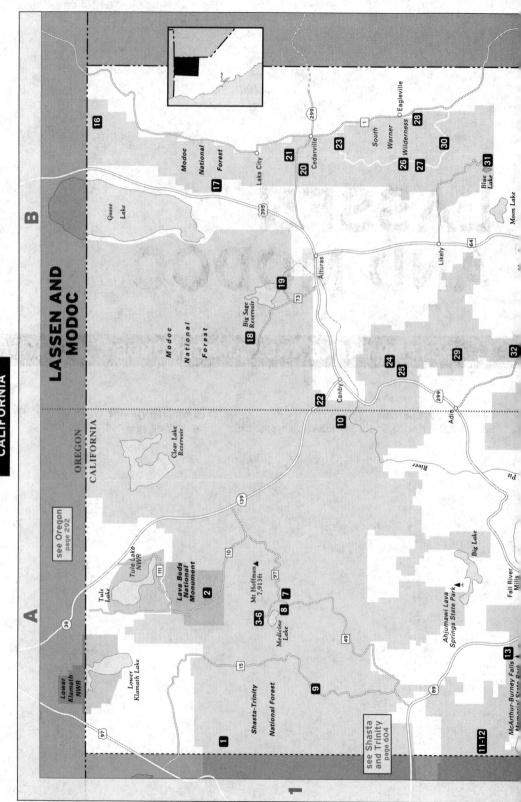

CALIFORNIA

LASSEN AND MODOC

see Oregon
page 292

see Shasta
and Trinity
page 604

OREGON

CALIFORNIA

Lower Klamath NWR

Lower Klamath Lake

Tule Lake NWR

Tule Lake

Clear Lake Reservoir

Goose Lake

Modoc National Forest

Big Sage Reservoir

Modoc National Forest

South Warner Wilderness

Lake City

Cedarville

Eagleville

Alturas

Canby

Likely

Adin

Blue Lake

Moon Lake

Big Lake

Fall River Mills

Pit River

Shasta-Trinity National Forest

Lava Beds National Monument

Mt Hoffman 7,913ft

Medicine Lake

Ahjumawi Lava Springs State Park

McArthur-Burney Falls State Park

97

139

111

15

10

97

49

89

395

299

73

299

64

1

16

17

18

19

20

21

22

23

24

25

26

27

28

29

30

31

32

10

1

2

3-6

7

8

9

1

13

11-12

A

B

1

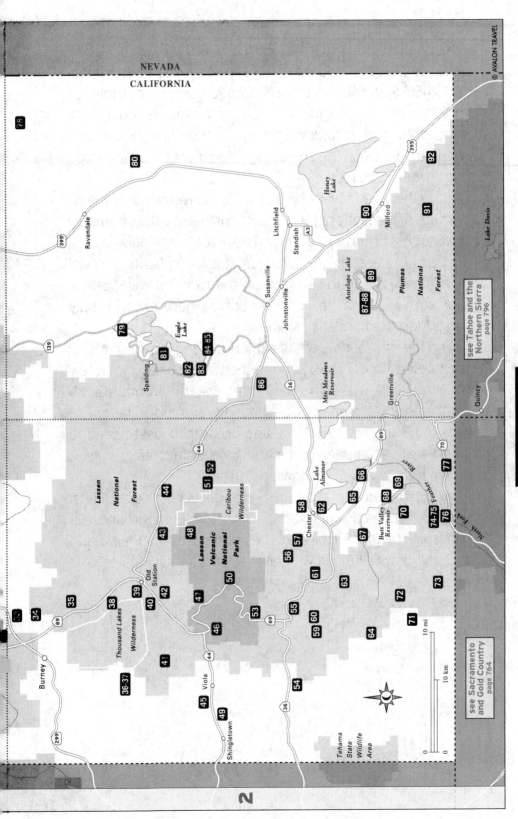

Mount Lassen and its awesome volcanic past seem to cast a shadow everywhere you go in this region. At 10,457 feet, the mountain's domed summit is visible for more than 100 miles in all directions. It blew its top in 1914, with continuing eruptions through 1918. Although now dormant, the volcanic-based geology dominates the landscape everywhere you look.

Of all the areas covered in this book, this region has the least number of romantic getaway spots. Instead it caters primarily to outdoors enthusiasts. And Lassen Volcanic National Park is one of the best places to lace up the hiking boots or spool new line on the reel. It's often off the radar of vacationers, making it one of the few national parks where you can enjoy the wilderness in relative solitude.

The national park is easily explored along the main route, the Lassen Park Highway. Along the way, you can pick a few trails for adventure. The best hikes are the Summit Climb (moderate to challenging), best done first thing in the morning, and Bumpass Hell (easy and great for kids) to see the sulfur vents and boiling mud pots. Another favorite for classic alpine beauty is the Shadow Lake Trail.

Unique features of the region include its pumice boulders, volcanic rock, and spring-fed streams from underground lava tubes. Highlights include the best still-water canoeing and fly-fishing at Fall River, Big Lake, and Ahjumawi State Park.

Ahjumawi is reached by canoe or powerboat only – a great boat-in campground with access to a matrix of clear, cold waters with giant trout.

Nearby is Burney Falls State Park, along with the Pit River and Lake Britton, which together make up one of Northern California's best recreation destinations for families. This is also one of the best areas for fly-fishing, especially at Hat Creek, Pit River, Burney Creek, and Manzanita Lake. For more beautiful settings, you can visit Lake Almanor and Eagle Lake, both of which provide lakeside campgrounds and excellent fishing and boating recreation.

And there's more. In remote Modoc County, you'll find Lava Beds National Monument and the South Warner Wilderness. Lava Beds is a stark, pretty, and often lonely place. It's sprinkled with small lakes full of trout, is home to large-antlered deer that migrate in after the first snow (and after the hunting season has closed), and features a unique volcanic habitat with huge flows of obsidian (dark, smooth, natural glass formed by the cooling of molten lava) and dacite (gray, craggy, volcanic flow). Lava Beds National Monument boasts about 500 caves and lava tubes, including the 6,000-foot Catacomb Tunnel. Nearby is pretty Medicine Lake, formed in a caldera, which provides good trout fishing, hiking, and exploring.

There are so many campgrounds that, no matter where you go, it seems you can always find a match for what you desire.

CALIFORNIA

1 SHAFTER

Scenic rating: 4

in Klamath National Forest

Map grid A1

This is a little-used camp, with trout fishing at nearby Butte Creek for small rainbows, primarily six- to eight-inchers. Little Orr Lake, about a 10-minute drive away on the southwest flank of Orr Mountain, provides fishing for bass and larger rainbow trout, 10- to 12-inchers, as well as a sprinkling of smaller brook trout. This camp is primitive and not well known, set in a juniper- and sage-filled landscape. The elevation is 4,300 feet. A great side trip is to the nearby Orr Mountain Lookout, where there are spectacular views of Mount Shasta. The road adjacent to the campground is paved, keeping the dust down—a Forest Service touch that is like gold in the summer.

RV sites, facilities: There are 10 sites for tents or RVs up to 28 feet (no hookups). Picnic tables and fire grills are provided. Drinking water and vault toilets are available. A boat ramp is available at Orr Lake. Garbage must be packed out. Leashed pets are permitted.

Reservations, fees: Reservations are not accepted. Sites are $6 per night. Open year-round, with limited services in winter.

Directions: From Redding, drive north on I-5 to Weed and the exit for Central Weed/Highway 97. Take that exit, turn right at the stop sign, drive through Weed and bear right (north) on Highway 97 and drive 40 miles to Ball Mountain Road. Turn right at Ball Mountain Road and drive 2.5 miles to a T with Old State Highway 97. Turn right and drive 4.25 miles (crossing railroad tracks) to the campground on the right side of the road.

Contact: Klamath National Forest, Goose-nest Ranger District, 530/398-4391, fax 530/398-5749.

2 INDIAN WELL

Scenic rating: 9

in Lava Beds National Monument

Map grid A1   BEST (

Lava Beds National Monument is a one-in-a-million spot, with more than 500 lava-tube caves, Schonchin Butte (a cinder cone with a hiking trail), Mammoth Crater, Native American petroglyphs and pictographs, battlefields and campsites from the Modoc War, and wildlife overlooks of Tule Lake. After winter's first snow, this is one of the best places in the West to photograph deer. Nearby is Klamath National Wildlife Refuge, the largest bald eagle wintering area in the lower 48. If you are new to the outdoors, an interpretive center is available to explain it all to you through informative displays. A visitors center is open year-round.

RV sites, facilities: There are 43 sites for tents or RVs up to 30 feet (no hookups). Picnic tables, fire rings, and cooking grills are provided. Drinking water and flush toilets are available. Some facilities are wheelchair-accessible. The town of Tulelake (30 miles north) is the nearest supply station. Leashed pets are permitted in the campground and roads only.

Reservations, fees: Reservations are not accepted. Sites are $10 per night plus $10 per vehicle park entrance fee. Maximum of eight campers per site. Open year-round.

Directions: From Redding, drive north on I-5 to the Central Weed/Highway 97 exit. Take that exit, turn right and continue for one mile to U.S. 97. Drive north on U.S. 97 for 54 miles to Highway 161. Turn east on Highway 161 and drive 20 miles to Hill Road. Turn right (south) and drive 18 miles to the visitors center and the campground entrance on the left. Turn left and drive 0.25 mile to the campground.

Contact: Lava Beds National Monument Visitor Center, 530/667-8113, www.nps.gov/labe.

3 MEDICINE

Scenic rating: 7

on Medicine Lake in Modoc National Forest

Map grid A1

Lakeside campsites tucked away in conifers make this camp a winner. Medicine Lake, at 640 acres, was formed in the crater of an old volcano and is surrounded by lodgepole pine and fir trees. The lake is stocked with rainbow and brook trout in the summer, gets quite cold in the fall, and freezes over in winter. All water sports are permitted. Many side trips are possible, including nearby Bullseye and Blanche Lakes and Ice Caves (both signed and off the access road) and Lava Beds National Monument just 15 miles north. At 6,700 feet, temperatures can drop in summer and the season is short.

RV sites, facilities: There are 22 sites for tents or RVs up to 30 feet (no hookups). Picnic tables and fire grills are provided. Drinking water and vault toilets are available. Ranger-guided cave tours, walks, and talks are available during the summer. A boat ramp is nearby. A café and bar are in Bartle; otherwise, no supplies are available within an hour's drive. Some facilities are wheelchair-accessible. Leashed pets are permitted.

Reservations, fees: Reservations are not accepted. Sites are $7 per vehicle per night. Open late May through early October, weather permitting.

Directions: From Redding, drive north on I-5 past Dunsmuir to Highway 89. Turn east on Highway 89 and drive 28 miles (just past Bartle) to Forest Road 15/Harris Springs Road. Turn left on Forest Road 15 and drive approximately five miles to the Y intersection with Forest Road 49/Medicine Lake Road. Turn right on Forest Road 49 and drive approximately 26 miles to the lake and campground access road.

Contact: Modoc National Forest, Doublehead Ranger District, 530/667-2246, fax 530/667-8609.

4 A. H. HOGUE

Scenic rating: 7

on Medicine Lake in Modoc National Forest

Map grid A1

This camp was created in 1990 when the original Medicine Lake Campground was divided in half. (For more information, see the Medicine listing.)

RV sites, facilities: There are 24 sites for tents or RVs up to 30 feet (no hookups). Picnic tables and fire grills are provided. Drinking water and vault toilets are available. A boat ramp is nearby. Some facilities are wheelchair-accessible. Leashed pets are permitted. A café and bar are in Bartle; otherwise, no supplies are available within an hour's drive.

Reservations, fees: Reservations are not accepted. Sites are $7 per vehicle per night. Open late May through early October, weather permitting.

Directions: From Redding, drive north on I-5 past Dunsmuir to Highway 89. Turn east on Highway 89 and drive 28 miles (just past Bartle) to Forest Road 15/Harris Springs Road. Turn left on Forest Road 15 and drive approximately five miles to the Y intersection with Forest Road 49/Medicine Lake Road. Turn right on Forest Road 49 and drive approximately 26 miles to the lake and campground access road.

Contact: Modoc National Forest, Doublehead Ranger District, 530/667-2246, fax 530/667-8609.

5 HEMLOCK

Scenic rating: 7

on Medicine Lake in Modoc National Forest

Map grid A1

This is one in a series of campgrounds on Medicine Lake operated by the Forest Service. A special attraction at Hemlock is the natural sand beach. (For more information, see the Medicine listing in this chapter.)

RV sites, facilities: There are 19 sites for tents or RVs up to 22 feet (no hookups). Picnic tables

CALIFORNIA

and fire grills are provided. Drinking water and vault toilets are available. A boat ramp is available nearby. Some facilities are wheelchair-accessible. Leashed pets are permitted. A café and bar are in Bartle; otherwise, no supplies are available within an hour's drive.

Reservations, fees: Reservations are not accepted. Sites are $7 per vehicle per night. Open late May through early October, weather permitting.

Directions: From Redding, drive north on I-5 past Dunsmuir to Highway 89. Turn east on Highway 89 and drive 28 miles (just past Bartle) to Forest Road 15/Harris Springs Road. Turn left on Forest Road 15 and drive approximately five miles to the Y intersection with Forest Road 49/Medicine Lake Road. Turn right on Forest Road 49 and drive approximately 26 miles to the lake and campground access road.

Contact: Modoc National Forest, Double-head Ranger District, 530/667-2246, fax 530/667-8609.

6 HEADQUARTERS

Scenic rating: 7

on Medicine Lake in Modoc National Forest

Map grid A1

This is one of four campgrounds set beside Medicine Lake. There is no lake access from this camp because of private property between the lake and campground. The elevation is 6,700 feet. (For more information, see the Medicine listing in this chapter.)

RV sites, facilities: There are 10 sites for tents or RVs up to 16 feet (no hookups). Picnic tables and fire grills are provided. Drinking water and vault toilets are available. A boat ramp is nearby. A café and bar are in Bartle; otherwise, no supplies are available within an hour's drive. Leashed pets are permitted.

Reservations, fees: Reservations are not accepted. Sites are $7 per vehicle per night. Open late May through early October, weather permitting.

Directions: From Redding, drive north on I-5 past Dunsmuir to Highway 89. Turn east on

Highway 89 and drive 28 miles (just past Bartle) to Forest Road 15/Harris Springs Road. Turn left on Forest Road 15 and drive approximately five miles to the Y intersection with Forest Road 49/Medicine Lake Road. Turn right on Forest Road 49 and drive approximately 26 miles to the lake and campground access road.

Contact: Modoc National Forest, Double-head Ranger District, 530/667-2246, fax 530/667-8609.

7 BULLSEYE LAKE

Scenic rating: 7

near Medicine Lake in Modoc National Forest

Map grid A1

This tiny lake gets overlooked every year, mainly because of its proximity to nearby Medicine Lake. Bullseye Lake is shallow, but because snow keeps it locked up until late May or early June, the water stays plenty cold for small trout through July. It is stocked with just 750 six- to eight-inch rainbow trout, not much to crow about—or to catch, for that matter. No boat motors are allowed. Nearby are some ice caves, created by ancient volcanic action. The place is small, quiet, and pretty, but most of all, small. This camp is set at an elevation of 6,500 feet.

RV sites, facilities: There are six sites for tents or RVs up to 22 feet (no hookups). Picnic tables and fire grills are provided. A vault toilet is available. No drinking water is available. Garbage must be packed out. Supplies are available in McCloud. A café and bar are in Bartle; otherwise, no supplies are available within an hour's drive. Leashed pets are permitted.

Reservations, fees: Reservations are not accepted. There is no fee for camping. Open late May through October, weather permitting.

Directions: From Redding, drive north on I-5 past Dunsmuir to Highway 89. Turn east on Highway 89 and drive 28 miles (just past Bartle) to Forest Road 15/Harris Springs Road. Turn left on Forest Road 15 and drive approximately five miles to the Y intersection with Forest Road 49/Medicine Lake Road. Turn right

CALIFORNIA

on Forest Road 49 and drive approximately 24 miles to the Bullseye Lake access road (if you reach Medicine Lake, you have gone about two miles too far). Turn right at the Bullseye Lake access road and drive a short distance past Blanche Lake, then turn right and drive a short distance to the lake.

Contact: Modoc National Forest, Double-head Ranger District, 530/667-2246, fax 530/667-8609.

8 PAYNE SPRINGS

Scenic rating: 8

near Medicine Lake in Modoc National Forest
Map grid A1

This camp is set by a small spring in a very pretty riparian area. It's small, but it is special.

RV sites, facilities: There are six dispersed sites for tents or RVs up to 20 feet (no hookups). Picnic tables and fire grills are provided. A vault toilet is available. No drinking water is available. Garbage must be packed out. A café and bar are in Bartle. Supplies are available in Tionesta, a 30-minute drive, or McCloud. Leashed pets are permitted.

Reservations, fees: Reservations are not accepted. There is no fee for camping. Open late May through October, weather permitting.

Directions: From Redding, drive north on I-5 drive past Dunsmuir to Highway 89. Turn east on Highway 89 and drive 28 miles (just past Bartle) to Forest Road 15/Harris Springs Road. Turn left on Forest Road 15 and drive approximately five miles to the Y intersection with Forest Road 49/Medicine Lake Road. Turn right on Forest Road 49 and drive 30 miles (0.2 mile past the Bullseye Lake access road) to the Payne Springs access road (if you reach Medicine Lake, you have gone too far). Turn left on the Payne Springs access road and drive a short distance to the campground.

Contact: Modoc National Forest, Double-head Ranger District, 530/667-2246, fax 530/667-8609.

9 HARRIS SPRINGS

Scenic rating: 3

in Shasta-Trinity National Forest
Map grid A1

This camp is a hidden spot in remote Shasta-Trinity National Forest, nestled in the long, mountainous ridge that runs east from Mount Shasta to Lava Beds National Monument. The camp is set at 4,800 feet, with a part-time fire station within a quarter mile on the opposite side of the access road. The area is best explored by four-wheel drive, venturing to a series of small buttes, mountaintops, and lookouts in the immediate area. A map of Shasta-Trinity National Forest is a must.

RV sites, facilities: There are 15 sites for tents or RVs up to 32 feet (no hookups). Picnic tables and fire grills are provided. There is no drinking water. Vault toilets are available. Garbage must be packed out. Leashed pets are permitted.

Reservations, fees: Reservations are not accepted. There is no fee for camping. Open late May through early October, weather permitting.

Directions: From Redding, drive north on I-5 past Dunsmuir to the junction with Highway 89. Turn east on Highway 89 and drive 28 miles (just past Bartle) to Forest Road 15/Harris Springs Road. Bear left on Forest Road 15 and drive five miles to the Y intersection with Harris Springs Road and Medicine Lake Road/Forest Road 49. Bear left at the Y, staying on Harris Springs Road/Forest Road 15, and drive 12 miles to a junction with a forest road signed for the Harris Springs Ranger Station. Turn right and drive a short distance, and look for the campground entrance on the right side of the road.

Contact: Shasta-Trinity National Forest, Mc-Cloud Ranger District, 530/964-2184, fax 530/964-2938.

CALIFORNIA

10 COTTONWOOD FLAT

Scenic rating: 6

in Modoc National Forest

Map grid A1

The camp is wooded and shady, set at 4,700 feet elevation in the rugged and remote Devil's Garden area of Modoc National Forest. The region is known for large mule deer, and Cottonwood Flat is well situated as a base camp for a hunting trip in the fall. The weather can get extremely cold early and late in the season.

RV sites, facilities: There are 10 sites for tents or RVs up to 16 feet (no hookups). Picnic tables and fire grills are provided. There is no drinking water. Vault toilets are available. Garbage must be packed out. Supplies are available within 10 miles in Canby. Leashed pets are permitted.

Reservations, fees: Reservations are not accepted. There is no fee for camping. Open May through October, weather permitting.

Directions: From Redding, drive east on Highway 299 for about 100 miles to Adin. Continue on Highway 299 for about 20 miles to the Canby Bridge at the Pit River and the junction with Forest Road 84. Turn left on Forest Road 84 and drive about eight miles to Forest Road 42N95. Turn right and drive 0.5 mile to the campground entrance on the left side of the road. Note: The access road is not recommended for RVs longer than 16 feet.

Contact: Modoc National Forest, Devil's Garden Ranger District, 530/233-5811, fax 530/233-8709.

11 DEADLUN

Scenic rating: 7

on Iron Canyon Reservoir in
Shasta-Trinity National Forest

Map grid A1

Deadlun is a pretty campground set in the forest, shaded and quiet, with a five-minute walk or one-minute drive to the Deadlun Creek arm of Iron Canyon Reservoir. Drive. If you have a canoe to launch or fishing equipment to carry, driving is the choice. Trout fishing is good here, both in April and May, then again in October and early November. One downer is that the shoreline is often very muddy here in March and early April. Because of an engineering error with the dam, the lake never fills completely, causing the lakeshore to be strewn with stumps and quite muddy after spring rains and snowmelt.

RV sites, facilities: There are 25 sites for tents or RVs up to 24 feet (no hookups). Picnic tables and fire grills are provided. Vault toilets are available. No drinking water is available. A small boat ramp is available one mile from the camp. Garbage must be packed out. Leashed pets are permitted.

Reservations, fees: Reservations are not accepted. There is no fee for camping. Open year-round.

Directions: From Redding, drive east on Highway 299 for 37 miles to Big Bend Road/County Road 7M01. Turn left and drive 17 miles to the town of Big Bend. Continue for five miles to the lake, bearing right at the T intersection, and continue for two miles (past the boat-launch turnoff) to the campground turnoff on the left side of the road. Turn left and drive one mile to the campground.

Contact: Shasta-Trinity National Forest, Shasta Lake Ranger District, 530/275-1587, fax 530/275-1512; Shasta Lake Visitor Center, 530/275-1589.

12 HAWKINS LANDING

Scenic rating: 7

on Iron Canyon Reservoir

Map grid A1

The adjacent boat ramp makes Hawkins Landing the better of the two camps at Iron Canyon Reservoir for campers with trailered boats (though Deadlun is far more secluded). Iron Canyon, with 15 miles of shoreline, provides good fishing for trout, has a resident bald eagle or two. One problem with this lake is the annual drawdown in late fall, which causes the shoreline to be extremely muddy in the spring. The lake usually rises high enough to make the boat ramp functional by mid-April. The best spot for swimming is near the earth dam, which is also a good put-in area for kayaks and canoes. This camp is set at an elevation of 2,700 feet.

RV sites, facilities: There are 10 sites for tents or RVs up to 30 feet (no hookups). Picnic tables and fire grills are provided. Drinking water, vault toilets, and a small boat ramp are available. Supplies can be obtained in Big Bend. Leashed pets are permitted.

Reservations, fees: Reservations are not accepted. Sites are $10 per night, $1 per pet per night, $3 per night for each additional vehicle, $7 per night for additional RV. Open mid-May through Labor Day weekend, weather permitting.

Directions: From Redding, drive east on Highway 299 for 37 miles to Big Bend Road. At Big Bend Road turn left and drive 15.2 miles to the town of Big Bend. Continue for 2.1 miles to Forest Road 38N11. Turn left and drive 3.3 miles to the Iron Canyon Reservoir Spillway. Turn right and drive 1.1 miles to a dirt road. Turn left and drive 0.3 mile to the campground.

Contact: PG&E Land Projects, 916/386-5164, www.pge.com/recreation.

13 NORTHSHORE

Scenic rating: 8

on Lake Britton
Map grid A1

This peaceful campground is set among the woodlands near the shore of Lake Britton, directly across the lake from McArthur-Burney Falls Memorial State Park. Boating and fishing are popular here, and once the water warms up in midsummer, swimming is also a winner. Boat rentals are available near the boat ramp. The lake has fair prospects for trout and is sometimes excellent for crappie. For side trips, the best trout fishing in the area is on the Pit River near Powerhouse Number Three. A hot

spring is available in Big Bend, about a 30-minute drive from camp. The elevation is 2,800 feet. Note: This is a bald eagle nesting area, and some areas are closed in spring when an active nest is verified.

RV sites, facilities: There are 30 sites for tents or RVs up to 30 feet (no hookups). Picnic tables and fire grills are provided. Drinking water and vault toilets are available. An unimproved boat ramp is available near the camp and an improved boat ramp is available in McArthur-Burney Falls State Park (about four miles away). Supplies can be obtained in Fall River Mills or Burney. Leashed pets are permitted.

Reservations, fees: Reservations are not accepted. Sites are $16 per night, $3 per night for each additional car, $7 per night per additional RV, $1 per pet per night. Open mid-May through mid-September, weather permitting.

Directions: From Redding, drive east on Highway 299 to Burney and then continue for five miles to Highway 89. Turn left (north) and drive 9.7 miles (past the state park entrance and over the Lake Britton Bridge) to Clark Creek Road. Turn left (west) and drive about a mile to the camp access road. Turn left and drive one mile to the camp.

Contact: PG&E Land Projects, 916/386-5164, www.pge.com/recreation.

14 McARTHUR-BURNEY FALLS MEMORIAL STATE PARK

Scenic rating: 9

in McArthur-Burney Falls Memorial State Park
Map grid A1

McArthur-Burney Falls Memorial State Park was originally formed by volcanic activity and features 910 acres of forest and five miles of stream and lake shore. The Headwaters horse camp is three miles from the main campground. (Non-equestrian campers may stay at the horse camp, but only tents are allowed.) The campground is pretty and set amid large ponderosa pines. Camping-style cabins were installed in 2008 and have been a hit here.

Burney Falls is a 129-foot waterfall, a beautiful cascade split at the top by a little grove of trees, with small trickles oozing and falling out of the adjacent moss-lined wall. Since it is fed primarily by a spring, it runs strong and glorious most of the year, producing 100 million gallons of water every day. The Headwaters Trail provides an outstanding hike, both to see the waterfall and Burney Creek, as well as for an easy adventure and fishing access to the stream. An excellent fly-fishing section of the Pit River is available below the dam. There are other stellar recreation options at this state park. At the end of the campground access road is a boat ramp for Lake Britton, with rentals available for canoes and paddleboats. This is a beautiful lake, with pretty canyon walls on its upper end, and good smallmouth bass (at rock piles) and crappie fishing (near the train trestle). There is also a good swimming beach. The Pacific Crest Trail is routed right through the park and provides an additional opportunity for a day hike, best explored downstream from the dam. Reservations for sites are essential during the summer.

RV sites, facilities: There are 128 sites for tents or RVs up to 32 feet (some with hookups), seven hike-in sites, and 24 wood cabins. Picnic tables, food lockers, and fire grills are provided. Drinking water, restrooms with flush toilets and showers, and a dump station are available. Vault toilets and a small horse corral are available at the horse camp. A grocery/gift store and boat rentals are available in the summer. Some facilities are wheelchair-accessible. Leashed pets are permitted, except on the trails and the beach.

Reservations, fees: Reservations are accepted for RV and tent sites and cabins at 800/444-PARK (800/444-7275) or www.reserveamerica.com ($8 reservation fee). RV and tent sites are $30 per night, cabins are $71.50 per night; $8 per night for each additional vehicle. Boat launching is $8 per day. Open year-round.

Directions: From Redding, drive east on Highway 299 to Burney and then continue for five miles to the junction with Highway 89. At Highway 89, turn north (left) and drive six miles to the campground entrance on the left side of the road.

Contact: McArthur-Burney Falls State Park, 530/335-2777, www.parks.ca.gov.

15 DUSTY CAMPGROUND

Scenic rating: 8

on Lake Britton

Map grid A1

This is one in a series of campgrounds near the north shore of Lake Britton. The lake has 18 miles of shoreline. (See Northshore listing in this chapter for more information.) The camp is set at an elevation of 2,800 feet. It provides an alternative to nearby McArthur-Burney Falls Memorial State Park, which is far more popular.

RV sites, facilities: There are seven sites for tents or RVs up to 30 feet (no hookups); two of the sites can accommodate groups of up to 25 people each. Fire rings are provided. Vault toilets are available. Drinking water is not available. Garbage must be packed out in winter. Some facilities are wheelchair-accessible. Leashed pets are permitted.

Reservations, fees: Reservations are not accepted. Sites are $6 per night, $3 per night for each additional vehicle, $7 per night per additional RV, $1 per pet per night, and $12 per night for double sites. Open year-round.

Directions: From Redding, drive east on Highway 299 to Burney and continue for five miles to the junction with Highway 89. Turn left (north) and drive 7.5 miles (past the state park entrance and over the Lake Britton Bridge) to the campground access road on the right (it will be confusing because the campground is on the left). Turn right and drive 0.75 mile (in the process crossing the highway) to the campground.

Contact: PG&E Land Projects, 916/386-5164, www.pge.com/recreation.

16 CAVE LAKE

Scenic rating: 8

in Modoc National Forest

Map grid B1

A pair of lakes can be discovered out here in the middle of nowhere, with Cave Lake on one end and Lily Lake on the other. Together they make a nice set, very quiet, extremely remote, with good fishing for rainbow trout and brook trout. A canoe, pram, or float tube can be ideal. No motors are permitted. Of the two lakes, it is nearby Lily Lake that is prettier and provides the better fishing. Cave Lake is set at 6,600 feet. By camping here, you become a member of the 5 Percent Club; that is, the 5 percent of campers who know of secret, isolated little spots such as this one.

RV sites, facilities: There are six sites for tents or RVs up to 15 feet (no hookups); trailers are not advised because of the steep access road. Picnic tables and fire grills are provided. There is no drinking water. Vault toilets are available. Garbage must be packed out. Motors (including electric) are prohibited on the lake. Supplies are available in New Pine Creek and Davis Creek. Leashed pets are permitted.

Reservations, fees: Reservations are not accepted. There is no fee for camping. Open July through October, weather permitting.

Directions: From Redding, drive east on Highway 299 for 146 miles to Alturas and U.S. 395. Turn north on U.S. 395 and drive 40 miles to Forest Road 2 (if you reach the town of New Pine Creek on the Oregon/California border, you have driven a mile too far). Turn right on Forest Road 2 (a steep dirt road—trailers are not recommended) and drive six miles to the campground entrance on the left side of the road, just beyond the Lily Lake picnic area.

Contact: Modoc National Forest, Warner Mountain Ranger District, 530/279-6116, fax 530/279-8309.

17 PLUM VALLEY

Scenic rating: 7

near the South Fork of Davis Creek in Modoc National Forest

Map grid B1

This secluded and primitive camp is set near the South Fork of Davis Creek, at 5,600 feet elevation. Davis Creek offers catch-and-release, barbless hook, no-bait fishing. You can, however, keep the brown trout. There are no other campgrounds within 15 miles.

RV sites, facilities: There are 15 sites for tents or RVs up to 15 feet (no hookups). Picnic tables and fire grills are provided. Vault toilets are available. No drinking water is available. Garbage must be packed out. Supplies are available in Davis Creek, about 3.5 miles away. Leashed pets are permitted.

Reservations, fees: Reservations are not accepted. There is no fee for camping. Open May through September.

Directions: From Alturas drive north on U.S. 395 for 18 miles to the town of Davis Creek and County Road 11. Turn right on County Road 11 and drive two miles to a Y. Bear right on Forest Road 45N35 and drive one mile to the signed entrance to the campground on the left side of the road.

Contact: Modoc National Forest, Warner Mountain Ranger District, 530/279-6116, fax 530/279-8309; Department of Fish and Game fishing information, 530/225-2146.

18 RESERVOIR C

Scenic rating: 6

near Alturas in Modoc National Forest

Map grid B1

It is one great adventure to explore the "alphabet lakes" in the remote Devil's Garden area of Modoc County. Reservoir C and Reservoir F provide the best of the lot, but the success can go up and down like a yo-yo, just like the water levels in the lakes. Reservoir C is stocked with both Eagle Lake trout and brown trout. A sidelight to this area is the number of primitive roads that are routed through Modoc National Forest, perfect for four-wheel-drivers. The elevation is 4,900 feet.

RV sites, facilities: There are six sites for tents or RVs up to 22 feet (no hookups). Picnic tables and fire grills are provided. Vault toilets and a primitive boat ramp are available. No drinking water is available. Garbage must be packed out. Some facilities are wheelchair-accessible. Leashed pets are permitted.

Reservations, fees: Reservations are not accepted. There is no fee for camping. Open May through September.

Directions: From Alturas drive west on Highway 299 for three miles to Crowder Flat Road/County Road 73. Turn right on Crowder Flat Road and drive 9.5 miles to Triangle Ranch Road/Forest Road 43N18. Turn left on Triangle Ranch Road and drive seven miles to Forest Road 44N32. Turn right on Forest Road 44N32, drive 0.5 mile, turn right on the access road for the lake and campground, and drive 0.5 mile to the camp at the end of the road.

Contact: Modoc National Forest, Doublehead Ranger District, 530/667-2246, fax 530/667-8309.

19 BIG SAGE RESERVOIR

Scenic rating: 5

in Modoc National Forest

Map grid B1

This is a do-it-yourself camp; that is, pick your own spot, bring your own water, and don't expect to see anybody else. This camp is set along Big Sage Reservoir—that's right, sagebrush country at 5,100 feet elevation. It is a big lake, covering 5,000 surface acres, and a boat ramp is adjacent to the campground. This is one of the better bass lakes in Modoc County. Catfish and crappie are also here. Water sports are allowed, except for personal watercraft. Swimming is not recommended

because of algae growth in midsummer, murky water, and muddy shoreline. Water levels can fluctuate greatly.

RV sites, facilities: There are six sites for tents or RVs up to 22 feet (no hookups). Picnic tables and fire grills are provided. Vault toilets are available. There is no drinking water. Some facilities are wheelchair-accessible. Garbage must be packed out. A boat ramp is available nearby. Leashed pets are permitted. Supplies can be obtained in Alturas, about eight miles away.

Reservations, fees: Reservations are not accepted. There is no fee for camping. Open May through September.

Directions: From Alturas, drive west on Highway 299 for three miles to Crowder Flat Road/County Road 73. Turn right on Crowder Flat Road and drive about five miles to County Road 180. Turn right on County Road 180 and drive four miles. Turn left at the access road for the campground and boat ramp and drive a short distance to the camp on the left side of the road.

Contact: Modoc National Forest, Doublehead Ranger District, 530/667-2246, fax 530/667-8309.

20 CEDAR PASS

Scenic rating: 5

on Cedar Pass in Modoc National Forest

Map grid B1

Cedar Pass is at 5,600 feet, set on the ridge between Cedar Mountain (8,152 feet) to the north and Payne Peak (7,618) to the south, high in the north Warner Mountains. Bear Creek enters Thomas Creek adjacent to the camp; both are small streams, but it's a pretty spot.

RV sites, facilities: There are 17 sites for tents or RVs up to 16 feet (no hookups). Picnic tables and fire grills are provided. Vault toilets are available. No drinking water is available. Garbage must be packed out. Supplies can be obtained in Cedarville or Alturas. Leashed pets are permitted.

Reservations, fees: Reservations are not

accepted. There is no fee for camping. Open late May through October, weather permitting.

Directions: From Redding drive east on Highway 299 to Alturas. In Alturas continue north on Highway 299/U.S. 395 for five miles to the split for Highway 299. Turn right on Highway 299 and drive about nine miles. Look for the signed entrance road on the right side of the road.

Contact: Modoc National Forest, Warner Mountain Ranger District, 530/279-6116, fax 530/279-8309.

21 STOUGH RESERVOIR

Scenic rating: 8

in Modoc National Forest
Map grid B1

Stough Reservoir looks like a large country pond where cattle might drink. You know why? Because it once actually was a cattle pond on a family ranch that has since been converted to Forest Service property. It is in the north Warner Mountains (not to be confused with the South Warner Wilderness), which features many back roads and remote four-wheel-drive routes. The camp is set at an elevation of 6,200 feet. Note that you may find this campground named "Stowe Reservoir" on some maps and in previous editions of this book. The name is now officially spelled "Stough Reservoir," after the family that originally owned the property.

RV sites, facilities: There are 14 sites for tents or RVs up to 22 feet (no hookups). Picnic tables and fire grills are provided. Drinking water and vault toilets are available. Garbage must be packed out. Leashed pets are permitted. Supplies can be obtained in Cedarville, six miles away.

Reservations, fees: Reservations are not accepted. There is no fee for camping. Open late May through early October, weather permitting.

Directions: From Redding, drive east on Highway 299 to Alturas. In Alturas, continue north on Highway 299/U.S. 395 for five miles to the split-off for Highway 299. Turn right on

Highway 299 and drive about 12 miles (just past Cedar Pass). Look for the signed entrance road on the left side of the road. Turn left and drive one mile to the campground on the left side of the road.

Contact: Modoc National Forest, Warner Mountain Ranger District, 530/279-6116, fax 530/279-8309.

22 HOWARD'S GULCH

Scenic rating: 6

near Duncan Reservoir in Modoc National Forest
Map grid B1

This is the nearest campground to Duncan Reservoir, three miles to the north and stocked with trout each year by the Department of Fish and Game. The camp is set in the typically sparse woods of Modoc National Forest, but a beautiful grove of aspen is three miles to the west on Highway 139, on the left side of the road. By the way, Highway 139 isn't much of a highway at all, but it is paved and will get you there. The elevation is 4,700 feet.

RV sites, facilities: There are 11 sites for tents or RVs up to 22 feet (no hookups). Picnic tables and fire grills are provided. Drinking water and vault toilets are available. Some facilities are wheelchair-accessible. Supplies are available within five miles in Canby. Leashed pets are permitted.

Reservations, fees: Reservations are not accepted. Sites are $6 per night. Open May through October, weather permitting.

Directions: From Redding, drive east on Highway 299 for about 100 miles to Adin. Continue on Highway 299 for about 25 miles to Highway 139. Turn left (northwest) on Highway 139 and drive six miles to the campground on the left side of the road.

Contact: Modoc National Forest, Devil's Garden Ranger District, 530/233-5811, fax 530/233-8709.

23 PEPPERDINE

Scenic rating: 5

in Modoc National Forest

Map grid B1

This camp is outstanding for hikers planning a backpacking trip into the adjacent South Warner Wilderness. The camp is at 6,680 feet, set along the south side of tiny Porter Reservoir, with a horse corral within walking distance. A trailhead out of camp provides direct access to the Summit Trail, the best hike in the South Warner Wilderness.

RV sites, facilities: There are five sites for tents or RVs up to 16 feet (no hookups). Picnic tables and fire grills are provided. Drinking water and vault toilets are available. Corrals are available with water for stock. Garbage must be packed out. Supplies are available in Cedarville or Alturas. Leashed pets are permitted.

Reservations, fees: Reservations are not accepted. There is no fee for camping. Open July through October, weather permitting.

Directions: In Alturas, drive south on U.S. 395 to the southern end of town and County Road 56. Turn left on County Road 56 and drive 13 miles to the Modoc Forest boundary and the junction with Parker Creek Road. Bear left on Parker Creek Road and continue for six miles to the signed campground access road on the right. Turn right and drive 0.5 mile to the campground on the left side of the road.

Contact: Modoc National Forest, Warner Mountain Ranger District, 530/279-6116, fax 530/279-8309.

24 UPPER RUSH CREEK

Scenic rating: 8

in Modoc National Forest

Map grid B1

Upper Rush Creek is a pretty campground, set along Rush Creek, a quiet, wooded spot that gets little use. It sits in the shadow of nearby Manzanita Mountain (7,036 feet elevation) to the east, where there is a Forest Service lookout

for a great view. To reach the lookout, drive back toward Highway 299 and when you reach the paved road, County Road 198, turn left and drive 0.5 mile to Forest Road 22. Turn left on Forest Road 22 and head up the hill. One mile from the summit, turn left at a four-way junction and drive to the top. You get dramatic views of the Warm Springs Valley to the north and the Likely Flats to the east, looking across miles and miles of open country.

RV sites, facilities: There are 13 sites for tents or RVs up to 22 feet (no hookups), but Lower Rush Creek is better for trailers. Picnic tables and fire grills are provided. Vault toilets are available. There is no drinking water. Supplies can be obtained about nine miles away in Adin or Canby. Leashed pets are permitted.

Reservations, fees: Reservations are not accepted. There is no camping fee. Open May through October, weather permitting.

Directions: From Redding, turn east on Highway 299 and drive to Adin. Continue east on Highway 299 for about seven miles to a signed campground turnoff on the right side of the road. Turn right and drive to the junction with Forest Road 40N05. Turn left and drive 2.5 miles to the campground at the end of the road.

Contact: Modoc National Forest, Big Valley Ranger District, 530/299-3215, fax 530/299-8409.

25 LOWER RUSH CREEK

Scenic rating: 6

on Rush Creek in Modoc National Forest

Map grid B1

This is one of two obscure campgrounds set a short distance from Highway 299 on Rush Creek in southern Modoc County. Lower Rush Creek is the first camp you will come to, with flat campsites surrounded by an outer fence and set along Rush Creek. This camp is better suited for trailers than the one at Upper Rush Creek. It is little known and little used. It's set at 4,400 feet elevation.

RV sites, facilities: There are 10 sites for tents

or RVs up to 22 feet (no hookups). Picnic tables and fire grills are provided. Vault toilets are available. There is no drinking water. Supplies are available in Adin or Canby. Leashed pets are permitted.

Reservations, fees: Reservations are not accepted. There is no camping fee. Open May through October, weather permitting.

Directions: From Redding, turn east on Highway 299 and drive to Adin. Continue east on Highway 299 for about seven miles to a signed campground turnoff on the right side of the road. Turn right and drive to the junction with Forest Road 40N05. Turn left and drive one mile to the campground on the right.

Contact: Modoc National Forest, Big Valley Ranger District, 530/299-3215, fax 530/299-8409.

26 SOUP SPRINGS

Scenic rating: 8

in Modoc National Forest
Map grid B1

This is a beautiful, quiet, wooded campground at a trailhead into the South Warner Wilderness. Soup Creek originates at Soup Springs in the meadow adjacent to the campground. The trailhead here is routed two miles into the wilderness, where it junctions with the Mill Creek Trail. From here, turn left for a beautiful walk along Mill Creek and into Mill Creek Meadow, an easy yet pristine stroll that can provide a serene experience. The elevation is 6,800 feet.

RV sites, facilities: There are 14 sites for tents or RVs up to 22 feet (no hookups). Picnic tables and fire grills are provided. Drinking water and vault toilets are available. Corrals are also available. Supplies can be obtained in Likely. Leashed pets are permitted.

Reservations, fees: Reservations are not accepted. Sites are $6 per night. Open June through October, weather permitting.

Directions: From Alturas, drive south on U.S. 395 for 17 miles to the town of Likely, where

you'll come to Jess Valley Road. Turn left on Jess Valley Road/County Road 64 and drive nine miles to the fork. Bear left on West Warner Road/Forest Road 5 and go 4.5 miles to Soup Loop Road. Turn right on Soup Loop Road/Forest Road 40N24 and continue on that gravel road for six miles to the campground entrance on the right.

Contact: Modoc National Forest, Warner Mountain Ranger District, 530/279-6116, fax 530/279-8309.

27 MILL CREEK FALLS

Scenic rating: 9

in Modoc National Forest
Map grid B1

This nice, wooded campground is a good base camp for a backpacking trip into the South Warner Wilderness. The camp is set on Mill Creek at 5,700 feet elevation. To see Mill Creek Falls, take the trail out of camp and bear left at the Y. To enter the interior of the South Warner Wilderness, bear right at the Y, after which the trail passes Clear Lake, heads to Poison Flat and Poison Creek, and then reaches a junction. Left will take you to the Mill Creek Trail; right will take you up to the Summit Trail. Take your pick. You can't go wrong.

RV sites, facilities: There are 19 sites for tents or RVs up to 22 feet (no hookups). Picnic tables and fire grills are provided. Drinking water and vault toilets are available. Supplies are available in Likely. Leashed pets are permitted.

Reservations, fees: Reservations are not accepted. Sites are $6 per night. Open June through October, weather permitting.

Directions: From Alturas drive 17 miles south on U.S. 395 to the town of Likely, where you'll come to Jess Valley Road. Turn left on Jess Valley Road/County Road 64 and drive nine miles to the fork. Bear left on West Warner Road/Forest Road 5 and drive 2.5 miles to Forest Road 40N46. Turn right on Forest Road 40N46 and drive two miles to the campground entrance at the end of the road.

CALIFORNIA

Contact: Modoc National Forest, Warner Mountain Ranger District, 530/279-6116, fax 530/279-8309.

28 EMERSON

Scenic rating: 6

in Modoc National Forest

Map grid B1

This tiny camp is virtually unknown, nestled at 6,000 feet on the eastern boundary of the South Warner Wilderness. Big alkali lakes and miles of the Nevada flats can be seen on the other side of the highway as you drive along the entrance road to the campground. A trailhead at this primitive setting is used by hikers and backpackers. Note that hitting the trail is a steep, sometimes wrenching climb for 4.5 miles to North Emerson Lake (poor to fair fishing). For many, this hike is a true butt-kicker.

RV sites, facilities: There are four sites for tents or RVs up to 16 feet (no hookups). Picnic tables and fire grills are provided. Vault toilets are available. No drinking water is available. Garbage must be packed out. Supplies can be obtained in Eagleville. Leashed pets are permitted.

Reservations, fees: Reservations are not accepted. There is no fee for camping. Open July through October, weather permitting.

Directions: From Alturas, drive north on U.S. 395/Highway 299 for about five miles to the junction with Highway 299. Turn right on Highway 299 and drive to Cedarville and County Road 1. Turn south on County Road 1 and drive to Eagleville. From Eagleville, continue south on County Road 1 for 1.5 miles to Forest Road 40N43/County Road 40. Turn right and drive three miles to the campground at the end of the road. The access road is steep, narrow, and very slick in wet weather. Trailers are not recommended.

Contact: Modoc National Forest, Warner Mountain Ranger District, 530/279-6116, fax 530/279-8309.

29 ASH CREEK

Scenic rating: 7

in Modoc National Forest

Map grid B1

This remote camp has stark beauty and is set at 4,800 feet along Ash Creek, a stream with small trout. This region of Modoc National Forest has an extensive network of backcountry roads, popular with deer hunters in the fall. The Ash Creek Wildlife Area is about 10 miles west of camp. Summer comes relatively late out here, and it can be cold and wet even in early June. Stash some extra clothes, just in case. That will probably guarantee nice weather.

RV sites, facilities: There are seven sites for tents or RVs up to 22 feet (no hookups). Picnic tables and fire grills are provided. Vault toilets are available. No drinking water is available. Garbage must be packed out. Supplies can be obtained in Adin. Leashed pets are permitted.

Reservations, fees: Reservations are not accepted. There is no fee for camping. Open May through October, weather permitting.

Directions: From Redding, turn east on Highway 299 and drive to Adin and Ash Valley Road. Turn right on Ash Valley Road/County Road 88/527 and drive eight miles. Turn left at the signed campground turnoff and drive a mile to the campground on the right side of the road.

Contact: Modoc National Forest, Big Valley Ranger District, 530/299-3215, fax 530/299-8409; Ash Creek Wildlife Area, 530/294-5824.

30 PATTERSON

Scenic rating: 4

in Modoc National Forest

Map grid B1

Patterson is set across the road from Patterson Meadow at 7,200 feet elevation. This beautiful landscape was burned by the Blue Fire of 2001, which enveloped 35,000 acres in the South Warners. During the past several years vegetation growth has improved the area's scenic beauty and it is now recovering.

There are both positives and negatives to the burn. The positives are a chance for much wider and longer views previously impossible, as well as the opportunity to watch the evolution of the landscape in a post-fire setting, as has been the case in Yellowstone for years. The negatives are the tree skeletons. The most affected area is to the east, especially on East Creek Trail, which rises through the burned area to a high, barren mountain rim.

RV sites, facilities: There are five sites for tents or RVs up to 20 feet (no hookups). Picnic tables and fire grills are provided. Drinking water and vault toilets are available. Garbage must be packed out. Supplies are available in Likely or Cedarville. Leashed pets are permitted.

Reservations, fees: Reservations are not accepted. There is no fee for camping. Open late July through October, weather permitting.

Directions: From Alturas drive 17 miles south on U.S. 395 to the town of Likely. Turn left on Jess Valley Road/County Road 64 and drive nine miles to the fork. Bear right on Forest Road 64 and drive for 16 miles to the campground on the left.

Contact: Modoc National Forest, Warner Mountain Ranger District, 530/279-6116, fax 530/279-8309.

31 BLUE LAKE

Scenic rating: 6

in Modoc National Forest
Map grid B1

The Blue Fire of 2001 burned 35,000 acres in this area, including the east and west slopes adjoining Blue Lake. Yet get this: The campground was untouched. It is a strange scene, a somewhat wooded campground (with some level campsites) near the shore of Blue Lake. The lake covers 160 acres and provides fishing for large brown trout and rainbow trout. A 5-mph speed limit assures quiet water for small boats and canoes. A trail circles the lake and takes less than an hour to hike. The elevation is 6,000 feet. Bald eagles have been spotted here. While their presence negates year-round use of six campsites otherwise

available, the trade-off is an unprecedented opportunity to view the national bird.

RV sites, facilities: There are 48 sites for tents or RVs up to 22 feet (no hookups). Picnic tables and fire grills are provided. Drinking water and vault toilets are available. Some facilities are wheelchair-accessible, including a paved boat launch and fishing pier. Supplies are available in Likely. Leashed pets are permitted.

Reservations, fees: Reservations are not accepted. Sites are $7 per night. Open June through October, weather permitting.

Directions: From Alturas, drive south on U.S. 395 for seven miles to the town of Likely, where you'll come to Jess Valley Road. Turn left on Jess Valley Road/County Road 64 and drive nine miles to the fork. At the fork, bear right on Forest Road 64 and drive seven miles to Forest Road 38N30. Turn right on Forest Road 38N30 and drive two miles to the campground.

Contact: Modoc National Forest, Warner Mountain Ranger District, 530/279-6116, fax 530/279-8309.

32 WILLOW CREEK

Scenic rating: 7

in Modoc National Forest
Map grid B1

This remote camp and picnic area is set at 5,200 feet along little Willow Creek amid pine, aspen, and willows. On the north side of the campground is Lower McBride Springs.

RV sites, facilities: There are eight sites for tents or RVs up to 22 feet (no hookups). Picnic tables and fire grills are provided. Drinking water and vault toilets are available. A wheelchair-accessible toilet is at the picnic area next to the campground. Leashed pets are permitted.

Reservations, fees: Reservations are not accepted. Sites are $7 per night. Open May through October, weather permitting.

Directions: From Redding, drive east on Highway 299 to Adin and Highway 139. Turn right on Highway 139 and drive 14 miles to the campground on the left side of the road.

Contact: Modoc National Forest, Big Valley Ranger District, 530/299-3215, fax 530/299-8409.

33 PIT RIVER

Scenic rating: 6

on the Pit River
Map grid A2

Very few out-of-towners know about this hidden campground set along the Pit River. It can provide a good base camp for a fishing trip adventure. The best stretch of trout water on the Pit is near Powerhouse Number Three. In addition to fishing there are many other recreation options. A parking area and trail along Hat Creek are available where the Highway 299 bridge crosses Hat Creek. Baum Lake, Crystal Lake, and the Cassel section of Hat Creek are all within five miles of this camp.

RV sites, facilities: There are seven sites for tents or RVs up to 40 feet (no hookups), and one double site for up to eight people. Picnic tables and fire rings are provided. Vault toilets, wheelchair-accessible fishing pier, and small-craft launch ramp are available. No drinking water is available. Garbage must be packed out. There are supplies and a coin laundry in Fall River Mills. Some facilities are wheelchair-accessible. Leashed pets are permitted.

Reservations, fees: Reservations are not accepted. Sites are $8 per night, and $12 per night for the double site. Open mid-April through mid-November.

Directions: From Redding, drive east on Highway 299 to Burney and continue for five miles to the junction with Highway 89. At the junction, continue straight on Highway 299, cross the Pit River Bridge, and drive about three miles to Pit One Powerhouse Road. Turn right and drive down the hill to the Pit River Lodge. Turn right and drive 0.5 mile to the campground.

Contact: Bureau of Land Management, Alturas Field Office, 530/233-4666, fax 530/233-5696.

34 CASSEL

Scenic rating: 8

on Hat Creek
Map grid A2

This camp is set at 3,200 feet in the beautiful Hat Creek Valley. It is an outstanding location for a fishing trip base camp, with nearby Crystal Lake, Baum Lake, and Hat Creek (all set in the Hat Creek Valley) providing trout fishing. This section of Hat Creek is well known for its challenging fly-fishing. A good source of fishing information is Vaughn's Sporting Goods in Burney. Baum Lake is ideal for car-top boats with electric motors.

RV sites, facilities: There are 27 sites for tents or RVs up to 30 feet (no hookups). Picnic tables and fire grills are provided. Drinking water and vault toilets are available. Some facilities are wheelchair-accessible. Leashed pets are permitted.

Reservations, fees: Reservations are not accepted. Sites are $16 per night, $3 per night for each additional vehicle, $7 per night per additional RV, $1 per pet per night. Open mid-April through mid-November, weather permitting.

Directions: From Redding, drive east on Highway 299 to Burney and continue for five miles to the junction with Highway 89. At the junction, continue straight on Highway 299 for two miles to Cassel Road. At Cassel Road, turn right and drive 3.6 miles to the campground entrance on the left.

Contact: PG&E Land Projects, 916/386-5164, www.pge.com/recreation.

35 HAT CREEK HEREFORD RANCH RV PARK AND CAMPGROUND

Scenic rating: 8

near Hat Creek
Map grid A2

This privately operated campground is set in a working cattle ranch. Campers are not allowed near the cattle pasture or cattle. Fishing is available in Hat Creek or in the nearby stocked trout pond. Swimming is also allowed in the pond. Sightseeing is excellent with Burney Falls, Lassen Volcanic National Park, and Subway Caves all within 30 miles.

RV sites, facilities: There are 40 tent sites and 40 RV sites with full or partial hookups (30 amps); some sites are pull-through. Picnic tables and fireplaces are provided. Restrooms with showers, a dump station, coin laundry, playground, modem hookups, wireless Internet access, and a convenience store are available. Some facilities are wheelchair-accessible. Leashed pets are permitted.

Reservations, fees: Reservations are recommended and can be made by telephone or website. RV sites are $24.75–27.50 per night, tent sites are $19.50–25.50 per night, $2 per night for more than two people, $1 per night per pet. Some credit cards accepted. Open April through October.

Directions: From Redding, drive east on Highway 299 to Burney and continue for five miles to the junction with Highway 89. Turn right (south) on Highway 89 and drive 12 miles to the second Doty Road Loop exit. Turn left and drive 0.5 mile to the park entrance on the right.

Contact: Hat Creek Hereford Ranch RV Park and Campground, 530/335-7171 or 877/459-9532, www.hatcreekrv.com.

36 OLD COW MEADOWS

Scenic rating: 7

in Latour Demonstration State Forest

Map grid A2

Nobody finds this campground without this book. You want quiet? You don't want to be bugged by anybody? This tiny camp, virtually unknown, is set at 5,900 feet in a wooded area along Old Cow Creek. Recreation options include all-terrain-vehicle use on existing roads and walking the dirt roads that crisscross the area.

RV sites, facilities: There are three sites for tents or RVs up to 25 feet (no hookups). Picnic tables and fire grills are provided. Vault toilets and drinking water are available. Garbage must be packed out. Some facilities are wheelchair-accessible. Leashed pets are permitted.

Reservations, fees: Reservations are not accepted. There is no fee for camping. Open June through October, weather permitting.

Directions: In Redding, turn east on Highway 44 and drive about 9.5 miles to Millville Road. Turn left on Millville Road and drive 0.5 mile to the intersection of Millville Road and Whitmore Road. Turn right on Whitmore Road and drive 13 miles, through Whitmore, until Whitmore Road becomes Tamarac Road. Continue for one mile to a fork at Bateman Road. Take the right fork on Bateman Road, drive 3.5 miles (where the road turns to gravel), and then continue 10 miles to Huckleberry Road. Turn right on Huckleberry Road and drive two miles to the campground.

Contact: Latour Demonstration State Forest, 530/225-2438, fax 530/225-2514.

37 SOUTH COW CREEK MEADOWS

Scenic rating: 6

in Latour Demonstration State Forest

Map grid A2

This camp is set in a pretty, wooded area next to a small meadow along South Cow Creek. It's used mostly in the fall for hunting, with off-highway-vehicle use on the surrounding roads in the summer. The camp is set at 5,600 feet. If you want to get away from it all without leaving your vehicle, this is one way to do it. The creek is a reliable water source, providing you use a water filtration pump.

RV sites, facilities: There are four sites for tents or RVs up to 30 feet (no hookups). Picnic tables and fire grills are provided. Vault toilets and drinking water are available. Garbage must be packed out. Some facilities are wheelchair-accessible. Leashed pets are permitted.

Reservations, fees: Reservations are not accepted. There is no fee for camping. Open June through October, weather permitting.

Directions: In Redding, turn east on Highway 44 and drive about 9.5 miles to Millville Road. Turn left on Millville Road and drive 0.5 mile to the intersection of Millville Road and Whitmore Road. Turn right on Whitmore Road and drive 13 miles, through Whitmore, until Whitmore Road becomes Tamarac Road. Continue for one mile to the fork at Bateman Road. Take the right fork on Bateman Road, drive 3.5 miles (where the road turns to gravel), and then continue for 11 miles to South Cow Creek Road. Turn right (east) and drive one mile to the campground.

Contact: Latour Demonstration State Forest, 530/225-2438, fax 530/225-2514.

38 BRIDGE CAMP

🚶 🎣 🐾 🚐 ⛺

Scenic rating: 7

on Hat Creek in Lassen National Forest

Map grid A2

This camp is one of four along Highway 89 in the area along Hat Creek. It is set at 4,000 feet elevation, with shaded sites and the stream within very short walking distance. Trout are stocked on this stretch of the creek, with fishing access available out of camp, as well as at Rocky and Cave Camps to the south and Honn to the north. In one weekend, anglers might hit all four.

RV sites, facilities: There are 25 sites for tents or RVs up to 22 feet (no hookups). Picnic tables and fire grills are provided. There is no drinking water. Vault toilets are available. A grocery store and propane gas are nearby. Leashed pets are permitted.

Reservations, fees: Reservations are not accepted. Sites are $10 per night, $5 per night for each additional vehicle. Open late April through October, weather permitting.

Directions: From Redding, drive east on Highway 299 to Burney and continue for five miles to the junction with Highway 89. Turn right

(south) on Highway 89 and drive 19 miles to the campground entrance on the right side of the road. If you reach Old Station, you have gone five miles too far.

Contact: Lassen National Forest, Hat Creek Ranger District, 530/336-5521, fax 530/336-5758; Department of Fish and Game fishing information, 530/225-2146.

39 CAVE CAMP

🚶 🎣 🐾 ♿ 🚐 ⛺

Scenic rating: 7

on Hat Creek in Lassen National Forest

Map grid A2

Cave Camp is set right along Hat Creek, with easy access off Highway 89 and an anglers' trail available along the stream. This stretch of Hat Creek is planted with rainbow trout twice per month by the Department of Fish and Game, starting with the opening of trout season on the last Saturday of April. Nearby side trips include Lassen Volcanic National Park, about a 15-minute drive to the south on Highway 89, and Subway Caves (turn left at the junction just across the road from the campground). A rare bonus at this camp is that wheelchair-accessible fishing is available.

RV sites, facilities: There are 46 sites for tents or RVs up to 22 feet (no hookups). Picnic tables and fire grills are provided. Drinking water and flush and vault toilets are available. Some facilities are wheelchair-accessible. Supplies can be obtained in Old Station. Leashed pets are permitted.

Reservations, fees: Reservations are not accepted. Sites are $16 per night, $5 per night for each additional vehicle. Open late April through October, weather permitting.

Directions: From Redding, drive east on Highway 299 to Burney and continue for five miles to the junction with Highway 89. Turn right (south) on Highway 89 and drive 23 miles to the campground entrance on the right side of the road. If you reach Old Station, you have gone one mile too far.

Contact: Lassen National Forest, Hat Creek

Ranger District, 530/336-5521, fax 530/336-5758; Department of Fish and Game fishing information, 530/225-2146.

40 HAT CREEK

Scenic rating: 7

on Hat Creek in Lassen National Forest

Map grid A2

This is one in a series of Forest Service camps set beside beautiful Hat Creek, a good trout stream stocked regularly by the Department of Fish and Game. The elevation is 4,300 feet. The proximity to Lassen Volcanic National Park to the south is a big plus. Supplies are available in the little town of Old Station one mile to the north.

RV sites, facilities: There are 75 sites for tents or RVs up to 30 feet, and three group camps for tents or RVs up to 30 feet that can accommodate up to 50 people each. No hookups. Picnic tables and fire grills are provided. Drinking water and vault toilets are available. A grocery store, dump station, coin laundry, and propane gas are nearby. There is an accessible fishing platform. Leashed pets are permitted.

Reservations, fees: Tent and RV sites are first-come, first-served. Reservations are required for group sites at 877/444-6777 or www.recreation. gov ($10 reservation fee). Tent and RV sites are $16 per night, $5 per night for each additional vehicle, $85 per night for group camps. Open late April through October, weather permitting.

Directions: From Redding, drive east on Highway 44 to the junction with Highway 89 (near the entrance to Lassen Volcanic National Park). Turn left (north) on Highway 89 and drive about 12 miles to the campground entrance on the left side of the road. Turn left and drive a short distance to the campground.

Contact: Lassen National Forest, Hat Creek Ranger District, 530/336-5521, fax 530/336-5758; Department of Fish and Game fishing information, 530/225-2146.

41 NORTH BATTLE CREEK RESERVOIR

Scenic rating: 7

on Battle Creek Reservoir

Map grid A2

This little-known lake is at 5,600 feet in elevation, largely surrounded by Lassen National Forest. No gas engines are permitted on the lake, making it ideal for canoes, rafts, and car-top aluminum boats equipped with electric motors. When the lake level is up in early summer, it is a pretty setting with good trout fishing.

RV sites, facilities: There are 10 sites for tents or RVs up to 30 feet (no hookups) and five walk-in tent sites. Picnic tables and fire grills are provided. Drinking water and vault toilets are available. A car-top boat launch is available nearby. Leashed pets are permitted.

Reservations, fees: Reservations are not accepted. Sites are $13 per night, $3 per night for each additional vehicle, $7 per additional RV per night, $1 per pet per night. Open mid-May through mid-September, weather permitting.

Directions: From Redding, drive east on Highway 44 to Viola. From Viola, continue east for 3.5 miles to Forest Road 32N17. Turn left on Forest Road 32N17 and drive five miles to Forest Road 32N31. Turn left and drive four miles to Forest Road 32N18. Turn right and drive 0.5 mile to the reservoir and the campground on the right side of the road.

Contact: PG&E Land Projects, 916/386-5164, www.pge.com/recreation.

42 BIG PINE CAMP

Scenic rating: 7

on Hat Creek in Lassen National Forest

Map grid A2

This campground is set on the headwaters of Hat Creek, a pretty spot amid ponderosa pines. The elevation is 4,500 feet. A dirt road out of camp parallels Hat Creek, providing access for trout fishing. A great vista point is set on the highway, a mile south of the campground entrance road. It is only a 10-minute drive south to the Highway 44 entrance station for Lassen Volcanic National Park.

RV sites, facilities: There are 19 sites for tents or RVs up to 22 feet (no hookups). Picnic tables and fire grills are provided. Drinking water (at two hand pumps) and vault toilets are available. A dump station, grocery store, and propane gas are nearby. Leashed pets are permitted.

Reservations, fees: Reservations are not accepted. Sites are $12 per night, $5 per night for each additional vehicle. Open late April through October, weather permitting.

Directions: From Redding, drive east on Highway 44 to the junction with Highway 89 (near the entrance to Lassen Volcanic National Park). Turn left (north) on Highway 89 and drive about eight miles (one mile past the vista point) to the campground entrance on the right side of the road. Turn right and drive 0.5 mile to the campground.

Contact: Lassen National Forest, Hat Creek Ranger District, 530/336-5521, fax 530/336-5758; Department of Fish and Game fishing information, 530/225-2146.

43 BUTTE CREEK

Scenic rating: 6

in Lassen National Forest

Map grid A2

This primitive, little-known spot is just three miles from the northern boundary of Lassen Volcanic National Park, set on little Butte Creek. The elevation is 5,600 feet. It is a four-mile drive south out of camp on Forest Road 18 to Butte Lake in Lassen Park and to the trailhead for a great hike up to the Cinder Cone (6,907 feet), with dramatic views of the Lassen wilderness.

RV sites, facilities: There are 20 sites for tents or RVs up to 22 feet (no hookups). Vault toilets are available. No drinking water is available. Garbage must be packed out. Leashed pets are permitted.

Reservations, fees: Reservations are not accepted. There is no fee for camping. Open May through October, weather permitting.

Directions: From Redding, drive east on Highway 44 to the junction with Highway 89 (near the entrance to Lassen Volcanic National Park). Turn north on Highway 89 and drive to Highway 44. Turn east (right) on Highway 44 and drive 11 miles to Forest Road 18. Turn right at Forest Road 18 and drive three miles to the campground on the left side of the road.

Contact: Lassen National Forest, Eagle Lake Ranger District, 530/257-4188, fax 530/252-5803.

44 BOGARD

Scenic rating: 6

in Lassen National Forest

Map grid A2

This little camp is set along Pine Creek, which flows through Pine Creek Valley at the foot of the Bogard Buttes. It is a relatively obscure camp that gets missed by many travelers. A bonus here are the beautiful aspens, breathtaking in fall. To the nearby west is a network of Forest Service roads, and beyond is the Caribou Wilderness.

RV sites, facilities: There are 11 sites for tents or RVs up to 25 feet (no hookups). Picnic tables and fire grills are provided. Drinking water and vault toilets are available. Leashed pets are permitted.

Reservations, fees: Reservations are not accepted. Sites are $13 per night. Open May through October, weather permitting.

Directions: From Redding, drive east on Highway 44 to the junction with Highway 89 (near the entrance to Lassen Volcanic National Park). Turn north on Highway 89 and drive to Highway 44. Turn east on Highway 44 and drive to the Bogard Work Center (about seven miles past Poison Lake) and the adjacent rest stop. Continue east on Highway 44 for two miles to a gravel road on the right side of the road (Forest Road 31N26). Turn right on Forest Road 31N26 and drive two miles. Turn right on Forest Road 31N21 and drive 0.5 mile to the campground at the end of the road.

Contact: Lassen National Forest, Eagle Lake Ranger District, 530/257-4188, fax 530/252-5803.

45 MACCUMBER RESERVOIR

Scenic rating: 7

on MacCumber Reservoir
Map grid A2

Here's a small lake, easy to reach from Redding, that is little known and rarely visited. MacCumber Reservoir is set at 3,500 feet and is stocked with rainbow trout each year, providing fair fishing. No gas motors are permitted here. That's fine—it guarantees quiet, calm water, ideal for car-top boats: prams, canoes, rafts, and small aluminum boats.

RV sites, facilities: There are seven sites for tents or RVs up to 30 feet (no hookups) and five walk-in tent sites. Picnic tables and fire grills are provided. Drinking water and vault toilets are available. Leashed pets are permitted.

Reservations, fees: Reservations are not accepted. Sites are $13 per night, $3 per night for each additional vehicle, $7 per night per additional RV, $1 per pet per night. Open mid-April through mid-September, weather permitting.

Directions: In Redding, turn east on Highway 44 and drive toward Viola to Lake MacCumber Road (if you reach Viola, you have gone four miles too far). Turn left at Lake MacCumber Road and drive two miles to the reservoir and campground.

Contact: PG&E Land Projects, 916/386-5164, fax 916/923-7044, www.pge.com/recreation.

46 MANZANITA LAKE

Scenic rating: 9

in Lassen Volcanic National Park
Map grid A2

Manzanita Lake, set at 5,890 feet, is one of the prettiest lakes in Lassen Volcanic National Park, and evening walks around the lake are beautiful. The campground, set among towering Ponderosa pines, is often crowded due to this great natural beauty.

Manzanita Lake provides good catch-and-release trout fishing for experienced fly fishers in prams and other nonpowered boats. Fishing regulations prohibit bait and lures with barbs. This is no place for a dad, mom, and a youngster to fish from shore with Power Bait; you'll end up with a citation. Swimming is permitted, but there are few takers.

Note: Small park model cabins are scheduled to be installed in 2009 and will likely be an instant hit.

RV sites, facilities: There are 179 sites for tents or RVs up to 35 feet (no hookups). Picnic tables, fire grills, and bear-proof food lockers are provided. Drinking water and flush toilets are available. A museum, visitors center, and small store, as well as propane gas, groceries, coin showers, dump station, and coin laundry are nearby. Ranger programs are offered in the summer. A boat launch is also nearby (no motors are permitted on boats at Manzanita Lake). Some facilities are wheelchair-accessible. Leashed pets are permitted at campsites only.

Reservations, fees: Reservations are accepted at 877/444-6777 or www.ReserveUSA.com ($10 reservation fee). Sites are $18 per night, $10 per vehicle park entrance fee. Some credit cards accepted. Open late May through late September, weather permitting (during the fall, it's open without drinking water until the camp is closed by snow).

Directions: From Redding, drive east on Highway 44 to the junction with Highway 89. Turn right (south) on Highway 89 and drive one mile to the entrance station to Lassen Volcanic National Park (the state highway becomes Lassen Park Highway/Main Park Road). Continue a short distance on Lassen Park Highway/Main Park Road to the campground entrance road. Turn right and drive 0.5 mile to the campground.

Contact: Lassen Volcanic National Park, 530/595-4444, fax 530/595-3262, www.nps.gov/lavo.

47 CRAGS

Scenic rating: 8

in Lassen Volcanic National Park

Map grid A2

Crags is sometimes overlooked as a prime spot at Lassen Volcanic National Park because there is no lake nearby. No problem, because even though this campground is small compared to the giant complex at Manzanita Lake, the campsites are more spacious, do not fill up as quickly, and many are backed by forest. In addition, Emigrant Trail runs out of camp, routing east and meeting pretty Lost Creek after a little more than a mile, a great short hike. Directly across from Crags are the towering Chaos Crags, topping out at 8,503 feet. The elevation here is 5,720 feet.

RV sites, facilities: There are 45 sites for tents or RVs up to 35 feet (no hookups). Picnic tables, fire rings, and bearproof food lockers are provided. Drinking water and vault toilets are available. Wheelchair access is limited. Leashed pets are permitted in the campground and on paved roads only.

Reservations, fees: Reservations are not accepted. Sites are $12 per night, $10 per vehicle park entrance fee. Open late June through early September.

Directions: From Redding, drive east on Highway 44 for 42 miles to the junction with Highway 89. Turn right and drive one mile to the entrance station at Lassen Volcanic National Park (the state highway becomes Lassen Park Highway/Main Park Road). Continue on Lassen Park Highway/Main Park Road for about five miles to the campground on the left side of the road.

Contact: Lassen Volcanic National Park, 530/595-4444, fax 530/595-3262, www.nps.gov/lavo.

48 BUTTE LAKE

Scenic rating: 9

in Lassen Volcanic National Park

Map grid A2

Butte Lake campground is situated in an open, volcanic setting with a sprinkling of lodgepole pine. The contrast of the volcanics against the emerald greens of the lake is beautiful and memorable. Cinder Cone Trail can provide an even better look. The trailhead is near the boat launch area, and it's a strenuous hike involving a climb of 800 feet over the course of two miles to the top of the Cinder Cone. The footing is often loose because of volcanic pebbles. At the rim, you can peer inside the Cinder Cone, as well as be rewarded with lake views and a long-distance vista. Trout fishing is poor at Butte Lake, as at nearly all the lakes at this national park, because trout have not been planted for years. The elevation is 6,100 feet, and the lake covers 212 acres.

RV sites, facilities: There are 101 sites for tents or RVs up to 35 feet (no hookups), one equestrian site, and six group tent sites that can accommodate 10–25 people each. Some sites are pull-through. Picnic tables, fire rings, and bearproof food lockers are provided. Drinking water and flush and vault toilets are available. A boat ramp is nearby. No motors are permitted on the lake. Some facilities are wheelchair-accessible. Leashed pets are permitted at campsites only.

Reservations, fees: Reservations are accepted for individual sites and are required for group sites at 877/444-6777 or www.recreation.gov ($10 reservation fee). Reservations are also required for equestrian sites at 530/335-7029. Tent and RV sites are $14 per night; equestrian sites are $14 per night plus $4 per horse per night; group sites are $50 per night, plus $10 park entrance fee per vehicle. Open mid-June through mid-September, weather permitting.

Directions: From Redding, drive east on Highway 44 to the junction with Highway 89. Bear north on Highway 89/44 and drive 13 miles to Old Station. Just past Old Station, turn right (east) on Highway 44 and drive 10 miles to

Forest Road 32N21/Butte Lake Road. Turn right and drive six miles to the campground.

Contact: Lassen Volcanic National Park, 530/595-4444, fax 530/595-3262, www.nps.gov/lavo.

49 MOUNT LASSEN/ SHINGLETOWN KOA

Scenic rating: 6

near Lassen Volcanic National Park

Map grid A2

This popular KOA camp is 14 miles from the entrance of Lassen Volcanic National Park and has pretty, wooded sites. Location is always the critical factor on vacations, and this park is set up perfectly for launching trips into Lassen Volcanic National Park. Hat Creek provides trout fishing along Highway 89, and just inside the Highway 44 entrance station at Lassen is Manzanita Lake, providing good fishing and hiking.

RV sites, facilities: There are 46 sites with full or partial hookups (30 and 50 amps) for tents or RVs up to 40 feet, including some pull-through sites, and five cabins. Picnic tables and fire grills are provided. Restroom with flush toilets and showers, playground, heated pool (summer only), dump station, convenience store, ice, firewood, coin laundry, video arcade and recreation room, dog run, and propane gas are available. Leashed pets are permitted.

Reservations, fees: Reservations are accepted with a deposit at 800/562-3403. Sites are $28–45 per night, $3–5 per person per night for more than two people. Some credit cards accepted. Open mid-March through November.

Directions: From Redding, turn east on Highway 44 and drive to Shingletown. In Shingletown, continue east for four miles and look for the park entrance on the right (signed KOA).

Contact: Mount Lassen/Shingletown KOA, 530/474-3133, www.koa.com.

50 SUMMIT LAKE: NORTH, SOUTH, AND EQUESTRIAN

Scenic rating: 9

in Lassen Volcanic National Park

Map grid A2   **BEST (**

Summit Lake is a beautiful spot where deer often visit in the evening on the adjacent meadow just east of the campground. The lake is small, just 15 acres, and since trout plants were suspended it has been just about fished out. Summit Lake is the most popular lake for swimming in the park. Evening walks around the lake are perfect for families. A more ambitious trail is routed out of camp and leads past lavish wildflower displays in early summer to a series of wilderness lakes. The campgrounds are set at an elevation of 6,695 feet.

RV sites, facilities: There are 46 sites for tents or RVs up to 35 feet at North Summit, 48 sites for tents or RVs up to 30 feet at South Summit, and one equestrian site for tents or RVs up to 35 feet that can accommodate up to 10 people and eight horses. No hookups. Picnic tables, fire rings, and bearproof food lockers are provided. Drinking water and toilets (flush toilets on the north side, pit toilets on the south side, and vault toilets at the equestrian site) are available. Some facilities are wheelchair-accessible. Ranger programs are sometimes offered in summer. Leashed pets are permitted at campsites only.

Reservations, fees: Reservations are accepted for individual sites at 877/444-6777 or www.recreation.gov ($10 reservation fee). Reservations are required for equestrian sites at 530/335-7029. Sites are $16 (South) to $18 (North) per night, $14 per night plus $4 per horse per night at the equestrian site, plus $10 park entrance fee per vehicle. Some credit cards accepted. Open late June through mid-September, weather permitting.

Directions: From Redding, drive east on Highway 44 to the junction with Highway 89. Turn south on Highway 89 and drive one mile to the entrance station to Lassen Volcanic National Park (where the state highway becomes Lassen

CALIFORNIA

Park Highway/Main Park Road). Continue on Lassen Park Highway/Main Park Road for 12 miles to the campground entrance on the left side of the road. The horse camp is located across the street from the other campsites.

Contact: Lassen Volcanic National Park, 530/595-4444, fax 530/595-3262, www.nps.gov/lavo.

51 SILVER BOWL

Scenic rating: 7

on Silver Lake in Lassen National Forest

Map grid A2

Silver Lake is a pretty lake set at 6,400 feet elevation at the edge of the Caribou Wilderness. There is an unimproved boat ramp at the southern end of the lake. It is occasionally planted by the Department of Fish and Game with Eagle Lake trout and brown trout, which provide a summer fishery for campers. A trailhead from adjacent Caribou Lake is routed west into the wilderness, with routes available both to Emerald Lake to the northwest, and Betty, Trail, and Shotoverin Lakes nearby to the southeast.

RV sites, facilities: There are 18 sites for tents or RVs up to 25 feet (no hookups). Picnic tables and fire grills are provided. Drinking water and vault toilets are available. Leashed pets are permitted.

Reservations, fees: Reservations are not accepted. Sites are $12 per night, $3 per night for each additional vehicle. Open late May through October, weather permitting.

Directions: From Red Bluff, drive east on Highway 36 to the junction with Highway 89. Continue east on Highway 36 past Lake Almanor to Westwood. In Westwood, turn left on County Road A21 and drive 12.5 miles to Silver Lake Road. Turn left on Silver Lake Road/County Road 110 and drive 8.5 miles north to Silver Lake. At Silver Lake, turn right and drive 0.75 mile to the campground.

Contact: Lassen National Forest, Almanor Ranger District, 530/258-2141, fax 530/258-5194.

52 ROCKY KNOLL

Scenic rating: 7

on Silver Lake in Lassen National Forest

Map grid A2

This is one of two camps at pretty Silver Lake, set at 6,400 feet elevation at the edge of the Caribou Wilderness. The other camp is Silver Bowl to the nearby north, which is larger and provides better access for hikers. This camp, however, is closer to the boat ramp, which is set at the south end of the lake. Silver Lake provides a good summer fishery for campers.

RV sites, facilities: There are 18 sites for tents or RVs up to 27 feet (no hookups). Picnic tables and fire grills are provided. Drinking water and vault toilets are available. Leashed pets are permitted.

Reservations, fees: Reservations are not accepted. Sites are $12 per night, $3 per night for each additional vehicle. Open late May through early November, weather permitting.

Directions: From Red Bluff, drive east on Highway 36 to the junction with Highway 89. Continue east on Highway 36 past Lake Almanor to Westwood. In Westwood, turn left on County Road A21 and drive 12.5 miles to Silver Lake Road. Turn left (west) on Silver Lake Road/County Road 110 and drive 8.5 miles to Silver Lake. At Silver Lake, turn left and drive 300 yards to the campground.

Contact: Lassen National Forest, Almanor Ranger District, 530/258-2141, fax 530/258-5194.

53 SOUTHWEST WALK-IN

Scenic rating: 8

in Lassen Volcanic National Park

Map grid A2

This pretty campground at 6,700 feet elevation re-opened in late fall 2008 after the new visitors center near the southwest entrance station was built. Well, both are stellar. So is the hiking. Just taking the short walk required to reach the camp will launch you into an orbit beyond most of the highway cruisers visiting Lassen. The 4.6-mile hike to Mill Creek Falls, the park's highest waterfall, begins at the campground. The Sulphur Works and Brokeoff Mountain trailheads are nearby, as is the new visitors center.

One must-see is Bumpass Hell. The trail is about seven miles north of the campground on the right side of the Lassen Park Highway/Main Park Road. This easy hike takes you past steam vents and boiling mud pots, all set in prehistoric-looking volcanic rock. Ranger-led programs are sometimes offered.

RV sites, facilities: There are 21 walk-in tent sites, and a large parking lot available for RVs of any length (no hookups). Picnic tables, fire rings, and bearproof food lockers are provided. Drinking water and restrooms with flush toilets are available in summer. Leashed pets are permitted in campground only.

Reservations, fees: Reservations are not accepted. Sites are $14 per night for tent campers, $10 per night for RV parking, plus $10 per vehicle park entrance fee. Open year-round, weather permitting.

Directions: From Red Bluff, take Highway 36 east for 48 miles to the junction with Highway 89. Turn left on Highway 89 (becomes Lassen Park Highway/Main Park Road) and drive to the park's entrance. Just after passing through the park entrance gate, look for the camp parking area on the right side of the road.

Contact: Lassen Volcanic National Park, 530/595-4444, fax 530/595-3262, www.nps.gov/lavo.

54 BATTLE CREEK

Scenic rating: 7

on Battle Creek in Lassen National Forest

Map grid A2

This pretty spot offers easy access and streamside camping along Battle Creek. The trout fishing can be good in May, June, and early July, when the creek is stocked with trout by the Department of Fish and Game. Many people drive right by without knowing there is a stream here and that the fishing can be good. The elevation is 4,800 feet.

RV sites, facilities: There are 50 sites for tents or RVs up to 30 feet (no hookups). Picnic tables and fire grills are provided. Drinking water, flush and vault toilets, and a day-use picnic area are available. Supplies can be obtained in the town of Mineral. Leashed pets are permitted.

Reservations, fees: Reservations are not accepted. Sites are $18 per night, $3 per night for each additional vehicle. Open late April through early November, weather permitting.

Directions: From Red Bluff, turn east on Highway 36 and drive 39 miles to the campground (if you reach Mineral, you have gone two miles too far).

Contact: Lassen National Forest, Almanor Ranger District, 530/258-2141, fax 530/258-5194; Department of Fish and Game fishing information, 530/225-2146.

55 CHILDS MEADOW RESORT

Scenic rating: 7

near Mill Creek

Map grid A2

Childs Meadow Resort is an 18-acre resort set at 5,000 feet elevation. It features many recreation options, including catch-and-release fishing one mile away at Mill Creek. There are also a number of trails nearby for horseback riding. The trailhead for Spencer Meadow Trail is just east of the resort along Highway 36. The trail provides a 12-mile route (one-way) to Spencer Meadow and an effervescent spring that is the source of Mill Creek.

RV sites, facilities: There are eight tent sites and 24 sites with full hookups (50 amps) for RVs of any length; most are pull-through. Cabins, park-model cabins, and a motel are also available. Picnic tables and fire rings are provided. Drinking water and restrooms with flush toilets and showers are available. A coin laundry, store, restaurant, group picnic area, meeting room, and horseshoes are on-site. Groups can be accommodated. Leashed pets are permitted.

Reservations, fees: Reservations are accepted at 888/595-3383. Sites are $18–25 per night, $10 per pet per night. Some credit cards accepted. Open mid-May through October, weather permitting.

Directions: From Red Bluff, drive east on Highway 36 for 43 miles to the town of Mineral. Continue east on Highway 36 for 10 miles to the resort on the left.

Contact: Childs Meadow Resort, 530/595-3383, www.childsmeadowresort.com.

56 DOMINGO SPRINGS

Scenic rating: 7

in Lassen National Forest
Map grid A2

This camp is named after a spring adjacent to the site. It is a small fountain that pours into the headwaters of the North Fork Feather River, a good trout stream. The Pacific Crest Trail is routed from this camp north for four miles to Little Willow Lake and the southern border of Lassen Volcanic National Park. The elevation is 5,060 feet.

RV sites, facilities: There are 18 sites for tents or RVs up to 27 feet (no hookups). Picnic tables and fire grills are provided. Drinking water and vault toilets are available. Leashed pets are permitted.

Reservations, fees: Reservations are not accepted. Sites are $14 per night, $3 per night for each additional vehicle. Open late May through early November, weather permitting.

Directions: From Red Bluff, take Highway 36 east to Chester and Feather River Drive. Turn left on Feather River Drive and drive 0.75 mile to County Road 312. Bear left and drive five miles to the Y with County Road 311 and County Road 312. Bear left on County Road 311 and drive two miles to the campground entrance road on the left.

Contact: Lassen National Forest, Almanor Ranger District, 530/258-2141, fax 530/258-5194.

57 HIGH BRIDGE

Scenic rating: 8

on the North Fork of the Feather River in Lassen National Forest
Map grid A2

This camp is set at an elevation of 5,200 feet, near where the South Cascades meet the North Sierra, and is ideal for many people. The result is that it is often full in July and August. The payoff includes a pretty, adjacent trout stream, the headwaters of the North Fork Feather. Trout fishing is often good here, including some rare large brown trout, a surprise considering the relatively small size of the stream. Nearby access to the Warner Valley/Drakesbad entrance of Lassen Volcanic National Park provides a must-do side trip. The area is wooded and the road dusty.

RV sites, facilities: There are 12 sites for tents or RVs up to 27 feet (no hookups). Picnic tables and fire grills are provided. Drinking water and vault toilets are available. Groceries and propane gas are available in Chester. Leashed pets are permitted.

Reservations, fees: Reservations are not accepted. Sites are $14 per night, $3 per night for each additional vehicle. Open late May through early November, weather permitting.

Directions: From Red Bluff, take Highway 36 east to Chester and Feather River Drive. Turn left on Feather River Drive and drive 0.75 mile to County Road 312. Bear left and drive five miles to the campground entrance road on the left.

Contact: Lassen National Forest, Almanor Ranger District, 530/258-2141, fax 530/258-5194; Department of Fish and Game fishing information, 530/225-2146.

58 LAST CHANCE CREEK

Scenic rating: 7

near Lake Almanor
Map grid A2

This secluded camp is set at 4,500 feet, adjacent to where Last Chance Creek empties into the north end of Lake Almanor. It is an unpublicized PG&E camp that is known primarily by locals and gets missed almost every time by out-of-towners. The adjacent lake area is a breeding ground in the spring for white pelicans, and the beauty of these birds in large flocks can be extraordinary.

RV sites, facilities: There are 12 sites for tents or RVs up to 30 feet (no hookups), and three group camps that can accommodate up to 100 people (total). Picnic tables and fire grills are provided. Drinking water and vault toilets are available. Leashed pets are permitted.

Reservations, fees: Reservations are not accepted for individual sites but are required for the group camps at 916/386-5164. Sites are $16 per night for individual sites, $3 per night for each additional vehicle, $7 per night for each additional RV, $60–120 per night for group sites, $1 per pet per night. Group sites require a two-night minimum stay and a three-night minimum on holidays. Open mid-May through September, weather permitting.

Directions: From Red Bluff, take Highway 36 east to Chester and continue for two miles over the causeway (at the north end of Lake Almanor). About 0.25 mile after crossing the causeway, turn left on the campground access road and drive 3.5 miles to the campground.

Contact: PG&E Land Projects, 916/386-5164, www.pge.com/recreation.

59 HOLE-IN-THE-GROUND

Scenic rating: 8

on Mill Creek in Lassen National Forest

Map grid A2

This is one of two campgrounds set along Mill Creek at 4,300 feet. Take your pick. The highlight here is a trail that follows along Mill Creek for many miles; it provides good fishing access. Rules mandate the use of artificials with a single barbless hook, and catch-and-release; check current fishing regulations. The result is a challenging but quality wild-trout fishery. Another option is to drive 0.5 mile to the end of the Forest Service road, where there is a parking area for a trail that is routed downstream along Mill Creek and into a state game refuge. To keep things easy, obtain a map of Lassen National Forest that details the recreational opportunities.

RV sites, facilities: There are 13 sites for tents or RVs up to 24 feet (no hookups). Picnic tables and fire grills are provided. Drinking water and vault toilets are available. Supplies are available in Mineral. Leashed pets are permitted.

Reservations, fees: Reservations are not accepted. Sites are $12 per night, $3 per night for each additional vehicle. Open late April through early November, weather permitting.

Directions: From Red Bluff, drive 43 miles east on Highway 36 to the town of Mineral and the junction with Highway 172. Turn right on Highway 172 and drive six miles to the town of Mill Creek. In Mill Creek, turn south onto Forest Road 28N06 (signed) and drive five miles to the campground access road. Turn left and drive 0.25 mile to the camp.

Contact: Lassen National Forest, Almanor Ranger District, 530/258-2141, fax 530/258-5194.

60 MILL CREEK RESORT

Scenic rating: 7

on Mill Creek near Lassen National Forest

Map grid A2

This is a great area, surrounded by Lassen National Forest and within close range of the southern Highway 89 entrance to Lassen Volcanic National Park. It is set at 4,800 feet along oft-bypassed Highway 172. A highlight here is Mill Creek (to reach it, turn south on the Forest Service road in town and drive to a parking area at the end of the road along the stream), where there is a great easy walk along the stream and fair trout fishing. Note that about half the campsites are taken by long-term renters.

RV sites, facilities: There are 14 sites for tents or RVs up to 35 feet, eight with full hookups (30 amps). Nine one- and two-bedroom cabins are also available. Picnic tables and fire rings are provided. Drinking water, vault toilets, seasonal showers, coin laundry, playground, a small grocery store, and a restaurant are also available. Some facilities are wheelchair-accessible. Leashed pets are permitted.

Reservations, fees: Reservations are accepted. Sites are $16–25 per night. Campsites are open May through October. Cabins are available year-round.

Directions: From Red Bluff, drive 43 miles east on Highway 36 to the town of Mineral and the junction with Highway 172. Turn right and drive six miles to the town of Mill Creek. In Mill Creek, look for the sign for Mill Creek Resort on the right side of the road.

Contact: Mill Creek Resort, 530/595-4449 or 888/595-4449, www.millcreekresort.net.

61 GURNSEY CREEK AND GROUP CAMPS

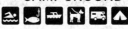

Scenic rating: 7

in Lassen National Forest

Map grid A2

This camp is set at 5,000 feet elevation in Lassen National Forest, with extremely easy access off Highway 36. The camp is on the headwaters of little Gurnsey Creek, a highlight of the surrounding Lost Creek Plateau. Gurnsey Creek runs downstream and pours into Deer Creek, a good trout stream with access along narrow, winding Highway 32 to the nearby south. The group camps are ideal spots for a Scout troop.

RV sites, facilities: There are 30 sites for tents or RVs up to 30 feet (no hookups). There are two group camps that can accommodate up to 20 people with tents or RVs up to 30 feet (no hookups). Picnic tables and fire grills are provided. Drinking water and vault toilets are available. Supplies are available in Mineral. Leashed pets are permitted.

Reservations, fees: Reservations are not accepted for individual sites, but are required for the group site at 877/444-6777 or www.recreation.gov ($10 reservation fee). Tent and RV sites are $14 per night, $3 per night for

each additional vehicle. Trout Group Camp is $56 per night and Rainbow Group Camp is $112 per night, with a two-night minimum stay required on weekends. Open May through October, weather permitting.

Directions: From Red Bluff, drive east on Highway 36 for 55 miles (five miles east of Childs Meadow). Turn left at the campground entrance road and drive a short distance to the campground.

Contact: Lassen National Forest, Almanor Ranger District, 530/258-2141, fax 530/258-5194.

62 NORTH SHORE CAMPGROUND

Scenic rating: 7

on Lake Almanor

Map grid A2

This is a large, privately developed park on the northern shoreline of beautiful Lake Almanor. The park has 37 acres and a mile of shoreline. The camp is set amid pine tree cover, and most of the sites are lakefront or lakeview. About half of the sites are filled with seasonal renters. The lending library here was once the original Chester jail, built in 1925. Alas, the jail itself busted out during a storm a few years ago and was found washed ashore at this campground, which converted it to its new use.

RV sites, facilities: There are 34 tent sites and 94 sites with partial hookups (30 amps) for RVs up to 40 feet; a few are pull-through. Two log cabins are also available. Picnic tables and fire rings are provided. Drinking water, restrooms with showers and flush toilets, coin laundry, general store, playground, lending library, modem access, Wi-Fi, propane, dump station, fish-cleaning station, horseshoes, boat ramp, boat dock, boat slips, and boat rentals are available. Leashed pets are permitted.

Reservations, fees: Reservations are accepted. RV sites are $36–48 per night, tent sites are $33 per night, $5 per person per night for more than two people (children under age 12 are free), $2 per pet per night. Monthly and seasonal rates available. Some credit cards accepted. Open April through October.

Directions: From Red Bluff, take Highway 36 east for 44 miles to the junction with Highway 89. Drive east on Highway 36/89; the camp is two miles past Chester on the right.

Contact: North Shore Campground, 530/258-3376, www.northshorecampground.com.

63 ELAM

Scenic rating: 7

on Deer Creek in Lassen National Forest
Map grid A2

Of the campgrounds set on Deer Creek along Highway 32, Elam gets the most use. It is the first stopping point visitors arrive at while heading west on narrow, curvy Highway 32, and it has an excellent day-use picnic area available. The stream here is stocked with rainbow trout in late spring and early summer, with good access for fishing. It is a pretty area, set where Elam Creek enters Deer Creek. A Forest Service Information Center is nearby in Chester. If the camp has too many people to suit your style, consider other more distant and primitive camps downstream on Deer Creek. The elevation here is 4,600 feet.

RV sites, facilities: There are 11 sites for tents or RVs up to 30 feet (no hookups). Picnic tables and fire grills are provided. Drinking water and vault toilets are available. Leashed pets are permitted.

Reservations, fees: Reservations are not accepted. Sites are $14 per night, $3 per night for each additional vehicle. Open mid-April through October, weather permitting.

Directions: From Red Bluff, take Highway 36 east for 44 miles to the junction with Highway 89. Continue east on Highway 36/89 to the junction with Highway 32. Turn south on Highway 32 and drive three miles to the campground on the right side of the road. Trailers are not recommended.

Contact: Lassen National Forest, Almanor Ranger District, 530/258-2141, fax 530/258-5194.

64 POTATO PATCH

Scenic rating: 7

on Deer Creek in Lassen National Forest
Map grid A2

You get good hiking and fishing at this camp. It is set beside Deer Creek at 3,400 feet elevation, with good access for trout fishing. This is a wild trout stream in this area, and the use of artificials with a single barbless hook and catch-and-release are required along most of the river; check DFG regulations. An excellent anglers'/swimmers' trail is available along the river.

RV sites, facilities: There are 32 sites for tents or RVs up to 27 feet (no hookups). Picnic tables and fire grills are provided. Drinking water and vault toilets are available. Leashed pets are permitted.

Reservations, fees: Reservations are not accepted. Sites are $14 per night, $3 per night for each additional vehicle. Open early April through early November, weather permitting.

Directions: From Red Bluff, take Highway 36 east for 44 miles to the junction with Highway 89. Continue east on Highway 36/89 to the junction with Highway 32. Turn south on Highway 32 and drive 11 miles to the campground on the right side of the road.

Contact: Lassen National Forest, Almanor Ranger District, 530/258-2141, fax 530/258-5194; Department of Fish and Game, 530/225-2146.

65 ROCKY POINT CAMPGROUND

Scenic rating: 7

on Lake Almanor
Map grid A2

What you get here is a series of four campgrounds along the southwest shore of Lake Almanor, provided by PG&E as mitigation for its hydroelectric activities on the Feather River system. The camps are set upstream from the dam, with boat ramps available on each side of the dam. This is a pretty spot, with giant Almanor ringed by lodgepole pine and firs. The lake is usually full, or close to it, well into summer, with Mount Lassen set in the distance to the north—bring your camera. The lake is 13 miles long and all water sports are permitted. The lake level remains full most of the year and much of the shoreline is wooded. Though it can take a day or two to find the fish, once that effort is made, fishing is good for large trout and salmon in the spring and fall and for smallmouth bass in the summer.

RV sites, facilities: There are 131 sites for tents or RVs up to 30 feet (no hookups). Picnic tables and fire grills are provided. Drinking water, vault toilets, and a dump station are available. Some facilities are wheelchair-accessible. Leashed pets are permitted.

Reservations, fees: Reservations are not accepted. Sites are $18 per night, $3 per night for each additional vehicle, $7 per night per additional RV, $1 per pet per night. Open May through September.

Directions: From Red Bluff, take Highway 36 east for 44 miles to the junction with Highway 89. Continue east on Highway 36/89 to Lake Almanor and the next junction with Highway 89 (two miles before reaching Chester). Turn right on Highway 89 and drive eight miles to the southwest end of Lake Almanor. Turn left at your choice of four campground entrances.

Contact: PG&E Land Projects, 916/386-5164, www.pge.com/recreation.

66 ALMANOR NORTH AND SOUTH

Scenic rating: 8

on Lake Almanor in Lassen National Forest

Map grid A2

This is one of Lake Almanor's best-known and most popular Forest Service campgrounds. It is set along the western shore of beautiful Almanor at 4,550 feet elevation, directly across from the beautiful Almanor Peninsula. There is an excellent view of Mount Lassen to the north, along with gorgeous sunrises. A 10-mile recreation trail runs right through the campground and is excellent for biking or hiking. This

section of the lake provides good fishing for smallmouth bass in the summer. Fishing in this lake is also good for rainbow trout, brown trout, and lake-raised salmon. There are two linked campgrounds, named North and South.

RV sites, facilities: There are 104 sites for tents or RVs up to 40 feet (no hookups), and a group camp for tents or RVs up to 40 feet that can accommodate up to 100 people. Picnic tables and fire grills are provided. Drinking water and vault toilets are available. A boat ramp and beach area are nearby. Some facilities are wheelchair-accessible. Leashed pets are permitted.

Reservations, fees: Reservations are accepted for individual sites and required for the group camp at 877/444-6777 or www.recreation.gov ($10 reservation fee). Sites are $18 per night, $5 per night for each additional vehicle, and $100 per night for the group camp. Open May through October, weather permitting.

Directions: From Red Bluff, take Highway 36 east for 44 miles to the junction with Highway 89. Continue east on Highway 36/89 to Lake Almanor and the next junction with Highway 89 (two miles before reaching Chester). Turn right on Highway 89 and drive six miles to County Road 310. Turn left on County Road 310 and drive 0.25 mile to the campground.

Contact: Lassen National Forest, Almanor Ranger District, 530/258-2141, fax 530/258-5194.

67 SOLDIER MEADOWS

Scenic rating: 7

on Soldier Creek in Lassen National Forest

Map grid A2

This camp is little known and primitive and is used primarily by anglers and hunters in season. The campsites here are shaded, set in forest on the edge of meadows, and near a stream. The latter is Soldier Creek, which is stocked with trout by the Department of Fish and Game; check fishing regulations. In the fall, early storms can drive deer through this area on their annual migration to their wintering habitat in the valley, making this a decent base camp for hunters. However, no early storms often mean no deer. The elevation is 4,890 feet.

RV sites, facilities: There are 15 sites for tents or RVs up to 25 feet (no hookups). Picnic tables and fire rings are provided. Vault toilets are available. No drinking water is available. Leashed pets are permitted.

Reservations, fees: Reservations are not accepted. Sites are $10 per night, $5 per night for each additional vehicle. Open late May through early November, weather permitting.

Directions: From Chester, drive south on Highway 89 for approximately six miles to Humboldt Road. Turn right on Humboldt Road and drive one mile, bear right at the fork, and continue five more miles to the intersection at Fanani Meadows. Turn right and drive one mile to the campground on the left.

Contact: Lassen National Forest, Almanor Ranger District, 530/258-2141, fax 530/258-5194.

68 PONDEROSA FLAT

Scenic rating: 7

on Butt Valley Reservoir

Map grid A2

This camp is set at the north end of Butt Valley Reservoir (more commonly called Butt Lake), the little brother to nearby Lake Almanor. It is a fairly popular camp, with the boat ramp a prime attraction, allowing campers/anglers a lakeside spot with easy access. Technically, Butt is the "afterbay" for Almanor, fed by a four-mile-long pipe with water from Almanor. What occurs is that pond smelt from Almanor get ground up in the Butt Lake powerhouse, providing a large amount of feed for trout at the head of the lake; that's why the trout often get huge at Butt Lake. The one downer here is that lake drawdowns are common, exposing tree stumps.

RV sites, facilities: There are 63 sites for tents or RVs up to 30 feet (no hookups), and an overflow camping area. Picnic tables and fire grills are provided. Drinking water, vault toilets,

and a boat ramp are available. Some facilities are wheelchair-accessible. Leashed pets are permitted.

Reservations, fees: Reservations are not accepted. Sites are $18 per night, $3 per night for each additional vehicle, $1 per pet per night. Open May through October, weather permitting.

Directions: From Red Bluff, take Highway 36 east for 44 miles to the junction with Highway 89. Continue east on Highway 36/89 to Lake Almanor and the next junction with Highway 89 (two miles before reaching Chester). Turn right on Highway 89 and drive about seven miles to Butt Valley Road. Turn right on Butt Valley Road and drive 3.2 miles to the campground on the right side of the road.

Contact: PG&E Land Projects, 916/386-5164, www.pge.com/recreation.

69 COOL SPRINGS

Scenic rating: 7

on Butt Valley Reservoir

Map grid A2

One of two camps at Butt Lake (officially known as Butt Valley Reservoir), Cool Springs is set about midway down the lake on its eastern shore, 2.5 miles south of Ponderosa Flat. Cool Springs Creek enters the lake near the camp. (See the Ponderosa Flat listing for more information about Butt Lake.)

RV sites, facilities: There are 25 sites for tents or RVs up to 30 feet (no hookups), and five walk-in tent sites. Picnic tables and fire grills are provided. Drinking water, vault toilets, and a boat ramp are available. Some facilities are wheelchair-accessible. Leashed pets are permitted.

Reservations, fees: Reservations are not accepted. Sites are $16 per night, $3 per night for each additional vehicle, $7 per night per additional RV, $1 per pet per night. Open May through October, weather permitting.

Directions: From Red Bluff, take Highway 36 east for 44 miles to the junction with Highway 89. Continue east on Highway 36/89 to Lake

Almanor and the next junction with Highway 89 (two miles before reaching Chester). Turn right on Highway 89 and drive about seven miles to Butt Valley Road. Turn right on Butt Valley Road and drive 5.7 miles to the campground on the right side of the road.

Contact: PG&E Land Projects, 916/386-5164, www.pge.com/recreation.

70 YELLOW CREEK

Scenic rating: 8

in Humbug Valley

Map grid A2

Yellow Creek is one of Cal Trout's pet projects. It's a beautiful stream for fly fishers, demanding the best from skilled anglers. This camp is set at 4,400 feet in Humbug Valley and provides access to this stretch of water. Another option is to fish Butt Creek, much easier fishing for small, planted rainbow trout, with access along the road on the way in.

RV sites, facilities: There are 10 sites for tents or RVs up to 30 feet (no hookups). Picnic tables and fire grills are provided. Drinking water and vault toilets are available. Leashed pets are permitted.

Reservations, fees: Reservations are not accepted. Sites are $16 per night, $3 per night for each additional vehicle, $7 per night per additional RV, $1 per pet per night. Open May through September.

Directions: From Red Bluff, take Highway 36 east for 44 miles to the junction with Highway 89. Continue east on Highway 36/89 for eight miles to Humbug Road. Turn right and drive 0.6 mile and bear left to stay on Humbug Road. Continue for 1.2 miles and bear right (signed for Longville) to stay on Humbug Road. Continue for 5.4 miles to Humbug Valley and a road intersection. Turn left to stay on Humbug Road and drive 1.2 miles (passing the Soda Springs Historic Site) to a fork. Bear right to stay on Humbug Road and drive 0.3 mile to the campground.

Contact: PG&E Land Projects, 916/386-5164, www.pge.com/recreation.

71 BUTTE MEADOWS

Scenic rating: 6

on Butte Creek in Lassen National Forest

Map grid A2

On hot summer days, when a cold stream sounds even better than a cold drink, Butte Meadows provides a hideout in the national forest east of Chico. This is a summer camp situated along Butte Creek, which is stocked with rainbow trout by the Department of Fish and Game. Nearby Doe Mill Ridge and the surrounding Lassen National Forest can provide good side-trip adventures. The camp elevation is 4,600 feet.

RV sites, facilities: There are 13 sites for tents or RVs up to 25 feet (no hookups). Fire grills and picnic tables are provided. Drinking water and vault toilets are available. Supplies are available in Butte Meadows. Leashed pets are permitted.

Reservations, fees: Reservations are not accepted. Sites are $12 per night, $3 per night for each additional vehicle. Open late April through early November, weather permitting.

Directions: From Chico, drive about 15 miles northeast on Highway 32 to the town of Forest Ranch. Continue on Highway 32 for another nine miles. Turn right on Humboldt Road and drive five miles to Butte Meadows.

Contact: Lassen National Forest, Almanor Ranger District, 530/258-2141, fax 530/258-5194; Department of Fish and Game fishing information, 530/225-2146.

72 CHERRY HILL

Scenic rating: 7

on Butte Creek in Lassen National Forest

Map grid A2

The camp is set along little Butte Creek at the foot of Cherry Hill, just downstream from the confluence of Colby Creek and Butte Creek. It is also on the western edge of the alpine zone in Lassen National Forest. A four-mile drive to the north, much of it along Colby Creek, will take visitors to the Colby Mountain Lookout at 6,002 feet for a dramatic view of the Ishi Wilderness to the west. Nearby to the south is Philbrook Reservoir.

RV sites, facilities: There are six walk-in tent sites and 19 sites for tents or RVs up to 30 feet (no hookups). Picnic tables and fire grills are provided. Drinking water and vault toilets are available. Supplies are available in the town of Butte Meadows. Leashed pets are permitted.

Reservations, fees: Reservations are not accepted. Sites are $12 per night, $3 per night for each additional vehicle. Open late April through early November, weather permitting.

Directions: From Chico, drive northeast on Highway 32 for approximately 24 miles to the junction with Humboldt Road (well past the town of Forest Ranch). Turn right and drive five miles to Butte Meadows. Continue on Humboldt Road for three miles to the campground on the right side of the road.

Contact: Lassen National Forest, Almanor Ranger District, 530/258-2141, fax 530/258-5194.

73 PHILBROOK RESERVOIR

Scenic rating: 7

in Lassen National Forest

Map grid A2

Philbrook Reservoir is set at 5,600 feet on the western mountain slopes above Chico, on the southwest edge of Lassen National Forest. It is a pretty lake, though subject to late-season drawdowns, with a scenic lookout a short distance from camp. Swimming beaches and a picnic area are bonuses. The lake is loaded with small trout—a dink here, a dink there, a dink everywhere.

RV sites, facilities: There are 20 sites for tents or RVs up to 30 feet (no hookups), and an overflow camping area. Picnic tables and fire grills are provided. Drinking water and vault toilets are available. Trailer and car-top boat launches are available. Some facilities are wheelchair-accessible. Leashed pets are permitted.

Reservations, fees: Reservations are not

accepted. Sites are $16 per night, $3 per night for each additional vehicle, $7 per night per additional RV, $1 per pet per night. Open May through September.

Directions: At Orland on I-5, take the Highway 32/Chico exit and drive to Chico and the junction with Highway 99. Turn south on Highway 99 and drive to Skyway Road/Paradise (in south Chico). Turn east on Skyway Road, drive through Paradise, and continue for 27 miles to Humbug Summit Road. Turn right and drive two miles to Philbrook Road. Turn right and drive 3.1 miles to the campground entrance road. Turn right and drive 0.5 mile to the campground. Note: Access roads are unpaved and often rough.

Contact: PG&E Land Projects, 916/386-5164, www.pge.com/recreation.

74 QUEEN LILY

Scenic rating: 7

on the North Fork of the Feather River in Plumas National Forest

Map grid A2

The North Fork Feather River is a prime destination for camping and trout fishing, especially for families. This is one of three camps along the river on Caribou Road. This stretch of river is well stocked. Insider's note: The first 150 yards of river below the dam at Caribou typically have large but elusive trout.

RV sites, facilities: There are 12 sites for tents or RVs up to 30 feet (no hookups). Picnic tables and fire grills are provided. Drinking water and vault toilets are available. A grocery store and coin laundry are available within three miles. Leashed pets are permitted.

Reservations, fees: Reservations are not accepted. Sites are $20 per night. Open May through September.

Directions: From Oroville, drive north on Highway 70 to Caribou Road (two miles past Belden). Turn left on Caribou Road and drive about three miles to the campground on the left side of the road.

Contact: Plumas National Forest, Mount Hough Ranger District, 530/283-0555, fax 530/283-1821; Northwest Park Management, 530/283-5559.

75 NORTH FORK

Scenic rating: 7

on the North Fork of the Feather River in Plumas National Forest

Map grid A2

This camp is between Queen Lily to the nearby north and Gansner Bar camp to the nearby south, all three set on the North Fork Feather River. The elevation is 2,600 feet. Fishing access is good and trout plants are decent, making for a good fishing/camping trip. Note: All three camps are extremely popular on summer weekends.

RV sites, facilities: There are 20 sites for tents or RVs up to 32 feet (no hookups). Picnic tables and fire grills are provided. Drinking water and vault toilets are available. A grocery store and coin laundry are available within three miles. Leashed pets are permitted.

Reservations, fees: Reservations are not accepted. Sites are $20 per night. Open May through September.

Directions: From Oroville, drive north on Highway 70 to Caribou Road (two miles past Belden at Gansner Ranch Ranger Station). Turn left on Caribou Road and drive about two miles to the campground on the left side of the road.

Contact: Plumas National Forest, Mount Hough Ranger District, 530/283-0555, fax 530/283-1821; Northwest Park Management, 530/283-5559.

76 GANSNER BAR

Scenic rating: 7

on the North Fork of the Feather River in Plumas National Forest

Map grid A2

Gansner Bar is the first of three camps along Caribou Road, which runs parallel to the North Fork Feather River. Of the three, this one receives the highest trout stocks of rainbow trout in the 10- to 12-inch class. Caribou Road runs upstream to Caribou Dam, with stream and fishing access along almost all of it. The camps often fill on summer weekends.

RV sites, facilities: There are 14 sites for tents or RVs up to 30 feet (no hookups). Picnic tables and fire grills are provided. Drinking water and vault toilets are available. A grocery store and coin laundry are available within one mile. Some facilities are wheelchair-accessible. Leashed pets are permitted.

Reservations, fees: Reservations are not accepted. Sites are $20 per night. Open April through October.

Directions: From Oroville, drive northeast on Highway 70 to Caribou Road (two miles past Belden). Turn left on Caribou Road and drive a short distance to the campground on the left side of the road.

Contact: Plumas National Forest, Mount Hough Ranger District, 530/283-0555, fax 530/283-1821; Northwest Park Management, 530/283-5559.

77 HALLSTED

Scenic rating: 7

on the North Fork of the Feather River in Plumas National Forest

Map grid A2

Easy highway access and a pretty trout stream right alongside have made this an extremely popular campground. It typically fills on summer weekends. Hallsted is set on the East Branch North Fork Feather River at 2,800 feet elevation. The river is stocked with trout by the Department of Fish and Game.

RV sites, facilities: There are 20 sites for tents or RVs up to 30 feet (no hookups). Picnic tables and fire grills are provided. Drinking water and vault toilets are available. A grocery store is within a quarter mile. Some facilities are wheelchair-accessible. Leashed pets are permitted.

Reservations, fees: Reservations are accepted

CALIFORNIA

at 877/444-6777 or www.recreation.gov ($10 reservation fee). Sites are $20 per night. Open May through September.

Directions: From Oroville, drive northeast on Highway 70 to Belden. Continue past Belden for about 12 miles to the campground entrance on the right side of the road. Turn right and drive 0.25 mile to the campground.

Contact: Plumas National Forest, Mount Hough Ranger District, 530/283-0555, fax 530/283-1821; Northwest Park Management, 530/283-5559.

78 DODGE RESERVOIR

Scenic rating: 6

near Ravendale

Map grid B2

This camp is set at 5,735 feet elevation near Dodge Reservoir, remote and little used. The lake covers 400 acres and is stocked with Eagle Lake trout. Those who know of this lake feel as if they know a secret, because the limit is two at Eagle Lake itself, but it is five here. Small boats can be launched from the shoreline, and though it can be windy, mornings are usually calm, ideal for canoes. The surrounding hillsides are sprinkled with sage and juniper. This camp is also popular with hunters who get drawn in the annual DFG lottery for tags for this zone. There is a very good chance that, along the entire length of road from the Madeline Plain into Dodge Reservoir, you'll see some wild horses. There's no sight quite like them. They are considered to be wild, but some will stay close to the road, while others will come no closer then 300 yards.

RV sites, facilities: There are 12 sites for tents or RVs up to 35 feet (no hookups). Picnic tables and fire pits are provided. A vault toilet is available. No drinking water is available. There is no developed boat ramp, but hand-launched boats are permitted. Leashed pets are permitted.

Reservations, fees: Reservations are not accepted. There is no fee for camping, but donations are encouraged. Open year-round, weather permitting.

Directions: From Susanville, drive north on U.S. 395 for 54 miles to Ravendale and County Road 502. Turn right on County Road 502 (Mail Route) and drive four miles, then bear left to stay on County Road 502. Continue four miles, then bear right to stay on County Road 502. Drive two miles to County Road 526. Continue straight onto County Road 526 and drive 4.5 miles to County Road 504. Turn left and drive two miles to County Road 506. Turn right and drive 7.5 miles to the access road for Dodge Reservoir. Turn left on the access road and drive one mile to the lake and camp. Note: The last mile of road before the turnoff to Dodge Reservoir can become impassable with just a small amount of rain or snow.

Contact: Bureau of Land Management, Eagle Lake Field Office, 530/257-0456, fax 530/257-4831, www.blm.gov/ca.

79 NORTH EAGLE LAKE

Scenic rating: 7

on Eagle Lake

Map grid B2

This camp provides direct access in the fall to the best fishing area of huge Eagle Lake. When the weather turns cold, the population of big Eagle Lake trout migrates to its favorite haunts just outside the tules, often in water only 5–8 feet deep. A boat ramp is about 1.5 miles to the southwest on Stone Road. In the summer this area is quite exposed and the lake can be hammered by west winds, which can howl from midday to sunset. The elevation is 5,100 feet.

RV sites, facilities: There are 20 sites for tents or RVs up to 35 feet (no hookups). Picnic tables and fire grills are provided. Drinking water and vault toilets are available. A private dump station and boat ramp are within 1.5 miles. Leashed pets are permitted.

Reservations, fees: Reservations are not accepted. Sites are $8 per night. Open Memorial Day through mid-November, weather permitting.

Directions: From Red Bluff, drive east on Highway 36 to Susanville. In Susanville, turn left (north) on Highway 139 and drive 29 miles to County Road A1. Turn left at County Road A1 and drive 0.5 mile to the campground on the right.

Contact: Bureau of Land Management, Eagle Lake Field Office, 530/257-0456, fax 530/257-4831, www.blm.gov/ca.

80 RAMHORN SPRINGS

Scenic rating: 3

south of Ravendale
Map grid B2

This camp is not even three miles off the biggest state highway in northeastern California, yet it feels remote and is little known. It is way out in Nowhere Land, near the flank of Shinn Peak (7,562 feet). There are large numbers of antelope in the area, along with a sprinkling of large mule deer. Hunters lucky enough to get a deer tag can use this camp for their base in the fall. It is also popular for upland game hunters in search of sage grouse and chukar.

RV sites, facilities: There are 10 sites for tents or RVs up to 35 feet (no hookups). Picnic tables and fire grills are provided. Vault toilets and a horse corral are available. There is no drinking water, although spring water, which can be filtered, is available. Leashed pets are permitted.

Reservations, fees: Reservations are not accepted. There is no fee for camping, but donations are encouraged. Open year-round, weather permitting.

Directions: From Red Bluff, drive east on Highway 36 to Susanville. In Susanville, turn north on U.S. 395 and drive 45 miles to Post Camp Road. Turn right on Post Camp Road (unmarked except for small recreation sign) and drive 2.5 miles east to the campground.

Contact: Bureau of Land Management, Eagle Lake Field Office, 530/257-0456, fax 530/257-4831, www.blm.gov/ca.

81 EAGLE LAKE RV PARK

Scenic rating: 7

near Susanville
Map grid B2

Eagle Lake RV Park has become something of a headquarters for anglers in pursuit of Eagle Lake trout, which typically range 18–22 inches. A nearby boat ramp provides access to Pelican Point and Eagle Point, where the fishing is often best in the summer. In the fall, the north end of the lake provides better prospects (see the North Eagle Lake listing in this chapter). This RV park has all the amenities, including a small store. That means no special trips into town, just vacation time, lounging beside Eagle Lake, maybe catching a big trout now and then. One downer: The wind typically howls here most summer afternoons. When the whitecaps are too big to deal with and surface conditions become choppy, get off the water; it can be dangerous here. Resident deer, including bucks with spectacular racks, can be like pets here on late summer evenings.

RV sites, facilities: There are 65 RV sites with full hookups (30 amps), including some pull-through sites, a separate grassy area for tents only, and cabin and RV rentals. Picnic tables and fire grills are provided. Restrooms with showers, coin laundry, satellite TV hookups, dump station, convenience store, propane gas, diesel, bait and tackle, video rentals, RV supplies, firewood, and recreation room are available. A boat ramp, dock, and boat slips are nearby. Some facilities are wheelchair-accessible. Leashed pets are permitted.

Reservations, fees: Reservations are recommended. RV sites are $36 per night, tent sites are $25 per night, $5 per day for each additional person, $1 per pet per night. Some credit cards accepted. Open late May through early November, weather permitting.

Directions: From Red Bluff, drive east on Highway 36 toward Susanville. Just before reaching Susanville, turn left on County Road A1 and drive approximately 25 miles to County Road 518 near Spalding Tract. Turn right on County Road 518 and drive through a small neighborhood to The Strand (the lake frontage road).

Turn right on The Strand and drive about eight blocks to Palmetto Way and the entrance to the store and the park entrance at 687-125 Palmetto Way. Register at the store.

Contact: Eagle Lake RV Park, 530/825-3133, www.eaglelakeandrv.com.

82 CHRISTIE

Scenic rating: 7

on Eagle Lake in Lassen National Forest

Map grid B2

This camp is set along the southern shore of Eagle Lake at 5,100 feet. Eagle Lake, with 100 miles of shoreline, is well known for its big trout (hooray) and big winds (boo). The camp offers some protection from the north winds. Its location is also good for seeing osprey in the Osprey Management Area, which covers a six-mile stretch of shoreline just two miles to the north above Wildcat Point. A nearby resort is a bonus. The nearest boat ramp is at Gallatin Marina. A five-mile-long paved trail runs from Christie to Aspen Grove Campground, perfect for hiking, cycling, and horseback riding.

RV sites, facilities: There are 69 individual sites and 10 double sites for tents or RVs up to 50 feet. No hookups. Picnic tables and fire grills are provided. Drinking water and flush toilets are available. Some facilities are wheelchair-accessible. A grocery store is nearby. A dump station is 2.5 miles away at Merrill Campground. Leashed pets are permitted. A campground host is on site.

Reservations, fees: Reservations are accepted at 877/444-6777 or www.recreation.gov ($10 reservation fee). Sites are $18–24 per night, $30 per night for "small group sites" (which are like double sites), $5 per night for each additional vehicle. Open May through October, weather permitting.

Directions: From Red Bluff, drive east on Highway 36 toward Susanville. Three miles before Susanville turn left on Eagle Lake Road/County Road A1 and drive 19.5 miles to the campground on the right side of the road.

Contact: Lassen National Forest, Eagle Lake

Ranger District, 530/257-4188, fax 530/252-5803.

83 MERRILL

Scenic rating: 8

on Eagle Lake in Lassen National Forest

Map grid B2

This is one of the largest, most developed Forest Service campgrounds in the entire county. It is set along the southern shore of huge Eagle Lake at 5,100 feet. The nearest boat launch is at Gallatin Marina, where there is a developed swim beach.

RV sites, facilities: There are 173 individual sites and two double sites with full or partial hookups (30 and 50 amps) for tents or RVs up to 50 feet. Picnic tables and fire rings are provided. Drinking water and flush toilets are available. A dump station is nearby. Some facilities are wheelchair-accessible. A grocery store and boat ramp are nearby. Leashed pets are permitted. A camp host is on site.

Reservations, fees: Reservations are accepted at 877/444-6777 or www.recreation.gov ($10 reservation fee). RV sites are $29–33 per night, double sites are $56 per night, tent sites are $18–19 per night. Open May through October, weather permitting.

Directions: From Red Bluff, drive east on Highway 36 toward Susanville. Three miles before Susanville, turn left on Eagle Lake Road/County Road A1 and drive 17.5 miles to the campground on the right side of the road.

Contact: Lassen National Forest, Eagle Lake Ranger District, 530/257-4188, fax 530/252-5803, camp host, 530/825-3450.

84 WEST EAGLE GROUP CAMPS

Scenic rating: 9

on Eagle Lake in Lassen National Forest

Map grid B2

If you are coming in a big group to Eagle Lake, you'd better get on the telephone first and reserve this camp. Then you can have your own private slice of solitude along the southern shore of Eagle Lake. Bring your boat; the Gallatin Marina and a swimming beach are only about a mile away. The elevation is 5,100 feet.

RV sites, facilities: There are two group camps for tents or RVs up to 35 feet (no hookups) that can accommodate 75–100 people each. Picnic tables and fire grills are provided. Drinking water, flush toilets, and picnic areas are available. A grocery store, dump station, and boat ramp are nearby. Leashed pets are permitted.

Reservations, fees: Reservations are required at 877/444-6777 or www.recreation.gov ($10 reservation fee). The sites are $100–125 per night. Open May through October, weather permitting.

Directions: From Red Bluff, drive east on Highway 36 toward Susanville. Three miles before Susanville, turn left on Eagle Lake Road/County Road A1 and drive 15.5 miles to County Road 231. Turn right on County Road 231 and drive 0.25 mile to the campground on the left side of the road.

Contact: Lassen National Forest, Eagle Lake Ranger District, 530/257-4188, fax 530/252-5803.

85 EAGLE

Scenic rating: 8

on Eagle Lake in Lassen National Forest
Map grid B2

Eagle is set just up the road from Aspen Grove, which is more popular because of the boat ramp nearby. Eagle Lake is one of the great trout lakes in California. The elevation is 5,100 feet.

RV sites, facilities: There are 50 individual sites and two double sites for tents or RVs up to 25 feet (no hookups). Picnic tables and fire grills are provided. Drinking water and flush toilets are available. Some facilities are wheelchair-accessible. There is a boat launch nearby at Gallatin Marina. Leashed pets are permitted.

Reservations, fees: Reservations are accepted

at 877/444-6777 or www.recreation.gov ($10 reservation fee). Sites are $18 per night, "small group sites" (which are like double sites) are $30 per night, $5 per night for each additional vehicle. Open May through October, weather permitting.

Directions: From Red Bluff, drive east on Highway 36 toward Susanville. Three miles before Susanville, turn left on Eagle Lake Road/County Road A1 and drive 15.5 miles to County Road 231. Turn right and drive 0.5 mile to the campground on the left side of the road.

Contact: Lassen National Forest, Eagle Lake Ranger District, 530/257-4188, fax 530/252-5803.

86 GOUMAZ

Scenic rating: 7

on the Susan River in Lassen National Forest
Map grid B2

This camp is set beside the Susan River, adjacent to historic Bizz Johnson Trail, a former route for a rail line that has been converted to a 25-mile trail. The trail runs from Susanville to Westwood, but this section provides access to many of its prettiest and most remote stretches as it runs in a half-circle around Pegleg Mountain (7,112 feet) to the east. It is an outstanding route for biking, hiking, and horseback riding in the summer and cross-country skiing in the winter. Equestrian campers are welcome here. The elevation is 5,200 feet.

RV sites, facilities: There are six sites for tents or RVs up to 25 feet (no hookups). Picnic tables and fire grills are provided. Drinking water and vault toilets are available. Equestrian facilities include water troughs and tie-lines. Leashed pets are permitted.

Reservations, fees: Reservations are not accepted. Sites are $13 per night, $5 per night for each additional vehicle. Open May through October, weather permitting.

Directions: From Red Bluff, drive east on Highway 36 past Lake Almanor to the junction with Highway 44. Turn west on Highway 44 and drive six miles (one mile past the Worley Ranch) to Goumaz Road/Forest Road 30N08. Turn left on Goumaz Road and drive about five miles to the campground entrance road on the right.

Contact: Lassen National Forest, Eagle Lake Ranger District, 530/257-4188, fax 530/252-5803.

87 BOULDER CREEK

Scenic rating: 7

at Antelope Lake in Plumas National Forest
Map grid B2

Antelope Lake is a pretty mountain lake circled by conifers, with nice campsites and good trout fishing. It is set at 5,000 feet elevation in remote eastern Plumas National Forest, far enough away so the marginally inclined never make the trip. Campgrounds are at each end of the lake (this one is just north of Lone Rock at the north end), with a boat ramp at Lost Cove on the east side of the lake. All water sports are permitted, and swimming is best near the campgrounds. The lake isn't huge, but it is big enough, with 15 miles of shoreline and little islands, coves, and peninsulas to give it an intimate feel.

RV sites, facilities: There are 70 sites for tents or RVs up to 40 feet (no hookups). Picnic tables and fire grills are provided. Drinking water and vault toilets are available. A dump station, boat ramp, and grocery store are nearby. Some facilities are wheelchair-accessible. Leashed pets are permitted.

Reservations, fees: Reservations are accepted at 877/444-6777 or www.recreation.gov ($10 reservation fee). Sites are $20 per night, double sites are $35 per night, $5 per night for each additional vehicle. Open May through early September.

Directions: From Red Bluff, drive east on Highway 36 to Susanville and U.S. 395. Turn south on U.S. 395 and drive about 10 miles (one mile past Janesville) to County Road 208. Turn right on County Road 208 (signed Antelope Lake) and drive about 15 miles to a Y (one mile

before Antelope Lake). Turn left at the Y and drive four miles to the campground entrance on the right side of the road (on the northwest end of the lake).

Contact: Plumas National Forest, Mount Hough Ranger District, 530/283-0555, fax 530/283-1821; Northwest Park Management, 530/283-5559.

88 LONE ROCK

Scenic rating: 9

at Antelope Lake in Plumas National Forest
Map grid B2

This camp provides an option to nearby Boulder Creek, to the immediate north at the northwest shore of Antelope Lake. (See the Boulder Creek listing for more information.) The elevation is 5,000 feet. Campfire programs are offered in the summer at the on-site amphitheater.

RV sites, facilities: There are 87 sites for tents or RVs up to 40 feet (no hookups). Picnic tables and fire grills are provided. Drinking water and vault toilets are available. A dump station, boat ramp, and grocery store are nearby. Some facilities are wheelchair-accessible. Leashed pets are permitted.

Reservations, fees: Reservations are accepted at 877/444-6777 or www.recreation.gov ($10 reservation fee). Sites are $18–20 per night. Open May through October.

Directions: From Red Bluff, drive east on Highway 36 to Susanville and U.S. 395. Go south on U.S. 395 and drive about 10 miles (one mile past Janesville) to County Road 208. Turn right on County Road 208 (signed Antelope Lake) and drive about 15 miles to a Y (one mile before Antelope Lake). Turn left at the Y and drive three miles to the campground entrance on the right side of the road (on the northwest end of the lake).

Contact: Plumas National Forest, Mount Hough Ranger District, 530/283-0555, fax 530/283-1821; Northwest Park Management, 530/283-5559.

CALIFORNIA

89 LONG POINT

🥾 🏊 🎣 🛶 🐴 ♿ 🚐 ⛺

Scenic rating: 7

at Antelope Lake in Plumas National Forest

Map grid B2

Long Point is a pretty camp set on a peninsula that extends well into Antelope Lake, facing Lost Cove. The lake's boat ramp is at Lost Cove, a three-mile drive around the northeast shore. Trout fishing is often good here for both rainbow and brown trout, and there is a nature trail. A group campground is set within this campground.

RV sites, facilities: There are 38 sites for tents or RVs up to 30 feet, and four group sites for tents or RVs up to 35 feet that can accommodate up to 25 people each. No hookups. Picnic tables and fire grills are provided. Drinking water and vault toilets are available. A grocery store, boat ramp, and dump stations are nearby. Some facilities are wheelchair-accessible. Leashed pets are permitted.

Reservations, fees: Reservations are accepted for individual sites and required for the group sites at 877/444-6777 or www.recreation.gov ($10 reservation fee). Sites are $20 per night, double sites are $35 per night, $75 per night for group sites. Open May through October.

Directions: From Red Bluff, drive east on Highway 36 to Susanville and U.S. 395. Go south on U.S. 395 and drive about 10 miles (one mile past Janesville) to County Road 208. Turn right on County Road 208 (signed Antelope Lake) and drive about 15 miles to a Y (one mile before Antelope Lake). Turn right at the Y and drive one mile to the campground entrance on the left side of the road.

Contact: Plumas National Forest, Mount Hough Ranger District, 530/283-0555, fax 530/283-1821; Northwest Park Management, 530/283-5559.

90 HONEY LAKE CAMPGROUND

🎣 🏕 🐴 ♿ 🚐 ⛺

Scenic rating: 4

near Milford

Map grid B2

For newcomers, Honey Lake is a strange-looking place—a vast, shallow lake set on the edge of the desert of the Great Basin. The campground is set at 4,385 feet elevation and covers 30 acres, most of it overlooking the lake. There are a few pine trees in the campground, and a waterfowl management area is along the north shore of the lake. This campground is popular with hunters. Equestrian facilities, including a corral and exercise ring, are available. Fishing for Eagle Lake trout is good here. The lake is 26 miles across, and on rare flat calm evenings, the sunsets are spectacular here.

RV sites, facilities: There are 44 pull-through sites for tents or RVs of any length, half with full or partial hookups (30 amps), plus 25 mobile homes and trailers. Picnic tables are provided. Restrooms with showers, coin laundry, dump station, propane gas, restaurant, gift and grocery store, playground, ice, video rentals, and a recreation room are available. Some facilities are wheelchair-accessible. Leashed pets are permitted.

Reservations, fees: Reservations are not accepted. Sites are $14.95–29.95 per night, $3.50 per person per night for more than two people. Long-term rentals are available. Some credit cards accepted. Open year-round.

Directions: From Susanville on U.S. 395, drive 17 miles south (if you reach Milford, you have gone two miles too far) to the campground on the west side of the highway. It is 65 miles north of Reno.

Contact: Honey Lake Campground, 530/253-2508.

91 CONKLIN PARK

Scenic rating: 4

on Willow Creek in Plumas National Forest

Map grid B2

This camp is along little Willow Creek on the northeastern border of the Dixie Mountain State Game Refuge. Much of the area is recovering from a fire that burned during the summer of 1989. Although the area has greened up, there remains significant evidence of the fire. The campground is little known, primitive, rarely used, and is not likely to change any time soon. The elevation is 5,900 feet.

RV sites, facilities: There are nine sites for tents or RVs up to 25 feet (no hookups). Picnic tables and fire grills are provided. Vault toilets are available. No drinking water is available. Garbage must be packed out. Leashed pets are permitted.

Reservations, fees: Reservations are not accepted. There is no fee for camping. Open May through October, weather permitting.

Directions: From Susanville on U.S. 395, drive south for 24 miles to Milford. In Milford turn right (east) on County Road 336 and drive about four miles to a Y. Bear to the right on Forest Road 70/26N70 and drive three miles. Turn right at the bridge at Willow Creek, turn left on Forest Road 70 (now paved), and drive three miles to the camp entrance road on the left side.

Contact: Plumas National Forest, Beckwourth Ranger District, 530/836-2575, fax 530/836-0493.

92 MEADOW VIEW

Scenic rating: 6

near Little Last Chance Creek in Plumas National Forest

Map grid B2

This little-known, primitive camp is set along the headwaters of Little Last Chance Creek, along the eastern border of the Dixie Mountain State Game Refuge. The access road continues along the creek and connects with primitive roads that enter the interior of the game refuge. Side-trip options include Frenchman Lake to the south and the drive up to Dixie Mountain, at 8,323 feet elevation. The camp elevation is 6,100 feet.

RV sites, facilities: There are six sites for tents or RVs up to 30 feet (no hookups). Picnic tables and fire grills are provided. Vault toilets are available. No drinking water is available. Garbage must be packed out. Leashed pets are permitted.

Reservations, fees: Reservations are not accepted. There is no fee for camping. Open May through October, weather permitting.

Directions: From Reno, drive north on U.S. 395 for 43 miles to Doyle. At Doyle, turn west on Doyle Grade Road/County Road 331 (a dirt road most of the way) and drive seven miles to the campground.

Contact: Plumas National Forest, Beckwourth Ranger District, 530/836-2575, fax 530/836-0493.

CALIFORNIA

MENDOCINO AND WINE COUNTRY

◖ BEST RV PARKS AND CAMPGROUNDS

◖ Fishing
Westside Regional Park, page 750.
Doran Regional Park, page 751.

◖ Wildlife-Viewing
MacKerricher State Park, page 718.
Caspar Beach RV Park, page 722.
Ocean Cove Campground, page 746.

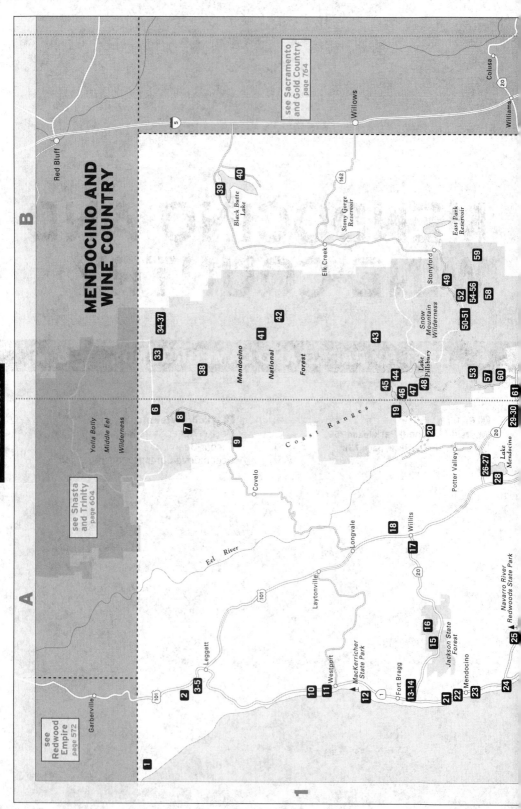

CALIFORNIA

MENDOCINO AND WINE COUNTRY

see Redwood Empire page 572

see Shasta and Trinity page 604

see Sacramento and Gold Country page 764

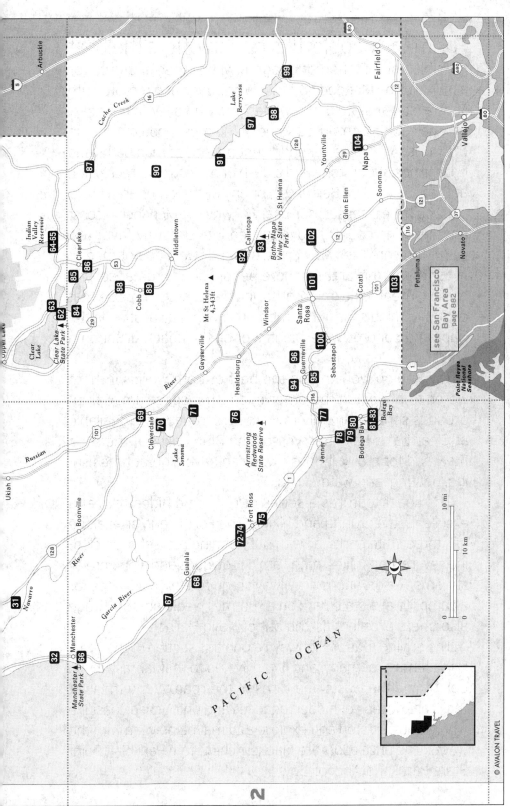

CALIFORNIA

PACIFIC OCEAN

© AVALON TRAVEL

For many people, this region offers the best possible combination of geography, weather, and outdoor activities. The Mendocino coast is dramatic and remote, with several stellar state parks, while Sonoma Valley, in the heart of wine country, produces some of the most popular wines in the world. Add in the self-indulgent options of mud baths and hot springs at Calistoga and a dash of mainstream recreation at Clear Lake, Lake Berryessa, or any of the other area lakes, and you have a capsule summary of why the Mendocino coast and the wine country have turned into getaway favorites.

But they are like two worlds, and the twain do not meet.

For many, this area is where people go for romance, fine cuisine, great wine, mineral springs, and anything else that comes to mind spur-of-the-moment. Such is a vacation in the Napa and Sonoma wine country, or on the beautiful Sonoma and Mendocino coast.

This region wouldn't be the best of both worlds if there weren't options on the other end of the spectrum. Campgrounds set up primarily for family recreation are available at Clear Lake, Lake Berryessa, and Blue Lakes. If the shoe fits – and for many, it does – you can have a great time fishing, boating, and waterskiing.

The coast features a series of romantic hideaways and excellent adventuring and hiking. The Fort Bragg area alone has three state parks, all with outstanding recreation, including several easy hikes, many amid redwoods and along pretty streams. Reservations are always required far in advance for a campsite at a state park on a summer weekend. Fort Bragg also offers excellent fishing out of Noyo Harbor.

The driving tour of Highway 1 along this section of the coast is the fantasy of many, and it can live up to that fantasy if you don't mind the twists and turns of the road. Along the way, there are dozens of hidden beaches and untouched coastline where you can stop and explore and maybe play tag with the waves. The prize spots are MacKerricher State Park, Salt Point State Park, and Anchor Bay.

1 NADELOS AND WAILAKI

Scenic rating: 7

in the King Range
Map grid A1

Nadelos and Wailaki campgrounds are set a short distance apart at 1,840 feet elevation near the South Fork Bear Creek at the southern end of the King Range National Conservation Area. This provides access to a rare geographic dynamic, where mountains and coast adjoin. Nearby Chemise Mountain, elevation 2,598 feet, is one of the highest points in California within two miles of the sea, and it provides a dramatic lookout on clear days. Nadelos is also one of the few camps with individual sites that can be reserved by a group.

RV sites, facilities: There are eight tent sites at Nadelos. There are 13 sites for tents or RVs up to 20 feet (no hookups) at Wailaki. Picnic tables and fire grills are provided. Drinking water and vault toilets are available. Some facilities are wheelchair-accessible. Leashed pets are permitted.

Reservations, fees: Reservations for individual sites are not accepted. Reservations for Nadelos are accepted at 707/986-5400. Individual sites are $8 per night; groups sites are $85 per night. Open year-round.

Directions: From Eureka, drive 60 miles south on U.S. 101 to the Redway exit. Take the Redway/Shelter Cove exit onto Redwood Drive into the town of Redway. Drive 2.5 miles (look on the right for the King Range Conservation Area sign) to Briceland-Thorne Road. Turn right on Briceland-Thorne Road (which will become Shelter Cove Road) and drive 17 miles to Chemise Mountain Road. Turn left (south) on Chemise Mountain Road and drive one mile to Nadelos Campground on the right. To reach Wailaki Campground from Nadelos, continue 0.4 mile to the camp on the right.

Contact: Bureau of Land Management, Arcata Field Office, 707/825-2300, fax 707/825-2301, www.ca.blm.gov/arcata.

2 REDWOODS RIVER RESORT

Scenic rating: 8

on the Eel River
Map grid A1

This resort is situated in a 21-acre grove of redwoods on U.S. 101 and features 1,500 feet of river access, including a sandy beach and two swimming holes. Many of the campsites are shaded. A hiking trail leads from the resort to the Eel River, a walk of just over a quarter mile. This is one in a series of both public and private campgrounds along the highway between Leggett and Garberville. Steelhead and salmon fishing are popular here in the winter, and the resort provides nearby access to state parks. The elevation is 700 feet.

RV sites, facilities: There are 14 tent sites and 27 sites with full hookups (30 amps) for RVs of any length; some sites are pull-through. Eight cabins and eight lodge rooms are also available. At campsites, picnic tables and fire rings are provided. Restrooms with showers, seasonal heated swimming pool, playground, recreation room, modem access, minimart, coin laundry, group kitchen, dump station, table tennis, basketball, volleyball, badminton, horseshoes, shuffleboard, group facilities, seasonal organized activities, and a seasonal evening campfire are available. Some facilities are wheelchair-accessible. Leashed pets are permitted, except in buildings.

Reservations, fees: Reservations are recommended in the summer. Sites are $22–40 per night, $4 per person per night for more than two people, $2 per pet per night. Off-season discounts available. Some credit cards accepted. Open year-round.

Directions: From the junction of U.S. 101 and Highway 1 in Leggett, drive north on U.S. 101 for seven miles to the campground entrance on the left.

Contact: Redwoods River Resort, 707/925-6249, www.redwoodriverresort.com.

CALIFORNIA

3 STANDISH-HICKEY STATE RECREATION AREA: REDWOOD CAMPGROUND

Scenic rating: 8

on the Eel River in Standish-Hickey
State Recreation Area

Map grid A1

This is one of three camps in Standish-Hickey State Recreation Area, and it is by far the most unusual. Reaching Redwood Campground requires driving over a temporary "summer bridge," which provides access to a pretty spot along the South Fork Eel River. In early September, out comes the bridge and up comes the river. The park covers 1,012 acres set in an inland river canyon; the South Fork Eel provides two miles of river frontage. Standish-Hickey is known as "the gateway to the tall trees country." The Grove Trail contains one of the few virgin stands of redwoods in this area. Note that two other campgrounds are available at this park, and that this camp is open only in summer. The elevation is 800 feet.

RV sites, facilities: There are 63 sites for tents or RVs up to 18 feet (no hookups). No trailers, including pop-up tent trailers, are permitted. Picnic tables, food lockers, and fire rings are provided. Drinking water and restrooms with coin showers and flush toilets are available. Some facilities are wheelchair-accessible. Leashed pets are permitted.

Reservations, fees: Reservations are accepted at 800/444-PARK (800/444-7275) or www.reserveamerica.com ($8 reservation fee). Sites are $45 per night, $8 per night for each additional vehicle. Open July through Labor Day weekend.

Directions: From the junction of U.S. 101 and Highway 1 in Leggett, drive north on U.S. 101 for one mile. The park entrance is on the west (left) side of the road.

Contact: Standish-Hickey State Recreation Area, 707/925-6482, fax 707/925-6402, www.parks.ca.gov.

4 STANDISH-HICKEY STATE RECREATION AREA: ROCK CREEK

Scenic rating: 8

on the Eel River in Standish-Hickey
State Recreation Area

Map grid A1

This is one of two main campgrounds set in a mixed redwood grove at Standish-Hickey State Recreation Area (the other is Hickey). It is the classic state park camp, with numbered sites, flat tent spaces, picnic tables, and food lockers. There are 12 miles of hiking trails in the park. Hiking is only fair, but most people enjoy the short tromp down to the nearby South Fork Eel River. In the winter, steelhead migrate through the area. (See the Redwood Campground listing for more details on this park.)

RV sites, facilities: There are 35 sites for tents or RVs up to 27 feet (no hookups) and trailers up to 24 feet, and one hike-in/bike-in site. Picnic tables, food lockers, and fire rings are provided. Drinking water and restrooms with coin showers and flush toilets are available. Some facilities are wheelchair-accessible. Leashed pets are permitted.

Reservations, fees: Reservations are accepted at 800/444-PARK (800/444-7275) or www.reserveamerica.com ($8 reservation fee). Sites are $35 per night, $8 per night for each additional vehicle, $3 per person per night for the hike-in/bike-in site. Open year-round.

Directions: From the junction of U.S. 101 and Highway 1 in Leggett, drive north on U.S. 101 for one mile. The park entrance is on the west (left) side of the road.

Contact: Standish-Hickey State Recreation Area, 707/925-6482, fax 707/925-6402, www.parks.ca.gov.

5 STANDISH-HICKEY STATE RECREATION AREA: HICKEY

Scenic rating: 8

on the Eel River in Standish-Hickey
State Recreation Area

Map grid A1

This is an ideal layover for U.S. 101 cruisers yearning to spend a night in the redwoods. The park is best known for its campsites set amid redwoods and for the nearby South Fork Eel River with its steelhead fishing in the winter. The elevation is 800 feet. Insider's tip: There's a great swimming hole on the Eel River in the summer. (See details about Standish-Hickey State Recreation Area in the Redwood Campground listing in this chapter.)

RV sites, facilities: There are 65 sites for tents or RVs up to 16 feet (no hookups) and trailers up to 24 feet. Picnic tables, food lockers, and fire rings are provided. Drinking water and restrooms with showers and flush toilets are available. A grocery store is available nearby. Some facilities are wheelchair-accessible. Leashed pets are permitted.

Reservations, fees: Reservations are accepted at 800/444-PARK (800/444-7275) or www.reserveamerica.com ($8 reservation fee). Sites are $35 per night, $8 per night for each additional vehicle. Hike-in/bike-in sites are $3 per night. Open year-round.

Directions: From the junction of U.S. 101 and Highway 1 in Leggett, drive north on U.S. 101 for one mile. The park entrance is on the west (left) side of the road.

Contact: Standish-Hickey State Recreation Area, 707/925-6482, fax 707/925-6402, www.parks.ca.gov.

6 HAMMERHORN LAKE

Scenic rating: 7

near Covelo in Mendocino National Forest

Map grid A1

Obscure and hidden, this is a veritable dot of a lake, just five acres, set at 3,500 feet in Mendocino National Forest. The lake is too small for motorized boats, but swimming is allowed. There is a spring at the south end of the lake; go out of the camp and hike along the edge of the lake—you can hear the water running out of the pipe often before you see it. The lake is set near the border of the Yolla Bolly Wilderness, with Green Springs Trailhead a few miles away to the northeast. A great side trip is the drive up to Anthony Peak.

RV sites, facilities: There are nine sites for tents or RVs up to 16 feet (no hookups). Picnic tables and fire grills are provided. Drinking water, vault toilets, and fishing piers are available. Garbage must be packed out. Some facilities are wheelchair-accessible. Supplies are available in Covelo. Leashed pets are permitted.

Reservations, fees: Reservations are not accepted. Sites are $8 per night. Open April through December.

Directions: From Willits, drive north on U.S. 101 for 13 miles to Longvale and the junction with Highway 162. Turn northeast on Highway 162 and drive to Covelo. Continue east on Highway 162 for nine miles to the Eel River Bridge. After crossing the bridge, turn left on Forest Road M1 and drive about 17 miles to Forest Road M21. Turn right and drive one mile to the campground entrance.

Contact: Mendocino National Forest, Covelo Ranger District, 707/983-6118, fax 707/983-8004.

7 HOWARDS MEADOWS AND HOWARD LAKE

Scenic rating: 8

in Mendocino National Forest

Map grid A1

Howard Lake is a small lake located deep in Mendocino National Forest. It is pretty and larger than Hammerhorn Lake to the north. Some years it is stocked with small trout. If the tiny campground at Howard Lake is occupied, the camp at Howard Meadows is within walking distance. The elevation is 3,500 feet.

CALIFORNIA

RV sites, facilities: There are four sites for tents or small RVs at Howard Lake, one of which is wheelchair accessible. There are eight campsites for tents or small RVs at Howard Meadows. Picnic tables and fire rings are provided. Vault toilets are available, but there is no drinking water. Garbage must be packed out.

Reservations, fees: Reservations are not accepted. There is no camping fee. Open April to December.

Directions: From Willits, drive north on U.S. 101 for 13 miles to Longvale and the junction with Highway 162. Turn northeast on Highway 162 and drive for nine miles to the Eel River Bridge. After crossing the bridge, turn left on Forest Service Road M1/Indian Dick Road. Drive 22 miles on Forest Service Road M1/Indian Dick Road to the campground.

Contact: Mendocino National Forest, Covelo Ranger District, 707/983-6118, fax 707/983-6004, www.fs.fed.us.

8 LITTLE DOE

Scenic rating: 5

near Howard Lake in Mendocino National Forest
Map grid A1

Little Howard Lake is tucked deep in the interior of Mendocino National Forest between Espee Ridge to the south and Little Doe Ridge to the north, at an elevation of 3,600 feet. For a drive-to lake, it is surprisingly remote and provides fair trout fishing, primitive camping, and an opportunity for car-top boating. The lake covers 15–20 acres, and swimming is allowed. Side trips include Hammerhorn Lake, about six miles away, and several four-wheel-drive roads that allow you to explore the area. A Forest Service map is recommended.

RV sites, facilities: There are 13 sites for tents or RVs up to 16 feet (no hookups). Picnic tables and fire pits are provided. Vault toilets are available. No drinking water is available. All garbage must be packed out. No gas motors allowed. Supplies are available in Covelo, 12 miles

away. Some facilities are wheelchair-accessible. Leashed pets are permitted.

Reservations, fees: Reservations are not accepted. There is no fee for camping. Open April through December.

Directions: From Willits, drive north on U.S. 101 for 13 miles to Longvale and the junction with Highway 162. Turn northeast on Highway 162 and drive to Covelo. Continue east on Highway 162 and drive for nine miles to the Eel River Bridge. After crossing the bridge, turn left on Forest Road M1 and drive about 11 miles to the campground.

Contact: Mendocino National Forest, Covelo Ranger District, 707/983-6118, fax 707/983-8004.

9 EEL RIVER

Scenic rating: 8

in Mendocino National Forest
Map grid A1

This is a little-known spot, set in oak woodlands at the confluence of the Middle Fork of the Eel River and Black Butte River. The elevation is 1,500 feet, and it's often extremely hot in summer. Eel River is an ancient Native American campsite and a major archaeological site. For this reason restoration has been limited and at times the camp is overgrown and weedy. Who cares, though? After all, you're camping.

RV sites, facilities: There are 15 sites for tents or RVs up to 21 feet (no hookups). Picnic tables and fire grills are provided. Drinking water and vault toilets are available. Garbage must be packed out. Leashed pets are permitted.

Reservations, fees: Reservations are not accepted. Sites are $8 per night. Open April through December.

Directions: From Willits, drive north on U.S. 101 for 13 miles to Longvale and the junction with Highway 162. Turn northeast on Highway 162 and drive to Covelo. Continue east on Highway 162 for 13 miles to the campground.

Contact: Mendocino National Forest, Covelo Ranger District, 707/983-6118, fax 707/983-8004.

10 WESTPORT-UNION LANDING STATE BEACH

Scenic rating: 8

near Westport overlooking the Pacific Ocean
Map grid A1

The northern Mendocino coast is remote, beautiful, and gets far less people pressure than the Fort Bragg area. That is the key to its appeal. These state park campsites are on an ocean bluff. It can get windy here, but the reward is the view. This park covers more than three miles of rugged and scenic coastline. Splendid views, colorful sunsets, and tree-covered mountains provide great photo opportunities. Several small sandy beaches, and one large beach at the mouth of Howard Creek, provide some good spots for surf fishing. Several species of rockfish and abalone can be taken when tides and ocean conditions are right. But note that the surf here can surge, discouraging all but the hardy. The park was named for two early-day communities, Westport and Union Landing, settlements well known for lumber and rail ties.

RV sites, facilities: There are 46 sites for tents or RVs of any length (no hookups); eight people maximum per site. Picnic tables and fire rings are provided. Drinking water and chemical flush toilets are available. A grocery store is nearby. Leashed pets are permitted.

Reservations, fees: Reservations are not accepted. Sites are $10–15 per night, $6 per night for each additional vehicle. Open year-round.

Directions: From Fort Bragg, drive north on Highway 1 to Westport. In Westport, continue north on Highway 1 for three miles to the campground entrance on the west side of the road.

Contact: California State Parks, Mendocino District, 707/937-5804, fax 707/937-2953, www.parks.ca.gov.

11 WESTPORT BEACH RV AND CAMPING

Scenic rating: 8

near Westport overlooking the Pacific Ocean
Map grid A1

Westport Beach RV and Camping is set above the beach near the mouth of Wages Creek, with both creekside and beach sites available. The 30-acre campground has a quarter mile of beach frontage. You will notice as you venture north from Fort Bragg that the number of vacationers in the area falls way off, providing a chance for quiet beaches and serene moments. The best nearby hiking is to the north out of the trailhead for the Sinkyone Wilderness.

RV sites, facilities: There are 75 sites with full hookups (20, 30, and 50 amps) for RVs of any length, 24 sites with no hookups for RVs of any length, 47 sites for tents only, and six group sites for tents or RVs (no hookups) that can accommodate 12–50 people each. Some RV sites are pull-through. A two-bedroom house is also available. Picnic tables and fire rings are provided at most sites. Drinking water, restrooms with coin showers and flush toilets, convenience store, coin laundry, telephone/modem access, playground, volleyball, shuffleboard, horseshoes, firewood, and ice are available. Some facilities are wheelchair-accessible. Leashed pets are permitted.

Reservations, fees: Reservations are accepted. Sites are $25–49 per night for RV sites, $25 per night per vehicle for tent and RV sites (including group sites) with no hookups, $5–6 per night per person for more than two people, $2 per pet per night. Monthly rates available. Some credit cards accepted. Open year-round.

Directions: From Fort Bragg, drive north on Highway 1 to Westport. In Westport, continue north on Highway 1 for 0.5 mile to the campground entrance on the west side of the highway.

Contact: Westport Beach RV and Camping, 707/964-2964, fax 707/964-8185, www.westportbeachrv.com.

CALIFORNIA

12 MACKERRICHER STATE PARK

Scenic rating: 9

north of Fort Bragg overlooking the Pacific Ocean

Map grid A1   **BEST (**

MacKerricher is a beautiful park on the Mendocino coast, a great destination for adventure and exploration. The camps are set in a coastal forest, with gorgeous walk-in sites. Nearby is a small beach, great tidepools, a rocky point where harbor seals hang out in the sun, a small lake (Cleone) with trout fishing, a great bike trail, and outstanding short hikes. The short jaunt around little Cleone Lake has many romantic spots, often tunneling through vegetation, then emerging for lake views. The coastal walk to the point to see seals and tidepools is equally captivating. For wheelchair users, there is a wheelchair-accessible trail to Laguna Point and also a route on a raised boardwalk that runs halfway around Cleone Lake, a former tidal lagoon. This park covers more than 1,530 acres of beach, bluff, headlands, dune, forest, and wetlands. That diverse landscape provides habitat for more than 90 species of bird, most in the vicinity of Cleone Lake. The headland supplies a prime vantage point for whale-watching in winter and spring.

RV sites, facilities: There are 142 sites for tents or RVs up to 35 feet (no hookups), 10 walk-in sites, and two group sites for up to 40–60 people each. Picnic tables, fire rings, and food lockers are provided. Drinking water, restroom with flush toilets and coin showers, picnic area, Wi-Fi, and a dump station are available. A seasonal junior ranger program with nature walks, campfire programs, and exhibits is offered. Some facilities are wheelchair-accessible. Leashed pets are permitted.

Reservations, fees: Reservations are accepted at 800/444-PARK (800/444-7275) or www. reserveamerica.com ($8 reservation fee). Sites are $20–25 per night, $6 per night for each additional vehicle. Group sites are $120–180 per night. Open year-round.

Directions: From Fort Bragg, drive north on Highway 1 for three miles to the campground entrance on the left side of the road.

Contact: MacKerricher State Park, 707/964-9112; Mendocino District, 707/937-5804, fax 707/937-2953, www.parks.ca.gov.

13 FORT BRAGG LEISURE TIME RV PARK

Scenic rating: 5

in Fort Bragg

Map grid A1

This privately operated park adjoins Jackson State Forest, with easy access for hiking and cycling trails. The park offers horseshoes, badminton, and a covered group picnic area. The drive from Willits to Fort Bragg on Highway 20 is always a favorite, a curving two-laner through redwoods, not too slow, not too fast, best seen from the saddle of a Harley-Davidson. At the end of it is the coast, and just three miles inland is this campground in the sunbelt, said to be out of the fog by breakfast. Within short drives are Noyo Harbor in Fort Bragg, Russian Gulch State Park, Mendocino to the south, and MacKerricher State Park to the north. In fact, there's so much in the area, you could explore for days. Note that about 10 percent of the sites are filled with permanent or long-term renters.

RV sites, facilities: There are 70 pull-through sites, many with full or partial hookups (30 amps), for tents or RVs up to 40 feet. Picnic tables and fire rings are provided. Restrooms with coin showers, satellite TV, modem access, dump station, fish-cleaning station, horseshoes, RV storage, and a coin laundry are available. Some facilities are wheelchair-accessible. Leashed pets are permitted.

Reservations, fees: Reservations are accepted at 800/700-8542. Sites are $23–34 per night, $5 per person per night for more than two people, $1 per night for each additional vehicle, $2 per night for first pet, and $1 per night for additional pet. Monthly and seasonal rates available. Some credit cards accepted. Open year-round.

Directions: In Fort Bragg at the junction of Highway 1 and Highway 20, turn east on

Highway 20 and drive 2.5 miles to the campground entrance on the right side of the road at 30801 Highway 20.

Contact: Fort Bragg Leisure Time RV Park, 707/964-5994.

14 POMO RV PARK AND CAMPGROUND

Scenic rating: 7

in Fort Bragg

Map grid A1

This park covers 17 acres of lush, native vegetation, including rhododendrons, near the ocean. It is one of several camps on the Fort Bragg and Mendocino coast, and groups are welcome. Nearby Noyo Harbor offers busy restaurants, deep-sea fishing, a boat ramp, harbor, and a nice walk out to the Noyo Harbor jetty. Huckleberry picking is also an option. Many of the RV spaces are quite wide at this park.

RV sites, facilities: There are 94 sites with full or partial hookups (30 and 50 amps) for RVs of any length, and 30 sites for tents. Some sites are pull-through. Picnic tables and fire rings are provided. Restrooms with coin showers, cable TV hookups, Wi-Fi, convenience store, firewood, ice, RV supplies, propane gas, coin laundry, dump station, fish-cleaning table, horseshoe pits, and large grass playing field are available. Some facilities are wheelchair accessible. Leashed pets are permitted.

Reservations, fees: Reservations are recommended in the summer. Sites are $25–40 per night, $3–5 per person per night for more than two people, $1 per pet per night. Open year-round.

Directions: In Fort Bragg at the junction of Highway 1 and Highway 20, drive south on Highway 1 for one mile to Tregoning Lane. Turn left (east) and drive a short distance to the park at the end of the road (17999 Tregoning Lane).

Contact: Pomo RV Park and Campground, 707/964-3373.

15 JACKSON DEMONSTRATION STATE FOREST, CAMP 1

Scenic rating: 7

near Fort Bragg

Map grid A1

Primitive campsites set in a vast forest of redwoods and Douglas fir are the prime attraction at Jackson Demonstration State Forest. Even though Highway 20 is a major connecting link to the coast in the summer, these camps get bypassed because they are primitive and largely unknown. Why? Because reaching them requires driving on dirt roads sometimes frequented by logging trucks, and there are few campground signs along the highway. This camp features lots of tree cover, with oaks, redwoods, and madrones. Most of the campsites are adjacent to the south fork of the north fork of the Noyo River, well known among locals, but completely missed by most others. A one-mile trail circles the campground; the trailhead is at the day-use area. A DFG hatchery is next to the campground, but note that no fishing is permitted in the river.

RV sites, facilities: There are 32 sites for tents or RVs up to 27 feet (no hookups), and one group site that can accommodate up to 150 people for tents or RVs up to 45 feet. Picnic tables and fire pits are provided. Vault toilets are available. No drinking water is available. A camp host is on site and can issue camping permits. Leashed pets are permitted.

Reservations, fees: Reservations are accepted only for the group site at 707/964-5674. There is no fee for camping. A camping permit is required and can be obtained from the camp host or the State Department of Forestry and Fire Protection office (802 N. Main St./Hwy. 1, Fort Bragg, CA). Campers are limited to 30 days per year and no more than 14 consecutive days. Open late May through September.

Directions: From Willits on U.S. 101, turn west on Highway 20 and drive 27 miles to Forest Road 350 (at Mile Marker 5.9). Turn right (north) and drive 1.3 miles to the campground.

Contact: Jackson Demonstration State Forest, 707/964-5674.

CALIFORNIA

16 JACKSON DEMONSTRATION STATE FOREST, DUNLAP

Scenic rating: 6

near Fort Bragg
Map grid A1

A highlight of Jackson Demonstration Forest is a 50-foot waterfall on Chamberlain Creek. Set in a steep canyon at the east end of the forest, amid giant firs and redwoods, it can be reached with a 10-minute walk. There are also extensive logging roads that are good yet challenging for mountain biking. What to do first? Get a map from the State Forestry Department. For driving, the roads are extremely dusty in summer and muddy in winter.

RV sites, facilities: There are 30 sites for tents or RVs up to 16 feet (no hookups), including eight equestrian sites across the road at Big River Camp. Picnic tables and fire rings are provided. Vault toilets are available. No drinking water is available. A camp host is on site and can issue camping permits. Leashed pets are permitted.

Reservations, fees: Reservations are not accepted for individual sites, but are required for equestrian sites at 707/964-5674. There is no fee for camping. A camping permit is required and can be obtained from the camp host or the State Department of Forestry and Fire Protection office (802 N. Main St./Hwy. 1, Fort Bragg, CA). Campers are limited to 30 days per year and no more than 14 consecutive days. Open late May through September.

Directions: From Willits on U.S. 101, turn west on Highway 20 and drive 17 miles. At Mile Marker 16.9 (just past the Chamberlain Bridge) continue driving for about 0.25 mile to the Dunlap camp entrance on the left.

Contact: Jackson Demonstration State Forest, 707/964-5674, fax 707/964-0941.

17 WILLITS-UKIAH KOA

Scenic rating: 3

near Willits
Map grid A1

This is an ideal spot to park your RV if you plan on taking the Skunk Train west to Fort Bragg. A depot for the train is within walking distance of the campground, and tickets are available at KOA. The campground, which has a western theme, also offers nightly entertainment in summer. The elevation is 1,377 feet.

RV sites, facilities: There are 21 sites for tents and 50 sites with full or partial hookups (30 and 50 amps) for RVs of any length. Many sites are pull-through. Twelve cabins and two lodges are also available. Groups can be accommodated. Picnic tables and fire rings are provided. Drinking water, restrooms with flush toilets and showers, Wi-Fi, a playground, seasonal heated swimming pool, hay rides, mini golf, basketball, volleyball, fishing pond, convenience store, RV supplies, coin laundry, and a dump station are available. Some facilities are wheelchair accessible. Leashed pets are permitted, with certain restrictions.

Reservations, fees: Reservations are accepted at 800/562-8542. RV sites are $35–56 per night, tent sites are $25–37 per night, $3–4 per person per night for more than two people. Some credit cards accepted. Open year-round.

Directions: From Willits at the junction of U.S. 101 and Highway 20, turn west on Highway 20 and drive 1.5 miles to the campground on the right at 1600 Highway 20.

Contact: Willits-Ukiah KOA, 707/459-6179, fax 707/459-1489, www.koa.com.

18 CREEKSIDE CABINS AND RV RESORT

Scenic rating: 5

north of Willits
Map grid A1

The privately operated park is in a pretty valley, primarily oak/bay woodlands with a sprinkling of conifers. It was previously known as Hidden

Valley Campground. The most popular nearby recreation option is taking the Skunk Train in Willits for the ride out to the coast at Fort Bragg. There are also two golf courses within six miles. Note that about half of the sites are occupied by long-term renters.

RV sites, facilities: There are 50 sites, including 35 with full or partial hookups (20 and 30 amps), for tents or RVs up to 38 feet. Picnic tables and fire grills are provided, and some sites provide satellite TV, telephone, and Wi-Fi access. Restrooms with showers, ice, a coin laundry, and a dump station are available. Leashed pets are permitted.

Reservations, fees: Reservations are accepted. Sites are $25–45 per night, $3 per person per night for more than two people. Open year-round.

Directions: From Willits on U.S. 101, drive north for 6.5 miles on U.S. 101 to the campground on the east (right) side of the road at 29801 N. Highway 101.

Contact: Creekside Cabins and RV Resort, 707/459-2521, www.creeksidecabinsandrvresort.com.

19 POGIE POINT

Scenic rating: 7

on Lake Pillsbury in Mendocino National Forest
Map grid A1

This camp is set beside Lake Pillsbury in Mendocino National Forest, in the back of a cove at the lake's northwest corner. When the lake is full, this spot is quite pretty. A boat ramp is about a quarter mile to the south, a bonus. The elevation is 1,900 feet. (For more information about Lake Pillsbury, see the Fuller Grove listing in this chapter.)

RV sites, facilities: There are 45 sites for tents or RVs up to 16 feet (no hookups). Picnic tables and fire grills are provided. Drinking water and vault toilets are available. Some facilities are wheelchair-accessible. Leashed pets are permitted.

Reservations, fees: Reservations are not accepted. Sites are $13 per night, $3 per night for each additional vehicle, $1 per pet per night. Open May through October.

Directions: From Ukiah on U.S. 101, drive north to the junction with Highway 20. Turn east (right) on Highway 20 and drive five miles. Turn northwest on East Potter Valley Road toward Lake Pillsbury. Drive 5.9 miles to the town of Potter Valley. Continue on East Potter Valley Road to Eel River Road. Turn right and drive 15 miles to the Eel River Information Kiosk at Lake Pillsbury. Continue for two miles to the campground access road. Turn right and drive a short distance to the campground.

Contact: Mendocino National Forest, Upper Lake Ranger District, 707/275-2361, fax 707/275-0676; PG&E Land Services, 916/386-5164, www.pge.com/recreation.

20 TROUT CREEK

Scenic rating: 7

near East Van Arsdale Reservoir
Map grid A1

Relatively few campers know about this spot. Most others looking over this area are setting up shop at nearby Lake Pillsbury to the east. But if you like to watch the water roll by, this could be your port of call since it sits at the confluence of Trout Creek and the Eel River (not far from the East Van Arsdale Reservoir). Boats can be hand-launched. Insider's tip: Nearby in Potter Valley to the south, the East Fork Russian River (Cold Creek) is stocked with trout during the summer. The elevation is 1,500 feet.

RV sites, facilities: There are 14 sites for tents or RVs up to 30 feet (no hookups), and three walk-in tent sites. Fire grills and picnic tables are provided. Drinking water and vault toilets are available. Leashed pets are permitted.

Reservations, fees: Reservations are not accepted. Sites are $13 per night, $3 per night for each additional vehicle, $1 per pet per night. Open mid-April through September, weather permitting.

Directions: From Ukiah on U.S. 101, drive north to the junction with Highway 20. Turn east (right) on Highway 20 and drive five miles to East Potter Valley Road (M8/Eel River

CALIFORNIA

Road). Turn northwest on East Potter Valley Road toward Lake Pillsbury and drive 5.9 miles to the town of Potter Valley. Continue on east Potter Valley Road to Eel River Road. Turn right and drive 4.5 miles to the Eel River Bridge. From the bridge, continue two miles to the campground entrance.

Contact: PG&E Land Services, 916/386-5164, www.pge.com/recreation.

21 CASPAR BEACH RV PARK

Scenic rating: 8

near Mendocino

Map grid A1 BEST

This privately operated park has opportunities for beachcombing, kayaking, fishing, abalone and scuba diving, and good lookouts for whale-watching. The park is across the road from the ocean and somewhat wooded, with a small, year-round creek running behind it. The park is about midway between Fort Bragg and Mendocino, with Fort Bragg five miles to the north. Note that some of the sites are filled with long-term renters.

RV sites, facilities: There are 59 sites with full or partial hookups (30 amps) for RVs up to 50 feet, 30 tent sites, and two group tent sites that can accommodate up to 20 people each. Some sites are pull-through. Picnic tables and fire rings are provided. Cable TV, Wi-Fi, restrooms with flush toilets and coin showers, dump station, fish cleaning station, convenience store, firewood, propane, playground, video arcade, video rentals, and a coin laundry are available. Some facilities are wheelchair accessible. Leashed pets are permitted.

Reservations, fees: Reservations are accepted. Sites are $25–35 per night, $3–5 per person per night for more than two people, $2 per pet per night. Group tent sites are $60 per night and $3–5 per person per night for more than six people. Monthly rates available. Some credit cards accepted. Open year-round.

Directions: From Mendocino on Highway 1, drive north for 3.5 miles to the Point Cabrillo

exit. Turn west on Point Cabrillo Drive and continue 0.75 mile to the campground on the left at 14441 Point Cabrillo Drive.

From Fort Bragg on Highway 1, drive south for 4.5 miles to Point Cabrillo Drive (Mile Marker 54.6). Turn right and continue 0.75 mile to the campground.

Contact: Caspar Beach RV Park, 707/964-3306, www.casparbeachrvpark.com.

22 RUSSIAN GULCH STATE PARK

Scenic rating: 9

north of Mendocino near the Pacific Ocean

Map grid A1

Russian Gulch State Park is set near some of California's most beautiful coastline, but the camp speaks to the woods, not the water, with the campsites set in a wooded canyon. They include some of the prettiest and most secluded drive-in sites available on the Mendocino coast. There is a great hike here, an easy hour-long walk to Russian Gulch Falls, a wispy 36-foot waterfall that cascades into a rock basin. While it's always pretty, it's awesome in late winter. Much of the route is accessible by bicycle, with a bike rack available where the trail narrows and turns to dirt. In addition, there are many more miles of hiking trails and a few miles of trails for cycling. The park covers more than 1,100 acres with about 1.5 miles of ocean frontage, its rugged headlands thrusting into the Pacific. It rivals Point Lobos for coastal beauty. And yet the park is better known for its heavily forested canyon, Russian Gulch Creek Canyon, and a headland that features the Devil's Punchbowl, a 100-foot-wide and 60-foot-deep blowhole where one can look right in and watch the sea surge. Swim, dive, rock fish, or explore the tidepools on the beach.

RV sites, facilities: There are 30 sites for tents or RVs up to 24 feet (no hookups), one hike-in/bike-in site, four equestrian sites, and one group site for up to 40 people. Picnic tables, fire grills, and food lockers are provided. Drinking water, coin showers, and flush toilets are available. A seasonal junior ranger program with nature walks, campfire programs and exhibits is also available. A day-use picnic area, beach access, and recreation hall are nearby. Some facilities are wheelchair-accessible. Leashed pets are permitted in the campground and on some trails.

Reservations, fees: Reservations are accepted at 800/444-PARK (800/444-7275) or www.reserveamerica.com ($8 reservation fee). Equestrian sites can be reserved at 707/937-5804. Sites are $35 per night for individual sites, $25 per night for equestrian sites, $8 per night for each additional vehicle, $140–280 per night for the group site, and $3 per night per person for hike-in/bike-in site. Open mid-March through October, weather permitting, with a two-night maximum stay for hike-in/bike-in campers.

Directions: From Mendocino, drive two miles north on Highway 1 to the campground entrance on the west side of the highway.

Contact: Russian Gulch State Park, 707/937-4296; Mendocino District, 707/937-5804, fax 707/937-2953, www.parks.ca.gov.

23 VAN DAMME STATE PARK

Scenic rating: 10

near Mendocino
Map grid A1

The campsites at Van Damme are extremely popular, usually requiring reservations, but with a bit of planning your reward is a base of operations in a beautiful park with redwoods and a remarkable fern understory. The hike-in site (about 1.75 miles) on Fern Canyon Trail are perfectly situated for those wishing to take one of the most popular hikes in the Mendocino area, with the trail crossing the Little River several times and weaving among old trees. Just across from the entrance to the park is a small but beautiful coastal bay with a pretty beach, ideal for launching sea kayaks. The park covers 1,831 acres. A sidelight is the Pygmy Forest, where mature cone-bearing cypress and pine trees are only six inches to eight feet tall. Another favorite is the Bog Trail, where skunk

cabbage grows in abundance, most striking when seen in May and June. Ten miles of trails extend through the Little River's fern-rich canyon, and a paved road is popular with cyclists and joggers. Abalone divers explore the waters off the beach. Kayak tours may be available at the beach parking lot in the summer.

RV sites, facilities: There are 74 sites for tents or RVs up to 35 feet (no hookups), 10 primitive environmental sites, one hike-in/bike-in site, and one group campsite for up to 50 people. Picnic tables, food lockers, and fire grills are provided. Drinking water, restrooms with flush toilets and coin showers, Wi-Fi, and a dump station are available. A seasonal junior ranger program with nature walks, campfire programs, and exhibits is also available. A grocery store and propane gas are available nearby. Some facilities are wheelchair-accessible. Leashed pets are permitted at campsites, but not in environmental sites.

Reservations, fees: Reservations are accepted ($8 reservation fee) at 800/444-PARK (800/444-7275) or www.reserveamerica.com. Sites are $35 per night, $8 per night for each additional vehicle, $10–15 per night for environmental sites, $160 per night for group site, $3 per night per person for hike-in/bike-in site. Open year-round.

Directions: From Mendocino on Highway 1, drive south for three miles to the town of Little River and the park entrance road on the left (east) side of the road.

Contact: Van Damme State Park, 707/937-4296; Mendocino District, 707/937-5804, fax 707/937-2953, www.parks.ca.gov.

24 NAVARRO RIVER REDWOODS STATE PARK: NAVARRO BEACH CAMPGROUND

Scenic rating: 6

near the mouth of the Navarro River
Map grid A1

Navarro Beach is a primitive campground that can bail out drivers stuck for a night without a spot. It is small and open, with no tree cover, set near the ocean and the Navarro River. The camps are just south of the Navarro River Bridge.

RV sites, facilities: There are 10 sites for tents or RVs up to 35 feet (no hookups). Picnic tables and fire grills are provided. No drinking water. Pit toilets are available. Leashed pets are permitted.

Reservations, fees: Reservations are not accepted. Sites are $10–15 per night, $6 per night for each additional vehicle. Open year-round.

Directions: Drive on U.S. 101 to the turnoff for Highway 128 (two miles north of Cloverdale). Turn west on Highway 128 and drive 55 miles to Highway 1. Turn south on Highway 1 and, almost immediately, take the exit for Navarro Bluffs Road. Drive a short distance on Navarro Bluffs Road to the campground (on the south side of the Navarro River Bridge).

Contact: Navarro River Redwoods State Park, c/o Hendy Woods State Park, 707/895-3141; Mendocino District, 707/937-5804, fax 707/937-2953, www.parks.ca.gov.

25 NAVARRO RIVER REDWOODS STATE PARK: PAUL M. DIMMICK CAMPGROUND

Scenic rating: 7

on the Navarro River in
Navarro River Redwoods State Park

Map grid A1

A pretty grove of second-growth redwood trees and the nearby Navarro River are the highlights of this campground at Navarro River Redwoods State Park. It's a nice spot but, alas, lacks any significant hiking trails that could make it an overall spectacular destination; all the trailheads along Highway 128 turn out to be just little spur routes from the road to the river. That is because the park consists of an 11-mile "redwood tunnel" along the Navarro River in its course to the ocean. The river provides swimming in summer, but is better suited for easy kayaking and canoeing in later winter and early spring.

RV sites, facilities: There are 25 sites for tents or RVs up to 30 feet (no hookups) and trailers

up to 24 feet. Picnic tables and fire grills are provided. Drinking water (summer only) and vault (summer) or pit (winter) toilets are available. Leashed pets are permitted.

Reservations, fees: Reservations are not accepted. Sites are $10–15 per night, $6 per night for each additional vehicle. Open year-round, weather permitting.

Directions: From Cloverdale on U.S. 101, drive north for two miles to Highway 128. Turn west on Highway 128 and drive approximately 50 miles. Look for the signed campground entrance on the left side of the road at Mile Marker 8.

Contact: Navarro River Redwoods State Park, c/o Hendy Woods State Park, 707/895-3141; Mendocino District, 707/987-5804, fax 707/937-2953, www.parks.ca.gov.

26 BUSHAY

Scenic rating: 7

at Lake Mendocino

Map grid A1

Bushay, on the northeast end of Lake Mendocino, is set on a point that provides a pretty southern exposure when the lake is full. The lake is five miles long and one mile wide. It offers fishing for striped bass, largemouth bass, smallmouth bass, crappie, catfish, and bluegill, as well as waterskiing and powerboating. A nearby visitors center features exhibits of local Native American history. The elevation is 750 feet, and the lake covers 1,750 acres and has 15 miles of shoreline. (For more information about Lake Mendocino, see the Chekaka listing in this chapter.)

RV sites, facilities: There are 164 sites for tents or RVs up to 35 feet (no hookups). There are three group sites for up to 120 people each. Picnic tables, fire rings, and lantern holders are provided. Drinking water, restrooms with showers, playground (in the adjacent day-use area), group facilities, and dump station are available. The boat ramp is two miles from camp near Kyen Campground. Some facilities are wheelchair-accessible. Leashed pets are permitted.

Reservations, fees: Reservations are accepted at 877/444-6777 or www.recreation.gov ($10 reservation fee). Sites are $20–35 per night, group sites are $140–200 per night. Boat launching is free with a camping pass. Open April through September.

Directions: From Ukiah, drive north on U.S. 101 for five miles to the Highway 20 turnoff. Drive five miles east on Highway 20. Just after crossing the Russian River bridge, turn left (Inlet Road) and drive approximately one mile to the campground.

Contact: U.S. Army Corps of Engineers, Lake Mendocino, 707/462-7581, fax 707/462-3372.

27 KYEN

Scenic rating: 7

at Lake Mendocino

Map grid A1

This camp is on the north shore of Lake Mendocino. With the access road off Highway 20 instead of U.S. 101 (as with Chekaka), Kyen can be overlooked by newcomers. A nearby boat ramp makes it especially attractive. (For more information, see the Bushay and Chekaka listings in this chapter.)

RV sites, facilities: There are 101 sites for tents or RVs up to 30 feet (no hookups). Picnic tables, fire grills, and lantern holders are provided. Restrooms with showers, playground (in the adjacent day-use area), dump station, and boat ramp are available. Some facilities are wheelchair-accessible. Leashed pets are permitted, except in some day-use areas.

Reservations, fees: Reservations are accepted at 877/444-6777 or www.recreation.gov ($10 reservation fee). Sites are $20–22 per night. Boat launching is free with a camping pass. Open year-round with limited winter facilities.

Directions: From Ukiah, drive north on U.S. 101 for five miles to the Highway 20 turnoff. Drive east on Highway 20 to Marina Drive. Turn right and drive 200 yards (past the boat ramp) to the campground.

Contact: U.S. Army Corps of Engineers, Lake Mendocino, 707/462-7581, fax 707/462-3372.

28 CHEKAKA

Scenic rating: 7

at Lake Mendocino

Map grid A1

Lake Mendocino is known for good striped-bass fishing, waterskiing, and boating. Nearby, upstream of the lake, is Potter Valley and the East Fork Russian River (also called Cold Creek), which provides trout fishing in the summer. A boat ramp adjacent to the dam is a bonus. The elevation is 750 feet. This campground sits beside the dam at the south end of Lake Mendocino, and the Kaweyo trailhead is nearby. Insider's tip: A newly installed 18-hole Frisbee-golf course is at the Chekaka overlook.

RV sites, facilities: There are 21 sites for tents or RVs up to 35 feet (no hookups). Picnic tables, lantern hangers, and fire grills are provided. Drinking water, vault toilets, and a playground are available. A boat ramp is nearby. Leashed pets are permitted.

Reservations, fees: Reservations are accepted at 877/444-6777 or www.recreation.gov ($10 reservation fee). Sites are $18 per night. Boat launching is free with a camping pass. Open early April through September.

Directions: From Ukiah, drive north on U.S. 101 to Lake Mendocino Drive. Exit right on Lake Mendocino Drive and continue to the first stoplight. Turn left on North State Street and drive to the next stoplight. Turn right (which will put you back on Lake Mendocino Drive) and drive about two miles to the signed entrance to the campground at Coyote Dam.

Contact: U.S. Army Corps of Engineers, Lake Mendocino, 707/462-7581, fax 707/462-3372.

29 PINE ACRES
BLUE LAKES RESORT

Scenic rating: 8

on Upper Blue Lake

Map grid A1

The Blue Lakes are often overlooked because of their proximity to Clear Lake. These lovely lakes offer good fishing for trout, especially in spring and early summer on Upper Blue Lake. Other fish species are bass, crappie, catfish, and bluegill. With a 5-mph speed limit in place, quiet boating is the rule. Lake frontage sites are available, and other bonuses are a sandy beach and a good swimming area. A lawn area is available for tent camping. Note that the RV sites are spaced very close together.

RV sites, facilities: There are 30 sites with full or partial hookups (30 amps) for RVs up to 40 feet, a lawn area for dispersed tent camping, six cabins, and four lodge rooms. Two RV sites are pull-through. Picnic tables and barbecues are provided. Restrooms with flush toilets and coin showers, dump station, group facilities, boat rentals, boat launching, moorings, boat ramp, fish-cleaning station, horseshoes, convenience store, fishing supplies, and lake frontage sites are available. Leashed pets are permitted, with certain restrictions.

Reservations, fees: Reservations are accepted for RV sites, cabins, and lodge rooms, not for tent camping. Sites are $23–30 per night, $2 per person per night for more than two people, $3.50 per night for each additional vehicle, $2 per pet per night. Boat launching is free for campers. Some credit cards accepted. Open year-round.

Directions: From Ukiah, drive north on U.S. 101 for five miles to the junction with Highway 20. Turn east on Highway 20 and drive about 13 miles to Irvine Avenue. Turn right on Irvine Avenue and drive one block to the end of the road and Blue Lakes Road. Turn right and drive a short distance to the resort on the right at 5328 Blue Lakes Road.

Contact: Pine Acres Blue Lakes Resort, 707/275-2811, www.bluelakepineacres.com.

30 NARROWS LODGE RESORT

Scenic rating: 8

on Upper Blue Lake

Map grid A1

One of several campgrounds in the immediate vicinity at Blue Lakes, this is a good fish camp

with boat docks and a fish-cleaning station. The Blue Lakes are often overlooked because of their proximity to Clear Lake, but they are a quiet and pretty alternative, with good trout fishing in the spring and early summer, and decent prospects year-round. The lakes are long and narrow with a primarily forested shoreline, and the elevation is 1,400 feet.

RV sites, facilities: There are 48 sites with full or partial hookups (50 amps) for tents or RVs of any length, three park-model cabins, two cabins, and 14 motel rooms. Picnic tables are provided. Restrooms with flush toilets and showers, dump station, modem access, recreation room, boat rentals, pier, boat ramp, boat slips, fishing supplies, picnic area, and ice are available. Leashed pets are allowed.

Reservations, fees: Reservations are accepted at 800/476-2776. Sites are $24–27 per night, $4 per person per night for more than two people, $3 per night for each additional vehicle, $3 per pet per night. Some credit cards accepted. Open year-round.

Directions: From Ukiah, drive north on U.S. 101 for five miles to the junction with Highway 20. Turn east on Highway 20 and drive about 13 miles to Blue Lakes Road. Turn right and drive one mile to the resort (5690 Blue Lakes Road).

Contact: Narrows Lodge Resort, 707/275-2718 or 800/476-2776, www.thenarrowsresort.com.

31 HENDY WOODS STATE PARK

Scenic rating: 7

near Boonville

Map grid A1

This is a remarkable setting where the flora changes from open valley grasslands and oaks to a cloaked redwood forest with old growth, as if you had waved a magic wand. The campsites are set in the forest, with a great trail routed amid the old redwoods and up to the Hermit Hut (a fallen redwood stump covered with branches), where a hobo lived for 18 years. No, it wasn't me. There are two virgin redwood groves in the park: Big Hendy (80 acres with a self-guided discovery trail available) and Little Hendy (20 acres). The Navarro River runs the park's length, but note that fishing is forbidden in the park and that catch-and-release fishing is the law from the bridge at the park entrance on downstream; check regulations. The park is in the middle of the Anderson Valley wine district, which will at first seem an unlikely place to find an 845-acre redwood park, and is not as cold and foggy as the coastal redwood parks.

RV sites, facilities: There are 92 sites for tents or RVs up to 35 feet (no hookups), two hike-in/bike-in sites, and four cabins. Picnic tables, food lockers, and fire grills are provided. Drinking water, flush toilets, coin showers, and a dump station are available. A seasonal junior ranger program with nature walks, campfire programs, and exhibits is also available. A grocery store and propane gas station are available nearby. Some facilities are wheelchair-accessible. Leashed pets are permitted.

Reservations, fees: Reservations are accepted at 800/444-PARK (800/444-7275) or www.reserveamerica.com ($8 reservation fee). Sites are $35 per night, $50 for cabins, $8 per night for each additional vehicle, $3 per person per night for hike-in/bike-in sites. Open year-round.

Directions: From Cloverdale on U.S. 101, turn northwest on Highway 128 and drive about 35 miles to Philo Greenwood Road. Turn left on Philo Greenwood Road and drive 0.5 mile to the park entrance on the left.

Contact: Hendy Woods State Park, 707/895-3141; Mendocino District, 707/937-5804, fax 707/937-2953, www.parks.ca.gov.

32 MANCHESTER BEACH KOA

Scenic rating: 7

north of Point Arena at Manchester State Beach
Map grid A1

This is a privately operated KOA park set beside Highway 1 and near the beautiful Manchester State Beach. A great plus here is the cute little log cabins, complete with electric heat. They

can provide a great sense of privacy, and after a good sleep, campers are ready to explore the adjacent state park.

RV sites, facilities: There are 57 tent sites and 43 sites with full or partial hookups (30 and 50 amps) for tents or RVs of any length. There are also two cottages and 27 cabins. Picnic tables, barbecues, and fire rings are provided. Drinking water, restrooms with flush toilets and showers, Wi-Fi, modem access, cable TV, heated seasonal pool, spa, recreation room, playground, dump station, convenience store, group facilities, ice, firewood, coin laundry, and propane gas are available. Some facilities are wheelchair-accessible. Leashed pets are permitted, with certain breeds prohibited; call for details.

Reservations, fees: Reservations are accepted at 800/562-4188. Sites are $28–61 per night, $3–5 per person per night for more than two people. Groups of 18 or more can reserve sites for $4–13 per person per night. Hike-in/bike-in sites are $9 per night. Some credit cards accepted. Open year-round.

Directions: From U.S. 101 in Petaluma, take the Washington Street exit. Turn west on Washington Street and drive through Petaluma (Washington Street becomes Bodega Highway) and continue for 17 miles to Highway 1. Continue straight (west) on Highway 1 for eight miles to Bodega Bay. Turn north on Highway 1 and drive 66 miles to Point Arena. Continue north on Highway 1 for about six miles to Kinney Road. Turn west (toward the ocean) and drive one mile to the campground at 44330 Kinney Road.

Contact: Manchester Beach KOA, 707/882-2375, fax 707/882-3104, www.manchesterbeachkoa.com.

33 GREEN SPRINGS FAMILY AND EQUESTRIAN CAMP

Scenic rating: 7

in Mendocino National Forest
Map grid B1

Green Springs is a wilderness trailhead camp and staging area, located at the southern border

CALIFORNIA

for the Yolla Bolly Wilderness. Green Springs is not a destination camp, but rather a launch point. From here, you can head north along the ridge into the Yolla Bolly, what is called the Eel Divide: All water running off the slope to the west runs into the Eel River watershed; all water running to the east runs into the Sacramento River watershed. This is a land of little-known peaks, small creeks, and few people. The elevation is 6,000 feet. There is a good swimming hole at nearby Rattlesnake Creek.

RV sites, facilities: There are four primitive sites for tents or small RVs. Picnic tables and fire rings are provided. Vault toilets are available, but there is no drinking water. Water is available from a spring; but must be boiled or treated before use. Horse corrals are available on a first-come first-served basis. Garbage must be packed out.

Reservations, fees: Reservations are not accepted. There is no camping fee.

Directions: From Willits, drive north on U.S. 101 for 13 miles to Longvale and the junction with Highway 162. Turn northeast on Highway 162 and drive to Covelo. Continue east on Highway 162 for nine miles to the Eel River Bridge. Drive across the bridge and turn left on Forest Service (FS) Road M1/Indian Dick Road. Drive about 17 miles on Forest Service Road M1/Indian Dick Road to FS Road M21. Turn right and drive seven miles to FS Road M2. Turn left on FS Road M2 and drive 1.5 miles to the Green Springs Trailhead on the left.

Contact: Mendocino National Forest, Covelo Ranger District, 707/983-6118, fax 707/983-6004, www.fs.fed.us.

34 THREE PRONG
🏃 🐕 5% 🚐 ⛺

Scenic rating: 6

in Mendocino National Forest

Map grid B1

Three Prong is a remote and primitive campground. The camp is situated near a large meadow and you'll have a view of fir and pine trees. It gets little use, except in fall as a base camp for hunters. That's about it. The elevation is 5,800 feet.

RV sites, facilities: There are six sites for tents or small RVs. Picnic tables and fire rings are provided. Vault toilets are available, but there is no drinking water. Garbage must be packed out.

Reservations, fees: Reservations are not accepted. There is no camping fee. Open June through October, weather permitting.

Directions: From Corning, take County Road A9 west for 20 miles to Paskenta and Forest Road 23N01. Turn west on Forest Road 23N01 and drive to Forest Road 24N13. Turn left on Forest Road 24N13 and drive to the campground.

Contact: Mendocino National Forest, Grindstone Ranger Station, 530/934-3316; Paskenta Work Station, 530/833-5544, fax 530/833-5448, www.fs.fed.us.

35 KINGSLEY GLADE
🏃 🐕 5% 🚐 ⛺

Scenic rating: 6

in Mendocino National Forest

Map grid B1

Kingsley Grade is located west of Paskenta and Red Bluff. You know what that means, right? Right—it gets smoking hot out here in summer. Like nearby Sugarfoot to the south, this is primarily a base camp for hunters working the eastern slopes of the Eel Divide in the fall. It is set in the transition zone where oaks give way to pines. The elevation is 4,500 feet.

RV sites, facilities: There are six sites for tents or small RVs. Picnic tables and fire rings are provided. Vault toilets are available, but there is no drinking water. Garbage must be packed out.

Reservations, fees: Reservations are not accepted. There is no camping fee. Open June through October, weather permitting.

Directions: From Corning, take County Road A9 west for 20 miles to Paskenta and Forest Road M2/Thomes Road. Turn west on Forest

Road M2/Thomes Road (Forest Road 23N01) and drive 18 miles to Forest Road 24N01. Turn left on Forest Road 24N01 and drive 4.3 miles to the campground.
Contact: Mendocino National Forest, Grindstone Ranger Station, 530/934-3316; Paskenta Work Station, 530/833-5544, fax 530/833-5448, www.fs.fed.us.

36 SUGARFOOT GLADE

Scenic rating: 6

in Mendocino National Forest
Map grid B1

On the east-facing slopes of the Eel Divide, there are a series of tiny campgrounds sprinkled in national forest land west of Paskenta and the Sacramento Valley. This one is small, primitive, and so remote that it seems to be in the middle of nowhere. Actually, that is perfect in the fall when hunters use it as a base camp. A small seasonal creek runs through the camp amid a landscape of ponderosa pines and oak trees.
RV sites, facilities: There are six sites for tents or small RVs. Picnic tables and fire rings are provided. Vault toilets are available, but there is no drinking water. Garbage must be packed out.
Reservations, fees: Reservations are not accepted. There is no camping fee. Open mid-May to mid-November.
Directions: From Corning, take County Road A9 west for 20 miles to Paskenta and Forest Road 23N01. Turn west on Forest Road 23N01 and drive to Forest Road 24N01. Turn left on Forest Road 24N01 and drive past Kingsley Glade Campground to Sugarfoot Glade Campground.
Contact: Mendocino National Forest, Grindstone Ranger Station, 530/934-3316; Paskenta Work Station, 530/833-5544, fax 530/833-5448, www.fs.fed.us.

37 WHITLOCK

Scenic rating: 4

in Mendocino National Forest
Map grid B1

This obscure Forest Service camp is often empty or close to it. It is set at 4,300 feet elevation, where conifers have taken over from the valley grasslands to the nearby east. The camp is situated amid good deer range and makes a good hunting base camp in the fall, with a network of Forest Service roads in the area. It is advisable to obtain a Forest Service map.
RV sites, facilities: There are three sites for tents or RVs up to 16 feet (no hookups). Picnic tables, fire rings, and stoves are provided. Vault toilets are available. Drinking water is not available. Garbage must be packed out. Some facilities are wheelchair-accessible. Leashed pets are permitted.
Reservations, fees: Reservations are not accepted. There is no fee for camping. Open late May through October.
Directions: From Corning on I-5, turn west onto County Road A9/Corning Road and drive 20 miles to Paskenta and Toomes Camp Road/County Road 122. Turn right (north) on Toomes Camp Road/County Road 122 and drive 14 miles to the campground on the right.
Contact: Mendocino National Forest, Grindstone Ranger District, Paskenta Work Station, 530/833-5544, fax 530/833-5448.

38 WELLS CABIN

Scenic rating: 6

in Mendocino National Forest
Map grid B1

You'll join the 5 Percent Club when you reach this spot. It is one mile from Anthony Peak Lookout (6,900 feet) where, on a clear day, you can get great views all the way to the Pacific Ocean and sweeping views of the Sacramento Valley to the east. This campground is hardly used during the summer and often provides a cool escape from the heat of the valley. The elevation is 6,300 feet.

RV sites, facilities: There are 25 sites for tents or small RVs up to 16 feet (no hookups). Picnic tables, stoves, and fire rings are provided. Vault toilets are available. Drinking water is not available. Garbage must be packed out. Leashed pets are permitted.

Reservations, fees: Reservations are not accepted. There is no fee for camping. Open late June through October, weather permitting.

Directions: From Corning on I-5, turn west on County Road A9 and drive 20 miles to Paskenta and Forest Road M4. Turn west on Forest Road M4 and drive to the junction with Forest Road 23N16. Turn right (north) and drive three miles to the campground.

Contact: Mendocino National Forest, Grindstone Ranger District, Paskenta Work Station, 530/833-5544, fax 530/833-5448.

39 BUCKHORN

Scenic rating: 7

on Black Butte Lake

Map grid B1

Black Butte Lake is set in the foothills of the north Sacramento Valley at 500 feet. It is one of the 10 best lakes in Northern California for crappie, best in spring. There can also be good fishing for largemouth, smallmouth, and spotted bass, channel catfish, bluegill, and sunfish. Recreation options include powerboating, sailboating, and sailboarding. A one-mile-long interpretive trail is available.

RV sites, facilities: There are 65 sites for tents or RVs up to 35 feet (no hookups) and a group site for 25–80 people. Picnic tables and fire grills are provided. Drinking water, restrooms with flush toilets and showers, dump station, fish-cleaning station, and a playground are available. A boat ramp is nearby. Some facilities are wheelchair-accessible. Leashed pets are permitted.

Reservations, fees: Reservations are accepted at 877/444-6777 or www.recreation.gov ($10 reservation fee). Individual sites are $15 per night, $10 per night from November through

March. The group site is $120 per night. Open year-round.

Directions: From I-5 in Orland, take the Black Butte Lake exit. Drive about 15 miles west on Road 200/Newville Road to Buckhorn Road. Turn left and drive a short distance to the campground on the north shore of the lake.

Contact: Black Butte Lake, U.S. Army Corps of Engineers, 530/865-4781, fax 530/865-5283.

40 ORLAND BUTTES

Scenic rating: 7

on Black Butte Lake

Map grid B1

Black Butte Lake isn't far from I-5, but a lot of campers zoom right by it. The lake has 40 miles of shoreline at 500 feet in elevation. All water sports are allowed. The prime time to visit is in late spring and early summer, when the bass and crappie fishing can be quite good. Three self-guided nature trails are in the immediate area, including Paul Thomas Trail, a short 0.25-mile walk to an overlook. (See the Buckhorn listing for more information.) Note: In late winter and early spring, this area is delightful as spring arrives. But from mid-June through August, expect very hot, dry weather.

RV sites, facilities: There are 35 sites for tents or RVs up to 35 feet (no hookups) and a group site for 25–60 people. Picnic tables and fire grills are provided. Drinking water, restrooms with showers, boat ramp, fish-cleaning station, and a dump station are available. Leashed pets are permitted.

Reservations, fees: Reservations are accepted at 877/444-6777 or www.recreation.gov ($10 reservation fee). Sites are $15 per night. Open April through early September.

Directions: From I-5 in Orland, take the Black Butte Lake exit. Drive west on Road 200/Newville Road for six miles to Road 206. Turn left and drive three miles to the camp entrance on the right.

Contact: Black Butte Lake, U.S. Army Corps of Engineers, 530/865-4781, fax 530/865-5283.

41 PLASKETT MEADOWS

Scenic rating: 7

in Mendocino National Forest
Map grid B1

This is a little-known camp in the mountains near Plaskett Lakes, a pair of connected dot-sized mountain lakes that form the headwaters of little Plaskett Creek. Trout fishing is best at the westernmost of the two lakes. No motors are permitted in the lakes and swimming is not recommended. The camp is set at an elevation of 6,000 feet.

RV sites, facilities: There are 32 sites for tents or RVs up to 16 feet (no hookups). Fire grills and picnic tables are provided. Drinking water and vault toilets are available. Leashed pets are permitted.

Reservations, fees: Reservations are not accepted. Sites are $10 per night. Open mid-May through mid-October.

Directions: In Willows on I-5, turn west on Highway 162 and drive toward the town of Elk Creek. Just after crossing the Stony Creek Bridge, turn north on County Road 306 and drive four miles to Alder Springs Road/Forest Highway 7. Turn left and drive 31 miles to the campground on the left.

Contact: Mendocino National Forest, Grindstone Ranger District, Stonyford Work Center, 530/963-3128, fax 530/963-3173.

42 ATCHISON CAMP

Scenic rating: 5

in Mendocino National Forest
Map grid B1

Very few people know about this little spot. Atchison Camp is set at an elevation of 3,900 feet in a remote national forest in an area that is hot and dry all summer long. There is a network of four-wheel-drive roads in the area. Hunters will use this camp as a base in the fall, then drive around in ATVs or pick-ups trucks looking for deer or places to hunt.

RV sites, facilities: There are three sites for tents or small RVs. Picnic tables and fire rings are provided. Pit toilets are available, but there is no drinking water. Garbage must be packed out.

Reservations, fees: Reservations are not accepted. There is no camping fee.

Directions: In Willows, take Highway 162 west to the town of Elk Creek. Just after crossing the Stony Creek Bridge, turn north on County Road 306 and drive four miles to Alder Springs Road/Forest Highway 7. Turn left (east) onto Alder Springs Road/Forest Highway 7 and drive about 26 miles to the campground.

Contact: Mendocino National Forest, Covelo Ranger District, 707/983-6118, fax 707/983-6004.

43 LOWER NYE

Scenic rating: 8

in Mendocino National Forest
Map grid B1

This camp is on the northern border of the Snow Mountain Wilderness. It is a good jump-off point for backpackers, or a spot for folks who don't want to be bugged by anybody. It is set at 3,300 feet on Skeleton Creek near the Eel River. It is advisable to obtain a detailed USGS topographic map.

RV sites, facilities: There are six sites for tents or RVs up to 16 feet (no hookups). Picnic tables and fire grills are provided. Vault toilets are available. No drinking water is available. Garbage must be packed out. Leashed pets are permitted.

Reservations, fees: Reservations are not accepted. There is no fee for camping. Open year-round, weather permitting.

Directions: From Ukiah on U.S. 101, drive north to the junction of Highway 20. Turn east on Highway 20 and drive to the town of Upper Lake and to Elk Mountain Road. Turn left on Elk Mountain Road (which becomes Forest Road M1) and drive 17 miles to Forest Road M-10/Bear Creek Road. Turn right (dirt road) on Forest Road M-10/Bear Creek Road and drive seven miles to Forest Road 18N04/

Rice Creek Road. Turn north on Forest Road 18N04/Rice Creek Road and drive 14 miles to the campground.

Contact: Mendocino National Forest, Upper Lake Ranger District, 707/275-2361, fax 707/275-0676.

44 SUNSET CAMPGROUND

Scenic rating: 7

on Lake Pillsbury in Mendocino National Forest
Map grid B1

This camp is on the northeast corner of Lake Pillsbury, and Pillsbury Pines boat launch and picnic area are less than a quarter mile to the south. Lakeshore Trail, an adjacent designated nature trail along the shore of the lake here, is accessible to hikers, equestrians, and bicyclists. However, a section of the trail is covered with water when the lake is full. The surrounding national forest offers side-trip possibilities.

RV sites, facilities: There are 54 sites for tents or RVs up to 16 feet (no hookups). Picnic tables and fire grills are provided. Drinking water and vault toilets are available. A boat ramp is nearby. Leashed pets are permitted.

Reservations, fees: Reservations are not accepted. Sites are $13 per night, $3 per night for each additional vehicle, $1 per pet per night. Open May through October.

Directions: From Ukiah on U.S. 101, drive north to the junction with Highway 20. Turn east (right) on Highway 20 and drive five miles. Turn northwest on East Potter Valley Road toward Lake Pillsbury. Drive 5.9 miles to the town of Potter Valley. Continue on East Potter Valley Road to Eel River Road. Turn right and drive 15 miles to the Eel River Information Kiosk at Lake Pillsbury. Continue east for 4.1 miles to Lake Pillsbury and the junction with Hall Mountain Road. Turn right and drive three miles to the camp entrance.

Contact: Mendocino National Forest, Upper Lake Ranger District, 707/275-2361, fax 707/275-0676; PG&E Land Services, 916/386-5164, www.pge.com/recreation.

45 OAK FLAT

Scenic rating: 6

near Lake Pillsbury in Mendocino National Forest
Map grid B1

This primitive camp provides an option if Lake Pillsbury's other camps are full. It is set at 1,850 feet elevation near the north shore of Lake Pillsbury in the heart of Mendocino National Forest. Nearby trails leading into the backcountry are detailed on a Forest Service map.

RV sites, facilities: There are 12 sites for tents or RVs up to 16 feet (no hookups). Picnic tables and fire grills are provided. Vault toilets are available. No drinking water is available. Garbage must be packed out. A boat ramp is at the lake. Leashed pets are permitted.

Reservations, fees: Reservations are not accepted. There is no fee for camping. Open year-round.

Directions: From Ukiah on U.S. 101, drive north to the junction with Highway 20. Turn east (right) on Highway 20 and drive five miles to East Potter Valley Road. Turn northwest on East Potter Valley Road toward Lake Pillsbury and drive 5.9 miles to the town of Potter Valley. Continue on East Potter Valley Road to Eel River Road. Turn right and drive 15 miles to the Eel River Information Kiosk at Lake Pillsbury. Continue for four miles around the north end of the lake and look for the camp entrance on the right side of the road.

Contact: Mendocino National Forest, Upper Lake Ranger District, 707/275-2361, fax 707/275-0676.

46 NAVY CAMP

Scenic rating: 7

on Lake Pillsbury in Mendocino National Forest
Map grid B1

This camp is used primarily as an overflow area, and is usually open on busy weekends and holidays. When Lake Pillsbury is full of water, this is an attractive camp. However, when the lake level is down, as is common in the fall, it can seem as if the camp is on the edge of a dust bowl. The camp is set in the lake's north cove, sheltered from north winds. Although the camp is in a pretty setting, there is little shade and a lot of poison oak.

RV sites, facilities: There are 20 sites for tents or RVs up to 16 feet (no hookups). Picnic tables are provided. Drinking water and vault toilets are available. A boat ramp is nearby at Fuller Grove. Some facilities are wheelchair-accessible. Leashed pets are permitted.

Reservations, fees: Reservations are not accepted. Sites are $12 per night, $3 per night for each additional vehicle, $1 per pet per night. Open Memorial Day weekend through Labor Day weekend for overflow camping.

Directions: From Ukiah on U.S. 101, drive north to the junction with Highway 20. Turn east (right) on Highway 20 and drive five miles to East Potter Valley Road. Turn northwest on East Potter Valley Road toward Lake Pillsbury and drive 5.9 miles to the town of Potter Valley. Continue on East Potter Valley Road to Eel River Road. Turn right and drive 15 miles to the Eel River Information Kiosk at Lake Pillsbury. Continue for four miles around the north end of the lake and look for the campground entrance on the right side of the road. The campground is on the north shore, just west of Oak Flat Camp.

Contact: Mendocino National Forest, Upper Lake Ranger District, 707/275-2361, fax 707/275-0676.

47 FULLER GROVE AND FULLER GROVE GROUP CAMP

🥾 🏊 🛶 🚤 🎣 🐕 🚐 ⛺

Scenic rating: 7

on Lake Pillsbury in Mendocino National Forest
Map grid B1

This is one of several campgrounds bordering Lake Pillsbury, which, at 2,000 acres, is by far the largest lake in Mendocino National Forest. Set at an elevation of 1,800 feet, Pillsbury is big and pretty when full, with 65 miles of shoreline. It has lakeside camping, good boat ramps, and, in the spring, good fishing for trout, and in

the warmer months, for bass. This camp is set along the northwest shore of the lake, with a boat ramp only about a quarter mile away to the north. There are numerous backcountry roads in the area, which provide access to a state game refuge to the north and the Snow Mountain Wilderness to the east.

RV sites, facilities: There are 30 sites for tents or RVs up to 16 feet (no hookups), and a group tent area for up to 60 people. Picnic tables and fire grills are provided. Drinking water and vault toilets are available. A boat ramp is nearby. Leashed pets are permitted.

Reservations, fees: Reservations are not accepted for individual sites but are required for the group site at 916/386-5164. Sites are $13 per night for individual sites, $3 per night for each additional vehicle, $1 per pet per night, and $100 per night for the group site with a two-night minimum stay required. Weekly rates are available. Open May through October.

Directions: From Ukiah on U.S. 101, drive north to the junction with Highway 20. Turn east (right) on Highway 20 and drive five miles to East Potter Valley Road. Turn northwest on East Potter Valley Road toward Lake Pillsbury and drive 5.9 miles to the town of Potter Valley. Continue on East Potter Valley Road to Eel River Road. Turn right and drive 15 miles to the Eel River Information Kiosk at Lake Pillsbury. Continue for 2.2 miles to the campground access road. Turn right and drive 0.25 mile to the campground; the group camp is adjacent to the boat ramp.

Contact: Mendocino National Forest, Upper Lake Ranger District, 707/275-2361, fax 707/275-0676; PG&E Land Services, 916/386-5164.

48 LAKE PILLSBURY RESORT

🥾 🏊 🎣 🚤 🐕 🏕 🚐 ⛺

Scenic rating: 6

on Lake Pillsbury in Mendocino National Forest
Map grid B1

This is a pretty spot beside the shore of Lake Pillsbury in the heart of Mendocino National Forest. It can be headquarters for a vacation involving

CALIFORNIA

boating, fishing, waterskiing, or exploring the surrounding national forest. A boat ramp, small marina, and full facilities make this place a prime attraction in a relatively remote location. This is the only resort on the lake that accepts reservations, and it has some lakefront sites.

RV sites, facilities: There are 41 sites for tents or RVs up to 26 feet (no hookups); two sites have full hookups (30 amps). Eight cabins are also available. Picnic tables and fire pits are provided. Drinking water, restrooms with flush toilets and coin showers, playground, boat rentals, fuel, boat dock, fishing supplies, and small marina are available. Leashed pets are permitted.

Reservations, fees: Reservations are recommended. Sites are $26.16–35.97 per night, $6 per person per night for more than two people, $6 per night for each additional vehicle, $8 per pet per night. Boat launching is $6 per day. Weekly rates available. Some credit cards accepted. Open May through October.

Directions: From Ukiah on U.S. 101, drive north to the junction with Highway 20. Turn east (right) on Highway 20 and drive five miles to East Potter Valley Road (toward Lake Pillsbury). Turn left (northwest) on East Potter Valley Road and drive 5.9 miles to the town of Potter Valley. Continue on East Potter Valley Road to Eel River Road. Turn right and drive 11 miles (unpaved road) to the stop sign. Turn right (still Eel River Road) and drive 0.2 mile to Kapranos Road. Turn left and drive about 1.5 miles to the resort at 2756 Kapranos Road.

Contact: Lake Pillsbury Resort, 707/743-9935, www.lprandm.com.

49 FOUTS AND SOUTH FORK

🚶 🐕 ♿ 🚐 ⛺

Scenic rating: 1

on Stony Creek in Mendocino National Forest

Map grid B1

These two adjoining camps are in a designated off-highway-vehicle (OHV) area and are used primarily by dirt bikers. So if you're looking for quiet, these camps are not for you. The landscape was largely vanquished by forest fire, though facilities have been restored, including drinking water at Fouts. Several OHV trails are nearby—North Fork, South Fork, and Mill Creek—and campers can ride their OHVs directly out of camp. To the west is the Snow Mountain Wilderness and excellent hiking trails; to the south is an extensive Forest Service road and OHV trail network. The elevation is 1,700 feet.

RV sites, facilities: There are 11 dispersed sites for tents or RVs up to 16 feet at Fouts (no hookups); there are five dispersed tent sites at South Fork. Picnic tables and fire grills are provided. Vault toilets and drinking water are available. Garbage must be packed out. Some facilities are wheelchair-accessible. Leashed pets are permitted.

Reservations, fees: Reservations are not accepted. Sites are $4 per night at South Fork, $5 per night at Fouts. Open year-round, although trails may be closed during wet weather.

Directions: From I-5 at Maxwell, turn west on Maxwell-Sites Road and drive to Sites. Turn left on Sites-Lodoga Road and continue to Lodoga. Turn right on Lodoga-Stonyford Road and loop around East Park Reservoir to reach Stonyford. From Stonyford, turn west on Fouts Springs Road/County Road M10 and drive about eight miles. Turn right (north) on Forest Road 18N03 and drive one mile to the campgrounds on your right.

Contact: Mendocino National Forest, Grindstone Ranger District, Stonyford Work Center, 530/963-3128, fax 530/963-3173.

50 GRAY PINE GROUP CAMP

🚶 🐕 🚐 ⛺

Scenic rating: 1

in Mendocino National Forest

Map grid B1

Similar to Fouts Campground, Gray Pine is set in an area of burned-out forest with many OHV trails nearby. It is near (but not on) Stony Creek. (See the Fouts listing for additional information.)

RV sites, facilities: There is one group site for tents or RVs up to 26 feet (no hookups) that can accommodate up to 75 people. Picnic tables and fire rings are provided. Drinking water, vault toilet, and group barbecue grill are available. Leashed pets are permitted.

Reservations, fees: Reservations are required ($10 reservation fee) at 877/444-6777 or www. recreation.gov. The camp is $75 per night. Open year-round, weather permitting.

Directions: From I-5 at Maxwell, turn west on Maxwell-Sites Road and drive to Sites. Turn left on Sites-Lodoga Road and continue to Lodoga. Turn right on Lodoga-Stonyford Road and loop around East Park Reservoir to reach Stonyford. From Stonyford, turn west on Fouts Springs Road/County Road M10 and drive about nine miles. Turn right on Forest Road 18N03 and drive less than a mile to the campground on your right.

Contact: Mendocino National Forest, Grindstone Ranger District, Stonyford Work Center, 530/963-3128, fax 530/963-3173.

51 DAVIS FLAT

Scenic rating: 1

in Mendocino National Forest

Map grid B1

Davis Flat is across the road from Fouts and South Fork campgrounds and was also a victim of forest fire. All three campgrounds are in a designated off-highway-vehicle area, so expect OHVers, especially in the winter; campers are allowed to ride their OHVs from the campground. This isn't the quietest camp around, but there is some good hiking in the area to the immediate west in the Snow Mountain Wilderness. The elevation is 1,700 feet.

RV sites, facilities: There are 60 dispersed sites for tents or RVs of any length (no hookups). Picnic tables and fire grills are provided. Drinking water and vault toilets are available. Garbage must be packed out. Some facilities are wheelchair-accessible. Leashed pets are permitted.

Reservations, fees: Reservations are not

accepted. Sites are $5 per night. Open year-round, weather permitting.

Directions: From I-5 at Maxwell, turn west on Maxwell-Sites Road and drive to Sites. Turn left on Sites-Lodoga Road and continue to Lodoga. Turn right on Lodoga-Stonyford Road and loop around East Park Reservoir to reach Stonyford. From Stonyford, turn west on Fouts Springs Road/County Road M10 and drive about nine miles to Forest Road 18N03. Turn right and drive one mile to the campground on your left.

Contact: Mendocino National Forest, Grindstone Ranger District, Stonyford Work Center, 530/963-3128, fax 530/963-3173.

52 DIXIE GLADE HORSE CAMP

Scenic rating: 6

near the Snow Mountain Wilderness in Mendocino National Forest

Map grid B1

Got a horse who likes to tromp? No? Then take a pass on this one. Yes? Then sign right up, because this is a trailhead camp for people preparing to head north by horseback into the adjacent Snow Mountain Wilderness.

RV sites, facilities: There are eight sites for tents or RVs up to 26 feet (no hookups). Picnic tables and fire grills are provided. Vault toilets are available. No drinking water is available. Garbage must be packed out. Some facilities are wheelchair-accessible. A horse corral and hitching rack are available. Water in horse troughs is usually available; check current status. Leashed pets are permitted.

Reservations, fees: Reservations are not accepted. Sites are $5 per night. Open year-round, weather permitting.

Directions: From I-5 at Maxwell, turn west on Maxwell-Sites Road and drive to Sites and Sites-Lodoga Road. Turn left on Sites-Lodoga Road and continue to Lodoga and Lodoga-Stonyford Road. Turn right on Lodoga-Stonyford Road and loop around East Park Reservoir to reach Stonyford and Fouts Springs Road. Turn west on Fouts Springs Road/County Road M10 and drive 13 miles to the camp on the right side of the road.

Contact: Mendocino National Forest, Grindstone Ranger District, Stonyford Work Center, 530/963-3128, fax 530/963-3173.

53 BEAR CREEK CAMPGROUND

Scenic rating: 7

in Mendocino National Forest
Map grid B1

This campground is a primitive spot out in the boondocks of Mendocino National Forest, set at 2,000 feet elevation. It's a pretty spot, too, set beside Bear Creek near its confluence with Blue Slides Creek. Trout fishing can be good here. It's about a 10-minute drive to Summit Springs trailhead at the southern end of the Snow Mountain Wilderness. There are also numerous OHV roads in this region.

RV sites, facilities: There are 16 sites for tents or RVs up to 22 feet (no hookups). Picnic tables and fire grills are provided. Vault toilets are available. No drinking water is available. Garbage must be packed out. Leashed pets are permitted.

Reservations, fees: Reservations are not accepted. There is no fee for camping. Open year-round, weather permitting.

Directions: From Ukiah on U.S. 101, drive north to the junction with Highway 20 at Calpella. Turn east on Highway 20 and drive to the town of Upper Lake and Mendenhall Avenue. Turn left on Mendenhall Avenue (which becomes Forest Road M1) and drive one mile to the stop sign and Forest Road M-1/Elk Mountain Road. Bear left on Forest Road M-1/Elk Mountain Road and drive 16 miles (the latter stretch is extremely twisty) to Forest Road M-10. Turn right (east) and drive eight miles to the campground entrance road on the left. Turn left and continue 0.5 mile to the camp. Note: Approximately five miles along Forest Road M-10, the Rice Fork of the Eel River must be forded. Access can be dangerous and sometimes impossible when the water is high; call for road conditions. High-clearance vehicles are recommended.

Contact: Mendocino National Forest, Upper Lake Ranger District, 707/275-2361, fax 707/275-0676.

54 MILL VALLEY

Scenic rating: 5

near Letts Lake in Mendocino National Forest
Map grid B1

This camp is set beside Lily Pond, a little, teeny guy, with larger Letts Lake just a mile away. Since Lily Pond does not have trout and Letts Lake does, this camp gets far less traffic than its counterpart. The area is crisscrossed with numerous creeks, OHV routes, and Forest Service roads, making it a great adventure for owners of four-wheel drives who are allowed to drive their OHVs from the campground. The elevation is 4,200 feet.

RV sites, facilities: There are 15 sites for tents or RVs up to 18 feet (no hookups). Picnic tables and fire stoves are provided. Vault toilets and drinking water are available. Leashed pets are permitted.

Reservations, fees: Reservations are not accepted. Sites are $10 per night. Open mid-April through October, weather permitting.

Directions: From I-5 at Maxwell, turn west on Maxwell-Sites Road and drive to Sites and Sites-Lodoga Road. Turn left on Sites-Lodoga Road and continue to Lodoga and Lodoga-Stonyford Road. Turn right on Lodoga-Stonyford Road and loop around East Park Reservoir to reach Stonyford and Fouts Springs Road. Turn west on Fouts Springs Road/County Road M10 and drive about 16 miles into national forest (where the road becomes Forest Service 17N02) to the camp access road on the left. Turn left and drive 0.25 mile to the camp.

Contact: Mendocino National Forest, Grindstone Ranger District, Stonyford Work Center, 530/963-3128, fax 530/963-3173.

55 LETTS LAKE COMPLEX

Scenic rating: 9

in Mendocino National Forest
Map grid B1

An increasingly popular spot is Letts Lake, a 35-acre, spring-fed lake set in a mixed conifer forest at 4,500 feet just south of the Snow Mountain Wilderness. There are four main loops, each with a separate campground: Main, Stirrup, Saddle, and Spillway. The complex is set on the east side of the lake. No motors are allowed at Letts Lake, making it ideal for canoes, rafts, and float tubes. Swimming is allowed, although the shoreline is rocky. This lake is stocked with rainbow trout in early summer and is known also for black bass. It's a designated historical landmark, the site where the homesteaders known as the Letts brothers were murdered. While that may not impress you, the views to the north of the Snow Mountain Wilderness will. In addition, there are several natural springs that can be fun to hunt up. By the way, after such a long drive to get here, don't let your eagerness cause you to stop at Lily Pond (on the left, one mile before reaching Letts Lake), because there are no trout in it.

RV sites, facilities: There are four campgrounds with 44 sites for tents or RVs up to 20 feet (no hookups). Picnic tables and fire rings are provided. Drinking water and vault toilets are available. A picnic area is nearby. Some facilities, including a fishing pier, are wheelchair-accessible. Leashed pets are permitted.

Reservations, fees: Reservations are not accepted. Sites are $12 per night and there is a 14-day limit. Open May through October.

Directions: From I-5 at Maxwell, turn west on Maxwell-Sites Road and drive to Sites and Sites-Lodoga Road. Turn left on Sites-Lodoga Road and continue to Lodoga and Lodoga-Stonyford Road. Turn right on Lodoga-Stonyford Road and loop around East Park Reservoir to reach Stonyford and Fouts Springs Road. Turn west on Fouts Springs Road/County Road M10 and drive about 18 miles into national forest (where

the road becomes Forest Service 17N02) to the campground on the east side of Letts Lake.

Contact: Mendocino National Forest, Grindstone Ranger District, Stonyford Work Center, 530/963-3128, fax 530/963-3173.

56 OLD MILL

Scenic rating: 5

near Mill Creek in Mendocino National Forest
Map grid B1

Little known and little used, this camp is set at 3,700 feet amid a mature stand of pine and fir on Trough Spring Ridge. It's at the site of—guess what?—an old mill. Expect some OHV company as drivers of OHVs are allowed to ride from camp.

RV sites, facilities: There are eight sites for tents and two sites for tents or RVs up to 16 feet (no hookups). Note that the access road is poor for RVs. Picnic tables and fire rings are provided. Vault toilets are available. No drinking water is available. Garbage must be packed out. Leashed pets are permitted.

Reservations, fees: Reservations are not accepted. There is no fee for camping. Open May through October.

Directions: From I-5 at Maxwell, turn west on Maxwell-Sites Road and drive to Sites and Sites-Lodoga Road. Turn left on Sites-Lodoga Road and continue to Lodoga and Lodoga-Stonyford Road. Turn right on Lodoga-Stonyford Road and loop around East Park Reservoir to reach Stonyford and Fouts Springs Road. Turn west on Fouts Springs Road/County Road M10 and drive about six miles to Forest Road M5. Turn left on Forest Road M5/Trough Springs Road and drive 7.5 miles on a narrow road to the campground on your right. (The access road is not recommended for RVs.)

Contact: Mendocino National Forest, Grindstone Ranger District, Stonyford Work Center, 530/963-3128, fax 530/963-3173.

57 DEER VALLEY CAMPGROUND

Scenic rating: 4

in Mendocino National Forest
Map grid B1

This one is way out there. It is used primarily in summer by OHV enthusiasts and in the fall by deer hunters. It is set at 3,700 feet in Deer Valley, about five miles from the East Fork of Middle Creek.

RV sites, facilities: There are 13 sites for tents or RVs up to 16 feet (no hookups). Picnic tables and fire grills are provided. Vault toilets are available. No drinking water is available. Garbage must be packed out. Leashed pets are permitted.

Reservations, fees: Reservations are not accepted. There is no fee for camping. Open year-round, weather permitting.

Directions: From Ukiah on U.S. 101, drive north to the junction with Highway 20. Turn east on Highway 20 and drive to the town of Upper Lake and Mendenhall Avenue. Turn left on Mendenhall Avenue (which becomes Forest Road M1) and drive 17 miles (the latter stretch is extremely twisty) to Forest Road 16N01. Turn right on Forest Road 16N01 and drive about four miles to the campground.

Contact: Mendocino National Forest, Upper Lake Ranger District, 707/275-2361, fax 707/275-0676.

58 CEDAR CAMP

Scenic rating: 6

in Mendocino National Forest
Map grid B1

This camp is set at 4,300 feet elevation, just below Goat Mountain (6,121 feet) to the west about a mile away. Why did anybody decide to build a campground way out here? Because a small spring starts nearby, creating a trickle that runs into the nearby headwaters of Little Stony Creek.

RV sites, facilities: There are five sites for tents or RVs up to 16 feet (no hookups). Note that the access road is poor for trailers. Picnic tables and fire grills are provided. A vault toilet is available. No drinking water is available. Garbage must be packed out. Leashed pets are permitted.

Reservations, fees: Reservations are not accepted. There is no fee for camping. Open mid-June through mid-October.

Directions: From I-5 at Maxwell, turn west on Maxwell-Sites Road and drive to Sites and Sites-Lodoga Road. Turn left on Sites-Lodoga Road and continue to Lodoga and Lodoga-Stonyford Road. Turn right on Lodoga-Stonyford Road and loop around East Park Reservoir to reach Stonyford and Fouts Springs Road. Turn west on Fouts Springs Road/County Road M10 and drive about six miles to County Road M5. Turn left on County Road M5 (Trough Springs Road) and drive 13 miles to the campground on your right.

Contact: Mendocino National Forest, Grindstone Ranger District, Stonyford Work Center, 530/963-3128, fax 530/963-3173.

59 LITTLE STONY CAMPGROUND

Scenic rating: 7

on Little Stony Creek in Mendocino National Forest
Map grid B1

This pretty spot is set in Little Stony Canyon, beside Little Stony Creek at 1,500 feet. Very few people know of the place, and you will find it is appropriately named: It is little, it is stony, and the little trout amid the stones fit right in. The camp provides streamside access and, with Goat Mountain Road running along most of the stream, it is easy to fish much of this creek in an evening. Expect heavy OHV use from fall through spring.

RV sites, facilities: There are eight sites for tents or RVs up to 16 feet, and two small group sites for up to eight people each. No hookups. Picnic tables and fire grills are provided. Vault toilets are available. No drinking water is available. Garbage must be packed out. A day-use area is nearby. Some facilities are wheelchair-accessible. Leashed pets are permitted.

Reservations, fees: Reservations are not

accepted. Sites are $5 per night. Open year-round.

Directions: From I-5 at Maxwell, turn west on Maxwell-Sites Road and drive to Sites. Turn left on Sites-Lodoga Road and continue to where the road crosses Stony Creek. Just after the bridge, turn left on Goat Mountain Road and drive four miles (a rough county road) to the campground on the left.

Contact: Mendocino National Forest, Grindstone Ranger District, Stonyford Work Center, 530/963-3128, fax 530/963-3173.

60 MIDDLE CREEK CAMPGROUND

Scenic rating: 6

in Mendocino National Forest

Map grid B1

Middle Creek campground—some call it CC Camp—is not widely known, but it's known well enough as an off-highway-vehicle staging area. An easy track for beginners on dirt bikes and OHVs is located here. The camp is set at 2,000 feet at the confluence of the West and East Forks of Middle Creek.

RV sites, facilities: There are 23 sites for tents or RVs up to 30 feet (no hookups). Picnic tables and fire grills are provided. Drinking water and vault toilets are available. Leashed pets are permitted.

Reservations, fees: Reservations are not accepted. Sites are $8 per night, $16 per night for a double site, $3 per night for each additional vehicle, $1 per pet per night. Open year-round.

Directions: From Ukiah on U.S. 101, drive north to the junction with Highway 20. Turn east on Highway 20 and drive to the town of Upper Lake and Mendenhall Avenue. Turn left on Mendenhall Avenue (which becomes Forest Road M1) and drive eight miles to the camp on the right side of the road.

Contact: Mendocino National Forest, Upper Lake Ranger District, 707/275-2361, fax 707/275-0676.

61 KELLY'S FAMILY KAMPGROUND AND RV PARK

Scenic rating: 6

on Scotts Creek near Clear Lake

Map grid B1

This privately operated park is set beside Scotts Creek, within short driving range of Blue Lakes to the north on Highway 20 and the north end of Clear Lake to the south. The staff is friendly here, and the owner has been running the place for more than 30 years. A bonus is a 1.5-acre pond that can be used for swimming. Fishing is available 1.5 miles away at Blue Lakes.

RV sites, facilities: There are 75 sites for tents or RVs up to 40 feet, many with partial hookups (30 amps). Picnic tables, fire pits, and barbecues are provided. Restrooms with flush toilets and coin showers, dump station, coin laundry, ice, volleyball, basketball, horseshoes, and a small camp store are available. Leashed pets are permitted.

Reservations, fees: Reservations are accepted. Sites are $22–27 per night, $2 per night for each additional vehicle, $1 per pet per night. Open April through October.

Directions: From Ukiah on U.S. 101, drive north to the junction with Highway 20. Turn east and drive 14 miles (five miles from Upper Lake) to Scotts Valley Road. Turn right (south) and drive 1.5 miles to the park on the left (at 8220 Scotts Valley Road).

Contact: Kelly's Family Kampground and RV Park, 707/263-5754.

62 CLEAR LAKE STATE PARK

Scenic rating: 9

in Kelseyville at Clear Lake

Map grid B1

If you have fallen in love with Clear Lake and its surrounding oak woodlands, it is difficult to find a better spot than at Clear Lake State Park. It is set on the western shore of Clear Lake, and though the oak woodlands flora means you can seem quite close to your camping neighbors, the proximity to quality boating, water sports, and fishing makes the lack of privacy worth it. Reservations are a necessity in summer. That stands to reason, with excellent bass fishing from boats beside a tule-lined shoreline near the park and good catfishing in the sloughs that run through the park. Some campsites have water frontage. The elevation is 1,500 feet. Clear Lake is the largest natural freshwater lake within California state borders, and it has 150 miles of shoreline. Despite its name, the lake is not clear but green, and in late summer, rather soupy with algae and water grass in certain areas. The high nutrients in the lake give rise to a flourishing aquatic food chain. With that comes the highest number of large bass of any lake in Northern California. A few short hiking trails are also available at the park. The self-guided Indian Nature Trail passes through the site of what was once a Pomo village. Rangers here are friendly, helpful, and provide reliable fishing information. Junior ranger programs and guided walks for bird and flower identification are also available.

RV sites, facilities: There are 147 sites for tents or RVs up to 35 feet (no hookups), two group sites for up to 40 people each, and two hike-in/bike-in sites. Picnic tables and fire rings are provided. Drinking water, restrooms with coin showers and flush toilets, and a dump station are available. A boat ramp, dock, fish-cleaning stations, boat battery charging station, visitors center, Wi-Fi, and swimming beach are nearby. A grocery store, coin laundry, propane gas, restaurant, and gas station are available within three miles. Some facilities, including the boat ramp, are wheelchair-accessible. Leashed pets are permitted in the campgrounds.

Reservations, fees: Reservations are accepted at 800/444-PARK (800/444-7275) or www.reserveamerica.com ($8 reservation fee). Sites are $30 per night, $8 per night for each additional vehicle, $75 per night for group site, $3 per person per night for hike-in/bike-in sites. Boat launching is $5 per day. Open year-round.

Directions: From Vallejo, drive north on Highway 29 to Lower Lake. Turn left on Highway 29 and drive seven miles to Soda Bay Road. Turn right on Soda Bay Road and drive 11 miles to the park entrance on the right side of the road.

From Kelseyville on Highway 29, take the Kelseyville exit and turn north on Main Street. Drive a short distance to State Street. Turn right and drive 0.25 mile to Gaddy Lane. Turn right on Gaddy Lane and drive about two miles to Soda Bay Road. Turn right and drive one mile to the park entrance on the left.

Contact: Clear Lake State Park, 707/279-4293, www.parks.ca.gov.

63 GLENHAVEN BEACH CAMP AND MARINA

Scenic rating: 6

on Clear Lake

Map grid B1

This makes a good base camp for boaters, waterskiers, and anglers. It is set on a peninsula on the eastern shore of Clear Lake, with nearby Indian Beach providing a good recreation and waterplay spot. In addition, it is a short boat ride out to Anderson Island, Weekend Island, and Buckingham Point, where bass fishing can be excellent along shaded tules. Note that in addition to the campsites listed, there are another 22 sites occupied by long-term or permanent renters.

RV sites, facilities: There are 23 sites with full or partial hookups (30 amps) for RVs up to 35 feet and tents. Picnic tables and fire rings are provided. Drinking water, restrooms with showers and flush toilets, marina with gas, pier, mooring, convenience store, bait and tackle, boat ramp, boat and personal watercraft rentals, and recreation room are available. A boat ramp and boat rentals are nearby. Leashed pets are permitted.

Reservations, fees: Reservations are accepted. Sites are $18–20 per night, $2 per person per night for more than two people. Some credit cards accepted. Open year-round.

Directions: From north of Ukiah on U.S. 101 (or I-5 at Williams), turn on Highway 20 and drive to Clear Lake and the town of Glenhaven (four miles northwest of Clearlake Oaks). In

Glenhaven, continue on Highway 20 to the camp (lakeside) at 9625 East Highway 20.

Contact: Glenhaven Beach Camp and Marina, 707/998-3406.

64 BLUE OAK

Scenic rating: 7

at Indian Valley Reservoir

Map grid B1

Indian Valley Reservoir is kind of like an ugly dog that you love more than anything because inside beats a heart that will never betray you. The camp is out in the middle of nowhere in oak woodlands, about a mile from the dam. It is primitive and little known. For many, that kind of isolation is perfect. The lake has 41 miles of shoreline, is long and narrow, and is set at 1,500 feet elevation. The boat speed limit is 10 mph. While there are good trails nearby, it is the outstanding fishing for bass, bluegill, and some kokanee salmon at the lake every spring and early summer that is the key reason to make the trip. In addition, in the spring, there is a great variety of wildflowers in and around the campground. A detailed map is available from the BLM.

RV sites, facilities: There are six sites for tents or RVs up to 20 feet (no hookups). Picnic tables and fire grills are provided. Drinking water and vault toilets are available. Some facilities are wheelchair-accessible. Leashed pets are permitted.

Reservations, fees: Reservations are not accepted. There is no fee for camping. There is a 14-day stay limit. Open year-round, weather permitting.

Directions: From Williams on I-5, turn west on Highway 20 and drive 25 miles into the foothills to Walker Ridge Road. Turn north (right) on Walker Ridge Road (a dirt road) and drive north for about four miles to a "major" intersection of two dirt roads. Turn left and drive about 2.5 miles toward the Indian Valley Dam. The Blue Oak campground is just off the road on the right, about 1.5 miles from Indian Valley Reservoir.

Contact: Bureau of Land Management, Ukiah Field Office, 707/468-4000, fax 707/468-4027.

65 INDIAN VALLEY CAMPGROUND

Scenic rating: 7

at Indian Valley Reservoir

Map grid B1

Of the lakes nestled in the foothills of the western Sacramento Valley, Indian Valley Reservoir is the most remote and often provides the best fishing. The drive in is long and slow, especially if you are towing a boat. In recent years, trolling for kokanee salmon has been excellent. In the spring, bass fishing can be better than at Clear Lake (to the west), with tons of submerged trees providing good structure. Lake draw-downs are a frequent problem from mid-summer to fall, and there have been several fires in the wilderness near the lake. (The Walker Ridge Fire of 2008 missed this camp.)

RV sites, facilities: There are 20 sites for tents and small RVs. Picnic tables and fire rings are provided. Flush toilets are available. Drinking water may not be available in some years, so call ahead. Leashed pets are permitted.

Reservations, fees: Reservations are not accepted. Sites are $12 per vehicle per night.

Directions: In Williams, take Highway 20 west for 15 miles to Walker Ridge Road. Turn north (right) on Walker Ridge Road (a dirt road) and continue north for about four miles to a "major" intersection of two dirt roads. Turn left and drive about five miles to the campground at the dam.

Contact: Yolo County Flood Control, 530/662-0265, www.ycfcwcd.org.

66 MANCHESTER STATE PARK

Scenic rating: 8

near Point Arena

Map grid A2

Manchester State Park is a beautiful park on the Sonoma coast, set near the Garcia River with the town of Point Arena to the nearby north providing a supply point. If you hit it during one of the rare times when the skies are clear and the wind is down, the entire area will seem aglow in magical sunbeams. The park features 760 acres of beach, sand dunes, and grasslands, with 18,000 feet of ocean frontage and five miles of gentle sandy beach stretching southward toward the Point Arena Lighthouse. The curved beach catches a large amount of driftwood and other debris. Alder Creek Trail is a great hike, routed north along beachfront to the mouth of Alder Creek and its beautiful coastal lagoon. This is where the San Andreas Fault heads off from land into the sea. In winter, the main attraction is steelhead fishing in the Garcia River. Spring and early summer see a variety of coastal wildflowers. The park provides habitat for tundra swans. The region near the park is grazing land for sheep and cattle. Sixteen campsites were closed in 2004 to protect an endangered species, the Point Arena mountain beaver.

RV sites, facilities: There are 18 sites for tents or RVs up to 32 feet, 10 environmental sites (a one-mile walk in), and one group site for up to 40 people and RVs up to 21 feet. No hookups. Picnic tables and fire grills are provided. Drinking water, vault toilets, and a dump station are available. The environmental sites have pit toilets, picnic tables and fire rings, but no drinking water, and garbage must be packed out. Leashed pets are permitted. No dogs in environmental sites.

Reservations, fees: Reservations are accepted only for the group site at 800/444-PARK (800/444-7275) or www.reserveamerica.com ($8 reservation fee). Sites are $15 per night, $6 per night for each additional vehicle, $15 per night for environmental sites, $90 per night for group site. Open year-round.

Directions: On U.S. 101 north of Santa Rosa, turn west on River Road and drive 16 miles to Guerneville and Highway 116. Continue west on Highway 116 and drive about 20 miles to Highway 1 at Jenner. Turn north on Highway 1 and drive 55 miles to Point Arena. From Point

Arena, continue north about five miles to Kinney Lane. Turn left and drive one mile to the campground entrance on the right.

Contact: Manchester State Park, 707/882-2463; Mendocino District, 707/937-5804, fax 707/937-2953, www.parks.ca.gov.

67 ANCHOR BAY CAMPGROUND

Scenic rating: 8

near Gualala

Map grid A2

This is a quiet and beautiful stretch of California coast. The six-acre campground is on the ocean side of Highway 1 north of Gualala, with sites set at ocean level as well as amid trees—take your pick. Nearby Gualala Regional Park, six miles to the south, provides an excellent easy hike, the headlands-to-beach loop with coastal views, a lookout of the Gualala River, and many giant cypress trees. In winter, the nearby Gualala River attracts large but elusive steelhead.

RV sites, facilities: There are 30 sites for tents or RVs up to 40 feet; 12 sites have partial hookups (15 amps). Picnic tables and fire pits are provided. Drinking water, restrooms with flush toilets and coin showers, Wi-Fi, fish-cleaning room, dive-gear washroom, ice, bait, firewood, picnic area, and a dump station are available. Leashed pets are permitted, with certain restrictions, at a maximum of two per site.

Reservations, fees: Reservations are recommended at 707/884-4222 ($10 reservation fee). Sites are $38–42 per night, $3–5 per person per night for more than two people, $20 per night for each additional vehicle, $3 per pet per stay. Boat launching is $5 per day. Some credit cards accepted. Open year-round.

Directions: From San Francisco, take U.S. 101 north to Cotati/Rhonert Park and the exit for Highway 116. Take that exit to Highway 116 west and drive 14 miles to River Road/Main Street (still Highway 116). Turn left and drive 12 miles to Highway 1 at Jenner. Turn north on Highway 1 and drive 38 miles to Gualala. Continue four miles north on Highway 1 to the campground on the left (west) side of the road.

Contact: Anchor Bay Campground, 707/884-4222, www.abcamp.com.

68 GUALALA POINT REGIONAL PARK

Scenic rating: 8

at Sonoma County Regional Park

Map grid A2

This is a dramatic spot near the ocean, close to the mouth of the Gualala River. The campground is on the east side of the highway, about 0.3 mile from the ocean. A trail along the bluff provides an easy hiking adventure; on the west side of the highway other trails to the beach are available.

RV sites, facilities: There are 18 sites for tents or RVs up to 25 feet (no hookups) and six hike-in/bike-in sites. Picnic tables and fire rings are provided. Drinking water, restrooms with flush toilets and coin showers, dump station, and firewood are available. Some facilities are wheelchair-accessible. Leashed pets are permitted with valid rabies certificate.

Reservations, fees: Reservations are accepted on weekdays at 707/565-2267 ($8 reservation fee). Sites are $20 per night, $5 per person per night for hike-in/bike-in site, $6 per night for each additional vehicle, $1 per pet per night. Open year-round.

Directions: On U.S. 101 north of Santa Rosa, turn west on River Road and drive 16 miles to Guerneville and Highway 116. Continue west on Highway 116 and drive about 20 miles to Highway 1 at Jenner. Turn north on Highway 1 and drive 38 miles to Gualala. Turn right at the park entrance (a day-use area is on the west side of the highway).

Contact: Gualala Point Regional Park 707/785-2377, www.sonomacounty.org/camping.

69 CLOVERDALE KOA

Scenic rating: 7

near the Russian River

Map grid A2

This KOA campground is set just above the Russian River in the Alexander Valley wine country, just south of Cloverdale. The park is both rustic and tidy. The hillside pool has a nice view. In addition, a fishing pond is stocked with largemouth bass, bluegill, and catfish. On moonless nights, this is a great place for stargazing. Bird-watching is another pastime in this area. The nearby Russian River is an excellent beginner's route in an inflatable kayak or canoe. The nearby winery in Asti makes for a popular side trip.

RV sites, facilities: There are 89 sites with full hookups (30 and 50 amps) for RVs of any length, 49 sites for tents, 18 cabins, and five lodges. Some sites are pull-through. Picnic tables and fire grills are provided. Restrooms with flush toilets and showers, Wi-Fi, solar-heated swimming pool, playground, dump station, coin laundry, recreation room, mini golf, nature trails, catch-and-release fish pond, weekend entertainment in the summer, and a convenience and gift store are available. Some facilities are wheelchair-accessible. Leashed pets are permitted, with certain restrictions.

Reservations, fees: Reservations are accepted at 800/562-4042. Sites are $35–65 per night, $10 per person per night for more than two people, $8.50 per night for each additional vehicle. Some credit cards accepted. Open year-round.

Directions: From Cloverdale on U.S. 101, take the Central Cloverdale exit, which puts you on Asti Road. Drive straight on Asti Road to 1st Street. Turn right (east) and drive a short distance to River Road. Turn right (south) and drive four miles to Asti Ridge Road. Turn left and drive to the campground entrance.

In summer/fall: South of Cloverdale on U.S. 101, take the Asti exit to Asti Road. Turn right (south) on Asti Road and drive 1.5 miles to Washington School Road. Turn left (east) and drive 1.5 miles to Asti Ridge Road. Turn right and drive to the campground entrance. Note:

CALIFORNIA

This route is usually open Memorial Day Weekend through late November, when a seasonal bridge is in place. Both routes are well signed.
Contact: Cloverdale KOA, 707/894-3337, www.winecountrykoa.com.

70 DUTCHER CREEK RV PARK & CAMPGROUND

Scenic rating: 6

in the Alexander Valley
Map grid A2

This RV park is set in foothill-style oak woodlands and provides a layover spot for those touring the Alexander Valley wine country. The Russian River is nearby, running north to south through Cloverdale, the Valley, and on to Healdsburg.

RV sites, facilities: There are 38 RV sites with full hookups (30 and 50-amp) and a limited number of tent sites. There is one pull-through site. Picnic tables are provided. Drinking water, a swimming pool, a coin laundry, and restrooms with flush toilets and showers are available. Leashed pets are permitted.

Reservations, fees: Reservations for RVs and tent sites are accepted at www.dutchercreekrv.com. Sites are $35 per night with monthly rates available. Open year-round.

Directions: From Highway 101 south of Cloverdale, take the Dutcher Creek Road exit and drive 0.2 mile to Theresa Drive. Turn west on Theresa Drive and drive 0.3 mile to the campground.

Contact: Dutcher Creek RV Park & Campground, 230 Theresa Drive, 707/894-4829, www.dutchercreekrv.com.

71 LAKE SONOMA RECREATION AREA

Scenic rating: 8

near Healdsburg
Map grid A2

Lake Sonoma is one of the best weekend vacation sites for Bay Area campers. The developed campground (Liberty Glen) is fine for car campers, but the boat-in sites are ideal for folks who desire a quiet and pretty lakeside setting. This is a big lake, extending nine miles north on the Dry Creek arm and four miles west on the Warm Springs Creek arm. There is an adjacent 8,000-acre wildlife area that was set aside to protect nesting peregrine falcons, as well as 40 miles of hiking trails. The lake is set at an elevation of 450 feet, with 53 miles of shoreline and hundreds of hidden coves. A sandy swimming beach is available at Yorty Creek, but there is no lifeguard. The water-skier versus angler conflict has been resolved by limiting high-speed boats to specified areas. Laws are strictly enforced, making this lake excellent for either sport. Wildlife-watching includes wild pigs, wild turkeys, blacktail deer, and river otters. The best fishing is in the protected coves of the Warm Springs and Dry Creek arms of the lake. Fish species include bass, catfish, rainbow trout, crappie, and sunfish. The visitors center is adjacent to a public fish hatchery. Steelhead come to spawn from the Russian River between late December and late March.

RV sites, facilities: There are 109 primitive boat-in sites around the lake, several hike-in sites, and 95 tent and RV sites (no hookups). There are five group sites including two boat-in, one equestrian, and two drive-in at Liberty Glen Campground 2.5 miles from the lake. Picnic tables, fire grills, vault toilets, lantern poles, and garbage bins are provided at the primitive sites, but no drinking water is available. At Liberty Glen, picnic tables, fire rings, lantern holders, and vault toilets are provided. A boat ramp and houseboat and boat rentals are available nearby. Saturday night campfire talks are held at an amphitheater during the summer. Some facilities are wheelchair-accessible. Campsites have limited facilities in winter. Leashed pets are permitted.

Reservations, fees: Reservations for the boat-in sites and group sites only are accepted at 877/444-6777 or www.recreation.gov ($10 reservation fee). Reservations for equestrian sites are accepted at 707/431-4590. Sites are $14 per night, $20 per night for double sites and equestrian sites, $10–14 per night for primitive sites, $40–56 per night for group campsites. A camping permit is required from the visitors center for boat-in sites. Open year-round.

Directions: From Santa Rosa, drive north on U.S. 101 to Healdsburg. In Healdsburg, take the Dry Creek Road exit, turn left, and drive northwest for 11 miles. After you cross a small bridge, the visitors center will be on your right.

To reach the Yorty Creek Boat Ramp: On U.S. 101 at the south end of Cloverdale, take the Cloverdale Boulevard exit to Cloverdale Boulevard. Turn right on Cloverdale Boulevard and drive one block to Treadway Street. Turn left and drive two blocks to Foothill Boulevard. Turn right and drive 0.75 mile to Hot Springs Road. Turn left and drive about five miles to the boat launch. Note: Hot Springs Road is narrow with many hairpin turns. Trailers are prohibited, but the launch provides access for canoes, kayaks, and car-top boats to boat-in sites nearby.

Contact: U.S. Army Corps of Engineers, Lake Sonoma Visitor Center, 707/431-4533, fax 707/431-1031; headquarters, 707/431-4590, fax 707/431-0313, www.spn.usace .army.mil/LakeSonoma; Lake Sonoma Marina, 707/433-2200.

72 SALT POINT STATE PARK

Scenic rating: 9

near Fort Ross

Map grid A2

This is a gorgeous piece of Sonoma coast, highlighted by Fisk Mill Cove, inshore kelp beds, outstanding short hikes, and abalone diving. In fact, this is one of the finest diving areas for red abalone in the state. There is also an underwater reserve for divers, which is a protected area. Unfortunately there are also diving accidents that are due to the occasional large surf, strong currents, and rocky shoreline. There are two campgrounds here, Gerstle Cove Campground and the much larger Woodside Campground. Great hikes include Bluff Trail and Stump Beach Trail (great views). During abalone season, this is one of the best and most popular spots on the Northern California coast. The Kruse Rhododendron Reserve is within the park and definitely worth the stroll. This is a 317-acre conservation reserve that features second-growth redwoods, Douglas firs, tan oak, and many rhododendrons, with five miles of hiking trails. After the fall rains, this area is popular for mushroom hunters (the Kruse Rhododendron Reserve is closed to mushroom picking). Mushroom hunters must park in the area open to picking and be limited to five pounds per day. Of course, this can be a dangerous hobby; only eat mushrooms you can identify as safe. But you knew that, right?

RV sites, facilities: At Gerstle Cove Campground, there are 30 sites for tents or RVs up to 31 feet (no hookups). At Woodside Campground, there are 79 sites for tents or RVs up to 31 feet (no hookups), 20 walk-in tent sites (about a 300-yard walk), 10 hike-in/bike-in sites, a group site that can accommodate up to 40 people, and a primitive overflow area for self-contained vehicles. Picnic tables and fire rings are provided. Drinking water and flush toilets are available. Summer interpretive programs are offered; firewood is available for purchase. The picnic area and one hiking trail are wheelchair-accessible. Leashed pets are permitted, except on trails.

Reservations, fees: Reservations are accepted at 800/444-PARK (800/444-7275) or www. reserveamerica.com ($8 reservation fee). Sites are $35 per night, $8 per night for each additional vehicle, $15 per night for walk-in and overflow sites, $3 per person per night for hike-in/bike-in sites, $200 for the group site. Open year-round.

Directions: On U.S. 101 north of Santa Rosa, turn west on River Road and drive 16 miles to Guerneville and Highway 116. Continue west on Highway 116 and drive 13.1 miles to Highway 1 at Jenner. Turn north on Highway 1 and drive about 20 miles to the park entrance;

CALIFORNIA

Woodside Campground on the right and Gerstle Cove on the left.

Contact: Salt Point State Park, 707/847-3221; Russian River District, 707/865-2391, fax 707/865-2046, www.parks.ca.gov.

73 OCEAN COVE CAMPGROUND

Scenic rating: 8

near Fort Ross

Map grid A2   BEST (

The highlights here are the campsites on a bluff overlooking the ocean. Alas, it can be foggy during the summer. A good side trip is to Fort Ross, with a stellar easy hike available on the Fort Ross Trail, which features a walk through an old colonial fort as well as great coastal views, excellent for whale-watching. There is also excellent hiking at Stillwater Cove Regional Park, just a mile to the south off Highway 1.

RV sites, facilities: There are 125 pull-through sites for tents or RVs of any length (no hookups) and three large group sites. Picnic tables and fire grills are provided. Drinking water, chemical toilets, and coin showers are available. A boat launch, grocery store, fishing supplies, and diving-gear sales are nearby. Leashed pets are permitted.

Reservations, fees: Reservations are not accepted for individual sites, but are required for group sites. Sites are $19 per night per vehicle, $2 per pet per night, $8 per day for boat launching. The group site is $190 per night for up to 10 vehicles. Some credit cards accepted. Open April through November.

Directions: From San Francisco, take U.S. 101 north to Cotati/Rhonert Park and the exit for Highway 116. Take that exit to Highway 116 west and drive 14 miles to River Road/Main Street (still Highway 116). Turn left and drive 12 miles to Highway 1 at Jenner. Turn north on Highway 1 and drive 17 miles north on Highway 1 (five miles north of Fort Ross) to the campground entrance on the left.

Contact: Ocean Cove Campground, 707/847-3422, www.oceancove.org.

74 STILLWATER COVE REGIONAL PARK

Scenic rating: 8

near Fort Ross

Map grid A2

Stillwater Cove has a dramatic rock-strewn cove and sits on a classic chunk of Sonoma coast. The campground is sometimes overlooked, since it is a county-operated park and not on the state park reservation system. One of the region's great hikes is available here: Stockoff Creek Loop, with the trailhead at the day-use parking lot. In a little more than a mile, the trail is routed through forest with both firs and redwoods, and then along a pretty stream. To get beach access, you will need to cross Highway 1 and then drop to the cove.

RV sites, facilities: There are 20 sites for tents or RVs up to 30 feet (no hookups), and a hike-in/bike-in site. Picnic tables and fire rings are provided. Drinking water, restrooms with flush toilets and coin showers, firewood, and a dump station are available. Supplies can be obtained in Ocean Cove (one mile north) and Fort Ross. Some facilities are wheelchair-accessible. Leashed pets are permitted with a valid rabies certificate.

Reservations, fees: Reservations are accepted at 707/565-2267 on weekdays ($8 reservation fee). Sites are $20 per night, $6 per night for each additional vehicle, $5 per person per night for the hike-in/bike-in site, and $1 per pet per night. Open year-round.

Directions: From San Francisco, take U.S. 101 north to Cotati/Rhonert Park and the exit for Highway 116. Take that exit to Highway 116 west and drive 14 miles to River Road/Main Street (still Highway 116). Turn left and drive 12 miles to Highway 1 at Jenner. Turn north on Highway 1 and drive 16 miles north on Highway 1 (four miles north of Fort Ross) to the park entrance.

Contact: Stillwater Cove Regional Park, Sonoma County, 707/847-3245; Sonoma County Regional Parks, 707/565-2041, www.sonomacounty.org/camping.

75 REEF

Scenic rating: 8

at Fort Ross State Historic Park

Map grid A2

The campground at Fort Ross is two miles south of the north entrance station, less than 0.25 mile from the ocean. The privacy and beauty of the campsites vary as much as in any state park in California. Some redwoods and pines provide cover, and some sites are open. The sites at the end of the road fill up very quickly. Though the weather is relatively benign, tents are needed for protection against moisture from fog. From camp, a trail leads down to a beach, more rocky than sandy, and a one-mile trail leads to the fort.

Fort Ross is just as its name announces: an old fort, in this case, an old Russian fort from 1812. As a destination site, Fort Ross is known as a popular abalone diving spot, with the best areas below the campground and at nearby Reef Terrace. It also provides good, easy hikes amid its 3,386 acres. The park features a museum in the visitors center, which is always a must-see for campers making the tour up Highway 1. Note: Mushroom picking is prohibited in this park.

RV sites, facilities: There are 20 sites for tents or RVs up to 18 feet (no hookups). Picnic tables, food lockers, and fire rings are provided. Drinking water and flush toilets are available. Supplies can be obtained nearby. A visitor center and guided tours and programs are available. Some facilities are wheelchair-accessible. Leashed pets are permitted.

Reservations, fees: Reservations are not accepted. Sites are $15 per night, $8 per night for each additional vehicle. Open April through November, weather permitting.

Directions: On U.S. 101 north of Santa Rosa, turn west on River Road and drive 16 miles to Guerneville and Highway 116. Continue west on Highway 116 and drive about 13 miles to Highway 1 at Jenner. Turn north on Highway 1 and drive 10 miles to the (Fort Ross Reef) campground entrance. To reach the main state park entrance, drive north for two miles.

Contact: Fort Ross State Historic Park, 707/847-3286 or 707/847-3708.

76 AUSTIN CREEK STATE RECREATION AREA

Scenic rating: 7

near the Russian River

Map grid A2

Austin Creek State Recreation Area and Armstrong Redwoods State Reserve are actually coupled, forming 7,000 acres of continuous parkland. Most visitors prefer the redwood park. The campground is called Bullfrog Pond, set near a pond with bluegill. The landscape features open woodlands and foothills with 22 miles of trails. The rugged topography provides a sense of isolation. The highlight at the recreation area is a system of hiking trails that lead to a series of small creeks: Schoolhouse Creek, Gilliam Creek, and Austin Creek. They involve pretty steep climbs, and in the summer it's hot here, with temperatures occasionally exceeding 100°F, so plan accordingly. Elevations range 150–1,900 feet on Marble Mine Ridge. All of the park's trails are open to horses and horseback-riding rentals are available in adjacent Armstrong Redwoods State Park. There are many attractive side-trip possibilities, including the adjacent Armstrong Redwoods, of course, but also canoeing on the Russian River (3.5 miles away), fishing (smallmouth bass in summer, steelhead in winter), and wine-tasting. Annual winter rainfall often exceeds 50 inches.

RV sites, facilities: There are 24 sites for tents or RVs up to 20 feet (no hookups), and three hike-in sites. (The access road is very steep and narrow.) Picnic tables and fire grills are provided. Drinking water and flush toilets are available. Some facilities are wheelchair-accessible.

CALIFORNIA

Leashed pets are permitted at the main campground only. There are also three primitive, hike-in, backcountry campsites (requiring a hike of 3.5–5.1 miles) with picnic tables, fire rings, and pit toilets, but no drinking water is available and no pets are permitted. Obtain a backcountry camping permit from the office.

Reservations, fees: Reservations are not accepted. Sites are $25 per night, $25 per night for hike-in sites, $8 per night for each additional vehicle. Open year-round, but expect occasional fire closures during the summer season.

Directions: On U.S. 101 north of Santa Rosa, turn west on River Road and drive 15 miles to Guerneville and Armstrong Woods Road. Turn right and drive 2.5 miles to the entrance of Armstrong Redwoods State Park. Check in at the kiosk, and continue 3.5 miles through Armstrong Redwoods to Austin Creek State Recreation Area and the campground. The final 2.5 miles are steep and narrow, and no trailers, towed vehicles, or vehicles over 20 feet are permitted.

Contact: Austin Creek State Recreation Area, 707/869-2015, fax 707/869-5629, www.parks.ca.gov.

77 CASINI RANCH FAMILY CAMPGROUND

Scenic rating: 8

on the Russian River

Map grid A2

Woods and water—this campground has both, with sites set near the Russian River in both sun-filled and shaded areas. Its location on the lower river makes a side trip to the coast easy, with Sonoma Coast State Beach about a 15-minute drive to the nearby west. No long-term rentals available.

RV sites, facilities: There are 225 sites for tents or RVs of any length; many have full or partial hookups (30 amps); some sites are pull-through. Youth group camping is available. Picnic tables and fire grills are provided. Restrooms with flush toilets and showers, playground, dump station, coin laundry, cable TV, Wi-Fi, game arcade, boat and canoe rentals, propane gas, group facilities, seasonal activities, and convenience store are available. Some facilities are wheelchair-accessible. Leashed pets are permitted.

Reservations, fees: Reservations are accepted at 800/451-8400. Sites are $28.34–37.06 per night, $3–12 per person per night for more than two people, $1 per pet per night. The group site is $5 per person per night. Weekly and monthly rates available. Some credit cards accepted. Open year-round.

Directions: On U.S. 101 north of Santa Rosa, turn west on River Road and drive 16 miles to Guerneville and Highway 116. Continue west on Highway 116 and drive eight miles to Duncan Mills and Moscow Road. Turn left (southeast) on Moscow Road and drive 0.6 mile to the campground on the left.

Contact: Casini Ranch Family Campground Store, 707/865-2255, www.casiniranch.com.

78 SONOMA COAST STATE BEACH: WRIGHTS BEACH

Scenic rating: 8

in Sonoma Coast State Beach

Map grid A2

This park provides more than its share of heaven and hell. This state park campground is at the north end of a beach that stretches south for about a mile, yet to the north it is steep and rocky. The campsites are considered a premium because of their location next to the beach. Because the campsites are often full, a key plus is an overflow area available for self-contained vehicles. Sonoma Coast State Beach stretches from Bodega Head to Vista Trail for 17 miles, separated by rock bluffs and headlands that form a series of beaches. More than a dozen access points from the highway allow you can reach the beach. There are many excellent side trips. The best is to the north, where you can explore dramatic Shell Beach (the turnoff is on the west side of Highway 1), or take Pomo Trail (the trailhead is on the east side of the highway, across from Shell Beach) up the adjacent foothills for sweeping views of the coast. That's the heaven. Now for the hell: Dozens of people have drowned here. Wrights Beach is not for swimming; rip currents, heavy surf, and surprise rogue waves can make even playing in the surf dangerous. Many rescues are made each year. The bluffs and coastal rocks can also be unstable and unsafe for climbing. Got it? 1. Stay clear of the water. 2. Don't climb the bluffs. Now it's up to you to get it right.

RV sites, facilities: There are 27 sites for tents or RVs up to 27 feet (no hookups), with a limit of eight people per site, and an overflow area for self-contained vehicles. Picnic tables, food lockers, and fire rings are provided. Drinking water and flush toilets are available. Showers and a dump station are available at nearby Bodega Dunes Campground. Leashed pets are permitted in the campground and on the beach.

Reservations, fees: Reservations are recommended at 800/444-PARK (800/444-7275) or www.reserveamerica.com ($8 reservation fee). Sites are $35 per night, $8 per night for each additional vehicle. Open year-round, weather permitting.

Directions: In Petaluma on U.S. 101, take the East Washington exit and turn west (this street becomes Bodega Avenue). Drive west through Petaluma and continue for 17 miles to Highway 1. Turn right (north) on Highway 1 and drive nine miles to Bodega Bay. From Bodega Bay, continue north for six miles to the campground entrance.

Contact: Sonoma Coast State Beach, 707/875-3483, www.parks.ca.gov.

79 BODEGA BAY RV PARK

🎣 🚐 🐕 ♿ 🚍

Scenic rating: 8

in Bodega Bay

Map grid A2

Bodega Bay RV Park is one of the oldest RV parks in the state, and there are few north-state coastal destinations better than Bodega Bay. Excellent seafood restaurants are available

within five minutes, and some of the best deep-sea fishing is available out of Bodega Bay Sportfishing. In addition, there is a great view of the ocean at nearby Bodega Head to the west. It is a 35-minute walk from the park to the beach.

RV sites, facilities: There are 85 sites, most with full hookups (30 and 50 amps), for RVs of any length; some sites are pull-through. No tents. Picnic tables are provided. Drinking water and restrooms with flush toilets and showers are available. Coin laundry, restaurant, group facilities, horseshoes, video arcade, bocce ball, Wi-Fi, and cable TV are available. Some facilities are wheelchair-accessible. Leashed pets are permitted.

Reservations, fees: Reservations are recommended at 800/201-6864. Sites are $31.08–45.51 per night, $5 per person per night for more than two people. Some credit cards accepted. Open year-round.

Directions: In Petaluma on U.S. 101, take the East Washington exit and turn west (this street becomes Bodega Avenue). Drive west through Petaluma and continue for 17 miles to Highway 1. Turn right (north) on Highway 1 and drive nine miles to Bodega Bay. In Bodega Bay, continue north for two miles to the RV park on the left at 2001 Highway 1.

Contact: Bodega Bay RV Park, 707/875-3701, www.bodegabayrvpark.com.

80 SONOMA COAST STATE BEACH: BODEGA DUNES

🥾 🚴 🏊 🎣 🐕 ♿ 🚍 ⛺

Scenic rating: 8

in Sonoma Coast State Beach

Map grid A2

Sonoma Coast State Beach features several great campgrounds, and if you like beaches, this one rates high. Bodega Dunes campground is set near Salmon Creek Beach, the closest beach to the campground and far safer than Wrights Beach. The beach stretches for miles, providing stellar beach walks and excellent beachcombing during low tides. For some campers, a foghorn sounding repeatedly through the night can make sleep difficult. The quietest sites here are among the dunes. A day-use area includes a wheelchair-accessible boardwalk that leads out to a sandy beach. In summer, campfire programs and junior ranger programs are often offered. To the nearby south is Bodega Bay, with a major deep-sea sportfishing operation—crowned by often excellent salmon fishing; check current fishing regulations. The town of Bodega Bay offers a full marina and restaurants.

RV sites, facilities: There are 98 sites for tents or RVs up to 31 feet (no hookups), and one hike-in/bike-in site. Picnic tables, food lockers, and fire grills are provided. Drinking water, restrooms with flush toilets and free showers, and a dump station are available. Laundry facilities, supplies, and horse rentals are available within one mile. Some facilities are wheelchair-accessible. Leashed pets are permitted at the campsites only.

Reservations, fees: Reservations are accepted at 800/444-PARK (800/444-7275) or www.reserveamerica.com ($8 reservation fee). Sites are $35 per night, $8 per night for each additional vehicle, $3 per person per night for hike-in/bike-in site. Open year-round.

Directions: In Santa Rosa on U.S. 101, turn west on Highway 12 and drive 10 miles to Sebastopol (Highway 12 becomes Bodega Highway). Continue straight (west) for 10 miles to Bodega. Continue for 0.5 mile to Highway 1. Turn right (north) on Highway 1 and drive five miles to Bodega Bay. Continue 0.5 mile north to the campground entrance on the left (west).

Contact: Sonoma Coast State Beach, 707/875-3483, www.parks.ca.gov.

81 WESTSIDE REGIONAL PARK

Scenic rating: 7

on Bodega Bay

Map grid A2   BEST (

This campground is on the west shore of Bodega Bay. One of the greatest boat launches on the coast is adjacent to the park on the south, providing access to prime fishing waters. Salmon

fishing is excellent from mid-June through August; check current fishing regulations. A small, protected beach (where kids can dig in the sand and wade) is available at the end of the road beyond the campground. Hiking trails can be found at the state beach nearby.

RV sites, facilities: There are 45 sites for tents or RVs of any length (no hookups); most sites are pull-through. Picnic tables and fire grills are provided. Drinking water, restrooms with flush toilets and coin showers, fish-cleaning station, firewood, dump station, and boat ramp are available. Supplies can be obtained in Bodega Bay. Some facilities are wheelchair-accessible. Leashed pets are permitted with valid rabies certificate.

Reservations, fees: Reservations are accepted on weekdays at 707/565-2267 ($7 reservation fee). Sites are $18 per night, $6 per night for each additional vehicle, $1 per pet per night. Open year-round.

Directions: In Petaluma on U.S. 101, take the East Washington exit and turn west (this street becomes Bodega Avenue). Drive west through Petaluma and continue for 17 miles to Highway 1 north. Merge right onto Highway 1 and drive north nine miles to Bodega Bay. In Bodega Bay, continue north to Eastshore Road. Turn left and drive one block to Bay Flat Road. Turn right and drive (becomes Westshore Road) two miles to the park on the left, 0.5 mile past Spud Point Marina.

Contact: Westside Regional Parks, Sonoma County Parks Department, 707/875-3540 or 707/565-2041, www.sonomacounty.org/camping.

82 PORTO BODEGA MARINA & RV PARK

Scenic rating: 7

in Bodega Bay

Map grid A2

This RV park is located a short distance from Bodega Bay. The sites are open, most with full hookups, and the park is designed as a base to launch getaways. Fishing is often excellent out of Bodega Bay, and charter boat operations and an excellent marina and boat ramp are nearby. Nearby Bodega Head is an excellent spot for short walks or to watch the sunset. Note that new owners acquired this RV park in 2008.

RV sites, facilities: There are 58 sites for RVs to 42 feet, 41 of which have full hookups (20, 30, and 50-amp). Picnic tables and fire pits are provided. Drinking water, restrooms with flush toilets, showers, boat launch, and a dump station are available. Restaurants and grocery stores are nearby. Leashed pets are permitted.

Reservations, fees: Reservations are recommended at 707/875-2354. Sites are $46.87 with hookups, $30.52 without, per night.

Directions: From Highway 101 in Santa Rosa, drive west on Highway 12 to Sebastopol, where Highway 12 becomes Bodega Highway. Continue west on Bodega Highway 11 miles to where Bodega Highway ends at Highway 1. Turn right and drive five miles into Bodega Bay. Turn left on Eastshore Road and drive one block to the intersection with Bay Flat Road. Drive straight through the intersection and bear right to the campground.

Contact: Porto Bodega Marina & RV Park, 1500 Bay Flat Road, 707/875-2354.

83 DORAN REGIONAL PARK

Scenic rating: 7

on Bodega Bay

Map grid A2 **BEST (**

This campground is set beside Doran Beach on Bodega Bay, which offers complete fishing and marina facilities. In season, it's also a popular clamming and crabbing spot. This park has a wide, somewhat sheltered sandy beach. Salmon fishing is often excellent during the summer at the Whistle Buoy offshore from Bodega Head, and rock fishing is good year-round offshore. Fishing is also available off the rock jetty in the park.

RV sites, facilities: There are 10 sites for tents and 128 sites for tents or RVs of any length (no hookups), one group tent site for up to 50 people, and one hike-in/bike-in site. Picnic tables and fire grills are provided. Drinking water, restrooms with flush toilets and coin showers, dump stations, fish-cleaning station, and boat ramp are available. Some facilities are wheelchair-accessible. Supplies can be obtained in Bodega Bay. Leashed pets are permitted with a valid rabies certificate.

Reservations, fees: Reservations are accepted on weekdays at 707/565-2267 ($8 reservation fee; $30–50 reservation fee for the group site). Sites are $20 per night, $6 per night for each additional vehicle, $5 per person per night for hike-in/bike-in site, $1 per pet per night. The group site is $3 per person per night with a minimum of $75 and a maximum of 15 vehicles. Open year-round.

Directions: In Petaluma on U.S. 101, take the East Washington exit and turn west (this street becomes Bodega Avenue). Drive west through Petaluma and continue for 17 miles to Highway 1. Merge right (north) on Highway 1 and drive toward Bodega Bay and Doran Park Road. Turn left onto the campground entrance road. If you reach the town of Bodega Bay, you have gone a mile too far.

Contact: Sonoma County Parks Department, 707/875-3540 or 707/565-2041, www.sonoma-county.org/camping.

84 EDGEWATER RESORT AND RV PARK

Scenic rating: 7

on Clear Lake

Map grid B2

Soda Bay is one of Clear Lake's prettiest and most intimate spots, and this camp provides excellent access. It also provides friendly, professional service. Both waterskiing and fishing for bass and bluegill are excellent in this part of the lake. The resort has 600 feet of lake frontage, including a 300-foot swimming beach and a 230-foot fishing pier. This resort specializes in groups and family reunions. Wine-tasting, casinos, and golfing are nearby. Insider's tip: This park is very pet friendly and has occasional doggie socials.

RV sites, facilities: There are 61 sites with full hookups (20, 30, and 50 amps) for tents or RVs of any length, and eight cabins. Picnic tables and fire grills are provided. Restrooms with showers, cable TV, modem access, clubhouse, group facilities, general store, coin laundry, seasonal heated swimming pool, horseshoes, volleyball, and table tennis are available. A seasonal swimming beach, pet station, dog run, bait and tackle, boat ramp, fishing pier, boat docking, fish-cleaning station, and watercraft rentals are available on the premises. Firewood is available for purchase. Leashed pets are permitted.

Reservations, fees: Reservations are accepted at 800/396-6224. Sites are $38.15–49.05 per night, $5 per person per night for more than two people, $5 per pet per night. Boat launching is $10 per day. Winter discounts and weekly rates are available. Some credit cards accepted. Open year-round.

Directions: In Kelseyville on Highway 29, take the Merritt Road exit and drive on Merritt Road for two miles (it becomes Gaddy Lane) to Soda Bay Road. Turn right on Soda Bay Road and drive three miles to the campground entrance on the left at 6420 Soda Bay Road.

Contact: Edgewater Resort and RV Park, 707/279-0208, www.edgewaterresort.net.

85 PINE DELL RESORT

Scenic rating: 6

on Clear Lake in Clearlake

Map grid B2

Pine Dell Resort is an RV park that provides use as a base camp for fishing or water sports. The park is set in flat, oak woodlands at the north end of Clear Lake.

RV sites, facilities: There are 30 RV sites with full hookups. Picnic tables are provided. Restrooms with flush toilets and showers, a coin laundry, boat ramp and pier, and a store and deli are available. Leashed pets are permitted.

Reservations, fees: Reservations are recommended at 707/994-2227. Sites are $28 per night; $15 per night for each additional vehicle.

Directions: In Clearlake Oaks, take Highway 20 east to Sulphur Bank Drive. Turn right (south) onto Sulphur Back Drive and continue to North Drive. Turn right (west) on North Drive and continue to Crestview Drive. Turn left on Crestview Drive and drive to Pine Dell Resort.

From Highway 53 in Clearlake, turn west onto Olympic Drive. Drive to the end of Olympic Drive, then turn right onto Lakeshore Drive, and continue for five miles to Pine Dell Resort.

Contact: Pine Dell Resort, 10909 Lakeshore Drive, 707/994-2227, www.pinedellresort.com.

86 SHAW'S SHADY ACRES

Scenic rating: 7

on Cache Creek

Map grid B2

Shaw's Shady Acres is set beside Cache Creek, just south of Clear Lake. Canoeing and kayaking are popular. The fishing for catfish is often quite good on summer nights in Cache Creek, a deep, green, slow-moving water that looks more like a slough in a Mississippi bayou than a creek. Waterfront campsites with scattered walnut, ash, and oak trees are available. Clear Lake (the lake, not the town) is a short drive to the north, and a state park is across the creek. In addition to the campsites mentioned, there are an additional 36 long-term or permanent sites.

RV sites, facilities: There are six RV sites with full hookups (30 amps) and two tents sites. Picnic tables and barbecues are provided. Restrooms with showers, dump station, fishing dock, fishing boat rentals, boat ramp, coin laundry, swimming pool (seasonal), recreation patio, fishing supplies, and convenience store are available. Leashed pets are allowed, with certain restrictions.

Reservations, fees: Reservations are recommended. Sites are $22 per night, $3 per person per night for more than two people, $0.50 per pet per night. Boat launching is $1–3 per day. Open year-round.

Directions: From the town of Lower Lake, drive north on Highway 53 for 1.3 miles to Old Highway 53. Turn left on Old Highway 53 and then almost immediately you will arrive at Cache Creek Way. Turn left and drive 0.25 mile to the park entrance at 7805 Cache Creek Way.

Contact: Shaw's Shady Acres, 707/994-2236.

87 CACHE CREEK CANYON REGIONAL PARK

Scenic rating: 7

near Rumsey

Map grid B2

This is the best campground in Yolo County, yet it's known by few out-of-towners. It is set at 1,300 feet elevation beside Cache Creek, which is the closest river to the Bay Area that provides white-water rafting opportunities. This section of river features primarily Class I and II water, ideal for inflatable kayaks and overnight trips. One rapid, Big Mother, is sometimes considered Class III, though that might be a stretch. Huge catfish are occasionally caught in this area.

RV sites, facilities: There are 45 sites for tents or RVs up to 42 feet (no hookups), including some pull-through sites, and four group sites that can accommodate 20–30 people. Picnic tables, barbecue pits, and fire rings are provided. Drinking water, restrooms with flush toilets, playground, and dump station are available. Some facilities are wheelchair-accessible. Leashed pets are permitted.

Reservations, fees: Reservations are accepted for group sites only at 530/406-4880. Sites are $20 per night, $6 per night for each additional vehicle, $2 per pet per night. Group sites are $165 per night. Off-season discounts available. Discount for Yolo County residents. Open year-round.

Directions: From Vacaville on I-80, turn north on I-505 and drive 21 miles to Madison and the junction with Highway 16 west. Turn northwest on Highway 16 and drive northwest for about 35 miles to the town of Rumsey. From Rumsey, continue west on Highway 16 for five miles to the park entrance on the left at 1475 State Highway 16.

Contact: Cache Creek Canyon Regional Park, Yolo County, 530/406-4880, fax 530/668-1801, www.yolocounty.org.

88 BOGGS MOUNTAIN DEMONSTRATION STATE FOREST

Scenic rating: 5

near Middletown

Map grid B2

This overlooked spot is set in a state forest that covers 3,500 acres of pine and Douglas fir. There are two adjoining campgrounds here. This is a popular destination for the region's equestrians. There are numerous trails for horses, hikers, and bikers. Remember: Equestrians have the right of way over hikers and bikers, and hikers have the right of way over bikers. Got it? The International Mountain Biking Association has chosen this as one of the top 10 riding areas in the country. There is a 14-mile trail system available that started as a series of hand-built fire lines. Note that in early fall, this area is open to deer hunting. Boggs is one of nine state forests managed with the purpose of demonstrating economical forest management, which means there is logging along with compatible recreation.

RV sites, facilities: There are 19 sites for tents or RVs up to 22 feet (no hookups). No drinking water is available. Picnic tables and fire pits are provided. Vault toilets are available. Garbage must be packed out. Coin laundry, pizza parlor, and gas station are available within two miles. Horses and leashed pets are permitted.

Reservations, fees: Reservations are not accepted. There is no fee for camping. Self-registration required. Open year-round.

CALIFORNIA

Directions: From Vallejo, drive north on Highway 29 past Calistoga to Middletown and the junction with Highway 175. Turn left (north) on Highway 175 and drive seven miles (through the town of Cobb) to Forestry Road. Turn right and drive one mile to the campgrounds on the left.

Contact: Boggs Mountain Demonstration State Forest, 707/928-4378.

89 JELLYSTONE RV PARK

Scenic rating: 7

near Cobb Mountain

Map grid B2

Kelsey Creek runs through this campground which has a trout creek, a pond with canoe and kayak rentals in summer, plus plenty of hiking and bird-watching opportunities. In addition, horseback riding and hot-air balloon rides are available nearby. The camp is set near Highway 175 between Middletown and Clear Lake, and while there is a parade of vacation traffic on Highway 29, relatively few people take the longer route on Highway 175. Cobb Mountain looms nearby. Golf courses are in the vicinity. (Those familiar with this area may remember this camp was formerly called Beaver Creek RV Park.)

RV sites, facilities: There are 97 sites with full hookups (30 and 50 amps) for RVs up to 40 feet, 10 tent sites, and four cabins. Most sites are pull-through. Picnic tables and fire rings are provided. Drinking water, restrooms with showers, group facilities, coin laundry, Wi-Fi and modem access, seasonal swimming pool, kayak and paddleboat rentals, boating pond, playground, horseshoes, miniature golf, recreation hall, picnic area, athletic field, basketball, volleyball, horseshoes, firewood, ice, propane, and camp store are available. Some facilities are wheelchair-accessible. Leashed pets are permitted.

Reservations, fees: Reservations are accepted. Sites are $35–45 per night, $5–8 per person per night for more than two people, $3 per pet per night. Some credit cards accepted. Open year-round.

Directions: From Vallejo, drive north on Highway 29 past Calistoga to Middletown and the junction with Highway 175. Turn north on Highway 175 (to Cobb) and drive 12 miles to Bottle Rock Road. Turn left and drive three miles to the campground entrance on the left side of the road at 14117 Bottle Rock Road.

Contact: Jellystone RV Park, 707/928-4322, www.jellystonecobbmtn.com.

90 LOWER HUNTING CREEK

Scenic rating: 4

near Lake Berryessa

Map grid B2

This little-known camp might seem, to the folks who wind up here accidentally, as if it's out in the middle of nowhere, and it turns out that it is. If you plan on spending a few days here, it's advisable to get information or a map of the surrounding area from the Bureau of Land Management before your trip. There are about 25 miles of trails for off-highway-vehicle exploration on the surrounding lands. In the fall, the area provides access for deer hunting with generally poor to fair results.

RV sites, facilities: There are five sites for tents or RVs up to 20 feet (no hookups) and an overflow area. Picnic tables and fire grills are provided. Shade shelters and vault toilets are available. No drinking water. Leashed pets are permitted.

Reservations, fees: Reservations are not accepted. There is no fee for camping. Open year-round.

Directions: In Lower Lake on Highway 29, turn southeast on Morgan Valley Road/Berryessa-Knoxville Road and drive 15 miles to Devilhead Road. Turn south and drive two miles to the campground.

Contact: Bureau of Land Management, Ukiah District, 707/468-4000, fax 707/468-4027.

91 PUTAH CREEK RESORT

Scenic rating: 7

on Lake Berryessa

Map grid B2

This campground is set at 400 feet elevation on the northern end of Lake Berryessa. The lake is well known for powerboats and water sports. The Putah Creek arm provides very good bass fishing in the spring and trout trolling in the summer. In the fall, the trout come to the surface and provide excellent fishing at the mouth of Pope Creek or Putah Creek. The resort has a small, rustic motel. There is a two-week camping limit in season. Also, there is an area within this resort filled with long-term RV sites. Note: As part of the Bureau of Land Management's Lake Berryessa transformation project, this campground and other recreation sites have a new concessionaire for 2009.

RV sites, facilities: There are 125 sites for tents, and 55 sites with full or partial hookups (30 and 50 amps) for RVs of any length; some sites are pull-through. Picnic tables and barbecues are provided. Vault toilets, dump station, coin laundry, two boat ramps, seasonal snack bar, motel, cocktail lounge, restaurant, propane gas, ice, and convenience store are available. Leashed pets are permitted, with some restrictions.

Reservations, fees: Reservations are accepted at 707/966-0794. Sites are $30–38 per vehicle per night, $2 per pet per night. Some credit cards accepted. Open year-round.

Directions: From Vallejo, drive north on I-80 to the Suisun Valley Road exit. Take Suisun Valley Road and drive north to Highway 121. Turn north on Highway 121 and drive five miles to Highway 128. Turn left on Highway 128 and drive five miles to Berryessa-Knoxville Road. Turn right and continue 13 miles to 7600 Knoxville Road.

Contact: Putah Creek Resort, 707/966-0775; store, 707/966-2116.

92 NAPA COUNTY FAIRGROUNDS

Scenic rating: 3

in Calistoga

Map grid B2

What this really is, folks, is just the county fairgrounds, converted to an RV park. It is open year-round, except when the county fair is in progress. Who knows, maybe you can win a stuffed animal. What is more likely, of course, is that you have come here for the health spas, with great natural hot springs, mud baths, and assorted goodies at the health resorts in Calistoga. The downtown is within walking distance. Nearby parks for hiking include Bothe–Napa Valley and Robert Louis Stevenson State Parks. Cycling, wine-tasting, and hot-air balloon rides are also popular.

RV sites, facilities: There are 78 sites with partial or full hookups (30 and 50 amps) for RVs, and a lawn area for tents. Some sites are pull-through. Group sites are available by reservation only with a 10-vehicle minimum. Restrooms with flush toilets and showers, picnic area, and dump station are available. No fires are permitted. A nine-hole golf course is adjacent to the campground area. Some facilities are wheelchair-accessible. Leashed pets are permitted.

Reservations, fees: Reservations are accepted and required for groups at 707/942-5221 or through website. Sites are $20–33 per night. Some credit cards accepted. Open year-round.

Directions: From Napa on Highway 29, drive north to Calistoga, turn right on Lincoln Avenue, and drive four blocks to Fairway. Turn left and drive about four blocks to the end of the road to the campground.

Contact: Napa County Fairgrounds, 707/942-5111, fax 707/942-5125, www.napacountyfairgrounds.com.

CALIFORNIA

93 BOTHE-NAPA VALLEY STATE PARK

Scenic rating: 7

near Calistoga

Map grid B2

It's always a stunner for newcomers to discover this beautiful park with redwoods and a pretty stream so close to the Napa Valley wine and spa country. Though the campsites are relatively exposed, they are set beneath a pretty oak/bay/madrone forest, with trailheads for hiking nearby. One trail is routed south from the day-use parking lot for 1.8 mile to the restored Bale Grist Mill, a giant waterwheel on a pretty creek. Weekend tours of the Bale Grist Mill are available in summer. Another, more scenic, route, the Redwood Trail, heads up Ritchey Canyon, amid redwoods and towering Douglas fir, and along Ritchey Creek, all of it beautiful and intimate. The park covers 2,000 acres. Most of it is rugged, with elevations ranging from 300 to 2,000 feet. In summer, temperatures can reach the 100s, which is why finding a redwood grove can be stunning. The park has more than 10 miles of trails. Those who explore will find that the forests are on the north-facing slopes while the south-facing slopes tend to be brushy. The geology here is primarily volcanic, yet the vegetation hides most of it. Bird-watchers will note that this is one of the few places where you can see six species of woodpeckers, including the star of the show, the pileated woodpecker (the size of a crow).

RV sites, facilities: There are 37 sites for tents or RVs up to 31 feet and trailers up to 24 feet (no hookups), nine walk-in (up to 50 feet) tent sites, one hike-in/bike-in site, and one group tent site for up to 30 people. Picnic tables and fire grills are provided. Drinking water, restrooms with flush toilets and coin showers, and seasonal swimming pool are available. Some facilities are wheelchair-accessible. Supplies can be obtained four miles away in Calistoga. Leashed pets are permitted, but not on trails.

Reservations, fees: Reservations are accepted at 800/444-PARK (800/444-7275) or www.reserveamerica.com ($8 reservation fee). Sites are $35 per night, $8 per night for each additional vehicle, $3 per person per night for hike-in/bike-in site, $100 per night for the group site, $2–5 pool fee (free for children five and under). Open year-round.

Directions: From Napa, drive north on Highway 29 to St. Helena then continue north for five miles (one mile past the entrance to Bale Grist Mill State Park) to the park entrance road on the left.

Contact: Bothe–Napa Valley State Park, 707/942-4575, www.parks.ca.gov.

94 JOHNSON'S BEACH & RESORT

Scenic rating: 7

on the Russian River in Guerneville

Map grid B2

Johnson's is located on the north bank of the Russian River in Guerneville. The resort offers canoes, kayaks, and paddleboats for rent, as well as beach chairs and a boat launch. This is often a good fishing spot for steelhead in early winter.

RV sites, facilities: There are 40 tent sites and six sites with partial 20-amp hookups for RVs to 32 feet. Picnic tables and fire rings are provided. Restrooms with flush toilets, coin showers, laundry room, game room and a sandy beach are available.

Reservations, fees: Reservations are not accepted; sites are first-come, first-served. Tent sites are $14 per night for two people, $2 per each additional vehicle; RV sites are $25–30 per night. Open mid-May to mid-October, weather permitting.

Directions: From Santa Rosa, take Highway 101 north to River Road. Turn left (west) on River Road and drive 15 miles to Church Street in Guerneville. Turn left (south) on Church Street and drive one block to the campground at the corner of Church and First Streets.

Contact: Johnson's Beach & Resort, 707/869-2022, www.johnsonsbeach.com.

95 HILTON PARK FAMILY CAMPGROUND

Scenic rating: 6

on the Russian River

Map grid B2

This lush, wooded park is set on the banks of the Russian River, with a choice of open or secluded sites. The highlight of the campground is a large, beautiful beach that offers access for swimming, fishing, and canoeing. You get a choice of many recreation options in the area.

RV sites, facilities: There are 37 tent sites, five sites with partial hookups (30 amps) for RVs up to 28 feet, eight camping cottages, and a "magic bus." Picnic tables and fire rings are provided. Restrooms with coin showers, dishwashing area, arcade, playground, coin laundry, camp store, firewood, and ice are available. A beach is nearby. Boat rentals are available within three miles. Leashed pets are permitted, with certain restrictions.

Reservations, fees: Reservations are recommended. Sites are $38.15–49.05 per night, $6 per person per night for more than two people, $6 per night for each additional vehicle, $6 per night per pet. Some credit cards accepted. Open May through October.

Directions: From U.S. 101 north of Santa Rosa, take the River Road/Guerneville exit. Drive west on River Road for 11.5 miles (one mile after the metal bridge) to the campground on the left side of the road (just before the Russian River Pub) at 10750 River Road.

Contact: Hilton Park Family Campground, 707/887-9206, www.hiltonparkcampground. com.

96 RIVER BEND RESORT

Scenic rating: 7

on the Russian River near Guerneville

Map grid B2

River Bend Resort provides direct access to the Russian River and has a small beach for swimming. Burke's Canoe Trips is located nearby

and Korbel Champagne Cellars is adjacent to the property. Guerneville is four miles away.

RV sites, facilities: There are 34 tent sites and 44 RV sites, 13 with full 20/30/50-amp hookups and 31 with water and electricity only. Picnic tables and fire pits are provided. Restrooms with flush toilets, showers, a dog walk, a general store, propane, and a sport court are available. Leashed pets are permitted with some restrictions.

Reservations, fees: Reservations are recommended. RV sites are $45 for full hookup sites, $40 for partial hookups, and $5 per night for additional vehicle. Tent sites are $30 per night for two people, $5 for each additional person. Pets are $3 per pet per night.

Directions: From Santa Rosa, take Highway 101 north to River Road. Turn left (west) on River Road and drive about 11 miles to River Bend Resort.

Contact: River Bend Resort, 11820 River Road, 707/887-7662, fax 707/887-0816, www.riverbendresort.net.

97 LAKE BERRYESSA MARINA RESORT

Scenic rating: 7

on Lake Berryessa

Map grid B2

With 165 miles of shoreline, Lake Berryessa is the Bay Area's backyard water-recreation headquarters—the number-one lake (in the greater Bay Area) for waterskiing, loafing, and fishing. All water sports are permitted, but the focus is on powerboating, wakeboarding, waterskiing, and tubing. This resort is set on the west shore of the main lake, one of several resorts at the lake. The addition of park-model cabins is a great plus here. Note: As part of the Bureau of Land Management's Lake Berryessa transformation project, this campground and other recreation sites have a new concessionaire for 2009.

RV sites, facilities: There are 37 sites with full hookups (30 amps) for RVs up to 40 feet, 67 tent sites, a group tent site for up to 20 people, and 15 park-model cabins. Picnic tables are provided, and fire grills are also provided at the tent sites. Restrooms with flush toilets and showers, dump station, coin laundry, full-service marina, watercraft and houseboat rentals, and convenience store are available. Leashed pets are permitted at RV sites, but prohibited at tent sites and cabins.

Reservations, fees: Reservations are recommended. RV sites are $30–35 per night, tent sites are $25–30 per night, the group site is $60 per night, $4 per person per night for more than two people, $1 per pet per night. Boat launching is $20 per day. Some credit cards accepted. Open year-round.

Directions: From Vallejo, drive west on I-80 to the Suisun Valley Road exit. Take Suisun Valley Road and drive north to Highway 121. Turn north on Highway 121 and drive five miles to Highway 128. Turn left on Highway 128 and drive five miles to Berryessa-Knoxville Road. Turn right and continue nine miles to 5800 Knoxville Road.

Contact: Lake Berryessa Marina Resort, 707/966-2161, fax 707/966-0761, www.lakeberryessa.com.

98 SPANISH FLAT RESORT

Scenic rating: 7

on Lake Berryessa

Map grid B2

This is one of the most popular spots at Lake Berryessa because many of the sites have lake views. This makes it a natural gathering place for waterskiers and powerboaters. On summer weekends, particularly holidays, it can get rowdy here. Berryessa, considered the Bay Area's backyard fishing hole, is the third-largest artificial lake in Northern California (Lakes Shasta and Oroville are larger). Trout fishing is good, and there are also bass and salmon. The elevation is approximately 500 feet. As at Lake Berryessa Marina Resort, the addition of park-model cabins has given this resort a nice touch. There are also an additional 180 RV sites filled with seasonal renters.

Note: As part of the Bureau of Land Management's Lake Berryessa transformation project, this campground and other recreation sites have a new concessionaire for 2009.

RV sites, facilities: There are 120 sites for tents or RVs up to 37 feet, two yurts, and 16 park-model cabins. Some sites have partial hookups (30 amps). Picnic tables and fire grills are provided. Restrooms with flush toilets and showers, drinking water, dump station, boat storage, picnic area, ATM, boat launch, full-service marina, boat rentals, and convenience store are available. A snack bar is open on summer weekends. Coin laundry, restaurant, and bar are available within one mile. Some facilities are wheelchair-accessible. Leashed pets are permitted.

Reservations, fees: Reservations are accepted ($4 reservation fee). Sites are $25 per night, $50 per night for yurts, $5 per day for boat launching, $2 per pet per night. Some credit cards accepted. Open year-round.

Directions: From Vallejo, drive north on I-80 to the Suisun Valley Road exit. Take that exit and turn left onto Suisun Valley Road and drive north for approximately 17 miles to Highway 121. Turn north (right) on Highway 121 and drive seven miles to Highway 128. Turn north (left) on Highway 128 and drive five miles to Berryessa-Knoxville Road. Turn right on Berryessa-Knoxville Road and continue 4.5 miles to 4290 Knoxville Road.

Contact: Spanish Flat Resort, 707/966-7700; Spanish Flat Marina, 707/966-7708, www.spanishflatresort.com.

99 LAKE SOLANO PARK

Scenic rating: 6

near Lake Berryessa

Map grid B2

Lake Solano provides a low-pressure option to nearby Lake Berryessa. It is a long, narrow lake set below the outlet at Monticello Dam at Lake Berryessa, technically called the afterbay. Compared to Berryessa, life here moves at a much slower pace and some people prefer it. The water temperature at Lake Solano is also much cooler than at Berryessa. The lake has fair trout fishing in the spring, and it is known among Bay Area anglers as the closest fly-fishing spot for trout in the region. No motors, including electric motors, are permitted on boats at the lake. The park covers 177 acres along the river. A swimming pond is available in summer, and a children's fishing pond (trout and bass) is open year-round. The gate closes at night; check in before dusk.

RV sites, facilities: There are 50 sites with no hookups for tents or RVs, and 41 sites with full or partial hookups (30 amps) for tents or RVs up to 38 feet; some sites are pull-through. Picnic tables and fire grills are provided. Drinking water, restrooms with flush toilets and showers, two dump stations, picnic area, boat ramp (summer weekends only), and boat rentals are available. A grocery store is within walking distance, and firewood and ice are sold on the premises. Some facilities are wheelchair-accessible. Leashed pets are permitted in the campground only.

Reservations, fees: Reservations are recommended. RV sites are $15–25 per night, tent sites are $15 per night, $10 per night for each additional vehicle, $1 per pet per night. Holiday rates are higher. Some credit cards accepted. Open year-round.

Directions: In Vacaville, turn north on I-505 and drive 11 miles to the junction of Highway 128. Turn west on Highway 128 and drive about five miles (past Winters) to Pleasant Valley Road. Turn left on Pleasant Valley Road and drive to the park at 8685 Pleasant Valley Road (well signed).

Contact: Lake Solano Park, 530/795-2990, fax 530/795-1408, www.solanocounty.com.

100 VILLAGE PARK

Scenic rating: 7

in Sebastopol

Map grid B2

Village Park is an RV layover spot on the banks of the Laguna de Santa Rosa wetlands complex in the Sonoma foothills near Santa Rosa. This is a developed RV park with direct access from the adjacent highway. If you get a site with a view of the open space to the other side, it rates better.

RV sites, facilities: There are 15 tent sites and 17 RV sites with partial 30-amp hookups for RVs to 40 feet. Picnic tables are provided. Open fires are not permitted. Restrooms with flush toilets, showers and a coin laundry are available. Leashed pets are permitted. Restaurants and stores are within walking distance.

Reservations, fees: Reservations are accepted. RV sites are $27.25 per night; tent sites are $21.80 per night; pets are $2 per pet per night.

Directions: From Santa Rosa, take Highway 101 north to Highway 12. Turn west on Highway 12 (which becomes Sebastopol Avenue while remaining Highway 12) and continue to Village Park on the left just past the Chevron station on the right.

Contact: Village Park, 6665 Sebastopol Avenue, 707/823-6348.

101 SPRING LAKE REGIONAL PARK

Scenic rating: 6

at Spring Lake near Santa Rosa

Map grid B2

Spring Lake is one of the few lakes in the greater Bay Area that provides lakeside camping. No gas-powered boats are permitted on this small, pretty lake, which keeps things fun and quiet for everybody. An easy trail along the west shore of the lake to the dam, then into adjoining Howarth Park, provides a pleasant evening stroll. This little lake is where a 24-pound world-record bass was reportedly caught, a story taken as a hoax by nearly all anglers.

RV sites, facilities: There are 29 sites for tents or RVs up to 40 feet (no hookups), and one group site for up to 75 people and 15 vehicles. Several sites are pull-through. Picnic tables and fire grills are provided. Drinking water, restrooms with flush toilets and showers, dump station, boat ramp (no gas-powered motorboats), and boat rentals (in summer) are available. Some facilities are wheelchair-accessible. A grocery store, coin laundry, firewood, and propane gas are available within five minutes. Leashed pets are permitted.

Reservations, fees: Reservations are accepted at 707/565-2267 ($8 reservation fee and $30–50 reservation fee for the group site). Sites are $20 per night, $6 per night for each additional vehicle, group site is $3 per person per night with a $75 minimum, $1 per pet per night. There is a 10-day camping limit. Open daily from May through September and on weekends and holidays only during off-season.

Directions: From Santa Rosa on U.S. 101, turn east on Highway 12 and drive two miles to the junction with Hoen Avenue. Continue straight (east) onto Hoen Avenue and drive one mile (crossing Summerfield Road) to Newanga Avenue. Turn left and drive 0.5 mile to the park entrance at 5585 Newanga Avenue.

Contact: Spring Lake Regional Park, 707/539-8092; Sonoma County Parks, 707/565-2041, www.sonomacounty.org/camping.

102 SUGARLOAF RIDGE STATE PARK

Scenic rating: 5

near Santa Rosa

Map grid B2

Sugarloaf Ridge State Park is a perfect example of a place that you can't make a final judgment about from your first glance. Your first glance will lead you to believe that this is just hot foothill country, with old ranch roads set in oak woodlands for horseback riding and sweaty hiking or biking. A little discovery here, however, is that a half-mile walk off the Canyon Trail will lead you to a 25-foot waterfall, beautifully set in a canyon, complete with a redwood canopy. A shortcut to this waterfall is available off the south side of the park's entrance road. Otherwise, it can be a long, hot, and challenging hike.

In all, there are 25 miles of trails here for hikers and equestrians. Hikers planning for a day of it should leave early, wear a hat, and bring plenty of water. Rangers report that some unprepared hikers have suffered heat stroke in summer, and many others have just plain suffered. In the off-season, when the air is cool and clear, the views from the ridge are eye-popping—visitors can see the Sierra Nevada, Golden Gate, and a thousand other points of scenic beauty from the top of Bald Mountain at 2,769 feet. For the less ambitious, a self-guided nature trail along Sonoma Creek begins at the campground.

RV sites, facilities: There are 47 sites for tents or RVs up to 27 feet (no hookups), and one group site for tents only for up to 50 people. Picnic tables, food lockers and fire grills are provided. Drinking water and flush toilets are available. Leashed pets are permitted in campsites only.

Reservations, fees: Reservations are recommended at 800/444-PARK (800/444-7275) or www.reserveamerica.com ($8 reservation fee). Sites are $30 per night, $8 per night for each additional vehicle, $165 per night for group site. Open year-round.

Directions: From Santa Rosa on U.S. 101, turn east on Highway 12 and drive seven miles to Adobe Canyon Road. Turn left and drive 3.5 miles to the park entrance at the end of the road.

Contact: Sugarloaf Ridge State Park, 707/833-5712, www.parks.ca.gov.

103 SAN FRANCISCO NORTH/ PETALUMA KOA

Scenic rating: 3

near Petaluma

Map grid B2

This campground is less than a mile from U.S. 101, yet it has a rural feel in a 60-acre farm setting. It's a good base camp for folks who require some quiet mental preparation before heading south to the Bay Area or to the nearby wineries, redwoods, and Russian River. The big plus here is that this KOA has the cute log cabins called "Kamping Kabins," providing privacy for those who want it. There are recreational activities and live music on Saturdays in summer. During October, a pumpkin patch and corn maze are open across the street from the park.

RV sites, facilities: There are 272 sites, most with full or partial hookups (30 and 50 amps) for RVs or tents, 34 cabins, and a lodge. Most sites are pull-through. Picnic tables and fire pits are provided. Restrooms with flush toilets and showers, cable TV hookups, modem access and free Wi-Fi, dump station, playground, recreation rooms, basketball, volleyball, heated seasonal swimming pool, spa, petting farm, shuffleboard, coin laundry, propane gas, and convenience store are available. Some facilities are wheelchair-accessible. Leashed pets are permitted, with certain restrictions.

Reservations, fees: Reservations are accepted at 800/562-1233 or through the website. Sites are $29.95–80 per night, $5–7 per person per night for more than two people. Some credit cards accepted. Open year-round.

Directions: From Petaluma on U.S. 101 north, take the Penngrove exit and drive west for 0.25 mile on Petaluma Boulevard to Stony Point Road. Turn right (north) on Stony Point Road and drive 0.25 mile to Rainsville Road. Turn left (west) on Rainsville Road and drive a short distance to the park entrance at 20 Rainsville Road.

Contact: San Francisco North/Petaluma KOA, 707/763-1492, www.petalumakoa.com.

104 NAPA VALLEY EXPOSITION RV PARK

Scenic rating: 2

in Napa

Map grid B2

This RV park is directly adjacent to the Napa Valley Exposition. When the fair is in operation in late July and early August, it is closed. The rest of the year it is simply a RV parking area, and it can come in handy.

RV sites, facilities: There are 45 sites with partial hookups (30 and 50 amps) for RVs of any length and a grassy area for at least 100 self-contained RVs. Some sites are pull-through. Picnic tables, restrooms with showers, coin laundry, and dump station are available. A camp host is on-site. A grocery store and restaurant are within walking distance. Some facilities are wheelchair-accessible. Leashed pets are permitted.

Reservations, fees: Reservations are not accepted for individual sites, but are required for groups at 707/253-4900, ext. 102. Sites are $35 per night. Open year-round, except during the fair.

Directions: From Napa on Highway 29, drive to the Napa/Lake Berryessa exit. Take that exit and turn right (east) and drive about one mile to Silverado/Highway 121. Turn right and drive less than one mile to the fairgrounds entrance on the left.

Contact: Napa Valley Exposition, 707/253-4900, fax 707/253-4943, www.napavalleyexpo.com.

SACRAMENTO AND GOLD COUNTRY

☾ **Fishing**
Lundborg Landing, page 785.

☾ **Prettiest Rivers**
Moonshine Campground, page 776.

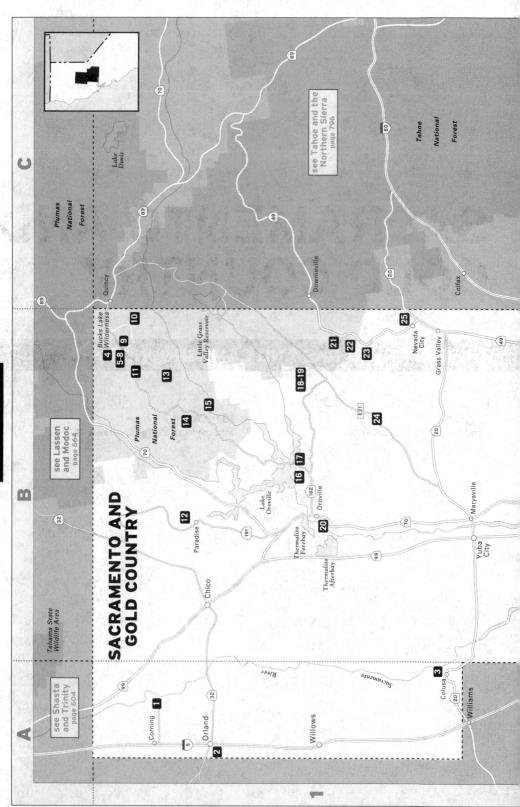

CALIFORNIA

SACRAMENTO AND GOLD COUNTRY

see Shasta and Trinity page 604

see Lassen and Modoc page 664

see Tahoe and the Northern Sierra page 796

Tehama State Wildlife Area

Plumas National Forest

Lake Davis

Tahoe National Forest

Bucks Lake Wilderness

Little Grass Valley Reservoir

Plumas National Forest

Lake Oroville

Thermalito Forebay

Thermalito Afterbay

Quincy

Downieville

Colfax

Nevada City

Grass Valley

Paradise

Chico

Corning

Orland

Willows

Colusa

Williams

Oroville

Marysville

Yuba City

Sacramento River

River

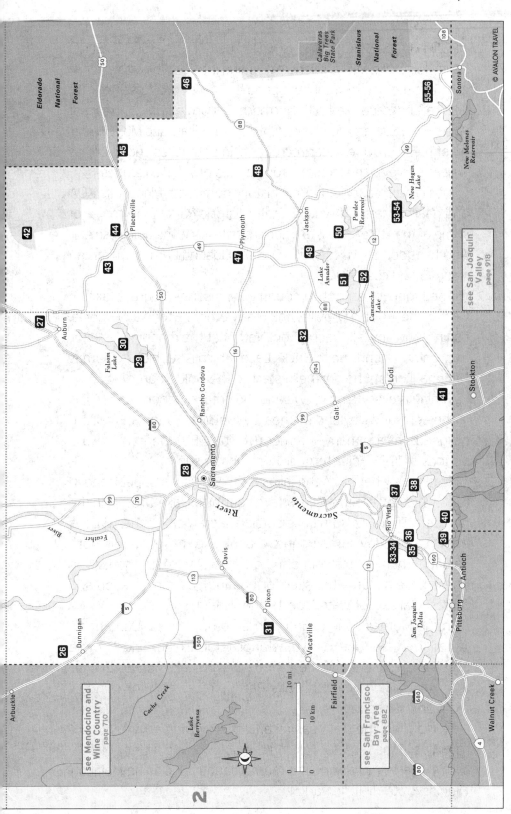

see Mendocino and Wine Country page 710

see San Francisco Bay Area page 882

see San Joaquin Valley page 918

CALIFORNIA

© AVALON TRAVEL

From a distance, this section of the Sacramento Valley looks like flat farmland extending into infinity, with a sprinkling of cities and towns interrupting the view. But a closer look reveals a landscape filled with Northern California's most significant rivers – the Sacramento, Feather, Yuba, American, and Mokelumne. All of these provide water recreation, in both lakes and rivers, as well as serve as the lifeblood for a series of wildlife refuges.

This is an area for California history buffs, with Placerville KOA and nearby Malakoff Diggins State Historic Park in the center of some of the state's most extraordinary history: the gold rush era. Another good deal is the Lake Oroville Floating Camps, which can sleep 15 and cost $100 a night.

The highlight of foothill country is its series of great lakes – Camanche, Rollins, Oroville, and many others – for water sports, fishing, and any lake recreation. Note that the mapping I use for this region extends up to Bucks Lake, which is set high in Plumas National Forest, the northern start to the Gold Country.

Timing is everything in love and the great outdoors, and so it is in the Central Valley and the nearby foothills. Spring and fall are gorgeous, as are many summer evenings. But there are always periods of 100°F-plus temperatures in the summer.

But that's what gives the lakes and rivers such appeal, and in turn, why they are treasured. Take your pick: Lake Oroville in the northern Sierra, Folsom Lake outside Sacramento... the list goes on. On a hot day, jumping into a cool lake makes water more valuable than gold, a cold drink on ice worth more than silver. These have become top sites for boating-based recreation and fantastic areas for water sports and fishing.

In the Mother Lode country, three other lakes – Camanche, Amador, and Pardee – are outstanding for fishing. Lake Oroville and Camanche Lake are best for bass while Lake Amador makes it for bluegill and catfish. Lake Pardee rates high for rainbow trout and salmon.

For touring, the state capital and nearby Old Sacramento are favorites. Others prefer reliving the gold-mining history of California's past or exploring the foothill country, including Malakoff Diggins State Historic Park.

1 WOODSON BRIDGE STATE RECREATION AREA

Scenic rating: 7

on the Sacramento River

Map grid A1

The campground at Woodson Bridge features direct access to the Sacramento River. The preserve itself is 328-acres of thick, riparian forest, including some of the only virgin habitat left on this 400-mile length of the Sacramento River. Boat-in sites, designed as camping spots for kayakers and canoeists, and a nearby boat ramp provide easy access for water sports, making this an ideal spot for campers with trailered boats. Note that waterskiing and personal watercraft are discouraged on this section of the river.

There are about two miles of hiking trails in the park; a beach is nearby. In June, the nearby Tehama Riffle is one of the best spots on the entire river for shad fishing. By mid-August, salmon start arriving, en route to their spawning grounds. Summer weather here is hot, with high temperatures commonly 85–100°F. In winter, look for bald eagles; in summer, the yellow-billed cuckoo builds nests here.

RV sites, facilities: There are 37 sites for tents or RVs up to 31 feet (no hookups) and five boat-in sites. One group site for up to 40 people is available. Picnic tables and fire grills are provided. Drinking water, coin showers, flush toilets, and boat launch (across the street) are available, and there is a camp host. Leashed pets are permitted.

Reservations, fees: Reservations are accepted at 800/444-PARK (800/444-7275) or www. reserveamerica.com ($8 reservation fee). Sites are $25 per night, $6 per night for each additional vehicle, $135 per night for the group camp. Open year-round.

Directions: From Corning, take the South Avenue exit off I-5 and drive six miles east to the campground on the left.

Contact: Woodson Bridge State Recreation Area, 530/839-2112, www.parks.ca.gov.

2 OLD ORCHARD RV PARK

Scenic rating: 4

near Orland

Map grid A1

Most folks use this as a layover spot while on long trips up or down I-5 in the Central Valley. If you're staying longer than a night, there are two side trips that have appeal for anglers. Nearby Black Butte Lake to the west, with crappie in the early summer, and the Sacramento River to the east, with salmon in the late summer and early fall, can add some spice to your trip. The elevation is 250 feet. Some sites are filled with long-term renters.

RV sites, facilities: There are 52 pull-through sites with partial or full hookups (30 and 50 amps) for RVs up to 60 feet, and six tent sites. Restrooms with showers, dump station, coin laundry, and modem access are available. All facilities are wheelchair-accessible. Leashed pets are permitted.

Reservations, fees: Reservations are accepted. Sites are $15–24 per night, $2 per person per night for more than two adults, $2 per night for 50-amp full hookup. Some credit cards accepted. Open year-round.

Directions: From Orland, take the Chico/Highway 32 exit west (Exit 619) off I-5. Drive west one block to County Road HH. Turn right on County Road HH and drive north one block to the park on the right at 4490 County Road HH.

Contact: Old Orchard RV Park, 877/481-9282, tel./fax 530/865-5335.

3 COLUSA-SACRAMENTO RIVER STATE RECREATION AREA

Scenic rating: 5

near Colusa

Map grid A1

This region of the Sacramento Valley is well known as a high-quality habitat for birds. This park covers 67 acres and features great bird-watching opportunities. Nearby Delevan and

Colusa National Wildlife Refuges are outstanding destinations for wildlife-viewing as well, and they provide good duck hunting in December. In summer the nearby Sacramento River is a bonus, with shad fishing in June and July, salmon fishing from August through October, sturgeon fishing in the winter, and striped-bass fishing in the spring. The landscape here features cottonwoods and willows along the Sacramento River.

RV sites, facilities: There are 10 sites for tents, four sites for tents or RVs up to 30 feet, and one group site for 10–40 people. No hookups. Picnic tables and barbecues are provided. Drinking water, restrooms with flush toilets and coin showers, boat ramp, Wi-Fi, and a dump station are available. Some facilities are wheelchair-accessible. A grocery store, restaurant, gas station, tackle shop, and coin laundry are nearby (within three blocks). Leashed pets are permitted.

Reservations, fees: Reservations for individual sites are accepted at 800/444-PARK (800/444-7275) or www.reserveamerica.com ($8 reservation fee). Group reservations are accepted at 530/458-4927. Sites are $25 per night, $6 per night for each additional vehicle, $100 per night for the group site, $6 for boat launch. Open year-round.

Directions: In Williams, at the junction of I-5 and Highway 20, drive east on Highway 20 for nine miles to the town of Colusa. Turn north (straight ahead) on 10th Street and drive two blocks, just over the levee, to the park.

Contact: Colusa–Sacramento River State Recreation Area, 530/458-4927, fax 530/458-8033, www.parks.ca.gov.

4 MILL CREEK

Scenic rating: 7

at Bucks Lake in Plumas National Forest

Map grid B1

When Bucks Lake is full, this is one of the prettiest spots on the lake. The camp is set deep in Mill Creek Cove, adjacent to where Mill Creek enters the northernmost point of Bucks Lake. A boat ramp is 0.5 mile away to the south,

providing boat access to one of the better trout fishing spots at the lake. Unfortunately, when the lake level falls, this camp is left high and dry, some distance from the water. All water sports are permitted on this 1,800-acre lake. The elevation is 5,200 feet.

RV sites, facilities: There are 10 sites for tents or RVs up to 27 feet (no hookups) and two walk-in tent sites. Picnic tables and fire grills are provided. Drinking water and vault toilets are available. Groceries are available within five miles. Leashed pets are permitted.

Reservations, fees: Reservations are not accepted. Sites are $20–22 per night. Open mid-May through September, weather permitting.

Directions: From Oroville, drive north on Highway 70 to the junction with Highway 89. Turn south on Highway 89/70 and drive 11 miles to Quincy. In Quincy, turn right at Bucks Lake Road and drive 17 miles to Bucks Lake and the junction with Bucks Lake Dam Road/Forest Road 33. Turn right, drive around the lake, cross over the dam, and continue for about three miles to the campground.

Contact: Plumas National Forest, Mount Hough Ranger District, 530/283-0555, fax 530/283-1821; Northwest Park Management, 530/283-5559.

5 SUNDEW

Scenic rating: 7

on Bucks Lake in Plumas National Forest

Map grid B1

Sundew Camp is set on the northern shore of Bucks Lake, just north of Bucks Lake Dam. A boat ramp is about two miles north at Sandy Point Day Use Area at the Mill Creek Cove, providing access to one of the better trout spots on the lake. You want fish? At Bucks Lake you can get fish—it's one of the state's top mountain trout lakes. Fish species include rainbow, brown, and Mackinaw trout. Sunrises are often spectacular from this camp, with the light glowing on the lake's surface.

RV sites, facilities: There are 19 sites for tents

or RVs up to 35 feet (no hookups). Picnic tables and fire grills are provided. Drinking water and vault toilets are available. Leashed pets are permitted. There is a boat ramp two miles north of the camp.

Reservations, fees: Reservations are not accepted. Sites are $20–22 per night. Open mid-May through September, weather permitting.

Directions: From Oroville, drive north on Highway 70 to the junction with Highway 89. Turn south on Highway 89/70 and drive 11 miles to Quincy. In Quincy, turn right at Bucks Lake Road and drive 17 miles to Bucks Lake and the junction with Bucks Lake Dam Road/Forest Road 33. Turn right, drive around the lake, cross over the dam, continue for 0.5 mile, and turn right at the campground access road.

Contact: Plumas National Forest, Mount Hough Ranger District, 530/283-0555, fax 530/283-1821; Northwest Park Management, 530/283-5559.

6 HUTCHINS GROUP CAMP

Scenic rating: 6

near Bucks Lake in Plumas National Forest

Map grid B1

This is a prime spot for a Scout outing or for any other large group that would like a pretty spot. An amphitheater is available. It is set at 5,200 feet elevation near Bucks and Lower Bucks Lakes. (For more information, see the Sundew, Lower Bucks, and Haskins Valley listings in this chapter.)

RV sites, facilities: There are three group sites for tents or RV up to 35 feet (no hookups) that can accommodate up to 25 people each. Picnic tables and fire grills are provided. Drinking water and vault toilets are available. A boat ramp is available. Leashed pets are permitted.

Reservations, fees: Reservations are required at 877/444-6777 or www.recreation.gov ($10 reservation fee). The group camp is $70 per night. Open May through October.

Directions: From Oroville, drive north on Highway 70 to the junction with Highway 89. Turn

south on Highway 89/70 and drive 11 miles to Quincy and Bucks Lake Road. Turn right at Bucks Lake Road and drive 17 miles to Bucks Lake and the junction with Bucks Lake Dam Road/Forest Road 33. Turn right, drive around the lake, cross over the dam, continue for a short distance, and turn right. Drive 0.5 mile, cross the stream (passing an intersection), and continue straight for 0.5 mile to the campground.

Contact: Plumas National Forest, Mount Hough Ranger District, 530/283-0555, fax 530/283-1821; Northwest Park Management, 530/283-5559.

7 LOWER BUCKS

Scenic rating: 7

on Lower Bucks Lake in Plumas National Forest

Map grid B1

This camp is on Lower Bucks Lake, which is actually the afterbay for Bucks Lake, set below the Bucks Lake Dam. It is a small, primitive, and quiet spot that is often overlooked because it is not on the main lake.

RV sites, facilities: There are six sites for tents or RVs up to 26 feet (no hookups). Picnic tables and fire rings are provided. Vault toilets are available. There is no drinking water. Leashed pets are permitted.

Reservations, fees: Reservations are not accepted. Sites are $16 per night. Open May through October.

Directions: From Oroville, drive north on Highway 70 to the junction with Highway 89. Turn south on Highway 89/70 and drive 11 miles to Quincy and Bucks Lake Road. Turn right at Bucks Lake Road and drive 17 miles to Bucks Lake and the junction with Bucks Lake Dam Road/Forest Road 33. Turn right and drive four miles around the lake, cross over the dam, drive 0.25 mile, and then turn left on the campground entrance road.

Contact: Plumas National Forest, Mount Hough Ranger District, 530/283-0555, fax 530/283-1821; Northwest Park Management, 530/283-5559.

CALIFORNIA

8 HASKINS VALLEY

Scenic rating: 7

on Bucks Lake
Map grid B1

This is the biggest and most popular of the campgrounds at Bucks Lake, a pretty alpine lake with excellent trout fishing and clean campgrounds. A boat ramp is available to the nearby north, along with Bucks Lodge. This camp is set deep in a cove at the extreme south end of the lake, where the water is quiet and sheltered from north winds. Bucks Lake, at 5,200 feet elevation, is well documented for excellent fishing for rainbow and Mackinaw trout, with high catch rates of rainbow trout and lake records in the 16-pound class. Insider's tip: This is the best lake in the region for sailboarding.

RV sites, facilities: There are 65 sites for tents or RVs up to 30 feet (no hookups). Picnic tables and fire grills are provided. Drinking water and vault toilets are available. A dump station and boat ramp are available nearby. Some facilities are wheelchair-accessible. Leashed pets are permitted.

Reservations, fees: Reservations are not accepted. Sites are $18 per night, $3 per night for each additional vehicle, $1 per pet per night. Open May to early October, weather permitting.

Directions: From Oroville, drive north on Highway 70 to the junction with Highway 89. Turn south on Highway 89/70 and drive 11 miles to Quincy. In Quincy, turn right at Bucks Lake Road and drive 16.5 miles to the campground entrance on the right side of the road.

Contact: PG&E Land Services, 916/386-5164, www.pge.com/recreation.

9 WHITEHORSE

Scenic rating: 7

near Bucks Lake in Plumas National Forest
Map grid B1

This campground is set along Bucks Creek, about two miles from the boat ramps and south shore concessions at Bucks Lake. The trout fishing can be quite good at Bucks Lake. The elevation is 5,200 feet. (For more information, see the Haskins Valley listing.)

RV sites, facilities: There are 20 sites for tents or RVs up to 27 feet (no hookups). Picnic tables and fire grills are provided. Drinking water and vault toilets are available. A grocery store and coin laundry are available within five miles. Leashed pets are permitted.

Reservations, fees: Reservations are not accepted. Sites are $16 per night. Open June through September.

Directions: From Oroville, drive north on Highway 70 to the junction with Highway 89. Turn south on Highway 89/70 and drive 11 miles to Quincy and Bucks Lake Road. Turn right at Bucks Lake Road and drive 14.5 miles to the campground entrance on the right side of the road.

Contact: Plumas National Forest, Mount Hough Ranger District, 530/283-0555, fax 530/283-1821; Northwest Park Management, 530/283-5559.

10 DEANES VALLEY

Scenic rating: 5

on Rock Creek in Plumas National Forest
Map grid B1

This secret spot is set on South Fork Rock Creek, deep in a valley at an elevation of 4,400 feet in Plumas National Forest. The trout here are very small natives. If you want a pure, quiet spot, great; if you want good fishing, not so great. The surrounding region has a network of backcountry roads, including routes passable only by four-wheel-drive vehicles; to explore these roads, get a map of Plumas National Forest.

RV sites, facilities: There are seven sites for tents or RVs up to 24 feet (no hookups). Picnic tables and fire grills are provided. Vault toilets are available. No drinking water is available. Garbage must be packed out. Leashed pets are permitted.

Reservations, fees: Reservations are not accepted. There is no fee for camping. Open April through October, weather permitting.

Directions: From Oroville, drive north on Highway 70 to the junction with Highway 89. Turn south on Highway 89/70 and drive 11 miles to Quincy and Bucks Lake Road. Turn right at Bucks Lake Road and drive 3.5 miles to Forest Road 24N28. Turn left and drive seven miles to the campground on the left.

Contact: Plumas National Forest, Mount Hough Ranger District, 530/283-0555, fax 530/283-1821.

11 GRIZZLY CREEK

Scenic rating: 4

near Bucks Lake in Plumas National Forest
Map grid B1

This is an alternative to the more developed, more crowded campgrounds at Bucks Lake. It is a small, primitive camp set near Grizzly Creek at 5,400 feet elevation. Nearby Bucks Lake provides good trout fishing, resorts, and boat rentals.

RV sites, facilities: There are eight sites for tents or RVs up to 35 feet (no hookups). Picnic tables and fire grills are provided. Drinking water and vault toilets are available. A boat ramp is available at Bucks Lake. A grocery store and coin laundry are available within five miles. Leashed pets are permitted.

Reservations, fees: Reservations are not accepted. Sites are $16 per night. Open June through October.

Directions: From Oroville, drive north on Highway 70 to the junction with Highway 89. Turn south on Highway 89/70 and drive 11 miles to Quincy and Bucks Lake Road. Turn right at Bucks Lake Road and drive 17 miles to Bucks Lake and the junction with Bucks Lake Dam Road/Forest Road 33. Turn right and drive one mile to the junction with Oroville-Quincy Road/Forest Road 36. Bear left and drive one mile to the campground on the right side of the road.

Contact: Plumas National Forest, Mount Hough Ranger District, 530/283-0555, fax 530/283-1821; Northwest Park Management, 530/283-5559.

12 QUAIL TRAILS VILLAGE RV AND MOBILE HOME PARK

Scenic rating: 4

near Paradise
Map grid B1

This is a rural motor-home campground, set near the west branch of the Feather River, with nearby Lake Oroville as the feature attraction. The Lime Saddle section of the Lake Oroville State Recreation Area is three miles away, with a beach, boat-launching facilities, and concessions. Note: About one-third of the sites are taken by long-term rentals.

RV sites, facilities: There are 20 pull-through sites with full hookups (30 amps) for RVs of any length, and five tent sites. Picnic tables are provided. Restrooms with showers and coin laundry are available. All facilities are wheelchair-accessible. Leashed pets up to 30 pounds are permitted.

Reservations, fees: Reservations are accepted. Sites are $30 per night. Weekly rates available. Open year-round.

Directions: From Oroville, drive north on Highway 70 for six miles to Pentz Road. Turn left and drive six miles south to the park on the left (5110 Pentz Road).

Contact: Quail Trails Village RV and Mobile Home Park, 530/877-6581, fax 530/876-0516, www.quailtrailsvillage.com.

13 LITTLE NORTH FORK

Scenic rating: 7

on the Middle Fork of the Feather River in Plumas National Forest

Map grid B1

Guaranteed quiet? You got it. This is a primitive camp in the outback that few know of. It is set

CALIFORNIA

along the Little North Fork of the Middle Fork of the Feather River at 4,000 feet elevation. The surrounding backcountry of Plumas National Forest features an incredible number of roads, giving four-wheel-drive owners a chance to get so lost they'll need this camp. Instead, get a map of Plumas National Forest before venturing out.

RV sites, facilities: There are 17 sites for tents or RVs up to 16 feet (no hookups). Picnic tables and fire grills are provided. Vault toilets are available. No drinking water is available. Garbage must be packed out. Leashed pets are permitted.

Reservations, fees: Reservations are not accepted. There is no fee for camping. Open May through October.

Directions: From Oroville, turn east on Highway 162/Oroville-Quincy Highway and drive 26.5 miles to the Brush Creek Work Center. Continue northeast on Oroville-Quincy Highway for about six miles to County Road 60. Turn right and drive about eight miles to the campground entrance road on the left side of the road. Turn left and drive 0.25 mile to the campground. Note: This route is long, twisty, bumpy, and narrow for most of the way.

Contact: Plumas National Forest, Feather River Ranger District, 530/534-6500, fax 530/532-1210.

14 ROGERS COW CAMP

🥾 🐕 5% 🚐 ⛺

Scenic rating: 4

in Plumas National Forest

Map grid B1

First note that the Oroville-Quincy "Highway" is actually a twisty Forest Service road, a backcountry route that connects Oroville to Quincy and passes Lake Oroville and Bucks Lake in the process. The road is paved, but it can still put you way out there in no-man's land, set in Plumas National Forest at 4,000 feet elevation. You want quiet, you got it. You want water, you bring it yourself. The camp is set near the headwaters of Coon Creek. There are no other natural destinations in the area, and I'm not

saying Coon Creek is anything to see. It's advisable to obtain a map of Plumas National Forest, which details all backcountry roads. There has been logging activity in the area.

RV sites, facilities: There are eight sites for tents or RVs up to 16 feet (no hookups). Picnic tables and fire grills are provided. Vault toilets are available. No drinking water is available. Garbage must be packed out. Leashed pets are permitted.

Reservations, fees: Reservations are not accepted. There is no fee for camping. Open May through September.

Directions: In Oroville, drive east on Highway 162/Oroville-Quincy Highway for 26.5 miles to the Brush Creek Work Center. Continue on Oroville-Quincy Highway for eight miles to the campground entrance road on the left side of the road. Turn left and drive a short distance to the camp.

Contact: Plumas National Forest, Feather River Ranger District, 530/534-6500, fax 530/532-1210.

15 MILSAP BAR

🥾 🚣 🎣 🐕 🚐 ⛺

Scenic rating: 8

on the Middle Fork of the Feather River in Plumas National Forest

Map grid B1

Among white-water river rafters, Milsap Bar is a well-known access point to the Middle Fork Feather River. This river country features a deep canyon, beautiful surroundings, and is formally recognized as the Feather Falls Scenic Area (named after the awesome 640-foot waterfall). Note that while no commercial raft companies are permitted to run this section of the Feather, private groups and individual use are permitted. The elevation is 1,600 feet.

RV sites, facilities: There are five sites for tents or RVs up to 16 feet (no hookups). Picnic tables and fire grills are provided. Vault toilets are available. No drinking water is available. Garbage must be packed out. Leashed pets are permitted.

Reservations, fees: Reservations are not accepted. There is no fee for camping. Open May through September.

Directions: In Oroville, drive east on Highway 162/Oroville-Quincy Highway for 26.5 miles to the Brush Creek Work Center and Bald Rock Road. Turn right on Bald Rock Road and drive for about 0.5 mile to Forest Road 22N62/Milsap Bar Road. Turn left and drive eight miles to the campground (a narrow, steep, mountain dirt road).

Contact: Plumas National Forest, Feather River Ranger District, 530/534-6500, fax 530/532-1210.

16 BIDWELL CANYON

Scenic rating: 7

on Lake Oroville

Map grid B1

Bidwell Canyon is a major destination at giant Lake Oroville as the campground is near a major marina and boat ramp. It is set along the southern shore of the lake, on a point directly adjacent to the massive Oroville Dam to the west. Many campers use this spot for boating headquarters. Lake Oroville is created from the tallest earth-filled dam in the country, rising 770 feet above the streambed of the Feather River. It creates a huge reservoir when full. It is popular for waterskiing, as the water is warm enough in the summer for all water sports, and there is enough room for both anglers and water-skiers. Fishing is excellent for spotted bass. What a lake—there are even floating toilets here (imagine that!). It is very hot in midsummer, with high temperatures ranging from the mid-80s to the low 100s. The area has four distinct seasons—spring is quite beautiful with many wildflowers and greenery. A must-see is the view from the 47-foot tower using the high-powered telescopes, where there is a panoramic view of the lake, Sierra Nevada, valley, foothills, and the Sutter Buttes. The Feather River Hatchery is nearby.

RV sites, facilities: There are 75 sites with full hookups (30 amps) for tents or RVs up to 40 feet

and trailers up to 31 feet (including boat trailers). Picnic tables and fire grills are provided. Drinking water, flush toilets, and coin showers are available. Boat rentals are available on the lake. A grocery store, boat ramp, marina with fuel and boat pumping station, snack bar, and propane gas are available within two miles. Leashed pets are permitted, except on trails or beaches.

Reservations, fees: Reservations are accepted at 800/444-PARK (800/444-7275) or www.reserveamerica.com ($8 reservation fee). Sites are $24 per night, $4 per night for each additional vehicle. Open year-round.

Directions: From Oroville, drive east on Oroville Dam Boulevard/Highway 162 (becomes the Olive Highway) for 6.8 miles to Kelly Ridge Road. Turn left (north) on Kelly Ridge Road and drive 1.5 miles to Arroyo Drive. Turn right and drive 0.25 mile to the campground.

Contact: Lake Oroville State Recreation Area, 530/538-2200; Lake Oroville Visitor Center, 530/538-2219, www.parks.ca.gov.

17 LOAFER CREEK FAMILY, GROUP, AND EQUESTRIAN CAMPS

Scenic rating: 7

on Lake Oroville

Map grid B1

These are three different campground areas that are linked, designed for individual use, groups, and equestrians, respectively. The camps are just across the water at Lake Oroville from Bidwell Canyon, but campers come here for more spacious sites. It's also a primary option for campers with boats, with the Loafer Creek boat ramp one mile away. So hey, this spot is no secret. A bonus here includes an extensive equestrian trail system right out of camp.

RV sites, facilities: There are 137 sites for tents or RVs up to 40 feet (no hookups) and trailers to 31 feet (including boat trailers), 15 equestrian sites with a two-horse limit per site, and six group sites for up to 25 people each. Picnic tables and fire grills are provided. Drinking water, restrooms with flush toilets and coin showers, laundry tubs, Wi-Fi, and a dump station are available. A tethering and feeding station is near each site for horses, and a horse-washing station is provided. Some facilities are wheelchair-accessible. Propane, groceries, boat rentals, and a boat ramp are available nearby. Leashed pets are permitted, but not on trails or beaches.

Reservations, fees: Reservations are accepted at 800/444-PARK (800/444-7275) or www.reserveamerica.com ($8 reservation fee). Sites are $13–18 per night for single sites, $4 per night for each additional vehicle, $60 per night for group sites, $30 per night for equestrian sites. Open year-round.

Directions: From Oroville, drive east on Oroville Dam Boulevard/Highway 162 (becomes the Olive Highway) for approximately eight miles to the signed campground entrance on the left.

Contact: Lake Oroville State Recreation Area, 530/538-2200; Lake Oroville Visitor Center, 530/538-2219, www.parks.ca.gov.

18 SLY CREEK

Scenic rating: 7

on Sly Creek Reservoir in Plumas National Forest
Map grid B1

Sly Creek Camp is set on Sly Creek Reservoir's southwestern shore near Lewis Flat, with a boat ramp about a mile to the north. Both camps at this lake are well situated for campers and anglers. This camp provides direct access to the lake's main body, with good trout fishing well upstream on the main lake arm. You get quiet water and decent fishing. The elevation is 3,530 feet.

RV sites, facilities: There are 26 sites for tents or RVs up to 40 feet (no hookups). Five walk-in tent cabins are also available. Picnic tables and fire grills are provided. Drinking water and vault toilets are available. A car-top boat launch and fish-cleaning stations are available on Sly Creek Reservoir. Some facilities are wheelchair-accessible. Leashed pets are permitted.

Reservations, fees: Reservations are not accepted. Sites are $20 per night. Open late April through mid-October, weather permitting.

Directions: From Oroville, drive east on Highway 162/Oroville Dam Boulevard for about eight miles (becomes the Olive Highway) to Forbestown Road. Turn right and drive through Forbestown to Challenge and LaPorte Road. Turn left on LaPorte Road and drive 15 miles to Forest Road 16 (signed for Sly Creek Reservoir). Turn left on Forest Road 16 and drive 4.5 miles to the campground on the eastern end of the lake.

Contact: Plumas National Forest, Feather River Ranger District, 530/534-6500, fax 530/532-1210; Northwest Park Management, 530/283-5559.

19 STRAWBERRY

Scenic rating: 7

on Sly Creek Reservoir in Plumas National Forest
Map grid B1

Sly Creek Reservoir is a long, narrow lake set in western Plumas National Forest. There are two campgrounds on opposite ends of the lake, with different directions to each. This camp is set in the back of a cove on the lake's eastern arm at an elevation of 3,530 feet, with a boat ramp nearby. This is a popular lake for trout fishing in the summer. You must bring your own drinking water. The water source (such as at the fish-cleaning station) has a high mineral content and strong smell.

RV sites, facilities: There are 27 sites for tents or RVs up to 40 feet (no hookups). Picnic tables and fire grills are provided. There is no drinking water. Vault toilets are available. A car-top boat launch and fish-cleaning station are available on Sly Creek Reservoir. Leashed pets are permitted.

Reservations, fees: Reservations are not accepted. Sites are $20 per night. Open late April to mid-October, weather permitting.

Directions: From Oroville, drive east on Highway 162/Oroville Dam Boulevard for about eight miles (becomes the Olive Highway) to Forbestown Road. Turn right and drive through Forbestown to Challenge and LaPorte Road. Turn left on LaPorte Road and drive 15 miles to Forest Road 16 (signed for Sly Creek Reservoir). Turn left on Forest Road 16 and drive two miles to the campground on the eastern end of the lake.

Contact: Plumas National Forest, Feather River Ranger District, 530/534-6500, fax 530/532-1210; Northwest Park Management, 530/283-5559.

20 DINGERVILLE USA

Scenic rating: 3

near Oroville
Map grid B1

You're right, they thought of this name all by themselves, needed no help. It is an RV park set in the Oroville foothill country—hot and dry in the summer, but with a variety of side trips nearby. It is adjacent to a wildlife area and the Feather River and within short range of Lake Oroville and the Thermalito Afterbay for boating, water sports, and fishing. The RV park is a clean, quiet campground with easy access from the highway. Some of the sites are occupied by long-term renters.

RV sites, facilities: There are 29 pull-through sites with full hookups (30 amps) for RVs of any length. No tents. Picnic tables are provided. Restrooms with showers, modem access, cable TV, seasonal swimming pool, coin laundry, horseshoe pit, and a nine-hole executive golf course are available. Some facilities are wheelchair-accessible. Leashed pets are permitted.

Reservations, fees: Reservations are recommended. Sites are $28 per night. Some credit cards accepted. Open year-round.

Directions: From Oroville, drive south on Highway 70 to the second Pacific Heights Road turnoff. Turn right at Pacific Heights Road and drive less than one mile to the campground on the left.

From Marysville, drive north on Highway 70

to Palermo-Welsh Road. Turn left on Palermo-Welsh Road and drive to Pacific Heights Road. Turn left (north) on Pacific Heights Road and drive 0.5 mile to the campground entrance on the right.

Contact: Dingerville USA, tel./fax 530/533-9343.

21 SCHOOLHOUSE

Scenic rating: 7

on Bullards Bar Reservoir
Map grid B1

Bullards Bar Reservoir is one of the better lakes in the Sierra Nevada for camping, primarily because the lake level tends to be higher here than at many other lakes. The camp is set on the southeast shore, with a trail out of the camp to a beautiful lookout of the lake. Bullards Bar is known for good fishing for trout and kokanee salmon, waterskiing, and all water sports. A concrete boat ramp is to the south at Cottage Creek. Boaters should consider the special boat-in camps at the lake. The elevation is 2,200 feet.

RV sites, facilities: There are 56 sites (12 double and 44 single sites) for tents or RVs of any length (no hookups). Single sites accommodate six people, double sites accommodate 12, and triple sites hold up to 18 people. Picnic tables, food lockers, and fire rings are provided. Drinking water and flush and vault toilets are available. A boat ramp and boat rentals are nearby. Some facilities are wheelchair-accessible. Supplies are available in North San Juan, Camptonville, Dobbins, and at the marina. Leashed pets are permitted.

Reservations, fees: Reservations and a camping permit are required from Emerald Cove Marina at 530/692-3200 ($8 reservation fee). Sites are $22 per night, $44 per night for a double site. Open mid-April through mid-October.

Directions: From Marysville, drive east on Highway 20 for 12 miles to Marysville Road (signed "Bullards Bar Reservoir"). Turn left on Marysville Road and drive 12 miles to Old

Marysville Road. Turn right on Old Marysville Road and drive 14 miles to the dam, then continue three miles to the campground entrance road on the left.

Contact: Emerald Cove Marina, 530/692-3200; Tahoe National Forest, Yuba River Ranger District, North, 530/288-3231, fax 530/288-0727, www.bullardsbar.com.

22 HORNSWOGGLE GROUP CAMP

Scenic rating: 7

on Bullards Bar Reservoir in Tahoe National Forest

Map grid B1

This camp is designed for group use. A concrete boat ramp is one mile north at the Dark Day Picnic Area. (For information about family campgrounds and boat-in sites, see the listings in this chapter that are located on Bullards Bar Reservoir.)

RV sites, facilities: There are five 25-person group sites and one 50-person group site for tents or RVs up to 50 feet (no hookups). Picnic tables, food lockers, and fire grills are provided. Drinking water and flush and vault toilets are available. A boat ramp is nearby. Supplies and boat rentals are available at the marina. Leashed pets are permitted.

Reservations, fees: Reservations and a camping permit are required from Emerald Cove Marina at 530/692-3200 ($8 reservation fee). Sites are $80–140 per night. Open April to mid-October.

Directions: From Auburn, drive north on Highway 49 to Nevada City and continue for 17 miles through the town of North San Juan. Continue on Highway 49 for approximately eight miles to Marysville Road. Turn left on Marysville Road and drive approximately five miles to the campground on the left.

Contact: Emerald Cove Marina, 530/692-3200; Tahoe National Forest, Yuba River Ranger District, North, 530/288-3231, fax 530/288-0727, www.bullardsbar.com.

23 MOONSHINE CAMPGROUND

Scenic rating: 7

near the Yuba River and Bullards Bar Reservoir

Map grid B1   BEST (

This campground features shaded sites and a swimming hole on the nearby Middle Fork Yuba River. Both are needed, with the weather hot here in the summer, at 1,430 feet elevation in the Sierra foothills. Gold panning is available here. It's a seven-mile drive to a three-lane boat ramp at Dark Day Picnic Area at Bullards Bar Reservoir, the featured side trip. Malakoff Diggins State Historic Park is 15 miles away. A few of the sites are occupied by seasonal renters.

RV sites, facilities: There are 25 sites with partial hookups (30 amps), for tents or RVs up to 30 feet. Picnic tables and fire rings are provided. Drinking water, vault toilets, ice, and firewood are available. Some facilities are wheelchair-accessible. A grocery store, café, deli, and propane gas are about three miles away in North San Juan. Leashed pets are permitted.

Reservations, fees: Reservations are required. Sites are $25–30 per night. Open May to early October, weather permitting.

Directions: From Auburn, drive north on Highway 49 to Nevada City and the exit for Downieville/Highway 49. Turn left and drive for 17 miles through the town of North San Juan. Continue on Highway 49 and cross a bridge over the Middle Fork Yuba River to Moonshine Road (immediately after bridge crossing). Turn left on Moonshine Road and drive 0.75 mile to the campground on the left.

Contact: Moonshine Campground, 530/288-3585.

24 COLLINS LAKE RECREATION AREA

Scenic rating: 8

near Marysville on Collins Lake

Map grid B1

Collins Lake is set in the foothill country east of Marysville at 1,200 feet elevation, ideal for the camper, boater, and angler. I counted 45 campsites set near the lakefront. This lake is becoming known as an outstanding destination for trophy-sized trout, especially in late spring through early summer, though fishing is often good year-round for know-hows. Other fish species are bass, crappie, bluegill, and catfish. The lake has 12 miles of shoreline and is quite pretty. In summer, warm water makes the lake exceptional for waterskiing (permitted from May through mid-October). There is a marina adjacent to the campground, and farther south is a 60-foot-wide swimming beach and boat ramp. Bonuses for anglers: No personal watercraft are allowed on the lake. A weekly fishing report is available at the camp's website. Insider's tip: Lakefront sites fill quickly; book early.

RV sites, facilities: There are 150 sites with full or partial hookups (30 amps) for RVs or tents, 60 sites with no hookups, five group tent sites, one RV group site, and a large overflow camping area. Some sites are pull-through. Four rental trailers and five cabins are also available. Picnic tables and barbecues are provided. Restrooms with flush toilets and coin showers, drinking water, portable toilets, dump station, playground, marina, boat ramp, boat rentals, berths, sandy swimming beach, beach volleyball, three group picnic areas, convenience store, coin laundry, firewood, ice, and propane gas are available. RV storage is also available. Some facilities are wheelchair-accessible. Leashed pets are permitted.

Reservations, fees: Reservations are accepted up to one year in advance (2-night minimum, $50 nonrefundable reservation deposit required). Sites are $20–45 per night, $10 per night for each additional vehicle, $2 per pet per night. Group tent sites are $9 per person per night with a $75–150 per night minimum, and group RV sites are $10 per person per night with a $200 minimum per night. Boat launching is $8 per day. Weekly and monthly rates available. Some credit cards accepted. Open year-round.

Directions: From Marysville, drive east on Highway 20 for about 12 miles to Marysville Road/Road E-21. Turn left (north) and drive

approximately 10 miles to the recreation area entrance road on the right. Turn right, drive 0.3 mile to the entrance station and store, and then continue to the campground. (For detailed directions from other areas, visit the website.)

Contact: Collins Lake Recreation Area, 530/692-1600 or 800/286-0576, www.collinslake.com.

25 NEVADA COUNTY FAIRGROUNDS

Scenic rating: 6

near Grass Valley

Map grid B1

The motto here is "California's Most Beautiful Fairgrounds," and that's right. The area is set at 2,300 feet in the Sierra foothills, with a good number of pines sprinkled about. The park is adjacent to the fairgrounds, and even though the fair runs for a week every August, the park is open year-round. However, check status before planning a trip because the campground is sometimes closed for scheduled activities. A caretaker at the park is available to answer any questions. Kids can fish at a small lake nearby. The Draft Horse Classic is held here every September and a country Christmas Faire is held Thanksgiving weekend.

RV sites, facilities: There are 130 sites with full or partial hookups (50 amps) for RVs of any length, and an open dirt and grassy area with no hookups available as an overflow area. No tents. Two dump stations, drinking water, restrooms with showers and flush toilets, and group facilities are available. Some facilities are wheelchair-accessible. Leashed pets are permitted.

Reservations, fees: Reservations are recommended. Sites are $20–28 per night. A seven-day limit is enforced. Some credit cards accepted. Open year-round.

Directions: From Auburn, drive north on Highway 49 to Grass Valley and the McKnight Way exit. Take that exit and turn left on McKnight Way and drive over the freeway to Freeman Lane (just past the shopping center on the

CALIFORNIA

left). Turn right on Freeman Lane and drive to the second stop sign and McCourtney Road. Continue straight on McCourtney Road and drive two blocks to the fairgrounds on the right. Continue to Gate 4.

Contact: Nevada County Fairgrounds, 530/273-6217, fax 530/273-1146, www.nevadacountyfair.com.

26 CAMPERS INN RV PARK AND GOLF COURSE

Scenic rating: 3

near Dunnigan

Map grid B2

This private park has a rural valley atmosphere and provides a layover for drivers cruising I-5. The park has a par-three golf course (nine holes), and it specializes in golf tournaments and group outings. The Sacramento River to the east is the closest body of water, but this section of river is hardly a premium side-trip destination. There are no nearby lakes.

RV sites, facilities: There are three tent sites and 72 sites with full or partial hookups (30 and 50 amps) for RVs of any length. Many sites are pull-through. Picnic tables are provided. Restrooms with flush toilets and showers, modem access, seasonal swimming pool, two clubhouses/meeting rooms, horseshoes, nine-hole golf course, coin laundry, propane gas, ice, and general store are available. Some facilities are wheelchair-accessible. Leashed pets are permitted.

Reservations, fees: Reservations are accepted. Sites are $19.80–22 per night. Some credit cards accepted. Open year-round.

Directions: From I-5 in Dunnigan, take the Dunnigan exit (Exit 556, just north of the I-505 cutoff). Drive west on County Road E4/Road 6 for a mile to County Road 88. Turn right and drive for 1.5 miles to the park.

Contact: Campers Inn RV Park and Golf Course, 530/724-3350 or 800/79-GOLF3 (800/794-6533), www.campersinnrv.com.

27 AUBURN STATE RECREATION AREA: MINERAL BAR

Scenic rating: 8

near Colfax

Map grid B2

This state park is a jewel in the valley foothill country, covering more than 42,000 acres along the North and Middle Forks of the American River. Formerly the domain of gold miners, the area is now home to wildlife as well as a wide variety of recreational opportunities. The Auburn SRA is composed of land set aside for the Auburn Dam, consisting of 40 miles along two forks of the American River.

Mineral Bar Camp is situated near the American River, which runs through the park, offering visitors opportunities to fish, boat, kayak, and raft. In addition, there are more than 100 miles of hiking, biking, and horseback-riding trails. Nearby Clementine Lake offers fishing (not stocked) and waterskiing, with a boat limit of 25 boats per day; the quota is reached every day on summer weekends. White-water rafting is extremely popular, with more than 30 private outfitters licensed for trips in sections of river through the park.

RV sites, facilities: There are 17 sites for tents or RVs up to 24 feet (no hookups). Picnic tables and fire grills are provided. Chemical toilets are available. No drinking water is available. Leashed pets are permitted.

Reservations, fees: Reservations are not accepted. Sites are $15 per night, $10 per night for each additional vehicle. Open year-round, with limited winter facilities.

Directions: From I-80 in Auburn, drive east for 15 miles to Colfax and the Canyon Way/Placer Hills Drive exit. Take that exit and turn left on Canyon Way and drive one mile to Iowa Hill Road. Turn right and drive three miles on a narrow paved road to the campground.

Contact: Auburn State Recreation Area, 530/885-4527, fax 530/885-2798, www.parks.ca.gov.

28 SACRAMENTO WEST/ OLD TOWN KOA

Scenic rating: 2

in West Sacramento

Map grid B2

This is the choice of car and RV campers touring California's capital and looking for a layover spot. It is in West Sacramento not far from the Capitol building, the railroad museum, Sutter's Fort, Old Sacramento, Crocker Museum, and shopping.

RV sites, facilities: There are 95 pull-through sites with full or partial hookups (30 and 50 amps) for RVs up to 45 feet, and 27 tent sites. Twelve cabins are also available. Restrooms with flush toilets and showers, Wi-Fi, cable TV, playground, fishing pond, seasonal swimming pool, coin laundry, propane gas, and convenience and gift store are available. Some facilities are wheelchair-accessible. Leashed pets are permitted, with certain restrictions.

Reservations, fees: Reservations are accepted at 800/562-2747. Sites are $30–80 per night. Some credit cards accepted. Open year-round.

Directions: From Sacramento, drive west on I-80 about four miles to the West Capitol Avenue exit. Exit and turn left onto West Capitol Avenue, going under the freeway to the second stoplight and the intersection with Lake Road. Turn left onto Lake Road and continue a half block to the camp on the right at 3951 Lake Road.

Contact: Sacramento West/Old Town KOA, 916/371-6771, www.sacramentokoa.com.

29 BEAL'S POINT

Scenic rating: 6

in Folsom Lake State Recreation Area

Map grid B2

Folsom Lake State Recreation Area is Sacramento's backyard vacation spot, a huge lake covering about 18,000 acres with 75 miles of shoreline, which means plenty of room for boating, waterskiing, fishing, and suntanning.

This camp is set on the lake's southwest side, just north of the dam, with a boat ramp nearby at Granite Bay. The lake has a productive trout fishery in the spring, a fast-growing population of kokanee salmon, and good prospects for bass in late spring and early summer. By summer wakeboarders and water-skiers usually take over the lake each day by about 10 A.M. One problem with this lake is that a minor water drawdown can cause major amounts of shoreline to become exposed on its upper arms. There are opportunities for hiking, biking, running, picnics, and horseback riding. A paved 32-mile-long trail, the American River Parkway, connects Folsom Lake with many Sacramento County parks before reaching Old Sacramento. This trail is outstanding for family biking and inline skating. Summers are hot and dry.

RV sites, facilities: There are 69 sites for tents or RVs up to 31 feet; some sites have full hookups (30 and 50 amps). Picnic tables and fire grills are provided. Drinking water, restrooms with flush toilets and showers, Wi-Fi, and a dump station are available. A bike path and horseback-riding facilities are nearby. Some facilities are wheelchair-accessible. There are boat rentals, moorings, summer snack bar, ice, and bait and tackle available at the Folsom Lake Marina. Leashed pets are permitted.

Reservations, fees: Reservations are accepted April through September at 800/444-PARK (800/444-7275) or www.reserveamerica.com ($8 reservation fee). Tent sites are $25 per night, RV sites are $45 per night, $10 per night for each additional vehicle. Open year-round; the park is open daily 7 A.M.–6 P.M.

Directions: From Sacramento, drive east on U.S. 50 to the Folsom Boulevard exit. Take that exit to the stop sign and Folsom Boulevard. Turn left and continue north on Folsom Boulevard for 3.5 miles (road name changes to Folsom-Auburn Road) to the park entrance on the right.

Contact: Folsom Lake State Recreation Area, 916/988-0205, fax 916/988-9062; Beal's Point Campground, 916/791-1531, www.parks.ca.gov.

CALIFORNIA

30 PENINSULA

Scenic rating: 6

in Folsom Lake State Recreation Area

Map grid B2

This is one of the big camps at Folsom Lake, but it is also more remote than the other camps, requiring a circuitous drive. It is set on the peninsula on the northeast shore, right where the North Fork American River arm of the lake enters the main lake area. A nearby boat ramp, marina, and boat rentals make this a great weekend spot. Fishing for bass and trout is often quite good in spring and early summer, and other species include catfish and perch. Water-skiing and wakeboarding are popular in the hot summer, and all water sports are allowed.

RV sites, facilities: There are 100 sites for tents or RVs up to 32 feet (no hookups). Picnic tables and fire grills are provided. Drinking water and restrooms with flush toilets are available. A bike path is nearby. Boat rentals, moorings, snack bar, ice, and bait and tackle are available at the Folsom Lake Marina. Leashed pets are permitted.

Reservations, fees: Reservations are accepted at 800/444-PARK (800/444-7275) or www.reserveamerica.com ($8 reservation fee). Sites are $30 per night, $10 per night for each additional vehicle. Open year-round; the park is open daily 7 A.M.–6 P.M.

Directions: From Placerville, drive east on U.S. 50 to the Spring Street/Highway 49 exit. Turn north on Highway 49 (toward the town of Coloma) and continue 8.3 miles into the town of Pilot Hill and Rattlesnake Bar Road. Turn left on Rattlesnake Bar Road and drive nine miles to the end of the road and the park entrance.

Contact: Folsom Lake State Recreation Area, 916/988-0205, fax 916/988-9062, www.parks.ca.gov.

31 VINEYARD RV PARK

Scenic rating: 2

in Vacaville

Map grid B2

This is one of two privately operated parks in the area set up primarily for RVs. It is in a eucalyptus grove, with clean, well-kept sites. If you are heading to the Bay Area, it is late in the day, and you don't have your destination set, this spot offers a chance to hole up for the night and formulate your travel plans. Note that about half of the sites are long-term rentals.

RV sites, facilities: There are 110 sites with full hookups (30 and 50 amps) for RVs of any length. No tents. Some sites are pull-through. Picnic tables are provided. Restrooms with flush toilets and showers, Wi-Fi, seasonal swimming pool, coin laundry, enclosed dog walk, and ice are available. Some facilities are wheelchair-accessible. Leashed pets are permitted, with certain restrictions.

Reservations, fees: Reservations are recommended at 866/447-8797. Sites are $44–48 per night, $1 per pet per night. Some credit cards accepted. Open year-round.

From Vacaville on I-80, turn north on I-505 and drive three miles to Midway Road. Turn right (east) on Midway Road and drive 0.5 mile to the second campground on the left at 4985 Midway Road.

Contact: Vineyard RV Park, 707/447-8797, www.vineyardrvpark.com.

32 RANCHO SECO RECREATION AREA

Scenic rating: 6

near Sacramento

Map grid B2

There is a shortage of campgrounds close to Sacramento, so this one about 35 miles from the state capital comes in handy. This public facility has a 160-acre lake that is surrounded by 400 acres of open space and includes trails for walking and bicycling. In 2006, a seven-mile loop nature trail opened next to the lake. The centerpiece of this recreation area is the lake, which is especially popular for fishing and sailboarding. The lake is stocked with rainbow trout, and fishing derbies are held during the winter. Other fish species include bass, bluegill, redear sunfish, crappie, and catfish. Live bait is prohibited and only electric motors are allowed. A bonus is that the lake level remains constant year-round, and since the lake is fed by the Folsom South Canal, the water is warm in summer. Swimming is popular and there is a large sandy beach with summer lifeguard service. Pedal boats and kayaks can also be rented on weekends in summer. Tent sites are situated along the lake. The Amanda Blake Memorial Wildlife Refuge is here, and visitors can observe exotic captive wildlife that has been rescued from circuses and other performing groups. Migratory birds, including bald eagles, winter at the lake. What are those two large towers? They're remnants of the now-closed Rancho Seco nuclear power–generating station.

RV sites, facilities: There are 20 tent sites, 18 sites with partial hookups (30 amps) for RVs of any length, and two group tent sites that can accommodate up to 200 people each. A couple of sites are pull-through. Picnic tables and fire grills are provided. Drinking water, restrooms with coin showers, dump station, swimming beach, six fishing piers, picnic areas, coin laundry, fish-cleaning station, horseshoe pit, recreation room, seasonal general store, weekend boat rentals, and boat launch are available. Supplies are available in Galt. Some facilities are wheelchair-accessible, including some fishing piers. Leashed pets are permitted.

Reservations, fees: Reservations are accepted at 916/732-4913. Sites are $10–15 per night, and the group tent site is $45 per night for the first 20 people, plus $1.50 per person per night for additional campers. There is a 14-day maximum stay. Open year-round.

Directions: From Sacramento, drive south on Highway 99 for approximately 25 miles to the Twin Cities Road/Highway 104 exit. Take that exit and drive east for 13 miles, past the two

towers, to the Rancho Seco Park exit. Turn right and continue to the lake and campground.

Contact: Rancho Seco Recreation Area, 209/748-2318, www.smud.org/about/recreation-rancho.html.

33 SANDY BEACH REGIONAL PARK

Scenic rating: 6

on the Sacramento River

Map grid B2

This is a surprisingly little-known park, especially considering it provides beach access to the Sacramento River. It is a popular spot for sunbathers in hot summer months, and the park has a sandy beach stretching for more than a half mile. Swimming is not allowed because there is no lifeguard; however, wading is permitted. Sailboarding and sailing are possible here. In winter, it is one of the few viable spots where you can fish from the shore for sturgeon; check fishing regulations. It also provides outstanding boating access to the Sacramento River, including one of the best fishing spots for striped bass in the fall, the Rio Vista Bridge.

RV sites, facilities: There are 42 sites with partial hookups (30 amps) for tents or RVs of any length. Picnic tables and fire pits are provided. Drinking water, restrooms with flush toilets and showers, a dump station, picnic areas, volleyball, horseshoes, firewood, and a boat ramp are available. A camp host is on-site. Some facilities are wheelchair-accessible. Supplies can be obtained nearby (within a mile). Leashed pets are permitted in the campground only.

Reservations, fees: Reservations are accepted. Sites are $21 per night, $7 per night for each additional vehicle, $1 per pet per night. Some credit cards accepted. Open year-round.

Directions: From I-80 in Fairfield, take the Highway 12 exit and drive southeast for 14 miles to Rio Vista and the intersection with Main Street. Turn right on Main Street and drive a short distance to 2nd Street. Turn right and drive 0.5 mile to Beach Drive. Turn left (west) and drive 0.5 mile to the park.

Contact: Sandy Beach Regional Park, 707/374-2097, fax 707/374-4972, www.solanocounty.com.

34 DELTA MARINA YACHT HARBOR AND RV

Scenic rating: 6

on the Sacramento River Delta

Map grid B2

This is a prime spot for boat campers. Summers are hot and breezy, and waterskiing is popular on the nearby Sacramento River. From November to March, the striped-bass fishing is quite good, often as close as just a half mile upriver at the Rio Vista Bridge. The boat launch at the harbor is a bonus, especially with night lighting. Some campsites have river frontage, and some sites are filled with long-term renters.

RV sites, facilities: There are 25 sites with full hookups (30 and 50 amps) for RVs up to 40 feet. No tents. Picnic tables and fire grills are provided. Restrooms with showers, cable TV, coin laundry, playground, boat ramp, fishing pier, marine repair service, pet restroom, restaurant, marine supplies and gift store, ice, and propane gas are available. Fuel is available 24 hours. Free boat launching for RV guests. Some facilities are wheelchair-accessible. Leashed pets are permitted.

Reservations, fees: Reservations are accepted. Sites are $25–35 per night. Two-week maximum stay in summer. Some credit cards accepted. Open year-round.

Directions: From Fairfield on I-80, take the Highway 12 exit and drive southeast for 14 miles to Rio Vista and the intersection with Main Street. Take the Main Street exit and drive a short distance to 2nd Street. Turn right on 2nd Street and drive to Marina Drive. Turn left on Marina Drive, and continue another short distance to the harbor.

Contact: Delta Marina Yacht Harbor and RV, 707/374-2315, fax 707/374-6471, www.delta-marina.com.

35 BRANNAN ISLAND STATE RECREATION AREA

Scenic rating: 7

on the Sacramento River

Map grid B2

This state park is perfectly designed for boaters, set in the heart of the Delta's vast waterways. You get year-round adventure: waterskiing, wakeboarding, and fishing for catfish are popular in the summer, and in the winter the immediate area is often good for striped-bass fishing. The proximity of the campgrounds to the boat launch deserves a medal. What many people do is tow a boat here, launch it, keep it docked, and then return to their site and set up; this allows them to come and go as they please, boating, fishing, and exploring in the Delta. There is a six-lane boat ramp that provides access to a maze of waterways amid many islands, marshes, sloughs, and rivers. Day-use areas include the Windy Cove sailboarding area. Though striped bass in winter and catfish in summer are the most favored fish here, sturgeon, bluegill, perch, bullhead, and bass are also caught. Some sections of the San Joaquin Delta are among the best bass fishing spots in California. A hiking/biking trail circles the park.

RV sites, facilities: There are 102 sites for tents or RVs up to 36 feet, eight walk-in sites, and six group sites for up to 30 people each. No hookups. Picnic tables and fire grills are provided. Drinking water, restrooms with coin showers (at campground and boat launch), boat berths, dump station, Wi-Fi, and a boat launch are available. Some facilities are wheelchair-accessible. Supplies can be obtained three miles away in Rio Vista. Leashed pets are permitted.

Reservations, fees: Reservations are accepted at 800/444-PARK (800/444-7275) or www.reserveamerica.com ($8 reservation fee). Sites are $25–40 per night, $8 per night for each additional vehicle, $100 per night for group sites. Boat launching is $5 per day. Open year-round.

Directions: In Fairfield on I-80, take the Highway 12 exit, drive southeast 14 miles to Rio

Vista, and continue to Highway 160. Turn right on Highway 160 and drive three miles to the park entrance on the left.

Contact: Brannan Island State Recreation Area, 916/777-6671; Entrance Kiosk, 916/777-7701; Goldfield District Office, 916/988-0205, www. parks.ca.gov.

36 SNUG HARBOR RESORT

Scenic rating: 7

near Rio Vista

Map grid B2

This year-round resort is an ideal resting place for families who enjoy waterskiing, wakeboarding, boating, biking, swimming, and fishing. After the ferry ride, it is only a few minutes to Snug Harbor, a gated marina resort on eight acres with a campground, RV hookups, and a separate area with cabins and cottages. Some say that the waterfront sites with docks give the place the feel of a Louisiana bayou, yet everything is clean and orderly, including a full-service marina, a store, and all facilities—and an excellent location to explore the boating paradise of the Delta. Anglers will find good prospects for striped bass, black bass, blue gill, steelhead, sturgeon, and catfish. The waterfront sites with docks are a bonus.

RV sites, facilities: There are 38 waterfront sites with docks and full hookups (30 and 50 amps) for RVs of any length, including four pull-through water-view sites with full hookups for RVs. There is one group site for RVs and 15 park-model cabins. Barbecues or burn barrels are provided. Restrooms with key-accessible showers, dump station, Wi-Fi, small convenience store, swimming beach, children's play area, volleyball, croquet, bocce ball, badminton, horseshoes, boat launch, and a full-service marina are available. Some facilities are wheelchair-accessible. Dogs are permitted on leash it some sites.

Reservations, fees: Reservations are recommended. Sites are $38–45 per night, $10 per night for each additional vehicle, $90 per night

for group site, $2 per pet per night. Boat launching is available for a one-time fee of $10. Some credit cards accepted. Open year-round.

Directions: From Fairfield, take Highway 12 east to Rio Vista and Front Street. Turn left on Front Street (before crossing the bridge) and drive under the bridge to River Road. Turn right on River Road and drive two miles to the Rio Vista/Real McCoy Ferry (signed Ryer Island). Take the ferry (free) across the Sacramento River to Ryer Island and Levee Road. Turn right on Levee Road and drive 4.5 miles to the Snug Harbor entrance on the right.

Contact: Snug Harbor Resort, 916/775-1455, fax 916/411-0124, www.snugharbor.net.

37 WESTGATE LANDING COUNTY PARK

Scenic rating: 6

on the San Joaquin River Delta near Stockton

Map grid B2

Summer temperatures typically reach the high 90s and low 100s here, and this county park provides a little shade and boating access to the South Fork Mokelumne River. On hot summer nights, some campers will stay up late and night fish for catfish. Between storms in winter, the area typically gets smothered in dense fog. The sites are not pull-through but semicircles, which work nearly as well for RV drivers.

RV sites, facilities: There are 14 sites for tents or RVs up to 32 feet (no hookups). Picnic tables and barbecues are provided. Drinking water and flush toilets are available. Groceries and propane gas are nearby. A fishing pier, 24 boat slips, and boat docking are available. Some facilities are wheelchair-accessible. Leashed pets are permitted, with a limit of two.

Reservations, fees: Reservations are accepted at least two weeks in advance ($10 reservation fee). Less than two weeks, sites are first come, first served. Sites are $15 per night, $5 per night for each additional vehicle, boat slips $15 per day, $1 per pet per night. Open year-round.

Directions: On I-5, drive to Lodi and Highway

12. Take Highway 12 west and drive about five miles to Glasscock Road. Turn right and drive about a mile to the park.

Contact: San Joaquin County Parks Department, 209/953-8800 or 209/331-7400, www.co.sanjoaquin.ca.us/parks.

38 STOCKTON DELTA KOA

Scenic rating: 6

near Stockton
Map grid B2

Some people may remember this campground by its previous name: Tower Park Resort. This huge resort is ideal for boat-in campers who desire a full-facility marina. The camp is set on Little Potato Slough near the Mokelumne River. In the summer, this is a popular waterskiing area. Some hot weekends are like a continuous party. Note that tents are now allowed here.

RV sites, facilities: There are 300 sites with full hookups (30 amps) for RVs up to 45 feet, 12 tent sites, and 13 park-model cabins. Picnic tables are provided. Restrooms with showers, dump station, pavilion, banquet room, boat rentals, overnight boat slips, boat storage, double boat launch, playground, swimming pool, spa, gas station, restaurant, coin laundry, gift shop, store, ice, and propane gas are available. Leashed pets are permitted, with certain restrictions.

Reservations, fees: Reservations are available, with a three-night minimum on summer holidays. Sites are $30–54 per night, maximum six people per site. Some credit cards accepted. Open year-round.

Directions: On I-5, drive to Lodi and Highway 12. Take Highway 12 west and drive about five miles to Tower Park Way (before first bridge). Turn left and drive a short distance to the park.

Contact: Stockton Delta KOA, 209/369-1041, fax 209/369-1301, www.koa.com or www.stocktondeltakoa.com.

39 EDDOS HARBOR AND RV PARK

Scenic rating: 6

on the San Joaquin River Delta
Map grid B2

This is an ideal spot for campers with boats. Eddos is set on the San Joaquin River and Gallagher Slough, upstream of the Antioch Bridge, in an outstanding region for fishing, powerboating, wakeboarding, and waterskiing. In summer, boaters have access to 1,000 miles of Delta waterways, with the best of them in a nearby spider web of rivers and sloughs off the San Joaquin to False River, Frank's Tract, and Old River. Hot weather and sheltered sloughs make this ideal for waterskiing. In the winter, a nearby fishing spot, as well as the mouth of the False River, attract striped bass. Many of the sites here are occupied by seasonal renters; plan well ahead for the summer.

RV sites, facilities: There are 44 sites with full hookups (30 and 50 amps) for RVs up to 40 feet. Picnic tables are provided. Restrooms with flush toilets and showers, launch ramp, boat storage, fuel dock, Wi-Fi, coin laundry, and a small grocery store are available. Some facilities are wheelchair-accessible. Leashed pets are permitted.

Reservations, fees: Reservations are recommended. Sites are $30–32 per night. Monthly rates available. Some credit cards accepted. Open year-round.

Directions: In Fairfield on I-80, take the Highway 12 exit and drive 14 miles southeast to Rio Vista and continue three miles to Highway 160 (at the signal just after the bridge). Turn right on Highway 160 and drive three miles to Sherman Island/East Levee Road, at the end of the drawbridge. Turn left on East Levee Road and drive 5.5 miles to the campground along the San Joaquin River. Note: If arriving by boat, look for the camp adjacent to Light 21.

Contact: Eddos Harbor and RV Park, 925/757-5314, www.eddosharbor.com.

40 LUNDBORG LANDING

Scenic rating: 6

on the San Joaquin River Delta

Map grid B2   **BEST (**

This park is set on Bethel Island in the heart of the California Delta. The boat ramp here provides immediate access to an excellent area for waterskiing, and it turns into a playland on hot summer days. In the fall and winter, the area often provides good striper fishing at nearby Frank's Tract, False River, and the San Joaquin River. The fishing for largemouth bass at Frank's Tract is rated among the best in North America. Catfishing in surrounding slough areas is also good year-round. The Delta Sportsman Shop at Bethel Island has reliable fishing information. Live webcams of Frank's Tract are available on the website. Note that some sites are occupied by long-term tenants.

RV sites, facilities: There are 70 sites with full hookups (30 and 50 amps) for RVs; some sites are pull-through and some sites allow tents. A large overflow area can handle up to 300 RVs and many tents. Several cabins are also available. Restrooms with showers, coin laundry, dump station, propane gas, modem access, playground, boat ramp, fishing pier, berthing, boat storage, fish-cleaning station, and full restaurant and bar are available. Some facilities are wheelchair-accessible. Leashed pets are permitted with some restrictions.

Reservations, fees: Reservations are accepted. Sites are $20–30 per night. Long-term rates available. Open year-round.

Directions: From Antioch, turn east on Highway 4 and drive to Oakley and East Cypress Road. Turn left on East Cypress Road, drive over the Bethel Island Bridge, and continue 0.5 mile to Gateway Road. Turn right on Gateway Road and drive two miles to the park entrance on the left (signed well, next to the tugboat).

Contact: Lundborg Landing, 925/684-9351, www.lundborglanding.com.

41 STOCKTON/LODI RV PARK

Scenic rating: 3

in Lodi

Map grid B2

This former KOA camp is in the heart of the San Joaquin Valley. The proximity to I-5 and Highway 99 makes it work for long-distance vacationers looking for a spot to park the rig for the night. The San Joaquin Delta is 15 miles to the west, with best access provided off Highway 12 to Isleton and Rio Vista; it's also a pretty drive.

RV sites, facilities: There are 102 sites—most pull-through and many with full hookups (30 and 50 amps)—for RVs of any length, 13 tent sites, and two cabins. Picnic tables are provided. Restrooms with showers, dump station, convenience store, propane gas, coin laundry, Wi-Fi, modem access, recreation room, seasonal swimming pool, bicycle rentals, and a playground are available. Some facilities are wheelchair-accessible. Leashed pets are permitted at campsites, with certain restrictions, but not in cabins.

Reservations, fees: Reservations are accepted at 800/562-1229. Sites are $26–34 per night, $2–4 per night for more than two people. Some credit cards accepted. Open year-round.

Directions: On I-5, drive to Eight Mile Road (Exit 481, five miles north of Stockton). Turn east and drive five miles to the campground at 2851 East Eight Mile Road.

Contact: Stockton/Lodi RV Park, tel./fax 209/941-2573 or 209/334-0309 (from Lodi), www.stknlodirv.com.

42 DRU BARNER EQUESTRIAN CAMP

Scenic rating: 7

near Georgetown in Eldorado National Forest

Map grid C2

This camp, set at 3,200 feet elevation in an area of pine and fir, is ideal for horses; there are miles of equestrian trails. Please note that wheat straw is not allowed at this campground.

CALIFORNIA

RV sites, facilities: There are 48 sites for tents or RVs up to 35 feet (no hookups). Picnic tables and fire rings are provided. Drinking water and flush and vault toilets are available. Five stock troughs and four hitching posts are also available. Some facilities are wheelchair-accessible. Leashed pets are permitted.

Reservations, fees: Reservations are not accepted. Sites are $8 per night, $5 per night for each additional vehicle. Open year-round.

Directions: From Sacramento on I-80, drive east to the north end of Auburn and the exit for Elm Avenue. Take that exit and turn left on Elm Avenue and drive about 0.1 mile to High Street. Turn left on High Street and drive through the signal that marks the continuation of High Street as Highway 49 and drive 3.5 miles on Highway 49 to the bridge. Turn right over the bridge and drive 2.5 miles into the town of Cool and Georgetown Road/Highway 193. Turn left and drive 14 miles into Georgetown to a four-way stop at Main Street. Turn left on Main Street and drive 5.5 miles (the road becomes Georgetown–Wentworth Springs Road/Forest Road 1) to Bottle Hill Bypass Road. Turn left on Bottle Hill Bypass Road and drive about a mile to the campground on the left.

Contact: Eldorado National Forest, Georgetown Ranger District, 530/333-4312, fax 530/333-5522.

43 CAMP LOTUS

Scenic rating: 7

on the American River near Coloma

Map grid C2

This is a great area with 0.5 mile of frontage on the South Fork of the American River. During spring and summer you'll see plenty of white-water rafters and kayakers here because this is a popular place for outfitters to put in and take out. Several swimming holes are in the immediate vicinity. The camp is situated on 23 acres at 700 feet elevation. There are a variety of trees at Camp Lotus, including pines, oaks, willows, and cottonwoods. Coloma, two miles away, is where

you'll find the Marshall Gold Discovery Site. Gold was discovered there in 1848, and the site features displays and exhibits on gold rush–era mining methods and the history of the California gold rush. Wineries are nearby, and gold panning, hiking, and fishing are also popular.

RV sites, facilities: There are 26 tent sites and 10 sites with partial hookups (20 and 30 amps) for tents or RVs of any length. A cabin and three lodge rooms are also available for rent. Picnic tables and fire grills are provided. Drinking water, restrooms with showers, Wi-Fi, dump station, general store with deli, volleyball, horseshoes, and raft and kayak put-in and take-out areas are available. Groups can be accommodated. Limited supplies are available in Coloma. Some facilities are wheelchair-accessible. Dogs are not permitted.

Reservations, fees: Reservations are accepted and required for weekends. Sites are $7–10 per person per night with a minimum campsite fee of $21–30 per night. Credit cards accepted. Open February through October.

Directions: From Sacramento, drive east on Highway 50 for approximately 30 miles (past Cameron Park) to Exit 37, the Ponderosa Road exit. Take that exit and drive north over the freeway to North Shingle Road. Turn right and drive 10 miles (the road becomes Lotus Road) to Bassi Road. Turn left and drive one mile to the campground entrance on the right.

Contact: Camp Lotus, 530/622-8672, www.camplotus.com.

44 PLACERVILLE KOA

Scenic rating: 5

near Placerville

Map grid C2

This is a classic KOA campground, complete with the cute little log cabins KOA calls "Kamping Kabins." The location of this camp is ideal for many, set near U.S. 50 in the Sierra foothills, the main route up to South Lake Tahoe. Nearby is Apple Hill, where from September to November it is a popular tourist attraction, when the local ranches and orchards sell produce and crafts, often with live music. In addition, the Marshall Gold Discovery Site is 10 miles north, where gold was discovered in 1848, setting off the 1849 gold rush. White-water rafting and gold panning are popular on the nearby American River.

RV sites, facilities: There are 70 sites with full or partial hookups (30 and 50 amps) for RVs of any length, 14 tent sites, including eight with electricity, 20 sites for tents or RVs, and eight cabins. Some sites are pull-through. Picnic tables and barbecues are provided. Restrooms with flush toilets and showers, drinking water, dump station, cable TV, modem access, Wi-Fi, recreation room, seasonal swimming pool, spa (some restrictions apply), playground, video arcade, basketball courts, 18-hole miniature golf course, convenience store, snack bar, dog run, petting zoo, fishing pond, bike rentals, pavilion cooking facilities, volleyball court, and horseshoe pits are available. Some facilities are wheelchair-accessible. Leashed pets are permitted, with certain restrictions.

Reservations, fees: Reservations are accepted at 800/562-4197. RV sites are $35–51, tent sites are $30–32, $4 per person per night for more than two people. Some credit cards accepted. Open year-round.

Directions: From U.S. 50 west of Placerville, take the exit for Shingle Springs Drive/Exit 39 (and not the Shingle Springs/Ponderosa Road exit). Drive one block to Rock Barn Road. Turn left and drive 0.5 mile to the campground at the end of the road.

Contact: Placerville KOA, 530/676-2267, www.koa.com or www.koaplacerville.com.

45 SLY PARK RECREATION AREA

Scenic rating: 7

on Jenkinson Lake

Map grid C2

Jenkinson Lake is set at 3,500 feet elevation in the lower reaches of Eldorado National Forest, with a climate that is perfect for waterskiing, wakeboarding, and fishing. The lake covers 640 acres and features eight miles of forested shoreline. Participants of these sports get along, with most water-skiers/wakeboarders motoring around the lake's main body, while anglers head upstream into the Hazel Creek arm of the lake for trout (in the spring) and bass (in the summer). Good news for anglers: Personal water-craft are not permitted. More good news: This is one of the better lakes in the Sierra for brown trout. There is a boat ramp at the campground, and another one located on the southwest end of the lake. The area also has several hiking trails, and the lake is good for swimming. There are nine miles of trails available for hiking, biking, and equestrians; an equestrian trail also circles the lake. A group camp is available for visitors with horses, complete with riding trails, hitching posts, and corrals. Note: No pets or babies with diapers are allowed in the lake.

RV sites, facilities: There are 164 sites for tents or RVs up to 40 feet (no hookups). There are five group sites that can accommodate 50–100 people and an equestrian camp called Black Oak, which has 12 sites and two youth-group areas. Picnic tables, fire rings, and barbecues are provided. Drinking water, vault toilets, boat rentals, and firewood are available. Two boat ramps are available nearby. Some facilities are wheelchair-accessible. A grocery store, snack bar, dump station, bait, and propane gas are available nearby. Leashed pets are permitted.

Reservations, fees: Reservations are accepted at least seven days in advance at 866/759-7275 or 530/644-2792 ($8 reservation fee). Sites are $27–35 per night, $220 per night for a group site, $110 per night for a youth group site, $13 per night for each additional vehicle. Boat launching is $3–8 per day. Reduced rates available in winter. Some credit cards accepted during the summer season. Open year-round.

Directions: From Sacramento, drive east on U.S. 50 to Pollock Pines and take the exit for Sly Park Road. Drive south for 4.5 miles to Jenkinson Lake and the campground entrance.

Contact: Sly Park Recreation Area, El Dorado Irrigation District, 530/644-2545, fax 530/644-1003, www.eid.org.

CALIFORNIA

46 PIPI

Scenic rating: 7

on the Middle Fork of the Cosumnes River in Eldorado National Forest

Map grid C2

This place is far enough out of the way to get missed by most campers. It is beside the Middle Fork of the Cosumnes River at 4,100 feet elevation. There are some good swimming holes in the area, but the water is cold and swift in early summer (after all, it's snowmelt). A trail/boardwalk along the river is wheelchair-accessible. Several sites border a pretty meadow in the back of the camp. This is also a gateway to a vast network of Forest Service roads to the north in Eldorado National Forest.

RV sites, facilities: There are 51 sites for tents or RVs up to 42 feet (no hookups), including two double sites. Picnic tables and fire grills are provided. Drinking water and vault toilets are available. Some facilities are wheelchair-accessible. Leashed pets are permitted.

Reservations, fees: Reservations are accepted at 877/444-6777 or www.recreation.gov ($10 reservation fee). Sites are $20 per night, $40 per night for double sites, $5 per night for each additional vehicle. Open May through mid-November, weather permitting.

Directions: From Jackson, drive east on Highway 88 to Pioneer and continue for nine miles to Omo Ranch Road. Turn left and drive 0.8 mile to North-South Road/Forest Road 6. Turn right and drive 5.9 miles to the campground on the right side of the road.

Contact: Eldorado National Forest, Amador Ranger District, 209/295-4251, fax 209/295-5998.

47 FAR HORIZONS 49ER VILLAGE RV RESORT

Scenic rating: 4

in Plymouth

Map grid C2

This is the granddaddy of RV parks, set on 23 acres in the heart of the Gold Country 40 miles east of Stockton and Sacramento. It is rarely crowded and offers warm pools and a huge spa. A bonus is the year-round heated, covered swimming pool. This resort is pet-friendly, and dogs receive a free milk bone at check-in. About one-fourth of the sites are occupied by annual renters. Wineries are nearby.

RV sites, facilities: There are 329 sites with full hookups (30 and 50 amps) for RVs up to 40 feet; some sites are pull-through. Eleven park-model cabins and an RV rental are also available. Restrooms with flush toilets and showers, cable TV, dump station, playground, two heated swimming pools, indoor spa, recreation room, TV lounge, recreation complex, modem access, Wi-Fi, business services, organized activities, café, gift shop, coin laundry, propane gas, and a general store are available. Some facilities are wheelchair-accessible. Leashed pets are permitted.

Reservations, fees: Reservations are recommended at 800/339-6981. Sites are $46–56 per night (holiday rates higher), $2 per night for each additional vehicle. Winter discounts are available. Some credit cards accepted. Open year-round.

Directions: From Sacramento, drive east on U.S. 50 to Watt Avenue. Turn south on Watt Avenue and drive to Highway 16. Turn left (east) on Highway 16/Jackson Road and drive approximately 30 miles to Highway 49 north/Jackson Road. Merge north on Highway 49 and drive two miles to the resort on the left side of the road at 18265 Highway 49. Note: This is a mile south of Main Street in Plymouth.

Contact: Far Horizons 49er Village RV Resort, 209/245-6981, www.49ervillage.com.

48 INDIAN GRINDING ROCK STATE HISTORIC PARK

Scenic rating: 7

near Jackson

Map grid C2

Indian Grinding Rock covers 135 acres of the Sierra foothills at an elevation of 2,400 feet.

Set in a small valley of meadows and oaks, the park contains a collection of limestone bedrock mortars, a reconstructed Miwok village with petroglyphs, a museum, and two nature trails. Interpretive talks are offered for groups (by reservation), while campers receive free access to the museum.

Local Native Americans schedule several ceremonies each year, including the Acorn Harvest Thanksgiving in September. In summer, expect warm and dry temperatures, often exceeding 90°F. Spring and fall are ideal, with winters cool, often right on the edge of snow (a few times) and rain (mostly) during storms.

RV sites, facilities: There are 23 sites for tents or RVs up to 27 feet (no hookups), and a group camp for up to 44 people that includes bark houses. Picnic tables, fire grills, and food lockers are provided. Drinking water and restrooms with flush toilets and coin showers are available. Some facilities are wheelchair-accessible. Leashed pets are permitted.

Reservations, fees: Reservations are not accepted for individual sites, but are required for the environmental group camp ($25 nonrefundable deposit required), which includes the bark houses. Tent and RV sites are $15–20 per night, $8 per night for each additional vehicle, $86 per night for the group camp. Open year-round.

Directions: From Jackson, drive east on Highway 88 for 11 miles to Pine Grove–Volcano Road. Turn left on Pine Grove–Volcano Road and drive 1.75 miles to the campground on the left.

Contact: Indian Grinding Rock State Historic Park, 209/296-7488, www.parks.ca.gov.

49 LAKE AMADOR RECREATION AREA

Scenic rating: 7

near Stockton

Map grid C2

Lake Amador is set in the foothill country east of Stockton at an elevation of 485 feet, covering 400 acres with 13 miles of shoreline. Everything here is set up for fishing, with large trout stocks from winter through late spring and the chance for huge bass. The lake record bass weighed 17 pounds, 1.25 ounces. The Carson Creek arm and Jackson Creek arm are the top spots. Night fishing is available. Waterskiing and personal watercraft are prohibited, and the speed limit is 5 mph. A bonus is a swimming pond. About half of the sites are lakefront with full hookups.

RV sites, facilities: There are 150 sites for tents or RVs of any length, and 13 group sites for 5–30 vehicles each; some sites have full hookups (30 and 50 amps). Picnic tables and fire grills are provided. Drinking water, restrooms with showers, dump station, boat ramp, boat rentals, fishing supplies (including bait and tackle), seasonal café, convenience store, propane gas, swimming pond, and a playground are available. Some facilities are wheelchair-accessible. Leashed pets are permitted.

Reservations, fees: Reservations are accepted in the summer ($5 reservation fee). Sites are $22–30 per night per vehicle, $4 per night for electricity. Boat launching is $7 per day and fishing is $8 per day. Some credit cards accepted. Open year-round.

Directions: From Stockton, turn east on Highway 88 and drive 24 miles to Clements. Just east of Clements, bear left on Highway 88 and drive nine miles to Jackson Valley Road. Turn right (well signed) and drive five miles to Lake Amador Drive. Turn right and drive over the dam to the campground office.

Contact: Lake Amador Recreation Area, 209/274-4739, www.lakeamador.com.

50 LAKE PARDEE MARINA

Scenic rating: 7

on Pardee Reservoir

Map grid C2

Many people think that Pardee is the prettiest lake in the Mother Lode country; it's a big lake covering 2,257 acres with 37 miles of shoreline.

CALIFORNIA

It is a beautiful sight in the spring when the lake is full and the surrounding hills are green and glowing. Waterskiing, personal watercraft, swimming, and all water/body contact are prohibited at the lake; it is set up expressly for fishing, with high catch rates for rainbow trout and kokanee salmon. During hot weather, attention turns to bass, both smallmouth and largemouth, as well as catfish and sunfish. The lake speed limit is 25 mph.

RV sites, facilities: There are 99 sites for tents or RVs up to 42 feet (no hookups), and 12 sites with full hookups (50 amps) for RVs. Picnic tables and fire grills are provided. Drinking water, restrooms with showers (in the hookup section), chemical toilets (in the no-hookup campground), dump station, full-service marina, fish-cleaning station, boat ramp, boat rentals, coin laundry, café, gas station, convenience store, propane gas, RV and boat storage, wading pool, and a seasonal swimming pool are available. Some facilities are wheelchair-accessible. Leashed pets are permitted.

Reservations, fees: Reservations are accepted. RV sites with full hookups are $29 per night, tent sites are $20 per night, $10 per night for each additional vehicle, $2.50 per pet per night. Boat launching is $7 per day. There is a daily fishing fee of $3.50. Monthly and seasonal rates available. Some credit cards accepted. Open February through October.

Directions: From Stockton, drive east on Highway 88/Waterloo Road for 17 miles to the town of Clements. One mile east of Clements, bear left on Highway 88 and drive 11 miles to Jackson Valley Road. Turn right and drive 3.4 miles to a four-way-stop sign at Buena Vista. Turn right and drive 3.1 miles to Stony Creek Road. Turn left and drive a mile to the campground on the right. (Driving directions from other areas are available on the marina's website.)

Contact: Lake Pardee Marina, 209/772-1472, fax 209/772-0985, www.pardeelakerecreation.com.

51 CAMANCHE LAKE NORTH

Scenic rating: 7

on Camanche Lake

Map grid C2

The sites at North Shore feature grassy spots with picnic tables set above the lake, and though there are few trees and the sites seem largely exposed, the lake view is quite pretty. The lake will beckon you and is excellent for boating and all water sports, with a full-service marina available. The warm, clean waters make for good waterskiing and wakeboarding (in specified areas), and fishing for trout in spring, bass in early summer, and crappie, bluegill, and catfish in summer. There are five miles of hiking and equestrian trails.

RV sites, facilities: There are 219 sites for tents or RVs of any length (no hookups), and four group sites for 12–72 people. Nine cottages, four triplexes, and motel rooms are also available. Picnic tables and fire grills are provided. Restrooms with showers, drinking water, dump station, boat ramp, boat rentals, coin laundry, convenience store, café, and a playground are available. Some facilities are wheelchair-accessible. Leashed pets are permitted.

Reservations, fees: Reservations are accepted at 866/763-5121 ($8.50 reservation fee). Sites are $26–30 per night, $10.50 per night for each additional vehicle with a maximum of two vehicles, $55–245 per night for a group site, $4 per pet per night. Boat launching is $7.50 per day. Group rates are available. Some credit cards accepted. Open year-round.

Directions: From Stockton, drive east on Highway 88/Waterloo Road for 17 miles to Clements. One mile east of Clements, bear left on Highway 88 and drive six miles to Liberty Road/North Camanche Parkway. Turn right and drive six miles to Camanche Road. Turn right and drive to the Camanche North Shore entrance gate.

Contact: Camanche Lake North, 209/763-5121, fax 209/763-5789, www.camancherecreation.com.

52 CAMANCHE LAKE SOUTH AND EQUESTRIAN CAMP

Scenic rating: 7

on Camanche Lake
Map grid C2

Camanche Lake is a huge, multifaceted facility, covering 7,700 acres with 53 miles of shoreline, set in the foothills east of Lodi at 325 feet elevation. It is the number-one recreation lake for waterskiing, wakeboarding, and personal watercraft (in specified areas), as well as swimming. In the spring and summer, it provides outstanding fishing for bass, trout, crappie, bluegill, and catfish. There are two campgrounds at the lake, and both have boat ramps nearby and full facilities. A new equestrian campground is open, and it's about one mile from the main campground area. This one at South Shore has a large, but exposed, overflow area for camping, a way to keep from getting stuck for a spot on popular weekends.

RV sites, facilities: There are 297 sites for tents or RVs of any length (no hookups), 99 sites with full hookups (30 and 50 amps) for RVs of any length, 25 double sites, five triple sites, two quad sites, seven equestrian sites, and 35 group sites for up to 16 people. Seven cottages are also available. Additionally, Miners Camp has 108 RV sites with full hookups (30 and 50 amps), 63 of which are long-term rentals. Picnic tables and fire grills are provided. Drinking water, restrooms with flush toilets and showers, chemical toilets, dump station, trout pond, marina, boat ramp, boat rentals, coin laundry, amphitheater with seasonal movies, basketball, tennis courts, and a convenience store are available. Some facilities are wheelchair-accessible. Leashed pets are permitted.

Reservations, fees: Reservations are accepted at 866/763-5178 ($8.50 reservation fee). Sites are $26–45 per night, $39–125 per night for equestrian sites, $240 per night for group site, $10.50 per night for each additional vehicle, $7.50 per day boat launch fee, $4 per pet per night. Monthly rates available, with a six-month limit. Some credit cards accepted. Open year-round.

Directions: From Stockton, drive east on Highway 88/Waterloo Road for 17 miles to Clements. One mile east of Clements, continue east on Highway 12 and drive six miles to South Camanche Parkway at Wallace. Continue straight and drive five miles to the entrance gate.

Contact: Camanche Lake South, 209/763-5178, www.camancherecreation.com.

53 OAK KNOLL AND GROUP CAMP

Scenic rating: 7

at New Hogan Lake
Map grid C2

This is one of two camps at New Hogan Lake. The reservoir was created by an Army Corps of Engineers dam project on the Calaveras River. (See the Acorn Campground listing for more information.)

RV sites, facilities: There are 50 sites for tents or RVs of any length, and a group site for tents or RVs of any length that can accommodate up to 50–60 people. No hookups. Fire grills and picnic tables are provided. Drinking water, vault toilets, and coin showers are available. A dump station and a four-lane boat ramp (at Fiddleneck) are nearby. A grocery store and propane gas are within five miles. Leashed pets are permitted.

Reservations, fees: Reservations are accepted at 877/444-6777 or www.recreation.gov ($10 reservation fee). Sites are $12 per night, and the group site is $100 per night. Open May through early September.

Directions: From Stockton, drive east on Highway 26 for about 30 miles to Valley Springs and Hogan Dam Road. Turn right and drive 1.5 miles to Hogan Parkway. Turn left and drive one mile to South Petersburg Road. Turn left and drive 0.5 mile to the campground on the right (adjacent to Acorn Campground).

Contact: U.S. Army Corps of Engineers, Sacramento District, 209/772-1343, fax 209/772-9352.

54 ACORN CAMPGROUND AND BOAT-IN

Scenic rating: 7

at New Hogan Lake

Map grid C2

New Hogan is a big lake in the foothill country east of Stockton, set at an elevation of 680 feet and covering 4,000 acres, with 50 miles of shoreline. Acorn is on the lake and operated by the Army Corps of Engineers. Boaters might also consider boat-in sites near Deer Flat on the eastern shore, and there is a group camp at Coyote Point. Boating and waterskiing are popular here, and all water sports are allowed. It's a decent lake for fishing, with a unique opportunity for striped bass, and it's OK for largemouth bass. Other species are crappie, bluegill, and catfish. There are bicycle trails and an eight-mile equestrian trail. An interpretive trail below the dam is worth checking out. Insider's tip: This is a wintering area for bald eagles.

RV sites, facilities: There are 127 sites for tents or RVs of any length (no hookups) and 30 boat-in sites. Fire pits and picnic tables are provided. Drinking water, restrooms with flush toilets and coin showers, pay telephones, fish-cleaning station, amphitheater, and a dump station are available. A two-lane, paved boat ramp and an 18-hole disc golf course are nearby. Nature walks and ranger programs are sometimes available. Groceries, a restaurant, and propane gas are within two miles. Some facilities are wheelchair accessible. Leashed pets are permitted.

Reservations, fees: Reservations are accepted at 877/444-6777 or www.recreation.gov. Sites are $14–18 per night, and boat-in sites are $10 per night. Some credit cards accepted. Open year-round, with reduced number of sites in winter; boat-in sites are open May through September.

Directions: From Stockton, drive east on Highway 26 for about 30 miles to Valley Springs and Hogan Dam Road. Turn right and drive 1.5 miles to Hogan Parkway. Turn left and drive one mile to South Petersburg Road. Turn left and drive 0.25 mile to the campground on the right.

Contact: U.S. Army Corps of Engineers, Sacramento District, 209/772-1343, fax 209/772-9352.

55 49ER RV RANCH

Scenic rating: 6

near Columbia

Map grid C2

This historic ranch/campground was originally built in 1852 as a dairy farm. Several original barns are still standing. The place has been brought up to date, of course, with a small store on the property providing last-minute supplies. Location is a plus, with the Columbia State Historic Park only 0.5 mile away, and the Stanislaus River arm of New Melones Lake within a five-minute drive. Live theater and wineries are nearby. The elevation is 2,100 feet. Note that there is a separate mobile home park on the premises.

RV sites, facilities: There are 42 sites with full hookups (50 amps) for trailers and RVs up to 50 feet. No tents. Picnic tables and cable TV are provided. Restrooms with showers, drinking water, coin laundry, convenience store, dump station, modem access, Wi-Fi, propane gas, and a large barn for group or club activities are available. Some facilities are wheelchair-accessible. Leashed pets are permitted.

Reservations, fees: Reservations are accepted by phone or website. Sites are $39.90 per night, $2.50 per person per night for more than two people, $3 per night for each additional vehicle. Group rates available. Open year-round.

Directions: From Sonora, turn north on Highway 49 and drive for 2.5 miles to Parrotts Ferry Road. Turn right and drive 1.7 miles to Columbia Street. Turn right and drive 0.4 mile to Pacific Street. Turn left and drive a block to Italian Bar Road. Turn right and drive 0.5 mile to the campground on the right.

Contact: 49er RV Ranch, tel./fax 209/532-4978, www.49rv.com.

56 MARBLE QUARRY RV PARK

Scenic rating: 6

near Columbia

Map grid C2

This is a family-oriented RV park set at 2,100 feet elevation in the Gold Country, within nearby range of several adventures. A 0.25-mile trail leads directly to Columbia State Historic Park, and the Stanislaus River arm of New Melones Lake is only five miles away.

RV sites, facilities: There are 85 sites with full or partial hookups (30 and 50 amps) for RVs up to 40 feet, a small area for tents, and three cabins of different sizes, including mid-size and executive cabins with kitchenettes. A few sites are pull-through. Picnic tables are provided. Restrooms with showers, satellite TV, seasonal swimming pool, coin laundry, Wi-Fi, convenience store, dump station, playground, two clubhouses, reading/TV room, group facilities, and propane gas are available. Some facilities are wheelchair-accessible. Leashed pets are permitted.

Reservations, fees: Reservations are accepted. RV sites are $35.50–39 per night, tent sites are $25.50 per night, $3.50 per person per night for more than two people. Some credit cards accepted. Open year-round.

Directions: From Sonora, turn north on Highway 49 and drive 2.5 miles to Parrotts Ferry Road (stop sign). Bear right on Parrotts Ferry Road and drive 1.5 miles to Columbia Street. Turn right and drive a short distance to Jackson Street. Turn right on Jackson Street and drive 0.25 mile (becomes Yankee Hill Road) to the campground on the right (at 11551 Yankee Hill Road).

Contact: Marble Quarry RV Park, 866/677-8464 or 209/532-9539, www.marblequarry.com.

CALIFORNIA

TAHOE AND THE NORTHERN SIERRA

◖ BEST RV PARKS AND CAMPGROUNDS

◖ Prettiest Lakes
Sardine Lake, page 811.
Donner Memorial State Park, page 829.
D. L. Bliss State Park, page 851.
Emerald Bay State Park and Boat-In, page 852.

◖ Prettiest Rivers
Indian Springs, page 828.

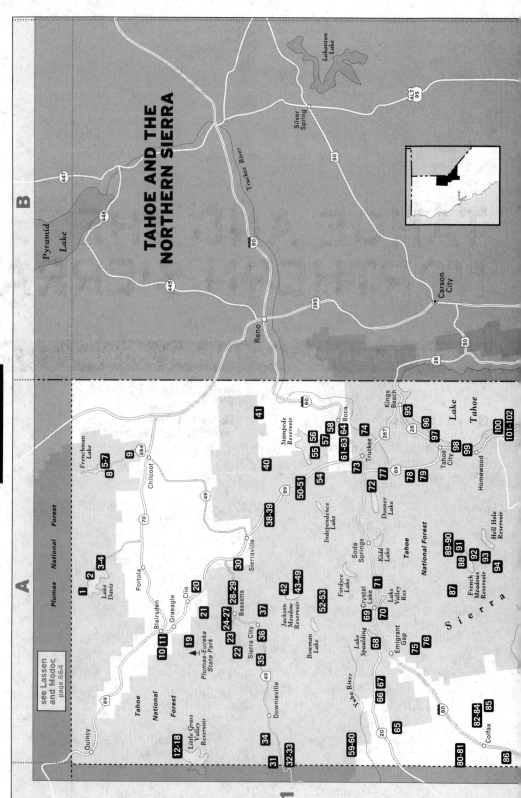

TAHOE AND THE NORTHERN SIERRA

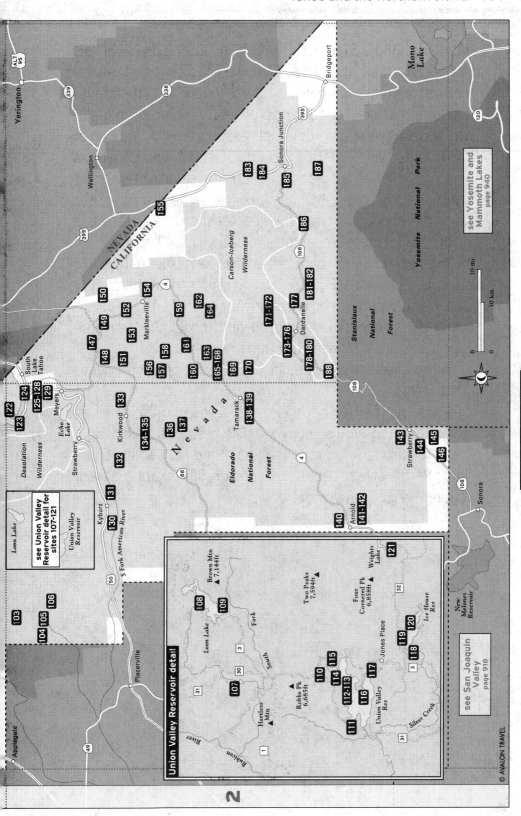

see Yosemite and Mammoth Lakes
page 940

Mono Lake

Yosemite National Park

Stanislaus National Forest

Bridgeport

Sonora Junction

Carson-Iceberg Wilderness

Markleeville

Dardanelle

South Lake Tahoe

Meyers

Echo Lake

Strawberry

Kirkwood

Tamarack

Eldorado National Forest

Nevada

Arnold

Strawberry

Sonora

New Melones Reservoir

Desolation Wilderness

Loon Lake

see Union Valley Reservoir detail for sites 107-121

Union Valley Reservoir

S Fork American River

Kyburz

Placerville

Applegate

Yerington

Wellington

NEVADA
CALIFORNIA

Union Valley Reservoir detail

Rubicon River

Hartless Mtn

Robbs Pk
6,685ft ▲

Loon Lake

Brown Mtn
▲ 7,144ft

South Fork

Two Peaks
7,591ft ▲

Four Cornered Pk
6,855ft ▲

Jones Place

Union Valley Res

Silver Creek

Wrights Lake

Ice House Res

see San Joaquin Valley
page 918

10 mi

10 km

© AVALON TRAVEL

Mount Tallac affords a view across Lake Tahoe like no other: a cobalt-blue expanse of water bordered by mountains that span miles of Sierra wildlands. The beauty is stunning. Lake Tahoe is one of the few places on earth where people feel an emotional response just by looking at it. Yosemite Valley, the giant sequoias, the Grand Canyon, a perfect sunset on the Pacific Ocean... these are a few other sights that occasionally can evoke the same response. But Tahoe often seems to strike the deepest chord. It can resonate inside you for weeks, even after a short visit.

"What about all the people?" you ask. It's true that people come here in droves. But I found many spots that I shared only with the chipmunks. You can enjoy these spots, too, if you're willing to read my books, hunt a bit, and, most important, time your trip to span Monday through Thursday.

This area has the widest range and number of campgrounds in California.

Tahoe and the Northern Sierra feature hundreds of lakes, including dozens you can drive to. The best for scenic beauty are Echo Lakes, Donner, Fallen Leaf, Sardine, Caples, Loon, Union Valley – well, I could go on and on. It is one of the most beautiful regions anywhere on earth.

The north end of the Northern Sierra starts near Bucks Lake, a great lake for trout fishing, and extends to Bear River Canyon (and Caples Lake, Silver Lake, and Bear River Reservoir). In between are the Lakes Basin Recreation Area (containing Gold, Sardine, Packer, and other lakes) in southern Plumas County; the Crystal Basin (featuring Union Valley Reservoir and Loon Lake, among others) in the Sierra foothills west of Tahoe; Lake Davis (with the highest catch rates for trout) near Portola; and the Carson River Canyon and Hope Valley south of Tahoe.

You could spend weeks exploring any of these places, having the time of your life, and still not get to Tahoe's magic. But it is Tahoe where the adventure starts for many, especially in the surrounding Tahoe National Forest and Desolation Wilderness.

One of California's greatest day trips from Tahoe is to Echo Lakes, where you can take a hikers shuttle boat across the two lakes to the Pacific Crest Trail, then hike a few miles into Desolation Wilderness and Aloha Lakes. Yet with so many wonderful ways to spend a day in this area, this day trip is hardly a blip on the radar.

With so many places and so little time, this region offers what can be the ultimate adventureland.

CALIFORNIA

1 LIGHTNING TREE

Scenic rating: 7

on Lake Davis in Plumas National Forest

Map grid A1

Lightning Tree campground is set near the shore of Lake Davis. Davis is a good-sized lake, with 32 miles of shoreline, set high in the northern Sierra at 5,775 feet. Lake Davis is one of the top mountain lakes in California for fishing, with large rainbow trout in the early summer and fall. This camp is perfectly situated for a fishing trip. It is at Lightning Tree Point on the lake's remote northeast shore, directly across the lake from Freeman Creek, one of the better spots for big trout. This lake is famous for pike; the Department of Fish and Game has twice poisoned the lake to kill them. In turn, the biggest trout plants in California history have been made here, with more than one million trout in 2008! There are three boat ramps on the lake.

RV sites, facilities: There are 40 sites for tents or RVs up to 50 feet (no hookups). Vault toilets and drinking water are available. Garbage must be packed out. A dump station and a car-top boat launch are nearby. Some facilities are wheelchair-accessible. Leashed pets are permitted.

Reservations, fees: Reservations are accepted at 877/444-6777 or www.recreation.gov ($10 reservation fee). Sites are $9 per night, $18 per night for a double site. Open May through October, weather permitting.

Directions: From Truckee, turn north on Highway 89 and drive to Sattley and County Road A23. Turn right on County Road A23 and drive 13 miles to Highway 70. Turn left on Highway 70 and drive one mile to Grizzly Road. Turn right on Grizzly Road and drive about six miles to Lake Davis. Continue north on Lake Davis Road along the lake's east shore and drive about five miles to the campground entrance on the left side of the road.

Contact: Plumas National Forest, Beckwourth Ranger District, 530/836-2575, fax 530/836-0493; Thousand Trails, 530/832-1076.

2 GRASSHOPPER FLAT

Scenic rating: 7

on Lake Davis in Plumas National Forest

Map grid A1

Grasshopper Flat provides a nearby alternative to Grizzly at Lake Davis, with the boat ramp at adjacent Honker Cove a primary attraction for campers with trailered boats for fishing. The camp is on the southeast end of the lake, at 5,800 feet elevation. Lake Davis is known for its large rainbow trout that bite best in early summer and fall. Swimming and powerboats are allowed, but no waterskiing or personal watercraft are permitted.

RV sites, facilities: There are 70 sites for tents or RVs up to 35 feet (no hookups). Picnic tables and fire grills are provided. Drinking water and restrooms with flush toilets and coin showers are available. A boat ramp, grocery store, and a dump station are nearby. Some facilities are wheelchair-accessible. Leashed pets are permitted.

Reservations, fees: Reservations are accepted at 877/444-6777 or www.recreation.gov ($10 reservation fee). Sites are $18 per night. Open May through October, weather permitting.

Directions: From Truckee, turn north on Highway 89 and drive to Sattley and County Road A23. Turn right on County Road A23 and drive 13 miles to Highway 70. Turn left on Highway 70 and drive one mile to Grizzly Road. Turn right on Grizzly Road and drive about six miles to Lake Davis. Continue north on Lake Davis Road for a mile (just past Grizzly) to the campground entrance on the left side of the road.

Contact: Plumas National Forest, Beckwourth Ranger District, 530/836-2575, fax 530/836-0493; Thousand Trails, 530/832-1076.

3 CROCKER

Scenic rating: 5

in Plumas National Forest

Map grid A1

Even though this camp is just four miles east of Lake Davis, it is little known and little used since there are three lakeside camps close by. This camp is set in Plumas National Forest at 5,900 feet elevation, and it is about a 15-minute drive north to the border of the Dixie Mountain State Game Refuge.

RV sites, facilities: There are 10 sites for tents or RVs up to 16 feet (no hookups). Picnic tables and fire grills are provided. Vault toilets are available. No drinking water is available. Garbage must be packed out. Leashed pets are permitted.

Reservations, fees: Reservations are not accepted. There is no fee for camping. Open May through October, weather permitting.

Directions: From Reno, drive north on U.S. 395 to the junction with Highway 70. Turn west on Highway 70 and drive to Beckwourth and County Road 111/Beckwourth-Genessee Road. Turn right on County Road 111 and drive six miles to the campground on the left side of the road.

Contact: Plumas National Forest, Beckwourth Ranger District, 530/836-2575, fax 530/836-0493; Thousand Trails, 530/832-1076.

4 GRIZZLY

Scenic rating: 7

on Lake Davis in Plumas National Forest

Map grid A1

This is one of the better developed campgrounds at Lake Davis and is a popular spot for camping anglers. Its proximity to the Grizzly Store, just over the dam to the south, makes getting last-minute supplies a snap. In addition, a boat ramp is to the north in Honker Cove, providing access to the southern reaches of the lake, including the island area, where trout trolling is good in early summer and fall. The elevation is 5,800 feet.

RV sites, facilities: There are 55 sites for tents or RVs up to 35 feet (no hookups). Picnic tables and fire grills are provided. Drinking water and flush toilets are available. A boat ramp, grocery store, and a dump station are nearby. Some facilities are wheelchair-accessible. Leashed pets are permitted.

Reservations, fees: Reservations are accepted at 877/444-6777 or www.recreation.gov ($10 reservation fee). Sites are $18 per night. Open May through October, weather permitting.

Directions: From Truckee, turn north on Highway 89 and drive to Sattley and County Road A23. Turn right on County Road A23 and drive 13 miles to Highway 70. Turn left on Highway 70 and drive one mile to Grizzly Road. Turn right on Grizzly Road and drive about six miles to Lake Davis. Continue north on Lake Davis Road for less than a mile to the campground entrance on the left side of the road.

Contact: Plumas National Forest, Beckwourth Ranger District, 530/836-2575, fax 530/836-0493; Thousand Trails, 530/832-1076.

5 BIG COVE

Scenic rating: 7

at Frenchman Lake in Plumas National Forest

Map grid A1

Big Cove is one of four camps at the southeastern end of Frenchman Lake, with a boat ramp available about a mile away near the Frenchman and Spring Creek camps. (For more information, see the Frenchman listing in this chapter.) A trail from the campground leads to the lakeshore. Another trail connects to the Spring Creek campground, a walk of 0.5 mile. The elevation is 5,800 feet.

RV sites, facilities: There are 38 sites for tents or RVs up to 50 feet (no hookups). Picnic tables and fire rings are provided. Drinking water and flush toilets are available. Some facilities are wheelchair-accessible. A boat ramp and dump station are nearby. A grocery store and propane gas are available seven miles away. Leashed pets are permitted.

Reservations, fees: Reservations are accepted at 877/444-6777 or www.recreation.gov ($10 reservation fee). Sites are $18–36 per night. Open May through October, weather permitting.

Directions: From Reno, drive north on U.S. 395 to the junction with Highway 70. Turn west on Highway 70 and drive to Chilcoot and the junction with Frenchman Lake Road. Turn right on Frenchman Lake Road and drive nine miles to the lake and to a Y. At the Y, turn right and drive two miles to Forest Road 24N01. Turn left and drive a short distance to the campground entrance on the left side of the road (on the east side of the lake).

Contact: Plumas National Forest, Beckwourth Ranger District, 530/836-2575, fax 530/836-0493; Thousand Trails, 530/832-1076.

6 SPRING CREEK

Scenic rating: 7

on Frenchman Lake in Plumas National Forest
Map grid A1

Frenchman Lake is set at 5,800 feet elevation, on the edge of high desert to the east and forest to the west. The lake has 21 miles of shoreline and is surrounded by a mix of sage and pines. All water sports are allowed. This camp is on the southeast end of the lake, where there are three other campgrounds, including a group camp and a boat ramp. The lake provides good fishing for stocked rainbow trout—best in the cove near the campgrounds. Trails lead out from the campground: One heads 0.25 mile to the Frenchman campground; the other a 0.5-mile route to Big Cove campground.

RV sites, facilities: There are 35 sites for tents or RVs up to 35 feet (no hookups). Picnic tables and fire grills are provided. Drinking water and vault toilets are available. Some facilities are wheelchair-accessible. A boat ramp and dump station are nearby. Leashed pets are permitted.

Reservations, fees: Reservations are accepted at 877/444-6777 or www.recreation.gov ($10 reservation fee). Sites are $18 per night. Open May through October, weather permitting.

Directions: From Reno, drive north on U.S. 395 to the junction with Highway 70. Turn west on Highway 70 and drive to Chilcoot and the junction with Frenchman Lake Road. Turn right on Frenchman Lake Road and drive nine miles to the lake and to a Y. At the Y, turn right and drive two miles to the campground on the left side of the road.

Contact: Plumas National Forest, Beckwourth Ranger District, 530/836-2575, fax 530/836-0493; Thousand Trails, 530/832-1076.

7 FRENCHMAN

Scenic rating: 7

on Frenchman Lake in Plumas National Forest
Map grid A1

This camp is on the southeast end of the lake, where there are three other campgrounds, including a group camp and a boat ramp. The best trout fishing is in the cove near the campgrounds and the two inlets, one along the west shore and one at the head of the lake. The proximity to Reno, only 35 miles away, keeps gambling in the back of the minds of many anglers. Because of water demands downstream, the lake often drops significantly by the end of summer. A trail from camp is routed 0.25 mile to the Spring Creek campground.

RV sites, facilities: There are 38 sites for tents or RVs up to 35 feet (no hookups). Picnic tables and fire grills are provided. Drinking water and vault toilets are available. A dump station and boat ramp are nearby. Leashed pets are permitted.

Reservations, fees: Reservations are accepted at 877/444-6777 or www.recreation.gov ($10 reservation fee). Sites are $18 per night. Open May through October, weather permitting.

Directions: From Reno, drive north on U.S. 395 to the junction with Highway 70. Turn west on Highway 70 and drive to Chilcoot and the junction with Frenchman Lake Road. Turn right on Frenchman Lake Road and drive nine miles to the lake and to a Y. At the Y, turn right and drive 1.5 miles to the campground on the left side of the road.

Contact: Plumas National Forest, Beckwourth Ranger District, 530/836-2575, fax 530/836-0493; Thousand Trails, 530/259-7606.

8 COTTONWOOD SPRINGS

Scenic rating: 7

near Frenchman Lake in Plumas National Forest

Map grid A1

Cottonwood Springs, elevation 5,800 feet, is largely an overflow camp at Frenchman Lake. It is the only camp at the lake with a group site. The more popular Frenchman, Big Cove, and Spring Creek camps are along the southeast shore of the lake near a boat ramp.

RV sites, facilities: There are 20 sites for tents or RVs up to 50 feet (no hookups), and two group sites for tents or RVs up to 35 feet that can accommodate 25–50 people each. Picnic tables and fire rings are provided. Drinking water and flush toilets are available. Some facilities are wheelchair-accessible. A boat ramp and dump station are nearby. Leashed pets are permitted.

Reservations, fees: Reservations are accepted for individual sites and are required for group sites at 877/444-6777 or www.recreation.gov ($10 reservation fee). Sites are $18 per night, $70–110 per night for groups. Open May through October, weather permitting.

Directions: From Reno, drive north on U.S. 395 to the junction with Highway 70. Turn west on Highway 70 and drive to Chilcoot and the junction with Frenchman Lake Road. Turn right on Frenchman Lake Road and drive nine miles to the lake and to a Y. At the Y, turn left and drive 1.5 miles to the campground on the right side of the road.

Contact: Plumas National Forest, Beckwourth Ranger District, 530/836-2575, fax 530/836-0493; Thousand Trails, 530/832-1076.

9 CHILCOOT

Scenic rating: 7

on Little Last Chance Creek in Plumas National Forest

Map grid A1

This small camp is set along Little Last Chance Creek at 5,400 feet elevation, about three miles downstream from Frenchman Lake. The stream provides good trout fishing, but access can be difficult at some spots because of brush.

RV sites, facilities: There are 40 sites for tents or RVs up to 35 feet (no hookups), and five walk-in sites for tents only. Picnic tables and fire rings are provided. Drinking water and flush toilets are available. Some facilities are wheelchair-accessible. A boat ramp, grocery store, and dump station are nearby. Leashed pets are permitted.

Reservations, fees: Reservations are accepted at 877/444-6777 or www.recreation.gov ($10 reservation fee). Sites are $18 per night. Open May through October, weather permitting.

Directions: From Reno, drive north on U.S. 395 to the junction with Highway 70. Turn west on Highway 70 and drive to Chilcoot and the junction with Frenchman Lake Road. Turn right on Frenchman Lake Road and drive six miles to the campground on the left side of the road.

Contact: Plumas National Forest, Beckwourth Ranger District, 530/836-2575, fax 530/836-0493; Thousand Trails, 530/832-1076.

10 LITTLE BEAR RV PARK

Scenic rating: 7

on the Feather River

Map grid A1

This is a privately operated RV park set near the Feather River. Nearby destinations include Plumas-Eureka State Park and the Lakes Basin Recreation Area. The elevation is 4,300 feet. About half of the sites are taken by full-season rentals.

RV sites, facilities: There are 97 sites with full

or partial hookups (30 amps) for RVs of any length, and 10 sleeping cabins. No tents are allowed. Picnic tables and fire rings are provided. Drinking water, restrooms with showers and flush toilets, coin laundry, convenience store, satellite TV, modem access, RV storage, propane, and ice are available. A dump station, clubhouse, table tennis, shuffleboard, and horseshoes are also available. Leashed pets are permitted at campsites; but no pets in the cabins.

Reservations, fees: Reservations are recommended. Sites are $27–29 per night, $4–8 per person per night for more than two people, $1 per pet per night. Weekly and monthly rates available. Open mid-April through late October.

Directions: In Truckee, drive north on Highway 89 to Graeagle. Continue north on Highway 89 for one mile to Little Bear Road. Turn left on Little Bear Road and drive a short distance to the campground on the right.

Contact: Little Bear RV Park, tel. 530/836-2774, fax 530/836-1810, www.littlebearrvpark.com.

11 MOVIN' WEST RV PARK

Scenic rating: 5

in Graeagle

Map grid A1

This RV park began life as a mobile home park. Approximately half of the sites are for permanent residents; the other half are for vacationers, with about half of those rented for the summer. The park has also become very popular with golfers. A nine-hole golf course is across the road and five other golf courses are within five miles. The elevation is 4,300 feet.

RV sites, facilities: There are 51 sites for RVs of any length with full (30 amps), partial, or no hookups, including five pull-through sites. There are also three tent sites and two cabins. Picnic tables and fire rings are provided. Drinking water, restrooms with flush toilets and showers, pay phone, cable TV, Wi-Fi, and a coin laundry are available. Propane gas, a nine-hole golf course, swimming pond, horse-

stable, and mini golf are nearby. Leashed pets are permitted.

Reservations, fees: Reservations are recommended. RV sites with full hookups are $29 per night or $25 per night with no hookups, tent sites are $25 per night, cabins are $40 per night, $5 per person per night for more than two people. Open May through October.

Directions: From Truckee, drive northwest on Highway 89 about 50 miles to Graeagle. Continue just past Graeagle to County Road A14 (Graeagle-Johnsville Road). Turn left and drive 0.25 mile northwest to the campground on the left.

Contact: Movin' West RV Park, 530/836-2614.

12 BLACK ROCK WALK-IN AND OVERFLOW

Scenic rating: 7

on Little Grass Valley Reservoir in Plumas National Forest

Map grid A1

This is the only campground on the west shore of Little Grass Valley Reservoir, with an adjacent boat ramp making it an attractive choice for anglers. The lake is set at 5,060 feet elevation in Plumas National Forest and provides lakeside camping and decent fishing for rainbow trout and kokanee salmon. If you don't like the company, there are seven other camps to choose from at the lake, all on the opposite eastern shore.

RV sites, facilities: There are 20 walk-in sites (a walk of a few yards to 0.1 mile) for tents or RVs up to 22 feet (no hookups). There is a parking lot for overflow camping for RVs up to 35 feet. Picnic tables and fire grills are provided. Drinking water, vault toilets, and a fish-cleaning station are available. A dump station, boat ramp, and grocery store are nearby. Leashed pets are permitted.

Reservations, fees: Reservations are not accepted. Sites are $20 per night. Open May through September, weather permitting.

Directions: From Oroville, drive east on

Highway 162/Oroville Dam Boulevard for about eight miles (becomes the Olive Highway) to Forbestown Road. Turn right and drive through Forbestown to Challenge and LaPorte Road. Turn left on LaPorte Road and drive to LaPorte. Continue two miles past LaPorte to the junction with County Road 514/Little Grass Valley Road. Turn left and drive about five miles to the campground access road on the west side of the lake. Turn right on the access road and drive 0.25 mile to the campground.

Contact: Plumas National Forest, Feather River Ranger District, 530/534-6500, fax 530/532-1210; Northwest Management, 530/283-5559.

13 HORSE CAMP

Scenic rating: 7

on Little Grass Valley Reservoir in Plumas National Forest

Map grid A1

This camp is reserved for equestrians only and thus it gets low use. This is a high-country forested campground set near Little Grass Valley Reservoir, but there is no lake view because of tree cover. Several trails are accessible from the campground, including the Pacific Crest Trail and Lakeshore Trail, as well as access to Bald Mountain (6,255 feet). The elevation at camp is 5,060 feet.

RV sites, facilities: There are 10 sites for tents or RVs up to 25 feet (no hookups) available for equestrian campers only. Picnic tables and fire grills are provided. Vault toilets are available. No drinking water is available. Hitching posts and a wheelchair-accessible mounting rack are available. A restaurant and deli are available five miles away in LaPorte. Leashed pets are permitted.

Reservations, fees: Reservations are accepted at 877/444-6777 or www.recreation.gov ($10 reservation fee). Sites are $20 per night. Open June through September.

Directions: From Oroville, drive east on Highway 162/Oroville Dam Boulevard for about eight miles (becomes the Olive Highway) to

Forbestown Road. Turn right and drive through Forbestown to Challenge and LaPorte Road. Turn left on LaPorte Road and drive to LaPorte. Continue on County Road 512 (which becomes County Road 514/Little Grass Valley Road) for three miles to Forest Road 22N57. Turn right and drive four miles (cross the bridge) to the campground on the left.

Contact: Plumas National Forest, Feather River Ranger District, 530/534-6500, fax 530/532-1210; Northwest Management, 530/283-5559.

14 PENINSULA TENT

Scenic rating: 9

on Little Grass Valley Reservoir in Plumas National Forest

Map grid A1

This camp, at 5,060 feet in elevation, is exceptional in that most of the campsites provide views of Little Grass Valley Reservoir, a pretty lake in national forest. The fishing can be excellent, especially for rainbow trout, brown trout, and kokanee salmon. The camp gets moderate use, and it is a pretty site with tents sprinkled amid white fir and pine. This is a good family campground. A 13.5-mile hiking trail circles the lake.

RV sites, facilities: There are 25 sites for tents or RVs up to 25 feet (no hookups). Picnic tables and fire rings are provided. Drinking water and flush toilets are available. A boat launch, fish-cleaning station, and a swimming beach are nearby. Leashed pets are permitted.

Reservations, fees: Reservations are not accepted. Sites are $20 per night. Open Memorial Day weekend through September, weather permitting.

Directions: From Oroville, drive east on Highway 162/Oroville Dam Boulevard for about eight miles (becomes the Olive Highway) to Forbestown Road. Turn right and drive through Forbestown to Challenge and LaPorte Road. Turn left on LaPorte Road and drive to LaPorte. Continue on County Road 512 (which becomes County Road 514/Little Grass Valley

Road) for three miles to Forest Road 22N57. Continue on Forest Road 514 for one mile to the campground entrance on right. Turn right and drive 0.25 mile to the campground.

Contact: Plumas National Forest, Feather River Ranger District, 530/534-6500, fax 530/532-1210; Northwest Management, 530/283-5559.

15 RUNNING DEER

Scenic rating: 7

on Little Grass Valley Reservoir in Plumas National Forest

Map grid A1

Little Grass Valley Reservoir is a pretty mountain lake set at 5,060 feet elevation in Plumas National Forest, providing lakeside camping, boating, and fishing for rainbow trout and kokanee salmon. Looking straight north from the camp is a spectacular view, gazing across the water and up at Bald Mountain, at 6,255 feet elevation. One of seven campgrounds on the eastern shore, this one is on the far northeastern end of the lake. A trailhead for the Pacific Crest Trail is nearby at little Fowler Lake about four miles north of Little Grass Valley Reservoir. Note that fish-cleaning stations are not available at Running Deer, but there is one nearby at Little Beaver.

RV sites, facilities: There are 40 sites for tents or RVs up to 40 feet (no hookups). Picnic tables and fire rings are provided. Drinking water and flush toilets are available. A fish-cleaning station, boat ramp, grocery store, and a dump station are nearby. Leashed pets are permitted.

Reservations, fees: Reservations are accepted at 877/444-6777 or www.recreation.gov ($10 reservation fee). Sites are $20–22 per night. Open late May through September.

Directions: From Oroville, drive east on Highway 162/Oroville Dam Boulevard for about eight miles (becomes the Olive Highway) to Forbestown Road. Turn right and drive through Forbestown to Challenge and LaPorte Road. Turn left on LaPorte Road and drive to LaPorte. Continue on County Road 512 (which

becomes County Road 514/Little Grass Valley Road) for three miles to Forest Road 22N57. Turn right and drive three miles to the campground on the left.

Contact: Plumas National Forest, Feather River Ranger District, 530/534-6500, fax 530/532-1210; Northwest Management, 530/283-5559.

16 WYANDOTTE

Scenic rating: 8

on Little Grass Valley Reservoir in Plumas National Forest

Map grid A1

Of the eight camps on Little Grass Valley Reservoir, this is the favorite. It is set at 5,100 feet elevation on a small peninsula that extends well into the lake, with a boat ramp nearby. All water sports are allowed. (For more information, see the Running Deer listing in this chapter.)

RV sites, facilities: There are 28 individual sites and two double sites for tents or RVs up to 40 feet (no hookups). Picnic tables and fire rings are provided. Drinking water and flush toilets are available. A dump station, boat ramp, fish-cleaning station, and grocery store are nearby. Leashed pets are permitted.

Reservations, fees: Reservations are not accepted. Sites are $20 per night, $35 per night for a double site. Open late May through mid-October, weather permitting.

Directions: From Oroville, drive east on Highway 162/Oroville Dam Boulevard for about eight miles (becomes the Olive Highway) to Forbestown Road. Turn right and drive through Forbestown to Challenge and LaPorte Road. Turn left on LaPorte Road and drive to LaPorte. Continue two miles past LaPorte to the junction with County Road 514/Little Grass Valley Road. Turn left and drive one mile to a junction. Turn left and drive one mile to the campground entrance road on the right.

Contact: Plumas National Forest, Feather River Ranger District, 530/534-6500, fax 530/532-1210; Northwest Management, 530/283-5559.

CALIFORNIA

17 LITTLE BEAVER

Scenic rating: 7

on Little Grass Valley Reservoir in
Plumas National Forest

Map grid A1

This is one of eight campgrounds on Little
Grass Valley Reservoir, set at 5,060 feet elevation. Take your pick. (For more information,
see the Running Deer listing in this chapter.)

RV sites, facilities: There are 120 sites for tents
or RVs up to 40 feet (no hookups). Picnic tables
and fire rings are provided. Drinking water
and flush toilets are available. A grocery store,
dump station, fish-cleaning station, and boat
ramp are nearby. Some facilities are wheelchair-
accessible. Leashed pets are permitted.

Reservations, fees: Reservations are not accepted. Sites are $20–22 per night. Open June
through mid-September, weather permitting.

Directions: From Oroville, drive east on Highway 162/Oroville Dam Boulevard for about
eight miles (becomes the Olive Highway)
to Forbestown Road. Turn right and drive
through Forbestown to Challenge and LaPorte
Road. Turn left on LaPorte Road and drive
to LaPorte. Continue two miles past LaPorte
to the junction with County Road 514/Little
Grass Valley Road. Turn left and drive one mile
to a junction. Turn right and drive two miles to
the campground entrance road on the left.

Contact: Plumas National Forest, Feather River
Ranger District, 530/534-6500, fax 530/532-
1210; Northwest Management, 530/283-5559.

18 RED FEATHER CAMP

Scenic rating: 7

on Little Grass Valley Reservoir in
Plumas National Forest

Map grid A1

This camp is well developed and popular, set
on the eastern shore of Little Grass Valley
Reservoir, just south of Running Deer and just
north of Little Beaver. Bears frequent this area,
so be sure to properly store your food and avoid

scented products. (For more information, see
the Running Deer listing in this chapter.)

RV sites, facilities: There are 60 sites for tents
or RVs up to 40 feet (no hookups). Picnic tables
and fire rings are provided. Drinking water and
flush toilets are available. A dump station, boat
ramp, fish-cleaning station, and grocery store
are nearby. Leashed pets are permitted.

Reservations, fees: Reservations are accepted at
877/444-6777 or www.recreation.gov ($10 reser-
vation fee). Sites are $20–22 per night. Open late
June through September, weather permitting.

Directions: From Oroville, drive east on Highway 162/Oroville Dam Boulevard for about
eight miles (becomes the Olive Highway)
to Forbestown Road. Turn right and drive
through Forbestown to Challenge and LaPorte
Road. Turn left on LaPorte Road and drive
to LaPorte. Continue two miles past LaPorte
to the junction with County Road 514/Little
Grass Valley Road. Turn left and drive one mile
to a junction. Turn right and drive three miles
to the campground entrance road on the left.

Contact: Plumas National Forest, Feather River
Ranger District, 530/534-6500, fax 530/532-
1210; Northwest Management, 530/283-5559.

19 PLUMAS-EUREKA STATE PARK

Scenic rating: 9

near Graeagle

Map grid A1

Plumas-Eureka State Park is a beautiful chunk
of parkland, featuring great hiking, a pretty
lake, and this well-maintained campground.
For newcomers to the area, Jamison Camp
at the southern end of the park makes for an
excellent first stop. So does the nearby hike to
Grass Lake, a first-class tromp that takes about
two hours and features a streamside walk along
Little Jamison Creek, with the chance to take a
five-minute cutoff to see 40-foot Jamison Falls.
A historic mine, park museum, blacksmith
shop, stable, and stamp mill are also here, with
campers allowed free admission to the museum.

Other must-see destinations in the park include Eureka Lake, and from there, the 1,100-foot climb to Eureka Peak (formerly known as Gold Mountain), at 7,447 feet, for a dramatic view of all the famous peaks in this region. Camp elevation is 5,200 feet. The park covers 5,500 acres. Fishing opportunities feature Madora and Eureka Lakes and Jamison Creek, best in May and June. The visitors center was originally constructed as a bunkhouse for miners. More than $8 million of gold was mined here.

RV sites, facilities: Upper Jamison Creek Campground has 67 sites for tents or RVs up to 30 feet (no hookups). At Camp Lisa, there is one group tent site for up to 50 people. Picnic tables, food lockers, and fire rings are provided. Drinking water and restrooms with flush toilets and free showers are available. Some facilities are wheelchair-accessible. A dump station is nearby, and a grocery store, coin laundry, and propane gas are available within five miles. Leashed pets are permitted.

Reservations, fees: Reservations are accepted at 800/444-7275 or www.reserveamerica.com ($8 reservation fee). (Note that Reserve America lists both camps under "Plumas-Eureka State Park" and not their camp names.) Sites are $35 per night, $8 per night for each additional vehicle, $225 per night for the group site. Open mid-May through mid-October, weather permitting.

Directions: In Truckee, drive north on Highway 89 to Graeagle. Just after passing Graeagle (one mile from the junction of Highway 70) turn left on County Road A14/Graeagle-Johnsville Road and drive west for about five miles to the park entrance on the left.

Contact: Plumas-Eureka State Park, 530/836-2380, fax 530/836-0498, www.parks.ca.gov.

20 CLIO'S RIVER'S EDGE RV PARK

Scenic rating: 7

on the Feather River

Map grid A1

This is a giant RV park set adjacent to a pretty and easily accessible stretch of the Feather River.

There are many possible side-trip destinations, including Plumas-Eureka State Park, Lakes Basin Recreation Area, and several nearby golf courses and a horseback-riding facility. The elevation is about 4,500 feet. Many of the sites are rented for the entire summer season.

RV sites, facilities: There are 220 sites with full hookups (50 amps) for RVs of any length. Some sites are pull-through. Picnic tables are provided. Drinking water, restrooms with flush toilets and coin showers, coin laundry, Wi-Fi, modem access, and cable TV are available. Some facilities are wheelchair-accessible. A grocery store is within three miles. Leashed pets are permitted, with certain restrictions.

Reservations, fees: Reservations are accepted. Sites are $30–35 per night, $5 per person per night for more than two people. Weekly and monthly rates are available. Some credit cards accepted. Open mid-April through October.

Directions: From Truckee, drive north on Highway 89 toward Graeagle and Blairsden. Near Clio (4.5 miles south of Highway 70 at Blairsden), look for the campground entrance on the right (0.2 mile south of Graeagle).

Contact: Clio's River's Edge, tel./fax 530/836-2375, www.riversedgervpark.net.

21 LAKES BASIN

Scenic rating: 8

in Plumas National Forest

Map grid A1

This camp is a great location for a base camp to explore the surrounding Lakes Basin Recreation Area. From nearby Gold Lake or Elwell Lodge, there are many short hikes to small pristine lakes. A must-do trip is the easy hike to Frazier Falls, only a mile round-trip to see the spectacular 176-foot waterfall, though the trail is crowded during the middle of the day. The trail to this waterfall is paved and is wheelchair-accessible. The camp elevation is 6,400 feet.

RV sites, facilities: There are 23 sites for tents or RVs up to 30 feet (no hookups). Picnic tables and fire grills are provided. Drinking water and vault toilets are available. Some facilities are wheelchair-accessible. Supplies are available in Graeagle. Leashed pets are permitted.

Reservations, fees: Reservations are accepted at 877/444-6777 or www.recreation.gov ($10 reservation fee). Sites are $16 per night and double sites are $32 per night. Open June through October, weather permitting.

Directions: From Truckee, drive north on Highway 89 toward Graeagle to the Gold Lake Highway (one mile before reaching Graeagle). Turn left on the Gold Lake Highway and drive about seven miles to the campground.

Contact: Plumas National Forest, Beckwourth Ranger District, 530/836-2575, fax 530/836-0493; Thousand Trails, 530/832-1076.

22 PACKSADDLE

Scenic rating: 6

near Packer Lake in Tahoe National Forest
Map grid A1

Packsaddle is a Forest Service site about a half mile from Packer Lake, with an additional 15 lakes within a five-mile radius, and one of America's truly great hiking trails nearby. The trail to the Sierra Buttes features a climb of 2,369 feet over the course of five miles. It is highlighted by a stairway with 176 steps that literally juts into open space, and crowned by an astounding view for hundreds of miles in all directions. Packer Lake, at 6,218 feet elevation, is at the foot of the dramatic Sierra Buttes and has lakefront log cabins, good trout fishing, and low-speed boating. The campground elevation is 6,000 feet.

RV sites, facilities: There are 15 sites for tents or RVs up to 35 feet (no hookups). Vault toilets and drinking water are available. Pack and saddle animals are permitted and corrals and hitching rails are available. Supplies are available in Bassetts and Sierra City. Some facilities are wheelchair-accessible. Leashed pets are permitted.

Reservations, fees: Reservations are accepted at 877/444-6777 or www.recreation.gov ($10 reservation fee). Sites are $20 per night, $5 per night for each additional vehicle. Open late May through September, weather permitting.

Directions: From Truckee, turn north on Highway 89 and drive 20 miles to Sierraville. At Sierraville, turn left on Highway 49 and drive about 10 miles to the Bassetts Store. Turn right on Gold Lake Road and drive 1.5 miles to Packer Lake Road. Turn left, drive a short distance, bear right at the fork, and drive 2.5 miles to the campground on the left.

Contact: Tahoe National Forest, Yuba River Ranger District, North, 530/288-3231, fax 530/288-0727; California Land Management, 530/587-9281 or 650/322-1181.

23 BERGER CREEK

Scenic rating: 6

in Tahoe National Forest
Map grid A1

Berger Creek provides an overflow alternative to nearby Diablo, which is also extremely primitive. On busy summer weekends, when an open campsite can be difficult to find at a premium location in the Lakes Basin Recreation Area, these two camps provide a safety valve to keep you from being stuck for the night. Nearby are Packer Lake, the trail to the Sierra Buttes, Sardine Lakes, and Sand Pond, all excellent destinations. The elevation is 5,900 feet.

RV sites, facilities: There are 10 sites for tents or RVs up to 16 feet (no hookups). Picnic tables and fire grills are provided. Vault toilets are available. No drinking water is available. Garbage must be packed out. Supplies are available in Bassetts and Sierra City. Leashed pets are permitted.

Reservations, fees: Reservations are not accepted. Sites are $16 per night, $5 per night for each additional vehicle. Open June through October, weather permitting.

Directions: From Truckee, turn north on Highway 89 and drive 20 miles to Sierraville. At Sierraville, turn left on Highway 49 and drive about 10 miles to the Bassetts Store. Turn right on Gold Lake Road and drive 1.5 miles to Packer Lake Road. Turn left, drive a short distance, bear right at the fork, and drive two miles to the campground on the left.

Contact: Tahoe National Forest, Yuba River Ranger District, North, 530/288-3231, fax 530/288-0727; California Land Management, 530/587-9281 or 650/322-1181.

24 SNAG LAKE

Scenic rating: 8

in Tahoe National Forest

Map grid A1

Snag Lake is an ideal little lake for camping anglers with canoes. There are no boat ramps and you can have the place virtually to yourself. It is set at 6,000 feet in elevation, an easy-to-reach lake in the Lakes Basin Recreation Area. Trout fishing is only fair, as in fair numbers and fair size, mainly rainbow trout in the 10- to 12-inch class. Note that campers here must provide their own drinking water.

RV sites, facilities: There are 12 sites for tents or RVs up to 16 feet (no hookups). Picnic tables and fire grills are provided. Vault toilets are available. No drinking water is available. Garbage must be packed out. Only hand boat launching is allowed. Supplies are available in Bassetts and Sierra City. Leashed pets are permitted.

Reservations, fees: Reservations are not accepted. There is no fee for camping. Open June through October, weather permitting.

Directions: From Truckee, turn north on Highway 89 and drive 20 miles to Sierraville. At Sierraville, turn left on Highway 49 and drive about 10 miles to the Bassetts Store. Turn right on Gold Lake Road and drive five miles to the campground on the left.

Contact: Tahoe National Forest, Yuba River Ranger District, North, 530/288-3231, fax 530/288-0727; California Land Management, 530/587-9281 or 650/322-1181.

25 DIABLO

Scenic rating: 8

on Packer Creek in Tahoe National Forest

Map grid A1

This is a developed camping area set on Packer Creek, about two miles from Packer Lake. This area is extremely beautiful with several lakes nearby, including the Sardine Lakes and Packer Lake, and this camp provides an overflow area when the more developed campgrounds have filled.

RV sites, facilities: There are eight sites for tents or RVs up to 30 feet (no hookups). Picnic tables and fire rings are provided. Vault toilets are available. No drinking water is available. Supplies are available in Bassetts and Sierra City. Leashed pets are permitted.

Reservations, fees: Reservations are accepted at 877/444-6777 or www.recreation.gov ($10 reservation fee). Sites are $16 per night, $5 per night for each additional vehicle. Open June through October, weather permitting.

Directions: From Truckee, turn north on Highway 89 and drive 20 miles to Sierraville. At Sierraville, turn left on Highway 49 and drive about 10 miles to the Bassetts Store. Turn right on Gold Lake Road and drive 1.5 miles to Packer Lake Road. Turn left, drive a short distance, bear right at the fork, and drive one mile to the campground on the right side of the road.

Contact: Tahoe National Forest, Yuba River Ranger District, North, 530/288-3231, fax 530/288-0727; California Land Management, 530/587-9281 or 650/322-1181.

26 SALMON CREEK

Scenic rating: 9

in Tahoe National Forest

Map grid A1

This campground is set at the confluence of Packer and Salmon Creeks, at 5,800 feet elevation, with easy access off the Gold Lakes Highway. It is near the Lakes Basin Recreation Area, with literally dozens of small lakes within five miles, plus great hiking, fishing, and low-speed boating.

RV sites, facilities: There are 31 sites for tents or RVs up to 30 feet (no hookups). Picnic tables and fire grills are provided. Drinking water and vault toilets are available. Supplies and a coin laundry are available in Sierra City. Leashed pets are permitted.

Reservations, fees: Reservations are accepted at 877/444-6777 or www.recreation.gov ($10 reservation fee). Sites are $20 per night, $5 per night for each additional vehicle. Open June through October.

Directions: From Truckee, turn north on Highway 89 and drive 20 miles to Sierraville and Highway 49. Turn left on Highway 49 and drive about 10 miles to the Bassetts Store and Gold Lake Road. Turn right on Gold Lake Road and drive two miles to the campground on the left side of the road.

Contact: Tahoe National Forest, Yuba River Ranger District, North, 530/288-3231, fax 530/288-0727; California Land Management, 530/587-9281 or 650/322-1181.

27 SARDINE LAKE

Scenic rating: 8

in Tahoe National Forest
Map grid A1   BEST

Lower Sardine Lake is a jewel set below the Sierra Buttes, one of the prettiest settings in California. The campground is actually about a mile east of the lake. Nearby is beautiful Sand Pond Interpretive Trail. A great hike is routed along the shore of Lower Sardine Lake to a hidden waterfall (in spring) that feeds the lake, and ambitious hikers can explore beyond and discover Upper Sardine Lake. Trout fishing is excellent in Lower Sardine Lake, with a primitive boat ramp available for small boats. The speed limit and small size of the lake keeps boaters slow and quiet. A small marina and boat rentals are available.

RV sites, facilities: There are 29 sites for tents or RVs up to 22 feet (no hookups). Picnic tables and fire grills are provided. Drinking water and vault toilets are available. Some facilities are wheelchair-accessible. Limited supplies are available at the Sardine Lake Lodge or in Bassetts. Leashed pets are permitted.

Reservations, fees: Reservations are accepted at 877/444-6777 or www.recreation.gov ($10 reservation fee). Sites are $20 per night, $5 per night for each additional vehicle, $40 per night for double sites. Open June through October, weather permitting.

Directions: From Truckee, drive north on Highway 89 for 20 miles to Sierraville. Turn left on Highway 49 and drive about 10 miles to the Bassetts Store. Turn right on Gold Lake Road and drive 1.5 miles to Packer Lake Road. Turn left, drive a short distance, then bear left at the fork (signed) and drive 0.5 mile to the campground on the left.

Contact: Tahoe National Forest, Yuba River Ranger District, North, 530/288-3231, fax 530/288-0727.

28 CHAPMAN CREEK

Scenic rating: 8

on the North Yuba River in Tahoe National Forest
Map grid A1

This campground is set along Chapman Creek at 6,000 feet, just across the highway from where it enters the North Yuba River. A good side trip is to hike Chapman Creek Trail, which leads out of camp to Beartrap Meadow or to Haskell Peak (8,107 feet).

RV sites, facilities: There are 29 sites for tents or RVs up to 22 feet (no hookups). Picnic tables and fire grills are provided. Drinking water and vault toilets are available. Supplies are available in Bassetts. Leashed pets are permitted.

Reservations, fees: Reservations are not accepted. Sites are $20 per night, $5 per night for each additional vehicle. Open June through October, weather permitting.

Directions: From Truckee, turn north on Highway 89 and drive 20 miles to Sierraville. At Sierraville, turn left on Highway 49, drive over Yuba Pass, and continue for four miles to the campground on the right.

Contact: Tahoe National Forest, Yuba River

Ranger District, North, 530/288-3231, fax 530/288-0727; California Land Management, 530/587-9281 or 650/322-1181.

29 SIERRA

Scenic rating: 7

on the North Yuba River in Tahoe National Forest

Map grid A1

This is an easy-to-reach spot set along the North Yuba River, used primarily as an overflow area from nearby Chapman Creek (a mile upstream). Nearby recreation options include Chapman Creek Trail, several waterfalls (see the Wild Plum listing in this chapter), and the nearby Lakes Basin Recreation Area to the north off the Gold Lake Highway. The elevation is 5,600 feet. Note: Bring your own drinking water.

RV sites, facilities: There are 16 sites for tents or RVs up to 22 feet (no hookups). Picnic tables and fire rings are provided. Vault toilets are available. No drinking water is available. Supplies are available in Bassetts. Leashed pets are permitted.

Reservations, fees: Reservations are accepted at 877/444-6777 or www.recreation.gov ($10 reservation fee). Sites are $16 per night, $5 per night for each additional vehicle. Open June through October, weather permitting.

Directions: From Truckee, turn north on Highway 89 and drive 20 miles to Sierraville. At Sierraville, turn left on Highway 49 and drive over Yuba Pass. Continue for five miles to the campground on the left side of the road.

Contact: Tahoe National Forest, Yuba River Ranger District, North, 530/288-3231, fax 530/288-0727; California Land Management, 530/587-9281 or 650/322-1181.

30 YUBA PASS

Scenic rating: 6

in Tahoe National Forest

Map grid A1

This camp is set right at Yuba Pass at an elevation of 6,700 feet. In the winter, the surrounding area is a Sno-Park, which gives it an unusual look in summer. Yuba Pass is a popular bird-watching area in the summer.

RV sites, facilities: There are 20 sites for tents or RVs up to 22 feet (no hookups). Picnic tables and fire grills are provided. Vault toilets are available. There is no drinking water. Supplies are available at Bassetts. Leashed pets are permitted.

Reservations, fees: Reservations are accepted at 877/444-6777 or www.recreation.gov ($10 reservation fee). Sites are $20 per night, $5 per night for each additional vehicle. Open late June through October, weather permitting.

Directions: From Truckee, drive north on Highway 89 past Sattley to the junction with Highway 49. Turn west on Highway 49 and drive about six miles to the campground on the left side of the road.

Contact: Tahoe National Forest, Yuba River Ranger District, North, 530/288-3231, fax 530/288-0727; California Land Management, 530/587-9281 or 650/322-1181.

31 CARLTON/CAL-IDA

Scenic rating: 7

on the North Yuba River in Tahoe National Forest

Map grid A1

Carlton is on the North Yuba River, and Cal-Ida is across the road. Both are right next door to Fiddle Creek.

RV sites, facilities: There are 30 sites at Carlton and 20 sites at Cal-Ida for tents or RVs up to 28 feet (no hookups). Picnic tables and fire grills are provided. Drinking water and vault toilets are available. Some facilities are wheelchair-accessible. Some supplies are available at the Indian Valley Outpost nearby. Leashed pets are permitted.

Reservations, fees: Reservations are accepted at 877/444-6777 or www.recreation.gov ($10 reservation fee). Sites are $20 per night, $5 per night for each additional vehicle. Open mid-April through November, weather permitting.

Directions: From Auburn, take Highway 49 north to Nevada City and continue on Highway 49 (the road jogs left, then narrows) to Camptonville. Continue northeast for nine miles to the campground entrance. The camping area at Carlton is one mile northeast of the Highway 49 bridge at Indian Valley. The camping area at Cal-Ida is just east of the Indian Valley Outpost on the Cal-Ida Road.

Contact: Tahoe National Forest, Yuba River Ranger District, North, 530/288-3231, fax 530/288-0727; California Land Management, 530/587-9281 or 650/322-1181.

32 INDIAN VALLEY

Scenic rating: 7

on the North Yuba River in Tahoe National Forest
Map grid A1

This is an easy-to-reach spot set at 2,200 feet beside the North Yuba River. Highway 49 runs adjacent to the Yuba River for miles eastward, providing easy access to the river in many areas. There are several other campgrounds in the immediate area (see the listing in this chapter for Cal-Ida, found within a mile).

RV sites, facilities: There are 17 sites for tents or RVs up to 22 feet (no hookups). Picnic tables and fire grills are provided. Drinking water and vault toilets are available. Limited supplies are available nearby at the Indian Valley Outpost. Some facilities are wheelchair-accessible. Leashed pets are permitted.

Reservations, fees: Reservations are accepted at 877/444-6777 or www.recreation.gov ($10 reservation fee). Sites are $20 per night, $5 per night for each additional vehicle. Open year-round.

Directions: From Auburn, take Highway 49 north to Nevada City and continue on Highway 49 (the road jogs left, then narrows) to Camptonville. Drive 10 miles to the camp entrance on the right.

Contact: Tahoe National Forest, Yuba River Ranger District, North, 530/288-3231, fax

530/288-0727; California Land Management, 530/587-9281 or 650/322-1181.

33 ROCKY REST

Scenic rating: 7

on the North Yuba River in Tahoe National Forest
Map grid A1

This is one in a series of campgrounds set at streamside on the North Yuba River. The elevation is 2,200 feet. A footbridge crosses the North Yuba River and provides an outstanding seven-mile hike.

RV sites, facilities: There are 10 dispersed camping sites for tents and RVs up to 16 feet (no hookups). Picnic tables and fire grills are provided. Drinking water and vault toilets are available. Limited supplies are nearby at the Indian Valley Outpost. Some facilities are wheelchair-accessible. Leashed pets are permitted.

Reservations, fees: Reservations are accepted at 877/444-6777 or www.recreation.gov ($10 reservation fee). Sites are $20 per night, $5 per night for each additional vehicle. Open mid-April through November, weather permitting.

Directions: From Auburn, take Highway 49 north to Nevada City and continue (the road jogs left, then narrows) to Camptonville. Continue on Highway 49 for 10 miles to the campground entrance on the right.

Contact: Tahoe National Forest, Yuba River Ranger District, North, 530/288-3231, fax 530/288-0727; California Land Management, 530/587-9281 or 650/322-1181.

34 RAMSHORN

Scenic rating: 7

on the North Yuba River in Tahoe National Forest
Map grid A1

This camp is set on Ramshorn Creek, just across the road from the North Yuba River. It's one in a series of camps on this stretch of the beautiful North Yuba River. One mile east is a well-known access point for white-water rafting trips on the Yuba. The camp's elevation is 2,200 feet.

RV sites, facilities: There are 16 sites for tents or RVs up to 22 feet (no hookups). Picnic tables and fire grills are provided. Vault toilets and drinking water are available. Supplies are available in Downieville. Leashed pets are permitted.

Reservations, fees: Reservations are accepted at 877/444-6777 or www.recreation.gov ($10 reservation fee). Sites are $20 per night, $5 per night for each additional vehicle per night. Open year-round.

Directions: From Auburn, take Highway 49 north to Nevada City and continue on Highway 49 (the road jogs left, then narrows) to Camptonville. Drive 15 miles north to the campground entrance on the left.

Contact: Tahoe National Forest, Yuba River Ranger District, North, 530/288-3231, fax 530/288-0727; California Land Management, 530/587-9281 or 650/322-1181.

35 UNION FLAT

Scenic rating: 8

on the North Yuba River in Tahoe National Forest

Map grid A1

Of all the campgrounds on the North Yuba River along Highway 49, this one has the best swimming. The camp has a nice swimming hole next to it, and the water is cold. Recreational mining is also an attraction here. The elevation is 3,400 feet.

RV sites, facilities: There are 11 sites for tents or RVs up to 35 feet (no hookups). Picnic tables and fire grills are provided. Drinking water and vault toilets are available. Some facilities are wheelchair-accessible. Supplies are available in Downieville. Leashed pets are permitted.

Reservations, fees: Reservations are accepted at 877/444-6777 or www.recreation.gov ($10 reservation fee). Sites are $20 per night, $5 per night for each additional vehicle, $40 for double sites. Open May through October, weather permitting.

Directions: From Auburn, take Highway 49 north to Nevada City and continue (the road jogs left, then narrows) to Downieville. Drive six miles east to the campground entrance on the right.

Contact: Tahoe National Forest, Yuba River Ranger District, North, 530/288-3231, fax 530/288-0727; California Land Management, 530/587-9281 or 650/322-1181.

36 LOGANVILLE

Scenic rating: 8

on the North Yuba River in Tahoe National Forest

Map grid A1

Sierra City is only two miles away, meaning you can make a quick getaway for a prepared meal or any food or drink you may need to add to your camp. Loganville is set on the North Yuba River, elevation 4,200 feet. It offers a good stretch of water in this region for trout fishing, with many pools set below miniature waterfalls.

RV sites, facilities: There are 20 sites for tents or RVs up to 22 feet (no hookups). Picnic tables and fire grills are provided. Drinking water and vault toilets are available. Supplies and a coin laundry are available in Sierra City. Leashed pets are permitted.

Reservations, fees: Reservations are accepted at 877/444-6777 or www.recreation.gov ($10 reservation fee). Sites are $20 per night, $5 per night for each additional vehicle. Open May through October, weather permitting.

Directions: From Auburn, take Highway 49 north to Nevada City and continue on Highway 49 (the road jogs left, then narrows) to Downieville. Drive 12 miles east to the campground entrance on the right (two miles west of Sierra City).

Contact: Tahoe National Forest, Yuba River Ranger District, North, 530/288-3231, fax 530/288-0727; California Land Management, 530/587-9281 or 650/322-1181.

37 WILD PLUM

Scenic rating: 8

on Haypress Creek in Tahoe National Forest

Map grid A1

This popular Forest Service campground is set on Haypress Creek at 4,400 feet. There are several hidden waterfalls in the area, which makes this a popular camp for the people who know of them. There's a scenic hike up Haypress Trail, which goes past a waterfall to Haypress Valley. Two other nearby waterfalls are Loves Falls (on the North Yuba on Highway 49 two miles east of Sierra City) and Hackmans Falls (remote, set in a ravine one mile south of Sierra City; no road access).

RV sites, facilities: There are 44 sites for tents or RVs up to 22 feet (no hookups). Picnic tables, food lockers, and fire grills are provided. Drinking water and vault toilets are available. Supplies and a coin laundry are available in Sierra City. Leashed pets are permitted.

Reservations, fees: Reservations are accepted at 877/444-6777 or www.recreation.gov ($10 reservation fee). Sites are $20 per night, $5 per night for each additional vehicle. Open May through October, weather permitting.

Directions: From Auburn, take Highway 49 north to Nevada City and continue (the road jogs left, then narrows) past Downieville to Sierra City at Wild Plum Road. Turn right on Wild Plum Road and drive two miles to the campground entrance road on the right.

Contact: Tahoe National Forest, Yuba River Ranger District, North, 530/288-3231, fax 530/288-0727; California Land Management, 530/587-9281 or 650/322-1181.

38 COLD CREEK

Scenic rating: 8

in Tahoe National Forest

Map grid A1

There are four small campgrounds along Highway 89 between Sierraville and Truckee, all within close range of side trips to Webber Lake, Independence Lake, and Sierra Hot Springs in Sierraville. Cold Creek is set just upstream of the confluence of Cottonwood Creek and Cold Creek, at 5,800 feet elevation.

RV sites, facilities: There are 13 sites for tents or RVs up to 22 feet (no hookups). Picnic tables and fire rings are provided. Vault toilets are available. There is no drinking water. Supplies are available in Sierraville. Leashed pets are permitted.

Reservations, fees: Reservations are accepted at 877/444-6777 or www.recreation.gov ($10 reservation fee). Sites are $12 per night, $5 per night for each additional vehicle. Open May through October.

Directions: From Truckee, drive north on Highway 89 for about 20 miles to the campground on the left side of the road. If you reach Sierraville, you have gone five miles too far.

Contact: Tahoe National Forest, Sierraville Ranger District, 530/994-3401, fax 530/994-3143; California Land Management, 530/587-9281 or 650/322-1181.

39 COTTONWOOD CREEK

Scenic rating: 7

in Tahoe National Forest

Map grid A1

This camp sits beside Cottonwood Creek at 5,800 feet elevation. An interpretive trail starts at the upper camp and makes a short loop, and there are several nearby side-trip options, including trout fishing on the Little Truckee River to the nearby south, visiting the Sierra Hot Springs out of Sierraville to the nearby north, or venturing into the surrounding Tahoe National Forest.

RV sites, facilities: There are 46 sites for tents or RVs up to 22 feet (no hookups). Picnic tables and fire rings are provided. Drinking water and vault toilets are available. Supplies are available in Sierraville. Some facilities are wheelchair-accessible. Leashed pets are permitted.

Reservations, fees: Reservations are accepted at 877/444-6777 or www.recreation.gov ($10

CALIFORNIA

reservation fee). Sites are $16 per night, $5 per night for each additional vehicle. Open mid-May through early October, weather permitting.

Directions: From Truckee, drive north on Highway 89 for about 20 miles to the campground entrance road on the right (0.5 mile past Cold Creek Camp).

Contact: Tahoe National Forest, Sierraville Ranger District, 530/994-3401, fax 530/994-3143; California Land Management, 530/587-9281 or 650/322-1181.

40 BEAR VALLEY

Scenic rating: 7

on Bear Valley Creek in Tahoe National Forest

Map grid A1

The surrounding national forest land was largely burned by the historic Cottonwood Fire of 1994, but the camp itself was saved. It is at 6,700 feet elevation, with a spring adjacent to the campground. The road leading southeast out of camp is routed to Sardine Peak Look-Out (8,134 feet), where there is a dramatic view of the region. There is an 18-mile loop OHV trail across the road from the campground.

RV sites, facilities: There are 10 sites for tents or RVs up to 16 feet (no hookups). Picnic tables and fire rings are provided. Vault toilets are available. There is no drinking water. Garbage must be packed out. Supplies are available in Sierraville. Leashed pets are permitted.

Reservations, fees: Reservations are not accepted. There is no fee for camping. Open May through October, weather permitting.

Directions: From Truckee, drive north on Highway 89 about 17 miles. Turn right on County Road 451 and drive northeast about six miles to the campground entrance on the right.

Contact: Tahoe National Forest, Sierraville Ranger District, 530/994-3401, fax 530/994-3143.

41 LOOKOUT

Scenic rating: 4

in Humboldt-Toiyabe National Forest

Map grid A1

This primitive camp is set in remote country near the California/Nevada border at 6,700 feet elevation. It is a former mining site, and the highlight here is a quartz crystal mine a short distance from the campground. Stampede Lake provides a side-trip option, about 10 miles to the southwest, over the rough dirt Henness Pass Road.

RV sites, facilities: There are 18 sites for tents or RVs up to 35 feet (no hookups), and a group site for up to 16 people. Picnic tables and fire grills are provided. Vault toilets are available. There is no drinking water. Garbage must be packed out. Leashed pets are permitted.

Reservations, fees: Reservations are accepted for individual sites and are required for the group site at 775/882-2766. Sites are $6 per night and the group site is $25 per night. Open June through September.

Directions: From Truckee on I-80, drive east across the state line into Nevada to Verdi. Take the Verdi exit and drive north through town to Bridge Street and then to Old Dog Valley Road. Drive north on Old Dog Valley Road for 11 miles to the campground.

Contact: Humboldt-Toiyabe National Forest, Carson Ranger District, 775/882-2766, fax 775/884-8199.

42 LITTLE LASIER MEADOWS EQUESTRIAN

Scenic rating: 7

near Jackson Meadows Reservoir

Map grid A1

This is the best camp in the area for those with horses. Little Lasier Meadows has open sites in the forest, adjacent to a meadow, and has a horse corral. Best of all, there is direct access to the Pacific Crest Trail. Nearby Jackson

Meadows Reservoir is very pretty and provides boating, fishing, and swimming.

RV sites, facilities: There are 11 sites for tents or RVs. Drinking water and vault toilets are available. Picnic tables, fire rings, horse corrals, and tie rails are provided. Water for horses is available.

Reservations, fees: Reservations are required ($10 reservation fee) at 877/444-6777 or recreation.gov. Sites are $20, $5 each additional vehicle per night. Open year-round, weather permitting.

Directions: From Truckee, drive north 17.5 miles on Highway 89 to Forest Road 7/Fiberboard Road. Turn left and drive 15 miles to the East Meadows turnoff. Cross the metal bridge and take the first left turn. Drive approximately two miles to the campground.

Contact: Tahoe National Forest, Truckee Ranger District, 530/587-3558, fax 530/587-6914; California Land Management, 530/587-9281.

43 SILVER TIP GROUP CAMP

Scenic rating: 7

at Jackson Meadow Reservoir in
Tahoe National Forest

Map grid A1

This group camp is set on the southwest edge of Jackson Meadow Reservoir at 6,100 feet elevation, in a pretty area with pine forest, high meadows, and the trademark granite look of the Sierra Nevada. A boat ramp and swimming beach are nearby at Woodcamp. (For more information, see the Woodcamp listing in this chapter.)

RV sites, facilities: There are two group sites for tents or RVs up to 22 feet (no hookups) that can accommodate up to 25 people each. Picnic tables and fire rings are provided. Drinking water and vault toilets are available. Obtain supplies in Truckee or Sierraville. A boat ramp is nearby. Leashed pets are permitted.

Reservations, fees: Reservations are required at 877/444-6777 or www.recreation.gov ($10 reservation fee). The camps are $72 per night. Open June through October, weather permitting.

Directions: From Truckee, drive north on Highway 89 for 17 miles to Forest Road 7. Turn left on Forest Road 7 and drive 16 miles to Jackson Meadow Reservoir. At the lake, continue across the dam around the west shoreline and then turn left at the campground access road. The entrance is on the right just after the Woodcamp campground.

Contact: Tahoe National Forest, Sierraville Ranger District, 530/994-3401, fax 530/994-3143; California Land Management, 530/587-9281 or 650/322-1181.

44 WOODCAMP

Scenic rating: 7

at Jackson Meadow Reservoir in
Tahoe National Forest

Map grid A1

Woodcamp and Pass Creek are the best camps for boaters at Jackson Meadow Reservoir because each is directly adjacent to a boat ramp. That is critical because fishing is far better by boat here than from shore, with a good mix of both rainbow and brown trout. The camp is set at 6,700 feet elevation along the lake's southwest shore, in a pretty spot with a swimming beach and short interpretive hiking trail nearby. All water sports are allowed. This is a beautiful lake in the Sierra Nevada, complete with pine forest and a classic granite backdrop.

RV sites, facilities: There are 20 sites for tents or RVs up to 22 feet (no hookups). Picnic tables and fire rings are provided. Drinking water, flush and vault toilets, food lockers, and firewood (fee) are available. Supplies are available in Truckee or Sierraville. A boat ramp is adjacent to the camp and a dump station is nearby. Leashed pets are permitted.

Reservations, fees: Reservations are accepted at 877/444-6777 or www.recreation.gov ($10 reservation fee). Sites are $20 per night, $5 per night for each additional vehicle. Open June through October, weather permitting.

Directions: From Truckee, drive north on Highway 89 for 17 miles to Forest Road 7. Turn left on Forest Road 7 and drive 16 miles to Jackson Meadow Reservoir. At the lake, continue across the dam around the west shoreline and then turn left at the campground access road. The entrance is on the right just before the Woodcamp boat ramp.

Contact: Tahoe National Forest, Sierraville Ranger District, 530/994-3401, fax 530/994-3143; California Land Management, 530/587-9281 or 650/322-1181.

45 FIR TOP

Scenic rating: 7

at Jackson Meadow Reservoir in
Tahoe National Forest

Map grid A1

Jackson Meadow is a great destination for a short vacation, and that's why there are so many campgrounds available; it's not exactly a secret. This camp is set above the lake, less than a mile from a boat ramp near Woodcamp. (See the Woodcamp and Pass Creek listings in this chapter for more information.) The elevation is 6,200 feet.

RV sites, facilities: There are 14 sites for tents or RVs up to 22 feet (no hookups). Picnic tables and fire rings are provided. Drinking water, flush and vault toilets, and food lockers are available. Supplies are available in Truckee or Sierraville. Leashed pets are permitted.

Reservations, fees: Reservations are accepted at 877/444-6777 or www.recreation.gov ($10 reservation fee). Sites are $20 per night, $5 per night for each additional vehicle. Open June through November, weather permitting.

Directions: From Truckee, drive north on Highway 89 for 17.5 miles to Forest Road 7. Turn left on Forest Road 7 and drive 16 miles to Jackson Meadow Reservoir. Continue across the dam and around the lake to the west side. Turn left at the campground access road. The campground entrance is on the right across from the entrance to the Woodcamp Picnic Area.

Contact: Tahoe National Forest, Sierraville Ranger District, 530/994-3401, fax 530/994-3143; California Land Management, 530/587-9281 or 650/322-1181.

46 FINDLEY

Scenic rating: 7

at Jackson Meadow Reservoir in
Tahoe National Forest

Map grid A1

Findley is set near Woodcamp Creek, 0.25 mile from where it pours into Jackson Meadow Reservoir. Though it is not a lakeside camp, it is quite pretty just the same, and within a mile of the boat ramp near Woodcamp. It is set at 6,300 feet elevation. This is one of several camps at the lake.

RV sites, facilities: There are 14 sites for tents or RVs up to 22 feet (no hookups). Picnic tables and fire rings are provided. Drinking water, flush and vault toilets, and food lockers are available. Supplies are available in Truckee or Sierraville. A boat ramp is nearby. Some facilities are wheelchair-accessible. Leashed pets are permitted.

Reservations, fees: Reservations are accepted at 877/444-6777 or www.recreation.gov ($10 reservation fee). Sites are $20 per night, $5 per night for each additional vehicle, $40 for double sites. Open May through October.

Directions: From Truckee, drive north on Highway 89 for 17 miles to Forest Road 7. Turn left on Forest Road 7 and drive 16 miles to Jackson Meadow Reservoir. Continue across the dam around the lake to the west side. Turn left at the campground access road and drive about 0.25 mile to the entrance on the left.

Contact: Tahoe National Forest, Sierraville Ranger District, 530/994-3401, fax 530/994-3143; California Land Management, 530/587-9281 or 650/322-1181.

CALIFORNIA

47 PASS CREEK

Scenic rating: 7

at Jackson Meadow Reservoir in
Tahoe National Forest

Map grid A1

This is the premium campground at Jackson Meadow Reservoir, a developed site with water, concrete boat ramp, swimming beach nearby at Aspen Creek Picnic Area, and access to the Pacific Crest Trail 0.5 mile to the east (you'll pass it on the way in). This lake has the trademark look of the high Sierra, and the bonus here is that lake levels are often kept higher than at other reservoirs on the western slopes of the Sierra Nevada. Trout stocks are excellent, with rainbow and brown trout planted each summer after ice-out. The elevation is 6,100 feet.

RV sites, facilities: There are 30 sites for tents or RVs up to 22 feet (no hookups). Picnic tables and fire rings are provided. Drinking water, flush and vault toilets, and food lockers are available. A dump station is nearby. A boat ramp is nearby. Supplies are available in Truckee or Sierraville. Leashed pets are permitted.

Reservations, fees: Reservations are accepted at 877/444-6777 or www.recreation.gov ($10 reservation fee). Sites are $20 per night, $5 per night for each additional vehicle. Open May through October, weather permitting.

Directions: From Truckee, drive north on Highway 89 for 17 miles to Forest Road 7. Turn left on Forest Road 7 and drive 16 miles to Jackson Meadow Reservoir; the campground is on the left at the north end of the lake.

Contact: Tahoe National Forest, Sierraville Ranger District, 530/994-3401, fax 530/994-3143; California Land Management, 530/587-9281 or 650/322-1181.

48 EAST MEADOW

Scenic rating: 7

at Jackson Meadow Reservoir in
Tahoe National Forest

Map grid A1

This camp is in a beautiful setting on the northeast side of Jackson Meadow Reservoir, on the edge of a sheltered cove. The Pacific Crest Trail passes right by camp, providing access for a day trip, though no stellar destinations are on this stretch of the PCT. The nearest boat ramp is at Pass Creek, two miles away. The elevation is 6,200 feet.

RV sites, facilities: There are 46 sites for tents or RVs up to 40 feet (no hookups). Picnic tables and fire rings are provided. Drinking water, flush and vault toilets, food lockers, and firewood (fee) are available. A dump station and boat ramp are near Pass Creek. Supplies are available in Truckee or Sierraville. Some facilities are wheelchair-accessible. Leashed pets are permitted.

Reservations, fees: Reservations are accepted at 877/444-6777 or www.recreation.gov ($10 reservation fee). The fee is $20 per night, $5 per night for each additional vehicle, $40 per night for double sites. Open May through October, weather permitting.

Directions: From Truckee, drive north on Highway 89 for 17 miles to Forest Road 7. Turn left on Forest Road 7 and drive 15 miles to the campground entrance road on the left (if you reach Pass Creek, you have gone too far). Turn left and drive a mile to the campground on the right.

Contact: Tahoe National Forest, Sierraville Ranger District, 530/994-3401, fax 530/994-3143; California Land Management, 530/587-9281 or 650/322-1181.

CALIFORNIA

49 ASPEN GROUP CAMP

Scenic rating: 7

at Jackson Meadow Reservoir in
Tahoe National Forest

Map grid A1

A boat ramp and easy access to adjacent Jackson Meadow Reservoir make this a premium group camp. The elevation is 6,100 feet.

RV sites, facilities: There are three group sites for tents or RVs up to 40 feet (no hookups) that can accommodate 25–50 people each. Picnic tables and fire grills are provided. Drinking water, vault toilets, food lockers, firewood (fee), and a campfire circle are available. A dump station is nearby. There is a boat ramp nearby at Pass Creek. Supplies are available in Truckee or Sierraville. Leashed pets are permitted.

Reservations, fees: Reservations are required at 877/444-6777 or www.recreation.gov ($10 reservation fee). Sites are $62–122 per night. Open mid-May through October, weather permitting.

Directions: From Truckee, drive north on Highway 89 for 17.5 miles to Forest Road 7. Turn left on Forest Road 7 and drive 16 miles (a mile past Pass Creek) to the campground entrance on the right.

Contact: Tahoe National Forest, Sierraville Ranger District, 530/994-3401, fax 530/994-3143; California Land Management, 530/587-9281 or 650/322-1181.

50 UPPER LITTLE TRUCKEE

Scenic rating: 7

on the Little Truckee River in Tahoe National Forest

Map grid A1

This camp is set along the Little Truckee River at 6,100 feet. The Little Truckee is a pretty trout stream, with easy access not only from this campground, but also from another three miles northward along Highway 89, then from another seven miles to the west along Forest Road 7, the route to Webber Lake. It is only about a 10-minute drive from this camp to reach Stampede Lake to the east.

RV sites, facilities: There are 26 sites for tents or RVs up to 30 feet (no hookups). Picnic tables and fire rings are provided. Drinking water and vault toilets are available. Supplies are available in Sierraville. Leashed pets are permitted.

Reservations, fees: Reservations are accepted at 877/444-6777 or www.recreation.gov ($10 reservation fee). Sites are $16 per night, $5 per night for each additional vehicle. Open mid-May through October, weather permitting.

Directions: From Truckee, drive north on Highway 89 for about 11 miles to the campground on the left, a short distance beyond Lower Little Truckee Camp.

Contact: Tahoe National Forest, Sierraville Ranger District, 530/994-3401, fax 530/994-3143; California Land Management, 530/587-9281 or 650/322-1181.

51 LOWER LITTLE TRUCKEE

Scenic rating: 7

on the Little Truckee River in Tahoe National Forest

Map grid A1

This pretty camp is set along Highway 89 and the Little Truckee River at 6,200 feet. (For more information, see the Upper Little Truckee listing in this chapter.)

RV sites, facilities: There are 15 sites for tents or RVs up to 20 feet (no hookups). Picnic tables and fire grills are provided. Drinking water and vault toilets are available. Supplies are available in Sierraville or Truckee. Leashed pets are permitted.

Reservations, fees: Reservations are accepted at 877/444-6777 or www.recreation.gov ($10 reservation fee). Sites are $16 per night, $5 per night for each additional vehicle. Open May through October, weather permitting.

Directions: From Truckee, drive north on Highway 89 for about 12 miles to the campground on the left. If you reach Upper Little Truckee Camp, you have gone 0.5 mile too far.

Contact: Tahoe National Forest, Sierraville Ranger District, 530/994-3401, fax 530/994-3143; California Land Management, 530/587-9281 or 650/322-1181.

CALIFORNIA

52 FAUCHERIE LAKE GROUP CAMP

Scenic rating: 7

near Bowman Lake in Tahoe National Forest

Map grid A1

Faucherie Lake is the kind of place that most people believe can be reached only by long, difficult hikes with a backpack. Guess again: Here it is, set in Sierra granite at 6,100 feet elevation, quiet and pristine, a classic alpine lake. It is ideal for car-top boating and has decent fishing for both rainbow and brown trout. The boating speed limit is 10 mph. This is a group camp on the lake's northern shore, a prime spot, with the outlet creek nearby. Note: Road washouts may require four-wheel drive.

RV sites, facilities: There is one group camp for tents or RVs up to 22 feet (no hookups) that can accommodate up to 25 people. Picnic tables and fire grills are provided. Vault toilets are available. No drinking water is available. Garbage must be packed out. A boat ramp is nearby. Leashed pets are permitted.

Reservations, fees: Reservations are required at 877/444-6777 or www.recreation.gov ($10 reservation fee). The camp is $55 per night. Open June through October, weather permitting.

Directions: From Sacramento, drive east on I-80 past Emigrant Gap to Highway 20. Turn west on Highway 20 and drive to Bowman Road/ Forest Road 18. Turn right and drive about 16 miles (much of the road is quite rough) to Bowman Lake and continue four miles to a Y. Bear right at the Y and drive about three miles to the campground at the end of the road.

Contact: Tahoe National Forest, Yuba River Ranger District, South, 530/265-4531, fax 530/478-6109; Big Bend Visitor Center, 530/426-3609, fax 530/426-1744.

53 CANYON CREEK

Scenic rating: 6

near Faucherie Lake in Tahoe National Forest

Map grid A1

This pretty spot is at 6,000 feet elevation in Tahoe National Forest, a mile from Sawmill Lake (which you pass on the way in) and a mile from pretty Faucherie Lake. It is set along Canyon Creek, the stream that connects those two lakes. Of the two, Faucherie provides better fishing and, because of that, there are fewer people at Sawmill. Take your pick. A trailhead is available at the north end of Sawmill Lake with a hike to several small alpine lakes, a great day or overnight backpacking trip.

RV sites, facilities: There are 20 sites for tents or RVs up to 16 feet (no hookups). Picnic tables and fire grills are provided. Vault toilets are available. No drinking water is available. Garbage must be packed out. Leashed pets are permitted.

Reservations, fees: Reservations are not accepted. There is no fee for camping. Open June through October, weather permitting.

Directions: From Sacramento, drive east on I-80 to Emigrant Gap. Take the off-ramp and head north on the short connector road to Highway 20. Turn west on Highway 20 and drive four miles to Bowman Road/Forest Road 18. Turn right and drive about 16 miles (nine of these miles are paved, but the rest is quite rough) to Bowman Lake and continue four miles to a Y. Bear right at the Y and drive about two miles to the campground on the right side of the road. (Occasionally the access route requires a four-wheel-drive vehicle.)

Contact: Tahoe National Forest, Yuba River Ranger District, South, 530/265-4531, fax 530/478-6109; Big Bend Visitor Center, 530/426-3609, fax 530/426-1744.

54 SAGEHEN CREEK

Scenic rating: 7

in Tahoe National Forest

Map grid A1

This is a small, primitive camp set at 6,500 feet beside little Sagehen Creek, just north of a miniature mountain range called the Sagehen Hills, which top out at 7,707 feet. Sagehen Creek provides an option when the camps along Highway 89 and at Stampede, Boca, and Prosser Creek have filled. In the fall, it is popular with campers as a base camp.

RV sites, facilities: There are 10 sites for tents or RVs up to 16 feet (no hookups). Picnic tables and fire grills are provided. Vault toilets are available. No drinking water is available. Garbage must be packed out. Leashed pets are permitted.

Reservations, fees: Reservations are not accepted. There is no fee for camping. Open mid-May to mid-October, weather permitting.

Directions: From Truckee, drive 8.5 miles north on Highway 89 to Sagehen Summit Road on the left. Turn left and drive four miles to the campground.

Contact: Tahoe National Forest, Truckee Ranger District, 530/587-3558, fax 530/587-6914.

55 LOGGER

Scenic rating: 7

at Stampede Lake in Tahoe National Forest

Map grid A1

Covering 3,400 acres and with 25 miles of shoreline, Stampede Lake is a huge lake by Sierra standards—the largest in the region after Lake Tahoe. It is set at 6,000 feet, surrounded by Sierra granite mountains and pines, and is big, and on days when the wind is down, quite beautiful. The campground is also huge, set along the lake's southern shore, a few minutes' drive from the Captain Roberts boat ramp. This camp is ideal for campers, boaters, and anglers. The lake is becoming one of the top fishing lakes in California for kokanee salmon (which can be caught only by trolling), and it also has some large Mackinaw trout and a sprinkling of planter-sized rainbow trout. All water sports are allowed. One problem at Stampede is receding water levels from midsummer through fall, a real pain, which puts the campsites some distance from the lake. Even when the lake is full, there are only a few "lakeside" campsites. However, the boat ramp has been extended to assist boaters during drawdowns.

RV sites, facilities: There are 252 sites for tents or RVs up to 32 feet (no hookups). Picnic tables and fire rings are provided. Drinking water, vault toilets, and a dump station are available. A concrete boat ramp is available one mile from camp. Some facilities are wheelchair-accessible. Leashed pets are permitted.

Reservations, fees: Reservations are accepted at 877/444-6777 or www.recreation.gov ($10 reservation fee). Sites are $20 per night, $5 per night for each additional vehicle. Open May through October.

Directions: From Truckee, drive east on I-80 for seven miles to the Boca-Hirschdale/County Road 270 exit. Take that exit and drive north on County Road 270 for about seven miles (past Boca Reservoir) to the junction with County Road S261 on the left. Turn left and drive 1.5 miles to the campground on the right.

Contact: Tahoe National Forest, Truckee Ranger District, 530/587-3558, fax 530/587-6914; California Land Management, 530/587-9281 or 650/322-1181.

56 EMIGRANT SPRINGS GROUP CAMP

Scenic rating: 7

at Stampede Lake in Tahoe National Forest

Map grid A1

Emigrant Group Camp is set at a beautiful spot on Stampede Lake, near a point along a cove on the southeastern corner of the lake. There is a beautiful view of the lake from the point, and a boat ramp is two miles to the east. Elevation is 6,000 feet. (See the Logger listing in this chapter for more information.)

CALIFORNIA

RV sites, facilities: There are four group sites for tents or RVs up to 32 feet (no hookups) that can accommodate 25–50 people each. Picnic tables and fire grills are provided. Drinking water and vault toilets are available. Bring your own firewood. A three-lane concrete boat ramp is available. Some facilities are wheelchair-accessible. Leashed pets are permitted.

Reservations, fees: Reservations are required at 877/444-6777 or www.recreation.gov ($10 reservation fee). The camp is $86–167 per night. Open May through September, weather permitting.

Directions: From Truckee, drive east on I-80 for seven miles to the Boca-Hirschdale/County Road 270 exit. Take that exit and drive north on County Road 270 for about seven miles (past Boca Reservoir) to the junction with County Road S261 on the left. Turn left and drive 1.5 miles to the campground access road on the right. Turn right and drive one mile to the camp on the left.

Contact: Tahoe National Forest, Truckee Ranger District, 530/587-3558, fax 530/587-6914; California Land Management, 530/587-9281 or 650/322-1181.

57 BOYINGTON MILL

Scenic rating: 7

on the Little Truckee River in Tahoe National Forest
Map grid A1

Boyington Mill is a little Forest Service camp set between Boca Reservoir to the nearby south and Stampede Lake to the nearby north, along a small inlet creek to the adjacent Little Truckee River. Though open all summer, it is most often used as an overflow camp when lakeside campsites at Boca, Stampede, and Prosser have already filled. The elevation is 5,700 feet.

RV sites, facilities: There are 10 sites for tents or RVs up to 32 feet (no hookups). Picnic tables and fire rings are provided. Vault toilets are available. No drinking water is available. Leashed pets are permitted.

Reservations, fees: Reservations are accepted at 877/444-6777 or www.recreation.gov ($10 reservation fee). Sites are $16 per night, $5 per night for each additional vehicle. Open May through October, weather permitting.

Directions: From Truckee, drive east on I-80 for seven miles. Take the Boca-Hirschdale exit and drive north on County Road 270 for four miles (past Boca Reservoir) to the campground.

Contact: Tahoe National Forest, Truckee Ranger District, 530/587-3558, fax 530/587-6914; California Land Management, 530/587-9281 or 650/322-1181.

58 BOCA REST CAMPGROUND

Scenic rating: 7

on Boca Reservoir in Tahoe National Forest
Map grid A1

The Boca Dam faces I-80, so the lake is out of sight of the zillions of highway travelers who would otherwise certainly stop here. Those who do stop find that the lake is very pretty, set at 5,700 feet elevation and covering 1,000 acres with deep, blue water and 14 miles of shoreline. All water sports are allowed. This camp is on the lake's northeastern shore, not far from the inlet to the Little Truckee River. The boat ramp is some distance away.

RV sites, facilities: There are 31 sites for tents or RVs up to 22 feet (no hookups). Picnic tables and fire grills are provided. Drinking water and vault toilets are available. A hand-launch boat ramp is also available. A concrete boat ramp is three miles away on the southwest shore of Boca Reservoir. Leashed pets are permitted.

Reservations, fees: Reservations are accepted at 877/444-6777 or www.recreation.gov ($10 reservation fee). Sites are $16 per night, $5 per night for each additional vehicle. Open May through October, weather permitting.

Directions: From Truckee, drive east on I-80 for seven miles to the Boca-Hirschdale exit. Take that exit and drive north on County Road 270 for about 2.5 miles to the campground on the left side of the road.

Contact: Tahoe National Forest, Truckee

Ranger District, 530/587-3558, fax 530/587-6914; California Land Management, 530/587-9281 or 650/322-1181.

59 MALAKOFF DIGGINS STATE HISTORIC PARK

Scenic rating: 7

near Nevada City

Map grid A1

This camp is set at 3,400 feet elevation near a small lake in the park, but the main attraction of the area is its gold-mining past. A trip here is like a walk through history. Gold-mining efforts at this site washed away entire mountains with powerful streams of water, leaving behind enormous cliffs. This practice began in the 1850s and continued for many years. Several major gold-mining operations combined hydraulic mining with giant sluice boxes. Hydraulic mining was a scourge to the land, of course, and was eventually put to an end due to litigation between mine operators and landowners downstream. Though the remains of the state's biggest hydraulic mine are now closed to public viewing, visitors can view exhibits on mining life.

The park also contains a 7,847-foot bedrock tunnel that served as a drain. Although this tunnel is not open to the public, a shorter tunnel is available for viewing. The visitors center has exhibits on life in the old mining town of North Bloomfield. Tours of the numerous historic sites are offered during the summer.

RV sites, facilities: There are 30 sites for tents or RVs up to 24 feet (no hookups), three cabins, and one group tent site for up to 50 people. Picnic tables and fire grills are provided. Drinking water and flush toilets (except mid-November through February) are available. Leashed pets are permitted.

Reservations, fees: Reservations are accepted Memorial Day through Labor Day at 800/444-PARK (800/444-7275) or www.reserveamerica.com ($8 reservation fee). Sites are $35 per night, $8 per night for each additional vehicle, $165

per night for the group site. The cabins are $40 per night. Open year-round.

Directions: From Auburn, drive north on Highway 49 to Nevada City and continue 11 miles to the junction of Tyler Foote Crossing Road. Turn right and drive approximately 11 miles (in the process the road changes names to Cruzon Grade and Back Bone Road) to Der Bec Road. Turn right on Der Bec Road and drive one mile to North Bloomfield Road. Turn right and drive two miles to the entrance on the right. The route is well signed; the last two miles are quite steep.

Contact: California State Parks, Goldrush District, tel./fax 530/265-2740, www.parks.ca.gov.

60 SOUTH YUBA

Scenic rating: 7

near the Yuba River

Map grid A1

This little-known BLM camp is set next to where little Kenebee Creek enters the Yuba River. The Yuba is about a mile away, with some great swimming holes and evening trout-fishing spots to explore. A good side trip is to nearby Malakoff Diggins State Historic Park and the town of North Bloomfield (about a 10-minute drive to the northeast on North Bloomfield Road), which is being completely restored to its 1850s character. Twelve-mile-long South Yuba Trail begins at the state park and features outstanding spring wildflower blooms. The elevation is 2,600 feet.

RV sites, facilities: There are 16 sites for tents or RVs up to 27 feet (no hookups). Picnic tables and fire grills are provided. Drinking water and vault toilets are available. Some facilities are wheelchair-accessible. Leashed pets are permitted.

Reservations, fees: Reservations are not accepted. Sites are $5 per night. Open April through mid-October, weather permitting.

Directions: From Auburn, turn north on Highway 49, drive to Nevada City, and then continue on Highway 49 (the highway jogs left in town) a short distance to North Bloomfield Road. Turn right and drive 10 miles to the one-lane bridge at Edward's Crossing. Cross the bridge and continue 1.5 miles to the campground on the right side of the road (the road becomes quite rough). This route is not recommended for RVs or trailers.

Alternate route for RVs or vehicles with trailers: From Auburn turn north on Highway 49 to Nevada City and continue on Highway 49 (the highway jogs left in town) to Tyler Foote Crossing Road. Turn right and drive to Grizzly Hills Road (just past North Columbia). Turn right and drive two miles to North Bloomfield Road. Bear right on North Bloomfield Road and drive 0.5 mile to the campground on the left.

Contact: The Bureau of Land Management, Folsom Field Office, 916/985-4474, fax 916/985-3259.

61 LAKESIDE

Scenic rating: 7

on Prosser Creek Reservoir in
Tahoe National Forest

Map grid A1

This primitive camp is in a deep cove in the northwestern end of Prosser Creek Reservoir, near the lake's headwaters. It is a gorgeous lake, set at 5,741 feet elevation, and a 10-mph speed limit keeps the fast boats out. The adjacent shore is decent for hand-launched, car-top boats, providing the lake level is up, and a concrete boat ramp is a mile down the road. Lots of trout are stocked here every year. The trout fishing is often quite good after the ice breaks up in late spring. Sound perfect? Unfortunately for many, the Prosser OHV Park is nearby and can be noisy.

RV sites, facilities: There are 30 sites for tents or RVs up to 33 feet (no hookups). Drinking water and vault toilets are available. A boat ramp is nearby. Leashed pets are permitted.

Reservations, fees: Reservations are accepted at 877/444-6777 or www.recreation.gov ($10 reservation fee). Sites are $16 per night, $5 per night for each additional vehicle. Open June through October, weather permitting.

Directions: From Truckee, drive north on Highway 89 for three miles to the campground entrance road on the right. Turn right and drive less than a mile to the campground.

Contact: Tahoe National Forest, Truckee Ranger District, 530/587-3558, fax 530/587-6914; California Land Management, 530/587-9281 or 650/322-1181.

62 PROSSER CAMPGROUND

Scenic rating: 9

at Prosser Reservoir

Map grid A1

This camp is set at an elevation of 5,800 feet on the west shore peninsula of Prosser Reservoir. Though water levels can be an issue in late summer and fall, this campground is gorgeous in late spring and early summer. The landscape consists of Sierra granite sprinkled with pines, and the contrast of the emerald water, granite shore, and cobalt sky can be very special. In spring and fall, look for rainbow trout up to 18 inches. In summer, anglers have a shot a 10- to 12-inch planters. A 10-mph speed limit for boaters keeps it quiet.

RV sites, facilities: There are 29 sites for tents and small RVs, and one group site. Drinking water and vault toilets are available. Picnic tables and fire grills are provided. A boat ramp is nearby.

Reservations, fees: Reservations are not accepted for individual sites, but are required for the group site at 877/444-6777 or recreation. gov ($10 reservation fee). Sites are $20, $113.85 for the group site, $5 each additional vehicle per night. A maximum stay of 14 days is enforced. Open late May through early September.

Directions: From Truckee, drive north on Highway 89 for four miles and turn right onto access road to Prosser Reservoir. This campground is past Lakeside Campground.

Contact: Tahoe National Forest, Truckee Ranger District, 530/587-3558, fax 530/587-6914, www.fs.fed.us.

CALIFORNIA

63 BOCA SPRINGS CAMPGROUND AND GROUP CAMP

Scenic rating: 7

in Tahoe National Forest

Map grid A1

Boca Springs is located just past the north end of Boca Lake, near the Little Truckee River and a short way beyond Lakeside Campground. Boca is known for good trolling for trout and large kokanee salmon. A Forest Road provides access to a good stretch of the Little Truckee River, which can also provide good fishing for small trout. The elevation is 5,800 feet.

RV sites, facilities: There are seven tent sites, eight sites for tents or RVs, and one group site. Some sites are pull-through. Drinking water and vault toilets are available. Picnic tables and fire grills are provided. Horses are permitted in the campground, and a watering trough is provided. Some facilities are wheelchair accessible.

Reservations, fees: Reservations are accepted ($10 reservation fee) at 877/444-6777 or recreation.gov. Sites are $16, $48.40 for the group site, $5 each additional vehicle fee. A maximum stay of 14 days is enforced. Open mid-May through September.

Directions: From Truckee, drive north on Highway 89 for four miles and turn right onto access road to Prosser Reservoir. This campground is past Lakeside Campground.

Contact: Tahoe National Forest, Truckee Ranger District, 530/587-3558, fax 530/587-6914.

64 BOCA

Scenic rating: 7

on Boca Reservoir in Tahoe National Forest

Map grid A1

Boca Reservoir is known as a "big fish factory," with some huge but rare brown trout and rainbow trout sprinkled among a growing fishery for kokanee salmon. The lake is set at 5,700 feet amid a few sparse pines. While the surrounding landscape is not in the drop-dead beautiful class, the lake can still seem a Sierra gem on a windless dawn out on a boat. It is within a few miles of I-80. The camp is the best choice for anglers/boaters, with a launch ramp set just down from the campground.

RV sites, facilities: There are 20 sites for tents or RVs up to 16 feet (no hookups). Picnic tables and fire grills are provided. Vault toilets are available. No drinking water is available. A concrete boat ramp is north of the campground on Boca Reservoir. Truckee is the nearest place for telephones and supplies. Leashed pets are permitted.

Reservations, fees: Reservations are accepted at 877/444-6777 or www.recreation.gov ($10 reservation fee). Sites are $16 per night, $5 per night for each additional vehicle. Open May through October, weather permitting.

Directions: From I-80 in Truckee, take the exit for Highway 89-North. At the stoplight, turn left onto Highway 89-North and drive approximately one mile to Prosser Dam Road. Turn right and drive 4.5 miles to Prosser-Boca Road. Turn right and drive approximately four miles to the camp on the left.

Contact: Tahoe National Forest, Truckee Ranger District, 530/587-3558, fax 530/587-6914; California Land Management, 530/587-9281 or 650/322-1181.

65 SCOTTS FLAT LAKE RECREATION AREA

Scenic rating: 8

near Grass Valley

Map grid A1

Scotts Flat Lake (at 3,100 feet elevation) is shaped like a large teardrop and is one of the prettier lakes in the Sierra foothills, with 7.5 miles of shoreline circled by forest. Rules prohibiting personal watercraft keep the place sane. The camp is set on the lake's north shore, largely protected from spring winds and within short range of the marina and one of the lake's two boat launches. Trout fishing is good here in the spring and early summer. When the lake heats up, waterskiing and powerboating become more popular. Sailing and sailboarding are also good during afternoon winds.

RV sites, facilities: There are 187 sites for tents or RVs up to 35 feet (no hookups). Picnic tables and fire pits are provided. Restrooms with flush toilets and coin showers, coin laundry, and a dump station are provided. A general store, bait and tackle, boat rentals, boat ramp, and a playground are also available. Groups can be accommodated. Some facilities are wheelchair-accessible. Leashed pets are permitted.

Reservations, fees: Reservations are recommended in the summer at 530/265-5302. Sites are $19–30 per night, $6.25 per night for each additional vehicle, $3 per pet per night, $6 boat launch fee. Maximum stay 14 days. Some credit cards accepted. Open year-round, weather permitting.

Directions: From Auburn, drive north on Highway 49 to Nevada City and the junction with Highway 20. Continue straight onto Highway 20 and drive five miles (east) to Scotts Flat Road. Turn right and drive four miles to the camp entrance road on the right (on the north shore of the lake).

Contact: Scotts Flat Lake Recreation Area, 530/265-5302 or 530/265-8861, fax 530/265-3777, www.scottsflatlake.net.

66 WHITE CLOUD

Scenic rating: 5

in Tahoe National Forest

Map grid A1

This camp is set along historic Pioneer Trail, which has turned into one of the top mountain-bike routes in the Sierra Nevada, easy and fast. The trail traces the route of the first wagon road opened by emigrants and gold seekers in 1850. It is best suited for mountain biking, with a lot of bikers taking the one-way downhill ride (with an extra car for a shuttle ride) from Bear Valley to Lone Grave. The Omega Overlook is the highlight, with dramatic views of granite cliffs and the Yuba River. The elevation is 4,200 feet.

RV sites, facilities: There are 46 sites for tents or RVs of any length (no hookups). Picnic tables and fire grills are provided. Drinking water, flush toilets, and vault toilets are available. Some facilities are wheelchair-accessible. Leashed pets are permitted.

Reservations, fees: Reservations are accepted at 877/444-6777 or www.recreation.gov ($10 reservation fee). Sites are $22 per night, $5 per night for each additional vehicle. Open May through October, weather permitting.

Directions: From Sacramento, drive east on I-80 to Emigrant Gap. Take the off-ramp and then head north on the short connector road to Highway 20. Turn west on Highway 20 and drive about 15 miles to the campground entrance on the left.

Contact: Tahoe National Forest, Yuba River Ranger District, South, 530/265-4531, fax 530/478-6109; Big Bend Visitor's Center, 530/426-3609, fax 530/426-1744.

67 SKILLMAN FAMILY, EQUESTRIAN, AND GROUP CAMP

Scenic rating: 5

in Tahoe National Forest

Map grid A1

Skillman Group Camp is set at 4,400 feet, on a loop access road just off Highway 20, and historic Pioneer Trail runs right through it. (See the White Cloud listing in this chapter for more information.)

RV sites, facilities: There are 16 sites for tents or RVs up to 25 feet (no hookups). This campground can also be used as a group camp for tents or RVs up to 25 feet and can accommodate up to 75 people. Picnic tables and fire grills are provided. Vault toilets and drinking water are available. Horse corrals, tie rails, troughs, and stock water are available. Leashed pets are permitted.

Reservations, fees: Reservations are accepted

at 877/444-6777 or www.recreation.gov ($10 reservation fee). Sites are $22 per night, double sites are $44 per night, and the group camp is $110–330 per night. Open May through October, weather permitting.

Directions: From Sacramento, drive east on I-80 past Emigrant Gap to Highway 20. Turn west on Highway 20 and drive 12 miles to the campground entrance on the left.

Contact: Tahoe National Forest, Yuba River Ranger District, South, 530/265-4531, fax 530/478-6109; Sierra Recreation Managers, 209/295-4512; Big Bend Visitor Center, 530/426-3609, fax 530/426-1744.

68 LAKE SPAULDING

Scenic rating: 8

near Emigrant Gap
Map grid A1

Lake Spaulding is set at 5,000 feet elevation in the Sierra Nevada, complete with huge boulders and a sprinkling of conifers. Its clear, pure, very cold water has startling effects on swimmers. The 772-acre lake is extremely pretty, with the Sierra granite backdrop looking as if it has been cut, chiseled, and smoothed. Just one problem: There's not much of a lake view from the campground, although there are a few sites with filtered views. In fact, the lake is about a quarter mile from the campground. The drive here is nearly a straight shot up I-80, so there will be plenty of company at the campground. All water sports are allowed, except personal watercraft. Fishing for kokanee salmon and rainbow trout is often good, as well as fishing for trout at the nearby South Fork Yuba River. There are many other lakes set in the mountain country to the immediate north that can make for excellent side trips, including Bowman, Weaver, and Faucherie Lakes.

RV sites, facilities: There are 25 sites (13 are walk-in) for tents or RVs up to 30 feet (no hookups) and an overflow area. Picnic tables and fire grills are provided. Drinking water, vault toilets, and picnic areas are available. A boat ramp is nearby. Supplies are available in Nevada City. Some facilities are wheelchair-accessible. Leashed pets are permitted.

Reservations, fees: Reservations are not accepted. Sites are $16 per night, $3 per night for each additional vehicle, $1 per pet per night, $7 per day for boat launching. Open mid-May through September, weather permitting.

Directions: From Sacramento, drive east on I-80 past Emigrant Gap to Highway 20. Drive west on Highway 20 for 2.3 miles to Lake Spaulding Road. Turn right on Lake Spaulding Road and drive 0.5 mile to the campground.

Contact: PG&E Land Projects, 916/386-5164; Big Bend Visitor Center, 530/426-3609, fax 530/426-1744, www.pge.com/recreation.

69 INDIAN SPRINGS

Scenic rating: 8

near the Yuba River in Tahoe National Forest
Map grid A1   BEST (

The camp is easy to reach from I-80 yet is in a beautiful setting at 5,600 feet along the South Fork Yuba River. This is a gorgeous stream, running deep blue-green and pure through a granite setting, complete with giant boulders and beautiful pools. Trout fishing is fair. There is a small beach nearby where you can go swimming, though the water is cold. There are also several lakes in the vicinity.

RV sites, facilities: There are 35 sites for tents or RVs up to 26 feet (no hookups). Picnic tables and fire grills are provided. Drinking water and vault toilets are available. A grocery store and propane gas are nearby. Some facilities are wheelchair-accessible. Leashed pets are permitted.

Reservations, fees: Reservations are accepted at 877/444-6777 or www.recreation.gov ($10 reservation fee). Sites are $22 per night, $5 per night for each additional vehicle. Open June through September, weather permitting.

Directions: From Sacramento, drive east on I-80 to Yuba Gap and continue for about three miles to the Eagle Lakes exit. Head north on

CALIFORNIA

Eagle Lakes Road for a mile to the campground on the left side of the road.

Contact: Tahoe National Forest, Yuba River Ranger District, South, 530/265-4531, fax 530/478-6109; Big Bend Visitor Center, 530/426-3609, fax 530/426-1744.

70 LODGEPOLE

Scenic rating: 8

on Lake Valley Reservoir in Tahoe National Forest
Map grid A1

Lake Valley Reservoir is set at 5,786 feet elevation and covers 300 acres. It is gorgeous when full, its shoreline sprinkled with conifers and boulders. The lake provides decent results for anglers, who have the best luck while trolling. A 15-mph speed limit prohibits waterskiing and personal watercraft, and that keeps the place quiet and peaceful. The camp is about a quarter mile from the lake's southwest shore and two miles from the boat ramp on the north shore. A trailhead from camp leads south up Monumental Ridge and to Monumental Creek (three miles, one-way) on the northwestern flank of Quartz Mountain (6,931 feet).

RV sites, facilities: There are 35 sites for tents or RVs up to 30 feet (no hookups). Picnic tables and fire grills are provided. Drinking water and vault toilets are available. A boat ramp is available nearby. Supplies can be obtained off I-80. Some facilities are wheelchair-accessible. Leashed pets are permitted.

Reservations, fees: Reservations are not accepted. Sites are $18 per night, $3 per night for each additional vehicle, $1 per pet per night. Open late May through September, weather permitting.

Directions: From I-80, take the Yuba Gap exit and drive south for 0.4 mile to Lake Valley Road. Turn right on Lake Valley Road and drive for 1.2 miles until the road forks. Bear right and continue for 1.5 miles to the campground entrance road to the right on another fork.

Contact: PG&E Land Projects, 916/386-5164, www.pge.com/recreation.

71 HAMPSHIRE ROCKS

Scenic rating: 8

on the Yuba River in Tahoe National Forest
Map grid A1

This camp sits along the South Fork of the Yuba River at 5,800 feet elevation, with easy access off I-80 and a nearby Forest Service information center. Fishing for trout is fair. There are some swimming holes, but the water is often very cold. Nearby lakes that can provide side trips include Sterling and Fordyce Lakes (drive-to) to the north, and the Loch Leven Lakes (hike-to) to the south.

RV sites, facilities: There are 31 sites for tents or RVs up to 22 feet (no hookups) and four walk-in tent sites. Picnic tables and fire grills are provided. Drinking water and vault toilets are available. A convenience store, restaurant, and propane gas are available nearby. Some facilities are wheelchair-accessible. Leashed pets are permitted.

Reservations, fees: Reservations are accepted at 877/444-6777 or www.recreation.gov ($10 reservation fee). Sites are $22 per night, $5 per night for each additional vehicle. Open June through September, weather permitting.

Directions: From Sacramento, drive east on I-80 to Cisco Grove and continue for a mile to the Big Bend exit. Take that exit (remaining just south of the highway), then turn left on the frontage road and drive east for two miles to the campground on the right.

Contact: Tahoe National Forest, Yuba River Ranger District, South, 530/265-4531, fax 530/478-6109; Big Bend Visitor Center, 530/426-3609, fax 530/426-1744.

72 DONNER MEMORIAL STATE PARK

Scenic rating: 9

on Donner Lake
Map grid A1   **BEST**

The remarkable beauty of Donner Lake often evokes a deep, heartfelt response. Nearly everybody passing by from nearby I-80 has looked down and seen it. The lake is big, three miles long and 0.75 mile wide, gemlike blue, and set near the Sierra crest at 5,900 feet. The area is well developed, with a number of cabins and access roads, and this state park is the feature destination. Along the southeastern end of the lake, it is extremely pretty, but the campsites are set in forest, not along the lake. Fishing is good here (typically only in the early morning), trolling for kokanee salmon or rainbow trout, with big Mackinaw and brown trout providing wild cards. The park features more than three miles of frontage of Donner Creek and Donner Lake, with 2.5 miles of hiking trails. Donner Lake itself has 7.5 miles of shoreline. The lake is open to all water sports, but there is no boat launch at the park; a public ramp is available in the northwest corner of the lake. Campers get free admission to Emigrant Trail Museum.

RV sites, facilities: There are 150 sites for tents or RVs up to 28 feet (no hookups) and trailers up to 24 feet, and two hike-in/bike-in sites. Picnic tables and fire pits are provided. Drinking water, coin showers, vault toilets, picnic area, and interpretive trail are available. Supplies are available about one mile away in Truckee. Some facilities are wheelchair-accessible. Leashed pets are permitted.

Reservations, fees: Reservations are accepted at 800/444-PARK (800/444-7275) or www.reserveamerica.com ($8 reservation fee). Sites are $35 per night, $8 per night for each additional vehicle, $3 per person per night for hike-in/bike-in sites. Open late May to mid-September, weather permitting.

Directions: From Auburn, drive east on I-80 just past Donner Lake to the Donner State Park exit. Take that exit and turn south (right) on Donner Pass Road and drive 0.5 mile to the park entrance on the left at the southeast end of the lake.

Contact: Donner Memorial State Park, 530/582-7892 or 530/582-7894. For boat-launching info, call 530/582-7720, www.parks.ca.gov.

73 COACHLAND RV PARK

Scenic rating: 6

in Truckee
Map grid A1

Truckee is the gateway to recreation at North Tahoe. Within minutes are Donner Lake, Prosser Creek Reservoir, Boca Reservoir, Stampede Lake, the Truckee River, and ski resorts. Squaw Valley is a short distance to the south off Highway 89, and Northstar is just off Highway 267. The park is set in a wooded area near I-80, providing easy access. The downtown Truckee area (with restaurants) is a half mile away. This is one of the few parks in the area that is open year-round. The elevation is 6,000 feet. One problem: Only 25 of the 131 sites are available for overnighters, with the rest taken by long-term rentals.

RV sites, facilities: There are 131 pull-through sites with full hookups (30 amps, 13 sites provide 50 amps) for trailers or RVs up to 40 feet. No tents. Picnic tables are provided. Restrooms with showers, coin laundry, cable TV, modem access, Wi-Fi, playground, horseshoes, athletic field, tetherball, clubhouse, and propane are available. Some facilities are wheelchair-accessible. Leashed pets are permitted.

Reservations, fees: Reservations are recommended. Sites are $41 per night, $1.50–3 per person per night for more than two people, $2 per night for each additional vehicle. Monthly rates available. Some credit cards accepted. Open year-round.

Directions: From eastbound I-80 in Truckee, take the 188A exit to Donner Pass Road. Turn north on Donner Pass Road and drive one block to Pioneer Trail. Turn left and drive a short distance to the park at 10100 Pioneer Trail on the left side of the road.

From westbound I-80 in Truckee, take the 188 exit to Highway 89. Turn right on Highway 89 and drive north one block to Donner Pass Road. Turn left and drive one block to Pioneer Trail. Turn right and continue to the park.

Contact: Coachland RV Park, 530/587-3071, fax 530/587-6976, www.coachlandrvpark.com.

74 MARTIS CREEK LAKE

Scenic rating: 7

near Truckee

Map grid A1

If only this lake weren't so often windy in the afternoon, it would be heaven to fly fishers in float tubes. To some it's heaven anyway, with Lahontan cutthroat trout growing to 25 inches here. This is a special catch-and-release fishery where anglers are permitted to use only artificial lures with single, barbless hooks. The setting is somewhat sparse and open—a small lake, 70 acres, on the eastern edge of the Martis Valley. No motors are permitted at the lake, making it ideal (when the wind is down) for float tubes or prams. Sailing, sailboarding, and swimming are permitted. There is no boat launch, but small boats can be hand-launched. The lake level can fluctuate daily, which, along with the wind, can be frustrating for those who show up expecting automatic perfection; that just isn't the way it is out there. At times, the lake level can even be very low. The elevation is 5,800 feet.

RV sites, facilities: There are 25 sites for tents or RVs up to 30 feet (no hookups). Some sites are pull-through. Picnic tables and fire grills are provided. Drinking water, vault toilets, tent pads, and pay phones are available. Some facilities are wheelchair-accessible. Supplies are available six minutes away in Truckee. Leashed pets are permitted.

Reservations, fees: Reservations accepted for the wheelchair-accessible sites only at 530/587-8113. Sites are $16 per night. Open late May through mid-October, weather permitting.

Directions: From Truckee, drive south on Highway 267 for about three miles (past the airport) to the lake entrance road on the left. Turn left and drive another 2.5 miles to the campground at the end of the road.

Contact: U.S. Army Corps of Engineers, Sacramento District, 530/587-8113, fax 530/587-8623.

75 NORTH FORK

Scenic rating: 7

on the North Fork of the American River in Tahoe National Forest

Map grid A1

This is gold-mining country, and this camp is set along the Little North Fork of the North Fork American River at 4,400 feet in elevation, where you might still find a few magic gold flecks. Unfortunately, they will probably be fool's gold, not the real stuff. This feeder stream is small and pretty, and the camp is fairly remote and overlooked by most. It is set on the edge of a network of backcountry Forest Service roads. To explore them, a map of Tahoe National Forest is a must.

RV sites, facilities: There are 17 sites for tents or RVs up to 16 feet (no hookups). Picnic tables and fire grills are provided. Drinking water and vault toilets are available. Supplies are available at Emigrant Gap, Cisco Grove, and Soda Springs. Leashed pets are permitted.

Reservations, fees: Reservations are accepted at 877/444-6777 or www.recreation.gov ($10 reservation fee). Sites are $18 per night, $5 per night for each additional vehicle. Open June through October, weather permitting.

Directions: From Sacramento, drive east on I-80 to the Emigrant Gap exit. Take that exit and drive south a short distance to Texas Hill Road/Forest Road 19. Turn right and drive about seven miles to the camp on the right.

Contact: Tahoe National Forest, Yuba River Ranger District, South, 530/265-4531, fax 530/478-6109; Big Bend Visitor Center, 530/426-3609, fax 530/426-1744.

76 TUNNEL MILL GROUP CAMP

Scenic rating: 7

on the North Fork of the American River in Tahoe National Forest

Map grid A1

This is a good spot for a Boy or Girl Scout camp-out. It's a rustic, quiet group camp set all by itself along the (take a deep breath) East Fork of the North Fork of the North Fork of the American River (whew). (See the North Fork listing in this chapter for more recreation information.) The elevation is 4,400 feet.

RV sites, facilities: There are two group sites for tents or RVs up to 40 feet (no hookups) that can accommodate up to 30 people each. Picnic tables and fire grills are provided. Vault toilets are available. No drinking water is available. Supplies are available at the Nyack exit near Emigrant Gap. Leashed pets are permitted.

Reservations, fees: Reservations are required at 877/444-6777 or www.recreation.gov ($10 reservation fee). The camp is $99 per night. Open June through October, weather permitting.

Directions: From Sacramento, drive east on I-80 to the Emigrant Gap exit. Drive south for a short distance to Texas Hill Road/Forest Road 19. Turn right and drive about nine miles to the campground on the right side of the road.

Contact: Tahoe National Forest, Yuba River Ranger District, South, 530/265-4531, fax 530/478-6109; Big Bend Visitor Center, 530/426-3609, fax 530/426-1744.

77 GRANITE FLAT

Scenic rating: 6

on the Truckee River in Tahoe National Forest
Map grid A1

This camp is set along the Truckee River at 5,800 feet elevation. The area is known for a ton of traffic on adjacent Highway 89, as well as decent trout fishing and, in the spring and early summer, rafting. It is about a 15-minute drive to Squaw Valley or Lake Tahoe. A bike route is also available along the Truckee River out of Tahoe City.

RV sites, facilities: There are 68 sites for tents or RVs up to 40 feet (no hookups) and seven walk-in tent sites. Picnic tables and fire grills are provided. Drinking water and vault toilets are available. Some facilities are wheelchair-accessible. Leashed pets are permitted.

Reservations, fees: Reservations are accepted

at 877/444-6777 or www.recreation.gov ($10 reservation fee). Sites are $18 per night, $5 per night for each additional vehicle. Open May through October, weather permitting.

Directions: From Truckee, drive south on Highway 89 for 1.5 miles to the campground entrance on the left.

Contact: Tahoe National Forest, Truckee Ranger District, 530/587-3558, fax 530/587-6914; California Land Management, 530/587-9281 or 650/322-1181.

78 GOOSE MEADOWS

Scenic rating: 6

on the Truckee River in Tahoe National Forest
Map grid A1

There are three campgrounds set along the Truckee River off Highway 89 between Truckee and Tahoe City. Goose Meadows provides good fishing access with decent prospects, despite the high number of vehicles roaring past on the adjacent highway. This stretch of river is also popular for rafting. The elevation is 5,800 feet.

RV sites, facilities: There are 24 sites for tents or RVs up to 30 feet (no hookups). Picnic tables and fire grills are provided. Drinking water and vault toilets are available. Supplies are available in Truckee and Tahoe City. Some facilities are wheelchair-accessible. Leashed pets are permitted.

Reservations, fees: Reservations are accepted at 877/444-6777 or www.recreation.gov ($10 reservation fee). Sites are $16 per night, $5 per night for each additional vehicle. Open May through October, weather permitting.

Directions: From Truckee, drive south on Highway 89 for four miles to the campground entrance on the left (river) side of the highway.

Contact: Tahoe National Forest, Truckee Ranger District, 530/587-3558, fax 530/587-6914; California Land Management, 530/587-9281 or 650/322-1181.

79 SILVER CREEK

Scenic rating: 8

on the Truckee River in Tahoe National Forest
Map grid A1

This pretty campground is set near where Silver Creek enters the Truckee River. The trout fishing is often good in this area. This is one of three campgrounds along Highway 89 and the Truckee River, between Truckee and Tahoe City. The elevation is 6,000 feet.

RV sites, facilities: There are 21 sites for tents or RVs up to 40 feet (no hookups) and seven walk-in tent sites. Picnic tables and fire grills are provided. Drinking water and vault toilets are available. Supplies are available in Truckee and Tahoe City. Some facilities are wheelchair-accessible. Leashed pets are permitted.

Reservations, fees: Reservations are accepted at 877/444-6777 or www.recreation.gov ($10 reservation fee). Sites are $16 per night, $5 per night for each additional vehicle. Open June through September, weather permitting.

Directions: From Truckee, drive south on Highway 89 for six miles to the campground entrance on the river side of the highway.

Contact: Tahoe National Forest, Truckee Ranger District, 530/587-3558, fax 530/587-6914; California Land Management, 530/587-9281 or 650/322-1181.

80 ORCHARD SPRINGS RESORT

Scenic rating: 7

on Rollins Lake
Map grid A1

Orchard Springs Resort is set on the shore of Rollins Lake among pine, oak, and cedar trees in the Sierra Nevada foothills. The summer heat makes the lake excellent for waterskiing, boating, and swimming. Spring and fall are great for trout and bass fishing.

RV sites, facilities: There are 90 tent sites and 16 sites with full hookups (30 amps) for tents or RVs up to 40 feet. Two sites are pull-through. Four camping cabins are also available. Picnic

tables, fire rings, and barbecues are provided. Drinking water, restrooms with flush toilets and showers, launch ramp, boat rentals, slips, bait and tackle, swimming beach, group picnic area, and a convenience store are available. Some facilities are wheelchair-accessible. Leashed pets are permitted.

Reservations, fees: Reservations are accepted. Sites are $29–39 per night, $6.25 per night for each additional vehicle unless towed, $5.75 per boat per night, $3 per pet per night. Some credit cards accepted. Open year-round.

Directions: From Auburn, drive northeast on I-80 for about 20 miles to the Colfax/Grass Valley exit. Take that exit and loop back over the freeway to the stop sign. Turn right and drive a short distance to Highway 174. Turn right and drive north on Highway 174 (a winding, two-lane road) for 3.7 miles (bear left at Giovanni's Restaurant) to Orchard Springs Road. Turn right on Orchard Springs Road and drive 0.5 mile to the road's end. Turn right at the gatehouse and continue to the campground.

Contact: Orchard Springs Resort, 530/346-2212, www.osresort.net.

81 PENINSULA CAMPING AND BOATING RESORT

Scenic rating: 8

on Rollins Lake
Map grid A1

Peninsula Campground is set on a point that extends into Rollins Lake, flanked on each side by two sprawling lake arms. The resort has 280 acres and 1.5 miles of lake frontage. A bonus is that you can boat directly from some of the lakefront sites. If you like boating, waterskiing, or swimming, you'll definitely like this place in the summer. All water sports are allowed. This is a family-oriented campground with lots of youngsters on summer vacation. Fishing is available for rainbow and brown trout, small- and largemouth bass, perch, crappie, and catfish.

RV sites, facilities: There are 78 sites for tents

or RVs up to 40 feet (no hookups), and three group sites for 16–40 people. Three cabins are also available. Picnic tables and fire pits are provided. Restrooms with flush toilets and showers, drinking water, Wi-Fi, dump station, boat rentals (fishing boats, patio boats, canoes, and kayaks), boat ramp, limited fishing licenses, fish-cleaning station, swimming beach, horseshoes, volleyball, and a convenience store are available. Marine gas is available on the lake. Leashed pets are permitted, but call for current status.

Reservations, fees: Reservations are accepted by phone or website. Sites are $26–32 per night, $10 per night for each additional vehicle, $65–160 per night for a group site, $3 per pet per night. Maximum 14-day stay. Some credit cards accepted. Open mid-April through September.

Directions: From Auburn, drive northeast on I-80 for about 20 miles to the Colfax/Grass Valley exit. Take that exit and loop back over the freeway to the stop sign. Turn right and drive a short distance to Highway 174. Turn right and drive north on Highway 174 (a winding, two-lane road) for eight miles to You Bet Road. Turn right and drive 4.3 miles (turning right again to stay on You Bet Road), and continue another 3.1 miles to the campground entrance at the end of the road.

Contact: Peninsula Camping and Boating Resort, 530/477-9413 or 866/4MY-CAMP (866/469-2267), www.penresort.com.

82 GIANT GAP

Scenic rating: 7

on Sugar Pine Reservoir in Tahoe National Forest

Map grid A1

This is a lakeside spot along the western shore of Sugar Pine Reservoir at 4,000 feet elevation in Tahoe National Forest. There is a ramp on the south shore for boaters. Note that a 10-mph speed limit is the law, making this lake ideal for anglers in search of quiet water. Other recreation notes: There's a little less than a mile

of paved trail, which goes through the day-use area. Big Reservoir (also known as Morning Star Lake), five miles to the east, is the only other lake in the region and also has a campground. The trout and bass fishing at Sugar Pine is fair—not usually great, not usually bad. Swimming is allowed; kayaking and canoeing are also popular.

RV sites, facilities: There are 30 sites for tents or RVs of any length (no hookups). Picnic tables and fire grills are provided. Drinking water and vault toilets are available. Some facilities are wheelchair-accessible. A dump station and boat ramp are on the south shore. Supplies can be obtained in Foresthill. Leashed pets are permitted.

Reservations, fees: Reservations are accepted at 877/444-6777 or www.recreation.gov ($10 reservation fee). Sites are $18 per night, $36 per night for a double site. Open May to mid-October, weather permitting.

Directions: From Sacramento, drive east on I-80 to the north end of Auburn and the Foresthill Road exit. Take that exit and drive east for 20 miles to Foresthill. Drive through Foresthill (road changes to Foresthill Divide Road) and continue for eight miles to Sugar Pine Road. Turn left and drive five miles to a fork. Turn right and drive one mile to the campground.

Contact: Tahoe National Forest, American River Ranger District, Foresthill Ranger Station, 530/367-2224, fax 530/367-2992.

83 SHIRTTAIL CREEK

Scenic rating: 7

on Sugar Pine Reservoir in Tahoe National Forest

Map grid A1

This camp is set near the little creek that feeds into the north end of Sugar Pine Reservoir. The boat ramp is all the way around the south side of the lake, near Forbes Creek Group Camp. (For recreation information, see the Giant Gap listing in this chapter.)

RV sites, facilities: There are 30 sites for tents or RVs of any length (no hookups, double and triple sites are available). Picnic tables and fire grills are provided. Drinking water and vault toilets are available. Some facilities are wheelchair-accessible. A dump station and boat ramp are on the south shore. Supplies can be obtained in Foresthill. Leashed pets are permitted.

Reservations, fees: Reservations are accepted at 877/444-6777 or www.recreation.gov ($10 reservation fee). Sites are $18 for single sites, $36 for double sites, $54 for triple site, per night. Open May through mid-October, weather permitting.

Directions: From Sacramento, drive east on I-80 to the north end of Auburn and the Foresthill Road exit. Take that exit and drive east for 20 miles to Foresthill. Drive through Foresthill (road changes to Foresthill Divide Road) and continue for eight miles to Sugar Pine Road. Turn left and drive five miles to the campground access road. Turn right (signed) and drive to the campground.

Contact: Tahoe National Forest, American River Ranger District, Foresthill Ranger Station, 530/367-2224, fax 530/367-2992.

84 BIG RESERVOIR/ MORNING STAR LAKE

Scenic rating: 7

on Big Reservoir in Tahoe National Forest

Map grid A1

Here's a quiet lake where only electric boat motors are allowed; no gas motors are permitted. That makes it ideal for canoeists, rowboaters, and tube floaters who don't like the idea of having to dodge water-skiers. The lake is stocked with rainbow trout; free fishing permits are required and can be obtained at the lake. Big Reservoir (also known as Morning Star Lake) is quite pretty with a nice beach and some lakefront campsites. The elevation is 4,000 feet.

RV sites, facilities: There are 100 sites for tents or RVs up to 40 feet (no hookups). Picnic tables and fire grills are provided. Drinking water, vault toilets, free showers, dump station, and firewood (fee) are available. There is a small

store near the campground and supplies are also available in Foresthill. Some facilities are wheelchair-accessible. Leashed pets are permitted.

Reservations, fees: Reservations are accepted at 530/367-2129. Sites are $23–35 per night. Fishing fees are charged. Open May through October, weather permitting.

Directions: From Sacramento, drive east on I-80 to the north end of Auburn and the Foresthill Road exit. Take that exit and drive east for 20 miles to Foresthill. Drive through Foresthill (road changes to Foresthill Divide Road) and continue for eight miles to Sugar Pine Road. Turn left and drive about three miles to Forest Road 24 (signed Big Reservoir). Continue straight onto Forest Road 24 and drive about three miles to the campground entrance road on the right.

Contact: Tahoe National Forest, American River Ranger District, Foresthill Ranger Station, 530/367-2224, fax 530/367-2992; concessionaire: DeAnza Placer Gold Mining Company, 530/367-2129.

85 FORBES CREEK GROUP CAMP

Scenic rating: 7

on Sugar Pine Reservoir in Tahoe National Forest

Map grid A1

The boat launch is nearby, but note: A 10-mph speed limit is the law. That makes for quiet water, perfect for anglers, canoeists, and other small boats. A paved trail circles the 160-acre lake. (For more information see the Giant Gap listing in this chapter.)

RV sites, facilities: There are two group campsites, Madrone and Rocky Ridge, for tents or RVs up to 45 feet (no hookups) that can accommodate up to 50 people each. Picnic tables and fire grills are provided. Drinking water and vault toilets are available. Some facilities are wheelchair-accessible. A campfire circle, central parking area, dump station, and a boat ramp are available nearby. Supplies can be obtained in Foresthill. Leashed pets are permitted.

Reservations, fees: Reservations are accepted

at 877/444-6777 or www.recreation.gov ($10 reservation fee). Sites are $120 per night. Open May through mid-October, weather permitting.

Directions: From Sacramento, drive east on I-80 to the north end of Auburn and the Foresthill Road exit. Take that exit and drive east for 20 miles to Foresthill. Drive through Foresthill (road changes to Forest-hill Divide Road) and continue for eight miles to Sugar Pine Road/ Forest Road 10. Turn left and drive five miles to the fork in the road (still Sugar Pine Road/ Forest Road 10). Bear left and drive approximately 4.5 miles to the boat ramp (still Sugar Pine Road/Forest Road 10). Turn right, head up the hill, and drive approximately seven miles to the camp.

Contact: Tahoe National Forest, American River Ranger District, Foresthill Ranger Station, 530/367-2224, fax 530/367-2992.

86 BEAR RIVER CAMPGROUND

Scenic rating: 7

near Colfax on Bear River

Map grid A1

This RV park is set in the Sierra foothills at 1,800 feet, near Bear River, and features riverfront campsites. The park covers 200 acres, offers five miles of hiking trails, and is set right on the Placer and Nevada County lines. It fills up on weekends and is popular with both locals and out-of-towners. In the spring, when everything is green, it can be a gorgeous landscape. Fishing is OK for rainbow and brown trout, smallmouth bass, and bluegill. Noncommercial gold panning is permitted, and some rafting is popular on the river. A 14-day maximum stay is enforced.

RV sites, facilities: There are 25 sites for tents or small RVs up to 40 feet (no hookups), and two group sites for tents or RVs up to 35 feet for 50–100 people. Picnic tables and fire rings are provided. Pit toilets are available. There is no drinking water. Supplies are available within

five miles in Colfax or Bowman. Leashed pets are permitted.

Reservations, fees: Reservations are accepted only for the group sites at 530/886-4901 ($5 reservation fee). Sites are $10 per night, $2 per night for each additional vehicle, $1 per pet per night, and $40–75 per night for group sites. A certificate of insurance is required for group sites. Open March through November.

Directions: From Sacramento, drive east on I-80 east of Auburn to West Weimar Crossroads exit. Take that exit on to Weimar Cross Road and drive north for 1.5 miles to Placer Hills Road. Turn right and drive 2.5 miles to Plum Tree Road. Turn left and drive one mile to the campground on the left. The access road is steep and narrow.

Contact: Bear River Campground, Placer County Facilities Services, 530/886-4901, www.placer.ca.gov.

87 ROBINSON FLAT

Scenic rating: 5

near French Meadows Reservoir in Tahoe National Forest

Map grid A1

This camp is set at 6,800 feet elevation in remote Tahoe National Forest, on the eastern flank of Duncan Peak (7,116 feet), with a two-mile drive south to Duncan Peak Lookout (7,182 feet). A trail out of camp follows along a small stream, a fork to Duncan Creek, in Little Robinsons Valley. French Meadows Reservoir is 15 miles southeast. An equestrian camp with seven sites is also available.

RV sites, facilities: There are seven sites for tents or RVs up to 25 feet, plus an equestrian camp with seven sites for tents or RVs up to 45 feet. No hookups. Picnic tables and fire grills are provided. Drinking water and vault toilets are available. Garbage must be packed out. Supplies are available in Foresthill. Some facilities are wheelchair-accessible. Leashed pets are permitted.

Reservations, fees: Reservations are not

accepted. There is no fee for camping. Open mid-May through October, weather permitting.

Directions: From Sacramento, drive east on I-80 to the north end of Auburn and the Foresthill Road exit. Take that exit and drive east to Foresthill (the road name changes to Foresthill Divide Road) and continue northeast (the road is narrow and curvy) for 27 miles to the junction with County Road 43. The campground is at the junction.

Contact: Tahoe National Forest, American River Ranger District, Foresthill Ranger Station, 530/367-2224, fax 530/367-2992.

88 LEWIS

Scenic rating: 7

on French Meadows Reservoir in Tahoe National Forest

Map grid A1

This camp is not right at lakeside but is just across the road from French Meadows Reservoir. It is still quite pretty, set along a feeder creek near the lake's northwest shore. A boat ramp is available only 0.5 mile to the south, and the adjacent McGuire boat ramp area has a trailhead that is routed along the lake's northern shoreline. This lake is big (2,000 acres) and pretty, created by a dam on the Middle Fork American River, with good fishing for rainbow trout.

RV sites, facilities: There are 40 sites for tents or RVs up to 45 feet (no hookups). Picnic tables and fire grills are provided. Drinking water and vault toilets are available. A concrete boat ramp is nearby. Supplies are available in Foresthill. Some facilities are wheelchair-accessible. Leashed pets are permitted.

Reservations, fees: Reservations are accepted at 877/444-6777 or www.recreation.gov ($10 reservation fee). Sites are $18 per night, $6 per night for each additional vehicle. Open mid-May through early September.

Directions: From Sacramento, drive east on I-80 to the north end of Auburn and the Foresthill

Road exit. Take that exit and drive east to Foresthill and Mosquito Ridge Road (Forest Road 96). Turn right (east) and drive 40 miles (curvy) to Anderson Dam and to a junction. Turn left (still Mosquito Ridge Road) and then continue along the southern shoreline of French Meadows Reservoir for five miles to a fork at the head of the lake. Bear left at the fork and drive 0.5 mile to the camp on the right side of the road.

Contact: Tahoe National Forest, American River Ranger District, Foresthill Ranger Station, 530/367-2224, fax 530/367-2992.

89 AHART

Scenic rating: 7

near French Meadows Reservoir in Tahoe National Forest

Map grid A1

This camp is a mile north of French Meadows Reservoir near where the Middle Fork of the American River enters the lake. It is on the Middle Fork and is primarily used for campers who would rather camp near this river than French Meadows Reservoir. Note: This is bear country in the summer.

RV sites, facilities: There are 12 sites for tents or RVs up to 40 feet (no hookups). Picnic tables and fire grills are provided. Vault toilets are available. No drinking water is available. Supplies are available in Foresthill. Some facilities are wheelchair-accessible. Leashed pets are permitted.

Reservations, fees: Reservations are not accepted. Sites are $16 per night, $6 per night for each additional vehicle. Open late May through October, weather permitting.

Directions: From Sacramento, drive east on I-80 to the north end of Auburn and the Foresthill Road exit. Take that exit and drive east to Foresthill and Mosquito Ridge Road (Forest Road 96). Turn right (east) and drive 40 miles (curvy) to Anderson Dam and to a junction. Turn left (still Mosquito Ridge Road) and then continue along the southern shoreline of French Meadows Reservoir for seven miles.

Contact: Tahoe National Forest, American River Ranger District, Foresthill Ranger Station, 530/367-2224, fax 530/367-2992.

90 GATES GROUP CAMP

Scenic rating: 7

on the North Fork of the American River in Tahoe National Forest

Map grid A1

This group camp is well secluded along the North Fork American River, just upstream from where it pours into French Meadows Reservoir. (For recreation options, see the French Meadows, Lewis, and Coyote Group Camp listings in this chapter.)

RV sites, facilities: There are three group sites for tents or RVs of any length (no hookups) that can accommodate 25–75 people each. Picnic tables and fire grills are provided. Drinking water, vault toilets, central parking, and a campfire circle are available. Obtain supplies in Foresthill. Leashed pets are permitted.

Reservations, fees: Reservations are required at 877/444-6777 or www.recreation.gov ($10 reservation fee). Sites are $75–135 per night. Open mid-May through October, weather permitting.

Directions: From Sacramento, drive east on I-80 to the north end of Auburn and the Foresthill Road exit. Take that exit and drive east to Foresthill and Mosquito Ridge Road (Forest Road 96). Turn right (east) and drive 40 miles (curvy) to Anderson Dam and to a junction. Turn left (still Mosquito Ridge Road) and continue along the southern shoreline of French Meadows Reservoir for five miles to a fork at the head of the lake. Bear left at the fork (Forest Road 68) and drive a mile to the camp at the end of the road.

Contact: Tahoe National Forest, American River Ranger District, Foresthill Ranger Station, 530/367-2224, fax 530/367-2992.

91 COYOTE GROUP CAMP

Scenic rating: 6

on French Meadows Reservoir in Tahoe National Forest

Map grid A1

This group camp is set right at the head of French Meadows Reservoir, at 5,300 feet elevation. A boat ramp is two miles to the south, just past Lewis on the lake's north shore. (For recreation options, see the French Meadows listing in this chapter.)

RV sites, facilities: There are three group sites for tents or RVs of any length (no hookups) that can accommodate 25–50 people each. Picnic tables and fire grills are provided. Drinking water and vault toilets are available. A campfire circle and central parking area are also available. Supplies are available in Foresthill. Leashed pets are permitted.

Reservations, fees: Reservations are required at 877/444-6777 or www.recreation.gov ($10 reservation fee). Sites are $75–110 per night. Open mid-May through October.

Directions: From Sacramento, drive east on I-80 to the north end of Auburn and the Foresthill Road exit. Take that exit and drive east to Foresthill and Mosquito Ridge Road (Forest Road 96). Turn right (east) and drive 40 miles (curvy) to Anderson Dam and to a junction. Turn left (still Mosquito Ridge Road) and then continue along the southern shoreline of French Meadows Reservoir for five miles to a fork at the head of the lake. Bear left at the fork and drive 0.5 mile to the camp on the left side of the road.

Contact: Tahoe National Forest, American River Ranger District, Foresthill Ranger Station, 530/367-2224, fax 530/367-2992.

92 FRENCH MEADOWS

Scenic rating: 7

on French Meadows Reservoir in Tahoe National Forest

Map grid A1

The nearby boat launch makes this the choice for boating campers. The camp is on French

Meadows Reservoir at 5,300 feet elevation. It is set on the lake's southern shore, with the boat ramp about a mile to the south (you'll see the entrance road on the way in). This is a big lake set in remote Tahoe National Forest in the North Fork American River Canyon with good trout fishing. All water sports are allowed. The lake level often drops in late summer, and then a lot of stumps and boulders start poking through the lake surface. This creates navigational hazards for boaters and water skiers, but it also makes it easier for the anglers to know where to find the fish. If the fish don't bite here, boaters should make the nearby side trip to pretty Hell Hole Reservoir to the south.

RV sites, facilities: There are 75 sites for tents or RVs up to 45 feet (no hookups). Picnic tables and fire grills are provided. Drinking water and vault toilets are available. Some facilities are wheelchair-accessible. A concrete boat ramp is nearby. Supplies are available in Foresthill. Leashed pets are permitted.

Reservations, fees: Reservations are accepted at 877/444-6777 or www.recreation.gov ($10 reservation fee). Sites are $18 per night, $6 per night for each additional vehicle. Open late May through October, weather permitting.

Directions: From Sacramento, drive east on I-80 to the north end of Auburn and the Foresthill Road exit. Take that exit and drive east to Foresthill and Mosquito Ridge Road (Forest Road 96). Turn right (east) and drive 40 miles (curvy) to Anderson Dam and to a junction. Turn left (still Mosquito Ridge Road) and then continue along the southern shoreline of French Meadows Reservoir for four miles to the campground.

Contact: Tahoe National Forest, American River Ranger District, Foresthill Ranger Station, 530/367-2224, fax 530/367-2992.

93 BIG MEADOWS

Scenic rating: 7

near Hell Hole Reservoir in Eldorado National Forest
Map grid A1

This camp sits on a meadow near the ridge above Hell Hole Reservoir, which is about two miles away.

RV sites, facilities: There are 54 sites for tents or RVs of any length (no hookups). Picnic tables are provided. Drinking water and flush and vault toilets are available. A boat ramp is nearby. Some facilities are wheelchair accessible. Leashed pets are permitted.

Reservations, fees: Reservations are not accepted. Sites are $10 per night, $5 per night for each additional vehicle. Open late May through early November, weather permitting.

Directions: From Sacramento, drive east on I-80 to the north end of Auburn. Take the Elm Avenue exit and turn left at the first stoplight onto Elm Avenue. Drive 0.1 mile, turn left on High Street, and continue through the signal where High Street merges with Highway 49. Continue on Highway 49 for about 3.5 miles, turn right over the bridge, and drive about 2.5 miles into the town of Cool. Turn left on Georgetown Road/Highway 193 and drive about 14 miles into Georgetown. At the four-way stop turn left on Main Street (which becomes Wentworth Springs/Forest Road 1) and drive about 25 miles. Turn left on Forest Road 2 and drive 21 miles to the campground on the left.

Contact: Eldorado National Forest, Georgetown Ranger District, 530/333-4312, fax 530/333-5522.

94 MIDDLE MEADOWS GROUP CAMP

Scenic rating: 7

on Long Canyon Creek in Eldorado National Forest
Map grid A1

This group camp is within range of several adventures. To the nearby east is Hell Hole Reservoir (you'll need a boat here to do it right), and to the nearby north is French Meadows Reservoir (you'll drive past the dam on the way in). Unfortunately, there isn't a heck of a lot to do at this camp other than watch the water flow by on adjacent Long Canyon Creek.

RV sites, facilities: There are two group sites for tents or RVs up to 16 feet (no hookups), including one that can accommodate 25–50 people. Picnic tables and fire grills are provided. Drinking water and flush and vault toilets are available. Supplies can be obtained in Foresthill. Leashed pets are permitted.

Reservations, fees: Reservations are accepted at 877/444-6777 or www.recreation.gov ($10 reservation fee). Sites are $25–50 per night. Open mid-May through mid-September, weather permitting.

Directions: From Sacramento, drive east on I-80 to the north end of Auburn. Take the Elm Avenue exit and turn left at the first stoplight onto Elm Avenue. Drive 0.1 mile, turn left on High Street, and continue through the signal where High Street merges with Highway 49. Travel on Highway 49 for about 3.5 miles, turn right over the bridge, and drive about 2.5 miles into the town of Cool. Turn left on Georgetown Road/Highway 193 and drive about 14 miles into Georgetown. At the four-way stop turn left on Main Street (which becomes Wentworth Springs/Forest Road 1) and drive about 25 miles. Turn left on Forest Road 2 and drive 19 miles to the campground on the right.

Contact: Eldorado National Forest, Georgetown Ranger District, 530/333-4312, fax 530/333-5522.

95 SANDY BEACH CAMPGROUND

Scenic rating: 8

on Lake Tahoe

Map grid A1

Sandy Beach Campground is set at 6,200 feet elevation near the northwest shore of Lake Tahoe. A nearby boat ramp provides access to one of the better fishing areas of the lake for Mackinaw trout. A public beach is across the road. But the water in Tahoe is always cold, and though a lot of people will get suntans on beaches next to the lake, swimmers need to be members of the Polar Bear Club. A short drive to the east will take you past the town of Kings Beach and into Nevada, where there are

some small casinos near the shore of Crystal Bay. Note that some sites fill up for the summer season.

RV sites, facilities: There are 27 sites with full or partial hookups (30 amps) for tents or RVs up to 40 feet. Some sites are pull-through. Picnic tables, barbecues, and fire rings are provided. Drinking water, restrooms with showers and flush toilets, and a dump station are available. A boat ramp is half a block away. A grocery store and propane gas are available nearby. Leashed pets are permitted.

Reservations, fees: Reservations are recommended. Sites are $20–25 per night for up to six people with two vehicles, two-dog limit. For weeklong stays, seventh night is free. Some credit cards accepted. Open May through October.

Directions: From Truckee, drive south on Highway 267 to Highway 28. Turn right and drive one mile to the park on the right side of the road (entrance well signed).

Contact: Sandy Beach Campground, 530/546-7682.

96 LAKE FOREST CAMPGROUND

Scenic rating: 8

on Lake Tahoe

Map grid A1

The north shore of Lake Tahoe provides beautiful lookouts and excellent boating access. The latter is a highlight of this camp, with a boat ramp nearby. From here it is a short cruise to Dollar Point and around the corner north to Carnelian Bay, one of the better stretches of water for trout fishing. The elevation is 6,200 feet. There is a 10-day camping limit.

RV sites, facilities: There are 20 sites for tents or RVs up to 20 feet (no hookups). Picnic tables and fire grills are provided. Drinking water and vault toilets are available. Some facilities are wheelchair-accessible. A grocery store, coin laundry, and propane gas are available within four miles. Leashed pets are permitted.

Reservations, fees: Reservations are not

accepted. Sites are $15 per night. Open May through October, weather permitting.

Directions: From Truckee, drive south on Highway 89 through Tahoe City to Highway 28. Bear north on Highway 28 and drive four miles to the campground entrance road (Lake Forest Road) on the right.

Contact: Tahoe City Public Utility District, Parks and Recreation, 530/583-3796, ext. 10, fax 530/583-8452.

97 TAHOE STATE RECREATION AREA

Scenic rating: 9

on Lake Tahoe
Map grid A1

This is a popular summer-only campground at the north shore of Lake Tahoe. The Tahoe State Recreation Area covers a large area just west of Highway 28 near Tahoe City. There are opportunities for hiking and horseback riding nearby (though not right at the park). It is also near shopping, restaurants, and, unfortunately, traffic jams in Tahoe City. A boat ramp is two miles to the northwest at nearby Lake Forest, and bike rentals are available in Tahoe City for rides along Highway 89 near the shore of the lake. For a more secluded site nearby at Tahoe, get reservations instead for Sugar Pine Point State Park, 11 miles south on Highway 89.

RV sites, facilities: There are 25 sites for tents or RVs up to 27 feet (no hookups) and trailers up to 24 feet. Picnic tables, food lockers, barbecues, and fire pits are provided. Drinking water, vault toilets, and coin showers are available. Firewood, other supplies, and a coin laundry are available within walking distance. Leashed pets are permitted.

Reservations, fees: Reservations are accepted at 800/444-PARK (800/444-7275) or www. reserveamerica.com ($8 reservation fee). Sites are $20–25 per night, $6 per night for each additional vehicle. Open May through October, weather permitting.

Directions: From Truckee, drive south on Highway 89 through Tahoe City. Turn north on Highway 28 and drive 0.9 mile to the campground entrance on the right side of the road.

Contact: Tahoe State Recreation Area, 530/583-3074; Sierra District, 530/525-7232, www. parks.ca.gov.

98 WILLIAM KENT

Scenic rating: 8

near Lake Tahoe in the Lake Tahoe Basin
Map grid A1

William Kent camp is a little pocket of peace set near the busy traffic of Highway 89 on the western shore corridor. It is on the west side of the highway, meaning visitors have to cross the highway to get lakeside access. The elevation is 6,300 feet, and the camp is wooded with primarily lodgepole pines. The drive here is awesome or ominous, depending on how you look at it, with the view of incredible Lake Tahoe to the east, the third-deepest blue lake in North America and the 10th-deepest lake in the world. But you often have a lot of time to look at it, since traffic rarely moves quickly.

RV sites, facilities: There are 55 tent sites and 36 sites for RVs up to 40 feet (no hookups). Picnic tables, food lockers, and fire grills are provided. Drinking water, flush toilets, and a dump station are available. A grocery store, coin laundry, and propane gas are available nearby. Some facilities are wheelchair-accessible. Leashed pets are permitted.

Reservations, fees: Reservations are accepted at 877/444-6777 or www.recreation.gov ($10 reservation fee). Sites are $20 per night, $5 per night for each additional vehicle. Open late May through mid-October, weather permitting.

Directions: From Truckee, drive south on Highway 89 to Tahoe City. Turn south on Highway 89 and drive three miles to the campground entrance on the right side of the road.

Contact: Lake Tahoe Basin Management Unit, 530/543-2600, fax 530/543-2693; Taylor Creek

Visitor Center, 530/543-2674; California Land Management, 530/583-3642.

99 KASPIAN

Scenic rating: 7

on Lake Tahoe

Map grid A1

As gorgeous and as huge as Lake Tahoe is, there are relatively few camps or even restaurants with lakeside settings. This is one of the few. Kaspian is set along the west shore of the lake at 6,235 feet elevation, near the little town of Tahoe Pines. A Forest Service road (03) is available adjacent to the camp on the west side of Highway 89, routed west into national forest (becoming quite rough) to a trailhead. From there you can hike up to Barker Peak (8,166 feet) for incredible views of Lake Tahoe, as well as access to the Pacific Crest Trail.

RV sites, facilities: There are nine walk-in sites for tents only. RVs up to 20 feet may use the parking lot on a space-available basis. Picnic tables and fire grills are provided. Drinking water, food lockers, and flush toilets are available. A grocery store, coin laundry, and propane gas are nearby. Leashed pets are permitted.

Reservations, fees: Reservations are accepted at 877/444-6777 or www.recreation.gov ($10 reservation fee). Sites are $15 per night, $5 per night for each additional vehicle. Open May through September, weather permitting.

Directions: From Truckee, drive south on Highway 89 to Tahoe City. Turn south on Highway 89 and drive four miles to the campground (signed) on the west side of the road. The tent sites require a walk-in of 50–100 feet.

Contact: Lake Tahoe Basin Management Unit, 530/543-2600, fax 530/543-2693; Taylor Creek Visitor Center, 530/543-2674; California Land Management, 530/583-3642.

100 SUGAR PINE POINT STATE PARK

Scenic rating: 10

on Lake Tahoe

Map grid A1

This is one of three beautiful and popular state parks on the west shore of Lake Tahoe. It is just north of Meeks Bay on General Creek, with almost two miles of lake frontage available, though the campground is on the opposite side of Highway 89. General Creek, a feeder stream to Lake Tahoe, is one of the clearest streams imaginable. A pretty trail is routed seven miles along the creek up to Lost Lake, just outside the northern boundary of the Desolation Wilderness. This stream also provides trout fishing from mid-July to mid-September. This park contains one of the finest remaining natural areas at Lake Tahoe. The park features dense forests of pine, fir, aspen, and juniper, covering more than 2,000 acres of beautiful landscape. There are many hiking trails and a swimming beach. There is also evidence of occupation by Washoe Indians, with bedrock mortars, or grinding rocks, near the Ehrman Mansion. The elevation is 6,200 feet.

RV sites, facilities: There are 175 sites for tents or RVs up to 32 feet and trailers up to 26 feet (no hookups). There are also 10 group sites for up to 40 people each. Picnic tables and fire rings are provided. Drinking water, restrooms with flush toilets and coin showers (except in winter), dump station, a day-use area, and nature center with bird display are available. A grocery store, coin laundry, and propane gas are available nearby. Some facilities are wheelchair-accessible. Leashed pets are permitted.

Reservations, fees: Reservations are accepted at 800/444-PARK (800/444-7275) or www.reserveamerica.com ($8 reservation fee). Sites are $35 per night, $8 per night for each additional vehicle, $75–165 per night for a group site. Open year-round.

Directions: From Truckee, drive south on Highway 89 through Tahoe City. Continue south on Highway 89 and drive 9.3 miles to the campground (signed) on the right (west) side of the road.

Contact: Sugar Pine Point State Park, 530/525-7982; Sierra District, 530/525-7232, www.parks.ca.gov.

101 MEEKS BAY

Scenic rating: 9

on Lake Tahoe

Map grid A1

Meeks Bay is a beautiful spot along the western shore of Lake Tahoe. A bicycle trail is available nearby and is routed along the lake's shore, but it requires occasionally crossing busy Highway 89.

RV sites, facilities: There are 40 sites for tents or RVs up to 20 feet (no hookups). Picnic tables, food lockers, and fire grills are provided. Drinking water and flush toilets are available. Coin laundry and groceries are available nearby. Leashed pets are permitted.

Reservations, fees: Reservations are accepted at 877/444-6777 or www.recreation.gov ($10 reservation fee). Sites are $20 per night, $5 per night for each additional vehicle. Open mid-May through mid-October, weather permitting.

Directions: In South Lake Tahoe at the junction of Highway 89 and U.S. 50, turn north on Highway 89 and drive 17 miles to the campground (signed) on the east side of Highway 89.

Contact: Lake Tahoe Basin Management Unit, 530/543-2600, fax 530/543-2693; Taylor Creek Visitor Center, 530/543-2674; California Land Management, 530/587-9281 or 650/322-1181.

102 MEEKS BAY RESORT AND MARINA

Scenic rating: 7

on Lake Tahoe

Map grid A1

Prime access for boating makes this a camp of choice for the boater/camper at Lake Tahoe. This campground is extremely popular and

often booked well ahead of time for July and August. A boat launch is on the premises, and access to Rubicon Bay and beyond to breathtaking Emerald Bay is possible, a six-mile trip one-way for boats. The resort is adjacent to a 20-mile paved bike trail, with a swimming beach also nearby. A 14-day stay limit is enforced.

RV sites, facilities: There are 22 sites with full hookups (50 amps) for RVs up to 60 feet, and 12 sites for tents. Some sites are pull-through. Lodge rooms, cabins, and a house are also available. Picnic tables and fire grills are provided. Restrooms with showers and flush toilets, snack bar, gift shop, and a camp store are available. A boat ramp, boat rentals (kayaks, canoes, and paddle boats), and boat slips are also available. No pets are allowed.

Reservations, fees: Reservations are accepted at 877/326-3357. RV sites are $45 per night, tent sites are $25 per night, $60 per night for boat slips, $25 to launch boats. Some credit cards accepted. Open May through September.

Directions: In South Lake Tahoe at the junction of Highway 89 and U.S. 50, turn north on Highway 89 and drive 17 miles to the campground on the right at 7941 Emerald Bay Road.

Contact: Meeks Bay Resort and Marina, 530/525-6946 or 988/326-3357, www.meeksbayresort.com.

103 AIRPORT FLAT

Scenic rating: 6

near Loon Lake in Eldorado National Forest

Map grid A2

Loon Lake is a gorgeous mountain lake in the Crystal Basin. Airport Flat provides an overflow area when the camps at Loon Lake (see listing in this chapter) are full. Trout fishing is good and Loon Lake, along with Ice House Reservoir, is a favorite spot whether for a weekend or a week. Smaller Gerle Creek Reservoir and Union Valley Reservoir are also in the area. The elevation is 5,300 feet.

RV sites, facilities: There are 16 sites for tents

or RVs. Vault toilets, picnic tables, fire rings, and bear-proof boxes are provided. No drinking water is available. Garbage must be packed out. All sites are wheelchair-accessible. Leashed pets are allowed.

Reservations, fees: Reservations are not accepted. There is no camping fee. Open Memorial Day weekend to mid-October.

Directions: From Placerville, drive east on U.S. 50 for 23 miles to Riverton and the junction with Ice House Road/Forest Road 3. Turn north and drive 27 miles (past Union Valley Reservoir) to a fork with Forest Road 30. Turn left toward Gerle Creek Reservoir and the campground is about three miles from the fork, on the right.

Contact: Eldorado National Forest, Pacific Ranger District, 530/644-2349, fax 530/647-5405, www.fs.fed.us.

104 PONDEROSA COVE

Scenic rating: 9

at Stumpy Meadows Reservoir

Map grid A2

Ponderosa Cove is located just east of the dam at Stumpy Meadows Reservoir, a pretty spot with lake views and good trout fishing in the spring and early summer. This is a beautiful lake, surrounded by forest, with clear water and good fishing. A 5-mph speed limit keeps the place quiet and calm. The elevation is 4,400 feet.

RV sites, facilities: There are 18 sites for tents and small RVs. Fire rings are provided. Drinking water and vault toilets are available. A boat launch and a dump station are nearby.

Reservations, fees: Reservations are not accepted. Sites are $12 per night.

Directions: From Sacramento, drive east on I-80 to the north end of Auburn. Take the Elm Avenue exit and at the first signal turn left onto Elm Avenue. Drive 0.1 mile, turn left on High Street, and continue through the signal where High Street merges with Highway 49. Drive on Highway 49 for about 3.5 miles, turn right over the bridge and drive about 2.5 miles into the

town of Cool. Turn left on Georgetown Road/Hwy 193 and drive about 14 miles into Georgetown. At the four-way stop, turn left on Main Street (which becomes Wentworth Springs/Forest Road 1) and drive about 16 miles.

Contact: Eldorado National Forest, Georgetown Ranger District, 530/333-4312, fax 530/333-5522.

105 STUMPY MEADOWS

Scenic rating: 7

on Stumpy Meadows Lake in Eldorado National Forest

Map grid A2

This is the camp of choice for visitors to Stumpy Meadows Lake. The first things visitors notice are the huge ponderosa pine trees, noted for their distinctive, mosaic-like bark. The lake is set at 4,400 feet elevation in Eldorado National Forest and covers 320 acres with water that is cold and clear. The lake has both rainbow and brown trout, and in the fall provides good fishing for big browns (they move up into the head of the lake, near where Pilot Creek enters).

RV sites, facilities: There are 40 sites for tents or RVs of any length (no hookups). Two of the sites are double units. Picnic tables and fire grills are provided. Drinking water and vault toilets are available. A boat ramp is nearby. Leashed pets are permitted.

Reservations, fees: Reservations are accepted at 877/444-6777 or www.recreation.gov ($10 reservation fee). Sites are $17 per night, $34 per night for double-unit sites, $5 per night for each additional vehicle. Boat launching is $8 per day. Open May through mid-October, weather permitting.

Directions: From Sacramento on I-80, drive east to the north end of Auburn. Turn left on Elm Avenue and drive about 0.1 mile. Turn left on High Street and drive through the signal that marks the continuation of High Street as Highway 49. Drive 3.5 miles on Highway 49, turn right over the bridge, and drive 2.5 miles into the town of Cool. Turn left on Georgetown

Road/Highway 193 and drive 14 miles into Georgetown. At the four-way stop, turn left on Main Street, which becomes Georgetown–Wentworth Springs Road/Forest Road 1. Drive about 18 miles to Stumpy Meadows Lake. Continue about a mile and turn right into Stumpy Meadows campground.

Contact: Eldorado National Forest, Georgetown Ranger District, 530/333-4312, fax 530/333-5522.

106 BLACK OAK GROUP CAMP

Scenic rating: 7

near Stumpy Meadows Lake in
Eldorado National Forest

Map grid A2

This group camp is set directly adjacent to Stumpy Meadows Campground. (See the Stumpy Meadows listing in this chapter for more information.) The boat ramp for the lake is just south of the Mark Edson Dam, near the picnic area. The elevation is 4,400 feet.

RV sites, facilities: There are three group sites for tents and one group site for RVs of any length (no hookups) that can accommodate 25–75 people each. Picnic tables and fire grills are provided. Drinking water and vault toilets are available. A boat ramp is nearby. Leashed pets are permitted.

Reservations, fees: Reservations are accepted at 877/444-6777 or www.recreation.gov ($10 reservation fee). Sites are $50–100 per night. Boat launching is $8 per day. Open mid-May through mid-September, weather permitting.

Directions: From Sacramento on I-80, drive east to the north end of Auburn. Turn left on Elm Avenue and drive about 0.1 mile. Turn left on High Street and drive through the signal that marks the continuation of High Street as Highway 49. Drive 3.5 miles on Highway 49, turn right over the bridge, and drive 2.5 miles into the town of Cool. Turn left on Georgetown Road/Highway 193 and drive 14 miles into Georgetown. At the four-way stop, turn left on Main Street, which becomes

Georgetown–Wentworth Springs Road/Forest Road 1. Drive about 18 miles to Stumpy Meadows Lake, and then continue for two miles to the north shore of the lake and the campground entrance road on the right.

Contact: Eldorado National Forest, Georgetown Ranger District, 530/333-4312, fax 530/333-5522.

107 GERLE CREEK

Scenic rating: 7

on Gerle Creek Reservoir in
Eldorado National Forest

Map grid A2

This is a small, pretty, but limited spot set along the northern shore of little Gerle Creek Reservoir at 5,231 feet elevation. The lake is ideal for canoes or other small boats because no motors are permitted and no boat ramp is available. That makes for quiet water. It is set in the Gerle Creek Canyon, which feeds into the South Fork Rubicon River. No trout plants are made at this lake, and fishing can be correspondingly poor. A wild brown trout population lives here, though. A network of Forest Service roads to the north can provide great exploring. A map of Eldorado National Forest is a must.

RV sites, facilities: There are 50 sites for tents or RVs up to 40 feet (no hookups). Picnic tables and fire grills are provided. Drinking water and vault toilets are available. Wheelchair-accessible trails and fishing pier are available nearby. Leashed pets are permitted.

Reservations, fees: Reservations are accepted at 877/444-6777 or www.recreation.gov ($10 reservation fee). Sites are $20 per night, $6 per night for each additional vehicle. Open mid-May through mid-October, weather permitting.

Directions: From Placerville, drive east on U.S. 50 for 23 miles to Riverton and the junction with Ice House Road/Forest Road 3. Turn north and drive 27 miles (past Union Valley Reservoir) to a fork with Forest Road 30. Turn left, drive two miles, bear left on the

CALIFORNIA

campground entrance road, and drive a mile to the campground.

Contact: Eldorado National Forest, Pacific Ranger District, 530/644-2349, fax 530/647-5405.

108 NORTHSHORE

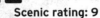

Scenic rating: 9

on Loon Lake in Eldorado National Forest
Map grid A2

The waterfront sites are in an extremely pretty setting on the northwestern shore of Loon Lake. There are few facilities, though, and no boat ramp; the boat ramp is near the Loon Lake campground and picnic area at the south end of the lake. (For more information, see the Loon Lake and Pleasant Hike-In/Boat-In listings.)

RV sites, facilities: There are 15 sites for tents or RVs up to 35 feet (no hookups). Picnic tables and fire grills are provided. Vault toilets are available. There is no drinking water. Some facilities are wheelchair-accessible. Leashed pets are permitted.

Reservations, fees: Reservations are not accepted. Sites are $10 per night, $6 per night for each additional vehicle. Open June through September, weather permitting.

Directions: From Placerville, drive east on U.S. 50 for 23 miles to Riverton and the junction with Ice House Road/Forest Road 3. Turn left and drive 34 miles to a fork at the foot of Loon Lake. Turn left and drive three miles to the campground.

Contact: Eldorado National Forest, Pacific Ranger District, 530/644-2349, fax 530/644-5405.

109 LOON LAKE

Scenic rating: 9

in Eldorado National Forest
Map grid A2

Loon Lake is set near the Sierra crest at 6,400 feet, covering 600 acres with depths up to 130 feet. This is the lake's primary campground, and it is easy to see why, with a picnic

area, beach (includes a small unit for changing clothes), and boat ramp adjacent to the camp. The lake provides good trout fishing, and the lake is stocked on a regular basis once the access road is clear of snow. Afternoon winds drive anglers off the lake but are cheered by sailboarders. An excellent trail is also available here, with the hike routed along the lake's eastern shore to Pleasant Hike-In/Boat-In, where there's a trailhead for the Desolation Wilderness.

RV sites, facilities: There are 53 sites for tents or RVs up to 40 feet, nine equestrian sites, and one group equestrian site for tents or RVs up to 40 feet that can accommodate up to 25 people. No hookups. Picnic tables and fire grills are provided. Drinking water and vault toilets are available. Tie lines are available for horses. A boat ramp and swimming beach are nearby. A dump station is two miles away. Some facilities are wheelchair-accessible. Leashed pets are permitted.

Reservations, fees: Reservations are accepted at 877/444-6777 or www.recreation.gov ($10 reservation fee). Sites are $20 per night, $40 per night for a double site, $6 per night for each additional vehicle. Open June through mid-October, weather permitting.

Directions: From Placerville, drive east on U.S. 50 for 23 miles to Riverton and the junction with Ice House Road/Forest Road 3. Turn left and drive 34 miles to a fork at the foot of Loon Lake. Turn right and drive one mile to the Loon Lake Picnic Area or boat ramp.

Contact: Eldorado National Forest, Pacific Ranger District, 530/644-2349, fax 530/644-5405.

110 BIG SILVER GROUP CAMP

Scenic rating: 7

on Big Silver Creek in Eldorado National Forest
Map grid A2

This camp was built along the Union Valley bike trail, less than a mile from Union Valley Reservoir. The paved bike trail stretches for miles both north and south of the campground and is wheelchair-accessible. It's a classic Sierra forest setting, with plenty of ponderosa pine on the north side of Big Silver Creek.

RV sites, facilities: There is one group site for tents or RVs up to 50 feet (no hookups) that can accommodate up to 50 people. Picnic tables and fire grills are provided. Vault toilets are available. No drinking water is available. There is also a group kitchen area with pedestal grills. Some facilities are wheelchair-accessible. Leashed pets are permitted.

Reservations, fees: Reservations are required at 877/444-6777 or www.recreation.gov ($10 reservation fee). The camp is $50 per night. Open late May through mid-October, weather permitting.

Directions: From Placerville, drive east on U.S. 50 for 23 miles to Riverton and the junction with Ice House Road/Forest Road 3. Turn left (north) and drive about 16 miles to the campground.

Contact: Eldorado National Forest, Pacific Ranger District, 530/644-2349, fax 530/647-5405.

111 WEST POINT

Scenic rating: 9

at Union Valley Reservoir in
Eldorado National Forest

Map grid A2

West Point is a pretty, primitive campground on the northwest shore of little Union Valley Reservoir. This is a pretty spot in the Crystal Basin that sometimes gets overlooked in the shadow of Loon Lake and Ice House Reservoir. But the camping, low-speed boating, and trout fishing can be excellent. Some surprise giant mackinaw trout and brown trout can provide a fish of a lifetime when the lake first opens in late spring. The elevation is 4,875 feet.

RV sites, facilities: There are eight sites for tents or RVs. Vault toilet and a boat launch are available. Fire rings are provided, but there are no grills or picnic tables. Drinking water is not available. Some sites are wheelchair-accessible.

Reservations, fees: Reservations are not accepted. There is no camping fee.

Directions: From Placerville, drive east on

Highway 50 for 23 miles to Riverton and the junction with Ice House Road/Forest Road 3. Turn north on Ice House Road, and drive 7 miles to Peavine Ridge Road. Turn left on Peavine Ridge Road and drive east for 3 miles to Bryant Springs Road. Turn right on Bryant Springs Road and drive north 5 miles to just past West Point Boat Ramp on the right.

Contact: Eldorado National Forest, Pacific Ranger District, 530/644-2349, fax 530/647-5405, www.fs.fed.us.

112 WOLF CREEK AND WOLF CREEK GROUP

Scenic rating: 9

on Union Valley Reservoir in
Eldorado National Forest

Map grid A2

Wolf Creek Camp is on the north shore of Union Valley Reservoir. Listen up? Notice that it's quieter? Yep. That's because there are not as many water-skiers in the vicinity. Why? The nearest boat ramp is three miles away. The view of the Crystal Range from the campground is drop-dead gorgeous. The elevation is 4,900 feet.

RV sites, facilities: There are 42 sites for tents or RVs up to 40 feet, and three group sites for tents or RVs up to 40 feet that can accommodate up to 50 people each. No hookups. Picnic tables and fire grills are provided. Drinking water and vault toilets are available. Some facilities are wheelchair-accessible. A boat ramp is three miles away at the campground at Yellowjacket. Leashed pets are permitted.

Reservations, fees: Reservations are accepted for individual sites and required for group sites at 877/444-6777 or www.recreation.gov ($10 reservation fee). Sites are $20 per night for a single site, $40 per night for a double site, $5 per night for each additional vehicle. Group sites are $100–150 per night. Open mid-May through mid-September, weather permitting.

Directions: From Placerville, drive east on U.S. 50 for 23 miles to Riverton and the junction with Ice House Road/Forest Road 3. Turn

CALIFORNIA

left (north) and drive 19 miles to Forest Road 12N78/Union Valley Road (at the head of Union Valley Reservoir). Turn left (west) and drive two miles to the campground.

Contact: Eldorado National Forest, Pacific Ranger District, 530/644-2349, fax 530/647-5405.

113 CAMINO COVE

Scenic rating: 10

on Union Valley Reservoir in Eldorado National Forest

Map grid A2

Camino Cove Camp is the nicest spot at Union Valley Reservoir, a slam dunk. It is set at the north end of the lake on a peninsula, absolutely beautiful, a tree-covered landscape and yet with sweeping views of the Crystal Basin. The nearest boat ramp is 1.5 miles to the west at West Point. If this camp is full, there is a small camp at West Point, with just eight sites. The elevation is 4,900 feet.

RV sites, facilities: There are 32 sites for tents or RVs up to 30 feet (no hookups). Fire rings are provided. Vault toilets are available. No drinking water is available. Garbage must be packed out. A swimming beach is nearby and a boat ramp is 1.5 miles away at the campground at West Point. Some facilities are wheelchair-accessible. Leashed pets are permitted.

Reservations, fees: Reservations are not accepted. There is no fee for camping. Open early May through October, weather permitting.

Directions: From Placerville, drive east on U.S. 50 for 23 miles to Riverton and the junction with Ice House Road/Forest Road 3. Turn north on Ice House Road and drive seven miles to Peavine Ridge Road. Turn left and drive three miles to Bryant Springs Road. Turn right and drive five miles north past the West Point boat ramp, and continue 1.5 miles east to the campground entrance on the right.

Contact: Eldorado National Forest, Pacific Ranger District, 530/644-2349, fax 530/647-5405.

114 YELLOWJACKET

Scenic rating: 8

on Union Valley Reservoir in Eldorado National Forest

Map grid A2

The camp is set at 4,900 feet elevation on the north shore of gorgeous Union Valley Reservoir. A boat launch adjacent to the camp makes this an ideal destination for trout-angling campers with boats. Union Valley Reservoir, a popular weekend destination for campers from the Central Valley, is stocked with brook trout and rainbow trout by the Department of Fish and Game.

RV sites, facilities: There are 40 sites for tents or RVs up to 30 feet (no hookups). Picnic tables and fire rings are provided. Drinking water and vault toilets are available. A boat ramp and dump station are nearby. Leashed pets are permitted.

Reservations, fees: Reservations are accepted at 877/444-6777 or www.recreation.gov ($10 reservation fee). Sites are $20 per night, $6 per night for each additional vehicle. Open mid-May through mid-September, weather permitting.

Directions: From Placerville, drive east on U.S. 50 for 23 miles to Riverton and the junction with Ice House Road/Forest Road 3. Turn left (north) and drive 19 miles to Forest Road 12N78/Union Valley Road (at the head of Union Valley Reservoir). Turn left (west) and drive one mile to Forest Road 12N33. Turn left (south) and drive 0.5 mile to the campground.

Contact: Eldorado National Forest, Pacific Ranger District, 530/644-2349, fax 530/647-5405.

115 WENCH CREEK AND WENCH CREEK GROUP

Scenic rating: 7

on Union Valley Reservoir in Eldorado National Forest

Map grid A2

Wench Creek is on the northeast shore of Union Valley Reservoir. (For more information, see the

Jones Fork and Peninsula Recreation Area listings in this chapter.) The elevation is 4,900 feet.

RV sites, facilities: There are 100 sites for tents or RVs up to 25 feet (no hookups), and two group tent sites for up to 50 people each. Picnic tables and fire grills are provided. Drinking water and vault toilets are available. A boat ramp is three miles away at the Yellowjacket campground. Leashed pets are permitted.

Reservations, fees: Reservations are not accepted for individual sites, but are accepted for group sites at 877/444-6777 or www.recreation. gov ($10 reservation fee). Sites are $20 per night, $6 per night for each additional vehicle. The group sites are $120 per night. Open mid-May through September.

Directions: From Placerville, drive east on U.S. 50 for 23 miles to Riverton and the junction with Ice House Road/Forest Road 3. Turn left and drive 15 miles to the campground entrance road (four miles past the turnoff for Sunset Camp). Turn left and drive a mile to the campground at the end of the road.

Contact: Eldorado National Forest, Pacific Ranger District, 530/644-2349, fax 530/647-5405.

116 PENINSULA RECREATION AREA

Scenic rating: 8

on Union Valley Reservoir in
Eldorado National Forest

Map grid A2

The two campgrounds here, Sunset and Fashoda, are the prettiest of all the camps at Union Valley Reservoir, set at the eastern tip of the peninsula that juts into the lake at the mouth of Jones Fork. A nearby boat ramp (you'll see it on the left on the way in) is a big plus, along with a picnic area and beach. All water sports are allowed. The lake has decent trout fishing, with brook trout, brown trout, rainbow trout, Mackinaw, kokanee salmon, and smallmouth bass. The place is gorgeous, set at 4,900 feet elevation in the Sierra Nevada.

RV sites, facilities: There are 131 sites for tents

or RVs up to 50 feet (no hookups) at Sunset Camp and 30 walk-in tent sites at Fashoda Camp. Picnic tables, fire rings, and fire grills are provided. Drinking water, coin showers (at Fashoda), vault toilets, boat ramp, and a dump station are available. Some facilities are wheelchair-accessible. Leashed pets are permitted.

Reservations, fees: Reservations are accepted at 877/444-6777 or www.recreation.gov ($10 reservation fee). Sites are $20 per night, $40 per night for a double site, $6 per night for each additional vehicle. Open late May through late September, weather permitting.

Directions: From Placerville, drive east on U.S. 50 for 23 miles to Riverton and the junction with Ice House Road/Forest Road 3. Turn left and drive 14 miles to the campground entrance road (a mile past the turnoff for Jones Fork Camp). Turn left and drive 1.5 miles to the campground at the end of the road.

Contact: Eldorado National Forest, Pacific Ranger District, 530/644-2349, fax 530/647-5405.

117 JONES FORK

Scenic rating: 7

on Union Valley Reservoir in
Eldorado National Forest

Map grid A2

The Crystal Basin Recreation Area is the most popular backcountry region for campers from the Sacramento area, and Union Valley Reservoir is the centerpiece. The area gets its name from the prominent granite Sierra ridge, which looks like crystal when it is covered with frozen snow. This is a big lake, set at 4,900 feet elevation, with numerous lakeside campgrounds and three boat ramps providing access. This is the first camp you will arrive at, set at the mouth of the Jones Fork Cove.

RV sites, facilities: There are 10 sites for tents or RVs up to 25 feet (no hookups). Picnic tables and fire rings are provided. Vault toilets are available. No drinking water is available. Leashed pets are permitted.

Reservations, fees: Reservations are not accepted.

Sites are $10 per night, $5 per night for each additional vehicle. Open June through October.

Directions: From Placerville, drive east on U.S. 50 for 23 miles to Riverton and the junction with Ice House Road/Forest Road 3. Turn left and drive 14 miles to the campground entrance road on the left (at the south end of Union Valley Reservoir). Turn left and drive 0.5 mile to the campground.

Contact: Eldorado National Forest, Pacific Ranger District, 530/644-2349, fax 530/647-5405.

118 ICE HOUSE UPPER AND LOWER

Scenic rating: 8

on Ice House Reservoir in Eldorado National Forest
Map grid A2

Along with Loon Lake and Union Valley Reservoir, Ice House Reservoir is a feature destination in the Crystal Basin Recreation Area. Ice House gets most of the anglers and Union Valley gets most of the campers. All water sports are allowed at Ice House, though. The camp is set on the lake's northwestern shore, at 5,500 feet elevation, just up from the dam and adjacent to the lake's boat ramp. The lake, created by a dam on South Fork Silver Creek, covers 650 acres with the deepest spot about 130 feet deep. It is stocked with rainbow trout, brook trout, and brown trout. A 2.5-mile bike trail connects Ice House to Northwind and Strawberry Point campgrounds.

RV sites, facilities: There are 83 sites for tents or RVs up to 30 feet (no hookups). Picnic tables and fire grills are provided. Drinking water, vault toilets, boat ramp, and a dump station are available. Some facilities are wheelchair-accessible. Leashed pets are permitted.

Reservations, fees: Reservations are accepted at 877/444-6777 or www.recreation.gov ($10 reservation fee). Sites are $20 per night, $40 per night for a double site, $6 per night for each additional vehicle. Open late May through mid-October, weather permitting.

Directions: From Placerville, drive east on U.S. 50 for 23 miles to Riverton and the junction with Ice House Road/Forest Road 3. Turn left

(north) and drive 11 miles to Forest Road 32/Ice House/Wrights Tie Road. Turn right (east) and drive 1.5 miles to the campground access road on the right.

Contact: Eldorado National Forest, Pacific Ranger District, 530/644-2349, fax 530/647-5405.

119 NORTHWIND

Scenic rating: 7

on Ice House Reservoir in Eldorado National Forest
Map grid A2

This camp sits on the north shore of Ice House Reservoir. It is slightly above the reservoir, offering prime views. A 2.5-mile bike trail connects Northwind with Ice House and Strawberry Point campgrounds. (See the Ice House listing for more information.)

RV sites, facilities: There are nine sites for tents or RVs up to 40 feet (no hookups). Picnic tables and fire grills are provided. Vault toilets are available. No drinking water is available. Some facilities are wheelchair-accessible. Leashed pets are permitted.

Reservations, fees: Reservations are not accepted. Sites are $10 per night, $5 per night for each additional vehicle. Open May through mid-October, weather permitting.

Directions: From Placerville, drive east on U.S. 50 for 23 miles to Riverton and the junction with Ice House Road/Forest Road 3. Turn left (north) and drive 11 miles to Forest Road 32/Ice House/Wrights Tie Road. Turn right (east) and drive three miles (two miles past the boat ramp) to the campground access road on the right.

Contact: Eldorado National Forest, Pacific Ranger District, 530/644-2349, fax 530/647-5405.

120 STRAWBERRY POINT

Scenic rating: 7

on Ice House Reservoir in Eldorado National Forest
Map grid A2

This camp is set on the north shore of Ice House Reservoir, at 5,400 feet elevation. A 2.5-

mile bike trail connects Strawberry Point with Northwind and Ice House campgrounds. (For more information, see the Ice House listing in this chapter.)

RV sites, facilities: There are 10 sites for tents or RVs up to 40 feet (no hookups). Picnic tables and fire grills are provided. Vault toilets are available. No drinking water is available. Some facilities are wheelchair-accessible. Leashed pets are permitted.

Reservations, fees: Reservations are not accepted. Sites are $10 per night, $5 per night for each additional vehicle. Open May through December, weather permitting.

Directions: From Placerville, drive east on U.S. 50 for 23 miles to Riverton and the junction with Ice House Road/Forest Road 3. Turn left (north) and drive 11 miles to Forest Road 32/Ice House/Wrights Tie Road. Turn right (east) and drive three miles (three miles past the boat ramp) to the campground access road on the road.

Contact: Eldorado National Forest, Pacific Ranger District, 530/644-2349, fax 530/647-5405.

121 WRIGHTS LAKE AND EQUESTRIAN

Scenic rating: 9

in Eldorado National Forest

Map grid A2

This high mountain lake (7,000 feet) has shoreline picnicking and good fishing and hiking. There is no boat ramp, and the rules do not permit motors, so it is ideal for canoes, rafts, prams, and people who like quiet. Swimming is allowed. Fishing is fair for both rainbow trout and brown trout. It is a classic alpine lake, though small (65 acres), with a trailhead for the Desolation Wilderness at its north end. From here it is only a three-mile hike to the beautiful Twin Lakes and Island Lake, set on the western flank of Mount Price (9,975 feet).

RV sites, facilities: There are 67 sites for tents or RVs up to 50 feet (no hookups) and 15 sites at the equestrian camp. Picnic tables and fire grills are provided. Drinking water and vault toilets

are available. Some facilities are wheelchair-accessible, including a boat dock. Leashed pets are permitted.

Reservations, fees: Reservations are accepted and are required for some sites in July and August at 877/444-6777 or www.recreation.gov ($10 reservation fee). Sites are $20 per night, $40 per night for a double site, $5 per night for each additional vehicle. Open late June through mid-October, weather permitting.

Directions: From Placerville, drive east on U.S. 50 for 23 miles to Riverton and the junction with Ice House Road/Forest Road 3. Turn left (north) and drive 11 miles to Forest Road 32/Ice House/Wrights Tie Road. Turn right (east) and drive nine miles to Forest Road 4/Wrights Lake Road. Turn left (north) and drive two miles to the campground on the right side of the road.

Contact: Eldorado National Forest, Pacific Ranger District, 530/644-2349, fax 530/644-5405.

122 D. L. BLISS STATE PARK

Scenic rating: 10

on Lake Tahoe

Map grid A2   BEST (

D. L. Bliss State Park is set on one of Lake Tahoe's most beautiful stretches of shoreline, from Emerald Point at the mouth of Emerald Bay northward to Rubicon Point, spanning about three miles. The camp is at the north end of the park, the sites nestled amid pine trees, with 80 percent of the campsites within 0.5–1 mile of the beach. The park is named for a pioneering lumberman, railroad owner, and banker of the region, whose family donated this 744-acre parcel to California in 1929. There are two great easy hiking trails. Rubicon Trail is one of Tahoe's most popular easy hikes, a meandering path just above the southwest shore of Lake Tahoe, wandering through pine, cedar, and fir, with breaks for fantastic panoramas of the lake, as well as spots where you can see nearly 100 feet into the lake. Don't be surprised if you are joined by a chipmunk circus, many begging, sitting upright, hoping for their nut for the day. While this trail is beautiful and solitary at dawn, by noon it can be crowded with hikers and chipmunks alike. Another trail, a great hike for youngsters, is Balancing Rock Trail, just a 0.5-mile romp, where after about 40 yards you arrive at this 130-ton, oblong granite boulder that is set on a tiny perch, and the whole thing seems to defy gravity. Some day it has to fall, right? Not yet. Rubicon Trail runs all the way past Emerald Point to Emerald Bay.

RV sites, facilities: There are 165 sites for tents or RVs up to 18 feet (no hookups) and trailers up to 15 feet, one hike-in/bike-in site, and a group site for up to 50 people. Picnic tables, fire grills, and food lockers are provided. Restrooms with coin showers and flush toilets are available. All water must sometimes be pump-filtered or boiled before use, depending on current water conditions. Some facilities are wheelchair-accessible. Leashed pets are permitted at campsites only.

Reservations, fees: Reservations are accepted at 800/444-PARK (800/444-7275) or www.reserveamerica.com ($8 reservation fee). Sites are $35 per night, $8 per night for each additional vehicle, $165 per night for group site, $6 per night for hike-in/bike-in site. Open late May through late September, weather permitting.

Directions: In South Lake Tahoe at the junction of Highway 89 and U.S. 50, turn north on Highway 89 and drive 10.5 miles to the state park turnoff on the right side of the road. Turn right (east) and drive to the park entrance. (If arriving from the north, drive from Tahoe City south on Highway 89 for 17 miles to the park entrance road.)

Contact: D. L. Bliss State Park, 530/525-7277; Sierra District, 530/525-7232, www.parks.ca.gov.

123 EMERALD BAY STATE PARK AND BOAT-IN

Scenic rating: 10

on Lake Tahoe

Map grid A2   **BEST (**

Emerald Bay is a place of rare and divine beauty, one of the most striking and popular state parks on the planet. With its deep cobalt-blue waters, awesome surrounding ridgelines, glimpses of Lake Tahoe out the mouth of the bay, and even a little island, there may be no place more perfect to run a boat or kayak.

There are boat-in camps on the northern side of Emerald Bay, set in pine forest with water views. Even when Tahoe is packed, there are times when you can paddle right up and find a site—though reservations at one of the 22 boat-in sites makes for a sure thing, of course. Drive-in campsites are available near Eagle Point at the mouth of Emerald Bay. Sites are also accessible via the Rubicon Trail from D. L. Bliss State Park.

Emerald Bay is a designated underwater park featuring Fanette Island, Tahoe's only island, and Vikingsholm, one of the greatest examples of Scandinavian architecture in North America. Vikingsholm is located along the shore about a mile's hike from the campground and tours are very popular. The park also has several short hiking trails.

RV sites, facilities: There are 100 sites for tents or RVs up to 21 feet (no hookups) and trailers up to 18 feet and 22 boat-in sites. Picnic tables and fire grills are provided. Drinking water and restrooms with flush toilets and coin showers are available. At boat-in sites, drinking water and vault toilets are available. Leashed pets are permitted in the campground and on asphalt, but not on trails.

Reservations, fees: Reservations are accepted at 800/444-PARK (800/444-7275) or www.reserveamerica.com ($8 reservation fee). Sites are $25–35 per night, $7 per night for each additional vehicle, $11–15 per night for boat-in sites. Open early June through mid-September, weather permitting.

Directions: In South Lake Tahoe at the junction of Highway 89 and U.S. 50, turn north on Highway 89 and drive 6.5 miles to the state park entrance turnoff on the right side of the road.

Contact: Emerald Bay State Park, 530/541-3030, or D. L. Bliss State Park, 530/525-7277, www.parks.ca.gov.

124 HISTORIC CAMP RICHARDSON RESORT

Scenic rating: 7

on Lake Tahoe

Map grid A2

Camp Richardson Resort is within minutes of boating, biking, gambling, and, in the winter, skiing and snowboarding. It's a take-your-pick deal. With cabins, restaurant, and live music (often nightly in summer) also on the property, this is a place that offers one big package. The campsites are set in the woods, not on the lake itself. From here you can gain access to an excellent bike route that runs for three miles, then loops around by the lake for another three miles, most of it flat and easy, all of it beautiful. Expect company. The elevation is 6,300 feet.

RV sites, facilities: There are 223 sites for tents, and 112 sites with full or partial hookups (30 amps) for RVs up to 35 feet, including two pull-through sites. Cabins, duplex units, inn rooms, and hotel rooms are also available. Picnic tables and fire pits are provided. Restrooms with showers and flush toilets, drinking water, dump station, group facilities, and playground are available. A full-service marina, boat ramp, boat rentals, swimming beach, bike rentals, general store, restaurant, ice cream parlor, and propane gas are nearby. Some facilities are wheelchair-accessible.

Reservations, fees: Reservations are accepted at 800/544-1801. Sites are $30–38 per night, $5 per night for each additional vehicle. Some credit cards accepted. Open June through October, with lodging available year-round.

Directions: In South Lake Tahoe at the junction of Highway 89 and U.S. 50, turn north on Highway 89 and drive 2.5 miles to the resort on the right side of the road.

Contact: Historic Camp Richardson Resort, 530/541-1801, www.camprichardson.com.

125 CAMP SHELLY

Scenic rating: 7

near Lake Tahoe in the Lake Tahoe Basin

Map grid A2

This campground is set near South Lake Tahoe within close range of an outstanding bicycle trail. The camp is set in the woods, with campfire programs available on Saturday night in summer. Nearby to the west is the drive to Inspiration Point and the incredible lookout of Emerald Bay, as well as the parking area for the short hike to Eagle Falls. Nearby to the east are Fallen Leaf Lake and the south shore of Lake Tahoe.

RV sites, facilities: There are 26 sites for tents or RVs up to 24 feet long and 10.5 feet high (no hookups). Picnic tables and fire grills are provided. Drinking water, restrooms with free showers and flush toilets, horseshoes, ping-pong, volleyball, and basketball are available. Some facilities are wheelchair-accessible. Groceries, propane, and a boat ramp are available nearby at Camp Richardson. Leashed pets are permitted.

Reservations, fees: Reservations can be made in person, 9 A.M.–4 P.M. Monday–Friday, at the Robert Livermore Community Center, 4444 East Avenue, Livermore, CA 94550. Reservations can also be made by mail, fax, or at the campground office, which is intermittently staffed during the season. A reservation form can be downloaded from the website. Sites are $30 per night, ($25 for Livermore residents), $5 per night for each additional vehicle. Open mid-June through Labor Day weekend.

Directions: In South Lake Tahoe at the junction of U.S. 50 and Highway 89, turn north on Highway 89, drive 2.5 miles to Camp Richardson, and then continue for 1.3 miles to the sign for Mount Tallac. Turn left at the sign for Mount Tallac Trailhead/Camp Shelly and drive to the campground on the right.

Contact: Camp Shelly, 530/541-6985; Livermore Area Recreation and Park District, 925/373-5700 or 925/960-2400, fax 925/960-2457, www.larpd.dst.ca.us.

CALIFORNIA

126 FALLEN LEAF CAMPGROUND

Scenic rating: 7

in the Lake Tahoe Basin

Map grid A2

This is a large camp near the north shore of Fallen Leaf Lake, set at 6,337 feet elevation. The lake is big (three miles long), quite deep (430 feet at its deepest point), and almost as blue as nearby Lake Tahoe. A concessionaire operates the campground. There are a variety of recreational opportunities, including boat rentals at the marina and horseback-riding at Camp Richardson Resort. Fishing is best in the fall for kokanee salmon. Because Fallen Leaf Lake is circled by forest—much of it private property— you will need a boat to fish or explore the lake. A visitors center is north of the Fallen Leaf Lake turnoff on Highway 89.

RV sites, facilities: There are 75 sites for tents and 130 sites for tents or RVs up to 40 feet (no hookups). Picnic tables, food lockers, and fire grills are provided. Drinking water, vault toilets, and coin showers are available. A boat ramp, coin laundry, and supplies are nearby. Some facilities are wheelchair-accessible. Leashed pets are permitted.

Reservations, fees: Reservations are accepted at 877/444-6777 or www.recreation.gov ($10 reservation fee). Sites are $25 per night, $5 per night for each additional vehicle. Open mid-May through mid-October, weather permitting.

Directions: In South Lake Tahoe at the junction of U.S. 50 and Highway 89, turn north on Highway 89 and drive two miles to the Fallen Leaf Lake turnoff. Turn left and drive 1.5 miles to the campground.

Contact: Lake Tahoe Basin Management Unit, 530/543-2600, fax 530/543-2693; Taylor Creek Visitor Center, 530/543-2674; California Land Management, 530/587-9281 or 650/322-1181; Fallen Leaf Lake Marina, 530/544-0787.

127 TAHOE VALLEY CAMPGROUND

Scenic rating: 5

near Lake Tahoe

Map grid A2

This is a massive, privately operated park near South Lake Tahoe. The nearby attractions include five golf courses, horseback riding, casinos, and, of course, "The Lake." Note that about half of the sites are filled with seasonal renters.

RV sites, facilities: There are 305 sites with full or partial hookups (30 and 50 amps) for RVs of any length, 77 sites for tents, and two group sites. Some RV sites are pull-through. Picnic tables and fire grills are provided. Restrooms with showers, cable TV, Wi-Fi, modem access, dump station, coin laundry, seasonal heated swimming pool, playground, tennis courts, grocery store, RV supplies, propane gas, ice, firewood, and recreation room are available. Some facilities are wheelchair-accessible. Leashed pets are permitted.

Reservations, fees: Reservations are recommended. Sites are $36–54 per night. Monthly rates available. Credit cards accepted. Open year-round.

Directions: Entering South Lake Tahoe on U.S. 50, drive east on U.S. 50 to Meyers. Continue on U.S. 50 about five miles beyond Meyers to the signed entrance on the right. Turn right on C Street and drive 1.5 blocks to the campground.

Contact: Tahoe Valley Campground, 530/541-2222, fax 530/541-1825, www.rvonthego.com.

128 CAMPGROUND BY THE LAKE

Scenic rating: 5

near Lake Tahoe

Map grid A2

This city-operated campground provides an option at South Lake Tahoe. It is set at 6,200 feet elevation, across the road from the lake, with pine trees and views of the lake.

RV sites, facilities: There are 175 sites for tents or RVs up to 40 feet, and one group site for up to 30 people. Some sites have partial hookups (30 and 50 amps) and/or are pull-through. One cabin is also available. Picnic tables, barbecues, and fire grills are provided. Drinking water, restrooms with flush toilets and showers, dump station, playground, and boat ramp (check current status) are available. An indoor ice-skating rink and a public indoor heated pool are nearby (fee for access). Some facilities are wheelchair-accessible. Supplies and a coin laundry are nearby. Leashed pets are permitted.

Reservations, fees: Reservations are accepted at 530/542-6096 ($3.50 reservation fee). Sites are $23–31 per night, $4 per night for each additional vehicle, $152.50 per night for the group site, $1 per pet per night. Weekly rates available. Some credit cards accepted. Open April through October, with a 14-day maximum stay.

Directions: If entering South Lake Tahoe on U.S. 50, drive east on U.S. 50 to Rufus Allen Boulevard. Turn right and drive 0.25 mile to the campground on the right side of the road.

Contact: Campground by the Lake, 530/542-6096; City of South Lake Tahoe, Parks and Recreation Department, 530/542-6055, www.recreationintahoe.com.

129 KOA SOUTH LAKE TAHOE

Scenic rating: 5

near Lake Tahoe

Map grid A2

Like so many KOA camps, this one is on the outskirts of a major destination area, in this case, South Lake Tahoe. It is within close range of gambling, fishing, hiking, and bike rentals. The camp is set at 6,300 feet elevation.

RV sites, facilities: There are 40 sites with full hookups (30 amps) for RVs up to 36 feet, and 16 sites with no hookups for tents and RVs. Some sites are pull-through. A lodge is also available. Picnic tables and fire grills are provided. Restrooms with showers, cable TV, Wi-Fi, dump station, recreation room, seasonal heated swimming pool, playground, coin laundry, convenience store, RV supplies, horseshoes, firewood, ice, and propane gas are available. Leashed pets are permitted.

Reservations, fees: Reservations are recommended at 800/562-3477. Sites are $36–66 per night, $5 per person per night for more than two people, $5 per night for each additional vehicle, $10–25 per boat per night, $5 per pet per night. Weekly and monthly rates available. Holiday rates are higher. Some credit cards accepted. Open April through mid-October.

Directions: From Sacramento, take U.S. 50 and drive east over the Sierra Nevada past Echo Summit to Meyers. As you enter Meyers, it will be the first campground on the right. Turn right and enter the campground.

Contact: KOA South Lake Tahoe, 530/577-3693, www.laketahoekoa.com.

130 SAND FLAT-AMERICAN RIVER

Scenic rating: 7

on the South Fork of the American River in Eldorado National Forest

Map grid A2

This first-come, first-served campground often gets filled up by U.S. 50 travelers. And why not? You get easy access, a well-signed exit, and a nice setting on the South Fork of the American River. The elevation is 3,900 feet. The river is very pretty here, but fishing is often poor. In winter, the snow level usually starts just a few miles uphill.

RV sites, facilities: There are 29 sites for tents or RVs of any length (no hookups) and six walk-in tent sites. Picnic tables and fire grills are provided. Drinking water and vault toilets are available. Groceries, restaurant, and gas are nearby. Some facilities are wheelchair-accessible. Leashed pets are permitted.

Reservations, fees: Reservations are not accepted. Sites are $16 per night, $32 per night for a double site, $6 per night for each additional vehicle. Open May through late October, weather permitting.

Directions: From Sacramento, drive east on U.S. 50 to Placerville and then continue 28 miles to the campground on the right. (If you reach the Kyburz store, you have driven about one mile too far.)

Contact: Eldorado National Forest, Placerville Ranger District, 530/644-2324, fax 530/647-5315.

131 CHINA FLAT

Scenic rating: 7

on the Silver Fork of the American River in Eldorado National Forest

Map grid A2

China Flat sits across the road from the Silver Fork American River, with a nearby access road that is routed along the river for a mile. This provides access for fishing, swimming, gold panning, and exploring. The elevation is 4,800 feet. The camp feels far off the beaten path, even though it is only five minutes from that parade of traffic on U.S. 50.

RV sites, facilities: There are 18 sites for tents or RVs of any length (no hookups). Picnic tables and fire grills are provided. Drinking water and vault toilets are available. Some facilities are wheelchair-accessible. Leashed pets are permitted.

Reservations, fees: Reservations are not accepted. Sites are $16 per night, $32 per night for double sites, $6 per night for each additional vehicle. Open May through October, weather permitting.

Directions: From Sacramento, drive east on U.S. 50 to Kyburz and Silver Fork Road. Turn right and drive three miles to the campground on the right side of the road.

Contact: Eldorado National Forest, Placerville Ranger District, 530/644-2324, fax 530/647-5315.

132 SILVER FORK

Scenic rating: 7

on the Silver Fork of the American River in Eldorado National Forest

Map grid A2

The tons of vacationers driving U.S. 50 along the South Fork American River always get frustrated when they try to fish or camp, because there are precious few opportunities for either. But, just 20 minutes off the highway, you can find both at Silver Fork Camp. The access road provides many fishing opportunities and the stream is stocked with rainbow trout by the state. The camp is set right along the river, at 5,500 feet elevation, in Eldorado National Forest.

RV sites, facilities: There are 35 sites for tents or RVs of any length (no hookups) and four double sites. Picnic tables and fire grills are provided. Drinking water and vault toilets are available. Some of the facilities are wheelchair-accessible. Leashed pets are permitted.

Reservations, fees: Reservations are not accepted. Sites are $16 per night, $32 per night for double sites, $6 per night for each additional vehicle. Open May through October, weather permitting.

Directions: From Sacramento, drive east on U.S. 50 to Kyburz and Silver Fork Road. Turn right and drive eight miles to the campground on the right side of the road.

Contact: Eldorado National Forest, Placerville Ranger District, 530/644-2324, fax 530/647-5315.

133 CAPLES LAKE

Scenic rating: 8

in Eldorado National Forest

Map grid A2

Caples Lake, in the high country at 7,800 feet, is a pretty lake right along Highway 88. It covers 600 acres, has a 5-mph speed limit, and provides good trout fishing and excellent hiking terrain. Swimming is allowed. The camp is set across the highway (a little two-laner) from the lake, with the Caples Lake Resort and boat rentals nearby. There is a parking area at the west end of the lake, and from here you can begin a great 3.5-mile hike to Emigrant Lake, in the Mokelumne Wilderness on the western flank of Mount Round Top (10,310 feet).

RV sites, facilities: There are 30 sites for tents or RVs up to 35 feet (no hookups), and six walk-in tent sites (requiring a 200-foot walk). Picnic tables and fire grills are provided. Drinking water and vault toilets are available. Groceries, propane gas, boat ramp, and boat rentals are nearby. Some facilities are wheelchair-accessible. Leashed pets are permitted.

Reservations, fees: Reservations are not accepted. Sites are $20 per night, $5 per night for each additional vehicle, $40 per night for a double site. Open June through mid-October, weather permitting.

Directions: From Jackson, drive east on Highway 88 for 63 miles (one mile past the entrance road to Kirkwood Ski Area) to the camp entrance road on the left.

Contact: Eldorado National Forest, Amador Ranger District, 209/295-4251, fax 209/295-5998; Caples Lake Resort, 209/258-8888.

134 SILVER LAKE WEST

Scenic rating: 9

on Silver Lake in Eldorado National Forest

Map grid A2

The Highway 88 corridor provides access to three excellent lakes: Lower Bear River Reservoir, Silver Lake, and Caples Lake. Silver Lake is difficult to pass by, with cabin rentals, pretty campsites, decent trout fishing, and excellent hiking. The lake is set at 7,200 feet elevation in a classic granite cirque just below the Sierra ridge. This camp is on the west side of Highway 88, across the road from the lake. A great hike starts at the trailhead on the east side of the lake, a two-mile tromp to little Hidden Lake, one of several nice hikes in the area. In addition, horseback-riding is available nearby at

Plasse's Resort. Note that bears frequent this campground, so store food properly and avoid scented products.

RV sites, facilities: There are 35 sites for tents or RVs up to 30 feet (no hookups). Picnic tables, food lockers, and fire pits are provided. Vault toilets and drinking water are available. A boat ramp and boat rentals are nearby. Leashed pets are permitted. There is a maximum of six people and two pets per site.

Reservations, fees: Reservations are not accepted. Sites are $20–24 per night, $6 per night for each additional vehicle, $2 per pet per night. Open Memorial Day Weekend through October, weather permitting.

Directions: From Jackson, drive east on Highway 88 for 50 miles (to the north end of Silver Lake) to the campground entrance road on the left.

Contact: Eldorado Irrigation District, 530/644-1960, fax 530/647-5155.

135 SILVER LAKE EAST

Scenic rating: 7

in Eldorado National Forest

Map grid A2

Silver Lake is an easy-to-reach alpine lake set at 7,200 feet, providing a beautiful setting, good trout fishing, and hiking. This camp is on the northeast side of the lake, with a boat ramp nearby. (See the Silver Lake West listing in this chapter for more information.)

RV sites, facilities: There are 62 sites for tents or RVs up to 40 feet (no hookups). Picnic tables and fire grills are provided. Drinking water and vault toilets are available. A grocery store, boat rentals, boat ramp, and propane gas are nearby. Leashed pets are permitted.

Reservations, fees: Reservations are accepted at 877/444-6777 or www.recreation.gov ($10 reservation fee). Sites are $22 per night, $5 per night for each additional vehicle, $44 per night for a double site. Open June through mid-October, weather permitting.

Directions: From Jackson, drive east on

Highway 88 for 50 miles (to the north end of Silver Lake) to the campground entrance road on the right.

Contact: Eldorado National Forest, Amador Ranger District, 209/295-4251, fax 209/295-5998; Silver Lake Resort, 209/258-8598.

136 BEAR RIVER LAKE RESORT

Scenic rating: 8

on Bear River Reservoir
Map grid A2

Bear River Lake Resort is a complete vacation service lodge, with everything you could ask for. A lot of people have been asking in recent years, making this a popular spot that often requires a reservation. The resort also sponsors fishing derbies in the summer and sweetens the pot considerably by stocking exceptionally large rainbow trout. Other fish species include brown trout and Mackinaw trout. The resort is set at 6,000 feet. The lake freezes over in the winter. (See the South Shore listing in this chapter for more information about Bear River Reservoir.)

RV sites, facilities: There are 152 sites with partial hookups (15 amps) for tents or RVs up to 35 feet, a group site for up to 60 people, and six rental trailers. Picnic tables and fire pits are provided. Restrooms with flush toilets and coin showers, drinking water, dump station, boat ramp, boat rentals, berthing, bait and tackle, fishing licenses, video arcade, playground, firewood, ice, propane gas, coin laundry, pay phone, restaurant and cocktail lounge, and grocery store are available. ATVs are permitted, but no motorcycles are allowed. Some facilities are wheelchair-accessible. Leashed pets are permitted at campsites, but not in lodging units.

Reservations, fees: Reservations are recommended. Sites are $33 per night, $5 per night for each additional vehicle with a maximum of two vehicles, $255 per night for the group site, $5 one-time pet fee. Some credit cards accepted. Open April through October.

Directions: From Stockton, drive east on Highway 88 for about 80 miles to the lake entrance on the right side of the road, 42 miles east of Jackson. Turn right and drive 2.5 miles to a junction (if you pass the dam, you have gone 0.25 mile too far). Turn left and drive 0.5 mile to the campground entrance on the right side of the road.

Contact: Bear River Lake Resort, 209/295-4868, www.bearrivercampground.com.

137 SOUTH SHORE

Scenic rating: 7

on Bear River Reservoir in
Eldorado National Forest
Map grid A2

Bear River Reservoir is set at 5,900 feet, which means it becomes ice-free earlier in the spring than its uphill neighbors to the east, Silver Lake and Caples Lake. It is a good-sized lake—725 acres—and cold and deep, too. All water sports are allowed. It gets double-barreled trout stocks, receiving fish from the state and from the operator of the lake's marina and lodge. This campground is on the lake's southern shore, just east of the dam. Explorers can drive south for five miles to Salt Springs Reservoir, which has a trailhead and parking area on the north side of the dam for a great day hike along the lake.

RV sites, facilities: There are 22 sites for tents or RVs up to 35 feet (no hookups). Picnic tables and fire grills are provided. Drinking water and vault toilets are available. A boat ramp, grocery store, boat rentals, and propane gas are available at nearby Bear River Lake Resort. Some facilities are wheelchair-accessible. Leashed pets are permitted.

Reservations, fees: Reservations are accepted at 877/444-6777 or www.recreation.gov ($10 reservation fee). Sites are $20 per night, $40 per night for double site. Open mid-May through mid-October, weather permitting.

Directions: From Stockton, drive east on Highway 88 for about 80 miles to the lake entrance on the right side of the road (well signed). Turn right and drive four miles (past the dam) to the campground entrance on the right side of the road.

Contact: Eldorado National Forest, Amador Ranger District, 209/295-4251, fax 209/295-5998.

138 WA KA LUU HEP YOO

Scenic rating: 8

on the Stanislaus River in
Stanislaus National Forest

Map grid A2

This is a riverside Forest Service campground that provides good trout fishing on the Stanislaus River and a put-in for white-water rafting. The highlight for most is the fishing here—one of the best spots on the Stanislaus, stocked by Fish and Game, and good for rainbow, brook, and brown trout. It is four miles downstream of Dorrington and was first opened in 1999 as part of the Sourgrass Recreation Complex. There are cultural sites and preserved artifacts, such as grinding rocks. It is a pretty streamside spot, with ponderosa pine and black oak providing good screening. A wheelchair-accessible trail is available along the stream. The camp is set at an elevation of 3,900 feet, but it feels higher. By the way, I was told that the name of the campground means "wild river."

RV sites, facilities: There are 49 sites for tents or RVs up to 50 feet (no hookups) and four walk-in tent sites. Picnic tables and fire grills are provided. Drinking water and restrooms with flush and vault toilets are available. Some facilities are wheelchair-accessible. Leashed pets are permitted.

Reservations, fees: Reservations are not accepted. Sites are $16 per night. Free campfire permits are required. Open Memorial Day weekend through October, weather permitting.

Directions: From Angels Camp, drive east on Highway 4, past Arnold to Dorrington and Boards Crossing Road. Turn right and drive four miles to the campground on the left (just before the bridge that crosses the Stanislaus River).

Contact: Stanislaus National Forest, Calaveras Ranger District, 209/795-1381, fax 209/795-6849.

139 BIG MEADOW AND BIG MEADOW GROUP CAMP

Scenic rating: 5

in Stanislaus National Forest

Map grid A2

Big Meadow is set at 6,460 feet elevation on the western slopes of the Sierra Nevada. There are a number of recreation attractions nearby, the most prominent being the North Fork Stanislaus River two miles to the south in a national forest, with access available from a four-wheel-drive road just east of camp, or on Spicer Reservoir Road (see the Stanislaus River listing in this chapter). Lake Alpine, a pretty lake popular for trout fishing, is nine miles east on Highway 4. Three mountain reservoirs—Spicer, Utica, and Union—are all within a 15-minute drive. Big Meadow is also a good base camp for hunting.

RV sites, facilities: There are 68 sites for tents or RVs up to 27 feet (no hookups), and one group tent site (requires a walk in of 100 feet) that can accommodate up to 25 people. Picnic tables and fire grills are provided. Drinking water and vault toilets are available. Groceries, coin laundry, and propane gas are within five miles. Leashed pets are permitted.

Reservations, fees: Reservations are accepted for individual sites and required for the group camp at 877/444-6777 or www.recreation.gov ($10 reservation fee). Sites are $17 per night, $45 per night for the group camp. Open June through October, weather permitting.

Directions: From Angels Camp on Highway 49, turn east on Highway 4 and drive about 30 miles (three miles past Ganns Meadows) to the campground on the right.

Contact: Stanislaus National Forest, Calaveras Ranger District, 209/795-1381, fax 209/795-6849.

CALIFORNIA

140 STANISLAUS RIVER

Scenic rating: 8

in Stanislaus National Forest

Map grid A2

As you might figure from its name, this camp provides excellent access to the adjacent North Fork Stanislaus River. The elevation is 6,200 feet, with timbered sites and the river just south of camp.

RV sites, facilities: There are 25 sites for tents or RVs up to 35 feet (no hookups). Fire grills and picnic tables are provided. Drinking water and vault toilets are available. Supplies are available in Bear Valley. Leashed pets are permitted.

Reservations, fees: Reservations are not accepted. Sites are $8 per night. Open June through October, weather permitting.

Directions: From Angels Camp on Highway 49, turn east on Highway 4 and drive about 44 miles to Spicer Reservoir Road. Turn right and drive four miles to the campground on the right side of the road.

Contact: Stanislaus National Forest, Calaveras Ranger District, 209/795-1381, fax 209/795-6849.

141 GOLDEN PINES RV RESORT AND CAMPGROUND

Scenic rating: 6

near Arnold

Map grid A2

This is a privately operated park set at 5,800 feet elevation on the slopes of the Sierra Nevada. The resort is surrounded by 400 acres of forest and has a self-guided nature trail. Nearby destinations include Stanislaus National Forest, the North Stanislaus River, and Calaveras Big Trees State Park (two miles away). The latter features 150 giant sequoias, along with the biggest stump you can imagine, and two easy hikes, one routed through the North Grove, another through the South Grove. The Bear Valley/Mount Reba ski resort is nearby. Note that about half the sites here are long-term vacation leases.

RV sites, facilities: There are 33 sites with full or partial hookups (30 amps) for RVs up to 42 feet, and 40 tent sites. Picnic tables, fire pits, and barbecues are provided. Drinking water, restrooms with showers, seasonal heated swimming pool, playground, horseshoes, table tennis, volleyball, group facilities, pay phone, coin laundry, and propane gas are available. Some facilities are wheelchair-accessible. Leashed pets are permitted.

Reservations, fees: Reservations are recommended. RV sites with full hookups are $35 per night, RV sites with partial hookups are $30 per night, tent sites are $20 per night, $2.50 per night for each additional vehicle, $2.50 one-time charge per pet. Some credit cards accepted. Open year-round.

Directions: From Angels Camp, turn northeast on Highway 4 and drive 22 miles to Arnold. Continue for seven miles to the campground entrance on the left.

Contact: Golden Pines RV Resort and Campground, 209/795-2820, www.goldenpinesrvresort.com.

142 NORTH GROVE

Scenic rating: 7

in Calaveras Big Trees State Park

Map grid A2

This is one of two campgrounds at Calaveras Big Trees State Park, the state park known for its two groves of giant sequoias (Sierra redwoods). The park covers 6,500 acres, preserving the extraordinary North Grove of giant sequoias. The grove includes the Discovery Tree. Through the years, additional acreage surrounding the grove has been added, providing a mixed conifer forest as a buffer around the giant sequoias. The trailhead for a hike on North Grove Loop is here; it's an easy 1.5-mile walk that is routed among 150 sequoias; the sweet fragrance of the huge trees fills the air. These trees are known for their massive diameter, not for their height, as is the case with coastal redwoods. Another hike, a five-miler, is in the South Grove, where the park's two largest sequoias (the Agassiz Tree and the Palace Hotel Tree) can be seen on a spur trail. A visitors center is open during peak periods, offering exhibits on the giant sequoia and natural history. The North Fork Stanislaus River runs near Highway 4, providing trout-fishing access. The Stanislaus (near the bridge) and Beaver Creek (about 10 miles away) are stocked with trout in late spring and early summer. In the winter, this is a popular spot for cross-country skiing and snowshoeing. The elevation is 4,800 feet.

RV sites, facilities: There are 51 sites for tents, 48 sites for RVs up to 30 feet (no hookups), five hike-in environmental sites, and two group sites for 40–60 people each. Fire grills, food lockers, and picnic tables are provided. Drinking water, restrooms with flush toilets and coin showers, firewood, and a dump station are available. Some facilities are wheelchair-accessible, including a nature trail and exhibits. No bicycles are allowed on the paths, but they are permitted on fire roads and paved roads. Leashed pets are permitted, but not on trails.

Reservations, fees: Reservations are accepted at 800/444-PARK (800/444-7275) or www.reserveamerica.com ($8 reservation fee). Sites are $35 per night, $8 per night for each additional vehicle, $135–200 per night for group sites, and $20 per night for environmental sites. Open year-round, with 12 sites available in winter.

Directions: From Angels Camp, drive east on Highway 4 for 23 miles to Arnold and then continue another four miles to the park entrance on the right.

Contact: Calaveras Big Trees State Park, 209/795-2334; Columbia State Park, 209/544-9128, www.parks.ca.gov.

143 OAK HOLLOW

Scenic rating: 7

in Calaveras Big Trees State Park

Map grid A2

This is one of two campgrounds at Calaveras Big Trees State Park. (See *North Grove* in this chapter for recreation information.)

RV sites, facilities: There are 23 sites for tents only, 18 sites for RVs up to 30 feet (no hookups), and two hike-in environmental sites. Picnic

tables, fire rings, and food lockers are provided. Drinking water and restrooms with flush toilets and coin showers are available. A dump station is available four miles away at North Grove. You can buy supplies in Dorrington or Arnold. Some facilities are wheelchair-accessible, including a nature trail and exhibits. Leashed pets are permitted in the campground, but not on trails.

Reservations, fees: Reservations are accepted at 800/444-PARK (800/444-7275) or www.reserveamerica.com ($8 reservation fee). Sites are $35 per night, $8 per night for each additional vehicle, and $20 per night for environmental sites. Open March through November.

Directions: From Angels Camp, drive east on Highway 4 for 23 miles to Arnold and then continue four miles to the park entrance on the right. Continue another four miles to the campground on the right.

Contact: Calaveras Big Trees State Park, 209/795-2334; Columbia State Park, 209/588-2198, www.parks.ca.gov.

144 BEARDSLEY

Scenic rating: 6

at Beardsley Reservoir in Stanislaus National Forest

Map grid A2

This lake is set in a deep canyon with a paved ramp, nice picnic area, and a fair beach. It is often an outstanding fishery early in the season for brown trout, and then once planted, good for catches of hatchery fish during the evening bite. In winter and spring, as soon as the gate is opened to the boat ramp access road, the fishing is best when the wind blows. This lake allows powerboats and all water sports. The water is generally warm enough for swimmers by midsummer. The camp is set at 3,400 feet elevation, but because it is near the bottom of the lake canyon, it actually feels much higher. Since the lake is a reservoir, it is subject to severe drawdowns in late summer. Bonus: There is more fishing nearby on the Middle Fork of the Stanislaus.

RV sites, facilities: There are 16 sites for tents or RVs up to 22 feet (no hookups). Fire rings are provided. Vault toilets are available. No drinking water is available. Garbage must be packed out. Leashed pets are permitted.

Reservations, fees: Reservations are not accepted. There is no fee for camping. Open May through October, weather permitting (the road is often gated at the top of the canyon when the boat ramp road at lake level is iced over).

Directions: From Sonora, drive east on Highway 108 for about 25 miles to Strawberry and the turnoff for Beardsley Reservoir/Forest Road 52. Turn left and drive seven miles to Beardsley Dam. Continue for 0.25 mile past the dam to the campground.

Contact: Stanislaus National Forest, Summit Ranger District, 209/965-3434, fax 209/965-3372.

145 FRASER FLAT

Scenic rating: 7

on the South Fork of the Stanislaus River in Stanislaus National Forest

Map grid A2

This camp is set along the South Fork of the Stanislaus River at an elevation of 4,800 feet. If the fish aren't biting, a short side trip via Forest Service roads will route you north into the main canyon of the Middle Fork Stanislaus. A map of Stanislaus National Forest is required for this adventure.

RV sites, facilities: There are 38 sites for tents or RVs up to 30 feet (no hookups). Picnic tables and fire grills are provided. Drinking water, vault toilets, and a wheelchair-accessible fishing pier are available. Some facilities are wheelchair-accessible. A grocery store and propane gas are nearby. Leashed pets are permitted.

Reservations, fees: Reservations are not accepted. Sites are $15 per night, $5 per night for each additional vehicle. Open May through October, weather permitting.

Directions: From Sonora, drive east on Highway 108 to Long Barn. Continue east for six miles to Spring Gap Road/Forest Road 4N01.

Turn left and drive three miles to the campground on the left side of the road.

Contact: Stanislaus National Forest, Mi-Wok Ranger District, 209/586-3234, fax 209/586-0643.

146 HULL CREEK

Scenic rating: 7

in Stanislaus National Forest

Map grid A2

This obscure camp borders little Hull Creek (too small for trout fishing) at 5,600 feet elevation in Stanislaus National Forest. This is a good spot for those wishing to test out four-wheel-drive vehicles, with an intricate set of Forest Service roads available to the east. To explore that area, a map of Stanislaus National Forest is essential.

RV sites, facilities: There are 18 sites for tents or RVs up to 22 feet (no hookups). Picnic tables and fire grills are provided. Drinking water and vault toilets are available. Leashed pets are permitted.

Reservations, fees: Reservations are not accepted. Sites are $5 per night. Open May through October, weather permitting.

Directions: From Sonora, drive east on Highway 108 to Long Barn and the Long Barn Fire Station and a signed turnoff for the campground at Road 31/Forest Road 3N01. Turn right and drive 12 miles to the campground on the left side of the road.

Contact: Stanislaus National Forest, Mi-Wok Ranger District, 209/586-3234, fax 209/586-0643.

147 SUGARPINE RV PARK

Scenic rating: 5

in Twain Harte

Map grid B2

Twain Harte is a beautiful little town, right at the edge of the snow line in winter, and right where pines take over the alpine landscape. This park is at the threshold of mountain country, with Pinecrest, Dodge Ridge, and Beardsley Reservoir nearby. It sits on 15 acres and features several walking paths. Note that only 17 of the RV sites are available for overnight campers; the other sites are rented as annual vacation leases. RVs and mobile homes are also for sale at the park.

RV sites, facilities: There are 78 sites with full hookups (20, 30, and 50 amps) for RVs up to 40 feet, 15 tent sites, and three park-model cabins. Picnic tables are provided. Restrooms with showers, cable TV, modem access, playground, seasonal swimming pool, horseshoes, volleyball, badminton, tetherball, basketball, coin laundry, group facilities, and convenience store are available. Some facilities are wheelchair-accessible. Leashed pets are permitted.

Reservations, fees: Reservations are accepted. Sites are $38 per night, $1 per pet per night, $3 per night for each additional vehicle, with exception for towed vehicles. Some credit cards accepted. Open year-round.

Directions: From Sonora, drive east on Highway 108 for 17 miles to the park on the right side of the road, three miles east of Twain Harte.

Contact: Sugarpine RV Park, 209/586-4631, fax 209/586-7738.

148 KIT CARSON

Scenic rating: 8

on the West Fork of the Carson River in Humboldt-Toiyabe National Forest

Map grid B2

This is one in a series of pristine, high-Sierra camps set along the West Fork of the Carson River. There's good trout fishing, thanks to regular stocks from the Department of Fish and Game. This is no secret, however, and the area from the Highway 89 bridge on downstream gets a lot of fishing pressure. The elevation is 6,900 feet.

RV sites, facilities: There are 12 sites for tents or RVs up to 22 feet (no hookups). Picnic tables and fire grills are provided. Drinking water and vault toilets are available. Leashed pets are permitted.

Reservations, fees: Reservations are not accepted. Sites are $14 per night. Open late-May through mid-September, weather permitting.

Directions: From Sacramento, drive east on U.S. 50 to the junction with Highway 89. Turn south on Highway 89 and drive over Luther Pass to the junction with Highway 88. Turn left and drive a mile to the campground on the left side of the road.

From Jackson, drive east on Highway 88 over Carson Pass and to the junction with Highway 89 and then continue for a mile to the campground on the left side of the road.

Contact: Humboldt-Toiyabe National Forest, Carson Ranger District, 775/882-2766, fax 775/884-8199.

149 SNOWSHOE SPRINGS

Scenic rating: 8

on the West Fork of the Carson River in Humboldt-Toiyabe National Forest

Map grid B2

Take your pick of this or the other three streamside camps on the West Fork of the Carson River. This one is at 6,100 feet elevation. Trout are plentiful but rarely grow very large.

RV sites, facilities: There are 19 sites for tents or RVs up to 16 feet (no hookups). Picnic tables and fire grills are provided. Drinking water and vault toilets are available. Leashed pets are permitted.

Reservations, fees: Reservations are not accepted. Sites are $14 per night. Open late May through mid-September.

Directions: From Sacramento, drive east on U.S. 50 to the junction with Highway 89. Turn south on Highway 89 and drive over Luther Pass to the junction with Highway 88. Turn left (east) and drive two miles to the campground on the right side of the road.

From Jackson, drive east on Highway 88 over Carson Pass to the junction with Highway 89 and continue for two miles to the campground on the right side of the road.

Contact: Humboldt-Toiyabe National Forest, Carson Ranger District, 775/882-2766, fax 775/884-8199.

150 CRYSTAL SPRINGS

Scenic rating: 8

on the West Fork of the Carson River in Humboldt-Toiyabe National Forest

Map grid B2

For many people, this camp is an ideal choice. It is set at an elevation of 6,000 feet, right alongside the West Fork of the Carson River. This stretch of water is stocked with trout by the Department of Fish and Game. Crystal Springs is easy to reach, just off Highway 88, and supplies can be obtained in nearby Woodfords or Markleeville. Grover Hot Springs State Park makes a good side-trip destination.

RV sites, facilities: There are 20 sites for tents or RVs up to 22 feet (no hookups). Picnic tables and fire grills are provided. Drinking water and vault toilets are available. Some facilities are wheelchair-accessible. Leashed pets are permitted.

Reservations, fees: Reservations are not accepted. Sites are $14 per night. Open late April to early October, weather permitting.

Directions: From Sacramento, drive east on U.S. 50 to the junction with Highway 89. Turn south on Highway 89 and drive over Luther Pass to the junction with Highway 88. Turn left (east) and drive 4.5 miles to the campground on the right side of the road.

From Jackson, drive east on Highway 88 over Carson Pass to the junction with Highway 89 and continue for 4.5 miles to the campground on the right side of the road.

Contact: Humboldt-Toiyabe National Forest, Carson Ranger District, 775/882-2766, fax 775/884-8199.

151 INDIAN CREEK RECREATION AREA

Scenic rating: 10

near Indian Creek Reservoir and Markleeville

Map grid B2

This beautiful campground is set amid sparse pines near Indian Creek Reservoir, elevation 5,600 feet. The campground is popular and often fills to capacity. This is an excellent lake for trout fishing, and the nearby Carson River is managed as a trophy trout fishery. The lake covers 160 acres, with a maximum speed for boats on the lake set at 5 mph. Sailing, sailboarding, and swimming are allowed. There are several good hikes in the vicinity as well. The best is a short trek, a one-mile climb to Summit Lake, with scenic views of the Indian Creek area. Summers are dry and warm here, with high temperatures typically in the 80s, and nights cool and comfortable. (There is little shade in the summer at the group site.) Bears provide an occasional visit. The lake freezes over in winter. It is about 35 miles to Carson City, Nevada, and two miles to Markleeville.

RV sites, facilities: There are 19 sites for tents or RVs up to 30 feet (no hookups), 10 walk-in sites for tents only, and a group tent site for up to 40 people. Picnic tables and fire grills are provided. Drinking water and restrooms with flush toilets and showers are available. A boat ramp is nearby. Some facilities are wheelchair-accessible. Leashed pets are permitted.

Reservations, fees: Reservations are not accepted for individual sites but are required for the group tent site at 775/885-6000. Sites are $20 per night, double sites are $32 per night, $14–20 per night for walk-in sites, $5 per night for each additional vehicle, $50 per night for group site. Open late April through mid-November, weather permitting.

Directions: From Sacramento, drive east on U.S. 50 over Echo Summit to Meyers and Highway 89. Turn south on Highway 89 and drive to Highway 88. Turn left (east) on Highway 88/89 and drive six miles to Woodfords and Highway 89. Turn right (south) on Highway 89 and drive about four miles to Airport Road. Turn left on

Airport Road and drive four miles to Indian Creek Reservoir. At the fork, bear left and drive to the campground on the west side of the lake.

From Markleeville, drive north on Highway 89 for about four miles to Airport Road. Turn right on Airport Road and drive about four miles to Indian Creek Reservoir. At the fork, bear left and drive to the campground on the west side of the lake.

Contact: Bureau of Land Management, Carson City Field Office, 775/885-6000, fax 775/885-6147.

152 HOPE VALLEY

Scenic rating: 7

near the Carson River in Humboldt-Toiyabe National Forest

Map grid B2

The West Fork of the Carson River runs right through Hope Valley, a pretty trout stream with a choice of four streamside campgrounds. Trout stocks are made near the campgrounds during summer. The campground at Hope Valley is just east of Carson Pass, at 7,300 feet elevation, in a very pretty area. A trailhead for the Pacific Crest Trail is three miles south of the campground. The primary nearby destination is Blue Lakes, about a 10-minute drive away. Insider's note: Little Tamarack Lake, set just beyond the turnoff for Lower Blue Lake, is excellent for swimming.

RV sites, facilities: There are 20 sites for tents or RVs up to 22 feet and a group site for tents or RVs up to 22 feet that can accommodate up to 16 people. No hookups. Picnic tables and fire grills are provided. Drinking water and vault toilets are available. Leashed pets are permitted.

Reservations, fees: Reservations are accepted for individual sites and are required for the group site at 877/444-6777 or www.recreation.gov ($10 reservation fee). Sites are $14 per night, $25 per night for the group camp. Open June through September.

Directions: From Sacramento, drive east on

U.S. 50 to the junction with Highway 89. Turn south on Highway 89 and drive over Luther Pass to the junction with Highway 88. Turn right (west) and drive two miles to Blue Lakes Road. Turn left (south) and drive 1.5 miles to the campground on the right side of the road.

From Jackson, drive east on Highway 88 over Carson Pass and continue east for five miles to Blue Lakes Road. Turn right (south) and drive 1.5 miles to the campground on the right side of the road.

Contact: Humboldt-Toiyabe National Forest, Carson Ranger District, 775/882-2766, fax 775/884-8199.

153 TURTLE ROCK PARK

Scenic rating: 5

near Woodfords

Map grid B2

Because it is administered at the county level, this pretty, wooded campground, set at 6,000 feet elevation, gets missed by a lot of folks. Most vacationers want the more pristine beauty of the nearby camps along the Carson River. But it doesn't get missed by mountain bikers, who travel here every July for the "Death Ride," a wild ride over several mountain passes. The camp always fills for this event. (If it snows, it closes, so call ahead if you're planning an autumn visit.) Nearby side trips include Grover Hot Springs and the hot springs in Markleeville.

RV sites, facilities: There are 28 sites for tents or RVs up to 34 feet (no hookups). Picnic tables and fire grills are provided. Drinking water, vault toilets, and showers are available. A recreation building is available for rent. A camp host is on-site. Some facilities are wheelchair-accessible. Coin laundry, groceries, and propane gas are available within two miles. Leashed pets are permitted.

Reservations, fees: Reservations are not accepted. Sites are $10–15 per night, $3 per night for each additional vehicle. Open May through mid-October, weather permitting.

Directions: From Sacramento, drive east on U.S. 50 to the junction with Highway 89. Turn south on Highway 89 and drive over Luther Pass to the junction with Highway 88. Turn left (east) and drive to Woodfords and the junction with Highway 89. Turn south on Highway 89 and drive 4.5 miles to the park entrance on the right side of the road.

Contact: Alpine County Public Works, 530/694-2140, www.alpinecountyca.gov.

154 GROVER HOT SPRINGS STATE PARK

Scenic rating: 8

near Markleeville

Map grid B2

This is a famous spot for folks who like the rejuvenating powers of hot springs. Some say they feel a glow about them for weeks after soaking here. When touring the South Tahoe/Carson Pass area, many vacationers take part of a day to make the trip to the hot springs. This park is set in alpine meadow at 5,900 feet elevation on the east side of the Sierra at the edge of the Great Basin, and surrounded by peaks that top 10,000 feet. The hot springs are green because of the mineral deposits at the bottom of the pools. The landscape is primarily pine forest and sagebrush. It is well known for the great fluctuations in weather, from serious blizzards to intense, dry heat, and from mild nights to awesome rim-rattling thunderstorms. High winds are occasional but legendary. During thunderstorms, the hot springs pools close because of the chance of lightning strikes. Yet they remain open in snow, even blizzards, when it can be a euphoric experience to sit in the steaming water. Note that the pools are closed for maintenance for two weeks in September. A forest fire near here remains in evidence. A 2.4-mile round-trip hike starts from the campground and continues to a series of small waterfalls. Side-trip options include a nature trail in the park and driving to the Carson River (where the water is a mite cooler) and fishing for trout.

RV sites, facilities: There are 26 sites for tents, and 50 sites for tents or RVs up to 27 feet (no hookups) and trailers up to 24 feet. Picnic tables, fire grills, and food lockers are provided. Restrooms with flush toilets and coin showers (summer only), drinking water, hot springs pool with wheelchair access, and heated swimming pool are available. A grocery store is four miles away, and a coin laundry is within 10 miles. Leashed pets are permitted.

Reservations, fees: Reservations are accepted at 800/444-PARK (800/444-7275) or www.reserveamerica.com ($8 reservation fee). Sites are $35 per night, $8 per night for each additional vehicle, pool fees are $3–5 per person per day. Open year-round, with reduced facilities in winter.

Directions: From Sacramento, drive east on U.S. 50 to the junction with Highway 89. Turn south on Highway 89 and drive over Luther Pass to the junction with Highway 88. Turn left and drive to Woodfords and the junction with Highway 89. Turn right (south) and drive six miles to Markleeville and the junction with Hot Springs Road. Turn right and drive four miles to the park entrance.

Contact: Grover Hot Springs State Park, 530/694-2248; Sierra District, 530/525-7232; pool information, 530/525-7232, www.parks.ca.gov.

155 MARKLEEVILLE

Scenic rating: 7

on Markleeville Creek in Humboldt-Toiyabe National Forest

Map grid B2

This is a pretty, streamside camp set at 5,500 feet along Markleeville Creek, a mile from the East Fork of the Carson River. The trout here are willing, but alas, are dinkers. This area is the transition zone where high mountains to the west give way to the high desert to the east. The hot springs in Markleeville and Grover Hot Springs State Park provide good side trips.

RV sites, facilities: There are 10 sites for tents or RVs up to 20 feet (no hookups). Trailers are not recommended because of road conditions. Picnic tables and fire grills are provided. Drinking water and vault toilets are available. A grocery store and restaurant are nearby. Leashed pets are permitted.

Reservations, fees: Reservations are not accepted. Sites are $14 per night. Open late April through September, weather permitting.

Directions: From Sacramento, drive east on U.S. 50 to the junction with Highway 89. Turn south on Highway 89 and drive over Luther Pass to the junction with Highway 88. Turn left and drive to Woodfords and the junction with Highway 89. Turn south, drive six miles to Markleeville, and continue for 0.5 mile to the campground on the left side of the highway.

Contact: Humboldt-Toiyabe National Forest, Carson Ranger District, 775/882-2766, fax 775/884-8199.

156 TOPAZ LAKE RV PARK

Scenic rating: 6

on Topaz Lake, near Markleeville
Map grid B2

Topaz Lake, set at 5,000 feet elevation, is one of the hidden surprises for California anglers. The surprise is the size of the rainbow trout, with one of the highest rates of 15- to 18-inch trout of any lake in the mountain country. All water sports are allowed on this 2,400-acre lake, and there is a swimming area. The campground itself is attractive, with a number of shade trees. The setting is on the edge of barren high desert, which also serves as the border between California and Nevada. Wind is a problem for small boats, especially in the early summer. Some of the sites here are rented for the entire season.

RV sites, facilities: There are 54 sites with full hookups (30 amps) for RVs up to 42 feet. Some sites are pull-through. Tents are allowed with RVs only, though tent-only sites are allowed during non-peak season. Picnic tables and cable TV are provided. Restrooms with coin showers, coin laundry, propane gas, small grocery store, fish-cleaning station, Wi-Fi, and modem access

are available. A 40-boat marina with courtesy launch and boat-trailer storage is available at lakeside. Some facilities are wheelchair-accessible. Leashed pets are permitted.

Reservations, fees: Reservations are recommended. Sites are $26–28 per night, $3 per person for more than two people. Monthly rates available. Some credit cards accepted. Open March through early October, weather permitting.

Directions: From Carson City, drive south on U.S. 395 for 45 miles to Topaz Lake and the campground on the left side of the road.

From Bridgeport, drive north on U.S. 395 for 45 miles to the campground on the right side of the road (0.3 mile south of the California/Nevada border).

Contact: Topaz Lake RV Park, 530/495-2357, fax 530/495-2118, www.topazlakervpark.com.

157 UPPER BLUE LAKE DAM AND EXPANSION

Scenic rating: 7

near Carson Pass
Map grid B2

These two camps are set across the road from each other along Upper Blue Lake, and are two of five camps in the area. The trout fishing is usually quite good here in early summer. (See the Lower Blue Lake listing in this chapter for more information.) These camps are three miles past the Lower Blue Lake campground. The elevation is 8,400 feet.

RV sites, facilities: There are 10 sites at Upper Blue Lake Dam and 15 sites at the expansion area for tents or RVs up to 25 feet. Picnic tables and fire grills are provided at Upper Blue Lake Dam only. Drinking water and vault toilets are available. Some facilities are wheelchair-accessible. Leashed pets are permitted.

Reservations, fees: Reservations are not accepted. Sites are $17 per night, $3 per night for each additional vehicle, $1 per pet per night. Open June through mid-September, weather permitting.

Directions: From Sacramento, drive east on

U.S. 50 to the junction with Highway 89. Turn south on Highway 89 and drive over Luther Pass to the junction with Highway 88. Turn right and drive 2.5 miles to Blue Lakes Road. Turn left and drive 12 miles to the junction at the south end of Lower Blue Lake. Turn right and drive three miles to the Upper Blue Lake Dam campground on the left side of the road or the expansion area on the right.

From Jackson, drive east on Highway 88 over Carson Pass and continue east for five miles to Blue Lakes Road. Turn right (south) and drive 12 miles to a junction at the south end of Lower Blue Lake. Turn right and drive three miles to the Upper Blue Lake Dam campground on the left side of the road or the expansion area on the right.

Contact: PG&E Land Projects, 916/386-5164, www.pge.com/recreation.

158 MIDDLE CREEK AND EXPANSION

Scenic rating: 7

near Carson Pass and Blue Lakes

Map grid B2

This tiny, captivating spot, set along the creek that connects Upper and Lower Blue Lakes, provides a take-your-pick deal for anglers. PG&E has expanded this facility and now offers a larger camping area about 200 yards from the original campground. (See the Lower Blue Lake listing in this chapter for more information.) The elevation is 8,200 feet.

RV sites, facilities: There are five sites for tents or RVs up to 30 feet at Middle Creek and 25 sites for tents or RVs up to 45 feet at the expansion area. No hookups. Picnic tables and fire grills are provided. Drinking water and vault toilets are available at the expansion area. Some facilities are wheelchair-accessible. Leashed pets are permitted.

Reservations, fees: Reservations are not accepted. Sites are $17 per night, $3 per night for each additional vehicle, $1 per pet per night. Open June through September, weather permitting.

Directions: From Sacramento, drive east on U.S. 50 to the junction with Highway 89. Turn south on Highway 89 and drive over Luther Pass to the junction with Highway 88. Turn right and drive 2.5 miles to Blue Lakes Road. Turn left and drive 12 miles to a junction at the south end of Lower Blue Lake. Turn right and drive 1.5 miles to the Middle Creek campground on the left side of the road and continue another 200 yards to reach the expansion area.

From Jackson, drive east on Highway 88 over Carson Pass and continue east for five miles to Blue Lakes Road. Turn right (south) and drive 12 miles (road becomes dirt) to a junction at the south end of Lower Blue Lake. Turn right and drive 1.5 miles to the Middle Creek campground on the left side of the road and continue another 200 yards to reach the expansion area.

Contact: PG&E Land Projects, 916/386-5164, www.pge.com/recreation.

159 LOWER BLUE LAKE

Scenic rating: 7

near Carson Pass

Map grid B2

This is the high country, at 8,400 feet, where the terrain is stark and steep and edged by volcanic ridgelines, and where the deep blue-green hue of lake water brightens the landscape. Lower Blue Lake provides a popular trout fishery, with rainbow, brook, and cutthroat trout all stocked regularly. The boat ramp is adjacent to the campground. The access road crosses the Pacific Crest Trail, providing a route to a series of small, pretty, hike-to lakes just outside the edge of the Mokelumne Wilderness.

RV sites, facilities: There are 17 sites for tents or RVs up to 25 feet (no hookups). Picnic tables and fire grills are provided. Drinking water and vault toilets are available. Leashed pets are permitted.

Reservations, fees: Reservations are not accepted. Sites are $18 per night, $3 per night for each additional vehicle, $1 per pet per night,

14-day occupancy limit. Open June through September, weather permitting.

Directions: From Sacramento, drive east on U.S. 50 to the junction with Highway 89. Turn south on Highway 89 and drive over Luther Pass to the junction with Highway 88. Turn right and drive 2.5 miles to Blue Lakes Road. Turn left and drive 12 miles to a junction at the south end of Lower Blue Lake. Turn right and drive a short distance to the campground on the left side of the road.

From Jackson, drive east on Highway 88 over Carson Pass and continue east for five miles to Blue Lakes Road. Turn right (south) and drive 12 miles to a junction at the south end of Lower Blue Lake. Turn right and drive a short distance to the campground on the left.

Contact: PG&E Land Projects, 916/386-5164, www.pge.com/recreation.

160 SILVER CREEK

Scenic rating: 6

in Humboldt-Toiyabe National Forest

Map grid B2

This pretty spot, set near Silver Creek, has easy access from Highway 4 and, in years without washouts, good fishing in early summer for small trout. It is in the remote high Sierra, east of Ebbetts Pass. A side trip to Ebbetts Pass features Kinney Lake, Pacific Crest Trail access, and a trailhead at the north end of the lake (on the west side of Highway 4) for a mile hike to Lower Kinney Lake. No bikes are permitted on the trails. The elevation is 6,800 feet.

RV sites, facilities: There are 22 sites for tents or RVs up to 22 feet (no hookups). Picnic tables and fire grills are provided. Drinking water and vault toilets are available. Some facilities are wheelchair-accessible. Leashed pets are permitted.

Reservations, fees: Reservations are accepted at 877/444-6777 or www.recreation.gov ($10 reservation fee). Sites are $15 per night. Open late May through early September, weather permitting.

Directions: From Angels Camp, drive east on Highway 4 all the way over Ebbetts Pass and continue for about six miles to the campground.

From Markleeville, drive south on Highway 89 to the junction with Highway 4. Turn west on Highway 4 (steep and winding) and drive about five miles to the campground.

Contact: Humboldt-Toiyabe National Forest, Carson Ranger District, 775/882-2766, fax 775/884-8199.

161 MOSQUITO LAKE

Scenic rating: 10

at Mosquito Lake in Stanislaus National Forest

Map grid B2

Mosquito Lake is in a pristine Sierra setting at 8,260 feet elevation, presenting remarkable beauty for a place that can be reached by car. Most people believe that Mosquito Lake is for day-use only, and that's why they crowd into nearby Lake Alpine Campground. But it's not just for day-use, and this camp is often overlooked because it is about a mile west of the little lake. The lake is small, a pretty emerald green, and even has a few small trout in it. The camp provides a few dispersed sites.

RV sites, facilities: There are eight sites for tents or RVs up to 16 feet (no hookups). Picnic tables and fire grills are provided. Vault toilets are available. No drinking water is available. Garbage must be packed out. Leashed pets are permitted.

Reservations, fees: Reservations are not accepted. Sites are $5 per night. A free campfire permit is required from the district office. Open June through September, weather permitting.

Directions: From Angels Camp, drive east on Highway 4 to Lake Alpine and continue for about six miles to the campground on the left side of the road.

Contact: Stanislaus National Forest, Calaveras Ranger District, 209/795-1381, fax 209/795-6849.

CALIFORNIA

162 HERMIT VALLEY

Scenic rating: 8

in Stanislaus National Forest

Map grid B2

This tiny, remote, little-known spot is set near the border of the Mokelumne Wilderness near where Grouse Creek enters the Mokelumne River, at 7,100 feet elevation. Looking north, there is a good view into Deer Valley. A primitive road, 0.5-mile west of camp, is routed through Deer Valley north for six miles to the Blue Lakes. On the opposite (south) side of the road from the camp there is a little-traveled hiking trail that is routed up Grouse Creek to Beaver Meadow and Willow Meadow near the border of the Carson-Iceberg Wilderness.

RV sites, facilities: There are 25 sites for tents or RVs up to 16 feet (no hookups). Vault toilets are available. No drinking water is available. Garbage must be packed out. Leashed pets are permitted.

Reservations, fees: Reservations are not accepted. There is no fee for camping. A free campfire permit is required from the district office. Open June through October, weather permitting.

Directions: From Angels Camp, drive east on Highway 4 to Lake Alpine and continue for about nine miles to the campground on the left side of the road (just east of the Mokelumne River Bridge). Note: Trailers are not recommended because of the steep access road.

Contact: Stanislaus National Forest, Calaveras Ranger District, 209/795-1381, fax 209/795-6849.

163 BLOOMFIELD

Scenic rating: 7

in Stanislaus National Forest

Map grid B2

This is a primitive and little-known camp set at 7,800 feet elevation near Ebbetts Pass. The North Fork Mokelumne River runs right by the camp, with good stream access for about a mile on each side of the camp. The access road continues south to Highland Lakes, a destination that provides car-top boating, fair fishing, and trailheads for hiking into the Carson-Iceberg Wilderness.

RV sites, facilities: There are 20 sites for tents or RVs up to 16 feet (no hookups). Picnic tables and fire rings are provided. Drinking water and vault toilets are available. Garbage must be packed out. Facilities and supplies are available at Lake Alpine Lodge, 25 minutes away. Leashed pets are permitted.

Reservations, fees: Reservations are not accepted. Sites are $8 per night. A free campfire permit is required from the district office. Open June through October, weather permitting.

Directions: From Angels Camp, drive east on Highway 4 to Lake Alpine and continue for about 15 miles to Forest Road 8N01 on the right side of the road (1.5 miles west of Ebbetts Pass). Turn right and drive two miles to the campground on the right side of the road. Note: Access roads are rough and not recommended for trailers.

Contact: Stanislaus National Forest, Calaveras Ranger District, 209/795-1381, fax 209/795-6849.

164 PACIFIC VALLEY

Scenic rating: 7

in Stanislaus National Forest
overlooking Pacific Creek

Map grid B2

This is a do-it-yourself special; that is, more of a general area for camping than a campground, set up for backpackers heading out on expeditions into the Carson-Iceberg Wilderness to the south. It is set at 7,600 feet elevation along Pacific Creek, a tributary to the Mokelumne River. The landscape is an open lodgepole forest with nearby meadow and a small stream. The trail from camp is routed south and reaches three forks within two miles. The best is routed deep into the wilderness, flanking Hiram Peak (9,760 feet), Airola Peak (9,938 feet), and Iceberg Peak (9,720 feet).

RV sites, facilities: There are 15 sites for tents or RVs up to 16 feet (no hookups). Picnic tables and fire grills are provided. Vault toilets are available. No drinking water is available. Garbage must be packed out. Leashed pets are permitted.

Reservations, fees: Reservations are not accepted. There is no fee for camping. A free campfire permit is required from the district office. Open June through October, weather permitting.

Directions: From Angels Camp, drive east on Highway 4 to Lake Alpine and continue for eight miles to a dirt road. Turn right (south) and drive about 0.5 mile to the campground. Note: Trailers are not recommended because of the rough roads.

Contact: Stanislaus National Forest, Calaveras Ranger District, 209/795-1381, fax 209/795-6849.

165 UPPER AND LOWER HIGHLAND LAKES

Scenic rating: 9

in Stanislaus National Forest

Map grid B2

This camp is set between Upper and Lower Highland Lakes, two beautiful alpine ponds that offer good fishing for small brook trout as well as spectacular panoramic views. The boat speed limit is 15 mph, and a primitive boat ramp is at Upper Highland Lake. Swimming is allowed, although the water is very cold. The elevation at this campground is 8,600 feet, with Hiram Peak (9,760 feet) looming to the nearby south. Several great trails are available from this camp. Day hikes include up Boulder Creek and Disaster Creek. For overnight backpacking, a trail that starts at the north end of Highland Lakes (a parking area is available) is routed east for two miles to Wolf Creek Pass, where it connects with the Pacific Crest Trail; from there, turn left or right—you can't lose. The access road is not recommended for trailers or large RVs.

RV sites, facilities: There are 35 sites for tents or RVs up to 16 feet (no hookups). Picnic tables and fire grills are provided. Drinking water and vault toilets are available. Garbage must be packed out. Leashed pets are permitted.

Reservations, fees: Reservations are not accepted. Sites are $8 per night. Open June through October, weather permitting.

Directions: From Angels Camp, drive east on Highway 4 to Arnold, past Lake Alpine, and continue for 14.5 miles to Forest Road 8N01 (one mile west of Ebbetts Pass). Turn right and drive 7.5 miles to the campground on the right side of the road. Note: The roads are rough and trailers are not recommended.

Contact: Stanislaus National Forest, Calaveras Ranger District, 209/795-1381, fax 209/795-6849.

166 PINE MARTEN

Scenic rating: 8

near Lake Alpine in Stanislaus National Forest

Map grid B2

Lake Alpine is a beautiful Sierra lake surrounded by granite and pines and set at 7,320 feet, just above where the snowplows stop in winter. This camp is on the northeast side, about a quarter mile from the shore. Fishing for rainbow trout is good in May and early June, before the summer crush. Despite the long drive to get here, the lake is becoming better known for its beauty, camping, and hiking. Lake Alpine has 180 surface acres and a 10-mph speed limit. A trailhead out of nearby Silver Valley Camp provides a two-mile hike to pretty Duck Lake and beyond into the Carson-Iceberg Wilderness.

RV sites, facilities: There are 32 sites for tents or RVs up to 27 feet (no hookups). Picnic tables and fire grills are provided. Drinking water and restrooms with flush toilets are available. A boat ramp is nearby. A grocery store, propane gas, and coin laundry are nearby. Some facilities are wheelchair-accessible. Leashed pets are permitted.

Reservations, fees: Reservations are not accepted. Sites are $20 per night. Open June through early October, weather permitting.

Directions: From Angels Camp, drive east on Highway 4 to Arnold and continue for 29 miles

CALIFORNIA

to Lake Alpine. Drive to the northeast end of the lake to the campground entrance on the right side of the road.

Contact: Stanislaus National Forest, Calaveras Ranger District, 209/795-1381, fax 209/795-6849.

167 SILVER VALLEY

Scenic rating: 8

on Lake Alpine in Stanislaus National Forest
Map grid B2

This is one of four camps at Lake Alpine. Silver Valley is on the northeast end of the lake at 7,400 feet elevation, with a trailhead nearby that provides access to the Carson-Iceberg Wilderness. (For recreation information, see the Pine Marten listing in this chapter.)

RV sites, facilities: There are 21 sites for tents or RVs up to 16 feet (no hookups). Picnic tables and fire grills are provided. Drinking water and vault toilets are available. Some facilities are wheelchair-accessible. A boat launch, grocery store, and coin laundry are nearby. Leashed pets are permitted.

Reservations, fees: Reservations are not accepted. Sites are $20 per night. A free campfire permit is required. Open June through October, weather permitting.

Directions: From Angels Camp, drive east on Highway 4 to Arnold and continue for 29 miles to Lake Alpine. Drive to the northeast end of the lake to the campground entrance on the right side of the road. Turn right and drive 0.5 mile to the campground.

Contact: Stanislaus National Forest, Calaveras Ranger District, 209/795-1381, fax 209/795-6849.

168 LAKE ALPINE CAMPGROUND

Scenic rating: 8

on Lake Alpine in Stanislaus National Forest
Map grid B2

This is the campground that is in the greatest demand at Lake Alpine, and it is easy to see why. It is very small, a boat ramp is adjacent to

the camp, you can get supplies at a small grocery store within walking distance, and during the evening rise you can often see the jumping trout from your campsite. Lake Alpine is one of the prettiest lakes you can drive to, set at 7,303 feet elevation amid pines and Sierra granite. A trailhead out of nearby Silver Valley Camp provides a two-mile hike to pretty Duck Lake and beyond into the Carson-Iceberg Wilderness.

RV sites, facilities: There are 25 sites for tents or RVs up to 27 feet (no hookups). Picnic tables and fire grills are provided. Drinking water, flush and vault toilets, and a boat launch are available. A grocery store, restaurant, coin showers, and a coin laundry are nearby. Some facilities are wheelchair-accessible. Leashed pets are permitted.

Reservations, fees: Reservations are not accepted. Sites are $20 per night. Open June through October, weather permitting.

Directions: From Angels Camp, drive east on Highway 4 to Arnold and continue for 29 miles to Lake Alpine. Just before reaching the lake turn right and drive 0.25 mile to the campground on the left.

Contact: Stanislaus National Forest, Calaveras Ranger District, 209/795-1381, fax 209/795-6849.

169 SILVER TIP

Scenic rating: 6

near Lake Alpine in Stanislaus National Forest
Map grid B2

This camp is just over 0.5 mile from the shore of Lake Alpine at an elevation of 7,350 feet. Why then would anyone camp here when there are campgrounds right at the lake? Two reasons: One, those lakeside camps are often full on summer weekends. Two, Highway 4 is snowplowed to this campground entrance, but not beyond. So in big snow years when the road is still closed in late spring and early summer, you can park your rig here to camp, then hike in to the lake. In the fall, it also makes for a base camp for hunters. (See the Lake Alpine Campground listing in this chapter for more information.)

RV sites, facilities: There are 23 sites for tents

or RVs up to 27 feet (no hookups). Picnic tables and fire grills are provided. Drinking water and flush toilets are available. A boat launch is about a mile away. A grocery store, coin laundry, and coin showers are nearby. Some facilities are wheelchair-accessible. Leashed pets are permitted.

Reservations, fees: Reservations are not accepted. Sites are $20 per night. Open June through early October, weather permitting.

Directions: From Angels Camp, drive east on Highway 4 to Arnold and continue for 29 miles to Lake Alpine. A mile before reaching the lake (adjacent to the Bear Valley/Mount Reba turnoff), turn right at the campground entrance on the right side of the road.

Contact: Stanislaus National Forest, Calaveras Ranger District, 209/795-1381, fax 209/795-6849.

170 SPICER RESERVOIR AND GROUP CAMP

Scenic rating: 8

near Spicer Reservoir in Stanislaus National Forest

Map grid B2

Set at 6,200 feet elevation and covering only 227 acres, Spicer Reservoir isn't big by reservoir standards, but it is surrounded by canyon walls and is quite pretty from a boat. Good trout fishing adds to the beauty. A boat ramp is available near the campground, and the lake speed limit is 10 mph. A trail links the east end of Spicer Reservoir to the Summit Lake trailhead, with the route bordering the north side of the reservoir. Note: This area can really get hammered with snow in big winters, so always check for access conditions in the spring and early summer before planning a trip.

RV sites, facilities: There are 60 sites for tents or RVs up to 50 feet (no hookups). There is one group site for tents or RVs up to 28 feet (no hookups) that can accommodate up to 60 people. Picnic tables and fire grills are provided. Drinking water and vault toilets, group facilities, and a primitive amphitheater are available. A boat ramp is nearby. Some facilities are wheelchair-accessible. Leashed pets are permitted.

Reservations, fees: Reservations are not accepted for individual sites, but are required for the group site at 209/295-4512. Sites are $20 per night. The group site is $140 per night. Open June through October, weather permitting.

Directions: From Angels Camp, drive east on Highway 4 for about 32 miles to Spicer Reservoir Road/Forest Road 7N01. Turn right, drive seven miles, bear right at a fork with a sharp right turn, and drive a mile to the campground at the west end of the lake.

Contact: Stanislaus National Forest, Calaveras Ranger District, 209/795-1381, fax 209/795-6849.

171 SAND FLAT- STANISLAUS RIVER

Scenic rating: 7

on the Clark Fork of the Stanislaus River in Stanislaus National Forest

Map grid B2

Sand Flat campground, at 6,200 feet, is only three miles (by vehicle on Clark Fork Road) from an outstanding trailhead for the Carson-Iceberg Wilderness. The camp is used primarily by late-arriving backpackers who camp for the night, get their gear in order, then head off on the trail. The trail is routed out of Iceberg Meadow, with a choice of heading north to Paradise Valley (unbelievably green and loaded with corn lilies along a creek) and onward to the Pacific Crest Trail, or east to Clark Fork and upstream to Clark Fork Meadow below Sonora Peak. Two choices, both winners.

RV sites, facilities: There are 53 sites for tents or RVs up to 22 feet (no hookups) and 15 walk-in tent sites. Picnic tables and fire grills are provided. Drinking water and vault toilets are available. You can buy supplies in Dardanelle. Some facilities are wheelchair-accessible. Leashed pets are permitted.

Reservations, fees: Reservations are not accepted. Sites are $11 per night per vehicle. Open May through early October, weather permitting.

Directions: From Sonora, drive east on Highway

CALIFORNIA

108 past the town of Strawberry to Clark Fork Road. Turn left on Clark Fork Road and drive six miles to the campground entrance on the right side of the road.

Contact: Stanislaus National Forest, Summit Ranger District, 209/965-3434, fax 209/965-3372.

172 CLARK FORK AND CLARK FORK HORSE

Scenic rating: 8

on the Clark Fork of the Stanislaus River in Stanislaus National Forest

Map grid B2

Clark Fork borders the Clark Fork of the Stanislaus River and is used by both drive-in vacationers and backpackers. A trailhead for hikers is 0.25 mile away on the north side of Clark Fork Road (a parking area is available here). From here the trail is routed up along Arnot Creek, skirting between Iceberg Peak on the left and Lightning Mountain on the right, for eight miles to Wolf Creek Pass and the junction with the Pacific Crest Trail. (For another nearby trailhead, see the Sand Flat–Stanislaus River listing in this chapter.)

RV sites, facilities: There are 88 sites for tents or RVs up to 40 feet, and at an adjacent area, 14 equestrian sites for tents or RVs up to 22 feet. No hookups. Picnic tables and fire grills are provided. Drinking water and flush toilets are available. At the equestrian site, no drinking water is available but there are water troughs. Some facilities are wheelchair-accessible. You can buy supplies in Dardanelle. Leashed pets are permitted.

Reservations, fees: Reservations are not accepted. Sites are $14–16 per night, horse camp fee is $9 per night, $5 per night for each additional vehicle. Open May through October, weather permitting.

Directions: From Sonora, drive east on Highway 108 past the town of Strawberry to Clark Fork Road. Turn left, drive five miles, turn right again, and drive 0.5 mile to the campground entrance on the right side of the road.

Contact: Stanislaus National Forest, Summit Ranger District, 209/965-3434, fax 209/965-3372.

173 FENCE CREEK

Scenic rating: 4

near the Middle Fork of the Stanislaus River in Stanislaus National Forest

Map grid B2

Fence Creek is a feeder stream to Clark Fork, which runs a mile downstream and joins with the Middle Fork Stanislaus River en route to Donnells Reservoir. The camp sits along little Fence Creek, at 5,600 feet elevation. Fence Creek Road continues east for another nine miles to an outstanding trailhead at Iceberg Meadow on the edge of the Carson-Iceberg Wilderness.

RV sites, facilities: There are 38 sites for tents or RVs up to 22 feet (no hookups). Picnic tables and fire grills are provided. Vault toilets are available. No drinking water is available. You can buy supplies in Pinecrest about 10 miles away. Leashed pets are permitted.

Reservations, fees: Reservations are not accepted. Sites are $6 per night. Open May through mid-October, weather permitting.

Directions: From Sonora, drive east on Highway 108 about 50 miles to Clark Ford Road. Turn left and drive a mile to Forest Road 6N06. Turn left again and drive 0.5 mile to the campground on the right.

Contact: Stanislaus National Forest, Summit Ranger District, 209/965-3434, fax 209/965-3372.

174 BOULDER FLAT

Scenic rating: 7

near the Middle Fork of the Stanislaus River in Stanislaus National Forest

Map grid B2

You want camping on the Stanislaus River? As you drive east on Highway 108, this is the first in a series of campgrounds along the Middle Fork Stanislaus. Boulder Flat is set at 5,600 feet elevation and offers easy access off the highway. Here's another bonus: This stretch of river is stocked with trout.

RV sites, facilities: There are 21 sites for tents

or RVs up to 22 feet (no hookups). Picnic tables and fire grills are provided. Drinking water and vault toilets are available. You can buy supplies in Dardanelle. Some facilities are wheelchair-accessible. Leashed pets are permitted.

Reservations, fees: Reservations are not accepted. Sites are $15–17 per night, $5 per night for each additional vehicle. Open May through October, weather permitting.

Directions: From Sonora, drive east on Highway 108 past the town of Strawberry to Clark Fork Road. At Clark Fork Road, continue east on Highway 108 for a mile to the campground on the left side of the road.

Contact: Stanislaus National Forest, Summit Ranger District, 209/965-3434, fax 209/965-3372.

175 BRIGHTMAN FLAT

Scenic rating: 7

on the Middle Fork of the Stanislaus River in Stanislaus National Forest

Map grid B2

This camp is on the Middle Fork of the Stanislaus River at 5,700 feet elevation, a mile east of Boulder Flat and two miles west of Dardanelle. Trout are small here and get fished hard.

RV sites, facilities: There are 33 sites for tents or RVs up to 22 feet (no hookups). Picnic tables and fire grills are provided. Vault toilets and drinking water are available. You can buy supplies in Dardanelle. Some facilities are wheelchair-accessible. Leashed pets are permitted.

Reservations, fees: Reservations are not accepted. Sites are $12 per night, $5 per night for each additional vehicle. Open May through October, weather permitting.

Directions: From Sonora, drive east on Highway 108 past the town of Strawberry to Clark Fork Road. At Clark Fork Road continue east on Highway 108 for two miles to the campground entrance on the left side of the road.

Contact: Stanislaus National Forest, Summit Ranger District, 209/965-3434, fax 209/965-3372.

176 DARDANELLE

Scenic rating: 7

on the Middle Fork of the Stanislaus River in Stanislaus National Forest

Map grid B2

This Forest Service camp is within walking distance of supplies in Dardanelle and is also right alongside the Middle Fork Stanislaus River. This section of river is stocked with trout by the Department of Fish and Game. The trail to see Columns of the Giants is just 1.5 miles to the east out of Pigeon Flat.

RV sites, facilities: There are 28 sites for tents or RVs up to 28 feet (no hookups). Picnic tables and fire grills are provided. Drinking water and vault toilets are available. You can buy supplies in Dardanelle. Some facilities are wheelchair-accessible. Leashed pets are permitted.

Reservations, fees: Reservations are not accepted. Sites are $17–21 per night, $5 per night for each additional vehicle. Open May through October, weather permitting.

Directions: From Sonora, drive east on Highway 108 past Strawberry to Dardanelle and the campground on the left side of the road.

Contact: Stanislaus National Forest, Summit Ranger District, 209/965-3434, fax 209/965-3372.

177 EUREKA VALLEY

Scenic rating: 8

on the Middle Fork of the Stanislaus River in Stanislaus National Forest

Map grid B2

There are about a half-dozen campgrounds on this stretch of the Middle Fork Stanislaus River near Dardanelle, at 6,100 feet elevation. The river runs along two sides of this campground, making it quite pretty. This stretch of river is planted with trout by the Department of Fish and Game, but it is hit pretty hard despite its relatively isolated location. A good short and easy hike is to Columns of the Giants, accessible on a 0.25-mile-long trail out of Pigeon Flat, a mile to the west.

RV sites, facilities: There are 28 sites for tents or RVs up to 22 feet (no hookups). Picnic tables and fire grills are provided. Drinking water and vault toilets are available. You can buy supplies in Dardanelle. Leashed pets are permitted.

Reservations, fees: Reservations are not accepted. Sites are $15 per night, $5 per night for each additional vehicle. Open May through October, weather permitting.

Directions: From Sonora, drive east on Highway 108 past the town of Strawberry to Dardanelle. Continue three miles east to the campground on the right.

Contact: Stanislaus National Forest, Summit Ranger District, 209/965-3434, fax 209/965-3372.

178 NIAGARA CREEK

Scenic rating: 6

in Stanislaus National Forest

Map grid B2

This camp is set beside Niagara Creek at 6,600 feet elevation, high in Stanislaus National Forest on the western slopes of the Sierra. It provides direct access to a network of roads in national forest, including routes to Double Dome Rock and another to Eagle Meadows. So if you have a four-wheel-drive vehicle or dirt bike, this is the place to come.

RV sites, facilities: There are 10 sites for tents or RVs up to 22 feet (no hookups); some are walk-in sites. Picnic tables and fire grills are provided. A vault toilet is available. No drinking water is available. You can buy supplies in Pinecrest about 10 miles away. Leashed pets are permitted.

Reservations, fees: Reservations are not accepted. Sites are $6 per night. Open May through October, weather permitting.

Directions: From Sonora, drive east on Highway 108 to the town of Strawberry and continue for about 15 miles to Eagle Meadows Road/Forest Road 5N01 on the right. Turn right and drive 0.5 mile to the campground on the left.

Contact: Stanislaus National Forest, Summit Ranger District, 209/965-3434, fax 209/965-3372.

179 MILL CREEK

Scenic rating: 7

on Mill Creek in Stanislaus National Forest

Map grid B2

This pretty little camp is set along Mill Creek at 6,200 feet elevation, high in Stanislaus National Forest, near a variety of outdoor recreation options. The camp is near the Middle Fork Stanislaus River, which is stocked with trout near Donnells. For hiking, there is an outstanding trailhead at Kennedy Meadow (east of Donnells). For fishing, both Beardsley Reservoir (boat necessary) and Pinecrest Lake (shoreline prospects fair) provide two nearby alternatives.

RV sites, facilities: There are 18 sites for tents or RVs up to 22 feet (no hookups). Picnic tables and fire grills are provided. Vault toilets are available. No drinking water is available. Leashed pets are permitted.

Reservations, fees: Reservations are not accepted. Sites are $6 per night. Open May through mid-October, weather permitting.

Directions: From Sonora, drive east on Highway 108 to Strawberry. From Strawberry continue east on Highway 108 about 13 miles to Forest Road 5N21. Turn right on Forest Road 5N21 and drive 0.1 mile to the campground access road (Forest Road 5N26) on the left.

Contact: Stanislaus National Forest, Summit Ranger District, 209/965-3434, fax 209/965-3372.

180 NIAGARA CREEK OFF-HIGHWAY VEHICLE

Scenic rating: 6

on Niagara Creek in Stanislaus National Forest

Map grid B2

This small, primitive camp along Niagara Creek is designed primarily for people with off-highway vehicles. Got it? It is set on Niagara Creek near Donnells Reservoir. The elevation is 6,600 feet.

RV sites, facilities: There are 10 sites for tents or RVs up to 22 feet (no hookups). Picnic tables and fire grills are provided. A vault toilet is available. No drinking water is available. You can buy supplies in Pinecrest about 10 miles away. Leashed pets are permitted.

Reservations, fees: Reservations are not accepted. Sites are $6 per night. Open May through October, weather permitting.

Directions: From Sonora, drive east on Highway 108 to Strawberry and continue for about 15 miles to Eagle Meadows Road/Forest Road 5N01. Turn right and drive 1.5 miles to the campground on the left (just after crossing the bridge at Niagara Creek).

Contact: Stanislaus National Forest, Summit Ranger District, 209/965-3434, fax 209/965-3372.

181 BAKER

Scenic rating: 7

on the Middle Fork of the Stanislaus River in Stanislaus National Forest

Map grid B2

Baker lies at the turnoff for the well-known and popular Kennedy Meadow trailhead for the Emigrant Wilderness. The camp is set along the Middle Fork Stanislaus River, at 6,200 feet elevation, downstream a short way from the confluence with Deadman Creek. The trailhead, with a nearby horse corral, is another two miles farther on the Kennedy Meadow access road. From here it is a 1.5-mile hike to a fork in the trail; right will take you two miles to Relief Reservoir, 7,226 feet, and left will route you up Kennedy Creek for five miles to pretty Kennedy Lake, just north of Kennedy Peak (10,716 feet).

RV sites, facilities: There are 44 sites for tents or RVs up to 22 feet (no hookups). Picnic tables and fire grills are provided. Drinking water and vault toilets are available. You can buy supplies in Dardanelle. Some facilities are wheelchair-accessible. Leashed pets are permitted.

Reservations, fees: Reservations are not accepted. Sites are $17–34 per night, $5 per night for each additional vehicle. Open May through mid-October, weather permitting.

Directions: From Sonora, drive east on Highway 108 past Strawberry to Dardanelle. From Dardanelle, continue 5.5 miles east to the campground on the right side of the road at the turnoff for Kennedy Meadow.

Contact: Stanislaus National Forest, Summit Ranger District, 209/965-3434, fax 209/965-3372.

182 DEADMAN

Scenic rating: 7

on the Middle Fork of the Stanislaus River in Stanislaus National Forest

Map grid B2

This is a popular trailhead camp and an ideal jump-off point for backpackers heading into the adjacent Emigrant Wilderness. The elevation is 6,200 feet. The camp is a short distance from Baker (see the Baker listing in this chapter for hiking destinations).

RV sites, facilities: There are 17 sites for tents or RVs up to 22 feet (no hookups). Picnic tables and fire grills are provided. Drinking water and vault toilets are available. You can buy supplies in Dardanelle. Some facilities are wheelchair-accessible. Leashed pets are permitted.

Reservations, fees: Reservations are not accepted. Sites are $17–34 per night, $5 per night for each additional vehicle. Open May through early October, weather permitting.

Directions: From Sonora, drive east on Highway 108 past the town of Strawberry to Dardanelle. From Dardanelle, continue 5.5 miles east to the Kennedy Meadow turnoff. Drive a mile on Kennedy Meadow Road to the campground, which is opposite the parking area for Kennedy Meadow Trail.

Contact: Stanislaus National Forest, Summit Ranger District, 209/965-3434, fax 209/965-3372.

183 BOOTLEG

Scenic rating: 6

on the Walker River in
Humboldt-Toiyabe National Forest

Map grid B2

Location is always key, and easy access off U.S. 395, the adjacent West Walker River, and good trout stocks in summer make this a popular spot. (See the Chris Flat and Sonora Bridge listings in this chapter for more information.) Note that this camp is on the west side of the highway, and anglers will have to cross the road to gain fishing access. The elevation is 6,600 feet.

RV sites, facilities: There are 63 sites for tents or RVs up to 35 feet (no hookups). Picnic tables and fire grills are provided. Drinking water and flush toilets are available. Leashed pets are permitted.

Reservations, fees: Reservations are accepted at 877/444-6777 or www.recreation.gov ($10 reservation fee). Sites are $17 per night, $6 per night for each additional vehicle. Open early May through mid-September, weather permitting.

Directions: From Carson City, drive south on U.S. 395 to Coleville and then continue south for 13 miles to the campground on the west side of the highway (six miles north of the junction of U.S. 395 and Highway 108).

Contact: Humboldt-Toiyabe National Forest, Bridgeport Ranger District, 760/932-7070, fax 760/932-5899.

184 CHRIS FLAT

Scenic rating: 7

on the Walker River in
Humboldt-Toiyabe National Forest

Map grid B2

This is one of two campgrounds set along U.S. 395 next to the West Walker River, a pretty trout stream with easy access and good stocks of rainbow trout. The plants are usually made at two campgrounds, resulting in good prospects

here at Chris Flat and west on Highway 108 at Sonora Bridge. The elevation is 6,600 feet.

RV sites, facilities: There are 15 sites for tents or RVs up to 30 feet (no hookups). Picnic tables and fire grills are provided. Drinking water (shut off during freezing temperatures) and vault toilets are available. Leashed pets are permitted.

Reservations, fees: Reservations are accepted at 877/444-6777 or www.recreation.gov ($10 reservation fee). Sites are $17 per night, $6 per night for each additional vehicle. Open April through mid-November, weather permitting.

Directions: From Carson City, drive south on U.S. 395 to Coleville and then continue south for 15 miles to the campground on the east side of the road (four miles north of the junction of U.S. 395 and Highway 108).

Contact: Humboldt-Toiyabe National Forest, Bridgeport Ranger District, 760/932-7070, fax 760/932-5899.

185 SONORA BRIDGE

Scenic rating: 7

near the Walker River in
Humboldt-Toiyabe National Forest

Map grid B2

The West Walker River is a pretty stream, flowing over boulders and into pools, and each year this stretch of river is well stocked with rainbow trout by the Department of Fish and Game. One of several campgrounds near the West Walker, Sonora Bridge is set at 6,800 feet elevation, about 0.5 mile from the river. The setting is in the transition zone from high mountains to high desert on the eastern edge of the Sierra Nevada.

RV sites, facilities: There are 23 sites for tents or RVs up to 35 feet (no hookups). Picnic tables and fire grills are provided. Drinking water and vault toilets are available. Leashed pets are permitted.

Reservations, fees: Reservations are accepted at 877/444-6777 or www.recreation.gov ($10 reservation fee). Sites are $15 per night, $6 per night for each additional vehicle. Open mid-May through mid-October, weather permitting.

Directions: From north of Bridgeport, at the junction of U.S. 395 and Highway 108, turn west on Highway 108 and drive one mile to the campground on the left.

Contact: Humboldt-Toiyabe National Forest, Bridgeport Ranger District, 760/932-7070, fax 760/932-5899.

186 LEAVITT MEADOWS

Scenic rating: 9

on the Walker River in
Humboldt-Toiyabe National Forest

Map grid B2

While Leavitt Meadows sits right beside Highway 108, a little winding two-laner, there are several nearby off-pavement destinations that make this camp a winner. The camp is set in the high eastern Sierra, east of Sonora Pass at 7,000 feet elevation, where Leavitt Creek and Brownie Creek enter the West Walker River. There is a pack station for horseback riding nearby. For four-wheel-drive owners, the most popular side trip is driving four miles west on Highway 108, then turning south and driving four miles to Leavitt Lake, where the trout fishing is sometimes spectacular, if you're trolling a gold Cripplure.

RV sites, facilities: There are 16 sites for tents or RVs up to 30 feet (no hookups). Picnic tables, food lockers, and fire grills are provided. Drinking water and vault toilets are available. Leashed pets are permitted.

Reservations, fees: Reservations are accepted at 877/444-6777 or www.recreation.gov ($10 reservation fee). Sites are $15 per night, $6 per night for each additional vehicle. Open April through mid-October, weather permitting.

Directions: From the junction of Highway 108 and U.S. 395 north of Bridgeport, turn west on Highway 108 and drive approximately seven miles to the campground on the left side of the road.

Contact: Humboldt-Toiyabe National Forest, Bridgeport Ranger District, 760/932-7070, fax 760/932-5899.

187 OBSIDIAN

Scenic rating: 6

on Molybdenite Creek in
Humboldt-Toiyabe National Forest

Map grid B2

This primitive, little-known camp at 7,800 feet elevation is set up for backpackers, with an adjacent trailhead providing a jump-off point into the wilderness; wilderness permits are required. The trail is routed up the Molybdenite Creek drainage and into the Hoover Wilderness.

RV sites, facilities: There are 14 sites for tents or RVs up to 30 feet (no hookups). Picnic tables and fire grills are provided. Vault toilets are available. No drinking water is available. Garbage must be packed out. Leashed pets are permitted.

Reservations, fees: Reservations are accepted at 877/444-6777 or www.recreation.gov ($10 reservation fee). Sites are $10 per night, $6 per night for each additional vehicle. Open June through October, weather permitting.

Directions: At the junction of U.S. 395 and Highway 108 (13 miles north of Bridgeport), drive south a short distance on U.S. 395 to an improved dirt road and a sign that says "Little Walker River Road." Turn west and drive four miles to the campground.

Contact: Humboldt-Toiyabe National Forest, Bridgeport Ranger District, 760/932-7070, fax 760/932-5899.

188 CASCADE CREEK

Scenic rating: 6

in Stanislaus National Forest

Map grid B2

This campground is set along Cascade Creek at an elevation of 6,000 feet. A Forest Service road about a quarter mile west of camp on the south side of the highway provides a side trip three miles up to Pikes Peak, at 7,236 feet.

RV sites, facilities: There are 14 sites for tents or RVs up to 22 feet (no hookups). Picnic tables and fire rings are provided. Pit and vault toilets are available. No drinking water is available. Supplies are available in Dardanelle. Leashed pets are permitted.

Reservations, fees: Reservations are not accepted. Sites are $6 per night. Open May through October, weather permitting.

Directions: From Sonora, drive east on Highway 108 to Strawberry and continue for 11 miles to the campground on the left side of the road.

Contact: Stanislaus National Forest, Summit Ranger District, 209/965-3434, fax 209/965-3372.

SAN FRANCISCO BAY AREA

(BEST RV PARKS AND CAMPGROUNDS

(**Coastal Sites**
San Francisco RV Resort, page 889.

(**Wildlife-Viewing**
Olema Ranch Campground, page 885.

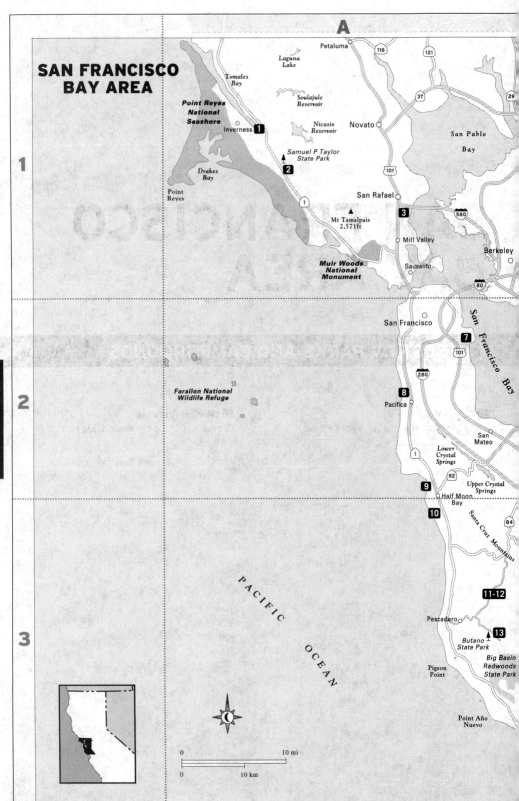

SAN FRANCISCO BAY AREA

Petaluma
116
121
37
29

Laguna Lake
Tomales Bay
Soulajule Reservoir

Point Reyes National Seashore
Inverness **1**

Nicasio Reservoir
Novato

San Pablo Bay

Samuel P Taylor State Park **2**

101

Drakes Bay

San Rafael
3
580

Point Reyes

1

Mt Tamalpais 2,571ft

Mill Valley
Berkeley

Muir Woods National Monument
Sausalito
80

San Francisco
7
101

Farallon National Wildlife Refuge
280

San Francisco Bay

2

8
Pacifica

San Mateo

Lower Crystal Springs
1
92
Upper Crystal Springs

9
Half Moon Bay
10
84

Santa Cruz Mountains

11-12

P A C I F I C   O C E A N

Pescadero
13

Butano State Park

Big Basin Redwoods State Park

Pigeon Point

3

Point Año Nuevo

CALIFORNIA

0   10 mi

0   10 km

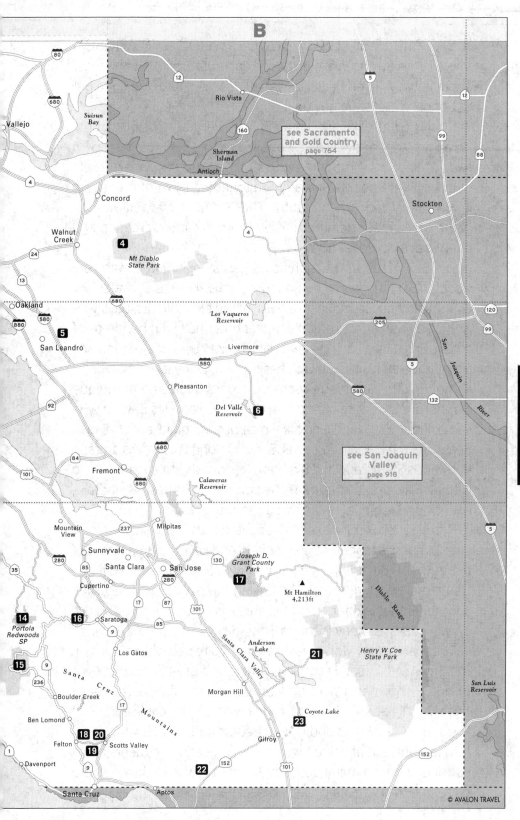

CALIFORNIA

© AVALON TRAVEL

It's ironic that many people who have chosen

to live in the Bay Area are often the ones who complain the most about it. We've even heard some say, "Some day I'm going to get out of here and start having a good time."

I wish I could take anyone who has ever had these thoughts on a little trip in my airplane and circle the Bay Area at 3,000 feet. What you see is that despite strips of roadways and pockets of cities where people are jammed together, most of the region is wild, unsettled, and beautiful. There is no metropolitan area in the world that offers better and more diverse recreation and open space so close to so many.

The Bay Area has 150 significant parks (including 12 with redwoods), 7,500 miles of hiking and biking trails, 45 lakes, 25 waterfalls, 100 miles of coast, mountains with incredible lookouts, bays with islands, and, in all, 1.2 million acres of greenbelt with hundreds of acres being added each year with land bought by money earmarked from property taxes. The land has no limit. Enjoy it.

Along with the unique recreation possibilities come unique campgrounds. There are boat-in camps at Tomales Bay, ferry-in camps on Angel Island, and hike-in camps at Point Reyes National Seashore, the Marin Headlands, Sunol-Ohlone Wilderness, Butano Redwoods State Park, and Big Basin Redwoods State Park – along with a sprinkling of the more traditional drive-in sites at state, county, and regional parks throughout the region.

Note that proximity to a metropolitan area means two things: The demand is higher, so plan ahead; and second, 85 percent of the park use occurs from 3 P.M. Friday to 5 P.M. Sunday, so if you visit at non-peak times it's like having the park to yourself. One shocker is that in spring and fall, there is a huge drop-off in use on weekdays, Sunday through Thursday.

There are many world-class landmarks to see while staying in the Bay Area. In San Francisco alone there are the Golden Gate Bridge, Fisherman's Wharf, Alcatraz, Ghirardelli Square, Chinatown, AT&T ballpark, the Crissy Field waterfront, cable cars, Fort Point, the Cliff House and Ocean Beach, and Fort Funston.

In fact, instead of going far away for a vacation, residents might consider what so many do from all over the world: Stay and discover the treasures in your own backyard.

1 OLEMA RANCH CAMPGROUND

Scenic rating: 4

in Olema

Map grid A1 BEST (

If location is everything, then this 32-acre campground should be rated a 10. Set in Olema, in a valley amid Marin's coastal foothills, it is an ideal jump-off spot for a Point Reyes adventure. Bird-watchers and wildlife-lovers will be happy here, with opportunities for Tule elk, deer, seals, sea lions, whales off shore.

The camp borders the Point Reyes National Seashore to the west and the Golden Gate National Recreation Area to the east, with Tomales Bay to the nearby north. There are several excellent trailheads available within a 10-minute drive along Highway 1 to the south. Note that the campsites are small, tightly placed, and I have received a few complaint letters about the ambience of the place.

RV sites, facilities: There are 203 sites, some with full or partial hookups (30 and 50 amps), for tents or RVs of any length, and a large area for up to 175 tents. Picnic tables and fire rings are provided. Drinking water, restrooms with showers, dump station, coin laundry, post office, ATM, firewood, ice, playground, RV supplies, propane, horseshoes, volleyball, shuffleboard, ping-pong, badminton, tetherball, Wi-Fi, modem access, meeting facilities, amphitheater, and a recreation hall (for groups of 25 or more only) are available. Some facilities are wheelchair-accessible. Leashed pets are permitted.

Reservations, fees: Reservations are accepted at 800/655-CAMP (800/655-2267). RV sites are $35–58 for per night, $2 per night for each additional vehicle, $1.50 per person per night for more than two people; tent sites are $30–44. Weekly rates available. No credit cards. Open year-round.

Directions: From U.S. 101 in Marin, take the San Anselmo/Sir Francis Drake Boulevard exit and drive west for about 22 miles to Highway 1 at Olema. Turn north (right) on Highway 1 and drive 0.25 mile to the campground on the left.

Contact: Olema Ranch Campground, 415/663-8001, fax 415/663-8135, www.olemaranch.com.

2 SAMUEL P. TAYLOR STATE PARK

Scenic rating: 9

near San Rafael

Map grid A1

This is a beautiful park, with campsites set amid redwoods, complete with a babbling brook running nearby. The park covers more than 2,700 acres of wooded countryside in the steep and rolling hills of Marin County. This features unique contrasts of coast redwoods and open grassland. Hikers will find 20 miles of hiking trails, a hidden waterfall, and some good mountain-biking routes on service roads. The paved bike path that runs through the park and parallels Lagunitas Creek is a terrific, easy ride. Trees include redwood, Douglas fir, oak, and madrone, and native wildflowers include buttercups, milkmaids, and Indian paintbrush. The section of the park on the north side of Sir Francis Drake has the best hiking in the park. Campsites are on the south side of the park, except for three sites on the north side.

RV sites, facilities: There are 25 sites for tents, 35 sites for tents or RVs up to 27 feet, two primitive sites for up to 10 people each, two group sites for 25 and 50 people, one hike-in/bike-in camp, and one equestrian site with corrals at Devil's Gulch Horse Camp. No hookups. Picnic tables, food lockers, and fire grills are provided. Drinking water, flush and pit toilets, and Wi-Fi are available. There are a small store and café two miles away in Lagunitas. Some facilities are wheelchair-accessible. Leashed pets are permitted in campsites only.

Reservations, fees: Reservations are accepted at 800/444-PARK (800/444-7275) or www.reserveamerica.com ($8 reservation fee). Sites are $35 per night and $8 per night for each additional vehicle, primitive groups sites are $23 per night, group sites $110–225 per night, equestrian camp

$75 per night, $3 per person per night for hike-in/bike-in site. Open year-round.

Directions: From U.S. 101 in Marin, take the Sir Francis Drake Boulevard exit and drive west for about 15 miles to the park entrance on the left side of the road.

Contact: Samuel P. Taylor State Park, 415/488-9897, fax 415/488-4315; Marin Sector, 415/898-4362, www.parks.ca.gov.

3 MARIN RV PARK

Scenic rating: 2

in Greenbrae
Map grid A1

For out-of-towners with RVs, this can make an ideal base camp for Marin County adventures. To the west are Mount Tamalpais State Park, Muir Woods National Monument, Samuel P. Taylor State Park, and Point Reyes National Seashore. To the nearby east is the Loch Lomond Marina on San Pablo Bay, where fishing trips can be arranged for striped bass and sturgeon; phone Loch Lomond Bait Shop, 415/456-0321. The park offers complete sightseeing information and easy access to buses and ferry service to San Francisco.

RV sites, facilities: There are 89 sites with full hookups (30 and 50 amps) for tents or RVs. Restrooms with showers, coin laundry, Wi-Fi, swimming pool, dump station, and RV supplies are available. Some facilities are wheelchair-accessible. Leashed pets are permitted.

Reservations, fees: Reservations are recommended. Sites are $48 per night for two people (July–Aug.) or $43 per night (Sept.–June), $2 per person per night for more than two people. Six people maximum per site. Weekly and monthly rates available in off-season. Some credit cards accepted. Open year-round.

Directions: From the south: From the Golden Gate Bridge, drive north on U.S. 101 for 10 miles to Lucky Drive (south of San Rafael). Exit and turn left on Redwood Highway (no sign) and drive three blocks north to the park entrance on the right.

From the north: From San Rafael, drive south on U.S. 101 to the Lucky Drive exit (450A). Take that exit to the first light at Tamal Vista. Turn left and drive to the next stoplight and Wornum Avenue. Turn left at Wornum Avenue and drive under the freeway to Redwood Highway (frontage road). Turn left and drive four blocks north to the park entrance.

Contact: Marin RV Park, 415/461-5199 or 888/461-5199, fax 415/925-1584, www.marin-rvpark.com.

4 MOUNT DIABLO STATE PARK

Scenic rating: 6

east of Oakland
Map grid B1

Mount Diablo, elevation 3,849 feet, provides one of the most all-encompassing lookouts anywhere in America, an awesome 360° on clear mornings. On crystal-clear days you can see the Sierra Nevada and its white, snowbound crest. Some claim to have seen Half Dome in Yosemite with binoculars. The drive to the summit is a must-do trip, and the weekend interpretive center right on top of the mountain is one of the best in the Bay Area. The camps at Mount Diablo are set in foothill/oak grassland country, with some shaded sites. Winter and spring are good times to visit, when the weather is still cool enough for good hiking trips. Most of the trails require long hikes, often including significant elevation gains and losses. No alcohol is permitted in the park. The park offers extensive but challenging hiking, biking, and horseback riding. A museum, visitors center, and gift shop is perched on the Diablo summit. Summers are hot and dry, and in late summer the park can be closed because of fire danger. In winter, snow occasionally falls on the peak—according to my logbook, during the first full moon in February.

RV sites, facilities: There are 64 sites in three campgrounds for tents or RVs up to 20 feet long (no hookups), five group sites for 20–50 people, and one group site for equestrian use. The

CALIFORNIA

equestrian site has hitching posts and a water trough. Picnic tables and fire grills are provided. Drinking water and flush and vault toilets are available. Showers are available at Juniper and Live Oak campgrounds. Leashed pets are permitted in campgrounds and picnic areas.

Reservations, fees: Reservations are accepted at 800/444-PARK (800/444-7275) or www.reserveamerica.com ($8 reservation fee). Sites are $30 per night, $10 per night for each additional vehicle, group sites are $65–165 per night. Open year-round.

Directions: From Danville on I-680, take the Diablo Road exit. Turn east on Diablo Road and drive three miles to Mount Diablo Scenic Boulevard. Turn left and continue 3.5 miles (the road becomes South Gate Road) to the park entrance station. Register at the kiosk, obtain a park map, and drive to the designated campground.

Contact: Mount Diablo State Park, 925/837-2525 or 925/837-0904; Diablo Vista District, 707/769-5652, www.mdia.org or www.parks.ca.gov.

5 ANTHONY CHABOT REGIONAL PARK

Scenic rating: 7

near Castro Valley

Map grid B2

The campground at Chabot Regional Park is set on a hilltop sheltered by eucalyptus, with good views and trails available. The best campsites are the walk-in units, requiring a walk of only a minute or so. Several provide views of Lake Chabot to the south 0.5 mile away. The 315-acre lake provides good trout fishing in the winter and spring, and a chance for huge but elusive largemouth bass. Huckleberry Trail is routed down from the campground (near walk-in site 20) to the lake at Honker Bay, a good fishing area. There is also a good 12-mile bike ride around the lake. In all, this 5,000-acre park includes 31 miles of hiking, biking, and riding trails. East Bay Skyline Trail runs the length

of the park. Boat rentals are available, but no swimming or water-body contact is permitted. A weekend marksmanship range is available at the park, and a golf course is nearby.

RV sites, facilities: There are 53 sites for tents and small RVs, 12 sites with full hookups (30 amps) for RVs, and 10 walk-in sites for tents only. Picnic tables and fire grills are provided. Restrooms with flush toilets and showers, drinking water, dump station, amphitheater, small marina, boat rentals, snack bar, picnic area, bait and tackle, and naturalist-led campfire programs are available. No boat launch, and gas motors and inflatables are prohibited. Leashed pets are permitted.

Reservations, fees: Reservations are accepted at 888/327-2757, x2 ($8 reservation fee) or reserveamerica.com ($8 reservation fee). Sites are $18–25 per night, $6 per night for each additional vehicle, $2 per pet per night. Some credit cards accepted. Open year-round.

Directions: From I-580 in the Oakland hills, drive to the 35th Avenue exit. Take that exit, and at the stop sign, turn east on 35th Avenue and drive up the hill and straight across Skyline Boulevard, where 35th Avenue becomes Redwood Road. Continue on Redwood Road for eight miles to the park and Marciel Road (campground entrance road) on the right.

Contact: Regional Park Headquarters, 888/327-2757; Anthony Chabot Regional Park, 510/639-4751; Chabot Equestrian Center, 510/569-4428, www.ebparks.org/parks.htm.

6 DEL VALLE REGIONAL PARK

Scenic rating: 7

near Livermore

Map grid B2

Of the 65 parks in the East Bay Regional Park District, it is Del Valle that provides the greatest variety of recreation at the highest quality. Del Valle Reservoir is the centerpiece, a five-mile-long, narrow lake that fills a canyon with 16 miles of shoreline, providing a good boat launch for powerboating (10 mph speed limit) and good fishing for trout (stocked), striped bass, panfish, and catfish. Two swimming beaches are popular in summer. The park offers boat tours of the natural history and lake ecology of the area. The sites are somewhat exposed because of the grassland habitat, but they fill anyway on most weekends and three-day holidays. A trailhead south of the lake provides access to Ohlone Wilderness Trail, and for the well conditioned, there is the 5.5-mile butt-kicker of a climb to Murietta Falls, gaining 1,600 feet in 1.5 miles. Murietta Falls is the Bay Area's highest waterfall, 100 feet tall, though its thin, silvery wisp is difficult to view directly and rarely evokes much emotional response after such an intense climb. Riding trails are also available in this 4,000-acre park.

RV sites, facilities: There are 150 sites, including 21 with water and sewer hookups for tents or RVs of any length, and two walk-in group areas for up to 75 people each. Group camps require a walk of 0.25–1 mile. Picnic tables and fire grills are provided. Drinking water, restrooms with flush toilets and showers, dump station, full marina, boat and sailboard rentals, seasonal campfire programs, swimming beaches, and a boat launch are available. Some facilities are wheelchair-accessible. Leashed pets are permitted.

Reservations, fees: Reservations are accepted at 888/327-2757 x2 ($8 reservation fee) or reserveamerica.com ($8 reservation fee). Sites are $18–23 per night, $6 per night for each additional vehicle, $2–4 per day boat launch fee, $2 per pet per night. Some credit cards accepted. Open year-round.

Directions: From I-580 east at Livermore, take the North Livermore Avenue exit and turn south (right if driving from San Francisco). Drive south and proceed through Livermore (road becomes South Livermore Avenue). Continue for 1.5 miles (the road then becomes Tesla Road) to Mines Road. Turn right on Mines Road and drive 3.5 miles to Del Valle Road. Continue straight on Del Valle Road for four miles to the park entrance.

Contact: Del Valle Regional Park, 925/373-0332;

East Bay Regional Park District, 888/327-2757, www.ebparks.org/parks.htm.

7 CANDLESTICK RV PARK

Scenic rating: 6

in San Francisco

Map grid A2

This RV park is set adjacent to Candlestick Park. It is five miles from downtown San Francisco and an ideal destination for out-of-towners who want to explore the city without having to drive, because the park offers tours and inexpensive shuttles to the downtown area. In addition, there are good hiking opportunities along the shoreline of the bay. On summer afternoons, when the wind howls at 20–30 mph here, sailboarders rip by. Rates are higher, much higher, on 49er game days, and the stadium is usually packed with 60,000 or more people.

RV sites, facilities: There are 165 sites with full hookups (30 and 50 amps) for trailers or RVs up to 42 feet, and 24 tent sites. Some sites are pull-through. Restrooms with showers, coin laundry, Wi-Fi, grocery store, game room, and RV washing are available. Shuttles and bus tours are also available. Some facilities are wheelchair-accessible. A security officer is posted at the entry station at night. Small leashed pets are permitted.

Reservations, fees: Reservations are recommended at 800/888-CAMP (800/888-2267). RV sites are $69–74 per night for two people, $5 per person per night for more than two people. Rates are higher on game days. Some credit cards accepted. Open year-round.

Directions: From San Francisco on U.S. 101, take the Candlestick Park exit (Exit 429A) to Gilman Road. Turn east on the stadium entrance road/Gilman Road and drive around the parking lot to the far end of the stadium (Gate 4).

Contact: Candlestick RV Park, 415/822-2299, fax 415/822-7638, www.sanfranciscorvpark.com.

CALIFORNIA

8 SAN FRANCISCO RV RESORT

Scenic rating: 8

in Pacifica

Map grid A2 BEST (

This is one of the best RV parks in the Bay Area. It is set on the bluffs just above the Pacific Ocean in Pacifica, complete with beach access, nearby fishing pier, and sometimes excellent surf fishing. There is also a nearby golf course and the chance for dramatic ocean sunsets. The park is kept clean and in good shape, and though there is too much asphalt, the proximity to the beach overcomes it. It is only 20 minutes from San Francisco.

RV sites, facilities: There are 182 sites with full hookups (50 amps) for RVs up to 45 feet. No tents. Restrooms with showers, heated swimming pool, year-round spa, playground, game room, group facilities, cable TV, Wi-Fi, modem access, convenience store, coin laundry, and propane gas are available. Some facilities are wheelchair-accessible. Leashed pets are permitted, with some exceptions.

Reservations, fees: Reservations are recommended at 650/355-7093. Sites are $56–88 per night. Some credit cards accepted. Open year-round.

Directions: From San Francisco, drive south on Highway 280 to Highway 1. Bear west on Highway 1 and drive into Pacifica to the Palmetto Drive exit. Take that exit and drive south to the stop sign (you will be on the west side of the highway). Continue straight ahead (the road becomes Palmetto Avenue) for about two blocks and look for the entrance to the park on the right side of the road at 700 Palmetto.

From the south, drive north on Highway 1 into Pacifica. Take the Manor Drive exit. At the stop sign, turn left on Oceana Avenue (you will be on the east side of the highway), and drive a block to another stop sign at Manor Drive. Turn left, drive a short distance over the highway to a stop sign at Palmetto Avenue. Turn left and drive about two blocks to the park on the right.

Contact: San Francisco RV Resort, 650/355-7093, fax 650/355-7102, www.sanfranciscorvresort.com.

9 HALF MOON BAY STATE BEACH

Scenic rating: 7

at Half Moon Bay

Map grid A2

In summer, this park often fills to capacity with campers touring Highway 1. The campground has level, grassy sites for tents, a clean parking area for RVs, and a state beach available just a short walk away. The feature here is four miles of broad, sandy beaches with three access points with parking. A visitors center is available. Side trips include Princeton and Pillar Point Marina, seven miles north on Highway 1, where fishing and whale-watching trips are possible. Typical weather is fog in summer, clear days in spring and fall, and wet and windy in the winter—yet occasionally there are drop-dead beautiful days in winter between storms, warm, clear, and windless. Temperatures range from lows in the mid-40s in winter to highs in the mid-60s in fall. One frustrating point: The weekend traffic on Highway 1 up and down the coast here is often jammed, with absolute gridlock during festivals.

RV sites, facilities: There are 52 sites for tents or RVs up to 40 feet (no hookups), four hike-in/bike-in sites, and one group site (for up to 50 people) two miles north of the main campground. Picnic tables, food lockers, and fire grills are provided. Restrooms with flush toilets and coin showers, drinking water, Wi-Fi, pay telephone, and dump station are available. Some facilities are wheelchair-accessible. Leashed pets are permitted, except on the beach.

Reservations, fees: Reservations are required at 800/444-PARK (800/444-7275) or www.reserveamerica.com ($8 reservation fee). Sites are $35 per night, $165 per night for group site, $3 per person per night for hike-in/bike-in sites, $10 per night for each additional vehicle. Open year-round.

Directions: Drive to Half Moon Bay to the

CALIFORNIA

junction of Highway 1 and Highway 92. Turn south on Highway 1 and drive two blocks to Kelly Avenue. Turn right on Kelly Avenue and drive 0.5 mile to the park entrance at the end of the road.

Contact: Half Moon Bay State Beach, 650/726-8820 or 650/726-8819; Santa Cruz District, 831/335-6318, www.parks.ca.gov.

10 PELICAN POINT RV PARK

Scenic rating: 7

in Half Moon Bay

Map grid A3

Pelican Point is set on an extended bluff near the ocean in a rural area on the southern outskirts Half Moon Bay. Fog is common on summer mornings. Sites consist of cement slabs with picnic tables; half of the RV sites are monthly rentals. The harbor has an excellent boat launch, a fish-cleaning station, party boat trips for salmon and rockfish and, in the winter, whale-watching trips. A beautiful golf course is nearby.

RV sites, facilities: There are 75 sites with full hookups (30 and 50 amps) for RVs up to 40 feet. Picnic tables are provided. Restrooms with showers, coin laundry, propane gas, small store, clubhouse, and dump station are available. All facilities are nearby, with restaurants in Half Moon Bay and 10 miles north in Princeton at Pillar Point Harbor. Leashed pets are permitted.

Reservations, fees: Reservations are accepted. Sites are $45–50 per night, $2 per night for each additional vehicle, $3.30 per person per night for more than two people, $1 per pet per night. Some credit cards accepted. Open year-round.

Directions: In Half Moon Bay, at the junction of Highway 1 and Highway 92, turn south on Highway 1 and drive 2.5 miles to Miramontes Point Road. Turn right and drive a short distance to the park entrance on the left.

Contact: Pelican Point RV Park, 650/726-9100.

11 JACK BROOK HORSE CAMPS

Scenic rating: 7

in Sam McDonald Park just outside La Honda

Map grid A3

This is a beautiful horse camp with access to a network of service roads. The park is filled with second-growth redwoods and then feeds north to rolling foothills. You get a mix of moist, cool redwoods in the canyons and rolling grassland foothills on the ridges. From the top, you also get views to the west across Butano Canyon to the coast.

RV sites, facilities: There are three group sites: two small sites for up to 10 people each and one larger site for up to 40 people. Some sites have 15 or 20-amp hookups. Picnic tables and barbecues are provided. Drinking water, flush toilets, showers, horse paddocks, tie posts, and a horse-wash rack are available. A shared outdoor kitchen is also provided. Open May 1 through mid-November, weather permitting.

Reservations, fees: Reservations are required at 650/363-4021 or www.eparks.net. The two smaller sites are $50–100 per night, $125–250 per night for the larger site.

Directions: From the Peninsula, take Highway 101 or 280 to Redwood City/Woodside and Highway 84. Take Highway 84 (Woodside-La Honda-San Gregorio Rd.) west to La Honda and continue one mile to Alpine Road. Turn left on Alpine Road and drive 1.1 miles to a Y with Pescadero Road. Bear right at the Y and drive 0.5 mile to the park entrance on the right.

From Highway 1: Take the Pescadero Road exit. Drive east on Pescadero Creek Road about 11 miles to the Jack Brook entrance or continue to the Sam McDonald Park entrance where horse trailers can be parked for entrance on horseback.

Contact: San Mateo County Parks and Recreation, 650/879-0238 or 650/363-4020, fax 650/599-1721, www.co.sanmateo.ca.us/.

CALIFORNIA

12 MEMORIAL COUNTY PARK

Scenic rating: 8

near La Honda

Map grid A3

This beautiful 500-acre redwood park is set on the western slopes of the Santa Cruz Mountains, tucked in a pocket between the tiny towns of La Honda and Loma Mar. The park is known for its family camping areas and Tan Oak and Mount Ellen nature trails. The campground features access to a nearby network of 50 miles of trails, with the best hike along the headwaters of Pescadero Creek. In late winter, it is sometimes possible to see steelhead spawn (no fishing permitted, of course). The trails link with others in nearby Portola State Park and Sam McDonald County Park, providing access to a vast recreation land. A swimming hole on Pescadero Creek next to the campground is popular during the summer. The camp is often filled on summer weekends, but the sites are spaced so it won't cramp your style.

RV sites, facilities: There are 156 sites for tents or RVs up to 35 feet, two group sites for tents or RVs up to 35 feet (no hookups) that can accommodate up to 75 people, and six areas for youth groups of up to 50 people. Picnic tables, food lockers, and fire grills are provided. Drinking water, restrooms with coin showers and flush toilets, amphitheater, picnic area, summer convenience store, visitors center, summer campfire programs, and firewood are available. A dump station is available from May through October. No smoking is allowed.

Reservations, fees: Reservations are required at 650/363-4021 or www.eparks.net ($7 reservation fee). Sites are $21 per vehicle per night, $8 per night for each additional vehicle. Group sites are $135 per night, plus $5 per vehicle per stay. Open year-round.

Directions: From Half Moon Bay at the junction of Highway 1 and Highway 92, drive south on Highway 1 for 18 miles to the Pescadero Road exit. Turn left (east) on Pescadero Road and drive about 10.5 miles to the park entrance on the right.

Contact: Memorial County Park, 650/879-0212 or 650/879-0238; San Mateo County Parks and Recreation, 650/363-4021, www.eparks.net or www.co.sanmateo.ca.us.

13 BUTANO STATE PARK

Scenic rating: 9

near Pescadero

Map grid A3

The campground at Butano is set in a canyon filled with a redwood forest, so pretty and with such good hiking that it has become popular enough to make reservations a must. The reason for its popularity is a series of exceptional hikes, including one to the Año Nuevo Lookout (well, the lookout is now blocked by trees, but there are glimpses of the ocean elsewhere along the way), Mill Ox Loop, and, for the ambitious, 11-mile Butano Rim Loop. The latter has a backpack camp with seven trail campsites (primitive with pit toilets available) requiring a 5.5-mile hike in the park's most remote area, where no drinking water is available. Creek water is within 0.5 mile of the campsites; bring a water purifier.

RV sites, facilities: There are 20 sites for tents or RVs up to 24 feet (no hookups), 18 walk-in sites, and seven hike-in sites (5.5 miles, with pit toilets available). Picnic tables, food lockers, and fire grills are provided. Drinking water and restrooms with flush toilets are available. Leashed pets are permitted in campsites, picnic areas, and on paved roads.

Reservations, fees: Reservations are accepted at 800/444-PARK (800/444-7275) or www.reserveamerica.com ($8 reservation fee). Sites are $35 per night, $10 per night for hike-in trail sites, $10 per night for each additional vehicle. Note: Reservations are not available for hike-in trail sites. Open year-round.

Note: At time of publication, the park was gated at the entrance and closed to vehicles. Restrooms and camping areas were scheduled closed until May 1, 2010.

Directions: Drive to Half Moon Bay and the

CALIFORNIA

junction of Highway 1 and Highway 92. Drive south on Highway 1 for 18 miles to the Pescadero Road exit. Turn left on Pescadero Road and drive three miles past the town of Pescadero to Cloverdale Road. Turn right and drive 4.5 miles to the park entrance on the left.

Contact: Butano State Park, 650/879-2040, fax 650/879-2173; Santa Cruz District, 831/335-6318, www.parks.ca.gov.

14 PORTOLA REDWOODS STATE PARK

🚶 🚴 🐕 🚐 ⛺

Scenic rating: 9

near Skyline Ridge

Map grid B3

Portola Redwoods State Park is very secluded since visitors are required to travel on an extremely slow and winding series of roads to reach it. The park features redwoods and a mixed evergreen and hardwood forest on the western slopes of the Santa Cruz Mountains, the headwaters of Pescadero Creek, and 18 miles of hiking trails. A literal highlight is a 300-foot-high redwood, one of the tallest trees in the Santa Cruz Mountains. In addition to redwoods, there are Douglas fir and live oak, as well as a riparian zone along the stream. A four-mile hike links up to nearby Pescadero Creek County Park (which, in turn, borders Memorial County Park). At times in the summer, a low fog will move in along the San Mateo coast, and from lookouts near Skyline, visitors can peer to the west at what seems like a pearlescent sea with little islands (hilltops) poking through (this view is available from the access road, not from campsites). Wild pigs are occasionally spotted here, with larger numbers at neighboring Pescadero Creek County Park. The Slate Creek Backpack Camp provides a little-known option.

RV sites, facilities: There are 56 sites for tents or RVs up to 24 feet (no hookups), four hike-in/bike-in sites, four walk-in sites, six hike-in backpack sites (three-mile hike), and four group sites for 25–50 people each. Picnic tables, storage lockers, and fire grills are provided. Drinking water, restrooms with flush toilets and coin showers, and firewood are available. There are nature hikes and campfire programs scheduled on weekends from Memorial Day through Labor Day. The nearest gas is 13 miles away. Leashed pets are permitted on paved surfaces only.

Reservations, fees: Reservations are accepted at 800/444-PARK (800/444-7275) or www.reserveamerica.com ($8 reservation fee). Sites are $35 per night, $10 per night for each additional vehicle, $3 per person per night for hike-in/bike-in sites, $10 per person per night for walk-in sites and hike-in backpack sites, $165–335 per night for group sites. Reservations for Slate Creek Backpack Camp are accepted at 831/338-8861. Open May through November; closed Sunday–Thursday, November –June.

Directions: From Palo Alto on I-280, turn west on Page Mill Road and drive (slow and twisty) to Skyline Boulevard/Highway 35. Cross Skyline and continue west on Alpine Road (very twisty) for about three miles to Portola State Park Road. Turn left on Portola State Park Road and drive about three miles to the park entrance at the end of the road.

Contact: Portola Redwoods State Park, 650/948-9098; Santa Cruz District, 831/335-6318, www.parks.ca.gov, www.santacruzstateparks.org.

15 BIG BASIN REDWOODS STATE PARK

🚶 🐕 ♿ 🚐 ⛺

Scenic rating: 10

near Santa Cruz

Map grid B3

Big Basin is one of the best state parks in California, featuring giant redwoods near the park headquarters, secluded campsites set in forest, and rare opportunities to stay in a tent cabin or a backpacking trail site. The park covers more than 18,000 acres of redwoods, much of it old-growth, including forest behemoths more than 1,000 years old. It is a great park for hikers, with four waterfalls making for stellar destinations. Sempervirens Falls, a long, narrow, silvery stream, is an easy 1.5-miles round-trip on Sequoia Trail. The famous Berry Creek Falls, a spectacular 70-foot cascade set in a beautiful canyon, is framed by redwoods. For hikers in good condition, figure two hours (4.7 miles) to reach Berry Creek Falls, five hours for the round-trip in and out, and six hours for the complete loop (12 miles) that extends into the park's most remote areas. Other waterfalls include Silver Falls and Golden Falls. There is also an easy nature loop trail near the park headquarters in the valley floor that is routed past several mammoth redwoods. This is California's oldest state park, established in 1902. It is home to the largest continuous stand of ancient coast redwoods south of Humboldt State Park in far Northern California. There are more than 80 miles of trails with elevations varying from 2,000 feet at the eastern Big Basin Rim on down to sea level. Rainfall averages 60 inches per year, most arriving from December through mid-March.

RV sites, facilities: There are 31 sites for tents or RVs up to 27 feet or trailers up to 24 feet (no hookups), 69 sites for tents only, 38 walk-in sites, 36 tent cabins (reservations required), two hike-in/bike-in sites, 52 hike-in campsites, and four group sites for 40–50 people. Picnic tables, food lockers, and fire grills are provided. Drinking water, restrooms with flush toilets and coin showers, dump station, firewood, and groceries are available. Some facilities are wheelchair-accessible. Leashed pets are allowed in campsites and on paved roads only.

Reservations, fees: Reservation are accepted at 800/444-PARK (800/444-7275) or www.reserveamerica.com ($8 reservation fee). Sites are $35 per night for individual sites and walk-in sites, $6 per night for each additional vehicle, $10 per person for hike-in sites, $3 per person per night for hike-in/bike-in sites, $180–224 per night for group sites. Reserve tent cabins at 831/338-4745. Open year-round; campground closed Sunday–Thursday, December–March.

Directions: From Santa Cruz, turn north on Highway 9 and drive 12 miles to Boulder Creek and Highway 236 (signed Big Basin). Turn west on Highway 236 and drive nine miles to the park headquarters.

Contact: Big Basin Redwoods State Park, 831/338-8860 or 831/338-8861; Santa Cruz District, 831/335-6318, www.santacruz-stateparks.org or www.parks.ca.gov.

16 SANBORN-SKYLINE COUNTY PARK

Scenic rating: 8

near Saratoga

Map grid B3

This is a pretty camp set in a redwood forest, semi-primitive, but like a world in a different orbit compared to the asphalt of San Jose and the rest of the Santa Clara Valley. These campgrounds get heavy use on summer weekends, of course. This is headquarters for a 3,688-acre park that stretches from the foothills of Saratoga up to the Skyline Ridge in the Santa Cruz Mountains. Fifteen miles of hiking trails are available, with a trailhead at camp. Most trails explore lush wooded slopes, with redwoods and tan oak. Dogs are prohibited at walk-in sites, but are allowed at the RV sites, the main park's grassy area, and day-use areas.

RV sites, facilities: There are 15 sites with full hookups (20 and 30 amps) for RVs up to 30 feet, a separate walk-in campground with 33 sites for tents, and a youth group area for up to 35 people. Picnic tables, food lockers, and fire pits are provided. Drinking water, restrooms with flush toilets and coin showers, dump station, a seasonal youth science center, and a one-mile nature trail are available. Some facilities are wheelchair-accessible. Leashed pets are permitted in RV campground and picnic areas only.

Reservations, fees: Reservations are required at 408/355-2201 (Mon.–Fri.) or at www.parkhere.org ($6 reservation fee). Tent sites are $10–20 per night, $25 for RV sites, $12 per night for walk-in, $40 for youth group area for up to 30 people for first night and then $10 per night,

CALIFORNIA

$144–216 per night for group camps. Check-in required before sunset; gates are locked at dusk. Some credit cards accepted. RV sites open year-round; walk-in sites open April through mid-October.

Directions: From San Jose, take Highway 17 south for six miles to Highway 9/Saratoga Avenue. Turn west and drive to Saratoga, then continue on Highway 9 for two miles to Sanborn Road. Turn left and drive one mile to the park on the right. Walk-in sites require a 0.1- to 0.5-mile walk from the parking area.

Contact: Sanborn-Skyline County Park, 408/867-9959, www.parkhere.org.

17 JOSEPH D. GRANT COUNTY PARK

Scenic rating: 7

near San Jose

Map grid B3

Grant Ranch is a great, wild playland covering more than 9,000 acres in the foothills of nearby Mount Hamilton to the east. It features 52 miles of hiking trails (horses permitted), 20 miles of old ranch roads that are perfect for mountain biking, a pretty lake (Grant Lake), and miles of foothills, canyons, oaks, and grasslands. The campground is set amid oak grasslands, is shaded, and can be used as a base camp for planning the day's recreation. The best hikes are to Halls Valley, especially in the winter and spring when there are many secret little creeks and miniature waterfalls in hidden canyons; Hotel Trail; and Cañada de Pala Trail, which drops to San Felipe Creek, the prettiest stream in the park. Warm-water fishing is available in the lake and several smaller ponds. A great side trip is the slow, curvy drive east to Lick Observatory for great views of the Santa Clara Valley. Wood fires are often banned in summer.

RV sites, facilities: There are 40 sites for tents or RVs up to 31 feet (no hookups). Picnic tables, food lockers, and fire pits are provided. Drinking water, restrooms with flush toilets and free showers, and dump station are available. Some

facilities are wheelchair accessible. Leashed pets are permitted.

Reservations, fees: Reservations are required at 408/355-2201 (Mon.–Fri.) or at www.parkhere.org ($6 reservation fee). Sites are $12–24 per night. Check-in required before sunset; gates are locked at dusk. Open year-round.

Directions: In San Jose at the junction of I-680 and U.S. 101, take I-680 north to the Alum Rock Avenue exit. Turn east and drive four miles to Mount Hamilton Road. Turn right and drive eight miles to the park headquarters entrance on the right side of the road.

Contact: Joseph D. Grant County Park, 408/274-6121, fax 408/270-4808, www.parkhere.org.

18 COTILLION GARDENS RV PARK

Scenic rating: 6

near Santa Cruz

Map grid B3

This is a pretty place with several possible side trips. It is set on the edge of the Santa Cruz Mountain redwoods, near Henry Cowell Redwoods State Park and the San Lorenzo River. The Santa Cruz Beach and Boardwalk is only a few minutes away by car, and Monterey is 45 miles away. Other side trips include the steam engine ride along the San Lorenzo River out of Roaring Camp Train Rides in Felton, and visiting Loch Lomond Reservoir near Ben Lomond for hiking, boat rentals, or fishing. A golf course is nearby. There is a mix of both overnighters and some long-term rentals at this park.

RV sites, facilities: There are 80 sites with full or partial hookups (30 amps) for RVs up to 36 feet, four sites for tents, and five camping cabins. One RV site is pull-through. Picnic tables and fire rings are provided. Restrooms with showers, dump station, cable TV, Wi-Fi, modem access, recreation room, heated seasonal swimming pool, and convenience store are available. Some facilities are wheelchair-accessible. Leashed pets are permitted.

Reservations, fees: Reservations are recommended. RV sites are $45–58 per night, $35 per night for tent sites, plus $3 per person per night for more than two people. Call for cabin prices. Some credit cards accepted. Open year-round.

Directions: From Los Gatos, drive west on Highway 17 for 20 miles toward Santa Cruz to the Mount Hermon Road exit/Scotts Valley (second exit in Scotts Valley). Take the Mount Hermon Road exit to the stoplight at Mount Hermon Road. Turn right on Mount Hermon Road and drive 3.5 miles to Felton and Graham Hill Road (Y intersection). Bear right onto Graham Hill Road, immediately move to the left lane, and drive 50 feet to Highway 9. Turn left on Highway 9 and drive 1.5 miles to the park on the left.

Contact: Cotillion Gardens RV Park, 831/335-7669.

19 HENRY COWELL REDWOODS STATE PARK

Scenic rating: 8

near Santa Cruz

Map grid B3

This state park near Santa Cruz has good hiking, good views, and a chance of fishing in the winter for steelhead. The 1,750-acre park features 20 miles of trails in the forest, where the old-growth redwoods are estimated at 1,400–1,800 years old. One great easy hike is a 15-minute walk to a lookout platform over Santa Cruz and the Pacific Ocean; the trailhead is near campsite 49. Another good hike is Eagle Creek Trail, a three-mile walk that heads along Eagle Creek and the San Lorenzo River, running through a classic redwood canyon. In winter, there is limited steelhead fishing in the San Lorenzo River. A side-trip option is taking the Roaring Camp Big Trees Railroad (831/335-4400), which is adjacent to camp. Insider's tips: Poison oak is prevalent in this park and around the campground. Alcohol is prohibited in the campground, but not in the day-use area.

RV sites, facilities: There are 111 sites for tents or RVs up to 35 feet (no hookups), and one bike-in site for up to eight people. Picnic tables and fire grills are provided. Drinking water, restrooms with flush toilets and coin showers, and Wi-Fi are available. Some facilities are wheelchair-accessible. A nature center, bookstore, and picnic area are nearby. Leashed pets are permitted, but must be kept inside tents or vehicles at night.

Reservations, fees: Reservations accepted mid-March through October at 800/444-PARK (800/444-7275) or www.reserveamerica.com ($8 reservation fee). Sites are $35 per night (maximum of eight people). The bike-in site is first come, first served, $3 per person per night. Day-use parking $10. Open March through October.

Directions: In Scotts Valley on Highway 17, take the Mount Hermon Road exit and drive west toward Felton to Lockwood Lane. Turn left on Lockwood Lane and drive about one mile to Graham Hill Road. Turn left on Graham Hill Road and drive 0.5 mile to the campground on the right.

Contact: Henry Cowell Redwoods State Park, 831/438-2396 or 831/335-4598, www.santacruzstateparks.org or www.parks.ca.gov.

20 SANTA CRUZ RANCH RV PARK

Scenic rating: 5

near Scotts Valley

Map grid B3

This camp is situated on 6.5 acres and is just a short hop from Santa Cruz and Monterey Bay. There are many side-trip options, making this a prime location for vacationers cruising the California coast. In Santa Cruz there are several quality restaurants, plus fishing trips and boat rentals at Santa Cruz Wharf, as well as the famous Santa Cruz Beach Boardwalk and amusement park. Discount tickets for local attractions are available in the office. Note that most of the

CALIFORNIA

sites are filled with long-term renters; a few sites are set aside for overnight vacationers.

RV sites, facilities: There are 25 pull-through sites with full hookups (30 amps) for RVs up to 43 feet and four sites for tents. Picnic tables are provided. Restrooms with showers, cable TV, coin laundry, free Wi-Fi and modem access, recreation and meeting room, hot tub, and seasonal heated swimming pool are available. No open fires. Leashed pets are permitted with approval.

Reservations, fees: Reservations are recommended. RV sites are $51 per night, tent sites are $37 per night, $3 per night for each additional vehicle. First pet is free and second pet is $1 per night. Weekly, monthly, and group rates available. Some credit cards accepted. Open year-round.

Directions: From Santa Cruz, at the junction of Highways 1 and 17, turn north on Highway 17 and drive three miles to the Mount Hermon/Big Basin exit. Take that exit north onto Mount Hermon Road and drive 0.5 mile to Scotts Valley Drive. Turn right and drive 0.7 mile to Disc Drive. Turn right and continue to 917 Disc Drive on the left. Note: Big rigs use Granite Creek exit, or call for best route.

Contact: Santa Cruz Ranch RV Park, 831/438-1288 or 800/546-1288, fax 831/438-2877, www.santacruzranchrv.com.

21 HENRY W. COE STATE PARK

Scenic rating: 8

near Gilroy

Map grid B3

This is the Bay Area's backyard wilderness, with 87,000 acres of wildlands, including a 23,300-acre wilderness area. There are more than 100 miles of ranch roads and 300 miles of hiking trails, a remarkable network that provides access to 140 ponds and small lakes, hidden streams, and a habitat that is paradise for fish, wildlife, and wild flora. In 2007, a wildfire burned about half of the park, but this grassland country is always quick to spring back to life.

The best camping introduction is at the drive-in campsites at park headquarters, set on a hilltop at 2,600 feet elevation that is ideal for stargazing and watching meteor showers. That provides a taste. If you like it, then come back for the full meal. It is the wilderness hike-in and bike-in sites where you will get the full flavor of the park. Before setting out for the outback, always consult with the rangers here—the ambitious plans of many hikers cause them to suffer dehydration and heatstroke. For wilderness trips, the best jump-off point is Coyote Creek or Hunting Hollow trailheads upstream of Coyote Reservoir near Gilroy. The park has excellent pond-style fishing but requires extremely long hikes (typically 10- to 25-mile round-trips) to reach the best lakes, including Mustang Pond, Jackrabbit Lake, Coit Lake, and Mississippi Lake. Expect hot weather in the summer; spring and early summer are the prime times. Even though the park may appear to be 120 square miles of oak foothills, the terrain is often steep, and making ridges often involves climbs of 1,500 feet. There are many great secrets to be discovered here, including Rooster Comb and Coyote Creek. At times on spring days, wild pigs seem to be everywhere. Golden eagles are also abundant. Bring a water purifier for hikes because there is no drinking water in the outback.

RV sites, facilities: There are 10 sites for tents and 10 sites for tents or RVs up to 24 feet (no hookups). There are also eight equestrian campsites, 82 hike-in/bike-in sites, and 10 group sites for 10–50 people. At the drive-in site at park headquarters, picnic tables and fire grills are provided. Drinking water and vault toilets are available. Leashed pets are permitted at the drive-in campgrounds only. At the horse camps, corrals and water troughs are available. At hike-in/bike-in sites, vault toilets are provided, but no drinking water is available. Garbage must be packed out at hike-in/bike-in camps.

Reservations, fees: Reservations are accepted at 800/444-PARK (800/444-7275) or www.reserveamerica.com ($8 reservation fee). Sites are $20 per night, $5 per night for each additional vehicle, $30 per night for group sites, $6–8 for each additional vehicle. No reservation for hike-in/bike-in or horse sites, $14 per night for horse sites, $3 per person per night for hike-in/bike-in sites. For hike-in/bike-in or horse sites, a wilderness permit is required from park headquarters. Make reservations for group sites at 408/779-2728 ($8 reservation fee). Open year-round.

Directions: From Morgan Hill on U.S. 101, take the East Dunne Avenue exit. Turn east and drive 13 miles (including over the bridge at Anderson Lake, then very twisty and narrow) to the park entrance.

Contact: Henry W. Coe State Park, 408/779-2728, www.coepark.org or www.parks.ca.gov.

22 MOUNT MADONNA COUNTY PARK

Scenic rating: 7

between Watsonville and Gilroy
Map grid B3

It's a twisty son-of-a-gun road to reach the top of Mount Madonna, but the views on clear days of Monterey Bay to the west and Santa Clara Valley to the east always make it worth the trip. In addition, a small herd of white deer are kept protected in a pen near the parking area for a rare chance to see unique wildlife. This 3,688-acre park is dominated by redwood forest, but at the lower slopes of Mount Madonna the landscape changes to oak woodland, dense chaparral, and grassy meadows. Ohlone Indians once lived here. There are many good hiking trails in the park; the best is Bayview Loop. The 20-mile trail system includes a one-mile self-guided nature trail. Elevation in the park reaches 1,896 feet. Free programs are offered at the amphitheater on Saturday evenings during the summer. Insider's note: Campsite 105 at Valley View is the only pull-through site. While no credit cards are accepted in person, there is a self-pay machine that accepts credit cards, a nice touch. The campsites are dispersed throughout four campgrounds.

RV sites, facilities: There are 118 sites with partial hookups (30 amps) for tents or RVs up to 31 feet and two group areas for up to 240 people. One site is pull-through. Five youth-group areas for 40–50 people each are also available; youth groups must have tax-exempt status. Picnic tables, food lockers, and fire pits are provided. Drinking water, restrooms with coin showers and flush toilets, dump station, seasonal live music, archery range, picnic areas, amphitheater, and visitors center are available. Some facilities are wheelchair-accessible. Leashed pets are permitted.

Reservations, fees: Reservations are required at 408/355-2201 (Mon.–Fri.) or at www.parkhere.org ($6 reservation fee). Sites are $24–25 per night, $150–450 per night for group areas and $40 per night for youth-group areas. Some credit cards accepted at self-serve machine. Open year-round.

Directions: From U.S. 101 in Gilroy, take the Hecker Pass Highway/Highway 152 exit west. Drive west seven miles to Pole Line Road and the park entrance on the right.

From Highway 1 in Watsonville, turn east onto Highway 152 and drive about 12 miles east to Pole Line Road and the park entrance on the left.

Contact: Mount Madonna County Park, 408/842-2341, fax 408/842-6642, www.parkhere.org.

23 COYOTE LAKE COUNTY PARK

Scenic rating: 7

near Gilroy
Map grid B3

Several campsites here are set on a bluff with a lake view. The campground is nestled in oaks, among 796 acres of parkland, furnishing some much-needed shade. Coyote Lake, a long, narrow lake set in a canyon just over the ridge east of U.S. 101, is a pretty surprise to newcomers. It covers 635 acres and is stocked with trout from late winter through spring; the lake also provides the top fishery for bass in the Bay

Area. Other species are bluegill and crappie. Both powerboating and non-motorized boating are allowed; the boat launch is one mile north of the visitors center. Swimming is prohibited. There are no longer hiking trails along the lakeshore, but more than 13 miles of multi-use trails (horses and mountain bikes are allowed) are available. Note: If you continue east about four miles on the access road that runs past the lake to the Coe State Park Hunting Hollow entrance, you'll come to two outstanding trailheads (one at a parking area, one at the Coyote Creek gate) into that park's wildlands. Wildlife, including deer and wild turkey, is abundant.

RV sites, facilities: There are 74 pull-through sites for tents or RVs up to 31 feet (no hookups). Picnic tables, food lockers, and fire pits are provided. Drinking water, flush toilets, and a boat ramp are available. A visitors center is also available. Some facilities are wheelchair-accessible. Leashed pets are permitted.

Reservations, fees: Reservations are required at 408/355-2201 (Mon.–Fri.) or at www.parkhere. org ($6 reservation fee). Sites are $12–25 per night, $6 per day for boat launching. Some credit cards accepted. Open year-round.

Directions: Drive on U.S. 101 to Gilroy and Leavesley Road. Take that exit and drive east on Leavesley Road for 1.75 miles to New Avenue. Turn left on New Avenue and drive 0.6 mile to Roop Road. Turn right on Roop Road and drive three miles to Coyote Reservoir Road. Turn left on Coyote Reservoir Road and drive to the campground.

Contact: Coyote Lake County Park, 408/842-7800, fax 408/842-6439, www.parkhere.org; Coyote Discount Bait and Tackle, 408/463-0711.

MONTEREY AND BIG SUR

BEST RV PARKS AND CAMPGROUNDS

☾ **Coastal Sites**
Seacliff State Beach, page 903.

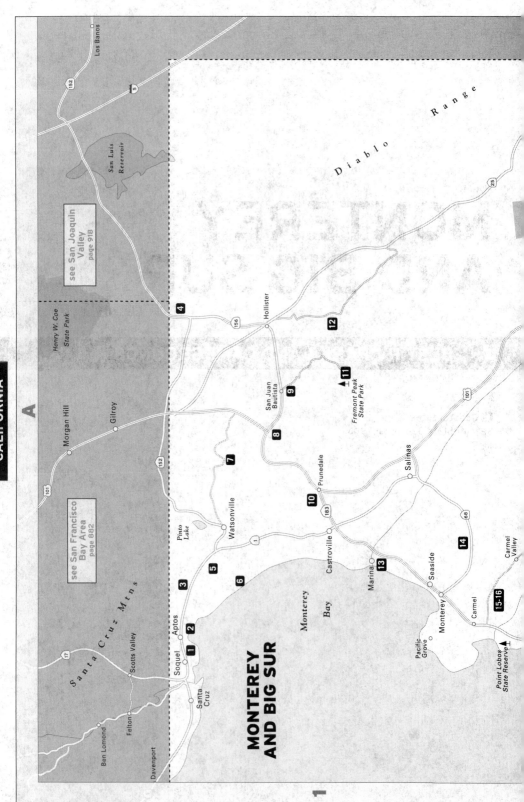

see San Joaquin Valley page 918

see San Francisco Bay Area page 882

CALIFORNIA

A

MONTEREY AND BIG SUR

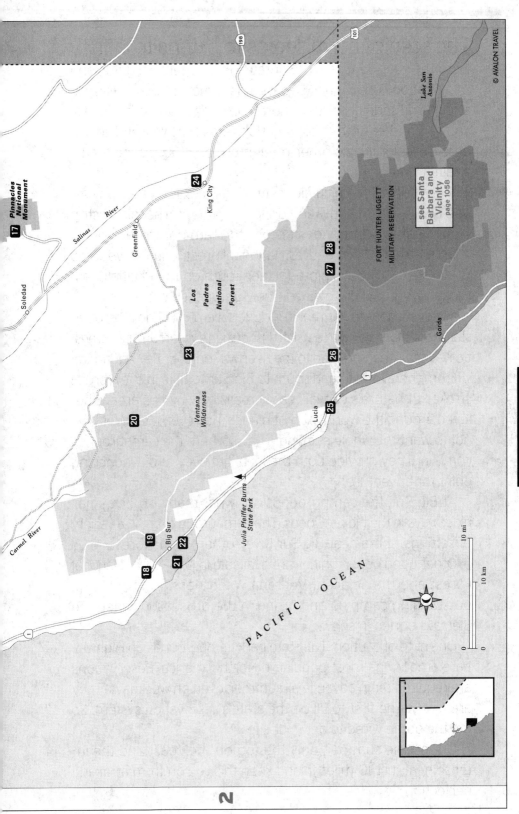

CALIFORNIA

The scenic charm seems to extend to infinity

from the seaside towns of Santa Cruz, Monterey, Big Sur, and San Simeon. The primary treasure is the coast, which is rock-strewn and sprinkled with inshore kelp beds, where occasionally you can find sea otters playing Pop Goes the Weasel. The sea here is a color like no other, often more of a tourmaline than a straight green or blue.

From Carmel to Lucia alone, touring Big Sur on Highway 1 is one of the most captivating drives anywhere. The inland strip along Highway 1 provides access to state parks, redwoods, coastal streams, Los Padres National Forest, and the Ventana Wilderness. As you explore farther south on the Pacific Coast Highway, you will discover a largely untouched coast.

Most vacations to this region include several must-do trips, often starting in Monterey with a visit to Fisherman's Wharf and its domesticated sea lions, and then to the nearby Monterey Bay Aquarium.

From there, most head south to Big Sur to take in a few brush strokes of nature's canvas, easily realizing why this area is beloved around the world. At first glance, however, it's impossible not to want the whole painting. That is where the campgrounds come in. They provide both the ideal getaway and a launching point for adventure.

At Big Sur, the campgrounds are what many expect: small hideaways in the big redwoods. The campgrounds are in a variety of settings, some near Big Sur River, others in the forest.

Other good opportunities are available in Los Padres National Forest and the adjacent Ventana Wilderness, which provide outstanding camping and hiking in the off-season, when the Sierra is buried in snow.

One note of caution: The state park campgrounds on Highway 1 are among the most popular in North America. Reservations are required far in advance all summer, even on weekdays. They are always the first to fill on the state's reservation system. So get the game wired to get your site.

During the summer, only the fog on the coast and the intense heat just 10 miles inland keep this region from attaining perfection.

1 NEW BRIGHTON STATE BEACH

Scenic rating: 10

near Capitola

Map grid A1

This is one in a series of state park camps set on the bluffs overlooking Monterey Bay. They are among the most popular and in-demand state campgrounds in California. Reservations are a necessity. This camp is set near a forest of Monterey pine and live oak. The summer is often foggy and cool, especially in the morning. Beach-combing, swimming, and surf fishing for perch provide recreation options, and skiff rentals are available at the nearby Capitola Wharf. The San Lorenzo River enters the ocean nearby.

RV sites, facilities: There are 111 sites for tents or RVs up to 36 feet, three group sites, and four hike-in/bike-in sites. Some sites have partial hookups (30 amps). Picnic tables, fire rings, and food lockers are provided. Drinking water, restrooms with coin showers and flush toilets, and visitors center are available. Dump stations, propane gas, groceries, coin laundry, restaurant, and gas station are available within 2.5 miles. Some facilities are wheelchair-accessible. Leashed pets are permitted.

Reservations, fees: Reservations are recommended and can be made at 800/444-PARK (800/444-7275) or www.reserveamerica.com ($8 reservation fee). Sites are $25–50 per night, $10 per night for each additional vehicle, $185 per night for group site, $3 per person per night for hike-in/bike-in site. Two-night maximum stay per month. Open year-round, weather permitting.

Directions: From Santa Cruz, drive south on Highway 1 for about five miles to the Park Avenue exit. Take that exit and turn right on Park Avenue and drive a short distance to McGregor Drive (a four-way stop). Turn left and drive a short distance to the park entrance on the right.

Contact: New Brighton State Beach, 831/464-6330 or 831/464-6329; California State Parks, Santa Cruz District, 831/335-6318, www.santacruzstateparks.org or www.parks.ca.gov.

2 SEACLIFF STATE BEACH

Scenic rating: 10

near Santa Cruz

Map grid A1 **BEST (**

Here is a very pretty spot on a beach along Monterey Bay. Beach walks are great, especially on clear evenings for dramatic sunsets. A visitors center is available in the summer. This is a popular layover for vacationers touring Highway 1 in the summer, but the best weather is from mid-August to early October. This is a popular beach for swimming and sunbathing, with a long stretch of sand backed by coastal bluffs. A structure many call the "old cement ship" nearby provides some fascination, but for safety reasons visitors are no longer allowed to walk on it. It is actually an old concrete freighter, the Palo Alto. Fishing is often good adjacent to the ship.

RV sites, facilities: There are 25 sites with full hookups (30 amps) for RVs up to 40 feet, and an overflow area that can accommodate 21 RVs up to 34 feet (no hookups). No tents. Picnic tables and fire grills are provided. Drinking water, restrooms with flush toilets and coin showers, and picnic area are available. Propane gas, groceries, and a coin laundry are nearby. Some facilities are wheelchair-accessible. Leashed pets are permitted in the camping area and on the beach.

Reservations, fees: Reservations are accepted at 800/444-PARK (800/444-7275) or www.reserveamerica.com ($8 reservation fee). Sites are $35–65 per night, and $10 per night for each additional vehicle. Open year-round, weather permitting.

Directions: From Santa Cruz, drive south on Highway 1 about six miles to State Park Drive/Seacliff Beach exit. Take that exit, turn west (right), and drive a short distance to the park entrance.

Contact: Seacliff State Beach, 831/685-6442 or 831/685-6500; California State Parks, Santa Cruz District, 831/429-2851, fax 831/429-2876, www.santacruzstateparks.org or www.parks.ca.gov.

CALIFORNIA

3 PINTO LAKE PARK

Scenic rating: 7

near Watsonville

Map grid A1

Pinto Lake can be a real find. Of the nine lakes in the nine Bay Area counties that offer camping, it is the only one where the RV campsites are actually near the lake. For the few who know about it, it's an offer that can't be refused. But note that no tent camping is permitted. The lake is best known as a fishing lake, with trout stocks and a small resident population of crappie and bluegill. Rainbow trout are stocked twice weekly in season. A 5-mph speed limit has been established for boaters, and no swimming or wading is permitted. The leash law for dogs is strictly enforced here.

RV sites, facilities: There are 28 sites with full hookups (30 amps) for RVs of any length. No tents. Picnic tables, cable TV, and barbecues are provided. A boat ramp, boat rentals, volleyball, softball field, and horseshoes are available nearby in the summer. Leashed pets are permitted. Most facilities are wheelchair-accessible. Open year-round.

Reservations, fees: Reservations are accepted. Sites are $28 per night, $2 per night per person for more than two people (children 12 and under are free), $2 per night for each additional vehicle, $2 per pet per night. Credit cards are not accepted.

Directions: From Santa Cruz, drive 17 miles south on Highway 1 to the exit for Watsonville/Gilroy–Highway 152. Take that exit onto Main Street, then immediately turn left on Green Valley Road and drive 2.7 miles (0.5 mile past Holohan intersection) to the entrance for the lake and campground on the left.

From Monterey, drive north on Highway 1 to the Green Valley Road exit. Take that exit and turn right at the Green Valley Road and drive 2.7 miles (0.5 mile past the Holohan intersection) to the entrance for the lake and campground.

Contact: Pinto Lake Park, City of Watsonville, 831/722-8129, www.pintolake.com.

4 CASA DE FRUTA RV ORCHARD RESORT

Scenic rating: 3

near Pacheco Pass

Map grid A1

This 80-acre RV park has a festival-like atmosphere to it, with country music and dancing every weekend in the summer and barbecues on Sunday. The resort is also busy during the Gilroy Garlic Festival in July and the Hollister Independence Rally, a motorcycle event held nearby during the Fourth of July weekend. Huge, but sparse, San Luis Reservoir is 20 miles to the east.

RV sites, facilities: There are 300 sites with full hookups (30 amps) for RVs; some sites are pull-through. Tent sites are also available. Picnic tables are provided. Restrooms with flush toilets and showers, dump station, Wi-Fi, satellite TV, coin laundry, playground, swimming pool, wading pool, outdoor dance floor, horseshoes, volleyball courts, baseball diamonds, wine- and cheese-tasting room, candy factory, bakery, fruit stand, 24-hour restaurant, motel, gift shop, carousel, narrow-gauge train ride through animal park, and a minimart are available. Some facilities are wheelchair-accessible. Leashed pets are permitted.

Reservations, fees: Reservations are accepted at 800/548-3813. Sites are $34–40 per night, $2 per person per night for more than two people, $3 per pet per night. Some credit cards accepted. Open year-round.

Directions: Drive on U.S. 101 to the junction with Highway 152 (near Gilroy). Take Highway 152 east and drive 13 miles to Casa de Fruta Parkway. Take that exit and drive a short distance to the resort.

Contact: Casa de Fruta RV Orchard Resort, 408/842-9316 or 800/548-3813, www.casadefruta.com.

5 SANTA CRUZ KOA

Scenic rating: 8

near Watsonville

Map grid A1

Bike rentals and nearby access to Manresa State Beach make this KOA campground a winner. The little log cabins are quite cute, and security is first class. It is a popular layover spot and weekend vacation destination. The only downer is the amount of asphalt.

RV sites, facilities: There are 180 sites, including five pull-through, with full or partial hookups (30 and 50 amps) for RVs up to 40 feet, six sites for tents only, 50 camping cabins, and three camping lodges. Picnic tables and fire grills are provided. Restrooms with showers, two dump stations, free Wi-Fi, modem access, swimming pool, spa, playground, two recreation rooms, bicycle rentals, miniature golf, convenience store, and propane gas are available. Some facilities are wheelchair-accessible. Leashed pets are permitted.

Reservations, fees: Reservations are advised by calling 800/562-7701. Sites are $76–135 for RVs, $113–135 per night for camping cabins, $225 per night for camping lodges. Some credit cards accepted. Open year-round.

Directions: From Santa Cruz, drive 12 miles southeast on Highway 1. Take the San Andreas Road exit and head southwest for 3.5 miles to 1186 San Andreas Road.

Contact: Santa Cruz KOA, 831/722-0551, fax 831/722-0989, www.santacruzkoa.com or www.koa.com.

6 SUNSET STATE BEACH

Scenic rating: 9

near Watsonville

Map grid A1

On clear evenings, the sunsets here look as if they are imported from Hawaii. The camp is set on a bluff along Monterey Bay. While there are no ocean views from the campsites, the location makes for easy, short walks down to the beach for beautiful shoreline walks. The beachfront features pine trees, bluffs, and expansive sand dunes. Large agricultural fields border the park. This area was once a good spot for clamming, but the clams have just about been fished out. The best weather is in late summer and fall. Spring can be windy here, and early summer is often foggy. Reservations are often needed well in advance to secure a spot.

RV sites, facilities: There are 91 sites for tents or RVs up to 31 feet (no hookups), one hike-in/bike-in site, and one group site for up to 50 people. Picnic tables, food lockers, and fire grills are provided. Drinking water, restrooms with flush toilets and coin showers, Wi-Fi, and firewood are available. Some facilities are wheelchair-accessible. Leashed pets are permitted, except on the beach.

Reservations, fees: Reservations are accepted at 800/444-PARK (800/444-7275) or www.reserveamerica.com ($8 reservation fee). Sites are $35 per night, $10 per night for each additional vehicle, $3 per person per night for hike-in/bike-in site, $335 per night for group site. Open year-round.

Directions: From Highway 1 near Watsonville, take the Riverside Drive exit toward the ocean to Beach Road. Drive 3.5 miles on Beach Road to the San Andreas Road exit. Turn right on San Andreas Road and drive about three miles to Sunset Beach Road. Turn left and drive a short distance to the park entrance.

Contact: Sunset State Beach, 831/763-7063; California State Parks, Santa Cruz District, 831/335-6318, www.santacruzstateparks.org or www.parks.ca.gov.

7 McALPINE LAKE AND PARK

Scenic rating: 5

near San Juan Bautista

Map grid A1

This is the only privately operated campground in the immediate region that has any spots for tenters. The camping cabins here look like miniature log cabins, quite cute and comfortable.

CALIFORNIA

In addition, the park has a 40-foot-deep lake stocked with trout, bass, bluegill, and catfish; no fishing license is required. The swimming pool was recently transformed into a trout-fishing pond. Other highlights of the park are its proximity to Mission San Juan Bautista and the relatively short drive to the Monterey-Carmel area.

RV sites, facilities: There are 40 sites for tents only, 27 sites with partial hookups (30 amps) for tents or RVs, 14 sites with full hookups (30 amps) for RVs, and four cabins. Picnic tables and fire grills are provided. Restrooms with flush toilets and showers, dump station, banquet facilities, fishing pond, bait and tackle, gold panning, coin laundry, propane gas, and groceries are available. Some facilities are wheelchair-accessible. Leashed pets are permitted.

Reservations, fees: Reservations are accepted. Sites are $27–35 per night, $5 per person per night for more than four people, $5 per night for each additional vehicle. Some credit cards accepted. Open year-round.

Directions: On U.S. 101, drive to the Highway 129 exit. Take Highway 129 west and drive 100 feet to Searle Road (frontage road). Turn left onto Searle Road and drive to the stop sign at Anzar. Turn left again on Anzar and drive under the freeway to the park entrance on the left (900 Anzar Road).

Contact: McAlpine Lake and Park, 831/623-4263, fax 831/623-4559, www.mcalpinelake.com.

8 MONTEREY VACATION RV PARK

Scenic rating: 4

near San Juan Bautista

Map grid A1

This RV park has an ideal location for many vacationers. It's a 10-minute drive to San Juan Bautista, 15 minutes to winery tours, 30 minutes to the Monterey Bay Aquarium, and 40 minutes to Monterey's Fisherman's Wharf and Cannery Row. It's set in an attractive spot with some trees, but the nearby attractions are what make it a clear winner. The park is next to the old stagecoach trail where famous outlaw Joaquin Murrieta once ambushed travelers. Note that about half of the sites are occupied by long-term renters.

RV sites, facilities: There are 88 sites with full hookups (30 amps) for RVs up to 40 feet; many are pull-through. No tents. Picnic tables and barbecues are provided at some sites. Restrooms with flush toilets and showers, spa, swimming pool, coin laundry, recreation halls, modem access (in office), and propane gas are available. Some facilities are wheelchair-accessible. Leashed pets up to 40 pounds are permitted, with certain restrictions.

Reservations, fees: Reservations are recommended for three-day holiday weekends; $27–35 per night, $3 per person per night for more than two people, $1 per pet per night. Some credit cards accepted (except on discounts). Open year-round.

Directions: On U.S. 101, drive toward San Juan Bautista (between Gilroy and Salinas). The park is on U.S. 101 two miles south of the Highway 156/San Juan Bautista exit at 1400 Highway 101.

Contact: Monterey Vacation RV Park, 831/726-9118, fax 831/726-1841.

9 MISSION FARM RV PARK

Scenic rating: 4

near San Juan Bautista

Map grid A1

The primary appeal of this RV park is that it is within easy walking distance of San Juan Bautista. The park is set beside a walnut orchard. Golfing and fishing are nearby.

RV sites, facilities: There are 144 sites with full hookups (30 amps) for RVs up to 33 feet. No tents. Picnic tables are provided. Restrooms with flush toilets and showers, barbecue area, coin laundry, and propane gas are available. Leashed pets are permitted; a dog run is available.

Reservations, fees: Reservations are recommended. Sites are $28–31 per night, $7 per person per night for more than two people, $2–4 per pet per night. Monthly rates available. Some credit cards accepted. Open year-round.

Directions: From U.S. 101 near San Juan Bautista, drive three miles east on U.S. 101/Highway 156. Merge onto Highway 156 East toward San Juan Bautista/Hollister and drive three miles to The Alameda. Turn right at The Alameda and drive one block to San Juan–Hollister Road. Turn left and drive 0.25 mile to the campground at 400 San Juan–Hollister Road.

Contact: Mission Farm RV Park, 831/623-4456.

10 CABANA HOLIDAY RV RESORT

Scenic rating: 3

near Salinas

Map grid A1

If Big Sur, Monterey, and Carmel are packed, this spot provides some overflow space. This is primarily an RV park; tent sites are noisy and not secluded, located right by the highway. Salinas is the artichoke capital of the world and about a half-hour drive from the Monterey area.

RV sites, facilities: There are 79 sites with full or partial hookups (30 amps) for RVs up to 40 feet; some sites are pull-through. Limited space for tents is available, and 21 cabins can be rented. Picnic tables are provided. Restrooms with showers, recreation room, swimming pool (heated and open mid-May through mid-October), playground, clubhouse, basketball court, and coin laundry are available. Some facilities are wheelchair-accessible. Leashed pets are permitted and must be attended and leashed at all times.

Reservations, fees: Reservations are recommended. RV sites are $45 per night and tents are $20 per night. Some credit cards accepted. Open year-round.

Directions: From Salinas, drive north on U.S. 101 for seven miles to Highway 156 West. Take the exit for Highway 156 West and drive over the overpass 0.2 mile to the Prunedale Road exit. Take that exit to Prunedale North Road. Turn right and drive a short distance to the campground entrance on the left.

Contact: Cabana Holiday, 831/663-2886 or 800/541-0085 (reservations), fax 831/663-1660, www.reynoldsresorts.com.

11 FREMONT PEAK STATE PARK

Scenic rating: 7

near San Juan Bautista

Map grid A1

Most vacationers in this region are heading to Monterey Bay and the surrounding environs. That's why Fremont Peak State Park is missed by a lot of folks. It is on a ridge (2,900 feet) with great views of Monterey Bay available on the trail going up Fremont Peak (3,169 feet) in the Gavilan Range. An observatory with a 30-inch telescope at the park is open to the public on specified Saturday evenings. There are views of the San Benito Valley, Salinas Valley, and the Santa Lucia Mountains. A picnic is held in the park each April to commemorate Captain John C. Frémont, his expeditions, and his raising of the U.S. flag in defiance of the Mexican government. Note: There is no access from this park to the adjacent Hollister Hills State Vehicular Recreation Area.

RV sites, facilities: There are 25 primitive sites for tents or RVs up to 25 feet (no hookups), and one group site for up to 50 people. Picnic tables and fire rings are provided. Drinking water and vault toilets are available. Some facilities are wheelchair-accessible. Leashed pets are permitted.

Reservations, fees: Reservations are accepted at 800/444-PARK (800/444-7275) or www.reserveamerica.com ($8 reservation fee). Sites are $25 per night, $6 per night for each additional vehicle, $100 per night for group site. Open March through November.

Directions: From Highway 156 in San Juan Bautista, drive to San Juan Canyon Road. Turn south on San Juan Canyon Road (unsigned except for state park directional sign) and drive 11 miles (narrow, twisty, not recommended for vehicles longer than 25 feet) to the park.

Contact: Fremont Peak State Park, 831/623-4255; Monterey State Park District, Gavilan Sector, 831/623-4526, or www.parks.ca.gov; observatory, 831/623-2465 or www.fpoa.net.

12 HOLLISTER HILLS STATE VEHICULAR RECREATION AREA

🏃 🚴 🐕 🚐 ⛺

Scenic rating: 4

near Hollister

Map grid A1

This unique park was designed for off-highway-vehicle enthusiasts. It provides 80 miles of trails for motorcycles and 40 miles of trails for four-wheel-drive vehicles. Some of the trails are accessible directly from the campground. All trails close at sunset. Note that there is no direct access to Fremont Peak State Park, bordering directly to the west. Elevations at the park range 800–2,600 feet. Visitors are advised to always call in advance when planning a trip because the area is sometimes closed for special events. A sidelight is that a 288-acre area is set aside for hiking and mountain biking. In addition, a self-guided natural history walk is routed into Azalea Canyon and along the San Andreas Fault.

RV sites, facilities: There are four campgrounds with a total of 125 sites for tents or RVs of any length (no hookups), and group sites for up to 300 people. Picnic tables and fire rings are provided. Drinking water, restrooms with flush toilets and showers, and a camp store are available. Leashed pets are permitted.

Reservations, fees: Reservations are not accepted. Sites are $10 per night per vehicle. Call for group rates. Day-use parking $5. Open year-round.

Directions: From Highway 156 west of Hollister, drive east to Union Road. Turn right (south) on Union Road and drive three miles

to Cienega Road. Turn right (south) on Cienega Road and drive five miles to the park on the right.

Contact: Hollister Hills State Vehicular Recreation Area, 831/637-3874, District Office, 831/637-8186; Fault Line Power Sports, park store, 831/637-9780, www.parks.ca.gov or www.ohv.parks.ca.gov.

13 MARINA DUNES RV PARK

🐕 🏕 ♿ 🚐 ⛺

Scenic rating: 4

near Monterey Bay

Map grid A1

This is a popular park for RV cruisers who are touring Highway 1 and want a layover spot near Monterey. This place fills the bill, open all year and in Marina, just a short drive from the many side-trip opportunities available in Monterey and Carmel. It is set in the sand dunes, about 300 yards from the ocean. Horseback riding, boat rentals, and golfing are nearby.

RV sites, facilities: There are 65 sites, most with full hookups (30 and 50 amps), for RVs of any length and 10 sites for tents. Picnic tables and barbecue grills are provided. Restrooms with showers, drinking water, coin laundry, cable TV, Wi-Fi, modem access, recreation room, playground, meeting room, picnic area, RV supplies, gift shop, and propane are available. Some facilities are wheelchair-accessible. Leashed pets are permitted.

Reservations, fees: Reservations are recommended. Sites are $50–75 per night, $5 per night for each additional vehicle. Credit cards accepted. Open year-round.

Directions: From Highway 1 in Marina, drive to the Reservation Road exit. Take that exit and drive west a short distance to Dunes Drive. Turn right on Dunes Drive and drive to the end of the road and the park entrance on the right.

Contact: Marina Dunes RV Park, 831/384-6914, fax 831/384-0285, www.marinadunesrv.com.

14 LAGUNA SECA RECREATION AREA

Scenic rating: 5

near Monterey

Map grid A1

This campground is just minutes away from the sights in Monterey and Carmel. It is situated in oak woodlands overlooking the world-famous Laguna Seca Raceway. There are three separate camping areas.

RV sites, facilities: There are 172 sites for tents or RVs up to 40 feet; most sites have partial hookups (30 amps). A large overflow area is also available for RVs and tents. Picnic tables and fire pits are provided. Restrooms with showers, dump station, pond, rifle and pistol range, clubhouse, and group camping and meeting facilities are available. Some facilities are wheelchair-accessible. Leashed pets are permitted.

Reservations, fees: Reservations are accepted at 831/755-4895 or 888/588-2267 ($5 reservation fee). Sites are $22–30 per night, $10 per night for each additional vehicle, $2 per pet per night. Some credit cards accepted. Open year-round.

Directions: From Monterey and Highway 101, drive east on Highway 68 for 6.5 miles to the park entrance on the left.

Contact: Laguna Seca Recreation Area, 831/758-3604 or fax 831/758-6818, www.co.monterey.ca.us/parks.

15 CARMEL BY THE RIVER RV PARK

Scenic rating: 8

on the Carmel River

Map grid A1

Location, location, location. That's what vacationers want. Well, this park is set on the Carmel River, minutes away from Carmel, Cannery Row, the Monterey Bay Aquarium, golf courses, and the beach. Hedges and flowers separate each RV site.

RV sites, facilities: There are 35 sites with full hookups (30 and 50 amps) for RVs up to 45 feet. No tents. Restrooms with showers, cable TV, Wi-Fi, recreational cabana, game room with pool tables, barbecue area, and river access are available. A convenience store and propane gas are nearby. Some facilities are wheelchair-accessible. Leashed pets are permitted.

Reservations, fees: Reservations are accepted for two or more nights. Sites are $60–65 per night, $2–3 per person per night for more than two people, $3 per night for each additional vehicle, $3 per pet per night. Open year-round.

Directions: In Carmel on Highway 1 drive to Carmel Valley Road. Take Carmel Valley Road southeast and drive 4.5 miles to Schulte Road. Turn right and drive to the end of the road (27680 Schulte Road in Carmel).

Contact: Carmel by the River RV Park, 831/624-9329, fax 831/624-8416, www.carmelrv.com.

16 SADDLE MOUNTAIN RV PARK AND CAMPGROUND

Scenic rating: 6

near the Carmel River

Map grid A1

This pretty park is set about 100 yards from the Carmel River amid a grove of oak trees. The park offers hiking trails, and if you want to make a buyer's swing into Carmel, it's only a five-mile drive. Note: The Carmel River is reduced to a trickle most of the year.

RV sites, facilities: There are 25 tent sites and 24 sites with full hookups (30 amps) for RVs up to 40 feet. Picnic tables, cable TV, Wi-Fi, and barbecue grills are provided. Restrooms with flush toilets and showers are available. A seasonal swimming pool, playground, horseshoe pits and a basketball court are available nearby. Some facilities are wheelchair-accessible. Leashed pets are permitted in the RV area only; check for current status of pet policy for campground.

Reservations, fees: Reservations are accepted. Tent sites are $30, $55 for RV sites, $5 per person per night for more than two people, $5 per night for each additional vehicle. Group rates available. Open year-round.

Directions: In Carmel on Highway 1 drive to Carmel Valley Road. Take Carmel Valley Road southeast and drive 4.5 miles to Schulte Road. Turn right and drive to the park at the end of the road.

Contact: Saddle Mountain RV Park and Campground, 831/624-1617, www.saddlemountain-camping.com.

17 PINNACLES CAMPGROUND

Scenic rating: 7

near Pinnacles National Monument
Map grid A2

This is the only camp at the Pinnacles National Monument, where there are more than 30 miles of hiking trails and two sets of talus caves. The jagged pinnacles for which the park was named were formed by the erosion of an ancient volcanic eruption and are popular for rock climbing. Pinnacles National Monument is like a different planet, and condors can sometimes be seen flying in the monument and over the campground. It's a 24,000-acre park with volcanic clusters and strange caves, all great for exploring. This is a popular place for astronomy buffs, and ranger-led dark sky viewings are offered occasionally. Campfire programs are held in the amphitheater most of the year. If you are planning to stay a weekend in the spring, arrive early on Friday evening to be sure you get a campsite. In the summer, beware of temperatures in the 90s and 100s. Also note that caves can be closed to access; always check with rangers.

RV sites, facilities: There are 103 sites for tents, 36 sites with partial hookups (30 amps) for RVs, and 13 group sites. Picnic tables and fire grills are provided. Drinking water, restrooms with showers and flush toilets, dump station, amphitheater, convenience store, and a swimming pool are available. Some facilities are wheelchair-accessible. Although discouraged, leashed pets are permitted, except on trails.

Reservations, fees: Reservations are accepted at 877/444-6777 or www.recreation.gov ($10 reservation fee). RV sites are $36 per night, $23 per night for tent sites. The group site is $75 per night for 1–10 people, $110 for 11–20 people. Some credit cards accepted. Open year-round, weather permitting.

Directions: From Hollister, drive south on Highway 25 for 32 miles to Highway 146 west (signed "Pinnacles"). Take Highway 146 and drive 2.5 miles to the campground.

Contact: Pinnacles Campground, 831/389-4462, www.npa.gov/pinn.

18 BIG SUR CAMPGROUND AND CABINS

Scenic rating: 8

on the Big Sur River
Map grid A2

This camp is in the redwoods near the Big Sur River. Campers can stay in the redwoods, hike on great trails through the forest at nearby state parks, or explore nearby Pfeiffer Beach. Nearby Los Padres National Forest and Ventana Wilderness in the mountains to the east provide access to remote hiking trails with ridge-top vistas. Cruising Highway 1 south to Lucia and back offers endless views of breathtaking coastal scenery.

RV sites, facilities: There are 40 sites with partial hookups (20 and 30 amps) for RVs up to 40 feet, 40 sites with no hookups for tents or RVs, 14 cabins, and four tent cabins. Picnic tables and fire grills are provided. Restrooms with flush toilets and showers, drinking water, dump station, playground, basketball, inner-tube rentals, convenience store, and coin laundry are available. Some facilities are wheelchair-accessible. Leashed pets are permitted at campsites. No pets in cabins.

Reservations, fees: Reservations are recommended. Tent sites are $40–50 per night, RV sites are $50–60 per night, $5 per person per night for more than two people, $10 per night for each additional vehicle with a maximum of two cars, $5 per pet per night. Some credit cards accepted. Open year-round.

Directions: From Carmel, drive 25 miles south on Highway 1 to the campground on the right side of the road (two miles north of the state park).

Contact: Big Sur Campground and Cabins, 831/667-2322, www.bigsurcamp.com.

19 PFEIFFER BIG SUR STATE PARK

Scenic rating: 10

in Big Sur

Map grid A2

This stretch of coast is one of the most beautiful anywhere. This is one of the most popular state parks in California, and it's easy to see why. You can have it all: fantastic coastal vistas along Highway 1, redwood forests and waterfalls in the Julia Pfeiffer Burns State Park (11.5 miles to the south), expansive beaches with elusive sea otters playing on the edge of kelp beds in Andrew Molera State Park (4.5 miles north), great restaurants such as Ventana Inn (a few miles south), and private, patrolled sites. Reservations are a necessity. Some campsites in this park are set along the Big Sur River. The park features 800 acres of alders, conifers, cottonwoods, maples, oaks, redwoods, sycamores, and willows, plus open meadows—just about everything, in other words. Wildlife includes raccoons, skunk, deer, squirrels, occasional bobcats and mountain lions, and many birds, among them water ouzels and belted kingfishers. Wild boar are spotted infrequently. A number of loop trails provide spectacular views of the Pacific Ocean and the Big Sur Gorge. Big Sur Lodge is within the park.

RV sites, facilities: There are 218 sites for tents or RVs up to 32 feet and trailers up to 27 feet, two hike-in/bike-in sites, and two group sites for up to 35 people. Picnic tables and fire grills are provided. Restrooms with flush toilets and showers, Wi-Fi, and drinking water are available. Groceries, a café, and propane gas are nearby. Some facilities are wheelchair-accessible. Leashed pets are permitted in the campground only.

Reservations, fees: Reservations are accepted at 800/444-PARK (800/444-7275) or www.reserveamerica.com ($8 reservation fee). Sites are $35 per night, $10 per night for each additional vehicle, $75 per night for group sites, $3 per person per night for hike-in/bike-in sites. Open year-round.

Directions: From Carmel, drive 26 miles south on Highway 1 to the park on the left (east side of highway).

Contact: Pfeiffer Big Sur State Park, 831/667-2315, fax 831/667-2886; California State Parks, Monterey District, 831/649-2836, www.parks.ca.gov.

20 CHINA CAMP

Scenic rating: 6

on Chews Ridge in Los Padres National Forest

Map grid A2

A lot of folks might find it difficult to believe that a spot that feels so remote can be so close to the manicured Carmel Valley. But here it is, one of two camps on Tassajara Road at an elevation of 4,500 feet. This one has a trail out of camp that is routed into the Ventana Wilderness. Tassajara Hot Springs, a private facility, is seven miles away at the end of Tassajara Road.

Note: The campground was used as a staging area during the 2008 fires. It is scheduled to reopen in summer 2009.

RV sites, facilities: There are six sites for tents or RVs up to 20 feet (no hookups). Picnic tables and fire grills are provided. Vault toilets are available. No drinking water is available. Leashed pets are permitted.

Reservations, fees: No reservations are accepted. There is no camping fee. Open April through November, weather permitting.

Directions: From Highway 1 in Carmel, turn east on Carmel Valley Road and drive about 22 miles. Turn right (south) on Tassajara Road/

CALIFORNIA

County Road 5007 and drive 11 miles to the campground on the right.

From Salinas, drive south on Highway 101 to Soledad. Continue south for approximately one mile to the exit for Arroyo Road. Take that exit and drive west on Arroyo Road (becomes Arroyo Seco Road) for 16.5 miles to Carmel Valley Road. Turn right and drive 17.5 miles to Tassajara Road. Turn left and drive 11 miles to the campground on the right.

Contact: Los Padres National Forest, Monterey Ranger District, 831/385-5434, fax 831/385-0628.

21 RIVERSIDE CAMPGROUND AND CABINS

Scenic rating: 8

on the Big Sur River
Map grid A2

This is one in a series of privately operated camps designed for Highway 1 cruisers touring the Big Sur area. This camp is set amid redwoods. Side trips include expansive beaches with sea otters playing on the edge of kelp beds (Andrew Molera State Park), redwood forests and waterfalls (Julia Pfeiffer Burns State Park), and several quality restaurants, including Nepenthe for those on a budget, and the Ventana Inn for those who can light cigars with $100 bills.

RV sites, facilities: There are 44 sites for tents or RVs up to 34 feet; 14 sites have partial hookups (20 amps). Cabins are also available. Picnic tables and fire pits are provided. Restrooms with coin showers, coin laundry, and firewood are available. A store is on-site. Leashed pets are permitted at campsites and in cabins.

Reservations, fees: Reservations are recommended at reservations@riversidecampground. com. Sites are $30 per night; premier sites are higher, plus $5 per person per night for more than two people, with a maximum of five people, $10 per night for each additional vehicle, with a maximum of two vehicles, $5 per

pet per night at tent and RV sites, $15 per pet per night in cabins. Some credit cards accepted. Open year-round, weather permitting.

Directions: From Carmel, drive 22 miles south on Highway 1 to the campground on the right.

Contact: Riverside Campground and Cabins, tel. 831/667-2414, fax 831/667-2648, www. riversidecampground.com.

22 FERNWOOD PARK

Scenic rating: 7

on the Big Sur River
Map grid A2

This RV park is on the banks of the Big Sur River in the redwoods of the beautiful Big Sur coast. Many of the sites are set along the river. There also are eight tent cabins. A highlight is that there is live music on Saturday nights in season. You can crown your trip with a dinner at the Ventana Inn (first-class—bring your bank with you). The park is adjacent to Pfeiffer Big Sur State Park.

RV sites, facilities: There are 13 sites for tents only, 31 sites with partial hookups (30 amps) for RVs up to 36 feet, 11 tent cabins, and a motel. Fire grills and picnic tables are provided. Restrooms with showers, grocery store, restaurant, and a bar are available. Leashed pets are permitted.

Reservations, fees: Reservations are accepted. Sites are $35 per night, $5 per person per night for more than two people (maximum of six), $5 per night for each additional vehicle, $5 per pet per night. Tent cabins are $60 per night, and $10 per person per night for more than two people. Discounts available in the off-season. Some credit cards accepted. Open year-round.

Directions: From Carmel, drive 26 miles south on Highway 1 to the campground on the right.

Contact: Fernwood Park, 831/667-2422, fax 831/667-2663, www.fernwoodbigsur.com.

CALIFORNIA

23 ARROYO SECO

Scenic rating: 5

along Arroyo Seco River in
Los Padres National Forest

Map grid A2

This pretty spot near the Arroyo Seco River is just outside the northern border of the Ventana Wilderness. The elevation is 900 feet. Arroyo Seco Group Camp is available to keep the pressure off this campground.

Note: The Arroyo Seco area recieved burn damage from the 2008 fires and is under recovery.

RV sites, facilities: There are 49 sites for tents or RVs up to 26 feet, plus a group site for 25–50 people. Picnic tables and fire grills are provided. Drinking water, restrooms with flush toilets and coin showers, and a dump station are available. Leashed pets are permitted.

Reservations, fees: Reservations are accepted for individual sites and required for group sites at 877/444-6777 or www.recreation.gov ($10 reservation fee). Sites are $20 per night, $5 per night for each additional vehicle, primitive sites are $15, group site is $75 per night. Open year-round.

Directions: Drive on U.S. 101 to the town of Greenfield and the Arroyo Seco Road/Elm Avenue exit. Turn west on Elm Avenue/Road G16 and drive six miles to Arroyo Seco Road. Turn left and drive 6.5 miles to Carmel Valley Road. Turn right and drive 3.5 miles to the campground.

Contact: Los Padres National Forest, Monterey Ranger District, 831/385-5434, fax 831/385-0628; Rocky Mountain Recreation Company, 831/674-5726.

24 SAN LORENZO COUNTY PARK

Scenic rating: 3

in King City

Map grid A2

A lot of folks cruising up and down the state on U.S. 101 can underestimate their travel time and find themselves caught out near King City, a small city about midpoint between Northern and Southern California. Well, don't sweat it, because San Lorenzo County Park offers a spot to overnight. It's set near the Salinas River, which isn't exactly the Mississippi, but it'll do. A museum complex captures the rural agricultural life of the valley. The park covers 200 acres, featuring playgrounds and ball fields.

RV sites, facilities: There are 99 sites with full or partial hookups (30 amps) for tents or RVs of any length; some sites are pull-through. Picnic tables and fire pits are provided. A dump station, restrooms with flush toilets and showers, picnic area, coin laundry, meeting facilities, playgrounds, horseshoes, volleyball, softball fields, walking trail, and computer kiosks are available. Leashed pets are permitted.

Reservations, fees: Reservations are accepted at 831/385-5964 ($5 reservation fee). Sites are $23–30 per night, $10 per night for each additional vehicle, $2 per pet per night. Off-season and group rates available. Open year-round.

Directions: From King City on U.S. 101, take the Broadway exit, turn onto Broadway, and drive to the park at 1160 Broadway.

Contact: San Lorenzo County Park, 831/385-5964, www.co.monterey.ca.us/parks.

25 KIRK CREEK

Scenic rating: 8

in Los Padres National Forest
near the Pacific Ocean

Map grid A2

This pretty camp is set along Kirk Creek where it empties into the Pacific Ocean. There is beach access through a footpath. Another trail from camp branches north through the Ventana Wilderness, which is sprinkled with little-used, hike-in, backcountry campsites. For gorgeous scenery without all the work, a quaint little café in Lucia provides open-air dining on a cliff-top deck, with a dramatic sweeping lookout over the coast.

RV sites, facilities: There are 33 sites for tents

CALIFORNIA

or RVs up to 30 feet (no hookups). Picnic tables and fire grills are provided. Drinking water and flush toilets are available. Leashed pets are permitted.

Reservations, fees: Reservations are accepted for 50 percent of the sites at 877/444-6777 or www.recreation.gov ($10 reservation fee). Sites are $22 per night, hike-in/bike-in sites are $5 per night. Open year-round.

Directions: From Monterey, drive south on Highway 1 to Lucia. From Lucia, continue south on Highway 1 for four miles to the campground on the right.

Contact: Parks Management Company, 805/434-1996, fax 805/434-1986, www.campone.com; Los Padres National Forest, Monterey Ranger District, 831/385-5434, fax 831/385-0628.

26 LIMEKILN STATE PARK

Scenic rating: 9

south of Big Sur

Map grid A2

Limekiln State Park provides spectacular views of the Big Sur coast. This camp provides a great layover spot in the Big Sur area of Highway 1, with drive-in campsites set near both the beach and the redwoods—take your pick. Several hiking trails are nearby, including one that is routed past some historic lime kilns, which were used in the late 1800s to make cement and bricks. Want more? A short rock hop on a spur trail (just off the main trail) leads to dramatic 100-foot Limekiln Falls, a gorgeous waterfall. This camp was originally called Limekiln Beach Redwoods and was privately operated. It became a state park in 1995. One remaining problem: Parking is limited. One big plus: From November 1 through March 21, Limekiln is off the reservation grid, with a limited number of sites available on a first-come, first-served basis.

Note: As of this writing, the park was closed due to the 2008 Chalk Fire.

RV sites, facilities: There are 10 sites for tents

and 18 sites for tents or RVs up to 24 feet (no hookups) and trailers up to 15 feet. Picnic tables and fire grills are provided. Drinking water, restrooms with showers and flush toilets, and firewood are available. Leashed pets are allowed, except on trails.

Reservations, fees: Reservations are accepted at 800/444-PARK (800/444-7275) or www.reserveamerica.com ($8 reservation fee). Sites are $35 per night, $12 per night for each additional vehicle. November 1 through March 21 some campsites are available on a first-come, first-served basis. Some credit cards accepted for reservations, but not at the park. Open year-round, weather and road conditions permitting.

Directions: From Big Sur, drive south on Highway 1 for 32 miles (past Lucia) to the park on the left.

Contact: Limekiln State Park, 831/667-2403; California State Parks, Monterey District, 831/649-2836, www.parks.ca.gov.

27 NACIMIENTO

Scenic rating: 4

in Los Padres National Forest

Map grid A2

This little-known spot is set near the Nacimiento River at 1,600 feet elevation. Most campers will head up Nacimiento-Ferguson Road to camp on a Friday night and get up Saturday morning to head off on a hiking or backpacking trip in the nearby Ventana Wilderness.

Note: The 2008 fire burned around the campground, but damage is not noticeable from the campsites.

RV sites, facilities: There are eight sites for tents or RVs up to 25 feet (no hookups). Picnic tables and fire grills are provided. Vault toilets are available. No drinking water is available. Leashed pets are permitted.

Reservations, fees: Reservations are not accepted. Sites are $10 per night. Open year-round.

Directions: From Monterey, drive south on Highway 1 to Lucia. From Lucia, continue south on Highway 1 for four miles to Nacimiento Road.

CALIFORNIA

Turn east (left) on Nacimiento Road and drive 11 winding miles to the campground on the right. **Contact:** Parks Management Company, 805/434-1996, fax 805/434-1986, or at www. campone.com; Los Padres National Forest, Monterey Ranger District, 831/385-5434, fax 831/385-0628.

28 PONDEROSA

Scenic rating: 4

in Los Padres National Forest

Map grid A2

As soon as you turn off Highway 1, you leave behind the crowds and enter a land that is largely unknown to people. This camp is set at 1,500 feet elevation in Los Padres National Forest, not far from the border of the Ventana Wilderness (good hiking and backpacking) and the Hunter Liggett Military Reservation (wild-pig hunting is allowed there with a permit). It is one in a series of small camps on Nacimiento-Ferguson Road.

Note: The fires of 2008 burned in the region here, but not in the campground. The Forest Service closed a few campsites near a creek, where there is potential for flooding, mud slides and erosion from heavy rains.

RV sites, facilities: There are 23 sites for tents or RVs up to 35 feet. Picnic tables and fire grills are provided. Vault toilets and drinking water are available. Leashed pets are permitted.

Reservations, fees: Reservations accepted at 877/444-6777 or www.recreation.gov. Sites are $15 per night. Open year-round.

Directions: From Monterey, drive south on Highway 1 to Lucia. From Lucia, continue south on Highway 1 for four miles to Nacimiento-Ferguson Road. Turn left on Nacimiento-Ferguson Road and drive about 12 miles to the campground on the right.

Contact: Parks Management Company, 805/434-1996, fax 805/434-1986, www. campone.com; Los Padres National Forest, Monterey Ranger District, 831/385-5434, fax 831/385-0628.

CALIFORNIA

SAN JOAQUIN VALLEY

CALIFORNIA

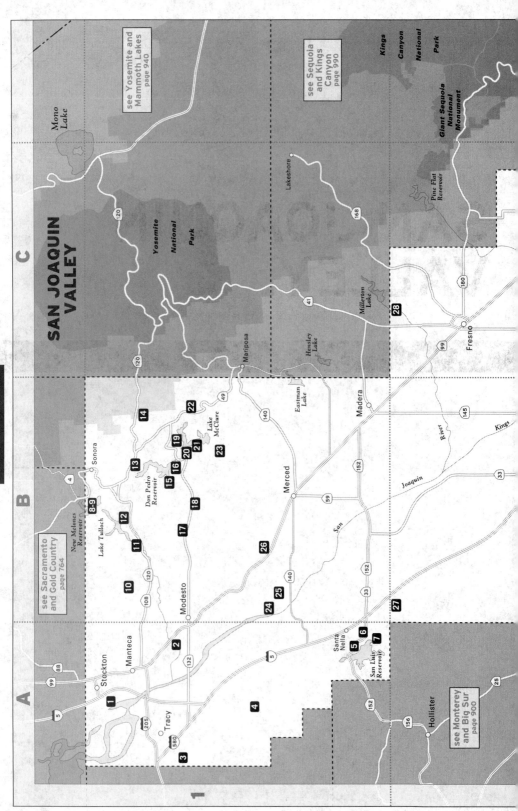

SAN JOAQUIN VALLEY

see Yosemite and Mammoth Lakes
page 940

see Sequoia and Kings Canyon
page 990

see Sacramento and Gold Country
page 764

see Monterey and Big Sur
page 900

Kings   Canyon   National   Park

Giant Sequoia National Monument

Mono Lake

Lakeshore

Pine Flat Reservoir

Yosemite National Park

Millerton Lake

Mariposa

Hensley Lake

Fresno

Eastman Lake

Madera

Lake McClure

Merced

Don Pedro Reservoir

Lake Tulloch

New Melones Reservoir

Sonora

Joaquin

San

Kings

River

Modesto

Manteca

Stockton

Tracy

Santa Nella

San Luis Reservoir

Hollister

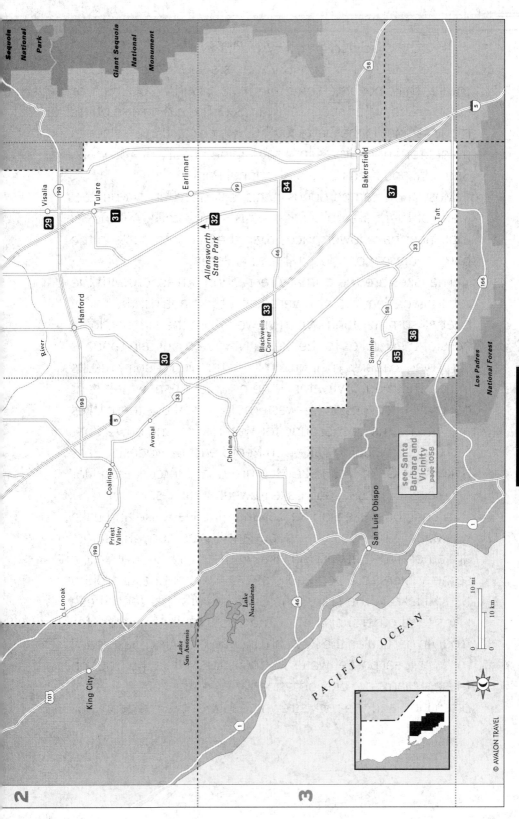

see Santa
Barbara and
Vicinity
page 1058

© AVALON TRAVEL

CALIFORNIA

The San Joaquin Valley is noted for its searing weather all summer long. But that is also when the lakes in the foothills become something like a Garden of Eden for boating and water-sports enthusiasts. The region also offers many settings in the Sierra foothills, which can serve as launch points for short drives into the alpine beauty of Yosemite, Sequoia, and Kings Canyon National Parks.

Most of the campgrounds in this region are family-oriented. Many of them are on access roads to Yosemite. A bonus is that most have lower prices than their counterparts in the park, and are more hospitable to children.

The lakes are the primary recreation attraction, with the refreshing, clean water revered as a tonic against the valley heat all summer long. When viewed from the air, the close-ness of these lakes to the Sierra Nevada mountain range is surprising to many. Their proximity to the high country results in cool, high-quality water – the product of snowmelt sent down river canyons on the western slope. Some of these lakes are among the best around for waterskiing and powerboat recreation, including Lake Don Pedro east of Modesto, Bass Lake near Oakhurst, Lake McClure near Merced, Pine Flat Lake east of Fresno, and Lake Kaweah near Visalia.

In addition, Lake Don Pedro, and Pine Flat Lake and Lake Kaweah in the nearby Sequoia and Kings Canyon region, are among the best fishing lakes in the entire Central Valley; some anglers rate Don Pedro as the number-one all-around fishing lake in the state. The Sierra rivers that feed these lakes (and others) also offer the opportunity to fly-fish for trout. In particular, the Kaweah and Kings Rivers boast many miles of ideal pocket water for fly fishers. While the trout on these streams are only occasionally large, the catch rates are often high and the rock-strewn beauty of the river canyons is exceptional.

1 DOS REIS COUNTY PARK

Scenic rating: 6

on the San Joaquin River near Stockton

Map grid A1

This is a nine-acre county park that has a quarter mile of San Joaquin River frontage, boat ramp, and nearby access to the eastern Delta near Stockton. Note that tent camping is available on weekends and holidays only. The sun gets scalding hot here in the summer, branding everything in sight. That's why boaters make quick work of getting in the water, then cooling off with water sports. In the winter, this area often has zero visibility from tule fog.

RV sites, facilities: There are 26 sites with full hookups (20 and 30 amps) for RVs of any length and tents; some sites are pull-through. Picnic tables and fire grills are provided. Restrooms with showers, children's play area, horseshoe pits, and boat ramp are available. A store, coin laundry, and propane gas are within three miles. Leashed pets are permitted, with a limit of two.

Reservations, fees: Reservations are required at least two weeks in advance. Sites are $20 per night, $5 per night for each additional vehicle, $1 per pet per night. Open year-round.

Directions: From I-5 and Stockton, drive south to the Lathrop exit. Turn west on Lathrop and drive 1.5 blocks to Manthy Road. Turn north (right) and drive 0.5 mile to Dos Reis Road. Turn left and drive to the campground at the end of the road.

Contact: San Joaquin County Parks Department, 209/953-8800 or 209/331-7400, www.co.sanjoaquin.ca.us/parks.

2 CASWELL MEMORIAL STATE PARK

Scenic rating: 7

on the Stanislaus River near Stockton

Map grid A1

Caswell Memorial State Park features shoreline frontage along the Stanislaus River, along with an additional 250 acres of parkland. The Stanislaus provides shoreline fishing for catfish on summer nights. Bass and crappie are also occasionally caught. Other recreation options here include an interpretive nature trail and swimming. Bird-watching is popular; look for red-shouldered and red-tail hawks. During warm months, bring mosquito repellent.

RV sites, facilities: There are 64 sites for tents or RVs up to 24 feet (no hookups), and one group site for up to 50 people. Picnic tables, food lockers, and fire grills are provided. Drinking water, flush toilets, showers, firewood, a swimming beach, and nature trails are available. Weekend interpretive programs and junior ranger programs are offered in the summer. Some facilities are wheelchair-accessible. Leashed pets are permitted.

Reservations, fees: Reservations are accepted for the summer at 800/444-PARK (800/444-7275) or www.reserveamerica.com ($8 reservation fee). Sites are $30 per night, and $8 per night for each additional vehicle; groups with up to 12 vehicles, $165 per night. Open year-round.

Directions: Drive on Highway 99 to Austin Road (1.5 miles south of Manteca). Turn south on Austin Road and drive four miles to the park entrance at the end of the road.

Contact: Caswell Memorial State Park, 209/599-3810, www.parks.ca.gov.

3 CARNEGIE STATE VEHICULAR RECREATION AREA

Scenic rating: 2

near Tracy

Map grid A1

This is a major state-run OHV area, with mainly dirt bikes and all-terrain vehicles. Don't show up without one, or its equivalent. This area is barren, ugly, and extremely noisy on weekends. It can get hot, windy, and dusty as well. But that's just what dirt bikers want, and they have it all to themselves. The main campground fills on most weekends from October through

May. The area covers 1,500 acres with challenging hill-type trail riding and a professionally designed motocross track. There is also a four-wheel-drive obstacle course. Elevations here rise to 1,800 feet, with summer temperatures peaking at 105°F. Winters are mild.

RV sites, facilities: There are 22 sites for tents or RVs of any length (no hookups). Picnic tables, shade ramadas, and fire rings are provided. Drinking water and flush toilets are available, but note that the drinking water (high in iron) might taste terrible, and you are advised to bring bottled water. Nearest supplies are 14 miles away. Some facilities are wheelchair-accessible. Leashed pets are permitted.

Reservations, fees: Reservations are not accepted. Sites are $10 per night. Open year-round, weather permitting.

Directions: From I-580 (south of Tracy), drive to Corral Hollow Road. Take that exit and drive west for six miles to the campground on the left.

Contact: Carnegie State Vehicular Recreation Area, 925/447-9027; Carnegie Sector Office, 925/447-0426, www.parks.ca.gov.

4 FRANK RAINES REGIONAL PARK

Scenic rating: 4

near Modesto

Map grid A1

This park is primarily a riding area for folks with dirt bikes, all-terrain vehicles, and dune buggies who take advantage of the rough-terrain riding course. About 850 acres of this 1,500-acre park are reserved for OHV use. Deer and pig hunting in season are also a possibility. A side-trip option is to visit Minniear Park, directly to the east, which is a day-use wilderness park with hiking trails and a creek. This area is very pretty in the spring when the foothills are still green and many wildflowers are blooming.

RV sites, facilities: There are 34 sites with full hookups (30 amps) for RVs or tents, and 20 sites with no hookups for tents or RVs. Some sites are pull-through. Fire grills and picnic tables are provided. Restrooms with showers, picnic area, baseball diamond, group facilities, nature trails, and a recreation hall are available. Bring your own drinking water or be prepared to boil or treat water before use. Some facilities are wheelchair-accessible. Leashed pets are permitted.

Reservations, fees: Reservations are not accepted. Sites are $14–20 per night, $5 per night for each additional vehicle, $3 per pet per night. Open mid-October through March.

Directions: On I-5, drive to the Patterson exit (south of the junction of I-5 and I-580). Turn west on the Patterson exit and drive onto Diablo Grande Parkway. Continue a short distance under the freeway to Del Puerto Canyon Road. Turn west (right) and drive 16 miles to the park and the campground on the right.

Contact: Stanislaus County Parks and Recreation Department, 866/648-7275 or 209/525-6750, www.co.stanislaus.ca.us/ER/PARKS/.

5 SAN LUIS CREEK

Scenic rating: 5

on San Luis Reservoir

Map grid A1

San Luis Creek Campground is near San Luis Reservoir. It is one in a series of camps operated by the state in the San Luis Reservoir State Recreation Area, adjacent to the reservoir and O'Neill Forebay, home of many of the biggest striped bass in California, including the world record for landlocked stripers.

RV sites, facilities: There are 53 sites with partial hookups (20 and 30 amps) for tents or RVs up to 35 feet, and two group sites for up to 30–60 people. Picnic tables and fire pits are provided. Drinking water, pit toilets, and a dump station are available. A boat ramp is nearby. Leashed pets are permitted.

Reservations, fees: Reservations are accepted at 800/444-PARK (800/444-7275) or www.reserveamerica.com ($8 reservation fee). Sites are $40 per night, $10 per night for each additional vehicle, $100–200 per night for group sites. Boast launch is $6. Open year-round.

Directions: Drive on Highway 152 to San Luis Reservoir (12 miles west of Los Banos) and the signed campground entrance road (15 miles west of Los Banos). Turn north and drive two miles to the campground on the left.

Contact: San Luis Reservoir State Recreation Area, 209/826-1196; Four Rivers Sector, 209/826-1197, fax 209/826-0284, www.parks. ca.gov.

6 MEDEIROS

Scenic rating: 5

on O'Neill Forebay near Santa Nella

Map grid A1

This is a vast, primitive campground set on the stark expanse of foothill country on O'Neill Forebay and near San Luis Reservoir. Some of the biggest striped bass in California history have been caught here at the forebay. It is best known for wind in the spring, hot weather in the summer, and low water levels in the fall. Striped-bass fishing is best in the fall when the wind is down and stripers will corral schools of bait fish near the lake surface. Sailboarding is decent. There's a large, developed, swimming beach on O'Neill Forebay, and boats can be launched four miles west of the campground at San Luis Creek. There used to be another boat ramp at Medeiros, but it's been closed since 9/11 and will not reopen. In addition to security concerns, there were problems with launching in low water conditions. The forebay can get congested on weekends and holidays; the reservoir is less crowded. The campground elevation is 225 feet. (See the Basalt listing for more information about San Luis.)

RV sites, facilities: There are 350 primitive sites for tents or RVs of any length (no hookups). Some shaded ramadas with fire grills and picnic tables are available. Drinking water and chemical toilets are available. A boat ramp is four miles away. Leashed pets are permitted.

Reservations, fees: Reservations are not accepted. Sites are $10 per night, and each additional vehicle is $6 per night. Boat launching is $6 per day. Open year-round.

Directions: Drive on Highway 152 to Highway 33 (about 10 miles west of Los Banos). Turn north (right) on Highway 33 and drive 0.25 mile to the campground entrance on the left.

Contact: San Luis Reservoir State Recreation Area, 209/826-1196; Four Rivers Sector, 209/826-1197, fax 209/826-0284, www.parks. ca.gov.

7 BASALT

Scenic rating: 5

on San Luis Reservoir

Map grid A1

San Luis Reservoir is a huge, man-made lake, covering 13,800 acres with 65 miles of shoreline, developed among stark foothills to provide a storage facility along the California Aqueduct. It fills by late winter and is used primarily by anglers, water-skiers, and sailboarders. When the Sacramento River Delta water pumps take the water, they also take the fish, filling this lake up with both. Striped-bass fishing is best in the fall when the stripers chase schools of bait fish on the lake surface. Spring and early summer can be quite windy, but that makes for good sailboarding. The adjacent O'Neill Forebay is the best recreation bet because of the boat launch and often good fishing. There is a visitors center at the Romero Overlook. The elevation is 575 feet. Summer temperatures can occasionally exceed 100°F, but evenings are usually pleasant. During winter, tule fog is common. Note that in spring and early summer, it can turn windy very quickly. Warning lights mark several spots at the reservoir and forebay.

RV sites, facilities: There are 79 sites for tents or RVs up to 30 feet (no hookups). Picnic tables and fire grills are provided. Drinking water, restrooms with flush toilets and coin showers, dump station, picnic areas, and a boat ramp are available. A store, coin laundry, gas station, restaurant, and propane gas are nearby (about 1.5 miles away). Some facilities are wheelchair-accessible. Leashed pets are permitted.

Reservations, fees: Reservations are accepted at 800/444-PARK (800/444-7275) or www.reserveamerica.com ($8 reservation fee). Sites are $30 per night, and $10 per night for each additional vehicle. Boat launching is $6 per day. Open year-round.

Directions: Drive on Highway 152 to San Luis Reservoir (12 miles west of Los Banos) and the Basalt campground entrance road. Turn south on Basalt Road and drive 2.5 miles to the campground on the left.

Contact: San Luis Reservoir State Recreation Area, 209/826-1196; Four Rivers Sector, 209/826-1197, fax 209/826-0284, www.parks.ca.gov.

8 GLORY HOLE

Scenic rating: 7

at New Melones Reservoir
Map grid B1

Glory Hole encompasses both Big Oak and Ironhorse campgrounds. This is one of two major recreation areas on New Melones Reservoir in the Sierra Nevada foothills, a popular spot with a boat ramp nearby for access to outstanding waterskiing and fishing. (See the *Tuttletown Recreation Area* listing in this chapter for more information.) Campfire programs are often offered at the amphitheater in summer. Camp hosts are usually on-site year-round.

RV sites, facilities: Big Oak has 55 sites for tents or RVs up to 40 feet (no hookups) and Ironhorse has 89 sites for tents or RVs of any length; 20 walk-in sites are for tents only. Picnic tables and fire grills are provided. Drinking water, restrooms with flush toilets and showers, marina, boat ramps, houseboat and boat rentals, swimming beach, amphitheater, and playground are available. Some facilities are wheelchair-accessible. Leashed pets are permitted.

Reservations, fees: Reservations are accepted at 877/444-6777 or www.recreation.gov ($10 reservation fee). Sites are $14–18 per night. Open year-round.

Directions: From Sonora, drive north on Highway 49 for about 15 miles (Glory Hole Market will be on the left side of the road) to Whittle Ranch Road. Turn left and drive five miles to the campground, with sites on both sides of the road.

Contact: U.S. Bureau of Reclamation, New Melones Visitor Center, 209/536-9094, fax 209/536-9652; New Melones Lake Marina, 209/785-3300; Glory Hole Sports, 209/736-4333.

9 TUTTLETOWN RECREATION AREA

Scenic rating: 7

at New Melones Reservoir
Map grid B1

Here is a mammoth camping area set on the giant New Melones Reservoir in the Sierra Nevada foothills, a beautiful sight when the lake is full. The lake is set in the valley foothills between the historic mining towns of Angels Camp and Sonora. New Melones is one of California's top recreation lakes. All water sports are permitted. Waterskiing and houseboating are particularly popular. Tuttletown encompasses three campgrounds (Acorn, Manzanita, and Chamise) and two group camping areas (Oak Knoll and Fiddleneck). New Melones is a huge reservoir that covers 12,500 acres and offers more than 100 miles of shoreline and good fishing. The elevation is 1,085 feet. A boat ramp is near camp. Although the lake's main body is huge, the better fishing is well up the lake's Stanislaus River arm (for trout) and in its coves (for bass and bluegill), where there are submerged trees providing perfect aquatic habitat. Trolling for kokanee salmon also has become popular. The lake level often drops dramatically in the fall.

RV sites, facilities: At Acorn there are 69 sites

for tents or RVs of any length (no hookups), at Chamise there are 36 tent sites, and at Manzanita there are 55 sites for tents or RVs of any length, 13 walk-in tent sites; Oak Knoll group site holds up to 80 people, and Fiddleneck group site up to 48 people. Picnic tables and fire grills are provided. Drinking water, restrooms with flush toilets and showers, dump station, playground, and boat ramp are available. Some facilities are wheelchair-accessible. Leashed pets are permitted.

Reservations, fees: Reservations are accepted at 877/444-6777 or www.recreation.gov. Sites are $14–18 per night, and the group fee is $128–160 per night. Open year-round.

Directions: From Sonora, drive north on Highway 49 to Reynolds Ferry Road. Turn left and drive about two miles to the entrance road to the campgrounds.

Contact: U.S. Bureau of Reclamation, New Melones Visitor Center, 209/536-9094, fax 209/536-9652.

10 WOODWARD RESERVOIR COUNTY PARK

Scenic rating: 7

near Oakdale
Map grid B1

This is one of the best sailing lakes in Northern California. Regattas are held through the year, and it is also very popular for sailboarding. Woodward's nickname, in fact, is "Windward Reservoir." Woodward Reservoir is a large lake covering 2,900 acres with 23 miles of shoreline, set in the rolling foothills just north of Oakdale. It is a good lake for both waterskiing and fishing, with minimal conflict between the two sports. All boating is allowed, and speedboats have the main lake body to let her rip. Trout fishing has improved and they are stocked here in winter. Bass fishing has been slow the past several years. Note that because this is one of the largest reservoirs near Modesto and Stockton, it gets lots of local traffic, especially on summer weekends. There are equestrian

facilities at this park, and horse camping is permitted in undeveloped sites only.

RV sites, facilities: There are 155 sites, 114 with partial hookups and four with full hookups (30 amps), for RVs or tents. Picnic tables and fire grills are provided. Drinking water is available intermittently; check for current status. A dump station, picnic shelter, three boat ramps, dry boat storage, restrooms with flush toilets and showers, and some equestrian facilities are available. Some facilities are wheelchair-accessible. Leashed pets are permitted.

Reservations, fees: Reservations are not accepted. Sites are $15–23 per night per vehicle, $7 per day boat launch fee, $3 per pet per night, $2 per horse per night. Holiday rates are higher. Open year-round.

Directions: Drive on Highway 120 to Oakdale (the road becomes Highway 108/120) and the junction with County Road J14/26 Mile Road. Turn left on 26 Mile Road and drive four miles to the park entrance at Woodward Reservoir (14528 26 Mile Road).

Contact: Woodward Reservoir County Park, 209/847-3304; Stanislaus County Parks, 209/525-6750, www.co.stanislaus.ca.us/ER/PARKS/.

11 SUNSHINE RAFT AND RV RESORT

Scenic rating: 7

at Knights Ferry on the Stanislaus River
Map grid B1

This is a privately run campground in the small historic town of Knights Ferry. The campground has a good number of trees. A nice touch is a restaurant overlooking the Stanislaus River. Side trips include tours of the covered bridge ("the longest west of the Mississippi") and several historic buildings and homes, all within walking distance of the park. River access and hiking trails are available at the east end of town. Two runs are available, the Goodwin Canyon Run, which is exciting, even scary and challenging, and the Knights Ferry

Run, an easy float. Raft and canoe rentals are also available nearby. This resort is popular with rafters and canoeists.

RV sites, facilities: There are 14 sites with partial hookups (30 amps) for tents or RVs up to 40 feet. A community fire pit, restrooms with showers, and a restaurant are available. No pets permitted.

Reservations, fees: Reservations are required with a deposit. Sites are $35 per night for RVs, $30 per night for tents. Some credit cards accepted. Open April through October.

Directions: From Oakdale, drive east on Highway 108 for approximately 12 miles to Knight's Ferry and Kennedy Road. Turn left and drive to a bridge, cross the bridge, and continue a short distance to Sonora Road/Main Street. Turn left and drive to the campground entrance at the River's Edge Restaurant.

Contact: Sunshine Raft and RV Resort, 800/829-7238, www.knightsferrycamping.com.

12 LAKE TULLOCH RV CAMPGROUND AND MARINA

Scenic rating: 7

on the south shore of Lake Tulloch

Map grid B1

This camp features tons of waterfront on Lake Tulloch, a dispersed tent area, and cabins with direct beach access. Unlike so many reservoirs in the foothill country, this one is nearly always full of water. In addition, it is a place where anglers and water-skiers live in harmony. That is because of the many coves and a six-mile-long arm with an enforced 5-mph speed limit. It's a big lake, shaped like a giant X with extended lake arms adding up to 55 miles of shoreline. The campground features mature oak trees that provide shade to most of the developed sites. A secret at Tulloch is that fishing is also good for crawdads. The elevation is 500 feet.

RV sites, facilities: There are 130 sites, including 31 boat sites and 30 with full or partial hookups (30 and 50 amps) for tents or RVs up to 35 feet, a large area for lakefront tent camping and self-contained RVs, and 10 waterfront cabins. Picnic tables and fire grills are provided. Drinking water, restrooms with flush toilets and showers, coin laundry, convenience store, dump station, playground, restaurant, volleyball, horseshoes, tetherball, ping-pong, swimming beach, marina, boat rentals, boat slips, fuel dock, and a boat launch are available. Some facilities are wheelchair-accessible. Leashed pets are permitted.

Reservations, fees: Reservations are accepted. The fee is $20–30 per night, $12 per night for the first vehicle, then $20 per each additional vehicle, and $1 per pet per night. Group rates are available. Boat launch fee is $5 (one time). Credit cards accepted. Open year-round.

Directions: From Manteca, drive east on Highway 120 (it becomes Highway 108/120) to Oakdale. Continue east for 13 miles to Tulloch Road on the left. Turn left and drive 4.6 miles to the campground entrance and gatehouse at the south shore of Lake Tulloch.

Contact: Lake Tulloch RV Campground and Marina, 209/881-0107 or 800/894-2267, www.laketullochcampground.com.

13 MOCCASIN POINT

Scenic rating: 7

at Lake Don Pedro

Map grid B1

This camp is at the northeastern end of Lake Don Pedro, adjacent to a boat ramp. Moccasin Point juts well into the lake, directly across from where the major Tuolumne River arm enters the lake. Don Pedro is a giant lake, with extended lake arms and nearly 13,000 surface acres and 160 miles of shoreline. It is one of the best boating and recreation lakes in California, but subject to drawdowns from midsummer through early fall. At different times, fishing is excellent for salmon, trout, or bass. Other species are redear sunfish, catfish, crappie, and bluegill. Houseboating and boat-in camping (bring sunscreen) provide options. The elevation is 800 feet.

RV sites, facilities: There are 50 sites for tents, 18 sites with full hookups (20 and 30 amps) for RVs of any length, and an overflow camping area. Some sites are pull-through. Picnic tables, food lockers, and barbecue units are provided at all sites. Drinking water, restrooms with showers, dump station, group picnic area, fish-cleaning station, propane gas, ice, small store, boat ramp, motorboat and houseboat rentals, fuel, moorings, and bait and tackle are available. Some facilities are wheelchair-accessible. Ground fires are prohibited. No pets are permitted.

Reservations, fees: Reservations are accepted for a minimum of two nights, or three nights on holidays, and can be made by telephone or website ($7 reservation fee). Sites are $20–30 per night, $6 per night for each additional vehicle. Boat launching is $7 per day. Some credit cards accepted. Open year-round.

Directions: From Manteca, drive east on Highway 120 (it becomes Highway 108/120) for 30 miles to the Highway 120/Yosemite exit. Bear right on Highway 120 and drive 11 miles to Jacksonville Road. Turn left on Jacksonville Road and drive a short distance to the campground on the right.

Contact: Don Pedro Recreation Agency, 209/852-2396; Moccasin Point Marina, 209/989-2206, www.donpedrolake.com.

14 THE PINES

Scenic rating: 4

in Stanislaus National Forest
Map grid B1

The Pines camp is set at 3,200 feet elevation on the western edge of Stanislaus National Forest, only 0.5 mile from the Groveland District Office and about five miles from the Tuolumne River, one of the best white-water rafting stretches in the Central Valley foothills. A Forest Service road is routed south of camp for two miles, climbing to Smith Peak Lookout (3,877

feet) and providing sweeping views to the west of the San Joaquin Valley foothills.

RV sites, facilities: There are 11 sites for tents or RVs up to 22 feet (no hookups), and two group sites for up to 50 people each. Picnic tables and fire grills are provided. Drinking water and vault toilets are available. A convenience store is nearby. Leashed pets are permitted.

Reservations, fees: Reservations are required for the group sites only at 877/444-6777 or www.recreation.gov ($10 reservation fee). Sites are $12 per night, $65 per night for group site. Open late April through October, weather permitting.

Directions: From Groveland, drive east on Highway 120 for nine miles (about a mile past the County Road J132 turnoff) to the signed campground entrance road on the right. Turn right onto the campground entrance road and drive a short distance to the camp.

Contact: Stanislaus National Forest, Groveland Ranger District, 209/962-7825, fax 209/962-7412.

15 BLUE OAKS

Scenic rating: 7

at Lake Don Pedro
Map grid B1

Blue Oaks is between the dam at Lake Don Pedro and Fleming Meadows. The on-site boat ramp to the east is a big plus here. (See the Fleming Meadows and Moccasin Point listings in this chapter for more information.)

RV sites, facilities: There are 195 sites for tents or RVs of any length; some sites have partial hookups (20 and 30 amps) and one is pull-through. Group camping is available. Picnic tables, food lockers, and barbecue units are provided. Drinking water, restrooms with flush toilets and showers, boat launch, fish-cleaning stations, and a dump station are available. Some facilities are wheelchair-accessible. A store, coin laundry, and propane gas are nearby at Fleming Meadows Marina. No ground fires are permitted. No pets are permitted.

CALIFORNIA

Reservations, fees: Reservations are accepted by telephone with a two-night minimum; three-night minimum on holidays ($7 reservation fee). Sites are $20–26 per night, $6 per night for each additional vehicle; group fee is $200 per night. Boat launching is $7 per day. Some credit cards accepted. Open Memorial Day weekend through Labor Day weekend.

Directions: From Manteca, take Highway 120 east to Oakdale (the road becomes Highway 120/108). Continue east on Highway 108 for 20 miles to La Grange Road/J59 (signed "Don Pedro Reservoir"). Turn right on La Grange Road and drive 10 miles to Bonds Flat Road. Turn left on Bonds Flat Road and drive 0.5 mile to the campground on the left.

Contact: Don Pedro Recreation Area, 209/852-2396, www.donpedrolake.com; Lake Don Pedro Marina, 209/852-2369.

16 FLEMING MEADOWS

Scenic rating: 7

on Lake Don Pedro
Map grid B1

Fleming Meadows is set on the shore of Lake Don Pedro, just east of the dam. A boat ramp is available in the campground on the southeast side of the dam. A sandy beach and concession stand are here. This is a big camp at the foot of a giant lake, where hot weather, warm water, waterskiing, and bass fishing make for weekend vacations. Don Pedro has many extended lake arms, providing 160 miles of shoreline and nearly 13,000 surface acres when full. (See the Moccasin Point listing in this chapter for more information.)

RV sites, facilities: There are 172 sites for tents or RVs of any length, including 50 walk-in sites for tents, and 91 sites with full hookups (20 and 30 amps) for RVs. A few sites are pull-through. Picnic tables, food lockers, and barbecues are provided. Drinking water, restrooms with flush toilets and showers, and a dump station are available. A coin laundry, store, ice, snack bar, group picnic areas, restaurant, swimming

lagoon, amphitheater, softball field, volleyball, bait and tackle, motorboat and houseboat rentals, boat ramp, mooring, boat storage, engine repairs, and propane gas are nearby. Some facilities are wheelchair-accessible. Ground fires are prohibited. No pets are permitted.

Reservations, fees: Reservations are accepted with a two-night minimum, and a three-night minimum on holidays ($7 reservation fee). Sites are $20–30 per night, $6 per night for each additional vehicle. Boat launching is $7 per day. Some credit cards accepted. Open year-round.

Directions: From Manteca, take Highway 120 east to Oakdale (the road becomes Highway 120/108). Continue east on Highway 108 for 20 miles to La Grange Road/J59 (signed "Don Pedro Reservoir"). Turn right on La Grange Road and drive 10 miles to Bonds Flat Road. Turn left on Bonds Flat Road and drive 2.5 miles to the campground on the left.

Contact: Don Pedro Recreation Area, 209/852-2396; Lake Don Pedro Marina, 209/852-2369, www.donpedrolake.com.

17 MODESTO RESERVOIR REGIONAL PARK AND BOAT-IN

Scenic rating: 7

on Modesto Reservoir
Map grid B1

Modesto Reservoir is a big lake, at 2,800 acres with 31 miles of shoreline, set in the hot foothill country. That's good because it is a popular place in the summer. Waterskiing is excellent in the main lake body. Sandy swimming beaches are available, and swimming is popular. Anglers head to the southern shore of the lake, which is loaded with submerged trees and coves and is also protected by a 5-mph speed limit. Fishing for bass is good, though the fish are often small. Wildlife viewing is good and waterfowl hunting is available in season. The elevation is 200 feet.

RV sites, facilities: There are 145 sites with full hookups (30 amps) for RVs up to 36 feet and 36 tent sites. Picnic tables and fire grills are provided. Drinking water, restrooms with flush toilets and showers, dump station, two boat ramps, store, snack bar, propane, gas, archery range, and radio-controlled glider field are available. Some facilities are wheelchair-accessible. No gas cans are permitted. No pets are allowed.

Reservations, fees: Reservations are not accepted. Sites are $15–23 per night, $2 surcharge per vehicle on holidays. Boat launching is $7 per day. Open year-round.

Directions: From Modesto, drive east on Highway 132 for 16 miles past Waterford to Reservoir Road. Turn left and drive to the campground at 18143 Reservoir Road.

Contact: Modesto Reservoir Regional Park, 209/525-6750, fax 209/525-6773, www.co.stanislaus.ca.us/ER/PARKS/.

18 TURLOCK LAKE STATE RECREATION AREA

Scenic rating: 6

east of Modesto
Map grid B1

This campground is on the shady south shore of the Tuolumne River, about one mile from Turlock Lake. Turlock Lake warms to 65–74°F in the summer, cooler than many Central Valley reservoirs, since the water entering this lake is released from the bottom of Don Pedro Reservoir. It often seems just right for boating and all water sports on hot summer days. The lake covers 3,500 surface acres and offers 26 miles of shoreline. A boat ramp is available near the camp, making it ideal for boaters/campers. Bass fishing is fair in the summer. In the late winter and spring, the lake is quite cold, fed by snowmelt from the Tuolumne River. Trout fishing is good year-round as a result. The elevation is 250 feet. The park is bordered by ranches, orchards, and mining tailings along the river.

RV sites, facilities: There are 48 sites for tents or RVs up to 27 feet (no hookups), 15 sites for tents, and one hike-in/bike-in site. Picnic tables, fire grills, and food lockers are provided.

Drinking water and restrooms with flush toilets and coin showers are available. A swimming beach and boat ramp are available nearby. The boat facilities are wheelchair-accessible. Leashed pets are permitted.

Reservations, fees: Reservations are accepted at 800/444-PARK (800/444-7275) or www.reserveamerica.com ($8 reservation fee). Sites are $30 per night, $10 per night for each additional vehicle, $5 per person per night for hike-in/bike-in site. Boat launching is $6 per day. Open year-round.

Directions: From Modesto, drive east on Highway 132 for 14 miles to Waterford, then continue eight miles on Highway 132 to Roberts Ferry Road. Turn right (south) and drive one mile to Lake Road. Turn left and drive two miles to the campground on the left.

Contact: Turlock Lake State Recreation Area, 209/874-2056 or 209/874-2008, www.parks.ca.gov.

19 McCLURE: HORSESHOE BEND RECREATION AREA

Scenic rating: 7

on Lake McClure
Map grid B1

Lake McClure is a unique, horseshoe-shaped lake in the foothill country west of Yosemite. It adjoins smaller Lake McSwain, connected by the Merced River. McClure is shaped like a giant H, with its lake arms providing 82 miles of shoreline, warm water for waterskiing, and fishing for bass (on the west half of the H near Cotton Creek) and for trout (on the east half of the H). There is a boat launch adjacent to the campground. It's one of four lakes in the immediate area; the others are Don Pedro Reservoir to the north and Modesto Reservoir and Turlock Lake to the west. The elevation is 900 feet.

RV sites, facilities: There are 110 sites for tents or RVs of any length, including 35 with partial hookups (30 amps). Picnic tables and barbecues are provided. Restrooms with showers, dump station, a boat ramp, fish-cleaning stations, picnic areas, swimming lagoon, store, and coin laundry are available. Some facilities are wheelchair-accessible. Leashed pets are permitted.

Reservations, fees: Reservations are accepted at 800/468-8889 ($6 reservation fee). Sites are $17–26 per night, $6–19 per night for each additional vehicle, $3 per pet per night. Boat launching is $6 per day. Some credit cards accepted. Open year-round.

Directions: From Modesto, drive east on Highway 132 for 31 miles to La Grange and then continue for about 17 miles (toward Coulterville) to the north end of Lake McClure and the campground entrance road on the right side of the road. Turn right and drive 0.5 mile to the campground.

Contact: Horseshoe Bend Recreation Area, 209/878-3452; Merced Irrigation District, 209/378-2521, www.lakemcclure.com.

20 BARRETT COVE RECREATION AREA

Scenic rating: 7

on Lake McClure

Map grid B1

Lake McClure is shaped like a giant H, with its lake arms providing 82 miles of shoreline. The lake is popular for water sports, including skiing, wakeboarding, houseboating, and fishing. Although swimming is not prohibited in the lake, you'll rarely see people swimming or playing along the shore, mainly because of the typically steep drop-offs. This camp is on the left side of the H, that is, on the western shore, within a park that provides a good boat ramp. This is the largest in a series of camps on Lake McClure. (See the Horseshoe Bend Recreation Area, McClure Point Recreation Area, and Bagby Recreation Area listings in this chapter for more information.)

RV sites, facilities: There are 275 sites for tents or RVs of any length, including 89 with full hookups (30 amps). Picnic tables and barbecues are provided. Restrooms with showers, boat ramps, dump station, swimming lagoon, and playground are available. A convenience store, coin laundry, marina, picnic areas, fish-cleaning stations, boat and houseboat rentals, and propane gas are also available on-site. Some facilities are wheelchair-accessible. Leashed pets are permitted.

Reservations, fees: Reservations are accepted at 800/468-8889 ($6 reservation fee). Sites are $17–26, $6 per night for each additional vehicle, $3 per pet per night. Boat launching is $6 per day. Some credit cards accepted. Open year-round.

Directions: From Modesto, drive east on Highway 132 for 31 miles to La Grange and then continue for about eight miles (toward Coulterville) to Merced Falls Road. Turn right and drive three miles to the campground entrance on the left. Turn left and drive a mile to the campground on the left side of the road.

Contact: Barrett Cove Recreation Area, 209/378-2611; Merced Irrigation District, 209/378-2521, fax 209/378-2519, www.lakemcclure.com.

21 McCLURE POINT RECREATION AREA

Scenic rating: 7

on Lake McClure

Map grid B1

McClure Point Recreation Area is the campground of choice for campers/boaters coming from the Turlock and Merced areas. It is a well-developed facility with an excellent boat ramp that provides access to the main body of Lake McClure. This is the best spot on the lake for waterskiing.

RV sites, facilities: There are 100 sites for tents or RVs up to 40 feet; 52 sites have partial hookups (30 amps). Picnic tables and barbecues are provided. Restrooms with showers, boat ramps, boat rentals, marina, fish-cleaning stations, picnic areas, swimming lagoon, and a coin laundry are available. A store is nearby. Leashed pets are permitted.

Reservations, fees: Reservations are accepted at 800/468-8889 ($6 reservation fee). Sites are $17–26 per night, $3 per pet per night. Boat launching is $6 per day. Open year-round.

Directions: From Turlock, drive east on County Road J16 for 19 miles to the junction with Highway 59. Continue east on Highway 59/County Road J16 for 4.5 miles to Snelling and bear right at Lake McClure Road. Drive approximately two miles to Lake McSwain Dam and continue for seven miles to the campground at the end of the road.

Contact: McClure Point and Bagby Recreation Area, 209/378-2521, fax 209/378-2519, www.lakemcclure.com.

22 BAGBY RECREATION AREA

Scenic rating: 7

on upper Lake McClure

Map grid B1

This is the most distant and secluded camp on Lake McClure. It is set near the Merced River as it enters the lake, way up adjacent to the Highway 49 bridge, nearly an hour's drive from the dam. Trout fishing is good in the area, and it makes sense; when the lake heats up in summer, the trout naturally congregate near the cool incoming flows of the Merced River.

RV sites, facilities: There are 30 sites for tents or RVs of any length, including 10 with partial hookups (30 amps). Drinking water, restrooms with flush toilets and coin showers, picnic areas, fish-cleaning stations, and a boat ramp are available. Leashed pets are permitted.

Reservations, fees: Reservations are accepted at 800/468-8889 ($6 reservation fee). Sites are $17–26, $6 per night for each additional vehicle, $3 per pet per night. Boat launching is $6 per day. Open year-round.

Directions: From Turlock, drive east on County Road J16 for 19 miles to the junction with Highway 59. Continue east on Highway 59/County Road J16 for 4.5 miles to Snelling and Merced Falls Road (continue straight, well signed). Drive 0.5 mile to Hornitos Road.

Turn right and drive eight miles (drive over the bridge) to Hornitos to a Y. Bear left at the Y in Hornitos (signed to Highway 49) and drive 10 miles to Highway 49. Turn left on Highway 49 and drive eight miles to the Bagby Bridge and entrance kiosk on the right.

Contact: McClure Point and Bagby Recreation Area, 209/378-2521, fax 209/378-2519, www.lakemcclure.com.

23 McSWAIN RECREATION AREA

Scenic rating: 7

near McSwain Dam on the Merced River

Map grid B1

Lake McSwain is actually the afterbay for adjacent Lake McClure, and this camp is near the McSwain Dam on the Merced River. Even though McClure and McSwain sit beside each other, each has its own identity. McSwain is low-key with a 10-mph speed limit. If you have a canoe or car-top boat, this lake is preferable to Lake McClure because waterskiing is not allowed. In terms of size, McSwain is like a puddle compared to the giant McClure, but unlike McClure, the water levels are kept up almost year-round at McSwain. The water is cold here and trout stocks are good in the spring. The lake is used primarily by anglers, and several fishing derbies are held here each year. The shoreline is favorable for swimming, and there is even a good sandy beach.

RV sites, facilities: There are 99 sites for tents or RVs up to 40 feet, including 65 with partial hookups (30 amps). The best access sites for large RVs are the pull-through sites in the G Loop. Picnic tables, barbecues, and electrical connections are provided. Drinking water, dump station, restrooms with showers, boat ramp, boat rentals, coin laundry, and a playground are available. A convenience store, marina, snack bar, fish-cleaning stations, picnic area, and propane gas are available nearby. Leashed pets are permitted.

Reservations, fees: Reservations are accepted at 800/468-8889 ($6 reservation fee). Sites are

CALIFORNIA

$20–26 per night, $3 per pet per night. Boat launching is $6 per day. Open year-round.

Directions: From Turlock, drive east on County Road J16 for 19 miles to the junction with Highway 59. Continue east on Highway 59/County Road J16 for 4.5 miles to Snelling. Continue straight ahead to Lake McClure Road and drive seven miles to the campground turn-off on the right.

Contact: Lake McSwain Recreation Area, 209/378-2521, fax 209/378-2519; Lake Mc-Swain Marina, 209/378-2534, www.lakemc-clure.com.

24 FISHERMAN'S BEND RIVER CAMPGROUND

Scenic rating: 5

on the San Joaquin River

Map grid B1

This small, privately operated campground is set along the San Joaquin River on the southern outskirts of the San Joaquin Delta country. The park offers shaded sites and direct river access for boaters. This section of river provides fishing for catfish on hot summer nights. Although many of the sites are rented seasonally or longer, about 10 sites are usually available for overnight campers.

RV sites, facilities: There are 38 pull-through sites with full hookups (30 amps) for RVs of any length, and 20 sites for tents only. Picnic tables are provided. Drinking water, restrooms with showers, dump station, coin laundry, boat ramp, fish-cleaning station, seasonal swimming pool, playground, and modem access are available. Some facilities are wheelchair-accessible. Leashed pets are permitted, with certain restrictions.

Reservations, fees: Reservations are accepted at 800/862-3731. Sites are $17–30 per night, $3 per person per night for more than three people. Monthly rates available. Some credit cards accepted. Open year-round.

Directions: Drive on I-5 to the exit for New-man/Stuhr Road (south of the junction of I-5

and I-580). Take that exit and turn east on County Road J18/Stuhr Road and drive 6.5 miles to Hills Ferry Road. Turn left and drive a mile to River Road. Turn left on River Road and drive to 26836 River Road on the right.

Contact: Fisherman's Bend River Campground, 209/862-3731.

25 GEORGE J. HATFIELD STATE RECREATION AREA WALK-IN

Scenic rating: 5

near Newman

Map grid B1

This is a small state park set in the heart of the San Joaquin Valley, near the confluence of the Merced River and the San Joaquin River, well known for hot summer days and foggy winter nights. The park has many trees. Swimming is popular in the summer. Fishing is good for catfish in the summer, and some folks will stay up late hoping a big channel catfish will take their bait. During the peak migration from late fall through winter and early spring, there can also be a good number of striped bass in the area. This park is more popular for day use than for camping. The campsites require a walk of about 100 feet. This campground may close during the winter; check current status before planning an off-season trip.

RV sites, facilities: There are 15 walk-in sites for tents, and a large group site for tents or RVs of any length. The group site has an electrical hookup (20 amps) and can accommodate up to 40 people. Picnic tables and fire grills are provided. Drinking water and flush toilets are available. Supplies can be obtained in Newman, five miles away. Leashed pets are permitted.

Reservations, fees: Reservations are accepted only for groups at 800/444-PARK (800/444-7275) or www.reserveamerica.com ($8 reservation fee). Sites are $10–14 per night, $8 per night for each additional vehicle, $100 per night for group site. Open year-round, weather permitting.

Directions: Drive on I-5 to the exit for Newman/

CALIFORNIA

Stuhr Road (south of the junction of I-5 and I-580). Take that exit and turn east on County Road J18/Stuhr Road and drive to Newman and the junction with Highway 33. Continue straight on Stuhr Road for 1.5 miles to Hills Ferry Road. Turn left and drive three miles to the park entrance on the right (just past the bridge over the San Joaquin River).

Contact: George J. Hatfield State Recreation Area, 209/632-1852; Four Rivers Sector, 209/826-1197, fax 209/826-0284, www.parks.ca.gov.

26 McCONNELL STATE RECREATION AREA

Scenic rating: 6

on the Merced River

Map grid B1

The weather gets scorching hot around these parts in the summer, and a lot of out-of-towners would pay a bunch for a little shade and a river to sit next to. That's what this park provides, with the Merced River flowing past, along with occasional mermaids on the beach. The park covers 70 acres and has many trees. Fishing is popular for catfish, black bass, and panfish. In high-water years the Merced River attracts salmon (in the fall); check current fishing regulations.

RV sites, facilities: There are 20 sites for tents or RVs up to 30 feet (no hookups), and two group sites for tents only for 25–50 people. Group sites have an electrical hookup (20 amps). Picnic tables, fire grills, and food lockers are provided. Drinking water, restrooms with flush toilets and coin showers, and a swimming beach are available. Firewood is available for purchase. Supplies can be obtained in Delhi, five miles away. Some sites are wheelchair-accessible. Leashed pets are permitted.

Reservations, fees: Reservations are accepted at 800/444-PARK (800/444-7275) or www.reserveamerica.com ($8 reservation fee). Sites are $25 per night, $8 per night for each additional vehicle, $90–145 per night for group sites. Open year-round.

Directions: From Modesto, drive south on Highway 99 to Delhi. Continue south for five miles to the South Avenue exit. Take that exit and turn east on South Avenue and drive 2.7 miles to Pepper Street. Turn right and drive one mile to McConnell Road. Turn right and drive a short distance to the park entrance at the end of the road.

Contact: McConnell State Recreation Area, 209/394-7755; Four Rivers Sector, 209/826-1197, fax 209/826-0284, www.parks.ca.gov.

27 LOS BANOS CREEK RESERVOIR

Scenic rating: 6

near Los Banos

Map grid B2

Los Banos Creek Reservoir is set in a long, narrow valley, covering 410 surface acres with 12 miles of shoreline. It provides a smaller, more low-key setting (a 5-mph speed limit is enforced) compared to the nearby giant, San Luis Reservoir. In spring, it can be quite windy and is a popular spot for sailboarding and sailing. It is also stocked with trout in late winter and spring, and some large bass have been caught here. The elevation is 330 feet. Although drinking water is available, campers are advised to bring their own water, as the water supply is limited.

RV sites, facilities: There are 15 sites for tents or RVs up to 30 feet (no hookups). Picnic tables, drinking water, and fire grills are provided. Chemical toilets and picnic areas are available. A boat ramp is nearby. Leashed pets are permitted.

Reservations, fees: Reservations are not accepted. The fee is $10 per night, and $6 per night for each additional vehicle. Boat launching is $6 per day. Open year-round, weather permitting.

Directions: Drive on Highway 152 to Volta Road (five miles west of Los Banos). Turn south on Volta Road and drive about a mile to Pioneer Road. Turn left on Pioneer Road and drive a mile to Canyon Road. Turn south (right) onto Canyon Road and drive about five miles to the park.

Contact: San Luis Reservoir State Recreation Area, 209/826-1196; Four Rivers Sector, 209/826-1197, fax 209/826-0284, www.parks. ca.gov.

28 LOST LAKE

Scenic rating: 7

on lower San Joaquin River
Map grid C2

Lost Lake campground is part of a Fresno County park. It is set in the foothills of the San Joaquin Valley, at an elevation of about 500 feet, along the lower San Joaquin River. The campground is broken out into two areas, with about half along the river. Many think this park is quite pretty. There is a lot of wildlife at this park, especially birds and deer. A self-guided hiking trail is routed into a nature study area. Easy canoeing is a plus, with no powerboats permitted. Trout fishing is available; check fishing regulations.

RV sites, facilities: There are 42 sites for tents, with most accessible for self-contained RVs up to 36 feet, and one group site for up to 80 people. Picnic tables and barbecues are provided. Drinking water, flush toilets, dump station, volleyball, softball, and playground are available. A restaurant and store are two miles away in Friant. Some facilities are wheelchair accessible. Leashed pets are permitted.

Reservations, fees: Reservations accepted for the group site only. Sites are $11 per night, $5 per night for each additional vehicle, and $80 per night for the group site. Open year-round.

Directions: From Fresno, drive north on Highway 41 for 24 miles to the first exit for Friant Road. Take that exit and drive 12 miles to the entrance road for Lost Lake. Turn left and drive a short distance to the campground.

Contact: Fresno County Parks Department, 559/488-3004, fax 559/262-4286.

29 VISALIA/FRESNO SOUTH KOA

Scenic rating: 3

west of Visalia
Map grid C2

This is a layover spot for Highway 99 cruisers. If you're looking for a spot to park your rig for the night, you can't get too picky around these parts. Most campers here are on their way to or from Sequoia and Kings Canyon National Parks. The swimming pool is a great bonus during the summer. Grassy shaded sites are available. Golf and tennis are nearby. Note that a few of the sites are occupied by monthly renters.

RV sites, facilities: There are 48 pull-through sites with full or partial hookups (30 and 50 amps), 20 sites for tents or RVs with no hookups, 20 sites for tents only, and eight cabins. Restrooms with showers, seasonal heated swimming pool, laundry facilities, playground, recreation room, free Wi-Fi, dog walk, store, gift shop, dump station, and propane gas are available. Leashed pets are permitted, with certain restrictions.

Reservations, fees: Reservations are accepted at 800/562-0544. Sites are $28–48 per night, $5 per person per night for more than two people. Some credit cards accepted. Open year-round.

Directions: From Highway 99 near Visalia, take the Goshen Avenue exit and drive 0.2 mile to Betty Drive/County Road 332. Turn left and drive 0.5 mile to County Road 76. Turn left and drive 0.5 mile (becomes Avenue 308) to the campground.

Contact: Visalia-Fresno KOA, 559/651-0544, www.koa.com.

30 TRAVELER'S RV PARK

Scenic rating: 2

near Kettleman City
Map grid C2

Being stuck in Kings County looking for a place to park an RV is no picnic. Unless, that is, you are lucky enough to know about Traveler's RV

Park. The spaces are wide open with long-distance views of the Sierra. It's the "only game in town." Visitors will find access to miles of open paths and roads for hiking or running. The restaurant is open 24 hours a day, and campers get a 10 percent discount. Some may remember this park as Kettleman City RV Park.

RV sites, facilities: There are 46 pull-through sites with full hookups (30 and 50 amps) for RVs up to 36 feet, and two tent sites. Picnic tables are provided. Restrooms with showers, coin laundry, playgrounds, swimming pool, dump station, dog run, tire and RV repair, and propane gas are available. A restaurant and snack bar are nearby. Some facilities are wheelchair-accessible. Leashed pets are permitted.

Reservations, fees: Reservations are accepted. Sites are $27–29 per night, $5 per night for each additional vehicle. Weekly and monthly rates available. Some credit cards accepted. Open year-round.

Directions: Drive on I-5 to the junction with Highway 41 (Kettleman Junction). Take Highway 41 north and drive 0.5 mile to Hubert Way. Turn left on Hubert Way and drive a short distance to Cyril Place. Turn right on Cyril Place and continue to the park entrance (30000 Cyril Place).

Contact: Traveler's RV Park, 559/386-0583.

31 SUN AND FUN RV PARK

Scenic rating: 2

near Tulare
Map grid C2

This RV park is just off Highway 99, exactly halfway between San Francisco and Los Angeles. Are you having fun yet? Anybody making the long drive up or down the state on Highway 99 will learn what a dry piece of life the San Joaquin Valley can seem in summer. That's why the swimming pool at this RV park can be a lifesaver. The park has a number of mature trees, providing an opportunity for shade. Note that most of the sites are filled with long-term

renters, but a few spaces are reserved for overnight campers.

RV sites, facilities: There are 53 sites with full hookups (30 and 50 amps) for RVs up to 45 feet. No tents. Picnic tables and barbecues are provided at some sites. Restrooms with showers, drinking water, cable TV, modem access, dump station, playground, swimming pool, spa, coin laundry, dog runs, and a recreation room are available. A golf course, restaurant, and store are nearby. Some facilities are wheelchair-accessible. Leashed pets are permitted.

Reservations, fees: Reservations are accepted. Sites are $26 per night. Monthly rates available. Open year-round.

Directions: From Tulare, drive south on Highway 99 for three miles to the Avenue 200 exit. Take Avenue 200 west and drive a short distance to the park (1000 Avenue 200).

Contact: Sun and Fun RV Park, 559/686-5779.

32 COLONEL ALLENSWORTH STATE HISTORIC PARK

Scenic rating: 2

near Earlimart
Map grid C3

What you have here is the old town of Allensworth, which has been restored as a historical park dedicated to the African American pioneers who founded it with Colonel Allen Allensworth. He was the highest-ranking army chaplain of his time. Allensworth is the sole town in California to be established, financed, and governed by African Americans. One museum is available at the school here and another is at the colonel's house with a 30-minute movie on the history of Allensworth. Tours are available by appointment. One frustrating element is that railroad tracks run alongside the park and it can be disruptive. There can be other problems—very hot weather in the summer, and since it is an open area, the wind can blow dust and sand. Are we having fun yet? One nice touch is the addition of shade ramadas at some

CALIFORNIA

campsites. A history note: This small farming community was founded in 1908, but a drop in the water table led to its demise.

RV sites, facilities: There are 15 sites for tents or RVs up to 35 feet (no hookups). Picnic tables and fire grills are provided. Restrooms with flush toilets and coin showers, drinking water, dump station, a visitors center, and picnic area are available. A store and coin laundry are 12 miles away in Delano. Some facilities are wheelchair-accessible. Leashed pets are permitted.

Reservations, fees: Reservations are accepted at 800/444-PARK (800/444-7275) or www. reserveamerica.com ($8 reservation fee). Sites are $10 per night for one vehicle; additional vehicles park in day-use area for $6. Open year-round.

Directions: From Fresno, drive south on Highway 99 about 60 miles to Earlimart and the Avenue 56 exit. Turn right (west) on Avenue 56 and drive seven miles to the Highway 43 turnoff. Turn left (south) on Highway 43 and drive two miles to Palmer Avenue. Turn right (and drive over the railroad tracks) to the park entrance.

Contact: Colonel Allensworth State Historic Park, 661/849-3433 or 661/849-2101, www. parks.ca.gov.

33 LOST HILLS RV PARK

Scenic rating: 2

near Kern National Wildlife Refuge
Map grid C3

The pickings can get slim around these parts when you're cruising on I-5, so if it's late, you'll likely be happy to find this camp (formerly known as Lost Hills KOA). The cabin that sleeps four is a nice plus. The nearby Kern National Wildlife Refuge, about a 15-minute drive away, offers a side-trip possibility. It's a waterfowl reserve that attracts ducks, geese, and other waterfowl in the fall and winter. An 18-hole golf course is also within 15 miles.

RV sites, facilities: There are 79 sites, all pull-through, with full hookups (30 and 50 amps)

for RVs, nine sites for tents only, an overflow area with 20 sites for tents and self-contained RVs. Picnic tables are provided. Restrooms with showers, drinking water, swimming pool, coin laundry, store, modem access, and propane gas are available. Restaurants are nearby. Some facilities are wheelchair-accessible. Leashed pets are permitted, with certain restrictions.

Reservations, fees: Reservations are accepted at 661/797-2719. Sites are $33–36 per night, and $3 per person per night for more than two people. Some credit cards accepted. Open year-round.

Directions: Drive on I-5 to the junction with Highway 46 (41 miles south of Avenal near Lost Hills). Turn west on Highway 46 and drive a short distance to the park entrance on the south side of the road (behind the Carl's Jr.).

Contact: Lost Hills RV Park, 661/797-2719.

34 BAKERSFIELD KOA

Scenic rating: 2

north of Bakersfield
Map grid C3

If you're stuck in the southern valley and the temperature makes you feel as if you're sitting in a cauldron, well, this spot provides a layover for the night near the town of Shafter. The closest golf course is eight miles away.

RV sites, facilities: There are 20 tent sites, 35 RV sites with full or partial hookups (30 and 50 amps), and two cabins. Picnic tables are provided. Restrooms with showers, drinking water, seasonal swimming pool, coin laundry, convenience store, dump station, and propane gas are available. Some facilities are wheelchair-accessible. Leashed pets are permitted.

Reservations, fees: Reservations are accepted at 800/562-1633. Sites are $30–35 per night, $2 per person per night for more than two people. Some credit cards accepted. Open year-round.

Directions: From Bakersfield, drive north on Highway 99 for 12 miles to the Shafter-Lerdo Highway exit. Take that exit and drive a mile west on Lerdo Highway to the park (5101 East Lerdo Highway in Shafter).

Contact: Bakersfield KOA, 661/399-3107, fax 661/399-8981, www.koa.com.

35 SELBY

🚶 🐕 5% 🚐 ⛺

Scenic rating: 6

at the Carrizo Plain National Monument, northeast of San Luis Obispo

Map grid C3

The Carrizo Plain is California's largest nature preserve, but because of its remote location, primitive setting, and lack of recreational lakes and streams, it remains largely unknown and is explored by few people. The feature attraction is to visit Soda Lake in the winter to see flocks of the endangered sandhill crane; the lake is a nesting area for these huge birds with seven-foot wingspans. Selby is a primitive camping area at the base of the Caliente Mountain Range, known for its scorching hot temperatures (hey, after all, "Caliente") during the summer. The top hiking destination in the region is Painted Rock, a 55-foot rock with Chumash pictographs. Other hiking trails are available.

RV sites, facilities: This is a primitive camping area with six designated sites for tents or RVs up to 25 feet (no hookups). Picnic tables, shade ramadas, and fire rings are provided. A chemical toilet is available. No drinking water is available. Garbage must be packed out. Nearest services are about 50 miles away. Leashed pets are permitted.

Reservations, fees: Reservations are not accepted. There is no fee for camping, but donations are encouraged. Group camping must be authorized by calling 661/391-6048. Open year-round.

Directions: From Bakersfield, drive west on Highway 58 for about 30 miles to McKittrick (where Highway 33 merges with Highway 58). Bear left on Highway 58/33, continuing through town, and drive west for approximately 10 miles to Seven-Mile Road. Turn west on Seven-Mile Road, and drive seven miles (six

miles will be on gravel/dirt road) to Soda Lake Road. Turn left on Soda Lake Road and drive about six miles to the Selby camping area on your right.

Contact: Bureau of Land Management, Bakersfield Field Office, 661/391-6000, fax 661/391-6041.

36 KCL

🚶 🐕 5% 🚐 ⛺

Scenic rating: 6

at the Carrizo Plain National Monument, northeast of San Luis Obispo

Map grid C3

KCL is the name of the old ranch headquarters in the Carrizo, of which remain old broken-down outbuildings, a corral, and not much else. Note that the buildings are off-limits to visitors. At least there are some trees here (in comparison, there are none at nearby Selby camp). The Carrizo Plain is best known for providing a habitat for many rare species of plants, animals, and insects, in addition to furnishing the winter nesting sites at Soda Lake for the awesome migration of giant sandhill cranes. These birds are often spotted north of this area. This campground is popular with hunters and birders because of its easy access to Soda Lake Road for daily outings. Dispersed camping is allowed throughout the national monument.

RV sites, facilities: This is a primitive camping area with eight sites for tents or RVs up to 25 feet (no hookups). Picnic tables and fire pits are provided. A pit toilet and corrals are available. No drinking water is available. Garbage must be packed out. The nearest services are about 50 miles away. Leashed pets are permitted.

Reservations, fees: Reservations are not accepted. There is no camping fee. Group camping must be authorized by calling 661/391-6048. Open year-round.

Directions: From Bakersfield, drive west on Highway 58 for about 30 miles to McKittrick (where Highway 33 merges with Highway 58). Bear left on Highway 58/33, continuing through town, and drive west for about 10 miles to Seven-Mile Road. Turn west on Seven-Mile Road, and drive seven miles (six miles will be on gravel/dirt road) to Soda Lake Road. Turn left on Soda Lake Road and drive 0.5 mile to the entrance of the Carrizo Plains National Monument. Continue about 15 miles to the KCL camping area on your right.

Contact: Bureau of Land Management, Bakersfield Field Office, 661/391-6000, fax 661/391-6041.

37 BUENA VISTA AQUATIC RECREATION AREA

Scenic rating: 6

near Bakersfield

Map grid C3

This is the showpiece of Kern County recreation. Buena Vista is actually two connected lakes fed by the West Side Canal: little Lake Evans to the west and larger Lake Webb to the east. Be certain to know the difference between the two: Lake Webb (875 acres) is open to all boating including personal watercraft, and fast boats towing skiers are a common sight in designated ski areas. The speed limit is 45 mph. Lake Evans (85 acres) is small, quiet, and has a strictly enforced 5-mph speed limit, an ideal lake for family water play and fishing. Swimming is prohibited at both lakes, but is allowed in the lagoons. Lake Webb is a catfish lake, while Lake Evans is stocked in season with trout, and also has bass, bluegill, catfish, and crappie. The elevation is 330 feet.

RV sites, facilities: There are 112 sites, some with full hookups (30 and 50 amps) for RVs or tents, and an overflow camping area. Picnic tables and fire grills are provided. Restrooms with flush toilets and showers, drinking water, playground, four boat ramps, store, dump station, and picnic shelters are available. Two swimming lagoons, marina, snack bar, fishing supplies, and groceries are available nearby. A PGA-rated golf course is two miles west. Some facilities are wheelchair-accessible. Leashed pets are permitted.

Reservations, fees: Reservations are accepted Monday through Friday at 661/868-7050 ($7 reservation fee). Sites are $26–39 per night, $7–15 per night for each additional vehicle, $4 per night per pet, $7 per night for boats. Some credit cards accepted. Open year-round.

Directions: From I-5 just south of Bakersfield, take Highway 119 west and drive two miles to Highway 43. Turn south (left) on Highway 43 and drive two miles to the campground at road's end.

Contact: Buena Vista Aquatic Recreation Area, Kern County Parks, 661/868-7000, www.co.kern.ca.us/parks/index.htm; Buena Vista concession, 661/763-1526.

CALIFORNIA

YOSEMITE AND MAMMOTH LAKES

☾ BEST RV PARKS AND CAMPGROUNDS

☾ Prettiest Lakes
Tuolumne Meadows, page 946.

☾ Wildlife-Viewing
White Wolf, page 946.
Tuolumne Meadows, page 946.

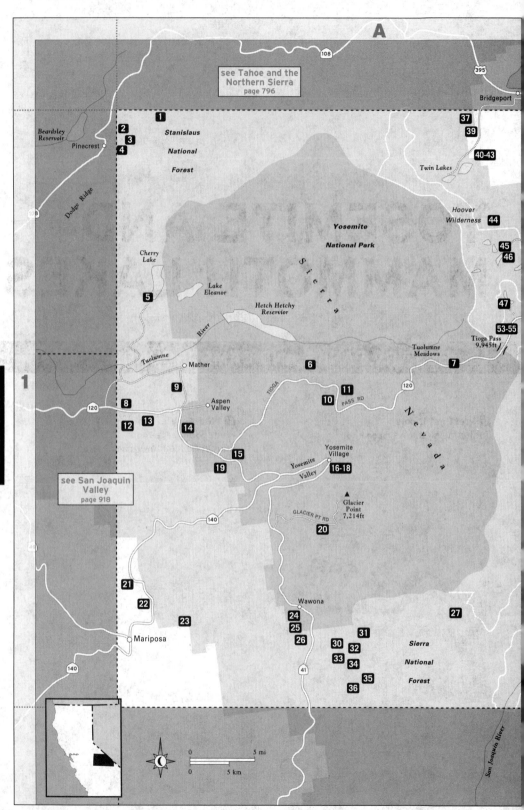

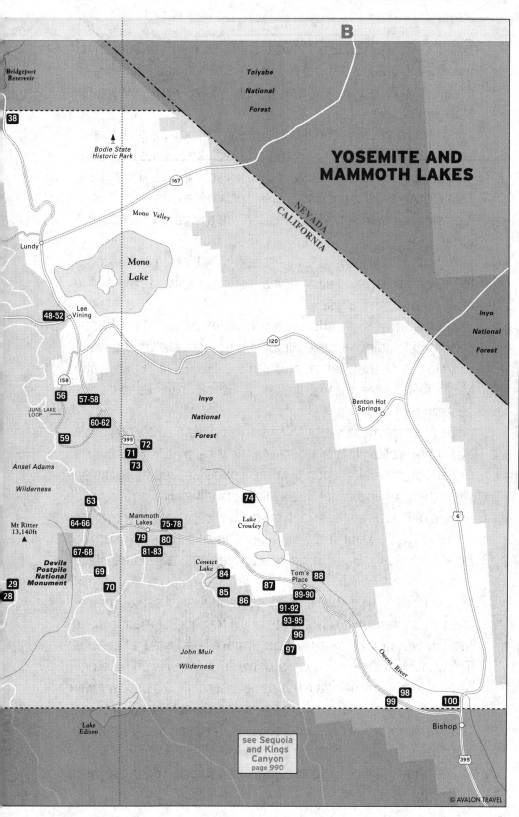

Some of nature's most perfect artwork and

the most profound natural phenomena imaginable have been created in Yosemite and the adjoining eastern Sierra near Mammoth Lakes.

Yosemite Valley is the world's greatest showpiece. It is also among the most highly visited and well-known destinations on earth. Many of the campgrounds listed in this section are within close driving proximity of Yosemite National Park. When it comes to cabin rentals in this region, the variety is extraordinary.

Anything in Yosemite, or in its sphere of influence, is going to be in high demand almost year-round, and the same is true near Mammoth Lakes.

Many family recreation opportunities exist at lake-based settings, including at Lake Alpine, Pinecrest Lake on the western slopes of the Sierra, and June Lake, Silver Lake, Lake Mary, Twin Lakes, Convict Lake, and Rock Creek Lake on the eastern Sierra.

Of course, most visits to this region start with a tour of Yosemite Valley. It is framed on one side by El Capitan, the Goliath of Yosemite, and the three-spired Cathedral Rocks on the other. As you enter the valley, Bridalveil Fall comes into view, a perfect free fall over the south canyon rim, then across a meadow. To your left you'll see the two-tiered Yosemite Falls, and finally, Half Dome, the single most awesome piece of rock in the world.

The irony is that this is all most people ever see of the region, even though it represents but a fraction of the fantastic land of wonder, adventure, and unparalleled natural beauty. Though 24,000 people jam into five square miles of Yosemite Valley each summer day, the park is actually 90 percent wilderness. Other landmark areas you can reach by car include the Wawona Grove of Giant Sequoias, Tenaya Lake, Tuolumne Meadows, and Hetch Hetchy.

But that's still only scratching the surface. For those who

hike, another world will open up: Yosemite has 318 lakes, dozens of pristine streams, the Grand Canyon of the Tuolumne River, Matterhorn Peak, Benson Lake (with the largest white-sand beach in the Sierra), and dozens of spectacular waterfalls.

If you explore beyond the park boundaries, the adventures just keep getting better. Over Tioga Pass, outside the park and just off Highway 120 (open seasonally, May–Sept.), are Tioga Lake, Ellery Lake, and Saddlebag Lake (10,087 feet), the latter of which is the highest lake in California accessible by car. To the east is Mono Lake and its weird tufa spires, which create a stark moonscape. Time your trip before the winter snows, or after the spring thaws, and you can traverse from alpine peaks to desert lows in a matter of hours.

The nearby June Lake Loop and Mammoth Lakes area is a launch point to another orbit. Both have small lakes with on-site cabin rentals, excellent fishing, great hiking and mountain biking for all levels, and phenomenal skiing and winter sports. In addition, just east of Mammoth Lakes airport is a series of hot springs, including a famous spot on Hot Creek, something of a legend in these parts.

More hiking and fishing opportunities abound at Devils Postpile National Monument, where you can hike to Rainbow Falls. At nearby Agnew Meadows, you'll find a trail that hugs the pristine San Joaquin River up to Thousand Island Lake and leads to the beautiful view from Banner and Ritter Peaks in the Ansel Adams Wilderness. Horseback riding is also popular in this area, with pack trips available from Reds Meadow.

In case you didn't already know, many of California's best lakes for a chance to catch giant rainbow and brown trout are in this region. They include Bridgeport Reservoir, Twin Lakes, June Lake, Convict Lake, and Crowley Lake in the eastern Sierra.

This region has it all: beauty, variety, and a chance at the hike or fish of a lifetime. There is nothing else like it.

CALIFORNIA

1 HERRING RESERVOIR

Scenic rating: 8

at Herring Lake in Stanislaus National Forest

Map grid A1

This is a pretty little spot, a rustic campground set near Herring Creek as it enters Herring Lake, set at an elevation of 7,350 feet. There is no boat ramp, but hand-launched boats, such as kayaks, canoes, rafts, prams, and float tubes, are ideal. The lake is shallow, with fair fishing for brook trout and rainbow trout. No horses are permitted.

RV sites, facilities: There are 42 sites for tents or RVs up to 22 feet (no hookups). Fire rings are provided. Vault toilets are available. No drinking water is available. Garbage must be packed out. Leashed pets are permitted.

Reservations, fees: Reservations are not accepted. There is no camping fee. Open May through October, weather permitting.

Directions: From Sonora, drive east on Highway 108 for about 25 miles to Strawberry. Continue past Strawberry for two miles to Herring Creek Road/Forest Road 4N12. Turn right and drive seven miles to Hamill Canyon Road/Forest Road 4N12. Bear right and drive 0.25 mile to Herring Creek Reservoir. Continue another 0.25 mile (cross the bridge) and turn right and drive to the campground. The road is rough and not recommended for RVs or low-clearance vehicles.

Contact: Stanislaus National Forest, Summit Ranger District, 209/965-3434, fax 209/965-3372.

2 PINECREST

Scenic rating: 7

near Pinecrest Lake in Stanislaus National Forest

Map grid A1

This monster-sized Forest Service camp is set near Pinecrest Lake. A launch ramp is available, and a 20-mph speed limit is enforced on the lake. A trail circles the lake and also branches off to nearby Catfish Lake. In early summer, there is good fishing for stocked rainbow trout. The elevation is 5,600 feet. Winter camping is allowed near the Pinecrest Day-Use Area. (For details about Pinecrest Lake, see the Meadowview listing in this chapter.)

RV sites, facilities: There are 200 sites for tents or RVs up to 22 feet (no hookups). Picnic tables and fire grills are provided. Drinking water and flush toilets are available. Garbage must be packed out. A grocery store, coin laundry, coin showers, boat ramp, and propane gas are nearby at Pinecrest Lake Resort. Some facilities are wheelchair-accessible. Leashed pets are permitted.

Reservations, fees: Reservations are required mid-May–mid-September at 877/444-6777 or www.recreation.gov ($10 reservation fee). Sites are $19 per night. Open May through October, weather permitting.

Directions: From Sonora, drive east on Highway 108 for about 30 miles to the signed turn for Pinecrest Lake on the right. Turn right and drive to the access road (0.7 mile past the turnoff signed "Pinecrest") for the campground. Turn right and drive a short distance to the campground.

Contact: Stanislaus National Forest, Summit Ranger District, 209/965-3434, fax 209/965-3372.

3 PIONEER TRAIL GROUP CAMP

Scenic rating: 8

near Pinecrest Lake in Stanislaus National Forest

Map grid A1

If you're going to Pinecrest Lake with a Scout troop, this is the spot, since it is set up specifically for groups. You get beautiful creek and lake views, with the camp set at an elevation of 5,700 feet. (For recreation information, see the Meadowview listing in this chapter.)

RV sites, facilities: There are three group areas for tents or RVs up to 22 feet (no hookups) that can accommodate 50–100 people each. Picnic tables and fire grills are provided. Drinking water and vault toilets are available. Garbage must be packed out. A grocery store, coin laundry, boat ramp, coin showers, and propane gas are nearby. Some facilities are wheelchair-accessible. Leashed pets are permitted.

Reservations, fees: Reservations are accepted at 877/444-6777 or www.recreation.gov ($10 reservation fee). Sites are $60–75 per night. Open May through October, weather permitting.

Directions: From Sonora, drive east on Highway 108 for about 30 miles to the signed road for Pinecrest Lake. Turn right at the sign and drive 0.5 mile to the signed road for Pinecrest/Dodge Ridge Road. Turn right and drive about a mile to the campground entrance on the left.

Contact: Stanislaus National Forest, Summit Ranger District, 209/965-3434, fax 209/965-3372.

4 MEADOWVIEW

Scenic rating: 7

near Pinecrest Lake in Stanislaus National Forest

Map grid A1

No secret here, folks. This camp is one mile from Pinecrest Lake, a popular weekend vacation area (and there's a trail that connects the camp with the town). Pinecrest Lake is set at 5,621 feet elevation, covers 300 acres and 2.5 miles of shoreline, has a sandy swimming beach, and has a 20-mph speed limit for boaters. The lake is the centerpiece of a fully developed family vacation area; boat rentals at the small marina are a big bonus. The lake is stocked with rainbow trout and also has a small resident population of brown trout. The easy hike around the lake is a popular walk. If you want something more ambitious, there is a cutoff on the north side of the lake that is routed one mile up to little Catfish Lake, which in reality is a set of shallow ponds surrounded by old-growth forest. The Dodge Ridge Ski Area is nearby, with many privately owned cabins in the area.

RV sites, facilities: There are 100 sites for tents or RVs up to 22 feet (no hookups). Picnic tables and fire grills are provided. Drinking water and

flush toilets are available. A grocery store, coin laundry, boat ramp, boat rentals, coin showers, and propane gas are nearby. Garbage must be packed out. Some facilities are wheelchair-accessible. Leashed pets are permitted.

Reservations, fees: Reservations are not accepted. Sites are $14 per night. Open May through September, weather permitting.

Directions: From Sonora, drive east on Highway 108 for about 30 miles to the signed road for Pinecrest Lake. Turn right at the sign and drive 0.5 mile to Pinecrest/Dodge Ridge Road. Turn right and drive about 200 yards to the campground entrance on the right side of the road.

Contact: Stanislaus National Forest, Summit Ranger District, 209/965-3434, fax 209/965-3372.

5 CHERRY VALLEY AND BOAT-IN

Scenic rating: 8

on Cherry Lake in Stanislaus National Forest

Map grid A1

Cherry Lake is a mountain lake surrounded by national forest at 4,700 feet elevation, just outside the western boundary of Yosemite National Park. It is much larger than most people anticipate and provides much better trout fishing than anything in Yosemite. The camp is on the southwest shore of the lake, a very pretty spot, about a mile ride to the boat launch on the west side of the Cherry Valley Dam. A bonus is that dispersed boat-in camping is allowed on the lake's east side. All water sports are allowed, yet because it takes a considerable drive to reach the lake, you won't find nearly the waterskiing traffic as at other regional lakes. Water levels can fluctuate here. The lake is bordered to the east by Kibbie Ridge; just on the other side are Yosemite Park and Lake Eleanor. Insider's tip: During periods of campfire restrictions, which is often most of the summer in this national forest, this campground is the only one in the area where campfires are permitted. A fire permit is required from the Forest Service.

RV sites, facilities: There are 45 sites for tents or RVs up to 22 feet (no hookups). Primitive boat-in camping is permitted on the lake's east side. Picnic tables and fire grills are provided. Drinking water and vault toilets are available. A boat ramp is nearby. Leashed pets are permitted.

Reservations, fees: Reservations are not accepted. Sites are $17 per night, $34 per night for double sites. There is no camping fee for boat-in sites. A 14-day limit is enforced. Open April through October, weather permitting.

Directions: From Groveland, drive east on Highway 120 for about 15 miles to Forest Road 1N07/Cherry Lake Road. Turn left and drive 20 miles to Cottonwood Road/Forest Road 1N04. Turn left and drive one mile to the campground entrance road. Turn right and drive one mile to the campground.

Contact: Stanislaus National Forest, Groveland Ranger District, 209/962-7825, fax 209/962-7412.

6 WHITE WOLF

Scenic rating: 8

in Yosemite National Park

Map grid A1   BEST (

This is one of Yosemite National Park's prime mountain camps for people who like to hike, either for great day hikes in the immediate area and beyond, or for overnight backpacking trips. The day hike to Lukens Lake is an easy two-mile trip, the payoff being this pretty little alpine lake set amid a meadow, pines, and granite. Just about everybody who camps at White Wolf makes the trip. Backpackers (wilderness permit required) can make the overnight trip into the Ten Lakes Basin, set below Grand Mountain and Colby Mountain. Bears are common at this camp, and campers are required to secure food in the bearproof lockers. The elevation is 8,000 feet.

RV sites, facilities: There are 74 sites for tents or RVs up to 27 feet (no hookups). Tent cabins are also available. Picnic tables, food lockers,

and fire grills are provided. Drinking water and flush toilets are available. Evening ranger programs are occasionally offered. A small store with a walk-up window and limited items is nearby. Leashed pets are permitted in the campground, but not on trails.

Reservations, fees: Reservations are not accepted. Sites are $14 per night, plus $20 park entrance fee per vehicle. Open July to early September, weather permitting.

Directions: From Merced, drive east on Highway 140 to the Arch Rock entrance station. Continue east to the Big Oak Flat Road junction (0.5 mile before entering Yosemite Valley). Turn left and drive 14 miles to Tioga Road. Turn right and drive 15 miles to White Wolf Road on the left. Turn left and drive a mile to the campground entrance road on the right.

Contact: Yosemite National Park, 209/372-0200, for an automated menu of recorded information, www.nps.gov/yose.

7 TUOLUMNE MEADOWS

Scenic rating: 8

in Yosemite National Park

Map grid A1   BEST (

This is Yosemite's biggest camp, and for the variety of nearby adventures, it might also be the best. It is set in the high country, at 8,600 feet, and can be used as a base camp for fishing, hiking, and horseback riding, or as a start-up point for a backpacking trip (wilderness permits required). This is one of the top trailheads in North America. There are two outstanding and easy day hikes from here, one heading north on the Pacific Crest Trail for the near-level walk to Tuolumne Falls and Glen Aulin, the other heading south up Lyell Fork (toward Donohue Pass), with good fishing for small brook trout. With a backpack (wilderness permit required), either route can be extended for as long as desired into remote and beautiful country. Tenaya Lake, one of the most beautiful lakes in Yosemite, is just a short drive (or shuttle hop) away. The campground is huge, and neighbors are guaranteed, but it is well wooded and feels somewhat secluded even with all the RVs and tents. There are lots of food-raiding bears in the area, so use of the food lockers is required.

RV sites, facilities: There are 304 sites for tents or RVs up to 35 feet (no hookups), four horse camps, and seven group sites that can accommodate 30 people each. There are also an additional 25 hike-in sites available for backpackers (no parking is available for backpacker campsites, often reserved for those hiking the Pacific Crest Trail, for which a wilderness permit is required). Picnic tables, fire grills, and food lockers are provided. Drinking water, flush toilets, and dump station are available. Showers and groceries are nearby. Leashed pets are permitted, except in group sites, horse camps, and backpacker sites.

Reservations, fees: Reservations are accepted at 877/444-6777 or www.recreation.gov ($10 reservation fee); half of the sites are available through reservations, the other half are first come, first served. Sites are $20 per night for individual sites, $5 per night per person for walk-in (backpack) sites, $25 per night for horse camp, and $40 per night for group sites, plus a $20 per vehicle park entrance fee. Open July through late-September, weather permitting.

Directions: From Merced, drive east on Highway 140 to the Arch Rock entrance station. Continue east to the Big Oak Flat Road junction (0.5 mile before entering Yosemite Valley). Turn left and drive 14 miles to Tioga Road. Turn right and drive 46 miles to the campground on the right side of the road.

From just south of Lee Vining at the junction of U.S. 395 and Highway 120, turn west and drive to the Tioga Pass entrance station for Yosemite National Park. Continue for about eight miles to the campground entrance on the left.

Contact: Yosemite National Park, 209/372-0200, for an automated menu of recorded information, www.nps.gov/yose.

8 SWEETWATER

Scenic rating: 4

near the South Fork of the Tuolumne River in Stanislaus National Forest

Map grid A1

This camp is set at 3,000 feet elevation, near the South Fork Tuolumne River, one of several camps along Highway 120 that provide a safety valve for campers who can't find space in Yosemite National Park to the east. Nearby, on the North Fork of the Tuolumne River, is a popular swimming area known as Rainbow Pools, with a waterfall and series of pools created by the river. Whitewater rafting and kayaking are also available a few miles from this camp; a Forest Service permit is required.

RV sites, facilities: There are 12 sites for tents or RVs up to 22 feet (no hookups). Picnic tables and fire grills are provided. Drinking water and vault toilets are available. Leashed pets are permitted.

Reservations, fees: Reservations are not accepted. Sites are $15 per night. A 14-day limit is enforced. Open April through October, weather permitting.

Directions: From Groveland, drive east on Highway 120 for about 15 miles (five miles past the Groveland District Office) to the campground on the left side of the road.

Contact: Stanislaus National Forest, Groveland Ranger District, 209/962-7825, fax 209/962-7412.

9 DIMOND "O"

Scenic rating: 7

in Stanislaus National Forest

Map grid A1

Dimond "O" is set at 4,400 feet elevation on the eastern side of Stanislaus National Forest—just two miles from the western border of Yosemite National Park.

RV sites, facilities: There are 36 sites for tents or RVs up to 22 feet (no hookups). Picnic tables and fire grills are provided. Drinking water

and vault toilets are available. Some facilities are wheelchair-accessible. Leashed pets are permitted.

Reservations, fees: Reservations are accepted at 877/444-6777 or www.recreation.gov ($10 reservation fee). Sites are $19 per night, double sites are $38 per night. Open April through October, weather permitting.

Directions: From Groveland, drive east on Highway 120 for 25 miles to Evergreen Road/Forest Road 12. Turn left on Evergreen Road and drive six miles to the campground.

Contact: Stanislaus National Forest, Groveland Ranger District, 209/962-7825, fax 209/962-7412.

10 YOSEMITE CREEK

Scenic rating: 9

on Yosemite Creek in Yosemite National Park
Map grid A1

This is the most remote drive-to camp in Yosemite National Park, a great alternative to camping in the valley or at Tuolumne Meadows, and the rough, curvy access road keeps many visitors away. It is set along Yosemite Creek at 7,659 feet elevation, with poor trout fishing but a trailhead for a spectacular hike. If you arrange a shuttle ride, you can make a great one-way trip down to the north side of the Yosemite Canyon rim, skirting past the top of Yosemite Falls (a side trip to Yosemite Point is a must!), then tackling the unbelievable descent into the valley, emerging at Camp 4 Walk-In. Note: The narrow entrance road is a remnant of "Old Tioga Road."

RV sites, facilities: There are 40 sites with no hookups for tents or small RVs. Picnic tables, food lockers (mandatory use), and fire grills are provided. Vault toilets are available. No drinking water is available. Leashed pets are permitted.

Reservations, fees: Reservations are not accepted. Sites are $10 per night, plus $20 park entrance fee per vehicle. A 14-day stay limit is enforced. Open July through early September, weather permitting.

Directions: From Merced, drive east on Highway 140 to the Arch Rock entrance station. Continue east to the Big Oak Flat Road junction (0.5 mile before entering Yosemite Valley). Turn left and drive 14 miles to Tioga Road. Turn right and drive about 30 miles (just beyond the White Wolf turnoff on the left) to Yosemite Creek Campground Road on the right. Turn right (RVs over 24 feet and trailers are not recommended) and drive five miles to the campground at the end of the road.

Contact: Yosemite National Park, 209/372-0200, for an automated menu of recorded information, www.nps.gov/yose.

11 PORCUPINE FLAT

Scenic rating: 6

near Yosemite Creek in Yosemite National Park
Map grid A1

Porcupine Flat, set at 8,100 feet elevation, is southwest of Mount Hoffman, one of the prominent nearby peaks along Tioga Road in Yosemite National Park. The trailhead for a hike to May Lake, set just below Mount Hoffman, is about five miles away on a signed turnoff on the north side of the road. There are several little peaks above the lake where hikers can gain great views, including one of the back side of Half Dome.

RV sites, facilities: There are 52 sites for tents or RVs up to 24 feet (no hookups). There is limited RV space. Picnic tables, fire rings, and food lockers (mandatory use) are provided. Pit toilets are available. No drinking water is available. No pets are allowed.

Reservations, fees: Reservations are not accepted. Sites are $10 per night, plus $20 park entrance fee per vehicle. Open July through mid-October, weather permitting.

Directions: From Merced, drive east on Highway 140 to the Arch Rock entrance station. Continue east to the Big Oak Flat Road junction (0.5 mile before entering Yosemite Valley). Turn left and drive 14 miles to Tioga Road. Turn right and drive about 25 miles to the campground on the left side of the road (16 miles west from Tuolumne Meadows).

Contact: Yosemite National Park, 209/372-0200, for an automated menu of recorded information, www.nps.gov/yose.

12 MOORE CREEK GROUP CAMP

Scenic rating: 6

in Stanislaus National Forest

Map grid A1

This group camp is set at 3,100 feet elevation, just past where the Sierra alpine zone takes over from foothill oak woodlands. It is near the access route (Highway 120) to the Crane Flat entrance station of Yosemite National Park.

RV sites, facilities: There is one group site for tents or RVs up to 30 feet (no hookups) that can accommodate up to 40 people. Picnic tables and fire grills are provided. No drinking water is available. No toilet is available and campers are required to bring a portable toilet with them. Garbage must be packed out. Leashed pets are permitted.

Reservations, fees: Reservations are required at Groveland Ranger District at 209/962-7825. There is no camping fee. Open year-round.

Directions: From Groveland, drive east on Highway 120 for about 12 miles to Buck Meadows Road. Turn right and drive 1.5 miles (the road becomes Forest Road 2S05) to the campground on the right.

Contact: Stanislaus National Forest, Groveland Ranger District, 209/962-7825, fax 209/962-7412.

13 YOSEMITE LAKES

Scenic rating: 6

on Tuolumne River at Groveland

Map grid A1

This is a 400-acre park set at 3,600 feet elevation along the South Fork Tuolumne River in the Sierra foothills near Groveland. Its proximity to Yosemite National Park, just five miles from the west entrance station, makes it ideal for many. The park is an affiliate of Thousand Trails, whose facilities usually are open only to members, but in this case, it is open to the general public on a limited basis. It is a family-oriented park with a large variety of recreation options and seasonal organized activities. Fishing and swimming are popular, and the river is stocked with trout. A plus is 24-hour security.

RV sites, facilities: There are 20 sites with full hookups (30 amps) for RVs of any length and 25 sites for tents available to the public (more sites available to Thousand Trails members only), and cabins, yurts, and a hostel. Picnic tables and fire rings are provided. Restrooms, drinking water, showers, flush toilets, fish-cleaning station, and coin laundry are available. A store, gas station, propane, and firewood are available. Kayak rentals, pedalboats, inner tubes, and bicycles are available for rent. Some facilities are wheelchair accessible. Leashed pets are permitted.

Reservations, fees: Reservations are accepted at 800/533-1001. Sites are $37–39.50 per night for RVs, $29.50–32 per night for tents. Credit cards accepted. Open year-round, weather permitting.

Directions: Drive east on Highway 120 to Groveland. From Groveland, continue east for 18 miles to the entrance road (signed) for Yosemite Lakes on the right. Turn right and drive a short distance to the park.

Contact: Yosemite Lakes, 209/962-0121, www.stayatyosemite.com.

14 HODGDON MEADOW

Scenic rating: 7

in Yosemite National Park

Map grid A1

Hodgdon Meadow is on the outskirts of Yosemite, just inside the park's borders at the Big Oak Flat (Highway 120) entrance station, at 4,900 feet in elevation. It is near a small feeder creek to the South Fork Tuolumne River. It is about a 20-minute drive on Highway 120 to a major junction, where a left turn takes you on Tioga Road and to Yosemite's high country, including Tuolumne Meadows, and where staying on Big Flat Road routes you toward Yosemite Valley (25 miles from the camp). Because of the presence of bears, use of food lockers is required.

RV sites, facilities: There are 105 sites for tents or RVs up to 24 feet (no hookups) and four group sites for 13–30 people each. Picnic tables, fire rings, and food lockers are provided. Drinking water and flush toilets are available. Leashed pets are permitted in the campground, but not in group camps or on trails.

Reservations, fees: Reservations are accepted at 877/444-6777 or www.recreation.gov, and are required April through mid-October ($10 reservation fee). Sites are $20 per night May through October, $14 remainder of year, group campsite $40 per night, plus $20 park entrance fee per vehicle. Open year-round, except for group sites.

Directions: From Groveland, drive east on Highway 120 to the Big Oak Flat entrance station for Yosemite National Park. Just after passing the entrance station, turn left and drive a short distance to the campground on the right.

Contact: Yosemite National Park, 209/372-0200, for an automated menu of recorded information, www.nps.gov/yose.

15 TAMARACK FLAT

Scenic rating: 7

on Tamarack Creek in Yosemite National Park

Map grid A1

The road to this campground looks something like the surface of the moon. Then you arrive and find one of the few primitive drive-to camps in Yosemite National Park, at 6,300 feet elevation. From the trailhead at camp, you can link up with El Capitan Trail and then hike across Ribbon Meadow on up to the north valley rim at El Capitan, at 7,569 feet elevation. This is the largest single piece of granite in the world, and standing atop it for both the

sensation and the divine view is a breathtaking experience. From camp, Yosemite Valley is 23 miles away. Note that the use of food lockers is now required.

RV sites, facilities: There are 52 sites for tents or RVs up to 24 feet (no hookups). Note that the access road is difficult. Picnic tables, food lockers, and fire grills are provided. Vault toilets are available. No drinking water is available. No pets are allowed.

Reservations, fees: Reservations are not accepted. Sites are $10 per night, plus $20 park entrance fee per vehicle. Open June through September.

Directions: From Merced, drive east on Highway 140 to the Arch Rock entrance station. Continue east to the Big Oak Flat Road junction (0.5 mile before entering Yosemite Valley). Turn left and drive 14 miles to Tioga Road. Turn right on Tioga Road and drive three miles to the campground entrance on the right side of the road. Turn right and drive 2.5 miles to the campground at the end of the road. Trailers and RVs are not advised.

Contact: Yosemite National Park, 209/372-0200, for an automated menu of recorded information, www.nps.gov/yose.

16 LOWER PINES

Scenic rating: 9

in Yosemite Valley in Yosemite National Park

Map grid A1

Lower Pines sits right along the Merced River, quite pretty, in the center of Yosemite Valley. Of course, the tents and RVs are jammed in quite close together. Within walking distance is the trail to Mirror Lake (a zoo on parade), as well as the trailhead at Happy Isles for the hike up to Vernal Fall and Nevada Fall. The park's shuttle bus picks up riders near the camp entrance.

RV sites, facilities: There are 60 sites for tents or RVs up to 40 feet, one double site for tents or RVs up to 40 feet, and two group camps. No hookups. Fire rings, picnic tables, and food lockers (mandatory use) are provided. Drinking water and flush toilets are available. A grocery store, coin laundry, propane gas, recycling center, dump station and horse and bike rentals are nearby. Leashed pets are permitted.

Reservations, fees: Reservations are required at 877/444-6777 or www.recreation.gov ($10 reservation fee). Sites are $20 per night, $30 per night for double or group sites, plus $20 park entrance fee per vehicle. There is a seven-day limit during the summer. Open late March through October, weather permitting.

Directions: From Merced, drive east on Highway 140 to the Arch Rock entrance station. Continue east to the Big Oak Flat Road junction (0.5 mile before entering Yosemite Valley). Continue into Yosemite Valley, drive past Curry Village (on the right) to the campground entrance on the left side of the road (just before Clarks Bridge).

Contact: Yosemite National Park, 209/372-0200, for an automated menu of recorded information, www.nps.gov/yose.

17 UPPER PINES

Scenic rating: 9

in Yosemite Valley in Yosemite National Park

Map grid A1

Of the campgrounds in Yosemite Valley, Upper Pines is the closest trailhead to paradise, providing you can get a campsite at the far south end of the camp. From here it is a short walk to Happy Isles trailhead and with it the chance to hike to Vernal Fall on Mist Trail (steep), or beyond to Nevada Fall (very steep) at the foot of Liberty Cap. But crowded this camp is, and you'd better expect it. People come from all over the world to camp here. Sometimes it appears as if they are from other worlds as well. The elevation is 4,000 feet.

RV sites, facilities: There are 238 sites for tents or RVs up to 35 feet (no hookups). Fire rings, picnic tables, and food lockers (mandatory use) are provided. Drinking water, flush toilets, and dump station are available. A grocery store, coin laundry, propane gas, recycling center, and horse

and bike rentals are nearby. Three sites provide wheelchair access. Leashed pets are permitted in the campgrounds, but not on trails.

Reservations, fees: Reservations are required at 877/444-6777 or www.recreation.gov ($10 reservation fee). Sites are $20 per night, plus $20 park entrance fee per vehicle. There is a seven-day limit during the summer. Open year-round.

Directions: From Merced, drive east on Highway 140 to the Arch Rock entrance station. Continue east to the Big Oak Flat Road junction (0.5 mile before entering Yosemite Valley). Continue into Yosemite Valley, drive past Curry Village (on the right) to the campground entrance on the right side of the road (just before Clarks Bridge).

Contact: Yosemite National Park, 209/372-0200, for an automated menu of recorded information, www.nps.gov/yose.

18 NORTH PINES

Scenic rating: 9

in Yosemite Valley in Yosemite National Park

Map grid A1

North Pines is set along the Merced River. A trail out of camp heads east and links with the paved road/trail to Mirror Lake, a virtual parade of people. If you continue hiking past Mirror Lake you will get astounding views of Half Dome and then leave the masses behind as you enter Tenaya Canyon. The elevation is 4,000 feet.

RV sites, facilities: There are 81 sites for tents or RVs up to 40 feet (no hookups). Picnic tables, fire grills, and food lockers (mandatory use) are provided. Drinking water and flush toilets are available. A grocery store, coin laundry, recycling center, propane gas, and horse and bike rentals are nearby. Leashed pets are allowed.

Reservations, fees: Reservations are required at 877/444-6777 or www.recreation.gov ($10 reservation fee). Sites are $20 per night, plus $20 park entrance fee per vehicle. Open April through September, weather permitting.

Directions: From Merced, drive east on Highway 140 to the Arch Rock entrance station. Continue east to the Big Oak Flat Road junction (0.5 mile before entering Yosemite Valley). Continue into Yosemite Valley, drive past Curry Village (on the right), continue past Upper and Lower Pines Campgrounds, and drive over Clarks Bridge to a junction at the horse stables. Turn left at the horse stables and drive a short distance to the campground on the right.

Contact: Yosemite National Park, 209/372-0200, for an automated menu of recorded information, www.nps.gov/yose.

19 CRANE FLAT

Scenic rating: 6

near Tuolumne Grove of Big Trees in Yosemite National Park

Map grid A1

Crane Flat is within a five-minute drive of the Tuolumne Grove of Big Trees and to the Merced Grove to the nearby west. This is the feature attraction in this part of Yosemite National Park, set near the western border in close proximity to the Big Oak Flat Entrance Station (Highway 120). The elevation is 6,200 feet. Yosemite Valley is about a 25-minute drive away.

RV sites, facilities: There are 166 sites for tents or RVs up to 35 feet (no hookups). Picnic tables, fire rings, and food lockers are provided. Drinking water and flush toilets are available. Groceries, propane gas, and a gas station are nearby. Leashed pets are allowed in the campground.

Reservations, fees: Reservations are required at 877/444-6777 or www.recreation.gov ($10 reservation fee). Sites are $20 per night, plus $20 park entrance fee per vehicle. Open July through September, weather permitting.

Directions: From Groveland, drive east on Highway 120 to the Big Oak Flat entrance station for Yosemite National Park. After passing through the entrance station, drive about 10 miles to the campground entrance road on the right. Turn right and drive 0.5 mile to the campground.

Contact: Yosemite National Park, 209/372-0200, for an automated menu of recorded information, www.nps.gov/yose.

20 BRIDALVEIL CREEK AND EQUESTRIAN AND GROUP CAMP

Scenic rating: 10

near Glacier Point in Yosemite National Park

Map grid A1

There may be no better view in the world than the one from Glacier Point, looking down into Yosemite Valley, where Half Dome stands like nature's perfect sculpture. Then there are the perfect views of Yosemite Fall, Nevada Fall, Vernal Fall, and several hundred square miles of Yosemite's wilderness backcountry. This is the closest camp to Glacier Point's drive-to vantage point, but it is also the closest camp to the best day hikes in the entire park. Along Glacier Point Road are trailheads to Sentinel Dome (incredible view of Yosemite Fall) and Taft Point (breathtaking drop, incredible view of El Capitan), and McGurk Meadow (one of the most pristine spots on Earth). At 7,200 feet, the camp is more than 3,000 feet higher than Yosemite Valley. A good day hike out of camp leads you to Ostrander Lake, just below Horse Ridge.

RV sites, facilities: There are 110 sites for tents or RVs up to 35 feet (no hookups), three equestrian sites, and two group sites for 13–30 people each. Picnic tables, fire rings, and food lockers (mandatory use) are provided. Drinking water and flush toilets are available. Leashed pets are permitted, except in group sites.

Reservations, fees: Reservations are not accepted for individual sites, but they are required for equestrian sites and group sites at 800/444-6777 or www.recreation.gov ($10 reservation fee). Sites are $14 per night, $25 per night for equestrian site, $40 per night for group site, plus $20 park entrance fee per vehicle. A 14-day stay limit is enforced. Open July through early September, weather permitting.

Directions: From Merced, drive east on Highway 140 to the Arch Rock entrance station. Continue east (past Big Oak Flat Road junction) to the junction with Wawona Road/Highway 41 (just before Yosemite Valley). Turn right on Highway 41/Wawona Road and drive about 10 miles to Glacier Point Road. Turn left on Glacier Point Road and drive about five miles (a few miles past Badger Pass Ski Area) to Peregoy Meadow and the campground access road on the right. Turn right and drive a short distance to the campground.

Contact: Yosemite National Park, 209/372-0200, for an automated menu of recorded information, www.nps.gov/yose.

21 MERCED RECREATION AREA

Scenic rating: 8

on the Merced River east of Briceburg

Map grid A1

What a spot: The campsites are along one of the prettiest sections of the Merced River, where you can enjoy great hiking, swimming, rafting, kayaking, and fishing, all on the same day. There are three campgrounds here: McCabe Flat, Willow Placer, and Railroad Flat. The access road out of camp leads downstream to the Yosemite Railroad Grade, which has been converted into a great trail. One of the best wildflower blooms anywhere in the Sierra foothills is found near here at Red Hills (just outside Chinese Camp), usually best in April. If you don't mind the cold water, swimming in the Merced River's pools can provide relief from summer heat. Evening fly-fishing is good in many of the same spots through July. But the true attraction on the Merced River is rafting and kayaking. An extraordinarily long stretch of river, 29 miles, can be run from the put-in at Red Bud Day-Use Area to the take-out at Bagby. A number of whitewater guide companies work this stretch of river.

RV sites, facilities: There are 21 walk-in tent sites and nine sites for tents or RVs up to 18 feet (no hookups). Picnic tables and fire grills are provided. Vault and pit toilets are available. No drinking water is available at the campsites (drinking water is available across from the Briceburg Bridge). Supplies are available in Mariposa. Some facilities are wheelchair-accessible. Leashed pets are permitted.

Reservations, fees: Reservations are not accepted. Sites are $10 per night. There is a 14-day limit. Open April through October, weather permitting.

Directions: From Merced, turn east on Highway 140 and drive 40 miles to Mariposa. Continue another 15 miles to Briceburg and the Briceburg Visitor Center on the left. Turn left at a road that is signed "BLM Camping Areas" (the road remains paved for about 150 yards). Drive over the Briceburg suspension bridge and turn left, traveling downstream on the road, parallel to the river. Drive 2.5 miles to McCabe Flat, 3.8 miles to Willow Placer, and 4.8 miles to Railroad Flat.

Contact: Bureau of Land Management, Folsom Field Office, 916/985-4474, fax 916/985-3259.

22 YOSEMITE-MARIPOSA KOA

Scenic rating: 7

near Mariposa

Map grid A1

A little duck pond, swimming pool, and proximity to Yosemite National Park make this one a winner. A shuttle bus service (fee) to the national park is a great bonus. The RV sites are lined up along the entrance road. A 10 P.M. "quiet time" helps ensure a good night's sleep. It's a one-hour drive to Yosemite Valley, and your best bet is to get there early to enjoy the spectacular beauty before the park is packed with people.

RV sites, facilities: There are 49 sites with full or partial hookups (30 and 50 amps) for RVs up to 40 feet, 26 tent sites, 12 cabins, and three lodges. Picnic tables and barbecues are provided; no wood fires. Restrooms with showers, dump station, Wi-Fi, telephone/modem access,

CALIFORNIA

coin laundry, convenience store, propane gas, seasonal swimming pool, train caboose with arcade, and playground are available. Some facilities are wheelchair accessible. Leashed pets are permitted in RV and tent sites only, with certain restrictions.

Reservations, fees: Reservations are accepted at 800/562-9391. Sites are $35–60 per night, $6 per person per night for more than two people, $5 per night for each additional vehicle, $2 per pet per night. Call for cabin and lodge prices. Some credit cards accepted. Open March through October.

Directions: From Merced, drive east on Highway 140 to Mariposa. Continue on Highway 140 for seven miles to Midpines and the campground entrance on the left at 6323 Highway 140.

Contact: Yosemite-Mariposa KOA, 209/966-2201, www.yosemitekoa.com.

23 JERSEYDALE

Scenic rating: 5

in Sierra National Forest

Map grid A1

This little camp gets overlooked by many visitors shut out of nearby Yosemite National Park simply because they don't realize it exists. Jerseydale is set southwest of the national park in Sierra National Forest, with two good side trips nearby. If you continue north on Jerseydale Road to its end (about six miles), you will come to a Forest Service road/trailhead that provides access east along a portion of the South Fork of the Merced River, where there is often good fishing, swimming, and rafting. In addition, a dirt road from the camp is routed east for many miles into the Chowchilla Mountains.

RV sites, facilities: There are 10 sites for tents or RVs up to 24 feet (no hookups). Picnic tables and fire grills are provided. Vault toilets are available. No drinking water. A few hitching posts are available and horses are permitted at these camps. Leashed pets are permitted.

Reservations, fees: Reservations are not accepted. There is no fee for camping. Open May through November.

Directions: From Mariposa, drive northeast on Highway 140 for about five miles to Triangle Road (if you reach Midpines, you have gone 1.5 miles too far). Turn right on Triangle Road and drive about six miles to Darrah and Jerseydale Road. Turn left and drive three miles to the campground on the left side of the road (adjacent to the Jerseydale Ranger Station).

Contact: Sierra National Forest, Bass Lake Ranger District, 559/877-2218, fax 559/877-3108.

24 WAWONA

Scenic rating: 9

on the South Fork of the Merced River in Yosemite National Park

Map grid A1

Wawona is an attractive alternative to the packed camps in Yosemite Valley, providing you don't mind the relatively long drives to the best destinations. The camp is pretty, set along the South Fork of the Merced River, with the sites more spacious than at most other drive-to camps in the park. The nearest attraction is the Mariposa Grove of Giant Sequoias, but get your visit in by 9 A.M., because after that it turns into a zoo, complete with shuttle train. The best nearby hike is a strenuous 10-mile round-trip to Chilnualna Falls, the prettiest sight in the southern region of the park; the trailhead is at the east end of Chilnualna Road in North Wawona. It's a 45-minute drive to either Glacier Point or Yosemite Valley.

RV sites, facilities: There are 93 sites for tents or RVs up to 35 feet (no hookups), one group tent site for 13–30 people each, and two horse camps. Picnic tables, fire grills, and food lockers (mandatory use) are provided. Drinking water and flush toilets are available. There are some stock-handling facilities for camping with pack animals; call for further information. A

CALIFORNIA

grocery store, dump station, propane gas, gas station, post office, restaurant, and seasonal horseback-riding facilities are nearby. Leashed pets are permitted, but not in group sites, horse camps, or on trails.

Reservations, fees: From May through September, reservations are required at 877/444-6777 or www.recreation.gov ($10 reservation fee). No reservations are needed from October to April. Sites are $20 per night, $14 per night in off-season; horse camps are $25 per night, group tent site is $40 per night; plus $20 park entrance fee per vehicle. A seven-day camping limit is enforced during the summer. Open year-round, and horse camp open April through October.

Directions: From Oakhurst, drive north on Highway 41 to the Wawona entrance of Yosemite National Park. Continue north on Highway 41 past Wawona (golf course on the left) and drive one mile to the campground entrance on the left.

Contact: Yosemite National Park, 209/372-0200, for an automated menu of recorded information, www.nps.gov/yose.

25 SUMMIT CAMP

Scenic rating: 5

in Sierra National Forest

Map grid A1

The prime attraction of tiny Summit Camp is its proximity to the Wawona entrance of Yosemite National Park. It sits along a twisty Forest Service road, perched in the Chowchilla Mountains at 5,800 feet, about three miles from Big Creek. It's a little-known alternative when the park campgrounds at Wawona are packed.

RV sites, facilities: There are six primitive sites for tents or RVs up to 16 feet (no hookups). Picnic tables and fire grills are provided. Vault toilets are available. No drinking water is available. Garbage must be packed out. Leashed pets are permitted.

Reservations, fees: Reservations are not accepted. There is no fee for camping. A 14-day limit is enforced. Open June through October, weather permitting.

Directions: From Oakhurst, drive north on Highway 41 toward the town of Fish Camp and to the gravel Forest Road 5S09X a mile before Fish Camp on the left. Turn left and drive six twisty miles to the campground on the left side of the road. High-clearance vehicles are required. Trailers are not advised.

Contact: Sierra National Forest, Bass Lake Ranger District, 559/877-2218, fax 559/877-3108.

26 SUMMERDALE

Scenic rating: 7

on the South Fork of the Merced River in Sierra National Forest

Map grid A1

You can't get much closer to Yosemite National Park. This camp is within a mile of the Wawona entrance to Yosemite, about a five-minute drive to the Mariposa Grove. If you don't mind its proximity to the highway, this is a pretty spot in its own right, set along Big Creek, a feeder stream to the South Fork Merced River. Some good swimming holes are in this area. The elevation is 5,000 feet.

RV sites, facilities: There are 79 sites for tents or RVs up to 24 feet (no hookups). Picnic tables and fire grills are provided. Vault toilets are available. No drinking water is available. A grocery store is nearby (within one mile). Some facilities are wheelchair-accessible. Leashed pets are permitted.

Reservations, fees: Reservations are accepted at 877/444-6777 or www.recreation.gov ($10 reservation fee). Sites are $19 per night, $5 per night for each additional vehicle. Open May through October, weather permitting.

Directions: From Oakhurst, drive north on Highway 41 to Fish Camp and continue for one mile to the campground entrance on the left side of the road.

Contact: Sierra National Forest, Bass Lake Ranger District, 559/877-2218, fax 559/877-3108.

CALIFORNIA

27 UPPER CHIQUITO

Scenic rating: 7

on Chiquito Creek in Sierra National Forest

Map grid A1

Upper Chiquito is set at 6,800 feet elevation on a major access road to Sierra National Forest and the western region of the Ansel Adams Wilderness, about 15 miles to the east. The camp is set on Upper Chiquito Creek. About a mile down the road (southwest) is a Forest Service spur road (turn north) that provides access to a trail that is routed up Chiquito Creek for three miles to gorgeous Chiquita Lake (another route with a longer drive and shorter hike is available out of Fresno Dome).

RV sites, facilities: There are 20 sites for tents or RVs up to 20 feet (no hookups). Picnic tables and fire rings are provided. Vault toilets are available. No drinking water is available. Garbage service is located at the entrance to the campground. Leashed pets are permitted.

Reservations, fees: Reservations are not accepted. There is no fee for camping. Open June through September, weather permitting.

Directions: From Fresno, drive north on Highway 41 for 50 miles to Yosemite Forks and County Road 222. Turn right on County Road 222 (keeping to the right at each of two Y intersections) and drive six miles to Pines Village and Beasore Road. Turn left onto Beasore Road and drive 16 miles to the campground.

Contact: Sierra National Forest, Bass Lake Ranger District, 559/877-2218, fax 559/877-3108.

28 CLOVER MEADOW

Scenic rating: 8

in Sierra National Forest

Map grid A1

This is one of two excellent jump-off camps in the area for backpackers; the other is Granite Creek. The camp is set at 7,000 feet elevation, adjacent to the Clover Meadow Ranger Station, where backcountry information is available. While a trail is available from camp heading east into the Ansel Adams Wilderness, most hikers drive about three miles farther northeast on Minarets Road to a trailhead for a five-mile hike to Cora Lakes.

RV sites, facilities: There are seven sites for tents or RVs up to 20 feet (no hookups). Picnic tables and fire rings are provided. Drinking water and vault toilets are available. Garbage must be packed out. Leashed pets are permitted.

Reservations, fees: Reservations are not accepted. There is no fee for camping. Open June through September, weather permitting.

Directions: From Fresno, drive north on Highway 41 for about 25 miles to North Fork Road/County Road 200. Turn right and drive northeast for 17.5 miles to Auberry Road/County Road 222. Turn left (north) and drive one mile to the town of North Fork and Mammoth Pool Road. Turn right and drive 1.5 miles to County Road 225 (still Mammoth Pool Road). Turn right and drive (the road eventually becomes Minarets Road) to the junction with Forest Road 4S81. Bear left (north) on Forest Road 4S81 and drive to the campground entrance road. Bear left (signed "Clover Meadow") and drive to the campground, adjacent to the Clover Meadow Ranger Station. The total distance from North Fork to the entrance road is about 63 miles; it's 20 miles north of the well-signed Mammoth Pool Reservoir on Minarets Road.

Contact: Sierra National Forest, Bass Lake Ranger District, 559/877-2218, fax 559/877-3108.

29 GRANITE CREEK AND EQUESTRIAN CAMP

Scenic rating: 6

in Sierra National Forest

Map grid A1

This camp is a good jump-off point for backpackers since a trail from camp leads north for five miles to Cora Lakes in the Ansel Adams Wilderness, with the option of continuing to more remote wilderness. Note that nearby Clover Meadow camp (see listing in this chapter) may be more desirable because it has both drinking water to tank up your canteens and a ranger station to obtain the latest trail information. In addition, the upper half of this campground is available for equestrians. The elevation is 6,900 feet.

RV sites, facilities: There are 20 sites for tents or RVs up to 20 feet (no hookups). Picnic tables and fire rings are provided. Vault toilets and a horse corral are available. No drinking water is available. Garbage must be packed out. Leashed pets are permitted.

Reservations, fees: Reservations are not accepted. There is no fee for camping. Open June through September, weather permitting.

Directions: From Fresno, drive north on Highway 41 for about 25 miles to North Fork Road/County Road 200. Turn right and drive northeast for 17.5 miles to Auberry Road/County Road 222. Turn left (north) and drive one mile to the town of North Fork and Mammoth Pool Road. Turn right and drive 1.5 miles to County Road 225 (still Mammoth Pool Road). Turn right and drive (the road eventually becomes Minarets Road) to the junction with Forest Road 4S81. Bear left (north) on Forest Road 4S81 and drive to the campground entrance road. Turn left (signed for Granite Creek) and drive 3.5 miles to the campground. (The total distance from North Fork to the entrance road is about 66.5 miles; it's 23.5 miles north of Mammoth Pool Reservoir on the well-signed Minarets Road.)

Contact: Sierra National Forest, Bass Lake Ranger District, 559/877-2218, fax 559/877-3108.

30 BIG SANDY

Scenic rating: 7

on Big Creek in Sierra National Forest
Map grid A1

It's only six miles from the highway and just eight miles from the southern entrance to Yosemite National Park. Add that up: Right, when Wawona is full in southern Yosemite, this camp provides a much-needed option. It's a pretty camp set on Big Creek in the Sierra National Forest, one of two camps in the immediate area. The elevation is 5,800 feet. If you head into Yosemite for the tour of giant

sequoias in Wawona, get there early, by 7:30 or 8:30 A.M., when the grove is still quiet and cool, and you will have the old, mammoth trees practically to yourself.

RV sites, facilities: There are 18 sites for tents or RVs up to 20 feet (no hookups). Picnic tables and fire grills are provided. Vault toilets are available. No drinking water is available. Leashed pets are permitted.

Reservations, fees: Reservations are not accepted. Sites are $16 per night, $5 per night for each additional vehicle. Open May through September, weather permitting.

Directions: From Oakhurst drive north on Highway 41 for 15 miles to Forest Road 6S07 (one mile before reaching Marriotts). Turn right on Forest Road 6S07 and drive about six miles (a slow, rough road) to the camp.

Contact: Sierra National Forest, Bass Lake Ranger District, 559/877-2218, fax 559/877-3108.

31 FRESNO DOME

Scenic rating: 7

on Big Creek in Sierra National Forest
Map grid A1

This camp is named after nearby Fresno Dome to the east, at 7,540 feet elevation the dominating feature in the surrounding landscape. The trailhead for a mile hike to its top is two miles curving down the road to the east. This camp is set at 6,400 feet on Big Creek in Sierra National Forest, a good option to nearby Yosemite National Park.

RV sites, facilities: There are 15 sites for tents or RVs up to 20 feet (no hookups). Picnic tables and fire grills are provided. Vault toilets are available. No drinking water is available. Garbage service is located near the entrance to the campground. Leashed pets are permitted.

Reservations, fees: Reservations are not accepted. Sites are $14 per night, $5 per night for each additional vehicle. A 14-day limit is enforced. Open June through mid-October, weather permitting.

Directions: From Oakhurst, drive north on

Highway 41 approximately five miles to Sky Ranch Road/Forest Road 6S10. Turn right and drive 12 miles to the campground on the left.

Contact: Sierra National Forest, Bass Lake Ranger District, 559/877-2218, fax 559/877-3108.

32 KELTY MEADOW AND EQUESTRIAN CAMP

Scenic rating: 6

on Willow Creek in Sierra National Forest

Map grid A1

This primitive campground is often used by campers with horses. It is at Kelty Meadow by Willow Creek. Side-trip options feature nearby Fresno Dome, the Nelder Grove of giant sequoias and, of course, the southern entrance to nearby Yosemite National Park. The elevation is 5,800 feet.

RV sites, facilities: There are 11 sites for tents or RVs up to 20 feet. Fire grills and picnic tables are provided. Vault toilets and hitching posts are available. No drinking water is available. Garbage service is located near the entrance to the campground. Leashed pets are permitted.

Reservations, fees: Reservations are required for equestrian sites at 877/444-6777 or www.recreation.gov ($10 reservation fee). Sites are $16 per night, $5 per night for each additional vehicle. Open June through September, weather permitting.

Directions: From Oakhurst on Highway 41, drive five miles north to Sky Ranch Road/Forest Road 6S10. Turn left (northeast) and drive approximately 10 miles to the campground.

Contact: Sierra National Forest, Bass Lake Ranger District, 559/877-2218, fax 559/877-3108.

33 NELDER GROVE

Scenic rating: 7

in Sierra National Forest

Map grid A1

Nelder Grove is a primitive spot, also pretty, yet it is a camp that is often overlooked. It is set amid the Nelder Grove of giant sequoias, the majestic mountain redwoods. There are two interpretive trails, each about a two-mile walk. Since the southern entrance to Yosemite National Park is just 10 miles away, Nelder Grove is overshadowed by Yosemite's Wawona Grove. The elevation is 5,300 feet. A good option.

RV sites, facilities: There are seven sites for tents or RVs up to 20 feet (no hookups). Picnic tables and fire grills are provided. Vault toilets are available. No drinking water is available. Garbage must be packed out. Leashed pets are permitted.

Reservations, fees: Reservations are not accepted. There is no fee for camping. Open May through September, weather permitting.

Directions: From Fresno, drive north on Highway 41 for 46 miles to the town of Oakhurst. Continue north on Highway 41 for five miles to Sky Ranch Road/Forest Road 6S10. Turn right (northeast) and drive about eight miles to Forest Road 6S47Y. Turn left and drive a short distance to the campground.

Contact: Sierra National Forest, Bass Lake Ranger District, 559/877-2218, fax 559/877-3108.

34 SOQUEL

Scenic rating: 7

on the North Fork of Willow Creek in Sierra National Forest

Map grid A1

Soquel is at 5,400 feet elevation on the North Fork of Willow Creek, an alternative to nearby Grey's Mountain in Sierra National Forest. When the camps are filled at Bass Lake, these two camps provide overflow areas as well as more primitive settings for those who are looking for more of a wilderness experience.

RV sites, facilities: There are 11 sites for tents or RVs up to 20 feet (no hookups). Picnic tables and fire grills are provided. Vault toilets are available. No drinking water is available. Leashed pets are permitted.

Reservations, fees: Reservations are accepted at 877/444-6777 or www.recreation.gov ($10 reservation fee). Sites are $16 per night, $5 per night for each additional vehicle. Open June through October, weather permitting.

Directions: From Fresno, drive north on Highway 41 for 46 miles to the town of Oakhurst. Continue north on Highway 41 for five miles to Sky Ranch Road/Forest Road 6S10. Turn right (east) and drive approximately five miles to Forest Road 6S40. Turn right and drive about three-quarters of a mile to the campground.

Contact: Sierra National Forest, Bass Lake Ranger District, 559/877-2218, fax 559/877-3108.

35 TEXAS FLAT GROUP CAMP

Scenic rating: 5

on the North Fork of Willow Creek in
Sierra National Forest

Map grid A1

If you are on your honeymoon, this definitely ain't the place to be. Unless you like the smell of horses, that is. It's a pretty enough spot, set along the North Fork of Willow Creek, but the camp is primitive and designed for groups with horses. This camp is 15 miles from the south entrance of Yosemite National Park and 15 miles north of Bass Lake. The elevation is 5,400 feet.

RV sites, facilities: There are four group sites for tents or RVs up to 20 feet (no hookups) that can accommodate 25–100 people each. Fire grills and picnic tables are provided. Vault toilets and a corral are available. No drinking water is available. Leashed pets are permitted.

Reservations, fees: Reservations are accepted at 877/444-6777 or www.recreation.gov ($10 reservation fee). Sites are $60.50–90.20 per night. A 14-day limit is enforced. Open June through November.

Directions: From Fresno, drive about 52 miles north on Highway 41 to Sky Ranch Road/County Road 632. Turn right (east) on Sky Ranch Road/Forest Road 6S10 and drive approximately five miles to Forest Road 6S40. Turn right and drive about three-quarters of a mile to Forest Road 6S08. Turn left and drive 2.5 miles to Forest Road 6S38 and the campground.

Contact: Sierra National Forest, Bass Lake Ranger District, 559/877-2218, fax 559/877-3108.

36 GREY'S MOUNTAIN

Scenic rating: 7

on Willow Creek in Sierra National Forest

Map grid A1

This is a small, primitive campground to keep in mind when all the campgrounds are filled at nearby Bass Lake. It is one of a series of campgrounds on Willow Creek. The elevation is 5,400 feet, set just below Sivels Mountain to the east at 5,813 feet.

RV sites, facilities: There are 26 sites for tents or RVs up to 20 feet (no hookups). Picnic tables and fire grills are provided. Vault toilets are available. No drinking water is available. Leashed pets are permitted.

Reservations, fees: Reservations are not accepted. Sites are $16 per night, $5 per night for each additional vehicle. Open May through November, weather permitting.

Directions: From Oakhurst, drive north on Highway 41 for approximately five miles to Sky Ranch Road/Forest Road 6S10. Turn right and drive five miles to Forest Road 6S40. Turn right and drive 0.75 mile to Forest Road 6S08 and the camp.

Contact: Sierra National Forest, Bass Lake Ranger District, 559/877-2218, fax 559/877-3108.

37 BUCKEYE

Scenic rating: 8

near Buckeye Creek in
Humboldt-Toiyabe National Forest

Map grid A1

Here's a little secret: A two-mile hike out of camp heads to the undeveloped Buckeye Hot Springs. That is what inspires campers to bypass the fishing at nearby Robinson Creek (three miles away) and Twin Lakes (six miles away). The camp feels remote and primitive, set at 7,000 feet elevation on the eastern slope of the Sierra near Buckeye Creek. Another secret is that rainbow trout are

Contact: Sierra National Forest, Bass Lake Ranger District, 559/877-2218, fax 559/877-3108.

planted at the little bridge that crosses Buckeye Creek near the campground. A trail that starts near camp is routed through Buckeye Canyon and into the Hoover Wilderness.

RV sites, facilities: There are 65 paved sites for tents or RVs up to 35 feet (no hookups). Picnic tables and fire grills are provided. Drinking water and vault and flush toilets are available. Some facilities are wheelchair-accessible. Leashed pets are permitted.

Reservations, fees: Reservations are not accepted. Sites are $15 per night, $5 per night for each additional vehicle. Open May through October, weather permitting.

Directions: On U.S. 395, drive to Bridgeport and the junction with Twin Lakes Road. Turn west and drive seven miles to Buckeye Road. Turn right (north) on Buckeye Road (dirt, often impassable when wet) and drive 3.5 miles to the campground.

Contact: Humboldt-Toiyabe National Forest, Bridgeport Ranger District, 760/932-7070, fax 760/932-5899; American Land and Leisure, 760/932-9888.

38 WILLOW SPRINGS RV PARK

Scenic rating: 6

near Bridgeport
Map grid A1

Willow Springs RV Park is set at 6,800 feet elevation along U.S. 395, which runs along the eastern Sierra from Carson City south to Bishop and beyond to Lone Pine. The park is one mile from the turnoff to Bodie ghost town. A nice touch to the place is a central campfire that has been in place for more than 50 years. The country is stark here on the edge of the high Nevada desert, but there are many side trips that give the area life. The most popular destinations are to the nearby south: Mono Lake, with its tufa towers and incredible populations of breeding gulls and waterfowl, and the Bodie ghost town. For trout fishing, there's Bridgeport Reservoir to the north (good trolling) and downstream to the East Walker River (fly-fishing), both excellent destinations, as well as Twin Lakes to the west (huge brown trout).

RV sites, facilities: There are 25 sites with full hookups (30 amps) for RVs of any length. No tents. A motel is also available. Picnic tables are provided. Restrooms with showers, coin laundry, and nightly campfires are available. A restaurant is within walking distance. Leashed pets are permitted.

Reservations, fees: Reservations are accepted. Sites are $30 per night, $5 per person per night for more than two people. Open May through October.

Directions: From Bridgeport on U.S. 395, drive five miles south to the park, which is on the east side of the highway.

Contact: Willow Springs RV Park, 760/932-7725.

39 HONEYMOON FLAT

Scenic rating: 8

on Robinson Creek in
Humboldt-Toiyabe National Forest

Map grid A1

The camp is set beside Robinson Creek at 7,000 feet elevation, in the transition zone between the Sierra Nevada range to the west and the high desert to the east. It is easy to reach on the access road to Twin Lakes, only three miles farther. The lake is famous for occasional huge brown trout. However, the fishing at Robinson Creek is also often quite good, thanks to large numbers of trout planted each year.

RV sites, facilities: There are 35 sites with no hookups for tents or RVs up to 35 feet. Picnic tables and fire grills are provided. Drinking water, food lockers, and vault toilets are available. Some facilities are wheelchair-accessible. Leashed pets are permitted.

Reservations, fees: Reservations are accepted at 877/444-6777 or www.recreation.gov ($10 reservation fee). Sites are $13.39–15 per night, $5 per night for each additional vehicle. Open mid-April through October.

Directions: On U.S. 395, drive to Bridgeport and the junction with Twin Lakes Road. Turn west and drive eight miles to the campground.

Contact: Humboldt-Toiyabe National Forest, Bridgeport Ranger District, 760/932-7070, fax 760/932-5899; American Land and Leisure, 760/932-9888.

40 PAHA

Scenic rating: 8

near Twin Lakes in
Humboldt-Toiyabe National Forest

Map grid A1

This is one in a series of camps near Robinson Creek and within close range of Twin Lakes. The elevation at the camp is 7,000 feet. (See the Lower Twin Lake and Honeymoon Flat listings in this chapter for more information.)

RV sites, facilities: There are 22 sites for tents or RVs up to 35 feet (no hookups). Picnic tables and fire grills are provided. Drinking water, flush toilets, and food lockers are available. Two boat launches, a store, coin showers, and a coin laundry are available nearby at Twin Lakes Resort. Leashed pets are permitted.

Reservations, fees: Reservations are accepted at 877/444-6777 or www.recreation.gov ($10 reservation fee). Sites are $15.18–30.36 per night, $5 per night for each additional vehicle. Open May through October, weather permitting.

Directions: On U.S. 395, drive to Bridgeport and the junction with Twin Lakes Road. Turn west and drive 10 miles to the campground.

Contact: Humboldt-Toiyabe National Forest, Bridgeport Ranger District, 760/932-7070, fax 760/932-5899; American Land and Leisure, 760/932-9888.

41 ROBINSON CREEK

Scenic rating: 9

near Twin Lakes in
Humboldt-Toiyabe National Forest

Map grid A1

This campground, one of a series in the area, is set at 7,000 feet elevation on Robinson Creek, not far from Twin Lakes. The campground is divided into two areas. (For recreation options, see the Lower Twin Lake and Honeymoon Flat listings in this chapter.)

RV sites, facilities: There are 54 paved sites for tents or RVs up to 35 feet (no hookups). Picnic tables, food lockers, and fire grills are provided. Drinking water and flush and vault toilets are available. Some facilities are wheelchair-accessible. An amphitheater is nearby. Boat launches, a store, coin laundry, and coin showers are nearby at Twin Lakes Resort. Leashed pets are permitted.

Reservations, fees: Reservations are accepted at 877/444-6777 or www.recreation.gov ($10 reservation fee). Sites are $15.18–30.36 per night, $5 per night for each additional vehicle. Open mid-April through October, weather permitting.

Directions: On U.S. 395, drive to Bridgeport and the junction with Twin Lakes Road. Turn west and drive 10 miles to the campground.

Contact: Humboldt-Toiyabe National Forest, Bridgeport Ranger District, 760/932-7070, fax 760/932-5899; American Land and Leisure, 760/932-9888.

42 CRAGS CAMPGROUND

Scenic rating: 8

on Robinson Creek in
Humboldt-Toiyabe National Forest

Map grid A1

Crags Campground is set at 7,100 feet elevation in the Sierra, one of a series of campgrounds along Robinson Creek near Lower Twin Lake. While this camp does not offer direct access to Lower Twin, home of giant brown trout, it is very close. (See the Lower Twin Lake and Honeymoon Flat listings in this chapter.)

RV sites, facilities: There are 52 sites for tents or RVs up to 45 feet (no hookups). Picnic tables, food lockers, and fire grills are provided. Drinking water and flush toilets are available. Some facilities are wheelchair-accessible. A boat launch (at Lower Twin Lake), store, coin laundry, and coin showers are within a half mile. Leashed pets are permitted.

Reservations, fees: Reservations are accepted at 877/444-6777 or www.recreation.gov ($10 reservation fee). Sites are $15.18–30.36 per night, $5 per night for each additional vehicle. A group site is $95 per night. Open mid-May through mid-November, weather permitting.

Directions: On U.S. 395, drive to Bridgeport and the junction with Twin Lakes Road. Turn west and drive 11 miles to South Twin Road (just before reaching Lower Twin Lake). Turn left and drive over the bridge at Robinson Creek to another road on the left. Turn left and drive a short distance to the campground.

Contact: Humboldt-Toiyabe National Forest, Bridgeport Ranger District, 760/932-7070, fax 760/932-5899; American Land and Leisure, 760/932-9888.

43 LOWER TWIN LAKE

Scenic rating: 9

in Humboldt-Toiyabe National Forest

Map grid A1

The Twin Lakes are actually two lakes, set high in the eastern Sierra at 7,000 feet elevation. Each lake is unique. Lower Twin, known as the fishing lake, with a 5-mph speed limit, has a full resort, marina, boat ramp, and some of the biggest brown trout in the West. The state-record brown—26.5 pounds—was caught here in 1985. Of course, most of the trout are your typical 10- to 12-inch planted rainbow trout, but nobody seems to mind, with the chance of a true monster-sized fish always in the back of the minds of anglers. Upper Twin Lake, with a resort and marina, is a primary destination for boaters, personal watercraft, water-skiers, swimmers, and sailboarders. These lakes are very popular in summer. An option for campers is an excellent trailhead for hiking near Mono Village at the head of Upper Twin Lake. Here you will find Barney Lake Trail, which is routed up the headwaters of Robinson Creek, steeply at times, to Barney Lake, an excellent day hike.

RV sites, facilities: There are 15 paved sites for tents or RVs up to 35 feet (no hookups). Picnic tables and fire grills are provided. Drinking water, flush toilets, and food lockers are available. A boat launch, store, coin showers, and a coin laundry are available nearby. Leashed pets are permitted.

Reservations, fees: Reservations are accepted at 877/444-6777 or www.recreation.gov ($10 reservation fee). Sites are $15.18–17 per night, $5 per night for each additional vehicle. Open early May through mid-October, weather permitting.

Directions: On U.S. 395, drive to Bridgeport and the junction with Twin Lakes Road. Turn west and drive 11 miles to South Twin Road (just before reaching Lower Twin Lake). Turn left and drive over the bridge at Robinson Creek and to the campground entrance road on the right.

Contact: Humboldt-Toiyabe National Forest, Bridgeport Ranger District, 760/932-7070, fax 760/932-5899; American Land and Leisure, 760/932-9888.

44 GREEN CREEK

Scenic rating: 7

in Humboldt-Toiyabe National Forest

Map grid A1

This camp is ideal for backpackers or campers who like to fish for trout in streams. That is because it is set at 7,500 feet, with a trailhead that leads into the Hoover Wilderness and to several high mountain lakes, including Green Lake, West Lake, and East Lake; the ambitious can hike beyond in remote northeastern Yosemite National Park. The camp is set along Green Creek, a fair trout stream with small rainbow trout.

RV sites, facilities: There are 11 sites for tents or RVs up to 35 feet and two group sites for tents or RVs of any length that can accommodate 25–30 people each. No hookups. Picnic tables and fire grills are provided. Drinking water and vault toilets are available. Leashed pets are permitted.

Reservations, fees: Reservations are not accepted for individual sites but are required for group sites at 877/444-6777 or www.recreation.gov ($10 reservation fee). Sites are $15.18 per night, $5 per night for each additional vehicle, and $46.43–58.04 per night for a group site. Open mid-May through early October, weather permitting.

Directions: From Bridgeport, drive south on U.S. 395 for four miles to Green Lakes Road (dirt). Turn right and drive seven miles to the campground.

Contact: Humboldt-Toiyabe National Forest, Bridgeport Ranger District, 760/932-7070, fax 760/932-5899; American Land and Leisure, 760/932-9888.

45 TRUMBULL LAKE

Scenic rating: 8

in Humboldt-Toiyabe National Forest

Map grid A1

This is a high-mountain camp (9,500 feet) at the gateway to a beautiful Sierra basin. Little Trumbull Lake is the first lake on the north side of Virginia Lakes Road, with Virginia Lakes set nearby, along with the Hoover Wilderness and access to many other small lakes by trail. A trail is available that is routed just north of Blue Lake, and then it leads west to Frog Lake, Summit Lake, and beyond into a remote area of Yosemite National Park. If you don't want to rough it, cabins, boat rentals, and a restaurant are available at Virginia Lakes Resort. No gas motors, swimming, and water/body contact is permitted at Virginia Lakes.

RV sites, facilities: There are 45 sites for tents or RVs up to 35 feet (no hookups). Picnic tables and fire grills are provided. Drinking water and pit toilets are available. A store is nearby at the resort. Some facilities are wheelchair-accessible. Leashed pets are permitted.

Reservations, fees: Reservations are accepted at 877/444-6777 or www.recreation.gov ($10 reservation fee). Sites are $13.39–45 per night, $5 per night for each additional vehicle. Open June through September, weather permitting.

Directions: From Bridgeport, drive south on U.S. 395 for 13.5 miles to Virginia Lakes Road. Turn right on Virginia Lakes Road and drive 6.5 miles to the campground entrance road.

Contact: Humboldt-Toiyabe National Forest, Bridgeport Ranger District, 760/932-7070, fax 760/932-5899; American Land and Leisure, 760/932-9888.

46 LUNDY CANYON CAMPGROUND

Scenic rating: 7

near Lundy Lake

Map grid A1

This camp is set high in the eastern Sierra at 7,400 feet elevation along pretty Lundy Creek, the mountain stream that feeds Lundy Lake and then runs downhill, eventually joining other creeks on its trip to nearby Mono Lake. Nearby Lundy Lake (at 7,800 feet elevation) is a long, narrow lake with good fishing for rainbow trout and brown trout. The water is clear and cold, even through the summer. There is a trailhead just west of the lake that is routed steeply up into the Hoover Wilderness to several small pretty lakes, passing two waterfalls about two miles in. A must-do side trip is visiting Mono Lake and its spectacular tufa towers, best done at the Mono Lake Tufa State Reserve along the southern shore of the lake.

RV sites, facilities: There are 50 sites for tents or RVs up to 24 feet (no hookups). Picnic tables and fire rings are provided. Pit toilets are available. No drinking water is available. You can buy supplies in Lee Vining, 8.5 miles away. Leashed pets are permitted.

Reservations, fees: Reservations are not accepted. Sites are $12 per night, with a limit of two vehicles and six people per site. Monthly rates available. Open May through mid-November.

Directions: From Lee Vining, drive north on U.S. 395 for seven miles to Lundy Lake Road. Turn left and drive a short distance to the campground.

CALIFORNIA

Contact: Mono County Public Works, 760/932-5440, fax 760/932-5441.

47 SADDLEBAG LAKE

Scenic rating: 10

in Inyo National Forest

Map grid A1

This camp is set in spectacular high country above tree line, the highest drive-to camp and lake in California, at 10,087 feet elevation. The camp is about a quarter mile from the lake, within walking range of the little store, boat rentals, and a one-minute drive for launching a boat at the ramp. The scenery is stark; everything is granite, ice, or water, with only a few lodgepole pines managing precarious toeholds, sprinkled across the landscape on the access road. An excellent trailhead is available for hiking, with the best hike routed out past little Hummingbird Lake to Lundy Pass. A hikers shuttle boat, which will ferry you across the lake, is a nice plus. Note that with the elevation and the high mountain pass, it can be windy and cold here, and some people find it difficult to catch their breath on simple hikes. In addition, RV users should note that level sites are extremely hard to come by.

RV sites, facilities: There are 20 sites for tents or RVs up to 30 feet (no hookups), and one group tent site for up to 25 people. Drinking water, fire grills, and picnic tables are provided. Flush toilets, boat rentals, and a primitive boat launch are available. A grocery store is nearby. Some facilities are wheelchair-accessible. Leashed pets are permitted.

Reservations, fees: Reservations are not accepted for individual sites, but are required for the group site at 877/444-6777 or www.recreation.gov ($10 reservation fee). Sites are $17 per night, $45 per night for the group site for up to 15 people, $60 per night for the group site for 16 people or more. Open late June through early September, weather permitting.

Directions: On U.S. 395, drive 0.5 mile south of Lee Vining and the junction with Highway 120. Turn west and drive about 11 miles to Saddlebag Lake Road. Turn right and drive 2.5 miles to the campground on the right.

From Merced, drive east on Highway 140 to the Arch Rock entrance station. Continue east to the Big Oak Flat Road junction (0.5 mile before entering Yosemite Valley). Turn left and drive 14 miles to Tioga Road. Turn right and drive about 65 miles (past Tuolumne Meadows) and through the Tioga Pass entrance station. Continue two miles to Saddlebag Lake Road. Turn left and drive 2.5 miles (rough road) to the campground on the right.

Contact: Inyo National Forest, Mono Basin Scenic Area Ranger Station and Visitor Center, 760/647-3044, fax 760/647-3046.

48 LOWER LEE VINING CAMP

Scenic rating: 7

near Lee Vining

Map grid A1

This former Mono County camp and its neighboring camps—Cattleguard, Moraine, Aspen, Big Bend, and Boulder—can be a godsend for vacationers who show up at Yosemite National Park and make the discovery that there are no sites left, a terrible experience for some late-night arrivals. But these Forest Service campgrounds provide a great safety valve, even if they are extremely primitive, on the edge of timber. Lee Vining Creek is the highlight, flowing right past the campgrounds along Highway 120, bound for Mono Lake to the nearby east. It is stocked regularly during the fishing season. A must-do side trip is venturing to the south shore of Mono Lake to walk amid the bizarre yet beautiful tufa towers. There is good rock-climbing and hiking in the area. Although sunshine is the norm, be prepared for all kinds of weather: It can snow every month of the year here. Short but lively thunderstorms are common in early summer. Other nearby trips are available to Mammoth Lakes, June Lake, and Bodie State Park.

RV sites, facilities: There are 54 sites for tents

or RVs up to 40 feet (no hookups). Picnic tables, food lockers, and fire rings are provided. Portable toilets are available. No drinking water is available. You can buy supplies in Lee Vining (about two miles away). Leashed pets are permitted.

Reservations, fees: Reservations are not accepted. Sites are $14 per night. Open May through October, weather permitting.

Directions: On U.S. 395, drive to just south of Lee Vining and the junction with Highway 120. Turn west on Highway 120 and drive about 2.5 miles. Turn left into the campground entrance.

Contact: Inyo National Forest, Mono Basin Scenic Area Ranger Station and Visitor Center, 760/647-3044, fax 760/647-3046.

49 CATTLEGUARD CAMP

Scenic rating: 7

near Lee Vining

Map grid A1

This camp is an alternative to Yosemite National Park. Though primitive, it has several advantages: It is quiet, gets more sun than the three neighboring camps (Lower Lee Vining, Moraine, and Boulder), and provides the best views of Dana Plateau. (For more information, see the Lower Lee Vining Camp listing in this chapter.)

RV sites, facilities: There are 15 sites for tents or RVs up to 40 feet (no hookups). Picnic tables, food lockers, and fire rings are provided. Pit toilets are available. No drinking water is available. You can buy supplies in Lee Vining (about two miles away). Leashed pets are permitted.

Reservations, fees: Reservations are not accepted. Sites are $14 per night. A 14-day limit is enforced. Open May through October, weather permitting.

Directions: On U.S. 395, drive to just south of Lee Vining and the junction with Highway 120. Turn west on Highway 120 and drive about three miles. Turn left into the campground entrance.

50 MORAINE CAMP

Scenic rating: 7

near Lee Vining

Map grid A1

This camp provides an alternative to Yosemite National Park. (For more information, see the Lower Lee Vining Camp listing in this chapter.)

RV sites, facilities: There are 20 sites for tents or RVs up to 40 feet (no hookups). Picnic tables and fire rings are provided. Pit toilets are available. There is no drinking water. You can buy supplies in Lee Vining (about two miles away). Leashed pets are permitted.

Reservations, fees: Reservations are not accepted. Sites are $14 per night. Open May through October, weather permitting.

Directions: On U.S. 395, drive to just south of Lee Vining and the junction with Highway 120. Turn west on Highway 120 and drive 3.5 miles to Poole Power Plant Road. Exit left onto Poole Power Plant Road and drive 0.25 mile to the campground entrance at the end of the road.

Contact: Inyo National Forest, Mono Basin Scenic Area Ranger Station and Visitor Center, 760/647-3044, fax 760/647-3046.

51 BIG BEND

Scenic rating: 8

on Lee Vining Creek in Inyo National Forest

Map grid A1

This camp is set in sparse but beautiful country along Lee Vining Creek at 7,800 feet elevation. Ancient pine trees are on site. It is an excellent bet for an overflow camp if Tuolumne Meadows in nearby Yosemite is packed. The view from the camp to the north features Mono Dome (10,614 feet) and Lee Vining Peak (11,691 feet).

CALIFORNIA

RV sites, facilities: There are 17 sites for tents or RVs up to 30 feet (no hookups). Picnic tables, food lockers, and fire grills are provided. Drinking water and vault toilets are available. Some facilities are wheelchair-accessible. Leashed pets are permitted.

Reservations, fees: Reservations are not accepted. Sites are $17 per night. A 14-day limit is enforced. Open late April through mid-October, weather permitting.

Directions: On U.S. 395, drive to just south of Lee Vining and the junction with Highway 120. Turn west on Highway 120 and drive about 3.5 miles to Poole Power Plant Road and the signed campground access road on the right. Turn right and drive a short distance to the camp.

Contact: Inyo National Forest, Mono Basin Scenic Area Ranger Station and Visitor Center, 760/647-3044, fax 760/647-3046.

52 ASPEN

Scenic rating: 8

on Lee Vining Creek

Map grid A1

This high-country, primitive camp is set along Lee Vining Creek at 7,500 feet elevation, on the eastern slopes of the Sierra just east of Yosemite National Park. Take the side trip to moonlike Mono Lake, best seen at the south shore's Tufa State Reserve.

RV sites, facilities: There are 56 sites for tents or RVs up to 40 feet (no hookups). Picnic tables and fire rings are provided. Portable toilets are available. Drinking water is available. You can buy supplies in Lee Vining. Leashed pets are permitted.

Reservations, fees: Reservations are not accepted. Sites are $14 per night. A 14-day limit is enforced. Open May through October, weather permitting.

Directions: On U.S. 395, drive to just south of Lee Vining and the junction with Highway 120. Turn west on Highway 120 and drive about 3.5 miles. Exit onto Poole Power Plant

Road. Turn left and drive about four miles west to the campground on the left.

Contact: Inyo National Forest, Mono Basin Scenic Area Ranger Station and Visitor Center, 760/647-3044, fax 760/647-3046.

53 JUNCTION

Scenic rating: 7

near Ellery and Tioga Lakes in Inyo National Forest

Map grid A1

Which way do you go? From Junction, any way you choose, you can't miss. Two miles to the north is Saddlebag Lake, the highest drive-to lake (10,087 feet) in California. Directly across the road is Ellery Lake, and a mile to the south is Tioga Lake, two beautiful, pristine waters with trout fishing. To the east is Mono Lake, and to the west is Yosemite National Park. From camp, it is a one-mile hike to Bennetville, a historic camp. Take your pick. Camp elevation is 9,600 feet.

RV sites, facilities: There are 13 sites for tents or RVs up to 30 feet (no hookups). Picnic tables, food lockers, and fire grills are provided. Pit toilets are available. No drinking water is available. Some facilities are wheelchair-accessible. Leashed pets are permitted.

Reservations, fees: Reservations are not accepted. Sites are $12 per night. Open early June through mid-October, weather permitting.

Directions: On U.S. 395, drive to just south of Lee Vining and the junction with Highway 120. Turn west on Highway 120 and drive about 10 miles to Saddlebag Road and the campground on the right side of the road.

From Merced, drive east on Highway 140 to the Arch Rock entrance station. Continue east to the Big Oak Flat Road junction (0.5 mile before entering Yosemite Valley). Turn left and drive 14 miles to Tioga Road. Turn right and drive about 65 miles (past Tuolumne Meadows) and through the Tioga Pass entrance station. Continue two miles to Saddlebag Lake Road and the campground on the left side of the road.

Contact: Inyo National Forest, Mono Basin

Scenic Area Ranger Station and Visitor Center, 760/647-3044, fax 760/647-3046.

54 TIOGA LAKE

Scenic rating: 9

in Inyo National Forest

Map grid A1

Tioga Lake is a dramatic sight, with gemlike blue waters encircled by Sierra granite at 9,700 feet elevation. Together with adjacent Ellery Lake, it makes a pair of gorgeous waters with near-lake camping, trout fishing (stocked with rainbow trout), and access to Yosemite National Park and Saddlebag Lake. Conditions here are much like those at neighboring Ellery. The only downers: It can get windy here (no foolin'!) and the camps fill quickly from the overflow crowds at Tuolumne Meadows. (See the Ellery Lake listing for more information.)

RV sites, facilities: There are 13 sites for tents or RVs up to 30 feet (no hookups). Picnic tables, food lockers, and fire grills are provided. Drinking water and pit toilets are available. Some facilities are wheelchair-accessible. Leashed pets are permitted.

Reservations, fees: Reservations are not accepted. Sites are $17 per night. Open early June through mid-October, weather permitting.

Directions: On U.S. 395, drive to just south of Lee Vining and the junction with Highway 120. Turn west on Highway 120 and drive about 11 miles (just past Ellery Lake) to the campground on the left side of the road.

From Merced, drive east on Highway 140 to the Arch Rock entrance station. Continue east to the Big Oak Flat Road junction (0.5 mile before entering Yosemite Valley). Turn left and drive 14 miles to Tioga Road. Turn right and drive about 65 miles (past Tuolumne Meadows) and through the Tioga Pass entrance station. Continue one mile to the campground entrance road on the right side of the road.

Contact: Inyo National Forest, Mono Basin Scenic Area Ranger Station and Visitor Center, 760/647-3044, fax 760/647-3046.

55 ELLERY LAKE

Scenic rating: 9

in Inyo National Forest

Map grid A1

Ellery Lake offers all the spectacular beauty of Yosemite but is two miles outside park borders. That means it is stocked with trout by the Department of Fish and Game (no lakes in Yosemite are planted, hence the lousy fishing). Just like neighboring Tioga Lake, here are deep-blue waters set in rock in the 9,500-foot-elevation range, one of the most pristine highway-access lake settings anywhere. Although there is no boat ramp, boats with small motors are allowed and can be hand-launched. Nearby Saddlebag Lake, the highest drive-to lake in California, is a common side trip. Whenever Tuolumne Meadows fills in Yosemite, this camp fills shortly thereafter. Camp elevation is 9,500 feet.

RV sites, facilities: There are 21 sites for tents or RVs up to 30 feet (no hookups). Picnic tables and fire grills are provided. Drinking water, food lockers, and pit toilets are available. A grocery store is nearby. Some facilities are wheelchair-accessible. Leashed pets are permitted.

Reservations, fees: Reservations are not accepted. Sites are $17 per night. Open early June through mid-October, weather permitting.

Directions: On U.S. 395, drive to just south of Lee Vining and the junction with Highway 120. Turn west on Highway 120 and drive about 10 miles to the campground on the left side of the road.

From Merced, drive east on Highway 140 to the Arch Rock entrance station. Continue east to the Big Oak Flat Road junction (0.5 mile before entering Yosemite Valley). Turn left and drive 14 miles to Tioga Road. Turn right and drive about 65 miles (past Tuolumne Meadows) and through the Tioga Pass entrance station. Continue four miles to the campground entrance road on the right.

Contact: Inyo National Forest, Mono Basin Scenic Area Ranger Station and Visitor Center, 760/647-3044, fax 760/647-3046.

CALIFORNIA

56 SILVER LAKE

Scenic rating: 9

in Inyo National Forest

Map grid A1

Silver Lake is set at 7,200 feet elevation, an 80-acre lake in the June Lake Loop with Carson Peak looming in the background. Boat rentals, fishing for trout at the lake, a beautiful trout stream (Rush Creek) next to the camp, and a nearby trailhead for wilderness hiking and horseback riding (rentals available) are the highlights. The camp is largely exposed and vulnerable to winds, the only downer. Within walking distance to the south is Silver Lake, always a pretty sight, especially when afternoon winds cause the lake surface to sparkle in crackling silvers. The lake speed limit is 10 mph. Swimming is not recommended because of the rocky shoreline. Just across the road from the camp is a great trailhead for the Ansel Adams Wilderness, with a two-hour hike that climbs to pretty Agnew Lake overlooking the June Lake basin; wilderness permit required for overnight use.

RV sites, facilities: There are 63 sites for tents or RVs up to 32 feet (no hookups). Picnic tables, food lockers, and fire rings are provided. Drinking water, flush toilets, and horseback-riding facilities are available. A grocery store, coin laundry, motorboat rentals, boat ramp, bait, café, boat fuel, and propane gas are nearby. Some facilities are wheelchair-accessible. Leashed pets are permitted.

Reservations, fees: Reservations are accepted at 877/444-6777 or www.recreation.gov ($10 reservation fee). Sites are $18 per night. A 14-day limit is enforced. Open late April through early November, weather permitting.

Directions: From Lee Vining on U.S. 395, drive south for six miles to the first Highway 158 north/June Lake Loop turnoff. Turn west (right) and drive nine miles (past Grant Lake) to Silver Lake. Just as you arrive at Silver Lake (a small store is on the right), turn left at the campground entrance.

Contact: Inyo National Forest, Mono Basin Scenic Area Ranger Station and Visitor Center, 760/647-3044, fax 760/647-3046.

57 OH! RIDGE

Scenic rating: 8

on June Lake in Inyo National Forest

Map grid A1

This is the largest of the campgrounds on June Lake. However, it is not the most popular since it is not right on the lakeshore, but back about a quarter mile or so from the north end of the lake. Regardless, it has the best views of the lake, with the ridge of the high Sierra providing a backdrop. The lake is a good one for trout fishing. The elevation is 7,600 feet.

RV sites, facilities: There are 148 sites for tents or RVs up to 40 feet (no hookups). Picnic tables and fire grills are provided. Drinking water, flush toilets, and a swimming beach are available. A grocery store, coin laundry, volleyball, amphitheater, boat ramp, boat and tackle rentals, moorings, and propane gas are nearby. Some facilities are wheelchair-accessible. Leashed pets are permitted.

Reservations, fees: Reservations are accepted at 877/444-6777 or www.recreation.gov ($10 reservation fee). Sites are $15–18 per night. Open late April through early November, weather permitting.

Directions: From Lee Vining, drive south on U.S. 395 (past the first Highway 158/June Lake Loop turnoff) to June Lake Junction (a gas station/store is on the west side of the road) and Highway 158 south. Turn west on Highway 158 south and drive two miles to Oh! Ridge Road. Turn right and drive a mile to the campground access road (signed). Turn left and drive to the campground.

Contact: Inyo National Forest, Mono Basin Scenic Area Ranger Station and Visitor Center, 760/647-3044, fax 760/647-3046.

CALIFORNIA

58 PINE CLIFF RESORT

Scenic rating: 7

at June Lake

Map grid A1

You'll find "kid heaven" at Pine Cliff Resort. This camp is in a pretty setting along the north shore of June Lake (7,600 feet elevation), the feature lake among four in the June Lake Loop. The campsites are nestled in pine trees, designed so each site accommodates different-sized rigs and families, and the campground is set about a quarter mile from June Lake. This is the only camp at June Lake Loop that has a swimming beach. The landscape is a pretty one, with the lake set below snowcapped peaks. The bonus is that June Lake gets large numbers of trout plants each summer, making it extremely popular with anglers. Of the lakes in the June Lake Loop, this is the one that has the most of everything—the most beauty, the most fish, the most developed accommodations, and, alas, the most people. This resort has been operated as a family business for more than 50 years.

RV sites, facilities: There are 154 sites with full hookups (20 and 30 amps) for RVs, 17 sites with partial hookups (20 and 30 amps) for tents or RVs, and 55 sites for tents; a few sites are pull-through. There are also 14 rental trailers. Picnic tables and fire rings are provided. Restrooms with flush toilets and coin showers, drinking water, coin laundry, basketball, volleyball, tetherball, horseshoes, convenience store, and propane gas are available. Some facilities are wheelchair-accessible. A primitive boat ramp, fish-cleaning facilities, and fuel are nearby. Leashed pets are permitted, with a maximum of two pets per site.

Reservations, fees: Reservations are recommended. Sites are $16–26 per night, $5 per night for each additional vehicle, $1 per person per night for more than four people. The first pet is free, and the second pet is $1 per night. Open mid-April through October.

Directions: From Lee Vining, drive south on U.S. 395 (passing the first Highway 158 north/June Lake Loop turnoff) to June Lake Junction (a sign is posted for "June Lake Village") and Highway 158 south. Turn right (west) on Highway 158 south and drive two miles to North Shore Drive (a sign is nearby for Pine Cliff Resort). Turn right and drive 0.5 mile to Pine Cliff Road. Turn left and drive 0.5 mile to the resort store on the right (route is well signed).

Contact: Pine Cliff Resort, 760/648-7558.

59 GULL LAKE

Scenic rating: 8

in Inyo National Forest

Map grid A1

Little Gull Lake, just 64 acres, is the smallest of the lakes on the June Lake Loop, but to many it is the prettiest. It is set at 7,600 feet, just west of June Lake and, with Carson Peak looming on the Sierra crest to the west, it is a dramatic and intimate setting. The lake is stocked with trout each summer, providing good fishing. A boat ramp is on the lake's southwest corner. Insider's tip: There is a rope swing at Gull Lake that youngsters love.

RV sites, facilities: There are 11 sites for tents or RVs up to 30 feet (no hookups). Drinking water, fire grills, and picnic tables are provided, and flush toilets are available. A grocery store, coin laundry, boat ramp, and propane gas are nearby. Some facilities are wheelchair-accessible. Leashed pets are permitted.

Reservations, fees: Reservations are not accepted. Sites are $18 per night. Open late April through early November, weather permitting.

Directions: From Lee Vining, drive south on U.S. 395 (past the first Highway 158/June Lake Loop turnoff) to June Lake Junction (a gas station/store is on the west side of the road) and Highway 158. Turn west on Highway 158 and drive three miles to the campground entrance on the right side of the road.

Contact: Inyo National Forest, Mono Basin Scenic Area Ranger Station and Visitor Center, 760/647-3044, fax 760/647-3046.

CALIFORNIA

60 REVERSED CREEK

in Inyo National Forest

Map grid A1

This camp is set at 7,600 feet elevation near pretty Reversed Creek, the only stream in the region that flows toward the mountains, not away from them. It is a small, tree-lined stream that provides decent trout fishing. The campsites are sheltered and set in a grove of aspen, but close enough to the road so you can still hear highway traffic. There are also cabins available for rent near here. Directly opposite the camp, on the other side of the road, is Gull Lake and the boat ramp. Two miles to the west, on the west side of the road, is the trailhead for the hike to Fern Lake on the edge of the Ansel Adams Wilderness, a little butt-kicker of a climb.

RV sites, facilities: There are 17 sites for tents or RVs up to 30 feet (no hookups). Picnic tables and fire grills are provided. Drinking water and flush toilets are available. A grocery store, coin laundry, and propane gas are nearby. Boating is available at nearby Silver Lake, two miles away. Some facilities are wheelchair-accessible. Leashed pets are permitted.

Reservations, fees: Reservations are not accepted. Sites are $18 per night. Open mid-May through October, weather permitting.

Directions: From Lee Vining, drive south on U.S. 395 (past the first Highway 158/June Lake Loop turnoff) to June Lake Junction (a gas station/store is on the west side of the road) and Highway 158 south. Turn right (west) on Highway 158 south and drive three miles to the campground on the left side of the road (across from Gull Lake).

Contact: Inyo National Forest, Mono Basin Scenic Area Ranger Station and Visitor Center, 760/647-3044, fax 760/647-3046.

61 JUNE LAKE

in Inyo National Forest

Map grid A1

June Lake gets the highest use of all the lakes in the June Lakes Loop, and it has the best swimming, best fishing, and best sailboarding. There are three campgrounds at pretty June Lake; this is one of the two operated by the Forest Service (the other is Oh! Ridge). This one is on the northeast shore of the lake at 7,600 feet elevation, a pretty spot with all supplies available just two miles to the south in the town of June Lake. The nearest boat launch is north of town. This is a good lake for trout fishing, receiving high numbers of stocked trout each year. A 10-mph speed limit is enforced.

RV sites, facilities: There are 28 sites for tents or RVs up to 32 feet (no hookups). Picnic tables, food lockers, and fire grills are provided. Drinking water, restrooms with flush toilets and coin showers, and boat ramp are available. A grocery store, coin laundry, boat and tackle rentals, moorings, and propane gas are nearby. Leashed pets are permitted.

Reservations, fees: Reservations are accepted at 877/444-6777 or www.recreation.gov ($10 reservation fee). Sites are $18 per night. Open late April through early November, weather permitting.

Directions: From Lee Vining, drive south on U.S. 395 (passing Highway 158 North) for 20 miles (six miles past Highway 158 north) to June Lake Junction (signed "June Lake Village") and Highway 158 south. Turn west (right) on Highway 158 south and drive two miles to June Lake. Turn right (signed) and drive a short distance to the campground.

Contact: Inyo National Forest, Mono Basin Scenic Area Ranger Station and Visitor Center, 760/647-3044, fax 760/647-3046.

CALIFORNIA

62 HARTLEY SPRINGS

Scenic rating: 8

in Inyo National Forest

Map grid A1

Even though this camp is only a five-minute drive from U.S. 395, those five minutes will take you into another orbit. It is set in a forest of Jeffrey pine and has the feel of a remote, primitive camp, set in a high-mountain environment at an elevation of 8,400 feet. About two miles to the immediate north, at 8,611 feet, is Obsidian Dome "Glass Flow," a craggy geologic formation that some people enjoy scrambling around and exploring; pick your access point carefully.

RV sites, facilities: There are 20 sites for tents or RVs up to 40 feet (no hookups). Picnic tables and fire grills are provided. Vault toilets are available. No drinking water is available. Garbage must be packed out. Leashed pets are permitted.

Reservations, fees: Reservations are not accepted. There is no fee for camping. (Note: This is one of four campgrounds in the Mono Basin Scenic Area that may impose a camping fee.) Open late May through early November, weather permitting.

Directions: From Lee Vining, drive south on U.S. 395 (passing the first Highway 158/June Lake Loop turnoff) for 10 miles to June Lake Junction. Continue south on U.S. 395 for six miles to Glass Creek Road (a dirt road on the west side of the highway). Turn west (right) and drive two miles to the campground entrance road on the left.

Contact: Inyo National Forest, Mono Basin Scenic Area Ranger Station and Visitor Center, 760/647-3044, fax 760/647-3046.

63 AGNEW MEADOWS AND EQUESTRIAN CAMP

Scenic rating: 9

in Inyo National Forest

Map grid A1

This is a perfect camp to use as a launching pad for a backpacking trip or day of fly-fishing for trout. It is set along the Upper San Joaquin River at 8,400 feet, with a trailhead for the Pacific Crest Trail available near the camp. From here you can hike seven miles to the gorgeous Thousand Island Lake, a beautiful lake sprinkled with islands set below Banner and Ritter Peaks in the spectacular Minarets. For day hiking, walk the River Trail, which is routed from Agnew Meadows along the San Joaquin. The trail provides access to excellent fishing with a chance at the grand slam of California trout—four species in a single day (though the trout are small).

RV sites, facilities: There are 21 sites for tents or RVs up to 45 feet, and four group sites for tents or RVs that can accommodate 10–20 people each. No hookups. Picnic tables and fire grills are provided. Drinking water, vault toilets, and horseback-riding facilities are available (three family sites have hitching racks where horse camping is permitted). Supplies can be obtained at Red's Meadow store. Leashed pets are permitted.

Reservations, fees: Reservations are not accepted for individual sites, but are required for equestrian sites and group sites at 877/444-6777 or www.recreation.gov ($10 reservation fee). Sites are $18 per night for individual sites, $15–30 per night group sites, $22 per night for equestrian site, plus $4–7 per person Reds Meadow/Agnew Meadows access fee. Open mid-June through mid-September, weather permitting.

Directions: On U.S. 395, drive to Mammoth Junction/Highway 203. Turn west on Highway 203 and drive four miles, through the town of Mammoth Lakes to Minaret Road (still Highway 203). Turn right and drive five miles to Minaret Station (past the Mammoth Mountain Ski Area). Continue for 2.6 miles to the campground entrance road on the right. Turn right and drive just under a mile to the campground. Note: The access road to the group sites is steep and narrow.

Note: Noncampers are required to use a shuttle bus (fee) from the shuttle bus terminal at Mammoth Mountain Main Lodge Gondola

Station 7 A.M.–7:30 P.M. Space is available for leashed dogs, bikes, and backpacks.

Contact: Inyo National Forest, Mammoth Ranger Station and Visitor Center, 760/924-5500, fax 760/924-5547.

64 PUMICE FLAT

Scenic rating: 8

on the San Joaquin River in Inyo National Forest

Map grid A1

Pumice Flat (7,700 feet elevation) provides roadside camping within short range of several adventures. A trail out of camp links with the Pacific Crest Trail, where you can hike along the Upper San Joaquin River for miles, with excellent access for fly-fishing, and head north into the Ansel Adams Wilderness. Devils Postpile National Monument is just two miles south, along with the trailhead for Rainbow Falls.

RV sites, facilities: There are 17 sites for tents or RVs up to 45 feet (no hookups). Picnic tables and fire grills are provided. Drinking water, vault toilets, and horseback-riding facilities are available. Limited supplies are available at a small store, or buy full supplies in Mammoth Lakes. Leashed pets are permitted.

Reservations, fees: Reservations are not accepted. Sites are $18 per night, plus $4–7 per person Reds Meadow/Agnew Meadows access fee. Open mid-June through mid-September, weather permitting.

Directions: On U.S. 395, drive to Mammoth Junction/Highway 203. Turn west on Highway 203 and drive four miles, through the town of Mammoth Lakes to Minaret Road (still Highway 203). Turn right and drive five miles to Minaret Station (past the Mammoth Mountain Ski Area). Continue for 5.1 miles to the campground on the right.

Note: Noncampers are required to use a shuttle bus (fee) from the shuttle bus terminal at Mammoth Mountain Main Lodge Gondola Station 7 A.M.–7:30 P.M. Space is available for leashed dogs, bikes, and backpacks.

Contact: Inyo National Forest, Mammoth Ranger Station and Visitor Center, 760/924-5500, fax 760/924-5547.

65 UPPER SODA SPRINGS

Scenic rating: 8

on the San Joaquin River in Inyo National Forest

Map grid A1

This is a premium location within earshot of the Upper San Joaquin River and within minutes of many first-class recreation options. The river is stocked with trout at this camp, with several good pools within short walking distance. Farther upstream, accessible by an excellent trail, are smaller wild trout that provide good fly-fishing prospects. Devils Postpile National Monument, a massive formation of ancient columnar jointed rock, is only three miles to the south. The Pacific Crest Trail passes right by the camp, providing a trailhead for access to numerous lakes in the Ansel Adams Wilderness. The elevation is 7,700 feet.

RV sites, facilities: There are 29 sites for tents or RVs up to 36 feet (no hookups). Picnic tables and fire grills are provided. Drinking water, flush toilets, and horseback-riding facilities are available. Limited supplies can be obtained at Red's Meadow store. Leashed pets are permitted.

Reservations, fees: Reservations are not accepted. Sites are $18 per night, plus $4–7 per person Reds Meadow/Agnew Meadows access fee. Open mid-June through mid-September, weather permitting.

Directions: On U.S. 395, drive to Mammoth Junction/Highway 203. Turn west on Highway 203 and drive four miles, through the town of Mammoth Lakes to Minaret Road (still Highway 203). Turn right and drive five miles to Minaret Station (past the Mammoth Mountain Ski Area). Continue for 5.1 miles to the campground entrance road on the right. Turn right and drive 0.25 mile to the campground.

Note: Noncampers are required to use a shuttle bus (fee) from the shuttle bus terminal at Mammoth Mountain Main Lodge Gondola Station 7 A.M.–7:30 P.M. Space is available for leashed dogs, bikes, and backpacks.

Contact: Inyo National Forest, Mammoth Ranger Station and Visitor Center, 760/924-5500, fax 760/924-5547.

66 PUMICE FLAT GROUP CAMP

🏃 🎣 🐕 🚐 ⛺

Scenic rating: 6

on the San Joaquin River in Inyo National Forest
Map grid A1

Pumice Flat Group Camp is set at 7,700 feet elevation near the Upper San Joaquin River, adjacent to Pumice Flat. (For recreation information, see the Pumice Flat listing in this chapter.)

RV sites, facilities: There are four group sites for tents or RVs up to 45 feet (no hookups) that can accommodate 20–50 people each. Picnic tables and fire grills are provided. Drinking water, flush toilets, and horseback-riding facilities are available. You can buy supplies in Mammoth Lakes. Leashed pets are permitted.

Reservations, fees: Reservations are accepted at 877/444-6777 or www.recreation.gov ($10 reservation fee). Sites are $40–110 per night per group, plus $4–7 per person Reds Meadow/Agnew Meadows access fee. Open mid-June through mid-September, weather permitting.

Directions: On U.S. 395, drive to Mammoth Junction/Highway 203. Turn west on Highway 203 and drive four miles, through the town of Mammoth Lakes to Minaret Road (still Highway 203). Turn right and drive five miles to Minaret Station (past the Mammoth Mountain Ski Area). Continue for 5.1 miles to the campground on the left side of the road.

Note: Noncampers are required to use a shuttle bus (fee) from the shuttle bus terminal at Mammoth Mountain Main Lodge Gondola Station 7 A.M.–7:30 P.M. Space is available for leashed dogs, bikes, and backpacks.

Contact: Inyo National Forest, Mammoth Ranger Station and Visitor Center, 760/924-5500, fax 760/924-5547.

67 MINARET FALLS

🏃 🎣 🐕 ♿ 🚐 ⛺

Scenic rating: 8

on the San Joaquin River in Inyo National Forest
Map grid A1

This camp has one of the prettiest settings of the series of camps along the Upper San Joaquin River and near Devils Postpile National Monument. It is set at 7,600 feet elevation near Minaret Creek, across from where beautiful Minaret Falls pours into the San Joaquin River. Devils Postpile National Monument, one of the best examples in the world of hexagonal, columnar jointed rock, is less than a mile from camp, where there is also a trail to awesome Rainbow Falls. The Pacific Crest Trail runs right through this area as well, and if you hike to the south, there is excellent streamside fishing access.

RV sites, facilities: There are 28 sites for tents or RVs up to 47 feet (no hookups). Picnic tables and fire grills are provided. Drinking water and vault toilets are available. Horseback-riding facilities are nearby. You can buy limited supplies at Red's Meadow store, or all supplies in Mammoth Lakes. Some facilities are wheelchair-accessible. Leashed pets are permitted.

Reservations, fees: Reservations are not accepted. Sites are $18 per night, plus $4–7 per person Reds Meadow/Agnew Meadows access fee. Open mid-June through mid-September, weather permitting.

Directions: On U.S. 395, drive to Mammoth Junction/Highway 203. Turn west on Highway 203 and drive four miles, through the town of Mammoth Lakes to Minaret Road (still Highway 203). Turn right and drive five miles to Minaret Station (past the Mammoth Mountain Ski Area). Continue for six miles to the campground entrance road on the right. Turn right and drive 0.25 mile to the campground.

Note: Noncampers are required to use a shuttle bus from the shuttle bus terminal at Mammoth Mountain Main Lodge Gondola Station 7 A.M.–7:30 P.M. Space is available for leashed dogs, bikes, and backpacks.

Contact: Inyo National Forest, Mammoth

CALIFORNIA

Ranger Station and Visitor Center, 760/924-5500, fax 760/924-5547.

68 DEVILS POSTPILE NATIONAL MONUMENT

Scenic rating: 9

near the San Joaquin River

Map grid A1

Devils Postpile is a spectacular and rare example of hexagonal, columnar jointed rock that looks like posts, hence the name. The camp is set at 7,600 feet elevation and provides nearby access for the easy hike to the Postpile. Guided walks are offered during the summer; call for details. If you keep walking, it is a 2.5-mile walk to Rainbow Falls, a breathtaking 101-foot cascade that produces rainbows in its floating mist, seen only from the trail alongside the waterfall looking downstream. The camp is also adjacent to the Middle Fork San Joaquin River and the Pacific Crest Trail.

RV sites, facilities: There are 21 sites for tents or RVs up to 25 feet (no hookups). Picnic tables, food lockers, and fire grills are provided. Drinking water and flush toilets are available. Some facilities are wheelchair-accessible. Leashed pets are permitted.

Reservations, fees: Reservations are not accepted. Sites are $18 per night, plus $4–7 per person Reds Meadow/Devils Postpile access fee. Open mid-June through mid-October, weather permitting, with a two-week maximum stay. Note: National Parks Pass and Golden Passport are not accepted.

Directions: On U.S. 395, drive to Mammoth Junction/Highway 203. Turn west on Highway 203 and drive four miles, through the town of Mammoth Lakes to Minaret Road (still Highway 203). Turn right and drive five miles to Minaret Station (past the Mammoth Mountain Ski Area). Continue for nine miles to the campground entrance road on the right.

Note: Noncampers are required to use a shuttle bus from the shuttle bus terminal at Mammoth Mountain Main Lodge Gondola

Station 7 A.M.–7:30 P.M. Space is available for leashed dogs, bikes, and backpacks.

Contact: Devils Postpile National Monument, 760/934-2289, www.nps.gov/depo.

69 RED'S MEADOW

Scenic rating: 6

in Inyo National Forest

Map grid A1

Red's Meadow has long been established as one of the best outfitters for horseback-riding trips. To get the feel of it, three-mile round-trip rides are available to Rainbow Falls. Multiday trips into the Ansel Adams Wilderness on the Pacific Crest Trail are also offered. A small restaurant is a bonus here, always a must-stop for long-distance hikers getting a shot to chomp their first hamburger in weeks, something like a bear finding a candy bar, quite a sight for the drive-in campers. The nearby Devils Postpile National Monument, Rainbow Falls, Minaret Falls, and San Joaquin River provide recreation options. The elevation is 7,600 feet.

RV sites, facilities: There are 56 sites for tents or RVs up to 30 feet (no hookups). Picnic tables, food lockers, and fire grills are provided. Drinking water, flush toilets, horseback riding, and natural hot springs are available. You can buy limited supplies at a small store. Leashed pets are permitted.

Reservations, fees: Reservations are not accepted. Sites are $18 per night, plus $4–7 per person Reds Meadow/Agnew Meadows access fee. Open mid-June through mid-September, weather permitting.

Directions: On U.S. 395, drive to Mammoth Junction/Highway 203. Turn west on Highway 203 and drive four miles, through the town of Mammoth Lakes to Minaret Road (still Highway 203). Turn right and drive five miles to Minaret Station (past the Mammoth Mountain Ski Area). Continue for 7.4 miles to the campground entrance on the left.

Note: Noncampers are required to use a shuttle bus from the shuttle bus terminal at Mammoth Mountain Main Lodge Gondola

Station 7 A.M.–7:30 P.M. Space is available for leashed dogs, bikes, and backpacks.

Contact: Inyo National Forest, Mammoth Ranger Station and Visitor Center, 760/924-5500, fax 760/924-5547.

70 LAKE GEORGE

Scenic rating: 8

in Inyo National Forest

Map grid A1

The sites here have views of Lake George, a beautiful lake in a rock basin set below the spectacular Crystal Crag. Lake George is at 9,000 feet elevation, a small lake fed by creeks coming from both Crystal Lake and TJ Lake. TJ Lake is only about a 20-minute walk from the campground, and Crystal Lake is about a 45-minute romp; both make excellent short hiking trips. Trout fishing at Lake George is decent—not great, not bad, but decent. Swimming is not allowed, but boats with small motors are permitted.

RV sites, facilities: There are 16 sites for tents or RVs up to 25 feet (no hookups). Picnic tables and fire grills are provided. Drinking water and flush toilets are available. A grocery store, coin laundry, coin showers, primitive boat launch, and propane gas are nearby. Leashed pets are permitted.

Reservations, fees: Reservations are not accepted. Sites are $19 per night with a seven-day limit. Open mid-June through mid-September, weather permitting.

Directions: From Lee Vining on U.S. 395, drive south for 25 miles to Mammoth Junction and Highway 203/Minaret Summit Road. Turn west on Highway 203 and drive four miles to Lake Mary Road. Continue straight through the intersection and drive four miles to Lake Mary Loop Drive. Turn left and drive 0.3 mile to Lake George Road. Turn right and drive 0.5 mile to the campground.

Contact: Inyo National Forest, Mammoth Ranger Station and Visitor Center, 760/924-5500, fax 760/924-5547.

71 GLASS CREEK

Scenic rating: 5

in Inyo National Forest

Map grid B1

This primitive camp is set along Glass Creek at 7,600 feet elevation, about a mile from Obsidian Dome to the nearby west. A trail follows Glass Creek past the southern edge of the dome, a craggy, volcanic formation that tops out at 8,611 feet elevation. That trail continues along Glass Creek, climbing to the foot of San Joaquin Mountain for a great view of the high desert to the east. Insider's tip: The Department of Fish and Game stocks Glass Creek with trout just once each June, right at the camp.

RV sites, facilities: There are 50 sites for tents or RVs up to 40 feet (no hookups). Picnic tables and fire grills are provided. Vault toilets are available. No drinking water is available. Some facilities are wheelchair-accessible. Leashed pets are permitted.

Reservations, fees: Reservations are not accepted. There is no fee for camping. (Note: This is one of four campgrounds in the Mono Basin Scenic Area that may impose a camping fee.) A 42-day limit is enforced. Open late April through early November, weather permitting.

Directions: From Lee Vining, drive south on U.S. 395 (past the first Highway 158/June Lake Loop turnoff) for 11 miles to June Lake Junction. Continue south on U.S. 395 for six miles to a Forest Service road (Glass Creek Road). Turn west (right) and drive 0.25 mile to the camp access road on the right. Turn right and continue 0.5 mile to the main camp at the end of the road. Two notes: 1. A primitive area with large RV sites can be used as an overflow area on the right side of the access road. 2. If arriving from the south on U.S. 395, a direct left turn to Glass Creek Road is impossible. Heading north you will pass the CalTrans Crestview Maintenance Station on the right. Continue north, make a U-turn when possible, and follow the above directions.

Contact: Inyo National Forest, Mono Basin Scenic Area Ranger Station and Visitor Center, 760/647-3044, fax 760/647-3046.

CALIFORNIA

72 BIG SPRINGS

Scenic rating: 5

on Deadman Creek in Inyo National Forest

Map grid B1

Big Springs, at 7,300 feet elevation, is set on the edge of the high desert on the east side of U.S. 395. The main attractions are Deadman Creek, which runs right by the camp, and Big Springs, which is set just on the opposite side of the river. There are several hot springs in the area, best reached by driving south on U.S. 395 to the Mammoth Lakes Airport and turning left on Hot Creek Road. As with all hot springs, use at your own risk.

RV sites, facilities: There are 26 sites for tents or RVs up to 40 feet (no hookups). Picnic tables and fire grills are provided. Vault toilets are available. No drinking water is available. Leashed pets are permitted.

Reservations, fees: Reservations are not accepted. There is no fee for camping. (Note: This is one of four campgrounds in the Mono Basin Scenic Area that may impose a camping fee.) A 21-day limit is enforced. Open late April through early November, weather permitting.

Directions: From Lee Vining, drive south on U.S. 395 (past the first Highway 158/June Lake Loop turnoff) to June Lake Junction. Continue south for about seven miles to Owens River Road. Turn east (left) and drive two miles to a fork. Bear left at the fork and drive 0.25 mile to the camp on the left side of the road.

Contact: Inyo National Forest, Mono Basin Scenic Area Ranger Station and Visitor Center, 760/647-3044, fax 760/647-3046.

73 DEADMAN

Scenic rating: 5

on Deadman Creek in Inyo National Forest

Map grid B1

This little-known camp is set at 7,800 feet elevation along little Deadman Creek. It is primitive and dusty in the summer, cold in the early summer and fall. From camp, hikers can drive west for three miles to the headwaters of Deadman Creek and to a trailhead for a route that runs past San Joaquin Mountain and beyond to little Yost Lake, a one-way hike of four miles.

RV sites, facilities: There are 30 sites for tents or RVs up to 30 feet. Nearby Obsidian Flat Group Camp can accommodate tents or RVs of any length and up to 50 people (no hookups). Picnic tables and fire grills are provided. Vault toilets are available. No drinking water is available. Garbage must be packed out. Leashed pets are permitted.

Reservations, fees: Reservations are not accepted. There is no camping fee for individual sites. (Note: This is one of four campgrounds in the Mono Basin Scenic Area that may impose a camping fee.) Obsidian Group is $20 per night; reservations are required at 877/444-6777 or www.recreation.gov. Open late May through early November, weather permitting.

Directions: From Lee Vining, drive south on U.S. 395 (past the first Highway 158/June Lake Loop turnoff) to June Lake Junction. Continue south for 6.5 miles to a Forest Service road (Deadman Creek Road) on the west (right) side of the road. Turn west (right) and drive two miles to the camp access road on the right. Turn right and drive 0.5 mile to the camp. Note: If you are arriving from the south on U.S. 395 and you reach the CalTrans Crestview Maintenance Station on the right, you have gone one mile too far; make a U-turn when possible and return for access.

Contact: Inyo National Forest, Mono Basin Scenic Area and Visitor Center, 760/647-3044, fax 760/647-3046.

74 BROWN'S OWENS RIVER CAMPGROUND

Scenic rating: 7

near the Owens River

Map grid B1

This camp is located along the upper Owens River, and is well situated for hiking, mountain biking, fishing, and swimming. The campground landscape is fairly sparse, so the campground can seem less intimate than those set in a forest. But this makes for great long-distance views of the White Mountains and for taking in those sunsets.

RV sites, facilities: There are 75 sites for tents or RVs up to any feet (no hookups). Some trailer rentals with full hookups are available. Picnic tables and fire rings are provided. Drinking water, flush and pit toilets, coin showers, coin laundry, a convenience store and cafe are available. Some facilities are wheelchair-accessible. Leashed pets are permitted.

Reservations, fees: Reservations are accepted. Sites are $17–20 per night.

Directions: From Mammoth Lakes on Highway 395/203, drive south on Highway 395 to Benton Crossing Road. Turn left and drive five miles to campground.

Contact: Brown's Owens River Campground, 760/920-0975, www.brownscampgrounds.com.

75 PINE GLEN

Scenic rating: 6

in Inyo National Forest
Map grid B1

This is a well-situated base camp for several side trips. The most popular is the trip to Devils Postpile National Monument, with a shuttle ride from the Mammoth Ski Area. Other nearby trips include exploring Inyo Craters and Mammoth Lakes. The elevation is 7,800 feet.

RV sites, facilities: There are 11 sites (used as overflow from Old Shady Rest and New Shady Rest campgrounds) and five group sites for tents or RVs up to 55 feet (no hookups) that can accommodate 25–30 people each. Picnic tables and fire grills are provided. Drinking water, flush toilets, and a dump station are available. A grocery store, coin laundry, propane gas, and horseback-riding facilities are nearby in Mammoth Lakes. Leashed pets are permitted.

Reservations, fees: Reservations are not accepted for individual sites but are required for group sites at 877/444-6777 or www.recreation.gov ($10 reservation fee). Sites are $18 per night, and group sites are $35–50 per night. Open late May through September, weather permitting.

Directions: From Lee Vining on U.S. 395, drive south for 25 miles to Mammoth Junction and Highway 203/Minaret Summit Road. Turn west on Highway 203 and drive about three miles to the Mammoth Lakes Visitor Center. Just past the visitor center, turn right on Old Sawmill Road and drive a short distance to the campground on the right.

Contact: Inyo National Forest, Mammoth Ranger Station and Visitor Center, 760/924-5500, fax 760/924-5547.

76 NEW SHADY REST

Scenic rating: 6

in Inyo National Forest
Map grid B1

This easy-to-reach camp is set at 7,800 feet elevation, not far from the Mammoth Mountain Ski Area. The surrounding Inyo National Forest provides many side-trip opportunities, including Devils Postpile National Monument (by shuttle available from near the Mammoth Mountain Ski Area), Upper San Joaquin River, and the Inyo National Forest backcountry trails, streams, and lakes.

RV sites, facilities: There are 95 sites for tents or RVs up to 38 feet (no hookups). Picnic tables and fire grills are provided. Drinking water and flush toilets are available. A dump station, playground, grocery store, coin laundry, and propane gas are nearby. Leashed pets are permitted.

Reservations, fees: Reservations are accepted at 877/444-6777 or www.recreation.gov ($10 reservation fee). Sites are $18 per night with a 14-day limit. Open mid-May through October, weather permitting.

Directions: From Lee Vining on U.S. 395, drive south for 25 miles to Mammoth Junction and

Highway 203/Minaret Summit Road. Turn west on Highway 203 and drive about three miles to the Mammoth Lakes Visitor Center. Just past the visitors center, turn right on Old Sawmill Road and drive a short distance to the campground on the right.

Contact: Inyo National Forest, Mammoth Ranger Station and Visitor Center, 760/924-5500, fax 760/924-5547.

77 OLD SHADY REST

Scenic rating: 6

in Inyo National Forest

Map grid B1

Names such as "Old Shady Rest" are usually reserved for mom-and-pop RV parks. The Forest Service respected tradition in officially naming this park what the locals have called it all along. Like New Shady Rest, this camp is near the Mammoth Lakes Visitor Center, with the same side trips available. It is one of three camps in the immediate vicinity. The elevation is 7,800 feet.

RV sites, facilities: There are 51 sites for tents or RVs up to 55 feet (no hookups). Picnic tables and fire grills are provided. Drinking water and flush toilets are available. A dump station, playground, grocery store, coin laundry, and propane gas are nearby. Leashed pets are permitted.

Reservations, fees: Reservations are accepted at 877/444-6777 or www.recreation.gov ($10 reservation fee). Sites are $18 per night with a 14-day limit. Open mid-June through early September, weather permitting.

Directions: From Lee Vining on U.S. 395, drive south for 25 miles to Mammoth Junction and Highway 203/Minaret Summit Road. Turn west on Highway 203 and drive about three miles to the Forest Service Visitor Center. Just past the visitors center, turn right and drive 0.3 mile to the campground on the left.

Contact: Inyo National Forest, Mammoth Ranger Station and Visitor Center, 760/924-5500, fax 760/924-5547.

78 MAMMOTH MOUNTAIN RV PARK

Scenic rating: 6

near Mammoth Lakes

Map grid B1

This RV park is just across the street from the Forest Service Visitor Center. Got a question? Someone there has got an answer. This camp is open year-round, making it a great place to stay for a ski trip.

RV sites, facilities: There are 185 sites, some with full hookups (50 amps), for tents or RVs up to 45 feet. Two cabins are also available. Picnic tables are provided. Fire pits are provided at some sites. Restrooms with showers, drinking water, cable TV, modem access, dump station, coin laundry, heated year-round swimming pool, seasonal recreation room, playground, RV supplies, and a spa are available. Some facilities are wheelchair-accessible. Supplies can be obtained in Mammoth Lakes, 0.25 mile away. Leashed pets are permitted, with certain restrictions.

Reservations, fees: Reservations are accepted at 800/582-4603. Sites are $21–40 per night, $3 per person per night for more than two people, $2 per night for each additional vehicle, $3 per pet per night. Some credit cards accepted. Open year-round.

Directions: From Lee Vining on U.S. 395, drive south for 25 miles to Mammoth Junction and Highway 203. Turn west on Highway 203 and drive three miles to the park on the left.

From Bishop, drive 40 miles north on Highway 395 to Mammoth Lakes exit. Turn west on Highway 203, go under the overpass, and drive three miles to the park on the left.

Contact: Mammoth Mountain RV Park, 760/934-3822, fax 760/934-1896, www.mammothrv.com.

79 TWIN LAKES

Scenic rating: 8

in Inyo National Forest

Map grid B1

From Twin Lakes, you can look southwest and see pretty Twin Falls, a wide cascade that runs into the head of upper Twin Lake. There are actually two camps here, one on each side of the access road, at 8,600 feet. Lower Twin Lake is a favorite for fly fishers in float tubes. Powerboats, swimming, and sailboarding are not permitted. Use is heavy at the campground. Often there will be people lined up waiting for another family's weeklong vacation to end so theirs can start. Excellent hiking trails are in the area.

RV sites, facilities: There are 94 sites for tents or RVs up to 40 feet (no hookups). Picnic tables and fire grills are provided. Drinking water, flush toilets, and a boat launch are available. A grocery store, coin laundry, coin showers, and propane gas are nearby. Some facilities are wheelchair-accessible. Leashed pets are permitted.

Reservations, fees: Reservations are accepted at 877/444-6777 or www.recreation.gov ($10 reservation fee). Sites are $19 per night. Open mid-May through late October, weather permitting.

Directions: From Lee Vining on U.S. 395, drive south for 25 miles to Mammoth Junction and Highway 203/Minaret Summit Road. Turn west on Highway 203 and drive four miles to Lake Mary Road. Continue straight through the intersection and drive 2.3 miles to Twin Lakes Loop Road. Turn right and drive 0.5 mile to the campground.

Contact: Inyo National Forest, Mammoth Ranger Station and Visitor Center, 760/924-5500, fax 760/924-5547.

80 SHERWIN CREEK

Scenic rating: 7

in Inyo National Forest

Map grid B1

This camp is set along little Sherwin Creek, at 7,600 feet elevation, a short distance from the town of Mammoth Lakes. If you drive a mile east on Sherwin Creek Road, then turn right at the short spur road, you will find a trailhead for a hike that is routed up six miles to Valentine Lake in the John Muir Wilderness, set on the northwest flank of Bloody Mountain.

RV sites, facilities: There are 87 sites for tents or RVs up to 34 feet (no hookups), and 15 walk-in sites for tents only. Picnic tables and fire grills are provided. Drinking water and flush toilets are available. Leashed pets are permitted.

Reservations, fees: Reservations are accepted at 877/444-6777 or www.recreation.gov ($10 reservation fee). Sites are $18 per night. Open early May through mid-September, weather permitting.

Directions: From Lee Vining on U.S. 395, drive south for 25 miles to Mammoth Junction and Highway 203/Minaret Summit Road. Turn west on Highway 203 and drive about three miles to the Mammoth Lakes Visitor Center and continue a short distance to Old Mammoth Road. Turn left and drive about a mile to Sherwin Creek. Turn south and drive two miles on largely unpaved road to the campground on the left side of the road.

Contact: Inyo National Forest, Mammoth Lakes Visitor Center, 760/924-5500, fax 760/924-5547.

81 LAKE MARY

Scenic rating: 9

in Inyo National Forest

Map grid B1

Lake Mary is the star of the Mammoth Lakes region. Of the 11 lakes in the area, this is the largest and most developed. It provides a resort, boat ramp, and boat rentals, and it receives the highest number of trout stocks. No water/body contact, including swimming, is allowed, and the speed limit is 10 mph. It is set at 8,900 feet elevation in a place of incredible natural beauty, one of the few spots that literally has it all. Of course, that often includes quite a few other people. If there are too many for you, an excellent trailhead is available at nearby Coldwater camp that routes you up to Emerald Lake.

RV sites, facilities: There are 48 sites for tents or RVs up to 30 feet (no hookups). Picnic tables, food lockers, and fire grills are provided. Drinking water and flush toilets are available. A grocery store, coin laundry, and propane gas are nearby. Leashed pets are permitted.

Reservations, fees: Reservations are not accepted. Sites are $19 per night with a 14-day limit. Open early June through mid-September, weather permitting.

Directions: Take U.S. 395 to Mammoth Junction and Highway 203. Turn west on Highway 203 and drive through the town of Mammoth Lakes to the junction of Minaret Road/Highway 203 and Lake Mary Road. Continue straight through the intersection and drive 3.6 miles to Lake Mary Loop Drive. Turn right and drive 0.5 mile to the campground entrance.

Contact: Inyo National Forest, Mammoth Ranger Station and Visitor Center, 760/924-5500, fax 760/924-5547.

82 PINE CITY

Scenic rating: 7

near Lake Mary in Inyo National Forest

Map grid B1

This camp is at the edge of Lake Mary at an elevation of 8,900 feet. It's popular for both families and fly fishers with float tubes. Swimming is not permitted.

RV sites, facilities: There are 10 sites for tents or RVs up to 40 feet (no hookups). Picnic tables and fire grills are provided. Drinking water and flush toilets are available. A grocery store, coin laundry, boat launch, boat rentals, and propane gas are nearby. Some facilities are wheelchair-accessible. Leashed pets are permitted.

Reservations, fees: Reservations are not accepted. Sites are $19 per night. Open early June through mid-September.

Directions: Take U.S. 395 to Mammoth Junction and Highway 203. Turn west on Highway

203 and drive through the town of Mammoth Lakes to the junction of Minaret Road/Highway 203 and Lake Mary Road. Continue straight through the intersection and drive 3.6 miles to Lake Mary Loop Drive. Turn left and drive 0.25 mile to the campground.

Contact: Inyo National Forest, Mammoth Ranger Station and Visitor Center, 760/924-5500, fax 760/924-5547.

83 COLDWATER

Scenic rating: 7

on Coldwater Creek in Inyo National Forest

Map grid B1

While this camp is not the first choice of many simply because there is no lake view, it has a special attraction all its own. First, it is a two-minute drive from the campground to Lake Mary, where there is a boat ramp, rentals, and good trout fishing. Second, at the end of the campground access road is a trailhead for two outstanding hikes. From the Y at the trailhead, if you head right, you will be routed up Coldwater Creek to Emerald Lake, a great little hike. If you head to the left, you will have a more ambitious trip to Arrowhead, Skelton, and Red Lakes, all within three miles. The elevation is 8,900 feet.

RV sites, facilities: There are 78 sites for tents or RVs up to 50 feet (no hookups). Picnic tables and fire grills are provided. Drinking water, flush toilets, and horse facilities are available. You can buy supplies in Mammoth Lakes. Leashed pets are permitted.

Reservations, fees: Reservations are accepted at 877/444-6777 or www.recreation.gov ($10 reservation fee). Sites are $19 per night, with a 14-day limit. Open mid-June through mid-September.

Directions: From Lee Vining on U.S. 395, drive south for 25 miles to Mammoth Junction and Highway 203/Minaret Summit Road. Turn west on Highway 203 and drive four miles to Lake Mary Road. Continue straight through the intersection and drive 3.6 miles to Lake

Mary Loop Drive. Turn left and drive 0.6 mile to the camp entrance road.

Contact: Inyo National Forest, Mammoth Ranger Station and Visitor Center, 760/924-5500, fax 760/924-5547.

84 CONVICT LAKE

Scenic rating: 7

in Inyo National Forest
Map grid B1

This is the most popular camp in the Mammoth area and it is frequently full. While the lake rates a 10 for scenic beauty, the camp itself is in a stark desert setting, out of sight of the lake, and it can get windy and cold due to the exposed sites. After driving on U.S. 395 to get here, it is always astonishing to clear the rise and see Convict Lake (7,583 feet) and its gem-like waters set in a mountain bowl beneath a back wall of high, jagged wilderness peaks. The camp is right beside Convict Creek, about a quarter mile from Convict Lake. Both provide very good trout fishing, including some rare monster-sized brown trout below the Convict Lake outlet. Fishing is often outstanding in Convict Lake, with a chance of hooking a 10- or 15-pound trout. The lake speed limit is 10 mph, and although swimming is allowed, it is not popular because of the cold, often choppy water. A trail is routed around the lake, providing a nice day hike. A bonus is an outstanding resort with a boat launch, boat rentals, cabin rentals, small store, restaurant, and bar. Horseback rides and hiking are also available, with a trail routed along the north side of the lake, then along upper Convict Creek (a stream crossing is required about three miles in), and into the John Muir Wilderness.

RV sites, facilities: There are 88 sites for tents or RVs up to 40 feet (no hookups). Rental cabins are also available through the Convict Lake Resort. Picnic tables and fire grills are provided. Drinking water and flush toilets are available. A dump station, boat ramp, store, restaurant, and horseback-riding facilities are available nearby. Some facilities are wheelchair-accessible. Leashed pets are permitted.

Reservations, fees: Reservations are accepted at 877/444-6777 or www.recreation.gov ($10 reservation fee). Sites are $18 per night. For cabin reservations, phone 760/934-3880 or 800/992-2260. Open mid-April through October, weather permitting; cabins open year-round.

Directions: From Lee Vining on U.S. 395, drive south for 31 miles (five miles past Mammoth Junction) to Convict Lake Road (adjacent to Mammoth Lakes Airport). Turn west (right) on Convict Lake Road and drive three miles to Convict Lake. Cross the dam and drive a short distance to the campground entrance road on the left. Turn left and drive 0.25 mile to the campground.

From Bishop, drive north on U.S. 395 for 35 miles to Convict Lake Road. Turn west (left) and drive three miles to the lake and campground.

Contact: Inyo National Forest, Mammoth Ranger Station and Visitor Center, 760/924-5500, fax 760/924-5547; Convict Lake Resort and Cabins, 800/992-2260.

85 McGEE CREEK RV PARK

Scenic rating: 6

near Crowley Lake
Map grid B1

This is a popular layover spot for folks visiting giant Crowley Lake. Crowley Lake is still one of the better lakes in the Sierra for trout fishing, with good prospects for large rainbow trout and brown trout, though the 20-pound brown trout that once made this lake famous are now mainly a legend. McGee Creek runs through the campground, and trout fishing is popular. Several trout ponds are also available; call for fees. Beautiful Convict Lake provides a nearby side-trip option. It is also about nine miles to Rock Creek Lake, a beautiful high-mountain destination. The elevation is 7,000 feet.

RV sites, facilities: There are 40 sites with full,

partial, or no hookups (50 amps) for tents or RVs up to 40 feet; some sites are pull-through. Picnic tables and fire pits are provided. Drinking water and restrooms with showers and vault toilets are available. Leashed pets are permitted.

Reservations, fees: Reservations are accepted. Sites are $20–30 per night, $3 per person per night for more than two people. Weekly and monthly rates available. Open late April through September, weather permitting.

Directions: From the junction of U.S. 395 and Highway 203 (the Mammoth Lakes turnoff), drive south on U.S. 395 for eight miles to the turnoff for McGee Creek Road. Take that exit and look for the park entrance on the left.

Contact: McGee Creek RV Park, 760/935-4233, www.mcgeecreekrvcampground.com.

86 McGEE CREEK

Scenic rating: 7

in Inyo National Forest

Map grid B1

This is a Forest Service camp at an elevation of 7,600 feet, set along little McGee Creek, a good location for fishing and hiking. There are few trees here. The stream is stocked with trout, and a trailhead is just up the road. From here you can hike along upper McGee Creek and into the John Muir Wilderness.

RV sites, facilities: There are 28 sites for tents or RVs up to 25 feet (no hookups). Picnic tables and fire grills are provided. Drinking water, vault toilets, and shade structures are available. Horseback-riding facilities are available nearby. Some facilities are wheelchair-accessible. Leashed pets are permitted.

Reservations, fees: Reservations are accepted at 877/444-6777 or www.recreation.gov ($10 reservation fee). Sites are $18 per night. Open mid-May through mid-October, weather permitting.

Directions: From Mammoth Lakes at the junction of U.S. 395 and Highway 203, drive south on U.S. 395 for 8.5 miles to McGee Creek

Road (signed). Turn right (toward the Sierra) and drive 1.5 miles on a narrow, windy road to the campground.

Contact: Inyo National Forest, White Mountain Ranger District, 760/873-2500, fax 760/873-2563; McGee Creek Pack Station, 760/935-4324.

87 CROWLEY LAKE

Scenic rating: 5

near Crowley Lake

Map grid B1

This large BLM camp is across U.S. 395 from the south shore of Crowley Lake. For many, Crowley is the trout-fishing capital of the eastern Sierra, with the annual opener (the last Saturday in April) a great celebration. Though the trout fishing can go through a lull in midsummer, it can become excellent again in the fall when the lake's population of big brown trout heads up to the top of the lake at the mouth of the Owens River. This is a large lake with 45 miles of shoreline. In the summer, water sports include swimming, waterskiing, wakeboarding, personal watercraft riding, and sailboarding. The surroundings are fairly stark; the elevation is 6,800 feet.

RV sites, facilities: There are 47 sites for tents or RVs of any length (no hookups). Picnic tables and fire grills are provided. Vault toilets are available. No drinking water is available. A grocery store, boat ramp, boat rentals, and horseback-riding facilities are nearby. Floating chemical toilets are available on the lake. Leashed pets are permitted.

Reservations, fees: Reservations are not accepted. Sites are $5 per night, and season passes are available for $300. Open late April through October, weather permitting.

Directions: Drive on U.S. 395 to the Crowley Lake Road exit (30 miles north of Bishop). Take that exit west (toward the Sierra) to Crowley Lake Road. Turn right on Crowley Lake Road and drive northwest for three miles to the campground entrance on the left (well signed).

Contact: Bureau of Land Management, Bishop Field Office, 760/872-4881, fax 760/872-5050; McGee Creek Pack Station, 760/935-4324.

88 TUFF

Scenic rating: 5

near Crowley Lake in Inyo National Forest

Map grid B1

Easy access off U.S. 395 makes this camp a winner, though it is not nearly as pretty as those up Rock Creek Road to the west of Tom's Place. The fact that you can get in and out of here quickly makes it ideal for campers planning fishing trips to nearby Crowley Lake. The elevation is 7,000 feet.

RV sites, facilities: There are 34 sites for tents or RVs up to 45 feet (no hookups). Picnic tables and fire grills are provided. Drinking water and flush toilets are available. Some facilities are wheelchair-accessible. Leashed pets are permitted.

Reservations, fees: Reservations are accepted at 877/444-6777 or www.recreation.gov ($10 reservation fee). Sites are $18 per night. A 21-day limit is enforced. Open late April through mid-October, weather permitting.

Directions: From Mammoth Lakes at the junction of U.S. 395 and Highway 203, drive south on U.S. 395 for 15.5 miles (one mile north of Tom's Place) to Rock Creek Road. Turn left (east) on Rock Creek Road and drive 0.5 mile to the campground.

Contact: Inyo National Forest, White Mountain Ranger District, 760/873-2500, fax 760/873-2563.

89 FRENCH CAMP

Scenic rating: 5

on Rock Creek near Crowley Lake in
Inyo National Forest

Map grid B1

French Camp is just a short hop from U.S. 395 and Tom's Place, right where the high Sierra

turns into high plateau country. Side-trip opportunities include boating and fishing on giant Crowley Lake and, to the west on Rock Creek Road, visiting little Rock Creek Lake 10 miles away. The elevation is 7,500 feet.

RV sites, facilities: There are 86 sites for tents or RVs up to 40 feet (no hookups). Picnic tables and fire grills are provided. Drinking water, flush toilets, and dump station are available. Leashed pets are permitted.

Reservations, fees: Reservations are accepted at 877/444-6777 or www.recreation.gov ($10 reservation fee). Sites are $18 per night. Open early May through October, weather permitting.

Directions: From Mammoth Lakes at the junction of U.S. 395 and Highway 203, drive south on U.S. 395 for 15 miles to Tom's Place and Rock Creek Road. Turn right (toward the Sierra) at Rock Creek Road and drive 0.25 mile to the campground on the right.

Contact: Inyo National Forest, White Mountain Ranger District, 760/873-2500, fax 760/873-2563.

90 HOLIDAY GROUP CAMP

Scenic rating: 5

near Crowley Lake in Inyo National Forest

Map grid B1

There's a story behind every name. Holiday is a group camp that is opened as an overflow camp unless reserved on holiday weekends. It is near Rock Creek, not far from Crowley Lake, with surroundings far more stark than the camps to the west on Rock Creek Road. The elevation is 7,500 feet.

RV sites, facilities: There are 35 sites for tents or RVs up to 16 feet (no hookups) or groups up to 100 people. Picnic tables and fire grills are provided. Drinking water and vault toilets are available. Some facilities are wheelchair-accessible. Leashed pets are permitted.

Reservations, fees: Reservations are required at 760/935-4339. As a group site, it is $135 per night. Open only when reserved by groups.

Directions: From Mammoth Lakes at the

junction of U.S. 395 and Highway 203, drive south on U.S. 395 for 15 miles south to Tom's Place and Rock Creek Road. Turn right (toward the Sierra) and drive 0.5 mile to the campground on the left.

Contact: Inyo National Forest, White Mountain Ranger District, 760/873-2500, fax 760/873-2563.

91 ASPEN GROUP CAMP

Scenic rating: 7

near Crowley Lake in Inyo National Forest

Map grid B1

This small group campground set on Rock Creek is used primarily as a base camp for anglers and campers heading to nearby Crowley Lake or venturing west to Rock Creek Lake. The elevation at the camp is 8,100 feet.

RV sites, facilities: There is one group camp for tents or RVs up to 25 feet (no hookups) that can accommodate up to 25 people. Picnic tables and fire grills are provided. Drinking water and flush toilets are available. Limited supplies are available in Tom's Place, three miles away. Some facilities are wheelchair-accessible. Leashed pets are permitted.

Reservations, fees: Reservations are required at 877/444-6777 or www.recreation.gov ($10 reservation fee). The group fee is $65 per night. Open mid-May through mid-October, weather permitting.

Directions: From Mammoth Lakes at the junction of U.S. 395 and Highway 203, drive south on U.S. 395 for 15 miles south to Tom's Place and Rock Creek Road. Turn right (toward the Sierra) at Rock Creek Road and drive three miles to the campground.

Contact: Inyo National Forest, White Mountain Ranger District, 760/873-2500, fax 760/873-2563; Recreation Resource Management, 760/935-4321.

92 IRIS MEADOW

Scenic rating: 5

near Crowley Lake in Inyo National Forest

Map grid B1

Iris Meadow, at 8,300 feet elevation on the flank of Red Mountain (11,472 feet), is the first in a series of five Forest Service camps set near Rock Creek Canyon on the road leading from Tom's Place up to pretty Rock Creek Lake. A bonus is that some of the campsites are next to the creek. Rock Creek is stocked with trout, and nearby Rock Creek Lake also provides fishing and boating for hand-launched boats. This camp also has access to a great trailhead for wilderness exploration.

RV sites, facilities: There are 14 sites for tents or RVs up to 40 feet (no hookups). Picnic tables and fire grills are provided. Drinking water and flush toilets are available. Limited supplies are available in Tom's Place, three miles away. Some facilities are wheelchair-accessible. Leashed pets are permitted.

Reservations, fees: Reservations are not accepted. Sites are $18 per night. Open late May through mid-September, weather permitting.

Directions: From Mammoth Lakes at the junction of U.S. 395 and Highway 203, drive south on U.S. 395 for 15 miles to Tom's Place and Rock Creek Road. Turn right (toward the Sierra) at Rock Creek Road and drive three miles to the campground.

Contact: Inyo National Forest, White Mountain Ranger District, 760/873-2500, fax 760/873-2563.

93 BIG MEADOW

Scenic rating: 8

near Crowley Lake in Inyo National Forest

Map grid B1

This is a smaller, quieter camp in the series of campgrounds along Rock Creek. Some of the campsites are along the creek. Beautiful Rock

CALIFORNIA

Creek Lake provides a nearby side trip. The elevation is 8,600 feet. In the fall, turning aspens make for spectacular colors.

RV sites, facilities: There are 11 sites for tents or RVs up to 22 feet (no hookups). Picnic tables and fire grills are provided. Drinking water and flush toilets are available. Limited supplies are available in Tom's Place, four miles away. Some facilities are wheelchair-accessible. Leashed pets are permitted.

Reservations, fees: Reservations are not accepted. Sites are $18 per night. Open early May through late October.

Directions: From Mammoth Lakes at the junction of U.S. 395 and Highway 203, drive south on U.S. 395 for 15 miles south to Tom's Place and Rock Creek Road. Turn right (toward the Sierra) at Rock Creek Road and drive four miles to the campground.

Contact: Inyo National Forest, White Mountain Ranger District, 760/873-2500, fax 760/873-2563.

94 PALISADE

Scenic rating: 8

near Crowley Lake in Inyo National Forest

Map grid B1

This shoe might just fit. Palisade, a tiny campground, provides a pretty spot along Rock Creek at 8,600 feet elevation, with many side-trip options. The closest is fishing for small trout on Rock Creek and at pretty Rock Creek Lake up the road to the west. Another option is horseback riding, and horse rentals are in the area. The area is loaded with aspens. Some of the campsites are directly on the creek.

RV sites, facilities: There are five sites for tents or RVs up to 30 feet (no hookups); this campground can also be used as a group site for up to 30 people. Picnic tables and fire grills are provided. Drinking water and flush toilets are available. Horseback-riding facilities are nearby.

Limited supplies are available in Tom's Place, five miles away. Leashed pets are permitted.

Reservations, fees: Reservations are accepted at 760/935-4339. Sites are $18 per night. The group price is $90 per night. Open mid-May through mid-September, weather permitting.

Directions: From Mammoth Lakes at the junction of U.S. 395 and Highway 203, drive south on U.S. 395 for 15 miles south to Tom's Place and Rock Creek Road. Turn right (toward the Sierra) at Rock Creek Road and drive five miles to the campground.

Contact: Inyo National Forest, White Mountain Ranger District, 760/873-2500, fax 760/873-2563; Rock Creek Pack Station, 760/935-4493; Recreation Resource Management, 760/935-4339.

95 EAST FORK

Scenic rating: 8

near Crowley Lake in Inyo National Forest

Map grid B1

This is a beautiful, popular campground set along East Fork Rock Creek at 9,000 feet elevation. The camp is only three miles from Rock Creek Lake, where there's an excellent trailhead. Mountain biking is popular in this area, and Lower Rock Creek and Sand Canyon have two of the most difficult and desirable trails around; they're suggested for experienced riders only.

RV sites, facilities: There are 138 sites for tents or RVs up to 40 feet (no hookups). Picnic tables and fire grills are provided. Drinking water and flush toilets are available. Limited supplies are available in Tom's Place and at Rock Creek Lakes Resort. Leashed pets are permitted.

Reservations, fees: Reservations are accepted at 877/444-6777 or www.recreation.gov ($10 reservation fee). Sites are $18 per night. Open early May through October.

Directions: From Mammoth Lakes at the junction of U.S. 395 and Highway 203, drive

CALIFORNIA

south on U.S. 395 for 15 miles south to Tom's Place and Rock Creek Road. Turn right (toward the Sierra) at Rock Creek Road and drive five miles to the campground access road on the left.

Contact: Inyo National Forest, White Mountain Ranger District, 760/873-2500, fax 760/873-2563.

96 PINE GROVE UPPER AND LOWER

Scenic rating: 8

near Crowley Lake in Inyo National Forest

Map grid B1

Pine Grove is one of the smaller camps in the series of campgrounds along Rock Creek. Of the five camps in this canyon, this one is the closest to Rock Creek Lake, just a two-mile drive away (Rock Creek Lake Campground is closer, of course). The aspens here are stunning in September, when miles of mountains turn to shimmering golds. Some of the campsites are along the creek. The elevation is 9,300 feet.

RV sites, facilities: There are 19 sites for tents or RVs up to 16 feet (no hookups). Picnic tables and fire grills are provided. Drinking water and flush toilets are available. Horseback-riding facilities are nearby. Limited supplies can be obtained in Tom's Place and at Rock Creek Lakes Resort. Leashed pets are permitted.

Reservations, fees: Reservations are not accepted. Sites are $18 per night. Open mid-May through mid-October.

Directions: From Mammoth Lakes at the junction of U.S. 395 and Highway 203, drive south on U.S. 395 for 15 miles south to Tom's Place and Rock Creek Road. Turn right (toward the Sierra) at Rock Creek Road and drive seven miles to the campground.

Contact: Inyo National Forest, White Mountain Ranger District, 760/873-2500, fax 760/873-2563.

97 ROCK CREEK LAKE

Scenic rating: 9

in Inyo National Forest

Map grid B1

Rock Creek Lake, set at an elevation of 9,600 feet, is a small but beautiful lake that features cool, clear water, small trout, and a great trailhead for access to the adjacent John Muir Wilderness, with 50 other lakes within a two-hour hike. The setting is drop-dead beautiful, hence the high rating for scenic beauty, but note that the campsites are set closely together, side by side, in a paved parking area. This 63-acre lake has a 5-mph speed limit and swimming is allowed. The lake is stocked with Alpers trout, and they are joined by resident brown trout in the 10- to 16-pound class. At times, especially afternoons in late spring, winds out of the west can be cold and pesky at the lake. If this campground is full, the nearby Mosquito Flat walk-in campground provides an option. Note that Mosquito Flat has a limit of one night and is designed as a staging area for wilderness backpacking trips, with tent camping only. Insider's tip: Rock Creek Lakes Resort has mouth-watering homemade pie available in the café.

RV sites, facilities: There are 28 sites for tents or RVs up to 22 feet (no hookups), and one group tent site for up to 50 people; some of the sites require a short walk-in. Picnic tables and fire grills are provided. Drinking water, flush toilets, an unimproved boat launch, and boat rentals are available. Horseback-riding facilities and a café are nearby. Limited supplies can be obtained in Tom's Place and at Rock Creek Lakes Resort. Leashed pets are permitted.

Reservations, fees: Reservations are accepted for individual sites and required for group sites at 877/444-6777 or www.recreation.gov ($10 reservation fee). Sites are $18 per night, $55–65 per night for a group site. Open mid-May through October, weather permitting.

Directions: From the junction of U.S. 395 and Highway 203 (the Mammoth Lakes turnoff), drive 15 miles south on U.S. 395 to

Tom's Place. Turn right (toward the Sierra) at Rock Creek Road and drive seven miles to the campground.

Contact: Inyo National Forest, White Mountain Ranger District, 760/873-2500, fax 760/873-2563; Rock Creek Pack Station, 760/935-4493.

98 PLEASANT VALLEY

Scenic rating: 7

near Pleasant Valley Reservoir
Map grid B1

Pleasant Valley County Campground is set near long, narrow Pleasant Valley Reservoir, created by the Owens River. A 15-minute walk from camp will take you to the lake. It is east of the Sierra range in the high desert plateau country; the elevation is 4,200 feet. That makes it available for year-round fishing, and trout are stocked. The Owens River passes through the park, providing wild trout fishing, with most anglers practicing catch-and-release fly-fishing. This is also near a major jump-off point for hiking, rock-climbing, and wilderness fishing at the Bishop Pass area to the west.

RV sites, facilities: There are 200 sites for tents or RVs of any length (no hookups). Picnic tables and fire grills are provided. Drinking water (hand-pumped well water) and vault toilets are available. Groups can be accommodated. Some facilities are wheelchair-accessible. Leashed pets are permitted.

Reservations, fees: Reservations are not accepted. Sites are $10 per night per vehicle. Open year-round.

Directions: Drive on U.S. 395 to Pleasant Valley Road (seven miles north of Bishop) on the east side of the road. Turn northeast and drive one mile to the park entrance.

Contact: Inyo County Parks Department, 760/873-5577, www.395.com/inyo/campgrounds.

99 PLEASANT VALLEY PIT CAMPGROUND

Scenic rating: 6

near Bishop off US 395
Map grid B1

This camp is set in a rocky desert area just south of Pleasant Valley Reservoir. It's a good spot for kids, with boulder scrambling the primary recreation, and is also a good area to see a variety of raptors. Few travelers on U.S. 395 know about the campground, operated by the Bureau of Land Management.

RV sites, facilities: There are 75 sites for tents or RVs (no hookups). Vault toilets and a dumpster are provided. There is a campground host, as well as law enforcement patrols, and the campground sees regular maintenance. Fires, charcoal grills, and portable stoves outside developed campgrounds require a permit, when allowed. Leashed pets are permitted.

Reservations, fees: Reservations are not accepted. The fee is $2 per night. There is a 60-day limit. Open November to early May, weather permitting.

Directions: From Bishop, drive north on U.S. 395 for about five miles to Pleasant Valley Road. Turn right on Pleasant Valley Road and proceed approximately one-half mile to the gravel road on the left (west) side of the road. Turn left on the gravel road and drive to the Pleasant Valley Pit Campground.

Contact: Bureau of Land Management, Bishop Field Office, 760/872-4881, fax 760/872-5050, www.blm.gov.

100 HIGHLANDS RV PARK

Scenic rating: 3

near Bishop
Map grid B1

This is a privately operated RV park near Bishop that is set up for U.S. 395 cruisers. There is a casino in town. A great side trip is up two-lane Highway 168 to Lake Sabrina. The elevation is

4,300 feet. Note that a few sites are occupied by long-term renters.

RV sites, facilities: There are 103 sites with full hookups (30 and 50 amps) for RVs of any length; many sites are pull-through. No tents. Picnic tables and cable TV are provided. Drinking water, restrooms with flush toilets and showers, dump station, social room with pool table, Wi-Fi, propane gas, ice, fish-cleaning station, and coin laundry are available. Supplies are available nearby. Some facilities are wheelchair-accessible. Leashed pets are permitted.

Reservations, fees: Reservations are recommended. Sites are $39 per night, $1 per person per night for more than two people. Weekly and monthly rates available. Some credit cards accepted. Open year-round.

Directions: From Bishop, drive two miles north on U.S. 395/North Sierra Highway to the campground on the right (east side of road) at 2275 North Sierra Highway.

Contact: Highlands RV Park, 760/873-7616.

SEQUOIA AND KINGS CANYON

☾ BEST RV PARKS AND CAMPGROUNDS

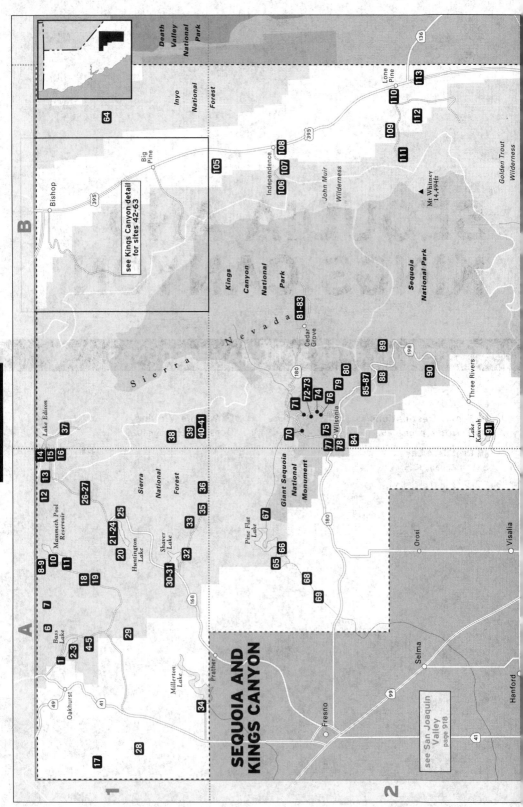

SEQUOIA AND
KINGS CANYON

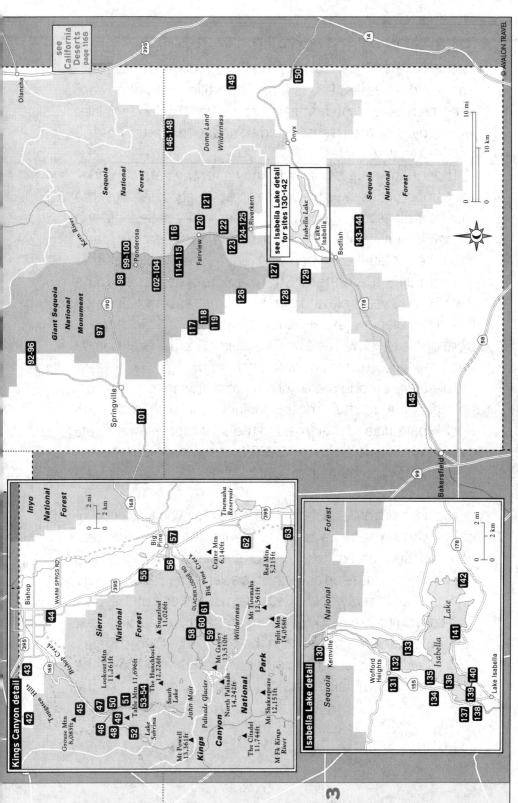

CALIFORNIA

3

There is no place on earth like the high Sierra,

from Mount Whitney north through Sequoia and Kings Canyon National Parks. This is a paradise filled with deep canyons, high peaks, and fantastic natural beauty, and sprinkled with groves of the largest living things in the history of the earth – giant sequoias.

Though the area is primarily known for the national parks, the campgrounds available span a great variety of settings. The most popular spots, though, are in the vicinity of Sequoia and Kings Canyon National Parks, or on the parks' access roads.

Sooner or later, everyone will want to see the biggest tree of them all – the General Sherman Tree, estimated to be 2,300-2,700 years old and with a circumference of 102.6 feet. It is in the Giant Forest at Sequoia National Park. To stand in front of it is to know true awe. That said, I find the Grant Grove and the Muir Grove even more enchanting.

These are among the highlights of a driving tour through both parks. A must for most is taking in the view from Moro Rock – parking and then making the 300-foot walk up a succession of stairs to reach the 6,725-foot summit. Here you can scan a series of mountain rims and granite peaks, highlighted by the Great Western Divide.

The drive out of Sequoia and into Kings Canyon features rim-of-the-world-type views as you first enter the Kings River canyon. You then descend to the bottom of the canyon, right along the Kings River, gaze up at the high glacial-carved canyon walls, and drive all the way out to Cedar Grove, the end of the road. The canyon rises 8,000 feet from the river to Spanish Peak, making it the deepest canyon in the continental United States.

Crystal Cave is another point of fascination. Among the formations are adjoined crystal columns that look like the sound pipes in the giant organ at the Mormon Tabernacle. Lights are placed strategically for perfect viewing.

This is only a start. Bears, marmots, and deer are abundant and are commonly seen in Sequoia, especially at Dorst Creek Campground. If you drive up to Mineral King and take a hike, it can seem like the marmot capital of the world.

But this region also harbors many wonderful secrets having nothing to do with the national parks. One of them, for instance, is the Muir Trail Ranch near Florence Lake. The ranch is set in the John Muir Wilderness and requires a trip by foot, boat, or horse to reach it. Other unique launching points for trips into the wilderness lie nearby.

On the western slopes of the Sierra, pretty lakes with good trout fishing include Edison, Florence, and Hume Lakes. Hidden spots in Sierra National Forest provide continual fortune hunts, especially up the Dinkey Creek drainage above Courtright Reservoir. On the eastern slopes, a series of small streams offers good vehicle access; here, too, you'll encounter the beautiful Rock Creek Lake, Sabrina and South Lakes (west of Bishop), and great wilderness trailheads at the end of almost every road.

The remote Golden Trout Wilderness on the southwest flank of Mount Whitney is one of the most pristine areas in California. Yet it is lost in the shadow of giant Whitney, elevation 14,497.6 feet, the highest point in the continental United States, where hiking has become so popular that reservations are required at each trailhead for overnight use, and quotas are enforced to ensure an undisturbed experience for each visitor.

In the Kernville area, there are campgrounds along the Kern River. Most choose this canyon for one reason: the outstanding white-water rafting and kayaking.

1 LUPINE-CEDAR BLUFF

Scenic rating: 8

on Bass Lake in Sierra National Forest

Map grid A1

Bass Lake is a popular vacation spot, a pretty lake, long and narrow, covering 1,200 acres when full and surrounded by national forest. The elevation is 3,500 feet. This is camping headquarters, with the only year-round individual sites at the lake. Though these camps are adjoining, the concessionaire treats them as separate camps, with Cedar Bluff reserved for RV camping only. Most of the campgrounds are filled on weekends and three-day holidays. Fishing is best in the spring for rainbow trout and largemouth bass, and by mid-June waterskiers have usually taken over. Boats must be registered at the Bass Lake observation tower after launching.

RV sites, facilities: There are 113 sites for tents or RVs up to 40 feet (no hookups) and several double sites at Lupine, with 62 sites at Cedar Bluff for RVs only. Picnic tables and fire grills are provided. Drinking water, flush toilets, and a camp host are available. Groceries, coin showers, and boat ramp are within two miles. Some facilities are wheelchair-accessible. Leashed pets are permitted.

Reservations, fees: Reservations are accepted at 877/444-6777 or www.recreation.gov ($10 reservation fee). Sites are $19.27–21 per night, $38.53–84 per night for double sites, $5 per night for each additional vehicle. Fees increase on holiday weekends. Open year-round.

Directions: From Fresno, drive north on Highway 41 to Oakhurst and continue 2.5 miles to Yosemite Forks and Bass Lake Road/County Road 222. Turn right at Bass Lake Road and drive eight miles (staying right at two forks) to the campground (on the south shore of Bass Lake).

Contact: Sierra National Forest, Bass Lake Ranger District, 559/877-2218, fax 559/877-3108; California Land Management, 559/642-3212.

2 RECREATION POINT GROUP AND CRANE VALLEY GROUP

Scenic rating: 8

on Bass Lake in Sierra National Forest

Map grid A1

Bass Lake is a long, narrow, mountain lake set in the Sierra foothills at 3,400 feet elevation. It's especially popular in the summer for waterskiing, personal watercraft riding, and swimming. There are two separate group camps at Bass Lake: Recreation Point and Crane Valley. There are no individual sites. Crane Valley is the better of the two because it has drinking water and flush toilets.

RV sites, facilities: At Recreation Point, there are 14 group sites for tents only that can accommodate 30–50 people. Drinking water and flush toilets are available. At Crane Valley, there are seven group sites for tents or RVs up to 45 feet (no hookups) that can accommodate 30–50 people each. Flush toilets are available, but there is no drinking water. Picnic tables and fire grills are provided at both camps. A store is nearby. Leashed pets are permitted.

Reservations, fees: Reservations are required at 877/444-6777 or www.recreation.gov ($10 reservation fee). At Recreation Point, sites are $113.76–189.91 per night; at Crane Valley, sites are $33.03–90 per night. Open year-round.

Directions: From Fresno, drive north on Highway 41 to Oakhurst and continue 2.5 miles to Yosemite Forks and Bass Lake Road/County Road 222. Turn right at Bass Lake Road and drive four miles to the campground.

Contact: Sierra National Forest, Bass Lake Ranger District, 559/877-2218, fax 559/877-3108; California Land Management, 559/642-3212.

3 FORKS

Scenic rating: 8

on Bass Lake in Sierra National Forest

Map grid A1

Bass Lake is set in a canyon. It's a long, narrow, deep lake that is popular for fishing in the spring and waterskiing in the summer. It's a pretty spot, set at 3,500 feet elevation in the Sierra National Forest. This is one of several camps at the lake. Boats must be registered at the Bass Lake observation tower after launching.

RV sites, facilities: There are 31 sites for tents or RVs up to 40 feet (no hookups). Picnic tables and fire grills are provided. Drinking water, flush toilets, and a camp host are available. A store, dump station, and coin laundry are nearby. Some facilities are wheelchair-accessible. Leashed pets are permitted.

Reservations, fees: Reservations are accepted at 877/444-6777 or www.recreation.gov ($10 reservation fee). Sites are $19.27–21 per night, $5 per night for each additional vehicle. Open May through September.

Directions: From Fresno, drive north on Highway 41 to Oakhurst and continue 2.5 miles to Yosemite Forks and Bass Lake Road/County Road 222. Turn right at Bass Lake Road and drive six miles (staying right at two forks) to the campground (on the south shore of Bass Lake). Note: The road is narrow and curvy.

Contact: Sierra National Forest, Bass Lake Ranger District, 559/877-2218, fax 559/877-3108; California Land Management, 559/642-3212.

4 SPRING COVE

Scenic rating: 8

on Bass Lake in Sierra National Forest

Map grid A1

This is one of several camps beside Bass Lake, a long, narrow reservoir in the Sierra foothill country. A bonus here is that the shoreline is quite sandy nearly all around the lake. That makes for good swimming and sunbathing. Expect hot weather in the summer. Boats must be registered at the Bass Lake observation tower after launching. The elevation is 3,400 feet.

RV sites, facilities: There are 63 sites for tents or RVs up to 35 feet (no hookups). Picnic tables and fire grills are provided. Drinking water, flush toilets, and camp host are available. Groceries and a boat ramp are nearby. Some

facilities are wheelchair-accessible. Leashed pets are permitted.

Reservations, fees: Reservations are accepted at 877/444-6777 or www.recreation.gov ($10 reservation fee). Sites are $19–21 per night, $5 per night for each additional vehicle. Open May through August.

Directions: From Fresno, drive north on Highway 41 to Oakhurst and continue 2.5 miles to Yosemite Forks and Bass Lake Road/County Road 222. Turn right at Bass Lake Road and drive 8.5 miles (staying right at two forks) to the campground (on the south shore of Bass Lake).

Contact: Sierra National Forest, Bass Lake Ranger District, 559/877-2218, fax 559/877-3108; California Land Management, 559/642-3212.

5 WISHON BASS LAKE

Scenic rating: 9

on Bass Lake in Sierra National Forest

Map grid A1

This camp on Wishon Point is the smallest, and many say the prettiest, of the camps at Bass Lake. The elevation is 3,400 feet.

RV sites, facilities: There are 47 sites for tents or RVs up to 30 feet (no hookups). Some sites are pull-through. Picnic tables and fire grills are provided. Drinking water and flush toilets are available. Groceries and a boat ramp are nearby. Some facilities are wheelchair-accessible. Leashed pets are permitted.

Reservations, fees: Reservations are accepted at 877/444-6777 or www.recreation.gov ($10 reservation fee). Single sites are $19.27 per night, double sites are $38.53, $5 per night for additional vehicle. Open June through September.

Directions: From Fresno, drive north on Highway 41 to Oakhurst and continue 2.5 miles to Yosemite Forks and Bass Lake Road/County Road 222. Turn right at Bass Lake Road and drive nine miles (staying right at two forks) to the campground (on the south shore of Bass Lake).

Contact: Sierra National Forest, Bass Lake Ranger District, 559/877-2218, fax 559/877-3108; California Land Management, 559/642-3212.

CALIFORNIA

6 CHILKOOT

Scenic rating: 7

near Bass Lake in Sierra National Forest

Map grid A1

A lot of people have heard of Bass Lake, but only the faithful know about Chilcoot Creek. That's where this camp is, but it's just two miles from Bass Lake. It provides a primitive option to use either as an overflow area for Bass Lake or for folks who don't want to get jammed into one of the Bass Lake campgrounds on a popular weekend. The elevation is 4,600 feet.

RV sites, facilities: There are 14 sites for tents or RVs up to 20 feet (no hookups). Picnic tables and fire grills are provided. Vault toilets are available. No drinking water is available. Groceries and a coin laundry are available at Bass Lake. Leashed pets are permitted.

Reservations, fees: Reservations are accepted at 877/444-6777 or www.recreation.gov ($10 reservation fee). Sites are $14–16 per night, $5 per night for each additional vehicle. Open early May through early September.

Directions: From Fresno, drive north on Highway 41 to Oakhurst and continue 2.5 miles to Yosemite Forks and Bass Lake Road/County Road 222. Turn right at Bass Lake Road and drive six miles to the town of Bass Lake and Beasore Road. Turn left at Beasore Road and drive 4.5 miles to the campground.

Contact: Sierra National Forest, Bass Lake Ranger District, 559/877-2218, fax 559/877-3108.

7 GAGGS CAMP

Scenic rating: 7

in Sierra National Forest

Map grid A1

The masses are not exactly beating a hot trail to this camp. It's a small, remote, and primitive spot, set along a little creek at 5,700 feet elevation, deep in the interior of Sierra National Forest. A Forest Service map is advisable. With that in hand, you can make the three-mile drive to Little Shuteye Pass, where the road is often gated in the winter (the gate is open when the look-out station is staffed); from here it is a three-mile trip to Shuteye Peak, at 8,351 feet, where there is a drop-dead gorgeous view of the surrounding landscape.

RV sites, facilities: There are 11 sites for tents or RVs up to 16 feet (no hookups). Picnic tables and fire grills are provided. Vault toilets are available. No drinking water is available. Garbage bins are located at campground entrance. Leashed pets are permitted.

Reservations, fees: Reservations are not accepted. Sites are $16 per night, $5 per night for each additional vehicle. Open June through October, weather permitting.

Directions: From Fresno, drive north on Highway 41 for about 25 miles to North Fork Road/County Road 200. Turn right and drive northeast for 17.5 miles to Auberry Road/County Road 222. Turn left (north) and drive one mile to the town of North Fork and Mammoth Pool Road. Turn right and drive 0.5 mile to Malum Ridge Road/County Road 274. Turn left (north) and drive 4.5 miles to Central Camp Road/Forest Road 6S42. Turn right and drive 11.5 miles (narrow, dirt road) to the campground on the right.

Contact: Sierra National Forest, Bass Lake Ranger District, 559/877-2218, fax 559/877-3108.

8 SODA SPRINGS

Scenic rating: 7

on the West Fork of Chiquito Creek in Sierra National Forest

Map grid A1

Soda Springs is set at 4,400 feet elevation on West Fork Chiquito Creek, about five miles from Mammoth Pool Reservoir. It is used primarily as an overflow area if the more developed camps with drinking water have filled up. As long as you remember that the camp is primitive, it is a good overflow option.

RV sites, facilities: There are 18 sites for tents or RVs up to 20 feet (no hookups). Picnic tables and fire grills are provided. Vault toilets are available.

No drinking water is available. A store and boat ramp are nearby. Leashed pets are permitted.

Reservations, fees: Reservations are not accepted. The fee is $16 per night for single sites, $32 per night for double sites, $5 per night for each additional vehicle. Open April through October, weather permitting.

Directions: From Fresno, drive north on Highway 41 for about 25 miles to North Fork Road/County Road 200. Turn right and drive northeast for 17.5 miles to Auberry Road/ County Road 222. Turn left (north) and drive one mile to the town of North Fork and Mammoth Pool Road. Turn right and drive 1.5 miles to County Road 225 (still Mammoth Pool Road). Turn right and drive 35 miles (the road becomes Minarets Road/Forest Road 81) to the campground.

Contact: Sierra National Forest, Bass Lake Ranger District, 559/877-2218, fax 559/877-3108.

9 LOWER CHIQUITO

Scenic rating: 7

on Chiquito Creek in Sierra National Forest

Map grid A1

Lower Chiquito is a primitive, little-known, pretty camp in Sierra National Forest, about eight miles from Mammoth Pool Reservoir. Mosquitoes can be abundant in summer. The elevation is 4,900 feet, with a very warm climate in summer. Note that Lower Chiquito is a long distance (a twisting, 30- to 40-minute drive) from Upper Chiquito, despite the similarity in names and streamside settings along the same creek.

RV sites, facilities: There are seven sites for tents or RVs up to 25 feet (no hookups). Picnic tables and fire grills are provided. Vault toilets are available. No drinking water is available. Leashed pets are permitted.

Reservations, fees: Reservations are not accepted. The fee is $16 per night for single sites, $32 per night for double sites, $5 per night for each additional vehicle. Open May through September, weather permitting.

Directions: From the town of North Fork (south of Bass Lake), drive east on Mammoth Pool Road/County Road 225 (it becomes Minarets Road/Forest Road 4S81). Bear left (north, still Minarets Road/Forest Road 4S81) and drive to Forest Road 6S71. Turn left on Forest Road 6S71 and drive three miles to the campground. (The distance is about 40 miles from North Fork.)

Contact: Sierra National Forest, Bass Lake Ranger District, 559/877-2218, fax 559/877-3108.

10 SWEETWATER

Scenic rating: 6

near Mammoth Pool Reservoir on Chiquito Creek in Sierra National Forest

Map grid A1

Sweetwater is small and primitive, but if the camp at Mammoth Pool Reservoir is filled up, this spot provides an alternative. It is set on Chiquito Creek, just a mile from the lake. The elevation is 3,800 feet. (See the Mammoth Pool listing in this chapter for more information.)

RV sites, facilities: There are 10 sites for tents or RVs up to 20 feet (no hookups). Picnic tables and fire grills are provided. Vault toilets are available. No drinking water is available. A store and boat ramp are within 1.5 miles. Leashed pets are permitted.

Reservations, fees: Reservations are accepted at 877/444-6777 or www.recreation.gov ($10 reservation fee). Sites are $14.68 per night, $5 per night per additional vehicle. Open mid-May through mid-September.

Directions: From Fresno, drive north on Highway 41 for about 25 miles to North Fork Road/County Road 200. Turn right and drive northeast for 17.5 miles to Auberry Road/County Road 222. Turn left (north) and drive one mile to the town of North Fork and Mammoth Pool Road. Turn right and drive 1.5 miles to County Road 225 (still Mammoth Pool Road). Turn right and drive about 37 miles (the road becomes Minarets Road/Forest Road 81) to a junction. Bear right (still Mammoth Pool Road) and drive 1.5 miles to the campground on the right. The drive from North Fork takes 1.5–2 hours.

Contact: Sierra National Forest, Bass Lake Ranger

District, 559/877-2218, fax 559/877-3108; California Land Management, 559/642-3212.

11 MAMMOTH POOL

Scenic rating: 7

near Mammoth Pool Reservoir in
Sierra National Forest

Map grid A1

Mammoth Pool was created by a dam in the San Joaquin River gorge, a steep canyon, resulting in a long, narrow lake with steep, high walls. The lake seems much higher than its official elevation of 3,330 feet, but that is because of the high ridges. This is the only drive-in camp at the lake, though there is a boat-in camp, China Camp, on the lake's upper reaches. Trout fishing can be good in the spring and early summer, with waterskiing dominant during warm weather. All water sports are allowed during part of the season, but get this: Water sports are restricted from May 1 to June 15 because of deer migrating across the lake—that's right, swimming—but the campgrounds here are still open. Note that the water level can drop significantly by late summer.

RV sites, facilities: There are 47 sites for tents or RVs up to 30 feet (no hookups). Picnic tables and fire grills are provided. Drinking water and flush toilets are available. A store and boat ramp are within a mile. Leashed pets are permitted.

Reservations, fees: Reservations are accepted at 877/444-6777 or www.recreation.gov ($10 reservation fee). Sites are $15.60 per night, $5 per night for each additional vehicle. Open mid-May through mid-September.

Directions: From Fresno, drive north on Highway 41 for about 25 miles to North Fork Road/County Road 200. Turn right and drive northeast for 17.5 miles to Auberry Road/County Road 222. Turn left (north) and drive one mile to the town of North Fork and Mammoth Pool Road. Turn right and drive 1.5 miles to County Road 225 (still Mammoth Pool Road). Turn right and drive about 37 miles (the road becomes Minarets Road/Forest Road 81) to a junction. Bear right (still Mammoth Pool Road) and drive three miles to Mammoth Pool Reservoir and the campground. The drive from North Fork takes 1.5–2 hours.

Contact: Sierra National Forest, Bass Lake Ranger District, 559/877-2218, fax 559/877-3108.

12 SAMPLE MEADOW

Scenic rating: 7

on Kaiser Creek in Sierra National Forest

Map grid A1

This is a pretty, secluded spot set at 7,800 feet elevation along Kaiser Creek, with nearby trailheads available for backpackers. While there is a trail out of camp, most hikers drive a mile down Forest Road 80 to the Rattlesnake Parking Area. From here, one trail is routed three miles southwest to Kaiser Ridge and Upper and Lower Twin Lakes in the Kaiser Wilderness, a great hike. Another trail is routed north for three miles to Rattlesnake Creek, and then enters the western slopes of the Ansel Adams Wilderness, with this section featuring a series of canyons, streams, and very few people.

RV sites, facilities: There are 16 sites for tents or RVs up to 16 feet (no hookups). Picnic tables and fire grills are provided. Vault toilets are available. No drinking water is available. Garbage must be packed out. Leashed pets are permitted.

Reservations, fees: Reservations are not accepted. There is no camping fee. Open June through October, weather permitting.

Directions: From Fresno, drive east on Highway 168 to Shaver Lake, and then continue 21 miles to Huntington Lake and Kaiser Pass Road/Forest Road 80. Bear right on Forest Road 80 and drive eight miles to a fork with Forest Road 7505. Turn left on Forest Road 7505 and drive 3.5 miles to a fork with the campground entrance road. Bear left at the campground entrance road and drive 0.25 mile to the campground. The road is narrow and curvy, with blind turns.

Contact: Sierra National Forest, High Sierra Ranger District, 559/855-5355, fax 559/855-5375.

13 PORTAL FOREBAY

Scenic rating: 8

on Forebay Lake in Sierra National Forest

Map grid A1

This small, primitive camp is set along the shore of little Forebay Lake at 7,200 feet elevation. The camp is pretty and provides a good hiking option, with a trailhead near the camp that is routed up Camp 61 Creek and then to Mono Creek, with a ford of Mono Creek required about two miles in. Another side trip is visiting Mono Hot Springs about five miles to the east, just off the road to Lake Edison.

RV sites, facilities: There are 11 sites for tents or RVs up to 16 feet (no hookups). Picnic tables and fire grills are provided. Vault toilets are available. No drinking water is available. Groceries are available nearby at Mono Hot Springs. Leashed pets are permitted.

Reservations, fees: Reservations are not accepted. Sites are $15 per night, $5 per night per each additional vehicle. Open June through September.

Directions: From Fresno, drive east on Highway 168 to Shaver Lake, and then continue 21 miles to Huntington Lake and Kaiser Pass Road/ Forest Road 80. Bear right on Forest Road 80 and drive eight miles to a fork with Forest Road 5. Stay right at the fork on Forest Road 80 and continue five miles to the campground entrance on the left. The road is narrow and curvy, with blind turns.

Contact: Sierra National Forest, High Sierra Ranger District, 559/855-5355, fax 559/855-5375; California Land Management, 559/893-2111.

14 VERMILLION

Scenic rating: 8

on Lake Edison in Sierra National Forest

Map grid A1

If you don't mind the drive, Lake Edison is a premium vacation destination. It is a large, high-mountain camp set just a few miles from the border of the John Muir Wilderness. The elevation is 7,700 feet. A 15-mph speed limit on the lake guarantees quiet water, and trout fishing is often quite good in early summer, with occasionally huge brown trout hooked. Swimming is allowed. A day-trip option is to hike the trail from the camp out along the north shore of Lake Edison for five miles to Quail Meadows, where it intersects with the Pacific Crest Trail in the John Muir Wilderness. A lodge at the lake provides meals and supplies, with a hikers boat shuttle available to the head of the lake. Hang out here for long and you are bound to see John Muir Trail hikers taking a break. Note that the drive in is long and extremely twisty on a narrow road. Also note that the lake level can drop dramatically here by late summer.

RV sites, facilities: There are 31 sites for tents or RVs up to 26 feet (no hookups). Picnic tables, fire grills, and food lockers are provided. Drinking water and vault toilets are available. A boat ramp, boat rentals, bait and tackle, horseback-riding facilities, convenience store, and restaurant are nearby. Leashed pets are permitted.

Reservations, fees: Reservations are accepted at 877/444-6777 or www.recreation.gov ($10 reservation fee). Sites are $17 per night, $5 per night for each additional vehicle. Open mid-June through mid-September.

Directions: From the town of Shaver Lake, drive east on Highway 168 for 21 miles to Kaiser Pass Road. Bear northeast on Kaiser Pass Road/Forest Road 80 (slow and curvy) to Mono Hot Springs (the road becomes Edison Lake Road). Continue on Kaiser Pass/Edison Lake Road for five miles to the campground. It is about 0.25 mile from the west shore of Lake Edison. Be warned that the access road is narrow with many blind turns and may be difficult for RVs.

Contact: Sierra National Forest, High Sierra Ranger District, 559/855-5355, fax 559/855-5375; California Land Management, 559/893-2111.

CALIFORNIA

15 MONO HOT SPRINGS

Scenic rating: 8

on the San Joaquin River in Sierra National Forest

Map grid A1

The campground is set in the Sierra at 7,400 feet elevation along the San Joaquin River directly adjacent to the Mono Hot Springs Resort. The hot springs are typically 104°F, with public pools (everybody wears swimming suits) available just above the river on one side, and the private resort (rock cabins available) with its private baths on the other. A small convenience store and excellent restaurant are available at the lodge. Many find the hot springs perfect, but for some the water is too hot. No problem; the best swimming lake in the Sierra Nevada, Dorris Lake, is a 15-minute walk past the lodge. Dorris is clear, clean, and not too cold since it too is fed by hot springs. There are walls on one side for fun jumps into deep water. The one downer: The drive in to the campground is long, slow, and hellacious, with many blind corners in narrow sections.

RV sites, facilities: There are 26 sites for tents or RVs up to 26 feet (no hookups). Picnic tables and fire grills are provided. Vault toilets are available. Drinking water is not available. You can buy supplies in Mono Hot Springs. Leashed pets are permitted.

Reservations, fees: Reservations are accepted at 877/444-6777 or www.recreation.gov ($10 reservation fee). Sites are $17 per night, $34 per night for double site, $5 per night for additional vehicle. Open June through mid-September, weather permitting.

Directions: From the town of Shaver Lake, drive east on Highway 168 for 21 miles to Kaiser Pass Road. Bear northeast on Kaiser Pass Road/Forest Road 80 (slow and curvy) to Mono Hot Springs Campground Road (signed). Turn left and drive a short distance to the campground. Be warned that the access road is narrow with many blind turns and may be difficult for RVs.

Contact: Sierra National Forest, High Sierra Ranger District, 559/855-5355, fax 559/855-5375; California Land Management, 559/893-2111.

16 MONO CREEK

Scenic rating: 6

near Lake Edison in Sierra National Forest

Map grid A1

Here's a beautiful spot in the forest near Mono Creek that makes for an overflow campground when the camps at Mono Hot Springs and Lake Edison are filled, or when you want a quieter, more remote spot. The camp is set at 7,400 feet elevation about three miles from Lake Edison, via a twisty and bumpy road. Edison has good evening trout fishing and a small restaurant. For side trips, the Mono Hot Springs Resort is three miles away (slow, curvy, and bumpy driving), and there are numerous trails nearby into the backcountry. A camp host is on-site.

RV sites, facilities: There are 14 sites for tents or RVs up to 16 feet (no hookups). Picnic tables, fire grills, and food lockers are provided. Vault toilets are available. Drinking water is not available. Limited supplies and small restaurants are at Lake Edison and Mono Hot Springs. Leashed pets are permitted.

Reservations, fees: Reservations are accepted at 877/444-6777 or www.recreation.gov ($10 reservation fee). Sites are $17 per night, $34 per night for double site, $5 per night for each additional vehicle. Open June through mid-September, weather permitting.

Directions: From the town of Shaver Lake, drive east on Highway 168 for 21 miles to Kaiser Pass Road. Bear northeast on Kaiser Pass Road/Forest Road 80 (slow and curvy) to Mono Hot Springs (the road becomes Edison Lake Road). Continue on Kaiser Pass/Edison Lake Road for three miles to the campground on the left.

Contact: Sierra National Forest, High Sierra Ranger District, 559/855-5355, fax 559/855-5375; California Land Management, 559/893-2111.

CALIFORNIA

17 CODORNIZ RECREATION AREA

Scenic rating: 6

on Eastman Lake

Map grid A1

Eastman Lake provides relief on your typical 90- and 100-degree summer day out here. It is tucked in the foothills of the San Joaquin Valley at an elevation of 650 feet and covers 1,800 surface acres. Shade shelters have been added at 12 of the more exposed campsites, a big plus. The warm water in summer makes it a good spot for a dip, thus it is a favorite for waterskiing, swimming, and, in the spring, fishing. Swimming is best at the large beach on the west side. The Department of Fish and Game has established a trophy bass program here, and fishing can be good in the appropriate season for rainbow trout, catfish, bluegill, and redear sunfish. Check fishing regulations, posted on all bulletin boards. The lake is also a designated "Watchable Wildlife" site; it is home to 163 species of birds and a nesting pair of bald eagles. A small area near the upper end of the lake is closed to boating to protect a bald eagle nest site. Some may remember the problem that Eastman Lake had with hydrilla, an invasive weed. The problem has been largely solved, and a buoy line has been placed at the mouth. No water activities are allowed upstream of this line. Mild winter temperatures are a tremendous plus at this lake.

RV sites, facilities: There are 62 sites for tents or RVs of any length (some have full hookups/50 amps and one is pull-through), three group sites for up to 200 people, three equestrian sites, and one group equestrian site. Picnic tables and fire grills are provided. Drinking water, flush toilets with showers, dump station, playground, horseshoe pits, volleyball court, Frisbee golf course, and two boat ramps are available. An equestrian staging area is available for overnight use, and there are seven miles of hiking, biking, and equestrian trails. Some facilities are wheelchair accessible. Leashed pets are permitted.

Reservations, fees: Reservations are accepted at 877/444-6777 or www.recreation.gov ($10 reservation fee). Sites are $14–22 per night, $55–75 per night for group sites, and $10–25 per night for equestrian sites. Open year-round.

Directions: Drive on Highway 99 to Chowchilla and the Avenue 26 exit. Take that exit and drive east for 17 miles to County Road 29. Turn left (north) on County Road 29 and drive eight miles to the lake.

Contact: U.S. Army Corps of Engineers, Sacramento District, Eastman Lake, 559/689-3255, fax 559/689-3408.

18 ROCK CREEK

Scenic rating: 6

in Sierra National Forest

Map grid A1

Drinking water is the big bonus here. It's easier to live with than the no-water situation at Fish Creek, the other camp in the immediate area. It is also why this camp tends to fill up on weekends. A side trip is the primitive road that heads southeast out of camp. It has a series of sharp turns as it heads east and drops down the canyon near where pretty Aspen Creek feeds into Rock Creek. The elevation at camp is 4,300 feet. (For the best camp in the immediate region, see the Mammoth Pool listing in this chapter.)

RV sites, facilities: There are 18 sites for tents or RVs up to 32 feet (no hookups). Picnic tables and fire grills are provided. Drinking water and vault toilets are available. A camp host is on-site. Leashed pets are permitted.

Reservations, fees: Reservations are accepted at 877/444-6777 or www.recreation.gov ($10 reservation fee). Sites are $17 per night, $34 per night for a double site, $5 per night per each additional vehicle. Open mid-May through mid-September, weather permitting.

Directions: From Fresno, drive north on Highway 41 for about 25 miles to North Fork Road/County Road 200. Turn right and drive northeast for 17.5 miles to Auberry Road/County

CALIFORNIA

Road 222. Turn left (north) and drive one mile to the town of North Fork and Mammoth Pool Road. Turn right and drive 1.5 miles to County Road 225 (still Mammoth Pool Road). Turn right and drive about 25 miles (the road becomes Minarets Road/Forest Road 81) to the campground on the right.

Contact: Sierra National Forest, Bass Lake Ranger District, 559/877-2218, fax 559/877-3108; California Land Management, 559/642-3212.

19 FISH CREEK

Scenic rating: 6

in Sierra National Forest

Map grid A1

This is a small, primitive camp set along Fish Creek at 4,600 feet elevation in the Sierra National Forest. It's a nearby option to Rock Creek, both set on the access road to Mammoth Pool Reservoir.

RV sites, facilities: There are seven sites for tents or RVs up to 16 feet (no hookups). Picnic tables and fire grills are provided. Vault toilets are available. No drinking water is available. Leashed pets are permitted.

Reservations, fees: Reservations are accepted at 877/444-6777 or www.recreation.gov ($10 reservation fee). Sites are $14.68–16 per night, $5 per night per each additional vehicle. Open mid-May through mid-September, weather permitting.

Directions: From Fresno, drive north on Highway 41 for about 25 miles to North Fork Road/County Road 200. Turn right and drive northeast for 17.5 miles to Auberry Road/County Road 222. Turn left (north) and drive one mile to the town of North Fork and Mammoth Pool Road. Turn right and drive 1.5 miles to County Road 225 (still Mammoth Pool Road). Turn right and drive about 21 miles (the road becomes Minarets Road/Forest Road 81) to the campground on the right.

Contact: Sierra National Forest, Bass Lake Ranger District, 559/877-2218, fax 559/877-3108.

20 UPPER AND LOWER BILLY CREEK

Scenic rating: 8

on Huntington Lake in Sierra National Forest

Map grid A1

Huntington Lake is at an elevation of 7,000 feet in the Sierra Nevada. These camps are at the west end of the lake along the north shore, where Billy Creek feeds the lake. Of these two adjacent campgrounds, Lower Billy Creek is smaller than Upper Billy and has lakeside sites available. The lake is four miles long and 0.5 mile wide, with 14 miles of shoreline, several resorts, boat rentals, and a trailhead for hiking into the Kaiser Wilderness.

RV sites, facilities: Upper Billy has 44 sites for tents or RVs up to 30 feet. Lower Billy has 13 sites for tents or RVs up to 30 feet. No hookups. Picnic tables and fire grills are provided. Drinking water and vault toilets are available at both camps; Upper Billy also has flush toilets available. A camp host is on-site. Campfire programs are often available. A small store is nearby. Leashed pets are permitted.

Reservations, fees: Reservations are accepted at 877/444-6777 or www.recreation.gov ($10 reservation fee). Sites are $19 per night, $5 per night for each additional vehicle. Open June through September, weather permitting.

Directions: From Fresno, drive east on Highway 168 to Shaver Lake, then continue 21 miles to Huntington Lake and Huntington Lake Road. Turn left on Huntington Lake Road and drive about five miles to the campgrounds on the left.

Contact: Sierra National Forest, High Sierra Ranger District, 559/855-5355, fax 559/855-5375; California Land Management, 559/893-2111.

21 CATAVEE

Scenic rating: 7

on Huntington Lake in Sierra National Forest

Map grid A1

Catavee is one of three camps in the immediate vicinity, set on the north shore at the eastern end of Huntington Lake. The camp sits near where Bear Creek enters the lake. Huntington Lake is a scenic, High Sierra Ranger District lake at 7,000 feet elevation, where visitors can enjoy fishing, hiking, and sailing. Sailboat regattas take place here regularly during the summer. All water sports are allowed. Nearby resorts offer boat rentals and guest docks, and a boat ramp is nearby. Tackle rentals and bait are also available. A trailhead near camp offers access to the Kaiser Wilderness.

RV sites, facilities: There are 23 sites for tents or RVs up to 30 feet (no hookups). Picnic tables and fire grills are provided. Drinking water and flush toilets are available. A camp host is on-site. Horseback-riding facilities and a small store are nearby. Some facilities are wheelchair-accessible. Leashed pets are permitted.

Reservations, fees: Reservations are accepted at 877/444-6777 or www.recreation.gov ($10 reservation fee). Sites are $21 per night, $5 per night for each additional vehicle. Open June through early September, weather permitting.

Directions: From Fresno, drive east on Highway 168 to Shaver Lake, then continue 21 miles to Huntington Lake and Huntington Lake Road. Turn left on Huntington Lake Road and drive one mile (just past Kinnikinnick) to the campground on the right.

Contact: Sierra National Forest, High Sierra Ranger District, 559/855-5355, fax 559/855-5375; California Land Management, 559/893-2111.

22 KINNIKINNICK

Scenic rating: 7

on Huntington Lake in Sierra National Forest

Map grid A1

Flip a coin; there are three camps in the immediate vicinity on the north shore of the east end of Huntington Lake and, with a boat ramp nearby, they are all favorites. Kinnikinnick is set between Catavee and Deer Creek Campgrounds. The elevation is 7,000 feet.

RV sites, facilities: There are 27 sites for tents or RVs up to 40 feet (no hookups). Picnic tables

and fire grills are provided. Drinking water and flush toilets are available. Horseback-riding facilities and a store are nearby. Some facilities are wheelchair-accessible. Leashed pets are permitted.

Reservations, fees: Reservations are accepted at 877/444-6777 or www.recreation.gov ($10 reservation fee). Sites are $21–46 per night, $5 per night for each additional vehicle. Open June through early September, weather permitting.

Directions: From Fresno, drive east on Highway 168 to Shaver Lake, then continue 21 miles to Huntington Lake and Huntington Lake Road. Turn left on Huntington Lake Road and drive one mile to the campground on the right.

Contact: Sierra National Forest, High Sierra Ranger District, 559/855-5355, fax 559/855-5375; California Land Management, 559/893-2111.

23 DEER CREEK

Scenic rating: 8

on Huntington Lake in Sierra National Forest

Map grid A1

This is one of the best camps at Huntington Lake, set near lakeside at Bear Cove with a boat ramp nearby. It is on the north shore of the lake's eastern end. Huntington Lake is four miles long and 0.5 mile wide, with 14 miles of shoreline, several resorts, boat rentals, and a trailhead for hiking into the Kaiser Wilderness. Two other campgrounds are nearby.

RV sites, facilities: There are 28 sites for tents or RVs up to 40 feet (no hookups). Picnic tables and fire grills are provided. Drinking water and flush toilets are available. A store and propane gas are nearby. Some facilities are wheelchair-accessible. Leashed pets are permitted.

Reservations, fees: Reservations are accepted at 877/444-6777 or www.recreation.gov ($10 reservation fee). Sites are $21 per night, $5 per night for each additional vehicle. Open mid-May through September, weather permitting.

Directions: From Fresno, drive east on Highway 168 to Shaver Lake, then continue 21 miles to Huntington Lake and Huntington Lake Road. Turn left on Huntington Lake Road and drive one mile to the campground entrance road on the left.

Contact: Sierra National Forest, High Sierra Ranger District, 559/855-5355, fax 559/855-5375; California Land management, 559/893-2111.

24 COLLEGE

Scenic rating: 7

on Huntington Lake in Sierra National Forest
Map grid A1

College is a beautiful site along the shore of the northeastern end of Huntington Lake, at 7,000 feet elevation. This camp is close to a small store in the town of Huntington Lake.

RV sites, facilities: There are 11 sites for tents or RVs up to 20 feet (no hookups). Picnic tables and fire grills are provided. Vault toilets and limited drinking water are available. Interpretive programs are offered. Horseback-riding facilities, store, and propane gas are nearby. Leashed pets are permitted.

Reservations, fees: Reservations are accepted at 877/444-6777 or www.recreation.gov ($10 reservation fee). Sites are $18–32 per night, $5 per night for each additional vehicle. Open June through early September, weather permitting.

Directions: From Fresno, drive east on Highway 168 to Shaver Lake, then continue 21 miles to Huntington Lake and Huntington Lake Road. Turn left on Huntington Lake Road and drive 0.5 mile to the campground.

Contact: Sierra National Forest, High Sierra Ranger District, 559/855-5355, fax 559/855-5375; California Land Management, 559/893-2111.

25 RANCHERIA

Scenic rating: 8

on Huntington Lake in Sierra National Forest
Map grid A1

This is the granddaddy of the camps at Huntington Lake, and also the easiest to reach.

It is along the shore of the lake's eastern end. A bonus here is nearby Rancheria Falls National Recreation Trail, which provides access to beautiful Rancheria Falls. Another side trip is the 15-minute drive to Bear Butte (the access road is across from the campground entrance) at 8,598 feet elevation, providing a sweeping view of the lake below. The elevation at camp is 7,000 feet.

RV sites, facilities: There are 146 sites for tents or RVs up to 40 feet (no hookups). Picnic tables and fire grills are provided. Drinking water and flush and vault toilets are available. A camp host is on-site. Interpretive programs are offered. A store and propane gas are nearby. Leashed pets are permitted.

Reservations, fees: Reservations are accepted at 877/444-6777 or www.recreation.gov ($10 reservation fee). Sites are $19–42 per night, $5 per night for each additional vehicle. Open year-round, weather permitting.

Directions: From Fresno, drive east on Highway 168 to Shaver Lake, then continue 20 miles to Huntington Lake and the campground on the left.

Contact: Sierra National Forest, High Sierra Ranger District, 559/855-5355, fax 559/855-5375; California Land Management, 559/893-2111.

26 BADGER FLAT

Scenic rating: 7

on Rancheria Creek in Sierra National Forest
Map grid A1

This camp is a good launching pad for backpackers. It is set at 8,200 feet elevation along Rancheria Creek. The trail leading out of the camp is routed into the Kaiser Wilderness to the north and Dinkey Lakes Wilderness to the south.

RV sites, facilities: There are 15 sites for tents or RVs up to 22 feet (no hookups). Fire grills and picnic tables are provided. Vault toilets and horseback-riding facilities are available. No drinking water is available. Leashed pets are permitted.

Reservations, fees: Reservations are not accepted. Sites are $17 per night, $5 per night for each additional vehicle. Open June through October, weather permitting.

Directions: From Fresno, drive east on Highway 168 to Shaver Lake, then continue 21 miles to Huntington Lake and Kaiser Pass Road/Forest Road 80. Turn right and drive four miles to the campground.

Contact: Sierra National Forest, High Sierra Ranger District, 559/855-5355, fax 559/855-5375; California Land Management, 559/893-2111.

27 BADGER FLAT GROUP AND HORSE CAMP

Scenic rating: 7

on Rancheria Creek in Sierra National Forest

Map grid A1

Badger Flat is a primitive site along Rancheria Creek at 8,200 feet elevation, about five miles east of Huntington Lake. It is a popular horse camp and a good jump-off spot for wilderness trekkers. A trail that passes through camp provides two options: Head south for three miles to enter the Dinkey Lakes Wilderness, or head north for two miles to enter the Kaiser Wilderness.

RV sites, facilities: There is one group site for tents or RVs up to 30 feet (no hookups) that can accommodate up to 100 people. Picnic tables, fire grills, and food lockers are provided. Vault toilets and horse facilities are available. No drinking water is available. A store is nearby. Leashed pets are permitted.

Reservations, fees: Reservations are required at 877/444-6777 or www.recreation.gov ($10 reservation fee). The fee is $275 per night. Open June through October, weather permitting.

Directions: From Fresno, drive east on Highway 168 to Shaver Lake, then continue 21 miles to Huntington Lake and Kaiser Pass Road/Forest Road 80. Turn right and drive five miles to the campground on the right.

Contact: Sierra National Forest, High Sierra Ranger District, 559/855-5355, fax 559/855-5375; California Land Management, 559/893-2111.

28 HIDDEN VIEW

Scenic rating: 5

north of Fresno on Hensley Lake

Map grid A1

Hensley Lake is popular with water-skiers and personal watercraft users in spring and summer, and it has good prospects for bass fishing as well. Hensley covers 1,500 surface acres with 24 miles of shoreline and, as long as water levels are maintained, makes for a wonderful water playland. Swimming is good, with the best spot at Buck Ridge on the east side of the lake, where there are picnic tables and trees for shade. The reservoir was created by a dam on the Fresno River. A nature trail is also here. The elevation is 540 feet.

RV sites, facilities: There are 55 sites for tents or RVs of any length, some with electric hookups (30 amps), and two group sites for 25–100 people. Picnic tables and fire grills are provided. Restrooms with flush toilets and showers, drinking water, dump station, playground, and boat ramp are available. Some facilities are wheelchair accessible. Leashed pets are permitted.

Reservations, fees: Reservations are accepted at 877/444-6777 or www.recreation.gov ($10 reservation fee). Sites are $14–20 per night, $50 per night for group sites. Boat launching is free for campers. Open year-round.

Directions: From Madera, drive northeast on Highway 145 for about six miles to County Road 400. Bear left on County Road 400 and drive to County Road 603 below the dam. Turn left and drive about two miles on County Road 603 to County Road 407. Turn right on County Road 407 and drive 0.5 mile to the campground.

Contact: U.S. Army Corps of Engineers, Sacramento District, Hensley Lake, 559/673-5151, fax 559/673-2044.

CALIFORNIA

29 SMALLEY COVE

Scenic rating: 7

on Kerckhoff Reservoir near Madera

Map grid A1

Kerckhoff Reservoir can get so hot that it might seem you could fry an egg on the rocks. Campers should be certain to have some kind of tarp they can set up as a sun screen. The lake is small and remote, and the use of boat motors more than five horsepower is prohibited. Most campers bring rafts or canoes, and there is a good swimming beach near the picnic area and campground. Fishing is not so good here. The elevation is 1,000 feet.

RV sites, facilities: There are five sites for tents or RVs up to 30 feet (no hookups). Picnic tables and fire grills are provided. Drinking water and vault toilets are available. Five group picnic sites are available. You can buy supplies in Auberry. Some facilities are wheelchair-accessible. Leashed pets are permitted.

Reservations, fees: Reservations are not accepted. Sites are $10 per night, $3 per night for each additional vehicle, $7 per night for additional RV, $1 per pet per night. Open year-round.

Directions: From Fresno, take Highway 41 north for three miles to the exit for Highway 168 east. Take that exit and drive east on Highway 168 for about 22 miles to Auberry Road. Turn left (north) and drive 2.8 miles to Powerhouse Road. Turn left and drive 8.5 miles to the campground.

Contact: PG&E Land Services, 916/386-5164, fax 916/386-5388, www.pge.com/recreation.

30 CAMP EDISON

Scenic rating: 8

on Shaver Lake

Map grid A1

Camp Edison is the best camp at Shaver Lake, set on a peninsula along the lake's western shore, with a boat ramp and marina. The lake is at an elevation of 5,370 feet in the Sierra, a pretty area that has become popular for its calm, warm days and cool water. Boat rentals and bait and tackle are available at the marina. Newcomers with youngsters will discover that the best area for swimming and playing in the water is on the east side of the lake. Though more distant, this part of the lake offers sandy beaches rather than rocky drop-offs.

RV sites, facilities: There are 252 sites for RVs or tents; some sites have full or partial hookups (20, 30, and 50 amps). During the summer season, six tent trailers also are available. Picnic tables, fire rings, and barbecues are provided. Restrooms with flush toilets and pay showers, drinking water, cable TV, Wi-Fi, general store, dump station, coin laundry, marina, boat ramp, and horseback-riding facilities are available. Some facilities are wheelchair-accessible. Leashed pets are permitted.

Reservations, fees: Reservations are required and must be made by fax or mail to: Camp Edison, PO Box 600, 42696 Tollhouse Road, Shaver Lake, CA 93664. Sites are $25–60 per night, $7.50–18 per night for each additional vehicle, $4 per person per night for more than two people, $6 per day for boat launching, $5 per pet per night. Tent trailers are $75 per night. Group rates are available. Open year-round with limited winter services.

Directions: From Fresno, take the exit for Highway 41 north and drive north on Highway 41 to the exit for Highway 180 east. Take that exit and drive east on Highway 180 to Highway 168 east. Take that exit and drive east on Highway 168 to the town of Shaver Lake. Continue one mile on Highway 168 to the campground entrance road on the right. Turn right and drive to the campground on the west shore of Shaver Lake.

Contact: Camp Edison, Southern California Edison, 559/841-3134, fax 559/841-3193, www.sce.com/campedison.

31 DORABELLE

Scenic rating: 7

on Shaver Lake in Sierra National Forest

Map grid A1

This is one of the few Forest Service camps in the state that is set up more for RVers than for tenters. The camp is along a long cove at the southwest corner of the lake, well protected from winds out of the northwest. Several hiking trails are available here. Shaver Lake is a popular lake for vacationers, and waterskiing and wakeboarding are extremely popular. It is well stocked with trout and kokanee salmon. Boat rentals and bait and tackle are available at the nearby marina. The elevation is 5,400 feet.

RV sites, facilities: There are 68 sites for tents or RVs up to 40 feet (no hookups). Picnic tables and fire grills are provided. Drinking water and vault toilets are available. A store is nearby. Leashed pets are permitted.

Reservations, fees: Reservations are accepted at 877/444-6777 or www.recreation.gov ($10 reservation fee). Sites are $19 per night, $5 per night for each additional vehicle. Open May through September, weather permitting.

Directions: From Fresno, drive east on Highway 168 to Dorabelle Road (on the right just as you enter the town of Shaver Lake). Turn right on Dorabelle Road and drive one mile to the campground at the southwest end of Shaver Lake.

Contact: Sierra National Forest, High Sierra Ranger District, 559/855-5355, fax 559/855-5375; California Land Management, 559/893-2111.

32 SWANSON MEADOW

Scenic rating: 4

near Shaver Lake in Sierra National Forest

Map grid A1

This is the smallest and most primitive of the camps near Shaver Lake; it is used primarily as an overflow area if lakeside camps are full. It is about two miles south of Shaver Lake at an elevation of 5,600 feet.

RV sites, facilities: There are eight sites for tents or RVs up to 30 feet (no hookups). Picnic tables and fire grills are provided. Vault toilets are available. No drinking water is available. A store is nearby. Leashed pets are permitted.

Reservations, fees: Reservations are not accepted. Sites are $17 per night, $5 per night for each additional vehicle. Open May through October, weather permitting.

Directions: From Fresno, drive east on Highway 168 to Dinkey Creek Road (on the right just as you enter the town of Shaver Lake). Turn right and drive three miles to the campground entrance road on the left. Turn left and drive a short distance to the campground.

Contact: Sierra National Forest, High Sierra Ranger District, 559/855-5355, fax 559/855-5375; California Land Management, 559/893-2111.

33 DINKEY CREEK AND GROUP CAMP

Scenic rating: 7

in Sierra National Forest

Map grid A1

This is a huge Forest Service camp set along Dinkey Creek at 5,700 feet elevation, well in the interior of Sierra National Forest. It is a popular camp for anglers who take the trail and hike upstream along the creek for small-trout fishing in a pristine setting. Backpackers occasionally lay over here before driving on to the Dinkey Lakes Parking Area, for hikes to Mystery Lake, Swede Lake, South Lake, and others in the nearby Dinkey Lakes Wilderness.

RV sites, facilities: There are 127 sites for tents or RVs up to 40 feet (no hookups), and one group site for up to 50 people. Picnic tables and fire grills are provided. Drinking water, flush and vault toilets, coin showers, and horseback-riding facilities are nearby. You can buy supplies in Dinkey Creek. Leashed pets are permitted.

Reservations, fees: Reservations are required at 877/444-6777 or www.recreation.gov ($10 reservation fee). Sites are $22–24 per night, $5 per night for each additional vehicle, $154 per night for the group site. Open May through September, weather permitting.

Directions: From Fresno, drive east on Highway 168 to Dinkey Creek Road (on the right just as you enter the town of Shaver Lake). Turn right and drive 13 miles to the campground. A map of Sierra National Forest is advised.

Contact: Sierra National Forest, High Sierra Ranger District, 559/855-5355, fax 559/855-5375; project office, 559/841-2705.

34 MILLERTON LAKE STATE RECREATION AREA

Scenic rating: 6

near Madera

Map grid A1

As the temperature gauge goes up in the summer, the value of Millerton Lake increases at the same rate. The lake is set at 578 feet in the foothills of the San Joaquin Valley, and the water is like gold here. The campground and recreation area are set on a peninsula along the north shore of the lake; there are sandy beach areas on both sides of the lake with boat ramps available near the campgrounds. It's a big lake, with 43 miles of shoreline, from a narrow lake inlet extending to an expansive main lake body. The irony at Millerton is that when the lake is filled to the brim, the beaches are covered, so ideal conditions are actually when the lake level is down a bit, typically from early summer on. Fishing for bass can be good here in spring. Catfish are popular for shoreliners on summer evenings. Waterskiing is very popular in summer, of course. Anglers head upstream, water-skiers downstream. The lake's south side has a huge day-use area. During winter, boat tours are available to view bald eagles. A note of history: The original Millerton County Courthouse, built in 1867, is in the park.

RV sites, facilities: There are 148 sites, 27 with full hookups, for tents or RVs up to 36 feet, 40 boat-in sites, and two group sites for 45–75 people. Picnic tables and fire grills are provided. Drinking water, restrooms with flush toilets and coin showers, dump station, picnic areas, full-service marina, snack bar, boat rentals, and boat ramps are available. You can buy supplies in Friant. Some facilities are wheelchair-accessible. Leashed pets are permitted.

Reservations, fees: Reservations are accepted at 800/444-7275 or www.reserveamerica.com ($8 reservation fee). Sites are $30–40 per night, $10 per night for each additional vehicle, $11 for boat-in sites, $150–200 per night for group sites. Boat launching is $7 per day. Open year-round.

Directions: Drive on Highway 99 to Madera at the exit for Highway 145 East. Take that exit east and drive on Highway 145 for 22 miles (six miles past the intersection with Highway 41) to the park entrance on the right.

Contact: Millerton Lake State Recreation Area, 559/822-2332, fax 559/822-2319, www.parks.ca.gov.

35 GIGANTEA

Scenic rating: 7

on Dinkey Creek in Sierra National Forest

Map grid A1

This primitive campground is set along Dinkey Creek adjacent to the McKinley Grove Botanical Area, which features a little-known grove of giant sequoias. The campground is set on a short loop spur road, and day visitors are better off stopping at the McKinley Grove Picnic Area. The elevation is 6,400 feet.

RV sites, facilities: There are 11 sites for tents or RVs up to 35 feet (no hookups). Picnic tables and fire grills are provided. Vault toilets are available. No drinking water is available. You can buy supplies in Dinkey Creek. Leashed pets are permitted.

Reservations, fees: Reservations are not accepted. Sites are $17 per night, $5 per night for each additional vehicle. Open May through September, weather permitting.

Directions: From Fresno, drive east on Highway 168 to Dinkey Creek Road (on the right just as you enter the town of Shaver Lake). Turn right and drive 13 miles to McKinley Grove Road/ Forest Road 40. Turn right and drive 6.5 miles to the campground.

Contact: Sierra National Forest, High Sierra Ranger District, 559/855-5355, fax 559/855-5375; California Land Management, 559/893-2111.

BUCK MEADOW

Scenic rating: 7

on Deer Creek in Sierra National Forest
Map grid A1

This is one of the three little-known, primitive camps in the area. It's set at 6,800 feet elevation along Deer Creek, about seven miles from Wishon Reservoir, a more popular destination.

RV sites, facilities: There are 10 sites for tents or RVs up to 35 feet (no hookups). Picnic tables and fire grills are provided. Vault toilets are available. No drinking water is available. Garbage must be packed out. Leashed pets are permitted.

Reservations, fees: Reservations are not accepted. Sites are $17 per night, $5 per night for each additional vehicle. Open June through September, weather permitting.

Directions: From Fresno, drive east on Highway 168 to Dinkey Creek Road (on the right just as you enter the town of Shaver Lake). Turn right and drive 13 miles to McKinley Grove Road (Forest Road 40). Turn right and drive eight miles to the campground.

Contact: Sierra National Forest, High Sierra Ranger District, 559/855-5355, fax 559/855-5375; California Land Management, 559/893-2111.

37 JACKASS MEADOW

Scenic rating: 7

on Florence Lake in Sierra National Forest
Map grid B1

Jackass Meadow is a pretty spot adjacent to Florence Lake, near the Upper San Joaquin River. There are good canoeing, rafting, and float-tubing possibilities, all high-Sierra style,

and swimming is allowed. The boat speed limit is 15 mph. The elevation is 7,200 feet. The lake is remote and can be reached only after a long, circuitous drive on a narrow road with many blind turns. A trailhead at the lake offers access to the wilderness and the John Muir Trail. A hikers water taxi is available.

RV sites, facilities: There are 44 sites for tents or RVs up to 23 feet (no hookups). Picnic tables and fire grills are provided. Drinking water and vault toilets are available. A boat launch, fishing boat rentals, and wheelchair-accessible fishing pier are available nearby. Leashed pets are permitted.

Reservations, fees: Reservations are accepted at 877/444-6777 or www.recreation.gov ($10 reservation fee). Sites are $17 per night, $34 per night for a double site, $5 per night for each additional vehicle. Open June through September, weather permitting.

Directions: From the town of Shaver Lake, drive east on Highway 168 for 21 miles to Kaiser Pass Road. Bear northeast on Kaiser Pass Road/Forest Road 80 (slow and curvy) to a junction (left goes to Mono Hot Springs and Lake Edison) with Florence Lake Road. Bear right at the junction and drive seven miles to the campground.

Contact: Sierra National Forest, High Sierra Ranger District, 559/855-5355, fax 559/855-5375; California Land Management, 559/893-2111.

38 TRAPPER SPRINGS

Scenic rating: 8

on Courtright Reservoir in Sierra National Forest
Map grid B1

Trapper Springs is on the west shore of Courtright Reservoir, set at 8,200 feet elevation on the west slope of the Sierra. Courtright is a great destination, with excellent camping, boating, fishing, and hiking into the nearby John Muir Wilderness. A 15-mph speed limit makes the lake ideal for fishing, canoeing, and rafting. Swimming is allowed, but the water is very cold. The lake level can drop dramatically by late summer. A trailhead a mile north of camp by car heads around the north end of the lake to a fork; to the left it is routed into the Dinkey Lakes Wilderness, and to the right it is routed to the head of the lake, then follows Dusy Creek in a long climb into spectacular country in the John Muir Wilderness. There are two driving routes to this lake, one from Shaver Lake and the other from Pine Flat Reservoir; both are very long, slow, and twisty drives.

RV sites, facilities: There are 70 sites for tents or RVs up to 35 feet (no hookups). Picnic tables and fire grills are provided. Drinking water and vault toilets are available. A boat ramp is nearby. Some facilities are wheelchair-accessible. Leashed pets are permitted.

Reservations, fees: Reservations are not accepted. Sites are $18 per night, $9 per night for additional RV, $3 per night for each additional vehicle, $1 per pet per night. Open June through October.

Directions: From Fresno, drive east on Highway 168 to Dinkey Creek Road (on the right just as you enter the town of Shaver Lake). Turn right and drive 13 miles to McKinley Grove Road/Forest Road 40. Turn right and drive 14 miles to Courtright Road. Turn left (north) and drive 12 miles to the campground entrance road on the right.

Contact: Sierra National Forest, High Sierra Ranger District, 559/855-5355, fax 559/855-5375; PG&E Land Services, 916/386-5164, fax 916/386-5388, www.pge.com/recreation.

39 WISHON VILLAGE RV RESORT

Scenic rating: 7

near Wishon Reservoir
Map grid B1

This privately operated mountain park is set near the shore of Wishon Reservoir, about one mile from the dam. Trout stocks often make for good fishing in early summer, and anglers with boats love the 15-mph speed limit, which keeps personal watercraft off the water. Backpackers and hikers can find a great trailhead at the south end of the lake at Coolidge Meadow, where a trail awaits that is routed to the Woodchuck Creek drainage and numerous lakes in the John Muir Wilderness. The elevation is 6,772 feet.

RV sites, facilities: There are 97 sites with full hookups (50 amps) for RVs up to 45 feet, and 26 sites for tents. A rental trailer is also available. Picnic tables and fire pits are provided. Restrooms with coin showers, drinking water, a general store, and Sunday church services are available. Coin laundry, ice, boat ramp, motorboat rentals, bait and tackle, boat slips, volleyball, horseshoes, and propane gas are nearby. Leashed pets are permitted.

Reservations, fees: Reservations are recommended. RV sites are $34 per night, $23 per night for tent sites, $5 per night for extra vehicle, $3 per person per night for more than two people, $3 per pet per night. Weekly and monthly rates available. Open May through October.

Directions: From Fresno, drive east on Highway 168 to Dinkey Creek Road (on the right just as you enter the town of Shaver Lake). Turn right and drive 13 miles to McKinley Grove Road (Forest Road 40). Turn right and drive 15 miles to the park (66500 McKinley Grove Road/Forest Road 40).

Contact: Wishon Village RV Resort, 559/865-5361, www.wishonvillage.com.

40 LILY PAD

Scenic rating: 7

near Wishon Reservoir in Sierra National Forest
Map grid B1

This is the smallest of the three camps at Wishon Reservoir. It is set along the southwest shore at 6,500 feet elevation, about a mile from both the lake and a good boat ramp. A 15-mph speed limit ensures quiet water, making this an ideal destination for families with canoes or rafts. The conditions at this lake are similar to those at Courtright Reservoir. There are two driving routes to this lake, one from Shaver Lake and the other from Pine Flat Reservoir; both are very long, slow, and twisty drives.

RV sites, facilities: There are 11 sites for tents or RVs up to 35 feet (no hookups), and four hike-in sites. Picnic tables and fire grills are provided. Drinking water and vault toilets are available. Groceries, boat rentals, boat ramp, and propane gas are nearby. Leashed pets are permitted.

Reservations, fees: Reservations are not accepted. Sites are $18 per night, $7 per night for additional RV, $3 per night for each additional vehicle, $1 per pet per night. Open May through October, weather permitting.

Directions: From Fresno, drive east on Highway 168 to Dinkey Creek Road (on the right just as you enter the town of Shaver Lake). Turn right and drive 13 miles to McKinley Grove Road (Forest Road 40). Turn right and drive 16 miles to the campground on the right.

Contact: Sierra National Forest, High Sierra Ranger District, 559/855-5355, fax 559/855-5375; PG&E Land Services, 916/386-5164, fax 916/386-5388, www.pge.com/recreation.

41 UPPER KINGS RIVER GROUP CAMP

Scenic rating: 8

on Wishon Reservoir

Map grid B1

Wishon Reservoir is a great place for a camping trip. When the lake is full, which is not often enough, the place has great natural beauty, set at 6,400 feet elevation and surrounded by national forest. The fishing is fair enough on summer evenings, and a 15-mph speed limit keeps the lake quiet. Swimming is allowed, but the water is very cold. A side-trip option is hiking from the trailhead at Woodchuck Creek, which within the span of a one-day hike takes you into the John Muir Wilderness and past three lakes—Woodchuck, Chimney, and Marsh. There are two driving routes to this lake, one from Shaver Lake and the other from Pine Flat Reservoir; both are very long, slow, and twisty drives.

RV sites, facilities: There is a group site for tents or RVs up to 40 feet (no hookups) that can accommodate up to 50 people. Picnic tables and fire grills are provided. Drinking water and vault toilets are available. Leashed pets are permitted.

Reservations, fees: Reservations are required at 916/386-5164. Sites are $150 per night. Open June through early October, weather permitting.

Directions: From Fresno, drive east on Highway 168 to Dinkey Creek Road (on the right just as you enter the town of Shaver Lake). Turn right and drive 13 miles to McKinley Grove Road/Forest Road 40. Turn right and drive to the Wishon Dam. The campground is near the base of the dam.

Contact: PG&E Land Services, 916/386-5164, fax 916/386-5388, www.pge.com/recreation.

42 HORTON CREEK

Scenic rating: 7

near Bishop

Map grid B1

This is a little-known, primitive BLM camp set along Horton Creek, northwest of Bishop. It can make a good base camp for hunters in the fall, with wild, rugged country to the west. The elevation is 4,975 feet.

RV sites, facilities: There are 53 sites for tents or RVs up to 30 feet (no hookups). Picnic tables and fire grills are provided. Pit toilets and garbage containers are available. No drinking water is available. Leashed pets are permitted.

Reservations, fees: Reservations are not accepted. Sites are $5 per night and there is a 14-day stay limit. Open early May through October, weather permitting.

Directions: Drive on U.S. 395 to Sawmill Road (eight miles north of Bishop). Turn left (northwest, toward the Sierra) and drive a very short distance to Round Valley Road. Turn right and drive approximately five miles to the campground entrance on the left.

Contact: Bureau of Land Management,

CALIFORNIA

Bishop Field Office, 760/872-4881, fax 760/872-5050.

43 BROWN'S MILLPOND CAMPGROUND

Scenic rating: 6

near Bishop

Map grid B1

This privately operated camp is adjacent to the Millpond Recreation Area, which offers ball fields, playgrounds, and a swimming lake. No powerboats are allowed. There are opportunities for sailing, archery, tennis, horseshoe games, and fishing.

RV sites, facilities: There are 75 sites for tents or RVs of any length; some sites have partial hookups (30 amps). Picnic tables and fire grills are provided. Restrooms with flush toilets and coin showers, drinking water, and coin laundry are available. A limit of one vehicle per site is enforced. Leashed pets are permitted.

Reservations, fees: Reservations are accepted. Sites are $20–25 per vehicle per night. Open March through October.

Directions: Drive on U.S. 395 to a road signed "Millpond/County Park" (seven miles north of Bishop). Turn southwest (toward the Sierra) at that road (Ed Powers Road) and drive 0.2 mile to Sawmill Road. Turn right and drive 0.8 mile to Millpond Road. Turn left and drive a short distance to the campground.

Contact: Brown's Millpond Campground, 760/873-5342, www.brownscampgrounds.com/millpond.html.

44 BROWN'S TOWN

Scenic rating: 5

near Bishop

Map grid B1

This privately operated campground is one of several in the vicinity of Bishop. It's all shade and grass, and it's next to the golf course.

RV sites, facilities: There are 106 sites with no hookups for tents or RVs of any length and 44 sites with partial hookups (30 amps) for tents or RVs. Some sites are pull-through. Picnic tables are provided, and fire grills are provided at most sites. Restrooms with flush toilets and coin showers, drinking water, cable TV at 10 sites, coin laundry, dump station, museum, convenience store, and snack bar are available. Leashed pets are permitted.

Reservations, fees: Reservations are accepted. Sites are $20–27 per night, $1 per person per night for more than two people. One-vehicle limit per site. Fourteen-day stay limit per season. Some credit cards accepted. Open March through Thanksgiving, weather permitting.

Directions: Drive on U.S. 395 to Schober Lane (one mile south of Bishop) and the campground entrance. Turn northwest (toward the Sierra) and into the campground.

Contact: Brown's Town, 760/873-8522, www.brownscampgrounds.com/browns.html.

45 BITTERBRUSH

Scenic rating: 7

near Bishop in the Inyo National Forest

Map grid B1

Bitterbrush opened in 2007 and is situated along Bishop Creek with piñon pines and sagebrush providing the scenery. In the fall, the aspens are spectacular in the canyon between here and beautiful Lake Sabrina. The elevation is 7,350 feet.

RV sites, facilities: There are 35 sites for tents or RVs to 35 feet (no hookups). Picnic tables, bear-proof lockers, and fire rings are provided. Drinking water (seasonal), vault toilets, and a dump station are available. Some facilities are wheelchair-accessible. Leashed pets are permitted.

Reservations, fees: Reservations are not accepted. Sites are $19 per night; free when water becomes unavailable. There is a maximum 14-day limit. Open year-round, weather permitting.

Directions: From Bishop drive west on Highway 168 for nine miles to the campground.

Contact: Inyo National Forest, White Mountain Ranger District, 760/873-2500, fax 760/873-2563, www.fs.fed.us.

46 FORKS

Scenic rating: 7

near South Lake in Inyo National Forest

Map grid B1

After a visit here, it's no mystery how the Forest Service named this camp. It is at the fork in the road, which gives you two options: You can turn south on South Lake Road and drive along the South Fork of Bishop Creek up to pretty South Lake, or you can keep driving on Highway 168 to another beautiful lake, Lake Sabrina, where hikers will find a trailhead that offers access to the John Muir Wilderness. The elevation is 7,800 feet.

RV sites, facilities: There are eight sites for tents only and 18 sites for RVs up to 30 feet (no hookups). Picnic tables and fire grills are provided. Drinking water and flush and vault toilets are available. Supplies are available in Bishop. Leashed pets are permitted.

Reservations, fees: Reservations are not accepted. Sites are $19 per night. Open late April through October, weather permitting.

Directions: Drive on U.S. 395 to Bishop and Highway 168. Turn west (toward the Sierra) on Highway 168 and drive 14 miles to South Lake Road. Turn left and drive 0.25 mile to the campground entrance on the right.

Contact: Inyo National Forest, White Mountain Ranger District, 760/873-2500, fax 760/873-2563; Rainbow Pack Outfitters, 760/873-8877.

47 BIG TREES

Scenic rating: 8

on Bishop Creek in Inyo National Forest

Map grid B1

This is a small Forest Service camp on Bishop Creek at 7,500 feet elevation. This section of

the stream is stocked with small trout by the Department of Fish and Game. Both South Lake and Lake Sabrina are about 10 miles away.

RV sites, facilities: There are nine sites for tents or RVs up to 30 feet (no hookups). Picnic tables and fire grills are provided. Drinking water and flush toilets are available. Horseback-riding facilities are approximately seven miles away. Supplies are available in Bishop. Leashed pets are permitted.

Reservations, fees: Reservations are not accepted. Sites are $16 per night. Open late April through October, weather permitting.

Directions: Drive on U.S. 395 to Bishop and Highway 168. Turn west (toward the Sierra) on Highway 168 and drive 11 miles to the campground access road on the left. Turn left and drive two miles on a dirt road to the campground.

Contact: Inyo National Forest, White Mountain Ranger District, 760/873-2500, fax 760/873-2563; Rainbow Pack Outfitters, 760/873-8877.

48 BISHOP PARK

Scenic rating: 6

near Lake Sabrina in Inyo National Forest

Map grid B1

Bishop Park Camp is one in a series of camps along Bishop Creek. This one is set just behind the summer community of Aspendell. It is about two miles from Lake Sabrina, an ideal day trip or jump-off spot for a backpacking expedition into the John Muir Wilderness. The elevation is 8,400 feet.

RV sites, facilities: There are 20 sites for tents or RVs up to 22 feet (no hookups), and a group tent site for up to 25 people. Picnic tables, fire grills, and food lockers are provided. Drinking water and flush toilets are available. Horseback-riding facilities are nearby. Supplies are available in Bishop. Some facilities are wheelchair-accessible. Leashed pets are permitted.

Reservations, fees: Reservations are not accepted for the family sites, but are required for the group site at 877/444-6777 or www.recreation.gov ($10 reservation fee). Sites are $19 per night, $60 per night for group site. Open mid-May through mid-October, weather permitting.

Directions: Drive on U.S. 395 to Bishop and Highway 168. Turn west (toward the Sierra) on Highway 168 and drive 15 miles to the campground.

Contact: Inyo National Forest, White Mountain Ranger District, 760/873-2500, fax 760/873-2563; Rainbow Pack Outfitters, 760/873-8877; campground management, 760/872-7018.

49 INTAKE AND INTAKE WALK-IN

Scenic rating: 7

on Sabrina Creek in Inyo National Forest

Map grid B1

This small camp, set at 8,200 feet elevation at a tiny reservoir on Bishop Creek, is about three miles from Lake Sabrina where a trailhead leads into the John Muir Wilderness. Nearby North Lake and South Lake provide side-trip options. All three are beautiful alpine lakes.

RV sites, facilities: There are 11 sites for tents or RVs up to 40 feet (no hookups), and five walk-in tent sites. Picnic tables, food lockers, and fire grills are provided. Drinking water and flush toilets are available. Supplies are available in Bishop. Leashed pets are permitted.

Reservations, fees: Reservations are not accepted. Sites are $19 per night. The walk-in sites are open year-round, weather permitting. Drive-in sites are open April through October, weather permitting.

Directions: Drive on U.S. 395 to Bishop and Highway 168. Turn west (toward the Sierra) on Highway 168 and drive 14.5 miles to the campground entrance.

Contact: Inyo National Forest, White Mountain Ranger District, 760/873-2500, fax 760/873-2563.

50 FOUR JEFFREY

Scenic rating: 8

near South Lake in Inyo National Forest

Map grid B1

The camp is set on the South Fork of Bishop Creek at 8,100 feet elevation, about four miles from South Lake. If you can arrange a trip in the fall, make sure you visit this camp. The fall colors are spectacular, with the aspen trees exploding in yellows and oranges. It is also the last camp on South Lake Road to be closed in the fall, and though nights are cold, it is well worth the trip. This is by far the largest of the Forest Service camps in the vicinity. There are three lakes in the area: North Lake, Lake Sabrina, and South Lake. South Lake is stocked with trout and has a 5-mph speed limit.

RV sites, facilities: There are 106 sites for tents or RVs up to 30 feet (no hookups). Picnic tables, food lockers, and fire grills are provided. Drinking water, flush toilets, and a dump station are available. Horseback-riding facilities are available nearby. A café, a small store, and fishing-boat rentals are available at South Lake. Supplies are available in Bishop. Some facilities are wheelchair-accessible. Leashed pets are permitted.

Reservations, fees: Reservations are accepted at 877/444-6777 or www.recreation.gov ($10 reservation fee). Sites are $19 per night. Open mid-April through October, weather permitting.

Directions: Drive on U.S. 395 to Bishop and Highway 168. Turn west (toward the Sierra) on Highway 168 and drive 14 miles to South Lake Road. Turn left and drive 0.5 mile to the campground.

Contact: Inyo National Forest, White Mountain Ranger District, 760/873-2500, fax 760/873-2563; Rainbow Pack Outfitters, 760/873-8877.

51 CREEKSIDE RV PARK

Scenic rating: 7

on the South Fork of Bishop Creek

Map grid B1

This privately operated park in the high country is set up primarily for RVs. A lot of folks are surprised to find it here. The South Fork of Bishop Creek runs through the park. A bonus is a fishing pond stocked with Alpers trout. North, Sabrina, and South Lakes are in the area. The elevation is 8,300 feet.

RV sites, facilities: There are 45 sites with full or partial hookups (20 and 30 amps) for RVs up to 35 feet, and four sites for tents. Fourteen rental trailers are also available. Restrooms with flush toilets and coin showers, drinking water, convenience store, propane, horseshoes, and fish-cleaning facilities are available. Leashed pets are permitted.

Reservations, fees: Reservations are accepted. RV sites are $39 per night, tent sites are $29 per night, $1 per person per night for more than two people, $5 per night for each additional vehicle, $5 per pet per night. Open May through October. Some credit cards accepted.

Directions: Drive on U.S. 395 to Bishop and Highway 168. Turn west (toward the Sierra) on Highway 168 and drive 14 miles to South Lake Road. Turn left and drive two miles to the campground entrance on the left (1949 South Lake Road).

Contact: Creekside RV Park, 760/873-4483, www.bishopcreeksidervpark.com.

52 SABRINA

Scenic rating: 8

near Lake Sabrina in Inyo National Forest

Map grid B1   **BEST(**

You get the best of both worlds at this camp. It is set at 9,000 feet elevation on Bishop Creek, just 0.5 mile from 200-acre Lake Sabrina, one of the prettiest alpine lakes in California that you can reach by car. A 10-mph boat speed limit is in effect. Sabrina is stocked with trout, including some big Alpers trout. Trails nearby

are routed into the high country of the John Muir Wilderness. Take your pick. Whatever your choice, it's a good one. By the way, Sabrina is pronounced "Sa-bry-na," not "Sa-bree-na."

RV sites, facilities: There are 18 sites for tents or RVs up to 30 feet (no hookups). Picnic tables and fire grills are provided. Drinking water and pit toilets are available. A boat ramp and boat rentals are nearby. Supplies are available in Bishop. Leashed pets are permitted.

Reservations, fees: Reservations are not accepted. Sites are $19 per night. Open mid-May through mid-September, weather permitting.

Directions: Drive on U.S. 395 to Bishop and Highway 168. Turn west (toward the Sierra) on Highway 168 and drive 17 miles (signed "Lake Sabrina" at a fork) to the campground.

Contact: Inyo National Forest, White Mountain Ranger District, 760/873-2500, fax 760/873-2563; Bishop Pack Outfitters, 760/873-4785.

53 WILLOW

Scenic rating: 8

on Bishop Creek in Inyo National Forest

Map grid B1

This is one in a series of pretty Forest Service camps set along the south fork of Bishop Creek. Willow is located near Mountain Glen (see listing in this chapter) at an elevation of 9,000 feet. Primitive and beautiful, this is a favorite. Just up the road is the trailhead to the Chocolate Lakes and Bishop Pass, as well as low-speed boating and fishing at Lake Sabrina and South Lake. A good spot to set up shop.

RV sites, facilities: There are 10 sites for tents or RVs to 25 feet (no hookups). Picnic tables, bear-proof, lockers, and fire rings are provided. Pit toilets are available. There is no drinking water. A nearby spring has water that looks good but must be treated before use. Leashed pets are permitted.

Reservations, fees: Reservations are not accepted. Sites are $18 per night. There is a 7-day stay limit. Open late May to late September.

Directions: From Bishop drive west 13 miles on

Highway 168 to South Lake Road. Turn left and drive 5.5 miles to the campground.

Contact: Inyo National Forest, White Mountain Ranger District, 760/873-2500, fax 760/873-2563.

54 MOUNTAIN GLEN

Scenic rating: 8

on Bishop Creek in Inyo National Forest

Map grid B1

Mountain Glen rests along the south fork of Bishop Creek. Jeffrey pines, piñon pines, aspen, and sagebrush green the campground, but come in mid-September when the aspens explode in a riot of colors, bringing the canyon to life. You can often have this place to yourself then. Little Bishop Creek is nearby and is stocked with small trout. The elevation is 8,200 feet.

RV sites, facilities: There are five sites for tents or RVs to 28 feet (no hookups). Picnic tables, bear-proof lockers, and fire rings are provided. Vault toilets are available, but there is no drinking water. Leashed pets are permitted.

Reservations, fees: Reservations are not accepted. Sites are $18 per night. There is a maximum 7-day limit. Open late May to late September.

Directions: From Bishop drive west 13 miles on Highway 168 to South Lake Road. Turn left and drive three miles to the campground.

Contact: Inyo National Forest, White Mountain Ranger District, 760/873-2500, fax 760/873-2563.

55 KEOUGH'S HOT SPRINGS

Scenic rating: 5

in Owens Valley on U.S. 305

Map grid B1

This private facility is the site of the Eastern Sierra's largest natural hot springs pool. The landscape is the stark high desert, but makes for sensational sunsets with colors sometimes refracting across what seems an infinite sky. With the public springs at Hot Creek now off limits, Keough's is a very good choice.

RV sites, facilities: There are 10 tent sites and 10 sites for RVs up to 40 feet (partial 30-amp hookups). Picnic tables are provided, and campers can bring their own above-ground fire pit. Drinking water, flush toilets, a snack bar, and a gift shop are available. Leashed pets are permitted.

Reservations, fees: Reservations are accepted. Sites are $20–25 per night. There is a maximum 14-day limit. Open year round, weather permitting.

Directions: From Bishop drive south on Highway 395 for seven miles to Keough's Hot Springs Road. Turn right on Keough's Hot Springs Road and drive one mile to the resort.

Contact: Keough's Hot Springs, 760/872-4670, www.keoughshotsprings.com.

56 BAKER CREEK CAMPGROUND

Scenic rating: 4

near Big Pine

Map grid B1

Because this is a county-operated RV park, it is often overlooked by campers who consider only camps on reservations systems. That makes this a good option for cruisers touring the eastern Sierra on U.S. 395. It's ideal for a quick overnighter, with easy access from Big Pine. The camp is set along Baker Creek at 4,000 feet elevation in the high plateau country of the eastern Sierra. An option is fair trout fishing during the evening bite on the creek.

RV sites, facilities: There are 70 sites for tents or RVs up to 40 feet (no hookups). Picnic tables and fire grills are provided. Vault toilets and hand-pumped well water are available. You can buy supplies about 1.5 miles away in Big Pine. Leashed pets are permitted.

Reservations, fees: Reservations are not accepted. The fee is $10 per vehicle per night. Open year-round, weather permitting.

Directions: Drive on U.S. 395 to Big Pine and Baker Creek Road. Turn west (toward the Sierra) on Baker Creek Road and drive a mile to the campground.

Contact: Inyo County Parks Department, 760/873-5577, www.inyocountycamping.com.

57 GLACIER VIEW

Scenic rating: 4

near Big Pine
Map grid B1

This is one of two county camps near the town of Big Pine, providing U.S. 395 cruisers with two options. The camp is set along the Big Pine Canal at 3,900 feet elevation. It is owned by the county but operated by a concessionaire, Brown's, which runs five small campgrounds in the area: Glacier View, Keough Hot Springs, Millpond, Brown's Owens River, and Brown's Town.

RV sites, facilities: There are 40 sites for tents or RVs of any length; some sites have partial hookups (30 amps) and/or are pull-through. Picnic tables and fire grills are provided. Restrooms with flush toilets and coin showers and drinking water are available. Supplies are available in Big Pine. Leashed pets are permitted.

Reservations, fees: Reservations are not accepted. Sites are $12–17 per vehicle per night. Open year-round.

Directions: Drive on U.S. 395 to the park entrance (0.5 mile north of Big Pine) on the southeast side of the road. Turn east (away from the Sierra) and enter the park.

Contact: Inyo County Parks Department, 760/873-5577, www.inyocountycamping.com.

58 PALISADE GLACIER AND CLYDE GLACIER GROUP CAMP

Scenic rating: 8

on Big Pine Creek in Inyo National Forest
Map grid B1

This is a trailhead camp set at 7,600 feet elevation, most popular for groups planning to rock-climb the Palisades. This climbing trip is for experienced mountaineers only; it's a dangerous expedition where risk of life can be included in

the bargain. Safer options include exploring the surrounding John Muir Wilderness.

RV sites, facilities: There are two group sites for tents or RVs up to 35 feet (no hookups) that can accommodate up to 35 people each. Picnic tables and fire grills are provided. Drinking water and vault toilets are available. Some facilities are wheelchair-accessible. Leashed pets are permitted.

Reservations, fees: Reservations are required at 877/444-6777 or www.recreation.gov ($10 reservation fee). Sites are $60 per night for the first 25 people. Open mid-May through mid-October.

Directions: Drive on U.S. 395 to Big Pine and Crocker Street/Glacier Lodge Road. Turn west (toward the Sierra) and drive nine miles (it becomes Glacier Lodge Road) to the campground on the left.

Contact: Inyo National Forest, White Mountain Ranger District, 760/873-2500, fax 760/873-2563.

59 BIG PINE CREEK

Scenic rating: 8

in Inyo National Forest
Map grid B1

This is another good spot for backpackers to launch a multiday trip. The camp is set along Big Pine Creek at 7,700 feet elevation, with trails near the camp that are routed to the numerous lakes in the high country of the John Muir Wilderness.

RV sites, facilities: There are 30 sites for tents or RVs up to 22 feet (no hookups). Picnic tables, food lockers, and fire grills are provided. Drinking water and pit toilets are available. Some facilities are wheelchair-accessible. Leashed pets are permitted.

Reservations, fees: Reservations are not accepted. Sites are $18 per night. Open early May through October, weather permitting.

Directions: Drive on U.S. 395 to Big Pine and Crocker Street/Glacier Lodge Road. Turn west (toward the Sierra) and drive nine miles (it becomes Glacier Lodge Road) to the campground.

Contact: Inyo National Forest, White Mountain Ranger District, 760/873-2500, fax 760/873-2563.

60 UPPER SAGE FLAT

Scenic rating: 8

on Big Pine Creek in Inyo National Forest

Map grid B1

This is one in a series of Forest Service camps in the area set up primarily for backpackers taking off on wilderness expeditions. Several trails are available nearby that lead into the John Muir Wilderness. The best of these is routed west past several lakes to the base of the Palisades, and beyond to John Muir Trail. Even starting at 7,600 feet, expect a steep climb.

RV sites, facilities: There are 28 sites for tents or RVs up to 35 feet (no hookups). Picnic tables, food lockers, and fire grills are provided. Drinking water and vault toilets are available. Some facilities are wheelchair-accessible. Leashed pets are permitted.

Reservations, fees: Reservations are accepted at 877/444-6777 or www.recreation.gov ($10 reservation fee). Sites are $18 per night. Open late April through mid-September, weather permitting.

Directions: Drive on U.S. 395 to Big Pine and Crocker Street/Glacier Lodge Road. Turn west (toward the Sierra) and drive 8.5 miles (it becomes Glacier Lodge Road) to the campground.

Contact: Inyo National Forest, White Mountain Ranger District, 760/873-2500, fax 760/873-2563.

61 SAGE FLAT

Scenic rating: 8

on Big Pine Creek near Big Pine in Inyo National Forest

Map grid B1

This camp, like the others in the immediate vicinity, is set up primarily for backpackers who are getting ready to head out on multiday expeditions into the nearby John Muir Wilderness. The trail is routed west past several lakes to the base of the Palisades, and beyond to John Muir Trail. Your hike from here will begin with a steep climb from the trailhead at 7,600 feet elevation. The camp is set along Big Pine Creek, which is stocked with small trout.

RV sites, facilities: There are 28 sites for tents or RVs up to 35 feet (no hookups). Picnic tables, food lockers, and fire grills are provided. Drinking water and pit toilets are available. Leashed pets are permitted.

Reservations, fees: Reservations are not accepted. Sites are $18 per night. Open late mid-April through mid-September, weather permitting.

Directions: Drive on U.S. 395 to Big Pine and Crocker Street/Glacier Lodge Road. Turn west (toward the Sierra) and drive eight miles (it becomes Glacier Lodge Road) to the campground.

Contact: Inyo National Forest, White Mountain Ranger District, 760/873-2500, fax 760/873-2563.

62 TINNEMAHA CAMPGROUND

Scenic rating: 6

near Big Pine

Map grid B1

This primitive, little-known (to out-of-towners) county park campground is on Tinnemaha Creek at 4,400 feet elevation. The creek is stocked with Alpers trout. Horse camping is allowed, but call ahead.

RV sites, facilities: There are 55 sites for tents or RVs of any length (no hookups). Picnic tables and fire grills are provided. Vault toilets are available. Limited drinking water is available with a hand pump. Stream water is available and must be boiled or pump-filtered before use. Leashed pets are permitted.

Reservations, fees: Reservations are not accepted. Sites are $10 per vehicle per night. Open year-round.

Directions: Drive on U.S. 395 to Tinnemaha Creek Road (seven miles south of Big Pine and

19.5 miles north of Independence). Turn west (toward the Sierra) on Fish Springs Road and drive 0.5 mile to Tinnemaha Creek Road. Turn west (left) and drive two miles to the park on the right.

Contact: Inyo County Parks Department, 760/873-5577, www.inyocountycamping.com.

63 TABOOSE CREEK CAMPGROUND

Scenic rating: 4

near Big Pine
Map grid B1

The eastern Sierra is stark country, but this little spot provides a stream (Taboose Creek) and some trees near the campground. There is an opportunity for trout fishing—fair, not spectacular. The easy access off U.S. 395 is a bonus. The hike up to Taboose Pass from here is one of the steepest grinds in the Sierra, but provides one-day access to the interior of the John Muir Wilderness. The elevation is 3,900 feet.

RV sites, facilities: There are 56 sites for tents or RVs up to 40 feet (no hookups). Picnic tables and fire grills are provided. Drinking water (hand-pumped from a well) and vault toilets are available. Supplies are available in Big Pine or Independence. Leashed pets are permitted.

Reservations, fees: Reservations are not accepted. The fee is $10 per vehicle per night. Open year-round.

Directions: Drive on U.S. 395 to Taboose Creek Road (11 miles south of Big Pine and 14 miles north of Independence). Turn west (toward the Sierra) on Taboose Creek Road and drive 2.5 miles to the campground (straight in).

Contact: Inyo County Parks Department, 760/873-5577, www.inyocountycamping.com.

64 GRANDVIEW

Scenic rating: 6

near Big Pine in Inyo National Forest
Map grid B1

This is a primitive and little-known camp, and the folks who find this area earn their solitude. It is in the White Mountains east of Bishop at 8,600 feet elevation along White Mountain Road. The road borders the Ancient Bristlecone Pine Forest to the east and leads north to jump-off spots for hikers heading up Mount Barcroft (13,023 feet) or White Mountain (14,246 feet, the third-highest mountain in California). A trail out of the camp leads up to an old mining site.

RV sites, facilities: There are 26 sites for tents or RVs up to 22 feet (no hookups). Picnic tables and fire grills are provided. Vault toilets are available. No drinking water is available. Garbage must be packed out. Leashed pets are permitted.

Reservations, fees: Reservations are not accepted. There is no camping fee, but donations are accepted. Open year-round, weather permitting.

Directions: From Big Pine on U.S. 395, turn east on Highway 168 and drive 13 miles. Turn north on White Mountain/Bristlecone Forest Road (Forest Road 4S01) and drive 5.5 miles to the campground.

Contact: Inyo National Forest, White Mountain Ranger District, 760/873-2500, fax 760/873-2563.

65 ISLAND PARK AND DEER CREEK POINT GROUP

Scenic rating: 7

on Pine Flat Lake
Map grid A2

These are two of four Army Corps of Engineer campgrounds available at Pine Flat Lake, a popular lake set in the foothill country east of Fresno. When Pine Flat is full, or close to full, it is very

CALIFORNIA

pretty. The lake is 21 miles long with 67 miles of shoreline and 4,270 surface acres. Right—a big lake with unlimited potential. Because the temperatures get warm here in spring, then smoking hot in summer, the lake is like Valhalla for boating and water sports. The fishing for white bass is often excellent in late winter and early spring and, after that, conditions are ideal for water sports. The elevation is 1,000 feet.

RV sites, facilities: There are 52 sites for tents or RVs of any length (no hookups), 60 overflow sites (at Island Park), and two group sites for 50 people each for tents or RVs up to 45 feet. Picnic tables and fire grills are provided. Restrooms with flush toilets and coin showers, drinking water, pay telephone, boat ramp, fish-cleaning station, and dump station are available. There is a seasonal store at the campground entrance. Boat rentals are available within five miles. Some facilities are wheelchair-accessible. Leashed pets are permitted.

Reservations, fees: Reservations are accepted for individual sites and required for the group sites at 877/444-6777 or www.recreation.gov ($10 reservation fee). Sites are $16 per night, $75 per night for group site. Boat launching is $3 per day. Open year-round.

Directions: From Fresno, drive east on Highway 180 for 17.5 miles to Trimmer Springs Road. Turn left and drive eight miles to the town of Piedra. Continue on Trimmer Springs Road for one mile to Pine Flat Road. Turn right and drive 0.25 mile to the park entrance (signed "Island Park").

Contact: U.S. Army Corps of Engineers, Sacramento District, Pine Flat Field Office, 559/787-2589, fax 559/787-2773.

66 LAKERIDGE CAMPING AND BOATING RESORT

Scenic rating: 7

on Pine Flat Lake

Map grid A2

Pine Flat Lake is a 20-mile-long reservoir with seemingly unlimited recreation potential. It is

an excellent lake for all water sports. It is in the foothills east of Fresno at 970 feet elevation, covering 4,912 surface acres with 67 miles of shoreline. The lake's proximity to Fresno has made it a top destination for boating and water sports. Fishing for white bass can be excellent in the spring and early summer. There are also rainbow trout, largemouth bass, smallmouth bass, bluegill, catfish, and black crappie. Note: A downer is that there are only a few sandy beaches, and the lake level can drop to as low as 20 percent full.

RV sites, facilities: There are 107 sites with full or partial hookups (50 amps) for tents or RVs up to 40 feet. Picnic tables and barbecue grills are available at some sites. Rest-rooms with showers, modem access, coin laundry, ice, horseshoes, and pay phone are available. A convenience store and boat and houseboat rentals are nearby. Leashed pets are permitted.

Reservations, fees: Reservations are recommended at 877/787-2260. Sites are $20–30 per night, $5 per pet per night. Some credit cards accepted. Open year-round.

Directions: From Fresno, drive east on Highway 180 for 17.5 miles to Trimmer Springs Road. Turn left and drive eight miles to the town of Piedra. Continue on Trimmer Springs Road for four miles to Sunnyslope Road. Turn right and drive one mile to the resort on the right.

Contact: Lakeridge Camping and Boating Resort, 559/787-2260, fax 559/787-2354; Pine Flat Marina, 559/787-2506.

67 KIRCH FLAT

Scenic rating: 8

on the Kings River in Sierra National Forest

Map grid A2

Kirch Flat is on the Kings River, about five miles from the head of Pine Flat Lake. This campground is a popular take-out spot for rafters and kayakers running the Middle Kings, putting in at Garnet Dike dispersed camping area and then making the 10-mile, Class III run downstream to Kirch Flat. The camp is set in the foothill country at 1,100 feet elevation, where the temperatures are often hot and the water cold.

RV sites, facilities: There are 17 sites for tents or RVs up to 22 feet (no hookups), and one group camp for up to 50 people. Picnic tables and fire grills are provided. Vault toilets are available. No drinking water is available. Leashed pets are permitted.

Reservations, fees: Reservations are not accepted for individual sites, but are required for the group site at 559/855-5355. There is no fee for individual sites; the group site is $50 per night. Reservation applications are open from March through July with a lottery to select the winners. Open year-round.

Directions: From Fresno, drive east on Highway 180 for 17.5 miles to Trimmer Springs Road. Turn left and drive 28 miles to Trimmer. Continue east on Trimmer Springs Road (along the north shore of Pine Flat Lake) and drive 18 miles to the campground on the right.

Contact: Sierra National Forest, High Sierra Ranger District, 559/855-5355, fax 559/855-5375.

68 PINE FLAT RECREATION AREA

Scenic rating: 7

near Pine Flat Lake

Map grid A2

This is a county park that is open all year, set below the dam of Pine Flat Lake, actually not on the lake at all. As a county park campground, it is often overlooked by out-of-towners.

RV sites, facilities: There are 52 pull-through sites for tents or RVs of any length (no hookups). Fire grills and picnic tables are provided. Restrooms with flush toilets, drinking water, dump station, and a wheelchair-accessible fishing area are available. A store, coin laundry, and propane gas are nearby (within a mile). Leashed pets are permitted.

Reservations, fees: Reservations are not accepted. Sites are $18 per night, $5 per night for each additional vehicle. Open year-round.

Directions: From Fresno, drive east on Highway 180 for 17.5 miles to Trimmer Springs Road. Turn left and drive eight miles to the town of Piedra. Continue on Trimmer Springs Road for one mile to Pine Flat Road. Turn right and drive three miles to the campground on the right.

Contact: Fresno County Parks Department, 559/488-3004, fax 559/262-4286.

69 CHOINUMNI

Scenic rating: 7

on lower Kings River

Map grid A2

This campground is set in the San Joaquin foothills on the Kings River, a pretty area. Since the campground is operated by Fresno County, it is off the radar of many visitors. Fishing, rafting, canoeing, and hiking are popular. The elevation is roughly 1,000 feet, surrounded by a landscape of oak woodlands and grassland foothills. The park is roughly 33 miles east of Fresno.

RV sites, facilities: There are 79 sites for tents or RVs of any length (no hookups), and one group site for up to 75 people. Some sites are pull-through. Picnic tables and fire rings are provided. Drinking water, flush toilets, and dump station are available. Canoe rentals are available nearby. No facilities within 10 miles. Leashed pets are permitted.

Reservations, fees: Reservations are accepted for the group site only. Sites are $18 per night, $5 per night for each additional vehicle, $110 per night for the group site. Open year-round.

Directions: From Fresno, drive east on Highway 180 for 17.5 miles to Piedra Road. Turn left on Piedra Road and drive eight miles to Trimmer Springs Road. Turn right on Trimmer Springs Road and drive one mile to Pine Flat Road. Turn right and drive 100 yards to the camp entrance on the right.

Contact: Fresno County Parks Department, 559/488-3004, fax 559/262-4286.

CALIFORNIA

70 PRINCESS

Scenic rating: 7

on Princess Meadow in
Giant Sequoia National Forest

Map grid B2

This mountain camp is at 5,900 feet elevation. It is popular because of its proximity to both Hume Lake and the star attractions at Kings Canyon National Park. Hume Lake is just four miles from the camp. The Grant Grove entrance to Kings Canyon National Park is only six miles away to the south, while continuing on Highway 180 to the east will take you into the heart of Kings Canyon.

RV sites, facilities: There are 90 sites for tents or RVs up to 22 feet (no hookups). Picnic tables and fire grills are provided. Drinking water, vault toilets, amphitheater, and dump station are available. A store is four miles away at Hume Lake. Leashed pets are permitted.

Reservations, fees: Reservations are accepted at 877/444-6777 or www.recreation.gov ($10 reservation fee). Sites are $17–19 per night, $34–38 per night for a double site, $5 per night for each additional vehicle, plus $20 per vehicle national park entrance fee. Prices are higher on holiday weekends. Open May through September, weather permitting.

Directions: From Fresno, drive east on Highway 180 for 55 miles to the Big Stump Entrance Station at Sequoia and Kings Canyon National Parks. Continue 1.5 miles to a junction (signed left for Grant Grove). Turn left and drive 1.5 miles to Grant Grove Village, then continue for 4.5 miles to the campground on the right.

Contact: Sequoia National Forest, Hume Lake Ranger District, 559/338-2251, fax 559/338-2131; California Land Management, 559/335-2232.

71 HUME LAKE

Scenic rating: 8

in Giant Sequoia National Forest

Map grid B2

For newcomers, Hume Lake is a surprise: a pretty lake, with great summer camps for teenagers. Canoeing and kayaking are excellent, and so is the trout fishing, especially near the dam. Swimming is allowed. A 5-mph speed limit is in effect on this 85-acre lake, and only electric motors are permitted. Another surprise is the adjacent religious camp center. The nearby entrances to Kings Canyon National Park adds a bonus. The elevation is 5,200 feet.

RV sites, facilities: There are 60 tent sites and 14 sites for tents or RVs up to 22 feet (no hookups). Picnic tables and fire grills are provided. Drinking water and flush toilets are available. A store, café, bicycle rentals, and boat rentals are nearby. Leashed pets are permitted.

Reservations, fees: Reservations are accepted at 877/444-6777 or www.recreation.gov ($10 reservation fee). Sites are $19–38 per night, $5 per night for each additional vehicle, plus $20 per vehicle national park entrance fee. Rates are higher on holiday weekends. Open mid-May through September, weather permitting.

Directions: From Fresno, drive east on Highway 180 for 55 miles to the Big Stump Entrance Station at Sequoia and Kings Canyon National Parks. Continue 1.5 miles to a junction (signed left for Grant Grove). Turn left and drive six miles to the Hume Lake Road junction. Turn right and drive three miles to Hume Lake and the campground entrance road. Turn right and drive 0.25 mile to the campground on the left.

Contact: Sequoia National Forest, Hume Lake Ranger District, 559/338-2251, fax 559/338-2131; California Land Management, 559/335-2232.

CALIFORNIA

72 ASPEN HOLLOW GROUP CAMP

Scenic rating: 6

near Hume Lake in Sequoia National Forest

Map grid B2

This large group camp is set at 5,200 feet elevation about a mile south of Hume Lake near a feeder to Tenmile Creek, the inlet stream to Hume Lake. Entrances to Kings Canyon National Park are nearby.

RV sites, facilities: This is a group camp for tents or RVs of any length (no hookups) that can accommodate up to 100 people. Picnic tables, food lockers, and fire grills are provided. Drinking water and vault toilets are available. A store is nearby. Some facilities are wheelchair-accessible. Leashed pets are permitted.

Reservations, fees: Reservations are required at 877/444-6777 or www.recreation.gov ($10 reservation fee). The fee is $181.50 per night, plus $20 per vehicle national park entrance fee. Open mid-May through mid-September, weather permitting.

Directions: From Fresno, drive east on Highway 180 for 55 miles to the Big Stump Entrance Station at Sequoia and Kings Canyon National Parks. Continue 1.5 miles to a junction (signed left for Grant Grove). Turn left and drive six miles to the Hume Lake Road junction. Turn right and drive three miles to Hume Lake and the campground entrance road. Turn right and drive around Hume Lake. Continue south one mile (past the lake) to the campground entrance road.

Contact: Sequoia National Forest, Hume Lake Ranger District, 559/338-2251, fax 559/338-2131.

73 LOGGER FLAT GROUP CAMP

Scenic rating: 7

on Tenmile Creek in Giant Sequoia National Forest

Map grid B2

This is the group-site alternative to Landslide campground. This camp is set near the confluence of Tenmile Creek and Landslide Creek at 5,300 feet elevation, about two miles upstream from Hume Lake. (For more information, see the Landslide listing in this chapter.)

RV sites, facilities: This is one group campsite for tents or RVs of any length (no hookups) that can accommodate up to 50 people. Picnic tables, food lockers, and fire ring are provided. Drinking water and vault toilets are available. A store is nearby. Some facilities are wheelchair-accessible. Leashed pets are permitted.

Reservations, fees: Reservations are required at 877/444-6777 or www.recreation.gov ($10 reservation fee). The fee is $93.50 per night, plus $20 per vehicle national park entrance fee. Open mid-May through mid-September, weather permitting.

Directions: From Fresno, drive east on Highway 180 for 55 miles to the Big Stump Entrance Station at Sequoia and Kings Canyon National Parks. Continue 1.5 miles to a junction (signed left for Grant Grove). Turn left and drive six miles to the Hume Lake Road junction. Turn right and drive three miles to Hume Lake and the campground entrance road. Turn right and drive around Hume Lake to Tenmile Road. Continue south three miles to the campground entrance on the right.

Contact: Sequoia National Forest, Hume Lake Ranger District, 559/338-2251, fax 559/338-2131.

74 LANDSLIDE

Scenic rating: 7

on Landslide Creek in
Giant Sequoia National Forest

Map grid B2

If you want quiet, you got it; few folks know about this camp. If you want a stream nearby, you got it; Landslide Creek runs right beside the camp. If you want a lake nearby, you got it; Hume Lake is just to the north. If you want a national park nearby, you got it; Kings Canyon National Park is nearby. Add it up: You got it. The elevation is 5,800 feet.

RV sites, facilities: There are eight sites for tents only and one site for RVs up to 22 feet (no hookups). Picnic tables and fire grills are provided. Drinking water and vault toilets are available. A store is nearby. Leashed pets are permitted.

Reservations, fees: Reservations are not accepted. Sites are $15 per night, $30 per night for a double site, $5 per night for each additional vehicle, plus $20 per vehicle national park entrance fee. Open May through September, weather permitting.

Directions: From Fresno, drive east on Highway 180 for 55 miles to the Big Stump Entrance Station at Sequoia and Kings Canyon National Parks. Continue 1.5 miles to a junction (signed left for Grant Grove). Turn right at Generals Highway and drive three miles to Hume Lake Road/Tenmile Road (Forest Road 13S09). Turn left and drive about seven miles (past Tenmile campground) to the campground on the left.

Contact: Sequoia National Forest, Hume Lake Ranger District, 559/338-2251, fax 559/338-2131.

75 CRYSTAL SPRINGS

Scenic rating: 5

in Kings Canyon National Park

Map grid B2

Directly to the south of this camp is the General Grant Grove and its giant sequoias. But continuing on Highway 180 provides access to the interior of Kings Canyon National Park, and this camp makes an ideal jump-off point. From here you can drive east, passing Cedar Grove Village, cruising along the Kings River, and finally coming to a dead-end loop, taking in the drop-dead gorgeous landscape of one of the deepest gorges in North America. One of the best hikes, but also the most demanding, is the 13-mile round-trip to Lookout Peak, out of the Cedar Grove Village area. It involves a 4,000-foot climb to 8,531 feet elevation, and with it a breathtaking view of Sierra ridges, Cedar Grove far below, and Kings Canyon.

RV sites, facilities: There are 36 sites for tents or RVs up to 22 feet (no hookups) and 14 group sites for 7–15 people each. Picnic tables, food

lockers, and fire grills are provided. Drinking water and flush toilets are available. A store and horseback-riding facilities are nearby. Evening ranger programs are often offered in the summer. Showers are available in Grant Grove Village during the summer season. Some facilities are wheelchair-accessible. Leashed pets are permitted, except on trails.

Reservations, fees: Reservations are not accepted. Sites are $18 per night, plus $20 per vehicle national park entrance fee; group sites are $35 per night. Open mid-May through mid-September, weather permitting.

Directions: From Fresno, drive east on Highway 180 for 55 miles to the Big Stump Entrance Station at Sequoia and Kings Canyon National Parks. Continue 1.5 miles to a junction (signed left for Grant Grove). Turn left and drive 1.5 miles to Grant Grove Village, then continue for 0.7 mile to the campground entrance on the right.

Contact: Sequoia and Kings Canyon National Parks, 559/565-3341, fax 559/565-3730; Kings Canyon Visitor Center, 559/565-4307, www.nps.gov/seki.

76 TENMILE

Scenic rating: 7

on Tenmile Creek in Giant Sequoia National Forest

Map grid B2

This is one of three small, primitive campgrounds along Tenmile Creek south (and upstream) of Hume Lake. RV campers are advised to use the lower campsites because they are larger. This one is about four miles from the lake at 5,800 feet elevation. It provides an alternative to camping in nearby Kings Canyon National Park.

RV sites, facilities: There are 13 sites for tents or RVs up to 22 feet (no hookups). Picnic tables and fire grills are provided. Vault toilets are available. No drinking water is available. Some facilities are wheelchair-accessible. Leashed pets are permitted.

Reservations, fees: Reservations are not

accepted. Sites are $15 per night, $30 per night for a double site, $5 per night per each additional vehicle, plus $20 per vehicle for national park entrance fee. Camping fees are higher on holiday weekends. Open May through mid-September, weather permitting.

Directions: From Fresno, drive east on Highway 180 for 55 miles to the Big Stump Entrance Station at Sequoia and Kings Canyon National Parks. Continue 1.5 miles to a junction (signed left for Grant Grove). Turn right at Generals Highway and drive three miles to Hume Lake Road/Tenmile Road (Forest Road 13S09). Turn left and drive about five miles to the campground on the left.

Contact: Sequoia National Forest, Hume Lake Ranger District, 559/338-2251, fax 559/338-2131.

77 AZALEA

Scenic rating: 7

in Kings Canyon National Park

Map grid B2

This camp is tucked just inside the western border of Kings Canyon National Park. It is set at 6,600 feet elevation, near the General Grant Grove of giant sequoias. (For information on several short, spectacular hikes among the giant sequoias, see the Sunset listing in this chapter.) Nearby Sequoia Lake is privately owned; no fishing, no swimming, no trespassing. To see the spectacular Kings Canyon, one of the deepest gorges in North America, re-enter the park on Highway 180.

RV sites, facilities: There are 110 sites for tents or RVs up to 30 feet (no hookups). Picnic tables, food lockers, and fire grills are provided. Drinking water and flush toilets are available. Evening ranger programs are often offered. A store and horseback-riding facilities are nearby. Showers are available in Grant Grove Village during the summer. Some facilities are wheelchair-accessible. Leashed pets are permitted, except on trails.

Reservations, fees: Reservations are not accepted. Sites are $18 per night, plus $20 per vehicle national park entrance fee. Open year-round.

Directions: From Fresno, drive east on Highway 180 for 55 miles to the Big Stump Entrance Station at Sequoia and Kings Canyon National Parks. Continue 1.5 miles to a junction (signed left for Grant Grove). Turn left and drive 1.5 miles to Grant Grove Village, then continue for 0.7 mile to the campground entrance on the left.

Contact: Sequoia and Kings Canyon National Parks, 559/565-3341, fax 559/565-3730; Kings Canyon Visitor Center, 559/565-4307; Grant Grove Horse Stables, 559/335-9292, www.nps.gov/seki.

78 SUNSET

Scenic rating: 7

in Kings Canyon National Park

Map grid B2

This is the biggest of the camps that are just inside the Sequoia National Park boundaries at Grant Grove Village, at 6,600 feet elevation. The nearby General Grant Grove of giant sequoias is the main attraction. There are many short, easy walks among the sequoias, each breathtakingly beautiful. They include Big Stump Trail, Sunset Trail, North Grove Loop, General Grant Tree, Manzanita and Azalea Loop, and Panoramic Point and Park Ridge Trail. Seeing the General Grant Tree is a rite of passage for newcomers; after a half-hour walk you arrive at a sequoia that is approximately 1,800 years old, 107 feet in circumference, and 267 feet tall.

RV sites, facilities: There are 157 sites for tents or RVs up to 30 feet (no hookups). Picnic, food lockers, and fire grills are provided. Drinking water and flush toilets are available. In the summer, evening ranger programs are often available. A store and horseback-riding facilities are nearby. Showers are available in Grant Grove Village during the summer. Some facilities are wheelchair-accessible. Leashed pets are permitted, except on trails.

CALIFORNIA

Reservations, fees: Reservations are not accepted. Sites are $18 per night, plus $20 per vehicle national park entrance fee. Open late May through mid-September, weather permitting.

Directions: From Fresno, drive east on Highway 180 for 55 miles to the Big Stump Entrance Station at Sequoia and Kings Canyon National Parks. Continue 1.5 miles to a junction (signed left for Grant Grove). Turn left (still Highway 180) and drive one mile to the campground entrance (0.5 mile before reaching Grant Grove Village).

Contact: Sequoia and Kings Canyon National Parks, 559/565-3341, fax 559/565-3730; Kings Canyon Visitor Center, 559/565-4307, www. nps.gov/seki.

79 BUCK ROCK

Scenic rating: 4

near Big Meadows Creek in
Giant Sequoia National Monument

Map grid B2

This is a remote camp that provides a little-known option to nearby Sequoia and Kings Canyon National Parks. If the national parks are full and you're stuck, this camp provides an insurance policy. The elevation is 7,500 feet.

RV sites, facilities: There are nine primitive sites for tents or RVs up to 25 feet (no hookups). Picnic tables and fire grills are provided. Vault toilets are available. No drinking water is available. Leashed pets are permitted.

Reservations, fees: Reservations are not accepted. There is no fee for camping, but there is a $20 per vehicle national park entrance fee. Open May to early September, weather permitting.

Directions: From Fresno, drive east on Highway 180 for 55 miles to the Big Stump Entrance Station at Sequoia and Kings Canyon National Parks. Continue 1.5 miles to a junction (signed left for Grant Grove). Turn right at Generals Highway and drive about five miles to Big Meadows Road/Forest Road 14S11. Turn left on Big Meadows Road and drive five miles to the campground entrance road on the left. Turn left and drive a short distance to the campground.

Contact: Sequoia National Forest, Hume Lake Ranger District, 559/338-2251, fax 559/338-2131.

80 BIG MEADOWS

Scenic rating: 7

on Big Meadows Creek in
Giant Sequoia National Monument

Map grid B2

This primitive, high-mountain camp (7,600 feet) is beside little Big Meadows Creek. Backpackers can use this as a launching pad, with the nearby trailhead (one mile down the road to the west) leading to the Jennie Lake Wilderness. Kings Canyon National Park, only a 12-mile drive away, is a nearby side trip.

RV sites, facilities: There are 40 sites along Big Meadows Creek and Big Meadows Road for tents or RVs up to 22 feet (no hookups). Picnic tables and fire grills are provided. Vault toilets are available. No drinking water is available. Leashed pets are permitted.

Reservations, fees: Reservations are not accepted. There is no fee for camping, but there is a $20 per vehicle national park entrance fee. Open May through early October, weather permitting.

Directions: From Fresno, drive east on Highway 180 for 55 miles to the Big Stump Entrance Station at Sequoia and Kings Canyon National Parks. Continue 1.5 miles to a junction (signed left for Grant Grove). Turn right at Generals Highway and drive about five miles to Big Meadows Road/Forest Road 14S11. Turn left on Big Meadows Road and drive five miles to the camp.

Contact: Sequoia National Forest, Hume Lake Ranger District, 559/338-2251, fax 559/338-2131.

81 SENTINEL

Scenic rating: 8

in Kings Canyon National Park

Map grid B2

This camp provides an alternative to nearby Sheep Creek (see listing in this chapter). They both tend to fill up quickly in the summer. It's a short walk to Cedar Grove Village, the center of activity in the park. The elevation is 4,600 feet. Hiking and trout fishing are excellent in the vicinity. The entrance road provides stunning rim-of-the-world views of Kings Canyon, and then drops to right along the Kings River. **RV sites, facilities:** There are 82 sites for tents or RVs up to 30 feet (no hookups). Picnic tables, food lockers, and fire grills are provided. Restrooms with flush toilets and drinking water are available. A store, coin showers, coin laundry, and snack bar are nearby. Some facilities are wheelchair-accessible. Leashed pets are permitted. **Reservations, fees:** Reservations are not accepted. Sites are $18 per night, plus $20 per vehicle national park entrance fee. Open late April through October, weather permitting. **Directions:** From Fresno, drive east on Highway 180 for 55 miles to the Big Stump Entrance Station at Sequoia and Kings Canyon National Parks. Continue 1.5 miles to a junction (signed left for Grant Grove). Turn left and drive 32 miles to the campground entrance on the left (near Cedar Grove Village). **Contact:** Sequoia and Kings Canyon National Parks, 559/565-3341, fax 559/565-3730; Cedar Grove Visitor Center, 559/565-3793, www.nps. gov/seki.

82 SHEEP CREEK

Scenic rating: 8

in Kings Canyon National Park

Map grid B2

This is one of the camps that always fills up quickly on summer weekends. It's a pretty spot and just a short walk from Cedar Grove Village. The camp is set along Sheep Creek at 4,600 feet elevation. **RV sites, facilities:** There are 111 sites for tents or RVs up to 30 feet (no hookups). Picnic tables and fire grills are provided. Restrooms with flush toilets and drinking water are available. A store, coin laundry, snack bar, and coin showers are available nearby. Leashed pets are permitted. **Reservations, fees:** Reservations are not

accepted. Sites are $18 per night, plus $20 per vehicle national park entrance fee. Open late April through mid-November. **Directions:** From Fresno, drive east on Highway 180 for 55 miles to the Big Stump Entrance Station at Sequoia and Kings Canyon National Parks. Continue 1.5 miles to a junction (signed left for Grant Grove). Turn left and drive 31.5 miles to the campground entrance on the left (near Cedar Grove Village). **Contact:** Sequoia and Kings Canyon National Parks, 559/565-3341, fax 559/565-3730; Cedar Grove Visitor Center, 559/565-3793, www.nps. gov/seki.

83 MORAINE

Scenic rating: 8

in Kings Canyon National Park

Map grid B2

This is one in a series of camps in the Cedar Grove Village area of Kings Canyon National Park. This camp is used only as an overflow area. Hikers should drive past the Cedar Grove Ranger Station to the end of the road at Copper Creek, a prime jump-off point for a spectacular hike. The elevation is 4,600 feet. **RV sites, facilities:** There are 120 sites for tents or RVs up to 30 feet (no hookups). Picnic tables and fire grills are provided. Drinking water and flush toilets are available. Coin showers, store, snack bar, and coin laundry are nearby. Leashed pets are permitted. **Reservations, fees:** Reservations are not accepted. Sites are $18 per night, plus $20 per vehicle national park entrance fee. Open May through October, weather permitting. **Directions:** From Fresno, drive east on Highway 180 for 55 miles to the Big Stump Entrance Station at Sequoia and Kings Canyon National Parks. Continue 1.5 miles to a junction (signed left for Grant Grove). Turn left and drive 33 miles to the campground entrance (one mile past the ranger station, near Cedar Village). **Contact:** Sequoia and Kings Canyon National Parks, 559/565-3341, fax 559/565-3730;

CALIFORNIA

Cedar Grove Visitor Center, 559/565-3793, www.nps.gov/seki.

84 ESHOM CREEK

Scenic rating: 7

on Eshom Creek in
Giant Sequoia National Monument

Map grid B2

The campground at Eshom Creek is just two miles outside the boundaries of Sequoia National Park. It is well hidden and a considerable distance from the crowds and sights in the park interior. It is set along Eshom Creek at an elevation of 4,800 feet. Many campers at Eshom Creek hike straight into the national park, with a trailhead at Redwood Saddle (just inside the park boundary) providing a route to see the Redwood Mountain Grove, Fallen Goliath, Hart Tree, and Hart Meadow in a sensational loop hike.

RV sites, facilities: There are 23 sites for tents or RVs up to 22 feet (no hookups), and five group sites for up to 12 people each. Picnic tables and fire grills are provided. Drinking water and vault toilets are available. Leashed pets are permitted.

Reservations, fees: Reservations are not accepted. Sites are $17 per night, $5 per night for each additional vehicle, $34 per night for group site. Camping fees are higher on holiday weekends. Open May through early October, weather permitting.

Directions: Drive on Highway 99 to Visalia and the exit for Highway 198 east. Take that exit and drive east on Highway 198 for 11 miles to Highway 245. Turn left (north) on Highway 245 and drive 18 miles to Badger and County Road 465. Turn right and drive eight miles to the campground.

Contact: Sequoia National Forest, Hume Lake Ranger District, 559/338-2251, fax 559/338-2131; California Land Management, 559/335-2232.

85 FIR GROUP CAMPGROUND

Scenic rating: 6

near Stony Creek in
Giant Sequoia National Monument

Map grid B2

This is the second of two large group camps in the area set along Stony Creek.

RV sites, facilities: This is a group camp for tents or RVs up to 45 feet (no hookups) that can accommodate up to 100 people. Picnic tables, food lockers, and fire grills are provided. Drinking water and vault toilets are available. A store and coin laundry are nearby. Leashed pets are permitted.

Reservations, fees: Reservations are required at 877/444-6777 or www.recreation.gov ($10 reservation fee). The fee is $181.50 per night, plus $20 per vehicle national park entrance fee. Fees are higher on holiday weekends. Open mid-May through mid-September, weather permitting.

Directions: From Fresno, drive east on Highway 180 for 55 miles to the Big Stump Entrance Station at Sequoia and Kings Canyon National Parks. Continue 1.5 miles to a junction (signed left for Grant Grove). Turn right at Generals Highway and drive about 14 miles to the campground entrance on the left.

Contact: Sequoia National Forest, Hume Lake Ranger District, 559/338-2251, fax 559/338-2131.

86 STONY CREEK

Scenic rating: 6

in Giant Sequoia National Monument

Map grid B2

Stony Creek Camp provides a good option if the national park camps are filled. It is set creekside at 6,400 feet elevation. Sequoia and Kings Canyon National Parks are nearby.

RV sites, facilities: There are 49 sites for tents or RVs up to 22 feet (no hookups). Picnic tables and fire grills are provided. Drinking water, food lockers, and flush toilets are available. A store and coin laundry are nearby. Leashed pets are permitted.

Reservations, fees: Reservations are accepted at 877/444-6777 or www.recreation.gov ($10 reservation fee). Sites are $19–38 per night, $5 per night for each additional vehicle, plus $20 per vehicle national park entrance fee; walk-in sites are $17 per night. Fees are higher on holiday weekends. Open May through early September, weather permitting.

Directions: From Fresno, drive east on Highway 180 for 55 miles to the Big Stump Entrance Station at Sequoia and Kings Canyon National Parks. Continue 1.5 miles to a junction (signed left for Grant Grove). Turn right at Generals Highway and drive about 13 miles to the campground entrance on the right.

Contact: Sequoia National Forest, Hume Lake Ranger District, 559/338-2251, fax 559/338-2131.

87 COVE GROUP CAMP

Scenic rating: 6

near Stony Creek in
Giant Sequoia National Monument

Map grid B2

This large group camp is beside Stony Creek. The elevation is 6,500 feet.

RV sites, facilities: This is a group camp for tents or RVs up to 22 feet (no hookups) that can accommodate up to 50 people. Picnic tables, food lockers, and fire grills are provided. Drinking water and vault toilets are available. A store and coin laundry are nearby. Leashed pets are permitted.

Reservations, fees: Reservations are required at 877/444-6777 or www.recreation.gov ($10 reservation fee). The fee is 93.50 per night, plus $20 per vehicle national park entrance fee. Open mid-May through mid-September, weather permitting.

Directions: From Fresno, drive east on Highway 180 for 55 miles to the Big Stump Entrance Station at Sequoia and Kings Canyon National Parks. Continue 1.5 miles to a junction (signed left for Grant Grove). Turn right at Generals Highway and drive about 14 miles to the campground entrance on the left (just past Fir Group Campground).

Contact: Sequoia National Forest, Hume Lake Ranger District, 559/338-2251, fax 559/338-2131.

88 DORST CREEK

Scenic rating: 7

on Dorst Creek in Sequoia National Park
Map grid B2   **BEST (**

This camp is set on Dorst Creek at 6,700 feet elevation, near a trail routed into the backcountry and through Muir Grove. It is one in a series of big, popular camps in Sequoia National Park. Dorst Creek is a favorite for families because the spacious sites are set beneath a forest canopy and the campground itself is huge. There is plenty of room to run around and youngsters are apt to make friends with kids from other sites. The hike to the Muir Grove of Giant Sequoias is an easy hike, not too hard for children and their parents.

Campers must keep food in a bear-proof food locker or you will get a ticket. The reason why? Things that go bump in the night swing through Dorst Creek camp all summer long. That's right, Mr. Bear (a whole bunch of them) makes food raids like UPS drivers on pick-up routes. That's why keeping your food in a bear-proof locker is not only a must, it's the law.

RV sites, facilities: There are 204 sites for tents or RVs up to 30 feet (no hookups) and five group sites for 12–50 people each. Picnic tables and fire grills are provided. Drinking water, flush toilets, and dump station are available. A store, coin showers, and coin laundry are eight miles away. Some facilities are wheelchair-accessible. Leashed pets are permitted.

Reservations, fees: Reservations are accepted at 877/444-6777 or www.recreation.gov ($10 reservation fee). Sites are $20 per night (includes reservation fee), plus $20 per vehicle national park entrance fee, $40–60 per night for group sites. Open Memorial Day through Labor Day, weather permitting.

Directions: From Fresno, drive east on Highway 180 for 55 miles to the Big Stump Entrance Station at Sequoia and Kings Canyon National

CALIFORNIA

Parks. Continue 1.5 miles to a junction (signed left for Grant Grove). Turn right at Generals Highway and drive about 25.5 miles to the campground entrance on the right.

Contact: Sequoia and Kings Canyon National Parks, 559/565-3341, fax 559/565-3730; Lodgepole Visitor Center, 559/565-4436, www.nps.gov/seki.

89 LODGEPOLE

Scenic rating: 8

on the Marble Fork of the Kaweah River in Sequoia National Park

Map grid B2

This giant, pretty camp on the Marble Fork of the Kaweah River is typically crowded. A bonus here is an excellent trailhead nearby that leads into the backcountry of Sequoia National Park. The elevation is 6,700 feet. For information on backcountry permits, phone the Mineral King Ranger Station, 559/565-3135.

RV sites, facilities: There are 214 sites for tents or RVs up to 40 feet (no hookups). Picnic tables and fire grills are provided. Restrooms with flush toilets, drinking water, dump station, gift shop, and evening ranger programs are available. A store, deli, coin showers, and coin laundry are nearby. Leashed pets are permitted.

Reservations, fees: Reservations are accepted at 877/444-6777 or www.recreation.gov ($10 reservation fee). Sites are $18–20 per night (includes reservation fee), plus $20 per vehicle national park entrance fee. Open year-round, with limited winter services.

Directions: From Fresno, drive east on Highway 180 for 55 miles to the Big Stump Entrance Station at Sequoia and Kings Canyon National Parks. Continue 1.5 miles to a junction (signed left for Grant Grove). Turn right at Generals Highway and drive about 25 miles to Lodgepole Village and the turnoff for Lodgepole Campground. Turn left and drive 0.25 mile (past Lodgepole Village) to the campground.

Contact: Sequoia and Kings Canyon National Parks, 559/565-3341, fax 559/565-3730; Lodgepole Visitor Center, 559/565-4436, www.nps.gov/seki.

90 POTWISHA

Scenic rating: 7

on the Marble Fork of the Kaweah River in Sequoia National Park

Map grid B2

This pretty spot on the Marble Fork of the Kaweah River is one of Sequoia National Park's smaller drive-to campgrounds. By looking at maps, newcomers may think it is a very short drive farther into the park to see the General Sherman Tree, Giant Forest, and the famous trailhead for the walk up Moro Rock. Nope. It's a slow, twisty drive, but with many pullouts for great views. A few miles east of the camp, visitors can find Buckeye Flat and a trail that is routed along Paradise Creek.

RV sites, facilities: There are 42 sites for tents or RVs up to 30 feet (no hookups). Picnic tables, food lockers, and fire grills are provided. Drinking water, flush toilets, dump station, and evening ranger programs are available. Some facilities are wheelchair-accessible. Leashed pets are permitted.

Reservations, fees: Reservations are not accepted. Sites are $18 per night, plus $20 per vehicle national park entrance fee. Open year-round.

Directions: From Visalia, drive east on Highway 198 for 36 miles to the Ash Mountain entrance station to Sequoia and Kings Canyon National Parks. Continue into the park (the road becomes Generals Highway) and drive four miles to the campground on the left. Vehicles of 22 feet or longer are not advised on Generals Highway from Potwisha to Giant Forest Village and are advised to use Highway 180 through the Big Stump entrance station.

Contact: Sequoia and Kings Canyon National Parks, 559/565-3341, fax 559/565-3730; Lodgepole Visitor Center, 559/565-4436, www.nps.gov/seki.

91 HORSE CREEK

Scenic rating: 6

on Lake Kaweah

Map grid B2

Lake Kaweah is a big lake, covering nearly 2,000 acres with 22 miles of shoreline. This camp is set on the southern shore of the lake. In the spring when the lake is full and the surrounding hills are green, you may even think you have found Valhalla. With such hot weather in the San Joaquin Valley, it's a boater's heaven, ideal for water-skiers. In spring, when the water is too cool for water sports, anglers can have the lake to themselves for good bass fishing. Other species include trout, catfish, and crappie. By early summer, it's crowded with personal watercraft and ski boats. The lake level fluctuates and flooding is a potential problem in some years. Another problem is that the water level drops a great deal during late summer, as thirsty farms suck up every drop they can get, killing prospects of developing beaches for swimming and wading. The elevation is 300 feet.

RV sites, facilities: There are 80 sites for tents or RVs up to 30 feet (no hookups). Picnic tables and fire grills are provided. Restrooms with flush toilets and showers, drinking water, playground, and a dump station are available. Two paved boat ramps are available at Kaweah Recreation Area and Lemon Hill Recreation Area. A store, coin laundry, boat and water-ski rentals, ice, snack bar, restaurant, gas station, and propane gas are nearby. Some facilities are wheelchair-accessible. Leashed pets are permitted.

Reservations, fees: Reservations are accepted at 877/444-6777 or www.recreation.gov ($10 reservation fee). Sites are $16 per night. Some credit cards accepted. Open year-round.

Directions: From Visalia, drive east on Highway 198 for 25 miles to Lake Kaweah's south shore and the camp on the left.

Contact: U.S. Army Corps of Engineers, Lake Kaweah, 559/597-2301, fax 559/597-2468.

92 BALCH PARK

Scenic rating: 6

near Mountain Home State Forest

Map grid B2

Balch Park is surrounded by Mountain Home State Forest and Giant Sequoia National Monument. A nearby grove of giant sequoias is a feature attraction. The elevation is 6,500 feet. Two stocked fishing ponds are also available.

RV sites, facilities: There are 70 sites for tents or RVs up to 40 feet (no hookups); some sites are pull-through. Picnic tables and fire grills are provided. Drinking water and flush toilets are available. Leashed pets are permitted.

Reservations, fees: Reservations are not accepted. Sites are $16 per night, $5 per night for each additional vehicle, $3 per pet per night. Open May through late October.

Directions: From Porterville, drive east on Highway 190 for 19 miles (a mile past the town of Springville) to Balch Park Road. Turn left (north) at Balch Park Road and drive three miles to Bear Creek Road. Turn east (right) and drive 15 miles (extremely slow and curvy) to the campground (RVs not recommended).

Alternate route for RV drivers: After turning north onto Balch Park Road, drive 40 miles (long and curvy) to the park.

Contact: Balch Park, Tulare County, 559/539-3896.

93 FRAZIER MILL

Scenic rating: 5

in Mountain Home State Forest

Map grid B2

Abundant old-growth sequoias are the prime attraction at this remote camp. The Wishon Fork of the Tule River is the largest of the several streams that pass through this forest. You can't beat the price.

RV sites, facilities: There are 49 sites for tents, with a few of these sites also for RVs up to 35 feet (no hookups). Picnic tables and fire grills are provided. Drinking water, food lockers, and vault toilets are available. Some facilities are wheelchair-accessible. Leashed pets are permitted.

Reservations, fees: Reservations are not accepted, except for the site that is wheelchair-accessible. There is no fee for camping. Open mid-May through early October, weather permitting.

Directions: From Porterville, drive east on Highway 190 for 19 miles (a mile past the town of Springville) to Balch Park Road. Turn left (north) at Balch Park Road and drive about 23 miles to the Mountain Home State Forest sign. Continue on Balch Park Road (the road is long and twisty) and follow the signs to the State Forest Headquarters (where free forest maps are available). The campgrounds are well signed from this point.

Contact: Mountain Home State Forest, 559/539-2321 (summer) or 559/539-2855 (winter).

94 SHAKE CAMP

Scenic rating: 6

in Mountain Home State Forest

Map grid B2

This is a little-known spot for horseback riding. Horses can be rented for the day, hour, or night. The camp is set at 6,500 feet elevation and there's a trailhead here for trips into the adjoining Sequoia National Forest and beyond to the east into the Golden Trout Wilderness. Hikers should note that the Balch Park Pack Station, a commercial outfitter, is nearby, so you can expect horse traffic on the trail.

RV sites, facilities: There are 11 sites for tents or RVs up to 20 feet (no hookups). Picnic tables and fire grills are provided. Drinking water, food lockers, and vault toilets are available. A public pack station with corrals is nearby. Some facilities are wheelchair-accessible. Leashed pets are permitted.

Reservations, fees: Reservations are not accepted. There is no fee for camping. Open mid-May through early October, weather permitting.

Directions: From Porterville, drive east on Highway 190 for 19 miles (a mile past the

town of Springville) to Balch Park Road. Turn left (north) at Balch Park Road and drive about 23 miles to the Mountain Home State Forest sign. Continue on Balch Park Road (the road is long and twisty) and follow the signs to the State Forest Headquarters (where free forest maps are available). The campgrounds are well signed from this point.

Contact: Mountain Home State Forest, 559/539-2321 (summer) or 559/539-2855 (winter); Balch Park Pack Station, 559/539-2227.

95 HEDRICK POND

Scenic rating: 6

in Mountain Home State Forest

Map grid B2

Mountain Home State Forest is highlighted by giant sequoias, and Hedrick Pond provides a fishing opportunity, as it's stocked occasionally in summer with rainbow trout. This camp is set at 6,200 feet elevation, one of five campgrounds in the immediate region. (See the Methuselah Group Camp listing in this chapter for recreation options.)

RV sites, facilities: There are 14 sites for tents or RVs up to 20 feet (no hookups). Picnic tables, food lockers, and fire grills are provided. Drinking water and vault toilets are available. Some facilities are wheelchair-accessible. Leashed pets are permitted.

Reservations, fees: Reservations are not accepted. There is no fee for camping. Open mid-May through October, weather permitting.

Directions: From Porterville, drive east on Highway 190 for 19 miles (a mile past the town of Springville) to Balch Park Road. Turn left (north) at Balch Park Road and drive about 23 miles to the Mountain Home State Forest sign. Continue on Balch Park Road (the road is long and twisty) and follow the signs to the State Forest Headquarters (where free forest maps are available). The campgrounds are well signed from this point.

Contact: Mountain Home State Forest, 559/539-2321 (summer) or 559/539-2855 (winter).

96 METHUSELAH GROUP CAMP

Scenic rating: 6

in Mountain Home State Forest

Map grid B2

This is one of the few group campgrounds anywhere in California that is free to users. But hey: Remember to bring water. The elevation is 5,900 feet. Mountain Home State Forest is best known for its remoteness, old-growth giant sequoias (hence the name of this camp, Methuselah), trails that provide access to small streams, and horseback trips into the surrounding Sequoia National Forest.

RV sites, facilities: There is one group site for tents or 1–2 RVs up to 20 feet (no hookups) that can accommodate 20–100 people. Fire grills and picnic tables are provided. Vault toilets are available. No drinking water is available. Garbage must be packed out. Leashed pets are permitted.

Reservations, fees: Reservations are required. There is no fee for camping. Open mid-May through early October, weather permitting.

Directions: From Porterville, drive east on Highway 190 for 19 miles (a mile past the town of Springville) to Balch Park Road. Turn left (north) at Balch Park Road and drive about 23 miles to the Mountain Home State Forest sign. Continue on Balch Park Road (the road is long and twisty) and follow the signs to the State Forest Headquarters (where free forest maps are available). The campgrounds are well signed from this point.

Contact: Mountain Home State Forest, 559/539-2321 (summer) or 559/539-2855 (winter).

97 WISHON

Scenic rating: 8

on the Tule River in
Giant Sequoia National Monument

Map grid B2

Wishon Camp is set at 3,900 feet elevation on the Middle Fork of the North Fork Tule River, just west of the Doyle Springs Summer Home Tract. Just down the road to the east, on the left side, is a parking area for a trailhead. The hike here is routed for a mile to the Tule River and then runs along the stream for about five miles, to Mountain Home State Forest.

RV sites, facilities: There are 39 sites for tents or RVs up to 22 feet (no hookups). Picnic tables and fire grills are provided. Drinking water and vault toilets are available. Leashed pets are permitted.

Reservations, fees: Reservations are accepted at 877/444-6777 or www.recreation.gov ($10 reservation fee). Sites are $17–38 per night, $5 per night for each additional vehicle. Fees are higher on holiday weekends. Open year-round.

Directions: From Porterville, drive east on Highway 190 for 25 miles to County Road 209/Wishon Drive. Turn left at County Road 208/Wishon Drive and drive 3.5 miles (narrow, curvy—RVs not advised).

Contact: Sequoia National Forest and Giant Sequoia National Monument, Western Divide Ranger District, 559/539-2607, fax 559/539-2067.

98 COY FLAT

Scenic rating: 4

in Giant Sequoia National Monument

Map grid B2

Coy Flat is set between Coy Creek and Bear Creek, small forks of the Tule River, at 5,000 feet elevation. The road out of camp is routed five miles (through Rogers' Camp, which is private property) to the Black Mountain Grove of redwoods, with some giant sequoias set just inside the border of the neighboring Tule River Indian Reservation. From camp, a hiking trail (Forest Trail 31S31) is routed east for two miles through the Belknap Camp Grove of sequoias and then turns and heads south for four miles to Slate Mountain, where it intersects with Summit National Recreation Trail, a steep butt-kicker of a hike that tops out at over 9,000 feet elevation.

RV sites, facilities: There are 20 sites for tents or RVs up to 22 feet (no hookups). Picnic tables and fire grills are provided. Drinking water

and vault toilets are available. Leashed pets are permitted.

Reservations, fees: Reservations are accepted at 877/444-6777 or www.recreation.gov ($10 reservation fee). Sites are $7–34 per night, $5 per night for each additional vehicle. Camping fees are higher for holiday weekends. Open mid-April through mid-November.

Directions: From Porterville, drive east on Highway 190 for 34 miles to Camp Nelson and Coy Flat Road. Turn right on Coy Flat Road and drive one mile to the campground.

Contact: Sequoia National Forest and Giant Sequoia National Monument, Western Divide Ranger District, 559/539-2607, fax 559/539-2067.

99 QUAKING ASPEN

Scenic rating: 4

in Giant Sequoia National Monument

Map grid B2

Quaking Aspen sits at a junction of Forest Service roads at 7,000 feet elevation, near the headwaters of Freeman Creek. A trailhead for Summit National Recreation Trail runs right through camp; it's a popular trip on horseback, heading deep into Sequoia National Forest. Another trailhead is 0.5 mile away on Forest Road 21S50. This hike is routed east along Freeman Creek and reaches the Freeman Grove of sequoias in four miles. This camp is in the vicinity of the Sequoia National Forest fire, named the McNalley Fire, which burned more than 100,000 acres to the east of this area in the summer of 2002. The fire started in the Kern River Canyon and then burned up the Kern Canyon north to Forks of the Kern and the surrounding environs. While 11 groves of giant sequoias here were saved, much of the surrounding forest several miles to the east of the camps was burned.

RV sites, facilities: There are 32 sites for tents or RVs up to 24 feet (no hookups). Picnic tables and fire grills are provided. Drinking water and vault toilets are available. An amphitheater is available. A store is nearby. Some facilities

are wheelchair-accessible. Leashed pets are permitted.

Reservations, fees: Reservations are accepted at 877/444-6777 or www.recreation.gov ($10 reservation fee). Sites are $17 per night, $5 per night for each additional vehicle. Fees are higher on holiday weekends. Open May through mid-November, weather permitting.

Directions: From Porterville, drive east on Highway 190 for 34 miles to Camp Nelson. Continue east on Highway 190 for 11 miles to the campground on the right.

Contact: Sequoia National Forest and Giant Sequoia National Monument, Western Divide Ranger District, 559/539-2607, fax 559/539-2067.

100 QUAKING ASPEN GROUP CAMP

Scenic rating: 4

at the headwaters of the South Fork of the Middle Fork Tule River in Giant Sequoia National Monument

Map grid B2

For groups, here is an alternative to nearby Peppermint. (See the Peppermint listing in this chapter for recreation options.) The elevation is 7,000 feet. (For details about this area, see the Quaking Aspen listing in this chapter.)

RV sites, facilities: There are seven group sites for tents or RVs up to 24 feet (no hookups) that can accommodate 12–50 people each. Picnic tables and fire grills are provided. Drinking water and vault toilets are available. A lodge with limited supplies is nearby. Some facilities are wheelchair-accessible. Leashed pets are permitted.

Reservations, fees: Reservations are required at 877/444-6777 or www.recreation.gov ($10 reservation fee). Sites are $24.75–104.50 per night, depending on group size. Open mid-May through mid-November.

Directions: From Porterville, drive east on Highway 190 for 34 miles to Camp Nelson. Continue east on Highway 190 for 11 miles to the campground on the right.

Contact: Sequoia National Forest and Giant

Sequoia National Monument, Western Divide Ranger District, 559/539-2607, fax 559/539-2067.

101 TULE

Scenic rating: 7

on Lake Success

Map grid B2

Lake Success is a big lake with many arms, providing 30 miles of shoreline and making the place seem like a dreamland for boaters on hot summer days. The lake is set in the foothill country, at an elevation of 650 feet, where day after day of 100-degree summer temperatures are common. That is why boating, waterskiing, and personal-watercraft riding are so popular—anything to get wet. In the winter and spring, fishing for trout and bass is good, including the chance for largemouth bass. No beaches are developed for swimming because of fluctuating water levels, though the day-use area has a decent sloped stretch of shore that is good for swimming. Lake Success is much shallower than most reservoirs, and the water can fluctuate from week to week, with major drawdowns during the summer. The wildlife area along the west side of the lake is worth exploring, and there is a nature trail below the dam. The campground is the centerpiece of the Tule Recreation Area.

RV sites, facilities: There are 104 sites for tents or RVs up to 35 feet; some sites have electrical hookups (30 and 50 amps). Picnic tables and fire grills are provided. Restrooms with flush toilets and showers, dump station, picnic areas, and playground are available. A store, marina, boat ramp, houseboat, boat and water-ski rentals, bait and tackle, propane gas, restaurant, and gas station are nearby. Leashed pets are permitted.

Reservations, fees: Reservations are accepted at 877/444-6777 or www.recreation.gov ($10 reservation fee). Sites are $16–21 per night. Open year-round.

Directions: Drive on Highway 65 to Porterville and the junction with Highway 190. Turn east on Highway 190 and drive eight miles to Lake Success and the campground entrance on the left.

Contact: U.S. Army Corps of Engineers, Sacramento District, 559/784-0215, fax 559/784-5469; Success Marina, 559/781-2078.

102 HOLEY MEADOW GROUP CAMP

Scenic rating: 7

on Double Bunk Creek in Giant Sequoia National Monument

Map grid B2

Holey Meadow is set at 6,400 feet elevation on the western slopes of the Sierra, near Redwood and Long Meadow. Parker Pass is a mile to the west, and if you drive on the Forest Service road over the pass, continue southwest (four miles from camp) to Cold Springs Saddle, and then turn east on the Forest Service spur road, it will take you two miles to Starvation Creek and the Starvation Creek Grove.

RV sites, facilities: There is a group site for tents or RVs up to 16 feet (no hookups) that can accommodate up to 60 people. Fire grills and picnic tables are provided. Vault toilets are available. There is no drinking water; water is available 2.5 miles away at Redwood Meadow campground. Leashed pets are permitted.

Reservations, fees: Reservations are required at 877/444-6777 or www.recreation.gov ($10 reservation fee). The camp is $121 per night. Open June through October.

Directions: Drive on Highway 99 to Earlimart (about eight miles north of Delano) and the exit for Avenue 56/County Road J22. Take that exit east and drive 39 miles to the town of California Hot Springs and Parker Pass Road/County Road M50. Turn left on Parker Pass Road and drive 12 miles to Western Divide Highway/County Road M107. Turn left on Western Divide Highway and drive 0.5 mile to the campground entrance.

Contact: Sequoia National Forest and Giant Sequoia National Monument, Western Divide Ranger District, 559/539-2607, fax 559/539-2067.

CALIFORNIA

103 REDWOOD MEADOW

Scenic rating: 7

near Parker Meadow Creek in
Giant Sequoia National Monument

Map grid B2

The highlight here is the 1.5-mile Trail of the Hundred Giants, which is routed through a grove of giant sequoias and is accessible for wheelchair hikers. This is the site where President Clinton proclaimed the Giant Sequoia National Monument in 2000. The camp is set near Parker Meadow Creek at 6,100 feet elevation. Despite its remoteness, this has become a popular place.

RV sites, facilities: There are 15 sites for tents or RVs up to 16 feet (no hookups). Picnic tables and fire grills are provided. Drinking water and vault toilets are available. Leashed pets are permitted.

Reservations, fees: Reservations are accepted at 877/444-6777 or www.recreation.gov ($10 reservation fee). Sites are $17 per night, $5 per night for each additional vehicle. Camping fees are higher on holiday weekends. Open June through October, weather permitting.

Directions: Drive on Highway 99 to Earlimart (about eight miles north of Delano) and the exit for Avenue 56/County Road J22. Take that exit east and drive 39 miles to the town of California Hot Springs and Parker Pass Road/County Road M50. Turn left on Parker Pass Road and drive 12 miles to Western Divide Highway/County Road M107. Turn left on Western Divide Highway and drive three miles to the campground entrance.

Contact: Sequoia National Forest and Giant Sequoia National Monument, Western Divide Ranger District, 559/539-2607, fax 559/539-2067.

104 LONG MEADOW GROUP CAMP

Scenic rating: 8

in Giant Sequoia National Monument

Map grid B2

Long Meadow is set on little Long Meadow Creek at an elevation of 6,000 feet, within a mile of the remote Cunningham Grove of redwoods to the east. Note that Redwood Meadow is just one mile to the west, where the Trail of the Hundred Giants is a feature attraction.

RV sites, facilities: There is one group site for tents or RVs up to 16 feet (no hookups) that can accommodate up to 25 people. Picnic tables and fire grills are provided. Vault toilets are available. No drinking water is available. Leashed pets are permitted.

Reservations, fees: Reservations are required at 877/444-6777 or www.recreation.gov ($10 reservation fee). The site is $55 per night. Open mid-May through mid-November.

Directions: Drive on Highway 99 to Earlimart (about eight miles north of Delano) and the exit for Avenue 56/County Road J22. Take that exit east and drive 39 miles to the town of California Hot Springs and Parker Pass Road/County Road M50. Turn left on Parker Pass Road and drive 12 miles to Western Divide Highway/County Road M107. Turn left on Western Divide Highway and drive four miles to the campground entrance.

Contact: Sequoia National Forest and Giant Sequoia National Monument, Western Divide Ranger District, 559/539-2607, fax 559/539-2067.

105 GOODALE CREEK

Scenic rating: 6

near Independence

Map grid B2

This obscure BLM camp is set along little Goodale Creek at 4,000 feet elevation. It is a good layover spot for U.S. 395 cruisers heading north. In hot summer months, snakes are occasionally spotted near this campground.

RV sites, facilities: There are 62 sites for tents or RVs up to 30 feet (no hookups). Picnic tables and fire rings are provided. Pit toilets are available. No drinking water is available. Leashed pets are permitted.

Reservations, fees: Reservations are not accepted. Sites are $5 per night. Maximum stay is 14 days. A LTVA Permit ($300) allows all season access to this and two other BLM campgrounds,

CALIFORNIA

Tuttle Creek (see listing in this chapter) and Crowley. Open early April through October, weather permitting.

Directions: Drive on U.S. 395 to Aberdeen Road (12 miles north of Independence). Turn west (toward the Sierra) on Aberdeen Road and drive two miles to the campground on the left.

Contact: Bureau of Land Management, Bishop Field Office, 760/872-4881, fax 760/872-5050.

106 ONION VALLEY

Scenic rating: 8

in Inyo National Forest

Map grid B2

Onion Valley is one of the best trailhead camps for backpackers in the Sierra. The camp is set at 9,200 feet elevation, and from here it's a 2,600-foot climb over the course of about three miles to awesome Kearsarge Pass (11,823 feet). From there you can camp at the Kearsarge Lakes, explore the Kearsarge Pinnacles, or join the John Muir Trail and venture to your choice of many wilderness lakes. A wilderness map and a free wilderness permit (if obtained from the ranger station) are your passports to the high country from this camp. For backpackers, trailhead reservations are required. Note: Bears frequent this camp almost every night of summer. Do not keep your food in your vehicle. Many cars have been severely damaged by bears. Use bear-proof food lockers at the campground and parking area, or use bear-proof food canisters as required in adjacent wilderness area.

RV sites, facilities: There are 29 sites for tents or RVs up to 16 feet (no hookups). Picnic tables and fire grills are provided. Drinking water and vault toilets are available. Leashed pets are permitted.

Reservations, fees: Reservations are accepted at 877/444-6777 or www.recreation.gov ($10 reservation fee). Sites are $13 per night. Maximum stay is 14 days. Open late May through September, weather permitting.

Directions: Drive on U.S. 395 to Independence and Market Street. Turn west (toward the Sierra) at Market Street (becomes Onion Valley

Road) and drive 15 miles to the campground at the road's end.

Contact: Inyo National Forest, Mount Whitney Ranger District, 760/876-6200, fax 760/876-6202; Interagency Visitor Center, 760/876-6222.

107 UPPER AND LOWER GRAY'S MEADOW

Scenic rating: 6

on Independence Creek in Inyo National Forest

Map grid B2

Gray's Meadow provides two adjacent camps that are set along Independence Creek. Upper Gray's is set at an elevation of 6,200 feet; Lower Gray's is 200 feet lower down canyon. The creek is stocked with small trout by the Department of Fish and Game. The highlight in the immediate area is the trailhead at the end of the road at Onion Valley camp. For U.S. 395 cruisers looking for a spot, this is a pretty alternative to the camps in Bishop.

RV sites, facilities: Lower Gray's has 52 sites for tents or RVs up to 34 feet (no hookups). Upper Gray's has 35 sites for tents or RVs. Picnic tables, food lockers, and fire grills are provided. Drinking water and flush toilets are available. Supplies and a coin laundry are in Independence. Leashed pets are permitted.

Reservations, fees: Reservations are accepted at 877/444-6777 or www.recreation.gov ($10 reservation fee). Sites are $13 per night. Open late March through mid-October, with a 14-day limit.

Directions: Drive on U.S. 395 to Independence and Market Street. Turn west (toward the Sierra) at Market Street (becomes Onion Valley Road) and drive five miles to the campground on the right.

Contact: Inyo National Forest, Mount Whitney Ranger District, 760/876-6200, fax 760/876-6202; Interagency Visitor Center, 760/876-6222.

CALIFORNIA

108 INDEPENDENCE CREEK CAMPGROUND

Scenic rating: 4

in Independence

Map grid B2

This unpublicized county park is often over-looked among U.S. 395 cruisers. It is set at 3,900 feet elevation just outside of Independence, which is spiraling downward into something resembling a ghost town. True to form, maintenance is sometimes lacking here. Independence Creek runs through the campground and a museum is within walking distance. At the rate it's going, the whole town could be a museum.

RV sites, facilities: There are 25 sites for tents or RVs up to 27 feet (no hookups). Picnic tables and fire grills are provided. Drinking water and vault toilets are available. Some facilities are wheelchair-accessible. Supplies and a coin laundry are available in Independence. Leashed pets are permitted.

Reservations, fees: Reservations are not accepted. Sites are $10 per vehicle per night. Open year-round.

Directions: Drive on U.S. 395 to Independence and Market Street. Turn west (toward the Sierra) at Market Street and drive one mile (outside the town limits) to the campground.

Contact: Inyo County Parks Department, 760/873-5577, www.inyocountycamping.com.

109 LONE PINE AND LONE PINE GROUP

Scenic rating: 8

near Mount Whitney in Inyo National Forest

Map grid B2

This is an alternative for campers preparing to hike Mount Whitney or start the John Muir Trail. It is set at 6,000 feet elevation, 2,000 feet below Whitney Portal (the hiking jump-off spot), providing a lower-elevation location for hikers to acclimate themselves to the altitude. The camp is set on Lone Pine Creek, with decent fishing and spectacular views of Mount

Whitney. Because of its exposure to the east, there are also beautiful sunrises, especially in fall.

RV sites, facilities: There are 43 sites for tents or RVs up to 35 feet (no hookups), and one group site for up to 15 people. Picnic tables and fire grills are provided. Drinking water and flush toilets are available. Supplies are available in Lone Pine. Leashed pets are permitted.

Reservations, fees: Reservations are accepted at 877/444-6777 or www.recreation.gov ($10 reservation fee). Sites are $15 per night, $5 per night per each additional vehicle, $50 per night for the group site. Open late April through mid-October, with a 14-day limit.

Directions: Drive on U.S. 395 to Lone Pine and Whitney Portal Road. Turn west (toward the Sierra) on Whitney Portal Road and drive six miles to the campground on the left.

Contact: Inyo National Forest, Mount Whitney Ranger District, 760/876-6200, fax 760/876-6202; Interagency Visitor Center, 760/876-6222.

110 PORTAGEE JOE CAMPGROUND

Scenic rating: 4

near Lone Pine

Map grid B2

This small, little-known county park provides an option for both Mount Whitney hikers and U.S. 395 cruisers. It is about five miles from Diaz Lake, set on a small creek at 3,750 feet, near the base of Mount Whitney. Very few out-of-towners know about this spot, a nice insurance policy if you find yourself stuck for a campsite in this region.

RV sites, facilities: There are 15 sites for tents or RVs up to 27 feet (no hookups). Picnic tables and fire grills are provided. Vault toilets and well water are available. Supplies and a coin laundry are available in Lone Pine. Leashed pets are permitted.

Reservations, fees: Reservations are not accepted. Sites are $10 per vehicle per night. Open year-round.

Directions: Drive on U.S. 395 to Lone Pine and Whitney Portal Road. Turn west (toward the Sierra) on Whitney Portal Road and drive one mile to Tuttle Creek Road. Turn left (south) at Tuttle Creek Road and drive 0.1 mile to the campground on the right.

Contact: Inyo County Parks Department, 760/878-0272 or 760/873-5577, www.inyo-countycamping.com.

111 WHITNEY PORTAL AND WHITNEY PORTAL GROUP

Scenic rating: 9

near Mount Whitney in Inyo National Forest

Map grid B2

This camp is home to a world-class trailhead. It is regarded as the number-one jump-off spot for the hike to the top of Mount Whitney, the highest spot in the continental United States, at 14,497.6 feet, as well as the start of the 211-mile John Muir Trail from Mount Whitney to Yosemite Valley. Hikers planning to scale the summit must have a wilderness permit, available by reservation at the Forest Service office in Lone Pine. The camp is at 8,000 feet elevation, and virtually everyone staying here plans to make the trek to the Whitney summit, a climb of 6,500 feet over the course of 10 miles. The trip includes an ascent over 100 switchbacks (often snow-covered in early summer) to top Wotan's Throne and reach Trail Crest (13,560 feet). Here you turn right and take Summit Trail, where the ridge is cut by huge notch windows providing a view down more than 10,000 feet to the little town of Lone Pine and the Owens Valley. When you sign the logbook on top, don't be surprised if you see my name in the registry. A plus at the campground is watching the JMT hikers arrive who are just finishing the trail from north to south—that is, from Yosemite to Whitney. There is no comparing the happy look of success when they drop their packs for the last time, head into the little store, and pick a favorite refreshment for celebration.

RV sites, facilities: There are 43 sites for tents or RVs up to 30 feet (no hookups), and three group sites for up to 15 people each. Picnic tables, food lockers, and fire grills are provided. Drinking water and flush toilets are available. Supplies are available in Lone Pine. Some facilities are wheelchair-accessible. Leashed pets are permitted.

Reservations, fees: Reservations are accepted at 877/444-6777 or www.recreation.gov ($10 reservation fee). Sites are $17 per night, $5 per night per each additional vehicle, $45–55 per night for a group site. One-night limit for walk-in tent sites; seven-day stay limit for group site. Open late May through mid-October.

Directions: Drive on U.S. 395 to Lone Pine and Whitney Portal Road. Turn west (toward the Sierra) on Whitney Portal Road and drive 13 miles to the campground on the left.

Contact: Inyo National Forest, Mount Whitney Ranger District, 760/876-6200, fax 760/876-6202; Interagency Visitor Center, 760/876-2222; California Land Management, 760/937-6070.

112 TUTTLE CREEK

Scenic rating: 4

near Mount Whitney

Map grid B2

This primitive BLM camp is set at the base of Mount Whitney along Tuttle Creek at 5,120 feet elevation and is shadowed by several impressive peaks (Mount Whitney, Lone Pine Peak, and Mount Williamson). It is often used as an overflow area if the camps farther up Whitney Portal Road are full. Note: This campground is often confused with a small county campground also on Tuttle Creek Road just off Whitney Portal Road.

RV sites, facilities: There are 85 sites for tents or RVs up to 30 feet (no hookups). Picnic tables and fire rings are provided. Pit toilets are available. No drinking water. Supplies are available in Lone Pine. Leashed pets are permitted.

Reservations, fees: Reservations are not

accepted. Sites are $5 per night; season passes are $300. Open early March through October.

Directions: Drive on U.S. 395 to Lone Pine and Whitney Portal Road. Turn west (toward the Sierra) on Whitney Portal Road and drive 3.5 miles to Horseshoe Meadow Road. Turn left and drive 1.5 miles to Tuttle Creek Road and the campground entrance (a dirt road) on the right.

Contact: Bureau of Land Management, Bishop Field Office, 760/872-4881, fax 760/873-5050.

113 DIAZ LAKE

Scenic rating: 6

near Lone Pine

Map grid B2

Diaz Lake, set at 3,650 feet elevation in the Owens Valley, is sometimes overlooked by visitors to nearby Mount Whitney. It's a small lake, just 85 acres, and it is popular for trout fishing in the spring when a speed limit of 15 mph is enforced. The lake is stocked with Alpers trout and also has a surprise population of bass. From May through October, when hot weather takes over and the speed limit is bumped up to 35 mph, you can say adios to the anglers and hola to waterskiers. Diaz Lake is extremely popular for waterskiing and swimming and it is sunny most of the year. A 20-foot limit is enforced for boats. A nine-hole golf course is nearby.

RV sites, facilities: There are 200 sites for tents or RVs of any length; some have partial hookups. Picnic tables and fire grills are provided. Restrooms with flush and vault toilets, drinking water (from a well), playground, and boat ramp are available. Supplies and a coin laundry are in Lone Pine. Leashed pets are permitted.

Reservations, fees: Group reservations are accepted at 760/876-5656. Sites are $10–14 per vehicle per night. Open year-round.

Directions: Drive on U.S. 395 to the Diaz Lake entrance (three miles south of Lone Pine) on the west side of the road.

Contact: Inyo County Parks Department, 760/878-0272 or 760/873-5577, www.inyo-countycamping.com.

114 PEPPERMINT

Scenic rating: 4

on Peppermint Creek in
Giant Sequoia National Monument

Map grid B3

This is one of two primitive campgrounds at Peppermint Creek, but a road does not directly connect the two camps. Several backcountry access roads snake throughout the area, as detailed on a Forest Service map, and exploring them can make for some self-styled fortune hunts. For the ambitious, hiking the two-mile trail at the end of nearby Forest Road 21S05 leads to a fantastic lookout at The Needles (8,245 feet). The camp elevation is 7,100 feet. There is fire damage in some of the surrounding area.

RV sites, facilities: There are 19 sites for tents or RVs up to 24 feet (no hookups). Picnic tables and fire rings are provided. Vault toilets are available. No drinking water is available. Garbage must be packed out. A lodge with limited supplies is nearby. Leashed pets are permitted.

Reservations, fees: Reservations are not accepted. There is no fee for camping. A fire permit is required. Open June through September, weather permitting.

Directions: From Porterville, drive east on Highway 190 for 34 miles to Camp Nelson. Continue east on Highway 190 for 15 miles to the campground entrance road.

Contact: Sequoia National Forest and Giant Sequoia National Monument, Western Divide Ranger District, 559/539-2607, fax 559/539-2067.

115 LOWER PEPPERMINT

Scenic rating: 2

in Giant Sequoia National Monument

Map grid B3

This is a little-known camp in Sequoia National Forest, set along Peppermint Creek at 5,300 feet elevation. This area has a vast network of backcountry roads, which are detailed on a Forest Service map. The camp is in the immediate vicinity of the Sequoia forest fire, named the McNalley Fire, which burned more than 100,000 acres in the summer of 2002. The fire started in the Kern River Canyon and then burned up the Kern Canyon north to Forks of the Kern.

RV sites, facilities: There are 17 sites for tents or RVs up to 22 feet (no hookups). Picnic tables and fire grills are provided. Drinking water and vault toilets are available. Leashed pets are permitted.

Reservations, fees: Reservations are not accepted. Sites are $17 per night. Open June through September.

Directions: From Bakersfield, drive east on Highway 178 for 40 miles to the town of Lake Isabella and Highway 155/Burlando Way. Turn left (north) and drive 10 miles to Kernville Sierra Way. Turn (north) and drive 24 miles to Johnsondale and Forest Road 22S82/Lloyd Meadow Road. Turn right and drive about 10.5 miles (paved road) to the campground.

Contact: Sequoia National Forest and Giant Sequoia National Monument, Western Divide Ranger District, 559/539-2607, fax 559/539-2067.

116 LIMESTONE

Scenic rating: 1

on the Kern River in Sequoia National Forest
Map grid B3

Set deep in the Sequoia National Forest at 3,800 feet, Limestone is a small campground along the Kern River, fed by snowmelt from Mount Whitney. This stretch of the Kern is extremely challenging and sensational for white-water rafting, with cold water and many of the rapids rated Class IV and Class V—for experts with guides only. The favored put-in is at the Johnsondale Bridge, and from here it's a 21-mile run to Kernville. The river pours into Isabella Lake many miles later. Two sections are unrunnable: Fairview Dam (Mile 2.5) and Salmon Falls (Mile 8). For nonrafters, South Creek Falls provides a side trip, one mile to the west. There is fire damage in some of the surrounding area.

RV sites, facilities: There are 22 sites for tents or RVs up to 30 feet (no hookups). Picnic tables and fire grills are provided. Vault toilets are available. No drinking water is available. Supplies and a coin laundry are in Kernville. Leashed pets are permitted.

Reservations, fees: Reservations are not accepted. Sites are $15 per night, $5 per night for each additional vehicle. Open April through November, weather permitting.

Directions: From Bakersfield, drive east on Highway 178 for about 40 miles to the town of Lake Isabella and Highway 155/Burlando Way. Turn left (north) and drive 10 miles to Kernville and the Kern River Highway/Sierra Way. Turn left on the Kern River Highway and drive 19 miles (two miles past Fairview) to the campground entrance.

Contact: Sequoia National Forest, Kern River Ranger District, Kernville Office, 760/376-3781, fax 760/376-3795.

117 LEAVIS FLAT

Scenic rating: 7

on Deer Creek in Giant Sequoia National Monument
Map grid B3

Leavis Flat is just inside the western border of Sequoia National Forest along Deer Creek, at an elevation of 3,000 feet. The highlight here is the adjacent California Hot Springs.

RV sites, facilities: There are nine sites for tents or RVs up to 16 feet (no hookups). Picnic tables and fire grills are provided. Drinking water and vault toilets are available. A store, coin laundry, and propane gas can be found nearby. Leashed pets are permitted.

Reservations, fees: Reservations are accepted at 877/444-6777 or www.recreation.gov ($10 reservation fee). Sites are $17–19 per night, $5 per night for each additional vehicle. Camping fees are higher on holiday weekends. Open year-round.

Directions: Drive on Highway 99 to Earlimart (about eight miles north of Delano) and the exit for Avenue 56/County Road J22. Take that exit east and drive 39 miles to the town of California Hot Springs and the campground.

Contact: Sequoia National Forest and Giant Sequoia National Monument, Western Divide Ranger District, 559/539-2607, fax 559/539-2067.

118 WHITE RIVER

Scenic rating: 7

in Giant Sequoia National Monument

Map grid B3

White River is set at 4,000 feet elevation, on the White River near where little Dark Canyon Creek enters it. A trail from camp follows downstream along the White River to the west for three miles, dropping into Ames Hole and Cove Canyon. The region's hot springs are about a 10-minute drive away to the north.

RV sites, facilities: There are 12 sites for tents or RVs up to 16 feet (no hookups). Picnic tables and fire grills are provided. Drinking water and vault toilets are available. Leashed pets are permitted.

Reservations, fees: Reservations are accepted at 877/444-6777 or www.recreation.gov ($10 reservation fee). Sites are $17–19 per night, $5 per night for each additional vehicle. Camping fees are higher on holiday weekends. Open mid-April through mid-October.

Directions: Drive on Highway 99 to Delano and the exit for Highway 155. Take that exit and drive east for about 40 miles to Jack Ranch Road (just west of Glennville). Turn left on Jack Ranch Road and drive about four miles to White River Road/Sugarloaf Drive. Turn right and drive 1.5 miles to Forest Road 24S05. Bear left and drive 0.75 mile to Idlewild, and continue (on this dirt road) for six miles to the campground.

Contact: Sequoia National Forest and Giant Sequoia National Monument, Western Divide Ranger District, 559/539-2607, fax 559/539-2067.

119 FROG MEADOW

Scenic rating: 6

near Giant Sequoia National Monument

Map grid B3

This small, primitive camp, set near Tobias Creek at 7,500 feet elevation, is in the center of a network of Forest Service roads that explore the surrounding Sequoia National Forest. The nearby feature destination is the Tobias Peak Lookout (8,284 feet), two miles directly south of the camp.

RV sites, facilities: There are 10 sites for tents or RVs up to 16 feet (no hookups). Vault toilets are available. No drinking water is available. Garbage must be packed out. Leashed pets are permitted.

Reservations, fees: Reservations are not accepted. There is no fee for camping. Open June through September, weather permitting.

Directions: Drive on Highway 99 to Delano and the exit for Highway 155. Take that exit and drive east for about 40 miles to Jack Ranch Road (just west of Glennville). Turn left on Jack Ranch Road and drive about four miles to White River Road/Sugarloaf Drive. Turn right on Sugarloaf Drive and drive 4.5 miles to Guernsey Mill/Sugarloaf Drive. Continue on Sugarloaf Road/Forest Road 23S16 for about seven miles to Forest Road 24S50 (a dirt road). Turn left on Forest Road 24S50 and drive four miles to Frog Meadow and the campground. The route is long, slow, and circuitous. A map of Sierra National Forest is required.

Contact: Sequoia National Forest and Giant Sequoia National Monument, Western Divide Ranger District, 559/539-2607, fax 559/539-2067.

120 FAIRVIEW

Scenic rating: 4

on the Kern River in Sequoia National Forest

Map grid B3

Fairview is one of six campgrounds set on the Upper Kern River above Isabella Lake and adjacent to the Kern River, one of the prime rafting and kayaking rivers in California. This camp sits at 3,500 feet elevation. Many of the rapids are rated Class IV and Class V—for experts with guides only. The favored put-in is at the Johnsondale Bridge, and from here it's a 21-mile run to Kernville. The river eventually pours into Isabella Lake. Two sections are un-runnable: Fairview Dam (Mile 2.5) and Salmon Falls (Mile 8). There is fire damage in some of the surrounding area.

RV sites, facilities: There are 55 sites for tents or RVs up to 45 feet (no hookups). Picnic tables and fire grills are provided. Drinking water, vault toilets, and a dump station are available. Supplies and a coin laundry are available in Kernville. Some facilities are wheelchair-accessible. Leashed pets are permitted.

Reservations, fees: Reservations are accepted at 877/444-6777 or www.recreation.gov ($10 reservation fee). Sites are $17–19 per night, $5 per night for each additional vehicle. Camping fees are higher on holiday weekends. Open April through October, weather permitting.

Directions: From Bakersfield, drive east on Highway 178 for about 40 miles to the town of Lake Isabella and Highway 155/Burlando Way. Turn left (north) and drive 10 miles to Kernville and the Kern River Highway/Sierra Way. Turn left on the Kern River Highway and drive 18 miles to the town of Fairview. Continue to the north end of town to the campground entrance.

Contact: Sequoia National Forest, Kern River Ranger District, Kernville Office, 760/376-3781, fax 760/376-3795.

121 HORSE MEADOW

🏃 🎣 🐕 🚐 ⛺

Scenic rating: 8

on Salmon Creek in Sequoia National Forest

Map grid B3

This is a little-known spot set along Salmon Creek at 7,600 feet elevation. It is a region known for big meadows, forests, backcountry roads, and plenty of horses. It is just west of the Dome Land Wilderness, and there is a series of three public pastures for horses in the area, as well as trails ideal for horseback riding. From camp, one such trail follows along Salmon Creek to the west to Salmon Falls, a favorite for the few who know of it. A more popular overnight trip is to head to a trailhead about five miles east, which provides a route to Manter Meadows in the Dome Lands.

RV sites, facilities: There are 41 sites for tents or RVs up to 22 feet (no hookups). Picnic tables and fire grills are provided. Drinking water and vault toilets are available. Garbage must be packed out. Leashed pets are permitted.

Reservations, fees: Reservations are not accepted. Sites are $17 per night, $5 per night for each additional vehicle. Open June through October, weather permitting.

Directions: From Bakersfield, drive east on Highway 178 for about 40 miles to the town of Lake Isabella and Highway 155/Burlando Way. Turn left (north) and drive 10 miles to Kernville and the Kern River Highway/Sierra Way. Turn left on the Kern River Highway for about 20 miles to Sherman Pass Road (signed "Highway 395/Black Rock Ranger Station"). Make a sharp right on Sherman Pass Road and drive about 6.5 miles to Cherry Hill Road/Forest Road 22S12 (there is a green gate with a sign that says "Horse Meadow/Big Meadow"). Turn right and drive about four miles (the road becomes dirt) and continue for another three miles (follow the signs) to the campground entrance road.

Contact: Sequoia National Forest, Kern River Ranger District, Kernville Office, 760/376-3781, fax 760/376-3795.

122 GOLDLEDGE

🎣 🐕 🚐 ⛺

Scenic rating: 7

on the Kern River in Sequoia National Forest

Map grid B3

This is another in the series of camps on the Kern River north of Isabella Lake. This one is set at 3,200 feet elevation.

CALIFORNIA

RV sites, facilities: There are 37 sites for tents or RVs up to 30 feet (no hookups). Picnic tables and fire grills are provided. Drinking water and vault toilets are available. Supplies and a coin laundry are available in Kernville. Leashed pets are permitted.

Reservations, fees: Reservations are accepted at 877/444-6777 or www.recreation.gov ($10 reservation fee). Sites are $17–10 per night, $5 per night for each additional vehicle. Camping fees are higher on holiday weekends. Open May through August.

Directions: From Bakersfield, drive east on Highway 178 for about 40 miles to the town of Lake Isabella and Highway 155/Burlando Way. Turn left (north) and drive 10 miles to Kernville and the Kern River Highway/Sierra Way. Turn left on the Kern River Highway and drive 10 miles to the campground.

Contact: Sequoia National Forest, Kern River Ranger District, Kernville Office, 760/376-3781, fax 760/376-3795.

123 HOSPITAL FLAT

Scenic rating: 8

on the North Fork of the Kern River in Sequoia National Forest

Map grid B3

It's kind of like the old shell game, trying to pick the best of the campgrounds along the North Fork of the Kern River. This one is seven miles north of Isabella Lake. The elevation is 2,800 feet. (For information on rafting on the Kern River, see the Fairview listing in this chapter.)

RV sites, facilities: There are 40 sites for tents or RVs up to 30 feet (no hookups), and one group site for up to 30 people. Picnic tables and fire grills are provided. Drinking water and vault toilets are available. Supplies and a coin laundry are available in Kernville. Some facilities are wheelchair-accessible. Leashed pets are permitted.

Reservations, fees: Reservations are accepted

for individual sites and required for the group site at 877/444-6777 or www.recreation.gov ($10 reservation fee). Sites are $17–19 per night, $5 per night for each additional vehicle. Camping fees are higher on holiday weekends. Open May through August.

Directions: From Bakersfield, drive east on Highway 178 for about 40 miles to the town of Lake Isabella and Highway 155/Burlando Way. Turn left (north) and drive 10 miles to Kernville and the Kern River Highway/Sierra Way. Turn left on the Kern River Highway and drive 6.5 miles to the campground.

Contact: Sequoia National Forest, Kern River Ranger District, Kernville Office, 760/376-3781, fax 760/376-3795.

124 CAMP THREE

Scenic rating: 9

on the North Fork of the Kern River in Sequoia National Forest

Map grid B3

This is the second in a series of camps along the North Fork Kern River north of Isabella Lake (in this case, five miles north of the lake). If you don't like this spot, Hospital Flat is just two miles upriver and Headquarters is just one mile downriver. The camp elevation is 2,800 feet. Note: In past editions, this was listed as "Camp 3." But if you are making an online reservation, you must spell it out or the camp will not be recognized.

RV sites, facilities: There are 52 sites for tents or RVs up to 30 feet (no hookups), and two group sites for up to 30 people. Picnic tables and fire grills are provided. Drinking water and vault toilets are available. A store and coin laundry are available in Kernville. Some facilities are wheelchair-accessible. Leashed pets are permitted.

Reservations, fees: Reservations are accepted for individual sites and required for the group sites at 877/444-6777 or www.recreation. gov ($10 reservation fee). Sites are $17–19 per night, $5 per night for each additional vehicle, $85 per night for a group site. Camping fees are higher on holiday weekends. Open May through August.

Directions: From Bakersfield, drive east on Highway 178 for about 40 miles to the town of Lake Isabella and Highway 155/Burlando Way. Turn left (north) and drive 10 miles to Kernville and the Kern River Highway/Sierra Way. Turn left on the Kern River Highway and drive five miles to the campground.

Contact: Sequoia National Forest, Kern River Ranger District, Kernville Office, 760/376-3781, fax 760/376-3795.

125 HEADQUARTERS

Scenic rating: 8

on the North Fork of the Kern River in Sequoia National Forest

Map grid B3

As you head north from Isabella Lake on Sierra Way, this is the first in a series of Forest Service campgrounds from which to take your pick, all of them set along the North Fork of the Kern River. The North Fork Kern is best known for offering prime white water for rafting and kayaking. The elevation is 2,800 feet.

RV sites, facilities: There are 44 sites for tents or RVs up to 27 feet (no hookups). Picnic tables and fire grills are provided. Drinking water and vault toilets are available. Some facilities are wheelchair-accessible. Supplies and a coin laundry are available in Kernville. Leashed pets are permitted.

Reservations, fees: Reservations are accepted at 877/444-6777 or www.recreation.gov ($10 reservation fee). Sites are $15 per night, $5 per night for each additional vehicle. Camping fees are higher on holiday weekends. Open year-round.

Directions: From Bakersfield, drive east on Highway 178 for about 40 miles to the town of Lake Isabella and Highway 155/Burlando Way. Turn left (north) and drive 10 miles to Kernville

and the Kern River Highway/Sierra Way. Turn left on the Kern River Highway and drive three miles to the campground.

Contact: Sequoia National Forest, Kern River Ranger District, Kernville Office, 760/376-3781, fax 760/376-3795.

126 PANORAMA

Scenic rating: 7

in Giant Sequoia National Monument

Map grid B3

This pretty spot is set at 7,200 feet elevation in a region of Sequoia National Forest filled with a network of backcountry roads. The camp is set in an inconspicuous spot and is easy to miss. A good side trip is to drive two miles south, turn left, and continue a short distance to a trailhead on the right side of the road for Portuguese Peak (a Forest Service map is strongly advised). From here, it's a one-mile butt-kicker to the top of Portuguese Peak, at 7,914 feet elevation.

RV sites, facilities: There are 10 sites for tents or RVs up to 16 feet (no hookups). No drinking water is available. Garbage must be packed out. Leashed pets are permitted.

Reservations, fees: Reservations are not accepted. There is no fee for camping. Open June through August.

Directions: Drive on Highway 99 to Delano and the exit for Highway 155. Take that exit and drive east for about 40 miles to Jack Ranch Road (just west of Glennville). Turn left on Jack Ranch Road and drive about four miles to White River Road/Sugarloaf Drive. Turn right on Sugarloaf Drive and drive 4.5 miles to Guernsey Mill/Sugarloaf Drive. Continue on Sugarloaf Road/Forest Road 23S16 for about six miles to the campground (paved all the way).

Contact: Sequoia National Forest and Giant Sequoia National Monument, Western Divide Ranger District, 559/539-2607, fax 559/539-2067.

127 GREENHORN MOUNTAIN PARK

Scenic rating: 7

near Shirley Meadows

Map grid B3

This county campground is near the Shirley Meadows Ski Area, a small ski park open on weekends in winter when there is sufficient snow. Greenhorn Mountain Park covers 160 acres, set at 6,000 feet elevation. The region is filled with a network of Forest Service roads, detailed on a map of Sequoia National Forest. Isabella Lake is a 15-minute drive to the east.

RV sites, facilities: There are 70 sites for tents or RVs up to 24 feet (no hookups). Fourteen cabins are also available as a group rental. Picnic tables and fire pits or fire rings are provided. Drinking water is available intermittently; check for current status. Restrooms with flush toilets and showers are available. Leashed pets are permitted.

Reservations, fees: No reservations accepted, except for groups of at least 40 people. Sites are $14 per night. Open spring through fall, weather permitting.

Directions: From Bakersfield, drive east on Highway 178 for about 40 miles to the town of Lake Isabella and Highway 155/Burlando Way. Turn left (north) and drive six miles to Wofford Heights. Turn left (west) on Highway 155 and drive 10 miles to the park on the left.

Contact: Kern County Parks, 661/868-7000, www.co.kern.ca.us/parks/.

128 ALDER CREEK

Scenic rating: 7

in Sequoia National Forest

Map grid B3

This primitive camp is just inside the western border of Sequoia National Forest, an obscure spot that requires traversing a very twisty and, at times, rough road. It is set at 3,900 feet elevation, just 0.25 mile upstream from where Alder Creek meets Slick Rock Creek. There is a trail out of the camp that runs north for two miles along Slick Rock Creek.

RV sites, facilities: There are 13 sites for tents or RVs up to 20 feet (no hookups). Picnic tables and fire grills are provided. Vault toilets are available. No drinking water is available. Garbage must be packed out. Leashed pets are permitted.

Reservations, fees: Reservations are not accepted. There is no fee for camping. Open May through October.

Directions: Drive on Highway 99 to Delano and the exit for Highway 155. Take that exit and drive east on Highway 155 for 41 miles to Glennville. Continue east for eight miles to Alder Creek Road. Turn right on Alder Creek Road and drive three miles to the campground.

Contact: Sequoia National Forest, Kern River Ranger District, Lake Isabella Office, 760/379-5646, fax 760/379-8597.

129 EVANS FLAT

Scenic rating: 4

in Sequoia National Forest

Map grid B3

Evans Flat is an obscure campground in the southwest region of Sequoia National Forest, about 10 miles west of Isabella Lake, with no other camps in the vicinity. You have to earn this one, but if you want solitude, Evans Flat can provide it. It is set at 6,100 feet elevation, with Woodward Peak 0.5 mile to the east. A natural spring is east of camp within walking distance. Note that this campsite is no longer designed as an equestrian site.

RV sites, facilities: There are 20 sites for tents or RVs up to 20 feet (no hookups). Fire grills and picnic tables are provided. A vault toilet is available. No drinking water is available. Garbage must be packed out. Leashed pets are permitted.

Reservations, fees: Reservations are not accepted. There is no fee for camping. Open May through October.

Directions: From Bakersfield, drive east on

Highway 178 for about 40 miles to the town of Lake Isabella and Highway 155. Turn left (north) and drive six miles to Wofford Heights. Turn left (west) on Highway 155 and drive seven miles to Rancheria Road. Turn left and drive 8.3 miles (first paved, then dirt) to the campground.

Contact: Sequoia National Forest, Kern River Ranger District, Lake Isabella office, 760/379-5646, fax 760/379-8597.

130 RIVERNOOK CAMPGROUND

Scenic rating: 7

on the North Fork of the Kern River

Map grid B3

This is a large, privately operated park set near Isabella Lake a few miles from the head of the lake. Boat rentals are available at one of the nearby marinas. An optional side trip is to visit Keysville, the first town to become established on the Kern River during the gold rush days. The elevation is 2,665 feet.

RV sites, facilities: There are 30 pull-through sites with full hookups (30 and 50 amps) for RVs, 41 sites with partial hookups for RVs, and 59 sites for tents. Picnic tables, fire rings, and drinking water are provided. Restrooms with flush toilets and showers, three dump stations, and cable TV are available. Some facilities are wheelchair-accessible. Leashed pets are permitted.

Reservations, fees: Reservations are recommended. Sites are $35–45 per night, $5 per person per night for more than two people. Some credit cards accepted. Open year-round.

Directions: From Bakersfield, drive east on Highway 178 for about 40 miles to the town of Lake Isabella and Highway 155/Burlando Way. Turn left (north) and drive 10 miles to Kernville and the Kern River Highway/Sierra Way. Turn left on Sierra Way and drive 0.5 mile to the park entrance (14001 Sierra Way).

Contact: Rivernook Campground, 760/376-2705, fax 760/376-2595.

131 LIVE OAK NORTH AND SOUTH

Scenic rating: 8

on Isabella Lake

Map grid B3

This is one of two camps set in the immediate area on Isabella Lake's northwest side; the other is Tillie Creek. Live Oak is on the west side of the road, Tillie Creek on the eastern, lake side of the road. (For recreation information, see the Tillie Creek listing in this chapter.)

RV sites, facilities: There are 150 sites for tents or RVs up to 30 feet (no hookups) and one group site for up to 100 people. Picnic tables and fire grills are provided. Drinking water and restrooms with coin showers and flush toilets are available. Supplies are available in nearby Wofford Heights. Leashed pets are permitted.

Reservations, fees: Reservations are accepted for individual sites and required for the group site at 877/444-6777 or www.recreation.gov ($10 reservation fee). Sites are $19–21 per night, $5 per night for each additional vehicle, $275 per night for group site for up to 100 people. Open May through September.

Directions: From Bakersfield, drive east on Highway 178 for about 40 miles to the town of Lake Isabella and Highway 155. Turn left (north) and drive six miles to the campground entrance road on the left (0.5 mile before reaching Wofford Heights).

Contact: Sequoia National Forest, Kern River Ranger District, Lake Isabella Office, 760/379-5646, fax 760/379-8597.

132 TILLIE CREEK

Scenic rating: 9

on Isabella Lake

Map grid B3

This is one of two camps (the other is Live Oak) near where Tillie Creek enters Isabella Lake, set on the northwest shore of the lake near the town of Wofford Heights. Isabella Lake is a large lake, and with it comes a dynamic

CALIFORNIA

array of campgrounds, marinas, and facilities. It is set at 2,650 feet elevation in the foothills east of Bakersfield, fed by the Kern River, and dominated by water sports of all kinds.

RV sites, facilities: There are 159 sites for tents or RVs up to 45 feet and four group sites for tents or RVs up to 45 feet that can accommodate 60–150 people each. No hookups. Picnic tables and fire grills are provided. Drinking water and restrooms with showers and flush toilets are available. Dump station, playground, amphitheater, and a fish-cleaning station are nearby. Supplies are nearby in Wofford Heights. Some facilities are wheelchair-accessible. Leashed pets are permitted.

Reservations, fees: Reservations are accepted for individual sites and required for group sites at 877/444-6777 or www.recreation.gov ($10 reservation fee). Sites are $19–21 per night, $5 per night for each additional vehicle, $137–242 per night for group sites. Open year-round.

Directions: From Bakersfield, drive east on Highway 178 for about 40 miles to the town of Lake Isabella and Highway 155. Turn left (north) and drive five miles to the campground (0.5 mile before reaching Wofford Heights).

Contact: Sequoia National Forest, Kern River Ranger District, Lake Isabella Office, 760/379-5646, fax 760/379-8597.

133 CAMP 9

Scenic rating: 8

on Isabella Lake
Map grid B3

This campground is primitive and sparsely covered, but it has several bonus features. It is set along the northeast shore of Isabella Lake, known for good boating, waterskiing in the summer, and fishing in the spring. Other options include great rafting and kayaking waters along the North Fork of the Kern River (north of the lake), a good bird-watching area at the South Fork Wildlife Area (along the east side of the lake), and an off-highway-motorcycle park

across the road from this campground. The elevation is 2,650 feet.

RV sites, facilities: There are 109 primitive sites for tents or RVs of any length (no hookups), and 11 group sites that can accommodate 40 people each. Picnic tables and fire rings are provided. Drinking water, flush and vault toilets, dump station, boat launch, and fish-cleaning station are available. Supplies and a coin laundry are nearby in Kernville. Some facilities are wheelchair-accessible. Leashed pets are permitted.

Reservations, fees: Reservations are accepted for individual sites and are required for the group site at 877/444-6777 or www.recreation.gov ($10 reservation fee). Sites are $17 per night, $5 per night for each additional vehicle, $75–160 per night for a group site. Open year-round.

Directions: From Bakersfield, drive east on Highway 178 for about 40 miles to the town of Lake Isabella and Highway 155. Turn right (south) and drive six miles to the campground entrance on the right (on the northeast shore of Isabella Lake). The campground entrance is just south of the small airport at Lake Isabella.

Contact: Sequoia National Forest, Kern River Ranger District, Lake Isabella Office, 760/379-5646, fax 760/379-8597.

134 HUNGRY GULCH

Scenic rating: 9

near Isabella Lake in Sequoia National Forest
Map grid B3

Hungry Gulch is on the western side of Isabella Lake, but across the road from the shore. Nearby Boulder Gulch camp, directly across the road, is an alternative. There are no boat ramps in the immediate area. (For details about Isabella Lake, see the Pioneer Point listing in this chapter.)

RV sites, facilities: There are 78 sites for tents or RVs up to 30 feet (no hookups). Picnic tables and fire grills are provided. Drinking water, restrooms with coin showers and flush toilets, and fish-cleaning station are available. A playground is nearby. Supplies and a coin laundry are available in Lake Isabella. Leashed pets are permitted.

Reservations, fees: Reservations are accepted at 877/444-6777 or www.recreation.gov ($10 reservation fee). Sites are $19–21 per night, $5 per night for each additional vehicle. Open April through September.

Directions: From Bakersfield, drive east on Highway 178 for about 40 miles to the town of Lake Isabella and Highway 155. Turn left (north) and drive four miles on Highway 155 to the campground.

Contact: Sequoia National Forest, Kern River Ranger District, Lake Isabella Office, 760/379-5646, fax 760/379-8597.

135 BOULDER GULCH

Scenic rating: 8

on Isabella Lake

Map grid B3

Boulder Gulch lies fairly near the western shore of Isabella Lake, across the road from Hungry Gulch. Take your pick. Isabella is one of the biggest lakes in Southern California and a prime destination point for Bakersfield area residents. Fishing for trout and bass is best in the spring. The lake is stocked with trout in winter, and other species are bluegill, catfish, and crappie. By the dog days of summer, when people are bow-wowin' at the heat, water-skiers take over, along with folks just looking to cool off. Like a lot of lakes in the valley, Isabella is subject to drawdowns. The elevation is 2,650 feet. (For more information, see the Pioneer Point listing in this chapter.)

RV sites, facilities: There are 58 sites for tents or RVs up to 45 feet (no hookups). Picnic tables and fire grills are provided. Restrooms with flush toilets and coin showers, drinking water, playground, marina, and fish-cleaning station are available. Supplies and a coin laundry are available in the town of Lake Isabella. Leashed pets are permitted.

Reservations, fees: Reservations are accepted at 877/444-6777 or www.recreation.gov ($10 reservation fee). Sites are $19–21 per night, $5 per night for each additional vehicle. Open April through September.

Directions: From Bakersfield, drive east on Highway 178 for about 40 miles to the town of Lake Isabella and Highway 155. Turn left (north) and drive four miles to the campground entrance.

Contact: Sequoia National Forest, Kern River Ranger District, Lake Isabella Office, 760/379-5646, fax 760/379-8597.

136 FRENCH GULCH GROUP CAMP

Scenic rating: 9

on Isabella Lake

Map grid B3

This is a large group camp on Isabella Lake at the southwest end of the lake about two miles north of Pioneer Point and the spillway. (For recreation information, see the Pioneer Point listing in this chapter.) The elevation is 2,700 feet.

RV sites, facilities: There is one large group site for tents or RVs of any length (no hookups) that can accommodate up to 100 people. Picnic tables and fire grills are provided. Drinking water and restrooms with flush toilets and solar-heated showers are available. A store, coin laundry, and propane gas are nearby. Leashed pets are permitted.

Reservations, fees: Reservations are required at 877/444-6777 or www.recreation.gov ($10 reservation fee). The fee is $275 per night. Open year-round.

Directions: From Bakersfield, drive east on Highway 178 for about 40 miles to the town of Lake Isabella and Highway 155. Turn left (north) and drive three miles to the campground entrance on the right.

Contact: Sequoia National Forest, Kern River Ranger District, Lake Isabella Office, 760/379-5646, fax 760/379-8597.

1 3 7 PIONEER POINT

Scenic rating: 9

on Isabella Lake in Sequoia National Forest

Map grid B3

Isabella Lake is one of the largest freshwater lakes in Southern California, and with it comes a dynamic array of campgrounds, marinas, and facilities. It is set at 2,650 feet elevation in the foothills east of Bakersfield, fed by the Kern River, and dominated by boating sports of all kinds. This camp is at the lake's southwest corner, between the spillway and the main dam, with a boat ramp available a mile to the east. Another camp, Main Dam, is nearby. Isabella is a first-class lake for waterskiing, but in the spring and early summer sailboarding is also excellent, best just east of the Auxiliary Dam. Boat rentals of all kinds are available at several marinas.

RV sites, facilities: There are 78 sites for tents or RVs up to 30 feet (no hookups). Picnic tables and fire grills are provided. Drinking water and restrooms with coin showers and flush toilets are available. A playground and fish-cleaning station are available nearby. A boat ramp is three miles from camp. Supplies and a coin laundry are available in the town of Lake Isabella. Leashed pets are permitted.

Reservations, fees: Reservations are accepted at 877/444-6777 or www.recreation.gov ($10 reservation fee). The fee is $17–21 per night, $5 per night for each additional vehicle. Open year-round.

Directions: From Bakersfield, drive east on Highway 178 for about 40 miles to the town of Lake Isabella and Highway 155. Turn left (north) and drive 2.5 miles north on Highway 155 to the campground.

Contact: Sequoia National Forest, Kern River Ranger District, Lake Isabella Office, 760/379-5646, fax 760/379-8597.

1 3 8 KEYESVILLE SPECIAL MANAGEMENT AREA

Scenic rating: 5

on the Kern River near Lake Isabella

Map grid B3

The Keyesville area originally was developed in the 1850s during the California gold rush; gold was first discovered in this area in 1851. Very few historical buildings remain, however, since much of the old town of Keyesville was comprised of tents and small shacks along trails. Today, this camp is used primarily by OHV enthusiasts and miners and is an alternative to the more crowded and developed campgrounds around Lake Isabella. The Kern River runs through this 7,133-acre BLM area and campsites are available near the river; dispersed camping is also allowed. The Sequoia National Forest borders this area to the north and west. Keyesville has multi-use trails and specific areas for recreational mining and OHV use. Hunting is allowed in season. Fishing for trout or bass is another option. Swimming is not recommended because of the swift water, undercurrents, and obstacles. A free permit is required for whitewater rafting and is available at the forest service office in Lake Isabella, 760/379-5646.

RV sites, facilities: There are several sites for tents or RVs up to 30 feet (no hookups); dispersed camping is also available. Picnic tables and fire rings are provided. Vault toilets are available. There is no drinking water. Garbage must be packed out. Leashed pets are permitted.

Reservations, fees: Reservations are not accepted. There is no fee for camping. A 14-day stay limit for every 30 days is enforced; 28 camping days maximum per year. Open year-round.

Directions: From Bakersfield, drive east on Highway 178 for approximately 40 miles to the town of Lake Isabella and Highway 155. Turn left (north) on Highway 155 and drive one mile to Keyesville Road. Turn left and drive 0.5 mile to the Special Management Area entrance.

Contact: Bureau of Land Management, Bakersfield Field Office, 661/391-6000, fax 661/391-6041.

139 MAIN DAM

Scenic rating: 8

on Isabella Lake

Map grid B3

This camp is on the south shore of Isabella Lake, just east of Pioneer Point and within a mile of a boat ramp. The elevation is 2,500 feet. This camp is used as an overflow area and is open only on holiday weekends. (For recreation information, see the Pioneer Point listing in this chapter.)

RV sites, facilities: There are 82 sites for tents or RVs up to 45 feet (no hookups). Picnic tables and fire grills are provided. Drinking water and flush and vault toilets are available. A dump station is nearby. Supplies and a coin laundry are available in the town of Lake Isabella. Leashed pets are permitted.

Reservations, fees: Reservations are not accepted. Sites are $17 per night, $5 per night for each additional vehicle. Open May through September, holiday weekends only.

Directions: From Bakersfield, drive east on Highway 178 for about 40 miles to the town of Lake Isabella and Highway 155. Turn left (north) and drive 1.5 miles to the campground.

Contact: Sequoia National Forest, Kern River Ranger District, Lake Isabella Office, 760/379-5646, fax 760/379-8597.

140 AUXILIARY DAM

Scenic rating: 8

on Isabella Lake

Map grid B3

This primitive camp was designed to be an overflow area if other camps at Isabella Lake are packed. It's the only camp directly on the shore of the lake, and many people like it. In addition,

a boat ramp is just a mile east for good lake access, and the sailboarding prospects adjacent to the campground are the best of the entire lake. The winds come up and sail right over the dam, creating a steady breeze in the afternoon that is not gusty. The elevation is 2,650 feet.

RV sites, facilities: There are a number of primitive, undesignated sites for tents or RVs of any length (no hookups). Drinking water and restrooms with flush toilets and coin showers are available. Supplies and a coin laundry are available in the town of Lake Isabella. Some facilities are wheelchair-accessible. Leashed pets are permitted.

Reservations, fees: Reservations are not accepted. Sites are $10 per night per vehicle May through September or $50 for a season pass. There is no fee for camping October through April. Open year-round.

Directions: From Bakersfield, drive east on Highway 178 for about 40 miles to the town of Lake Isabella. Continue east on Highway 178 for one mile to the campground entrance.

Contact: Sequoia National Forest, Kern River Ranger District, Lake Isabella Office, 760/379-5646, fax 760/379-8597.

141 PARADISE COVE

Scenic rating: 6

on Isabella Lake

Map grid B3

Paradise Cove is on the southeast shore of Isabella Lake at 2,600 feet elevation. A boat ramp is about two miles away to the west, near the South Fork Picnic Area. While the camp is not directly at the lakeshore, it does overlook the broadest expanse of the lake. This part of the lake is relatively undeveloped compared to the areas near Wofford Heights and the dam.

RV sites, facilities: There are 58 sites for tents and a primitive area for up to 80 RVs of any length (no hookups). Picnic tables and fire grills are provided at some sites. Drinking water, restrooms with flush toilets and coin showers,

CALIFORNIA

dump station, and fish-cleaning station are available. A camp host is on-site. Some facilities are wheelchair-accessible. Supplies, dump station, and coin laundry are available in Mountain Mesa. Leashed pets are permitted.

Reservations, fees: Reservations are accepted at 877/444-6777 or www.recreation.gov ($10 reservation fee). Sites are $19–21 per night, $5 per night for each additional vehicle. Open year-round.

Directions: From Bakersfield, drive east on Highway 178 for about 40 miles to the town of Lake Isabella. Continue east on Highway 178 for six miles to the campground entrance.

Contact: Sequoia National Forest, Kern River Ranger District, Lake Isabella Office, 760/379-5646, fax 760/379-8597.

142 KOA LAKE ISABELLA

Scenic rating: 4

on Isabella Lake

Map grid B3

This KOA camp provides a good, clean option to the Forest Service camps on the southern end of Isabella Lake, Southern California's largest lake. It is set in South Fork Valley (elevation 2,600 feet), east of the lake off Highway 178. The nearest boat ramp is at South Fork Picnic Area (about a five-minute drive to the west), where there is also a good view of the lake.

RV sites, facilities: There are 70 sites with full or partial hookups (30 amps) for tents or RVs up to 40 feet; some sites are pull-through. Picnic tables and fire rings are provided. Restrooms with flush toilets and showers, drinking water, playground, seasonal swimming pool, coin laundry, recreation room, pub, convenience store, dump station, firewood, and propane gas are available. Leashed pets are permitted with some restrictions.

Reservations, fees: Reservations are accepted. RV sites are $48 per night, tent sites are $28 per night, $4 per person per night for more than two people. Some credit cards accepted. Open year-round.

Directions: From Bakersfield, drive east on Highway 178 for about 40 miles to the town of Lake Isabella. Continue east on Highway 178 for 10 miles to the campground entrance on the left (well signed).

Contact: KOA Lake Isabella, 760/378-2001 or 800/562-2085, www.koa.com.

143 SANDY FLAT

Scenic rating: 6

on the Kern River in Sequoia National Forest

Map grid B3

This camp is opened as an overflow camp if Hobo is filled. It is about a mile from Hobo. It is a low-use campground, with less shade than Hobo; some sites are shaded, others, well, nope. It is used primarily as a boat launch area for kayakers and rafters. Fishing is fair for catfish, bass, and rainbow trout. The river is stocked with trout in the summer.

RV sites, facilities: There are 35 sites for tents or RVs up to 24 feet (no hookups), including six walk-in sites. Fire rings and picnic tables are provided. Vault toilets and drinking water are available. Some facilities are wheelchair-accessible. Leashed pets are permitted.

Reservations, fees: Reservations are not accepted. Sites are $17 per night, $5 per night for each additional vehicle. Open May through September.

Directions: From Bakersfield, drive east on Highway 178 for 35 miles to Borel Road (five miles from Lake Isabella). Turn right (south) at Borel Road and drive 0.3 mile to Old Kern Canyon Road. Turn right and drive one mile to the campground on your right.

Contact: Sequoia National Forest, Kern River Ranger District, Lake Isabella Office, 760/379-5646, fax 760/379-8597.

CALIFORNIA

144 HOBO

Scenic rating: 7

on the Kern River in Sequoia National Forest

Map grid B3

The secret is out about Hobo: It is set adjacent to a mineral hot springs, that is, an open-air springs, with room for about 10 people at once. The camp is also situated along the lower Kern River, about 10 miles downstream of the dam at Isabella Lake. Rafters sometimes use this camp as a put-in spot for an 18-mile run to the takeout at Democrat Picnic Area, a challenging Class IV run. The elevation is 2,300 feet.

RV sites, facilities: There are 35 sites for tents or RVs up to 24 feet (no hookups). Fire grills and picnic tables are provided. Drinking water, vault toilets, showers, and dump station are available. Leashed pets are permitted.

Reservations, fees: Reservations are accepted at 877/444-6777 or www.recreation.gov ($10 reservation fee). The fee is $17–19 per night for the first vehicle, $5 per night for each additional vehicle. Open year-round.

Directions: From Bakersfield, drive east on Highway 178 for 35 miles to Borel Road (five miles from Lake Isabella). Turn right (south) at Borel Road and drive 0.3 mile to Old Kern Road. Turn right and drive two miles to the campground on your right.

Contact: Sequoia National Forest, Kern River Ranger District, Lake Isabella Office, 760/379-5646, fax 760/379-8597.

145 KERN RIVER CAMPGROUND

Scenic rating: 7

at Lake Ming

Map grid B3

The campground is set at Lake Ming, a small but exciting place. The lake covers just 205 surface acres, and with the weather so hot, the hot jet boats can make it a wild affair here. It's become a popular spot for southern valley residents, only a 15-minute drive from Bakersfield. It is so popular for water sports that every year, beginning in March, the lake is closed to the public one weekend per month for private boat races and water-skiing competitions. The lake is restricted to sailing and sailboarding on the second weekend of every month and on Tuesday and Thursday afternoons. All other boating, including water-skiing, is permitted on the remaining days. All boats are required to have a permit; boaters may buy one at the park. Swimming is not allowed because there is a parasite in the water that has been known to cause swimmer's itch. Yikes. The lake is stocked with rainbow trout in the winter months, and they join a sprinkling of bluegill, catfish, crappie, and bass. The elevation is 450 feet. Maximum stay is 10 days.

RV sites, facilities: There are 50 sites for tents or RVs up to 28 feet. Picnic tables and fire rings are provided. Restrooms with flush toilets and coin showers, drinking water, dump station, playground, concession stand, picnic area, and boat ramp are available. Some facilities are wheelchair-accessible. A store is nearby. Leashed pets are permitted.

Reservations, fees: Reservations are not accepted. Sites are $10–22 per night, $6–10 per night per each additional vehicle, $4 per night per pet. Discounts available in winter. Open year-round.

Directions: From Bakersfield, drive east on Highway 178 for 11 miles to Alfred Harrell Highway. Turn left (north) on Alfred Harrell Highway and drive four miles to Lake Ming Road. Turn right on Lake Ming Road and follow the signs to the campground on the right, 0.25 mile west of the lake.

Contact: Kern County Parks and Recreation Department, 661/868-7000, www.co.kern.ca.us/parks.

146 TROY MEADOWS

Scenic rating: 7

on Fish Creek in Sequoia National Forest

Map grid B3

Obscure? Yes, but what the heck, it gives you an idea of what is possible out in the boondocks.

CALIFORNIA

The camp is set at 7,800 feet elevation right along Fish Creek. Black Rock Ranger Station is available two miles northwest. You are advised to stop there before any backcountry trips. Note that off-highway vehicles (OHVs) are allowed in this area. Also note that Jackass National Recreation Trail is a short drive to the east; it runs north aside Jackass Creek to its headwaters just below Jackass Peak (9,245 feet).

RV sites, facilities: There are 73 sites for tents or RVs up to 30 feet (no hookups). Picnic tables and fire grills are provided. Drinking water and vault toilets are available. Garbage must be packed out. Some facilities are wheelchair-accessible. Leashed pets are permitted.

Reservations, fees: Reservations are not accepted. Sites are $17 per night, $5 per night per each additional vehicle. Open June through October, weather permitting.

Directions: Drive on U.S. 395 to Ninemile Canyon Road (four miles north of the town of Pearsonville, 48 miles south of Lone Pine). Turn west on Ninemile Canyon Road and drive 31 miles (the road becomes Sherman Pass Road) to the campground.

Contact: Sequoia National Forest, Kern River Ranger District, Kernville Office, 760/376-3781, fax 760/376-3795.

147 FISH CREEK

Scenic rating: 8

in Sequoia National Forest

Map grid B3

This is a pretty spot set at the confluence of Fish Creek and Jackass Creek. The elevation is 7,500 feet. The nearby trails are used by off-highway vehicles, which can make this a noisy campground during the day.

RV sites, facilities: There are 40 sites for tents or RVs up to 24 feet (no hookups). Picnic tables and fire grills are provided. Drinking water and vault toilets are available. Garbage must be packed out. Leashed pets are permitted.

Reservations, fees: Reservations are not accepted. Sites are $17 per night, $5 per night per each additional vehicle. Open June through October, weather permitting.

Directions: Drive on U.S. 395 to Ninemile Canyon Road (four miles north of the town of Pearsonville, 48 miles south of Lone Pine). Turn west on Ninemile Canyon Road and drive 28 miles (the road becomes Sherman Pass Road) to the campground.

Contact: Sequoia National Forest, Kern River Ranger District, Kernville Office, 760/376-3781, fax 760/376-3795.

148 KENNEDY MEADOW

Scenic rating: 8

on the South Fork of the Kern River in Sequoia National Forest

Map grid B3

This is a pretty Forest Service campground set amid piñon pine and sage country, with the Pacific Crest Trail running by the camp. That makes it a great trailhead camp, as well as a refreshing stopover for PCT through-hikers. A highlight is the nearby South Fork Kern River, which provides fishing for rainbow trout. The camp receives moderate use and is a lifesaver for PCT through-hikers.

RV sites, facilities: There are 35 sites for tents or RVs up to 30 feet (no hookups) and three sites for RVs of any length. Picnic tables and fire rings are provided. Drinking water (seasonal) and vault toilets are available. Garbage must be packed out. Leashed pets are permitted.

Reservations, fees: Reservations are not accepted. Sites are $17 per night, $5 per night per each additional vehicle. Open year-round, weather permitting.

Directions: Drive on U.S. 395 to Ninemile Canyon Road (four miles north of the town of Pearsonville, 48 miles south of Lone Pine). Turn west on Ninemile Canyon Road and drive 21 miles to a small store. Bear right at the store (still Ninemile Canyon Road) and continue for three miles to the campground.

Contact: Sequoia National Forest, Kern River Ranger District, Kernville Office, 760/376-3781, fax 760/376-3795.

149 CHIMNEY CREEK

Scenic rating: 5

on the Pacific Crest Trail

Map grid B3

This BLM camp is set at 5,900 feet elevation along the headwaters of Chimney Creek, on the southern flank of Chimney Peak (7,990 feet) two miles to the north. This is a trailhead camp for the Pacific Crest Trail, one of its relatively obscure sections. The PCT heads north from camp and in 10 miles skirts the eastern border of Dome Land Wilderness.

RV sites, facilities: There are 32 sites for tents or RVs up to 25 feet (no hookups). Picnic tables and fire grills are provided. Vault toilets are available. No drinking water is available. Garbage must be packed out. Horses and leashed pets are permitted.

Reservations, fees: Reservations are not accepted. There is no fee for camping, but donations are encouraged. Open year-round.

Directions: Drive on U.S. 395 to Ninemile Canyon Road (four miles north of the town of Pearsonville, 48 miles south of Lone Pine). Turn west on Ninemile Canyon Road and drive 11 miles to the BLM Work Station and Cane Brake Road. Turn left on Cane Brake Road (the dirt road opposite the BLM station) and drive three miles to the camp on the left.

Contact: Bureau of Land Management, Bakersfield Field Office, 661/391-6000, fax 661/391-6041.

150 WALKER PASS WALK-IN

Scenic rating: 6

on the Pacific Crest Trail southwest of Death Valley National Park

Map grid B3

Long-distance hikers on the Pacific Crest Trail treat this camp as if they were arriving at Valhalla. That's because it is set right on the trail and, better yet, drinking water is usually available (for updates on water availability, call the BLM at 661/391-6120). Out here in the desert there aren't many places where you can act like a camel and suck up all the liquid you can hold. The camp is set at 5,200 feet elevation, southwest of Death Valley National Park. And if you guessed it was named for Joe Walker, the West's greatest trailblazer and one of my heroes, well, right you are. If you arrive by car instead of on the PCT, use this spot as a base camp. Because of its desert remoteness, very few hikers start trips from this location.

RV sites, facilities: There are two sites for tents or RVs up to 20 feet (no hookups) with limited parking and 11 walk-in sites for tents only. Picnic tables and fire rings are provided. Drinking water (spring through fall) and pit toilets are available. Hitching racks and corrals are available. Garbage must be packed out. Leashed pets are permitted.

Reservations, fees: Reservations are not accepted. There is no fee for camping, but donations are encouraged. A 14-day stay limit is enforced. Open year-round.

Directions: From Bakersfield, drive east on Highway 178 for about 40 miles to the town of Lake Isabella. Continue east on Highway 178 to Onyx and continue 14 miles to Walker Pass and the right side of the road (where a sign is posted for the Pacific Crest Trail). Park and walk 0.25 mile to the campground.

Contact: Bureau of Land Management, Bakersfield Field Office, 661/391-6000, fax 661/391-6041.

CALIFORNIA

SANTA BARBARA AND VICINITY

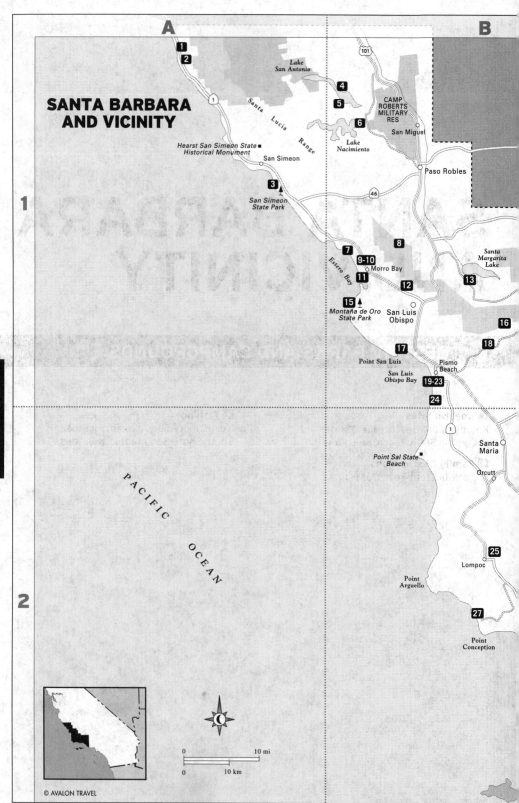

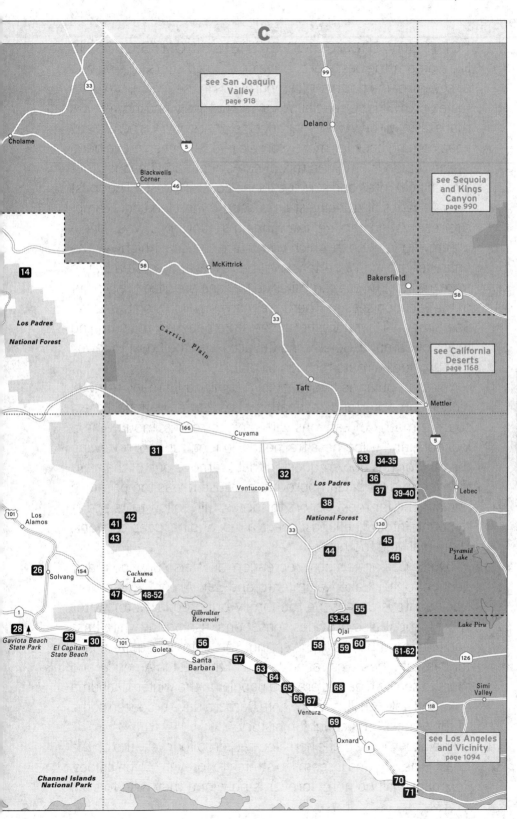

C

see San Joaquin
Valley
page 918

see Sequoia
and Kings
Canyon
page 990

see California
Deserts
page 1168

see Los Angeles
and Vicinity
page 1094

CALIFORNIA

Cholame

Blackwells
Corner

Delano

McKittrick

Bakersfield

14

Los Padres

National Forest

Carrizo Plain

Taft

Mettler

166 Cuyama

31

32 Ventucopa

33 **34-35**

36

37 **39-40**

Lebec

Los Padres

38

National Forest

Los
Alamos

41 **42**

43

44

138

45

46

*Pyramid
Lake*

26 Solvang

154

*Cachuma
Lake*

47 **48-52**

*Gilbraltar
Reservoir*

55

53-54

Ojai

Lake Piru

28

*Gaviota Beach
State Park*

29 **30**

El Capitan
State Beach

101 Goleta

56

Santa
Barbara

57

58

59 **60**

61-62

126

Simi
Valley

118

63

64

65

66 **67**

68

Ventura

69

Oxnard

1

70

71

*Channel Islands
National Park*

For many, this region of the California coast is like a dream, the best place to live on earth. Visitors, picking one or several of the dozens of campgrounds in the region, can get a taste of why it is so special. What you will likely find, however, is that a taste will only whet your appetite. That's how it is here. Many keep coming back for more. Some eventually even move here.

The region is a unique mix of sun-swept sand beaches that stretch 200 miles and surprise inland coastal forests. The coast offers a series of stunning state beaches, where getting a campsite reservation can feel like winning the lottery. If you have a dream trip in mind in which you cruise the coast highway the entire length, you'd better have the reservation system wired from the start. These campsites go fast and are filled every night of the vacation season. There are many highlights on the coast: San Simeon, Hearst Castle, all the state beaches, the stunning towns of Cambria, Goleta, and Cayucos, and the Coast Highway that provides a route through all of it.

Yet as popular as the coast is, just inland lie many remote, hidden campsites and destinations. Los Padres National Forest spans a matrix of canyons with small streams, mountaintop lookouts, and wilderness trailheads. In fact, rangers reviewing the text for this book requested that I remove one of the trails highlighted from a campground because it was too primitive and difficult for most visitors to successfully follow to its end at a mountaintop. The landscape is a mix of pine, deep canyons, chaparral, and foothills.

Two of California's best recreation lakes also provide major destinations – Lake Nacimiento and San Antonio Reservoir. Nacimiento is one of the top family-oriented lakes for water sports, and it also provides sensational fishing for white bass and largemouth bass in the spring. San Antonio is a great lake for bass, at times even rating as one of the best in America, and tours to see bald eagles are also popular in the winter. Cachuma Lake and Lake Casitas near Santa Barbara have produced some of the largest bass caught in history.

The ocean is dramatic here, the backdrop for every trip on the Coast Highway, and it seems to stretch to forever. Maybe it does. For many visiting here, forever is how long they wish to stay.

1 PLASKETT CREEK

Scenic rating: 8

in Los Padres National Forest
overlooking the Pacific Ocean

Map grid A1

This is a premium coastal camp for Highway 1 cruisers, set at an elevation of just 100 feet along little Plaskett Creek above the Pacific Ocean. It is slightly farther south of Big Sur than most are willing to drive from Monterey, and is often overlooked as a result. The campground provides access to Sand Dollar Beach. A little café in Lucia provides open-air dining with a dramatic lookout over the coast.

RV sites, facilities: There are 44 sites for tents or RVs up to 30 feet (no hookups). Picnic tables and fire grills are provided. Drinking water and flush toilets are available. Leashed pets are permitted.

Reservations, fees: Reservations are accepted at 877/444-6777 or www.recreation.gov ($10 reservation fee). Some sites are first come, first served. Sites are $22 per night, $5 per night per person for bicyclists, $5 per person per extra vehicle. Open year-round.

Directions: From Monterey, drive south on Highway 1 to Lucia. From Lucia, continue south on Highway 1 for 9.5 miles to the campground on the left.

Contact: Los Padres National Forest, Monterey Ranger District, 831/385-5434, fax 831/385-0628; Parks Management Company, 805/434-1996, fax 805/434-1986, www.campone.com.

2 PLASKETT CREEK GROUP CAMP

Scenic rating: 8

in Los Padres National Forest
overlooking the Pacific Ocean

Map grid A1

This is one of two prime coastal camps in the immediate area along Highway 1, which is one of the prettiest drives in the West. The camp is for small groups and is set beside little Plaskett Creek. For a premium day trip, drive north five miles to Nacimiento-Ferguson Road, turn east, and drive into Los Padres National Forest and to the border of the Ventana Wilderness. Coastal views and hikes are first-class.

RV sites, facilities: There are three group sites for tents or RVs up to 30 feet (no hookups) that can accommodate up to 40 people each. Picnic tables and fire grills are provided. Drinking water and vault toilets are available. Leashed pets are permitted.

Reservations, fees: Reservations are required at 877/444-6777 or www.recreation.gov ($10 reservation fee). Groups sites are $80 per night. Open year-round.

Directions: From Monterey, drive south on Highway 1 to Lucia. From Lucia, continue south on Highway 1 for 9.5 miles to the campground on the left.

Contact: Los Padres National Forest, Monterey Ranger District, 831/385-5434, fax 831/385-0628; Parks Management Company, 805/434-1996, fax 805/434-1986, www.campone.com.

3 SAN SIMEON STATE PARK

Scenic rating: 9

in San Simeon State Park

Map grid A1

Hearst Castle is only five miles northeast, so San Simeon Creek is a natural for visitors planning to take the tour; for a tour reservation, phone 800/444-4445. San Simeon Creek campground is set across the highway from the ocean, with easy access under the highway to the beach. San Simeon Creek, while not exactly the Mississippi, runs through the campground and adds a nice touch. Washburn campground provides another option at this park; though it has better views, the sites are exposed and can be windy. It is one mile inland on a plateau overlooking the Pacific Ocean and Santa Lucia Mountains. The best hike in the area is from Leffingwell Landing to Moonstone Beach, featuring sweeping views of the coast from ocean bluffs and a good chance to see passing whales. There are three preserves in the park, including a wintering site for monarch butterfly populations, and it has an archaeological site dating from more than 5,800 years ago. In the summer, junior ranger programs and interpretive programs are offered.

RV sites, facilities: At San Simeon Creek camp, there are 115 sites for tents or RVs up to 35 feet (no hookups), 10 sites for tents only, and two hike-in/bike-in sites. Picnic tables and fire grills are provided. Drinking water, dump station, and restrooms with flush toilets and coin showers are available. At Washburn camp, there are 70 sites for tents or RVs up to 31 feet (no hookups). Picnic tables and fire grills are provided. Drinking water, chemical flush toilets, and firewood are available. A grocery store, coin laundry, gas station, restaurants, and propane gas are two miles away in Cambria. Some facilities are wheelchair-accessible. Leashed pets are permitted in the campgrounds only.

Reservations, fees: Reservations are accepted March 30 through September 30 at 800/444-PARK (800/444-7275) or www.reserveamerica.com ($8 reservation fee). Sites are $20–25 per night at San Simeon Creek, $11–15 per night at Washburn, $3 per night for each additional vehicle, $2 per person per night for hike-in/bike-in sites. Open year-round.

Directions: From Cambria, drive two miles north on Highway 1 to San Simeon Creek Road. Turn east and drive 0.2 mile to the park entrance on the right.

Contact: San Simeon State Park, 805/927-2035, www.parks.ca.gov.

4 NORTH SHORE SAN ANTONIO

🚶 🚴 🏊 🛶 ⛴ 🐕 🚐 ⛺

Scenic rating: 7

on Lake San Antonio

Map grid B1   **BEST (**

Lake San Antonio makes a great year-round destination for adventure. It is a big, warm-water lake, long and narrow, set at an elevation of 780 feet in the foothills north of Paso Robles. The camp features four miles of shoreline camping, with the bonus of primitive sites along Pleyto Points. The lake is 16 miles long, covers 5,500 surface acres, and has 60 miles of shoreline and average summer water temperatures in the 70s, making it an ideal place for fun in the sun. It is one of the top lakes in California for bass fishing, best in spring and early summer. It is also good for striped bass, catfish, crappie, sunfish, and bluegill. It provides the best wintering habitat in the region for bald eagles, and eagle-watching tours are available from the south shore of the lake. Of course, the size of the lake, along with hot temperatures all summer, make waterskiing and water sports absolutely first-class. Note that boat rentals are not available here, but are at South Shore. Equestrian trails are also available.

RV sites, facilities: There are 200 sites with no hookups for tents or RVs of any length, 24 sites with full or partial hookups (30 amps) for tents or RVs of any length, and up to 1,800 primitive dispersed sites near the shoreline. Mobile home rentals are also available. Fire grills and picnic tables are provided. Restrooms with showers, drinking water, dump station, boat ramp, hitching posts, general store, volleyball, and fishing licenses are available. Leashed pets are permitted.

Reservations, fees: Reservations are accepted at 805/472-2456 or 888/588-2267 ($5 reservation fee). Sites are $27–32 per night, $15 per night for each additional vehicle, $2 per pet per night. Boat launching is $6 per day. Off-season discounts available. Some credit cards accepted. Open year-round.

Directions: On U.S. 101, drive to the Jolon Road/G14 exit (just north of King City). Take that exit and turn south on Jolon Road and drive 27 miles to Pleyto Road (curvy road). Turn right and drive three miles to the North Shore entrance of the lake. Note: When arriving from the south or east on U.S. 101 near Paso Robles, it is faster to take the G18/Jolon Road exit.

Contact: North Shore, 805/472-2456, www.co.monterey.ca.us/parks.

5 SOUTH SHORE SAN ANTONIO

Scenic rating: 7

on Lake San Antonio

Map grid B1   **BEST (**

Harris Creek, Redondo Vista, and Lynch are the three campgrounds set near each other along the south shore of Lake San Antonio, a 16-mile reservoir that provides good bass fishing in the spring and waterskiing in the summer. There are also 26 miles of good biking and hiking trails in the park. A museum and a visitors center are available at the park's administration building. In the winter, the Monterey County Department of Parks offers a unique eagle-watching program here, which includes boat tours. (See the North Shore listing for more details about the lake.)

RV sites, facilities: There are three campgrounds here: Redondo has 173 sites with no hookups for tents or RVs and 86 sites with full hookups (30 amps) for tents or RVs; Lynch has 52 sites for tents and 54 sites with partial hookups for tents or RVs; Harris Creek has 88 sites for tents and 26 sites with partial hookups for tents or RVs. Mobile-home rentals are also available. Picnic tables and fire grills are provided. Drinking water and flush toilets are available. Restrooms with showers, dump station, marina, boat ramp, boat rentals, boat slips, bait and tackle, playground, recreation room, coin laundry, general store, and fishing licenses are available nearby. Leashed pets are permitted.

Reservations, fees: Reservations are accepted for Redondo sites only at 888/588-2267. Sites are $25–35 per night, $15 per night for each additional vehicle, $2 per pet per night. All other sites are first come, first served. Boat launching is $6 per day. Some credit cards accepted. Off-season discounts available. Group reservations available at 805/472-2311 ($40 reservation fee). Open year-round.

Directions: From the north, on U.S. 101 (just north of King City), take the Jolon Road/G14 exit. Turn south on Jolon Road and drive 21 miles to Lockwood and Interlake Road (G14). Turn right and drive 18 miles to San Antonio

Lake Road. Turn left and drive three miles to the South Shore entrance of the lake.

From the south, drive on U.S. 101 to Paso Robles and the 24th Street exit (G14 west). Take that exit and drive 14 miles to Lake Nacimiento Drive. Turn right and drive across Lake Nacimiento Dam to Interlake Road. Turn left and drive seven miles to Lake San Antonio Road. Turn right and drive three miles to the South Shore entrance.

Contact: South Shore, 805/472-2311, www.co.monterey.ca.us/parks.

6 LAKE NACIMIENTO RESORT

Scenic rating: 8

at Lake Nacimiento

Map grid B1

This is the only game in town at Nacimiento, and the management plays it well. It's an outstanding operation, with headquarters for a great fishing or water-sports trip. The fishing for white bass and largemouth bass can be incredible. And the water play is also great, with such a big lake, 70-degree temperatures, and some of the best waterskiing in California. The lake has 165 miles of shoreline with an incredible number of arms, many ideal for bass fishing. Nacimiento hosts about 25 fishing tournaments per year. Not only is bass fishing good, but there are also opportunities for trout (in cool months) and bluegill and catfish (in warm months). The resort has a lakeview restaurant open during the summer, and the campsites provide limited tree cover with pines and oaks. Two camps are on the lake's shore, and the rest are set back about 0.75 mile from the lake. Lakeview lodging is also available.

RV sites, facilities: There are a series of campgrounds with 297 sites with no hookups for tents or RVs of any length, 40 sites with full hookups for RVs up to 35 feet, and 12 group sites for 15–40 people each. Nineteen lodges, eight trailers, and two mobile homes are also available for rent. Picnic tables and fire grills are provided. Drinking water, restrooms with showers and flush toilets, dump station, boat ramp, boat docks, boat rentals, playground, seasonal swimming pool, seasonal restaurant, coin laundry, general store, fishing licenses, swimming beaches, basketball and volleyball courts, and horseshoe pits are available. Leashed pets are permitted.

Reservations, fees: Reservations are accepted. Sites are $30–40 per vehicle per night, $10 per pet per night. Some credit cards accepted. Open year-round.

Directions: From U.S. 101 north, drive to Paso Robles and the 46E exit; from U.S. 101 south, drive to Paso Robles and the 24th Street exit (same exit, different names depending on which direction you're coming from). Turn west on 24th Street (becomes Lake Nacimiento Drive/G14) and drive for nine miles. Bear right on Lake Nacimiento Drive and continue for seven miles to the resort entrance on the left. Note: If you cross the Lake Nacimiento dam, you've gone too far.

Contact: Lake Nacimiento Resort, 805/238-3256 or 800/323-3839, www.nacimientoresort.com.

7 MORRO STRAND STATE BEACH

🏊 🎣 🐕 🚐 ⛺

Scenic rating: 7

near Morro Bay
Map grid B1

A ton of Highway 1 cruisers plan to stay overnight at this state park. It is set along the ocean near Morro Bay, right on the beach, a pretty spot year-round. The park features a three-mile stretch of beach that connects the southern and northern entrances to the state beach. Fishing, jogging, sailboarding, and kite flying are popular. Side trips include the Morro Bay Wildlife Refuge, the Museum of Natural History, or an ocean-fishing trip out of Morro Bay. (See the Morro Bay State Park listing in this chapter for more information.)

RV sites, facilities: There are 76 sites for tents or RVs up to 24 feet (no hookups). Picnic tables and fire grills are provided. Drinking water and flush toilets are available. Cold, outdoor

showers are also available. Supplies and a coin laundry are in Morro Bay. Leashed pets are permitted, but not on the beach.

Reservations, fees: Reservations are accepted at 800/444-PARK (800/444-7275) or www.reserveamerica.com ($8 reservation fee). Sites are $20–25 per night, $6 per night for each additional vehicle. Open year-round.

Directions: On Highway 1, drive to Morro Bay. Take the Yerba Buena Street/Morro Strand State Beach exit. Turn west on Yerba Buena Street and drive one block to the campground.

Contact: Morro Strand State Beach, 805/772-8812; San Luis Obispo Coast District, 805/927-2065, www.parks.ca.gov.

8 CERRO ALTO

🥾 🚲 🐕 ♿ 🚐 ⛺

Scenic rating: 7

near San Luis Obispo
Map grid B1

This camp is set near Morro Creek, which runs most of the year but can disappear in late summer in dry years. Some sites are along the creek, nicely spaced, with sycamore and bay trees peppering the hillside. There are numerous hiking and mountain-biking trails. The best of these is Cerro Alto Trail, which is accessible from camp and then is routed four miles up to Cuesta Ridge for sweeping views of Morro Bay.

RV sites, facilities: There are 22 sites for tents or RVs up to 30 feet (no hookups). Picnic tables and fire grills are provided. Drinking water and vault toilets are available. A camp host and pay phone are nearby. Some facilities are wheelchair-accessible. Leashed pets permitted.

Reservations, fees: Reservations are not accepted. Sites are $18 per night. Open year-round, weather permitting.

Directions: From U.S. 101 at Atascadero, take the Highway 41 west exit. Drive west on Highway 41 for eight miles to the campground on the left.

Contact: Los Padres National Forest, Santa Lucia Ranger District, 805/925-9538, fax 805/961-5781.

9 RANCHO COLINA RV PARK

Scenic rating: 6

in Morro Bay

Map grid B1

This privately operated RV park is one of several camping options in the Morro Bay area. Folks who park here typically stroll the boardwalk, exploring the little shops. (For recreation, see the Morro Bay State Park listing in this chapter.) About 20 percent of the sites here are long-term rentals.

RV sites, facilities: There are 57 sites with full hookups (30 amps) for RVs up to 40 feet. No tents. Picnic tables are provided. Restrooms with showers, laundry facilities, and a recreation room are available. You can buy supplies nearby. Leashed pets are permitted.

Reservations, fees: Reservations are accepted. Sites are $32 per night. Monthly rates available. Some credit cards accepted. Open year-round.

Directions: From Morro Bay on Highway 1, drive one mile east on Atascadero Road/Highway 41 to the park at 1045 Atascadero Road.

Contact: Rancho Colina RV Park, 805/772-8420.

10 MORRO DUNES TRAVEL TRAILER PARK AND RESORT CAMPING

Scenic rating: 6

in Morro Bay

Map grid B1

A wide array of side-trip possibilities and great natural beauty make Morro Bay an attractive destination. Most visitors will walk the boardwalk, try at least one of the coastal restaurants, and then head to Morro Bay State Park for hiking or sea kayaking. Other folks will head straight to the port for fishing, or just explore the area before heading north to San Simeon for the Hearst Castle tour. (See the Morro Bay State Park listing for more information.)

RV sites, facilities: There are 178 sites with full or partial hookups (30 amps) for RVs of any length, and 18 sites for tents. Some sites are pull-through. Picnic tables and fire grills are provided. Restrooms with showers, drinking water, cable TV, Wi-Fi, modem access, coin laundry, general store, clubhouse, RV storage, RV supplies and repair, recreation hall, group facilities, horseshoes, basketball, firewood, ice, and dump station are available. Propane gas, golf course, playground, and boat rentals are nearby. Some facilities are wheelchair-accessible. Leashed pets are permitted.

Reservations, fees: Reservations are accepted. RV sites are $30–40 per night, tent sites are $28 per night, $1 per person per night for more than two people, $1 per pet per night. Weekly and monthly rates are available during the winter. Some credit cards accepted. Open year-round.

Directions: Drive on Highway 1 to Morro Bay and the exit for Highway 41. Take that exit and turn west on Atascadero Road/Highway 41 and drive 0.5 mile to 1700 Embarcadero/Atascadero Road.

Contact: Morro Dunes Travel Trailer Park and Resort Camping, 805/772-2722, fax 805/772-2372, www.morrodunes.com.

11 MORRO BAY STATE PARK

Scenic rating: 9

in Morro Bay

Map grid B1

Reservations are strongly advised at this popular campground. This is one of the premium stopover spots for folks cruising on Highway 1. The park offers a wide range of activities and exhibits covering the natural and cultural history of the area. The park features lagoon and natural bay habitat. The most prominent feature is Morro Rock. A "morro" is a small volcanic peak, and there are nine of them along the local coast. The top hike at the park climbs one of them, Black Hill, and rewards hikers with sensational coastal views. The park has a marina and golf course, with opportunities for sailing, fishing, and bird-watching. Activities include beach walks, kayaking in Morro Bay, ocean fishing on a party boat, and touring Hearst Castle.

RV sites, facilities: There are 95 sites for tents or RVs up to 31 feet (no hookups), 27 sites with partial hookups (15 and 30 amps) for RVs up to 35 feet, five hike-in/bike-in sites, and two group sites for 25–35 people. Picnic tables, food lockers, and fire rings are provided. Restrooms with flush toilets and coin showers, drinking water, dump station, Wi-Fi, museum exhibits, nature walks, and interpretive programs are available. A coin laundry, grocery store, propane gas, boat ramp, mooring, boat rentals, gas stations, and food service are available in Morro Bay. Some facilities are wheelchair-accessible. Leashed pets are permitted, but not on the beach.

Reservations, fees: Reservations are accepted at 800/444-PARK (800/444-7275) or www. reserveamerica.com ($8 reservation fee). Sites are $35–50 per night, $8 per night for each additional vehicle, $5 per person per night for hike-in/bike-in sites, $100–165 per night for group sites. Open year-round.

Directions: On Highway 1, drive to Morro Bay and take the exit for Los Osos–Baywood Park/ Morro Bay State Park. Turn south and drive one mile to State Park Road. Turn right and drive one mile to the park entrance on the right.

Contact: Morro Bay State Park, 805/772-7434; San Luis Obispo Coast District, 805/927-2065, www.parks.ca.gov.

12 EL CHORRO REGIONAL PARK

Scenic rating: 6

near San Luis Obispo

Map grid B1

North of Morro Bay on the way to San Simeon and Hearst Castle, this can be a prime spot for RV travelers. Note that the campground isn't in the state park reservation system, which means there are times when coastal state parks can be jammed full and this regional park may still have space. Morro Bay, six miles away, provides many possible side trips. The park has full recreational facilities, including a golf course,

volleyball, horseshoe pits, softball fields, hiking trails, and botanical gardens. Note that there's a men's prison about four miles away. For some people, this can be a real turnoff.

RV sites, facilities: There are 63 sites for tents or RVs up to 40 feet and some undesignated overflow sites; 44 sites have full hookups and the remaining sites have no hookups. Some primitive sites are pull-through. Fire grills and picnic tables are provided. Restrooms with flush toilets and showers, drinking water, playground, picnic area, off-leash dog area, and recreational facilities are available. Supplies and a coin laundry are nearby in San Luis Obispo. Leashed pets are permitted.

Reservations, fees: Reservations are accepted for groups only (minimum of three campsites). Sites are $18–29 per night, $10 per night for each additional vehicle, $3 per pet per night. Weekly rates available. Two-week maximum stay. Some credit cards accepted. Open year-round.

Directions: From San Luis Obispo, drive 4.5 miles north on Highway 1 to the park entrance on the right side of the highway.

Contact: El Chorro Regional Park, 805/781-5930, fax 805/781-1102, www.slocountyparks.com.

13 SANTA MARGARITA KOA

Scenic rating: 6

near Santa Margarita Lake

Map grid B1

Santa Margarita Lake should have a sign at its entrance that proclaims, "Fishing Only!" That's because the rules here do not allow waterskiing or any water contact, including swimming, wading, using float tubes, or sailboarding. The excellent prospects for bass fishing, along with the prohibitive rules, make this lake a favorite among anglers. Santa Margarita Lake covers nearly 800 acres, most of it long and narrow and set in a dammed-up valley in the foothill country at an elevation of 1,300 feet, just below the Santa Lucia Mountains. Horseback riding is available nearby.

RV sites, facilities: There are 100 sites for tents or RVs up to 40 feet; most have full or partial hookups (30 and 50 amps) and two are pull-through. Eleven cabins are also available. Picnic tables and fire grills are provided. Restrooms with flush toilets and showers, drinking water, Wi-Fi, modem access, seasonal swimming pool, playground, coin laundry, convenience store, dump station, and propane gas are available. Leashed pets are permitted.

Reservations, fees: Reservations are accepted at 800/562-5619. RV sites are $33–49 per night, tent sites are $25–35 per night, cabins are $54–89 per night, $3–4 per person per night for more than two people. Some credit cards accepted. Open year-round.

Directions: From San Luis Obispo, drive north on U.S. 101 for eight miles to the Highway 58/Santa Margarita Lake exit. Take that exit and drive through the town of Santa Margarita to Estrada. Turn right on Estrada and drive eight miles (Estrada becomes Pozo Road) to Santa Margarita Lake Road. Turn left and drive 0.5 mile to the campground on the right.

Contact: Santa Margarita KOA, 805/438-5618, fax 805/438-3576, www.koa.com.

14 LA PANZA

Scenic rating: 3

in Los Padres National Forest
Map grid B1

This primitive spot sits at 2,200 feet elevation in the La Panza Range, an oak woodland area that is crisscrossed by numerous off-highway-vehicle and hiking trails and small streams. Some of the trails are not maintained. The Machesna Mountain Wilderness is to the south. Water is scarce.

RV sites, facilities: There are 15 sites for tents or RVs up to 16 feet (no hookups). Picnic tables and fire grills are provided. Vault toilets are available. There is no drinking water. Garbage must be packed out. Leashed pets are permitted.

Reservations, fees: Reservations are not accepted. There is no camping fee. An Adventure Pass ($30 annual fee or a $5 daily fee) per parked vehicle is required. Open year-round.

Directions: From San Luis Obispo, drive eight

miles north on U.S. 101. Turn east on Highway 58 and drive four miles (two miles past Santa Margarita). Turn southeast on Pozo Road and drive for 16 miles to the town of Pozo and Pozo Grade Road. Turn right and drive five miles to Red Hill Road. Turn right and drive one mile to the camp on the left.

Contact: Los Padres National Forest, Santa Lucia Ranger District, 805/925-9538, fax 805/961-5781.

15 MONTAÑA DE ORO STATE PARK

Scenic rating: 9

near Morro Bay
Map grid B1

This sprawling chunk of primitive land includes coastline, 8,500 acres of foothills, and 1,373-foot Valencia Peak. The name means "Mountain of Gold," named for the golden wildflowers that bloom here in the spring. The camp is perched near a bluff, and while there are no sweeping views from campsites, they await nearby. Bluffs Trail is one of the best easy coastal walks anywhere, offering stunning views of the ocean and cliffs and, in the spring, tons of wildflowers over the course of just 1.5 miles. Another hiking option at the park is to climb Valencia Peak, a little butt-kicker of an ascent that tops out at 1,373 feet, providing more panoramic coastal views. These are the two best hikes among 50 miles of trails for horses, mountain bikers, and hikers, with trails accessible right out of the campground.

RV sites, facilities: There are 48 sites for tents or RVs up to 27 feet (no hookups), four walk-in (50- to 150-yard walk) environmental sites, four equestrian sites, and two group equestrian sites for up to 50 people and 25 horses. Picnic tables and fire grills are provided, but fires are not allowed at the environmental sites. Vault toilets are available. Drinking water is available only at the main campground; stock water is available at the equestrian campground. There is limited corral space and single-site equestrian camps with two stalls each. Garbage from equestrian and environmental sites must be packed out. Supplies and a coin laundry are available five miles away in the town of Los Osos. Leashed pets are permitted, except at the environmental sites and on trails.

Reservations, fees: Reservations are accepted at 800/444-PARK (800/444-7275) or www.reserveamerica.com ($8 reservation fee). Sites are $11–15 per night, $25–30 for equestrian sites, $6 per night for each additional vehicle, $75 per night for group sites. Open year-round.

Directions: From Morro Bay, drive two miles south on Highway 1. Turn on South Bay Boulevard and drive four miles to Los Osos. Turn right on Los Osos Valley Road and drive five miles (it becomes Pecho Valley Road) to the park.

Contact: Montaña de Oro State Park, 805/528-0513; San Luis Obispo Coast District, 805/927-2065, www.parks.ca.gov.

16 HI MOUNTAIN

Scenic rating: 4

in Los Padres National Forest
Map grid B1

At an elevation of 2,800 feet, this camp is on the edge of the Santa Lucia Wilderness. You can reach the Hi Mountain Lookout if you continue driving 1.5 miles past the campground. The Lookout has awesome 360-degree views from the 3,180-foot summit.

RV sites, facilities: There are 11 sites for tents or RVs up to 16 feet (no hookups). Note that trailers are not recommended. Picnic tables and fire grills are provided. Vault toilets are available. There is no drinking water. Garbage must be packed out. Leashed pets are permitted.

Reservations, fees: No reservations are accepted. There is no camping fee. An Adventure Pass ($30 annual fee or a $5 daily fee) per parked vehicle is required. Open year-round, weather permitting (road may be closed during heavy rains).

Directions: From San Luis Obispo, drive eight miles north on U.S. 101. Turn east on Highway 58 and drive four miles (four miles past Santa Margarita) to Pozo Road/Santa Margarita Lake. Turn right (southeast) and drive 16 miles to the town of Pozo and Hi Mountain Road. Turn right on Hi Mountain Road (next to the Pozo fire station) and drive four miles to the campground.

Contact: Los Padres National Forest, Santa Lucia Ranger District, 805/925-9538, fax 805/961-5781.

17 AVILA HOT SPRINGS SPA AND RV PARK

Scenic rating: 6

on San Luis Obispo Bay
Map grid B1

The hot mineral pool here is a featured attraction. This is a natural mineral hot springs with an artesian well that produces water directly into the spas at 104°F. A pizza kitchen and snack bar are available as well. Nearby recreation options include Avila State Beach and Pismo State Beach.

RV sites, facilities: There are 11 sites with full hookups for RVs, 22 tent sites in three areas, and 28 cabins (26 are rented monthly, two are rented nightly). Picnic tables and fire grills (at some sites) are provided. Restrooms with showers, cable TV, laundry, heated swimming pool, hot mineral pool, spa, dump station, recreation room, arcade, pizza kitchen, and group barbecue pits are available. An 18-hole golf course is nearby. Leashed pets are permitted. Some facilities are wheelchair-accessible.

Reservations, fees: Reservations are accepted at 805/595-2359. Sites are $45 per night, $5 per night for each additional vehicle. Some credit cards accepted. Open year-round.

Directions: From San Luis Obispo, drive south on U.S. 101 for nine miles to the Avila Beach Drive exit. Take that exit and drive a short distance to the park at 250 Avila Beach Drive.

Contact: Avila Hot Springs Spa and RV Park, 805/595-2359, www.avilahotsprings.com.

18 LOPEZ LAKE RECREATION AREA

Scenic rating: 7

near Arroyo Grande

Map grid B1

Lopez Lake has become an example of how to do something right, with specially marked areas set aside exclusively for waterskiing, personal watercraft, and sailboarding, and the rest of the lake designated for fishing and low-speed boating. There are also full facilities for swimming, with a big swimming beach and two giant water slides, a children's wading pool, and a nice beach area. Another bonus is the scenic boat tours available on Saturdays, which get plenty of takers. A 25-mile trail system provides opportunities for biking, hiking, and horseback riding. That makes it perfect for just about everyone and, with good bass fishing, the lake has become very popular, especially on spring weekends when the bite is on. Other species include trout, bluegill, crappie, and catfish. Lopez Lake is set amid oak woodlands southeast of San Luis Obispo. The lake is shaped something like a horseshoe, has 940 surface acres with 22 miles of shoreline when full, and gets excellent weather most of the year. Features of the park in summer are ranger-led hikes and campfire shows. Many campsites overlook the lake or are nestled among oaks.

RV sites, facilities: There are 143 sites with full hookups (20 and 30 amps) for tents or RVs, 211 sites for tents, an overflow site with no hookups for tents or RVs of any length, and six group sites for 30–100 people each. An equestrian camp with four corrals will accommodate up to 10 vehicles. Picnic tables and fire rings are provided. Restrooms with showers, playground, children's wading pool, coin laundry, convenience store, ice, snack bar, marina, boat ramp, mooring, boat fuel (dry land fueling only), tackle, boat rentals, and water slides are available. Some facilities are wheelchair-accessible. Leashed pets are permitted.

Reservations, fees: Reservations are required by phone or website ($7 reservation fee). Sites are $18–29 per night, $10 per night for each additional vehicle, $108–264 per night for a group site, $3 per dog per night. Boat launching is $6 per day. Group rates available. Two-week maximum stay in summer. Some credit cards accepted. Open year-round.

Directions: From Arroyo Grande on U.S. 101, take the Grand Avenue exit. Turn east and drive through Arroyo Grande to Lopez Drive. Turn left (northeast) on Lopez Drive and drive 10 miles to the park.

Contact: Lopez Lake Recreation Area, 805/788-2381; Lopez Lake Marina, 805/489-1006, www.slocountyparks.com.

19 PISMO STATE BEACH: NORTH BEACH

Scenic rating: 7

in Pismo State Beach

Map grid B1

Pismo State Beach is nationally renowned for its beaches, dunes, and, in the good old days, clamming. The adjacent tree-lined dunes make for great walks or, for kids, great rolls. The beach is popular with bird-watchers, and the habitat supports the largest wintering colony of monarch butterflies in the United States. Plan on a reservation and having plenty of company in summer. This is an exceptionally popular state beach, either as an ultimate destination or as a stopover for folks cruising Highway 1. There are four restaurants and ATV rentals within two blocks. A trolley service provides a shuttle to the surrounding community. The clamming on minus low tides was legendary. Poaching has devastated the clamming here, with no legal clams taken for years.

RV sites, facilities: There are 103 sites for tents or RVs up to 36 feet (no hookups). Fire grills and picnic tables are provided. Restrooms with showers and flush toilets, drinking water, Wi-Fi, and a dump station are available. Horseback-riding facilities, grocery store, ATV rentals, restaurants, coin laundry, and propane gas are nearby. Some facilities are wheelchair-

CALIFORNIA

accessible. Leashed pets are permitted at the campground and on the beach.

Reservations, fees: Reservations are accepted at 800/444-PARK (800/444-7275) or www.reserveamerica.com ($8 reservation fee). Sites are $35 per night, and $10 per night for each additional vehicle. Open year-round.

Directions: On Highway 1 in Pismo Beach, take the North Beach/State Campground exit (well signed) and drive to the park entrance.

Contact: Pismo State Beach, 805/773-7220, www.parks.ca.gov.

20 PISMO COAST VILLAGE RV RESORT

Scenic rating: 7

in Pismo Beach

Map grid B1

This big-time RV park gets a lot of use by Highway 1 cruisers. Set near the ocean, its location is a plus. Pismo Beach is well known for its sand dunes and beautiful coastal frontage.

RV sites, facilities: There are 400 sites with full hookups (30 and 50 amps) for RVs up to 40 feet. No tents. Picnic tables, fire rings, and satellite TV are provided. Restrooms with showers, modem access, free Wi-Fi, playgrounds, heated swimming pool, coin laundry, convenience store, firewood, ice, recreation room, propane gas, seasonal recreation programs, restaurant, RV supplies and repair, bicycle rentals, and a nine-hole miniature golf course are available. Some facilities are wheelchair-accessible. Leashed pets are permitted, with restrictions on certain breeds.

Reservations, fees: Reservations are accepted at 888/RV-BEACH (888/782-3224). Sites are $39–51 per night. Group discounts available in the off-season. There is a 29-day maximum stay. Some credit cards accepted. Open year-round.

Directions: In Pismo Beach, drive on Highway 1/Pacific Coast Highway to the park at 165 South Dolliver Street/Highway 1.

Contact: Pismo Coast Village, 805/773-1811, fax 805/773-1507, www.pismocoastvillage.com.

21 LE SAGE RIVIERA

Scenic rating: 6

near Pismo State Beach

Map grid B1

This is a year-round RV park that can serve as headquarters for folks who are interested in visiting several nearby attractions, including neighboring Pismo State Beach and Lopez Lake, 10 miles to the east. The park is set on the ocean side of Highway 1, 250 yards from the beach. Note that many sites are filled with seasonal renters.

RV sites, facilities: There are 60 sites with full hookups (30 and 50 amps) for RVs up to 55 feet; many are pull-through. No tents. Picnic tables are provided. Restrooms with showers, drinking water, and coin laundry are available. Stores, restaurants, and golf courses are nearby. Some facilities are wheelchair-accessible. Leashed pets are permitted with certain restrictions.

Reservations, fees: Reservations are accepted. Sites are $32–47 per night from May through Labor Day Weekend, $27–37 the rest of the year, $3 per night for each additional vehicle. Holiday rates are higher. Some credit cards accepted. Open year-round.

Directions: In Pismo Beach on Highway 1, drive south on Highway 1 for 0.5 mile to the park on the right (west side) to 319 North Highway 1 (in Grover Beach).

Contact: Le Sage Riviera, 805/489-5506, fax 805/489-2103, www.lesageriviera.com.

22 OCEANO MEMORIAL PARK AND CAMPGROUND

Scenic rating: 7

in Oceano

Map grid B1

This San Luis Obispo county park is extremely busy during the summer and busy the rest of the year. The location is a bonus; it's set within a quarter mile of the Pismo State Beach entrance, the site of great sand dunes and wide-open ocean frontage. Oceano has a fishing lagoon.

RV sites, facilities: There are 24 sites for tents or RVs up to 40 feet (full hookups). No pull-through sites. Picnic tables and fire grills are provided. Drinking water, restrooms with coin showers and flush toilets, basketball court, horseshoes, athletic field, and picnic area are available. A playground, coin laundry, grocery store, and propane gas are available nearby. Leashed pets are permitted.

Reservations, fees: Reservations accepted at 805/781-4900 ($7 reservation fee). RV sites are $22–29 per night, $18 per night for tents, $10 per night for each additional vehicle, $3 per pet per night. Weekly rates are available. Four-week maximum stay. Open year-round.

Directions: From Pismo Beach, drive south on U.S. 101 to the Pismo Beach/Grand Avenue exit west to Highway 1. Take that exit and turn south on Highway 1 and drive 1.5 miles to Pier Avenue. Turn right on Pier Avenue and drive a short distance to Norswing. Turn left and drive to the end of the street and Mendel Avenue. Turn right and drive to Air Park Drive. Turn right and drive to the park on the right.

Contact: Oceano Memorial Park and Campground, 805/781-5930, fax 805/781-1102, www.slocountyparks.com.

23 PISMO STATE BEACH: OCEANO

Scenic rating: 6

in Pismo State Beach

Map grid B1

This is a prized state beach campground, with Pismo Beach and its sand dunes and coastal frontage a centerpiece for the state park system. Its location on the central coast on Highway 1, as well as its beauty and recreational opportunities, make it extremely popular. It fills to capacity most nights, and reservations are usually a necessity. (For more information on Pismo State Beach, see the Pismo State Beach: North Beach listing in this chapter.)

RV sites, facilities: There are 40 sites for tents or RVs up to 31 feet (no hookups), 42 sites with partial hookups for trailers and RVs up to 36 feet. Picnic tables and fire grills are provided. Drinking water and restrooms with flush toilets and coin showers are available. Horseback-riding facilities, grocery store, coin laundry, dump station, restaurants, and gas stations are nearby. Some facilities are wheelchair accessible, including a fishing overlook at Oceano Lagoon. Leashed pets are permitted at the campground and beach.

Reservations, fees: Reservations are accepted at 800/444-PARK (800/444-7275) or www.reserveamerica.com ($8 reservation fee). Sites are $35–50 per night, $10 per night for additional vehicle. Open year-round.

Directions: From Pismo Beach, drive two miles south on Highway 1 to Pier Avenue. Turn right and drive 0.2 mile to the campground entrance.

Contact: Pismo State Beach, 805/473-7220, www.parks.ca.gov.

24 OCEANO DUNES STATE VEHICULAR RECREATION AREA

Scenic rating: 6

south of Pismo Beach

Map grid B1

This is "national headquarters" for all-terrain vehicles (ATVs)—you know, those three- and four-wheeled motorcycles that turn otherwise normal people into lunatics. The camps are along one to three miles of beach and 1,500 acres of open sand dunes, and since not many make the walk to the campsites, four-wheel drives or ATVs are needed for access. The area covers 3,600 acres, including 5.5 miles of beach open for vehicles and 1,500 acres of sand dunes available for OHVs. They roam wild on the dunes here; that's the law, so don't go planning a quiet stroll. If you don't like 'em, you are strongly advised to go elsewhere. If this is your game, have fun and try to keep from killing yourself. Each fall, the "National Sand Drags" are held here. More than one million people

CALIFORNIA

visit each year. High tides can limit access. A beach towing service for RVs and trailers is available. Activities include swimming, surfing, surf fishing, horseback riding, and bird- and nutcase-watching.

RV sites, facilities: There are 1,000 sites for tents or RVs of any length (no hookups). Chemical and vault toilets are provided. There is no drinking water. Drinking water, horseback-riding facilities, grocery store, coin laundry, restaurants, gas stations, Wi-Fi, and dump station are available nearby. Leashed pets are permitted at the campground and beach.

Reservations, fees: Reservations are accepted at 800/444-PARK (800/444-7275) or www.reserveamerica.com ($8 reservation fee). Sites are $10 per night per vehicle. Day-use parking $5. Open year-round.

Directions: Drive on U.S. 101 to Arroyo Grande and take the Grand Avenue exit. Turn left (toward the beach) on Grand Avenue and drive four miles until the road ends at the North Entrance beach camping area. The South Entrance is one mile south. To get there from Highway 1, take Pier Avenue.

Contact: Oceano Dunes, 805/473-7220 or 805/773-7170, fax 805/473-7234, www.ohv.parks.ca.gov or www.parks.ca.gov.

25 RIVER PARK

Scenic rating: 4

in Lompoc
Map grid B2

River Park is set next to the lower Santa Ynez River, which looks quite a bit different than it does up in Los Padres National Forest. A small fishing lake within the 45-acre park is stocked with trout and catfish. A camp host and resident ranger are on-site. Side-trip possibilities include the nearby La Purisima Mission State Historic Park and Jalama Beach. Before checking in here you'd better get a lesson in how to pronounce Lompoc. It's "Lom-Poke." If you arrive and say, "Hey, it's great to be in Lom-Pock," they might just tell ya to get on back to the other cowpokes.

RV sites, facilities: There are 35 sites for RVs up to 40 feet (full hookups), a group camping area for tents or RVs, and an open area for up to five tents. No pull-through sites. Picnic tables and barbecues are provided. Restrooms with flush toilets and coin showers, drinking water, dump station, fishing pond, trail, sand volleyball, horseshoes, group facilities, and playground are available. Supplies and a coin laundry are nearby. Leashed pets are permitted with certain restrictions.

Reservations, fees: Reservations are not accepted for family sites but are required for groups at 805/875-8036. Sites are $5–20 per night, $10 per night for each additional vehicle, $5 per night for hike-in/bike-in sites, $1 per pet per night. Group fees are $5 per night per tent, $10 per night per RV, with a $25 minimum. Weekly rates available. Some credit cards accepted. Open year-round.

Directions: In Lompoc, drive to the junction of Highway 246 and Sweeney Road at the southwest edge of town and continue to the park at 401 East Highway 246.

Contact: Lompoc Parks and Recreation Department, 805/875-8100, fax 805/736-5195, www.ci.lompoc.ca.us.

26 FLYING FLAGS RV RESORT AND CAMPGROUND

Scenic rating: 3

near Solvang
Map grid B2

This is one of the few privately operated parks in the area that welcomes tenters as well as RVers. Nearby side trips include the Santa Ynez Mission, just east of Solvang. The town of Solvang is of interest. It was originally a small Danish settlement that has expanded since the 1920s yet managed to keep its cultural heritage intact through the years. The town is exceptionally clean, an example of how to do something right. Wineries and casinos are nearby.

RV sites, facilities: There are 256 sites with full or partial hookups (30 and 50 amps) for RVs of any length and 100 sites for tents. Most sites are pull-through. Picnic tables are provided. Restrooms with showers, cable TV, playground, heated swimming pool, spa, coin laundry, convenience store, dump station, ice, recreation room, modem access, free Wi-Fi, arcade, five clubhouses, group facilities, and propane gas are available. A nine-hole golf course, boat launch, and boat rentals are nearby. Some facilities are wheelchair-accessible. Leashed pets are permitted with certain restrictions.

Reservations, fees: Reservations are accepted by phone or website. Sites are $24–88 in summer, $22–98 on holidays, $22–68 in winter, $3 per person per night for more than two people, $5 per night for each additional vehicle, $1 per pet per night for more than two dogs. Holiday rates are higher. Monthly rates available. Open year-round. Some credit cards accepted.

Directions: From Santa Barbara, drive 45 miles north on U.S. 101 to Highway 246. Turn west (left) on Highway 246 and drive about 0.5 mile to Avenue of the Flags (a four-way stop). Turn left on Avenue of the Flags and drive about one block to the campground entrance on the left at 180 Avenue of the Flags.

Contact: Flying Flags RV Resort and Campground, 805/688-3716, fax 805/688-9245, www.flyingflags.com.

27 JALAMA BEACH COUNTY PARK

Scenic rating: 8

near Lompoc

Map grid B2

This is a pretty spot set where Jalama Creek empties into the ocean, about five miles north of Point Conception and just south of Vandenberg Air Force Base. The area is known for its sunsets and beachcombing. The camp is so popular that a waiting list is common in summer. Activities include surfing, sailboarding, and fishing for perch, cabezon, kelp bass, and halibut.

RV sites, facilities: There are 98 sites for tents

or RVs up to 40 feet, and two group sites for 7–15 vehicles each. Some sites have electrical (30 amps) hookups. Picnic tables and fire pits are provided. Restrooms with flush toilets and showers, drinking water, dump station, general store, snack bar, bait and tackle, picnic area, firewood, and ice are available. Note that the nearest gas station is 20 miles away. Some facilities are wheelchair-accessible. Leashed pets are permitted, but a vaccination certificate is required.

Reservations, fees: Reservations are not accepted for individual sites. Group reservations are required at 805/934-6211 ($25 reservation fee). Sites are $18–30 per night, $10 per night for each additional vehicle, $126–325 per night for a group site, $3 per pet per night. Weekly rates available in the off-season. Some credit cards accepted. Open year-round.

Directions: From Lompoc, drive about five miles south on Highway 1. Turn southwest on Jalama Road and drive 14 miles to the park.

Contact: Jalama Beach County Park, 805/736-6316 or 805/736-3504, fax 805/735-8020, www.santabarbaraparks.org.

28 GAVIOTA STATE PARK

Scenic rating: 10

near Santa Barbara

Map grid B2

This is the granddaddy, the biggest of the three state beaches along U.S. 101 northwest of Santa Barbara. Spectacular and beautiful, the park covers 2,700 acres, providing trails for hiking and horseback riding, as well as a mile-long stretch of stunning beach frontage. Gaviota means "seagull" and was first named by the soldiers of the Portola Expedition in 1769, who learned why you always wear a hat (or a helmet) when they are passing overhead. The ambitious can hike the beach to get more seclusion. Trails to Gaviota Overlook (1.5 miles) and Gaviota Peak (3.2 miles one-way) provide lookouts with drop-dead gorgeous views of the coast and Channel Islands. Want more? There is also a 0.5-mile trail to the hot springs. This park is known for being windy and for shade being hard to find. Unfortunately, a railroad trestle crosses above the day-use parking lot. You know what that means? Of course you do. It means trains run through here day and night, and with them, noise. This is a popular beach for swimming and surf fishing, as well as boat launching and fishing from the pier.

RV sites, facilities: There are 41 sites for tents or RVs up to 30 feet (no hookups) and an area for hike-in/bike-in sites. Picnic tables and fire grills are provided. Restrooms with flush toilets and coin showers, drinking water, summer lifeguard service, and boat hoist (two-ton maximum weight) are available. A convenience store (open summer only) is nearby. Some facilities are wheelchair-accessible. Leashed pets are permitted at campsites.

Reservations, fees: Reservations are accepted for about half the sites from Memorial Day weekend through Labor Day weekend at 800/444-PARK (800/444-7275) or www.reserveamerica.com ($8 reservation fee). Sites are $35 per night, $10 per night for each additional vehicle, $3 per person per night for hike-in/bike-in sites. Boat launching is $8 per day. One-week maximum stay in summer and two-week maximum in winter. Open year-round.

Directions: From Santa Barbara, drive north on U.S. 101 for 30 miles to the Gaviota State Beach exit. Take that exit and turn west and drive a short distance to the park entrance.

Contact: Gaviota State Park, Channel Coast District, 805/968-1033 or 805/585-1850, www.parks.ca.gov.

29 REFUGIO STATE BEACH

Scenic rating: 9

near Santa Barbara

Map grid B2   BEST (

Refugio State Beach is the smallest of the three beautiful state beaches along U.S. 101 north of Santa Barbara. The others are Gaviota and El Capitán, which also have campgrounds. Palm

trees planted close to Refugio Creek provide a unique look to this beach and campground. This is a great spot for family campers with bikes, with a paved two-mile bike trail connecting Refugio campground with El Capitán. Fishing is often good in this area of the coast. As with all state beaches and private camps on the Coast Highway, reservations are strongly advised and often a necessity throughout the vacation season.

RV sites, facilities: There are 67 sites for tents or RVs up to 30 feet (no hookups), one hike-in/bike-in site, and three group sites for tents or RVs that can accommodate up to 80 people and 25 vehicles. Picnic tables and fire grills are provided. Restrooms with flush toilets and coin showers, drinking water, summer lifeguard service, summer convenience store, and food services are available. Some facilities are wheelchair-accessible. Leashed pets are permitted at campsites.

Reservations, fees: Reservations are accepted at 800/444-PARK (800/444-7275) or www.reserveamerica.com ($8 reservation fee). Sites are $35 per night, $10 per night for each additional vehicle, $3–5 per night per person for hike-in/bike-in sites, $185 per night for the group site. One-week maximum stay in summer and two-week maximum stay in winter. Open year-round, weather permitting.

Directions: From Santa Barbara, drive northwest on U.S. 101 for 23 miles to the Refugio State Beach exit. Take that exit and turn west (left) and drive a short distance to the campground entrance.

Contact: Refugio State Beach, Channel Coast District, 805/968-1033 or 805/585-1850, www.parks.ca.gov.

30 EL CAPITÁN STATE BEACH

Scenic rating: 10

near Santa Barbara

Map grid B2   BEST (

This is one in a series of beautiful state beaches along the Santa Barbara coast. El Capitán has a sandy beach and rocky tidepools. The water is warm, the swimming good. A stairway descends from the bluffs to the beach, a beautiful setting, and sycamores and oaks line El Capitán Creek. A paved, two-mile bicycle trail is routed to Refugio State Beach, a great family trip. This is a perfect layover for Coast Highway vacationers, and reservations are usually required to assure a spot. Refugio State Beach to the north is another camping option.

RV sites, facilities: There are 130 sites for tents or RVs up to 40 feet, one hike-in/bike-in site, two group sites for tents or RVs that can accommodate 50–125 people each, and three group sites for tents only that can accommodate 50–125 people each. No hookups. Picnic tables and fire grills are provided. Restrooms with flush toilets and coin showers, drinking water, summer lifeguard service, and a summer convenience store are available. Some facilities are wheelchair-accessible. Leashed pets are permitted in the campgrounds, but not on the beach.

Reservations, fees: Reservations are accepted at 800/444-PARK (800/444-7275) or www.reserveamerica.com ($8 reservation fee). Sites are $35 per night, $10 per night for each additional vehicle, $3 per person per night for hike-in/bike-in sites, $165–420 per night for group sites. One-week maximum stay in summer and two-week maximum in winter. Open year-round, weather permitting.

Directions: From Santa Barbara, drive north on U.S. 101 for 20 miles to the El Capitán State Beach exit. Turn west (left) and drive a short distance to the campground entrance.

Contact: El Capitán State Beach, Channel Coast District, 805/968-1033 or 805/585-1850, www.parks.ca.gov.

31 ALISO PARK

Scenic rating: 6

in Los Padres National Forest

Map grid C2

This primitive, quiet camp is set at the foot of the Sierra Madre at 3,200 feet, directly below McPherson Peak (5,749 feet). It is just inside the

northeast boundary of Los Padres National Forest, making it easily accessible from Highway 166.

RV sites, facilities: There are 10 sites for tents or RVs up to 28 feet (no hookups). Picnic tables and fire grills are provided. Pit toilets are available. Drinking water is not available. Garbage must be packed out. Some facilities are wheelchair-accessible. Leashed pets are permitted.

Reservations, fees: Reservations are not accepted and there is no camping fee. An Adventure Pass ($30 annual fee or $5 daily pass) per parked vehicle is required. Open year-round.

Directions: From Santa Maria, drive east on Highway 166 for 59 miles to Aliso Canyon Road/Forest Road 10N04. Turn right on Aliso Canyon Road/Forest Road 10N04 and drive south about six miles to the campground at the end of the road.

Contact: Los Padres National Forest, Mount Piños Ranger District, 661/245-3731, fax 661/245-1526.

32 BALLINGER

Scenic rating: 3

in Los Padres National Forest

Map grid C2

Ballinger Camp is right inside the boundary of Los Padres National Forest in the Mount Piños Ranger District, just six miles east of Highway 33. During the week, this camp receives very little use. On weekends, it gets moderate, even heavy use at times, from OHV owners. Note that the California "green sticker" is required to ride OHVs here. The camp is set at an elevation of 3,000 feet.

RV sites, facilities: There are 20 sites for tents or RVs up to 32 feet (no hookups). Picnic tables and fire grills are provided. Vault toilets are available. No drinking water is available. Garbage must be packed out. Leashed pets are permitted.

Reservations, fees: Reservations are not accepted and there is no camping fee. An Adventure Pass ($30 annual fee or $5 daily pass) per parked vehicle is required. Open year-round.

CALIFORNIA

Directions: From Maricopa, drive southwest on Highway 166 about 14 miles to Highway 33. Turn south on Highway 33 and drive about 3.5 miles to Ballinger Canyon Road/Forest Road 9N10. Turn left (east) and drive three miles to the campground.

Contact: Los Padres National Forest, Mount Piños Ranger District, 661/245-3731, fax 661/245-1526.

33 VALLE VISTA

Scenic rating: 8

in Los Padres National Forest

Map grid C2

The view of the southern San Joaquin Valley and the snow-capped Sierra is the highlight of this primitive camp. It is set at 4,800 feet elevation, near the boundary of Los Padres National Forest. Visitors have an opportunity to view condors here, and you can usually spot a few buzzards, er, turkey vultures, circling around. If you don't bring your own water, they might just start circling you. Little-known fact: This camp sits exactly on the border of Kern County and Ventura County.

RV sites, facilities: There are seven sites for tents or RVs up to 22 feet (no hookups). Picnic tables and fire grills are provided. Pit toilets are available. No drinking water is available. Garbage must be packed out. Leashed pets are permitted.

Reservations, fees: Reservations are not accepted and there is no camping fee. An Adventure Pass ($30 annual fee or $5 daily pass) per parked vehicle is required. Open year-round.

Directions: From Maricopa, drive south on Highway 166 about nine miles to Cerro Noroeste Road. Turn left and drive 12 miles to the campground on the left.

Contact: Los Padres National Forest, Mount Piños Ranger District, 661/245-3731, fax 661/245-1526.

34 CABALLO

Scenic rating: 4

in Los Padres National Forest

Map grid C2

Caballo is set at 5,850 feet elevation on a small creek that is the headwaters for Santiago Creek, on the northern flank of Mount Abel. The creek flows only about 10 days a year, usually before the opening of the campground, so do not count on it for water. It is one of several primitive camps in the immediate area—a take-your-pick offer. But it's an offer not many folks even know about.

RV sites, facilities: There are six sites for tents or RVs up to 16 feet (no hookups). Picnic tables and fire grills are provided. Pit toilets are available. No drinking water is available. Garbage must be packed out. Leashed pets are permitted.

Reservations, fees: Reservations are not accepted and there is no camping fee. An Adventure Pass ($30 annual fee or $5 daily pass) per parked vehicle is required. Open early May through October, weather permitting.

Directions: Drive on I-5 to just south of Lebec to the Frazier Park exit. Take that exit and drive west on Frazier Mountain Road to the town of Lake of the Woods and Cuddy Valley Road. Continue straight on Cuddy Valley Road for six miles to Mil Potrero Highway (signed "Pine Mountain Club"). Turn right and drive 10 miles to Forest Road 9N27. Turn right and drive a short distance to the campground. Note: To reach Marian campground, continue for another mile.

Contact: Los Padres National Forest, Mount Piños Ranger District, 661/245-3731, fax 661/245-1526.

35 MARIAN

Scenic rating: 4

in Los Padres National Forest

Map grid C2

Marian is extremely primitive, set on the outskirts of Los Padres National Forest at 6,600 feet elevation, between Brush Mountain to the immediate northwest and San Emigdio Mountain to the immediate southeast. A primitive route out of camp leads three miles to the San Emigdio summit, at 7,495 feet elevation. A network of Forest Service roads provides access to a number of other camps in the area, as well as to Mount Abel (8,286 feet) and Mount Piños (8,831 feet). If the access gate is locked, reaching this camp requires a two-mile hike; nearby Toad Springs and Caballo are smaller but more easily accessible. Note that not only is no drinking water available, but there are no toilets either.

RV sites, facilities: There are five sites for tents or RVs up to 16 feet (no hookups). Picnic tables and fire grills are provided. No drinking water or toilets are available, so bring your own. Garbage must be packed out. Leashed pets are permitted.

Reservations, fees: Reservations are not accepted and there is no camping fee. An Adventure Pass ($30 annual fee or $5 daily pass) per parked vehicle is required. Open early May through October, weather permitting.

Directions: Drive on I-5 to just south of Lebec to the Frazier Park exit. Take that exit and drive west on Frazier Mountain Road to the town of Lake of the Woods and Cuddy Valley Road. Continue straight on Cuddy Valley Road for six miles to Mil Potrero Highway (signed "Pine Mountain Club"). Turn right and drive 10 miles to Forest Road 9N27. Turn right and drive one mile (passing Caballo campground) to the camp. Note: Four-wheel-drive or high-clearance vehicles are recommended.

Contact: Los Padres National Forest, Mount Piños Ranger District, 661/245-3731, fax 661/245-1526.

36 TOAD SPRINGS

Scenic rating: 8

in Los Padres National Forest

Map grid C2

Toad Springs is set at 5,700 feet elevation near Apache Saddle, on the northwest flank of Mount Abel (8,286 feet). It is at the head of Quatal Canyon with a spectacular badlands landscape. No water or toilets are available, so forget this one for your honeymoon. Note that a landslide destroyed a primitive trail (about a mile out of camp) that once was routed south out of camp for six miles to Mesa Springs and a trail camp. It is considered too dangerous for use.

RV sites, facilities: There are five sites for tents or RVs up to 16 feet (no hookups). Picnic tables and fire grills are provided. No drinking water or toilet is available, so bring your own. Garbage must be packed out. Leashed pets are permitted.

Reservations, fees: Reservations are not accepted and there is no camping fee. An Adventure Pass ($30 annual fee or $5 daily pass) per parked vehicle is required. Open early May through October, weather permitting.

Directions: Drive on I-5 to just south of Lebec to the Frazier Park exit. Take that exit and drive west on Frazier Mountain Road to the town of Lake of the Woods and Cuddy Valley Road. Continue straight on Cuddy Valley Road for six miles to Mil Potrero Highway (signed "Pine Mountain Club"). Turn right and drive 10 miles to the campground on the left.

Contact: Los Padres National Forest, Mount Piños Ranger District, 661/245-3731, fax 661/245-1526.

37 CAMPO ALTO

Scenic rating: 6

in Los Padres National Forest

Map grid C2

Campo Alto means "High Camp," and you'll find when you visit that the name fits. The camp is set high (8,250 feet) on Cerro Noroeste/Mount Abel in Los Padres National Forest. Don't show up thirsty, as there's no drinking water. About half a mile from camp there is a trailhead on the southeast side of the road. From here, you can hike two miles to Grouse Mountain, and in another mile, reach remote, hike-in Sheep Camp.

RV sites, facilities: There are 17 sites for tents

or RVs up to 22 feet (no hookups). Picnic tables and fire grills (stoves) are provided. Pit toilets are available. No drinking water is available. Garbage must be packed out. Some facilities are wheelchair-accessible. Leashed pets are permitted.

Reservations, fees: Reservations are not accepted and there is no camping fee. An Adventure Pass ($30 annual fee or $5 daily pass) per parked vehicle is required. Open May through October, weather permitting.

Directions: Drive on I-5 to just south of Lebec to the Frazier Park exit. Take that exit and drive west on Frazier Mountain Road to the town of Lake of the Woods and Cuddy Valley Road. Continue straight on Cuddy Valley Road and drive six miles to Mil Potrero Highway (signed "Pine Mountain Club"). Turn right and drive nine miles to Cerro Noroeste Road (Forest Road 9N07). Turn left and drive nine miles to the campground.

Contact: Los Padres National Forest, Mount Piños Ranger District, 661/245-3731, fax 661/245-1526.

38 NETTLE SPRINGS

Scenic rating: 4

in Los Padres National Forest

Map grid C2

This remote camp borders the Chumash Wilderness, set near the end of a Forest Service road in Apache Canyon. A mile east of camp, via the access road, is a primitive trailhead on the left side. This trail is routed four miles to Mesa Springs and a trail camp. The elevation is 4,400 feet.

RV sites, facilities: There are 11 sites for tents or RVs up to 22 feet (no hookups). Picnic tables and fire grills are provided. Pit toilets and drinking water are available. Garbage must be packed out. Leashed pets are permitted.

Reservations, fees: Reservations are not accepted and there is no camping fee. An Adventure Pass ($30 annual fee or $5 daily pass) per parked vehicle is required. Open year-round.

Directions: From Maricopa, drive 14 miles south on Highway 166 to the Highway 33 exit. Turn south on Highway 33 and drive about 13 miles to Apache Canyon Road (Forest Road 8N06). Turn left and drive about 11 miles to the campground. Note: The last 10 miles are rough; high-clearance vehicles are advised.

Contact: Los Padres National Forest, Mount Piños Ranger District, 661/245-3731, fax 661/245-1526.

39 MOUNT PIÑOS

Scenic rating: 7

in Los Padres National Forest

Map grid C2

This camp is set at 7,800 feet elevation, one of three camps on the eastern flank of Mount Piños (8,831 feet). This is one of the few places on earth where it is possible to see flying California condors, the largest bird in North America. Note that a once-popular drive to the top of Mount Piños for beautiful and sweeping views is now closed after being recognized as a Chumash holy site. There's access to the Mount Piños summit trail 2.5 miles away on Mil Potrero Highway at the Chula Vista parking area. From there it's about two miles to the summit, which is a designated botanical area. July and August usually are the best months for wildflower displays. McGill (see listing in this chapter) provides a nearby camping alternative.

RV sites, facilities: There are 19 sites for tents or RVs up to 16 feet (no hookups). Picnic tables and fire grills are provided. Pit toilets and drinking water are available. Some facilities are wheelchair-accessible. Leashed pets are permitted.

Reservations, fees: Reservations are not accepted. Sites are $14 per night. Open late May through October, weather permitting.

Directions: Drive on I-5 to just south of Lebec to the Frazier Park exit. Take that exit and drive west on Frazier Mountain Road to the town of Lake of the Woods and Cuddy Valley Road.

Continue straight on Cuddy Valley Road and drive about six miles to Mount Piños Highway. Bear left and drive five miles (the road name changes several times, but stay on the main road) to the campground.

Contact: Los Padres National Forest, Mount Piños Ranger District, 661/245-3731, fax 661/245-1526.

40 McGILL

Scenic rating: 6

near Mount Piños in Los Padres National Forest
Map grid C2

The camp is set at 7,400 feet elevation, about four miles from the top of nearby Mount Piños. Although the road is closed to the top of Mount Piños, there are numerous hiking and biking trails in the area that provide spectacular views. On clear days, there are vantage points to the high Sierra, the San Joaquin Valley, and Antelope Valley.

RV sites, facilities: There are 73 sites for tents or RVs up to 16 feet (no hookups), and two group sites for 60 and 80 people. Picnic tables and fire grills are provided. Pit toilets are available. There is no drinking water. Some facilities are wheelchair-accessible. Leashed pets are permitted.

Reservations, fees: Reservations are required for group sites at 877/444-6777 or www.recreation.gov ($10 reservation fee). Sites are $14 per night, $75 per night for a group site. Open late May through October.

Directions: Drive on I-5 to just south of Lebec to the Frazier Park exit. Take that exit and drive west on Frazier Mountain Road to the town of Lake of the Woods and Cuddy Valley Road. Continue straight on Cuddy Valley Road and drive about six miles to Mount Piños Highway. Bear left and drive about five miles to the campground on the right.

Contact: Los Padres National Forest, Mount Piños Ranger District, 661/245-3731, fax 661/245-1526.

41 DAVY BROWN

Scenic rating: 7

on Davy Brown Creek in Los Padres National Forest
Map grid C2

This is a pretty spot, set along little Davy Brown Creek at 2,100 feet elevation, deep in Los Padres National Forest. The border of the San Rafael Wilderness and an excellent trailhead are just two miles down the road (along Davy Brown Creek) to the northeast at Nira (see the Nira listing in this chapter for hiking options).

RV sites, facilities: There are 13 sites for tents or RVs up to 25 feet (no hookups). Picnic tables and fire grills are provided. Vault toilets are available. No drinking water is available. Garbage must be packed out. Leashed pets are permitted.

Reservations, fees: Reservations are not accepted and there is no camping fee. An Adventure Pass ($30 annual fee or $5 daily pass) per parked vehicle is required. Open year-round.

Directions: From U.S. 101 in Santa Barbara, take Highway 154 and drive northeast for 22 miles to Armour Ranch Road. Turn right on Armour Ranch Road and drive 1.5 miles to Happy Canyon Road. Turn right on Happy Canyon Road/County Route 3350 and drive 11 miles to Cachuma Saddle. Continue straight (north) on Sunset Valley/Cachuma Road/Forest Road 8N09 for four miles to the campground.

Contact: Los Padres National Forest, Santa Lucia Ranger District, 805/925-9538, fax 805/961-5781.

42 NIRA

Scenic rating: 8

on Manzana Creek in Los Padres National Forest
Map grid C2

Nira is a premium jump-off spot for backpackers, set at 1,000 feet elevation along Manzana Creek, on the border of the San Rafael Wilderness. A primary wilderness trailhead is available, routed east into the San Rafael Wilderness through Lost Valley, along Fish Creek, and to Manzana Creek (and beyond), all in just six miles, with a series of hike-in camps available as the trail enters the wilderness interior. Today's history lesson? This camp was originally an NRA (National Recovery Act) camp during the Depression, hence the name Nira.

RV sites, facilities: There are 11 sites for tents or RVs up to 16 feet (no hookups). Picnic tables and fire grills are provided. Vault toilets and horse-hitching posts are available. No drinking water is available. Garbage must be packed out. Some facilities are wheelchair-accessible. Leashed pets are permitted.

Reservations, fees: Reservations are not accepted and there is no camping fee. An Adventure Pass ($30 annual fee or $5 daily pass) per parked vehicle is required. Open year-round, but access roads may be closed during and after heavy rains.

Directions: From U.S. 101 in Santa Barbara, take Highway 154 northeast and drive 22 miles to Armour Ranch Road. Turn right on Armour Ranch Road and drive 1.5 miles to Happy Canyon Road. Turn right on Happy Canyon Road and drive 11 miles to Cachuma Saddle. Continue straight (north) on Sunset Valley/Cachuma Road/Forest Road 8N09 for six miles to the campground.

Contact: Los Padres National Forest, Santa Lucia Ranger District, 805/925-9538, fax 805/961-5781.

43 FIGUEROA

Scenic rating: 7

in Los Padres National Forest

Map grid C2

This is one of the more attractive camps in Los Padres National Forest. It is set at 3,500 feet elevation beneath an unusual stand of oak and huge manzanita trees and offers a view of the Santa Ynez Valley. Nearby attractions include the Piño Alto Picnic Area, 2.5 miles away, offering a panoramic view of the adjacent wildlands with a 0.5-mile, wheelchair-accessible nature

trail. An exceptional view is also available from the nearby Figueroa fire lookout. Though it requires a circuitous 10-mile ride around Figueroa Mountain to get there, Nira to the east provides the best trailhead in this area for the San Rafael Wilderness.

RV sites, facilities: There are 32 sites for tents or RVs up to 25 feet (no hookups). Picnic tables and fire grills are provided. Vault toilets are available. No drinking water is available. Garbage must be packed out. Leashed pets are permitted.

Reservations, fees: Reservations are not accepted and there is no camping fee. An Adventure Pass ($30 annual fee or $5 daily pass) per parked vehicle is required. Open year-round.

Directions: Drive on Highway 154 to Los Olivos and Figueroa Mountain Road. Turn northeast on Figueroa Mountain Road and drive 12.5 miles to the campground.

Contact: Los Padres National Forest, Santa Lucia Ranger District, 805/925-9538, fax 805/961-5781.

44 REYES CREEK FAMILY AND EQUESTRIAN CAMP

Scenic rating: 7

in Los Padres National Forest

Map grid C2

This developed Forest Service camp sits at the end of an old spur, Forest Road 7N11. The camp is set at 3,960 feet elevation along Reyes Creek, which is stocked with trout in early summer. The Piedra Blanca/Gene Marshall Trail is routed out of camp to the south and climbs three miles to Upper Reyes backpack camp, and beyond, up a ridge and down to Bear-trap Creek and several trail camps along that creek. In all, the trail covers approximately 20 miles.

RV sites, facilities: There are 30 sites for tents or RVs up to 22 feet (no hookups). Picnic tables and fire grills are provided. Pit toilets, drinking water, and a corral are available. Garbage must be packed out. A small store, bar, and café are nearby. Some facilities are wheelchair-accessible. Leashed pets are permitted.

Reservations, fees: Reservations are not accepted and there is no camping fee. An Adventure Pass ($30 annual fee or $5 daily pass) per parked vehicle is required. Open year-round.

Directions: From Ojai, drive north on Highway 33 for 36 miles to Lockwood Valley Road. Turn right on Lockwood Valley Road (Ozena Road) and drive about 3.5 miles to Forest Road 7N11. Turn right and drive about 1.5 miles to the village of Camp Scheideck and a T intersection. Bear left at the T intersection and drive 0.25 mile to the campground.

Contact: Los Padres National Forest, Mount Piños Ranger District, 661/245-3731, fax 661/245-1526.

45 PINE SPRINGS

Scenic rating: 6

near San Guillermo Mountain in
Los Padres National Forest

Map grid C2

This primitive camp is set at 5,800 feet elevation on a short spur road that dead-ends on the east flank of San Guillermo Mountain (6,569 feet). Pine Springs feeds the tiny headwaters of Guillermo Creek at this spot. This is a quiet spot. It gets little use, primarily in the fall by hunters.

RV sites, facilities: There are 12 sites for tents or RVs up to 22 feet (no hookups). Picnic tables and fire grills are provided. Pit toilets and drinking water are available. Garbage must be packed out. Leashed pets are permitted.

Reservations, fees: Reservations are not accepted and there is no camping fee. An Adventure Pass ($30 annual fee or $5 daily pass) per parked vehicle is required. Open early May through October, weather permitting.

Directions: Drive on I-5 to just south of Lebec to the Frazier Park exit. Take that exit and drive west on Frazier Mountain Road to the town of Lake of the Woods and Lockwood Valley Road. Turn left on Lockwood Valley Road (take the left fork) and drive about 12 miles to Grade Valley Road (Forest Road 7N03). Turn left and drive 3.5 miles to Forest Road 7N03A. Turn right and drive one mile to the campground.

Contact: Los Padres National Forest, Mount Piños Ranger District, 661/245-3731, fax 661/245-1526.

46 THORN MEADOWS FAMILY AND EQUESTRIAN CAMP

Scenic rating: 7

on Piru Creek in Los Padres National Forest

Map grid C2

The reward at Thorn Meadows is a small, quiet spot along Piru Creek at 5,000 feet elevation, deep in Los Padres National Forest. A trail out of camp leads three miles up to Thorn Point, a magnificent 6,935-foot lookout. It is by far the best view in the area, worth the 2,000-foot climb, and on a clear day you can see the Channel Islands.

RV sites, facilities: There are five sites for tents or RVs up to 16 feet (no hookups). Picnic tables and fire grills are provided. Pit toilets, drinking water and a double split corral are available. Garbage must be packed out. Leashed pets are permitted.

Reservations, fees: Reservations are not accepted and there is no camping fee. An Adventure Pass ($30 annual fee or $5 daily pass) per parked vehicle is required. Open early May through October, weather permitting.

Directions: Drive on I-5 to just south of Lebec and the Frazier Park exit. Take that exit and drive west on Frazier Mountain Road to the town of Lake of the Woods and Lockwood Valley Road. Turn left on Lockwood Valley Road and drive about 12 miles to Mutau Flat Road (Forest Road 7N03/Grade Valley Road). Turn left and drive seven miles to Forest Road 7N03B. Turn right and drive one mile to the campground.

Contact: Los Padres National Forest, Mount Piños Ranger District, 661/245-3731, fax 661/245-1526.

CALIFORNIA

47 CACHUMA LAKE RECREATION AREA

Scenic rating: 7

near Santa Barbara

Map grid C2

Cachuma has become one of the best lakes in America for fishing big bass, and the ideal climate makes it a winner for camping as well. Cachuma is set at 750 feet elevation in the foothills northwest of Santa Barbara, a big, beautiful lake covering 3,200 acres. In low-rain years the drawdowns are so significant that you'd hardly recognize the place. The rules are perfect for fishing: No waterskiing, personal watercraft riding, swimming, canoeing, kayaking, or sailboarding is permitted; for fishing boats there is a 5-mph speed limit in the coves and a 40-mph limit elsewhere. After fishing, picnicking and camping come in a distant second and third in popularity, respectively. Note: All boats must be inspected for Quagga and Zebra mussels prior to launch, along with other requirements designed to prevent the spread of invasive mussels.

RV sites, facilities: There are 420 sites for tents or RVs of any length, and nine group areas for 8–30 vehicles. Some sites have full or partial hookups (30 amps) and/or are pull-through. Yurts are also available. Picnic tables and fire pits are provided. Drinking water, restrooms with flush toilets and coin showers, and coin laundry are available. Playground, general store, propane gas, seasonal swimming pool, full-service marina, fishing piers, bait and tackle, boat ramp, mooring, boat fuel, boat and water bike rentals, bicycle rentals, nature cruises, miniature golf, dump station, group facilities, RV storage, gas station, ice, and snack bar are nearby. Watercraft under 10 feet and inflatables under 12 feet are prohibited on the lake. Leashed pets are permitted, but they must be kept at least 50 feet from the lake.

Reservations, fees: Reservations are accepted only for groups and yurts at 805/686-5050 ($5 reservation fee). Sites are $18–30 per night, $10 per night for each additional vehicle, $160–600 per night for group sites, $3 per pet per night. Some credit cards accepted. Open year-round.

Directions: From Santa Barbara, drive 18 miles north on Highway 154 to the campground entrance on the right.

Contact: Cachuma Lake Recreation Area, Santa Barbara County, 805/686-5054; Cachuma Marina and Boat Rentals, 805/688-4040; Cachuma Boat Tours, 805/686-5050, www.cachuma.com.

48 FREMONT

Scenic rating: 7

near the Santa Ynez River in Los Padres National Forest

Map grid C2

As you travel west to east, Fremont is the first in a series of Forest Service campgrounds near the Santa Ynez River. This one is just inside the boundary of Los Padres National Forest at 900 feet elevation, nine miles east of Cachuma Lake to the west.

RV sites, facilities: There are 15 sites for tents or RVs up to 22 feet (no hookups). Picnic tables and fire grills are provided. Drinking water and flush toilets are available. Some facilities are wheelchair-accessible. Groceries are available within two miles and propane gas is available at Cachuma Lake nine miles away. Leashed pets are permitted.

Reservations, fees: Reservations are accepted at 877/444-6777 or www.recreation.gov ($10 reservation fee). Sites are $15 per night, $5 per night for each additional vehicle. Open early April through late October.

Directions: From Santa Barbara, drive northwest on Highway 154 for about 10 miles to Paradise Road/Forest Road 5N18. Turn right on Paradise Road/Forest Road 5N18 and drive 2.5 miles to the campground on the right.

Contact: Los Padres National Forest, Santa Barbara Ranger District, 805/967-3481, fax 805/967-7312; Rocky Mountain Recreation Company, 805/521-1319.

CALIFORNIA

49 LOS PRIETOS

Scenic rating: 7

near the Santa Ynez River in
Los Padres National Forest

Map grid C2

Los Prietos is set across from the Santa Ynez River at an elevation of 1,000 feet, just upstream from nearby Fremont campground to the west. There are several nice hiking trails nearby; the best starts near the Los Prietos Ranger Station, heading south for two miles to Wellhouse Falls (get specific directions and a map at the ranger station). River access is available 0.25 mile away at the White Rock day-use area.

RV sites, facilities: There are 37 sites for tents or RVs up to 22 feet (no hookups). Picnic tables and fire grills are provided. Drinking water and flush toilets are available. Some facilities are wheelchair-accessible. Leashed pets are permitted.

Reservations, fees: Reservations are accepted at 877/444-6777 or www.recreation.gov ($10 reservation fee). The fee is $15 per night, $5 per night for each additional vehicle. Open early April through late October.

Directions: From Santa Barbara, take Highway 154 and drive 10 miles northeast to Paradise Road/Forest Road 5N18. Turn right on Paradise Road/Forest Road 5N18 and drive 3.8 miles to the campground.

Contact: Los Padres National Forest, Santa Barbara Ranger District, 805/967-3481, fax 805/967-7312; Rocky Mountain Recreation, 805/521-1319.

50 UPPER OSO FAMILY AND EQUESTRIAN CAMP

Scenic rating: 7

near the Santa Ynez River in
Los Padres National Forest

Map grid C2

This is one of the Forest Service campgrounds in the Santa Ynez Recreation Area. It is set in Oso Canyon at 1,100 feet elevation, one mile from the Santa Ynez River. This is a prime spot for equestrians, with horse corrals available at adjacent campsites. Note that at high water this campground can become inaccessible. A mile north of camp is the Santa Cruz trailhead for a hike that is routed north up Oso Canyon for a mile, then three miles up to Happy Hollow, and beyond that to a trail camp just west of Little Pine Mountain, elevation 4,508 feet. A trailhead into the San Rafael Wilderness is nearby, and once on the trail, you'll find many primitive sites in the backcountry.

RV sites, facilities: There are 25 sites for tents or RVs up to 22 feet (no hookups). Picnic tables and fire grills are provided. Drinking water and flush toilets are available. Some facilities are wheelchair-accessible. Many sites have horse corrals. Leashed pets are permitted.

Reservations, fees: Reservations are accepted at 877/444-6777 or www.recreation.gov ($10 reservation fee). Sites are $15 per night, $20 per night for equestrian sites, $5 per night for each additional vehicle. Open year-round, weather permitting.

Directions: From Santa Barbara, take Highway 154 and drive 10 miles northeast to Paradise Road/Forest Road 5N18. Turn right on Paradise Road/Forest Road 5N18 and drive six miles to Upper Oso Road. Turn left on Upper Oso Road and drive one mile to the campground at the end of the road.

Contact: Los Padres National Forest, Santa Barbara Ranger District, 805/967-3481, fax 805/967-7312; Rocky Mountain Recreation, 805/521-1319.

51 PARADISE

Scenic rating: 7

near the Santa Ynez River in
Los Padres National Forest

Map grid C2

Here is yet another option among the camps along the Santa Ynez River. As you drive east it is the second camp you will come to, just after Fremont. Trout are usually planted upriver of

CALIFORNIA

the campground during the spring. The best hiking trailheads nearby are at Upper Oso Camp and the Sage Hill Group Campground. Cachuma Lake is six miles to the west.

RV sites, facilities: There are 14 sites for tents or RVs up to 22 feet. Picnic tables and fire grills are provided. Drinking water and flush toilets are available. Groceries are available nearby. Some facilities are wheelchair-accessible. Leashed pets are permitted.

Reservations, fees: Reservations are accepted at 877/444-6777 or www.recreation.gov ($10 reservation fee). Sites are $15 per night, $5 per night for each additional vehicle. Open year-round.

Directions: From Santa Barbara, take Highway 154 and drive 10 miles northeast to Paradise Road/Forest Road 5N18. Turn right on Paradise Road/Forest Road 5N18 and drive three miles to the campground on the right.

Contact: Los Padres National Forest, Santa Barbara Ranger District, 805/967-3481, fax 805/967-7312; Rocky Mountain Recreation, 805/521-1319.

52 SAGE HILL GROUP AND EQUESTRIAN CAMP

Scenic rating: 7

on the Santa Ynez River in
Los Padres National Forest

Map grid C2

This is another in the series of camps along the Santa Ynez River in Los Padres National Forest. This one, set at 2,000 feet elevation, was designed for large groups as well as equestrians, with horse corrals available next to one group site. A 3.5-mile loop trail starts at the back end of Sage Hill Group Camp. The first mile is a self-guided interpretive trail.

RV sites, facilities: There are five group areas for tents or RVs up to 32 feet (no hookups) that can accommodate 25–50 people each. Picnic tables and fire grills are provided. Flush toilets are available. No drinking water is available.

Horse corrals are in one group site. Some facilities are wheelchair-accessible. Leashed pets are permitted.

Reservations, fees: Reservations are required at 877/444-6777 or www.recreation.gov ($10 reservation fee). Sites are $75–100 per night. Open year-round, weather permitting.

Directions: From Santa Barbara, take Highway 154 and drive 10 miles northeast to Paradise Road/Forest Road 5N18. Turn right on Paradise Road/Forest Road 5N18 and drive five miles to the ranger station and the campground entrance road. Turn left and drive 0.5 mile to the campground.

Contact: Los Padres National Forest, Santa Barbara Ranger District, 805/967-3481, fax 805/967-7312; Rocky Mountain Recreation, 805/521-1319.

53 HOLIDAY GROUP CAMP

Scenic rating: 7

on Matilija Creek in Los Padres National Forest

Map grid C2

This group site, set at 2,000 feet elevation, is near the North Fork of the Matilija. It's only three miles uphill from Matilija Reservoir.

RV sites, facilities: There is one group site for tents or RVs up to 22 feet (no hookups) that can accommodate up to 75 people. Picnic tables and fire grills are provided. Drinking water and vault toilets are available. Garbage must be packed out. Leashed pets are permitted.

Reservations, fees: Reservations are required at 877/444-6777 or www.recreation.gov ($10 reservation fee). The fee is $75–100 per night, $5 per night per each additional vehicle. Open year-round.

Directions: From Ojai, drive northwest on Highway 33 for nine miles to the campground entrance on the right.

Contact: Rocky Mountain Recreation, 805/640-1977.

54 WHEELER GORGE

Scenic rating: 7

on Matilija Creek in Los Padres National Forest

Map grid C2

This developed Forest Service camp is set at 2,000 feet elevation and is one of the more popular spots in the area. The North Fork of the Matilija runs beside the camp and provides some fair trout fishing in the spring and good swimming holes in early summer. Interpretive programs are also available, a nice plus, and a nature trail is adjacent to the campground.

RV sites, facilities: There are 68 sites for tents or RVs up to 35 feet (no hookups), including six double sites. Picnic tables and fire grills are provided. Pit toilets are available. Drinking water is available intermittently; check for current status. Garbage must be packed out. Some facilities are wheelchair-accessible. Leashed pets are permitted.

Reservations, fees: Reservations are accepted at 877/444-6777 or www.recreation.gov ($10 reservation fee). Sites are $20 per night, $5 per night for each additional vehicle. Open year-round.

Directions: From Ojai, drive northwest on Highway 33 for 8.5 miles to the campground entrance on the left.

Contact: Rocky Mountain Recreation, 805/640-1977.

55 ROSE VALLEY

Scenic rating: 8

in Los Padres National Forest

Map grid C2

The short walk to Rose Valley Falls, a 300-foot waterfall that provides a happy surprise, makes this camp a sure winner in late winter and spring. The walk to the waterfall is just 0.5-mile round-trip. Note that there are two views of it: a long-distance view of the entire waterfall, and at the base a view of just the lower tier. It is one of the scenic highlights in this section of Los Padres National Forest. The camp is set at 3,400 feet elevation next to Rose Valley Creek, about two miles from Sespe Creek. If this campground is full, there is another campground, Middle Lion, two miles beyond Rose Valley camp.

RV sites, facilities: There are nine sites for tents or RVs up to 30 feet (no hookups). Picnic tables and fire grills are provided. Vault toilets are available. There is no drinking water. Horseback-riding facilities are nearby. Garbage must be packed out. Some facilities are wheelchair-accessible. Leashed pets are permitted.

Reservations, fees: Reservations are not accepted and there is no camping fee. An Adventure Pass ($30 annual fee or $5 daily pass) per parked vehicle is required. Open year-round, weather permitting.

Directions: From Ojai, drive north on Highway 33 for 15 miles to Sespe River Road/Rose Valley Road. Turn right on Sespe River Road/Rose Valley Road and drive 5.5 miles to the campground entrance.

Contact: Los Padres National Forest, Ojai Ranger District, 805/646-4348, fax 805/646-0484.

56 SANTA BARBARA SUNRISE RV PARK

Scenic rating: 3

in Santa Barbara

Map grid C2

RV cruisers get a little of two worlds here. For one thing, the park is close to the beach; for another, the downtown shopping area isn't too far away, either. This is the only RV park in Santa Barbara. It is close to the highway, so noise can be a problem for RVs that are less than soundproof. In addition, access is difficult for RVs over 30 feet.

RV sites, facilities: There are 33 sites with full hookups (20, 30 and 50 amps) for RVs up to 45 feet, including 10 pull-through sites. No tents. Picnic tables, restrooms with free showers, cable TV, free Wi-Fi, and coin laundry are available. A grocery store, golf course, tennis

CALIFORNIA

courts, and propane gas are nearby. Leashed pets are permitted.

Reservations, fees: Reservations are accepted up to 45 days in advance. Sites are $45 per night, $5 per person per night for more than two people, $5 per night for each additional vehicle, $5 per pet per night. Some credit cards accepted. Open year-round.

Directions: In Santa Barbara on U.S. 101 northbound, drive to the Salinas Street exit. Take that exit and drive to the park (well signed) at 516 South Salinas Street, near the highway exit.

In Santa Barbara on U.S. 101 southbound, drive to the Milpas Street exit. Take that exit and turn left on Milpas Street. Drive under the freeway to Carpinteria Street. Turn right and drive 0.5 mile to Salinas Street. Turn right and drive 0.5 mile to the park on the right.

Contact: Santa Barbara Sunrise RV Park, 805/966-9954 or 800/345-5018, fax 805/966-7950.

57 CARPINTERIA STATE BEACH

Scenic rating: 8

near Santa Barbara
Map grid C2

First, plan on reservations, and then, plan on plenty of neighbors. This state beach is one pretty spot, and a lot of folks cruising up the coast like the idea of taking off their boots here for a while. This is an urban park; that is, it is within walking distance of downtown, restaurants, and shopping. You can love it or hate it, but this camp is almost always full. It features one mile of beach. Harbor seals can be seen December through May, along with an occasional passing gray whale. Tidepools here are protected and contain starfish, sea anemones, crabs, snails, octopus, and sea urchins. In the summer, the visitors center features a living tidepool exhibit. Other state beaches to the nearby north are El Capitán State Beach and Refugio State Beach, both with campgrounds.

RV sites, facilities: There are 65 sites for tents, 79 sites with full or partial hookups (30 amps) for RVs up to 30 feet, 29 sites with partial hookups for RVs up to 35 feet, 38 sites with no hookups for RVs up to 21 feet, one hike-in/bike-in site, and seven group sites that can accommodate 25–65 people each. Picnic tables and fire rings are provided. Drinking water, restrooms with flush toilets and coin showers, and a picnic area are available. A convenience store, coin laundry, restaurants, and propane gas are nearby in the town of Carpinteria. Some facilities are wheelchair-accessible. Leashed pets are permitted, except on the beach.

Reservations, fees: Reservations are accepted at 800/444-PARK (800/444-7275) or www.reserveamerica.com ($8 reservation fee). Sites are $35–50 per night, $10 per night for each additional vehicle, $5 per person per night for hike-in/bike-in site, $140–335 per night for group sites. Open year-round, except for group sites.

Note: At time of publication, there was a planned midweek closure of the Anacapa campground (27 sites) and reduced services.

Directions: From Santa Barbara, drive south on U.S. 101 for 12 miles to Carpinteria and the Casitas Pass Road exit. Take that exit and turn right on Casitas Pass Road and drive about a block to Carpinteria Avenue. Turn right and drive a short distance to Palm Avenue. Turn left and drive about six blocks to the campground at the end of Palm Avenue.

Contact: Carpinteria State Beach, 805/684-2811; Channel Coast District, 805/968-1033, www.parks.ca.gov.

58 LAKE CASITAS RECREATION AREA

Scenic rating: 7

north of Ventura
Map grid C2

Lake Casitas is known as one of Southern California's world-class fish factories, with more 10-pound bass produced here than anywhere and including the former state record, a bass that weighed 21 pounds, 3 ounces. Other fish species include catfish, crappie, and sunfish.

Fishing at night is permitted on select weekends. The ideal climate in the foothill country gives the fish a nine-month growing season and provides excellent weather for camping. Casitas is north of Ventura at an elevation of 567 feet in the foothills bordering Los Padres National Forest. The lake has 32 miles of shoreline with a huge number of sheltered coves, covering 2,710 acres. The lake is managed primarily for anglers. Waterskiing, personal watercraft, and swimming are not permitted. The park holds many special events, including the Ojai Wine Festival and the Ojai Renaissance Festival.

Note that private boats were banned in 2008 to prevent the spread of Quagga and Zebra mussels; the ban may be extended through 2009 and beyond, or a new program will be established that requires searches, cleaning, and proof of residence or other restrictions. Canoes and kayaks are included in the ban.

RV sites, facilities: There are 400 sites for tents or RVs of any length and a group site for a minimum of 10 vehicles; some sites have full or partial hookups (30 and 50 amps) and/or are pull-through. Trailer rentals are also available. Picnic tables and fire rings are provided. Restrooms with flush toilets and showers, drinking water, two dump stations, playgrounds, general store, picnic areas, propane, ice, snack bar, water playground, bike rentals, and full-service marina (including boat ramps, boat rentals, slips, fuel, tackle, and bait) are available. Some facilities are wheelchair-accessible. Leashed pets are permitted, except on the lake or boats.

Reservations, fees: Reservations are accepted at 805/649-1122 ($8 reservation fee, $75 fee for group sites). Sites are $19–50 per night, $10 per night for each additional vehicle, $2 per pet per night. The group site is $19–25 per vehicle per night with a two-night, 10-vehicle minimum. Some credit cards accepted. Open year-round.

Directions: From Ventura, drive north on Highway 33 for 10.5 miles to Highway 150/Baldwin Road. Turn left (west) on Highway 150 and drive three miles to Santa Ana Road. Turn left and drive to the lake and campground entrance at 11311 Santa Ana Road.

Contact: Lake Casitas Recreation Area, 805/649-2233, fax 805/649-4661; Lake Casitas Marina, 805/649-2043; Nature Cruises, 805/640-6844, ext. 654, www.lakecasitas.info.

59 CAMP COMFORT PARK

Scenic rating: 4

on San Antonio Creek north of Ventura

Map grid C2

This Ventura County park gets missed by many. It's set in a residential area in the Ojai Valley foothill country at 1,000 feet elevation. San Antonio Creek runs through the park and there are shade trees. Lake Casitas Recreation Area is 10 miles away.

RV sites, facilities: There are 15 sites with full hookups (30 and 50 amps) for tents or RVs up to 34 feet. Picnic tables and fire pits are provided. Restrooms with flush toilets and showers, drinking water, coin laundry, cable TV, picnic areas, group facilities, clubhouse, and playground are available. Supplies are nearby. Leashed pets are permitted in the campground only.

Reservations, fees: Reservations are accepted ($10 reservation fee, $20 for groups). Sites are $40 per night, $1 per pet per night. Open year-round.

Directions: From Ventura, take Highway 33 north to North Creek Road. Turn right and drive 4.5 miles to the park at 11969 North Creek Road.

Contact: Camp Comfort Park, 805/654-3951, www.portal.countyofventura.org.

60 DENNISON CAMPGROUND

Scenic rating: 8

in Ojai

Map grid C2

Dennison Campground is located in the foothills of Ojai. This is a nice, calm place to relax, with shade trees and an outstanding view of the Ojai Valley. As a county park, it is often overlooked by out-of-towners. Lake Casitas, known for huge but hard-to-catch bass, is located to the west.

Campsite, facilities: There are 46 sites for tents or RVs up to 25 feet (no hookups). Picnic tables and fire pits are provided. Drinking water, restrooms with flush toilets and coin showers, horseshoe pits, a playground, and a camp host are available.

Reservations, fees: Reservations are accepted ($10 reservation fee, $20 for groups). Sites are $20 per night. Open year-round.

Directions: From Ventura, drive north on Highway 33 for 13 miles to E. Ojai Ave. Continue on E. Ojai Ave. for 3.5 miles to a slight right on Ojai Santa Paula Rd (Highway 150). Continue 1.5 miles to Dennison Park.

Contact: Ventura County Parks Department, 805/654-3951, http://portal.countyofventura.org.

61 FAR WEST RESORT

Scenic rating: 7

on Santa Paula Creek east of Ventura

Map grid C2

Far West Resort is set near little Santa Paula Creek in the foothill country adjacent to Steckel County Park. For those who want a well-developed park with a lot of amenities, the shoe fits. Note that at one time the two campgrounds, Far West Resort and Steckel County Park, were linked. No more, and for good reason. Far West Resort is a tight ship where the gates close at 10 P.M. and quiet time assures campers of a good night's sleep. It is a good place to bring a family. Steckel County Park, on the other hand, has a campground with so many problems that I removed it from the book. Steckel is a beautiful place gone bad, crime-ridden and scary for most visitors, with partying, fights, and loud noise. So what do you do? Go next door to Far West where the inmates aren't running the asylum, and the days are fun and nights are peaceful.

RV sites, facilities: There are 72 sites with full or partial hookups (20, 30, and 50 amps) for RVs up to 42 feet, and a tent area for up to 400 people. Picnic tables and fire rings are provided.

Restrooms with flush toilets and showers, drinking water, coin laundry, Wi-Fi for RVs, dump station, clubhouse, petting zoo, video room, RV storage, and horseshoes are available. Supplies are nearby. Leashed pets are permitted.

Reservations, fees: Reservations are accepted for RV sites and required for the tent area. RV sites are $31.75 per night with partial hookups, $36 per night with full hookups, $3 per night for each additional vehicle, $1 per pet per night, $3 per person per night for group sites. Tent sites are $18 per night. Group rates are $25 per RV for six RVs. Weekly and monthly rates available. Some credit cards accepted. Open year-round for RVs; tent sites closed November through February.

Directions: From Ventura, drive east on Highway 126 for 14 miles to Highway 150. Turn northwest on Highway 150 and drive five miles to the resort entrance on the right.

Contact: Far West Resort, 805/933-3200.

62 RIVER VIEW CAMPGROUND

Scenic rating: 7

in Steckel Park

Map grid C2

Santa Paula Creek flows through Steckel Park, a pretty county park that has put some work into their campground. It offers enough shade trees so that you don't feel jammed in, an aviary, fishing, and hiking. To the near north is the Sespe Wilderness, fronted by Santa Paula Ridge and the Topatopa Mountains. This area is also a refuge for the California condor.

RV sites, facilities: There are 50 sites for tents and RVs; some sites have full 20-, 30-, and 50-amp hookups. Picnic tables and fire pits are provided. Drinking water, restrooms with flush toilets and coin showers, horseshoe pits, a playground, a softball field, and a camp host are available.

Reservations, fees: Reservations are accepted ($10 individual, $20 group reservation fee). Sites are $20–36 per night. Open year-round.

Directions: From Ventura, drive east on Highway 126 for 14 miles to Highway 150. Turn left (northwest) on Highway 150 and drive five miles to the campground entrance on right.

Contact: Ventura County Parks Department, 805/654-3951, http://portal.countyofventura.org.

63 HOBSON COUNTY PARK

Scenic rating: 6

north of Ventura

Map grid C2

This county park is at the end of Rincon Parkway, kind of like a crowded cul-de-sac, with easy access to the beach and many side-trip possibilities. There is a great reef here for exploring at low tides. Emma Wood State Beach, San Buenaventura State Beach, and McGrath State Beach are all within 11 miles of the park.

RV sites, facilities: There are 31 sites for tents or RVs up to 34 feet; some sites have full hookups, including cable TV. Picnic tables and fire pits are provided. Restrooms with flush toilets and coin showers, drinking water, and snack bar are available. Leashed pets are permitted, but not on the beach.

Reservations, fees: Reservations are accepted November through March ($10 reservation fee, $20 for groups). Sites are $30–45 per night, $1 per pet per night. Open year-round.

Directions: From Ventura, drive northwest on U.S. 101 for three miles to the State Beaches exit. Take that exit and turn north on West Pacific Highway and drive five miles to the campground on the left.

Contact: Ventura County Parks Department, 805/654-3951, www.portal.countyofventura.org.

64 FARIA COUNTY PARK

Scenic rating: 7

north of Ventura

Map grid C2

This county park provides a possible base of operations for beach adventures, including surf fishing. It is set along the ocean, with Emma

Wood State Beach, San Buenaventura State Beach, and McGrath State Beach all within 10 miles of the park.

RV sites, facilities: There are 42 sites for tents or RVs up to 34 feet; some sites have full hookups (30 amps), including cable TV. Picnic tables and fire pits are provided. Restrooms with flush toilets and coin showers, drinking water, playground, and snack bar are available. Leashed pets are permitted.

Reservations, fees: Reservations are not accepted. Sites are $30–45 per night, $1 per pet per night. Open year-round.

Directions: From Ventura, drive north on U.S. 101 for three miles to the State Beaches exit. Take that exit and turn north on West Pacific Highway and drive four miles to the campground.

Contact: Ventura County Parks Department, 805/654-3951, www.portal.countyofventura.org.

65 RINCON PARKWAY

Scenic rating: 5

north of Ventura

Map grid C2

This is basically an RV park near the ocean, where the sites are created by parking end-to-end along old Highway 1. It is not quiet. Passing trains across the highway vie for noise honors with the surf. Emma Wood State Beach, San Buenaventura State Beach, and McGrath State Beach are all within 10 miles. Two activities you can do here are surf fish and watch great sunsets.

RV sites, facilities: There are 127 sites for RVs up to 40 feet (no hookups). No tents. Supplies are available nearby. Leashed pets are allowed, but not on the beach.

Reservations, fees: Reservations are not accepted. Sites are $25 per night per vehicle. Open year-round.

Directions: From Ventura, drive northwest on U.S. 101 for three miles to the State Beaches exit. Take that exit and turn north on West Pacific Highway and drive 4.5 miles to the campground on the left.

CALIFORNIA

Contact: Ventura County Parks Department, 805/654-3951, www.portal.countyofventura. org.

66 EMMA WOOD STATE BEACH

Scenic rating: 8

north of Ventura

Map grid C2

This is more of a parking lot than a campground with individual sites. And oh, what a place to camp: It is set along the ocean, a pretty spot with tidepools full of all kinds of little marine critters waiting to be discovered. It is also just a short drive from the town of Ventura and the Mission San Buenaventura. One downer, a big one for many: noise from passing trains. Another downer: no toilets at night, so you must have a self-contained vehicle. The gate closes at 10 p.m. and reopens at 6 a.m.

RV sites, facilities: There are 90 sites for RVs up to 40 feet (no hookups). No tents. Chemical toilets are available for day use only. No drinking water is available. Supplies and a coin laundry are three miles away. Leashed pets are permitted, but not on the beach.

Reservations, fees: Reservations are required mid-May through Labor Day weekend at 800/444-7275 or www.reserveamerica.com ($8 reservation fee). Sites are $20–30 per night, $10 per night for each additional vehicle. Open year-round, weather and tides permitting.

Note: At time of publication, the state park service planned to close 30 sites on the North Beach camping loop (reopening weekends and holidays, as needed).

Directions: From Ventura drive north on U.S. 101 for three miles to the State Beaches exit. Take that exit, drive under the freeway, and continue less than a mile to the park entrance on the left.

Contact: Emma Wood State Beach, Channel Coast District, 805/968-1033 or 805/585-1850, www.parks.ca.gov.

67 EMMA WOOD STATE BEACH: VENTURA RIVER GROUP CAMP

Scenic rating: 1

at Emma Wood State Beach near Ventura

Map grid C2

This is an extremely noisy area and the campsites are also downright ugly. It is set near the freeway and railroad tracks, and you get a lot of noise from both. It's not popular either. What you have here is mainly a dry riverbed. It is saved somewhat by a freshwater marsh at the southwest end of the beach that attracts red-tailed hawks, songbirds, and raccoons.

RV sites, facilities: There are four group tent sites for up to 30 people each, one group site for RVs of any length that can accommodate up to 50 people, and five hike-in/bike-in sites. Picnic tables and fire rings are provided. Drinking water, chemical toilets, and cold showers are available. Leashed pets are permitted in the campground, but not on the beach. Supplies are within one mile.

Reservations, fees: Reservations are required for the group sites at 800/444-PARK (800/444-7275) or www.reserveamerica.com ($8 reservation fee). The fee is $66–186 per night, $5 per person per night for hike-in/bike-in sites. Open year-round.

Directions: On U.S. 101 in Ventura, take the Main Street exit and turn west. Drive one mile on Main Street to the campground on the left.

Contact: Emma Wood State Beach, Channel Coast District, 805/968-1033 or 805/585-1850, www.parks.ca.gov.

68 FOSTER PARK

Scenic rating: 7

in Ventura

Map grid C2

The Ventura River meanders through this park, which offers two campgrounds: Red Mountain and Residence. The park has shade trees, a small amphitheater, an equestrian area, and is close to the trailhead for the Ojai Valley trail. Fishing and hiking round out the recreation options.

RV sites, facilities: There are 21 sites for tents and RVs at Red Mountain and 27 sites for tents and RVs at Residence; some sites have 20, 30, and 50-amp hookups. Picnic tables and fire pits are provided, and there is an area for group barbecues. Drinking water, restrooms with flush toilets, a playground, horseshoe pits, and a camp host are available.

Reservations, fees: Reservations are accepted ($10 individual, $20 group reservation fee). Sites are $20–34 per night. Open year-round.

Directions: From Ventura, drive north on Highway 33 for 4.5 miles to the N. Ventura Ave exit (immediately before the freeway ends). Turn right on N. Ventura and then right again almost immediately onto Casitas Vista. The park entrance is at 438 Casitas Vista Road.

Contact: Ventura County Parks Department, 805/654-3951, http://portal.countyofventura.org.

69 McGRATH STATE BEACH

🚶 🚴 🏊 🛶 🎣 🐕 ♿ 🚐 ⛺

Scenic rating: 9

south of Ventura
Map grid C2

This is a pretty spot just south of Ventura Harbor. Campsites are about 400 yards from the beach. This park features two miles of beach frontage, as well as lush riverbanks and sand dunes along the ocean shore. That gives rise to some of the best bird-watching in California. The north tip of the park borders the Santa Clara River Estuary Natural Preserve, where the McGrath State Beach Nature Trail provides an easy walk (wheelchair-accessible) along the Santa Clara River as it feeds into the estuary and then into the ocean. Rangers caution all considering swimming here to beware of strong currents and rip tides; they can be deadly. Note that the park and campground can close on short notice during winter because of river floodings; check status before planning a trip here. Ventura Harbor and the Channel Islands National Park Visitor Center are nearby side trips.

RV sites, facilities: There are 174 sites for tents or RVs up to 30 feet (no hookups); 29 of the sites can be used as group sites. There is also a hike-in/bike-in site. Picnic tables and fire grills are provided. Restrooms with flush toilets and coin showers, drinking water, and a dump station are available. A lifeguard service is provided in summer. Supplies and a coin laundry are nearby. Some facilities are wheelchair-accessible. Leashed pets are permitted in campsites only.

Reservations, fees: Reservations are accepted for individual sites at 800/444-PARK (800/444-7275) or www.reserveamerica.com ($8 reservation fee). Sites are $35 per night, $10 per night for each additional vehicle, $5 per person per night for hike-in/bike-in site. For group prices and reservations, phone 805/648-3918. Open year-round, weather and river conditions permitting.

Directions: Drive on U.S. 101 to south of Ventura and the Seaward exit. Take that exit and drive to the stoplight and Harbor Boulevard. Turn west on Harbor Boulevard and drive four miles to the park (signed).

Contact: McGrath State Beach or Emma Wood State Beach, Channel Coast District, 805/968-1033 or 805/585-1850, www.parks.ca.gov.

70 POINT MUGU STATE PARK: THORNHILL BROOME AND LA JOLLA CAMPS

🚶 🏊 🎣 🎿 🐕 ♿ 🚐 ⛺

Scenic rating: 7

in Point Mugu State Park
Map grid C2

Point Mugu State Park is known for its rocky bluffs, sandy beaches, rugged hills, and uplands. There are two major river canyons and wide grassy valleys sprinkled with sycamores, oaks, and a few native walnut trees. Of the campgrounds at Point Mugu, Thornhill Broome campground is more attractive than Sycamore Canyon (see listing in this chapter) for many visitors because it is on the ocean side of the highway (Big Sycamore is on the north side of the highway). It is a 2.5-mile walk to reach La Jolla Valley. While the beachfront is pretty and you can always just lie there in the sun and pretend you're a beached whale, the park's expanse on the east side of the highway in the Santa Monica Mountains provides more recreation. That includes two stellar hikes, the 9.5-mile Big Sycamore Canyon Loop and the seven-mile La Jolla Valley Loop. In all, the park covers 14,980 acres, far more than the obvious strip of beachfront. The park has more than 70 miles of hiking trails and five miles of ocean shoreline. Swimming, body surfing, and surf fishing are available on the beach.

RV sites, facilities: There are 65 primitive sites at Thornhill Broome for tents or RVs up to 31 feet (no hookups), one group site at La Jolla Canyon Group Walk-In for up to 50 people, and 10 environmental walk-in sites and one hike-in group camp for up to 25 people at La Jolla Valley and Group Walk-In. Picnic tables and fire rings are provided at some sites; no open fires are allowed at the environmental walk-in sites. Drinking water and chemical toilets are available at Thornhill Broome. Drinking water, flush toilets, and showers are available at La Jolla Canyon. La Jolla Valley has chemical toilets but no water and no fires; camp stoves are allowed. Supplies can be obtained nearby. No park entry after 10 P.M. Note that nearby Big Sycamore has a dump station and nature center. Some facilities are wheelchair-accessible. Leashed pets are permitted, but not at the La Jolla Valley campground or on trails.

Reservations, fees: Except for environmental sites, reservations are accepted at 800/444-PARK (800/444-7275) or www.reserveamerica.com ($8 reservation fee). Sites are $25 per night at Thornhill Broome, $8 per night for each additional vehicle, $3 per person per night for environmental sites and group site at La Jolla Valley, $165 per night for group site at La Jolla Canyon. Open year-round, but subject to closure during inclement weather and fire season.

Directions: From Oxnard, drive 15 miles south on Highway 1 to the camp entrance: on the right for Thornhill Broome, on the left for La Jolla Valley and La Jolla Canyon Group.

Contact: California State Parks, Angeles District, 818/880-0363, www.parks.ca.gov.

71 POINT MUGU STATE PARK: SYCAMORE CANYON

Scenic rating: 6

in Point Mugu State Park

Map grid C2

While this camp is across the highway from the ocean, it is also part of Point Mugu State Park, which covers 14,980 acres. That gives you plenty of options. One of the best is taking the Big Sycamore Canyon Loop, a long hiking route with great views that starts right at the camp. In all, it's a 9.5-mile loop that climbs to a ridge top and offers beautiful views of nearby canyons and long-distance vistas of the coast. Note: The front gate closes at 10 P.M. and re-opens at 7 A.M.

RV sites, facilities: There are 55 sites for tents or RVs up to 31 feet (no hookups), and one hike-in/bike-in site. Picnic tables and fire grills are provided. Restrooms with flush toilets and coin showers, drinking water, and a dump station are available. A weekend nature center is within walking distance. Supplies can be obtained nearby. Some facilities are wheelchair-accessible. Leashed pets are permitted at campsites and on the beach, but not on trails.

Reservations, fees: Reservations are accepted at 800/444-PARK (800/444-7275) or www.reserveamerica.com ($8 reservation fee). Sites are $35 per night, $12 per night for each additional vehicle, $3 per person per night for hike-in/bike-in site. Open year-round.

Directions: From Oxnard, drive south on Highway 1 for 16 miles to the camp on the left.

Contact: California State Parks, Angeles District, 818/880-0363, www.parks.ca.gov.

LOS ANGELES AND VICINITY

(BEST RV PARKS AND CAMPGROUNDS

(Family Destinations
Newport Dunes Waterfront Resort, page 1121.

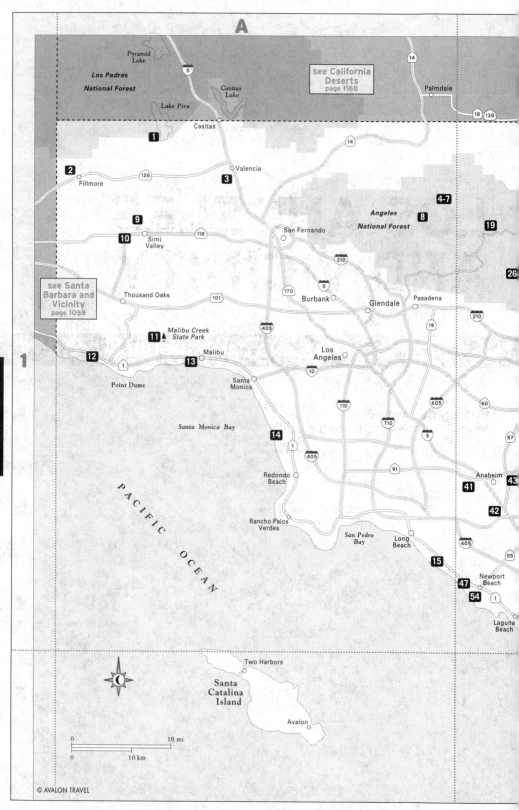

A

Pyramid Lake

Los Padres National Forest

5

Casitas Lake

see California Deserts page 1168

14

Palmdale

18 138

Lake Piru

Casitas

1

126

Valencia

3

14

2

Fillmore

Angeles National Forest

4-7

8

19

9

10

Simi Valley

118

San Fernando

210

26

see Santa Barbara and Vicinity page 1058

Thousand Oaks

101

170

5

Burbank

Glendale

Pasadena

210

19

Malibu Creek State Park

11

405

Los Angeles

12

1

Malibu

13

Santa Monica

10

110

605

60

Point Dume

Santa Monica Bay

14

1

710

5

57

405

91

Anaheim

43

Redondo Beach

41

42

55

Rancho Palos Verdes

San Pedro Bay

Long Beach

405

15

Newport Beach

47

PACIFIC OCEAN

54

1

Laguna Beach

Two Harbors

Santa Catalina Island

Avalon

0   10 mi

0   10 km

© AVALON TRAVEL

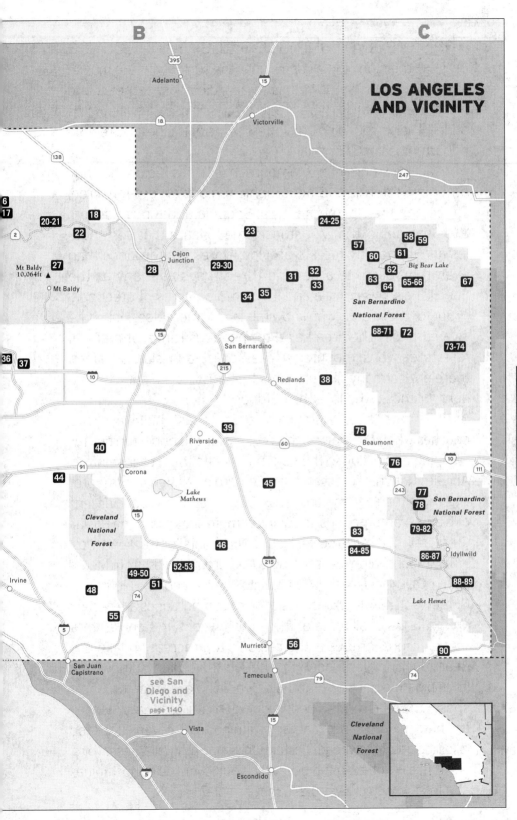

LOS ANGELES AND VICINITY

CALIFORNIA

The stereotypical image of the region you see on TV – the blonde in a convertible, the surfer with the movie-star jawline – is so flawed as to be ridiculous, pathetic, and laughable. And while there are some classic beaches, lifeguards and all, the surrounding area offers some of the best recreation opportunities in California.

In fact, there are more campgrounds in this region than any other in California's 16 geographic regions except for three: Tahoe and the Northern Sierra, Sequoia and Kings Canyon, and Shasta and Trinity. It stuns some to learn that Los Angeles and its nearby forests provide more campgrounds than even the Yosemite area, and three times as many as the San Francisco Bay Area and its 1.2 million acres of greenbelt.

But for those of us who know this landscape, it does not come as a surprise. The area has a tremendous range of national forests, canyons, mountains, lakes, coast, and islands. In fact, there are so many hidden gems that it is like a giant treasure hunt for those who love the outdoors.

While most people first think of the coast, highways, and beaches when envisioning this region, it is the opportunities for camping and hiking in the national forests that surprise most. Angeles National Forest and San Bernardino National Forest provide more than one million acres, 1,000 miles of trails, and dozens of hidden campgrounds, including remote sites along the Pacific Crest Trail, that make perfect launching points for weekend trips.

The mountaintop views are incredible, probably best from Mount Baldy (10,064 feet), Mount San Jacinto (10,834 feet), and Mount San Gorgonio (11,490 feet). A series of great campgrounds are nestled on the flanks of all three of these destinations. It is only a start.

Even more famous is the region's top recreation lake, Big Bear, for fishing and boating. Though the region is known for its population density – and Big Bear is no exception on weekends – the relatively few people on weekdays, especially Monday to Thursday mornings, can be stunning to discover. Other top lakes include Arrowhead, Castaic, and several smaller reservoirs.

Yet this is not even the best of it. Look over the opportunities and take your pick. People? What people?

❶ KENNEY GROVE PARK AND GROUP CAMPGROUND

Scenic rating: 4

near Fillmore

Map grid A1

A lot of folks miss this spot, a park tucked away among orchards, coast live oaks, and eucalyptus groves, with several group campgrounds. This is a privately leased facility on Ventura County property. It's just far enough off the highway to allow for some privacy.

RV sites, facilities: This is a group camp with 33 sites with partial hookups (30 amps) for RVs up to 40 feet and 18 sites for tents. No pull-through sites. Picnic tables and fire pits are provided. Drinking water, restrooms with flush toilets and showers, amphitheater, softball field, horseshoes, and playground are available. Supplies and a coin laundry are nearby. Leashed pets are permitted.

Reservations, fees: Reservations are required and a minimum of five sites must be reserved. Sites are $24 per night for tents, $20 per night for RVs, $1 per pet per night. Open year-round.

Directions: From Ventura, drive east on Highway 126 for 22 miles to Old Telegraph Road (before the town of Fillmore). Turn left on Old Telegraph Road and drive 0.6 mile to 7th Street. Turn left (northwest) and drive 0.3 mile to North Oak Avenue. Turn right and drive one-half mile to the park on the left.

Contact: Kenney Grove, tel./fax 805/524-0750.

❷ LAKE PIRU RECREATION AREA

Scenic rating: 7

on Lake Piru

Map grid A1

Things can get crazy at Lake Piru, but it's usually a happy crazy, not an insane crazy. Lake Piru (1,055 feet elevation) is shaped like a teardrop and covers 1,200 acres when full. This is a lake set up for waterskiing, with lots of fast boats. All others be forewarned: The rules prohibit boats under 12 feet or over 26 feet, as well as personal watercraft. Canoes and kayaks over eight feet are permitted in a special-use area. Bass and trout fishing can be quite good in the spring before the water-skiers take over. From Memorial Day weekend through Labor Day weekend, there is a designated swimming area, safe from the boats. The tent sites here consist of roughly 40-by-40-foot areas amid trees.

RV sites, facilities: There are 235 sites with partial hookups (30 and 50 amps) for tents or RVs up to 40 feet, seven sites with full hookups (30 and 50 amps) for RVs, and three group camps with no hookups for tents or RVs that can accommodate 4–12 vehicles. Fire pits and picnic tables are provided. Restrooms with flush toilets and showers, drinking water, dump station, convenience store, coin laundry, picnic area, boat storage, propane, fish-cleaning station, seasonal snack bar, ice, full-service marina, boat ramp, temporary mooring, boat rentals, and bait and tackle are available. Some facilities are wheelchair-accessible. Leashed pets are permitted, but not in the lake.

Reservations, fees: Reservations are accepted for individual sites and required for group sites at 805/521-1572 ($7 reservation fee for individual sites; $20 reservation fee and $50 key charge for group sites). Sites are $19–42 per night, $2 per pet per night. Group sites are $96 minimum per night for up to four vehicles (with a two-night minimum), and $24 per night for each additional vehicle. Holiday rates are higher. Credit cards accepted. Open year-round.

Directions: From Ventura, drive east on Highway 126 for about 30 miles to the Lake Piru Recreation Area/Piru Canyon Road exit. Take that exit and drive northeast on Piru Canyon Road for about six miles to the campground at the end of the road.

Contact: Lake Piru Recreation Area, 805/521-1500; Lake Piru Marina, 805/521-1231, www.visitcatalinaisland.org.

3 VALENCIA TRAVEL VILLAGE

Scenic rating: 5

in Valencia

Map grid A1

This huge RV park is in the scenic San Fernando foothills, just five minutes from Six Flags Magic Mountain. Lake Piru and Lake Castaic are only 15 minutes away. The camp was built on a 65-acre horse ranch. Note: There are about 300 permanent residents here, so temporary camping space may be limited.

RV sites, facilities: There are 379 sites, including about 300 with permanent residents, with full or partial hookups (30 and 50 amps) for RVs; most are pull-through. No tents. Picnic tables and fire pits (some sites) are provided. A market, two heated swimming pools, spa, lounge, video and games arcade, playground, shuffleboard, horseshoes, volleyball courts, coin laundry, Wi-Fi, modem access, propane, and dump station are available. Some facilities are wheelchair-accessible. Leashed pets are permitted.

Reservations, fees: Reservations are recommended at 888/LUV-TORV (888/588-8678). Sites are $51 per night, $2 per person per night for more than two people. Weekly and monthly rates are available. Some credit cards accepted. Open year-round.

Directions: Drive on I-5 to Santa Clarita and Highway 126 west/Henry Mayo Road. Take that exit and drive west on Highway 126 for one mile to the camp on the left.

Contact: Valencia Travel Village, 661/257-3333.

4 HORSE FLATS

Scenic rating: 7

near the San Gabriel Wilderness in Angeles National Forest

Map grid A1

This is one of several options in the immediate area: Chilao, Bandido Group Camp, and Coulter Group Camp are the other three. Horse Flats is set at 5,700 feet elevation along a national recreation trail (Silver Moccasin Trail) and is about two miles by trail to the Chilao Visitor Center. Two trails into the San Gabriel Wilderness are nearby.

RV sites, facilities: There are 25 sites for tents or RVs up to 22 feet (no hookups). Picnic tables and fire pits are provided. Vault toilets, hitching rails, and horse corrals are available. No drinking water is available. Some facilities are wheelchair-accessible. Leashed pets are permitted.

Reservations, fees: Reservations are not accepted. Sites are $12 per night. Open April through mid-November, weather permitting.

Directions: From Pasadena, drive north on I-210 for four miles to the exit for Highway 2/Angeles Crest Highway. Take that exit and drive northeast on Highway 2 for 30 miles to Santa Clara Divide Road/Forest Road 3N17 at Three Points (signed). Turn left and drive three miles to Horse Flats Road. Turn left and drive one mile to the campground.

Contact: Angeles National Forest, Los Angeles River Ranger District, 818/899-1900, fax 818/896-6727; Chilao Visitor Center (weekends only), 626/796-5541.

5 BANDIDO GROUP CAMP

Scenic rating: 6

near the Pacific Crest Trail in Angeles National Forest

Map grid A1

This is a base camp for groups preparing to hike into the surrounding wilderness. A trail out of the camp heads east and intersects with the Pacific Crest Trail a little over two miles away at Three Points, a significant PCT junction. Before heading out visitors must check in and register with the rangers at the Los Angeles River Ranger District office, two miles west of Three Points on Highway 2. The elevation is 5,840 feet.

RV sites, facilities: There is one group camp for tents or RVs up to 40 feet (no hookups) that accommodates up to 120 people. Picnic tables and fire rings are provided. There is no drinking water. Vault toilets, corrals, and water troughs are available. Leashed pets are permitted.

Reservations, fees: Reservations are required at 877/444-6777 or www.recreation.gov ($10 reservation fee). The camp is $100 per night with a 60-person maximum, $200 per night with 120-person maximum. Open April through mid-November, weather permitting.

Directions: From Pasadena, drive north on I-210 for four miles to the exit for Highway 2/Angeles Crest Highway. Take that exit and drive northeast on Highway 2 for 30 miles to Santa Clara Divide Road/Forest Road 3N17 at Three Points (signed). Turn left and drive two miles to the campground on the left.

Contact: Angeles National Forest, Los Angeles River Ranger District, 818/899-1900, fax 818/896-6727; Chilao Visitor Center (weekends only), 626/796-5541.

6 CHILAO CAMPGROUND

🥾 🐕 ♿ 🚐 ⛺

Scenic rating: 6

near the San Gabriel Wilderness in
Angeles National Forest

Map grid A1

This popular trailhead camp gets a lot of use. And it's easy to see why, with the Chilao Visitor Center nearby (have any questions—here's where you ask them) and a national recreation trail running right by the camp. Access to the Pacific Crest Trail is three miles north at Three Points (five miles if hiking the Silver Moccasin Trail), and parking is available there. An Adventure Pass is required to park at all trailheads. The elevation is 5,300 feet. Note: There is frequent bear activity, so use precautions.

RV sites, facilities: There are 84 sites for tents or RVs up to 28 feet (no hookups), with one site for RVs up to 36 feet. Picnic tables and fire rings are provided. Drinking water and vault toilets are available. Some facilities are wheelchair-accessible. Leashed pets are permitted.

Reservations, fees: Reservations are not accepted. Sites are $12 per night. Open April through mid-November, weather permitting.

Directions: From Pasadena, drive north on I-210 for four miles to the exit for Highway 2/Angeles Crest Highway. Take that exit and drive northeast on Highway 2 for 27 miles to the campground entrance road (signed) on the left.

Contact: Angeles National Forest, Los Angeles River Ranger District, 818/899-1900, fax 818/896-6727; Chilao Visitor Center (weekends only), 626/796-5541.

7 COULTER GROUP CAMP

🥾 🐕 ♿ 🚐 ⛺

Scenic rating: 6

near the San Gabriel Wilderness in
Angeles National Forest

Map grid A1

This is a popular group camp set near both a visitors center and a trailhead for the Pacific Crest Trail. Access to the PCT is 3.5 miles north at Three Points (5.5 miles if hiking the Silver Moccasin Trail), and parking is available. An Adventure Pass is required to park at the trailheads. The elevation is 5,300 feet. It is close to Chilao Campground.

RV sites, facilities: There is one group site for up to 50 people (no hookups). Four picnic tables, a barbecue pit, fire ring, vault toilet, and drinking water are available. Some facilities are wheelchair-accessible. Leashed pets are permitted.

Reservations, fees: Reservations are required at 877/444-6777 or www.recreation.gov ($10 reservation fee). The camp is $100 per night. Open April through mid-November, weather permitting.

Directions: From Pasadena, drive north on I-210 for four miles to the exit for Highway 2/Angeles Crest Highway. Take that exit and drive northeast on Highway 2 for 27 miles to the campground entrance road on the left (enter through the Litle Pines Loop at Chilao Campground).

Contact: Angeles National Forest, Los

Angeles River Ranger District, 818/899-1900, fax 818/896-6727.

8 MONTE CRISTO

Scenic rating: 7

on Mill Creek in Angeles National Forest

Map grid A1

This is a Forest Service camp on Mill Creek at 3,600 feet elevation, just west of Iron Mountain. The camp is situated under sycamore trees, which provide great color in the fall. In most years Mill Creek flows six months out of the year.

RV sites, facilities: There are 19 sites for tents or RVs up to 30 feet (no hookups). Picnic tables and fire grills are provided. Vault toilets are available. There is no drinking water. Some facilities are wheelchair-accessible. Leashed pets are permitted.

Reservations, fees: Reservations are not accepted. Sites are $8 per night. Open year-round.

Directions: From Pasadena, drive north on I-210 for four miles to the exit for Highway 2/Angeles Crest Highway. Take that exit and drive northeast on Highway 2 for nine miles to Angeles Forest Highway/County Road N3. Turn left on Angeles Forest Highway and drive about ten miles to the campground on the right.

Contact: Angeles National Forest, Los Angeles River Ranger District, 818/899-1900, fax 818/896-6727.

9 TAPO CANYON COUNTY PARK

Scenic rating: 7

off Tapo Canyon Road in Simi Valley

Map grid A1

Camping at Tapo Canyon reopened in 2008 after being closed for several years. The campground features a large undeveloped area for tents, and slots with hookups for RVs. Highlights are a grassy picnic area and an arena for horseback riding; a camp host is a plus. This county park has quickly become a favorite site for youth groups.

RV sites, facilities: There are 16 sites with hookups (20-, 30-, and 50-amps) for RVs of any length and a large undeveloped tent area for groups. Picnic tables and fire rings are provided. Drinking water, restrooms with flush toilets, and coin showers are available. A dump station, equestrian arena, horse watering station, and hitching posts are also available. A camp host is on site.

Reservations, fees: Reservations are accepted for the individual sites and required for the group sites at 805/654-3951. Individual sites are $37 per night. Call for group rates.

Directions: From Highway 101 north of Thousand Oaks, turn north on Highway 23 and drive eight miles to Highway 118. Merge onto Highway 118 East and drive 4.1 miles to Tapo Canyon Road, Exit 27. Take that exit and turn left onto Tapo Canyon Road. Drive three miles to the campground.

Contact: Tapo Canyon Park, Ventura, 805/654-3951, http//portal.countyofventura.org.

10 OAK PARK

Scenic rating: 3

in Simi Valley near Moorpark

Map grid A1

One of the frustrations of trying to find a camp for the night is that so many state and national park campgrounds are full from reservations, especially at the state beaches. The county parks often provide a safety valve, and Oak Park certainly applies. But not always, and that's the catch. This is an oft-overlooked county park set in the foothill country of Simi Valley. The park has many trails offering good hiking possibilities. The camp is somewhat secluded, more so than many expect. The catch? Sometimes the entire campground is rented to a single group. Note: Gates close at dusk and reopen at 8 A.M.

RV sites, facilities: There are 16 sites with partial hookups (20 and 30 amps) for RVs, a group area for up to 13 RVs, and a large tent area with no hookups that can accommodate up to 140 people. Picnic tables and fire pits are provided.

Restrooms with flush toilets, drinking water, group facilities, clubhouse, and dump station are available. Horseshoe pits, a playground, and basketball and volleyball courts are available nearby. Supplies and a coin laundry are within two miles. Leashed pets are permitted.

Reservations, fees: Reservations are accepted. Sites are $10 per night for tents, $30 per night for RVs, $1 per pet per night, off-season discounts available. Open year-round, except Christmas Day.

Directions: From Ventura, drive south on U.S. 101 to Highway 23. Turn north on Highway 23 (which becomes Highway 123 East) and drive about three miles to the Collins Street exit. Continue straight through the intersection (it becomes Old Los Angeles Avenue) and drive 1.5 miles to the park entrance on the left.

Contact: Oak Park, 805/654-3951, www.portal. countyofventura.org.

11 MALIBU CREEK STATE PARK

Scenic rating: 9

near Malibu

Map grid A1

If you plan on staying here, be sure to get your reservation in early. This 6,600-acre state park is just a few miles out of Malibu between Highway 1 and U.S. 101, two major thoroughfares for vacationers. Despite its popularity, the park manages to retain a natural setting, with miles of trails for hiking, biking, and horseback riding, and inspiring scenic views. The park offers 15 miles of streamside trail through oak and sycamore woodlands and also some chaparral-covered slopes. It is an ideal spot for a break on a coastal road trip. This park was once used as a setting for the filming of some movies and TV shows, including Planet of the Apes and M*A*S*H.

RV sites, facilities: There are 62 sites for tents or RVs up to 30 feet (no hookups) and a group tent site for up to 60 people. Picnic tables are provided. No wood fires are permitted in the summer, but propane and charcoal barbecues

are allowed. Drinking water and restrooms with flush toilets and coin showers are available. Some facilities are wheelchair-accessible. Leashed pets are permitted, but only in the campground area.

Reservations, fees: Reservations are accepted at 800/444-PARK (800/444-7275) or www. reserveamerica.com ($8 reservation fee). Sites are $35 per night, $12 per night for each additional vehicle, $200 per night for group site. Open year-round.

Directions: From U.S. 101: Drive on U.S. 101 to the exit for Las Virgenes Canyon Road (on the western border of Calabasas). Take that exit south and drive on Las Virgenes Canyon Road/ County Road N1 for four miles to the park entrance on the right.

From Highway 1: Drive on Highway 1 to Malibu and Malibu Canyon Road. Turn north on Malibu Canyon Road and drive north for 5.5 miles (the road becomes Las Virgenes Canyon Road/County Road N1) to the park entrance on the left.

Contact: Malibu Creek State Park, 818/880-0367, fax 818/706-3869, www.parks.ca.gov.

12 LEO CARRILLO STATE PARK

Scenic rating: 8

north of Malibu

Map grid A1

The camping area at this state park is set in a canyon, and reservations are essential during the summer and on weekends the remainder of the year. Large sycamore trees shade the campsites. The Nicholas Flat Trail provides an excellent hike to the Willow Creek Overlook for beautiful views of the beach. In addition, a pedestrian tunnel provides access to a wonderful coastal spot with sea caves, tunnels, tidepools, and patches of beach. This park features 1.5 miles of beach for swimming, surfing, and surf fishing. In the summer, lifeguards are posted at the beach. Many will remember a beach camp that was once popular here. Well, that sucker is gone, wiped out by a storm.

RV sites, facilities: There are 127 sites for tents or RVs up to 31 feet (no hookups), one hike-in/bike-in area for up to 24 people, and one group tent site for up to 50 people. Picnic tables and fire rings are provided. Restrooms with flush toilets and coin showers, drinking water, a dump station, a seasonal visitors center, Wi-Fi, summer programs, and a summer convenience store are available. Some facilities are wheelchair-accessible. Leashed pets are permitted. Front gates close at 10 P.M. and reopen at 7 A.M.

Reservations, fees: Reservations are recommended at 800/444-PARK (800/444-7275) or www.reserveamerica.com ($8 reservation fee). Sites are $35 per night, $12 per night for each additional vehicle, $3 per person per night for hike-in/bike-in site, $165 per night for group tent site. Open year-round.

Directions: From Santa Monica, drive north on Highway 1 for 28 miles to the park entrance (signed) on the right.

From Oxnard, drive south on Highway 1 for 20 miles to the park entrance (signed) on the left.

Contact: California State Parks, Angeles District, 818/880-0350 or fax 818/880-6165, www.parks.ca.gov.

13 MALIBU BEACH RV PARK

Scenic rating: 7

in Malibu

Map grid A1

This is one of the few privately developed RV parks in the region that provides some sites for tent campers as well. It's one of the nicer spots in the area, set on a bluff overlooking the Pacific Ocean, near both Malibu Pier (for fishing) and Paradise Cove. Each RV site and many of the tent sites have views of either the ocean or adjacent mountains. Sites with ocean views are charged a small premium. Whale-watching is best in March and April, and then again in October and November. Dolphin-watching is popular year-round.

RV sites, facilities: There are 35 sites for tents (four-person maximum per site) and 140 sites with full or partial hookups (30 and 50 amps) for RVs; some sites are pull-through. Picnic tables and barbecue grills are provided. Restrooms with showers, spa, recreation room, playground, coin laundry, Wi-Fi, modem access, dog walk area, propane gas, ice, cable TV, dump station, and convenience store are available. Some facilities are wheelchair-accessible. Leashed pets are permitted, except in the tent area, and certain breeds are prohibited.

Reservations, fees: Reservations are recommended at 800/622-6052. Sites are $29–77 for RV sites, $25 per night for tent sites with ocean view, $20 for tent sites with no views, $10 per night for each additional vehicle, $5 per person per night for more than two people, $3 per pet per night. Credit cards accepted. Open year-round.

Directions: Drive on Pacific Coast Highway/Highway 1 to the Malibu area. The park is two miles north of the intersection of Highway 1 and Malibu Canyon Road on the east side of the road.

Contact: Malibu Beach RV Park, 310/456-6052, www.maliburv.com.

14 DOCKWEILER BEACH RV PARK

Scenic rating: 6

near Manhattan Beach

Map grid A1

This layover spot for coast cruisers is just a hop from the beach and the Pacific Ocean. There is access to a 26-mile-long coastal bike path.

RV sites, facilities: There are 117 sites with full hookups (20, 30, and 50 amps) for RVs up to 37 feet. No tents. Picnic tables and barbecue grills are provided. Restrooms with flush toilets and showers, dump station, and coin laundry are available. Some facilities are wheelchair-accessible. You can buy supplies nearby. Leashed pets are permitted, with a two-dog limit.

Reservations, fees: Reservations are accepted

at 310/322-4951 or 800/950-7275 ($7 reservation fee). Sites are $24–32 per night, $2 per pet per night. Open year-round, except in January. Some credit cards accepted.

Directions: From Santa Monica, take I-405 south to the 105/Imperial Highway. Take the 105 and continue as it becomes Imperial Highway. When road name changes to Imperial Highway, drive west for four miles to the park (signed) on the left.

Contact: Dockweiler Beach RV Park, Los Angeles County, 310/322-7036.

15 BOLSA CHICA STATE BEACH

Scenic rating: 7

near Huntington Beach

Map grid A1

This state beach extends three miles from Seal Beach to Huntington Beach City Pier. A bikeway connects it with Huntington State Beach, seven miles to the south. Across the road from Bolsa Chica is the 1,000-acre Bolsa Chica Ecological Preserve, managed by the Department of Fish and Game. The campground consists of basically a beachfront parking lot, but a popular one at that. A great little walk is available at the adjacent Bolsa Chica State Reserve, a 1.5-mile loop that provides an escape from the parking lot and entry into the 530-acre nature reserve, complete with egrets, pelicans, and many shorebirds. Lifeguard service is available during the summer. This camp has a seven-day maximum stay during the summer and a 14-day maximum stay during the winter. Surf fishing is popular here for perch, cabezon, small sharks, and croaker. There are also occasional runs of grunion, a small fish that spawns in hordes on the sandy beaches of Southern California.

RV sites, facilities: There are 56 sites with full hookups (30 and 50 amps) available in a parking lot configuration for RVs up to 48 feet. No tents. Fire rings are provided. Restrooms with flush toilets and coin showers, drinking water, Wi-Fi, dump station, picnic areas, bicycle trail, volleyball, basketball, and food service

(seasonal) are available. Some facilities are wheelchair-accessible, including a paved ramp for wheelchair access to the beach. Leashed pets are permitted at campsites.

Reservations, fees: Reservations are accepted at 800/444-PARK (800/444-7275) or www.reserveamerica.com ($8 reservation fee). Sites are $50–65 per night, $15 per night for each additional vehicle. Open year-round; gates close at 9 P.M. daily.

Directions: From Huntington Beach, drive 1.5 miles north on Highway 1 to the park entrance at 21601 Pacific Coast Highway.

Contact: Bolsa Chica State Beach, 714/846-3460, www.parks.ca.gov.

16 SYCAMORE FLATS

Scenic rating: 7

on Big Rock Creek in Angeles National Forest

Map grid B1

Sycamore Flats is a developed camp just inside the northern boundary of Angeles National Forest, set at 4,200 feet on the southwest flank of Pinyon Ridge. While there are no trails leading out from this camp, a trailhead is at South Fork, which is two miles to the south.

RV sites, facilities: There are 11 sites for tents or RVs up to 18 feet (no hookups). Picnic tables and fire grills are provided. Vault toilets are available. There is no drinking water. Garbage must be packed out. Leashed pets are permitted. There is no drinking water in dry years.

Reservations, fees: Reservations are not accepted. There is no fee for camping. An Adventure Pass ($30 annual fee or a $5 daily pass) is required. Open year-round, weather permitting.

Directions: From Palmdale (at the junction of Highway 14 and Highway 138), take Highway 138 southeast and drive about 10 miles to Pearblossom and Longview Road. Turn south (right) and drive a short distance to Avenue W/Valyermo Road. Turn left on Avenue W/Valyermo Road and drive about 20 miles into the national forest (past the ranger station) to

Big Rock Road. Turn right on Big Rock Road and drive about two miles to the campground entrance.

Contact: Angeles National Forest, Santa Clara/Mojave Rivers Ranger District, 661/296-9710, fax 661/295-5829.

17 SOUTH FORK

Scenic rating: 7

on Big Rock Creek in Angeles National Forest
Map grid B1

This is an excellent trailhead camp set at 4,500 feet elevation along South Fork Creek. One trail climbs 2.2 miles to the west to Devils Punchbowl County Park, topping out at Devils Chair (the trail includes a steep descent and climb). There are two other options: One is routed south along Big Rock Creek, and the other heads east on High Desert National Recreation Trail (also called Manzanita Trail).

RV sites, facilities: There are 21 sites for tents or RVs up to 16 feet (no hookups). Picnic tables and fire rings are provided. Vault toilets are available. No drinking water is available. Garbage must be packed out. Leashed pets are permitted.

Reservations, fees: Reservations are not accepted. An Adventure Pass ($30 annual fee or a $5 daily pass) is required. Open year-round, weather permitting.

Directions: From Palmdale (at the junction of Highway 14 and Highway 138), take Highway 138 southeast and drive about 10 miles to Pearblossom and Longview Road. Turn south (right) and drive a short distance to Avenue W/Valyermo Road. Turn left on Avenue W/Valyermo Road and drive about 20 miles into the national forest (past the ranger station) to Big Rock Road. Turn right on Big Rock Road and drive about two miles up the canyon (past the Sycamore Flat campground entrance) to the South Fork campground entrance.

Contact: Angeles National Forest, Santa Clara/Mojave River Ranger District, 661/296-9710, fax 661/295-5829.

18 TABLE MOUNTAIN

Scenic rating: 6

in Angeles National Forest
Map grid B1

This is a family campground that accommodates both tents and RVs. The road leading in is a paved two-lane county road, easily accessible by any vehicle. The nearby Big Pines Visitor Information Center, one mile to the south, can provide maps and information on road conditions. The camp elevation is 7,200 feet. A rough road for four-wheel-drive rigs is available out of camp that leads north along the Table Mountain Ridge.

RV sites, facilities: There are 115 sites for tents or RVs up to 32 feet (no hookups). Picnic tables and fire pits are provided. Drinking water, vault toilets, and an amphitheater (available for groups by reservation) are available. Leashed pets are permitted.

Reservations, fees: Reservations are accepted at 877/444-6777 or www.recreation.gov ($10 reservation fee). Sites are $13 per night. Open May through November, weather permitting.

Directions: Drive on I-15 to Cajon Junction (north of San Bernardino) and the exit for Highway 138 west. Take that exit and drive west on Highway 138 to Angeles Crest Highway/Highway 2. Turn west on Angeles Crest Highway and drive five miles to Wrightwood, then continue for three miles to Big Pines and Table Mountain Road. Turn right on Table Mountain Road and drive one mile to the campground.

Contact: Angeles National Forest, Santa Clara/Mojave Rivers Ranger District, 661/296-9710, fax 661/295-5829; Big Pines Visitor Center, 760/249-3504.

19 BUCKHORN

Scenic rating: 9

near Snowcrest Ridge in Angeles National Forest
Map grid B1

This is a prime jump-off spot for backpackers in Angeles National Forest. The camp is set at 6,300 feet elevation among huge pine and cedar trees, along a small creek near Mount Waterman (8,038 feet). A great day hike begins here, a tromp down to Cooper Canyon and the PCT; hikers will be rewarded by beautiful Cooper Falls on this three-hour round-trip. Want a weekend trip? You got it: The Burkhart National Recreational Trail descends into Caruthers Canyon where hikers can access the High Desert National Recreational Trail. From here, you can head east to Devil's Punchbowl County Park to Vincent's Gap and the Pacific Crest Trail.

RV sites, facilities: There are 38 sites for tents or RVs up to 18 feet (no hookups). Picnic tables and fire pits are provided. Drinking water and vault toilets are available. Leashed pets are permitted.

Reservations, fees: Reservations are not accepted. Sites are $12 per night. Open April through mid-November, weather permitting.

Directions: From Pasadena, drive north on I-210 for four miles to the exit for Highway 2/Angeles Crest Highway. Take that exit and drive northeast on Highway 2 for 35 miles to the signed campground entrance.

Contact: Angeles National Forest, Los Angeles River Ranger District, 818/899-1900, fax 818/896-6727.

20 MOUNTAIN OAK

Scenic rating: 4

near Jackson Lake in Angeles National Forest
Map grid B1

This is one of four camps within a mile of little Jackson Lake on Big Pines Highway. The others are Lake, Peavine, and Apple Tree. This camp is about 0.25 mile northwest of the lake. The elevation is 6,200 feet.

RV sites, facilities: There are 17 sites for tents or RVs up to 18 feet (no hookups). Picnic tables and fire pits are provided. Vault and flush toilets are available. There is no drinking water. Groceries and propane gas are nearby. Leashed pets are permitted.

Reservations, fees: Reservations are accepted

at 877/444-6777 or www.recreation.gov ($10 reservation fee). Sites are $13 per night. Open May through November, weather permitting.

Directions: Drive on I-15 to Cajon Junction (north of San Bernardino) and the exit for Highway 138 west. Take that exit and drive west on Highway 138 to Angeles Crest Highway/Highway 2. Turn west on Angeles Crest Highway and drive five miles to Wrightwood, and then continue for three miles to Big Pines and Big Pines Highway/County Road N4. Bear right on Big Pines Highway and drive three miles to the campground.

Contact: Angeles National Forest, Santa Clara/Mojave Rivers Ranger District, 661/296-9710, fax 661/295-5829.

21 LAKE

Scenic rating: 8

on Jackson Lake in Angeles National Forest
Map grid B1

This is a pretty setting on the southeast shore of little Jackson Lake. Of the four camps within a mile, this is the only one right beside the lake. The elevation is 6,100 feet.

RV sites, facilities: There are eight sites for tents or RVs up to 18 feet (no hookups). Picnic tables and fire pits are provided. Vault toilets are available. There is no drinking water. Leashed pets are permitted. Some facilities are wheelchair-accessible.

Reservations, fees: Reservations are accepted at 877/444-6777 or www.recreation.gov ($10 reservation fee). Sites are $13 per night. Open May through November, weather permitting.

Directions: Drive on I-15 to Cajon Junction (north of San Bernardino) and the exit for Highway 138 west. Take that exit and drive west on Highway 138 to Angeles Crest Highway/Highway 2. Turn west on Angeles Crest Highway and drive five miles to Wrightwood, and then continue for three miles to Big Pines and Big Pines Highway/County Road N4. Bear right on Big Pines Highway and drive 2.5 miles to the campground.

CALIFORNIA

Contact: Angeles National Forest, Santa Clara/Mojave Rivers Ranger District, 661/296-9710, fax 661/295-5829.

22 BLUE RIDGE

Scenic rating: 8

on the Pacific Crest Trail in Angeles National Forest
Map grid B1

Blue Ridge is set high in Angeles National Forest at 8,000 feet elevation and makes a jump-off spot for a multiday backpacking trip. The Pacific Crest Trail runs right alongside the camp. Guffy, also aside the PCT, provides an option two miles to the southeast. Note that some of the surrounding area is closed to vehicles to protect the yellow-legged frog.

RV sites, facilities: There are eight sites for tents or RVs up to 20 feet. Picnic tables and fire rings are provided. Vault toilets are available. No drinking water is available. Garbage must be packed out. Leashed pets are permitted.

Reservations, fees: Reservations are not accepted. There is no fee for camping. An Adventure Pass ($30 annual fee or a $5 daily pass) is required. Open May through November, weather permitting.

Directions: Drive on I-15 to Cajon Junction (north of San Bernardino) and the exit for Highway 138 west. Take that exit and drive west on Highway 138 to Angeles Crest Highway/Highway 2. Turn west on Angeles Crest Highway and drive five miles to Wrightwood, and then continue for three miles to Big Pines. Bear left (still on Angeles Crest Highway) and drive 1.5 miles to Blue Ridge Road (adjacent to Inspiration Point). Turn left on Blue Ridge Road and drive three miles to the campground.

Contact: Angeles National Forest, Santa Clara/Mojave Rivers Ranger District, 661/296-9710, fax 661/295-5829.

23 MOJAVE RIVER FORKS REGIONAL PARK

Scenic rating: 5

near Silverwood Lake
Map grid B1

Full hookups are a bonus for RV drivers, as is the park's proximity to Silverwood Lake—which is only nine miles away but does not have any sites with hookups. The sites here are well spaced, but the nearby "river" is usually dry. The elevation at this 840-acre park is 3,200 feet.

RV sites, facilities: There are 25 sites with full hookups (20 and 30 amps) for RVs up to 40 feet, 25 sites with no hookups for RVs, 30 sites for tents only, and four group sites for 200–300 people each. Several sites are pull-through. Picnic tables and fire grills are provided. Restrooms with flush toilets and showers, drinking water, and a dump station are available. Leashed pets are permitted.

Reservations, fees: Reservations are accepted for individual sites and required for group sites. Sites are $13–20 per night, $5 per night for each additional vehicle, $1 per pet per night. Some credit cards accepted. Campers must show proof of current vehicle registration and insurance. Open year-round.

Directions: Drive on I-15 to Cajon Junction (north of San Bernardino) and the exit for Highway 138/Silverwood. Take that exit east and drive nine miles to a fork with Highway 173. Bear left at the fork on Highway 173 and drive six miles to the park on the right.

Contact: Mojave River Forks Regional Park, 760/389-2322, www.co.sanbernardino.ca.us/parks.

24 BIG PINE FLATS

Scenic rating: 6

in San Bernardino National Forest
Map grid B1

This is a favorite staging area for OHV users, with many OHV trails nearby. It is a pretty spot set at 6,800 feet elevation in San Bernardino National Forest and provides a little of both worlds: You are surrounded by wildlands near Redondo Ridge, yet you're not a long drive (about 45 minutes) from Big Bear Lake to the south. Any questions? The firefighters at Big Pine Flats Fire Station, just across the road, can answer them.

RV sites, facilities: There are 17 sites for tents or RVs up to 32 feet (no hookups). Picnic tables and fire grills are provided. Vault toilets are available. No drinking water is available. Leashed pets are permitted.

Reservations, fees: Reservations are not accepted. Sites are $18 per night. Open mid-May through mid-October.

Directions: Drive on Highway 30 to the junction with Highway 330 (east of San Bernardino near Highland). Take Highway 330 north (signed "Mountain Resorts") and drive 35 miles to the dam on Big Bear Lake and a fork with Highway 38. Continue straight on Highway 38 and drive about four miles to the town of Fawnskin and Rim of the World Highway. Turn left and drive seven miles (after 0.5 mile it becomes Forest Road 3N14, a dirt road) to Big Pine Flats Fire Station and the campground on the right.

Contact: San Bernardino National Forest, Mountaintop Ranger District, Big Bear Ranger Station/Discovery Center, 909/382-2790, fax 909/866-1781.

25 BIG PINE GROUP AND EQUESTRIAN

Scenic rating: 3

in San Bernardino National Forest

Map grid B1

This camp is adjacent to the Big Pine Flats Fire Station and is used by equestrians and OHV riders. A trailhead for the Pacific Crest Trail is about two miles to the southeast of the camp via Forest Road 3N14. The elevation is 6,700 feet.

RV sites, facilities: There is one group camp

for tents or RVs up to 32 feet (no hookups) that can accommodate up to 60 people. Picnic tables and fire grills are provided. Vault toilets and drinking water are available. Horse facilities include corrals and water troughs. Leashed pets are permitted.

Reservations, fees: Reservations are required at 877/444-6777 or www.recreation.gov ($10 reservation fee). The camp is $75 per night. Open mid-May through mid-November.

Directions: Drive on Highway 30 to the junction with Highway 330 (east of San Bernardino near Highland). Take Highway 330 north (signed "Mountain Resorts") and drive 35 miles to the dam on Big Bear Lake and a fork with Highway 38. Continue straight on Highway 38 and drive about four miles to the town of Fawnskin and Rim of the World Highway. Turn left and drive seven miles (after 0.5 mile it becomes Forest Road 3N14, a dirt road) to Forest Road 3N16. Turn left and drive 0.25 mile to the campground on the right.

Contact: San Bernardino National Forest, Mountaintop Ranger District, Big Bear Ranger Station/Discovery Center, 909/382-2790, fax 909/866-1781.

26 COLDBROOK

Scenic rating: 5

on the North Fork of the San Gabriel River in Angeles National Forest

Map grid B1

This campground was closed for three years, but is expected to reopen in 2009 or 2010; check for current status before planning a trip. This roadside camp is set along the North Fork San Gabriel River, with little Crystal Lake to the north. A secret waterfall is hidden off the road, about three miles north on Soldier Creek. To find it, park at the deep bending turn in the road at Soldier Creek, then hike uphill for less than a mile. It's just like a treasure hunt, and it's always a welcome surprise to find the waterfall. The elevation is 3,300 feet. Note that there is some damage from a 2002 wildfire and a 2005 flood.

RV sites, facilities: There are 20 sites for tents or RVs up to 22 feet (no hookups). Picnic tables and fire rings are provided. Vault toilets are available. No drinking water is available. Garbage must be packed out. Leashed pets are permitted.

Reservations, fees: Reservations are not accepted. Camping is free. An Adventure Pass ($30 annual fee or a $5 daily pass) is required. Open year-round.

Directions: Drive on I-210 to Azusa and the exit for Azusa Canyon and San Gabriel Canyon Road/Highway 39. Take that exit and drive north on San Gabriel Canyon Road for 18 miles to the campground entrance.

Contact: Angeles National Forest, San Gabriel River Ranger District, 626/335-1251 or 909/982-2821, fax 626/914-3790.

27 MANKER FLATS

Scenic rating: 7

near Mount Baldy in Angeles National Forest
Map grid B1

This camp is best known for its proximity to Mount Baldy and the nearby trailhead to reach San Antonio Falls. The trail to San Antonio Falls starts at an elevation of 6,160 feet, 0.3 mile up the road on the left. From here, it's a 1.5-mile saunter on a ski park maintenance road to the waterfall, a pretty 80-footer. The wild and ambitious can continue six more miles and climb to the top of Mount Baldy (10,064 feet) for breathtaking 360-degree views. Making this all-day butt-kicker is like a baptism for Southern California hikers.

RV sites, facilities: There are 21 sites for tents or RVs up to 16 feet (no hookups). Picnic tables and fire grills are provided. Drinking water and flush toilets are available. Leashed pets are permitted. There is no drinking water in dry years.

Reservations, fees: Reservations are not accepted. Sites are $12 per night, $5 per night for each additional vehicle. Open May through September.

Directions: Drive on I-10 to Ontario and the exit for Highway 83. Take that exit and drive north on Highway 83 to Mount Baldy Road. Continue north on Mount Baldy Road for nine miles to the campground.

Contact: Angeles National Forest, San Gabriel River Ranger District, 626/335-1251 or 909/982-2821, fax 626/914-3790.

28 APPLE WHITE

Scenic rating: 5

near Lytle Creek in San Bernardino National Forest
Map grid B1

Nothing like a little insiders' know-how, especially at this camp, set at 3,300 feet elevation near Lytle Creek. You can reach the Middle Fork of Lytle Creek by driving north from Fontana via Serra Avenue to the Lytle Creek area. To get to the stretch of water that is stocked with trout by the Department of Fish and Game, turn west on Middle Fork Road, which is 1.5 miles before the campground at Apple White. The first mile upstream is stocked repeatedly every other week in spring and early summer.

RV sites, facilities: There are 44 sites for tents or RVs up to 30 feet (no hookups). Picnic tables and fire grills are provided. Restrooms with flush toilets and drinking water are available. A store is nearby. Some facilities are wheelchair-accessible. Leashed pets are permitted.

Reservations, fees: Reservations are not accepted. Sites are $10 per night, double sites are $15 per night, $3 per night for each additional vehicle. Open year-round.

Directions: Drive to Ontario and the junction of I-10 and I-15. Take I-15 north and drive 11 miles to the Sierra Avenue exit. Take that exit and turn left, go under the freeway, and continue north (into the national forest) for about nine miles to the campground on the right.

Contact: San Bernardino National Forest, Front Country Ranger District, Lytle Creek Ranger Station, 909/382-2850, fax 909/887-8197.

SILVERWOOD LAKE STATE RECREATION AREA: MESA

Scenic rating: 6

on Silverwood Lake

Map grid B1

The Old Fire did extensive damage to this park in 2003. The prettiest part of the recreation area was destroyed by fire, along with damage to a section of this campground. Sites 1–13 were burned and there is no shade, so bring your own. This state park campground is on the west side of Silverwood Lake at 3,355 feet elevation, bordered by San Bernardino National Forest to the south and high desert to the north. The hot weather and proximity to San Bernardino make it a winner with boaters, who have 1,000 surface acres of water and 13 miles of shoreline to explore. All water sports are allowed. It's a great lake for waterskiing (35-mph speed limit), water sports (5-mph speed limit in major coves), and sailboarding, with afternoon winds usually strong in the spring and early summer. Note that the quota on boats is enforced, with a maximum of 166 boats per day, and that boat-launch reservations are required on summer weekends and holidays. There are also designated areas for boating, waterskiing, and fishing to reduce conflicts. Fishing varies dramatically according to season, with trout planted in the cool months, and largemouth bass, bluegill, striped bass, catfish, and crappie caught the rest of the year. A large sandy swimming beach is available on the lake's southeast side at the Sawpit Recreation Area. The park also has a modest trail system with both nature and bike trails. Note that because of the 2003 wildfire, Miller Canyon is accessible only by foot. It is off-limits during bald eagle nesting season. A bonus is that there are also some hike-in/bike-in campsites.

RV sites, facilities: There are 131 sites for tents or RVs up to 22 feet (no hookups), with a few for RVs of any length, and four hike-in/bike-in sites. Some sites are pull-through. Picnic tables and fire rings (fire restriction may be in effect) are provided. Restrooms with flush toilets and coin showers, drinking water, Wi-Fi, dump station, boat ramp, marina, boat rentals, and small store are available. Some facilities are wheelchair-accessible. Leashed pets are permitted.

Reservations, fees: Reservations are accepted at 800/444-PARK (800/444-7275) or www.reserveamerica.com ($8 reservation fee). Sites are $35 per night, $10 per night for each additional vehicle, $2 per night per person for hike-in/bike-in sites. Boat launch is $8. Open year-round; closed Wednesdays and Thursdays.

Directions: Drive on I-15 to Cajon Junction (north of San Bernardino) and the exit for Highway 138 east. Take that exit and drive east on Highway 138 for 12 miles to the park entrance on the right.

Contact: Silverwood Lake State Recreation Area, 760/389-2303 or 760/389-2281; Silverwood Lake Marina, 760/389-2299, www.parks.ca.gov.

SILVERWOOD LAKE STATE RECREATION AREA: WEST FORK GROUP CAMPS

Scenic rating: 4

at Silverwood Lake

Map grid B1

A catastrophic fire in 2003 destroyed a good part of this group camp area, along with what many consider to be the prettiest part of the state recreation area. The Old Fire burned one of the group camps and the equestrian camp here. There are now two group camps at this site, located about 2.5 miles from the lake. There is extensive burn damage evident in this area, and work is ongoing to repair some of the damage. (For information on Silverwood Lake, see the Mesa listing in this chapter.) These group campgrounds are about 2.5 miles from the lake.

RV sites, facilities: There are three group camps for RVs of any length (no hookups) or tents that can accommodate up to 100 people each. Picnic tables and fire rings (fire restriction

CALIFORNIA

may be in effect) are provided. Rest-rooms with flush toilets and coin showers and drinking water are available. Some facilities are wheelchair-accessible. Shaded picnic areas, fishing, hiking, swimming, boating, food service, and a store are available nearby. A dump station is available at Mesa campground. Leashed pets are permitted.

Reservations, fees: Reservations are required at 800/444-PARK (800/444-7275) or www.reserveamerica.com ($8 reservation fee). The camp is $300 per night. Day-use parking $10. Open April through October.

Directions: Drive on I-15 to Cajon Junction (north of San Bernardino) and the exit for Highway 138 east. Take that exit and drive east on Highway 138 for 12 miles to the park entrance on the right.

Contact: Silverwood Lake State Recreation Area, 760/389-2303 or 760/389-2281, www.parks.ca.gov.

31 NORTH SHORE

Scenic rating: 8

on Lake Arrowhead in
San Bernardino National Forest

Map grid B1

Of the two camps at Lake Arrowhead, this one is preferable. It is set at 5,300 feet elevation near the northeastern shore of the lake, which provides decent trout fishing in the spring and early summer from a boat. Note that this is a private lake, and there is no shore access. To the nearby north, Deep Creek in San Bernardino National Forest is well worth exploring; a hike along the stream to fish for small trout (catch-and-release only) or see a unique set of small waterfalls is highly recommended.

RV sites, facilities: There are 27 sites for tents or RVs up to 22 feet (no hookups). Picnic tables and fire rings are provided. Drinking water and flush toilets are available. A store is nearby. Some facilities are wheelchair-accessible. Leashed pets are permitted.

Reservations, fees: Reservations are accepted

at 877/444-6777 or www.recreation.gov ($10 reservation fee). Sites are $17 per night, $5 per night for each additional vehicle. Open May through September.

Directions: Drive on Highway 30 to San Bernardino and the Waterman exit. Take that exit and drive north on Waterman Avenue until it becomes Highway 18. Continue on Highway 18/Rim of the World Highway and drive 17 miles to Highway 173. Turn left on Highway 173 and drive north for 1.6 miles to the stop sign. Turn right (still on Highway 173) and drive 2.9 miles to Hospital Road. Turn right and continue 0.1 mile to the top of the small hill. Turn left just past the hospital entrance and continue a short distance to the campground.

Contact: San Bernardino National Forest, Mountaintop Ranger District, Arrowhead Ranger Station, 909/382-2782, fax 909/337-1104.

32 CRAB FLATS

Scenic rating: 4

near Crab Creek in San Bernardino National Forest

Map grid B1

Four-wheel-drive cowboys and dirt-bike enthusiasts often make this a base camp, known as a staging area for off-highway vehicles. It is a developed Forest Service camp set at a fork in the road at 6,200 feet elevation. A challenging jeep road and motorcycle trail is available from here, heading west into Deep Creek Canyon. Note that Tent Peg Group camp is just 0.5 mile to the west on Forest Road 3N34 (hiking trails are available there).

Note: Tent Peg, Crab Flats, and Green Valley were damaged in the 2008 Glide Fire, but the site is still open for camping.

RV sites, facilities: There are 29 sites for tents or RVs up to 16 feet (no hookups). Picnic tables and fire rings are provided. Drinking water and vault toilets are available. Leashed pets are permitted.

Reservations, fees: Reservations are accepted

at 877/444-6777 or www.recreation.gov ($10 reservation fee). Sites are $16 per night. Open mid-May through October.

Directions: From San Bernardino, drive east on Highway 30 to the junction with Highway 330 (east of San Bernardino near Highland). Take Highway 330 north (signed "Mountain Resorts") and drive to Running Springs and the junction with Highway 18. Turn east on Highway 18 and drive to Green Valley Road. Turn left on Green Valley Road and drive three miles to Forest Road 3N16 (a dirt road). Turn left and drive four miles (you will cross two creeks that vary in depth depending on season; high clearance is recommended but is typically not necessary) to an intersection. Bear left at the intersection and drive a very short distance to the campground entrance on the right.

Contact: San Bernardino National Forest, Mountaintop Ranger District, Arrowhead Ranger Station, 909/382-2782, fax 909/337-1104.

33 GREEN VALLEY

Scenic rating: 4

near Green Valley Lake in
San Bernardino National Forest

Map grid B1

This camp sits along Green Valley Creek at an elevation of 7,000 feet. Little Green Valley Lake is a mile to the west; it is privately owned, but public access is allowed. It's quiet and intimate at this lake, and kayaks and rowboats can be rented. The lake is stocked with trout by the Department of Fish and Game and it is also a good spot to take a flying leap and belly flop when water levels are high enough.

Note: Tent Peg, Crab Flats, and Green Valley were damaged in the 2008 Glide Fire, but the site is still open for camping.

RV sites, facilities: There are 38 sites for tents or RVs up to 22 feet (no hookups). Picnic tables and fire grills are provided. Drinking water and flush toilets are available. A store and coin laundry are nearby. Leashed pets are permitted.

Reservations, fees: Reservations are accepted at 877/444-6777 or www.recreation.gov ($10 reservation fee). Sites are $18 per night, $5 per night for each additional vehicle. Open May through October.

Directions: From San Bernardino, take Highway 30 east to the junction with Highway 330 (east of San Bernardino near Highland). Take Highway 330 north (signed "Mountain Resorts") and drive to Running Springs and the junction with Highway 18. Turn east on Highway 18 and drive to Green Valley Lake Road. Turn left on Green Valley Lake Road and drive five miles to the campground (one mile past the town of Green Valley Lake).

Contact: San Bernardino National Forest, Mountaintop Ranger District, Arrowhead Ranger Station, 909/382-2782, fax 909/337-1104.

34 CAMP SWITZERLAND

Scenic rating: 7

near Lake Gregory
Map grid B1

Well, it really doesn't look much like Switzerland, but this camp is set in a wooded canyon at 4,500 feet elevation below the dam at little Lake Gregory. Since it is well below the dam, there are no lake views or even much of a sense that the lake is nearby. Yet it is only a short distance away. Lake Gregory covers just 120 acres, and while no privately owned boats are permitted here, boats can be rented at the marina. No gas motors are permitted at the lake, but electric motors are allowed. Trout and steelhead are stocked. It is surrounded by the San Bernardino National Forest. A large swimming beach is available on the south shore (about three-quarters of a mile away) with a water slide and dressing rooms.

RV sites, facilities: There are 40 sites with full or partial hookups (30 amps) for tents or RVs up to 25 feet. Two cabins are also available. Picnic tables are provided. Restrooms with flush toilets and coin showers and drinking water are available. A store and propane gas are nearby. Leashed pets are permitted, with some restrictions.

Reservations, fees: Reservations are accepted ($10 reservation fee). Sites are $27–32 per night, plus $8 per adult and $3 per child per night for more than two people, $10 per night for each additional vehicle, $10 per pet per night. Open year-round, weather permitting.

Directions: Drive on Highway 210 to San Bernardino and the Waterman Avenue exit. Take that exit and drive north on Waterman Avenue until it becomes Highway 18. Continue on Highway 18 to Crestline/Highway 138. Turn north (left) on Highway 138 and drive two miles to Lake Drive. Continue straight and drive three miles to the campground entrance (signed, just past the fire station, below the dam at the north end of Lake Gregory).

Contact: Camp Switzerland, 909/338-2731.

35 DOGWOOD

Scenic rating: 6

near Lake Arrowhead in
San Bernardino National Forest

Map grid B1

So close, yet so far—that's the paradox between Lake Arrowhead and Dogwood. The lake is just a mile away, but there is no public access. The lake is ringed by gated trophy homes. The elevation is 5,600 feet. Any questions? The rangers at the Arrowhead Ranger Station, about 1.5 miles down the road to the east, can answer them.

RV sites, facilities: There are 94 sites for tents or RVs up to 40 feet (no hookups); some sites have partial hookups (30 amps). Picnic tables and fire grills are provided. Drinking water, restrooms with flush toilets and coin showers, and a dump station are available. A store is nearby. Some facilities are wheelchair-accessible. Leashed pets are permitted.

Reservations, fees: Reservations are accepted at 877/444-6777 or www.recreation.gov ($10 reservation fee). Sites are $26–31 per night,

$5 per night for each additional vehicle. Open mid-May through October.

Directions: Drive on Highway 30 to San Bernardino and Highway 18 (two miles east of the junction of Highway 30 and Highway 215). Turn north on Highway 18 and drive 15 miles to Rim of the World Highway. Continue on Highway 18 for 0.3 mile to the road immediately after Daley Canyon Road. Turn left and make an immediate right on the Daley Canyon access road. Drive a short distance to the campground entrance on the left.

Contact: San Bernardino National Forest, Mountaintop Ranger District, Arrowhead Ranger Station, 909/382-2782, fax 909/337-1104.

36 LOS ANGELES/POMONA/ FAIRPLEX KOA

Scenic rating: 4

in Pomona

Map grid B1

This is what you might call an urban RV park. Then again, the L.A. County Fairgrounds are right across the street, and there's something going on there every weekend. Frank G. Bonnelli Regional Park, which includes Puddingstone Lake, is only 15 minutes away. Note that about 100 of the sites are occupied by permanent residents.

RV sites, facilities: There are 159 pull-through sites with full hookups (50 amps) for RVs, 27 sites with partial hookups for RVs, and 11 tent sites. Two cabins are also available. Restrooms with showers, heated pool and spa, convenience store, dump station, dog walk, and coin laundry are available. Some facilities are wheelchair-accessible. Leashed pets are permitted, with certain restrictions.

Reservations, fees: Reservations are accepted. Sites are $37–60.50 per night, $27.95 per night for tent sites, $2 per night for each additional vehicle, $5.50 per person per night for more than two people. Some credit cards accepted. Open year-round.

Directions: Drive on I-10 to the exit for Fairplex Drive (five miles west of Pomona). Take that exit north (toward the mountain) and drive two miles to McKinley Avenue. Turn right on McKinley Avenue and drive one mile to White Avenue. Turn left and drive about 0.5 mile (0.2 mile south of Arrow Street) to the park on the right (2200 North White Avenue).

Contact: Los Angeles/Pomona/Fairplex KOA, 909/593-8915, www.koa.com.

37 EAST SHORE RV PARK

Scenic rating: 7

at Puddingstone Lake

Map grid B1

Considering how close Puddingstone Lake is to so many people, the quality of fishing and waterskiing might be a surprise to newcomers. The lake covers 250 acres and is an excellent recreation facility. For the most part, rules permit waterskiing and personal watercraft between 10 A.M. and sunset, making it an excellent lake for fishing for bass and trout (in season) during the morning and evening. All water sports are allowed here, with specific days and hours for powerboating and personal watercraft. A ski beach is available on the north shore, and there is a large, sandy swimming beach on the southwest shore about a mile away. The lake is just south of Raging Waters in San Dimas and is bordered to the south by Bonnelli Regional Park; there are also a golf course and equestrian facilities adjacent. The park has roughly 50 monthly residents. Insider's tip: There is a nice tent site available on a hilltop with trees that provides more privacy.

RV sites, facilities: There are 518 sites with full hookups (20, 30, and 50 amps) for RVs of any length, 25 walk-in sites for tents, and three group tent sites. Some sites are pull-through. Restrooms with showers, cable TV, Wi-Fi, modem access, recreation room, swimming pools, general store, playground, basketball, volleyball, horseshoes, propane gas delivery, 24-hour ranger service, and coin laundry are

available. A hot-tub facility is nearby. Some facilities are wheelchair-accessible. Leashed pets are permitted at RV sites, but not at tent sites.

Reservations, fees: Reservations are accepted. RV sites are $43–47 per night for up to two people, $8 per night for each additional person. Tent sites are $24 per night for up to three people, $3 per night for each additional person, $10 per person per night for premium tent sites, $3 per pet per night. Monthly and seasonal rates available. Some credit cards accepted. Open year-round.

Directions: Drive on I-10 to the exit for Fairplex Drive (five miles west of Pomona). Take that exit north to Via Verde (the first traffic light). Turn left on Via Verde and drive to the first stop sign at Campers View. Turn right on Campers View and drive into the park.

Contact: East Shore RV Park, 909/599-8355 or 800/809-3778, www.eastshorervpark.com.

38 YUCAIPA REGIONAL PARK

Scenic rating: 7

near Redlands

Map grid B1

This is a great family-oriented county park, complete with water slides and paddleboats for the kids and fishing access and hiking trails for adults. Three lakes are stocked weekly with catfish in the summer and trout in the winter, the closest thing around to an insurance policy for anglers. Spectacular scenic views of the Yucaipa Valley, the San Bernardino Mountains, and Mount San Gorgonio are possible from the park. The park covers 885 acres in the foothills of the San Bernardino Mountains. A one-acre swimming lagoon and two water slides make this a favorite for youngsters. The Yucaipa Adobe and Mousley Museum of Natural History is nearby.

RV sites, facilities: There are 42 sites for RVs of any length and nine sites for tents. All sites have full hookups (20, 30, and 50 amps) and/or are pull-through. Picnic tables and fire rings are provided at most sites. Drinking water and

CALIFORNIA

restrooms with flush toilets and showers are available, and shade ramadas are available at tent sites. A seasonal swimming lagoon and water slides, fishing ponds, seasonal paddleboat and aquacycle rentals, pay phone, seasonal snack bar, picnic shelters, playground, volleyball (bring net), horseshoes, group facilities, bait shop, and dump station are nearby. The water slide is open Memorial Day weekend through Labor Day weekend. Some facilities are wheelchair-accessible. Leashed pets are permitted.

Reservations, fees: Reservations are accepted ($5 reservation fee). Sites are $18 per night for tent sites, $27 per night per vehicle for RV sites, $1 per pet per night. Weekly and youth group rates available. Some credit cards accepted. Additional charges apply for fishing, swimming, and use of the water slide. Proof of vehicle registration required for campers. Maximum 14-day stay in any 30-day period. Open year-round.

Directions: Drive on I-10 to Redlands and the exit for Yucaipa Boulevard. Take that exit and drive east on Yucaipa Boulevard to Oak Glen Road. Turn left and continue two miles to the park on the left.

Contact: Yucaipa Regional Park, 909/790-3127, fax 909/790-3121, www.co.sanbernardino.ca.us/parks.

39 RANCHO JURUPA PARK

Scenic rating: 4

near Riverside
Map grid B1

Lord, it gets hot in the summertime, but there is shade and grass here at this 200-acre park. The setting is along the Santa Ana River, amid cottonwood trees and meadows. This Riverside County park stocks trout and catfish in a three-acre fishing lake. Hiking, cycling, and equestrian trails are also available in the park. Shaded picnic sites are a plus. Summer visitors will find that the nearest lake for swimming and water sports is Lake Perris, about a 20-minute drive away. The elevation is 780 feet.

RV sites, facilities: There are 67 sites with full or partial hookups (30 and 50 amps) for tents or RVs of any length. Picnic tables and fire grills are provided. Drinking water, flush toilets with showers, and a dump station are available. Some facilities are wheelchair-accessible. Leashed pets are permitted.

Reservations, fees: Reservations are accepted for the individual sites and required for the group camp at 800/234-7275 ($7 reservation fee, $15 for group camp). Sites are $18–20 per night, $225 per night for the group camp, $1 per pet per night. Weekly rates available. A fishing fee is charged. Some credit cards accepted. Open year-round, with a maximum 14-day stay in a 28-day period.

Directions: Drive on I-215 to Riverside and Highway 60. Take Highway 60 east and drive seven miles to Rubidoux Boulevard. Turn left on Rubidoux Boulevard and drive 0.5 mile to Mission Boulevard. Turn left on Mission Boulevard and drive about one mile to Crestmore Road. Turn right and drive 1.5 miles to the park gate on the left (4800 Crestmore Road).

Contact: Rancho Jurupa Park, 951/684-7032, fax 951/955-4305, www.riversidecountyparks.org.

40 PRADO REGIONAL PARK
Scenic rating: 6

on Prado Park Lake near Corona
Map grid B1

Prado Park Lake is the centerpiece of a 2,280-acre recreation-oriented park that features hiking trails, an equestrian center, athletic fields, shooting range, dog-training facility, and 36-hole golf course. The lake is small and used primarily for paddling small boats and fishing, which is best in the winter and early spring when trout are planted, and then in early summer for catfish and bass. Gas motors, inflatables, sailboarding, swimming, and water/body contact are not permitted. The shooting facility, the site of the 1984 Olympic shooting venue, is outstanding.

CALIFORNIA

RV sites, facilities: There are 75 sites with full hookups (30 and 50 amps) for RVs of any length, 15 tent sites, and nine group sites. Most sites are pull-through. Picnic tables and fire rings are provided. Restrooms with showers, coin laundry, pay phone, snack bar, picnic area, playground, group facilities, boat ramp, and bait shop are available. A playing field with softball, soccer, and horseshoes is on-site. Some facilities are wheelchair-accessible. Leashed pets are permitted.

Reservations, fees: Reservations accepted ($5 reservation fee, $10 for group sites). Sites are $22 per night, $5 per night for each additional vehicle, $1 per pet per night. Group sites are $3 per person per night with a 20-person minimum. Weekly rates available. A fee is charged for fishing. Campers must show proof of vehicle registration and insurance. Some credit cards accepted. Open year-round, with a maximum 14-day stay in a 30-day period.

Directions: Drive on Highway 91 to Highway 71 (west of Norco and Riverside). Take Highway 71 north and drive four miles to Highway 83/Euclid Avenue. Turn right on Euclid Avenue and drive one mile to the park entrance on the right.

Contact: Prado Regional Park, 909/597-4260, fax 909/393-8428, www.co.sanbernardino.ca.us/parks.

41 ANAHEIM RV VILLAGE

Scenic rating: 1

near Disneyland

Map grid B1

This is one of the most popular RV parks for visitors to Disneyland and other nearby attractions. It is easy to see why, with the park just 0.5 mile from Disneyland. A shuttle service is available to Disneyland for a fee.

RV sites, facilities: There are 289 sites with full hookups (20, 30, and 50 amps) for tents or RVs up to 45 feet, with several 60-foot concrete pads for RVs with trailers; some sites are pull-through. Picnic tables are provided. Restrooms with showers, Wi-Fi, playground, game room, heated swimming pool, coin laundry,

convenience store, dump station, ice, recreation room, RV wash rack, and propane gas are available. Some facilities are wheelchair-accessible. Leashed pets are permitted.

Reservations, fees: Reservations are recommended. Sites are $35–75 per night, $2 per person per night for more than two people, $5 per night for each additional vehicle. Pets are free. Some credit cards accepted. Open year-round.

Directions: Take I-5 to Anaheim and the exit for Ball Road. Take that exit and drive on Ball Road for about one block to the park on the left.

Directions for RVs from I-5 South: Drive on I-5 south to Disney Way/Anaheim Boulevard (Exit 109B). Turn left (east) on Disney Way and drive to Anaheim Boulevard. Turn left on Anaheim Boulevard. and drive to Ball. Turn left on Ball and drive to park.

Directions for RVs from I-5 North: Drive on I-5 north to Katella Avenue/Disney Way (Exit 109). Take that exit and drive across Katella to Anaheim Boulevard. Turn right on Anaheim Boulevard and drive to Ball. Turn left on Ball and drive to park.

Contact: Anaheim RV Village, 333 West Ball Road, 714/991-0100, fax 714/991-1363, www.ahaheimrvvillage.com.

42 C. C. CAMPERLAND

Scenic rating: 1

near Disneyland

Map grid B1

Camperland is nine blocks south of Disneyland, and that right there is the number-one appeal. The Crystal Cathedral is one mile away, and Knott's Berry Farm is also close by. An outdoor sink for washing dishes and a pet restroom are bonuses.

RV sites, facilities: There are 70 sites with full hookups (30 and 50 amps) for tents or RVs up to 40 feet. No pull-through sites. Picnic tables are provided. Restrooms with showers, swimming pool, coin laundry, dump station, and ice are available. Leashed pets are permitted with certain restrictions, except in the tent area.

Reservations, fees: Reservations are accepted. Sites are $46–68 per night for RVs, $34–38 per night for tents, $3 per person per night for more than two people, $3 per night for each additional vehicle, $3 per pet per night. Some credit cards accepted. Open year-round.

Directions: Drive on I-5 to Garden Grove and the exit for Harbor Boulevard/Anaheim south. Take that exit and drive south on Harbor Boulevard for 1.5 miles to the park on the left (12262 Harbor Boulevard).

Contact: C. C. Camperland, 714/750-6747, www.cccamperland.com.

43 ORANGELAND RV PARK

Scenic rating: 1

near Disneyland

Map grid B1

This park is about three miles east of Disneyland. If the other RV parks near Disneyland are filled, this is a useful alternative. Note that about half of the sites are filled with long-term renters.

RV sites, facilities: There are 203 sites for RVs of any length (full hookups); some sites are pull-through. No tents. Picnic tables are provided. Restrooms with showers, two fire grills, playground, heated swimming pool, spa, exercise room, coin laundry, convenience store, modem access, Wi-Fi, car wash, shuffleboard court, billiards, dump station, ice, and recreation room are available. Some facilities are wheelchair-accessible. Leashed pets are permitted, with certain restrictions.

Reservations, fees: Reservations are recommended. Sites are $60–75 per night, $1 per pet per night. Monthly rates available. Some credit cards accepted. Open year-round.

Directions: Drive on I-5 to Anaheim and the exit for Katella Avenue. Take that exit east for Katella Avenue and drive two miles (passing Anaheim Stadium and the Santa Ana River) to Struck Avenue. Turn right and drive 200 yards to the park on the right (1600 West Struck Avenue).

Contact: Orangeland RV Park, 714/633-0414, fax 714/633-9012, www.orangeland.com.

44 CANYON RV PARK GROUP CAMPGROUND

Scenic rating: 6

near Yorba Linda

Map grid B1

The group campground is set in a mature grove of cottonwood and sycamore trees, with natural riparian wildland areas and open spaces nearby. It is near the Santa Ana River (swimming or wading at the lake or creek is prohibited). The Santa Ana River Bicycle Trail runs through this park, which runs from Orange in Riverside County to Huntington Beach and the Pacific Ocean. Side-trip possibilities include Chino Hills State Park (Fr.–Sun., 8 A.M.–5 P.M.) to the north, Cleveland National Forest to the south, and Lake Matthews to the southeast. The park is also close to Disneyland and Knott's Berry Farm. Canyon RV Park is a private group campground operating under a long-term lease from Orange County. It is at Featherly Regional Park.

RV sites, facilities: There are 140 sites with full hookups (30 and 50 amps) for RVs up to 40 feet. Nine cabins are also available. Picnic tables and fire pits are provided. Restrooms with flush toilets and showers, modem access, two dump stations, seasonal swimming pool, horseshoes, firewood, ice, and two playgrounds are available. A visitors center and two amphitheaters are on-site. A convenience store, coin laundry, and propane are also available. Restaurants are nearby. Some facilities are wheelchair-accessible. Leashed pets are permitted, with some restrictions.

Reservations, fees: Reservations are accepted by phone, fax, or website. Sites are $35–45 per night, $10 per night for tents allowed within RV sites, $5 per night for each additional vehicle, $1–2 per person per night for more than two people, $1 per dog per night. Call for youth-group rates. Some credit cards accepted. Open year-round.

Directions: Drive on I-5 to Highway 91 in Anaheim. Take Highway 91 east and drive 13 miles to the exit for Gypsum Canyon Road. Take that exit to Gypsum Canyon Road. Turn left, drive under the freeway, and drive about one block to the park entrance on the left.

Contact: Canyon RV Park, 714/637-0210, fax 714/637-9317, www.canyonrvpark.com.

45 LAKE PERRIS STATE RECREATION AREA

Scenic rating: 7

on Lake Perris

Map grid B1

Lake Perris is a great recreation lake with first-class fishing for spotted bass, and many fishing records have been set here. In the summer, it's an excellent destination for boating and water sports. It is set at 1,500 feet elevation in Moreno Valley, just southwest of the Badlands foothills. The lake has a roundish shape, covering 2,200 acres, with an island that provides a unique boat-in picnic site. There are large ski beaches on the northeast and southeast shores and a designated sailing cove on the northwest side, an ideal spot for various water sports; inflatables are not permitted. Swimming is also excellent, but it's allowed only at the developed beaches a short distance from the campground. The recreation area covers 8,300 acres and includes 10 miles of paved bike trails, including a great route that circles the lake, 15 miles of equestrian trails, and five miles of hiking trails. Summer campfire and junior ranger programs are offered. There is also a special area for scuba diving, and a rock-climbing area is just south of the dam.

RV sites, facilities: There are 177 sites for tents only, 254 sites with partial hookups (30 amps) for tents or RVs up to 31 feet, seven primitive horse camps with corrals and water troughs, and six group sites with no hookups for 25–100 people each. Picnic tables and fire grills are available. Restrooms with flush toilets and coin showers, drinking water, Wi-Fi, dump station, playground, convenience store, two swimming beaches, boat launch, and fishing boat rentals are available. Some facilities are wheelchair-accessible. Leashed pets are permitted, with certain restrictions, except at the beach or in the water.

Reservations, fees: Reservations are accepted for individual sites at 800/444-PARK (800/444-7275) or www.reserveamerica.com ($8 reservation fee). Sites are $30–45 per night, $21 per night for equestrian sites, $10 per night for each additional vehicle; $180 per night for group sites plus $10 per vehicle. Boat launch is $5. Reserve group and equestrian sites at 951/940-5603. Open year-round; closed Tuesdays and Wednesdays.

Directions: From Riverside, drive southeast on Highway 215/60 for about five miles to the 215/60 split. Bear south on 215 at the split and drive six miles to Ramona Expressway. Turn left (east) and drive 3.5 miles to Lake Perris Drive. Turn left and drive 0.75 mile to the park entrance.

Contact: Lake Perris State Recreation Area, 951/657-0676, or Lake Perris Marina, 951/657-2179, www.parks.ca.gov.

46 PALM VIEW RV PARK

Scenic rating: 5

near Lake Elsinore

Map grid B1

This privately operated RV park is in a quiet valley at 700 feet elevation and has a duck pond. The sites are fairly rustic, with some shade trees. The park's recreation area offers basketball, volleyball, horseshoes, tether-ball, and a playground. For you wonderful goofballs, bungee jumping and parachuting are available in the town of Perris. Note that 50 percent of the sites are occupied by long-term renters.

RV sites, facilities: There are 41 sites with full hookups (30 amps) for RVs, nine tent sites, and a group tent area that can accommodate up to 200 people. Some sites are pull-through. Picnic tables and fire rings are provided. Restrooms, dump station, recreation area, modem access, seasonal swimming pool, coin laundry, playground, convenience store, ice, and firewood are available. Leashed pets are permitted.

Reservations, fees: Reservations are accepted. Sites are $25–30 per night. The group area is $5

CALIFORNIA

per person per night. Monthly rates available. Open year-round.

Directions: Drive to the junction of I-15 and Highway 74. At that junction, take Highway 74/Central Avenue and drive east on Highway 74 for 4.5 miles to River Road. Turn right (south) and drive one mile to the park on the left (22200 River Road).

Contact: Palm View RV Park, 951/657-7791, fax 951/657-7673.

47 SUNSET VISTA RV PARK

Scenic rating: 7

in Huntington Beach

Map grid B1

This RV park is operated by the city of Huntington Beach, and is a helpful layover for Highway 1 cruisers. Bolsa Chica State Beach provides an alternative spot to park an RV. The best nearby adventure is the short loop walk at Bolsa Chica State Reserve (see the Bolsa Chica State Beach listing in this chapter for more information).

RV sites, facilities: There are 46 sites with partial hookups (30 and 50 amps) for RVs up to 40 feet. Fire rings are provided. Drinking water, outdoor cold showers, flush toilets, and dump station are available. Supplies are available within a mile. Leashed pets are permitted.

Reservations, fees: Reservations are accepted by mail only. Print out the reservation form at www.surfcityhb.org and mail to 103 Pacific Coast Highway, Huntington Beach, CA 92648. Sites are $50 per night. Open October through May.

Directions: Drive on I-405 to Huntington Beach and the exit for Beach Boulevard. Take that exit west and drive on Beach Boulevard to Highway 1/Pacific Coast Highway. Turn right (north) and drive approximately one mile to 1st Street. Turn left and drive a short distance to the park entrance.

Contact: Huntington Beach, Parks Department, 714/536-5286.

48 O'NEILL REGIONAL PARK AND EQUESTRIAN CAMP

Scenic rating: 6

near Cleveland National Forest

Map grid B1

This Orange County park is just far enough off the main drag to get missed by most of the RV cruisers on I-5. It is set near Trabuco Canyon, adjacent to Cleveland National Forest to the east. About 70 percent of the campsites are set under a canopy of sycamore and oak, and, in general, the park is heavily wooded. The park covers 3,800 acres and features 18 miles of trails, including those accessible by equestrians. Several roads near this park lead to trailheads into Cleveland National Forest. Occasional mountain lion warnings are posted by rangers. The elevation is 1,000 feet.

RV sites, facilities: There are 79 sites for tents and RVs of any length (no hookups), six equestrian sites for up to two horses per site, and two group camping areas for 20–130 people each. A few sites are pull-through. Picnic tables and fire rings are provided. Restrooms with flush toilets and showers, drinking water, playground, picnic area, amphitheater, horseshoes, firewood, and a dump station are available. Horse corral, water faucets, and an arena are available at equestrian sites. An interpretive center is open on weekends. A store is nearby. Some facilities are wheelchair-accessible. Leashed pets are permitted.

Reservations, fees: Reservations are recommended for individual sites and required for group sites ($12 reservation fee). Reservations are not accepted for equestrian sites. Sites are $15 per night, $5 per night for each additional vehicle, $2 per pet per night, $3 per horse per night. The group site is $15 per vehicle per night, plus a $12 processing fee. Some credit cards accepted. Open year-round.

Directions: From I-5 in Laguna Hills, take the County Road S18/El Toro Road exit and drive east (past El Toro) for 7.5 miles. Turn right onto Live Oak Canyon Road/County Road S19 and drive about three miles to the park on the right.

Contact: O'Neill Regional Park, 949/923-2260 or 949/923-2256, www.ocparks.com.

49 FALCON GROUP CAMPS

Scenic rating: 4

in the Santa Ana Mountains in
Cleveland National Forest

Map grid B1

At an elevation of 3,300 feet, Falcon is near the trailheads for the San Juan and Chiquito Trails, which both lead into the backcountry and the Santa Ana Mountains. There are three group campgrounds here, with limited parking at Lupine and Yarrow Campgrounds.

RV sites, facilities: There are three group sites for tents or RVs (no hookups). Sage Camp accommodates 30 people and RVs up to 40 feet, Lupine Camp accommodates 40 people and RVs up to 20 feet, and Yarrow Camp accommodates 70 people and RVs up to 30 feet. Picnic tables and fire rings are provided. Drinking water and vault toilets are available. A store is within five miles. Leashed pets are permitted.

Reservations, fees: Reservations are required at 877/444-6777 or www.recreation.gov ($10 reservation fee). Sites are $50–100 per night. Open year-round, weather permitting.

Directions: Drive on I-15 to Lake Elsinore and the Central exit to Highway 74 west. Take that exit and drive west on Highway 74 for 12 miles (the road becomes Grand Avenue for a couple of miles in Lake Elsinore, then bears right) to Forest Road 6S05 (Long Canyon Road). Turn right and drive approximately 4.5 miles to the campground entrance on the left.

Contact: Cleveland National Forest, Trabuco Ranger District, 951/736-1811, fax 951/736-3002.

50 BLUE JAY

Scenic rating: 4

in the Santa Ana Mountains in
Cleveland National Forest

Map grid B1

The few hikers who know of this spot like it and keep coming back, provided they time their hikes when temperatures are cool. The trailheads to San Juan Trail and Chiquito Trail

(which is accessed from the San Juan Trail), both of which lead into the backcountry and the Santa Ana Mountains, are adjacent to the camp. A Forest Service map is strongly advised. The elevation is 3,400 feet.

RV sites, facilities: There are 50 sites for tents or RVs up to 20 feet (no hookups). Picnic tables and fire rings are provided. Drinking water and vault toilets are available. A store is within five miles. Leashed pets are permitted.

Reservations, fees: Reservations are not accepted. Sites are $15 per night. Open year-round, weather permitting.

Directions: From Lake Elsinore, take Route 74 south for 5.7 miles to the sign for Bue Jay campground. Turn right and proceed 5.1 miles to the capground on the right.

Contact: Cleveland National Forest, Trabuco Ranger District, 951/736-1811, fax 951/736-3002.

51 EL CARISO NORTH CAMPGROUND

Scenic rating: 5

near Lake Elsinore in Cleveland National Forest

Map grid B1

This pretty, shaded spot at 2,600 feet elevation is just inside the border of Cleveland National Forest, with Lake Elsinore to the east. On the drive in there are great views to the east, looking down at Lake Elsinore and across the desert country. Hikers should head west to the Upper San Juan Campground.

RV sites, facilities: There are 18 sites for tents or RVs up to 32 feet (no hookups). Picnic tables and fire rings are provided. Drinking water and vault toilets are available. Leashed pets are permitted.

Reservations, fees: Reservations are not accepted. Sites are $15 per night. Open year-round, weather permitting.

Directions: Drive on I-15 to Lake Elsinore and the Central exit to Highway 74 west. Take that exit and drive west on Highway 74 for 12 miles (the road becomes Grand Avenue for a couple of miles in Lake Elsinore, then bears right) to the campground on the right.

Drive on I-5 to San Juan Capistrano and Highway 74/Ortega Highway. Turn east on the Ortega Highway and drive 24 miles northeast (into national forest) to the campground.

Contact: Cleveland National Forest, Trabuco Ranger District, 951/736-1811, fax 951/736-3002.

52 LAKE ELSINORE WEST MARINA AND RV RESORT

Scenic rating: 7

on Lake Elsinore
Map grid B1

This privately operated RV park has 1,000 feet of lake frontage, and boat rentals are nearby. Note that about a third of the sites are occupied by long-term renters. (For information about Lake Elsinore, see the Lake Elsinore Campground and Recreation Area listing in this chapter.)

RV sites, facilities: There are 195 sites with full hookups (50 amps) for RVs up to 40 feet. No tents. Picnic tables and cable TV are provided. Restrooms with showers, dump station, horseshoe pit, clubhouse, modem access, convenience store, group facilities, propane, and boat ramp are available. Some facilities are wheelchair-accessible. Leashed pets are permitted, with some restrictions.

Reservations, fees: Reservations are accepted at 800/328-6844. Sites are $40 per night, $3–5 per person per night for more than two people, $1 per pet per night. Some credit cards accepted. Open year-round.

Directions: Drive to the junction of I-15 and Highway 74. At that junction, take Highway 74 west/Central Avenue and drive west for four miles to the entrance to the park on the left (32700 Riverside Drive).

Contact: Lake Elsinore West Marina, 951/678-1300 or 800/328-6844, fax 951/678-6377, www.lakeelsinoremarina.com.

53 LAKE ELSINORE CAMPGROUND AND RECREATION AREA

Scenic rating: 7

on Lake Elsinore
Map grid B1

The weather is hot and dry enough in this region to make the water in Lake Elsinore more valuable than gold. Elsinore is a huge, wide lake, where water-skiers, personal-watercraft riders, and sailboarders can find a slice of heaven. This camp is set along the north shore, where there are also several trails for hiking, biking, and horseback riding. There is a designated area near the campground for swimming and water play; a gently sloping lake bottom is a big plus here. Fishing has improved greatly in recent years and the lake is stocked with trout and striped bass. Other fish species include channel catfish, crappie, and bluegill. Night fishing is available. Anglers have a chance to fish for Whiskers, a very special catfish. It is a hybrid channel catfish that was stocked in 2000. It is a genetic cross between a blue and channel catfish, meaning that Whiskers could grow to more than 100 pounds. If you catch Whiskers, it's worth $200 in prize money. If you like thrill sports, hang gliding and parachuting are also available at the lake and, as you scan across the water, you can often look up and see these daredevils soaring overhead. The recreation area covers 3,300 acres and has 15 miles of shoreline. The elevation is 1,239 feet. While the lake is huge when full, in low-rain years Elsinore's water level can be subject to extreme and erratic fluctuations. Boaters planning to visit this lake should call first to get the latest on water levels and quality.

RV sites, facilities: There are nine primitive sites and 185 sites for tents or RVs up to 40 feet; several sites have full hookups (30 amps). Fire pits are provided. Picnic tables are provided at some sites. Restrooms with flush toilets and showers, drinking water, picnic area, and dump station are available. Supplies and coin laundry are nearby. Some facilities are wheelchair-accessible. Leashed pets are permitted.

Reservations, fees: Reservations are accepted at 800/416-6992. Sites are $25–30 per night, $5 per pet per night. Some credit cards accepted. Open year-round.

Directions: Drive to the junction of I-15 and Highway 74. At that junction, take Highway 74 west/Central Avenue. Drive a short distance on Central Avenue to Collier. Turn right on Collier and drive 0.25 mile to Riverside Drive. Turn left and drive approximately 1.5 miles to the campground on the left.

Contact: Lake Elsinore Campground, 951/471-1212; City of Lake Elsinore, 951/674-3124.

54 NEWPORT DUNES WATERFRONT RESORT

Scenic rating: 9

in Newport Beach

Map grid B1   **BEST (**

This five-star resort is set in a pretty spot on the bay, with a beach, boat ramp, and storage area providing bonuses. The resort received the "Mega Park of the Year Award 2003" from the California Travel Parks Association. It is situated on 100 acres of Newport Bay beach, beautiful and private, without public access. It features one mile of beach and a swimming lagoon, beachfront sites, and 24-hour security. A one-mile promenade circles the resort and is popular for cycling and inline skating. Nearby to the west is Corona del Mar State Beach, and to the south, Crystal Cove State Park. The park is five minutes' walking distance from Balboa Island and is next to the largest estuary in California, the Upper Newport Bay Ecological Reserve.

RV sites, facilities: There are 382 sites with full hookups (30 and 50 amps) for tents or RVs up to 50 feet. Cottages are also available. Picnic tables are provided. Restrooms with showers, heated swimming pool and spa, waveless saltwater lagoon, 440-slip marina, satellite TV, Wi-Fi, organized activities, beach volleyball, coin laundry, market, waterfront restaurant, café, fitness center, game room/video arcade, group facilities, dog run, playground, RV and boat storage, RV and boat wash, and marina with boat launch ramp are available. Boat, kayak, sailboard, and bicycle rentals are available, along with lessons for various water sports. Some facilities are wheelchair-accessible. Leashed pets are permitted, with some restrictions, including a maximum of two leashed pets; no pit bulls or rottweilers, and no pets in the cottages. No smoking in cottages.

Reservations, fees: Reservations are accepted up to two years in advance (up to one year in advance for the week of July 4) at 800/765-7661. Tent sites are 84–100 per night, RV sites are $84–415 per night with discounts between Labor Day and Memorial Day, $8 per night for each additional vehicle, $2 per pet per night. Monthly rates available. Note that long-term stays are limited to five and a half months. Some credit cards accepted. Open year-round.

Directions: Drive on I-405 to the exit for Highway 55. Take that exit south and drive on Highway 55 to Highway 73. Turn south on Highway 73 and drive three miles to the Jamboree Road exit. Take that exit, turn right, and drive south on Jamboree Road for five miles to Back Bay Drive. Turn right and drive a short distance to the resort on the left.

Contact: Newport Dunes Waterfront Resort, 949/729-3863, fax 949/729-1133, www.newportdunes.com.

55 CASPERS WILDERNESS PARK FAMILY, GROUP, AND EQUESTRIAN CAMP

Scenic rating: 6

on the San Juan Creek

Map grid B1

This is an 8,500-acre protected wilderness preserve that is best known for coastal stands of live oak and magnificent stands of California sycamore. Highway 74 provides access to this regional park. It is a popular spot for picnics, day hikes, horseback riding, and cycling. Since the campground is not listed with any of the computer-based reservation services, it is overlooked by most out-of-town travelers. A highlight is 30 miles of trails. Much of the land is pristine and protected in its native state. It is bordered to the south by the San Juan Creek and to the east by the Cleveland National Forest and the San Mateo Canyon Wilderness, adding to its protection.

RV sites, facilities: There are 42 sites with partial hookups (no electrical) for tents or RVs of any length, 23 equestrian sites, six group sites for 40–60 people each, and 13 sites in an overflow area for tents and RVs. Picnic tables, fire pits, and barbecues are provided. Drinking water, restrooms with flush toilets and showers, dump station, corrals, stables, amphitheater, museum with interpretive programs, and playground are available. Some facilities are wheelchair-accessible. Pets are not allowed.

Reservations, fees: Reservations are required at 800/600-1600. Sites are $13–15 per night, $3 per horse per night. Some credit cards accepted. Open year-round.

Directions: Drive on I-5 to San Juan Capistrano and Highway 74/Ortega Highway. Turn east on Ortega Highway and drive 7.5 miles northeast to the signed park entrance on the left.

Contact: Caspers Wilderness Park, Orange County, 949/923-2210, fax 949/728-0346, www.ocparks.com.

56 LAKE SKINNER RECREATION AREA

Scenic rating: 7

on Lake Skinner

Map grid B1

Lake Skinner is set within a Riverside County park at an elevation of 1,470 feet in sparse foothill country, where the water can sparkle, and it covers 1,200 surface acres. There is a speed limit of 10 mph and only four-stroke engines are allowed. Unlike nearby Lake Elsinore, which is dominated by fast boats and water-skiers, no water-contact sports are permitted here; hence no waterskiing, no swimming, no sailboarding. However, a half-acre swimming pool is available in the summer. Afternoon winds make for great sailing, and you can count on consistent midday breezes. The fishing can be good. Many fish are stocked at this lake, including trophy-sized bass and trout, along with catfish and bluegill. The fishing records here include a 39.5-pound striped bass, 33-pound catfish, and 14-pound, 8-ounce largemouth bass. The recreation area also provides hiking trails.

RV sites, facilities: There are 213 sites for tents or RVs of any length, an overflow area, and three group camping areas; many sites have full or partial hookups (50 amps) and/or are pull-through. Picnic tables and fire grills are provided. Restrooms with flush toilets and coin showers, drinking water, playground, convenience store, picnic area, group facilities, ice, bait, dump station, swimming pool (in the summer), boat ramp, marina, mooring, boat rentals, and propane gas are available. Some facilities are wheelchair-accessible. Leashed pets are permitted.

Reservations, fees: Reservations are accepted at 800/234-7275 ($7–15 reservation fee). Sites are $17–20 per night, $12 per night for overflow area, $200–225 per night for group sites, $1 per pet per night. Some credit cards accepted. Open year-round.

Directions: Drive on I-15 to Temecula and the exit for Rancho California. Take that exit and drive northeast 9.5 miles to the park entrance on the right.

Contact: Lake Skinner Recreation Area, 951/926-1541, www.riversidecountyparks.org.

57 HANNA FLAT

Scenic rating: 5

near Big Bear Lake in San Bernardino National Forest

Map grid C1

Over the years, Hanna Flat has been one of the largest, best maintained, and most popular of the Forest Service camps in the Big Bear Lake District (Serrano Campground is the most popular). The camp is set at 7,000 feet elevation on the slopes on the north side of Big Bear Lake, just under three miles from the lake. Big Bear is a beautiful mountain lake covering more than 3,000 acres, with 22 miles of shoreline and often excellent trout fishing and waterskiing. A trailhead for the Pacific Crest Trail is a mile by road north of the camp.

Note: Hanna Flat was closed for repair after the 2007 Butler Fire, but has been such a popular campground that it will be repaired and reopened in 2009 or 2010.

RV sites, facilities: There are 88 sites for tents or RVs up to 32 feet (no hookups). Picnic tables and fire grills are provided. Drinking water and flush toilets are available. Some facilities are wheelchair-accessible. Leashed pets are permitted.

Reservations, fees: Reservations are accepted at 877/444-6777 or www.recreation.gov ($10 reservation fee). Sites are $22 per night, $5 per night for each additional vehicle. Open May through September.

Directions: Drive on Highway 30 to the junction with Highway 330 (east of San Bernardino near Highland). Take Highway 330 north (signed "Mountain Resorts") and drive 28 miles (Highway 330 becomes Highway 18/Rim of the World Highway) to the Big Bear Lake Dam and a fork with Highway 38 and Highway 18. Continue straight on Highway 38 and drive approximately four miles to the town of Fawnskin and Rim of the World Highway. Turn left and drive three miles (after 0.5 mile, it becomes Forest Road 3N14, a dirt road) to the campground on the left.

Contact: San Bernardino National Forest, Mountaintop Ranger District, Big Bear Ranger Station/Discovery Center, 909/382-2790, fax 909/866-1781.

58 HOLCOMB VALLEY

Scenic rating: 7

near the Pacific Crest Trail in
San Bernardino National Forest

Map grid C1

This camp is set near the Holcomb Valley Historic Area, at 7,400 feet elevation in the

mountains about four miles north of Big Bear Lake. On the way in on Van Dusen Canyon Road you will pass a trailhead for the Pacific Crest Trail (two miles southeast of the camp). From here you can make the two-mile climb southwest to Bertha Peak, at 8,198 feet, overlooking Big Bear to the south.

RV sites, facilities: There are 22 sites for tents or RVs up to 32 feet (no hookups). Picnic tables and fire grills are provided. Pit toilets are available. No drinking water is available. Leashed pets are permitted.

Reservations, fees: Reservations are not accepted. Sites are $14 per night. Open year-round.

Directions: Drive on Highway 30 to the junction with Highway 330 (east of San Bernardino near Highland). Take Highway 330 north (signed "Mountain Resorts") and drive 28 miles (Highway 330 becomes Highway 18/Rim of the World Highway) to the Big Bear Lake Dam and a fork with Highway 38 and Highway 18. Continue straight on Highway 38 and drive about 10 miles to Van Dusen Canyon Road/Forest Road 3N09. Turn left and drive three miles (a dirt road) to Forest Road 3N16. Turn left and drive to the campground on the right.

Contact: San Bernardino National Forest, Mountaintop Ranger District, Big Bear Ranger Station/Discovery Center, 909/382-2790, fax 909/866-1781.

59 TANGLEWOOD GROUP CAMP

Scenic rating: 4

on the Pacific Crest Trail in
San Bernardino National Forest

Map grid C1

This primitive group camp is off an old spur road with the trailhead for the Pacific Crest Trail—the primary highlight. It is set at 7,400 feet elevation in a flat but wooded area northeast of Big Bear Lake. It is about a 10- to 15-minute drive from Big Bear City.

RV sites, facilities: There is one group campsite for tents or RVs up to 32 feet (no hookups) that can accommodate up to 40 people. Picnic tables

CALIFORNIA

and fire grills are provided. Vault toilets are available. No drinking water is available. Some facilities are wheelchair-accessible. Leashed pets are permitted.

Reservations, fees: Reservations are required at 877/444-6777 or www.recreation.gov ($10 reservation fee). The fee is $75 per night. Open mid-May through September.

Directions: Drive on Highway 30 to the junction with Highway 330 (east of San Bernardino near Highland). Take Highway 330 north (signed "Mountain Resorts") and drive 28 miles (Highway 330 becomes Highway 18/Rim of the World Highway) to the Big Bear Lake Dam and a fork with Highway 38 and Highway 18. Continue straight on Highway 38 and drive about 10 miles to Van Dusen Canyon Road/Forest Road 3N09. Turn left (dirt road) and drive four miles to Forest Road 3N16. Turn right and drive 1.7 miles to Forest Road 3N79. Turn right and drive 0.5 mile to the campground. Trailers are not recommended.

Contact: San Bernardino National Forest, Mountaintop Ranger District, Big Bear Ranger Station/Discovery Center, 909/382-2790, fax 909/866-1781.

60 GRAY'S PEAK GROUP CAMP

Scenic rating: 4

near Big Bear Lake in
San Bernardino National Forest

Map grid C1

The appeal of this primitive group camp is its proximity to Big Bear Lake, with the camp just three miles northwest of the lake, set at 7,200 feet elevation. Gray's Peak (7,952 feet) is about a mile south of the camp, but there is no direct access to the peak. The drive is not recommended for trailers or large RVs.

Note: This camp was closed for repair after the 2007 Butler Fire, but will be repaired and reopened in 2009 or 2010.

RV sites, facilities: There is one group campsite for tents and RVs up to 16 feet (no hookups) that can accommodate up to 40 people. Picnic

tables and fire grills are provided. Vault toilets are available. No drinking water is available. Leashed pets are permitted.

Reservations, fees: Reservations are required at 877/444-6777 or www.recreation.gov ($10 reservation fee). The camp is $75 per night. Open mid-May through mid-October.

Directions: Drive on Highway 30 to the junction with Highway 330 (east of San Bernardino near Highland). Take Highway 330 north (signed "Mountain Resorts") and drive 28 miles (Highway 330 becomes Highway 18/Rim of the World Highway) to the Big Bear Lake Dam and a fork with Highway 38 and Highway 18. Continue straight on Highway 38 and drive about four miles to the town of Fawnskin and Rim of the World Highway. Turn left and drive 1.2 miles (after 0.5 mile, it becomes Forest Road 3N14, a dirt road) to Forest Road 2N13. Turn left and drive about a mile to the campground on the right.

Contact: San Bernardino National Forest, Mountaintop Ranger District, Big Bear Ranger Station/Discovery Center, 909/382-2790, fax 909/866-1781.

61 SERRANO

Scenic rating: 8

on Big Bear Lake in San Bernardino National Forest

Map grid C1

This campground opened in the 1990s and became the first National Forest campground to offer state-of-the-art restrooms and hot showers. That is why it costs more to camp here. Regardless, it has since become the most popular campground in the region. Location is also a big plus, as this is one of the few camps at Big Bear within walking distance of the lakeshore. It covers 60 acres, another big plus. Another bonus is a paved trail that is wheelchair-accessible. Want more? Big Bear is the jewel of Southern California lakes, the Lake Tahoe of the South, with outstanding trout fishing and waterskiing. All water sports are allowed. The lake is stocked with trout and catfish, and it also has large- and smallmouth bass, crappie, bluegill, and sunfish. Swimming is excellent at this lake, with large, sandy beaches around the shoreline. However, the water is cold. A trailhead for the Pacific Crest Trail is nearby, and Canada is only 2,200 miles away. The elevation is 6,800 feet.

RV sites, facilities: There are 132 sites for tents or RVs up to 35 feet; some sites have full hookups (30 amps). Picnic tables and fire rings are provided. Restrooms with flush toilets and coin showers, drinking water, and a dump station are available. A store is nearby. Some facilities are wheelchair-accessible. Leashed pets are permitted.

Reservations, fees: Reservations are accepted at 877/444-6777 or www.recreation.gov ($10 reservation fee). Sites are $26–36 per night, $52 per night for double sites. Open April through November.

Directions: Drive on Highway 30 to the junction with Highway 330 (east of San Bernardino near Highland). Take Highway 330 north (signed "Mountain Resorts") and drive 28 miles (Highway 330 becomes Highway 18/Rim of the World Highway) to the Big Bear Lake Dam and a fork with Highway 38 and Highway 18. Continue straight on Highway 38 and drive about 2.5 miles to Fawnskin and North Shore Lane (signed "Serrano Campground"). Turn right on North Shore Lane and drive to the campground entrance.

Contact: San Bernardino National Forest, Mountaintop Ranger District, Big Bear Ranger Station/Discovery Center, 909/382-2790, fax 909/866-1781.

62 HOLLOWAY'S MARINA AND RV PARK

Scenic rating: 6

on Big Bear Lake

Map grid C1

This privately operated RV park (no tent sites) is a good choice at Big Bear Lake with boat rentals, ramp, and full marina available. Big Bear is the jewel of Southern California's lakes, covering more than 3,000 surface acres with 22 miles

of shoreline. Its cool waters make for excellent trout fishing, and yet, by summer, it has heated up enough to make for superb waterskiing. A bonus in the summer is that a breeze off the lake keeps the temperature in the mid-80s. Note that about one-third of the sites are occupied by long-term renters. (For details about the lake, see the Serrano listing in this chapter.)

RV sites, facilities: There are 116 sites with full hookups (30 and 50 amps) for RVs up to 40 feet. No tents. Picnic tables and fire grills are provided. Restrooms with flush toilets and showers, drinking water, dump station, cable TV, convenience store, ice, propane gas, coin laundry, playground, and full marina with boat rentals are on the premises. A pirate ship tour is available. Leashed pets are permitted, including on rental boats.

Reservations, fees: Reservations are accepted at 800/448-5335. Sites are $45–60 per night, $5 per night for each additional vehicle. Monthly rates available. Some credit cards accepted. Open year-round, weather permitting.

Directions: Drive on Highway 30 to the junction with Highway 330 (east of San Bernardino near Highland). Take Highway 330 north (signed "Mountain Resorts") and drive 28 miles (Highway 330 becomes Highway 18/Rim of the World Highway) to the Big Bear Lake Dam and a fork with Highway 38 and Highway 18. Turn left on Highway 18 and drive three miles to Edgemoor Road. Turn left at Edgemoor Road and drive 0.25 mile to the park entrance on the left.

Contact: Holloway's Marina and RV Park, 909/866-5706 or 800/448-5335, fax 909/866-5436, www.800bigbearboating.com.

63 BLUFF MESA GROUP CAMP

Scenic rating: 7

near Big Bear Lake in
San Bernardino National Forest

Map grid C1

Bluff Mesa Group Camp is one of several camps south of Big Bear Lake. A highlight here is the

CALIFORNIA

trailhead (signed on the access road on the way in) for the 0.5-mile walk to the Champion Lodgepole Pine, the largest lodgepole pine in the world: 400 years old, 112 feet tall, with a circumference of 20 feet. Many Forest Service roads are available nearby for self-planned side trips. The elevation is 7,600 feet.

RV sites, facilities: There is one group campsite for tents or RVs up to 20 feet (no hookups) that can accommodate up to 40 people. Picnic tables and fire grills are provided. Vault toilets are available. No drinking water is available. Leashed pets are permitted.

Reservations, fees: Reservations are required at 877/444-6777 or www.recreation.gov ($10 reservation fee). The fee is $66 per night. Open mid-May through mid-October.

Directions: Drive on Highway 30 to the junction with Highway 330 (east of San Bernardino near Highland). Take Highway 330 north (signed "Mountain Resorts") and drive 28 miles (Highway 330 becomes Highway 18/Rim of the World Highway) to the Big Bear Lake Dam and a fork with Highway 38 and Highway 18. Turn right at Highway 18 and drive about four miles to Mill Creek Road. Turn right on Mill Creek Road and drive about 1.5 miles to the sign at the top of the hill and Forest Road 2N10. Turn right on Forest Road 2N10 and drive three miles (dirt road) to Forest Road 2N86. Turn right on Forest Road 2N86 and drive 0.25 mile to the campground.

Contact: San Bernardino National Forest, Mountaintop Ranger District, Big Bear Ranger Station/Discovery Center, 909/382-2790, fax 909/866-1781.

64 BOULDER GROUP CAMP

Scenic rating: 6

near Big Bear Lake in
San Bernardino National Forest

Map grid C1

This is a primitive camp at 7,500 feet elevation, just far enough away from some prime attractions to make you wish you could move the camp to a slightly different spot. The headwaters of Metcalf Creek are hidden in the forest on the other side of the road, tiny Cedar Lake is about a half-mile drive north, and Big Bear Lake is about two miles north. You get the idea.

RV sites, facilities: There is one group campsite for tents and RVs up to 20 feet (no hookups) that can accommodate up to 40 people. Picnic tables and fire grills are provided. Vault toilets are available. No drinking water is available. A store and coin laundry are nearby. Leashed pets are permitted.

Reservations, fees: Reservations are required at 877/444-6777 or www.recreation.gov ($10 reservation fee). The camp is $66 per night. Open mid-May through mid-October.

Directions: Drive on Highway 30 to the junction with Highway 330 (east of San Bernardino near Highland). Take Highway 330 north (signed "Mountain Resorts") and drive 28 miles (Highway 330 becomes Highway 18/Rim of the World Highway) to the Big Bear Lake Dam and a fork with Highway 38 and Highway 18. Turn right at Highway 18 and drive about four miles to Mill Creek Road. Turn right on Mill Creek Road and drive about 1.5 miles to the sign at the top of the hill and Forest Road 2N10. Turn right on Forest Road 2N10 and drive about two miles to the campground entrance road (Forest Road 2M10B). Turn right and drive to the camp.

Contact: San Bernardino National Forest, Mountaintop Ranger District, Big Bear Ranger Station/Discovery Center, 909/382-2790, fax 909/866-1781.

65 PINEKNOT

Scenic rating: 6

near Big Bear Lake in
San Bernardino National Forest

Map grid C1

This popular, developed Forest Service camp is set just east of Big Bear Lake Village (on the southern shore of the lake) about two miles from the lake. It is a popular spot for mountain biking, with several ideal routes available. Of the camps at Big Bear, this is the closest to supplies. The elevation is 7,000 feet. (For details about the lake, see the Serrano listing in this chapter.)

RV sites, facilities: There are 52 sites for tents or RVs up to 35 feet (no hookups). Picnic tables and fire grills are provided. Drinking water and flush toilets are available. A store and coin laundry are nearby. Some facilities are wheelchair-accessible. Leashed pets are permitted.

Reservations, fees: Reservations are accepted at 877/444-6777 or www.recreation.gov ($10 reservation fee). Sites are $21 per night. Open May through mid-October.

Directions: Drive on Highway 30 to the junction with Highway 330 (east of San Bernardino near Highland). Take Highway 330 north (signed "Mountain Resorts") and drive 28 miles (Highway 330 becomes Highway 18/ Rim of the World Highway) to the Big Bear Lake Dam and a fork with Highway 38 and Highway 18. Turn right at Highway 18 and drive about six miles to Summit Boulevard. Turn right and drive through the parking area to the road on the left (just before the gate to the ski area). Turn left and drive 0.25 mile to the campground on the right.

Contact: San Bernardino National Forest, Mountaintop Ranger District, Big Bear Ranger Station/Discovery Center, 909/382-2790, fax 909/866-1781.

66 BUTTERCUP GROUP CAMP

Scenic rating: 5

near the town of Big Bear Lake in San Bernardino National Forest

Map grid C1

This is a forested camp designed for large groups looking for a developed site near Big Bear Lake. It is about four miles from the southeast side of the lake, just outside the Snow Summit Ski Area. The elevation is 7,000 feet.

RV sites, facilities: There is one group campsite for tents or RVs up to 25 feet (no hookups) that

can accommodate up to 40 people. Picnic tables and fire rings are provided. Drinking water and vault toilets are available. A store and coin laundry are nearby. Leashed pets are permitted.

Reservations, fees: Reservations are required at 877/444-6777 or www.recreation.gov ($10 reservation fee). The camp is $99 per night. Open mid-May through mid-October.

Directions: Drive on Highway 30 to the junction with Highway 330 (east of San Bernardino near Highland). Take Highway 330 north (signed "Mountain Resorts") and drive 28 miles (Highway 330 becomes Highway 18/Rim of the World Highway) to the Big Bear Lake Dam and a fork with Highway 38 and Highway 18. Turn right at Highway 18 and drive about six miles to Summit Boulevard. Turn right and drive through the parking area to the road on the left (just before the gate to the ski area). Turn left and drive 0.5 mile (past Pineknot Camp) to the campground on the right.

Contact: San Bernardino National Forest, Mountaintop Ranger District, Big Bear Ranger Station/Discovery Center, 909/382-2790, fax 909/866-1781.

67 JUNIPER SPRINGS GROUP CAMP

Scenic rating: 3

in San Bernardino National Forest

Map grid C1

This is a little-known group camp, set at 7,700 feet elevation in a desertlike area about 10 miles east of Big Bear Lake. It is little known because there are not a lot of reasons to camp here. You need to be creative. Got a Scrabble game? Want to watch the junipers grow? Or maybe watch the features of the land change colors as the day passes? You get the idea.

RV sites, facilities: There is one group camp for tents and RVs up to 20 feet (no hookups) that can accommodate up to 40 people. Picnic tables and fire grills are provided. Vault toilets are available. No drinking water is available. Leashed pets are permitted.

Reservations, fees: Reservations are required at 877/444-6777 or www.recreation.gov ($10 reservation fee). The camp is $60 per night. Open year-round.

Directions: Drive on I-10 to Redlands and Highway 38. Take Highway 38 northeast and drive about 40 miles (1.5 miles past Onyx Summit) to Forest Road 2N01 on the right. Turn right (dirt road) and drive three miles to a Forest Service road (opposite the sign on the left posted Forest Road 2N04). Turn right and drive into the campground.

Contact: San Bernardino National Forest, Mountaintop Ranger District, Big Bear Ranger Station/Discovery Center, 909/382-2790, fax 909/866-1781.

68 COUNCIL GROUP CAMP

Scenic rating: 5

near Jenks Lake and the San Gorgonio Wilderness in San Bernardino National Forest

Map grid C1

This is a group camp in a pretty wooded area 0.5 mile from little Jenks Lake (there is a nice, easy walk around the lake) and a few miles north of the northern border of the San Gorgonio Wilderness. There are several other camps in the area.

RV sites, facilities: There is one group campsite for tents or RVs up to 22 feet (no hookups) that can accommodate up to 50 people. Picnic tables and fire rings are provided. Drinking water and vault toilets are available. Some facilities are wheelchair-accessible. Leashed pets are permitted.

Reservations, fees: Reservations are required at 877/444-6777 or www.recreation.gov ($10 reservation fee). The camp is $130 per night. Open May through mid-November.

Directions: Drive on I-10 to Redlands and Highway 38. Take Highway 38 northeast and drive 26 miles to the campground on the left, just past the Barton Flats Visitor Center.

Contact: San Bernardino National Forest, Mountaintop Ranger District, Big Bear Ranger Station/Discovery Center, 909/382-2790, fax 909/866-1781.

69 BARTON FLATS

Scenic rating: 7

near Jenks Lake in San Bernardino National Forest

Map grid C1

This is one of the more developed Forest Service camps in San Bernardino National Forest. The camp is set at 6,500 feet elevation, about two miles from Jenks Lake, a small, pretty lake with good hiking and a picnic area. Barton Creek, a small stream, runs nearby, although it may be waterless in late summer. The San Gorgonio Wilderness, one mile to the south, is accessible via Forest Service roads to the wilderness area trailhead. Permits are required for overnight camping within the wilderness boundaries and are available at Forest Service ranger stations. For those driving in on Highway 38, stop at the Mill Creek Ranger Station in Redlands.

RV sites, facilities: There are 52 sites for tents or RVs of any length (no hookups). Picnic tables and fire grills are provided. Drinking water and restrooms with coin showers and flush toilets are available. Some facilities are wheelchair-accessible. Leashed pets are permitted.

Reservations, fees: Reservations are accepted at 877/444-6777 or www.recreation.gov ($10 reservation fee). Sites are $25 per night, $40 per night for multifamily sites, $5 per night for each additional vehicle. Open May through mid-November.

Directions: Drive on I-10 to Redlands and Highway 38. Take Highway 38 northeast and drive 27.5 miles to the campground on the left.

Contact: San Bernardino National Forest, Mountaintop Ranger District, Big Bear Ranger Station/Discovery Center, 909/382-2790, fax 909/866-1781.

70 SAN GORGONIO

Scenic rating: 7

near the San Gorgonio Wilderness in
San Bernardino National Forest

Map grid C1

San Gorgonio is one in a series of Forest Service camps along Highway 38 and about 2.5 miles from Jenks Lake. (See the Barton Flats listing in this chapter for details.) The elevation is 6,500 feet.

RV sites, facilities: There are 53 sites for tents or RVs of any length (no hookups). Picnic tables and fire grills are provided. Drinking water and restrooms with flush toilets and coin showers are available. Some facilities are wheelchair-accessible. Leashed pets are permitted.

Reservations, fees: Reservations are accepted at 877/444-6777 or www.recreation.gov ($10 reservation fee). Sites are $25 per night, $40 per night for multifamily sites, $5 per night for each additional vehicle. Open mid-May through mid-October.

Directions: Drive on I-10 to Redlands and Highway 38. Take Highway 38 northeast and drive 28 miles to the campground.

Contact: San Bernardino National Forest, Mountaintop Ranger District, Big Bear Ranger Station/Discovery Center, 909/382-2790, fax 909/866-1781.

71 OSO AND LOBO GROUP

Scenic rating: 6

near the San Gorgonio Wilderness in
San Bernardino National Forest

Map grid C1

Oso and Lobo Group Camps are set directly adjacent to each other at 6,600 feet elevation. The camps are about three-quarters of a mile from the Santa Ana River. Little Jenks Lake is two miles away to the west, and the northern border of the San Gorgonio Wilderness is just a few miles to the south.

RV sites, facilities: There are two group sites for tents or RVs of any length (no hookups) that can accommodate 75–100 people each. Picnic tables and fire grills are provided. Drinking water and flush toilets are available. Leashed pets are permitted.

Reservations, fees: Reservations are required at 877/444-6777 or www.recreation.gov ($10 reservation fee). The fee is $190–250 per night. Open May through mid-October, weather permitting.

Directions: From I-10 in Redlands, drive 29 miles east on Highway 38 to the campground entrance road on the left.

Contact: San Bernardino National Forest, Mountaintop Ranger District, Big Bear Ranger Station/Discovery Center, 909/382-2790, fax 909/866-1781.

72 SOUTH FORK

Scenic rating: 7

near the Santa Ana River in
San Bernardino National Forest

Map grid C1

This is an easy-access Forest Service camp just off Highway 38, set at 6,400 feet elevation near the headwaters of two rivers, the South Fork River and the Santa Ana River. It is part of the series of camps in the immediate area, just north of the San Gorgonio Wilderness. This one is a four-mile drive from little Jenks Lake. (See the Barton Flats listing in this chapter for more details.)

RV sites, facilities: There are 24 sites for tents or RVs up to 25 feet (no hookups). Picnic tables and fire rings are provided. Drinking water and vault toilets are available. Leashed pets are permitted.

Reservations, fees: Reservations are accepted at 877/444-6777 or www.recreation.gov ($10 reservation fee). Sites are $20 per night, $5 per night for each additional vehicle. Open mid-May through September.

Directions: Drive on I-10 to Redlands and Highway 38. Take Highway 38 northeast and drive 29.5 miles to the campground entrance road.

Contact: San Bernardino National Forest, Mountaintop Ranger District, Big Bear Ranger Station/Discovery Center, 909/382-2790, fax 909/866-1781.

CALIFORNIA

73 HEART BAR FAMILY AND SKYLINE GROUP CAMPS

Scenic rating: 4

in San Bernardino National Forest

Map grid C1

It's a good thing there is drinking water at this camp. Why? Because Heart Bar Creek often isn't much more than a trickle and can't be relied on for water. The camp is set at 6,900 feet elevation near Big Meadows and Aspen Grove. A challenging butt-kicker of a hike has a trailhead about 0.5 mile away to the north off a spur road, midway between the camp and the fire station. The trail here is routed along Wildhorse Creek to Sugarloaf Mountain (9,952 feet, about 8–9 miles one-way to the top). Insider's note: Just past the midway point on the trail to Sugarloaf Mountain is a trail camp on Wildhorse Creek.

RV sites, facilities: There are 95 sites for tents or RVs up to 40 feet (no hookups), and one group tent site for up to 25 people. Picnic tables and fire grills are provided. Drinking water and vault toilets are available. Some facilities are wheelchair-accessible. Leashed pets are permitted.

Reservations, fees: Reservations are accepted for individual sites and required for the group site at 877/444-6777 or www.recreation.gov ($10 reservation fee). Sites are $20 per night, $30 per night for multifamily sites, $70 per night for the group site. Open mid-May through early October.

Directions: Drive on I-10 to Redlands and Highway 38. Take Highway 38 northeast and drive 33.5 miles to Forest Road 1N02. Turn right and drive one mile to the campground.

Contact: San Bernardino National Forest, Mountaintop Ranger District, Big Bear Ranger Station/Discovery Center, 909/382-2790, fax 909/866-1781.

74 HEART BAR EQUESTRIAN GROUP AND WILD HORSE EQUESTRIAN

Scenic rating: 5

in San Bernardino National Forest

Map grid C1

You might not meet Mr. Ed here, but bring an apple anyway. Heart Bar is a horse camp on Heart Bar Creek, less than a mile east of Heart Bar Family Camp. Wild Horse is just 0.1 mile before Heart Bar Family Camp. A good trail that leads into the San Gorgonio Wilderness starts four miles down the road at Fish Creek Meadows. It is routed west for three miles to Fish Creek and then up Grinnell Mountain to the north peak of the Ten Thousand Foot Ridge. A wilderness permit is required. The elevation is 7,000 feet.

RV sites, facilities: Heart Bar has one group campsite for tents or RVs up to 22 feet (no hookups) and can accommodate up to 65 people. Wild Horse has 11 equestrian sites, including two double sites. Picnic tables and fire grills are provided. Flush toilets are available. No drinking water is available. Water is available for horses. Heart Bar has 46 corrals. Leashed pets are permitted.

Reservations, fees: Reservations are required at 877/444-6777 or www.recreation.gov ($10 reservation fee). Sites are $25 per night for equestrian sites at Wild Horse and $250 per night for the group camp at Heart Bar. Open May through early October.

Directions: Drive on I-10 to Redlands and Highway 38. Take Highway 38 northeast and drive 33.5 miles to Forest Road 1N02. Turn right and drive a mile to the Heart Bar Group Campground on the right. Continue for 0.1 mile to the Wild Horse camp on the left. To reach Heart Bar Group Equestrian Campground, continue another 0.1 mile.

Contact: San Bernardino National Forest, Mountaintop Ranger District, Big Bear Ranger Station/Discovery Center, 909/382-2790, fax 909/866-1781.

CALIFORNIA

75 BOGART PARK/FAMILY, GROUP, AND EQUESTRIAN

Scenic rating: 4

in Cherry Valley

Map grid C1

This county park is overlooked by many vacationers on I-10, and it is as pretty as it gets for this area. There are two miles of horse trails and some hiking trails for a recreation option during the cooler months. It covers 414 acres of Riverside County foothills set at the north end of Cherry Valley. The elevation is 2,800 feet. Bears frequent this area, so store your food properly and avoid scented products.

RV sites, facilities: There are 26 sites for tents or RVs up to 40 feet (no hookups), a group campground for tents that can accommodate up to 100 people, and a group equestrian campground. Fire grills and picnic tables are provided. Drinking water and flush toilets are available. The equestrian camp has corrals and water troughs. Supplies are available in Beaumont. Some facilities are wheelchair-accessible. Leashed pets are permitted.

Reservations, fees: Reservations are accepted and required for group sites at 800/234-7275 ($7–15 reservation fee). Sites are $12 per night, $120 per night for the group equestrian camp, $144 per night for the group camp, $1 per night per pet or horse. Open year-round, but closed on Tuesday and Wednesday.

Directions: Drive on I-10 to Beaumont and the exit for Beaumont Avenue. Take that exit north and drive four miles to Brookside. Turn right and drive 0.5 mile to Cherry Avenue. Turn left at Cherry Avenue and drive to the park on the right (9600 Cherry Avenue).

Contact: Bogart Park, 951/845-3818; Riverside County Parks, 800/234-7275, www.riversidecountyparks.org.

76 PINE RANCH RV PARK

Scenic rating: 2

in Banning

Map grid C1

Banning may not seem like a hotbed of civilization at first glance, but this clean, comfortable park is a good spot to make camp while exploring some of the area's hidden attractions, including Agua Caliente Indian Canyons and the Lincoln Shrine. It is set at 2,400 feet elevation, 22 miles from Palm Springs. A good side trip is to head south on curving "Highway" 240 up to Vista Point in the San Bernardino National Forest. Note: In 2008, there were 13 permanent residents here.

RV sites, facilities: There are 106 sites with full hookups (30 and 50 amps) for RVs; many sites are pull-through. No tents. Picnic tables and fire grills are provided. Restrooms with showers, cable TV, playground, heated swimming pool, coin laundry, Wi-Fi, dump station, ice, horseshoes, and propane gas are available. Leashed pets are permitted, with certain restrictions.

Reservations, fees: Reservations are recommended at 800/562-4110. Sites are $33–38 per night, $2 per person per night for more than two people with a maximum of eight people per site, $1 per night for each additional vehicle. Some credit cards accepted. Open year-round.

Directions: Drive on I-10 to Banning and the exit for Highway 243. Take that exit south and take 8th Street south for one block to Lincoln. Turn left on Lincoln and drive two blocks to San Gorgonio. Turn right and drive one mile to the park (1455 South San Gorgonio Avenue).

Contact: Pine Ranch RV Park, 951/849-7513, fax 951/849-7998, www.reynoldsresorts.com.

CALIFORNIA

77 BLACK MOUNTAIN GROUP CAMP

Scenic rating: 6

near Mount San Jacinto in
San Bernardino National Forest

Map grid C1

This is a beautiful scenic area, particularly to the north on the edge of the San Jacinto Wilderness and to the east of Mount San Jacinto State Park. The camp is set at 7,500 feet elevation and is within a mile of a trailhead for the Pacific Crest Trail. Here you can turn southeast and hike along Fuller Ridge for another mile to the border of Mount San Jacinto State Park. Note that Black Mountain Lookout is just a two-mile drive, close to Boulder Basin Camp.

RV sites, facilities: There is one group camp for tents and RVs up to 16 feet (no hookups) that can accommodate up to 100 people. Picnic tables and fire rings are provided. Drinking water and vault toilets are available. Leashed pets are permitted.

Reservations, fees: Reservations are required at 877/444-6777 or www.recreation.gov ($10 reservation fee). The camp is $60–120 per night. Open May through mid-October.

Directions: Drive on I-10 to Banning and Highway 243/Pinesto Palms Scenic Highway. Turn south on Pinesto Palms Scenic Highway and drive about 15 miles to Forest Road 4S01. Turn left on Forest Road 4S01 and drive eight miles (a narrow dirt road) to the campground on the right. Trailers are not advised.

Contact: San Bernardino National Forest, San Jacinto Ranger District, 909/382-2922, fax 951/659-2107.

78 BOULDER BASIN

Scenic rating: 8

near the San Jacinto Wilderness in
San Bernardino National Forest

Map grid C1

This camp is on the top of the world for these parts: 7,300 feet elevation, adjacent to the Black Mountain Fire Lookout with great views in all directions and highlighted by Tahquitz Peak (8,828 feet) 10 miles to the southeast. Boulder Basin is also near the San Jacinto Wilderness (to the northeast) and makes a good trailhead camp for hikers. A trail starting at Black Mountain Lookout leads west, dropping steeply into a canyon and also into a designated scenic area.

RV sites, facilities: There are 34 sites for tents or RVs up to 15 feet (no hookups). Note that trailers and RVs are not recommended. Picnic tables and fire rings are provided. Drinking water and vault toilets are available. Leashed pets are permitted.

Reservations, fees: Reservations are accepted at 877/444-6777 or www.recreation.gov ($10 reservation fee). Sites are $10 per night. Open May through mid-October.

Directions: Drive on I-10 to Banning and Highway 243/Pinesto Palms Scenic Highway. Turn south on Pinesto Palms Scenic Highway and drive about 15 miles to Forest Road 4S01/Black Mountain Road. Turn left and drive six miles (a narrow dirt road) to the campground on the right. RVs not advised.

Contact: San Bernardino National Forest, San Jacinto Ranger District, 909/382-2922, fax 951/659-2107.

79 DARK CANYON

Scenic rating: 7

in the San Jacinto Mountains in
San Bernardino National Forest

Map grid C1

This pretty setting is on the slopes of the San Jacinto Mountains at 5,800 feet elevation. Hikers can drive to the Seven Pines Trailhead less than a mile north of camp at the end of Forest Road 4S02. The trail leads east for three miles into Mount San Jacinto State Park to Deer Springs, where there is a trail camp and a junction with the Pacific Crest Trail. A wilderness permit is required.

RV sites, facilities: There are 17 sites for tents or RVs up to 17 feet (no hookups). Picnic tables and fire grills are provided. Drinking water and vault toilets are available. Leashed pets are permitted.

Reservations, fees: Reservations are accepted at 877/444-6777 or www.recreation.gov ($10 reservation fee). Sites are $12 per night. Open mid-May through mid-September.

Directions: Drive on I-10 to Banning and Highway 243/Pinesto Palms Scenic Highway. Turn south on Pinesto Palms Scenic Highway and drive about 13 miles to Forest Road 4S02. Turn left on Forest Road 4S02 and drive three miles (narrow paved road) to the campground.

Contact: San Bernardino National Forest, San Jacinto Ranger District, 909/382-2922, fax 951/659-2107.

80 MARION MOUNTAIN

Scenic rating: 7

in San Bernardino National Forest

Map grid C1

You get good lookouts and a developed campground at this spot. Nearby Black Mountain is a good side trip that includes a drive-to scenic lookout point. In addition, there are several trailheads in the area. The best one starts near this camp and heads up the slopes to Marion Mountain and east into adjacent Mount San Jacinto State Park. The elevation is 6,400 feet.

RV sites, facilities: There are 24 sites for tents or RVs up to 15 feet (no hookups). Picnic tables and fire grills are provided. Drinking water and vault toilets are available. Leashed pets are permitted.

Reservations, fees: Reservations are accepted at 877/444-6777 or www.recreation.gov ($10 reservation fee). Sites are $10 per night. Open mid-May through mid-October.

Directions: Drive on I-10 to Banning and Highway 243/Pinesto Palms Scenic Highway. Turn south on Pinesto Palms Scenic Highway and drive about 13 miles south to Forest Road 4S02. Turn left on Forest Road 4S02 and drive two miles (narrow paved road) to the campground.

Contact: San Bernardino National Forest, San Jacinto Ranger District, 909/382-2922, fax 951/659-2107.

81 FERN BASIN

Scenic rating: 7

near Mount San Jacinto State Park in San Bernardino National Forest

Map grid C1

This is a nearby alternative to Stone Creek (you'll pass it on the way in) and Dark Canyon (another three miles in). Marion Mountain Trailhead is accessible within 0.5 mile of the campground by driving east on Forest Road 4S02.

RV sites, facilities: There are 22 sites for tents or RVs up to 15 feet (no hookups). Picnic tables and fire rings are provided. Drinking water and vault toilets are available. Leashed pets are permitted.

Reservations, fees: Reservations are accepted at 877/444-6777 or www.recreation.gov ($10 reservation fee). Sites are $10 per night. Open mid-May through mid-October.

Directions: Drive on I-10 to Banning and Highway 243/Pinesto Palms Scenic Highway. Turn south on Pinesto Palms Scenic Highway and drive about 13 miles south to Forest Road 4S02. Turn left on Forest Road 4S02 and drive one mile (narrow paved road) to the campground on the left.

Contact: San Bernardino National Forest, San Jacinto Ranger District, 909/382-2922, fax 951/659-2107.

82 MOUNT SAN JACINTO STATE PARK: STONE CREEK

Scenic rating: 7

in Mount San Jacinto State Park

Map grid C1

This is a wooded camp set in Mount San Jacinto State Park. The elevation is 5,900 feet, 0.25 mile off the main road along Stone Creek, just outside the national forest boundary. It is less than a mile from Fern Basin and less than three miles from Dark Canyon. The best trailhead in the immediate area is Seven Pines Trail out of Marion Mountain Camp, one-half mile from this camp.

RV sites, facilities: There are 26 sites for tents, and 21 sites for tents or RVs up to 24 feet (no hookups). Picnic tables and fire rings are provided. Drinking water and vault toilets are available. Supplies and coin laundry are three miles away in Pine Cove. Some facilities are wheelchair-accessible. Leashed pets are permitted.

Reservations, fees: Reservations are accepted at 800/444-PARK (800/444-7275) or www. reserveamerica.com ($8 reservation fee). Sites are $15–25 per night, $8 per night for each additional vehicle. Open year-round.

Directions: Drive on I-10 to Banning and Highway 243/Idyllwild Panoramic Highway. Turn south on Idyllwild Panoramic Highway and drive about 13 miles south to the park entrance on the left.

Contact: Mount San Jacinto State Park, 951/659-2607; Inland Empire District, 951/443-2423, www.parks.ca.gov.

83 GOLDEN VILLAGE PALMS RV RESORT

Scenic rating: 5

in Hemet

Map grid C1

This RV resort is for those ages 55 and over. It is the biggest RV park in Southern California. The grounds are lush, with gravel pads for RVs. It is set near Diamond Valley Lake, about 10 miles south, a new lake that is the largest reservoir in Southern California. A golf course is nearby, Lake Hemet is 20 miles east, and winery tours are available in Temecula, a 30-minute drive. About 250 of the 1,019 sites are rented on a year-round basis.

RV sites, facilities: There are 1,019 sites with full hookups (20, 30, and 50 amps) for RVs up to 45 feet; some sites are pull-through. No tent sites. Restrooms with flush toilets and showers,

drinking water, cable TV, modem access, Wi-Fi, business services, three heated swimming pools, three spas, recreation room, fitness center, billiard room, coin laundry, large clubhouse, banquet and meeting rooms, organized activities, pavilion, church services, library, ballroom, shuffleboard, nine-hole putting green, volleyball courts, and horseshoe pits are available. A day-use area with propane barbecues is also available. Leashed pets are permitted.

Reservations, fees: Reservations are accepted at 800/323-9610. Sites are $40–53 per night, $10 per person per night for more than two people. Weekly, monthly, and annual rates available. Open year-round.

Directions: Drive to the junction of I-215 and Highway 74 (near Perris). At that junction, take Highway 74 east and drive 14 miles to Hemet (the highway becomes Florida Avenue in Hemet) and continue to the resort on the left.

Contact: Golden Village Palms RV Resort, 951/925-2518, www.goldenvillagepalms.com.

84 CASA DEL SOL RV PARK RESORT

Scenic rating: 3

in Hemet

Map grid C1

Hemet is a retirement town, so if you want excitement, the four lakes in the area are the best place to look for it: Lake Perris to the northwest, Diamond Valley Lake and Lake Skinner to the south, and Lake Hemet to the east. The elevation at this 20-acre resort is 1,575 feet. Note that many of the sites are taken by year-round or long-term rentals.

RV sites, facilities: There are 358 sites with full hookups (30 and 50 amps) for RVs up to 40 feet. No tents. Restrooms with flush toilets and showers, drinking water, cable TV, telephone and modem access, ice, library, heated swimming pool, spa, recreation room, exercise room, billiard room, shuffleboard courts, golf driving cage, dog runs, and coin laundry are available. Leashed pets are permitted.

Reservations, fees: Reservations are accepted at 888/925-2516. Sites are $39 per night, $5 per person per night for more than two people. Weekly and monthly rates available; discounts available. Some credit cards accepted. Open year-round.

Directions: Drive to the junction of I-215 and Highway 74 (near Perris). At that junction, take Highway 74 east and drive 15 miles to Hemet (the highway becomes Florida Avenue in Hemet) and drive to Kirby Avenue. Turn right (south) on Kirby Avenue and drive a half block to the resort (2750 West Acacia Avenue).

Contact: Casa del Sol RV Park Resort, 951/925-2515, www.casadelsolrvpark.com.

85 MOUNTAIN VALLEY RV RESORT

Scenic rating: 3

in Hemet

Map grid C1

This is one of three RV parks in the Hemet area. Four lakes in the area provide side-trip possibilities: Lake Perris to the northwest, Lake Skinner and Diamond Valley Lake to the south, and Lake Hemet to the east. Golf courses are nearby.

RV sites, facilities: There are 170 sites with full hookups (30 and 50 amps) for RVs up to 40 feet. No tents or campers. Restrooms with flush toilets and showers, cable TV, drinking water, a fireside room, heated swimming pool, enclosed spa, fitness center, golf driving cage, card-access laundry, billiards room, meeting room, group facilities, computer kiosk, Wi-Fi, and telephone hookups are available. A store and propane gas are nearby. Some facilities are wheelchair-accessible. Leashed pets are permitted, with some breeds prohibited.

Reservations, fees: Reservations are accepted at 800/926-5593. Sites are $33 per night, $5 per person per night for more than two people, $2 per pet per night. Weekly, monthly, and annual rates available. Some credit cards accepted. Open year-round.

Directions: Drive to the junction of I-215 and Highway 74 (near Perris). At that junction, take Highway 74 east and drive 15 miles to Hemet (the highway becomes Florida Avenue in Hemet) and continue to South Lyon Avenue. Turn right on South Lyon Avenue and drive to the park at the corner of Lyon and South Acacia (235 South Lyon).

Contact: Mountain Valley RV Resort, 951/925-5812, www.mountainvalleyrvp.com.

86 IDYLLWILD COUNTY PARK

Scenic rating: 6

near San Bernardino National Forest

Map grid C1

This Riverside County park covers 202 acres, set at 5,300 feet elevation and surrounded by Mount San Jacinto State Park, San Jacinto Wilderness, and the San Bernardino National Forest lands. That provides plenty of options for visitors. The park has equestrian trails and an interpretive trail. The top hike in the region is the ambitious climb up the western slopes to the top of Mount San Jacinto (10,804 feet), a terrible challenge of a butt-kicker that provides one of the most astounding views in all the land. (The best route, however, is out of Palm Springs, taking the aerial tramway, which will get you to 8,516 feet elevation before you hike out the rest.)

RV sites, facilities: There are 83 sites for tents or RVs up to 40 feet (no hookups). Fire grills and picnic tables are provided. Drinking water and restrooms with flush toilets and coin showers are available. A store, coin laundry, and propane gas are nearby. There is no drinking water in dry years. Some facilities are wheelchair-accessible. Leashed pets are permitted.

Reservations, fees: Reservations are accepted at 800/234-PARK (800/234-7275; $6.50 reservation fee). Sites are $17 per night, $1 per pet per night. Some credit cards accepted. Open year-round.

Directions: Drive on I-10 to Banning and Highway 243/Idyllwild Panoramic Highway. Turn south on Idyllwild Panoramic Highway and drive to Idyllwild and Riverside County Playground Road. Turn west on Riverside County Playground Road and drive 0.5 mile (follow the signs) to the park entrance on the right.

Contact: Idyllwild County Park, 951/659-2656, www.riversidecountyparks.org.

87 MOUNT SAN JACINTO STATE PARK: IDYLLWILD

Scenic rating: 8

in Mount San Jacinto State Park

Map grid C1

This is a prime spot for hikers and one of the better jump-off points for trekking in the area, set at 5,400 feet elevation. There are no trails from this campground. But 0.5 mile north is Deer Spring Trail, which is connected with the Pacific Crest Trail and then climbs on to Mount San Jacinto (10,834 feet) and its astounding lookout.

RV sites, facilities: There are 11 sites for tents only, 10 sites for tents or RVs up to 18 feet, eight sites for RVs only up to 24 feet, and three hike-in/bike-in sites. Two of the sites have full hookups. Fire grills and picnic tables are provided. Drinking water, restrooms with flush toilets and coin showers, and Wi-Fi are available. Supplies and coin laundry (100 yards) are nearby. Some facilities are wheelchair-accessible. Leashed pets are permitted.

Reservations, fees: Reservations are accepted at 800/444-PARK (800/444-7275) or www.reserveamerica.com ($8 reservation fee). Sites are $15–25 per night, $8 per night for each additional vehicle, $3 per person per night for hike-in/bike-in site. Open year-round.

Directions: In Idyllwild, drive to the north end of town on Highway 243 to the park entrance on the left (next to the fire station). Note: From I-10 in Banning, take the A Street exit onto Highway 243. Drive south for 23.8 miles to the campground on the right, just before Idyllwild.

From I-10 in Banning, take the A Street exit onto Highway 243. Drive south on Highway 243 for 23.8 miles to the campground on the right, just before the town of Idyllwild.

Contact: Mount San Jacinto State Park, 951/659-2607; Inland Empire District, 951/443-2423, www.parks.ca.gov.

88 LAKE HEMET

Scenic rating: 7

near Hemet

Map grid C1

Lake Hemet covers 420 acres, is set at 4,340 feet elevation, and sits near San Bernardino National Forest just west of Garner Valley. Many campsites have lake views. It provides a good camping/fishing destination, with large stocks of trout each year, and yep, catch rates are good. The lake also has bass, bluegill, and catfish. Boating rules prohibit boats under 10 feet, canoes, sailboats, inflatables, and swimming—no swimming or wading at Lake Hemet. The boat speed limit is 10 mph.

RV sites, facilities: There are 275 sites for RVs up to 40 feet, and 250 dry sites for tents. All sites have full hookups (20 amps). Picnic tables and fire rings are provided. Restrooms with flush toilets and coin showers, drinking water, dump station, playground, horseshoes, boat ramp, boat rentals, convenience store, coin laundry, and propane gas are available. No generators permitted at campsites. Some facilities are wheelchair-accessible. Leashed pets are permitted.

Reservations, fees: Reservations are not accepted. Sites are $21–27 per vehicle per night, $4 per person per night for more than two people, $3 per pet per night. Some credit cards accepted. Open year-round.

Directions: From Palm Desert, drive southwest on Highway 74 for 33 miles (near Lake Hemet) to the campground entrance on the left. For directions if arriving from the west (several options), phone 951/659-2680, ext. 2.

Contact: Lake Hemet, 951/659-2680, www.lakehemet.org.

89 HURKEY CREEK PARK

🏃 🎣 🐕 🚼 ♿ 🚐 ⛺

Scenic rating: 5

near Lake Hemet

Map grid C1

This large Riverside County park is just east (across the road) of Lake Hemet, beside Hurkey Creek (which runs in winter and spring). The highlight, of course, is the nearby lake, known for good fishing in the spring. No swimming is permitted. The camp elevation is 4,800 feet. The park covers 59 acres.

RV sites, facilities: There are 130 sites and five group sites for tents or RVs up to 40 feet (no hookups) that can accommodate up to 100 people each. Fire grills and picnic tables are provided. Drinking water, restrooms with flush toilets and coin showers, a playground, and picnic areas are available. Some facilities are wheelchair-accessible. A dump station is available at nearby Lake Hemet. Leashed pets are permitted.

Reservations, fees: Reservations are accepted for individual sites and required for the group sites at 800/234-PARK (800/234-7275; $7–15 reservation fee). Sites are $17 per night, $1 per pet per night. Group sites are $175 per night for up to 40 people, plus $4 per person per night for more than 40 people. Some credit cards accepted. Open year-round.

Directions: From Palm Desert, drive southwest on Highway 74 for 32 miles (near Lake Hemet) to the campground entrance on the right.

Contact: Hurkey Creek Park, 951/659-2050, www.riversidecountyparks.org.

90 ANZA RV RESORT

🎣 🐕 🚐 ⛺

Scenic rating: 4

near Anza

Map grid C1

This is a year-round RV park set at 4,100 feet elevation, with many nearby recreation options. Lake Hemet is 16 miles away, with hiking, motorbiking, and jeep trails nearby in San Bernardino National Forest. Pacific Crest Trail hikers are welcome to clean up and to arrange for food and mail pick-up. Note that most sites are filled with long-term renters.

RV sites, facilities: There are 116 sites for tents and RVs; many have full hookups (30 and 50 amps) and some sites are pull-through. Picnic tables are provided. Restrooms with showers, catch-and-release fishing pond, horseshoe pits, coin laundry, convenience store, dump station, ice, recreation room, modem access, and propane gas are available. Leashed pets are permitted, with certain restrictions.

Reservations, fees: Reservations are accepted. Sites are $20 per night on Fridays and Saturdays, $18 per night the rest of week, $1 per person per night for more than two people. No credit cards accepted. Open year-round.

Directions: From Palm Desert, drive west on Highway 74 for 24 miles to Highway 371. Turn left on Highway 371 and drive west to the town of Anza and Kirby Road. Turn left on Kirby Road and drive 3.5 miles to the campground on the left at Terwilliger Road (look for the covered wagon out front).

Contact: Anza RV Resort, 951/763-4819, fax 951/763-0619.

CALIFORNIA

SAN DIEGO AND VICINITY

(BEST RV PARKS AND CAMPGROUNDS

(Coastal Sites
South Carlsbad State Beach, page 1147.

(Fishing
Campland on the Bay, page 1149.

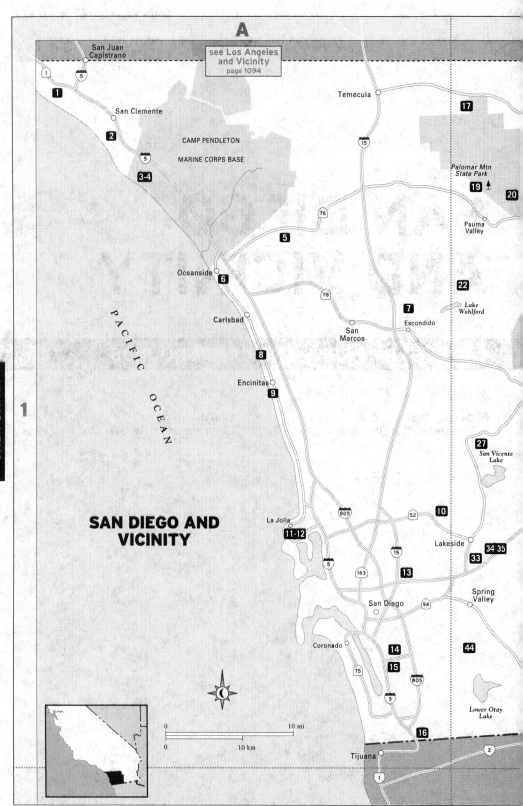

CALIFORNIA

1

SAN DIEGO AND VICINITY

PACIFIC OCEAN

San Juan Capistrano

see Los Angeles and Vicinity page 1094

Temecula

San Clemente

CAMP PENDLETON

MARINE CORPS BASE

Palomar Mtn State Park

Pauma Valley

Oceanside

Carlsbad

San Marcos

Escondido

Lake Wohlford

Encinitas

San Vicente Lake

La Jolla

Lakeside

San Diego

Spring Valley

Coronado

Lower Otay Lake

Tijuana

0   10 mi

0   10 km

San Diego was picked as one of the best regions to live in America in an unofficial vote at a national conference for the Outdoors Writers Association of America.

It is easy to understand why: the weather, the ocean and beaches, the lakes and fishing, Cleveland National Forest, the state parks, the mountains, the hiking, the biking, and the water sports. What more could anyone ask for? For many, the answer is you don't ask for more, because it does not get any better than this.

The weather is near perfect. It fits a warm coastal environment with an azure-tinted sea that borders foothills and mountains. In a relatively small geographic spread, you get it all.

The ocean here is warm and beautiful, with 70 miles of beaches and often sensational fishing offshore for albacore, yellowtail, and marlin. The foothills provide canyon settings for many lakes, including Lower Otay, Morena, Barrett, El Capitan, Cuyamaca, San Vicente, Hodges, Henshaw, and several more – with some of the biggest lake-record bass ever caught in the world.

Cleveland National Forest provides a surprise for many – remote mountains with canyons, hidden streams, small campgrounds, and a terrain with a forest of fir, cedar, and

CALIFORNIA

hardwoods such as oak. A landmark is Palomar Mountain, with several campgrounds at Palomar State Park and nearby in the national forest. This is a great family destination. Long-distance views, stargazing, and watching meteor showers from the 5,000-foot ridges and lookouts set on the edge of Anza-Borrego Desert to the nearby east are all among the best anywhere in the state.

For more urban pursuits, San Diego's Mission Bay Park offers a fantastic network of recreation opportunities, with trails for biking and inline skating, and beaches and boating access.

Everywhere you go, you will find campgrounds and parks, from primitive to deluxe. Some of the more remote sections of Cleveland National Forest, as well as Cuyamaca Rancho State Park, provide access to wildlands and primitive campsites. There are developed RV parks in the San Diego area that cost as much as fine hotel rooms in other parts of the state, and they're worth it, like silver dollars in a sea of pennies.

The region is one of the few that provides year-round recreation at a stellar level.

If you could live anywhere in America, where would it be? Well, that's what makes it so special to explore and visit, camping along the way.

CALIFORNIA

1 DOHENY STATE BEACH

Scenic rating: 10

on Dana Point Harbor

Map grid A1

Some campsites are within steps of the beach. Yet this state beach is right in town, set at the entrance to Dana Point Harbor. It is a pretty spot with easy access off the highway. Reservations are needed to guarantee a site at this popular campground. A lifeguard service is available in the summer, and campfire and junior ranger programs are also offered. A day-use area has a lawn with picnic area and volleyball courts. Bonfire rings are set up on the beach. Surfing is popular, but note that it is permitted at the north end of the beach only. San Juan Capistrano provides a nearby side trip, just three miles away.

RV sites, facilities: There are 115 sites for tents or RVs up to 35 feet (no hookups), and one hike-in/bike-in site. Picnic tables and fire grills are provided. Drinking water, restrooms with flush toilets and coin showers, dump station, Wi-Fi, aquarium, and seasonal snack bar are available. Propane gas and gasoline are nearby. Some facilities are wheelchair-accessible. Leashed pets are permitted in campground only, not on the beach.

Reservations, fees: Reservations are accepted at www.reserveamerica.com ($8 reservation fee). The fee is $40 per night, $15 per night for each additional vehicle, $3 per person per night for hike-in/bike-in site (photo ID required). Open year-round.

Directions: Drive on I-5 to the exit for Pacific Coast Highway/Camino de las Ramblas (three miles south of San Juan Capistrano). Take that exit and drive to Dana Point/Harbor Drive (second light). Turn left and drive one block to the park entrance. Doheny State Beach is about one mile from I-5.

Contact: Doheny State Beach, 949/496-6172; Orange Coast District, San Clemente Sector, 949/492-0802, www.parks.ca.gov.

2 SAN CLEMENTE STATE BEACH

Scenic rating: 8

near San Clemente

Map grid A1

The campground at San Clemente State Beach is set on a bluff, not on a beach. A few campsites here have ocean views. Surfing is popular on the north end of a one-mile beach. The beach is popular for swimming, body surfing, and skin diving. Of the three local state beaches that provide easy access and beachfront camping, this one offers full hookups. The others are Doheny State Beach to the north and San Onofre State Beach to the south. A feature at this park is a two-mile long interpretive trail, along with hike-in/bike-in campsites. Surfing camp is held here during the summer.

RV sites, facilities: There are 160 sites, 56 with full hookups (30 amps), for tents or RVs up to 40 feet, two hike-in/bike-in sites, and one group site with no hookups for tents or RVs for up to 50 people and 20 vehicles. Picnic tables and fire grills are provided. Restrooms with flush toilets and coin showers, dump station, Wi-Fi, summer lifeguard service, and summer programs are available. A store, coin laundry, and propane gas are nearby. Some facilities are wheelchair-accessible. Leashed pets are permitted in the campground only.

Reservations, fees: Reservations are accepted at www.reserveamerica.com ($8 reservation fee). The fee is $35–60 per night, $15 per night for each additional vehicle, $280 per night for the group site, $3 per person per night for hike-in/bike-in sites. Open year-round.

Directions: From I-5 in San Clemente, take the Avenida Calafia exit. Drive west for a short distance to the park entrance on the left.

Contact: San Clemente State Beach, 949/492-3156; Orange Coast District, 949/492-0802, www.parks.ca.gov.

CALIFORNIA

3 SAN ONOFRE STATE BEACH: BLUFF AREA

Scenic rating: 7

near San Clemente

Map grid A1

This camp may appear perfect at first glance, but nope, it is very noisy. Both the highway and train tracks are within very close range. You can practically feel the ground rumble, and that's not all: With Camp Pendleton just on the other side of the freeway, there is considerable noise from helicopters and other operations. Too bad. This is one of three parks set along the beach near San Clemente, just off the busy Coast Highway. The campground is set on top of a 90-foot bluff. This state beach covers more than 3,000 acres, featuring 3.5 miles of sandy beaches and access trails on the neighboring bluffs. This area is one of the most popular in California for surfing, and is also good for swimming. The shadow of the San Onofre Nuclear Power Plant is nearby. Other state beaches in the area are San Clemente State Beach and Doheny State Beach, both situated to the north.

RV sites, facilities: There are 176 sites for tents or RVs up to 30 feet (no hookups), and one group site for up to 50 people. Picnic tables and fire rings are provided. Drinking water, flush toilets, and cold outdoor showers are available. A store, coin laundry, and propane gas are available within about five miles. Some facilities are wheelchair-accessible. Leashed pets are permitted at the campground and beach, but must stay on designated trails to access the beach.

Reservations, fees: Reservations are accepted at www.reserveamerica.com ($8 reservation fee). The fee is $35 per night, $15 per night for each additional vehicle, $225 per night for the group site. Open March through October, weather permitting.

Directions: From San Clemente, drive south on I-5 for three miles to the Basilone Road exit. Take that exit and drive south on Basilone Road for two miles to the park.

Contact: San Onofre State Beach, 949/492-4872; Orange Coast District Office, 949/492-0802 or 949/366-8500, www.parks.ca.gov.

4 SAN ONOFRE STATE BEACH: SAN MATEO

Scenic rating: 9

near San Clemente

Map grid A1

This state beach is considered one of the best surf breaks in the United States—it's well known as the outstanding Trestles Surfing Area. The camp is set inland and includes a nature trail, featuring a marshy area where San Mateo Creek meets the shoreline. Although this is a state beach, the camp is relatively far from the ocean; it is a 1.5-mile walk to the beach. But it sure is a lot quieter than the nearby option, Bluff Area campground.

RV sites, facilities: There are 159 sites for tents or RVs up to 35 feet; 67 sites have partial hookups (30 amps). Picnic tables and fire grills are provided. A dump station and restrooms with coin showers and flush toilets are available. A store, propane gas, and coin laundry are nearby. Some facilities are wheelchair-accessible. Leashed pets are permitted.

Reservations, fees: Reservations are accepted at www.reserveamerica.com ($8 reservation fee). The fee is $35–60 per night, $15 per night for each additional vehicle. Open year-round.

Directions: Drive on I-5 to the southern end of San Clemente and the Cristianitos Road exit. Take that exit and drive east on Cristianitos Road for 1.5 miles to the park entrance on the right.

Contact: San Onofre State Beach, 949/492-4872; Orange Coast District Office, 949/492-0802 or 949/366-8500, www.parks.ca.gov.

5 GUAJOME COUNTY PARK

Scenic rating: 5

in Oceanside

Map grid A1

Guajome means "home of the frog" and, yep, so it is with little Guajome Lake and the adjacent marsh, both of which can be explored on a delightful two-mile hike. The lake provides a bit of fishing for warm-water species, mainly sunfish and catfish. Swimming is prohibited. Because of the wetlands, a huge variety of birds stop here on their migratory journeys, making this a favorite area for bird-watching. A historic adobe house in the park is a must-see. The park covers 557 acres and features several miles of trails for hiking and horseback riding, and a nearby museum with antique gas and steam engines and farm engines.

RV sites, facilities: There are 35 sites with full hookups (30 amps) for tents or RVs up to 45 feet; a few sites are pull-through. Picnic tables and fire grills are provided. Drinking water, restrooms with flush toilets and showers, dump station, and playground are available. An enclosed pavilion and gazebo can be reserved for groups. A store and propane gas are nearby. Leashed pets are permitted.

Reservations, fees: Reservations are accepted at 877/565-3600 ($5 reservation fee). Sites are $20 per night, $2 per night per each additional vehicle, $1 per pet per night. Some credit cards accepted. Open year-round.

Directions: From Oceanside, drive east on Highway 76/Mission Avenue for seven miles to Guajome Lakes Road. Turn right (south) on Guajome Lakes Road and drive to the entrance.

Contact: San Diego County Parks Department, Guajome County Park, 760/724-4489, www.sdparks.org.

6 PARADISE BY THE SEA RV RESORT

Scenic rating: 7

in Oceanside

Map grid A1

This is a classic oceanfront RV resort, but no tenters need apply. It's an easy walk to the beach. The main coastal rail line runs adjacent to the resort, so expect some noise. For boaters, Oceanside Marina to the immediate north is the place to go. Oceanside is an excellent headquarters for deep-sea fishing, with charter trips available; contact Helgren's Sportfishing (760/722-2133) to arrange charters. Legoland is four miles from the resort, and the Wave Waterpark and Mission San Luis Rey are seven miles away. Camp Pendleton, a huge Marine Corps training complex, is to the north.

RV sites, facilities: There are 102 sites with full hookups (30 amps) for RVs up to 40 feet; a few sites are pull-through. No tents. Picnic tables are provided. Restrooms, flush toilets, showers, cable TV, Wi-Fi, heated swimming pool, spa, clubhouse, banquet room, coin laundry, RV supplies, and convenience store are available. Boat rentals are nearby. Leashed pets are permitted, with certain breeds prohibited.

Reservations, fees: Reservations are recommended. Sites are $89–109 in summer, $44–49 in off-season, $5 per person ($3 in off-season) per night for more than two people, $15 per night ($5 in off-season) for each additional vehicle, $1.50 per pet per night. There is a 90-day limit per stay. Credit cards accepted. Open year-round.

Directions: Drive on I-5 to Oceanside and the Oceanside Boulevard exit. Take that exit and drive west on Oceanside Boulevard for 0.5 mile to South Coast Highway. Turn left on South Coast Highway and drive to the park on the right (1537 South Coast Highway).

Contact: Paradise by the Sea RV Resort, 760/439-1376, fax 760/439-1919, www.paradisebythesearvresort.com.

7 DIXON LAKE RECREATION AREA

Scenic rating: 7

near Escondido

Map grid A1

Little Dixon Lake is the centerpiece of a regional park in the Escondido foothills. The camp is set at an elevation of 1,405 feet, about 400 feet above the lake's shoreline. No private boats or swimming are permitted, and a 5-mph speed limit for rental boats keeps things quiet. The water is clear, with fair bass fishing (a few huge lunkers). "Dottie," a 25 lb. 1 oz. bass, was snagged and released in 2006, then floated up dead from old age in 2008. The best success for bass is in the spring, with trout fishing best in the winter and early spring. Catfish are stocked in the summer, trout in winter and spring. In the summer, the lake is open at night for fishing for catfish. A pretty and easy hike is Jack Creek Nature Trail, a one-mile walk to a seasonal 20-foot waterfall. Note that no wood fires are permitted, but charcoal and gas are allowed.

RV sites, facilities: There are 45 sites for tents or RVs up to 35 feet; 11 sites have full hookups (30 amps). A cabin is also available. Picnic tables, fire grills, and food lockers are provided. Drinking water, restrooms with flush toilets and showers, picnic shelters, boat rentals, bait, ice, snack bar, and playground are available. Some facilities are wheelchair- accessible. No pets are allowed.

Reservations, fees: Reservations are accepted at 760/741-3328 ($5 reservation fee). Sites are $20–25 per night. Groups can be accommodated. Some credit cards accepted. Open year-round.

Directions: Drive on I-15 to the exit for El Norte Parkway (four miles north of Escondido). Take that exit northeast and drive four miles to La Honda Drive. Turn left and drive about one mile to Dixon Lake.

Contact: Dixon Lake Recreation Area, City of Escondido, 760/839-4680, www.dixonlake. com or www.lakedixon.com.

8 SOUTH CARLSBAD STATE BEACH

Scenic rating: 9

near Carlsbad

Map grid A1   BEST (

No reservation? Then likely you can forget about staying here. This is a beautiful state beach and, as big as it is, the sites go fast to the coastal cruisers who reserved a spot. The campground is set on a bluff, with half the sites overlooking the ocean. The nearby beach is accessible by a series of stairs. This is a phenomenal place for scuba diving and snorkeling, with

a nearby reef available. This is also a popular spot for surfing and body surfing. Legoland is one mile away.

RV sites, facilities: There are 222 sites for tents or RVs up to 35 feet (no hookups). Picnic tables and fire rings are provided. Drinking water, restrooms with flush toilets and coin showers, Wi-Fi, and dump station are available. A lifeguard service is provided in summer. Supplies and a coin laundry are available in Carlsbad. Some facilities are wheelchair-accessible. Leashed pets are permitted, but not on the beach.

Reservations, fees: Reservations are accepted at www.reserveamerica.com ($8 reservation fee). Sites are $35–50 per night, $10 per night for each additional vehicle. Open year-round, with limited facilities in the winter.

Directions: Drive on I-5 to Carlsbad and the exit for Palomar Airport Road. Take that exit and drive west for 0.3 mile to Carlsbad Boulevard South. Turn south on Carlsbad Boulevard South and drive three miles to Poinsettia Avenue and the park entrance on the right.

Contact: South Carlsbad State Beach, 760/438-3143; San Diego Coast District, 619/688-3260, www.parks.ca.gov.

9 SAN ELIJO STATE BEACH

Scenic rating: 9

in Cardiff by the Sea

Map grid A1

As with South Carlsbad State Beach, about half the sites here overlook the ocean—that is, these are bluff-top campgrounds. The swimming and surfing are good, with a reef nearby for snorkeling and diving. What more could you ask for? Well, for one thing, how about not so many trains? Yep, train tracks run nearby and the trains roll by several times a day. So much for tranquility. Regardless, it is a beautiful beach just north of the small town of Cardiff by the Sea. As at all state beaches, reservations are usually required to get a spot between Memorial Day weekend and Labor Day weekend. Nearby San Elijo Lagoon at Solana Beach is an ecological preserve. Though this is near a developed area, there are numerous white egrets, as well as occasional herons and other marine birds.

RV sites, facilities: There are 144 sites for tents or RVs up to 22 feet (no hookups), 26 sites for tents or RVs up to 24 feet (full hookups), and one hike-in/bike-in site. Picnic tables and fire rings are provided. Drinking water, restrooms with flush toilets and coin showers, Wi-Fi, coin laundry, dump station, and small store are available. A lifeguard service is available in the summer. Some facilities are wheelchair-accessible. Leashed pets are permitted, but not on the beach.

Reservations, fees: Reservations are accepted aat www.reserveamerica.com ($8 reservation fee). Sites are $35–50 per night, $10 per night for each additional vehicle, $3 per person per night for hike-in/bike-in site. Open year-round.

Directions: Drive on I-5 to Encinitas and the Encinitas Boulevard exit. Take that exit and drive west on Encinitas Boulevard for one mile to U.S. 101 (South Coast Highway). Turn south (left) on U.S. 101 and drive two miles to the park on the right.

Contact: San Elijo State Beach, 760/753-5091; San Diego Coast District, 619/688-3260 or 760/720-7005, www.parks.ca.gov.

10 SANTEE LAKES RECREATION PRESERVE

Scenic rating: 8

near Santee

Map grid A1

This is a 190-acre park built around a complex of seven lakes. Some campsites are lakefront. The park is best known for its fishing. The lakes are stocked with large numbers of trout and catfish, with fantastic lake records including a 39-pound catfish, 13-pound rainbow trout, 13.9-pound largemouth bass, and 2.5-pound bluegill. Rowboats, pedal boats, kayaks, and canoes are available for rent. So how many lakes can you boat on? Answer: Only one, Lake 5. Fishing is now allowed on all lakes, and float tubing is permitted on four lakes for campers only. No swimming or water/body contact is allowed here, and no private motorized boats are permitted. This small regional park is 20 miles east of San Diego. It receives more than 100,000 visitors per year. The camp is set at 400 feet elevation. The Carlton Oaks Country Club is 0.5-mile away and open to the public. In 2007, Santa Lakes Recreation Preserve was voted "Best Campground in San Diego County," in a poll of San Diego Union-Tribune readers.

RV sites, facilities: There are 300 sites with full hookups (50 amps) for RVs of any length, and tents are allowed at some sites. Some sites are pull-through. Picnic tables are provided and some sites have barbecue grills. Restrooms with flush toilets and showers, drinking water, dump station, boat rentals, playground, seasonal swimming pool, general store, picnic area, amphitheater, RV storage, recreation center, Wi-Fi, pay phone, propane, and coin laundry are available. Some facilities are wheelchair-accessible. Leashed pets are permitted in the campground.

Reservations, fees: Reservations are accepted by website or at 619/596-3141. Sites are $34–44 per night, $2.50 per night for each additional vehicle, $1.50 per pet per night. Weekly and monthly rates available. Some credit cards accepted. Open year-round.

Directions: Drive on I-8 to El Cajon and Highway 67. Take the Highway 67 exit north (toward Santee) and drive one mile to Bradley Avenue. Take that exit and drive a short distance to Bradley Avenue. Turn left and drive one mile to Cuyamaca Street. Turn right and drive 1.6 miles to Mission Gorge Road. Turn left (west) and drive 0.3 mile to Fanita Parkway. Turn right and drive a short distance to the campground entrance on the left at 9310 Fanita Parkway.

Contact: Santee Lakes Recreation Preserve, Padre Dam Municipal Water District, 619/596-3141, www.santeelakes.com.

11 CAMPLAND ON THE BAY

Scenic rating: 6

on Mission Bay

Map grid A1   **BEST (**

No kidding, this is one of the biggest campgrounds on this side of the galaxy. The place has a prime location: The park overlooks Kendall Frost Wildlife Preserve and is set on Mission Bay, a beautiful spot and a boater's paradise; it includes a private beach. Waterskiing, sailboarding, and ocean access for deep-sea fishing are preeminent. SeaWorld, just north of San Diego, offers a premium side trip. There used to be numerous complaints about poor communications and customer services support, as well as staff shortages and safety issues. These problems appear to have been addressed by management, and the situation has improved.

RV sites, facilities: There are more than 558 sites, most with full or partial hookups (30 and 50 amps) for tents or RVs up to 45 feet. Picnic tables and fire pits are provided. Restrooms with flush toilets and showers, drinking water, cable TV, phone and modem access, Wi-Fi, swimming pools, spa, recreation hall, arcade, playground, café, dump station, coin laundry, grocery store, amphitheater, RV and boat storage, RV supplies, propane gas, boat ramp, marina, boat docks, water toy rentals, boat and bike rentals, and organized activities and events are available. Leashed pets are permitted, with certain restrictions.

Reservations, fees: Reservations are accepted up to two years in advance at 800/422-9386 ($25 site guarantee fee); tent sites are $39–84 per night, RV sites are $46–249.90 per night; $7 per night for each additional vehicle or boats and trailers, $3 per night per pet. Weekly rates are available during the winter. Some credit cards accepted. Open year-round.

Directions: Drive on I-5 south to San Diego and the Balboa-Garnet exit. Take that exit to Mission Bay Drive and drive to Grand Avenue. Turn right and drive one mile to Olney Street. Turn left on Olney Street and drive to Pacific Beach Drive. Turn left and drive a short distance to the campground entrance.

From northbound I-5 in San Diego, take the Grand-Garnet exit. Stay in the left lane to Grand Avenue. Turn left on Grand Avenue and drive to Olney Street. Turn left on Olney Street and continue as above.

Contact: Campland on the Bay, 800/422-9386, administration office, 858/581-4200, www.campland.com.

12 SANTA FE PARK RV RESORT

Scenic rating: 3

in San Diego

Map grid A1

This resort is a short drive from a variety of side trips, including the San Diego Zoo, SeaWorld, the historic San Diego Mission and Presidio Park, golf courses, beaches, sportfishing, and Tijuana.

RV sites, facilities: There are 129 sites with full hookups (20 and 30 amps) for RVs up to 40 feet (at three pull-through sites). No tent camping is allowed. Picnic tables and barbecues are provided. Restrooms with flush toilets and showers, drinking water, playground, heated swimming pool, spa, dump station, satellite TV, Wi-Fi, recreation room, mini theater, fitness center, and coin laundry are available. Some facilities are wheelchair-accessible. Leashed pets under 25 pounds are permitted, with some restrictions.

Reservations, fees: Reservations are accepted by website or at 800/959-3787. Sites are $45–69 per night, $3 per pet per night. Monthly rates available. Some credit cards accepted. Open year-round.

Directions: Drive on I-5 south to San Diego and Exit 23 for Balboa-Garnet. Take that exit, get in the left lane, and drive a short distance to the second stoplight and Damon Street. Turn left and drive 0.25 mile to Santa Fe Street. Turn left and drive 1.4 miles to the resort on the right (5707 Santa Fe Street).

On northbound I-5, drive to Exit 23 for Grand-Garnet. Take that exit and continue as it feeds to East Mission Bay Drive. Continue

CALIFORNIA

through four traffic signals to Damon Street. Turn right and drive 0.25 mile to Santa Fe Street. Turn left and drive 1.4 miles to the resort on the right (5707 Santa Fe Street). Note: Disregard the "Not a through street" sign on Santa Fe.

Contact: Santa Fe Park RV Resort, 858/272-4051 or 800/959-3787, fax 858/272-2845, www.santafepark.com.

13 MISSION TRAILS REGIONAL PARK

Scenic rating: 7

near San Diego

Map grid A1

Kumeyaay Lake and its campground are the centerpiece of this more than 6,000-acre park, which is only eight miles northeast of downtown San Diego. The park includes chaparral, oak woodland, mountains, and grasslands. Fishing is permitted for bass, bluegill, crappie, catfish, and carp; catch-and-release fishing is recommended. There are more than 40 miles of trails for hiking, biking, and horseback riding. Bird-watching is good in this park. Interpretive programs and organized activities are offered.

RV sites, facilities: There are 46 sites for tents or RVs up to 40 feet (no hookups). Picnic tables, tent pads, and fire boxes are provided. Restrooms with flush toilets and solar-heated showers, dump station, amphitheater, picnic area, and firewood are available. Alcoholic beverages are prohibited. Some facilities are wheelchair-accessible. Leashed pets are permitted.

Reservations, fees: Reservations are accepted at www.mtrp.org/campground. The fee is $14 per night, $4 per night for each additional vehicle, $3 per pet per night. Open Thursday through Sunday, year-round; campground closed Monday through Wednesday.

Directions: From I-8 in San Diego, take the Mission Gorge/Fairmount exit. Turn north on Mission Gorge Road and drive 6.5 miles to the northern (Kumeyaay Lake) entrance and Father Junipero Serra Trail. Turn left on Father

Junipero Serra Trail and drive 0.2 mile to the lake and campground on the right.

Contact: Mission Trails Regional Park, City of San Diego, 619/668-2748, Visitors Center, 619/668-3281, www.mtrp.org.

14 SAN DIEGO METROPOLITAN KOA

Scenic rating: 2

in Chula Vista

Map grid A1

This is one in a series of parks set up primarily for RVs cruising I-5. Chula Vista is between Mexico and San Diego, allowing visitors to make side trips east to Lower Otay Lake, north to the San Diego attractions, south to Tijuana, or "around the corner" on Highway 75 to Silver Strand State Beach. Nearby San Diego Bay is beautiful, with excellent waterskiing (in designated areas), sailboarding, and a great swimming beach.

RV sites, facilities: There are 180 sites for RVs of any length (full hookups), 63 sites for tents, and 27 cabins. Many sites are pull-through. Picnic tables and barbecue grills are provided. Restrooms with flush toilets and showers, drinking water, modem access, Wi-Fi, playground, dump station, coin laundry, heated swimming pool, spa, bike rentals, propane gas, seasonal organized activities, and convenience store are available. Some facilities are wheelchair-accessible. Leashed pets are permitted.

Reservations, fees: Reservations are accepted at 800/562-KAMP (800/562-5267). Sites are $30–49 per night for tents, $38–67 per night for RVs, $5 per night for each additional vehicle, $4 per person per night for more than two people. Some credit cards accepted. Open year-round.

Directions: Drive on I-5 to Chula Vista and the exit for E Street. Take that exit and drive east on E Street for three miles to 2nd Avenue. Turn left (north) on 2nd Avenue and drive 0.75 mile to the park on the right (111 North 2nd Avenue).

Contact: San Diego Metropolitan KOA,

619/427-3601, fax 619/427-3622, www.san
diegokoa.com.

15 CHULA VISTA RV RESORT

Scenic rating: 6

in Chula Vista

Map grid A1

This RV park is about 50 yards from San Diego
Bay, a beautiful, calm piece of water where
waterskiing is permitted in designated areas.
An excellent swimming beach is available, and
conditions in the afternoon for sailboarding are
also excellent. Bike paths are nearby.

RV sites, facilities: There are 237 sites with full
hookups (30 and 50 amps) for RVs. Some sites
are pull-through. No tents. Picnic tables and
cable TV are provided. Restrooms with flush
toilets and showers, drinking water, Wi-Fi,
modem access, fitness center, playgrounds,
heated swimming pool and spa, game room,
two waterfront restaurants, marina, fishing
pier, free boat launch, coin laundry, propane
gas, bicycle rentals, car rentals, picnic area,
meeting rooms, and general store are available. Some facilities are wheelchair-accessible.
Leashed pets up to 20 pounds are permitted,
with certain restrictions.

Reservations, fees: Reservations are accepted at
800/770-2878 or www.chulavistarv.com. Sites
are $54–70 in summer, $45–59 in off-season,
$3 per night per additional person for more
than four people, $3 per night for each addi-
tional vehicle, $1 per pet per night. Boat slips
are $36 per night if the boat is under 40 feet.
Weekly and monthly rates are available. Some
credit cards accepted. Open year-round.

Directions: Drive on I-5 to Chula Vista and the
exit for J Street/Marina Parkway. Take that exit,
turn left, and drive 0.5 mile west to Sandpiper
Way. Turn left and drive a short distance to the
park on the left (460 Sandpiper Way).

Contact: Chula Vista RV Resort, 619/422-0111,
fax 619/422-8872, www.chulavistarv.com.

16 LA PACIFICA RV RESORT

Scenic rating: 1

in San Ysidro

Map grid A1

This RV park is less than two miles from the
Mexican border. Note that many sites are filled
with long-term renters, but some sites are available for overnight use.

RV sites, facilities: There are 177 sites with
full hookups (30 and 50 amps) for RVs up to
40 feet. No tents. Many sites are pull-through.
Picnic tables are provided at most sites. Restrooms with flush toilets and showers, heated
swimming pool, whirlpool, clubhouse, video
and book library, cable TV, phone and modem
hookups, Wi-Fi, recreation room, dump station,
coin laundry, and propane gas are available. All
facilities are wheelchair-accessible. Leashed pets
are permitted with restrictions.

Reservations, fees: Reservations are accepted
at 888/786-6997. The fee is $40 per night.
Weekly and monthly rates available. Credit
cards accepted. Open year-round.

Directions: From the San Diego area, drive
south on I-5 to San Ysidro and the exit for
Dairymart Road. Take that exit east to Dairymart Road and drive a short distance to San
Ysidro Boulevard. Turn left and drive to the
park on the left (1010 San Ysidro Boulevard).

Contact: La Pacifica RV Resort, 619/428-4411,
fax 619/428-4413, www.lapacificarvresortpark.
com.

17 DRIPPING SPRINGS

Scenic rating: 7

near the Agua Tibia Wilderness in
Cleveland National Forest

Map grid B1

This is one of the premium Forest Service
camps available, set just inside the national
forest border near Vail Lake and adjacent to the
Agua Tibia Wilderness. Dripping Springs Trail
is routed south out of camp, starting at 1,600

feet elevation and climbing near the peak of Agua Tibia Mountain, at 4,779 feet.

RV sites, facilities: There are 33 sites for tents or RVs up to 22 feet (no hookups). Equestrian sites are available. Picnic tables and fire rings are provided. There is no drinking water. Vault toilets are available. Supplies are nearby in Temecula. Leashed pets are permitted.

Reservations, fees: Reservations are not accepted. The fee is $12 per night. Open June through February. Closed March through May for protection of an endangered species, the arroyo southwestern toad.

Directions: From I-15 in Temecula, drive 11 miles southeast on Highway 79 to the campground.

Contact: Cleveland National Forest, Palomar Ranger District, 760/788-0250, fax 760/788-6130.

18 OAK GROVE

🚶 🚲 🏊 🐕 🏕 ♿ 🚐 ⛺

Scenic rating: 4

near Temecula Creek in Cleveland National Forest
Map grid B1

Oak Grove camp is on the northeastern fringe of Cleveland National Forest at 2,800 feet elevation. Easy access from Highway 79 makes this a popular camp. The Palomar Observatory is five miles up the mountain to the west, but there is no direct way to reach it from the campground and it cannot be viewed from camp. Lake Henshaw is about a half-hour drive to the south. A boat ramp and boat rentals are available there. Note that some areas in the vicinity were burned by 2007 wildfires.

RV sites, facilities: There are 81 sites for tents or RVs up to 27 feet (no hookups). Picnic tables and fire grills are provided. Drinking water and flush toilets are available. Propane gas and groceries are nearby. Leashed pets are permitted.

Reservations, fees: Reservations are not accepted. Sites are $10–20 per night. Open year-round.

Directions: Drive on I-15 to the Highway 79 exit. Take that exit and drive south on Highway

79 to Aguanga. Continue southeast on Highway 79 for 6.5 miles to the camp entrance.

Contact: Cleveland National Forest, Palomar Ranger District, 760/788-0250, fax 760/788-6130.

19 PALOMAR MOUNTAIN STATE PARK

🚶 🚲 🏊 🐕 🏕 ♿ 🚐 ⛺

Scenic rating: 3

near the Palomar Observatory
Map grid B1

The 2007 Poomacha Fire damaged this campground. Before the fire, Reserve America named Palomar one of the top 100 family campgrounds in the United States. The long-distance views are still spectacular, of course, and there is some fishing in Doane Pond (state fishing laws are in effect here—great for youngsters learning to fish).

This developed state park is a short drive from the Palomar Observatory (not part of the park). At the Palomar Observatory you'll find the 200-inch Hale Telescope, America's largest telescope. This is a private, working telescope, run by the California Institute of Technology. Observatory tours are available, and the telescope can be viewed (but not used) by the public. There are four other campgrounds in the immediate area that are a short distance from the observatory. The elevation is 4,700 feet.

Note: At time of publication, all trails remained closed. There are 14 miles of trails, including several loop trails, often featuring long-distance views. Hikes include Boucher Trail (4 miles) and Lower Doane Valley Trail (3 miles); the view from Boucher Lookout is stunning, at 5,438 feet elevation looking out over the valley below.

RV sites, facilities: There are 31 sites for tents or RVs up to 27 feet (no hookups) and trailers up to 24 feet, three group sites for 15–25 people, and one hike-in/bike-in site. Picnic tables, fire grills, and food lockers are provided. Drinking water and restrooms with flush toilets and coin showers are available. Some facilities are wheelchair-accessible. Leashed pets are permitted in the campground, but not on trails.

Reservations, fees: Reservations are accepted at www.reserveamerica.com ($8 reservation fee). Sites are $30 per night, $8 per night for each additional vehicle, $90–145 per night for group sites. Fishing license required for fishing pond; buy before arrival. Open April–October, weather permitting.

Directions: Drive on I-15 to the Highway 76 exit (east of Oceanside). Take that exit and drive east on Highway 76 for approximately 25 miles to County Road S6 (which brings you to the top of Palomar Mountain). At the top of the mountain, turn left, drive about 50 feet to State Park Road/County Road S7. Turn left on State Park Road/County Road S7 and drive about 3.5 miles to the park entrance.

Contact: Palomar Mountain State Park, 760/742-3462, Colorado Desert District, 760/767-4087; Palomar Observatory, 760/742-2119, www.parks.ca.gov.

20 OBSERVATORY

🏃 🏕 ♿ 🚐 ⛺

Scenic rating: 4

near the Palomar Observatory in
Cleveland National Forest

Map grid B1

The Poomacha Fire in 2007 damaged this campground. Call before planning a trip.

This popular Forest Service camp is used primarily as a layover spot for campers visiting the nearby Palomar Observatory, housing the largest telescope in America. There are four other camps in the immediate area. The elevation is 4,800 feet. The trailhead for Observatory Trail starts at this camp. This two-hour hike from the campground to the observatory includes one short, steep climb, highlighted by a vista deck with a sweeping view of Mendenhall Valley, and then onward to the top and to the viewing area to catch a glimpse of the telescope. Tours are available, but the telescope itself is not available to the public for use.

RV sites, facilities: There are 42 sites for tents

or RVs up to 27 feet (no hookups). Picnic tables and fire grills are provided. Drinking water and restrooms with flush toilets and coin showers are available. Some facilities are wheelchair-accessible. Leashed pets are permitted.

Reservations, fees: Reservations are not accepted. Sites are $12 per night, double sites are $20 per night. Open May through November.

Directions: Drive on I-15 to the Highway 76 exit (east of Oceanside). Take that exit and drive east on Highway 76 for 25 miles to County Road S6 (which brings you to the top of Palomar Mountain). Turn left on County Road S6 and drive about 8.5 miles to the campground entrance on the right. The road is not recommended for trailers.

Contact: Cleveland National Forest, Palomar Ranger District, 760/788-0250, fax 760/788-6130.

21 OAK KNOLL CAMPGROUND

🏃 🏊 🏕 🚣 🚐 ⛺

Scenic rating: 4

near the Palomar Observatory

Map grid B1

The 2007 Poomacha Fire damaged this area.

The camp is set at 3,000 feet elevation in San Diego County foothill country among giant old California oaks. It is at the western base of Palomar Mountain, and to visit the Palomar Observatory and its awesome 200-inch telescope requires a remarkably twisty 10-mile drive up the mountain (the telescope is not open to the public, but the observatory is open). The campground management suggests you bring your telescope or borrow one of theirs for nighttime stargazing. A good side trip is the Boucher Lookout in Palomar Mountain State Park. Trailheads for hikes on Palomar Mountain include Observatory Trail (starting at Observatory) and Doane Valley Loop (starting in Palomar Mountain State Park).

RV sites, facilities: There are 46 sites for tents or RVs up to 30 feet, including 15 for RVs up to 40 feet; many sites have full or partial hookups (30 amps). Picnic tables and fire barrels are provided. Drinking water, restrooms with flush

CALIFORNIA

toilets and coin showers, dump station, library, video arcade, Wi-Fi, recreation hall, pavilion, seasonal activities, playground, swimming pool, baseball diamond, horseshoes, basketball court, coin laundry, propane gas, and convenience store are available. Leashed pets are permitted, with certain restrictions.

Reservations, fees: Reservations are accepted. Sites are $25–35 per night, $5 per person per night for more than two people, $5 per night for each additional vehicle, $3 per pet per night. Monthly rates available. Open year-round.

Directions: Drive on I-15 to the Highway 76 exit (east of Oceanside). Take that exit and drive east on Highway 76 for 21 miles to South Grade Road/County Road S6. Turn left and drive a short distance to the campground on the left.

Contact: Oak Knoll Campground, 760/742-3437, www.oakknoll.net.

22 WOODS VALLEY KAMPGROUND

Scenic rating: 5

near Lake Wohlford

Map grid B1

This privately operated park is situated on 20 acres and is popular with families. Lake Wohlford is about 10 miles to the south and has a lake speed limit of 5 mph. The lake is stocked with rainbow trout, brown trout, steelhead, channel catfish, and blue catfish. Insider's tip: A bald eagle winters at Lake Wohlford.

RV sites, facilities: There are 59 sites for RVs of any length, and 30 sites for tents. Many of the RV sites have partial hookups and some have full hookups (30 amps). Picnic tables and fire barrels are provided. Drinking water, restrooms with flush toilets and showers, dump station, coin laundry, swimming pool, catch-and-release fishing pond, small animal farm, playground, volleyball, horseshoes, recreation hall, group facilities, and supplies are available. Leashed pets are permitted, with some dogs prohibited.

Reservations, fees: Reservations are accepted.

Sites are $31–45 per night, $3 per night for each additional vehicle, $3 per pet per night. Monthly rates available. Open year-round.

Directions: From San Diego, drive north on I-15 to the Escondido area and take the Via Rancho Parkway exit and continue to Via Rancho Parkway. Turn right (name changes to Bear Valley Parkway) and drive approximately nine miles to a T intersection and Valley Parkway. Turn right on Valley Parkway and drive approximately six miles (name changes to Valley Center Road) to Woods Valley Road. Turn right and drive 2.2 miles to the park on the left.

Contact: Woods Valley Kampground, 760/749-2905, www.woodsvalley.com.

23 LAKE HENSHAW RESORT

Scenic rating: 7

near Santa Ysabel

Map grid B1

Lake Henshaw is the biggest lake in San Diego County, with 25 miles of shoreline, yet it has only one camp. It's a good one, with the cabin rentals a big plus. The camp is on the southern corner of the lake, at 2,727 feet elevation near Cleveland National Forest. Swimming, water/body contact, canoes, and rafts are not permitted and a 10-mph speed limit is in effect. The fishing is best for catfish, especially in the summer, and at times decent for bass, with the lake-record bass weighing 14 pounds, four ounces. Other fish species are trout, bluegill, and crappie. Like many reservoirs, Lake Henshaw is sometimes plagued by low water levels. A mobile home park is also on the premises.

RV sites, facilities: There are four acres of open sites for tents or RVs of any length (no hookups), and 25 sites with full hookups (20 amps) for tents or RVs up to 28 feet. Picnic tables and fire pits are provided. Restrooms with flush toilets and showers, cabins, swimming pool, spa, picnic area, clubhouse, playground, dump station, coin laundry, propane gas, boat and motor rentals, boat launch, bait and tackle, café, and convenience store are available. Some facilities are wheelchair-accessible. A golf course is 10 miles away. Leashed pets are permitted.

Reservations, fees: Reservations are not accepted. Sites are $20–25 per night, $2 per pet per night, and $7.50 per person per day for lake use. Boat launching is $5 per day. Some credit cards accepted. Open year-round.

Directions: From Santa Ysabel, drive seven miles north on Highway 79 to Highway 76. Turn east on Highway 76 and drive four miles to the campground on the left.

Contact: Lake Henshaw Resort, 760/782-3487 or 760/782-3501.

24 STAGECOACH TRAILS

Scenic rating: 6

near Julian

Map grid B1

You want space? You got space. That includes 600,000 acres of public lands bordering this RV campground, making Stagecoach Trails Resort ideal for those who love horseback riding and hiking. Forty corrals and two round pens at the campground let you know right away that this camp is very horse-friendly. It is more than a horse camp, however, with amenities for various types of campers. The resort provides the perfect jumping-off place for trips into neighboring Anza-Borrego Desert State Park and onto the Pacific Crest Trail, which is 2.5 miles away. The resort's name comes from its proximity to the old Wells Fargo Butterfield Stage Route. While the scenic rating merits a 6, if the rating were based purely on cleanliness, professionalism, and friendliness, this resort would rate a 10.

RV sites, facilities: There are 250 sites with full hookups (30 amps) for RVs of any length, and a large dispersed camping area for tents. Most RV sites are pull-through. Picnic tables and fire rings are provided. Drinking water, restrooms with flush toilets and showers, a heated pool, 40 horse corrals, a roping area, guided horseback riding, convenience store, ATM, coin laundry, group facilities, horseshoe pits, shuffleboard, 24-hour security, and propane

gas are available. Some facilities are wheelchair-accessible. Leashed pets are permitted.

Reservations, fees: Reservations are accepted at 877/TWO-CAMP (877/896-2267). Sites are $36 per night, $5 per person per night for more than two people, $5 per night per horse. Some credit cards accepted. Open year-round.

Directions: From Santa Ysabel, turn north on Highway 79 and drive 14 miles to County Road S2/San Felipe Road. Turn right and drive 17 miles to Highway 78. Turn right (west, toward Julian) and drive 0.3 mile to County Road S2 (Great Southern Overland Stage Route). Turn left and drive four miles to the resort on the right (at Mile Marker 21 on Road S2). Note: There are various ways to get here. Since equestrian campers towing horse trailers and other campers may need alternate directions, and those not towing rigs might want shortcut directions, call the resort for driving details.

Contact: Stagecoach Trails Park, 760/765-2197, www.stagecoachtrails.com.

25 PINEZANITA RV PARK AND CAMPGROUNDS

Scenic rating: 6

near Julian

Map grid B1

Set at an elevation of 4,680 feet in dense pine and oak, this camp has had the same owners, the Stanley family, for more than 30 years. The fishing pond is a great attraction for kids (no license is required); no swimming allowed. The pond is stocked with bluegill and catfish, some of which are 12 inches or longer. Two possible side trips include Lake Cuyamaca, five miles to the south, and William Heise County Park, about 10 miles to the north as the crow flies. Note that while the 2003 wildfires burned the area adjacent to the park, Pinezanita itself sustained no damage.

RV sites, facilities: There are 210 sites with full or partial hookups (30 and 50 amps) for RVs, 32 sites for tents, and three cottages. Picnic tables and fire rings are provided. Restrooms with flush toilets and showers, drinking water, a general store, ice, propane, bait and tackle, fishing pond, and dump station are available. Leashed pets are permitted, but not in the cottages.

Reservations, fees: Reservations are accepted. Sites are $25 per night per vehicle, $2 per night per person for more than two people, $5 per night for hookups, and $2 per night per pet, with a maximum of three pets. Some credit cards accepted. Open year-round.

Directions: From El Cajon, drive east on I-8 to Highway 79 (near Descanso Junction). Turn north on Highway 79 and drive 20 miles to Julian and the campground on the left.

Contact: Pinezanita RV Park and Campgrounds, 760/765-0429, www.pinezanita.com.

26 WILLIAM HEISE COUNTY PARK

Scenic rating: 6

near Julian

Map grid B1

This is a beautiful county park, set at 4,200 feet elevation, that offers hiking trails and a playground, all amid woodlands with a mix of oak and pine. Cabins provide a bonus opportunity for those who do not want to tent camp. A great hike starts right at camp (at the tent camping area), signed "Nature Trail." It joins Canyon Oak Trail and, after little more than a mile, links with Desert View Trail. Here you will reach an overlook with a view of the Anza-Borrego Desert and the Salton Sea. The park features more than 900 acres of mountain forests of oak, pine, and cedar. A popular equestrian trail is Kelly Ditch Trail, which is linked to Cuyamaca Rancho State Park and Lake Cuyamaca. The vast Anza-Borrego Desert State Park lies to the east, and the historic mining town of Julian is five miles away. Julian is known for its Apple Day Festival each fall. Note: Wildfires damaged some of this area.

RV sites, facilities: There are 20 sites for tents or RVs up to 40 feet with partial hookups (30

amps), 37 sites for tents or RVs up to 40 feet (full hookups), 42 sites for tents only, two group sites for up to 30 people each, and four cabins. Picnic tables and fire grills are provided. Restrooms with flush toilets and showers, drinking water, coin laundry, dump station, picnic areas, and a playground are available. Supplies are available five miles away in Julian. Leashed pets are permitted.

Reservations, fees: Reservations are accepted at 877/565-3600 ($5 reservation fee). Sites are $15–20 per night, group sites are $25–50 per night, cabins are $45 per night, $1 per pet per night. Some credit cards accepted. Open year-round.

Directions: From El Cajon, drive east on I-8 to Highway 79 (near Descanso Junction). Turn north on Highway 79 and drive to Julian and Highway 78. Turn west (left) on Highway 78 and drive to Pine Hills Road. Turn left (south) on Pine Hills Road and drive two miles to Frisius Drive. Turn left (south) on Frisius Drive and drive two miles to the park.

Contact: San Diego County Parks Department, 760/765-0650, www.sdparks.org.

27 DOS PICOS COUNTY PARK

Scenic rating: 4

near Ramona

Map grid B1

Dos Picos means "two peaks" and is the highlight of a landscape featuring old groves of oaks and steep, boulder-strewn mountain slopes. Some of the oaks are 300 years old. The park covers 78 acres and has a nature trail. As a county park, this camp is often missed. The park is quite picturesque, with plenty of shade trees and a small pond. Fishing is allowed in the pond, but swimming is prohibited. Several nearby recreation options are in the area, including Lake Poway and Lake Sutherland. The elevation is 1,500 feet. Note that this park was partially damaged by the Cedar Fire of 2003, although the campground is intact.

RV sites, facilities: There are two sites with

full hookups (30 amps), 61 sites with partial hookups, 11 sites with no hookups, one youth group area for up to 25 people, and a caravan area for tents or RVs. Picnic tables and fire grills are provided. Restrooms with flush toilets and showers, drinking water, dump station, playground, horseshoes, and soccer field are available. Supplies and a coin laundry are one mile away in Ramona. Leashed pets are permitted.

Reservations, fees: Reservations are accepted at 877/565-3600 ($5 reservation fee). Sites are $15–20 per night, $25 per night for the group area, $1 per pet per night. Some credit cards accepted. Open year-round.

Directions: Drive on I-8 to El Cajon and the exit for Highway 67. Take that exit and drive north on Highway 67 for 22 miles to Mussey Grade Road. Turn right (a sharp turn) on Mussey Grade Road and drive two miles to the park.

Contact: San Diego County Parks Department, Dos Picos County Park, 760/789-2220, fax 760/789-8435, www.sdparks.org.

28 CUYAMACA RANCHO STATE PARK: PASO PICACHO

Scenic rating: 2

in Cuyamaca Rancho State Park

Map grid B1

This camp is set at 4,900 feet elevation in Cuyamaca Rancho State Park, best known for Cuyamaca Peak, at 6,512 feet. Stonewall Peak Trail is accessible from across the street. This is a five-mile (sun-exposed) round-trip, featuring the climb to the summit at 5,730 feet. There are long-distance views from here, highlighted by the Salton Sea and the Anza-Borrego State Desert. It's the most popular hike in the park, a fair to moderate grade, and completed by a lot of families. Another, more ambitious, hike is the trail up to Cuyamaca Peak, starting at the southern end of the campground, a 6.5-mile round-trip tromp (alas, on a paved road; at least it's closed to traffic) with a climb of 1,600 feet in the process. The view from the

top is breathtaking, with the Pacific Ocean and Mexico visible to the west and south, respectively. Cuyamaca means "The Rain Beyond." Wildfires damaged some of this area.

RV sites, facilities: There are 85 sites for tents or RVs up to 30 feet long and 10 feet tall (no hookups), five cabins, a nature den cabin, four wood cabins, two group tent sites for up to 60 people each, and one hike-in/bike-in site. Fire grills and picnic tables are provided. Restrooms with flush toilets and coin showers, drinking water, Wi-Fi, and dump station are available. Supplies are nearby in Cuyamaca. Leashed pets are permitted.

Reservations, fees: Reservations are accepted at 800/444-PARK (800/444-7275) or www.recreation.gov ($8 reservation fee). Sites are $30 per night, $335 per night for group sites, $75 per night for nature den cabin, $70 per night for cabins, $3 per person per night for hike-in/bike-in site. Day-use parking $8. Open year-round.

Directions: From El Cajon, drive east on I-8 to Highway 79 (near Descanso Junction). Turn north (left) and drive 13.5 miles to the park entrance on the left.

Contact: Cuyamaca Rancho State Park, 760/765-0755, fax 760/765-3021, www.parks.ca.gov.

29 CUYAMACA RANCHO STATE PARK: GREEN VALLEY

Scenic rating: 2

in Cuyamaca Rancho State Park

Map grid B1

Green Valley is the southernmost camp in Cuyamaca Rancho State Park, which was 98 percent burned in the 2003 Cedar Fire. The camp is set at 3,900 feet elevation, with Cuyamaca Peak (6,512 feet) looming overhead to the northwest. A trailhead is available (look for the picnic area) at the camp for an easy five-minute walk to Green Valley Falls, and it can be continued out to the Sweetwater River in a 1.5-mile round-trip. The park covers 25,000 acres with trails for hiking, mountain biking, and horseback riding.

Note: Green Valley was closed to camping in 2008 due to tree hazards. Call prior to planning a trip.

RV sites, facilities: There are 81 sites for tents or RVs up to 30 feet long and 10 feet tall (no hookups), and one hike-in/bike-in site. Picnic tables and fire grills are provided. Restrooms with flush toilets and coin showers, drinking water, Wi-Fi, and dump station are available. A store and propane gas are nearby. Some facilities are wheelchair-accessible. Leashed pets are permitted.

Reservations, fees: Reservations are accepted at 800/444-PARK (800/444-7275) or www.reserveamerica.com ($8 reservation fee). Sites are $15–20 per night, $6 per night for each additional vehicle, $3 per person per night for hike-in/bike-in site. Open mid-May through November.

Directions: From El Cajon, drive east on I-8 to Highway 79 (near Descanso Junction). Turn north (left) on Highway 79 and drive seven miles to the campground entrance on the left (near Mile Marker 4).

Contact: Cuyamaca Rancho State Park, 760/765-3020, fax 760/765-3021, www.parks.ca.gov or www.cuyamaca.us.

30 LAGUNA
🚶 🐕 ♿ 🚐 ⛺

Scenic rating: 4

near Little Laguna Lake in Cleveland National Forest

Map grid B1

Laguna is set on Little Laguna Lake, one of the few lakes in America where "Little" is part of its official name. That's because for years everybody always referred to it as "Little Laguna Lake," and it became official. Yep, it's a "little" lake all right, a relative speck, and the lake can occasionally dry up. The camp is on its eastern side at an elevation of 5,550 feet. A trailhead for the Pacific Crest Trail is a mile north on the Sunrise Highway.

Big Laguna Lake, which is actually a pretty small lake, is one mile to the west.

RV sites, facilities: There are 103 sites for tents, and 73 sites for tents or RVs up to 50 feet (no hookups). Picnic tables and fire grills are provided. Drinking water and restrooms with flush toilets and coin showers are available. A store and propane gas are nearby. Some facilities are wheelchair-accessible. Leashed pets are permitted.

Reservations, fees: Reservations are accepted at 877/444-6777 or www.recreation.gov ($10 reservation fee). Sites are $17 per night. Open year-round.

Directions: From San Diego, drive east on I-8 about 50 miles to the Laguna Junction exit for the Sunrise Highway. Turn north on the Sunrise Highway and drive 11 miles to the town of Mount Laguna. Continue north on Sunrise Highway for 2.5 miles to the campground entrance road on the left.

Contact: Cleveland National Forest, Descanso Ranger District, 619/445-6235, fax 619/445-1753; Laguna Mountain Visitor Center, 619/473-8547.

31 EL PRADO GROUP CAMP
🚶 🐕 🚐 ⛺

Scenic rating: 3

in Cleveland National Forest

Map grid B1

El Prado Group Camp is directly adjacent to Laguna and is an alternative to nearby Horse Heaven Group Camp. Five separate group sites are available. The elevation is 5,500 feet.

RV sites, facilities: There are five group sites for tents or RVs up to 27 feet (no hookups) that can accommodate 30–50 people each. Picnic tables and fire grills are provided. Drinking water and vault toilets are available. You can buy supplies in Mount Laguna. Leashed pets are permitted.

Reservations, fees: Reservations are required at 877/444-6777 or www.recreation.gov ($10 reservation fee). Sites are $45–75 per night.

Open Memorial Day weekend through mid-October, weather permitting.

Directions: From San Diego, drive east on I-8 about 50 miles to the Laguna Junction exit for the Sunrise Highway. Turn north on the Sunrise Highway and drive 11 miles to the town of Mount Laguna. Continue north on Sunrise Highway for 2.5 miles to the campground entrance road on the left.

Contact: Cleveland National Forest, Descanso Ranger District, 619/445-6235, fax 619/445-1753.

32 HORSE HEAVEN GROUP CAMP

Scenic rating: 3

near the Pacific Crest Trail in Cleveland National Forest

Map grid B1

Horse Heaven is set on the northeastern border of Cleveland National Forest at 5,500 feet elevation, near Mount Laguna in the Laguna Recreation Area. The Pacific Crest Trail passes near the camp. Laguna and El Prado Group Camp provide nearby options. Side-trip possibilities include visiting Little Laguna Lake to the immediate west and Desert View Picnic Area to the south at Mount Laguna.

RV sites, facilities: There are three group sites for tents or RVs up to 27 feet (no hookups) that can accommodate 40–100 people each. Picnic tables and fire grills are provided. Drinking water and vault toilets are available. You can buy supplies in Mount Laguna. Leashed pets are permitted.

Reservations, fees: Reservations are required at 877/444-6777 or www.recreation.gov ($10 reservation fee). Sites are $60–150 per night. Open Memorial Day weekend through Labor Day weekend.

Directions: From San Diego, drive east on I-8 about 50 miles to the Laguna Junction exit for the Sunrise Highway. Turn north on the Sunrise Highway and drive 11 miles to the town of Mount Laguna. Continue north on Sunrise

Highway for two miles to the campground entrance road on the left.

Contact: Cleveland National Forest, Descanso Ranger District, 619/445-6235, fax 619/445-1753.

33 VACATIONER RV RESORT

Scenic rating: 2

near El Cajon

Map grid B1

This well-maintained resort is 25 minutes from San Diego, 40 minutes from Mexico. Discount tickets to area attractions such as the San Diego Zoo, SeaWorld, and the Wild Animal Park are available. There is the very real chance of getting highway noise if you have a site at the back of the park. The RV sites are on asphalt and gravel, and there are many shade trees. The elevation is 260 feet.

RV sites, facilities: There are 147 sites with full hookups (30 and 50 amps) for RVs up to 40 feet, including 13 pull-through sites. No tent camping is allowed. Restrooms with flush toilets and showers, drinking water, coin laundry, recreation room, horseshoe pits, telephone and modem access, Wi-Fi, heated swimming pool, spa, cable TV, free video library, RV storage, and picnic area with barbecues are available. A store is nearby. Some facilities are wheelchair-accessible. Leashed pets up to 20 pounds are permitted, with certain restrictions.

Reservations, fees: Reservations are accepted at 866/490-5844. Sites are $32–45 per night, $2 per person per night for more than two people, $2 per night for each additional vehicle, $2 per pet per night. Some credit cards accepted. Open year-round.

Directions: From El Cajon, drive east on I-8 for three miles to the Greenfield Drive exit. Take that exit, turn north and drive 100 feet to East Main Street. Turn left (west) and drive 0.5 mile to the park on the left.

Contact: Vacationer RV Resort, 866/490-5844 or 619/442-0904, fax 619/442-4378, www.vacationerrv.com.

CALIFORNIA

34 RANCHO LOS COCHES RV PARK

Scenic rating: 2

near Lake Jennings

Map grid B1

This is not your typical RV park. This place has plenty of charm and a private setting. There is an abundance of history here, too. The park land was once the smallest Mexican land grant of the 19th century. The former ranch was also once a station for the Jackass Mail and Butterfield Stage routes. Windmill House, built in 1925, is featured prominently on the property and is a local historic landmark. Nearby Lake Jennings provides an option for boaters and anglers and also has a less developed camp on its northeast shore. Vista Point on the southeastern side of the lake provides a side trip. (For more information, see the Lake Jennings County Park listing in this chapter.) Casinos are nearby.

RV sites, facilities: There are 142 sites with full hookups (30 and 50 amps) for RVs up to 45 feet and four tent areas. Restrooms with flush toilets and showers, drinking water, cable TV, dump station, heated swimming pool, spa, recreation hall, fitness room, horseshoes, table tennis, Wi-Fi, and coin laundry are available. A store and gas station are one mile away. Leashed pets are permitted.

Reservations, fees: Reservations are accepted by website or at 800/630-0448. Sites are $36–43 per night for RVs (depending on size), $25 per night for tents, $3 per person per night for more than two people. Weekly and monthly rates available. Open year-round.

Directions: From El Cajon, drive east on I-8 to the Los Coches Road exit. Take that exit, and drive under the freeway to Highway 8 Business Route. Turn right on Highway 8 Business Route and drive 0.25 mile to the park entrance on the left (13468 Highway 8 Business).

Contact: Rancho Los Coches RV Park, 619/443-2025, fax 619/443-8440, www.rancholoscochesrv.com.

35 LAKE JENNINGS COUNTY PARK

Scenic rating: 6

on Lake Jennings

Map grid B1

Lake Jennings, at 108 acres, is a nice little backyard fishing hole and recreation area set at 700 feet elevation, with easy access from I-8. Most people come here for the fishing; the lake is stocked with trout and catfish. It has quality prospects for giant catfish, as well as largemouth bass, bluegill, and, in cool months, rainbow trout. The lake-record blue catfish is 60 pounds. Note that while shore fishing is available on a daily basis, boats are permitted on the lake November through August, Friday through Sunday. Night fishing is allowed on weekends during the summer. A fishing permit is required. The highlights here are evening picnics, summer catfishing, and a boat ramp and rentals. Swimming and water/body contact are prohibited. Miles of hiking trails are routed through chaparral-covered hills. Only one camp is available right at the lake, and this is it. Note that though some of this park was damaged in the Cedar Fire of 2003, the campground was unaffected.

RV sites, facilities: There are 30 sites with full hookups (30 amps) for RVs up to 35 feet, 35 sites with partial hookups (20 amps) for RVs up to 25 feet, 25 tent sites, and a youth group area for up to 35 people. Some sites are pull-through. Picnic tables and fire grills are provided. Restrooms with flush toilets and showers, drinking water, nature trail, clubhouse, horseshoes, and dump station are available. A store is nearby. Leashed pets are permitted.

Reservations, fees: Reservations are accepted at 877/565-3600 ($5 reservation fee). Sites are $15–25 per night, $25 per night for the group area, $1 per pet per night. A fee is charged for fishing. Open year-round.

Directions: From San Diego, drive east on I-8 for 21 miles to Lake Jennings Park Road. Turn north (left) on Lake Jennings Park Road and drive one mile to the park entrance.

Contact: San Diego County Parks Department, 858/694-3049, fax 858/495-5841, www.sdparks.org; Lake Jennings Entrance Station, 619/443-2004.

36 WOODED HILL GROUP

Scenic rating: 4

near the Pacific Crest Trail in
Cleveland National Forest

Map grid B1

This camp is set on the southern flank of Mount Laguna. The Pacific Crest Trail is within one mile of Burnt Rancheria Campground, a mile up the road to the northwest. The elevation is 6,000 feet.

RV sites, facilities: There is one group site for tents or RVs up to 27 feet (no hookups) that can accommodate up to 100 people. Picnic tables and fire grills are provided. Drinking water and vault toilets are available. A store is nearby. Leashed pets are permitted.

Reservations, fees: Reservations are required at 877/444-6777 or www.recreation.gov ($10 reservation fee). Sites are $165 per night. Open Memorial Day weekend through Labor Day weekend.

Directions: From San Diego, drive east on I-8 about 50 miles to the Laguna Junction exit for the Sunrise Highway. Turn north on the Sunrise Highway and drive about eight miles to the campground entrance road on the left.

Contact: Cleveland National Forest, Descanso Ranger District, 619/445-6235, fax 619/445-1753.

37 BURNT RANCHERIA

Scenic rating: 6

near the Pacific Crest Trail in
Cleveland National Forest

Map grid B1

Burnt Rancheria is set high on the slopes of Mount Laguna in Cleveland National Forest, at an elevation of 6,000 feet. Remodeled in 2005, it is quiet and private with large, roomy sites.

The Pacific Crest Trail is approximately one mile from camp. Desert View Picnic Area, a mile to the north, provides a good side trip. Wooded Hill Group Campground is one mile away.

RV sites, facilities: There are 58 sites for tents or RVs up to 50 feet (no hookups), and 51 sites for tents only. Picnic tables and fire grills are provided. Vault and flush toilets and coin showers are available. Drinking water is available. Some facilities are wheelchair-accessible. Supplies are nearby in Mount Laguna. Leashed pets are permitted.

Reservations, fees: Reservations are accepted at 877/444-6777 or www.recreation.gov ($10 reservation fee). Sites are $17 per night. Open mid-April through October, weather permitting.

Directions: From San Diego, drive east on I-8 about 50 miles to the Laguna Junction exit for the Sunrise Highway. Turn north on the Sunrise Highway and drive about 10 miles north to the campground entrance road on the right.

Contact: Cleveland National Forest, Descanso Ranger District, 619/445-6235, fax 619/445-1753.

38 CIBBETS FLAT

Scenic rating: 4

on Troy Canyon Creek in Cleveland National Forest

Map grid B1

Cibbets Flat is at the southern flank of the Laguna Mountains near Troy Canyon Creek, and Kitchen Creek runs adjacent to the camp. It is an obscure, fairly remote camp and staging area for the Pacific Crest Trail. A trailhead for the PCT is a mile southeast of camp, used mostly by hikers heading north across the Laguna Mountains. The elevation is 4,200 feet.

RV sites, facilities: There are 25 sites for tents or RVs up to 27 feet (no hookups). Picnic tables and fire grills are provided. Drinking water and vault toilets are available. Leashed pets are permitted.

Reservations, fees: Reservations are not accepted. Sites are $10 per night. Open year-round.

Directions: From El Cajon, drive east on I-8 for about 50 miles to Boulder Oaks, then continue a short distance to the exit for Kitchen Creek/Cameron Station. Turn north on Kitchen Creek Road and drive 4.5 miles to the campground entrance on the right.

Contact: Cleveland National Forest, Descanso Ranger District, 619/445-6235, fax 619/445-1753.

39 COTTONWOOD

Scenic rating: 4

in the McCain Valley Recreation Area
Map grid B1

This camp is set on the western edge of the McCain Valley Recreation Area. Like most Bureau of Land Management camps, it is little known and little used. It is occasionally frequented by backcountry horseback riders. The elevation is 4,000 feet.

RV sites, facilities: There are 29 sites for tents or RVs up to 35 feet (no hookups). Picnic tables and fire grills are provided. Drinking water and vault toilets are available. Two group horse corrals are also available. Leashed pets are permitted.

Reservations, fees: Reservations are not accepted. Sites are $6 per night. Open year-round.

Directions: From El Cajon, drive east on I-8 for 70 miles to the Boulevard/Campo exit. Take that exit right, then at the frontage road, turn left immediately and drive east (just south of the interstate) for two miles to McCain Valley Road. Turn left on McCain Valley Road and drive about 13 miles to the campground.

Contact: Bureau of Land Management, El Centro Field Office, 760/337-4400, fax 760/337-4490.

40 BOBCAT MEADOWS

Scenic rating: 6

in Cleveland National Forest
Map grid B1

This camp, along with nearby Corral Canyon, caters primarily to OHV users. The camp is shaded with live oaks and is a 10-minute drive

from Corral Canyon camp. This camp is similar, but it has no water. The more spacious sites and privacy can make up for that. The elevation is 3,800 feet.

RV sites, facilities: There are 20 sites for tents or RVs up to 27 feet (no hookups). Fire pits are provided. Vault toilets are available. No drinking water is available. Garbage must be packed out. Leashed pets are permitted.

Reservations, fees: Reservations are not accepted and there is no camping fee. An Adventure Pass ($30 annual fee or $5 daily fee per parked vehicle) is required. Open year-round.

Directions: From El Cajon, drive east on I-8 to Pine Valley, then continue east for four miles to Buckman Springs Road. Take the Buckman Springs off-ramp, turn right (south) on Buckman Springs Road, and drive 3.6 miles to Corral Canyon Road, signed "Camp Morena." Turn right and drive 6.2 miles (the road becomes Forest Service Road 17S04) to Four Corners Trailhead. Bear left (Forest Service Road 17S04) and drive a mile to the campground on the left.

Contact: Cleveland National Forest, Descanso Ranger District, 619/445-6235, fax 619/445-1753.

41 CORRAL CANYON

Scenic rating: 6

in Cleveland National Forest
Map grid B1

This is a primitive camp set adjacent to a network of OHV trails leading 24 miles into the Corral Canyon area, hence the name. Most of the routes lead into a chaparral landscape. The camp is set at 3,500 feet elevation and is used primarily by the OHV crowd. The availability of drinking water at this campground is a big plus.

RV sites, facilities: There are 20 sites for tents or RVs up to 27 feet (no hookups). Picnic tables and fire rings are provided. Drinking water and vault toilets are available. Garbage must be packed out. Leashed pets are permitted.

Reservations, fees: Reservations are not accepted and there is no camping fee. An Adventure

Pass ($30 annual fee or $5 daily fee per parked vehicle) is required. Open year-round.

Directions: From El Cajon, drive east on I-8 to Pine Valley, then continue east for four miles to Buckman Springs Road. Take the Buckman Springs off-ramp, turn right (south) on Buckman Springs Road, and drive 3.6 miles to Corral Canyon Road, signed "Camp Morena." Turn right and drive 6.2 miles (the road becomes Forest Service Road 17S04) to the Four Corners Trailhead. Continue straight on Corral Canyon Road for one mile to the campground on the right.

Contact: Cleveland National Forest, Descanso Ranger District, 619/445-6235, fax 619/445-1753.

42 BOULDER OAKS EQUESTRIAN

Scenic rating: 4

near Lake Morena in Cleveland National Forest

Map grid B1

Boulder Oaks is easy to reach, just off I-8, yet it is a very small camp with an important trailhead for the Pacific Crest Trail running right by it. This camp also is designed as a trailhead camp for equestrians. The elevation is 3,300 feet, set in the southern end of Cleveland National Forest and the Laguna Mountains. This campground is closed March 1 to approximately mid-June to protect the breeding activity of the arroyo southwestern toad, an endangered species.

RV sites, facilities: There are 19 sites for tents or RVs up to 27 feet (no hookups) and 17 equestrian sites. Picnic tables and fire grills are provided. Drinking water and vault toilets are available. Leashed pets are permitted.

Reservations, fees: Reservations are not accepted for individual sites. Reservations are required for equestrian sites at 877/444-6777 or www.recreation.gov ($10 reservation fee). Sites are $10 per night for individual sites, $12–24 per night for equestrian sites. Open mid-June through February.

Directions: From El Cajon, drive east on I-8 to Pine Valley, then continue east for four miles

to Buckman Springs Road. Take the Buckman Springs off-ramp, turn right (south) on Buckman Springs Road, and drive a short distance to a four-way stop sign at Old Highway 80. Turn left and drive 2.5 miles to the campground.

Contact: Cleveland National Forest, Descanso Ranger District, 619/445-6235, fax 619/445-1753.

43 LARK CANYON OHV

Scenic rating: 5

in the McCain Valley Recreation Area

Map grid B1

This is a small camp that few know of, set at 4,000 feet elevation in the McCain Valley National Cooperative and Recreation Area. It is near a popular off-highway-vehicle area. Many dirt bikers use it as their base camp.

RV sites, facilities: There are 15 sites for tents or RVs up to 35 feet (no hookups). Picnic tables and fire grills are provided. Vault toilets are available. Drinking water is available. Garbage must be packed out. Leashed pets are permitted.

Reservations, fees: Reservations are not accepted. The fee is $6 per night. Open year-round.

Directions: From El Cajon, drive east on I-8 for 70 miles to the Boulevard/Campo exit. Take that exit right, then at the frontage road, turn left immediately and drive east (just south of the interstate) for two miles to McCain Valley Road. Turn left at McCain Valley Road and drive three miles to the campground.

Contact: Bureau of Land Management, El Centro Field Office, 760/337-4400, fax 760/337-4490.

44 SWEETWATER SUMMIT REGIONAL PARK

Scenic rating: 7

near Sweetwater Reservoir in Bonita

Map grid B1

This regional park overlooks the Sweetwater Reservoir in Bonita. The campground is set right on the summit, overlooking the

CALIFORNIA

Sweetwater Valley. This camp has equestrian sites with corrals for the horses. There are 15 miles of trails in the park for hiking, mountain biking, and horseback riding. There are several golf courses nearby and it is 15 minutes from Tijuana. The Chula Vista Nature Center is nearby on the shore of south San Diego Bay.

RV sites, facilities: There are 46 sites with partial hookups (20 amps) for tents or RVs up to 45 feet, including 15 equestrian sites with corrals. Picnic tables and fire grills are provided. Restrooms with flush toilets and showers, drinking water, covered pavilion, and dump station are available. Leashed pets are permitted.

Reservations, fees: Reservations are accepted at 858/565-3600 or 877/565-3600 ($5 reservation fee). Sites are $20 per night, $2 per horse per night, $1 per pet per night. Open year-round.

Directions: From San Diego, drive south on I-805 for 10 miles to Bonita Road. Turn east on Bonita Road and drive to San Miguel Road. Bear right on San Miguel Road and drive two miles to the park entrance on the left.

Contact: San Diego County Parks Department, Sweetwater Summit Regional Park, 619/472-7572, fax 619/472-7571, www.sdparks.org.

45 LAKE MORENA COUNTY PARK

Scenic rating: 7

near Campo

Map grid B1

Lake Morena is like a silver dollar in a field of pennies. Yes, it is out in the boondocks, but it's well worth the trip. The county park camp is set on the southern shore at an elevation of 3,200 feet. The landscape is chaparral, oak woodlands, and grasslands, and the campsites are set in a grove of oaks. When full, the lake covers 1,500 surface acres, but water levels can fluctuate wildly. Bass fishing can be excellent, so if you like to fish for bass, don't miss it. Catch rates for bass can be very good, and some bass are big; the lake record for largemouth bass weighed 19 pounds, three ounces, and

the lake record for trout weighed nine pounds, six ounces. Boat rentals are available nearby; motor boats are allowed only on Fridays and Saturdays. No swimming or powerboating allowed. The lake is just south of Cleveland National Forest and only seven or eight miles from the California–Mexico border. The Pacific Crest Trail passes through the park, and the surrounding national forest has hiking and horseback-riding trails. San Diego is about a 45-minute drive from the campground.

RV sites, facilities: There are 86 sites and a group area for tents or RVs of any length; many sites have full hookups (30 amps). Ten cabins are also available. Picnic tables and fire grills are provided. Restrooms with flush toilets, showers, and drinking water are available. A store, boat ramp, and rowboat rentals are nearby. Leashed pets are permitted.

Reservations, fees: Reservations are accepted at 858/565-3600 or 877/565-3600 ($5 reservation fee). Sites are $15–20 per night, $25–50 per night for the group area, $1 per pet per night, $6 per day for boat launching. Open year-round.

Directions: From El Cajon, drive east on I-8 to Pine Valley, then continue east for four miles to the exit for Buckman Springs Road/County Road S1. Take that exit, turn south (right), and drive 5.5 miles to Oak Drive. Turn right (south) on Oak Drive and drive 1.5 miles to Lake Morena Drive. Turn left on Lake Morena Drive and drive to the park entrance on the right.

Contact: San Diego County Parks Department, Lake Morena County Park, 619/579-4101, fax 619/478-5327, www.sdparks.org.

46 LAKE MORENA RV PARK

Scenic rating: 6

near Campo

Map grid B1

This camp is near the southern side of Lake Morena, a great lake for fishing and off-season vacations. It is one of three camps near the lake and the best for RVs. Lake Morena, at

3,200 feet elevation, is a large reservoir in the San Diego County foothills and is known for big bass. It is also known for fluctuating water levels. Swimming is prohibited at this lake. (See the Lake Morena County Park listing in this chapter for information on Lake Morena.)

RV sites, facilities: There are 41 sites with full or partial hookups (30 and 50 amps) for RVs up to 40 feet. No tents. Picnic tables are provided. Restrooms with flush toilets and showers, dump station, nine-hole pitch-and-putt golf course, propane gas, and coin laundry are available. Some facilities are wheelchair-accessible. Leashed pets are permitted.

Reservations, fees: Reservations are recommended. Sites are $28 per night. Some credit cards accepted. Open year-round.

Directions: From El Cajon, drive east on I-8 to Buckman Springs Road. Take the Buckman Springs off-ramp, turn right (south) on Buckman Springs Road, and drive 5.5 miles to Oak Drive. Turn right on Oak Drive and drive 1.5 miles to Lake Morena Drive. Turn left on Lake Morena Drive and drive a short distance to the park on the right (2330 Lake Morena Drive).

Contact: Lake Morena RV Park, 619/478-5677, fax 619/478-5031.

47 POTRERO COUNTY PARK

Scenic rating: 3

near the Mexican border

Map grid B1

If you are looking for a spot to hole up for the night before getting through customs, this is the place. This park covers 115 acres, set at an elevation of 2,300 feet. It is a broad valley peppered with coastal live oaks amid grassy meadows and rocky foothills. The average summer high temperature is in the 90° F range, and the average winter low is 34° F. There is occasional light snowfall in the winter. Potrero means "pasturing place." Some of the summer grazers are rattlesnakes, occasionally spotted here. Side trips include the railroad museum and century-old historic stone store in Campo, and the Mexican community of Tecate. In fact, it is just a heartbeat away from the customs inspection station in Tecate. A good side trip is to the nearby Tecate Mission Chapel, where you can pray that the guards do not rip your vehicle up in the search for contraband. Insider's tip: In the spring you may hear the evening call of the Pacific tree frog.

RV sites, facilities: There are 39 sites with partial hookups (20, 30, and 50 amps) for RVs up to 45 feet, 10 tent sites, and a group site for up to 45 people. Picnic tables and fire grills are provided. Restrooms with flush toilets and showers, drinking water, playground, and dump station are available. Picnic areas, ball fields, and a dance pavilion are available. You can buy supplies in Potrero. Leashed pets are permitted.

Reservations, fees: Reservations are accepted at 858/565-3600 or 877/565-3600 ($5 reservation fee). Sites are $15–20 per night, $25–50 per night for the group site, $1 per pet per night. Open year-round.

Directions: From El Cajon, drive east on Highway 94 for 42 miles (near the junction of Highway 188) to Potrero Valley Road. Turn north on Potrero Valley Road and drive one mile to Potrero Park Road. Turn right (east) on Potrero Park Road and drive one mile to the park entrance.

Contact: San Diego County Parks Department, 619/478-5212, fax 619/478-2060, www.sdparks.org.

48 OUTDOOR WORLD RETREAT

Scenic rating: 4

in Boulevard

Map grid B1

This retreat sits on 163 acres and has hiking trails. The elevation is 3,800 feet. The town of Boulevard is centrally situated for a wide variety of recreation possibilities. About 10 miles to the north is Mount Laguna, with hiking trails available. About 30 minutes to the south is the nearest point of entry to Mexico at Tecate. Fishing at Lake Morena or Lake Cuyamaca is also a possibility, as is soaking in nearby hot springs. A casino is four miles away. A train museum is available in Campo, about 16 miles away.

RV sites, facilities: There are 151 sites with full hookups (20, 30, and 50 amps) for tents or RVs up to 45 feet, a primitive tent camping area, and a group camping area for up to 1,000 people. Some sites are pull-through. Picnic tables and fire rings are provided at some sites. A clubhouse, rest-rooms with showers, horseshoes, volleyball court, coin laundry, gift shop, general store, Wi-Fi, group campfire area, and organized activities and classes are available. A swimming pool and hot tub are available May through September. Golf carts are allowed. Some facilities are wheelchair-accessible. Leashed pets are permitted, with some breeds prohibited.

Reservations, fees: Reservations are accepted by website or at 888/703-0009. Sites are $37 per night, $3 per person per night for more than two people, $3 per night for each additional vehicle. Weekly, monthly, and group rates available. Credit cards accepted. Open year-round.

Directions: From El Cajon, drive east on I-8 for approximately 50 miles (past Alpine) to the Crestwood/Live Oak Springs Road exit. Take that exit and turn east and drive 0.5 mile to Church Street. Turn right and drive 4.2 miles to Highway 94. Turn left (east) and drive 1.1 miles to the resort on the right.

Contact: Outdoor World Retreat, 619/766-4480, www.outdoorworldrvpark.com.

CALIFORNIA DESERTS

☾ BEST RV PARKS AND CAMPGROUNDS

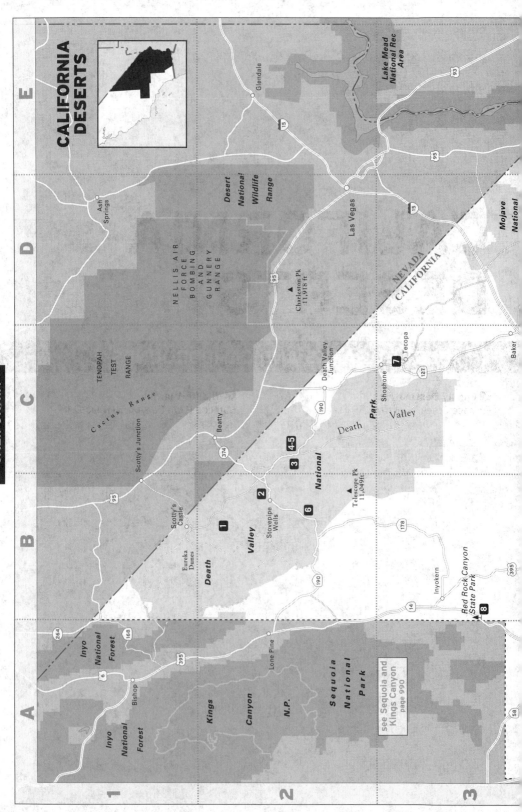

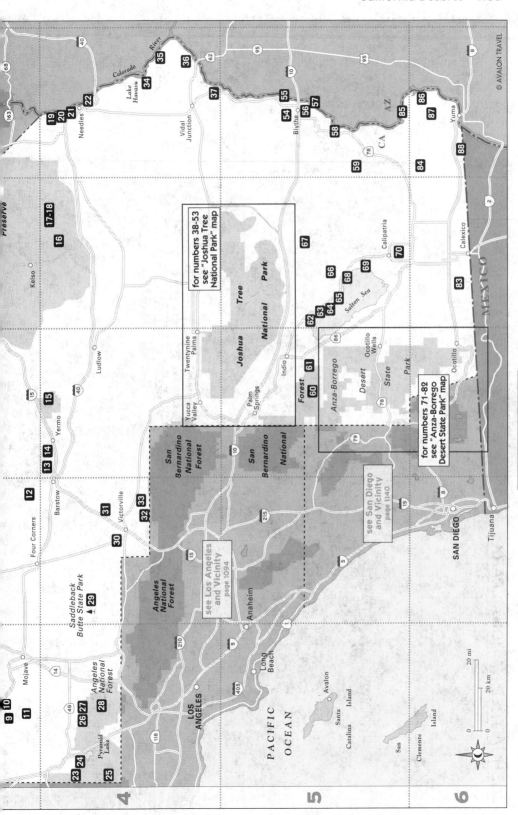

© AVALON TRAVEL

CALIFORNIA

for numbers 38-53
see "Joshua Tree
National Park" map

for numbers 71-82
see "Anza-Borrego
Desert State Park" map

see San Diego
and Vicinity
page 1140

see Los Angeles
and Vicinity
page 1094

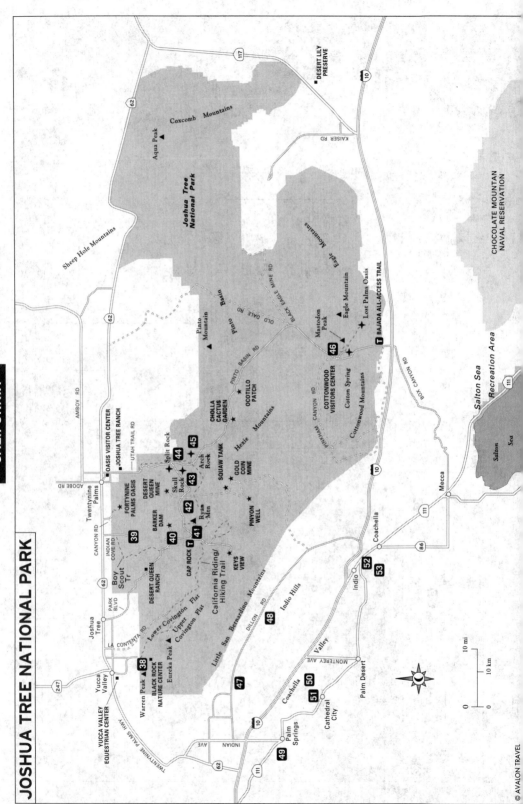

ANZA-BORREGO DESERT STATE PARK

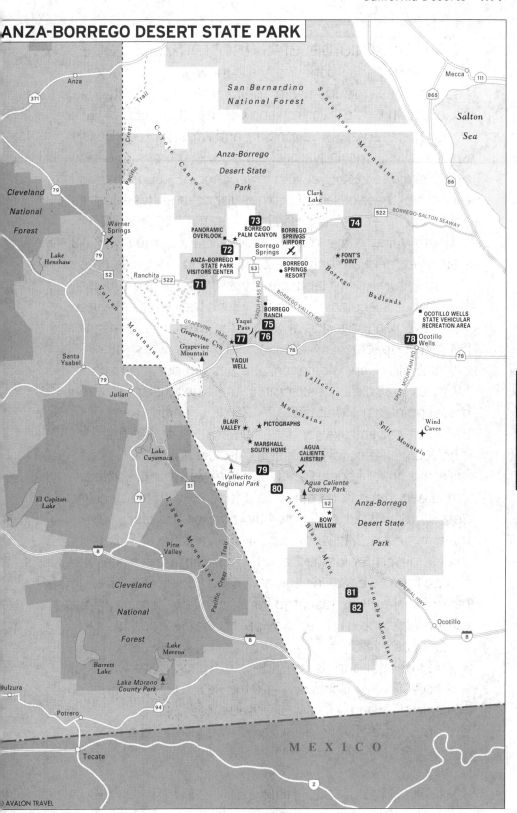

CALIFORNIA

The California deserts encompass a series

of state and regional parks located in the Mojave and Colorado Deserts. These include two of California's most spectacular national parks – Joshua Tree and Death Valley – plus Mojave National Preserve, the Salton Sea, and Anza-Borrego Desert State Park, California's largest state park. There is no region in California so vast – yet with fewer people – than the broad expanse of these deserts. Each has distinct qualities, separate and special, yet they are also joined at the edges.

Death Valley is the largest national park in the lower 48 states, yet there are only nine campgrounds. Because of the sparse nature of the land, campers should arrive self-contained; that is, equipped with everything they need. It is often warm even on the fringe of winter, the wildflowers are small but can be spectacular in spring, and the highways – and everything else – are wide open, at times without another soul for miles in all directions. Some of the highlights include the lowest point in the United States, 282 feet below sea level, at Badwater in Death Valley National Park. Yet also in the park is Telescope Peak, towering at 11,049 feet. Crazy? Oh yeah.

Joshua Tree National Park features a sweeping desert landscape edged by mountains and peppered with the peculiar Joshua tree. It is best known by most as the place where the high desert (Mojave Desert, 4,000 feet elevation) meets the low desert (Colorado Desert). This transition creates the setting for a diversity in vegetation and habitat. The strange piles of rocks often appear to have been left there by an ancient prehistoric giant, as if chipped, chiseled, and then left in rows and piles.

The national park is far different than Mojave National Preserve. The highlights here are the Kelso Dunes, a series of volcanic cliffs and a forest of Joshua trees. It is remote and explored by relatively few visitors. The Mojave is a point of national significance because it is where three major land-scapes join: the Sonoran Desert, the Colorado Desert, and the Mojave Desert.

Anza-Borrego Desert State Park is so big that it seems to stretch to forever – and that is because it does. The park covers 600,000 acres, the largest state park in California. The landscape features virtually every type of desert terrain, but most obvious are canyons, badlands, and barren ridges. In spring, the blooming cholla can be impressive. This is habitat for the endangered desert bighorn, and seeing one can be the highlight of a lifetime of wildlife-viewing.

The nearby Salton Sea and the endless BLM desert land provide one of the most distinct (and strange) lakes and terrain on earth. The Salton Sea, created in an accident from a broken dike, is one of the largest inland seas in the world. The BLM's desert land is under BLM control only because no other agency wanted it.

Surprisingly, what often attracts people here for the first time is boating, water sports, and recreation – or partying – on the Colorado River. On big weekends, it can even seem as if there is a party within close vicinity of every boat ramp on the river. Campgrounds are available throughout for the best access to the water.

Of course, summer is well known for the blazing temperatures, over 100°F about every day and occasionally hitting 120°F and up. But that is not when people visit here – they visit in fall, winter, and spring. Throughout this region, you'll find campgrounds sprinkled in most of the best spots. Some are extremely remote. Some consist of nothing but flat parking areas. Some are simple staging areas for OHV riders, and some serve as base camps for weekend parties. Somewhere amid all this, a place like no other, you will likely be able to find a match for your desires.

CALIFORNIA

1 MESQUITE SPRING

Scenic rating: 7

in Death Valley National Park

Map grid B2

Mesquite Spring is the northernmost and often the prettiest campground in Death Valley, providing you time it right. If you are a lover of desert beauty, then you must make this trip in late winter or early spring, when all kinds of tiny wildflowers can bring the stark valley floor to life. The key is soil moisture, courtesy of rains in November and December. The elevation is 1,800 feet. Mesquite Spring campground is within short range of two side trips. It is five miles (past the Grapevine Entrance Station) to Ubehebe Crater, a scenic point, and four miles to Scotty's Castle, a historic building, where tours are available.

RV sites, facilities: There are 30 sites for tents or RVs up to 30 feet (no hookups). Picnic tables and fire grills are provided. Drinking water, flush toilets, and a dump station are available. Some facilities are wheelchair-accessible. Leashed pets are permitted.

Reservations, fees: Reservations are not accepted. Sites are $12 per night, plus a $20 park entrance fee that is valid for seven days. Visitors may pay the entrance fee and obtain a park brochure at the Furnace Creek, Grapevine, Stovepipe Wells, or Beatty Ranger Stations. Open year-round.

Directions: From Furnace Creek Visitor Center, drive north on Highway 190 for 19 miles to Scotty's Castle Road. Turn right (east) and drive 33 miles (just before the Grapevine entrance station and three miles before reaching Scotty's Castle) to the campground entrance road on the left. Turn left and drive two miles to the campground.

Contact: Death Valley National Park, 760/786-3200, fax 760/786-3283, www.nps.gov/deva.

2 STOVEPIPE WELLS

Scenic rating: 4

in Death Valley National Park

Map grid B2

Stovepipe Wells is on the major highway through Death Valley. The RV sites consist of an enormous asphalt area with sites simply marked on it. There is no shelter or shade. But note: Get fuel here because prices are usually lower than at Furnace Creek. An unusual trail is available off the highway within a short distance; look for the sign for the Mosaic Canyon Trail parking area. From here you can take the easy one-mile walk up a beautiful canyon, where the walls are marble and seem as if they are polished. Rock scramblers can extend the trip for another mile. The elevation is at sea level on the edge of a large expanse of Death Valley below sea level.

RV sites, facilities: There are 18 sites for tents only and 172 sites for RVs of any length (no hookups). Picnic tables and fire rings are provided at the tent sites. Drinking water, restrooms with flush toilets and coin showers, dump station, swimming pool (extra fee), camp store, and gasoline are available. Some facilities are wheelchair-accessible. Leashed pets are permitted at campsites only.

Reservations, fees: Reservations are not accepted. Sites are $12 per night, plus a $20 park entrance fee per vehicle that is valid for seven days. Open mid-October through mid-April.

Directions: In Stovepipe Wells Village, drive west on Highway 190 to the signed entrance (just before the general store) on the right.

Contact: Death Valley National Park, 760/786-3200, fax 760/786-3283, www.nps.gov/deva.

3 FURNACE CREEK

Scenic rating: 5

in Death Valley National Park

Map grid C2   BEST (

This is a well-developed national park site that provides a good base camp for exploring Death

Valley, especially for newcomers and families. The nearby visitors center includes Death Valley Museum and offers maps and suggestions for hikes and drives in this unique wildland. This camp offers shady sites, a rarity in Death Valley, but they are packed close together and noise may be a factor when the campground is full. It's open all year, but keep in mind that the daytime summer temperatures commonly exceed 120°F, making this area virtually uninhabitable in the summer. The elevation is 190 feet below sea level.

RV sites, facilities: There are 136 sites for tents or RVs up to 35 feet (no hookups), and two group sites for up to 10 vehicles and 40 people each. Picnic tables and fire rings are provided. Drinking water, flush toilets, dump station, and evening ranger programs are available. Campfires are not permitted during the summer. Some facilities are wheelchair-accessible. Leashed pets are permitted at campsites only.

Reservations, fees: Reservations are recommended mid-October through mid-April at 877/444-6777 or www.recreation.gov ($10 reservation fee); sites are first-come, first-served the rest of the year. Sites are $12–18 per night (includes reservation fee), plus a $20 park entrance fee per vehicle that is valid for seven days. Group sites are $50 per night. Open year-round.

Directions: From the intersection of Highways 190 and 267 (38 miles east of Stovepipe Wells), continue south on Highway 190 for 16 miles to the signed campground entrance on the left.

Contact: Death Valley National Park, 760/786-3200, fax 760/786-3283, www.nps.gov/deva.

4 TEXAS SPRING

Scenic rating: 2

in Death Valley National Park
Map grid C2

Although this camp is slightly more protected than Sunset camp, there's limited shade and no shelter. The lower half of the campground is for tents only. It is open only in winter. The upper

end of the camp has trails that provide access to the historic springs and a viewing area. The nearby visitors center, which features the Death Valley Museum, offers maps and suggestions for hikes and drives. The lowest point in the United States, Badwater, set 282 feet below sea level, is to the southwest. This camp has one truly unique feature: bathrooms that are listed on the National Historic Register.

RV sites, facilities: There are 92 sites for tents or RVs of any length (no hookups). Picnic tables and fire rings are provided. Drinking water, flush toilets, and a dump station are available. Campfires are not permitted in the summer. Some facilities are wheelchair-accessible. Leashed pets are permitted.

Reservations, fees: No reservations are accepted. Sites are $14 per night, plus a $20 park entrance fee per vehicle that is valid for seven days. Open mid-October through mid-April.

Directions: From Furnace Creek Ranch, drive south on Highway 190 for 0.25 mile to the signed campground entrance on the left.

Contact: Death Valley National Park, 760/786-3200, fax 760/786-3283, www.nps.gov/deva.

5 SUNSET

Scenic rating: 4

in Death Valley National Park
Map grid C2

This camp is another enormous section of asphalt where the campsites consist of white lines for borders. Sunset is one of several options for campers in the Furnace Creek area of Death Valley, with an elevation of 190 feet below sea level. It is advisable to make your first stop at the nearby visitors center for maps and suggested hikes (according to your level of fitness) and drives.

RV sites, facilities: There are 270 sites for RVs of any length (no hookups). Drinking water, flush toilets, and a dump station are available. Campfires are not permitted in the summer. Some facilities are wheelchair-accessible. Leashed pets are permitted at campsites.

Reservations, fees: No reservations are accepted. Sites are $12 per night, plus a $20 park entrance fee per vehicle that is valid for seven days. Open mid-October through mid-April.

Directions: From Furnace Creek Ranch, turn south on Highway 190 and drive 0.25 mile to the signed campground entrance and turn left into the campground.

Contact: Death Valley National Park, 760/786-3200, fax 760/786-3283, www.nps.gov/deva.

6 WILDROSE

Scenic rating: 4

in Death Valley National Park

Map grid B2

Wildrose is set on the road that heads out to the primitive country of the awesome Panamint Range, eventually coming within range of Telescope Peak, the highest point in Death Valley National Park (11,049 feet). The elevation at the camp is 4,100 feet.

RV sites, facilities: There are 23 sites for tents or RVs up to 25 feet (no hookups). Picnic tables and fire rings are provided. Drinking water (April through November only) and pit toilets are available. Campfires are not permitted during the summer. Leashed pets are permitted at campsites only.

Reservations, fees: No reservations are accepted and there is no camping fee; however, there is a $20 park entrance fee per vehicle that is valid for seven days. Open year-round.

Directions: From Stovepipe Wells Village, drive south on Highway 190 for eight miles to Emigrant Canyon Road (just past the Emigrant rest area). Turn left (east) on Emigrant Canyon Road and drive 22 miles to the campground entrance on the left.

Contact: Death Valley National Park, 760/786-3200, fax 760/786-3283, www.nps.gov/deva.

7 TECOPA HOT SPRINGS PARK

Scenic rating: 3

north of Tecopa

Map grid C3

This Inyo County campground is out there in no-man's land, and if it weren't for the hot springs and the good rockhounding, all you'd see around here would be a few skeletons. Regardless, it's quite an attraction in the winter, when the warm climate is a plus and the nearby mineral baths are worth taking a dunk in. Rockhounds will enjoy looking for amethysts, opals, and petrified wood in the nearby areas. The elevation is 1,500 feet. Nobody gets here by accident.

RV sites, facilities: There are 250 sites for tents or RVs of any length (with partial hookups of 30 amps). Some sites are pull-through. Picnic tables and fire grills are provided. Restrooms with flush toilets and showers and a dump station are available. There is no drinking water. Groceries and propane gas are available within 10 miles. Leashed pets are permitted.

Reservations, fees: Reservations are accepted. Sites are $14–17 per vehicle per night. Weekly and monthly rates are available. Open year-round.

Directions: From Baker, drive north on Highway 127 for 58 miles to a county road signed "Tecopa Hot Springs" (south of the junction of Highway 178 and Highway 127). Turn right (east) and drive five miles to the park and campground entrance.

Contact: Tecopa Hot Springs Park, 760/852-4481.

8 RED ROCK CANYON STATE PARK

Scenic rating: 8

near Mojave

Map grid B3

This unique state park is one of the prettiest spots in the region year-round. What makes it worthwhile in any season is the chance to see wondrous geologic formations, most of them tinted red. The park also has paleontology sites, as well as remnants of some 1890s-era mining operations. A great, easy hike is the two-mile walk to Red Cliffs Natural Preserve, where there are awesome 300-foot cliffs and columns, painted red by the iron in the soil. Part of this area is closed February through June to protect nesting raptors. For those who don't hike, a must is driving up Jawbone Canyon Road to see Jawbone and Last Chance Canyons. Hikers have it better. The park also has excellent wildflower blooms March through May. A primitive OHV trail also is available; check regulations. The elevation is 2,600 feet.

RV sites, facilities: There are 50 sites for tents or RVs up to 30 feet (no hookups). Picnic tables and fire grills are provided. Drinking water, pit toilets, picnic area, seasonal exhibits, seasonal campfire program, and a seasonal nature trail are available. In spring and fall, nature walks led by rangers are available. Some facilities are wheelchair-accessible. Leashed pets are permitted in the campground only.

Reservations, fees: Reservations are not accepted. Sites are $12 per night, and $6 for each additional vehicle. Self-register prior to parking. Open year-round.

Directions: Drive on Highway 14 to the town of Mojave (50 miles east of the Los Angeles Basin area). Continue northeast on Highway 14 for 25 miles to the park entrance on the left.

Contact: Red Rock Canyon State Park, 661/320-4001, www.parks.ca.gov.

9 BRITE VALLEY AQUATIC RECREATION AREA

Scenic rating: 7

at Brite Lake

Map grid A3

Brite Valley Lake is a speck of a water hole (90 acres) on the northern flank of the Tehachapi Mountains in Kern County, at an elevation of 4,000 feet. No gas motors are permitted on the lake, so it's perfect for canoes, kayaks, or inflatables. No swimming is permitted. Use is moderate, primarily by picnickers and anglers. The lake is stocked with trout in the spring and catfish in the summer. Other species include bluegill. A golf course is nearby.

RV sites, facilities: There are 12 sites with partial hookups (20 amps) for RVs of any length and a tent camping area. Picnic tables and fire grills are provided. Drinking water, restroom with flush toilets and showers, dump station, playground, picnic pavilions (available by reservation), and fish-cleaning station are available. Supplies are available about eight miles away in Tehachapi. Leashed pets are permitted.

Reservations, fees: Reservations are not accepted. Sites are $15–30 per night for each vehicle. Boat launching is $5 per day. Open year-round.

Directions: From Bakersfield, drive east on Highway 58 for 40 miles toward the town of Tehachapi. Take the Highway 202 exit and drive three miles west to Banducci Road. Turn left and drive for about one mile to the park on the right.

Contact: Tehachapi Valley Recreation and Parks District, 661/822-3228, fax 661/823-8529.

10 INDIAN HILL RANCH AND RV PARK

Scenic rating: 7

near Tehachapi

Map grid A3

This is a unique park with two seasonal ponds stocked with largemouth bass and catfish. Crappie and bluegill are other fish species. The campground is open year-round and offers spacious, private sites with oak trees and a view of Brite Valley. A bonus is the hiking trails in the park. The elevation is 5,000 feet. Although this area is known for being windy, this campground is somewhat sheltered from the wind.

RV sites, facilities: There are 46 sites for RVs, including 37 sites with full hookups; nearly half are pull-through. Tents are allowed only in sites without hookups. Picnic tables and fire pits are provided. Restroom with flush toilets and showers (seasonal), dump station, coin laundry, Wi-Fi, propane, and two stocked fishing ponds are available. Small leashed pets are permitted, with certain restrictions.

Reservations, fees: Reservations are accepted. Sites are $20–40 per night. Monthly and group rates available. No credit cards accepted. Open year-round, with some sites closed November through mid-May.

Directions: Drive on Highway 58 to Tehachapi and Exit 148 for Tehachapi/Highway 202. Take that exit to Tucker Road. Turn right and drive south one mile to Highway 202/Valley Boulevard. Turn right (west) and drive four miles to Banducci Road. Turn left and drive 0.75 mile to Arosa Road. Turn left and drive 1.7 miles to the park at 18061 Arosa Road.

Contact: Indian Hill Ranch and RV Park, 661/822-6613, www.indianhillranch.com.

11 TEHACHAPI MOUNTAIN PARK

Scenic rating: 6

southwest of Tehachapi

Map grid A3

This county park is overlooked by most out-of-towners. It is a pretty spot covering 5,000 acres, set on the slopes of the Tehachapi Mountains, with elevations in the park ranging from 5,500 to 7,000 feet. The roads to the campgrounds are steep, but the sites are flat. Trails for hikers and equestrians are available, but no horses are allowed at the campground. An interpretive trail, Nuooah Nature Trail, is available. This park is popular not only in spring, but also in winter, with the elevations sometimes high enough to get snow (chains often required for access). The park lies eight miles southwest of the town of Tehachapi on the southern side of Highway 58 between Mojave and Bakersfield. Woody's Peak, at almost 8,000 feet, overlooks the park from its dominion in the Tehachapi Mountains, the dividing line between the San Joaquin Valley and the Los Angeles Basin.

RV sites, facilities: There are 61 sites for tents or RVs of any length (no hookups), a group campsite for up to 40 people, a group campsite for up to 150 people, and group lodging with 10 cabins for a minimum of 40 people. Picnic tables and fire grills are provided. Drinking water (natural spring) and chemical toilets are available. Some facilities are wheelchair-accessible. Leashed pets are permitted.

Reservations, fees: Reservations are not accepted for individual sites, but are required for the group sites and group cabins at 661/868-7002. Sites are $14 per night per vehicle, $60–275 per night for the group site, and $2 per pet per night. Open year-round, weather permitting.

Directions: In Tehachapi, take Tehachapi Boulevard to the Cury Street exit. Take that exit south and drive about three miles to Highline Road. Turn right on Highline Road and drive two miles to Water Canyon Road. Turn left on Water Canyon Road and drive three miles to the park.

Contact: Kern County Parks Department info line, 661/868-7000, www.co.kern.ca.us/parks/index.htm.

12 OWL CANYON

Scenic rating: 3

near Barstow

Map grid B3

The primary attraction of Owl Canyon camp is that the surrounding desert is sprinkled with exposed fossils of ancient animals. Guess they couldn't find any water. Well, if people try hiking here without a full canteen, there may soon be some human skeletons out here, too. Actually, rangers say that the general public is unlikely to spot fossils here because it takes some basic scientific knowledge to identify them. The sparse BLM land out here is kind of like an ugly dog you learn to love: After a while, when you look closely, you learn it has a heart of gold. This region is best visited in the spring and fall, of course, when hiking allows a fresh, new look at what may appear to some as a wasteland. The beauty is in the detail of it—tiny critters and tiny flowers seen against the unfenced vastness, with occasional fossils yet to be discovered. The elevation is 2,600 feet.

RV sites, facilities: There are 31 sites for tents or RVs of any length (no hookups). Picnic tables and fire grills are provided. Vault toilets are available. There is no drinking water. Leashed pets are permitted.

Reservations, fees: Reservations are not accepted. Sites are $6 per night. Open year-round.

Directions: Drive on I-15 to Barstow to the exit for 1st Street. Take that exit and drive north on 1st Street (crossing the Mojave River Bridge) for 0.75 mile to Irwin Road. Turn left and drive eight miles to Fossil Bed Road. Turn left and drive two miles to the campground on the right.

Contact: Bureau of Land Management, Barstow Field Office, 760/252-6000, fax 760/252-6099.

13 CALICO GHOST TOWN REGIONAL PARK

Scenic rating: 4

near Barstow

Map grid C4

Let me tell you about this ghost town: There are probably more people here now than there have ever been. In the 1880s and 1890s it was a booming silver mine town, and there are still remnants of that. Alas, it now has lots of restaurants and shops. Recreation options include riding on a narrow-gauge railroad, touring what was once the largest silver mine in California, and watching an old-style melodrama with villains and heroes. This is a 480-acre park with self-guided tours, hiking trails, gold panning, summer entertainment, and museum, with festivals held throughout the year. Whatever you do, don't take any artifacts you may come across, such as an old nail, a jar, or anything; you will be doomed with years of bad luck. No foolin'. A park representative told the story of a man from the East Coast who nabbed a

beautiful rock on his visit. He then was plagued with years of bad luck, including broken bones, disappointment in his love life, and several family deaths. In desperation, he flew back to California and returned the rock to its rightful place.

RV sites, facilities: There are 253 sites for tents and RVs up to 45 feet; 104 sites have full or partial hookups (20, 30, and 50 amps) and some sites are pull-through. There are also three group camping areas, six cabins, and a bunkhouse. Fire pits are provided. Restrooms with flush toilets and showers, drinking water, and three dump stations are available. Pay phone, restaurants, and shops are on-site. Groceries, propane gas, and laundry facilities are 10 miles away. Some facilities are wheelchair-accessible. Leashed pets are permitted.

Reservations, fees: Reservations are accepted at 800/TO-CALICO (800/862-2542) 8 A.M.–3 P.M. ($2 reservation fee). Sites are $20–25 per night, $1 per pet per night. Some credit cards accepted. Open year-round.

Directions: From Barstow, drive northeast on I-15 for seven miles to the exit for Ghost Town Road. Take that exit and drive north on Ghost Town Road for three miles to the park on the left.

Contact: Calico Ghost Town Regional Park, San Bernardino County, 760/254-2122, fax 760/254-2047, www.calicotown.com.

14 BARSTOW CALICO KOA

Scenic rating: 3

near Barstow

Map grid C4

Don't blame me if you end up way out here. Actually, for vacationers making the long-distance grind of a drive on I-15, this KOA can seem like the promised land. It has received awards for its cleanliness, and a nightly quiet time ensures that you have a chance to get rested. Vegetation screening between sites enhance privacy. But hey, as long as you're here, you might as well take a side trip to Calico Ghost Town, about three miles to the northeast at the foot of the Calico Mountains. A unique side trip is the Calico Early Man Site, about five miles to the north; tours are available. Primitive stone tools are believed to have been discovered here in 1942. Rockhounding, hiking, and an outlet mall are other nearby options. The elevation is 1,900 feet.

RV sites, facilities: There are 78 sites with full or partial hookups (30 and 50 amps) for tents or RVs of any length; many are pull-through. Picnic tables and fire grills are provided. Drinking water, restrooms with flush toilets and showers, dump station, modem access, playground, heated swimming pool, recreation room, convenience store, propane gas, ice, and coin laundry are available. Some facilities are wheelchair-accessible. Leashed pets are permitted.

Reservations, fees: Reservations are accepted at 800/KOA-0059 (800/562-0059). Sites are $26–46 per night, $3.50 per person per night for more than two people. Some credit cards accepted. Open year-round.

Directions: From Barstow, drive northeast on I-15 for seven miles to the exit for Ghost Town Road. Take that exit and drive left under the freeway to a frontage road at the Shell gas station. Turn left at the frontage road and drive 0.25 mile to the campground on the right.

Contact: Barstow Calico KOA, 760/254-2311, fax 760/254-2247, www.koa.com.

15 AFTON CANYON

Scenic rating: 6

near Barstow in the East Mojave National Scenic Area

Map grid C4

This camp is set at 1,400 feet elevation in a desert riparian habitat along the Mojave River. This is one of several Bureau of Land Management tracts near the Mojave National Preserve. Side-trip options include the Rainbow Basin Natural Area (about an hour's drive), Soda Springs, and the Calico Early Man Site. Remember, rivers in the desert are not like rivers in cooler climates. There are no fish worth eating.

RV sites, facilities: There are 22 sites for tents or RVs up to 30 feet (no hookups). Picnic tables and fire rings are provided. Vault toilets are available. Drinking water is available intermittently, so bring your own water. Leashed pets are permitted.

Reservations, fees: Reservations are not accepted. Sites are $6 per night. Open year-round.

Directions: From Barstow, drive east on I-15 for 37 miles to Afton Road. Turn right (south) and drive three miles to the campground. Note: Four-wheel-drive or high-clearance vehicles are recommended since the access road can be rough and have washouts.

Contact: Bureau of Land Management, Barstow Field Office, 760/252-6000, fax 760/252-6099.

16 PROVIDENCE MOUNTAINS STATE RECREATION AREA

Scenic rating: 8

near Mitchell Caverns

Map grid D4

This remote desert park, set at 4,300 feet elevation, offers guided tours of Mitchell Caverns ($2–4 tour fee, discounts available), caverns made of classic limestone formations These tours are available daily from early September through Memorial Day weekend, and on weekends from Memorial Day through early September. It's a good idea to make a reservation for the tour at 760/928-2586. The cavern tours are the reason most people visit and camp at this park. There are additional recreational opportunities. From the campground Nina Mora Overlook Trail is a short (0.25-mile) walk to a lookout of the Marble Mountains and the valley below. Another short hike with a great view is the steep, one-mile hike (one-way) on Crystal Springs Trail, the best of the bunch. Another hike is Mary Beale, an interpretive trail accessible from the visitors center, a one-mile loop.

RV sites, facilities: There are six sites for tents or RVs up to 31 feet (no hookups). Picnic tables and fire grills are provided. Drinking water and flush toilets are available. A pay phone is nearby. Leashed pets are permitted in the campground only.

Reservations, fees: Reservations are not accepted. Sites are $12 per night, $5 per night for each additional vehicle. Open year-round.

Directions: Drive on I-40 to Essex Road (near Essex, 116 miles east of Barstow). Take that road and drive north on Essex Road for 16 miles to the park at road's end.

Contact: Providence Mountains State Recreation Area, 760/928-2586; Mojave Desert Information Center, 661/942-0662, fax 661/940-7327, www.parks.ca.gov.

17 MID HILLS

Scenic rating: 4

in the Mojave National Preserve
Map grid D4

This is a primitive campground set among the junipers and piñon trees in a mountainous area at 5,600 feet elevation. It is one of two little-known camps in the vast desert that is now managed by the National Park Service. About two-thirds of the campsites were burned in the 2005 Hackberry Fire; most of the piñon and juniper trees burned as well. There is an eight-mile one-way trail that starts across from the entrance to Mid Hills and is routed down to the Hole-in-the-Wall Campground. It a pleasant walk in spring and fall.

RV sites, facilities: There are 26 sites for tents or RVs up to 22 feet (no hookups). Picnic tables and fire grills are provided. Drinking water and vault toilets are available. Leashed pets are permitted.

Reservations, fees: Reservations are not accepted. Sites are $12 per night. Open year-round.

Directions: Drive on I-40 to Essex Road (near Essex, 116 miles east of Barstow). Take that exit and drive north on Essex Road for 10 miles to Black Canyon Road. Turn north and drive nine miles (at Hole-in-the-Wall campground, the road becomes dirt) and continue seven miles to Wild Horse Canyon Road. Turn left and drive

two miles (rough, dirt road) to the campground on the right.

Contact: Mojave National Preserve, 760/252-6100, fax 760/252-6174, www.nps.gov/moja.

18 HOLE-IN-THE-WALL (AND BLACK CANYON GROUP AND HORSE CAMP)

Scenic rating: 6

in the Mojave National Preserve
Map grid D4

This is the largest and best-known of the camps in the vast Mojave National Preserve. There are three camps: a family camp across the street from a group camp and an equestrian camp. All are set at 4,400 feet elevation. An interesting side trip is to the Mitchell Caverns in the nearby Providence Mountains State Recreation Area.

RV sites, facilities: There are 35 sites for tents or RVs of any length (no hookups), one group site for up to 50 people, and an equestrian camp. Picnic tables and fire grills are provided. Drinking water, vault toilets, and a dump station are available. Leashed pets are permitted.

Reservations, fees: Reservations are not accepted. Sites are $12 per night. Make reservations for group camp and horse camp at 760/928-2572; $25 per night, including horse corral if needed. Open year-round.

Directions: Drive on I-40 to Essex Road (near Essex, 116 miles east of Barstow). Take that exit and drive north on Essex Road for 10 miles to Black Canyon Road. Turn north and drive nine miles to the campgrounds.

Contact: Mojave National Preserve, 760/252-6100, fax 760/252-6174, www.nps.gov/moja.

19 RAINBO BEACH RESORT

Scenic rating: 6

on the Colorado River
Map grid E4

The big bonus here is the full marina, making this resort on the Colorado River the headquarters for boaters and water-skiers. And headquarters it is, with tons of happy folks who are extremely well lubed, both inside and out. This resort boasts 800 feet of river frontage. A 70-site mobile home park is adjacent to the RV park. (For boating details, see the Needles Marina Park listing in this chapter.)

RV sites, facilities: There are 64 sites with full hookups (30 and 50 amps) for RVs. Some sites are pull-through. Picnic tables are provided. Restrooms with showers, coin laundry, heated swimming pool, spa, recreation room, and a restaurant are available. A boat dock is nearby. Leashed pets are permitted.

Reservations, fees: Reservations are accepted. Sites are $25–28 per night. Seasonal rates available. Some credit cards accepted. Open year-round.

Directions: Drive on I-40 to Needles and River Road. Turn north on River Road and drive 1.5 miles to the resort on the right.

Contact: Rainbo Beach Resort, 760/326-3101, fax 760/326-5085.

20 NEEDLES MARINA PARK

Scenic rating: 6

on the Colorado River

Map grid E4

Bring your suntan lotion and a beach towel. This section of the Colorado River is a big tourist spot where the body oil and beer can flow faster than the river. There are a ton of hot bodies and hot boats, and waterskiing dominates the adjacent calm-water section of the Colorado River. However, note that upstream of the Needles-area put-in is the prime area for waterskiing. Downstream is the chance for canoeing or kayaking. Meanwhile, there's also an 18-hole golf course adjacent to the camp, but most folks head for the river. Compared to the surrounding desert, this park is almost a golden paradise. A mobile home park is adjacent to the RV park.

RV sites, facilities: There are 158 sites with full hookups (30 and 50 amps) for tents or RVs, and

six cabins. Some sites are pull-through. Picnic tables are provided. Restrooms with flush toilets and showers, drinking water, heated pool, spa, recreation room, Wi-Fi, modem access, playground, picnic area, boat ramp, boat slips, store, gas, and laundry facilities are available. Leashed pets are permitted.

Reservations, fees: Reservations are accepted. Sites are $34–36 per night, $4.50 per night for air conditioning, $5 per pet per night. Some credit cards accepted. Open year-round.

Directions: Drive on I-40 to Needles and the exit for J Street. Take that exit and drive to Broadway. Turn left on Broadway and drive 0.75 mile to Needles Highway. Turn right (north) on Needles Highway and drive 0.5 mile to the park on the left.

Contact: Needles Marina Park, 760/326-2197, fax 760/326-4125, www.needlesmarinapark.com.

21 NEEDLES KOA

Scenic rating: 2

near the Colorado River

Map grid E4

At least you've got the Needles KOA out here, complete with swimming pool, where you can get a new start. Side trips include venturing to the nearby Colorado River or heading north to Lake Mead. Of course, you could always go to Las Vegas. Nah.

RV sites, facilities: There are 93 pull-through sites with full hookups (30 and 50 amps), and 18 pull-through sites with partial hookups (30 and 50 amps) for tents or RVs of any length. Five cabins are also available. Restrooms with flush toilets and showers, drinking water, recreation room, swimming pool, playground, store, snack bar, propane gas, and coin laundry are available. Some facilities are wheelchair-accessible. Leashed pets are permitted.

Reservations, fees: Reservations are accepted at 800/562-3407. Sites are $22–32 per night, $2 per person per night for more than two people. Credit cards accepted. Open year-round.

Directions: Drive on I-40 to Needles and the exit for West Broadway. Take that exit to Needles Highway. Turn northwest on Needles Highway and drive 0.75 mile to National Old Trails Highway. Turn left and drive one mile to the park on the right (5400 National Old Trails Highway).

Contact: Needles KOA, 760/326-4207, fax 760/326-6329, www.koa.com.

22 MOABI REGIONAL PARK

Scenic rating: 7

on the Colorado River

Map grid E4

Campsites are situated in the main area of the park along 2.5 miles of shoreline peninsula. The park features 24 group areas. The adjacent Colorado River provides the main attraction, the only thing liquid around these parts that isn't contained in a can or bottle. The natural response when you see it is to jump in the water, and everybody does so, with or without a boat. You'll see lots of wild and crazy types having the times of their lives on the water. The boating season is a long one here, courtesy of that desert climate. Fishing is good for catfish, smallmouth bass, bluegill, striped bass, and sometimes crappie.

RV sites, facilities: There is a large grassy area for tents and more than 600 sites for RVs or tents—155 with full or partial hookups (20, 30, and 50 amps), and a few are pull-through. There are also 24 group camping areas. Picnic tables and fire grills are provided at most sites. Restrooms with flush toilets and showers, coin laundry, store, ice, dump station, covered picnic area, marina, bait, and boat ramp are available. Volleyball, basketball, horseshoes, and putting green are also available. An 18-hole golf course is nearby. Some facilities are wheelchair-accessible. Leashed pets are permitted.

Reservations, fees: Reservations are accepted. Sites are $15–35 per night per vehicle, $1 per pet per night. Long-term rates available in the winter, with limit of five months. Some credit cards accepted. Open year-round.

Directions: From Needles, drive east on I-40 for 11 miles to Park Moabi Road. Turn left on Park Moabi Road and continue 0.5 mile to the park entrance at the end of the road.

Contact: Moabi Regional Park Marina, 760/326-3831, fax 760/326-3272; San Bernardino County, 760/326-4777, www.co.san-bernardino.ca.us/parks/moabi.htm.

23 KINGS

Scenic rating: 5

near Piru Creek in Los Padres National Forest

Map grid A4

The Hungry Valley State Vehicular Recreation Area is just five miles to the east. Figure it out: Right, this is a primitive but well-placed camp for four-wheel-drive and off-highway vehicles. The camp is near Piru Creek, off a short spur road, so it feels remote yet is close to one of California's top off-road areas.

RV sites, facilities: There are seven sites for tents or RVs up to 16 feet (no hookups). Picnic tables and fire grills are provided. Vault toilets are available. No drinking water is available. Garbage must be packed out. Leashed pets are permitted.

Reservations, fees: No reservations are accepted and there is no camping fee. An Adventure Pass ($30 annual fee or $5 daily fee) per parked vehicle is required. Open year-round.

Directions: Drive on I-5 to south of Gorman and the Gorman–Hungry Valley Road exit (the northern exit for the Hungry Valley Recreation Area). Take that exit and turn south on Hungry Valley Road (Forest Road 8N01) and drive six miles to Gold Hill Road (Forest Road 8N01). Turn right and drive six miles to Forest Road 18N01A. Turn left and drive 0.75 mile to the campground.

Contact: Los Padres National Forest, Mount Piños Ranger District, 661/245-3731, fax 661/245-1526.

CALIFORNIA

24 LOS ALAMOS

Scenic rating: 4

near Pyramid Lake in Angeles National Forest

Map grid A4

Los Alamos is set at an elevation of 2,600 feet near the southern border of the Hungry Valley State Vehicular Recreation Area, and about 2.5 miles north of Pyramid Lake. Pyramid Lake is a big lake, covering 1,300 acres with 20 miles of shoreline, and is extremely popular for waterskiing and fast boating (35 mph speed limit), as well as for sailboarding (best at the northern launch point), fishing (best in the spring and early summer and in the fall for striped bass), and swimming. A lifeguard is on duty at the boat launch area during the summer season.

RV sites, facilities: There are 93 sites and three group sites for tents or RVs up to 40 feet (no hookups) that can accommodate up to 25 people each. Picnic tables and fire pits are provided. Drinking water and flush toilets are available. A boat ramp is at the Emigrant Landing Picnic Area. Some facilities are wheelchair-accessible. Leashed pets are permitted.

Reservations, fees: Reservations are not accepted for individual sites, but are required for group sites at 661/248-6725. Sites are $14 per night, $7 per night per each additional vehicle, $65 per night for a group site. Open year-round.

Directions: Drive on I-5 to eight miles south of Gorman and the Smokey Bear Road exit. Take the Smokey Bear Road exit and drive west about three-quarters of a mile and follow the signs to the campground.

Contact: Recreation Resource Management, 661/248-6725; National Forest, Santa Clara/Mojave Rivers Ranger District, 661/296-9710, fax 661/296-5847.

25 HALF MOON

Scenic rating: 7

near Piru Creek in Los Padres National Forest

Map grid A4

Half Moon is a primitive camp set along Piru Creek at 4,700 feet elevation. Adjacent to camp, Forest Road 7N13 follows the creek for a few miles, then dead-ends at a trailhead that continues along more remote stretches of this little stream. Hikers should also consider the trail to nearby Thorn Point for a beautiful lookout.

RV sites, facilities: There are 10 sites for tents or RVs up to 22 feet (no hookups). Picnic tables and fire grills are provided. Pit toilets are available. No drinking water is available. Garbage must be packed out. Leashed pets are permitted.

Reservations, fees: No reservations are accepted and there is no camping fee. An Adventure Pass ($30 annual fee or $5 daily pas) per parked vehicle is required. Open seasonally, weather permitting.

Directions: Drive on I-5 to just south of Lebec and the Frazier Park exit. Take that exit and drive west on Frazier Mountain Road to the town of Lake of the Woods and Lockwood Valley Road. Turn left on Lockwood Valley Road and drive about 12 miles to Grade Valley Road (Forest Road 7N03). Turn left and drive 11 miles to the campground on the left. High-clearance or four-wheel-drive vehicles are recommended; access requires crossing a creek in which the current can be fairly fast and high, especially in the spring.

Contact: Los Padres National Forest, Mount Piños Ranger District, 661/245-3731, fax 661/245-1526.

26 SAWMILL

Scenic rating: 7

on the Pacific Crest Trail in Angeles National Forest

Map grid A4

This is a classic hikers trailhead camp. It is set at 5,200 feet elevation, right on the Pacific Crest Trail and just one mile from the junction with Burnt Peak Canyon Trail. For a good day hike, head southeast on the Pacific Crest Trail for one mile to Burnt Peak Canyon Trail, turn right (southwest), and hike just over a mile to Burnt Peak, at 5,788 feet elevation. Note that this camp is inaccessible after the first snow. Nearby Upper Shake provides an alternative.

RV sites, facilities: There are eight sites for tents or RVs up to 16 feet (no hookups). Note that RVs are not recommended. Picnic tables and fire pits are provided. Vault toilets are available. No drinking water is available. Garbage must be packed out. Leashed pets are permitted.

Reservations, fees: No reservations are accepted and there is no camping fee. An Adventure Pass ($30 annual fee or $5 daily pass) per parked vehicle is required. Open May through October, weather permitting.

Directions: Drive on I-5 to the Tehachapis near the small town of Castaic and Lake Hughes Road. Turn northeast on Lake Hughes Road and drive 27 miles to the town of Lake Hughes and Pine Canyon Road/County Road N2. Turn left on Pine Canyon Road and drive 10 miles to Bushnell Summit Road. Turn left and drive two miles to the campground on the left.

Contact: Angeles National Forest, Santa Clara/Mojave Rivers Ranger District, 661/296-9710, fax 661/296-5847.

27 UPPER SHAKE

Scenic rating: 7

on the Pacific Crest Trail in Angeles National Forest

Map grid A4

Upper Shake, like nearby Sawmill, is right on the Pacific Crest Trail. The elevation is 4,400 feet. Hikers who plan on heading to Burnt Peak are better off departing from Sawmill (less than two miles to the west). This camp is used primarily as a jump-off point for those heading east on the PCT; Lake Hughes is the nearest destination, less than four miles away, and a mile after that is Lake Elizabeth. The camp is inaccessible after the first snow.

RV sites, facilities: There are 18 sites for tents or RVs up to 22 feet (no hookups). Picnic tables and fire pits are provided. Vault toilets are available. No drinking water is available. Garbage must be packed out. Leashed pets are permitted.

Reservations, fees: No reservations are accepted and there is no camping fee. An Adventure Pass ($30 annual fee or $5 daily pass) per parked vehicle is required. Open May through October, weather permitting.

Directions: Drive on I-5 to the Tehachapis near the small town of Castaic and Lake Hughes Road. Turn northeast on Lake Hughes Road and drive 27 miles to the town of Lake Hughes and Pine Canyon Road/County Road N2. Turn left on Pine Canyon Road and drive about 5.5 miles to the entrance road on the left.

Contact: Angeles National Forest, Santa Clara/Mojave Rivers Ranger District, 661/296-9710, fax 661/296-5847.

28 COTTONWOOD

Scenic rating: 5

near the Warm Springs Mountain Lookout in Angeles National Forest

Map grid A4

Cottonwood Camp is set at 2,680 feet elevation in remote Angeles National Forest along a small stream. The camp is on the north flank of Warm Springs Mountain. A great side trip is to the Warm Springs Mountain Lookout (4,023 feet), about a five-mile drive. Drive south on Forest Road 7N09 for three miles, turn right (west) on Forest Road 6N32, and drive for 1.5 miles to Forest Road 7N13. Turn left (south) and drive a mile to the summit.

RV sites, facilities: There are 22 sites for tents

or RVs up to 22 feet (no hookups). Picnic tables and fire pits are provided. Vault toilets are available. No drinking water is available. Garbage must be packed out. Supplies are less than four miles away in the town of Lake Hughes. Leashed pets are permitted.

Reservations, fees: No reservations are accepted and there is no camping fee. An Adventure Pass ($30 annual fee or $5 daily pass) per parked vehicle is required. Open year-round, weather permitting.

Directions: Drive on I-5 to the Tehachapis near the small town of Castaic and Lake Hughes Road. Turn northeast on Lake Hughes Road and drive 27 miles to the campground on the right.

Contact: Angeles National Forest, Santa Clara/Mojave Rivers Ranger District, 661/296-9710, fax 661/296-5847.

29 SADDLEBACK BUTTE STATE PARK

Scenic rating: 8

near Lancaster

Map grid B4

This 3,000-acre park was originally established to preserve ancient Joshua trees. In fact, it used to be called Joshua Tree State Park, but folks kept getting it confused with Joshua Tree National Park, so it was renamed. The terrain is sparsely vegetated and desertlike, with excellent hiking trails up the nearby buttes. The best hike is Saddleback Loop, a five-mile trip that features a 1,000-foot climb to Saddleback Summit at 3,651 feet. On rare clear days, there are fantastic views in all directions, including the Antelope Valley California Poppy Preserve, the surrounding mountains, and the Mojave Desert. On the typical hazy day, the poppy preserve might as well be on the moon; you can't even come close to seeing it. The elevation is 2,700 feet.

RV sites, facilities: There are 50 sites for tents or RVs up to 30 feet (no hookups). A group camp is available for up to 30 people. Picnic tables, shade ramadas, and fire grills are provided. Drinking water, flush toilets, and dump station

are available. A visitors center is nearby. Some facilities are wheelchair-accessible. Leashed pets are permitted in the campground only.

Reservations, fees: Reservations are not accepted for individual sites, but the group camp may be reserved at 800/444-PARK (800/444-7275) or www.reserveamerica.com ($8 reservation fee). Sites are $12 per night, $6 per night for each additional vehicle, $66 per night for the group site. Open year-round.

Directions: Drive north on Highway 14 to Lancaster and the exit for Avenue J. Take that exit and drive east on Avenue J for 17 miles to the park entrance on the right.

Or drive south on Highway 14 to Lancaster to the exit for 20th Street west. Take that exit, turn left, and drive to Avenue J. Turn east on Avenue J and drive 17 miles to the park entrance on the right.

Contact: Saddleback Butte State Park, Mojave Desert Information Center, 661/942-0662, fax 661/940-7327, www.parks.ca.gov.

30 DESERT WILLOW RV PARK

Scenic rating: 2

in Hesperia

Map grid B4

This is an RV park for I-15 cruisers looking to make a stop. Silverwood Lake, a 1,000-acre recreation lake with fishing, boating, and water sports, is 18 miles to the south. The elevation is 3,200 feet.

RV sites, facilities: There are 176 sites with full hookups (30 and 50 amps) for RVs up to 70 feet; some sites are pull-through. No tents. Note that only 17 sites are available for overnight campers. Restrooms with showers, cable TV hookups, ice, coin laundry, propane gas, swimming pool, indoor spa, billiard room, exercise room, and library are on the premises. Some facilities are wheelchair-accessible. Leashed pets are permitted.

Reservations, fees: Reservations are accepted at 800/900-8114. Sites are $35 per night. Monthly rates available. Open year-round.

Directions: Drive on I-15 to Hesperia and Exit 143. Take that exit to Main Street. Turn west and drive to the park on the right (12624 Main Street West).

Contact: Desert Willow RV Park, 760/949-0377, fax 760/949-4334.

31 SHADY OASIS VICTORVILLE

Scenic rating: 3

near Victorville
Map grid B4

Most long-distance trips on I-15 are grueling endurance tests with drivers making the mistake of trying to get a decent night's sleep at a roadside rest stop. Why endure the torture, especially with Shady Oasis way out here, in Victorville of all places? Where the heck is Victorville? If you are exhausted and lucky enough to find the place, you won't be making any jokes about it. Note: There are about 50 permanent residents at this former KOA.

RV sites, facilities: There are 136 sites for tents or RVs of any length, many with full or partial hookups (50 amps) and some pull-through. There are also eight cabins. Picnic tables and fire grills are provided. Drinking water, restrooms with flush toilets and showers, recreation room, seasonal heated swimming pool, playground, modem access, convenience store, propane gas, and coin laundry are available. Some facilities are wheelchair-accessible. Leashed pets are permitted.

Reservations, fees: Reservations are accepted at 760/245-6867. Sites are $26–46 per night, $3 per person for more than two people, $1 per night for each additional vehicle. Some credit cards accepted. Open year-round.

Directions: Drive on I-15 to Victorville and Stoddard Wells Road (north of Victorville). Turn south on Stoddard Wells Road and drive a short distance to the campground (16530 Stoddard Wells Road).

Contact: Shady Oasis Victorville, 760/245-6867, fax 760/243-2108.

32 HESPERIA LAKE CAMPGROUND

Scenic rating: 5

in Hesperia
Map grid B4

This is a slightly more rustic alternative to Desert Willow RV Park in Hesperia. There is a small lake/pond for recreational fishing and there is a small fishing fee, but no fishing license is required. Boating and swimming are not allowed, but youngsters usually get a kick out of feeding the ducks and geese that live at the pond.

RV sites, facilities: There are 52 sites with partial hookups (30 and 50 amps) for tents or RVs up to 40 feet. Picnic tables and fire pits are provided. Drinking water, restrooms with flush toilets and showers, a playground, and a fishing pond are available. Some facilities are wheelchair-accessible. Leashed pets are permitted.

Reservations, fees: Reservations are accepted at 800/521-6332. Sites are $35 per night, $2 per night per pet, $15 to fish at the pond. Some credit cards accepted. Open year-round.

Directions: Drive on I-15 to Hesperia and the exit for Main Street. Take that exit and drive east on Main Street for 9.5 miles (the road curves and becomes Arrowhead Lake Road) to the park on the left.

Contact: Hesperia Lake Campground, 760/244-5951 or 800/521-6332.

33 MOJAVE NARROWS REGIONAL PARK

Scenic rating: 7

on the Mojave River
Map grid B4

Almost no one except the locals knows about this little county park. It is like an oasis in the Mojave Desert. There are actually two small lakes here: the larger Horseshoe Lake and Pelican Lake. No private boats are allowed and rental rowboats and pedal boats are available on weekends. Swimming and water/body contact are prohibited. It is set at 2,000 feet elevation and provides a few recreation options, including a pond stocked in season with trout and catfish, horseback-riding facilities, and equestrian trails. Hiking includes a wheelchair-accessible trail. The Mojave River level fluctuates here, almost disappearing in some years in summer and early fall. One of the big events of the year here, the Huck Finn Jubilee, is on Father's Day in June. Note: The gate closes each evening.

RV sites, facilities: There are 110 sites for tents or RVs of any length; seven pull-through, 42 with full hookups (15 and 30 amps). Fourteen group areas are also available. Picnic tables and barbecue grills are provided. Drinking water, restrooms with flush toilets and showers, dump station, snack bar, playground, picnic shelters, bait, boat rentals, horse rentals, and horseback-riding facilities are available. A store, propane gas, and coin laundry are available three miles from the campground. Leashed pets are permitted.

Reservations, fees: Reservations accepted for RVs and groups. Sites are $15–22 per night, $1 per night per pet, $5 per day fishing fee. Weekly and group rates available. Some credit cards accepted. Open year-round.

Directions: Drive on I-15 to Victorville and the exit for Bear Valley Road. Take that exit and drive east on Bear Valley Road for six miles to Ridgecrest. Turn left on Ridgecrest, drive three miles, and make a left into the park.

Contact: Mojave Narrows Regional Park, 760/245-2226, fax 760/245-7887, www.co.sanbernardino.ca.us/parks/mojave.htm.

34 HAVASU LANDING RESORT AND CASINO

Scenic rating: 6

on western shore of Lake Havasu

Map grid E4

Situated on the western shore of Lake Havasu, this full-service resort is run by the Chemehuevi Indian Tribe. It even includes a casino with slot machines and a card room. The resort is situated in a desert landscape in the Chemehuevi Valley. A boat shuttle operates from the resort to the London Bridge and Havasu City, Arizona. A mobile-home park is within the resort and an airstrip is nearby. Some of the RV sites are rented for the entire winter. Permits are required for off-road vehicles and can be obtained at the resort. This is one of the most popular boating areas in the southwestern United States. The lake is 45 miles long, covers 19,300 acres, and is at the low elevation of 482 feet. Havasu was created when the Parker Dam was built across the Colorado River.

RV sites, facilities: There are 180 sites with full hookups (30 and 50 amps) for RVs up to 35 feet, three large tent camping areas, and mobile home and RV rentals. Picnic tables, restrooms with flush toilets and showers, a dump station, coin laundry, picnic areas, restaurant and lounge, casino, 24-hour security, 24-hour marina with gas dock, bait and tackle, general store and deli, boat launches, boat slips, fish-cleaning room, dry storage, boat shuttle, and boat launch and retrieval service are available. An airport is nearby. Leashed pets are permitted.

Reservations, fees: Reservations are accepted at 800/307-3610. Sites are $25–30 per night for RV sites, $15–20 per night for tent sites, $2 per person per night for more than two people, and $6 per night for each additional vehicle. Holiday rates are higher. Weekly and monthly rates are available. A boat-launch fee is charged. Some credit cards accepted. Two ATMs are on-site. Open year-round.

Directions: From Needles, drive south on Highway 95 for 19 miles to Havasu Lake Road. Turn left and drive 17.5 miles to the resort on the right.

From Blythe, drive north on Highway 95 for 79 miles to Havasu Lake Road. Turn right and drive 17.5 miles to the resort on the right.

Contact: Havasu Landing Resort and Casino, 760/858-4593 or 800/307-3610, www.havasu-landing.com. For general information about Lake Havasu, contact the Lake Havasu Tourism Bureau, 928/453-3444 or 800/2-HAVASU (800/242-8278), www.golakehavasu.com; Lake

Havasu Area Chamber of Commerce, 928/855-4115, www.havasuchamber.com.

35 BLACK MEADOW LANDING

Scenic rating: 6

south of Lake Havasu on the Colorado River

Map grid E4

This area of the Colorado River attracts a lot of people, so reservations are highly recommended. Hot weather, warm water, and proximity to Las Vegas make this one of the top camping and boating hot spots in the West. Vacationers are here year-round, although fewer people use it in the late winter. Black Meadow Landing is a large resort with hundreds of RV sites, lodging, and a long list of amenities. Once you arrive, everything you need for a stay should be available within the resort.

RV sites, facilities: There are 350 sites with full hookups (30 amps) for RVs up to 40 feet and tent camping is available. Park-model cabins, kitchen cabins, and a motel are also available. Restrooms with flush toilets and showers, drinking water, picnic tables, picnic areas, horseshoe pit, restaurant, convenience store, recreation room (winter only), bait and tackle, propane, full-service marina, boat launch, boat slips, boat and RV storage, a swimming lagoon, and a five-hole golf course are available. Leashed pets are permitted.

Reservations, fees: Reservations are accepted at 800/7-HAVASU (800/742-8278). Sites are $25–60 per night, $6 per person per night for more than two people, $25 per night for tent sites, and $6 per night for each additional vehicle. Monthly rates are available. Some credit cards accepted. Open year-round.

Directions: From Southern California, take I-10 east to Blythe and turn north on U.S. 95. Continue to Vidal Junction at the intersection of U.S. 95 and Highway 62. Turn east on Highway 62 and drive to Earp and Parker Dam Road. Continue straight on Parker Dam Road and drive to a Y intersection and Black Meadow Landing Road (near Parker Dam).

Bear left on Black Meadow Landing Road and drive approximately nine miles to the resort at the end of the road.

From Northern California, drive to Barstow and I-40. Turn east on I-40 and drive to Needles. Continue east on I-40 to Arizona Highway 95. Drive south on Arizona Highway 95 to Lake Havasu City. Continue south to the Parker Dam turnoff. Turn west and drive across the dam to a Y intersection and Black Meadow Landing Road. Bear right on Black Meadow Landing Road and drive approximately nine miles to the resort at the end of the road. Note: Towed vehicles are not allowed to cross the dam.

Contact: Black Meadow Landing, 760/663-4901, www.blackmeadowlanding.com. For general information about the Colorado River and Lake Havasu, contact the Lake Havasu Tourism Bureau, 928/453-3444 or 800/2-HAVASU (800/242-8278), www.golakehavasu.com; Lake Havasu Area Chamber of Commerce, 928/855-4115, www.havasuchamber.com.

36 RIVERLAND RV PARK

Scenic rating: 6

on the Colorado River near Parker Dam

Map grid E4

This resort is in the middle of a very popular boating area, particularly for waterskiing. Summer is the busiest time because of the sunshine and warm water. In the winter, although temperatures can get pretty cold, around 40°F at night, the campground fills with retirees from the snow and rain country. Even though the resort is way out there on the Colorado River, there are plenty of services, including a convenience store, swimming beach, and full-service marina. Insider's tip: One of the best spots for catfish is a few miles down the road below Parker Dam.

RV sites, facilities: There are 60 sites with full hookups (50 amps) for RVs up to 40 feet. Picnic tables are provided. A park-model cabin is available. Restrooms with flush toilets and showers, drinking water, cable television, Wi-Fi, convenience store, coin laundry, full-service marina, boat launch, boat slips, boat and RV storage, swimming beach, fishing pier, bait, recreation room (winter only), and horseshoe pits are available. An ATM is within five miles and an 18-hole golf course is about 20 minutes away in Arizona. Leashed pets are permitted with restrictions.

Reservations, fees: Reservations are accepted at 760/663-3733. Sites are $35 per night on Friday and Saturday, $30 per night Sunday through Thursday, $40 on holidays. Monthly rates are available November through May. Some credit cards accepted. Open year-round.

Directions: From Southern California, take I-10 east to Blythe and turn north on U.S. 95. Continue to Vidal Junction at the intersection of U.S. 95 and Highway 62. Turn east on Highway 62 and drive to Earp and Parker Dam Road. Continue straight on Parker Dam Road and drive five miles to the resort on the right.

Contact: Riverland RV Park, 760/663-3733, www.reynoldsresorts.com.

37 LOST LAKE RESORT

Scenic rating: 6

on the Colorado River in Parker Valley
Map grid E4

If you're looking for a remote spot on the Colorado River, this is it. This is kind of like an oasis in the middle of the desert. Direct access to the Colorado River is provided, and this is one of the few places around that sell fishing licenses for this stretch of the Colorado River. The Parker Valley section of the river is part of the Colorado River Indian Reservation, and the tribe requires that all anglers obtain a permit. One of the best spots for big catfish, including large flathead catfish and channel catfish, is below Parker Dam. If you catch a razorback sucker, a rare event, it must be released. It is an endangered species. Note that about half of the sites are filled with long-term or permanent renters.

RV sites, facilities: There are 150 sites with full

hookups (30 amps), including four premium sites. Tent camping is available. Picnic tables are provided at most sites. Restrooms with flush toilets, showers, coin laundry, convenience store, café, recreation room (winter only), boat and RV storage, boat launch, bait and tackle, fishing licenses, and full-service marina are available. Leashed pets are permitted.

Reservations, fees: Reservations are accepted at 760/664-4413. Sites are $30 per night per vehicle; the premium sites are $40 per night. Monthly rates are available in winter. Some credit cards accepted. Open year-round.

Directions: From Southern California, take I-10 east to Blythe and turn north on U.S. 95. Drive for 31 miles to the resort on the right.

Contact: Lost Lake Resort, 760/664-4413.

38 BLACK ROCK CANYON AND HORSE CAMP

Scenic rating: 4

in Joshua Tree National Park
See Joshua Tree National Park map, page 1170

This is the fanciest darn public campground this side of the desert. Why, it actually has drinking water. The camp is set at the mouth of Black Rock Canyon, at 4,000 feet elevation, which provides good winter hiking possibilities amid unique (in other words, weird) rock formations, about a half-hour drive from the campground. Show up in summer and you'll trade your gold for a sip of water. The camp is set near the excellent Black Rock Canyon Visitor Center and a trailhead for a four-mile round-trip hike to a rock wash. If you scramble onward, the route continues all the way to the top of Eureka Peak, at 5,518 feet, an 11-mile round-trip. But hey, why not just drive there?

RV sites, facilities: There are 100 sites for tents or RVs up to 35 feet (no hookups), and 15 equestrian sites for up to six people and four horses per site. Picnic tables and fire grills are provided. Drinking water, flush toilets, and dump station are available. The horse camp has hitching posts and a water faucet and no tents are allowed. Some facilities are wheelchair-accessible. Leashed pets are permitted, but not on trails.

Reservations, fees: Reservations are accepted at 877/444-6777 or www.recreation.gov ($10 reservation fee). Sites are $15 per night, plus $15 park entrance fee per vehicle. Open year-round, weather permitting.

Directions: From the junction of I-10 and Highway 62 near Palm Springs, drive northeast on Highway 62 for 22.5 miles to Yucca Valley and Joshua Lane. Turn right (south) on Joshua Lane and drive about five miles to the campground.

Contact: Joshua Tree National Park, 760/367-5500 or 760/362-4367; Black Rock Nature Center, 760/367-3001, www.nps.gov/jotr.

39 INDIAN COVE CAMPGROUND

Scenic rating: 4

in Joshua Tree National Park

See Joshua Tree National Park map, page 1170

This is one of the campgrounds near the northern border of Joshua Tree National Park. The vast desert park, covering 1,238 square miles, is best known for its unique granite formations and scraggly-looking trees. If you had to withstand the summer heat here, you'd look scraggly too. Drinking water is available at the Indian Cove Ranger Station.

RV sites, facilities: There are 101 sites for tents or RVs up to 35 feet (no hookups), and a group camp with 13 sites for tents only for up to 60 people. Drinking water is available at the Indian Cove Ranger Station. Vault toilets, picnic tables, and fire grills are provided. Gas, groceries, and laundry services are available in Twentynine Palms (seven miles) or Joshua Tree (12 miles). Leashed pets are permitted, but not on trails.

Reservations, fees: Reservations are accepted at 800/365-CAMP (800/365-2267) or at http://reservations.nps.gov. Sites are $15 per night, $25–40 per night for group sites, plus $15 per vehicle park entrance fee. Open year-round.

Directions: From the junction of I-10 and Highway 62 near Palm Springs, drive northeast on Highway 62 for 22 miles to Yucca Valley, continue to the small town of Joshua Tree, and then continue nine miles to Indian Cove Road. Turn right and drive three miles to the campground.

Contact: Joshua Tree National Park, 760/367-5500 or 760/362-4367, fax 760/367-5546, www.nps.gov/jotr.

40 HIDDEN VALLEY

Scenic rating: 7

in Joshua Tree National Park

See Joshua Tree National Park map, page 1170

This is one of California's top campgrounds for rock-climbers. Set at 4,200 feet elevation in the high desert country, this is one of several camping options in the area. A trailhead is available two miles from camp at Barker Dam, an easy one-mile loop that features the Wonderland of Rocks. The hike takes you next to a small lake with magical reflections of rock formations off its surface. The RV sites here are snatched up quickly and this campground fills almost daily with rock-climbers.

RV sites, facilities: There are 45 sites for tents or RVs up to 25 feet (no hookups). Picnic tables and fire grills are provided. Vault toilets are available. No drinking water is available. Leashed pets are permitted.

Reservations, fees: No reservations are accepted. Sites are $10 per night, and $15 park entrance fee per vehicle. Open year-round.

Directions: From the junction of I-10 and Highway 62 near Palm Springs, drive northeast on Highway 62 for 22 miles to Yucca Valley, then continue to the small town of Joshua Tree and Park Boulevard. Turn south on Park Boulevard and drive 14 miles to the campground on the left.

Contact: Joshua Tree National Park, 760/367-5500 or 760/362-4367, fax 760/367-5546, www.nps.gov/jotr.

CALIFORNIA

41 RYAN

Scenic rating: 4

in Joshua Tree National Park

See Joshua Tree National Park map, page 1170

This is one of the high desert camps in the immediate area (see also the *Jumbo Rocks* listing in this chapter). Joshua Tree National Park is a forbidding paradise: huge, hot, and waterless (most of the time). The unique rock formations look as if some great artist made them with a chisel. The elevation is 4,300 feet. The best hike in the park starts here—a three-mile round-trip to Ryan Mountain is a 1,000-foot climb to the top at 5,470 feet elevation. The view is simply drop-dead gorgeous, not only of San Jacinto, Tahquitz, and San Gorgonio peaks, but of several beautiful rock-studded valleys as well as the Wonderland of Rocks.

RV sites, facilities: There are 31 sites for tents or RVs up to 25 feet (no hookups). Picnic tables and fire grills are provided. Vault toilets are available. No drinking water is available. Hitching posts are available (bring water for the horses). Leashed pets are permitted.

Reservations, fees: Reservations are accepted for equestrian sites only at 760/367-5541. Sites are $10 per night, and there is a $15 park entrance fee per vehicle. Open year-round.

Directions: From the junction of I-10 and Highway 62 near Palm Springs, drive northeast on Highway 62 to Twentynine Palms and Utah Trail. Turn right (south) on Utah Trail and drive about 20 miles to the campground entrance on the left.

Contact: Joshua Tree National Park, 760/367-5500 or 760/362-4367, fax 760/367-5546, www.nps.gov/jotr.

42 SHEEP PASS GROUP CAMP

Scenic rating: 4

in Joshua Tree National Park

See Joshua Tree National Park map, page 1170

Several campgrounds are in this stretch of high desert. Ryan campground (see listing in this chapter), just a couple of miles down the road, has an excellent trailhead for a trek to Ryan Mountain, the best hike in the park. Temperatures are routinely over 100°F here in the summer. (For details on this area, see the *White Tank* listing in this chapter.)

RV sites, facilities: There are six group camps for tents or RVs up to 25 feet (no hookups) that can accommodate 20–50 people each. Picnic tables and fire grills are provided. Vault toilets are available. No drinking water is available. Leashed pets are permitted.

Reservations, fees: Reservations are accepted at 877/444-6777 or at www.recreation.gov ($10 reservation fee). Sites are $25–40 per night, plus $15 park entrance fee per vehicle. Open year-round.

Directions: From the junction of I-10 and Highway 62 near Palm Springs, drive northeast on Highway 62 to Twentynine Palms and Utah Trail. Turn right (south) on Utah Trail and drive about 16 miles to the campground on the left.

Contact: Joshua Tree National Park, 760/367-5500 or 760/362-4367, fax 760/367-5546, www.nps.gov/jotr.

43 JUMBO ROCKS

Scenic rating: 4

in Joshua Tree National Park

See Joshua Tree National Park map, page 1170

Joshua Tree National Park covers more than 1,238 square miles. It is striking high-desert country with unique granite formations that seem to change color at different times of the day. At 4,400 feet, this camp is one of the higher ones in the park, with adjacent boulders and rock formations that look as if they have been strewn about by an angry giant. It is a popular site for rock-climbing.

RV sites, facilities: There are 125 sites for tents or RVs up to 35 feet (no hookups). Picnic tables and fire grills are provided. Vault toilets are available. No drinking water is available. Leashed pets are permitted.

Reservations, fees: Reservations are not accepted. Sites are $10, and there is a $15 park entrance fee per vehicle. Open year-round.

Directions: From the junction of I-10 and Highway 62 near Palm Springs, drive northeast on Highway 62 to Twentynine Palms and Utah Trail. Turn right (south) on Utah Trail and drive about nine miles to the campground on the left side of the road.

Contact: Joshua Tree National Park, 760/367-5500 or 760/362-4367, fax 760/367-5546, www.nps.gov/jotr.

44 BELLE

Scenic rating: 4

in Joshua Tree National Park

See Joshua Tree National Park map, page 1170

This camp is at 3,800 feet elevation in rocky high country. It is one of six camps in the immediate area. (For more details, see the *White Tank* listing in this chapter.)

RV sites, facilities: There are 18 sites for tents or RVs up to 35 feet (no hookups). Picnic tables and fire grills are provided. Vault toilets are available. No drinking water is available. Leashed pets are permitted.

Reservations, fees: No reservations are accepted. Sites are $10 per night, and there is a $15 park entrance fee per vehicle. Open year-round.

Directions: From the junction of I-10 and Highway 62 near Palm Springs, drive northeast on Highway 62 to Twentynine Palms and Utah Trail. Turn right (south) on Utah Trail and drive eight miles to Pinto Basin Road. Turn left (heading toward I-10) and drive about 1.5 miles to the campground on the left.

Contact: Joshua Tree National Park, 760/367-5500 or 760/362-4367, fax 760/367-5546, www.nps.gov/jotr.

45 WHITE TANK

Scenic rating: 4

in Joshua Tree National Park

See Joshua Tree National Park map, page 1170

Joshua Tree National Park is a unique area where the high and low desert meet. Winter is a good time to explore the beautiful boulder piles and rock formations amid scraggly Joshua trees. There are several trails in the area, with the best near Black Rock Campground, Hidden Valley, and Cottonwood. The elevation is 3,800 feet.

RV sites, facilities: There are 15 sites for tents or RVs up to 25 feet (no hookups). Picnic tables and fire grills are provided. Vault toilets are available. No drinking water is available. Leashed pets are permitted.

Reservations, fees: No reservations are accepted. Sites are $10 per night, and there is $15 park entrance fee per vehicle. Open year-round.

Directions: From the junction of I-10 and Highway 62 near Palm Springs, drive northeast on Highway 62 to Twentynine Palms and Utah Trail. Turn right (south) on Utah Trail and drive eight miles to Pinto Basin Road. Turn left (heading toward I-10) and drive three miles to the campground on the left.

Contact: Joshua Tree National Park, 760/367-5500 or 760/362-4367, fax 760/367-5546, www.nps.gov/jotr.

46 COTTONWOOD

Scenic rating: 4

in Joshua Tree National Park

See Joshua Tree National Park map, page 1170

If you enter Joshua Tree National Park at its southern access point, this is the first camp you will reach. The park visitors center, where maps are available, is a mandatory stop. This park is vast, high-desert country, highlighted by unique rock formations, occasional scraggly trees, and vegetation that manages to survive the bleak, roasting summers. This camp is set at 3,000 feet elevation. A trailhead is available here for an easy one-mile nature trail, where small signs have been posted to identify different types of vegetation. You'll notice, however, that they all look like cacti (the plants, not the signs, heh, heh).

RV sites, facilities: There are 62 sites for tents or RVs up to 35 feet (no hookups), and a group campground with three sites for 15–20 people each. Picnic tables and fire grills are provided. Drinking water and flush toilets are available. Some facilities are wheelchair-accessible. Leashed pets are permitted.

Reservations, fees: Reservations are accepted for group sites only at 877/444-6777 or www. recreation.gov ($10 reservation fee). Sites are $15 per night, and group sites are $30 per night. Park entrance fee is $15 per vehicle. Open year-round.

Directions: From Indio, drive east on I-10 for 35 miles to the exit for Pinto Basin Road/Twentynine Palms (near Chiriaco Summit). Take that exit and drive north for seven miles (entering the park) to the campground on the right.

Contact: Joshua Tree National Park, 760/367-5500 or 760/362-4367, fax 760/367-5546, www.nps.gov/jotr.

47 SAM'S FAMILY SPA

Scenic rating: 3

near Palm Springs

See Joshua Tree National Park map, page 1170

Hot mineral pools attract swarms of winter vacationers to the Palm Springs area. The therapeutic pools are partially enclosed. This 50-acre park, set 13 miles outside of Palm Springs, provides an alternative to the more crowded spots. And this is one of the few parks in the area that allows tent campers. A mobile-home park is adjacent to the RV park. The elevation of Sam's Family Spa is 1,000 feet. (For information on the tramway ride to Desert View west of Palm Springs, or the hike to Mount San Jacinto, see the Sky Valley Resort listing in this chapter.)

RV sites, facilities: There are 170 sites for tents and RVs up to 42 feet (with full hookups of 30 and 50 amps). Four mobile-home rentals and a motel are also available. Picnic tables are provided. There is a separate area with barbecues. Restrooms with showers, playground, heated swimming pool, heated wading pool, four hot mineral pools, sauna, Wi-Fi, coin laundry, and convenience store are available. Some facilities

are wheelchair-accessible. Leashed pets are permitted in the campground only.

Reservations, fees: Reservations are accepted online only; no telephone reservations. Sites are $40 per night. Weekly and monthly rates available. Some credit cards accepted. Open year-round.

Directions: Drive on I-10 to the Palm Springs Area and the Palm Drive exit (to Desert Hot Springs). Take that exit and drive north on Palm Drive for about two miles to Dillon Road. Turn right (east) on Dillon Road and drive 4.5 miles to the park on the right (70–875 Dillon Road).

Contact: Sam's Family Spa, 760/329-6457, fax 760/329-8267, www.samsfamilyspa.com.

48 SKY VALLEY RESORT

Scenic rating: 2

near Palm Springs

See Joshua Tree National Park map, page 1170

This 140-acre park is much like a small town, complete with RV homes, an RV park, and park-model rentals and seasonal restaurants. One of the best adventures in California is just west of Palm Springs, taking the aerial tram up from Chino Canyon to Desert View, a ride/climb of 2,600 feet for remarkable views to the east across the desert below. An option from there is hiking the flank of Mount San Jacinto, including making the ascent to the summit (10,804 feet), a round-trip butt-kicker of nearly 12 miles. Golf courses are nearby. Note that there are 260 permanent residents.

RV sites, facilities: There are 618 sites with full hookups (30 and 50 amps) for RVs up to 42 feet. No tents allowed. Restrooms with showers, cable TV, four swimming pools, nine natural hot mineral whirlpools, two laundry rooms, two large recreation rooms, fitness centers, children's playroom, seasonal grocery store, chapel program, seasonal tennis and golf lessons, pickleball court, business center with modem access, Wi-Fi, social director, shuffleboard, tennis, horseshoes, crafts room, and walking paths are available. Propane gas is nearby. Some facilities are wheelchair-accessible. Leashed pets are permitted.

Reservations, fees: Reservations are accepted at 888/893-7727 or by website. Sites are $48–49 per night, $38–39.50 in off-season, $5 per person per night for more than two people. Monthly rates available. Some credit cards accepted. Open year-round.

Directions: Drive on I-10 to the Palm Springs area and the Palm Drive exit (to Desert Hot Springs). Take that exit and drive north on Palm Drive for three miles to Dillon Road. Turn right on Dillon Road and drive 8.5 miles to the park on the right (74–711 Dillon Road).

Contact: Sky Valley Resort, 760/329-2909, fax 760/329-9473, www.skyvalleyresort.com.

49 HAPPY TRAVELER RV PARK

Scenic rating: 1

in Palm Springs

See Joshua Tree National Park map, page 1170

Are we having fun yet? They are at Happy Traveler, which is within walking distance of Palm Springs shopping areas and restaurants. The Palm Springs Air Museum has a collection of World War II aircraft. A casino is one mile away.

RV sites, facilities: There are 130 sites with full hookups (30 and 50 amps) for RVs up to 40 feet. No tents or tent trailers. Picnic tables are provided. Restrooms with showers, cable TV, Wi-Fi, swimming pool, spa, clubhouse, shuffleboard, propane, seasonal activities, and coin laundry are available. Leashed pets are permitted with restrictions, including a maximum of two pets.

Reservations, fees: Reservations are accepted. Sites are $38 per night. Monthly rates available. Credit cards are not accepted. Open year-round.

Directions: Drive on I-10 to Palm Springs and Highway 111/Palm Canyon Drive. Take Palm Canyon Drive and drive 12 miles south to Mesquite Avenue. Turn right on Mesquite Avenue and drive to the park on the left (211 West Mesquite).

Contact: Happy Traveler RV Park, 760/325-8518, www.happytravelerrv.com.

50 OUTDOOR RESORT OF PALM SPRINGS

Scenic rating: 6

near Palm Springs

See Joshua Tree National Park map, page 1170

This is considered a five-star resort, beautifully landscaped, huge, and offering many activities: swimming pools galore, 27-hole golf course, tons of tennis courts, spas, and on and on. The 137-acre park is four miles from Palm Springs. Note that this is a lot-ownership park with lots for sale. About a quarter of the sites are available for rent to vacationers. One of the best adventures in California is just west of Palm Springs: taking the aerial tram up from Chino Canyon to Desert View, a ride/climb of 2,600 feet for remarkable views to the east across the desert below.

RV sites, facilities: There are 1,213 sites with full hookups (30 and 50 amps) for RVs up to 45 feet. No tent camping. RV rentals are also available. Restrooms with showers, eight swimming pools, spas, 14 lighted tennis courts, 27-hole golf course, two clubhouses, snack bar, café, beauty salon, coin laundry, Wi-Fi, modem access, convenience store, shuffleboard, and planned activities are available. Some facilities are wheelchair-accessible. Leashed pets are permitted.

Reservations, fees: Reservations are accepted at 800/843-3131 (California only). Sites are $67–77 per night, $1 per pet per night with a two-pet maximum. RV rentals are $95–115 per night. Monthly rates available. Some credit cards accepted. Open year-round.

Directions: Drive on I-10 to the Palm Springs area and continue to Cathedral City and the exit for Date Palm Drive. Take that exit and drive south on Date Palm Drive for two miles to Ramon Road. Turn left and drive to the resort on the right (69–411 Ramon Road).

Contact: Outdoor Resort, 760/324-4005, www.outdoorresort.com.

CALIFORNIA

51 PALM SPRINGS OASIS RV PARK

Scenic rating: 2

in Cathedral City

See Joshua Tree National Park map, page 1170

This popular wintering spot is for RV cruisers looking to hole up in the Palm Springs area for awhile. Palm Springs is only six miles away. This is a seniors-only park, meaning that you need to be at the magic age of 55 or above to qualify for a stay.

RV sites, facilities: There are 140 sites with full hookups (30 and 50 amps) for RVs up to 45 feet. No tents. Restrooms with showers, cable TV, Wi-Fi, modem access, two swimming pools, spa, tennis courts, coin laundry, and propane gas are available. An 18-hole golf course is adjacent to the park. Some facilities are wheelchair-accessible. Children and people under age 55 are not allowed. Leashed pets are permitted, with a two-pet maximum.

Reservations, fees: Reservations are accepted. Sites are $41 per night, $2 per person per night for more than two people. Weekly and monthly rates available. Some credit cards accepted. Open year-round.

Directions: Drive on I-10 to the Palm Springs area and continue to Cathedral City and the exit for Date Palm Drive. Take that exit and drive south on Date Palm Drive for four miles to Gerald Ford Drive and the park on the left corner (36–100 Date Palm Drive).

Contact: Palm Springs Oasis RV Park, 760/328-4813 or 800/680-0144, fax 760/328-8455.

52 INDIAN WELLS RV RESORT

Scenic rating: 2

in Indio

See Joshua Tree National Park map, page 1170

Indio is a good-sized town midway between the Salton Sea to the south and Palm Springs to the north, which is about 20 miles away. In the summer, it is one of the hottest places in America. In the winter, it is a favorite for "snowbirds," that is, RV and trailer owners from the snow country who migrate south for the winter. About half of the sites are filled with long-term renters.

RV sites, facilities: There are 381 sites with full hookups (50 amps) for RVs up to 45 feet; most are pull-through. No tents. Restrooms with showers, cable TV, Wi-Fi, three swimming pools, two therapy pools, horseshoes, basketball, volleyball, shuffleboard courts, putting green, planned activities, ice, dog run, picnic area, and coin laundry are available. Some facilities are wheelchair-accessible. Leashed pets are permitted, with a maximum of two.

Reservations, fees: Reservations are accepted at 800/789-0895. Sites are $46 per night, $2.50 per person per night for more than two people. Weekly and monthly rates available. Some credit cards accepted. Open year-round.

Directions: Drive on I-10 to Indio and the exit for Jefferson Street. Take that exit, stay in the right lane, and drive to the light at Jefferson. Turn right at Jefferson and drive south for three miles to the park on the left (47–340 Jefferson Street).

Contact: Indian Wells RV Resort, 760/347-0895, fax 760/775-1147, www.carefreervresorts.com.

53 OUTDOOR RESORTS INDIO

Scenic rating: 7

in Indio

See Joshua Tree National Park map, page 1170

For owners of tour buses, motor coaches, and lavish RVs, it doesn't get any better than this in Southern California. Only RVers in Class A motor homes are allowed here. This resort bills itself as the "ultimate RV resort" and has been featured on the Travel Channel and in the Wall Street Journal. About 25 percent of the sites are available for rent; the other sites are owned by RVers. This park is set close to golf, shopping, and restaurants. Jeep tours of the surrounding desert canyons and organized recreation events are offered.

RV sites, facilities: There are 419 sites with full hookups (50 amps) for Class A motor homes with a minimum length of 28 feet. No trailers or pickup-truck campers. Restrooms with showers, cable TV, Wi-Fi, modem access, swimming pools, tennis courts, sauna, spas, massage service, hair salon, café, fitness center, clubhouse, coin laundry, and 18-hole golf course are available. Some facilities are wheelchair-accessible. Leashed pets are permitted, with a two-pet maximum.

Reservations, fees: Reservations are accepted. The winter rates are $65–75 per night, plus $5 for electricity; summer rates are $40–50 per night, plus $7 for electricity. Some credit cards accepted. Open year-round.

Directions: Drive on I-10 to Indio and the exit for Indio Boulevard/Jefferson Street. Take that exit, stay in the right lane, and drive to the light at Jefferson. Turn right at Jefferson and drive south for three miles to Avenue 48. Turn left and drive 0.25 mile to the park on the left side of the road (80–394 Avenue 48).

Contact: Outdoor Resorts Indio, 760/775-7255 or 800/892-2992 (outside California), www.outdoorresortsindio.com.

54 MIDLAND LONG TERM VISITOR AREA

Scenic rating: 4

west of Blythe

Map grid E5

Like its neighbor to the south (Mule Mountain), this camp is attractive to snowbirds, rockhounds (geodes and agates can be collected), and stargazers. The campground is on the southwest slope of the Big Maria Mountains, a designated wilderness, set at an elevation of 250 feet. The campsites are situated on flattened desert pavements consisting of alluvium. The desert landscape is extremely stark.

RV sites, facilities: There are numerous dispersed sites for tents or RVs of any length (no hookups). No drinking water or toilets are available. A dump station is nearby and is available

mid-September through mid-April. Leashed pets are permitted.

Reservations, fees: Reservations are not accepted. The fee is $40 for up to 14 nights, $180 per season. Fees charged September 15 through April 15. Summer is free, with a 14-day limit. Open year-round.

Directions: From Blythe, drive east on I-10 a short distance to Lovekin Boulevard. Turn left and drive about eight miles to the campground on the right.

Contact: Bureau of Land Management, Palm Springs Field Office, 760/251-4800, fax 760/251-4899, www.blm.gov/ca.

55 MAYFLOWER COUNTY PARK

Scenic rating: 6

on the Colorado River

Map grid E5

The Colorado River is the fountain of life around these parts and, for campers, the main attraction of this county park. It is a popular spot for waterskiing. There is river access here in the Blythe area. Fishing is good for channel and flathead catfish, striped bass, large- and smallmouth bass, bluegill, and crappie. This span of water is flanked by agricultural lands, although there are several developed recreation areas on the California side of the river south of Blythe near Palo Verde.

RV sites, facilities: There are 25 tent sites and 152 sites for RVs of any length (with partial hookups of 30 and 50 amps). Picnic tables and fire grills are provided. Drinking water, restrooms with flush toilets and free showers, dump station, and boat ramp are available. Some facilities are wheelchair-accessible. Leashed pets are permitted.

Reservations, fees: Reservations are not accepted. Sites are $16–18 per night, $2 boat launch fee, $1 per pet per night. Monthly rates available. Some credit cards accepted. Open year-round.

Directions: Drive on I-10 to Blythe and Highway 95. Take Highway 95 north (it becomes

Intake Boulevard) and drive 3.5 miles to 6th Avenue. Turn right at 6th Avenue and drive 2.5 miles to Colorado River Road. Bear left and drive 0.5 mile to the park entrance.

Contact: Mayflower County Park, 760/922-4665, fax 760/922-9177, www.riversidecountyparks.org.

56 BLYTHE/ COLORADO RIVER KOA

Scenic rating: 6

near the Colorado River
Map grid E5

This RV park is set up for camper-boaters who want to hunker down for awhile along the Colorado River and cool off. Access to the park is easy off I-10, and a marina is available, both big pluses for those showing up with trailered boats. Swimming lagoons are another bonus. A golf course is within 10 miles. Note that about half of the sites are rented year-round.

RV sites, facilities: There are 287 sites for RVs of any length (with full hookups of 30 and 50 amps); some sites are pull-through. Tents are allowed, and seven park-model cabins are available. Picnic tables are provided. Restrooms with showers, heated swimming pool, spa, cable TV, Wi-Fi, modem access, coin laundry, telephone room, convenience store, card room, 24-hour security, RV and boat storage, arcade, recreation center, boat ramps, boat fuel, and propane gas are available. Some facilities are wheelchair-accessible. Leashed pets are permitted, with certain restrictions.

Reservations, fees: Reservations are accepted at 800/562-3948. Sites are $55.37 per night on Friday and Saturday, $45.37 per night Sunday through Thursday, $2 per person for more than four adults, $10 per night for each additional vehicle. Tent sites are $20 per night. Holiday rates are higher. Monthly rates available. Credit cards accepted. Open year-round.

Directions: Drive on I-10 to Blythe and continue east for two miles to the exit for Riviera Drive. Take that exit east and drive two miles to the park on the right (14100 Riviera Drive).

Contact: Blythe/Colorado River KOA, 14100 Riviera Dr., 760/922-5350, fax 760/922-1134, www.koa.com.

57 DESTINY McINTYRE RV RESORT

Scenic rating: 3

on the Colorado River
Map grid E5

This RV park sits on the outskirts of Blythe on the Colorado River, with this stretch of river providing good conditions for boating, water-skiing, and other water sports. A swimming lagoon is a big plus, along with riverfront beach access. Fishing is an option, with a variety of fish, including striped bass, largemouth bass, and catfish, providing fair results.

RV sites, facilities: There are 40 tent sites and 160 sites with full hookups (30 and 50 amps) for RVs of any length, including 11 pull-through sites. Picnic tables and fire rings are provided. Drinking water, restrooms with flush toilets and showers, dump station, propane gas, store, bait, ice, and boat ramp and boat fuel are available. Some facilities are wheelchair-accessible. Leashed pets are permitted November through April only.

Reservations, fees: Reservations are accepted at 800/RV-DESTINY (800/783-3784). Sites are $20–37 per night or $10–19 during off-season (Nov.–Mar.), $4 per person per night for more than two people, $10 per night for each additional vehicle. Monthly rates available. Some credit cards accepted. Open year-round.

Directions: Drive on I-10 to Blythe to the exit for Intake Boulevard south. Take that exit and drive south on Intake Boulevard for 6.5 miles to the junction with 26th Avenue (it takes off to the right) and the park entrance on the left. Turn left and enter the park.

Contact: Destiny McIntyre RV Resort, 760/922-8205, fax 760/922-5695, www.destinyrv.com/mcintyrervresort.htm.

58 PALO VERDE COUNTY PARK

Scenic rating: 5

near the Colorado River

Map grid E5

This is the only game in town, with no other camp around for many miles. It is set near a bend in the Colorado River, not far from the Cibola National Wildlife Refuge. A boat ramp is available at the park, making it a launch point for adventure. This stretch of river is a good one for powerboating and waterskiing. The best facilities for visitors are available here and on the west side of the river between Palo Verde and Blythe, with nothing available on the east side of the river.

RV sites, facilities: There are 20 sites for tents or RVs of any length (no hookups). Picnic tables, fire rings, restrooms with flush toilets, and shade ramadas are available. No drinking water. A boat ramp is available. A store, coin laundry, and propane gas are available in Palo Verde. Leashed pets are permitted.

Reservations, fees: Reservations are not accepted. There is no fee for camping. A three-day limit is enforced. Open year-round.

Directions: Drive on I-10 to Highway 78 (two miles west of Blythe). Take Highway 78 south and drive about 20 miles (three miles past Palo Verde) to the park entrance road on the east side.

Contact: Palo Verde County Park, Imperial County, 760/482-4462.

59 MULE MOUNTAIN LONG TERM VISITOR AREA

Scenic rating: 4

west of Blythe

Map grid E5

Mule Mountain is out in the middle of nowhere, but rockhounds and stargazers have found it anyway; it's ideal for both activities. There are two campgrounds, Coon Hollow and Wiley's Well, along with dispersed camping. Rockhounding, in particular, can be outstanding, with several geode and agate beds nearby. Hobby rock-collecting is permitted. Commercial rock-poaching is not. The site, ideal for winter camping, attracts snowbirds and is set in a desert landscape at an elevation of 150 feet. Bradshaw Trail runs east to west through the visitors area.

RV sites, facilities: There are 28 sites at Coon Hollow and 14 sites at Wiley's Well for tents or RVs up to 35 feet (no hookups). Picnic tables and fire grills are provided. Vault toilets are available. No drinking water is available. A dump station is nearby, halfway between the two campgrounds, and is available mid-September through mid-April. Leashed pets are permitted.

Reservations, fees: Reservations are not accepted. Sites are $40 for up to 14 nights, $180 per season, with a 14-day stay limit every 28 days. Open year-round.

Directions: From Blythe, drive west on I-10 about 15 miles to Wiley's Well Road. Turn left (south) and drive about nine miles (the road turns to dirt) to Wiley's Well. Continue another three miles to reach Coon Hollow. Dispersed camping is allowed once you pass the sign that indicates you're in the visitors center.

Contact: Bureau of Land Management, Palm Springs Field Office, 760/251-4800, fax 760/251-4899, www.blm.gov.

60 PINYON FLAT

Scenic rating: 6

near Cahuilla Tewanet Vista Point in San Bernardino National Forest

Map grid C5

The Cahuilla Tewanet Vista Point is just two miles east of the camp and provides a good, easy side trip, along with a sweeping view to the east of the desert on clear days. A primitive trail is available two miles away to the southeast via Forest Road 7S01 off a short spur road (look for it on the left side of the road). This hike crosses a mix of sparse forest and high-desert terrain for 10 miles, passing Cactus Spring five miles in.

Desert bighorn sheep are sometimes spotted in this area. The elevation is 4,000 feet.

RV sites, facilities: There are 18 sites for tents or RVs up to 15 feet (no hookups). Picnic tables and fire rings are provided. Drinking water and vault toilets are available. Some facilities are wheelchair-accessible. Leashed pets are permitted.

Reservations, fees: Reservations are not accepted. Sites are $8 per night. Open year-round.

Directions: Drive on I-10 to Palm Springs and Highway 111. Turn south on Highway 111 and drive to Rancho Mirage and Highway 74. Turn right (south) on Highway 74 and drive 14 miles (a slow, twisty road) to the campground on the right.

Contact: San Bernardino National Forest, San Jacinto Ranger District, 909/382-2921, fax 951/659-2107.

61 LAKE CAHUILLA COUNTY PARK

Scenic rating: 7

near Indio

Map grid C5

Lake Cahuilla covers just 135 acres, but those are the most loved 135 acres for miles in all directions. After all, water out here is as scarce as polar bears. This 710-acre Riverside County park provides large palm trees and a 10-acre beach and water-play area. In the winter it is stocked with trout, and in the summer with catfish. Other species include largemouth and striped bass, crappie, and carp to 30 pounds. No swimming is allowed. Only car-top boats are permitted (no gas motors), and a speed limit of 10 mph is enforced. An equestrian camp is also available, complete with corrals. Equestrian and hiking trails are available on nearby public land. Morrow Trail is popular, and the trailhead is near the park's ranger station. A warning: The wind can really howl through here, and temperatures well over 100°F are typical in the summer.

RV sites, facilities: There are 55 sites with partial hookups (30 and 50 amps) and 10 sites with no hookups for RVs, a primitive camping area with no hookups for tents or RVs, and a large group area with horse corrals. Maximum RV length is 45 feet. Fire grills and picnic tables are provided. Restrooms with showers, dump station, seasonal swimming pool, and a primitive (hand-launch) beach boat launch are available. No gas motors are allowed. Some facilities are wheelchair-accessible. Leashed pets are permitted.

Reservations, fees: Reservations are accepted at 800/234-PARK (800/234-7275; $8 reservation fee). Sites are $13–18 per night, $1 per pet per night. Weekly rates are available during the winter. Maximum stay is two weeks. Some credit cards accepted. Open year-round, closed Tuesday, Wednesday, and Thursday May through October.

Directions: Drive on I-10 to Indio and the exit for Monroe Street. Take that exit and drive south on Monroe Street to Avenue 58. Turn right (west) and drive two miles to the park at the end of the road.

Contact: Lake Cahuilla County Park, 760/564-4712, fax 760/564-2506, www.riversidecountyparks.org.

62 HEADQUARTERS

Scenic rating: 5

in the Salton Sea State Recreation Area

Map grid D5

This is the northernmost camp on the shore of the giant Salton Sea, one of the campgrounds at the Salton Sea State Recreation Area. Salton Sea is a vast, shallow, and unique lake, the center of a 360-square-mile basin and one of the world's inland seas. Salton Sea was created in 1905 when a dike broke, and in turn, the basin was flooded with saltwater. The lake is 35 miles long, but it has an average depth of just 15 feet. It is set at the recreation area headquarters, just south of the town of Desert Beach at an elevation of 227 feet below sea level. Fishing for tilapia is popular, and it is also one of Southern California's most popular boating areas. Because of the low altitude, atmospheric pressure allows high performance for many ski boats. If winds are hazardous, a red beacon on the northeast shore of the lake will flash. If you see it, get to the nearest shore. The Salton Sea is about a three-hour drive from Los Angeles. Use is moderate year-round, but lowest in the summer because of temperatures that can hover in the 110°F range for days.

RV sites, facilities: There are 25 sites with no hookups for tents or RVs, 15 with full hookups (30 amps) for RVs up to 40 feet, and several hike-in/bike-in sites. Picnic tables, fire grills, and shade ramadas are provided. Drinking water, restrooms with flush toilets and coin showers, dump station, fish cleaning station, and visitors center with Wi-Fi access are available. A store is within two miles. Some facilities are wheelchair-accessible. Leashed pets are permitted in the campgrounds and on roadways only.

Reservations, fees: Reservations are accepted at 800/444-PARK (800/444-7275) or www. reserveamerica.com ($8 reservation fee). Sites are $30 per night, and $2 per person per night for hike-in/bike-in sites. Boat launching is $3 per day. Open year-round.

Directions: From the Los Angeles area, take I-10 east to Indio and the exit for the Highway 86 Expressway. Take that exit and drive south for 12 miles to 66th Avenue. Turn left and drive less than one mile to Mecca and Highway 111. Turn right (south) on Highway 111 and drive 12 miles to the entrance on the right.

Contact: Salton Sea State Recreation Area, 760/393-3052 or 760/393-3059, www.parks. ca.gov.

63 MECCA BEACH

Scenic rating: 4

in the Salton Sea State Recreation Area
Map grid D5

This is one of the camps set in the Salton Sea State Recreation Area on the northeastern

shore of the lake. The big attractions here are the waterfront sites, which are not available at nearby Headquarters campground (see listing in this chapter).

RV sites, facilities: There are 110 sites, 10 with full hookups (30 amps) for tents or RVs of any length, and several hike-in/bike-in sites. Picnic tables and fire grills are provided. Drinking water, restrooms with flush toilets and showers, amphitheater, and a fish cleaning station are available. A dump station is one mile north of Headquarters campground and a store is within 3.5 miles. Some facilities are wheelchair-accessible. Leashed pets are permitted in the campgrounds and roadways only.

Reservations, fees: Reservations are accepted at 800/444-PARK (800/444-7275) or www. reserveamerica.com ($8 reservation fee). Sites are $20 per night, $2 per person per night for hike-in/bike-in sites. Boat launching is $3 per day. Open year-round.

Directions: From the Los Angeles area, take I-10 east to Indio and the exit for the Highway 86 Expressway. Take that exit and drive south for 12 miles to 66th Avenue. Turn left and drive less than one mile to Mecca and Highway 111. Turn right (south) on Highway 111 and drive 12.5 miles to the entrance on the right.

Contact: Salton Sea State Recreation Area, 760/393-3052 or 760/393-3059, www.parks. ca.gov.

64 CORVINA BEACH

Scenic rating: 5

in the Salton Sea State Recreation Area
Map grid D5

This is by far the biggest of the campgrounds on the Salton Sea. The campground is actually more of an open area on hard-packed dirt, best for parking an RV. (For details about the Salton Sea, see the Headquarters listing in this chapter.)

RV sites, facilities: There are 250 primitive sites in an open area for tents or RVs of any length (no hookups) and some hike-in/bike-in sites.

Drinking water and chemical toilets are available. Fires are permitted in metal containers only. A store and gas station are available within five miles. Leashed pets are permitted in the campground and on roadways only.

Reservations, fees: Reservations are not accepted. Sites are $7 per night, $2 per person per night for hike-in/bike-in sites. Boat launching is $3 per day. Open year-round.

Directions: From the Los Angeles area, take I-10 east to Indio and the exit for the Highway 86 Expressway. Take that exit and drive south for 12 miles to 66th Avenue. Turn left and drive less than one mile to Mecca and Highway 111. Turn right (south) on Highway 111 and drive 14 miles to the entrance on the right.

Contact: Salton Sea State Recreation Area, 760/393-3052 or 760/393-3059, www.parks.ca.gov.

65 SALT CREEK PRIMITIVE AREA

Scenic rating: 4

in the Salton Sea State Recreation Area

Map grid D5

Waterfront campsites are a bonus at this campground, even though the campground consists of just an open area on hard-packed dirt. Birding hikes are available during winter months. Several trails leave from camp, or nearby the camp, and head 1–2 miles to the Bat Cave Buttes, which are in the Durmid Hills on Bureau of Land Management property. There are bats in the numerous caves to explore, although the nearby OHV traffic has reduced their numbers. From the buttes, which are up to 100 feet above sea level, hikers can see both the north and south ends of the Salton Sea simultaneously. This is the only easily accessible place to view both shores of the Salton Sea. Many people believe the buttes are the southernmost point of the San Andreas Fault; the fault does not exist above ground south of here. (For details on the Salton Sea State Recreation Area, see the Headquarters listing in this chapter.)

RV sites, facilities: There are 200 primitive

sites for tents or RVs of any length (no hookups) and several hike-in/bike-in sites. Drinking water and chemical toilets are available. Fires are permitted in metal containers only. Leashed pets are permitted in the campgrounds and on roadways only.

Reservations, fees: Reservations are not accepted. Sites are $7 per night, $2 per person per night for hike-in/bike-in sites. Open year-round.

Directions: From the Los Angeles area, take I-10 east to Indio and the exit for the Highway 86 Expressway. Take that exit and drive south for 12 miles to 66th Avenue. Turn left and drive less than one mile to Mecca and Highway 111. Turn right (south) on Highway 111 and drive 17.5 miles to the entrance on the right.

Contact: Salton Sea State Recreation Area, 760/393-3052 or 760/393-3059, www.parks.ca.gov.

66 FOUNTAIN OF YOUTH SPA

Scenic rating: 4

near the Salton Sea

Map grid D5

Natural artesian steam rooms are the highlight here, but close inspection reveals that nobody seems to be getting any younger. This is a vast private park on 90 acres, set near the Salton Sea. Though this park has 1,000 sites for RVs, almost half of the sites have seasonal renters. This park is popular with snowbird campers and about 2,000 people live here during the winter. (See the Red Hill Marina County Park listing in this chapter for side-trip options.)

RV sites, facilities: There are 835 sites with full hookups (30 and 50 amps) and 165 sites with no hookups for tents or RVs. Restrooms with flush toilets and showers, cable TV, natural artesian steam rooms, swimming pools, artesian mineral water spa, three freshwater spas, recreation halls, dump stations, fitness room, library, picnic areas, nine-hole desert-style golf course, horseshoes, organized activities, craft and sewing room, Wi-Fi, modem access, coin laundry, beauty parlor, masseur, church services, propane gas, and groceries are available. Some facilities are wheelchair-accessible. Leashed pets are permitted.

Reservations, fees: No reservations accepted. Winter rates are $15–42 per night, summer rates are $15–35 per night, $1 per person per night for more than two people. Weekly and monthly rates available. Some credit cards accepted. Open year-round.

Directions: From the Los Angeles area, take I-10 east to Indio and the exit for the Highway 86 Expressway. Take that exit and drive south for 12 miles to Avenue 62. Turn right and drive less than one mile to Highway 111. Turn left (south) on Highway 111 and drive 44 miles to Hot Mineral Spa Road. Turn left (north) on Hot Mineral Spa Road and drive approximately four miles to Spa Road. Turn right and drive approximately 1.5 miles to the park on the left.

From Calipatria, drive north on Highway 111 to Niland, and then continue north for 15 miles to Hot Mineral Spa Road. Turn right (north) on Hot Mineral Spa Road and drive approximately four miles to Spa Road. Turn right and drive about 1.5 miles to the park on the left.

Contact: Fountain of Youth Spa, 888/8000-SPA (888/800-0772) or 760/354-1340, fax 760/354-1558, www.foyspa.com.

67 CORN SPRINGS
🚶 🐕 🚐 ⛺

Scenic rating: 4

in BLM desert

Map grid D5

Just think: If you spend a night here, you can say to darn near anybody, "I've camped someplace you haven't." I don't know whether to offer my condolences or congratulations, but Corn Springs offers a primitive spot in the middle of nowhere in desert country. A 0.5-mile interpretive trail can easily be walked in tennis shoes. It is divided into 11 stops with different vegetation, wildlife habitat, and cultural

notes at each stop. The side trip to Joshua Tree National Park to the north (40-minute drive to closest entrance) is also well worth the adventure. So is the aerial tram ride available west of Palm Springs (one-hour drive) for an incredible view of the desert. On the other hand, if it's a summer afternoon, tell me, just how do you spend the day here when it's 115°F?

RV sites, facilities: There are nine sites for tents or RVs up to 22 feet (no hookups) and one group site for tents or RVs (one or two only) up to 22 feet that can accommodate up to 25 people. Picnic tables and fire grills are provided. Drinking water, shade ramadas, and vault toilets are available. Leashed pets are permitted.

Reservations, fees: Reservations are not accepted. Sites are $6 per night. Open year-round.

Directions: From Indio, drive east on I-10 for 60 miles to the Corn Springs Road exit. Take that exit to Old Chuckwalla Valley Road. Turn right (south) onto Old Chuckwalla Valley Road and drive 0.5 mile to Corn Springs Road. Turn right and drive 10 miles on a dirt road to the campground on the left.

Contact: Bureau of Land Management, Palm Springs Field Office, 760/251-4800, fax 760/251-4899, www.blm.gov/ca.

68 BOMBAY BEACH
🚶 🚴 🏊 🛶 🚐 🐕 ♿ 🚙 ⛺

Scenic rating: 5

in the Salton Sea State Recreation Area

Map grid D5

All in all, this is a strange-looking place, with the Salton Sea, a vast body of water, surrounded by stark, barren countryside. This camp is set in a bay along the northeastern shoreline, where a beach and nature trails are available. The campground is a flat, open area. Nearby to the south is the Wister Waterfowl Management Area. The Salton Sea is California's unique saltwater lake set below sea level, with fishing for tilapia a possibility.

RV sites, facilities: There are 200 sites for tents or RVs of any length (no hookups) and several hike-in/bike-in sites. Drinking water and chemical toilets are available. Fires are permitted in metal containers only. A store, restaurant, marina, and boat launch are available nearby in Bombay Beach. Leashed pets are permitted.

Reservations, fees: Reservations are not accepted. Sites are $7 per night, $2 per person per night for hike-in/bike-in sites. Open year-round.

Directions: From the Los Angeles area, take I-10 east to Indio and the exit for the Highway 86 Expressway. Take that exit and drive south for 12 miles to 66th Avenue. Turn left and drive less than one mile to Mecca and Highway 111. Turn right (south) on Highway 111 and drive 25 miles to the campground entrance on the right.

From Calipatria, drive north on Highway 111 to Niland, then continue north 18 miles to the entrance on the left.

Contact: Salton Sea State Recreation Area, 760/393-3052 or 760/393-3059, www.parks.ca.gov.

69 RED HILL MARINA COUNTY PARK

Scenic rating: 3

near the Salton Sea
Map grid D5

It's called Red Hill Marina, but you won't find a marina here; it washed away in the mid-1970s. This county park is near the south end of the Salton Sea, one of the weirdest places on earth. Set 228 feet below sea level, it's a vast body of water covering 360 square miles, 35 miles long, but with an average depth of just 15 feet. It's an extremely odd place to swim, as you bob around effortlessly in the highly saline water. Note that swimming is not recommended in this park because of the muddy shore. Fishing is often good for corvina in spring and early summer. Hundreds of species of birds stop by this area as they travel along the Pacific Flyway. Several wildlife refuges are in the immediate area, including two separate chunks of the Imperial Wildfowl Management Area, to the

west and south, and the huge Wister Waterfowl Management Area, northwest of Niland. (For side-trip options, see the Bombay Beach listing in this chapter.)

RV sites, facilities: There are 40 sites for RVs or tents; some sites have partial hookups. Picnic tables, cabanas, and barbecue pits are provided. Restrooms with flush toilets and showers, a concession stand, beer, bait, fishing and hunting licenses, and a boat launch are available. The water at this park is not certified for drinking. Leashed pets are permitted.

Reservations, fees: Reservations are not accepted. Sites are $7–12 per night, $2 per night for each additional vehicle. Monthly rates available. Open year-round.

Directions: From Mecca, drive south on Highway 111 to Niland, and continue to Sinclair Road. Turn right and drive 3.5 miles to Garst Road. Turn right and drive 1.5 miles to the end of Garst Road at Red Hill Road. Turn left on Red Hill Road and drive to the park at the end of the road.

From El Centro, drive north on Highway 111 to Brawley and Highway 78/Main Street. Turn west (left) on Highway 78/Main Street and drive a short distance to Highway 111. Turn right (north) and drive to Calipatria. Continue north on Highway 111 just outside of Calipatria to Sinclair Road. Turn left on Sinclair Road and drive to Garst Road. Turn right and drive 1.5 miles to where it ends at Red Hill Road. Turn left at Red Hill Road and drive to the end of the road and the marina and the campground.

Contact: Red Hill Marina, tel./fax 760/348-2310.

70 WIEST LAKE COUNTY PARK

Scenic rating: 4

on Wiest Lake
Map grid D5

This is a developed county park along the southern shore of Wiest Lake, which adjoins the Imperial Wildfowl Management Area to the north. Wiest Lake is just 50 acres, set 110 feet below sea level, and a prized area with such desolate country in the surrounding region. Waterskiing and sailboarding can be excellent, although few take advantage of the latter. Swimming is allowed when lifeguards are on duty. The lake is most popular for fishing, with trout planted in winter and catfish in summer. The lake also has bass and bluegill. The Salton Sea, about a 20-minute drive to the northwest, is a worthy side trip.

RV sites, facilities: There are 20 tent sites and 24 sites with full hookups (50 amps) for RVs up to 45 feet. Picnic tables and fire grills are provided. There is no drinking water. Restrooms with flush toilets and showers, a boat ramp, and a dump station are available. A store, coin laundry, and propane gas are available within five miles. Leashed pets are permitted.

Reservations, fees: Reservations are not accepted. Sites are $7–12 per night, $2 per night for each additional vehicle. Monthly rates available. Open year-round.

Directions: From El Centro, drive north on Highway 111 to Brawley and Highway 78/Main Street. Turn west (left) on Highway 78/Main Street and drive a short distance to Highway 111. Turn right (north) on Highway 111 and drive four miles to Rutherford Road (well signed). Turn right (east) and drive two miles to the park entrance on the right.

Contact: Wiest Lake County Park, tel./fax 760/344-3712.

71 CULP VALLEY PRIMITIVE CAMP AREA

Scenic rating: 4

near Peña Springs in
Anza-Borrego Desert State Park

See Anza-Borrego Desert State Park map, page 1171

Culp Valley is set near Peña Springs, which is more of a mudhole than a spring. A 600-yard hike takes you to an overlook of Hellhole Canyon and an eastern view of the Borrego Valley. The elevation at this campground is 3,400 feet.

RV sites, facilities: This is a primitive, open camping area for tents or small RVs of any length (no hookups). Vault toilets are available. No drinking water is available. Fires are permitted in metal containers. Garbage and ashes must be packed out. Leashed pets are permitted in the campground, but not on trails.

Reservations, fees: Reservations are not accepted. There is no fee for camping. Day-use parking is $8. Open year-round.

Directions: From Julian, at the junction of Highway 78 and Highway 79, drive east on Highway 78 (steep and curvy) for 10 miles to Highway S2. Turn left (north) and drive 16 miles to Highway S22/Borrego Salton Seaway. Turn right (east) and drive 10 miles to the campground entrance road on the left.

Contact: Anza-Borrego Desert State Park, Visitor Center, 760/767-4205; Colorado Desert District, 760/767-5311, fax 760/767-7492, www.parks.ca.gov.

72 BORREGO PALM CANYON

Scenic rating: 4

in Anza-Borrego Desert State Park

See Anza-Borrego Desert map, page 1171 **BEST**

Anza-Borrego Desert State Park is one of the largest state parks in the continental United States, covering more than 600,000 acres and with 500 miles of dirt roads. Borrego Palm Canyon is one of the best camps in the park, with two excellent hikes available. The short hike into Borrego Palm Canyon is like being transported to another world, from the desert to the tropics, complete with a small waterfall, a rare sight in these parts. Panorama Overlook Trail also starts here. An excellent visitors center is available, offering an array of exhibits and a slide show. The park is appropriately named for the desert bighorn sheep (*borrego* in Spanish) that live in the mountains and are often viewed from the Palm Canyon Nature Trail adjacent to the campground. The elevation is 760 feet.

RV sites, facilities: There are 29 sites for tents or RVs up to 25 feet (no hookups), 50 sites with full hookups (30 amps) for RVs up to 35 feet, and five group tent sites for up to 24 people each. Picnic tables and fire grills are provided. Drinking water, restrooms with flush toilets and showers, and dump station are available. A store, coin laundry, and propane gas are nearby. Some facilities are wheelchair-accessible. Leashed pets are permitted.

Reservations, fees: Reservations are accepted at 800/444-PARK (800/444-7275) or www.recreation.gov ($8 reservation fee). Sites are $20–35 per night, $50–80 per night for group sites. Day-use parking is $8. Open year-round.

Directions: From Julian, at the junction of Highway 78 and Highway 79, drive east on Highway 78 (steep and curvy) for 19.5 miles to Yaqui Pass Road/County Road S3. Turn left (north) and drive eight miles to Borrego Springs and Palm Canyon Drive. Turn left (west) and drive 4.5 miles to the campground entrance road on the right.

Contact: Anza-Borrego Desert State Park, Visitor Center, 760/767-4205; Colorado Desert District, 760/767-5311, fax 760/767-7492, www.parks.ca.gov.

73 VERN WHITAKER HORSE CAMP

🚶 🐴 🚐 ⛺

Scenic rating: 5

in Anza-Borrego Desert State Park

See Anza-Borrego Desert State Park map, page 1171

This camp is popular during spring and fall, with lighter use during the winter. The 30 miles of horse trails attract equestrian campers. Campers are expected to clean up after their horses, and garbage bins are available for manure.

RV sites, facilities: There are 10 equestrian sites for tents or RVs up to 24 feet (no hookups). Picnic tables and fire grills are provided. Restrooms with flush toilets, an outdoor shower, drinking water, picnic areas, group gathering area, horse-washing station, and horse corrals are available. Leashed pets are permitted in the campground, but not on trails or in wilderness.

Reservations, fees: Reservations are accepted

at 800/444-PARK (800/444-7275) or www.recreation.gov ($8 reservation fee). Sites are $30 per night, which includes two horses; $2 per additional horse per night. Day-use parking is $8. Open October through May.

Directions: From Julian, at the junction of Highway 78 and Highway 79, drive east on Highway 78 (steep and curvy) for 19.5 miles to Yaqui Pass Road/County Road 53. Turn left (north) and drive eight miles to Palm Canyon Drive. Turn left and drive to Borrego Springs and bear right (at the traffic circle) onto northbound Borrego Springs Road. Drive four miles on Borrego Springs Road to Henderson Canyon Road. Bear right and drive a short distance to the campground entrance road (look for the metal sign). Turn left and continue four miles to the camp. Note: Part of the last four miles are on a private road; please respect the property owner's rights.

Contact: Anza-Borrego Desert State Park, Visitor Center, 760/767-4205; Colorado Desert District, 760/767-5311, fax 760/767-7492, www.parks.ca.gov.

74 ARROYO SALADO PRIMITIVE CAMP AREA

🚶 🐴 🚐 ⛺

Scenic rating: 5

in Anza-Borrego Desert State Park

See Anza-Borrego Desert State Park map, page 1171

This camp is a primitive spot set along (and named after) an ephemeral stream, the Arroyo Salado. About eight miles to the west is the trailhead for Thimble Trail, which is routed south into a wash in the Borrego Badlands. The elevation is 880 feet.

RV sites, facilities: This is a primitive, open camping area for tents or small RVs of any length (no hookups). Vault toilets are available. No drinking water is available. Fires are allowed in metal containers. Garbage and ashes must be packed out. Open fires are not allowed. Leashed pets are permitted in the campground, but not on trails or in wilderness.

Reservations, fees: Reservations are not

accepted. There is no fee for camping. Day-use parking is $8. Open year-round.

Directions: From Julian, at the junction of Highway 78 (steep and curvy) and Highway 79, drive east on Highway 78 for 19.5 miles to Yaqui Pass Road/County Road S3. Turn left (north) and drive eight miles to Borrego Springs and Palm Canyon Drive. Turn right on Palm Canyon Drive (becomes Highway 522) and drive 20 miles (past Fonts Point) to the campground entrance on the right.

Contact: Anza-Borrego Desert State Park, Visitor Center, 760/767-4205; Colorado Desert District, 760/767-5311, fax 760/767-7492, www.parks.ca.gov.

75 YAQUI PASS PRIMITIVE CAMP AREA

Scenic rating: 1

in Anza-Borrego Desert State Park

See Anza-Borrego Desert State Park map, page 1171

This extremely primitive area is set beside rough Yaqui Pass Road at an elevation of 1,730 feet. The camping area is a large, open, sloping area of asphalt, where it is darn near impossible to get an RV level. The trailhead for Kenyon Loop Trail is to the immediate south. This spot is often overlooked because the Tamarisk Grove camp nearby provides shade, drinking water, and a feature trail.

RV sites, facilities: This is a primitive, open camping area for tents or small RVs of any length (no hookups). No drinking water or toilets are available. No open fires are allowed. Garbage must be packed out. Leashed pets are permitted, but not on trails or in wilderness.

Reservations, fees: Reservations are not accepted. There is no fee for camping. Day-use parking is $8. Open year-round.

Directions: From Julian, at the junction of Highway 78 and Highway 79, drive east on Highway 78 (steep and curvy) for 19.5 miles to Yaqui Pass Road/County Road S3. Turn left (north) and drive 2.5 miles to the campground entrance on the right. The access road

is rough and the camping area has few level areas for large RVs, so only small RVs are recommended.

Contact: Anza-Borrego Desert State Park, Visitor Center, 760/767-4205; Colorado Desert District, 760/767-5311, fax 760/767-7492, www.parks.ca.gov.

76 YAQUI WELL PRIMITIVE CAMP AREA

Scenic rating: 2

in Anza-Borrego Desert State Park

See Anza-Borrego Desert State Park map, page 1171

This camp is used primarily as an overflow area if the more developed Tamarisk Grove camp is full. Cactus Loop Trail, a 2.5-mile loop hike that passes seven varieties of cacti, starts at Tamarisk Grove. The elevation is 1,400 feet.

RV sites, facilities: This is a primitive, open camping area for tents or small RVs of any length (no hookups). Vault toilets are available. No drinking water is available. Fires are permitted in metal containers. Garbage and ashes must be packed out. Open fires are not permitted. Leashed pets are permitted, but not on trails or in wilderness.

Reservations, fees: Reservations are not accepted. There is no fee for camping. Day-use parking is $8. Open year-round.

Directions: From Julian, at the junction of Highway 78 and Highway 79, drive east on Highway 78 (steep and curvy) for 19.5 miles to Yaqui Pass Road/County Road S3. Turn left (north) and drive a short distance to the campground entrance road on the left. The access road is rough and the camping area has few level areas for large RVs, so only small RVs are recommended.

Contact: Anza-Borrego Desert State Park, Visitor Center, 760/767-4205; Colorado Desert District, 760/767-5311, fax 760/767-7492, www.parks.ca.gov.

77 TAMARISK GROVE

Scenic rating: 7

in Anza-Borrego Desert State Park

See Anza-Borrego Desert State Park map, page 1171

This is the number-one campground in Anza-Borrego Desert State Park, and it is easy to see why: Big tamarisk trees provide shade, and the park provides limited drinking water (recommended that you bring your own water as a backup). It is one of three camps in the immediate area, so if this camp is full, primitive Yaqui Well to the immediate west and Yaqui Pass to the north on Yaqui Pass Road provide alternatives. Cactus Loop Trail, with the trailhead just north of camp, provides a hiking option. This is a 1.5-mile loop that passes seven varieties of cacti, some as tall as people. The elevation is 1,400 feet at this campground.

RV sites, facilities: There are 27 sites for tents or RVs up to 21 feet (no hookups). Picnic tables and fire grills are provided. Restrooms with flush toilets and coin showers and limited drinking water are available. Some facilities are wheelchair-accessible. Leashed pets are permitted in the campground, but not on trails or in wilderness.

Reservations, fees: Reservations are accepted at www.reserveamerica.com ($8 reservation fee). Sites are $20 per night, $8 per night for each additional vehicle. Open October through May, from 2 P.M. Friday to noon Sunday.

Directions: From Julian, at the junction of Highway 78 and Highway 79, drive east on Highway 78 (steep and curvy) for 19.5 miles to Yaqui Pass Road/County Road S3. Turn left (north) and drive 0.5 mile to the campground on the right.

Contact: Anza-Borrego Desert State Park, Visitor Center, 760/767-4205; Colorado Desert District, 760/767-5311, fax 760/767-7492, www.parks.ca.gov.

78 OCOTILLO WELLS STATE VEHICLE RECREATION AREA

Scenic rating: 4

in Ocotillo Wells

See Anza-Borrego Desert State Park map, page 1171

This can be a wild place, a giant OHV camp where the population of Ocotillo Wells can go from 10 to 5,000 overnight, no kidding. Yet if you arrive when there is no off-road event, it can also be a lonely, extremely remote destination. Some locals call the OHV crowd "escapees" and watch stunned as they arrive every February for two or three weeks. OHV events are held here occasionally as well. Mountain bikers also use these trails. One great side note is that annually there is "Desert Cleanup Day," when OHV users will clean up the place; date changes every year. The non-OHV crowd can still use this camp, but most come in the winter on weekdays, when activity is lower. The landscape is barren desert, dry as an iguana's back. A few shade ramadas are provided. The area covers 72,000 acres, ranging from below sea level to an elevation of 400 feet. It is adjacent to Anza-Borrego Desert State Park, another 600,000 acres of wildlands. The wash-and-ridge terrain includes a butte with dunes, a sand bowl, a blow sand dune, and springs. After wet winters, the blooms of wildflowers can be excellent. While this area is well known as a wild play area for the OHV crowd, it is also a place where on most days you can literally disappear and see no one. All drivers should watch for soft ground. Many vehicles get stuck here and have to be towed out. Also, dispersed camping is allowed in most of these state park lands.

RV sites, facilities: There are 60 dispersed primitive sites for tents or RVs of any length (no hookups). Picnic tables and fire rings are provided. Chemical toilets and shade ramadas are available. There is no drinking water. A coin-shower building is available near the ranger station, and another is 3.5 miles east at Holmes Camp. A store, restaurants, propane, and auto supplies are available four miles away in Ocotillo Wells. A gas station is seven miles from the ranger station. Leashed pets are permitted.

Reservations, fees: Reservations are not accepted. There is no fee for camping. Day-use parking is $5. Open year-round.

Directions: From Julian, at the junction of Highway 78 and Highway 79, drive east on Highway 78 for 31.5 miles to Ranger Station Road. Turn left and drive 0.25 mile to the ranger station.

Note: For an alternate route that avoids curvy sections of Highway 78, from Santa Ysabel, turn north on Highway 79 and drive 14 miles to County Road S2/San Felipe Road. Turn right and drive 17 miles to Highway 78. Turn right and continue to Ranger Station Road.

Contact: Ocotillo Wells SVRA, 760/767-5391, fax 760/767-4951, www.parks.ca.gov or www.ohv.parks.ca.gov.

79 VALLECITO COUNTY PARK

Scenic rating: 3

near Anza-Borrego Desert State Park

See Anza-Borrego Desert State Park map, page 1171

This county park in the desert gets little attention in the face of the other nearby attractions. This is a 71-acre park built around a sod reconstruction of the historic Vallecito Stage Station. It was part of the Butterfield Overland Stage from 1858 to 1861. The route carried mail and passengers from Missouri to San Francisco in 25 days, covering 2,800 miles. Vallecito means "little valley." It provides a quiet alternative to some of the busier campgrounds in the desert. One bonus is that it is usually 10 degrees cooler here than at Agua Caliente. A covered picnic area is a big plus. Other nearby destinations include Agua Caliente Hot Springs, Anza-Borrego Desert State Park to the east, and Lake Cuyamaca and Cuyamaca Rancho State Park about 35 miles away. The elevation is 1,500 feet.

RV sites, facilities: There are 44 sites for tents or RVs up to 40 feet (no hookups), one group area for up to 15 RVs, and one youth camping area for up to 35 people. Picnic tables, fire rings, and barbecues are provided. Drinking water, flush toilets, and a playground are available. Leashed pets are permitted.

Reservations, fees: Reservations are available at 877/565-3600 ($5 reservation fee). Sites are $15 per night, $100–200 per night for the group area, $25 per night for the youth group area, $1 per pet per night. Some credit cards accepted. Open Labor Day weekend through Memorial Day weekend; closed June, July, and August.

Directions: From El Cajon, drive east on I-8 for about 75 miles to the town of Ocotillo (the first town after crossing from San Diego County to Imperial County) and County Road S2/Imperial Highway. Turn north (left) on County Road S2/Imperial Highway and drive 30 miles to the park entrance.

Contact: San Diego County Parks Department, 858/694-3049, fax 858/495-5841, www.sdparks.org.

80 AGUA CALIENTE REGIONAL PARK

Scenic rating: 3

near Anza-Borrego Desert State Park

See Anza-Borrego Desert State Park map, page 1171

This is a popular park in winter. It has two naturally fed pools: A large outdoor thermal pool is kept at its natural 90°F, and an indoor pool is heated to 102°F and outfitted with jets. Everything is hot here. The weather is hot, the coffee is hot, and the water is hot. And hey, that's what "Agua Caliente" means—hot water, named after the nearby hot springs. Anza-Borrego Desert State Park is also nearby. If you would like to see some cold water, Lake Cuyamaca and Cuyamaca Rancho State Park are about 35 miles away. The elevation is 1,350 feet. The park covers 910 acres with several miles of hiking trails.

RV sites, facilities: There are 106 sites with full or partial hookups (30 amps) for RVs up to 40 feet, 35 sites with no hookups for tents or RVs, and a group area for up to 100 people. Picnic tables and fire grills are provided. Restrooms with flush toilets and showers, drinking water, outdoor and indoor pools, picnic area, and a playground with horseshoes and shuffleboard are available. Groceries and propane gas are nearby. Some facilities are wheelchair-accessible. No pets are allowed.

Reservations, fees: Reservations are accepted at 877/565-3600 ($5 reservation fee). Sites are $15–25 per night, and the group area is $100–200 per night. Some credit cards accepted. Open Labor Day weekend through Memorial Day weekend; closed June, July, and August.

Directions: From El Cajon, drive east on I-8 about 75 miles to the town of Ocotillo (the first town after crossing from San Diego County to Imperial County) and County Road S2/Imperial Highway. Turn north (left) on County Road S2/Imperial Highway and drive 25 miles to the park entrance.

From Julian, take Highway 78 east and drive 12 miles to County Road S2/San Felipe Road. Turn right on County Road S2/San Felipe Road and drive 21 miles south to the park entrance.

Contact: San Diego County Parks Department, 858/694-3049, fax 858/495-5841, www.sdparks.org.

81 MOUNTAIN PALM SPRINGS PRIMITIVE CAMP AREA

Scenic rating: 4

in Anza-Borrego Desert State Park

See Anza-Borrego Desert State Park map, page 1171

A plus for this camping area is easy access from County Road S2, but no water is a giant minus. Regardless of pros and cons, only hikers will get the full benefit of the area. A trail leads south to Bow Willow Creek (and Bow Willow) and onward into Bow Willow Canyon. The Carrizo Badlands Overlook is on the southeast side of Sweeney Pass, about a 10-minute drive south on County Road S2. The elevation is 760 feet.

RV sites, facilities: This is a primitive, open camping area for tents or RVs of any length (no hookups). Vault toilets are available. No drinking water is available. Fires are permitted in metal containers. Garbage and ashes must be packed out. Leashed pets are permitted, but not on trails or in wilderness.

Reservations, fees: Reservations are not accepted. There is no fee for camping. Day-use parking is $8. Open year-round.

Directions: From El Cajon, drive east on I-8 for about 75 miles to the town of Ocotillo (the first town after crossing from San Diego County to Imperial County) and County Road S2/Imperial Highway. Turn north (left) on County Road S2/Imperial Highway and drive 27.5 miles to the campground entrance road on the left (about 0.5 mile past the Bow Willow campground turnoff). Turn left and continue 0.75 mile to the camp.

Contact: Anza-Borrego Desert State Park, Visitor Center, 760/767-4205; Colorado Desert District, 760/767-5311, fax 760/767-7492, www.parks.ca.gov.

82 BOW WILLOW

Scenic rating: 4

near Bow Willow Canyon in Anza-Borrego Desert State Park

See Anza-Borrego Desert State Park map, page 1171

Bow Willow Canyon is a rugged setting that can be explored by hiking the trail that starts at this camp. A short distance east of the camp, the trail forks to the south to Rockhouse Canyon. For a good side trip, drive back to County Road S2 and head south over Sweeney Pass for the view at the Carrizo Badlands Overlook.

RV sites, facilities: There are 16 sites for tents or RVs up to 24 feet (no hookups). Picnic tables, fire rings, and shade ramadas are provided. Limited drinking water and vault toilets are available. Leashed pets are permitted in the campground, but not on trails.

Reservations, fees: Reservations are not accepted. Sites are $7 per night. Day-use parking is $8. Open year-round.

Directions: From El Cajon, drive east on I-8 about 75 miles to the town of Ocotillo (the first town after crossing from San Diego County to Imperial County) and County Road S2/Imperial Highway. Turn north (left) on County Road S2/Imperial Highway and drive 27 miles to the gravel campground entrance road on the left.

Contact: Anza-Borrego Desert State Park, Visitor Center, 760/767-4205; Colorado Desert District, 760/767-5311, fax 760/767-7492, www.parks.ca.gov.

83 RIO BEND RV AND GOLF RESORT

Scenic rating: 5

near El Centro
Map grid D6

This resort is set at 50 feet below sea level near Mount Signal, about a 20-minute drive south of the Salton Sea. For some, this region is a godforsaken wasteland, but hey, that makes arriving at this park all the more like coming to a mirage in the desert. This resort is a combination RV park and year-round community with park models for sale. Management does what it can to offer visitors recreational options, including a nine-hole golf course. It's hot out here, sizzling most of the year, but dry and cool in the winter, the best time to visit.

RV sites, facilities: There are 500 sites for RVs of any length, including 460 pull-through sites with full hookups (30 and 50 amps). Group sites have partial hookups. Picnic tables are provided. Cable TV and restrooms with showers are available. Two small, stocked lakes for catch-and-release fishing, a convenience store, café, heated swimming pool, spa, shuffleboard, volleyball, horseshoes, bocce ball, pet park, nine-hole golf course, library, pool table, club room, organized activities, and modem access are available on a seasonal basis. Some facilities are wheelchair-accessible. A small store is nearby. Leashed pets are permitted.

Reservations, fees: Reservations are accepted. Sites are $50 per night in winter, $38 per night in summer, $3 per person for more than two people. Weekly, monthly, and annual rates available. Some credit cards accepted. Open year-round.

Directions: From El Centro, drive west on I-8 for seven miles to the Drew Road exit. Take that exit and drive south on Drew Road for

0.25 mile to the park on the right (1589 Drew Road).

Contact: Rio Bend RV and Golf Resort, 760/352-7061 or 800/545-6481, www.riobend-rvgolfresort.com.

84 IMPERIAL SAND DUNES RECREATION AREA

Scenic rating: 1

east of Brawley
Map grid E6

Gecko, Roadrunner, and Midway campgrounds are three of the many camping options at Imperial Sand Dunes Recreation Area. There isn't a tree within a million miles of this camp. People who wind up here all have the same thing in common: They're ready to ride across the dunes in their dune buggies or off-highway vehicles. The dune season is on a weather-permitting basis. Note that several areas are off-limits to motorized vehicles and camping because of plant and habitat protection; hiking in these areas is allowed. There are opportunities for hiking on this incredible moonscape. Other recreation options include watching the sky and waiting for a cloud to show up. A gecko, by the way, is a harmless little lizard. I've had them crawl on the sides of my tent. Nice little fellows.

RV sites, facilities: There are numerous dispersed sites for tents or RVs of any length (no hookups). Vault toilets and a trash bin are available. No drinking water is available. A few sites have camping pads. Leashed pets are permitted.

Reservations, fees: Reservations are not accepted. Sites are $25 per week, $90 per season, if purchased from the vendor. Permits purchased onsite cost $40 per week, $120 per season, with a 14-day stay limit every 28 days. Open year-round.

Directions: From Brawley, drive east on Highway 78 for 27 miles to Gecko Road. Turn south on Gecko Road and drive three miles to the campground entrance on the left. To reach

Roadrunner Camp, continue for two miles to the campground at the end of the road.

Contact: Bureau of Land Management, El Centro Field Office, 760/337-4400, fax 760/337-4490. For more information on closed areas, contact the Imperial Sand Dunes ranger station at 760/344-4400.

85 PICACHO STATE RECREATION AREA

Scenic rating: 6

near Taylor Lake on the Colorado River

Map grid E5

To get here, you really have to want it. Picacho State Recreation Area is way out there, requiring a long drive north out of Winterhaven on a spindly little road. The camp is on the southern side of Taylor Lake on the Colorado River. The park is the best deal around for many miles, though, with boat ramps, waterskiing, good bass fishing, and, occasionally, crazy folks having the time of their lives. The sun and water make a good combination. This recreation area includes eight miles of the lower Colorado River. Park wildlife includes wild burros and bighorn sheep, with thousands of migratory waterfowl on the Pacific Flyway occasionally taking up residence. More than 100 years ago, Picacho was a gold-mining town with a population of 2,500 people. Visitors should always carry extra water and essential supplies.

RV sites, facilities: There are 54 sites for tents or RVs up to 35 feet (no hookups), a group site for up to 100 people, and two boat-in group sites. Picnic tables and fire grills are provided. Drinking water, pit toilets, dump station, solar showers, and two boat launches are available. Some facilities are wheelchair-accessible. Leashed pets are permitted.

Reservations, fees: Reservations are accepted for group sites only at 760/996-2963. Sites are $10 per night. Group sites are $37 per night for up to 12 vehicles. Boat-in group sites are

$45 per night for up to 15 people, and $3 per person per night for additional people. Day-use parking $8. Open year-round.

Directions: From El Centro, drive east on I-8 to Winterhaven and the exit for Winterhaven/4th Avenue. Take that exit to Winterhaven Drive. Turn left on Winterhaven Drive and drive 0.5 mile to County Road S24/Picacho Road. Turn right and drive 24 miles (crossing rail tracks, driving under a railroad bridge, and over the American Canal, the road becoming dirt for the last 18 miles) to the campground. The road is not suitable for large RVs. The drive takes 1–2 hours from Winterhaven. In summer, thunderstorms can cause flash flooding, making short sections of the road impassable.

Contact: Picacho State Recreation Area, c/o Salton Sea State Recreation Area, 760/996-2963 (reservations), www.parks.ca.gov.

86 SQUAW LAKE

Scenic rating: 6

near the Colorado River

Map grid E6

Take your pick. There are two camps near the Colorado River in this area (the other is Senator Wash). This one is near Squaw Lake, created by the nearby Imperial Dam on the Colorado River. These sites provides opportunities for swimming, fishing, boating, and hiking, featuring direct boat access to the Colorado River. Wildlife includes numerous waterfowl, as well as quail, coyotes, and reptiles. A speed limit of 5 mph is enforced on the lake; no wakes permitted. The no-wake zone ends at the Colorado River.

RV sites, facilities: There are 125 sites for RVs of any length (no hookups) and dispersed sites for tents. Picnic tables and barbecue grills are provided. Four restrooms with flush toilets and outdoor showers are available. Drinking water is available at a central location. Two boat ramps are nearby. Some facilities are wheelchair-accessible. Leashed pets are permitted.

Reservations, fees: Reservations are not accepted. Sites are $15 per night. There is a year-round maximum 14-day limit for every 28 days. Open year-round.

Directions: Drive on I-8 to Yuma, Arizona, and the exit for 4th Avenue. Take that exit and drive to Imperial Highway/County Road S24. Turn north and drive 22 miles to Senator Wash Road. Turn left and drive about four miles (well signed) to the lake and campground on the right.

Contact: Bureau of Land Management, Yuma Field Office, 928/317-3200, fax 928/317-3250.

87 SENATOR WASH RECREATION AREA

Scenic rating: 6

near Senator Wash Reservoir

Map grid E6

Senator Wash Reservoir Recreation Area features two campgrounds, named (surprise) Senator Wash South Shore and Senator Wash North Shore. This recreation area is approximately 50 acres, with many trees of various types and several secluded camping areas. At Senator Wash North Shore (where there are fewer facilities than at South Shore), campsites are both on the water as well as further inland. Gravel beaches provide access to the reservoir. Boat ramps are nearby. This spot provides boating, fishing, OHV riding, wildlife-viewing, and opportunities for solitude and sightseeing.

RV sites, facilities: There are numerous dispersed sites for tents or RVs of any length (no hookups). No drinking water is available. At South Shore, there are restrooms with flush toilets, outdoor showers, and drinking water. A buoyed swimming area and boat ramp providing boat-in access to campsites at North Shore is available about 0.25 mile from South Shore. At North Shore, there are two vault toilets, but no drinking water; boat ramp is approximately 0.25 mile away. Some facilities are wheelchair-accessible. No camping at the boat ramp. Leashed pets are permitted.

Reservations, fees: Reservations are not accepted. Sites are $15 per night. There is a year-round maximum 14-day limit for every 28 days. Open year-round.

Directions: Drive on I-8 to Yuma, Arizona, and the exit for 4th Avenue. Take that exit and drive to Imperial Highway/County Road S24. Turn north and drive 22 miles to Senator Wash Road. Turn left and drive about three miles south to Mesa Campground. Turn left and drive 200 yards to the South Shore Campground access road on the right. Turn right and drive to the reservoir and campground.

Contact: Bureau of Land Management, Yuma Field Office, 928/317-3200, fax 928/317-3250.

88 MIDWAY

Scenic rating: 6

in the Imperial Sand Dunes Recreation Area

Map grid E6

This is off-highway-vehicle headquarters, a place where people bring their three-wheelers, four-wheelers, and motorcycles. That's because a large area has been set aside just for this type of recreation. Good news is that this area has become more family-oriented because of increased enforcement, eliminating much of the lawlessness and lunatic behavior of the past. As you drive in, you will enter the Buttercup Recreation Area, which is part of the Imperial Sand Dunes Recreation Area. You camp almost anywhere you like, and nobody beefs. Note that several areas are off-limits to motorized vehicles and camping because of plant and habitat protection; hiking in these areas is allowed. (See the Imperial Sand Dunes Recreation Area listing in this chapter for more options.)

RV sites, facilities: There are several primitive sites for tents or RVs of any length (no hookups). Vault toilets and a trash bin are available. No drinking water is available. Leashed pets are permitted.

Reservations, fees: Reservations are not accepted. Sites are $25 per week, $90 per season. Permits purchased onsite cost $40 per week, $120 per season. Open year-round, weather permitting.

Directions: From El Centro, drive east on I-8 for about 40 miles to Gray's Wells Road (signed Sand Dunes). Take that exit and drive (it bears to the right) to a stop sign. Continue straight on Gray's Wells Road and drive three miles to another stop sign. To reach Buttercup Recreation Area, turn left and drive a short distance. To reach Midway, continue straight on Gray's Wells Road for 1.5 miles (the road turns from pavement to dirt and then dead-ends); camping is permitted anywhere in this region.

Contact: Bureau of Land Management, El Centro Field Office, 760/337-4400, fax 760/337-4490. For more information on closed areas, contact the Imperial Sand Dunes ranger station at 760/344-4400.

RESOURCES

NATIONAL FORESTS

The U.S. Forest Service provides many secluded camps and allows camping anywhere except where it is specifically prohibited. If you ever want to clear the cobwebs from your head and get away from it all, this is the way to go.

Many Forest Service campgrounds are remote and have no drinking water. You usually don't need to check in or make reservations, and sometimes there is no fee. At many Forest Service campgrounds that provide drinking water, the camping fee is often only a few dollars, with payment made on the honor system. Because most of these camps are in mountain areas, they are subject to winter closure due to snow or mud.

Dogs are permitted in national forests with no extra charge. Leashes are required for all dogs in some places. Always carry documentation of current vaccinations.

Northwest Forest Pass (Oregon and Washington)

A Northwest Forest Pass is required for certain activities in some national forests and at North Cascades National Park. The pass is required for parking at participating trailheads, non-developed camping areas, boat launches, picnic areas, and visitors centers.

Daily passes cost $5 per vehicle; annual passes are $30 per vehicle. Combined recreation passes for Washington and Oregon are also available. You can buy Northwest Forest Passes at national forest offices and dozens of retail outlets and online vendors. Holders of Golden Age and Golden Access (not Golden Eagle) cards can buy the Northwest Forest Pass at a 50 percent discount at national forest offices only, or at retail outlets for the retail price. Major credit cards are accepted at most retail and online outlets and at some Forest Service offices.

More information about the Northwest Forest Pass program, including a listing of retail and online vendors, can be obtained at 503/808-6008 or www.fs.fed.us/r6/passespermits.

National Forest Adventure Pass (California)

Angeles, Cleveland, Los Padres, and San Bernardino National Forests require an Adventure Pass for each vehicle parked in any of the 34 recreation areas managed by the Forest Service in Southern California. Daily passes cost $5; annual passes are available for $30. You can buy Adventure Passes at national forest offices in Southern California and dozens of retail outlets and online vendors. The new charges are use fees, not entrance fees. Golden Age and Golden Access Passes are honored in lieu of an Adventure Pass.

When you buy an annual Adventure Pass, you can also buy an annual second-vehicle Adventure Pass for $5. Major credit cards are accepted at most retail and online outlets and at some forest service offices. You can buy Adventure Passes by telephone at 909/382-2622, -2623, -2621, or by mail at San Bernardino National Forest, Pass Program Headquarters, 602 S. Tippecanoe Avenue, San Bernardino, CA 92408-2607. Checks should be made payable to USDA Forest Service.

You will not need an Adventure Pass while traveling through these forests, nor when you've paid other types of fees such as camping or ski pass fees. However, if you are camping in these forests and you leave the campground in your vehicle and park outside the campground for recreation, such as at a trailhead, day-use area, near a fishing stream, etc., you will need an Adventure Pass for your vehicle. You also need an Adventure Pass if camping at a no-fee campground. More information about the Adventure Pass program, including a listing of retail and online vendors, can be obtained at website www.fs.fed.us/r5/sanbernardino/ap/.

America the Beautiful Pass (Interagency Pass)

An America the Beautiful Pass (Interagency Pass) is available for $80 annually in lieu of a Northwest Forest Pass or an Adventure Pass. The America the Beautiful Pass is honored nationwide at all Forest Service, National Park Service, Bureau of Land Management, Bureau of Reclamation, and U.S. Fish and Wildlife Service sites charging entrance or standard amenity fees. Valid for 12 months from the month of purchase, the America the Beautiful Pass is available at most national forest or grassland offices or online at http://store.usgs.gov.

National Forest Reservations

Some of the more popular camps, and most of the group camps, are on a reservation system. Reservations can be made up to 240 days in advance and up to 360 days in advance for groups. To reserve a site, call 877/444-6777 or visit www.recreation.gov. The reservation fee is usually $10 for a campsite in a national forest, but group site reservation fees are higher. Major credit cards are accepted. Holders of America the Beautiful (Interagency Pass), Golden Age or Golden Access passports receive a 50 percent discount for campground fees, except for group sites.

National Forest Maps

National Forest maps are among the best you can get for the price. They detail all backcountry streams, lakes, hiking trails, and logging roads for access. They cost $9–12 or more and can be obtained in person at Forest Service offices or by contacting:

U.S. Forest Service
National Forest Store
Attn: Map Sales
P.O. Box 8268
Missoula, MT 59807
406/329-3024
fax 406/329-3030
www.fs.fed.us/recreation/nationalforeststore/
or
www.nationalforeststore.com

STATE FORESTS
Oregon
Oregon Department of Forestry
2600 State Street
Salem, OR 97310
503/945-7200
egov.oregon.gov/ODF

Tillamook State Forest, Forest Grove District
801 Gales Creek Road
Forest Grove, OR 97116-1199
503/357-2191
http://oregon.gov/ODF/TSF/tsf.shtml

Tillamook State Forest, Tillamook District
5005 3rd Street
Tillamook, OR 97141-2999
503/842-2545
http://oregon.gov/ODF/TSF/tsf.shtml

California
Jackson Demonstration State Forest
802 North Main Street
Fort Bragg, CA 95437
707/964-5674
fax 707/964-0941

Mountain Home Demonstration State Forest
P.O. Box 517
Springville, CA 93265
559/539-2321 (summer)
559/539-2855 (winter)

COUNTY/REGIONAL PARK DEPARTMENTS
Del Norte County Parks
840 9th Street, Suite 11
Crescent City, CA 95531
707/464-7230
fax 707/464-5824
www.co.delnorte.ca.us

East Bay Regional Park District
P.O. Box 5381
Oakland, CA 94605-0381
510/562-PARK (510/562-7275)
or 510/544-2200
fax 510/635-3478
www.ebparks.org

Humboldt County Parks
1106 2nd Street
Eureka, CA 95501
707/445-7651
fax 707/445-7409
www.co.humboldt.ca.us/

Marin Municipal Water District
220 Nellen Avenue
Corte Madera, CA 94925
415/945-1455
fax 415/927-4953
www.marinwater.org

**Midpeninsula Regional
Open Space District**
330 Distel Circle
Los Altos, CA 94022-1404
650/691-1200
fax 650/691-0485
www.openspace.org

Pacific Gas and Electric Company
Corporate Real Estate/Recreation
5555 Florin-Perkins Road, Room 100
Sacramento, CA 95826
916/386-5164
fax 916/923-7044
www.pge.com/recreation

Sacramento County Regional Parks
3711 Branch Center Road
Sacramento, CA 95827
916/875-6961
fax 916/875-6050
www.sacparks.net

**San Diego County Parks and
Recreation Department**
2454 Heritage Park Row
San Diego, CA 92110
858/694-3049
fax 619/260-6492
www.co.san-diego.ca.us/parks

**San Luis Obispo County
Parks Department**
1087 Santa Rosa Street
San Luis Obispo, CA 93408
805/781-5930
fax 805/781-1102
www.slocountyparks.org

**San Mateo County Parks and
Recreation Department**
455 County Center, 4th floor
Redwood City, CA 94063-1646
650/363-4020
fax 650/599-1721
www.eparks.net

**Santa Barbara County Parks and
Recreation Department**
610 Mission Canyon Road
Santa Barbara, CA 93105
805/568-2461
fax 805/568-2459
www.sbparks.com

Santa Clara County Parks Department
298 Garden Hill Drive
Los Gatos, CA 95032-7669
408/355-2200
fax 408/355-2290
www.parkhere.org

Sonoma County Regional Parks
2300 County Center Drive, Suite 120-A
Santa Rosa, CA 95403
707/565-2041
fax 707/579-8247
www.sonomacounty.org/parks

INFORMATION SERVICES

Lake County Visitor Information Center
P.O. Box 1025
6110 East Highway 20
Lucerne, CA 95458
707/274-5652 or 800/525-3743
fax 707/274-5664
www.lakecounty.com

Mammoth Lakes Visitors Bureau
P.O. Box 48
2520 Main St.
Mammoth Lakes, CA 93546
888/GO-MAMMOTH (888/466-2666)
or 760/934-2712
fax 760/934-7066
www.visitmammoth.com

Mount Shasta Visitors Bureau
300 Pine Street
Mount Shasta, CA 96067
530/926-4865 or 800/926-4865
fax 530/926-0976
www.mtshastachamber.com

The Nature Conservancy of California
201 Mission Street, 4th floor
San Francisco, CA 94105-1832
415/777-0487
fax 415/777-0244
www.nature.org

Plumas County Visitors Bureau
550 Crescent Street
P.O. Box 4120
Quincy, CA 95971
530/283-6345 or 800/326-2247
fax 530/283-5465
www.plumascounty.org

Shasta Cascade Wonderland Association
1699 Highway 273
Anderson, CA 96007
530/365-7500 or 800/474-2782
fax 530/365-1258
www.shastacascade.com

FOREST SERVICE INFORMATION

Forest Service personnel are most helpful for obtaining camping or hiking trail information. Unless you are buying a map or Adventure Pass, it is advisable to phone in advance to get the best service.

For specific information on individual national forests, contact the following offices:

Washington

Colville National Forest
765 South Main St.
Colville, WA 99114
509/684-7000
www.fs.fed.us/r6/colville

Gifford Pinchot National Forest
10600 NE 51st Cir.
Vancouver, WA 98682
360/891-5000
fax 360/891-5045
www.fs.fed.us/gpnf

Mount Baker-Snoqualmie National Forest
2930 Wetmore Ave.
Everett, WA 98201
425/783-6000 or 800/627-0062
www.fs.fed.us/r6/mbs

Okanogan and Wenatchee National Forests
215 Melody Ln.
Wenatchee, WA 98801
509/664-9200
www.fs.fed.us/r6/wenatchee

Olympic National Forest
1835 Black Lake Blvd. SW
Olympia, WA 98512-5623
360/956-2402
fax 360/956-2330
www.fs.fed.us/r6/Olympic

Umatilla National Forest
Pomeroy Ranger District
71 West Main St.
Pomeroy, WA 99347
509/843-1891
www.fs.fed.us/r6/uma/

Walla Walla Ranger District
1415 West Rose St.
Walla Walla, WA 99362
509/522-6290
www.fs.fed.us/r6/uma/

Oregon

U.S. Forest Service
Pacific Northwest Region 6
333 SW 1st Avenue
Portland, OR 97204-3440
503/808-2468
www.fs.fed.us/r6
or
P.O. Box 3623
Portland, OR 97208-3623

Deschutes National Forest
1001 SW Emkay Drive
Bend, OR 97702
541/383-5300
www.fs.fed.us/r6/centraloregon/

Fremont-Winema National Forests
HC 10 Box 337
1301 South G Street
Lakeview, OR 97630
541/947-2151
www.fs.fed.us/r6/frewin/

Malheur National Forest
P.O. Box 909
431 Patterson Bridge Road
John Day, OR 97845
541/575-3000
www.fs.fed.us/r6/malheur/

Mount Hood National Forest
16400 Champion Way
Sandy, OR 97055
503/668-1700
www.fs.fed.us/r6/mthood/

Ochoco National Forest
3160 NE 3rd Street
Prineville, OR 97754
541/416-6500
www.fs.fed.us/r6/centraloregon/

Rogue River-Siskiyou National Forest
3040 Biddle Road
Medford, OR 97504
541/618-2200
www.fs.fed.us/r6/rogue-siskiyou/

Siuslaw National Forest
P.O. Box 1148
4077 SW Research Way
Corvallis, OR 97339
541/750-7000
fax 541/750-7234
www.fs.fed.us/r6/siuslaw/

Umatilla National Forest
2517 SW Hailey Avenue
Pendleton, OR 97801
541/278-3716
www.fs.fed.us/r6/uma/

Umpqua National Forest
2900 NW Stewart Parkway
Roseburg, OR 97471
541/672-6601
www.fs.fed.us/r6/umpqua/

Wallowa-Whitman National Forest
P.O. Box 907
1550 Dewey Avenue
Baker City, OR 97814
541/523-6391
www.fs.fed.us/r6/w-w/

Willamette National Forest
3106 Pierce Parkway, Ste. D
Springfield, OR 97477
541/225-6300
www.fs.fed.us/r6/willamette/

California

USDA Forest Service
Pacific Southwest Region
1323 Club Drive
Vallejo, CA 94592
707/562-USFS (707/562-8737)
fax 707/562-9130
www.fs.fed.us/r5

Angeles National Forest
701 North Santa Anita Avenue
Arcadia, CA 91006
626/574-1613
fax 626/574-5233
www.fs.fed.us/r5/angeles

Cleveland National Forest
10845 Rancho Bernardo Road, No. 200
San Diego, CA 92127-2107
858/673-6180
fax 858/673-6192
www.fs.fed.us/r5/cleveland

Eldorado National Forest
100 Forni Road
Placerville, CA 95667
530/622-5061
fax 530/621-5297
www.fs.fed.us/r5/eldorado

Humboldt-Toiyabe National Forest
1200 Franklin Way
Sparks, NV 89431
775/331-6444
fax 775/355-5399
www.fs.fed.us/r4/htnf

Inyo National Forest
351 Pacu Lane, Suite 200
Bishop, CA 93514
760/873-2400
fax 760/873-2458
www.fs.fed.us/r5/inyo

Klamath National Forest
1312 Fairlane Road
Yreka, CA 96097-9549
530/842-6131
fax 530/841-4571
www.fs.fed.us/r5/klamath

Lake Tahoe Basin Management Unit
35 College Drive
South Lake Tahoe, CA 96150
530/543-2600
fax 530/543-2693
www.fs.fed.us/r5/ltbmu

Lassen National Forest
2550 Riverside Drive
Susanville, CA 96130
530/257-2151
fax 530/252-6448
www.r5.fs.fed.us/r5/lassen

Los Padres National Forest
6755 Hollister Avenue, Suite 150
Goleta, CA 93117
805/968-6640
fax 805/961-5729
www.fs.fed.us/r5/lospadres

Mendocino National Forest
825 North Humboldt Avenue
Willows, CA 95988
530/934-3316
fax 530/934-7384
www.fs.fed.us/r5/mendocino

Modoc National Forest
800 West 12th Street
Alturas, CA 96101
530/233-5811
fax 530/233-8709
www.fs.fed.us/r5/modoc

Plumas National Forest
P.O. Box 11500
159 Lawrence Street
Quincy, CA 95971
530/283-2050
fax 530/283-7746
www.fs.fed.us/r5/plumas

San Bernardino National Forest
602 South Tippecanoe Avenue
San Bernardino, CA 92408-2607
909/382-2600
fax 909/383-5770
www.fs.fed.us/r5/sanbernardino

Sequoia National Forest
Giant Sequoia National Monument
1839 South Newcomb Street
Porterville, CA 93257
559/784-1500
fax 559/781-4744
www.fs.fed.us/r5/sequoia

Shasta-Trinity National Forest
3644 Avtech Parkway
Redding, CA 96002
530/226-2500
fax 530/226-2470
www.fs.fed.us/r5/shastatrinity

Sierra National Forest
1600 Tollhouse Road
Clovis, CA 93611
559/297-0706
fax 559/294-4809
www.fs.fed.us/r5/sierra

Six Rivers National Forest
1330 Bayshore Way
Eureka, CA 95501
707/442-1721
fax 707/442-9242
www.fs.fed.us/r5/sixrivers

Stanislaus National Forest
19777 Greenley Road
Sonora, CA 95370
209/532-3671
fax 209/533-1890
www.fs.fed.us/r5/stanislaus

Tahoe National Forest
631 Coyote Street
Nevada City, CA 95959
530/265-4531
fax 530/478-6109
www.fs.fed.us/r5/tahoe

NATIONAL PARKS AND RECREATION AREAS

The national parks and recreation areas on the west coast are natural wonders, ranging from the rugged Mount Rainier National Park to the breathtaking Columbia River Gorge to the spectacular yet crowded Yosemite Valley. Reservations for campsites are available at some of the campgrounds at these parks and recreation areas. Various discounts are available for holders of Golden Age and Golden Access passports, including a 50 percent reduction of camping fees (group camps not included).

For information about each of the national parks, contact the parks directly:

Washington

Lake Roosevelt National Recreation Area
1008 Crest Dr.
Coulee Dam, WA 99116-1259
or
1368 South Kettle Park Rd.
Kettle Falls, WA 99141
509/633-9441
fax 509/633-9332
www.nps.gov/laro

Mount Rainier National Park
55210 238th Ave. East
Ashford, WA 98304
360/569-2211
fax 360/569-2170
www.nps.gov/mora

**Mount St. Helens
National Volcanic Monument**
Headquarters, 42218 NE Yale Bridge Rd.
Amboy, WA 98601
360/449-7800

Mount St. Helens Visitor Center
360/274-0962
fax 360/449-7801
www.fs.fed.us/gpnf/mshnvm

North Cascades National Park
810 State Route 20
Sedro-Woolley, WA 98284-1239
Visitor Information 360/854-7200
Wilderness Information 360/854-7245
fax 360/856-1934
www.nps.gov/noca

Olympic National Park
600 East Park Avenue
Port Angeles, WA 98362-6798
360/565-3130 or 800/833-6388
fax 360/565-3015
www.nps.gov/olym

Oregon
Columbia River Gorge National Scenic Area
902 Wasco Avenue, Suite 200
Hood River, OR 97031
541/308-1700
www.fs.fed.us/r6/columbia/forest/

Crater Lake National Park
P.O. Box 7
Crater Lake, OR 97604
541/594-3100
www.nps.gov/crla/

Crooked River National Grassland
813 SW Highway 97
Madras, OR 97741
541/475-9272
www.fs.fed.us/r6/centraloregon

Hells Canyon National Recreation Area
Wallowa Mountains Visitor Center
88401 Highway 82
Enterprise, OR 97828
541/426-5546
www.fs.fed.us/hellscanyon/

Oregon Dunes National Recreation Area
855 Highway Avenue
Reedsport, OR 97467
541/271-6000
www.fs.fed.us/r6/siuslaw/

California
Reservations for campsites are available five months in advance for many of the national parks in California. In addition to campground fees, expect to pay a park entrance fee of $20 per vehicle, or as low as $5 per person for hike-in/bike-in (you can buy an annual National Parks Pass that waives entrance fees). This entrance fee is valid for seven days. For an additional fee, an America the Beautiful sticker can be added to the National Parks Pass, thereby eliminating entrance fees at sites managed by the U.S. Fish and Wildlife Service, the U.S. Forest Service, and the Bureau of Land Management.

For reservations, call 877/444-6777 or visit www.recreation.gov ($10 reservation fee). Major credit cards are accepted.

National Park Service
Pacific West Region
One Jackson Center
1111 Jackson Street, Suite 700
Oakland, CA 94607
510/817-1304
www.nps.gov

Cabrillo National Monument
1800 Cabrillo Memorial Drive
San Diego, CA 92106-3601
619/557-5450
fax 619/226-6311
www.nps.gov/cabr

Channel Islands National Park
1901 Spinnaker Drive
Ventura, CA 93001
805/658-5730
fax 805/658-5799
www.nps.gov/chis

Death Valley National Park
P.O. Box 579
Death Valley, CA 92328-0579
760/786-3200
fax 760/786-3283
www.nps.gov/deva

Devils Postpile National Monument
P.O. Box 3999
Mammoth Lakes, CA 93546
760/934-2289 (summer only)
fax 760/934-8896 (summer only)
www.nps.gov/depo
For year-round information, contact Sequoia and Kings Canyon National Parks.

Golden Gate National Recreation Area
Fort Mason, Building 201
San Francisco, CA 94123-0022
415/561-4700
www.nps.gov/goga

Joshua Tree National Park
74485 National Park Drive
Twentynine Palms, CA 92277-3597
760/367-5500
fax 760/367-6392
www.nps.gov/jotr

Lassen Volcanic National Park
P.O. Box 100
Mineral, CA 96063-0100
530/595-4444
fax 530/595-3262
www.nps.gov/lavo

Lava Beds National Monument
1 Indian Well Headquarters
Tulelake, CA 96134
530/667-2282
fax 530/667-2737
www.nps.gov/labe

Mojave National Preserve
2701 Barstow Road
Barstow, CA 92311
760/252-6100
fax 760/252-6174
www.nps.gov/moja

Pinnacles National Monument
5000 Highway 146
Paicines, CA 95043
831/389-4485
fax 831/389-4489
www.nps.gov/pinn

Point Reyes National Seashore
Point Reyes Station
CA 94956-9799
415/464-5100
fax 415/464-5149
www.nps.gov/pore

Redwood National and State Parks
1111 2nd Street
Crescent City, CA 95531
707/464-6101
fax 707/464-1812
www.nps.gov/redw

**Santa Monica Mountains
National Recreation Area**
401 West Hillcrest Drive
Thousand Oaks, CA 91360
805/370-2301
fax 805/370-1850
www.nps.gov/samo

Sequoia and Kings Canyon National Parks
47050 Generals Highway
Three Rivers, CA 93271-9700
559/565-3341
fax 559/565-3730
www.nps.gov/seki

Smith River National Recreation Area
P.O. Box 228
Gasquet, CA 95543
707/457-3131
fax 707/457-3794
www.fs.fed.us/r5/sixrivers

Whiskeytown National Recreation Area
P.O. Box 188
Whiskeytown, CA 96095
530/246-1225 or 530/242-3400
fax 530/246-5154
www.nps.gov/whis

Yosemite National Park
P.O. Box 577
Yosemite National Park, CA 95389
209/372-0200 for 24-hour recorded message
www.nps.gov/yose

STATE PARKS

The state parks system provides many popular camping spots in spectacular settings. The camps include drive-in numbered sites, tent spaces, and picnic tables, with restrooms provided. Reservations are often a necessity during the summer. Although some parks are well known, there are still some little-known gems in the state parks system where campers can enjoy seclusion, even in the summer.

State park fees have increased significantly since 2008, but camping in a state park is still a good deal. Many of the campgrounds along the coastline are particularly popular in summer and require planning to secure a campsite.

Washington

Many of the state park campgrounds are on a reservation system, and campsites can be booked up to nine months in advance at these parks. Reservations can be made at 888/CAMP-OUT (888/226-7688) or at www.parks.wa.gov/reservations/. The reservation number is open 7 A.M.–8 P.M. (Pacific Standard Time) every day of the year except Christmas Day and New Year's Day, with shortened hours on Christmas Eve and New Year's Eve. Major credit cards are accepted for reservations, and credit cards are accepted at some of the parks during the summer. A $6.50 reservation fee is charged for a campsite reservation made online, $8.50 for one made by phone. The reservation fee for group sites is $25. Discounts are available for pass holders of Disability, Senior Citizen Limited Income, Off-Season Senior Citizen, and Disabled Veteran Lifetime.

**Washington State Parks and
Recreation Commission**
7150 Cleanwater Ln.
P.O. Box 42650
Olympia, WA 98504-2650
360/902-8844
www.parks.wa.gov

Oregon

Reservations can be made for 44 Oregon state parks through Reserve America at 800/452-5687 or online at www.reserveamerica.com. A nonrefundable reservation fee of $8 and the first night's fee will be required as a deposit, charged to a MasterCard or Visa credit card (debit cards linked to MasterCard or Visa also accepted).

**Oregon Parks and Recreation Department:
State Parks**
725 Summer St. NE, Ste. C
Salem, OR 97301
800/551-6949
www.oregon.gov/OPRD/PARKS/index.shtml

California

Reservations can be made at 800/444-PARK (800/444-7275) or online at www.reserveamerica.com. There are also hike-in/bike-in sites at many of the parks, and they are available on a first-come, first-served basis. The reservation fee is usually $8 for a campsite. Major credit cards are accepted for reservations but are generally not accepted in person at the parks.

Camping discounts of 50 percent are available for holders of the Disabled Discount Pass, and free camping is allowed for holders of the Disabled Veteran/Prisoner of War Pass.

For general information about California State Parks, contact:

**California Department of Parks and
Recreation**
Public Information Office
P.O. Box 942896
1416 9th Street
Sacramento, CA 94296
916/653-6995 or 800/777-0369
fax 916/653-6995
www.parks.ca.gov

DEPARTMENT OF NATURAL RESOURCES

The Department of Natural Resources manages more than five million acres of public land in Washington. All of it is managed under the concept of "multiple use," designed to provide the greatest number of recreational opportunities while still protecting natural resources.

The campgrounds in these areas are among the most primitive, remote, and least known of the camps listed in this book. The campsites are usually free, and campers are asked to remove all litter and trash from the area, leaving only footprints behind. Due to budget cutbacks, some of these campgrounds have been closed in recent years; expect more closures in the future.

In addition to maps of the area it manages, the Department of Natural Resources also has Washington public lands maps, U.S. Geological Survey maps, and U.S. Army Corps of Engineers maps. For information, contact the

Department of Natural Resources at its state or regional addresses:

State of Washington Department of Natural Resources
1111 Washington St. SE
P.O. Box 47000
Olympia, WA 98504-7000
360/902-1000
fax 360/902-1775
www.dnr.wa.gov

Northeast Region
225 South Silke Rd.
P.O. Box 190
Colville, WA 99114-0190
509/684-7474
fax 509/684-7484

Northwest Region
919 North Township St.
Sedro Woolley, WA 98284-9384
360/856-3500
fax 360/856-2150

Olympic Region
411 Tillicum Ln.
Forks, WA 98331-9271
360/374-2800
fax 360/374-5446

Pacific Cascade Region
601 Bond Rd.
P.O. Box 280
Castle Rock, WA 98611-0280
360/577-2025
fax 360/274-4196

Southeast Region
713 Bowers Rd.
Ellensburg, WA 98926-9301
509/925-8510

South Puget Sound Region
950 Farman Ave. North
Enumclaw, WA 98022-9282
360/825-1631
fax 360/825-1672

U.S. ARMY CORPS OF ENGINEERS

Some of the family camps and most of the group camps operated by the U.S. Army Corps of Engineers are on a reservation system. Reservations can be made up to 240 days in advance and up to 360 days in advance for groups. To reserve a site, call 877/444-6777 or visit www.recreation.gov. The reservation fee is usually $10 for a campsite, but group site reservation fees are higher. Major credit cards are accepted. Holders of Golden Age or Golden Access passports receive a 50 percent discount for campground fees, except for group sites.

Washington

Walla Walla District
201 North 3rd Ave.
Walla Walla, WA 99362-1876
509/527-7020
www.nww.usace.army.mil

Oregon

Portland District
333 SW 1st Ave.
Portland, OR 97204
503/808-6008
www.blm.gov
or
P.O. Box 2946
Portland, OR 97208-2946
503/808-4510
www.nwp.usace.army.mil

California

Los Angeles District
915 Wilshire Boulevard, Suite 980
Los Angeles, CA 90017-3401
213/452-3908
fax 213/452-4209
www.spl.usace.army.mil

Sacramento District
1325 J Street
Sacramento, CA 95814
916/557-5100
www.spk.usace.army.mil

South Pacific Division
333 Market Street
San Francisco, CA 94105
415/977-8272
fax 415/977-8316
www.spn.usace.army.mil

BUREAU OF LAND MANAGEMENT (BLM)

Most BLM campgrounds are primitive and in remote areas. Often, there is no fee charged for camping. Holders of Golden Age or Golden Access passports receive a 50 percent discount at BLM campgrounds with fees (group camps excluded).

Oregon

333 SW 1st Avenue
Portland, OR 97204
503/808-6008
www.blm.gov/or
or
P.O. Box 2965
Portland, OR 97208-2946
503/808-4510

Burns District
28910 Highway 20 West
Hines, OR 97738
541/573-4400
fax 541/573-4411
www.blm.gov/or/districts/burns

Coos Bay District
1300 Airport Lane
North Bend, OR 97459
541/756-0100
www.blm.gov/or/districts/coosbay

Eugene District
3106 Pierce Parkway, Ste. E
Springfield, OR 97477
541/683-6600
fax 541/683-6981
www.blm.gov/or/districts/eugene
or
P.O. Box 10226
Eugene, OR 97440

Lakeview District
1301 South G Street
Lakeview, OR 97630
541/947-2177
fax 541/947-6399
www.blm.gov/or/districts/lakeview

Medford District
3040 Biddle Road
Medford, OR 97504
541/618-2200
fax 541/618-2400
www.blm.gov/or/districts/medford

Prineville District
3050 NE 3rd Street
Prineville, OR 97754
541/416-6700
fax 541/416-6798
www.blm.gov/or/districts/prineville

Roseburg District
777 NW Garden Valley Boulevard
Roseburg, OR 97471
541/440-4930
fax 541/440-4948
www.blm.gov/or/districts/roseburg

Salem District
1717 Fabry Road SE
Salem, OR 97306
503/375-5646
fax 503/375-5622
www.blm.gov/or/districts/salem

Vale District
100 Oregon Street
Vale, OR 97918
541/473-3144
www.blm.gov/or/districts/vale

California

California State Office
2800 Cottage Way, Suite W-1834
Sacramento, CA 95825-1886
916/978-4400
fax 916/978-4416
www.blm.gov/ca

California Desert District Office
22835 Calle San Juan de los Lagos
Moreno Valley, CA 92553
951/697-5200
fax 951/697-5299
www.blm.gov/ca/cdd

Alturas Field Office
708 West 12th Street
Alturas, CA 96101
530/233-4666
fax 530/233-5696
www.blm.gov/ca/alturas

Arcata Field Office
1695 Heindon Road
Arcata, CA 95521-4573
707/825-2300
fax 707/825-2301
www.blm.gov/ca/arcata

Bakersfield Field Office
3801 Pegasus Drive
Bakersfield, CA 93308
661/391-6000
fax 661/391-6041
www.blm.gov/ca/bakersfield

Barstow Field Office
2601 Barstow Road
Barstow, CA 92311
760/252-6000
fax 760/252-6098
www.blm.gov/ca/barstow

Bishop Field Office
351 Pacu Lane, Suite 100
Bishop, CA 93514
760/872-5000
fax 760/872-5050
www.blm.gov/ca/bishop

Eagle Lake Field Office
2950 Riverside Drive
Susanville, CA 96130
530/257-0456
fax 530/257-4831
www.blm.gov/ca/eaglelake

El Centro Field Office
1661 South 4th Street
El Centro, CA 92243
760/337-4400
fax 760/337-4490
www.blm.gov/ca/elcentro

Folsom Field Office
63 Natoma Street
Folsom, CA 95630
916/985-4474
fax 916/985-3259
www.blm.gov/ca/folsom

Hollister Field Office
20 Hamilton Court
Hollister, CA 95023
831/630-5000
fax 831/630-5055
www.blm.gov/ca/hollister

Palm Springs/South Coast Field Office
P.O. Box 581260
North Palm Springs, CA 92258-1260
760/251-4800
fax 760/251-4899
www.blm.gov/ca/palmsprings

Redding Field Office
355 Hemsted Drive
Redding, CA 96002
530/224-2100
fax 530/224-2172
www.blm.gov/ca/redding

Ridgecrest Field Office
300 South Richmond Road
Ridgecrest, CA 93555
760/384-5400
fax 760/384-5499
www.blm.gov/ca/ridgecrest

Ukiah Field Office
2550 North State Street
Ukiah, CA 95482
707/468-4000
fax 707/468-4027
www.blm.gov/ca/ukiah

OTHER VALUABLE RESOURCES

U.S. Fish and Wildlife Service
1849 C Street NW
Washington, DC 20240
www.fws.gov

Washington

Tacoma Power
P.O. Box 11007
Tacoma, WA 98411
Fishing and Recreation Hotline
888/502-8690
www.mytpu.org/tacomapower/parks-rec

Washington Department of Fish and Wildlife
600 Capitol Way North
Olympia, WA 98501-1091
360/902-2200
www.wdfw.wa.gov

Washington State Department of Transportation
Washington State Highway Information
800/695-ROAD (800/695-7623)
Greater Seattle Area Information
206/DOT-HIWY (206/368-4499)
www.wsdot.wa.gov

Oregon

Oregon Department of Fish and Wildlife
3406 Cherry Avenue
Salem, OR 97303
503/947-6000
www.dfw.state.or.us

Oregon State Department of Transportation
888/275-6368
www.oregon.gov/ODOT/

California

California Department of Fish and Game
1416 9th Street, 12th floor
Sacramento, CA 95814
916/445-0411
www.dfg.ca.gov

California Department of Transportation
1120 N St.
or
P.O. Box 942873
Sacramento, CA 94273-0001
916/654-5266
www.dot.ca.gov

MAP RESOURCES

Map Link
30 South La Patera Lane, Unit 5
Goleta, CA 93117
805/692-6777 or 800/962-1394
fax 805/692-6787
www.maplink.com

Olmsted and Bros. Map Company
P.O. Box 5351
Berkeley, CA 94705
tel./fax 510/658-6534

Tom Harrison Maps
2 Falmouth Cove
San Rafael, CA 94901-4465
tel./fax 415/456-7940
www.tomharrisonmaps.com

U.S. Forest Service
National Forest Store
Attn: Map Sales
P.O. Box 8268
Missoula, MT 59807
406/329-3024
fax 406/329-3030
www.nationalforeststore.com

U.S. Geological Survey
Branch of Information Services
P.O. Box 25286, Bldg. 810, MS 306,
    Federal Center
Denver, CO 80225
888/ASK-USGS (888/275-8747)
or 303/202-4700
www.usgs.gov

Index

XYZ

Acknowledgments

The following state and federal resource experts provided critical information and galley reviews regarding changes in reservations, fees, directions, and recreational opportunities. I am extremely grateful for their timely help and expert advice.

WASHINGTON

U.S. Forest Service

Nan Berger, Colville National Forest, Newport Ranger District

Eric McQuay, Colville National Forest, Republic Ranger District

Wendy Zoodsma, Colville National Forest, Sullivan Lake Ranger District

Carmen Nielsen, Colville National Forest, Three Rivers Ranger District

Amber Malandry, Gifford Pinchot National Forest, Cowlitz Ranger District

Julie Knutson and Byron Carlisle, Gifford Pinchot National Forest, Mount Adams Ranger District

Diane Tharp, Gifford Pinchot National Forest, Mount St. Helens National Volcanic Monument

Shayla Hooper, Mt. Baker/Snoqualmie National Forest, Darrington Ranger District

Ann Dunphy, Mt. Baker/Snoqualmie National Forest, Mt. Baker Ranger District

Pam Young, Mt. Baker/Snoqualmie National Forest, Skykomish Ranger District

Linda Belcher, Christina Perez, Kelly Underwood, Okanogan and Wenatchee National Forests, Chelan Ranger District

Kim Larned, Okanogan and Wenatchee National Forests, Cle Elum Ranger District

Monte Bowe, Okanogan and Wenatchee National Forests, Entiat Ranger District

Terri Halstead, Okanogan and Wenatchee National Forests, Lake Wenatchee Ranger District

Mary Anderson, Okanogan and Wenatchee National Forests, Leavenworth Ranger District

Kathy Corrigan, Okanogan and Wenatchee National Forests, Methow Valley Ranger District

Kevin Hill, Mike Rowan, Okanogan and Wenatchee National Forests, Naches Ranger District

Joseph Cox, Okanogan and Wenatchee National Forests, Tonasket Ranger District

Peggy Dressler, Susie Graham, Olympic National Forest, Hood Canal Ranger District

Nancy Petrick, Olympic National Forest, Pacific Ranger District

Pete Erban, Olympic National Forest, Pacific Ranger District, Quinault Office

Ruth Forcier, Umatilla National Forest, Pomeroy Ranger District

U.S. Army Corps of Engineers

Jesus Navarro, Walla Walla District

Kathy Johnston, Central Ferry Park

Wayne O'Neal, Chief Timothy Park

National Parks

Lorie Carstensen, Lake Roosevelt National Recreation Area

Mindy Garvin, Daniel Keebler, Mare Staton, Mount Rainier National Park

Aaron Pouliot, North Cascades National Park

Benjamin Komar, Josh McLean, Kirran Peart, Olympic National Park

State Parks

Linda Burnett, Joyce Riley, State Park Information

Morris Shook, Alta Lake State Park

Breeanne Jordan, Beacon Rock State Park

Kathy Stermolle, Belfair State Park

Nancy Wallwork, Brooks Memorial State Park

Tom Riggs, Camano Island State Park

Tracy Zuern, Cape Disappointment State Park

Fritz Osborne, Columbia Hills State Park

Ryan Layton, Conconully State Park

Don Robertson, Curlew Lake State Park

John Wennes, Daroga State Park

Douglas Hinton, Dosewallips State Park

Peggy Russell, Fay Bainbridge State Park

Shaun Bristol, Fields Spring State Park

Brett Bayne, Fort Casey State Park

Lori Bond, Fort Flagler State Park

Steve Shively, Fort Worden State Park

James Mitchell, Ginkgo–Wanapum State Park

Candace Rodda, Grayland Beach State Park

Reuben Stuart, Ike Kinswa State Park

Roy Salisbury, Illahee State Park

Chris Patterson, Jarrell Cove and Hope Island State Parks

Kristie Cronin, Joemma Beach State Park

Karlene Herron, Kanaskat–Palmer State Park

Vern Matzen, Kitsap Memorial State Park

Matthew Smith, Kopachuck State Park

Carina Silva, Lake Chelan State Park

Teri Milbert, Lake Easton State Park

Brian Hageman, Lake Sylvia State Park

Gary Lentz, Lewis and Clark Trail State Park

Roy Torgerson, Manchester State Park

Kim Shupe, Maryhill State Park

Jim Schmidt, Ocean City State Park

Georgia Nelson, Osoyoos Lake State Park

Daniel Cox, Pacific Beach State Park

Cynthia Brown, Potholes State Park

Becky Meyer, Potlatch State Park

Dave Rush, Rainbow Falls State Park

Lori Cobb, Riverside State Park

William Hoppe, San Juan Marine Area

Brad Muir, Seaquest State Park

Arnold Hampton, Schafer State Park

Steve Gilstrom, Sequim Bay State Park

Patty Anderson, South Whidbey State Park

Tina O'Brian, Spencer Spit State Park

Stacy Czebotar, Twanoh State Park

Dennis Mills, Twenty–Five Mile Creek State Park

Tyler Vanderpool, Twin Harbors State Park

Rick Halstead, Wenatchee Confluence State Park

Bryce Erickson, Yakima Sportsman State Park

State Department of Natural Resources

Brett Walker, Northeast Region

Jim Cahill, Stan Kurowski, Candace Johnson and Christ Thompsen, Northwest Region

Erin Kreutz, Mike Williams, Southeast Region

Nancy Barker, Karen Robertson, Jesse Sims, South Puget Sound Region

Nick Cronquist, Brian Poehlein, Pacific Cascade Region

Cathryn Baker, Olympic Region

Other

Cathy Mether, Mike Miller, City of Auburn

Tracey Paddock, City of Chehalis

Blanca Anderson, City of Entiat

Hank Nydam, City of Oak Harbor

Randy Juette, Naches Valley Chamber of Commerce

Erin Grasseth, Port of Wahkiakum No. 2

Lori Peña, Clallam County

Ron Curran, Pend Oreille County Public Works

Kyle Peninger, Skagit County

Marcie Allen, Linda McCrea, Joe Miller, Snohomish County

Jeanne Blackburn, Wenberg County Park

Janel Goebel, Terry Jeffries, Ernie Miller, Whitman County Parks and Recreation

Rhonda Dow, Shawn DuFault, Kaly Harward, HooDoo Recreation

Gale Bridges, Tisa Pelletier, Trish Stanfield, Tacoma Power

OREGON

U.S. Forest Service

Ronda Bishop, Deschutes National Forest, Bend–Fort Rock Ranger District

Bob Hennings, Deschutes National Forest, Sisters Ranger District

Larry Hills, Fremont–Winema National Forests, Bly and Lakeview Ranger Districts

Doug Uran, Fremont–Winema National Forests, Silver Lake Ranger District

Phil McNeil, Klamath National Forest, Happy Camp/Oak Knoll Ranger District

Shannon Winegar, Terry Rittner, Malheur National Forest, Prairie City Ranger District

Jacquelyn Oakes, Mount Hood National Forest, Clackamas River and Zigzag Ranger Districts

Katherine Martin, Ochoco National Forest, Paulina Ranger District

Nancy Schwieger, Siskiyou National Forest, Gold Beach Ranger District

David Wickwire, Siskiyou National Forest, Galice Ranger Districts

Diana Dunn, Siuslaw National Forest, Central Coast Ranger District–Oregon Dunes National Recreation Area

Vicky Mugnai, Siuslaw National Forest, Waldport Ranger District

Kathy Rankin, Umatilla National Forest, Heppner Ranger District

Janelle Lacey, Umatilla National Forest, North Fork John Day Ranger District

Jeff Bloom, Umatilla National Forest, Walla Walla Ranger District

Dennis Scott, Umpqua National Forest, North Umpqua Ranger District

Mike Montgomery, Wallowa–Whitman National Forest, LaGrande Ranger District

Yvonne Santiago, Wallowa–Whitman National Forest, Wallowa Valley Ranger District/Eagle Cap Ranger District/Hells Canyon National Recreation Area

Annie Moore, Wallowa–Whitman National Forest, Whitman Ranger District

Jennifer McDonald, Willamette National Forest, McKenzie Ranger District

Bureau of Land Management

Dennis Byrd, Ashland Resource Area

Kevin McCoy, Brett Paige, Baker City Office

Trish Lindemann, Medford District

Greg Currie, Prineville District

Greg Morgan, Roseburg District

Traci Meredith, Salem District

Deb Drake, Tillamook District

David Draheim, Vale District

National Parks, Recreation Areas, and Refuges

Edan Lira, Columbia River Gorge National Scenic Area

State Parks

Chris Havel, Oregon State Parks media services

Rick Duda, Milo McIver State Park

Linda Brege, Deschutes State Recreation Area

Larry Moniz, Goose Lake State Park

Mary Nulty, Carl G. Washburne State Park

Other

Bill Doran, Metro Regional Parks and Green Spaces

Kirsti Cason, Morrow County Parks

Clara Johnson, Crook County Parks and Recreation

Kristi Mosier, Lane County, Richardson Park

Lynn Studley, Portland General Electric

Christie Harris, Linn County Parks

Jill Hammond, Jackson County Parks

Ken Hill, Port of Siuslaw

Kathy Hammons, Douglas County Parks

Alisha Howard, Josephine County Parks

CALIFORNIA

U.S. Forest Service

Jerry Reponen, Los Angeles River Ranger District, Angeles National Forest

Patrick Hersey, San Gabriel Ranger District, Angeles National Forest

Kirsten Johansen, Santa Clara–Mojave Ranger District, Angeles National Forest

Ann Carey, Descanso Ranger District, Cleveland National Forest

Jeff Wells, Palomar Ranger District, Cleveland National Forest

Jake Rodriguez, Trabuco Ranger District, Cleveland National Forest

Billy Brown, Amador Ranger District, Eldorado National Forest

John Jue, Georgetown Ranger District, Eldorado National Forest

Melanie Hornsby, Pacific Ranger District, Eldorado National Forest

Joyce Pratt, Placerville Ranger District, Eldorado National Forest

Paul Kohler and Jeff Weiss, Bridgeport Ranger District, Humboldt–Toiyabe National Forest

Ed diCarlo and Jeff Weiss, Carson Ranger District, Humboldt–Toiyabe National Forest

Kitty VanStelle, Mammoth Lakes Ranger Station and Visitor Center, Inyo National Forest

Jon Kacnierski, Mono Basin Scenic Area and Visitor Center, Inyo National Forest

Kendrah Madrid, Mount Whitney Ranger District, Inyo National Forest

Barbara Torres, White Mountain Ranger District, Inyo National Forest

Laura Allen, Goosenest Ranger District, Klamath National Forest

Alan Vandiver, Happy Camp and Oak Knoll Ranger Districts, Klamath National Forest

Ray Haupt, Scott River and Salmon River Ranger Districts, Klamath National Forest

Kathy Gibson, Almanor Ranger District, Lassen National Forest

Lisa Sedlacek and Ben Fox, Eagle Lake Ranger District, Lassen National Forest

Mary Lou Schmierer, Hat Creek Ranger District, Lassen National Forest

Nicole Karres, Monterey Ranger District, Los Padres National Forest

Rick Howell, Mount PiÒos Ranger District, Los Padres National Forest

Joe Sigorino, Ojai Ranger District, Los Padres National Forest

Jim Lopez, Santa Barbara Ranger District, Los Padres National Forest

Helen Tarbet, Santa Lucia Ranger District, Los Padres National Forest

Larry Razzano, Covelo Ranger District, Mendocino National Forest

Gary Hayton, Grindstone Ranger District, Mendocino National Forest

Ray Linnet, Red Bluff Recreation Area, Mendocino National Forest

Debbie McIntosh, Upper Lake Ranger District, Mendocino National Forest

Jean Breakfield, Big Valley Ranger District, Modoc National Forest

Stephen Riley, Devilís Garden Ranger District, Modoc National Forest

Mike Kegg, Doublehead Ranger District, Modoc National Forest

Kathy Kempa, Warner Mountain Ranger District, Modoc National Forest

Pandora Valle, Bill Benson, and Judy Schaber, Beckwourth Ranger District, Plumas National Forest

Mary August, Feather River Ranger District, Plumas National Forest

Amy Furlong and Estres Wellings, Mount Hough Ranger District, Plumas National Forest

Jonathan Cook-Fisher and Audrey Scranton, Mountaintop Ranger Station, San Bernardino National Forest

Roman Rodriguez, San Jacinto Ranger District, San Bernardino National Forest

Carol Hallacy, Hume Lake Ranger District, Sequoia National Forest

Sherry Montgomery, Kern River Ranger District, Kernville, Sequoia National Forest

Geri Adams, Kern River Ranger District, Lake Isabella, Sequoia National Forest

Carol Zeigler, Tule River–Hot Springs Ranger District, Sequoia National Forest

J. Sharon Heywood, Shasta–Trinity National Forest

Cindy Beckstead, Big Bar Ranger District, Shasta–Trinity National Forest

Pat Smith, Hayfork Ranger District, Shasta–Trinity National Forest

Jeff Thompson, McCloud Ranger District, Shasta–Trinity National Forest

Don Lee, Mount Shasta Ranger District, Shasta–Trinity National Forest

Cathy Southwick, Shasta Lake Ranger District, Shasta–Trinity National Forest

Fay Mok, Weaverville Ranger District, Shasta–Trinity National Forest

Judy Hanevold, Yolla Bolly Ranger District, Shasta–Trinity National Forest

Edward C. Cole, Sierra National Forest

Dave Martin, Bass Lake Ranger District, Sierra National Forest

Ray Porter, High Sierra Ranger District, Sierra National Forest

Tyrone Kelley, Six Rivers National Forest

Ann Garland, Lower Trinity Ranger District, Six Rivers National Forest

Roberto Delgado, Mad River Ranger District, Six Rivers National Forest

Bill Rice, Orleans Ranger District, Six Rivers National Forest

Tom Quinn, Six Rivers National Forest, Smith River National Recreation Area

Kevin Purcell, Calaveras Ranger District, Stanislaus National Forest

Jan Cargill, Groveland Ranger District, Stanislaus National Forest

Bill Seib, Mi-Wok Ranger District, Stanislaus National Forest

Emily Ellis, Summit Ranger District, Stanislaus National Forest

Jan Welsh, American River Ranger District, Foresthill Ranger Station, Tahoe National Forest

Susanne Johnson, Lake Tahoe Basin Management Unit, Tahoe National Forest

Mary Westmoreland and Jeff Wiley, Sierraville Ranger District, Tahoe National Forest

Heather Newell, Yuba River Ranger District, North, Tahoe National Forest

Rene Smith, Yuba River Ranger District, South, Tahoe National Forest

U.S. Army Corps of Engineers

Mike Acheson, Lake Sonoma Recreation Area, San Francisco District

Phil Deffenbaugh, Lake Kaweah, Sacramento District

Tom Ehrke, Hensley Lake, Sacramento District

Hector Galvan, Island Park and Deer Creek Point Campgrounds, Sacramento District

Kathy Guynes, Englebright Lake, Sacramento District

Denice Hogan, Black Butte Lake, Sacramento District

Joanne Jackson, Cordoniz Recreation Area, Sacramento District

Valerie Mavis, Lake Mendocino, San Francisco District

Donna Nelson, Acorn and Oak Knoll Campgrounds, Sacramento District

Dwayne Urquhart, Tule Campground, Sacramento District

Dale Verner, Martis Creek Lake, Sacramento District

Bureau of Land Management

Claude Singleton, Alturas Field Office

Clarence Killingsworth, Arcata Field Office

Steve Larsen and Kenneth Hock, Bakersfield Field Office

Bob Raver, Barstow Field Office

Marian Ardohain and Amy Tischman, Merced Irrigation District

Steve Benson, Huntington Beach City Parks

Tim Bolla, Richard Chandler, and Marilea Linne, Solano County Parks

Gail Brown, Brown's Campgrounds

Christopher Burdette, The Presidio Trust

Cheryl Bynum and Martha Martinez, Imperial County Parks

Debbie Campbell, City of South Lake Tahoe

Liz Castillo, Riverside County Parks

Julie Cloherty, San Diego County Parks

Peggy Davidson, Nevada Irrigation District

Anna Diaz and Ann Springer, San Luis Obispo County Parks

Brent Doan, Lake Casitas Municipal Water District

Joy Feller, Nevada County Fairgrounds

Irene Flores, Karen Montanye, Juisa Powell, and Mary Sheehan, San Bernardino Regional Parks

Clay Garland, Santa Barbara County Parks

Colleen Ghiglia, Lompoc Parks and Recreation

Patty Guida, New Melones Visitors Center, U.S. Bureau of Reclamation

Sherie Harral, Shasta Dam, U.S. Bureau of Reclamation

JosÈ Gutierrez, Sacramento Municipal Utility District

Heidi Gutnecht, City of San Diego

Chuck Hamilton and Ychelle Tillemans, Inyo County Parks

Darlene Hennings, Placer County Facilities Services

Connie Jackson, Marty Johnson, and Danae Schmidt, Stanislaus County Parks and Recreation

Sara Johnston and Karen White, United Water Conservation District

Bill Kromer, Sierra Recreation Management

Tracy Kves, Northern California Power Agency

Donna LaGraffe, Sonoma County Regional Parks

Jim Langley and Jay Vanderpool, California Land Management

Cynthia McDonald, Joy Vandell, Ross Jackson, and Mike Drury, Pacific Gas and Electric

Kathy McGadden, Greg Smith, and Jim Spreng, Monterey County Parks

Bill Minor, Humboldt County Public Works

Janet Morrison, Fresno County Parks

Dave Moore, San Mateo County Parks

Julie Ola, Alpine County Public Works Department

John Parsons, Stancy Perich, and John Wilbanks, Kern County Parks and Recreation

Don Pearson, Eldorado Irrigation District

Darla Pence and Melissa Brosnan-Torrise, PG&E Land Projects

Pam Phelps, City of Escondido

Christina Phillips, Hoopa Valley Tribal Council

Neil Pilegard, Tulare County Parks and Recreation

Patty Sereni, Napa County Fairgrounds

Ron Slimm, Orange County Parks

Cookie Hanlon, San Joaquin County Parks

Pat Sotelo, Livermore Area Recreation and Park District

Laurie Swanson, Tahoe City Public Utilities District

Sue Vanderschans, Turlock Irrigation District

Ron Vandyck, Ventura County Parks

Roberta Warden, El Dorado Irrigation District

Amy Welch, Mono County Public Works

Jerry Wright, Yolo County Parks